# City Crime Rankings
# 2015

# *State FactFinder Series*

## *State Rankings*
## *City Crime Rankings*

### *SAGE Stats online database, featuring State Stats and Local Stats*

What is **SAGE Stats**? **SAGE Stats** is a new website from SAGE Publications that delivers a dynamic and engaging user experience that is unmatched in other resources. SAGE Stats draws together the statistics from the *State Rankings* series of books by CQ Press (*SAGE State Stats*) and a new collection of data by county, city, and metro Area (*SAGE Local Stats*). Featuring data from more than 80 different government and nongovernment sources and backed by a rich collection of more than 6,000 current and historical data series on popular topics of research interest, **SAGE Stats** uniquely allows users to discover, view, and export key information measures for the 50 states and the District of Columbia, over 1400 cities, over 3000 counties, and over 900 metro areas. Check it out online at http://data.sagepub.com/sagestats

**SAGE Stats** makes research easy by providing in one place annual measures dating back more than 15 years. Data series are displayed in a clear and consistent format with detailed source information. Numerous topics are covered in categories including Agriculture; Crime and Law Enforcement; Defense; Demographics; Economics; Education; Employment and Labor; Geography, Energy, and the Environment; Health and Medicine; Religion; Social Welfare; Taxes and Government Finance; Transportation. The City Crime Rankings data since 1993 are featured in **SAGE Stats**!

The benefit of **SAGE Stats** is in its ease of use and clean and concise presentation of data and trends. An intuitive interface lets users easily browse by location or by topic, and then compare across locations or across time. Users can then share, save, and export data. **SAGE Stats** also features SAGE's CiteNow!® function for generating source citations in APA, MLA, Chicago, or Bluebook styles.

Users can:

- Analyze data patterns by comparing across locations, data series, and time

- Create and export custom visuals including line charts, scatter plots, and maps

- Generate tables and download data for statistical research

- Toggle user display between interactive visual and tabular data view

- Engage a moveable timeline to discover trends

- Explore interactive maps featuring zoom and hover functions

- Export data across single-click download of complete data series and multiple series

Ongoing updates to **SAGE Stats** throughout the year ensure that users have the most current data available.

# City Crime Rankings 2015

*Crime in Metropolitan America*

**Kathleen O'Leary Morgan**
**and**
**Scott Morgan**
*with*
**Rachel Boba Santos**

Los Angeles | London | New Delhi
Singapore | Washington DC | Boston

Los Angeles | London | New Delhi
Singapore | Washington DC | Boston

*For information:*

SAGE Publications, Inc.
2455 Teller Road
Thousand Oaks, California 91320
E-mail: order@sagepub.com

SAGE Publications Ltd.
1 Oliver's Yard
55 City Road
London, EC1Y 1SP
United Kingdom

SAGE Publications India Pvt. Ltd.
B 1/I 1 Mohan Cooperative Industrial Area
Mathura Road, New Delhi 110 044
India

SAGE Publications Asia-Pacific Pte. Ltd.
3 Church Street
#10-04 Samsung Hub
Singapore 049483

Printed in the United States of America.

Developmental Editor:      John Martino
Production Editor:         Tracy Buyan
Proofreader:               Laura Webb
Cover Designer:            Michael Dubowe
Marketing Manager:         Carmel Schrire

ISBN 978-1-4833-8507-5 (paper)

15 16 17 18 19 10 9 8 7 6 5 4 3 2 1

# Contents

# Detailed Table of Contents

## III. METROPOLITAN AND CITY POPULATIONS

## APPENDIX

---

**Please note the following for Tables 13–16 and 53–56**

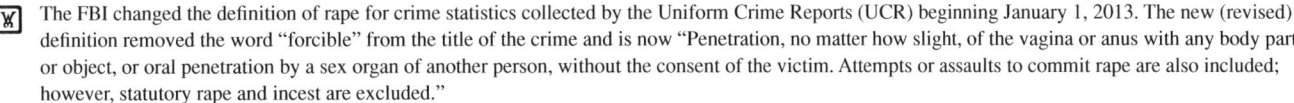 The FBI changed the definition of rape for crime statistics collected by the Uniform Crime Reports (UCR) beginning January 1, 2013. The new (revised) definition removed the word "forcible" from the title of the crime and is now "Penetration, no matter how slight, of the vagina or anus with any body part or object, or oral penetration by a sex organ of another person, without the consent of the victim. Attempts or assaults to commit rape are also included; however, statutory rape and incest are excluded."

The previous (legacy) definition had been "The carnal knowledge of a female forcibly and against her will. While the definition includes assaults or attempts to commit rape by force or threat of force, it does not include statutory rape (without force) or other sex offenses."

Regarding the change, the FBI wrote "Proponents of the new definition state the changes will broaden the scope of the previously narrow . . . definition by capturing gender neutrality, the penetration of any bodily orifice, penetration by any object or body part, and offenses in which physical force is not involved. Now instances in which offenders sodomize victims of the same gender will be counted as rape for statistical purposes."

Not all jurisdictions, however, have begun collecting rape statistics under the revised definition, and so the 2013 statistics include some cities with rapes collected under the revised definition and others with rapes collected under the legacy definition. Because there has only been one year of any data collection under the revised definition, all trends in this summary and the book are based on the legacy definition. The tables showing the one and five year percent change in rape rates for cities use a double asterisk (**) to indicate which cities used the legacy definition. Because cities within the same metro area used different definitions, it is not possible to have comparable numbers to show trends. Accordingly, the two tables showing one- and five-year percent change in rape rates are omitted from the metro section of this book.

# Introduction

*City Crime Rankings 2015* analyzes the latest (2013) FBI crime statistics for U.S. metropolitan areas and cities with populations of 75,000 or more. *City Crime Rankings* starts off by describing the data and methodology used in the rankings; it then provides a comparative analysis of cities and metropolitan areas, a distribution analysis of comparison scores and rates, and additional information and caveats regarding the analyzed data. The data and their limitations, the methodology, and the results of the comparative analysis of six types of reported crime are discussed.[1] Also presented are charts illustrating the distribution of values for selected analyses along with the related statistics for the median, mean, standard deviation, minimum value, and maximum value. Lastly, the definitions of crimes based on the FBI's coding system are presented with supporting facts and caveats that provide context to the numbers presented in this volume.

The two main sections of the book, Metropolitan Area Crime Statistics and City Crime Statistics, report the statistics for 377 metropolitan areas and 442 cities with populations of 75,000 or more. Each section has forty tables, presented in both alphabetical and rank order, that compare the actual numbers of reported crimes, crime rates, and percent changes over periods of one year and five years.[2] Each table spans four pages with the first two pages displaying the metro areas and cities in alphabetical order and the third and fourth pages displaying them in rank order. In addition, City Crime Statistics presents the actual numbers, rates, and percent change in police officers employed per capita by law enforcement agencies in each city.

To be included in this edition, cities must have reported crime data to the FBI for 2013. Metropolitan areas must have met two criteria: first, their central city or cities must have submitted twelve months of data in 2013, and second, at least 75% of all law enforcement agencies located in a specific metro area must have reported crime statistics for 2013. (The cities and metro areas not meeting these requirements were excluded from this edition of *City Crime Rankings* and are listed in the Missing Cities and Metro Areas section.)

The Metropolitan and City Populations Appendix presents population data for the cities and metro areas included in *City Crime Rankings*. The section consists of a description for each metropolitan area, including a list of cities and counties, a county index for 2013, tables illustrating rates for each reported crime category for the past twenty years with an examination of national trends and perspective of crime in the United States, and a summary of the 2013 national, metropolitan, and city crime statistics.

## Purpose of This Book

The purpose of *City Crime Rankings* is to serve as a resource for researchers, city and law enforcement officials, and the community. The book provides the means by which individuals can compare local communities to other similar communities through contrast with the national level of reported crime—more specifically, crime rates per 100,000 for individual types of reported crime, for violent and property crime categories, and for overall crime.

In editions prior to the 2009–2010 edition, the terms *safest* and *dangerous* were used to describe the cities and metropolitan areas with the lowest and highest rankings in the comparative analysis, respectively. Even though the rankings are still provided, these terms are no longer used because perceptions of safety and danger are just that—perceptions. The data analyzed here are *reported crime* and *population*, which together constitute only two factors considered when determining safety or risk of crime victimization. Thus, the analyses in this book are purely descriptive. At no time do we attempt to explain why reported

---

[1] The FBI changed the definition of rape for crime statistics beginning January 1, 2013. The new definition removed the word "forcible" from the title of the crime and is now "Penetration, no matter how slight, of the vagina or anus with any body part or object, or oral penetration by a sex organ of another person, without the consent of the victim. Attempts or assaults to commit rape are also included; however, statutory rape and incest are excluded." The previous definition had been "The carnal knowledge of a female forcibly and against her will. While the definition includes assaults or attempts to commit rape by force or threat of force, it does not include statutory rape (without force) or other sex offenses." Not all jurisdictions have made the change and the 2013 statistics include rapes collected under both the revised definition and the legacy definition. Because there has only been one year of any data collection under the revised definition all trends in this summary and the book are based on the legacy definition.

[2] Two of the metro area tables (15 and 16) are omitted from this edition due to the difficulty in comparing trends in rape statistics following the changed definition of rape explained in the previous footnote.

crime rates are higher or lower from one community to the next. These explanations—currently sought by criminologists and other social science researchers—are beyond the scope of this book.

Consequently, to enhance the usefulness of *City Crime Rankings,* a new section was introduced in the 2009–2010 edition and is continued in subsequent editions. The "Distribution Analysis" section (see page xii) provides histograms of the comparison score and reported crime rate distributions as well as such measures of central tendency as median, mean, standard deviation, and minimum and maximum values for each distribution. Because the rank ordering of scores and crime rates does not illustrate the relative difference between metro areas' and cities' values, this analysis is provided so the reader can better understand how the values are distributed and where a particular metro area's or city's ranking falls in comparison to others.

These statistics are used in a variety of ways, by a range of audiences, including the following:

- Law enforcement agencies use them to help identify crime problems for further study.
- City governments compare their cities' crime levels to those of other jurisdictions to determine how their rates appear in comparison.
- The federal government uses this type of analysis to allocate grant funding.
- The media report these results to report and compare crime rates across cities and years.

In addition, it is important to examine the statistics of a city along with its metro area when using *City Crime Rankings.* Although a city's scores and rates are useful for understanding the crime levels within the boundaries of that city and for making comparisons to other law enforcement jurisdictions, criminals and opportunities for crime do not adhere to city boundaries, but rather spill over to adjacent (i.e., metro) areas. In fact, crime rates and comparison scores tend to be lower in metro areas than in individual cities because many of the more populous cities are geographically small and include central business, retail, and industrial areas where residential population is low. These nonresidential areas contain more victims and targets (e.g., commuters, merchandise, vehicles) than do residential areas, so their crime rates appear higher when population is used as the denominator in the calculation of the crime rate. Researchers who study low-population areas within cities often use other denominators to determine rates, such as number of vehicles parked in lots for auto theft, number of businesses for commercial burglary, or square footage of retail establishments for shoplifting and theft (Santos, 2012).

However, these variables are not easily obtained for all U.S. cities. By expanding the geographic unit from city to metro area to include business, retail, industrial, and residential areas, using population of the entire area as a basis for determining rate is more practical. Thus, combining a major city with its suburbs provides an overall view of how crime is present in interrelated communities. For example, the table below compares the city of Boston, MA, with its metro area, showing differences between the city and its metro area for each variable with the city having higher crime rates. Thus, city statistics and metro-area statistics both serve useful purposes and should be considered together when examining a city situated within a metro area.

## The Data and Their Limitations

The data featured in *City Crime Rankings* come from the FBI publication *Crime in the United States* (2014), which is available every fall (e.g., November 2014) and presents information for the previous year (e.g., 2013). This report is based on data collected through the Uniform Crime Reporting (UCR) Program, which began in 1930. The purpose of the UCR Program has been to develop reliable information about crime reported to law enforcement that can be used by law enforcement as well as by criminologists, sociologists, legislators, municipal planners, and the media for a variety of research and planning purposes. Although the program is voluntary, in 2013 more than 18,000 city, university and college, county, state, tribal, and federal law enforcement agencies provide information representing 98% of the population (FBI, 2014a).

Although law enforcement agencies collect common information on crimes reported to and discovered by them, each state has slightly different criminal laws, and each law enforcement agency has its own policies and procedures for recording activity. These differences make it very difficult to compare statistics across agencies. To classify criminal activity consistently, the UCR Program was created. The UCR Program provides national standards for the uniform classification of crimes and arrests (for further details, visit the FBI's website at http://www.fbi.gov/stats-services/crimestats). Notably, the UCR crime definitions are distinct and do not conform to federal or state laws.

There are well-documented criticisms of the UCR data that must be considered when using these data for any purpose. But while the nature of the data and their limitations should be understood, they should not preclude researchers, practitioners, and others from using the data to understand crime and guide policy decisions. The following is a brief discussion of the major issues and concerns surrounding UCR data.

While individual law enforcement agencies classify reported crimes based on the laws of their own states and jurisdictions, these agencies reclassify these crimes according to UCR definitions when reporting them and provide aggregate counts of (a) particular crimes (known as Part I crimes: murder, rape, robbery, aggravated assault, burglary, larceny-theft, motor vehicle theft, and arson) and (b) arrests for all crimes. Note that the FBI does not report the aggregate counts of Part II crimes—including simple assault, fraud, prostitution, and DUI—it reports only the

| | 2013 Population | Comparison Score | Overall Crime Rate | Violent Crime Rate | Property Crime Rate |
|---|---|---|---|---|---|
| Boston, MA, City | 643,799 | 59.76 | 3,555.5 | 782.4 | 2,773.1 |
| Boston, MA, Metro | 1,942,405 | –24.29 | 2,595.6 | 503.0 | 2,092.6 |

arrests that occur. Thus, when statistics about reported violent and property crime are published in this or any other book or article, they are only based on the eight Part I crimes.

In addition, UCR reporting requires the use of a hierarchical coding system that means if two crimes happen during one incident, only one is counted. For example, if one person is the victim of both rape and robbery, only the rape will be counted, or if a car is stolen out of a locked garage, it is considered a burglary, not a burglary and an auto theft. The UCR Program has specific rules for coding that are not detailed here; however, the result is that the actual number of reported crimes might be underestimated in that the number of incidents is counted and not the number of unique crimes that occur.

The factor of actual versus reported crime is probably the most important one to consider when interpreting statistics based on UCR data. That is, the data provided to the FBI contain only those crimes reported or known to law enforcement as opposed to all crime that has actually occurred. We know from victimization surveys that not all crimes are reported to law enforcement (Truman & Langton, 2014) and that different types of crimes are reported at different levels. The Bureau of Justice Statistics estimates from the National Crime Victimization Survey that violent crime was reported to police 45.6% in 2013, 44.2% in 2012, and 50.3% in 2004. Property crime was reported 36.1% in 2013, 33.5% in 2012, and 39.2% in 2004 (Truman & Langton, 2014). When UCR data are analyzed, we must recognize that the data do not represent the actual amount of crime. However, if the data are collected accurately and consistently, they can be used, with caution, to make comparisons across geographic areas and over time.

Additional criticisms of the UCR data include inaccuracy due to inputting errors and handling of missing data (Lynch & Jarvis, 2008; Maltz, 1999), pressure on some law enforcement agencies to "doctor" the numbers, and the use of aggregate numbers that mask other factors such as time of day, location, and circumstance of the crime (e.g., whether the crime is committed by a stranger or family member). Yet, the UCR data are the most comprehensive and consistently collected data on crime in the United States. In most cases, analysis of UCR data begins the conversation, and additional in-depth analysis of crime in local areas is required to really understand the nature and context of crime problems (Santos, 2012).

## Methodology

As noted above, the crimes tracked by the UCR Program include the violent crimes of murder, rape, robbery, and aggravated assault and the property crimes of burglary, larceny-theft, motor vehicle theft, and arson. This combination of crimes are also sometimes known as *Crime Index* offenses; the index is simply the total of the eight main offense categories. The FBI discontinued use of this measure in 2004 because its officials and advisory board of criminologists concluded that the index was no longer a true indicator of crime. The primary concern was that the Crime Index was inflated by a high number of larceny-thefts, which account for nearly 60% of reported crime, thereby diminishing the focus on more serious but less frequently reported offenses, such as murder and rape. The consensus of the FBI and its advisory groups was that the Crime Index no longer served its purpose and that a more meaningful index should be developed.

While the FBI considers how it will replace the Crime Index, *City Crime Rankings* continues to provide total crime numbers, rates, and trends for U.S. cities and metropolitan areas as a service to readers. We offer a cautionary note, however, that in 2013, larceny-theft comprised 70% of property crime and 61% of all reported crimes.

Our analyses are conducted on two geographic units: the city and the metropolitan statistical area (MSA) as provided by the FBI. The cities included in these analyses are those with populations of 75,000 or more. According to the FBI in 2013,

Each MSA contains a principal city or urbanized area with a population of at least 50,000 inhabitants. MSAs include the principal city; the county in which the city is located; and other adjacent counties that have, as defined by the OMB, a high degree of economic and social integration with the principal city and county as measured through commuting. In the UCR Program, counties within an MSA are considered metropolitan. In addition, MSAs may cross state boundaries.

In 2013, approximately 85.2 percent of the nation's population lived in MSAs. Some presentations in this publication refer to Metropolitan Divisions, which are subdivisions of an MSA that consists of a core with "a population of at least 2.5 million persons. A Metropolitan Division consists of one or more main/secondary counties that represent an employment center or centers, plus adjacent counties associated with the main county or counties through commuting ties," (Federal Register 65 [249]). Also, some tables reference suburban areas, which are subdivisions of MSAs that exclude the principal cities but include all the remaining cities (those having fewer than 50,000 inhabitants) and the unincorporated areas of the MSAs. (FBI, 2014b).

The methodology used to produce the statistics presented in this book is fairly straightforward. In the first analysis, a score is calculated for each metropolitan area and city; this score is a summary of the percent differences of the reported crime rate from the national rate of six crime types (excluding larceny-theft and arson). Because this formula is unique to this book, it is described in detail below. The rest of the analyses are simple calculations of reported crime rates per 100,000 population and percent change for one year and five years. Lastly, all the analyses present a ranking that is a simple sort of the values computed for the analysis and numbered from highest to lowest. In case of a tie, the rankings are listed alphabetically. Parentheses indicate negative numbers and rates (except in the data distribution charts). Data reported as "NA" are not available or could not be calculated. The national totals and rates appearing at the top of each table are for the entire United States, including both metropolitan and nonmetropolitan areas. Specific totals for metropolitan areas and larger cities are provided in the Appendix.

## Comparison Score Methodology

The methodology for determining the city and metro area comparison crime rate rankings involves a multistep process in which the reported crime per 100,000 population rate are compared to the national reported crime per 100,000 population rate and then indexed to create a summary score and ranking across six areas

**Example: City A, Population 150,000**

| | Murder | Rape | Robbery | Aggravated Assault | Burglary | Motor Vehicle Theft |
|---|---|---|---|---|---|---|
| City Rate | 7.33 | 20.67 | 84.00 | 250.00 | 638.00 | 116.67 |
| National Rate | 4.8 | 27.5 | 119.1 | 252.3 | 699.6 | 238.8 |
| Percent Difference | 52.71 | (24.84) | (29.47) | (0.91) | (8.81) | (51.14) |
| | | | | | | |
| Percent Difference | 52.71 | (24.84) | (29.47) | (0.91) | (8.81) | (51.14) |
| Weighting Factor | .1667 | .1667 | .1667 | .1667 | .1667 | .1667 |
| Resulting Score | 8.62 | (4.31) | (5.08) | (0.32) | (1.63) | (8.69) |

of reported violent and property crime. The methodology used for this edition of the book has been used for the past thirteen editions and is described here in detail.

Reported crime rates per 100,000 population in 2013 across six crime categories—murder, rape (legacy definition), robbery, aggravated assault, burglary, and motor vehicle theft—were examined in this analysis. Larceny-theft was removed from this analysis because of the aforementioned concerns noted by the FBI and others. Cities with populations of 75,000 or more that reported data for the six categories of crime measured were included in the analysis. There is no population minimum for metropolitan areas. In all, 441 cities and 368 metro areas were included in the results.

The following are steps for the comparison score calculation and examples that illustrate the calculations:

1. For each of the six categories of reported crime, the crime rate per 100,000 residents of a city or metropolitan area is calculated from the reported crime and population data provided to the FBI by local law enforcement agencies for a particular type of crime. In the example below, the calculation for murder is 11 divided by 150,000 multiplied by 100,000, which results in a 7.33 per capita reported murder rate per 100,000 people for that year.

2. The percent difference between the metro area or city rate and the national rate for each of the six crimes is then computed. The use of percent difference for each crime separately eliminates weighting more frequent crimes more heavily (e.g., a city may have 1 murder and 1,500 burglaries). Negative numbers are displayed in parentheses here and throughout the analysis tables. The formula for this calculation is:

$$\frac{\text{Metro Area Rate or City Rate} - \text{National Rate}}{\text{National Rate}} \times 100$$

3. The number is then scaled to be one-sixth of the index to make it comparable to scores in the previous editions of this book. A number of years ago, each of the six crimes was weighted based on the results of a telephone survey that determined which crimes were of greatest concern to Americans. The polls indicated that most Americans believed crimes such as burglary are more likely to happen in their lives than more serious crimes such as murder. Thus, burglary received the highest weight, and murder received the lowest weight in the formula. In subsequent years, the polling was discontinued and, consequently, the weights were eliminated. However, equal weight is assigned to the crimes during this step in the analysis so that future scores would be more closely comparable to the scores with the weighted factors.

4. The final comparison score for each metro area and city is the sum of the individual scores for the six crimes. In this case, the sum is –11.41. The interpretation of these scores is that the higher a metro area or city score, the further above the national score; the lower the score, the further below the national score; and a score of zero is equal to the national score.

5. The scores are then sorted from highest to lowest to produce the rankings. Note that the rankings do not indicate the actual difference between the scores, only their order. The 21st Annual America's Cities and Metropolitan Areas with the Highest and Lowest Crimes Rates tables on pages [xx–xxvii] provide the results of the metro area and city scores. The Metropolitan and Cities Comparison Scores Distribution Analysis for 2013 on pages [xiii–xvi] provides the results of the distribution of these scores.

This methodology results in a score for each metro area and city that compares its rate to the national rates, providing a means to gauge crime trends in communities.

## References

FBI. (2014a). *Crime in the United States*. Retrieved December 15, 2014, from http://www.fbi.gov/about-us/cjis/ucr/crime-in-the-u.s/2013/crime-in-the-u.s.-2013/cius-home

FBI. (2014b). *Area definitions*. Retrieved December 15, 2014, from http://www.fbi.gov/about-us/cjis/ucr/crime-in-the-u.s/2013/crime-in-the-u.s.-2013/area-definitions

Lynch, J. P., & Jarvis, J. P. (2008). Missing data and imputation in the Uniform Crime Reports and the effects on national estimates. *Journal of Contemporary Criminal Justice, 24*, 69–85.

Maltz, M. (1999). *Bridging gaps in police crime data*. Washington, DC: Bureau of Justice Statistics.

Santos, R. B. (2012). *Crime analysis with crime mapping*. Thousand Oaks, CA: Sage.

Truman, J. L., & Langton, L. (2014). *Criminal victimization, 2013*. Washington, DC: Bureau of Justice Statistics.

# Distribution Analysis

This section presents charts depicting the distributions of the comparison scores as well as the individual and collective reported crime rates shown in *City Crime Rankings* to provide a mechanism of comparison beyond the rankings included in each analysis. The histograms in this section illustrate the distribution of values for the comparison score analyses as well as for the overall, violent, and property crime rate analyses. Along with each histogram, measures of central tendency, such as median, mean, standard deviation, and minimum and maximum values, are reported to provide further description of each distribution.

In each histogram (formatted as area charts for easier viewing), the values of the scores or rates are shown along the bottom (x-axis) and the frequency of cases (i.e., metro areas or cities) are shown along the left (y-axis). The values along the bottom are ranges for which the frequency of cases is totaled. These ranges and frequencies are different for each distribution, in this case, each histogram.

The median indicates the middle value of the distribution, meaning that 50% of the metro areas or cities have scores or rates above that value, and 50% have scores or rates below it. The mean is the average value of the distribution, and the standard deviation, described generally, is the measure of spread of all the values from the mean. The minimum and maximum values are the lowest and highest values of the distribution, respectively.

These statistics are based on a normal curve, so one standard deviation above and below the mean contains 68% of the distribution, two standard deviations above and below the mean contain 95% of the distribution, and three standard deviations above and below the mean contain 99.7% of the distribution. The use of these statistics is purely descriptive, but it does help the reader assess the distribution as a whole as well as illustrate where an individual value sits in terms of all the other values. For example, if a score is two or three standard deviations above or below the mean, it may be considered an outlier because it falls with only 5% or .3% of the values, respectively.

For example, Figure 1 depicts the comparison scores for metro areas in 2013. The median is –6.4, the mean is –0.4, the standard deviation is 40.8, the minimum value is –72.7, and the maximum value is 205.6. These statistics are interpreted as follows:

- The lowest comparison score for metro areas is –72.7.
- The highest comparison score for metro areas is 194.2.
- The range of scores (maximum minus minimum) is 205.6.
- 50% of the metro areas have comparison scores lower than –6.4, and 50% have scores higher than –6.4.
- The average comparison score for metro areas is –0.4 and the standard deviation is 40.8.
- 68% of the metro areas have scores between –41.2 and 40.4.
- 95% of the metro areas have scores between –81.2 and 82.0.
- 99.7% of the metro areas have scores between –122.8 and 122.0. (The fact that the lower end of this range (–122.8) and the 95% range (–81.2) is less than the minimum value of the distribution (–72.7) indicates the distribution is skewed in that there are very high outliers).

Assessing the score of –61.50 for the metropolitan area of Elizabethtown-Fort Knox, KY, for example, reveals that it is in the lower 50% of all the scores (below the median of –6.4) and falls between the first and second standard deviation below the mean indicating that it is within the 95% interval of the distribution.

The remainder of this section presents a total of eight charts and sets of statistics for both metropolitan areas and cities in the categories listed here:

1. Comparison Score
2. Overall Reported Crime
3. Reported Violent Crime
4. Reported Property Crime

A word of caution: These distribution analysis charts and statistics are provided to help the reader understand the nature of the values within each analysis, but the analyses are still based on data that must be interpreted within the constraints noted earlier. These charts are only descriptions of the data and do not provide predictions or explanations of why these values are different.

**Figure 1  Metropolitan Areas Comparison Score Distribution Analysis for 2013**

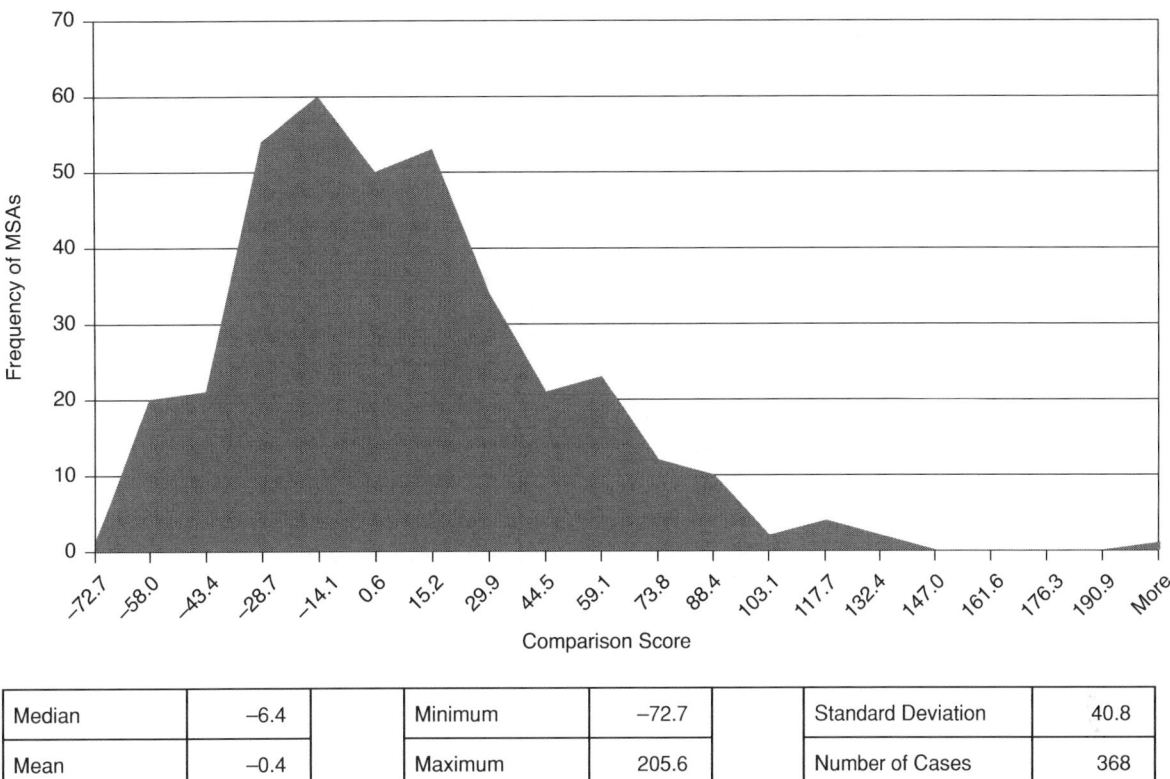

| Median | −6.4 | | Minimum | −72.7 | | Standard Deviation | 40.8 |
| Mean | −0.4 | | Maximum | 205.6 | | Number of Cases | 368 |

**Figure 2  Cities Comparison Score Distribution Analysis for 2013**

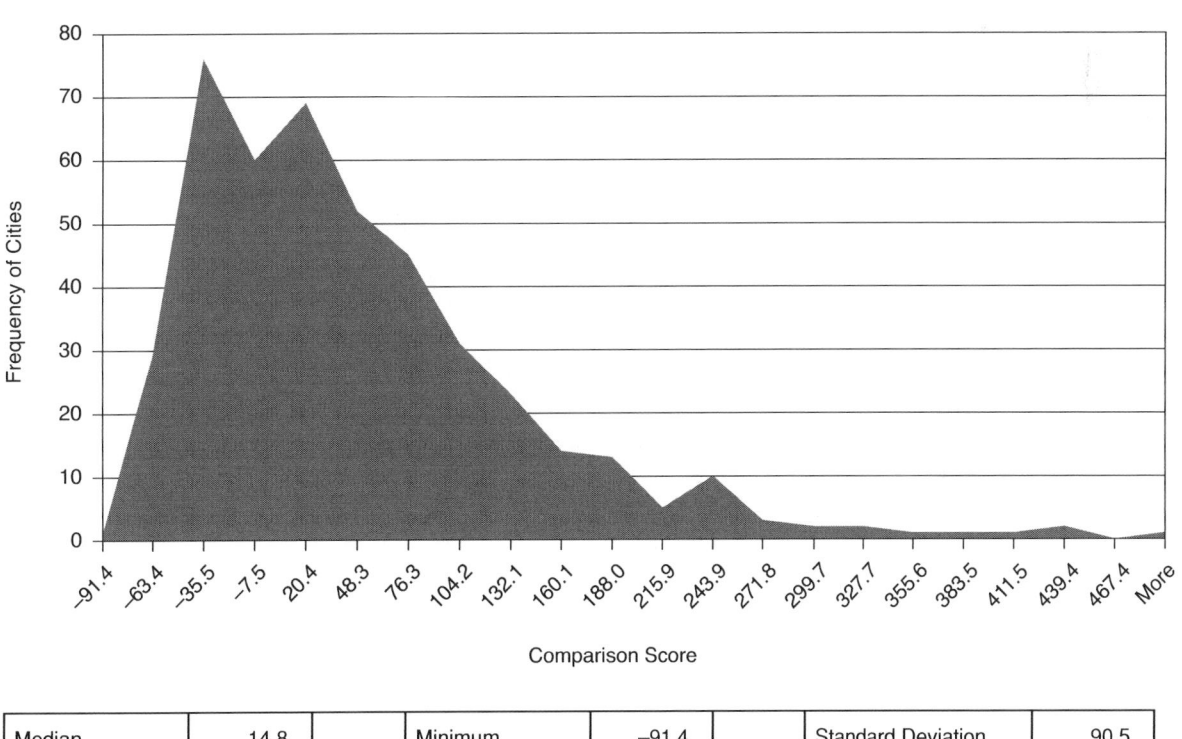

| Median | 14.8 | | Minimum | −91.4 | | Standard Deviation | 90.5 |
| Mean | 34.1 | | Maximum | 495.3 | | Number of Cases | 441 |

**Figure 3  Metropolitan Areas Overall Reported Crime Rate Distribution Analysis for 2013**

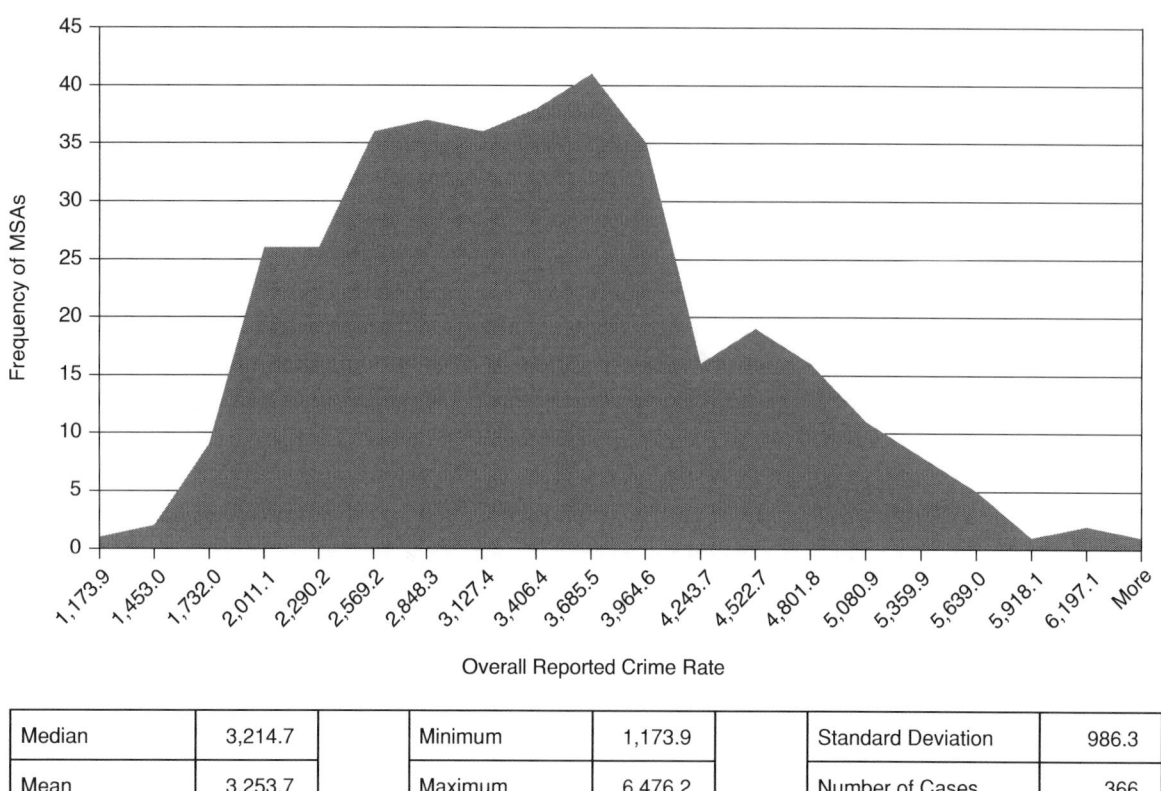

| Median | 3,214.7 | | Minimum | 1,173.9 | | Standard Deviation | 986.3 |
| Mean | 3,253.7 | | Maximum | 6,476.2 | | Number of Cases | 366 |

**Figure 4  Cities Overall Reported Crime Rate Distribution Analysis for 2013**

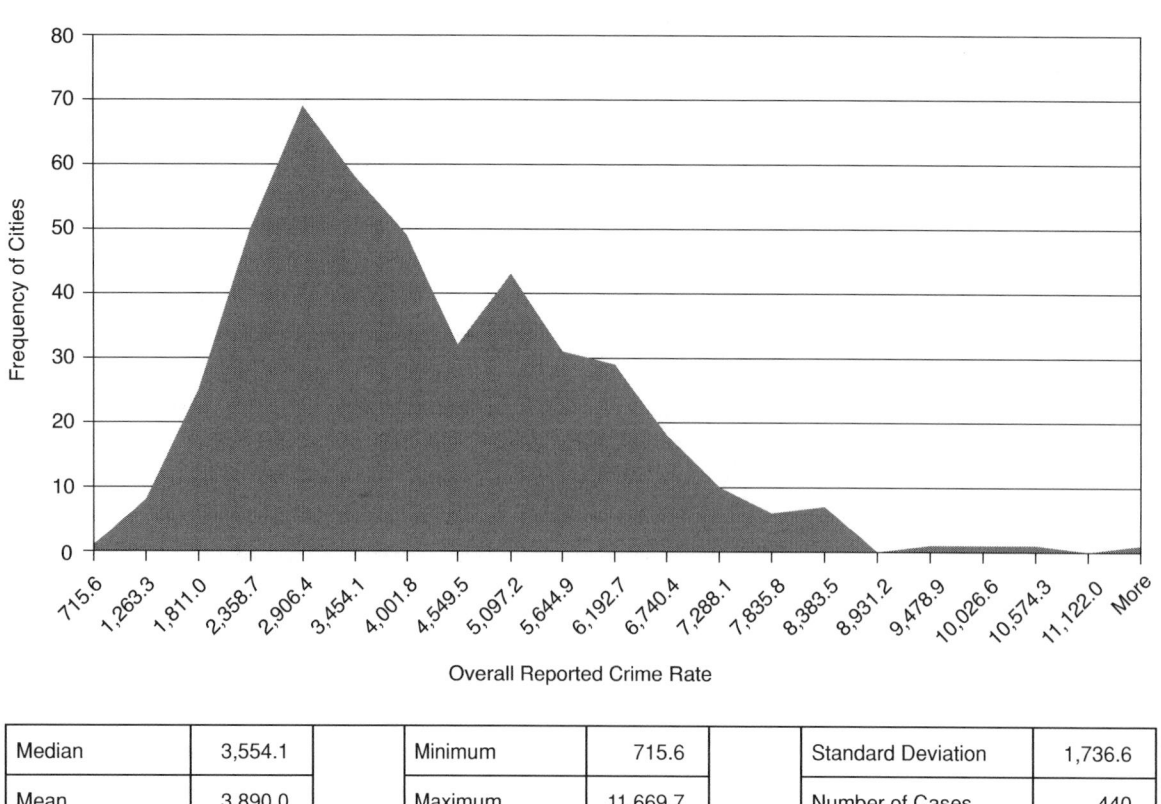

| Median | 3,554.1 | | Minimum | 715.6 | | Standard Deviation | 1,736.6 |
| Mean | 3,890.0 | | Maximum | 11,669.7 | | Number of Cases | 440 |

## Figure 5  Metropolitan Areas Reported Violent Crime Rate Distribution Analysis for 2013

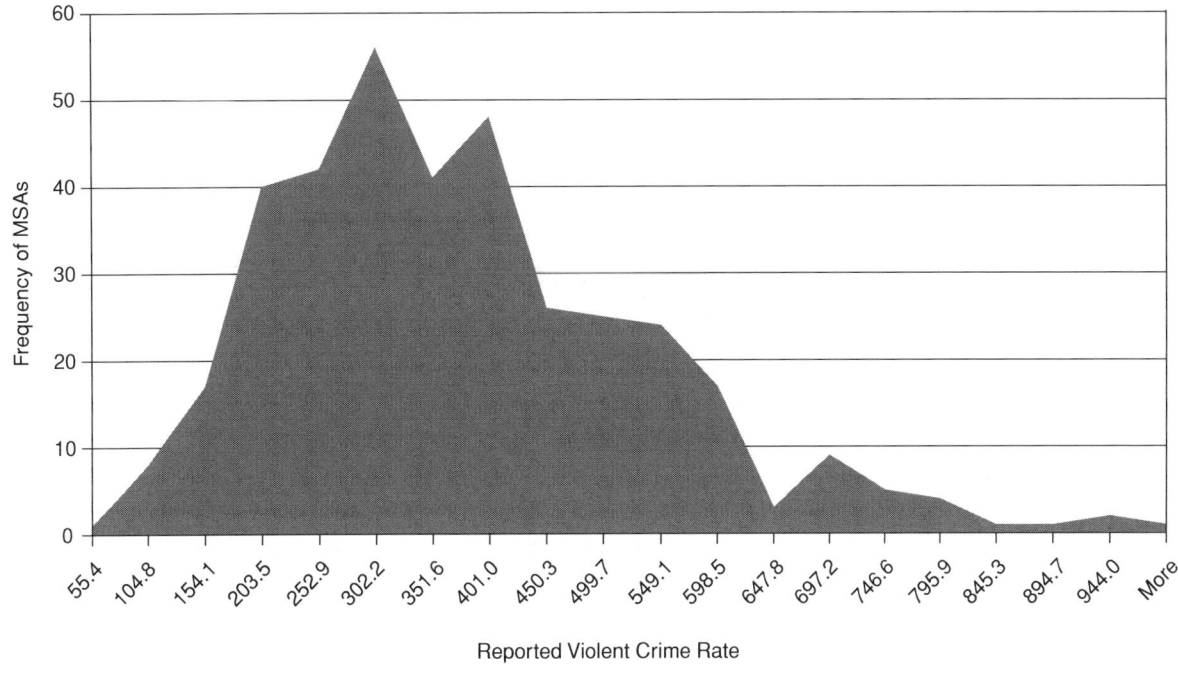

| Median | 331.9 | Minimum | 55.4 | Standard Deviation | 166.9 |
|---|---|---|---|---|---|
| Mean | 355.9 | Maximum | 1,047.8 | Number of Cases | 372 |

## Figure 6  Cities Reported Violent Crime Rate Distribution Analysis for 2013

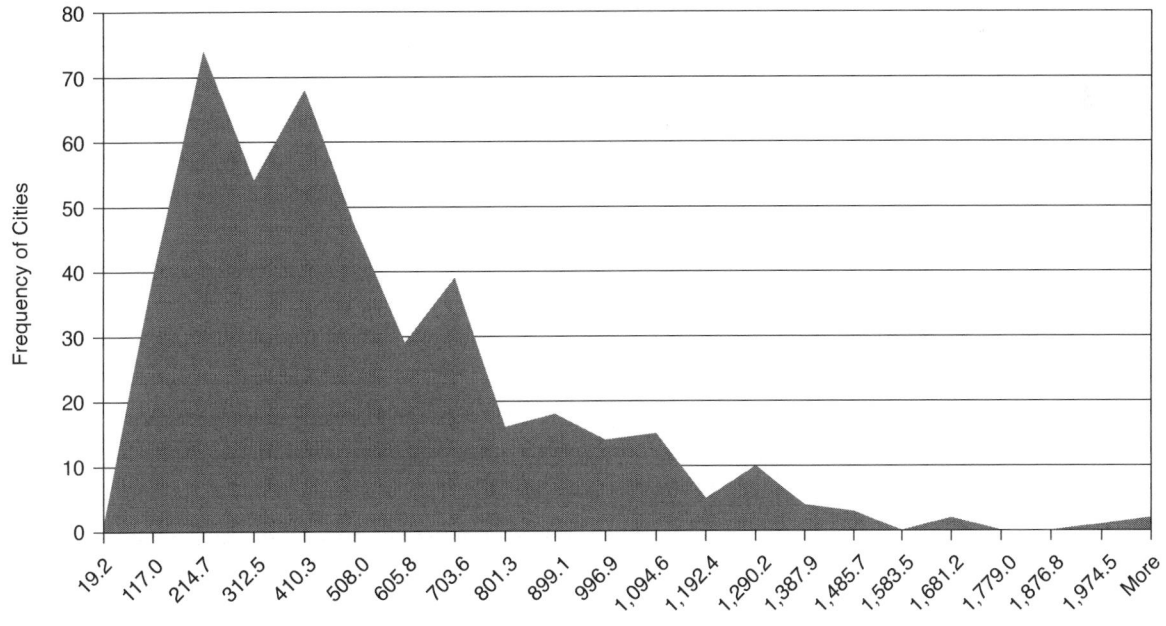

| Median | 386.7 | Minimum | 19.2 | Standard Deviation | 348.8 |
|---|---|---|---|---|---|
| Mean | 476.4 | Maximum | 2,072.3 | Number of Cases | 441 |

**Figure 7  Metropolitan Areas Reported Property Crime Rate Distribution Analysis for 2013**

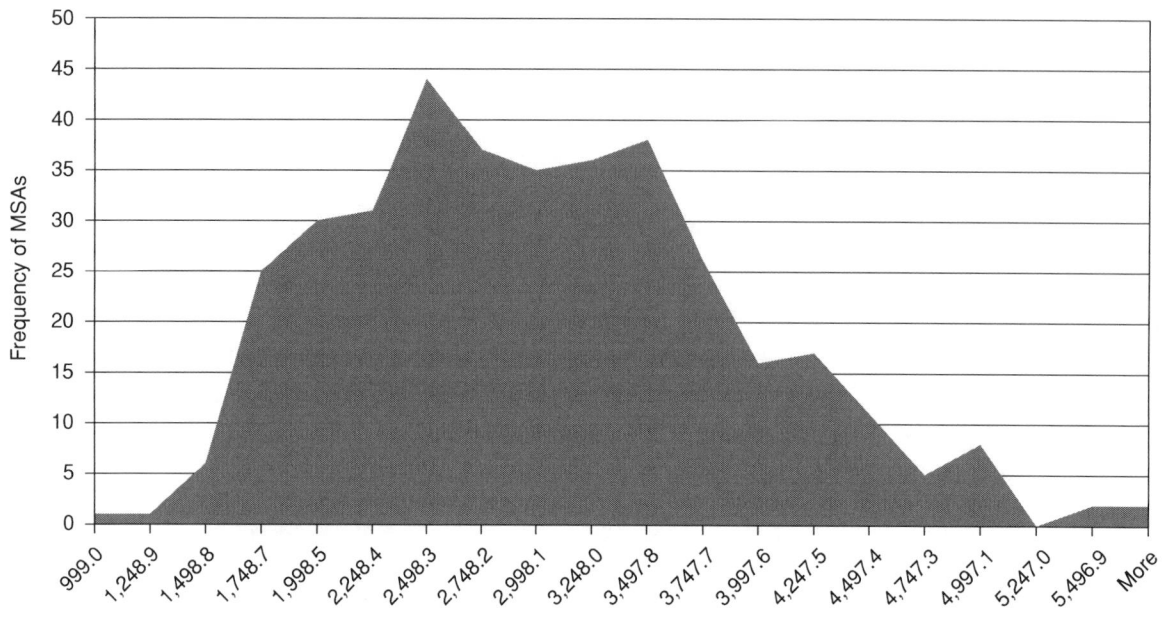

| Median | 2,830.2 | Minimum | 999.0 | Standard Deviation | 876.1 |
| Mean | 2,900.6 | Maximum | 5,746.8 | Number of Cases | 371 |

**Figure 8  Cities Reported Property Crime Rate Distribution Analysis for 2013**

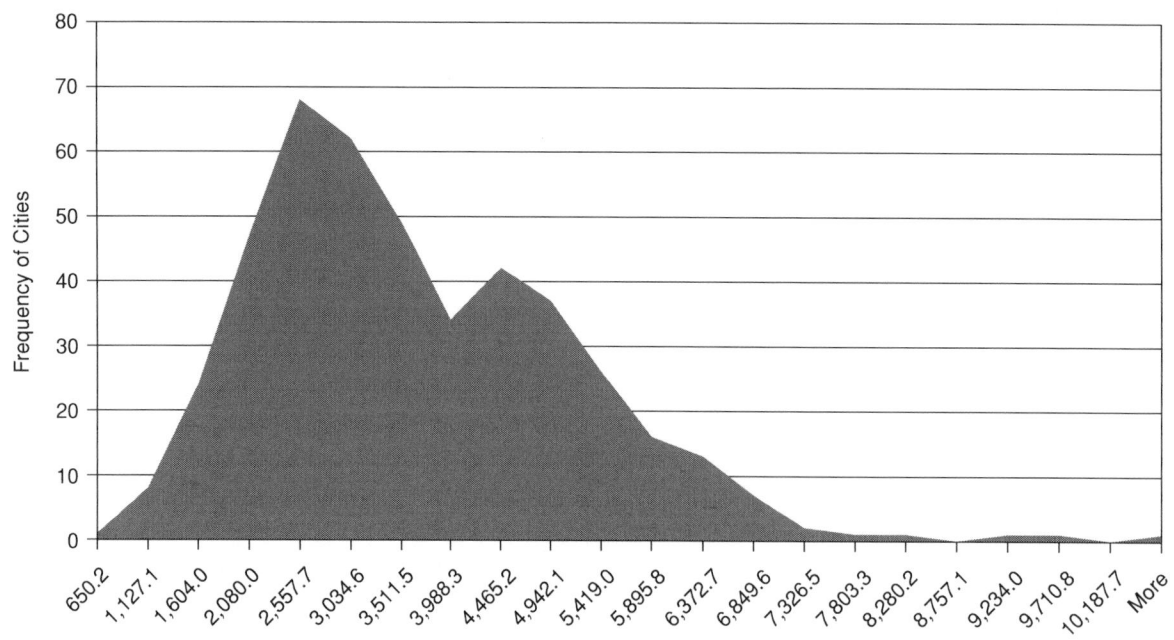

| Median | 3,108.9 | Minimum | 650.2 | Standard Deviation | 1,489.1 |
| Mean | 3,415.1 | Maximum | 10,664.6 | Number of Cases | 441 |

## Notes Regarding City and Metro Crime Data

To be included in the comparative analysis, cities and metro areas must report data for six crime categories: murder, rape robbery, aggravated assault, burglary, and motor vehicle theft. All metro areas and all cities with populations of 75,000 or more that reported crime data to the FBI were included. A number of cities and metropolitan areas did not report complete crime information for 2013. This information is delineated below.

### Missing Cities

The data collection method used by the city of Chicago, IL, for the offenses of rape and aggravated assault did not meet the Federal Bureau of Investigation's Uniform Crime Reporting (UCR) guidelines in 2013. Given that the rape and aggravated assault numbers were not available, Chicago is not included in the comparative analysis.

The FBI did not report crime data for fifteen other cities with populations larger than 75,000. Crime statistics for these cities were unavailable for a number of reasons, ranging from general reporting difficulties and computer issues to changes in reporting systems. Below is a list of cities with populations greater than 75,000 (according to the U.S. Census Bureau) but for which no information was available in the FBI's 2013 Uniform Crime Report. These cities are: Asheville, NC; Augusta-Richmond County, GA; Avondale, AZ; Bellingham, WA; Camden, NJ; Columbus, OH; Deltona, FL; Durham, NC; Honolulu, HI; Kalamazoo, MI; Montgomery, AL; Palm Coast, FL; Parma, OH; Rio Rancho, NM; and West Jordan, UT.

### Missing Metropolitan Areas

For crime figures to be reported for a metropolitan area, 12 months of complete data must be submitted for 75 percent of agencies and for the principal city or cities within that area. Nine metropolitan areas are not included in the comparative analysis because of missing data for specific offenses. Rape statistics were not available for the Chicago (greater), IL-IN-WI and Chicago-Naperville, IL M.D. metropolitan areas. Aggravated assault statistics were not available for Brunswick, GA; Indianapolis, IN; and Louisville, KY-IN metropolitan areas. Burglary statistics were not available for Ogden-Clearfield, UT and St. George, UT metropolitan areas. Motor vehicle theft statistics were not available for Phoenix-Mesa-Scottsdale, AZ and Visalia-Porterville, CA metropolitan areas.

Another group of metropolitan areas were not included in the comparative analysis because the FBI did not report data for them in its 2013 Crime in the United States report. These metropolitan areas are: Asheville, NC; Auburn-Opelika, AL; Battle Creek, MI; Beckley, WV; Bellingham, WA; Burlington-South Burlington, VT; Charleston, WV; Cleveland-Elyria, OH; Columbus, OH; Danville, IL; Durham-Chapel Hill, NC; Elkhart-Goshen, IN; Evansville, IN-KY; Harrisburg-Carlisle, PA; Hattiesburg, MS; Hickory-Lenoir-Morganton, NC; Honolulu, HI; Huntington-Ashland, WV-KY-OH; Ithaca, NY; Jacksonville, NC; Kalamazoo-Portage, MI; Killeen-Temple, TX; Michigan City-La Porte, IN; Midland, MI; Montgomery, AL; Pine Bluff, AR; Santa Fe, NM; Sierra Vista-Douglas, AZ; Valdosta, GA; Walla Walla, WA; Waterloo-Cedar Falls, IA; Weirton-Steubenville, WV-OH; Wenatchee, WA; Wheeling, WV-OH; and Youngstown-Warren-Boardman, OH-PA.

## An Overview of 2013 Crime

Crimes are reported by police agencies to the FBI as part of the Uniform Crime Reporting (UCR) Program. More than 18,000 city, county, college and university, state, tribal, and federal law enforcement agencies participated in the program in 2013. Law enforcement agencies active in the program represented more than 98 percent of the total U.S. population in 2013.

Larcenies and thefts accounted for 61.3 percent of crimes, burglaries accounted for 19.7 percent, aggravated assaults for 7.4 percent, motor vehicle thefts for 7.1 percent, robberies for 3.5 percent, rapes for 0.8 percent, and murders for 0.14 percent. The national 2013 total crime rate of 3,098.6 crimes per 100,000 people is 4.8 percent lower than in 2012.

### Violent Crime

Violent crimes include offenses of murder, rape, robbery, and aggravated assault. A total of 1,163,146 such crimes were committed in 2013. Of these, 62.3 percent were aggravated assaults, 29.7 percent were robberies, 6.9 percent were rapes, and 1.2 percent were murders. The 2013 national violent crime rate was 367.9 violent crimes per 100,000 population, 5.1 percent lower than in 2012.

Five- and ten-year trends show the 2013 violent crime rate was 14.8 percent lower than it was in 2009 and 20.6 percent lower than in 2004. Actual numbers of violent crimes dropped 12.3 percent from 2009 levels and 14.5 percent lower than in 2004.

Among those violent crimes for which weapons information was available, firearms were involved in 69.0 percent of murders, 40.0 percent of robberies, and 21.6 percent of aggravated assaults.

### Murder

Murder and nonnegligent manslaughter, as defined by the FBI, involve the willful (nonnegligent) killing of one human being by another. There were 14,196 murders in 2013. The national murder rate was 4.5 per 100,000 population in 2013, down 5.1 percent from 2012. Five-year trends show the 2013 murder rate was 10.5 percent lower than in 2009. A ten-year comparison of murder rates shows a drop of 18.3 percent from levels recorded in 2004.

Of those murders for which complete weapons data were available, 69.0 percent involved firearms. FBI data showed that 24.4 percent of murders were committed in conjunction with felonies or suspected felonies such as robberies, drug deals, and rapes. Among murders for which the relationship between the victim and offender was known, strangers committed 19.2 percent of those murders in 2013. Approximately 78 percent of murder victims were male, 43.9 percent were white, and 53.6 percent were black.

Gary, IN, had the highest murder rate in 2013 of any reporting city with more than 75,000 in population. The city's murder rate of 68.5 murders per 100,000 population was well above the national rate of 4.5 murders per 100,000 population.

### Rape

The FBI changed the definition of rape for crime statistics beginning January 1, 2013. The new definition removed the word "forcible" from the title of the crime and is now "Penetration, no matter how slight, of the vagina or anus with any body part or object, or oral penetration by a sex organ of another person, without the consent of the victim. Attempts or assaults to commit rape are also included; however, statutory rape and incest are excluded."

The previous definition had been "The carnal knowledge of a female forcibly and against her will. While the definition includes assaults or attempts to commit rape by force or threat of force, it does not include statutory rape (without force) or other sex offenses."

Not all jurisdictions, however, have begun collecting rape statistics under the revised definition, and so the 2013 statistics include some cities with rapes collected under the revised definition and others with rapes collected under the legacy definition. Because there has only been one year of any data collection under the revised definition all trends in this summary and the book are based on the legacy definition.

Using the legacy definition of rape an estimated 49.7 of every 100,000 females in the United States were reported rape victims in 2013. Although the FBI's legacy definition of rape limited victims to female victims, the 2013 national rape rate of 25.2 per 100,000 applies to the entire U.S. population, both males and females. This national rape rate dropped 7.0 percent from levels recorded in 2012 and decreased 13.2 percent from 2009 levels.

Under the legacy definition a total of 79,770 rapes were reported to the FBI by law enforcement agencies in 2013. For rapes for which additional data were reported, 93.9 percent constituted rapes by force. The remainder included attempts or assaults to commit forcible rape. The FBI estimates that using the expanded revised definition of rape there were 108,612 rapes nationally in 2013 with a rate of 34.4 rapes per 100,000 population.

## Robbery

Robbery is the taking or attempt to take anything by force or threat of force. The 345,031 robberies that occurred in 2013 represented a decrease of 2.8 percent from levels recorded in 2012. The national rate of 109.1 robberies per 100,000 population is lower as well, having decreased 3.5 percent from 2012.

The average dollar loss per robbery was $1,170. Banks lost an average of $3,542 per robbery. An estimated 42.5 percent of robberies occurred on streets or highways, 20.7 percent took place in commercial establishments, 16.6 percent were at residences, and 1.9 percent were at banks. The remaining robbery locations were termed "miscellaneous."

Firearms of various types were used in 40.0 percent of robberies in 2013. Strong-arm tactics were used in 43.6 percent of robberies, knives or cutting instruments were used in 7.6 percent, and other dangerous weapons were involved in the remaining 8.9 percent.

## Aggravated Assault

Aggravated assault is the unlawful attack by one person upon another for the purpose of inflicting severe bodily injury. This type of assault usually involves the use of a dangerous weapon. The FBI aggravated assault data includes attempts.

The 724,129 aggravated assaults that occurred in 2013 represent a 5.0 percent decrease from 2012 levels. The nation's 2013 rate of 229.1 aggravated assaults per 100,000 population is a 5.6 percent decrease from 2012. Aggravated assault rates fell 13.4 percent from 2009 levels and 20.6 percent from 2004 levels.

Assailants chose a variety of weapons with which to carry out their attacks in 2013. An estimated 27 percent were committed with "personal weapons" (e.g., hands or feet), 21.6 percent with firearms, 19.1 percent with knives, and 32.2 percent of assaults with "other" weapons.

## Property Crime

Property crime includes the crimes of burglary, larceny-theft, motor vehicle theft, and arson. These offenses involve the taking of money or property, but there is no force or threat of force against the victims. While arson is considered a property crime, data for arson offenses are not included in this book. The vast majority of crimes committed in the United States are property crimes; in 2013 they accounted for approximately 88.1 percent of all crimes reported.

A total of 8,632,512 property crimes occurred in the United States in 2013. The national property crime rate measured 2,730.7 property crimes per 100,000 population. Property crime decreased from 2012 to 2013 in both number and rate: the number of property crimes fell 4.1 percent from 2012, while the rate decreased 4.8 percent. Five-year trends show that property crime rates decreased 7.5 percent from 2009. A ten-year comparison shows a decline of 16.3 percent from 2004.

Property crimes accounted for an estimated $16.6 billion in losses in 2013. Larceny-thefts accounted for 69.6 percent of all property crimes, burglaries for 22.3 percent, and motor vehicle thefts for 8.1 percent.

## Burglary

Burglary is defined as the unlawful entry of a structure to commit a felony or theft. The use of force to gain entry is not required for an offense to be classified as burglary. The FBI tracks data for three types of burglaries: forcible entry, unlawful entry where no force is used, and attempted forcible entry. Burglary accounted for 22.3 percent of the estimated number of property crimes committed in 2013.

A total of 1,928,465 burglaries were reported in 2013, a decrease of 8.6 percent from 2012. The year's burglary rate of 610.0 burglaries per 100,000 population is 9.3 percent lower than in 2012. Five- and ten-year trends show that burglary rates have decreased 15.0 percent since 2009 and 16.5 percent since 2004.

Burglaries of residential properties accounted for 74.0 percent of all burglary offenses. Burglary offenses cost victims an estimated $4.5 billion in lost property. The average dollar loss per burglary offense was $2,322.

## Larceny-Theft

Larceny-theft is the unlawful taking of property from another person. It includes crimes such as shoplifting, pick-pocketing, purse-snatching, thefts from motor vehicles, thefts of motor vehicle parts and accessories, and bicycle thefts. No use of force, violence, or fraud is involved in these offenses. This category does not include embezzlement, "con" games, forgery, or worthless check writing.

A total of 6,004,453 thefts occurred in 2013, down 2.7 percent from 2012. This number represents 69.6 percent of property crimes reported for the year. The national rate of 1,899.4 larcenies and thefts per 100,000 population represents a 3.4 percent decrease from 2012 levels. Five- and ten-year trends show that larceny-theft rates have decreased 8.0 percent since 2009 and are down 19.6 percent from 2004.

The average value of property stolen in 2013 was $1,259. Total losses from larceny-thefts were estimated to be $7.6 billion.

## Motor Vehicle Theft

The motor vehicle theft category includes the stealing of automobiles, trucks, buses, motorcycles, motor scooters, snowmobiles, and so on. The definition does not include the taking of a motor vehicle for temporary use by those persons having lawful access to the vehicle.

A total of 699,954 motor vehicle thefts were committed in 2013. This represents a 3.3 percent decrease from 2012. The national rate of 221.3 vehicles stolen per 100,000 population represents a decrease of 4.0 percent from the prior year.

The total estimated value of these thefts was $4.1 billion, or an average of $5,972 per stolen vehicle. Automobiles were the most frequently stolen vehicle type, accounting for 73.9 percent of all those stolen.

## Police Officers

Nationwide, a total of 626,942 sworn police officers were on the job in 2013, with an additional 275,468 civilian employees assisting. This equates to 2.3 full-time officers per 1,000 population. This is a 0.9 percent decrease from 2012 in the rate of police officers and a 4.5% decrease from 2009.

Only police officers on each city's primary police force are reported in this volume. Many cities have a number of overlapping law enforcement agencies. For example, New York City has its Transit Police, Port Authority Police, and officials in other special law enforcement agencies. Those officers are not covered in *City Crime Rankings*.

## Miscellaneous Notes Regarding City and Metro Crime Data

- 2013 crime statistics are not comparable to 2012 data for 25 Metropolitan Statistical Areas (M.S.A.) and to 2009 data for 65 M.S.A. areas. Most are missing because of incomplete data from prior years. Some of these are because of changes in reporting practices. A few M.S.A.s for the 2009 to 2013 period are not compatible because the federal government redefines its M.S.A.s every ten years following a decennial census. This was done in 2012 based on the 2010 census. As a result, new M.S.A.s were created and significant changes were made in some existing M.S.A.s. The 2012 data are comparable to the 2013 data, but where the changes created a five-year population change of twenty percent or greater, the editors determined that the data were not comparable. As a result, five-year trends are not available for these metro areas.
- The population estimates reported in *City Crime Rankings 2015* are provided by the FBI. These estimates sometimes differ from those reported by the U.S. Census Bureau.
- The FBI changed the definition of rape for crime statistics collected by the Uniform Crime Reports (UCR) beginning January 1, 2013. The new (revised) definition removed the word "forcible" from the title of the crime and is now "Penetration, no matter how slight, of the vagina or anus with any body part or object, or oral penetration by a sex organ of another person, without the consent of the victim. Attempts or assaults to commit rape are also included; however, statutory rape and incest are excluded."

  The previous (legacy) definition had been "The carnal knowledge of a female forcibly and against her will. While the definition includes assaults or attempts to commit rape by force or threat of force, it does not include statutory rape (without force) or other sex offenses."

Regarding the change, the FBI wrote, "Proponents of the new definition state the changes will broaden the scope of the previously narrow . . . definition by capturing gender neutrality, the penetration of any bodily orifice, penetration by any object or body part, and offenses in which physical force is not involved. Now instances in which offenders sodomize victims of the same gender will be counted as rape for statistical purposes."

Not all jurisdictions, however, have begun collecting rape statistics under the revised definition, and so the 2013 statistics include some cities with rapes collected under the revised definition and others with rapes collected under the legacy definition. Because there has only been one year of any data collection under the revised definition, all trends in this summary and the book are based on the legacy definition. The tables showing the one- and five-year percent change in rape rates for cities use a double asterisk (**) to indicate which cities used the legacy definition. Because cities within the same metro area used different definitions, it is not possible to have comparable numbers to show trends. Accordingly, the two tables showing one- and five-year percent change in rape rates are omitted from the metro section of this book.

All national figures that include rape (e.g., Crimes, Violent Crimes, and Rape) are based on the legacy definition of rape.

- Rape and aggravated assault data were not reported for either the city or the metro area of Chicago, IL, because they did not meet UCR guidelines (either the legacy or the revised). Thus this information, as well as violent crime and overall crime statistics, are not available for these areas.
- Larceny-theft data were not reported for either the city or the metro area of Toledo, OH, because they did not meet UCR guidelines. Thus this information, as well as property crime and overall crime statistics, are not available for these areas.
- The Hamilton Township, NJ, data are for the township by that name located in Mercer County.
- Honolulu, HI, has a combined city-county government. Therefore, the population and crime data provided in this book include areas outside the principal city of Honolulu.
- Charlotte, NC, crime and population data include Mecklenburg County.
- Indianapolis, IN, crime and population data include Marion County.
- Louisville, KY, data include offenses reported by the Louisville and Jefferson County Police Departments.
- Las Vegas, NV, has a metropolitan police department and its crime and population numbers include areas outside of the principal city of Las Vegas.
- Savannah, GA, crime and population data include Chatham County.
- Toms River Township, NJ, was formerly known as Dover Township.
- The city of Camden, NJ, no longer has a city police department. The new Camden County Police Department is not included in the *City Crime Rankings 2015*. The Camden, NJ, M.D. remains included in the Metropolitan Crime Rankings.
- The population shown for the city of Mobile, AL, includes 55,819 inhabitants from the jurisdiction of the Mobile County Sheriff's Department.
- *City Crime Rankings 2015* also provides rankings for Metropolitan Divisions (M.D.s). These are subdivisions of eleven large Metropolitan Statistical Areas. For example, Philadelphia, PA M.D. is a Metro Division that falls within the Philadelphia (greater) PA-NJ-MD-DE M.S.A. Both are listed in the Metropolitan Crime Rankings.

# 2014 Metropolitan Crime Rate Rankings*

| RANK | METROPOLITAN AREA | SCORE | RANK | METROPOLITAN AREA | SCORE | RANK | METROPOLITAN AREA | SCORE |
|---|---|---|---|---|---|---|---|---|
| 140 | Abilene, TX | (17.84) | 37 | Cheyenne, WY | (46.18) | 283 | Gary, IN M.D. | 26.40 |
| 204 | Akron, OH | 0.40 | NA | Chicago (greater), IL-IN-WI** | NA | 9 | Gettysburg, PA | (66.21) |
| 59 | Albany-Schenectady-Troy, NY | (38.28) | NA | Chicago-Naperville, IL M.D.** | NA | 1 | Glens Falls, NY | (72.65) |
| 312 | Albany, GA | 42.40 | 272 | Chico, CA | 19.07 | 226 | Goldsboro, NC | 5.16 |
| 40 | Albany, OR | (43.60) | 194 | Cincinnati, OH-KY-IN | (1.25) | 93 | Grand Forks, ND-MN | (29.76) |
| 359 | Albuquerque, NM | 87.24 | 219 | Clarksville, TN-KY | 3.17 | 134 | Grand Island, NE | (19.00) |
| 349 | Alexandria, LA | 70.99 | 173 | Cleveland, TN | (10.39) | 240 | Grand Junction, CO | 8.61 |
| 55 | Allentown, PA-NJ | (39.14) | 186 | Coeur d'Alene, ID | (5.57) | 181 | Grand Rapids-Wyoming, MI | (7.49) |
| 35 | Altoona, PA | (46.96) | 131 | College Station-Bryan, TX | (20.35) | 187 | Grants Pass, OR | (5.46) |
| 323 | Amarillo, TX | 50.99 | 311 | Colorado Springs, CO | 41.98 | 89 | Great Falls, MT | (30.62) |
| 47 | Ames, IA | (42.39) | 180 | Columbia, MO | (8.12) | 97 | Greeley, CO | (28.48) |
| 52 | Anaheim-Santa Ana-Irvine, CA M.D. | (40.38) | 303 | Columbia, SC | 37.55 | 27 | Green Bay, WI | (52.78) |
| 361 | Anchorage, AK | 101.36 | 340 | Columbus, GA-AL | 61.38 | 203 | Greensboro-High Point, NC | 0.10 |
| 161 | Ann Arbor, MI | (12.05) | 153 | Columbus, IN | (16.01) | 324 | Greenville-Anderson, SC | 51.11 |
| 317 | Anniston-Oxford, AL | 46.81 | 285 | Corpus Christi, TX | 26.98 | 256 | Greenville, NC | 14.06 |
| 2 | Appleton, WI | (71.39) | 11 | Corvallis, OR | (64.13) | 198 | Gulfport-Biloxi-Pascagoula, MS | (0.62) |
| 107 | Athens-Clarke County, GA | (26.04) | 184 | Crestview-Fort Walton Beach, FL | (7.06) | 76 | Hagerstown-Martinsburg, MD-WV | (33.24) |
| 277 | Atlanta, GA | 21.38 | 141 | Cumberland, MD-WV | (17.52) | 364 | Hammond, LA | 108.98 |
| 170 | Atlantic City, NJ | (10.45) | 235 | Dallas (greater), TX | 7.56 | 234 | Hanford-Corcoran, CA | 7.50 |
| 251 | Augusta, GA-SC | 13.31 | 239 | Dallas-Plano-Irving, TX M.D. | 8.60 | 17 | Harrisonburg, VA | (60.34) |
| 112 | Austin-Round Rock, TX | (25.57) | 79 | Dalton, GA | (32.95) | 124 | Hartford, CT | (22.33) |
| 353 | Bakersfield, CA | 75.96 | 41 | Daphne-Fairhope-Foley, AL | (43.52) | 230 | Hilton Head Island, SC | 5.72 |
| 322 | Baltimore, MD | 49.96 | 138 | Davenport, IA-IL | (18.13) | 171 | Hinesville, GA | (10.43) |
| 30 | Bangor, ME | (48.69) | 243 | Dayton, OH | 9.53 | 149 | Homosassa Springs, FL | (16.28) |
| 179 | Barnstable Town, MA | (8.33) | 120 | Decatur, AL | (22.92) | 355 | Hot Springs, AR | 80.34 |
| 299 | Baton Rouge, LA | 36.49 | 167 | Decatur, IL | (11.04) | 228 | Houma, LA | 5.26 |
| 265 | Bay City, MI | 17.08 | 207 | Deltona-Daytona Beach, FL | 0.77 | 313 | Houston, TX | 43.77 |
| 308 | Beaumont-Port Arthur, TX | 40.87 | 246 | Denver-Aurora, CO | 10.00 | 293 | Huntsville, AL | 28.92 |
| 53 | Bend, OR | (40.22) | 127 | Des Moines-West Des Moines, IA | (21.92) | 56 | Idaho Falls, ID | (38.94) |
| 199 | Billings, MT | (0.58) | 346 | Detroit (greater), MI | 69.33 | NA | Indianapolis, IN** | NA |
| 67 | Binghamton, NY | (35.19) | 368 | Detroit-Dearborn-Livonia, MI M.D. | 205.58 | 105 | Iowa City, IA | (26.51) |
| 330 | Birmingham-Hoover, AL | 53.97 | 253 | Dothan, AL | 13.71 | 282 | Jacksonville, FL | 25.54 |
| 196 | Bismarck, ND | (1.09) | 209 | Dover, DE | 1.21 | 266 | Jackson, MI | 17.24 |
| 39 | Blacksburg, VA | (43.68) | 24 | Dubuque, IA | (55.37) | 302 | Jackson, MS | 36.76 |
| 132 | Bloomington, IL | (20.16) | 130 | Duluth, MN-WI | (20.68) | 351 | Jackson, TN | 74.20 |
| 123 | Bloomington, IN | (22.57) | 19 | Dutchess-Putnam, NY M.D. | (59.60) | 95 | Janesville, WI | (29.34) |
| 29 | Bloomsburg-Berwick, PA | (50.37) | 158 | East Stroudsburg, PA | (12.98) | 38 | Jefferson City, MO | (45.72) |
| 69 | Boise City, ID | (35.06) | 14 | Eau Claire, WI | (61.36) | 115 | Johnson City, TN | (24.88) |
| 117 | Boston (greater), MA-NH | (24.29) | 160 | El Centro, CA | (12.29) | 94 | Johnstown, PA | (29.74) |
| 214 | Boston, MA M.D. | 2.26 | 81 | El Paso, TX | (32.20) | 225 | Jonesboro, AR | 5.04 |
| 87 | Boulder, CO | (30.84) | 23 | Elgin, IL M.D. | (55.68) | 202 | Joplin, MO | (0.08) |
| 72 | Bowling Green, KY | (34.34) | 13 | Elizabethtown-Fort Knox, KY | (61.50) | 135 | Kahului-Wailuku-Lahaina, HI | (18.77) |
| 168 | Bremerton-Silverdale, WA | (11.00) | 8 | Elmira, NY | (66.62) | 190 | Kankakee, IL | (2.50) |
| 60 | Bridgeport-Stamford, CT | (37.83) | 90 | Erie, PA | (30.60) | 314 | Kansas City, MO-KS | 44.34 |
| 100 | Brownsville-Harlingen, TX | (28.27) | 136 | Eugene, OR | (18.28) | 106 | Kennewick-Richland, WA | (26.24) |
| NA | Brunswick, GA** | NA | 327 | Fairbanks, AK | 52.86 | 114 | Kingsport, TN-VA | (25.04) |
| 205 | Buffalo-Niagara Falls, NY | 0.42 | 116 | Fargo, ND-MN | (24.86) | 20 | Kingston, NY | (58.55) |
| 164 | Burlington, NC | (11.20) | 280 | Farmington, NM | 23.01 | 189 | Knoxville, TN | (2.88) |
| 45 | California-Lexington Park, MD | (42.59) | 163 | Fayetteville-Springdale, AR-MO | (11.51) | 125 | Kokomo, IN | (22.19) |
| 44 | Cambridge-Newton, MA M.D. | (43.01) | 325 | Fayetteville, NC | 51.39 | 18 | La Crosse, WI-MN | (59.88) |
| 175 | Camden, NJ M.D. | (10.00) | 113 | Flagstaff, AZ | (25.38) | 92 | Lafayette, IN | (29.97) |
| 177 | Canton, OH | (8.75) | 363 | Flint, MI | 108.03 | 241 | Lafayette, LA | 8.84 |
| 147 | Cape Coral-Fort Myers, FL | (16.41) | 221 | Florence-Muscle Shoals, AL | 4.15 | 356 | Lake Charles, LA | 81.93 |
| 250 | Cape Girardeau, MO-IL | 12.86 | 296 | Florence, SC | 32.62 | 28 | Lake Co.-Kenosha Co., IL-WI M.D. | (51.02) |
| 128 | Carbondale-Marion, IL | (21.88) | 34 | Fond du Lac, WI | (47.59) | 152 | Lake Havasu City-Kingman, AZ | (16.02) |
| 73 | Carson City, NV | (34.04) | 50 | Fort Collins, CO | (41.57) | 183 | Lakeland, FL | (7.27) |
| 61 | Casper, WY | (37.66) | 270 | Fort Lauderdale, FL M.D. | 18.24 | 31 | Lancaster, PA | (48.37) |
| 70 | Cedar Rapids, IA | (34.81) | 197 | Fort Smith, AR-OK | (0.71) | 252 | Lansing-East Lansing, MI | 13.52 |
| 33 | Chambersburg-Waynesboro, PA | (47.77) | 218 | Fort Wayne, IN | 3.12 | 162 | Laredo, TX | (11.73) |
| 233 | Champaign-Urbana, IL | 7.26 | 232 | Fort Worth-Arlington, TX M.D. | 6.01 | 176 | Las Cruces, NM | (8.78) |
| 245 | Charleston-North Charleston, SC | 9.74 | 332 | Fresno, CA | 55.28 | 345 | Las Vegas-Henderson, NV | 69.18 |
| 210 | Charlotte-Concord-Gastonia, NC-SC | 1.36 | 357 | Gadsden, AL | 82.85 | 174 | Lawrence, KS | (10.01) |
| 57 | Charlottesville, VA | (38.78) | 248 | Gainesville, FL | 10.74 | 358 | Lawton, OK | 85.43 |
| 269 | Chattanooga, TN-GA | 18.16 | 77 | Gainesville, GA | (33.23) | 21 | Lebanon, PA | (58.52) |

Note: All listings are for Metropolitan Statistical Areas (M.S.A.s) except for those ending with "M.D." Listings with "M.D." are Metropolitan Divisions which are smaller parts of eleven large M.S.A.s. See explanatory note at beginning of metropolitan area section.

| RANK | METROPOLITAN AREA | SCORE | RANK | METROPOLITAN AREA | SCORE | RANK | METROPOLITAN AREA | SCORE |
|---|---|---|---|---|---|---|---|---|
| 75 | Lewiston-Auburn, ME | (33.56) | 291 | Omaha-Council Bluffs, NE-IA | 28.82 | 16 | Sheboygan, WI | (61.06) |
| 43 | Lewiston, ID-WA | (43.35) | 286 | Orlando, FL | 27.08 | 139 | Sherman-Denison, TX | (17.86) |
| 227 | Lexington-Fayette, KY | 5.23 | 5 | Oshkosh-Neenah, WI | (69.98) | 289 | Shreveport-Bossier City, LA | 28.10 |
| 236 | Lima, OH | 7.62 | 63 | Owensboro, KY | (37.45) | 25 | Silver Spring-Frederick, MD M.D. | (55.08) |
| 155 | Lincoln, NE | (14.93) | 66 | Oxnard-Thousand Oaks, CA | (35.79) | 122 | Sioux City, IA-NE-SD | (22.82) |
| 350 | Little Rock, AR | 73.83 | 263 | Palm Bay-Melbourne, FL | 15.75 | 169 | Sioux Falls, SD | (10.66) |
| 6 | Logan, UT-ID | (69.94) | 276 | Panama City, FL | 21.29 | 244 | South Bend-Mishawaka, IN-MI | 9.60 |
| 262 | Longview, TX | 15.46 | 96 | Parkersburg-Vienna, WV | (28.94) | 257 | Spartanburg, SC | 14.28 |
| 304 | Longview, WA | 37.96 | 292 | Pensacola, FL | 28.85 | 335 | Spokane, WA | 57.48 |
| 259 | Los Angeles County, CA M.D. | 15.01 | 159 | Peoria, IL | (12.38) | 366 | Springfield, IL | 124.08 |
| 212 | Los Angeles (greater), CA | 1.87 | 281 | Philadelphia (greater) PA-NJ-MD-DE | 24.62 | 298 | Springfield, MA | 33.36 |
| NA | Louisville, KY-IN** | NA | 367 | Philadelphia, PA M.D. | 127.16 | 321 | Springfield, MO | 49.54 |
| 310 | Lubbock, TX | 41.89 | NA | Phoenix-Mesa-Scottsdale, AZ** | NA | 284 | Springfield, OH | 26.65 |
| 41 | Lynchburg, VA | (43.52) | 82 | Pittsburgh, PA | (32.17) | 3 | State College, PA | (71.21) |
| 328 | Macon, GA | 52.89 | 165 | Pittsfield, MA | (11.19) | 51 | Staunton-Waynesboro, VA | (41.55) |
| 341 | Madera, CA | 62.04 | 68 | Pocatello, ID | (35.14) | 352 | Stockton-Lodi, CA | 74.47 |
| 49 | Madison, WI | (41.91) | 118 | Port St. Lucie, FL | (24.00) | 65 | St. Cloud, MN | (36.22) |
| 133 | Manchester-Nashua, NH | (19.32) | 143 | Portland-Vancouver, OR-WA | (17.24) | NA | St. George, UT** | NA |
| 85 | Manhattan, KS | (31.13) | 32 | Portland, ME | (48.19) | 249 | St. Joseph, MO-KS | 12.51 |
| 83 | Mankato-North Mankato, MN | (31.79) | 48 | Prescott, AZ | (41.96) | 268 | St. Louis, MO-IL | 17.50 |
| 182 | Mansfield, OH | (7.31) | 188 | Providence-Warwick, RI-MA | (5.42) | 338 | Sumter, SC | 60.06 |
| 156 | McAllen-Edinburg-Mission, TX | (14.87) | 12 | Provo-Orem, UT | (61.67) | 103 | Syracuse, NY | (27.16) |
| 148 | Medford, OR | (16.31) | 360 | Pueblo, CO | 95.50 | 316 | Tacoma, WA M.D. | 45.00 |
| 365 | Memphis, TN-MS-AR | 109.53 | 36 | Punta Gorda, FL | (46.48) | 305 | Tallahassee, FL | 38.54 |
| 343 | Merced, CA | 64.02 | 54 | Racine, WI | (39.92) | 193 | Tampa-St Petersburg, FL | (1.53) |
| 301 | Miami (greater), FL | 36.73 | 62 | Raleigh, NC | (37.63) | 145 | Terre Haute, IN | (16.88) |
| 339 | Miami-Dade County, FL M.D. | 60.38 | 220 | Rapid City, SD | 3.72 | 297 | Texarkana, TX-AR | 33.28 |
| 110 | Midland, TX | (25.73) | 111 | Reading, PA | (25.58) | 22 | The Villages, FL | (57.41) |
| 318 | Milwaukee, WI | 46.86 | 348 | Redding, CA | 70.43 | 300 | Toledo, OH | 36.63 |
| 142 | Minneapolis-St. Paul, MN-WI | (17.42) | 238 | Reno, NV | 8.24 | 229 | Topeka, KS | 5.37 |
| 108 | Missoula, MT | (25.88) | 144 | Richmond, VA | (17.03) | 267 | Trenton, NJ | 17.25 |
| 347 | Mobile, AL | 69.60 | 271 | Riverside-San Bernardino, CA | 18.93 | 294 | Tucson, AZ | 30.19 |
| 342 | Modesto, CA | 62.53 | 119 | Roanoke, VA | (23.60) | 331 | Tulsa, OK | 55.27 |
| 326 | Monroe, LA | 52.13 | 26 | Rochester, MN | (55.01) | 261 | Tuscaloosa, AL | 15.29 |
| 222 | Monroe, MI | 4.75 | 129 | Rochester, NY | (20.85) | 151 | Tyler, TX | (16.13) |
| 15 | Montgomery County, PA M.D. | (61.19) | 334 | Rockford, IL | 56.01 | 86 | Utica-Rome, NY | (30.85) |
| 91 | Morgantown, WV | (30.12) | 45 | Rockingham County, NH M.D. | (42.59) | 336 | Vallejo-Fairfield, CA | 58.11 |
| 121 | Morristown, TN | (22.86) | 307 | Rocky Mount, NC | 40.33 | 278 | Victoria, TX | 22.67 |
| 208 | Mount Vernon-Anacortes, WA | 0.79 | 231 | Rome, GA | 5.98 | 279 | Vineland-Bridgeton, NJ | 22.72 |
| 97 | Muncie, IN | (28.48) | 258 | Sacramento, CA | 14.67 | 201 | Virginia Beach-Norfolk, VA-NC | (0.52) |
| 320 | Muskegon, MI | 49.33 | 362 | Saginaw, MI | 103.88 | NA | Visalia-Porterville, CA** | NA |
| 315 | Myrtle Beach, SC-NC | 44.90 | 154 | Salem, OR | (15.65) | 195 | Waco, TX | (1.10) |
| 99 | Napa, CA | (28.42) | 319 | Salinas, CA | 48.78 | 191 | Warner Robins, GA | (2.36) |
| 58 | Naples-Marco Island, FL | (38.73) | 237 | Salisbury, MD-DE | 7.71 | 101 | Warren-Troy, MI M.D. | (27.71) |
| 264 | Nashville-Davidson, TN | 15.94 | 290 | Salt Lake City, UT | 28.65 | 150 | Washington (greater) DC-VA-MD-WV | (16.18) |
| 10 | Nassau-Suffolk, NY M.D. | (65.41) | 223 | San Angelo, TX | 4.79 | 185 | Washington, DC-VA-MD-WV M.D. | (5.73) |
| 137 | New Bern, NC | (18.25) | 295 | San Antonio, TX | 30.49 | 4 | Watertown-Fort Drum, NY | (70.61) |
| 200 | New Haven-Milford, CT | (0.57) | 178 | San Diego, CA | (8.40) | 7 | Wausau, WI | (66.81) |
| 344 | New Orleans, LA | 69.13 | 337 | San Francisco (greater), CA | 58.76 | 260 | West Palm Beach, FL M.D. | 15.25 |
| 109 | New York (greater), NY-NJ-PA | (25.87) | 309 | San Francisco-Redwood, CA M.D. | 41.47 | 223 | Wichita Falls, TX | 4.79 |
| 126 | New York-Jersey City, NY-NJ M.D. | (21.95) | 210 | San Jose, CA | 1.36 | 306 | Wichita, KS | 40.10 |
| 215 | Newark, NJ-PA M.D. | 2.28 | 157 | San Luis Obispo, CA | (13.42) | 74 | Williamsport, PA | (33.77) |
| 288 | Niles-Benton Harbor, MI | 27.27 | 71 | San Rafael, CA M.D. | (34.70) | 253 | Wilmington, DE-MD-NJ M.D. | 13.71 |
| 192 | North Port-Sarasota-Bradenton, FL | (1.81) | 247 | Santa Cruz-Watsonville, CA | 10.56 | 217 | Wilmington, NC | 2.99 |
| 172 | Norwich-New London, CT | (10.40) | 165 | Santa Maria-Santa Barbara, CA | (11.19) | 80 | Winchester, VA-WV | (32.83) |
| 354 | Oakland-Hayward, CA M.D. | 77.91 | 102 | Santa Rosa, CA | (27.41) | 216 | Winston-Salem, NC | 2.91 |
| 206 | Ocala, FL | 0.45 | 273 | Savannah, GA | 19.58 | 146 | Worcester, MA-CT | (16.61) |
| 78 | Ocean City, NJ | (32.96) | 88 | Scranton--Wilkes-Barre, PA | (30.66) | 287 | Yakima, WA | 27.16 |
| 329 | Odessa, TX | 53.15 | 275 | Seattle (greater), WA | 21.28 | 64 | York-Hanover, PA | (36.42) |
| NA | Ogden-Clearfield, UT** | NA | 255 | Seattle-Bellevue-Everett, WA M.D. | 14.04 | 274 | Yuba City, CA | 19.96 |
| 333 | Oklahoma City, OK | 55.60 | 84 | Sebastian-Vero Beach, FL | (31.68) | 242 | Yuma, AZ | 9.39 |
| 104 | Olympia, WA | (27.10) | 213 | Sebring, FL | 1.97 | | | |

Source: CQ Press using reported data from the F.B.I. "Crime in the United States 2013"
*Includes murder, rape, robbery, aggravated assault, burglary, and motor vehicle theft. A negative score (in parentheses) indicates a composite crime number below the national rate, a positive number is above the national rate. **Not available.

# 2014 Metropolitan Crime Rate Rankings* (continued)

| RANK | METROPOLITAN AREA | SCORE | RANK | METROPOLITAN AREA | SCORE | RANK | METROPOLITAN AREA | SCORE |
|---|---|---|---|---|---|---|---|---|
| 1 | Glens Falls, NY | (72.65) | 65 | St. Cloud, MN | (36.22) | 129 | Rochester, NY | (20.85) |
| 2 | Appleton, WI | (71.39) | 66 | Oxnard-Thousand Oaks, CA | (35.79) | 130 | Duluth, MN-WI | (20.68) |
| 3 | State College, PA | (71.21) | 67 | Binghamton, NY | (35.19) | 131 | College Station-Bryan, TX | (20.35) |
| 4 | Watertown-Fort Drum, NY | (70.61) | 68 | Pocatello, ID | (35.14) | 132 | Bloomington, IL | (20.16) |
| 5 | Oshkosh-Neenah, WI | (69.98) | 69 | Boise City, ID | (35.06) | 133 | Manchester-Nashua, NH | (19.32) |
| 6 | Logan, UT-ID | (69.94) | 70 | Cedar Rapids, IA | (34.81) | 134 | Grand Island, NE | (19.00) |
| 7 | Wausau, WI | (66.81) | 71 | San Rafael, CA M.D. | (34.70) | 135 | Kahului-Wailuku-Lahaina, HI | (18.77) |
| 8 | Elmira, NY | (66.62) | 72 | Bowling Green, KY | (34.34) | 136 | Eugene, OR | (18.28) |
| 9 | Gettysburg, PA | (66.21) | 73 | Carson City, NV | (34.04) | 137 | New Bern, NC | (18.25) |
| 10 | Nassau-Suffolk, NY M.D. | (65.41) | 74 | Williamsport, PA | (33.77) | 138 | Davenport, IA-IL | (18.13) |
| 11 | Corvallis, OR | (64.13) | 75 | Lewiston-Auburn, ME | (33.56) | 139 | Sherman-Denison, TX | (17.86) |
| 12 | Provo-Orem, UT | (61.67) | 76 | Hagerstown-Martinsburg, MD-WV | (33.24) | 140 | Abilene, TX | (17.84) |
| 13 | Elizabethtown-Fort Knox, KY | (61.50) | 77 | Gainesville, GA | (33.23) | 141 | Cumberland, MD-WV | (17.52) |
| 14 | Eau Claire, WI | (61.36) | 78 | Ocean City, NJ | (32.96) | 142 | Minneapolis-St. Paul, MN-WI | (17.42) |
| 15 | Montgomery County, PA M.D. | (61.19) | 79 | Dalton, GA | (32.95) | 143 | Portland-Vancouver, OR-WA | (17.24) |
| 16 | Sheboygan, WI | (61.06) | 80 | Winchester, VA-WV | (32.83) | 144 | Richmond, VA | (17.03) |
| 17 | Harrisonburg, VA | (60.34) | 81 | El Paso, TX | (32.20) | 145 | Terre Haute, IN | (16.88) |
| 18 | La Crosse, WI-MN | (59.88) | 82 | Pittsburgh, PA | (32.17) | 146 | Worcester, MA-CT | (16.61) |
| 19 | Dutchess-Putnam, NY M.D. | (59.60) | 83 | Mankato-North Mankato, MN | (31.79) | 147 | Cape Coral-Fort Myers, FL | (16.41) |
| 20 | Kingston, NY | (58.55) | 84 | Sebastian-Vero Beach, FL | (31.68) | 148 | Medford, OR | (16.31) |
| 21 | Lebanon, PA | (58.52) | 85 | Manhattan, KS | (31.13) | 149 | Homosassa Springs, FL | (16.28) |
| 22 | The Villages, FL | (57.41) | 86 | Utica-Rome, NY | (30.85) | 150 | Washington (greater) DC-VA-MD-WV | (16.18) |
| 23 | Elgin, IL M.D. | (55.68) | 87 | Boulder, CO | (30.84) | 151 | Tyler, TX | (16.13) |
| 24 | Dubuque, IA | (55.37) | 88 | Scranton--Wilkes-Barre, PA | (30.66) | 152 | Lake Havasu City-Kingman, AZ | (16.02) |
| 25 | Silver Spring-Frederick, MD M.D. | (55.08) | 89 | Great Falls, MT | (30.62) | 153 | Columbus, IN | (16.01) |
| 26 | Rochester, MN | (55.01) | 90 | Erie, PA | (30.60) | 154 | Salem, OR | (15.65) |
| 27 | Green Bay, WI | (52.78) | 91 | Morgantown, WV | (30.12) | 155 | Lincoln, NE | (14.93) |
| 28 | Lake Co.-Kenosha Co., IL-WI M.D. | (51.02) | 92 | Lafayette, IN | (29.97) | 156 | McAllen-Edinburg-Mission, TX | (14.87) |
| 29 | Bloomsburg-Berwick, PA | (50.37) | 93 | Grand Forks, ND-MN | (29.76) | 157 | San Luis Obispo, CA | (13.42) |
| 30 | Bangor, ME | (48.69) | 94 | Johnstown, PA | (29.74) | 158 | East Stroudsburg, PA | (12.98) |
| 31 | Lancaster, PA | (48.37) | 95 | Janesville, WI | (29.34) | 159 | Peoria, IL | (12.38) |
| 32 | Portland, ME | (48.19) | 96 | Parkersburg-Vienna, WV | (28.94) | 160 | El Centro, CA | (12.29) |
| 33 | Chambersburg-Waynesboro, PA | (47.77) | 97 | Greeley, CO | (28.48) | 161 | Ann Arbor, MI | (12.05) |
| 34 | Fond du Lac, WI | (47.59) | 97 | Muncie, IN | (28.48) | 162 | Laredo, TX | (11.73) |
| 35 | Altoona, PA | (46.96) | 99 | Napa, CA | (28.42) | 163 | Fayetteville-Springdale, AR-MO | (11.51) |
| 36 | Punta Gorda, FL | (46.48) | 100 | Brownsville-Harlingen, TX | (28.27) | 164 | Burlington, NC | (11.20) |
| 37 | Cheyenne, WY | (46.18) | 101 | Warren-Troy, MI M.D. | (27.71) | 165 | Pittsfield, MA | (11.19) |
| 38 | Jefferson City, MO | (45.72) | 102 | Santa Rosa, CA | (27.41) | 165 | Santa Maria-Santa Barbara, CA | (11.19) |
| 39 | Blacksburg, VA | (43.68) | 103 | Syracuse, NY | (27.16) | 167 | Decatur, IL | (11.04) |
| 40 | Albany, OR | (43.60) | 104 | Olympia, WA | (27.10) | 168 | Bremerton-Silverdale, WA | (11.00) |
| 41 | Daphne-Fairhope-Foley, AL | (43.52) | 105 | Iowa City, IA | (26.51) | 169 | Sioux Falls, SD | (10.66) |
| 41 | Lynchburg, VA | (43.52) | 106 | Kennewick-Richland, WA | (26.24) | 170 | Atlantic City, NJ | (10.45) |
| 43 | Lewiston, ID-WA | (43.35) | 107 | Athens-Clarke County, GA | (26.04) | 171 | Hinesville, GA | (10.43) |
| 44 | Cambridge-Newton, MA M.D. | (43.01) | 108 | Missoula, MT | (25.88) | 172 | Norwich-New London, CT | (10.40) |
| 45 | California-Lexington Park, MD | (42.59) | 109 | New York (greater), NY-NJ-PA | (25.87) | 173 | Cleveland, TN | (10.39) |
| 45 | Rockingham County, NH M.D. | (42.59) | 110 | Midland, TX | (25.73) | 174 | Lawrence, KS | (10.01) |
| 47 | Ames, IA | (42.39) | 111 | Reading, PA | (25.58) | 175 | Camden, NJ M.D. | (10.00) |
| 48 | Prescott, AZ | (41.96) | 112 | Austin-Round Rock, TX | (25.57) | 176 | Las Cruces, NM | (8.78) |
| 49 | Madison, WI | (41.91) | 113 | Flagstaff, AZ | (25.38) | 177 | Canton, OH | (8.75) |
| 50 | Fort Collins, CO | (41.57) | 114 | Kingsport, TN-VA | (25.04) | 178 | San Diego, CA | (8.40) |
| 51 | Staunton-Waynesboro, VA | (41.55) | 115 | Johnson City, TN | (24.88) | 179 | Barnstable Town, MA | (8.33) |
| 52 | Anaheim-Santa Ana-Irvine, CA M.D. | (40.38) | 116 | Fargo, ND-MN | (24.86) | 180 | Columbia, MO | (8.12) |
| 53 | Bend, OR | (40.22) | 117 | Boston (greater), MA-NH | (24.29) | 181 | Grand Rapids-Wyoming, MI | (7.49) |
| 54 | Racine, WI | (39.92) | 118 | Port St. Lucie, FL | (24.00) | 182 | Mansfield, OH | (7.31) |
| 55 | Allentown, PA-NJ | (39.14) | 119 | Roanoke, VA | (23.60) | 183 | Lakeland, FL | (7.27) |
| 56 | Idaho Falls, ID | (38.94) | 120 | Decatur, AL | (22.92) | 184 | Crestview-Fort Walton Beach, FL | (7.06) |
| 57 | Charlottesville, VA | (38.78) | 121 | Morristown, TN | (22.86) | 185 | Washington, DC-VA-MD-WV M.D. | (5.73) |
| 58 | Naples-Marco Island, FL | (38.73) | 122 | Sioux City, IA-NE-SD | (22.82) | 186 | Coeur d'Alene, ID | (5.57) |
| 59 | Albany-Schenectady-Troy, NY | (38.28) | 123 | Bloomington, IN | (22.57) | 187 | Grants Pass, OR | (5.46) |
| 60 | Bridgeport-Stamford, CT | (37.83) | 124 | Hartford, CT | (22.33) | 188 | Providence-Warwick, RI-MA | (5.42) |
| 61 | Casper, WY | (37.66) | 125 | Kokomo, IN | (22.19) | 189 | Knoxville, TN | (2.88) |
| 62 | Raleigh, NC | (37.63) | 126 | New York-Jersey City, NY-NJ M.D. | (21.95) | 190 | Kankakee, IL | (2.50) |
| 63 | Owensboro, KY | (37.45) | 127 | Des Moines-West Des Moines, IA | (21.92) | 191 | Warner Robins, GA | (2.36) |
| 64 | York-Hanover, PA | (36.42) | 128 | Carbondale-Marion, IL | (21.88) | 192 | North Port-Sarasota-Bradenton, FL | (1.81) |

Note: All listings are for Metropolitan Statistical Areas (M.S.A.s) except for those ending with "M.D." Listings with "M.D." are Metropolitan Divisions which are smaller parts of eleven large M.S.A.s. See explanatory note at beginning of metropolitan area section.

| RANK | METROPOLITAN AREA | SCORE | RANK | METROPOLITAN AREA | SCORE | RANK | METROPOLITAN AREA | SCORE |
|---|---|---|---|---|---|---|---|---|
| 193 | Tampa-St Petersburg, FL | (1.53) | 255 | Seattle-Bellevue-Everett, WA M.D. | 14.04 | 317 | Anniston-Oxford, AL | 46.81 |
| 194 | Cincinnati, OH-KY-IN | (1.25) | 256 | Greenville, NC | 14.06 | 318 | Milwaukee, WI | 46.86 |
| 195 | Waco, TX | (1.10) | 257 | Spartanburg, SC | 14.28 | 319 | Salinas, CA | 48.78 |
| 196 | Bismarck, ND | (1.09) | 258 | Sacramento, CA | 14.67 | 320 | Muskegon, MI | 49.33 |
| 197 | Fort Smith, AR-OK | (0.71) | 259 | Los Angeles County, CA M.D. | 15.01 | 321 | Springfield, MO | 49.54 |
| 198 | Gulfport-Biloxi-Pascagoula, MS | (0.62) | 260 | West Palm Beach, FL M.D. | 15.25 | 322 | Baltimore, MD | 49.96 |
| 199 | Billings, MT | (0.58) | 261 | Tuscaloosa, AL | 15.29 | 323 | Amarillo, TX | 50.99 |
| 200 | New Haven-Milford, CT | (0.57) | 262 | Longview, TX | 15.46 | 324 | Greenville-Anderson, SC | 51.11 |
| 201 | Virginia Beach-Norfolk, VA-NC | (0.52) | 263 | Palm Bay-Melbourne, FL | 15.75 | 325 | Fayetteville, NC | 51.39 |
| 202 | Joplin, MO | (0.08) | 264 | Nashville-Davidson, TN | 15.94 | 326 | Monroe, LA | 52.13 |
| 203 | Greensboro-High Point, NC | 0.10 | 265 | Bay City, MI | 17.08 | 327 | Fairbanks, AK | 52.86 |
| 204 | Akron, OH | 0.40 | 266 | Jackson, MI | 17.24 | 328 | Macon, GA | 52.89 |
| 205 | Buffalo-Niagara Falls, NY | 0.42 | 267 | Trenton, NJ | 17.25 | 329 | Odessa, TX | 53.15 |
| 206 | Ocala, FL | 0.45 | 268 | St. Louis, MO-IL | 17.50 | 330 | Birmingham-Hoover, AL | 53.97 |
| 207 | Deltona-Daytona Beach, FL | 0.77 | 269 | Chattanooga, TN-GA | 18.16 | 331 | Tulsa, OK | 55.27 |
| 208 | Mount Vernon-Anacortes, WA | 0.79 | 270 | Fort Lauderdale, FL M.D. | 18.24 | 332 | Fresno, CA | 55.28 |
| 209 | Dover, DE | 1.21 | 271 | Riverside-San Bernardino, CA | 18.93 | 333 | Oklahoma City, OK | 55.60 |
| 210 | Charlotte-Concord-Gastonia, NC-SC | 1.36 | 272 | Chico, CA | 19.07 | 334 | Rockford, IL | 56.01 |
| 210 | San Jose, CA | 1.36 | 273 | Savannah, GA | 19.58 | 335 | Spokane, WA | 57.48 |
| 212 | Los Angeles (greater), CA | 1.87 | 274 | Yuba City, CA | 19.96 | 336 | Vallejo-Fairfield, CA | 58.11 |
| 213 | Sebring, FL | 1.97 | 275 | Seattle (greater), WA | 21.28 | 337 | San Francisco (greater), CA | 58.76 |
| 214 | Boston, MA M.D. | 2.26 | 276 | Panama City, FL | 21.29 | 338 | Sumter, SC | 60.06 |
| 215 | Newark, NJ-PA M.D. | 2.28 | 277 | Atlanta, GA | 21.38 | 339 | Miami-Dade County, FL M.D. | 60.38 |
| 216 | Winston-Salem, NC | 2.91 | 278 | Victoria, TX | 22.67 | 340 | Columbus, GA-AL | 61.38 |
| 217 | Wilmington, NC | 2.99 | 279 | Vineland-Bridgeton, NJ | 22.72 | 341 | Madera, CA | 62.04 |
| 218 | Fort Wayne, IN | 3.12 | 280 | Farmington, NM | 23.01 | 342 | Modesto, CA | 62.53 |
| 219 | Clarksville, TN-KY | 3.17 | 281 | Philadelphia (greater) PA-NJ-MD-DE | 24.62 | 343 | Merced, CA | 64.02 |
| 220 | Rapid City, SD | 3.72 | 282 | Jacksonville, FL | 25.54 | 344 | New Orleans, LA | 69.13 |
| 221 | Florence-Muscle Shoals, AL | 4.15 | 283 | Gary, IN M.D. | 26.40 | 345 | Las Vegas-Henderson, NV | 69.18 |
| 222 | Monroe, MI | 4.75 | 284 | Springfield, OH | 26.65 | 346 | Detroit (greater), MI | 69.33 |
| 223 | San Angelo, TX | 4.79 | 285 | Corpus Christi, TX | 26.98 | 347 | Mobile, AL | 69.60 |
| 223 | Wichita Falls, TX | 4.79 | 286 | Orlando, FL | 27.08 | 348 | Redding, CA | 70.43 |
| 225 | Jonesboro, AR | 5.04 | 287 | Yakima, WA | 27.16 | 349 | Alexandria, LA | 70.99 |
| 226 | Goldsboro, NC | 5.16 | 288 | Niles-Benton Harbor, MI | 27.27 | 350 | Little Rock, AR | 73.83 |
| 227 | Lexington-Fayette, KY | 5.23 | 289 | Shreveport-Bossier City, LA | 28.10 | 351 | Jackson, TN | 74.20 |
| 228 | Houma, LA | 5.26 | 290 | Salt Lake City, UT | 28.65 | 352 | Stockton-Lodi, CA | 74.47 |
| 229 | Topeka, KS | 5.37 | 291 | Omaha-Council Bluffs, NE-IA | 28.82 | 353 | Bakersfield, CA | 75.96 |
| 230 | Hilton Head Island, SC | 5.72 | 292 | Pensacola, FL | 28.85 | 354 | Oakland-Hayward, CA M.D. | 77.91 |
| 231 | Rome, GA | 5.98 | 293 | Huntsville, AL | 28.92 | 355 | Hot Springs, AR | 80.34 |
| 232 | Fort Worth-Arlington, TX M.D. | 6.01 | 294 | Tucson, AZ | 30.19 | 356 | Lake Charles, LA | 81.93 |
| 233 | Champaign-Urbana, IL | 7.26 | 295 | San Antonio, TX | 30.49 | 357 | Gadsden, AL | 82.85 |
| 234 | Hanford-Corcoran, CA | 7.50 | 296 | Florence, SC | 32.62 | 358 | Lawton, OK | 85.43 |
| 235 | Dallas (greater), TX | 7.56 | 297 | Texarkana, TX-AR | 33.28 | 359 | Albuquerque, NM | 87.24 |
| 236 | Lima, OH | 7.62 | 298 | Springfield, MA | 33.36 | 360 | Pueblo, CO | 95.50 |
| 237 | Salisbury, MD-DE | 7.71 | 299 | Baton Rouge, LA | 36.49 | 361 | Anchorage, AK | 101.36 |
| 238 | Reno, NV | 8.24 | 300 | Toledo, OH | 36.63 | 362 | Saginaw, MI | 103.88 |
| 239 | Dallas-Plano-Irving, TX M.D. | 8.60 | 301 | Miami (greater), FL | 36.73 | 363 | Flint, MI | 108.03 |
| 240 | Grand Junction, CO | 8.61 | 302 | Jackson, MS | 36.76 | 364 | Hammond, LA | 108.98 |
| 241 | Lafayette, LA | 8.84 | 303 | Columbia, SC | 37.55 | 365 | Memphis, TN-MS-AR | 109.53 |
| 242 | Yuma, AZ | 9.39 | 304 | Longview, WA | 37.96 | 366 | Springfield, IL | 124.08 |
| 243 | Dayton, OH | 9.53 | 305 | Tallahassee, FL | 38.54 | 367 | Philadelphia, PA M.D. | 127.16 |
| 244 | South Bend-Mishawaka, IN-MI | 9.60 | 306 | Wichita, KS | 40.10 | 368 | Detroit-Dearborn-Livonia, MI M.D. | 205.58 |
| 245 | Charleston-North Charleston, SC | 9.74 | 307 | Rocky Mount, NC | 40.33 | NA | Brunswick, GA** | NA |
| 246 | Denver-Aurora, CO | 10.00 | 308 | Beaumont-Port Arthur, TX | 40.87 | NA | Chicago (greater), IL-IN-WI** | NA |
| 247 | Santa Cruz-Watsonville, CA | 10.56 | 309 | San Francisco-Redwood, CA M.D. | 41.47 | NA | Chicago-Naperville, IL M.D.** | NA |
| 248 | Gainesville, FL | 10.74 | 310 | Lubbock, TX | 41.89 | NA | Indianapolis, IN** | NA |
| 249 | St. Joseph, MO-KS | 12.51 | 311 | Colorado Springs, CO | 41.98 | NA | Louisville, KY-IN** | NA |
| 250 | Cape Girardeau, MO-IL | 12.86 | 312 | Albany, GA | 42.40 | NA | Ogden-Clearfield, UT** | NA |
| 251 | Augusta, GA-SC | 13.31 | 313 | Houston, TX | 43.77 | NA | Phoenix-Mesa-Scottsdale, AZ** | NA |
| 252 | Lansing-East Lansing, MI | 13.52 | 314 | Kansas City, MO-KS | 44.34 | NA | St. George, UT** | NA |
| 253 | Dothan, AL | 13.71 | 315 | Myrtle Beach, SC-NC | 44.90 | NA | Visalia-Porterville, CA** | NA |
| 253 | Wilmington, DE-MD-NJ M.D. | 13.71 | 316 | Tacoma, WA M.D. | 45.00 | | | |

Source: CQ Press using reported data from the F.B.I. "Crime in the United States 2013"
*Includes murder, rape, robbery, aggravated assault, burglary, and motor vehicle theft.  A negative score (in parentheses) indicates a composite crime number below the national rate, a positive number is above the national rate. **Not available.

# 2014 City Crime Rate Rankings*

| RANK | CITY | SCORE | RANK | CITY | SCORE | RANK | CITY | SCORE |
|---|---|---|---|---|---|---|---|---|
| 181 | Abilene, TX | (1.23) | 172 | Chino, CA | (5.43) | 117 | Fullerton, CA | (30.62) |
| 388 | Akron, OH | 135.00 | 112 | Chula Vista, CA | (32.18) | 262 | Gainesville, FL | 32.54 |
| 129 | Alameda, CA | (25.39) | 210 | Cicero, IL | 9.78 | 127 | Garden Grove, CA | (26.32) |
| 368 | Albany, GA | 106.12 | 419 | Cincinnati, OH | 220.76 | 161 | Garland, TX | (9.30) |
| 298 | Albany, NY | 55.65 | 244 | Citrus Heights, CA | 23.22 | 440 | Gary, IN | 418.85 |
| 379 | Albuquerque, NM | 117.92 | 6 | Clarkstown, NY | (80.65) | 16 | Gilbert, AZ | (74.03) |
| 92 | Alexandria, VA | (41.00) | 233 | Clarksville, TN | 19.75 | 264 | Glendale, AZ | 34.17 |
| 106 | Alhambra, CA | (35.86) | 258 | Clearwater, FL | 28.60 | 22 | Glendale, CA | (68.40) |
| 334 | Allentown, PA | 78.88 | 436 | Cleveland, OH | 331.31 | 199 | Grand Prairie, TX | 6.89 |
| 13 | Allen, TX | (76.37) | 63 | Clifton, NJ | (50.74) | 304 | Grand Rapids, MI | 60.82 |
| 351 | Amarillo, TX | 90.11 | 202 | Clinton Twnshp, MI | 7.84 | 28 | Greece, NY | (65.23) |
| 9 | Amherst, NY | (78.19) | 136 | Clovis, CA | (22.17) | 245 | Greeley, CO | 23.87 |
| 200 | Anaheim, CA | 7.35 | 110 | College Station, TX | (33.29) | 180 | Green Bay, WI | (1.37) |
| 364 | Anchorage, AK | 104.21 | 7 | Colonie, NY | (79.58) | 281 | Greensboro, NC | 44.54 |
| 113 | Ann Arbor, MI | (31.96) | 316 | Colorado Springs, CO | 67.59 | 291 | Greenville, NC | 51.40 |
| 406 | Antioch, CA | 166.77 | 218 | Columbia, MO | 12.32 | 307 | Gresham, OR | 62.40 |
| 4 | Arlington Heights, IL | (83.74) | 355 | Columbia, SC | 93.98 | 88 | Hamilton Twnshp, NJ | (43.40) |
| 241 | Arlington, TX | 22.53 | 354 | Columbus, GA | 93.25 | 372 | Hammond, IN | 110.91 |
| 74 | Arvada, CO | (47.76) | 430 | Compton, CA | 248.62 | 223 | Hampton, VA | 16.82 |
| 166 | Athens-Clarke, GA | (8.67) | 197 | Concord, CA | 6.36 | 410 | Hartford, CT | 173.21 |
| 421 | Atlanta, GA | 222.14 | 131 | Concord, NC | (24.64) | 329 | Hawthorne, CA | 74.42 |
| 277 | Aurora, CO | 41.72 | 53 | Coral Springs, FL | (54.06) | 326 | Hayward, CA | 73.31 |
| 98 | Aurora, IL | (38.65) | 121 | Corona, CA | (29.92) | 337 | Hemet, CA | 80.51 |
| 183 | Austin, TX | (0.82) | 269 | Corpus Christi, TX | 37.15 | 107 | Henderson, NV | (35.12) |
| 336 | Bakersfield, CA | 79.86 | 145 | Costa Mesa, CA | (17.44) | 212 | Hesperia, CA | 10.03 |
| 191 | Baldwin Park, CA | 2.35 | 102 | Cranston, RI | (37.59) | 169 | Hialeah, FL | (5.77) |
| 434 | Baltimore, MD | 300.20 | 378 | Dallas, TX | 117.88 | 253 | High Point, NC | 27.07 |
| 398 | Baton Rouge, LA | 152.59 | 96 | Daly City, CA | (39.01) | 70 | Hillsboro, OR | (48.39) |
| 396 | Beaumont, TX | 144.65 | 78 | Danbury, CT | (46.08) | 324 | Hollywood, FL | 71.73 |
| 39 | Beaverton, OR | (60.09) | 306 | Davenport, IA | 61.44 | 51 | Hoover, AL | (54.52) |
| 72 | Bellevue, WA | (48.35) | 158 | Davie, FL | (10.94) | 389 | Houston, TX | 135.27 |
| 215 | Bellflower, CA | 10.84 | 416 | Dayton, OH | 192.65 | 80 | Huntington Beach, CA | (45.20) |
| 85 | Bend, OR | (43.70) | 196 | Dearborn, MI | 5.59 | 371 | Huntsville, AL | 107.73 |
| 299 | Berkeley, CA | 56.78 | 208 | Decatur, IL | 9.15 | 315 | Independence, MO | 67.29 |
| 147 | Bethlehem, PA | (16.34) | 198 | Deerfield Beach, FL | 6.46 | 418 | Indianapolis, IN | 213.59 |
| 256 | Billings, MT | 27.92 | 155 | Denton, TX | (12.61) | 308 | Indio, CA | 64.36 |
| 433 | Birmingham, AL | 296.02 | 350 | Denver, CO | 90.08 | 352 | Inglewood, CA | 90.93 |
| 221 | Bloomington, IL | 14.82 | 290 | Des Moines, IA | 50.23 | 11 | Irvine, CA | (77.80) |
| 173 | Bloomington, IN | (4.50) | 441 | Detroit, MI | 495.29 | 109 | Irving, TX | (33.96) |
| 50 | Bloomington, MN | (54.62) | 261 | Downey, CA | 31.88 | 313 | Jacksonville, FL | 66.85 |
| 101 | Boca Raton, FL | (37.71) | 220 | Duluth, MN | 13.38 | 428 | Jackson, MS | 243.05 |
| 141 | Boise, ID | (21.07) | 193 | Edinburg, TX | 3.05 | 274 | Jersey City, NJ | 38.35 |
| 302 | Boston, MA | 59.76 | 42 | Edison Twnshp, NJ | (59.26) | 19 | Johns Creek, GA | (69.74) |
| 105 | Boulder, CO | (36.11) | 25 | Edmond, OK | (66.29) | 190 | Joliet, IL | 0.80 |
| 18 | Brick Twnshp, NJ | (69.90) | 213 | El Cajon, CA | 10.04 | 230 | Jurupa Valley, CA | 18.82 |
| 377 | Bridgeport, CT | 117.03 | 185 | El Monte, CA | (0.36) | 387 | Kansas City, KS | 134.23 |
| 393 | Brockton, MA | 140.42 | 115 | El Paso, TX | (31.03) | 431 | Kansas City, MO | 252.21 |
| 86 | Broken Arrow, OK | (43.50) | 128 | Elgin, IL | (25.50) | 170 | Kennewick, WA | (5.70) |
| 189 | Brooklyn Park, MN | 0.45 | 367 | Elizabeth, NJ | 105.56 | 144 | Kenosha, WI | (17.83) |
| 130 | Brownsville, TX | (25.27) | 56 | Elk Grove, CA | (53.57) | 273 | Kent, WA | 38.18 |
| 188 | Bryan, TX | 0.38 | 255 | Erie, PA | 27.66 | 275 | Killeen, TX | 38.97 |
| 162 | Buena Park, CA | (9.27) | 240 | Escondido, CA | 22.22 | 381 | Knoxville, TN | 123.85 |
| 417 | Buffalo, NY | 195.60 | 206 | Eugene, OR | 8.95 | 285 | Lafayette, LA | 46.90 |
| 55 | Burbank, CA | (53.75) | 89 | Evanston, IL | (43.01) | 35 | Lake Forest, CA | (60.84) |
| 123 | Cambridge, MA | (29.41) | 278 | Evansville, IN | 43.26 | 282 | Lakeland, FL | 45.47 |
| 29 | Canton Twnshp, MI | (64.45) | 332 | Everett, WA | 75.87 | 20 | Lakewood Twnshp, NJ | (69.54) |
| 37 | Cape Coral, FL | (60.11) | 250 | Fairfield, CA | 25.03 | 157 | Lakewood, CA | (11.09) |
| 79 | Carlsbad, CA | (45.33) | 342 | Fall River, MA | 85.49 | 279 | Lakewood, CO | 43.47 |
| 2 | Carmel, IN | (86.55) | 209 | Fargo, ND | 9.29 | 243 | Lancaster, CA | 23.14 |
| 60 | Carrollton, TX | (51.87) | 40 | Farmington Hills, MI | (59.75) | 392 | Lansing, MI | 140.34 |
| 232 | Carson, CA | 19.39 | 204 | Fayetteville, AR | 8.52 | 150 | Laredo, TX | (13.84) |
| 14 | Cary, NC | (76.00) | 359 | Fayetteville, NC | 96.43 | 257 | Largo, FL | 28.51 |
| 177 | Cedar Rapids, IA | (1.77) | 322 | Federal Way, WA | 70.87 | 179 | Las Cruces, NM | (1.47) |
| 84 | Centennial, CO | (43.90) | 1 | Fishers, IN | (91.35) | 347 | Las Vegas, NV | 88.37 |
| 268 | Champaign, IL | 37.02 | 439 | Flint, MI | 411.49 | 187 | Lawrence, KS | (0.01) |
| 87 | Chandler, AZ | (43.41) | 211 | Fontana, CA | 9.90 | 376 | Lawrence, MA | 116.08 |
| 111 | Charleston, SC | (32.72) | 91 | Fort Collins, CO | (41.64) | 390 | Lawton, OK | 135.90 |
| 276 | Charlotte, NC | 40.77 | 373 | Fort Lauderdale, FL | 112.94 | 48 | League City, TX | (56.60) |
| 385 | Chattanooga, TN | 128.77 | 331 | Fort Smith, AR | 75.85 | 30 | Lee's Summit, MO | (63.44) |
| 57 | Cheektowaga, NY | (53.15) | 280 | Fort Wayne, IN | 44.48 | 165 | Lewisville, TX | (8.90) |
| 134 | Chesapeake, VA | (23.07) | 311 | Fort Worth, TX | 66.36 | 247 | Lexington, KY | 24.06 |
| NA | Chicago, IL** | NA | 83 | Fremont, CA | (44.40) | 171 | Lincoln, NE | (5.45) |
| 237 | Chico, CA | 20.88 | 327 | Fresno, CA | 73.56 | 427 | Little Rock, AR | 234.09 |
| 21 | Chino Hills, CA | (69.37) | 17 | Frisco, TX | (72.72) | 104 | Livermore, CA | (36.64) |

| RANK | CITY | SCORE | RANK | CITY | SCORE | RANK | CITY | SCORE |
|---|---|---|---|---|---|---|---|---|
| 59 | Livonia, MI | (52.46) | 148 | Pasadena, CA | (15.37) | 300 | South Gate, CA | 56.82 |
| 296 | Long Beach, CA | 54.14 | 203 | Pasadena, TX | 8.44 | 184 | Sparks, NV | (0.39) |
| 156 | Longmont, CO | (12.59) | 397 | Paterson, NJ | 144.95 | 239 | Spokane Valley, WA | 21.83 |
| 284 | Longview, TX | 45.82 | 76 | Pearland, TX | (46.72) | 408 | Spokane, WA | 168.30 |
| 238 | Los Angeles, CA | 21.47 | 46 | Pembroke Pines, FL | (56.71) | 340 | Springfield, IL | 82.29 |
| 287 | Louisville, KY | 47.56 | 66 | Peoria, AZ | (48.98) | 411 | Springfield, MA | 174.45 |
| 260 | Lowell, MA | 31.46 | 320 | Peoria, IL | 69.52 | 422 | Springfield, MO | 223.85 |
| 297 | Lubbock, TX | 55.12 | 409 | Philadelphia, PA | 171.49 | 100 | Stamford, CT | (37.95) |
| 164 | Lynchburg, VA | (8.94) | 335 | Phoenix, AZ | 79.11 | 58 | Sterling Heights, MI | (52.99) |
| 289 | Lynn, MA | 49.97 | 338 | Pittsburgh, PA | 80.63 | 405 | Stockton, CA | 165.69 |
| 407 | Macon, GA | 168.16 | 71 | Plano, TX | (48.36) | 125 | St. George, UT | (27.68) |
| 149 | Madison, WI | (14.23) | 160 | Plantation, FL | (9.71) | 294 | St. Joseph, MO | 52.40 |
| 309 | Manchester, NH | 65.14 | 361 | Pomona, CA | 99.11 | 437 | St. Louis, MO | 366.60 |
| 52 | McAllen, TX | (54.14) | 358 | Pompano Beach, FL | 94.79 | 365 | St. Paul, MN | 105.44 |
| 68 | McKinney, TX | (48.48) | 36 | Port St. Lucie, FL | (60.81) | 374 | St. Petersburg, FL | 114.20 |
| 251 | Medford, OR | 25.36 | 271 | Portland, OR | 37.29 | 207 | Suffolk, VA | 9.04 |
| 345 | Melbourne, FL | 87.61 | 353 | Portsmouth, VA | 91.49 | 26 | Sugar Land, TX | (66.11) |
| 429 | Memphis, TN | 246.19 | 343 | Providence, RI | 86.32 | 90 | Sunnyvale, CA | (42.89) |
| 116 | Menifee, CA | (30.71) | 122 | Provo, UT | (29.42) | 154 | Sunrise, FL | (12.62) |
| 301 | Merced, CA | 56.95 | 404 | Pueblo, CO | 165.32 | 32 | Surprise, AZ | (63.31) |
| 45 | Meridian, ID | (56.93) | 133 | Quincy, MA | (23.08) | 380 | Syracuse, NY | 120.68 |
| 214 | Mesa, AZ | 10.65 | 226 | Racine, WI | 18.04 | 400 | Tacoma, WA | 159.86 |
| 229 | Mesquite, TX | 18.68 | 168 | Raleigh, NC | (6.71) | 348 | Tallahassee, FL | 88.99 |
| 375 | Miami Beach, FL | 115.58 | 8 | Ramapo, NY | (78.84) | 252 | Tampa, FL | 25.77 |
| 382 | Miami Gardens, FL | 125.34 | 118 | Rancho Cucamon., CA | (30.44) | 95 | Temecula, CA | (39.49) |
| 403 | Miami, FL | 164.10 | 383 | Reading, PA | 127.28 | 224 | Tempe, AZ | 17.17 |
| 126 | Midland, TX | (26.77) | 314 | Redding, CA | 66.93 | 182 | Thornton, CO | (1.15) |
| 426 | Milwaukee, WI | 229.50 | 152 | Redwood City, CA | (13.40) | 15 | Thousand Oaks, CA | (74.90) |
| 402 | Minneapolis, MN | 163.55 | 259 | Reno, NV | 30.25 | 395 | Toledo, OH | 144.60 |
| 186 | Miramar, FL | (0.07) | 263 | Renton, WA | 32.65 | 27 | Toms River Twnshp, NJ | (65.36) |
| 5 | Mission Viejo, CA | (83.42) | 288 | Rialto, CA | 48.74 | 293 | Topeka, KS | 51.86 |
| 49 | Mission, TX | (56.15) | 77 | Richardson, TX | (46.23) | 73 | Torrance, CA | (48.32) |
| 333 | Mobile, AL | 77.62 | 424 | Richmond, CA | 226.46 | 81 | Tracy, CA | (44.74) |
| 366 | Modesto, CA | 105.49 | 362 | Richmond, VA | 100.40 | 432 | Trenton, NJ | 283.86 |
| 228 | Moreno Valley, CA | 18.32 | 254 | Riverside, CA | 27.23 | 23 | Troy, MI | (67.29) |
| 67 | Mountain View, CA | (48.55) | 266 | Roanoke, VA | 36.75 | 330 | Tucson, AZ | 75.57 |
| 242 | Murfreesboro, TN | 22.71 | 103 | Rochester, MN | (37.27) | 414 | Tulsa, OK | 188.33 |
| 31 | Murrieta, CA | (63.35) | 401 | Rochester, NY | 161.01 | 292 | Tuscaloosa, AL | 51.46 |
| 135 | Nampa, ID | (22.61) | 413 | Rockford, IL | 178.60 | 41 | Tustin, CA | (59.74) |
| 142 | Napa, CA | (20.19) | 75 | Roseville, CA | (47.29) | 217 | Tyler, TX | 11.13 |
| 3 | Naperville, IL | (84.61) | 64 | Roswell, GA | (49.31) | 163 | Upland, CA | (9.23) |
| 146 | Nashua, NH | (16.44) | 44 | Round Rock, TX | (57.15) | 195 | Upper Darby Twnshp, PA | 4.63 |
| 357 | Nashville, TN | 94.65 | 325 | Sacramento, CA | 71.86 | 93 | Vacaville, CA | (40.01) |
| 391 | New Bedford, MA | 138.51 | 219 | Salem, OR | 12.54 | 425 | Vallejo, CA | 228.44 |
| 415 | New Haven, CT | 190.82 | 386 | Salinas, CA | 131.53 | 248 | Vancouver, WA | 24.08 |
| 423 | New Orleans, LA | 225.20 | 399 | Salt Lake City, UT | 154.65 | 167 | Ventura, CA | (6.99) |
| 37 | New Rochelle, NY | (60.11) | 174 | San Angelo, TX | (4.15) | 317 | Victorville, CA | 68.71 |
| 176 | New York, NY | (1.98) | 318 | San Antonio, TX | 69.20 | 108 | Virginia Beach, VA | (34.74) |
| 435 | Newark, NJ | 316.46 | 420 | San Bernardino, CA | 221.00 | 272 | Visalia, CA | 37.91 |
| 47 | Newport Beach, CA | (56.61) | 205 | San Diego, CA | 8.68 | 192 | Vista, CA | 2.40 |
| 236 | Newport News, VA | 20.40 | 370 | San Francisco, CA | 106.79 | 227 | Waco, TX | 18.24 |
| 12 | Newton, MA | (76.67) | 265 | San Jose, CA | 36.63 | 305 | Warren, MI | 61.30 |
| 328 | Norfolk, VA | 73.93 | 346 | San Leandro, CA | 87.82 | 120 | Warwick, RI | (30.04) |
| 143 | Norman, OK | (20.13) | 94 | San Marcos, CA | (39.91) | 412 | Washington, DC | 178.17 |
| 363 | North Charleston, SC | 101.88 | 97 | San Mateo, CA | (38.88) | 246 | Waterbury, CT | 23.95 |
| 310 | North Las Vegas, NV | 65.74 | 132 | Sandy Springs, GA | (23.40) | 201 | Waukegan, IL | 7.82 |
| 231 | Norwalk, CA | 18.86 | 114 | Sandy, UT | (31.17) | 139 | West Covina, CA | (21.60) |
| 69 | Norwalk, CT | (48.40) | 178 | Santa Ana, CA | (1.60) | 360 | West Palm Beach, FL | 97.01 |
| 438 | Oakland, CA | 410.19 | 159 | Santa Barbara, CA | (10.53) | 339 | West Valley, UT | 82.22 |
| 175 | Oceanside, CA | (3.76) | 82 | Santa Clara, CA | (44.44) | 267 | Westland, MI | 36.79 |
| 323 | Odessa, TX | 71.59 | 43 | Santa Clarita, CA | (58.78) | 138 | Westminster, CA | (21.95) |
| 10 | O'Fallon, MO | (78.07) | 283 | Santa Maria, CA | 45.81 | 119 | Westminster, CO | (30.16) |
| 295 | Ogden, UT | 53.26 | 216 | Santa Monica, CA | 11.01 | 151 | Whittier, CA | (13.75) |
| 394 | Oklahoma City, OK | 143.60 | 124 | Santa Rosa, CA | (27.85) | 249 | Wichita Falls, TX | 24.64 |
| 61 | Olathe, KS | (51.53) | 286 | Savannah, GA | 47.02 | 341 | Wichita, KS | 85.15 |
| 356 | Omaha, NE | 93.99 | 65 | Scottsdale, AZ | (49.15) | 321 | Wilmington, NC | 70.04 |
| 235 | Ontario, CA | 20.33 | 137 | Scranton, PA | (21.96) | 312 | Winston-Salem, NC | 66.60 |
| 62 | Orange, CA | (51.04) | 319 | Seattle, WA | 69.25 | 33 | Woodbridge Twnshp, NJ | (62.27) |
| 24 | Orem, UT | (66.60) | 344 | Shreveport, LA | 87.08 | 303 | Worcester, MA | 60.23 |
| 369 | Orlando, FL | 106.22 | 34 | Simi Valley, CA | (62.21) | 349 | Yakima, WA | 89.68 |
| 54 | Overland Park, KS | (54.00) | 234 | Sioux City, IA | 20.02 | 153 | Yonkers, NY | (12.81) |
| 194 | Oxnard, CA | 3.89 | 222 | Sioux Falls, SD | 16.01 | 270 | Yuma, AZ | 37.21 |
| 140 | Palm Bay, FL | (21.08) | 99 | Somerville, MA | (38.54) | | | |
| 225 | Palmdale, CA | 17.75 | 384 | South Bend, IN | 127.65 | | | |

Source: CQ Press using reported data from the F.B.I. "Crime in the United States 2013"

*Includes murder, rape, robbery, aggravated assault, burglary, and motor vehicle theft. A negative score (in parentheses) indicates a composite crime number below the national rate, a positive number is above the national rate. **Not available.

# 2014 City Crime Rate Rankings* (continued)

| RANK | CITY | SCORE | RANK | CITY | SCORE | RANK | CITY | SCORE |
|------|------|-------|------|------|-------|------|------|-------|
| 1 | Fishers, IN | (91.35) | 75 | Roseville, CA | (47.29) | 149 | Madison, WI | (14.23) |
| 2 | Carmel, IN | (86.55) | 76 | Pearland, TX | (46.72) | 150 | Laredo, TX | (13.84) |
| 3 | Naperville, IL | (84.61) | 77 | Richardson, TX | (46.23) | 151 | Whittier, CA | (13.75) |
| 4 | Arlington Heights, IL | (83.74) | 78 | Danbury, CT | (46.08) | 152 | Redwood City, CA | (13.40) |
| 5 | Mission Viejo, CA | (83.42) | 79 | Carlsbad, CA | (45.33) | 153 | Yonkers, NY | (12.81) |
| 6 | Clarkstown, NY | (80.65) | 80 | Huntington Beach, CA | (45.20) | 154 | Sunrise, FL | (12.62) |
| 7 | Colonie, NY | (79.58) | 81 | Tracy, CA | (44.74) | 155 | Denton, TX | (12.61) |
| 8 | Ramapo, NY | (78.84) | 82 | Santa Clara, CA | (44.44) | 156 | Longmont, CO | (12.59) |
| 9 | Amherst, NY | (78.19) | 83 | Fremont, CA | (44.40) | 157 | Lakewood, CA | (11.09) |
| 10 | O'Fallon, MO | (78.07) | 84 | Centennial, CO | (43.90) | 158 | Davie, FL | (10.94) |
| 11 | Irvine, CA | (77.80) | 85 | Bend, OR | (43.70) | 159 | Santa Barbara, CA | (10.53) |
| 12 | Newton, MA | (76.67) | 86 | Broken Arrow, OK | (43.50) | 160 | Plantation, FL | (9.71) |
| 13 | Allen, TX | (76.37) | 87 | Chandler, AZ | (43.41) | 161 | Garland, TX | (9.30) |
| 14 | Cary, NC | (76.00) | 88 | Hamilton Twnshp, NJ | (43.40) | 162 | Buena Park, CA | (9.27) |
| 15 | Thousand Oaks, CA | (74.90) | 89 | Evanston, IL | (43.01) | 163 | Upland, CA | (9.23) |
| 16 | Gilbert, AZ | (74.03) | 90 | Sunnyvale, CA | (42.89) | 164 | Lynchburg, VA | (8.94) |
| 17 | Frisco, TX | (72.72) | 91 | Fort Collins, CO | (41.64) | 165 | Lewisville, TX | (8.90) |
| 18 | Brick Twnshp, NJ | (69.90) | 92 | Alexandria, VA | (41.00) | 166 | Athens-Clarke, GA | (8.67) |
| 19 | Johns Creek, GA | (69.74) | 93 | Vacaville, CA | (40.01) | 167 | Ventura, CA | (6.99) |
| 20 | Lakewood Twnshp, NJ | (69.54) | 94 | San Marcos, CA | (39.91) | 168 | Raleigh, NC | (6.71) |
| 21 | Chino Hills, CA | (69.37) | 95 | Temecula, CA | (39.49) | 169 | Hialeah, FL | (5.77) |
| 22 | Glendale, CA | (68.40) | 96 | Daly City, CA | (39.01) | 170 | Kennewick, WA | (5.70) |
| 23 | Troy, MI | (67.29) | 97 | San Mateo, CA | (38.88) | 171 | Lincoln, NE | (5.45) |
| 24 | Orem, UT | (66.60) | 98 | Aurora, IL | (38.65) | 172 | Chino, CA | (5.43) |
| 25 | Edmond, OK | (66.29) | 99 | Somerville, MA | (38.54) | 173 | Bloomington, IN | (4.50) |
| 26 | Sugar Land, TX | (66.11) | 100 | Stamford, CT | (37.95) | 174 | San Angelo, TX | (4.15) |
| 27 | Toms River Twnshp, NJ | (65.36) | 101 | Boca Raton, FL | (37.71) | 175 | Oceanside, CA | (3.76) |
| 28 | Greece, NY | (65.23) | 102 | Cranston, RI | (37.59) | 176 | New York, NY | (1.98) |
| 29 | Canton Twnshp, MI | (64.45) | 103 | Rochester, MN | (37.27) | 177 | Cedar Rapids, IA | (1.77) |
| 30 | Lee's Summit, MO | (63.44) | 104 | Livermore, CA | (36.64) | 178 | Santa Ana, CA | (1.60) |
| 31 | Murrieta, CA | (63.35) | 105 | Boulder, CO | (36.11) | 179 | Las Cruces, NM | (1.47) |
| 32 | Surprise, AZ | (63.31) | 106 | Alhambra, CA | (35.86) | 180 | Green Bay, WI | (1.37) |
| 33 | Woodbridge Twnshp, NJ | (62.27) | 107 | Henderson, NV | (35.12) | 181 | Abilene, TX | (1.23) |
| 34 | Simi Valley, CA | (62.21) | 108 | Virginia Beach, VA | (34.74) | 182 | Thornton, CO | (1.15) |
| 35 | Lake Forest, CA | (60.84) | 109 | Irving, TX | (33.96) | 183 | Austin, TX | (0.82) |
| 36 | Port St. Lucie, FL | (60.81) | 110 | College Station, TX | (33.29) | 184 | Sparks, NV | (0.39) |
| 37 | Cape Coral, FL | (60.11) | 111 | Charleston, SC | (32.72) | 185 | El Monte, CA | (0.36) |
| 37 | New Rochelle, NY | (60.11) | 112 | Chula Vista, CA | (32.18) | 186 | Miramar, FL | (0.07) |
| 39 | Beaverton, OR | (60.09) | 113 | Ann Arbor, MI | (31.96) | 187 | Lawrence, KS | (0.01) |
| 40 | Farmington Hills, MI | (59.75) | 114 | Sandy, UT | (31.17) | 188 | Bryan, TX | 0.38 |
| 41 | Tustin, CA | (59.74) | 115 | El Paso, TX | (31.03) | 189 | Brooklyn Park, MN | 0.45 |
| 42 | Edison Twnshp, NJ | (59.26) | 116 | Menifee, CA | (30.71) | 190 | Joliet, IL | 0.80 |
| 43 | Santa Clarita, CA | (58.78) | 117 | Fullerton, CA | (30.62) | 191 | Baldwin Park, CA | 2.35 |
| 44 | Round Rock, TX | (57.15) | 118 | Rancho Cucamon., CA | (30.44) | 192 | Vista, CA | 2.40 |
| 45 | Meridian, ID | (56.93) | 119 | Westminster, CO | (30.16) | 193 | Edinburg, TX | 3.05 |
| 46 | Pembroke Pines, FL | (56.71) | 120 | Warwick, RI | (30.04) | 194 | Oxnard, CA | 3.89 |
| 47 | Newport Beach, CA | (56.61) | 121 | Corona, CA | (29.92) | 195 | Upper Darby Twnshp, PA | 4.63 |
| 48 | League City, TX | (56.60) | 122 | Provo, UT | (29.42) | 196 | Dearborn, MI | 5.59 |
| 49 | Mission, TX | (56.15) | 123 | Cambridge, MA | (29.41) | 197 | Concord, CA | 6.36 |
| 50 | Bloomington, MN | (54.62) | 124 | Santa Rosa, CA | (27.85) | 198 | Deerfield Beach, FL | 6.46 |
| 51 | Hoover, AL | (54.52) | 125 | St. George, UT | (27.68) | 199 | Grand Prairie, TX | 6.89 |
| 52 | McAllen, TX | (54.14) | 126 | Midland, TX | (26.77) | 200 | Anaheim, CA | 7.35 |
| 53 | Coral Springs, FL | (54.06) | 127 | Garden Grove, CA | (26.32) | 201 | Waukegan, IL | 7.82 |
| 54 | Overland Park, KS | (54.00) | 128 | Elgin, IL | (25.50) | 202 | Clinton Twnshp, MI | 7.84 |
| 55 | Burbank, CA | (53.75) | 129 | Alhambra, CA | (25.39) | 203 | Pasadena, TX | 8.44 |
| 56 | Elk Grove, CA | (53.57) | 130 | Brownsville, TX | (25.27) | 204 | Fayetteville, AR | 8.52 |
| 57 | Cheektowaga, NY | (53.15) | 131 | Concord, NC | (24.64) | 205 | San Diego, CA | 8.68 |
| 58 | Sterling Heights, MI | (52.99) | 132 | Sandy Springs, GA | (23.40) | 206 | Eugene, OR | 8.95 |
| 59 | Livonia, MI | (52.46) | 133 | Quincy, MA | (23.08) | 207 | Suffolk, VA | 9.04 |
| 60 | Carrollton, TX | (51.87) | 134 | Chesapeake, VA | (23.07) | 208 | Decatur, IL | 9.15 |
| 61 | Olathe, KS | (51.53) | 135 | Nampa, ID | (22.61) | 209 | Fargo, ND | 9.29 |
| 62 | Orange, CA | (51.04) | 136 | Clovis, CA | (22.17) | 210 | Cicero, IL | 9.78 |
| 63 | Clifton, NJ | (50.74) | 137 | Scranton, PA | (21.96) | 211 | Fontana, CA | 9.90 |
| 64 | Roswell, GA | (49.31) | 138 | Westminster, CA | (21.95) | 212 | Hesperia, CA | 10.03 |
| 65 | Scottsdale, AZ | (49.15) | 139 | West Covina, CA | (21.60) | 213 | El Cajon, CA | 10.04 |
| 66 | Peoria, AZ | (48.98) | 140 | Palm Bay, FL | (21.08) | 214 | Mesa, AZ | 10.65 |
| 67 | Mountain View, CA | (48.55) | 141 | Boise, ID | (21.07) | 215 | Bellflower, CA | 10.84 |
| 68 | McKinney, TX | (48.48) | 142 | Napa, CA | (20.19) | 216 | Santa Monica, CA | 11.01 |
| 69 | Norwalk, CT | (48.40) | 143 | Norman, OK | (20.13) | 217 | Tyler, TX | 11.13 |
| 70 | Hillsboro, OR | (48.39) | 144 | Kenosha, WI | (17.83) | 218 | Columbia, MO | 12.32 |
| 71 | Plano, TX | (48.36) | 145 | Costa Mesa, CA | (17.44) | 219 | Salem, OR | 12.54 |
| 72 | Bellevue, WA | (48.35) | 146 | Nashua, NH | (16.44) | 220 | Duluth, MN | 13.38 |
| 73 | Torrance, CA | (48.32) | 147 | Bethlehem, PA | (16.34) | 221 | Bloomington, IL | 14.82 |
| 74 | Arvada, CO | (47.76) | 148 | Pasadena, CA | (15.37) | 222 | Sioux Falls, SD | 16.01 |

| RANK | CITY | SCORE | RANK | CITY | SCORE | RANK | CITY | SCORE |
|---|---|---|---|---|---|---|---|---|
| 223 | Hampton, VA | 16.82 | 297 | Lubbock, TX | 55.12 | 371 | Huntsville, AL | 107.73 |
| 224 | Tempe, AZ | 17.17 | 298 | Albany, NY | 55.65 | 372 | Hammond, IN | 110.91 |
| 225 | Palmdale, CA | 17.75 | 299 | Berkeley, CA | 56.78 | 373 | Fort Lauderdale, FL | 112.94 |
| 226 | Racine, WI | 18.04 | 300 | South Gate, CA | 56.82 | 374 | St. Petersburg, FL | 114.20 |
| 227 | Waco, TX | 18.24 | 301 | Merced, CA | 56.95 | 375 | Miami Beach, FL | 115.58 |
| 228 | Moreno Valley, CA | 18.32 | 302 | Boston, MA | 59.76 | 376 | Lawrence, MA | 116.08 |
| 229 | Mesquite, TX | 18.68 | 303 | Worcester, MA | 60.23 | 377 | Bridgeport, CT | 117.03 |
| 230 | Jurupa Valley, CA | 18.82 | 304 | Grand Rapids, MI | 60.82 | 378 | Dallas, TX | 117.88 |
| 231 | Norwalk, CA | 18.86 | 305 | Warren, MI | 61.30 | 379 | Albuquerque, NM | 117.92 |
| 232 | Carson, CA | 19.39 | 306 | Davenport, IA | 61.44 | 380 | Syracuse, NY | 120.68 |
| 233 | Clarksville, TN | 19.75 | 307 | Gresham, OR | 62.40 | 381 | Knoxville, TN | 123.85 |
| 234 | Sioux City, IA | 20.02 | 308 | Indio, CA | 64.36 | 382 | Miami Gardens, FL | 125.34 |
| 235 | Ontario, CA | 20.33 | 309 | Manchester, NH | 65.14 | 383 | Reading, PA | 127.28 |
| 236 | Newport News, VA | 20.40 | 310 | North Las Vegas, NV | 65.74 | 384 | South Bend, IN | 127.65 |
| 237 | Chico, CA | 20.88 | 311 | Fort Worth, TX | 66.36 | 385 | Chattanooga, TN | 128.77 |
| 238 | Los Angeles, CA | 21.47 | 312 | Winston-Salem, NC | 66.60 | 386 | Salinas, CA | 131.53 |
| 239 | Spokane Valley, WA | 21.83 | 313 | Jacksonville, FL | 66.85 | 387 | Kansas City, KS | 134.23 |
| 240 | Escondido, CA | 22.22 | 314 | Redding, CA | 66.93 | 388 | Akron, OH | 135.00 |
| 241 | Arlington, TX | 22.53 | 315 | Independence, MO | 67.29 | 389 | Houston, TX | 135.27 |
| 242 | Murfreesboro, TN | 22.71 | 316 | Colorado Springs, CO | 67.59 | 390 | Lawton, OK | 135.90 |
| 243 | Lancaster, CA | 23.14 | 317 | Victorville, CA | 68.71 | 391 | New Bedford, MA | 138.51 |
| 244 | Citrus Heights, CA | 23.22 | 318 | San Antonio, TX | 69.20 | 392 | Lansing, MI | 140.34 |
| 245 | Greeley, CO | 23.87 | 319 | Seattle, WA | 69.25 | 393 | Brockton, MA | 140.42 |
| 246 | Waterbury, CT | 23.95 | 320 | Peoria, IL | 69.52 | 394 | Oklahoma City, OK | 143.60 |
| 247 | Lexington, KY | 24.06 | 321 | Wilmington, NC | 70.04 | 395 | Toledo, OH | 144.60 |
| 248 | Vancouver, WA | 24.08 | 322 | Federal Way, WA | 70.87 | 396 | Beaumont, TX | 144.65 |
| 249 | Wichita Falls, TX | 24.64 | 323 | Odessa, TX | 71.59 | 397 | Paterson, NJ | 144.95 |
| 250 | Fairfield, CA | 25.03 | 324 | Hollywood, FL | 71.73 | 398 | Baton Rouge, LA | 152.59 |
| 251 | Medford, OR | 25.36 | 325 | Sacramento, CA | 71.86 | 399 | Salt Lake City, UT | 154.65 |
| 252 | Tampa, FL | 25.77 | 326 | Hayward, CA | 73.31 | 400 | Tacoma, WA | 159.86 |
| 253 | High Point, NC | 27.07 | 327 | Fresno, CA | 73.56 | 401 | Rochester, NY | 161.01 |
| 254 | Riverside, CA | 27.23 | 328 | Norfolk, VA | 73.93 | 402 | Minneapolis, MN | 163.55 |
| 255 | Erie, PA | 27.66 | 329 | Hawthorne, CA | 74.42 | 403 | Miami, FL | 164.10 |
| 256 | Billings, MT | 27.92 | 330 | Tucson, AZ | 75.57 | 404 | Pueblo, CO | 165.32 |
| 257 | Largo, FL | 28.51 | 331 | Fort Smith, AR | 75.85 | 405 | Stockton, CA | 165.69 |
| 258 | Clearwater, FL | 28.60 | 332 | Everett, WA | 75.87 | 406 | Antioch, CA | 166.77 |
| 259 | Reno, NV | 30.25 | 333 | Mobile, AL | 77.62 | 407 | Macon, GA | 168.16 |
| 260 | Lowell, MA | 31.46 | 334 | Allentown, PA | 78.88 | 408 | Spokane, WA | 168.30 |
| 261 | Downey, CA | 31.88 | 335 | Phoenix, AZ | 79.11 | 409 | Philadelphia, PA | 171.49 |
| 262 | Gainesville, FL | 32.54 | 336 | Bakersfield, CA | 79.86 | 410 | Hartford, CT | 173.21 |
| 263 | Renton, WA | 32.65 | 337 | Hemet, CA | 80.51 | 411 | Springfield, MA | 174.45 |
| 264 | Glendale, AZ | 34.17 | 338 | Pittsburgh, PA | 80.63 | 412 | Washington, DC | 178.17 |
| 265 | San Jose, CA | 36.63 | 339 | West Valley, UT | 82.22 | 413 | Rockford, IL | 178.60 |
| 266 | Roanoke, VA | 36.75 | 340 | Springfield, IL | 82.29 | 414 | Tulsa, OK | 188.33 |
| 267 | Westland, MI | 36.79 | 341 | Wichita, KS | 85.15 | 415 | New Haven, CT | 190.82 |
| 268 | Champaign, IL | 37.02 | 342 | Fall River, MA | 85.49 | 416 | Dayton, OH | 192.65 |
| 269 | Corpus Christi, TX | 37.15 | 343 | Providence, RI | 86.32 | 417 | Buffalo, NY | 195.60 |
| 270 | Yuma, AZ | 37.21 | 344 | Shreveport, LA | 87.08 | 418 | Indianapolis, IN | 213.59 |
| 271 | Portland, OR | 37.29 | 345 | Melbourne, FL | 87.61 | 419 | Cincinnati, OH | 220.76 |
| 272 | Visalia, CA | 37.91 | 346 | San Leandro, CA | 87.82 | 420 | San Bernardino, CA | 221.00 |
| 273 | Kent, WA | 38.18 | 347 | Las Vegas, NV | 88.37 | 421 | Atlanta, GA | 222.14 |
| 274 | Jersey City, NJ | 38.35 | 348 | Tallahassee, FL | 88.99 | 422 | Springfield, MO | 223.85 |
| 275 | Killeen, TX | 38.97 | 349 | Yakima, WA | 89.68 | 423 | New Orleans, LA | 225.20 |
| 276 | Charlotte, NC | 40.77 | 350 | Denver, CO | 90.08 | 424 | Richmond, CA | 226.46 |
| 277 | Aurora, CO | 41.72 | 351 | Amarillo, TX | 90.11 | 425 | Vallejo, CA | 228.44 |
| 278 | Evansville, IN | 43.26 | 352 | Inglewood, CA | 90.93 | 426 | Milwaukee, WI | 229.50 |
| 279 | Lakewood, CO | 43.47 | 353 | Portsmouth, VA | 91.49 | 427 | Little Rock, AR | 234.09 |
| 280 | Fort Wayne, IN | 44.48 | 354 | Columbus, GA | 93.25 | 428 | Jackson, MS | 243.05 |
| 281 | Greensboro, NC | 44.54 | 355 | Columbia, SC | 93.98 | 429 | Memphis, TN | 246.19 |
| 282 | Lakeland, FL | 45.47 | 356 | Omaha, NE | 93.99 | 430 | Compton, CA | 248.62 |
| 283 | Santa Maria, CA | 45.81 | 357 | Nashville, TN | 94.65 | 431 | Kansas City, MO | 252.21 |
| 284 | Longview, TX | 45.82 | 358 | Pompano Beach, FL | 94.79 | 432 | Trenton, NJ | 283.86 |
| 285 | Lafayette, LA | 46.90 | 359 | Fayetteville, NC | 96.43 | 433 | Birmingham, AL | 296.02 |
| 286 | Savannah, GA | 47.02 | 360 | West Palm Beach, FL | 97.01 | 434 | Baltimore, MD | 300.20 |
| 287 | Louisville, KY | 47.56 | 361 | Pomona, CA | 99.11 | 435 | Newark, NJ | 316.46 |
| 288 | Rialto, CA | 48.74 | 362 | Richmond, VA | 100.40 | 436 | Cleveland, OH | 331.31 |
| 289 | Lynn, MA | 49.97 | 363 | North Charleston, SC | 101.88 | 437 | St. Louis, MO | 366.60 |
| 290 | Des Moines, IA | 50.23 | 364 | Anchorage, AK | 104.21 | 438 | Oakland, CA | 410.19 |
| 291 | Greenville, NC | 51.40 | 365 | St. Paul, MN | 105.44 | 439 | Flint, MI | 411.49 |
| 292 | Tuscaloosa, AL | 51.46 | 366 | Modesto, CA | 105.49 | 440 | Gary, IN | 418.85 |
| 293 | Topeka, KS | 51.86 | 367 | Elizabeth, NJ | 105.56 | 441 | Detroit, MI | 495.29 |
| 294 | St. Joseph, MO | 52.40 | 368 | Albany, GA | 106.12 | NA | Chicago, IL** | NA |
| 295 | Ogden, UT | 53.26 | 369 | Orlando, FL | 106.22 | | | |
| 296 | Long Beach, CA | 54.14 | 370 | San Francisco, CA | 106.79 | | | |

Source: CQ Press using reported data from the F.B.I. "Crime in the United States 2013"

*Includes murder, rape, robbery, aggravated assault, burglary, and motor vehicle theft. A negative score (in parentheses) indicates a composite crime number below the national rate, a positive number is above the national rate. **Not available.

# About the Editors

**Scott Morgan and Kathleen O'Leary Morgan** founded Morgan Quitno Press in 1990. They edited more than 2,700 annual state and city statistical reference publications before selling the titles to CQ Press in 2007. They also edited a monthly journal, *State Statistical Trends* for six years. They have continued to edit a number of the publications continued by CQ Press as well as an ever-growing online database (*State Stats*).

Scott received both a BS and a law degree from the University of Kansas. He previously worked on the staffs of two U.S. Senators as well as the Senate Judiciary Committee. He represented the Senate on the Federal Election Commission and served as Chief Counsel for Senator Bob Dole's presidential campaign in 1988. He was Chief Counsel for Governor Mike Hayden in Kansas until 1990.

Kathleen received a BS and a master's in Public Administration from the University of Kansas. She served in a number of media and legislative positions within the U.S. Department of Transportation, where she also served as deputy director of congressional affairs.

**Rachel Boba Santos** is an associate professor at Florida Atlantic University in the School of Criminology and Criminal Justice. She works with police departments and conducts research on police accountability, the effectiveness of crime reduction efforts by police, and crime analysis.

# I. Metropolitan Area Crime Statistics

---

**Please note the following for Tables 1 through 40 and 85 through 87:**

- All listings are for Metropolitan Statistical Areas (M.S.A.s) except for those ending with "M.D."
- Listings with "M.D." are Metropolitan Divisions, which are smaller parts of eleven large M.S.A.s. These eleven M.S.A.s divided into M.D.s are identified using "(greater)" following the metropolitan area name.
- For example, the "Dallas (greater)" M.S.A. includes the two M.D.s of Dallas-Plano-Irving and Fort Worth-Arlington. The data for the M.D.s are included in the data for the overall M.S.A. as well.
- The name of a M.S.A. or M.D. is subject to change based on the changing proportional size of the large cities included within it. Percent changes are calculated in this book if the M.S.A. or M.D. has not substantially changed, despite the changes in name. Furthermore, the Office of Management and Budget (OMB) redefined a number of M.S.A.s in 2013; if the redefined M.S.A. had a population change of 5% or greater from the previous definition, its data are treated as not comparable and are not included in the tables showing change over time.
- Some M.S.A. and M.D. names are abbreviated to preserve space within the tables.

# 1. Crimes in 2013
## National Total = 9,795,658 Crimes*

| RANK | METROPOLITAN AREA | CRIMES | RANK | METROPOLITAN AREA | CRIMES | RANK | METROPOLITAN AREA | CRIMES |
|---|---|---|---|---|---|---|---|---|
| 234 | Abilene, TX | 6,082 | 327 | Cheyenne, WY | 2,824 | 92 | Gary, IN M.D. | 23,380 |
| 97 | Akron, OH | 22,654 | NA | Chicago (greater), IL-IN-WI** | NA | 364 | Gettysburg, PA | 1,383 |
| 99 | Albany-Schenectady-Troy, NY | 22,513 | NA | Chicago-Naperville, IL M.D.** | NA | 355 | Glens Falls, NY | 2,177 |
| 189 | Albany, GA | 8,146 | 213 | Chico, CA | 6,857 | 255 | Goldsboro, NC | 5,034 |
| 290 | Albany, OR | 4,115 | 36 | Cincinnati, OH-KY-IN | 73,338 | 347 | Grand Forks, ND-MN | 2,350 |
| 57 | Albuquerque, NM | 47,171 | 193 | Clarksville, TN-KY | 8,043 | 322 | Grand Island, NE | 3,056 |
| 184 | Alexandria, LA | 8,615 | 287 | Cleveland, TN | 4,254 | 283 | Grand Junction, CO | 4,312 |
| 108 | Allentown, PA-NJ | 19,716 | 277 | Coeur d'Alene, ID | 4,448 | 95 | Grand Rapids-Wyoming, MI | 22,836 |
| 345 | Altoona, PA | 2,439 | 215 | College Station-Bryan, TX | 6,781 | 308 | Grants Pass, OR | 3,500 |
| 162 | Amarillo, TX | 10,284 | 88 | Colorado Springs, CO | 24,731 | 320 | Great Falls, MT | 3,131 |
| 357 | Ames, IA | 2,089 | 230 | Columbia, MO | 6,181 | 233 | Greeley, CO | 6,092 |
| 41 | Anaheim-Santa Ana-Irvine, CA M.D. | 67,692 | 72 | Columbia, SC | 33,436 | 226 | Green Bay, WI | 6,313 |
| 126 | Anchorage, AK | 15,544 | 120 | Columbus, GA-AL | 16,870 | 83 | Greensboro-High Point, NC | 28,145 |
| 185 | Ann Arbor, MI | 8,488 | 328 | Columbus, IN | 2,822 | 64 | Greenville-Anderson, SC | 39,112 |
| 256 | Anniston-Oxford, AL | 4,991 | 102 | Corpus Christi, TX | 21,146 | 218 | Greenville, NC | 6,722 |
| 309 | Appleton, WI | 3,463 | 348 | Corvallis, OR | 2,323 | 131 | Gulfport-Biloxi-Pascagoula, MS | 14,947 |
| 220 | Athens-Clarke County, GA | 6,617 | 211 | Crestview-Fort Walton Beach, FL | 6,973 | 225 | Hagerstown-Martinsburg, MD-WV | 6,327 |
| 8 | Atlanta, GA | 205,014 | 323 | Cumberland, MD-WV | 3,029 | 192 | Hammond, LA | 8,044 |
| 173 | Atlantic City, NJ | 9,424 | 7 | Dallas (greater), TX | 229,588 | 277 | Hanford-Corcoran, CA | 4,448 |
| 94 | Augusta, GA-SC | 22,927 | 13 | Dallas-Plano-Irving, TX M.D. | 144,607 | 354 | Harrisonburg, VA | 2,188 |
| 42 | Austin-Round Rock, TX | 64,830 | 282 | Dalton, GA | 4,333 | 86 | Hartford, CT | 25,236 |
| 65 | Bakersfield, CA | 38,350 | 251 | Daphne-Fairhope-Foley, AL | 5,319 | 219 | Hilton Head Island, SC | 6,630 |
| 22 | Baltimore, MD | 101,026 | 154 | Davenport, IA-IL | 10,994 | 343 | Hinesville, GA | 2,489 |
| 276 | Bangor, ME | 4,479 | 82 | Dayton, OH | 28,844 | 315 | Homosassa Springs, FL | 3,297 |
| 232 | Barnstable Town, MA | 6,144 | 285 | Decatur, AL | 4,291 | 244 | Hot Springs, AR | 5,637 |
| 70 | Baton Rouge, LA | 35,323 | 316 | Decatur, IL | 3,228 | 201 | Houma, LA | 7,366 |
| 340 | Bay City, MI | 2,568 | 104 | Deltona-Daytona Beach, FL | 20,976 | 5 | Houston, TX | 254,251 |
| 125 | Beaumont-Port Arthur, TX | 15,818 | 30 | Denver-Aurora, CO | 82,829 | 121 | Huntsville, AL | 16,682 |
| 269 | Bend, OR | 4,616 | 117 | Des Moines-West Des Moines, IA | 18,085 | 333 | Idaho Falls, ID | 2,745 |
| 209 | Billings, MT | 7,030 | 15 | Detroit (greater), MI | 135,291 | NA | Indianapolis, IN** | NA |
| 202 | Binghamton, NY | 7,327 | 26 | Detroit-Dearborn-Livonia, MI M.D. | 87,118 | 303 | Iowa City, IA | 3,652 |
| 55 | Birmingham-Hoover, AL | 48,431 | 262 | Dothan, AL | 4,841 | 49 | Jacksonville, FL | 51,878 |
| 314 | Bismarck, ND | 3,356 | 241 | Dover, DE | 5,831 | 270 | Jackson, MI | 4,609 |
| 299 | Blacksburg, VA | 3,770 | 358 | Dubuque, IA | 2,047 | 110 | Jackson, MS | 19,522 |
| 272 | Bloomington, IL | 4,556 | 163 | Duluth, MN-WI | 10,191 | 237 | Jackson, TN | 5,984 |
| 263 | Bloomington, IN | 4,832 | 240 | Dutchess-Putnam, NY M.D. | 5,960 | 281 | Janesville, WI | 4,354 |
| 361 | Bloomsburg-Berwick, PA | 1,706 | 265 | East Stroudsburg, PA | 4,744 | 301 | Jefferson City, MO | 3,669 |
| 143 | Boise City, ID | 12,471 | 325 | Eau Claire, WI | 2,980 | 242 | Johnson City, TN | 5,817 |
| 21 | Boston (greater), MA-NH | 105,037 | 222 | El Centro, CA | 6,445 | 330 | Johnstown, PA | 2,793 |
| 52 | Boston, MA M.D. | 50,417 | 101 | El Paso, TX | 21,256 | 260 | Jonesboro, AR | 4,890 |
| 196 | Boulder, CO | 7,737 | 158 | Elgin, IL M.D. | 10,660 | 191 | Joplin, MO | 8,106 |
| 291 | Bowling Green, KY | 4,025 | 346 | Elizabethtown-Fort Knox, KY | 2,353 | 231 | Kahului-Wailuku-Lahaina, HI | 6,154 |
| 188 | Bremerton-Silverdale, WA | 8,276 | 353 | Elmira, NY | 2,199 | 317 | Kankakee, IL | 3,222 |
| 119 | Bridgeport-Stamford, CT | 17,170 | 200 | Erie, PA | 7,376 | 33 | Kansas City, MO-KS | 76,297 |
| 124 | Brownsville-Harlingen, TX | 15,853 | 134 | Eugene, OR | 13,892 | 214 | Kennewick-Richland, WA | 6,839 |
| NA | Brunswick, GA** | NA | 362 | Fairbanks, AK | 1,666 | 174 | Kingsport, TN-VA | 9,290 |
| 68 | Buffalo-Niagara Falls, NY | 35,927 | 245 | Fargo, ND-MN | 5,636 | 307 | Kingston, NY | 3,575 |
| 247 | Burlington, NC | 5,562 | 313 | Farmington, NM | 3,380 | 80 | Knoxville, TN | 29,833 |
| 336 | California-Lexington Park, MD | 2,731 | 138 | Fayetteville-Springdale, AR-MO | 13,252 | 337 | Kokomo, IN | 2,680 |
| 58 | Cambridge-Newton, MA M.D. | 45,429 | 106 | Fayetteville, NC | 20,417 | 338 | La Crosse, WI-MN | 2,674 |
| 73 | Camden, NJ M.D. | 33,264 | 268 | Flagstaff, AZ | 4,620 | 229 | Lafayette, IN | 6,194 |
| 148 | Canton, OH | 11,897 | 129 | Flint, MI | 15,424 | 112 | Lafayette, LA | 19,116 |
| 122 | Cape Coral-Fort Myers, FL | 16,584 | 261 | Florence-Muscle Shoals, AL | 4,847 | 153 | Lake Charles, LA | 11,015 |
| 310 | Cape Girardeau, MO-IL | 3,459 | 161 | Florence, SC | 10,394 | 123 | Lake Co.-Kenosha Co., IL-WI M.D. | 16,183 |
| 304 | Carbondale-Marion, IL | 3,628 | 360 | Fond du Lac, WI | 1,851 | 203 | Lake Havasu City-Kingman, AZ | 7,319 |
| 366 | Carson City, NV | 1,057 | 199 | Fort Collins, CO | 7,458 | 107 | Lakeland, FL | 20,402 |
| 341 | Casper, WY | 2,536 | 38 | Fort Lauderdale, FL M.D. | 71,798 | 156 | Lancaster, PA | 10,750 |
| 216 | Cedar Rapids, IA | 6,749 | 168 | Fort Smith, AR-OK | 9,861 | 145 | Lansing-East Lansing, MI | 12,216 |
| 319 | Chambersburg-Waynesboro, PA | 3,161 | 137 | Fort Wayne, IN | 13,551 | 147 | Laredo, TX | 12,012 |
| 210 | Champaign-Urbana, IL | 7,014 | 29 | Fort Worth-Arlington, TX M.D. | 84,981 | 206 | Las Cruces, NM | 7,098 |
| 87 | Charleston-North Charleston, SC | 24,952 | 62 | Fresno, CA | 41,566 | 35 | Las Vegas-Henderson, NV | 74,851 |
| 32 | Charlotte-Mecklenburg, NC-SC | 78,849 | 254 | Gadsden, AL | 5,049 | 274 | Lawrence, KS | 4,523 |
| 266 | Charlottesville, VA | 4,717 | 172 | Gainesville, FL | 9,475 | 224 | Lawton, OK | 6,404 |
| 90 | Chattanooga, TN-GA | 23,705 | 275 | Gainesville, GA | 4,491 | 334 | Lebanon, PA | 2,736 |

Note: All listings are for Metropolitan Statistical Areas (M.S.A.s) except for those ending with "M.D." Listings with "M.D." are Metropolitan Divisions which are smaller parts of eleven large M.S.A.s. See explanatory note at beginning of metropolitan area section.

| RANK | METROPOLITAN AREA | CRIMES | RANK | METROPOLITAN AREA | CRIMES | RANK | METROPOLITAN AREA | CRIMES |
|---|---|---|---|---|---|---|---|---|
| 321 | Lewiston-Auburn, ME | 3,079 | 77 | Omaha-Council Bluffs, NE-IA | 32,462 | 351 | Sheboygan, WI | 2,225 |
| 356 | Lewiston, ID-WA | 2,163 | 25 | Orlando, FL | 89,547 | 311 | Sherman-Denison, TX | 3,418 |
| 111 | Lexington-Fayette, KY | 19,474 | 318 | Oshkosh-Neenah, WI | 3,187 | 113 | Shreveport-Bossier City, LA | 18,360 |
| 293 | Lima, OH | 3,969 | 331 | Owensboro, KY | 2,749 | 96 | Silver Spring-Frederick, MD M.D. | 22,777 |
| 152 | Lincoln, NE | 11,057 | 118 | Oxnard-Thousand Oaks, CA | 18,029 | 253 | Sioux City, IA-NE-SD | 5,089 |
| 63 | Little Rock, AR | 40,259 | 114 | Palm Bay-Melbourne, FL | 18,282 | 223 | Sioux Falls, SD | 6,425 |
| 363 | Logan, UT-ID | 1,603 | 187 | Panama City, FL | 8,283 | 157 | South Bend-Mishawaka, IN-MI | 10,734 |
| 190 | Longview, TX | 8,118 | 341 | Parkersburg-Vienna, WV | 2,536 | 149 | Spartanburg, SC | 11,540 |
| 279 | Longview, WA | 4,419 | 115 | Pensacola, FL | 18,215 | 75 | Spokane, WA | 32,718 |
| 4 | Los Angeles County, CA M.D. | 268,803 | 164 | Peoria, IL | 10,163 | 166 | Springfield, IL | 9,901 |
| 2 | Los Angeles (greater), CA | 336,495 | 10 | Philadelphia (greater) PA-NJ-MD-DE | 179,587 | 100 | Springfield, MA | 21,530 |
| NA | Louisville, KY-IN** | NA | 28 | Philadelphia, PA M.D. | 85,911 | 98 | Springfield, MO | 22,639 |
| 132 | Lubbock, TX | 14,754 | NA | Phoenix-Mesa-Scottsdale, AZ** | NA | 221 | Springfield, OH | 6,465 |
| 270 | Lynchburg, VA | 4,609 | 51 | Pittsburgh, PA | 50,740 | 349 | State College, PA | 2,311 |
| 146 | Macon, GA | 12,036 | 306 | Pittsfield, MA | 3,596 | 350 | Staunton-Waynesboro, VA | 2,240 |
| 259 | Madera, CA | 4,951 | 335 | Pocatello, ID | 2,732 | 71 | Stockton-Lodi, CA | 33,583 |
| 128 | Madison, WI | 15,524 | 151 | Port St. Lucie, FL | 11,205 | 257 | St. Cloud, MN | 4,989 |
| 160 | Manchester-Nashua, NH | 10,467 | 34 | Portland-Vancouver, OR-WA | 75,071 | NA | St. George, UT** | NA |
| 359 | Manhattan, KS | 1,937 | 142 | Portland, ME | 12,538 | 248 | St. Joseph, MO-KS | 5,560 |
| 329 | Mankato-North Mankato, MN | 2,807 | 264 | Prescott, AZ | 4,812 | 27 | St. Louis, MO-IL | 86,965 |
| 236 | Mansfield, OH | 6,010 | 61 | Providence-Warwick, RI-MA | 43,293 | 267 | Sumter, SC | 4,644 |
| 76 | McAllen-Edinburg-Mission, TX | 32,616 | 155 | Provo-Orem, UT | 10,929 | 116 | Syracuse, NY | 18,107 |
| 182 | Medford, OR | 8,912 | 167 | Pueblo, CO | 9,898 | 66 | Tacoma, WA M.D. | 37,934 |
| 40 | Memphis, TN-MS-AR | 69,860 | 297 | Punta Gorda, FL | 3,799 | 130 | Tallahassee, FL | 15,065 |
| 170 | Merced, CA | 9,651 | 252 | Racine, WI | 5,156 | 24 | Tampa-St Petersburg, FL | 89,859 |
| 6 | Miami (greater), FL | 247,278 | 78 | Raleigh, NC | 30,278 | 238 | Terre Haute, IN | 5,976 |
| 16 | Miami-Dade County, FL M.D. | 127,011 | 295 | Rapid City, SD | 3,956 | 217 | Texarkana, TX-AR | 6,726 |
| 273 | Midland, TX | 4,547 | 179 | Reading, PA | 9,018 | 365 | The Villages, FL | 1,228 |
| 45 | Milwaukee, WI | 57,379 | 208 | Redding, CA | 7,044 | NA | Toledo, OH** | NA |
| 23 | Minneapolis-St. Paul, MN-WI | 99,147 | 139 | Reno, NV | 13,042 | 177 | Topeka, KS | 9,126 |
| 300 | Missoula, MT | 3,708 | 74 | Richmond, VA | 32,790 | 180 | Trenton, NJ | 9,009 |
| 103 | Mobile, AL | 21,111 | 14 | Riverside-San Bernardino, CA | 137,369 | 48 | Tucson, AZ | 52,811 |
| 93 | Modesto, CA | 23,254 | 186 | Roanoke, VA | 8,351 | 67 | Tulsa, OK | 36,427 |
| 169 | Monroe, LA | 9,806 | 298 | Rochester, MN | 3,784 | 183 | Tuscaloosa, AL | 8,693 |
| 294 | Monroe, MI | 3,958 | 81 | Rochester, NY | 29,226 | 207 | Tyler, TX | 7,068 |
| 69 | Montgomery County, PA M.D. | 35,842 | 140 | Rockford, IL | 12,763 | 205 | Utica-Rome, NY | 7,258 |
| 339 | Morgantown, WV | 2,673 | 175 | Rockingham County, NH M.D. | 9,191 | 127 | Vallejo-Fairfield, CA | 15,534 |
| 296 | Morristown, TN | 3,848 | 227 | Rocky Mount, NC | 6,235 | 305 | Victoria, TX | 3,622 |
| 250 | Mount Vernon-Anacortes, WA | 5,446 | 280 | Rome, GA | 4,356 | 195 | Vineland-Bridgeton, NJ | 7,768 |
| 292 | Muncie, IN | 4,023 | 39 | Sacramento, CA | 70,448 | 46 | Virginia Beach-Norfolk, VA-NC | 56,790 |
| 212 | Muskegon, MI | 6,917 | 243 | Saginaw, MI | 5,796 | NA | Visalia-Porterville, CA** | NA |
| 109 | Myrtle Beach, SC-NC | 19,652 | 136 | Salem, OR | 13,758 | 171 | Waco, TX | 9,546 |
| 324 | Napa, CA | 2,991 | 141 | Salinas, CA | 12,734 | 194 | Warner Robins, GA | 8,024 |
| 235 | Naples-Marco Island, FL | 6,021 | 133 | Salisbury, MD-DE | 14,249 | 56 | Warren-Troy, MI M.D. | 48,173 |
| 44 | Nashville-Davidson, TN | 57,853 | 47 | Salt Lake City, UT | 53,715 | 12 | Washington (greater) DC-VA-MD-WV | 148,591 |
| 60 | Nassau-Suffolk, NY M.D. | 44,810 | 284 | San Angelo, TX | 4,301 | 17 | Washington, DC-VA-MD-WV M.D. | 125,814 |
| 286 | New Bern, NC | 4,283 | 19 | San Antonio, TX | 110,708 | 344 | Watertown-Fort Drum, NY | 2,453 |
| 84 | New Haven-Milford, CT | 25,847 | 31 | San Diego, CA | 81,453 | 352 | Wausau, WI | 2,212 |
| 59 | New Orleans, LA | 44,931 | 9 | San Francisco (greater), CA | 185,816 | 54 | West Palm Beach, FL M.D. | 48,469 |
| 1 | New York (greater), NY-NJ-PA | 398,764 | 37 | San Francisco-Redwood, CA M.D. | 73,129 | 239 | Wichita Falls, TX | 5,967 |
| 3 | New York-Jersey City, NY-NJ M.D. | 296,994 | 53 | San Jose, CA | 50,050 | 79 | Wichita, KS | 29,977 |
| 50 | Newark, NJ-PA M.D. | 51,000 | 204 | San Luis Obispo, CA | 7,277 | 332 | Williamsport, PA | 2,748 |
| 258 | Niles-Benton Harbor, MI | 4,967 | 249 | San Rafael, CA M.D. | 5,503 | 89 | Wilmington, DE-MD-NJ M.D. | 24,570 |
| 91 | North Port-Sarasota-Bradenton, FL | 23,690 | 176 | Santa Cruz-Watsonville, CA | 9,142 | 159 | Wilmington, NC | 10,504 |
| 289 | Norwich-New London, CT | 4,145 | 150 | Santa Maria-Santa Barbara, CA | 11,240 | 326 | Winchester, VA-WV | 2,848 |
| 20 | Oakland-Hayward, CA M.D. | 107,184 | 165 | Santa Rosa, CA | 10,000 | 85 | Winston-Salem, NC | 25,497 |
| NA | Ocala, FL** | NA | 144 | Savannah, GA | 12,394 | 105 | Worcester, MA-CT | 20,632 |
| 288 | Ocean City, NJ | 4,206 | 135 | Scranton--Wilkes-Barre, PA | 13,834 | 178 | Yakima, WA | 9,084 |
| 198 | Odessa, TX | 7,496 | 11 | Seattle (greater), WA | 156,432 | 181 | York-Hanover, PA | 8,966 |
| NA | Ogden-Clearfield, UT** | NA | 18 | Seattle-Bellevue-Everett, WA M.D. | 118,498 | 246 | Yuba City, CA | 5,597 |
| 43 | Oklahoma City, OK | 58,654 | 312 | Sebastian-Vero Beach, FL | 3,402 | 228 | Yuma, AZ | 6,229 |
| 197 | Olympia, WA | 7,526 | 302 | Sebring, FL | 3,656 | | | |

Source: CQ Press using reported data from the F.B.I. "Crime in the United States 2013"
*Includes murder, rape, robbery, aggravated assault, burglary, larceny-theft, and motor vehicle theft. The FBI changed the definition of rape beginning with 2013 data. Not all cities have made the change so the metro area figures reported here include rape figures based on differing definitions of rape. See note on page vii. **Not available.

# 1. Crimes in 2013 (continued)
## National Total = 9,795,658 Crimes*

| RANK | METROPOLITAN AREA | CRIMES | RANK | METROPOLITAN AREA | CRIMES | RANK | METROPOLITAN AREA | CRIMES |
|---|---|---|---|---|---|---|---|---|
| 1 | New York (greater), NY-NJ-PA | 398,764 | 65 | Bakersfield, CA | 38,350 | 129 | Flint, MI | 15,424 |
| 2 | Los Angeles (greater), CA | 336,495 | 66 | Tacoma, WA M.D. | 37,934 | 130 | Tallahassee, FL | 15,065 |
| 3 | New York-Jersey City, NY-NJ M.D. | 296,994 | 67 | Tulsa, OK | 36,427 | 131 | Gulfport-Biloxi-Pascagoula, MS | 14,947 |
| 4 | Los Angeles County, CA M.D. | 268,803 | 68 | Buffalo-Niagara Falls, NY | 35,927 | 132 | Lubbock, TX | 14,754 |
| 5 | Houston, TX | 254,251 | 69 | Montgomery County, PA M.D. | 35,842 | 133 | Salisbury, MD-DE | 14,249 |
| 6 | Miami (greater), FL | 247,278 | 70 | Baton Rouge, LA | 35,323 | 134 | Eugene, OR | 13,892 |
| 7 | Dallas (greater), TX | 229,588 | 71 | Stockton-Lodi, CA | 33,583 | 135 | Scranton--Wilkes-Barre, PA | 13,834 |
| 8 | Atlanta, GA | 205,014 | 72 | Columbia, SC | 33,436 | 136 | Salem, OR | 13,758 |
| 9 | San Francisco (greater), CA | 185,816 | 73 | Camden, NJ M.D. | 33,264 | 137 | Fort Wayne, IN | 13,551 |
| 10 | Philadelphia (greater) PA-NJ-MD-DE | 179,587 | 74 | Richmond, VA | 32,790 | 138 | Fayetteville-Springdale, AR-MO | 13,252 |
| 11 | Seattle (greater), WA | 156,432 | 75 | Spokane, WA | 32,718 | 139 | Reno, NV | 13,042 |
| 12 | Washington (greater) DC-VA-MD-WV | 148,591 | 76 | McAllen-Edinburg-Mission, TX | 32,616 | 140 | Rockford, IL | 12,763 |
| 13 | Dallas-Plano-Irving, TX M.D. | 144,607 | 77 | Omaha-Council Bluffs, NE-IA | 32,462 | 141 | Salinas, CA | 12,734 |
| 14 | Riverside-San Bernardino, CA | 137,369 | 78 | Raleigh, NC | 30,278 | 142 | Portland, ME | 12,538 |
| 15 | Detroit (greater), MI | 135,291 | 79 | Wichita, KS | 29,977 | 143 | Boise City, ID | 12,471 |
| 16 | Miami-Dade County, FL M.D. | 127,011 | 80 | Knoxville, TN | 29,833 | 144 | Savannah, GA | 12,394 |
| 17 | Washington, DC-VA-MD-WV M.D. | 125,814 | 81 | Rochester, NY | 29,226 | 145 | Lansing-East Lansing, MI | 12,216 |
| 18 | Seattle-Bellevue-Everett, WA M.D. | 118,498 | 82 | Dayton, OH | 28,844 | 146 | Macon, GA | 12,036 |
| 19 | San Antonio, TX | 110,708 | 83 | Greensboro-High Point, NC | 28,145 | 147 | Laredo, TX | 12,012 |
| 20 | Oakland-Hayward, CA M.D. | 107,184 | 84 | New Haven-Milford, CT | 25,847 | 148 | Canton, OH | 11,897 |
| 21 | Boston (greater), MA-NH | 105,037 | 85 | Winston-Salem, NC | 25,497 | 149 | Spartanburg, SC | 11,540 |
| 22 | Baltimore, MD | 101,026 | 86 | Hartford, CT | 25,236 | 150 | Santa Maria-Santa Barbara, CA | 11,240 |
| 23 | Minneapolis-St. Paul, MN-WI | 99,147 | 87 | Charleston-North Charleston, SC | 24,952 | 151 | Port St. Lucie, FL | 11,205 |
| 24 | Tampa-St Petersburg, FL | 89,859 | 88 | Colorado Springs, CO | 24,731 | 152 | Lincoln, NE | 11,057 |
| 25 | Orlando, FL | 89,547 | 89 | Wilmington, DE-MD-NJ M.D. | 24,570 | 153 | Lake Charles, LA | 11,015 |
| 26 | Detroit-Dearborn-Livonia, MI M.D. | 87,118 | 90 | Chattanooga, TN-GA | 23,705 | 154 | Davenport, IA-IL | 10,994 |
| 27 | St. Louis, MO-IL | 86,965 | 91 | North Port-Sarasota-Bradenton, FL | 23,690 | 155 | Provo-Orem, UT | 10,929 |
| 28 | Philadelphia, PA M.D. | 85,911 | 92 | Gary, IN M.D. | 23,380 | 156 | Lancaster, PA | 10,750 |
| 29 | Fort Worth-Arlington, TX M.D. | 84,981 | 93 | Modesto, CA | 23,254 | 157 | South Bend-Mishawaka, IN-MI | 10,734 |
| 30 | Denver-Aurora, CO | 82,829 | 94 | Augusta, GA-SC | 22,927 | 158 | Elgin, IL M.D. | 10,660 |
| 31 | San Diego, CA | 81,453 | 95 | Grand Rapids-Wyoming, MI | 22,836 | 159 | Wilmington, NC | 10,504 |
| 32 | Charlotte-Mecklenburg, NC-SC | 78,849 | 96 | Silver Spring-Frederick, MD M.D. | 22,777 | 160 | Manchester-Nashua, NH | 10,467 |
| 33 | Kansas City, MO-KS | 76,297 | 97 | Akron, OH | 22,654 | 161 | Florence, SC | 10,394 |
| 34 | Portland-Vancouver, OR-WA | 75,071 | 98 | Springfield, MO | 22,639 | 162 | Amarillo, TX | 10,284 |
| 35 | Las Vegas-Henderson, NV | 74,851 | 99 | Albany-Schenectady-Troy, NY | 22,513 | 163 | Duluth, MN-WI | 10,191 |
| 36 | Cincinnati, OH-KY-IN | 73,338 | 100 | Springfield, MA | 21,530 | 164 | Peoria, IL | 10,163 |
| 37 | San Francisco-Redwood, CA M.D. | 73,129 | 101 | El Paso, TX | 21,256 | 165 | Santa Rosa, CA | 10,000 |
| 38 | Fort Lauderdale, FL M.D. | 71,798 | 102 | Corpus Christi, TX | 21,146 | 166 | Springfield, IL | 9,901 |
| 39 | Sacramento, CA | 70,448 | 103 | Mobile, AL | 21,111 | 167 | Pueblo, CO | 9,898 |
| 40 | Memphis, TN-MS-AR | 69,860 | 104 | Deltona-Daytona Beach, FL | 20,976 | 168 | Fort Smith, AR-OK | 9,861 |
| 41 | Anaheim-Santa Ana-Irvine, CA M.D. | 67,692 | 105 | Worcester, MA-CT | 20,632 | 169 | Monroe, LA | 9,806 |
| 42 | Austin-Round Rock, TX | 64,830 | 106 | Fayetteville, NC | 20,417 | 170 | Merced, CA | 9,651 |
| 43 | Oklahoma City, OK | 58,654 | 107 | Lakeland, FL | 20,402 | 171 | Waco, TX | 9,546 |
| 44 | Nashville-Davidson, TN | 57,853 | 108 | Allentown, PA-NJ | 19,716 | 172 | Gainesville, FL | 9,475 |
| 45 | Milwaukee, WI | 57,379 | 109 | Myrtle Beach, SC-NC | 19,652 | 173 | Atlantic City, NJ | 9,424 |
| 46 | Virginia Beach-Norfolk, VA-NC | 56,790 | 110 | Jackson, MS | 19,522 | 174 | Kingsport, TN-VA | 9,290 |
| 47 | Salt Lake City, UT | 53,715 | 111 | Lexington-Fayette, KY | 19,474 | 175 | Rockingham County, NH M.D. | 9,191 |
| 48 | Tucson, AZ | 52,811 | 112 | Lafayette, LA | 19,116 | 176 | Santa Cruz-Watsonville, CA | 9,142 |
| 49 | Jacksonville, FL | 51,878 | 113 | Shreveport-Bossier City, LA | 18,360 | 177 | Topeka, KS | 9,126 |
| 50 | Newark, NJ-PA M.D. | 51,000 | 114 | Palm Bay-Melbourne, FL | 18,282 | 178 | Yakima, WA | 9,084 |
| 51 | Pittsburgh, PA | 50,740 | 115 | Pensacola, FL | 18,215 | 179 | Reading, PA | 9,018 |
| 52 | Boston, MA M.D. | 50,417 | 116 | Syracuse, NY | 18,107 | 180 | Trenton, NJ | 9,009 |
| 53 | San Jose, CA | 50,050 | 117 | Des Moines-West Des Moines, IA | 18,085 | 181 | York-Hanover, PA | 8,966 |
| 54 | West Palm Beach, FL M.D. | 48,469 | 118 | Oxnard-Thousand Oaks, CA | 18,029 | 182 | Medford, OR | 8,912 |
| 55 | Birmingham-Hoover, AL | 48,431 | 119 | Bridgeport-Stamford, CT | 17,170 | 183 | Tuscaloosa, AL | 8,693 |
| 56 | Warren-Troy, MI M.D. | 48,173 | 120 | Columbus, GA-AL | 16,870 | 184 | Alexandria, LA | 8,615 |
| 57 | Albuquerque, NM | 47,171 | 121 | Huntsville, AL | 16,682 | 185 | Ann Arbor, MI | 8,488 |
| 58 | Cambridge-Newton, MA M.D. | 45,429 | 122 | Cape Coral-Fort Myers, FL | 16,584 | 186 | Roanoke, VA | 8,351 |
| 59 | New Orleans, LA | 44,931 | 123 | Lake Co.-Kenosha Co., IL-WI M.D. | 16,183 | 187 | Panama City, FL | 8,283 |
| 60 | Nassau-Suffolk, NY M.D. | 44,810 | 124 | Brownsville-Harlingen, TX | 15,853 | 188 | Bremerton-Silverdale, WA | 8,276 |
| 61 | Providence-Warwick, RI-MA | 43,293 | 125 | Beaumont-Port Arthur, TX | 15,818 | 189 | Albany, GA | 8,146 |
| 62 | Fresno, CA | 41,566 | 126 | Anchorage, AK | 15,544 | 190 | Longview, TX | 8,118 |
| 63 | Little Rock, AR | 40,259 | 127 | Vallejo-Fairfield, CA | 15,534 | 191 | Joplin, MO | 8,106 |
| 64 | Greenville-Anderson, SC | 39,112 | 128 | Madison, WI | 15,524 | 192 | Hammond, LA | 8,044 |

Note: All listings are for Metropolitan Statistical Areas (M.S.A.s) except for those ending with "M.D." Listings with "M.D." are Metropolitan Divisions which are smaller parts of eleven large M.S.A.s. See explanatory note at beginning of metropolitan area section.

| RANK | METROPOLITAN AREA | CRIMES | RANK | METROPOLITAN AREA | CRIMES | RANK | METROPOLITAN AREA | CRIMES |
|---|---|---|---|---|---|---|---|---|
| 193 | Clarksville, TN-KY | 8,043 | 255 | Goldsboro, NC | 5,034 | 317 | Kankakee, IL | 3,222 |
| 194 | Warner Robins, GA | 8,024 | 256 | Anniston-Oxford, AL | 4,991 | 318 | Oshkosh-Neenah, WI | 3,187 |
| 195 | Vineland-Bridgeton, NJ | 7,768 | 257 | St. Cloud, MN | 4,989 | 319 | Chambersburg-Waynesboro, PA | 3,161 |
| 196 | Boulder, CO | 7,737 | 258 | Niles-Benton Harbor, MI | 4,967 | 320 | Great Falls, MT | 3,131 |
| 197 | Olympia, WA | 7,526 | 259 | Madera, CA | 4,951 | 321 | Lewiston-Auburn, ME | 3,079 |
| 198 | Odessa, TX | 7,496 | 260 | Jonesboro, AR | 4,890 | 322 | Grand Island, NE | 3,056 |
| 199 | Fort Collins, CO | 7,458 | 261 | Florence-Muscle Shoals, AL | 4,847 | 323 | Cumberland, MD-WV | 3,029 |
| 200 | Erie, PA | 7,376 | 262 | Dothan, AL | 4,841 | 324 | Napa, CA | 2,991 |
| 201 | Houma, LA | 7,366 | 263 | Bloomington, IN | 4,832 | 325 | Eau Claire, WI | 2,980 |
| 202 | Binghamton, NY | 7,327 | 264 | Prescott, AZ | 4,812 | 326 | Winchester, VA-WV | 2,848 |
| 203 | Lake Havasu City-Kingman, AZ | 7,319 | 265 | East Stroudsburg, PA | 4,744 | 327 | Cheyenne, WY | 2,824 |
| 204 | San Luis Obispo, CA | 7,277 | 266 | Charlottesville, VA | 4,717 | 328 | Columbus, IN | 2,822 |
| 205 | Utica-Rome, NY | 7,258 | 267 | Sumter, SC | 4,644 | 329 | Mankato-North Mankato, MN | 2,807 |
| 206 | Las Cruces, NM | 7,098 | 268 | Flagstaff, AZ | 4,620 | 330 | Johnstown, PA | 2,793 |
| 207 | Tyler, TX | 7,068 | 269 | Bend, OR | 4,616 | 331 | Owensboro, KY | 2,749 |
| 208 | Redding, CA | 7,044 | 270 | Jackson, MI | 4,609 | 332 | Williamsport, PA | 2,748 |
| 209 | Billings, MT | 7,030 | 270 | Lynchburg, VA | 4,609 | 333 | Idaho Falls, ID | 2,745 |
| 210 | Champaign-Urbana, IL | 7,014 | 272 | Bloomington, IL | 4,556 | 334 | Lebanon, PA | 2,736 |
| 211 | Crestview-Fort Walton Beach, FL | 6,973 | 273 | Midland, TX | 4,547 | 335 | Pocatello, ID | 2,732 |
| 212 | Muskegon, MI | 6,917 | 274 | Lawrence, KS | 4,523 | 336 | California-Lexington Park, MD | 2,731 |
| 213 | Chico, CA | 6,857 | 275 | Gainesville, GA | 4,491 | 337 | Kokomo, IN | 2,680 |
| 214 | Kennewick-Richland, WA | 6,839 | 276 | Bangor, ME | 4,479 | 338 | La Crosse, WI-MN | 2,674 |
| 215 | College Station-Bryan, TX | 6,781 | 277 | Coeur d'Alene, ID | 4,448 | 339 | Morgantown, WV | 2,673 |
| 216 | Cedar Rapids, IA | 6,749 | 277 | Hanford-Corcoran, CA | 4,448 | 340 | Bay City, MI | 2,568 |
| 217 | Texarkana, TX-AR | 6,726 | 279 | Longview, WA | 4,419 | 341 | Casper, WY | 2,536 |
| 218 | Greenville, NC | 6,722 | 280 | Rome, GA | 4,356 | 341 | Parkersburg-Vienna, WV | 2,536 |
| 219 | Hilton Head Island, SC | 6,630 | 281 | Janesville, WI | 4,354 | 343 | Hinesville, GA | 2,489 |
| 220 | Athens-Clarke County, GA | 6,617 | 282 | Dalton, GA | 4,333 | 344 | Watertown-Fort Drum, NY | 2,453 |
| 221 | Springfield, OH | 6,465 | 283 | Grand Junction, CO | 4,312 | 345 | Altoona, PA | 2,439 |
| 222 | El Centro, CA | 6,445 | 284 | San Angelo, TX | 4,301 | 346 | Elizabethtown-Fort Knox, KY | 2,353 |
| 223 | Sioux Falls, SD | 6,425 | 285 | Decatur, AL | 4,291 | 347 | Grand Forks, ND-MN | 2,350 |
| 224 | Lawton, OK | 6,404 | 286 | New Bern, NC | 4,283 | 348 | Corvallis, OR | 2,323 |
| 225 | Hagerstown-Martinsburg, MD-WV | 6,327 | 287 | Cleveland, TN | 4,254 | 349 | State College, PA | 2,311 |
| 226 | Green Bay, WI | 6,313 | 288 | Ocean City, NJ | 4,206 | 350 | Staunton-Waynesboro, VA | 2,240 |
| 227 | Rocky Mount, NC | 6,235 | 289 | Norwich-New London, CT | 4,145 | 351 | Sheboygan, WI | 2,225 |
| 228 | Yuma, AZ | 6,229 | 290 | Albany, OR | 4,115 | 352 | Wausau, WI | 2,212 |
| 229 | Lafayette, IN | 6,194 | 291 | Bowling Green, KY | 4,025 | 353 | Elmira, NY | 2,199 |
| 230 | Columbia, MO | 6,181 | 292 | Muncie, IN | 4,023 | 354 | Harrisonburg, VA | 2,188 |
| 231 | Kahului-Wailuku-Lahaina, HI | 6,154 | 293 | Lima, OH | 3,969 | 355 | Glens Falls, NY | 2,177 |
| 232 | Barnstable Town, MA | 6,144 | 294 | Monroe, MI | 3,958 | 356 | Lewiston, ID-WA | 2,163 |
| 233 | Greeley, CO | 6,092 | 295 | Rapid City, SD | 3,956 | 357 | Ames, IA | 2,089 |
| 234 | Abilene, TX | 6,082 | 296 | Morristown, TN | 3,848 | 358 | Dubuque, IA | 2,047 |
| 235 | Naples-Marco Island, FL | 6,021 | 297 | Punta Gorda, FL | 3,799 | 359 | Manhattan, KS | 1,937 |
| 236 | Mansfield, OH | 6,010 | 298 | Rochester, MN | 3,784 | 360 | Fond du Lac, WI | 1,851 |
| 237 | Jackson, TN | 5,984 | 299 | Blacksburg, VA | 3,770 | 361 | Bloomsburg-Berwick, PA | 1,706 |
| 238 | Terre Haute, IN | 5,976 | 300 | Missoula, MT | 3,708 | 362 | Fairbanks, AK | 1,666 |
| 239 | Wichita Falls, TX | 5,967 | 301 | Jefferson City, MO | 3,669 | 363 | Logan, UT-ID | 1,603 |
| 240 | Dutchess-Putnam, NY M.D. | 5,960 | 302 | Sebring, FL | 3,656 | 364 | Gettysburg, PA | 1,383 |
| 241 | Dover, DE | 5,831 | 303 | Iowa City, IA | 3,652 | 365 | The Villages, FL | 1,228 |
| 242 | Johnson City, TN | 5,817 | 304 | Carbondale-Marion, IL | 3,628 | 366 | Carson City, NV | 1,057 |
| 243 | Saginaw, MI | 5,796 | 305 | Victoria, TX | 3,622 | NA | Brunswick, GA** | NA |
| 244 | Hot Springs, AR | 5,637 | 306 | Pittsfield, MA | 3,596 | NA | Chicago (greater), IL-IN-WI** | NA |
| 245 | Fargo, ND-MN | 5,636 | 307 | Kingston, NY | 3,575 | NA | Chicago-Naperville, IL M.D.** | NA |
| 246 | Yuba City, CA | 5,597 | 308 | Grants Pass, OR | 3,500 | NA | Indianapolis, IN** | NA |
| 247 | Burlington, NC | 5,562 | 309 | Appleton, WI | 3,463 | NA | Louisville, KY-IN** | NA |
| 248 | St. Joseph, MO-KS | 5,560 | 310 | Cape Girardeau, MO-IL | 3,459 | NA | Ocala, FL** | NA |
| 249 | San Rafael, CA M.D. | 5,503 | 311 | Sherman-Denison, TX | 3,418 | NA | Ogden-Clearfield, UT** | NA |
| 250 | Mount Vernon-Anacortes, WA | 5,446 | 312 | Sebastian-Vero Beach, FL | 3,402 | NA | Phoenix-Mesa-Scottsdale, AZ** | NA |
| 251 | Daphne-Fairhope-Foley, AL | 5,319 | 313 | Farmington, NM | 3,380 | NA | St. George, UT** | NA |
| 252 | Racine, WI | 5,156 | 314 | Bismarck, ND | 3,356 | NA | Toledo, OH** | NA |
| 253 | Sioux City, IA-NE-SD | 5,089 | 315 | Homosassa Springs, FL | 3,297 | NA | Visalia-Porterville, CA** | NA |
| 254 | Gadsden, AL | 5,049 | 316 | Decatur, IL | 3,228 | | | |

Source: CQ Press using reported data from the F.B.I. "Crime in the United States 2013"

*Includes murder, rape, robbery, aggravated assault, burglary, larceny-theft, and motor vehicle theft. The FBI changed the definition of rape beginning with 2013 data. Not all cities have made the change so the metro area figures reported here include rape figures based on differing definitions of rape. See note on page vii. **Not available.

# 2. Crime Rate in 2013
## National Rate = 3,098.6 Crimes per 100,000 Population*

| RANK | METROPOLITAN AREA | RATE | RANK | METROPOLITAN AREA | RATE | RANK | METROPOLITAN AREA | RATE |
|---|---|---|---|---|---|---|---|---|
| 128 | Abilene, TX | 3,617.7 | 212 | Cheyenne, WY | 2,952.9 | 171 | Gary, IN M.D. | 3,301.7 |
| 183 | Akron, OH | 3,220.3 | NA | Chicago (greater), IL-IN-WI** | NA | 364 | Gettysburg, PA | 1,363.3 |
| 267 | Albany-Schenectady-Troy, NY | 2,567.4 | NA | Chicago-Naperville, IL M.D.** | NA | 356 | Glens Falls, NY | 1,694.7 |
| 14 | Albany, GA | 5,176.5 | 197 | Chico, CA | 3,083.7 | 74 | Goldsboro, NC | 4,024.5 |
| 146 | Albany, OR | 3,453.5 | 150 | Cincinnati, OH-KY-IN | 3,432.6 | 301 | Grand Forks, ND-MN | 2,338.4 |
| 12 | Albuquerque, NM | 5,226.0 | 222 | Clarksville, TN-KY | 2,883.6 | 124 | Grand Island, NE | 3,631.3 |
| 5 | Alexandria, LA | 5,569.6 | 131 | Cleveland, TN | 3,588.3 | 219 | Grand Junction, CO | 2,889.2 |
| 296 | Allentown, PA-NJ | 2,379.3 | 196 | Coeur d'Alene, ID | 3,084.1 | 306 | Grand Rapids-Wyoming, MI | 2,256.2 |
| 342 | Altoona, PA | 1,919.4 | 228 | College Station-Bryan, TX | 2,859.1 | 66 | Grants Pass, OR | 4,208.6 |
| 82 | Amarillo, TX | 3,950.8 | 121 | Colorado Springs, CO | 3,643.3 | 97 | Great Falls, MT | 3,809.2 |
| 304 | Ames, IA | 2,273.2 | 127 | Columbia, MO | 3,620.5 | 305 | Greeley, CO | 2,267.5 |
| 310 | Anaheim-Santa Ana-Irvine, CA M.D. | 2,170.5 | 65 | Columbia, SC | 4,214.9 | 326 | Green Bay, WI | 2,018.4 |
| 20 | Anchorage, AK | 4,941.6 | 10 | Columbus, GA-AL | 5,343.0 | 99 | Greensboro-High Point, NC | 3,793.1 |
| 293 | Ann Arbor, MI | 2,403.2 | 137 | Columbus, IN | 3,523.0 | 40 | Greenville-Anderson, SC | 4,588.4 |
| 60 | Anniston-Oxford, AL | 4,269.7 | 31 | Corpus Christi, TX | 4,784.3 | 94 | Greenville, NC | 3,855.4 |
| 361 | Appleton, WI | 1,509.2 | 251 | Corvallis, OR | 2,671.6 | 88 | Gulfport-Biloxi-Pascagoula, MS | 3,908.6 |
| 163 | Athens-Clarke County, GA | 3,351.5 | 239 | Crestview-Fort Walton Beach, FL | 2,760.0 | 285 | Hagerstown-Martinsburg, MD-WV | 2,454.7 |
| 104 | Atlanta, GA | 3,719.9 | 205 | Cumberland, MD-WV | 2,979.5 | 1 | Hammond, LA | 6,476.2 |
| 154 | Atlantic City, NJ | 3,413.3 | 159 | Dallas (greater), TX | 3,369.3 | 214 | Hanford-Corcoran, CA | 2,940.7 |
| 81 | Augusta, GA-SC | 3,953.4 | 184 | Dallas-Plano-Irving, TX M.D. | 3,209.0 | 357 | Harrisonburg, VA | 1,687.1 |
| 147 | Austin-Round Rock, TX | 3,449.8 | 200 | Dalton, GA | 3,032.1 | 282 | Hartford, CT | 2,464.9 |
| 47 | Bakersfield, CA | 4,447.9 | 240 | Daphne-Fairhope-Foley, AL | 2,751.4 | 160 | Hilton Head Island, SC | 3,369.2 |
| 120 | Baltimore, MD | 3,645.5 | 226 | Davenport, IA-IL | 2,864.6 | 203 | Hinesville, GA | 3,000.1 |
| 218 | Bangor, ME | 2,917.4 | 130 | Dayton, OH | 3,592.0 | 297 | Homosassa Springs, FL | 2,367.9 |
| 230 | Barnstable Town, MA | 2,846.5 | 237 | Decatur, AL | 2,780.8 | 4 | Hot Springs, AR | 5,801.6 |
| 56 | Baton Rouge, LA | 4,309.4 | 215 | Decatur, IL | 2,937.9 | 138 | Houma, LA | 3,518.9 |
| 292 | Bay City, MI | 2,404.9 | 142 | Deltona-Daytona Beach, FL | 3,501.1 | 72 | Houston, TX | 4,047.8 |
| 91 | Beaumont-Port Arthur, TX | 3,895.5 | 198 | Denver-Aurora, CO | 3,075.3 | 96 | Huntsville, AL | 3,839.3 |
| 234 | Bend, OR | 2,811.5 | 199 | Des Moines-West Des Moines, IA | 3,032.5 | 331 | Idaho Falls, ID | 1,995.5 |
| 61 | Billings, MT | 4,264.6 | 191 | Detroit (greater), MI | 3,148.7 | NA | Indianapolis, IN** | NA |
| 209 | Binghamton, NY | 2,956.0 | 25 | Detroit-Dearborn-Livonia, MI M.D. | 4,876.5 | 303 | Iowa City, IA | 2,276.2 |
| 63 | Birmingham-Hoover, AL | 4,252.3 | 175 | Dothan, AL | 3,267.3 | 102 | Jacksonville, FL | 3,724.5 |
| 245 | Bismarck, ND | 2,701.2 | 149 | Dover, DE | 3,435.5 | 223 | Jackson, MI | 2,871.7 |
| 318 | Blacksburg, VA | 2,100.0 | 315 | Dubuque, IA | 2,137.8 | 161 | Jackson, MS | 3,366.6 |
| 291 | Bloomington, IL | 2,405.4 | 122 | Duluth, MN-WI | 3,637.5 | 41 | Jackson, TN | 4,578.3 |
| 211 | Bloomington, IN | 2,953.6 | 362 | Dutchess-Putnam, NY M.D. | 1,500.5 | 244 | Janesville, WI | 2,711.4 |
| 329 | Bloomsburg-Berwick, PA | 2,005.4 | 233 | East Stroudsburg, PA | 2,818.6 | 287 | Jefferson City, MO | 2,437.2 |
| 340 | Boise City, ID | 1,925.0 | 350 | Eau Claire, WI | 1,811.9 | 220 | Johnson City, TN | 2,887.7 |
| 308 | Boston (greater), MA-NH | 2,244.8 | 126 | El Centro, CA | 3,621.7 | 332 | Johnstown, PA | 1,982.6 |
| 264 | Boston, MA M.D. | 2,595.6 | 274 | El Paso, TX | 2,523.7 | 87 | Jonesboro, AR | 3,910.7 |
| 278 | Boulder, CO | 2,493.1 | 355 | Elgin, IL M.D. | 1,694.9 | 37 | Joplin, MO | 4,653.1 |
| 283 | Bowling Green, KY | 2,462.7 | 360 | Elizabethtown-Fort Knox, KY | 1,561.4 | 95 | Kahului-Wailuku-Lahaina, HI | 3,854.7 |
| 182 | Bremerton-Silverdale, WA | 3,221.6 | 281 | Elmira, NY | 2,469.7 | 229 | Kankakee, IL | 2,855.3 |
| 346 | Bridgeport-Stamford, CT | 1,864.2 | 258 | Erie, PA | 2,630.1 | 103 | Kansas City, MO-KS | 3,722.9 |
| 101 | Brownsville-Harlingen, TX | 3,775.1 | 90 | Eugene, OR | 3,898.7 | 276 | Kennewick-Richland, WA | 2,500.5 |
| NA | Brunswick, GA** | NA | 30 | Fairbanks, AK | 4,795.5 | 201 | Kingsport, TN-VA | 3,004.1 |
| 190 | Buffalo-Niagara Falls, NY | 3,165.2 | 272 | Fargo, ND-MN | 2,536.9 | 335 | Kingston, NY | 1,966.4 |
| 132 | Burlington, NC | 3,583.5 | 254 | Farmington, NM | 2,649.9 | 143 | Knoxville, TN | 3,500.1 |
| 280 | California-Lexington Park, MD | 2,476.1 | 243 | Fayetteville-Springdale, AR-MO | 2,715.3 | 181 | Kokomo, IN | 3,224.7 |
| 336 | Cambridge-Newton, MA M.D. | 1,963.9 | 9 | Fayetteville, NC | 5,400.3 | 334 | La Crosse, WI-MN | 1,967.4 |
| 256 | Camden, NJ M.D. | 2,645.5 | 158 | Flagstaff, AZ | 3,372.3 | 208 | Lafayette, IN | 2,971.1 |
| 213 | Canton, OH | 2,944.5 | 108 | Flint, MI | 3,702.3 | 75 | Lafayette, LA | 4,006.3 |
| 273 | Cape Coral-Fort Myers, FL | 2,527.1 | 173 | Florence-Muscle Shoals, AL | 3,299.5 | 8 | Lake Charles, LA | 5,460.1 |
| 134 | Cape Girardeau, MO-IL | 3,547.3 | 19 | Florence, SC | 5,017.7 | 347 | Lake Co.-Kenosha Co., IL-WI M.D. | 1,860.9 |
| 227 | Carbondale-Marion, IL | 2,863.8 | 349 | Fond du Lac, WI | 1,815.5 | 133 | Lake Havasu City-Kingman, AZ | 3,568.6 |
| 341 | Carson City, NV | 1,924.0 | 298 | Fort Collins, CO | 2,360.8 | 174 | Lakeland, FL | 3,275.6 |
| 189 | Casper, WY | 3,170.3 | 92 | Fort Lauderdale, FL M.D. | 3,894.9 | 324 | Lancaster, PA | 2,033.3 |
| 270 | Cedar Rapids, IA | 2,560.4 | 140 | Fort Smith, AR-OK | 3,510.1 | 261 | Lansing-East Lansing, MI | 2,617.4 |
| 321 | Chambersburg-Waynesboro, PA | 2,084.5 | 186 | Fort Wayne, IN | 3,195.4 | 43 | Laredo, TX | 4,568.4 |
| 204 | Champaign-Urbana, IL | 2,994.6 | 115 | Fort Worth-Arlington, TX M.D. | 3,682.2 | 172 | Las Cruces, NM | 3,300.1 |
| 139 | Charleston-North Charleston, SC | 3,510.2 | 52 | Fresno, CA | 4,355.6 | 114 | Las Vegas-Henderson, NV | 3,694.8 |
| 156 | Charlotte-Mecklenburg, NC-SC | 3,385.4 | 27 | Gadsden, AL | 4,838.7 | 76 | Lawrence, KS | 3,989.5 |
| 319 | Charlottesville, VA | 2,099.6 | 141 | Gainesville, FL | 3,502.5 | 29 | Lawton, OK | 4,798.9 |
| 49 | Chattanooga, TN-GA | 4,380.1 | 294 | Gainesville, GA | 2,397.8 | 327 | Lebanon, PA | 2,016.4 |

Note: All listings are for Metropolitan Statistical Areas (M.S.A.s) except for those ending with "M.D." Listings with "M.D." are Metropolitan Divisions which are smaller parts of eleven large M.S.A.s. See explanatory note at beginning of metropolitan area section.

| RANK | METROPOLITAN AREA | RATE | RANK | METROPOLITAN AREA | RATE | RANK | METROPOLITAN AREA | RATE |
|---|---|---|---|---|---|---|---|---|
| 225 | Lewiston-Auburn, ME | 2,865.0 | 123 | Omaha-Council Bluffs, NE-IA | 3,632.6 | 339 | Sheboygan, WI | 1,935.6 |
| 144 | Lewiston, ID-WA | 3,498.9 | 80 | Orlando, FL | 3,960.2 | 236 | Sherman-Denison, TX | 2,785.0 |
| 78 | Lexington-Fayette, KY | 3,979.8 | 345 | Oshkosh-Neenah, WI | 1,880.4 | 69 | Shreveport-Bossier City, LA | 4,083.6 |
| 100 | Lima, OH | 3,779.9 | 299 | Owensboro, KY | 2,359.1 | 351 | Silver Spring-Frederick, MD M.D. | 1,810.1 |
| 136 | Lincoln, NE | 3,526.4 | 314 | Oxnard-Thousand Oaks, CA | 2,144.6 | 202 | Sioux City, IA-NE-SD | 3,003.4 |
| 6 | Little Rock, AR | 5,567.3 | 167 | Palm Bay-Melbourne, FL | 3,321.0 | 253 | Sioux Falls, SD | 2,658.9 |
| 365 | Logan, UT-ID | 1,234.4 | 50 | Panama City, FL | 4,378.5 | 162 | South Bend-Mishawaka, IN-MI | 3,362.8 |
| 105 | Longview, TX | 3,719.2 | 241 | Parkersburg-Vienna, WV | 2,744.7 | 129 | Spartanburg, SC | 3,611.1 |
| 55 | Longview, WA | 4,325.2 | 89 | Pensacola, FL | 3,905.2 | 2 | Spokane, WA | 6,113.6 |
| 250 | Los Angeles County, CA M.D. | 2,682.0 | 252 | Peoria, IL | 2,668.8 | 36 | Springfield, IL | 4,661.7 |
| 269 | Los Angeles (greater), CA | 2,560.6 | 206 | Philadelphia (greater) PA-NJ-MD-DE | 2,975.2 | 151 | Springfield, MA | 3,426.6 |
| NA | Louisville, KY-IN** | NA | 71 | Philadelphia, PA M.D. | 4,063.0 | 18 | Springfield, MO | 5,053.2 |
| 23 | Lubbock, TX | 4,905.4 | NA | Phoenix-Mesa-Scottsdale, AZ** | NA | 33 | Springfield, OH | 4,713.7 |
| 352 | Lynchburg, VA | 1,794.6 | 313 | Pittsburgh, PA | 2,149.3 | 363 | State College, PA | 1,487.1 |
| 15 | Macon, GA | 5,168.0 | 238 | Pittsfield, MA | 2,766.7 | 344 | Staunton-Waynesboro, VA | 1,881.3 |
| 179 | Madera, CA | 3,240.8 | 180 | Pocatello, ID | 3,233.9 | 32 | Stockton-Lodi, CA | 4,738.8 |
| 279 | Madison, WI | 2,479.7 | 268 | Port St. Lucie, FL | 2,565.0 | 263 | St. Cloud, MN | 2,604.8 |
| 265 | Manchester-Nashua, NH | 2,590.9 | 178 | Portland-Vancouver, OR-WA | 3,242.3 | NA | St. George, UT** | NA |
| 337 | Manhattan, KS | 1,949.8 | 290 | Portland, ME | 2,415.9 | 54 | St. Joseph, MO-KS | 4,329.3 |
| 231 | Mankato-North Mankato, MN | 2,842.4 | 307 | Prescott, AZ | 2,246.0 | 194 | St. Louis, MO-IL | 3,101.9 |
| 21 | Mansfield, OH | 4,909.0 | 246 | Providence-Warwick, RI-MA | 2,697.7 | 59 | Sumter, SC | 4,272.2 |
| 77 | McAllen-Edinburg-Mission, TX | 3,981.2 | 338 | Provo-Orem, UT | 1,946.5 | 242 | Syracuse, NY | 2,739.2 |
| 57 | Medford, OR | 4,286.1 | 3 | Pueblo, CO | 6,098.6 | 38 | Tacoma, WA M.D. | 4,627.6 |
| 13 | Memphis, TN-MS-AR | 5,183.3 | 302 | Punta Gorda, FL | 2,317.4 | 79 | Tallahassee, FL | 3,976.4 |
| 119 | Merced, CA | 3,648.8 | 255 | Racine, WI | 2,648.0 | 192 | Tampa-St Petersburg, FL | 3,128.6 |
| 64 | Miami (greater), FL | 4,229.4 | 275 | Raleigh, NC | 2,502.6 | 145 | Terre Haute, IN | 3,454.4 |
| 28 | Miami-Dade County, FL M.D. | 4,828.3 | 235 | Rapid City, SD | 2,807.2 | 45 | Texarkana, TX-AR | 4,477.3 |
| 217 | Midland, TX | 2,918.9 | 309 | Reading, PA | 2,179.2 | 366 | The Villages, FL | 1,173.9 |
| 118 | Milwaukee, WI | 3,651.3 | 85 | Redding, CA | 3,929.7 | NA | Toledo, OH** | NA |
| 224 | Minneapolis-St. Paul, MN-WI | 2,868.8 | 207 | Reno, NV | 2,975.1 | 93 | Topeka, KS | 3,890.6 |
| 170 | Missoula, MT | 3,309.2 | 257 | Richmond, VA | 2,639.5 | 286 | Trenton, NJ | 2,439.6 |
| 16 | Mobile, AL | 5,098.4 | 193 | Riverside-San Bernardino, CA | 3,127.7 | 11 | Tucson, AZ | 5,282.8 |
| 48 | Modesto, CA | 4,432.8 | 249 | Roanoke, VA | 2,682.4 | 98 | Tulsa, OK | 3,794.1 |
| 7 | Monroe, LA | 5,500.0 | 353 | Rochester, MN | 1,792.2 | 107 | Tuscaloosa, AL | 3,709.3 |
| 260 | Monroe, MI | 2,623.0 | 247 | Rochester, NY | 2,695.3 | 176 | Tyler, TX | 3,254.1 |
| 348 | Montgomery County, PA M.D. | 1,841.6 | 109 | Rockford, IL | 3,701.5 | 288 | Utica-Rome, NY | 2,435.6 |
| 333 | Morgantown, WV | 1,974.7 | 311 | Rockingham County, NH M.D. | 2,170.1 | 116 | Vallejo-Fairfield, CA | 3,667.4 |
| 164 | Morristown, TN | 3,336.3 | 68 | Rocky Mount, NC | 4,105.9 | 111 | Victoria, TX | 3,699.8 |
| 42 | Mount Vernon-Anacortes, WA | 4,576.3 | 44 | Rome, GA | 4,531.7 | 22 | Vineland-Bridgeton, NJ | 4,907.7 |
| 153 | Muncie, IN | 3,421.5 | 188 | Sacramento, CA | 3,182.5 | 168 | Virginia Beach-Norfolk, VA-NC | 3,320.0 |
| 70 | Muskegon, MI | 4,074.4 | 216 | Saginaw, MI | 2,926.9 | NA | Visalia-Porterville, CA** | NA |
| 24 | Myrtle Beach, SC-NC | 4,893.1 | 148 | Salem, OR | 3,448.7 | 113 | Waco, TX | 3,696.7 |
| 317 | Napa, CA | 2,136.7 | 210 | Salinas, CA | 2,955.4 | 58 | Warner Robins, GA | 4,285.5 |
| 354 | Naples-Marco Island, FL | 1,786.5 | 112 | Salisbury, MD-DE | 3,698.5 | 343 | Warren-Troy, MI M.D. | 1,919.1 |
| 169 | Nashville-Davidson, TN | 3,314.2 | 34 | Salt Lake City, UT | 4,704.6 | 277 | Washington (greater) DC-VA-MD-WV | 2,500.2 |
| 359 | Nassau-Suffolk, NY M.D. | 1,568.9 | 110 | San Angelo, TX | 3,700.9 | 248 | Washington, DC-VA-MD-WV M.D. | 2,685.5 |
| 165 | New Bern, NC | 3,323.8 | 26 | San Antonio, TX | 4,874.9 | 328 | Watertown-Fort Drum, NY | 2,016.2 |
| 185 | New Haven-Milford, CT | 3,195.7 | 271 | San Diego, CA | 2,540.5 | 358 | Wausau, WI | 1,638.0 |
| 125 | New Orleans, LA | 3,626.0 | 67 | San Francisco (greater), CA | 4,130.1 | 135 | West Palm Beach, FL M.D. | 3,530.8 |
| 330 | New York (greater), NY-NJ-PA | 2,000.1 | 39 | San Francisco-Redwood, CA M.D. | 4,626.4 | 83 | Wichita Falls, TX | 3,945.0 |
| 320 | New York-Jersey City, NY-NJ M.D. | 2,093.6 | 262 | San Jose, CA | 2,613.9 | 35 | Wichita, KS | 4,704.4 |
| 323 | Newark, NJ-PA M.D. | 2,042.1 | 259 | San Luis Obispo, CA | 2,628.8 | 300 | Williamsport, PA | 2,340.0 |
| 187 | Niles-Benton Harbor, MI | 3,184.4 | 316 | San Rafael, CA M.D. | 2,137.4 | 152 | Wilmington, DE-MD-NJ M.D. | 3,421.9 |
| 177 | North Port-Sarasota-Bradenton, FL | 3,252.4 | 155 | Santa Cruz-Watsonville, CA | 3,407.9 | 84 | Wilmington, NC | 3,936.0 |
| 232 | Norwich-New London, CT | 2,836.1 | 266 | Santa Maria-Santa Barbara, CA | 2,589.0 | 312 | Winchester, VA-WV | 2,159.5 |
| 73 | Oakland-Hayward, CA M.D. | 4,028.0 | 325 | Santa Rosa, CA | 2,020.8 | 86 | Winston-Salem, NC | 3,911.6 |
| NA | Ocala, FL** | NA | 157 | Savannah, GA | 3,381.8 | 289 | Worcester, MA-CT | 2,419.0 |
| 51 | Ocean City, NJ | 4,375.2 | 284 | Scranton--Wilkes-Barre, PA | 2,455.8 | 117 | Yakima, WA | 3,652.9 |
| 17 | Odessa, TX | 5,083.8 | 53 | Seattle (greater), WA | 4,346.8 | 322 | York-Hanover, PA | 2,045.4 |
| NA | Ogden-Clearfield, UT** | NA | 62 | Seattle-Bellevue-Everett, WA M.D. | 4,264.0 | 166 | Yuba City, CA | 3,323.4 |
| 46 | Oklahoma City, OK | 4,458.6 | 295 | Sebastian-Vero Beach, FL | 2,397.6 | 195 | Yuma, AZ | 3,085.5 |
| 221 | Olympia, WA | 2,884.1 | 105 | Sebring, FL | 3,719.2 | | | |

Source: CQ Press using reported data from the F.B.I. "Crime in the United States 2013"

*Includes murder, rape, robbery, aggravated assault, burglary, larceny-theft, and motor vehicle theft. The FBI changed the definition of rape beginning with 2013 data. Not all cities have made the change so the metro area figures reported here include rape figures based on differing definitions of rape. See note on page vii. **Not available.

## 2. Crime Rate in 2013 (continued)
## National Rate = 3,098.6 Crimes per 100,000 Population*

| RANK | METROPOLITAN AREA | RATE | RANK | METROPOLITAN AREA | RATE | RANK | METROPOLITAN AREA | RATE |
|---|---|---|---|---|---|---|---|---|
| 1 | Hammond, LA | 6,476.2 | 65 | Columbia, SC | 4,214.9 | 129 | Spartanburg, SC | 3,611.1 |
| 2 | Spokane, WA | 6,113.6 | 66 | Grants Pass, OR | 4,208.6 | 130 | Dayton, OH | 3,592.0 |
| 3 | Pueblo, CO | 6,098.6 | 67 | San Francisco (greater), CA | 4,130.1 | 131 | Cleveland, TN | 3,588.3 |
| 4 | Hot Springs, AR | 5,801.6 | 68 | Rocky Mount, NC | 4,105.9 | 132 | Burlington, NC | 3,583.5 |
| 5 | Alexandria, LA | 5,569.6 | 69 | Shreveport-Bossier City, LA | 4,083.6 | 133 | Lake Havasu City-Kingman, AZ | 3,568.6 |
| 6 | Little Rock, AR | 5,567.3 | 70 | Muskegon, MI | 4,074.4 | 134 | Cape Girardeau, MO-IL | 3,547.3 |
| 7 | Monroe, LA | 5,500.0 | 71 | Philadelphia, PA M.D. | 4,063.0 | 135 | West Palm Beach, FL M.D. | 3,530.8 |
| 8 | Lake Charles, LA | 5,460.1 | 72 | Houston, TX | 4,047.8 | 136 | Lincoln, NE | 3,526.4 |
| 9 | Fayetteville, NC | 5,400.3 | 73 | Oakland-Hayward, CA M.D. | 4,028.0 | 137 | Columbus, IN | 3,523.0 |
| 10 | Columbus, GA-AL | 5,343.0 | 74 | Goldsboro, NC | 4,024.5 | 138 | Houma, LA | 3,518.9 |
| 11 | Tucson, AZ | 5,282.8 | 75 | Lafayette, LA | 4,006.3 | 139 | Charleston-North Charleston, SC | 3,510.2 |
| 12 | Albuquerque, NM | 5,226.0 | 76 | Lawrence, KS | 3,989.5 | 140 | Fort Smith, AR-OK | 3,510.1 |
| 13 | Memphis, TN-MS-AR | 5,183.3 | 77 | McAllen-Edinburg-Mission, TX | 3,981.2 | 141 | Gainesville, FL | 3,502.5 |
| 14 | Albany, GA | 5,176.5 | 78 | Lexington-Fayette, KY | 3,979.8 | 142 | Deltona-Daytona Beach, FL | 3,501.1 |
| 15 | Macon, GA | 5,168.0 | 79 | Tallahassee, FL | 3,976.4 | 143 | Knoxville, TN | 3,500.1 |
| 16 | Mobile, AL | 5,098.4 | 80 | Orlando, FL | 3,960.2 | 144 | Lewiston, ID-WA | 3,498.9 |
| 17 | Odessa, TX | 5,083.8 | 81 | Augusta, GA-SC | 3,953.4 | 145 | Terre Haute, IN | 3,454.4 |
| 18 | Springfield, MO | 5,053.2 | 82 | Amarillo, TX | 3,950.8 | 146 | Albany, OR | 3,453.5 |
| 19 | Florence, SC | 5,017.7 | 83 | Wichita Falls, TX | 3,945.0 | 147 | Austin-Round Rock, TX | 3,449.8 |
| 20 | Anchorage, AK | 4,941.6 | 84 | Wilmington, NC | 3,936.0 | 148 | Salem, OR | 3,448.7 |
| 21 | Mansfield, OH | 4,909.0 | 85 | Redding, CA | 3,929.7 | 149 | Dover, DE | 3,435.5 |
| 22 | Vineland-Bridgeton, NJ | 4,907.7 | 86 | Winston-Salem, NC | 3,911.6 | 150 | Cincinnati, OH-KY-IN | 3,432.6 |
| 23 | Lubbock, TX | 4,905.4 | 87 | Jonesboro, AR | 3,910.7 | 151 | Springfield, MA | 3,426.6 |
| 24 | Myrtle Beach, SC-NC | 4,893.1 | 88 | Gulfport-Biloxi-Pascagoula, MS | 3,908.6 | 152 | Wilmington, DE-MD-NJ M.D. | 3,421.9 |
| 25 | Detroit-Dearborn-Livonia, MI M.D. | 4,876.5 | 89 | Pensacola, FL | 3,905.2 | 153 | Muncie, IN | 3,421.5 |
| 26 | San Antonio, TX | 4,874.9 | 90 | Eugene, OR | 3,898.7 | 154 | Atlantic City, NJ | 3,413.3 |
| 27 | Gadsden, AL | 4,838.7 | 91 | Beaumont-Port Arthur, TX | 3,895.5 | 155 | Santa Cruz-Watsonville, CA | 3,407.9 |
| 28 | Miami-Dade County, FL M.D. | 4,828.3 | 92 | Fort Lauderdale, FL M.D. | 3,894.9 | 156 | Charlotte-Mecklenburg, NC-SC | 3,385.4 |
| 29 | Lawton, OK | 4,798.9 | 93 | Topeka, KS | 3,890.6 | 157 | Savannah, GA | 3,381.8 |
| 30 | Fairbanks, AK | 4,795.5 | 94 | Greenville, NC | 3,855.4 | 158 | Flagstaff, AZ | 3,372.3 |
| 31 | Corpus Christi, TX | 4,784.3 | 95 | Kahului-Wailuku-Lahaina, HI | 3,854.7 | 159 | Dallas (greater), TX | 3,369.3 |
| 32 | Stockton-Lodi, CA | 4,738.8 | 96 | Huntsville, AL | 3,839.3 | 160 | Hilton Head Island, SC | 3,369.2 |
| 33 | Springfield, OH | 4,713.7 | 97 | Great Falls, MT | 3,809.2 | 161 | Jackson, MS | 3,366.6 |
| 34 | Salt Lake City, UT | 4,704.6 | 98 | Tulsa, OK | 3,794.1 | 162 | South Bend-Mishawaka, IN-MI | 3,362.8 |
| 35 | Wichita, KS | 4,704.4 | 99 | Greensboro-High Point, NC | 3,793.1 | 163 | Athens-Clarke County, GA | 3,351.5 |
| 36 | Springfield, IL | 4,661.7 | 100 | Lima, OH | 3,779.9 | 164 | Morristown, TN | 3,336.3 |
| 37 | Joplin, MO | 4,653.1 | 101 | Brownsville-Harlingen, TX | 3,775.1 | 165 | New Bern, NC | 3,323.8 |
| 38 | Tacoma, WA M.D. | 4,627.6 | 102 | Jacksonville, FL | 3,724.5 | 166 | Yuba City, CA | 3,323.4 |
| 39 | San Francisco-Redwood, CA M.D. | 4,626.4 | 103 | Kansas City, MO-KS | 3,722.9 | 167 | Palm Bay-Melbourne, FL | 3,321.0 |
| 40 | Greenville-Anderson, SC | 4,588.4 | 104 | Atlanta, GA | 3,719.9 | 168 | Virginia Beach-Norfolk, VA-NC | 3,320.0 |
| 41 | Jackson, TN | 4,578.3 | 105 | Longview, TX | 3,719.2 | 169 | Nashville-Davidson, TN | 3,314.2 |
| 42 | Mount Vernon-Anacortes, WA | 4,576.3 | 105 | Sebring, FL | 3,719.2 | 170 | Missoula, MT | 3,309.2 |
| 43 | Laredo, TX | 4,568.4 | 107 | Tuscaloosa, AL | 3,709.3 | 171 | Gary, IN M.D. | 3,301.7 |
| 44 | Rome, GA | 4,531.7 | 108 | Flint, MI | 3,702.3 | 172 | Las Cruces, NM | 3,300.1 |
| 45 | Texarkana, TX-AR | 4,477.3 | 109 | Rockford, IL | 3,701.5 | 173 | Florence-Muscle Shoals, AL | 3,299.9 |
| 46 | Oklahoma City, OK | 4,458.6 | 110 | San Angelo, TX | 3,700.9 | 174 | Lakeland, FL | 3,275.6 |
| 47 | Bakersfield, CA | 4,447.9 | 111 | Victoria, TX | 3,699.8 | 175 | Dothan, AL | 3,267.3 |
| 48 | Modesto, CA | 4,432.8 | 112 | Salisbury, MD-DE | 3,698.5 | 176 | Tyler, TX | 3,254.1 |
| 49 | Chattanooga, TN-GA | 4,380.1 | 113 | Waco, TX | 3,696.7 | 177 | North Port-Sarasota-Bradenton, FL | 3,252.4 |
| 50 | Panama City, FL | 4,378.5 | 114 | Las Vegas-Henderson, NV | 3,694.8 | 178 | Portland-Vancouver, OR-WA | 3,242.3 |
| 51 | Ocean City, NJ | 4,375.2 | 115 | Fort Worth-Arlington, TX M.D. | 3,682.2 | 179 | Madera, CA | 3,240.8 |
| 52 | Fresno, CA | 4,355.6 | 116 | Vallejo-Fairfield, CA | 3,667.4 | 180 | Pocatello, ID | 3,233.9 |
| 53 | Seattle (greater), WA | 4,346.8 | 117 | Yakima, WA | 3,652.9 | 181 | Kokomo, IN | 3,224.7 |
| 54 | St. Joseph, MO-KS | 4,329.3 | 118 | Milwaukee, WI | 3,651.3 | 182 | Bremerton-Silverdale, WA | 3,221.6 |
| 55 | Longview, WA | 4,325.2 | 119 | Merced, CA | 3,648.8 | 183 | Akron, OH | 3,220.3 |
| 56 | Baton Rouge, LA | 4,309.4 | 120 | Baltimore, MD | 3,645.5 | 184 | Dallas-Plano-Irving, TX M.D. | 3,209.0 |
| 57 | Medford, OR | 4,286.1 | 121 | Colorado Springs, CO | 3,643.3 | 185 | New Haven-Milford, CT | 3,195.7 |
| 58 | Warner Robins, GA | 4,285.5 | 122 | Duluth, MN-WI | 3,637.5 | 186 | Fort Wayne, IN | 3,195.4 |
| 59 | Sumter, SC | 4,272.2 | 123 | Omaha-Council Bluffs, NE-IA | 3,632.6 | 187 | Niles-Benton Harbor, MI | 3,184.4 |
| 60 | Anniston-Oxford, AL | 4,269.7 | 124 | Grand Island, NE | 3,631.3 | 188 | Sacramento, CA | 3,182.5 |
| 61 | Billings, MT | 4,264.6 | 125 | New Orleans, LA | 3,626.0 | 189 | Casper, WY | 3,170.3 |
| 62 | Seattle-Bellevue-Everett, WA M.D. | 4,264.0 | 126 | El Centro, CA | 3,621.7 | 190 | Buffalo-Niagara Falls, NY | 3,165.2 |
| 63 | Birmingham-Hoover, AL | 4,252.3 | 127 | Columbia, MO | 3,620.5 | 191 | Detroit (greater), MI | 3,148.7 |
| 64 | Miami (greater), FL | 4,229.4 | 128 | Abilene, TX | 3,617.7 | 192 | Tampa-St Petersburg, FL | 3,128.6 |

Note: All listings are for Metropolitan Statistical Areas (M.S.A.s) except for those ending with "M.D." Listings with "M.D." are Metropolitan Divisions which are smaller parts of eleven large M.S.A.s. See explanatory note at beginning of metropolitan area section.

| RANK | METROPOLITAN AREA | RATE | RANK | METROPOLITAN AREA | RATE | RANK | METROPOLITAN AREA | RATE |
|---|---|---|---|---|---|---|---|---|
| 193 | Riverside-San Bernardino, CA | 3,127.7 | 255 | Racine, WI | 2,648.0 | 317 | Napa, CA | 2,136.7 |
| 194 | St. Louis, MO-IL | 3,101.9 | 256 | Camden, NJ M.D. | 2,645.5 | 318 | Blacksburg, VA | 2,100.0 |
| 195 | Yuma, AZ | 3,085.5 | 257 | Richmond, VA | 2,639.5 | 319 | Charlottesville, VA | 2,099.6 |
| 196 | Coeur d'Alene, ID | 3,084.1 | 258 | Erie, PA | 2,630.1 | 320 | New York-Jersey City, NY-NJ M.D. | 2,093.6 |
| 197 | Chico, CA | 3,083.7 | 259 | San Luis Obispo, CA | 2,628.8 | 321 | Chambersburg-Waynesboro, PA | 2,084.5 |
| 198 | Denver-Aurora, CO | 3,075.3 | 260 | Monroe, MI | 2,623.0 | 322 | York-Hanover, PA | 2,045.4 |
| 199 | Des Moines-West Des Moines, IA | 3,032.5 | 261 | Lansing-East Lansing, MI | 2,617.4 | 323 | Newark, NJ-PA M.D. | 2,042.1 |
| 200 | Dalton, GA | 3,032.1 | 262 | San Jose, CA | 2,613.9 | 324 | Lancaster, PA | 2,033.3 |
| 201 | Kingsport, TN-VA | 3,004.1 | 263 | St. Cloud, MN | 2,604.8 | 325 | Santa Rosa, CA | 2,020.8 |
| 202 | Sioux City, IA-NE-SD | 3,003.4 | 264 | Boston, MA M.D. | 2,595.6 | 326 | Green Bay, WI | 2,018.4 |
| 203 | Hinesville, GA | 3,000.1 | 265 | Manchester-Nashua, NH | 2,590.9 | 327 | Lebanon, PA | 2,016.4 |
| 204 | Champaign-Urbana, IL | 2,994.6 | 266 | Santa Maria-Santa Barbara, CA | 2,589.0 | 328 | Watertown-Fort Drum, NY | 2,016.2 |
| 205 | Cumberland, MD-WV | 2,979.5 | 267 | Albany-Schenectady-Troy, NY | 2,567.4 | 329 | Bloomsburg-Berwick, PA | 2,005.4 |
| 206 | Philadelphia (greater) PA-NJ-MD-DE | 2,975.2 | 268 | Port St. Lucie, FL | 2,565.0 | 330 | New York (greater), NY-NJ-PA | 2,000.1 |
| 207 | Reno, NV | 2,975.1 | 269 | Los Angeles (greater), CA | 2,560.6 | 331 | Idaho Falls, ID | 1,995.5 |
| 208 | Lafayette, IN | 2,971.1 | 270 | Cedar Rapids, IA | 2,560.4 | 332 | Johnstown, PA | 1,982.6 |
| 209 | Binghamton, NY | 2,956.0 | 271 | San Diego, CA | 2,540.5 | 333 | Morgantown, WV | 1,974.7 |
| 210 | Salinas, CA | 2,955.4 | 272 | Fargo, ND-MN | 2,536.9 | 334 | La Crosse, WI-MN | 1,967.4 |
| 211 | Bloomington, IN | 2,953.6 | 273 | Cape Coral-Fort Myers, FL | 2,527.1 | 335 | Kingston, NY | 1,966.4 |
| 212 | Cheyenne, WY | 2,952.9 | 274 | El Paso, TX | 2,523.7 | 336 | Cambridge-Newton, MA M.D. | 1,963.9 |
| 213 | Canton, OH | 2,944.5 | 275 | Raleigh, NC | 2,502.6 | 337 | Manhattan, KS | 1,949.8 |
| 214 | Hanford-Corcoran, CA | 2,940.7 | 276 | Kennewick-Richland, WA | 2,500.5 | 338 | Provo-Orem, UT | 1,946.5 |
| 215 | Decatur, IL | 2,937.9 | 277 | Washington (greater) DC-VA-MD-WV | 2,500.2 | 339 | Sheboygan, WI | 1,935.6 |
| 216 | Saginaw, MI | 2,926.9 | 278 | Boulder, CO | 2,493.1 | 340 | Boise City, ID | 1,925.0 |
| 217 | Midland, TX | 2,918.9 | 279 | Madison, WI | 2,479.7 | 341 | Carson City, NV | 1,924.0 |
| 218 | Bangor, ME | 2,917.4 | 280 | California-Lexington Park, MD | 2,476.1 | 342 | Altoona, PA | 1,919.4 |
| 219 | Grand Junction, CO | 2,889.2 | 281 | Elmira, NY | 2,469.7 | 343 | Warren-Troy, MI M.D. | 1,919.1 |
| 220 | Johnson City, TN | 2,887.7 | 282 | Hartford, CT | 2,464.9 | 344 | Staunton-Waynesboro, VA | 1,881.3 |
| 221 | Olympia, WA | 2,884.1 | 283 | Bowling Green, KY | 2,462.7 | 345 | Oshkosh-Neenah, WI | 1,880.4 |
| 222 | Clarksville, TN-KY | 2,883.6 | 284 | Scranton--Wilkes-Barre, PA | 2,455.8 | 346 | Bridgeport-Stamford, CT | 1,864.2 |
| 223 | Jackson, MI | 2,871.7 | 285 | Hagerstown-Martinsburg, MD-WV | 2,454.7 | 347 | Lake Co.-Kenosha Co., IL-WI M.D. | 1,860.9 |
| 224 | Minneapolis-St. Paul, MN-WI | 2,868.8 | 286 | Trenton, NJ | 2,439.6 | 348 | Montgomery County, PA M.D. | 1,841.6 |
| 225 | Lewiston-Auburn, ME | 2,865.0 | 287 | Jefferson City, MO | 2,437.2 | 349 | Fond du Lac, WI | 1,815.5 |
| 226 | Davenport, IA-IL | 2,864.6 | 288 | Utica-Rome, NY | 2,435.6 | 350 | Eau Claire, WI | 1,811.9 |
| 227 | Carbondale-Marion, IL | 2,863.8 | 289 | Worcester, MA-CT | 2,419.0 | 351 | Silver Spring-Frederick, MD M.D. | 1,810.1 |
| 228 | College Station-Bryan, TX | 2,859.1 | 290 | Portland, ME | 2,415.9 | 352 | Lynchburg, VA | 1,794.6 |
| 229 | Kankakee, IL | 2,855.3 | 291 | Bloomington, IL | 2,405.4 | 353 | Rochester, MN | 1,792.2 |
| 230 | Barnstable Town, MA | 2,846.5 | 292 | Bay City, MI | 2,404.9 | 354 | Naples-Marco Island, FL | 1,786.5 |
| 231 | Mankato-North Mankato, MN | 2,842.4 | 293 | Ann Arbor, MI | 2,403.2 | 355 | Elgin, IL M.D. | 1,694.9 |
| 232 | Norwich-New London, CT | 2,836.1 | 294 | Gainesville, GA | 2,397.8 | 356 | Glens Falls, NY | 1,694.7 |
| 233 | East Stroudsburg, PA | 2,818.6 | 295 | Sebastian-Vero Beach, FL | 2,397.6 | 357 | Harrisonburg, VA | 1,687.1 |
| 234 | Bend, OR | 2,811.5 | 296 | Allentown, PA-NJ | 2,379.3 | 358 | Wausau, WI | 1,638.0 |
| 235 | Rapid City, SD | 2,807.2 | 297 | Homosassa Springs, FL | 2,367.9 | 359 | Nassau-Suffolk, NY M.D. | 1,568.9 |
| 236 | Sherman-Denison, TX | 2,785.0 | 298 | Fort Collins, CO | 2,360.8 | 360 | Elizabethtown-Fort Knox, KY | 1,561.4 |
| 237 | Decatur, AL | 2,780.8 | 299 | Owensboro, KY | 2,359.1 | 361 | Appleton, WI | 1,509.2 |
| 238 | Pittsfield, MA | 2,766.7 | 300 | Williamsport, PA | 2,340.0 | 362 | Dutchess-Putnam, NY M.D. | 1,500.5 |
| 239 | Crestview-Fort Walton Beach, FL | 2,760.0 | 301 | Grand Forks, ND-MN | 2,338.4 | 363 | State College, PA | 1,487.1 |
| 240 | Daphne-Fairhope-Foley, AL | 2,751.4 | 302 | Punta Gorda, FL | 2,317.4 | 364 | Gettysburg, PA | 1,363.3 |
| 241 | Parkersburg-Vienna, WV | 2,744.7 | 303 | Iowa City, IA | 2,276.2 | 365 | Logan, UT-ID | 1,234.4 |
| 242 | Syracuse, NY | 2,739.2 | 304 | Ames, IA | 2,273.2 | 366 | The Villages, FL | 1,173.9 |
| 243 | Fayetteville-Springdale, AR-MO | 2,715.3 | 305 | Greeley, CO | 2,267.5 | NA | Brunswick, GA** | NA |
| 244 | Janesville, WI | 2,711.4 | 306 | Grand Rapids-Wyoming, MI | 2,256.2 | NA | Chicago (greater), IL-IN-WI** | NA |
| 245 | Bismarck, ND | 2,701.2 | 307 | Prescott, AZ | 2,246.0 | NA | Chicago-Naperville, IL M.D.** | NA |
| 246 | Providence-Warwick, RI-MA | 2,697.7 | 308 | Boston (greater), MA-NH | 2,244.8 | NA | Indianapolis, IN** | NA |
| 247 | Rochester, NY | 2,695.3 | 309 | Reading, PA | 2,179.2 | NA | Louisville, KY-IN** | NA |
| 248 | Washington, DC-VA-MD-WV M.D. | 2,685.5 | 310 | Anaheim-Santa Ana-Irvine, CA M.D. | 2,170.5 | NA | Ocala, FL** | NA |
| 249 | Roanoke, VA | 2,682.4 | 311 | Rockingham County, NH M.D. | 2,170.1 | NA | Ogden-Clearfield, UT** | NA |
| 250 | Los Angeles County, CA M.D. | 2,682.0 | 312 | Winchester, VA-WV | 2,159.5 | NA | Phoenix-Mesa-Scottsdale, AZ** | NA |
| 251 | Corvallis, OR | 2,671.6 | 313 | Pittsburgh, PA | 2,149.3 | NA | St. George, UT** | NA |
| 252 | Peoria, IL | 2,668.8 | 314 | Oxnard-Thousand Oaks, CA | 2,144.6 | NA | Toledo, OH** | NA |
| 253 | Sioux Falls, SD | 2,658.9 | 315 | Dubuque, IA | 2,137.8 | NA | Visalia-Porterville, CA** | NA |
| 254 | Farmington, NM | 2,649.9 | 316 | San Rafael, CA M.D. | 2,137.4 | | | |

Source: CQ Press using reported data from the F.B.I. "Crime in the United States 2013"

*Includes murder, rape, robbery, aggravated assault, burglary, larceny-theft, and motor vehicle theft. The FBI changed the definition of rape beginning with 2013 data. Not all cities have made the change so the metro area figures reported here include rape figures based on differing definitions of rape. See note on page vii. **Not available.

# 3. Percent Change in Crime Rate: 2012 to 2013
## National Percent Change = 4.8% Decrease*

| RANK | METROPOLITAN AREA | % CHANGE | RANK | METROPOLITAN AREA | % CHANGE | RANK | METROPOLITAN AREA | % CHANGE |
|---|---|---|---|---|---|---|---|---|
| 13 | Abilene, TX | 8.4 | 169 | Cheyenne, WY | (5.7) | 154 | Gary, IN M.D. | (5.0) |
| 124 | Akron, OH | (3.9) | NA | Chicago (greater), IL-IN-WI** | NA | NA | Gettysburg, PA** | NA |
| 175 | Albany-Schenectady-Troy, NY | (6.0) | NA | Chicago-Naperville, IL M.D.** | NA | 219 | Glens Falls, NY | (7.6) |
| 71 | Albany, GA | (1.1) | 14 | Chico, CA | 8.1 | 229 | Goldsboro, NC | (8.0) |
| 18 | Albany, OR | 5.9 | 144 | Cincinnati, OH-KY-IN | (4.7) | NA | Grand Forks, ND-MN** | NA |
| NA | Albuquerque, NM** | NA | 169 | Clarksville, TN-KY | (5.7) | 80 | Grand Island, NE | (1.7) |
| NA | Alexandria, LA** | NA | 55 | Cleveland, TN | 0.4 | 256 | Grand Junction, CO | (9.8) |
| 87 | Allentown, PA-NJ | (1.9) | 274 | Coeur d'Alene, ID | (11.3) | NA | Grand Rapids-Wyoming, MI** | NA |
| 55 | Altoona, PA | 0.4 | 210 | College Station-Bryan, TX | (7.1) | NA | Grants Pass, OR** | NA |
| 214 | Amarillo, TX | (7.4) | NA | Colorado Springs, CO** | NA | 154 | Great Falls, MT | (5.0) |
| 163 | Ames, IA | (5.4) | 96 | Columbia, MO | (2.6) | 237 | Greeley, CO | (8.6) |
| 262 | Anaheim-Santa Ana-Irvine, CA M.D. | (10.3) | NA | Columbia, SC** | NA | 144 | Green Bay, WI | (4.7) |
| 6 | Anchorage, AK | 11.6 | 35 | Columbus, GA-AL | 2.4 | 111 | Greensboro-High Point, NC | (3.2) |
| 283 | Ann Arbor, MI | (12.0) | 160 | Columbus, IN | (5.2) | 40 | Greenville-Anderson, SC | 2.2 |
| 303 | Anniston-Oxford, AL | (16.1) | NA | Corpus Christi, TX** | NA | 69 | Greenville, NC | (1.0) |
| 271 | Appleton, WI | (11.1) | 2 | Corvallis, OR | 19.4 | NA | Gulfport-Biloxi-Pascagoula, MS** | NA |
| 258 | Athens-Clarke County, GA | (10.0) | 278 | Crestview-Fort Walton Beach, FL | (11.6) | 121 | Hagerstown-Martinsburg, MD-WV | (3.8) |
| 87 | Atlanta, GA | (1.9) | 211 | Cumberland, MD-WV | (7.2) | 124 | Hammond, LA | (3.9) |
| NA | Atlantic City, NJ** | NA | 135 | Dallas (greater), TX | (4.3) | 12 | Hanford-Corcoran, CA | 8.5 |
| 235 | Augusta, GA-SC | (8.4) | 186 | Dallas-Plano-Irving, TX M.D. | (6.3) | 10 | Harrisonburg, VA | 9.7 |
| 214 | Austin-Round Rock, TX | (7.4) | 57 | Dalton, GA | 0.2 | 257 | Hartford, CT | (9.9) |
| 121 | Bakersfield, CA | (3.8) | 157 | Daphne-Fairhope-Foley, AL | (5.1) | 162 | Hilton Head Island, SC | (5.3) |
| 48 | Baltimore, MD | 1.1 | 110 | Davenport, IA-IL | (3.1) | 267 | Hinesville, GA | (10.6) |
| 169 | Bangor, ME | (5.7) | 96 | Dayton, OH | (2.6) | 80 | Homosassa Springs, FL | (1.7) |
| 229 | Barnstable Town, MA | (8.0) | 289 | Decatur, AL | (12.6) | NA | Hot Springs, AR** | NA |
| NA | Baton Rouge, LA** | NA | 127 | Decatur, IL | (4.0) | 71 | Houma, LA | (1.1) |
| 17 | Bay City, MI | 6.9 | 104 | Deltona-Daytona Beach, FL | (2.9) | NA | Houston, TX** | NA |
| 32 | Beaumont-Port Arthur, TX | 3.1 | 64 | Denver-Aurora, CO | (0.3) | 66 | Huntsville, AL | (0.7) |
| NA | Bend, OR** | NA | NA | Des Moines-West Des Moines, IA** | NA | 96 | Idaho Falls, ID | (2.6) |
| 7 | Billings, MT | 11.2 | 144 | Detroit (greater), MI | (4.7) | NA | Indianapolis, IN** | NA |
| 66 | Binghamton, NY | (0.7) | 79 | Detroit-Dearborn-Livonia, MI M.D. | (1.6) | 42 | Iowa City, IA | 2.0 |
| 95 | Birmingham-Hoover, AL | (2.5) | 197 | Dothan, AL | (6.8) | 183 | Jacksonville, FL | (6.2) |
| 102 | Bismarck, ND | (2.7) | 308 | Dover, DE | (19.1) | NA | Jackson, MI** | NA |
| 262 | Blacksburg, VA | (10.3) | NA | Dubuque, IA** | NA | 249 | Jackson, MS | (9.3) |
| 111 | Bloomington, IL | (3.2) | NA | Duluth, MN-WI** | NA | 34 | Jackson, TN | 2.5 |
| 291 | Bloomington, IN | (13.6) | 287 | Dutchess-Putnam, NY M.D. | (12.3) | 298 | Janesville, WI | (15.6) |
| 273 | Bloomsburg-Berwick, PA | (11.2) | 203 | East Stroudsburg, PA | (6.9) | 246 | Jefferson City, MO | (9.2) |
| 282 | Boise City, ID | (11.8) | NA | Eau Claire, WI** | NA | 287 | Johnson City, TN | (12.3) |
| 127 | Boston (greater), MA-NH | (4.0) | 214 | El Centro, CA | (7.4) | 75 | Johnstown, PA | (1.3) |
| 108 | Boston, MA M.D. | (3.0) | 203 | El Paso, TX | (6.9) | 39 | Jonesboro, AR | 2.3 |
| 91 | Boulder, CO | (2.0) | 219 | Elgin, IL M.D. | (7.6) | 53 | Joplin, MO | 0.8 |
| 190 | Bowling Green, KY | (6.4) | 23 | Elizabethtown-Fort Knox, KY | 4.1 | 143 | Kahului-Wailuku-Lahaina, HI | (4.6) |
| 179 | Bremerton-Silverdale, WA | (6.1) | 251 | Elmira, NY | (9.4) | 232 | Kankakee, IL | (8.3) |
| 267 | Bridgeport-Stamford, CT | (10.6) | 226 | Erie, PA | (7.9) | 179 | Kansas City, MO-KS | (6.1) |
| 269 | Brownsville-Harlingen, TX | (11.0) | 116 | Eugene, OR | (3.5) | 157 | Kennewick-Richland, WA | (5.1) |
| NA | Brunswick, GA** | NA | 134 | Fairbanks, AK | (4.2) | 265 | Kingsport, TN-VA | (10.5) |
| 175 | Buffalo-Niagara Falls, NY | (6.0) | NA | Fargo, ND-MN** | NA | 239 | Kingston, NY | (8.7) |
| 172 | Burlington, NC | (5.8) | 296 | Farmington, NM | (15.4) | 265 | Knoxville, TN | (10.5) |
| 277 | California-Lexington Park, MD | (11.5) | 203 | Fayetteville-Springdale, AR-MO | (6.9) | 27 | Kokomo, IN | 3.7 |
| 144 | Cambridge-Newton, MA M.D. | (4.7) | 226 | Fayetteville, NC | (7.9) | NA | La Crosse, WI-MN** | NA |
| 245 | Camden, NJ M.D. | (9.1) | 104 | Flagstaff, AZ | (2.9) | 65 | Lafayette, IN | (0.5) |
| 255 | Canton, OH | (9.6) | 307 | Flint, MI | (18.6) | NA | Lafayette, LA** | NA |
| 186 | Cape Coral-Fort Myers, FL | (6.3) | 84 | Florence-Muscle Shoals, AL | (1.8) | NA | Lake Charles, LA** | NA |
| 304 | Cape Girardeau, MO-IL | (16.8) | 160 | Florence, SC | (5.2) | 283 | Lake Co.-Kenosha Co., IL-WI M.D. | (12.0) |
| NA | Carbondale-Marion, IL** | NA | 218 | Fond du Lac, WI | (7.5) | 87 | Lake Havasu City-Kingman, AZ | (1.9) |
| 290 | Carson City, NV | (12.8) | 285 | Fort Collins, CO | (12.1) | 149 | Lakeland, FL | (4.8) |
| 80 | Casper, WY | (1.7) | 232 | Fort Lauderdale, FL M.D. | (8.3) | NA | Lancaster, PA** | NA |
| NA | Cedar Rapids, IA** | NA | 30 | Fort Smith, AR-OK | 3.2 | 45 | Lansing-East Lansing, MI | 1.5 |
| NA | Chambersburg-Waynesboro, PA** | NA | 43 | Fort Wayne, IN | 1.9 | 96 | Laredo, TX | (2.6) |
| 164 | Champaign-Urbana, IL | (5.5) | 66 | Fort Worth-Arlington, TX M.D. | (0.7) | 93 | Las Cruces, NM | (2.4) |
| 152 | Charleston-North Charleston, SC | (4.9) | 286 | Fresno, CA | (12.2) | 51 | Las Vegas-Henderson, NV | 0.9 |
| NA | Charlotte-Mecklenburg, NC-SC** | NA | 60 | Gadsden, AL | (0.1) | 251 | Lawrence, KS | (9.4) |
| 78 | Charlottesville, VA | (1.4) | 246 | Gainesville, FL | (9.2) | 124 | Lawton, OK | (3.9) |
| NA | Chattanooga, TN-GA** | NA | 141 | Gainesville, GA | (4.5) | 157 | Lebanon, PA | (5.1) |

Note: All listings are for Metropolitan Statistical Areas (M.S.A.s) except for those ending with "M.D." Listings with "M.D." are Metropolitan Divisions which are smaller parts of eleven large M.S.A.s. See explanatory note at beginning of metropolitan area section.

| RANK | METROPOLITAN AREA | % CHANGE | RANK | METROPOLITAN AREA | % CHANGE | RANK | METROPOLITAN AREA | % CHANGE |
|---|---|---|---|---|---|---|---|---|
| 260 | Lewiston-Auburn, ME | (10.2) | 121 | Omaha-Council Bluffs, NE-IA | (3.8) | 298 | Sheboygan, WI | (15.6) |
| 116 | Lewiston, ID-WA | (3.5) | 84 | Orlando, FL | (1.8) | 301 | Sherman-Denison, TX | (15.7) |
| 251 | Lexington-Fayette, KY | (9.4) | 293 | Oshkosh-Neenah, WI | (14.7) | NA | Shreveport-Bossier City, LA** | NA |
| 240 | Lima, OH | (8.9) | 305 | Owensboro, KY | (17.0) | 179 | Silver Spring-Frederick, MD M.D. | (6.1) |
| 254 | Lincoln, NE | (9.5) | 35 | Oxnard-Thousand Oaks, CA | 2.4 | 29 | Sioux City, IA-NE-SD | 3.4 |
| 135 | Little Rock, AR | (4.3) | 196 | Palm Bay-Melbourne, FL | (6.7) | 135 | Sioux Falls, SD | (4.3) |
| 313 | Logan, UT-ID | (24.2) | 131 | Panama City, FL | (4.1) | 120 | South Bend-Mishawaka, IN-MI | (3.6) |
| 241 | Longview, TX | (9.0) | 296 | Parkersburg-Vienna, WV | (15.4) | 131 | Spartanburg, SC | (4.1) |
| 11 | Longview, WA | 9.5 | 222 | Pensacola, FL | (7.7) | 24 | Spokane, WA | 3.9 |
| 113 | Los Angeles County, CA M.D. | (3.3) | 294 | Peoria, IL | (15.1) | 116 | Springfield, IL | (3.5) |
| 149 | Los Angeles (greater), CA | (4.8) | NA | Philadelphia (greater) PA-NJ-MD-DE** | NA | 102 | Springfield, MA | (2.7) |
| NA | Louisville, KY-IN** | NA | NA | Philadelphia, PA M.D.** | NA | 69 | Springfield, MO | (1.0) |
| 190 | Lubbock, TX | (6.4) | NA | Phoenix-Mesa-Scottsdale, AZ** | NA | 15 | Springfield, OH | 7.3 |
| 219 | Lynchburg, VA | (7.6) | NA | Pittsburgh, PA** | NA | 87 | State College, PA | (1.9) |
| 47 | Macon, GA | 1.2 | 26 | Pittsfield, MA | 3.8 | 96 | Staunton-Waynesboro, VA | (2.6) |
| 50 | Madera, CA | 1.0 | 3 | Pocatello, ID | 16.0 | 183 | Stockton-Lodi, CA | (6.2) |
| NA | Madison, WI** | NA | 152 | Port St. Lucie, FL | (4.9) | NA | St. Cloud, MN** | NA |
| 45 | Manchester-Nashua, NH | 1.5 | 164 | Portland-Vancouver, OR-WA | (5.5) | NA | St. George, UT** | NA |
| 278 | Manhattan, KS | (11.6) | 203 | Portland, ME | (6.9) | 172 | St. Joseph, MO-KS | (5.8) |
| NA | Mankato-North Mankato, MN** | NA | 190 | Prescott, AZ | (6.4) | 212 | St. Louis, MO-IL | (7.3) |
| 61 | Mansfield, OH | (0.2) | 149 | Providence-Warwick, RI-MA | (4.8) | 295 | Sumter, SC | (15.3) |
| 96 | McAllen-Edinburg-Mission, TX | (2.6) | 51 | Provo-Orem, UT | 0.9 | 108 | Syracuse, NY | (3.0) |
| 21 | Medford, OR | 4.6 | 8 | Pueblo, CO | 11.0 | NA | Tacoma, WA M.D.** | NA |
| 138 | Memphis, TN-MS-AR | (4.4) | 116 | Punta Gorda, FL | (3.5) | 104 | Tallahassee, FL | (2.9) |
| 309 | Merced, CA | (19.7) | 260 | Racine, WI | (10.2) | 138 | Tampa-St Petersburg, FL | (4.4) |
| 174 | Miami (greater), FL | (5.9) | 226 | Raleigh, NC | (7.9) | 274 | Terre Haute, IN | (11.3) |
| 141 | Miami-Dade County, FL M.D. | (4.5) | 312 | Rapid City, SD | (20.8) | 222 | Texarkana, TX-AR | (7.7) |
| 30 | Midland, TX | 3.2 | 298 | Reading, PA | (15.6) | 203 | The Villages, FL | (6.9) |
| 197 | Milwaukee, WI | (6.8) | 208 | Redding, CA | (7.0) | NA | Toledo, OH** | NA |
| NA | Minneapolis-St. Paul, MN-WI** | NA | 84 | Reno, NV | (1.8) | 236 | Topeka, KS | (8.5) |
| 197 | Missoula, MT | (6.8) | 175 | Richmond, VA | (6.0) | 237 | Trenton, NJ | (8.6) |
| 19 | Mobile, AL | 5.1 | 222 | Riverside-San Bernardino, CA | (7.7) | NA | Tucson, AZ** | NA |
| 208 | Modesto, CA | (7.0) | 154 | Roanoke, VA | (5.0) | 75 | Tulsa, OK | (1.3) |
| 9 | Monroe, LA | 10.2 | NA | Rochester, MN** | NA | 58 | Tuscaloosa, AL | 0.1 |
| 278 | Monroe, MI | (11.6) | 229 | Rochester, NY | (8.0) | 241 | Tyler, TX | (9.0) |
| 114 | Montgomery County, PA M.D. | (3.4) | 281 | Rockford, IL | (11.7) | 183 | Utica-Rome, NY | (6.2) |
| 269 | Morgantown, WV | (11.0) | 179 | Rockingham County, NH M.D. | (6.1) | 40 | Vallejo-Fairfield, CA | 2.2 |
| 274 | Morristown, TN | (11.3) | 75 | Rocky Mount, NC | (1.3) | 127 | Victoria, TX | (4.0) |
| 22 | Mount Vernon-Anacortes, WA | 4.2 | 24 | Rome, GA | 3.9 | 44 | Vineland-Bridgeton, NJ | 1.6 |
| 71 | Muncie, IN | (1.1) | 164 | Sacramento, CA | (5.5) | 93 | Virginia Beach-Norfolk, VA-NC | (2.4) |
| NA | Muskegon, MI** | NA | 212 | Saginaw, MI | (7.3) | NA | Visalia-Porterville, CA** | NA |
| NA | Myrtle Beach, SC-NC** | NA | 59 | Salem, OR | 0.0 | 164 | Waco, TX | (5.5) |
| 271 | Napa, CA | (11.1) | 28 | Salinas, CA | 3.5 | 35 | Warner Robins, GA | 2.4 |
| 194 | Naples-Marco Island, FL | (6.6) | 80 | Salisbury, MD-DE | (1.7) | 241 | Warren-Troy, MI M.D. | (9.0) |
| 222 | Nashville-Davidson, TN | (7.7) | 48 | Salt Lake City, UT | 1.1 | 138 | Washington (greater) DC-VA-MD-WV | (4.4) |
| 197 | Nassau-Suffolk, NY M.D. | (6.8) | NA | San Angelo, TX** | NA | 131 | Washington, DC-VA-MD-WV M.D. | (4.1) |
| 302 | New Bern, NC | (16.0) | 127 | San Antonio, TX | (4.0) | 311 | Watertown-Fort Drum, NY | (20.2) |
| 186 | New Haven-Milford, CT | (6.3) | 74 | San Diego, CA | (1.2) | 258 | Wausau, WI | (10.0) |
| 104 | New Orleans, LA | (2.9) | NA | San Francisco (greater), CA** | NA | 175 | West Palm Beach, FL M.D. | (6.0) |
| NA | New York (greater), NY-NJ-PA** | NA | 4 | San Francisco-Redwood, CA M.D. | 15.8 | 193 | Wichita Falls, TX | (6.5) |
| NA | New York-Jersey City, NY-NJ M.D.** | NA | 246 | San Jose, CA | (9.2) | 61 | Wichita, KS | (0.2) |
| 194 | Newark, NJ-PA M.D. | (6.6) | 53 | San Luis Obispo, CA | 0.8 | 61 | Williamsport, PA | (0.2) |
| NA | Niles-Benton Harbor, MI** | NA | NA | San Rafael, CA M.D.** | NA | 262 | Wilmington, DE-MD-NJ M.D. | (10.3) |
| 197 | North Port-Sarasota-Bradenton, FL | (6.8) | 197 | Santa Cruz-Watsonville, CA | (6.8) | 186 | Wilmington, NC | (6.3) |
| 35 | Norwich-New London, CT | 2.4 | 164 | Santa Maria-Santa Barbara, CA | (5.5) | 291 | Winchester, VA-WV | (13.6) |
| NA | Oakland-Hayward, CA M.D.** | NA | 114 | Santa Rosa, CA | (3.4) | 214 | Winston-Salem, NC | (7.4) |
| NA | Ocala, FL** | NA | 92 | Savannah, GA | (2.2) | 144 | Worcester, MA-CT | (4.7) |
| 241 | Ocean City, NJ | (9.0) | NA | Scranton--Wilkes-Barre, PA** | NA | 306 | Yakima, WA | (17.9) |
| 5 | Odessa, TX | 13.9 | NA | Seattle (greater), WA** | NA | 232 | York-Hanover, PA | (8.3) |
| NA | Ogden-Clearfield, UT** | NA | 20 | Seattle-Bellevue-Everett, WA M.D. | 4.8 | 32 | Yuba City, CA | 3.1 |
| 249 | Oklahoma City, OK | (9.3) | 310 | Sebastian-Vero Beach, FL | (20.0) | 16 | Yuma, AZ | 7.2 |
| NA | Olympia, WA** | NA | 1 | Sebring, FL | 19.5 | | | |

Source: CQ Press using reported data from the F.B.I. "Crime in the United States 2013"
*Includes murder, rape, robbery, aggravated assault, burglary, larceny-theft, and motor vehicle theft. The FBI changed the definition of rape beginning with 2013 data. Not all cities have made the change so the metro area figures reported here include rape figures based on differing definitions of rape. See note on page vii. **Not available.

# 3. Percent Change in Crime Rate: 2012 to 2013 (continued)
## National Percent Change = 4.8% Decrease*

| RANK | METROPOLITAN AREA | % CHANGE | RANK | METROPOLITAN AREA | % CHANGE | RANK | METROPOLITAN AREA | % CHANGE |
|---|---|---|---|---|---|---|---|---|
| 1 | Sebring, FL | 19.5 | 65 | Lafayette, IN | (0.5) | 127 | San Antonio, TX | (4.0) |
| 2 | Corvallis, OR | 19.4 | 66 | Binghamton, NY | (0.7) | 127 | Victoria, TX | (4.0) |
| 3 | Pocatello, ID | 16.0 | 66 | Fort Worth-Arlington, TX M.D. | (0.7) | 131 | Panama City, FL | (4.1) |
| 4 | San Francisco-Redwood, CA M.D. | 15.8 | 66 | Huntsville, AL | (0.7) | 131 | Spartanburg, SC | (4.1) |
| 5 | Odessa, TX | 13.9 | 69 | Greenville, NC | (1.0) | 131 | Washington, DC-VA-MD-WV M.D. | (4.1) |
| 6 | Anchorage, AK | 11.6 | 69 | Springfield, MO | (1.0) | 134 | Fairbanks, AK | (4.2) |
| 7 | Billings, MT | 11.2 | 71 | Albany, GA | (1.1) | 135 | Dallas (greater), TX | (4.3) |
| 8 | Pueblo, CO | 11.0 | 71 | Houma, LA | (1.1) | 135 | Little Rock, AR | (4.3) |
| 9 | Monroe, LA | 10.2 | 71 | Muncie, IN | (1.1) | 135 | Sioux Falls, SD | (4.3) |
| 10 | Harrisonburg, VA | 9.7 | 74 | San Diego, CA | (1.2) | 138 | Memphis, TN-MS-AR | (4.4) |
| 11 | Longview, WA | 9.5 | 75 | Johnstown, PA | (1.3) | 138 | Tampa-St Petersburg, FL | (4.4) |
| 12 | Hanford-Corcoran, CA | 8.5 | 75 | Rocky Mount, NC | (1.3) | 138 | Washington (greater) DC-VA-MD-WV | (4.4) |
| 13 | Abilene, TX | 8.4 | 75 | Tulsa, OK | (1.3) | 141 | Gainesville, GA | (4.5) |
| 14 | Chico, CA | 8.1 | 78 | Charlottesville, VA | (1.4) | 141 | Miami-Dade County, FL M.D. | (4.5) |
| 15 | Springfield, OH | 7.3 | 79 | Detroit-Dearborn-Livonia, MI M.D. | (1.6) | 143 | Kahului-Wailuku-Lahaina, HI | (4.6) |
| 16 | Yuma, AZ | 7.2 | 80 | Casper, WY | (1.7) | 144 | Cambridge-Newton, MA M.D. | (4.7) |
| 17 | Bay City, MI | 6.9 | 80 | Grand Island, NE | (1.7) | 144 | Cincinnati, OH-KY-IN | (4.7) |
| 18 | Albany, OR | 5.9 | 80 | Homosassa Springs, FL | (1.7) | 144 | Detroit (greater), MI | (4.7) |
| 19 | Mobile, AL | 5.1 | 80 | Salisbury, MD-DE | (1.7) | 144 | Green Bay, WI | (4.7) |
| 20 | Seattle-Bellevue-Everett, WA M.D. | 4.8 | 84 | Florence-Muscle Shoals, AL | (1.8) | 144 | Worcester, MA-CT | (4.7) |
| 21 | Medford, OR | 4.6 | 84 | Orlando, FL | (1.8) | 149 | Lakeland, FL | (4.8) |
| 22 | Mount Vernon-Anacortes, WA | 4.2 | 84 | Reno, NV | (1.8) | 149 | Los Angeles (greater), CA | (4.8) |
| 23 | Elizabethtown-Fort Knox, KY | 4.1 | 87 | Allentown, PA-NJ | (1.9) | 149 | Providence-Warwick, RI-MA | (4.8) |
| 24 | Rome, GA | 3.9 | 87 | Atlanta, GA | (1.9) | 152 | Charleston-North Charleston, SC | (4.9) |
| 24 | Spokane, WA | 3.9 | 87 | Lake Havasu City-Kingman, AZ | (1.9) | 152 | Port St. Lucie, FL | (4.9) |
| 26 | Pittsfield, MA | 3.8 | 87 | State College, PA | (1.9) | 154 | Gary, IN M.D. | (5.0) |
| 27 | Kokomo, IN | 3.7 | 91 | Boulder, CO | (2.0) | 154 | Great Falls, MT | (5.0) |
| 28 | Salinas, CA | 3.5 | 92 | Savannah, GA | (2.2) | 154 | Roanoke, VA | (5.0) |
| 29 | Sioux City, IA-NE-SD | 3.4 | 93 | Las Cruces, NM | (2.4) | 157 | Daphne-Fairhope-Foley, AL | (5.1) |
| 30 | Fort Smith, AR-OK | 3.2 | 93 | Virginia Beach-Norfolk, VA-NC | (2.4) | 157 | Kennewick-Richland, WA | (5.1) |
| 30 | Midland, TX | 3.2 | 95 | Birmingham-Hoover, AL | (2.5) | 157 | Lebanon, PA | (5.1) |
| 32 | Beaumont-Port Arthur, TX | 3.1 | 96 | Columbia, MO | (2.6) | 160 | Columbus, IN | (5.2) |
| 32 | Yuba City, CA | 3.1 | 96 | Dayton, OH | (2.6) | 160 | Florence, SC | (5.2) |
| 34 | Jackson, TN | 2.5 | 96 | Idaho Falls, ID | (2.6) | 162 | Hilton Head Island, SC | (5.3) |
| 35 | Columbus, GA-AL | 2.4 | 96 | Laredo, TX | (2.6) | 163 | Ames, IA | (5.4) |
| 35 | Norwich-New London, CT | 2.4 | 96 | McAllen-Edinburg-Mission, TX | (2.6) | 164 | Champaign-Urbana, IL | (5.5) |
| 35 | Oxnard-Thousand Oaks, CA | 2.4 | 96 | Staunton-Waynesboro, VA | (2.6) | 164 | Portland-Vancouver, OR-WA | (5.5) |
| 35 | Warner Robins, GA | 2.4 | 102 | Bismarck, ND | (2.7) | 164 | Sacramento, CA | (5.5) |
| 39 | Jonesboro, AR | 2.3 | 102 | Springfield, MA | (2.7) | 164 | Santa Maria-Santa Barbara, CA | (5.5) |
| 40 | Greenville-Anderson, SC | 2.2 | 104 | Deltona-Daytona Beach, FL | (2.9) | 164 | Waco, TX | (5.5) |
| 40 | Vallejo-Fairfield, CA | 2.2 | 104 | Flagstaff, AZ | (2.9) | 169 | Bangor, ME | (5.7) |
| 42 | Iowa City, IA | 2.0 | 104 | New Orleans, LA | (2.9) | 169 | Cheyenne, WY | (5.7) |
| 43 | Fort Wayne, IN | 1.9 | 104 | Tallahassee, FL | (2.9) | 169 | Clarksville, TN-KY | (5.7) |
| 44 | Vineland-Bridgeton, NJ | 1.6 | 108 | Boston, MA M.D. | (3.0) | 172 | Burlington, NC | (5.8) |
| 45 | Lansing-East Lansing, MI | 1.5 | 108 | Syracuse, NY | (3.0) | 172 | St. Joseph, MO-KS | (5.8) |
| 45 | Manchester-Nashua, NH | 1.5 | 110 | Davenport, IA-IL | (3.1) | 174 | Miami (greater), FL | (5.9) |
| 47 | Macon, GA | 1.2 | 111 | Bloomington, IL | (3.2) | 175 | Albany-Schenectady-Troy, NY | (6.0) |
| 48 | Baltimore, MD | 1.1 | 111 | Greensboro-High Point, NC | (3.2) | 175 | Buffalo-Niagara Falls, NY | (6.0) |
| 48 | Salt Lake City, UT | 1.1 | 113 | Los Angeles County, CA M.D. | (3.3) | 175 | Richmond, VA | (6.0) |
| 50 | Madera, CA | 1.0 | 114 | Montgomery County, PA M.D. | (3.4) | 175 | West Palm Beach, FL M.D. | (6.0) |
| 51 | Las Vegas-Henderson, NV | 0.9 | 114 | Santa Rosa, CA | (3.4) | 179 | Bremerton-Silverdale, WA | (6.1) |
| 51 | Provo-Orem, UT | 0.9 | 116 | Eugene, OR | (3.5) | 179 | Kansas City, MO-KS | (6.1) |
| 53 | Joplin, MO | 0.8 | 116 | Lewiston, ID-WA | (3.5) | 179 | Rockingham County, NH M.D. | (6.1) |
| 53 | San Luis Obispo, CA | 0.8 | 116 | Punta Gorda, FL | (3.5) | 179 | Silver Spring-Frederick, MD M.D. | (6.1) |
| 55 | Altoona, PA | 0.4 | 116 | Springfield, IL | (3.5) | 183 | Jacksonville, FL | (6.2) |
| 55 | Cleveland, TN | 0.4 | 120 | South Bend-Mishawaka, IN-MI | (3.6) | 183 | Stockton-Lodi, CA | (6.2) |
| 57 | Dalton, GA | 0.2 | 121 | Bakersfield, CA | (3.8) | 183 | Utica-Rome, NY | (6.2) |
| 58 | Tuscaloosa, AL | 0.1 | 121 | Hagerstown-Martinsburg, MD-WV | (3.8) | 186 | Cape Coral-Fort Myers, FL | (6.3) |
| 59 | Salem, OR | 0.0 | 121 | Omaha-Council Bluffs, NE-IA | (3.8) | 186 | Dallas-Plano-Irving, TX M.D. | (6.3) |
| 60 | Gadsden, AL | (0.1) | 124 | Akron, OH | (3.9) | 186 | New Haven-Milford, CT | (6.3) |
| 61 | Mansfield, OH | (0.2) | 124 | Hammond, LA | (3.9) | 186 | Wilmington, NC | (6.3) |
| 61 | Wichita, KS | (0.2) | 124 | Lawton, OK | (3.9) | 190 | Bowling Green, KY | (6.4) |
| 61 | Williamsport, PA | (0.2) | 127 | Boston (greater), MA-NH | (4.0) | 190 | Lubbock, TX | (6.4) |
| 64 | Denver-Aurora, CO | (0.3) | 127 | Decatur, IL | (4.0) | 190 | Prescott, AZ | (6.4) |

Note: All listings are for Metropolitan Statistical Areas (M.S.A.s) except for those ending with "M.D." Listings with "M.D." are Metropolitan Divisions which are smaller parts of eleven large M.S.A.s. See explanatory note at beginning of metropolitan area section.

| RANK | METROPOLITAN AREA | % CHANGE | RANK | METROPOLITAN AREA | % CHANGE | RANK | METROPOLITAN AREA | % CHANGE |
|---|---|---|---|---|---|---|---|---|
| 193 | Wichita Falls, TX | (6.5) | 255 | Canton, OH | (9.6) | NA | Baton Rouge, LA** | NA |
| 194 | Naples-Marco Island, FL | (6.6) | 256 | Grand Junction, CO | (9.8) | NA | Bend, OR** | NA |
| 194 | Newark, NJ-PA M.D. | (6.6) | 257 | Hartford, CT | (9.9) | NA | Brunswick, GA** | NA |
| 196 | Palm Bay-Melbourne, FL | (6.7) | 258 | Athens-Clarke County, GA | (10.0) | NA | Carbondale-Marion, IL** | NA |
| 197 | Dothan, AL | (6.8) | 258 | Wausau, WI | (10.0) | NA | Cedar Rapids, IA** | NA |
| 197 | Milwaukee, WI | (6.8) | 260 | Lewiston-Auburn, ME | (10.2) | NA | Chambersburg-Waynesboro, PA** | NA |
| 197 | Missoula, MT | (6.8) | 260 | Racine, WI | (10.2) | NA | Charlotte-Mecklenburg, NC-SC** | NA |
| 197 | Nassau-Suffolk, NY M.D. | (6.8) | 262 | Anaheim-Santa Ana-Irvine, CA M.D. | (10.3) | NA | Chattanooga, TN-GA** | NA |
| 197 | North Port-Sarasota-Bradenton, FL | (6.8) | 262 | Blacksburg, VA | (10.3) | NA | Chicago (greater), IL-IN-WI** | NA |
| 197 | Santa Cruz-Watsonville, CA | (6.8) | 262 | Wilmington, DE-MD-NJ M.D. | (10.3) | NA | Chicago-Naperville, IL M.D.** | NA |
| 203 | East Stroudsburg, PA | (6.9) | 265 | Kingsport, TN-VA | (10.5) | NA | Colorado Springs, CO** | NA |
| 203 | El Paso, TX | (6.9) | 265 | Knoxville, TN | (10.5) | NA | Columbia, SC** | NA |
| 203 | Fayetteville-Springdale, AR-MO | (6.9) | 267 | Bridgeport-Stamford, CT | (10.6) | NA | Corpus Christi, TX** | NA |
| 203 | Portland, ME | (6.9) | 267 | Hinesville, GA | (10.6) | NA | Des Moines-West Des Moines, IA** | NA |
| 203 | The Villages, FL | (6.9) | 269 | Brownsville-Harlingen, TX | (11.0) | NA | Dubuque, IA** | NA |
| 208 | Modesto, CA | (7.0) | 269 | Morgantown, WV | (11.0) | NA | Duluth, MN-WI** | NA |
| 208 | Redding, CA | (7.0) | 271 | Appleton, WI | (11.1) | NA | Eau Claire, WI** | NA |
| 210 | College Station-Bryan, TX | (7.1) | 271 | Napa, CA | (11.1) | NA | Fargo, ND-MN** | NA |
| 211 | Cumberland, MD-WV | (7.2) | 273 | Bloomsburg-Berwick, PA | (11.2) | NA | Gettysburg, PA** | NA |
| 212 | Saginaw, MI | (7.3) | 274 | Coeur d'Alene, ID | (11.3) | NA | Grand Forks, ND-MN** | NA |
| 212 | St. Louis, MO-IL | (7.3) | 274 | Morristown, TN | (11.3) | NA | Grand Rapids-Wyoming, MI** | NA |
| 214 | Amarillo, TX | (7.4) | 274 | Terre Haute, IN | (11.3) | NA | Grants Pass, OR** | NA |
| 214 | Austin-Round Rock, TX | (7.4) | 277 | California-Lexington Park, MD | (11.5) | NA | Gulfport-Biloxi-Pascagoula, MS** | NA |
| 214 | El Centro, CA | (7.4) | 278 | Crestview-Fort Walton Beach, FL | (11.6) | NA | Hot Springs, AR** | NA |
| 214 | Winston-Salem, NC | (7.4) | 278 | Manhattan, KS | (11.6) | NA | Houston, TX** | NA |
| 218 | Fond du Lac, WI | (7.5) | 278 | Monroe, MI | (11.6) | NA | Indianapolis, IN** | NA |
| 219 | Elgin, IL M.D. | (7.6) | 281 | Rockford, IL | (11.7) | NA | Jackson, MI** | NA |
| 219 | Glens Falls, NY | (7.6) | 282 | Boise City, ID | (11.8) | NA | La Crosse, WI-MN** | NA |
| 219 | Lynchburg, VA | (7.6) | 283 | Ann Arbor, MI | (12.0) | NA | Lafayette, LA** | NA |
| 222 | Nashville-Davidson, TN | (7.7) | 283 | Lake Co.-Kenosha Co., IL-WI M.D. | (12.0) | NA | Lake Charles, LA** | NA |
| 222 | Pensacola, FL | (7.7) | 285 | Fort Collins, CO | (12.1) | NA | Lancaster, PA** | NA |
| 222 | Riverside-San Bernardino, CA | (7.7) | 286 | Fresno, CA | (12.2) | NA | Louisville, KY-IN** | NA |
| 222 | Texarkana, TX-AR | (7.7) | 287 | Dutchess-Putnam, NY M.D. | (12.3) | NA | Madison, WI** | NA |
| 226 | Erie, PA | (7.9) | 287 | Johnson City, TN | (12.3) | NA | Mankato-North Mankato, MN** | NA |
| 226 | Fayetteville, NC | (7.9) | 289 | Decatur, AL | (12.6) | NA | Minneapolis-St. Paul, MN-WI** | NA |
| 226 | Raleigh, NC | (7.9) | 290 | Carson City, NV | (12.8) | NA | Muskegon, MI** | NA |
| 229 | Barnstable Town, MA | (8.0) | 291 | Bloomington, IN | (13.6) | NA | Myrtle Beach, SC-NC** | NA |
| 229 | Goldsboro, NC | (8.0) | 291 | Winchester, VA-WV | (13.6) | NA | New York (greater), NY-NJ-PA** | NA |
| 229 | Rochester, NY | (8.0) | 293 | Oshkosh-Neenah, WI | (14.7) | NA | New York-Jersey City, NY-NJ M.D.** | NA |
| 232 | Fort Lauderdale, FL M.D. | (8.3) | 294 | Peoria, IL | (15.1) | NA | Niles-Benton Harbor, MI** | NA |
| 232 | Kankakee, IL | (8.3) | 295 | Sumter, SC | (15.3) | NA | Oakland-Hayward, CA M.D.** | NA |
| 232 | York-Hanover, PA | (8.3) | 296 | Farmington, NM | (15.4) | NA | Ocala, FL** | NA |
| 235 | Augusta, GA-SC | (8.4) | 296 | Parkersburg-Vienna, WV | (15.4) | NA | Ogden-Clearfield, UT** | NA |
| 236 | Topeka, KS | (8.5) | 298 | Janesville, WI | (15.6) | NA | Olympia, WA** | NA |
| 237 | Greeley, CO | (8.6) | 298 | Reading, PA | (15.6) | NA | Philadelphia (greater) PA-NJ-MD-DE** | NA |
| 237 | Trenton, NJ | (8.6) | 298 | Sheboygan, WI | (15.6) | NA | Philadelphia, PA M.D.** | NA |
| 239 | Kingston, NY | (8.7) | 301 | Sherman-Denison, TX | (15.7) | NA | Phoenix-Mesa-Scottsdale, AZ** | NA |
| 240 | Lima, OH | (8.9) | 302 | New Bern, NC | (16.0) | NA | Pittsburgh, PA** | NA |
| 241 | Longview, TX | (9.0) | 303 | Anniston-Oxford, AL | (16.1) | NA | Rochester, MN** | NA |
| 241 | Ocean City, NJ | (9.0) | 304 | Cape Girardeau, MO-IL | (16.8) | NA | San Angelo, TX** | NA |
| 241 | Tyler, TX | (9.0) | 305 | Owensboro, KY | (17.0) | NA | San Francisco (greater), CA** | NA |
| 241 | Warren-Troy, MI M.D. | (9.0) | 306 | Yakima, WA | (17.9) | NA | San Rafael, CA M.D.** | NA |
| 245 | Camden, NJ M.D. | (9.1) | 307 | Flint, MI | (18.6) | NA | Scranton--Wilkes-Barre, PA** | NA |
| 246 | Gainesville, FL | (9.2) | 308 | Dover, DE | (19.1) | NA | Seattle (greater), WA** | NA |
| 246 | Jefferson City, MO | (9.2) | 309 | Merced, CA | (19.7) | NA | Shreveport-Bossier City, LA** | NA |
| 246 | San Jose, CA | (9.2) | 310 | Sebastian-Vero Beach, FL | (20.0) | NA | St. Cloud, MN** | NA |
| 249 | Jackson, MS | (9.3) | 311 | Watertown-Fort Drum, NY | (20.2) | NA | St. George, UT** | NA |
| 249 | Oklahoma City, OK | (9.3) | 312 | Rapid City, SD | (20.8) | NA | Tacoma, WA M.D.** | NA |
| 251 | Elmira, NY | (9.4) | 313 | Logan, UT-ID | (24.2) | NA | Toledo, OH** | NA |
| 251 | Lawrence, KS | (9.4) | NA | Albuquerque, NM** | NA | NA | Tucson, AZ** | NA |
| 251 | Lexington-Fayette, KY | (9.4) | NA | Alexandria, LA** | NA | NA | Visalia-Porterville, CA** | NA |
| 254 | Lincoln, NE | (9.5) | NA | Atlantic City, NJ** | NA | | | |

Source: CQ Press using reported data from the F.B.I. "Crime in the United States 2013"

*Includes murder, rape, robbery, aggravated assault, burglary, larceny-theft, and motor vehicle theft. The FBI changed the definition of rape beginning with 2013 data. Not all cities have made the change so the metro area figures reported here include rape figures based on differing definitions of rape. See note on page vii. **Not available.

# 4. Percent Change in Crime Rate: 2009 to 2013
## National Percent Change = 10.8% Decrease*

| RANK | METROPOLITAN AREA | % CHANGE | RANK | METROPOLITAN AREA | % CHANGE | RANK | METROPOLITAN AREA | % CHANGE |
|---|---|---|---|---|---|---|---|---|
| 129 | Abilene, TX | (9.0) | 172 | Cheyenne, WY | (13.9) | NA | Gary, IN M.D.** | NA |
| 147 | Akron, OH | (11.2) | NA | Chicago (greater), IL-IN-WI** | NA | NA | Gettysburg, PA** | NA |
| 139 | Albany-Schenectady-Troy, NY | (10.3) | NA | Chicago-Naperville, IL M.D.** | NA | 63 | Glens Falls, NY | (0.9) |
| 32 | Albany, GA | 5.6 | 103 | Chico, CA | (6.1) | 201 | Goldsboro, NC | (16.9) |
| NA | Albany, OR** | NA | 99 | Cincinnati, OH-KY-IN | (5.9) | NA | Grand Forks, ND-MN** | NA |
| 37 | Albuquerque, NM | 4.8 | 195 | Clarksville, TN-KY | (16.4) | NA | Grand Island, NE** | NA |
| 30 | Alexandria, LA | 6.4 | 64 | Cleveland, TN | (1.2) | 179 | Grand Junction, CO | (14.4) |
| 115 | Allentown, PA-NJ | (7.6) | 45 | Coeur d'Alene, ID | 3.2 | NA | Grand Rapids-Wyoming, MI** | NA |
| 153 | Altoona, PA | (11.6) | 284 | College Station-Bryan, TX | (40.2) | NA | Grants Pass, OR** | NA |
| 272 | Amarillo, TX | (28.1) | 16 | Colorado Springs, CO | 10.8 | 29 | Great Falls, MT | 6.8 |
| 234 | Ames, IA | (20.8) | 48 | Columbia, MO | 1.8 | 171 | Greeley, CO | (13.8) |
| 86 | Anaheim-Santa Ana-Irvine, CA M.D. | (3.8) | 149 | Columbia, SC | (11.3) | 94 | Green Bay, WI | (5.2) |
| 18 | Anchorage, AK | 9.2 | 225 | Columbus, GA-AL | (20.0) | 235 | Greensboro-High Point, NC | (20.9) |
| 225 | Ann Arbor, MI | (20.0) | 61 | Columbus, IN | (0.7) | NA | Greenville-Anderson, SC** | NA |
| 248 | Anniston-Oxford, AL | (22.6) | 185 | Corpus Christi, TX | (15.5) | NA | Greenville, NC** | NA |
| 277 | Appleton, WI | (28.9) | 124 | Corvallis, OR | (8.4) | NA | Gulfport-Biloxi-Pascagoula, MS** | NA |
| 249 | Athens-Clarke County, GA | (23.8) | NA | Crestview-Fort Walton Beach, FL** | NA | 67 | Hagerstown-Martinsburg, MD-WV | (1.4) |
| 107 | Atlanta, GA | (6.5) | 120 | Cumberland, MD-WV | (8.0) | NA | Hammond, LA** | NA |
| 169 | Atlantic City, NJ | (13.6) | 245 | Dallas (greater), TX | (22.1) | NA | Hanford-Corcoran, CA** | NA |
| 243 | Augusta, GA-SC | (21.9) | 252 | Dallas-Plano-Irving, TX M.D. | (24.0) | 52 | Harrisonburg, VA | 0.9 |
| 239 | Austin-Round Rock, TX | (21.3) | 90 | Dalton, GA | (4.6) | 222 | Hartford, CT | (19.2) |
| 60 | Bakersfield, CA | (0.3) | NA | Daphne-Fairhope-Foley, AL** | NA | NA | Hilton Head Island, SC** | NA |
| 131 | Baltimore, MD | (9.3) | NA | Davenport, IA-IL** | NA | 281 | Hinesville, GA | (30.1) |
| 187 | Bangor, ME | (15.7) | 87 | Dayton, OH | (4.0) | NA | Homosassa Springs, FL** | NA |
| 233 | Barnstable Town, MA | (20.7) | NA | Decatur, AL** | NA | 189 | Hot Springs, AR | (16.0) |
| 167 | Baton Rouge, LA | (13.4) | NA | Decatur, IL** | NA | 94 | Houma, LA | (5.2) |
| 160 | Bay City, MI | (12.4) | 205 | Deltona-Daytona Beach, FL | (17.1) | 194 | Houston, TX | (16.2) |
| 164 | Beaumont-Port Arthur, TX | (13.1) | 73 | Denver-Aurora, CO | (2.2) | 89 | Huntsville, AL | (4.4) |
| 42 | Bend, OR | 3.7 | 58 | Des Moines-West Des Moines, IA | (0.2) | 218 | Idaho Falls, ID | (18.4) |
| 20 | Billings, MT | 8.8 | 185 | Detroit (greater), MI | (15.5) | NA | Indianapolis, IN** | NA |
| 22 | Binghamton, NY | 8.7 | 141 | Detroit-Dearborn-Livonia, MI M.D. | (10.6) | 47 | Iowa City, IA | 3.0 |
| 192 | Birmingham-Hoover, AL | (16.1) | NA | Dothan, AL** | NA | 261 | Jacksonville, FL | (25.6) |
| 13 | Bismarck, ND | 17.4 | 211 | Dover, DE | (17.9) | 92 | Jackson, MI | (5.1) |
| 256 | Blacksburg, VA | (24.8) | 242 | Dubuque, IA | (21.8) | 238 | Jackson, MS | (21.1) |
| NA | Bloomington, IL** | NA | NA | Duluth, MN-WI** | NA | 225 | Jackson, TN | (20.0) |
| 112 | Bloomington, IN | (7.2) | NA | Dutchess-Putnam, NY M.D.** | NA | 162 | Janesville, WI | (12.8) |
| NA | Bloomsburg-Berwick, PA** | NA | NA | East Stroudsburg, PA** | NA | 83 | Jefferson City, MO | (3.5) |
| 167 | Boise City, ID | (13.4) | 188 | Eau Claire, WI | (15.9) | 122 | Johnson City, TN | (8.2) |
| 155 | Boston (greater), MA-NH | (12.0) | NA | El Centro, CA** | NA | NA | Johnstown, PA** | NA |
| 164 | Boston, MA M.D. | (13.1) | 257 | El Paso, TX | (24.9) | 115 | Jonesboro, AR | (7.6) |
| 101 | Boulder, CO | (6.0) | NA | Elgin, IL M.D.** | NA | NA | Joplin, MO** | NA |
| NA | Bowling Green, KY** | NA | NA | Elizabethtown-Fort Knox, KY** | NA | NA | Kahului-Wailuku-Lahaina, HI** | NA |
| 26 | Bremerton-Silverdale, WA | 7.9 | 49 | Elmira, NY | 1.7 | NA | Kankakee, IL** | NA |
| 216 | Bridgeport-Stamford, CT | (18.3) | 57 | Erie, PA | 0.0 | NA | Kansas City, MO-KS** | NA |
| 262 | Brownsville-Harlingen, TX | (26.0) | 147 | Eugene, OR | (11.2) | 129 | Kennewick-Richland, WA | (9.0) |
| NA | Brunswick, GA** | NA | 77 | Fairbanks, AK | (3.0) | 231 | Kingsport, TN-VA | (20.3) |
| 145 | Buffalo-Niagara Falls, NY | (10.9) | NA | Fargo, ND-MN** | NA | 119 | Kingston, NY | (7.9) |
| 201 | Burlington, NC | (16.9) | 204 | Farmington, NM | (17.0) | 163 | Knoxville, TN | (13.0) |
| NA | California-Lexington Park, MD** | NA | 76 | Fayetteville-Springdale, AR-MO | (2.7) | 128 | Kokomo, IN | (8.9) |
| NA | Cambridge-Newton, MA M.D.** | NA | 179 | Fayetteville, NC | (14.4) | NA | La Crosse, WI-MN** | NA |
| 101 | Camden, NJ M.D. | (6.0) | 138 | Flagstaff, AZ | (10.1) | 84 | Lafayette, IN | (3.6) |
| NA | Canton, OH** | NA | 223 | Flint, MI | (19.3) | NA | Lafayette, LA** | NA |
| 259 | Cape Coral-Fort Myers, FL | (25.2) | 74 | Florence-Muscle Shoals, AL | (2.4) | 53 | Lake Charles, LA | 0.7 |
| 71 | Cape Girardeau, MO-IL | (1.6) | 181 | Florence, SC | (14.7) | NA | Lake Co.-Kenosha Co., IL-WI M.D.** | NA |
| NA | Carbondale-Marion, IL** | NA | 107 | Fond du Lac, WI | (6.5) | 67 | Lake Havasu City-Kingman, AZ | (1.4) |
| 239 | Carson City, NV | (21.3) | 246 | Fort Collins, CO | (22.4) | 243 | Lakeland, FL | (21.9) |
| 251 | Casper, WY | (23.9) | 172 | Fort Lauderdale, FL M.D. | (13.9) | NA | Lancaster, PA** | NA |
| 183 | Cedar Rapids, IA | (15.1) | 80 | Fort Smith, AR-OK | (3.2) | 170 | Lansing-East Lansing, MI | (13.7) |
| NA | Chambersburg-Waynesboro, PA** | NA | 33 | Fort Wayne, IN | 5.1 | 275 | Laredo, TX | (28.6) |
| NA | Champaign-Urbana, IL** | NA | 220 | Fort Worth-Arlington, TX M.D. | (18.8) | 135 | Las Cruces, NM | (9.7) |
| NA | Charleston-North Charleston, SC** | NA | 55 | Fresno, CA | 0.4 | 125 | Las Vegas-Henderson, NV | (8.6) |
| NA | Charlotte-Mecklenburg, NC-SC** | NA | 9 | Gadsden, AL | 22.4 | 195 | Lawrence, KS | (16.4) |
| 263 | Charlottesville, VA | (26.1) | 283 | Gainesville, FL | (31.0) | 199 | Lawton, OK | (16.7) |
| 140 | Chattanooga, TN-GA | (10.4) | 106 | Gainesville, GA | (6.4) | 23 | Lebanon, PA | 8.6 |

Note: All listings are for Metropolitan Statistical Areas (M.S.A.s) except for those ending with "M.D." Listings with "M.D." are Metropolitan Divisions which are smaller parts of eleven large M.S.A.s. See explanatory note at beginning of metropolitan area section.

| RANK | METROPOLITAN AREA | % CHANGE | RANK | METROPOLITAN AREA | % CHANGE | RANK | METROPOLITAN AREA | % CHANGE |
|---|---|---|---|---|---|---|---|---|
| 14 | Lewiston-Auburn, ME | 15.1 | 81 | Omaha-Council Bluffs, NE-IA | (3.3) | 273 | Sheboygan, WI | (28.4) |
| 17 | Lewiston, ID-WA | 9.9 | 184 | Orlando, FL | (15.4) | 237 | Sherman-Denison, TX | (21.0) |
| 40 | Lexington-Fayette, KY | 3.8 | 274 | Oshkosh-Neenah, WI | (28.5) | NA | Shreveport-Bossier City, LA** | NA |
| 241 | Lima, OH | (21.5) | 229 | Owensboro, KY | (20.1) | 282 | Silver Spring-Frederick, MD M.D. | (30.2) |
| 142 | Lincoln, NE | (10.8) | 64 | Oxnard-Thousand Oaks, CA | (1.2) | 18 | Sioux City, IA-NE-SD | 9.2 |
| 123 | Little Rock, AR | (8.3) | 205 | Palm Bay-Melbourne, FL | (17.1) | 27 | Sioux Falls, SD | 7.8 |
| 246 | Logan, UT-ID | (22.4) | 154 | Panama City, FL | (11.8) | 255 | South Bend-Mishawaka, IN-MI | (24.6) |
| 277 | Longview, TX | (28.9) | NA | Parkersburg-Vienna, WV** | NA | 216 | Spartanburg, SC | (18.3) |
| 25 | Longview, WA | 8.2 | 56 | Pensacola, FL | 0.1 | 4 | Spokane, WA | 31.7 |
| 142 | Los Angeles County, CA M.D. | (10.8) | NA | Peoria, IL** | NA | NA | Springfield, IL** | NA |
| 133 | Los Angeles (greater), CA | (9.6) | 114 | Philadelphia (greater) PA-NJ-MD-DE | (7.4) | 51 | Springfield, MA | 1.1 |
| NA | Louisville, KY-IN** | NA | NA | Philadelphia, PA M.D.** | NA | 37 | Springfield, MO | 4.8 |
| 229 | Lubbock, TX | (20.1) | NA | Phoenix-Mesa-Scottsdale, AZ** | NA | 28 | Springfield, OH | 7.2 |
| 199 | Lynchburg, VA | (16.7) | NA | Pittsburgh, PA** | NA | 252 | State College, PA | (24.0) |
| 87 | Macon, GA | (4.0) | 39 | Pittsfield, MA | 4.3 | NA | Staunton-Waynesboro, VA** | NA |
| 5 | Madera, CA | 26.8 | 20 | Pocatello, ID | 8.8 | 97 | Stockton-Lodi, CA | (5.7) |
| NA | Madison, WI** | NA | 232 | Port St. Lucie, FL | (20.5) | NA | St. Cloud, MN** | NA |
| 40 | Manchester-Nashua, NH | 3.8 | 50 | Portland-Vancouver, OR-WA | 1.4 | NA | St. George, UT** | NA |
| 254 | Manhattan, KS | (24.5) | 99 | Portland, ME | (5.9) | 35 | St. Joseph, MO-KS | 5.0 |
| NA | Mankato-North Mankato, MN** | NA | 105 | Prescott, AZ | (6.3) | NA | St. Louis, MO-IL** | NA |
| 11 | Mansfield, OH | 18.6 | 120 | Providence-Warwick, RI-MA | (8.0) | 24 | Sumter, SC | 8.3 |
| 264 | McAllen-Edinburg-Mission, TX | (26.3) | 178 | Provo-Orem, UT | (14.2) | 67 | Syracuse, NY | (1.4) |
| 2 | Medford, OR | 59.3 | 1 | Pueblo, CO | 71.7 | 92 | Tacoma, WA M.D. | (5.1) |
| 198 | Memphis, TN-MS-AR | (16.6) | 258 | Punta Gorda, FL | (25.0) | 127 | Tallahassee, FL | (8.8) |
| 126 | Merced, CA | (8.7) | 182 | Racine, WI | (14.8) | 280 | Tampa-St Petersburg, FL | (29.8) |
| 209 | Miami (greater), FL | (17.4) | 176 | Raleigh, NC | (14.1) | NA | Terre Haute, IN** | NA |
| 189 | Miami-Dade County, FL M.D. | (16.0) | 136 | Rapid City, SD | (9.9) | 137 | Texarkana, TX-AR | (10.0) |
| 249 | Midland, TX | (23.8) | 214 | Reading, PA | (18.1) | NA | The Villages, FL** | NA |
| 152 | Milwaukee, WI | (11.4) | 10 | Redding, CA | 20.5 | NA | Toledo, OH** | NA |
| NA | Minneapolis-St. Paul, MN-WI** | NA | 235 | Reno, NV | (20.9) | 145 | Topeka, KS | (10.9) |
| 12 | Missoula, MT | 18.2 | 160 | Richmond, VA | (12.4) | 91 | Trenton, NJ | (4.7) |
| 132 | Mobile, AL | (9.5) | 85 | Riverside-San Bernardino, CA | (3.7) | NA | Tucson, AZ** | NA |
| 98 | Modesto, CA | (5.8) | 174 | Roanoke, VA | (14.0) | 158 | Tulsa, OK | (12.2) |
| NA | Monroe, LA** | NA | NA | Rochester, MN** | NA | 264 | Tuscaloosa, AL | (26.3) |
| 54 | Monroe, MI | 0.5 | 155 | Rochester, NY | (12.0) | 269 | Tyler, TX | (27.5) |
| NA | Montgomery County, PA M.D.** | NA | NA | Rockford, IL** | NA | 142 | Utica-Rome, NY | (10.8) |
| 268 | Morgantown, WV | (27.2) | 31 | Rockingham County, NH M.D. | 6.3 | 75 | Vallejo-Fairfield, CA | (2.6) |
| 110 | Morristown, TN | (6.7) | 211 | Rocky Mount, NC | (17.9) | 279 | Victoria, TX | (29.0) |
| 81 | Mount Vernon-Anacortes, WA | (3.3) | 8 | Rome, GA | 23.8 | 6 | Vineland-Bridgeton, NJ | 26.7 |
| 46 | Muncie, IN | 3.1 | 176 | Sacramento, CA | (14.1) | NA | Virginia Beach-Norfolk, VA-NC** | NA |
| 149 | Muskegon, MI | (11.3) | 269 | Saginaw, MI | (27.5) | NA | Visalia-Porterville, CA** | NA |
| NA | Myrtle Beach, SC-NC** | NA | 43 | Salem, OR | 3.6 | 266 | Waco, TX | (26.4) |
| 218 | Napa, CA | (18.4) | 133 | Salinas, CA | (9.6) | NA | Warner Robins, GA** | NA |
| 208 | Naples-Marco Island, FL | (17.3) | NA | Salisbury, MD-DE** | NA | 224 | Warren-Troy, MI M.D. | (19.4) |
| 209 | Nashville-Davidson, TN | (17.4) | 115 | Salt Lake City, UT | (7.6) | 225 | Washington (greater) DC-VA-MD-WV | (20.0) |
| 201 | Nassau-Suffolk, NY M.D. | (16.9) | 221 | San Angelo, TX | (19.0) | 213 | Washington, DC-VA-MD-WV M.D. | (18.0) |
| NA | New Bern, NC** | NA | 214 | San Antonio, TX | (18.1) | NA | Watertown-Fort Drum, NY** | NA |
| 174 | New Haven-Milford, CT | (14.0) | 113 | San Diego, CA | (7.3) | 158 | Wausau, WI | (12.2) |
| NA | New Orleans, LA** | NA | 33 | San Francisco (greater), CA | 5.1 | 260 | West Palm Beach, FL M.D. | (25.3) |
| 104 | New York (greater), NY-NJ-PA | (6.2) | 7 | San Francisco-Redwood, CA M.D. | 25.5 | 189 | Wichita Falls, TX | (16.0) |
| NA | New York-Jersey City, NY-NJ M.D.** | NA | 77 | San Jose, CA | (3.0) | 64 | Wichita, KS | (1.2) |
| 166 | Newark, NJ-PA M.D. | (13.3) | 35 | San Luis Obispo, CA | 5.0 | 15 | Williamsport, PA | 11.9 |
| 111 | Niles-Benton Harbor, MI | (6.9) | NA | San Rafael, CA M.D.** | NA | 157 | Wilmington, DE-MD-NJ M.D. | (12.1) |
| 271 | North Port-Sarasota-Bradenton, FL | (27.8) | 195 | Santa Cruz-Watsonville, CA | (16.4) | NA | Wilmington, NC** | NA |
| 96 | Norwich-New London, CT | (5.4) | 79 | Santa Maria-Santa Barbara, CA | (3.1) | 192 | Winchester, VA-WV | (16.1) |
| 72 | Oakland-Hayward, CA M.D. | (1.8) | 207 | Santa Rosa, CA | (17.2) | NA | Winston-Salem, NC** | NA |
| NA | Ocala, FL** | NA | 267 | Savannah, GA | (27.0) | 109 | Worcester, MA-CT | (6.6) |
| 118 | Ocean City, NJ | (7.7) | NA | Scranton--Wilkes-Barre, PA** | NA | NA | Yakima, WA** | NA |
| 44 | Odessa, TX | 3.4 | 70 | Seattle (greater), WA | (1.5) | 149 | York-Hanover, PA | (11.3) |
| NA | Ogden-Clearfield, UT** | NA | 58 | Seattle-Bellevue-Everett, WA M.D. | (0.2) | 3 | Yuba City, CA | 32.4 |
| NA | Oklahoma City, OK** | NA | 276 | Sebastian-Vero Beach, FL | (28.7) | 62 | Yuma, AZ | (0.8) |
| NA | Olympia, WA** | NA | NA | Sebring, FL** | NA | | | |

Source: CQ Press using reported data from the F.B.I. "Crime in the United States 2013"

*Includes murder, rape, robbery, aggravated assault, burglary, larceny-theft, and motor vehicle theft. The FBI changed the definition of rape beginning with 2013 data. Not all cities have made the change so the metro area figures reported here include rape figures based on differing definitions of rape. See note on page vii. **Not available.

# 4. Percent Change in Crime Rate: 2009 to 2013 (continued)
## National Percent Change = 10.8% Decrease*

| RANK | METROPOLITAN AREA | % CHANGE | RANK | METROPOLITAN AREA | % CHANGE | RANK | METROPOLITAN AREA | % CHANGE |
|---|---|---|---|---|---|---|---|---|
| 1 | Pueblo, CO | 71.7 | 64 | Oxnard-Thousand Oaks, CA | (1.2) | 129 | Abilene, TX | (9.0) |
| 2 | Medford, OR | 59.3 | 64 | Wichita, KS | (1.2) | 129 | Kennewick-Richland, WA | (9.0) |
| 3 | Yuba City, CA | 32.4 | 67 | Hagerstown-Martinsburg, MD-WV | (1.4) | 131 | Baltimore, MD | (9.3) |
| 4 | Spokane, WA | 31.7 | 67 | Lake Havasu City-Kingman, AZ | (1.4) | 132 | Mobile, AL | (9.5) |
| 5 | Madera, CA | 26.8 | 67 | Syracuse, NY | (1.4) | 133 | Los Angeles (greater), CA | (9.6) |
| 6 | Vineland-Bridgeton, NJ | 26.7 | 70 | Seattle (greater), WA | (1.5) | 133 | Salinas, CA | (9.6) |
| 7 | San Francisco-Redwood, CA M.D. | 25.5 | 71 | Cape Girardeau, MO-IL | (1.6) | 135 | Las Cruces, NM | (9.7) |
| 8 | Rome, GA | 23.8 | 72 | Oakland-Hayward, CA M.D. | (1.8) | 136 | Rapid City, SD | (9.9) |
| 9 | Gadsden, AL | 22.4 | 73 | Denver-Aurora, CO | (2.2) | 137 | Texarkana, TX-AR | (10.0) |
| 10 | Redding, CA | 20.5 | 74 | Florence-Muscle Shoals, AL | (2.4) | 138 | Flagstaff, AZ | (10.1) |
| 11 | Mansfield, OH | 18.6 | 75 | Vallejo-Fairfield, CA | (2.6) | 139 | Albany-Schenectady-Troy, NY | (10.3) |
| 12 | Missoula, MT | 18.2 | 76 | Fayetteville-Springdale, AR-MO | (2.7) | 140 | Chattanooga, TN-GA | (10.4) |
| 13 | Bismarck, ND | 17.4 | 77 | Fairbanks, AK | (3.0) | 141 | Detroit-Dearborn-Livonia, MI M.D. | (10.6) |
| 14 | Lewiston-Auburn, ME | 15.1 | 77 | San Jose, CA | (3.0) | 142 | Lincoln, NE | (10.8) |
| 15 | Williamsport, PA | 11.9 | 79 | Santa Maria-Santa Barbara, CA | (3.1) | 142 | Los Angeles County, CA M.D. | (10.8) |
| 16 | Colorado Springs, CO | 10.8 | 80 | Fort Smith, AR-OK | (3.2) | 142 | Utica-Rome, NY | (10.8) |
| 17 | Lewiston, ID-WA | 9.9 | 81 | Mount Vernon-Anacortes, WA | (3.3) | 145 | Buffalo-Niagara Falls, NY | (10.9) |
| 18 | Anchorage, AK | 9.2 | 81 | Omaha-Council Bluffs, NE-IA | (3.3) | 145 | Topeka, KS | (10.9) |
| 18 | Sioux City, IA-NE-SD | 9.2 | 83 | Jefferson City, MO | (3.5) | 147 | Akron, OH | (11.2) |
| 20 | Billings, MT | 8.8 | 84 | Lafayette, IN | (3.6) | 147 | Eugene, OR | (11.2) |
| 20 | Pocatello, ID | 8.8 | 85 | Riverside-San Bernardino, CA | (3.7) | 149 | Columbia, SC | (11.3) |
| 22 | Binghamton, NY | 8.7 | 86 | Anaheim-Santa Ana-Irvine, CA M.D. | (3.8) | 149 | Muskegon, MI | (11.3) |
| 23 | Lebanon, PA | 8.6 | 87 | Dayton, OH | (4.0) | 149 | York-Hanover, PA | (11.3) |
| 24 | Sumter, SC | 8.3 | 87 | Macon, GA | (4.0) | 152 | Milwaukee, WI | (11.4) |
| 25 | Longview, WA | 8.2 | 89 | Huntsville, AL | (4.4) | 153 | Altoona, PA | (11.6) |
| 26 | Bremerton-Silverdale, WA | 7.9 | 90 | Dalton, GA | (4.6) | 154 | Panama City, FL | (11.8) |
| 27 | Sioux Falls, SD | 7.8 | 91 | Trenton, NJ | (4.7) | 155 | Boston (greater), MA-NH | (12.0) |
| 28 | Springfield, OH | 7.2 | 92 | Jackson, MI | (5.1) | 155 | Rochester, NY | (12.0) |
| 29 | Great Falls, MT | 6.8 | 92 | Tacoma, WA M.D. | (5.1) | 157 | Wilmington, DE-MD-NJ M.D. | (12.1) |
| 30 | Alexandria, LA | 6.4 | 94 | Green Bay, WI | (5.2) | 158 | Tulsa, OK | (12.2) |
| 31 | Rockingham County, NH M.D. | 6.3 | 94 | Houma, LA | (5.2) | 158 | Wausau, WI | (12.2) |
| 32 | Albany, GA | 5.6 | 96 | Norwich-New London, CT | (5.4) | 160 | Bay City, MI | (12.4) |
| 33 | Fort Wayne, IN | 5.1 | 97 | Stockton-Lodi, CA | (5.7) | 160 | Richmond, VA | (12.4) |
| 33 | San Francisco (greater), CA | 5.1 | 98 | Modesto, CA | (5.8) | 162 | Janesville, WI | (12.8) |
| 35 | San Luis Obispo, CA | 5.0 | 99 | Cincinnati, OH-KY-IN | (5.9) | 163 | Knoxville, TN | (13.0) |
| 35 | St. Joseph, MO-KS | 5.0 | 99 | Portland, ME | (5.9) | 164 | Beaumont-Port Arthur, TX | (13.1) |
| 37 | Albuquerque, NM | 4.8 | 101 | Boulder, CO | (6.0) | 164 | Boston, MA M.D. | (13.1) |
| 37 | Springfield, MO | 4.8 | 101 | Camden, NJ M.D. | (6.0) | 166 | Newark, NJ-PA M.D. | (13.3) |
| 39 | Pittsfield, MA | 4.3 | 103 | Chico, CA | (6.1) | 167 | Baton Rouge, LA | (13.4) |
| 40 | Lexington-Fayette, KY | 3.8 | 104 | New York (greater), NY-NJ-PA | (6.2) | 167 | Boise City, ID | (13.4) |
| 40 | Manchester-Nashua, NH | 3.8 | 105 | Prescott, AZ | (6.3) | 169 | Atlantic City, NJ | (13.6) |
| 42 | Bend, OR | 3.7 | 106 | Gainesville, GA | (6.4) | 170 | Lansing-East Lansing, MI | (13.7) |
| 43 | Salem, OR | 3.6 | 107 | Atlanta, GA | (6.5) | 171 | Greeley, CO | (13.8) |
| 44 | Odessa, TX | 3.4 | 107 | Fond du Lac, WI | (6.5) | 172 | Cheyenne, WY | (13.9) |
| 45 | Coeur d'Alene, ID | 3.2 | 109 | Worcester, MA-CT | (6.6) | 172 | Fort Lauderdale, FL M.D. | (13.9) |
| 46 | Muncie, IN | 3.1 | 110 | Morristown, TN | (6.7) | 174 | New Haven-Milford, CT | (14.0) |
| 47 | Iowa City, IA | 3.0 | 111 | Niles-Benton Harbor, MI | (6.9) | 174 | Roanoke, VA | (14.0) |
| 48 | Columbia, MO | 1.8 | 112 | Bloomington, IN | (7.2) | 176 | Raleigh, NC | (14.1) |
| 49 | Elmira, NY | 1.7 | 113 | San Diego, CA | (7.3) | 176 | Sacramento, CA | (14.1) |
| 50 | Portland-Vancouver, OR-WA | 1.4 | 114 | Philadelphia (greater) PA-NJ-MD-DE | (7.4) | 178 | Provo-Orem, UT | (14.2) |
| 51 | Springfield, MA | 1.1 | 115 | Allentown, PA-NJ | (7.6) | 179 | Fayetteville, NC | (14.4) |
| 52 | Harrisonburg, VA | 0.9 | 115 | Jonesboro, AR | (7.6) | 179 | Grand Junction, CO | (14.4) |
| 53 | Lake Charles, LA | 0.7 | 115 | Salt Lake City, UT | (7.6) | 181 | Florence, SC | (14.7) |
| 54 | Monroe, MI | 0.5 | 118 | Ocean City, NJ | (7.7) | 182 | Racine, WI | (14.8) |
| 55 | Fresno, CA | 0.4 | 119 | Kingston, NY | (7.9) | 183 | Cedar Rapids, IA | (15.1) |
| 56 | Pensacola, FL | 0.1 | 120 | Cumberland, MD-WV | (8.0) | 184 | Orlando, FL | (15.4) |
| 57 | Erie, PA | 0.0 | 120 | Providence-Warwick, RI-MA | (8.0) | 185 | Corpus Christi, TX | (15.5) |
| 58 | Des Moines-West Des Moines, IA | (0.2) | 122 | Johnson City, TN | (8.2) | 185 | Detroit (greater), MI | (15.5) |
| 58 | Seattle-Bellevue-Everett, WA M.D. | (0.2) | 123 | Little Rock, AR | (8.3) | 187 | Bangor, ME | (15.7) |
| 60 | Bakersfield, CA | (0.3) | 124 | Corvallis, OR | (8.4) | 188 | Eau Claire, WI | (15.9) |
| 61 | Columbus, IN | (0.7) | 125 | Las Vegas-Henderson, NV | (8.6) | 189 | Hot Springs, AR | (16.0) |
| 62 | Yuma, AZ | (0.8) | 126 | Merced, CA | (8.7) | 189 | Miami-Dade County, FL M.D. | (16.0) |
| 63 | Glens Falls, NY | (0.9) | 127 | Tallahassee, FL | (8.8) | 189 | Wichita Falls, TX | (16.0) |
| 64 | Cleveland, TN | (1.2) | 128 | Kokomo, IN | (8.9) | 192 | Birmingham-Hoover, AL | (16.1) |

Note: All listings are for Metropolitan Statistical Areas (M.S.A.s) except for those ending with "M.D." Listings with "M.D." are Metropolitan Divisions which are smaller parts of eleven large M.S.A.s. See explanatory note at beginning of metropolitan area section.

| RANK | METROPOLITAN AREA | % CHANGE | RANK | METROPOLITAN AREA | % CHANGE | RANK | METROPOLITAN AREA | % CHANGE |
|---|---|---|---|---|---|---|---|---|
| 192 | Winchester, VA-WV | (16.1) | 255 | South Bend-Mishawaka, IN-MI | (24.6) | NA | Grand Rapids-Wyoming, MI** | NA |
| 194 | Houston, TX | (16.2) | 256 | Blacksburg, VA | (24.8) | NA | Grants Pass, OR** | NA |
| 195 | Clarksville, TN-KY | (16.4) | 257 | El Paso, TX | (24.9) | NA | Greenville-Anderson, SC** | NA |
| 195 | Lawrence, KS | (16.4) | 258 | Punta Gorda, FL | (25.0) | NA | Greenville, NC** | NA |
| 195 | Santa Cruz-Watsonville, CA | (16.4) | 259 | Cape Coral-Fort Myers, FL | (25.2) | NA | Gulfport-Biloxi-Pascagoula, MS** | NA |
| 198 | Memphis, TN-MS-AR | (16.6) | 260 | West Palm Beach, FL M.D. | (25.3) | NA | Hammond, LA** | NA |
| 199 | Lawton, OK | (16.7) | 261 | Jacksonville, FL | (25.6) | NA | Hanford-Corcoran, CA** | NA |
| 199 | Lynchburg, VA | (16.7) | 262 | Brownsville-Harlingen, TX | (26.0) | NA | Hilton Head Island, SC** | NA |
| 201 | Burlington, NC | (16.9) | 263 | Charlottesville, VA | (26.1) | NA | Homosassa Springs, FL** | NA |
| 201 | Goldsboro, NC | (16.9) | 264 | McAllen-Edinburg-Mission, TX | (26.3) | NA | Indianapolis, IN** | NA |
| 201 | Nassau-Suffolk, NY M.D. | (16.9) | 264 | Tuscaloosa, AL | (26.3) | NA | Johnstown, PA** | NA |
| 204 | Farmington, NM | (17.0) | 266 | Waco, TX | (26.4) | NA | Joplin, MO** | NA |
| 205 | Deltona-Daytona Beach, FL | (17.1) | 267 | Savannah, GA | (27.0) | NA | Kahului-Wailuku-Lahaina, HI** | NA |
| 205 | Palm Bay-Melbourne, FL | (17.1) | 268 | Morgantown, WV | (27.2) | NA | Kankakee, IL** | NA |
| 207 | Santa Rosa, CA | (17.2) | 269 | Saginaw, MI | (27.5) | NA | Kansas City, MO-KS** | NA |
| 208 | Naples-Marco Island, FL | (17.3) | 269 | Tyler, TX | (27.5) | NA | La Crosse, WI-MN** | NA |
| 209 | Miami (greater), FL | (17.4) | 271 | North Port-Sarasota-Bradenton, FL | (27.8) | NA | Lafayette, LA** | NA |
| 209 | Nashville-Davidson, TN | (17.4) | 272 | Amarillo, TX | (28.1) | NA | Lake Co.-Kenosha Co., IL-WI M.D.** | NA |
| 211 | Dover, DE | (17.9) | 273 | Sheboygan, WI | (28.4) | NA | Lancaster, PA** | NA |
| 211 | Rocky Mount, NC | (17.9) | 274 | Oshkosh-Neenah, WI | (28.5) | NA | Louisville, KY-IN** | NA |
| 213 | Washington, DC-VA-MD-WV M.D. | (18.0) | 275 | Laredo, TX | (28.6) | NA | Madison, WI** | NA |
| 214 | Reading, PA | (18.1) | 276 | Sebastian-Vero Beach, FL | (28.7) | NA | Mankato-North Mankato, MN** | NA |
| 214 | San Antonio, TX | (18.1) | 277 | Appleton, WI | (28.9) | NA | Minneapolis-St. Paul, MN-WI** | NA |
| 216 | Bridgeport-Stamford, CT | (18.3) | 277 | Longview, TX | (28.9) | NA | Monroe, LA** | NA |
| 216 | Spartanburg, SC | (18.3) | 279 | Victoria, TX | (29.0) | NA | Montgomery County, PA M.D.** | NA |
| 218 | Idaho Falls, ID | (18.4) | 280 | Tampa-St Petersburg, FL | (29.8) | NA | Myrtle Beach, SC-NC** | NA |
| 218 | Napa, CA | (18.4) | 281 | Hinesville, GA | (30.1) | NA | New Bern, NC** | NA |
| 220 | Fort Worth-Arlington, TX M.D. | (18.8) | 282 | Silver Spring-Frederick, MD M.D. | (30.2) | NA | New Orleans, LA** | NA |
| 221 | San Angelo, TX | (19.0) | 283 | Gainesville, FL | (31.0) | NA | New York-Jersey City, NY-NJ M.D.** | NA |
| 222 | Hartford, CT | (19.2) | 284 | College Station-Bryan, TX | (40.2) | NA | Ocala, FL** | NA |
| 223 | Flint, MI | (19.3) | NA | Albany, OR** | NA | NA | Ogden-Clearfield, UT** | NA |
| 224 | Warren-Troy, MI M.D. | (19.4) | NA | Bloomington, IL** | NA | NA | Oklahoma City, OK** | NA |
| 225 | Ann Arbor, MI | (20.0) | NA | Bloomsburg-Berwick, PA** | NA | NA | Olympia, WA** | NA |
| 225 | Columbus, GA-AL | (20.0) | NA | Bowling Green, KY** | NA | NA | Parkersburg-Vienna, WV** | NA |
| 225 | Jackson, TN | (20.0) | NA | Brunswick, GA** | NA | NA | Peoria, IL** | NA |
| 225 | Washington (greater) DC-VA-MD-WV | (20.0) | NA | California-Lexington Park, MD** | NA | NA | Philadelphia, PA M.D.** | NA |
| 229 | Lubbock, TX | (20.1) | NA | Cambridge-Newton, MA M.D.** | NA | NA | Phoenix-Mesa-Scottsdale, AZ** | NA |
| 229 | Owensboro, KY | (20.1) | NA | Canton, OH** | NA | NA | Pittsburgh, PA** | NA |
| 231 | Kingsport, TN-VA | (20.3) | NA | Carbondale-Marion, IL** | NA | NA | Rochester, MN** | NA |
| 232 | Port St. Lucie, FL | (20.5) | NA | Chambersburg-Waynesboro, PA** | NA | NA | Rockford, IL** | NA |
| 233 | Barnstable Town, MA | (20.7) | NA | Champaign-Urbana, IL** | NA | NA | Salisbury, MD-DE** | NA |
| 234 | Ames, IA | (20.8) | NA | Charleston-North Charleston, SC** | NA | NA | San Rafael, CA M.D.** | NA |
| 235 | Greensboro-High Point, NC | (20.9) | NA | Charlotte-Mecklenburg, NC-SC** | NA | NA | Scranton--Wilkes-Barre, PA** | NA |
| 235 | Reno, NV | (20.9) | NA | Chicago (greater), IL-IN-WI** | NA | NA | Sebring, FL** | NA |
| 237 | Sherman-Denison, TX | (21.0) | NA | Chicago-Naperville, IL M.D.** | NA | NA | Shreveport-Bossier City, LA** | NA |
| 238 | Jackson, MS | (21.1) | NA | Crestview-Fort Walton Beach, FL** | NA | NA | Springfield, IL** | NA |
| 239 | Austin-Round Rock, TX | (21.3) | NA | Daphne-Fairhope-Foley, AL** | NA | NA | Staunton-Waynesboro, VA** | NA |
| 239 | Carson City, NV | (21.3) | NA | Davenport, IA-IL** | NA | NA | St. Cloud, MN** | NA |
| 241 | Lima, OH | (21.5) | NA | Decatur, AL** | NA | NA | St. George, UT** | NA |
| 242 | Dubuque, IA | (21.8) | NA | Decatur, IL** | NA | NA | St. Louis, MO-IL** | NA |
| 243 | Augusta, GA-SC | (21.9) | NA | Dothan, AL** | NA | NA | Terre Haute, IN** | NA |
| 243 | Lakeland, FL | (21.9) | NA | Duluth, MN-WI** | NA | NA | The Villages, FL** | NA |
| 245 | Dallas (greater), TX | (22.1) | NA | Dutchess-Putnam, NY M.D.** | NA | NA | Toledo, OH** | NA |
| 246 | Fort Collins, CO | (22.4) | NA | East Stroudsburg, PA** | NA | NA | Tucson, AZ** | NA |
| 246 | Logan, UT-ID | (22.4) | NA | El Centro, CA** | NA | NA | Virginia Beach-Norfolk, VA-NC** | NA |
| 248 | Anniston-Oxford, AL | (22.6) | NA | Elgin, IL M.D.** | NA | NA | Visalia-Porterville, CA** | NA |
| 249 | Athens-Clarke County, GA | (23.8) | NA | Elizabethtown-Fort Knox, KY** | NA | NA | Warner Robins, GA** | NA |
| 249 | Midland, TX | (23.8) | NA | Fargo, ND-MN** | NA | NA | Watertown-Fort Drum, NY** | NA |
| 251 | Casper, WY | (23.9) | NA | Gary, IN M.D.** | NA | NA | Wilmington, NC** | NA |
| 252 | Dallas-Plano-Irving, TX M.D. | (24.0) | NA | Gettysburg, PA** | NA | NA | Winston-Salem, NC** | NA |
| 252 | State College, PA | (24.0) | NA | Grand Forks, ND-MN** | NA | NA | Yakima, WA** | NA |
| 254 | Manhattan, KS | (24.5) | NA | Grand Island, NE** | NA | | | |

Source: CQ Press using reported data from the F.B.I. "Crime in the United States 2013"

*Includes murder, rape, robbery, aggravated assault, burglary, larceny-theft, and motor vehicle theft. The FBI changed the definition of rape beginning with 2013 data. Not all cities have made the change so the metro area figures reported here include rape figures based on differing definitions of rape. See note on page vii. **Not available.

# 5. Violent Crimes in 2013
## National Total = 1,163,146 Violent Crimes*

| RANK | METROPOLITAN AREA | CRIMES | RANK | METROPOLITAN AREA | CRIMES | RANK | METROPOLITAN AREA | CRIMES |
|---|---|---|---|---|---|---|---|---|
| 246 | Abilene, TX | 560 | 344 | Cheyenne, WY | 198 | 103 | Gary, IN M.D. | 2,385 |
| 120 | Akron, OH | 2,091 | NA | Chicago (greater), IL-IN-WI** | NA | 370 | Gettysburg, PA | 100 |
| 108 | Albany-Schenectady-Troy, NY | 2,338 | NA | Chicago-Naperville, IL M.D.** | NA | 365 | Glens Falls, NY | 126 |
| 176 | Albany, GA | 1,031 | 232 | Chico, CA | 634 | 265 | Goldsboro, NC | 489 |
| 371 | Albany, OR | 97 | 50 | Cincinnati, OH-KY-IN | 6,094 | 338 | Grand Forks, ND-MN | 210 |
| 46 | Albuquerque, NM | 6,700 | 178 | Clarksville, TN-KY | 1,030 | 354 | Grand Island, NE | 156 |
| 156 | Alexandria, LA | 1,228 | 257 | Cleveland, TN | 519 | 270 | Grand Junction, CO | 465 |
| 138 | Allentown, PA-NJ | 1,536 | 272 | Coeur d'Alene, ID | 459 | 84 | Grand Rapids-Wyoming, MI | 3,057 |
| 320 | Altoona, PA | 271 | 199 | College Station-Bryan, TX | 881 | 363 | Grants Pass, OR | 136 |
| 148 | Amarillo, TX | 1,365 | 96 | Colorado Springs, CO | 2,504 | 346 | Great Falls, MT | 184 |
| 361 | Ames, IA | 140 | 244 | Columbia, MO | 568 | 207 | Greeley, CO | 795 |
| 51 | Anaheim-Santa Ana-Irvine, CA M.D. | 6,042 | 67 | Columbia, SC | 4,585 | 230 | Green Bay, WI | 644 |
| 97 | Anchorage, AK | 2,497 | 152 | Columbus, GA-AL | 1,304 | 94 | Greensboro-High Point, NC | 2,557 |
| 172 | Ann Arbor, MI | 1,079 | 358 | Columbus, IN | 148 | 65 | Greenville-Anderson, SC | 4,793 |
| 235 | Anniston-Oxford, AL | 622 | 109 | Corpus Christi, TX | 2,314 | 206 | Greenville, NC | 799 |
| 319 | Appleton, WI | 285 | 369 | Corvallis, OR | 104 | 170 | Gulfport-Biloxi-Pascagoula, MS | 1,085 |
| 251 | Athens-Clarke County, GA | 537 | 175 | Crestview-Fort Walton Beach, FL | 1,044 | 241 | Hagerstown-Martinsburg, MD-WV | 600 |
| 11 | Atlanta, GA | 21,444 | 316 | Cumberland, MD-WV | 296 | 169 | Hammond, LA | 1,087 |
| 157 | Atlantic City, NJ | 1,225 | 10 | Dallas (greater), TX | 22,682 | 214 | Hanford-Corcoran, CA | 725 |
| 131 | Augusta, GA-SC | 1,672 | 22 | Dallas-Plano-Irving, TX M.D. | 14,328 | 351 | Harrisonburg, VA | 166 |
| 58 | Austin-Round Rock, TX | 5,099 | 305 | Dalton, GA | 344 | 92 | Hartford, CT | 2,706 |
| 60 | Bakersfield, CA | 4,969 | 281 | Daphne-Fairhope-Foley, AL | 427 | 190 | Hilton Head Island, SC | 955 |
| 15 | Baltimore, MD | 17,552 | 147 | Davenport, IA-IL | 1,387 | 333 | Hinesville, GA | 230 |
| 361 | Bangor, ME | 140 | 116 | Dayton, OH | 2,182 | 248 | Homosassa Springs, FL | 542 |
| 192 | Barnstable Town, MA | 941 | 312 | Decatur, AL | 301 | 272 | Hot Springs, AR | 459 |
| 69 | Baton Rouge, LA | 4,173 | 284 | Decatur, IL | 422 | 233 | Houma, LA | 626 |
| 309 | Bay City, MI | 316 | 106 | Deltona-Daytona Beach, FL | 2,353 | 5 | Houston, TX | 35,112 |
| 117 | Beaumont-Port Arthur, TX | 2,177 | 39 | Denver-Aurora, CO | 8,848 | 119 | Huntsville, AL | 2,101 |
| 300 | Bend, OR | 364 | 136 | Des Moines-West Des Moines, IA | 1,597 | 335 | Idaho Falls, ID | 218 |
| 277 | Billings, MT | 439 | 9 | Detroit (greater), MI | 24,475 | NA | Indianapolis, IN** | NA |
| 252 | Binghamton, NY | 536 | 14 | Detroit-Dearborn-Livonia, MI M.D. | 18,719 | 269 | Iowa City, IA | 473 |
| 52 | Birmingham-Hoover, AL | 6,034 | 243 | Dothan, AL | 587 | 45 | Jacksonville, FL | 6,904 |
| 262 | Bismarck, ND | 494 | 209 | Dover, DE | 774 | 228 | Jackson, MI | 651 |
| 310 | Blacksburg, VA | 314 | 356 | Dubuque, IA | 153 | 114 | Jackson, MS | 2,191 |
| 237 | Bloomington, IL | 610 | 227 | Duluth, MN-WI | 654 | 159 | Jackson, TN | 1,209 |
| 282 | Bloomington, IN | 426 | 231 | Dutchess-Putnam, NY M.D. | 642 | 296 | Janesville, WI | 368 |
| 337 | Bloomsburg-Berwick, PA | 214 | 236 | East Stroudsburg, PA | 618 | 282 | Jefferson City, MO | 426 |
| 144 | Boise City, ID | 1,453 | 340 | Eau Claire, WI | 205 | 225 | Johnson City, TN | 660 |
| 19 | Boston (greater), MA-NH | 16,586 | 248 | El Centro, CA | 542 | 324 | Johnstown, PA | 253 |
| 32 | Boston, MA M.D. | 9,770 | 87 | El Paso, TX | 2,925 | 274 | Jonesboro, AR | 454 |
| 226 | Boulder, CO | 658 | 168 | Elgin, IL M.D. | 1,108 | 255 | Joplin, MO | 521 |
| 331 | Bowling Green, KY | 236 | 367 | Elizabethtown-Fort Knox, KY | 118 | 276 | Kahului-Wailuku-Lahaina, HI | 450 |
| 219 | Bremerton-Silverdale, WA | 707 | 357 | Elmira, NY | 151 | 33 | Kansas City, MO-KS | 9,601 |
| 111 | Bridgeport-Stamford, CT | 2,252 | 223 | Erie, PA | 687 | 240 | Kennewick-Richland, WA | 603 |
| 182 | Brownsville-Harlingen, TX | 1,009 | 222 | Eugene, OR | 691 | 188 | Kingsport, TN-VA | 976 |
| NA | Brunswick, GA** | NA | 330 | Fairbanks, AK | 237 | 317 | Kingston, NY | 294 |
| 63 | Buffalo-Niagara Falls, NY | 4,883 | 244 | Fargo, ND-MN | 568 | 81 | Knoxville, TN | 3,103 |
| 242 | Burlington, NC | 593 | 234 | Farmington, NM | 625 | 335 | Kokomo, IN | 218 |
| 328 | California-Lexington Park, MD | 242 | 133 | Fayetteville-Springdale, AR-MO | 1,633 | 350 | La Crosse, WI-MN | 167 |
| 49 | Cambridge-Newton, MA M.D. | 6,103 | 126 | Fayetteville, NC | 1,853 | 254 | Lafayette, IN | 522 |
| 71 | Camden, NJ M.D. | 4,034 | 275 | Flagstaff, AZ | 451 | 113 | Lafayette, LA | 2,201 |
| 171 | Canton, OH | 1,080 | 86 | Flint, MI | 3,004 | 157 | Lake Charles, LA | 1,225 |
| 115 | Cape Coral-Fort Myers, FL | 2,184 | 256 | Florence-Muscle Shoals, AL | 520 | 149 | Lake Co.-Kenosha Co., IL-WI M.D. | 1,361 |
| 267 | Cape Girardeau, MO-IL | 478 | 186 | Florence, SC | 984 | 278 | Lake Havasu City-Kingman, AZ | 437 |
| 294 | Carbondale-Marion, IL | 377 | 342 | Fond du Lac, WI | 200 | 110 | Lakeland, FL | 2,287 |
| 364 | Carson City, NV | 133 | 229 | Fort Collins, CO | 646 | 194 | Lancaster, PA | 905 |
| 349 | Casper, WY | 169 | 42 | Fort Lauderdale, FL M.D. | 8,078 | 125 | Lansing-East Lansing, MI | 1,893 |
| 250 | Cedar Rapids, IA | 539 | 166 | Fort Smith, AR-OK | 1,122 | 164 | Laredo, TX | 1,133 |
| 333 | Chambersburg-Waynesboro, PA | 230 | 165 | Fort Wayne, IN | 1,129 | 217 | Las Cruces, NM | 716 |
| 167 | Champaign-Urbana, IL | 1,118 | 41 | Fort Worth-Arlington, TX M.D. | 8,354 | 23 | Las Vegas-Henderson, NV | 13,735 |
| 95 | Charleston-North Charleston, SC | 2,555 | 64 | Fresno, CA | 4,868 | 295 | Lawrence, KS | 371 |
| 35 | Charlotte-Mecklenburg, NC-SC | 9,419 | 238 | Gadsden, AL | 607 | 191 | Lawton, OK | 950 |
| 280 | Charlottesville, VA | 430 | 143 | Gainesville, FL | 1,466 | 327 | Lebanon, PA | 243 |
| 89 | Chattanooga, TN-GA | 2,759 | 318 | Gainesville, GA | 293 | | | |

Note: All listings are for Metropolitan Statistical Areas (M.S.A.s) except for those ending with "M.D." Listings with "M.D." are Metropolitan Divisions which are smaller parts of eleven large M.S.A.s. See explanatory note at beginning of metropolitan area section.

| RANK | METROPOLITAN AREA | CRIMES | RANK | METROPOLITAN AREA | CRIMES | RANK | METROPOLITAN AREA | CRIMES |
|---|---|---|---|---|---|---|---|---|
| 355 | Lewiston-Auburn, ME | 155 | 76 | Omaha-Council Bluffs, NE-IA | 3,462 | 352 | Sheboygan, WI | 163 |
| 368 | Lewiston, ID-WA | 113 | 25 | Orlando, FL | 12,212 | 306 | Sherman-Denison, TX | 327 |
| 154 | Lexington-Fayette, KY | 1,256 | 321 | Oshkosh-Neenah, WI | 270 | 101 | Shreveport-Bossier City, LA | 2,394 |
| 289 | Lima, OH | 402 | 353 | Owensboro, KY | 161 | 104 | Silver Spring-Frederick, MD M.D. | 2,383 |
| 176 | Lincoln, NE | 1,031 | 135 | Oxnard-Thousand Oaks, CA | 1,629 | 285 | Sioux City, IA-NE-SD | 419 |
| 62 | Little Rock, AR | 4,886 | 88 | Palm Bay-Melbourne, FL | 2,889 | 220 | Sioux Falls, SD | 705 |
| 372 | Logan, UT-ID | 72 | 187 | Panama City, FL | 977 | 185 | South Bend-Mishawaka, IN-MI | 985 |
| 195 | Longview, TX | 904 | 322 | Parkersburg-Vienna, WV | 269 | 141 | Spartanburg, SC | 1,481 |
| 301 | Longview, WA | 362 | 105 | Pensacola, FL | 2,379 | 123 | Spokane, WA | 1,963 |
| 4 | Los Angeles County, CA M.D. | 40,384 | 153 | Peoria, IL | 1,303 | 134 | Springfield, IL | 1,631 |
| 3 | Los Angeles (greater), CA | 46,426 | 7 | Philadelphia (greater) PA-NJ-MD-DE | 30,030 | 78 | Springfield, MA | 3,281 |
| NA | Louisville, KY-IN** | NA | 12 | Philadelphia, PA M.D. | 19,827 | 102 | Springfield, MO | 2,388 |
| 122 | Lubbock, TX | 1,979 | 18 | Phoenix-Mesa-Scottsdale, AZ | 17,212 | 267 | Springfield, OH | 478 |
| 263 | Lynchburg, VA | 491 | 44 | Pittsburgh, PA | 6,913 | 359 | State College, PA | 144 |
| 196 | Macon, GA | 900 | 293 | Pittsfield, MA | 383 | 343 | Staunton-Waynesboro, VA | 199 |
| 181 | Madera, CA | 1,017 | 328 | Pocatello, ID | 242 | 59 | Stockton-Lodi, CA | 4,980 |
| 150 | Madison, WI | 1,359 | 142 | Port St. Lucie, FL | 1,470 | 308 | St. Cloud, MN | 322 |
| 163 | Manchester-Nashua, NH | 1,137 | 54 | Portland-Vancouver, OR-WA | 5,810 | 339 | St. George, UT | 208 |
| 345 | Manhattan, KS | 192 | 210 | Portland, ME | 757 | 271 | St. Joseph, MO-KS | 462 |
| 348 | Mankato-North Mankato, MN | 179 | 253 | Prescott, AZ | 525 | 26 | St. Louis, MO-IL | 12,103 |
| 332 | Mansfield, OH | 233 | 56 | Providence-Warwick, RI-MA | 5,428 | 213 | Sumter, SC | 730 |
| 107 | McAllen-Edinburg-Mission, TX | 2,349 | 290 | Provo-Orem, UT | 394 | 129 | Syracuse, NY | 1,710 |
| 212 | Medford, OR | 732 | 174 | Pueblo, CO | 1,063 | 73 | Tacoma, WA M.D. | 3,675 |
| 24 | Memphis, TN-MS-AR | 13,389 | 291 | Punta Gorda, FL | 390 | 112 | Tallahassee, FL | 2,206 |
| 137 | Merced, CA | 1,555 | 303 | Racine, WI | 354 | 28 | Tampa-St Petersburg, FL | 11,388 |
| 6 | Miami (greater), FL | 31,507 | 93 | Raleigh, NC | 2,653 | 311 | Terre Haute, IN | 302 |
| 17 | Miami-Dade County, FL M.D. | 17,247 | 259 | Rapid City, SD | 517 | 201 | Texarkana, TX-AR | 839 |
| 278 | Midland, TX | 437 | 155 | Reading, PA | 1,229 | 347 | The Villages, FL | 183 |
| 36 | Milwaukee, WI | 9,226 | 162 | Redding, CA | 1,150 | 79 | Toledo, OH | 3,233 |
| 34 | Minneapolis-St. Paul, MN-WI | 9,466 | 132 | Reno, NV | 1,657 | 202 | Topeka, KS | 819 |
| 312 | Missoula, MT | 301 | 85 | Richmond, VA | 3,029 | 139 | Trenton, NJ | 1,518 |
| 99 | Mobile, AL | 2,426 | 21 | Riverside-San Bernardino, CA | 14,637 | 68 | Tucson, AZ | 4,334 |
| 90 | Modesto, CA | 2,716 | 211 | Roanoke, VA | 742 | 61 | Tulsa, OK | 4,962 |
| 179 | Monroe, LA | 1,026 | 312 | Rochester, MN | 301 | 197 | Tuscaloosa, AL | 892 |
| 288 | Monroe, MI | 414 | 82 | Rochester, NY | 3,075 | 239 | Tyler, TX | 605 |
| 91 | Montgomery County, PA M.D. | 2,713 | 98 | Rockford, IL | 2,452 | 224 | Utica-Rome, NY | 669 |
| 296 | Morgantown, WV | 368 | 218 | Rockingham County, NH M.D. | 713 | 121 | Vallejo-Fairfield, CA | 2,001 |
| 296 | Morristown, TN | 368 | 202 | Rocky Mount, NC | 819 | 266 | Victoria, TX | 485 |
| 323 | Mount Vernon-Anacortes, WA | 254 | 296 | Rome, GA | 368 | 200 | Vineland-Bridgeton, NJ | 854 |
| 307 | Muncie, IN | 323 | 37 | Sacramento, CA | 9,207 | 57 | Virginia Beach-Norfolk, VA-NC | 5,192 |
| 205 | Muskegon, MI | 800 | 140 | Saginaw, MI | 1,490 | 118 | Visalia-Porterville, CA | 2,151 |
| 124 | Myrtle Beach, SC-NC | 1,956 | 193 | Salem, OR | 932 | 198 | Waco, TX | 887 |
| 287 | Napa, CA | 417 | 127 | Salinas, CA | 1,794 | 215 | Warner Robins, GA | 720 |
| 208 | Naples-Marco Island, FL | 785 | 130 | Salisbury, MD-DE | 1,706 | 55 | Warren-Troy, MI M.D. | 5,756 |
| 31 | Nashville-Davidson, TN | 10,405 | 70 | Salt Lake City, UT | 4,071 | 13 | Washington (greater) DC-VA-MD-WV | 19,675 |
| 72 | Nassau-Suffolk, NY M.D. | 3,994 | 315 | San Angelo, TX | 299 | 16 | Washington, DC-VA-MD-WV M.D. | 17,292 |
| 303 | New Bern, NC | 354 | 30 | San Antonio, TX | 10,439 | 360 | Watertown-Fort Drum, NY | 143 |
| 80 | New Haven-Milford, CT | 3,112 | 29 | San Diego, CA | 11,177 | 365 | Wausau, WI | 126 |
| 53 | New Orleans, LA | 5,872 | 8 | San Francisco (greater), CA | 25,131 | 48 | West Palm Beach, FL M.D. | 6,182 |
| 1 | New York (greater), NY-NJ-PA | 77,802 | 38 | San Francisco-Redwood, CA M.D. | 8,940 | 259 | Wichita Falls, TX | 517 |
| 2 | New York-Jersey City, NY-NJ M.D. | 64,668 | 66 | San Jose, CA | 4,783 | 74 | Wichita, KS | 3,621 |
| 40 | Newark, NJ-PA M.D. | 8,498 | 173 | San Luis Obispo, CA | 1,069 | 341 | Williamsport, PA | 201 |
| 221 | Niles-Benton Harbor, MI | 700 | 263 | San Rafael, CA M.D. | 491 | 77 | Wilmington, DE-MD-NJ M.D. | 3,456 |
| 82 | North Port-Sarasota-Bradenton, FL | 3,075 | 183 | Santa Cruz-Watsonville, CA | 1,002 | 189 | Wilmington, NC | 966 |
| 247 | Norwich-New London, CT | 555 | 146 | Santa Maria-Santa Barbara, CA | 1,416 | 326 | Winchester, VA-WV | 245 |
| 20 | Oakland-Hayward, CA M.D. | 15,700 | 128 | Santa Rosa, CA | 1,782 | 100 | Winston-Salem, NC | 2,423 |
| 144 | Ocala, FL | 1,453 | 161 | Savannah, GA | 1,158 | 75 | Worcester, MA-CT | 3,602 |
| 325 | Ocean City, NJ | 251 | 151 | Scranton--Wilkes-Barre, PA | 1,308 | 216 | Yakima, WA | 719 |
| 160 | Odessa, TX | 1,189 | 27 | Seattle (greater), WA | 11,643 | 184 | York-Hanover, PA | 986 |
| 180 | Ogden-Clearfield, UT | 1,018 | 43 | Seattle-Bellevue-Everett, WA M.D. | 7,968 | 261 | Yuba City, CA | 516 |
| 47 | Oklahoma City, OK | 6,617 | 285 | Sebastian-Vero Beach, FL | 419 | 204 | Yuma, AZ | 816 |
| 258 | Olympia, WA | 518 | 292 | Sebring, FL | 388 | | | |

Source: Reported data from the F.B.I. "Crime in the United States 2013"

*Includes murder, rape, robbery, and aggravated assault. The FBI changed the definition of rape beginning with 2013 data. Not all cities have made the change so the metro area figures reported here include rape figures based on differing definitions of rape. See note on page vii.

**Not available.

# 5. Violent Crimes in 2013 (continued)
## National Total = 1,163,146 Violent Crimes*

| RANK | METROPOLITAN AREA | CRIMES | RANK | METROPOLITAN AREA | CRIMES | RANK | METROPOLITAN AREA | CRIMES |
|---|---|---|---|---|---|---|---|---|
| 1 | New York (greater), NY-NJ-PA | 77,802 | 65 | Greenville-Anderson, SC | 4,793 | 129 | Syracuse, NY | 1,710 |
| 2 | New York-Jersey City, NY-NJ M.D. | 64,668 | 66 | San Jose, CA | 4,783 | 130 | Salisbury, MD-DE | 1,706 |
| 3 | Los Angeles (greater), CA | 46,426 | 67 | Columbia, SC | 4,585 | 131 | Augusta, GA-SC | 1,672 |
| 4 | Los Angeles County, CA M.D. | 40,384 | 68 | Tucson, AZ | 4,334 | 132 | Reno, NV | 1,657 |
| 5 | Houston, TX | 35,112 | 69 | Baton Rouge, LA | 4,173 | 133 | Fayetteville-Springdale, AR-MO | 1,633 |
| 6 | Miami (greater), FL | 31,507 | 70 | Salt Lake City, UT | 4,071 | 134 | Springfield, IL | 1,631 |
| 7 | Philadelphia (greater) PA-NJ-MD-DE | 30,030 | 71 | Camden, NJ M.D. | 4,034 | 135 | Oxnard-Thousand Oaks, CA | 1,629 |
| 8 | San Francisco (greater), CA | 25,131 | 72 | Nassau-Suffolk, NY M.D. | 3,994 | 136 | Des Moines-West Des Moines, IA | 1,597 |
| 9 | Detroit (greater), MI | 24,475 | 73 | Tacoma, WA M.D. | 3,675 | 137 | Merced, CA | 1,555 |
| 10 | Dallas (greater), TX | 22,682 | 74 | Wichita, KS | 3,621 | 138 | Allentown, PA-NJ | 1,536 |
| 11 | Atlanta, GA | 21,444 | 75 | Worcester, MA-CT | 3,602 | 139 | Trenton, NJ | 1,518 |
| 12 | Philadelphia, PA M.D. | 19,827 | 76 | Omaha-Council Bluffs, NE-IA | 3,462 | 140 | Saginaw, MI | 1,490 |
| 13 | Washington (greater) DC-VA-MD-WV | 19,675 | 77 | Wilmington, DE-MD-NJ M.D. | 3,456 | 141 | Spartanburg, SC | 1,481 |
| 14 | Detroit-Dearborn-Livonia, MI M.D. | 18,719 | 78 | Springfield, MA | 3,281 | 142 | Port St. Lucie, FL | 1,470 |
| 15 | Baltimore, MD | 17,552 | 79 | Toledo, OH | 3,233 | 143 | Gainesville, FL | 1,466 |
| 16 | Washington, DC-VA-MD-WV M.D. | 17,292 | 80 | New Haven-Milford, CT | 3,112 | 144 | Boise City, ID | 1,453 |
| 17 | Miami-Dade County, FL M.D. | 17,247 | 81 | Knoxville, TN | 3,103 | 144 | Ocala, FL | 1,453 |
| 18 | Phoenix-Mesa-Scottsdale, AZ | 17,212 | 82 | North Port-Sarasota-Bradenton, FL | 3,075 | 146 | Santa Maria-Santa Barbara, CA | 1,416 |
| 19 | Boston (greater), MA-NH | 16,586 | 82 | Rochester, NY | 3,075 | 147 | Davenport, IA-IL | 1,387 |
| 20 | Oakland-Hayward, CA M.D. | 15,700 | 84 | Grand Rapids-Wyoming, MI | 3,057 | 148 | Amarillo, TX | 1,365 |
| 21 | Riverside-San Bernardino, CA | 14,637 | 85 | Richmond, VA | 3,029 | 149 | Lake Co.-Kenosha Co., IL-WI M.D. | 1,361 |
| 22 | Dallas-Plano-Irving, TX M.D. | 14,328 | 86 | Flint, MI | 3,004 | 150 | Madison, WI | 1,359 |
| 23 | Las Vegas-Henderson, NV | 13,735 | 87 | El Paso, TX | 2,925 | 151 | Scranton--Wilkes-Barre, PA | 1,308 |
| 24 | Memphis, TN-MS-AR | 13,389 | 88 | Palm Bay-Melbourne, FL | 2,889 | 152 | Columbus, GA-AL | 1,304 |
| 25 | Orlando, FL | 12,212 | 89 | Chattanooga, TN-GA | 2,759 | 153 | Peoria, IL | 1,303 |
| 26 | St. Louis, MO-IL | 12,103 | 90 | Modesto, CA | 2,716 | 154 | Lexington-Fayette, KY | 1,256 |
| 27 | Seattle (greater), WA | 11,643 | 91 | Montgomery County, PA M.D. | 2,713 | 155 | Reading, PA | 1,229 |
| 28 | Tampa-St Petersburg, FL | 11,388 | 92 | Hartford, CT | 2,706 | 156 | Alexandria, LA | 1,228 |
| 29 | San Diego, CA | 11,177 | 93 | Raleigh, NC | 2,653 | 157 | Atlantic City, NJ | 1,225 |
| 30 | San Antonio, TX | 10,439 | 94 | Greensboro-High Point, NC | 2,557 | 157 | Lake Charles, LA | 1,225 |
| 31 | Nashville-Davidson, TN | 10,405 | 95 | Charleston-North Charleston, SC | 2,555 | 159 | Jackson, TN | 1,209 |
| 32 | Boston, MA M.D. | 9,770 | 96 | Colorado Springs, CO | 2,504 | 160 | Odessa, TX | 1,189 |
| 33 | Kansas City, MO-KS | 9,601 | 97 | Anchorage, AK | 2,497 | 161 | Savannah, GA | 1,158 |
| 34 | Minneapolis-St. Paul, MN-WI | 9,466 | 98 | Rockford, IL | 2,452 | 162 | Redding, CA | 1,150 |
| 35 | Charlotte-Mecklenburg, NC-SC | 9,419 | 99 | Mobile, AL | 2,426 | 163 | Manchester-Nashua, NH | 1,137 |
| 36 | Milwaukee, WI | 9,226 | 100 | Winston-Salem, NC | 2,423 | 164 | Laredo, TX | 1,133 |
| 37 | Sacramento, CA | 9,207 | 101 | Shreveport-Bossier City, LA | 2,394 | 165 | Fort Wayne, IN | 1,129 |
| 38 | San Francisco-Redwood, CA M.D. | 8,940 | 102 | Springfield, MO | 2,388 | 166 | Fort Smith, AR-OK | 1,122 |
| 39 | Denver-Aurora, CO | 8,848 | 103 | Gary, IN M.D. | 2,385 | 167 | Champaign-Urbana, IL | 1,118 |
| 40 | Newark, NJ-PA M.D. | 8,498 | 104 | Silver Spring-Frederick, MD M.D. | 2,383 | 168 | Elgin, IL M.D. | 1,108 |
| 41 | Fort Worth-Arlington, TX M.D. | 8,354 | 105 | Pensacola, FL | 2,379 | 169 | Hammond, LA | 1,087 |
| 42 | Fort Lauderdale, FL M.D. | 8,078 | 106 | Deltona-Daytona Beach, FL | 2,353 | 170 | Gulfport-Biloxi-Pascagoula, MS | 1,085 |
| 43 | Seattle-Bellevue-Everett, WA M.D. | 7,968 | 107 | McAllen-Edinburg-Mission, TX | 2,349 | 171 | Canton, OH | 1,080 |
| 44 | Pittsburgh, PA | 6,913 | 108 | Albany-Schenectady-Troy, NY | 2,338 | 172 | Ann Arbor, MI | 1,079 |
| 45 | Jacksonville, FL | 6,904 | 109 | Corpus Christi, TX | 2,314 | 173 | San Luis Obispo, CA | 1,069 |
| 46 | Albuquerque, NM | 6,700 | 110 | Lakeland, FL | 2,287 | 174 | Pueblo, CO | 1,063 |
| 47 | Oklahoma City, OK | 6,617 | 111 | Bridgeport-Stamford, CT | 2,252 | 175 | Crestview-Fort Walton Beach, FL | 1,044 |
| 48 | West Palm Beach, FL M.D. | 6,182 | 112 | Tallahassee, FL | 2,206 | 176 | Albany, GA | 1,031 |
| 49 | Cambridge-Newton, MA M.D. | 6,103 | 113 | Lafayette, LA | 2,201 | 176 | Lincoln, NE | 1,031 |
| 50 | Cincinnati, OH-KY-IN | 6,094 | 114 | Jackson, MS | 2,191 | 178 | Clarksville, TN-KY | 1,030 |
| 51 | Anaheim-Santa Ana-Irvine, CA M.D. | 6,042 | 115 | Cape Coral-Fort Myers, FL | 2,184 | 179 | Monroe, LA | 1,026 |
| 52 | Birmingham-Hoover, AL | 6,034 | 116 | Dayton, OH | 2,182 | 180 | Ogden-Clearfield, UT | 1,018 |
| 53 | New Orleans, LA | 5,872 | 117 | Beaumont-Port Arthur, TX | 2,177 | 181 | Madera, CA | 1,017 |
| 54 | Portland-Vancouver, OR-WA | 5,810 | 118 | Visalia-Porterville, CA | 2,151 | 182 | Brownsville-Harlingen, TX | 1,009 |
| 55 | Warren-Troy, MI M.D. | 5,756 | 119 | Huntsville, AL | 2,101 | 183 | Santa Cruz-Watsonville, CA | 1,002 |
| 56 | Providence-Warwick, RI-MA | 5,428 | 120 | Akron, OH | 2,091 | 184 | York-Hanover, PA | 986 |
| 57 | Virginia Beach-Norfolk, VA-NC | 5,192 | 121 | Vallejo-Fairfield, CA | 2,001 | 185 | South Bend-Mishawaka, IN-MI | 985 |
| 58 | Austin-Round Rock, TX | 5,099 | 122 | Lubbock, TX | 1,979 | 186 | Florence, SC | 984 |
| 59 | Stockton-Lodi, CA | 4,980 | 123 | Spokane, WA | 1,963 | 187 | Panama City, FL | 977 |
| 60 | Bakersfield, CA | 4,969 | 124 | Myrtle Beach, SC-NC | 1,956 | 188 | Kingsport, TN-VA | 976 |
| 61 | Tulsa, OK | 4,962 | 125 | Lansing-East Lansing, MI | 1,893 | 189 | Wilmington, NC | 966 |
| 62 | Little Rock, AR | 4,886 | 126 | Fayetteville, NC | 1,853 | 190 | Hilton Head Island, SC | 955 |
| 63 | Buffalo-Niagara Falls, NY | 4,883 | 127 | Salinas, CA | 1,794 | 191 | Lawton, OK | 950 |
| 64 | Fresno, CA | 4,868 | 128 | Santa Rosa, CA | 1,782 | 192 | Barnstable Town, MA | 941 |

Note: All listings are for Metropolitan Statistical Areas (M.S.A.s) except for those ending with "M.D." Listings with "M.D." are Metropolitan Divisions which are smaller parts of eleven large M.S.A.s. See explanatory note at beginning of metropolitan area section.

| RANK | METROPOLITAN AREA | CRIMES | RANK | METROPOLITAN AREA | CRIMES | RANK | METROPOLITAN AREA | CRIMES |
|---|---|---|---|---|---|---|---|---|
| 193 | Salem, OR | 932 | 255 | Joplin, MO | 521 | 317 | Kingston, NY | 294 |
| 194 | Lancaster, PA | 905 | 256 | Florence-Muscle Shoals, AL | 520 | 318 | Gainesville, GA | 293 |
| 195 | Longview, TX | 904 | 257 | Cleveland, TN | 519 | 319 | Appleton, WI | 285 |
| 196 | Macon, GA | 900 | 258 | Olympia, WA | 518 | 320 | Altoona, PA | 271 |
| 197 | Tuscaloosa, AL | 892 | 259 | Rapid City, SD | 517 | 321 | Oshkosh-Neenah, WI | 270 |
| 198 | Waco, TX | 887 | 259 | Wichita Falls, TX | 517 | 322 | Parkersburg-Vienna, WV | 269 |
| 199 | College Station-Bryan, TX | 881 | 261 | Yuba City, CA | 516 | 323 | Mount Vernon-Anacortes, WA | 254 |
| 200 | Vineland-Bridgeton, NJ | 854 | 262 | Bismarck, ND | 494 | 324 | Johnstown, PA | 253 |
| 201 | Texarkana, TX-AR | 839 | 263 | Lynchburg, VA | 491 | 325 | Ocean City, NJ | 251 |
| 202 | Rocky Mount, NC | 819 | 263 | San Rafael, CA M.D. | 491 | 326 | Winchester, VA-WV | 245 |
| 202 | Topeka, KS | 819 | 265 | Goldsboro, NC | 489 | 327 | Lebanon, PA | 243 |
| 204 | Yuma, AZ | 816 | 266 | Victoria, TX | 485 | 328 | California-Lexington Park, MD | 242 |
| 205 | Muskegon, MI | 800 | 267 | Cape Girardeau, MO-IL | 478 | 328 | Pocatello, ID | 242 |
| 206 | Greenville, NC | 799 | 267 | Springfield, OH | 478 | 330 | Fairbanks, AK | 237 |
| 207 | Greeley, CO | 795 | 269 | Iowa City, IA | 473 | 331 | Bowling Green, KY | 236 |
| 208 | Naples-Marco Island, FL | 785 | 270 | Grand Junction, CO | 465 | 332 | Mansfield, OH | 233 |
| 209 | Dover, DE | 774 | 271 | St. Joseph, MO-KS | 462 | 333 | Chambersburg-Waynesboro, PA | 230 |
| 210 | Portland, ME | 757 | 272 | Coeur d'Alene, ID | 459 | 333 | Hinesville, GA | 230 |
| 211 | Roanoke, VA | 742 | 272 | Hot Springs, AR | 459 | 335 | Idaho Falls, ID | 218 |
| 212 | Medford, OR | 732 | 274 | Jonesboro, AR | 454 | 335 | Kokomo, IN | 218 |
| 213 | Sumter, SC | 730 | 275 | Flagstaff, AZ | 451 | 337 | Bloomsburg-Berwick, PA | 214 |
| 214 | Hanford-Corcoran, CA | 725 | 276 | Kahului-Wailuku-Lahaina, HI | 450 | 338 | Grand Forks, ND-MN | 210 |
| 215 | Warner Robins, GA | 720 | 277 | Billings, MT | 439 | 339 | St. George, UT | 208 |
| 216 | Yakima, WA | 719 | 278 | Lake Havasu City-Kingman, AZ | 437 | 340 | Eau Claire, WI | 205 |
| 217 | Las Cruces, NM | 716 | 278 | Midland, TX | 437 | 341 | Williamsport, PA | 201 |
| 218 | Rockingham County, NH M.D. | 713 | 280 | Charlottesville, VA | 430 | 342 | Fond du Lac, WI | 200 |
| 219 | Bremerton-Silverdale, WA | 707 | 281 | Daphne-Fairhope-Foley, AL | 427 | 343 | Staunton-Waynesboro, VA | 199 |
| 220 | Sioux Falls, SD | 705 | 282 | Bloomington, IN | 426 | 344 | Cheyenne, WY | 198 |
| 221 | Niles-Benton Harbor, MI | 700 | 282 | Jefferson City, MO | 426 | 345 | Manhattan, KS | 192 |
| 222 | Eugene, OR | 691 | 284 | Decatur, IL | 422 | 346 | Great Falls, MT | 184 |
| 223 | Erie, PA | 687 | 285 | Sebastian-Vero Beach, FL | 419 | 347 | The Villages, FL | 183 |
| 224 | Utica-Rome, NY | 669 | 285 | Sioux City, IA-NE-SD | 419 | 348 | Mankato-North Mankato, MN | 179 |
| 225 | Johnson City, TN | 660 | 287 | Napa, CA | 417 | 349 | Casper, WY | 169 |
| 226 | Boulder, CO | 658 | 288 | Monroe, MI | 414 | 350 | La Crosse, WI-MN | 167 |
| 227 | Duluth, MN-WI | 654 | 289 | Lima, OH | 402 | 351 | Harrisonburg, VA | 166 |
| 228 | Jackson, MI | 651 | 290 | Provo-Orem, UT | 394 | 352 | Sheboygan, WI | 163 |
| 229 | Fort Collins, CO | 646 | 291 | Punta Gorda, FL | 390 | 353 | Owensboro, KY | 161 |
| 230 | Green Bay, WI | 644 | 292 | Sebring, FL | 388 | 354 | Grand Island, NE | 156 |
| 231 | Dutchess-Putnam, NY M.D. | 642 | 293 | Pittsfield, MA | 383 | 355 | Lewiston-Auburn, ME | 155 |
| 232 | Chico, CA | 634 | 294 | Carbondale-Marion, IL | 377 | 356 | Dubuque, IA | 153 |
| 233 | Houma, LA | 626 | 295 | Lawrence, KS | 371 | 357 | Elmira, NY | 151 |
| 234 | Farmington, NM | 625 | 296 | Janesville, WI | 368 | 358 | Columbus, IN | 148 |
| 235 | Anniston-Oxford, AL | 622 | 296 | Morgantown, WV | 368 | 359 | State College, PA | 144 |
| 236 | East Stroudsburg, PA | 618 | 296 | Morristown, TN | 368 | 360 | Watertown-Fort Drum, NY | 143 |
| 237 | Bloomington, IL | 610 | 296 | Rome, GA | 368 | 361 | Ames, IA | 140 |
| 238 | Gadsden, AL | 607 | 300 | Bend, OR | 364 | 361 | Bangor, ME | 140 |
| 239 | Tyler, TX | 605 | 301 | Kankakee, IL | 362 | 363 | Grants Pass, OR | 136 |
| 240 | Kennewick-Richland, WA | 603 | 301 | Longview, WA | 362 | 364 | Carson City, NV | 133 |
| 241 | Hagerstown-Martinsburg, MD-WV | 600 | 303 | New Bern, NC | 354 | 365 | Glens Falls, NY | 126 |
| 242 | Burlington, NC | 593 | 303 | Racine, WI | 354 | 365 | Wausau, WI | 126 |
| 243 | Dothan, AL | 587 | 305 | Dalton, GA | 344 | 367 | Elizabethtown-Fort Knox, KY | 118 |
| 244 | Columbia, MO | 568 | 306 | Sherman-Denison, TX | 327 | 368 | Lewiston, ID-WA | 113 |
| 244 | Fargo, ND-MN | 568 | 307 | Muncie, IN | 323 | 369 | Corvallis, OR | 104 |
| 246 | Abilene, TX | 560 | 308 | St. Cloud, MN | 322 | 370 | Gettysburg, PA | 100 |
| 247 | Norwich-New London, CT | 555 | 309 | Bay City, MI | 316 | 371 | Albany, OR | 97 |
| 248 | El Centro, CA | 542 | 310 | Blacksburg, VA | 314 | 372 | Logan, UT-ID | 72 |
| 248 | Homosassa Springs, FL | 542 | 311 | Terre Haute, IN | 302 | NA | Brunswick, GA** | NA |
| 250 | Cedar Rapids, IA | 539 | 312 | Decatur, AL | 301 | NA | Chicago (greater), IL-IN-WI** | NA |
| 251 | Athens-Clarke County, GA | 537 | 312 | Missoula, MT | 301 | NA | Chicago-Naperville, IL M.D.** | NA |
| 252 | Binghamton, NY | 536 | 312 | Rochester, MN | 301 | NA | Indianapolis, IN** | NA |
| 253 | Prescott, AZ | 525 | 315 | San Angelo, TX | 299 | NA | Louisville, KY-IN** | NA |
| 254 | Lafayette, IN | 522 | 316 | Cumberland, MD-WV | 296 | | | |

Source: Reported data from the F.B.I. "Crime in the United States 2013"

*Includes murder, rape, robbery, and aggravated assault. The FBI changed the definition of rape beginning with 2013 data. Not all cities have made the change so the metro area figures reported here include rape figures based on differing definitions of rape. See note on page vii.

**Not available.

# 6. Violent Crime Rate in 2013
## National Rate = 367.9 Violent Crimes per 100,000 Population*

| RANK | METROPOLITAN AREA | RATE | RANK | METROPOLITAN AREA | RATE | RANK | METROPOLITAN AREA | RATE |
|---|---|---|---|---|---|---|---|---|
| 182 | Abilene, TX | 333.1 | 303 | Cheyenne, WY | 207.0 | 178 | Gary, IN M.D. | 336.8 |
| 214 | Akron, OH | 297.2 | NA | Chicago (greater), IL-IN-WI** | NA | 364 | Gettysburg, PA | 98.6 |
| 252 | Albany-Schenectady-Troy, NY | 266.6 | NA | Chicago-Naperville, IL M.D.** | NA | 365 | Glens Falls, NY | 98.1 |
| 23 | Albany, GA | 655.2 | 231 | Chico, CA | 285.1 | 127 | Goldsboro, NC | 390.9 |
| 369 | Albany, OR | 81.4 | 230 | Cincinnati, OH-KY-IN | 285.2 | 302 | Grand Forks, ND-MN | 209.0 |
| 11 | Albuquerque, NM | 742.3 | 147 | Clarksville, TN-KY | 369.3 | 320 | Grand Island, NE | 185.4 |
| 7 | Alexandria, LA | 793.9 | 100 | Cleveland, TN | 437.8 | 203 | Grand Junction, CO | 311.6 |
| 320 | Allentown, PA-NJ | 185.4 | 199 | Coeur d'Alene, ID | 318.3 | 209 | Grand Rapids-Wyoming, MI | 302.0 |
| 298 | Altoona, PA | 213.3 | 146 | College Station-Bryan, TX | 371.5 | 339 | Grants Pass, OR | 163.5 |
| 57 | Amarillo, TX | 524.4 | 149 | Colorado Springs, CO | 368.9 | 289 | Great Falls, MT | 223.9 |
| 347 | Ames, IA | 152.3 | 186 | Columbia, MO | 332.7 | 216 | Greeley, CO | 295.9 |
| 312 | Anaheim-Santa Ana-Irvine, CA M.D. | 193.7 | 35 | Columbia, SC | 578.0 | 304 | Green Bay, WI | 205.9 |
| 8 | Anchorage, AK | 793.8 | 113 | Columbus, GA-AL | 413.0 | 172 | Greensboro-High Point, NC | 344.6 |
| 206 | Ann Arbor, MI | 305.5 | 322 | Columbus, IN | 184.8 | 41 | Greenville-Anderson, SC | 562.3 |
| 53 | Anniston-Oxford, AL | 532.1 | 58 | Corpus Christi, TX | 523.5 | 91 | Greenville, NC | 458.3 |
| 360 | Appleton, WI | 124.2 | 362 | Corvallis, OR | 119.6 | 232 | Gulfport-Biloxi-Pascagoula, MS | 283.7 |
| 245 | Athens-Clarke County, GA | 272.0 | 112 | Crestview-Fort Walton Beach, FL | 413.2 | 282 | Hagerstown-Martinsburg, MD-WV | 232.8 |
| 130 | Atlanta, GA | 389.1 | 223 | Cumberland, MD-WV | 291.2 | 5 | Hammond, LA | 875.1 |
| 97 | Atlantic City, NJ | 443.7 | 183 | Dallas (greater), TX | 332.9 | 79 | Hanford-Corcoran, CA | 479.3 |
| 226 | Augusta, GA-SC | 288.3 | 200 | Dallas-Plano-Irving, TX M.D. | 318.0 | 358 | Harrisonburg, VA | 128.0 |
| 248 | Austin-Round Rock, TX | 271.3 | 275 | Dalton, GA | 240.7 | 256 | Hartford, CT | 264.3 |
| 36 | Bakersfield, CA | 576.3 | 291 | Daphne-Fairhope-Foley, AL | 220.9 | 76 | Hilton Head Island, SC | 485.3 |
| 26 | Baltimore, MD | 633.4 | 158 | Davenport, IA-IL | 361.4 | 239 | Hinesville, GA | 277.2 |
| 368 | Bangor, ME | 91.2 | 247 | Dayton, OH | 271.7 | 129 | Homosassa Springs, FL | 389.3 |
| 101 | Barnstable Town, MA | 436.0 | 309 | Decatur, AL | 195.1 | 83 | Hot Springs, AR | 472.4 |
| 66 | Baton Rouge, LA | 509.1 | 136 | Decatur, IL | 384.1 | 210 | Houma, LA | 299.1 |
| 216 | Bay City, MI | 295.9 | 125 | Deltona-Daytona Beach, FL | 392.7 | 42 | Houston, TX | 559.0 |
| 50 | Beaumont-Port Arthur, TX | 536.1 | 190 | Denver-Aurora, CO | 328.5 | 77 | Huntsville, AL | 483.5 |
| 290 | Bend, OR | 221.7 | 250 | Des Moines-West Des Moines, IA | 267.8 | 344 | Idaho Falls, ID | 158.5 |
| 254 | Billings, MT | 266.3 | 38 | Detroit (greater), MI | 569.6 | NA | Indianapolis, IN** | NA |
| 296 | Binghamton, NY | 216.2 | 1 | Detroit-Dearborn-Livonia, MI M.D. | 1,047.8 | 219 | Iowa City, IA | 294.8 |
| 55 | Birmingham-Hoover, AL | 529.8 | 123 | Dothan, AL | 396.2 | 70 | Jacksonville, FL | 495.7 |
| 121 | Bismarck, ND | 397.6 | 92 | Dover, DE | 456.0 | 115 | Jackson, MI | 405.6 |
| 329 | Blacksburg, VA | 174.9 | 342 | Dubuque, IA | 159.8 | 143 | Jackson, MS | 377.8 |
| 195 | Bloomington, IL | 322.1 | 280 | Duluth, MN-WI | 233.4 | 4 | Jackson, TN | 925.0 |
| 260 | Bloomington, IN | 260.4 | 341 | Dutchess-Putnam, NY M.D. | 161.6 | 285 | Janesville, WI | 229.2 |
| 265 | Bloomsburg-Berwick, PA | 251.6 | 150 | East Stroudsburg, PA | 367.2 | 234 | Jefferson City, MO | 283.0 |
| 288 | Boise City, ID | 224.3 | 359 | Eau Claire, WI | 124.6 | 191 | Johnson City, TN | 327.6 |
| 163 | Boston (greater), MA-NH | 354.5 | 207 | El Centro, CA | 304.6 | 326 | Johnstown, PA | 179.6 |
| 67 | Boston, MA M.D. | 503.0 | 171 | El Paso, TX | 347.3 | 155 | Jonesboro, AR | 363.1 |
| 300 | Boulder, CO | 212.0 | 328 | Elgin, IL M.D. | 176.2 | 210 | Joplin, MO | 299.1 |
| 350 | Bowling Green, KY | 144.4 | 370 | Elizabethtown-Fort Knox, KY | 78.3 | 235 | Kahului-Wailuku-Lahaina, HI | 281.9 |
| 240 | Bremerton-Silverdale, WA | 275.2 | 334 | Elmira, NY | 169.6 | 196 | Kankakee, IL | 320.8 |
| 272 | Bridgeport-Stamford, CT | 244.5 | 270 | Erie, PA | 245.0 | 87 | Kansas City, MO-KS | 468.5 |
| 276 | Brownsville-Harlingen, TX | 240.3 | 310 | Eugene, OR | 193.9 | 292 | Kennewick-Richland, WA | 220.5 |
| NA | Brunswick, GA** | NA | 16 | Fairbanks, AK | 682.2 | 202 | Kingsport, TN-VA | 315.6 |
| 106 | Buffalo-Niagara Falls, NY | 430.2 | 264 | Fargo, ND-MN | 255.7 | 340 | Kingston, NY | 161.7 |
| 139 | Burlington, NC | 382.1 | 74 | Farmington, NM | 490.0 | 154 | Knoxville, TN | 364.1 |
| 293 | California-Lexington Park, MD | 219.4 | 180 | Fayetteville-Springdale, AR-MO | 334.6 | 258 | Kokomo, IN | 262.3 |
| 257 | Cambridge-Newton, MA M.D. | 263.8 | 73 | Fayetteville, NC | 490.1 | 361 | La Crosse, WI-MN | 122.9 |
| 196 | Camden, NJ M.D. | 320.8 | 188 | Flagstaff, AZ | 329.2 | 267 | Lafayette, IN | 250.4 |
| 251 | Canton, OH | 267.3 | 12 | Flint, MI | 721.1 | 89 | Lafayette, LA | 461.3 |
| 185 | Cape Coral-Fort Myers, FL | 332.8 | 165 | Florence-Muscle Shoals, AL | 354.0 | 27 | Lake Charles, LA | 607.2 |
| 72 | Cape Girardeau, MO-IL | 490.2 | 81 | Florence, SC | 475.0 | 345 | Lake Co.-Kenosha Co., IL-WI M.D. | 156.5 |
| 213 | Carbondale-Marion, IL | 297.6 | 308 | Fond du Lac, WI | 196.2 | 299 | Lake Havasu City-Kingman, AZ | 213.1 |
| 274 | Carson City, NV | 242.1 | 305 | Fort Collins, CO | 204.5 | 150 | Lakeland, FL | 367.2 |
| 301 | Casper, WY | 211.3 | 99 | Fort Lauderdale, FL M.D. | 438.2 | 332 | Lancaster, PA | 171.2 |
| 305 | Cedar Rapids, IA | 204.5 | 120 | Fort Smith, AR-OK | 399.4 | 115 | Lansing-East Lansing, MI | 405.6 |
| 348 | Chambersburg-Waynesboro, PA | 151.7 | 255 | Fort Wayne, IN | 266.2 | 104 | Laredo, TX | 430.9 |
| 80 | Champaign-Urbana, IL | 477.3 | 156 | Fort Worth-Arlington, TX M.D. | 362.0 | 183 | Las Cruces, NM | 332.9 |
| 161 | Charleston-North Charleston, SC | 359.4 | 63 | Fresno, CA | 510.1 | 17 | Las Vegas-Henderson, NV | 678.0 |
| 117 | Charlotte-Mecklenburg, NC-SC | 404.4 | 34 | Gadsden, AL | 581.7 | 192 | Lawrence, KS | 327.2 |
| 314 | Charlottesville, VA | 191.4 | 45 | Gainesville, FL | 541.9 | 13 | Lawton, OK | 711.9 |
| 65 | Chattanooga, TN-GA | 509.8 | 346 | Gainesville, GA | 156.4 | 327 | Lebanon, PA | 179.1 |

Note: All listings are for Metropolitan Statistical Areas (M.S.A.s) except for those ending with "M.D." Listings with "M.D." are Metropolitan Divisions which are smaller parts of eleven large M.S.A.s. See explanatory note at beginning of metropolitan area section.

| RANK | METROPOLITAN AREA | RATE | RANK | METROPOLITAN AREA | RATE | RANK | METROPOLITAN AREA | RATE |
|---|---|---|---|---|---|---|---|---|
| 351 | Lewiston-Auburn, ME | 144.2 | 131 | Omaha-Council Bluffs, NE-IA | 387.4 | 353 | Sheboygan, WI | 141.8 |
| 323 | Lewiston, ID-WA | 182.8 | 46 | Orlando, FL | 540.1 | 253 | Sherman-Denison, TX | 266.4 |
| 263 | Lexington-Fayette, KY | 256.7 | 343 | Oshkosh-Neenah, WI | 159.3 | 52 | Shreveport-Bossier City, LA | 532.5 |
| 137 | Lima, OH | 382.8 | 357 | Owensboro, KY | 138.2 | 318 | Silver Spring-Frederick, MD M.D. | 189.4 |
| 189 | Lincoln, NE | 328.8 | 311 | Oxnard-Thousand Oaks, CA | 193.8 | 269 | Sioux City, IA-NE-SD | 247.3 |
| 18 | Little Rock, AR | 675.7 | 56 | Palm Bay-Melbourne, FL | 524.8 | 222 | Sioux Falls, SD | 291.8 |
| 372 | Logan, UT-ID | 55.4 | 62 | Panama City, FL | 516.5 | 204 | South Bend-Mishawaka, IN-MI | 308.6 |
| 111 | Longview, TX | 414.2 | 224 | Parkersburg-Vienna, WV | 291.1 | 88 | Spartanburg, SC | 463.4 |
| 164 | Longview, WA | 354.3 | 64 | Pensacola, FL | 510.0 | 153 | Spokane, WA | 366.8 |
| 119 | Los Angeles County, CA M.D. | 402.9 | 174 | Peoria, IL | 342.2 | 9 | Springfield, IL | 767.9 |
| 166 | Los Angeles (greater), CA | 353.3 | 69 | Philadelphia (greater) PA-NJ-MD-DE | 497.5 | 59 | Springfield, MA | 522.2 |
| NA | Louisville, KY-IN** | NA | 3 | Philadelphia, PA M.D. | 937.7 | 51 | Springfield, MO | 533.0 |
| 21 | Lubbock, TX | 658.0 | 126 | Phoenix-Mesa-Scottsdale, AZ | 392.3 | 170 | Springfield, OH | 348.5 |
| 315 | Lynchburg, VA | 191.2 | 221 | Pittsburgh, PA | 292.8 | 367 | State College, PA | 92.7 |
| 132 | Macon, GA | 386.4 | 220 | Pittsfield, MA | 294.7 | 337 | Staunton-Waynesboro, VA | 167.1 |
| 20 | Madera, CA | 665.7 | 229 | Pocatello, ID | 286.5 | 15 | Stockton-Lodi, CA | 702.7 |
| 295 | Madison, WI | 217.1 | 179 | Port St. Lucie, FL | 336.5 | 336 | St. Cloud, MN | 168.1 |
| 236 | Manchester-Nashua, NH | 281.4 | 266 | Portland-Vancouver, OR-WA | 250.9 | 354 | St. George, UT | 140.6 |
| 313 | Manhattan, KS | 193.3 | 349 | Portland, ME | 145.9 | 160 | St. Joseph, MO-KS | 359.7 |
| 325 | Mankato-North Mankato, MN | 181.3 | 270 | Prescott, AZ | 245.0 | 103 | St. Louis, MO-IL | 431.7 |
| 317 | Mansfield, OH | 190.3 | 177 | Providence-Warwick, RI-MA | 338.2 | 19 | Sumter, SC | 671.6 |
| 227 | McAllen-Edinburg-Mission, TX | 286.7 | 371 | Provo-Orem, UT | 70.2 | 261 | Syracuse, NY | 258.7 |
| 167 | Medford, OR | 352.0 | 24 | Pueblo, CO | 655.0 | 96 | Tacoma, WA M.D. | 448.3 |
| 2 | Memphis, TN-MS-AR | 993.4 | 278 | Punta Gorda, FL | 237.9 | 33 | Tallahassee, FL | 582.3 |
| 30 | Merced, CA | 587.9 | 324 | Racine, WI | 181.8 | 122 | Tampa-St Petersburg, FL | 396.5 |
| 49 | Miami (greater), FL | 538.9 | 294 | Raleigh, NC | 219.3 | 331 | Terre Haute, IN | 174.6 |
| 22 | Miami-Dade County, FL M.D. | 655.6 | 152 | Rapid City, SD | 366.9 | 44 | Texarkana, TX-AR | 558.5 |
| 237 | Midland, TX | 280.5 | 215 | Reading, PA | 297.0 | 329 | The Villages, FL | 174.9 |
| 31 | Milwaukee, WI | 587.1 | 25 | Redding, CA | 641.6 | 54 | Toledo, OH | 530.3 |
| 244 | Minneapolis-St. Paul, MN-WI | 273.9 | 142 | Reno, NV | 378.0 | 168 | Topeka, KS | 349.2 |
| 249 | Missoula, MT | 268.6 | 273 | Richmond, VA | 243.8 | 114 | Trenton, NJ | 411.1 |
| 32 | Mobile, AL | 585.9 | 181 | Riverside-San Bernardino, CA | 333.3 | 102 | Tucson, AZ | 433.5 |
| 60 | Modesto, CA | 517.7 | 277 | Roanoke, VA | 238.3 | 61 | Tulsa, OK | 516.8 |
| 37 | Monroe, LA | 575.5 | 352 | Rochester, MN | 142.6 | 140 | Tuscaloosa, AL | 380.6 |
| 243 | Monroe, MI | 274.4 | 233 | Rochester, NY | 283.6 | 238 | Tyler, TX | 278.5 |
| 356 | Montgomery County, PA M.D. | 139.4 | 14 | Rockford, IL | 711.1 | 287 | Utica-Rome, NY | 224.5 |
| 246 | Morgantown, WV | 271.9 | 335 | Rockingham County, NH M.D. | 168.3 | 83 | Vallejo-Fairfield, CA | 472.4 |
| 198 | Morristown, TN | 319.1 | 48 | Rocky Mount, NC | 539.3 | 71 | Victoria, TX | 495.4 |
| 297 | Mount Vernon-Anacortes, WA | 213.4 | 137 | Rome, GA | 382.8 | 47 | Vineland-Bridgeton, NJ | 539.5 |
| 241 | Muncie, IN | 274.7 | 110 | Sacramento, CA | 415.9 | 208 | Virginia Beach-Norfolk, VA-NC | 303.5 |
| 86 | Muskegon, MI | 471.2 | 10 | Saginaw, MI | 752.4 | 85 | Visalia-Porterville, CA | 472.2 |
| 75 | Myrtle Beach, SC-NC | 487.0 | 279 | Salem, OR | 233.6 | 173 | Waco, TX | 343.5 |
| 212 | Napa, CA | 297.9 | 109 | Salinas, CA | 416.4 | 135 | Warner Robins, GA | 384.5 |
| 281 | Naples-Marco Island, FL | 232.9 | 98 | Salisbury, MD-DE | 442.8 | 284 | Warren-Troy, MI M.D. | 229.3 |
| 28 | Nashville-Davidson, TN | 596.1 | 162 | Salt Lake City, UT | 356.6 | 187 | Washington (greater) DC-VA-MD-WV | 331.1 |
| 355 | Nassau-Suffolk, NY M.D. | 139.8 | 262 | San Angelo, TX | 257.3 | 148 | Washington, DC-VA-MD-WV M.D. | 369.1 |
| 241 | New Bern, NC | 274.7 | 90 | San Antonio, TX | 459.7 | 363 | Watertown-Fort Drum, NY | 117.5 |
| 134 | New Haven-Milford, CT | 384.8 | 169 | San Diego, CA | 348.6 | 366 | Wausau, WI | 93.3 |
| 82 | New Orleans, LA | 473.9 | 43 | San Francisco (greater), CA | 558.6 | 94 | West Palm Beach, FL M.D. | 450.3 |
| 128 | New York (greater), NY-NJ-PA | 390.2 | 40 | San Francisco-Redwood, CA M.D. | 565.6 | 175 | Wichita Falls, TX | 341.8 |
| 93 | New York-Jersey City, NY-NJ M.D. | 455.9 | 268 | San Jose, CA | 249.8 | 39 | Wichita, KS | 568.3 |
| 176 | Newark, NJ-PA M.D. | 340.3 | 133 | San Luis Obispo, CA | 386.2 | 332 | Williamsport, PA | 171.2 |
| 95 | Niles-Benton Harbor, MI | 448.8 | 316 | San Rafael, CA M.D. | 190.7 | 78 | Wilmington, DE-MD-NJ M.D. | 481.3 |
| 108 | North Port-Sarasota-Bradenton, FL | 422.2 | 144 | Santa Cruz-Watsonville, CA | 373.5 | 156 | Wilmington, NC | 362.0 |
| 141 | Norwich-New London, CT | 379.7 | 193 | Santa Maria-Santa Barbara, CA | 326.2 | 319 | Winchester, VA-WV | 185.8 |
| 29 | Oakland-Hayward, CA M.D. | 590.0 | 159 | Santa Rosa, CA | 360.1 | 145 | Winston-Salem, NC | 371.7 |
| 105 | Ocala, FL | 430.3 | 201 | Savannah, GA | 316.0 | 107 | Worcester, MA-CT | 422.3 |
| 259 | Ocean City, NJ | 261.1 | 283 | Scranton--Wilkes-Barre, PA | 232.2 | 225 | Yakima, WA | 289.1 |
| 6 | Odessa, TX | 806.4 | 194 | Seattle (greater), WA | 323.5 | 286 | York-Hanover, PA | 224.9 |
| 338 | Ogden-Clearfield, UT | 164.0 | 227 | Seattle-Bellevue-Everett, WA M.D. | 286.7 | 205 | Yuba City, CA | 306.4 |
| 67 | Oklahoma City, OK | 503.0 | 218 | Sebastian-Vero Beach, FL | 295.3 | 118 | Yuma, AZ | 404.2 |
| 307 | Olympia, WA | 198.5 | 124 | Sebring, FL | 394.7 | | | |

Source: Reported data from the F.B.I. "Crime in the United States 2013"

*Includes murder, rape, robbery, and aggravated assault. The FBI changed the definition of rape beginning with 2013 data. Not all cities have made the change so the metro area figures reported here include rape figures based on differing definitions of rape. See note on page vii.

**Not available.

# 6. Violent Crime Rate in 2013 (continued)
## National Rate = 367.9 Violent Crimes per 100,000 Population*

| RANK | METROPOLITAN AREA | RATE | RANK | METROPOLITAN AREA | RATE | RANK | METROPOLITAN AREA | RATE |
|---|---|---|---|---|---|---|---|---|
| 1 | Detroit-Dearborn-Livonia, MI M.D. | 1,047.8 | 65 | Chattanooga, TN-GA | 509.8 | 129 | Homosassa Springs, FL | 389.3 |
| 2 | Memphis, TN-MS-AR | 993.4 | 66 | Baton Rouge, LA | 509.1 | 130 | Atlanta, GA | 389.1 |
| 3 | Philadelphia, PA M.D. | 937.7 | 67 | Boston, MA M.D. | 503.0 | 131 | Omaha-Council Bluffs, NE-IA | 387.4 |
| 4 | Jackson, TN | 925.0 | 67 | Oklahoma City, OK | 503.0 | 132 | Macon, GA | 386.4 |
| 5 | Hammond, LA | 875.1 | 69 | Philadelphia (greater) PA-NJ-MD-DE | 497.5 | 133 | San Luis Obispo, CA | 386.2 |
| 6 | Odessa, TX | 806.4 | 70 | Jacksonville, FL | 495.7 | 134 | New Haven-Milford, CT | 384.8 |
| 7 | Alexandria, LA | 793.9 | 71 | Victoria, TX | 495.4 | 135 | Warner Robins, GA | 384.5 |
| 8 | Anchorage, AK | 793.8 | 72 | Cape Girardeau, MO-IL | 490.2 | 136 | Decatur, IL | 384.1 |
| 9 | Springfield, IL | 767.9 | 73 | Fayetteville, NC | 490.1 | 137 | Lima, OH | 382.8 |
| 10 | Saginaw, MI | 752.4 | 74 | Farmington, NM | 490.0 | 137 | Rome, GA | 382.8 |
| 11 | Albuquerque, NM | 742.3 | 75 | Myrtle Beach, SC-NC | 487.0 | 139 | Burlington, NC | 382.1 |
| 12 | Flint, MI | 721.1 | 76 | Hilton Head Island, SC | 485.3 | 140 | Tuscaloosa, AL | 380.6 |
| 13 | Lawton, OK | 711.9 | 77 | Huntsville, AL | 483.5 | 141 | Norwich-New London, CT | 379.7 |
| 14 | Rockford, IL | 711.1 | 78 | Wilmington, DE-MD-NJ M.D. | 481.3 | 142 | Reno, NV | 378.0 |
| 15 | Stockton-Lodi, CA | 702.7 | 79 | Hanford-Corcoran, CA | 479.3 | 143 | Jackson, MS | 377.8 |
| 16 | Fairbanks, AK | 682.2 | 80 | Champaign-Urbana, IL | 477.3 | 144 | Santa Cruz-Watsonville, CA | 373.5 |
| 17 | Las Vegas-Henderson, NV | 678.0 | 81 | Florence, SC | 475.0 | 145 | Winston-Salem, NC | 371.7 |
| 18 | Little Rock, AR | 675.7 | 82 | New Orleans, LA | 473.9 | 146 | College Station-Bryan, TX | 371.5 |
| 19 | Sumter, SC | 671.6 | 83 | Hot Springs, AR | 472.4 | 147 | Clarksville, TN-KY | 369.3 |
| 20 | Madera, CA | 665.7 | 83 | Vallejo-Fairfield, CA | 472.4 | 148 | Washington, DC-VA-MD-WV M.D. | 369.1 |
| 21 | Lubbock, TX | 658.0 | 85 | Visalia-Porterville, CA | 472.2 | 149 | Colorado Springs, CO | 368.9 |
| 22 | Miami-Dade County, FL M.D. | 655.6 | 86 | Muskegon, MI | 471.2 | 150 | East Stroudsburg, PA | 367.2 |
| 23 | Albany, GA | 655.2 | 87 | Kansas City, MO-KS | 468.5 | 150 | Lakeland, FL | 367.2 |
| 24 | Pueblo, CO | 655.0 | 88 | Spartanburg, SC | 463.4 | 152 | Rapid City, SD | 366.9 |
| 25 | Redding, CA | 641.6 | 89 | Lafayette, LA | 461.3 | 153 | Spokane, WA | 366.8 |
| 26 | Baltimore, MD | 633.4 | 90 | San Antonio, TX | 459.7 | 154 | Knoxville, TN | 364.1 |
| 27 | Lake Charles, LA | 607.2 | 91 | Greenville, NC | 458.3 | 155 | Jonesboro, AR | 363.1 |
| 28 | Nashville-Davidson, TN | 596.1 | 92 | Dover, DE | 456.0 | 156 | Fort Worth-Arlington, TX M.D. | 362.0 |
| 29 | Oakland-Hayward, CA M.D. | 590.0 | 93 | New York-Jersey City, NY-NJ M.D. | 455.9 | 156 | Wilmington, NC | 362.0 |
| 30 | Merced, CA | 587.9 | 94 | West Palm Beach, FL M.D. | 450.3 | 158 | Davenport, IA-IL | 361.4 |
| 31 | Milwaukee, WI | 587.1 | 95 | Niles-Benton Harbor, MI | 448.8 | 159 | Santa Rosa, CA | 360.1 |
| 32 | Mobile, AL | 585.9 | 96 | Tacoma, WA M.D. | 448.3 | 160 | St. Joseph, MO-KS | 359.7 |
| 33 | Tallahassee, FL | 582.3 | 97 | Atlantic City, NJ | 443.7 | 161 | Charleston-North Charleston, SC | 359.4 |
| 34 | Gadsden, AL | 581.7 | 98 | Salisbury, MD-DE | 442.8 | 162 | Salt Lake City, UT | 356.6 |
| 35 | Columbia, SC | 578.0 | 99 | Fort Lauderdale, FL M.D. | 438.2 | 163 | Boston (greater), MA-NH | 354.5 |
| 36 | Bakersfield, CA | 576.3 | 100 | Cleveland, TN | 437.8 | 164 | Longview, WA | 354.3 |
| 37 | Monroe, LA | 575.5 | 101 | Barnstable Town, MA | 436.0 | 165 | Florence-Muscle Shoals, AL | 354.0 |
| 38 | Detroit (greater), MI | 569.6 | 102 | Tucson, AZ | 433.5 | 166 | Los Angeles (greater), CA | 353.3 |
| 39 | Wichita, KS | 568.3 | 103 | St. Louis, MO-IL | 431.7 | 167 | Medford, OR | 352.0 |
| 40 | San Francisco-Redwood, CA M.D. | 565.6 | 104 | Laredo, TX | 430.9 | 168 | Topeka, KS | 349.2 |
| 41 | Greenville-Anderson, SC | 562.3 | 105 | Ocala, FL | 430.3 | 169 | San Diego, CA | 348.6 |
| 42 | Houston, TX | 559.0 | 106 | Buffalo-Niagara Falls, NY | 430.2 | 170 | Springfield, OH | 348.5 |
| 43 | San Francisco (greater), CA | 558.6 | 107 | Worcester, MA-CT | 422.3 | 171 | El Paso, TX | 347.3 |
| 44 | Texarkana, TX-AR | 558.5 | 108 | North Port-Sarasota-Bradenton, FL | 422.2 | 172 | Greensboro-High Point, NC | 344.6 |
| 45 | Gainesville, FL | 541.9 | 109 | Salinas, CA | 416.4 | 173 | Waco, TX | 343.5 |
| 46 | Orlando, FL | 540.1 | 110 | Sacramento, CA | 415.9 | 174 | Peoria, IL | 342.2 |
| 47 | Vineland-Bridgeton, NJ | 539.5 | 111 | Longview, TX | 414.2 | 175 | Wichita Falls, TX | 341.8 |
| 48 | Rocky Mount, NC | 539.3 | 112 | Crestview-Fort Walton Beach, FL | 413.2 | 176 | Newark, NJ-PA M.D. | 340.3 |
| 49 | Miami (greater), FL | 538.9 | 113 | Columbus, GA-AL | 413.0 | 177 | Providence-Warwick, RI-MA | 338.2 |
| 50 | Beaumont-Port Arthur, TX | 536.1 | 114 | Trenton, NJ | 411.1 | 178 | Gary, IN M.D. | 336.8 |
| 51 | Springfield, MO | 533.0 | 115 | Jackson, MI | 405.6 | 179 | Port St. Lucie, FL | 336.5 |
| 52 | Shreveport-Bossier City, LA | 532.5 | 115 | Lansing-East Lansing, MI | 405.6 | 180 | Fayetteville-Springdale, AR-MO | 334.6 |
| 53 | Anniston-Oxford, AL | 532.1 | 117 | Charlotte-Mecklenburg, NC-SC | 404.4 | 181 | Riverside-San Bernardino, CA | 333.3 |
| 54 | Toledo, OH | 530.3 | 118 | Yuma, AZ | 404.2 | 182 | Abilene, TX | 333.1 |
| 55 | Birmingham-Hoover, AL | 529.8 | 119 | Los Angeles County, CA M.D. | 402.9 | 183 | Dallas (greater), TX | 332.9 |
| 56 | Palm Bay-Melbourne, FL | 524.8 | 120 | Fort Smith, AR-OK | 399.4 | 183 | Las Cruces, NM | 332.9 |
| 57 | Amarillo, TX | 524.4 | 121 | Bismarck, ND | 397.6 | 185 | Cape Coral-Fort Myers, FL | 332.8 |
| 58 | Corpus Christi, TX | 523.5 | 122 | Tampa-St Petersburg, FL | 396.5 | 186 | Columbia, MO | 332.7 |
| 59 | Springfield, MA | 522.2 | 123 | Dothan, AL | 396.2 | 187 | Washington (greater) DC-VA-MD-WV | 331.1 |
| 60 | Modesto, CA | 517.7 | 124 | Sebring, FL | 394.7 | 188 | Flagstaff, AZ | 329.2 |
| 61 | Tulsa, OK | 516.8 | 125 | Deltona-Daytona Beach, FL | 392.7 | 189 | Lincoln, NE | 328.8 |
| 62 | Panama City, FL | 516.5 | 126 | Phoenix-Mesa-Scottsdale, AZ | 392.3 | 190 | Denver-Aurora, CO | 328.5 |
| 63 | Fresno, CA | 510.1 | 127 | Goldsboro, NC | 390.9 | 191 | Johnson City, TN | 327.6 |
| 64 | Pensacola, FL | 510.0 | 128 | New York (greater), NY-NJ-PA | 390.2 | 192 | Lawrence, KS | 327.2 |

Note: All listings are for Metropolitan Statistical Areas (M.S.A.s) except for those ending with "M.D." Listings with "M.D." are Metropolitan Divisions which are smaller parts of eleven large M.S.A.s. See explanatory note at beginning of metropolitan area section.

| RANK | METROPOLITAN AREA | RATE | RANK | METROPOLITAN AREA | RATE | RANK | METROPOLITAN AREA | RATE |
|---|---|---|---|---|---|---|---|---|
| 193 | Santa Maria-Santa Barbara, CA | 326.2 | 255 | Fort Wayne, IN | 266.2 | 317 | Mansfield, OH | 190.3 |
| 194 | Seattle (greater), WA | 323.5 | 256 | Hartford, CT | 264.3 | 318 | Silver Spring-Frederick, MD M.D. | 189.4 |
| 195 | Bloomington, IL | 322.1 | 257 | Cambridge-Newton, MA M.D. | 263.8 | 319 | Winchester, VA-WV | 185.8 |
| 196 | Camden, NJ M.D. | 320.8 | 258 | Kokomo, IN | 262.3 | 320 | Allentown, PA-NJ | 185.4 |
| 196 | Kankakee, IL | 320.8 | 259 | Ocean City, NJ | 261.1 | 320 | Grand Island, NE | 185.4 |
| 198 | Morristown, TN | 319.1 | 260 | Bloomington, IN | 260.4 | 322 | Columbus, IN | 184.8 |
| 199 | Coeur d'Alene, ID | 318.3 | 261 | Syracuse, NY | 258.7 | 323 | Lewiston, ID-WA | 182.8 |
| 200 | Dallas-Plano-Irving, TX M.D. | 318.0 | 262 | San Angelo, TX | 257.3 | 324 | Racine, WI | 181.8 |
| 201 | Savannah, GA | 316.0 | 263 | Lexington-Fayette, KY | 256.7 | 325 | Mankato-North Mankato, MN | 181.3 |
| 202 | Kingsport, TN-VA | 315.6 | 264 | Fargo, ND-MN | 255.7 | 326 | Johnstown, PA | 179.6 |
| 203 | Grand Junction, CO | 311.6 | 265 | Bloomsburg-Berwick, PA | 251.6 | 327 | Lebanon, PA | 179.1 |
| 204 | South Bend-Mishawaka, IN-MI | 308.6 | 266 | Portland-Vancouver, OR-WA | 250.9 | 328 | Elgin, IL M.D. | 176.2 |
| 205 | Yuba City, CA | 306.4 | 267 | Lafayette, IN | 250.4 | 329 | Blacksburg, VA | 174.9 |
| 206 | Ann Arbor, MI | 305.5 | 268 | San Jose, CA | 249.8 | 329 | The Villages, FL | 174.9 |
| 207 | El Centro, CA | 304.6 | 269 | Sioux City, IA-NE-SD | 247.3 | 331 | Terre Haute, IN | 174.6 |
| 208 | Virginia Beach-Norfolk, VA-NC | 303.5 | 270 | Erie, PA | 245.0 | 332 | Lancaster, PA | 171.2 |
| 209 | Grand Rapids-Wyoming, MI | 302.0 | 270 | Prescott, AZ | 245.0 | 332 | Williamsport, PA | 171.2 |
| 210 | Houma, LA | 299.1 | 272 | Bridgeport-Stamford, CT | 244.5 | 334 | Elmira, NY | 169.6 |
| 210 | Joplin, MO | 299.1 | 273 | Richmond, VA | 243.8 | 335 | Rockingham County, NH M.D. | 168.3 |
| 212 | Napa, CA | 297.9 | 274 | Carson City, NV | 242.1 | 336 | St. Cloud, MN | 168.1 |
| 213 | Carbondale-Marion, IL | 297.6 | 275 | Dalton, GA | 240.7 | 337 | Staunton-Waynesboro, VA | 167.1 |
| 214 | Akron, OH | 297.2 | 276 | Brownsville-Harlingen, TX | 240.3 | 338 | Ogden-Clearfield, UT | 164.0 |
| 215 | Reading, PA | 297.0 | 277 | Roanoke, VA | 238.3 | 339 | Grants Pass, OR | 163.5 |
| 216 | Bay City, MI | 295.9 | 278 | Punta Gorda, FL | 237.9 | 340 | Kingston, NY | 161.7 |
| 216 | Greeley, CO | 295.9 | 279 | Salem, OR | 233.6 | 341 | Dutchess-Putnam, NY M.D. | 161.6 |
| 218 | Sebastian-Vero Beach, FL | 295.3 | 280 | Duluth, MN-WI | 233.4 | 342 | Dubuque, IA | 159.8 |
| 219 | Iowa City, IA | 294.8 | 281 | Naples-Marco Island, FL | 232.9 | 343 | Oshkosh-Neenah, WI | 159.3 |
| 220 | Pittsfield, MA | 294.7 | 282 | Hagerstown-Martinsburg, MD-WV | 232.8 | 344 | Idaho Falls, ID | 158.5 |
| 221 | Pittsburgh, PA | 292.8 | 283 | Scranton--Wilkes-Barre, PA | 232.2 | 345 | Lake Co.-Kenosha Co., IL-WI M.D. | 156.5 |
| 222 | Sioux Falls, SD | 291.8 | 284 | Warren-Troy, MI M.D. | 229.3 | 346 | Gainesville, GA | 156.4 |
| 223 | Cumberland, MD-WV | 291.2 | 285 | Janesville, WI | 229.2 | 347 | Ames, IA | 152.3 |
| 224 | Parkersburg-Vienna, WV | 291.1 | 286 | York-Hanover, PA | 224.9 | 348 | Chambersburg-Waynesboro, PA | 151.7 |
| 225 | Yakima, WA | 289.1 | 287 | Utica-Rome, NY | 224.5 | 349 | Portland, ME | 145.9 |
| 226 | Augusta, GA-SC | 288.3 | 288 | Boise City, ID | 224.3 | 350 | Bowling Green, KY | 144.4 |
| 227 | McAllen-Edinburg-Mission, TX | 286.7 | 289 | Great Falls, MT | 223.9 | 351 | Lewiston-Auburn, ME | 144.2 |
| 227 | Seattle-Bellevue-Everett, WA M.D. | 286.7 | 290 | Bend, OR | 221.7 | 352 | Rochester, MN | 142.6 |
| 229 | Pocatello, ID | 286.5 | 291 | Daphne-Fairhope-Foley, AL | 220.9 | 353 | Sheboygan, WI | 141.8 |
| 230 | Cincinnati, OH-KY-IN | 285.2 | 292 | Kennewick-Richland, WA | 220.5 | 354 | St. George, UT | 140.6 |
| 231 | Chico, CA | 285.1 | 293 | California-Lexington Park, MD | 219.4 | 355 | Nassau-Suffolk, NY M.D. | 139.8 |
| 232 | Gulfport-Biloxi-Pascagoula, MS | 283.7 | 294 | Raleigh, NC | 219.3 | 356 | Montgomery County, PA M.D. | 139.4 |
| 233 | Rochester, NY | 283.6 | 295 | Madison, WI | 217.1 | 357 | Owensboro, KY | 138.2 |
| 234 | Jefferson City, MO | 283.0 | 296 | Binghamton, NY | 216.2 | 358 | Harrisonburg, VA | 128.0 |
| 235 | Kahului-Wailuku-Lahaina, HI | 281.9 | 297 | Mount Vernon-Anacortes, WA | 213.4 | 359 | Eau Claire, WI | 124.6 |
| 236 | Manchester-Nashua, NH | 281.4 | 298 | Altoona, PA | 213.3 | 360 | Appleton, WI | 124.2 |
| 237 | Midland, TX | 280.5 | 299 | Lake Havasu City-Kingman, AZ | 213.1 | 361 | La Crosse, WI-MN | 122.9 |
| 238 | Tyler, TX | 278.5 | 300 | Boulder, CO | 212.0 | 362 | Corvallis, OR | 119.6 |
| 239 | Hinesville, GA | 277.2 | 301 | Casper, WY | 211.3 | 363 | Watertown-Fort Drum, NY | 117.5 |
| 240 | Bremerton-Silverdale, WA | 275.2 | 302 | Grand Forks, ND-MN | 209.0 | 364 | Gettysburg, PA | 98.6 |
| 241 | Muncie, IN | 274.7 | 303 | Cheyenne, WY | 207.0 | 365 | Glens Falls, NY | 98.1 |
| 241 | New Bern, NC | 274.7 | 304 | Green Bay, WI | 205.9 | 366 | Wausau, WI | 93.3 |
| 243 | Monroe, MI | 274.4 | 305 | Cedar Rapids, IA | 204.5 | 367 | State College, PA | 92.7 |
| 244 | Minneapolis-St. Paul, MN-WI | 273.9 | 305 | Fort Collins, CO | 204.5 | 368 | Bangor, ME | 91.2 |
| 245 | Athens-Clarke County, GA | 272.0 | 307 | Olympia, WA | 198.5 | 369 | Albany, OR | 81.4 |
| 246 | Morgantown, WV | 271.9 | 308 | Fond du Lac, WI | 196.2 | 370 | Elizabethtown-Fort Knox, KY | 78.3 |
| 247 | Dayton, OH | 271.7 | 309 | Decatur, AL | 195.1 | 371 | Provo-Orem, UT | 70.2 |
| 248 | Austin-Round Rock, TX | 271.3 | 310 | Eugene, OR | 193.9 | 372 | Logan, UT-ID | 55.4 |
| 249 | Missoula, MT | 268.6 | 311 | Oxnard-Thousand Oaks, CA | 193.8 | NA | Brunswick, GA** | NA |
| 250 | Des Moines-West Des Moines, IA | 267.8 | 312 | Anaheim-Santa Ana-Irvine, CA M.D. | 193.7 | NA | Chicago (greater), IL-IN-WI** | NA |
| 251 | Canton, OH | 267.3 | 313 | Manhattan, KS | 193.3 | NA | Chicago-Naperville, IL M.D.** | NA |
| 252 | Albany-Schenectady-Troy, NY | 266.6 | 314 | Charlottesville, VA | 191.4 | NA | Indianapolis, IN** | NA |
| 253 | Sherman-Denison, TX | 266.4 | 315 | Lynchburg, VA | 191.2 | NA | Louisville, KY-IN** | NA |
| 254 | Billings, MT | 266.3 | 316 | San Rafael, CA M.D. | 190.7 | | | |

Source: Reported data from the F.B.I. "Crime in the United States 2013"

*Includes murder, rape, robbery, and aggravated assault. The FBI changed the definition of rape beginning with 2013 data. Not all cities have made the change so the metro area figures reported here include rape figures based on differing definitions of rape. See note on page vii.

**Not available.

# 7. Percent Change in Violent Crime Rate: 2012 to 2013
## National Percent Change = 5.1% Decrease*

| RANK | METROPOLITAN AREA | % CHANGE | RANK | METROPOLITAN AREA | % CHANGE | RANK | METROPOLITAN AREA | % CHANGE |
|---|---|---|---|---|---|---|---|---|
| 79 | Abilene, TX | 1.4 | 289 | Cheyenne, WY | (14.3) | 54 | Gary, IN M.D. | 5.3 |
| 207 | Akron, OH | (6.4) | NA | Chicago (greater), IL-IN-WI** | NA | NA | Gettysburg, PA** | NA |
| 96 | Albany-Schenectady-Troy, NY | (0.1) | NA | Chicago-Naperville, IL M.D.** | NA | 331 | Glens Falls, NY | (36.4) |
| 135 | Albany, GA | (2.2) | 226 | Chico, CA | (7.3) | 240 | Goldsboro, NC | (8.4) |
| 329 | Albany, OR | (30.3) | 92 | Cincinnati, OH-KY-IN | 0.2 | NA | Grand Forks, ND-MN** | NA |
| 18 | Albuquerque, NM | 15.1 | 304 | Clarksville, TN-KY | (16.3) | 298 | Grand Island, NE | (15.7) |
| NA | Alexandria, LA** | NA | 319 | Cleveland, TN | (19.7) | 110 | Grand Junction, CO | (0.7) |
| 275 | Allentown, PA-NJ | (12.1) | 38 | Coeur d'Alene, ID | 8.4 | NA | Grand Rapids-Wyoming, MI** | NA |
| 296 | Altoona, PA | (15.4) | 210 | College Station-Bryan, TX | (6.5) | NA | Grants Pass, OR** | NA |
| 101 | Amarillo, TX | (0.3) | 138 | Colorado Springs, CO | (2.4) | 148 | Great Falls, MT | (2.9) |
| 65 | Ames, IA | 3.9 | 269 | Columbia, MO | (11.4) | 86 | Greeley, CO | 1.0 |
| 274 | Anaheim-Santa Ana-Irvine, CA M.D. | (12.0) | NA | Columbia, SC** | NA | 264 | Green Bay, WI | (10.9) |
| 134 | Anchorage, AK | (2.1) | 192 | Columbus, GA-AL | (5.6) | 215 | Greensboro-High Point, NC | (6.7) |
| 67 | Ann Arbor, MI | 3.7 | 47 | Columbus, IN | 6.9 | 123 | Greenville-Anderson, SC | (1.4) |
| 223 | Anniston-Oxford, AL | (7.2) | 217 | Corpus Christi, TX | (6.8) | 25 | Greenville, NC | 12.5 |
| 317 | Appleton, WI | (19.4) | 40 | Corvallis, OR | 7.8 | NA | Gulfport-Biloxi-Pascagoula, MS** | NA |
| 294 | Athens-Clarke County, GA | (15.1) | 254 | Crestview-Fort Walton Beach, FL | (10.2) | 189 | Hagerstown-Martinsburg, MD-WV | (5.3) |
| 178 | Atlanta, GA | (4.8) | 281 | Cumberland, MD-WV | (12.8) | 244 | Hammond, LA | (8.9) |
| NA | Atlantic City, NJ** | NA | 156 | Dallas (greater), TX | (3.4) | 151 | Hanford-Corcoran, CA | (3.0) |
| 237 | Augusta, GA-SC | (7.9) | 142 | Dallas-Plano-Irving, TX M.D. | (2.6) | 154 | Harrisonburg, VA | (3.1) |
| 226 | Austin-Round Rock, TX | (7.3) | 230 | Dalton, GA | (7.4) | 232 | Hartford, CT | (7.5) |
| 104 | Bakersfield, CA | (0.4) | 221 | Daphne-Fairhope-Foley, AL | (7.1) | 213 | Hilton Head Island, SC | (6.6) |
| 74 | Baltimore, MD | 2.0 | 148 | Davenport, IA-IL | (2.9) | 311 | Hinesville, GA | (17.9) |
| 86 | Bangor, ME | 1.0 | 218 | Dayton, OH | (6.9) | 10 | Homosassa Springs, FL | 18.8 |
| 54 | Barnstable Town, MA | 5.3 | 324 | Decatur, AL | (25.7) | NA | Hot Springs, AR** | NA |
| NA | Baton Rouge, LA** | NA | 101 | Decatur, IL | (0.3) | 73 | Houma, LA | 2.7 |
| 118 | Bay City, MI | (1.2) | 144 | Deltona-Daytona Beach, FL | (2.7) | 104 | Houston, TX | (0.4) |
| 82 | Beaumont-Port Arthur, TX | 1.3 | 144 | Denver-Aurora, CO | (2.7) | 226 | Huntsville, AL | (7.3) |
| NA | Bend, OR** | NA | 230 | Des Moines-West Des Moines, IA | (7.4) | 158 | Idaho Falls, ID | (3.5) |
| 207 | Billings, MT | (6.4) | 112 | Detroit (greater), MI | (0.8) | NA | Indianapolis, IN** | NA |
| 287 | Binghamton, NY | (14.0) | 98 | Detroit-Dearborn-Livonia, MI M.D. | (0.2) | 29 | Iowa City, IA | 11.2 |
| 203 | Birmingham-Hoover, AL | (6.2) | 72 | Dothan, AL | 2.8 | 156 | Jacksonville, FL | (3.4) |
| 28 | Bismarck, ND | 12.2 | 298 | Dover, DE | (15.7) | NA | Jackson, MI** | NA |
| 51 | Blacksburg, VA | 5.9 | 110 | Dubuque, IA | (0.7) | 138 | Jackson, MS | (2.4) |
| 92 | Bloomington, IL | 0.2 | NA | Duluth, MN-WI** | NA | 158 | Jackson, TN | (3.5) |
| 43 | Bloomington, IN | 7.5 | 271 | Dutchess-Putnam, NY M.D. | (11.5) | 169 | Janesville, WI | (4.2) |
| 1 | Bloomsburg-Berwick, PA | 54.4 | 203 | East Stroudsburg, PA | (6.2) | 246 | Jefferson City, MO | (9.0) |
| 49 | Boise City, ID | 6.2 | NA | Eau Claire, WI** | NA | 61 | Johnson City, TN | 4.6 |
| 98 | Boston (greater), MA-NH | (0.2) | 59 | El Centro, CA | 4.9 | 316 | Johnstown, PA | (19.2) |
| 79 | Boston, MA M.D. | 1.4 | 278 | El Paso, TX | (12.5) | 30 | Jonesboro, AR | 11.1 |
| 54 | Boulder, CO | 5.3 | 163 | Elgin, IL M.D. | (3.9) | 305 | Joplin, MO | (16.4) |
| 89 | Bowling Green, KY | 0.6 | 70 | Elizabethtown-Fort Knox, KY | 3.3 | 36 | Kahului-Wailuku-Lahaina, HI | 8.9 |
| 77 | Bremerton-Silverdale, WA | 1.7 | 330 | Elmira, NY | (31.8) | 195 | Kankakee, IL | (5.7) |
| 313 | Bridgeport-Stamford, CT | (18.6) | 107 | Erie, PA | (0.5) | 166 | Kansas City, MO-KS | (4.0) |
| 210 | Brownsville-Harlingen, TX | (6.5) | 312 | Eugene, OR | (18.0) | 197 | Kennewick-Richland, WA | (5.8) |
| NA | Brunswick, GA** | NA | 2 | Fairbanks, AK | 29.0 | 308 | Kingsport, TN-VA | (16.9) |
| 147 | Buffalo-Niagara Falls, NY | (2.8) | NA | Fargo, ND-MN** | NA | 48 | Kingston, NY | 6.3 |
| 276 | Burlington, NC | (12.2) | 325 | Farmington, NM | (25.9) | 283 | Knoxville, TN | (13.6) |
| 226 | California-Lexington Park, MD | (7.3) | 259 | Fayetteville-Springdale, AR-MO | (10.7) | 123 | Kokomo, IN | (1.4) |
| 169 | Cambridge-Newton, MA M.D. | (4.2) | 135 | Fayetteville, NC | (2.2) | NA | La Crosse, WI-MN** | NA |
| 189 | Camden, NJ M.D. | (5.3) | 129 | Flagstaff, AZ | (1.8) | 269 | Lafayette, IN | (11.4) |
| 251 | Canton, OH | (9.8) | 320 | Flint, MI | (20.5) | NA | Lafayette, LA** | NA |
| 175 | Cape Coral-Fort Myers, FL | (4.7) | 74 | Florence-Muscle Shoals, AL | 2.0 | NA | Lake Charles, LA** | NA |
| 26 | Cape Girardeau, MO-IL | 12.4 | 279 | Florence, SC | (12.7) | 142 | Lake Co.-Kenosha Co., IL-WI M.D. | (2.6) |
| NA | Carbondale-Marion, IL** | NA | 261 | Fond du Lac, WI | (10.8) | 10 | Lake Havasu City-Kingman, AZ | 18.8 |
| 71 | Carson City, NV | 3.0 | 261 | Fort Collins, CO | (10.8) | 61 | Lakeland, FL | 4.6 |
| 42 | Casper, WY | 7.7 | 248 | Fort Lauderdale, FL M.D. | (9.3) | NA | Lancaster, PA** | NA |
| 17 | Cedar Rapids, IA | 15.3 | 141 | Fort Smith, AR-OK | (2.5) | 22 | Lansing-East Lansing, MI | 14.0 |
| NA | Chambersburg-Waynesboro, PA** | NA | 65 | Fort Wayne, IN | 3.9 | 107 | Laredo, TX | (0.5) |
| 240 | Champaign-Urbana, IL | (8.4) | 178 | Fort Worth-Arlington, TX M.D. | (4.8) | 127 | Las Cruces, NM | (1.5) |
| 292 | Charleston-North Charleston, SC | (14.9) | 191 | Fresno, CA | (5.5) | 144 | Las Vegas-Henderson, NV | (2.7) |
| NA | Charlotte-Mecklenburg, NC-SC** | NA | 46 | Gadsden, AL | 7.2 | 267 | Lawrence, KS | (11.3) |
| 27 | Charlottesville, VA | 12.3 | 213 | Gainesville, FL | (6.6) | 123 | Lawton, OK | (1.4) |
| NA | Chattanooga, TN-GA** | NA | 257 | Gainesville, GA | (10.4) | 301 | Lebanon, PA | (16.0) |

Note: All listings are for Metropolitan Statistical Areas (M.S.A.s) except for those ending with "M.D." Listings with "M.D." are Metropolitan Divisions which are smaller parts of eleven large M.S.A.s. See explanatory note at beginning of metropolitan area section.

| RANK | METROPOLITAN AREA | % CHANGE | RANK | METROPOLITAN AREA | % CHANGE | RANK | METROPOLITAN AREA | % CHANGE |
|------|-------------------|----------|------|-------------------|----------|------|-------------------|----------|
| 120 | Lewiston-Auburn, ME | (1.3) | 178 | Omaha-Council Bluffs, NE-IA | (4.8) | 301 | Sheboygan, WI | (16.0) |
| 85 | Lewiston, ID-WA | 1.1 | 115 | Orlando, FL | (1.1) | 53 | Sherman-Denison, TX | 5.5 |
| 286 | Lexington-Fayette, KY | (13.9) | 306 | Oshkosh-Neenah, WI | (16.6) | NA | Shreveport-Bossier City, LA** | NA |
| 327 | Lima, OH | (27.2) | 35 | Owensboro, KY | 9.4 | 202 | Silver Spring-Frederick, MD M.D. | (6.1) |
| 221 | Lincoln, NE | (7.1) | 135 | Oxnard-Thousand Oaks, CA | (2.2) | 15 | Sioux City, IA-NE-SD | 16.3 |
| 78 | Little Rock, AR | 1.6 | 138 | Palm Bay-Melbourne, FL | (2.4) | 162 | Sioux Falls, SD | (3.8) |
| 67 | Logan, UT-ID | 3.7 | 69 | Panama City, FL | 3.5 | 120 | South Bend-Mishawaka, IN-MI | (1.3) |
| 169 | Longview, TX | (4.2) | 283 | Parkersburg-Vienna, WV | (13.6) | 59 | Spartanburg, SC | 4.9 |
| 8 | Longview, WA | 20.6 | 281 | Pensacola, FL | (12.8) | 52 | Spokane, WA | 5.6 |
| 250 | Los Angeles County, CA M.D. | (9.7) | 307 | Peoria, IL | (16.8) | 24 | Springfield, IL | 13.6 |
| 252 | Los Angeles (greater), CA | (10.1) | NA | Philadelphia (greater) PA-NJ-MD-DE** | NA | 63 | Springfield, MA | 4.5 |
| NA | Louisville, KY-IN** | NA | NA | Philadelphia, PA M.D.** | NA | 31 | Springfield, MO | 10.7 |
| 242 | Lubbock, TX | (8.6) | 161 | Phoenix-Mesa-Scottsdale, AZ | (3.6) | 9 | Springfield, OH | 19.1 |
| 7 | Lynchburg, VA | 22.8 | NA | Pittsburgh, PA** | NA | 178 | State College, PA | (4.8) |
| 151 | Macon, GA | (3.0) | 295 | Pittsfield, MA | (15.3) | 84 | Staunton-Waynesboro, VA | 1.2 |
| 32 | Madera, CA | 10.0 | 6 | Pocatello, ID | 23.8 | 321 | Stockton-Lodi, CA | (21.0) |
| NA | Madison, WI** | NA | 173 | Port St. Lucie, FL | (4.4) | NA | St. Cloud, MN** | NA |
| 23 | Manchester-Nashua, NH | 13.7 | 200 | Portland-Vancouver, OR-WA | (5.9) | 309 | St. George, UT | (17.2) |
| 318 | Manhattan, KS | (19.5) | 33 | Portland, ME | 9.8 | 21 | St. Joseph, MO-KS | 14.4 |
| NA | Mankato-North Mankato, MN** | NA | 322 | Prescott, AZ | (25.0) | 218 | St. Louis, MO-IL | (6.9) |
| 148 | Mansfield, OH | (2.9) | 104 | Providence-Warwick, RI-MA | (0.4) | 273 | Sumter, SC | (11.9) |
| 254 | McAllen-Edinburg-Mission, TX | (10.2) | 112 | Provo-Orem, UT | (0.8) | 292 | Syracuse, NY | (14.9) |
| 39 | Medford, OR | 7.9 | 4 | Pueblo, CO | 28.3 | 64 | Tacoma, WA M.D. | 4.2 |
| 201 | Memphis, TN-MS-AR | (6.0) | 151 | Punta Gorda, FL | (3.0) | 185 | Tallahassee, FL | (5.1) |
| 300 | Merced, CA | (15.9) | 326 | Racine, WI | (26.4) | 154 | Tampa-St Petersburg, FL | (3.1) |
| 175 | Miami (greater), FL | (4.7) | 266 | Raleigh, NC | (11.2) | 235 | Terre Haute, IN | (7.8) |
| 115 | Miami-Dade County, FL M.D. | (1.1) | 168 | Rapid City, SD | (4.1) | 314 | Texarkana, TX-AR | (18.8) |
| 264 | Midland, TX | (10.9) | 261 | Reading, PA | (10.8) | 82 | The Villages, FL | 1.3 |
| 74 | Milwaukee, WI | 2.0 | 267 | Redding, CA | (11.3) | 283 | Toledo, OH | (13.6) |
| NA | Minneapolis-St. Paul, MN-WI** | NA | 173 | Reno, NV | (4.4) | 303 | Topeka, KS | (16.1) |
| 223 | Missoula, MT | (7.2) | 92 | Richmond, VA | 0.2 | 235 | Trenton, NJ | (7.8) |
| 50 | Mobile, AL | 6.1 | 249 | Riverside-San Bernardino, CA | (9.6) | 247 | Tucson, AZ | (9.1) |
| 197 | Modesto, CA | (5.8) | 205 | Roanoke, VA | (6.3) | 178 | Tulsa, OK | (4.8) |
| 5 | Monroe, LA | 26.3 | NA | Rochester, MN** | NA | 183 | Tuscaloosa, AL | (4.9) |
| 118 | Monroe, MI | (1.2) | 101 | Rochester, NY | (0.3) | 328 | Tyler, TX | (28.8) |
| 197 | Montgomery County, PA M.D. | (5.8) | 163 | Rockford, IL | (3.9) | 244 | Utica-Rome, NY | (8.9) |
| 192 | Morgantown, WV | (5.6) | 16 | Rockingham County, NH M.D. | 15.4 | 45 | Vallejo-Fairfield, CA | 7.3 |
| 315 | Morristown, TN | (18.9) | 276 | Rocky Mount, NC | (12.2) | 175 | Victoria, TX | (4.7) |
| 34 | Mount Vernon-Anacortes, WA | 9.7 | 57 | Rome, GA | 5.2 | 128 | Vineland-Bridgeton, NJ | (1.7) |
| 57 | Muncie, IN | 5.2 | 195 | Sacramento, CA | (5.7) | 88 | Virginia Beach-Norfolk, VA-NC | 0.9 |
| NA | Muskegon, MI** | NA | 237 | Saginaw, MI | (7.9) | 115 | Visalia-Porterville, CA | (1.1) |
| NA | Myrtle Beach, SC-NC** | NA | 123 | Salem, OR | (1.4) | 296 | Waco, TX | (15.4) |
| 290 | Napa, CA | (14.4) | 184 | Salinas, CA | (5.0) | 132 | Warner Robins, GA | (1.9) |
| 210 | Naples-Marco Island, FL | (6.5) | 166 | Salisbury, MD-DE | (4.0) | 96 | Warren-Troy, MI M.D. | (0.1) |
| 258 | Nashville-Davidson, TN | (10.5) | 36 | Salt Lake City, UT | 8.9 | 107 | Washington (greater) DC-VA-MD-WV | (0.5) |
| 279 | Nassau-Suffolk, NY M.D. | (12.7) | NA | San Angelo, TX** | NA | 91 | Washington, DC-VA-MD-WV M.D. | 0.3 |
| 192 | New Bern, NC | (5.6) | 12 | San Antonio, TX | 17.7 | 332 | Watertown-Fort Drum, NY | (37.0) |
| 220 | New Haven-Milford, CT | (7.0) | 215 | San Diego, CA | (6.7) | 323 | Wausau, WI | (25.2) |
| 132 | New Orleans, LA | (1.9) | 79 | San Francisco (greater), CA | 1.4 | 233 | West Palm Beach, FL M.D. | (7.6) |
| NA | New York (greater), NY-NJ-PA** | NA | 18 | San Francisco-Redwood, CA M.D. | 15.1 | 259 | Wichita Falls, TX | (10.7) |
| NA | New York-Jersey City, NY-NJ M.D.** | NA | 243 | San Jose, CA | (8.8) | 44 | Wichita, KS | 7.4 |
| 40 | Newark, NJ-PA M.D. | 7.8 | 14 | San Luis Obispo, CA | 17.0 | 185 | Williamsport, PA | (5.1) |
| NA | Niles-Benton Harbor, MI** | NA | 92 | San Rafael, CA M.D. | 0.2 | 272 | Wilmington, DE-MD-NJ M.D. | (11.7) |
| 205 | North Port-Sarasota-Bradenton, FL | (6.3) | 172 | Santa Cruz-Watsonville, CA | (4.3) | 129 | Wilmington, NC | (1.8) |
| 207 | Norwich-New London, CT | (6.4) | 291 | Santa Maria-Santa Barbara, CA | (14.5) | 120 | Winchester, VA-WV | (1.3) |
| 185 | Oakland-Hayward, CA M.D. | (5.1) | 114 | Santa Rosa, CA | (1.0) | 234 | Winston-Salem, NC | (7.7) |
| 254 | Ocala, FL | (10.2) | 158 | Savannah, GA | (3.5) | 90 | Worcester, MA-CT | 0.5 |
| 98 | Ocean City, NJ | (0.2) | NA | Scranton--Wilkes-Barre, PA** | NA | 310 | Yakima, WA | (17.3) |
| 129 | Odessa, TX | (1.8) | 163 | Seattle (greater), WA | (3.9) | 252 | York-Hanover, PA | (10.1) |
| 13 | Ogden-Clearfield, UT | 17.1 | 223 | Seattle-Bellevue-Everett, WA M.D. | (7.2) | 288 | Yuba City, CA | (14.1) |
| 239 | Oklahoma City, OK | (8.3) | 185 | Sebastian-Vero Beach, FL | (5.1) | 20 | Yuma, AZ | 14.6 |
| NA | Olympia, WA** | NA | 3 | Sebring, FL | 28.9 | | | |

Source: CQ Press using reported data from the F.B.I. "Crime in the United States 2013"

*Includes murder, rape, robbery, and aggravated assault. The FBI changed the definition of rape beginning with 2013 data. Not all cities have made the change so the metro area figures reported here include rape figures based on differing definitions of rape. See note on page vii.

**Not available.

# 7. Percent Change in Violent Crime Rate: 2012 to 2013 (continued)
## National Percent Change = 5.1% Decrease*

| RANK | METROPOLITAN AREA | % CHANGE | RANK | METROPOLITAN AREA | % CHANGE | RANK | METROPOLITAN AREA | % CHANGE |
|---|---|---|---|---|---|---|---|---|
| 1 | Bloomsburg-Berwick, PA | 54.4 | 65 | Ames, IA | 3.9 | 129 | Flagstaff, AZ | (1.8) |
| 2 | Fairbanks, AK | 29.0 | 65 | Fort Wayne, IN | 3.9 | 129 | Odessa, TX | (1.8) |
| 3 | Sebring, FL | 28.9 | 67 | Ann Arbor, MI | 3.7 | 129 | Wilmington, NC | (1.8) |
| 4 | Pueblo, CO | 28.3 | 67 | Logan, UT-ID | 3.7 | 132 | New Orleans, LA | (1.9) |
| 5 | Monroe, LA | 26.3 | 69 | Panama City, FL | 3.5 | 132 | Warner Robins, GA | (1.9) |
| 6 | Pocatello, ID | 23.8 | 70 | Elizabethtown-Fort Knox, KY | 3.3 | 134 | Anchorage, AK | (2.1) |
| 7 | Lynchburg, VA | 22.8 | 71 | Carson City, NV | 3.0 | 135 | Albany, GA | (2.2) |
| 8 | Longview, WA | 20.6 | 72 | Dothan, AL | 2.8 | 135 | Fayetteville, NC | (2.2) |
| 9 | Springfield, OH | 19.1 | 73 | Houma, LA | 2.7 | 135 | Oxnard-Thousand Oaks, CA | (2.2) |
| 10 | Homosassa Springs, FL | 18.8 | 74 | Baltimore, MD | 2.0 | 138 | Colorado Springs, CO | (2.4) |
| 10 | Lake Havasu City-Kingman, AZ | 18.8 | 74 | Florence-Muscle Shoals, AL | 2.0 | 138 | Jackson, MS | (2.4) |
| 12 | San Antonio, TX | 17.7 | 74 | Milwaukee, WI | 2.0 | 138 | Palm Bay-Melbourne, FL | (2.4) |
| 13 | Ogden-Clearfield, UT | 17.1 | 77 | Bremerton-Silverdale, WA | 1.7 | 141 | Fort Smith, AR-OK | (2.5) |
| 14 | San Luis Obispo, CA | 17.0 | 78 | Little Rock, AR | 1.6 | 142 | Dallas-Plano-Irving, TX M.D. | (2.6) |
| 15 | Sioux City, IA-NE-SD | 16.3 | 79 | Abilene, TX | 1.4 | 142 | Lake Co.-Kenosha Co., IL-WI M.D. | (2.6) |
| 16 | Rockingham County, NH M.D. | 15.4 | 79 | Boston, MA M.D. | 1.4 | 144 | Deltona-Daytona Beach, FL | (2.7) |
| 17 | Cedar Rapids, IA | 15.3 | 79 | San Francisco (greater), CA | 1.4 | 144 | Denver-Aurora, CO | (2.7) |
| 18 | Albuquerque, NM | 15.1 | 82 | Beaumont-Port Arthur, TX | 1.3 | 144 | Las Vegas-Henderson, NV | (2.7) |
| 18 | San Francisco-Redwood, CA M.D. | 15.1 | 82 | The Villages, FL | 1.3 | 147 | Buffalo-Niagara Falls, NY | (2.8) |
| 20 | Yuma, AZ | 14.6 | 84 | Staunton-Waynesboro, VA | 1.2 | 148 | Davenport, IA-IL | (2.9) |
| 21 | St. Joseph, MO-KS | 14.4 | 85 | Lewiston, ID-WA | 1.1 | 148 | Great Falls, MT | (2.9) |
| 22 | Lansing-East Lansing, MI | 14.0 | 86 | Bangor, ME | 1.0 | 148 | Mansfield, OH | (2.9) |
| 23 | Manchester-Nashua, NH | 13.7 | 86 | Greeley, CO | 1.0 | 151 | Hanford-Corcoran, CA | (3.0) |
| 24 | Springfield, IL | 13.6 | 88 | Virginia Beach-Norfolk, VA-NC | 0.9 | 151 | Macon, GA | (3.0) |
| 25 | Greenville, NC | 12.5 | 89 | Bowling Green, KY | 0.6 | 151 | Punta Gorda, FL | (3.0) |
| 26 | Cape Girardeau, MO-IL | 12.4 | 90 | Worcester, MA-CT | 0.5 | 154 | Harrisonburg, VA | (3.1) |
| 27 | Charlottesville, VA | 12.3 | 91 | Washington, DC-VA-MD-WV M.D. | 0.3 | 154 | Tampa-St Petersburg, FL | (3.1) |
| 28 | Bismarck, ND | 12.2 | 92 | Bloomington, IL | 0.2 | 156 | Dallas (greater), TX | (3.4) |
| 29 | Iowa City, IA | 11.2 | 92 | Cincinnati, OH-KY-IN | 0.2 | 156 | Jacksonville, FL | (3.4) |
| 30 | Jonesboro, AR | 11.1 | 92 | Richmond, VA | 0.2 | 158 | Idaho Falls, ID | (3.5) |
| 31 | Springfield, MO | 10.7 | 92 | San Rafael, CA M.D. | 0.2 | 158 | Jackson, TN | (3.5) |
| 32 | Madera, CA | 10.0 | 96 | Albany-Schenectady-Troy, NY | (0.1) | 158 | Savannah, GA | (3.5) |
| 33 | Portland, ME | 9.8 | 96 | Warren-Troy, MI M.D. | (0.1) | 161 | Phoenix-Mesa-Scottsdale, AZ | (3.6) |
| 34 | Mount Vernon-Anacortes, WA | 9.7 | 98 | Boston (greater), MA-NH | (0.2) | 162 | Sioux Falls, SD | (3.8) |
| 35 | Owensboro, KY | 9.4 | 98 | Detroit-Dearborn-Livonia, MI M.D. | (0.2) | 163 | Elgin, IL M.D. | (3.9) |
| 36 | Kahului-Wailuku-Lahaina, HI | 8.9 | 98 | Ocean City, NJ | (0.2) | 163 | Rockford, IL | (3.9) |
| 36 | Salt Lake City, UT | 8.9 | 101 | Amarillo, TX | (0.3) | 163 | Seattle (greater), WA | (3.9) |
| 38 | Coeur d'Alene, ID | 8.4 | 101 | Decatur, IL | (0.3) | 166 | Kansas City, MO-KS | (4.0) |
| 39 | Medford, OR | 7.9 | 101 | Rochester, NY | (0.3) | 166 | Salisbury, MD-DE | (4.0) |
| 40 | Corvallis, OR | 7.8 | 104 | Bakersfield, CA | (0.4) | 168 | Rapid City, SD | (4.1) |
| 40 | Newark, NJ-PA M.D. | 7.8 | 104 | Houston, TX | (0.4) | 169 | Cambridge-Newton, MA M.D. | (4.2) |
| 42 | Casper, WY | 7.7 | 104 | Providence-Warwick, RI-MA | (0.4) | 169 | Janesville, WI | (4.2) |
| 43 | Bloomington, IN | 7.5 | 107 | Erie, PA | (0.5) | 169 | Longview, TX | (4.2) |
| 44 | Wichita, KS | 7.4 | 107 | Laredo, TX | (0.5) | 172 | Santa Cruz-Watsonville, CA | (4.3) |
| 45 | Vallejo-Fairfield, CA | 7.3 | 107 | Washington (greater) DC-VA-MD-WV | (0.5) | 173 | Port St. Lucie, FL | (4.4) |
| 46 | Gadsden, AL | 7.2 | 110 | Dubuque, IA | (0.7) | 173 | Reno, NV | (4.4) |
| 47 | Columbus, IN | 6.9 | 110 | Grand Junction, CO | (0.7) | 175 | Cape Coral-Fort Myers, FL | (4.7) |
| 48 | Kingston, NY | 6.3 | 112 | Detroit (greater), MI | (0.8) | 175 | Miami (greater), FL | (4.7) |
| 49 | Boise City, ID | 6.2 | 112 | Provo-Orem, UT | (0.8) | 175 | Victoria, TX | (4.7) |
| 50 | Mobile, AL | 6.1 | 114 | Santa Rosa, CA | (1.0) | 178 | Atlanta, GA | (4.8) |
| 51 | Blacksburg, VA | 5.9 | 115 | Miami-Dade County, FL M.D. | (1.1) | 178 | Fort Worth-Arlington, TX M.D. | (4.8) |
| 52 | Spokane, WA | 5.6 | 115 | Orlando, FL | (1.1) | 178 | Omaha-Council Bluffs, NE-IA | (4.8) |
| 53 | Sherman-Denison, TX | 5.5 | 115 | Visalia-Porterville, CA | (1.1) | 178 | State College, PA | (4.8) |
| 54 | Barnstable Town, MA | 5.3 | 118 | Bay City, MI | (1.2) | 178 | Tulsa, OK | (4.8) |
| 54 | Boulder, CO | 5.3 | 118 | Monroe, MI | (1.2) | 183 | Tuscaloosa, AL | (4.9) |
| 54 | Gary, IN M.D. | 5.3 | 120 | Lewiston-Auburn, ME | (1.3) | 184 | Salinas, CA | (5.0) |
| 57 | Muncie, IN | 5.2 | 120 | South Bend-Mishawaka, IN-MI | (1.3) | 185 | Oakland-Hayward, CA M.D. | (5.1) |
| 57 | Rome, GA | 5.2 | 120 | Winchester, VA-WV | (1.3) | 185 | Sebastian-Vero Beach, FL | (5.1) |
| 59 | El Centro, CA | 4.9 | 123 | Greenville-Anderson, SC | (1.4) | 185 | Tallahassee, FL | (5.1) |
| 59 | Spartanburg, SC | 4.9 | 123 | Kokomo, IN | (1.4) | 185 | Williamsport, PA | (5.1) |
| 61 | Johnson City, TN | 4.6 | 123 | Lawton, OK | (1.4) | 189 | Camden, NJ M.D. | (5.3) |
| 61 | Lakeland, FL | 4.6 | 123 | Salem, OR | (1.4) | 189 | Hagerstown-Martinsburg, MD-WV | (5.3) |
| 63 | Springfield, MA | 4.5 | 127 | Las Cruces, NM | (1.5) | 191 | Fresno, CA | (5.5) |
| 64 | Tacoma, WA M.D. | 4.2 | 128 | Vineland-Bridgeton, NJ | (1.7) | 192 | Columbus, GA-AL | (5.6) |

Note: All listings are for Metropolitan Statistical Areas (M.S.A.s) except for those ending with "M.D." Listings with "M.D." are Metropolitan Divisions which are smaller parts of eleven large M.S.A.s. See explanatory note at beginning of metropolitan area section.

| RANK | METROPOLITAN AREA | % CHANGE | RANK | METROPOLITAN AREA | % CHANGE | RANK | METROPOLITAN AREA | % CHANGE |
|---|---|---|---|---|---|---|---|---|
| 192 | Morgantown, WV | (5.6) | 254 | McAllen-Edinburg-Mission, TX | (10.2) | 317 | Appleton, WI | (19.4) |
| 192 | New Bern, NC | (5.6) | 254 | Ocala, FL | (10.2) | 318 | Manhattan, KS | (19.5) |
| 195 | Kankakee, IL | (5.7) | 257 | Gainesville, GA | (10.4) | 319 | Cleveland, TN | (19.7) |
| 195 | Sacramento, CA | (5.7) | 258 | Nashville-Davidson, TN | (10.5) | 320 | Flint, MI | (20.5) |
| 197 | Kennewick-Richland, WA | (5.8) | 259 | Fayetteville-Springdale, AR-MO | (10.7) | 321 | Stockton-Lodi, CA | (21.0) |
| 197 | Modesto, CA | (5.8) | 259 | Wichita Falls, TX | (10.7) | 322 | Prescott, AZ | (25.0) |
| 197 | Montgomery County, PA M.D. | (5.8) | 261 | Fond du Lac, WI | (10.8) | 323 | Wausau, WI | (25.2) |
| 200 | Portland-Vancouver, OR-WA | (5.9) | 261 | Fort Collins, CO | (10.8) | 324 | Decatur, AL | (25.7) |
| 201 | Memphis, TN-MS-AR | (6.0) | 261 | Reading, PA | (10.8) | 325 | Farmington, NM | (25.9) |
| 202 | Silver Spring-Frederick, MD M.D. | (6.1) | 264 | Green Bay, WI | (10.9) | 326 | Racine, WI | (26.4) |
| 203 | Birmingham-Hoover, AL | (6.2) | 264 | Midland, TX | (10.9) | 327 | Lima, OH | (27.2) |
| 203 | East Stroudsburg, PA | (6.2) | 266 | Raleigh, NC | (11.2) | 328 | Tyler, TX | (28.8) |
| 205 | North Port-Sarasota-Bradenton, FL | (6.3) | 267 | Lawrence, KS | (11.3) | 329 | Albany, OR | (30.3) |
| 205 | Roanoke, VA | (6.3) | 267 | Redding, CA | (11.3) | 330 | Elmira, NY | (31.8) |
| 207 | Akron, OH | (6.4) | 269 | Columbia, MO | (11.4) | 331 | Glens Falls, NY | (36.4) |
| 207 | Billings, MT | (6.4) | 269 | Lafayette, IN | (11.4) | 332 | Watertown-Fort Drum, NY | (37.0) |
| 207 | Norwich-New London, CT | (6.4) | 271 | Dutchess-Putnam, NY M.D. | (11.5) | NA | Alexandria, LA** | NA |
| 210 | Brownsville-Harlingen, TX | (6.5) | 272 | Wilmington, DE-MD-NJ M.D. | (11.7) | NA | Atlantic City, NJ** | NA |
| 210 | College Station-Bryan, TX | (6.5) | 273 | Sumter, SC | (11.9) | NA | Baton Rouge, LA** | NA |
| 210 | Naples-Marco Island, FL | (6.5) | 274 | Anaheim-Santa Ana-Irvine, CA M.D. | (12.0) | NA | Bend, OR** | NA |
| 213 | Gainesville, FL | (6.6) | 275 | Allentown, PA-NJ | (12.1) | NA | Brunswick, GA** | NA |
| 213 | Hilton Head Island, SC | (6.6) | 276 | Burlington, NC | (12.2) | NA | Carbondale-Marion, IL** | NA |
| 215 | Greensboro-High Point, NC | (6.7) | 276 | Rocky Mount, NC | (12.2) | NA | Chambersburg-Waynesboro, PA** | NA |
| 215 | San Diego, CA | (6.7) | 278 | El Paso, TX | (12.5) | NA | Charlotte-Mecklenburg, NC-SC** | NA |
| 217 | Corpus Christi, TX | (6.8) | 279 | Florence, SC | (12.7) | NA | Chattanooga, TN-GA** | NA |
| 218 | Dayton, OH | (6.9) | 279 | Nassau-Suffolk, NY M.D. | (12.7) | NA | Chicago (greater), IL-IN-WI** | NA |
| 218 | St. Louis, MO-IL | (6.9) | 281 | Cumberland, MD-WV | (12.8) | NA | Chicago-Naperville, IL M.D.** | NA |
| 220 | New Haven-Milford, CT | (7.0) | 281 | Pensacola, FL | (12.8) | NA | Columbia, SC** | NA |
| 221 | Daphne-Fairhope-Foley, AL | (7.1) | 283 | Knoxville, TN | (13.6) | NA | Duluth, MN-WI** | NA |
| 221 | Lincoln, NE | (7.1) | 283 | Parkersburg-Vienna, WV | (13.6) | NA | Eau Claire, WI** | NA |
| 223 | Anniston-Oxford, AL | (7.2) | 283 | Toledo, OH | (13.6) | NA | Fargo, ND-MN** | NA |
| 223 | Missoula, MT | (7.2) | 286 | Lexington-Fayette, KY | (13.9) | NA | Gettysburg, PA** | NA |
| 223 | Seattle-Bellevue-Everett, WA M.D. | (7.2) | 287 | Binghamton, NY | (14.0) | NA | Grand Forks, ND-MN** | NA |
| 226 | Austin-Round Rock, TX | (7.3) | 288 | Yuba City, CA | (14.1) | NA | Grand Rapids-Wyoming, MI** | NA |
| 226 | California-Lexington Park, MD | (7.3) | 289 | Cheyenne, WY | (14.3) | NA | Grants Pass, OR** | NA |
| 226 | Chico, CA | (7.3) | 290 | Napa, CA | (14.4) | NA | Gulfport-Biloxi-Pascagoula, MS** | NA |
| 226 | Huntsville, AL | (7.3) | 291 | Santa Maria-Santa Barbara, CA | (14.5) | NA | Hot Springs, AR** | NA |
| 230 | Dalton, GA | (7.4) | 292 | Charleston-North Charleston, SC | (14.9) | NA | Indianapolis, IN** | NA |
| 230 | Des Moines-West Des Moines, IA | (7.4) | 292 | Syracuse, NY | (14.9) | NA | Jackson, MI** | NA |
| 232 | Hartford, CT | (7.5) | 294 | Athens-Clarke County, GA | (15.1) | NA | La Crosse, WI-MN** | NA |
| 233 | West Palm Beach, FL M.D. | (7.6) | 295 | Pittsfield, MA | (15.3) | NA | Lafayette, LA** | NA |
| 234 | Winston-Salem, NC | (7.7) | 296 | Altoona, PA | (15.4) | NA | Lake Charles, LA** | NA |
| 235 | Terre Haute, IN | (7.8) | 296 | Waco, TX | (15.4) | NA | Lancaster, PA** | NA |
| 235 | Trenton, NJ | (7.8) | 298 | Dover, DE | (15.7) | NA | Louisville, KY-IN** | NA |
| 237 | Augusta, GA-SC | (7.9) | 298 | Grand Island, NE | (15.7) | NA | Madison, WI** | NA |
| 237 | Saginaw, MI | (7.9) | 300 | Merced, CA | (15.9) | NA | Mankato-North Mankato, MN** | NA |
| 239 | Oklahoma City, OK | (8.3) | 301 | Lebanon, PA | (16.0) | NA | Minneapolis-St. Paul, MN-WI** | NA |
| 240 | Champaign-Urbana, IL | (8.4) | 301 | Sheboygan, WI | (16.0) | NA | Muskegon, MI** | NA |
| 240 | Goldsboro, NC | (8.4) | 303 | Topeka, KS | (16.1) | NA | Myrtle Beach, SC-NC** | NA |
| 242 | Lubbock, TX | (8.6) | 304 | Clarksville, TN-KY | (16.3) | NA | New York (greater), NY-NJ-PA** | NA |
| 243 | San Jose, CA | (8.8) | 305 | Joplin, MO | (16.4) | NA | New York-Jersey City, NY-NJ M.D.** | NA |
| 244 | Hammond, LA | (8.9) | 306 | Oshkosh-Neenah, WI | (16.6) | NA | Niles-Benton Harbor, MI** | NA |
| 244 | Utica-Rome, NY | (8.9) | 307 | Peoria, IL | (16.8) | NA | Olympia, WA** | NA |
| 246 | Jefferson City, MO | (9.0) | 308 | Kingsport, TN-VA | (16.9) | NA | Philadelphia (greater) PA-NJ-MD-DE** | NA |
| 247 | Tucson, AZ | (9.1) | 309 | St. George, UT | (17.2) | NA | Philadelphia, PA M.D.** | NA |
| 248 | Fort Lauderdale, FL M.D. | (9.3) | 310 | Yakima, WA | (17.3) | NA | Pittsburgh, PA** | NA |
| 249 | Riverside-San Bernardino, CA | (9.6) | 311 | Hinesville, GA | (17.9) | NA | Rochester, MN** | NA |
| 250 | Los Angeles County, CA M.D. | (9.7) | 312 | Eugene, OR | (18.0) | NA | San Angelo, TX** | NA |
| 251 | Canton, OH | (9.8) | 313 | Bridgeport-Stamford, CT | (18.6) | NA | Scranton--Wilkes-Barre, PA** | NA |
| 252 | Los Angeles (greater), CA | (10.1) | 314 | Texarkana, TX-AR | (18.8) | NA | Shreveport-Bossier City, LA** | NA |
| 252 | York-Hanover, PA | (10.1) | 315 | Morristown, TN | (18.9) | NA | St. Cloud, MN** | NA |
| 254 | Crestview-Fort Walton Beach, FL | (10.2) | 316 | Johnstown, PA | (19.2) | | | |

Source: CQ Press using reported data from the F.B.I. "Crime in the United States 2013"

*Includes murder, rape, robbery, and aggravated assault. The FBI changed the definition of rape beginning with 2013 data. Not all cities have made the change so the metro area figures reported here include rape figures based on differing definitions of rape. See note on page vii.

**Not available.

# 8. Percent Change in Violent Crime Rate: 2009 to 2013
## National Percent Change = 14.8% Decrease*

| RANK | METROPOLITAN AREA | % CHANGE | RANK | METROPOLITAN AREA | % CHANGE | RANK | METROPOLITAN AREA | % CHANGE |
|---|---|---|---|---|---|---|---|---|
| 259 | Abilene, TX | (28.2) | 48 | Cheyenne, WY | 2.8 | NA | Gary, IN M.D.** | NA |
| 174 | Akron, OH | (16.8) | NA | Chicago (greater), IL-IN-WI** | NA | NA | Gettysburg, PA** | NA |
| 157 | Albany-Schenectady-Troy, NY | (14.0) | NA | Chicago-Naperville, IL M.D.** | NA | 110 | Glens Falls, NY | (7.5) |
| 28 | Albany, GA | 13.1 | 273 | Chico, CA | (32.2) | 151 | Goldsboro, NC | (13.6) |
| NA | Albany, OR** | NA | 173 | Cincinnati, OH-KY-IN | (16.6) | NA | Grand Forks, ND-MN** | NA |
| 27 | Albuquerque, NM | 13.8 | 166 | Clarksville, TN-KY | (16.0) | NA | Grand Island, NE** | NA |
| 20 | Alexandria, LA | 18.4 | 275 | Cleveland, TN | (32.4) | 45 | Grand Junction, CO | 3.8 |
| 231 | Allentown, PA-NJ | (23.9) | 107 | Coeur d'Alene, ID | (7.3) | NA | Grand Rapids-Wyoming, MI** | NA |
| 229 | Altoona, PA | (23.5) | 140 | College Station-Bryan, TX | (12.6) | NA | Grants Pass, OR** | NA |
| 221 | Amarillo, TX | (22.3) | 188 | Colorado Springs, CO | (18.3) | 203 | Great Falls, MT | (20.0) |
| 289 | Ames, IA | (41.6) | 179 | Columbia, MO | (17.3) | 40 | Greeley, CO | 7.8 |
| 216 | Anaheim-Santa Ana-Irvine, CA M.D. | (21.3) | 233 | Columbia, SC | (24.0) | 37 | Green Bay, WI | 8.8 |
| 104 | Anchorage, AK | (7.0) | 208 | Columbus, GA-AL | (20.8) | 256 | Greensboro-High Point, NC | (28.1) |
| 94 | Ann Arbor, MI | (5.1) | 3 | Columbus, IN | 71.1 | NA | Greenville-Anderson, SC** | NA |
| 246 | Anniston-Oxford, AL | (26.7) | 204 | Corpus Christi, TX | (20.3) | NA | Greenville, NC** | NA |
| 41 | Appleton, WI | 7.5 | 90 | Corvallis, OR | (4.6) | NA | Gulfport-Biloxi-Pascagoula, MS** | NA |
| 263 | Athens-Clarke County, GA | (29.0) | NA | Crestview-Fort Walton Beach, FL** | NA | 75 | Hagerstown-Martinsburg, MD-WV | (2.0) |
| 129 | Atlanta, GA | (11.5) | 282 | Cumberland, MD-WV | (36.6) | NA | Hammond, LA** | NA |
| 180 | Atlantic City, NJ | (17.4) | 194 | Dallas (greater), TX | (19.0) | NA | Hanford-Corcoran, CA** | NA |
| 271 | Augusta, GA-SC | (30.5) | 206 | Dallas-Plano-Irving, TX M.D. | (20.7) | 171 | Harrisonburg, VA | (16.5) |
| 230 | Austin-Round Rock, TX | (23.8) | 184 | Dalton, GA | (17.9) | 123 | Hartford, CT | (10.2) |
| 84 | Bakersfield, CA | (4.0) | NA | Daphne-Fairhope-Foley, AL** | NA | NA | Hilton Head Island, SC** | NA |
| 136 | Baltimore, MD | (12.3) | NA | Davenport, IA-IL** | NA | 288 | Hinesville, GA | (40.8) |
| 34 | Bangor, ME | 9.5 | 189 | Dayton, OH | (18.5) | NA | Homosassa Springs, FL** | NA |
| 99 | Barnstable Town, MA | (6.3) | NA | Decatur, AL** | NA | 240 | Hot Springs, AR | (25.2) |
| 249 | Baton Rouge, LA | (27.0) | NA | Decatur, IL** | NA | 273 | Houma, LA | (32.2) |
| 98 | Bay City, MI | (6.2) | 261 | Deltona-Daytona Beach, FL | (28.9) | 209 | Houston, TX | (20.9) |
| 57 | Beaumont-Port Arthur, TX | 0.3 | 95 | Denver-Aurora, CO | (5.3) | 18 | Huntsville, AL | 19.2 |
| 44 | Bend, OR | 4.9 | 78 | Des Moines-West Des Moines, IA | (2.7) | 293 | Idaho Falls, ID | (46.1) |
| 25 | Billings, MT | 15.1 | 145 | Detroit (greater), MI | (13.3) | NA | Indianapolis, IN** | NA |
| 33 | Binghamton, NY | 9.9 | 113 | Detroit-Dearborn-Livonia, MI M.D. | (8.1) | 56 | Iowa City, IA | 0.9 |
| 67 | Birmingham-Hoover, AL | (0.9) | NA | Dothan, AL** | NA | 260 | Jacksonville, FL | (28.7) |
| 1 | Bismarck, ND | 92.4 | 254 | Dover, DE | (27.9) | 89 | Jackson, MI | (4.5) |
| 137 | Blacksburg, VA | (12.4) | 294 | Dubuque, IA | (58.7) | 82 | Jackson, MS | (3.4) |
| NA | Bloomington, IL** | NA | NA | Duluth, MN-WI** | NA | 11 | Jackson, TN | 29.3 |
| 96 | Bloomington, IN | (5.8) | NA | Dutchess-Putnam, NY M.D.** | NA | 107 | Janesville, WI | (7.3) |
| NA | Bloomsburg-Berwick, PA** | NA | NA | East Stroudsburg, PA** | NA | 121 | Jefferson City, MO | (9.9) |
| 87 | Boise City, ID | (4.3) | 47 | Eau Claire, WI | 3.1 | 88 | Johnson City, TN | (4.4) |
| 128 | Boston (greater), MA-NH | (11.4) | NA | El Centro, CA** | NA | NA | Johnstown, PA** | NA |
| 144 | Boston, MA M.D. | (13.1) | 212 | El Paso, TX | (21.1) | 106 | Jonesboro, AR | (7.1) |
| 142 | Boulder, CO | (12.7) | NA | Elgin, IL M.D.** | NA | NA | Joplin, MO** | NA |
| NA | Bowling Green, KY** | NA | NA | Elizabethtown-Fort Knox, KY** | NA | NA | Kahului-Wailuku-Lahaina, HI** | NA |
| 284 | Bremerton-Silverdale, WA | (37.7) | 111 | Elmira, NY | (7.9) | NA | Kankakee, IL** | NA |
| 224 | Bridgeport-Stamford, CT | (23.1) | 70 | Erie, PA | (1.2) | 140 | Kansas City, MO-KS | (12.6) |
| 256 | Brownsville-Harlingen, TX | (28.1) | 281 | Eugene, OR | (36.1) | 191 | Kennewick-Richland, WA | (18.8) |
| NA | Brunswick, GA** | NA | 118 | Fairbanks, AK | (9.3) | 171 | Kingsport, TN-VA | (16.5) |
| 169 | Buffalo-Niagara Falls, NY | (16.4) | NA | Fargo, ND-MN** | NA | 278 | Kingston, NY | (33.9) |
| 162 | Burlington, NC | (15.2) | 279 | Farmington, NM | (34.0) | 245 | Knoxville, TN | (26.4) |
| NA | California-Lexington Park, MD** | NA | 36 | Fayetteville-Springdale, AR-MO | 9.4 | 10 | Kokomo, IN | 30.8 |
| NA | Cambridge-Newton, MA M.D.** | NA | 133 | Fayetteville, NC | (11.9) | NA | La Crosse, WI-MN** | NA |
| 121 | Camden, NJ M.D. | (9.9) | 63 | Flagstaff, AZ | (0.5) | 46 | Lafayette, IN | 3.6 |
| NA | Canton, OH** | NA | 100 | Flint, MI | (6.5) | NA | Lafayette, LA** | NA |
| 212 | Cape Coral-Fort Myers, FL | (21.1) | 20 | Florence-Muscle Shoals, AL | 18.4 | 191 | Lake Charles, LA | (18.8) |
| 13 | Cape Girardeau, MO-IL | 26.5 | 286 | Florence, SC | (38.5) | NA | Lake Co.-Kenosha Co., IL-WI M.D.** | NA |
| NA | Carbondale-Marion, IL** | NA | 16 | Fond du Lac, WI | 20.7 | 104 | Lake Havasu City-Kingman, AZ | (7.0) |
| 246 | Carson City, NV | (26.7) | 236 | Fort Collins, CO | (24.5) | 214 | Lakeland, FL | (21.2) |
| 80 | Casper, WY | (3.0) | 201 | Fort Lauderdale, FL M.D. | (19.8) | NA | Lancaster, PA** | NA |
| 69 | Cedar Rapids, IA | (1.0) | 109 | Fort Smith, AR-OK | (7.4) | 64 | Lansing-East Lansing, MI | (0.7) |
| NA | Chambersburg-Waynesboro, PA** | NA | 39 | Fort Wayne, IN | 8.1 | 239 | Laredo, TX | (25.1) |
| NA | Champaign-Urbana, IL** | NA | 166 | Fort Worth-Arlington, TX M.D. | (16.0) | 193 | Las Cruces, NM | (18.9) |
| 290 | Charleston-North Charleston, SC | (41.7) | 59 | Fresno, CA | (0.2) | 169 | Las Vegas-Henderson, NV | (16.4) |
| NA | Charlotte-Mecklenburg, NC-SC** | NA | 5 | Gadsden, AL | 64.5 | 216 | Lawrence, KS | (21.3) |
| 127 | Charlottesville, VA | (11.3) | 272 | Gainesville, FL | (31.5) | 267 | Lawton, OK | (30.1) |
| 151 | Chattanooga, TN-GA | (13.6) | 145 | Gainesville, GA | (13.3) | 43 | Lebanon, PA | 5.5 |

Note: All listings are for Metropolitan Statistical Areas (M.S.A.s) except for those ending with "M.D." Listings with "M.D." are Metropolitan Divisions which are smaller parts of eleven large M.S.A.s. See explanatory note at beginning of metropolitan area section.

| RANK | METROPOLITAN AREA | % CHANGE | RANK | METROPOLITAN AREA | % CHANGE | RANK | METROPOLITAN AREA | % CHANGE |
|---|---|---|---|---|---|---|---|---|
| 91 | Lewiston-Auburn, ME | (4.8) | 72 | Omaha-Council Bluffs, NE-IA | (1.7) | 52 | Sheboygan, WI | 2.3 |
| 26 | Lewiston, ID-WA | 14.3 | 209 | Orlando, FL | (20.9) | 97 | Sherman-Denison, TX | (6.1) |
| 290 | Lexington-Fayette, KY | (41.7) | 275 | Oshkosh-Neenah, WI | (32.4) | NA | Shreveport-Bossier City, LA** | NA |
| 254 | Lima, OH | (27.9) | 60 | Owensboro, KY | (0.3) | 228 | Silver Spring-Frederick, MD M.D. | (23.4) |
| 184 | Lincoln, NE | (17.9) | 227 | Oxnard-Thousand Oaks, CA | (23.3) | 143 | Sioux City, IA-NE-SD | (13.0) |
| 159 | Little Rock, AR | (14.4) | 219 | Palm Bay-Melbourne, FL | (21.8) | 9 | Sioux Falls, SD | 37.7 |
| 256 | Logan, UT-ID | (28.1) | 158 | Panama City, FL | (14.3) | 174 | South Bend-Mishawaka, IN-MI | (16.8) |
| 243 | Longview, TX | (26.1) | NA | Parkersburg-Vienna, WV** | NA | 235 | Spartanburg, SC | (24.2) |
| 4 | Longview, WA | 67.1 | 220 | Pensacola, FL | (22.0) | 79 | Spokane, WA | (2.8) |
| 251 | Los Angeles County, CA M.D. | (27.4) | NA | Peoria, IL** | NA | NA | Springfield, IL** | NA |
| 248 | Los Angeles (greater), CA | (26.8) | 151 | Philadelphia (greater) PA-NJ-MD-DE | (13.6) | 72 | Springfield, MA | (1.7) |
| NA | Louisville, KY-IN** | NA | NA | Philadelphia, PA M.D.** | NA | 14 | Springfield, MO | 25.9 |
| 221 | Lubbock, TX | (22.3) | 61 | Phoenix-Mesa-Scottsdale, AZ | (0.4) | 61 | Springfield, OH | (0.4) |
| 265 | Lynchburg, VA | (29.1) | NA | Pittsburgh, PA** | NA | 242 | State College, PA | (26.0) |
| 135 | Macon, GA | (12.2) | 269 | Pittsfield, MA | (30.4) | NA | Staunton-Waynesboro, VA** | NA |
| 7 | Madera, CA | 46.6 | 23 | Pocatello, ID | 16.1 | 145 | Stockton-Lodi, CA | (13.3) |
| NA | Madison, WI** | NA | 190 | Port St. Lucie, FL | (18.7) | NA | St. Cloud, MN** | NA |
| 12 | Manchester-Nashua, NH | 27.0 | 101 | Portland-Vancouver, OR-WA | (6.6) | 34 | St. George, UT | 9.5 |
| 292 | Manhattan, KS | (44.2) | 38 | Portland, ME | 8.6 | 134 | St. Joseph, MO-KS | (12.1) |
| NA | Mankato-North Mankato, MN** | NA | 224 | Prescott, AZ | (23.1) | NA | St. Louis, MO-IL** | NA |
| 77 | Mansfield, OH | (2.2) | 120 | Providence-Warwick, RI-MA | (9.7) | 55 | Sumter, SC | 1.1 |
| 266 | McAllen-Edinburg-Mission, TX | (29.5) | 112 | Provo-Orem, UT | (8.0) | 151 | Syracuse, NY | (13.6) |
| 2 | Medford, OR | 80.4 | 30 | Pueblo, CO | 11.9 | 162 | Tacoma, WA M.D. | (15.2) |
| 148 | Memphis, TN-MS-AR | (13.4) | 238 | Punta Gorda, FL | (24.6) | 234 | Tallahassee, FL | (24.1) |
| 131 | Merced, CA | (11.6) | 285 | Racine, WI | (38.3) | 277 | Tampa-St Petersburg, FL | (32.7) |
| 206 | Miami (greater), FL | (20.7) | 214 | Raleigh, NC | (21.2) | NA | Terre Haute, IN** | NA |
| 182 | Miami-Dade County, FL M.D. | (17.8) | 22 | Rapid City, SD | 17.8 | 241 | Texarkana, TX-AR | (25.9) |
| 216 | Midland, TX | (21.3) | 82 | Reading, PA | (3.4) | NA | The Villages, FL** | NA |
| 19 | Milwaukee, WI | 18.8 | 116 | Redding, CA | (9.0) | 92 | Toledo, OH | (4.9) |
| NA | Minneapolis-St. Paul, MN-WI** | NA | 249 | Reno, NV | (27.0) | 168 | Topeka, KS | (16.2) |
| 42 | Missoula, MT | 6.5 | 174 | Richmond, VA | (16.8) | 123 | Trenton, NJ | (10.2) |
| 196 | Mobile, AL | (19.2) | 198 | Riverside-San Bernardino, CA | (19.5) | 71 | Tucson, AZ | (1.3) |
| 74 | Modesto, CA | (1.8) | 205 | Roanoke, VA | (20.4) | 174 | Tulsa, OK | (16.8) |
| NA | Monroe, LA** | NA | NA | Rochester, MN** | NA | 200 | Tuscaloosa, AL | (19.7) |
| 15 | Monroe, MI | 23.5 | 81 | Rochester, NY | (3.1) | 280 | Tyler, TX | (35.2) |
| NA | Montgomery County, PA M.D.** | NA | NA | Rockford, IL** | NA | 194 | Utica-Rome, NY | (19.0) |
| 209 | Morgantown, WV | (20.9) | 8 | Rockingham County, NH M.D. | 43.4 | 103 | Vallejo-Fairfield, CA | (6.8) |
| 116 | Morristown, TN | (9.0) | 199 | Rocky Mount, NC | (19.6) | 126 | Victoria, TX | (11.0) |
| 32 | Mount Vernon-Anacortes, WA | 11.3 | 151 | Rome, GA | (13.6) | 65 | Vineland-Bridgeton, NJ | (0.8) |
| 252 | Muncie, IN | (27.6) | 187 | Sacramento, CA | (18.2) | NA | Virginia Beach-Norfolk, VA-NC** | NA |
| 31 | Muskegon, MI | 11.7 | 196 | Saginaw, MI | (19.2) | 114 | Visalia-Porterville, CA | (8.6) |
| NA | Myrtle Beach, SC-NC** | NA | 67 | Salem, OR | (0.9) | 283 | Waco, TX | (36.8) |
| 54 | Napa, CA | 1.6 | 202 | Salinas, CA | (19.9) | NA | Warner Robins, GA** | NA |
| 263 | Naples-Marco Island, FL | (29.0) | NA | Salisbury, MD-DE** | NA | 186 | Warren-Troy, MI M.D. | (18.1) |
| 119 | Nashville-Davidson, TN | (9.6) | 50 | Salt Lake City, UT | 2.5 | 181 | Washington (greater) DC-VA-MD-WV | (17.7) |
| 224 | Nassau-Suffolk, NY M.D. | (23.1) | 268 | San Angelo, TX | (30.2) | 178 | Washington, DC-VA-MD-WV M.D. | (17.2) |
| NA | New Bern, NC** | NA | 76 | San Antonio, TX | (2.1) | NA | Watertown-Fort Drum, NY** | NA |
| 159 | New Haven-Milford, CT | (14.4) | 182 | San Diego, CA | (17.8) | 287 | Wausau, WI | (40.5) |
| 150 | New Orleans, LA | (13.5) | 65 | San Francisco (greater), CA | (0.8) | 261 | West Palm Beach, FL M.D. | (28.9) |
| 53 | New York (greater), NY-NJ-PA | 2.2 | 24 | San Francisco-Redwood, CA M.D. | 15.9 | 161 | Wichita Falls, TX | (15.1) |
| NA | New York-Jersey City, NY-NJ M.D.** | NA | 148 | San Jose, CA | (13.4) | 129 | Wichita, KS | (11.5) |
| 125 | Newark, NJ-PA M.D. | (10.8) | 6 | San Luis Obispo, CA | 48.3 | 132 | Williamsport, PA | (11.7) |
| 29 | Niles-Benton Harbor, MI | 12.6 | NA | San Rafael, CA M.D.** | NA | 231 | Wilmington, DE-MD-NJ M.D. | (23.9) |
| 253 | North Port-Sarasota-Bradenton, FL | (27.8) | 223 | Santa Cruz-Watsonville, CA | (22.5) | NA | Wilmington, NC** | NA |
| 115 | Norwich-New London, CT | (8.9) | 269 | Santa Maria-Santa Barbara, CA | (30.4) | 51 | Winchester, VA-WV | 2.4 |
| 85 | Oakland-Hayward, CA M.D. | (4.2) | 138 | Santa Rosa, CA | (12.5) | NA | Winston-Salem, NC** | NA |
| 236 | Ocala, FL | (24.5) | 244 | Savannah, GA | (26.3) | 85 | Worcester, MA-CT | (4.2) |
| 101 | Ocean City, NJ | (6.6) | NA | Scranton--Wilkes-Barre, PA** | NA | NA | Yakima, WA** | NA |
| 17 | Odessa, TX | 20.3 | 165 | Seattle (greater), WA | (15.8) | 92 | York-Hanover, PA | (4.9) |
| 58 | Ogden-Clearfield, UT | 0.2 | 164 | Seattle-Bellevue-Everett, WA M.D. | (15.7) | 151 | Yuba City, CA | (13.6) |
| NA | Oklahoma City, OK** | NA | 138 | Sebastian-Vero Beach, FL | (12.5) | 48 | Yuma, AZ | 2.8 |
| NA | Olympia, WA** | NA | NA | Sebring, FL** | NA | | | |

Source: CQ Press using reported data from the F.B.I. "Crime in the United States 2013"
*Includes murder, rape, robbery, and aggravated assault. The FBI changed the definition of rape beginning with 2013 data. Not all cities have made the change so the metro area figures reported here include rape figures based on differing definitions of rape. See note on page vii.
**Not available.

# 8. Percent Change in Violent Crime Rate: 2009 to 2013 (continued)
## National Percent Change = 14.8% Decrease*

| RANK | METROPOLITAN AREA | % CHANGE | RANK | METROPOLITAN AREA | % CHANGE | RANK | METROPOLITAN AREA | % CHANGE |
|---|---|---|---|---|---|---|---|---|
| 1 | Bismarck, ND | 92.4 | 65 | San Francisco (greater), CA | (0.8) | 129 | Atlanta, GA | (11.5) |
| 2 | Medford, OR | 80.4 | 65 | Vineland-Bridgeton, NJ | (0.8) | 129 | Wichita, KS | (11.5) |
| 3 | Columbus, IN | 71.1 | 67 | Birmingham-Hoover, AL | (0.9) | 131 | Merced, CA | (11.6) |
| 4 | Longview, WA | 67.1 | 67 | Salem, OR | (0.9) | 132 | Williamsport, PA | (11.7) |
| 5 | Gadsden, AL | 64.5 | 69 | Cedar Rapids, IA | (1.0) | 133 | Fayetteville, NC | (11.9) |
| 6 | San Luis Obispo, CA | 48.3 | 70 | Erie, PA | (1.2) | 134 | St. Joseph, MO-KS | (12.1) |
| 7 | Madera, CA | 46.6 | 71 | Tucson, AZ | (1.3) | 135 | Macon, GA | (12.2) |
| 8 | Rockingham County, NH M.D. | 43.4 | 72 | Omaha-Council Bluffs, NE-IA | (1.7) | 136 | Baltimore, MD | (12.3) |
| 9 | Sioux Falls, SD | 37.7 | 72 | Springfield, MA | (1.7) | 137 | Blacksburg, VA | (12.4) |
| 10 | Kokomo, IN | 30.8 | 74 | Modesto, CA | (1.8) | 138 | Santa Rosa, CA | (12.5) |
| 11 | Jackson, TN | 29.3 | 75 | Hagerstown-Martinsburg, MD-WV | (2.0) | 138 | Sebastian-Vero Beach, FL | (12.5) |
| 12 | Manchester-Nashua, NH | 27.0 | 76 | San Antonio, TX | (2.1) | 140 | College Station-Bryan, TX | (12.6) |
| 13 | Cape Girardeau, MO-IL | 26.5 | 77 | Mansfield, OH | (2.2) | 140 | Kansas City, MO-KS | (12.6) |
| 14 | Springfield, MO | 25.9 | 78 | Des Moines-West Des Moines, IA | (2.7) | 142 | Boulder, CO | (12.7) |
| 15 | Monroe, MI | 23.5 | 79 | Spokane, WA | (2.8) | 143 | Sioux City, IA-NE-SD | (13.0) |
| 16 | Fond du Lac, WI | 20.7 | 80 | Casper, WY | (3.0) | 144 | Boston, MA M.D. | (13.1) |
| 17 | Odessa, TX | 20.3 | 81 | Rochester, NY | (3.1) | 145 | Detroit (greater), MI | (13.3) |
| 18 | Huntsville, AL | 19.2 | 82 | Jackson, MS | (3.4) | 145 | Gainesville, GA | (13.3) |
| 19 | Milwaukee, WI | 18.8 | 82 | Reading, PA | (3.4) | 145 | Stockton-Lodi, CA | (13.3) |
| 20 | Alexandria, LA | 18.4 | 84 | Bakersfield, CA | (4.0) | 148 | Memphis, TN-MS-AR | (13.4) |
| 20 | Florence-Muscle Shoals, AL | 18.4 | 85 | Oakland-Hayward, CA M.D. | (4.2) | 148 | San Jose, CA | (13.4) |
| 22 | Rapid City, SD | 17.8 | 85 | Worcester, MA-CT | (4.2) | 150 | New Orleans, LA | (13.5) |
| 23 | Pocatello, ID | 16.1 | 87 | Boise City, ID | (4.3) | 151 | Chattanooga, TN-GA | (13.6) |
| 24 | San Francisco-Redwood, CA M.D. | 15.9 | 88 | Johnson City, TN | (4.4) | 151 | Goldsboro, NC | (13.6) |
| 25 | Billings, MT | 15.1 | 89 | Jackson, MI | (4.5) | 151 | Philadelphia (greater) PA-NJ-MD-DE | (13.6) |
| 26 | Lewiston, ID-WA | 14.3 | 90 | Corvallis, OR | (4.6) | 151 | Rome, GA | (13.6) |
| 27 | Albuquerque, NM | 13.8 | 91 | Lewiston-Auburn, ME | (4.8) | 151 | Syracuse, NY | (13.6) |
| 28 | Albany, GA | 13.1 | 92 | Toledo, OH | (4.9) | 151 | Yuba City, CA | (13.6) |
| 29 | Niles-Benton Harbor, MI | 12.6 | 92 | York-Hanover, PA | (4.9) | 157 | Albany-Schenectady-Troy, NY | (14.0) |
| 30 | Pueblo, CO | 11.9 | 94 | Ann Arbor, MI | (5.1) | 158 | Panama City, FL | (14.3) |
| 31 | Muskegon, MI | 11.7 | 95 | Denver-Aurora, CO | (5.3) | 159 | Little Rock, AR | (14.4) |
| 32 | Mount Vernon-Anacortes, WA | 11.3 | 96 | Bloomington, IN | (5.8) | 159 | New Haven-Milford, CT | (14.4) |
| 33 | Binghamton, NY | 9.9 | 97 | Sherman-Denison, TX | (6.1) | 161 | Wichita Falls, TX | (15.1) |
| 34 | Bangor, ME | 9.5 | 98 | Bay City, MI | (6.2) | 162 | Burlington, NC | (15.2) |
| 34 | St. George, UT | 9.5 | 99 | Barnstable Town, MA | (6.3) | 162 | Tacoma, WA M.D. | (15.2) |
| 36 | Fayetteville-Springdale, AR-MO | 9.4 | 100 | Flint, MI | (6.5) | 164 | Seattle-Bellevue-Everett, WA M.D. | (15.7) |
| 37 | Green Bay, WI | 8.8 | 101 | Ocean City, NJ | (6.6) | 165 | Seattle (greater), WA | (15.8) |
| 38 | Portland, ME | 8.6 | 101 | Portland-Vancouver, OR-WA | (6.6) | 166 | Clarksville, TN-KY | (16.0) |
| 39 | Fort Wayne, IN | 8.1 | 103 | Vallejo-Fairfield, CA | (6.8) | 166 | Fort Worth-Arlington, TX M.D. | (16.0) |
| 40 | Greeley, CO | 7.8 | 104 | Anchorage, AK | (7.0) | 168 | Topeka, KS | (16.2) |
| 41 | Appleton, WI | 7.5 | 104 | Lake Havasu City-Kingman, AZ | (7.0) | 169 | Buffalo-Niagara Falls, NY | (16.4) |
| 42 | Missoula, MT | 6.5 | 106 | Jonesboro, AR | (7.1) | 169 | Las Vegas-Henderson, NV | (16.4) |
| 43 | Lebanon, PA | 5.5 | 107 | Coeur d'Alene, ID | (7.3) | 171 | Harrisonburg, VA | (16.5) |
| 44 | Bend, OR | 4.9 | 107 | Janesville, WI | (7.3) | 171 | Kingsport, TN-VA | (16.5) |
| 45 | Grand Junction, CO | 3.8 | 109 | Fort Smith, AR-OK | (7.4) | 173 | Cincinnati, OH-KY-IN | (16.6) |
| 46 | Lafayette, IN | 3.6 | 110 | Glens Falls, NY | (7.5) | 174 | Akron, OH | (16.8) |
| 47 | Eau Claire, WI | 3.1 | 111 | Elmira, NY | (7.9) | 174 | Richmond, VA | (16.8) |
| 48 | Cheyenne, WY | 2.8 | 112 | Provo-Orem, UT | (8.0) | 174 | South Bend-Mishawaka, IN-MI | (16.8) |
| 48 | Yuma, AZ | 2.8 | 113 | Detroit-Dearborn-Livonia, MI M.D. | (8.1) | 174 | Tulsa, OK | (16.8) |
| 50 | Salt Lake City, UT | 2.5 | 114 | Visalia-Porterville, CA | (8.6) | 178 | Washington, DC-VA-MD-WV M.D. | (17.2) |
| 51 | Winchester, VA-WV | 2.4 | 115 | Norwich-New London, CT | (8.9) | 179 | Columbia, MO | (17.3) |
| 52 | Sheboygan, WI | 2.3 | 116 | Morristown, TN | (9.0) | 180 | Atlantic City, NJ | (17.4) |
| 53 | New York (greater), NY-NJ-PA | 2.2 | 116 | Redding, CA | (9.0) | 181 | Washington (greater) DC-VA-MD-WV | (17.7) |
| 54 | Napa, CA | 1.6 | 118 | Fairbanks, AK | (9.3) | 182 | Miami-Dade County, FL M.D. | (17.8) |
| 55 | Sumter, SC | 1.1 | 119 | Nashville-Davidson, TN | (9.6) | 182 | San Diego, CA | (17.8) |
| 56 | Iowa City, IA | 0.9 | 120 | Providence-Warwick, RI-MA | (9.7) | 184 | Dalton, GA | (17.9) |
| 57 | Beaumont-Port Arthur, TX | 0.3 | 121 | Camden, NJ M.D. | (9.9) | 184 | Lincoln, NE | (17.9) |
| 58 | Ogden-Clearfield, UT | 0.2 | 121 | Jefferson City, MO | (9.9) | 186 | Warren-Troy, MI M.D. | (18.1) |
| 59 | Fresno, CA | (0.2) | 123 | Hartford, CT | (10.2) | 187 | Sacramento, CA | (18.2) |
| 60 | Owensboro, KY | (0.3) | 123 | Trenton, NJ | (10.2) | 188 | Colorado Springs, CO | (18.3) |
| 61 | Phoenix-Mesa-Scottsdale, AZ | (0.4) | 125 | Newark, NJ-PA M.D. | (10.8) | 189 | Dayton, OH | (18.5) |
| 61 | Springfield, OH | (0.4) | 126 | Victoria, TX | (11.0) | 190 | Port St. Lucie, FL | (18.7) |
| 63 | Flagstaff, AZ | (0.5) | 127 | Charlottesville, VA | (11.3) | 191 | Kennewick-Richland, WA | (18.8) |
| 64 | Lansing-East Lansing, MI | (0.7) | 128 | Boston (greater), MA-NH | (11.4) | 191 | Lake Charles, LA | (18.8) |

Note: All listings are for Metropolitan Statistical Areas (M.S.A.s) except for those ending with "M.D." Listings with "M.D." are Metropolitan Divisions which are smaller parts of eleven large M.S.A.s. See explanatory note at beginning of metropolitan area section.

| RANK | METROPOLITAN AREA | % CHANGE | RANK | METROPOLITAN AREA | % CHANGE | RANK | METROPOLITAN AREA | % CHANGE |
|---|---|---|---|---|---|---|---|---|
| 193 | Las Cruces, NM | (18.9) | 254 | Lima, OH | (27.9) | NA | East Stroudsburg, PA** | NA |
| 194 | Dallas (greater), TX | (19.0) | 256 | Brownsville-Harlingen, TX | (28.1) | NA | El Centro, CA** | NA |
| 194 | Utica-Rome, NY | (19.0) | 256 | Greensboro-High Point, NC | (28.1) | NA | Elgin, IL M.D.** | NA |
| 196 | Mobile, AL | (19.2) | 256 | Logan, UT-ID | (28.1) | NA | Elizabethtown-Fort Knox, KY** | NA |
| 196 | Saginaw, MI | (19.2) | 259 | Abilene, TX | (28.2) | NA | Fargo, ND-MN** | NA |
| 198 | Riverside-San Bernardino, CA | (19.5) | 260 | Jacksonville, FL | (28.7) | NA | Gary, IN M.D.** | NA |
| 199 | Rocky Mount, NC | (19.6) | 261 | Deltona-Daytona Beach, FL | (28.9) | NA | Gettysburg, PA** | NA |
| 200 | Tuscaloosa, AL | (19.7) | 261 | West Palm Beach, FL M.D. | (28.9) | NA | Grand Forks, ND-MN** | NA |
| 201 | Fort Lauderdale, FL M.D. | (19.8) | 263 | Athens-Clarke County, GA | (29.0) | NA | Grand Island, NE** | NA |
| 202 | Salinas, CA | (19.9) | 263 | Naples-Marco Island, FL | (29.0) | NA | Grand Rapids-Wyoming, MI** | NA |
| 203 | Great Falls, MT | (20.0) | 265 | Lynchburg, VA | (29.1) | NA | Grants Pass, OR** | NA |
| 204 | Corpus Christi, TX | (20.3) | 266 | McAllen-Edinburg-Mission, TX | (29.5) | NA | Greenville-Anderson, SC** | NA |
| 205 | Roanoke, VA | (20.4) | 267 | Lawton, OK | (30.1) | NA | Greenville, NC** | NA |
| 206 | Dallas-Plano-Irving, TX M.D. | (20.7) | 268 | San Angelo, TX | (30.2) | NA | Gulfport-Biloxi-Pascagoula, MS** | NA |
| 206 | Miami (greater), FL | (20.7) | 269 | Pittsfield, MA | (30.4) | NA | Hammond, LA** | NA |
| 208 | Columbus, GA-AL | (20.8) | 269 | Santa Maria-Santa Barbara, CA | (30.4) | NA | Hanford-Corcoran, CA** | NA |
| 209 | Houston, TX | (20.9) | 271 | Augusta, GA-SC | (30.5) | NA | Hilton Head Island, SC** | NA |
| 209 | Morgantown, WV | (20.9) | 272 | Gainesville, FL | (31.5) | NA | Homosassa Springs, FL** | NA |
| 209 | Orlando, FL | (20.9) | 273 | Chico, CA | (32.2) | NA | Indianapolis, IN** | NA |
| 212 | Cape Coral-Fort Myers, FL | (21.1) | 273 | Houma, LA | (32.2) | NA | Johnstown, PA** | NA |
| 212 | El Paso, TX | (21.1) | 275 | Cleveland, TN | (32.4) | NA | Joplin, MO** | NA |
| 214 | Lakeland, FL | (21.2) | 275 | Oshkosh-Neenah, WI | (32.4) | NA | Kahului-Wailuku-Lahaina, HI** | NA |
| 214 | Raleigh, NC | (21.2) | 277 | Tampa-St Petersburg, FL | (32.7) | NA | Kankakee, IL** | NA |
| 216 | Anaheim-Santa Ana-Irvine, CA M.D. | (21.3) | 278 | Kingston, NY | (33.9) | NA | La Crosse, WI-MN** | NA |
| 216 | Lawrence, KS | (21.3) | 279 | Farmington, NM | (34.0) | NA | Lafayette, LA** | NA |
| 216 | Midland, TX | (21.3) | 280 | Tyler, TX | (35.2) | NA | Lake Co.-Kenosha Co., IL-WI M.D.** | NA |
| 219 | Palm Bay-Melbourne, FL | (21.8) | 281 | Eugene, OR | (36.1) | NA | Lancaster, PA** | NA |
| 220 | Pensacola, FL | (22.0) | 282 | Cumberland, MD-WV | (36.6) | NA | Louisville, KY-IN** | NA |
| 221 | Amarillo, TX | (22.3) | 283 | Waco, TX | (36.8) | NA | Madison, WI** | NA |
| 221 | Lubbock, TX | (22.3) | 284 | Bremerton-Silverdale, WA | (37.7) | NA | Mankato-North Mankato, MN** | NA |
| 223 | Santa Cruz-Watsonville, CA | (22.5) | 285 | Racine, WI | (38.3) | NA | Minneapolis-St. Paul, MN-WI** | NA |
| 224 | Bridgeport-Stamford, CT | (23.1) | 286 | Florence, SC | (38.5) | NA | Monroe, LA** | NA |
| 224 | Nassau-Suffolk, NY M.D. | (23.1) | 287 | Wausau, WI | (40.5) | NA | Montgomery County, PA M.D.** | NA |
| 224 | Prescott, AZ | (23.1) | 288 | Hinesville, GA | (40.8) | NA | Myrtle Beach, SC-NC** | NA |
| 227 | Oxnard-Thousand Oaks, CA | (23.3) | 289 | Ames, IA | (41.6) | NA | New Bern, NC** | NA |
| 228 | Silver Spring-Frederick, MD M.D. | (23.4) | 290 | Charleston-North Charleston, SC | (41.7) | NA | New York-Jersey City, NY-NJ M.D.** | NA |
| 229 | Altoona, PA | (23.5) | 290 | Lexington-Fayette, KY | (41.7) | NA | Oklahoma City, OK** | NA |
| 230 | Austin-Round Rock, TX | (23.8) | 292 | Manhattan, KS | (44.2) | NA | Olympia, WA** | NA |
| 231 | Allentown, PA-NJ | (23.9) | 293 | Idaho Falls, ID | (46.1) | NA | Parkersburg-Vienna, WV** | NA |
| 231 | Wilmington, DE-MD-NJ M.D. | (23.9) | 294 | Dubuque, IA | (58.7) | NA | Peoria, IL** | NA |
| 233 | Columbia, SC | (24.0) | NA | Albany, OR** | NA | NA | Philadelphia, PA M.D.** | NA |
| 234 | Tallahassee, FL | (24.1) | NA | Bloomington, IL** | NA | NA | Pittsburgh, PA** | NA |
| 235 | Spartanburg, SC | (24.2) | NA | Bloomsburg-Berwick, PA** | NA | NA | Rochester, MN** | NA |
| 236 | Fort Collins, CO | (24.5) | NA | Bowling Green, KY** | NA | NA | Rockford, IL** | NA |
| 236 | Ocala, FL | (24.5) | NA | Brunswick, GA** | NA | NA | Salisbury, MD-DE** | NA |
| 238 | Punta Gorda, FL | (24.6) | NA | California-Lexington Park, MD** | NA | NA | San Rafael, CA M.D.** | NA |
| 239 | Laredo, TX | (25.1) | NA | Cambridge-Newton, MA M.D.** | NA | NA | Scranton--Wilkes-Barre, PA** | NA |
| 240 | Hot Springs, AR | (25.2) | NA | Canton, OH** | NA | NA | Sebring, FL** | NA |
| 241 | Texarkana, TX-AR | (25.9) | NA | Carbondale-Marion, IL** | NA | NA | Shreveport-Bossier City, LA** | NA |
| 242 | State College, PA | (26.0) | NA | Chambersburg-Waynesboro, PA** | NA | NA | Springfield, IL** | NA |
| 243 | Longview, TX | (26.1) | NA | Champaign-Urbana, IL** | NA | NA | Staunton-Waynesboro, VA** | NA |
| 244 | Savannah, GA | (26.3) | NA | Charlotte-Mecklenburg, NC-SC** | NA | NA | St. Cloud, MN** | NA |
| 245 | Knoxville, TN | (26.4) | NA | Chicago (greater), IL-IN-WI** | NA | NA | St. Louis, MO-IL** | NA |
| 246 | Anniston-Oxford, AL | (26.7) | NA | Chicago-Naperville, IL M.D.** | NA | NA | Terre Haute, IN** | NA |
| 246 | Carson City, NV | (26.7) | NA | Crestview-Fort Walton Beach, FL** | NA | NA | The Villages, FL** | NA |
| 248 | Los Angeles (greater), CA | (26.8) | NA | Daphne-Fairhope-Foley, AL** | NA | NA | Virginia Beach-Norfolk, VA-NC** | NA |
| 249 | Baton Rouge, LA | (27.0) | NA | Davenport, IA-IL** | NA | NA | Warner Robins, GA** | NA |
| 249 | Reno, NV | (27.0) | NA | Decatur, AL** | NA | NA | Watertown-Fort Drum, NY** | NA |
| 251 | Los Angeles County, CA M.D. | (27.4) | NA | Decatur, IL** | NA | NA | Wilmington, NC** | NA |
| 252 | Muncie, IN | (27.6) | NA | Dothan, AL** | NA | NA | Winston-Salem, NC** | NA |
| 253 | North Port-Sarasota-Bradenton, FL | (27.8) | NA | Duluth, MN-WI** | NA | NA | Yakima, WA** | NA |
| 254 | Dover, DE | (27.9) | NA | Dutchess-Putnam, NY M.D.** | NA | | | |

Source: CQ Press using reported data from the F.B.I. "Crime in the United States 2013"

*Includes murder, rape, robbery, and aggravated assault. The FBI changed the definition of rape beginning with 2013 data. Not all cities have made the change so the metro area figures reported here include rape figures based on differing definitions of rape. See note on page vii.

**Not available.

# 9. Murders in 2013
## National Total = 14,196 Murders*

| RANK | METROPOLITAN AREA | MURDERS | RANK | METROPOLITAN AREA | MURDERS | RANK | METROPOLITAN AREA | MURDERS |
|---|---|---|---|---|---|---|---|---|
| 336 | Abilene, TX | 1 | 336 | Cheyenne, WY | 1 | 48 | Gary, IN M.D. | 82 |
| 89 | Akron, OH | 36 | 2 | Chicago (greater), IL-IN-WI | 608 | 361 | Gettysburg, PA | 0 |
| 117 | Albany-Schenectady-Troy, NY | 24 | 5 | Chicago-Naperville, IL M.D. | 496 | 336 | Glens Falls, NY | 1 |
| 189 | Albany, GA | 9 | 161 | Chico, CA | 13 | 202 | Goldsboro, NC | 8 |
| 336 | Albany, OR | 1 | 36 | Cincinnati, OH-KY-IN | 103 | 336 | Grand Forks, ND-MN | 1 |
| 68 | Albuquerque, NM | 53 | 152 | Clarksville, TN-KY | 14 | 336 | Grand Island, NE | 1 |
| 165 | Alexandria, LA | 12 | 336 | Cleveland, TN | 1 | 258 | Grand Junction, CO | 4 |
| 117 | Allentown, PA-NJ | 24 | 281 | Coeur d'Alene, ID | 3 | 117 | Grand Rapids-Wyoming, MI | 24 |
| 303 | Altoona, PA | 2 | 243 | College Station-Bryan, TX | 5 | 281 | Grants Pass, OR | 3 |
| 189 | Amarillo, TX | 9 | 81 | Colorado Springs, CO | 42 | 361 | Great Falls, MT | 0 |
| 361 | Ames, IA | 0 | 243 | Columbia, MO | 5 | 303 | Greeley, CO | 2 |
| 72 | Anaheim-Santa Ana-Irvine, CA M.D. | 51 | 88 | Columbia, SC | 37 | 303 | Green Bay, WI | 2 |
| 149 | Anchorage, AK | 15 | 104 | Columbus, GA-AL | 30 | 91 | Greensboro-High Point, NC | 35 |
| 176 | Ann Arbor, MI | 11 | 243 | Columbus, IN | 5 | 79 | Greenville-Anderson, SC | 46 |
| 202 | Anniston-Oxford, AL | 8 | 117 | Corpus Christi, TX | 24 | 176 | Greenville, NC | 11 |
| 336 | Appleton, WI | 1 | 361 | Corvallis, OR | 0 | 165 | Gulfport-Biloxi-Pascagoula, MS | 12 |
| 303 | Athens-Clarke County, GA | 2 | 214 | Crestview-Fort Walton Beach, FL | 7 | 202 | Hagerstown-Martinsburg, MD-WV | 8 |
| 12 | Atlanta, GA | 324 | 258 | Cumberland, MD-WV | 4 | 165 | Hammond, LA | 12 |
| 202 | Atlantic City, NJ | 8 | 13 | Dallas (greater), TX | 303 | 226 | Hanford-Corcoran, CA | 6 |
| 100 | Augusta, GA-SC | 32 | 21 | Dallas-Plano-Irving, TX M.D. | 213 | 336 | Harrisonburg, VA | 1 |
| 70 | Austin-Round Rock, TX | 52 | 303 | Dalton, GA | 2 | 91 | Hartford, CT | 35 |
| 59 | Bakersfield, CA | 61 | 336 | Daphne-Fairhope-Foley, AL | 1 | 226 | Hilton Head Island, SC | 6 |
| 14 | Baltimore, MD | 278 | 214 | Davenport, IA-IL | 7 | 243 | Hinesville, GA | 5 |
| 226 | Bangor, ME | 6 | 80 | Dayton, OH | 44 | 243 | Homosassa Springs, FL | 5 |
| 303 | Barnstable Town, MA | 2 | 214 | Decatur, AL | 7 | 189 | Hot Springs, AR | 9 |
| 46 | Baton Rouge, LA | 84 | 243 | Decatur, IL | 5 | 125 | Houma, LA | 23 |
| 303 | Bay City, MI | 2 | 113 | Deltona-Daytona Beach, FL | 26 | 10 | Houston, TX | 373 |
| 91 | Beaumont-Port Arthur, TX | 35 | 37 | Denver-Aurora, CO | 99 | 110 | Huntsville, AL | 27 |
| 281 | Bend, OR | 3 | 152 | Des Moines-West Des Moines, IA | 14 | 281 | Idaho Falls, ID | 3 |
| 258 | Billings, MT | 4 | 8 | Detroit (greater), MI | 411 | 28 | Indianapolis, IN | 148 |
| 202 | Binghamton, NY | 8 | 11 | Detroit-Dearborn-Livonia, MI M.D. | 364 | 361 | Iowa City, IA | 0 |
| 40 | Birmingham-Hoover, AL | 93 | 189 | Dothan, AL | 9 | 37 | Jacksonville, FL | 99 |
| 281 | Bismarck, ND | 3 | 258 | Dover, DE | 4 | 243 | Jackson, MI | 5 |
| 303 | Blacksburg, VA | 2 | 361 | Dubuque, IA | 0 | 63 | Jackson, MS | 58 |
| 258 | Bloomington, IL | 4 | 258 | Duluth, MN-WI | 4 | 176 | Jackson, TN | 11 |
| 281 | Bloomington, IN | 3 | 165 | Dutchess-Putnam, NY M.D. | 12 | 303 | Janesville, WI | 2 |
| 336 | Bloomsburg-Berwick, PA | 1 | 202 | East Stroudsburg, PA | 8 | 303 | Jefferson City, MO | 2 |
| 226 | Boise City, ID | 6 | 303 | Eau Claire, WI | 2 | 214 | Johnson City, TN | 7 |
| 45 | Boston (greater), MA-NH | 86 | 303 | El Centro, CA | 2 | 165 | Johnstown, PA | 12 |
| 57 | Boston, MA M.D. | 62 | 165 | El Paso, TX | 12 | 303 | Jonesboro, AR | 2 |
| 303 | Boulder, CO | 2 | 189 | Elgin, IL M.D. | 9 | 258 | Joplin, MO | 4 |
| 303 | Bowling Green, KY | 2 | 303 | Elizabethtown-Fort Knox, KY | 2 | 336 | Kahului-Wailuku-Lahaina, HI | 1 |
| 303 | Bremerton-Silverdale, WA | 2 | 361 | Elmira, NY | 0 | 226 | Kankakee, IL | 6 |
| 152 | Bridgeport-Stamford, CT | 14 | 258 | Erie, PA | 4 | 27 | Kansas City, MO-KS | 152 |
| 226 | Brownsville-Harlingen, TX | 6 | 258 | Eugene, OR | 4 | 189 | Kennewick-Richland, WA | 9 |
| 214 | Brunswick, GA | 7 | 361 | Fairbanks, AK | 0 | 243 | Kingsport, TN-VA | 5 |
| 60 | Buffalo-Niagara Falls, NY | 59 | 258 | Fargo, ND-MN | 4 | 281 | Kingston, NY | 3 |
| 281 | Burlington, NC | 3 | 226 | Farmington, NM | 6 | 102 | Knoxville, TN | 31 |
| 281 | California-Lexington Park, MD | 3 | 165 | Fayetteville-Springdale, AR-MO | 12 | 303 | Kokomo, IN | 2 |
| 133 | Cambridge-Newton, MA M.D. | 21 | 104 | Fayetteville, NC | 30 | 303 | La Crosse, WI-MN | 2 |
| 46 | Camden, NJ M.D. | 84 | 281 | Flagstaff, AZ | 3 | 281 | Lafayette, IN | 3 |
| 165 | Canton, OH | 12 | 64 | Flint, MI | 57 | 117 | Lafayette, LA | 24 |
| 115 | Cape Coral-Fort Myers, FL | 25 | 243 | Florence-Muscle Shoals, AL | 5 | 152 | Lake Charles, LA | 14 |
| 214 | Cape Girardeau, MO-IL | 7 | 176 | Florence, SC | 11 | 133 | Lake Co.-Kenosha Co., IL-WI M.D. | 21 |
| 281 | Carbondale-Marion, IL | 3 | 336 | Fond du Lac, WI | 1 | 189 | Lake Havasu City-Kingman, AZ | 9 |
| 258 | Carson City, NV | 4 | 303 | Fort Collins, CO | 2 | 135 | Lakeland, FL | 20 |
| 281 | Casper, WY | 3 | 49 | Fort Lauderdale, FL M.D. | 80 | 189 | Lancaster, PA | 9 |
| 258 | Cedar Rapids, IA | 4 | 226 | Fort Smith, AR-OK | 6 | 149 | Lansing-East Lansing, MI | 15 |
| 258 | Chambersburg-Waynesboro, PA | 4 | 96 | Fort Wayne, IN | 34 | 258 | Laredo, TX | 4 |
| 189 | Champaign-Urbana, IL | 9 | 42 | Fort Worth-Arlington, TX M.D. | 90 | 202 | Las Cruces, NM | 8 |
| 72 | Charleston-North Charleston, SC | 51 | 64 | Fresno, CA | 57 | 33 | Las Vegas-Henderson, NV | 116 |
| 31 | Charlotte-Mecklenburg, NC-SC | 122 | 202 | Gadsden, AL | 8 | 336 | Lawrence, KS | 1 |
| 258 | Charlottesville, VA | 4 | 185 | Gainesville, FL | 10 | 161 | Lawton, OK | 13 |
| 129 | Chattanooga, TN-GA | 22 | 214 | Gainesville, GA | 7 | 303 | Lebanon, PA | 2 |

Note: All listings are for Metropolitan Statistical Areas (M.S.A.s) except for those ending with "M.D." Listings with "M.D." are Metropolitan Divisions which are smaller parts of eleven large M.S.A.s. See explanatory note at beginning of metropolitan area section.

| RANK | METROPOLITAN AREA | MURDERS | RANK | METROPOLITAN AREA | MURDERS | RANK | METROPOLITAN AREA | MURDERS |
|---|---|---|---|---|---|---|---|---|
| 336 | Lewiston-Auburn, ME | 1 | 75 | Omaha-Council Bluffs, NE-IA | 47 | 336 | Sheboygan, WI | 1 |
| 361 | Lewiston, ID-WA | 0 | 43 | Orlando, FL | 89 | 214 | Sherman-Denison, TX | 7 |
| 117 | Lexington-Fayette, KY | 24 | 361 | Oshkosh-Neenah, WI | 0 | 91 | Shreveport-Bossier City, LA | 35 |
| 281 | Lima, OH | 3 | 361 | Owensboro, KY | 0 | 152 | Silver Spring-Frederick, MD M.D. | 14 |
| 243 | Lincoln, NE | 5 | 96 | Oxnard-Thousand Oaks, CA | 34 | 258 | Sioux City, IA-NE-SD | 4 |
| 67 | Little Rock, AR | 56 | 135 | Palm Bay-Melbourne, FL | 20 | 281 | Sioux Falls, SD | 3 |
| 336 | Logan, UT-ID | 1 | 202 | Panama City, FL | 8 | 176 | South Bend-Mishawaka, IN-MI | 11 |
| 165 | Longview, TX | 12 | 361 | Parkersburg-Vienna, WV | 0 | 189 | Spartanburg, SC | 9 |
| 336 | Longview, WA | 1 | 107 | Pensacola, FL | 29 | 135 | Spokane, WA | 20 |
| 4 | Los Angeles County, CA M.D. | 543 | 129 | Peoria, IL | 22 | 91 | Springfield, IL | 35 |
| 3 | Los Angeles (greater), CA | 594 | 7 | Philadelphia (greater) PA-NJ-MD-DE | 426 | 108 | Springfield, MA | 28 |
| 57 | Louisville, KY-IN | 62 | 14 | Philadelphia, PA M.D. | 278 | 152 | Springfield, MO | 14 |
| 189 | Lubbock, TX | 9 | 22 | Phoenix-Mesa-Scottsdale, AZ | 212 | 226 | Springfield, OH | 6 |
| 243 | Lynchburg, VA | 5 | 39 | Pittsburgh, PA | 97 | 361 | State College, PA | 0 |
| 125 | Macon, GA | 23 | 336 | Pittsfield, MA | 1 | 303 | Staunton-Waynesboro, VA | 2 |
| 161 | Madera, CA | 13 | 336 | Pocatello, ID | 1 | 75 | Stockton-Lodi, CA | 47 |
| 176 | Madison, WI | 11 | 149 | Port St. Lucie, FL | 15 | 303 | St. Cloud, MN | 2 |
| 185 | Manchester-Nashua, NH | 10 | 100 | Portland-Vancouver, OR-WA | 32 | 303 | St. George, UT | 2 |
| 226 | Manhattan, KS | 6 | 226 | Portland, ME | 6 | 303 | St. Joseph, MO-KS | 2 |
| 303 | Mankato-North Mankato, MN | 2 | 281 | Prescott, AZ | 3 | 24 | St. Louis, MO-IL | 203 |
| 336 | Mansfield, OH | 1 | 83 | Providence-Warwick, RI-MA | 40 | 214 | Sumter, SC | 7 |
| 129 | McAllen-Edinburg-Mission, TX | 22 | 226 | Provo-Orem, UT | 6 | 108 | Syracuse, NY | 28 |
| 258 | Medford, OR | 4 | 243 | Pueblo, CO | 5 | 115 | Tacoma, WA M.D. | 25 |
| 29 | Memphis, TN-MS-AR | 139 | 336 | Punta Gorda, FL | 1 | 141 | Tallahassee, FL | 17 |
| 110 | Merced, CA | 27 | 303 | Racine, WI | 2 | 30 | Tampa-St Petersburg, FL | 123 |
| 9 | Miami (greater), FL | 383 | 98 | Raleigh, NC | 33 | 226 | Terre Haute, IN | 6 |
| 17 | Miami-Dade County, FL M.D. | 229 | 303 | Rapid City, SD | 2 | 226 | Texarkana, TX-AR | 6 |
| 226 | Midland, TX | 6 | 176 | Reading, PA | 11 | 303 | The Villages, FL | 2 |
| 34 | Milwaukee, WI | 110 | 185 | Redding, CA | 10 | 104 | Toledo, OH | 30 |
| 44 | Minneapolis-St. Paul, MN-WI | 87 | 125 | Reno, NV | 23 | 161 | Topeka, KS | 13 |
| 336 | Missoula, MT | 1 | 52 | Richmond, VA | 77 | 83 | Trenton, NJ | 40 |
| 83 | Mobile, AL | 40 | 19 | Riverside-San Bernardino, CA | 219 | 54 | Tucson, AZ | 71 |
| 98 | Modesto, CA | 33 | 361 | Rochester, MN | 0 | 56 | Tulsa, OK | 64 |
| 141 | Monroe, LA | 17 | 70 | Rochester, NY | 52 | 145 | Tuscaloosa, AL | 16 |
| 243 | Monroe, MI | 5 | 113 | Rockford, IL | 26 | 202 | Tyler, TX | 8 |
| 117 | Montgomery County, PA M.D. | 24 | 281 | Rockingham County, NH M.D. | 3 | 141 | Utica-Rome, NY | 17 |
| 336 | Morgantown, WV | 1 | 145 | Rocky Mount, NC | 16 | 102 | Vallejo-Fairfield, CA | 31 |
| 303 | Morristown, TN | 2 | 258 | Rome, GA | 4 | 281 | Victoria, TX | 3 |
| 258 | Mount Vernon-Anacortes, WA | 4 | 41 | Sacramento, CA | 91 | 258 | Vineland-Bridgeton, NJ | 4 |
| 361 | Muncie, IN | 0 | 87 | Saginaw, MI | 38 | 32 | Virginia Beach-Norfolk, VA-NC | 118 |
| 185 | Muskegon, MI | 10 | 152 | Salem, OR | 14 | 81 | Visalia-Porterville, CA | 42 |
| 152 | Myrtle Beach, SC-NC | 14 | 75 | Salinas, CA | 47 | 214 | Waco, TX | 7 |
| 303 | Napa, CA | 2 | 176 | Salisbury, MD-DE | 11 | 202 | Warner Robins, GA | 8 |
| 165 | Naples-Marco Island, FL | 12 | 135 | Salt Lake City, UT | 20 | 75 | Warren-Troy, MI M.D. | 47 |
| 60 | Nashville-Davidson, TN | 59 | 243 | San Angelo, TX | 5 | 18 | Washington (greater) DC-VA-MD-WV | 222 |
| 72 | Nassau-Suffolk, NY M.D. | 51 | 35 | San Antonio, TX | 105 | 23 | Washington, DC-VA-MD-WV M.D. | 208 |
| 336 | New Bern, NC | 1 | 54 | San Diego, CA | 71 | 361 | Watertown-Fort Drum, NY | 0 |
| 110 | New Haven-Milford, CT | 27 | 20 | San Francisco (greater), CA | 216 | 303 | Wausau, WI | 2 |
| 16 | New Orleans, LA | 235 | 60 | San Francisco-Redwood, CA M.D. | 59 | 53 | West Palm Beach, FL M.D. | 74 |
| 1 | New York (greater), NY-NJ-PA | 688 | 64 | San Jose, CA | 57 | 214 | Wichita Falls, TX | 7 |
| 6 | New York-Jersey City, NY-NJ M.D. | 448 | 243 | San Luis Obispo, CA | 5 | 129 | Wichita, KS | 22 |
| 25 | Newark, NJ-PA M.D. | 177 | 303 | San Rafael, CA M.D. | 2 | 226 | Williamsport, PA | 6 |
| 281 | Niles-Benton Harbor, MI | 3 | 176 | Santa Cruz-Watsonville, CA | 11 | 83 | Wilmington, DE-MD-NJ M.D. | 40 |
| 135 | North Port-Sarasota-Bradenton, FL | 20 | 226 | Santa Maria-Santa Barbara, CA | 6 | 189 | Wilmington, NC | 9 |
| 258 | Norwich-New London, CT | 4 | 189 | Santa Rosa, CA | 9 | 281 | Winchester, VA-WV | 3 |
| 26 | Oakland-Hayward, CA M.D. | 155 | 89 | Savannah, GA | 36 | 125 | Winston-Salem, NC | 23 |
| 141 | Ocala, FL | 17 | 117 | Scranton--Wilkes-Barre, PA | 24 | 152 | Worcester, MA-CT | 14 |
| 361 | Ocean City, NJ | 0 | 50 | Seattle (greater), WA | 78 | 145 | Yakima, WA | 16 |
| 281 | Odessa, TX | 3 | 68 | Seattle-Bellevue-Everett, WA M.D. | 53 | 140 | York-Hanover, PA | 19 |
| 202 | Ogden-Clearfield, UT | 8 | 258 | Sebastian-Vero Beach, FL | 4 | 214 | Yuba City, CA | 7 |
| 50 | Oklahoma City, OK | 78 | 258 | Sebring, FL | 4 | 165 | Yuma, AZ | 12 |
| 281 | Olympia, WA | 3 | | | | | | |

Source: Reported data from the F.B.I. "Crime in the United States 2013"
*Includes nonnegligent manslaughter.

# 9. Murders in 2013 (continued)
## National Total = 14,196 Murders*

| RANK | METROPOLITAN AREA | MURDERS | RANK | METROPOLITAN AREA | MURDERS | RANK | METROPOLITAN AREA | MURDERS |
|---|---|---|---|---|---|---|---|---|
| 1 | New York (greater), NY-NJ-PA | 688 | 64 | Fresno, CA | 57 | 129 | Chattanooga, TN-GA | 22 |
| 2 | Chicago (greater), IL-IN-WI | 608 | 64 | San Jose, CA | 57 | 129 | McAllen-Edinburg-Mission, TX | 22 |
| 3 | Los Angeles (greater), CA | 594 | 67 | Little Rock, AR | 56 | 129 | Peoria, IL | 22 |
| 4 | Los Angeles County, CA M.D. | 543 | 68 | Albuquerque, NM | 53 | 129 | Wichita, KS | 22 |
| 5 | Chicago-Naperville, IL M.D. | 496 | 68 | Seattle-Bellevue-Everett, WA M.D. | 53 | 133 | Cambridge-Newton, MA M.D. | 21 |
| 6 | New York-Jersey City, NY-NJ M.D. | 448 | 70 | Austin-Round Rock, TX | 52 | 133 | Lake Co.-Kenosha Co., IL-WI M.D. | 21 |
| 7 | Philadelphia (greater) PA-NJ-MD-DE | 426 | 70 | Rochester, NY | 52 | 135 | Lakeland, FL | 20 |
| 8 | Detroit (greater), MI | 411 | 72 | Anaheim-Santa Ana-Irvine, CA M.D. | 51 | 135 | North Port-Sarasota-Bradenton, FL | 20 |
| 9 | Miami (greater), FL | 383 | 72 | Charleston-North Charleston, SC | 51 | 135 | Palm Bay-Melbourne, FL | 20 |
| 10 | Houston, TX | 373 | 72 | Nassau-Suffolk, NY M.D. | 51 | 135 | Salt Lake City, UT | 20 |
| 11 | Detroit-Dearborn-Livonia, MI M.D. | 364 | 75 | Omaha-Council Bluffs, NE-IA | 47 | 135 | Spokane, WA | 20 |
| 12 | Atlanta, GA | 324 | 75 | Salinas, CA | 47 | 140 | York-Hanover, PA | 19 |
| 13 | Dallas (greater), TX | 303 | 75 | Stockton-Lodi, CA | 47 | 141 | Monroe, LA | 17 |
| 14 | Baltimore, MD | 278 | 75 | Warren-Troy, MI M.D. | 47 | 141 | Ocala, FL | 17 |
| 14 | Philadelphia, PA M.D. | 278 | 79 | Greenville-Anderson, SC | 46 | 141 | Tallahassee, FL | 17 |
| 16 | New Orleans, LA | 235 | 80 | Dayton, OH | 44 | 141 | Utica-Rome, NY | 17 |
| 17 | Miami-Dade County, FL M.D. | 229 | 81 | Colorado Springs, CO | 42 | 145 | Roanoke, VA | 16 |
| 18 | Washington (greater) DC-VA-MD-WV | 222 | 81 | Visalia-Porterville, CA | 42 | 145 | Rocky Mount, NC | 16 |
| 19 | Riverside-San Bernardino, CA | 219 | 83 | Mobile, AL | 40 | 145 | Tuscaloosa, AL | 16 |
| 20 | San Francisco (greater), CA | 216 | 83 | Providence-Warwick, RI-MA | 40 | 145 | Yakima, WA | 16 |
| 21 | Dallas-Plano-Irving, TX M.D. | 213 | 83 | Trenton, NJ | 40 | 149 | Anchorage, AK | 15 |
| 22 | Phoenix-Mesa-Scottsdale, AZ | 212 | 83 | Wilmington, DE-MD-NJ M.D. | 40 | 149 | Lansing-East Lansing, MI | 15 |
| 23 | Washington, DC-VA-MD-WV M.D. | 208 | 87 | Saginaw, MI | 38 | 149 | Port St. Lucie, FL | 15 |
| 24 | St. Louis, MO-IL | 203 | 88 | Columbia, SC | 37 | 152 | Bridgeport-Stamford, CT | 14 |
| 25 | Newark, NJ-PA M.D. | 177 | 89 | Akron, OH | 36 | 152 | Clarksville, TN-KY | 14 |
| 26 | Oakland-Hayward, CA M.D. | 155 | 89 | Savannah, GA | 36 | 152 | Des Moines-West Des Moines, IA | 14 |
| 27 | Kansas City, MO-KS | 152 | 91 | Beaumont-Port Arthur, TX | 35 | 152 | Lake Charles, LA | 14 |
| 28 | Indianapolis, IN | 148 | 91 | Greensboro-High Point, NC | 35 | 152 | Myrtle Beach, SC-NC | 14 |
| 29 | Memphis, TN-MS-AR | 139 | 91 | Hartford, CT | 35 | 152 | Salem, OR | 14 |
| 30 | Tampa-St Petersburg, FL | 123 | 91 | Shreveport-Bossier City, LA | 35 | 152 | Silver Spring-Frederick, MD M.D. | 14 |
| 31 | Charlotte-Mecklenburg, NC-SC | 122 | 91 | Springfield, IL | 35 | 152 | Springfield, MO | 14 |
| 32 | Virginia Beach-Norfolk, VA-NC | 118 | 96 | Fort Wayne, IN | 34 | 152 | Worcester, MA-CT | 14 |
| 33 | Las Vegas-Henderson, NV | 116 | 96 | Oxnard-Thousand Oaks, CA | 34 | 161 | Chico, CA | 13 |
| 34 | Milwaukee, WI | 110 | 98 | Modesto, CA | 33 | 161 | Lawton, OK | 13 |
| 35 | San Antonio, TX | 105 | 98 | Raleigh, NC | 33 | 161 | Madera, CA | 13 |
| 36 | Cincinnati, OH-KY-IN | 103 | 100 | Augusta, GA-SC | 32 | 161 | Topeka, KS | 13 |
| 37 | Denver-Aurora, CO | 99 | 100 | Portland-Vancouver, OR-WA | 32 | 165 | Alexandria, LA | 12 |
| 37 | Jacksonville, FL | 99 | 102 | Knoxville, TN | 31 | 165 | Canton, OH | 12 |
| 39 | Pittsburgh, PA | 97 | 102 | Vallejo-Fairfield, CA | 31 | 165 | Dutchess-Putnam, NY M.D. | 12 |
| 40 | Birmingham-Hoover, AL | 93 | 104 | Columbus, GA-AL | 30 | 165 | El Paso, TX | 12 |
| 41 | Sacramento, CA | 91 | 104 | Fayetteville, NC | 30 | 165 | Fayetteville-Springdale, AR-MO | 12 |
| 42 | Fort Worth-Arlington, TX M.D. | 90 | 104 | Toledo, OH | 30 | 165 | Gulfport-Biloxi-Pascagoula, MS | 12 |
| 43 | Orlando, FL | 89 | 107 | Pensacola, FL | 29 | 165 | Hammond, LA | 12 |
| 44 | Minneapolis-St. Paul, MN-WI | 87 | 108 | Springfield, MA | 28 | 165 | Johnstown, PA | 12 |
| 45 | Boston (greater), MA-NH | 86 | 108 | Syracuse, NY | 28 | 165 | Longview, TX | 12 |
| 46 | Baton Rouge, LA | 84 | 110 | Huntsville, AL | 27 | 165 | Naples-Marco Island, FL | 12 |
| 46 | Camden, NJ M.D. | 84 | 110 | Merced, CA | 27 | 165 | Yuma, AZ | 12 |
| 48 | Gary, IN M.D. | 82 | 110 | New Haven-Milford, CT | 27 | 176 | Ann Arbor, MI | 11 |
| 49 | Fort Lauderdale, FL M.D. | 80 | 113 | Deltona-Daytona Beach, FL | 26 | 176 | Florence, SC | 11 |
| 50 | Oklahoma City, OK | 78 | 113 | Rockford, IL | 26 | 176 | Greenville, NC | 11 |
| 50 | Seattle (greater), WA | 78 | 115 | Cape Coral-Fort Myers, FL | 25 | 176 | Jackson, TN | 11 |
| 52 | Richmond, VA | 77 | 115 | Tacoma, WA M.D. | 25 | 176 | Madison, WI | 11 |
| 53 | West Palm Beach, FL M.D. | 74 | 117 | Albany-Schenectady-Troy, NY | 24 | 176 | Reading, PA | 11 |
| 54 | San Diego, CA | 71 | 117 | Allentown, PA-NJ | 24 | 176 | Salisbury, MD-DE | 11 |
| 54 | Tucson, AZ | 71 | 117 | Corpus Christi, TX | 24 | 176 | Santa Cruz-Watsonville, CA | 11 |
| 56 | Tulsa, OK | 64 | 117 | Grand Rapids-Wyoming, MI | 24 | 176 | South Bend-Mishawaka, IN-MI | 11 |
| 57 | Boston, MA M.D. | 62 | 117 | Lafayette, LA | 24 | 185 | Gainesville, FL | 10 |
| 57 | Louisville, KY-IN | 62 | 117 | Lexington-Fayette, KY | 24 | 185 | Manchester-Nashua, NH | 10 |
| 59 | Bakersfield, CA | 61 | 117 | Montgomery County, PA M.D. | 24 | 185 | Muskegon, MI | 10 |
| 60 | Buffalo-Niagara Falls, NY | 59 | 117 | Scranton--Wilkes-Barre, PA | 24 | 185 | Redding, CA | 10 |
| 60 | Nashville-Davidson, TN | 59 | 125 | Houma, LA | 23 | 189 | Albany, GA | 9 |
| 60 | San Francisco-Redwood, CA M.D. | 59 | 125 | Macon, GA | 23 | 189 | Amarillo, TX | 9 |
| 63 | Jackson, MS | 58 | 125 | Reno, NV | 23 | 189 | Champaign-Urbana, IL | 9 |
| 64 | Flint, MI | 57 | 125 | Winston-Salem, NC | 23 | 189 | Dothan, AL | 9 |

Note: All listings are for Metropolitan Statistical Areas (M.S.A.s) except for those ending with "M.D." Listings with "M.D." are Metropolitan Divisions which are smaller parts of eleven large M.S.A.s. See explanatory note at beginning of metropolitan area section.

| RANK | METROPOLITAN AREA | MURDERS | RANK | METROPOLITAN AREA | MURDERS | RANK | METROPOLITAN AREA | MURDERS |
|---|---|---|---|---|---|---|---|---|
| 189 | Elgin, IL M.D. | 9 | 243 | Pueblo, CO | 5 | 303 | Green Bay, WI | 2 |
| 189 | Hot Springs, AR | 9 | 243 | San Angelo, TX | 5 | 303 | Janesville, WI | 2 |
| 189 | Kennewick-Richland, WA | 9 | 243 | San Luis Obispo, CA | 5 | 303 | Jefferson City, MO | 2 |
| 189 | Lake Havasu City-Kingman, AZ | 9 | 258 | Billings, MT | 4 | 303 | Jonesboro, AR | 2 |
| 189 | Lancaster, PA | 9 | 258 | Bloomington, IL | 4 | 303 | Kokomo, IN | 2 |
| 189 | Lubbock, TX | 9 | 258 | Carson City, NV | 4 | 303 | La Crosse, WI-MN | 2 |
| 189 | Santa Rosa, CA | 9 | 258 | Cedar Rapids, IA | 4 | 303 | Lebanon, PA | 2 |
| 189 | Spartanburg, SC | 9 | 258 | Chambersburg-Waynesboro, PA | 4 | 303 | Mankato-North Mankato, MN | 2 |
| 189 | Wilmington, NC | 9 | 258 | Charlottesville, VA | 4 | 303 | Morristown, TN | 2 |
| 202 | Anniston-Oxford, AL | 8 | 258 | Cumberland, MD-WV | 4 | 303 | Napa, CA | 2 |
| 202 | Atlantic City, NJ | 8 | 258 | Dover, DE | 4 | 303 | Racine, WI | 2 |
| 202 | Binghamton, NY | 8 | 258 | Duluth, MN-WI | 4 | 303 | Rapid City, SD | 2 |
| 202 | East Stroudsburg, PA | 8 | 258 | Erie, PA | 4 | 303 | San Rafael, CA M.D. | 2 |
| 202 | Gadsden, AL | 8 | 258 | Eugene, OR | 4 | 303 | Staunton-Waynesboro, VA | 2 |
| 202 | Goldsboro, NC | 8 | 258 | Fargo, ND-MN | 4 | 303 | St. Cloud, MN | 2 |
| 202 | Hagerstown-Martinsburg, MD-WV | 8 | 258 | Grand Junction, CO | 4 | 303 | St. George, UT | 2 |
| 202 | Las Cruces, NM | 8 | 258 | Joplin, MO | 4 | 303 | St. Joseph, MO-KS | 2 |
| 202 | Ogden-Clearfield, UT | 8 | 258 | Laredo, TX | 4 | 303 | The Villages, FL | 2 |
| 202 | Panama City, FL | 8 | 258 | Medford, OR | 4 | 303 | Wausau, WI | 2 |
| 202 | Tyler, TX | 8 | 258 | Mount Vernon-Anacortes, WA | 4 | 336 | Abilene, TX | 1 |
| 202 | Warner Robins, GA | 8 | 258 | Norwich-New London, CT | 4 | 336 | Albany, OR | 1 |
| 214 | Brunswick, GA | 7 | 258 | Rome, GA | 4 | 336 | Appleton, WI | 1 |
| 214 | Cape Girardeau, MO-IL | 7 | 258 | Sebastian-Vero Beach, FL | 4 | 336 | Bloomsburg-Berwick, PA | 1 |
| 214 | Crestview-Fort Walton Beach, FL | 7 | 258 | Sebring, FL | 4 | 336 | Cheyenne, WY | 1 |
| 214 | Davenport, IA-IL | 7 | 258 | Sioux City, IA-NE-SD | 4 | 336 | Cleveland, TN | 1 |
| 214 | Decatur, AL | 7 | 258 | Vineland-Bridgeton, NJ | 4 | 336 | Daphne-Fairhope-Foley, AL | 1 |
| 214 | Gainesville, GA | 7 | 281 | Bend, OR | 3 | 336 | Fond du Lac, WI | 1 |
| 214 | Johnson City, TN | 7 | 281 | Bismarck, ND | 3 | 336 | Glens Falls, NY | 1 |
| 214 | Sherman-Denison, TX | 7 | 281 | Bloomington, IN | 3 | 336 | Grand Forks, ND-MN | 1 |
| 214 | Sumter, SC | 7 | 281 | Burlington, NC | 3 | 336 | Grand Island, NE | 1 |
| 214 | Waco, TX | 7 | 281 | California-Lexington Park, MD | 3 | 336 | Harrisonburg, VA | 1 |
| 214 | Wichita Falls, TX | 7 | 281 | Carbondale-Marion, IL | 3 | 336 | Kahului-Wailuku-Lahaina, HI | 1 |
| 214 | Yuba City, CA | 7 | 281 | Casper, WY | 3 | 336 | Lawrence, KS | 1 |
| 226 | Bangor, ME | 6 | 281 | Coeur d'Alene, ID | 3 | 336 | Lewiston-Auburn, ME | 1 |
| 226 | Boise City, ID | 6 | 281 | Flagstaff, AZ | 3 | 336 | Logan, UT-ID | 1 |
| 226 | Brownsville-Harlingen, TX | 6 | 281 | Grants Pass, OR | 3 | 336 | Longview, WA | 1 |
| 226 | Farmington, NM | 6 | 281 | Idaho Falls, ID | 3 | 336 | Mansfield, OH | 1 |
| 226 | Fort Smith, AR-OK | 6 | 281 | Kingston, NY | 3 | 336 | Missoula, MT | 1 |
| 226 | Hanford-Corcoran, CA | 6 | 281 | Lafayette, IN | 3 | 336 | Morgantown, WV | 1 |
| 226 | Hilton Head Island, SC | 6 | 281 | Lima, OH | 3 | 336 | New Bern, NC | 1 |
| 226 | Kankakee, IL | 6 | 281 | Niles-Benton Harbor, MI | 3 | 336 | Pittsfield, MA | 1 |
| 226 | Manhattan, KS | 6 | 281 | Odessa, TX | 3 | 336 | Pocatello, ID | 1 |
| 226 | Midland, TX | 6 | 281 | Olympia, WA | 3 | 336 | Punta Gorda, FL | 1 |
| 226 | Portland, ME | 6 | 281 | Prescott, AZ | 3 | 336 | Sheboygan, WI | 1 |
| 226 | Provo-Orem, UT | 6 | 281 | Rockingham County, NH M.D. | 3 | 361 | Ames, IA | 0 |
| 226 | Santa Maria-Santa Barbara, CA | 6 | 281 | Sioux Falls, SD | 3 | 361 | Corvallis, OR | 0 |
| 226 | Springfield, OH | 6 | 281 | Victoria, TX | 3 | 361 | Dubuque, IA | 0 |
| 226 | Terre Haute, IN | 6 | 281 | Winchester, VA-WV | 3 | 361 | Elmira, NY | 0 |
| 226 | Texarkana, TX-AR | 6 | 303 | Altoona, PA | 2 | 361 | Fairbanks, AK | 0 |
| 226 | Williamsport, PA | 6 | 303 | Athens-Clarke County, GA | 2 | 361 | Gettysburg, PA | 0 |
| 243 | College Station-Bryan, TX | 5 | 303 | Barnstable Town, MA | 2 | 361 | Great Falls, MT | 0 |
| 243 | Columbia, MO | 5 | 303 | Bay City, MI | 2 | 361 | Iowa City, IA | 0 |
| 243 | Columbus, IN | 5 | 303 | Blacksburg, VA | 2 | 361 | Lewiston, ID-WA | 0 |
| 243 | Decatur, IL | 5 | 303 | Boulder, CO | 2 | 361 | Muncie, IN | 0 |
| 243 | Florence-Muscle Shoals, AL | 5 | 303 | Bowling Green, KY | 2 | 361 | Ocean City, NJ | 0 |
| 243 | Hinesville, GA | 5 | 303 | Bremerton-Silverdale, WA | 2 | 361 | Oshkosh-Neenah, WI | 0 |
| 243 | Homosassa Springs, FL | 5 | 303 | Dalton, GA | 2 | 361 | Owensboro, KY | 0 |
| 243 | Jackson, MI | 5 | 303 | Eau Claire, WI | 2 | 361 | Parkersburg-Vienna, WV | 0 |
| 243 | Kingsport, TN-VA | 5 | 303 | El Centro, CA | 2 | 361 | Rochester, MN | 0 |
| 243 | Lincoln, NE | 5 | 303 | Elizabethtown-Fort Knox, KY | 2 | 361 | State College, PA | 0 |
| 243 | Lynchburg, VA | 5 | 303 | Fort Collins, CO | 2 | 361 | Watertown-Fort Drum, NY | 0 |
| 243 | Monroe, MI | 5 | 303 | Greeley, CO | 2 | | | |

Source: Reported data from the F.B.I. "Crime in the United States 2013"
*Includes nonnegligent manslaughter.

# 10. Murder Rate in 2013
## National Rate = 4.5 Murders per 100,000 Population*

| RANK | METROPOLITAN AREA | RATE | RANK | METROPOLITAN AREA | RATE | RANK | METROPOLITAN AREA | RATE |
|---|---|---|---|---|---|---|---|---|
| 353 | Abilene, TX | 0.6 | 326 | Cheyenne, WY | 1.0 | 7 | Gary, IN M.D. | 11.6 |
| 107 | Akron, OH | 5.1 | 62 | Chicago (greater), IL-IN-WI | 6.4 | 361 | Gettysburg, PA | 0.0 |
| 223 | Albany-Schenectady-Troy, NY | 2.7 | 55 | Chicago-Naperville, IL M.D. | 6.8 | 340 | Glens Falls, NY | 0.8 |
| 87 | Albany, GA | 5.7 | 84 | Chico, CA | 5.8 | 62 | Goldsboro, NC | 6.4 |
| 340 | Albany, OR | 0.8 | 117 | Cincinnati, OH-KY-IN | 4.8 | 326 | Grand Forks, ND-MN | 1.0 |
| 78 | Albuquerque, NM | 5.9 | 110 | Clarksville, TN-KY | 5.0 | 311 | Grand Island, NE | 1.2 |
| 35 | Alexandria, LA | 7.8 | 340 | Cleveland, TN | 0.8 | 223 | Grand Junction, CO | 2.7 |
| 214 | Allentown, PA-NJ | 2.9 | 253 | Coeur d'Alene, ID | 2.1 | 238 | Grand Rapids-Wyoming, MI | 2.4 |
| 282 | Altoona, PA | 1.6 | 253 | College Station-Bryan, TX | 2.1 | 173 | Grants Pass, OR | 3.6 |
| 178 | Amarillo, TX | 3.5 | 68 | Colorado Springs, CO | 6.2 | 361 | Great Falls, MT | 0.0 |
| 361 | Ames, IA | 0.0 | 214 | Columbia, MO | 2.9 | 350 | Greeley, CO | 0.7 |
| 282 | Anaheim-Santa Ana-Irvine, CA M.D. | 1.6 | 123 | Columbia, SC | 4.7 | 353 | Green Bay, WI | 0.6 |
| 117 | Anchorage, AK | 4.8 | 23 | Columbus, GA-AL | 9.5 | 123 | Greensboro-High Point, NC | 4.7 |
| 201 | Ann Arbor, MI | 3.1 | 68 | Columbus, IN | 6.2 | 97 | Greenville-Anderson, SC | 5.4 |
| 55 | Anniston-Oxford, AL | 6.8 | 97 | Corpus Christi, TX | 5.4 | 66 | Greenville, NC | 6.3 |
| 360 | Appleton, WI | 0.4 | 361 | Corvallis, OR | 0.0 | 201 | Gulfport-Biloxi-Pascagoula, MS | 3.1 |
| 326 | Athens-Clarke County, GA | 1.0 | 219 | Crestview-Fort Walton Beach, FL | 2.8 | 201 | Hagerstown-Martinsburg, MD-WV | 3.1 |
| 78 | Atlanta, GA | 5.9 | 157 | Cumberland, MD-WV | 3.9 | 19 | Hammond, LA | 9.7 |
| 214 | Atlantic City, NJ | 2.9 | 134 | Dallas (greater), TX | 4.4 | 154 | Hanford-Corcoran, CA | 4.0 |
| 93 | Augusta, GA-SC | 5.5 | 123 | Dallas-Plano-Irving, TX M.D. | 4.7 | 340 | Harrisonburg, VA | 0.8 |
| 219 | Austin-Round Rock, TX | 2.8 | 295 | Dalton, GA | 1.4 | 186 | Hartford, CT | 3.4 |
| 47 | Bakersfield, CA | 7.1 | 359 | Daphne-Fairhope-Foley, AL | 0.5 | 208 | Hilton Head Island, SC | 3.0 |
| 15 | Baltimore, MD | 10.0 | 267 | Davenport, IA-IL | 1.8 | 75 | Hinesville, GA | 6.0 |
| 157 | Bangor, ME | 3.9 | 93 | Dayton, OH | 5.5 | 173 | Homosassa Springs, FL | 3.6 |
| 333 | Barnstable Town, MA | 0.9 | 130 | Decatur, AL | 4.5 | 25 | Hot Springs, AR | 9.3 |
| 13 | Baton Rouge, LA | 10.2 | 127 | Decatur, IL | 4.6 | 8 | Houma, LA | 11.0 |
| 259 | Bay City, MI | 1.9 | 138 | Deltona-Daytona Beach, FL | 4.3 | 78 | Houston, TX | 5.9 |
| 28 | Beaumont-Port Arthur, TX | 8.6 | 165 | Denver-Aurora, CO | 3.7 | 68 | Huntsville, AL | 6.2 |
| 267 | Bend, OR | 1.8 | 246 | Des Moines-West Des Moines, IA | 2.3 | 249 | Idaho Falls, ID | 2.2 |
| 238 | Billings, MT | 2.4 | 22 | Detroit (greater), MI | 9.6 | 39 | Indianapolis, IN | 7.6 |
| 196 | Binghamton, NY | 3.2 | 1 | Detroit-Dearborn-Livonia, MI M.D. | 20.4 | 361 | Iowa City, IA | 0.0 |
| 32 | Birmingham-Hoover, AL | 8.2 | 74 | Dothan, AL | 6.1 | 47 | Jacksonville, FL | 7.1 |
| 238 | Bismarck, ND | 2.4 | 238 | Dover, DE | 2.4 | 201 | Jackson, MI | 3.1 |
| 320 | Blacksburg, VA | 1.1 | 361 | Dubuque, IA | 0.0 | 15 | Jackson, MS | 10.0 |
| 253 | Bloomington, IL | 2.1 | 295 | Duluth, MN-WI | 1.4 | 31 | Jackson, TN | 8.4 |
| 267 | Bloomington, IN | 1.8 | 208 | Dutchess-Putnam, NY M.D. | 3.0 | 311 | Janesville, WI | 1.2 |
| 311 | Bloomsburg-Berwick, PA | 1.2 | 117 | East Stroudsburg, PA | 4.8 | 308 | Jefferson City, MO | 1.3 |
| 333 | Boise City, ID | 0.9 | 311 | Eau Claire, WI | 1.2 | 178 | Johnson City, TN | 3.5 |
| 267 | Boston (greater), MA-NH | 1.8 | 320 | El Centro, CA | 1.1 | 29 | Johnstown, PA | 8.5 |
| 196 | Boston, MA M.D. | 3.2 | 295 | El Paso, TX | 1.4 | 282 | Jonesboro, AR | 1.6 |
| 353 | Boulder, CO | 0.6 | 295 | Elgin, IL M.D. | 1.4 | 246 | Joplin, MO | 2.3 |
| 311 | Bowling Green, KY | 1.2 | 308 | Elizabethtown-Fort Knox, KY | 1.3 | 353 | Kahului-Wailuku-Lahaina, HI | 0.6 |
| 340 | Bremerton-Silverdale, WA | 0.8 | 361 | Elmira, NY | 0.0 | 101 | Kankakee, IL | 5.3 |
| 289 | Bridgeport-Stamford, CT | 1.5 | 295 | Erie, PA | 1.4 | 41 | Kansas City, MO-KS | 7.4 |
| 295 | Brownsville-Harlingen, TX | 1.4 | 320 | Eugene, OR | 1.1 | 193 | Kennewick-Richland, WA | 3.3 |
| 68 | Brunswick, GA | 6.2 | 361 | Fairbanks, AK | 0.0 | 282 | Kingsport, TN-VA | 1.6 |
| 104 | Buffalo-Niagara Falls, NY | 5.2 | 267 | Fargo, ND-MN | 1.8 | 278 | Kingston, NY | 1.7 |
| 259 | Burlington, NC | 1.9 | 123 | Farmington, NM | 4.7 | 173 | Knoxville, TN | 3.6 |
| 223 | California-Lexington Park, MD | 2.7 | 233 | Fayetteville-Springdale, AR-MO | 2.5 | 238 | Kokomo, IN | 2.4 |
| 333 | Cambridge-Newton, MA M.D. | 0.9 | 34 | Fayetteville, NC | 7.9 | 289 | La Crosse, WI-MN | 1.5 |
| 58 | Camden, NJ M.D. | 6.7 | 249 | Flagstaff, AZ | 2.2 | 295 | Lafayette, IN | 1.4 |
| 208 | Canton, OH | 3.0 | 5 | Flint, MI | 13.7 | 110 | Lafayette, LA | 5.0 |
| 162 | Cape Coral-Fort Myers, FL | 3.8 | 186 | Florence-Muscle Shoals, AL | 3.4 | 53 | Lake Charles, LA | 6.9 |
| 44 | Cape Girardeau, MO-IL | 7.2 | 101 | Florence, SC | 5.3 | 238 | Lake Co.-Kenosha Co., IL-WI M.D. | 2.4 |
| 238 | Carbondale-Marion, IL | 2.4 | 326 | Fond du Lac, WI | 1.0 | 134 | Lake Havasu City-Kingman, AZ | 4.4 |
| 42 | Carson City, NV | 7.3 | 353 | Fort Collins, CO | 0.6 | 196 | Lakeland, FL | 3.2 |
| 162 | Casper, WY | 3.8 | 138 | Fort Lauderdale, FL M.D. | 4.3 | 278 | Lancaster, PA | 1.7 |
| 289 | Cedar Rapids, IA | 1.5 | 253 | Fort Smith, AR-OK | 2.1 | 196 | Lansing-East Lansing, MI | 3.2 |
| 232 | Chambersburg-Waynesboro, PA | 2.6 | 33 | Fort Wayne, IN | 8.0 | 289 | Laredo, TX | 1.5 |
| 162 | Champaign-Urbana, IL | 3.8 | 157 | Fort Worth-Arlington, TX M.D. | 3.9 | 165 | Las Cruces, NM | 3.7 |
| 44 | Charleston-North Charleston, SC | 7.2 | 75 | Fresno, CA | 6.0 | 87 | Las Vegas-Henderson, NV | 5.7 |
| 104 | Charlotte-Mecklenburg, NC-SC | 5.2 | 37 | Gadsden, AL | 7.7 | 333 | Lawrence, KS | 0.9 |
| 267 | Charlottesville, VA | 1.8 | 165 | Gainesville, FL | 3.7 | 19 | Lawton, OK | 9.7 |
| 149 | Chattanooga, TN-GA | 4.1 | 165 | Gainesville, GA | 3.7 | 289 | Lebanon, PA | 1.5 |

Note: All listings are for Metropolitan Statistical Areas (M.S.A.s) except for those ending with "M.D." Listings with "M.D." are Metropolitan Divisions which are smaller parts of eleven large M.S.A.s. See explanatory note at beginning of metropolitan area section.

| RANK | METROPOLITAN AREA | RATE | RANK | METROPOLITAN AREA | RATE | RANK | METROPOLITAN AREA | RATE |
|---|---|---|---|---|---|---|---|---|
| 333 | Lewiston-Auburn, ME | 0.9 | 101 | Omaha-Council Bluffs, NE-IA | 5.3 | 333 | Sheboygan, WI | 0.9 |
| 361 | Lewiston, ID-WA | 0.0 | 157 | Orlando, FL | 3.9 | 87 | Sherman-Denison, TX | 5.7 |
| 114 | Lexington-Fayette, KY | 4.9 | 361 | Oshkosh-Neenah, WI | 0.0 | 35 | Shreveport-Bossier City, LA | 7.8 |
| 214 | Lima, OH | 2.9 | 361 | Owensboro, KY | 0.0 | 320 | Silver Spring-Frederick, MD M.D. | 1.1 |
| 282 | Lincoln, NE | 1.6 | 154 | Oxnard-Thousand Oaks, CA | 4.0 | 238 | Sioux City, IA-NE-SD | 2.4 |
| 37 | Little Rock, AR | 7.7 | 173 | Palm Bay-Melbourne, FL | 3.6 | 311 | Sioux Falls, SD | 1.2 |
| 340 | Logan, UT-ID | 0.8 | 145 | Panama City, FL | 4.2 | 186 | South Bend-Mishawaka, IN-MI | 3.4 |
| 93 | Longview, TX | 5.5 | 361 | Parkersburg-Vienna, WV | 0.0 | 219 | Spartanburg, SC | 2.8 |
| 326 | Longview, WA | 1.0 | 68 | Pensacola, FL | 6.2 | 165 | Spokane, WA | 3.7 |
| 97 | Los Angeles County, CA M.D. | 5.4 | 84 | Peoria, IL | 5.8 | 4 | Springfield, IL | 16.5 |
| 130 | Los Angeles (greater), CA | 4.5 | 47 | Philadelphia (greater) PA-NJ-MD-DE | 7.1 | 130 | Springfield, MA | 4.5 |
| 114 | Louisville, KY-IN | 4.9 | 6 | Philadelphia, PA M.D. | 13.1 | 201 | Springfield, MO | 3.1 |
| 208 | Lubbock, TX | 3.0 | 117 | Phoenix-Mesa-Scottsdale, AZ | 4.8 | 134 | Springfield, OH | 4.4 |
| 259 | Lynchburg, VA | 1.9 | 149 | Pittsburgh, PA | 4.1 | 361 | State College, PA | 0.0 |
| 17 | Macon, GA | 9.9 | 340 | Pittsfield, MA | 0.8 | 278 | Staunton-Waynesboro, VA | 1.7 |
| 29 | Madera, CA | 8.5 | 311 | Pocatello, ID | 1.2 | 60 | Stockton-Lodi, CA | 6.6 |
| 267 | Madison, WI | 1.8 | 186 | Port St. Lucie, FL | 3.4 | 326 | St. Cloud, MN | 1.0 |
| 233 | Manchester-Nashua, NH | 2.5 | 295 | Portland-Vancouver, OR-WA | 1.4 | 295 | St. George, UT | 1.4 |
| 75 | Manhattan, KS | 6.0 | 311 | Portland, ME | 1.2 | 282 | St. Joseph, MO-KS | 1.6 |
| 257 | Mankato-North Mankato, MN | 2.0 | 295 | Prescott, AZ | 1.4 | 44 | St. Louis, MO-IL | 7.2 |
| 340 | Mansfield, OH | 0.8 | 233 | Providence-Warwick, RI-MA | 2.5 | 62 | Sumter, SC | 6.4 |
| 223 | McAllen-Edinburg-Mission, TX | 2.7 | 320 | Provo-Orem, UT | 1.1 | 145 | Syracuse, NY | 4.2 |
| 259 | Medford, OR | 1.9 | 201 | Pueblo, CO | 3.1 | 208 | Tacoma, WA M.D. | 3.0 |
| 12 | Memphis, TN-MS-AR | 10.3 | 353 | Punta Gorda, FL | 0.6 | 130 | Tallahassee, FL | 4.5 |
| 13 | Merced, CA | 10.2 | 326 | Racine, WI | 1.0 | 138 | Tampa-St Petersburg, FL | 4.3 |
| 60 | Miami (greater), FL | 6.6 | 223 | Raleigh, NC | 2.7 | 178 | Terre Haute, IN | 3.5 |
| 27 | Miami-Dade County, FL M.D. | 8.7 | 295 | Rapid City, SD | 1.4 | 154 | Texarkana, TX-AR | 4.0 |
| 157 | Midland, TX | 3.9 | 223 | Reading, PA | 2.7 | 259 | The Villages, FL | 1.9 |
| 52 | Milwaukee, WI | 7.0 | 91 | Redding, CA | 5.6 | 114 | Toledo, OH | 4.9 |
| 233 | Minneapolis-St. Paul, MN-WI | 2.5 | 104 | Reno, NV | 5.2 | 93 | Topeka, KS | 5.5 |
| 333 | Missoula, MT | 0.9 | 68 | Richmond, VA | 6.2 | 10 | Trenton, NJ | 10.8 |
| 19 | Mobile, AL | 9.7 | 110 | Riverside-San Bernardino, CA | 5.0 | 47 | Tucson, AZ | 7.1 |
| 66 | Modesto, CA | 6.3 | 107 | Roanoke, VA | 5.1 | 58 | Tulsa, OK | 6.7 |
| 23 | Monroe, LA | 9.5 | 361 | Rochester, MN | 0.0 | 55 | Tuscaloosa, AL | 6.8 |
| 193 | Monroe, MI | 3.3 | 117 | Rochester, NY | 4.8 | 165 | Tyler, TX | 3.7 |
| 311 | Montgomery County, PA M.D. | 1.2 | 40 | Rockford, IL | 7.5 | 87 | Utica-Rome, NY | 5.7 |
| 350 | Morgantown, WV | 0.7 | 350 | Rockingham County, NH M.D. | 0.7 | 42 | Vallejo-Fairfield, CA | 7.3 |
| 278 | Morristown, TN | 1.7 | 11 | Rocky Mount, NC | 10.5 | 201 | Victoria, TX | 3.1 |
| 186 | Mount Vernon-Anacortes, WA | 3.4 | 145 | Rome, GA | 4.2 | 233 | Vineland-Bridgeton, NJ | 2.5 |
| 361 | Muncie, IN | 0.0 | 149 | Sacramento, CA | 4.1 | 53 | Virginia Beach-Norfolk, VA-NC | 6.9 |
| 78 | Muskegon, MI | 5.9 | 2 | Saginaw, MI | 19.2 | 26 | Visalia-Porterville, CA | 9.2 |
| 178 | Myrtle Beach, SC-NC | 3.5 | 178 | Salem, OR | 3.5 | 223 | Waco, TX | 2.7 |
| 295 | Napa, CA | 1.4 | 9 | Salinas, CA | 10.9 | 138 | Warner Robins, GA | 4.3 |
| 173 | Naples-Marco Island, FL | 3.6 | 214 | Salisbury, MD-DE | 2.9 | 259 | Warren-Troy, MI M.D. | 1.9 |
| 186 | Nashville-Davidson, TN | 3.4 | 267 | Salt Lake City, UT | 1.8 | 165 | Washington (greater) DC-VA-MD-WV | 3.7 |
| 267 | Nassau-Suffolk, NY M.D. | 1.8 | 138 | San Angelo, TX | 4.3 | 134 | Washington, DC-VA-MD-WV M.D. | 4.4 |
| 340 | New Bern, NC | 0.8 | 127 | San Antonio, TX | 4.6 | 361 | Watertown-Fort Drum, NY | 0.0 |
| 193 | New Haven-Milford, CT | 3.3 | 249 | San Diego, CA | 2.2 | 289 | Wausau, WI | 1.5 |
| 3 | New Orleans, LA | 19.0 | 117 | San Francisco (greater), CA | 4.8 | 97 | West Palm Beach, FL M.D. | 5.4 |
| 178 | New York (greater), NY-NJ-PA | 3.5 | 165 | San Francisco-Redwood, CA M.D. | 3.7 | 127 | Wichita Falls, TX | 4.6 |
| 196 | New York-Jersey City, NY-NJ M.D. | 3.2 | 208 | San Jose, CA | 3.0 | 178 | Wichita, KS | 3.5 |
| 47 | Newark, NJ-PA M.D. | 7.1 | 267 | San Luis Obispo, CA | 1.8 | 107 | Williamsport, PA | 5.1 |
| 259 | Niles-Benton Harbor, MI | 1.9 | 340 | San Rafael, CA M.D. | 0.8 | 91 | Wilmington, DE-MD-NJ M.D. | 5.6 |
| 223 | North Port-Sarasota-Bradenton, FL | 2.7 | 149 | Santa Cruz-Watsonville, CA | 4.1 | 186 | Wilmington, NC | 3.4 |
| 223 | Norwich-New London, CT | 2.7 | 295 | Santa Maria-Santa Barbara, CA | 1.4 | 246 | Winchester, VA-WV | 2.3 |
| 84 | Oakland-Hayward, CA M.D. | 5.8 | 267 | Santa Rosa, CA | 1.8 | 178 | Winston-Salem, NC | 3.5 |
| 110 | Ocala, FL | 5.0 | 18 | Savannah, GA | 9.8 | 282 | Worcester, MA-CT | 1.6 |
| 361 | Ocean City, NJ | 0.0 | 138 | Scranton--Wilkes-Barre, PA | 4.3 | 62 | Yakima, WA | 6.4 |
| 257 | Odessa, TX | 2.0 | 249 | Seattle (greater), WA | 2.2 | 138 | York-Hanover, PA | 4.3 |
| 308 | Ogden-Clearfield, UT | 1.3 | 259 | Seattle-Bellevue-Everett, WA M.D. | 1.9 | 145 | Yuba City, CA | 4.2 |
| 78 | Oklahoma City, OK | 5.9 | 219 | Sebastian-Vero Beach, FL | 2.8 | 78 | Yuma, AZ | 5.9 |
| 320 | Olympia, WA | 1.1 | 149 | Sebring, FL | 4.1 | | | |

Source: Reported data from the F.B.I. "Crime in the United States 2013"
*Includes murder, rape, robbery, aggravated assault, burglary, larceny-theft, and motor vehicle theft.

# 10. Murder Rate in 2013 (continued)
## National Rate = 4.5 Murders per 100,000 Population*

| RANK | METROPOLITAN AREA | RATE | RANK | METROPOLITAN AREA | RATE | RANK | METROPOLITAN AREA | RATE |
|---|---|---|---|---|---|---|---|---|
| 1 | Detroit-Dearborn-Livonia, MI M.D. | 20.4 | 62 | Yakima, WA | 6.4 | 127 | Wichita Falls, TX | 4.6 |
| 2 | Saginaw, MI | 19.2 | 66 | Greenville, NC | 6.3 | 130 | Decatur, AL | 4.5 |
| 3 | New Orleans, LA | 19.0 | 66 | Modesto, CA | 6.3 | 130 | Los Angeles (greater), CA | 4.5 |
| 4 | Springfield, IL | 16.5 | 68 | Brunswick, GA | 6.2 | 130 | Springfield, MA | 4.5 |
| 5 | Flint, MI | 13.7 | 68 | Colorado Springs, CO | 6.2 | 130 | Tallahassee, FL | 4.5 |
| 6 | Philadelphia, PA M.D. | 13.1 | 68 | Columbus, IN | 6.2 | 134 | Dallas (greater), TX | 4.4 |
| 7 | Gary, IN M.D. | 11.6 | 68 | Huntsville, AL | 6.2 | 134 | Lake Havasu City-Kingman, AZ | 4.4 |
| 8 | Houma, LA | 11.0 | 68 | Pensacola, FL | 6.2 | 134 | Springfield, OH | 4.4 |
| 9 | Salinas, CA | 10.9 | 68 | Richmond, VA | 6.2 | 134 | Washington, DC-VA-MD-WV M.D. | 4.4 |
| 10 | Trenton, NJ | 10.8 | 74 | Dothan, AL | 6.1 | 138 | Deltona-Daytona Beach, FL | 4.3 |
| 11 | Rocky Mount, NC | 10.5 | 75 | Fresno, CA | 6.0 | 138 | Fort Lauderdale, FL M.D. | 4.3 |
| 12 | Memphis, TN-MS-AR | 10.3 | 75 | Hinesville, GA | 6.0 | 138 | San Angelo, TX | 4.3 |
| 13 | Baton Rouge, LA | 10.2 | 75 | Manhattan, KS | 6.0 | 138 | Scranton--Wilkes-Barre, PA | 4.3 |
| 13 | Merced, CA | 10.2 | 78 | Albuquerque, NM | 5.9 | 138 | Tampa-St Petersburg, FL | 4.3 |
| 15 | Baltimore, MD | 10.0 | 78 | Atlanta, GA | 5.9 | 138 | Warner Robins, GA | 4.3 |
| 15 | Jackson, MS | 10.0 | 78 | Houston, TX | 5.9 | 138 | York-Hanover, PA | 4.3 |
| 17 | Macon, GA | 9.9 | 78 | Muskegon, MI | 5.9 | 145 | Panama City, FL | 4.2 |
| 18 | Savannah, GA | 9.8 | 78 | Oklahoma City, OK | 5.9 | 145 | Rome, GA | 4.2 |
| 19 | Hammond, LA | 9.7 | 78 | Yuma, AZ | 5.9 | 145 | Syracuse, NY | 4.2 |
| 19 | Lawton, OK | 9.7 | 84 | Chico, CA | 5.8 | 145 | Yuba City, CA | 4.2 |
| 19 | Mobile, AL | 9.7 | 84 | Oakland-Hayward, CA M.D. | 5.8 | 149 | Chattanooga, TN-GA | 4.1 |
| 22 | Detroit (greater), MI | 9.6 | 84 | Peoria, IL | 5.8 | 149 | Pittsburgh, PA | 4.1 |
| 23 | Columbus, GA-AL | 9.5 | 87 | Albany, GA | 5.7 | 149 | Sacramento, CA | 4.1 |
| 23 | Monroe, LA | 9.5 | 87 | Las Vegas-Henderson, NV | 5.7 | 149 | Santa Cruz-Watsonville, CA | 4.1 |
| 25 | Hot Springs, AR | 9.3 | 87 | Sherman-Denison, TX | 5.7 | 149 | Sebring, FL | 4.1 |
| 26 | Visalia-Porterville, CA | 9.2 | 87 | Utica-Rome, NY | 5.7 | 154 | Hanford-Corcoran, CA | 4.0 |
| 27 | Miami-Dade County, FL M.D. | 8.7 | 91 | Redding, CA | 5.6 | 154 | Oxnard-Thousand Oaks, CA | 4.0 |
| 28 | Beaumont-Port Arthur, TX | 8.6 | 91 | Wilmington, DE-MD-NJ M.D. | 5.6 | 154 | Texarkana, TX-AR | 4.0 |
| 29 | Johnstown, PA | 8.5 | 93 | Augusta, GA-SC | 5.5 | 157 | Bangor, ME | 3.9 |
| 29 | Madera, CA | 8.5 | 93 | Dayton, OH | 5.5 | 157 | Cumberland, MD-WV | 3.9 |
| 31 | Jackson, TN | 8.4 | 93 | Longview, TX | 5.5 | 157 | Fort Worth-Arlington, TX M.D. | 3.9 |
| 32 | Birmingham-Hoover, AL | 8.2 | 93 | Topeka, KS | 5.5 | 157 | Midland, TX | 3.9 |
| 33 | Fort Wayne, IN | 8.0 | 97 | Corpus Christi, TX | 5.4 | 157 | Orlando, FL | 3.9 |
| 34 | Fayetteville, NC | 7.9 | 97 | Greenville-Anderson, SC | 5.4 | 162 | Cape Coral-Fort Myers, FL | 3.8 |
| 35 | Alexandria, LA | 7.8 | 97 | Los Angeles County, CA M.D. | 5.4 | 162 | Casper, WY | 3.8 |
| 35 | Shreveport-Bossier City, LA | 7.8 | 97 | West Palm Beach, FL M.D. | 5.4 | 162 | Champaign-Urbana, IL | 3.8 |
| 37 | Gadsden, AL | 7.7 | 101 | Florence, SC | 5.3 | 165 | Denver-Aurora, CO | 3.7 |
| 37 | Little Rock, AR | 7.7 | 101 | Kankakee, IL | 5.3 | 165 | Gainesville, FL | 3.7 |
| 39 | Indianapolis, IN | 7.6 | 101 | Omaha-Council Bluffs, NE-IA | 5.3 | 165 | Gainesville, GA | 3.7 |
| 40 | Rockford, IL | 7.5 | 104 | Buffalo-Niagara Falls, NY | 5.2 | 165 | Las Cruces, NM | 3.7 |
| 41 | Kansas City, MO-KS | 7.4 | 104 | Charlotte-Mecklenburg, NC-SC | 5.2 | 165 | San Francisco-Redwood, CA M.D. | 3.7 |
| 42 | Carson City, NV | 7.3 | 104 | Reno, NV | 5.2 | 165 | Spokane, WA | 3.7 |
| 42 | Vallejo-Fairfield, CA | 7.3 | 107 | Akron, OH | 5.1 | 165 | Tyler, TX | 3.7 |
| 44 | Cape Girardeau, MO-IL | 7.2 | 107 | Roanoke, VA | 5.1 | 165 | Washington (greater) DC-VA-MD-WV | 3.7 |
| 44 | Charleston-North Charleston, SC | 7.2 | 107 | Williamsport, PA | 5.1 | 173 | Grants Pass, OR | 3.6 |
| 44 | St. Louis, MO-IL | 7.2 | 110 | Clarksville, TN-KY | 5.0 | 173 | Homosassa Springs, FL | 3.6 |
| 47 | Bakersfield, CA | 7.1 | 110 | Lafayette, LA | 5.0 | 173 | Knoxville, TN | 3.6 |
| 47 | Jacksonville, FL | 7.1 | 110 | Ocala, FL | 5.0 | 173 | Naples-Marco Island, FL | 3.6 |
| 47 | Newark, NJ-PA M.D. | 7.1 | 110 | Riverside-San Bernardino, CA | 5.0 | 173 | Palm Bay-Melbourne, FL | 3.6 |
| 47 | Philadelphia (greater) PA-NJ-MD-DE | 7.1 | 114 | Lexington-Fayette, KY | 4.9 | 178 | Amarillo, TX | 3.5 |
| 47 | Tucson, AZ | 7.1 | 114 | Louisville, KY-IN | 4.9 | 178 | Johnson City, TN | 3.5 |
| 52 | Milwaukee, WI | 7.0 | 114 | Toledo, OH | 4.9 | 178 | Myrtle Beach, SC-NC | 3.5 |
| 53 | Lake Charles, LA | 6.9 | 117 | Anchorage, AK | 4.8 | 178 | New York (greater), NY-NJ-PA | 3.5 |
| 53 | Virginia Beach-Norfolk, VA-NC | 6.9 | 117 | Cincinnati, OH-KY-IN | 4.8 | 178 | Salem, OR | 3.5 |
| 55 | Anniston-Oxford, AL | 6.8 | 117 | East Stroudsburg, PA | 4.8 | 178 | Terre Haute, IN | 3.5 |
| 55 | Chicago-Naperville, IL M.D. | 6.8 | 117 | Phoenix-Mesa-Scottsdale, AZ | 4.8 | 178 | Wichita, KS | 3.5 |
| 55 | Tuscaloosa, AL | 6.8 | 117 | Rochester, NY | 4.8 | 178 | Winston-Salem, NC | 3.5 |
| 58 | Camden, NJ M.D. | 6.7 | 117 | San Francisco (greater), CA | 4.8 | 186 | Florence-Muscle Shoals, AL | 3.4 |
| 58 | Tulsa, OK | 6.7 | 123 | Columbia, SC | 4.7 | 186 | Hartford, CT | 3.4 |
| 60 | Miami (greater), FL | 6.6 | 123 | Dallas-Plano-Irving, TX M.D. | 4.7 | 186 | Mount Vernon-Anacortes, WA | 3.4 |
| 60 | Stockton-Lodi, CA | 6.6 | 123 | Farmington, NM | 4.7 | 186 | Nashville-Davidson, TN | 3.4 |
| 62 | Chicago (greater), IL-IN-WI | 6.4 | 123 | Greensboro-High Point, NC | 4.7 | 186 | Port St. Lucie, FL | 3.4 |
| 62 | Goldsboro, NC | 6.4 | 127 | Decatur, IL | 4.6 | 186 | South Bend-Mishawaka, IN-MI | 3.4 |
| 62 | Sumter, SC | 6.4 | 127 | San Antonio, TX | 4.6 | 186 | Wilmington, NC | 3.4 |

Note: All listings are for Metropolitan Statistical Areas (M.S.A.s) except for those ending with "M.D." Listings with "M.D." are Metropolitan Divisions which are smaller parts of eleven large M.S.A.s. See explanatory note at beginning of metropolitan area section.

| RANK | METROPOLITAN AREA | RATE | RANK | METROPOLITAN AREA | RATE | RANK | METROPOLITAN AREA | RATE |
|---|---|---|---|---|---|---|---|---|
| 193 | Kennewick-Richland, WA | 3.3 | 253 | College Station-Bryan, TX | 2.1 | 311 | Pocatello, ID | 1.2 |
| 193 | Monroe, MI | 3.3 | 253 | Fort Smith, AR-OK | 2.1 | 311 | Portland, ME | 1.2 |
| 193 | New Haven-Milford, CT | 3.3 | 257 | Mankato-North Mankato, MN | 2.0 | 311 | Sioux Falls, SD | 1.2 |
| 196 | Binghamton, NY | 3.2 | 257 | Odessa, TX | 2.0 | 320 | Blacksburg, VA | 1.1 |
| 196 | Boston, MA M.D. | 3.2 | 259 | Bay City, MI | 1.9 | 320 | El Centro, CA | 1.1 |
| 196 | Lakeland, FL | 3.2 | 259 | Burlington, NC | 1.9 | 320 | Eugene, OR | 1.1 |
| 196 | Lansing-East Lansing, MI | 3.2 | 259 | Lynchburg, VA | 1.9 | 320 | Olympia, WA | 1.1 |
| 196 | New York-Jersey City, NY-NJ M.D. | 3.2 | 259 | Medford, OR | 1.9 | 320 | Provo-Orem, UT | 1.1 |
| 201 | Ann Arbor, MI | 3.1 | 259 | Niles-Benton Harbor, MI | 1.9 | 320 | Silver Spring-Frederick, MD M.D. | 1.1 |
| 201 | Gulfport-Biloxi-Pascagoula, MS | 3.1 | 259 | Seattle-Bellevue-Everett, WA M.D. | 1.9 | 326 | Athens-Clarke County, GA | 1.0 |
| 201 | Hagerstown-Martinsburg, MD-WV | 3.1 | 259 | The Villages, FL | 1.9 | 326 | Cheyenne, WY | 1.0 |
| 201 | Jackson, MI | 3.1 | 259 | Warren-Troy, MI M.D. | 1.9 | 326 | Fond du Lac, WI | 1.0 |
| 201 | Pueblo, CO | 3.1 | 267 | Bend, OR | 1.8 | 326 | Grand Forks, ND-MN | 1.0 |
| 201 | Springfield, MO | 3.1 | 267 | Bloomington, IN | 1.8 | 326 | Longview, WA | 1.0 |
| 201 | Victoria, TX | 3.1 | 267 | Boston (greater), MA-NH | 1.8 | 326 | Racine, WI | 1.0 |
| 208 | Canton, OH | 3.0 | 267 | Charlottesville, VA | 1.8 | 326 | St. Cloud, MN | 1.0 |
| 208 | Dutchess-Putnam, NY M.D. | 3.0 | 267 | Davenport, IA-IL | 1.8 | 333 | Barnstable Town, MA | 0.9 |
| 208 | Hilton Head Island, SC | 3.0 | 267 | Fargo, ND-MN | 1.8 | 333 | Boise City, ID | 0.9 |
| 208 | Lubbock, TX | 3.0 | 267 | Madison, WI | 1.8 | 333 | Cambridge-Newton, MA M.D. | 0.9 |
| 208 | San Jose, CA | 3.0 | 267 | Nassau-Suffolk, NY M.D. | 1.8 | 333 | Lawrence, KS | 0.9 |
| 208 | Tacoma, WA M.D. | 3.0 | 267 | Salt Lake City, UT | 1.8 | 333 | Lewiston-Auburn, ME | 0.9 |
| 214 | Allentown, PA-NJ | 2.9 | 267 | San Luis Obispo, CA | 1.8 | 333 | Missoula, MT | 0.9 |
| 214 | Atlantic City, NJ | 2.9 | 267 | Santa Rosa, CA | 1.8 | 333 | Sheboygan, WI | 0.9 |
| 214 | Columbia, MO | 2.9 | 278 | Kingston, NY | 1.7 | 340 | Albany, OR | 0.8 |
| 214 | Lima, OH | 2.9 | 278 | Lancaster, PA | 1.7 | 340 | Bremerton-Silverdale, WA | 0.8 |
| 214 | Salisbury, MD-DE | 2.9 | 278 | Morristown, TN | 1.7 | 340 | Cleveland, TN | 0.8 |
| 219 | Austin-Round Rock, TX | 2.8 | 278 | Staunton-Waynesboro, VA | 1.7 | 340 | Glens Falls, NY | 0.8 |
| 219 | Crestview-Fort Walton Beach, FL | 2.8 | 282 | Altoona, PA | 1.6 | 340 | Harrisonburg, VA | 0.8 |
| 219 | Sebastian-Vero Beach, FL | 2.8 | 282 | Anaheim-Santa Ana-Irvine, CA M.D. | 1.6 | 340 | Logan, UT-ID | 0.8 |
| 219 | Spartanburg, SC | 2.8 | 282 | Jonesboro, AR | 1.6 | 340 | Mansfield, OH | 0.8 |
| 223 | Albany-Schenectady-Troy, NY | 2.7 | 282 | Kingsport, TN-VA | 1.6 | 340 | New Bern, NC | 0.8 |
| 223 | California-Lexington Park, MD | 2.7 | 282 | Lincoln, NE | 1.6 | 340 | Pittsfield, MA | 0.8 |
| 223 | Grand Junction, CO | 2.7 | 282 | St. Joseph, MO-KS | 1.6 | 340 | San Rafael, CA M.D. | 0.8 |
| 223 | McAllen-Edinburg-Mission, TX | 2.7 | 282 | Worcester, MA-CT | 1.6 | 350 | Greeley, CO | 0.7 |
| 223 | North Port-Sarasota-Bradenton, FL | 2.7 | 289 | Bridgeport-Stamford, CT | 1.5 | 350 | Morgantown, WV | 0.7 |
| 223 | Norwich-New London, CT | 2.7 | 289 | Cedar Rapids, IA | 1.5 | 350 | Rockingham County, NH M.D. | 0.7 |
| 223 | Raleigh, NC | 2.7 | 289 | La Crosse, WI-MN | 1.5 | 353 | Abilene, TX | 0.6 |
| 223 | Reading, PA | 2.7 | 289 | Laredo, TX | 1.5 | 353 | Boulder, CO | 0.6 |
| 223 | Waco, TX | 2.7 | 289 | Lebanon, PA | 1.5 | 353 | Fort Collins, CO | 0.6 |
| 232 | Chambersburg-Waynesboro, PA | 2.6 | 289 | Wausau, WI | 1.5 | 353 | Green Bay, WI | 0.6 |
| 233 | Fayetteville-Springdale, AR-MO | 2.5 | 295 | Brownsville-Harlingen, TX | 1.4 | 353 | Kahului-Wailuku-Lahaina, HI | 0.6 |
| 233 | Manchester-Nashua, NH | 2.5 | 295 | Dalton, GA | 1.4 | 353 | Punta Gorda, FL | 0.6 |
| 233 | Minneapolis-St. Paul, MN-WI | 2.5 | 295 | Duluth, MN-WI | 1.4 | 359 | Daphne-Fairhope-Foley, AL | 0.5 |
| 233 | Providence-Warwick, RI-MA | 2.5 | 295 | El Paso, TX | 1.4 | 360 | Appleton, WI | 0.4 |
| 233 | Vineland-Bridgeton, NJ | 2.5 | 295 | Elgin, IL M.D. | 1.4 | 361 | Ames, IA | 0.0 |
| 238 | Billings, MT | 2.4 | 295 | Erie, PA | 1.4 | 361 | Corvallis, OR | 0.0 |
| 238 | Bismarck, ND | 2.4 | 295 | Lafayette, IN | 1.4 | 361 | Dubuque, IA | 0.0 |
| 238 | Carbondale-Marion, IL | 2.4 | 295 | Napa, CA | 1.4 | 361 | Elmira, NY | 0.0 |
| 238 | Dover, DE | 2.4 | 295 | Portland-Vancouver, OR-WA | 1.4 | 361 | Fairbanks, AK | 0.0 |
| 238 | Grand Rapids-Wyoming, MI | 2.4 | 295 | Prescott, AZ | 1.4 | 361 | Gettysburg, PA | 0.0 |
| 238 | Kokomo, IN | 2.4 | 295 | Rapid City, SD | 1.4 | 361 | Great Falls, MT | 0.0 |
| 238 | Lake Co.-Kenosha Co., IL-WI M.D. | 2.4 | 295 | Santa Maria-Santa Barbara, CA | 1.4 | 361 | Iowa City, IA | 0.0 |
| 238 | Sioux City, IA-NE-SD | 2.4 | 295 | St. George, UT | 1.4 | 361 | Lewiston, ID-WA | 0.0 |
| 246 | Des Moines-West Des Moines, IA | 2.3 | 308 | Elizabethtown-Fort Knox, KY | 1.3 | 361 | Muncie, IN | 0.0 |
| 246 | Joplin, MO | 2.3 | 308 | Jefferson City, MO | 1.3 | 361 | Ocean City, NJ | 0.0 |
| 246 | Winchester, VA-WV | 2.3 | 308 | Ogden-Clearfield, UT | 1.3 | 361 | Oshkosh-Neenah, WI | 0.0 |
| 249 | Flagstaff, AZ | 2.2 | 311 | Bloomsburg-Berwick, PA | 1.2 | 361 | Owensboro, KY | 0.0 |
| 249 | Idaho Falls, ID | 2.2 | 311 | Bowling Green, KY | 1.2 | 361 | Parkersburg-Vienna, WV | 0.0 |
| 249 | San Diego, CA | 2.2 | 311 | Eau Claire, WI | 1.2 | 361 | Rochester, MN | 0.0 |
| 249 | Seattle (greater), WA | 2.2 | 311 | Grand Island, NE | 1.2 | 361 | State College, PA | 0.0 |
| 253 | Bloomington, IL | 2.1 | 311 | Janesville, WI | 1.2 | 361 | Watertown-Fort Drum, NY | 0.0 |
| 253 | Coeur d'Alene, ID | 2.1 | 311 | Montgomery County, PA M.D. | 1.2 | | | |

Source: Reported data from the F.B.I. "Crime in the United States 2013"
*Includes murder, rape, robbery, aggravated assault, burglary, larceny-theft, and motor vehicle theft.

# 11. Percent Change in Murder Rate: 2012 to 2013
## National Percent Change = 5.1% Decrease*

| RANK | METROPOLITAN AREA | % CHANGE | RANK | METROPOLITAN AREA | % CHANGE | RANK | METROPOLITAN AREA | % CHANGE |
|---|---|---|---|---|---|---|---|---|
| 307 | Abilene, TX | (66.7) | 295 | Cheyenne, WY | (52.4) | 77 | Gary, IN M.D. | 24.7 |
| 64 | Akron, OH | 34.2 | 184 | Chicago (greater), IL-IN-WI | (9.9) | NA | Gettysburg, PA** | NA |
| 118 | Albany-Schenectady-Troy, NY | 3.8 | 211 | Chicago-Naperville, IL M.D. | (17.1) | 324 | Glens Falls, NY | (85.2) |
| 126 | Albany, GA | 1.8 | 89 | Chico, CA | 18.4 | 302 | Goldsboro, NC | (60.0) |
| NA | Albany, OR*** | NA | 60 | Cincinnati, OH-KY-IN | 37.1 | 129 | Grand Forks, ND-MN | 0.0 |
| 129 | Albuquerque, NM | 0.0 | 228 | Clarksville, TN-KY | (21.9) | NA | Grand Island, NE*** | NA |
| 63 | Alexandria, LA | 34.5 | 323 | Cleveland, TN | (81.0) | 223 | Grand Junction, CO | (20.6) |
| 257 | Allentown, PA-NJ | (29.3) | 12 | Coeur d'Alene, ID | 200.0 | NA | Grand Rapids-Wyoming, MI** | NA |
| 306 | Altoona, PA | (66.0) | 218 | College Station-Bryan, TX | (19.2) | NA | Grants Pass, OR** | NA |
| 210 | Amarillo, TX | (16.7) | 27 | Colorado Springs, CO | 106.7 | 326 | Great Falls, MT | (100.0) |
| 129 | Ames, IA | 0.0 | 41 | Columbia, MO | 61.1 | 314 | Greeley, CO | (69.6) |
| 173 | Anaheim-Santa Ana-Irvine, CA M.D. | (5.9) | NA | Columbia, SC** | NA | 318 | Green Bay, WI | (73.9) |
| 129 | Anchorage, AK | 0.0 | 47 | Columbus, GA-AL | 53.2 | 227 | Greensboro-High Point, NC | (21.7) |
| 23 | Ann Arbor, MI | 121.4 | 4 | Columbus, IN | 376.9 | 207 | Greenville-Anderson, SC | (15.6) |
| 65 | Anniston-Oxford, AL | 33.3 | 125 | Corpus Christi, TX | 1.9 | 163 | Greenville, NC | (1.6) |
| 129 | Appleton, WI | 0.0 | 326 | Corvallis, OR | (100.0) | NA | Gulfport-Biloxi-Pascagoula, MS** | NA |
| 312 | Athens-Clarke County, GA | (67.7) | 20 | Crestview-Fort Walton Beach, FL | 133.3 | 94 | Hagerstown-Martinsburg, MD-WV | 14.8 |
| 168 | Atlanta, GA | (3.3) | 129 | Cumberland, MD-WV | 0.0 | 104 | Hammond, LA | 9.0 |
| 317 | Atlantic City, NJ | (73.4) | 111 | Dallas (greater), TX | 7.3 | 45 | Hanford-Corcoran, CA | 53.8 |
| 264 | Augusta, GA-SC | (32.9) | 112 | Dallas-Plano-Irving, TX M.D. | 6.8 | 129 | Harrisonburg, VA | 0.0 |
| 72 | Austin-Round Rock, TX | 27.3 | 289 | Dalton, GA | (50.0) | 172 | Hartford, CT | (5.6) |
| 176 | Bakersfield, CA | (6.6) | 325 | Daphne-Fairhope-Foley, AL | (88.4) | 316 | Hilton Head Island, SC | (72.7) |
| 114 | Baltimore, MD | 5.3 | 259 | Davenport, IA-IL | (30.8) | 81 | Hinesville, GA | 22.4 |
| 238 | Bangor, ME | (25.0) | 56 | Dayton, OH | 41.0 | 120 | Homosassa Springs, FL | 2.9 |
| 37 | Barnstable Town, MA | 80.0 | 10 | Decatur, AL | 246.2 | NA | Hot Springs, AR** | NA |
| 198 | Baton Rouge, LA | (13.6) | 204 | Decatur, IL | (14.8) | 16 | Houma, LA | 155.8 |
| 26 | Bay City, MI | 111.1 | 69 | Deltona-Daytona Beach, FL | 30.3 | 119 | Houston, TX | 3.5 |
| 51 | Beaumont-Port Arthur, TX | 48.3 | 170 | Denver-Aurora, CO | (5.1) | 84 | Huntsville, AL | 21.6 |
| NA | Bend, OR** | NA | 40 | Des Moines-West Des Moines, IA | 64.3 | NA | Idaho Falls, ID*** | NA |
| 76 | Billings, MT | 26.3 | 194 | Detroit (greater), MI | (11.9) | 75 | Indianapolis, IN | 26.7 |
| 96 | Binghamton, NY | 14.3 | 200 | Detroit-Dearborn-Livonia, MI M.D. | (14.3) | 326 | Iowa City, IA | (100.0) |
| 196 | Birmingham-Hoover, AL | (12.8) | 217 | Dothan, AL | (18.7) | 192 | Jacksonville, FL | (11.3) |
| 251 | Bismarck, ND | (27.3) | 129 | Dover, DE | 0.0 | NA | Jackson, MI** | NA |
| 129 | Blacksburg, VA | 0.0 | 326 | Dubuque, IA | (100.0) | 242 | Jackson, MS | (25.4) |
| 7 | Bloomington, IL | 320.0 | 129 | Duluth, MN-WI | 0.0 | 205 | Jackson, TN | (15.2) |
| 255 | Bloomington, IN | (28.0) | 17 | Dutchess-Putnam, NY M.D. | 150.0 | 275 | Janesville, WI | (36.8) |
| 286 | Bloomsburg-Berwick, PA | (47.8) | 29 | East Stroudsburg, PA | 100.0 | 270 | Jefferson City, MO | (35.0) |
| 214 | Boise City, ID | (18.2) | NA | Eau Claire, WI** | NA | 58 | Johnson City, TN | 40.0 |
| 200 | Boston (greater), MA-NH | (14.3) | 271 | El Centro, CA | (35.3) | 28 | Johnstown, PA | 102.4 |
| 197 | Boston, MA M.D. | (13.5) | 299 | El Paso, TX | (57.6) | 311 | Jonesboro, AR | (67.3) |
| NA | Boulder, CO*** | NA | 72 | Elgin, IL M.D. | 27.3 | 263 | Joplin, MO | (32.4) |
| 294 | Bowling Green, KY | (52.0) | 33 | Elizabethtown-Fort Knox, KY | 85.7 | 322 | Kahului-Wailuku-Lahaina, HI | (80.6) |
| 300 | Bremerton-Silverdale, WA | (57.9) | 326 | Elmira, NY | (100.0) | 236 | Kankakee, IL | (24.3) |
| 301 | Bridgeport-Stamford, CT | (58.3) | 304 | Erie, PA | (64.1) | 169 | Kansas City, MO-KS | (3.9) |
| 297 | Brownsville-Harlingen, TX | (54.8) | 284 | Eugene, OR | (45.0) | 5 | Kennewick-Richland, WA | 371.4 |
| 193 | Brunswick, GA | (11.4) | 326 | Fairbanks, AK | (100.0) | 283 | Kingsport, TN-VA | (44.8) |
| 101 | Buffalo-Niagara Falls, NY | 10.6 | 29 | Fargo, ND-MN | 100.0 | 11 | Kingston, NY | 240.0 |
| 248 | Burlington, NC | (26.9) | 129 | Farmington, NM | 0.0 | 185 | Knoxville, TN | (10.0) |
| NA | California-Lexington Park, MD*** | NA | 106 | Fayetteville-Springdale, AR-MO | 8.7 | 289 | Kokomo, IN | (50.0) |
| 71 | Cambridge-Newton, MA M.D. | 28.6 | 129 | Fayetteville, NC | 0.0 | NA | La Crosse, WI-MN** | NA |
| 116 | Camden, NJ M.D. | 4.7 | 234 | Flagstaff, AZ | (24.1) | 14 | Lafayette, IN | 180.0 |
| 175 | Canton, OH | (6.3) | 209 | Flint, MI | (16.0) | 258 | Lafayette, LA | (30.6) |
| 285 | Cape Coral-Fort Myers, FL | (45.7) | 129 | Florence-Muscle Shoals, AL | 0.0 | NA | Lake Charles, LA** | NA |
| 55 | Cape Girardeau, MO-IL | 41.2 | 261 | Florence, SC | (31.2) | 15 | Lake Co.-Kenosha Co., IL-WI M.D. | 166.7 |
| NA | Carbondale-Marion, IL** | NA | NA | Fond du Lac, WI*** | NA | 242 | Lake Havasu City-Kingman, AZ | (25.4) |
| NA | Carson City, NV*** | NA | 277 | Fort Collins, CO | (40.0) | 288 | Lakeland, FL | (49.2) |
| 166 | Casper, WY | (2.6) | 165 | Fort Lauderdale, FL M.D. | (2.3) | NA | Lancaster, PA** | NA |
| 129 | Cedar Rapids, IA | 0.0 | 238 | Fort Smith, AR-OK | (25.0) | 173 | Lansing-East Lansing, MI | (5.9) |
| NA | Chambersburg-Waynesboro, PA** | NA | 57 | Fort Wayne, IN | 40.4 | 292 | Laredo, TX | (51.6) |
| 22 | Champaign-Urbana, IL | 123.5 | 107 | Fort Worth-Arlington, TX M.D. | 8.3 | 99 | Las Cruces, NM | 12.1 |
| 120 | Charleston-North Charleston, SC | 2.9 | 238 | Fresno, CA | (25.0) | 88 | Las Vegas-Henderson, NV | 18.7 |
| NA | Charlotte-Mecklenburg, NC-SC** | NA | 8 | Gadsden, AL | 305.3 | NA | Lawrence, KS*** | NA |
| 265 | Charlottesville, VA | (33.3) | 129 | Gainesville, FL | 0.0 | 161 | Lawton, OK | (1.0) |
| NA | Chattanooga, TN-GA** | NA | 166 | Gainesville, GA | (2.6) | 262 | Lebanon, PA | (31.8) |

Note: All listings are for Metropolitan Statistical Areas (M.S.A.s) except for those ending with "M.D." Listings with "M.D." are Metropolitan Divisions which are smaller parts of eleven large M.S.A.s. See explanatory note at beginning of metropolitan area section.

| RANK | METROPOLITAN AREA | % CHANGE |
|---|---|---|
| NA | Lewiston-Auburn, ME*** | NA |
| 129 | Lewiston, ID-WA | 0.0 |
| 67 | Lexington-Fayette, KY | 32.4 |
| 303 | Lima, OH | (61.3) |
| 80 | Lincoln, NE | 23.1 |
| 206 | Little Rock, AR | (15.4) |
| NA | Logan, UT-ID*** | NA |
| 49 | Longview, TX | 52.8 |
| 319 | Longview, WA | (74.4) |
| 185 | Los Angeles County, CA M.D. | (10.0) |
| 185 | Los Angeles (greater), CA | (10.0) |
| 226 | Louisville, KY-IN | (21.0) |
| 238 | Lubbock, TX | (25.0) |
| 212 | Lynchburg, VA | (17.4) |
| 185 | Macon, GA | (10.0) |
| 2 | Madera, CA | 553.8 |
| NA | Madison, WI** | NA |
| 1 | Manchester-Nashua, NH | 1,150.0 |
| 3 | Manhattan, KS | 500.0 |
| NA | Mankato-North Mankato, MN*** | NA |
| 307 | Mansfield, OH | (66.7) |
| 250 | McAllen-Edinburg-Mission, TX | (27.0) |
| 129 | Medford, OR | 0.0 |
| 189 | Memphis, TN-MS-AR | (10.4) |
| 92 | Merced, CA | 15.9 |
| 115 | Miami (greater), FL | 4.8 |
| 110 | Miami-Dade County, FL M.D. | 7.4 |
| 95 | Midland, TX | 14.7 |
| 128 | Milwaukee, WI | 1.4 |
| 97 | Minneapolis-St. Paul, MN-WI | 13.6 |
| NA | Missoula, MT*** | NA |
| 195 | Mobile, AL | (12.6) |
| 199 | Modesto, CA | (13.7) |
| 47 | Monroe, LA | 53.2 |
| 129 | Monroe, MI | 0.0 |
| 200 | Montgomery County, PA M.D. | (14.3) |
| 314 | Morgantown, WV | (69.6) |
| 269 | Morristown, TN | (34.6) |
| 29 | Mount Vernon-Anacortes, WA | 100.0 |
| 326 | Muncie, IN | (100.0) |
| NA | Muskegon, MI** | NA |
| NA | Myrtle Beach, SC-NC** | NA |
| 129 | Napa, CA | 0.0 |
| 29 | Naples-Marco Island, FL | 100.0 |
| 265 | Nashville-Davidson, TN | (33.3) |
| 129 | Nassau-Suffolk, NY M.D. | 0.0 |
| 305 | New Bern, NC | (65.2) |
| 221 | New Haven-Milford, CT | (19.5) |
| 177 | New Orleans, LA | (7.8) |
| 178 | New York (greater), NY-NJ-PA | (7.9) |
| 208 | New York-Jersey City, NY-NJ M.D. | (15.8) |
| 103 | Newark, NJ-PA M.D. | 9.2 |
| NA | Niles-Benton Harbor, MI** | NA |
| 298 | North Port-Sarasota-Bradenton, FL | (55.0) |
| 223 | Norwich-New London, CT | (20.6) |
| 252 | Oakland-Hayward, CA M.D. | (27.5) |
| 220 | Ocala, FL | (19.4) |
| 326 | Ocean City, NJ | (100.0) |
| 281 | Odessa, TX | (42.9) |
| 33 | Ogden-Clearfield, UT | 85.7 |
| 246 | Oklahoma City, OK | (26.3) |
| NA | Olympia, WA** | NA |

| RANK | METROPOLITAN AREA | % CHANGE |
|---|---|---|
| 108 | Omaha-Council Bluffs, NE-IA | 8.2 |
| 229 | Orlando, FL | (22.0) |
| 129 | Oshkosh-Neenah, WI | 0.0 |
| 129 | Owensboro, KY | 0.0 |
| 42 | Oxnard-Thousand Oaks, CA | 60.0 |
| 265 | Palm Bay-Melbourne, FL | (33.3) |
| 225 | Panama City, FL | (20.8) |
| 326 | Parkersburg-Vienna, WV | (100.0) |
| 70 | Pensacola, FL | 29.2 |
| 79 | Peoria, IL | 23.4 |
| 212 | Philadelphia (greater) PA-NJ-MD-DE | (17.4) |
| 229 | Philadelphia, PA M.D. | (22.0) |
| 182 | Phoenix-Mesa-Scottsdale, AZ | (9.4) |
| NA | Pittsburgh, PA** | NA |
| NA | Pittsfield, MA*** | NA |
| 307 | Pocatello, ID | (66.7) |
| 62 | Port St. Lucie, FL | 36.0 |
| 279 | Portland-Vancouver, OR-WA | (41.7) |
| 200 | Portland, ME | (14.3) |
| 320 | Prescott, AZ | (75.0) |
| 117 | Providence-Warwick, RI-MA | 4.2 |
| 43 | Provo-Orem, UT | 57.1 |
| 274 | Pueblo, CO | (36.7) |
| 129 | Punta Gorda, FL | 0.0 |
| 312 | Racine, WI | (67.7) |
| 50 | Raleigh, NC | 50.0 |
| 293 | Rapid City, SD | (51.7) |
| 278 | Reading, PA | (41.3) |
| 54 | Redding, CA | 43.6 |
| 33 | Reno, NV | 85.7 |
| 181 | Richmond, VA | (8.8) |
| 83 | Riverside-San Bernardino, CA | 22.0 |
| 52 | Roanoke, VA | 45.7 |
| 326 | Rochester, MN | (100.0) |
| 86 | Rochester, NY | 20.0 |
| 24 | Rockford, IL | 120.6 |
| 307 | Rockingham County, NH M.D. | (66.7) |
| 93 | Rocky Mount, NC | 15.4 |
| 218 | Rome, GA | (19.2) |
| 109 | Sacramento, CA | 7.9 |
| 74 | Saginaw, MI | 27.2 |
| 113 | Salem, OR | 6.1 |
| 122 | Salinas, CA | 2.8 |
| 244 | Salisbury, MD-DE | (25.6) |
| 214 | Salt Lake City, UT | (18.2) |
| NA | San Angelo, TX** | NA |
| 183 | San Antonio, TX | (9.8) |
| 271 | San Diego, CA | (35.3) |
| 245 | San Francisco (greater), CA | (26.2) |
| 252 | San Francisco-Redwood, CA M.D. | (27.5) |
| 129 | San Jose, CA | 0.0 |
| 214 | San Luis Obispo, CA | (18.2) |
| NA | San Rafael, CA M.D.*** | NA |
| 100 | Santa Cruz-Watsonville, CA | 10.8 |
| 129 | Santa Maria-Santa Barbara, CA | 0.0 |
| 21 | Santa Rosa, CA | 125.0 |
| 58 | Savannah, GA | 40.0 |
| NA | Scranton--Wilkes-Barre, PA** | NA |
| 234 | Seattle (greater), WA | (24.1) |
| 248 | Seattle-Bellevue-Everett, WA M.D. | (26.9) |
| 9 | Sebastian-Vero Beach, FL | 300.0 |
| 61 | Sebring, FL | 36.7 |

| RANK | METROPOLITAN AREA | % CHANGE |
|---|---|---|
| 321 | Sheboygan, WI | (79.1) |
| 19 | Sherman-Denison, TX | 137.5 |
| 53 | Shreveport-Bossier City, LA | 44.4 |
| 180 | Silver Spring-Frederick, MD M.D. | (8.3) |
| 129 | Sioux City, IA-NE-SD | 0.0 |
| 65 | Sioux Falls, SD | 33.3 |
| 296 | South Bend-Mishawaka, IN-MI | (54.7) |
| 246 | Spartanburg, SC | (26.3) |
| 170 | Spokane, WA | (5.1) |
| 17 | Springfield, IL | 150.0 |
| 25 | Springfield, MA | 114.3 |
| 276 | Springfield, MO | (38.0) |
| 82 | Springfield, OH | 22.2 |
| 326 | State College, PA | (100.0) |
| 129 | Staunton-Waynesboro, VA | 0.0 |
| 287 | Stockton-Lodi, CA | (48.0) |
| NA | St. Cloud, MN** | NA |
| 265 | St. George, UT | (33.3) |
| 129 | St. Joseph, MO-KS | 0.0 |
| 162 | St. Louis, MO-IL | (1.4) |
| 280 | Sumter, SC | (42.3) |
| 36 | Syracuse, NY | 82.6 |
| 231 | Tacoma, WA M.D. | (23.1) |
| 232 | Tallahassee, FL | (23.7) |
| 102 | Tampa-St Petersburg, FL | 10.3 |
| 233 | Terre Haute, IN | (23.9) |
| 237 | Texarkana, TX-AR | (24.5) |
| NA | The Villages, FL*** | NA |
| 260 | Toledo, OH | (31.0) |
| 254 | Topeka, KS | (27.6) |
| 44 | Trenton, NJ | 54.3 |
| 78 | Tucson, AZ | 24.6 |
| 90 | Tulsa, OK | 17.5 |
| 85 | Tuscaloosa, AL | 21.4 |
| 68 | Tyler, TX | 32.1 |
| 6 | Utica-Rome, NY | 338.5 |
| 104 | Vallejo-Fairfield, CA | 9.0 |
| 289 | Victoria, TX | (50.0) |
| 282 | Vineland-Bridgeton, NJ | (43.2) |
| 127 | Virginia Beach-Norfolk, VA-NC | 1.5 |
| 98 | Visalia-Porterville, CA | 12.2 |
| 256 | Waco, TX | (28.9) |
| 129 | Warner Robins, GA | 0.0 |
| 87 | Warren-Troy, MI M.D. | 18.8 |
| 122 | Washington (greater) DC-VA-MD-WV | 2.8 |
| 124 | Washington, DC-VA-MD-WV M.D. | 2.3 |
| 326 | Watertown-Fort Drum, NY | (100.0) |
| 129 | Wausau, WI | 0.0 |
| 164 | West Palm Beach, FL M.D. | (1.8) |
| 129 | Wichita Falls, TX | 0.0 |
| 178 | Wichita, KS | (7.9) |
| 12 | Williamsport, PA | 200.0 |
| 222 | Wilmington, DE-MD-NJ M.D. | (20.0) |
| 190 | Wilmington, NC | (10.5) |
| 46 | Winchester, VA-WV | 53.3 |
| 38 | Winston-Salem, NC | 75.0 |
| 129 | Worcester, MA-CT | 0.0 |
| 191 | Yakima, WA | (11.1) |
| 91 | York-Hanover, PA | 16.2 |
| 273 | Yuba City, CA | (35.4) |
| 39 | Yuma, AZ | 73.5 |

Source: CQ Press using reported data from the F.B.I. "Crime in the United States 2013"

*Includes nonnegligent manslaughter.  **Not available.  ***These metro areas had murder rates of 0 in 2012 but had at least one murder in 2013.  Calculating percent increase from zero results in an infinite number.  This is shown as "NA."

# 11. Percent Change in Murder Rate: 2012 to 2013 (continued)
## National Percent Change = 5.1% Decrease*

| RANK | METROPOLITAN AREA | % CHANGE | RANK | METROPOLITAN AREA | % CHANGE | RANK | METROPOLITAN AREA | % CHANGE |
|---|---|---|---|---|---|---|---|---|
| 1 | Manchester-Nashua, NH | 1,150.0 | 65 | Anniston-Oxford, AL | 33.3 | 129 | Albuquerque, NM | 0.0 |
| 2 | Madera, CA | 553.8 | 65 | Sioux Falls, SD | 33.3 | 129 | Ames, IA | 0.0 |
| 3 | Manhattan, KS | 500.0 | 67 | Lexington-Fayette, KY | 32.4 | 129 | Anchorage, AK | 0.0 |
| 4 | Columbus, IN | 376.9 | 68 | Tyler, TX | 32.1 | 129 | Appleton, WI | 0.0 |
| 5 | Kennewick-Richland, WA | 371.4 | 69 | Deltona-Daytona Beach, FL | 30.3 | 129 | Blacksburg, VA | 0.0 |
| 6 | Utica-Rome, NY | 338.5 | 70 | Pensacola, FL | 29.2 | 129 | Cedar Rapids, IA | 0.0 |
| 7 | Bloomington, IL | 320.0 | 71 | Cambridge-Newton, MA M.D. | 28.6 | 129 | Cumberland, MD-WV | 0.0 |
| 8 | Gadsden, AL | 305.3 | 72 | Austin-Round Rock, TX | 27.3 | 129 | Dover, DE | 0.0 |
| 9 | Sebastian-Vero Beach, FL | 300.0 | 72 | Elgin, IL M.D. | 27.3 | 129 | Duluth, MN-WI | 0.0 |
| 10 | Decatur, AL | 246.2 | 74 | Saginaw, MI | 27.2 | 129 | Farmington, NM | 0.0 |
| 11 | Kingston, NY | 240.0 | 75 | Indianapolis, IN | 26.7 | 129 | Fayetteville, NC | 0.0 |
| 12 | Coeur d'Alene, ID | 200.0 | 76 | Billings, MT | 26.3 | 129 | Florence-Muscle Shoals, AL | 0.0 |
| 12 | Williamsport, PA | 200.0 | 77 | Gary, IN M.D. | 24.7 | 129 | Gainesville, FL | 0.0 |
| 14 | Lafayette, IN | 180.0 | 78 | Tucson, AZ | 24.6 | 129 | Grand Forks, ND-MN | 0.0 |
| 15 | Lake Co.-Kenosha Co., IL-WI M.D. | 166.7 | 79 | Peoria, IL | 23.4 | 129 | Harrisonburg, VA | 0.0 |
| 16 | Houma, LA | 155.8 | 80 | Lincoln, NE | 23.1 | 129 | Lewiston, ID-WA | 0.0 |
| 17 | Dutchess-Putnam, NY M.D. | 150.0 | 81 | Hinesville, GA | 22.4 | 129 | Medford, OR | 0.0 |
| 17 | Springfield, IL | 150.0 | 82 | Springfield, OH | 22.2 | 129 | Monroe, MI | 0.0 |
| 19 | Sherman-Denison, TX | 137.5 | 83 | Riverside-San Bernardino, CA | 22.0 | 129 | Napa, CA | 0.0 |
| 20 | Crestview-Fort Walton Beach, FL | 133.3 | 84 | Huntsville, AL | 21.6 | 129 | Nassau-Suffolk, NY M.D. | 0.0 |
| 21 | Santa Rosa, CA | 125.0 | 85 | Tuscaloosa, AL | 21.4 | 129 | Oshkosh-Neenah, WI | 0.0 |
| 22 | Champaign-Urbana, IL | 123.5 | 86 | Rochester, NY | 20.0 | 129 | Owensboro, KY | 0.0 |
| 23 | Ann Arbor, MI | 121.4 | 87 | Warren-Troy, MI M.D. | 18.8 | 129 | Punta Gorda, FL | 0.0 |
| 24 | Rockford, IL | 120.6 | 88 | Las Vegas-Henderson, NV | 18.7 | 129 | San Jose, CA | 0.0 |
| 25 | Springfield, MA | 114.3 | 89 | Chico, CA | 18.4 | 129 | Santa Maria-Santa Barbara, CA | 0.0 |
| 26 | Bay City, MI | 111.1 | 90 | Tulsa, OK | 17.5 | 129 | Sioux City, IA-NE-SD | 0.0 |
| 27 | Colorado Springs, CO | 106.7 | 91 | York-Hanover, PA | 16.2 | 129 | Staunton-Waynesboro, VA | 0.0 |
| 28 | Johnstown, PA | 102.4 | 92 | Merced, CA | 15.9 | 129 | St. Joseph, MO-KS | 0.0 |
| 29 | East Stroudsburg, PA | 100.0 | 93 | Rocky Mount, NC | 15.4 | 129 | Warner Robins, GA | 0.0 |
| 29 | Fargo, ND-MN | 100.0 | 94 | Hagerstown-Martinsburg, MD-WV | 14.8 | 129 | Wausau, WI | 0.0 |
| 29 | Mount Vernon-Anacortes, WA | 100.0 | 95 | Midland, TX | 14.7 | 129 | Wichita Falls, TX | 0.0 |
| 29 | Naples-Marco Island, FL | 100.0 | 96 | Binghamton, NY | 14.3 | 129 | Worcester, MA-CT | 0.0 |
| 33 | Elizabethtown-Fort Knox, KY | 85.7 | 97 | Minneapolis-St. Paul, MN-WI | 13.6 | 161 | Lawton, OK | (1.0) |
| 33 | Ogden-Clearfield, UT | 85.7 | 98 | Visalia-Porterville, CA | 12.2 | 162 | St. Louis, MO-IL | (1.4) |
| 33 | Reno, NV | 85.7 | 99 | Las Cruces, NM | 12.1 | 163 | Greenville, NC | (1.6) |
| 36 | Syracuse, NY | 82.6 | 100 | Santa Cruz-Watsonville, CA | 10.8 | 164 | West Palm Beach, FL M.D. | (1.8) |
| 37 | Barnstable Town, MA | 80.0 | 101 | Buffalo-Niagara Falls, NY | 10.6 | 165 | Fort Lauderdale, FL M.D. | (2.3) |
| 38 | Winston-Salem, NC | 75.0 | 102 | Tampa-St Petersburg, FL | 10.3 | 166 | Casper, WY | (2.6) |
| 39 | Yuma, AZ | 73.5 | 103 | Newark, NJ-PA M.D. | 9.2 | 166 | Gainesville, GA | (2.6) |
| 40 | Des Moines-West Des Moines, IA | 64.3 | 104 | Hammond, LA | 9.0 | 168 | Atlanta, GA | (3.3) |
| 41 | Columbia, MO | 61.1 | 104 | Vallejo-Fairfield, CA | 9.0 | 169 | Kansas City, MO-KS | (3.9) |
| 42 | Oxnard-Thousand Oaks, CA | 60.0 | 106 | Fayetteville-Springdale, AR-MO | 8.7 | 170 | Denver-Aurora, CO | (5.1) |
| 43 | Provo-Orem, UT | 57.1 | 107 | Fort Worth-Arlington, TX M.D. | 8.3 | 170 | Spokane, WA | (5.1) |
| 44 | Trenton, NJ | 54.3 | 108 | Omaha-Council Bluffs, NE-IA | 8.2 | 172 | Hartford, CT | (5.6) |
| 45 | Hanford-Corcoran, CA | 53.8 | 109 | Sacramento, CA | 7.9 | 173 | Anaheim-Santa Ana-Irvine, CA M.D. | (5.9) |
| 46 | Winchester, VA-WV | 53.3 | 110 | Miami-Dade County, FL M.D. | 7.4 | 173 | Lansing-East Lansing, MI | (5.9) |
| 47 | Columbus, GA-AL | 53.2 | 111 | Dallas (greater), TX | 7.3 | 175 | Canton, OH | (6.3) |
| 47 | Monroe, LA | 53.2 | 112 | Dallas-Plano-Irving, TX M.D. | 6.8 | 176 | Bakersfield, CA | (6.6) |
| 49 | Longview, TX | 52.8 | 113 | Salem, OR | 6.1 | 177 | New Orleans, LA | (7.8) |
| 50 | Raleigh, NC | 50.0 | 114 | Baltimore, MD | 5.3 | 178 | New York (greater), NY-NJ-PA | (7.9) |
| 51 | Beaumont-Port Arthur, TX | 48.3 | 115 | Miami (greater), FL | 4.8 | 178 | Wichita, KS | (7.9) |
| 52 | Roanoke, VA | 45.7 | 116 | Camden, NJ M.D. | 4.7 | 180 | Silver Spring-Frederick, MD M.D. | (8.3) |
| 53 | Shreveport-Bossier City, LA | 44.4 | 117 | Providence-Warwick, RI-MA | 4.2 | 181 | Richmond, VA | (8.8) |
| 54 | Redding, CA | 43.6 | 118 | Albany-Schenectady-Troy, NY | 3.8 | 182 | Phoenix-Mesa-Scottsdale, AZ | (9.4) |
| 55 | Cape Girardeau, MO-IL | 41.2 | 119 | Houston, TX | 3.5 | 183 | San Antonio, TX | (9.8) |
| 56 | Dayton, OH | 41.0 | 120 | Charleston-North Charleston, SC | 2.9 | 184 | Chicago (greater), IL-IN-WI | (9.9) |
| 57 | Fort Wayne, IN | 40.4 | 120 | Homosassa Springs, FL | 2.9 | 185 | Knoxville, TN | (10.0) |
| 58 | Johnson City, TN | 40.0 | 122 | Salinas, CA | 2.8 | 185 | Los Angeles County, CA M.D. | (10.0) |
| 58 | Savannah, GA | 40.0 | 122 | Washington (greater) DC-VA-MD-WV | 2.8 | 185 | Los Angeles (greater), CA | (10.0) |
| 60 | Cincinnati, OH-KY-IN | 37.1 | 124 | Washington, DC-VA-MD-WV M.D. | 2.3 | 185 | Macon, GA | (10.0) |
| 61 | Sebring, FL | 36.7 | 125 | Corpus Christi, TX | 1.9 | 189 | Memphis, TN-MS-AR | (10.4) |
| 62 | Port St. Lucie, FL | 36.0 | 126 | Albany, GA | 1.8 | 190 | Wilmington, NC | (10.5) |
| 63 | Alexandria, LA | 34.5 | 127 | Virginia Beach-Norfolk, VA-NC | 1.5 | 191 | Yakima, WA | (11.1) |
| 64 | Akron, OH | 34.2 | 128 | Milwaukee, WI | 1.4 | 192 | Jacksonville, FL | (11.3) |

Note: All listings are for Metropolitan Statistical Areas (M.S.A.s) except for those ending with "M.D." Listings with "M.D." are Metropolitan Divisions which are smaller parts of eleven large M.S.A.s. See explanatory note at beginning of metropolitan area section.

| RANK | METROPOLITAN AREA | % CHANGE | RANK | METROPOLITAN AREA | % CHANGE | RANK | METROPOLITAN AREA | % CHANGE |
|---|---|---|---|---|---|---|---|---|
| 193 | Brunswick, GA | (11.4) | 255 | Bloomington, IN | (28.0) | 317 | Atlantic City, NJ | (73.4) |
| 194 | Detroit (greater), MI | (11.9) | 256 | Waco, TX | (28.9) | 318 | Green Bay, WI | (73.9) |
| 195 | Mobile, AL | (12.6) | 257 | Allentown, PA-NJ | (29.3) | 319 | Longview, WA | (74.4) |
| 196 | Birmingham-Hoover, AL | (12.8) | 258 | Lafayette, LA | (30.6) | 320 | Prescott, AZ | (75.0) |
| 197 | Boston, MA M.D. | (13.5) | 259 | Davenport, IA-IL | (30.8) | 321 | Sheboygan, WI | (79.1) |
| 198 | Baton Rouge, LA | (13.6) | 260 | Toledo, OH | (31.0) | 322 | Kahului-Wailuku-Lahaina, HI | (80.6) |
| 199 | Modesto, CA | (13.7) | 261 | Florence, SC | (31.2) | 323 | Cleveland, TN | (81.0) |
| 200 | Boston (greater), MA-NH | (14.3) | 262 | Lebanon, PA | (31.8) | 324 | Glens Falls, NY | (85.2) |
| 200 | Detroit-Dearborn-Livonia, MI M.D. | (14.3) | 263 | Joplin, MO | (32.4) | 325 | Daphne-Fairhope-Foley, AL | (88.4) |
| 200 | Montgomery County, PA M.D. | (14.3) | 264 | Augusta, GA-SC | (32.9) | 326 | Corvallis, OR | (100.0) |
| 200 | Portland, ME | (14.3) | 265 | Charlottesville, VA | (33.3) | 326 | Dubuque, IA | (100.0) |
| 204 | Decatur, IL | (14.8) | 265 | Nashville-Davidson, TN | (33.3) | 326 | Elmira, NY | (100.0) |
| 205 | Jackson, TN | (15.2) | 265 | Palm Bay-Melbourne, FL | (33.3) | 326 | Fairbanks, AK | (100.0) |
| 206 | Little Rock, AR | (15.4) | 265 | St. George, UT | (33.3) | 326 | Great Falls, MT | (100.0) |
| 207 | Greenville-Anderson, SC | (15.6) | 269 | Morristown, TN | (34.6) | 326 | Iowa City, IA | (100.0) |
| 208 | New York-Jersey City, NY-NJ M.D. | (15.8) | 270 | Jefferson City, MO | (35.0) | 326 | Muncie, IN | (100.0) |
| 209 | Flint, MI | (16.0) | 271 | El Centro, CA | (35.3) | 326 | Ocean City, NJ | (100.0) |
| 210 | Amarillo, TX | (16.7) | 271 | San Diego, CA | (35.3) | 326 | Parkersburg-Vienna, WV | (100.0) |
| 211 | Chicago-Naperville, IL M.D. | (17.1) | 273 | Yuba City, CA | (35.4) | 326 | Rochester, MN | (100.0) |
| 212 | Lynchburg, VA | (17.4) | 274 | Pueblo, CO | (36.7) | 326 | State College, PA | (100.0) |
| 212 | Philadelphia (greater) PA-NJ-MD-DE | (17.4) | 275 | Janesville, WI | (36.8) | 326 | Watertown-Fort Drum, NY | (100.0) |
| 214 | Boise City, ID | (18.2) | 276 | Springfield, MO | (38.0) | NA | Albany, OR*** | NA |
| 214 | Salt Lake City, UT | (18.2) | 277 | Fort Collins, CO | (40.0) | NA | Bend, OR** | NA |
| 214 | San Luis Obispo, CA | (18.2) | 278 | Reading, PA | (41.3) | NA | Boulder, CO*** | NA |
| 217 | Dothan, AL | (18.7) | 279 | Portland-Vancouver, OR-WA | (41.7) | NA | California-Lexington Park, MD*** | NA |
| 218 | College Station-Bryan, TX | (19.2) | 280 | Sumter, SC | (42.3) | NA | Carbondale-Marion, IL** | NA |
| 218 | Rome, GA | (19.2) | 281 | Odessa, TX | (42.9) | NA | Carson City, NV** | NA |
| 220 | Ocala, FL | (19.4) | 282 | Vineland-Bridgeton, NJ | (43.2) | NA | Chambersburg-Waynesboro, PA** | NA |
| 221 | New Haven-Milford, CT | (19.5) | 283 | Kingsport, TN-VA | (44.8) | NA | Charlotte-Mecklenburg, NC-SC** | NA |
| 222 | Wilmington, DE-MD-NJ M.D. | (20.0) | 284 | Eugene, OR | (45.0) | NA | Chattanooga, TN-GA** | NA |
| 223 | Grand Junction, CO | (20.6) | 285 | Cape Coral-Fort Myers, FL | (45.7) | NA | Columbia, SC** | NA |
| 223 | Norwich-New London, CT | (20.6) | 286 | Bloomsburg-Berwick, PA | (47.8) | NA | Eau Claire, WI** | NA |
| 225 | Panama City, FL | (20.8) | 287 | Stockton-Lodi, CA | (48.0) | NA | Fond du Lac, WI*** | NA |
| 226 | Louisville, KY-IN | (21.0) | 288 | Lakeland, FL | (49.2) | NA | Gettysburg, PA** | NA |
| 227 | Greensboro-High Point, NC | (21.7) | 289 | Dalton, GA | (50.0) | NA | Grand Island, NE*** | NA |
| 228 | Clarksville, TN-KY | (21.9) | 289 | Kokomo, IN | (50.0) | NA | Grand Rapids-Wyoming, MI** | NA |
| 229 | Orlando, FL | (22.0) | 289 | Victoria, TX | (50.0) | NA | Grants Pass, OR** | NA |
| 229 | Philadelphia, PA M.D. | (22.0) | 292 | Laredo, TX | (51.6) | NA | Gulfport-Biloxi-Pascagoula, MS** | NA |
| 231 | Tacoma, WA M.D. | (23.1) | 293 | Rapid City, SD | (51.7) | NA | Hot Springs, AR** | NA |
| 232 | Tallahassee, FL | (23.7) | 294 | Bowling Green, KY | (52.0) | NA | Idaho Falls, ID*** | NA |
| 233 | Terre Haute, IN | (23.9) | 295 | Cheyenne, WY | (52.4) | NA | Jackson, MI** | NA |
| 234 | Flagstaff, AZ | (24.1) | 296 | South Bend-Mishawaka, IN-MI | (54.7) | NA | La Crosse, WI-MN** | NA |
| 234 | Seattle (greater), WA | (24.1) | 297 | Brownsville-Harlingen, TX | (54.8) | NA | Lake Charles, LA** | NA |
| 236 | Kankakee, IL | (24.3) | 298 | North Port-Sarasota-Bradenton, FL | (55.0) | NA | Lancaster, PA** | NA |
| 237 | Texarkana, TX-AR | (24.5) | 299 | El Paso, TX | (57.6) | NA | Lawrence, KS*** | NA |
| 238 | Bangor, ME | (25.0) | 300 | Bremerton-Silverdale, WA | (57.9) | NA | Lewiston-Auburn, ME*** | NA |
| 238 | Fort Smith, AR-OK | (25.0) | 301 | Bridgeport-Stamford, CT | (58.3) | NA | Logan, UT-ID*** | NA |
| 238 | Fresno, CA | (25.0) | 302 | Goldsboro, NC | (60.0) | NA | Madison, WI** | NA |
| 238 | Lubbock, TX | (25.0) | 303 | Lima, OH | (61.3) | NA | Mankato-North Mankato, MN*** | NA |
| 242 | Jackson, MS | (25.4) | 304 | Erie, PA | (64.1) | NA | Missoula, MT*** | NA |
| 242 | Lake Havasu City-Kingman, AZ | (25.4) | 305 | New Bern, NC | (65.2) | NA | Muskegon, MI** | NA |
| 244 | Salisbury, MD-DE | (25.6) | 306 | Altoona, PA | (66.0) | NA | Myrtle Beach, SC-NC** | NA |
| 245 | San Francisco (greater), CA | (26.2) | 307 | Abilene, TX | (66.7) | NA | Niles-Benton Harbor, MI** | NA |
| 246 | Oklahoma City, OK | (26.3) | 307 | Mansfield, OH | (66.7) | NA | Olympia, WA** | NA |
| 246 | Spartanburg, SC | (26.3) | 307 | Pocatello, ID | (66.7) | NA | Pittsburgh, PA** | NA |
| 248 | Burlington, NC | (26.9) | 307 | Rockingham County, NH M.D. | (66.7) | NA | Pittsfield, MA*** | NA |
| 248 | Seattle-Bellevue-Everett, WA M.D. | (26.9) | 311 | Jonesboro, AR | (67.3) | NA | San Angelo, TX** | NA |
| 250 | McAllen-Edinburg-Mission, TX | (27.0) | 312 | Athens-Clarke County, GA | (67.7) | NA | San Rafael, CA M.D.*** | NA |
| 251 | Bismarck, ND | (27.3) | 312 | Racine, WI | (67.7) | NA | Scranton--Wilkes-Barre, PA** | NA |
| 252 | Oakland-Hayward, CA M.D. | (27.5) | 314 | Greeley, CO | (69.6) | NA | St. Cloud, MN** | NA |
| 252 | San Francisco-Redwood, CA M.D. | (27.5) | 314 | Morgantown, WV | (69.6) | NA | The Villages, FL*** | NA |
| 254 | Topeka, KS | (27.6) | 316 | Hilton Head Island, SC | (72.7) | | | |

Source: CQ Press using reported data from the F.B.I. "Crime in the United States 2013"
*Includes nonnegligent manslaughter.  **Not available.  ***These metro areas had murder rates of 0 in 2012 but had at least one murder in 2013.  Calculating percent increase from zero results in an infinite number.  This is shown as "NA."

# 12. Percent Change in Murder Rate: 2009 to 2013
## National Percent Change = 10.5% Decrease*

| RANK | METROPOLITAN AREA | % CHANGE | RANK | METROPOLITAN AREA | % CHANGE | RANK | METROPOLITAN AREA | % CHANGE |
|---|---|---|---|---|---|---|---|---|
| 292 | Abilene, TX | (86.4) | 288 | Cheyenne, WY | (77.8) | NA | Gary, IN M.D.** | NA |
| 76 | Akron, OH | 27.5 | NA | Chicago (greater), IL-IN-WI** | NA | NA | Gettysburg, PA** | NA |
| 141 | Albany-Schenectady-Troy, NY | (3.6) | NA | Chicago-Naperville, IL M.D.** | NA | NA | Glens Falls, NY*** | NA |
| 109 | Albany, GA | 5.6 | 73 | Chico, CA | 28.9 | 252 | Goldsboro, NC | (48.0) |
| NA | Albany, OR** | NA | 94 | Cincinnati, OH-KY-IN | 17.1 | NA | Grand Forks, ND-MN*** | NA |
| 205 | Albuquerque, NM | (25.3) | 224 | Clarksville, TN-KY | (33.3) | NA | Grand Island, NE** | NA |
| 85 | Alexandria, LA | 20.0 | 281 | Cleveland, TN | (69.2) | 24 | Grand Junction, CO | 92.9 |
| 116 | Allentown, PA-NJ | 0.0 | 51 | Coeur d'Alene, ID | 50.0 | NA | Grand Rapids-Wyoming, MI** | NA |
| 224 | Altoona, PA | (33.3) | 167 | College Station-Bryan, TX | (12.5) | NA | Grants Pass, OR** | NA |
| 228 | Amarillo, TX | (34.0) | 27 | Colorado Springs, CO | 87.9 | 293 | Great Falls, MT | (100.0) |
| 116 | Ames, IA | 0.0 | 44 | Columbia, MO | 61.1 | 285 | Greeley, CO | (74.1) |
| 220 | Anaheim-Santa Ana-Irvine, CA M.D. | (30.4) | 207 | Columbia, SC | (25.4) | 275 | Green Bay, WI | (62.5) |
| 110 | Anchorage, AK | 4.3 | 38 | Columbus, GA-AL | 69.6 | 143 | Greensboro-High Point, NC | (4.1) |
| 29 | Ann Arbor, MI | 82.4 | NA | Columbus, IN*** | NA | NA | Greenville-Anderson, SC** | NA |
| 74 | Anniston-Oxford, AL | 28.3 | 207 | Columbia, SC | (25.4) | NA | Greenville, NC** | NA |
| 284 | Appleton, WI | (71.4) | 51 | Corpus Christi, TX | 50.0 | NA | Gulfport-Biloxi-Pascagoula, MS** | NA |
| 291 | Athens-Clarke County, GA | (82.8) | 293 | Corvallis, OR | (100.0) | 12 | Hagerstown-Martinsburg, MD-WV | 181.8 |
| 116 | Athens-Clarke County, GA | 0.0 | NA | Crestview-Fort Walton Beach, FL** | NA | NA | Hammond, LA** | NA |
| 116 | Atlanta, GA | 0.0 | 22 | Cumberland, MD-WV | 95.0 | NA | Hanford-Corcoran, CA** | NA |
| 279 | Atlantic City, NJ | (67.0) | 156 | Dallas (greater), TX | (8.3) | 264 | Harrisonburg, VA | (52.9) |
| 216 | Augusta, GA-SC | (29.5) | 170 | Dallas-Plano-Irving, TX M.D. | (13.0) | 209 | Hartford, CT | (26.1) |
| 95 | Austin-Round Rock, TX | 16.7 | 153 | Dalton, GA | (6.7) | NA | Hilton Head Island, SC** | NA |
| 198 | Bakersfield, CA | (22.8) | NA | Daphne-Fairhope-Foley, AL** | NA | 18 | Hinesville, GA | 106.9 |
| 160 | Baltimore, MD | (9.9) | NA | Davenport, IA-IL** | NA | NA | Homosassa Springs, FL** | NA |
| 57 | Bangor, ME | 44.4 | 136 | Dayton, OH | (1.8) | 155 | Hot Springs, AR | (7.9) |
| 255 | Barnstable Town, MA | (50.0) | 5 | Decatur, AL | 246.2 | 45 | Houma, LA | 59.4 |
| 212 | Baton Rouge, LA | (27.1) | 42 | Decatur, IL | 64.3 | 205 | Houston, TX | (25.3) |
| 222 | Bay City, MI | (32.1) | 97 | Deltona-Daytona Beach, FL | 13.2 | 90 | Huntsville, AL | 19.2 |
| 37 | Beaumont-Port Arthur, TX | 72.0 | 149 | Denver-Aurora, CO | (5.1) | 61 | Idaho Falls, ID | 37.5 |
| 51 | Bend, OR | 50.0 | 25 | Des Moines-West Des Moines, IA | 91.7 | 92 | Indianapolis, IN | 18.8 |
| 85 | Billings, MT | 20.0 | 146 | Detroit (greater), MI | (5.0) | 293 | Iowa City, IA | (100.0) |
| 267 | Binghamton, NY | (54.3) | 134 | Detroit-Dearborn-Livonia, MI M.D. | (1.0) | 193 | Jacksonville, FL | (22.0) |
| 164 | Birmingham-Hoover, AL | (11.8) | 11 | Dothan, AL | 190.5 | 234 | Jackson, MI | (38.0) |
| 174 | Bismarck, ND | (14.3) | 142 | Dover, DE | (4.0) | 80 | Jackson, MS | 23.5 |
| 289 | Blacksburg, VA | (78.0) | 293 | Dubuque, IA | (100.0) | 231 | Jackson, TN | (36.4) |
| NA | Bloomington, IL** | NA | 195 | Duluth, MN-WI | (22.2) | 280 | Janesville, WI | (67.6) |
| 99 | Bloomington, IN | 12.5 | NA | Dutchess-Putnam, NY M.D.** | NA | 274 | Jefferson City, MO | (61.8) |
| NA | Bloomsburg-Berwick, PA** | NA | NA | East Stroudsburg, PA** | NA | 233 | Johnson City, TN | (37.5) |
| 245 | Boise City, ID | (43.8) | 19 | Eau Claire, WI | 100.0 | NA | Johnstown, PA** | NA |
| 201 | Boston (greater), MA-NH | (25.0) | 239 | El Centro, CA | (38.9) | 229 | Jonesboro, AR | (36.0) |
| 183 | Boston, MA M.D. | (17.9) | 224 | El Paso, TX | (33.3) | NA | Joplin, MO** | NA |
| 286 | Boulder, CO | (75.0) | NA | Elgin, IL M.D.** | NA | NA | Kahului-Wailuku-Lahaina, HI** | NA |
| NA | Bowling Green, KY** | NA | NA | Elizabethtown-Fort Knox, KY** | NA | NA | Kankakee, IL** | NA |
| 264 | Bremerton-Silverdale, WA | (52.9) | 293 | Elmira, NY | (100.0) | 152 | Kansas City, MO-KS | (6.3) |
| 201 | Bridgeport-Stamford, CT | (25.0) | 272 | Erie, PA | (61.1) | 1 | Kennewick-Richland, WA | 725.0 |
| 219 | Brownsville-Harlingen, TX | (30.0) | 116 | Eugene, OR | 0.0 | 261 | Kingsport, TN-VA | (51.5) |
| 270 | Brunswick, GA | (60.0) | 116 | Fairbanks, AK | 0.0 | 7 | Kingston, NY | 240.0 |
| 196 | Buffalo-Niagara Falls, NY | (22.4) | 31 | Fargo, ND-MN | 80.0 | 184 | Knoxville, TN | (18.2) |
| 217 | Burlington, NC | (29.6) | 21 | Farmington, NM | 95.8 | 15 | Kokomo, IN | 140.0 |
| NA | California-Lexington Park, MD** | NA | 55 | Fayetteville-Springdale, AR-MO | 47.1 | NA | La Crosse, WI-MN** | NA |
| NA | Cambridge-Newton, MA M.D.** | NA | 187 | Fayetteville, NC | (18.6) | NA | Lafayette, IN*** | NA |
| 40 | Camden, NJ M.D. | 67.5 | 266 | Flagstaff, AZ | (53.2) | NA | Lafayette, LA** | NA |
| NA | Canton, OH** | NA | 69 | Flint, MI | 33.0 | 217 | Lake Charles, LA | (29.6) |
| 243 | Cape Coral-Fort Myers, FL | (42.4) | 213 | Florence-Muscle Shoals, AL | (29.2) | NA | Lake Co.-Kenosha Co., IL-WI M.D.** | NA |
| 6 | Cape Girardeau, MO-IL | 242.9 | 248 | Florence, SC | (46.5) | 104 | Lake Havasu City-Kingman, AZ | 10.0 |
| NA | Carbondale-Marion, IL** | NA | 255 | Fond du Lac, WI | (50.0) | 208 | Lakeland, FL | (25.6) |
| NA | Carson City, NV*** | NA | 282 | Fort Collins, CO | (70.0) | NA | Lancaster, PA** | NA |
| NA | Casper, WY*** | NA | 116 | Fort Lauderdale, FL M.D. | 0.0 | 81 | Lansing-East Lansing, MI | 23.1 |
| 3 | Cedar Rapids, IA | 275.0 | 236 | Fort Smith, AR-OK | (38.2) | 290 | Laredo, TX | (78.6) |
| NA | Chambersburg-Waynesboro, PA** | NA | 50 | Fort Wayne, IN | 50.9 | 106 | Las Cruces, NM | 8.8 |
| NA | Champaign-Urbana, IL** | NA | 101 | Fort Worth-Arlington, TX M.D. | 11.4 | 187 | Las Vegas-Henderson, NV | (18.6) |
| 72 | Charleston-North Charleston, SC | 30.9 | 190 | Fresno, CA | (20.0) | NA | Lawrence, KS*** | NA |
| NA | Charlotte-Mecklenburg, NC-SC** | NA | 14 | Gadsden, AL | 165.5 | 83 | Lawton, OK | 21.3 |
| 4 | Charlottesville, VA | 260.0 | 62 | Gainesville, FL | 37.0 | 287 | Lebanon, PA | (75.4) |
| 161 | Chattanooga, TN-GA | (10.9) | 58 | Gainesville, GA | 42.3 | | | |

Note: All listings are for Metropolitan Statistical Areas (M.S.A.s) except for those ending with "M.D." Listings with "M.D." are Metropolitan Divisions which are smaller parts of eleven large M.S.A.s. See explanatory note at beginning of metropolitan area section.

| RANK | METROPOLITAN AREA | % CHANGE | RANK | METROPOLITAN AREA | % CHANGE | RANK | METROPOLITAN AREA | % CHANGE |
|---|---|---|---|---|---|---|---|---|
| NA | Lewiston-Auburn, ME*** | NA | 65 | Omaha-Council Bluffs, NE-IA | 35.9 | 250 | Sheboygan, WI | (47.1) |
| 293 | Lewiston, ID-WA | (100.0) | 210 | Orlando, FL | (26.4) | 35 | Sherman-Denison, TX | 72.7 |
| 43 | Lexington-Fayette, KY | 63.3 | 116 | Oshkosh-Neenah, WI | 0.0 | 180 | Shreveport-Bossier City, LA | (17.0) |
| 254 | Lima, OH | (49.1) | 293 | Owensboro, KY | (100.0) | 239 | Silver Spring-Frederick, MD M.D. | (38.9) |
| 81 | Lincoln, NE | 23.1 | 102 | Oxnard-Thousand Oaks, CA | 11.1 | 174 | Sioux City, IA-NE-SD | (14.3) |
| 111 | Little Rock, AR | 4.1 | 201 | Palm Bay-Melbourne, FL | (25.0) | 9 | Sioux Falls, SD | 200.0 |
| NA | Logan, UT-ID*** | NA | 199 | Panama City, FL | (23.6) | 244 | South Bend-Mishawaka, IN-MI | (43.3) |
| 223 | Longview, TX | (32.9) | NA | Parkersburg-Vienna, WV** | NA | 241 | Spartanburg, SC | (39.1) |
| 116 | Longview, WA | 0.0 | 47 | Pensacola, FL | 55.0 | 32 | Spokane, WA | 76.2 |
| 200 | Los Angeles County, CA M.D. | (23.9) | NA | Peoria, IL** | NA | NA | Springfield, IL** | NA |
| 201 | Los Angeles (greater), CA | (25.0) | 139 | Philadelphia (greater) PA-NJ-MD-DE | (2.7) | 70 | Springfield, MA | 32.4 |
| 161 | Louisville, KY-IN | (10.9) | NA | Philadelphia, PA M.D.** | NA | 36 | Springfield, MO | 72.2 |
| 242 | Lubbock, TX | (41.2) | 159 | Phoenix-Mesa-Scottsdale, AZ | (9.4) | 49 | Springfield, OH | 51.7 |
| 146 | Lynchburg, VA | (5.0) | NA | Pittsburgh, PA** | NA | 293 | State College, PA | (100.0) |
| 134 | Macon, GA | (1.0) | 249 | Pittsfield, MA | (46.7) | NA | Staunton-Waynesboro, VA** | NA |
| 2 | Madera, CA | 325.0 | 105 | Pocatello, ID | 9.1 | 165 | Stockton-Lodi, CA | (12.0) |
| NA | Madison, WI** | NA | 181 | Port St. Lucie, FL | (17.1) | 157 | St. Cloud, MN | (9.1) |
| 41 | Manchester-Nashua, NH | 66.7 | 224 | Portland-Vancouver, OR-WA | (33.3) | 116 | St. George, UT | 0.0 |
| 28 | Manhattan, KS | 87.5 | 263 | Portland, ME | (52.0) | 255 | St. Joseph, MO-KS | (50.0) |
| 30 | Mankato-North Mankato, MN | 81.8 | 116 | Prescott, AZ | 0.0 | 139 | St. Louis, MO-IL | (2.7) |
| 278 | Mansfield, OH | (66.7) | 173 | Providence-Warwick, RI-MA | (13.8) | 246 | Sumter, SC | (44.3) |
| 255 | McAllen-Edinburg-Mission, TX | (50.0) | 46 | Provo-Orem, UT | 57.1 | 78 | Syracuse, NY | 27.3 |
| 26 | Medford, OR | 90.0 | 277 | Pueblo, CO | (64.8) | 179 | Tacoma, WA M.D. | (16.7) |
| 177 | Memphis, TN-MS-AR | (14.9) | 282 | Punta Gorda, FL | (70.0) | 79 | Tallahassee, FL | 25.0 |
| 137 | Merced, CA | (1.9) | 270 | Racine, WI | (60.0) | 89 | Tampa-St Petersburg, FL | 19.4 |
| 145 | Miami (greater), FL | (4.3) | 93 | Raleigh, NC | 17.4 | NA | Terre Haute, IN** | NA |
| 116 | Miami-Dade County, FL M.D. | 0.0 | 167 | Rapid City, SD | (12.5) | 276 | Texarkana, TX-AR | (63.6) |
| 38 | Midland, TX | 69.6 | 221 | Reading, PA | (30.8) | NA | The Villages, FL** | NA |
| 67 | Milwaukee, WI | 34.6 | 8 | Redding, CA | 229.4 | 158 | Toledo, OH | (9.3) |
| 55 | Minneapolis-St. Paul, MN-WI | 47.1 | 84 | Reno, NV | 20.9 | 232 | Topeka, KS | (36.8) |
| 116 | Missoula, MT | 0.0 | 107 | Richmond, VA | 6.9 | 16 | Trenton, NJ | 134.8 |
| 103 | Mobile, AL | 10.2 | 138 | Riverside-San Bernardino, CA | (2.0) | 71 | Tucson, AZ | 31.5 |
| 213 | Modesto, CA | (29.2) | 76 | Roanoke, VA | 27.5 | 194 | Tulsa, OK | (22.1) |
| NA | Monroe, LA** | NA | 293 | Rochester, MN | (100.0) | 115 | Tuscaloosa, AL | 1.5 |
| 116 | Monroe, MI | 0.0 | 68 | Rochester, NY | 33.3 | 48 | Tyler, TX | 54.2 |
| NA | Montgomery County, PA M.D.** | NA | NA | Rockford, IL** | NA | 17 | Utica-Rome, NY | 111.1 |
| 269 | Morgantown, WV | (58.8) | 116 | Rockingham County, NH M.D. | 0.0 | 54 | Vallejo-Fairfield, CA | 49.0 |
| 197 | Morristown, TN | (22.7) | 59 | Rocky Mount, NC | 40.0 | 90 | Victoria, TX | 19.2 |
| 63 | Mount Vernon-Anacortes, WA | 36.0 | 66 | Rome, GA | 35.5 | 260 | Vineland-Bridgeton, NJ | (51.0) |
| 293 | Muncie, IN | (100.0) | 112 | Sacramento, CA | 2.5 | NA | Virginia Beach-Norfolk, VA-NC** | NA |
| 34 | Muskegon, MI | 73.5 | 13 | Saginaw, MI | 174.3 | 75 | Visalia-Porterville, CA | 27.8 |
| NA | Myrtle Beach, SC-NC** | NA | 23 | Salem, OR | 94.4 | 262 | Waco, TX | (51.8) |
| 19 | Napa, CA | 100.0 | 169 | Salinas, CA | (12.8) | NA | Warner Robins, GA** | NA |
| 184 | Naples-Marco Island, FL | (18.2) | NA | Salisbury, MD-DE** | NA | 146 | Warren-Troy, MI M.D. | (5.0) |
| 259 | Nashville-Davidson, TN | (50.7) | 150 | Salt Lake City, UT | (5.3) | 237 | Washington (greater) DC-VA-MD-WV | (38.3) |
| 184 | Nassau-Suffolk, NY M.D. | (18.2) | 251 | San Angelo, TX | (47.6) | 234 | Washington, DC-VA-MD-WV M.D. | (38.0) |
| NA | New Bern, NC** | NA | 211 | San Antonio, TX | (27.0) | NA | Watertown-Fort Drum, NY** | NA |
| 171 | New Haven-Milford, CT | (13.2) | 165 | San Diego, CA | (12.0) | 116 | Wausau, WI | 0.0 |
| 163 | New Orleans, LA | (11.2) | 215 | San Francisco (greater), CA | (29.4) | 192 | West Palm Beach, FL M.D. | (20.6) |
| 176 | New York (greater), NY-NJ-PA | (14.6) | 116 | San Francisco-Redwood, CA M.D. | 0.0 | 238 | Wichita Falls, TX | (38.7) |
| NA | New York-Jersey City, NY-NJ M.D.** | NA | 85 | San Jose, CA | 20.0 | 187 | Wichita, KS | (18.6) |
| 98 | Newark, NJ-PA M.D. | 12.7 | 85 | San Luis Obispo, CA | 20.0 | 9 | Williamsport, PA | 200.0 |
| 116 | Niles-Benton Harbor, MI | 0.0 | NA | San Rafael, CA M.D.** | NA | 100 | Wilmington, DE-MD-NJ M.D. | 12.0 |
| 268 | North Port-Sarasota-Bradenton, FL | (55.7) | 112 | Santa Cruz-Watsonville, CA | 2.5 | 63 | Wilmington, NC | 36.0 |
| 154 | Norwich-New London, CT | (6.9) | 253 | Santa Maria-Santa Barbara, CA | (48.1) | 144 | Winchester, VA-WV | (4.2) |
| 230 | Oakland-Hayward, CA M.D. | (36.3) | 150 | Santa Rosa, CA | (5.3) | NA | Winston-Salem, NC** | NA |
| 60 | Ocala, FL | 38.9 | 108 | Savannah, GA | 6.5 | 190 | Worcester, MA-CT | (20.0) |
| 293 | Ocean City, NJ | (100.0) | NA | Scranton--Wilkes-Barre, PA** | NA | NA | Yakima, WA** | NA |
| 273 | Odessa, TX | (61.5) | 178 | Seattle (greater), WA | (15.4) | 114 | York-Hanover, PA | 2.4 |
| 116 | Ogden-Clearfield, UT | 0.0 | 182 | Seattle-Bellevue-Everett, WA M.D. | (17.4) | 33 | Yuba City, CA | 75.0 |
| 171 | Oklahoma City, OK | (13.2) | 247 | Sebastian-Vero Beach, FL | (46.2) | 96 | Yuma, AZ | 15.7 |
| NA | Olympia, WA** | NA | NA | Sebring, FL** | NA | | | |

Source: CQ Press using reported data from the F.B.I. "Crime in the United States 2013"

*Includes nonnegligent manslaughter.  **Not available.  ***These metro areas had murder rates of 0 in 2009 but had at least one murder in 2013.  Calculating percent increase from zero results in an infinite number.  This is shown as "NA."

# 12. Percent Change in Murder Rate: 2009 to 2013 (continued)
## National Percent Change = 10.5% Decrease*

| RANK | METROPOLITAN AREA | % CHANGE | RANK | METROPOLITAN AREA | % CHANGE | RANK | METROPOLITAN AREA | % CHANGE |
|---|---|---|---|---|---|---|---|---|
| 1 | Kennewick-Richland, WA | 725.0 | 65 | Omaha-Council Bluffs, NE-IA | 35.9 | 116 | Prescott, AZ | 0.0 |
| 2 | Madera, CA | 325.0 | 66 | Rome, GA | 35.5 | 116 | Rockingham County, NH M.D. | 0.0 |
| 3 | Cedar Rapids, IA | 275.0 | 67 | Milwaukee, WI | 34.6 | 116 | San Francisco-Redwood, CA M.D. | 0.0 |
| 4 | Charlottesville, VA | 260.0 | 68 | Rochester, NY | 33.3 | 116 | St. George, UT | 0.0 |
| 5 | Decatur, AL | 246.2 | 69 | Flint, MI | 33.0 | 116 | Wausau, WI | 0.0 |
| 6 | Cape Girardeau, MO-IL | 242.9 | 70 | Springfield, MA | 32.4 | 134 | Detroit-Dearborn-Livonia, MI M.D. | (1.0) |
| 7 | Kingston, NY | 240.0 | 71 | Tucson, AZ | 31.5 | 134 | Macon, GA | (1.0) |
| 8 | Redding, CA | 229.4 | 72 | Charleston-North Charleston, SC | 30.9 | 136 | Dayton, OH | (1.8) |
| 9 | Sioux Falls, SD | 200.0 | 73 | Chico, CA | 28.9 | 137 | Merced, CA | (1.9) |
| 9 | Williamsport, PA | 200.0 | 74 | Anniston-Oxford, AL | 28.3 | 138 | Riverside-San Bernardino, CA | (2.0) |
| 11 | Dothan, AL | 190.5 | 75 | Visalia-Porterville, CA | 27.8 | 139 | Philadelphia (greater) PA-NJ-MD-DE | (2.7) |
| 12 | Hagerstown-Martinsburg, MD-WV | 181.8 | 76 | Akron, OH | 27.5 | 139 | St. Louis, MO-IL | (2.7) |
| 13 | Saginaw, MI | 174.3 | 76 | Roanoke, VA | 27.5 | 141 | Albany-Schenectady-Troy, NY | (3.6) |
| 14 | Gadsden, AL | 165.5 | 78 | Syracuse, NY | 27.3 | 142 | Dover, DE | (4.0) |
| 15 | Kokomo, IN | 140.0 | 79 | Tallahassee, FL | 25.0 | 143 | Greensboro-High Point, NC | (4.1) |
| 16 | Trenton, NJ | 134.8 | 80 | Jackson, MS | 23.5 | 144 | Winchester, VA-WV | (4.2) |
| 17 | Utica-Rome, NY | 111.1 | 81 | Lansing-East Lansing, MI | 23.1 | 145 | Miami (greater), FL | (4.3) |
| 18 | Hinesville, GA | 106.9 | 81 | Lincoln, NE | 23.1 | 146 | Detroit (greater), MI | (5.0) |
| 19 | Eau Claire, WI | 100.0 | 83 | Lawton, OK | 21.3 | 146 | Lynchburg, VA | (5.0) |
| 19 | Napa, CA | 100.0 | 84 | Reno, NV | 20.9 | 146 | Warren-Troy, MI M.D. | (5.0) |
| 21 | Farmington, NM | 95.8 | 85 | Alexandria, LA | 20.0 | 149 | Denver-Aurora, CO | (5.1) |
| 22 | Cumberland, MD-WV | 95.0 | 85 | Billings, MT | 20.0 | 150 | Salt Lake City, UT | (5.3) |
| 23 | Salem, OR | 94.4 | 85 | San Jose, CA | 20.0 | 150 | Santa Rosa, CA | (5.3) |
| 24 | Grand Junction, CO | 92.9 | 85 | San Luis Obispo, CA | 20.0 | 152 | Kansas City, MO-KS | (6.3) |
| 25 | Des Moines-West Des Moines, IA | 91.7 | 89 | Tampa-St Petersburg, FL | 19.4 | 153 | Dalton, GA | (6.7) |
| 26 | Medford, OR | 90.0 | 90 | Huntsville, AL | 19.2 | 154 | Norwich-New London, CT | (6.9) |
| 27 | Colorado Springs, CO | 87.9 | 90 | Victoria, TX | 19.2 | 155 | Hot Springs, AR | (7.9) |
| 28 | Manhattan, KS | 87.5 | 92 | Indianapolis, IN | 18.8 | 156 | Dallas (greater), TX | (8.3) |
| 29 | Ann Arbor, MI | 82.4 | 93 | Raleigh, NC | 17.4 | 157 | St. Cloud, MN | (9.1) |
| 30 | Mankato-North Mankato, MN | 81.8 | 94 | Cincinnati, OH-KY-IN | 17.1 | 158 | Toledo, OH | (9.3) |
| 31 | Fargo, ND-MN | 80.0 | 95 | Austin-Round Rock, TX | 16.7 | 159 | Phoenix-Mesa-Scottsdale, AZ | (9.4) |
| 32 | Spokane, WA | 76.2 | 96 | Yuma, AZ | 15.7 | 160 | Baltimore, MD | (9.9) |
| 33 | Yuba City, CA | 75.0 | 97 | Deltona-Daytona Beach, FL | 13.2 | 161 | Chattanooga, TN-GA | (10.9) |
| 34 | Muskegon, MI | 73.5 | 98 | Newark, NJ-PA M.D. | 12.7 | 161 | Louisville, KY-IN | (10.9) |
| 35 | Sherman-Denison, TX | 72.7 | 99 | Bloomington, IN | 12.5 | 163 | New Orleans, LA | (11.2) |
| 36 | Springfield, MO | 72.2 | 100 | Wilmington, DE-MD-NJ M.D. | 12.0 | 164 | Birmingham-Hoover, AL | (11.8) |
| 37 | Beaumont-Port Arthur, TX | 72.0 | 101 | Fort Worth-Arlington, TX M.D. | 11.4 | 165 | San Diego, CA | (12.0) |
| 38 | Columbus, GA-AL | 69.6 | 102 | Oxnard-Thousand Oaks, CA | 11.1 | 165 | Stockton-Lodi, CA | (12.0) |
| 38 | Midland, TX | 69.6 | 103 | Mobile, AL | 10.2 | 167 | College Station-Bryan, TX | (12.5) |
| 40 | Camden, NJ M.D. | 67.5 | 104 | Lake Havasu City-Kingman, AZ | 10.0 | 167 | Rapid City, SD | (12.5) |
| 41 | Manchester-Nashua, NH | 66.7 | 105 | Pocatello, ID | 9.1 | 169 | Salinas, CA | (12.8) |
| 42 | Decatur, IL | 64.3 | 106 | Las Cruces, NM | 8.8 | 170 | Dallas-Plano-Irving, TX M.D. | (13.0) |
| 43 | Lexington-Fayette, KY | 63.3 | 107 | Richmond, VA | 6.9 | 171 | New Haven-Milford, CT | (13.2) |
| 44 | Columbia, MO | 61.1 | 108 | Savannah, GA | 6.5 | 171 | Oklahoma City, OK | (13.2) |
| 45 | Houma, LA | 59.4 | 109 | Albany, GA | 5.6 | 173 | Providence-Warwick, RI-MA | (13.8) |
| 46 | Provo-Orem, UT | 57.1 | 110 | Anchorage, AK | 4.3 | 174 | Bismarck, ND | (14.3) |
| 47 | Pensacola, FL | 55.0 | 111 | Little Rock, AR | 4.1 | 174 | Sioux City, IA-NE-SD | (14.3) |
| 48 | Tyler, TX | 54.2 | 112 | Sacramento, CA | 2.5 | 176 | New York (greater), NY-NJ-PA | (14.6) |
| 49 | Springfield, OH | 51.7 | 112 | Santa Cruz-Watsonville, CA | 2.5 | 177 | Memphis, TN-MS-AR | (14.9) |
| 50 | Fort Wayne, IN | 50.9 | 114 | York-Hanover, PA | 2.4 | 178 | Seattle (greater), WA | (15.4) |
| 51 | Bend, OR | 50.0 | 115 | Tuscaloosa, AL | 1.5 | 179 | Tacoma, WA M.D. | (16.7) |
| 51 | Coeur d'Alene, ID | 50.0 | 116 | Allentown, PA-NJ | 0.0 | 180 | Shreveport-Bossier City, LA | (17.0) |
| 51 | Corpus Christi, TX | 50.0 | 116 | Ames, IA | 0.0 | 181 | Port St. Lucie, FL | (17.1) |
| 54 | Vallejo-Fairfield, CA | 49.0 | 116 | Atlanta, GA | 0.0 | 182 | Seattle-Bellevue-Everett, WA M.D. | (17.4) |
| 55 | Fayetteville-Springdale, AR-MO | 47.1 | 116 | Eugene, OR | 0.0 | 183 | Boston, MA M.D. | (17.9) |
| 55 | Minneapolis-St. Paul, MN-WI | 47.1 | 116 | Fairbanks, AK | 0.0 | 184 | Knoxville, TN | (18.2) |
| 57 | Bangor, ME | 44.4 | 116 | Fort Lauderdale, FL M.D. | 0.0 | 184 | Naples-Marco Island, FL | (18.2) |
| 58 | Gainesville, GA | 42.3 | 116 | Longview, WA | 0.0 | 184 | Nassau-Suffolk, NY M.D. | (18.2) |
| 59 | Rocky Mount, NC | 40.0 | 116 | Miami-Dade County, FL M.D. | 0.0 | 187 | Fayetteville, NC | (18.6) |
| 60 | Ocala, FL | 38.9 | 116 | Missoula, MT | 0.0 | 187 | Las Vegas-Henderson, NV | (18.6) |
| 61 | Idaho Falls, ID | 37.5 | 116 | Monroe, MI | 0.0 | 187 | Wichita, KS | (18.6) |
| 62 | Gainesville, FL | 37.0 | 116 | Niles-Benton Harbor, MI | 0.0 | 190 | Fresno, CA | (20.0) |
| 63 | Mount Vernon-Anacortes, WA | 36.0 | 116 | Ogden-Clearfield, UT | 0.0 | 190 | Worcester, MA-CT | (20.0) |
| 63 | Wilmington, NC | 36.0 | 116 | Oshkosh-Neenah, WI | 0.0 | 192 | West Palm Beach, FL M.D. | (20.6) |

Note: All listings are for Metropolitan Statistical Areas (M.S.A.s) except for those ending with "M.D." Listings with "M.D." are Metropolitan Divisions which are smaller parts of eleven large M.S.A.s. See explanatory note at beginning of metropolitan area section.

| RANK | METROPOLITAN AREA | % CHANGE | RANK | METROPOLITAN AREA | % CHANGE | RANK | METROPOLITAN AREA | % CHANGE |
|---|---|---|---|---|---|---|---|---|
| 193 | Jacksonville, FL | (22.0) | 255 | Barnstable Town, MA | (50.0) | NA | Chicago (greater), IL-IN-WI** | NA |
| 194 | Tulsa, OK | (22.1) | 255 | Fond du Lac, WI | (50.0) | NA | Chicago-Naperville, IL M.D.** | NA |
| 195 | Duluth, MN-WI | (22.2) | 255 | McAllen-Edinburg-Mission, TX | (50.0) | NA | Columbus, IN*** | NA |
| 196 | Buffalo-Niagara Falls, NY | (22.4) | 255 | St. Joseph, MO-KS | (50.0) | NA | Crestview-Fort Walton Beach, FL** | NA |
| 197 | Morristown, TN | (22.7) | 259 | Nashville-Davidson, TN | (50.7) | NA | Daphne-Fairhope-Foley, AL** | NA |
| 198 | Bakersfield, CA | (22.8) | 260 | Vineland-Bridgeton, NJ | (51.0) | NA | Davenport, IA-IL** | NA |
| 199 | Panama City, FL | (23.6) | 261 | Kingsport, TN-VA | (51.5) | NA | Dutchess-Putnam, NY M.D.** | NA |
| 200 | Los Angeles County, CA M.D. | (23.9) | 262 | Waco, TX | (51.8) | NA | East Stroudsburg, PA** | NA |
| 201 | Boston (greater), MA-NH | (25.0) | 263 | Portland, ME | (52.0) | NA | Elgin, IL M.D.** | NA |
| 201 | Bridgeport-Stamford, CT | (25.0) | 264 | Bremerton-Silverdale, WA | (52.9) | NA | Elizabethtown-Fort Knox, KY** | NA |
| 201 | Los Angeles (greater), CA | (25.0) | 264 | Harrisonburg, VA | (52.9) | NA | Gary, IN M.D.** | NA |
| 201 | Palm Bay-Melbourne, FL | (25.0) | 266 | Flagstaff, AZ | (53.2) | NA | Gettysburg, PA** | NA |
| 205 | Albuquerque, NM | (25.3) | 267 | Binghamton, NY | (54.3) | NA | Glens Falls, NY*** | NA |
| 205 | Houston, TX | (25.3) | 268 | North Port-Sarasota-Bradenton, FL | (55.7) | NA | Grand Forks, ND-MN*** | NA |
| 207 | Columbia, SC | (25.4) | 269 | Morgantown, WV | (58.8) | NA | Grand Island, NE** | NA |
| 208 | Lakeland, FL | (25.6) | 270 | Brunswick, GA | (60.0) | NA | Grand Rapids-Wyoming, MI** | NA |
| 209 | Hartford, CT | (26.1) | 270 | Racine, WI | (60.0) | NA | Grants Pass, OR** | NA |
| 210 | Orlando, FL | (26.4) | 272 | Erie, PA | (61.1) | NA | Greenville-Anderson, SC** | NA |
| 211 | San Antonio, TX | (27.0) | 273 | Odessa, TX | (61.5) | NA | Greenville, NC** | NA |
| 212 | Baton Rouge, LA | (27.1) | 274 | Jefferson City, MO | (61.8) | NA | Gulfport-Biloxi-Pascagoula, MS** | NA |
| 213 | Florence-Muscle Shoals, AL | (29.2) | 275 | Green Bay, WI | (62.5) | NA | Hammond, LA** | NA |
| 213 | Modesto, CA | (29.2) | 276 | Texarkana, TX-AR | (63.6) | NA | Hanford-Corcoran, CA** | NA |
| 215 | San Francisco (greater), CA | (29.4) | 277 | Pueblo, CO | (64.8) | NA | Hilton Head Island, SC** | NA |
| 216 | Augusta, GA-SC | (29.5) | 278 | Mansfield, OH | (66.7) | NA | Homosassa Springs, FL** | NA |
| 217 | Burlington, NC | (29.6) | 279 | Atlantic City, NJ | (67.0) | NA | Johnstown, PA** | NA |
| 217 | Lake Charles, LA | (29.6) | 280 | Janesville, WI | (67.6) | NA | Joplin, MO** | NA |
| 219 | Brownsville-Harlingen, TX | (30.0) | 281 | Cleveland, TN | (69.2) | NA | Kahului-Wailuku-Lahaina, HI** | NA |
| 220 | Anaheim-Santa Ana-Irvine, CA M.D. | (30.4) | 282 | Fort Collins, CO | (70.0) | NA | Kankakee, IL** | NA |
| 221 | Reading, PA | (30.8) | 282 | Punta Gorda, FL | (70.0) | NA | La Crosse, WI-MN** | NA |
| 222 | Bay City, MI | (32.1) | 284 | Appleton, WI | (71.4) | NA | Lafayette, IN*** | NA |
| 223 | Longview, TX | (32.9) | 285 | Greeley, CO | (74.1) | NA | Lafayette, LA** | NA |
| 224 | Altoona, PA | (33.3) | 286 | Boulder, CO | (75.0) | NA | Lake Co.-Kenosha Co., IL-WI M.D.** | NA |
| 224 | Clarksville, TN-KY | (33.3) | 287 | Lebanon, PA | (75.4) | NA | Lancaster, PA** | NA |
| 224 | El Paso, TX | (33.3) | 288 | Cheyenne, WY | (77.8) | NA | Lawrence, KS*** | NA |
| 224 | Portland-Vancouver, OR-WA | (33.3) | 289 | Blacksburg, VA | (78.0) | NA | Lewiston-Auburn, ME*** | NA |
| 228 | Amarillo, TX | (34.0) | 290 | Laredo, TX | (78.6) | NA | Logan, UT-ID*** | NA |
| 229 | Jonesboro, AR | (36.0) | 291 | Athens-Clarke County, GA | (82.8) | NA | Madison, WI** | NA |
| 230 | Oakland-Hayward, CA M.D. | (36.3) | 292 | Abilene, TX | (86.4) | NA | Monroe, LA** | NA |
| 231 | Jackson, TN | (36.4) | 293 | Corvallis, OR | (100.0) | NA | Montgomery County, PA M.D.** | NA |
| 232 | Topeka, KS | (36.8) | 293 | Dubuque, IA | (100.0) | NA | Myrtle Beach, SC-NC** | NA |
| 233 | Johnson City, TN | (37.5) | 293 | Elmira, NY | (100.0) | NA | New Bern, NC** | NA |
| 234 | Jackson, MI | (38.0) | 293 | Great Falls, MT | (100.0) | NA | New York-Jersey City, NY-NJ M.D.** | NA |
| 234 | Washington, DC-VA-MD-WV M.D. | (38.0) | 293 | Iowa City, IA | (100.0) | NA | Olympia, WA** | NA |
| 236 | Fort Smith, AR-OK | (38.2) | 293 | Lewiston, ID-WA | (100.0) | NA | Parkersburg-Vienna, WV** | NA |
| 237 | Washington (greater) DC-VA-MD-WV | (38.3) | 293 | Muncie, IN | (100.0) | NA | Peoria, IL** | NA |
| 238 | Wichita Falls, TX | (38.7) | 293 | Ocean City, NJ | (100.0) | NA | Philadelphia, PA M.D.** | NA |
| 239 | El Centro, CA | (38.9) | 293 | Owensboro, KY | (100.0) | NA | Pittsburgh, PA** | NA |
| 239 | Silver Spring-Frederick, MD M.D. | (38.9) | 293 | Rochester, MN | (100.0) | NA | Rockford, IL** | NA |
| 241 | Spartanburg, SC | (39.1) | 293 | State College, PA | (100.0) | NA | Salisbury, MD-DE** | NA |
| 242 | Lubbock, TX | (41.2) | NA | Albany, OR** | NA | NA | San Rafael, CA M.D.** | NA |
| 243 | Cape Coral-Fort Myers, FL | (42.4) | NA | Bloomington, IL** | NA | NA | Scranton--Wilkes-Barre, PA** | NA |
| 244 | South Bend-Mishawaka, IN-MI | (43.3) | NA | Bloomsburg-Berwick, PA** | NA | NA | Sebring, FL** | NA |
| 245 | Boise City, ID | (43.8) | NA | Bowling Green, KY** | NA | NA | Springfield, IL** | NA |
| 246 | Sumter, SC | (44.3) | NA | California-Lexington Park, MD** | NA | NA | Staunton-Waynesboro, VA** | NA |
| 247 | Sebastian-Vero Beach, FL | (46.2) | NA | Cambridge-Newton, MA M.D.** | NA | NA | Terre Haute, IN** | NA |
| 248 | Florence, SC | (46.5) | NA | Canton, OH** | NA | NA | The Villages, FL** | NA |
| 249 | Pittsfield, MA | (46.7) | NA | Carbondale-Marion, IL** | NA | NA | Virginia Beach-Norfolk, VA-NC** | NA |
| 250 | Sheboygan, WI | (47.1) | NA | Carson City, NV*** | NA | NA | Warner Robins, GA** | NA |
| 251 | San Angelo, TX | (47.6) | NA | Casper, WY*** | NA | NA | Watertown-Fort Drum, NY** | NA |
| 252 | Goldsboro, NC | (48.0) | NA | Chambersburg-Waynesboro, PA** | NA | NA | Winston-Salem, NC** | NA |
| 253 | Santa Maria-Santa Barbara, CA | (48.1) | NA | Champaign-Urbana, IL** | NA | NA | Yakima, WA** | NA |
| 254 | Lima, OH | (49.1) | NA | Charlotte-Mecklenburg, NC-SC** | NA | | | |

Source: CQ Press using reported data from the F.B.I. "Crime in the United States 2013"

*Includes nonnegligent manslaughter.  **Not available.  ***These metro areas had murder rates of 0 in 2009 but had at least one murder in 2013.  Calculating percent increase from zero results in an infinite number.  This is shown as "NA."

# 13. Rapes in 2013
## National Total = 79,770 Rapes*

| RANK | METROPOLITAN AREA | RAPES | RANK | METROPOLITAN AREA | RAPES | RANK | METROPOLITAN AREA | RAPES |
|---|---|---|---|---|---|---|---|---|
| 294 | Abilene, TX | 43 | 352 | Cheyenne, WY | 20 | 142 | Gary, IN M.D. | 146 |
| 83 | Akron, OH | 270 | NA | Chicago (greater), IL-IN-WI** | NA | 344 | Gettysburg, PA | 25 |
| 156 | Albany-Schenectady-Troy, NY | 131 | NA | Chicago-Naperville, IL M.D.** | NA | 361 | Glens Falls, NY | 16 |
| 307 | Albany, GA | 37 | 216 | Chico, CA | 79 | 374 | Goldsboro, NC | 5 |
| 357 | Albany, OR | 18 | 37 | Cincinnati, OH-KY-IN | 691 | 267 | Grand Forks, ND-MN | 54 |
| 46 | Albuquerque, NM | 573 | 154 | Clarksville, TN-KY | 133 | 296 | Grand Island, NE | 41 |
| 280 | Alexandria, LA | 48 | 307 | Cleveland, TN | 37 | 149 | Grand Junction, CO | 136 |
| 119 | Allentown, PA-NJ | 170 | 214 | Coeur d'Alene, ID | 80 | 39 | Grand Rapids-Wyoming, MI | 672 |
| 314 | Altoona, PA | 36 | 220 | College Station-Bryan, TX | 78 | 369 | Grants Pass, OR | 11 |
| 95 | Amarillo, TX | 221 | 54 | Colorado Springs, CO | 498 | 316 | Great Falls, MT | 35 |
| 280 | Ames, IA | 48 | 220 | Columbia, MO | 78 | 167 | Greeley, CO | 119 |
| 60 | Anaheim-Santa Ana-Irvine, CA M.D. | 424 | 73 | Columbia, SC | 325 | 225 | Green Bay, WI | 76 |
| 61 | Anchorage, AK | 419 | 238 | Columbus, GA-AL | 70 | 149 | Greensboro-High Point, NC | 136 |
| 107 | Ann Arbor, MI | 187 | 348 | Columbus, IN | 23 | 55 | Greenville-Anderson, SC | 478 |
| 248 | Anniston-Oxford, AL | 64 | 102 | Corpus Christi, TX | 198 | 326 | Greenville, NC | 33 |
| 305 | Appleton, WI | 38 | 368 | Corvallis, OR | 13 | 148 | Gulfport-Biloxi-Pascagoula, MS | 137 |
| 271 | Athens-Clarke County, GA | 52 | 166 | Crestview-Fort Walton Beach, FL | 120 | 280 | Hagerstown-Martinsburg, MD-WV | 48 |
| 20 | Atlanta, GA | 1,077 | 322 | Cumberland, MD-WV | 34 | 261 | Hammond, LA | 57 |
| 305 | Atlantic City, NJ | 38 | 2 | Dallas (greater), TX | 2,169 | 316 | Hanford-Corcoran, CA | 35 |
| 116 | Augusta, GA-SC | 171 | 12 | Dallas-Plano-Irving, TX M.D. | 1,323 | 322 | Harrisonburg, VA | 34 |
| 59 | Austin-Round Rock, TX | 437 | 326 | Dalton, GA | 33 | 86 | Hartford, CT | 259 |
| 116 | Bakersfield, CA | 171 | 280 | Daphne-Fairhope-Foley, AL | 48 | 208 | Hilton Head Island, SC | 84 |
| 43 | Baltimore, MD | 647 | 143 | Davenport, IA-IL | 145 | 361 | Hinesville, GA | 16 |
| 348 | Bangor, ME | 23 | 70 | Dayton, OH | 330 | 288 | Homosassa Springs, FL | 46 |
| 194 | Barnstable Town, MA | 89 | 307 | Decatur, AL | 37 | 238 | Hot Springs, AR | 70 |
| 111 | Baton Rouge, LA | 180 | 354 | Decatur, IL | 19 | 296 | Houma, LA | 41 |
| 167 | Bay City, MI | 119 | 111 | Deltona-Daytona Beach, FL | 180 | 10 | Houston, TX | 1,441 |
| 173 | Beaumont-Port Arthur, TX | 116 | 11 | Denver-Aurora, CO | 1,427 | 107 | Huntsville, AL | 187 |
| 288 | Bend, OR | 46 | 124 | Des Moines-West Des Moines, IA | 159 | 280 | Idaho Falls, ID | 48 |
| 276 | Billings, MT | 49 | 3 | Detroit (greater), MI | 2,161 | 31 | Indianapolis, IN | 807 |
| 266 | Binghamton, NY | 55 | 19 | Detroit-Dearborn-Livonia, MI M.D. | 1,122 | 198 | Iowa City, IA | 88 |
| 53 | Birmingham-Hoover, AL | 506 | 251 | Dothan, AL | 62 | 45 | Jacksonville, FL | 583 |
| 233 | Bismarck, ND | 72 | 190 | Dover, DE | 92 | 149 | Jackson, MI | 136 |
| 216 | Blacksburg, VA | 79 | 361 | Dubuque, IA | 16 | 130 | Jackson, MS | 154 |
| 191 | Bloomington, IL | 91 | 165 | Duluth, MN-WI | 121 | 257 | Jackson, TN | 58 |
| 255 | Bloomington, IN | 59 | 296 | Dutchess-Putnam, NY M.D. | 41 | 241 | Janesville, WI | 69 |
| 357 | Bloomsburg-Berwick, PA | 18 | 276 | East Stroudsburg, PA | 49 | 354 | Jefferson City, MO | 19 |
| 76 | Boise City, ID | 313 | 322 | Eau Claire, WI | 34 | 288 | Johnson City, TN | 46 |
| 14 | Boston (greater), MA-NH | 1,308 | 334 | El Centro, CA | 30 | 364 | Johnstown, PA | 15 |
| 41 | Boston, MA M.D. | 656 | 91 | El Paso, TX | 236 | 248 | Jonesboro, AR | 64 |
| 123 | Boulder, CO | 162 | 137 | Elgin, IL M.D. | 150 | 244 | Joplin, MO | 66 |
| 233 | Bowling Green, KY | 72 | 316 | Elizabethtown-Fort Knox, KY | 35 | 292 | Kahului-Wailuku-Lahaina, HI | 45 |
| 167 | Bremerton-Silverdale, WA | 119 | 372 | Elmira, NY | 7 | 267 | Kankakee, IL | 54 |
| 115 | Bridgeport-Stamford, CT | 175 | 194 | Erie, PA | 89 | 26 | Kansas City, MO-KS | 862 |
| 160 | Brownsville-Harlingen, TX | 126 | 180 | Eugene, OR | 105 | 198 | Kennewick-Richland, WA | 88 |
| 354 | Brunswick, GA | 19 | 316 | Fairbanks, AK | 35 | 177 | Kingsport, TN-VA | 113 |
| 90 | Buffalo-Niagara Falls, NY | 241 | 188 | Fargo, ND-MN | 93 | 332 | Kingston, NY | 31 |
| 326 | Burlington, NC | 33 | 187 | Farmington, NM | 94 | 86 | Knoxville, TN | 259 |
| 373 | California-Lexington Park, MD | 6 | 85 | Fayetteville-Springdale, AR-MO | 265 | 357 | Kokomo, IN | 18 |
| 57 | Cambridge-Newton, MA M.D. | 456 | 202 | Fayetteville, NC | 86 | 341 | La Crosse, WI-MN | 26 |
| 100 | Camden, NJ M.D. | 201 | 261 | Flagstaff, AZ | 57 | 253 | Lafayette, IN | 60 |
| 146 | Canton, OH | 138 | 66 | Flint, MI | 341 | 205 | Lafayette, LA | 85 |
| 137 | Cape Coral-Fort Myers, FL | 150 | 233 | Florence-Muscle Shoals, AL | 72 | 170 | Lake Charles, LA | 118 |
| 348 | Cape Girardeau, MO-IL | 23 | 200 | Florence, SC | 87 | 106 | Lake Co.-Kenosha Co., IL-WI M.D. | 188 |
| 338 | Carbondale-Marion, IL | 27 | 301 | Fond du Lac, WI | 40 | 316 | Lake Havasu City-Kingman, AZ | 35 |
| 375 | Carson City, NV | 0 | 146 | Fort Collins, CO | 138 | 113 | Lakeland, FL | 177 |
| 369 | Casper, WY | 11 | 47 | Fort Lauderdale, FL M.D. | 568 | 155 | Lancaster, PA | 132 |
| 229 | Cedar Rapids, IA | 74 | 158 | Fort Smith, AR-OK | 129 | 75 | Lansing-East Lansing, MI | 314 |
| 316 | Chambersburg-Waynesboro, PA | 35 | 163 | Fort Wayne, IN | 124 | 214 | Laredo, TX | 80 |
| 171 | Champaign-Urbana, IL | 117 | 29 | Fort Worth-Arlington, TX M.D. | 846 | 225 | Las Cruces, NM | 76 |
| 98 | Charleston-North Charleston, SC | 202 | 122 | Fresno, CA | 163 | 27 | Las Vegas-Henderson, NV | 855 |
| 50 | Charlotte-Mecklenburg, NC-SC | 535 | 210 | Gadsden, AL | 83 | 261 | Lawrence, KS | 57 |
| 194 | Charlottesville, VA | 89 | 175 | Gainesville, FL | 115 | 191 | Lawton, OK | 91 |
| 163 | Chattanooga, TN-GA | 124 | 292 | Gainesville, GA | 45 | 366 | Lebanon, PA | 14 |

Note: All listings are for Metropolitan Statistical Areas (M.S.A.s) except for those ending with "M.D." Listings with "M.D." are Metropolitan Divisions which are smaller parts of eleven large M.S.A.s. See explanatory note at beginning of metropolitan area section.

| RANK | METROPOLITAN AREA | RAPES | RANK | METROPOLITAN AREA | RAPES | RANK | METROPOLITAN AREA | RAPES |
|---|---|---|---|---|---|---|---|---|
| 288 | Lewiston-Auburn, ME | 46 | 64 | Omaha-Council Bluffs, NE-IA | 342 | 338 | Sheboygan, WI | 27 |
| 369 | Lewiston, ID-WA | 11 | 23 | Orlando, FL | 939 | 341 | Sherman-Denison, TX | 26 |
| 109 | Lexington-Fayette, KY | 185 | 352 | Oshkosh-Neenah, WI | 20 | 156 | Shreveport-Bossier City, LA | 131 |
| 275 | Lima, OH | 50 | 265 | Owensboro, KY | 56 | 133 | Silver Spring-Frederick, MD M.D. | 153 |
| 135 | Lincoln, NE | 152 | 205 | Oxnard-Thousand Oaks, CA | 85 | 250 | Sioux City, IA-NE-SD | 63 |
| 79 | Little Rock, AR | 294 | 81 | Palm Bay-Melbourne, FL | 277 | 124 | Sioux Falls, SD | 159 |
| 326 | Logan, UT-ID | 33 | 193 | Panama City, FL | 90 | 127 | South Bend-Mishawaka, IN-MI | 158 |
| 202 | Longview, TX | 86 | 307 | Parkersburg-Vienna, WV | 37 | 141 | Spartanburg, SC | 147 |
| 182 | Longview, WA | 101 | 103 | Pensacola, FL | 197 | 88 | Spokane, WA | 253 |
| 7 | Los Angeles County, CA M.D. | 1,752 | 205 | Peoria, IL | 85 | 127 | Springfield, IL | 158 |
| 1 | Los Angeles (greater), CA | 2,176 | 4 | Philadelphia (greater) PA-NJ-MD-DE | 2,158 | 71 | Springfield, MA | 329 |
| 82 | Louisville, KY-IN | 271 | 9 | Philadelphia, PA M.D. | 1,461 | 67 | Springfield, MO | 340 |
| 173 | Lubbock, TX | 116 | 15 | Phoenix-Mesa-Scottsdale, AZ | 1,292 | 267 | Springfield, OH | 54 |
| 210 | Lynchburg, VA | 83 | 63 | Pittsburgh, PA | 367 | 307 | State College, PA | 37 |
| 233 | Macon, GA | 72 | 228 | Pittsfield, MA | 75 | 271 | Staunton-Waynesboro, VA | 52 |
| 255 | Madera, CA | 59 | 346 | Pocatello, ID | 24 | 153 | Stockton-Lodi, CA | 135 |
| 121 | Madison, WI | 166 | 200 | Port St. Lucie, FL | 87 | 194 | St. Cloud, MN | 89 |
| 110 | Manchester-Nashua, NH | 182 | 35 | Portland-Vancouver, OR-WA | 715 | 257 | St. George, UT | 58 |
| 337 | Manhattan, KS | 28 | 135 | Portland, ME | 152 | 230 | St. Joseph, MO-KS | 73 |
| 307 | Mankato-North Mankato, MN | 37 | 271 | Prescott, AZ | 52 | 22 | St. Louis, MO-IL | 981 |
| 276 | Mansfield, OH | 49 | 38 | Providence-Warwick, RI-MA | 683 | 274 | Sumter, SC | 51 |
| 103 | McAllen-Edinburg-Mission, TX | 197 | 130 | Provo-Orem, UT | 154 | 159 | Syracuse, NY | 128 |
| 233 | Medford, OR | 72 | 116 | Pueblo, CO | 171 | 64 | Tacoma, WA M.D. | 342 |
| 44 | Memphis, TN-MS-AR | 617 | 304 | Punta Gorda, FL | 39 | 94 | Tallahassee, FL | 223 |
| 220 | Merced, CA | 78 | 336 | Racine, WI | 29 | 24 | Tampa-St Petersburg, FL | 890 |
| 6 | Miami (greater), FL | 1,824 | 130 | Raleigh, NC | 154 | 296 | Terre Haute, IN | 41 |
| 30 | Miami-Dade County, FL M.D. | 813 | 181 | Rapid City, SD | 104 | 220 | Texarkana, TX-AR | 78 |
| 344 | Midland, TX | 25 | 186 | Reading, PA | 96 | 364 | The Villages, FL | 15 |
| 51 | Milwaukee, WI | 533 | 208 | Redding, CA | 84 | 97 | Toledo, OH | 209 |
| 16 | Minneapolis-St. Paul, MN-WI | 1,226 | 149 | Reno, NV | 136 | 276 | Topeka, KS | 49 |
| 286 | Missoula, MT | 47 | 89 | Richmond, VA | 249 | 332 | Trenton, NJ | 31 |
| 120 | Mobile, AL | 169 | 33 | Riverside-San Bernardino, CA | 758 | 68 | Tucson, AZ | 333 |
| 160 | Modesto, CA | 126 | 185 | Roanoke, VA | 98 | 48 | Tulsa, OK | 565 |
| 286 | Monroe, LA | 47 | 245 | Rochester, MN | 65 | 216 | Tuscaloosa, AL | 79 |
| 178 | Monroe, MI | 108 | 98 | Rochester, NY | 202 | 261 | Tyler, TX | 57 |
| 80 | Montgomery County, PA M.D. | 283 | 101 | Rockford, IL | 199 | 257 | Utica-Rome, NY | 58 |
| 245 | Morgantown, WV | 65 | 105 | Rockingham County, NH M.D. | 196 | 216 | Vallejo-Fairfield, CA | 79 |
| 314 | Morristown, TN | 36 | 346 | Rocky Mount, NC | 24 | 238 | Victoria, TX | 70 |
| 301 | Mount Vernon-Anacortes, WA | 40 | 338 | Rome, GA | 27 | 296 | Vineland-Bridgeton, NJ | 41 |
| 322 | Muncie, IN | 34 | 56 | Sacramento, CA | 469 | 49 | Virginia Beach-Norfolk, VA-NC | 563 |
| 124 | Muskegon, MI | 159 | 139 | Saginaw, MI | 149 | 202 | Visalia-Porterville, CA | 86 |
| 92 | Myrtle Beach, SC-NC | 230 | 184 | Salem, OR | 100 | 176 | Waco, TX | 114 |
| 307 | Napa, CA | 37 | 212 | Salinas, CA | 82 | 326 | Warner Robins, GA | 33 |
| 212 | Naples-Marco Island, FL | 82 | 114 | Salisbury, MD-DE | 176 | 21 | Warren-Troy, MI M.D. | 1,039 |
| 34 | Nashville-Davidson, TN | 747 | 42 | Salt Lake City, UT | 654 | 13 | Washington (greater) DC-VA-MD-WV | 1,321 |
| 188 | Nassau-Suffolk, NY M.D. | 93 | 230 | San Angelo, TX | 73 | 17 | Washington, DC-VA-MD-WV M.D. | 1,168 |
| 331 | New Bern, NC | 32 | 25 | San Antonio, TX | 889 | 366 | Watertown-Fort Drum, NY | 14 |
| 129 | New Haven-Milford, CT | 156 | 40 | San Diego, CA | 668 | 360 | Wausau, WI | 17 |
| 74 | New Orleans, LA | 321 | 28 | San Francisco (greater), CA | 853 | 58 | West Palm Beach, FL M.D. | 443 |
| 5 | New York (greater), NY-NJ-PA | 1,920 | 77 | San Francisco-Redwood, CA M.D. | 295 | 295 | Wichita Falls, TX | 42 |
| 8 | New York-Jersey City, NY-NJ M.D. | 1,557 | 62 | San Jose, CA | 414 | 69 | Wichita, KS | 332 |
| 93 | Newark, NJ-PA M.D. | 229 | 179 | San Luis Obispo, CA | 106 | 334 | Williamsport, PA | 30 |
| 144 | Niles-Benton Harbor, MI | 144 | 280 | San Rafael, CA M.D. | 48 | 96 | Wilmington, DE-MD-NJ M.D. | 213 |
| 77 | North Port-Sarasota-Bradenton, FL | 295 | 220 | Santa Cruz-Watsonville, CA | 78 | 245 | Wilmington, NC | 65 |
| 253 | Norwich-New London, CT | 60 | 133 | Santa Maria-Santa Barbara, CA | 153 | 252 | Winchester, VA-WV | 61 |
| 52 | Oakland-Hayward, CA M.D. | 510 | 160 | Santa Rosa, CA | 126 | 145 | Winston-Salem, NC | 142 |
| 140 | Ocala, FL | 148 | 242 | Savannah, GA | 68 | 84 | Worcester, MA-CT | 267 |
| 351 | Ocean City, NJ | 22 | 171 | Scranton--Wilkes-Barre, PA | 117 | 230 | Yakima, WA | 73 |
| 257 | Odessa, TX | 58 | 18 | Seattle (greater), WA | 1,136 | 182 | York-Hanover, PA | 101 |
| 71 | Ogden-Clearfield, UT | 329 | 32 | Seattle-Bellevue-Everett, WA M.D. | 794 | 267 | Yuba City, CA | 54 |
| 36 | Oklahoma City, OK | 695 | 301 | Sebastian-Vero Beach, FL | 40 | 242 | Yuma, AZ | 68 |
| 225 | Olympia, WA | 76 | 341 | Sebring, FL | 26 | | | |

Source: Reported data from the F.B.I. "Crime in the United States 2013"  *Revised definition: Rape is penetration, no matter how slight, of the vagina or anus with any body part or object, or oral penetration by a sex organ of another person, without the consent of the victim. Attempts or assaults to commit rape are also included; however, statutory rape and incest are excluded.  Not all cities have made the change so the metro area figures reported here include rape figures based on differing definitions of rape. See note on page vii. **Not available.

# 13. Rapes in 2013 (continued)
## National Total = 79,770 Rapes*

| RANK | METROPOLITAN AREA | RAPES | RANK | METROPOLITAN AREA | RAPES | RANK | METROPOLITAN AREA | RAPES |
|---|---|---|---|---|---|---|---|---|
| 1 | Los Angeles (greater), CA | 2,176 | 64 | Tacoma, WA M.D. | 342 | 129 | New Haven-Milford, CT | 156 |
| 2 | Dallas (greater), TX | 2,169 | 66 | Flint, MI | 341 | 130 | Jackson, MS | 154 |
| 3 | Detroit (greater), MI | 2,161 | 67 | Springfield, MO | 340 | 130 | Provo-Orem, UT | 154 |
| 4 | Philadelphia (greater) PA-NJ-MD-DE | 2,158 | 68 | Tucson, AZ | 333 | 130 | Raleigh, NC | 154 |
| 5 | New York (greater), NY-NJ-PA | 1,920 | 69 | Wichita, KS | 332 | 133 | Santa Maria-Santa Barbara, CA | 153 |
| 6 | Miami (greater), FL | 1,824 | 70 | Dayton, OH | 330 | 133 | Silver Spring-Frederick, MD M.D. | 153 |
| 7 | Los Angeles County, CA M.D. | 1,752 | 71 | Ogden-Clearfield, UT | 329 | 135 | Lincoln, NE | 152 |
| 8 | New York-Jersey City, NY-NJ M.D. | 1,557 | 71 | Springfield, MA | 329 | 135 | Portland, ME | 152 |
| 9 | Philadelphia, PA M.D. | 1,461 | 73 | Columbia, SC | 325 | 137 | Cape Coral-Fort Myers, FL | 150 |
| 10 | Houston, TX | 1,441 | 74 | New Orleans, LA | 321 | 137 | Elgin, IL M.D. | 150 |
| 11 | Denver-Aurora, CO | 1,427 | 75 | Lansing-East Lansing, MI | 314 | 139 | Saginaw, MI | 149 |
| 12 | Dallas-Plano-Irving, TX M.D. | 1,323 | 76 | Boise City, ID | 313 | 140 | Ocala, FL | 148 |
| 13 | Washington (greater) DC-VA-MD-WV | 1,321 | 77 | North Port-Sarasota-Bradenton, FL | 295 | 141 | Spartanburg, SC | 147 |
| 14 | Boston (greater), MA-NH | 1,308 | 77 | San Francisco-Redwood, CA M.D. | 295 | 142 | Gary, IN M.D. | 146 |
| 15 | Phoenix-Mesa-Scottsdale, AZ | 1,292 | 79 | Little Rock, AR | 294 | 143 | Davenport, IA-IL | 145 |
| 16 | Minneapolis-St. Paul, MN-WI | 1,226 | 80 | Montgomery County, PA M.D. | 283 | 144 | Niles-Benton Harbor, MI | 144 |
| 17 | Washington, DC-VA-MD-WV M.D. | 1,168 | 81 | Palm Bay-Melbourne, FL | 277 | 145 | Winston-Salem, NC | 142 |
| 18 | Seattle (greater), WA | 1,136 | 82 | Louisville, KY-IN | 271 | 146 | Canton, OH | 138 |
| 19 | Detroit-Dearborn-Livonia, MI M.D. | 1,122 | 83 | Akron, OH | 270 | 146 | Fort Collins, CO | 138 |
| 20 | Atlanta, GA | 1,077 | 84 | Worcester, MA-CT | 267 | 148 | Gulfport-Biloxi-Pascagoula, MS | 137 |
| 21 | Warren-Troy, MI M.D. | 1,039 | 85 | Fayetteville-Springdale, AR-MO | 265 | 149 | Grand Junction, CO | 136 |
| 22 | St. Louis, MO-IL | 981 | 86 | Hartford, CT | 259 | 149 | Greensboro-High Point, NC | 136 |
| 23 | Orlando, FL | 939 | 86 | Knoxville, TN | 259 | 149 | Jackson, MI | 136 |
| 24 | Tampa-St Petersburg, FL | 890 | 88 | Spokane, WA | 253 | 149 | Reno, NV | 136 |
| 25 | San Antonio, TX | 889 | 89 | Richmond, VA | 249 | 153 | Stockton-Lodi, CA | 135 |
| 26 | Kansas City, MO-KS | 862 | 90 | Buffalo-Niagara Falls, NY | 241 | 154 | Clarksville, TN-KY | 133 |
| 27 | Las Vegas-Henderson, NV | 855 | 91 | El Paso, TX | 236 | 155 | Lancaster, PA | 132 |
| 28 | San Francisco (greater), CA | 853 | 92 | Myrtle Beach, SC-NC | 230 | 156 | Albany-Schenectady-Troy, NY | 131 |
| 29 | Fort Worth-Arlington, TX M.D. | 846 | 93 | Newark, NJ-PA M.D. | 229 | 156 | Shreveport-Bossier City, LA | 131 |
| 30 | Miami-Dade County, FL M.D. | 813 | 94 | Tallahassee, FL | 223 | 158 | Fort Smith, AR-OK | 129 |
| 31 | Indianapolis, IN | 807 | 95 | Amarillo, TX | 221 | 159 | Syracuse, NY | 128 |
| 32 | Seattle-Bellevue-Everett, WA M.D. | 794 | 96 | Wilmington, DE-MD-NJ M.D. | 213 | 160 | Brownsville-Harlingen, TX | 126 |
| 33 | Riverside-San Bernardino, CA | 758 | 97 | Toledo, OH | 209 | 160 | Modesto, CA | 126 |
| 34 | Nashville-Davidson, TN | 747 | 98 | Charleston-North Charleston, SC | 202 | 160 | Santa Rosa, CA | 126 |
| 35 | Portland-Vancouver, OR-WA | 715 | 98 | Rochester, NY | 202 | 163 | Chattanooga, TN-GA | 124 |
| 36 | Oklahoma City, OK | 695 | 100 | Camden, NJ M.D. | 201 | 163 | Fort Wayne, IN | 124 |
| 37 | Cincinnati, OH-KY-IN | 691 | 101 | Rockford, IL | 199 | 165 | Duluth, MN-WI | 121 |
| 38 | Providence-Warwick, RI-MA | 683 | 102 | Corpus Christi, TX | 198 | 166 | Crestview-Fort Walton Beach, FL | 120 |
| 39 | Grand Rapids-Wyoming, MI | 672 | 103 | McAllen-Edinburg-Mission, TX | 197 | 167 | Bay City, MI | 119 |
| 40 | San Diego, CA | 668 | 103 | Pensacola, FL | 197 | 167 | Bremerton-Silverdale, WA | 119 |
| 41 | Boston, MA M.D. | 656 | 105 | Rockingham County, NH M.D. | 196 | 167 | Greeley, CO | 119 |
| 42 | Salt Lake City, UT | 654 | 106 | Lake Co.-Kenosha Co., IL-WI M.D. | 188 | 170 | Lake Charles, LA | 118 |
| 43 | Baltimore, MD | 647 | 107 | Ann Arbor, MI | 187 | 171 | Champaign-Urbana, IL | 117 |
| 44 | Memphis, TN-MS-AR | 617 | 107 | Huntsville, AL | 187 | 171 | Scranton--Wilkes-Barre, PA | 117 |
| 45 | Jacksonville, FL | 583 | 109 | Lexington-Fayette, KY | 185 | 173 | Beaumont-Port Arthur, TX | 116 |
| 46 | Albuquerque, NM | 573 | 110 | Manchester-Nashua, NH | 182 | 173 | Lubbock, TX | 116 |
| 47 | Fort Lauderdale, FL M.D. | 568 | 111 | Baton Rouge, LA | 180 | 175 | Gainesville, FL | 115 |
| 48 | Tulsa, OK | 565 | 111 | Deltona-Daytona Beach, FL | 180 | 176 | Waco, TX | 114 |
| 49 | Virginia Beach-Norfolk, VA-NC | 563 | 113 | Lakeland, FL | 177 | 177 | Kingsport, TN-VA | 113 |
| 50 | Charlotte-Mecklenburg, NC-SC | 535 | 114 | Salisbury, MD-DE | 176 | 178 | Monroe, MI | 108 |
| 51 | Milwaukee, WI | 533 | 115 | Bridgeport-Stamford, CT | 175 | 179 | San Luis Obispo, CA | 106 |
| 52 | Oakland-Hayward, CA M.D. | 510 | 116 | Augusta, GA-SC | 171 | 180 | Eugene, OR | 105 |
| 53 | Birmingham-Hoover, AL | 506 | 116 | Bakersfield, CA | 171 | 181 | Rapid City, SD | 104 |
| 54 | Colorado Springs, CO | 498 | 116 | Pueblo, CO | 171 | 182 | Longview, WA | 101 |
| 55 | Greenville-Anderson, SC | 478 | 119 | Allentown, PA-NJ | 170 | 182 | York-Hanover, PA | 101 |
| 56 | Sacramento, CA | 469 | 120 | Mobile, AL | 169 | 184 | Salem, OR | 100 |
| 57 | Cambridge-Newton, MA M.D. | 456 | 121 | Madison, WI | 166 | 185 | Roanoke, VA | 98 |
| 58 | West Palm Beach, FL M.D. | 443 | 122 | Fresno, CA | 163 | 186 | Reading, PA | 96 |
| 59 | Austin-Round Rock, TX | 437 | 123 | Boulder, CO | 162 | 187 | Farmington, NM | 94 |
| 60 | Anaheim-Santa Ana-Irvine, CA M.D. | 424 | 124 | Des Moines-West Des Moines, IA | 159 | 188 | Fargo, ND-MN | 93 |
| 61 | Anchorage, AK | 419 | 124 | Muskegon, MI | 159 | 188 | Nassau-Suffolk, NY M.D. | 93 |
| 62 | San Jose, CA | 414 | 124 | Sioux Falls, SD | 159 | 190 | Dover, DE | 92 |
| 63 | Pittsburgh, PA | 367 | 127 | South Bend-Mishawaka, IN-MI | 158 | 191 | Bloomington, IL | 91 |
| 64 | Omaha-Council Bluffs, NE-IA | 342 | 127 | Springfield, IL | 158 | 191 | Lawton, OK | 91 |

Note: All listings are for Metropolitan Statistical Areas (M.S.A.s) except for those ending with "M.D." Listings with "M.D." are Metropolitan Divisions which are smaller parts of eleven large M.S.A.s. See explanatory note at beginning of metropolitan area section.

| RANK | METROPOLITAN AREA | RAPES | RANK | METROPOLITAN AREA | RAPES | RANK | METROPOLITAN AREA | RAPES |
|---|---|---|---|---|---|---|---|---|
| 193 | Panama City, FL | 90 | 255 | Bloomington, IN | 59 | 316 | Elizabethtown-Fort Knox, KY | 35 |
| 194 | Barnstable Town, MA | 89 | 255 | Madera, CA | 59 | 316 | Fairbanks, AK | 35 |
| 194 | Charlottesville, VA | 89 | 257 | Jackson, TN | 58 | 316 | Great Falls, MT | 35 |
| 194 | Erie, PA | 89 | 257 | Odessa, TX | 58 | 316 | Hanford-Corcoran, CA | 35 |
| 194 | St. Cloud, MN | 89 | 257 | St. George, UT | 58 | 316 | Lake Havasu City-Kingman, AZ | 35 |
| 198 | Iowa City, IA | 88 | 257 | Utica-Rome, NY | 58 | 322 | Cumberland, MD-WV | 34 |
| 198 | Kennewick-Richland, WA | 88 | 261 | Flagstaff, AZ | 57 | 322 | Eau Claire, WI | 34 |
| 200 | Florence, SC | 87 | 261 | Hammond, LA | 57 | 322 | Harrisonburg, VA | 34 |
| 200 | Port St. Lucie, FL | 87 | 261 | Lawrence, KS | 57 | 322 | Muncie, IN | 34 |
| 202 | Fayetteville, NC | 86 | 261 | Tyler, TX | 57 | 326 | Burlington, NC | 33 |
| 202 | Longview, TX | 86 | 265 | Owensboro, KY | 56 | 326 | Dalton, GA | 33 |
| 202 | Visalia-Porterville, CA | 86 | 266 | Binghamton, NY | 55 | 326 | Greenville, NC | 33 |
| 205 | Lafayette, LA | 85 | 267 | Grand Forks, ND-MN | 54 | 326 | Logan, UT-ID | 33 |
| 205 | Oxnard-Thousand Oaks, CA | 85 | 267 | Kankakee, IL | 54 | 326 | Warner Robins, GA | 33 |
| 205 | Peoria, IL | 85 | 267 | Springfield, OH | 54 | 331 | New Bern, NC | 32 |
| 208 | Hilton Head Island, SC | 84 | 267 | Yuba City, CA | 54 | 332 | Kingston, NY | 31 |
| 208 | Redding, CA | 84 | 271 | Athens-Clarke County, GA | 52 | 332 | Trenton, NJ | 31 |
| 210 | Gadsden, AL | 83 | 271 | Prescott, AZ | 52 | 334 | El Centro, CA | 30 |
| 210 | Lynchburg, VA | 83 | 271 | Staunton-Waynesboro, VA | 52 | 334 | Williamsport, PA | 30 |
| 212 | Naples-Marco Island, FL | 82 | 274 | Sumter, SC | 51 | 336 | Racine, WI | 29 |
| 212 | Salinas, CA | 82 | 275 | Lima, OH | 50 | 337 | Manhattan, KS | 28 |
| 214 | Coeur d'Alene, ID | 80 | 276 | Billings, MT | 49 | 338 | Carbondale-Marion, IL | 27 |
| 214 | Laredo, TX | 80 | 276 | East Stroudsburg, PA | 49 | 338 | Rome, GA | 27 |
| 216 | Blacksburg, VA | 79 | 276 | Mansfield, OH | 49 | 338 | Sheboygan, WI | 27 |
| 216 | Chico, CA | 79 | 276 | Topeka, KS | 49 | 341 | La Crosse, WI-MN | 26 |
| 216 | Tuscaloosa, AL | 79 | 280 | Alexandria, LA | 48 | 341 | Sebring, FL | 26 |
| 216 | Vallejo-Fairfield, CA | 79 | 280 | Ames, IA | 48 | 341 | Sherman-Denison, TX | 26 |
| 220 | College Station-Bryan, TX | 78 | 280 | Daphne-Fairhope-Foley, AL | 48 | 344 | Gettysburg, PA | 25 |
| 220 | Columbia, MO | 78 | 280 | Hagerstown-Martinsburg, MD-WV | 48 | 344 | Midland, TX | 25 |
| 220 | Merced, CA | 78 | 280 | Idaho Falls, ID | 48 | 346 | Pocatello, ID | 24 |
| 220 | Santa Cruz-Watsonville, CA | 78 | 280 | San Rafael, CA M.D. | 48 | 346 | Rocky Mount, NC | 24 |
| 220 | Texarkana, TX-AR | 78 | 286 | Missoula, MT | 47 | 348 | Bangor, ME | 23 |
| 225 | Green Bay, WI | 76 | 286 | Monroe, LA | 47 | 348 | Cape Girardeau, MO-IL | 23 |
| 225 | Las Cruces, NM | 76 | 288 | Bend, OR | 46 | 348 | Columbus, IN | 23 |
| 225 | Olympia, WA | 76 | 288 | Homosassa Springs, FL | 46 | 351 | Ocean City, NJ | 22 |
| 228 | Pittsfield, MA | 75 | 288 | Johnson City, TN | 46 | 352 | Cheyenne, WY | 20 |
| 229 | Cedar Rapids, IA | 74 | 288 | Lewiston-Auburn, ME | 46 | 352 | Oshkosh-Neenah, WI | 20 |
| 230 | San Angelo, TX | 73 | 292 | Gainesville, GA | 45 | 354 | Brunswick, GA | 19 |
| 230 | St. Joseph, MO-KS | 73 | 292 | Kahului-Wailuku-Lahaina, HI | 45 | 354 | Decatur, IL | 19 |
| 230 | Yakima, WA | 73 | 294 | Abilene, TX | 43 | 354 | Jefferson City, MO | 19 |
| 233 | Bismarck, ND | 72 | 295 | Wichita Falls, TX | 42 | 357 | Albany, OR | 18 |
| 233 | Bowling Green, KY | 72 | 296 | Dutchess-Putnam, NY M.D. | 41 | 357 | Bloomsburg-Berwick, PA | 18 |
| 233 | Florence-Muscle Shoals, AL | 72 | 296 | Grand Island, NE | 41 | 357 | Kokomo, IN | 18 |
| 233 | Macon, GA | 72 | 296 | Houma, LA | 41 | 360 | Wausau, WI | 17 |
| 233 | Medford, OR | 72 | 296 | Terre Haute, IN | 41 | 361 | Dubuque, IA | 16 |
| 238 | Columbus, GA-AL | 70 | 296 | Vineland-Bridgeton, NJ | 41 | 361 | Glens Falls, NY | 16 |
| 238 | Hot Springs, AR | 70 | 301 | Fond du Lac, WI | 40 | 361 | Hinesville, GA | 16 |
| 238 | Victoria, TX | 70 | 301 | Mount Vernon-Anacortes, WA | 40 | 364 | Johnstown, PA | 15 |
| 241 | Janesville, WI | 69 | 301 | Sebastian-Vero Beach, FL | 40 | 364 | The Villages, FL | 15 |
| 242 | Savannah, GA | 68 | 304 | Punta Gorda, FL | 39 | 366 | Lebanon, PA | 14 |
| 242 | Yuma, AZ | 68 | 305 | Appleton, WI | 38 | 366 | Watertown-Fort Drum, NY | 14 |
| 244 | Joplin, MO | 66 | 305 | Atlantic City, NJ | 38 | 368 | Corvallis, OR | 13 |
| 245 | Morgantown, WV | 65 | 307 | Albany, GA | 37 | 369 | Casper, WY | 11 |
| 245 | Rochester, MN | 65 | 307 | Cleveland, TN | 37 | 369 | Grants Pass, OR | 11 |
| 245 | Wilmington, NC | 65 | 307 | Decatur, AL | 37 | 369 | Lewiston, ID-WA | 11 |
| 248 | Anniston-Oxford, AL | 64 | 307 | Mankato-North Mankato, MN | 37 | 372 | Elmira, NY | 7 |
| 248 | Jonesboro, AR | 64 | 307 | Napa, CA | 37 | 373 | California-Lexington Park, MD | 6 |
| 250 | Sioux City, IA-NE-SD | 63 | 307 | Parkersburg-Vienna, WV | 37 | 374 | Goldsboro, NC | 5 |
| 251 | Dothan, AL | 62 | 307 | State College, PA | 37 | 375 | Carson City, NV | 0 |
| 252 | Winchester, VA-WV | 61 | 314 | Altoona, PA | 36 | NA | Chicago (greater), IL-IN-WI** | NA |
| 253 | Lafayette, IN | 60 | 314 | Morristown, TN | 36 | NA | Chicago-Naperville, IL M.D.** | NA |
| 253 | Norwich-New London, CT | 60 | 316 | Chambersburg-Waynesboro, PA | 35 | | | |

Source: Reported data from the F.B.I. "Crime in the United States 2013"  *Revised definition: Rape is penetration, no matter how slight, of the vagina or anus with any body part or object, or oral penetration by a sex organ of another person, without the consent of the victim. Attempts or assaults to commit rape are also included; however, statutory rape and incest are excluded.  Not all cities have made the change so the metro area figures reported here include rape figures based on differing definitions of rape. See note on page vii. **Not available.

# 14. Rape Rate in 2013
## National Rate = 25.2 Rapes per 100,000 Population*

| RANK | METROPOLITAN AREA | RATE | RANK | METROPOLITAN AREA | RATE | RANK | METROPOLITAN AREA | RATE |
|---|---|---|---|---|---|---|---|---|
| 238 | Abilene, TX | 25.6 | 295 | Cheyenne, WY | 20.9 | 300 | Gary, IN M.D. | 20.6 |
| 137 | Akron, OH | 38.4 | NA | Chicago (greater), IL-IN-WI** | NA | 248 | Gettysburg, PA | 24.6 |
| 348 | Albany-Schenectady-Troy, NY | 14.9 | NA | Chicago-Naperville, IL M.D.** | NA | 359 | Glens Falls, NY | 12.5 |
| 262 | Albany, GA | 23.5 | 150 | Chico, CA | 35.5 | 373 | Goldsboro, NC | 4.0 |
| 345 | Albany, OR | 15.1 | 169 | Cincinnati, OH-KY-IN | 32.3 | 45 | Grand Forks, ND-MN | 53.7 |
| 27 | Albuquerque, NM | 63.5 | 69 | Clarksville, TN-KY | 47.7 | 62 | Grand Island, NE | 48.7 |
| 182 | Alexandria, LA | 31.0 | 179 | Cleveland, TN | 31.2 | 8 | Grand Junction, CO | 91.1 |
| 301 | Allentown, PA-NJ | 20.5 | 40 | Coeur d'Alene, ID | 55.5 | 25 | Grand Rapids-Wyoming, MI | 66.4 |
| 216 | Altoona, PA | 28.3 | 167 | College Station-Bryan, TX | 32.9 | 355 | Grants Pass, OR | 13.2 |
| 9 | Amarillo, TX | 84.9 | 18 | Colorado Springs, CO | 73.4 | 103 | Great Falls, MT | 42.6 |
| 51 | Ames, IA | 52.2 | 84 | Columbia, MO | 45.7 | 90 | Greeley, CO | 44.3 |
| 354 | Anaheim-Santa Ana-Irvine, CA M.D. | 13.6 | 122 | Columbia, SC | 41.0 | 250 | Green Bay, WI | 24.3 |
| 1 | Anchorage, AK | 133.2 | 280 | Columbus, GA-AL | 22.2 | 326 | Greensboro-High Point, NC | 18.3 |
| 48 | Ann Arbor, MI | 52.9 | 210 | Columbus, IN | 28.7 | 39 | Greenville-Anderson, SC | 56.1 |
| 41 | Anniston-Oxford, AL | 54.8 | 87 | Corpus Christi, TX | 44.8 | 318 | Greenville, NC | 18.9 |
| 339 | Appleton, WI | 16.6 | 346 | Corvallis, OR | 15.0 | 148 | Gulfport-Biloxi-Pascagoula, MS | 35.8 |
| 233 | Athens-Clarke County, GA | 26.3 | 72 | Crestview-Fort Walton Beach, FL | 47.5 | 322 | Hagerstown-Martinsburg, MD-WV | 18.6 |
| 307 | Atlanta, GA | 19.5 | 164 | Cumberland, MD-WV | 33.4 | 81 | Hammond, LA | 45.9 |
| 352 | Atlantic City, NJ | 13.8 | 174 | Dallas (greater), TX | 31.8 | 268 | Hanford-Corcoran, CA | 23.1 |
| 196 | Augusta, GA-SC | 29.5 | 200 | Dallas-Plano-Irving, TX M.D. | 29.4 | 234 | Harrisonburg, VA | 26.2 |
| 264 | Austin-Round Rock, TX | 23.3 | 268 | Dalton, GA | 23.1 | 242 | Hartford, CT | 25.3 |
| 304 | Bakersfield, CA | 19.8 | 246 | Daphne-Fairhope-Foley, AL | 24.8 | 102 | Hilton Head Island, SC | 42.7 |
| 264 | Baltimore, MD | 23.3 | 141 | Davenport, IA-IL | 37.8 | 310 | Hinesville, GA | 19.3 |
| 346 | Bangor, ME | 15.0 | 120 | Dayton, OH | 41.1 | 166 | Homosassa Springs, FL | 33.0 |
| 119 | Barnstable Town, MA | 41.2 | 253 | Decatur, AL | 24.0 | 19 | Hot Springs, AR | 72.0 |
| 283 | Baton Rouge, LA | 22.0 | 331 | Decatur, IL | 17.3 | 306 | Houma, LA | 19.6 |
| 2 | Bay City, MI | 111.4 | 192 | Deltona-Daytona Beach, FL | 30.0 | 273 | Houston, TX | 22.9 |
| 211 | Beaumont-Port Arthur, TX | 28.6 | 46 | Denver-Aurora, CO | 53.0 | 98 | Huntsville, AL | 43.0 |
| 222 | Bend, OR | 28.0 | 227 | Des Moines-West Des Moines, IA | 26.7 | 155 | Idaho Falls, ID | 34.9 |
| 194 | Billings, MT | 29.7 | 56 | Detroit (greater), MI | 50.3 | 116 | Indianapolis, IN | 41.5 |
| 280 | Binghamton, NY | 22.2 | 28 | Detroit-Dearborn-Livonia, MI M.D. | 62.8 | 41 | Iowa City, IA | 54.8 |
| 88 | Birmingham-Hoover, AL | 44.4 | 113 | Dothan, AL | 41.8 | 110 | Jacksonville, FL | 41.9 |
| 33 | Bismarck, ND | 58.0 | 44 | Dover, DE | 54.2 | 10 | Jackson, MI | 84.7 |
| 93 | Blacksburg, VA | 44.0 | 337 | Dubuque, IA | 16.7 | 228 | Jackson, MS | 26.6 |
| 66 | Bloomington, IL | 48.0 | 97 | Duluth, MN-WI | 43.2 | 88 | Jackson, TN | 44.4 |
| 147 | Bloomington, IN | 36.1 | 365 | Dutchess-Putnam, NY M.D. | 10.3 | 98 | Janesville, WI | 43.0 |
| 291 | Bloomsburg-Berwick, PA | 21.2 | 204 | East Stroudsburg, PA | 29.1 | 357 | Jefferson City, MO | 12.6 |
| 64 | Boise City, ID | 48.3 | 299 | Eau Claire, WI | 20.7 | 277 | Johnson City, TN | 22.8 |
| 222 | Boston (greater), MA-NH | 28.0 | 336 | El Centro, CA | 16.9 | 364 | Johnstown, PA | 10.6 |
| 160 | Boston, MA M.D. | 33.8 | 222 | El Paso, TX | 28.0 | 55 | Jonesboro, AR | 51.2 |
| 51 | Boulder, CO | 52.2 | 257 | Elgin, IL M.D. | 23.8 | 140 | Joplin, MO | 37.9 |
| 91 | Bowling Green, KY | 44.1 | 266 | Elizabethtown-Fort Knox, KY | 23.2 | 217 | Kahului-Wailuku-Lahaina, HI | 28.2 |
| 77 | Bremerton-Silverdale, WA | 46.3 | 371 | Elmira, NY | 7.9 | 68 | Kankakee, IL | 47.9 |
| 314 | Bridgeport-Stamford, CT | 19.0 | 175 | Erie, PA | 31.7 | 108 | Kansas City, MO-KS | 42.1 |
| 192 | Brownsville-Harlingen, TX | 30.0 | 196 | Eugene, OR | 29.5 | 172 | Kennewick-Richland, WA | 32.2 |
| 337 | Brunswick, GA | 16.7 | 4 | Fairbanks, AK | 100.7 | 146 | Kingsport, TN-VA | 36.5 |
| 291 | Buffalo-Niagara Falls, NY | 21.2 | 110 | Fargo, ND-MN | 41.9 | 333 | Kingston, NY | 17.1 |
| 289 | Burlington, NC | 21.3 | 17 | Farmington, NM | 73.7 | 190 | Knoxville, TN | 30.4 |
| 372 | California-Lexington Park, MD | 5.4 | 43 | Fayetteville-Springdale, AR-MO | 54.3 | 285 | Kokomo, IN | 21.7 |
| 305 | Cambridge-Newton, MA M.D. | 19.7 | 278 | Fayetteville, NC | 22.7 | 313 | La Crosse, WI-MN | 19.1 |
| 341 | Camden, NJ M.D. | 16.0 | 115 | Flagstaff, AZ | 41.6 | 209 | Lafayette, IN | 28.8 |
| 158 | Canton, OH | 34.2 | 11 | Flint, MI | 81.9 | 327 | Lafayette, LA | 17.8 |
| 273 | Cape Coral-Fort Myers, FL | 22.9 | 61 | Florence-Muscle Shoals, AL | 49.0 | 32 | Lake Charles, LA | 58.5 |
| 261 | Cape Girardeau, MO-IL | 23.6 | 109 | Florence, SC | 42.0 | 286 | Lake Co.-Kenosha Co., IL-WI M.D. | 21.6 |
| 289 | Carbondale-Marion, IL | 21.3 | 132 | Fond du Lac, WI | 39.2 | 333 | Lake Havasu City-Kingman, AZ | 17.1 |
| 375 | Carson City, NV | 0.0 | 95 | Fort Collins, CO | 43.7 | 213 | Lakeland, FL | 28.4 |
| 352 | Casper, WY | 13.8 | 188 | Fort Lauderdale, FL M.D. | 30.8 | 244 | Lancaster, PA | 25.0 |
| 220 | Cedar Rapids, IA | 28.1 | 81 | Fort Smith, AR-OK | 45.9 | 24 | Lansing-East Lansing, MI | 67.3 |
| 268 | Chambersburg-Waynesboro, PA | 23.1 | 203 | Fort Wayne, IN | 29.2 | 190 | Laredo, TX | 30.4 |
| 59 | Champaign-Urbana, IL | 50.0 | 145 | Fort Worth-Arlington, TX M.D. | 36.7 | 152 | Las Cruces, NM | 35.3 |
| 213 | Charleston-North Charleston, SC | 28.4 | 333 | Fresno, CA | 17.1 | 106 | Las Vegas-Henderson, NV | 42.2 |
| 271 | Charlotte-Mecklenburg, NC-SC | 23.0 | 12 | Gadsden, AL | 79.5 | 56 | Lawrence, KS | 50.3 |
| 128 | Charlottesville, VA | 39.6 | 105 | Gainesville, FL | 42.5 | 23 | Lawton, OK | 68.2 |
| 273 | Chattanooga, TN-GA | 22.9 | 253 | Gainesville, GA | 24.0 | 365 | Lebanon, PA | 10.3 |

Note: All listings are for Metropolitan Statistical Areas (M.S.A.s) except for those ending with "M.D." Listings with "M.D." are Metropolitan Divisions which are smaller parts of eleven large M.S.A.s. See explanatory note at beginning of metropolitan area section.

| RANK | METROPOLITAN AREA | RATE | RANK | METROPOLITAN AREA | RATE | RANK | METROPOLITAN AREA | RATE |
|------|-------------------|------|------|-------------------|------|------|-------------------|------|
| 100 | Lewiston-Auburn, ME | 42.8 | 138 | Omaha-Council Bluffs, NE-IA | 38.3 | 262 | Sheboygan, WI | 23.5 |
| 327 | Lewiston, ID-WA | 17.8 | 116 | Orlando, FL | 41.5 | 291 | Sherman-Denison, TX | 21.2 |
| 141 | Lexington-Fayette, KY | 37.8 | 361 | Oshkosh-Neenah, WI | 11.8 | 204 | Shreveport-Bossier City, LA | 29.1 |
| 70 | Lima, OH | 47.6 | 65 | Owensboro, KY | 48.1 | 360 | Silver Spring-Frederick, MD M.D. | 12.2 |
| 63 | Lincoln, NE | 48.5 | 367 | Oxnard-Thousand Oaks, CA | 10.1 | 144 | Sioux City, IA-NE-SD | 37.2 |
| 124 | Little Rock, AR | 40.7 | 56 | Palm Bay-Melbourne, FL | 50.3 | 26 | Sioux Falls, SD | 65.8 |
| 241 | Logan, UT-ID | 25.4 | 70 | Panama City, FL | 47.6 | 60 | South Bend-Mishawaka, IN-MI | 49.5 |
| 129 | Longview, TX | 39.4 | 126 | Parkersburg-Vienna, WV | 40.0 | 80 | Spartanburg, SC | 46.0 |
| 5 | Longview, WA | 98.9 | 106 | Pensacola, FL | 42.2 | 73 | Spokane, WA | 47.3 |
| 330 | Los Angeles County, CA M.D. | 17.5 | 279 | Peoria, IL | 22.3 | 15 | Springfield, IL | 74.4 |
| 339 | Los Angeles (greater), CA | 16.6 | 148 | Philadelphia (greater) PA-NJ-MD-DE | 35.8 | 50 | Springfield, MA | 52.4 |
| 286 | Louisville, KY-IN | 21.6 | 22 | Philadelphia, PA M.D. | 69.1 | 13 | Springfield, MO | 75.9 |
| 135 | Lubbock, TX | 38.6 | 196 | Phoenix-Mesa-Scottsdale, AZ | 29.5 | 129 | Springfield, OH | 39.4 |
| 169 | Lynchburg, VA | 32.3 | 344 | Pittsburgh, PA | 15.5 | 257 | State College, PA | 23.8 |
| 185 | Macon, GA | 30.9 | 34 | Pittsfield, MA | 57.7 | 95 | Staunton-Waynesboro, VA | 43.7 |
| 135 | Madera, CA | 38.6 | 213 | Pocatello, ID | 28.4 | 314 | Stockton-Lodi, CA | 19.0 |
| 229 | Madison, WI | 26.5 | 303 | Port St. Lucie, FL | 19.9 | 76 | St. Cloud, MN | 46.5 |
| 86 | Manchester-Nashua, NH | 45.1 | 185 | Portland-Vancouver, OR-WA | 30.9 | 132 | St. George, UT | 39.2 |
| 217 | Manhattan, KS | 28.2 | 202 | Portland, ME | 29.3 | 38 | St. Joseph, MO-KS | 56.8 |
| 143 | Mankato-North Mankato, MN | 37.5 | 250 | Prescott, AZ | 24.3 | 154 | St. Louis, MO-IL | 35.0 |
| 126 | Mansfield, OH | 40.0 | 103 | Providence-Warwick, RI-MA | 42.6 | 74 | Sumter, SC | 46.9 |
| 253 | McAllen-Edinburg-Mission, TX | 24.0 | 226 | Provo-Orem, UT | 27.4 | 309 | Syracuse, NY | 19.4 |
| 156 | Medford, OR | 34.6 | 3 | Pueblo, CO | 105.4 | 114 | Tacoma, WA M.D. | 41.7 |
| 83 | Memphis, TN-MS-AR | 45.8 | 257 | Punta Gorda, FL | 23.8 | 30 | Tallahassee, FL | 58.9 |
| 196 | Merced, CA | 29.5 | 348 | Racine, WI | 14.9 | 182 | Tampa-St Petersburg, FL | 31.0 |
| 179 | Miami (greater), FL | 31.2 | 356 | Raleigh, NC | 12.7 | 260 | Terre Haute, IN | 23.7 |
| 185 | Miami-Dade County, FL M.D. | 30.9 | 16 | Rapid City, SD | 73.8 | 54 | Texarkana, TX-AR | 51.9 |
| 341 | Midland, TX | 16.0 | 266 | Reading, PA | 23.2 | 351 | The Villages, FL | 14.3 |
| 159 | Milwaukee, WI | 33.9 | 74 | Redding, CA | 46.9 | 157 | Toledo, OH | 34.3 |
| 150 | Minneapolis-St. Paul, MN-WI | 35.5 | 182 | Reno, NV | 31.0 | 295 | Topeka, KS | 20.9 |
| 110 | Missoula, MT | 41.9 | 302 | Richmond, VA | 20.0 | 370 | Trenton, NJ | 8.4 |
| 123 | Mobile, AL | 40.8 | 331 | Riverside-San Bernardino, CA | 17.3 | 165 | Tucson, AZ | 33.3 |
| 253 | Modesto, CA | 24.0 | 177 | Roanoke, VA | 31.5 | 31 | Tulsa, OK | 58.8 |
| 230 | Monroe, LA | 26.4 | 188 | Rochester, MN | 30.8 | 161 | Tuscaloosa, AL | 33.7 |
| 20 | Monroe, MI | 71.6 | 322 | Rochester, NY | 18.6 | 234 | Tyler, TX | 26.2 |
| 350 | Montgomery County, PA M.D. | 14.5 | 34 | Rockford, IL | 57.7 | 307 | Utica-Rome, NY | 19.5 |
| 66 | Morgantown, WV | 48.0 | 77 | Rockingham County, NH M.D. | 46.3 | 320 | Vallejo-Fairfield, CA | 18.7 |
| 179 | Morristown, TN | 31.2 | 343 | Rocky Mount, NC | 15.8 | 21 | Victoria, TX | 71.5 |
| 163 | Mount Vernon-Anacortes, WA | 33.6 | 220 | Rome, GA | 28.1 | 236 | Vineland-Bridgeton, NJ | 25.9 |
| 208 | Muncie, IN | 28.9 | 291 | Sacramento, CA | 21.2 | 167 | Virginia Beach-Norfolk, VA-NC | 32.9 |
| 6 | Muskegon, MI | 93.7 | 14 | Saginaw, MI | 75.2 | 318 | Visalia-Porterville, CA | 18.9 |
| 36 | Myrtle Beach, SC-NC | 57.3 | 243 | Salem, OR | 25.1 | 91 | Waco, TX | 44.1 |
| 230 | Napa, CA | 26.4 | 314 | Salinas, CA | 19.0 | 329 | Warner Robins, GA | 17.6 |
| 250 | Naples-Marco Island, FL | 24.3 | 84 | Salisbury, MD-DE | 45.7 | 118 | Warren-Troy, MI M.D. | 41.4 |
| 100 | Nashville-Davidson, TN | 42.8 | 36 | Salt Lake City, UT | 57.3 | 280 | Washington (greater) DC-VA-MD-WV | 22.2 |
| 374 | Nassau-Suffolk, NY M.D. | 3.3 | 28 | San Angelo, TX | 62.8 | 245 | Washington, DC-VA-MD-WV M.D. | 24.9 |
| 246 | New Bern, NC | 24.8 | 134 | San Antonio, TX | 39.1 | 362 | Watertown-Fort Drum, NY | 11.5 |
| 310 | New Haven-Milford, CT | 19.3 | 297 | San Diego, CA | 20.8 | 357 | Wausau, WI | 12.6 |
| 236 | New Orleans, LA | 25.9 | 314 | San Francisco (greater), CA | 19.0 | 169 | West Palm Beach, FL M.D. | 32.3 |
| 368 | New York (greater), NY-NJ-PA | 9.6 | 320 | San Francisco-Redwood, CA M.D. | 18.7 | 225 | Wichita Falls, TX | 27.8 |
| 363 | New York-Jersey City, NY-NJ M.D. | 11.0 | 286 | San Jose, CA | 21.6 | 53 | Wichita, KS | 52.1 |
| 369 | Newark, NJ-PA M.D. | 9.2 | 138 | San Luis Obispo, CA | 38.3 | 239 | Williamsport, PA | 25.5 |
| 7 | Niles-Benton Harbor, MI | 92.3 | 322 | San Rafael, CA M.D. | 18.6 | 194 | Wilmington, DE-MD-NJ M.D. | 29.7 |
| 125 | North Port-Sarasota-Bradenton, FL | 40.5 | 204 | Santa Cruz-Watsonville, CA | 29.1 | 249 | Wilmington, NC | 24.4 |
| 120 | Norwich-New London, CT | 41.1 | 153 | Santa Maria-Santa Barbara, CA | 35.2 | 77 | Winchester, VA-WV | 46.3 |
| 312 | Oakland-Hayward, CA M.D. | 19.2 | 239 | Santa Rosa, CA | 25.5 | 284 | Winston-Salem, NC | 21.8 |
| 94 | Ocala, FL | 43.8 | 322 | Savannah, GA | 18.6 | 178 | Worcester, MA-CT | 31.3 |
| 273 | Ocean City, NJ | 22.9 | 297 | Scranton--Wilkes-Barre, PA | 20.8 | 200 | Yakima, WA | 29.4 |
| 131 | Odessa, TX | 39.3 | 176 | Seattle (greater), WA | 31.6 | 271 | York-Hanover, PA | 23.0 |
| 46 | Ogden-Clearfield, UT | 53.0 | 211 | Seattle-Bellevue-Everett, WA M.D. | 28.6 | 173 | Yuba City, CA | 32.1 |
| 49 | Oklahoma City, OK | 52.8 | 217 | Sebastian-Vero Beach, FL | 28.2 | 161 | Yuma, AZ | 33.7 |
| 204 | Olympia, WA | 29.1 | 230 | Sebring, FL | 26.4 | | | |

Source: Reported data from the F.B.I. "Crime in the United States 2013"  *Revised definition: Rape is penetration, no matter how slight, of the vagina or anus with any body part or object, or oral penetration by a sex organ of another person, without the consent of the victim. Attempts or assaults to commit rape are also included; however, statutory rape and incest are excluded.  Not all cities have made the change so the metro area figures reported here include rape figures based on differing definitions of rape. See note on page vii. **Not available.

# 14. Rape Rate in 2013 (continued)
## National Rate = 25.2 Rapes per 100,000 Population*

| RANK | METROPOLITAN AREA | RATE | RANK | METROPOLITAN AREA | RATE | RANK | METROPOLITAN AREA | RATE |
|---|---|---|---|---|---|---|---|---|
| 1 | Anchorage, AK | 133.2 | 65 | Owensboro, KY | 48.1 | 129 | Longview, TX | 39.4 |
| 2 | Bay City, MI | 111.4 | 66 | Bloomington, IL | 48.0 | 129 | Springfield, OH | 39.4 |
| 3 | Pueblo, CO | 105.4 | 66 | Morgantown, WV | 48.0 | 131 | Odessa, TX | 39.3 |
| 4 | Fairbanks, AK | 100.7 | 68 | Kankakee, IL | 47.9 | 132 | Fond du Lac, WI | 39.2 |
| 5 | Longview, WA | 98.9 | 69 | Clarksville, TN-KY | 47.7 | 132 | St. George, UT | 39.2 |
| 6 | Muskegon, MI | 93.7 | 70 | Lima, OH | 47.6 | 134 | San Antonio, TX | 39.1 |
| 7 | Niles-Benton Harbor, MI | 92.3 | 70 | Panama City, FL | 47.6 | 135 | Lubbock, TX | 38.6 |
| 8 | Grand Junction, CO | 91.1 | 72 | Crestview-Fort Walton Beach, FL | 47.5 | 135 | Madera, CA | 38.6 |
| 9 | Amarillo, TX | 84.9 | 73 | Spokane, WA | 47.3 | 137 | Akron, OH | 38.4 |
| 10 | Jackson, MI | 84.7 | 74 | Redding, CA | 46.9 | 138 | Omaha-Council Bluffs, NE-IA | 38.3 |
| 11 | Flint, MI | 81.9 | 74 | Sumter, SC | 46.9 | 138 | San Luis Obispo, CA | 38.3 |
| 12 | Gadsden, AL | 79.5 | 76 | St. Cloud, MN | 46.5 | 140 | Joplin, MO | 37.9 |
| 13 | Springfield, MO | 75.9 | 77 | Bremerton-Silverdale, WA | 46.3 | 141 | Davenport, IA-IL | 37.8 |
| 14 | Saginaw, MI | 75.2 | 77 | Rockingham County, NH M.D. | 46.3 | 141 | Lexington-Fayette, KY | 37.8 |
| 15 | Springfield, IL | 74.4 | 77 | Winchester, VA-WV | 46.3 | 143 | Mankato-North Mankato, MN | 37.5 |
| 16 | Rapid City, SD | 73.8 | 80 | Spartanburg, SC | 46.0 | 144 | Sioux City, IA-NE-SD | 37.2 |
| 17 | Farmington, NM | 73.7 | 81 | Fort Smith, AR-OK | 45.9 | 145 | Fort Worth-Arlington, TX M.D. | 36.7 |
| 18 | Colorado Springs, CO | 73.4 | 81 | Hammond, LA | 45.9 | 146 | Kingsport, TN-VA | 36.5 |
| 19 | Hot Springs, AR | 72.0 | 83 | Memphis, TN-MS-AR | 45.8 | 147 | Bloomington, IN | 36.1 |
| 20 | Monroe, MI | 71.6 | 84 | Columbia, MO | 45.7 | 148 | Gulfport-Biloxi-Pascagoula, MS | 35.8 |
| 21 | Victoria, TX | 71.5 | 84 | Salisbury, MD-DE | 45.7 | 148 | Philadelphia (greater) PA-NJ-MD-DE | 35.8 |
| 22 | Philadelphia, PA M.D. | 69.1 | 86 | Manchester-Nashua, NH | 45.1 | 150 | Chico, CA | 35.5 |
| 23 | Lawton, OK | 68.2 | 87 | Corpus Christi, TX | 44.8 | 150 | Minneapolis-St. Paul, MN-WI | 35.5 |
| 24 | Lansing-East Lansing, MI | 67.3 | 88 | Birmingham-Hoover, AL | 44.4 | 152 | Las Cruces, NM | 35.3 |
| 25 | Grand Rapids-Wyoming, MI | 66.4 | 88 | Jackson, TN | 44.4 | 153 | Santa Maria-Santa Barbara, CA | 35.2 |
| 26 | Sioux Falls, SD | 65.8 | 90 | Greeley, CO | 44.3 | 154 | St. Louis, MO-IL | 35.0 |
| 27 | Albuquerque, NM | 63.5 | 91 | Bowling Green, KY | 44.1 | 155 | Idaho Falls, ID | 34.9 |
| 28 | Detroit-Dearborn-Livonia, MI M.D. | 62.8 | 91 | Waco, TX | 44.1 | 156 | Medford, OR | 34.6 |
| 28 | San Angelo, TX | 62.8 | 93 | Blacksburg, VA | 44.0 | 157 | Toledo, OH | 34.3 |
| 30 | Tallahassee, FL | 58.9 | 94 | Ocala, FL | 43.8 | 158 | Canton, OH | 34.2 |
| 31 | Tulsa, OK | 58.8 | 95 | Fort Collins, CO | 43.7 | 159 | Milwaukee, WI | 33.9 |
| 32 | Lake Charles, LA | 58.5 | 95 | Staunton-Waynesboro, VA | 43.7 | 160 | Boston, MA M.D. | 33.8 |
| 33 | Bismarck, ND | 58.0 | 97 | Duluth, MN-WI | 43.2 | 161 | Tuscaloosa, AL | 33.7 |
| 34 | Pittsfield, MA | 57.7 | 98 | Huntsville, AL | 43.0 | 161 | Yuma, AZ | 33.7 |
| 34 | Rockford, IL | 57.7 | 98 | Janesville, WI | 43.0 | 163 | Mount Vernon-Anacortes, WA | 33.6 |
| 36 | Myrtle Beach, SC-NC | 57.3 | 100 | Lewiston-Auburn, ME | 42.8 | 164 | Cumberland, MD-WV | 33.4 |
| 36 | Salt Lake City, UT | 57.3 | 100 | Nashville-Davidson, TN | 42.8 | 165 | Tucson, AZ | 33.3 |
| 38 | St. Joseph, MO-KS | 56.8 | 102 | Hilton Head Island, SC | 42.7 | 166 | Homosassa Springs, FL | 33.0 |
| 39 | Greenville-Anderson, SC | 56.1 | 103 | Great Falls, MT | 42.6 | 167 | College Station-Bryan, TX | 32.9 |
| 40 | Coeur d'Alene, ID | 55.5 | 103 | Providence-Warwick, RI-MA | 42.6 | 167 | Virginia Beach-Norfolk, VA-NC | 32.9 |
| 41 | Anniston-Oxford, AL | 54.8 | 105 | Gainesville, FL | 42.5 | 169 | Cincinnati, OH-KY-IN | 32.3 |
| 41 | Iowa City, IA | 54.8 | 106 | Las Vegas-Henderson, NV | 42.2 | 169 | Lynchburg, VA | 32.3 |
| 43 | Fayetteville-Springdale, AR-MO | 54.3 | 106 | Pensacola, FL | 42.2 | 169 | West Palm Beach, FL M.D. | 32.3 |
| 44 | Dover, DE | 54.2 | 108 | Kansas City, MO-KS | 42.1 | 172 | Kennewick-Richland, WA | 32.2 |
| 45 | Grand Forks, ND-MN | 53.7 | 109 | Florence, SC | 42.0 | 173 | Yuba City, CA | 32.1 |
| 46 | Denver-Aurora, CO | 53.0 | 110 | Fargo, ND-MN | 41.9 | 174 | Dallas (greater), TX | 31.8 |
| 46 | Ogden-Clearfield, UT | 53.0 | 110 | Jacksonville, FL | 41.9 | 175 | Erie, PA | 31.7 |
| 48 | Ann Arbor, MI | 52.9 | 110 | Missoula, MT | 41.9 | 176 | Seattle (greater), WA | 31.6 |
| 49 | Oklahoma City, OK | 52.8 | 113 | Dothan, AL | 41.8 | 177 | Roanoke, VA | 31.5 |
| 50 | Springfield, MA | 52.4 | 114 | Tacoma, WA M.D. | 41.7 | 178 | Worcester, MA-CT | 31.3 |
| 51 | Ames, IA | 52.2 | 115 | Flagstaff, AZ | 41.6 | 179 | Cleveland, TN | 31.2 |
| 51 | Boulder, CO | 52.2 | 116 | Indianapolis, IN | 41.5 | 179 | Miami (greater), FL | 31.2 |
| 53 | Wichita, KS | 52.1 | 116 | Orlando, FL | 41.5 | 179 | Morristown, TN | 31.2 |
| 54 | Texarkana, TX-AR | 51.9 | 118 | Warren-Troy, MI M.D. | 41.4 | 182 | Alexandria, LA | 31.0 |
| 55 | Jonesboro, AR | 51.2 | 119 | Barnstable Town, MA | 41.2 | 182 | Reno, NV | 31.0 |
| 56 | Detroit (greater), MI | 50.3 | 120 | Dayton, OH | 41.1 | 182 | Tampa-St Petersburg, FL | 31.0 |
| 56 | Lawrence, KS | 50.3 | 120 | Norwich-New London, CT | 41.1 | 185 | Macon, GA | 30.9 |
| 56 | Palm Bay-Melbourne, FL | 50.3 | 122 | Columbia, SC | 41.0 | 185 | Miami-Dade County, FL M.D. | 30.9 |
| 59 | Champaign-Urbana, IL | 50.0 | 123 | Mobile, AL | 40.8 | 185 | Portland-Vancouver, OR-WA | 30.9 |
| 60 | South Bend-Mishawaka, IN-MI | 49.5 | 124 | Little Rock, AR | 40.7 | 188 | Fort Lauderdale, FL M.D. | 30.8 |
| 61 | Florence-Muscle Shoals, AL | 49.0 | 125 | North Port-Sarasota-Bradenton, FL | 40.5 | 188 | Rochester, MN | 30.8 |
| 62 | Grand Island, NE | 48.7 | 126 | Mansfield, OH | 40.0 | 190 | Knoxville, TN | 30.4 |
| 63 | Lincoln, NE | 48.5 | 126 | Parkersburg-Vienna, WV | 40.0 | 190 | Laredo, TX | 30.4 |
| 64 | Boise City, ID | 48.3 | 128 | Charlottesville, VA | 39.6 | 192 | Brownsville-Harlingen, TX | 30.0 |

Note: All listings are for Metropolitan Statistical Areas (M.S.A.s) except for those ending with "M.D." Listings with "M.D." are Metropolitan Divisions which are smaller parts of eleven large M.S.A.s. See explanatory note at beginning of metropolitan area section.

| RANK | METROPOLITAN AREA | RATE | RANK | METROPOLITAN AREA | RATE | RANK | METROPOLITAN AREA | RATE |
|---|---|---|---|---|---|---|---|---|
| 192 | Deltona-Daytona Beach, FL | 30.0 | 253 | McAllen-Edinburg-Mission, TX | 24.0 | 314 | Stockton-Lodi, CA | 19.0 |
| 194 | Billings, MT | 29.7 | 253 | Modesto, CA | 24.0 | 318 | Greenville, NC | 18.9 |
| 194 | Wilmington, DE-MD-NJ M.D. | 29.7 | 257 | Elgin, IL M.D. | 23.8 | 318 | Visalia-Porterville, CA | 18.9 |
| 196 | Augusta, GA-SC | 29.5 | 257 | Punta Gorda, FL | 23.8 | 320 | San Francisco-Redwood, CA M.D. | 18.7 |
| 196 | Eugene, OR | 29.5 | 257 | State College, PA | 23.8 | 320 | Vallejo-Fairfield, CA | 18.7 |
| 196 | Merced, CA | 29.5 | 260 | Terre Haute, IN | 23.7 | 322 | Hagerstown-Martinsburg, MD-WV | 18.6 |
| 196 | Phoenix-Mesa-Scottsdale, AZ | 29.5 | 261 | Cape Girardeau, MO-IL | 23.6 | 322 | Rochester, NY | 18.6 |
| 200 | Dallas-Plano-Irving, TX M.D. | 29.4 | 262 | Albany, GA | 23.5 | 322 | San Rafael, CA M.D. | 18.6 |
| 200 | Yakima, WA | 29.4 | 262 | Sheboygan, WI | 23.5 | 322 | Savannah, GA | 18.6 |
| 202 | Portland, ME | 29.3 | 264 | Austin-Round Rock, TX | 23.3 | 326 | Greensboro-High Point, NC | 18.3 |
| 203 | Fort Wayne, IN | 29.2 | 264 | Baltimore, MD | 23.3 | 327 | Lafayette, LA | 17.8 |
| 204 | East Stroudsburg, PA | 29.1 | 266 | Elizabethtown-Fort Knox, KY | 23.2 | 327 | Lewiston, ID-WA | 17.8 |
| 204 | Olympia, WA | 29.1 | 266 | Reading, PA | 23.2 | 329 | Warner Robins, GA | 17.6 |
| 204 | Santa Cruz-Watsonville, CA | 29.1 | 268 | Chambersburg-Waynesboro, PA | 23.1 | 330 | Los Angeles County, CA M.D. | 17.5 |
| 204 | Shreveport-Bossier City, LA | 29.1 | 268 | Dalton, GA | 23.1 | 331 | Decatur, IL | 17.3 |
| 208 | Muncie, IN | 28.9 | 268 | Hanford-Corcoran, CA | 23.1 | 331 | Riverside-San Bernardino, CA | 17.3 |
| 209 | Lafayette, IN | 28.8 | 271 | Charlotte-Mecklenburg, NC-SC | 23.0 | 333 | Fresno, CA | 17.1 |
| 210 | Columbus, IN | 28.7 | 271 | York-Hanover, PA | 23.0 | 333 | Kingston, NY | 17.1 |
| 211 | Beaumont-Port Arthur, TX | 28.6 | 273 | Cape Coral-Fort Myers, FL | 22.9 | 333 | Lake Havasu City-Kingman, AZ | 17.1 |
| 211 | Seattle-Bellevue-Everett, WA M.D. | 28.6 | 273 | Chattanooga, TN-GA | 22.9 | 336 | El Centro, CA | 16.9 |
| 213 | Charleston-North Charleston, SC | 28.4 | 273 | Houston, TX | 22.9 | 337 | Brunswick, GA | 16.7 |
| 213 | Lakeland, FL | 28.4 | 273 | Ocean City, NJ | 22.9 | 337 | Dubuque, IA | 16.7 |
| 213 | Pocatello, ID | 28.4 | 277 | Johnson City, TN | 22.8 | 339 | Appleton, WI | 16.6 |
| 216 | Altoona, PA | 28.3 | 278 | Fayetteville, NC | 22.7 | 339 | Los Angeles (greater), CA | 16.6 |
| 217 | Kahului-Wailuku-Lahaina, HI | 28.2 | 279 | Peoria, IL | 22.3 | 341 | Camden, NJ M.D. | 16.0 |
| 217 | Manhattan, KS | 28.2 | 280 | Binghamton, NY | 22.2 | 341 | Midland, TX | 16.0 |
| 217 | Sebastian-Vero Beach, FL | 28.2 | 280 | Columbus, GA-AL | 22.2 | 343 | Rocky Mount, NC | 15.8 |
| 220 | Cedar Rapids, IA | 28.1 | 280 | Washington (greater) DC-VA-MD-WV | 22.2 | 344 | Pittsburgh, PA | 15.5 |
| 220 | Rome, GA | 28.1 | 283 | Baton Rouge, LA | 22.0 | 345 | Albany, OR | 15.1 |
| 222 | Bend, OR | 28.0 | 284 | Winston-Salem, NC | 21.8 | 346 | Bangor, ME | 15.0 |
| 222 | Boston (greater), MA-NH | 28.0 | 285 | Kokomo, IN | 21.7 | 346 | Corvallis, OR | 15.0 |
| 222 | El Paso, TX | 28.0 | 286 | Lake Co.-Kenosha Co., IL-WI M.D. | 21.6 | 348 | Albany-Schenectady-Troy, NY | 14.9 |
| 225 | Wichita Falls, TX | 27.8 | 286 | Louisville, KY-IN | 21.6 | 348 | Racine, WI | 14.9 |
| 226 | Provo-Orem, UT | 27.4 | 286 | San Jose, CA | 21.6 | 350 | Montgomery County, PA M.D. | 14.5 |
| 227 | Des Moines-West Des Moines, IA | 26.7 | 289 | Burlington, NC | 21.3 | 351 | The Villages, FL | 14.3 |
| 228 | Jackson, MS | 26.6 | 289 | Carbondale-Marion, IL | 21.3 | 352 | Atlantic City, NJ | 13.8 |
| 229 | Madison, WI | 26.5 | 291 | Bloomsburg-Berwick, PA | 21.2 | 352 | Casper, WY | 13.8 |
| 230 | Monroe, LA | 26.4 | 291 | Buffalo-Niagara Falls, NY | 21.2 | 354 | Anaheim-Santa Ana-Irvine, CA M.D. | 13.6 |
| 230 | Napa, CA | 26.4 | 291 | Sacramento, CA | 21.2 | 355 | Grants Pass, OR | 13.2 |
| 230 | Sebring, FL | 26.4 | 291 | Sherman-Denison, TX | 21.2 | 356 | Raleigh, NC | 12.7 |
| 233 | Athens-Clarke County, GA | 26.3 | 295 | Cheyenne, WY | 20.9 | 357 | Jefferson City, MO | 12.6 |
| 234 | Harrisonburg, VA | 26.2 | 295 | Topeka, KS | 20.9 | 357 | Wausau, WI | 12.6 |
| 234 | Tyler, TX | 26.2 | 297 | San Diego, CA | 20.8 | 359 | Glens Falls, NY | 12.5 |
| 236 | New Orleans, LA | 25.9 | 297 | Scranton--Wilkes-Barre, PA | 20.8 | 360 | Silver Spring-Frederick, MD M.D. | 12.2 |
| 236 | Vineland-Bridgeton, NJ | 25.9 | 299 | Eau Claire, WI | 20.7 | 361 | Oshkosh-Neenah, WI | 11.8 |
| 238 | Abilene, TX | 25.6 | 300 | Gary, IN M.D. | 20.6 | 362 | Watertown-Fort Drum, NY | 11.5 |
| 239 | Santa Rosa, CA | 25.5 | 301 | Allentown, PA-NJ | 20.5 | 363 | New York-Jersey City, NY-NJ M.D. | 11.0 |
| 239 | Williamsport, PA | 25.5 | 302 | Richmond, VA | 20.0 | 364 | Johnstown, PA | 10.6 |
| 241 | Logan, UT-ID | 25.4 | 303 | Port St. Lucie, FL | 19.9 | 365 | Dutchess-Putnam, NY M.D. | 10.3 |
| 242 | Hartford, CT | 25.3 | 304 | Bakersfield, CA | 19.8 | 365 | Lebanon, PA | 10.3 |
| 243 | Salem, OR | 25.1 | 305 | Cambridge-Newton, MA M.D. | 19.7 | 367 | Oxnard-Thousand Oaks, CA | 10.1 |
| 244 | Lancaster, PA | 25.0 | 306 | Houma, LA | 19.6 | 368 | New York (greater), NY-NJ-PA | 9.6 |
| 245 | Washington, DC-VA-MD-WV M.D. | 24.9 | 307 | Atlanta, GA | 19.5 | 369 | Newark, NJ-PA M.D. | 9.2 |
| 246 | Daphne-Fairhope-Foley, AL | 24.8 | 307 | Utica-Rome, NY | 19.5 | 370 | Trenton, NJ | 8.4 |
| 246 | New Bern, NC | 24.8 | 309 | Syracuse, NY | 19.4 | 371 | Elmira, NY | 7.9 |
| 248 | Gettysburg, PA | 24.6 | 310 | Hinesville, GA | 19.3 | 372 | California-Lexington Park, MD | 5.4 |
| 249 | Wilmington, NC | 24.4 | 310 | New Haven-Milford, CT | 19.3 | 373 | Goldsboro, NC | 4.0 |
| 250 | Green Bay, WI | 24.3 | 312 | Oakland-Hayward, CA M.D. | 19.2 | 374 | Nassau-Suffolk, NY M.D. | 3.3 |
| 250 | Naples-Marco Island, FL | 24.3 | 313 | La Crosse, WI-MN | 19.1 | 375 | Carson City, NV | 0.0 |
| 250 | Prescott, AZ | 24.3 | 314 | Bridgeport-Stamford, CT | 19.0 | NA | Chicago (greater), IL-IN-WI** | NA |
| 253 | Decatur, AL | 24.0 | 314 | Salinas, CA | 19.0 | NA | Chicago-Naperville, IL M.D.** | NA |
| 253 | Gainesville, GA | 24.0 | 314 | San Francisco (greater), CA | 19.0 | | | |

Source: Reported data from the F.B.I. "Crime in the United States 2013"  *Revised definition: Rape is penetration, no matter how slight, of the vagina or anus with any body part or object, or oral penetration by a sex organ of another person, without the consent of the victim. Attempts or assaults to commit rape are also included; however, statutory rape and incest are excluded.  Not all cities have made the change so the metro area figures reported here include rape figures based on differing definitions of rape. See note on page vii. **Not available.

# 17. Robberies in 2013
## National Total = 345,031 Robberies*

| RANK | METROPOLITAN AREA | ROBBERY | RANK | METROPOLITAN AREA | ROBBERY | RANK | METROPOLITAN AREA | ROBBERY |
|---|---|---|---|---|---|---|---|---|
| 222 | Abilene, TX | 128 | 373 | Cheyenne, WY | 13 | 91 | Gary, IN M.D. | 801 |
| 100 | Akron, OH | 695 | 5 | Chicago (greater), IL-IN-WI | 15,998 | 365 | Gettysburg, PA | 17 |
| 97 | Albany-Schenectady-Troy, NY | 716 | 7 | Chicago-Naperville, IL M.D. | 14,569 | 373 | Glens Falls, NY | 13 |
| 174 | Albany, GA | 223 | 210 | Chico, CA | 148 | 239 | Goldsboro, NC | 104 |
| 321 | Albany, OR | 45 | 40 | Cincinnati, OH-KY-IN | 2,716 | 346 | Grand Forks, ND-MN | 27 |
| 69 | Albuquerque, NM | 1,239 | 202 | Clarksville, TN-KY | 164 | 376 | Grand Island, NE | 10 |
| 190 | Alexandria, LA | 188 | 332 | Cleveland, TN | 37 | 310 | Grand Junction, CO | 54 |
| 114 | Allentown, PA-NJ | 540 | 340 | Coeur d'Alene, ID | 31 | 104 | Grand Rapids-Wyoming, MI | 655 |
| 338 | Altoona, PA | 34 | 226 | College Station-Bryan, TX | 122 | 332 | Grants Pass, OR | 37 |
| 161 | Amarillo, TX | 250 | 131 | Colorado Springs, CO | 464 | 360 | Great Falls, MT | 19 |
| 371 | Ames, IA | 15 | 222 | Columbia, MO | 128 | 265 | Greeley, CO | 83 |
| 48 | Anaheim-Santa Ana-Irvine, CA M.D. | 1,993 | 89 | Columbia, SC | 838 | 237 | Green Bay, WI | 105 |
| 116 | Anchorage, AK | 528 | 115 | Columbus, GA-AL | 532 | 92 | Greensboro-High Point, NC | 796 |
| 205 | Ann Arbor, MI | 161 | 356 | Columbus, IN | 21 | 95 | Greenville-Anderson, SC | 739 |
| 241 | Anniston-Oxford, AL | 103 | 138 | Corpus Christi, TX | 432 | 173 | Greenville, NC | 225 |
| 360 | Appleton, WI | 19 | 347 | Corvallis, OR | 25 | 159 | Gulfport-Biloxi-Pascagoula, MS | 282 |
| 215 | Athens-Clarke County, GA | 134 | 224 | Crestview-Fort Walton Beach, FL | 125 | 194 | Hagerstown-Martinsburg, MD-WV | 181 |
| 11 | Atlanta, GA | 8,714 | 293 | Cumberland, MD-WV | 67 | 208 | Hammond, LA | 156 |
| 117 | Atlantic City, NJ | 520 | 15 | Dallas (greater), TX | 8,229 | 225 | Hanford-Corcoran, CA | 123 |
| 110 | Augusta, GA-SC | 612 | 20 | Dallas-Plano-Irving, TX M.D. | 5,984 | 365 | Harrisonburg, VA | 17 |
| 79 | Austin-Round Rock, TX | 1,001 | 339 | Dalton, GA | 33 | 78 | Hartford, CT | 1,046 |
| 67 | Bakersfield, CA | 1,285 | 293 | Daphne-Fairhope-Foley, AL | 67 | 215 | Hilton Head Island, SC | 134 |
| 19 | Baltimore, MD | 6,303 | 162 | Davenport, IA-IL | 247 | 316 | Hinesville, GA | 51 |
| 308 | Bangor, ME | 56 | 87 | Dayton, OH | 885 | 286 | Homosassa Springs, FL | 69 |
| 272 | Barnstable Town, MA | 78 | 329 | Decatur, AL | 39 | 275 | Hot Springs, AR | 74 |
| 64 | Baton Rouge, LA | 1,388 | 260 | Decatur, IL | 87 | 221 | Houma, LA | 130 |
| 343 | Bay City, MI | 29 | 133 | Deltona-Daytona Beach, FL | 457 | 6 | Houston, TX | 14,656 |
| 107 | Beaumont-Port Arthur, TX | 628 | 46 | Denver-Aurora, CO | 2,125 | 129 | Huntsville, AL | 466 |
| 324 | Bend, OR | 41 | 162 | Des Moines-West Des Moines, IA | 247 | 349 | Idaho Falls, ID | 24 |
| 263 | Billings, MT | 84 | 17 | Detroit (greater), MI | 7,058 | 28 | Indianapolis, IN | 4,162 |
| 207 | Binghamton, NY | 158 | 21 | Detroit-Dearborn-Livonia, MI M.D. | 5,873 | 280 | Iowa City, IA | 71 |
| 54 | Birmingham-Hoover, AL | 1,712 | 239 | Dothan, AL | 104 | 57 | Jacksonville, FL | 1,646 |
| 355 | Bismarck, ND | 22 | 212 | Dover, DE | 146 | 265 | Jackson, MI | 83 |
| 358 | Blacksburg, VA | 20 | 332 | Dubuque, IA | 37 | 80 | Jackson, MS | 995 |
| 242 | Bloomington, IL | 102 | 230 | Duluth, MN-WI | 115 | 201 | Jackson, TN | 168 |
| 254 | Bloomington, IN | 90 | 206 | Dutchess-Putnam, NY M.D. | 160 | 282 | Janesville, WI | 70 |
| 375 | Bloomsburg-Berwick, PA | 11 | 307 | East Stroudsburg, PA | 57 | 310 | Jefferson City, MO | 54 |
| 263 | Boise City, ID | 84 | 352 | Eau Claire, WI | 23 | 282 | Johnson City, TN | 70 |
| 27 | Boston (greater), MA-NH | 4,464 | 235 | El Centro, CA | 110 | 293 | Johnstown, PA | 67 |
| 36 | Boston, MA M.D. | 2,933 | 124 | El Paso, TX | 496 | 293 | Jonesboro, AR | 67 |
| 275 | Boulder, CO | 74 | 178 | Elgin, IL M.D. | 217 | 279 | Joplin, MO | 73 |
| 273 | Bowling Green, KY | 76 | 352 | Elizabethtown-Fort Knox, KY | 23 | 248 | Kahului-Wailuku-Lahaina, HI | 97 |
| 237 | Bremerton-Silverdale, WA | 105 | 332 | Elmira, NY | 37 | 254 | Kankakee, IL | 90 |
| 85 | Bridgeport-Stamford, CT | 943 | 172 | Erie, PA | 228 | 44 | Kansas City, MO-KS | 2,381 |
| 164 | Brownsville-Harlingen, TX | 244 | 166 | Eugene, OR | 242 | 257 | Kennewick-Richland, WA | 88 |
| 232 | Brunswick, GA | 113 | 324 | Fairbanks, AK | 41 | 275 | Kingsport, TN-VA | 74 |
| 51 | Buffalo-Niagara Falls, NY | 1,744 | 286 | Fargo, ND-MN | 69 | 314 | Kingston, NY | 52 |
| 211 | Burlington, NC | 147 | 305 | Farmington, NM | 60 | 108 | Knoxville, TN | 626 |
| 301 | California-Lexington Park, MD | 62 | 252 | Fayetteville-Springdale, AR-MO | 91 | 290 | Kokomo, IN | 68 |
| 63 | Cambridge-Newton, MA M.D. | 1,400 | 93 | Fayetteville, NC | 767 | 343 | La Crosse, WI-MN | 29 |
| 60 | Camden, NJ M.D. | 1,516 | 310 | Flagstaff, AZ | 54 | 260 | Lafayette, IN | 87 |
| 126 | Canton, OH | 482 | 98 | Flint, MI | 699 | 118 | Lafayette, LA | 513 |
| 113 | Cape Coral-Fort Myers, FL | 577 | 251 | Florence-Muscle Shoals, AL | 93 | 165 | Lake Charles, LA | 243 |
| 244 | Cape Girardeau, MO-IL | 100 | 202 | Florence, SC | 164 | 142 | Lake Co.-Kenosha Co., IL-WI M.D. | 411 |
| 290 | Carbondale-Marion, IL | 68 | 365 | Fond du Lac, WI | 17 | 280 | Lake Havasu City-Kingman, AZ | 71 |
| 365 | Carson City, NV | 17 | 297 | Fort Collins, CO | 66 | 143 | Lakeland, FL | 396 |
| 365 | Casper, WY | 17 | 35 | Fort Lauderdale, FL M.D. | 2,981 | 151 | Lancaster, PA | 340 |
| 246 | Cedar Rapids, IA | 99 | 229 | Fort Smith, AR-OK | 116 | 147 | Lansing-East Lansing, MI | 383 |
| 269 | Chambersburg-Waynesboro, PA | 80 | 122 | Fort Wayne, IN | 499 | 181 | Laredo, TX | 211 |
| 175 | Champaign-Urbana, IL | 220 | 45 | Fort Worth-Arlington, TX M.D. | 2,245 | 252 | Las Cruces, NM | 91 |
| 119 | Charleston-North Charleston, SC | 505 | 71 | Fresno, CA | 1,221 | 26 | Las Vegas-Henderson, NV | 4,716 |
| 41 | Charlotte-Mecklenburg, NC-SC | 2,665 | 228 | Gadsden, AL | 119 | 274 | Lawrence, KS | 75 |
| 248 | Charlottesville, VA | 97 | 168 | Gainesville, FL | 238 | 200 | Lawton, OK | 169 |
| 125 | Chattanooga, TN-GA | 491 | 286 | Gainesville, GA | 69 | 250 | Lebanon, PA | 96 |

Note: All listings are for Metropolitan Statistical Areas (M.S.A.s) except for those ending with "M.D." Listings with "M.D." are Metropolitan Divisions which are smaller parts of eleven large M.S.A.s. See explanatory note at beginning of metropolitan area section.

| RANK | METROPOLITAN AREA | ROBBERY | RANK | METROPOLITAN AREA | ROBBERY | RANK | METROPOLITAN AREA | ROBBERY |
|---|---|---|---|---|---|---|---|---|
| 336 | Lewiston-Auburn, ME | 36 | 88 | Omaha-Council Bluffs, NE-IA | 851 | 360 | Sheboygan, WI | 19 |
| 356 | Lewiston, ID-WA | 21 | 39 | Orlando, FL | 2,788 | 323 | Sherman-Denison, TX | 43 |
| 112 | Lexington-Fayette, KY | 584 | 343 | Oshkosh-Neenah, WI | 29 | 130 | Shreveport-Bossier City, LA | 465 |
| 257 | Lima, OH | 88 | 314 | Owensboro, KY | 52 | 83 | Silver Spring-Frederick, MD M.D. | 953 |
| 179 | Lincoln, NE | 214 | 111 | Oxnard-Thousand Oaks, CA | 607 | 321 | Sioux City, IA-NE-SD | 45 |
| 68 | Little Rock, AR | 1,270 | 127 | Palm Bay-Melbourne, FL | 470 | 290 | Sioux Falls, SD | 68 |
| 377 | Logan, UT-ID | 0 | 202 | Panama City, FL | 164 | 136 | South Bend-Mishawaka, IN-MI | 448 |
| 187 | Longview, TX | 190 | 372 | Parkersburg-Vienna, WV | 14 | 157 | Spartanburg, SC | 292 |
| 303 | Longview, WA | 61 | 132 | Pensacola, FL | 458 | 102 | Spokane, WA | 659 |
| 4 | Los Angeles County, CA M.D. | 16,783 | 153 | Peoria, IL | 332 | 150 | Springfield, IL | 351 |
| 3 | Los Angeles (greater), CA | 18,776 | 9 | Philadelphia (greater) PA-NJ-MD-DE | 11,921 | 86 | Springfield, MA | 913 |
| 52 | Louisville, KY-IN | 1,741 | 13 | Philadelphia, PA M.D. | 8,367 | 139 | Springfield, MO | 427 |
| 145 | Lubbock, TX | 390 | 22 | Phoenix-Mesa-Scottsdale, AZ | 5,057 | 175 | Springfield, OH | 220 |
| 256 | Lynchburg, VA | 89 | 49 | Pittsburgh, PA | 1,976 | 352 | State College, PA | 23 |
| 155 | Macon, GA | 308 | 313 | Pittsfield, MA | 53 | 347 | Staunton-Waynesboro, VA | 25 |
| 218 | Madera, CA | 132 | 342 | Pocatello, ID | 30 | 61 | Stockton-Lodi, CA | 1,477 |
| 149 | Madison, WI | 369 | 169 | Port St. Lucie, FL | 234 | 317 | St. Cloud, MN | 50 |
| 146 | Manchester-Nashua, NH | 384 | 56 | Portland-Vancouver, OR-WA | 1,702 | 365 | St. George, UT | 17 |
| 358 | Manhattan, KS | 20 | 195 | Portland, ME | 178 | 257 | St. Joseph, MO-KS | 88 |
| 329 | Mankato-North Mankato, MN | 39 | 340 | Prescott, AZ | 31 | 37 | St. Louis, MO-IL | 2,860 |
| 234 | Mansfield, OH | 111 | 66 | Providence-Warwick, RI-MA | 1,293 | 236 | Sumter, SC | 108 |
| 128 | McAllen-Edinburg-Mission, TX | 469 | 320 | Provo-Orem, UT | 49 | 120 | Syracuse, NY | 503 |
| 219 | Medford, OR | 131 | 177 | Pueblo, CO | 219 | 84 | Tacoma, WA M.D. | 950 |
| 31 | Memphis, TN-MS-AR | 3,468 | 337 | Punta Gorda, FL | 35 | 135 | Tallahassee, FL | 455 |
| 171 | Merced, CA | 231 | 184 | Racine, WI | 197 | 42 | Tampa-St Petersburg, FL | 2,607 |
| 10 | Miami (greater), FL | 11,062 | 90 | Raleigh, NC | 820 | 286 | Terre Haute, IN | 69 |
| 18 | Miami-Dade County, FL M.D. | 6,370 | 317 | Rapid City, SD | 50 | 227 | Texarkana, TX-AR | 120 |
| 282 | Midland, TX | 70 | 140 | Reading, PA | 423 | 349 | The Villages, FL | 24 |
| 30 | Milwaukee, WI | 3,692 | 192 | Redding, CA | 184 | 77 | Toledo, OH | 1,057 |
| 32 | Minneapolis-St. Paul, MN-WI | 3,341 | 144 | Reno, NV | 391 | 197 | Topeka, KS | 176 |
| 328 | Missoula, MT | 40 | 74 | Richmond, VA | 1,128 | 101 | Trenton, NJ | 685 |
| 103 | Mobile, AL | 658 | 25 | Riverside-San Bernardino, CA | 4,736 | 70 | Tucson, AZ | 1,225 |
| 94 | Modesto, CA | 741 | 198 | Roanoke, VA | 173 | 75 | Tulsa, OK | 1,093 |
| 182 | Monroe, LA | 199 | 308 | Rochester, MN | 56 | 170 | Tuscaloosa, AL | 233 |
| 301 | Monroe, MI | 62 | 72 | Rochester, NY | 1,211 | 270 | Tyler, TX | 79 |
| 81 | Montgomery County, PA M.D. | 964 | 133 | Rockford, IL | 457 | 209 | Utica-Rome, NY | 149 |
| 317 | Morgantown, WV | 50 | 219 | Rockingham County, NH M.D. | 131 | 96 | Vallejo-Fairfield, CA | 718 |
| 329 | Morristown, TN | 39 | 187 | Rocky Mount, NC | 190 | 303 | Victoria, TX | 61 |
| 298 | Mount Vernon-Anacortes, WA | 64 | 270 | Rome, GA | 79 | 148 | Vineland-Bridgeton, NJ | 382 |
| 244 | Muncie, IN | 100 | 38 | Sacramento, CA | 2,848 | 58 | Virginia Beach-Norfolk, VA-NC | 1,537 |
| 212 | Muskegon, MI | 146 | 187 | Saginaw, MI | 190 | 137 | Visalia-Porterville, CA | 438 |
| 141 | Myrtle Beach, SC-NC | 416 | 179 | Salem, OR | 214 | 193 | Waco, TX | 182 |
| 265 | Napa, CA | 83 | 104 | Salinas, CA | 655 | 185 | Warner Robins, GA | 192 |
| 231 | Naples-Marco Island, FL | 114 | 154 | Salisbury, MD-DE | 315 | 73 | Warren-Troy, MI M.D. | 1,185 |
| 47 | Nashville-Davidson, TN | 2,013 | 81 | Salt Lake City, UT | 964 | 12 | Washington (greater) DC-VA-MD-WV | 8,399 |
| 53 | Nassau-Suffolk, NY M.D. | 1,715 | 349 | San Angelo, TX | 24 | 16 | Washington, DC-VA-MD-WV M.D. | 7,446 |
| 282 | New Bern, NC | 70 | 43 | San Antonio, TX | 2,430 | 363 | Watertown-Fort Drum, NY | 18 |
| 65 | New Haven-Milford, CT | 1,350 | 34 | San Diego, CA | 3,054 | 363 | Wausau, WI | 18 |
| 50 | New Orleans, LA | 1,805 | 8 | San Francisco (greater), CA | 13,255 | 55 | West Palm Beach, FL M.D. | 1,711 |
| 1 | New York (greater), NY-NJ-PA | 31,094 | 24 | San Francisco-Redwood, CA M.D. | 4,780 | 215 | Wichita Falls, TX | 134 |
| 2 | New York-Jersey City, NY-NJ M.D. | 24,197 | 59 | San Jose, CA | 1,533 | 122 | Wichita, KS | 499 |
| 23 | Newark, NJ-PA M.D. | 5,022 | 268 | San Luis Obispo, CA | 81 | 306 | Williamsport, PA | 59 |
| 232 | Niles-Benton Harbor, MI | 113 | 214 | San Rafael, CA M.D. | 136 | 76 | Wilmington, DE-MD-NJ M.D. | 1,074 |
| 106 | North Port-Sarasota-Bradenton, FL | 646 | 182 | Santa Cruz-Watsonville, CA | 199 | 156 | Wilmington, NC | 298 |
| 247 | Norwich-New London, CT | 98 | 158 | Santa Maria-Santa Barbara, CA | 285 | 324 | Winchester, VA-WV | 41 |
| 14 | Oakland-Hayward, CA M.D. | 8,339 | 166 | Santa Rosa, CA | 242 | 109 | Winston-Salem, NC | 622 |
| 199 | Ocala, FL | 170 | 121 | Savannah, GA | 500 | 99 | Worcester, MA-CT | 696 |
| 298 | Ocean City, NJ | 64 | 152 | Scranton--Wilkes-Barre, PA | 333 | 186 | Yakima, WA | 191 |
| 196 | Odessa, TX | 177 | 29 | Seattle (greater), WA | 4,032 | 160 | York-Hanover, PA | 271 |
| 191 | Ogden-Clearfield, UT | 185 | 33 | Seattle-Bellevue-Everett, WA M.D. | 3,082 | 262 | Yuba City, CA | 85 |
| 62 | Oklahoma City, OK | 1,430 | 324 | Sebastian-Vero Beach, FL | 41 | 275 | Yuma, AZ | 74 |
| 243 | Olympia, WA | 101 | 300 | Sebring, FL | 63 | | | |

Source: Reported data from the F.B.I. "Crime in the United States 2013"

*Robbery is the taking of anything of value by force or threat of force. Attempts are included.

# 17. Robberies in 2013 (continued)
## National Total = 345,031 Robberies*

| RANK | METROPOLITAN AREA | ROBBERY | RANK | METROPOLITAN AREA | ROBBERY | RANK | METROPOLITAN AREA | ROBBERY |
|---|---|---|---|---|---|---|---|---|
| 1 | New York (greater), NY-NJ-PA | 31,094 | 65 | New Haven-Milford, CT | 1,350 | 129 | Huntsville, AL | 466 |
| 2 | New York-Jersey City, NY-NJ M.D. | 24,197 | 66 | Providence-Warwick, RI-MA | 1,293 | 130 | Shreveport-Bossier City, LA | 465 |
| 3 | Los Angeles (greater), CA | 18,776 | 67 | Bakersfield, CA | 1,285 | 131 | Colorado Springs, CO | 464 |
| 4 | Los Angeles County, CA M.D. | 16,783 | 68 | Little Rock, AR | 1,270 | 132 | Pensacola, FL | 458 |
| 5 | Chicago (greater), IL-IN-WI | 15,998 | 69 | Albuquerque, NM | 1,239 | 133 | Deltona-Daytona Beach, FL | 457 |
| 6 | Houston, TX | 14,656 | 70 | Tucson, AZ | 1,225 | 133 | Rockford, IL | 457 |
| 7 | Chicago-Naperville, IL M.D. | 14,569 | 71 | Fresno, CA | 1,221 | 135 | Tallahassee, FL | 455 |
| 8 | San Francisco (greater), CA | 13,255 | 72 | Rochester, NY | 1,211 | 136 | South Bend-Mishawaka, IN-MI | 448 |
| 9 | Philadelphia (greater) PA-NJ-MD-DE | 11,921 | 73 | Warren-Troy, MI M.D. | 1,185 | 137 | Visalia-Porterville, CA | 438 |
| 10 | Miami (greater), FL | 11,062 | 74 | Richmond, VA | 1,128 | 138 | Corpus Christi, TX | 432 |
| 11 | Atlanta, GA | 8,714 | 75 | Tulsa, OK | 1,093 | 139 | Springfield, MO | 427 |
| 12 | Washington (greater) DC-VA-MD-WV | 8,399 | 76 | Wilmington, DE-MD-NJ M.D. | 1,074 | 140 | Reading, PA | 423 |
| 13 | Philadelphia, PA M.D. | 8,367 | 77 | Toledo, OH | 1,057 | 141 | Myrtle Beach, SC-NC | 416 |
| 14 | Oakland-Hayward, CA M.D. | 8,339 | 78 | Hartford, CT | 1,046 | 142 | Lake Co.-Kenosha Co., IL-WI M.D. | 411 |
| 15 | Dallas (greater), TX | 8,229 | 79 | Austin-Round Rock, TX | 1,001 | 143 | Lakeland, FL | 396 |
| 16 | Washington, DC-VA-MD-WV M.D. | 7,446 | 80 | Jackson, MS | 995 | 144 | Reno, NV | 391 |
| 17 | Detroit (greater), MI | 7,058 | 81 | Montgomery County, PA M.D. | 964 | 145 | Lubbock, TX | 390 |
| 18 | Miami-Dade County, FL M.D. | 6,370 | 81 | Salt Lake City, UT | 964 | 146 | Manchester-Nashua, NH | 384 |
| 19 | Baltimore, MD | 6,303 | 83 | Silver Spring-Frederick, MD M.D. | 953 | 147 | Lansing-East Lansing, MI | 383 |
| 20 | Dallas-Plano-Irving, TX M.D. | 5,984 | 84 | Tacoma, WA M.D. | 950 | 148 | Vineland-Bridgeton, NJ | 382 |
| 21 | Detroit-Dearborn-Livonia, MI M.D. | 5,873 | 85 | Bridgeport-Stamford, CT | 943 | 149 | Madison, WI | 369 |
| 22 | Phoenix-Mesa-Scottsdale, AZ | 5,057 | 86 | Springfield, MA | 913 | 150 | Springfield, IL | 351 |
| 23 | Newark, NJ-PA M.D. | 5,022 | 87 | Dayton, OH | 885 | 151 | Lancaster, PA | 340 |
| 24 | San Francisco-Redwood, CA M.D. | 4,780 | 88 | Omaha-Council Bluffs, NE-IA | 851 | 152 | Scranton--Wilkes-Barre, PA | 333 |
| 25 | Riverside-San Bernardino, CA | 4,736 | 89 | Columbia, SC | 838 | 153 | Peoria, IL | 332 |
| 26 | Las Vegas-Henderson, NV | 4,716 | 90 | Raleigh, NC | 820 | 154 | Salisbury, MD-DE | 315 |
| 27 | Boston (greater), MA-NH | 4,464 | 91 | Gary, IN M.D. | 801 | 155 | Macon, GA | 308 |
| 28 | Indianapolis, IN | 4,162 | 92 | Greensboro-High Point, NC | 796 | 156 | Wilmington, NC | 298 |
| 29 | Seattle (greater), WA | 4,032 | 93 | Fayetteville, NC | 767 | 157 | Spartanburg, SC | 292 |
| 30 | Milwaukee, WI | 3,692 | 94 | Modesto, CA | 741 | 158 | Santa Maria-Santa Barbara, CA | 285 |
| 31 | Memphis, TN-MS-AR | 3,468 | 95 | Greenville-Anderson, SC | 739 | 159 | Gulfport-Biloxi-Pascagoula, MS | 282 |
| 32 | Minneapolis-St. Paul, MN-WI | 3,341 | 96 | Vallejo-Fairfield, CA | 718 | 160 | York-Hanover, PA | 271 |
| 33 | Seattle-Bellevue-Everett, WA M.D. | 3,082 | 97 | Albany-Schenectady-Troy, NY | 716 | 161 | Amarillo, TX | 250 |
| 34 | San Diego, CA | 3,054 | 98 | Flint, MI | 699 | 162 | Davenport, IA-IL | 247 |
| 35 | Fort Lauderdale, FL M.D. | 2,981 | 99 | Worcester, MA-CT | 696 | 162 | Des Moines-West Des Moines, IA | 247 |
| 36 | Boston, MA M.D. | 2,933 | 100 | Akron, OH | 695 | 164 | Brownsville-Harlingen, TX | 244 |
| 37 | St. Louis, MO-IL | 2,860 | 101 | Trenton, NJ | 685 | 165 | Lake Charles, LA | 243 |
| 38 | Sacramento, CA | 2,848 | 102 | Spokane, WA | 659 | 166 | Eugene, OR | 242 |
| 39 | Orlando, FL | 2,788 | 103 | Mobile, AL | 658 | 166 | Santa Rosa, CA | 242 |
| 40 | Cincinnati, OH-KY-IN | 2,716 | 104 | Grand Rapids-Wyoming, MI | 655 | 168 | Gainesville, FL | 238 |
| 41 | Charlotte-Mecklenburg, NC-SC | 2,665 | 104 | Salinas, CA | 655 | 169 | Port St. Lucie, FL | 234 |
| 42 | Tampa-St Petersburg, FL | 2,607 | 106 | North Port-Sarasota-Bradenton, FL | 646 | 170 | Tuscaloosa, AL | 233 |
| 43 | San Antonio, TX | 2,430 | 107 | Beaumont-Port Arthur, TX | 628 | 171 | Merced, CA | 231 |
| 44 | Kansas City, MO-KS | 2,381 | 108 | Knoxville, TN | 626 | 172 | Erie, PA | 228 |
| 45 | Fort Worth-Arlington, TX M.D. | 2,245 | 109 | Winston-Salem, NC | 622 | 173 | Greenville, NC | 225 |
| 46 | Denver-Aurora, CO | 2,125 | 110 | Augusta, GA-SC | 612 | 174 | Albany, GA | 223 |
| 47 | Nashville-Davidson, TN | 2,013 | 111 | Oxnard-Thousand Oaks, CA | 607 | 175 | Champaign-Urbana, IL | 220 |
| 48 | Anaheim-Santa Ana-Irvine, CA M.D. | 1,993 | 112 | Lexington-Fayette, KY | 584 | 175 | Springfield, OH | 220 |
| 49 | Pittsburgh, PA | 1,976 | 113 | Cape Coral-Fort Myers, FL | 577 | 177 | Pueblo, CO | 219 |
| 50 | New Orleans, LA | 1,805 | 114 | Allentown, PA-NJ | 540 | 178 | Elgin, IL M.D. | 217 |
| 51 | Buffalo-Niagara Falls, NY | 1,744 | 115 | Columbus, GA-AL | 532 | 179 | Lincoln, NE | 214 |
| 52 | Louisville, KY-IN | 1,741 | 116 | Anchorage, AK | 528 | 179 | Salem, OR | 214 |
| 53 | Nassau-Suffolk, NY M.D. | 1,715 | 117 | Atlantic City, NJ | 520 | 181 | Laredo, TX | 211 |
| 54 | Birmingham-Hoover, AL | 1,712 | 118 | Lafayette, LA | 513 | 182 | Monroe, LA | 199 |
| 55 | West Palm Beach, FL M.D. | 1,711 | 119 | Charleston-North Charleston, SC | 505 | 182 | Santa Cruz-Watsonville, CA | 199 |
| 56 | Portland-Vancouver, OR-WA | 1,702 | 120 | Syracuse, NY | 503 | 184 | Racine, WI | 197 |
| 57 | Jacksonville, FL | 1,646 | 121 | Savannah, GA | 500 | 185 | Warner Robins, GA | 192 |
| 58 | Virginia Beach-Norfolk, VA-NC | 1,537 | 122 | Fort Wayne, IN | 499 | 186 | Yakima, WA | 191 |
| 59 | San Jose, CA | 1,533 | 122 | Wichita, KS | 499 | 187 | Longview, TX | 190 |
| 60 | Camden, NJ M.D. | 1,516 | 124 | El Paso, TX | 496 | 187 | Rocky Mount, NC | 190 |
| 61 | Stockton-Lodi, CA | 1,477 | 125 | Chattanooga, TN-GA | 491 | 187 | Saginaw, MI | 190 |
| 62 | Oklahoma City, OK | 1,430 | 126 | Canton, OH | 482 | 190 | Alexandria, LA | 188 |
| 63 | Cambridge-Newton, MA M.D. | 1,400 | 127 | Palm Bay-Melbourne, FL | 470 | 191 | Ogden-Clearfield, UT | 185 |
| 64 | Baton Rouge, LA | 1,388 | 128 | McAllen-Edinburg-Mission, TX | 469 | 192 | Redding, CA | 184 |

Note: All listings are for Metropolitan Statistical Areas (M.S.A.s) except for those ending with "M.D." Listings with "M.D." are Metropolitan Divisions which are smaller parts of eleven large M.S.A.s. See explanatory note at beginning of metropolitan area section.

| RANK | METROPOLITAN AREA | ROBBERY | RANK | METROPOLITAN AREA | ROBBERY | RANK | METROPOLITAN AREA | ROBBERY |
|------|-------------------|---------|------|-------------------|---------|------|-------------------|---------|
| 193 | Waco, TX | 182 | 254 | Kankakee, IL | 90 | 317 | Morgantown, WV | 50 |
| 194 | Hagerstown-Martinsburg, MD-WV | 181 | 256 | Lynchburg, VA | 89 | 317 | Rapid City, SD | 50 |
| 195 | Portland, ME | 178 | 257 | Kennewick-Richland, WA | 88 | 317 | St. Cloud, MN | 50 |
| 196 | Odessa, TX | 177 | 257 | Lima, OH | 88 | 320 | Provo-Orem, UT | 49 |
| 197 | Topeka, KS | 176 | 257 | St. Joseph, MO-KS | 88 | 321 | Albany, OR | 45 |
| 198 | Roanoke, VA | 173 | 260 | Decatur, IL | 87 | 321 | Sioux City, IA-NE-SD | 45 |
| 199 | Ocala, FL | 170 | 260 | Lafayette, IN | 87 | 323 | Sherman-Denison, TX | 43 |
| 200 | Lawton, OK | 169 | 262 | Yuba City, CA | 85 | 324 | Bend, OR | 41 |
| 201 | Jackson, TN | 168 | 263 | Billings, MT | 84 | 324 | Fairbanks, AK | 41 |
| 202 | Clarksville, TN-KY | 164 | 263 | Boise City, ID | 84 | 324 | Sebastian-Vero Beach, FL | 41 |
| 202 | Florence, SC | 164 | 265 | Greeley, CO | 83 | 324 | Winchester, VA-WV | 41 |
| 202 | Panama City, FL | 164 | 265 | Jackson, MI | 83 | 328 | Missoula, MT | 40 |
| 205 | Ann Arbor, MI | 161 | 265 | Napa, CA | 83 | 329 | Decatur, AL | 39 |
| 206 | Dutchess-Putnam, NY M.D. | 160 | 268 | San Luis Obispo, CA | 81 | 329 | Mankato-North Mankato, MN | 39 |
| 207 | Binghamton, NY | 158 | 269 | Chambersburg-Waynesboro, PA | 80 | 329 | Morristown, TN | 39 |
| 208 | Hammond, LA | 156 | 270 | Rome, GA | 79 | 332 | Cleveland, TN | 37 |
| 209 | Utica-Rome, NY | 149 | 270 | Tyler, TX | 79 | 332 | Dubuque, IA | 37 |
| 210 | Chico, CA | 148 | 272 | Barnstable Town, MA | 78 | 332 | Elmira, NY | 37 |
| 211 | Burlington, NC | 147 | 273 | Bowling Green, KY | 76 | 332 | Grants Pass, OR | 37 |
| 212 | Dover, DE | 146 | 274 | Lawrence, KS | 75 | 336 | Lewiston-Auburn, ME | 36 |
| 212 | Muskegon, MI | 146 | 275 | Boulder, CO | 74 | 337 | Punta Gorda, FL | 35 |
| 214 | San Rafael, CA M.D. | 136 | 275 | Hot Springs, AR | 74 | 338 | Altoona, PA | 34 |
| 215 | Athens-Clarke County, GA | 134 | 275 | Kingsport, TN-VA | 74 | 339 | Dalton, GA | 33 |
| 215 | Hilton Head Island, SC | 134 | 275 | Yuma, AZ | 74 | 340 | Coeur d'Alene, ID | 31 |
| 215 | Wichita Falls, TX | 134 | 279 | Joplin, MO | 73 | 340 | Prescott, AZ | 31 |
| 218 | Madera, CA | 132 | 280 | Iowa City, IA | 71 | 342 | Pocatello, ID | 30 |
| 219 | Medford, OR | 131 | 280 | Lake Havasu City-Kingman, AZ | 71 | 343 | Bay City, MI | 29 |
| 219 | Rockingham County, NH M.D. | 131 | 282 | Janesville, WI | 70 | 343 | La Crosse, WI-MN | 29 |
| 221 | Houma, LA | 130 | 282 | Johnson City, TN | 70 | 343 | Oshkosh-Neenah, WI | 29 |
| 222 | Abilene, TX | 128 | 282 | Midland, TX | 70 | 346 | Grand Forks, ND-MN | 27 |
| 222 | Columbia, MO | 128 | 282 | New Bern, NC | 70 | 347 | Corvallis, OR | 25 |
| 224 | Crestview-Fort Walton Beach, FL | 125 | 286 | Fargo, ND-MN | 69 | 347 | Staunton-Waynesboro, VA | 25 |
| 225 | Hanford-Corcoran, CA | 123 | 286 | Gainesville, GA | 69 | 349 | Idaho Falls, ID | 24 |
| 226 | College Station-Bryan, TX | 122 | 286 | Homosassa Springs, FL | 69 | 349 | San Angelo, TX | 24 |
| 227 | Texarkana, TX-AR | 120 | 286 | Terre Haute, IN | 69 | 349 | The Villages, FL | 24 |
| 228 | Gadsden, AL | 119 | 290 | Carbondale-Marion, IL | 68 | 352 | Eau Claire, WI | 23 |
| 229 | Fort Smith, AR-OK | 116 | 290 | Kokomo, IN | 68 | 352 | Elizabethtown-Fort Knox, KY | 23 |
| 230 | Duluth, MN-WI | 115 | 290 | Sioux Falls, SD | 68 | 352 | State College, PA | 23 |
| 231 | Naples-Marco Island, FL | 114 | 293 | Cumberland, MD-WV | 67 | 355 | Bismarck, ND | 22 |
| 232 | Brunswick, GA | 113 | 293 | Daphne-Fairhope-Foley, AL | 67 | 356 | Columbus, IN | 21 |
| 232 | Niles-Benton Harbor, MI | 113 | 293 | Johnstown, PA | 67 | 356 | Lewiston, ID-WA | 21 |
| 234 | Mansfield, OH | 111 | 293 | Jonesboro, AR | 67 | 358 | Blacksburg, VA | 20 |
| 235 | El Centro, CA | 110 | 297 | Fort Collins, CO | 66 | 358 | Manhattan, KS | 20 |
| 236 | Sumter, SC | 108 | 298 | Mount Vernon-Anacortes, WA | 64 | 360 | Appleton, WI | 19 |
| 237 | Bremerton-Silverdale, WA | 105 | 298 | Ocean City, NJ | 64 | 360 | Great Falls, MT | 19 |
| 237 | Green Bay, WI | 105 | 300 | Sebring, FL | 63 | 360 | Sheboygan, WI | 19 |
| 239 | Dothan, AL | 104 | 301 | California-Lexington Park, MD | 62 | 363 | Watertown-Fort Drum, NY | 18 |
| 239 | Goldsboro, NC | 104 | 301 | Monroe, MI | 62 | 363 | Wausau, WI | 18 |
| 241 | Anniston-Oxford, AL | 103 | 303 | Longview, WA | 61 | 365 | Carson City, NV | 17 |
| 242 | Bloomington, IL | 102 | 303 | Victoria, TX | 61 | 365 | Casper, WY | 17 |
| 243 | Olympia, WA | 101 | 305 | Farmington, NM | 60 | 365 | Fond du Lac, WI | 17 |
| 244 | Cape Girardeau, MO-IL | 100 | 306 | Williamsport, PA | 59 | 365 | Gettysburg, PA | 17 |
| 244 | Muncie, IN | 100 | 307 | East Stroudsburg, PA | 57 | 365 | Harrisonburg, VA | 17 |
| 246 | Cedar Rapids, IA | 99 | 308 | Bangor, ME | 56 | 365 | St. George, UT | 17 |
| 247 | Norwich-New London, CT | 98 | 308 | Rochester, MN | 56 | 371 | Ames, IA | 15 |
| 248 | Charlottesville, VA | 97 | 310 | Flagstaff, AZ | 54 | 372 | Parkersburg-Vienna, WV | 14 |
| 248 | Kahului-Wailuku-Lahaina, HI | 97 | 310 | Grand Junction, CO | 54 | 373 | Cheyenne, WY | 13 |
| 250 | Lebanon, PA | 96 | 310 | Jefferson City, MO | 54 | 373 | Glens Falls, NY | 13 |
| 251 | Florence-Muscle Shoals, AL | 93 | 313 | Pittsfield, MA | 53 | 375 | Bloomsburg-Berwick, PA | 11 |
| 252 | Fayetteville-Springdale, AR-MO | 91 | 314 | Kingston, NY | 52 | 376 | Grand Island, NE | 10 |
| 252 | Las Cruces, NM | 91 | 314 | Owensboro, KY | 52 | 377 | Logan, UT-ID | 0 |
| 254 | Bloomington, IN | 90 | 316 | Hinesville, GA | 51 | | | |

Source: Reported data from the F.B.I. "Crime in the United States 2013"
*Robbery is the taking of anything of value by force or threat of force.  Attempts are included.

# 18. Robbery Rate in 2013
## National Rate = 109.1 Robberies per 100,000 Population*

| RANK | METROPOLITAN AREA | RATE | RANK | METROPOLITAN AREA | RATE | RANK | METROPOLITAN AREA | RATE |
|---|---|---|---|---|---|---|---|---|
| 184 | Abilene, TX | 76.1 | 366 | Cheyenne, WY | 13.6 | 94 | Gary, IN M.D. | 113.1 |
| 122 | Akron, OH | 98.8 | 31 | Chicago (greater), IL-IN-WI | 167.7 | 356 | Gettysburg, PA | 16.8 |
| 168 | Albany-Schenectady-Troy, NY | 81.7 | 17 | Chicago-Naperville, IL M.D. | 198.7 | 374 | Glens Falls, NY | 10.1 |
| 52 | Albany, GA | 141.7 | 208 | Chico, CA | 66.6 | 163 | Goldsboro, NC | 83.1 |
| 291 | Albany, OR | 37.8 | 68 | Cincinnati, OH-KY-IN | 127.1 | 331 | Grand Forks, ND-MN | 26.9 |
| 57 | Albuquerque, NM | 137.3 | 236 | Clarksville, TN-KY | 58.8 | 371 | Grand Island, NE | 11.9 |
| 76 | Alexandria, LA | 121.5 | 318 | Cleveland, TN | 31.2 | 298 | Grand Junction, CO | 36.2 |
| 213 | Allentown, PA-NJ | 65.2 | 344 | Coeur d'Alene, ID | 21.5 | 214 | Grand Rapids-Wyoming, MI | 64.7 |
| 332 | Altoona, PA | 26.8 | 253 | College Station-Bryan, TX | 51.4 | 271 | Grants Pass, OR | 44.5 |
| 128 | Amarillo, TX | 96.0 | 201 | Colorado Springs, CO | 68.4 | 341 | Great Falls, MT | 23.1 |
| 359 | Ames, IA | 16.3 | 187 | Columbia, MO | 75.0 | 321 | Greeley, CO | 30.9 |
| 218 | Anaheim-Santa Ana-Irvine, CA M.D. | 63.9 | 107 | Columbia, SC | 105.6 | 315 | Green Bay, WI | 33.6 |
| 29 | Anchorage, AK | 167.9 | 28 | Columbus, GA-AL | 168.5 | 104 | Greensboro-High Point, NC | 107.3 |
| 268 | Ann Arbor, MI | 45.6 | 335 | Columbus, IN | 26.2 | 153 | Greenville-Anderson, SC | 86.7 |
| 147 | Anniston-Oxford, AL | 88.1 | 124 | Corpus Christi, TX | 97.7 | 64 | Greenville, NC | 129.0 |
| 376 | Appleton, WI | 8.3 | 327 | Corvallis, OR | 28.8 | 190 | Gulfport-Biloxi-Pascagoula, MS | 73.7 |
| 204 | Athens-Clarke County, GA | 67.9 | 260 | Crestview-Fort Walton Beach, FL | 49.5 | 198 | Hagerstown-Martinsburg, MD-WV | 70.2 |
| 40 | Atlanta, GA | 158.1 | 211 | Cumberland, MD-WV | 65.9 | 70 | Hammond, LA | 125.6 |
| 20 | Atlantic City, NJ | 188.3 | 77 | Dallas (greater), TX | 120.8 | 170 | Hanford-Corcoran, CA | 81.3 |
| 108 | Augusta, GA-SC | 105.5 | 60 | Dallas-Plano-Irving, TX M.D. | 132.8 | 368 | Harrisonburg, VA | 13.1 |
| 249 | Austin-Round Rock, TX | 53.3 | 341 | Dalton, GA | 23.1 | 115 | Hartford, CT | 102.2 |
| 48 | Bakersfield, CA | 149.0 | 305 | Daphne-Fairhope-Foley, AL | 34.7 | 203 | Hilton Head Island, SC | 68.1 |
| 12 | Baltimore, MD | 227.4 | 215 | Davenport, IA-IL | 64.4 | 227 | Hinesville, GA | 61.5 |
| 296 | Bangor, ME | 36.5 | 100 | Dayton, OH | 110.2 | 259 | Homosassa Springs, FL | 49.6 |
| 299 | Barnstable Town, MA | 36.1 | 337 | Decatur, AL | 25.3 | 183 | Hot Springs, AR | 76.2 |
| 27 | Baton Rouge, LA | 169.3 | 177 | Decatur, IL | 79.2 | 224 | Houma, LA | 62.1 |
| 330 | Bay City, MI | 27.2 | 182 | Deltona-Daytona Beach, FL | 76.3 | 10 | Houston, TX | 233.3 |
| 42 | Beaumont-Port Arthur, TX | 154.7 | 179 | Denver-Aurora, CO | 78.9 | 105 | Huntsville, AL | 107.2 |
| 338 | Bend, OR | 25.0 | 279 | Des Moines-West Des Moines, IA | 41.4 | 354 | Idaho Falls, ID | 17.4 |
| 254 | Billings, MT | 51.0 | 35 | Detroit (greater), MI | 164.3 | 13 | Indianapolis, IN | 213.8 |
| 219 | Binghamton, NY | 63.7 | 2 | Detroit-Dearborn-Livonia, MI M.D. | 328.7 | 272 | Iowa City, IA | 44.3 |
| 46 | Birmingham-Hoover, AL | 150.3 | 198 | Dothan, AL | 70.2 | 84 | Jacksonville, FL | 118.2 |
| 353 | Bismarck, ND | 17.7 | 156 | Dover, DE | 86.0 | 252 | Jackson, MI | 51.7 |
| 373 | Blacksburg, VA | 11.1 | 290 | Dubuque, IA | 38.6 | 24 | Jackson, MS | 171.6 |
| 243 | Bloomington, IL | 53.9 | 282 | Duluth, MN-WI | 41.0 | 66 | Jackson, TN | 128.5 |
| 241 | Bloomington, IN | 55.0 | 285 | Dutchess-Putnam, NY M.D. | 40.3 | 273 | Janesville, WI | 43.6 |
| 370 | Bloomsburg-Berwick, PA | 12.9 | 312 | East Stroudsburg, PA | 33.9 | 300 | Jefferson City, MO | 35.9 |
| 369 | Boise City, ID | 13.0 | 365 | Eau Claire, WI | 14.0 | 305 | Johnson City, TN | 34.7 |
| 130 | Boston (greater), MA-NH | 95.4 | 225 | El Centro, CA | 61.8 | 263 | Johnstown, PA | 47.6 |
| 45 | Boston, MA M.D. | 151.0 | 234 | El Paso, TX | 58.9 | 246 | Jonesboro, AR | 53.6 |
| 340 | Boulder, CO | 23.8 | 309 | Elgin, IL M.D. | 34.5 | 276 | Joplin, MO | 41.9 |
| 267 | Bowling Green, KY | 46.5 | 360 | Elizabethtown-Fort Knox, KY | 15.3 | 228 | Kahului-Wailuku-Lahaina, HI | 60.8 |
| 283 | Bremerton-Silverdale, WA | 40.9 | 278 | Elmira, NY | 41.6 | 176 | Kankakee, IL | 79.8 |
| 114 | Bridgeport-Stamford, CT | 102.4 | 170 | Erie, PA | 81.3 | 87 | Kansas City, MO-KS | 116.2 |
| 237 | Brownsville-Harlingen, TX | 58.1 | 204 | Eugene, OR | 67.9 | 317 | Kennewick-Richland, WA | 32.2 |
| 121 | Brunswick, GA | 99.3 | 85 | Fairbanks, AK | 118.0 | 339 | Kingsport, TN-VA | 23.9 |
| 43 | Buffalo-Niagara Falls, NY | 153.6 | 319 | Fargo, ND-MN | 31.1 | 328 | Kingston, NY | 28.6 |
| 136 | Burlington, NC | 94.7 | 266 | Farmington, NM | 47.0 | 192 | Knoxville, TN | 73.4 |
| 239 | California-Lexington Park, MD | 56.2 | 352 | Fayetteville-Springdale, AR-MO | 18.6 | 166 | Kokomo, IN | 81.8 |
| 229 | Cambridge-Newton, MA M.D. | 60.5 | 15 | Fayetteville, NC | 202.9 | 346 | La Crosse, WI-MN | 21.3 |
| 78 | Camden, NJ M.D. | 120.6 | 288 | Flagstaff, AZ | 39.4 | 277 | Lafayette, IN | 41.7 |
| 82 | Canton, OH | 119.3 | 30 | Flint, MI | 167.8 | 103 | Lafayette, LA | 107.5 |
| 149 | Cape Coral-Fort Myers, FL | 87.9 | 221 | Florence-Muscle Shoals, AL | 63.3 | 79 | Lake Charles, LA | 120.5 |
| 111 | Cape Girardeau, MO-IL | 102.6 | 177 | Florence, SC | 79.2 | 264 | Lake Co.-Kenosha Co., IL-WI M.D. | 47.3 |
| 245 | Carbondale-Marion, IL | 53.7 | 357 | Fond du Lac, WI | 16.7 | 308 | Lake Havasu City-Kingman, AZ | 34.6 |
| 321 | Carson City, NV | 30.9 | 349 | Fort Collins, CO | 20.9 | 220 | Lakeland, FL | 63.6 |
| 346 | Casper, WY | 21.3 | 36 | Fort Lauderdale, FL M.D. | 161.7 | 216 | Lancaster, PA | 64.3 |
| 292 | Cedar Rapids, IA | 37.6 | 280 | Fort Smith, AR-OK | 41.3 | 165 | Lansing-East Lansing, MI | 82.1 |
| 250 | Chambersburg-Waynesboro, PA | 52.8 | 86 | Fort Wayne, IN | 117.7 | 173 | Laredo, TX | 80.2 |
| 137 | Champaign-Urbana, IL | 93.9 | 125 | Fort Worth-Arlington, TX M.D. | 97.3 | 275 | Las Cruces, NM | 42.3 |
| 195 | Charleston-North Charleston, SC | 71.0 | 67 | Fresno, CA | 127.9 | 11 | Las Vegas-Henderson, NV | 232.8 |
| 91 | Charlotte-Mecklenburg, NC-SC | 114.4 | 92 | Gadsden, AL | 114.0 | 210 | Lawrence, KS | 66.2 |
| 274 | Charlottesville, VA | 43.2 | 148 | Gainesville, FL | 88.0 | 69 | Lawton, OK | 126.6 |
| 141 | Chattanooga, TN-GA | 90.7 | 294 | Gainesville, GA | 36.8 | 196 | Lebanon, PA | 70.8 |

Note: All listings are for Metropolitan Statistical Areas (M.S.A.s) except for those ending with "M.D." Listings with "M.D." are Metropolitan Divisions which are smaller parts of eleven large M.S.A.s. See explanatory note at beginning of metropolitan area section.

| RANK | METROPOLITAN AREA | RATE | RANK | METROPOLITAN AREA | RATE | RANK | METROPOLITAN AREA | RATE |
|---|---|---|---|---|---|---|---|---|
| 316 | Lewiston-Auburn, ME | 33.5 | 134 | Omaha-Council Bluffs, NE-IA | 95.2 | 358 | Sheboygan, WI | 16.5 |
| 311 | Lewiston, ID-WA | 34.0 | 73 | Orlando, FL | 123.3 | 304 | Sherman-Denison, TX | 35.0 |
| 82 | Lexington-Fayette, KY | 119.3 | 355 | Oshkosh-Neenah, WI | 17.1 | 110 | Shreveport-Bossier City, LA | 103.4 |
| 161 | Lima, OH | 83.8 | 270 | Owensboro, KY | 44.6 | 186 | Silver Spring-Frederick, MD M.D. | 75.7 |
| 202 | Lincoln, NE | 68.3 | 194 | Oxnard-Thousand Oaks, CA | 72.2 | 333 | Sioux City, IA-NE-SD | 26.6 |
| 22 | Little Rock, AR | 175.6 | 158 | Palm Bay-Melbourne, FL | 85.4 | 329 | Sioux Falls, SD | 28.1 |
| 377 | Logan, UT-ID | 0.0 | 153 | Panama City, FL | 86.7 | 55 | South Bend-Mishawaka, IN-MI | 140.3 |
| 152 | Longview, TX | 87.0 | 361 | Parkersburg-Vienna, WV | 15.2 | 138 | Spartanburg, SC | 91.4 |
| 231 | Longview, WA | 59.7 | 123 | Pensacola, FL | 98.2 | 74 | Spokane, WA | 123.1 |
| 32 | Los Angeles County, CA M.D. | 167.5 | 151 | Peoria, IL | 87.2 | 34 | Springfield, IL | 165.3 |
| 51 | Los Angeles (greater), CA | 142.9 | 18 | Philadelphia (greater) PA-NJ-MD-DE | 197.5 | 50 | Springfield, MA | 145.3 |
| 56 | Louisville, KY-IN | 138.5 | 1 | Philadelphia, PA M.D. | 395.7 | 132 | Springfield, MO | 95.3 |
| 63 | Lubbock, TX | 129.7 | 89 | Phoenix-Mesa-Scottsdale, AZ | 115.3 | 37 | Springfield, OH | 160.4 |
| 305 | Lynchburg, VA | 34.7 | 162 | Pittsburgh, PA | 83.7 | 362 | State College, PA | 14.8 |
| 62 | Macon, GA | 132.3 | 284 | Pittsfield, MA | 40.8 | 348 | Staunton-Waynesboro, VA | 21.0 |
| 155 | Madera, CA | 86.4 | 302 | Pocatello, ID | 35.5 | 14 | Stockton-Lodi, CA | 208.4 |
| 234 | Madison, WI | 58.9 | 246 | Port St. Lucie, FL | 53.6 | 336 | St. Cloud, MN | 26.1 |
| 135 | Manchester-Nashua, NH | 95.1 | 191 | Portland-Vancouver, OR-WA | 73.5 | 372 | St. George, UT | 11.5 |
| 351 | Manhattan, KS | 20.1 | 310 | Portland, ME | 34.3 | 200 | St. Joseph, MO-KS | 68.5 |
| 287 | Mankato-North Mankato, MN | 39.5 | 364 | Prescott, AZ | 14.5 | 117 | St. Louis, MO-IL | 102.0 |
| 141 | Mansfield, OH | 90.7 | 172 | Providence-Warwick, RI-MA | 80.6 | 119 | Sumter, SC | 99.4 |
| 238 | McAllen-Edinburg-Mission, TX | 57.2 | 375 | Provo-Orem, UT | 8.7 | 184 | Syracuse, NY | 76.1 |
| 222 | Medford, OR | 63.0 | 59 | Pueblo, CO | 134.9 | 88 | Tacoma, WA M.D. | 115.9 |
| 6 | Memphis, TN-MS-AR | 257.3 | 345 | Punta Gorda, FL | 21.4 | 80 | Tallahassee, FL | 120.1 |
| 150 | Merced, CA | 87.3 | 118 | Racine, WI | 101.2 | 139 | Tampa-St Petersburg, FL | 90.8 |
| 19 | Miami (greater), FL | 189.2 | 206 | Raleigh, NC | 67.8 | 286 | Terre Haute, IN | 39.9 |
| 7 | Miami-Dade County, FL M.D. | 242.2 | 302 | Rapid City, SD | 35.5 | 175 | Texarkana, TX-AR | 79.9 |
| 269 | Midland, TX | 44.9 | 115 | Reading, PA | 102.2 | 343 | The Villages, FL | 22.9 |
| 9 | Milwaukee, WI | 234.9 | 111 | Redding, CA | 102.6 | 23 | Toledo, OH | 173.4 |
| 126 | Minneapolis-St. Paul, MN-WI | 96.7 | 144 | Reno, NV | 89.2 | 187 | Topeka, KS | 75.0 |
| 301 | Missoula, MT | 35.7 | 139 | Richmond, VA | 90.8 | 21 | Trenton, NJ | 185.5 |
| 38 | Mobile, AL | 158.9 | 102 | Riverside-San Bernardino, CA | 107.8 | 75 | Tucson, AZ | 122.5 |
| 53 | Modesto, CA | 141.3 | 240 | Roanoke, VA | 55.6 | 93 | Tulsa, OK | 113.8 |
| 98 | Monroe, LA | 111.6 | 334 | Rochester, MN | 26.5 | 119 | Tuscaloosa, AL | 99.4 |
| 281 | Monroe, MI | 41.1 | 96 | Rochester, NY | 111.7 | 297 | Tyler, TX | 36.4 |
| 260 | Montgomery County, PA M.D. | 49.5 | 61 | Rockford, IL | 132.5 | 258 | Utica-Rome, NY | 50.0 |
| 293 | Morgantown, WV | 36.9 | 321 | Rockingham County, NH M.D. | 30.9 | 26 | Vallejo-Fairfield, CA | 169.5 |
| 313 | Morristown, TN | 33.8 | 71 | Rocky Mount, NC | 125.1 | 223 | Victoria, TX | 62.3 |
| 244 | Mount Vernon-Anacortes, WA | 53.8 | 164 | Rome, GA | 82.2 | 8 | Vineland-Bridgeton, NJ | 241.3 |
| 159 | Muncie, IN | 85.0 | 65 | Sacramento, CA | 128.7 | 143 | Virginia Beach-Norfolk, VA-NC | 89.9 |
| 156 | Muskegon, MI | 86.0 | 129 | Saginaw, MI | 95.9 | 127 | Visalia-Porterville, CA | 96.1 |
| 109 | Myrtle Beach, SC-NC | 103.6 | 246 | Salem, OR | 53.6 | 197 | Waco, TX | 70.5 |
| 232 | Napa, CA | 59.3 | 44 | Salinas, CA | 152.0 | 113 | Warner Robins, GA | 102.5 |
| 313 | Naples-Marco Island, FL | 33.8 | 166 | Salisbury, MD-DE | 81.8 | 265 | Warren-Troy, MI M.D. | 47.2 |
| 89 | Nashville-Davidson, TN | 115.3 | 160 | Salt Lake City, UT | 84.4 | 53 | Washington (greater) DC-VA-MD-WV | 141.3 |
| 230 | Nassau-Suffolk, NY M.D. | 60.0 | 350 | San Angelo, TX | 20.7 | 38 | Washington, DC-VA-MD-WV M.D. | 158.9 |
| 242 | New Bern, NC | 54.3 | 106 | San Antonio, TX | 107.0 | 362 | Watertown-Fort Drum, NY | 14.8 |
| 33 | New Haven-Milford, CT | 166.9 | 132 | San Diego, CA | 95.3 | 72 | West Palm Beach, FL M.D. | 124.6 |
| 49 | New Orleans, LA | 145.7 | 5 | San Francisco (greater), CA | 294.6 | 146 | Wichita Falls, TX | 88.6 |
| 41 | New York (greater), NY-NJ-PA | 156.0 | 4 | San Francisco-Redwood, CA M.D. | 302.4 | 180 | Wichita, KS | 78.3 |
| 25 | New York-Jersey City, NY-NJ M.D. | 170.6 | 174 | San Jose, CA | 80.1 | 257 | Williamsport, PA | 50.2 |
| 16 | Newark, NJ-PA M.D. | 201.1 | 325 | San Luis Obispo, CA | 29.3 | 47 | Wilmington, DE-MD-NJ M.D. | 149.6 |
| 193 | Niles-Benton Harbor, MI | 72.4 | 250 | San Rafael, CA M.D. | 52.8 | 96 | Wilmington, NC | 111.7 |
| 145 | North Port-Sarasota-Bradenton, FL | 88.7 | 189 | Santa Cruz-Watsonville, CA | 74.2 | 319 | Winchester, VA-WV | 31.1 |
| 207 | Norwich-New London, CT | 67.1 | 212 | Santa Maria-Santa Barbara, CA | 65.6 | 130 | Winston-Salem, NC | 95.4 |
| 3 | Oakland-Hayward, CA M.D. | 313.4 | 262 | Santa Rosa, CA | 48.9 | 169 | Worcester, MA-CT | 81.6 |
| 256 | Ocala, FL | 50.3 | 58 | Savannah, GA | 136.4 | 181 | Yakima, WA | 76.8 |
| 208 | Ocean City, NJ | 66.6 | 233 | Scranton--Wilkes-Barre, PA | 59.1 | 225 | York-Hanover, PA | 61.8 |
| 81 | Odessa, TX | 120.0 | 95 | Seattle (greater), WA | 112.0 | 255 | Yuba City, CA | 50.5 |
| 324 | Ogden-Clearfield, UT | 29.8 | 99 | Seattle-Bellevue-Everett, WA M.D. | 110.9 | 295 | Yuma, AZ | 36.7 |
| 101 | Oklahoma City, OK | 108.7 | 326 | Sebastian-Vero Beach, FL | 28.9 | | | |
| 289 | Olympia, WA | 38.7 | 217 | Sebring, FL | 64.1 | | | |

Source: Reported data from the F.B.I. "Crime in the United States 2013"
*Robbery is the taking of anything of value by force or threat of force. Attempts are included.

# 18. Robbery Rate in 2013 (continued)
## National Rate = 109.1 Robberies per 100,000 Population*

| RANK | METROPOLITAN AREA | RATE | RANK | METROPOLITAN AREA | RATE | RANK | METROPOLITAN AREA | RATE |
|---|---|---|---|---|---|---|---|---|
| 1 | Philadelphia, PA M.D. | 395.7 | 65 | Sacramento, CA | 128.7 | 129 | Saginaw, MI | 95.9 |
| 2 | Detroit-Dearborn-Livonia, MI M.D. | 328.7 | 66 | Jackson, TN | 128.5 | 130 | Boston (greater), MA-NH | 95.4 |
| 3 | Oakland-Hayward, CA M.D. | 313.4 | 67 | Fresno, CA | 127.9 | 130 | Winston-Salem, NC | 95.4 |
| 4 | San Francisco-Redwood, CA M.D. | 302.4 | 68 | Cincinnati, OH-KY-IN | 127.1 | 132 | San Diego, CA | 95.3 |
| 5 | San Francisco (greater), CA | 294.6 | 69 | Lawton, OK | 126.6 | 132 | Springfield, MO | 95.3 |
| 6 | Memphis, TN-MS-AR | 257.3 | 70 | Hammond, LA | 125.6 | 134 | Omaha-Council Bluffs, NE-IA | 95.2 |
| 7 | Miami-Dade County, FL M.D. | 242.2 | 71 | Rocky Mount, NC | 125.1 | 135 | Manchester-Nashua, NH | 95.1 |
| 8 | Vineland-Bridgeton, NJ | 241.3 | 72 | West Palm Beach, FL M.D. | 124.6 | 136 | Burlington, NC | 94.7 |
| 9 | Milwaukee, WI | 234.9 | 73 | Orlando, FL | 123.3 | 137 | Champaign-Urbana, IL | 93.9 |
| 10 | Houston, TX | 233.3 | 74 | Spokane, WA | 123.1 | 138 | Spartanburg, SC | 91.4 |
| 11 | Las Vegas-Henderson, NV | 232.8 | 75 | Tucson, AZ | 122.5 | 139 | Richmond, VA | 90.8 |
| 12 | Baltimore, MD | 227.4 | 76 | Alexandria, LA | 121.5 | 139 | Tampa-St Petersburg, FL | 90.8 |
| 13 | Indianapolis, IN | 213.8 | 77 | Dallas (greater), TX | 120.8 | 141 | Chattanooga, TN-GA | 90.7 |
| 14 | Stockton-Lodi, CA | 208.4 | 78 | Camden, NJ M.D. | 120.6 | 141 | Mansfield, OH | 90.7 |
| 15 | Fayetteville, NC | 202.9 | 79 | Lake Charles, LA | 120.5 | 143 | Virginia Beach-Norfolk, VA-NC | 89.9 |
| 16 | Newark, NJ-PA M.D. | 201.1 | 80 | Tallahassee, FL | 120.1 | 144 | Reno, NV | 89.2 |
| 17 | Chicago-Naperville, IL M.D. | 198.7 | 81 | Odessa, TX | 120.0 | 145 | North Port-Sarasota-Bradenton, FL | 88.7 |
| 18 | Philadelphia (greater) PA-NJ-MD-DE | 197.5 | 82 | Canton, OH | 119.3 | 146 | Wichita Falls, TX | 88.6 |
| 19 | Miami (greater), FL | 189.2 | 82 | Lexington-Fayette, KY | 119.3 | 147 | Anniston-Oxford, AL | 88.1 |
| 20 | Atlantic City, NJ | 188.3 | 84 | Jacksonville, FL | 118.2 | 148 | Gainesville, FL | 88.0 |
| 21 | Trenton, NJ | 185.5 | 85 | Fairbanks, AK | 118.0 | 149 | Cape Coral-Fort Myers, FL | 87.9 |
| 22 | Little Rock, AR | 175.6 | 86 | Fort Wayne, IN | 117.7 | 150 | Merced, CA | 87.3 |
| 23 | Toledo, OH | 173.4 | 87 | Kansas City, MO-KS | 116.2 | 151 | Peoria, IL | 87.2 |
| 24 | Jackson, MS | 171.6 | 88 | Tacoma, WA M.D. | 115.9 | 152 | Longview, TX | 87.0 |
| 25 | New York-Jersey City, NY-NJ M.D. | 170.6 | 89 | Nashville-Davidson, TN | 115.3 | 153 | Greenville-Anderson, SC | 86.7 |
| 26 | Vallejo-Fairfield, CA | 169.5 | 89 | Phoenix-Mesa-Scottsdale, AZ | 115.3 | 153 | Panama City, FL | 86.7 |
| 27 | Baton Rouge, LA | 169.3 | 91 | Charlotte-Mecklenburg, NC-SC | 114.4 | 155 | Madera, CA | 86.4 |
| 28 | Columbus, GA-AL | 168.5 | 92 | Gadsden, AL | 114.0 | 156 | Dover, DE | 86.0 |
| 29 | Anchorage, AK | 167.9 | 93 | Tulsa, OK | 113.8 | 156 | Muskegon, MI | 86.0 |
| 30 | Flint, MI | 167.8 | 94 | Gary, IN M.D. | 113.1 | 158 | Palm Bay-Melbourne, FL | 85.4 |
| 31 | Chicago (greater), IL-IN-WI | 167.7 | 95 | Seattle (greater), WA | 112.0 | 159 | Muncie, IN | 85.0 |
| 32 | Los Angeles County, CA M.D. | 167.5 | 96 | Rochester, NY | 111.7 | 160 | Salt Lake City, UT | 84.4 |
| 33 | New Haven-Milford, CT | 166.9 | 96 | Wilmington, NC | 111.7 | 161 | Lima, OH | 83.8 |
| 34 | Springfield, IL | 165.3 | 98 | Monroe, LA | 111.6 | 162 | Pittsburgh, PA | 83.7 |
| 35 | Detroit (greater), MI | 164.3 | 99 | Seattle-Bellevue-Everett, WA M.D. | 110.9 | 163 | Goldsboro, NC | 83.1 |
| 36 | Fort Lauderdale, FL M.D. | 161.7 | 100 | Dayton, OH | 110.2 | 164 | Rome, GA | 82.2 |
| 37 | Springfield, OH | 160.4 | 101 | Oklahoma City, OK | 108.7 | 165 | Lansing-East Lansing, MI | 82.1 |
| 38 | Mobile, AL | 158.9 | 102 | Riverside-San Bernardino, CA | 107.8 | 166 | Kokomo, IN | 81.8 |
| 38 | Washington, DC-VA-MD-WV M.D. | 158.9 | 103 | Lafayette, LA | 107.5 | 166 | Salisbury, MD-DE | 81.8 |
| 40 | Atlanta, GA | 158.1 | 104 | Greensboro-High Point, NC | 107.3 | 168 | Albany-Schenectady-Troy, NY | 81.7 |
| 41 | New York (greater), NY-NJ-PA | 156.0 | 105 | Huntsville, AL | 107.2 | 169 | Worcester, MA-CT | 81.6 |
| 42 | Beaumont-Port Arthur, TX | 154.7 | 106 | San Antonio, TX | 107.0 | 170 | Erie, PA | 81.3 |
| 43 | Buffalo-Niagara Falls, NY | 153.6 | 107 | Columbia, SC | 105.6 | 170 | Hanford-Corcoran, CA | 81.3 |
| 44 | Salinas, CA | 152.0 | 108 | Augusta, GA-SC | 105.5 | 172 | Providence-Warwick, RI-MA | 80.6 |
| 45 | Boston, MA M.D. | 151.0 | 109 | Myrtle Beach, SC-NC | 103.6 | 173 | Laredo, TX | 80.2 |
| 46 | Birmingham-Hoover, AL | 150.3 | 110 | Shreveport-Bossier City, LA | 103.4 | 174 | San Jose, CA | 80.1 |
| 47 | Wilmington, DE-MD-NJ M.D. | 149.6 | 111 | Cape Girardeau, MO-IL | 102.6 | 175 | Texarkana, TX-AR | 79.9 |
| 48 | Bakersfield, CA | 149.0 | 111 | Redding, CA | 102.6 | 176 | Kankakee, IL | 79.8 |
| 49 | New Orleans, LA | 145.7 | 113 | Warner Robins, GA | 102.5 | 177 | Decatur, IL | 79.2 |
| 50 | Springfield, MA | 145.3 | 114 | Bridgeport-Stamford, CT | 102.4 | 177 | Florence, SC | 79.2 |
| 51 | Los Angeles (greater), CA | 142.9 | 115 | Hartford, CT | 102.2 | 179 | Denver-Aurora, CO | 78.9 |
| 52 | Albany, GA | 141.7 | 115 | Reading, PA | 102.2 | 180 | Wichita, KS | 78.3 |
| 53 | Modesto, CA | 141.3 | 117 | St. Louis, MO-IL | 102.0 | 181 | Yakima, WA | 76.8 |
| 53 | Washington (greater) DC-VA-MD-WV | 141.3 | 118 | Racine, WI | 101.2 | 182 | Deltona-Daytona Beach, FL | 76.3 |
| 55 | South Bend-Mishawaka, IN-MI | 140.3 | 119 | Sumter, SC | 99.4 | 183 | Hot Springs, AR | 76.2 |
| 56 | Louisville, KY-IN | 138.5 | 119 | Tuscaloosa, AL | 99.4 | 184 | Abilene, TX | 76.1 |
| 57 | Albuquerque, NM | 137.3 | 121 | Brunswick, GA | 99.3 | 184 | Syracuse, NY | 76.1 |
| 58 | Savannah, GA | 136.4 | 122 | Akron, OH | 98.8 | 186 | Silver Spring-Frederick, MD M.D. | 75.7 |
| 59 | Pueblo, CO | 134.9 | 123 | Pensacola, FL | 98.2 | 187 | Columbia, MO | 75.0 |
| 60 | Dallas-Plano-Irving, TX M.D. | 132.8 | 124 | Corpus Christi, TX | 97.7 | 187 | Topeka, KS | 75.0 |
| 61 | Rockford, IL | 132.5 | 125 | Fort Worth-Arlington, TX M.D. | 97.3 | 189 | Santa Cruz-Watsonville, CA | 74.2 |
| 62 | Macon, GA | 132.3 | 126 | Minneapolis-St. Paul, MN-WI | 96.7 | 190 | Gulfport-Biloxi-Pascagoula, MS | 73.7 |
| 63 | Lubbock, TX | 129.7 | 127 | Visalia-Porterville, CA | 96.1 | 191 | Portland-Vancouver, OR-WA | 73.5 |
| 64 | Greenville, NC | 129.0 | 128 | Amarillo, TX | 96.0 | 192 | Knoxville, TN | 73.4 |

Note: All listings are for Metropolitan Statistical Areas (M.S.A.s) except for those ending with "M.D." Listings with "M.D." are Metropolitan Divisions which are smaller parts of eleven large M.S.A.s. See explanatory note at beginning of metropolitan area section.

| RANK | METROPOLITAN AREA | RATE | RANK | METROPOLITAN AREA | RATE | RANK | METROPOLITAN AREA | RATE |
|---|---|---|---|---|---|---|---|---|
| 193 | Niles-Benton Harbor, MI | 72.4 | 255 | Yuba City, CA | 50.5 | 317 | Kennewick-Richland, WA | 32.2 |
| 194 | Oxnard-Thousand Oaks, CA | 72.2 | 256 | Ocala, FL | 50.3 | 318 | Cleveland, TN | 31.2 |
| 195 | Charleston-North Charleston, SC | 71.0 | 257 | Williamsport, PA | 50.2 | 319 | Fargo, ND-MN | 31.1 |
| 196 | Lebanon, PA | 70.8 | 258 | Utica-Rome, NY | 50.0 | 319 | Winchester, VA-WV | 31.1 |
| 197 | Waco, TX | 70.5 | 259 | Homosassa Springs, FL | 49.6 | 321 | Carson City, NV | 30.9 |
| 198 | Dothan, AL | 70.2 | 260 | Crestview-Fort Walton Beach, FL | 49.5 | 321 | Greeley, CO | 30.9 |
| 198 | Hagerstown-Martinsburg, MD-WV | 70.2 | 260 | Montgomery County, PA M.D. | 49.5 | 321 | Rockingham County, NH M.D. | 30.9 |
| 200 | St. Joseph, MO-KS | 68.5 | 262 | Santa Rosa, CA | 48.9 | 324 | Ogden-Clearfield, UT | 29.8 |
| 201 | Colorado Springs, CO | 68.4 | 263 | Johnstown, PA | 47.6 | 325 | San Luis Obispo, CA | 29.3 |
| 202 | Lincoln, NE | 68.3 | 264 | Lake Co.-Kenosha Co., IL-WI M.D. | 47.3 | 326 | Sebastian-Vero Beach, FL | 28.9 |
| 203 | Hilton Head Island, SC | 68.1 | 265 | Warren-Troy, MI M.D. | 47.2 | 327 | Corvallis, OR | 28.8 |
| 204 | Athens-Clarke County, GA | 67.9 | 266 | Farmington, NM | 47.0 | 328 | Kingston, NY | 28.6 |
| 204 | Eugene, OR | 67.9 | 267 | Bowling Green, KY | 46.5 | 329 | Sioux Falls, SD | 28.1 |
| 206 | Raleigh, NC | 67.8 | 268 | Ann Arbor, MI | 45.6 | 330 | Bay City, MI | 27.2 |
| 207 | Norwich-New London, CT | 67.1 | 269 | Midland, TX | 44.9 | 331 | Grand Forks, ND-MN | 26.9 |
| 208 | Chico, CA | 66.6 | 270 | Owensboro, KY | 44.6 | 332 | Altoona, PA | 26.8 |
| 208 | Ocean City, NJ | 66.6 | 271 | Grants Pass, OR | 44.5 | 333 | Sioux City, IA-NE-SD | 26.6 |
| 210 | Lawrence, KS | 66.2 | 272 | Iowa City, IA | 44.3 | 334 | Rochester, MN | 26.5 |
| 211 | Cumberland, MD-WV | 65.9 | 273 | Janesville, WI | 43.6 | 335 | Columbus, IN | 26.2 |
| 212 | Santa Maria-Santa Barbara, CA | 65.6 | 274 | Charlottesville, VA | 43.2 | 336 | St. Cloud, MN | 26.1 |
| 213 | Allentown, PA-NJ | 65.2 | 275 | Las Cruces, NM | 42.3 | 337 | Decatur, AL | 25.3 |
| 214 | Grand Rapids-Wyoming, MI | 64.7 | 276 | Joplin, MO | 41.9 | 338 | Bend, OR | 25.0 |
| 215 | Davenport, IA-IL | 64.4 | 277 | Lafayette, IN | 41.7 | 339 | Kingsport, TN-VA | 23.9 |
| 216 | Lancaster, PA | 64.3 | 278 | Elmira, NY | 41.6 | 340 | Boulder, CO | 23.8 |
| 217 | Sebring, FL | 64.1 | 279 | Des Moines-West Des Moines, IA | 41.4 | 341 | Dalton, GA | 23.1 |
| 218 | Anaheim-Santa Ana-Irvine, CA M.D. | 63.9 | 280 | Fort Smith, AR-OK | 41.3 | 341 | Great Falls, MT | 23.1 |
| 219 | Binghamton, NY | 63.7 | 281 | Monroe, MI | 41.1 | 343 | The Villages, FL | 22.9 |
| 220 | Lakeland, FL | 63.6 | 282 | Duluth, MN-WI | 41.0 | 344 | Coeur d'Alene, ID | 21.5 |
| 221 | Florence-Muscle Shoals, AL | 63.3 | 283 | Bremerton-Silverdale, WA | 40.9 | 345 | Punta Gorda, FL | 21.4 |
| 222 | Medford, OR | 63.0 | 284 | Pittsfield, MA | 40.8 | 346 | Casper, WY | 21.3 |
| 223 | Victoria, TX | 62.3 | 285 | Dutchess-Putnam, NY M.D. | 40.3 | 346 | La Crosse, WI-MN | 21.3 |
| 224 | Houma, LA | 62.1 | 286 | Terre Haute, IN | 39.9 | 348 | Staunton-Waynesboro, VA | 21.0 |
| 225 | El Centro, CA | 61.8 | 287 | Mankato-North Mankato, MN | 39.5 | 349 | Fort Collins, CO | 20.9 |
| 225 | York-Hanover, PA | 61.8 | 288 | Flagstaff, AZ | 39.4 | 350 | San Angelo, TX | 20.7 |
| 227 | Hinesville, GA | 61.5 | 289 | Olympia, WA | 38.7 | 351 | Manhattan, KS | 20.1 |
| 228 | Kahului-Wailuku-Lahaina, HI | 60.8 | 290 | Dubuque, IA | 38.6 | 352 | Fayetteville-Springdale, AR-MO | 18.6 |
| 229 | Cambridge-Newton, MA M.D. | 60.5 | 291 | Albany, OR | 37.8 | 353 | Bismarck, ND | 17.7 |
| 230 | Nassau-Suffolk, NY M.D. | 60.0 | 292 | Cedar Rapids, IA | 37.6 | 354 | Idaho Falls, ID | 17.4 |
| 231 | Longview, WA | 59.7 | 293 | Morgantown, WV | 36.9 | 355 | Oshkosh-Neenah, WI | 17.1 |
| 232 | Napa, CA | 59.3 | 294 | Gainesville, GA | 36.8 | 356 | Gettysburg, PA | 16.8 |
| 233 | Scranton--Wilkes-Barre, PA | 59.1 | 295 | Yuma, AZ | 36.7 | 357 | Fond du Lac, WI | 16.7 |
| 234 | El Paso, TX | 58.9 | 296 | Bangor, ME | 36.5 | 358 | Sheboygan, WI | 16.5 |
| 234 | Madison, WI | 58.9 | 297 | Tyler, TX | 36.4 | 359 | Ames, IA | 16.3 |
| 236 | Clarksville, TN-KY | 58.8 | 298 | Grand Junction, CO | 36.2 | 360 | Elizabethtown-Fort Knox, KY | 15.3 |
| 237 | Brownsville-Harlingen, TX | 58.1 | 299 | Barnstable Town, MA | 36.1 | 361 | Parkersburg-Vienna, WV | 15.2 |
| 238 | McAllen-Edinburg-Mission, TX | 57.2 | 300 | Jefferson City, MO | 35.9 | 362 | State College, PA | 14.8 |
| 239 | California-Lexington Park, MD | 56.2 | 301 | Missoula, MT | 35.7 | 362 | Watertown-Fort Drum, NY | 14.8 |
| 240 | Roanoke, VA | 55.6 | 302 | Pocatello, ID | 35.5 | 364 | Prescott, AZ | 14.5 |
| 241 | Bloomington, IN | 55.0 | 302 | Rapid City, SD | 35.5 | 365 | Eau Claire, WI | 14.0 |
| 242 | New Bern, NC | 54.3 | 304 | Sherman-Denison, TX | 35.0 | 366 | Cheyenne, WY | 13.6 |
| 243 | Bloomington, IL | 53.9 | 305 | Daphne-Fairhope-Foley, AL | 34.7 | 367 | Wausau, WI | 13.3 |
| 244 | Mount Vernon-Anacortes, WA | 53.8 | 305 | Johnson City, TN | 34.7 | 368 | Harrisonburg, VA | 13.1 |
| 245 | Carbondale-Marion, IL | 53.7 | 305 | Lynchburg, VA | 34.7 | 369 | Boise City, ID | 13.0 |
| 246 | Jonesboro, AR | 53.6 | 308 | Lake Havasu City-Kingman, AZ | 34.6 | 370 | Bloomsburg-Berwick, PA | 12.9 |
| 246 | Port St. Lucie, FL | 53.6 | 309 | Elgin, IL M.D. | 34.5 | 371 | Grand Island, NE | 11.9 |
| 246 | Salem, OR | 53.6 | 310 | Portland, ME | 34.3 | 372 | St. George, UT | 11.5 |
| 249 | Austin-Round Rock, TX | 53.3 | 311 | Lewiston, ID-WA | 34.0 | 373 | Blacksburg, VA | 11.1 |
| 250 | Chambersburg-Waynesboro, PA | 52.8 | 312 | East Stroudsburg, PA | 33.9 | 374 | Glens Falls, NY | 10.1 |
| 250 | San Rafael, CA M.D. | 52.8 | 313 | Morristown, TN | 33.8 | 375 | Provo-Orem, UT | 8.7 |
| 252 | Jackson, MI | 51.7 | 313 | Naples-Marco Island, FL | 33.8 | 376 | Appleton, WI | 8.3 |
| 253 | College Station-Bryan, TX | 51.4 | 315 | Green Bay, WI | 33.6 | 377 | Logan, UT-ID | 0.0 |
| 254 | Billings, MT | 51.0 | 316 | Lewiston-Auburn, ME | 33.5 | | | |

Source: Reported data from the F.B.I. "Crime in the United States 2013"

*Robbery is the taking of anything of value by force or threat of force. Attempts are included.

# 19. Percent Change in Robbery Rate: 2012 to 2013
## National Percent Change = 3.5% Decrease*

| RANK | METROPOLITAN AREA | % CHANGE | RANK | METROPOLITAN AREA | % CHANGE | RANK | METROPOLITAN AREA | % CHANGE |
|---|---|---|---|---|---|---|---|---|
| 185 | Abilene, TX | (5.5) | 347 | Cheyenne, WY | (52.6) | 52 | Gary, IN M.D. | 13.9 |
| 184 | Akron, OH | (5.4) | 222 | Chicago (greater), IL-IN-WI | (9.0) | NA | Gettysburg, PA** | NA |
| 120 | Albany-Schenectady-Troy, NY | 2.5 | 237 | Chicago-Naperville, IL M.D. | (10.5) | 293 | Glens Falls, NY | (17.9) |
| 260 | Albany, GA | (12.5) | 249 | Chico, CA | (11.3) | 189 | Goldsboro, NC | (5.7) |
| 74 | Albany, OR | 7.1 | 170 | Cincinnati, OH-KY-IN | (3.6) | 149 | Grand Forks, ND-MN | (0.7) |
| 139 | Albuquerque, NM | 0.6 | 233 | Clarksville, TN-KY | (10.1) | 348 | Grand Island, NE | (52.8) |
| 68 | Alexandria, LA | 7.9 | 335 | Cleveland, TN | (33.2) | 29 | Grand Junction, CO | 22.7 |
| 308 | Allentown, PA-NJ | (23.5) | 14 | Coeur d'Alene, ID | 38.7 | NA | Grand Rapids-Wyoming, MI** | NA |
| 233 | Altoona, PA | (10.1) | 101 | College Station-Bryan, TX | 4.3 | NA | Grants Pass, OR** | NA |
| 245 | Amarillo, TX | (10.9) | 297 | Colorado Springs, CO | (19.2) | 319 | Great Falls, MT | (26.9) |
| 1 | Ames, IA | 83.1 | 332 | Columbia, MO | (30.9) | 271 | Greeley, CO | (13.7) |
| 213 | Anaheim-Santa Ana-Irvine, CA M.D. | (7.5) | NA | Columbia, SC** | NA | 101 | Green Bay, WI | 4.3 |
| 87 | Anchorage, AK | 6.1 | 131 | Columbus, GA-AL | 1.3 | 213 | Greensboro-High Point, NC | (7.5) |
| 278 | Ann Arbor, MI | (15.1) | 294 | Columbus, IN | (18.1) | 105 | Greenville-Anderson, SC | 4.1 |
| 302 | Anniston-Oxford, AL | (20.5) | 109 | Corpus Christi, TX | 3.8 | 79 | Greenville, NC | 6.7 |
| 346 | Appleton, WI | (48.8) | 16 | Corvallis, OR | 38.5 | NA | Gulfport-Biloxi-Pascagoula, MS** | NA |
| 314 | Athens-Clarke County, GA | (25.9) | 181 | Crestview-Fort Walton Beach, FL | (4.8) | 90 | Hagerstown-Martinsburg, MD-WV | 5.4 |
| 120 | Atlanta, GA | 2.5 | 11 | Cumberland, MD-WV | 42.3 | 282 | Hammond, LA | (15.4) |
| 64 | Atlantic City, NJ | 8.8 | 136 | Dallas (greater), TX | 0.8 | 39 | Hanford-Corcoran, CA | 19.0 |
| 278 | Augusta, GA-SC | (15.1) | 130 | Dallas-Plano-Irving, TX M.D. | 1.5 | 341 | Harrisonburg, VA | (42.3) |
| 297 | Austin-Round Rock, TX | (19.2) | 310 | Dalton, GA | (24.3) | 256 | Hartford, CT | (12.3) |
| 159 | Bakersfield, CA | (2.4) | 272 | Daphne-Fairhope-Foley, AL | (14.3) | 309 | Hilton Head Island, SC | (23.7) |
| 86 | Baltimore, MD | 6.2 | 140 | Davenport, IA-IL | 0.5 | 52 | Hinesville, GA | 13.9 |
| 215 | Bangor, ME | (7.8) | 263 | Dayton, OH | (12.9) | 46 | Homosassa Springs, FL | 15.3 |
| 136 | Barnstable Town, MA | 0.8 | 350 | Decatur, AL | (57.9) | NA | Hot Springs, AR** | NA |
| 189 | Baton Rouge, LA | (5.7) | 305 | Decatur, IL | (21.0) | 146 | Houma, LA | (0.5) |
| 327 | Bay City, MI | (29.0) | 151 | Deltona-Daytona Beach, FL | (0.9) | 87 | Houston, TX | 6.1 |
| 109 | Beaumont-Port Arthur, TX | 3.8 | 202 | Denver-Aurora, CO | (6.5) | 285 | Huntsville, AL | (16.4) |
| NA | Bend, OR** | NA | 281 | Des Moines-West Des Moines, IA | (15.2) | 5 | Idaho Falls, ID | 58.2 |
| 35 | Billings, MT | 19.7 | 140 | Detroit (greater), MI | 0.5 | 63 | Indianapolis, IN | 9.1 |
| 55 | Binghamton, NY | 12.7 | 138 | Detroit-Dearborn-Livonia, MI M.D. | 0.7 | 6 | Iowa City, IA | 46.7 |
| 166 | Birmingham-Hoover, AL | (3.4) | 265 | Dothan, AL | (13.2) | 132 | Jacksonville, FL | 1.2 |
| 307 | Bismarck, ND | (21.7) | 247 | Dover, DE | (11.0) | NA | Jackson, MI** | NA |
| 342 | Blacksburg, VA | (44.5) | 3 | Dubuque, IA | 59.5 | 82 | Jackson, MS | 6.5 |
| 84 | Bloomington, IL | 6.3 | 267 | Duluth, MN-WI | (13.3) | 282 | Jackson, TN | (15.4) |
| 2 | Bloomington, IN | 61.8 | 206 | Dutchess-Putnam, NY M.D. | (6.7) | 320 | Janesville, WI | (27.1) |
| 216 | Bloomsburg-Berwick, PA | (7.9) | 340 | East Stroudsburg, PA | (39.2) | 219 | Jefferson City, MO | (8.2) |
| 329 | Boise City, ID | (29.7) | NA | Eau Claire, WI** | NA | 118 | Johnson City, TN | 2.7 |
| 122 | Boston (greater), MA-NH | 2.4 | 217 | El Centro, CA | (8.0) | 10 | Johnstown, PA | 42.9 |
| 134 | Boston, MA M.D. | 1.1 | 163 | El Paso, TX | (3.0) | 311 | Jonesboro, AR | (24.9) |
| 328 | Boulder, CO | (29.2) | 158 | Elgin, IL M.D. | (2.3) | 269 | Joplin, MO | (13.6) |
| 230 | Bowling Green, KY | (9.9) | 345 | Elizabethtown-Fort Knox, KY | (47.2) | 284 | Kahului-Wailuku-Lahaina, HI | (16.0) |
| 178 | Bremerton-Silverdale, WA | (4.4) | 297 | Elmira, NY | (19.2) | 101 | Kankakee, IL | 4.3 |
| 154 | Bridgeport-Stamford, CT | (1.4) | 118 | Erie, PA | 2.7 | 159 | Kansas City, MO-KS | (2.4) |
| 116 | Brownsville-Harlingen, TX | 3.0 | 212 | Eugene, OR | (7.4) | 265 | Kennewick-Richland, WA | (13.2) |
| 289 | Brunswick, GA | (17.3) | 96 | Fairbanks, AK | 4.7 | 333 | Kingsport, TN-VA | (31.5) |
| 165 | Buffalo-Niagara Falls, NY | (3.3) | 52 | Fargo, ND-MN | 13.9 | 17 | Kingston, NY | 38.2 |
| 84 | Burlington, NC | 6.3 | 70 | Farmington, NM | 7.8 | 290 | Knoxville, TN | (17.7) |
| 36 | California-Lexington Park, MD | 19.6 | 278 | Fayetteville-Springdale, AR-MO | (15.1) | 68 | Kokomo, IN | 7.9 |
| 123 | Cambridge-Newton, MA M.D. | 2.2 | 124 | Fayetteville, NC | 1.8 | NA | La Crosse, WI-MN** | NA |
| 182 | Camden, NJ M.D. | (5.0) | 178 | Flagstaff, AZ | (4.4) | 178 | Lafayette, IN | (4.4) |
| 295 | Canton, OH | (18.2) | 322 | Flint, MI | (27.7) | 43 | Lafayette, LA | 16.8 |
| 125 | Cape Coral-Fort Myers, FL | 1.7 | 108 | Florence-Muscle Shoals, AL | 3.9 | NA | Lake Charles, LA** | NA |
| 19 | Cape Girardeau, MO-IL | 36.6 | 301 | Florence, SC | (19.6) | 72 | Lake Co.-Kenosha Co., IL-WI M.D. | 7.7 |
| NA | Carbondale-Marion, IL** | NA | 23 | Fond du Lac, WI | 31.5 | 28 | Lake Havasu City-Kingman, AZ | 24.0 |
| 27 | Carson City, NV | 24.1 | 269 | Fort Collins, CO | (13.6) | 204 | Lakeland, FL | (6.6) |
| 18 | Casper, WY | 37.4 | 275 | Fort Lauderdale, FL M.D. | (14.8) | NA | Lancaster, PA** | NA |
| 170 | Cedar Rapids, IA | (3.6) | 83 | Fort Smith, AR-OK | 6.4 | 25 | Lansing-East Lansing, MI | 29.9 |
| NA | Chambersburg-Waynesboro, PA** | NA | 94 | Fort Wayne, IN | 4.9 | 58 | Laredo, TX | 11.7 |
| 177 | Champaign-Urbana, IL | (4.3) | 152 | Fort Worth-Arlington, TX M.D. | (1.3) | 117 | Las Cruces, NM | 2.9 |
| 303 | Charleston-North Charleston, SC | (20.8) | 272 | Fresno, CA | (14.3) | 91 | Las Vegas-Henderson, NV | 5.1 |
| NA | Charlotte-Mecklenburg, NC-SC** | NA | 245 | Gadsden, AL | (10.9) | 24 | Lawrence, KS | 31.1 |
| 21 | Charlottesville, VA | 32.5 | 202 | Gainesville, FL | (6.5) | 166 | Lawton, OK | (3.4) |
| NA | Chattanooga, TN-GA** | NA | 324 | Gainesville, GA | (28.3) | 9 | Lebanon, PA | 44.2 |

Note: All listings are for Metropolitan Statistical Areas (M.S.A.s) except for those ending with "M.D." Listings with "M.D." are Metropolitan Divisions which are smaller parts of eleven large M.S.A.s. See explanatory note at beginning of metropolitan area section.

| RANK | METROPOLITAN AREA | % CHANGE | RANK | METROPOLITAN AREA | % CHANGE | RANK | METROPOLITAN AREA | % CHANGE |
|---|---|---|---|---|---|---|---|---|
| 344 | Lewiston-Auburn, ME | (45.4) | 237 | Omaha-Council Bluffs, NE-IA | (10.5) | 287 | Sheboygan, WI | (17.1) |
| 22 | Lewiston, ID-WA | 31.8 | 128 | Orlando, FL | 1.6 | 232 | Sherman-Denison, TX | (10.0) |
| 296 | Lexington-Fayette, KY | (18.3) | 36 | Oshkosh-Neenah, WI | 19.6 | 260 | Shreveport-Bossier City, LA | (12.5) |
| 314 | Lima, OH | (25.9) | 73 | Owensboro, KY | 7.5 | 210 | Silver Spring-Frederick, MD M.D. | (7.1) |
| 94 | Lincoln, NE | 4.9 | 155 | Oxnard-Thousand Oaks, CA | (1.8) | 249 | Sioux City, IA-NE-SD | (11.3) |
| 105 | Little Rock, AR | 4.1 | 209 | Palm Bay-Melbourne, FL | (6.9) | 189 | Sioux Falls, SD | (5.7) |
| 352 | Logan, UT-ID | (100.0) | 189 | Panama City, FL | (5.7) | 55 | South Bend-Mishawaka, IN-MI | 12.7 |
| 76 | Longview, TX | 6.9 | 351 | Parkersburg-Vienna, WV | (58.5) | 70 | Spartanburg, SC | 7.8 |
| 201 | Longview, WA | (6.4) | 274 | Pensacola, FL | (14.7) | 144 | Spokane, WA | (0.4) |
| 252 | Los Angeles County, CA M.D. | (11.7) | 292 | Peoria, IL | (17.8) | 48 | Springfield, IL | 15.1 |
| 251 | Los Angeles (greater), CA | (11.4) | 197 | Philadelphia (greater) PA-NJ-MD-DE | (6.1) | 61 | Springfield, MA | 10.6 |
| 134 | Louisville, KY-IN | 1.1 | 174 | Philadelphia, PA M.D. | (4.1) | 58 | Springfield, MO | 11.7 |
| 41 | Lubbock, TX | 18.4 | 225 | Phoenix-Mesa-Scottsdale, AZ | (9.4) | 32 | Springfield, OH | 21.3 |
| 7 | Lynchburg, VA | 46.4 | NA | Pittsburgh, PA** | NA | 50 | Staunton-Waynesboro, VA | 14.8 |
| 146 | Macon, GA | (0.5) | 237 | Pittsfield, MA | (10.5) | 277 | State College, PA | (14.9) |
| 174 | Madera, CA | (4.1) | 38 | Pocatello, ID | 19.5 | 317 | Stockton-Lodi, CA | (26.5) |
| NA | Madison, WI** | NA | 312 | Port St. Lucie, FL | (25.2) | NA | St. Cloud, MN** | NA |
| 15 | Manchester-Nashua, NH | 38.6 | 196 | Portland-Vancouver, OR-WA | (5.9) | 343 | St. George, UT | (45.0) |
| 316 | Manhattan, KS | (26.4) | 236 | Portland, ME | (10.2) | 195 | St. Joseph, MO-KS | (5.8) |
| 42 | Mankato-North Mankato, MN | 17.2 | 336 | Prescott, AZ | (33.8) | 221 | St. Louis, MO-IL | (8.5) |
| 166 | Mansfield, OH | (3.4) | 218 | Providence-Warwick, RI-MA | (8.1) | 112 | Sumter, SC | 3.6 |
| 157 | McAllen-Edinburg-Mission, TX | (2.2) | 330 | Provo-Orem, UT | (29.8) | 254 | Syracuse, NY | (12.0) |
| 4 | Medford, OR | 58.3 | 66 | Pueblo, CO | 8.2 | 113 | Tacoma, WA M.D. | 3.3 |
| 230 | Memphis, TN-MS-AR | (9.9) | 189 | Punta Gorda, FL | (5.7) | 317 | Tallahassee, FL | (26.5) |
| 331 | Merced, CA | (30.8) | 256 | Racine, WI | (12.3) | 174 | Tampa-St Petersburg, FL | (4.1) |
| 173 | Miami (greater), FL | (4.0) | 241 | Raleigh, NC | (10.8) | 326 | Terre Haute, IN | (28.8) |
| 100 | Miami-Dade County, FL M.D. | 4.4 | 241 | Rapid City, SD | (10.8) | 237 | Texarkana, TX-AR | (10.5) |
| 29 | Midland, TX | 22.7 | 256 | Reading, PA | (12.3) | 152 | The Villages, FL | (1.3) |
| 78 | Milwaukee, WI | 6.8 | 60 | Redding, CA | 11.5 | 275 | Toledo, OH | (14.8) |
| 76 | Minneapolis-St. Paul, MN-WI | 6.9 | 206 | Reno, NV | (6.7) | 323 | Topeka, KS | (28.1) |
| 105 | Missoula, MT | 4.1 | 172 | Richmond, VA | (3.9) | 228 | Trenton, NJ | (9.7) |
| 144 | Mobile, AL | (0.4) | 248 | Riverside-San Bernardino, CA | (11.1) | 288 | Tucson, AZ | (17.2) |
| 199 | Modesto, CA | (6.2) | 99 | Roanoke, VA | 4.5 | 226 | Tulsa, OK | (9.6) |
| 62 | Monroe, LA | 9.6 | 189 | Rochester, MN | (5.7) | 161 | Tuscaloosa, AL | (2.7) |
| 338 | Monroe, MI | (36.4) | 51 | Rochester, NY | 14.4 | 333 | Tyler, TX | (31.5) |
| 74 | Montgomery County, PA M.D. | 7.1 | 303 | Rockford, IL | (20.8) | 262 | Utica-Rome, NY | (12.7) |
| 125 | Morgantown, WV | 1.7 | 7 | Rockingham County, NH M.D. | 46.4 | 67 | Vallejo-Fairfield, CA | 8.0 |
| 349 | Morristown, TN | (54.0) | 40 | Rocky Mount, NC | 18.7 | 47 | Victoria, TX | 15.2 |
| 13 | Mount Vernon-Anacortes, WA | 39.4 | 12 | Rome, GA | 39.8 | 33 | Vineland-Bridgeton, NJ | 21.0 |
| 169 | Muncie, IN | (3.5) | 164 | Sacramento, CA | (3.2) | 255 | Virginia Beach-Norfolk, VA-NC | (12.1) |
| NA | Muskegon, MI** | NA | 306 | Saginaw, MI | (21.1) | 92 | Visalia-Porterville, CA | 5.0 |
| NA | Myrtle Beach, SC-NC** | NA | 80 | Salem, OR | 6.6 | 290 | Waco, TX | (17.7) |
| 44 | Napa, CA | 16.5 | 220 | Salinas, CA | (8.3) | 156 | Warner Robins, GA | (2.0) |
| 313 | Naples-Marco Island, FL | (25.6) | 259 | Salisbury, MD-DE | (12.4) | 104 | Warren-Troy, MI M.D. | 4.2 |
| 226 | Nashville-Davidson, TN | (9.6) | 48 | Salt Lake City, UT | 15.1 | 199 | Washington (greater) DC-VA-MD-WV | (6.2) |
| 206 | Nassau-Suffolk, NY M.D. | (6.7) | NA | San Angelo, TX** | NA | 197 | Washington, DC-VA-MD-WV M.D. | (6.1) |
| 125 | New Bern, NC | 1.7 | 57 | San Antonio, TX | 12.5 | 337 | Watertown-Fort Drum, NY | (35.1) |
| 143 | New Haven-Milford, CT | 0.2 | 187 | San Diego, CA | (5.6) | 325 | Wausau, WI | (28.5) |
| 113 | New Orleans, LA | 3.3 | 65 | San Francisco (greater), CA | 8.4 | 241 | West Palm Beach, FL M.D. | (10.8) |
| 162 | New York (greater), NY-NJ-PA | (2.9) | 45 | San Francisco-Redwood, CA M.D. | 15.7 | 268 | Wichita Falls, TX | (13.4) |
| 204 | New York-Jersey City, NY-NJ M.D. | (6.6) | 229 | San Jose, CA | (9.8) | 183 | Wichita, KS | (5.2) |
| 34 | Newark, NJ-PA M.D. | 20.6 | 115 | San Luis Obispo, CA | 3.2 | 321 | Williamsport, PA | (27.6) |
| NA | Niles-Benton Harbor, MI** | NA | 263 | San Rafael, CA M.D. | (12.9) | 300 | Wilmington, DE-MD-NJ M.D. | (19.3) |
| 187 | North Port-Sarasota-Bradenton, FL | (5.6) | 233 | Santa Cruz-Watsonville, CA | (10.1) | 211 | Wilmington, NC | (7.3) |
| 149 | Norwich-New London, CT | (0.7) | 223 | Santa Maria-Santa Barbara, CA | (9.1) | 20 | Winchester, VA-WV | 35.8 |
| 92 | Oakland-Hayward, CA M.D. | 5.0 | 109 | Santa Rosa, CA | 3.8 | 80 | Winston-Salem, NC | 6.6 |
| 98 | Ocala, FL | 4.6 | 252 | Savannah, GA | (11.7) | 89 | Worcester, MA-CT | 5.6 |
| 31 | Ocean City, NJ | 22.0 | NA | Scranton--Wilkes-Barre, PA** | NA | 223 | Yakima, WA | (9.1) |
| 96 | Odessa, TX | 4.7 | 132 | Seattle (greater), WA | 1.2 | 241 | York-Hanover, PA | (10.8) |
| 26 | Ogden-Clearfield, UT | 24.7 | 140 | Seattle-Bellevue-Everett, WA M.D. | 0.5 | 128 | Yuba City, CA | 1.6 |
| 185 | Oklahoma City, OK | (5.5) | 339 | Sebastian-Vero Beach, FL | (36.5) | 146 | Yuma, AZ | (0.5) |
| NA | Olympia, WA** | NA | 286 | Sebring, FL | (16.8) | | | |

Source: CQ Press using reported data from the F.B.I. "Crime in the United States 2013"
*Includes murder, rape, robbery, aggravated assault, burglary, larceny-theft, and motor vehicle theft.
**Not available.

# 19. Percent Change in Robbery Rate: 2012 to 2013 (continued)
## National Percent Change = 3.5% Decrease*

| RANK | METROPOLITAN AREA | % CHANGE | RANK | METROPOLITAN AREA | % CHANGE | RANK | METROPOLITAN AREA | % CHANGE |
|---|---|---|---|---|---|---|---|---|
| 1 | Ames, IA | 83.1 | 65 | San Francisco (greater), CA | 8.4 | 128 | Yuba City, CA | 1.6 |
| 2 | Bloomington, IN | 61.8 | 66 | Pueblo, CO | 8.2 | 130 | Dallas-Plano-Irving, TX M.D. | 1.5 |
| 3 | Dubuque, IA | 59.5 | 67 | Vallejo-Fairfield, CA | 8.0 | 131 | Columbus, GA-AL | 1.3 |
| 4 | Medford, OR | 58.3 | 68 | Alexandria, LA | 7.9 | 132 | Jacksonville, FL | 1.2 |
| 5 | Idaho Falls, ID | 58.2 | 68 | Kokomo, IN | 7.9 | 132 | Seattle (greater), WA | 1.2 |
| 6 | Iowa City, IA | 46.7 | 70 | Farmington, NM | 7.8 | 134 | Boston, MA M.D. | 1.1 |
| 7 | Lynchburg, VA | 46.4 | 70 | Spartanburg, SC | 7.8 | 134 | Louisville, KY-IN | 1.1 |
| 7 | Rockingham County, NH M.D. | 46.4 | 72 | Lake Co.-Kenosha Co., IL-WI M.D. | 7.7 | 136 | Barnstable Town, MA | 0.8 |
| 9 | Lebanon, PA | 44.2 | 73 | Owensboro, KY | 7.5 | 136 | Dallas (greater), TX | 0.8 |
| 10 | Johnstown, PA | 42.9 | 74 | Albany, OR | 7.1 | 138 | Detroit-Dearborn-Livonia, MI M.D. | 0.7 |
| 11 | Cumberland, MD-WV | 42.3 | 74 | Montgomery County, PA M.D. | 7.1 | 139 | Albuquerque, NM | 0.6 |
| 12 | Rome, GA | 39.8 | 76 | Longview, TX | 6.9 | 140 | Davenport, IA-IL | 0.5 |
| 13 | Mount Vernon-Anacortes, WA | 39.4 | 76 | Minneapolis-St. Paul, MN-WI | 6.9 | 140 | Detroit (greater), MI | 0.5 |
| 14 | Coeur d'Alene, ID | 38.7 | 78 | Milwaukee, WI | 6.8 | 140 | Seattle-Bellevue-Everett, WA M.D. | 0.5 |
| 15 | Manchester-Nashua, NH | 38.6 | 79 | Greenville, NC | 6.7 | 143 | New Haven-Milford, CT | 0.2 |
| 16 | Corvallis, OR | 38.5 | 80 | Salem, OR | 6.6 | 144 | Mobile, AL | (0.4) |
| 17 | Kingston, NY | 38.2 | 80 | Winston-Salem, NC | 6.6 | 144 | Spokane, WA | (0.4) |
| 18 | Casper, WY | 37.4 | 82 | Jackson, MS | 6.5 | 146 | Houma, LA | (0.5) |
| 19 | Cape Girardeau, MO-IL | 36.6 | 83 | Fort Smith, AR-OK | 6.4 | 146 | Macon, GA | (0.5) |
| 20 | Winchester, VA-WV | 35.8 | 84 | Bloomington, IL | 6.3 | 146 | Yuma, AZ | (0.5) |
| 21 | Charlottesville, VA | 32.5 | 84 | Burlington, NC | 6.3 | 149 | Grand Forks, ND-MN | (0.7) |
| 22 | Lewiston, ID-WA | 31.8 | 86 | Baltimore, MD | 6.2 | 149 | Norwich-New London, CT | (0.7) |
| 23 | Fond du Lac, WI | 31.5 | 87 | Anchorage, AK | 6.1 | 151 | Deltona-Daytona Beach, FL | (0.9) |
| 24 | Lawrence, KS | 31.1 | 87 | Houston, TX | 6.1 | 152 | Fort Worth-Arlington, TX M.D. | (1.3) |
| 25 | Lansing-East Lansing, MI | 29.9 | 89 | Worcester, MA-CT | 5.6 | 152 | The Villages, FL | (1.3) |
| 26 | Ogden-Clearfield, UT | 24.7 | 90 | Hagerstown-Martinsburg, MD-WV | 5.4 | 154 | Bridgeport-Stamford, CT | (1.4) |
| 27 | Carson City, NV | 24.1 | 91 | Las Vegas-Henderson, NV | 5.1 | 155 | Oxnard-Thousand Oaks, CA | (1.8) |
| 28 | Lake Havasu City-Kingman, AZ | 24.0 | 92 | Oakland-Hayward, CA M.D. | 5.0 | 156 | Warner Robins, GA | (2.0) |
| 29 | Grand Junction, CO | 22.7 | 92 | Visalia-Porterville, CA | 5.0 | 157 | McAllen-Edinburg-Mission, TX | (2.2) |
| 29 | Midland, TX | 22.7 | 94 | Fort Wayne, IN | 4.9 | 158 | Elgin, IL M.D. | (2.3) |
| 31 | Ocean City, NJ | 22.0 | 94 | Lincoln, NE | 4.9 | 159 | Bakersfield, CA | (2.4) |
| 32 | Springfield, OH | 21.3 | 96 | Fairbanks, AK | 4.7 | 159 | Kansas City, MO-KS | (2.4) |
| 33 | Vineland-Bridgeton, NJ | 21.0 | 96 | Odessa, TX | 4.7 | 161 | Tuscaloosa, AL | (2.7) |
| 34 | Newark, NJ-PA M.D. | 20.6 | 98 | Ocala, FL | 4.6 | 162 | New York (greater), NY-NJ-PA | (2.9) |
| 35 | Billings, MT | 19.7 | 99 | Roanoke, VA | 4.5 | 163 | El Paso, TX | (3.0) |
| 36 | California-Lexington Park, MD | 19.6 | 100 | Miami-Dade County, FL M.D. | 4.4 | 164 | Sacramento, CA | (3.2) |
| 36 | Oshkosh-Neenah, WI | 19.6 | 101 | College Station-Bryan, TX | 4.3 | 165 | Buffalo-Niagara Falls, NY | (3.3) |
| 38 | Pocatello, ID | 19.5 | 101 | Green Bay, WI | 4.3 | 166 | Birmingham-Hoover, AL | (3.4) |
| 39 | Hanford-Corcoran, CA | 19.0 | 101 | Kankakee, IL | 4.3 | 166 | Lawton, OK | (3.4) |
| 40 | Rocky Mount, NC | 18.7 | 104 | Warren-Troy, MI M.D. | 4.2 | 166 | Mansfield, OH | (3.4) |
| 41 | Lubbock, TX | 18.4 | 105 | Greenville-Anderson, SC | 4.1 | 169 | Muncie, IN | (3.5) |
| 42 | Mankato-North Mankato, MN | 17.2 | 105 | Little Rock, AR | 4.1 | 170 | Cedar Rapids, IA | (3.6) |
| 43 | Lafayette, LA | 16.8 | 105 | Missoula, MT | 4.1 | 170 | Cincinnati, OH-KY-IN | (3.6) |
| 44 | Napa, CA | 16.5 | 108 | Florence-Muscle Shoals, AL | 3.9 | 172 | Richmond, VA | (3.9) |
| 45 | San Francisco-Redwood, CA M.D. | 15.7 | 109 | Beaumont-Port Arthur, TX | 3.8 | 173 | Miami (greater), FL | (4.0) |
| 46 | Homosassa Springs, FL | 15.3 | 109 | Corpus Christi, TX | 3.8 | 174 | Madera, CA | (4.1) |
| 47 | Victoria, TX | 15.2 | 109 | Santa Rosa, CA | 3.8 | 174 | Philadelphia, PA M.D. | (4.1) |
| 48 | Salt Lake City, UT | 15.1 | 112 | Sumter, SC | 3.6 | 174 | Tampa-St Petersburg, FL | (4.1) |
| 48 | Springfield, IL | 15.1 | 113 | New Orleans, LA | 3.3 | 177 | Champaign-Urbana, IL | (4.3) |
| 50 | Staunton-Waynesboro, VA | 14.8 | 113 | Tacoma, WA M.D. | 3.3 | 178 | Bremerton-Silverdale, WA | (4.4) |
| 51 | Rochester, NY | 14.4 | 115 | San Luis Obispo, CA | 3.2 | 178 | Flagstaff, AZ | (4.4) |
| 52 | Fargo, ND-MN | 13.9 | 116 | Brownsville-Harlingen, TX | 3.0 | 178 | Lafayette, IN | (4.4) |
| 52 | Gary, IN M.D. | 13.9 | 117 | Las Cruces, NM | 2.9 | 181 | Crestview-Fort Walton Beach, FL | (4.8) |
| 52 | Hinesville, GA | 13.9 | 118 | Erie, PA | 2.7 | 182 | Camden, NJ M.D. | (5.0) |
| 55 | Binghamton, NY | 12.7 | 118 | Johnson City, TN | 2.7 | 183 | Wichita, KS | (5.2) |
| 55 | South Bend-Mishawaka, IN-MI | 12.7 | 120 | Albany-Schenectady-Troy, NY | 2.5 | 184 | Akron, OH | (5.4) |
| 57 | San Antonio, TX | 12.5 | 120 | Atlanta, GA | 2.5 | 185 | Abilene, TX | (5.5) |
| 58 | Laredo, TX | 11.7 | 122 | Boston (greater), MA-NH | 2.4 | 185 | Oklahoma City, OK | (5.5) |
| 58 | Springfield, MO | 11.7 | 123 | Cambridge-Newton, MA M.D. | 2.2 | 187 | North Port-Sarasota-Bradenton, FL | (5.6) |
| 60 | Redding, CA | 11.5 | 124 | Fayetteville, NC | 1.8 | 187 | San Diego, CA | (5.6) |
| 61 | Springfield, MA | 10.6 | 125 | Cape Coral-Fort Myers, FL | 1.7 | 189 | Baton Rouge, LA | (5.7) |
| 62 | Monroe, LA | 9.6 | 125 | Morgantown, WV | 1.7 | 189 | Goldsboro, NC | (5.7) |
| 63 | Indianapolis, IN | 9.1 | 125 | New Bern, NC | 1.7 | 189 | Panama City, FL | (5.7) |
| 64 | Atlantic City, NJ | 8.8 | 128 | Orlando, FL | 1.6 | 189 | Punta Gorda, FL | (5.7) |

Note: All listings are for Metropolitan Statistical Areas (M.S.A.s) except for those ending with "M.D." Listings with "M.D." are Metropolitan Divisions which are smaller parts of eleven large M.S.A.s. See explanatory note at beginning of metropolitan area section.

| RANK | METROPOLITAN AREA | % CHANGE | RANK | METROPOLITAN AREA | % CHANGE | RANK | METROPOLITAN AREA | % CHANGE |
|---|---|---|---|---|---|---|---|---|
| 189 | Rochester, MN | (5.7) | 255 | Virginia Beach-Norfolk, VA-NC | (12.1) | 317 | Stockton-Lodi, CA | (26.5) |
| 189 | Sioux Falls, SD | (5.7) | 256 | Hartford, CT | (12.3) | 317 | Tallahassee, FL | (26.5) |
| 195 | St. Joseph, MO-KS | (5.8) | 256 | Racine, WI | (12.3) | 319 | Great Falls, MT | (26.9) |
| 196 | Portland-Vancouver, OR-WA | (5.9) | 256 | Reading, PA | (12.3) | 320 | Janesville, WI | (27.1) |
| 197 | Philadelphia (greater) PA-NJ-MD-DE | (6.1) | 259 | Salisbury, MD-DE | (12.4) | 321 | Williamsport, PA | (27.6) |
| 197 | Washington, DC-VA-MD-WV M.D. | (6.1) | 260 | Albany, GA | (12.5) | 322 | Flint, MI | (27.7) |
| 199 | Modesto, CA | (6.2) | 260 | Shreveport-Bossier City, LA | (12.5) | 323 | Topeka, KS | (28.1) |
| 199 | Washington (greater) DC-VA-MD-WV | (6.2) | 262 | Utica-Rome, NY | (12.7) | 324 | Gainesville, GA | (28.3) |
| 201 | Longview, WA | (6.4) | 263 | Dayton, OH | (12.9) | 325 | Wausau, WI | (28.5) |
| 202 | Denver-Aurora, CO | (6.5) | 263 | San Rafael, CA M.D. | (12.9) | 326 | Terre Haute, IN | (28.8) |
| 202 | Gainesville, FL | (6.5) | 265 | Dothan, AL | (13.2) | 327 | Bay City, MI | (29.0) |
| 204 | Lakeland, FL | (6.6) | 265 | Kennewick-Richland, WA | (13.2) | 328 | Boulder, CO | (29.2) |
| 204 | New York-Jersey City, NY-NJ M.D. | (6.6) | 267 | Duluth, MN-WI | (13.3) | 329 | Boise City, ID | (29.7) |
| 206 | Dutchess-Putnam, NY M.D. | (6.7) | 268 | Wichita Falls, TX | (13.4) | 330 | Provo-Orem, UT | (29.8) |
| 206 | Nassau-Suffolk, NY M.D. | (6.7) | 269 | Fort Collins, CO | (13.6) | 331 | Merced, CA | (30.8) |
| 206 | Reno, NV | (6.7) | 269 | Joplin, MO | (13.6) | 332 | Columbia, MO | (30.9) |
| 209 | Palm Bay-Melbourne, FL | (6.9) | 271 | Greeley, CO | (13.7) | 333 | Kingsport, TN-VA | (31.5) |
| 210 | Silver Spring-Frederick, MD M.D. | (7.1) | 272 | Daphne-Fairhope-Foley, AL | (14.3) | 333 | Tyler, TX | (31.5) |
| 211 | Wilmington, NC | (7.3) | 272 | Fresno, CA | (14.3) | 335 | Cleveland, TN | (33.2) |
| 212 | Eugene, OR | (7.4) | 274 | Pensacola, FL | (14.7) | 336 | Prescott, AZ | (33.8) |
| 213 | Anaheim-Santa Ana-Irvine, CA M.D. | (7.5) | 275 | Fort Lauderdale, FL M.D. | (14.8) | 337 | Watertown-Fort Drum, NY | (35.1) |
| 213 | Greensboro-High Point, NC | (7.5) | 275 | Toledo, OH | (14.8) | 338 | Monroe, MI | (36.4) |
| 215 | Bangor, ME | (7.8) | 277 | State College, PA | (14.9) | 339 | Sebastian-Vero Beach, FL | (36.5) |
| 216 | Bloomsburg-Berwick, PA | (7.9) | 278 | Ann Arbor, MI | (15.1) | 340 | East Stroudsburg, PA | (39.2) |
| 217 | El Centro, CA | (8.0) | 278 | Augusta, GA-SC | (15.1) | 341 | Harrisonburg, VA | (42.3) |
| 218 | Providence-Warwick, RI-MA | (8.1) | 278 | Fayetteville-Springdale, AR-MO | (15.1) | 342 | Blacksburg, VA | (44.5) |
| 219 | Jefferson City, MO | (8.2) | 281 | Des Moines-West Des Moines, IA | (15.2) | 343 | St. George, UT | (45.0) |
| 220 | Salinas, CA | (8.3) | 282 | Hammond, LA | (15.4) | 344 | Lewiston-Auburn, ME | (45.4) |
| 221 | St. Louis, MO-IL | (8.5) | 282 | Jackson, TN | (15.4) | 345 | Elizabethtown-Fort Knox, KY | (47.2) |
| 222 | Chicago (greater), IL-IN-WI | (9.0) | 284 | Kahului-Wailuku-Lahaina, HI | (16.0) | 346 | Appleton, WI | (48.8) |
| 223 | Santa Maria-Santa Barbara, CA | (9.1) | 285 | Huntsville, AL | (16.4) | 347 | Cheyenne, WY | (52.6) |
| 223 | Yakima, WA | (9.1) | 286 | Sebring, FL | (16.8) | 348 | Grand Island, NE | (52.8) |
| 225 | Phoenix-Mesa-Scottsdale, AZ | (9.4) | 287 | Sheboygan, WI | (17.1) | 349 | Morristown, TN | (54.0) |
| 226 | Nashville-Davidson, TN | (9.6) | 288 | Tucson, AZ | (17.2) | 350 | Decatur, AL | (57.9) |
| 226 | Tulsa, OK | (9.6) | 289 | Brunswick, GA | (17.3) | 351 | Parkersburg-Vienna, WV | (58.5) |
| 228 | Trenton, NJ | (9.7) | 290 | Knoxville, TN | (17.7) | 352 | Logan, UT-ID | (100.0) |
| 229 | San Jose, CA | (9.8) | 290 | Waco, TX | (17.7) | NA | Bend, OR** | NA |
| 230 | Bowling Green, KY | (9.9) | 292 | Peoria, IL | (17.8) | NA | Carbondale-Marion, IL** | NA |
| 230 | Memphis, TN-MS-AR | (9.9) | 293 | Glens Falls, NY | (17.9) | NA | Chambersburg-Waynesboro, PA** | NA |
| 232 | Sherman-Denison, TX | (10.0) | 294 | Columbus, IN | (18.1) | NA | Charlotte-Mecklenburg, NC-SC** | NA |
| 233 | Altoona, PA | (10.1) | 295 | Canton, OH | (18.2) | NA | Chattanooga, TN-GA** | NA |
| 233 | Clarksville, TN-KY | (10.1) | 296 | Lexington-Fayette, KY | (18.3) | NA | Columbia, SC** | NA |
| 233 | Santa Cruz-Watsonville, CA | (10.1) | 297 | Austin-Round Rock, TX | (19.2) | NA | Eau Claire, WI** | NA |
| 236 | Portland, ME | (10.2) | 297 | Colorado Springs, CO | (19.2) | NA | Gettysburg, PA** | NA |
| 237 | Chicago-Naperville, IL M.D. | (10.5) | 297 | Elmira, NY | (19.2) | NA | Grand Rapids-Wyoming, MI** | NA |
| 237 | Omaha-Council Bluffs, NE-IA | (10.5) | 300 | Wilmington, DE-MD-NJ M.D. | (19.3) | NA | Grants Pass, OR** | NA |
| 237 | Pittsfield, MA | (10.5) | 301 | Florence, SC | (19.6) | NA | Gulfport-Biloxi-Pascagoula, MS** | NA |
| 237 | Texarkana, TX-AR | (10.5) | 302 | Anniston-Oxford, AL | (20.5) | NA | Hot Springs, AR** | NA |
| 241 | Raleigh, NC | (10.8) | 303 | Charleston-North Charleston, SC | (20.8) | NA | Jackson, MI** | NA |
| 241 | Rapid City, SD | (10.8) | 303 | Rockford, IL | (20.8) | NA | La Crosse, WI-MN** | NA |
| 241 | West Palm Beach, FL M.D. | (10.8) | 305 | Decatur, IL | (21.0) | NA | Lake Charles, LA** | NA |
| 241 | York-Hanover, PA | (10.8) | 306 | Saginaw, MI | (21.1) | NA | Lancaster, PA** | NA |
| 245 | Amarillo, TX | (10.9) | 307 | Bismarck, ND | (21.7) | NA | Madison, WI** | NA |
| 245 | Gadsden, AL | (10.9) | 308 | Allentown, PA-NJ | (23.5) | NA | Muskegon, MI** | NA |
| 247 | Dover, DE | (11.0) | 309 | Hilton Head Island, SC | (23.7) | NA | Myrtle Beach, SC-NC** | NA |
| 248 | Riverside-San Bernardino, CA | (11.1) | 310 | Dalton, GA | (24.3) | NA | Niles-Benton Harbor, MI** | NA |
| 249 | Chico, CA | (11.3) | 311 | Jonesboro, AR | (24.9) | NA | Olympia, WA** | NA |
| 249 | Sioux City, IA-NE-SD | (11.3) | 312 | Port St. Lucie, FL | (25.2) | NA | Pittsburgh, PA** | NA |
| 251 | Los Angeles (greater), CA | (11.4) | 313 | Naples-Marco Island, FL | (25.6) | NA | San Angelo, TX** | NA |
| 252 | Los Angeles County, CA M.D. | (11.7) | 314 | Athens-Clarke County, GA | (25.9) | NA | Scranton--Wilkes-Barre, PA** | NA |
| 252 | Savannah, GA | (11.7) | 314 | Lima, OH | (25.9) | NA | St. Cloud, MN** | NA |
| 254 | Syracuse, NY | (12.0) | 316 | Manhattan, KS | (26.4) | | | |

Source: CQ Press using reported data from the F.B.I. "Crime in the United States 2013"

*Includes murder, rape, robbery, aggravated assault, burglary, larceny-theft, and motor vehicle theft.

**Not available.

# 20. Percent Change in Robbery Rate: 2009 to 2013
## National Percent Change = 18.0% Decrease*

| RANK | METROPOLITAN AREA | % CHANGE | RANK | METROPOLITAN AREA | % CHANGE | RANK | METROPOLITAN AREA | % CHANGE |
|---|---|---|---|---|---|---|---|---|
| 132 | Abilene, TX | (16.8) | 310 | Cheyenne, WY | (59.5) | NA | Gary, IN M.D.** | NA |
| 190 | Akron, OH | (24.4) | NA | Chicago (greater), IL-IN-WI** | NA | NA | Gettysburg, PA** | NA |
| 161 | Albany-Schenectady-Troy, NY | (20.9) | NA | Chicago-Naperville, IL M.D.** | NA | 34 | Glens Falls, NY | 18.8 |
| 85 | Albany, GA | (6.8) | 163 | Chico, CA | (21.1) | 221 | Goldsboro, NC | (28.3) |
| NA | Albany, OR** | NA | 174 | Cincinnati, OH-KY-IN | (22.7) | 154 | Grand Forks, ND-MN | (20.2) |
| 83 | Albuquerque, NM | (6.6) | 139 | Clarksville, TN-KY | (17.9) | NA | Grand Island, NE** | NA |
| 91 | Alexandria, LA | (8.6) | 231 | Cleveland, TN | (29.3) | 189 | Grand Junction, CO | (24.1) |
| 243 | Allentown, PA-NJ | (33.2) | 258 | Coeur d'Alene, ID | (37.1) | NA | Grand Rapids-Wyoming, MI** | NA |
| 276 | Altoona, PA | (42.2) | 256 | College Station-Bryan, TX | (36.8) | NA | Grants Pass, OR** | NA |
| 245 | Amarillo, TX | (34.0) | 180 | Colorado Springs, CO | (23.4) | 305 | Great Falls, MT | (53.7) |
| 227 | Ames, IA | (28.8) | 225 | Columbia, MO | (28.6) | 107 | Greeley, CO | (13.0) |
| 247 | Anaheim-Santa Ana-Irvine, CA M.D. | (34.1) | 191 | Columbia, SC | (24.8) | 48 | Green Bay, WI | 6.7 |
| 79 | Anchorage, AK | (5.6) | 232 | Columbus, GA-AL | (29.4) | 285 | Greensboro-High Point, NC | (44.4) |
| 227 | Ann Arbor, MI | (28.8) | 209 | Columbus, IN | (26.4) | NA | Greenville-Anderson, SC** | NA |
| 271 | Anniston-Oxford, AL | (41.5) | 151 | Corpus Christi, TX | (19.8) | NA | Greenville, NC** | NA |
| 254 | Appleton, WI | (36.6) | 78 | Corvallis, OR | (5.3) | NA | Gulfport-Biloxi-Pascagoula, MS** | NA |
| 201 | Athens-Clarke County, GA | (25.5) | NA | Crestview-Fort Walton Beach, FL** | NA | 23 | Hagerstown-Martinsburg, MD-WV | 27.9 |
| 100 | Atlanta, GA | (10.2) | 20 | Cumberland, MD-WV | 39.0 | NA | Hammond, LA** | NA |
| 139 | Atlantic City, NJ | (17.9) | 191 | Dallas (greater), TX | (24.8) | NA | Hanford-Corcoran, CA** | NA |
| 283 | Augusta, GA-SC | (43.9) | 202 | Dallas-Plano-Irving, TX M.D. | (25.6) | 307 | Harrisonburg, VA | (55.1) |
| 289 | Austin-Round Rock, TX | (45.6) | 137 | Dalton, GA | (17.8) | 98 | Hartford, CT | (10.0) |
| 93 | Bakersfield, CA | (8.8) | NA | Daphne-Fairhope-Foley, AL** | NA | NA | Hilton Head Island, SC** | NA |
| 80 | Baltimore, MD | (5.7) | NA | Davenport, IA-IL** | NA | 306 | Hinesville, GA | (55.0) |
| 71 | Bangor, ME | (2.9) | 191 | Dayton, OH | (24.8) | NA | Homosassa Springs, FL** | NA |
| 273 | Barnstable Town, MA | (41.8) | 308 | Decatur, AL | (55.5) | 295 | Hot Springs, AR | (46.5) |
| 126 | Baton Rouge, LA | (16.1) | 293 | Decatur, IL | (45.9) | 300 | Houma, LA | (49.7) |
| 301 | Bay City, MI | (49.9) | 290 | Deltona-Daytona Beach, FL | (45.7) | 123 | Houston, TX | (15.5) |
| 90 | Beaumont-Port Arthur, TX | (8.5) | 87 | Denver-Aurora, CO | (7.4) | 165 | Huntsville, AL | (21.5) |
| 24 | Bend, OR | 27.6 | 158 | Des Moines-West Des Moines, IA | (20.5) | 31 | Idaho Falls, ID | 20.8 |
| 57 | Billings, MT | 3.0 | 121 | Detroit (greater), MI | (15.4) | 101 | Indianapolis, IN | (10.5) |
| 10 | Binghamton, NY | 67.2 | 98 | Detroit-Dearborn-Livonia, MI M.D. | (10.0) | 71 | Iowa City, IA | (2.9) |
| 172 | Birmingham-Hoover, AL | (22.2) | 287 | Dothan, AL | (45.2) | 277 | Jacksonville, FL | (42.6) |
| 15 | Bismarck, ND | 45.1 | 218 | Dover, DE | (27.5) | 177 | Jackson, MI | (22.8) |
| 311 | Blacksburg, VA | (66.6) | 6 | Dubuque, IA | 110.9 | 115 | Jackson, MS | (14.8) |
| NA | Bloomington, IL** | NA | 234 | Duluth, MN-WI | (30.4) | 191 | Jackson, TN | (24.8) |
| 42 | Bloomington, IN | 9.6 | NA | Dutchess-Putnam, NY M.D.** | NA | 248 | Janesville, WI | (35.0) |
| NA | Bloomsburg-Berwick, PA** | NA | NA | East Stroudsburg, PA** | NA | 145 | Jefferson City, MO | (18.8) |
| 259 | Boise City, ID | (37.2) | 47 | Eau Claire, WI | 6.9 | 174 | Johnson City, TN | (22.7) |
| 112 | Boston (greater), MA-NH | (14.4) | 54 | El Centro, CA | 3.7 | NA | Johnstown, PA** | NA |
| 142 | Boston, MA M.D. | (18.2) | 109 | El Paso, TX | (13.5) | 179 | Jonesboro, AR | (23.2) |
| 266 | Boulder, CO | (39.7) | NA | Elgin, IL M.D.** | NA | NA | Joplin, MO** | NA |
| NA | Bowling Green, KY** | NA | NA | Elizabethtown-Fort Knox, KY** | NA | NA | Kahului-Wailuku-Lahaina, HI** | NA |
| 89 | Bremerton-Silverdale, WA | (7.5) | 25 | Elmira, NY | 25.3 | NA | Kankakee, IL** | NA |
| 186 | Bridgeport-Stamford, CT | (23.9) | 17 | Erie, PA | 41.1 | 157 | Kansas City, MO-KS | (20.3) |
| 168 | Brownsville-Harlingen, TX | (21.8) | 104 | Eugene, OR | (12.7) | 168 | Kennewick-Richland, WA | (21.8) |
| 240 | Brunswick, GA | (32.4) | 75 | Fairbanks, AK | (4.5) | 279 | Kingsport, TN-VA | (42.8) |
| 154 | Buffalo-Niagara Falls, NY | (20.2) | 21 | Fargo, ND-MN | 37.6 | 296 | Kingston, NY | (46.8) |
| 104 | Burlington, NC | (12.7) | 22 | Farmington, NM | 29.5 | 286 | Knoxville, TN | (44.5) |
| NA | California-Lexington Park, MD** | NA | 130 | Fayetteville-Springdale, AR-MO | (16.6) | 7 | Kokomo, IN | 88.9 |
| NA | Cambridge-Newton, MA M.D.** | NA | 45 | Fayetteville, NC | 8.0 | NA | La Crosse, WI-MN** | NA |
| 93 | Camden, NJ M.D. | (8.8) | 134 | Flagstaff, AZ | (17.1) | 84 | Lafayette, IN | (6.7) |
| NA | Canton, OH** | NA | 123 | Flint, MI | (15.5) | NA | Lafayette, LA** | NA |
| 209 | Cape Coral-Fort Myers, FL | (26.4) | 61 | Florence-Muscle Shoals, AL | 1.6 | 111 | Lake Charles, LA | (13.7) |
| 9 | Cape Girardeau, MO-IL | 71.6 | 288 | Florence, SC | (45.3) | NA | Lake Co.-Kenosha Co., IL-WI M.D.** | NA |
| NA | Carbondale-Marion, IL** | NA | 2 | Fond du Lac, WI | 138.6 | 64 | Lake Havasu City-Kingman, AZ | (0.3) |
| 250 | Carson City, NV | (35.2) | 273 | Fort Collins, CO | (41.8) | 262 | Lakeland, FL | (38.2) |
| 65 | Casper, WY | (0.5) | 128 | Fort Lauderdale, FL M.D. | (16.2) | NA | Lancaster, PA** | NA |
| 154 | Cedar Rapids, IA | (20.2) | 223 | Fort Smith, AR-OK | (28.5) | 60 | Lansing-East Lansing, MI | 2.1 |
| NA | Chambersburg-Waynesboro, PA** | NA | 76 | Fort Wayne, IN | (4.8) | 260 | Laredo, TX | (37.3) |
| NA | Champaign-Urbana, IL** | NA | 166 | Fort Worth-Arlington, TX M.D. | (21.7) | 184 | Las Cruces, NM | (23.8) |
| 309 | Charleston-North Charleston, SC | (55.7) | 147 | Fresno, CA | (19.2) | 139 | Las Vegas-Henderson, NV | (17.9) |
| NA | Charlotte-Mecklenburg, NC-SC** | NA | 52 | Gadsden, AL | 4.7 | 102 | Lawrence, KS | (11.3) |
| 237 | Charlottesville, VA | (31.2) | 265 | Gainesville, FL | (39.5) | 170 | Lawton, OK | (22.0) |
| 197 | Chattanooga, TN-GA | (25.2) | 59 | Gainesville, GA | 2.5 | 5 | Lebanon, PA | 114.5 |

Note: All listings are for Metropolitan Statistical Areas (M.S.A.s) except for those ending with "M.D." Listings with "M.D." are Metropolitan Divisions which are smaller parts of eleven large M.S.A.s. See explanatory note at beginning of metropolitan area section.

| RANK | METROPOLITAN AREA | % CHANGE |
|---|---|---|
| 262 | Lewiston-Auburn, ME | (38.2) |
| 8 | Lewiston, ID-WA | 71.7 |
| 113 | Lexington-Fayette, KY | (14.6) |
| 297 | Lima, OH | (47.3) |
| 58 | Lincoln, NE | 2.7 |
| 71 | Little Rock, AR | (2.9) |
| 312 | Logan, UT-ID | (100.0) |
| 227 | Longview, TX | (28.8) |
| 12 | Longview, WA | 53.5 |
| 241 | Los Angeles County, CA M.D. | (32.6) |
| 242 | Los Angeles (greater), CA | (32.9) |
| 87 | Louisville, KY-IN | (7.4) |
| 43 | Lubbock, TX | 9.1 |
| 172 | Lynchburg, VA | (22.2) |
| 191 | Macon, GA | (24.8) |
| 149 | Madera, CA | (19.6) |
| NA | Madison, WI** | NA |
| 11 | Manchester-Nashua, NH | 62.3 |
| 298 | Manhattan, KS | (48.2) |
| 3 | Mankato-North Mankato, MN | 131.0 |
| 18 | Mansfield, OH | 40.0 |
| 262 | McAllen-Edinburg-Mission, TX | (38.2) |
| 1 | Medford, OR | 277.2 |
| 213 | Memphis, TN-MS-AR | (26.9) |
| 163 | Merced, CA | (21.1) |
| 158 | Miami (greater), FL | (20.5) |
| 115 | Miami-Dade County, FL M.D. | (14.8) |
| 244 | Midland, TX | (33.8) |
| 51 | Milwaukee, WI | 5.2 |
| 69 | Minneapolis-St. Paul, MN-WI | (2.8) |
| 38 | Missoula, MT | 14.1 |
| 294 | Mobile, AL | (46.4) |
| 55 | Modesto, CA | 3.3 |
| NA | Monroe, LA** | NA |
| 36 | Monroe, MI | 16.4 |
| NA | Montgomery County, PA M.D.** | NA |
| 131 | Morgantown, WV | (16.7) |
| 282 | Morristown, TN | (43.2) |
| 33 | Mount Vernon-Anacortes, WA | 20.1 |
| 217 | Muncie, IN | (27.4) |
| 182 | Muskegon, MI | (23.6) |
| NA | Myrtle Beach, SC-NC** | NA |
| 113 | Napa, CA | (14.6) |
| 290 | Naples-Marco Island, FL | (45.7) |
| 204 | Nashville-Davidson, TN | (25.7) |
| 182 | Nassau-Suffolk, NY M.D. | (23.6) |
| NA | New Bern, NC** | NA |
| 85 | New Haven-Milford, CT | (6.8) |
| 77 | New Orleans, LA | (5.0) |
| 66 | New York (greater), NY-NJ-PA | (1.7) |
| NA | New York-Jersey City, NY-NJ M.D.** | NA |
| 50 | Newark, NJ-PA M.D. | 6.1 |
| 35 | Niles-Benton Harbor, MI | 18.3 |
| 249 | North Port-Sarasota-Bradenton, FL | (35.1) |
| 219 | Norwich-New London, CT | (27.9) |
| 40 | Oakland-Hayward, CA M.D. | 13.1 |
| 254 | Ocala, FL | (36.6) |
| 96 | Ocean City, NJ | (9.5) |
| 207 | Odessa, TX | (25.9) |
| 150 | Ogden-Clearfield, UT | (19.7) |
| 106 | Oklahoma City, OK | (12.8) |
| NA | Olympia, WA** | NA |

| RANK | METROPOLITAN AREA | % CHANGE |
|---|---|---|
| 170 | Omaha-Council Bluffs, NE-IA | (22.0) |
| 216 | Orlando, FL | (27.3) |
| 268 | Oshkosh-Neenah, WI | (40.8) |
| 32 | Owensboro, KY | 20.2 |
| 184 | Oxnard-Thousand Oaks, CA | (23.8) |
| 178 | Palm Bay-Melbourne, FL | (23.1) |
| 128 | Panama City, FL | (16.2) |
| NA | Parkersburg-Vienna, WV** | NA |
| 238 | Pensacola, FL | (32.1) |
| NA | Peoria, IL** | NA |
| 126 | Philadelphia (greater) PA-NJ-MD-DE | (16.1) |
| NA | Philadelphia, PA M.D.** | NA |
| 135 | Phoenix-Mesa-Scottsdale, AZ | (17.3) |
| NA | Pittsburgh, PA** | NA |
| 14 | Pittsfield, MA | 48.9 |
| 4 | Pocatello, ID | 124.7 |
| 284 | Port St. Lucie, FL | (44.1) |
| 108 | Portland-Vancouver, OR-WA | (13.1) |
| 180 | Portland, ME | (23.4) |
| 252 | Prescott, AZ | (35.3) |
| 143 | Providence-Warwick, RI-MA | (18.4) |
| 279 | Provo-Orem, UT | (42.8) |
| 25 | Pueblo, CO | 25.3 |
| 299 | Punta Gorda, FL | (48.3) |
| 188 | Racine, WI | (24.0) |
| 238 | Raleigh, NC | (32.1) |
| 52 | Rapid City, SD | 4.7 |
| 97 | Reading, PA | (9.6) |
| 16 | Redding, CA | 43.3 |
| 233 | Reno, NV | (30.3) |
| 235 | Richmond, VA | (31.0) |
| 153 | Riverside-San Bernardino, CA | (20.1) |
| 206 | Roanoke, VA | (25.8) |
| 148 | Rochester, MN | (19.5) |
| 49 | Rochester, NY | 6.6 |
| NA | Rockford, IL** | NA |
| 13 | Rockingham County, NH M.D. | 50.0 |
| 281 | Rocky Mount, NC | (43.1) |
| 132 | Rome, GA | (16.8) |
| 197 | Sacramento, CA | (25.2) |
| 272 | Saginaw, MI | (41.7) |
| 39 | Salem, OR | 13.6 |
| 81 | Salinas, CA | (5.8) |
| NA | Salisbury, MD-DE** | NA |
| 66 | Salt Lake City, UT | (1.7) |
| 302 | San Angelo, TX | (50.5) |
| 213 | San Antonio, TX | (26.9) |
| 230 | San Diego, CA | (28.9) |
| 41 | San Francisco (greater), CA | 11.4 |
| 28 | San Francisco-Redwood, CA M.D. | 22.7 |
| 82 | San Jose, CA | (6.0) |
| 209 | San Luis Obispo, CA | (26.4) |
| NA | San Rafael, CA M.D.** | NA |
| 125 | Santa Cruz-Watsonville, CA | (15.8) |
| 62 | Santa Maria-Santa Barbara, CA | 1.2 |
| 222 | Santa Rosa, CA | (28.4) |
| 250 | Savannah, GA | (35.2) |
| NA | Scranton--Wilkes-Barre, PA** | NA |
| 166 | Seattle (greater), WA | (21.7) |
| 158 | Seattle-Bellevue-Everett, WA M.D. | (20.5) |
| 303 | Sebastian-Vero Beach, FL | (51.8) |
| NA | Sebring, FL** | NA |

| RANK | METROPOLITAN AREA | % CHANGE |
|---|---|---|
| 269 | Sheboygan, WI | (40.9) |
| 261 | Sherman-Denison, TX | (37.4) |
| 225 | Shreveport-Bossier City, LA | (28.6) |
| 215 | Silver Spring-Frederick, MD M.D. | (27.1) |
| 102 | Sioux City, IA-NE-SD | (11.3) |
| 19 | Sioux Falls, SD | 39.8 |
| 68 | South Bend-Mishawaka, IN-MI | (2.2) |
| 207 | Spartanburg, SC | (25.9) |
| 46 | Spokane, WA | 7.7 |
| NA | Springfield, IL** | NA |
| 27 | Springfield, MA | 22.9 |
| 30 | Springfield, MO | 21.7 |
| 63 | Springfield, OH | 0.5 |
| 109 | State College, PA | (13.5) |
| NA | Staunton-Waynesboro, VA** | NA |
| 146 | Stockton-Lodi, CA | (19.1) |
| 37 | St. Cloud, MN | 15.0 |
| 92 | St. George, UT | (8.7) |
| 186 | St. Joseph, MO-KS | (23.9) |
| 235 | St. Louis, MO-IL | (31.0) |
| 204 | Sumter, SC | (25.7) |
| 95 | Syracuse, NY | (9.1) |
| 196 | Tacoma, WA M.D. | (25.0) |
| 220 | Tallahassee, FL | (28.0) |
| 273 | Tampa-St Petersburg, FL | (41.8) |
| NA | Terre Haute, IN** | NA |
| 304 | Texarkana, TX-AR | (52.0) |
| NA | The Villages, FL** | NA |
| 118 | Toledo, OH | (15.0) |
| 290 | Topeka, KS | (45.7) |
| 69 | Trenton, NJ | (2.8) |
| 151 | Tucson, AZ | (19.8) |
| 121 | Tulsa, OK | (15.4) |
| 212 | Tuscaloosa, AL | (26.5) |
| 253 | Tyler, TX | (35.8) |
| 199 | Utica-Rome, NY | (25.3) |
| 115 | Vallejo-Fairfield, CA | (14.8) |
| 137 | Victoria, TX | (17.8) |
| 29 | Vineland-Bridgeton, NJ | 22.5 |
| NA | Virginia Beach-Norfolk, VA-NC** | NA |
| 118 | Visalia-Porterville, CA | (15.0) |
| 257 | Waco, TX | (37.0) |
| NA | Warner Robins, GA** | NA |
| 174 | Warren-Troy, MI M.D. | (22.7) |
| 200 | Washington (greater) DC-VA-MD-WV | (25.4) |
| 202 | Washington, DC-VA-MD-WV M.D. | (25.6) |
| NA | Watertown-Fort Drum, NY** | NA |
| 56 | Wausau, WI | 3.1 |
| 267 | West Palm Beach, FL M.D. | (40.7) |
| 162 | Wichita Falls, TX | (21.0) |
| 136 | Wichita, KS | (17.7) |
| 144 | Williamsport, PA | (18.6) |
| 223 | Wilmington, DE-MD-NJ M.D. | (28.5) |
| 74 | Wilmington, NC | (4.0) |
| 270 | Winchester, VA-WV | (41.1) |
| NA | Winston-Salem, NC** | NA |
| 44 | Worcester, MA-CT | 8.5 |
| NA | Yakima, WA** | NA |
| 278 | York-Hanover, PA | (42.7) |
| 120 | Yuba City, CA | (15.3) |
| 245 | Yuma, AZ | (34.0) |

Source: CQ Press using reported data from the F.B.I. "Crime in the United States 2013"
*Robbery is the taking of anything of value by force or threat of force. Attempts are included.
**Not available.

# 20. Percent Change in Robbery Rate: 2009 to 2013 (continued)
## National Percent Change = 18.0% Decrease*

| RANK | METROPOLITAN AREA | % CHANGE | RANK | METROPOLITAN AREA | % CHANGE | RANK | METROPOLITAN AREA | % CHANGE |
|---|---|---|---|---|---|---|---|---|
| 1 | Medford, OR | 277.2 | 65 | Casper, WY | (0.5) | 128 | Panama City, FL | (16.2) |
| 2 | Fond du Lac, WI | 138.6 | 66 | New York (greater), NY-NJ-PA | (1.7) | 130 | Fayetteville-Springdale, AR-MO | (16.6) |
| 3 | Mankato-North Mankato, MN | 131.0 | 66 | Salt Lake City, UT | (1.7) | 131 | Morgantown, WV | (16.7) |
| 4 | Pocatello, ID | 124.7 | 68 | South Bend-Mishawaka, IN-MI | (2.2) | 132 | Abilene, TX | (16.8) |
| 5 | Lebanon, PA | 114.5 | 69 | Minneapolis-St. Paul, MN-WI | (2.8) | 132 | Rome, GA | (16.8) |
| 6 | Dubuque, IA | 110.9 | 69 | Trenton, NJ | (2.8) | 134 | Flagstaff, AZ | (17.1) |
| 7 | Kokomo, IN | 88.9 | 71 | Bangor, ME | (2.9) | 135 | Phoenix-Mesa-Scottsdale, AZ | (17.3) |
| 8 | Lewiston, ID-WA | 71.7 | 71 | Iowa City, IA | (2.9) | 136 | Wichita, KS | (17.7) |
| 9 | Cape Girardeau, MO-IL | 71.6 | 71 | Little Rock, AR | (2.9) | 137 | Dalton, GA | (17.8) |
| 10 | Binghamton, NY | 67.2 | 74 | Wilmington, NC | (4.0) | 137 | Victoria, TX | (17.8) |
| 11 | Manchester-Nashua, NH | 62.3 | 75 | Fairbanks, AK | (4.5) | 139 | Atlantic City, NJ | (17.9) |
| 12 | Longview, WA | 53.5 | 76 | Fort Wayne, IN | (4.8) | 139 | Clarksville, TN-KY | (17.9) |
| 13 | Rockingham County, NH M.D. | 50.0 | 77 | New Orleans, LA | (5.0) | 139 | Las Vegas-Henderson, NV | (17.9) |
| 14 | Pittsfield, MA | 48.9 | 78 | Corvallis, OR | (5.3) | 142 | Boston, MA M.D. | (18.2) |
| 15 | Bismarck, ND | 45.1 | 79 | Anchorage, AK | (5.6) | 143 | Providence-Warwick, RI-MA | (18.4) |
| 16 | Redding, CA | 43.3 | 80 | Baltimore, MD | (5.7) | 144 | Williamsport, PA | (18.6) |
| 17 | Erie, PA | 41.1 | 81 | Salinas, CA | (5.8) | 145 | Jefferson City, MO | (18.8) |
| 18 | Mansfield, OH | 40.0 | 82 | San Jose, CA | (6.0) | 146 | Stockton-Lodi, CA | (19.1) |
| 19 | Sioux Falls, SD | 39.8 | 83 | Albuquerque, NM | (6.6) | 147 | Fresno, CA | (19.2) |
| 20 | Cumberland, MD-WV | 39.0 | 84 | Lafayette, IN | (6.7) | 148 | Rochester, MN | (19.5) |
| 21 | Fargo, ND-MN | 37.6 | 85 | Albany, GA | (6.8) | 149 | Madera, CA | (19.6) |
| 22 | Farmington, NM | 29.5 | 85 | New Haven-Milford, CT | (6.8) | 150 | Ogden-Clearfield, UT | (19.7) |
| 23 | Hagerstown-Martinsburg, MD-WV | 27.9 | 87 | Denver-Aurora, CO | (7.4) | 151 | Corpus Christi, TX | (19.8) |
| 24 | Bend, OR | 27.6 | 87 | Louisville, KY-IN | (7.4) | 151 | Tucson, AZ | (19.8) |
| 25 | Elmira, NY | 25.3 | 89 | Bremerton-Silverdale, WA | (7.5) | 153 | Riverside-San Bernardino, CA | (20.1) |
| 25 | Pueblo, CO | 25.3 | 90 | Beaumont-Port Arthur, TX | (8.5) | 154 | Buffalo-Niagara Falls, NY | (20.2) |
| 27 | Springfield, MA | 22.9 | 91 | Alexandria, LA | (8.6) | 154 | Cedar Rapids, IA | (20.2) |
| 28 | San Francisco-Redwood, CA M.D. | 22.7 | 92 | St. George, UT | (8.7) | 154 | Grand Forks, ND-MN | (20.2) |
| 29 | Vineland-Bridgeton, NJ | 22.5 | 93 | Bakersfield, CA | (8.8) | 157 | Kansas City, MO-KS | (20.3) |
| 30 | Springfield, MO | 21.7 | 93 | Camden, NJ M.D. | (8.8) | 158 | Des Moines-West Des Moines, IA | (20.5) |
| 31 | Idaho Falls, ID | 20.8 | 95 | Syracuse, NY | (9.1) | 158 | Miami (greater), FL | (20.5) |
| 32 | Owensboro, KY | 20.2 | 96 | Ocean City, NJ | (9.5) | 158 | Seattle-Bellevue-Everett, WA M.D. | (20.5) |
| 33 | Mount Vernon-Anacortes, WA | 20.1 | 97 | Reading, PA | (9.6) | 161 | Albany-Schenectady-Troy, NY | (20.9) |
| 34 | Glens Falls, NY | 18.8 | 98 | Detroit-Dearborn-Livonia, MI M.D. | (10.0) | 162 | Wichita Falls, TX | (21.0) |
| 35 | Niles-Benton Harbor, MI | 18.3 | 98 | Hartford, CT | (10.0) | 163 | Chico, CA | (21.1) |
| 36 | Monroe, MI | 16.4 | 100 | Atlanta, GA | (10.2) | 163 | Merced, CA | (21.1) |
| 37 | St. Cloud, MN | 15.0 | 101 | Indianapolis, IN | (10.5) | 165 | Huntsville, AL | (21.5) |
| 38 | Missoula, MT | 14.1 | 102 | Lawrence, KS | (11.3) | 166 | Fort Worth-Arlington, TX M.D. | (21.7) |
| 39 | Salem, OR | 13.6 | 102 | Sioux City, IA-NE-SD | (11.3) | 166 | Seattle (greater), WA | (21.7) |
| 40 | Oakland-Hayward, CA M.D. | 13.1 | 104 | Burlington, NC | (12.7) | 168 | Brownsville-Harlingen, TX | (21.8) |
| 41 | San Francisco (greater), CA | 11.4 | 104 | Eugene, OR | (12.7) | 168 | Kennewick-Richland, WA | (21.8) |
| 42 | Bloomington, IN | 9.6 | 106 | Oklahoma City, OK | (12.8) | 170 | Lawton, OK | (22.0) |
| 43 | Lubbock, TX | 9.1 | 107 | Greeley, CO | (13.0) | 170 | Omaha-Council Bluffs, NE-IA | (22.0) |
| 44 | Worcester, MA-CT | 8.5 | 108 | Portland-Vancouver, OR-WA | (13.1) | 172 | Birmingham-Hoover, AL | (22.2) |
| 45 | Fayetteville, NC | 8.0 | 109 | El Paso, TX | (13.5) | 172 | Lynchburg, VA | (22.2) |
| 46 | Spokane, WA | 7.7 | 109 | State College, PA | (13.5) | 174 | Cincinnati, OH-KY-IN | (22.7) |
| 47 | Eau Claire, WI | 6.9 | 111 | Lake Charles, LA | (13.7) | 174 | Johnson City, TN | (22.7) |
| 48 | Green Bay, WI | 6.7 | 112 | Boston (greater), MA-NH | (14.4) | 174 | Warren-Troy, MI M.D. | (22.7) |
| 49 | Rochester, NY | 6.6 | 113 | Lexington-Fayette, KY | (14.6) | 177 | Jackson, MI | (22.8) |
| 50 | Newark, NJ-PA M.D. | 6.1 | 113 | Napa, CA | (14.6) | 178 | Palm Bay-Melbourne, FL | (23.1) |
| 51 | Milwaukee, WI | 5.2 | 115 | Jackson, MS | (14.8) | 179 | Jonesboro, AR | (23.2) |
| 52 | Gadsden, AL | 4.7 | 115 | Miami-Dade County, FL M.D. | (14.8) | 180 | Colorado Springs, CO | (23.4) |
| 52 | Rapid City, SD | 4.7 | 115 | Vallejo-Fairfield, CA | (14.8) | 180 | Portland, ME | (23.4) |
| 54 | El Centro, CA | 3.7 | 118 | Toledo, OH | (15.0) | 182 | Muskegon, MI | (23.6) |
| 55 | Modesto, CA | 3.3 | 118 | Visalia-Porterville, CA | (15.0) | 182 | Nassau-Suffolk, NY M.D. | (23.6) |
| 56 | Wausau, WI | 3.1 | 120 | Yuba City, CA | (15.3) | 184 | Las Cruces, NM | (23.8) |
| 57 | Billings, MT | 3.0 | 121 | Detroit (greater), MI | (15.4) | 184 | Oxnard-Thousand Oaks, CA | (23.8) |
| 58 | Lincoln, NE | 2.7 | 121 | Tulsa, OK | (15.4) | 186 | Bridgeport-Stamford, CT | (23.9) |
| 59 | Gainesville, GA | 2.5 | 123 | Flint, MI | (15.5) | 186 | St. Joseph, MO-KS | (23.9) |
| 60 | Lansing-East Lansing, MI | 2.1 | 123 | Houston, TX | (15.5) | 188 | Racine, WI | (24.0) |
| 61 | Florence-Muscle Shoals, AL | 1.6 | 125 | Santa Cruz-Watsonville, CA | (15.8) | 189 | Grand Junction, CO | (24.1) |
| 62 | Santa Maria-Santa Barbara, CA | 1.2 | 126 | Baton Rouge, LA | (16.1) | 190 | Akron, OH | (24.4) |
| 63 | Springfield, OH | 0.5 | 126 | Philadelphia (greater) PA-NJ-MD-DE | (16.1) | 191 | Columbia, SC | (24.8) |
| 64 | Lake Havasu City-Kingman, AZ | (0.3) | 128 | Fort Lauderdale, FL M.D. | (16.2) | 191 | Dallas (greater), TX | (24.8) |

Note: All listings are for Metropolitan Statistical Areas (M.S.A.s) except for those ending with "M.D." Listings with "M.D." are Metropolitan Divisions which are smaller parts of eleven large M.S.A.s. See explanatory note at beginning of metropolitan area section.

| RANK | METROPOLITAN AREA | % CHANGE | RANK | METROPOLITAN AREA | % CHANGE | RANK | METROPOLITAN AREA | % CHANGE |
|---|---|---|---|---|---|---|---|---|
| 191 | Dayton, OH | (24.8) | 254 | Ocala, FL | (36.6) | NA | California-Lexington Park, MD** | NA |
| 191 | Jackson, TN | (24.8) | 256 | College Station-Bryan, TX | (36.8) | NA | Cambridge-Newton, MA M.D.** | NA |
| 191 | Macon, GA | (24.8) | 257 | Waco, TX | (37.0) | NA | Canton, OH** | NA |
| 196 | Tacoma, WA M.D. | (25.0) | 258 | Coeur d'Alene, ID | (37.1) | NA | Carbondale-Marion, IL** | NA |
| 197 | Chattanooga, TN-GA | (25.2) | 259 | Boise City, ID | (37.2) | NA | Chambersburg-Waynesboro, PA** | NA |
| 197 | Sacramento, CA | (25.2) | 260 | Laredo, TX | (37.3) | NA | Champaign-Urbana, IL** | NA |
| 199 | Utica-Rome, NY | (25.3) | 261 | Sherman-Denison, TX | (37.4) | NA | Charlotte-Mecklenburg, NC-SC** | NA |
| 200 | Washington (greater) DC-VA-MD-WV | (25.4) | 262 | Lakeland, FL | (38.2) | NA | Chicago (greater), IL-IN-WI** | NA |
| 201 | Athens-Clarke County, GA | (25.5) | 262 | Lewiston-Auburn, ME | (38.2) | NA | Chicago-Naperville, IL M.D.** | NA |
| 202 | Dallas-Plano-Irving, TX M.D. | (25.6) | 262 | McAllen-Edinburg-Mission, TX | (38.2) | NA | Crestview-Fort Walton Beach, FL** | NA |
| 202 | Washington, DC-VA-MD-WV M.D. | (25.6) | 265 | Gainesville, FL | (39.5) | NA | Daphne-Fairhope-Foley, AL** | NA |
| 204 | Nashville-Davidson, TN | (25.7) | 266 | Boulder, CO | (39.7) | NA | Davenport, IA-IL** | NA |
| 204 | Sumter, SC | (25.7) | 267 | West Palm Beach, FL M.D. | (40.7) | NA | Dutchess-Putnam, NY M.D.** | NA |
| 206 | Roanoke, VA | (25.8) | 268 | Oshkosh-Neenah, WI | (40.8) | NA | East Stroudsburg, PA** | NA |
| 207 | Odessa, TX | (25.9) | 269 | Sheboygan, WI | (40.9) | NA | Elgin, IL M.D.** | NA |
| 207 | Spartanburg, SC | (25.9) | 270 | Winchester, VA-WV | (41.1) | NA | Elizabethtown-Fort Knox, KY** | NA |
| 209 | Cape Coral-Fort Myers, FL | (26.4) | 271 | Anniston-Oxford, AL | (41.5) | NA | Gary, IN M.D.** | NA |
| 209 | Columbus, IN | (26.4) | 272 | Saginaw, MI | (41.7) | NA | Gettysburg, PA** | NA |
| 209 | San Luis Obispo, CA | (26.4) | 273 | Barnstable Town, MA | (41.8) | NA | Grand Island, NE** | NA |
| 212 | Tuscaloosa, AL | (26.5) | 273 | Fort Collins, CO | (41.8) | NA | Grand Rapids-Wyoming, MI** | NA |
| 213 | Memphis, TN-MS-AR | (26.9) | 273 | Tampa-St Petersburg, FL | (41.8) | NA | Grants Pass, OR** | NA |
| 213 | San Antonio, TX | (26.9) | 276 | Altoona, PA | (42.2) | NA | Greenville-Anderson, SC** | NA |
| 215 | Silver Spring-Frederick, MD M.D. | (27.1) | 277 | Jacksonville, FL | (42.6) | NA | Greenville, NC** | NA |
| 216 | Orlando, FL | (27.3) | 278 | York-Hanover, PA | (42.7) | NA | Gulfport-Biloxi-Pascagoula, MS** | NA |
| 217 | Muncie, IN | (27.4) | 279 | Kingsport, TN-VA | (42.8) | NA | Hammond, LA** | NA |
| 218 | Dover, DE | (27.5) | 279 | Provo-Orem, UT | (42.8) | NA | Hanford-Corcoran, CA** | NA |
| 219 | Norwich-New London, CT | (27.9) | 281 | Rocky Mount, NC | (43.1) | NA | Hilton Head Island, SC** | NA |
| 220 | Tallahassee, FL | (28.0) | 282 | Morristown, TN | (43.2) | NA | Homosassa Springs, FL** | NA |
| 221 | Goldsboro, NC | (28.3) | 283 | Augusta, GA-SC | (43.9) | NA | Johnstown, PA** | NA |
| 222 | Santa Rosa, CA | (28.4) | 284 | Port St. Lucie, FL | (44.1) | NA | Joplin, MO** | NA |
| 223 | Fort Smith, AR-OK | (28.5) | 285 | Greensboro-High Point, NC | (44.4) | NA | Kahului-Wailuku-Lahaina, HI** | NA |
| 223 | Wilmington, DE-MD-NJ M.D. | (28.5) | 286 | Knoxville, TN | (44.5) | NA | Kankakee, IL** | NA |
| 225 | Columbia, MO | (28.6) | 287 | Dothan, AL | (45.2) | NA | La Crosse, WI-MN** | NA |
| 225 | Shreveport-Bossier City, LA | (28.6) | 288 | Florence, SC | (45.3) | NA | Lafayette, LA** | NA |
| 227 | Ames, IA | (28.8) | 289 | Austin-Round Rock, TX | (45.6) | NA | Lake Co.-Kenosha Co., IL-WI M.D.** | NA |
| 227 | Ann Arbor, MI | (28.8) | 290 | Deltona-Daytona Beach, FL | (45.7) | NA | Lancaster, PA** | NA |
| 227 | Longview, TX | (28.8) | 290 | Naples-Marco Island, FL | (45.7) | NA | Madison, WI** | NA |
| 230 | San Diego, CA | (28.9) | 290 | Topeka, KS | (45.7) | NA | Monroe, LA** | NA |
| 231 | Cleveland, TN | (29.3) | 293 | Decatur, IL | (45.9) | NA | Montgomery County, PA M.D.** | NA |
| 232 | Columbus, GA-AL | (29.4) | 294 | Mobile, AL | (46.4) | NA | Myrtle Beach, SC-NC** | NA |
| 233 | Reno, NV | (30.3) | 295 | Hot Springs, AR | (46.5) | NA | New Bern, NC** | NA |
| 234 | Duluth, MN-WI | (30.4) | 296 | Kingston, NY | (46.8) | NA | New York-Jersey City, NY-NJ M.D.** | NA |
| 235 | Richmond, VA | (31.0) | 297 | Lima, OH | (47.3) | NA | Olympia, WA** | NA |
| 235 | St. Louis, MO-IL | (31.0) | 298 | Manhattan, KS | (48.2) | NA | Parkersburg-Vienna, WV** | NA |
| 237 | Charlottesville, VA | (31.2) | 299 | Punta Gorda, FL | (48.3) | NA | Peoria, IL** | NA |
| 238 | Pensacola, FL | (32.1) | 300 | Houma, LA | (49.7) | NA | Philadelphia, PA M.D.** | NA |
| 238 | Raleigh, NC | (32.1) | 301 | Bay City, MI | (49.9) | NA | Pittsburgh, PA** | NA |
| 240 | Brunswick, GA | (32.4) | 302 | San Angelo, TX | (50.5) | NA | Rockford, IL** | NA |
| 241 | Los Angeles County, CA M.D. | (32.6) | 303 | Sebastian-Vero Beach, FL | (51.8) | NA | Salisbury, MD-DE** | NA |
| 242 | Los Angeles (greater), CA | (32.9) | 304 | Texarkana, TX-AR | (52.0) | NA | San Rafael, CA M.D.** | NA |
| 243 | Allentown, PA-NJ | (33.2) | 305 | Great Falls, MT | (53.7) | NA | Scranton--Wilkes-Barre, PA** | NA |
| 244 | Midland, TX | (33.8) | 306 | Hinesville, GA | (55.0) | NA | Sebring, FL** | NA |
| 245 | Amarillo, TX | (34.0) | 307 | Harrisonburg, VA | (55.1) | NA | Springfield, IL** | NA |
| 245 | Yuma, AZ | (34.0) | 308 | Decatur, AL | (55.5) | NA | Staunton-Waynesboro, VA** | NA |
| 247 | Anaheim-Santa Ana-Irvine, CA M.D. | (34.1) | 309 | Charleston-North Charleston, SC | (55.7) | NA | Terre Haute, IN** | NA |
| 248 | Janesville, WI | (35.0) | 310 | Cheyenne, WY | (59.5) | NA | The Villages, FL** | NA |
| 249 | North Port-Sarasota-Bradenton, FL | (35.1) | 311 | Blacksburg, VA | (66.6) | NA | Virginia Beach-Norfolk, VA-NC** | NA |
| 250 | Carson City, NV | (35.2) | 312 | Logan, UT-ID | (100.0) | NA | Warner Robins, GA** | NA |
| 250 | Savannah, GA | (35.2) | NA | Albany, OR** | NA | NA | Watertown-Fort Drum, NY** | NA |
| 252 | Prescott, AZ | (35.3) | NA | Bloomington, IL** | NA | NA | Winston-Salem, NC** | NA |
| 253 | Tyler, TX | (35.8) | NA | Bloomsburg-Berwick, PA** | NA | NA | Yakima, WA** | NA |
| 254 | Appleton, WI | (36.6) | NA | Bowling Green, KY** | NA | | | |

Source: CQ Press using reported data from the F.B.I. "Crime in the United States 2013"

*Robbery is the taking of anything of value by force or threat of force. Attempts are included.

**Not available.

# 21. Aggravated Assaults in 2013
## National Total = 724,149 Aggravated Assaults*

| RANK | METROPOLITAN AREA | ASSAULTS | RANK | METROPOLITAN AREA | ASSAULTS | RANK | METROPOLITAN AREA | ASSAULTS |
|---|---|---|---|---|---|---|---|---|
| 246 | Abilene, TX | 388 | 326 | Cheyenne, WY | 164 | 117 | Gary, IN M.D. | 1,356 |
| 132 | Akron, OH | 1,090 | NA | Chicago (greater), IL-IN-WI** | NA | 367 | Gettysburg, PA | 58 |
| 109 | Albany-Schenectady-Troy, NY | 1,467 | NA | Chicago-Naperville, IL M.D.** | NA | 357 | Glens Falls, NY | 96 |
| 166 | Albany, GA | 762 | 244 | Chico, CA | 394 | 249 | Goldsboro, NC | 372 |
| 372 | Albany, OR | 33 | 70 | Cincinnati, OH-KY-IN | 2,584 | 342 | Grand Forks, ND-MN | 128 |
| 39 | Albuquerque, NM | 4,835 | 173 | Clarksville, TN-KY | 719 | 353 | Grand Island, NE | 104 |
| 141 | Alexandria, LA | 980 | 222 | Cleveland, TN | 444 | 291 | Grand Junction, CO | 271 |
| 160 | Allentown, PA-NJ | 802 | 263 | Coeur d'Alene, ID | 345 | 90 | Grand Rapids-Wyoming, MI | 1,706 |
| 310 | Altoona, PA | 199 | 178 | College Station-Bryan, TX | 676 | 360 | Grants Pass, OR | 85 |
| 148 | Amarillo, TX | 885 | 108 | Colorado Springs, CO | 1,500 | 340 | Great Falls, MT | 130 |
| 363 | Ames, IA | 77 | 257 | Columbia, MO | 357 | 191 | Greeley, CO | 591 |
| 51 | Anaheim-Santa Ana-Irvine, CA M.D. | 3,574 | 58 | Columbia, SC | 3,385 | 216 | Green Bay, WI | 461 |
| 106 | Anchorage, AK | 1,535 | 179 | Columbus, GA-AL | 672 | 100 | Greensboro-High Point, NC | 1,590 |
| 172 | Ann Arbor, MI | 720 | 356 | Columbus, IN | 99 | 52 | Greenville-Anderson, SC | 3,530 |
| 220 | Anniston-Oxford, AL | 447 | 95 | Corpus Christi, TX | 1,660 | 204 | Greenville, NC | 530 |
| 301 | Appleton, WI | 227 | 366 | Corvallis, OR | 66 | 184 | Gulfport-Biloxi-Pascagoula, MS | 654 |
| 261 | Athens-Clarke County, GA | 349 | 161 | Crestview-Fort Walton Beach, FL | 792 | 254 | Hagerstown-Martinsburg, MD-WV | 363 |
| 11 | Atlanta, GA | 11,329 | 314 | Cumberland, MD-WV | 191 | 153 | Hammond, LA | 862 |
| 183 | Atlantic City, NJ | 659 | 9 | Dallas (greater), TX | 11,981 | 198 | Hanford-Corcoran, CA | 561 |
| 154 | Augusta, GA-SC | 857 | 29 | Dallas-Plano-Irving, TX M.D. | 6,808 | 346 | Harrisonburg, VA | 114 |
| 50 | Austin-Round Rock, TX | 3,609 | 288 | Dalton, GA | 276 | 116 | Hartford, CT | 1,366 |
| 55 | Bakersfield, CA | 3,452 | 276 | Daphne-Fairhope-Foley, AL | 311 | 170 | Hilton Head Island, SC | 731 |
| 15 | Baltimore, MD | 10,324 | 139 | Davenport, IA-IL | 988 | 329 | Hinesville, GA | 158 |
| 369 | Bangor, ME | 55 | 146 | Dayton, OH | 923 | 232 | Homosassa Springs, FL | 422 |
| 163 | Barnstable Town, MA | 772 | 304 | Decatur, AL | 218 | 280 | Hot Springs, AR | 306 |
| 71 | Baton Rouge, LA | 2,521 | 276 | Decatur, IL | 311 | 227 | Houma, LA | 432 |
| 324 | Bay City, MI | 166 | 93 | Deltona-Daytona Beach, FL | 1,690 | 5 | Houston, TX | 18,642 |
| 115 | Beaumont-Port Arthur, TX | 1,398 | 36 | Denver-Aurora, CO | 5,197 | 113 | Huntsville, AL | 1,421 |
| 289 | Bend, OR | 274 | 124 | Des Moines-West Des Moines, IA | 1,177 | 332 | Idaho Falls, ID | 143 |
| 282 | Billings, MT | 302 | 8 | Detroit (greater), MI | 14,845 | NA | Indianapolis, IN** | NA |
| 272 | Binghamton, NY | 315 | 10 | Detroit-Dearborn-Livonia, MI M.D. | 11,360 | 274 | Iowa City, IA | 314 |
| 49 | Birmingham-Hoover, AL | 3,723 | 238 | Dothan, AL | 412 | 41 | Jacksonville, FL | 4,576 |
| 242 | Bismarck, ND | 397 | 203 | Dover, DE | 532 | 229 | Jackson, MI | 427 |
| 306 | Blacksburg, VA | 213 | 355 | Dubuque, IA | 100 | 140 | Jackson, MS | 984 |
| 237 | Bloomington, IL | 413 | 236 | Duluth, MN-WI | 414 | 142 | Jackson, TN | 972 |
| 289 | Bloomington, IN | 274 | 228 | Dutchess-Putnam, NY M.D. | 429 | 301 | Janesville, WI | 227 |
| 319 | Bloomsburg-Berwick, PA | 184 | 206 | East Stroudsburg, PA | 504 | 258 | Jefferson City, MO | 351 |
| 135 | Boise City, ID | 1,050 | 330 | Eau Claire, WI | 146 | 202 | Johnson City, TN | 537 |
| 13 | Boston (greater), MA-NH | 10,728 | 241 | El Centro, CA | 400 | 328 | Johnstown, PA | 159 |
| 33 | Boston, MA M.D. | 6,119 | 77 | El Paso, TX | 2,181 | 271 | Jonesboro, AR | 321 |
| 234 | Boulder, CO | 420 | 169 | Elgin, IL M.D. | 732 | 248 | Joplin, MO | 378 |
| 359 | Bowling Green, KY | 86 | 367 | Elizabethtown-Fort Knox, KY | 58 | 278 | Kahului-Wailuku-Lahaina, HI | 307 |
| 211 | Bremerton-Silverdale, WA | 481 | 351 | Elmira, NY | 107 | 308 | Kankakee, IL | 212 |
| 127 | Bridgeport-Stamford, CT | 1,120 | 253 | Erie, PA | 366 | 32 | Kansas City, MO-KS | 6,206 |
| 186 | Brownsville-Harlingen, TX | 633 | 264 | Eugene, OR | 340 | 235 | Kennewick-Richland, WA | 418 |
| NA | Brunswick, GA** | NA | 327 | Fairbanks, AK | 161 | 162 | Kingsport, TN-VA | 784 |
| 65 | Buffalo-Niagara Falls, NY | 2,839 | 240 | Fargo, ND-MN | 402 | 309 | Kingston, NY | 208 |
| 239 | Burlington, NC | 410 | 214 | Farmington, NM | 465 | 76 | Knoxville, TN | 2,187 |
| 323 | California-Lexington Park, MD | 171 | 119 | Fayetteville-Springdale, AR-MO | 1,265 | 340 | Kokomo, IN | 130 |
| 45 | Cambridge-Newton, MA M.D. | 4,226 | 144 | Fayetteville, NC | 970 | 350 | La Crosse, WI-MN | 110 |
| 74 | Camden, NJ M.D. | 2,233 | 266 | Flagstaff, AZ | 337 | 249 | Lafayette, IN | 372 |
| 219 | Canton, OH | 448 | 85 | Flint, MI | 1,907 | 102 | Lafayette, LA | 1,579 |
| 112 | Cape Coral-Fort Myers, FL | 1,432 | 260 | Florence-Muscle Shoals, AL | 350 | 155 | Lake Charles, LA | 850 |
| 262 | Cape Girardeau, MO-IL | 348 | 171 | Florence, SC | 722 | 168 | Lake Co.-Kenosha Co., IL-WI M.D. | 741 |
| 287 | Carbondale-Marion, IL | 279 | 333 | Fond du Lac, WI | 142 | 270 | Lake Havasu City-Kingman, AZ | 322 |
| 347 | Carson City, NV | 112 | 223 | Fort Collins, CO | 440 | 92 | Lakeland, FL | 1,694 |
| 336 | Casper, WY | 138 | 43 | Fort Lauderdale, FL M.D. | 4,449 | 231 | Lancaster, PA | 424 |
| 255 | Cedar Rapids, IA | 362 | 151 | Fort Smith, AR-OK | 871 | 123 | Lansing-East Lansing, MI | 1,181 |
| 348 | Chambersburg-Waynesboro, PA | 111 | 213 | Fort Wayne, IN | 472 | 156 | Laredo, TX | 838 |
| 163 | Champaign-Urbana, IL | 772 | 37 | Fort Worth-Arlington, TX M.D. | 5,173 | 201 | Las Cruces, NM | 541 |
| 87 | Charleston-North Charleston, SC | 1,797 | 56 | Fresno, CA | 3,427 | 24 | Las Vegas-Henderson, NV | 8,048 |
| 34 | Charlotte-Mecklenburg, NC-SC | 6,097 | 242 | Gadsden, AL | 397 | 300 | Lawrence, KS | 238 |
| 298 | Charlottesville, VA | 240 | 131 | Gainesville, FL | 1,103 | 177 | Lawton, OK | 677 |
| 80 | Chattanooga, TN-GA | 2,122 | 322 | Gainesville, GA | 172 | 338 | Lebanon, PA | 131 |

Note: All listings are for Metropolitan Statistical Areas (M.S.A.s) except for those ending with "M.D." Listings with "M.D." are Metropolitan Divisions which are smaller parts of eleven large M.S.A.s. See explanatory note at beginning of metropolitan area section.

| RANK | METROPOLITAN AREA | ASSAULTS | RANK | METROPOLITAN AREA | ASSAULTS | RANK | METROPOLITAN AREA | ASSAULTS |
|---|---|---|---|---|---|---|---|---|
| 364 | Lewiston-Auburn, ME | 72 | 75 | Omaha-Council Bluffs, NE-IA | 2,222 | 345 | Sheboygan, WI | 116 |
| 362 | Lewiston, ID-WA | 81 | 22 | Orlando, FL | 8,396 | 296 | Sherman-Denison, TX | 251 |
| 215 | Lexington-Fayette, KY | 463 | 303 | Oshkosh-Neenah, WI | 221 | 89 | Shreveport-Bossier City, LA | 1,763 |
| 292 | Lima, OH | 261 | 370 | Owensboro, KY | 53 | 120 | Silver Spring-Frederick, MD M.D. | 1,263 |
| 182 | Lincoln, NE | 660 | 147 | Oxnard-Thousand Oaks, CA | 903 | 278 | Sioux City, IA-NE-SD | 307 |
| 61 | Little Rock, AR | 3,266 | 80 | Palm Bay-Melbourne, FL | 2,122 | 212 | Sioux Falls, SD | 475 |
| 371 | Logan, UT-ID | 38 | 174 | Panama City, FL | 715 | 252 | South Bend-Mishawaka, IN-MI | 368 |
| 187 | Longview, TX | 616 | 304 | Parkersburg-Vienna, WV | 218 | 136 | Spartanburg, SC | 1,033 |
| 310 | Longview, WA | 199 | 91 | Pensacola, FL | 1,695 | 137 | Spokane, WA | 1,031 |
| 4 | Los Angeles County, CA M.D. | 21,306 | 152 | Peoria, IL | 864 | 133 | Springfield, IL | 1,087 |
| 3 | Los Angeles (greater), CA | 24,880 | 7 | Philadelphia (greater) PA-NJ-MD-DE | 15,525 | 83 | Springfield, MA | 2,011 |
| NA | Louisville, KY-IN** | NA | 18 | Philadelphia, PA M.D. | 9,721 | 99 | Springfield, MO | 1,607 |
| 110 | Lubbock, TX | 1,464 | 14 | Phoenix-Mesa-Scottsdale, AZ | 10,651 | 312 | Springfield, OH | 198 |
| 274 | Lynchburg, VA | 314 | 42 | Pittsburgh, PA | 4,473 | 361 | State College, PA | 84 |
| 207 | Macon, GA | 497 | 294 | Pittsfield, MA | 254 | 344 | Staunton-Waynesboro, VA | 120 |
| 158 | Madera, CA | 813 | 316 | Pocatello, ID | 187 | 60 | Stockton-Lodi, CA | 3,321 |
| 158 | Madison, WI | 813 | 126 | Port St. Lucie, FL | 1,134 | 320 | St. Cloud, MN | 181 |
| 198 | Manchester-Nashua, NH | 561 | 59 | Portland-Vancouver, OR-WA | 3,361 | 338 | St. George, UT | 131 |
| 336 | Manhattan, KS | 138 | 233 | Portland, ME | 421 | 283 | St. Joseph, MO-KS | 299 |
| 354 | Mankato-North Mankato, MN | 101 | 225 | Prescott, AZ | 439 | 23 | St. Louis, MO-IL | 8,059 |
| 364 | Mansfield, OH | 72 | 57 | Providence-Warwick, RI-MA | 3,412 | 196 | Sumter, SC | 564 |
| 94 | McAllen-Edinburg-Mission, TX | 1,661 | 318 | Provo-Orem, UT | 185 | 134 | Syracuse, NY | 1,051 |
| 205 | Medford, OR | 525 | 180 | Pueblo, CO | 668 | 73 | Tacoma, WA M.D. | 2,358 |
| 19 | Memphis, TN-MS-AR | 9,165 | 272 | Punta Gorda, FL | 315 | 107 | Tallahassee, FL | 1,511 |
| 121 | Merced, CA | 1,219 | 343 | Racine, WI | 126 | 25 | Tampa-St Petersburg, FL | 7,768 |
| 6 | Miami (greater), FL | 18,238 | 96 | Raleigh, NC | 1,646 | 317 | Terre Haute, IN | 186 |
| 16 | Miami-Dade County, FL M.D. | 9,835 | 256 | Rapid City, SD | 361 | 185 | Texarkana, TX-AR | 635 |
| 267 | Midland, TX | 336 | 176 | Reading, PA | 699 | 333 | The Villages, FL | 142 |
| 38 | Milwaukee, WI | 4,891 | 150 | Redding, CA | 872 | 84 | Toledo, OH | 1,937 |
| 40 | Minneapolis-St. Paul, MN-WI | 4,812 | 130 | Reno, NV | 1,107 | 194 | Topeka, KS | 581 |
| 306 | Missoula, MT | 213 | 104 | Richmond, VA | 1,575 | 166 | Trenton, NJ | 762 |
| 105 | Mobile, AL | 1,559 | 20 | Riverside-San Bernardino, CA | 8,924 | 68 | Tucson, AZ | 2,705 |
| 86 | Modesto, CA | 1,816 | 218 | Roanoke, VA | 455 | 62 | Tulsa, OK | 3,240 |
| 165 | Monroe, LA | 763 | 321 | Rochester, MN | 180 | 196 | Tuscaloosa, AL | 564 |
| 299 | Monroe, MI | 239 | 98 | Rochester, NY | 1,610 | 216 | Tyler, TX | 461 |
| 111 | Montgomery County, PA M.D. | 1,442 | 88 | Rockford, IL | 1,770 | 221 | Utica-Rome, NY | 445 |
| 295 | Morgantown, WV | 252 | 247 | Rockingham County, NH M.D. | 383 | 125 | Vallejo-Fairfield, CA | 1,173 |
| 286 | Morristown, TN | 291 | 192 | Rocky Mount, NC | 589 | 258 | Victoria, TX | 351 |
| 330 | Mount Vernon-Anacortes, WA | 146 | 293 | Rome, GA | 258 | 229 | Vineland-Bridgeton, NJ | 427 |
| 315 | Muncie, IN | 189 | 35 | Sacramento, CA | 5,799 | 64 | Virginia Beach-Norfolk, VA-NC | 2,974 |
| 210 | Muskegon, MI | 485 | 129 | Saginaw, MI | 1,113 | 101 | Visalia-Porterville, CA | 1,585 |
| 118 | Myrtle Beach, SC-NC | 1,296 | 188 | Salem, OR | 604 | 193 | Waco, TX | 584 |
| 284 | Napa, CA | 295 | 138 | Salinas, CA | 1,010 | 209 | Warner Robins, GA | 487 |
| 195 | Naples-Marco Island, FL | 577 | 122 | Salisbury, MD-DE | 1,204 | 54 | Warren-Troy, MI M.D. | 3,485 |
| 26 | Nashville-Davidson, TN | 7,586 | 72 | Salt Lake City, UT | 2,433 | 17 | Washington (greater) DC-VA-MD-WV | 9,733 |
| 78 | Nassau-Suffolk, NY M.D. | 2,135 | 313 | San Angelo, TX | 197 | 21 | Washington, DC-VA-MD-WV M.D. | 8,470 |
| 296 | New Bern, NC | 251 | 28 | San Antonio, TX | 7,015 | 348 | Watertown-Fort Drum, NY | 111 |
| 102 | New Haven-Milford, CT | 1,579 | 27 | San Diego, CA | 7,384 | 358 | Wausau, WI | 89 |
| 53 | New Orleans, LA | 3,511 | 12 | San Francisco (greater), CA | 10,807 | 47 | West Palm Beach, FL M.D. | 3,954 |
| 1 | New York (greater), NY-NJ-PA | 44,100 | 48 | San Francisco-Redwood, CA M.D. | 3,806 | 268 | Wichita Falls, TX | 334 |
| 2 | New York-Jersey City, NY-NJ M.D. | 38,466 | 66 | San Jose, CA | 2,779 | 67 | Wichita, KS | 2,768 |
| 63 | Newark, NJ-PA M.D. | 3,070 | 149 | San Luis Obispo, CA | 877 | 352 | Williamsport, PA | 106 |
| 223 | Niles-Benton Harbor, MI | 440 | 281 | San Rafael, CA M.D. | 305 | 79 | Wilmington, DE-MD-NJ M.D. | 2,129 |
| 82 | North Port-Sarasota-Bradenton, FL | 2,114 | 175 | Santa Cruz-Watsonville, CA | 714 | 190 | Wilmington, NC | 594 |
| 245 | Norwich-New London, CT | 393 | 142 | Santa Maria-Santa Barbara, CA | 972 | 335 | Winchester, VA-WV | 140 |
| 30 | Oakland-Hayward, CA M.D. | 6,696 | 114 | Santa Rosa, CA | 1,405 | 97 | Winston-Salem, NC | 1,636 |
| 128 | Ocala, FL | 1,118 | 200 | Savannah, GA | 554 | 69 | Worcester, MA-CT | 2,625 |
| 325 | Ocean City, NJ | 165 | 157 | Scranton--Wilkes-Barre, PA | 834 | 225 | Yakima, WA | 439 |
| 145 | Odessa, TX | 951 | 31 | Seattle (greater), WA | 6,397 | 189 | York-Hanover, PA | 595 |
| 208 | Ogden-Clearfield, UT | 496 | 46 | Seattle-Bellevue-Everett, WA M.D. | 4,039 | 251 | Yuba City, CA | 370 |
| 44 | Oklahoma City, OK | 4,414 | 268 | Sebastian-Vero Beach, FL | 334 | 181 | Yuma, AZ | 662 |
| 265 | Olympia, WA | 338 | 284 | Sebring, FL | 295 | | | |

Source: Reported data from the F.B.I. "Crime in the United States 2013"

*Aggravated assault is an attack for the purpose of inflicting severe bodily injury.

**Not available.

# 21. Aggravated Assaults in 2013 (continued)
## National Total = 724,149 Aggravated Assaults*

| RANK | METROPOLITAN AREA | ASSAULTS | RANK | METROPOLITAN AREA | ASSAULTS | RANK | METROPOLITAN AREA | ASSAULTS |
|---|---|---|---|---|---|---|---|---|
| 1 | New York (greater), NY-NJ-PA | 44,100 | 65 | Buffalo-Niagara Falls, NY | 2,839 | 129 | Saginaw, MI | 1,113 |
| 2 | New York-Jersey City, NY-NJ M.D. | 38,466 | 66 | San Jose, CA | 2,779 | 130 | Reno, NV | 1,107 |
| 3 | Los Angeles (greater), CA | 24,880 | 67 | Wichita, KS | 2,768 | 131 | Gainesville, FL | 1,103 |
| 4 | Los Angeles County, CA M.D. | 21,306 | 68 | Tucson, AZ | 2,705 | 132 | Akron, OH | 1,090 |
| 5 | Houston, TX | 18,642 | 69 | Worcester, MA-CT | 2,625 | 133 | Springfield, IL | 1,087 |
| 6 | Miami (greater), FL | 18,238 | 70 | Cincinnati, OH-KY-IN | 2,584 | 134 | Syracuse, NY | 1,051 |
| 7 | Philadelphia (greater) PA-NJ-MD-DE | 15,525 | 71 | Baton Rouge, LA | 2,521 | 135 | Boise City, ID | 1,050 |
| 8 | Detroit (greater), MI | 14,845 | 72 | Salt Lake City, UT | 2,433 | 136 | Spartanburg, SC | 1,033 |
| 9 | Dallas (greater), TX | 11,981 | 73 | Tacoma, WA M.D. | 2,358 | 137 | Spokane, WA | 1,031 |
| 10 | Detroit-Dearborn-Livonia, MI M.D. | 11,360 | 74 | Camden, NJ M.D. | 2,233 | 138 | Salinas, CA | 1,010 |
| 11 | Atlanta, GA | 11,329 | 75 | Omaha-Council Bluffs, NE-IA | 2,222 | 139 | Davenport, IA-IL | 988 |
| 12 | San Francisco (greater), CA | 10,807 | 76 | Knoxville, TN | 2,187 | 140 | Jackson, MS | 984 |
| 13 | Boston (greater), MA-NH | 10,728 | 77 | El Paso, TX | 2,181 | 141 | Alexandria, LA | 980 |
| 14 | Phoenix-Mesa-Scottsdale, AZ | 10,651 | 78 | Nassau-Suffolk, NY M.D. | 2,135 | 142 | Jackson, TN | 972 |
| 15 | Baltimore, MD | 10,324 | 79 | Wilmington, DE-MD-NJ M.D. | 2,129 | 142 | Santa Maria-Santa Barbara, CA | 972 |
| 16 | Miami-Dade County, FL M.D. | 9,835 | 80 | Chattanooga, TN-GA | 2,122 | 144 | Fayetteville, NC | 970 |
| 17 | Washington (greater) DC-VA-MD-WV | 9,733 | 80 | Palm Bay-Melbourne, FL | 2,122 | 145 | Odessa, TX | 951 |
| 18 | Philadelphia, PA M.D. | 9,721 | 82 | North Port-Sarasota-Bradenton, FL | 2,114 | 146 | Dayton, OH | 923 |
| 19 | Memphis, TN-MS-AR | 9,165 | 83 | Springfield, MA | 2,011 | 147 | Oxnard-Thousand Oaks, CA | 903 |
| 20 | Riverside-San Bernardino, CA | 8,924 | 84 | Toledo, OH | 1,937 | 148 | Amarillo, TX | 885 |
| 21 | Washington, DC-VA-MD-WV M.D. | 8,470 | 85 | Flint, MI | 1,907 | 149 | San Luis Obispo, CA | 877 |
| 22 | Orlando, FL | 8,396 | 86 | Modesto, CA | 1,816 | 150 | Redding, CA | 872 |
| 23 | St. Louis, MO-IL | 8,059 | 87 | Charleston-North Charleston, SC | 1,797 | 151 | Fort Smith, AR-OK | 871 |
| 24 | Las Vegas-Henderson, NV | 8,048 | 88 | Rockford, IL | 1,770 | 152 | Peoria, IL | 864 |
| 25 | Tampa-St Petersburg, FL | 7,768 | 89 | Shreveport-Bossier City, LA | 1,763 | 153 | Hammond, LA | 862 |
| 26 | Nashville-Davidson, TN | 7,586 | 90 | Grand Rapids-Wyoming, MI | 1,706 | 154 | Augusta, GA-SC | 857 |
| 27 | San Diego, CA | 7,384 | 91 | Pensacola, FL | 1,695 | 155 | Lake Charles, LA | 850 |
| 28 | San Antonio, TX | 7,015 | 92 | Lakeland, FL | 1,694 | 156 | Laredo, TX | 838 |
| 29 | Dallas-Plano-Irving, TX M.D. | 6,808 | 93 | Deltona-Daytona Beach, FL | 1,690 | 157 | Scranton--Wilkes-Barre, PA | 834 |
| 30 | Oakland-Hayward, CA M.D. | 6,696 | 94 | McAllen-Edinburg-Mission, TX | 1,661 | 158 | Madera, CA | 813 |
| 31 | Seattle (greater), WA | 6,397 | 95 | Corpus Christi, TX | 1,660 | 158 | Madison, WI | 813 |
| 32 | Kansas City, MO-KS | 6,206 | 96 | Raleigh, NC | 1,646 | 160 | Allentown, PA-NJ | 802 |
| 33 | Boston, MA M.D. | 6,119 | 97 | Winston-Salem, NC | 1,636 | 161 | Crestview-Fort Walton Beach, FL | 792 |
| 34 | Charlotte-Mecklenburg, NC-SC | 6,097 | 98 | Rochester, NY | 1,610 | 162 | Kingsport, TN-VA | 784 |
| 35 | Sacramento, CA | 5,799 | 99 | Springfield, MO | 1,607 | 163 | Barnstable Town, MA | 772 |
| 36 | Denver-Aurora, CO | 5,197 | 100 | Greensboro-High Point, NC | 1,590 | 163 | Champaign-Urbana, IL | 772 |
| 37 | Fort Worth-Arlington, TX M.D. | 5,173 | 101 | Visalia-Porterville, CA | 1,585 | 165 | Monroe, LA | 763 |
| 38 | Milwaukee, WI | 4,891 | 102 | Lafayette, LA | 1,579 | 166 | Albany, GA | 762 |
| 39 | Albuquerque, NM | 4,835 | 102 | New Haven-Milford, CT | 1,579 | 166 | Trenton, NJ | 762 |
| 40 | Minneapolis-St. Paul, MN-WI | 4,812 | 104 | Richmond, VA | 1,575 | 168 | Lake Co.-Kenosha Co., IL-WI M.D. | 741 |
| 41 | Jacksonville, FL | 4,576 | 105 | Mobile, AL | 1,559 | 169 | Elgin, IL M.D. | 732 |
| 42 | Pittsburgh, PA | 4,473 | 106 | Anchorage, AK | 1,535 | 170 | Hilton Head Island, SC | 731 |
| 43 | Fort Lauderdale, FL M.D. | 4,449 | 107 | Tallahassee, FL | 1,511 | 171 | Florence, SC | 722 |
| 44 | Oklahoma City, OK | 4,414 | 108 | Colorado Springs, CO | 1,500 | 172 | Ann Arbor, MI | 720 |
| 45 | Cambridge-Newton, MA M.D. | 4,226 | 109 | Albany-Schenectady-Troy, NY | 1,467 | 173 | Clarksville, TN-KY | 719 |
| 46 | Seattle-Bellevue-Everett, WA M.D. | 4,039 | 110 | Lubbock, TX | 1,464 | 174 | Panama City, FL | 715 |
| 47 | West Palm Beach, FL M.D. | 3,954 | 111 | Montgomery County, PA M.D. | 1,442 | 175 | Santa Cruz-Watsonville, CA | 714 |
| 48 | San Francisco-Redwood, CA M.D. | 3,806 | 112 | Cape Coral-Fort Myers, FL | 1,432 | 176 | Reading, PA | 699 |
| 49 | Birmingham-Hoover, AL | 3,723 | 113 | Huntsville, AL | 1,421 | 177 | Lawton, OK | 677 |
| 50 | Austin-Round Rock, TX | 3,609 | 114 | Santa Rosa, CA | 1,405 | 178 | College Station-Bryan, TX | 676 |
| 51 | Anaheim-Santa Ana-Irvine, CA M.D. | 3,574 | 115 | Beaumont-Port Arthur, TX | 1,398 | 179 | Columbus, GA-AL | 672 |
| 52 | Greenville-Anderson, SC | 3,530 | 116 | Hartford, CT | 1,366 | 180 | Pueblo, CO | 668 |
| 53 | New Orleans, LA | 3,511 | 117 | Gary, IN M.D. | 1,356 | 181 | Yuma, AZ | 662 |
| 54 | Warren-Troy, MI M.D. | 3,485 | 118 | Myrtle Beach, SC-NC | 1,296 | 182 | Lincoln, NE | 660 |
| 55 | Bakersfield, CA | 3,452 | 119 | Fayetteville-Springdale, AR-MO | 1,265 | 183 | Atlantic City, NJ | 659 |
| 56 | Fresno, CA | 3,427 | 120 | Silver Spring-Frederick, MD M.D. | 1,263 | 184 | Gulfport-Biloxi-Pascagoula, MS | 654 |
| 57 | Providence-Warwick, RI-MA | 3,412 | 121 | Merced, CA | 1,219 | 185 | Texarkana, TX-AR | 635 |
| 58 | Columbia, SC | 3,385 | 122 | Salisbury, MD-DE | 1,204 | 186 | Brownsville-Harlingen, TX | 633 |
| 59 | Portland-Vancouver, OR-WA | 3,361 | 123 | Lansing-East Lansing, MI | 1,181 | 187 | Longview, TX | 616 |
| 60 | Stockton-Lodi, CA | 3,321 | 124 | Des Moines-West Des Moines, IA | 1,177 | 188 | Salem, OR | 604 |
| 61 | Little Rock, AR | 3,266 | 125 | Vallejo-Fairfield, CA | 1,173 | 189 | York-Hanover, PA | 595 |
| 62 | Tulsa, OK | 3,240 | 126 | Port St. Lucie, FL | 1,134 | 190 | Wilmington, NC | 594 |
| 63 | Newark, NJ-PA M.D. | 3,070 | 127 | Bridgeport-Stamford, CT | 1,120 | 191 | Greeley, CO | 591 |
| 64 | Virginia Beach-Norfolk, VA-NC | 2,974 | 128 | Ocala, FL | 1,118 | 192 | Rocky Mount, NC | 589 |

Note: All listings are for Metropolitan Statistical Areas (M.S.A.s) except for those ending with "M.D." Listings with "M.D." are Metropolitan Divisions which are smaller parts of eleven large M.S.A.s. See explanatory note at beginning of metropolitan area section.

| RANK | METROPOLITAN AREA | ASSAULTS | RANK | METROPOLITAN AREA | ASSAULTS | RANK | METROPOLITAN AREA | ASSAULTS |
|---|---|---|---|---|---|---|---|---|
| 193 | Waco, TX | 584 | 255 | Cedar Rapids, IA | 362 | 317 | Terre Haute, IN | 186 |
| 194 | Topeka, KS | 581 | 256 | Rapid City, SD | 361 | 318 | Provo-Orem, UT | 185 |
| 195 | Naples-Marco Island, FL | 577 | 257 | Columbia, MO | 357 | 319 | Bloomsburg-Berwick, PA | 184 |
| 196 | Sumter, SC | 564 | 258 | Jefferson City, MO | 351 | 320 | St. Cloud, MN | 181 |
| 196 | Tuscaloosa, AL | 564 | 258 | Victoria, TX | 351 | 321 | Rochester, MN | 180 |
| 198 | Hanford-Corcoran, CA | 561 | 260 | Florence-Muscle Shoals, AL | 350 | 322 | Gainesville, GA | 172 |
| 198 | Manchester-Nashua, NH | 561 | 261 | Athens-Clarke County, GA | 349 | 323 | California-Lexington Park, MD | 171 |
| 200 | Savannah, GA | 554 | 262 | Cape Girardeau, MO-IL | 348 | 324 | Bay City, MI | 166 |
| 201 | Las Cruces, NM | 541 | 263 | Coeur d'Alene, ID | 345 | 325 | Ocean City, NJ | 165 |
| 202 | Johnson City, TN | 537 | 264 | Eugene, OR | 340 | 326 | Cheyenne, WY | 164 |
| 203 | Dover, DE | 532 | 265 | Olympia, WA | 338 | 327 | Fairbanks, AK | 161 |
| 204 | Greenville, NC | 530 | 266 | Flagstaff, AZ | 337 | 328 | Johnstown, PA | 159 |
| 205 | Medford, OR | 525 | 267 | Midland, TX | 336 | 329 | Hinesville, GA | 158 |
| 206 | East Stroudsburg, PA | 504 | 268 | Sebastian-Vero Beach, FL | 334 | 330 | Eau Claire, WI | 146 |
| 207 | Macon, GA | 497 | 268 | Wichita Falls, TX | 334 | 330 | Mount Vernon-Anacortes, WA | 146 |
| 208 | Ogden-Clearfield, UT | 496 | 270 | Lake Havasu City-Kingman, AZ | 322 | 332 | Idaho Falls, ID | 143 |
| 209 | Warner Robins, GA | 487 | 271 | Jonesboro, AR | 321 | 333 | Fond du Lac, WI | 142 |
| 210 | Muskegon, MI | 485 | 272 | Binghamton, NY | 315 | 333 | The Villages, FL | 142 |
| 211 | Bremerton-Silverdale, WA | 481 | 272 | Punta Gorda, FL | 315 | 335 | Winchester, VA-WV | 140 |
| 212 | Sioux Falls, SD | 475 | 274 | Iowa City, IA | 314 | 336 | Casper, WY | 138 |
| 213 | Fort Wayne, IN | 472 | 274 | Lynchburg, VA | 314 | 336 | Manhattan, KS | 138 |
| 214 | Farmington, NM | 465 | 276 | Daphne-Fairhope-Foley, AL | 311 | 338 | Lebanon, PA | 131 |
| 215 | Lexington-Fayette, KY | 463 | 276 | Decatur, IL | 311 | 338 | St. George, UT | 131 |
| 216 | Green Bay, WI | 461 | 278 | Kahului-Wailuku-Lahaina, HI | 307 | 340 | Great Falls, MT | 130 |
| 216 | Tyler, TX | 461 | 278 | Sioux City, IA-NE-SD | 307 | 340 | Kokomo, IN | 130 |
| 218 | Roanoke, VA | 455 | 280 | Hot Springs, AR | 306 | 342 | Grand Forks, ND-MN | 128 |
| 219 | Canton, OH | 448 | 281 | San Rafael, CA M.D. | 305 | 343 | Racine, WI | 126 |
| 220 | Anniston-Oxford, AL | 447 | 282 | Billings, MT | 302 | 344 | Staunton-Waynesboro, VA | 120 |
| 221 | Utica-Rome, NY | 445 | 283 | St. Joseph, MO-KS | 299 | 345 | Sheboygan, WI | 116 |
| 222 | Cleveland, TN | 444 | 284 | Napa, CA | 295 | 346 | Harrisonburg, VA | 114 |
| 223 | Fort Collins, CO | 440 | 284 | Sebring, FL | 295 | 347 | Carson City, NV | 112 |
| 223 | Niles-Benton Harbor, MI | 440 | 286 | Morristown, TN | 291 | 348 | Chambersburg-Waynesboro, PA | 111 |
| 225 | Prescott, AZ | 439 | 287 | Carbondale-Marion, IL | 279 | 348 | Watertown-Fort Drum, NY | 111 |
| 225 | Yakima, WA | 439 | 288 | Dalton, GA | 276 | 350 | La Crosse, WI-MN | 110 |
| 227 | Houma, LA | 432 | 289 | Bend, OR | 274 | 351 | Elmira, NY | 107 |
| 228 | Dutchess-Putnam, NY M.D. | 429 | 289 | Bloomington, IN | 274 | 352 | Williamsport, PA | 106 |
| 229 | Jackson, MI | 427 | 291 | Grand Junction, CO | 271 | 353 | Grand Island, NE | 104 |
| 229 | Vineland-Bridgeton, NJ | 427 | 292 | Lima, OH | 261 | 354 | Mankato-North Mankato, MN | 101 |
| 231 | Lancaster, PA | 424 | 293 | Rome, GA | 258 | 355 | Dubuque, IA | 100 |
| 232 | Homosassa Springs, FL | 422 | 294 | Pittsfield, MA | 254 | 356 | Columbus, IN | 99 |
| 233 | Portland, ME | 421 | 295 | Morgantown, WV | 252 | 357 | Glens Falls, NY | 96 |
| 234 | Boulder, CO | 420 | 296 | New Bern, NC | 251 | 358 | Wausau, WI | 89 |
| 235 | Kennewick-Richland, WA | 418 | 296 | Sherman-Denison, TX | 251 | 359 | Bowling Green, KY | 86 |
| 236 | Duluth, MN-WI | 414 | 298 | Charlottesville, VA | 240 | 360 | Grants Pass, OR | 85 |
| 237 | Bloomington, IL | 413 | 299 | Monroe, MI | 239 | 361 | State College, PA | 84 |
| 238 | Dothan, AL | 412 | 300 | Lawrence, KS | 238 | 362 | Lewiston, ID-WA | 81 |
| 239 | Burlington, NC | 410 | 301 | Appleton, WI | 227 | 363 | Ames, IA | 77 |
| 240 | Fargo, ND-MN | 402 | 301 | Janesville, WI | 227 | 364 | Lewiston-Auburn, ME | 72 |
| 241 | El Centro, CA | 400 | 303 | Oshkosh-Neenah, WI | 221 | 364 | Mansfield, OH | 72 |
| 242 | Bismarck, ND | 397 | 304 | Decatur, AL | 218 | 366 | Corvallis, OR | 66 |
| 242 | Gadsden, AL | 397 | 304 | Parkersburg-Vienna, WV | 218 | 367 | Elizabethtown-Fort Knox, KY | 58 |
| 244 | Chico, CA | 394 | 306 | Blacksburg, VA | 213 | 367 | Gettysburg, PA | 58 |
| 245 | Norwich-New London, CT | 393 | 306 | Missoula, MT | 213 | 369 | Bangor, ME | 55 |
| 246 | Abilene, TX | 388 | 308 | Kankakee, IL | 212 | 370 | Owensboro, KY | 53 |
| 247 | Rockingham County, NH M.D. | 383 | 309 | Kingston, NY | 208 | 371 | Logan, UT-ID | 38 |
| 248 | Joplin, MO | 378 | 310 | Altoona, PA | 199 | 372 | Albany, OR | 33 |
| 249 | Goldsboro, NC | 372 | 310 | Longview, WA | 199 | NA | Brunswick, GA** | NA |
| 249 | Lafayette, IN | 372 | 312 | Springfield, OH | 198 | NA | Chicago (greater), IL-IN-WI** | NA |
| 251 | Yuba City, CA | 370 | 313 | San Angelo, TX | 197 | NA | Chicago-Naperville, IL M.D.** | NA |
| 252 | South Bend-Mishawaka, IN-MI | 368 | 314 | Cumberland, MD-WV | 191 | NA | Indianapolis, IN** | NA |
| 253 | Erie, PA | 366 | 315 | Muncie, IN | 189 | NA | Louisville, KY-IN** | NA |
| 254 | Hagerstown-Martinsburg, MD-WV | 363 | 316 | Pocatello, ID | 187 | | | |

Source: Reported data from the F.B.I. "Crime in the United States 2013"

*Aggravated assault is an attack for the purpose of inflicting severe bodily injury.

**Not available.

# 22. Aggravated Assault Rate in 2013
## National Rate = 229.1 Aggravated Assaults per 100,000 Population*

| RANK | METROPOLITAN AREA | RATE | RANK | METROPOLITAN AREA | RATE | RANK | METROPOLITAN AREA | RATE |
|---|---|---|---|---|---|---|---|---|
| 164 | Abilene, TX | 230.8 | 243 | Cheyenne, WY | 171.5 | 218 | Gary, IN M.D. | 191.5 |
| 265 | Akron, OH | 154.9 | NA | Chicago (greater), IL-IN-WI** | NA | 364 | Gettysburg, PA | 57.2 |
| 251 | Albany-Schenectady-Troy, NY | 167.3 | NA | Chicago-Naperville, IL M.D.** | NA | 357 | Glens Falls, NY | 74.7 |
| 17 | Albany, GA | 484.2 | 236 | Chico, CA | 177.2 | 96 | Goldsboro, NC | 297.4 |
| 372 | Albany, OR | 27.7 | 311 | Cincinnati, OH-KY-IN | 120.9 | 302 | Grand Forks, ND-MN | 127.4 |
| 8 | Albuquerque, NM | 535.7 | 130 | Clarksville, TN-KY | 257.8 | 305 | Grand Island, NE | 123.6 |
| 6 | Alexandria, LA | 633.6 | 45 | Cleveland, TN | 374.5 | 229 | Grand Junction, CO | 181.6 |
| 336 | Allentown, PA-NJ | 96.8 | 156 | Coeur d'Alene, ID | 239.2 | 249 | Grand Rapids-Wyoming, MI | 168.6 |
| 261 | Altoona, PA | 156.6 | 104 | College Station-Bryan, TX | 285.0 | 331 | Grants Pass, OR | 102.2 |
| 63 | Amarillo, TX | 340.0 | 175 | Colorado Springs, CO | 221.0 | 259 | Great Falls, MT | 158.2 |
| 350 | Ames, IA | 83.8 | 195 | Columbia, MO | 209.1 | 178 | Greeley, CO | 220.0 |
| 318 | Anaheim-Santa Ana-Irvine, CA M.D. | 114.6 | 27 | Columbia, SC | 426.7 | 276 | Green Bay, WI | 147.4 |
| 14 | Anchorage, AK | 488.0 | 188 | Columbus, GA-AL | 212.8 | 185 | Greensboro-High Point, NC | 214.3 |
| 201 | Ann Arbor, MI | 203.9 | 305 | Columbus, IN | 123.6 | 30 | Greenville-Anderson, SC | 414.1 |
| 40 | Anniston-Oxford, AL | 382.4 | 44 | Corpus Christi, TX | 375.6 | 91 | Greenville, NC | 304.0 |
| 335 | Appleton, WI | 98.9 | 355 | Corvallis, OR | 75.9 | 245 | Gulfport-Biloxi-Pascagoula, MS | 171.0 |
| 237 | Athens-Clarke County, GA | 176.8 | 82 | Crestview-Fort Walton Beach, FL | 313.5 | 284 | Hagerstown-Martinsburg, MD-WV | 140.8 |
| 198 | Atlanta, GA | 205.6 | 223 | Cumberland, MD-WV | 187.9 | 2 | Hammond, LA | 694.0 |
| 157 | Atlantic City, NJ | 238.7 | 239 | Dallas (greater), TX | 175.8 | 50 | Hanford-Corcoran, CA | 370.9 |
| 274 | Augusta, GA-SC | 147.8 | 269 | Dallas-Plano-Irving, TX M.D. | 151.1 | 347 | Harrisonburg, VA | 87.9 |
| 217 | Austin-Round Rock, TX | 192.0 | 212 | Dalton, GA | 193.1 | 296 | Hartford, CT | 133.4 |
| 33 | Bakersfield, CA | 400.4 | 255 | Daphne-Fairhope-Foley, AL | 160.9 | 48 | Hilton Head Island, SC | 371.5 |
| 47 | Baltimore, MD | 372.5 | 131 | Davenport, IA-IL | 257.4 | 219 | Hinesville, GA | 190.4 |
| 369 | Bangor, ME | 35.8 | 317 | Dayton, OH | 114.9 | 92 | Homosassa Springs, FL | 303.1 |
| 56 | Barnstable Town, MA | 357.7 | 283 | Decatur, AL | 141.3 | 81 | Hot Springs, AR | 314.9 |
| 90 | Baton Rouge, LA | 307.6 | 107 | Decatur, IL | 283.0 | 196 | Houma, LA | 206.4 |
| 263 | Bay City, MI | 155.5 | 109 | Deltona-Daytona Beach, FL | 282.1 | 97 | Houston, TX | 296.8 |
| 62 | Beaumont-Port Arthur, TX | 344.3 | 213 | Denver-Aurora, CO | 193.0 | 71 | Huntsville, AL | 327.0 |
| 252 | Bend, OR | 166.9 | 205 | Des Moines-West Des Moines, IA | 197.4 | 329 | Idaho Falls, ID | 104.0 |
| 227 | Billings, MT | 183.2 | 61 | Detroit (greater), MI | 345.5 | NA | Indianapolis, IN** | NA |
| 303 | Binghamton, NY | 127.1 | 5 | Detroit-Dearborn-Livonia, MI M.D. | 635.9 | 207 | Iowa City, IA | 195.7 |
| 72 | Birmingham-Hoover, AL | 326.9 | 111 | Dothan, AL | 278.1 | 69 | Jacksonville, FL | 328.5 |
| 76 | Bismarck, ND | 319.5 | 83 | Dover, DE | 313.4 | 122 | Jackson, MI | 266.0 |
| 313 | Blacksburg, VA | 118.6 | 328 | Dubuque, IA | 104.4 | 246 | Jackson, MS | 169.7 |
| 181 | Bloomington, IL | 218.0 | 274 | Duluth, MN-WI | 147.8 | 1 | Jackson, TN | 743.7 |
| 250 | Bloomington, IN | 167.5 | 323 | Dutchess-Putnam, NY M.D. | 108.0 | 282 | Janesville, WI | 141.4 |
| 183 | Bloomsburg-Berwick, PA | 216.3 | 95 | East Stroudsburg, PA | 299.4 | 162 | Jefferson City, MO | 233.2 |
| 254 | Boise City, ID | 162.1 | 345 | Eau Claire, WI | 88.8 | 120 | Johnson City, TN | 266.6 |
| 166 | Boston (greater), MA-NH | 229.3 | 169 | El Centro, CA | 224.8 | 320 | Johnstown, PA | 112.9 |
| 80 | Boston, MA M.D. | 315.0 | 129 | El Paso, TX | 258.9 | 133 | Jonesboro, AR | 256.7 |
| 295 | Boulder, CO | 135.3 | 315 | Elgin, IL M.D. | 116.4 | 182 | Joplin, MO | 217.0 |
| 366 | Bowling Green, KY | 52.6 | 368 | Elizabethtown-Fort Knox, KY | 38.5 | 215 | Kahului-Wailuku-Lahaina, HI | 192.3 |
| 225 | Bremerton-Silverdale, WA | 187.2 | 312 | Elmira, NY | 120.2 | 223 | Kankakee, IL | 187.9 |
| 310 | Bridgeport-Stamford, CT | 121.6 | 298 | Erie, PA | 130.5 | 93 | Kansas City, MO-KS | 302.8 |
| 270 | Brownsville-Harlingen, TX | 150.7 | 338 | Eugene, OR | 95.4 | 266 | Kennewick-Richland, WA | 152.8 |
| NA | Brunswick, GA** | NA | 19 | Fairbanks, AK | 463.4 | 137 | Kingsport, TN-VA | 253.5 |
| 146 | Buffalo-Niagara Falls, NY | 250.1 | 231 | Fargo, ND-MN | 180.9 | 319 | Kingston, NY | 114.4 |
| 123 | Burlington, NC | 264.2 | 51 | Farmington, NM | 364.6 | 134 | Knoxville, TN | 256.6 |
| 264 | California-Lexington Park, MD | 155.0 | 128 | Fayetteville-Springdale, AR-MO | 259.2 | 262 | Kokomo, IN | 156.4 |
| 228 | Cambridge-Newton, MA M.D. | 182.7 | 134 | Fayetteville, NC | 256.6 | 352 | La Crosse, WI-MN | 80.9 |
| 235 | Camden, NJ M.D. | 177.6 | 150 | Flagstaff, AZ | 246.0 | 233 | Lafayette, IN | 178.4 |
| 322 | Canton, OH | 110.9 | 22 | Flint, MI | 457.7 | 67 | Lafayette, LA | 330.9 |
| 180 | Cape Coral-Fort Myers, FL | 218.2 | 158 | Florence-Muscle Shoals, AL | 238.3 | 29 | Lake Charles, LA | 421.3 |
| 57 | Cape Girardeau, MO-IL | 356.9 | 58 | Florence, SC | 348.5 | 349 | Lake Co.-Kenosha Co., IL-WI M.D. | 85.2 |
| 177 | Carbondale-Marion, IL | 220.2 | 285 | Fond du Lac, WI | 139.3 | 260 | Lake Havasu City-Kingman, AZ | 157.0 |
| 201 | Carson City, NV | 203.9 | 285 | Fort Collins, CO | 139.3 | 113 | Lakeland, FL | 272.0 |
| 241 | Casper, WY | 172.5 | 152 | Fort Lauderdale, FL M.D. | 241.4 | 353 | Lancaster, PA | 80.2 |
| 291 | Cedar Rapids, IA | 137.3 | 87 | Fort Smith, AR-OK | 310.0 | 138 | Lansing-East Lansing, MI | 253.0 |
| 359 | Chambersburg-Waynesboro, PA | 73.2 | 321 | Fort Wayne, IN | 111.3 | 77 | Laredo, TX | 318.7 |
| 68 | Champaign-Urbana, IL | 329.6 | 170 | Fort Worth-Arlington, TX M.D. | 224.1 | 144 | Las Cruces, NM | 251.5 |
| 139 | Charleston-North Charleston, SC | 252.8 | 53 | Fresno, CA | 359.1 | 35 | Las Vegas-Henderson, NV | 397.3 |
| 125 | Charlotte-Mecklenburg, NC-SC | 261.8 | 41 | Gadsden, AL | 380.5 | 194 | Lawrence, KS | 209.9 |
| 326 | Charlottesville, VA | 106.8 | 32 | Gainesville, FL | 407.7 | 13 | Lawton, OK | 507.3 |
| 36 | Chattanooga, TN-GA | 392.1 | 341 | Gainesville, GA | 91.8 | 337 | Lebanon, PA | 96.5 |

Note: All listings are for Metropolitan Statistical Areas (M.S.A.s) except for those ending with "M.D." Listings with "M.D." are Metropolitan Divisions which are smaller parts of eleven large M.S.A.s. See explanatory note at beginning of metropolitan area section.

| RANK | METROPOLITAN AREA | RATE | RANK | METROPOLITAN AREA | RATE | RANK | METROPOLITAN AREA | RATE |
|------|-------------------|------|------|-------------------|------|------|-------------------|------|
| 360 | Lewiston-Auburn, ME | 67.0 | 147 | Omaha-Council Bluffs, NE-IA | 248.6 | 332 | Sheboygan, WI | 100.9 |
| 297 | Lewiston, ID-WA | 131.0 | 49 | Orlando, FL | 371.3 | 200 | Sherman-Denison, TX | 204.5 |
| 339 | Lexington-Fayette, KY | 94.6 | 299 | Oshkosh-Neenah, WI | 130.4 | 36 | Shreveport-Bossier City, LA | 392.1 |
| 147 | Lima, OH | 248.6 | 367 | Owensboro, KY | 45.5 | 334 | Silver Spring-Frederick, MD M.D. | 100.4 |
| 193 | Lincoln, NE | 210.5 | 325 | Oxnard-Thousand Oaks, CA | 107.4 | 230 | Sioux City, IA-NE-SD | 181.2 |
| 23 | Little Rock, AR | 451.6 | 39 | Palm Bay-Melbourne, FL | 385.5 | 206 | Sioux Falls, SD | 196.6 |
| 371 | Logan, UT-ID | 29.3 | 42 | Panama City, FL | 378.0 | 316 | South Bend-Mishawaka, IN-MI | 115.3 |
| 108 | Longview, TX | 282.2 | 159 | Parkersburg-Vienna, WV | 235.9 | 73 | Spartanburg, SC | 323.3 |
| 210 | Longview, WA | 194.8 | 52 | Pensacola, FL | 363.4 | 214 | Spokane, WA | 192.7 |
| 189 | Los Angeles County, CA M.D. | 212.6 | 167 | Peoria, IL | 226.9 | 12 | Springfield, IL | 511.8 |
| 222 | Los Angeles (greater), CA | 189.3 | 132 | Philadelphia (greater) PA-NJ-MD-DE | 257.2 | 75 | Springfield, MA | 320.1 |
| NA | Louisville, KY-IN** | NA | 21 | Philadelphia, PA M.D. | 459.7 | 54 | Springfield, MO | 358.7 |
| 15 | Lubbock, TX | 486.8 | 151 | Phoenix-Mesa-Scottsdale, AZ | 242.8 | 281 | Springfield, OH | 144.4 |
| 309 | Lynchburg, VA | 122.3 | 221 | Pittsburgh, PA | 189.5 | 365 | State College, PA | 54.1 |
| 186 | Macon, GA | 213.4 | 208 | Pittsfield, MA | 195.4 | 333 | Staunton-Waynesboro, VA | 100.8 |
| 9 | Madera, CA | 532.2 | 173 | Pocatello, ID | 221.3 | 18 | Stockton-Lodi, CA | 468.6 |
| 300 | Madison, WI | 129.9 | 127 | Port St. Lucie, FL | 259.6 | 340 | St. Cloud, MN | 94.5 |
| 288 | Manchester-Nashua, NH | 138.9 | 279 | Portland-Vancouver, OR-WA | 145.2 | 346 | St. George, UT | 88.6 |
| 288 | Manhattan, KS | 138.9 | 351 | Portland, ME | 81.1 | 163 | St. Joseph, MO-KS | 232.8 |
| 330 | Mankato-North Mankato, MN | 102.3 | 199 | Prescott, AZ | 204.9 | 102 | St. Louis, MO-IL | 287.4 |
| 363 | Mansfield, OH | 58.8 | 189 | Providence-Warwick, RI-MA | 212.6 | 10 | Sumter, SC | 518.8 |
| 204 | McAllen-Edinburg-Mission, TX | 202.7 | 370 | Provo-Orem, UT | 32.9 | 257 | Syracuse, NY | 159.0 |
| 140 | Medford, OR | 252.5 | 31 | Pueblo, CO | 411.6 | 101 | Tacoma, WA M.D. | 287.7 |
| 3 | Memphis, TN-MS-AR | 680.0 | 216 | Punta Gorda, FL | 192.2 | 34 | Tallahassee, FL | 398.8 |
| 20 | Merced, CA | 460.9 | 362 | Racine, WI | 64.7 | 116 | Tampa-St Petersburg, FL | 270.5 |
| 85 | Miami (greater), FL | 311.9 | 292 | Raleigh, NC | 136.0 | 324 | Terre Haute, IN | 107.5 |
| 46 | Miami-Dade County, FL M.D. | 373.9 | 136 | Rapid City, SD | 256.2 | 28 | Texarkana, TX-AR | 422.7 |
| 184 | Midland, TX | 215.7 | 248 | Reading, PA | 168.9 | 293 | The Villages, FL | 135.7 |
| 86 | Milwaukee, WI | 311.2 | 16 | Redding, CA | 486.6 | 78 | Toledo, OH | 317.7 |
| 287 | Minneapolis-St. Paul, MN-WI | 139.2 | 140 | Reno, NV | 252.5 | 149 | Topeka, KS | 247.7 |
| 220 | Missoula, MT | 190.1 | 304 | Richmond, VA | 126.8 | 197 | Trenton, NJ | 206.3 |
| 43 | Mobile, AL | 376.5 | 203 | Riverside-San Bernardino, CA | 203.2 | 115 | Tucson, AZ | 270.6 |
| 60 | Modesto, CA | 346.2 | 277 | Roanoke, VA | 146.1 | 64 | Tulsa, OK | 337.5 |
| 26 | Monroe, LA | 427.9 | 348 | Rochester, MN | 85.3 | 154 | Tuscaloosa, AL | 240.7 |
| 258 | Monroe, MI | 158.4 | 272 | Rochester, NY | 148.5 | 191 | Tyler, TX | 212.2 |
| 358 | Montgomery County, PA M.D. | 74.1 | 11 | Rockford, IL | 513.3 | 271 | Utica-Rome, NY | 149.3 |
| 226 | Morgantown, WV | 186.2 | 343 | Rockingham County, NH M.D. | 90.4 | 112 | Vallejo-Fairfield, CA | 276.9 |
| 142 | Morristown, TN | 252.3 | 38 | Rocky Mount, NC | 387.9 | 55 | Victoria, TX | 358.5 |
| 308 | Mount Vernon-Anacortes, WA | 122.7 | 119 | Rome, GA | 268.4 | 117 | Vineland-Bridgeton, NJ | 269.8 |
| 256 | Muncie, IN | 160.7 | 124 | Sacramento, CA | 262.0 | 240 | Virginia Beach-Norfolk, VA-NC | 173.9 |
| 103 | Muskegon, MI | 285.7 | 7 | Saginaw, MI | 562.0 | 59 | Visalia-Porterville, CA | 347.9 |
| 74 | Myrtle Beach, SC-NC | 322.7 | 267 | Salem, OR | 151.4 | 168 | Waco, TX | 226.2 |
| 192 | Napa, CA | 210.7 | 161 | Salinas, CA | 234.4 | 126 | Warner Robins, GA | 260.1 |
| 244 | Naples-Marco Island, FL | 171.2 | 84 | Salisbury, MD-DE | 312.5 | 290 | Warren-Troy, MI M.D. | 138.8 |
| 24 | Nashville-Davidson, TN | 434.6 | 187 | Salt Lake City, UT | 213.1 | 253 | Washington (greater) DC-VA-MD-WV | 163.8 |
| 356 | Nassau-Suffolk, NY M.D. | 74.8 | 247 | San Angelo, TX | 169.5 | 232 | Washington, DC-VA-MD-WV M.D. | 180.8 |
| 210 | New Bern, NC | 194.8 | 88 | San Antonio, TX | 308.9 | 342 | Watertown-Fort Drum, NY | 91.2 |
| 209 | New Haven-Milford, CT | 195.2 | 165 | San Diego, CA | 230.3 | 361 | Wausau, WI | 65.9 |
| 106 | New Orleans, LA | 283.3 | 155 | San Francisco (greater), CA | 240.2 | 100 | West Palm Beach, FL M.D. | 288.0 |
| 174 | New York (greater), NY-NJ-PA | 221.2 | 153 | San Francisco-Redwood, CA M.D. | 240.8 | 176 | Wichita Falls, TX | 220.8 |
| 114 | New York-Jersey City, NY-NJ M.D. | 271.2 | 280 | San Jose, CA | 145.1 | 25 | Wichita, KS | 434.4 |
| 307 | Newark, NJ-PA M.D. | 122.9 | 79 | San Luis Obispo, CA | 316.8 | 344 | Williamsport, PA | 90.3 |
| 109 | Niles-Benton Harbor, MI | 282.1 | 314 | San Rafael, CA M.D. | 118.5 | 98 | Wilmington, DE-MD-NJ M.D. | 296.5 |
| 99 | North Port-Sarasota-Bradenton, FL | 290.2 | 121 | Santa Cruz-Watsonville, CA | 266.2 | 172 | Wilmington, NC | 222.6 |
| 118 | Norwich-New London, CT | 268.9 | 171 | Santa Maria-Santa Barbara, CA | 223.9 | 327 | Winchester, VA-WV | 106.2 |
| 143 | Oakland-Hayward, CA M.D. | 251.6 | 105 | Santa Rosa, CA | 283.9 | 145 | Winston-Salem, NC | 251.0 |
| 66 | Ocala, FL | 331.1 | 268 | Savannah, GA | 151.2 | 89 | Worcester, MA-CT | 307.8 |
| 242 | Ocean City, NJ | 171.6 | 273 | Scranton--Wilkes-Barre, PA | 148.1 | 238 | Yakima, WA | 176.5 |
| 4 | Odessa, TX | 645.0 | 234 | Seattle (greater), WA | 177.8 | 293 | York-Hanover, PA | 135.7 |
| 354 | Ogden-Clearfield, UT | 79.9 | 278 | Seattle-Bellevue-Everett, WA M.D. | 145.3 | 179 | Yuba City, CA | 219.7 |
| 65 | Oklahoma City, OK | 335.5 | 160 | Sebastian-Vero Beach, FL | 235.4 | 70 | Yuma, AZ | 327.9 |
| 301 | Olympia, WA | 129.5 | 94 | Sebring, FL | 300.1 | | | |

Source: Reported data from the F.B.I. "Crime in the United States 2013"

*Aggravated assault is an attack for the purpose of inflicting severe bodily injury.

**Not available.

# 22. Aggravated Assault Rate in 2013 (continued)
## National Rate = 229.1 Aggravated Assaults per 100,000 Population*

| RANK | METROPOLITAN AREA | RATE | RANK | METROPOLITAN AREA | RATE | RANK | METROPOLITAN AREA | RATE |
|---|---|---|---|---|---|---|---|---|
| 1 | Jackson, TN | 743.7 | 65 | Oklahoma City, OK | 335.5 | 129 | El Paso, TX | 258.9 |
| 2 | Hammond, LA | 694.0 | 66 | Ocala, FL | 331.1 | 130 | Clarksville, TN-KY | 257.8 |
| 3 | Memphis, TN-MS-AR | 680.0 | 67 | Lafayette, LA | 330.9 | 131 | Davenport, IA-IL | 257.4 |
| 4 | Odessa, TX | 645.0 | 68 | Champaign-Urbana, IL | 329.6 | 132 | Philadelphia (greater) PA-NJ-MD-DE | 257.2 |
| 5 | Detroit-Dearborn-Livonia, MI M.D. | 635.9 | 69 | Jacksonville, FL | 328.5 | 133 | Jonesboro, AR | 256.7 |
| 6 | Alexandria, LA | 633.6 | 70 | Yuma, AZ | 327.9 | 134 | Fayetteville, NC | 256.6 |
| 7 | Saginaw, MI | 562.0 | 71 | Huntsville, AL | 327.0 | 134 | Knoxville, TN | 256.6 |
| 8 | Albuquerque, NM | 535.7 | 72 | Birmingham-Hoover, AL | 326.9 | 136 | Rapid City, SD | 256.2 |
| 9 | Madera, CA | 532.2 | 73 | Spartanburg, SC | 323.3 | 137 | Kingsport, TN-VA | 253.5 |
| 10 | Sumter, SC | 518.8 | 74 | Myrtle Beach, SC-NC | 322.7 | 138 | Lansing-East Lansing, MI | 253.0 |
| 11 | Rockford, IL | 513.3 | 75 | Springfield, MA | 320.1 | 139 | Charleston-North Charleston, SC | 252.8 |
| 12 | Springfield, IL | 511.8 | 76 | Bismarck, ND | 319.5 | 140 | Medford, OR | 252.5 |
| 13 | Lawton, OK | 507.3 | 77 | Laredo, TX | 318.7 | 140 | Reno, NV | 252.5 |
| 14 | Anchorage, AK | 488.0 | 78 | Toledo, OH | 317.7 | 142 | Morristown, TN | 252.3 |
| 15 | Lubbock, TX | 486.8 | 79 | San Luis Obispo, CA | 316.8 | 143 | Oakland-Hayward, CA M.D. | 251.6 |
| 16 | Redding, CA | 486.5 | 80 | Boston, MA M.D. | 315.0 | 144 | Las Cruces, NM | 251.5 |
| 17 | Albany, GA | 484.2 | 81 | Hot Springs, AR | 314.9 | 145 | Winston-Salem, NC | 251.0 |
| 18 | Stockton-Lodi, CA | 468.6 | 82 | Crestview-Fort Walton Beach, FL | 313.5 | 146 | Buffalo-Niagara Falls, NY | 250.1 |
| 19 | Fairbanks, AK | 463.4 | 83 | Dover, DE | 313.4 | 147 | Lima, OH | 248.6 |
| 20 | Merced, CA | 460.9 | 84 | Salisbury, MD-DE | 312.5 | 147 | Omaha-Council Bluffs, NE-IA | 248.6 |
| 21 | Philadelphia, PA M.D. | 459.7 | 85 | Miami (greater), FL | 311.9 | 149 | Topeka, KS | 247.7 |
| 22 | Flint, MI | 457.7 | 86 | Milwaukee, WI | 311.2 | 150 | Flagstaff, AZ | 246.0 |
| 23 | Little Rock, AR | 451.6 | 87 | Fort Smith, AR-OK | 310.0 | 151 | Phoenix-Mesa-Scottsdale, AZ | 242.8 |
| 24 | Nashville-Davidson, TN | 434.6 | 88 | San Antonio, TX | 308.9 | 152 | Fort Lauderdale, FL M.D. | 241.4 |
| 25 | Wichita, KS | 434.4 | 89 | Worcester, MA-CT | 307.8 | 153 | San Francisco-Redwood, CA M.D. | 240.8 |
| 26 | Monroe, LA | 427.9 | 90 | Baton Rouge, LA | 307.6 | 154 | Tuscaloosa, AL | 240.7 |
| 27 | Columbia, SC | 426.7 | 91 | Greenville, NC | 304.0 | 155 | San Francisco (greater), CA | 240.2 |
| 28 | Texarkana, TX-AR | 422.7 | 92 | Homosassa Springs, FL | 303.1 | 156 | Coeur d'Alene, ID | 239.2 |
| 29 | Lake Charles, LA | 421.3 | 93 | Kansas City, MO-KS | 302.8 | 157 | Atlantic City, NJ | 238.7 |
| 30 | Greenville-Anderson, SC | 414.1 | 94 | Sebring, FL | 300.1 | 158 | Florence-Muscle Shoals, AL | 238.3 |
| 31 | Pueblo, CO | 411.6 | 95 | East Stroudsburg, PA | 299.4 | 159 | Parkersburg-Vienna, WV | 235.9 |
| 32 | Gainesville, FL | 407.7 | 96 | Goldsboro, NC | 297.4 | 160 | Sebastian-Vero Beach, FL | 235.4 |
| 33 | Bakersfield, CA | 400.4 | 97 | Houston, TX | 296.8 | 161 | Salinas, CA | 234.4 |
| 34 | Tallahassee, FL | 398.8 | 98 | Wilmington, DE-MD-NJ M.D. | 296.5 | 162 | Jefferson City, MO | 233.2 |
| 35 | Las Vegas-Henderson, NV | 397.3 | 99 | North Port-Sarasota-Bradenton, FL | 290.2 | 163 | St. Joseph, MO-KS | 232.8 |
| 36 | Chattanooga, TN-GA | 392.1 | 100 | West Palm Beach, FL M.D. | 288.0 | 164 | Abilene, TX | 230.8 |
| 36 | Shreveport-Bossier City, LA | 392.1 | 101 | Tacoma, WA M.D. | 287.7 | 165 | San Diego, CA | 230.3 |
| 38 | Rocky Mount, NC | 387.9 | 102 | St. Louis, MO-IL | 287.4 | 166 | Boston (greater), MA-NH | 229.3 |
| 39 | Palm Bay-Melbourne, FL | 385.5 | 103 | Muskegon, MI | 285.7 | 167 | Peoria, IL | 226.9 |
| 40 | Anniston-Oxford, AL | 382.4 | 104 | College Station-Bryan, TX | 285.0 | 168 | Waco, TX | 226.2 |
| 41 | Gadsden, AL | 380.5 | 105 | Santa Rosa, CA | 283.9 | 169 | El Centro, CA | 224.8 |
| 42 | Panama City, FL | 378.0 | 106 | New Orleans, LA | 283.3 | 170 | Fort Worth-Arlington, TX M.D. | 224.1 |
| 43 | Mobile, AL | 376.5 | 107 | Decatur, IL | 283.0 | 171 | Santa Maria-Santa Barbara, CA | 223.9 |
| 44 | Corpus Christi, TX | 375.6 | 108 | Longview, TX | 282.2 | 172 | Wilmington, NC | 222.6 |
| 45 | Cleveland, TN | 374.5 | 109 | Deltona-Daytona Beach, FL | 282.1 | 173 | Pocatello, ID | 221.3 |
| 46 | Miami-Dade County, FL M.D. | 373.9 | 109 | Niles-Benton Harbor, MI | 282.1 | 174 | New York (greater), NY-NJ-PA | 221.2 |
| 47 | Baltimore, MD | 372.5 | 111 | Dothan, AL | 278.1 | 175 | Colorado Springs, CO | 221.0 |
| 48 | Hilton Head Island, SC | 371.5 | 112 | Vallejo-Fairfield, CA | 276.9 | 176 | Wichita Falls, TX | 220.8 |
| 49 | Orlando, FL | 371.3 | 113 | Lakeland, FL | 272.0 | 177 | Carbondale-Marion, IL | 220.2 |
| 50 | Hanford-Corcoran, CA | 370.9 | 114 | New York-Jersey City, NY-NJ M.D. | 271.2 | 178 | Greeley, CO | 220.0 |
| 51 | Farmington, NM | 364.6 | 115 | Tucson, AZ | 270.6 | 179 | Yuba City, CA | 219.7 |
| 52 | Pensacola, FL | 363.4 | 116 | Tampa-St Petersburg, FL | 270.5 | 180 | Cape Coral-Fort Myers, FL | 218.2 |
| 53 | Fresno, CA | 359.1 | 117 | Vineland-Bridgeton, NJ | 269.8 | 181 | Bloomington, IL | 218.0 |
| 54 | Springfield, MO | 358.7 | 118 | Norwich-New London, CT | 268.9 | 182 | Joplin, MO | 217.0 |
| 55 | Victoria, TX | 358.5 | 119 | Rome, GA | 268.4 | 183 | Bloomsburg-Berwick, PA | 216.3 |
| 56 | Barnstable Town, MA | 357.7 | 120 | Johnson City, TN | 266.6 | 184 | Midland, TX | 215.7 |
| 57 | Cape Girardeau, MO-IL | 356.9 | 121 | Santa Cruz-Watsonville, CA | 266.2 | 185 | Greensboro-High Point, NC | 214.3 |
| 58 | Florence, SC | 348.5 | 122 | Jackson, MI | 266.0 | 186 | Macon, GA | 213.4 |
| 59 | Visalia-Porterville, CA | 347.9 | 123 | Burlington, NC | 264.2 | 187 | Salt Lake City, UT | 213.1 |
| 60 | Modesto, CA | 346.2 | 124 | Sacramento, CA | 262.0 | 188 | Columbus, GA-AL | 212.8 |
| 61 | Detroit (greater), MI | 345.5 | 125 | Charlotte-Mecklenburg, NC-SC | 261.8 | 189 | Los Angeles County, CA M.D. | 212.6 |
| 62 | Beaumont-Port Arthur, TX | 344.3 | 126 | Warner Robins, GA | 260.1 | 189 | Providence-Warwick, RI-MA | 212.6 |
| 63 | Amarillo, TX | 340.0 | 127 | Port St. Lucie, FL | 259.6 | 191 | Tyler, TX | 212.2 |
| 64 | Tulsa, OK | 337.5 | 128 | Fayetteville-Springdale, AR-MO | 259.2 | 192 | Napa, CA | 210.7 |

Note: All listings are for Metropolitan Statistical Areas (M.S.A.s) except for those ending with "M.D." Listings with "M.D." are Metropolitan Divisions which are smaller parts of eleven large M.S.A.s. See explanatory note at beginning of metropolitan area section.

| RANK | METROPOLITAN AREA | RATE | RANK | METROPOLITAN AREA | RATE | RANK | METROPOLITAN AREA | RATE |
|---|---|---|---|---|---|---|---|---|
| 193 | Lincoln, NE | 210.5 | 255 | Daphne-Fairhope-Foley, AL | 160.9 | 317 | Dayton, OH | 114.9 |
| 194 | Lawrence, KS | 209.9 | 256 | Muncie, IN | 160.7 | 318 | Anaheim-Santa Ana-Irvine, CA M.D. | 114.6 |
| 195 | Columbia, MO | 209.1 | 257 | Syracuse, NY | 159.0 | 319 | Kingston, NY | 114.4 |
| 196 | Houma, LA | 206.4 | 258 | Monroe, MI | 158.4 | 320 | Johnstown, PA | 112.9 |
| 197 | Trenton, NJ | 206.3 | 259 | Great Falls, MT | 158.2 | 321 | Fort Wayne, IN | 111.3 |
| 198 | Atlanta, GA | 205.6 | 260 | Lake Havasu City-Kingman, AZ | 157.0 | 322 | Canton, OH | 110.9 |
| 199 | Prescott, AZ | 204.9 | 261 | Altoona, PA | 156.6 | 323 | Dutchess-Putnam, NY M.D. | 108.0 |
| 200 | Sherman-Denison, TX | 204.5 | 262 | Kokomo, IN | 156.4 | 324 | Terre Haute, IN | 107.5 |
| 201 | Ann Arbor, MI | 203.9 | 263 | Bay City, MI | 155.5 | 325 | Oxnard-Thousand Oaks, CA | 107.4 |
| 201 | Carson City, NV | 203.9 | 264 | California-Lexington Park, MD | 155.0 | 326 | Charlottesville, VA | 106.8 |
| 203 | Riverside-San Bernardino, CA | 203.2 | 265 | Akron, OH | 154.9 | 327 | Winchester, VA-WV | 106.2 |
| 204 | McAllen-Edinburg-Mission, TX | 202.7 | 266 | Kennewick-Richland, WA | 152.8 | 328 | Dubuque, IA | 104.4 |
| 205 | Des Moines-West Des Moines, IA | 197.4 | 267 | Salem, OR | 151.4 | 329 | Idaho Falls, ID | 104.0 |
| 206 | Sioux Falls, SD | 196.6 | 268 | Savannah, GA | 151.2 | 330 | Mankato-North Mankato, MN | 102.3 |
| 207 | Iowa City, IA | 195.7 | 269 | Dallas-Plano-Irving, TX M.D. | 151.1 | 331 | Grants Pass, OR | 102.2 |
| 208 | Pittsfield, MA | 195.4 | 270 | Brownsville-Harlingen, TX | 150.7 | 332 | Sheboygan, WI | 100.9 |
| 209 | New Haven-Milford, CT | 195.2 | 271 | Utica-Rome, NY | 149.3 | 333 | Staunton-Waynesboro, VA | 100.8 |
| 210 | Longview, WA | 194.8 | 272 | Rochester, NY | 148.5 | 334 | Silver Spring-Frederick, MD M.D. | 100.4 |
| 210 | New Bern, NC | 194.8 | 273 | Scranton--Wilkes-Barre, PA | 148.1 | 335 | Appleton, WI | 98.9 |
| 212 | Dalton, GA | 193.1 | 274 | Augusta, GA-SC | 147.8 | 336 | Allentown, PA-NJ | 96.8 |
| 213 | Denver-Aurora, CO | 193.0 | 274 | Duluth, MN-WI | 147.8 | 337 | Lebanon, PA | 96.5 |
| 214 | Spokane, WA | 192.7 | 276 | Green Bay, WI | 147.4 | 338 | Eugene, OR | 95.4 |
| 215 | Kahului-Wailuku-Lahaina, HI | 192.3 | 277 | Roanoke, VA | 146.1 | 339 | Lexington-Fayette, KY | 94.6 |
| 216 | Punta Gorda, FL | 192.2 | 278 | Seattle-Bellevue-Everett, WA M.D. | 145.3 | 340 | St. Cloud, MN | 94.5 |
| 217 | Austin-Round Rock, TX | 192.0 | 279 | Portland-Vancouver, OR-WA | 145.2 | 341 | Gainesville, GA | 91.8 |
| 218 | Gary, IN M.D. | 191.5 | 280 | San Jose, CA | 145.1 | 342 | Watertown-Fort Drum, NY | 91.2 |
| 219 | Hinesville, GA | 190.4 | 281 | Springfield, OH | 144.4 | 343 | Rockingham County, NH M.D. | 90.4 |
| 220 | Missoula, MT | 190.1 | 282 | Janesville, WI | 141.4 | 344 | Williamsport, PA | 90.3 |
| 221 | Pittsburgh, PA | 189.5 | 283 | Decatur, AL | 141.3 | 345 | Eau Claire, WI | 88.8 |
| 222 | Los Angeles (greater), CA | 189.3 | 284 | Hagerstown-Martinsburg, MD-WV | 140.8 | 346 | St. George, UT | 88.6 |
| 223 | Cumberland, MD-WV | 187.9 | 285 | Fond du Lac, WI | 139.3 | 347 | Harrisonburg, VA | 87.9 |
| 223 | Kankakee, IL | 187.9 | 285 | Fort Collins, CO | 139.3 | 348 | Rochester, MN | 85.3 |
| 225 | Bremerton-Silverdale, WA | 187.2 | 287 | Minneapolis-St. Paul, MN-WI | 139.2 | 349 | Lake Co.-Kenosha Co., IL-WI M.D. | 85.2 |
| 226 | Morgantown, WV | 186.2 | 288 | Manchester-Nashua, NH | 138.9 | 350 | Ames, IA | 83.8 |
| 227 | Billings, MT | 183.2 | 288 | Manhattan, KS | 138.9 | 351 | Portland, ME | 81.1 |
| 228 | Cambridge-Newton, MA M.D. | 182.7 | 290 | Warren-Troy, MI M.D. | 138.8 | 352 | La Crosse, WI-MN | 80.9 |
| 229 | Grand Junction, CO | 181.6 | 291 | Cedar Rapids, IA | 137.3 | 353 | Lancaster, PA | 80.2 |
| 230 | Sioux City, IA-NE-SD | 181.2 | 292 | Raleigh, NC | 136.0 | 354 | Ogden-Clearfield, UT | 79.9 |
| 231 | Fargo, ND-MN | 180.9 | 293 | The Villages, FL | 135.7 | 355 | Corvallis, OR | 75.9 |
| 232 | Washington, DC-VA-MD-WV M.D. | 180.8 | 293 | York-Hanover, PA | 135.7 | 356 | Nassau-Suffolk, NY M.D. | 74.8 |
| 233 | Lafayette, IN | 178.4 | 295 | Boulder, CO | 135.3 | 357 | Glens Falls, NY | 74.7 |
| 234 | Seattle (greater), WA | 177.8 | 296 | Hartford, CT | 133.4 | 358 | Montgomery County, PA M.D. | 74.1 |
| 235 | Camden, NJ M.D. | 177.6 | 297 | Lewiston, ID-WA | 131.0 | 359 | Chambersburg-Waynesboro, PA | 73.2 |
| 236 | Chico, CA | 177.2 | 298 | Erie, PA | 130.5 | 360 | Lewiston-Auburn, ME | 67.0 |
| 237 | Athens-Clarke County, GA | 176.8 | 299 | Oshkosh-Neenah, WI | 130.4 | 361 | Wausau, WI | 65.9 |
| 238 | Yakima, WA | 176.5 | 300 | Madison, WI | 129.9 | 362 | Racine, WI | 64.7 |
| 239 | Dallas (greater), TX | 175.8 | 301 | Olympia, WA | 129.5 | 363 | Mansfield, OH | 58.8 |
| 240 | Virginia Beach-Norfolk, VA-NC | 173.9 | 302 | Grand Forks, ND-MN | 127.4 | 364 | Gettysburg, PA | 57.2 |
| 241 | Casper, WY | 172.5 | 303 | Binghamton, NY | 127.1 | 365 | State College, PA | 54.1 |
| 242 | Ocean City, NJ | 171.6 | 304 | Richmond, VA | 126.8 | 366 | Bowling Green, KY | 52.6 |
| 243 | Cheyenne, WY | 171.5 | 305 | Columbus, IN | 123.6 | 367 | Owensboro, KY | 45.5 |
| 244 | Naples-Marco Island, FL | 171.2 | 305 | Grand Island, NE | 123.6 | 368 | Elizabethtown-Fort Knox, KY | 38.5 |
| 245 | Gulfport-Biloxi-Pascagoula, MS | 171.0 | 307 | Newark, NJ-PA M.D. | 122.9 | 369 | Bangor, ME | 35.8 |
| 246 | Jackson, MS | 169.7 | 308 | Mount Vernon-Anacortes, WA | 122.7 | 370 | Provo-Orem, UT | 32.9 |
| 247 | San Angelo, TX | 169.5 | 309 | Lynchburg, VA | 122.3 | 371 | Logan, UT-ID | 29.3 |
| 248 | Reading, PA | 168.9 | 310 | Bridgeport-Stamford, CT | 121.6 | 372 | Albany, OR | 27.7 |
| 249 | Grand Rapids-Wyoming, MI | 168.6 | 311 | Cincinnati, OH-KY-IN | 120.9 | NA | Brunswick, GA** | NA |
| 250 | Bloomington, IN | 167.5 | 312 | Elmira, NY | 120.2 | NA | Chicago (greater), IL-IN-WI** | NA |
| 251 | Albany-Schenectady-Troy, NY | 167.3 | 313 | Blacksburg, VA | 118.6 | NA | Chicago-Naperville, IL M.D.** | NA |
| 252 | Bend, OR | 166.9 | 314 | San Rafael, CA M.D. | 118.5 | NA | Indianapolis, IN** | NA |
| 253 | Washington (greater) DC-VA-MD-WV | 163.8 | 315 | Elgin, IL M.D. | 116.4 | NA | Louisville, KY-IN** | NA |
| 254 | Boise City, ID | 162.1 | 316 | South Bend-Mishawaka, IN-MI | 115.3 | | | |

Source: Reported data from the F.B.I. "Crime in the United States 2013"
*Aggravated assault is an attack for the purpose of inflicting severe bodily injury.
**Not available.

# 23. Percent Change in Aggravated Assault Rate: 2012 to 2013
## National Percent Change = 5.6% Decrease*

| RANK | METROPOLITAN AREA | % CHANGE | RANK | METROPOLITAN AREA | % CHANGE | RANK | METROPOLITAN AREA | % CHANGE |
|---|---|---|---|---|---|---|---|---|
| 44 | Abilene, TX | 5.1 | 106 | Cheyenne, WY | (2.3) | 70 | Gary, IN M.D. | 0.7 |
| 207 | Akron, OH | (8.7) | NA | Chicago (greater), IL-IN-WI** | NA | NA | Gettysburg, PA** | NA |
| 73 | Albany-Schenectady-Troy, NY | 0.5 | NA | Chicago-Naperville, IL M.D.** | NA | 334 | Glens Falls, NY | (34.5) |
| 68 | Albany, GA | 0.9 | 205 | Chico, CA | (8.6) | 154 | Goldsboro, NC | (5.7) |
| 338 | Albany, OR | (54.2) | 52 | Cincinnati, OH-KY-IN | 3.2 | 295 | Grand Forks, ND-MN | (18.0) |
| 17 | Albuquerque, NM | 16.1 | 319 | Clarksville, TN-KY | (23.7) | 244 | Grand Island, NE | (12.1) |
| NA | Alexandria, LA** | NA | 306 | Cleveland, TN | (19.2) | 257 | Grand Junction, CO | (13.2) |
| 154 | Allentown, PA-NJ | (5.7) | 85 | Coeur d'Alene, ID | (0.3) | NA | Grand Rapids-Wyoming, MI** | NA |
| 270 | Altoona, PA | (14.4) | 208 | College Station-Bryan, TX | (8.8) | NA | Grants Pass, OR** | NA |
| 185 | Amarillo, TX | (7.7) | 90 | Colorado Springs, CO | (1.1) | 234 | Great Falls, MT | (11.3) |
| 118 | Ames, IA | (3.3) | 240 | Columbia, MO | (11.9) | 132 | Greeley, CO | (4.5) |
| 281 | Anaheim-Santa Ana-Irvine, CA M.D. | (16.0) | NA | Columbia, SC** | NA | 277 | Green Bay, WI | (15.6) |
| 234 | Anchorage, AK | (11.3) | 259 | Columbus, GA-AL | (13.3) | 165 | Greensboro-High Point, NC | (6.3) |
| 50 | Ann Arbor, MI | 3.5 | 38 | Columbus, IN | 6.1 | 175 | Greenville-Anderson, SC | (6.9) |
| 227 | Anniston-Oxford, AL | (10.3) | 188 | Corpus Christi, TX | (7.8) | 15 | Greenville, NC | 17.6 |
| 289 | Appleton, WI | (17.4) | 25 | Corvallis, OR | 13.3 | NA | Gulfport-Biloxi-Pascagoula, MS** | NA |
| 179 | Athens-Clarke County, GA | (7.1) | 277 | Crestview-Fort Walton Beach, FL | (15.6) | 246 | Hagerstown-Martinsburg, MD-WV | (12.5) |
| 224 | Atlanta, GA | (9.9) | 329 | Cumberland, MD-WV | (26.5) | 185 | Hammond, LA | (7.7) |
| NA | Atlantic City, NJ** | NA | 205 | Dallas (greater), TX | (8.6) | 131 | Hanford-Corcoran, CA | (4.4) |
| 112 | Augusta, GA-SC | (2.9) | 208 | Dallas-Plano-Irving, TX M.D. | (8.8) | 73 | Harrisonburg, VA | 0.5 |
| 125 | Austin-Round Rock, TX | (3.8) | 182 | Dalton, GA | (7.2) | 232 | Hartford, CT | (11.2) |
| 73 | Bakersfield, CA | 0.5 | 211 | Daphne-Fairhope-Foley, AL | (9.1) | 129 | Hilton Head Island, SC | (4.3) |
| 84 | Baltimore, MD | (0.2) | 165 | Davenport, IA-IL | (6.3) | 295 | Hinesville, GA | (18.0) |
| 33 | Bangor, ME | 8.2 | 179 | Dayton, OH | (7.1) | 21 | Homosassa Springs, FL | 15.6 |
| 58 | Barnstable Town, MA | 2.5 | 326 | Decatur, AL | (24.9) | NA | Hot Springs, AR** | NA |
| NA | Baton Rouge, LA** | NA | 20 | Decatur, IL | 15.7 | 103 | Houma, LA | (2.2) |
| 310 | Bay City, MI | (21.0) | 193 | Deltona-Daytona Beach, FL | (7.9) | 136 | Houston, TX | (4.7) |
| 67 | Beaumont-Port Arthur, TX | 1.0 | 162 | Denver-Aurora, CO | (6.1) | 221 | Huntsville, AL | (9.8) |
| NA | Bend, OR** | NA | 147 | Des Moines-West Des Moines, IA | (5.4) | 251 | Idaho Falls, ID | (12.8) |
| 268 | Billings, MT | (14.2) | 149 | Detroit (greater), MI | (5.5) | NA | Indianapolis, IN** | NA |
| 325 | Binghamton, NY | (24.6) | 112 | Detroit-Dearborn-Livonia, MI M.D. | (2.9) | 96 | Iowa City, IA | (1.5) |
| 232 | Birmingham-Hoover, AL | (11.2) | 37 | Dothan, AL | 6.8 | 196 | Jacksonville, FL | (8.2) |
| 23 | Bismarck, ND | 14.8 | 321 | Dover, DE | (24.2) | NA | Jackson, MI** | NA |
| 42 | Blacksburg, VA | 5.6 | 136 | Dubuque, IA | (4.7) | 142 | Jackson, MS | (5.1) |
| 134 | Bloomington, IL | (4.6) | 175 | Duluth, MN-WI | (6.9) | 109 | Jackson, TN | (2.5) |
| 103 | Bloomington, IN | (2.2) | 281 | Dutchess-Putnam, NY M.D. | (16.0) | 158 | Janesville, WI | (5.9) |
| 1 | Bloomsburg-Berwick, PA | 95.6 | 94 | East Stroudsburg, PA | (1.4) | 196 | Jefferson City, MO | (8.2) |
| 71 | Boise City, ID | 0.6 | NA | Eau Claire, WI** | NA | 71 | Johnson City, TN | 0.6 |
| 121 | Boston (greater), MA-NH | (3.5) | 36 | El Centro, CA | 7.1 | 332 | Johnstown, PA | (31.1) |
| 89 | Boston, MA M.D. | (0.5) | 275 | El Paso, TX | (15.5) | 13 | Jonesboro, AR | 20.8 |
| 156 | Boulder, CO | (5.8) | 83 | Elgin, IL M.D. | 0.0 | 295 | Joplin, MO | (18.0) |
| 271 | Bowling Green, KY | (14.5) | 6 | Elizabethtown-Fort Knox, KY | 29.6 | 9 | Kahului-Wailuku-Lahaina, HI | 23.6 |
| 66 | Bremerton-Silverdale, WA | 1.1 | 335 | Elmira, NY | (36.8) | 242 | Kankakee, IL | (12.0) |
| 255 | Bridgeport-Stamford, CT | (13.1) | 77 | Erie, PA | 0.4 | 184 | Kansas City, MO-KS | (7.6) |
| 263 | Brownsville-Harlingen, TX | (13.5) | 321 | Eugene, OR | (24.2) | 188 | Kennewick-Richland, WA | (7.8) |
| NA | Brunswick, GA** | NA | 4 | Fairbanks, AK | 43.2 | 303 | Kingsport, TN-VA | (18.5) |
| 108 | Buffalo-Niagara Falls, NY | (2.4) | 109 | Fargo, ND-MN | (2.5) | 77 | Kingston, NY | 0.4 |
| 293 | Burlington, NC | (17.7) | 331 | Farmington, NM | (28.5) | 262 | Knoxville, TN | (13.4) |
| 259 | California-Lexington Park, MD | (13.3) | 250 | Fayetteville-Springdale, AR-MO | (12.7) | 125 | Kokomo, IN | (3.8) |
| 188 | Cambridge-Newton, MA M.D. | (7.8) | 132 | Fayetteville, NC | (4.5) | NA | La Crosse, WI-MN** | NA |
| 144 | Camden, NJ M.D. | (5.2) | 128 | Flagstaff, AZ | (4.2) | 248 | Lafayette, IN | (12.6) |
| 145 | Canton, OH | (5.3) | 320 | Flint, MI | (23.9) | NA | Lafayette, LA** | NA |
| 203 | Cape Coral-Fort Myers, FL | (8.5) | 156 | Florence-Muscle Shoals, AL | (5.8) | NA | Lake Charles, LA** | NA |
| 40 | Cape Girardeau, MO-IL | 5.7 | 275 | Florence, SC | (15.5) | 165 | Lake Co.-Kenosha Co., IL-WI M.D. | (6.3) |
| NA | Carbondale-Marion, IL** | NA | 284 | Fond du Lac, WI | (16.6) | 14 | Lake Havasu City-Kingman, AZ | 20.3 |
| 116 | Carson City, NV | (3.0) | 310 | Fort Collins, CO | (21.0) | 38 | Lakeland, FL | 6.1 |
| 54 | Casper, WY | 2.8 | 216 | Fort Lauderdale, FL M.D. | (9.5) | NA | Lancaster, PA** | NA |
| 8 | Cedar Rapids, IA | 24.7 | 145 | Fort Smith, AR-OK | (5.3) | 48 | Lansing-East Lansing, MI | 4.1 |
| NA | Chambersburg-Waynesboro, PA** | NA | 87 | Fort Wayne, IN | (0.4) | 102 | Laredo, TX | (1.9) |
| 196 | Champaign-Urbana, IL | (8.2) | 196 | Fort Worth-Arlington, TX M.D. | (8.2) | 64 | Las Cruces, NM | 1.3 |
| 272 | Charleston-North Charleston, SC | (14.8) | 96 | Fresno, CA | (1.5) | 202 | Las Vegas-Henderson, NV | (8.3) |
| NA | Charlotte-Mecklenburg, NC-SC** | NA | 50 | Gadsden, AL | 3.5 | 312 | Lawrence, KS | (21.4) |
| 112 | Charlottesville, VA | (2.9) | 149 | Gainesville, FL | (5.5) | 185 | Lawton, OK | (7.7) |
| NA | Chattanooga, TN-GA** | NA | 196 | Gainesville, GA | (8.2) | 333 | Lebanon, PA | (33.1) |

Note: All listings are for Metropolitan Statistical Areas (M.S.A.s) except for those ending with "M.D." Listings with "M.D." are Metropolitan Divisions which are smaller parts of eleven large M.S.A.s. See explanatory note at beginning of metropolitan area section.

| RANK | METROPOLITAN AREA | % CHANGE | RANK | METROPOLITAN AREA | % CHANGE | RANK | METROPOLITAN AREA | % CHANGE |
|---|---|---|---|---|---|---|---|---|
| 2 | Lewiston-Auburn, ME | 53.3 | 122 | Omaha-Council Bluffs, NE-IA | (3.6) | 295 | Sheboygan, WI | (18.0) |
| 103 | Lewiston, ID-WA | (2.2) | 134 | Orlando, FL | (4.6) | 29 | Sherman-Denison, TX | 10.5 |
| 290 | Lexington-Fayette, KY | (17.5) | 303 | Oshkosh-Neenah, WI | (18.5) | NA | Shreveport-Bossier City, LA** | NA |
| 327 | Lima, OH | (26.1) | 308 | Owensboro, KY | (20.3) | 152 | Silver Spring-Frederick, MD M.D. | (5.6) |
| 161 | Lincoln, NE | (6.0) | 111 | Oxnard-Thousand Oaks, CA | (2.6) | 17 | Sioux City, IA-NE-SD | 16.1 |
| 60 | Little Rock, AR | 2.2 | 136 | Palm Bay-Melbourne, FL | (4.7) | 129 | Sioux Falls, SD | (4.3) |
| 221 | Logan, UT-ID | (9.8) | 47 | Panama City, FL | 4.3 | 307 | South Bend-Mishawaka, IN-MI | (19.9) |
| 179 | Longview, TX | (7.1) | 237 | Parkersburg-Vienna, WV | (11.6) | 79 | Spartanburg, SC | 0.3 |
| 7 | Longview, WA | 25.2 | 269 | Pensacola, FL | (14.3) | 73 | Spokane, WA | 0.5 |
| 194 | Los Angeles County, CA M.D. | (8.0) | 290 | Peoria, IL | (17.5) | 33 | Springfield, IL | 8.2 |
| 213 | Los Angeles (greater), CA | (9.3) | NA | Philadelphia (greater) PA-NJ-MD-DE** | NA | 118 | Springfield, MA | (3.3) |
| NA | Louisville, KY-IN** | NA | NA | Philadelphia, PA M.D.** | NA | 54 | Springfield, MO | 2.8 |
| 252 | Lubbock, TX | (12.9) | 96 | Phoenix-Mesa-Scottsdale, AZ | (1.5) | 16 | Springfield, OH | 16.3 |
| 19 | Lynchburg, VA | 15.9 | NA | Pittsburgh, PA** | NA | 188 | State College, PA | (7.8) |
| 173 | Macon, GA | (6.8) | 314 | Pittsfield, MA | (22.1) | 300 | Staunton-Waynesboro, VA | (18.3) |
| 32 | Madera, CA | 8.4 | 10 | Pocatello, ID | 21.9 | 295 | Stockton-Lodi, CA | (18.0) |
| NA | Madison, WI** | NA | 40 | Port St. Lucie, FL | 5.7 | NA | St. Cloud, MN** | NA |
| 112 | Manchester-Nashua, NH | (2.9) | 158 | Portland-Vancouver, OR-WA | (5.9) | 323 | St. George, UT | (24.3) |
| 317 | Manhattan, KS | (23.0) | 12 | Portland, ME | 21.4 | 43 | St. Joseph, MO-KS | 5.5 |
| 280 | Mankato-North Mankato, MN | (15.9) | 328 | Prescott, AZ | (26.3) | 216 | St. Louis, MO-IL | (9.5) |
| 195 | Mansfield, OH | (8.1) | 122 | Providence-Warwick, RI-MA | (3.6) | 292 | Sumter, SC | (17.6) |
| 248 | McAllen-Edinburg-Mission, TX | (12.6) | 315 | Provo-Orem, UT | (22.6) | 288 | Syracuse, NY | (17.3) |
| 62 | Medford, OR | 1.5 | 27 | Pueblo, CO | 11.8 | 53 | Tacoma, WA M.D. | 3.1 |
| 139 | Memphis, TN-MS-AR | (4.8) | 182 | Punta Gorda, FL | (7.2) | 85 | Tallahassee, FL | (0.3) |
| 273 | Merced, CA | (15.2) | 337 | Racine, WI | (40.2) | 149 | Tampa-St Petersburg, FL | (5.5) |
| 188 | Miami (greater), FL | (7.8) | 227 | Raleigh, NC | (10.3) | 48 | Terre Haute, IN | 4.1 |
| 173 | Miami-Dade County, FL M.D. | (6.8) | 35 | Rapid City, SD | 8.0 | 324 | Texarkana, TX-AR | (24.4) |
| 286 | Midland, TX | (16.8) | 229 | Reading, PA | (10.7) | 57 | The Villages, FL | 2.6 |
| 142 | Milwaukee, WI | (5.1) | 273 | Redding, CA | (15.2) | 257 | Toledo, OH | (13.2) |
| 99 | Minneapolis-St. Paul, MN-WI | (1.6) | 210 | Reno, NV | (9.0) | 246 | Topeka, KS | (12.5) |
| 252 | Missoula, MT | (12.9) | 100 | Richmond, VA | (1.8) | 164 | Trenton, NJ | (6.2) |
| 45 | Mobile, AL | 4.5 | 225 | Riverside-San Bernardino, CA | (10.2) | 169 | Tucson, AZ | (6.4) |
| 152 | Modesto, CA | (5.6) | 279 | Roanoke, VA | (15.8) | 171 | Tulsa, OK | (6.7) |
| 5 | Monroe, LA | 29.8 | 31 | Rochester, MN | 8.5 | 218 | Tuscaloosa, AL | (9.6) |
| 117 | Monroe, MI | (3.1) | 171 | Rochester, NY | (6.7) | 330 | Tyler, TX | (27.6) |
| 252 | Montgomery County, PA M.D. | (12.9) | 69 | Rockford, IL | 0.8 | 242 | Utica-Rome, NY | (12.0) |
| 294 | Morgantown, WV | (17.9) | 92 | Rockingham County, NH M.D. | (1.2) | 28 | Vallejo-Fairfield, CA | 11.2 |
| 265 | Morristown, TN | (13.7) | 305 | Rocky Mount, NC | (19.1) | 245 | Victoria, TX | (12.2) |
| 81 | Mount Vernon-Anacortes, WA | 0.2 | 100 | Rome, GA | (1.8) | 286 | Vineland-Bridgeton, NJ | (16.8) |
| 92 | Muncie, IN | (1.2) | 170 | Sacramento, CA | (6.5) | 61 | Virginia Beach-Norfolk, VA-NC | 1.6 |
| NA | Muskegon, MI** | NA | 213 | Saginaw, MI | (9.3) | 90 | Visalia-Porterville, CA | (1.1) |
| NA | Myrtle Beach, SC-NC** | NA | 158 | Salem, OR | (5.9) | 283 | Waco, TX | (16.3) |
| 318 | Napa, CA | (23.1) | 106 | Salinas, CA | (2.3) | 94 | Warner Robins, GA | (1.4) |
| 221 | Naples-Marco Island, FL | (9.8) | 147 | Salisbury, MD-DE | (5.4) | 230 | Warren-Troy, MI M.D. | (10.9) |
| 255 | Nashville-Davidson, TN | (13.1) | 54 | Salt Lake City, UT | 2.8 | 63 | Washington (greater) DC-VA-MD-WV | 1.4 |
| 285 | Nassau-Suffolk, NY M.D. | (16.7) | NA | San Angelo, TX** | NA | 59 | Washington, DC-VA-MD-WV M.D. | 2.4 |
| 211 | New Bern, NC | (9.1) | 11 | San Antonio, TX | 21.6 | 336 | Watertown-Fort Drum, NY | (39.6) |
| 266 | New Haven-Milford, CT | (13.9) | 175 | San Diego, CA | (6.9) | 313 | Wausau, WI | (21.5) |
| 140 | New Orleans, LA | (4.9) | 140 | San Francisco (greater), CA | (4.9) | 196 | West Palm Beach, FL M.D. | (8.2) |
| NA | New York (greater), NY-NJ-PA** | NA | 24 | San Francisco-Redwood, CA M.D. | 14.1 | 225 | Wichita Falls, TX | (10.2) |
| NA | New York-Jersey City, NY-NJ M.D.** | NA | 215 | San Jose, CA | (9.4) | 30 | Wichita, KS | 9.3 |
| 165 | Newark, NJ-PA M.D. | (6.3) | 22 | San Luis Obispo, CA | 15.5 | 45 | Williamsport, PA | 4.5 |
| NA | Niles-Benton Harbor, MI** | NA | 79 | San Rafael, CA M.D. | 0.3 | 218 | Wilmington, DE-MD-NJ M.D. | (9.6) |
| 220 | North Port-Sarasota-Bradenton, FL | (9.7) | 120 | Santa Cruz-Watsonville, CA | (3.4) | 82 | Wilmington, NC | 0.1 |
| 238 | Norwich-New London, CT | (11.7) | 300 | Santa Maria-Santa Barbara, CA | (18.3) | 308 | Winchester, VA-WV | (20.3) |
| 259 | Oakland-Hayward, CA M.D. | (13.3) | 87 | Santa Rosa, CA | (0.4) | 264 | Winston-Salem, NC | (13.6) |
| 240 | Ocala, FL | (11.9) | 65 | Savannah, GA | 1.2 | 122 | Worcester, MA-CT | (3.6) |
| 230 | Ocean City, NJ | (10.9) | NA | Scranton--Wilkes-Barre, PA** | NA | 316 | Yakima, WA | (22.7) |
| 127 | Odessa, TX | (4.0) | 203 | Seattle (greater), WA | (8.5) | 239 | York-Hanover, PA | (11.8) |
| 162 | Ogden-Clearfield, UT | (6.1) | 267 | Seattle-Bellevue-Everett, WA M.D. | (14.0) | 302 | Yuba City, CA | (18.4) |
| 236 | Oklahoma City, OK | (11.5) | 175 | Sebastian-Vero Beach, FL | (6.9) | 26 | Yuma, AZ | 12.5 |
| NA | Olympia, WA** | NA | 3 | Sebring, FL | 50.1 | | | |

Source: CQ Press using reported data from the F.B.I. "Crime in the United States 2013"

*Aggravated assault is an attack for the purpose of inflicting severe bodily injury.

**Not available.

# 23. Percent Change in Aggravated Assault Rate: 2012 to 2013 (continued)
## National Percent Change = 5.6% Decrease*

| RANK | METROPOLITAN AREA | % CHANGE | RANK | METROPOLITAN AREA | % CHANGE | RANK | METROPOLITAN AREA | % CHANGE |
|---|---|---|---|---|---|---|---|---|
| 1 | Bloomsburg-Berwick, PA | 95.6 | 65 | Savannah, GA | 1.2 | 129 | Hilton Head Island, SC | (4.3) |
| 2 | Lewiston-Auburn, ME | 53.3 | 66 | Bremerton-Silverdale, WA | 1.1 | 129 | Sioux Falls, SD | (4.3) |
| 3 | Sebring, FL | 50.1 | 67 | Beaumont-Port Arthur, TX | 1.0 | 131 | Hanford-Corcoran, CA | (4.4) |
| 4 | Fairbanks, AK | 43.2 | 68 | Albany, GA | 0.9 | 132 | Fayetteville, NC | (4.5) |
| 5 | Monroe, LA | 29.8 | 69 | Rockford, IL | 0.8 | 132 | Greeley, CO | (4.5) |
| 6 | Elizabethtown-Fort Knox, KY | 29.6 | 70 | Gary, IN M.D. | 0.7 | 134 | Bloomington, IL | (4.6) |
| 7 | Longview, WA | 25.2 | 71 | Boise City, ID | 0.6 | 134 | Orlando, FL | (4.6) |
| 8 | Cedar Rapids, IA | 24.7 | 71 | Johnson City, TN | 0.6 | 136 | Dubuque, IA | (4.7) |
| 9 | Kahului-Wailuku-Lahaina, HI | 23.6 | 73 | Albany-Schenectady-Troy, NY | 0.5 | 136 | Houston, TX | (4.7) |
| 10 | Pocatello, ID | 21.9 | 73 | Bakersfield, CA | 0.5 | 136 | Palm Bay-Melbourne, FL | (4.7) |
| 11 | San Antonio, TX | 21.6 | 73 | Harrisonburg, VA | 0.5 | 139 | Memphis, TN-MS-AR | (4.8) |
| 12 | Portland, ME | 21.4 | 73 | Spokane, WA | 0.5 | 140 | New Orleans, LA | (4.9) |
| 13 | Jonesboro, AR | 20.8 | 77 | Erie, PA | 0.4 | 140 | San Francisco (greater), CA | (4.9) |
| 14 | Lake Havasu City-Kingman, AZ | 20.3 | 77 | Kingston, NY | 0.4 | 142 | Jackson, MS | (5.1) |
| 15 | Greenville, NC | 17.6 | 79 | San Rafael, CA M.D. | 0.3 | 142 | Milwaukee, WI | (5.1) |
| 16 | Springfield, OH | 16.3 | 79 | Spartanburg, SC | 0.3 | 144 | Camden, NJ M.D. | (5.2) |
| 17 | Albuquerque, NM | 16.1 | 81 | Mount Vernon-Anacortes, WA | 0.2 | 145 | Canton, OH | (5.3) |
| 17 | Sioux City, IA-NE-SD | 16.1 | 82 | Wilmington, NC | 0.1 | 145 | Fort Smith, AR-OK | (5.3) |
| 19 | Lynchburg, VA | 15.9 | 83 | Elgin, IL M.D. | 0.0 | 147 | Des Moines-West Des Moines, IA | (5.4) |
| 20 | Decatur, IL | 15.7 | 84 | Baltimore, MD | (0.2) | 147 | Salisbury, MD-DE | (5.4) |
| 21 | Homosassa Springs, FL | 15.6 | 85 | Coeur d'Alene, ID | (0.3) | 149 | Detroit (greater), MI | (5.5) |
| 22 | San Luis Obispo, CA | 15.5 | 85 | Tallahassee, FL | (0.3) | 149 | Gainesville, FL | (5.5) |
| 23 | Bismarck, ND | 14.8 | 87 | Fort Wayne, IN | (0.4) | 149 | Tampa-St Petersburg, FL | (5.5) |
| 24 | San Francisco-Redwood, CA M.D. | 14.1 | 87 | Santa Rosa, CA | (0.4) | 152 | Modesto, CA | (5.6) |
| 25 | Corvallis, OR | 13.3 | 89 | Boston, MA M.D. | (0.5) | 152 | Silver Spring-Frederick, MD M.D. | (5.6) |
| 26 | Yuma, AZ | 12.5 | 90 | Colorado Springs, CO | (1.1) | 154 | Allentown, PA-NJ | (5.7) |
| 27 | Pueblo, CO | 11.8 | 90 | Visalia-Porterville, CA | (1.1) | 154 | Goldsboro, NC | (5.7) |
| 28 | Vallejo-Fairfield, CA | 11.2 | 92 | Muncie, IN | (1.2) | 156 | Boulder, CO | (5.8) |
| 29 | Sherman-Denison, TX | 10.5 | 92 | Rockingham County, NH M.D. | (1.2) | 156 | Florence-Muscle Shoals, AL | (5.8) |
| 30 | Wichita, KS | 9.3 | 94 | East Stroudsburg, PA | (1.4) | 158 | Janesville, WI | (5.9) |
| 31 | Rochester, MN | 8.5 | 94 | Warner Robins, GA | (1.4) | 158 | Portland-Vancouver, OR-WA | (5.9) |
| 32 | Madera, CA | 8.4 | 96 | Fresno, CA | (1.5) | 158 | Salem, OR | (5.9) |
| 33 | Bangor, ME | 8.2 | 96 | Iowa City, IA | (1.5) | 161 | Lincoln, NE | (6.0) |
| 33 | Springfield, IL | 8.2 | 96 | Phoenix-Mesa-Scottsdale, AZ | (1.5) | 162 | Denver-Aurora, CO | (6.1) |
| 35 | Rapid City, SD | 8.0 | 99 | Minneapolis-St. Paul, MN-WI | (1.6) | 162 | Ogden-Clearfield, UT | (6.1) |
| 36 | El Centro, CA | 7.1 | 100 | Richmond, VA | (1.8) | 164 | Trenton, NJ | (6.2) |
| 37 | Dothan, AL | 6.8 | 100 | Rome, GA | (1.8) | 165 | Davenport, IA-IL | (6.3) |
| 38 | Columbus, IN | 6.1 | 102 | Laredo, TX | (1.9) | 165 | Greensboro-High Point, NC | (6.3) |
| 38 | Lakeland, FL | 6.1 | 103 | Bloomington, IN | (2.2) | 165 | Lake Co.-Kenosha Co., IL-WI M.D. | (6.3) |
| 40 | Cape Girardeau, MO-IL | 5.7 | 103 | Houma, LA | (2.2) | 165 | Newark, NJ-PA M.D. | (6.3) |
| 40 | Port St. Lucie, FL | 5.7 | 103 | Lewiston, ID-WA | (2.2) | 169 | Tucson, AZ | (6.4) |
| 42 | Blacksburg, VA | 5.6 | 106 | Cheyenne, WY | (2.3) | 170 | Sacramento, CA | (6.5) |
| 43 | St. Joseph, MO-KS | 5.5 | 106 | Salinas, CA | (2.3) | 171 | Rochester, NY | (6.7) |
| 44 | Abilene, TX | 5.1 | 108 | Buffalo-Niagara Falls, NY | (2.4) | 171 | Tulsa, OK | (6.7) |
| 45 | Mobile, AL | 4.5 | 109 | Fargo, ND-MN | (2.5) | 173 | Macon, GA | (6.8) |
| 45 | Williamsport, PA | 4.5 | 109 | Jackson, TN | (2.5) | 173 | Miami-Dade County, FL M.D. | (6.8) |
| 47 | Panama City, FL | 4.3 | 111 | Oxnard-Thousand Oaks, CA | (2.6) | 175 | Duluth, MN-WI | (6.9) |
| 48 | Lansing-East Lansing, MI | 4.1 | 112 | Augusta, GA-SC | (2.9) | 175 | Greenville-Anderson, SC | (6.9) |
| 48 | Terre Haute, IN | 4.1 | 112 | Charlottesville, VA | (2.9) | 175 | San Diego, CA | (6.9) |
| 50 | Ann Arbor, MI | 3.5 | 112 | Detroit-Dearborn-Livonia, MI M.D. | (2.9) | 175 | Sebastian-Vero Beach, FL | (6.9) |
| 50 | Gadsden, AL | 3.5 | 112 | Manchester-Nashua, NH | (2.9) | 179 | Athens-Clarke County, GA | (7.1) |
| 52 | Cincinnati, OH-KY-IN | 3.2 | 116 | Carson City, NV | (3.0) | 179 | Dayton, OH | (7.1) |
| 53 | Tacoma, WA M.D. | 3.1 | 117 | Monroe, MI | (3.1) | 179 | Longview, TX | (7.1) |
| 54 | Casper, WY | 2.8 | 118 | Ames, IA | (3.3) | 182 | Dalton, GA | (7.2) |
| 54 | Salt Lake City, UT | 2.8 | 118 | Springfield, MA | (3.3) | 182 | Punta Gorda, FL | (7.2) |
| 54 | Springfield, MO | 2.8 | 120 | Santa Cruz-Watsonville, CA | (3.4) | 184 | Kansas City, MO-KS | (7.6) |
| 57 | The Villages, FL | 2.6 | 121 | Boston (greater), MA-NH | (3.5) | 185 | Amarillo, TX | (7.7) |
| 58 | Barnstable Town, MA | 2.5 | 122 | Omaha-Council Bluffs, NE-IA | (3.6) | 185 | Hammond, LA | (7.7) |
| 59 | Washington, DC-VA-MD-WV M.D. | 2.4 | 122 | Providence-Warwick, RI-MA | (3.6) | 185 | Lawton, OK | (7.7) |
| 60 | Little Rock, AR | 2.2 | 122 | Worcester, MA-CT | (3.6) | 188 | Cambridge-Newton, MA M.D. | (7.8) |
| 61 | Virginia Beach-Norfolk, VA-NC | 1.6 | 125 | Austin-Round Rock, TX | (3.8) | 188 | Corpus Christi, TX | (7.8) |
| 62 | Medford, OR | 1.5 | 125 | Kokomo, IN | (3.8) | 188 | Kennewick-Richland, WA | (7.8) |
| 63 | Washington (greater) DC-VA-MD-WV | 1.4 | 127 | Odessa, TX | (4.0) | 188 | Miami (greater), FL | (7.8) |
| 64 | Las Cruces, NM | 1.3 | 128 | Flagstaff, AZ | (4.2) | 188 | State College, PA | (7.8) |

Note: All listings are for Metropolitan Statistical Areas (M.S.A.s) except for those ending with "M.D." Listings with "M.D." are Metropolitan Divisions which are smaller parts of eleven large M.S.A.s. See explanatory note at beginning of metropolitan area section.

| RANK | METROPOLITAN AREA | % CHANGE | RANK | METROPOLITAN AREA | % CHANGE | RANK | METROPOLITAN AREA | % CHANGE |
|---|---|---|---|---|---|---|---|---|
| 193 | Deltona-Daytona Beach, FL | (7.9) | 255 | Bridgeport-Stamford, CT | (13.1) | 317 | Manhattan, KS | (23.0) |
| 194 | Los Angeles County, CA M.D. | (8.0) | 255 | Nashville-Davidson, TN | (13.1) | 318 | Napa, CA | (23.1) |
| 195 | Mansfield, OH | (8.1) | 257 | Grand Junction, CO | (13.2) | 319 | Clarksville, TN-KY | (23.7) |
| 196 | Champaign-Urbana, IL | (8.2) | 257 | Toledo, OH | (13.2) | 320 | Flint, MI | (23.9) |
| 196 | Fort Worth-Arlington, TX M.D. | (8.2) | 259 | California-Lexington Park, MD | (13.3) | 321 | Dover, DE | (24.2) |
| 196 | Gainesville, GA | (8.2) | 259 | Columbus, GA-AL | (13.3) | 321 | Eugene, OR | (24.2) |
| 196 | Jacksonville, FL | (8.2) | 259 | Oakland-Hayward, CA M.D. | (13.3) | 323 | St. George, UT | (24.3) |
| 196 | Jefferson City, MO | (8.2) | 262 | Knoxville, TN | (13.4) | 324 | Texarkana, TX-AR | (24.4) |
| 196 | West Palm Beach, FL M.D. | (8.2) | 263 | Brownsville-Harlingen, TX | (13.5) | 325 | Binghamton, NY | (24.6) |
| 202 | Las Vegas-Henderson, NV | (8.3) | 264 | Winston-Salem, NC | (13.6) | 326 | Decatur, AL | (24.9) |
| 203 | Cape Coral-Fort Myers, FL | (8.5) | 265 | Morristown, TN | (13.7) | 327 | Lima, OH | (26.1) |
| 203 | Seattle (greater), WA | (8.5) | 266 | New Haven-Milford, CT | (13.9) | 328 | Prescott, AZ | (26.3) |
| 205 | Chico, CA | (8.6) | 267 | Seattle-Bellevue-Everett, WA M.D. | (14.0) | 329 | Cumberland, MD-WV | (26.5) |
| 205 | Dallas (greater), TX | (8.6) | 268 | Billings, MT | (14.2) | 330 | Tyler, TX | (27.6) |
| 207 | Akron, OH | (8.7) | 269 | Pensacola, FL | (14.3) | 331 | Farmington, NM | (28.5) |
| 208 | College Station-Bryan, TX | (8.8) | 270 | Altoona, PA | (14.4) | 332 | Johnstown, PA | (31.1) |
| 208 | Dallas-Plano-Irving, TX M.D. | (8.8) | 271 | Bowling Green, KY | (14.5) | 333 | Lebanon, PA | (33.1) |
| 210 | Reno, NV | (9.0) | 272 | Charleston-North Charleston, SC | (14.8) | 334 | Glens Falls, NY | (34.5) |
| 211 | Daphne-Fairhope-Foley, AL | (9.1) | 273 | Merced, CA | (15.2) | 335 | Elmira, NY | (36.8) |
| 211 | New Bern, NC | (9.1) | 273 | Redding, CA | (15.2) | 336 | Watertown-Fort Drum, NY | (39.6) |
| 213 | Los Angeles (greater), CA | (9.3) | 275 | El Paso, TX | (15.5) | 337 | Racine, WI | (40.2) |
| 213 | Saginaw, MI | (9.3) | 275 | Florence, SC | (15.5) | 338 | Albany, OR | (54.2) |
| 215 | San Jose, CA | (9.4) | 277 | Crestview-Fort Walton Beach, FL | (15.6) | NA | Alexandria, LA** | NA |
| 216 | Fort Lauderdale, FL M.D. | (9.5) | 277 | Green Bay, WI | (15.6) | NA | Atlantic City, NJ** | NA |
| 216 | St. Louis, MO-IL | (9.5) | 279 | Roanoke, VA | (15.8) | NA | Baton Rouge, LA** | NA |
| 218 | Tuscaloosa, AL | (9.6) | 280 | Mankato-North Mankato, MN | (15.9) | NA | Bend, OR** | NA |
| 218 | Wilmington, DE-MD-NJ M.D. | (9.6) | 281 | Anaheim-Santa Ana-Irvine, CA M.D. | (16.0) | NA | Brunswick, GA** | NA |
| 220 | North Port-Sarasota-Bradenton, FL | (9.7) | 281 | Dutchess-Putnam, NY M.D. | (16.0) | NA | Carbondale-Marion, IL** | NA |
| 221 | Huntsville, AL | (9.8) | 283 | Waco, TX | (16.3) | NA | Chambersburg-Waynesboro, PA** | NA |
| 221 | Logan, UT-ID | (9.8) | 284 | Fond du Lac, WI | (16.6) | NA | Charlotte-Mecklenburg, NC-SC** | NA |
| 221 | Naples-Marco Island, FL | (9.8) | 285 | Nassau-Suffolk, NY M.D. | (16.7) | NA | Chattanooga, TN-GA** | NA |
| 224 | Atlanta, GA | (9.9) | 286 | Midland, TX | (16.8) | NA | Chicago (greater), IL-IN-WI** | NA |
| 225 | Riverside-San Bernardino, CA | (10.2) | 286 | Vineland-Bridgeton, NJ | (16.8) | NA | Chicago-Naperville, IL M.D.** | NA |
| 225 | Wichita Falls, TX | (10.2) | 288 | Syracuse, NY | (17.3) | NA | Columbia, SC** | NA |
| 227 | Anniston-Oxford, AL | (10.3) | 289 | Appleton, WI | (17.4) | NA | Eau Claire, WI** | NA |
| 227 | Raleigh, NC | (10.3) | 290 | Lexington-Fayette, KY | (17.5) | NA | Gettysburg, PA** | NA |
| 229 | Reading, PA | (10.7) | 290 | Peoria, IL | (17.5) | NA | Grand Rapids-Wyoming, MI** | NA |
| 230 | Ocean City, NJ | (10.9) | 292 | Sumter, SC | (17.6) | NA | Grants Pass, OR** | NA |
| 230 | Warren-Troy, MI M.D. | (10.9) | 293 | Burlington, NC | (17.7) | NA | Gulfport-Biloxi-Pascagoula, MS** | NA |
| 232 | Birmingham-Hoover, AL | (11.2) | 294 | Morgantown, WV | (17.9) | NA | Hot Springs, AR** | NA |
| 232 | Hartford, CT | (11.2) | 295 | Grand Forks, ND-MN | (18.0) | NA | Indianapolis, IN** | NA |
| 234 | Anchorage, AK | (11.3) | 295 | Hinesville, GA | (18.0) | NA | Jackson, MI** | NA |
| 234 | Great Falls, MT | (11.3) | 295 | Joplin, MO | (18.0) | NA | La Crosse, WI-MN** | NA |
| 236 | Oklahoma City, OK | (11.5) | 295 | Sheboygan, WI | (18.0) | NA | Lafayette, LA** | NA |
| 237 | Parkersburg-Vienna, WV | (11.6) | 295 | Stockton-Lodi, CA | (18.0) | NA | Lake Charles, LA** | NA |
| 238 | Norwich-New London, CT | (11.7) | 300 | Santa Maria-Santa Barbara, CA | (18.3) | NA | Lancaster, PA** | NA |
| 239 | York-Hanover, PA | (11.8) | 300 | Staunton-Waynesboro, VA | (18.3) | NA | Louisville, KY-IN** | NA |
| 240 | Columbia, MO | (11.9) | 302 | Yuba City, CA | (18.4) | NA | Madison, WI** | NA |
| 240 | Ocala, FL | (11.9) | 303 | Kingsport, TN-VA | (18.5) | NA | Muskegon, MI** | NA |
| 242 | Kankakee, IL | (12.0) | 303 | Oshkosh-Neenah, WI | (18.5) | NA | Myrtle Beach, SC-NC** | NA |
| 242 | Utica-Rome, NY | (12.0) | 305 | Rocky Mount, NC | (19.1) | NA | New York (greater), NY-NJ-PA** | NA |
| 244 | Grand Island, NE | (12.1) | 306 | Cleveland, TN | (19.2) | NA | New York-Jersey City, NY-NJ M.D.** | NA |
| 245 | Victoria, TX | (12.2) | 307 | South Bend-Mishawaka, IN-MI | (19.9) | NA | Niles-Benton Harbor, MI** | NA |
| 246 | Hagerstown-Martinsburg, MD-WV | (12.5) | 308 | Owensboro, KY | (20.3) | NA | Olympia, WA** | NA |
| 246 | Topeka, KS | (12.5) | 308 | Winchester, VA-WV | (20.3) | NA | Philadelphia (greater) PA-NJ-MD-DE** | NA |
| 248 | Lafayette, IN | (12.6) | 310 | Bay City, MI | (21.0) | NA | Philadelphia, PA M.D.** | NA |
| 248 | McAllen-Edinburg-Mission, TX | (12.6) | 310 | Fort Collins, CO | (21.0) | NA | Pittsburgh, PA** | NA |
| 250 | Fayetteville-Springdale, AR-MO | (12.7) | 312 | Lawrence, KS | (21.4) | NA | San Angelo, TX** | NA |
| 251 | Idaho Falls, ID | (12.8) | 313 | Wausau, WI | (21.5) | NA | Scranton--Wilkes-Barre, PA** | NA |
| 252 | Lubbock, TX | (12.9) | 314 | Pittsfield, MA | (22.1) | NA | Shreveport-Bossier City, LA** | NA |
| 252 | Missoula, MT | (12.9) | 315 | Provo-Orem, UT | (22.6) | NA | St. Cloud, MN** | NA |
| 252 | Montgomery County, PA M.D. | (12.9) | 316 | Yakima, WA | (22.7) | | | |

Source: CQ Press using reported data from the F.B.I. "Crime in the United States 2013"
*Aggravated assault is an attack for the purpose of inflicting severe bodily injury.
**Not available.

# 24. Percent Change in Aggravated Assault Rate: 2009 to 2013
## National Percent Change = 13.4% Decrease*

| RANK | METROPOLITAN AREA | % CHANGE | RANK | METROPOLITAN AREA | % CHANGE | RANK | METROPOLITAN AREA | % CHANGE |
|---|---|---|---|---|---|---|---|---|
| 187 | Abilene, TX | (18.8) | 11 | Cheyenne, WY | 44.6 | NA | Gary, IN M.D.** | NA |
| 138 | Akron, OH | (13.0) | NA | Chicago (greater), IL-IN-WI** | NA | NA | Gettysburg, PA** | NA |
| 118 | Albany-Schenectady-Troy, NY | (9.5) | NA | Chicago-Naperville, IL M.D.** | NA | 138 | Glens Falls, NY | (13.0) |
| 16 | Albany, GA | 26.8 | 286 | Chico, CA | (39.4) | 91 | Goldsboro, NC | (5.1) |
| NA | Albany, OR** | NA | 150 | Cincinnati, OH-KY-IN | (13.8) | 125 | Grand Forks, ND-MN | (10.3) |
| 29 | Albuquerque, NM | 19.4 | 203 | Clarksville, TN-KY | (20.5) | NA | Grand Island, NE** | NA |
| 18 | Alexandria, LA | 25.6 | 280 | Cleveland, TN | (35.1) | 116 | Grand Junction, CO | (9.4) |
| 210 | Allentown, PA-NJ | (21.2) | 86 | Coeur d'Alene, ID | (4.1) | NA | Grand Rapids-Wyoming, MI** | NA |
| 213 | Altoona, PA | (21.3) | 87 | College Station-Bryan, TX | (4.4) | NA | Grants Pass, OR** | NA |
| 264 | Amarillo, TX | (29.2) | 231 | Colorado Springs, CO | (24.3) | 218 | Great Falls, MT | (21.7) |
| 301 | Ames, IA | (58.4) | 225 | Columbia, MO | (23.3) | 57 | Greeley, CO | 5.7 |
| 138 | Anaheim-Santa Ana-Irvine, CA M.D. | (13.0) | 240 | Columbia, SC | (25.8) | 26 | Green Bay, WI | 20.5 |
| 164 | Anchorage, AK | (15.4) | 172 | Columbus, GA-AL | (16.4) | 181 | Greensboro-High Point, NC | (17.7) |
| 80 | Ann Arbor, MI | (3.3) | 3 | Columbus, IN | 95.6 | NA | Greenville-Anderson, SC** | NA |
| 240 | Anniston-Oxford, AL | (25.8) | 200 | Corpus Christi, TX | (20.2) | NA | Greenville, NC** | NA |
| 31 | Appleton, WI | 17.9 | 68 | Corvallis, OR | 0.5 | NA | Gulfport-Biloxi-Pascagoula, MS** | NA |
| 269 | Athens-Clarke County, GA | (31.5) | NA | Crestview-Fort Walton Beach, FL** | NA | 149 | Hagerstown-Martinsburg, MD-WV | (13.7) |
| 138 | Atlanta, GA | (13.0) | 298 | Cumberland, MD-WV | (50.6) | NA | Hammond, LA** | NA |
| 151 | Atlantic City, NJ | (13.9) | 185 | Dallas (greater), TX | (18.3) | NA | Hanford-Corcoran, CA** | NA |
| 181 | Augusta, GA-SC | (17.7) | 202 | Dallas-Plano-Irving, TX M.D. | (20.3) | 133 | Harrisonburg, VA | (12.1) |
| 169 | Austin-Round Rock, TX | (16.2) | 195 | Dalton, GA | (19.5) | 163 | Hartford, CT | (15.0) |
| 73 | Bakersfield, CA | (0.6) | NA | Daphne-Fairhope-Foley, AL** | NA | NA | Hilton Head Island, SC** | NA |
| 178 | Baltimore, MD | (17.2) | NA | Davenport, IA-IL** | NA | 270 | Hinesville, GA | (31.8) |
| 20 | Bangor, ME | 23.9 | 199 | Dayton, OH | (20.1) | NA | Homosassa Springs, FL** | NA |
| 78 | Barnstable Town, MA | (2.7) | NA | Decatur, AL** | NA | 259 | Hot Springs, AR | (27.9) |
| 274 | Baton Rouge, LA | (33.3) | 277 | Decatur, IL | (33.9) | 252 | Houma, LA | (27.2) |
| 184 | Bay City, MI | (18.2) | 244 | Deltona-Daytona Beach, FL | (25.9) | 235 | Houston, TX | (24.6) |
| 48 | Beaumont-Port Arthur, TX | 8.6 | 106 | Denver-Aurora, CO | (8.0) | 12 | Huntsville, AL | 40.9 |
| 71 | Bend, OR | (0.3) | 45 | Des Moines-West Des Moines, IA | 9.5 | 300 | Idaho Falls, ID | (57.1) |
| 35 | Billings, MT | 16.2 | 183 | Detroit (greater), MI | (17.8) | NA | Indianapolis, IN** | NA |
| 87 | Binghamton, NY | (4.4) | 130 | Detroit-Dearborn-Livonia, MI M.D. | (11.6) | 104 | Iowa City, IA | (7.8) |
| 41 | Birmingham-Hoover, AL | 11.3 | NA | Dothan, AL** | NA | 259 | Jacksonville, FL | (27.9) |
| 2 | Bismarck, ND | 102.2 | 272 | Dover, DE | (31.9) | 101 | Jackson, MI | (7.3) |
| 74 | Blacksburg, VA | (1.8) | 303 | Dubuque, IA | (69.9) | 28 | Jackson, MS | 20.1 |
| NA | Bloomington, IL** | NA | 58 | Duluth, MN-WI | 5.5 | 10 | Jackson, TN | 48.5 |
| 146 | Bloomington, IN | (13.3) | NA | Dutchess-Putnam, NY M.D.** | NA | 98 | Janesville, WI | (6.7) |
| NA | Bloomsburg-Berwick, PA** | NA | NA | East Stroudsburg, PA** | NA | 94 | Jefferson City, MO | (5.3) |
| 110 | Boise City, ID | (8.5) | 51 | Eau Claire, WI | 7.5 | 76 | Johnson City, TN | (2.0) |
| 146 | Boston (greater), MA-NH | (13.3) | NA | El Centro, CA** | NA | NA | Johnstown, PA** | NA |
| 138 | Boston, MA M.D. | (13.0) | 228 | El Paso, TX | (23.7) | 104 | Jonesboro, AR | (7.8) |
| 230 | Boulder, CO | (24.1) | NA | Elgin, IL M.D.** | NA | NA | Joplin, MO** | NA |
| NA | Bowling Green, KY** | NA | NA | Elizabethtown-Fort Knox, KY** | NA | NA | Kahului-Wailuku-Lahaina, HI** | NA |
| 293 | Bremerton-Silverdale, WA | (42.6) | 111 | Elmira, NY | (8.6) | NA | Kankakee, IL** | NA |
| 240 | Bridgeport-Stamford, CT | (25.8) | 113 | Erie, PA | (9.2) | 144 | Kansas City, MO-KS | (13.1) |
| 281 | Brownsville-Harlingen, TX | (35.7) | 297 | Eugene, OR | (50.2) | 179 | Kennewick-Richland, WA | (17.5) |
| NA | Brunswick, GA** | NA | 72 | Fairbanks, AK | (0.4) | 166 | Kingsport, TN-VA | (15.9) |
| 156 | Buffalo-Niagara Falls, NY | (14.4) | 20 | Fargo, ND-MN | 23.9 | 279 | Kingston, NY | (34.7) |
| 154 | Burlington, NC | (14.1) | 284 | Farmington, NM | (38.2) | 207 | Knoxville, TN | (20.8) |
| NA | California-Lexington Park, MD** | NA | 38 | Fayetteville-Springdale, AR-MO | 13.5 | 32 | Kokomo, IN | 17.6 |
| NA | Cambridge-Newton, MA M.D.** | NA | 209 | Fayetteville, NC | (21.0) | NA | La Crosse, WI-MN** | NA |
| 135 | Camden, NJ M.D. | (12.5) | 54 | Flagstaff, AZ | 6.8 | 65 | Lafayette, IN | 2.5 |
| NA | Canton, OH** | NA | 123 | Flint, MI | (9.8) | NA | Lafayette, LA** | NA |
| 208 | Cape Coral-Fort Myers, FL | (20.9) | 37 | Florence-Muscle Shoals, AL | 14.4 | 205 | Lake Charles, LA | (20.6) |
| 25 | Cape Girardeau, MO-IL | 20.7 | 291 | Florence, SC | (39.7) | NA | Lake Co.-Kenosha Co., IL-WI M.D.** | NA |
| NA | Carbondale-Marion, IL** | NA | 40 | Fond du Lac, WI | 11.9 | 116 | Lake Havasu City-Kingman, AZ | (9.4) |
| 253 | Carson City, NV | (27.4) | 235 | Fort Collins, CO | (24.6) | 176 | Lakeland, FL | (16.8) |
| 55 | Casper, WY | 6.7 | 238 | Fort Lauderdale, FL M.D. | (25.6) | NA | Lancaster, PA** | NA |
| 63 | Cedar Rapids, IA | 2.9 | 100 | Fort Smith, AR-OK | (6.9) | 112 | Lansing-East Lansing, MI | (8.8) |
| NA | Chambersburg-Waynesboro, PA** | NA | 30 | Fort Wayne, IN | 18.8 | 219 | Laredo, TX | (22.0) |
| NA | Champaign-Urbana, IL** | NA | 169 | Fort Worth-Arlington, TX M.D. | (16.2) | 210 | Las Cruces, NM | (21.2) |
| 286 | Charleston-North Charleston, SC | (39.4) | 44 | Fresno, CA | 10.2 | 176 | Las Vegas-Henderson, NV | (16.8) |
| NA | Charlotte-Mecklenburg, NC-SC** | NA | 1 | Gadsden, AL | 103.5 | 249 | Lawrence, KS | (26.3) |
| 118 | Charlottesville, VA | (9.5) | 267 | Gainesville, FL | (30.4) | 278 | Lawton, OK | (34.2) |
| 127 | Chattanooga, TN-GA | (10.7) | 231 | Gainesville, GA | (24.3) | 189 | Lebanon, PA | (18.9) |

Note: All listings are for Metropolitan Statistical Areas (M.S.A.s) except for those ending with "M.D." Listings with "M.D." are Metropolitan Divisions which are smaller parts of eleven large M.S.A.s. See explanatory note at beginning of metropolitan area section.

| RANK | METROPOLITAN AREA | % CHANGE | RANK | METROPOLITAN AREA | % CHANGE | RANK | METROPOLITAN AREA | % CHANGE |
|---|---|---|---|---|---|---|---|---|
| 53 | Lewiston-Auburn, ME | 7.0 | 46 | Omaha-Council Bluffs, NE-IA | 8.7 | 33 | Sheboygan, WI | 16.9 |
| 23 | Lewiston, ID-WA | 22.2 | 215 | Orlando, FL | (21.5) | 96 | Sherman-Denison, TX | (5.4) |
| 302 | Lexington-Fayette, KY | (64.6) | 270 | Oshkosh-Neenah, WI | (31.8) | NA | Shreveport-Bossier City, LA** | NA |
| 165 | Lima, OH | (15.7) | 253 | Owensboro, KY | (27.4) | 217 | Silver Spring-Frederick, MD M.D. | (21.6) |
| 251 | Lincoln, NE | (26.7) | 224 | Oxnard-Thousand Oaks, CA | (23.2) | 203 | Sioux City, IA-NE-SD | (20.5) |
| 179 | Little Rock, AR | (17.5) | 249 | Palm Bay-Melbourne, FL | (26.3) | 8 | Sioux Falls, SD | 52.2 |
| 294 | Logan, UT-ID | (43.5) | 160 | Panama City, FL | (14.7) | 285 | South Bend-Mishawaka, IN-MI | (38.3) |
| 253 | Longview, TX | (27.4) | NA | Parkersburg-Vienna, WV** | NA | 258 | Spartanburg, SC | (27.8) |
| 7 | Longview, WA | 65.5 | 200 | Pensacola, FL | (20.2) | 186 | Spokane, WA | (18.4) |
| 227 | Los Angeles County, CA M.D. | (23.5) | 158 | Philadelphia (greater) PA-NJ-MD-DE | (14.5) | NA | Springfield, IL** | NA |
| 221 | Los Angeles (greater), CA | (22.3) | NA | Philadelphia, PA M.D.** | NA | 134 | Springfield, MA | (12.3) |
| NA | Louisville, KY-IN** | NA | 46 | Phoenix-Mesa-Scottsdale, AZ | 8.7 | 34 | Springfield, MO | 16.6 |
| 261 | Lubbock, TX | (28.4) | NA | Pittsburgh, PA** | NA | 92 | Springfield, OH | (5.2) |
| 283 | Lynchburg, VA | (38.0) | 296 | Pittsfield, MA | (44.9) | 289 | State College, PA | (39.6) |
| 107 | Macon, GA | (8.1) | 36 | Pocatello, ID | 15.5 | NA | Staunton-Waynesboro, VA** | NA |
| 6 | Madera, CA | 65.9 | 115 | Port St. Lucie, FL | (9.3) | 126 | Stockton-Lodi, CA | (10.5) |
| NA | Madison, WI** | NA | 70 | Portland-Vancouver, OR-WA | 0.1 | 171 | St. Cloud, MN | (16.3) |
| 58 | Manchester-Nashua, NH | 5.5 | 15 | Portland, ME | 34.5 | 92 | St. George, UT | (5.2) |
| 295 | Manhattan, KS | (44.3) | 247 | Prescott, AZ | (26.2) | 223 | St. Joseph, MO-KS | (23.0) |
| 48 | Mankato-North Mankato, MN | 8.6 | 145 | Providence-Warwick, RI-MA | (13.2) | 80 | St. Louis, MO-IL | (3.3) |
| 282 | Mansfield, OH | (36.1) | 196 | Provo-Orem, UT | (19.6) | 62 | Sumter, SC | 3.2 |
| 257 | McAllen-Edinburg-Mission, TX | (27.7) | 109 | Pueblo, CO | (8.4) | 173 | Syracuse, NY | (16.6) |
| 5 | Medford, OR | 68.1 | 246 | Punta Gorda, FL | (26.1) | 132 | Tacoma, WA M.D. | (12.0) |
| 107 | Memphis, TN-MS-AR | (8.1) | 299 | Racine, WI | (53.3) | 256 | Tallahassee, FL | (27.5) |
| 124 | Merced, CA | (10.1) | 156 | Raleigh, NC | (14.4) | 273 | Tampa-St Petersburg, FL | (32.4) |
| 229 | Miami (greater), FL | (23.8) | 9 | Rapid City, SD | 50.4 | NA | Terre Haute, IN** | NA |
| 221 | Miami-Dade County, FL M.D. | (22.3) | 89 | Reading, PA | (4.7) | 193 | Texarkana, TX-AR | (19.2) |
| 137 | Midland, TX | (12.6) | 161 | Redding, CA | (14.8) | NA | The Villages, FL** | NA |
| 17 | Milwaukee, WI | 26.4 | 263 | Reno, NV | (28.9) | 67 | Toledo, OH | 1.5 |
| 131 | Minneapolis-St. Paul, MN-WI | (11.7) | 113 | Richmond, VA | (9.2) | 65 | Topeka, KS | 2.5 |
| 64 | Missoula, MT | 2.7 | 194 | Riverside-San Bernardino, CA | (19.3) | 166 | Trenton, NJ | (15.9) |
| 99 | Mobile, AL | (6.8) | 247 | Roanoke, VA | (26.2) | 50 | Tucson, AZ | 7.6 |
| 79 | Modesto, CA | (3.2) | 197 | Rochester, MN | (19.7) | 220 | Tulsa, OK | (22.2) |
| NA | Monroe, LA** | NA | 103 | Rochester, NY | (7.7) | 206 | Tuscaloosa, AL | (20.7) |
| 24 | Monroe, MI | 21.8 | NA | Rockford, IL** | NA | 275 | Tyler, TX | (33.4) |
| NA | Montgomery County, PA M.D.** | NA | 22 | Rockingham County, NH M.D. | 22.8 | 198 | Utica-Rome, NY | (20.0) |
| 276 | Morgantown, WV | (33.5) | 94 | Rocky Mount, NC | (5.3) | 68 | Vallejo-Fairfield, CA | 0.5 |
| 84 | Morristown, TN | (3.7) | 158 | Rome, GA | (14.5) | 161 | Victoria, TX | (14.8) |
| 27 | Mount Vernon-Anacortes, WA | 20.2 | 148 | Sacramento, CA | (13.6) | 173 | Vineland-Bridgeton, NJ | (16.6) |
| 226 | Muncie, IN | (23.4) | 213 | Saginaw, MI | (21.3) | NA | Virginia Beach-Norfolk, VA-NC** | NA |
| 41 | Muskegon, MI | 11.3 | 77 | Salem, OR | (2.6) | 90 | Visalia-Porterville, CA | (4.9) |
| NA | Myrtle Beach, SC-NC** | NA | 239 | Salinas, CA | (25.7) | 286 | Waco, TX | (39.4) |
| 56 | Napa, CA | 6.5 | NA | Salisbury, MD-DE** | NA | NA | Warner Robins, GA** | NA |
| 266 | Naples-Marco Island, FL | (30.3) | 75 | Salt Lake City, UT | (1.9) | 244 | Warren-Troy, MI M.D. | (25.9) |
| 97 | Nashville-Davidson, TN | (6.5) | 268 | San Angelo, TX | (31.4) | 151 | Washington (greater) DC-VA-MD-WV | (13.9) |
| 210 | Nassau-Suffolk, NY M.D. | (21.2) | 39 | San Antonio, TX | 12.3 | 138 | Washington, DC-VA-MD-WV M.D. | (13.0) |
| NA | New Bern, NC** | NA | 135 | San Diego, CA | (12.5) | NA | Watertown-Fort Drum, NY** | NA |
| 215 | New Haven-Milford, CT | (21.5) | 122 | San Francisco (greater), CA | (9.7) | 292 | Wausau, WI | (41.5) |
| 187 | New Orleans, LA | (18.8) | 43 | San Francisco-Redwood, CA M.D. | 10.4 | 237 | West Palm Beach, FL M.D. | (25.4) |
| 60 | New York (greater), NY-NJ-PA | 5.4 | 191 | San Jose, CA | (19.0) | 128 | Wichita Falls, TX | (11.5) |
| NA | New York-Jersey City, NY-NJ M.D.** | NA | 4 | San Luis Obispo, CA | 70.5 | 128 | Wichita, KS | (11.5) |
| 262 | Newark, NJ-PA M.D. | (28.5) | NA | San Rafael, CA M.D.** | NA | 82 | Williamsport, PA | (3.4) |
| 52 | Niles-Benton Harbor, MI | 7.2 | 240 | Santa Cruz-Watsonville, CA | (25.8) | 234 | Wilmington, DE-MD-NJ M.D. | (24.5) |
| 265 | North Port-Sarasota-Bradenton, FL | (30.2) | 289 | Santa Maria-Santa Barbara, CA | (39.6) | NA | Wilmington, NC** | NA |
| 84 | Norwich-New London, CT | (3.7) | 101 | Santa Rosa, CA | (7.3) | 19 | Winchester, VA-WV | 24.2 |
| 168 | Oakland-Hayward, CA M.D. | (16.1) | 189 | Savannah, GA | (18.9) | NA | Winston-Salem, NC** | NA |
| 233 | Ocala, FL | (24.4) | NA | Scranton--Wilkes-Barre, PA** | NA | 118 | Worcester, MA-CT | (9.5) |
| 82 | Ocean City, NJ | (3.4) | 151 | Seattle (greater), WA | (13.9) | NA | Yakima, WA** | NA |
| 14 | Odessa, TX | 35.5 | 155 | Seattle-Bellevue-Everett, WA M.D. | (14.3) | 13 | York-Hanover, PA | 39.8 |
| 192 | Ogden-Clearfield, UT | (19.1) | 118 | Sebastian-Vero Beach, FL | (9.5) | 175 | Yuba City, CA | (16.7) |
| NA | Oklahoma City, OK** | NA | NA | Sebring, FL** | NA | 61 | Yuma, AZ | 4.6 |
| NA | Olympia, WA** | NA | | | | | | |

Source: CQ Press using reported data from the F.B.I. "Crime in the United States 2013"
*Aggravated assault is an attack for the purpose of inflicting severe bodily injury.
**Not available.

# 24. Percent Change in Aggravated Assault Rate: 2009 to 2013 (continued)
## National Percent Change = 13.4% Decrease*

| RANK | METROPOLITAN AREA | % CHANGE | RANK | METROPOLITAN AREA | % CHANGE | RANK | METROPOLITAN AREA | % CHANGE |
|---|---|---|---|---|---|---|---|---|
| 1 | Gadsden, AL | 103.5 | 65 | Lafayette, IN | 2.5 | 128 | Wichita, KS | (11.5) |
| 2 | Bismarck, ND | 102.2 | 65 | Topeka, KS | 2.5 | 130 | Detroit-Dearborn-Livonia, MI M.D. | (11.6) |
| 3 | Columbus, IN | 95.6 | 67 | Toledo, OH | 1.5 | 131 | Minneapolis-St. Paul, MN-WI | (11.7) |
| 4 | San Luis Obispo, CA | 70.5 | 68 | Corvallis, OR | 0.5 | 132 | Tacoma, WA M.D. | (12.0) |
| 5 | Medford, OR | 68.1 | 68 | Vallejo-Fairfield, CA | 0.5 | 133 | Harrisonburg, VA | (12.1) |
| 6 | Madera, CA | 65.9 | 70 | Portland-Vancouver, OR-WA | 0.1 | 134 | Springfield, MA | (12.3) |
| 7 | Longview, WA | 65.5 | 71 | Bend, OR | (0.3) | 135 | Camden, NJ M.D. | (12.5) |
| 8 | Sioux Falls, SD | 52.2 | 72 | Fairbanks, AK | (0.4) | 135 | San Diego, CA | (12.5) |
| 9 | Rapid City, SD | 50.4 | 73 | Bakersfield, CA | (0.6) | 137 | Midland, TX | (12.6) |
| 10 | Jackson, TN | 48.5 | 74 | Blacksburg, VA | (1.8) | 138 | Akron, OH | (13.0) |
| 11 | Cheyenne, WY | 44.6 | 75 | Salt Lake City, UT | (1.9) | 138 | Anaheim-Santa Ana-Irvine, CA M.D. | (13.0) |
| 12 | Huntsville, AL | 40.9 | 76 | Johnson City, TN | (2.0) | 138 | Atlanta, GA | (13.0) |
| 13 | York-Hanover, PA | 39.8 | 77 | Salem, OR | (2.6) | 138 | Boston, MA M.D. | (13.0) |
| 14 | Odessa, TX | 35.5 | 78 | Barnstable Town, MA | (2.7) | 138 | Glens Falls, NY | (13.0) |
| 15 | Portland, ME | 34.5 | 79 | Modesto, CA | (3.2) | 138 | Washington, DC-VA-MD-WV M.D. | (13.0) |
| 16 | Albany, GA | 26.8 | 80 | Ann Arbor, MI | (3.3) | 144 | Kansas City, MO-KS | (13.1) |
| 17 | Milwaukee, WI | 26.4 | 80 | St. Louis, MO-IL | (3.3) | 145 | Providence-Warwick, RI-MA | (13.2) |
| 18 | Alexandria, LA | 25.6 | 82 | Ocean City, NJ | (3.4) | 146 | Bloomington, IN | (13.3) |
| 19 | Winchester, VA-WV | 24.2 | 82 | Williamsport, PA | (3.4) | 146 | Boston (greater), MA-NH | (13.3) |
| 20 | Bangor, ME | 23.9 | 84 | Morristown, TN | (3.7) | 148 | Sacramento, CA | (13.6) |
| 20 | Fargo, ND-MN | 23.9 | 84 | Norwich-New London, CT | (3.7) | 149 | Hagerstown-Martinsburg, MD-WV | (13.7) |
| 22 | Rockingham County, NH M.D. | 22.8 | 86 | Coeur d'Alene, ID | (4.1) | 150 | Cincinnati, OH-KY-IN | (13.8) |
| 23 | Lewiston, ID-WA | 22.2 | 87 | Binghamton, NY | (4.4) | 151 | Atlantic City, NJ | (13.9) |
| 24 | Monroe, MI | 21.8 | 87 | College Station-Bryan, TX | (4.4) | 151 | Seattle (greater), WA | (13.9) |
| 25 | Cape Girardeau, MO-IL | 20.7 | 89 | Reading, PA | (4.7) | 151 | Washington (greater) DC-VA-MD-WV | (13.9) |
| 26 | Green Bay, WI | 20.5 | 90 | Visalia-Porterville, CA | (4.9) | 154 | Burlington, NC | (14.1) |
| 27 | Mount Vernon-Anacortes, WA | 20.2 | 91 | Goldsboro, NC | (5.1) | 155 | Seattle-Bellevue-Everett, WA M.D. | (14.3) |
| 28 | Jackson, MS | 20.1 | 92 | Springfield, OH | (5.2) | 156 | Buffalo-Niagara Falls, NY | (14.4) |
| 29 | Albuquerque, NM | 19.4 | 92 | St. George, UT | (5.2) | 156 | Raleigh, NC | (14.4) |
| 30 | Fort Wayne, IN | 18.8 | 94 | Jefferson City, MO | (5.3) | 158 | Philadelphia (greater) PA-NJ-MD-DE | (14.5) |
| 31 | Appleton, WI | 17.9 | 94 | Rocky Mount, NC | (5.3) | 158 | Rome, GA | (14.5) |
| 32 | Kokomo, IN | 17.6 | 96 | Sherman-Denison, TX | (5.4) | 160 | Panama City, FL | (14.7) |
| 33 | Sheboygan, WI | 16.9 | 97 | Nashville-Davidson, TN | (6.5) | 161 | Redding, CA | (14.8) |
| 34 | Springfield, MO | 16.6 | 98 | Janesville, WI | (6.7) | 161 | Victoria, TX | (14.8) |
| 35 | Billings, MT | 16.2 | 99 | Mobile, AL | (6.8) | 163 | Hartford, CT | (15.0) |
| 36 | Pocatello, ID | 15.5 | 100 | Fort Smith, AR-OK | (6.9) | 164 | Anchorage, AK | (15.4) |
| 37 | Florence-Muscle Shoals, AL | 14.4 | 101 | Jackson, MI | (7.3) | 165 | Lima, OH | (15.7) |
| 38 | Fayetteville-Springdale, AR-MO | 13.5 | 101 | Santa Rosa, CA | (7.3) | 166 | Kingsport, TN-VA | (15.9) |
| 39 | San Antonio, TX | 12.3 | 103 | Rochester, NY | (7.7) | 166 | Trenton, NJ | (15.9) |
| 40 | Fond du Lac, WI | 11.9 | 104 | Iowa City, IA | (7.8) | 168 | Oakland-Hayward, CA M.D. | (16.1) |
| 41 | Birmingham-Hoover, AL | 11.3 | 104 | Jonesboro, AR | (7.8) | 169 | Austin-Round Rock, TX | (16.2) |
| 41 | Muskegon, MI | 11.3 | 106 | Denver-Aurora, CO | (8.0) | 169 | Fort Worth-Arlington, TX M.D. | (16.2) |
| 43 | San Francisco-Redwood, CA M.D. | 10.4 | 107 | Macon, GA | (8.1) | 171 | St. Cloud, MN | (16.3) |
| 44 | Fresno, CA | 10.2 | 107 | Memphis, TN-MS-AR | (8.1) | 172 | Columbus, GA-AL | (16.4) |
| 45 | Des Moines-West Des Moines, IA | 9.5 | 109 | Pueblo, CO | (8.4) | 173 | Syracuse, NY | (16.6) |
| 46 | Omaha-Council Bluffs, NE-IA | 8.7 | 110 | Boise City, ID | (8.5) | 173 | Vineland-Bridgeton, NJ | (16.6) |
| 46 | Phoenix-Mesa-Scottsdale, AZ | 8.7 | 111 | Elmira, NY | (8.6) | 175 | Yuba City, CA | (16.7) |
| 48 | Beaumont-Port Arthur, TX | 8.6 | 112 | Lansing-East Lansing, MI | (8.8) | 176 | Lakeland, FL | (16.8) |
| 48 | Mankato-North Mankato, MN | 8.6 | 113 | Erie, PA | (9.2) | 176 | Las Vegas-Henderson, NV | (16.8) |
| 50 | Tucson, AZ | 7.6 | 113 | Richmond, VA | (9.2) | 178 | Baltimore, MD | (17.2) |
| 51 | Eau Claire, WI | 7.5 | 115 | Port St. Lucie, FL | (9.3) | 179 | Kennewick-Richland, WA | (17.5) |
| 52 | Niles-Benton Harbor, MI | 7.2 | 116 | Grand Junction, CO | (9.4) | 179 | Little Rock, AR | (17.5) |
| 53 | Lewiston-Auburn, ME | 7.0 | 116 | Lake Havasu City-Kingman, AZ | (9.4) | 181 | Augusta, GA-SC | (17.7) |
| 54 | Flagstaff, AZ | 6.8 | 118 | Albany-Schenectady-Troy, NY | (9.5) | 181 | Greensboro-High Point, NC | (17.7) |
| 55 | Casper, WY | 6.7 | 118 | Charlottesville, VA | (9.5) | 183 | Detroit (greater), MI | (17.8) |
| 56 | Napa, CA | 6.5 | 118 | Sebastian-Vero Beach, FL | (9.5) | 184 | Bay City, MI | (18.2) |
| 57 | Greeley, CO | 5.7 | 118 | Worcester, MA-CT | (9.5) | 185 | Dallas (greater), TX | (18.3) |
| 58 | Duluth, MN-WI | 5.5 | 122 | San Francisco (greater), CA | (9.7) | 186 | Spokane, WA | (18.4) |
| 58 | Manchester-Nashua, NH | 5.5 | 123 | Flint, MI | (9.8) | 187 | Abilene, TX | (18.8) |
| 60 | New York (greater), NY-NJ-PA | 5.4 | 124 | Merced, CA | (10.1) | 187 | New Orleans, LA | (18.8) |
| 61 | Yuma, AZ | 4.6 | 125 | Grand Forks, ND-MN | (10.3) | 189 | Lebanon, PA | (18.9) |
| 62 | Sumter, SC | 3.2 | 126 | Stockton-Lodi, CA | (10.5) | 189 | Savannah, GA | (18.9) |
| 63 | Cedar Rapids, IA | 2.9 | 127 | Chattanooga, TN-GA | (10.7) | 191 | San Jose, CA | (19.0) |
| 64 | Missoula, MT | 2.7 | 128 | Wichita Falls, TX | (11.5) | 192 | Ogden-Clearfield, UT | (19.1) |

Note: All listings are for Metropolitan Statistical Areas (M.S.A.s) except for those ending with "M.D." Listings with "M.D." are Metropolitan Divisions which are smaller parts of eleven large M.S.A.s. See explanatory note at beginning of metropolitan area section.

| RANK | METROPOLITAN AREA | % CHANGE | RANK | METROPOLITAN AREA | % CHANGE | RANK | METROPOLITAN AREA | % CHANGE |
|---|---|---|---|---|---|---|---|---|
| 193 | Texarkana, TX-AR | (19.2) | 253 | Owensboro, KY | (27.4) | NA | Chicago-Naperville, IL M.D.** | NA |
| 194 | Riverside-San Bernardino, CA | (19.3) | 256 | Tallahassee, FL | (27.5) | NA | Crestview-Fort Walton Beach, FL** | NA |
| 195 | Dalton, GA | (19.5) | 257 | McAllen-Edinburg-Mission, TX | (27.7) | NA | Daphne-Fairhope-Foley, AL** | NA |
| 196 | Provo-Orem, UT | (19.6) | 258 | Spartanburg, SC | (27.8) | NA | Davenport, IA-IL** | NA |
| 197 | Rochester, MN | (19.7) | 259 | Hot Springs, AR | (27.9) | NA | Decatur, AL** | NA |
| 198 | Utica-Rome, NY | (20.0) | 259 | Jacksonville, FL | (27.9) | NA | Dothan, AL** | NA |
| 199 | Dayton, OH | (20.1) | 261 | Lubbock, TX | (28.4) | NA | Dutchess-Putnam, NY M.D.** | NA |
| 200 | Corpus Christi, TX | (20.2) | 262 | Newark, NJ-PA M.D. | (28.5) | NA | East Stroudsburg, PA** | NA |
| 200 | Pensacola, FL | (20.2) | 263 | Reno, NV | (28.9) | NA | El Centro, CA** | NA |
| 202 | Dallas-Plano-Irving, TX M.D. | (20.3) | 264 | Amarillo, TX | (29.2) | NA | Elgin, IL M.D.** | NA |
| 203 | Clarksville, TN-KY | (20.5) | 265 | North Port-Sarasota-Bradenton, FL | (30.2) | NA | Elizabethtown-Fort Knox, KY** | NA |
| 203 | Sioux City, IA-NE-SD | (20.5) | 266 | Naples-Marco Island, FL | (30.3) | NA | Gary, IN M.D.** | NA |
| 205 | Lake Charles, LA | (20.6) | 267 | Gainesville, FL | (30.4) | NA | Gettysburg, PA** | NA |
| 206 | Tuscaloosa, AL | (20.7) | 268 | San Angelo, TX | (31.4) | NA | Grand Island, NE** | NA |
| 207 | Knoxville, TN | (20.8) | 269 | Athens-Clarke County, GA | (31.5) | NA | Grand Rapids-Wyoming, MI** | NA |
| 208 | Cape Coral-Fort Myers, FL | (20.9) | 270 | Hinesville, GA | (31.8) | NA | Grants Pass, OR** | NA |
| 209 | Fayetteville, NC | (21.0) | 270 | Oshkosh-Neenah, WI | (31.8) | NA | Greenville-Anderson, SC** | NA |
| 210 | Allentown, PA-NJ | (21.2) | 272 | Dover, DE | (31.9) | NA | Greenville, NC** | NA |
| 210 | Las Cruces, NM | (21.2) | 273 | Tampa-St Petersburg, FL | (32.4) | NA | Gulfport-Biloxi-Pascagoula, MS** | NA |
| 210 | Nassau-Suffolk, NY M.D. | (21.2) | 274 | Baton Rouge, LA | (33.3) | NA | Hammond, LA** | NA |
| 213 | Altoona, PA | (21.3) | 275 | Tyler, TX | (33.4) | NA | Hanford-Corcoran, CA** | NA |
| 213 | Saginaw, MI | (21.3) | 276 | Morgantown, WV | (33.5) | NA | Hilton Head Island, SC** | NA |
| 215 | New Haven-Milford, CT | (21.5) | 277 | Decatur, IL | (33.9) | NA | Homosassa Springs, FL** | NA |
| 215 | Orlando, FL | (21.5) | 278 | Lawton, OK | (34.2) | NA | Indianapolis, IN** | NA |
| 217 | Silver Spring-Frederick, MD M.D. | (21.6) | 279 | Kingston, NY | (34.7) | NA | Johnstown, PA** | NA |
| 218 | Great Falls, MT | (21.7) | 280 | Cleveland, TN | (35.1) | NA | Joplin, MO** | NA |
| 219 | Laredo, TX | (22.0) | 281 | Brownsville-Harlingen, TX | (35.7) | NA | Kahului-Wailuku-Lahaina, HI** | NA |
| 220 | Tulsa, OK | (22.2) | 282 | Mansfield, OH | (36.1) | NA | Kankakee, IL** | NA |
| 221 | Los Angeles (greater), CA | (22.3) | 283 | Lynchburg, VA | (38.0) | NA | La Crosse, WI-MN** | NA |
| 221 | Miami-Dade County, FL M.D. | (22.3) | 284 | Farmington, NM | (38.2) | NA | Lafayette, LA** | NA |
| 223 | St. Joseph, MO-KS | (23.0) | 285 | South Bend-Mishawaka, IN-MI | (38.3) | NA | Lake Co.-Kenosha Co., IL-WI M.D.** | NA |
| 224 | Oxnard-Thousand Oaks, CA | (23.2) | 286 | Charleston-North Charleston, SC | (39.4) | NA | Lancaster, PA** | NA |
| 225 | Columbia, MO | (23.3) | 286 | Chico, CA | (39.4) | NA | Louisville, KY-IN** | NA |
| 226 | Muncie, IN | (23.4) | 286 | Waco, TX | (39.4) | NA | Madison, WI** | NA |
| 227 | Los Angeles County, CA M.D. | (23.5) | 289 | Santa Maria-Santa Barbara, CA | (39.6) | NA | Monroe, LA** | NA |
| 228 | El Paso, TX | (23.7) | 289 | State College, PA | (39.6) | NA | Montgomery County, PA M.D.** | NA |
| 229 | Miami (greater), FL | (23.8) | 291 | Florence, SC | (39.7) | NA | Myrtle Beach, SC-NC** | NA |
| 230 | Boulder, CO | (24.1) | 292 | Wausau, WI | (41.5) | NA | New Bern, NC** | NA |
| 231 | Colorado Springs, CO | (24.3) | 293 | Bremerton-Silverdale, WA | (42.6) | NA | New York-Jersey City, NY-NJ M.D.** | NA |
| 231 | Gainesville, GA | (24.3) | 294 | Logan, UT-ID | (43.5) | NA | Oklahoma City, OK** | NA |
| 233 | Ocala, FL | (24.4) | 295 | Manhattan, KS | (44.3) | NA | Olympia, WA** | NA |
| 234 | Wilmington, DE-MD-NJ M.D. | (24.5) | 296 | Pittsfield, MA | (44.9) | NA | Parkersburg-Vienna, WV** | NA |
| 235 | Fort Collins, CO | (24.6) | 297 | Eugene, OR | (50.2) | NA | Peoria, IL** | NA |
| 235 | Houston, TX | (24.6) | 298 | Cumberland, MD-WV | (50.6) | NA | Philadelphia, PA M.D.** | NA |
| 237 | West Palm Beach, FL M.D. | (25.4) | 299 | Racine, WI | (53.3) | NA | Pittsburgh, PA** | NA |
| 238 | Fort Lauderdale, FL M.D. | (25.6) | 300 | Idaho Falls, ID | (57.1) | NA | Rockford, IL** | NA |
| 239 | Salinas, CA | (25.7) | 301 | Ames, IA | (58.4) | NA | Salisbury, MD-DE** | NA |
| 240 | Anniston-Oxford, AL | (25.8) | 302 | Lexington-Fayette, KY | (64.6) | NA | San Rafael, CA M.D.** | NA |
| 240 | Bridgeport-Stamford, CT | (25.8) | 303 | Dubuque, IA | (69.9) | NA | Scranton--Wilkes-Barre, PA** | NA |
| 240 | Columbia, SC | (25.8) | NA | Albany, OR** | NA | NA | Sebring, FL** | NA |
| 240 | Santa Cruz-Watsonville, CA | (25.8) | NA | Bloomington, IL** | NA | NA | Shreveport-Bossier City, LA** | NA |
| 244 | Deltona-Daytona Beach, FL | (25.9) | NA | Bloomsburg-Berwick, PA** | NA | NA | Springfield, IL** | NA |
| 244 | Warren-Troy, MI M.D. | (25.9) | NA | Bowling Green, KY** | NA | NA | Staunton-Waynesboro, VA** | NA |
| 246 | Punta Gorda, FL | (26.1) | NA | Brunswick, GA** | NA | NA | Terre Haute, IN** | NA |
| 247 | Prescott, AZ | (26.2) | NA | California-Lexington Park, MD** | NA | NA | The Villages, FL** | NA |
| 247 | Roanoke, VA | (26.2) | NA | Cambridge-Newton, MA M.D.** | NA | NA | Virginia Beach-Norfolk, VA-NC** | NA |
| 249 | Lawrence, KS | (26.3) | NA | Canton, OH** | NA | NA | Warner Robins, GA** | NA |
| 249 | Palm Bay-Melbourne, FL | (26.3) | NA | Carbondale-Marion, IL** | NA | NA | Watertown-Fort Drum, NY** | NA |
| 251 | Lincoln, NE | (26.7) | NA | Chambersburg-Waynesboro, PA** | NA | NA | Wilmington, NC** | NA |
| 252 | Houma, LA | (27.2) | NA | Champaign-Urbana, IL** | NA | NA | Winston-Salem, NC** | NA |
| 253 | Carson City, NV | (27.4) | NA | Charlotte-Mecklenburg, NC-SC** | NA | NA | Yakima, WA** | NA |
| 253 | Longview, TX | (27.4) | NA | Chicago (greater), IL-IN-WI** | NA | | | |

Source: CQ Press using reported data from the F.B.I. "Crime in the United States 2013"

*Aggravated assault is an attack for the purpose of inflicting severe bodily injury.

**Not available.

# 25. Property Crimes in 2013
## National Total = 8,632,512 Property Crimes*

| RANK | METROPOLITAN AREA | CRIMES | RANK | METROPOLITAN AREA | CRIMES | RANK | METROPOLITAN AREA | CRIMES |
|---|---|---|---|---|---|---|---|---|
| 235 | Abilene, TX | 5,522 | 332 | Cheyenne, WY | 2,626 | 95 | Gary, IN M.D. | 20,995 |
| 98 | Akron, OH | 20,563 | 5 | Chicago (greater), IL-IN-WI | 223,102 | 369 | Gettysburg, PA | 1,283 |
| 102 | Albany-Schenectady-Troy, NY | 20,175 | 10 | Chicago-Naperville, IL M.D. | 177,733 | 357 | Glens Falls, NY | 2,051 |
| 196 | Albany, GA | 7,115 | 213 | Chico, CA | 6,223 | 258 | Goldsboro, NC | 4,545 |
| 279 | Albany, OR | 4,018 | 36 | Cincinnati, OH-KY-IN | 67,244 | 354 | Grand Forks, ND-MN | 2,140 |
| 62 | Albuquerque, NM | 40,471 | 198 | Clarksville, TN-KY | 7,013 | 322 | Grand Island, NE | 2,900 |
| 192 | Alexandria, LA | 7,387 | 294 | Cleveland, TN | 3,735 | 292 | Grand Junction, CO | 3,847 |
| 111 | Allentown, PA-NJ | 18,180 | 282 | Coeur d'Alene, ID | 3,989 | 103 | Grand Rapids-Wyoming, MI | 19,779 |
| 352 | Altoona, PA | 2,168 | 222 | College Station-Bryan, TX | 5,900 | 306 | Grants Pass, OR | 3,364 |
| 167 | Amarillo, TX | 8,919 | 92 | Colorado Springs, CO | 22,227 | 318 | Great Falls, MT | 2,947 |
| 362 | Ames, IA | 1,949 | 234 | Columbia, MO | 5,613 | 241 | Greeley, CO | 5,297 |
| 41 | Anaheim-Santa Ana-Irvine, CA M.D. | 61,650 | 80 | Columbia, SC | 28,851 | 233 | Green Bay, WI | 5,669 |
| 134 | Anchorage, AK | 13,047 | 122 | Columbus, GA-AL | 15,566 | 87 | Greensboro-High Point, NC | 25,588 |
| 191 | Ann Arbor, MI | 7,409 | 330 | Columbus, IN | 2,674 | 68 | Greenville-Anderson, SC | 34,319 |
| 263 | Anniston-Oxford, AL | 4,369 | 104 | Corpus Christi, TX | 18,832 | 220 | Greenville, NC | 5,923 |
| 313 | Appleton, WI | 3,178 | 351 | Corvallis, OR | 2,219 | 130 | Gulfport-Biloxi-Pascagoula, MS | 13,862 |
| 217 | Athens-Clarke County, GA | 6,080 | 219 | Crestview-Fort Walton Beach, FL | 5,929 | 227 | Hagerstown-Martinsburg, MD-WV | 5,727 |
| 9 | Atlanta, GA | 183,570 | 329 | Cumberland, MD-WV | 2,733 | 200 | Hammond, LA | 6,957 |
| 179 | Atlantic City, NJ | 8,199 | 8 | Dallas (greater), TX | 206,906 | 295 | Hanford-Corcoran, CA | 3,723 |
| 93 | Augusta, GA-SC | 21,255 | 14 | Dallas-Plano-Irving, TX M.D. | 130,279 | 361 | Harrisonburg, VA | 2,022 |
| 44 | Austin-Round Rock, TX | 59,731 | 282 | Dalton, GA | 3,989 | 90 | Hartford, CT | 22,530 |
| 70 | Bakersfield, CA | 33,381 | 253 | Daphne-Fairhope-Foley, AL | 4,892 | 230 | Hilton Head Island, SC | 5,675 |
| 25 | Baltimore, MD | 83,474 | 161 | Davenport, IA-IL | 9,607 | 348 | Hinesville, GA | 2,259 |
| 264 | Bangor, ME | 4,339 | 84 | Dayton, OH | 26,662 | 327 | Homosassa Springs, FL | 2,755 |
| 243 | Barnstable Town, MA | 5,203 | 281 | Decatur, AL | 3,990 | 245 | Hot Springs, AR | 5,178 |
| 73 | Baton Rouge, LA | 31,150 | 325 | Decatur, IL | 2,806 | 205 | Houma, LA | 6,740 |
| 349 | Bay City, MI | 2,252 | 106 | Deltona-Daytona Beach, FL | 18,623 | 6 | Houston, TX | 219,139 |
| 131 | Beaumont-Port Arthur, TX | 13,641 | 30 | Denver-Aurora, CO | 73,981 | 127 | Huntsville, AL | 14,581 |
| 271 | Bend, OR | 4,252 | 117 | Des Moines-West Des Moines, IA | 16,488 | 338 | Idaho Falls, ID | 2,527 |
| 207 | Billings, MT | 6,591 | 17 | Detroit (greater), MI | 110,816 | 35 | Indianapolis, IN | 67,521 |
| 204 | Binghamton, NY | 6,791 | 34 | Detroit-Dearborn-Livonia, MI M.D. | 68,399 | 312 | Iowa City, IA | 3,179 |
| 58 | Birmingham-Hoover, AL | 42,397 | 270 | Dothan, AL | 4,254 | 53 | Jacksonville, FL | 44,974 |
| 323 | Bismarck, ND | 2,862 | 250 | Dover, DE | 5,057 | 286 | Jackson, MI | 3,958 |
| 302 | Blacksburg, VA | 3,456 | 363 | Dubuque, IA | 1,894 | 114 | Jackson, MS | 17,331 |
| 288 | Bloomington, IL | 3,946 | 164 | Duluth, MN-WI | 9,537 | 255 | Jackson, TN | 4,775 |
| 262 | Bloomington, IN | 4,406 | 240 | Dutchess-Putnam, NY M.D. | 5,318 | 285 | Janesville, WI | 3,986 |
| 367 | Bloomsburg-Berwick, PA | 1,492 | 275 | East Stroudsburg, PA | 4,126 | 310 | Jefferson City, MO | 3,243 |
| 147 | Boise City, ID | 11,018 | 326 | Eau Claire, WI | 2,775 | 246 | Johnson City, TN | 5,157 |
| 24 | Boston (greater), MA-NH | 88,451 | 221 | El Centro, CA | 5,903 | 337 | Johnstown, PA | 2,540 |
| 61 | Boston, MA M.D. | 40,647 | 108 | El Paso, TX | 18,331 | 260 | Jonesboro, AR | 4,436 |
| 197 | Boulder, CO | 7,079 | 162 | Elgin, IL M.D. | 9,552 | 188 | Joplin, MO | 7,585 |
| 293 | Bowling Green, KY | 3,789 | 350 | Elizabethtown-Fort Knox, KY | 2,235 | 229 | Kahului-Wailuku-Lahaina, HI | 5,704 |
| 189 | Bremerton-Silverdale, WA | 7,569 | 359 | Elmira, NY | 2,048 | 324 | Kankakee, IL | 2,860 |
| 124 | Bridgeport-Stamford, CT | 14,918 | 206 | Erie, PA | 6,689 | 37 | Kansas City, MO-KS | 66,696 |
| 125 | Brownsville-Harlingen, TX | 14,844 | 133 | Eugene, OR | 13,201 | 212 | Kennewick-Richland, WA | 6,236 |
| 261 | Brunswick, GA | 4,421 | 368 | Fairbanks, AK | 1,429 | 175 | Kingsport, TN-VA | 8,314 |
| 74 | Buffalo-Niagara Falls, NY | 31,044 | 249 | Fargo, ND-MN | 5,068 | 307 | Kingston, NY | 3,281 |
| 252 | Burlington, NC | 4,969 | 327 | Farmington, NM | 2,755 | 83 | Knoxville, TN | 26,730 |
| 342 | California-Lexington Park, MD | 2,489 | 143 | Fayetteville-Springdale, AR-MO | 11,619 | 343 | Kokomo, IN | 2,462 |
| 63 | Cambridge-Newton, MA M.D. | 39,326 | 107 | Fayetteville, NC | 18,564 | 339 | La Crosse, WI-MN | 2,507 |
| 78 | Camden, NJ M.D. | 29,230 | 273 | Flagstaff, AZ | 4,169 | 232 | Lafayette, IN | 5,672 |
| 150 | Canton, OH | 10,817 | 141 | Flint, MI | 12,420 | 116 | Lafayette, LA | 16,915 |
| 128 | Cape Coral-Fort Myers, FL | 14,400 | 265 | Florence-Muscle Shoals, AL | 4,327 | 158 | Lake Charles, LA | 9,790 |
| 317 | Cape Girardeau, MO-IL | 2,981 | 165 | Florence, SC | 9,410 | 126 | Lake Co.-Kenosha Co., IL-WI M.D. | 14,822 |
| 309 | Carbondale-Marion, IL | 3,251 | 365 | Fond du Lac, WI | 1,651 | 202 | Lake Havasu City-Kingman, AZ | 6,882 |
| 371 | Carson City, NV | 924 | 203 | Fort Collins, CO | 6,812 | 112 | Lakeland, FL | 18,115 |
| 344 | Casper, WY | 2,367 | 40 | Fort Lauderdale, FL M.D. | 63,720 | 156 | Lancaster, PA | 9,845 |
| 214 | Cedar Rapids, IA | 6,210 | 171 | Fort Smith, AR-OK | 8,739 | 152 | Lansing-East Lansing, MI | 10,323 |
| 319 | Chambersburg-Waynesboro, PA | 2,931 | 140 | Fort Wayne, IN | 12,422 | 149 | Laredo, TX | 10,879 |
| 223 | Champaign-Urbana, IL | 5,896 | 28 | Fort Worth-Arlington, TX M.D. | 76,627 | 210 | Las Cruces, NM | 6,382 |
| 91 | Charleston-North Charleston, SC | 22,397 | 66 | Fresno, CA | 36,698 | 43 | Las Vegas-Henderson, NV | 61,116 |
| 32 | Charlotte-Mecklenburg, NC-SC | 69,430 | 259 | Gadsden, AL | 4,442 | 274 | Lawrence, KS | 4,152 |
| 267 | Charlottesville, VA | 4,287 | 183 | Gainesville, FL | 8,009 | 236 | Lawton, OK | 5,454 |
| 96 | Chattanooga, TN-GA | 20,946 | 272 | Gainesville, GA | 4,198 | 340 | Lebanon, PA | 2,493 |

Note: All listings are for Metropolitan Statistical Areas (M.S.A.s) except for those ending with "M.D." Listings with "M.D." are Metropolitan Divisions which are smaller parts of eleven large M.S.A.s. See explanatory note at beginning of metropolitan area section.

| RANK | METROPOLITAN AREA | CRIMES | RANK | METROPOLITAN AREA | CRIMES | RANK | METROPOLITAN AREA | CRIMES |
|---|---|---|---|---|---|---|---|---|
| 320 | Lewiston-Auburn, ME | 2,924 | 79 | Omaha-Council Bluffs, NE-IA | 29,000 | 356 | Sheboygan, WI | 2,062 |
| 358 | Lewiston, ID-WA | 2,050 | 27 | Orlando, FL | 77,335 | 315 | Sherman-Denison, TX | 3,091 |
| 110 | Lexington-Fayette, KY | 18,218 | 321 | Oshkosh-Neenah, WI | 2,917 | 120 | Shreveport-Bossier City, LA | 15,966 |
| 298 | Lima, OH | 3,567 | 334 | Owensboro, KY | 2,588 | 100 | Silver Spring-Frederick, MD M.D. | 20,394 |
| 155 | Lincoln, NE | 10,026 | 118 | Oxnard-Thousand Oaks, CA | 16,400 | 256 | Sioux City, IA-NE-SD | 4,670 |
| 67 | Little Rock, AR | 35,373 | 123 | Palm Bay-Melbourne, FL | 15,393 | 228 | Sioux Falls, SD | 5,720 |
| 366 | Logan, UT-ID | 1,531 | 193 | Panama City, FL | 7,306 | 159 | South Bend-Mishawaka, IN-MI | 9,749 |
| 195 | Longview, TX | 7,214 | 347 | Parkersburg-Vienna, WV | 2,267 | 154 | Spartanburg, SC | 10,059 |
| 278 | Longview, WA | 4,057 | 121 | Pensacola, FL | 15,836 | 75 | Spokane, WA | 30,755 |
| 4 | Los Angeles County, CA M.D. | 228,419 | 168 | Peoria, IL | 8,860 | 177 | Springfield, IL | 8,270 |
| 2 | Los Angeles (greater), CA | 290,069 | 12 | Philadelphia (greater) PA-NJ-MD-DE | 149,557 | 109 | Springfield, MA | 18,249 |
| 55 | Louisville, KY-IN | 43,134 | 38 | Philadelphia, PA M.D. | 66,084 | 101 | Springfield, MO | 20,251 |
| 137 | Lubbock, TX | 12,775 | NA | Phoenix-Mesa-Scottsdale, AZ** | NA | 218 | Springfield, OH | 5,987 |
| 276 | Lynchburg, VA | 4,118 | 54 | Pittsburgh, PA | 43,827 | 353 | State College, PA | 2,167 |
| 146 | Macon, GA | 11,136 | 311 | Pittsfield, MA | 3,213 | 360 | Staunton-Waynesboro, VA | 2,041 |
| 289 | Madera, CA | 3,934 | 341 | Pocatello, ID | 2,490 | 81 | Stockton-Lodi, CA | 28,603 |
| 129 | Madison, WI | 14,165 | 160 | Port St. Lucie, FL | 9,735 | 257 | St. Cloud, MN | 4,667 |
| 166 | Manchester-Nashua, NH | 9,330 | 33 | Portland-Vancouver, OR-WA | 69,261 | NA | St. George, UT** | NA |
| 364 | Manhattan, KS | 1,745 | 142 | Portland, ME | 11,781 | 247 | St. Joseph, MO-KS | 5,098 |
| 331 | Mankato-North Mankato, MN | 2,628 | 267 | Prescott, AZ | 4,287 | 29 | St. Louis, MO-IL | 74,862 |
| 226 | Mansfield, OH | 5,777 | 65 | Providence-Warwick, RI-MA | 37,865 | 291 | Sumter, SC | 3,914 |
| 76 | McAllen-Edinburg-Mission, TX | 30,267 | 151 | Provo-Orem, UT | 10,535 | 119 | Syracuse, NY | 16,397 |
| 180 | Medford, OR | 8,180 | 169 | Pueblo, CO | 8,835 | 69 | Tacoma, WA M.D. | 34,259 |
| 45 | Memphis, TN-MS-AR | 56,471 | 304 | Punta Gorda, FL | 3,409 | 135 | Tallahassee, FL | 12,859 |
| 182 | Merced, CA | 8,096 | 254 | Racine, WI | 4,802 | 26 | Tampa-St Petersburg, FL | 78,471 |
| 7 | Miami (greater), FL | 215,771 | 82 | Raleigh, NC | 27,625 | 231 | Terre Haute, IN | 5,674 |
| 19 | Miami-Dade County, FL M.D. | 109,764 | 303 | Rapid City, SD | 3,439 | 225 | Texarkana, TX-AR | 5,887 |
| 277 | Midland, TX | 4,110 | 186 | Reading, PA | 7,789 | 370 | The Villages, FL | 1,045 |
| 50 | Milwaukee, WI | 48,153 | 224 | Redding, CA | 5,894 | NA | Toledo, OH** | NA |
| 23 | Minneapolis-St. Paul, MN-WI | 89,681 | 144 | Reno, NV | 11,385 | 176 | Topeka, KS | 8,307 |
| 305 | Missoula, MT | 3,407 | 77 | Richmond, VA | 29,761 | 190 | Trenton, NJ | 7,491 |
| 105 | Mobile, AL | 18,685 | 16 | Riverside-San Bernardino, CA | 122,732 | 49 | Tucson, AZ | 48,477 |
| 99 | Modesto, CA | 20,538 | 187 | Roanoke, VA | 7,609 | 72 | Tulsa, OK | 31,465 |
| 170 | Monroe, LA | 8,780 | 300 | Rochester, MN | 3,483 | 185 | Tuscaloosa, AL | 7,801 |
| 299 | Monroe, MI | 3,544 | 86 | Rochester, NY | 26,151 | 209 | Tyler, TX | 6,463 |
| 71 | Montgomery County, PA M.D. | 33,129 | 153 | Rockford, IL | 10,311 | 208 | Utica-Rome, NY | 6,589 |
| 346 | Morgantown, WV | 2,305 | 173 | Rockingham County, NH M.D. | 8,478 | 132 | Vallejo-Fairfield, CA | 13,533 |
| 301 | Morristown, TN | 3,480 | 238 | Rocky Mount, NC | 5,416 | 314 | Victoria, TX | 3,137 |
| 244 | Mount Vernon-Anacortes, WA | 5,192 | 284 | Rome, GA | 3,988 | 201 | Vineland-Bridgeton, NJ | 6,914 |
| 296 | Muncie, IN | 3,700 | 42 | Sacramento, CA | 61,241 | 47 | Virginia Beach-Norfolk, VA-NC | 51,598 |
| 216 | Muskegon, MI | 6,117 | 266 | Saginaw, MI | 4,306 | NA | Visalia-Porterville, CA** | NA |
| 113 | Myrtle Beach, SC-NC | 17,696 | 136 | Salem, OR | 12,826 | 172 | Waco, TX | 8,659 |
| 335 | Napa, CA | 2,574 | 148 | Salinas, CA | 10,940 | 194 | Warner Robins, GA | 7,304 |
| 242 | Naples-Marco Island, FL | 5,236 | 138 | Salisbury, MD-DE | 12,543 | 57 | Warren-Troy, MI M.D. | 42,417 |
| 51 | Nashville-Davidson, TN | 47,448 | 48 | Salt Lake City, UT | 49,644 | 15 | Washington (greater) DC-VA-MD-WV | 128,916 |
| 60 | Nassau-Suffolk, NY M.D. | 40,816 | 280 | San Angelo, TX | 4,002 | 20 | Washington, DC-VA-MD-WV M.D. | 108,522 |
| 290 | New Bern, NC | 3,929 | 21 | San Antonio, TX | 100,269 | 345 | Watertown-Fort Drum, NY | 2,310 |
| 89 | New Haven-Milford, CT | 22,735 | 31 | San Diego, CA | 70,276 | 355 | Wausau, WI | 2,086 |
| 64 | New Orleans, LA | 39,059 | 11 | San Francisco (greater), CA | 160,685 | 59 | West Palm Beach, FL M.D. | 42,287 |
| 1 | New York (greater), NY-NJ-PA | 320,962 | 39 | San Francisco-Redwood, CA M.D. | 64,189 | 237 | Wichita Falls, TX | 5,450 |
| 3 | New York-Jersey City, NY-NJ M.D. | 232,326 | 52 | San Jose, CA | 45,267 | 85 | Wichita, KS | 26,356 |
| 56 | Newark, NJ-PA M.D. | 42,502 | 215 | San Luis Obispo, CA | 6,208 | 336 | Williamsport, PA | 2,547 |
| 269 | Niles-Benton Harbor, MI | 4,267 | 251 | San Rafael, CA M.D. | 5,012 | 94 | Wilmington, DE-MD-NJ M.D. | 21,114 |
| 97 | North Port-Sarasota-Bradenton, FL | 20,615 | 181 | Santa Cruz-Watsonville, CA | 8,140 | 163 | Wilmington, NC | 9,538 |
| 297 | Norwich-New London, CT | 3,590 | 157 | Santa Maria-Santa Barbara, CA | 9,824 | 333 | Winchester, VA-WV | 2,603 |
| 22 | Oakland-Hayward, CA M.D. | 91,484 | 178 | Santa Rosa, CA | 8,218 | 88 | Winston-Salem, NC | 23,074 |
| NA | Ocala, FL** | NA | 145 | Savannah, GA | 11,236 | 115 | Worcester, MA-CT | 17,030 |
| 287 | Ocean City, NJ | 3,955 | 139 | Scranton--Wilkes-Barre, PA | 12,526 | 174 | Yakima, WA | 8,365 |
| 211 | Odessa, TX | 6,307 | 13 | Seattle (greater), WA | 144,789 | 184 | York-Hanover, PA | 7,980 |
| NA | Ogden-Clearfield, UT** | NA | 18 | Seattle-Bellevue-Everett, WA M.D. | 110,530 | 248 | Yuba City, CA | 5,081 |
| 46 | Oklahoma City, OK | 52,037 | 316 | Sebastian-Vero Beach, FL | 2,983 | 239 | Yuma, AZ | 5,413 |
| 199 | Olympia, WA | 7,008 | 308 | Sebring, FL | 3,268 | | | |

Source: Reported data from the F.B.I. "Crime in the United States 2013"

*Property crimes are offenses of burglary, larceny-theft, and motor vehicle theft. Attempts are included.

**Not available.

# 25. Property Crimes in 2013 (continued)
## National Total = 8,632,512 Property Crimes*

| RANK | METROPOLITAN AREA | CRIMES | RANK | METROPOLITAN AREA | CRIMES | RANK | METROPOLITAN AREA | CRIMES |
|---|---|---|---|---|---|---|---|---|
| 1 | New York (greater), NY-NJ-PA | 320,962 | 65 | Providence-Warwick, RI-MA | 37,865 | 129 | Madison, WI | 14,165 |
| 2 | Los Angeles (greater), CA | 290,069 | 66 | Fresno, CA | 36,698 | 130 | Gulfport-Biloxi-Pascagoula, MS | 13,862 |
| 3 | New York-Jersey City, NY-NJ M.D. | 232,326 | 67 | Little Rock, AR | 35,373 | 131 | Beaumont-Port Arthur, TX | 13,641 |
| 4 | Los Angeles County, CA M.D. | 228,419 | 68 | Greenville-Anderson, SC | 34,319 | 132 | Vallejo-Fairfield, CA | 13,533 |
| 5 | Chicago (greater), IL-IN-WI | 223,102 | 69 | Tacoma, WA M.D. | 34,259 | 133 | Eugene, OR | 13,201 |
| 6 | Houston, TX | 219,139 | 70 | Bakersfield, CA | 33,381 | 134 | Anchorage, AK | 13,047 |
| 7 | Miami (greater), FL | 215,771 | 71 | Montgomery County, PA M.D. | 33,129 | 135 | Tallahassee, FL | 12,859 |
| 8 | Dallas (greater), TX | 206,906 | 72 | Tulsa, OK | 31,465 | 136 | Salem, OR | 12,826 |
| 9 | Atlanta, GA | 183,570 | 73 | Baton Rouge, LA | 31,150 | 137 | Lubbock, TX | 12,775 |
| 10 | Chicago-Naperville, IL M.D. | 177,733 | 74 | Buffalo-Niagara Falls, NY | 31,044 | 138 | Salisbury, MD-DE | 12,543 |
| 11 | San Francisco (greater), CA | 160,685 | 75 | Spokane, WA | 30,755 | 139 | Scranton--Wilkes-Barre, PA | 12,526 |
| 12 | Philadelphia (greater) PA-NJ-MD-DE | 149,557 | 76 | McAllen-Edinburg-Mission, TX | 30,267 | 140 | Fort Wayne, IN | 12,422 |
| 13 | Seattle (greater), WA | 144,789 | 77 | Richmond, VA | 29,761 | 141 | Flint, MI | 12,420 |
| 14 | Dallas-Plano-Irving, TX M.D. | 130,279 | 78 | Camden, NJ M.D. | 29,230 | 142 | Portland, ME | 11,781 |
| 15 | Washington (greater) DC-VA-MD-WV | 128,916 | 79 | Omaha-Council Bluffs, NE-IA | 29,000 | 143 | Fayetteville-Springdale, AR-MO | 11,619 |
| 16 | Riverside-San Bernardino, CA | 122,732 | 80 | Columbia, SC | 28,851 | 144 | Reno, NV | 11,385 |
| 17 | Detroit (greater), MI | 110,816 | 81 | Stockton-Lodi, CA | 28,603 | 145 | Savannah, GA | 11,236 |
| 18 | Seattle-Bellevue-Everett, WA M.D. | 110,530 | 82 | Raleigh, NC | 27,625 | 146 | Macon, GA | 11,136 |
| 19 | Miami-Dade County, FL M.D. | 109,764 | 83 | Knoxville, TN | 26,730 | 147 | Boise City, ID | 11,018 |
| 20 | Washington, DC-VA-MD-WV M.D. | 108,522 | 84 | Dayton, OH | 26,662 | 148 | Salinas, CA | 10,940 |
| 21 | San Antonio, TX | 100,269 | 85 | Wichita, KS | 26,356 | 149 | Laredo, TX | 10,879 |
| 22 | Oakland-Hayward, CA M.D. | 91,484 | 86 | Rochester, NY | 26,151 | 150 | Canton, OH | 10,817 |
| 23 | Minneapolis-St. Paul, MN-WI | 89,681 | 87 | Greensboro-High Point, NC | 25,588 | 151 | Provo-Orem, UT | 10,535 |
| 24 | Boston (greater), MA-NH | 88,451 | 88 | Winston-Salem, NC | 23,074 | 152 | Lansing-East Lansing, MI | 10,323 |
| 25 | Baltimore, MD | 83,474 | 89 | New Haven-Milford, CT | 22,735 | 153 | Rockford, IL | 10,311 |
| 26 | Tampa-St Petersburg, FL | 78,471 | 90 | Hartford, CT | 22,530 | 154 | Spartanburg, SC | 10,059 |
| 27 | Orlando, FL | 77,335 | 91 | Charleston-North Charleston, SC | 22,397 | 155 | Lincoln, NE | 10,026 |
| 28 | Fort Worth-Arlington, TX M.D. | 76,627 | 92 | Colorado Springs, CO | 22,227 | 156 | Lancaster, PA | 9,845 |
| 29 | St. Louis, MO-IL | 74,862 | 93 | Augusta, GA-SC | 21,255 | 157 | Santa Maria-Santa Barbara, CA | 9,824 |
| 30 | Denver-Aurora, CO | 73,981 | 94 | Wilmington, DE-MD-NJ M.D. | 21,114 | 158 | Lake Charles, LA | 9,790 |
| 31 | San Diego, CA | 70,276 | 95 | Gary, IN M.D. | 20,995 | 159 | South Bend-Mishawaka, IN-MI | 9,749 |
| 32 | Charlotte-Mecklenburg, NC-SC | 69,430 | 96 | Chattanooga, TN-GA | 20,946 | 160 | Port St. Lucie, FL | 9,735 |
| 33 | Portland-Vancouver, OR-WA | 69,261 | 97 | North Port-Sarasota-Bradenton, FL | 20,615 | 161 | Davenport, IA-IL | 9,607 |
| 34 | Detroit-Dearborn-Livonia, MI M.D. | 68,399 | 98 | Akron, OH | 20,563 | 162 | Elgin, IL M.D. | 9,552 |
| 35 | Indianapolis, IN | 67,521 | 99 | Modesto, CA | 20,538 | 163 | Wilmington, NC | 9,538 |
| 36 | Cincinnati, OH-KY-IN | 67,244 | 100 | Silver Spring-Frederick, MD M.D. | 20,394 | 164 | Duluth, MN-WI | 9,537 |
| 37 | Kansas City, MO-KS | 66,696 | 101 | Springfield, MO | 20,251 | 165 | Florence, SC | 9,410 |
| 38 | Philadelphia, PA M.D. | 66,084 | 102 | Albany-Schenectady-Troy, NY | 20,175 | 166 | Manchester-Nashua, NH | 9,330 |
| 39 | San Francisco-Redwood, CA M.D. | 64,189 | 103 | Grand Rapids-Wyoming, MI | 19,779 | 167 | Amarillo, TX | 8,919 |
| 40 | Fort Lauderdale, FL M.D. | 63,720 | 104 | Corpus Christi, TX | 18,832 | 168 | Peoria, IL | 8,860 |
| 41 | Anaheim-Santa Ana-Irvine, CA M.D. | 61,650 | 105 | Mobile, AL | 18,685 | 169 | Pueblo, CO | 8,835 |
| 42 | Sacramento, CA | 61,241 | 106 | Deltona-Daytona Beach, FL | 18,623 | 170 | Monroe, LA | 8,780 |
| 43 | Las Vegas-Henderson, NV | 61,116 | 107 | Fayetteville, NC | 18,564 | 171 | Fort Smith, AR-OK | 8,739 |
| 44 | Austin-Round Rock, TX | 59,731 | 108 | El Paso, TX | 18,331 | 172 | Waco, TX | 8,659 |
| 45 | Memphis, TN-MS-AR | 56,471 | 109 | Springfield, MA | 18,249 | 173 | Rockingham County, NH M.D. | 8,478 |
| 46 | Oklahoma City, OK | 52,037 | 110 | Lexington-Fayette, KY | 18,218 | 174 | Yakima, WA | 8,365 |
| 47 | Virginia Beach-Norfolk, VA-NC | 51,598 | 111 | Allentown, PA-NJ | 18,180 | 175 | Kingsport, TN-VA | 8,314 |
| 48 | Salt Lake City, UT | 49,644 | 112 | Lakeland, FL | 18,115 | 176 | Topeka, KS | 8,307 |
| 49 | Tucson, AZ | 48,477 | 113 | Myrtle Beach, SC-NC | 17,696 | 177 | Springfield, IL | 8,270 |
| 50 | Milwaukee, WI | 48,153 | 114 | Jackson, MS | 17,331 | 178 | Santa Rosa, CA | 8,218 |
| 51 | Nashville-Davidson, TN | 47,448 | 115 | Worcester, MA-CT | 17,030 | 179 | Atlantic City, NJ | 8,199 |
| 52 | San Jose, CA | 45,267 | 116 | Lafayette, LA | 16,915 | 180 | Medford, OR | 8,180 |
| 53 | Jacksonville, FL | 44,974 | 117 | Des Moines-West Des Moines, IA | 16,488 | 181 | Santa Cruz-Watsonville, CA | 8,140 |
| 54 | Pittsburgh, PA | 43,827 | 118 | Oxnard-Thousand Oaks, CA | 16,400 | 182 | Merced, CA | 8,096 |
| 55 | Louisville, KY-IN | 43,134 | 119 | Syracuse, NY | 16,397 | 183 | Gainesville, FL | 8,009 |
| 56 | Newark, NJ-PA M.D. | 42,502 | 120 | Shreveport-Bossier City, LA | 15,966 | 184 | York-Hanover, PA | 7,980 |
| 57 | Warren-Troy, MI M.D. | 42,417 | 121 | Pensacola, FL | 15,836 | 185 | Tuscaloosa, AL | 7,801 |
| 58 | Birmingham-Hoover, AL | 42,397 | 122 | Columbus, GA-AL | 15,566 | 186 | Reading, PA | 7,789 |
| 59 | West Palm Beach, FL M.D. | 42,287 | 123 | Palm Bay-Melbourne, FL | 15,393 | 187 | Roanoke, VA | 7,609 |
| 60 | Nassau-Suffolk, NY M.D. | 40,816 | 124 | Bridgeport-Stamford, CT | 14,918 | 188 | Joplin, MO | 7,585 |
| 61 | Boston, MA M.D. | 40,647 | 125 | Brownsville-Harlingen, TX | 14,844 | 189 | Bremerton-Silverdale, WA | 7,569 |
| 62 | Albuquerque, NM | 40,471 | 126 | Lake Co.-Kenosha Co., IL-WI M.D. | 14,822 | 190 | Trenton, NJ | 7,491 |
| 63 | Cambridge-Newton, MA M.D. | 39,326 | 127 | Huntsville, AL | 14,581 | 191 | Ann Arbor, MI | 7,409 |
| 64 | New Orleans, LA | 39,059 | 128 | Cape Coral-Fort Myers, FL | 14,400 | 192 | Alexandria, LA | 7,387 |

Note: All listings are for Metropolitan Statistical Areas (M.S.A.s) except for those ending with "M.D." Listings with "M.D." are Metropolitan Divisions which are smaller parts of eleven large M.S.A.s. See explanatory note at beginning of metropolitan area section.

| RANK | METROPOLITAN AREA | CRIMES | RANK | METROPOLITAN AREA | CRIMES | RANK | METROPOLITAN AREA | CRIMES |
|---|---|---|---|---|---|---|---|---|
| 193 | Panama City, FL | 7,306 | 255 | Jackson, TN | 4,775 | 317 | Cape Girardeau, MO-IL | 2,981 |
| 194 | Warner Robins, GA | 7,304 | 256 | Sioux City, IA-NE-SD | 4,670 | 318 | Great Falls, MT | 2,947 |
| 195 | Longview, TX | 7,214 | 257 | St. Cloud, MN | 4,667 | 319 | Chambersburg-Waynesboro, PA | 2,931 |
| 196 | Albany, GA | 7,115 | 258 | Goldsboro, NC | 4,545 | 320 | Lewiston-Auburn, ME | 2,924 |
| 197 | Boulder, CO | 7,079 | 259 | Gadsden, AL | 4,442 | 321 | Oshkosh-Neenah, WI | 2,917 |
| 198 | Clarksville, TN-KY | 7,013 | 260 | Jonesboro, AR | 4,436 | 322 | Grand Island, NE | 2,900 |
| 199 | Olympia, WA | 7,008 | 261 | Brunswick, GA | 4,421 | 323 | Bismarck, ND | 2,862 |
| 200 | Hammond, LA | 6,957 | 262 | Bloomington, IN | 4,406 | 324 | Kankakee, IL | 2,860 |
| 201 | Vineland-Bridgeton, NJ | 6,914 | 263 | Anniston-Oxford, AL | 4,369 | 325 | Decatur, IL | 2,806 |
| 202 | Lake Havasu City-Kingman, AZ | 6,882 | 264 | Bangor, ME | 4,339 | 326 | Eau Claire, WI | 2,775 |
| 203 | Fort Collins, CO | 6,812 | 265 | Florence-Muscle Shoals, AL | 4,327 | 327 | Farmington, NM | 2,755 |
| 204 | Binghamton, NY | 6,791 | 266 | Saginaw, MI | 4,306 | 327 | Homosassa Springs, FL | 2,755 |
| 205 | Houma, LA | 6,740 | 267 | Charlottesville, VA | 4,287 | 329 | Cumberland, MD-WV | 2,733 |
| 206 | Erie, PA | 6,689 | 267 | Prescott, AZ | 4,287 | 330 | Columbus, IN | 2,674 |
| 207 | Billings, MT | 6,591 | 269 | Niles-Benton Harbor, MI | 4,267 | 331 | Mankato-North Mankato, MN | 2,628 |
| 208 | Utica-Rome, NY | 6,589 | 270 | Dothan, AL | 4,254 | 332 | Cheyenne, WY | 2,626 |
| 209 | Tyler, TX | 6,463 | 271 | Bend, OR | 4,252 | 333 | Winchester, VA-WV | 2,603 |
| 210 | Las Cruces, NM | 6,382 | 272 | Gainesville, GA | 4,198 | 334 | Owensboro, KY | 2,588 |
| 211 | Odessa, TX | 6,307 | 273 | Flagstaff, AZ | 4,169 | 335 | Napa, CA | 2,574 |
| 212 | Kennewick-Richland, WA | 6,236 | 274 | Lawrence, KS | 4,152 | 336 | Williamsport, PA | 2,547 |
| 213 | Chico, CA | 6,223 | 275 | East Stroudsburg, PA | 4,126 | 337 | Johnstown, PA | 2,540 |
| 214 | Cedar Rapids, IA | 6,210 | 276 | Lynchburg, VA | 4,118 | 338 | Idaho Falls, ID | 2,527 |
| 215 | San Luis Obispo, CA | 6,208 | 277 | Midland, TX | 4,110 | 339 | La Crosse, WI-MN | 2,507 |
| 216 | Muskegon, MI | 6,117 | 278 | Longview, WA | 4,057 | 340 | Lebanon, PA | 2,493 |
| 217 | Athens-Clarke County, GA | 6,080 | 279 | Albany, OR | 4,018 | 341 | Pocatello, ID | 2,490 |
| 218 | Springfield, OH | 5,987 | 280 | San Angelo, TX | 4,002 | 342 | California-Lexington Park, MD | 2,489 |
| 219 | Crestview-Fort Walton Beach, FL | 5,929 | 281 | Decatur, AL | 3,990 | 343 | Kokomo, IN | 2,462 |
| 220 | Greenville, NC | 5,923 | 282 | Coeur d'Alene, ID | 3,989 | 344 | Casper, WY | 2,367 |
| 221 | El Centro, CA | 5,903 | 282 | Dalton, GA | 3,989 | 345 | Watertown-Fort Drum, NY | 2,310 |
| 222 | College Station-Bryan, TX | 5,900 | 284 | Rome, GA | 3,988 | 346 | Morgantown, WV | 2,305 |
| 223 | Champaign-Urbana, IL | 5,896 | 285 | Janesville, WI | 3,986 | 347 | Parkersburg-Vienna, WV | 2,267 |
| 224 | Redding, CA | 5,894 | 286 | Jackson, MI | 3,958 | 348 | Hinesville, GA | 2,259 |
| 225 | Texarkana, TX-AR | 5,887 | 287 | Ocean City, NJ | 3,955 | 349 | Bay City, MI | 2,252 |
| 226 | Mansfield, OH | 5,777 | 288 | Bloomington, IL | 3,946 | 350 | Elizabethtown-Fort Knox, KY | 2,235 |
| 227 | Hagerstown-Martinsburg, MD-WV | 5,727 | 289 | Madera, CA | 3,934 | 351 | Corvallis, OR | 2,219 |
| 228 | Sioux Falls, SD | 5,720 | 290 | New Bern, NC | 3,929 | 352 | Altoona, PA | 2,168 |
| 229 | Kahului-Wailuku-Lahaina, HI | 5,704 | 291 | Sumter, SC | 3,914 | 353 | State College, PA | 2,167 |
| 230 | Hilton Head Island, SC | 5,675 | 292 | Grand Junction, CO | 3,847 | 354 | Grand Forks, ND-MN | 2,140 |
| 231 | Terre Haute, IN | 5,674 | 293 | Bowling Green, KY | 3,789 | 355 | Wausau, WI | 2,086 |
| 232 | Lafayette, IN | 5,672 | 294 | Cleveland, TN | 3,735 | 356 | Sheboygan, WI | 2,062 |
| 233 | Green Bay, WI | 5,669 | 295 | Hanford-Corcoran, CA | 3,723 | 357 | Glens Falls, NY | 2,051 |
| 234 | Columbia, MO | 5,613 | 296 | Muncie, IN | 3,700 | 358 | Lewiston, ID-WA | 2,050 |
| 235 | Abilene, TX | 5,522 | 297 | Norwich-New London, CT | 3,590 | 359 | Elmira, NY | 2,048 |
| 236 | Lawton, OK | 5,454 | 298 | Lima, OH | 3,567 | 360 | Staunton-Waynesboro, VA | 2,041 |
| 237 | Wichita Falls, TX | 5,450 | 299 | Monroe, MI | 3,544 | 361 | Harrisonburg, VA | 2,022 |
| 238 | Rocky Mount, NC | 5,416 | 300 | Rochester, MN | 3,483 | 362 | Ames, IA | 1,949 |
| 239 | Yuma, AZ | 5,413 | 301 | Morristown, TN | 3,480 | 363 | Dubuque, IA | 1,894 |
| 240 | Dutchess-Putnam, NY M.D. | 5,318 | 302 | Blacksburg, VA | 3,456 | 364 | Manhattan, KS | 1,745 |
| 241 | Greeley, CO | 5,297 | 303 | Rapid City, SD | 3,439 | 365 | Fond du Lac, WI | 1,651 |
| 242 | Naples-Marco Island, FL | 5,236 | 304 | Punta Gorda, FL | 3,409 | 366 | Logan, UT-ID | 1,531 |
| 243 | Barnstable Town, MA | 5,203 | 305 | Missoula, MT | 3,407 | 367 | Bloomsburg-Berwick, PA | 1,492 |
| 244 | Mount Vernon-Anacortes, WA | 5,192 | 306 | Grants Pass, OR | 3,364 | 368 | Fairbanks, AK | 1,429 |
| 245 | Hot Springs, AR | 5,178 | 307 | Kingston, NY | 3,281 | 369 | Gettysburg, PA | 1,283 |
| 246 | Johnson City, TN | 5,157 | 308 | Sebring, FL | 3,268 | 370 | The Villages, FL | 1,045 |
| 247 | St. Joseph, MO-KS | 5,098 | 309 | Carbondale-Marion, IL | 3,251 | 371 | Carson City, NV | 924 |
| 248 | Yuba City, CA | 5,081 | 310 | Jefferson City, MO | 3,243 | NA | Ocala, FL** | NA |
| 249 | Fargo, ND-MN | 5,068 | 311 | Pittsfield, MA | 3,213 | NA | Ogden-Clearfield, UT** | NA |
| 250 | Dover, DE | 5,057 | 312 | Iowa City, IA | 3,179 | NA | Phoenix-Mesa-Scottsdale, AZ** | NA |
| 251 | San Rafael, CA M.D. | 5,012 | 313 | Appleton, WI | 3,178 | NA | St. George, UT** | NA |
| 252 | Burlington, NC | 4,969 | 314 | Victoria, TX | 3,137 | NA | Toledo, OH** | NA |
| 253 | Daphne-Fairhope-Foley, AL | 4,892 | 315 | Sherman-Denison, TX | 3,091 | NA | Visalia-Porterville, CA** | NA |
| 254 | Racine, WI | 4,802 | 316 | Sebastian-Vero Beach, FL | 2,983 | | | |

Source: Reported data from the F.B.I. "Crime in the United States 2013"

*Property crimes are offenses of burglary, larceny-theft, and motor vehicle theft.  Attempts are included.

**Not available.

# 26. Property Crime Rate in 2013
## National Rate = 2,730.7 Property Crimes per 100,000 Population*

| RANK | METROPOLITAN AREA | RATE | RANK | METROPOLITAN AREA | RATE | RANK | METROPOLITAN AREA | RATE |
|---|---|---|---|---|---|---|---|---|
| 120 | Abilene, TX | 3,284.6 | 198 | Cheyenne, WY | 2,745.9 | 171 | Gary, IN M.D. | 2,964.9 |
| 180 | Akron, OH | 2,923.1 | 260 | Chicago (greater), IL-IN-WI | 2,339.0 | 369 | Gettysburg, PA | 1,264.7 |
| 267 | Albany-Schenectady-Troy, NY | 2,300.8 | 248 | Chicago-Naperville, IL M.D. | 2,424.3 | 359 | Glens Falls, NY | 1,596.6 |
| 15 | Albany, GA | 4,521.3 | 189 | Chico, CA | 2,798.6 | 72 | Goldsboro, NC | 3,633.6 |
| 103 | Albany, OR | 3,372.1 | 139 | Cincinnati, OH-KY-IN | 3,147.4 | 298 | Grand Forks, ND-MN | 2,129.4 |
| 18 | Albuquerque, NM | 4,483.7 | 232 | Clarksville, TN-KY | 2,514.3 | 92 | Grand Island, NE | 3,445.9 |
| 12 | Alexandria, LA | 4,775.7 | 137 | Cleveland, TN | 3,150.5 | 221 | Grand Junction, CO | 2,577.6 |
| 289 | Allentown, PA-NJ | 2,193.9 | 194 | Coeur d'Alene, ID | 2,765.8 | 316 | Grand Rapids-Wyoming, MI | 1,954.2 |
| 341 | Altoona, PA | 1,706.1 | 234 | College Station-Bryan, TX | 2,487.6 | 41 | Grants Pass, OR | 4,045.1 |
| 96 | Amarillo, TX | 3,426.4 | 123 | Colorado Springs, CO | 3,274.4 | 77 | Great Falls, MT | 3,585.3 |
| 299 | Ames, IA | 2,120.9 | 119 | Columbia, MO | 3,287.8 | 315 | Greeley, CO | 1,971.6 |
| 313 | Anaheim-Santa Ana-Irvine, CA M.D. | 1,976.8 | 71 | Columbia, SC | 3,636.9 | 333 | Green Bay, WI | 1,812.5 |
| 34 | Anchorage, AK | 4,147.8 | 5 | Columbus, GA-AL | 4,930.0 | 91 | Greensboro-High Point, NC | 3,448.5 |
| 302 | Ann Arbor, MI | 2,097.7 | 109 | Columbus, IN | 3,338.2 | 43 | Greenville-Anderson, SC | 4,026.1 |
| 62 | Anniston-Oxford, AL | 3,737.6 | 27 | Corpus Christi, TX | 4,260.8 | 99 | Greenville, NC | 3,397.1 |
| 367 | Appleton, WI | 1,385.0 | 226 | Corvallis, OR | 2,552.0 | 73 | Gulfport-Biloxi-Pascagoula, MS | 3,624.9 |
| 146 | Athens-Clarke County, GA | 3,079.5 | 259 | Crestview-Fort Walton Beach, FL | 2,346.8 | 282 | Hagerstown-Martinsburg, MD-WV | 2,221.9 |
| 110 | Atlanta, GA | 3,330.8 | 209 | Cumberland, MD-WV | 2,688.3 | 2 | Hammond, LA | 5,601.1 |
| 169 | Atlantic City, NJ | 2,969.6 | 155 | Dallas (greater), TX | 3,036.4 | 241 | Hanford-Corcoran, CA | 2,461.4 |
| 68 | Augusta, GA-SC | 3,665.1 | 183 | Dallas-Plano-Irving, TX M.D. | 2,891.0 | 360 | Harrisonburg, VA | 1,559.1 |
| 134 | Austin-Round Rock, TX | 3,178.5 | 192 | Dalton, GA | 2,791.4 | 287 | Hartford, CT | 2,200.6 |
| 56 | Bakersfield, CA | 3,871.6 | 229 | Daphne-Fairhope-Foley, AL | 2,530.5 | 184 | Hilton Head Island, SC | 2,883.9 |
| 161 | Baltimore, MD | 3,012.1 | 233 | Davenport, IA-IL | 2,503.2 | 203 | Hinesville, GA | 2,722.9 |
| 187 | Bangor, ME | 2,826.2 | 113 | Dayton, OH | 3,320.3 | 311 | Homosassa Springs, FL | 1,978.6 |
| 250 | Barnstable Town, MA | 2,410.5 | 219 | Decatur, AL | 2,585.7 | 4 | Hot Springs, AR | 5,329.2 |
| 61 | Baton Rouge, LA | 3,800.3 | 225 | Decatur, IL | 2,553.8 | 128 | Houma, LA | 3,219.8 |
| 300 | Bay City, MI | 2,109.0 | 144 | Deltona-Daytona Beach, FL | 3,108.4 | 88 | Houston, TX | 3,488.8 |
| 105 | Beaumont-Port Arthur, TX | 3,359.4 | 197 | Denver-Aurora, CO | 2,746.8 | 106 | Huntsville, AL | 3,355.8 |
| 218 | Bend, OR | 2,589.8 | 195 | Des Moines-West Des Moines, IA | 2,764.7 | 331 | Idaho Falls, ID | 1,837.0 |
| 45 | Billings, MT | 3,998.3 | 220 | Detroit (greater), MI | 2,579.1 | 89 | Indianapolis, IN | 3,468.7 |
| 199 | Binghamton, NY | 2,739.8 | 60 | Detroit-Dearborn-Livonia, MI M.D. | 3,828.7 | 310 | Iowa City, IA | 1,981.4 |
| 64 | Birmingham-Hoover, AL | 3,722.5 | 185 | Dothan, AL | 2,871.1 | 127 | Jacksonville, FL | 3,228.8 |
| 266 | Bismarck, ND | 2,303.6 | 167 | Dover, DE | 2,979.5 | 240 | Jackson, MI | 2,466.1 |
| 320 | Blacksburg, VA | 1,925.1 | 312 | Dubuque, IA | 1,978.0 | 164 | Jackson, MS | 2,988.8 |
| 304 | Bloomington, IL | 2,083.3 | 98 | Duluth, MN-WI | 3,404.1 | 70 | Jackson, TN | 3,653.3 |
| 207 | Bloomington, IN | 2,693.2 | 368 | Dutchess-Putnam, NY M.D. | 1,338.9 | 235 | Janesville, WI | 2,482.2 |
| 338 | Bloomsburg-Berwick, PA | 1,753.8 | 244 | East Stroudsburg, PA | 2,451.4 | 297 | Jefferson City, MO | 2,154.2 |
| 346 | Boise City, ID | 1,700.7 | 349 | Eau Claire, WI | 1,687.3 | 224 | Johnson City, TN | 2,560.1 |
| 323 | Boston (greater), MA-NH | 1,890.3 | 115 | El Centro, CA | 3,317.1 | 335 | Johnstown, PA | 1,803.0 |
| 303 | Boston, MA M.D. | 2,092.6 | 291 | El Paso, TX | 2,176.4 | 83 | Jonesboro, AR | 3,547.6 |
| 271 | Boulder, CO | 2,281.1 | 363 | Elgin, IL M.D. | 1,518.7 | 24 | Joplin, MO | 4,354.0 |
| 263 | Bowling Green, KY | 2,318.3 | 364 | Elizabethtown-Fort Knox, KY | 1,483.1 | 79 | Kahului-Wailuku-Lahaina, HI | 3,572.8 |
| 176 | Bremerton-Silverdale, WA | 2,946.4 | 268 | Elmira, NY | 2,300.1 | 228 | Kankakee, IL | 2,534.5 |
| 355 | Bridgeport-Stamford, CT | 1,619.7 | 252 | Erie, PA | 2,385.1 | 125 | Kansas City, MO-KS | 3,254.4 |
| 87 | Brownsville-Harlingen, TX | 3,534.8 | 65 | Eugene, OR | 3,704.8 | 272 | Kennewick-Richland, WA | 2,280.0 |
| 55 | Brunswick, GA | 3,886.8 | 38 | Fairbanks, AK | 4,113.3 | 208 | Kingsport, TN-VA | 2,688.5 |
| 201 | Buffalo-Niagara Falls, NY | 2,735.0 | 270 | Fargo, ND-MN | 2,281.2 | 334 | Kingston, NY | 1,804.7 |
| 131 | Burlington, NC | 3,201.4 | 295 | Farmington, NM | 2,159.9 | 141 | Knoxville, TN | 3,136.0 |
| 277 | California-Lexington Park, MD | 2,256.7 | 253 | Fayetteville-Springdale, AR-MO | 2,380.7 | 172 | Kokomo, IN | 2,962.4 |
| 347 | Cambridge-Newton, MA M.D. | 1,700.1 | 7 | Fayetteville, NC | 4,910.2 | 328 | La Crosse, WI-MN | 1,844.5 |
| 262 | Camden, NJ M.D. | 2,324.7 | 153 | Flagstaff, AZ | 3,043.1 | 205 | Lafayette, IN | 2,720.7 |
| 212 | Canton, OH | 2,677.2 | 165 | Flint, MI | 2,981.2 | 84 | Lafayette, LA | 3,545.0 |
| 288 | Cape Coral-Fort Myers, FL | 2,194.3 | 177 | Florence-Muscle Shoals, AL | 2,945.9 | 9 | Lake Charles, LA | 4,852.9 |
| 150 | Cape Girardeau, MO-IL | 3,057.1 | 14 | Florence, SC | 4,542.7 | 342 | Lake Co.-Kenosha Co., IL-WI M.D. | 1,704.4 |
| 223 | Carbondale-Marion, IL | 2,566.2 | 356 | Fond du Lac, WI | 1,619.3 | 107 | Lake Havasu City-Kingman, AZ | 3,355.5 |
| 350 | Carson City, NV | 1,681.9 | 296 | Fort Collins, CO | 2,156.3 | 181 | Lakeland, FL | 2,908.4 |
| 174 | Casper, WY | 2,959.0 | 90 | Fort Lauderdale, FL M.D. | 3,456.7 | 326 | Lancaster, PA | 1,862.1 |
| 257 | Cedar Rapids, IA | 2,355.9 | 143 | Fort Smith, AR-OK | 3,110.7 | 284 | Lansing-East Lansing, MI | 2,211.8 |
| 319 | Chambersburg-Waynesboro, PA | 1,932.8 | 179 | Fort Wayne, IN | 2,929.2 | 35 | Laredo, TX | 4,137.5 |
| 231 | Champaign-Urbana, IL | 2,517.3 | 114 | Fort Worth-Arlington, TX M.D. | 3,320.2 | 170 | Las Cruces, NM | 2,967.2 |
| 136 | Charleston-North Charleston, SC | 3,150.8 | 59 | Fresno, CA | 3,845.5 | 159 | Las Vegas-Henderson, NV | 3,016.8 |
| 166 | Charlotte-Mecklenburg, NC-SC | 2,981.0 | 28 | Gadsden, AL | 4,257.0 | 69 | Lawrence, KS | 3,662.3 |
| 321 | Charlottesville, VA | 1,908.2 | 173 | Gainesville, FL | 2,960.6 | 39 | Lawton, OK | 4,087.0 |
| 57 | Chattanooga, TN-GA | 3,870.3 | 279 | Gainesville, GA | 2,241.4 | 330 | Lebanon, PA | 1,837.3 |

Note: All listings are for Metropolitan Statistical Areas (M.S.A.s) except for those ending with "M.D." Listings with "M.D." are Metropolitan Divisions which are smaller parts of eleven large M.S.A.s. See explanatory note at beginning of metropolitan area section.

| RANK | METROPOLITAN AREA | RATE | RANK | METROPOLITAN AREA | RATE | RANK | METROPOLITAN AREA | RATE |
|---|---|---|---|---|---|---|---|---|
| 204 | Lewiston-Auburn, ME | 2,720.8 | 126 | Omaha-Council Bluffs, NE-IA | 3,245.2 | 336 | Sheboygan, WI | 1,793.8 |
| 116 | Lewiston, ID-WA | 3,316.1 | 97 | Orlando, FL | 3,420.1 | 230 | Sherman-Denison, TX | 2,518.6 |
| 63 | Lexington-Fayette, KY | 3,723.1 | 339 | Oshkosh-Neenah, WI | 1,721.1 | 82 | Shreveport-Bossier City, LA | 3,551.1 |
| 99 | Lima, OH | 3,397.1 | 283 | Owensboro, KY | 2,220.9 | 354 | Silver Spring-Frederick, MD M.D. | 1,620.7 |
| 132 | Lincoln, NE | 3,197.6 | 317 | Oxnard-Thousand Oaks, CA | 1,950.8 | 196 | Sioux City, IA-NE-SD | 2,756.1 |
| 8 | Little Rock, AR | 4,891.6 | 190 | Palm Bay-Melbourne, FL | 2,796.2 | 254 | Sioux Falls, SD | 2,367.1 |
| 370 | Logan, UT-ID | 1,179.0 | 58 | Panama City, FL | 3,862.0 | 151 | South Bend-Mishawaka, IN-MI | 3,054.2 |
| 117 | Longview, TX | 3,305.0 | 243 | Parkersburg-Vienna, WV | 2,453.6 | 138 | Spartanburg, SC | 3,147.7 |
| 47 | Longview, WA | 3,970.9 | 101 | Pensacola, FL | 3,395.2 | 1 | Spokane, WA | 5,746.8 |
| 273 | Los Angeles County, CA M.D. | 2,279.1 | 261 | Peoria, IL | 2,326.6 | 54 | Springfield, IL | 3,893.8 |
| 286 | Los Angeles (greater), CA | 2,207.3 | 237 | Philadelphia (greater) PA-NJ-MD-DE | 2,477.7 | 182 | Springfield, MA | 2,904.4 |
| 95 | Louisville, KY-IN | 3,430.4 | 142 | Philadelphia, PA M.D. | 3,125.3 | 16 | Springfield, MO | 4,520.2 |
| 29 | Lubbock, TX | 4,247.4 | NA | Phoenix-Mesa-Scottsdale, AZ** | NA | 22 | Springfield, OH | 4,365.2 |
| 358 | Lynchburg, VA | 1,603.4 | 327 | Pittsburgh, PA | 1,856.5 | 366 | State College, PA | 1,394.4 |
| 11 | Macon, GA | 4,781.6 | 238 | Pittsfield, MA | 2,472.0 | 340 | Staunton-Waynesboro, VA | 1,714.2 |
| 222 | Madera, CA | 2,575.1 | 175 | Pocatello, ID | 2,947.4 | 42 | Stockton-Lodi, CA | 4,036.1 |
| 276 | Madison, WI | 2,262.6 | 280 | Port St. Lucie, FL | 2,228.5 | 247 | St. Cloud, MN | 2,436.7 |
| 265 | Manchester-Nashua, NH | 2,309.5 | 162 | Portland-Vancouver, OR-WA | 2,991.4 | NA | St. George, UT** | NA |
| 337 | Manhattan, KS | 1,756.5 | 274 | Portland, ME | 2,270.0 | 48 | St. Joseph, MO-KS | 3,969.6 |
| 214 | Mankato-North Mankato, MN | 2,661.1 | 308 | Prescott, AZ | 2,001.0 | 213 | St. Louis, MO-IL | 2,670.2 |
| 13 | Mansfield, OH | 4,718.7 | 256 | Providence-Warwick, RI-MA | 2,359.5 | 76 | Sumter, SC | 3,600.6 |
| 66 | McAllen-Edinburg-Mission, TX | 3,694.5 | 325 | Provo-Orem, UT | 1,876.3 | 236 | Syracuse, NY | 2,480.5 |
| 50 | Medford, OR | 3,934.1 | 3 | Pueblo, CO | 5,443.6 | 31 | Tacoma, WA M.D. | 4,179.3 |
| 30 | Memphis, TN-MS-AR | 4,189.9 | 305 | Punta Gorda, FL | 2,079.5 | 102 | Tallahassee, FL | 3,394.1 |
| 149 | Merced, CA | 3,060.9 | 239 | Racine, WI | 2,466.2 | 202 | Tampa-St Petersburg, FL | 2,732.1 |
| 67 | Miami (greater), FL | 3,690.5 | 269 | Raleigh, NC | 2,283.3 | 121 | Terre Haute, IN | 3,279.8 |
| 32 | Miami-Dade County, FL M.D. | 4,172.7 | 246 | Rapid City, SD | 2,440.3 | 51 | Texarkana, TX-AR | 3,918.8 |
| 215 | Midland, TX | 2,638.4 | 324 | Reading, PA | 1,882.3 | 371 | The Villages, FL | 999.0 |
| 148 | Milwaukee, WI | 3,064.2 | 118 | Redding, CA | 3,288.1 | NA | Toledo, OH** | NA |
| 217 | Minneapolis-St. Paul, MN-WI | 2,594.9 | 216 | Reno, NV | 2,597.1 | 85 | Topeka, KS | 3,541.4 |
| 154 | Missoula, MT | 3,040.6 | 251 | Richmond, VA | 2,395.7 | 306 | Trenton, NJ | 2,028.5 |
| 17 | Mobile, AL | 4,512.5 | 191 | Riverside-San Bernardino, CA | 2,794.4 | 10 | Tucson, AZ | 4,849.3 |
| 52 | Modesto, CA | 3,915.1 | 245 | Roanoke, VA | 2,444.1 | 122 | Tulsa, OK | 3,277.3 |
| 6 | Monroe, LA | 4,924.5 | 352 | Rochester, MN | 1,649.6 | 111 | Tuscaloosa, AL | 3,328.7 |
| 258 | Monroe, MI | 2,348.6 | 249 | Rochester, NY | 2,411.7 | 168 | Tyler, TX | 2,975.6 |
| 344 | Montgomery County, PA M.D. | 1,702.2 | 163 | Rockford, IL | 2,990.4 | 285 | Utica-Rome, NY | 2,211.1 |
| 343 | Morgantown, WV | 1,702.8 | 307 | Rockingham County, NH M.D. | 2,001.8 | 133 | Vallejo-Fairfield, CA | 3,195.0 |
| 157 | Morristown, TN | 3,017.2 | 81 | Rocky Mount, NC | 3,566.6 | 130 | Victoria, TX | 3,204.4 |
| 23 | Mount Vernon-Anacortes, WA | 4,362.9 | 33 | Rome, GA | 4,148.9 | 21 | Vineland-Bridgeton, NJ | 4,368.2 |
| 140 | Muncie, IN | 3,146.8 | 193 | Sacramento, CA | 2,766.6 | 160 | Virginia Beach-Norfolk, VA-NC | 3,016.5 |
| 74 | Muskegon, MI | 3,603.2 | 292 | Saginaw, MI | 2,174.5 | NA | Visalia-Porterville, CA** | NA |
| 20 | Myrtle Beach, SC-NC | 4,406.1 | 129 | Salem, OR | 3,215.1 | 108 | Waco, TX | 3,353.2 |
| 329 | Napa, CA | 1,838.8 | 227 | Salinas, CA | 2,539.0 | 53 | Warner Robins, GA | 3,901.0 |
| 361 | Naples-Marco Island, FL | 1,553.6 | 124 | Salisbury, MD-DE | 3,255.7 | 348 | Warren-Troy, MI M.D. | 1,689.8 |
| 206 | Nashville-Davidson, TN | 2,718.1 | 25 | Salt Lake City, UT | 4,348.0 | 293 | Washington (greater) DC-VA-MD-WV | 2,169.1 |
| 365 | Nassau-Suffolk, NY M.D. | 1,429.1 | 93 | San Angelo, TX | 3,443.6 | 264 | Washington, DC-VA-MD-WV M.D. | 2,316.4 |
| 152 | New Bern, NC | 3,049.1 | 19 | San Antonio, TX | 4,415.2 | 322 | Watertown-Fort Drum, NY | 1,898.7 |
| 188 | New Haven-Milford, CT | 2,810.9 | 290 | San Diego, CA | 2,191.9 | 362 | Wausau, WI | 1,544.7 |
| 135 | New Orleans, LA | 3,152.1 | 80 | San Francisco (greater), CA | 3,571.5 | 145 | West Palm Beach, FL M.D. | 3,080.5 |
| 357 | New York (greater), NY-NJ-PA | 1,609.9 | 40 | San Francisco-Redwood, CA M.D. | 4,060.8 | 74 | Wichita Falls, TX | 3,603.2 |
| 353 | New York-Jersey City, NY-NJ M.D. | 1,637.7 | 255 | San Jose, CA | 2,364.1 | 36 | Wichita, KS | 4,136.1 |
| 345 | Newark, NJ-PA M.D. | 1,701.8 | 278 | San Luis Obispo, CA | 2,242.6 | 294 | Williamsport, PA | 2,168.8 |
| 200 | Niles-Benton Harbor, MI | 2,735.6 | 318 | San Rafael, CA M.D. | 1,946.7 | 178 | Wilmington, DE-MD-NJ M.D. | 2,940.6 |
| 186 | North Port-Sarasota-Bradenton, FL | 2,830.2 | 156 | Santa Cruz-Watsonville, CA | 3,034.4 | 78 | Wilmington, NC | 3,574.0 |
| 242 | Norwich-New London, CT | 2,456.4 | 275 | Santa Maria-Santa Barbara, CA | 2,262.8 | 314 | Winchester, VA-WV | 1,973.7 |
| 94 | Oakland-Hayward, CA M.D. | 3,438.0 | 351 | Santa Rosa, CA | 1,660.7 | 86 | Winston-Salem, NC | 3,539.9 |
| NA | Ocala, FL** | NA | 147 | Savannah, GA | 3,065.8 | 309 | Worcester, MA-CT | 1,996.7 |
| 37 | Ocean City, NJ | 4,114.1 | 281 | Scranton--Wilkes-Barre, PA | 2,223.6 | 104 | Yakima, WA | 3,363.8 |
| 26 | Odessa, TX | 4,277.4 | 44 | Seattle (greater), WA | 4,023.3 | 332 | York-Hanover, PA | 1,820.5 |
| NA | Ogden-Clearfield, UT** | NA | 46 | Seattle-Bellevue-Everett, WA M.D. | 3,977.3 | 158 | Yuba City, CA | 3,017.0 |
| 49 | Oklahoma City, OK | 3,955.6 | 301 | Sebastian-Vero Beach, FL | 2,102.3 | 211 | Yuma, AZ | 2,681.3 |
| 210 | Olympia, WA | 2,685.6 | 112 | Sebring, FL | 3,324.5 | | | |

Source: Reported data from the F.B.I. "Crime in the United States 2013"
*Property crimes are offenses of burglary, larceny-theft, and motor vehicle theft. Attempts are included.
**Not available.

# 26. Property Crime Rate in 2013 (continued)
## National Rate = 2,730.7 Property Crimes per 100,000 Population*

| RANK | METROPOLITAN AREA | RATE | RANK | METROPOLITAN AREA | RATE | RANK | METROPOLITAN AREA | RATE |
|---|---|---|---|---|---|---|---|---|
| 1 | Spokane, WA | 5,746.8 | 65 | Eugene, OR | 3,704.8 | 129 | Salem, OR | 3,215.1 |
| 2 | Hammond, LA | 5,601.1 | 66 | McAllen-Edinburg-Mission, TX | 3,694.5 | 130 | Victoria, TX | 3,204.4 |
| 3 | Pueblo, CO | 5,443.6 | 67 | Miami (greater), FL | 3,690.5 | 131 | Burlington, NC | 3,201.4 |
| 4 | Hot Springs, AR | 5,329.2 | 68 | Augusta, GA-SC | 3,665.1 | 132 | Lincoln, NE | 3,197.6 |
| 5 | Columbus, GA-AL | 4,930.0 | 69 | Lawrence, KS | 3,662.3 | 133 | Vallejo-Fairfield, CA | 3,195.0 |
| 6 | Monroe, LA | 4,924.5 | 70 | Jackson, TN | 3,653.3 | 134 | Austin-Round Rock, TX | 3,178.5 |
| 7 | Fayetteville, NC | 4,910.2 | 71 | Columbia, SC | 3,636.9 | 135 | New Orleans, LA | 3,152.1 |
| 8 | Little Rock, AR | 4,891.6 | 72 | Goldsboro, NC | 3,633.6 | 136 | Charleston-North Charleston, SC | 3,150.8 |
| 9 | Lake Charles, LA | 4,852.9 | 73 | Gulfport-Biloxi-Pascagoula, MS | 3,624.9 | 137 | Cleveland, TN | 3,150.5 |
| 10 | Tucson, AZ | 4,849.3 | 74 | Muskegon, MI | 3,603.2 | 138 | Spartanburg, SC | 3,147.7 |
| 11 | Macon, GA | 4,781.6 | 74 | Wichita Falls, TX | 3,603.2 | 139 | Cincinnati, OH-KY-IN | 3,147.4 |
| 12 | Alexandria, LA | 4,775.7 | 76 | Sumter, SC | 3,600.6 | 140 | Muncie, IN | 3,146.8 |
| 13 | Mansfield, OH | 4,718.7 | 77 | Great Falls, MT | 3,585.3 | 141 | Knoxville, TN | 3,136.0 |
| 14 | Florence, SC | 4,542.7 | 78 | Wilmington, NC | 3,574.0 | 142 | Philadelphia, PA M.D. | 3,125.3 |
| 15 | Albany, GA | 4,521.3 | 79 | Kahului-Wailuku-Lahaina, HI | 3,572.8 | 143 | Fort Smith, AR-OK | 3,110.7 |
| 16 | Springfield, MO | 4,520.2 | 80 | San Francisco (greater), CA | 3,571.5 | 144 | Deltona-Daytona Beach, FL | 3,108.4 |
| 17 | Mobile, AL | 4,512.5 | 81 | Rocky Mount, NC | 3,566.6 | 145 | West Palm Beach, FL M.D. | 3,080.5 |
| 18 | Albuquerque, NM | 4,483.7 | 82 | Shreveport-Bossier City, LA | 3,551.1 | 146 | Athens-Clarke County, GA | 3,079.5 |
| 19 | San Antonio, TX | 4,415.2 | 83 | Jonesboro, AR | 3,547.6 | 147 | Savannah, GA | 3,065.8 |
| 20 | Myrtle Beach, SC-NC | 4,406.1 | 84 | Lafayette, LA | 3,545.0 | 148 | Milwaukee, WI | 3,064.2 |
| 21 | Vineland-Bridgeton, NJ | 4,368.2 | 85 | Topeka, KS | 3,541.4 | 149 | Merced, CA | 3,060.9 |
| 22 | Springfield, OH | 4,365.2 | 86 | Winston-Salem, NC | 3,539.9 | 150 | Cape Girardeau, MO-IL | 3,057.1 |
| 23 | Mount Vernon-Anacortes, WA | 4,362.9 | 87 | Brownsville-Harlingen, TX | 3,534.8 | 151 | South Bend-Mishawaka, IN-MI | 3,054.2 |
| 24 | Joplin, MO | 4,354.0 | 88 | Houston, TX | 3,488.8 | 152 | New Bern, NC | 3,049.1 |
| 25 | Salt Lake City, UT | 4,348.0 | 89 | Indianapolis, IN | 3,468.7 | 153 | Flagstaff, AZ | 3,043.1 |
| 26 | Odessa, TX | 4,277.4 | 90 | Fort Lauderdale, FL M.D. | 3,456.7 | 154 | Missoula, MT | 3,040.6 |
| 27 | Corpus Christi, TX | 4,260.8 | 91 | Greensboro-High Point, NC | 3,448.5 | 155 | Dallas (greater), TX | 3,036.4 |
| 28 | Gadsden, AL | 4,257.0 | 92 | Grand Island, NE | 3,445.9 | 156 | Santa Cruz-Watsonville, CA | 3,034.4 |
| 29 | Lubbock, TX | 4,247.4 | 93 | San Angelo, TX | 3,443.6 | 157 | Morristown, TN | 3,017.2 |
| 30 | Memphis, TN-MS-AR | 4,189.9 | 94 | Oakland-Hayward, CA M.D. | 3,438.0 | 158 | Yuba City, CA | 3,017.0 |
| 31 | Tacoma, WA M.D. | 4,179.3 | 95 | Louisville, KY-IN | 3,430.4 | 159 | Las Vegas-Henderson, NV | 3,016.8 |
| 32 | Miami-Dade County, FL M.D. | 4,172.7 | 96 | Amarillo, TX | 3,426.4 | 160 | Virginia Beach-Norfolk, VA-NC | 3,016.5 |
| 33 | Rome, GA | 4,148.9 | 97 | Orlando, FL | 3,420.1 | 161 | Baltimore, MD | 3,012.1 |
| 34 | Anchorage, AK | 4,147.8 | 98 | Duluth, MN-WI | 3,404.1 | 162 | Portland-Vancouver, OR-WA | 2,991.4 |
| 35 | Laredo, TX | 4,137.5 | 99 | Greenville, NC | 3,397.1 | 163 | Rockford, IL | 2,990.4 |
| 36 | Wichita, KS | 4,136.1 | 99 | Lima, OH | 3,397.1 | 164 | Jackson, MS | 2,988.8 |
| 37 | Ocean City, NJ | 4,114.1 | 101 | Pensacola, FL | 3,395.2 | 165 | Flint, MI | 2,981.2 |
| 38 | Fairbanks, AK | 4,113.3 | 102 | Tallahassee, FL | 3,394.1 | 166 | Charlotte-Mecklenburg, NC-SC | 2,981.0 |
| 39 | Lawton, OK | 4,087.0 | 103 | Albany, OR | 3,372.1 | 167 | Dover, DE | 2,979.5 |
| 40 | San Francisco-Redwood, CA M.D. | 4,060.8 | 104 | Yakima, WA | 3,363.8 | 168 | Tyler, TX | 2,975.6 |
| 41 | Grants Pass, OR | 4,045.1 | 105 | Beaumont-Port Arthur, TX | 3,359.4 | 169 | Atlantic City, NJ | 2,969.6 |
| 42 | Stockton-Lodi, CA | 4,036.1 | 106 | Huntsville, AL | 3,355.8 | 170 | Las Cruces, NM | 2,967.2 |
| 43 | Greenville-Anderson, SC | 4,026.1 | 107 | Lake Havasu City-Kingman, AZ | 3,355.5 | 171 | Gary, IN M.D. | 2,964.9 |
| 44 | Seattle (greater), WA | 4,023.3 | 108 | Waco, TX | 3,353.2 | 172 | Kokomo, IN | 2,962.4 |
| 45 | Billings, MT | 3,998.3 | 109 | Columbus, IN | 3,338.2 | 173 | Gainesville, FL | 2,960.6 |
| 46 | Seattle-Bellevue-Everett, WA M.D. | 3,977.3 | 110 | Atlanta, GA | 3,330.8 | 174 | Casper, WY | 2,959.0 |
| 47 | Longview, WA | 3,970.9 | 111 | Tuscaloosa, AL | 3,328.7 | 175 | Pocatello, ID | 2,947.4 |
| 48 | St. Joseph, MO-KS | 3,969.6 | 112 | Sebring, FL | 3,324.5 | 176 | Bremerton-Silverdale, WA | 2,946.4 |
| 49 | Oklahoma City, OK | 3,955.6 | 113 | Dayton, OH | 3,320.3 | 177 | Florence-Muscle Shoals, AL | 2,945.9 |
| 50 | Medford, OR | 3,934.1 | 114 | Fort Worth-Arlington, TX M.D. | 3,320.2 | 178 | Wilmington, DE-MD-NJ M.D. | 2,940.6 |
| 51 | Texarkana, TX-AR | 3,918.8 | 115 | El Centro, CA | 3,317.1 | 179 | Fort Wayne, IN | 2,929.2 |
| 52 | Modesto, CA | 3,915.1 | 116 | Lewiston, ID-WA | 3,316.1 | 180 | Akron, OH | 2,923.1 |
| 53 | Warner Robins, GA | 3,901.0 | 117 | Longview, TX | 3,305.0 | 181 | Lakeland, FL | 2,908.4 |
| 54 | Springfield, IL | 3,893.8 | 118 | Redding, CA | 3,288.1 | 182 | Springfield, MA | 2,904.4 |
| 55 | Brunswick, GA | 3,886.8 | 119 | Columbia, MO | 3,287.8 | 183 | Dallas-Plano-Irving, TX M.D. | 2,891.0 |
| 56 | Bakersfield, CA | 3,871.6 | 120 | Abilene, TX | 3,284.6 | 184 | Hilton Head Island, SC | 2,883.9 |
| 57 | Chattanooga, TN-GA | 3,870.3 | 121 | Terre Haute, IN | 3,279.8 | 185 | Dothan, AL | 2,871.1 |
| 58 | Panama City, FL | 3,862.0 | 122 | Tulsa, OK | 3,277.3 | 186 | North Port-Sarasota-Bradenton, FL | 2,830.2 |
| 59 | Fresno, CA | 3,845.5 | 123 | Colorado Springs, CO | 3,274.4 | 187 | Bangor, ME | 2,826.2 |
| 60 | Detroit-Dearborn-Livonia, MI M.D. | 3,828.7 | 124 | Salisbury, MD-DE | 3,255.7 | 188 | New Haven-Milford, CT | 2,810.9 |
| 61 | Baton Rouge, LA | 3,800.3 | 125 | Kansas City, MO-KS | 3,254.4 | 189 | Chico, CA | 2,798.6 |
| 62 | Anniston-Oxford, AL | 3,737.6 | 126 | Omaha-Council Bluffs, NE-IA | 3,245.2 | 190 | Palm Bay-Melbourne, FL | 2,796.2 |
| 63 | Lexington-Fayette, KY | 3,723.1 | 127 | Jacksonville, FL | 3,228.8 | 191 | Riverside-San Bernardino, CA | 2,794.4 |
| 64 | Birmingham-Hoover, AL | 3,722.5 | 128 | Houma, LA | 3,219.8 | 192 | Dalton, GA | 2,791.4 |

Note: All listings are for Metropolitan Statistical Areas (M.S.A.s) except for those ending with "M.D." Listings with "M.D." are Metropolitan Divisions which are smaller parts of eleven large M.S.A.s. See explanatory note at beginning of metropolitan area section.

| RANK | METROPOLITAN AREA | RATE | RANK | METROPOLITAN AREA | RATE | RANK | METROPOLITAN AREA | RATE |
|---|---|---|---|---|---|---|---|---|
| 193 | Sacramento, CA | 2,766.6 | 255 | San Jose, CA | 2,364.1 | 317 | Oxnard-Thousand Oaks, CA | 1,950.8 |
| 194 | Coeur d'Alene, ID | 2,765.8 | 256 | Providence-Warwick, RI-MA | 2,359.5 | 318 | San Rafael, CA M.D. | 1,946.7 |
| 195 | Des Moines-West Des Moines, IA | 2,764.7 | 257 | Cedar Rapids, IA | 2,355.9 | 319 | Chambersburg-Waynesboro, PA | 1,932.8 |
| 196 | Sioux City, IA-NE-SD | 2,756.1 | 258 | Monroe, MI | 2,348.6 | 320 | Blacksburg, VA | 1,925.1 |
| 197 | Denver-Aurora, CO | 2,746.8 | 259 | Crestview-Fort Walton Beach, FL | 2,346.8 | 321 | Charlottesville, VA | 1,908.2 |
| 198 | Cheyenne, WY | 2,745.9 | 260 | Chicago (greater), IL-IN-WI | 2,339.0 | 322 | Watertown-Fort Drum, NY | 1,898.7 |
| 199 | Binghamton, NY | 2,739.8 | 261 | Peoria, IL | 2,326.6 | 323 | Boston (greater), MA-NH | 1,890.3 |
| 200 | Niles-Benton Harbor, MI | 2,735.6 | 262 | Camden, NJ M.D. | 2,324.7 | 324 | Reading, PA | 1,882.2 |
| 201 | Buffalo-Niagara Falls, NY | 2,735.0 | 263 | Bowling Green, KY | 2,318.3 | 325 | Provo-Orem, UT | 1,876.3 |
| 202 | Tampa-St Petersburg, FL | 2,732.1 | 264 | Washington, DC-VA-MD-WV M.D. | 2,316.4 | 326 | Lancaster, PA | 1,862.1 |
| 203 | Hinesville, GA | 2,722.9 | 265 | Manchester-Nashua, NH | 2,309.5 | 327 | Pittsburgh, PA | 1,856.5 |
| 204 | Lewiston-Auburn, ME | 2,720.8 | 266 | Bismarck, ND | 2,303.6 | 328 | La Crosse, WI-MN | 1,844.5 |
| 205 | Lafayette, IN | 2,720.7 | 267 | Albany-Schenectady-Troy, NY | 2,300.8 | 329 | Napa, CA | 1,838.8 |
| 206 | Nashville-Davidson, TN | 2,718.1 | 268 | Elmira, NY | 2,300.1 | 330 | Lebanon, PA | 1,837.3 |
| 207 | Bloomington, IN | 2,693.2 | 269 | Raleigh, NC | 2,283.3 | 331 | Idaho Falls, ID | 1,837.0 |
| 208 | Kingsport, TN-VA | 2,688.5 | 270 | Fargo, ND-MN | 2,281.2 | 332 | York-Hanover, PA | 1,820.5 |
| 209 | Cumberland, MD-WV | 2,688.3 | 271 | Boulder, CO | 2,281.1 | 333 | Green Bay, WI | 1,812.5 |
| 210 | Olympia, WA | 2,685.6 | 272 | Kennewick-Richland, WA | 2,280.0 | 334 | Kingston, NY | 1,804.7 |
| 211 | Yuma, AZ | 2,681.3 | 273 | Los Angeles County, CA M.D. | 2,279.1 | 335 | Johnstown, PA | 1,803.0 |
| 212 | Canton, OH | 2,677.2 | 274 | Portland, ME | 2,270.0 | 336 | Sheboygan, WI | 1,793.8 |
| 213 | St. Louis, MO-IL | 2,670.2 | 275 | Santa Maria-Santa Barbara, CA | 2,262.8 | 337 | Manhattan, KS | 1,756.5 |
| 214 | Mankato-North Mankato, MN | 2,661.1 | 276 | Madison, WI | 2,262.6 | 338 | Bloomsburg-Berwick, PA | 1,753.8 |
| 215 | Midland, TX | 2,638.4 | 277 | California-Lexington Park, MD | 2,256.7 | 339 | Oshkosh-Neenah, WI | 1,721.1 |
| 216 | Reno, NV | 2,597.1 | 278 | San Luis Obispo, CA | 2,242.6 | 340 | Staunton-Waynesboro, VA | 1,714.2 |
| 217 | Minneapolis-St. Paul, MN-WI | 2,594.9 | 279 | Gainesville, GA | 2,241.4 | 341 | Altoona, PA | 1,706.1 |
| 218 | Bend, OR | 2,589.8 | 280 | Port St. Lucie, FL | 2,228.5 | 342 | Lake Co.-Kenosha Co., IL-WI M.D. | 1,704.4 |
| 219 | Decatur, AL | 2,585.7 | 281 | Scranton--Wilkes-Barre, PA | 2,223.6 | 343 | Morgantown, WV | 1,702.8 |
| 220 | Detroit (greater), MI | 2,579.1 | 282 | Hagerstown-Martinsburg, MD-WV | 2,221.9 | 344 | Montgomery County, PA M.D. | 1,702.2 |
| 221 | Grand Junction, CO | 2,577.6 | 283 | Owensboro, KY | 2,220.9 | 345 | Newark, NJ-PA M.D. | 1,701.8 |
| 222 | Madera, CA | 2,575.1 | 284 | Lansing-East Lansing, MI | 2,211.8 | 346 | Boise City, ID | 1,700.7 |
| 223 | Carbondale-Marion, IL | 2,566.2 | 285 | Utica-Rome, NY | 2,211.1 | 347 | Cambridge-Newton, MA M.D. | 1,700.1 |
| 224 | Johnson City, TN | 2,560.1 | 286 | Los Angeles (greater), CA | 2,207.3 | 348 | Warren-Troy, MI M.D. | 1,689.8 |
| 225 | Decatur, IL | 2,553.8 | 287 | Hartford, CT | 2,200.6 | 349 | Eau Claire, WI | 1,687.3 |
| 226 | Corvallis, OR | 2,552.0 | 288 | Cape Coral-Fort Myers, FL | 2,194.3 | 350 | Carson City, NV | 1,681.9 |
| 227 | Salinas, CA | 2,539.0 | 289 | Allentown, PA-NJ | 2,193.9 | 351 | Santa Rosa, CA | 1,660.7 |
| 228 | Kankakee, IL | 2,534.5 | 290 | San Diego, CA | 2,191.9 | 352 | Rochester, MN | 1,649.6 |
| 229 | Daphne-Fairhope-Foley, AL | 2,530.5 | 291 | El Paso, TX | 2,176.4 | 353 | New York-Jersey City, NY-NJ M.D. | 1,637.7 |
| 230 | Sherman-Denison, TX | 2,518.6 | 292 | Saginaw, MI | 2,174.5 | 354 | Silver Spring-Frederick, MD M.D. | 1,620.7 |
| 231 | Champaign-Urbana, IL | 2,517.3 | 293 | Washington (greater) DC-VA-MD-WV | 2,169.1 | 355 | Bridgeport-Stamford, CT | 1,619.7 |
| 232 | Clarksville, TN-KY | 2,514.3 | 294 | Williamsport, PA | 2,168.8 | 356 | Fond du Lac, WI | 1,619.3 |
| 233 | Davenport, IA-IL | 2,503.2 | 295 | Farmington, NM | 2,159.9 | 357 | New York (greater), NY-NJ-PA | 1,609.9 |
| 234 | College Station-Bryan, TX | 2,487.6 | 296 | Fort Collins, CO | 2,156.3 | 358 | Lynchburg, VA | 1,603.4 |
| 235 | Janesville, WI | 2,482.2 | 297 | Jefferson City, MO | 2,154.2 | 359 | Glens Falls, NY | 1,596.6 |
| 236 | Syracuse, NY | 2,480.5 | 298 | Grand Forks, ND-MN | 2,129.4 | 360 | Harrisonburg, VA | 1,559.1 |
| 237 | Philadelphia (greater) PA-NJ-MD-DE | 2,477.7 | 299 | Ames, IA | 2,120.9 | 361 | Naples-Marco Island, FL | 1,553.6 |
| 238 | Pittsfield, MA | 2,472.0 | 300 | Bay City, MI | 2,109.0 | 362 | Wausau, WI | 1,544.7 |
| 239 | Racine, WI | 2,466.2 | 301 | Sebastian-Vero Beach, FL | 2,102.3 | 363 | Elgin, IL M.D. | 1,518.7 |
| 240 | Jackson, MI | 2,466.1 | 302 | Ann Arbor, MI | 2,097.7 | 364 | Elizabethtown-Fort Knox, KY | 1,483.1 |
| 241 | Hanford-Corcoran, CA | 2,461.4 | 303 | Boston, MA M.D. | 2,092.6 | 365 | Nassau-Suffolk, NY M.D. | 1,429.1 |
| 242 | Norwich-New London, CT | 2,456.4 | 304 | Bloomington, IL | 2,083.3 | 366 | State College, PA | 1,394.4 |
| 243 | Parkersburg-Vienna, WV | 2,453.6 | 305 | Punta Gorda, FL | 2,079.5 | 367 | Appleton, WI | 1,385.0 |
| 244 | East Stroudsburg, PA | 2,451.4 | 306 | Trenton, NJ | 2,028.5 | 368 | Dutchess-Putnam, NY M.D. | 1,338.9 |
| 245 | Roanoke, VA | 2,444.1 | 307 | Rockingham County, NH M.D. | 2,001.8 | 369 | Gettysburg, PA | 1,264.7 |
| 246 | Rapid City, SD | 2,440.3 | 308 | Prescott, AZ | 2,001.0 | 370 | Logan, UT-ID | 1,179.0 |
| 247 | St. Cloud, MN | 2,436.7 | 309 | Worcester, MA-CT | 1,996.7 | 371 | The Villages, FL | 999.0 |
| 248 | Chicago-Naperville, IL M.D. | 2,424.3 | 310 | Iowa City, IA | 1,981.4 | NA | Ocala, FL** | NA |
| 249 | Rochester, NY | 2,411.7 | 311 | Homosassa Springs, FL | 1,978.6 | NA | Ogden-Clearfield, UT** | NA |
| 250 | Barnstable Town, MA | 2,410.5 | 312 | Dubuque, IA | 1,978.0 | NA | Phoenix-Mesa-Scottsdale, AZ** | NA |
| 251 | Richmond, VA | 2,395.7 | 313 | Anaheim-Santa Ana-Irvine, CA M.D. | 1,976.8 | NA | St. George, UT** | NA |
| 252 | Erie, PA | 2,385.1 | 314 | Winchester, VA-WV | 1,973.7 | NA | Toledo, OH** | NA |
| 253 | Fayetteville-Springdale, AR-MO | 2,380.7 | 315 | Greeley, CO | 1,971.6 | NA | Visalia-Porterville, CA** | NA |
| 254 | Sioux Falls, SD | 2,367.1 | 316 | Grand Rapids-Wyoming, MI | 1,954.2 | | | |

Source: Reported data from the F.B.I. "Crime in the United States 2013"

*Property crimes are offenses of burglary, larceny-theft, and motor vehicle theft.  Attempts are included.

**Not available.

# 27. Percent Change in Property Crime Rate: 2012 to 2013
## National Percent Change = 4.8% Decrease*

| RANK | METROPOLITAN AREA | % CHANGE | RANK | METROPOLITAN AREA | % CHANGE | RANK | METROPOLITAN AREA | % CHANGE |
|---|---|---|---|---|---|---|---|---|
| 11 | Abilene, TX | 9.2 | 152 | Cheyenne, WY | (4.9) | 186 | Gary, IN M.D. | (6.0) |
| 120 | Akron, OH | (3.7) | 294 | Chicago (greater), IL-IN-WI | (12.6) | NA | Gettysburg, PA** | NA |
| 206 | Albany-Schenectady-Troy, NY | (6.6) | 301 | Chicago-Naperville, IL M.D. | (13.6) | 152 | Glens Falls, NY | (4.9) |
| 73 | Albany, GA | (1.0) | 10 | Chico, CA | 9.9 | 235 | Goldsboro, NC | (7.9) |
| 17 | Albany, OR | 7.3 | 166 | Cincinnati, OH-KY-IN | (5.2) | 148 | Grand Forks, ND-MN | (4.8) |
| NA | Albuquerque, NM** | NA | 127 | Clarksville, TN-KY | (3.9) | 71 | Grand Island, NE | (0.8) |
| NA | Alexandria, LA** | NA | 31 | Cleveland, TN | 4.0 | 284 | Grand Junction, CO | (10.8) |
| 72 | Allentown, PA-NJ | (0.9) | 298 | Coeur d'Alene, ID | (13.1) | NA | Grand Rapids-Wyoming, MI** | NA |
| 40 | Altoona, PA | 2.8 | 224 | College Station-Bryan, TX | (7.2) | NA | Grants Pass, OR** | NA |
| 242 | Amarillo, TX | (8.4) | NA | Colorado Springs, CO** | NA | 166 | Great Falls, MT | (5.2) |
| 186 | Ames, IA | (6.0) | 82 | Columbia, MO | (1.6) | 268 | Greeley, CO | (9.8) |
| 272 | Anaheim-Santa Ana-Irvine, CA M.D. | (10.1) | NA | Columbia, SC** | NA | 132 | Green Bay, WI | (4.0) |
| 6 | Anchorage, AK | 14.6 | 38 | Columbus, GA-AL | 3.2 | 105 | Greensboro-High Point, NC | (2.8) |
| 303 | Ann Arbor, MI | (13.9) | 178 | Columbus, IN | (5.8) | 42 | Greenville-Anderson, SC | 2.7 |
| 317 | Anniston-Oxford, AL | (17.2) | NA | Corpus Christi, TX** | NA | 100 | Greenville, NC | (2.6) |
| 278 | Appleton, WI | (10.3) | 1 | Corvallis, OR | 20.0 | NA | Gulfport-Biloxi-Pascagoula, MS** | NA |
| 260 | Athens-Clarke County, GA | (9.5) | 289 | Crestview-Fort Walton Beach, FL | (11.8) | 120 | Hagerstown-Martinsburg, MD-WV | (3.7) |
| 82 | Atlanta, GA | (1.6) | 201 | Cumberland, MD-WV | (6.5) | 112 | Hammond, LA | (3.1) |
| 100 | Atlantic City, NJ | (2.6) | 140 | Dallas (greater), TX | (4.4) | 8 | Hanford-Corcoran, CA | 11.0 |
| 242 | Augusta, GA-SC | (8.4) | 209 | Dallas-Plano-Irving, TX M.D. | (6.7) | 9 | Harrisonburg, VA | 10.9 |
| 227 | Austin-Round Rock, TX | (7.4) | 51 | Dalton, GA | 0.9 | 276 | Hartford, CT | (10.2) |
| 137 | Bakersfield, CA | (4.3) | 152 | Daphne-Fairhope-Foley, AL | (4.9) | 164 | Hilton Head Island, SC | (5.1) |
| 51 | Baltimore, MD | 0.9 | 115 | Davenport, IA-IL | (3.2) | 265 | Hinesville, GA | (9.7) |
| 180 | Bangor, ME | (5.9) | 95 | Dayton, OH | (2.3) | 152 | Homosassa Springs, FL | (4.9) |
| 272 | Barnstable Town, MA | (10.1) | 286 | Decatur, AL | (11.5) | NA | Hot Springs, AR** | NA |
| NA | Baton Rouge, LA** | NA | 143 | Decatur, IL | (4.5) | 78 | Houma, LA | (1.4) |
| 16 | Bay City, MI | 8.2 | 108 | Deltona-Daytona Beach, FL | (2.9) | NA | Houston, TX** | NA |
| 37 | Beaumont-Port Arthur, TX | 3.4 | 65 | Denver-Aurora, CO | 0.0 | 61 | Huntsville, AL | 0.3 |
| NA | Bend, OR** | NA | NA | Des Moines-West Des Moines, IA** | NA | 97 | Idaho Falls, ID | (2.5) |
| 7 | Billings, MT | 12.6 | 171 | Detroit (greater), MI | (5.5) | 171 | Indianapolis, IN | (5.5) |
| 59 | Binghamton, NY | 0.5 | 87 | Detroit-Dearborn-Livonia, MI M.D. | (1.9) | 55 | Iowa City, IA | 0.8 |
| 89 | Birmingham-Hoover, AL | (2.0) | 235 | Dothan, AL | (7.9) | 206 | Jacksonville, FL | (6.6) |
| 148 | Bismarck, ND | (4.8) | 323 | Dover, DE | (19.6) | NA | Jackson, MI** | NA |
| 288 | Blacksburg, VA | (11.6) | NA | Dubuque, IA** | NA | 276 | Jackson, MS | (10.2) |
| 120 | Bloomington, IL | (3.7) | 15 | Duluth, MN-WI | 8.4 | 27 | Jackson, TN | 4.2 |
| 309 | Bloomington, IN | (15.3) | 293 | Dutchess-Putnam, NY M.D. | (12.5) | 315 | Janesville, WI | (16.5) |
| 313 | Bloomsburg-Berwick, PA | (16.3) | 216 | East Stroudsburg, PA | (7.0) | 255 | Jefferson City, MO | (9.2) |
| 302 | Boise City, ID | (13.8) | NA | Eau Claire, WI** | NA | 304 | Johnson City, TN | (14.0) |
| 146 | Boston (greater), MA-NH | (4.7) | 242 | El Centro, CA | (8.4) | 51 | Johnstown, PA | 0.9 |
| 132 | Boston, MA M.D. | (4.0) | 186 | El Paso, TX | (6.0) | 48 | Jonesboro, AR | 1.5 |
| 100 | Boulder, CO | (2.6) | 237 | Elgin, IL M.D. | (8.0) | 44 | Joplin, MO | 2.2 |
| 212 | Bowling Green, KY | (6.8) | 27 | Elizabethtown-Fort Knox, KY | 4.2 | 171 | Kahului-Wailuku-Lahaina, HI | (5.5) |
| 212 | Bremerton-Silverdale, WA | (6.8) | 218 | Elmira, NY | (7.1) | 247 | Kankakee, IL | (8.6) |
| 258 | Bridgeport-Stamford, CT | (9.3) | 247 | Erie, PA | (8.6) | 199 | Kansas City, MO-KS | (6.4) |
| 285 | Brownsville-Harlingen, TX | (11.3) | 100 | Eugene, OR | (2.6) | 158 | Kennewick-Richland, WA | (5.0) |
| 180 | Brunswick, GA | (5.9) | 239 | Fairbanks, AK | (8.1) | 265 | Kingsport, TN-VA | (9.7) |
| 201 | Buffalo-Niagara Falls, NY | (6.5) | 27 | Fargo, ND-MN | 4.2 | 268 | Kingston, NY | (9.8) |
| 158 | Burlington, NC | (5.0) | 295 | Farmington, NM | (12.7) | 272 | Knoxville, TN | (10.1) |
| 289 | California-Lexington Park, MD | (11.8) | 197 | Fayetteville-Springdale, AR-MO | (6.3) | 30 | Kokomo, IN | 4.1 |
| 148 | Cambridge-Newton, MA M.D. | (4.8) | 242 | Fayetteville, NC | (8.4) | NA | La Crosse, WI-MN** | NA |
| 263 | Camden, NJ M.D. | (9.6) | 109 | Flagstaff, AZ | (3.0) | 57 | Lafayette, IN | 0.6 |
| 263 | Canton, OH | (9.6) | 320 | Flint, MI | (18.1) | NA | Lafayette, LA** | NA |
| 201 | Cape Coral-Fort Myers, FL | (6.5) | 93 | Florence-Muscle Shoals, AL | (2.2) | NA | Lake Charles, LA** | NA |
| 324 | Cape Girardeau, MO-IL | (20.1) | 137 | Florence, SC | (4.3) | 295 | Lake Co.-Kenosha Co., IL-WI M.D. | (12.7) |
| NA | Carbondale-Marion, IL** | NA | 218 | Fond du Lac, WI | (7.1) | 109 | Lake Havasu City-Kingman, AZ | (3.0) |
| 306 | Carson City, NV | (14.7) | 292 | Fort Collins, CO | (12.2) | 180 | Lakeland, FL | (5.9) |
| 95 | Casper, WY | (2.3) | 240 | Fort Lauderdale, FL M.D. | (8.2) | NA | Lancaster, PA** | NA |
| NA | Cedar Rapids, IA** | NA | 31 | Fort Smith, AR-OK | 4.0 | 69 | Lansing-East Lansing, MI | (0.5) |
| NA | Chambersburg-Waynesboro, PA** | NA | 46 | Fort Wayne, IN | 1.7 | 105 | Laredo, TX | (2.8) |
| 152 | Champaign-Urbana, IL | (4.9) | 67 | Fort Worth-Arlington, TX M.D. | (0.2) | 97 | Las Cruces, NM | (2.5) |
| 119 | Charleston-North Charleston, SC | (3.6) | 298 | Fresno, CA | (13.1) | 46 | Las Vegas-Henderson, NV | 1.7 |
| NA | Charlotte-Mecklenburg, NC-SC** | NA | 73 | Gadsden, AL | (1.0) | 255 | Lawrence, KS | (9.2) |
| 100 | Charlottesville, VA | (2.6) | 265 | Gainesville, FL | (9.7) | 140 | Lawton, OK | (4.4) |
| NA | Chattanooga, TN-GA** | NA | 134 | Gainesville, GA | (4.1) | 124 | Lebanon, PA | (3.8) |

Note: All listings are for Metropolitan Statistical Areas (M.S.A.s) except for those ending with "M.D." Listings with "M.D." are Metropolitan Divisions which are smaller parts of eleven large M.S.A.s. See explanatory note at beginning of metropolitan area section.

| RANK | METROPOLITAN AREA | % CHANGE | RANK | METROPOLITAN AREA | % CHANGE | RANK | METROPOLITAN AREA | % CHANGE |
|------|-------------------|----------|------|-------------------|----------|------|-------------------|----------|
| 282 | Lewiston-Auburn, ME | (10.6) | 120 | Omaha-Council Bluffs, NE-IA | (3.7) | 310 | Sheboygan, WI | (15.5) |
| 124 | Lewiston, ID-WA | (3.8) | 87 | Orlando, FL | (1.9) | 318 | Sherman-Denison, TX | (17.5) |
| 254 | Lexington-Fayette, KY | (9.1) | 305 | Oshkosh-Neenah, WI | (14.5) | NA | Shreveport-Bossier City, LA** | NA |
| 194 | Lima, OH | (6.2) | 321 | Owensboro, KY | (18.2) | 189 | Silver Spring-Frederick, MD M.D. | (6.1) |
| 268 | Lincoln, NE | (9.8) | 39 | Oxnard-Thousand Oaks, CA | 2.9 | 43 | Sioux City, IA-NE-SD | 2.4 |
| 158 | Little Rock, AR | (5.0) | 229 | Palm Bay-Melbourne, FL | (7.5) | 137 | Sioux Falls, SD | (4.3) |
| 328 | Logan, UT-ID | (25.1) | 164 | Panama City, FL | (5.1) | 124 | South Bend-Mishawaka, IN-MI | (3.8) |
| 260 | Longview, TX | (9.5) | 311 | Parkersburg-Vienna, WV | (15.6) | 168 | Spartanburg, SC | (5.3) |
| 13 | Longview, WA | 8.6 | 215 | Pensacola, FL | (6.9) | 35 | Spokane, WA | 3.8 |
| 91 | Los Angeles County, CA M.D. | (2.1) | 308 | Peoria, IL | (14.9) | 197 | Springfield, IL | (6.3) |
| 127 | Los Angeles (greater), CA | (3.9) | 218 | Philadelphia (greater) PA-NJ-MD-DE | (7.1) | 127 | Springfield, MA | (3.9) |
| 77 | Louisville, KY-IN | (1.3) | 180 | Philadelphia, PA M.D. | (5.9) | 93 | Springfield, MO | (2.2) |
| 189 | Lubbock, TX | (6.1) | NA | Phoenix-Mesa-Scottsdale, AZ** | NA | 19 | Springfield, OH | 6.5 |
| 278 | Lynchburg, VA | (10.3) | NA | Pittsburgh, PA** | NA | 86 | State College, PA | (1.7) |
| 48 | Macon, GA | 1.5 | 18 | Pittsfield, MA | 6.7 | 109 | Staunton-Waynesboro, VA | (3.0) |
| 75 | Madera, CA | (1.1) | 5 | Pocatello, ID | 15.2 | 112 | Stockton-Lodi, CA | (3.1) |
| NA | Madison, WI** | NA | 158 | Port St. Lucie, FL | (5.0) | NA | St. Cloud, MN** | NA |
| 62 | Manchester-Nashua, NH | 0.2 | 171 | Portland-Vancouver, OR-WA | (5.5) | NA | St. George, UT** | NA |
| 283 | Manhattan, KS | (10.7) | 234 | Portland, ME | (7.8) | 225 | St. Joseph, MO-KS | (7.3) |
| 146 | Mankato-North Mankato, MN | (4.7) | 117 | Prescott, AZ | (3.5) | 225 | St. Louis, MO-IL | (7.3) |
| 66 | Mansfield, OH | (0.1) | 169 | Providence-Warwick, RI-MA | (5.4) | 312 | Sumter, SC | (15.9) |
| 89 | McAllen-Edinburg-Mission, TX | (2.0) | 51 | Provo-Orem, UT | 0.9 | 82 | Syracuse, NY | (1.6) |
| 26 | Medford, OR | 4.4 | 11 | Pueblo, CO | 9.2 | NA | Tacoma, WA M.D.** | NA |
| 134 | Memphis, TN-MS-AR | (4.1) | 117 | Punta Gorda, FL | (3.5) | 97 | Tallahassee, FL | (2.5) |
| 325 | Merced, CA | (20.4) | 249 | Racine, WI | (8.7) | 144 | Tampa-St Petersburg, FL | (4.6) |
| 189 | Miami (greater), FL | (6.1) | 231 | Raleigh, NC | (7.6) | 286 | Terre Haute, IN | (11.5) |
| 158 | Miami-Dade County, FL M.D. | (5.0) | 327 | Rapid City, SD | (22.8) | 180 | Texarkana, TX-AR | (5.9) |
| 23 | Midland, TX | 5.0 | 314 | Reading, PA | (16.4) | 241 | The Villages, FL | (8.3) |
| 242 | Milwaukee, WI | (8.4) | 189 | Redding, CA | (6.1) | NA | Toledo, OH** | NA |
| NA | Minneapolis-St. Paul, MN-WI** | NA | 80 | Reno, NV | (1.5) | 233 | Topeka, KS | (7.7) |
| 209 | Missoula, MT | (6.7) | 201 | Richmond, VA | (6.5) | 249 | Trenton, NJ | (8.7) |
| 23 | Mobile, AL | 5.0 | 229 | Riverside-San Bernardino, CA | (7.5) | NA | Tucson, AZ** | NA |
| 218 | Modesto, CA | (7.1) | 152 | Roanoke, VA | (4.9) | 70 | Tulsa, OK | (0.7) |
| 13 | Monroe, LA | 8.6 | 199 | Rochester, MN | (6.4) | 56 | Tuscaloosa, AL | 0.7 |
| 295 | Monroe, MI | (12.7) | 251 | Rochester, NY | (8.8) | 201 | Tyler, TX | (6.5) |
| 115 | Montgomery County, PA M.D. | (3.2) | 300 | Rockford, IL | (13.4) | 180 | Utica-Rome, NY | (5.9) |
| 289 | Morgantown, WV | (11.8) | 231 | Rockingham County, NH M.D. | (7.6) | 48 | Vallejo-Fairfield, CA | 1.5 |
| 280 | Morristown, TN | (10.5) | 57 | Rocky Mount, NC | 0.6 | 127 | Victoria, TX | (3.9) |
| 33 | Mount Vernon-Anacortes, WA | 3.9 | 35 | Rome, GA | 3.8 | 45 | Vineland-Bridgeton, NJ | 2.1 |
| 82 | Muncie, IN | (1.6) | 169 | Sacramento, CA | (5.4) | 105 | Virginia Beach-Norfolk, VA-NC | (2.8) |
| NA | Muskegon, MI** | NA | 218 | Saginaw, MI | (7.1) | NA | Visalia-Porterville, CA** | NA |
| NA | Myrtle Beach, SC-NC** | NA | 64 | Salem, OR | 0.1 | 140 | Waco, TX | (4.4) |
| 280 | Napa, CA | (10.5) | 23 | Salinas, CA | 5.0 | 40 | Warner Robins, GA | 2.8 |
| 206 | Naples-Marco Island, FL | (6.6) | 78 | Salisbury, MD-DE | (1.4) | 271 | Warren-Troy, MI M.D. | (10.0) |
| 216 | Nashville-Davidson, TN | (7.0) | 59 | Salt Lake City, UT | 0.5 | 158 | Washington (greater) DC-VA-MD-WV | (5.0) |
| 194 | Nassau-Suffolk, NY M.D. | (6.2) | NA | San Angelo, TX** | NA | 148 | Washington, DC-VA-MD-WV M.D. | (4.8) |
| 316 | New Bern, NC | (16.8) | 178 | San Antonio, TX | (5.8) | 322 | Watertown-Fort Drum, NY | (18.8) |
| 194 | New Haven-Milford, CT | (6.2) | 67 | San Diego, CA | (0.2) | 252 | Wausau, WI | (8.9) |
| 112 | New Orleans, LA | (3.1) | NA | San Francisco (greater), CA** | NA | 176 | West Palm Beach, FL M.D. | (5.7) |
| 175 | New York (greater), NY-NJ-PA | (5.6) | 4 | San Francisco-Redwood, CA M.D. | 15.9 | 189 | Wichita Falls, TX | (6.1) |
| 144 | New York-Jersey City, NY-NJ M.D. | (4.6) | 255 | San Jose, CA | (9.2) | 75 | Wichita, KS | (1.1) |
| 253 | Newark, NJ-PA M.D. | (9.0) | 80 | San Luis Obispo, CA | (1.5) | 62 | Williamsport, PA | 0.2 |
| NA | Niles-Benton Harbor, MI** | NA | NA | San Rafael, CA M.D.** | NA | 272 | Wilmington, DE-MD-NJ M.D. | (10.1) |
| 212 | North Port-Sarasota-Bradenton, FL | (6.8) | 218 | Santa Cruz-Watsonville, CA | (7.1) | 209 | Wilmington, NC | (6.7) |
| 33 | Norwich-New London, CT | 3.9 | 134 | Santa Maria-Santa Barbara, CA | (4.1) | 306 | Winchester, VA-WV | (14.7) |
| NA | Oakland-Hayward, CA M.D.** | NA | 127 | Santa Rosa, CA | (3.9) | 227 | Winston-Salem, NC | (7.4) |
| NA | Ocala, FL** | NA | 91 | Savannah, GA | (2.1) | 176 | Worcester, MA-CT | (5.7) |
| 260 | Ocean City, NJ | (9.5) | NA | Scranton--Wilkes-Barre, PA** | NA | 319 | Yakima, WA | (17.9) |
| 3 | Odessa, TX | 17.5 | NA | Seattle (greater), WA** | NA | 237 | York-Hanover, PA | (8.0) |
| NA | Ogden-Clearfield, UT** | NA | 21 | Seattle-Bellevue-Everett, WA M.D. | 5.8 | 22 | Yuba City, CA | 5.3 |
| 259 | Oklahoma City, OK | (9.4) | 326 | Sebastian-Vero Beach, FL | (21.8) | 20 | Yuma, AZ | 6.2 |
| NA | Olympia, WA** | NA | 2 | Sebring, FL | 18.4 | | | |

Source: CQ Press using reported data from the F.B.I. "Crime in the United States 2013"

*Property crimes are offenses of burglary, larceny-theft, and motor vehicle theft. Attempts are included.

**Not available.

# 27. Percent Change in Property Crime Rate: 2012 to 2013 (continued)
## National Percent Change = 4.8% Decrease*

| RANK | METROPOLITAN AREA | % CHANGE | RANK | METROPOLITAN AREA | % CHANGE | RANK | METROPOLITAN AREA | % CHANGE |
|---|---|---|---|---|---|---|---|---|
| 1 | Corvallis, OR | 20.0 | 65 | Denver-Aurora, CO | 0.0 | 127 | Santa Rosa, CA | (3.9) |
| 2 | Sebring, FL | 18.4 | 66 | Mansfield, OH | (0.1) | 127 | Springfield, MA | (3.9) |
| 3 | Odessa, TX | 17.5 | 67 | Fort Worth-Arlington, TX M.D. | (0.2) | 127 | Victoria, TX | (3.9) |
| 4 | San Francisco-Redwood, CA M.D. | 15.9 | 67 | San Diego, CA | (0.2) | 132 | Boston, MA M.D. | (4.0) |
| 5 | Pocatello, ID | 15.2 | 69 | Lansing-East Lansing, MI | (0.5) | 132 | Green Bay, WI | (4.0) |
| 6 | Anchorage, AK | 14.6 | 70 | Tulsa, OK | (0.7) | 134 | Gainesville, GA | (4.1) |
| 7 | Billings, MT | 12.6 | 71 | Grand Island, NE | (0.8) | 134 | Memphis, TN-MS-AR | (4.1) |
| 8 | Hanford-Corcoran, CA | 11.0 | 72 | Allentown, PA-NJ | (0.9) | 134 | Santa Maria-Santa Barbara, CA | (4.1) |
| 9 | Harrisonburg, VA | 10.9 | 73 | Albany, GA | (1.0) | 137 | Bakersfield, CA | (4.3) |
| 10 | Chico, CA | 9.9 | 73 | Gadsden, AL | (1.0) | 137 | Florence, SC | (4.3) |
| 11 | Abilene, TX | 9.2 | 75 | Madera, CA | (1.1) | 137 | Sioux Falls, SD | (4.3) |
| 11 | Pueblo, CO | 9.2 | 75 | Wichita, KS | (1.1) | 140 | Dallas (greater), TX | (4.4) |
| 13 | Longview, WA | 8.6 | 77 | Louisville, KY-IN | (1.3) | 140 | Lawton, OK | (4.4) |
| 13 | Monroe, LA | 8.6 | 78 | Houma, LA | (1.4) | 140 | Waco, TX | (4.4) |
| 15 | Duluth, MN-WI | 8.4 | 78 | Salisbury, MD-DE | (1.4) | 143 | Decatur, IL | (4.5) |
| 16 | Bay City, MI | 8.2 | 80 | Reno, NV | (1.5) | 144 | New York-Jersey City, NY-NJ M.D. | (4.6) |
| 17 | Albany, OR | 7.3 | 80 | San Luis Obispo, CA | (1.5) | 144 | Tampa-St Petersburg, FL | (4.6) |
| 18 | Pittsfield, MA | 6.7 | 82 | Atlanta, GA | (1.6) | 146 | Boston (greater), MA-NH | (4.7) |
| 19 | Springfield, OH | 6.5 | 82 | Columbia, MO | (1.6) | 146 | Mankato-North Mankato, MN | (4.7) |
| 20 | Yuma, AZ | 6.2 | 82 | Muncie, IN | (1.6) | 148 | Bismarck, ND | (4.8) |
| 21 | Seattle-Bellevue-Everett, WA M.D. | 5.8 | 82 | Syracuse, NY | (1.6) | 148 | Cambridge-Newton, MA M.D. | (4.8) |
| 22 | Yuba City, CA | 5.3 | 86 | State College, PA | (1.7) | 148 | Grand Forks, ND-MN | (4.8) |
| 23 | Midland, TX | 5.0 | 87 | Detroit-Dearborn-Livonia, MI M.D. | (1.9) | 148 | Washington, DC-VA-MD-WV M.D. | (4.8) |
| 23 | Mobile, AL | 5.0 | 87 | Orlando, FL | (1.9) | 152 | Champaign-Urbana, IL | (4.9) |
| 23 | Salinas, CA | 5.0 | 89 | Birmingham-Hoover, AL | (2.0) | 152 | Cheyenne, WY | (4.9) |
| 26 | Medford, OR | 4.4 | 89 | McAllen-Edinburg-Mission, TX | (2.0) | 152 | Daphne-Fairhope-Foley, AL | (4.9) |
| 27 | Elizabethtown-Fort Knox, KY | 4.2 | 91 | Los Angeles County, CA M.D. | (2.1) | 152 | Glens Falls, NY | (4.9) |
| 27 | Fargo, ND-MN | 4.2 | 91 | Savannah, GA | (2.1) | 152 | Homosassa Springs, FL | (4.9) |
| 27 | Jackson, TN | 4.2 | 93 | Florence-Muscle Shoals, AL | (2.2) | 152 | Roanoke, VA | (4.9) |
| 30 | Kokomo, IN | 4.1 | 93 | Springfield, MO | (2.2) | 158 | Burlington, NC | (5.0) |
| 31 | Cleveland, TN | 4.0 | 95 | Casper, WY | (2.3) | 158 | Kennewick-Richland, WA | (5.0) |
| 31 | Fort Smith, AR-OK | 4.0 | 95 | Dayton, OH | (2.3) | 158 | Little Rock, AR | (5.0) |
| 33 | Mount Vernon-Anacortes, WA | 3.9 | 97 | Idaho Falls, ID | (2.5) | 158 | Miami-Dade County, FL M.D. | (5.0) |
| 33 | Norwich-New London, CT | 3.9 | 97 | Las Cruces, NM | (2.5) | 158 | Port St. Lucie, FL | (5.0) |
| 35 | Rome, GA | 3.8 | 97 | Tallahassee, FL | (2.5) | 158 | Washington (greater) DC-VA-MD-WV | (5.0) |
| 35 | Spokane, WA | 3.8 | 100 | Atlantic City, NJ | (2.6) | 164 | Hilton Head Island, SC | (5.1) |
| 37 | Beaumont-Port Arthur, TX | 3.4 | 100 | Boulder, CO | (2.6) | 164 | Panama City, FL | (5.1) |
| 38 | Columbus, GA-AL | 3.2 | 100 | Charlottesville, VA | (2.6) | 166 | Cincinnati, OH-KY-IN | (5.2) |
| 39 | Oxnard-Thousand Oaks, CA | 2.9 | 100 | Eugene, OR | (2.6) | 166 | Great Falls, MT | (5.2) |
| 40 | Altoona, PA | 2.8 | 100 | Greenville, NC | (2.6) | 168 | Spartanburg, SC | (5.3) |
| 40 | Warner Robins, GA | 2.8 | 105 | Greensboro-High Point, NC | (2.8) | 169 | Providence-Warwick, RI-MA | (5.4) |
| 42 | Greenville-Anderson, SC | 2.7 | 105 | Laredo, TX | (2.8) | 169 | Sacramento, CA | (5.4) |
| 43 | Sioux City, IA-NE-SD | 2.4 | 105 | Virginia Beach-Norfolk, VA-NC | (2.8) | 171 | Detroit (greater), MI | (5.5) |
| 44 | Joplin, MO | 2.2 | 108 | Deltona-Daytona Beach, FL | (2.9) | 171 | Indianapolis, IN | (5.5) |
| 45 | Vineland-Bridgeton, NJ | 2.1 | 109 | Flagstaff, AZ | (3.0) | 171 | Kahului-Wailuku-Lahaina, HI | (5.5) |
| 46 | Fort Wayne, IN | 1.7 | 109 | Lake Havasu City-Kingman, AZ | (3.0) | 171 | Portland-Vancouver, OR-WA | (5.5) |
| 46 | Las Vegas-Henderson, NV | 1.7 | 109 | Staunton-Waynesboro, VA | (3.0) | 175 | New York (greater), NY-NJ-PA | (5.6) |
| 48 | Jonesboro, AR | 1.5 | 112 | Hammond, LA | (3.1) | 176 | West Palm Beach, FL M.D. | (5.7) |
| 48 | Macon, GA | 1.5 | 112 | New Orleans, LA | (3.1) | 176 | Worcester, MA-CT | (5.7) |
| 48 | Vallejo-Fairfield, CA | 1.5 | 112 | Stockton-Lodi, CA | (3.1) | 178 | Columbus, IN | (5.8) |
| 51 | Baltimore, MD | 0.9 | 115 | Davenport, IA-IL | (3.2) | 178 | San Antonio, TX | (5.8) |
| 51 | Dalton, GA | 0.9 | 115 | Montgomery County, PA M.D. | (3.2) | 180 | Bangor, ME | (5.9) |
| 51 | Johnstown, PA | 0.9 | 117 | Prescott, AZ | (3.5) | 180 | Brunswick, GA | (5.9) |
| 51 | Provo-Orem, UT | 0.9 | 117 | Punta Gorda, FL | (3.5) | 180 | Lakeland, FL | (5.9) |
| 55 | Iowa City, IA | 0.8 | 119 | Charleston-North Charleston, SC | (3.6) | 180 | Philadelphia, PA M.D. | (5.9) |
| 56 | Tuscaloosa, AL | 0.7 | 120 | Akron, OH | (3.7) | 180 | Texarkana, TX-AR | (5.9) |
| 57 | Lafayette, IN | 0.6 | 120 | Bloomington, IL | (3.7) | 180 | Utica-Rome, NY | (5.9) |
| 57 | Rocky Mount, NC | 0.6 | 120 | Hagerstown-Martinsburg, MD-WV | (3.7) | 186 | Ames, IA | (6.0) |
| 59 | Binghamton, NY | 0.5 | 120 | Omaha-Council Bluffs, NE-IA | (3.7) | 186 | El Paso, TX | (6.0) |
| 59 | Salt Lake City, UT | 0.5 | 124 | Lebanon, PA | (3.8) | 186 | Gary, IN M.D. | (6.0) |
| 61 | Huntsville, AL | 0.3 | 124 | Lewiston, ID-WA | (3.8) | 189 | Lubbock, TX | (6.1) |
| 62 | Manchester-Nashua, NH | 0.2 | 124 | South Bend-Mishawaka, IN-MI | (3.8) | 189 | Miami (greater), FL | (6.1) |
| 62 | Williamsport, PA | 0.2 | 127 | Clarksville, TN-KY | (3.9) | 189 | Redding, CA | (6.1) |
| 64 | Salem, OR | 0.1 | 127 | Los Angeles (greater), CA | (3.9) | 189 | Silver Spring-Frederick, MD M.D. | (6.1) |

Note: All listings are for Metropolitan Statistical Areas (M.S.A.s) except for those ending with "M.D." Listings with "M.D." are Metropolitan Divisions which are smaller parts of eleven large M.S.A.s. See explanatory note at beginning of metropolitan area section.

| RANK | METROPOLITAN AREA | % CHANGE | RANK | METROPOLITAN AREA | % CHANGE | RANK | METROPOLITAN AREA | % CHANGE |
|------|-------------------|----------|------|-------------------|----------|------|-------------------|----------|
| 189 | Wichita Falls, TX | (6.1) | 255 | Jefferson City, MO | (9.2) | 317 | Anniston-Oxford, AL | (17.2) |
| 194 | Lima, OH | (6.2) | 255 | Lawrence, KS | (9.2) | 318 | Sherman-Denison, TX | (17.5) |
| 194 | Nassau-Suffolk, NY M.D. | (6.2) | 255 | San Jose, CA | (9.2) | 319 | Yakima, WA | (17.9) |
| 194 | New Haven-Milford, CT | (6.2) | 258 | Bridgeport-Stamford, CT | (9.3) | 320 | Flint, MI | (18.1) |
| 197 | Fayetteville-Springdale, AR-MO | (6.3) | 259 | Oklahoma City, OK | (9.4) | 321 | Owensboro, KY | (18.2) |
| 197 | Springfield, IL | (6.3) | 260 | Athens-Clarke County, GA | (9.5) | 322 | Watertown-Fort Drum, NY | (18.8) |
| 199 | Kansas City, MO-KS | (6.4) | 260 | Longview, TX | (9.5) | 323 | Dover, DE | (19.6) |
| 199 | Rochester, MN | (6.4) | 260 | Ocean City, NJ | (9.5) | 324 | Cape Girardeau, MO-IL | (20.1) |
| 201 | Buffalo-Niagara Falls, NY | (6.5) | 263 | Camden, NJ M.D. | (9.6) | 325 | Merced, CA | (20.4) |
| 201 | Cape Coral-Fort Myers, FL | (6.5) | 263 | Canton, OH | (9.6) | 326 | Sebastian-Vero Beach, FL | (21.8) |
| 201 | Cumberland, MD-WV | (6.5) | 265 | Gainesville, FL | (9.7) | 327 | Rapid City, SD | (22.8) |
| 201 | Richmond, VA | (6.5) | 265 | Hinesville, GA | (9.7) | 328 | Logan, UT-ID | (25.1) |
| 201 | Tyler, TX | (6.5) | 265 | Kingsport, TN-VA | (9.7) | NA | Albuquerque, NM** | NA |
| 206 | Albany-Schenectady-Troy, NY | (6.6) | 268 | Greeley, CO | (9.8) | NA | Alexandria, LA** | NA |
| 206 | Jacksonville, FL | (6.6) | 268 | Kingston, NY | (9.8) | NA | Baton Rouge, LA** | NA |
| 206 | Naples-Marco Island, FL | (6.6) | 268 | Lincoln, NE | (9.8) | NA | Bend, OR** | NA |
| 209 | Dallas-Plano-Irving, TX M.D. | (6.7) | 271 | Warren-Troy, MI M.D. | (10.0) | NA | Carbondale-Marion, IL** | NA |
| 209 | Missoula, MT | (6.7) | 272 | Anaheim-Santa Ana-Irvine, CA M.D. | (10.1) | NA | Cedar Rapids, IA** | NA |
| 209 | Wilmington, NC | (6.7) | 272 | Barnstable Town, MA | (10.1) | NA | Chambersburg-Waynesboro, PA** | NA |
| 212 | Bowling Green, KY | (6.8) | 272 | Knoxville, TN | (10.1) | NA | Charlotte-Mecklenburg, NC-SC** | NA |
| 212 | Bremerton-Silverdale, WA | (6.8) | 272 | Wilmington, DE-MD-NJ M.D. | (10.1) | NA | Chattanooga, TN-GA** | NA |
| 212 | North Port-Sarasota-Bradenton, FL | (6.8) | 276 | Hartford, CT | (10.2) | NA | Colorado Springs, CO** | NA |
| 215 | Pensacola, FL | (6.9) | 276 | Jackson, MS | (10.2) | NA | Columbia, SC** | NA |
| 216 | East Stroudsburg, PA | (7.0) | 278 | Appleton, WI | (10.3) | NA | Corpus Christi, TX** | NA |
| 216 | Nashville-Davidson, TN | (7.0) | 278 | Lynchburg, VA | (10.3) | NA | Des Moines-West Des Moines, IA** | NA |
| 218 | Elmira, NY | (7.1) | 280 | Morristown, TN | (10.5) | NA | Dubuque, IA** | NA |
| 218 | Fond du Lac, WI | (7.1) | 280 | Napa, CA | (10.5) | NA | Eau Claire, WI** | NA |
| 218 | Modesto, CA | (7.1) | 282 | Lewiston-Auburn, ME | (10.6) | NA | Gettysburg, PA** | NA |
| 218 | Philadelphia (greater) PA-NJ-MD-DE | (7.1) | 283 | Manhattan, KS | (10.7) | NA | Grand Rapids-Wyoming, MI** | NA |
| 218 | Saginaw, MI | (7.1) | 284 | Grand Junction, CO | (10.8) | NA | Grants Pass, OR** | NA |
| 218 | Santa Cruz-Watsonville, CA | (7.1) | 285 | Brownsville-Harlingen, TX | (11.3) | NA | Gulfport-Biloxi-Pascagoula, MS** | NA |
| 224 | College Station-Bryan, TX | (7.2) | 286 | Decatur, AL | (11.5) | NA | Hot Springs, AR** | NA |
| 225 | St. Joseph, MO-KS | (7.3) | 286 | Terre Haute, IN | (11.5) | NA | Houston, TX** | NA |
| 225 | St. Louis, MO-IL | (7.3) | 288 | Blacksburg, VA | (11.6) | NA | Jackson, MI** | NA |
| 227 | Austin-Round Rock, TX | (7.4) | 289 | California-Lexington Park, MD | (11.8) | NA | La Crosse, WI-MN** | NA |
| 227 | Winston-Salem, NC | (7.4) | 289 | Crestview-Fort Walton Beach, FL | (11.8) | NA | Lafayette, LA** | NA |
| 229 | Palm Bay-Melbourne, FL | (7.5) | 289 | Morgantown, WV | (11.8) | NA | Lake Charles, LA** | NA |
| 229 | Riverside-San Bernardino, CA | (7.5) | 292 | Fort Collins, CO | (12.2) | NA | Lancaster, PA** | NA |
| 231 | Raleigh, NC | (7.6) | 293 | Dutchess-Putnam, NY M.D. | (12.5) | NA | Madison, WI** | NA |
| 231 | Rockingham County, NH M.D. | (7.6) | 294 | Chicago (greater), IL-IN-WI | (12.6) | NA | Minneapolis-St. Paul, MN-WI** | NA |
| 233 | Topeka, KS | (7.7) | 295 | Farmington, NM | (12.7) | NA | Muskegon, MI** | NA |
| 234 | Portland, ME | (7.8) | 295 | Lake Co.-Kenosha Co., IL-WI M.D. | (12.7) | NA | Myrtle Beach, SC-NC** | NA |
| 235 | Dothan, AL | (7.9) | 295 | Monroe, MI | (12.7) | NA | Niles-Benton Harbor, MI** | NA |
| 235 | Goldsboro, NC | (7.9) | 298 | Coeur d'Alene, ID | (13.1) | NA | Oakland-Hayward, CA M.D.** | NA |
| 237 | Elgin, IL M.D. | (8.0) | 298 | Fresno, CA | (13.1) | NA | Ocala, FL** | NA |
| 237 | York-Hanover, PA | (8.0) | 300 | Rockford, IL | (13.4) | NA | Ogden-Clearfield, UT** | NA |
| 239 | Fairbanks, AK | (8.1) | 301 | Chicago-Naperville, IL M.D. | (13.6) | NA | Olympia, WA** | NA |
| 240 | Fort Lauderdale, FL M.D. | (8.2) | 302 | Boise City, ID | (13.8) | NA | Phoenix-Mesa-Scottsdale, AZ** | NA |
| 241 | The Villages, FL | (8.3) | 303 | Ann Arbor, MI | (13.9) | NA | Pittsburgh, PA** | NA |
| 242 | Amarillo, TX | (8.4) | 304 | Johnson City, TN | (14.0) | NA | San Angelo, TX** | NA |
| 242 | Augusta, GA-SC | (8.4) | 305 | Oshkosh-Neenah, WI | (14.5) | NA | San Francisco (greater), CA** | NA |
| 242 | El Centro, CA | (8.4) | 306 | Carson City, NV | (14.7) | NA | San Rafael, CA M.D.** | NA |
| 242 | Fayetteville, NC | (8.4) | 306 | Winchester, VA-WV | (14.7) | NA | Scranton--Wilkes-Barre, PA** | NA |
| 242 | Milwaukee, WI | (8.4) | 308 | Peoria, IL | (14.9) | NA | Seattle (greater), WA** | NA |
| 247 | Erie, PA | (8.6) | 309 | Bloomington, IN | (15.3) | NA | Shreveport-Bossier City, LA** | NA |
| 247 | Kankakee, IL | (8.6) | 310 | Sheboygan, WI | (15.5) | NA | St. Cloud, MN** | NA |
| 249 | Racine, WI | (8.7) | 311 | Parkersburg-Vienna, WV | (15.6) | NA | St. George, UT** | NA |
| 249 | Trenton, NJ | (8.7) | 312 | Sumter, SC | (15.9) | NA | Tacoma, WA M.D.** | NA |
| 251 | Rochester, NY | (8.8) | 313 | Bloomsburg-Berwick, PA | (16.3) | NA | Toledo, OH** | NA |
| 252 | Wausau, WI | (8.9) | 314 | Reading, PA | (16.4) | NA | Tucson, AZ** | NA |
| 253 | Newark, NJ-PA M.D. | (9.0) | 315 | Janesville, WI | (16.5) | NA | Visalia-Porterville, CA** | NA |
| 254 | Lexington-Fayette, KY | (9.1) | 316 | New Bern, NC | (16.8) | | | |

Source: CQ Press using reported data from the F.B.I. "Crime in the United States 2013"
*Property crimes are offenses of burglary, larceny-theft, and motor vehicle theft. Attempts are included.
**Not available.

# 28. Percent Change in Property Crime Rate: 2009 to 2013
## National Percent Change = 10.2% Decrease*

| RANK | METROPOLITAN AREA | % CHANGE | RANK | METROPOLITAN AREA | % CHANGE | RANK | METROPOLITAN AREA | % CHANGE |
|---|---|---|---|---|---|---|---|---|
| 115 | Abilene, TX | (6.5) | 192 | Cheyenne, WY | (14.9) | NA | Gary, IN M.D.** | NA |
| 154 | Akron, OH | (10.6) | NA | Chicago (greater), IL-IN-WI** | NA | NA | Gettysburg, PA** | NA |
| 147 | Albany-Schenectady-Troy, NY | (9.9) | NA | Chicago-Naperville, IL M.D.** | NA | 69 | Glens Falls, NY | (0.5) |
| 38 | Albany, GA | 4.6 | 82 | Chico, CA | (2.2) | 220 | Goldsboro, NC | (17.3) |
| NA | Albany, OR** | NA | 100 | Cincinnati, OH-KY-IN | (4.8) | 140 | Grand Forks, ND-MN | (9.3) |
| 47 | Albuquerque, NM | 3.5 | 214 | Clarksville, TN-KY | (16.4) | NA | Grand Island, NE** | NA |
| 38 | Alexandria, LA | 4.6 | 33 | Cleveland, TN | 5.6 | 208 | Grand Junction, CO | (16.2) |
| 108 | Allentown, PA-NJ | (5.9) | 38 | Coeur d'Alene, ID | 4.6 | NA | Grand Rapids-Wyoming, MI** | NA |
| 147 | Altoona, PA | (9.9) | 299 | College Station-Bryan, TX | (42.9) | NA | Grants Pass, OR** | NA |
| 288 | Amarillo, TX | (28.9) | 15 | Colorado Springs, CO | 15.5 | 24 | Great Falls, MT | 9.1 |
| 230 | Ames, IA | (18.7) | 42 | Columbia, MO | 4.3 | 213 | Greeley, CO | (16.3) |
| 76 | Anaheim-Santa Ana-Irvine, CA M.D. | (1.7) | 138 | Columbia, SC | (8.9) | 116 | Green Bay, WI | (6.6) |
| 17 | Anchorage, AK | 13.0 | 237 | Columbus, GA-AL | (19.9) | 239 | Greensboro-High Point, NC | (20.1) |
| 253 | Ann Arbor, MI | (21.8) | 86 | Columbus, IN | (3.0) | NA | Greenville-Anderson, SC** | NA |
| 255 | Anniston-Oxford, AL | (21.9) | 191 | Corpus Christi, TX | (14.8) | NA | Greenville, NC** | NA |
| 297 | Appleton, WI | (31.0) | 135 | Corvallis, OR | (8.6) | NA | Gulfport-Biloxi-Pascagoula, MS** | NA |
| 263 | Athens-Clarke County, GA | (23.3) | NA | Crestview-Fort Walton Beach, FL** | NA | 71 | Hagerstown-Martinsburg, MD-WV | (1.4) |
| 108 | Atlanta, GA | (5.9) | 88 | Cumberland, MD-WV | (3.3) | NA | Hammond, LA** | NA |
| 171 | Atlantic City, NJ | (12.9) | 260 | Dallas (greater), TX | (22.4) | NA | Hanford-Corcoran, CA** | NA |
| 250 | Augusta, GA-SC | (21.1) | 266 | Dallas-Plano-Irving, TX M.D. | (24.3) | 51 | Harrisonburg, VA | 2.7 |
| 249 | Austin-Round Rock, TX | (21.0) | 88 | Dalton, GA | (3.3) | 239 | Hartford, CT | (20.1) |
| 62 | Bakersfield, CA | 0.3 | NA | Daphne-Fairhope-Foley, AL** | NA | NA | Hilton Head Island, SC** | NA |
| 135 | Baltimore, MD | (8.6) | NA | Davenport, IA-IL** | NA | 287 | Hinesville, GA | (28.8) |
| 214 | Bangor, ME | (16.4) | 84 | Dayton, OH | (2.6) | NA | Homosassa Springs, FL** | NA |
| 261 | Barnstable Town, MA | (22.8) | 231 | Decatur, AL | (18.8) | 195 | Hot Springs, AR | (15.1) |
| 159 | Baton Rouge, LA | (11.2) | 272 | Decatur, IL | (25.4) | 75 | Houma, LA | (1.6) |
| 177 | Bay City, MI | (13.2) | 198 | Deltona-Daytona Beach, FL | (15.4) | 197 | Houston, TX | (15.3) |
| 192 | Beaumont-Port Arthur, TX | (14.9) | 78 | Denver-Aurora, CO | (1.8) | 119 | Huntsville, AL | (7.0) |
| 46 | Bend, OR | 3.6 | 63 | Des Moines-West Des Moines, IA | 0.1 | 189 | Idaho Falls, ID | (14.6) |
| 27 | Billings, MT | 8.4 | 205 | Detroit (greater), MI | (16.0) | 142 | Indianapolis, IN | (9.4) |
| 26 | Binghamton, NY | 8.6 | 161 | Detroit-Dearborn-Livonia, MI M.D. | (11.3) | 48 | Iowa City, IA | 3.3 |
| 226 | Birmingham-Hoover, AL | (17.9) | NA | Dothan, AL** | NA | 270 | Jacksonville, FL | (25.1) |
| 20 | Bismarck, ND | 10.0 | 208 | Dover, DE | (16.2) | 103 | Jackson, MI | (5.2) |
| 276 | Blacksburg, VA | (25.8) | 201 | Dubuque, IA | (15.7) | 262 | Jackson, MS | (22.9) |
| NA | Bloomington, IL** | NA | 66 | Duluth, MN-WI | (0.1) | 281 | Jackson, TN | (27.1) |
| 123 | Bloomington, IN | (7.3) | NA | Dutchess-Putnam, NY M.D.** | NA | 177 | Janesville, WI | (13.2) |
| NA | Bloomsburg-Berwick, PA** | NA | NA | East Stroudsburg, PA** | NA | 83 | Jefferson City, MO | (2.5) |
| 186 | Boise City, ID | (14.5) | 218 | Eau Claire, WI | (17.0) | 135 | Johnson City, TN | (8.6) |
| 169 | Boston (greater), MA-NH | (12.1) | NA | El Centro, CA** | NA | NA | Johnstown, PA** | NA |
| 175 | Boston, MA M.D. | (13.1) | 274 | El Paso, TX | (25.5) | 125 | Jonesboro, AR | (7.7) |
| 104 | Boulder, CO | (5.3) | NA | Elgin, IL M.D.** | NA | NA | Joplin, MO** | NA |
| NA | Bowling Green, KY** | NA | NA | Elizabethtown-Fort Knox, KY** | NA | NA | Kahului-Wailuku-Lahaina, HI** | NA |
| 14 | Bremerton-Silverdale, WA | 15.8 | 53 | Elmira, NY | 2.5 | NA | Kankakee, IL** | NA |
| 223 | Bridgeport-Stamford, CT | (17.5) | 63 | Erie, PA | 0.1 | NA | Kansas City, MO-KS** | NA |
| 277 | Brownsville-Harlingen, TX | (25.9) | 140 | Eugene, OR | (9.3) | 129 | Kennewick-Richland, WA | (7.9) |
| 216 | Brunswick, GA | (16.5) | 80 | Fairbanks, AK | (1.9) | 244 | Kingsport, TN-VA | (20.7) |
| 151 | Buffalo-Niagara Falls, NY | (10.0) | 156 | Fargo, ND-MN | (11.0) | 99 | Kingston, NY | (4.5) |
| 219 | Burlington, NC | (17.1) | 166 | Farmington, NM | (11.8) | 159 | Knoxville, TN | (11.2) |
| NA | California-Lexington Park, MD** | NA | 95 | Fayetteville-Springdale, AR-MO | (4.2) | 161 | Kokomo, IN | (11.3) |
| NA | Cambridge-Newton, MA M.D.** | NA | 190 | Fayetteville, NC | (14.7) | NA | La Crosse, WI-MN** | NA |
| 106 | Camden, NJ M.D. | (5.5) | 157 | Flagstaff, AZ | (11.1) | 95 | Lafayette, IN | (4.2) |
| NA | Canton, OH** | NA | 253 | Flint, MI | (21.8) | NA | Lafayette, LA** | NA |
| 275 | Cape Coral-Fort Myers, FL | (25.7) | 98 | Florence-Muscle Shoals, AL | (4.4) | 45 | Lake Charles, LA | 3.8 |
| 102 | Cape Girardeau, MO-IL | (5.0) | 157 | Florence, SC | (11.1) | NA | Lake Co.-Kenosha Co., IL-WI M.D.** | NA |
| NA | Carbondale-Marion, IL** | NA | 139 | Fond du Lac, WI | (9.0) | 70 | Lake Havasu City-Kingman, AZ | (1.0) |
| 242 | Carson City, NV | (20.4) | 258 | Fort Collins, CO | (22.2) | 256 | Lakeland, FL | (22.0) |
| 268 | Casper, WY | (25.0) | 175 | Fort Lauderdale, FL M.D. | (13.1) | NA | Lancaster, PA** | NA |
| 208 | Cedar Rapids, IA | (16.2) | 84 | Fort Smith, AR-OK | (2.6) | 204 | Lansing-East Lansing, MI | (15.8) |
| NA | Chambersburg-Waynesboro, PA** | NA | 37 | Fort Wayne, IN | 4.8 | 288 | Laredo, TX | (28.9) |
| NA | Champaign-Urbana, IL** | NA | 233 | Fort Worth-Arlington, TX M.D. | (19.1) | 134 | Las Cruces, NM | (8.5) |
| NA | Charleston-North Charleston, SC** | NA | 60 | Fresno, CA | 0.5 | 116 | Las Vegas-Henderson, NV | (6.6) |
| NA | Charlotte-Mecklenburg, NC-SC** | NA | 12 | Gadsden, AL | 18.3 | 205 | Lawrence, KS | (16.0) |
| 283 | Charlottesville, VA | (27.3) | 295 | Gainesville, FL | (30.9) | 184 | Lawton, OK | (13.9) |
| 147 | Chattanooga, TN-GA | (9.9) | 108 | Gainesville, GA | (5.9) | 25 | Lebanon, PA | 8.9 |

Note: All listings are for Metropolitan Statistical Areas (M.S.A.s) except for those ending with "M.D." Listings with "M.D." are Metropolitan Divisions which are smaller parts of eleven large M.S.A.s. See explanatory note at beginning of metropolitan area section.

| RANK | METROPOLITAN AREA | % CHANGE | RANK | METROPOLITAN AREA | % CHANGE | RANK | METROPOLITAN AREA | % CHANGE |
|---|---|---|---|---|---|---|---|---|
| 13 | Lewiston-Auburn, ME | 16.4 | 90 | Omaha-Council Bluffs, NE-IA | (3.5) | 292 | Sheboygan, WI | (30.0) |
| 23 | Lewiston, ID-WA | 9.7 | 186 | Orlando, FL | (14.5) | 259 | Sherman-Denison, TX | (22.3) |
| 21 | Lexington-Fayette, KY | 9.8 | 286 | Oshkosh-Neenah, WI | (28.2) | 155 | Shreveport-Bossier City, LA | (10.7) |
| 245 | Lima, OH | (20.8) | 250 | Owensboro, KY | (21.1) | 295 | Silver Spring-Frederick, MD M.D. | (30.9) |
| 151 | Lincoln, NE | (10.0) | 55 | Oxnard-Thousand Oaks, CA | 1.8 | 18 | Sioux City, IA-NE-SD | 11.8 |
| 123 | Little Rock, AR | (7.3) | 208 | Palm Bay-Melbourne, FL | (16.2) | 35 | Sioux Falls, SD | 5.0 |
| 257 | Logan, UT-ID | (22.1) | 164 | Panama City, FL | (11.4) | 272 | South Bend-Mishawaka, IN-MI | (25.4) |
| 290 | Longview, TX | (29.2) | NA | Parkersburg-Vienna, WV** | NA | 221 | Spartanburg, SC | (17.4) |
| 36 | Longview, WA | 4.9 | 38 | Pensacola, FL | 4.6 | 4 | Spokane, WA | 34.7 |
| 120 | Los Angeles County, CA M.D. | (7.1) | NA | Peoria, IL** | NA | NA | Springfield, IL** | NA |
| 111 | Los Angeles (greater), CA | (6.1) | 111 | Philadelphia (greater) PA-NJ-MD-DE | (6.1) | 56 | Springfield, MA | 1.7 |
| 49 | Louisville, KY-IN | 3.1 | NA | Philadelphia, PA M.D.** | NA | 51 | Springfield, MO | 2.7 |
| 236 | Lubbock, TX | (19.7) | NA | Phoenix-Mesa-Scottsdale, AZ** | NA | 29 | Springfield, OH | 7.8 |
| 192 | Lynchburg, VA | (14.9) | NA | Pittsburgh, PA** | NA | 264 | State College, PA | (23.9) |
| 87 | Macon, GA | (3.2) | 19 | Pittsfield, MA | 10.9 | NA | Staunton-Waynesboro, VA** | NA |
| 9 | Madera, CA | 22.5 | 28 | Pocatello, ID | 8.1 | 95 | Stockton-Lodi, CA | (4.2) |
| NA | Madison, WI** | NA | 245 | Port St. Lucie, FL | (20.8) | 33 | St. Cloud, MN | 5.6 |
| 57 | Manchester-Nashua, NH | 1.5 | 54 | Portland-Vancouver, OR-WA | 2.1 | NA | St. George, UT** | NA |
| 252 | Manhattan, KS | (21.4) | 118 | Portland, ME | (6.7) | 31 | St. Joseph, MO-KS | 6.9 |
| 147 | Mankato-North Mankato, MN | (9.9) | 92 | Prescott, AZ | (3.7) | 201 | St. Louis, MO-IL | (15.7) |
| 10 | Mansfield, OH | 19.6 | 125 | Providence-Warwick, RI-MA | (7.7) | 21 | Sumter, SC | 9.8 |
| 278 | McAllen-Edinburg-Mission, TX | (26.1) | 186 | Provo-Orem, UT | (14.5) | 65 | Syracuse, NY | 0.0 |
| 2 | Medford, OR | 57.7 | 1 | Pueblo, CO | 83.5 | 93 | Tacoma, WA M.D. | (3.9) |
| 221 | Memphis, TN-MS-AR | (17.4) | 268 | Punta Gorda, FL | (25.0) | 106 | Tallahassee, FL | (5.5) |
| 131 | Merced, CA | (8.1) | 170 | Racine, WI | (12.3) | 291 | Tampa-St Petersburg, FL | (29.3) |
| 217 | Miami (greater), FL | (16.9) | 179 | Raleigh, NC | (13.3) | NA | Terre Haute, IN** | NA |
| 201 | Miami-Dade County, FL M.D. | (15.7) | 173 | Rapid City, SD | (13.0) | 120 | Texarkana, TX-AR | (7.1) |
| 265 | Midland, TX | (24.0) | 239 | Reading, PA | (20.1) | NA | The Villages, FL** | NA |
| 199 | Milwaukee, WI | (15.5) | 7 | Redding, CA | 28.6 | NA | Toledo, OH** | NA |
| 173 | Minneapolis-St. Paul, MN-WI | (13.0) | 237 | Reno, NV | (19.9) | 153 | Topeka, KS | (10.3) |
| 11 | Missoula, MT | 19.4 | 167 | Richmond, VA | (11.9) | 90 | Trenton, NJ | (3.5) |
| 131 | Mobile, AL | (8.1) | 71 | Riverside-San Bernardino, CA | (1.4) | NA | Tucson, AZ** | NA |
| 113 | Modesto, CA | (6.3) | 179 | Roanoke, VA | (13.3) | 165 | Tulsa, OK | (11.5) |
| NA | Monroe, LA** | NA | 247 | Rochester, MN | (20.9) | 280 | Tuscaloosa, AL | (27.0) |
| 76 | Monroe, MI | (1.7) | 171 | Rochester, NY | (12.9) | 279 | Tyler, TX | (26.7) |
| NA | Montgomery County, PA M.D.** | NA | NA | Rockford, IL** | NA | 145 | Utica-Rome, NY | (9.8) |
| 285 | Morgantown, WV | (28.1) | 43 | Rockingham County, NH M.D. | 4.0 | 80 | Vallejo-Fairfield, CA | (1.9) |
| 114 | Morristown, TN | (6.4) | 225 | Rocky Mount, NC | (17.6) | 298 | Victoria, TX | (31.1) |
| 93 | Mount Vernon-Anacortes, WA | (3.9) | 6 | Rome, GA | 29.0 | 5 | Vineland-Bridgeton, NJ | 31.2 |
| 30 | Muncie, IN | 7.1 | 181 | Sacramento, CA | (13.4) | NA | Virginia Beach-Norfolk, VA-NC** | NA |
| 182 | Muskegon, MI | (13.6) | 292 | Saginaw, MI | (30.0) | NA | Visalia-Porterville, CA** | NA |
| NA | Myrtle Beach, SC-NC** | NA | 44 | Salem, OR | 3.9 | 271 | Waco, TX | (25.2) |
| 247 | Napa, CA | (20.9) | 125 | Salinas, CA | (7.7) | NA | Warner Robins, GA** | NA |
| 196 | Naples-Marco Island, FL | (15.2) | NA | Salisbury, MD-DE** | NA | 235 | Warren-Troy, MI M.D. | (19.6) |
| 232 | Nashville-Davidson, TN | (18.9) | 133 | Salt Lake City, UT | (8.3) | 242 | Washington (greater) DC-VA-MD-WV | (20.4) |
| 208 | Nassau-Suffolk, NY M.D. | (16.2) | 227 | San Angelo, TX | (18.0) | 229 | Washington, DC-VA-MD-WV M.D. | (18.2) |
| NA | New Bern, NC** | NA | 234 | San Antonio, TX | (19.5) | NA | Watertown-Fort Drum, NY** | NA |
| 185 | New Haven-Milford, CT | (14.0) | 105 | San Diego, CA | (5.4) | 144 | Wausau, WI | (9.6) |
| NA | New Orleans, LA** | NA | 32 | San Francisco (greater), CA | 6.0 | 267 | West Palm Beach, FL M.D. | (24.8) |
| 130 | New York (greater), NY-NJ-PA | (8.0) | 8 | San Francisco-Redwood, CA M.D. | 26.9 | 207 | Wichita Falls, TX | (16.1) |
| NA | New York-Jersey City, NY-NJ M.D.** | NA | 78 | San Jose, CA | (1.8) | 61 | Wichita, KS | 0.4 |
| 183 | Newark, NJ-PA M.D. | (13.8) | 66 | San Luis Obispo, CA | (0.1) | 16 | Williamsport, PA | 14.3 |
| 142 | Niles-Benton Harbor, MI | (9.4) | NA | San Rafael, CA M.D.** | NA | 145 | Wilmington, DE-MD-NJ M.D. | (9.8) |
| 284 | North Port-Sarasota-Bradenton, FL | (27.8) | 200 | Santa Cruz-Watsonville, CA | (15.6) | NA | Wilmington, NC** | NA |
| 100 | Norwich-New London, CT | (4.8) | 50 | Santa Maria-Santa Barbara, CA | 2.8 | 223 | Winchester, VA-WV | (17.5) |
| 71 | Oakland-Hayward, CA M.D. | (1.4) | 228 | Santa Rosa, CA | (18.1) | NA | Winston-Salem, NC** | NA |
| NA | Ocala, FL** | NA | 281 | Savannah, GA | (27.1) | 120 | Worcester, MA-CT | (7.1) |
| 128 | Ocean City, NJ | (7.8) | NA | Scranton--Wilkes-Barre, PA** | NA | NA | Yakima, WA** | NA |
| 59 | Odessa, TX | 0.8 | 68 | Seattle (greater), WA | (0.2) | 168 | York-Hanover, PA | (12.0) |
| NA | Ogden-Clearfield, UT** | NA | 58 | Seattle-Bellevue-Everett, WA M.D. | 1.1 | 3 | Yuba City, CA | 40.0 |
| 161 | Oklahoma City, OK | (11.3) | 294 | Sebastian-Vero Beach, FL | (30.5) | 71 | Yuma, AZ | (1.4) |
| NA | Olympia, WA** | NA | NA | Sebring, FL** | NA | | | |

Source: CQ Press using reported data from the F.B.I. "Crime in the United States 2013"

*Property crimes are offenses of burglary, larceny-theft, and motor vehicle theft. Attempts are included.

**Not available.

## 28. Percent Change in Property Crime Rate: 2009 to 2013 (continued)
## National Percent Change = 10.2% Decrease*

| RANK | METROPOLITAN AREA | % CHANGE | RANK | METROPOLITAN AREA | % CHANGE | RANK | METROPOLITAN AREA | % CHANGE |
|---|---|---|---|---|---|---|---|---|
| 1 | Pueblo, CO | 83.5 | 65 | Syracuse, NY | 0.0 | 129 | Kennewick-Richland, WA | (7.9) |
| 2 | Medford, OR | 57.7 | 66 | Duluth, MN-WI | (0.1) | 130 | New York (greater), NY-NJ-PA | (8.0) |
| 3 | Yuba City, CA | 40.0 | 66 | San Luis Obispo, CA | (0.1) | 131 | Merced, CA | (8.1) |
| 4 | Spokane, WA | 34.7 | 68 | Seattle (greater), WA | (0.2) | 131 | Mobile, AL | (8.1) |
| 5 | Vineland-Bridgeton, NJ | 31.2 | 69 | Glens Falls, NY | (0.5) | 133 | Salt Lake City, UT | (8.3) |
| 6 | Rome, GA | 29.0 | 70 | Lake Havasu City-Kingman, AZ | (1.0) | 134 | Las Cruces, NM | (8.5) |
| 7 | Redding, CA | 28.6 | 71 | Hagerstown-Martinsburg, MD-WV | (1.4) | 135 | Baltimore, MD | (8.6) |
| 8 | San Francisco-Redwood, CA M.D. | 26.9 | 71 | Oakland-Hayward, CA M.D. | (1.4) | 135 | Corvallis, OR | (8.6) |
| 9 | Madera, CA | 22.5 | 71 | Riverside-San Bernardino, CA | (1.4) | 135 | Johnson City, TN | (8.6) |
| 10 | Mansfield, OH | 19.6 | 71 | Yuma, AZ | (1.4) | 138 | Columbia, SC | (8.9) |
| 11 | Missoula, MT | 19.4 | 75 | Houma, LA | (1.6) | 139 | Fond du Lac, WI | (9.0) |
| 12 | Gadsden, AL | 18.3 | 76 | Anaheim-Santa Ana-Irvine, CA M.D. | (1.7) | 140 | Eugene, OR | (9.3) |
| 13 | Lewiston-Auburn, ME | 16.4 | 76 | Monroe, MI | (1.7) | 140 | Grand Forks, ND-MN | (9.3) |
| 14 | Bremerton-Silverdale, WA | 15.8 | 78 | Denver-Aurora, CO | (1.8) | 142 | Indianapolis, IN | (9.4) |
| 15 | Colorado Springs, CO | 15.5 | 78 | San Jose, CA | (1.8) | 142 | Niles-Benton Harbor, MI | (9.4) |
| 16 | Williamsport, PA | 14.3 | 80 | Fairbanks, AK | (1.9) | 144 | Wausau, WI | (9.6) |
| 17 | Anchorage, AK | 13.0 | 80 | Vallejo-Fairfield, CA | (1.9) | 145 | Utica-Rome, NY | (9.8) |
| 18 | Sioux City, IA-NE-SD | 11.8 | 82 | Chico, CA | (2.2) | 145 | Wilmington, DE-MD-NJ M.D. | (9.8) |
| 19 | Pittsfield, MA | 10.9 | 83 | Jefferson City, MO | (2.5) | 147 | Albany-Schenectady-Troy, NY | (9.9) |
| 20 | Bismarck, ND | 10.0 | 84 | Dayton, OH | (2.6) | 147 | Altoona, PA | (9.9) |
| 21 | Lexington-Fayette, KY | 9.8 | 84 | Fort Smith, AR-OK | (2.6) | 147 | Chattanooga, TN-GA | (9.9) |
| 21 | Sumter, SC | 9.8 | 86 | Columbus, IN | (3.0) | 147 | Mankato-North Mankato, MN | (9.9) |
| 23 | Lewiston, ID-WA | 9.7 | 87 | Macon, GA | (3.2) | 151 | Buffalo-Niagara Falls, NY | (10.0) |
| 24 | Great Falls, MT | 9.1 | 88 | Cumberland, MD-WV | (3.3) | 151 | Lincoln, NE | (10.0) |
| 25 | Lebanon, PA | 8.9 | 88 | Dalton, GA | (3.3) | 153 | Topeka, KS | (10.3) |
| 26 | Binghamton, NY | 8.6 | 90 | Omaha-Council Bluffs, NE-IA | (3.5) | 154 | Akron, OH | (10.6) |
| 27 | Billings, MT | 8.4 | 90 | Trenton, NJ | (3.5) | 155 | Shreveport-Bossier City, LA | (10.7) |
| 28 | Pocatello, ID | 8.1 | 92 | Prescott, AZ | (3.7) | 156 | Fargo, ND-MN | (11.0) |
| 29 | Springfield, OH | 7.8 | 93 | Mount Vernon-Anacortes, WA | (3.9) | 157 | Flagstaff, AZ | (11.1) |
| 30 | Muncie, IN | 7.1 | 93 | Tacoma, WA M.D. | (3.9) | 157 | Florence, SC | (11.1) |
| 31 | St. Joseph, MO-KS | 6.9 | 95 | Fayetteville-Springdale, AR-MO | (4.2) | 159 | Baton Rouge, LA | (11.2) |
| 32 | San Francisco (greater), CA | 6.0 | 95 | Lafayette, IN | (4.2) | 159 | Knoxville, TN | (11.2) |
| 33 | Cleveland, TN | 5.6 | 95 | Stockton-Lodi, CA | (4.2) | 161 | Detroit-Dearborn-Livonia, MI M.D. | (11.3) |
| 33 | St. Cloud, MN | 5.6 | 98 | Florence-Muscle Shoals, AL | (4.4) | 161 | Kokomo, IN | (11.3) |
| 35 | Sioux Falls, SD | 5.0 | 99 | Kingston, NY | (4.5) | 161 | Oklahoma City, OK | (11.3) |
| 36 | Longview, WA | 4.9 | 100 | Cincinnati, OH-KY-IN | (4.8) | 164 | Panama City, FL | (11.4) |
| 37 | Fort Wayne, IN | 4.8 | 100 | Norwich-New London, CT | (4.8) | 165 | Tulsa, OK | (11.5) |
| 38 | Albany, GA | 4.6 | 102 | Cape Girardeau, MO-IL | (5.0) | 166 | Farmington, NM | (11.8) |
| 38 | Alexandria, LA | 4.6 | 103 | Jackson, MI | (5.2) | 167 | Richmond, VA | (11.9) |
| 38 | Coeur d'Alene, ID | 4.6 | 104 | Boulder, CO | (5.3) | 168 | York-Hanover, PA | (12.0) |
| 38 | Pensacola, FL | 4.6 | 105 | San Diego, CA | (5.4) | 169 | Boston (greater), MA-NH | (12.1) |
| 42 | Columbia, MO | 4.3 | 106 | Camden, NJ M.D. | (5.5) | 170 | Racine, WI | (12.3) |
| 43 | Rockingham County, NH M.D. | 4.0 | 106 | Tallahassee, FL | (5.5) | 171 | Atlantic City, NJ | (12.9) |
| 44 | Salem, OR | 3.9 | 108 | Allentown, PA-NJ | (5.9) | 171 | Rochester, NY | (12.9) |
| 45 | Lake Charles, LA | 3.8 | 108 | Atlanta, GA | (5.9) | 173 | Minneapolis-St. Paul, MN-WI | (13.0) |
| 46 | Bend, OR | 3.6 | 108 | Gainesville, GA | (5.9) | 173 | Rapid City, SD | (13.0) |
| 47 | Albuquerque, NM | 3.5 | 111 | Los Angeles (greater), CA | (6.1) | 175 | Boston, MA M.D. | (13.1) |
| 48 | Iowa City, IA | 3.3 | 111 | Philadelphia (greater) PA-NJ-MD-DE | (6.1) | 175 | Fort Lauderdale, FL M.D. | (13.1) |
| 49 | Louisville, KY-IN | 3.1 | 113 | Modesto, CA | (6.3) | 177 | Bay City, MI | (13.2) |
| 50 | Santa Maria-Santa Barbara, CA | 2.8 | 114 | Morristown, TN | (6.4) | 177 | Janesville, WI | (13.2) |
| 51 | Harrisonburg, VA | 2.7 | 115 | Abilene, TX | (6.5) | 179 | Raleigh, NC | (13.3) |
| 51 | Springfield, MO | 2.7 | 116 | Green Bay, WI | (6.6) | 179 | Roanoke, VA | (13.3) |
| 53 | Elmira, NY | 2.5 | 116 | Las Vegas-Henderson, NV | (6.6) | 181 | Sacramento, CA | (13.4) |
| 54 | Portland-Vancouver, OR-WA | 2.1 | 118 | Portland, ME | (6.7) | 182 | Muskegon, MI | (13.6) |
| 55 | Oxnard-Thousand Oaks, CA | 1.8 | 119 | Huntsville, AL | (7.0) | 183 | Newark, NJ-PA M.D. | (13.8) |
| 56 | Springfield, MA | 1.7 | 120 | Los Angeles County, CA M.D. | (7.1) | 184 | Lawton, OK | (13.9) |
| 57 | Manchester-Nashua, NH | 1.5 | 120 | Texarkana, TX-AR | (7.1) | 185 | New Haven-Milford, CT | (14.0) |
| 58 | Seattle-Bellevue-Everett, WA M.D. | 1.1 | 120 | Worcester, MA-CT | (7.1) | 186 | Boise City, ID | (14.5) |
| 59 | Odessa, TX | 0.8 | 123 | Bloomington, IN | (7.3) | 186 | Orlando, FL | (14.5) |
| 60 | Fresno, CA | 0.5 | 123 | Little Rock, AR | (7.3) | 186 | Provo-Orem, UT | (14.5) |
| 61 | Wichita, KS | 0.4 | 125 | Jonesboro, AR | (7.7) | 189 | Idaho Falls, ID | (14.6) |
| 62 | Bakersfield, CA | 0.3 | 125 | Providence-Warwick, RI-MA | (7.7) | 190 | Fayetteville, NC | (14.7) |
| 63 | Des Moines-West Des Moines, IA | 0.1 | 125 | Salinas, CA | (7.7) | 191 | Corpus Christi, TX | (14.8) |
| 63 | Erie, PA | 0.1 | 128 | Ocean City, NJ | (7.8) | 192 | Beaumont-Port Arthur, TX | (14.9) |

Note: All listings are for Metropolitan Statistical Areas (M.S.A.s) except for those ending with "M.D." Listings with "M.D." are Metropolitan Divisions which are smaller parts of eleven large M.S.A.s. See explanatory note at beginning of metropolitan area section.

| RANK | METROPOLITAN AREA | % CHANGE | RANK | METROPOLITAN AREA | % CHANGE | RANK | METROPOLITAN AREA | % CHANGE |
|---|---|---|---|---|---|---|---|---|
| 192 | Cheyenne, WY | (14.9) | 255 | Anniston-Oxford, AL | (21.9) | NA | Dothan, AL** | NA |
| 192 | Lynchburg, VA | (14.9) | 256 | Lakeland, FL | (22.0) | NA | Dutchess-Putnam, NY M.D.** | NA |
| 195 | Hot Springs, AR | (15.1) | 257 | Logan, UT-ID | (22.1) | NA | East Stroudsburg, PA** | NA |
| 196 | Naples-Marco Island, FL | (15.2) | 258 | Fort Collins, CO | (22.2) | NA | El Centro, CA** | NA |
| 197 | Houston, TX | (15.3) | 259 | Sherman-Denison, TX | (22.3) | NA | Elgin, IL M.D.** | NA |
| 198 | Deltona-Daytona Beach, FL | (15.4) | 260 | Dallas (greater), TX | (22.4) | NA | Elizabethtown-Fort Knox, KY** | NA |
| 199 | Milwaukee, WI | (15.5) | 261 | Barnstable Town, MA | (22.8) | NA | Gary, IN M.D.** | NA |
| 200 | Santa Cruz-Watsonville, CA | (15.6) | 262 | Jackson, MS | (22.9) | NA | Gettysburg, PA** | NA |
| 201 | Dubuque, IA | (15.7) | 263 | Athens-Clarke County, GA | (23.3) | NA | Grand Island, NE** | NA |
| 201 | Miami-Dade County, FL M.D. | (15.7) | 264 | State College, PA | (23.9) | NA | Grand Rapids-Wyoming, MI** | NA |
| 201 | St. Louis, MO-IL | (15.7) | 265 | Midland, TX | (24.0) | NA | Grants Pass, OR** | NA |
| 204 | Lansing-East Lansing, MI | (15.8) | 266 | Dallas-Plano-Irving, TX M.D. | (24.3) | NA | Greenville-Anderson, SC** | NA |
| 205 | Detroit (greater), MI | (16.0) | 267 | West Palm Beach, FL M.D. | (24.8) | NA | Greenville, NC** | NA |
| 205 | Lawrence, KS | (16.0) | 268 | Casper, WY | (25.0) | NA | Gulfport-Biloxi-Pascagoula, MS** | NA |
| 207 | Wichita Falls, TX | (16.1) | 268 | Punta Gorda, FL | (25.0) | NA | Hammond, LA** | NA |
| 208 | Cedar Rapids, IA | (16.2) | 270 | Jacksonville, FL | (25.1) | NA | Hanford-Corcoran, CA** | NA |
| 208 | Dover, DE | (16.2) | 271 | Waco, TX | (25.2) | NA | Hilton Head Island, SC** | NA |
| 208 | Grand Junction, CO | (16.2) | 272 | Decatur, IL | (25.4) | NA | Homosassa Springs, FL** | NA |
| 208 | Nassau-Suffolk, NY M.D. | (16.2) | 272 | South Bend-Mishawaka, IN-MI | (25.4) | NA | Johnstown, PA** | NA |
| 208 | Palm Bay-Melbourne, FL | (16.2) | 274 | El Paso, TX | (25.5) | NA | Joplin, MO** | NA |
| 213 | Greeley, CO | (16.3) | 275 | Cape Coral-Fort Myers, FL | (25.7) | NA | Kahului-Wailuku-Lahaina, HI** | NA |
| 214 | Bangor, ME | (16.4) | 276 | Blacksburg, VA | (25.8) | NA | Kankakee, IL** | NA |
| 214 | Clarksville, TN-KY | (16.4) | 277 | Brownsville-Harlingen, TX | (25.9) | NA | Kansas City, MO-KS** | NA |
| 216 | Brunswick, GA | (16.5) | 278 | McAllen-Edinburg-Mission, TX | (26.1) | NA | La Crosse, WI-MN** | NA |
| 217 | Miami (greater), FL | (16.9) | 279 | Tyler, TX | (26.7) | NA | Lafayette, LA** | NA |
| 218 | Eau Claire, WI | (17.0) | 280 | Tuscaloosa, AL | (27.0) | NA | Lake Co.-Kenosha Co., IL-WI M.D.** | NA |
| 219 | Burlington, NC | (17.1) | 281 | Jackson, TN | (27.1) | NA | Lancaster, PA** | NA |
| 220 | Goldsboro, NC | (17.3) | 281 | Savannah, GA | (27.1) | NA | Madison, WI** | NA |
| 221 | Memphis, TN-MS-AR | (17.4) | 283 | Charlottesville, VA | (27.3) | NA | Monroe, LA** | NA |
| 221 | Spartanburg, SC | (17.4) | 284 | North Port-Sarasota-Bradenton, FL | (27.8) | NA | Montgomery County, PA M.D.** | NA |
| 223 | Bridgeport-Stamford, CT | (17.5) | 285 | Morgantown, WV | (28.1) | NA | Myrtle Beach, SC-NC** | NA |
| 223 | Winchester, VA-WV | (17.5) | 286 | Oshkosh-Neenah, WI | (28.2) | NA | New Bern, NC** | NA |
| 225 | Rocky Mount, NC | (17.6) | 287 | Hinesville, GA | (28.8) | NA | New Orleans, LA** | NA |
| 226 | Birmingham-Hoover, AL | (17.9) | 288 | Amarillo, TX | (28.9) | NA | New York-Jersey City, NY-NJ M.D.** | NA |
| 227 | San Angelo, TX | (18.0) | 288 | Laredo, TX | (28.9) | NA | Ocala, FL** | NA |
| 228 | Santa Rosa, CA | (18.1) | 290 | Longview, TX | (29.2) | NA | Ogden-Clearfield, UT** | NA |
| 229 | Washington, DC-VA-MD-WV M.D. | (18.2) | 291 | Tampa-St Petersburg, FL | (29.3) | NA | Olympia, WA** | NA |
| 230 | Ames, IA | (18.7) | 292 | Saginaw, MI | (30.0) | NA | Parkersburg-Vienna, WV** | NA |
| 231 | Decatur, AL | (18.8) | 292 | Sheboygan, WI | (30.0) | NA | Peoria, IL** | NA |
| 232 | Nashville-Davidson, TN | (18.9) | 294 | Sebastian-Vero Beach, FL | (30.5) | NA | Philadelphia, PA M.D.** | NA |
| 233 | Fort Worth-Arlington, TX M.D. | (19.1) | 295 | Gainesville, FL | (30.9) | NA | Phoenix-Mesa-Scottsdale, AZ** | NA |
| 234 | San Antonio, TX | (19.5) | 295 | Silver Spring-Frederick, MD M.D. | (30.9) | NA | Pittsburgh, PA** | NA |
| 235 | Warren-Troy, MI M.D. | (19.6) | 297 | Appleton, WI | (31.0) | NA | Rockford, IL** | NA |
| 236 | Lubbock, TX | (19.7) | 298 | Victoria, TX | (31.1) | NA | Salisbury, MD-DE** | NA |
| 237 | Columbus, GA-AL | (19.9) | 299 | College Station-Bryan, TX | (42.9) | NA | San Rafael, CA M.D.** | NA |
| 237 | Reno, NV | (19.9) | NA | Albany, OR** | NA | NA | Scranton--Wilkes-Barre, PA** | NA |
| 239 | Greensboro-High Point, NC | (20.1) | NA | Bloomington, IL** | NA | NA | Sebring, FL** | NA |
| 239 | Hartford, CT | (20.1) | NA | Bloomsburg-Berwick, PA** | NA | NA | Springfield, IL** | NA |
| 239 | Reading, PA | (20.1) | NA | Bowling Green, KY** | NA | NA | Staunton-Waynesboro, VA** | NA |
| 242 | Carson City, NV | (20.4) | NA | California-Lexington Park, MD** | NA | NA | St. George, UT** | NA |
| 242 | Washington (greater) DC-VA-MD-WV | (20.4) | NA | Cambridge-Newton, MA M.D.** | NA | NA | Terre Haute, IN** | NA |
| 244 | Kingsport, TN-VA | (20.7) | NA | Canton, OH** | NA | NA | The Villages, FL** | NA |
| 245 | Lima, OH | (20.8) | NA | Carbondale-Marion, IL** | NA | NA | Toledo, OH** | NA |
| 245 | Port St. Lucie, FL | (20.8) | NA | Chambersburg-Waynesboro, PA** | NA | NA | Tucson, AZ** | NA |
| 247 | Napa, CA | (20.9) | NA | Champaign-Urbana, IL** | NA | NA | Virginia Beach-Norfolk, VA-NC** | NA |
| 247 | Rochester, MN | (20.9) | NA | Charleston-North Charleston, SC** | NA | NA | Visalia-Porterville, CA** | NA |
| 249 | Austin-Round Rock, TX | (21.0) | NA | Charlotte-Mecklenburg, NC-SC** | NA | NA | Warner Robins, GA** | NA |
| 250 | Augusta, GA-SC | (21.1) | NA | Chicago (greater), IL-IN-WI** | NA | NA | Watertown-Fort Drum, NY** | NA |
| 250 | Owensboro, KY | (21.1) | NA | Chicago-Naperville, IL M.D.** | NA | NA | Wilmington, NC** | NA |
| 252 | Manhattan, KS | (21.4) | NA | Crestview-Fort Walton Beach, FL** | NA | NA | Winston-Salem, NC** | NA |
| 253 | Ann Arbor, MI | (21.8) | NA | Daphne-Fairhope-Foley, AL** | NA | NA | Yakima, WA** | NA |
| 253 | Flint, MI | (21.8) | NA | Davenport, IA-IL** | NA | | | |

Source: CQ Press using reported data from the F.B.I. "Crime in the United States 2013"

*Property crimes are offenses of burglary, larceny-theft, and motor vehicle theft. Attempts are included.

**Not available.

# 29. Burglaries in 2013
## National Total = 1,928,465 Burglaries*

| RANK | METROPOLITAN AREA | BURGLARY | RANK | METROPOLITAN AREA | BURGLARY | RANK | METROPOLITAN AREA | BURGLARY |
|---|---|---|---|---|---|---|---|---|
| 236 | Abilene, TX | 1,323 | 349 | Cheyenne, WY | 441 | 110 | Gary, IN M.D. | 4,240 |
| 94 | Akron, OH | 5,122 | 8 | Chicago (greater), IL-IN-WI | 40,196 | 369 | Gettysburg, PA | 291 |
| 121 | Albany-Schenectady-Troy, NY | 3,738 | 12 | Chicago-Naperville, IL M.D. | 31,574 | 362 | Glens Falls, NY | 344 |
| 171 | Albany, GA | 2,010 | 194 | Chico, CA | 1,685 | 220 | Goldsboro, NC | 1,413 |
| 302 | Albany, OR | 750 | 32 | Cincinnati, OH-KY-IN | 16,013 | 357 | Grand Forks, ND-MN | 351 |
| 48 | Albuquerque, NM | 10,350 | 181 | Clarksville, TN-KY | 1,823 | 311 | Grand Island, NE | 680 |
| 169 | Alexandria, LA | 2,033 | 291 | Cleveland, TN | 833 | 330 | Grand Junction, CO | 560 |
| 122 | Allentown, PA-NJ | 3,724 | 276 | Coeur d'Alene, ID | 916 | 104 | Grand Rapids-Wyoming, MI | 4,482 |
| 353 | Altoona, PA | 396 | 239 | College Station-Bryan, TX | 1,317 | 300 | Grants Pass, OR | 772 |
| 172 | Amarillo, TX | 1,998 | 100 | Colorado Springs, CO | 4,768 | 347 | Great Falls, MT | 451 |
| 365 | Ames, IA | 331 | 283 | Columbia, MO | 889 | 283 | Greeley, CO | 889 |
| 47 | Anaheim-Santa Ana-Irvine, CA M.D. | 10,416 | 85 | Columbia, SC | 5,927 | 266 | Green Bay, WI | 1,024 |
| 222 | Anchorage, AK | 1,398 | 109 | Columbus, GA-AL | 4,245 | 73 | Greensboro-High Point, NC | 7,251 |
| 208 | Ann Arbor, MI | 1,508 | 359 | Columbus, IN | 350 | 64 | Greenville-Anderson, SC | 8,631 |
| 231 | Anniston-Oxford, AL | 1,366 | 120 | Corpus Christi, TX | 3,750 | 185 | Greenville, NC | 1,761 |
| 346 | Appleton, WI | 459 | 370 | Corvallis, OR | 290 | 125 | Gulfport-Biloxi-Pascagoula, MS | 3,639 |
| 226 | Athens-Clarke County, GA | 1,384 | 250 | Crestview-Fort Walton Beach, FL | 1,197 | 235 | Hagerstown-Martinsburg, MD-WV | 1,332 |
| 6 | Atlanta, GA | 44,591 | 319 | Cumberland, MD-WV | 631 | 155 | Hammond, LA | 2,421 |
| 189 | Atlantic City, NJ | 1,741 | 5 | Dallas (greater), TX | 47,789 | 288 | Hanford-Corcoran, CA | 858 |
| 91 | Augusta, GA-SC | 5,179 | 14 | Dallas-Plano-Irving, TX M.D. | 30,918 | 356 | Harrisonburg, VA | 361 |
| 50 | Austin-Round Rock, TX | 10,035 | 285 | Dalton, GA | 878 | 114 | Hartford, CT | 3,998 |
| 46 | Bakersfield, CA | 10,728 | 269 | Daphne-Fairhope-Foley, AL | 939 | 238 | Hilton Head Island, SC | 1,321 |
| 29 | Baltimore, MD | 16,662 | 174 | Davenport, IA-IL | 1,984 | 316 | Hinesville, GA | 651 |
| 293 | Bangor, ME | 812 | 77 | Dayton, OH | 6,921 | 315 | Homosassa Springs, FL | 653 |
| 183 | Barnstable Town, MA | 1,785 | 263 | Decatur, AL | 1,050 | 205 | Hot Springs, AR | 1,547 |
| 67 | Baton Rouge, LA | 7,921 | 281 | Decatur, IL | 892 | 219 | Houma, LA | 1,414 |
| 341 | Bay City, MI | 502 | 112 | Deltona-Daytona Beach, FL | 4,142 | 2 | Houston, TX | 49,639 |
| 113 | Beaumont-Port Arthur, TX | 4,075 | 42 | Denver-Aurora, CO | 12,472 | 134 | Huntsville, AL | 3,190 |
| 318 | Bend, OR | 632 | 127 | Des Moines-West Des Moines, IA | 3,536 | 334 | Idaho Falls, ID | 535 |
| 249 | Billings, MT | 1,206 | 17 | Detroit (greater), MI | 26,226 | 27 | Indianapolis, IN | 17,235 |
| 236 | Binghamton, NY | 1,323 | 25 | Detroit-Dearborn-Livonia, MI M.D. | 17,401 | 329 | Iowa City, IA | 576 |
| 44 | Birmingham-Hoover, AL | 11,366 | 258 | Dothan, AL | 1,127 | 53 | Jacksonville, FL | 9,453 |
| 330 | Bismarck, ND | 560 | 301 | Dover, DE | 769 | 281 | Jackson, MI | 892 |
| 332 | Blacksburg, VA | 558 | 342 | Dubuque, IA | 481 | 90 | Jackson, MS | 5,277 |
| 289 | Bloomington, IL | 852 | 188 | Duluth, MN-WI | 1,742 | 245 | Jackson, TN | 1,263 |
| 271 | Bloomington, IN | 935 | 273 | Dutchess-Putnam, NY M.D. | 927 | 279 | Janesville, WI | 899 |
| 365 | Bloomsburg-Berwick, PA | 331 | 257 | East Stroudsburg, PA | 1,138 | 308 | Jefferson City, MO | 709 |
| 158 | Boise City, ID | 2,303 | 343 | Eau Claire, WI | 475 | 254 | Johnson City, TN | 1,146 |
| 30 | Boston (greater), MA-NH | 16,370 | 215 | El Centro, CA | 1,435 | 325 | Johnstown, PA | 600 |
| 68 | Boston, MA M.D. | 7,902 | 156 | El Paso, TX | 2,364 | 217 | Jonesboro, AR | 1,423 |
| 247 | Boulder, CO | 1,232 | 209 | Elgin, IL M.D. | 1,496 | 214 | Joplin, MO | 1,451 |
| 299 | Bowling Green, KY | 775 | 338 | Elizabethtown-Fort Knox, KY | 519 | 268 | Kahului-Wailuku-Lahaina, HI | 948 |
| 176 | Bremerton-Silverdale, WA | 1,931 | 357 | Elmira, NY | 351 | 321 | Kankakee, IL | 620 |
| 135 | Bridgeport-Stamford, CT | 2,955 | 191 | Erie, PA | 1,711 | 40 | Kansas City, MO-KS | 13,843 |
| 141 | Brownsville-Harlingen, TX | 2,761 | 150 | Eugene, OR | 2,552 | 243 | Kennewick-Richland, WA | 1,293 |
| 248 | Brunswick, GA | 1,209 | 375 | Fairbanks, AK | 125 | 203 | Kingsport, TN-VA | 1,558 |
| 80 | Buffalo-Niagara Falls, NY | 6,525 | 262 | Fargo, ND-MN | 1,098 | 326 | Kingston, NY | 590 |
| 240 | Burlington, NC | 1,311 | 322 | Farmington, NM | 618 | 83 | Knoxville, TN | 6,302 |
| 317 | California-Lexington Park, MD | 640 | 152 | Fayetteville-Springdale, AR-MO | 2,490 | 328 | Kokomo, IN | 581 |
| 75 | Cambridge-Newton, MA M.D. | 7,234 | 88 | Fayetteville, NC | 5,514 | 348 | La Crosse, WI-MN | 443 |
| 79 | Camden, NJ M.D. | 6,597 | 344 | Flagstaff, AZ | 473 | 253 | Lafayette, IN | 1,158 |
| 145 | Canton, OH | 2,680 | 103 | Flint, MI | 4,576 | 117 | Lafayette, LA | 3,814 |
| 118 | Cape Coral-Fort Myers, FL | 3,779 | 270 | Florence-Muscle Shoals, AL | 937 | 123 | Lake Charles, LA | 3,659 |
| 303 | Cape Girardeau, MO-IL | 738 | 165 | Florence, SC | 2,146 | 138 | Lake Co.-Kenosha Co., IL-WI M.D. | 2,886 |
| 265 | Carbondale-Marion, IL | 1,045 | 373 | Fond du Lac, WI | 250 | 179 | Lake Havasu City-Kingman, AZ | 1,861 |
| 374 | Carson City, NV | 202 | 272 | Fort Collins, CO | 934 | 98 | Lakeland, FL | 4,929 |
| 355 | Casper, WY | 377 | 34 | Fort Lauderdale, FL M.D. | 15,934 | 189 | Lancaster, PA | 1,741 |
| 223 | Cedar Rapids, IA | 1,395 | 164 | Fort Smith, AR-OK | 2,154 | 153 | Lansing-East Lansing, MI | 2,488 |
| 337 | Chambersburg-Waynesboro, PA | 528 | 136 | Fort Wayne, IN | 2,939 | 207 | Laredo, TX | 1,536 |
| 221 | Champaign-Urbana, IL | 1,400 | 28 | Fort Worth-Arlington, TX M.D. | 16,871 | 218 | Las Cruces, NM | 1,421 |
| 107 | Charleston-North Charleston, SC | 4,422 | 58 | Fresno, CA | 9,102 | 23 | Las Vegas-Henderson, NV | 18,568 |
| 33 | Charlotte-Mecklenburg, NC-SC | 15,963 | 233 | Gadsden, AL | 1,337 | 320 | Lawrence, KS | 622 |
| 313 | Charlottesville, VA | 675 | 204 | Gainesville, FL | 1,548 | 196 | Lawton, OK | 1,663 |
| 105 | Chattanooga, TN-GA | 4,469 | 278 | Gainesville, GA | 901 | 354 | Lebanon, PA | 378 |

Note: All listings are for Metropolitan Statistical Areas (M.S.A.s) except for those ending with "M.D." Listings with "M.D." are Metropolitan Divisions which are smaller parts of eleven large M.S.A.s. See explanatory note at beginning of metropolitan area section.

| RANK | METROPOLITAN AREA | BURGLARY | RANK | METROPOLITAN AREA | BURGLARY | RANK | METROPOLITAN AREA | BURGLARY |
|---|---|---|---|---|---|---|---|---|
| 309 | Lewiston-Auburn, ME | 703 | 89 | Omaha-Council Bluffs, NE-IA | 5,492 | 371 | Sheboygan, WI | 261 |
| 351 | Lewiston, ID-WA | 426 | 19 | Orlando, FL | 19,952 | 305 | Sherman-Denison, TX | 730 |
| 116 | Lexington-Fayette, KY | 3,816 | 350 | Oshkosh-Neenah, WI | 429 | 126 | Shreveport-Bossier City, LA | 3,572 |
| 275 | Lima, OH | 921 | 336 | Owensboro, KY | 529 | 129 | Silver Spring-Frederick, MD M.D. | 3,470 |
| 205 | Lincoln, NE | 1,547 | 133 | Oxnard-Thousand Oaks, CA | 3,210 | 292 | Sioux City, IA-NE-SD | 826 |
| 59 | Little Rock, AR | 9,031 | 119 | Palm Bay-Melbourne, FL | 3,751 | 256 | Sioux Falls, SD | 1,141 |
| 372 | Logan, UT-ID | 256 | 216 | Panama City, FL | 1,433 | 154 | South Bend-Mishawaka, IN-MI | 2,483 |
| 187 | Longview, TX | 1,747 | 327 | Parkersburg-Vienna, WV | 585 | 149 | Spartanburg, SC | 2,563 |
| 277 | Longview, WA | 910 | 115 | Pensacola, FL | 3,882 | 81 | Spokane, WA | 6,426 |
| 4 | Los Angeles County, CA M.D. | 48,172 | 162 | Peoria, IL | 2,185 | 186 | Springfield, IL | 1,759 |
| 1 | Los Angeles (greater), CA | 58,588 | 16 | Philadelphia (greater) PA-NJ-MD-DE | 28,621 | 99 | Springfield, MA | 4,817 |
| 51 | Louisville, KY-IN | 10,034 | 43 | Philadelphia, PA M.D. | 12,411 | 124 | Springfield, MO | 3,655 |
| 137 | Lubbock, TX | 2,934 | 11 | Phoenix-Mesa-Scottsdale, AZ | 32,071 | 192 | Springfield, OH | 1,694 |
| 303 | Lynchburg, VA | 738 | 63 | Pittsburgh, PA | 8,669 | 368 | State College, PA | 316 |
| 139 | Macon, GA | 2,878 | 267 | Pittsfield, MA | 1,017 | 363 | Staunton-Waynesboro, VA | 341 |
| 213 | Madera, CA | 1,454 | 361 | Pocatello, ID | 346 | 72 | Stockton-Lodi, CA | 7,538 |
| 157 | Madison, WI | 2,345 | 148 | Port St. Lucie, FL | 2,590 | 323 | St. Cloud, MN | 605 |
| 197 | Manchester-Nashua, NH | 1,654 | 45 | Portland-Vancouver, OR-WA | 11,002 | NA | St. George, UT** | NA |
| 364 | Manhattan, KS | 335 | 159 | Portland, ME | 2,270 | 264 | St. Joseph, MO-KS | 1,046 |
| 335 | Mankato-North Mankato, MN | 530 | 280 | Prescott, AZ | 894 | 35 | St. Louis, MO-IL | 15,095 |
| 195 | Mansfield, OH | 1,678 | 62 | Providence-Warwick, RI-MA | 8,780 | 229 | Sumter, SC | 1,382 |
| 82 | McAllen-Edinburg-Mission, TX | 6,417 | 242 | Provo-Orem, UT | 1,296 | 130 | Syracuse, NY | 3,367 |
| 255 | Medford, OR | 1,145 | 166 | Pueblo, CO | 2,117 | 65 | Tacoma, WA M.D. | 8,546 |
| 31 | Memphis, TN-MS-AR | 16,117 | 298 | Punta Gorda, FL | 784 | 132 | Tallahassee, FL | 3,257 |
| 167 | Merced, CA | 2,097 | 211 | Racine, WI | 1,476 | 24 | Tampa-St Petersburg, FL | 17,794 |
| 7 | Miami (greater), FL | 44,416 | 76 | Raleigh, NC | 6,976 | 228 | Terre Haute, IN | 1,383 |
| 22 | Miami-Dade County, FL M.D. | 18,943 | 294 | Rapid City, SD | 811 | 212 | Texarkana, TX-AR | 1,465 |
| 296 | Midland, TX | 788 | 177 | Reading, PA | 1,890 | 367 | The Villages, FL | 330 |
| 54 | Milwaukee, WI | 9,259 | 223 | Redding, CA | 1,395 | 78 | Toledo, OH | 6,728 |
| 36 | Minneapolis-St. Paul, MN-WI | 15,050 | 151 | Reno, NV | 2,504 | 193 | Topeka, KS | 1,689 |
| 340 | Missoula, MT | 507 | 87 | Richmond, VA | 5,533 | 175 | Trenton, NJ | 1,936 |
| 96 | Mobile, AL | 4,953 | 9 | Riverside-San Bernardino, CA | 33,572 | 71 | Tucson, AZ | 7,550 |
| 93 | Modesto, CA | 5,133 | 261 | Roanoke, VA | 1,104 | 66 | Tulsa, OK | 8,439 |
| 144 | Monroe, LA | 2,698 | 307 | Rochester, MN | 714 | 170 | Tuscaloosa, AL | 2,018 |
| 287 | Monroe, MI | 869 | 86 | Rochester, NY | 5,619 | 201 | Tyler, TX | 1,578 |
| 95 | Montgomery County, PA M.D. | 5,034 | 142 | Rockford, IL | 2,723 | 241 | Utica-Rome, NY | 1,301 |
| 339 | Morgantown, WV | 518 | 246 | Rockingham County, NH M.D. | 1,234 | 101 | Vallejo-Fairfield, CA | 4,666 |
| 314 | Morristown, TN | 658 | 180 | Rocky Mount, NC | 1,843 | 306 | Victoria, TX | 717 |
| 251 | Mount Vernon-Anacortes, WA | 1,195 | 286 | Rome, GA | 875 | 183 | Vineland-Bridgeton, NJ | 1,785 |
| 310 | Muncie, IN | 700 | 37 | Sacramento, CA | 14,681 | 57 | Virginia Beach-Norfolk, VA-NC | 9,109 |
| 233 | Muskegon, MI | 1,337 | 230 | Saginaw, MI | 1,373 | 106 | Visalia-Porterville, CA | 4,458 |
| 111 | Myrtle Beach, SC-NC | 4,163 | 168 | Salem, OR | 2,042 | 163 | Waco, TX | 2,160 |
| 323 | Napa, CA | 605 | 143 | Salinas, CA | 2,706 | 199 | Warner Robins, GA | 1,641 |
| 259 | Naples-Marco Island, FL | 1,121 | 131 | Salisbury, MD-DE | 3,355 | 61 | Warren-Troy, MI M.D. | 8,825 |
| 49 | Nashville-Davidson, TN | 10,270 | 70 | Salt Lake City, UT | 7,780 | 26 | Washington (greater) DC-VA-MD-WV | 17,341 |
| 84 | Nassau-Suffolk, NY M.D. | 5,948 | 294 | San Angelo, TX | 811 | 39 | Washington, DC-VA-MD-WV M.D. | 13,871 |
| 210 | New Bern, NC | 1,488 | 21 | San Antonio, TX | 19,295 | 360 | Watertown-Fort Drum, NY | 348 |
| 128 | New Haven-Milford, CT | 3,485 | 38 | San Diego, CA | 13,970 | 345 | Wausau, WI | 467 |
| 69 | New Orleans, LA | 7,853 | 15 | San Francisco (greater), CA | 30,011 | 52 | West Palm Beach, FL M.D. | 9,539 |
| 3 | New York (greater), NY-NJ-PA | 49,360 | 56 | San Francisco-Redwood, CA M.D. | 9,137 | 244 | Wichita Falls, TX | 1,267 |
| 10 | New York-Jersey City, NY-NJ M.D. | 33,236 | 60 | San Jose, CA | 8,960 | 92 | Wichita, KS | 5,165 |
| 55 | Newark, NJ-PA M.D. | 9,249 | 198 | San Luis Obispo, CA | 1,642 | 333 | Williamsport, PA | 541 |
| 260 | Niles-Benton Harbor, MI | 1,118 | 232 | San Rafael, CA M.D. | 1,354 | 102 | Wilmington, DE-MD-NJ M.D. | 4,579 |
| 97 | North Port-Sarasota-Bradenton, FL | 4,932 | 200 | Santa Cruz-Watsonville, CA | 1,640 | 146 | Wilmington, NC | 2,669 |
| 297 | Norwich-New London, CT | 787 | 161 | Santa Maria-Santa Barbara, CA | 2,249 | 352 | Winchester, VA-WV | 406 |
| 20 | Oakland-Hayward, CA M.D. | 19,520 | 182 | Santa Rosa, CA | 1,804 | 74 | Winston-Salem, NC | 7,235 |
| 178 | Ocala, FL | 1,866 | 140 | Savannah, GA | 2,854 | 108 | Worcester, MA-CT | 4,381 |
| 290 | Ocean City, NJ | 844 | 147 | Scranton--Wilkes-Barre, PA | 2,639 | 160 | Yakima, WA | 2,267 |
| 252 | Odessa, TX | 1,165 | 13 | Seattle (greater), WA | 31,505 | 226 | York-Hanover, PA | 1,384 |
| NA | Ogden-Clearfield, UT** | NA | 18 | Seattle-Bellevue-Everett, WA M.D. | 22,959 | 225 | Yuba City, CA | 1,389 |
| 41 | Oklahoma City, OK | 12,856 | 311 | Sebastian-Vero Beach, FL | 680 | 202 | Yuma, AZ | 1,577 |
| 172 | Olympia, WA | 1,998 | 274 | Sebring, FL | 926 | | | |

Source: Reported data from the F.B.I. "Crime in the United States 2013"
*Burglary is the unlawful entry of a structure to commit a felony or theft. Attempts are included.
**Not available.

# 29. Burglaries in 2013 (continued)
## National Total = 1,928,465 Burglaries*

| RANK | METROPOLITAN AREA | BURGLARY | RANK | METROPOLITAN AREA | BURGLARY | RANK | METROPOLITAN AREA | BURGLARY |
|---|---|---|---|---|---|---|---|---|
| 1 | Los Angeles (greater), CA | 58,588 | 65 | Tacoma, WA M.D. | 8,546 | 129 | Silver Spring-Frederick, MD M.D. | 3,470 |
| 2 | Houston, TX | 49,639 | 66 | Tulsa, OK | 8,439 | 130 | Syracuse, NY | 3,367 |
| 3 | New York (greater), NY-NJ-PA | 49,360 | 67 | Baton Rouge, LA | 7,921 | 131 | Salisbury, MD-DE | 3,355 |
| 4 | Los Angeles County, CA M.D. | 48,172 | 68 | Boston, MA M.D. | 7,902 | 132 | Tallahassee, FL | 3,257 |
| 5 | Dallas (greater), TX | 47,789 | 69 | New Orleans, LA | 7,853 | 133 | Oxnard-Thousand Oaks, CA | 3,210 |
| 6 | Atlanta, GA | 44,591 | 70 | Salt Lake City, UT | 7,780 | 134 | Huntsville, AL | 3,190 |
| 7 | Miami (greater), FL | 44,416 | 71 | Tucson, AZ | 7,550 | 135 | Bridgeport-Stamford, CT | 2,955 |
| 8 | Chicago (greater), IL-IN-WI | 40,196 | 72 | Stockton-Lodi, CA | 7,538 | 136 | Fort Wayne, IN | 2,939 |
| 9 | Riverside-San Bernardino, CA | 33,572 | 73 | Greensboro-High Point, NC | 7,251 | 137 | Lubbock, TX | 2,934 |
| 10 | New York-Jersey City, NY-NJ M.D. | 33,236 | 74 | Winston-Salem, NC | 7,235 | 138 | Lake Co.-Kenosha Co., IL-WI M.D. | 2,886 |
| 11 | Phoenix-Mesa-Scottsdale, AZ | 32,071 | 75 | Cambridge-Newton, MA M.D. | 7,234 | 139 | Macon, GA | 2,878 |
| 12 | Chicago-Naperville, IL M.D. | 31,574 | 76 | Raleigh, NC | 6,976 | 140 | Savannah, GA | 2,854 |
| 13 | Seattle (greater), WA | 31,505 | 77 | Dayton, OH | 6,921 | 141 | Brownsville-Harlingen, TX | 2,761 |
| 14 | Dallas-Plano-Irving, TX M.D. | 30,918 | 78 | Toledo, OH | 6,728 | 142 | Rockford, IL | 2,723 |
| 15 | San Francisco (greater), CA | 30,011 | 79 | Camden, NJ M.D. | 6,597 | 143 | Salinas, CA | 2,706 |
| 16 | Philadelphia (greater) PA-NJ-MD-DE | 28,621 | 80 | Buffalo-Niagara Falls, NY | 6,525 | 144 | Monroe, LA | 2,698 |
| 17 | Detroit (greater), MI | 26,226 | 81 | Spokane, WA | 6,426 | 145 | Canton, OH | 2,680 |
| 18 | Seattle-Bellevue-Everett, WA M.D. | 22,959 | 82 | McAllen-Edinburg-Mission, TX | 6,417 | 146 | Wilmington, NC | 2,669 |
| 19 | Orlando, FL | 19,952 | 83 | Knoxville, TN | 6,302 | 147 | Scranton--Wilkes-Barre, PA | 2,639 |
| 20 | Oakland-Hayward, CA M.D. | 19,520 | 84 | Nassau-Suffolk, NY M.D. | 5,948 | 148 | Port St. Lucie, FL | 2,590 |
| 21 | San Antonio, TX | 19,295 | 85 | Columbia, SC | 5,927 | 149 | Spartanburg, SC | 2,563 |
| 22 | Miami-Dade County, FL M.D. | 18,943 | 86 | Rochester, NY | 5,619 | 150 | Eugene, OR | 2,552 |
| 23 | Las Vegas-Henderson, NV | 18,568 | 87 | Richmond, VA | 5,533 | 151 | Reno, NV | 2,504 |
| 24 | Tampa-St Petersburg, FL | 17,794 | 88 | Fayetteville, NC | 5,514 | 152 | Fayetteville-Springdale, AR-MO | 2,490 |
| 25 | Detroit-Dearborn-Livonia, MI M.D. | 17,401 | 89 | Omaha-Council Bluffs, NE-IA | 5,492 | 153 | Lansing-East Lansing, MI | 2,488 |
| 26 | Washington (greater) DC-VA-MD-WV | 17,341 | 90 | Jackson, MS | 5,277 | 154 | South Bend-Mishawaka, IN-MI | 2,483 |
| 27 | Indianapolis, IN | 17,235 | 91 | Augusta, GA-SC | 5,179 | 155 | Hammond, LA | 2,421 |
| 28 | Fort Worth-Arlington, TX M.D. | 16,871 | 92 | Wichita, KS | 5,165 | 156 | El Paso, TX | 2,364 |
| 29 | Baltimore, MD | 16,662 | 93 | Modesto, CA | 5,133 | 157 | Madison, WI | 2,345 |
| 30 | Boston (greater), MA-NH | 16,370 | 94 | Akron, OH | 5,122 | 158 | Boise City, ID | 2,303 |
| 31 | Memphis, TN-MS-AR | 16,117 | 95 | Montgomery County, PA M.D. | 5,034 | 159 | Portland, ME | 2,270 |
| 32 | Cincinnati, OH-KY-IN | 16,013 | 96 | Mobile, AL | 4,953 | 160 | Yakima, WA | 2,267 |
| 33 | Charlotte-Mecklenburg, NC-SC | 15,963 | 97 | North Port-Sarasota-Bradenton, FL | 4,932 | 161 | Santa Maria-Santa Barbara, CA | 2,249 |
| 34 | Fort Lauderdale, FL M.D. | 15,934 | 98 | Lakeland, FL | 4,929 | 162 | Peoria, IL | 2,185 |
| 35 | St. Louis, MO-IL | 15,095 | 99 | Springfield, MA | 4,817 | 163 | Waco, TX | 2,160 |
| 36 | Minneapolis-St. Paul, MN-WI | 15,050 | 100 | Colorado Springs, CO | 4,768 | 164 | Fort Smith, AR-OK | 2,154 |
| 37 | Sacramento, CA | 14,681 | 101 | Vallejo-Fairfield, CA | 4,666 | 165 | Florence, SC | 2,146 |
| 38 | San Diego, CA | 13,970 | 102 | Wilmington, DE-MD-NJ M.D. | 4,579 | 166 | Pueblo, CO | 2,117 |
| 39 | Washington, DC-VA-MD-WV M.D. | 13,871 | 103 | Flint, MI | 4,576 | 167 | Merced, CA | 2,097 |
| 40 | Kansas City, MO-KS | 13,843 | 104 | Grand Rapids-Wyoming, MI | 4,482 | 168 | Salem, OR | 2,042 |
| 41 | Oklahoma City, OK | 12,856 | 105 | Chattanooga, TN-GA | 4,469 | 169 | Alexandria, LA | 2,033 |
| 42 | Denver-Aurora, CO | 12,472 | 106 | Visalia-Porterville, CA | 4,458 | 170 | Tuscaloosa, AL | 2,018 |
| 43 | Philadelphia, PA M.D. | 12,411 | 107 | Charleston-North Charleston, SC | 4,422 | 171 | Albany, GA | 2,010 |
| 44 | Birmingham-Hoover, AL | 11,366 | 108 | Worcester, MA-CT | 4,381 | 172 | Amarillo, TX | 1,998 |
| 45 | Portland-Vancouver, OR-WA | 11,002 | 109 | Columbus, GA-AL | 4,245 | 172 | Olympia, WA | 1,998 |
| 46 | Bakersfield, CA | 10,728 | 110 | Gary, IN M.D. | 4,240 | 174 | Davenport, IA-IL | 1,984 |
| 47 | Anaheim-Santa Ana-Irvine, CA M.D. | 10,416 | 111 | Myrtle Beach, SC-NC | 4,163 | 175 | Trenton, NJ | 1,936 |
| 48 | Albuquerque, NM | 10,350 | 112 | Deltona-Daytona Beach, FL | 4,142 | 176 | Bremerton-Silverdale, WA | 1,931 |
| 49 | Nashville-Davidson, TN | 10,270 | 113 | Beaumont-Port Arthur, TX | 4,075 | 177 | Reading, PA | 1,890 |
| 50 | Austin-Round Rock, TX | 10,035 | 114 | Hartford, CT | 3,998 | 178 | Ocala, FL | 1,866 |
| 51 | Louisville, KY-IN | 10,034 | 115 | Pensacola, FL | 3,882 | 179 | Lake Havasu City-Kingman, AZ | 1,861 |
| 52 | West Palm Beach, FL M.D. | 9,539 | 116 | Lexington-Fayette, KY | 3,816 | 180 | Rocky Mount, NC | 1,843 |
| 53 | Jacksonville, FL | 9,453 | 117 | Lafayette, LA | 3,814 | 181 | Clarksville, TN-KY | 1,823 |
| 54 | Milwaukee, WI | 9,259 | 118 | Cape Coral-Fort Myers, FL | 3,779 | 182 | Santa Rosa, CA | 1,804 |
| 55 | Newark, NJ-PA M.D. | 9,249 | 119 | Palm Bay-Melbourne, FL | 3,751 | 183 | Barnstable Town, MA | 1,785 |
| 56 | San Francisco-Redwood, CA M.D. | 9,137 | 120 | Corpus Christi, TX | 3,750 | 183 | Vineland-Bridgeton, NJ | 1,785 |
| 57 | Virginia Beach-Norfolk, VA-NC | 9,109 | 121 | Albany-Schenectady-Troy, NY | 3,738 | 185 | Greenville, NC | 1,761 |
| 58 | Fresno, CA | 9,102 | 122 | Allentown, PA-NJ | 3,724 | 186 | Springfield, IL | 1,759 |
| 59 | Little Rock, AR | 9,031 | 123 | Lake Charles, LA | 3,659 | 187 | Longview, TX | 1,747 |
| 60 | San Jose, CA | 8,960 | 124 | Springfield, MO | 3,655 | 188 | Duluth, MN-WI | 1,742 |
| 61 | Warren-Troy, MI M.D. | 8,825 | 125 | Gulfport-Biloxi-Pascagoula, MS | 3,639 | 189 | Atlantic City, NJ | 1,741 |
| 62 | Providence-Warwick, RI-MA | 8,780 | 126 | Shreveport-Bossier City, LA | 3,572 | 189 | Lancaster, PA | 1,741 |
| 63 | Pittsburgh, PA | 8,669 | 127 | Des Moines-West Des Moines, IA | 3,536 | 191 | Erie, PA | 1,711 |
| 64 | Greenville-Anderson, SC | 8,631 | 128 | New Haven-Milford, CT | 3,485 | 192 | Springfield, OH | 1,694 |

Note: All listings are for Metropolitan Statistical Areas (M.S.A.s) except for those ending with "M.D." Listings with "M.D." are Metropolitan Divisions which are smaller parts of eleven large M.S.A.s. See explanatory note at beginning of metropolitan area section.

| RANK | METROPOLITAN AREA | BURGLARY | RANK | METROPOLITAN AREA | BURGLARY | RANK | METROPOLITAN AREA | BURGLARY |
|---|---|---|---|---|---|---|---|---|
| 193 | Topeka, KS | 1,689 | 255 | Medford, OR | 1,145 | 317 | California-Lexington Park, MD | 640 |
| 194 | Chico, CA | 1,685 | 256 | Sioux Falls, SD | 1,141 | 318 | Bend, OR | 632 |
| 195 | Mansfield, OH | 1,678 | 257 | East Stroudsburg, PA | 1,138 | 319 | Cumberland, MD-WV | 631 |
| 196 | Lawton, OK | 1,663 | 258 | Dothan, AL | 1,127 | 320 | Lawrence, KS | 622 |
| 197 | Manchester-Nashua, NH | 1,654 | 259 | Naples-Marco Island, FL | 1,121 | 321 | Kankakee, IL | 620 |
| 198 | San Luis Obispo, CA | 1,642 | 260 | Niles-Benton Harbor, MI | 1,118 | 322 | Farmington, NM | 618 |
| 199 | Warner Robins, GA | 1,641 | 261 | Roanoke, VA | 1,104 | 323 | Napa, CA | 605 |
| 200 | Santa Cruz-Watsonville, CA | 1,640 | 262 | Fargo, ND-MN | 1,098 | 323 | St. Cloud, MN | 605 |
| 201 | Tyler, TX | 1,578 | 263 | Decatur, AL | 1,050 | 325 | Johnstown, PA | 600 |
| 202 | Yuma, AZ | 1,577 | 264 | St. Joseph, MO-KS | 1,046 | 326 | Kingston, NY | 590 |
| 203 | Kingsport, TN-VA | 1,558 | 265 | Carbondale-Marion, IL | 1,045 | 327 | Parkersburg-Vienna, WV | 585 |
| 204 | Gainesville, FL | 1,548 | 266 | Green Bay, WI | 1,024 | 328 | Kokomo, IN | 581 |
| 205 | Hot Springs, AR | 1,547 | 267 | Pittsfield, MA | 1,017 | 329 | Iowa City, IA | 576 |
| 205 | Lincoln, NE | 1,547 | 268 | Kahului-Wailuku-Lahaina, HI | 948 | 330 | Bismarck, ND | 560 |
| 207 | Laredo, TX | 1,536 | 269 | Daphne-Fairhope-Foley, AL | 939 | 330 | Grand Junction, CO | 560 |
| 208 | Ann Arbor, MI | 1,508 | 270 | Florence-Muscle Shoals, AL | 937 | 332 | Blacksburg, VA | 558 |
| 209 | Elgin, IL M.D. | 1,496 | 271 | Bloomington, IN | 935 | 333 | Williamsport, PA | 541 |
| 210 | New Bern, NC | 1,488 | 272 | Fort Collins, CO | 934 | 334 | Idaho Falls, ID | 535 |
| 211 | Racine, WI | 1,476 | 273 | Dutchess-Putnam, NY M.D. | 927 | 335 | Mankato-North Mankato, MN | 530 |
| 212 | Texarkana, TX-AR | 1,465 | 274 | Sebring, FL | 926 | 336 | Owensboro, KY | 529 |
| 213 | Madera, CA | 1,454 | 275 | Lima, OH | 921 | 337 | Chambersburg-Waynesboro, PA | 528 |
| 214 | Joplin, MO | 1,451 | 276 | Coeur d'Alene, ID | 916 | 338 | Elizabethtown-Fort Knox, KY | 519 |
| 215 | El Centro, CA | 1,435 | 277 | Longview, WA | 910 | 339 | Morgantown, WV | 518 |
| 216 | Panama City, FL | 1,433 | 278 | Gainesville, GA | 901 | 340 | Missoula, MT | 507 |
| 217 | Jonesboro, AR | 1,423 | 279 | Janesville, WI | 899 | 341 | Bay City, MI | 502 |
| 218 | Las Cruces, NM | 1,421 | 280 | Prescott, AZ | 894 | 342 | Dubuque, IA | 481 |
| 219 | Houma, LA | 1,414 | 281 | Decatur, IL | 892 | 343 | Eau Claire, WI | 475 |
| 220 | Goldsboro, NC | 1,413 | 281 | Jackson, MI | 892 | 344 | Flagstaff, AZ | 473 |
| 221 | Champaign-Urbana, IL | 1,400 | 283 | Columbia, MO | 889 | 345 | Wausau, WI | 467 |
| 222 | Anchorage, AK | 1,398 | 283 | Greeley, CO | 889 | 346 | Appleton, WI | 459 |
| 223 | Cedar Rapids, IA | 1,395 | 285 | Dalton, GA | 878 | 347 | Great Falls, MT | 451 |
| 223 | Redding, CA | 1,395 | 286 | Rome, GA | 875 | 348 | La Crosse, WI-MN | 443 |
| 225 | Yuba City, CA | 1,389 | 287 | Monroe, MI | 869 | 349 | Cheyenne, WY | 441 |
| 226 | Athens-Clarke County, GA | 1,384 | 288 | Hanford-Corcoran, CA | 858 | 350 | Oshkosh-Neenah, WI | 429 |
| 226 | York-Hanover, PA | 1,384 | 289 | Bloomington, IL | 852 | 351 | Lewiston, ID-WA | 426 |
| 228 | Terre Haute, IN | 1,383 | 290 | Ocean City, NJ | 844 | 352 | Winchester, VA-WV | 406 |
| 229 | Sumter, SC | 1,382 | 291 | Cleveland, TN | 833 | 353 | Altoona, PA | 396 |
| 230 | Saginaw, MI | 1,373 | 292 | Sioux City, IA-NE-SD | 826 | 354 | Lebanon, PA | 378 |
| 231 | Anniston-Oxford, AL | 1,366 | 293 | Bangor, ME | 812 | 355 | Casper, WY | 377 |
| 232 | San Rafael, CA M.D. | 1,354 | 294 | Rapid City, SD | 811 | 356 | Harrisonburg, VA | 361 |
| 233 | Gadsden, AL | 1,337 | 294 | San Angelo, TX | 811 | 357 | Elmira, NY | 351 |
| 233 | Muskegon, MI | 1,337 | 296 | Midland, TX | 788 | 357 | Grand Forks, ND-MN | 351 |
| 235 | Hagerstown-Martinsburg, MD-WV | 1,332 | 297 | Norwich-New London, CT | 787 | 359 | Columbus, IN | 350 |
| 236 | Abilene, TX | 1,323 | 298 | Punta Gorda, FL | 784 | 360 | Watertown-Fort Drum, NY | 348 |
| 236 | Binghamton, NY | 1,323 | 299 | Bowling Green, KY | 775 | 361 | Pocatello, ID | 346 |
| 238 | Hilton Head Island, SC | 1,321 | 300 | Grants Pass, OR | 772 | 362 | Glens Falls, NY | 344 |
| 239 | College Station-Bryan, TX | 1,317 | 301 | Dover, DE | 769 | 363 | Staunton-Waynesboro, VA | 341 |
| 240 | Burlington, NC | 1,311 | 302 | Albany, OR | 750 | 364 | Manhattan, KS | 335 |
| 241 | Utica-Rome, NY | 1,301 | 303 | Cape Girardeau, MO-IL | 738 | 365 | Ames, IA | 331 |
| 242 | Provo-Orem, UT | 1,296 | 303 | Lynchburg, VA | 738 | 365 | Bloomsburg-Berwick, PA | 331 |
| 243 | Kennewick-Richland, WA | 1,293 | 305 | Sherman-Denison, TX | 730 | 367 | The Villages, FL | 330 |
| 244 | Wichita Falls, TX | 1,267 | 306 | Victoria, TX | 717 | 368 | State College, PA | 316 |
| 245 | Jackson, TN | 1,263 | 307 | Rochester, MN | 714 | 369 | Gettysburg, PA | 291 |
| 246 | Rockingham County, NH M.D. | 1,234 | 308 | Jefferson City, MO | 709 | 370 | Corvallis, OR | 290 |
| 247 | Boulder, CO | 1,232 | 309 | Lewiston-Auburn, ME | 703 | 371 | Sheboygan, WI | 261 |
| 248 | Brunswick, GA | 1,209 | 310 | Muncie, IN | 700 | 372 | Logan, UT-ID | 256 |
| 249 | Billings, MT | 1,206 | 311 | Grand Island, NE | 680 | 373 | Fond du Lac, WI | 250 |
| 250 | Crestview-Fort Walton Beach, FL | 1,197 | 311 | Sebastian-Vero Beach, FL | 680 | 374 | Carson City, NV | 202 |
| 251 | Mount Vernon-Anacortes, WA | 1,195 | 313 | Charlottesville, VA | 675 | 375 | Fairbanks, AK | 125 |
| 252 | Odessa, TX | 1,165 | 314 | Morristown, TN | 658 | NA | Ogden-Clearfield, UT** | NA |
| 253 | Lafayette, IN | 1,158 | 315 | Homosassa Springs, FL | 653 | NA | St. George, UT** | NA |
| 254 | Johnson City, TN | 1,146 | 316 | Hinesville, GA | 651 | | | |

Source: Reported data from the F.B.I. "Crime in the United States 2013"

*Burglary is the unlawful entry of a structure to commit a felony or theft. Attempts are included.

**Not available.

# 30. Burglary Rate in 2013
## National Rate = 610.0 Burglaries per 100,000 Population*

| RANK | METROPOLITAN AREA | RATE | RANK | METROPOLITAN AREA | RATE | RANK | METROPOLITAN AREA | RATE |
|---|---|---|---|---|---|---|---|---|
| 108 | Abilene, TX | 787.0 | 274 | Cheyenne, WY | 461.1 | 192 | Gary, IN M.D. | 598.8 |
| 139 | Akron, OH | 728.1 | 298 | Chicago (greater), IL-IN-WI | 421.4 | 355 | Gettysburg, PA | 286.9 |
| 296 | Albany-Schenectady-Troy, NY | 426.3 | 294 | Chicago-Naperville, IL M.D. | 430.7 | 362 | Glens Falls, NY | 267.8 |
| 11 | Albany, GA | 1,277.3 | 125 | Chico, CA | 757.8 | 26 | Goldsboro, NC | 1,129.7 |
| 180 | Albany, OR | 629.4 | 130 | Cincinnati, OH-KY-IN | 749.5 | 324 | Grand Forks, ND-MN | 349.3 |
| 24 | Albuquerque, NM | 1,146.7 | 173 | Clarksville, TN-KY | 653.6 | 94 | Grand Island, NE | 808.0 |
| 8 | Alexandria, LA | 1,314.3 | 145 | Cleveland, TN | 702.7 | 311 | Grand Junction, CO | 375.2 |
| 282 | Allentown, PA-NJ | 449.4 | 176 | Coeur d'Alene, ID | 635.1 | 286 | Grand Rapids-Wyoming, MI | 442.8 |
| 345 | Altoona, PA | 311.6 | 221 | College Station-Bryan, TX | 555.3 | 56 | Grants Pass, OR | 928.3 |
| 117 | Amarillo, TX | 767.6 | 146 | Colorado Springs, CO | 702.4 | 225 | Great Falls, MT | 548.7 |
| 317 | Ames, IA | 360.2 | 240 | Columbia, MO | 520.7 | 335 | Greeley, CO | 330.9 |
| 331 | Anaheim-Santa Ana-Irvine, CA M.D. | 334.0 | 131 | Columbia, SC | 747.1 | 337 | Green Bay, WI | 327.4 |
| 285 | Anchorage, AK | 444.4 | 7 | Columbus, GA-AL | 1,344.4 | 46 | Greensboro-High Point, NC | 977.2 |
| 295 | Ann Arbor, MI | 427.0 | 288 | Columbus, IN | 436.9 | 37 | Greenville-Anderson, SC | 1,012.5 |
| 22 | Anniston-Oxford, AL | 1,168.6 | 77 | Corpus Christi, TX | 848.4 | 38 | Greenville, NC | 1,010.0 |
| 374 | Appleton, WI | 200.0 | 332 | Corvallis, OR | 333.5 | 54 | Gulfport-Biloxi-Pascagoula, MS | 951.6 |
| 148 | Athens-Clarke County, GA | 701.0 | 264 | Crestview-Fort Walton Beach, FL | 473.8 | 244 | Hagerstown-Martinsburg, MD-WV | 516.8 |
| 93 | Atlanta, GA | 809.1 | 184 | Cumberland, MD-WV | 620.7 | 1 | Hammond, LA | 1,949.1 |
| 179 | Atlantic City, NJ | 630.6 | 147 | Dallas (greater), TX | 701.3 | 217 | Hanford-Corcoran, CA | 567.3 |
| 62 | Augusta, GA-SC | 893.0 | 156 | Dallas-Plano-Irving, TX M.D. | 686.1 | 360 | Harrisonburg, VA | 278.4 |
| 231 | Austin-Round Rock, TX | 534.0 | 187 | Dalton, GA | 614.4 | 305 | Hartford, CT | 390.5 |
| 15 | Bakersfield, CA | 1,244.3 | 255 | Daphne-Fairhope-Foley, AL | 485.7 | 166 | Hilton Head Island, SC | 671.3 |
| 191 | Baltimore, MD | 601.2 | 243 | Davenport, IA-IL | 516.9 | 109 | Hinesville, GA | 784.7 |
| 236 | Bangor, ME | 528.9 | 73 | Dayton, OH | 861.9 | 270 | Homosassa Springs, FL | 469.0 |
| 84 | Barnstable Town, MA | 827.0 | 160 | Decatur, AL | 680.4 | 3 | Hot Springs, AR | 1,592.2 |
| 50 | Baton Rouge, LA | 966.4 | 91 | Decatur, IL | 811.8 | 164 | Houma, LA | 675.5 |
| 269 | Bay City, MI | 470.1 | 154 | Deltona-Daytona Beach, FL | 691.3 | 104 | Houston, TX | 790.3 |
| 40 | Beaumont-Port Arthur, TX | 1,003.6 | 273 | Denver-Aurora, CO | 463.1 | 133 | Huntsville, AL | 734.2 |
| 308 | Bend, OR | 384.9 | 198 | Des Moines-West Des Moines, IA | 592.9 | 307 | Idaho Falls, ID | 388.9 |
| 136 | Billings, MT | 731.6 | 189 | Detroit (greater), MI | 610.4 | 64 | Indianapolis, IN | 885.4 |
| 232 | Binghamton, NY | 533.7 | 49 | Detroit-Dearborn-Livonia, MI M.D. | 974.0 | 319 | Iowa City, IA | 359.0 |
| 42 | Birmingham-Hoover, AL | 997.9 | 122 | Dothan, AL | 760.6 | 161 | Jacksonville, FL | 678.6 |
| 280 | Bismarck, ND | 450.7 | 278 | Dover, DE | 453.1 | 219 | Jackson, MI | 555.8 |
| 346 | Blacksburg, VA | 310.8 | 251 | Dubuque, IA | 502.3 | 60 | Jackson, MS | 910.0 |
| 281 | Bloomington, IL | 449.8 | 183 | Duluth, MN-WI | 621.8 | 51 | Jackson, TN | 966.3 |
| 213 | Bloomington, IN | 571.5 | 369 | Dutchess-Putnam, NY M.D. | 233.4 | 218 | Janesville, WI | 559.8 |
| 306 | Bloomsburg-Berwick, PA | 389.1 | 163 | East Stroudsburg, PA | 676.1 | 268 | Jefferson City, MO | 471.0 |
| 320 | Boise City, ID | 355.5 | 353 | Eau Claire, WI | 288.8 | 216 | Johnson City, TN | 568.9 |
| 323 | Boston (greater), MA-NH | 349.9 | 95 | El Centro, CA | 806.4 | 297 | Johnstown, PA | 425.9 |
| 302 | Boston, MA M.D. | 406.8 | 358 | El Paso, TX | 280.7 | 25 | Jonesboro, AR | 1,138.0 |
| 303 | Boulder, CO | 397.0 | 367 | Elgin, IL M.D. | 237.8 | 81 | Joplin, MO | 832.9 |
| 262 | Bowling Green, KY | 474.2 | 328 | Elizabethtown-Fort Knox, KY | 344.4 | 196 | Kahului-Wailuku-Lahaina, HI | 593.8 |
| 129 | Bremerton-Silverdale, WA | 751.7 | 304 | Elmira, NY | 394.2 | 224 | Kankakee, IL | 549.4 |
| 340 | Bridgeport-Stamford, CT | 320.8 | 190 | Erie, PA | 610.1 | 164 | Kansas City, MO-KS | 675.5 |
| 171 | Brownsville-Harlingen, TX | 657.5 | 144 | Eugene, OR | 716.2 | 265 | Kennewick-Richland, WA | 472.7 |
| 33 | Brunswick, GA | 1,062.9 | 318 | Fairbanks, AK | 359.8 | 250 | Kingsport, TN-VA | 503.8 |
| 210 | Buffalo-Niagara Falls, NY | 574.9 | 252 | Fargo, ND-MN | 494.2 | 339 | Kingston, NY | 324.5 |
| 78 | Burlington, NC | 844.6 | 256 | Farmington, NM | 484.5 | 132 | Knoxville, TN | 739.4 |
| 204 | California-Lexington Park, MD | 580.3 | 247 | Fayetteville-Springdale, AR-MO | 510.2 | 149 | Kokomo, IN | 699.1 |
| 344 | Cambridge-Newton, MA M.D. | 312.7 | 5 | Fayetteville, NC | 1,458.5 | 338 | La Crosse, WI-MN | 325.9 |
| 238 | Camden, NJ M.D. | 524.7 | 327 | Flagstaff, AZ | 345.3 | 220 | Lafayette, IN | 555.5 |
| 168 | Canton, OH | 663.3 | 31 | Flint, MI | 1,098.4 | 99 | Lafayette, LA | 799.3 |
| 207 | Cape Coral-Fort Myers, FL | 575.9 | 174 | Florence-Muscle Shoals, AL | 637.9 | 2 | Lake Charles, LA | 1,813.8 |
| 127 | Cape Girardeau, MO-IL | 756.8 | 36 | Florence, SC | 1,036.0 | 334 | Lake Co.-Kenosha Co., IL-WI M.D. | 331.9 |
| 87 | Carbondale-Marion, IL | 824.9 | 366 | Fond du Lac, WI | 245.2 | 61 | Lake Havasu City-Kingman, AZ | 907.4 |
| 314 | Carson City, NV | 367.7 | 350 | Fort Collins, CO | 295.7 | 103 | Lakeland, FL | 791.4 |
| 267 | Casper, WY | 471.3 | 72 | Fort Lauderdale, FL M.D. | 864.4 | 336 | Lancaster, PA | 329.3 |
| 235 | Cedar Rapids, IA | 529.2 | 118 | Fort Smith, AR-OK | 766.7 | 233 | Lansing-East Lansing, MI | 533.1 |
| 325 | Chambersburg-Waynesboro, PA | 348.2 | 153 | Fort Wayne, IN | 693.0 | 203 | Laredo, TX | 584.2 |
| 193 | Champaign-Urbana, IL | 597.7 | 137 | Fort Worth-Arlington, TX M.D. | 731.0 | 170 | Las Cruces, NM | 660.7 |
| 182 | Charleston-North Charleston, SC | 622.1 | 52 | Fresno, CA | 953.8 | 57 | Las Vegas-Henderson, NV | 916.5 |
| 157 | Charlotte-Mecklenburg, NC-SC | 685.4 | 10 | Gadsden, AL | 1,281.3 | 226 | Lawrence, KS | 548.6 |
| 348 | Charlottesville, VA | 300.5 | 212 | Gainesville, FL | 572.2 | 14 | Lawton, OK | 1,246.2 |
| 86 | Chattanooga, TN-GA | 825.8 | 257 | Gainesville, GA | 481.1 | 359 | Lebanon, PA | 278.6 |

Note: All listings are for Metropolitan Statistical Areas (M.S.A.s) except for those ending with "M.D." Listings with "M.D." are Metropolitan Divisions which are smaller parts of eleven large M.S.A.s. See explanatory note at beginning of metropolitan area section.

| RANK | METROPOLITAN AREA | RATE | RANK | METROPOLITAN AREA | RATE | RANK | METROPOLITAN AREA | RATE |
|---|---|---|---|---|---|---|---|---|
| 172 | Lewiston-Auburn, ME | 654.1 | 186 | Omaha-Council Bluffs, NE-IA | 614.6 | 371 | Sheboygan, WI | 227.1 |
| 155 | Lewiston, ID-WA | 689.1 | 65 | Orlando, FL | 882.4 | 195 | Sherman-Denison, TX | 594.8 |
| 113 | Lexington-Fayette, KY | 779.8 | 364 | Oshkosh-Neenah, WI | 253.1 | 101 | Shreveport-Bossier City, LA | 794.5 |
| 68 | Lima, OH | 877.1 | 277 | Owensboro, KY | 454.0 | 361 | Silver Spring-Frederick, MD M.D. | 275.8 |
| 253 | Lincoln, NE | 493.4 | 310 | Oxnard-Thousand Oaks, CA | 381.8 | 254 | Sioux City, IA-NE-SD | 487.5 |
| 13 | Little Rock, AR | 1,248.9 | 158 | Palm Bay-Melbourne, FL | 681.4 | 266 | Sioux Falls, SD | 472.2 |
| 375 | Logan, UT-ID | 197.1 | 126 | Panama City, FL | 757.5 | 116 | South Bend-Mishawaka, IN-MI | 777.9 |
| 97 | Longview, TX | 800.4 | 178 | Parkersburg-Vienna, WV | 633.1 | 96 | Spartanburg, SC | 802.0 |
| 63 | Longview, WA | 890.7 | 82 | Pensacola, FL | 832.3 | 19 | Spokane, WA | 1,200.7 |
| 258 | Los Angeles County, CA M.D. | 480.6 | 211 | Peoria, IL | 573.8 | 83 | Springfield, IL | 828.2 |
| 283 | Los Angeles (greater), CA | 445.8 | 262 | Philadelphia (greater) PA-NJ-MD-DE | 474.2 | 118 | Springfield, MA | 766.7 |
| 100 | Louisville, KY-IN | 798.0 | 202 | Philadelphia, PA M.D. | 586.9 | 89 | Springfield, MO | 815.8 |
| 47 | Lubbock, TX | 975.5 | 137 | Phoenix-Mesa-Scottsdale, AZ | 731.0 | 17 | Springfield, OH | 1,235.1 |
| 354 | Lynchburg, VA | 287.3 | 315 | Pittsburgh, PA | 367.2 | 373 | State College, PA | 203.3 |
| 16 | Macon, GA | 1,235.8 | 111 | Pittsfield, MA | 782.4 | 356 | Staunton-Waynesboro, VA | 286.4 |
| 53 | Madera, CA | 951.7 | 300 | Pocatello, ID | 409.6 | 32 | Stockton-Lodi, CA | 1,063.7 |
| 312 | Madison, WI | 374.6 | 198 | Port St. Lucie, FL | 592.9 | 341 | St. Cloud, MN | 315.9 |
| 301 | Manchester-Nashua, NH | 409.4 | 261 | Portland-Vancouver, OR-WA | 475.2 | NA | St. George, UT** | NA |
| 330 | Manhattan, KS | 337.2 | 287 | Portland, ME | 437.4 | 90 | St. Joseph, MO-KS | 814.5 |
| 230 | Mankato-North Mankato, MN | 536.7 | 299 | Prescott, AZ | 417.3 | 229 | St. Louis, MO-IL | 538.4 |
| 6 | Mansfield, OH | 1,370.6 | 227 | Providence-Warwick, RI-MA | 547.1 | 12 | Sumter, SC | 1,271.4 |
| 110 | McAllen-Edinburg-Mission, TX | 783.3 | 370 | Provo-Orem, UT | 230.8 | 248 | Syracuse, NY | 509.3 |
| 223 | Medford, OR | 550.7 | 9 | Pueblo, CO | 1,304.4 | 34 | Tacoma, WA M.D. | 1,042.5 |
| 21 | Memphis, TN-MS-AR | 1,195.8 | 260 | Punta Gorda, FL | 478.2 | 75 | Tallahassee, FL | 859.7 |
| 102 | Merced, CA | 792.8 | 124 | Racine, WI | 758.0 | 185 | Tampa-St Petersburg, FL | 619.5 |
| 123 | Miami (greater), FL | 759.7 | 206 | Raleigh, NC | 576.6 | 98 | Terre Haute, IN | 799.4 |
| 141 | Miami-Dade County, FL M.D. | 720.1 | 209 | Rapid City, SD | 575.5 | 48 | Texarkana, TX-AR | 975.2 |
| 249 | Midland, TX | 505.8 | 276 | Reading, PA | 456.7 | 343 | The Villages, FL | 315.5 |
| 200 | Milwaukee, WI | 589.2 | 115 | Redding, CA | 778.2 | 29 | Toledo, OH | 1,103.5 |
| 291 | Minneapolis-St. Paul, MN-WI | 435.5 | 214 | Reno, NV | 571.2 | 141 | Topeka, KS | 720.1 |
| 279 | Missoula, MT | 452.5 | 284 | Richmond, VA | 445.4 | 239 | Trenton, NJ | 524.2 |
| 20 | Mobile, AL | 1,196.2 | 121 | Riverside-San Bernardino, CA | 764.4 | 128 | Tucson, AZ | 755.3 |
| 44 | Modesto, CA | 978.5 | 321 | Roanoke, VA | 354.6 | 66 | Tulsa, OK | 879.0 |
| 4 | Monroe, LA | 1,513.2 | 329 | Rochester, MN | 338.2 | 74 | Tuscaloosa, AL | 861.1 |
| 207 | Monroe, MI | 575.9 | 241 | Rochester, NY | 518.2 | 140 | Tyler, TX | 726.5 |
| 363 | Montgomery County, PA M.D. | 258.7 | 106 | Rockford, IL | 789.7 | 289 | Utica-Rome, NY | 436.6 |
| 309 | Morgantown, WV | 382.7 | 352 | Rockingham County, NH M.D. | 291.4 | 30 | Vallejo-Fairfield, CA | 1,101.6 |
| 215 | Morristown, TN | 570.5 | 18 | Rocky Mount, NC | 1,213.7 | 135 | Victoria, TX | 732.4 |
| 39 | Mount Vernon-Anacortes, WA | 1,004.2 | 59 | Rome, GA | 910.3 | 27 | Vineland-Bridgeton, NJ | 1,127.7 |
| 194 | Muncie, IN | 595.3 | 169 | Sacramento, CA | 663.2 | 234 | Virginia Beach-Norfolk, VA-NC | 532.5 |
| 107 | Muskegon, MI | 787.6 | 152 | Saginaw, MI | 693.3 | 43 | Visalia-Porterville, CA | 978.6 |
| 35 | Myrtle Beach, SC-NC | 1,036.5 | 246 | Salem, OR | 511.9 | 80 | Waco, TX | 836.5 |
| 292 | Napa, CA | 432.2 | 181 | Salinas, CA | 628.0 | 69 | Warner Robins, GA | 876.4 |
| 333 | Naples-Marco Island, FL | 332.6 | 71 | Salisbury, MD-DE | 870.8 | 322 | Warren-Troy, MI M.D. | 351.6 |
| 201 | Nashville-Davidson, TN | 588.3 | 158 | Salt Lake City, UT | 681.4 | 351 | Washington (greater) DC-VA-MD-WV | 291.8 |
| 372 | Nassau-Suffolk, NY M.D. | 208.3 | 150 | San Angelo, TX | 697.8 | 349 | Washington, DC-VA-MD-WV M.D. | 296.1 |
| 23 | New Bern, NC | 1,154.8 | 76 | San Antonio, TX | 849.6 | 357 | Watertown-Fort Drum, NY | 286.0 |
| 293 | New Haven-Milford, CT | 430.9 | 290 | San Diego, CA | 435.7 | 326 | Wausau, WI | 345.8 |
| 177 | New Orleans, LA | 633.8 | 167 | San Francisco (greater), CA | 667.0 | 151 | West Palm Beach, FL M.D. | 694.9 |
| 365 | New York (greater), NY-NJ-PA | 247.6 | 205 | San Francisco-Redwood, CA M.D. | 578.0 | 79 | Wichita Falls, TX | 837.7 |
| 368 | New York-Jersey City, NY-NJ M.D. | 234.3 | 272 | San Jose, CA | 467.9 | 92 | Wichita, KS | 810.6 |
| 313 | Newark, NJ-PA M.D. | 370.3 | 197 | San Luis Obispo, CA | 593.2 | 275 | Williamsport, PA | 460.7 |
| 143 | Niles-Benton Harbor, MI | 716.8 | 237 | San Rafael, CA M.D. | 525.9 | 175 | Wilmington, DE-MD-NJ M.D. | 637.7 |
| 162 | North Port-Sarasota-Bradenton, FL | 677.1 | 188 | Santa Cruz-Watsonville, CA | 611.3 | 41 | Wilmington, NC | 1,000.1 |
| 228 | Norwich-New London, CT | 538.5 | 242 | Santa Maria-Santa Barbara, CA | 518.0 | 347 | Winchester, VA-WV | 307.9 |
| 134 | Oakland-Hayward, CA M.D. | 733.6 | 316 | Santa Rosa, CA | 364.5 | 28 | Winston-Salem, NC | 1,110.0 |
| 222 | Ocala, FL | 552.6 | 114 | Savannah, GA | 778.7 | 245 | Worcester, MA-CT | 513.7 |
| 67 | Ocean City, NJ | 878.0 | 271 | Scranton--Wilkes-Barre, PA | 468.5 | 58 | Yakima, WA | 911.6 |
| 105 | Odessa, TX | 790.1 | 70 | Seattle (greater), WA | 875.4 | 342 | York-Hanover, PA | 315.7 |
| NA | Ogden-Clearfield, UT** | NA | 85 | Seattle-Bellevue-Everett, WA M.D. | 826.2 | 88 | Yuba City, CA | 824.8 |
| 45 | Oklahoma City, OK | 977.3 | 259 | Sebastian-Vero Beach, FL | 479.2 | 112 | Yuma, AZ | 781.2 |
| 120 | Olympia, WA | 765.7 | 55 | Sebring, FL | 942.0 | | | |

Source: Reported data from the F.B.I. "Crime in the United States 2013"

*Burglary is the unlawful entry of a structure to commit a felony or theft. Attempts are included.

**Not available.

# 30. Burglary Rate in 2013 (continued)
## National Rate = 610.0 Burglaries per 100,000 Population*

| RANK | METROPOLITAN AREA | RATE | RANK | METROPOLITAN AREA | RATE | RANK | METROPOLITAN AREA | RATE |
|---|---|---|---|---|---|---|---|---|
| 1 | Hammond, LA | 1,949.1 | 65 | Orlando, FL | 882.4 | 129 | Bremerton-Silverdale, WA | 751.7 |
| 2 | Lake Charles, LA | 1,813.8 | 66 | Tulsa, OK | 879.0 | 130 | Cincinnati, OH-KY-IN | 749.5 |
| 3 | Hot Springs, AR | 1,592.2 | 67 | Ocean City, NJ | 878.0 | 131 | Columbia, SC | 747.1 |
| 4 | Monroe, LA | 1,513.2 | 68 | Lima, OH | 877.1 | 132 | Knoxville, TN | 739.4 |
| 5 | Fayetteville, NC | 1,458.5 | 69 | Warner Robins, GA | 876.4 | 133 | Huntsville, AL | 734.2 |
| 6 | Mansfield, OH | 1,370.6 | 70 | Seattle (greater), WA | 875.4 | 134 | Oakland-Hayward, CA M.D. | 733.6 |
| 7 | Columbus, GA-AL | 1,344.4 | 71 | Salisbury, MD-DE | 870.8 | 135 | Victoria, TX | 732.4 |
| 8 | Alexandria, LA | 1,314.3 | 72 | Fort Lauderdale, FL M.D. | 864.4 | 136 | Billings, MT | 731.6 |
| 9 | Pueblo, CO | 1,304.4 | 73 | Dayton, OH | 861.9 | 137 | Fort Worth-Arlington, TX M.D. | 731.0 |
| 10 | Gadsden, AL | 1,281.3 | 74 | Tuscaloosa, AL | 861.1 | 137 | Phoenix-Mesa-Scottsdale, AZ | 731.0 |
| 11 | Albany, GA | 1,277.3 | 75 | Tallahassee, FL | 859.7 | 139 | Akron, OH | 728.1 |
| 12 | Sumter, SC | 1,271.4 | 76 | San Antonio, TX | 849.6 | 140 | Tyler, TX | 726.5 |
| 13 | Little Rock, AR | 1,248.9 | 77 | Corpus Christi, TX | 848.4 | 141 | Miami-Dade County, FL M.D. | 720.1 |
| 14 | Lawton, OK | 1,246.2 | 78 | Burlington, NC | 844.6 | 141 | Topeka, KS | 720.1 |
| 15 | Bakersfield, CA | 1,244.3 | 79 | Wichita Falls, TX | 837.7 | 143 | Niles-Benton Harbor, MI | 716.8 |
| 16 | Macon, GA | 1,235.8 | 80 | Waco, TX | 836.5 | 144 | Eugene, OR | 716.2 |
| 17 | Springfield, OH | 1,235.1 | 81 | Joplin, MO | 832.9 | 145 | Cleveland, TN | 702.7 |
| 18 | Rocky Mount, NC | 1,213.7 | 82 | Pensacola, FL | 832.3 | 146 | Colorado Springs, CO | 702.4 |
| 19 | Spokane, WA | 1,200.7 | 83 | Springfield, IL | 828.2 | 147 | Dallas (greater), TX | 701.3 |
| 20 | Mobile, AL | 1,196.2 | 84 | Barnstable Town, MA | 827.0 | 148 | Athens-Clarke County, GA | 701.0 |
| 21 | Memphis, TN-MS-AR | 1,195.8 | 85 | Seattle-Bellevue-Everett, WA M.D. | 826.2 | 149 | Kokomo, IN | 699.1 |
| 22 | Anniston-Oxford, AL | 1,168.6 | 86 | Chattanooga, TN-GA | 825.8 | 150 | San Angelo, TX | 697.8 |
| 23 | New Bern, NC | 1,154.8 | 87 | Carbondale-Marion, IL | 824.9 | 151 | West Palm Beach, FL M.D. | 694.9 |
| 24 | Albuquerque, NM | 1,146.7 | 88 | Yuba City, CA | 824.8 | 152 | Saginaw, MI | 693.3 |
| 25 | Jonesboro, AR | 1,138.0 | 89 | Springfield, MO | 815.8 | 153 | Fort Wayne, IN | 693.0 |
| 26 | Goldsboro, NC | 1,129.7 | 90 | St. Joseph, MO-KS | 814.5 | 154 | Deltona-Daytona Beach, FL | 691.3 |
| 27 | Vineland-Bridgeton, NJ | 1,127.7 | 91 | Decatur, IL | 811.8 | 155 | Lewiston, ID-WA | 689.1 |
| 28 | Winston-Salem, NC | 1,110.0 | 92 | Wichita, KS | 810.6 | 156 | Dallas-Plano-Irving, TX M.D. | 686.1 |
| 29 | Toledo, OH | 1,103.5 | 93 | Atlanta, GA | 809.1 | 157 | Charlotte-Mecklenburg, NC-SC | 685.4 |
| 30 | Vallejo-Fairfield, CA | 1,101.6 | 94 | Grand Island, NE | 808.0 | 158 | Palm Bay-Melbourne, FL | 681.4 |
| 31 | Flint, MI | 1,098.4 | 95 | El Centro, CA | 806.4 | 158 | Salt Lake City, UT | 681.4 |
| 32 | Stockton-Lodi, CA | 1,063.7 | 96 | Spartanburg, SC | 802.0 | 160 | Decatur, AL | 680.4 |
| 33 | Brunswick, GA | 1,062.9 | 97 | Longview, TX | 800.4 | 161 | Jacksonville, FL | 678.6 |
| 34 | Tacoma, WA M.D. | 1,042.5 | 98 | Terre Haute, IN | 799.4 | 162 | North Port-Sarasota-Bradenton, FL | 677.1 |
| 35 | Myrtle Beach, SC-NC | 1,036.5 | 99 | Lafayette, LA | 799.3 | 163 | East Stroudsburg, PA | 676.1 |
| 36 | Florence, SC | 1,036.0 | 100 | Louisville, KY-IN | 798.0 | 164 | Houma, LA | 675.5 |
| 37 | Greenville-Anderson, SC | 1,012.5 | 101 | Shreveport-Bossier City, LA | 794.5 | 164 | Kansas City, MO-KS | 675.5 |
| 38 | Greenville, NC | 1,010.0 | 102 | Merced, CA | 792.8 | 166 | Hilton Head Island, SC | 671.3 |
| 39 | Mount Vernon-Anacortes, WA | 1,004.2 | 103 | Lakeland, FL | 791.4 | 167 | San Francisco (greater), CA | 667.0 |
| 40 | Beaumont-Port Arthur, TX | 1,003.6 | 104 | Houston, TX | 790.3 | 168 | Canton, OH | 663.3 |
| 41 | Wilmington, NC | 1,000.1 | 105 | Odessa, TX | 790.1 | 169 | Sacramento, CA | 663.2 |
| 42 | Birmingham-Hoover, AL | 997.9 | 106 | Rockford, IL | 789.7 | 170 | Las Cruces, NM | 660.7 |
| 43 | Visalia-Porterville, CA | 978.6 | 107 | Muskegon, MI | 787.6 | 171 | Brownsville-Harlingen, TX | 657.5 |
| 44 | Modesto, CA | 978.5 | 108 | Abilene, TX | 787.0 | 172 | Lewiston-Auburn, ME | 654.1 |
| 45 | Oklahoma City, OK | 977.3 | 109 | Hinesville, GA | 784.7 | 173 | Clarksville, TN-KY | 653.6 |
| 46 | Greensboro-High Point, NC | 977.2 | 110 | McAllen-Edinburg-Mission, TX | 783.3 | 174 | Florence-Muscle Shoals, AL | 637.9 |
| 47 | Lubbock, TX | 975.5 | 111 | Pittsfield, MA | 782.4 | 175 | Wilmington, DE-MD-NJ M.D. | 637.7 |
| 48 | Texarkana, TX-AR | 975.2 | 112 | Yuma, AZ | 781.2 | 176 | Coeur d'Alene, ID | 635.1 |
| 49 | Detroit-Dearborn-Livonia, MI M.D. | 974.0 | 113 | Lexington-Fayette, KY | 779.8 | 177 | New Orleans, LA | 633.8 |
| 50 | Baton Rouge, LA | 966.4 | 114 | Savannah, GA | 778.7 | 178 | Parkersburg-Vienna, WV | 633.1 |
| 51 | Jackson, TN | 966.3 | 115 | Redding, CA | 778.2 | 179 | Atlantic City, NJ | 630.6 |
| 52 | Fresno, CA | 953.8 | 116 | South Bend-Mishawaka, IN-MI | 777.9 | 180 | Albany, OR | 629.4 |
| 53 | Madera, CA | 951.7 | 117 | Amarillo, TX | 767.6 | 181 | Salinas, CA | 628.0 |
| 54 | Gulfport-Biloxi-Pascagoula, MS | 951.6 | 118 | Fort Smith, AR-OK | 766.7 | 182 | Charleston-North Charleston, SC | 622.1 |
| 55 | Sebring, FL | 942.0 | 118 | Springfield, MA | 766.7 | 183 | Duluth, MN-WI | 621.8 |
| 56 | Grants Pass, OR | 928.3 | 120 | Olympia, WA | 765.7 | 184 | Cumberland, MD-WV | 620.7 |
| 57 | Las Vegas-Henderson, NV | 916.5 | 121 | Riverside-San Bernardino, CA | 764.4 | 185 | Tampa-St Petersburg, FL | 619.5 |
| 58 | Yakima, WA | 911.6 | 122 | Dothan, AL | 760.6 | 186 | Omaha-Council Bluffs, NE-IA | 614.6 |
| 59 | Rome, GA | 910.3 | 123 | Miami (greater), FL | 759.7 | 187 | Dalton, GA | 614.4 |
| 60 | Jackson, MS | 910.0 | 124 | Racine, WI | 758.0 | 188 | Santa Cruz-Watsonville, CA | 611.3 |
| 61 | Lake Havasu City-Kingman, AZ | 907.4 | 125 | Chico, CA | 757.8 | 189 | Detroit (greater), MI | 610.4 |
| 62 | Augusta, GA-SC | 893.0 | 126 | Panama City, FL | 757.5 | 190 | Erie, PA | 610.1 |
| 63 | Longview, WA | 890.7 | 127 | Cape Girardeau, MO-IL | 756.8 | 191 | Baltimore, MD | 601.2 |
| 64 | Indianapolis, IN | 885.4 | 128 | Tucson, AZ | 755.3 | 192 | Gary, IN M.D. | 598.8 |

Note: All listings are for Metropolitan Statistical Areas (M.S.A.s) except for those ending with "M.D." Listings with "M.D." are Metropolitan Divisions which are smaller parts of eleven large M.S.A.s. See explanatory note at beginning of metropolitan area section.

| RANK | METROPOLITAN AREA | RATE | RANK | METROPOLITAN AREA | RATE | RANK | METROPOLITAN AREA | RATE |
|---|---|---|---|---|---|---|---|---|
| 193 | Champaign-Urbana, IL | 597.7 | 255 | Daphne-Fairhope-Foley, AL | 485.7 | 317 | Ames, IA | 360.2 |
| 194 | Muncie, IN | 595.3 | 256 | Farmington, NM | 484.5 | 318 | Fairbanks, AK | 359.8 |
| 195 | Sherman-Denison, TX | 594.8 | 257 | Gainesville, GA | 481.1 | 319 | Iowa City, IA | 359.0 |
| 196 | Kahului-Wailuku-Lahaina, HI | 593.8 | 258 | Los Angeles County, CA M.D. | 480.6 | 320 | Boise City, ID | 355.5 |
| 197 | San Luis Obispo, CA | 593.2 | 259 | Sebastian-Vero Beach, FL | 479.2 | 321 | Roanoke, VA | 354.6 |
| 198 | Des Moines-West Des Moines, IA | 592.9 | 260 | Punta Gorda, FL | 478.2 | 322 | Warren-Troy, MI M.D. | 351.6 |
| 198 | Port St. Lucie, FL | 592.9 | 261 | Portland-Vancouver, OR-WA | 475.2 | 323 | Boston (greater), MA-NH | 349.9 |
| 200 | Milwaukee, WI | 589.2 | 262 | Bowling Green, KY | 474.2 | 324 | Grand Forks, ND-MN | 349.3 |
| 201 | Nashville-Davidson, TN | 588.3 | 262 | Philadelphia (greater) PA-NJ-MD-DE | 474.2 | 325 | Chambersburg-Waynesboro, PA | 348.2 |
| 202 | Philadelphia, PA M.D. | 586.9 | 264 | Crestview-Fort Walton Beach, FL | 473.8 | 326 | Wausau, WI | 345.8 |
| 203 | Laredo, TX | 584.2 | 265 | Kennewick-Richland, WA | 472.7 | 327 | Flagstaff, AZ | 345.3 |
| 204 | California-Lexington Park, MD | 580.3 | 266 | Sioux Falls, SD | 472.2 | 328 | Elizabethtown-Fort Knox, KY | 344.4 |
| 205 | San Francisco-Redwood, CA M.D. | 578.0 | 267 | Casper, WY | 471.3 | 329 | Rochester, MN | 338.2 |
| 206 | Raleigh, NC | 576.6 | 268 | Jefferson City, MO | 471.0 | 330 | Manhattan, KS | 337.2 |
| 207 | Cape Coral-Fort Myers, FL | 575.9 | 269 | Bay City, MI | 470.1 | 331 | Anaheim-Santa Ana-Irvine, CA M.D. | 334.0 |
| 207 | Monroe, MI | 575.9 | 270 | Homosassa Springs, FL | 469.0 | 332 | Corvallis, OR | 333.5 |
| 209 | Rapid City, SD | 575.5 | 271 | Scranton--Wilkes-Barre, PA | 468.5 | 333 | Naples-Marco Island, FL | 332.6 |
| 210 | Buffalo-Niagara Falls, NY | 574.9 | 272 | San Jose, CA | 467.9 | 334 | Lake Co.-Kenosha Co., IL-WI M.D. | 331.9 |
| 211 | Peoria, IL | 573.8 | 273 | Denver-Aurora, CO | 463.1 | 335 | Greeley, CO | 330.9 |
| 212 | Gainesville, FL | 572.2 | 274 | Cheyenne, WY | 461.1 | 336 | Lancaster, PA | 329.3 |
| 213 | Bloomington, IN | 571.5 | 275 | Williamsport, PA | 460.7 | 337 | Green Bay, WI | 327.4 |
| 214 | Reno, NV | 571.2 | 276 | Reading, PA | 456.7 | 338 | La Crosse, WI-MN | 325.9 |
| 215 | Morristown, TN | 570.5 | 277 | Owensboro, KY | 454.0 | 339 | Kingston, NY | 324.5 |
| 216 | Johnson City, TN | 568.2 | 278 | Dover, DE | 453.1 | 340 | Bridgeport-Stamford, CT | 320.8 |
| 217 | Hanford-Corcoran, CA | 567.3 | 279 | Missoula, MT | 452.5 | 341 | St. Cloud, MN | 315.9 |
| 218 | Janesville, WI | 559.8 | 280 | Bismarck, ND | 450.7 | 342 | York-Hanover, PA | 315.7 |
| 219 | Jackson, MI | 555.8 | 281 | Bloomington, IL | 449.8 | 343 | The Villages, FL | 315.5 |
| 220 | Lafayette, IN | 555.5 | 282 | Allentown, PA-NJ | 449.4 | 344 | Cambridge-Newton, MA M.D. | 312.7 |
| 221 | College Station-Bryan, TX | 555.3 | 283 | Los Angeles (greater), CA | 445.8 | 345 | Altoona, PA | 311.6 |
| 222 | Ocala, FL | 552.6 | 284 | Richmond, VA | 445.4 | 346 | Blacksburg, VA | 310.8 |
| 223 | Medford, OR | 550.7 | 285 | Anchorage, AK | 444.4 | 347 | Winchester, VA-WV | 307.9 |
| 224 | Kankakee, IL | 549.4 | 286 | Grand Rapids-Wyoming, MI | 442.8 | 348 | Charlottesville, VA | 300.5 |
| 225 | Great Falls, MT | 548.7 | 287 | Portland, ME | 437.4 | 349 | Washington, DC-VA-MD-WV M.D. | 296.1 |
| 226 | Lawrence, KS | 548.6 | 288 | Columbus, IN | 436.9 | 350 | Fort Collins, CO | 295.7 |
| 227 | Providence-Warwick, RI-MA | 547.1 | 289 | Utica-Rome, NY | 436.6 | 351 | Washington (greater) DC-VA-MD-WV | 291.8 |
| 228 | Norwich-New London, CT | 538.5 | 290 | San Diego, CA | 435.7 | 352 | Rockingham County, NH M.D. | 291.4 |
| 229 | St. Louis, MO-IL | 538.4 | 291 | Minneapolis-St. Paul, MN-WI | 435.5 | 353 | Eau Claire, WI | 288.8 |
| 230 | Mankato-North Mankato, MN | 536.7 | 292 | Napa, CA | 432.2 | 354 | Lynchburg, VA | 287.3 |
| 231 | Austin-Round Rock, TX | 534.0 | 293 | New Haven-Milford, CT | 430.9 | 355 | Gettysburg, PA | 286.9 |
| 232 | Binghamton, NY | 533.7 | 294 | Chicago-Naperville, IL M.D. | 430.7 | 356 | Staunton-Waynesboro, VA | 286.4 |
| 233 | Lansing-East Lansing, MI | 533.1 | 295 | Ann Arbor, MI | 427.0 | 357 | Watertown-Fort Drum, NY | 286.0 |
| 234 | Virginia Beach-Norfolk, VA-NC | 532.5 | 296 | Albany-Schenectady-Troy, NY | 426.3 | 358 | El Paso, TX | 280.7 |
| 235 | Cedar Rapids, IA | 529.2 | 297 | Johnstown, PA | 425.9 | 359 | Lebanon, PA | 278.6 |
| 236 | Bangor, ME | 528.9 | 298 | Chicago (greater), IL-IN-WI | 421.4 | 360 | Harrisonburg, VA | 278.4 |
| 237 | San Rafael, CA M.D. | 525.9 | 299 | Prescott, AZ | 417.3 | 361 | Silver Spring-Frederick, MD M.D. | 275.8 |
| 238 | Camden, NJ M.D. | 524.7 | 300 | Pocatello, ID | 409.6 | 362 | Glens Falls, NY | 267.8 |
| 239 | Trenton, NJ | 524.2 | 301 | Manchester-Nashua, NH | 409.4 | 363 | Montgomery County, PA M.D. | 258.7 |
| 240 | Columbia, MO | 520.7 | 302 | Boston, MA M.D. | 406.8 | 364 | Oshkosh-Neenah, WI | 253.1 |
| 241 | Rochester, NY | 518.2 | 303 | Boulder, CO | 397.0 | 365 | New York (greater), NY-NJ-PA | 247.6 |
| 242 | Santa Maria-Santa Barbara, CA | 518.0 | 304 | Elmira, NY | 394.2 | 366 | Fond du Lac, WI | 245.2 |
| 243 | Davenport, IA-IL | 516.9 | 305 | Hartford, CT | 390.5 | 367 | Elgin, IL M.D. | 237.8 |
| 244 | Hagerstown-Martinsburg, MD-WV | 516.8 | 306 | Bloomsburg-Berwick, PA | 389.1 | 368 | New York-Jersey City, NY-NJ M.D. | 234.3 |
| 245 | Worcester, MA-CT | 513.7 | 307 | Idaho Falls, ID | 388.9 | 369 | Dutchess-Putnam, NY M.D. | 233.4 |
| 246 | Salem, OR | 511.9 | 308 | Bend, OR | 384.9 | 370 | Provo-Orem, UT | 230.8 |
| 247 | Fayetteville-Springdale, AR-MO | 510.2 | 309 | Morgantown, WV | 382.7 | 371 | Sheboygan, WI | 227.1 |
| 248 | Syracuse, NY | 509.3 | 310 | Oxnard-Thousand Oaks, CA | 381.8 | 372 | Nassau-Suffolk, NY M.D. | 208.3 |
| 249 | Midland, TX | 505.8 | 311 | Grand Junction, CO | 375.2 | 373 | State College, PA | 203.3 |
| 250 | Kingsport, TN-VA | 503.8 | 312 | Madison, WI | 374.6 | 374 | Appleton, WI | 200.0 |
| 251 | Dubuque, IA | 502.3 | 313 | Newark, NJ-PA M.D. | 370.3 | 375 | Logan, UT-ID | 197.1 |
| 252 | Fargo, ND-MN | 494.2 | 314 | Carson City, NV | 367.7 | NA | Ogden-Clearfield, UT** | NA |
| 253 | Lincoln, NE | 493.4 | 315 | Pittsburgh, PA | 367.2 | NA | St. George, UT** | NA |
| 254 | Sioux City, IA-NE-SD | 487.5 | 316 | Santa Rosa, CA | 364.5 | | | |

Source: Reported data from the F.B.I. "Crime in the United States 2013"
*Burglary is the unlawful entry of a structure to commit a felony or theft. Attempts are included.
**Not available.

# 31. Percent Change in Burglary Rate: 2012 to 2013
## National Percent Change = 9.3% Decrease*

| RANK | METROPOLITAN AREA | % CHANGE | RANK | METROPOLITAN AREA | % CHANGE | RANK | METROPOLITAN AREA | % CHANGE |
|---|---|---|---|---|---|---|---|---|
| 23 | Abilene, TX | 6.8 | 50 | Cheyenne, WY | 2.0 | 259 | Gary, IN M.D. | (15.4) |
| 179 | Akron, OH | (10.5) | 309 | Chicago (greater), IL-IN-WI | (21.1) | NA | Gettysburg, PA** | NA |
| 197 | Albany-Schenectady-Troy, NY | (11.2) | 310 | Chicago-Naperville, IL M.D. | (22.1) | 239 | Glens Falls, NY | (13.8) |
| 84 | Albany, GA | (2.6) | 221 | Chico, CA | (12.2) | 214 | Goldsboro, NC | (11.9) |
| 26 | Albany, OR | 5.9 | 117 | Cincinnati, OH-KY-IN | (5.6) | 204 | Grand Forks, ND-MN | (11.5) |
| NA | Albuquerque, NM** | NA | 119 | Clarksville, TN-KY | (5.8) | 2 | Grand Island, NE | 30.0 |
| 18 | Alexandria, LA | 8.7 | 31 | Cleveland, TN | 5.1 | 88 | Grand Junction, CO | (2.9) |
| 29 | Allentown, PA-NJ | 5.4 | 312 | Coeur d'Alene, ID | (22.5) | NA | Grand Rapids-Wyoming, MI** | NA |
| 47 | Altoona, PA | 2.5 | 203 | College Station-Bryan, TX | (11.4) | NA | Grants Pass, OR** | NA |
| 253 | Amarillo, TX | (15.0) | NA | Colorado Springs, CO** | NA | 8 | Great Falls, MT | 15.6 |
| 327 | Ames, IA | (27.6) | 263 | Columbia, MO | (15.5) | 259 | Greeley, CO | (15.4) |
| 230 | Anaheim-Santa Ana-Irvine, CA M.D. | (12.8) | NA | Columbia, SC** | NA | 297 | Green Bay, WI | (19.7) |
| 11 | Anchorage, AK | 12.7 | 14 | Columbus, GA-AL | 11.0 | 84 | Greensboro-High Point, NC | (2.6) |
| 336 | Ann Arbor, MI | (36.3) | 194 | Columbus, IN | (11.1) | 33 | Greenville-Anderson, SC | 4.7 |
| 296 | Anniston-Oxford, AL | (19.2) | NA | Corpus Christi, TX** | NA | 81 | Greenville, NC | (2.2) |
| 206 | Appleton, WI | (11.6) | 177 | Corvallis, OR | (10.4) | NA | Gulfport-Biloxi-Pascagoula, MS** | NA |
| 228 | Athens-Clarke County, GA | (12.6) | 199 | Crestview-Fort Walton Beach, FL | (11.3) | 199 | Hagerstown-Martinsburg, MD-WV | (11.3) |
| 133 | Atlanta, GA | (7.2) | 147 | Cumberland, MD-WV | (8.4) | 172 | Hammond, LA | (9.9) |
| 88 | Atlantic City, NJ | (2.9) | 179 | Dallas (greater), TX | (10.5) | 20 | Hanford-Corcoran, CA | 8.3 |
| 216 | Augusta, GA-SC | (12.0) | 208 | Dallas-Plano-Irving, TX M.D. | (11.7) | 61 | Harrisonburg, VA | 0.1 |
| 237 | Austin-Round Rock, TX | (13.5) | 154 | Dalton, GA | (8.6) | 270 | Hartford, CT | (16.1) |
| 80 | Bakersfield, CA | (2.1) | 119 | Daphne-Fairhope-Foley, AL | (5.8) | 240 | Hilton Head Island, SC | (14.0) |
| 112 | Baltimore, MD | (5.2) | 63 | Davenport, IA-IL | (0.1) | 265 | Hinesville, GA | (15.7) |
| 184 | Bangor, ME | (10.7) | 105 | Dayton, OH | (4.6) | 229 | Homosassa Springs, FL | (12.7) |
| 294 | Barnstable Town, MA | (19.0) | 303 | Decatur, AL | (20.6) | NA | Hot Springs, AR** | NA |
| 97 | Baton Rouge, LA | (3.5) | 283 | Decatur, IL | (17.5) | 94 | Houma, LA | (3.2) |
| 10 | Bay City, MI | 14.3 | 157 | Deltona-Daytona Beach, FL | (8.7) | NA | Houston, TX** | NA |
| 49 | Beaumont-Port Arthur, TX | 2.2 | 135 | Denver-Aurora, CO | (7.3) | 233 | Huntsville, AL | (13.2) |
| NA | Bend, OR** | NA | NA | Des Moines-West Des Moines, IA** | NA | 7 | Idaho Falls, ID | 15.8 |
| 4 | Billings, MT | 18.7 | 224 | Detroit (greater), MI | (12.4) | 179 | Indianapolis, IN | (10.5) |
| 102 | Binghamton, NY | (4.1) | 224 | Detroit-Dearborn-Livonia, MI M.D. | (12.4) | 218 | Iowa City, IA | (12.1) |
| 194 | Birmingham-Hoover, AL | (11.1) | 299 | Dothan, AL | (19.8) | 159 | Jacksonville, FL | (8.8) |
| 33 | Bismarck, ND | 4.7 | 338 | Dover, DE | (38.4) | NA | Jackson, MI** | NA |
| 320 | Blacksburg, VA | (23.9) | NA | Dubuque, IA** | NA | 276 | Jackson, MS | (16.6) |
| 67 | Bloomington, IL | (0.8) | 24 | Duluth, MN-WI | 6.7 | 249 | Jackson, TN | (14.5) |
| 169 | Bloomington, IN | (9.5) | 259 | Dutchess-Putnam, NY M.D. | (15.4) | 56 | Janesville, WI | 1.6 |
| 189 | Bloomsburg-Berwick, PA | (10.9) | 103 | East Stroudsburg, PA | (4.3) | 138 | Jefferson City, MO | (8.1) |
| 249 | Boise City, ID | (14.5) | NA | Eau Claire, WI** | NA | 318 | Johnson City, TN | (23.3) |
| 221 | Boston (greater), MA-NH | (12.2) | 333 | El Centro, CA | (31.0) | 127 | Johnstown, PA | (6.7) |
| 175 | Boston, MA M.D. | (10.2) | 68 | El Paso, TX | (1.3) | 189 | Jonesboro, AR | (10.9) |
| 43 | Boulder, CO | 3.1 | 322 | Elgin, IL M.D. | (24.8) | 77 | Joplin, MO | (2.0) |
| 269 | Bowling Green, KY | (16.0) | 14 | Elizabethtown-Fort Knox, KY | 11.0 | 208 | Kahului-Wailuku-Lahaina, HI | (11.7) |
| 132 | Bremerton-Silverdale, WA | (7.1) | 204 | Elmira, NY | (11.5) | 189 | Kankakee, IL | (10.9) |
| 159 | Bridgeport-Stamford, CT | (8.8) | 111 | Erie, PA | (5.0) | 176 | Kansas City, MO-KS | (10.3) |
| 182 | Brownsville-Harlingen, TX | (10.6) | 86 | Eugene, OR | (2.7) | 154 | Kennewick-Richland, WA | (8.6) |
| 173 | Brunswick, GA | (10.0) | 268 | Fairbanks, AK | (15.9) | 286 | Kingsport, TN-VA | (18.2) |
| 218 | Buffalo-Niagara Falls, NY | (12.1) | 1 | Fargo, ND-MN | 33.6 | 291 | Kingston, NY | (18.6) |
| 162 | Burlington, NC | (9.1) | 138 | Farmington, NM | (8.1) | 285 | Knoxville, TN | (18.1) |
| 274 | California-Lexington Park, MD | (16.4) | 167 | Fayetteville-Springdale, AR-MO | (9.3) | 252 | Kokomo, IN | (14.9) |
| 244 | Cambridge-Newton, MA M.D. | (14.2) | 301 | Fayetteville, NC | (20.2) | NA | La Crosse, WI-MN** | NA |
| 244 | Camden, NJ M.D. | (14.2) | 259 | Flagstaff, AZ | (15.4) | 91 | Lafayette, IN | (3.0) |
| 329 | Canton, OH | (28.2) | 321 | Flint, MI | (24.2) | 74 | Lafayette, LA | (1.9) |
| 206 | Cape Coral-Fort Myers, FL | (11.6) | 323 | Florence-Muscle Shoals, AL | (25.1) | NA | Lake Charles, LA** | NA |
| 168 | Cape Girardeau, MO-IL | (9.4) | 288 | Florence, SC | (18.4) | 240 | Lake Co.-Kenosha Co., IL-WI M.D. | (14.0) |
| NA | Carbondale-Marion, IL** | NA | 62 | Fond du Lac, WI | 0.0 | 41 | Lake Havasu City-Kingman, AZ | 3.7 |
| 332 | Carson City, NV | (30.7) | 277 | Fort Collins, CO | (16.7) | 264 | Lakeland, FL | (15.6) |
| 314 | Casper, WY | (23.0) | 184 | Fort Lauderdale, FL M.D. | (10.7) | NA | Lancaster, PA** | NA |
| NA | Cedar Rapids, IA** | NA | 91 | Fort Smith, AR-OK | (3.0) | 129 | Lansing-East Lansing, MI | (6.8) |
| NA | Chambersburg-Waynesboro, PA** | NA | 9 | Fort Wayne, IN | 14.9 | 277 | Laredo, TX | (16.7) |
| 293 | Champaign-Urbana, IL | (18.7) | 138 | Fort Worth-Arlington, TX M.D. | (8.1) | 281 | Las Cruces, NM | (17.3) |
| 77 | Charleston-North Charleston, SC | (2.0) | 240 | Fresno, CA | (14.0) | 37 | Las Vegas-Henderson, NV | 4.3 |
| NA | Charlotte-Mecklenburg, NC-SC** | NA | 48 | Gadsden, AL | 2.4 | 274 | Lawrence, KS | (16.4) |
| 288 | Charlottesville, VA | (18.4) | 317 | Gainesville, FL | (23.2) | 94 | Lawton, OK | (3.2) |
| NA | Chattanooga, TN-GA** | NA | 99 | Gainesville, GA | (3.6) | 88 | Lebanon, PA | (2.9) |

Note: All listings are for Metropolitan Statistical Areas (M.S.A.s) except for those ending with "M.D." Listings with "M.D." are Metropolitan Divisions which are smaller parts of eleven large M.S.A.s. See explanatory note at beginning of metropolitan area section.

| RANK | METROPOLITAN AREA | % CHANGE | RANK | METROPOLITAN AREA | % CHANGE | RANK | METROPOLITAN AREA | % CHANGE |
|---|---|---|---|---|---|---|---|---|
| 149 | Lewiston-Auburn, ME | (8.5) | 68 | Omaha-Council Bluffs, NE-IA | (1.3) | 334 | Sheboygan, WI | (35.7) |
| 51 | Lewiston, ID-WA | 1.9 | 161 | Orlando, FL | (8.9) | 327 | Sherman-Denison, TX | (27.6) |
| 235 | Lexington-Fayette, KY | (13.4) | 337 | Oshkosh-Neenah, WI | (37.0) | 52 | Shreveport-Bossier City, LA | 1.8 |
| 184 | Lima, OH | (10.7) | 284 | Owensboro, KY | (17.8) | 54 | Silver Spring-Frederick, MD M.D. | 1.7 |
| 247 | Lincoln, NE | (14.4) | 45 | Oxnard-Thousand Oaks, CA | 3.0 | 96 | Sioux City, IA-NE-SD | (3.4) |
| 169 | Little Rock, AR | (9.5) | 107 | Palm Bay-Melbourne, FL | (4.8) | 72 | Sioux Falls, SD | (1.8) |
| 335 | Logan, UT-ID | (35.9) | 257 | Panama City, FL | (15.3) | 286 | South Bend-Mishawaka, IN-MI | (18.2) |
| 193 | Longview, TX | (11.0) | 177 | Parkersburg-Vienna, WV | (10.4) | 112 | Spartanburg, SC | (5.2) |
| 21 | Longview, WA | 8.1 | 253 | Pensacola, FL | (15.0) | 93 | Spokane, WA | (3.1) |
| 82 | Los Angeles County, CA M.D. | (2.3) | 300 | Peoria, IL | (19.9) | 291 | Springfield, IL | (18.6) |
| 104 | Los Angeles (greater), CA | (4.4) | 266 | Philadelphia (greater) PA-NJ-MD-DE | (15.8) | 149 | Springfield, MA | (8.5) |
| 109 | Louisville, KY-IN | (4.9) | 235 | Philadelphia, PA M.D. | (13.4) | 100 | Springfield, MO | (3.7) |
| 255 | Lubbock, TX | (15.1) | 189 | Phoenix-Mesa-Scottsdale, AZ | (10.9) | 87 | Springfield, OH | (2.8) |
| 311 | Lynchburg, VA | (22.4) | NA | Pittsburgh, PA** | NA | 199 | State College, PA | (11.3) |
| 60 | Macon, GA | 0.5 | 16 | Pittsfield, MA | 10.1 | 3 | Staunton-Waynesboro, VA | 22.2 |
| 197 | Madera, CA | (11.2) | 30 | Pocatello, ID | 5.2 | 129 | Stockton-Lodi, CA | (6.8) |
| NA | Madison, WI** | NA | 116 | Port St. Lucie, FL | (5.5) | NA | St. Cloud, MN** | NA |
| 109 | Manchester-Nashua, NH | (4.9) | 174 | Portland-Vancouver, OR-WA | (10.1) | NA | St. George, UT** | NA |
| 107 | Manhattan, KS | (4.8) | 171 | Portland, ME | (9.6) | 234 | St. Joseph, MO-KS | (13.3) |
| 22 | Mankato-North Mankato, MN | 7.4 | 118 | Prescott, AZ | (5.7) | 199 | St. Louis, MO-IL | (11.3) |
| 133 | Mansfield, OH | (7.2) | 154 | Providence-Warwick, RI-MA | (8.6) | 240 | Sumter, SC | (14.0) |
| 74 | McAllen-Edinburg-Mission, TX | (1.9) | 101 | Provo-Orem, UT | (3.8) | 271 | Syracuse, NY | (16.2) |
| 12 | Medford, OR | 12.0 | 54 | Pueblo, CO | 1.7 | NA | Tacoma, WA M.D.** | NA |
| 143 | Memphis, TN-MS-AR | (8.2) | 249 | Punta Gorda, FL | (14.5) | 307 | Tallahassee, FL | (21.0) |
| 313 | Merced, CA | (22.6) | 40 | Racine, WI | 3.8 | 149 | Tampa-St Petersburg, FL | (8.5) |
| 182 | Miami (greater), FL | (10.6) | 124 | Raleigh, NC | (6.4) | 238 | Terre Haute, IN | (13.7) |
| 208 | Miami-Dade County, FL M.D. | (11.7) | 27 | Rapid City, SD | 5.7 | 162 | Texarkana, TX-AR | (9.1) |
| 36 | Midland, TX | 4.4 | 315 | Reading, PA | (23.1) | 214 | The Villages, FL | (11.9) |
| 138 | Milwaukee, WI | (8.1) | 302 | Redding, CA | (20.4) | 303 | Toledo, OH | (20.6) |
| NA | Minneapolis-St. Paul, MN-WI** | NA | 136 | Reno, NV | (7.4) | 162 | Topeka, KS | (9.1) |
| 17 | Missoula, MT | 8.9 | 231 | Richmond, VA | (12.9) | 307 | Trenton, NJ | (21.0) |
| 13 | Mobile, AL | 11.2 | 223 | Riverside-San Bernardino, CA | (12.3) | 166 | Tucson, AZ | (9.2) |
| 137 | Modesto, CA | (7.7) | 331 | Roanoke, VA | (29.7) | 127 | Tulsa, OK | (6.7) |
| 5 | Monroe, LA | 18.4 | 157 | Rochester, MN | (8.7) | 97 | Tuscaloosa, AL | (3.5) |
| 297 | Monroe, MI | (19.7) | 184 | Rochester, NY | (10.7) | 280 | Tyler, TX | (16.9) |
| 231 | Montgomery County, PA M.D. | (12.9) | 247 | Rockford, IL | (14.4) | 218 | Utica-Rome, NY | (12.1) |
| 83 | Morgantown, WV | (2.5) | 216 | Rockingham County, NH M.D. | (12.0) | 25 | Vallejo-Fairfield, CA | 6.6 |
| 282 | Morristown, TN | (17.4) | 66 | Rocky Mount, NC | (0.4) | 212 | Victoria, TX | (11.8) |
| 121 | Mount Vernon-Anacortes, WA | (6.1) | 122 | Rome, GA | (6.2) | 224 | Vineland-Bridgeton, NJ | (12.4) |
| 315 | Muncie, IN | (23.1) | 106 | Sacramento, CA | (4.7) | 63 | Virginia Beach-Norfolk, VA-NC | (0.1) |
| NA | Muskegon, MI** | NA | 306 | Saginaw, MI | (20.9) | 57 | Visalia-Porterville, CA | 1.4 |
| NA | Myrtle Beach, SC-NC** | NA | 129 | Salem, OR | (6.8) | 122 | Waco, TX | (6.2) |
| 149 | Napa, CA | (8.5) | 143 | Salinas, CA | (8.2) | 32 | Warner Robins, GA | 5.0 |
| 288 | Naples-Marco Island, FL | (18.4) | 37 | Salisbury, MD-DE | 4.3 | 194 | Warren-Troy, MI M.D. | (11.1) |
| 143 | Nashville-Davidson, TN | (8.2) | 19 | Salt Lake City, UT | 8.6 | 126 | Washington (greater) DC-VA-MD-WV | (6.6) |
| 271 | Nassau-Suffolk, NY M.D. | (16.2) | NA | San Angelo, TX** | NA | 147 | Washington, DC-VA-MD-WV M.D. | (8.4) |
| 326 | New Bern, NC | (27.3) | 138 | San Antonio, TX | (8.1) | 329 | Watertown-Fort Drum, NY | (28.2) |
| 277 | New Haven-Milford, CT | (16.7) | 74 | San Diego, CA | (1.9) | 115 | Wausau, WI | (5.3) |
| 224 | New Orleans, LA | (12.4) | NA | San Francisco (greater), CA** | NA | 149 | West Palm Beach, FL M.D. | (8.5) |
| 256 | New York (greater), NY-NJ-PA | (15.2) | 42 | San Francisco-Redwood, CA M.D. | 3.6 | 273 | Wichita Falls, TX | (16.3) |
| 257 | New York-Jersey City, NY-NJ M.D. | (15.3) | 112 | San Jose, CA | (5.2) | 70 | Wichita, KS | (1.5) |
| 244 | Newark, NJ-PA M.D. | (14.2) | 39 | San Luis Obispo, CA | 3.9 | 35 | Williamsport, PA | 4.6 |
| NA | Niles-Benton Harbor, MI** | NA | NA | San Rafael, CA M.D.** | NA | 319 | Wilmington, DE-MD-NJ M.D. | (23.7) |
| 188 | North Port-Sarasota-Bradenton, FL | (10.8) | 63 | Santa Cruz-Watsonville, CA | (0.1) | 77 | Wilmington, NC | (2.0) |
| 6 | Norwich-New London, CT | 17.7 | 143 | Santa Maria-Santa Barbara, CA | (8.2) | 325 | Winchester, VA-WV | (26.3) |
| 212 | Oakland-Hayward, CA M.D. | (11.8) | 71 | Santa Rosa, CA | (1.7) | 162 | Winston-Salem, NC | (9.1) |
| 124 | Ocala, FL | (6.4) | 59 | Savannah, GA | 0.9 | 208 | Worcester, MA-CT | (11.7) |
| 295 | Ocean City, NJ | (19.1) | NA | Scranton--Wilkes-Barre, PA** | NA | 323 | Yakima, WA | (25.1) |
| 43 | Odessa, TX | 3.1 | NA | Seattle (greater), WA** | NA | 28 | York-Hanover, PA | 5.5 |
| NA | Ogden-Clearfield, UT** | NA | 72 | Seattle-Bellevue-Everett, WA M.D. | (1.8) | 52 | Yuba City, CA | 1.8 |
| 266 | Oklahoma City, OK | (15.8) | 305 | Sebastian-Vero Beach, FL | (20.7) | 58 | Yuma, AZ | 1.1 |
| NA | Olympia, WA** | NA | 45 | Sebring, FL | 3.0 | | | |

Source: CQ Press using reported data from the F.B.I. "Crime in the United States 2013"

*Burglary is the unlawful entry of a structure to commit a felony or theft. Attempts are included.

**Not available.

## 31. Percent Change in Burglary Rate: 2012 to 2013 (continued)
## National Percent Change = 9.3% Decrease*

| RANK | METROPOLITAN AREA | % CHANGE | RANK | METROPOLITAN AREA | % CHANGE | RANK | METROPOLITAN AREA | % CHANGE |
|---|---|---|---|---|---|---|---|---|
| 1 | Fargo, ND-MN | 33.6 | 63 | Virginia Beach-Norfolk, VA-NC | (0.1) | 129 | Lansing-East Lansing, MI | (6.8) |
| 2 | Grand Island, NE | 30.0 | 66 | Rocky Mount, NC | (0.4) | 129 | Salem, OR | (6.8) |
| 3 | Staunton-Waynesboro, VA | 22.2 | 67 | Bloomington, IL | (0.8) | 129 | Stockton-Lodi, CA | (6.8) |
| 4 | Billings, MT | 18.7 | 68 | El Paso, TX | (1.3) | 132 | Bremerton-Silverdale, WA | (7.1) |
| 5 | Monroe, LA | 18.4 | 68 | Omaha-Council Bluffs, NE-IA | (1.3) | 133 | Atlanta, GA | (7.2) |
| 6 | Norwich-New London, CT | 17.7 | 70 | Wichita, KS | (1.5) | 133 | Mansfield, OH | (7.2) |
| 7 | Idaho Falls, ID | 15.8 | 71 | Santa Rosa, CA | (1.7) | 135 | Denver-Aurora, CO | (7.3) |
| 8 | Great Falls, MT | 15.6 | 72 | Seattle-Bellevue-Everett, WA M.D. | (1.8) | 136 | Reno, NV | (7.4) |
| 9 | Fort Wayne, IN | 14.9 | 72 | Sioux Falls, SD | (1.8) | 137 | Modesto, CA | (7.7) |
| 10 | Bay City, MI | 14.3 | 74 | Lafayette, LA | (1.9) | 138 | Farmington, NM | (8.1) |
| 11 | Anchorage, AK | 12.7 | 74 | McAllen-Edinburg-Mission, TX | (1.9) | 138 | Fort Worth-Arlington, TX M.D. | (8.1) |
| 12 | Medford, OR | 12.0 | 74 | San Diego, CA | (1.9) | 138 | Jefferson City, MO | (8.1) |
| 13 | Mobile, AL | 11.2 | 77 | Charleston-North Charleston, SC | (2.0) | 138 | Milwaukee, WI | (8.1) |
| 14 | Columbus, GA-AL | 11.0 | 77 | Joplin, MO | (2.0) | 138 | San Antonio, TX | (8.1) |
| 14 | Elizabethtown-Fort Knox, KY | 11.0 | 77 | Wilmington, NC | (2.0) | 143 | Memphis, TN-MS-AR | (8.2) |
| 16 | Pittsfield, MA | 10.1 | 80 | Bakersfield, CA | (2.1) | 143 | Nashville-Davidson, TN | (8.2) |
| 17 | Missoula, MT | 8.9 | 81 | Greenville, NC | (2.2) | 143 | Salinas, CA | (8.2) |
| 18 | Alexandria, LA | 8.7 | 82 | Los Angeles County, CA M.D. | (2.3) | 143 | Santa Maria-Santa Barbara, CA | (8.2) |
| 19 | Salt Lake City, UT | 8.6 | 83 | Morgantown, WV | (2.5) | 147 | Cumberland, MD-WV | (8.4) |
| 20 | Hanford-Corcoran, CA | 8.3 | 84 | Albany, GA | (2.6) | 147 | Washington, DC-VA-MD-WV M.D. | (8.4) |
| 21 | Longview, WA | 8.1 | 84 | Greensboro-High Point, NC | (2.6) | 149 | Lewiston-Auburn, ME | (8.5) |
| 22 | Mankato-North Mankato, MN | 7.4 | 86 | Eugene, OR | (2.7) | 149 | Napa, CA | (8.5) |
| 23 | Abilene, TX | 6.8 | 87 | Springfield, OH | (2.8) | 149 | Springfield, MA | (8.5) |
| 24 | Duluth, MN-WI | 6.7 | 88 | Atlantic City, NJ | (2.9) | 149 | Tampa-St Petersburg, FL | (8.5) |
| 25 | Vallejo-Fairfield, CA | 6.6 | 88 | Grand Junction, CO | (2.9) | 149 | West Palm Beach, FL M.D. | (8.5) |
| 26 | Albany, OR | 5.9 | 88 | Lebanon, PA | (2.9) | 154 | Dalton, GA | (8.6) |
| 27 | Rapid City, SD | 5.7 | 91 | Fort Smith, AR-OK | (3.0) | 154 | Kennewick-Richland, WA | (8.6) |
| 28 | York-Hanover, PA | 5.5 | 91 | Lafayette, IN | (3.0) | 154 | Providence-Warwick, RI-MA | (8.6) |
| 29 | Allentown, PA-NJ | 5.4 | 93 | Spokane, WA | (3.1) | 157 | Deltona-Daytona Beach, FL | (8.7) |
| 30 | Pocatello, ID | 5.2 | 94 | Houma, LA | (3.2) | 157 | Rochester, MN | (8.7) |
| 31 | Cleveland, TN | 5.1 | 94 | Lawton, OK | (3.2) | 159 | Bridgeport-Stamford, CT | (8.8) |
| 32 | Warner Robins, GA | 5.0 | 96 | Sioux City, IA-NE-SD | (3.4) | 159 | Jacksonville, FL | (8.8) |
| 33 | Bismarck, ND | 4.7 | 97 | Baton Rouge, LA | (3.5) | 161 | Orlando, FL | (8.9) |
| 33 | Greenville-Anderson, SC | 4.7 | 97 | Tuscaloosa, AL | (3.5) | 162 | Burlington, NC | (9.1) |
| 35 | Williamsport, PA | 4.6 | 99 | Gainesville, GA | (3.6) | 162 | Texarkana, TX-AR | (9.1) |
| 36 | Midland, TX | 4.4 | 100 | Springfield, MO | (3.7) | 162 | Topeka, KS | (9.1) |
| 37 | Las Vegas-Henderson, NV | 4.3 | 101 | Provo-Orem, UT | (3.8) | 162 | Winston-Salem, NC | (9.1) |
| 37 | Salisbury, MD-DE | 4.3 | 102 | Binghamton, NY | (4.1) | 166 | Tucson, AZ | (9.2) |
| 39 | San Luis Obispo, CA | 3.9 | 103 | East Stroudsburg, PA | (4.3) | 167 | Fayetteville-Springdale, AR-MO | (9.3) |
| 40 | Racine, WI | 3.8 | 104 | Los Angeles (greater), CA | (4.4) | 168 | Cape Girardeau, MO-IL | (9.4) |
| 41 | Lake Havasu City-Kingman, AZ | 3.7 | 105 | Dayton, OH | (4.6) | 169 | Bloomington, IN | (9.5) |
| 42 | San Francisco-Redwood, CA M.D. | 3.6 | 106 | Sacramento, CA | (4.7) | 169 | Little Rock, AR | (9.5) |
| 43 | Boulder, CO | 3.1 | 107 | Manhattan, KS | (4.8) | 171 | Portland, ME | (9.6) |
| 43 | Odessa, TX | 3.1 | 107 | Palm Bay-Melbourne, FL | (4.8) | 172 | Hammond, LA | (9.9) |
| 45 | Oxnard-Thousand Oaks, CA | 3.0 | 109 | Louisville, KY-IN | (4.9) | 173 | Brunswick, GA | (10.0) |
| 45 | Sebring, FL | 3.0 | 109 | Manchester-Nashua, NH | (4.9) | 174 | Portland-Vancouver, OR-WA | (10.1) |
| 47 | Altoona, PA | 2.5 | 111 | Erie, PA | (5.0) | 175 | Boston, MA M.D. | (10.2) |
| 48 | Gadsden, AL | 2.4 | 112 | Baltimore, MD | (5.2) | 176 | Kansas City, MO-KS | (10.3) |
| 49 | Beaumont-Port Arthur, TX | 2.2 | 112 | San Jose, CA | (5.2) | 177 | Corvallis, OR | (10.4) |
| 50 | Cheyenne, WY | 2.0 | 112 | Spartanburg, SC | (5.2) | 177 | Parkersburg-Vienna, WV | (10.4) |
| 51 | Lewiston, ID-WA | 1.9 | 115 | Wausau, WI | (5.3) | 179 | Akron, OH | (10.5) |
| 52 | Shreveport-Bossier City, LA | 1.8 | 116 | Port St. Lucie, FL | (5.5) | 179 | Dallas (greater), TX | (10.5) |
| 52 | Yuba City, CA | 1.8 | 117 | Cincinnati, OH-KY-IN | (5.6) | 179 | Indianapolis, IN | (10.5) |
| 54 | Pueblo, CO | 1.7 | 118 | Prescott, AZ | (5.7) | 182 | Brownsville-Harlingen, TX | (10.6) |
| 54 | Silver Spring-Frederick, MD M.D. | 1.7 | 119 | Clarksville, TN-KY | (5.8) | 182 | Miami (greater), FL | (10.6) |
| 56 | Janesville, WI | 1.6 | 119 | Daphne-Fairhope-Foley, AL | (5.8) | 184 | Bangor, ME | (10.7) |
| 57 | Visalia-Porterville, CA | 1.4 | 121 | Mount Vernon-Anacortes, WA | (6.1) | 184 | Fort Lauderdale, FL M.D. | (10.7) |
| 58 | Yuma, AZ | 1.1 | 122 | Rome, GA | (6.2) | 184 | Lima, OH | (10.7) |
| 59 | Savannah, GA | 0.9 | 122 | Waco, TX | (6.2) | 184 | Rochester, NY | (10.7) |
| 60 | Macon, GA | 0.5 | 124 | Ocala, FL | (6.4) | 188 | North Port-Sarasota-Bradenton, FL | (10.8) |
| 61 | Harrisonburg, VA | 0.1 | 124 | Raleigh, NC | (6.4) | 189 | Bloomsburg-Berwick, PA | (10.9) |
| 62 | Fond du Lac, WI | 0.0 | 126 | Washington (greater) DC-VA-MD-WV | (6.6) | 189 | Jonesboro, AR | (10.9) |
| 63 | Davenport, IA-IL | (0.1) | 127 | Johnstown, PA | (6.7) | 189 | Kankakee, IL | (10.9) |
| 63 | Santa Cruz-Watsonville, CA | (0.1) | 127 | Tulsa, OK | (6.7) | 189 | Phoenix-Mesa-Scottsdale, AZ | (10.9) |

Note: All listings are for Metropolitan Statistical Areas (M.S.A.s) except for those ending with "M.D." Listings with "M.D." are Metropolitan Divisions which are smaller parts of eleven large M.S.A.s. See explanatory note at beginning of metropolitan area section.

| RANK | METROPOLITAN AREA | % CHANGE | RANK | METROPOLITAN AREA | % CHANGE | RANK | METROPOLITAN AREA | % CHANGE |
|---|---|---|---|---|---|---|---|---|
| 193 | Longview, TX | (11.0) | 255 | Lubbock, TX | (15.1) | 317 | Gainesville, FL | (23.2) |
| 194 | Birmingham-Hoover, AL | (11.1) | 256 | New York (greater), NY-NJ-PA | (15.2) | 318 | Johnson City, TN | (23.3) |
| 194 | Columbus, IN | (11.1) | 257 | New York-Jersey City, NY-NJ M.D. | (15.3) | 319 | Wilmington, DE-MD-NJ M.D. | (23.7) |
| 194 | Warren-Troy, MI M.D. | (11.1) | 257 | Panama City, FL | (15.3) | 320 | Blacksburg, VA | (23.9) |
| 197 | Albany-Schenectady-Troy, NY | (11.2) | 259 | Dutchess-Putnam, NY M.D. | (15.4) | 321 | Flint, MI | (24.2) |
| 197 | Madera, CA | (11.2) | 259 | Flagstaff, AZ | (15.4) | 322 | Elgin, IL M.D. | (24.8) |
| 199 | Crestview-Fort Walton Beach, FL | (11.3) | 259 | Gary, IN M.D. | (15.4) | 323 | Florence-Muscle Shoals, AL | (25.1) |
| 199 | Hagerstown-Martinsburg, MD-WV | (11.3) | 259 | Greeley, CO | (15.4) | 323 | Yakima, WA | (25.1) |
| 199 | State College, PA | (11.3) | 263 | Columbia, MO | (15.5) | 325 | Winchester, VA-WV | (26.3) |
| 199 | St. Louis, MO-IL | (11.3) | 264 | Lakeland, FL | (15.6) | 326 | New Bern, NC | (27.3) |
| 203 | College Station-Bryan, TX | (11.4) | 265 | Hinesville, GA | (15.7) | 327 | Ames, IA | (27.6) |
| 204 | Elmira, NY | (11.5) | 266 | Oklahoma City, OK | (15.8) | 327 | Sherman-Denison, TX | (27.6) |
| 204 | Grand Forks, ND-MN | (11.5) | 266 | Philadelphia (greater) PA-NJ-MD-DE | (15.8) | 329 | Canton, OH | (28.2) |
| 206 | Appleton, WI | (11.6) | 268 | Fairbanks, AK | (15.9) | 329 | Watertown-Fort Drum, NY | (28.2) |
| 206 | Cape Coral-Fort Myers, FL | (11.6) | 269 | Bowling Green, KY | (16.0) | 331 | Roanoke, VA | (29.7) |
| 208 | Dallas-Plano-Irving, TX M.D. | (11.7) | 270 | Hartford, CT | (16.1) | 332 | Carson City, NV | (30.7) |
| 208 | Kahului-Wailuku-Lahaina, HI | (11.7) | 271 | Nassau-Suffolk, NY M.D. | (16.2) | 333 | El Centro, CA | (31.0) |
| 208 | Miami-Dade County, FL M.D. | (11.7) | 271 | Syracuse, NY | (16.2) | 334 | Sheboygan, WI | (35.7) |
| 208 | Worcester, MA-CT | (11.7) | 273 | Wichita Falls, TX | (16.3) | 335 | Logan, UT-ID | (35.9) |
| 212 | Oakland-Hayward, CA M.D. | (11.8) | 274 | California-Lexington Park, MD | (16.4) | 336 | Ann Arbor, MI | (36.3) |
| 212 | Victoria, TX | (11.8) | 274 | Lawrence, KS | (16.4) | 337 | Oshkosh-Neenah, WI | (37.0) |
| 214 | Goldsboro, NC | (11.9) | 276 | Jackson, MS | (16.6) | 338 | Dover, DE | (38.4) |
| 214 | The Villages, FL | (11.9) | 277 | Fort Collins, CO | (16.7) | NA | Albuquerque, NM** | NA |
| 216 | Augusta, GA-SC | (12.0) | 277 | Laredo, TX | (16.7) | NA | Bend, OR** | NA |
| 216 | Rockingham County, NH M.D. | (12.0) | 277 | New Haven-Milford, CT | (16.7) | NA | Carbondale-Marion, IL** | NA |
| 218 | Buffalo-Niagara Falls, NY | (12.1) | 280 | Tyler, TX | (16.9) | NA | Cedar Rapids, IA** | NA |
| 218 | Iowa City, IA | (12.1) | 281 | Las Cruces, NM | (17.3) | NA | Chambersburg-Waynesboro, PA** | NA |
| 218 | Utica-Rome, NY | (12.1) | 282 | Morristown, TN | (17.4) | NA | Charlotte-Mecklenburg, NC-SC** | NA |
| 221 | Boston (greater), MA-NH | (12.2) | 283 | Decatur, IL | (17.5) | NA | Chattanooga, TN-GA** | NA |
| 221 | Chico, CA | (12.2) | 284 | Owensboro, KY | (17.8) | NA | Colorado Springs, CO** | NA |
| 223 | Riverside-San Bernardino, CA | (12.3) | 285 | Knoxville, TN | (18.1) | NA | Columbia, SC** | NA |
| 224 | Detroit (greater), MI | (12.4) | 286 | Kingsport, TN-VA | (18.2) | NA | Corpus Christi, TX** | NA |
| 224 | Detroit-Dearborn-Livonia, MI M.D. | (12.4) | 286 | South Bend-Mishawaka, IN-MI | (18.2) | NA | Des Moines-West Des Moines, IA** | NA |
| 224 | New Orleans, LA | (12.4) | 288 | Charlottesville, VA | (18.4) | NA | Dubuque, IA** | NA |
| 224 | Vineland-Bridgeton, NJ | (12.4) | 288 | Florence, SC | (18.4) | NA | Eau Claire, WI** | NA |
| 228 | Athens-Clarke County, GA | (12.6) | 288 | Naples-Marco Island, FL | (18.4) | NA | Gettysburg, PA** | NA |
| 229 | Homosassa Springs, FL | (12.7) | 291 | Kingston, NY | (18.6) | NA | Grand Rapids-Wyoming, MI** | NA |
| 230 | Anaheim-Santa Ana-Irvine, CA M.D. | (12.8) | 291 | Springfield, IL | (18.6) | NA | Grants Pass, OR** | NA |
| 231 | Montgomery County, PA M.D. | (12.9) | 293 | Champaign-Urbana, IL | (18.7) | NA | Gulfport-Biloxi-Pascagoula, MS** | NA |
| 231 | Richmond, VA | (12.9) | 294 | Barnstable Town, MA | (19.0) | NA | Hot Springs, AR** | NA |
| 233 | Huntsville, AL | (13.2) | 295 | Ocean City, NJ | (19.1) | NA | Houston, TX** | NA |
| 234 | St. Joseph, MO-KS | (13.3) | 296 | Anniston-Oxford, AL | (19.2) | NA | Jackson, MI** | NA |
| 235 | Lexington-Fayette, KY | (13.4) | 297 | Green Bay, WI | (19.7) | NA | La Crosse, WI-MN** | NA |
| 235 | Philadelphia, PA M.D. | (13.4) | 297 | Monroe, MI | (19.7) | NA | Lake Charles, LA** | NA |
| 237 | Austin-Round Rock, TX | (13.5) | 299 | Dothan, AL | (19.8) | NA | Lancaster, PA** | NA |
| 238 | Terre Haute, IN | (13.7) | 300 | Peoria, IL | (19.9) | NA | Madison, WI** | NA |
| 239 | Glens Falls, NY | (13.8) | 301 | Fayetteville, NC | (20.2) | NA | Minneapolis-St. Paul, MN-WI** | NA |
| 240 | Fresno, CA | (14.0) | 302 | Redding, CA | (20.4) | NA | Muskegon, MI** | NA |
| 240 | Hilton Head Island, SC | (14.0) | 303 | Decatur, AL | (20.6) | NA | Myrtle Beach, SC-NC** | NA |
| 240 | Lake Co.-Kenosha Co., IL-WI M.D. | (14.0) | 303 | Toledo, OH | (20.6) | NA | Niles-Benton Harbor, MI** | NA |
| 240 | Sumter, SC | (14.0) | 305 | Sebastian-Vero Beach, FL | (20.7) | NA | Ogden-Clearfield, UT** | NA |
| 244 | Cambridge-Newton, MA M.D. | (14.2) | 306 | Saginaw, MI | (20.9) | NA | Olympia, WA** | NA |
| 244 | Camden, NJ M.D. | (14.2) | 307 | Tallahassee, FL | (21.0) | NA | Pittsburgh, PA** | NA |
| 244 | Newark, NJ-PA M.D. | (14.2) | 307 | Trenton, NJ | (21.0) | NA | San Angelo, TX** | NA |
| 247 | Lincoln, NE | (14.4) | 309 | Chicago (greater), IL-IN-WI | (21.1) | NA | San Francisco (greater), CA** | NA |
| 247 | Rockford, IL | (14.4) | 310 | Chicago-Naperville, IL M.D. | (22.1) | NA | San Rafael, CA M.D.** | NA |
| 249 | Boise City, ID | (14.5) | 311 | Lynchburg, VA | (22.4) | NA | Scranton--Wilkes-Barre, PA** | NA |
| 249 | Jackson, TN | (14.5) | 312 | Coeur d'Alene, ID | (22.5) | NA | Seattle (greater), WA** | NA |
| 249 | Punta Gorda, FL | (14.5) | 313 | Merced, CA | (22.6) | NA | St. Cloud, MN** | NA |
| 252 | Kokomo, IN | (14.9) | 314 | Casper, WY | (23.0) | NA | St. George, UT** | NA |
| 253 | Amarillo, TX | (15.0) | 315 | Muncie, IN | (23.1) | NA | Tacoma, WA M.D.** | NA |
| 253 | Pensacola, FL | (15.0) | 315 | Reading, PA | (23.1) | | | |

Source: CQ Press using reported data from the F.B.I. "Crime in the United States 2013"

*Burglary is the unlawful entry of a structure to commit a felony or theft. Attempts are included.

**Not available.

# 32. Percent Change in Burglary Rate: 2009 to 2013
## National Percent Change = 15.0% Decrease*

| RANK | METROPOLITAN AREA | % CHANGE | RANK | METROPOLITAN AREA | % CHANGE | RANK | METROPOLITAN AREA | % CHANGE |
|---|---|---|---|---|---|---|---|---|
| 157 | Abilene, TX | (15.6) | 14 | Cheyenne, WY | 23.4 | NA | Gary, IN M.D.** | NA |
| 161 | Akron, OH | (16.3) | NA | Chicago (greater), IL-IN-WI** | NA | NA | Gettysburg, PA** | NA |
| 121 | Albany-Schenectady-Troy, NY | (10.8) | NA | Chicago-Naperville, IL M.D.** | NA | 62 | Glens Falls, NY | 3.0 |
| 85 | Albany, GA | (3.1) | 86 | Chico, CA | (3.2) | 222 | Goldsboro, NC | (23.8) |
| NA | Albany, OR** | NA | 95 | Cincinnati, OH-KY-IN | (4.5) | 207 | Grand Forks, ND-MN | (22.0) |
| 44 | Albuquerque, NM | 6.8 | 284 | Clarksville, TN-KY | (36.5) | NA | Grand Island, NE** | NA |
| 36 | Alexandria, LA | 9.4 | 83 | Cleveland, TN | (2.6) | 275 | Grand Junction, CO | (33.2) |
| 47 | Allentown, PA-NJ | 5.3 | 76 | Coeur d'Alene, ID | (0.5) | NA | Grand Rapids-Wyoming, MI** | NA |
| 133 | Altoona, PA | (12.2) | 305 | College Station-Bryan, TX | (49.5) | NA | Grants Pass, OR** | NA |
| 273 | Amarillo, TX | (32.6) | 43 | Colorado Springs, CO | 7.0 | 5 | Great Falls, MT | 50.8 |
| 242 | Ames, IA | (26.8) | 114 | Columbia, MO | (8.6) | 280 | Greeley, CO | (34.4) |
| 110 | Anaheim-Santa Ana-Irvine, CA M.D. | (7.8) | 209 | Columbia, SC | (22.2) | 183 | Green Bay, WI | (19.0) |
| 202 | Anchorage, AK | (21.3) | 192 | Columbus, GA-AL | (19.6) | 238 | Greensboro-High Point, NC | (26.2) |
| 291 | Ann Arbor, MI | (38.0) | 81 | Columbus, IN | (2.5) | NA | Greenville-Anderson, SC** | NA |
| 245 | Anniston-Oxford, AL | (27.2) | 192 | Corpus Christi, TX | (19.6) | NA | Greenville, NC** | NA |
| 262 | Appleton, WI | (29.4) | 254 | Corvallis, OR | (28.5) | NA | Gulfport-Biloxi-Pascagoula, MS** | NA |
| 298 | Athens-Clarke County, GA | (43.5) | NA | Crestview-Fort Walton Beach, FL** | NA | 66 | Hagerstown-Martinsburg, MD-WV | 1.6 |
| 175 | Atlanta, GA | (18.0) | 190 | Cumberland, MD-WV | (19.4) | NA | Hammond, LA** | NA |
| 86 | Atlantic City, NJ | (3.2) | 260 | Dallas (greater), TX | (29.0) | NA | Hanford-Corcoran, CA** | NA |
| 253 | Augusta, GA-SC | (28.2) | 258 | Dallas-Plano-Irving, TX M.D. | (28.9) | 27 | Harrisonburg, VA | 12.1 |
| 270 | Austin-Round Rock, TX | (32.1) | 59 | Dalton, GA | 3.4 | 207 | Hartford, CT | (22.0) |
| 40 | Bakersfield, CA | 7.7 | NA | Daphne-Fairhope-Foley, AL** | NA | NA | Hilton Head Island, SC** | NA |
| 122 | Baltimore, MD | (11.0) | NA | Davenport, IA-IL** | NA | 302 | Hinesville, GA | (45.6) |
| 167 | Bangor, ME | (16.8) | 97 | Dayton, OH | (5.7) | NA | Homosassa Springs, FL** | NA |
| 269 | Barnstable Town, MA | (31.4) | 136 | Decatur, AL | (12.6) | 235 | Hot Springs, AR | (25.7) |
| 150 | Baton Rouge, LA | (14.7) | 297 | Decatur, IL | (42.1) | 31 | Houma, LA | 10.8 |
| 163 | Bay City, MI | (16.5) | 258 | Deltona-Daytona Beach, FL | (28.9) | 220 | Houston, TX | (23.7) |
| 140 | Beaumont-Port Arthur, TX | (13.1) | 142 | Denver-Aurora, CO | (13.4) | 215 | Huntsville, AL | (22.8) |
| 176 | Bend, OR | (18.2) | 37 | Des Moines-West Des Moines, IA | 8.5 | 92 | Idaho Falls, ID | (4.1) |
| 22 | Billings, MT | 17.4 | 243 | Detroit (greater), MI | (27.0) | 158 | Indianapolis, IN | (15.7) |
| 8 | Binghamton, NY | 38.2 | 247 | Detroit-Dearborn-Livonia, MI M.D. | (27.3) | 108 | Iowa City, IA | (7.5) |
| 185 | Birmingham-Hoover, AL | (19.1) | NA | Dothan, AL** | NA | 293 | Jacksonville, FL | (39.0) |
| 2 | Bismarck, ND | 56.5 | 303 | Dover, DE | (46.7) | 78 | Jackson, MI | (1.9) |
| 300 | Blacksburg, VA | (44.9) | 203 | Dubuque, IA | (21.5) | 243 | Jackson, MS | (27.0) |
| NA | Bloomington, IL** | NA | 51 | Duluth, MN-WI | 4.5 | 245 | Jackson, TN | (27.2) |
| 265 | Bloomington, IN | (30.0) | NA | Dutchess-Putnam, NY M.D.** | NA | 50 | Janesville, WI | 4.6 |
| NA | Bloomsburg-Berwick, PA** | NA | NA | East Stroudsburg, PA** | NA | 55 | Jefferson City, MO | 3.8 |
| 172 | Boise City, ID | (17.5) | 156 | Eau Claire, WI | (15.5) | 205 | Johnson City, TN | (21.9) |
| 163 | Boston (greater), MA-NH | (16.5) | 223 | El Centro, CA | (23.9) | NA | Johnstown, PA** | NA |
| 112 | Boston, MA M.D. | (8.3) | 229 | El Paso, TX | (24.6) | 236 | Jonesboro, AR | (25.8) |
| 145 | Boulder, CO | (14.0) | NA | Elgin, IL M.D.** | NA | NA | Joplin, MO** | NA |
| NA | Bowling Green, KY** | NA | NA | Elizabethtown-Fort Knox, KY** | NA | NA | Kahului-Wailuku-Lahaina, HI** | NA |
| 17 | Bremerton-Silverdale, WA | 21.4 | 118 | Elmira, NY | (10.2) | NA | Kankakee, IL** | NA |
| 135 | Bridgeport-Stamford, CT | (12.4) | 77 | Erie, PA | (1.8) | NA | Kansas City, MO-KS** | NA |
| 264 | Brownsville-Harlingen, TX | (29.6) | 212 | Eugene, OR | (22.3) | 67 | Kennewick-Richland, WA | 1.2 |
| 163 | Brunswick, GA | (16.5) | 279 | Fairbanks, AK | (34.2) | 296 | Kingsport, TN-VA | (41.2) |
| 155 | Buffalo-Niagara Falls, NY | (15.4) | 84 | Fargo, ND-MN | (2.7) | 160 | Kingston, NY | (16.2) |
| 204 | Burlington, NC | (21.7) | 149 | Farmington, NM | (14.4) | 215 | Knoxville, TN | (22.8) |
| NA | California-Lexington Park, MD** | NA | 120 | Fayetteville-Springdale, AR-MO | (10.5) | 111 | Kokomo, IN | (7.9) |
| NA | Cambridge-Newton, MA M.D.** | NA | 226 | Fayetteville, NC | (24.3) | NA | La Crosse, WI-MN** | NA |
| 73 | Camden, NJ M.D. | 0.1 | 240 | Flagstaff, AZ | (26.7) | 74 | Lafayette, IN | (0.1) |
| NA | Canton, OH** | NA | 183 | Flint, MI | (19.0) | NA | Lafayette, LA** | NA |
| 294 | Cape Coral-Fort Myers, FL | (40.3) | 218 | Florence-Muscle Shoals, AL | (23.4) | 123 | Lake Charles, LA | (11.1) |
| 18 | Cape Girardeau, MO-IL | 20.0 | 231 | Florence, SC | (24.9) | NA | Lake Co.-Kenosha Co., IL-WI M.D.** | NA |
| NA | Carbondale-Marion, IL** | NA | 54 | Fond du Lac, WI | 3.9 | 38 | Lake Havasu City-Kingman, AZ | 8.3 |
| 232 | Carson City, NV | (25.3) | 282 | Fort Collins, CO | (35.0) | 270 | Lakeland, FL | (32.1) |
| 287 | Casper, WY | (37.2) | 96 | Fort Lauderdale, FL M.D. | (5.2) | NA | Lancaster, PA** | NA |
| 195 | Cedar Rapids, IA | (19.8) | 128 | Fort Smith, AR-OK | (11.5) | 171 | Lansing-East Lansing, MI | (17.4) |
| NA | Chambersburg-Waynesboro, PA** | NA | 49 | Fort Wayne, IN | 4.8 | 290 | Laredo, TX | (37.9) |
| NA | Champaign-Urbana, IL** | NA | 261 | Fort Worth-Arlington, TX M.D. | (29.2) | 148 | Las Cruces, NM | (14.1) |
| NA | Charleston-North Charleston, SC** | NA | 31 | Fresno, CA | 10.8 | 65 | Las Vegas-Henderson, NV | 1.7 |
| NA | Charlotte-Mecklenburg, NC-SC** | NA | 4 | Gadsden, AL | 53.2 | 226 | Lawrence, KS | (24.3) |
| 114 | Charlottesville, VA | (8.6) | 306 | Gainesville, FL | (50.2) | 138 | Lawton, OK | (12.8) |
| 187 | Chattanooga, TN-GA | (19.2) | 220 | Gainesville, GA | (23.7) | 145 | Lebanon, PA | (14.0) |

Note: All listings are for Metropolitan Statistical Areas (M.S.A.s) except for those ending with "M.D." Listings with "M.D." are Metropolitan Divisions which are smaller parts of eleven large M.S.A.s. See explanatory note at beginning of metropolitan area section.

| RANK | METROPOLITAN AREA | % CHANGE | RANK | METROPOLITAN AREA | % CHANGE | RANK | METROPOLITAN AREA | % CHANGE |
|---|---|---|---|---|---|---|---|---|
| 6 | Lewiston-Auburn, ME | 42.0 | 75 | Omaha-Council Bluffs, NE-IA | (0.4) | 301 | Sheboygan, WI | (45.4) |
| 11 | Lewiston, ID-WA | 25.9 | 187 | Orlando, FL | (19.2) | 224 | Sherman-Denison, TX | (24.1) |
| 70 | Lexington-Fayette, KY | 0.8 | 304 | Oshkosh-Neenah, WI | (47.1) | 177 | Shreveport-Bossier City, LA | (18.3) |
| 277 | Lima, OH | (33.4) | 201 | Owensboro, KY | (20.7) | 145 | Silver Spring-Frederick, MD M.D. | (14.0) |
| 153 | Lincoln, NE | (15.0) | 59 | Oxnard-Thousand Oaks, CA | 3.4 | 109 | Sioux City, IA-NE-SD | (7.7) |
| 174 | Little Rock, AR | (17.6) | 125 | Palm Bay-Melbourne, FL | (11.3) | 20 | Sioux Falls, SD | 19.0 |
| 199 | Logan, UT-ID | (20.2) | 251 | Panama City, FL | (27.8) | 256 | South Bend-Mishawaka, IN-MI | (28.7) |
| 254 | Longview, TX | (28.5) | NA | Parkersburg-Vienna, WV** | NA | 162 | Spartanburg, SC | (16.4) |
| 28 | Longview, WA | 12.0 | 68 | Pensacola, FL | 0.9 | 7 | Spokane, WA | 38.8 |
| 102 | Los Angeles County, CA M.D. | (6.2) | NA | Peoria, IL** | NA | NA | Springfield, IL** | NA |
| 104 | Los Angeles (greater), CA | (6.6) | 97 | Philadelphia (greater) PA-NJ-MD-DE | (5.7) | 53 | Springfield, MA | 4.0 |
| 104 | Louisville, KY-IN | (6.6) | NA | Philadelphia, PA M.D.** | NA | 94 | Springfield, MO | (4.4) |
| 288 | Lubbock, TX | (37.5) | 130 | Phoenix-Mesa-Scottsdale, AZ | (11.9) | 30 | Springfield, OH | 10.9 |
| 189 | Lynchburg, VA | (19.3) | NA | Pittsburgh, PA** | NA | 209 | State College, PA | (22.2) |
| 97 | Macon, GA | (5.7) | 39 | Pittsfield, MA | 7.8 | NA | Staunton-Waynesboro, VA** | NA |
| 15 | Madera, CA | 23.1 | 34 | Pocatello, ID | 9.8 | 88 | Stockton-Lodi, CA | (3.4) |
| NA | Madison, WI** | NA | 250 | Port St. Lucie, FL | (27.6) | 52 | St. Cloud, MN | 4.3 |
| 68 | Manchester-Nashua, NH | 0.9 | 35 | Portland-Vancouver, OR-WA | 9.6 | NA | St. George, UT** | NA |
| 212 | Manhattan, KS | (22.3) | 126 | Portland, ME | (11.4) | 172 | St. Joseph, MO-KS | (17.5) |
| 46 | Mankato-North Mankato, MN | 5.5 | 191 | Prescott, AZ | (19.5) | 140 | St. Louis, MO-IL | (13.1) |
| 24 | Mansfield, OH | 14.8 | 106 | Providence-Warwick, RI-MA | (7.3) | 45 | Sumter, SC | 6.5 |
| 239 | McAllen-Edinburg-Mission, TX | (26.3) | 247 | Provo-Orem, UT | (27.3) | 167 | Syracuse, NY | (16.8) |
| 1 | Medford, OR | 75.2 | 9 | Pueblo, CO | 32.9 | 48 | Tacoma, WA M.D. | 5.2 |
| 196 | Memphis, TN-MS-AR | (20.0) | 274 | Punta Gorda, FL | (33.0) | 283 | Tallahassee, FL | (35.9) |
| 150 | Merced, CA | (14.7) | 57 | Racine, WI | 3.6 | 286 | Tampa-St Petersburg, FL | (37.1) |
| 217 | Miami (greater), FL | (23.3) | 169 | Raleigh, NC | (16.9) | NA | Terre Haute, IN** | NA |
| 263 | Miami-Dade County, FL M.D. | (29.5) | 10 | Rapid City, SD | 32.1 | 228 | Texarkana, TX-AR | (24.5) |
| 295 | Midland, TX | (40.5) | 143 | Reading, PA | (13.5) | NA | The Villages, FL** | NA |
| 81 | Milwaukee, WI | (2.5) | 88 | Redding, CA | (3.4) | 252 | Toledo, OH | (28.1) |
| 194 | Minneapolis-St. Paul, MN-WI | (19.7) | 234 | Reno, NV | (25.6) | 249 | Topeka, KS | (27.4) |
| 12 | Missoula, MT | 25.7 | 180 | Richmond, VA | (18.9) | 23 | Trenton, NJ | 15.4 |
| 166 | Mobile, AL | (16.7) | 79 | Riverside-San Bernardino, CA | (2.1) | 90 | Tucson, AZ | (3.7) |
| 132 | Modesto, CA | (12.1) | 268 | Roanoke, VA | (31.0) | 154 | Tulsa, OK | (15.3) |
| NA | Monroe, LA** | NA | 61 | Rochester, MN | 3.2 | 285 | Tuscaloosa, AL | (36.8) |
| 71 | Monroe, MI | 0.6 | 101 | Rochester, NY | (6.1) | 180 | Tyler, TX | (18.9) |
| NA | Montgomery County, PA M.D.** | NA | NA | Rockford, IL** | NA | 93 | Utica-Rome, NY | (4.2) |
| 272 | Morgantown, WV | (32.3) | 91 | Rockingham County, NH M.D. | (3.9) | 40 | Vallejo-Fairfield, CA | 7.7 |
| 214 | Morristown, TN | (22.5) | 205 | Rocky Mount, NC | (21.9) | 288 | Victoria, TX | (37.5) |
| 19 | Mount Vernon-Anacortes, WA | 19.5 | 29 | Rome, GA | 11.2 | 13 | Vineland-Bridgeton, NJ | 24.7 |
| 139 | Muncie, IN | (13.0) | 144 | Sacramento, CA | (13.6) | NA | Virginia Beach-Norfolk, VA-NC** | NA |
| 100 | Muskegon, MI | (5.8) | 299 | Saginaw, MI | (44.3) | 64 | Visalia-Porterville, CA | 2.1 |
| NA | Myrtle Beach, SC-NC** | NA | 103 | Salem, OR | (6.3) | 218 | Waco, TX | (23.4) |
| 185 | Napa, CA | (19.1) | 179 | Salinas, CA | (18.8) | NA | Warner Robins, GA** | NA |
| 170 | Naples-Marco Island, FL | (17.3) | NA | Salisbury, MD-DE** | NA | 200 | Warren-Troy, MI M.D. | (20.5) |
| 224 | Nashville-Davidson, TN | (24.1) | 137 | Salt Lake City, UT | (12.7) | 237 | Washington (greater) DC-VA-MD-WV | (26.1) |
| 159 | Nassau-Suffolk, NY M.D. | (15.9) | 267 | San Angelo, TX | (30.8) | 256 | Washington, DC-VA-MD-WV M.D. | (28.7) |
| NA | New Bern, NC** | NA | 233 | San Antonio, TX | (25.4) | NA | Watertown-Fort Drum, NY** | NA |
| 180 | New Haven-Milford, CT | (18.9) | 117 | San Diego, CA | (9.7) | 129 | Wausau, WI | (11.7) |
| NA | New Orleans, LA** | NA | 72 | San Francisco (greater), CA | 0.5 | 275 | West Palm Beach, FL M.D. | (33.2) |
| 126 | New York (greater), NY-NJ-PA | (11.4) | 42 | San Francisco-Redwood, CA M.D. | 7.1 | 196 | Wichita Falls, TX | (20.0) |
| NA | New York-Jersey City, NY-NJ M.D.** | NA | 26 | San Jose, CA | 13.1 | 116 | Wichita, KS | (9.6) |
| 131 | Newark, NJ-PA M.D. | (12.0) | 33 | San Luis Obispo, CA | 10.3 | 21 | Williamsport, PA | 18.6 |
| 25 | Niles-Benton Harbor, MI | 14.4 | NA | San Rafael, CA M.D.** | NA | 133 | Wilmington, DE-MD-NJ M.D. | (12.2) |
| 265 | North Port-Sarasota-Bradenton, FL | (30.0) | 123 | Santa Cruz-Watsonville, CA | (11.1) | 178 | Wilmington, NC | (18.5) |
| 16 | Norwich-New London, CT | 22.8 | 113 | Santa Maria-Santa Barbara, CA | (8.5) | 278 | Winchester, VA-WV | (34.0) |
| 80 | Oakland-Hayward, CA M.D. | (2.4) | 152 | Santa Rosa, CA | (14.8) | NA | Winston-Salem, NC** | NA |
| 209 | Ocala, FL | (22.2) | 240 | Savannah, GA | (26.7) | 63 | Worcester, MA-CT | 2.5 |
| 198 | Ocean City, NJ | (20.1) | NA | Scranton--Wilkes-Barre, PA** | NA | NA | Yakima, WA** | NA |
| 281 | Odessa, TX | (34.6) | 55 | Seattle (greater), WA | 3.8 | 106 | York-Hanover, PA | (7.3) |
| NA | Ogden-Clearfield, UT** | NA | 58 | Seattle-Bellevue-Everett, WA M.D. | 3.5 | 3 | Yuba City, CA | 54.0 |
| 230 | Oklahoma City, OK | (24.8) | 292 | Sebastian-Vero Beach, FL | (38.2) | 118 | Yuma, AZ | (10.2) |
| NA | Olympia, WA** | NA | NA | Sebring, FL** | NA | | | |

Source: CQ Press using reported data from the F.B.I. "Crime in the United States 2013"
*Burglary is the unlawful entry of a structure to commit a felony or theft.  Attempts are included.
**Not available.

## 32. Percent Change in Burglary Rate: 2009 to 2013 (continued)
## National Percent Change = 15.0% Decrease*

| RANK | METROPOLITAN AREA | % CHANGE | RANK | METROPOLITAN AREA | % CHANGE | RANK | METROPOLITAN AREA | % CHANGE |
|---|---|---|---|---|---|---|---|---|
| 1 | Medford, OR | 75.2 | 65 | Las Vegas-Henderson, NV | 1.7 | 129 | Wausau, WI | (11.7) |
| 2 | Bismarck, ND | 56.5 | 66 | Hagerstown-Martinsburg, MD-WV | 1.6 | 130 | Phoenix-Mesa-Scottsdale, AZ | (11.9) |
| 3 | Yuba City, CA | 54.0 | 67 | Kennewick-Richland, WA | 1.2 | 131 | Newark, NJ-PA M.D. | (12.0) |
| 4 | Gadsden, AL | 53.2 | 68 | Manchester-Nashua, NH | 0.9 | 132 | Modesto, CA | (12.1) |
| 5 | Great Falls, MT | 50.8 | 68 | Pensacola, FL | 0.9 | 133 | Altoona, PA | (12.2) |
| 6 | Lewiston-Auburn, ME | 42.0 | 70 | Lexington-Fayette, KY | 0.8 | 133 | Wilmington, DE-MD-NJ M.D. | (12.2) |
| 7 | Spokane, WA | 38.8 | 71 | Monroe, MI | 0.6 | 135 | Bridgeport-Stamford, CT | (12.4) |
| 8 | Binghamton, NY | 38.2 | 72 | San Francisco (greater), CA | 0.5 | 136 | Decatur, AL | (12.6) |
| 9 | Pueblo, CO | 32.9 | 73 | Camden, NJ M.D. | 0.1 | 137 | Salt Lake City, UT | (12.7) |
| 10 | Rapid City, SD | 32.1 | 74 | Lafayette, IN | (0.1) | 138 | Lawton, OK | (12.8) |
| 11 | Lewiston, ID-WA | 25.9 | 75 | Omaha-Council Bluffs, NE-IA | (0.4) | 139 | Muncie, IN | (13.0) |
| 12 | Missoula, MT | 25.7 | 76 | Coeur d'Alene, ID | (0.5) | 140 | Beaumont-Port Arthur, TX | (13.1) |
| 13 | Vineland-Bridgeton, NJ | 24.7 | 77 | Erie, PA | (1.8) | 140 | St. Louis, MO-IL | (13.1) |
| 14 | Cheyenne, WY | 23.4 | 78 | Jackson, MI | (1.9) | 142 | Denver-Aurora, CO | (13.4) |
| 15 | Madera, CA | 23.1 | 79 | Riverside-San Bernardino, CA | (2.1) | 143 | Reading, PA | (13.5) |
| 16 | Norwich-New London, CT | 22.8 | 80 | Oakland-Hayward, CA M.D. | (2.4) | 144 | Sacramento, CA | (13.6) |
| 17 | Bremerton-Silverdale, WA | 21.4 | 81 | Columbus, IN | (2.5) | 145 | Boulder, CO | (14.0) |
| 18 | Cape Girardeau, MO-IL | 20.0 | 81 | Milwaukee, WI | (2.5) | 145 | Lebanon, PA | (14.0) |
| 19 | Mount Vernon-Anacortes, WA | 19.5 | 83 | Cleveland, TN | (2.6) | 145 | Silver Spring-Frederick, MD M.D. | (14.0) |
| 20 | Sioux Falls, SD | 19.0 | 84 | Fargo, ND-MN | (2.7) | 148 | Las Cruces, NM | (14.1) |
| 21 | Williamsport, PA | 18.6 | 85 | Albany, GA | (3.1) | 149 | Farmington, NM | (14.4) |
| 22 | Billings, MT | 17.4 | 86 | Atlantic City, NJ | (3.2) | 150 | Baton Rouge, LA | (14.7) |
| 23 | Trenton, NJ | 15.4 | 86 | Chico, CA | (3.2) | 150 | Merced, CA | (14.7) |
| 24 | Mansfield, OH | 14.8 | 88 | Redding, CA | (3.4) | 152 | Santa Rosa, CA | (14.8) |
| 25 | Niles-Benton Harbor, MI | 14.4 | 88 | Stockton-Lodi, CA | (3.4) | 153 | Lincoln, NE | (15.0) |
| 26 | San Jose, CA | 13.1 | 90 | Tucson, AZ | (3.7) | 154 | Tulsa, OK | (15.3) |
| 27 | Harrisonburg, VA | 12.1 | 91 | Rockingham County, NH M.D. | (3.9) | 155 | Buffalo-Niagara Falls, NY | (15.4) |
| 28 | Longview, WA | 12.0 | 92 | Idaho Falls, ID | (4.1) | 156 | Eau Claire, WI | (15.5) |
| 29 | Rome, GA | 11.2 | 93 | Utica-Rome, NY | (4.2) | 157 | Abilene, TX | (15.6) |
| 30 | Springfield, OH | 10.9 | 94 | Springfield, MO | (4.4) | 158 | Indianapolis, IN | (15.7) |
| 31 | Fresno, CA | 10.8 | 95 | Cincinnati, OH-KY-IN | (4.5) | 159 | Nassau-Suffolk, NY M.D. | (15.9) |
| 31 | Houma, LA | 10.8 | 96 | Fort Lauderdale, FL M.D. | (5.2) | 160 | Kingston, NY | (16.2) |
| 33 | San Luis Obispo, CA | 10.3 | 97 | Dayton, OH | (5.7) | 161 | Akron, OH | (16.3) |
| 34 | Pocatello, ID | 9.8 | 97 | Macon, GA | (5.7) | 162 | Spartanburg, SC | (16.4) |
| 35 | Portland-Vancouver, OR-WA | 9.6 | 97 | Philadelphia (greater) PA-NJ-MD-DE | (5.7) | 163 | Bay City, MI | (16.5) |
| 36 | Alexandria, LA | 9.4 | 100 | Muskegon, MI | (5.8) | 163 | Boston (greater), MA-NH | (16.5) |
| 37 | Des Moines-West Des Moines, IA | 8.5 | 101 | Rochester, NY | (6.1) | 163 | Brunswick, GA | (16.5) |
| 38 | Lake Havasu City-Kingman, AZ | 8.3 | 102 | Los Angeles County, CA M.D. | (6.2) | 166 | Mobile, AL | (16.7) |
| 39 | Pittsfield, MA | 7.8 | 103 | Salem, OR | (6.3) | 167 | Bangor, ME | (16.8) |
| 40 | Bakersfield, CA | 7.7 | 104 | Los Angeles (greater), CA | (6.6) | 167 | Syracuse, NY | (16.8) |
| 40 | Vallejo-Fairfield, CA | 7.7 | 104 | Louisville, KY-IN | (6.6) | 169 | Raleigh, NC | (16.9) |
| 42 | San Francisco-Redwood, CA M.D. | 7.1 | 106 | Providence-Warwick, RI-MA | (7.3) | 170 | Naples-Marco Island, FL | (17.3) |
| 43 | Colorado Springs, CO | 7.0 | 106 | York-Hanover, PA | (7.3) | 171 | Lansing-East Lansing, MI | (17.4) |
| 44 | Albuquerque, NM | 6.8 | 108 | Iowa City, IA | (7.5) | 172 | Boise City, ID | (17.5) |
| 45 | Sumter, SC | 6.5 | 109 | Sioux City, IA-NE-SD | (7.7) | 172 | St. Joseph, MO-KS | (17.5) |
| 46 | Mankato-North Mankato, MN | 5.5 | 110 | Anaheim-Santa Ana-Irvine, CA M.D. | (7.8) | 174 | Little Rock, AR | (17.6) |
| 47 | Allentown, PA-NJ | 5.3 | 111 | Kokomo, IN | (7.9) | 175 | Atlanta, GA | (18.0) |
| 48 | Tacoma, WA M.D. | 5.2 | 112 | Boston, MA M.D. | (8.3) | 176 | Bend, OR | (18.2) |
| 49 | Fort Wayne, IN | 4.8 | 113 | Santa Maria-Santa Barbara, CA | (8.5) | 177 | Shreveport-Bossier City, LA | (18.3) |
| 50 | Janesville, WI | 4.6 | 114 | Charlottesville, VA | (8.6) | 178 | Wilmington, NC | (18.5) |
| 51 | Duluth, MN-WI | 4.5 | 114 | Columbia, MO | (8.6) | 179 | Salinas, CA | (18.8) |
| 52 | St. Cloud, MN | 4.3 | 116 | Wichita, KS | (9.6) | 180 | New Haven-Milford, CT | (18.9) |
| 53 | Springfield, MA | 4.0 | 117 | San Diego, CA | (9.7) | 180 | Richmond, VA | (18.9) |
| 54 | Fond du Lac, WI | 3.9 | 118 | Elmira, NY | (10.2) | 180 | Tyler, TX | (18.9) |
| 55 | Jefferson City, MO | 3.8 | 118 | Yuma, AZ | (10.2) | 183 | Flint, MI | (19.0) |
| 55 | Seattle (greater), WA | 3.8 | 120 | Fayetteville-Springdale, AR-MO | (10.5) | 183 | Green Bay, WI | (19.0) |
| 57 | Racine, WI | 3.6 | 121 | Albany-Schenectady-Troy, NY | (10.8) | 185 | Birmingham-Hoover, AL | (19.1) |
| 58 | Seattle-Bellevue-Everett, WA M.D. | 3.5 | 122 | Baltimore, MD | (11.0) | 185 | Napa, CA | (19.1) |
| 59 | Dalton, GA | 3.4 | 123 | Lake Charles, LA | (11.1) | 187 | Chattanooga, TN-GA | (19.2) |
| 59 | Oxnard-Thousand Oaks, CA | 3.4 | 123 | Santa Cruz-Watsonville, CA | (11.1) | 187 | Orlando, FL | (19.2) |
| 61 | Rochester, MN | 3.2 | 125 | Palm Bay-Melbourne, FL | (11.3) | 189 | Lynchburg, VA | (19.3) |
| 62 | Glens Falls, NY | 3.0 | 126 | New York (greater), NY-NJ-PA | (11.4) | 190 | Cumberland, MD-WV | (19.4) |
| 63 | Worcester, MA-CT | 2.5 | 126 | Portland, ME | (11.4) | 191 | Prescott, AZ | (19.5) |
| 64 | Visalia-Porterville, CA | 2.1 | 128 | Fort Smith, AR-OK | (11.5) | 192 | Columbus, GA-AL | (19.6) |

Note: All listings are for Metropolitan Statistical Areas (M.S.A.s) except for those ending with "M.D." Listings with "M.D." are Metropolitan Divisions which are smaller parts of eleven large M.S.A.s. See explanatory note at beginning of metropolitan area section.

| RANK | METROPOLITAN AREA | % CHANGE | RANK | METROPOLITAN AREA | % CHANGE | RANK | METROPOLITAN AREA | % CHANGE |
|---|---|---|---|---|---|---|---|---|
| 192 | Corpus Christi, TX | (19.6) | 254 | Longview, TX | (28.5) | NA | Charleston-North Charleston, SC** | NA |
| 194 | Minneapolis-St. Paul, MN-WI | (19.7) | 256 | South Bend-Mishawaka, IN-MI | (28.7) | NA | Charlotte-Mecklenburg, NC-SC** | NA |
| 195 | Cedar Rapids, IA | (19.8) | 256 | Washington, DC-VA-MD-WV M.D. | (28.7) | NA | Chicago (greater), IL-IN-WI** | NA |
| 196 | Memphis, TN-MS-AR | (20.0) | 258 | Dallas-Plano-Irving, TX M.D. | (28.9) | NA | Chicago-Naperville, IL M.D.** | NA |
| 196 | Wichita Falls, TX | (20.0) | 258 | Deltona-Daytona Beach, FL | (28.9) | NA | Crestview-Fort Walton Beach, FL** | NA |
| 198 | Ocean City, NJ | (20.1) | 260 | Dallas (greater), TX | (29.0) | NA | Daphne-Fairhope-Foley, AL** | NA |
| 199 | Logan, UT-ID | (20.2) | 261 | Fort Worth-Arlington, TX M.D. | (29.2) | NA | Davenport, IA-IL** | NA |
| 200 | Warren-Troy, MI M.D. | (20.5) | 262 | Appleton, WI | (29.4) | NA | Dothan, AL** | NA |
| 201 | Owensboro, KY | (20.7) | 263 | Miami-Dade County, FL M.D. | (29.5) | NA | Dutchess-Putnam, NY M.D.** | NA |
| 202 | Anchorage, AK | (21.3) | 264 | Brownsville-Harlingen, TX | (29.6) | NA | East Stroudsburg, PA** | NA |
| 203 | Dubuque, IA | (21.5) | 265 | Bloomington, IN | (30.0) | NA | Elgin, IL M.D.** | NA |
| 204 | Burlington, NC | (21.7) | 265 | North Port-Sarasota-Bradenton, FL | (30.0) | NA | Elizabethtown-Fort Knox, KY** | NA |
| 205 | Johnson City, TN | (21.9) | 267 | San Angelo, TX | (30.8) | NA | Gary, IN M.D.** | NA |
| 205 | Rocky Mount, NC | (21.9) | 268 | Roanoke, VA | (31.0) | NA | Gettysburg, PA** | NA |
| 207 | Grand Forks, ND-MN | (22.0) | 269 | Barnstable Town, MA | (31.4) | NA | Grand Island, NE** | NA |
| 207 | Hartford, CT | (22.0) | 270 | Austin-Round Rock, TX | (32.1) | NA | Grand Rapids-Wyoming, MI** | NA |
| 209 | Columbia, SC | (22.2) | 270 | Lakeland, FL | (32.1) | NA | Grants Pass, OR** | NA |
| 209 | Ocala, FL | (22.2) | 272 | Morgantown, WV | (32.3) | NA | Greenville-Anderson, SC** | NA |
| 209 | State College, PA | (22.2) | 273 | Amarillo, TX | (32.6) | NA | Greenville, NC** | NA |
| 212 | Eugene, OR | (22.3) | 274 | Punta Gorda, FL | (33.0) | NA | Gulfport-Biloxi-Pascagoula, MS** | NA |
| 212 | Manhattan, KS | (22.3) | 275 | Grand Junction, CO | (33.2) | NA | Hammond, LA** | NA |
| 214 | Morristown, TN | (22.5) | 275 | West Palm Beach, FL M.D. | (33.2) | NA | Hanford-Corcoran, CA** | NA |
| 215 | Huntsville, AL | (22.8) | 277 | Lima, OH | (33.4) | NA | Hilton Head Island, SC** | NA |
| 215 | Knoxville, TN | (22.8) | 278 | Winchester, VA-WV | (34.0) | NA | Homosassa Springs, FL** | NA |
| 217 | Miami (greater), FL | (23.3) | 279 | Fairbanks, AK | (34.2) | NA | Johnstown, PA** | NA |
| 218 | Florence-Muscle Shoals, AL | (23.4) | 280 | Greeley, CO | (34.4) | NA | Joplin, MO** | NA |
| 218 | Waco, TX | (23.4) | 281 | Odessa, TX | (34.6) | NA | Kahului-Wailuku-Lahaina, HI** | NA |
| 220 | Gainesville, GA | (23.7) | 282 | Fort Collins, CO | (35.0) | NA | Kankakee, IL** | NA |
| 220 | Houston, TX | (23.7) | 283 | Tallahassee, FL | (35.9) | NA | Kansas City, MO-KS** | NA |
| 222 | Goldsboro, NC | (23.8) | 284 | Clarksville, TN-KY | (36.5) | NA | La Crosse, WI-MN** | NA |
| 223 | El Centro, CA | (23.9) | 285 | Tuscaloosa, AL | (36.8) | NA | Lafayette, LA** | NA |
| 224 | Nashville-Davidson, TN | (24.1) | 286 | Tampa-St Petersburg, FL | (37.1) | NA | Lake Co.-Kenosha Co., IL-WI M.D.** | NA |
| 224 | Sherman-Denison, TX | (24.1) | 287 | Casper, WY | (37.2) | NA | Lancaster, PA** | NA |
| 226 | Fayetteville, NC | (24.3) | 288 | Lubbock, TX | (37.5) | NA | Madison, WI** | NA |
| 226 | Lawrence, KS | (24.3) | 288 | Victoria, TX | (37.5) | NA | Monroe, LA** | NA |
| 228 | Texarkana, TX-AR | (24.5) | 290 | Laredo, TX | (37.9) | NA | Montgomery County, PA M.D.** | NA |
| 229 | El Paso, TX | (24.6) | 291 | Ann Arbor, MI | (38.0) | NA | Myrtle Beach, SC-NC** | NA |
| 230 | Oklahoma City, OK | (24.8) | 292 | Sebastian-Vero Beach, FL | (38.2) | NA | New Bern, NC** | NA |
| 231 | Florence, SC | (24.9) | 293 | Jacksonville, FL | (39.0) | NA | New Orleans, LA** | NA |
| 232 | Carson City, NV | (25.3) | 294 | Cape Coral-Fort Myers, FL | (40.3) | NA | New York-Jersey City, NY-NJ M.D.** | NA |
| 233 | San Antonio, TX | (25.4) | 295 | Midland, TX | (40.5) | NA | Ogden-Clearfield, UT** | NA |
| 234 | Reno, NV | (25.6) | 296 | Kingsport, TN-VA | (41.2) | NA | Olympia, WA** | NA |
| 235 | Hot Springs, AR | (25.7) | 297 | Decatur, IL | (42.1) | NA | Parkersburg-Vienna, WV** | NA |
| 236 | Jonesboro, AR | (25.8) | 298 | Athens-Clarke County, GA | (43.5) | NA | Peoria, IL** | NA |
| 237 | Washington (greater) DC-VA-MD-WV | (26.1) | 299 | Saginaw, MI | (44.3) | NA | Philadelphia, PA M.D.** | NA |
| 238 | Greensboro-High Point, NC | (26.2) | 300 | Blacksburg, VA | (44.9) | NA | Pittsburgh, PA** | NA |
| 239 | McAllen-Edinburg-Mission, TX | (26.3) | 301 | Sheboygan, WI | (45.4) | NA | Rockford, IL** | NA |
| 240 | Flagstaff, AZ | (26.7) | 302 | Hinesville, GA | (45.6) | NA | Salisbury, MD-DE** | NA |
| 240 | Savannah, GA | (26.7) | 303 | Dover, DE | (46.7) | NA | San Rafael, CA M.D.** | NA |
| 242 | Ames, IA | (26.8) | 304 | Oshkosh-Neenah, WI | (47.1) | NA | Scranton--Wilkes-Barre, PA** | NA |
| 243 | Detroit (greater), MI | (27.0) | 305 | College Station-Bryan, TX | (49.5) | NA | Sebring, FL** | NA |
| 243 | Jackson, MS | (27.0) | 306 | Gainesville, FL | (50.2) | NA | Springfield, IL** | NA |
| 245 | Anniston-Oxford, AL | (27.2) | NA | Albany, OR** | NA | NA | Staunton-Waynesboro, VA** | NA |
| 245 | Jackson, TN | (27.2) | NA | Bloomington, IL** | NA | NA | St. George, UT** | NA |
| 247 | Detroit-Dearborn-Livonia, MI M.D. | (27.3) | NA | Bloomsburg-Berwick, PA** | NA | NA | Terre Haute, IN** | NA |
| 247 | Provo-Orem, UT | (27.3) | NA | Bowling Green, KY** | NA | NA | The Villages, FL** | NA |
| 249 | Topeka, KS | (27.4) | NA | California-Lexington Park, MD** | NA | NA | Virginia Beach-Norfolk, VA-NC** | NA |
| 250 | Port St. Lucie, FL | (27.6) | NA | Cambridge-Newton, MA M.D.** | NA | NA | Warner Robins, GA** | NA |
| 251 | Panama City, FL | (27.8) | NA | Canton, OH** | NA | NA | Watertown-Fort Drum, NY** | NA |
| 252 | Toledo, OH | (28.1) | NA | Carbondale-Marion, IL** | NA | NA | Winston-Salem, NC** | NA |
| 253 | Augusta, GA-SC | (28.2) | NA | Chambersburg-Waynesboro, PA** | NA | NA | Yakima, WA** | NA |
| 254 | Corvallis, OR | (28.5) | NA | Champaign-Urbana, IL** | NA | | | |

Source: CQ Press using reported data from the F.B.I. "Crime in the United States 2013"

*Burglary is the unlawful entry of a structure to commit a felony or theft. Attempts are included.

**Not available.

# 33. Larceny-Thefts in 2013
## National Total = 6,004,453 Larceny-Thefts*

| RANK | METROPOLITAN AREA | THEFTS | RANK | METROPOLITAN AREA | THEFTS | RANK | METROPOLITAN AREA | THEFTS |
|---|---|---|---|---|---|---|---|---|
| 237 | Abilene, TX | 3,907 | 330 | Cheyenne, WY | 2,069 | 101 | Gary, IN M.D. | 14,663 |
| 103 | Akron, OH | 14,520 | 4 | Chicago (greater), IL-IN-WI | 163,715 | 373 | Gettysburg, PA | 952 |
| 93 | Albany-Schenectady-Troy, NY | 15,787 | 9 | Chicago-Naperville, IL M.D. | 129,707 | 356 | Glens Falls, NY | 1,676 |
| 205 | Albany, GA | 4,813 | 248 | Chico, CA | 3,642 | 281 | Goldsboro, NC | 2,906 |
| 277 | Albany, OR | 2,976 | 34 | Cincinnati, OH-KY-IN | 48,133 | 354 | Grand Forks, ND-MN | 1,681 |
| 65 | Albuquerque, NM | 26,272 | 203 | Clarksville, TN-KY | 4,912 | 326 | Grand Island, NE | 2,092 |
| 202 | Alexandria, LA | 4,922 | 297 | Cleveland, TN | 2,669 | 268 | Grand Junction, CO | 3,101 |
| 106 | Allentown, PA-NJ | 13,655 | 288 | Coeur d'Alene, ID | 2,845 | 102 | Grand Rapids-Wyoming, MI | 14,563 |
| 353 | Altoona, PA | 1,698 | 221 | College Station-Bryan, TX | 4,383 | 316 | Grants Pass, OR | 2,229 |
| 175 | Amarillo, TX | 6,178 | 95 | Colorado Springs, CO | 15,228 | 311 | Great Falls, MT | 2,374 |
| 364 | Ames, IA | 1,561 | 216 | Columbia, MO | 4,497 | 233 | Greeley, CO | 4,056 |
| 40 | Anaheim-Santa Ana-Irvine, CA M.D. | 44,001 | 78 | Columbia, SC | 20,246 | 217 | Green Bay, WI | 4,474 |
| 127 | Anchorage, AK | 10,722 | 131 | Columbus, GA-AL | 9,914 | 86 | Greensboro-High Point, NC | 17,164 |
| 189 | Ann Arbor, MI | 5,525 | 322 | Columbus, IN | 2,142 | 69 | Greenville-Anderson, SC | 23,089 |
| 291 | Anniston-Oxford, AL | 2,814 | 104 | Corpus Christi, TX | 14,382 | 236 | Greenville, NC | 3,958 |
| 299 | Appleton, WI | 2,651 | 345 | Corvallis, OR | 1,849 | 135 | Gulfport-Biloxi-Pascagoula, MS | 9,485 |
| 220 | Athens-Clarke County, GA | 4,422 | 218 | Crestview-Fort Walton Beach, FL | 4,469 | 230 | Hagerstown-Martinsburg, MD-WV | 4,125 |
| 10 | Atlanta, GA | 120,386 | 334 | Cumberland, MD-WV | 2,031 | 226 | Hammond, LA | 4,210 |
| 173 | Atlantic City, NJ | 6,226 | 8 | Dallas (greater), TX | 141,174 | 310 | Hanford-Corcoran, CA | 2,413 |
| 105 | Augusta, GA-SC | 14,369 | 16 | Dallas-Plano-Irving, TX M.D. | 86,363 | 361 | Harrisonburg, VA | 1,603 |
| 37 | Austin-Round Rock, TX | 46,713 | 285 | Dalton, GA | 2,879 | 88 | Hartford, CT | 16,853 |
| 89 | Bakersfield, CA | 16,851 | 244 | Daphne-Fairhope-Foley, AL | 3,749 | 232 | Hilton Head Island, SC | 4,077 |
| 25 | Baltimore, MD | 59,726 | 157 | Davenport, IA-IL | 7,240 | 366 | Hinesville, GA | 1,499 |
| 254 | Bangor, ME | 3,439 | 85 | Dayton, OH | 18,329 | 337 | Homosassa Springs, FL | 1,989 |
| 263 | Barnstable Town, MA | 3,219 | 296 | Decatur, AL | 2,698 | 258 | Hot Springs, AR | 3,370 |
| 73 | Baton Rouge, LA | 22,194 | 346 | Decatur, IL | 1,832 | 198 | Houma, LA | 5,087 |
| 359 | Bay City, MI | 1,636 | 108 | Deltona-Daytona Beach, FL | 13,372 | 6 | Houston, TX | 146,202 |
| 142 | Beaumont-Port Arthur, TX | 8,811 | 29 | Denver-Aurora, CO | 53,466 | 130 | Huntsville, AL | 10,393 |
| 253 | Bend, OR | 3,443 | 117 | Des Moines-West Des Moines, IA | 11,762 | 347 | Idaho Falls, ID | 1,828 |
| 207 | Billings, MT | 4,733 | 24 | Detroit (greater), MI | 65,422 | 42 | Indianapolis, IN | 43,790 |
| 195 | Binghamton, NY | 5,313 | 48 | Detroit-Dearborn-Livonia, MI M.D. | 35,484 | 305 | Iowa City, IA | 2,466 |
| 61 | Birmingham-Hoover, AL | 27,971 | 282 | Dothan, AL | 2,896 | 53 | Jacksonville, FL | 33,478 |
| 327 | Bismarck, ND | 2,081 | 231 | Dover, DE | 4,104 | 280 | Jackson, MI | 2,910 |
| 293 | Blacksburg, VA | 2,795 | 369 | Dubuque, IA | 1,332 | 129 | Jackson, MS | 10,615 |
| 274 | Bloomington, IL | 2,995 | 156 | Duluth, MN-WI | 7,365 | 261 | Jackson, TN | 3,276 |
| 262 | Bloomington, IN | 3,239 | 224 | Dutchess-Putnam, NY M.D. | 4,281 | 278 | Janesville, WI | 2,969 |
| 372 | Bloomsburg-Berwick, PA | 1,129 | 284 | East Stroudsburg, PA | 2,886 | 308 | Jefferson City, MO | 2,418 |
| 146 | Boise City, ID | 8,186 | 318 | Eau Claire, WI | 2,212 | 242 | Johnson City, TN | 3,828 |
| 23 | Boston (greater), MA-NH | 66,047 | 238 | El Centro, CA | 3,886 | 344 | Johnstown, PA | 1,853 |
| 59 | Boston, MA M.D. | 29,920 | 97 | El Paso, TX | 15,006 | 283 | Jonesboro, AR | 2,892 |
| 190 | Boulder, CO | 5,514 | 150 | Elgin, IL M.D. | 7,792 | 185 | Joplin, MO | 5,639 |
| 289 | Bowling Green, KY | 2,837 | 358 | Elizabethtown-Fort Knox, KY | 1,640 | 223 | Kahului-Wailuku-Lahaina, HI | 4,314 |
| 196 | Bremerton-Silverdale, WA | 5,126 | 357 | Elmira, NY | 1,670 | 321 | Kankakee, IL | 2,160 |
| 128 | Bridgeport-Stamford, CT | 10,644 | 206 | Erie, PA | 4,804 | 39 | Kansas City, MO-KS | 44,456 |
| 121 | Brownsville-Harlingen, TX | 11,587 | 133 | Eugene, OR | 9,643 | 214 | Kennewick-Richland, WA | 4,533 |
| 270 | Brunswick, GA | 3,045 | 371 | Fairbanks, AK | 1,190 | 169 | Kingsport, TN-VA | 6,385 |
| 70 | Buffalo-Niagara Falls, NY | 23,046 | 246 | Fargo, ND-MN | 3,694 | 301 | Kingston, NY | 2,636 |
| 256 | Burlington, NC | 3,433 | 338 | Farmington, NM | 1,969 | 84 | Knoxville, TN | 18,890 |
| 352 | California-Lexington Park, MD | 1,730 | 145 | Fayetteville-Springdale, AR-MO | 8,631 | 349 | Kokomo, IN | 1,753 |
| 60 | Cambridge-Newton, MA M.D. | 29,160 | 112 | Fayetteville, NC | 12,166 | 336 | La Crosse, WI-MN | 1,994 |
| 76 | Camden, NJ M.D. | 21,144 | 249 | Flagstaff, AZ | 3,594 | 227 | Lafayette, IN | 4,202 |
| 154 | Canton, OH | 7,434 | 160 | Flint, MI | 7,059 | 115 | Lafayette, LA | 12,074 |
| 132 | Cape Coral-Fort Myers, FL | 9,808 | 267 | Florence-Muscle Shoals, AL | 3,103 | 187 | Lake Charles, LA | 5,620 |
| 323 | Cape Girardeau, MO-IL | 2,136 | 165 | Florence, SC | 6,729 | 123 | Lake Co.-Kenosha Co., IL-WI M.D. | 11,553 |
| 331 | Carbondale-Marion, IL | 2,065 | 367 | Fond du Lac, WI | 1,355 | 210 | Lake Havasu City-Kingman, AZ | 4,616 |
| 375 | Carson City, NV | 654 | 186 | Fort Collins, CO | 5,631 | 111 | Lakeland, FL | 12,280 |
| 343 | Casper, WY | 1,879 | 41 | Fort Lauderdale, FL M.D. | 43,855 | 149 | Lancaster, PA | 7,814 |
| 219 | Cedar Rapids, IA | 4,435 | 177 | Fort Smith, AR-OK | 6,162 | 158 | Lansing-East Lansing, MI | 7,114 |
| 312 | Chambersburg-Waynesboro, PA | 2,314 | 139 | Fort Wayne, IN | 8,967 | 140 | Laredo, TX | 8,952 |
| 222 | Champaign-Urbana, IL | 4,326 | 27 | Fort Worth-Arlington, TX M.D. | 54,811 | 209 | Las Cruces, NM | 4,637 |
| 91 | Charleston-North Charleston, SC | 16,271 | 75 | Fresno, CA | 21,257 | 50 | Las Vegas-Henderson, NV | 34,302 |
| 33 | Charlotte-Mecklenburg, NC-SC | 49,867 | 292 | Gadsden, AL | 2,805 | 260 | Lawrence, KS | 3,334 |
| 254 | Charlottesville, VA | 3,439 | 179 | Gainesville, FL | 6,095 | 251 | Lawton, OK | 3,541 |
| 99 | Chattanooga, TN-GA | 14,833 | 273 | Gainesville, GA | 3,005 | 332 | Lebanon, PA | 2,049 |

Note: All listings are for Metropolitan Statistical Areas (M.S.A.s) except for those ending with "M.D." Listings with "M.D." are Metropolitan Divisions which are smaller parts of eleven large M.S.A.s. See explanatory note at beginning of metropolitan area section.

| RANK | METROPOLITAN AREA | THEFTS | RANK | METROPOLITAN AREA | THEFTS | RANK | METROPOLITAN AREA | THEFTS |
|---|---|---|---|---|---|---|---|---|
| 324 | Lewiston-Auburn, ME | 2,122 | 81 | Omaha-Council Bluffs, NE-IA | 19,422 | 350 | Sheboygan, WI | 1,740 |
| 365 | Lewiston, ID-WA | 1,531 | 30 | Orlando, FL | 52,808 | 319 | Sherman-Denison, TX | 2,189 |
| 107 | Lexington-Fayette, KY | 13,384 | 309 | Oshkosh-Neenah, WI | 2,416 | 122 | Shreveport-Bossier City, LA | 11,562 |
| 304 | Lima, OH | 2,499 | 340 | Owensboro, KY | 1,932 | 92 | Silver Spring-Frederick, MD M.D. | 15,861 |
| 147 | Lincoln, NE | 8,153 | 119 | Oxnard-Thousand Oaks, CA | 11,690 | 250 | Sioux City, IA-NE-SD | 3,549 |
| 68 | Little Rock, AR | 23,982 | 126 | Palm Bay-Melbourne, FL | 10,952 | 225 | Sioux Falls, SD | 4,262 |
| 370 | Logan, UT-ID | 1,227 | 188 | Panama City, FL | 5,551 | 166 | South Bend-Mishawaka, IN-MI | 6,707 |
| 199 | Longview, TX | 5,080 | 362 | Parkersburg-Vienna, WV | 1,586 | 162 | Spartanburg, SC | 6,898 |
| 287 | Longview, WA | 2,859 | 125 | Pensacola, FL | 11,099 | 77 | Spokane, WA | 20,999 |
| 7 | Los Angeles County, CA M.D. | 141,312 | 171 | Peoria, IL | 6,377 | 183 | Springfield, IL | 5,703 |
| 3 | Los Angeles (greater), CA | 185,313 | 11 | Philadelphia (greater) PA-NJ-MD-DE | 110,663 | 113 | Springfield, MA | 12,130 |
| 56 | Louisville, KY-IN | 30,252 | 36 | Philadelphia, PA M.D. | 47,212 | 96 | Springfield, MO | 15,113 |
| 141 | Lubbock, TX | 8,908 | 14 | Phoenix-Mesa-Scottsdale, AZ | 97,363 | 234 | Springfield, OH | 4,010 |
| 265 | Lynchburg, VA | 3,174 | 54 | Pittsburgh, PA | 33,343 | 348 | State College, PA | 1,824 |
| 153 | Macon, GA | 7,445 | 325 | Pittsfield, MA | 2,095 | 360 | Staunton-Waynesboro, VA | 1,623 |
| 341 | Madera, CA | 1,930 | 333 | Pocatello, ID | 2,044 | 87 | Stockton-Lodi, CA | 17,069 |
| 124 | Madison, WI | 11,386 | 163 | Port St. Lucie, FL | 6,740 | 243 | St. Cloud, MN | 3,812 |
| 155 | Manchester-Nashua, NH | 7,366 | 32 | Portland-Vancouver, OR-WA | 51,388 | 329 | St. George, UT | 2,070 |
| 368 | Manhattan, KS | 1,336 | 137 | Portland, ME | 9,173 | 245 | St. Joseph, MO-KS | 3,722 |
| 335 | Mankato-North Mankato, MN | 1,995 | 266 | Prescott, AZ | 3,158 | 28 | St. Louis, MO-IL | 53,631 |
| 235 | Mansfield, OH | 3,974 | 67 | Providence-Warwick, RI-MA | 26,013 | 315 | Sumter, SC | 2,277 |
| 72 | McAllen-Edinburg-Mission, TX | 22,286 | 144 | Provo-Orem, UT | 8,784 | 110 | Syracuse, NY | 12,385 |
| 164 | Medford, OR | 6,739 | 178 | Pueblo, CO | 6,112 | 74 | Tacoma, WA M.D. | 21,446 |
| 46 | Memphis, TN-MS-AR | 36,837 | 303 | Punta Gorda, FL | 2,511 | 138 | Tallahassee, FL | 8,995 |
| 208 | Merced, CA | 4,657 | 264 | Racine, WI | 3,180 | 26 | Tampa-St Petersburg, FL | 56,266 |
| 5 | Miami (greater), FL | 156,375 | 82 | Raleigh, NC | 19,369 | 240 | Terre Haute, IN | 3,861 |
| 18 | Miami-Dade County, FL M.D. | 82,490 | 306 | Rapid City, SD | 2,442 | 229 | Texarkana, TX-AR | 4,132 |
| 269 | Midland, TX | 3,056 | 193 | Reading, PA | 5,421 | 374 | The Villages, FL | 658 |
| 51 | Milwaukee, WI | 33,908 | 257 | Redding, CA | 3,396 | NA | Toledo, OH** | NA |
| 21 | Minneapolis-St. Paul, MN-WI | 68,642 | 151 | Reno, NV | 7,666 | 181 | Topeka, KS | 5,932 |
| 294 | Missoula, MT | 2,730 | 71 | Richmond, VA | 22,329 | 204 | Trenton, NJ | 4,867 |
| 109 | Mobile, AL | 12,504 | 22 | Riverside-San Bernardino, CA | 67,684 | 45 | Tucson, AZ | 37,897 |
| 116 | Modesto, CA | 11,936 | 174 | Roanoke, VA | 6,180 | 79 | Tulsa, OK | 19,762 |
| 182 | Monroe, LA | 5,846 | 302 | Rochester, MN | 2,625 | 192 | Tuscaloosa, AL | 5,422 |
| 306 | Monroe, MI | 2,442 | 80 | Rochester, NY | 19,517 | 213 | Tyler, TX | 4,539 |
| 63 | Montgomery County, PA M.D. | 26,866 | 159 | Rockford, IL | 7,088 | 197 | Utica-Rome, NY | 5,101 |
| 354 | Morgantown, WV | 1,681 | 161 | Rockingham County, NH M.D. | 6,967 | 167 | Vallejo-Fairfield, CA | 6,473 |
| 298 | Morristown, TN | 2,652 | 259 | Rocky Mount, NC | 3,361 | 313 | Victoria, TX | 2,312 |
| 247 | Mount Vernon-Anacortes, WA | 3,659 | 279 | Rome, GA | 2,923 | 201 | Vineland-Bridgeton, NJ | 4,939 |
| 290 | Muncie, IN | 2,821 | 44 | Sacramento, CA | 38,144 | 43 | Virginia Beach-Norfolk, VA-NC | 39,937 |
| 211 | Muskegon, MI | 4,553 | 295 | Saginaw, MI | 2,708 | 148 | Visalia-Porterville, CA | 7,870 |
| 114 | Myrtle Beach, SC-NC | 12,124 | 134 | Salem, OR | 9,640 | 176 | Waco, TX | 6,168 |
| 351 | Napa, CA | 1,732 | 180 | Salinas, CA | 6,036 | 194 | Warner Robins, GA | 5,376 |
| 239 | Naples-Marco Island, FL | 3,884 | 143 | Salisbury, MD-DE | 8,793 | 58 | Warren-Troy, MI M.D. | 29,938 |
| 49 | Nashville-Davidson, TN | 34,923 | 47 | Salt Lake City, UT | 36,244 | 13 | Washington (greater) DC-VA-MD-WV | 100,567 |
| 55 | Nassau-Suffolk, NY M.D. | 32,803 | 275 | San Angelo, TX | 2,994 | 17 | Washington, DC-VA-MD-WV M.D. | 84,706 |
| 314 | New Bern, NC | 2,298 | 20 | San Antonio, TX | 73,269 | 342 | Watertown-Fort Drum, NY | 1,880 |
| 90 | New Haven-Milford, CT | 16,783 | 38 | San Diego, CA | 45,034 | 363 | Wausau, WI | 1,565 |
| 62 | New Orleans, LA | 27,676 | 12 | San Francisco (greater), CA | 102,174 | 57 | West Palm Beach, FL M.D. | 30,030 |
| 1 | New York (greater), NY-NJ-PA | 250,083 | 35 | San Francisco-Redwood, CA M.D. | 47,520 | 241 | Wichita Falls, TX | 3,844 |
| 2 | New York-Jersey City, NY-NJ M.D. | 186,419 | 66 | San Jose, CA | 26,038 | 83 | Wichita, KS | 18,910 |
| 64 | Newark, NJ-PA M.D. | 26,580 | 228 | San Luis Obispo, CA | 4,167 | 339 | Williamsport, PA | 1,949 |
| 276 | Niles-Benton Harbor, MI | 2,983 | 272 | San Rafael, CA M.D. | 3,009 | 94 | Wilmington, DE-MD-NJ M.D. | 15,441 |
| 98 | North Port-Sarasota-Bradenton, FL | 14,885 | 191 | Santa Cruz-Watsonville, CA | 5,477 | 169 | Wilmington, NC | 6,385 |
| 300 | Norwich-New London, CT | 2,650 | 168 | Santa Maria-Santa Barbara, CA | 6,429 | 328 | Winchester, VA-WV | 2,072 |
| 31 | Oakland-Hayward, CA M.D. | 51,645 | 184 | Santa Rosa, CA | 5,693 | 100 | Winston-Salem, NC | 14,769 |
| NA | Ocala, FL** | NA | 152 | Savannah, GA | 7,512 | 118 | Worcester, MA-CT | 11,758 |
| 271 | Ocean City, NJ | 3,044 | 136 | Scranton--Wilkes-Barre, PA | 9,359 | 200 | Yakima, WA | 4,958 |
| 215 | Odessa, TX | 4,498 | 15 | Seattle (greater), WA | 94,993 | 172 | York-Hanover, PA | 6,334 |
| 120 | Ogden-Clearfield, UT | 11,614 | 19 | Seattle-Bellevue-Everett, WA M.D. | 73,547 | 286 | Yuba City, CA | 2,866 |
| 52 | Oklahoma City, OK | 33,747 | 317 | Sebastian-Vero Beach, FL | 2,215 | 252 | Yuma, AZ | 3,449 |
| 212 | Olympia, WA | 4,548 | 320 | Sebring, FL | 2,186 | | | |

Source: Reported data from the F.B.I. "Crime in the United States 2013"

*Larceny-theft is the unlawful taking of property. Attempts are included.

**Not available.

# 33. Larceny-Thefts in 2013 (continued)
## National Total = 6,004,453 Larceny-Thefts*

| RANK | METROPOLITAN AREA | THEFTS | RANK | METROPOLITAN AREA | THEFTS | RANK | METROPOLITAN AREA | THEFTS |
|---|---|---|---|---|---|---|---|---|
| 1 | New York (greater), NY-NJ-PA | 250,083 | 65 | Albuquerque, NM | 26,272 | 129 | Jackson, MS | 10,615 |
| 2 | New York-Jersey City, NY-NJ M.D. | 186,419 | 66 | San Jose, CA | 26,038 | 130 | Huntsville, AL | 10,393 |
| 3 | Los Angeles (greater), CA | 185,313 | 67 | Providence-Warwick, RI-MA | 26,013 | 131 | Columbus, GA-AL | 9,914 |
| 4 | Chicago (greater), IL-IN-WI | 163,715 | 68 | Little Rock, AR | 23,982 | 132 | Cape Coral-Fort Myers, FL | 9,808 |
| 5 | Miami (greater), FL | 156,375 | 69 | Greenville-Anderson, SC | 23,089 | 133 | Eugene, OR | 9,643 |
| 6 | Houston, TX | 146,202 | 70 | Buffalo-Niagara Falls, NY | 23,046 | 134 | Salem, OR | 9,640 |
| 7 | Los Angeles County, CA M.D. | 141,312 | 71 | Richmond, VA | 22,329 | 135 | Gulfport-Biloxi-Pascagoula, MS | 9,485 |
| 8 | Dallas (greater), TX | 141,174 | 72 | McAllen-Edinburg-Mission, TX | 22,286 | 136 | Scranton--Wilkes-Barre, PA | 9,359 |
| 9 | Chicago-Naperville, IL M.D. | 129,707 | 73 | Baton Rouge, LA | 22,194 | 137 | Portland, ME | 9,173 |
| 10 | Atlanta, GA | 120,386 | 74 | Tacoma, WA M.D. | 21,446 | 138 | Tallahassee, FL | 8,995 |
| 11 | Philadelphia (greater) PA-NJ-MD-DE | 110,663 | 75 | Fresno, CA | 21,257 | 139 | Fort Wayne, IN | 8,967 |
| 12 | San Francisco (greater), CA | 102,174 | 76 | Camden, NJ M.D. | 21,144 | 140 | Laredo, TX | 8,952 |
| 13 | Washington (greater) DC-VA-MD-WV | 100,567 | 77 | Spokane, WA | 20,999 | 141 | Lubbock, TX | 8,908 |
| 14 | Phoenix-Mesa-Scottsdale, AZ | 97,363 | 78 | Columbia, SC | 20,246 | 142 | Beaumont-Port Arthur, TX | 8,811 |
| 15 | Seattle (greater), WA | 94,993 | 79 | Tulsa, OK | 19,762 | 143 | Salisbury, MD-DE | 8,793 |
| 16 | Dallas-Plano-Irving, TX M.D. | 86,363 | 80 | Rochester, NY | 19,517 | 144 | Provo-Orem, UT | 8,784 |
| 17 | Washington, DC-VA-MD-WV M.D. | 84,706 | 81 | Omaha-Council Bluffs, NE-IA | 19,422 | 145 | Fayetteville-Springdale, AR-MO | 8,631 |
| 18 | Miami-Dade County, FL M.D. | 82,490 | 82 | Raleigh, NC | 19,369 | 146 | Boise City, ID | 8,186 |
| 19 | Seattle-Bellevue-Everett, WA M.D. | 73,547 | 83 | Wichita, KS | 18,910 | 147 | Lincoln, NE | 8,153 |
| 20 | San Antonio, TX | 73,269 | 84 | Knoxville, TN | 18,890 | 148 | Visalia-Porterville, CA | 7,870 |
| 21 | Minneapolis-St. Paul, MN-WI | 68,642 | 85 | Dayton, OH | 18,329 | 149 | Lancaster, PA | 7,814 |
| 22 | Riverside-San Bernardino, CA | 67,684 | 86 | Greensboro-High Point, NC | 17,164 | 150 | Elgin, IL M.D. | 7,792 |
| 23 | Boston (greater), MA-NH | 66,047 | 87 | Stockton-Lodi, CA | 17,069 | 151 | Reno, NV | 7,666 |
| 24 | Detroit (greater), MI | 65,422 | 88 | Hartford, CT | 16,853 | 152 | Savannah, GA | 7,512 |
| 25 | Baltimore, MD | 59,726 | 89 | Bakersfield, CA | 16,851 | 153 | Macon, GA | 7,445 |
| 26 | Tampa-St Petersburg, FL | 56,266 | 90 | New Haven-Milford, CT | 16,783 | 154 | Canton, OH | 7,434 |
| 27 | Fort Worth-Arlington, TX M.D. | 54,811 | 91 | Charleston-North Charleston, SC | 16,271 | 155 | Manchester-Nashua, NH | 7,366 |
| 28 | St. Louis, MO-IL | 53,631 | 92 | Silver Spring-Frederick, MD M.D. | 15,861 | 156 | Duluth, MN-WI | 7,365 |
| 29 | Denver-Aurora, CO | 53,466 | 93 | Albany-Schenectady-Troy, NY | 15,787 | 157 | Davenport, IA-IL | 7,240 |
| 30 | Orlando, FL | 52,808 | 94 | Wilmington, DE-MD-NJ M.D. | 15,441 | 158 | Lansing-East Lansing, MI | 7,114 |
| 31 | Oakland-Hayward, CA M.D. | 51,645 | 95 | Colorado Springs, CO | 15,228 | 159 | Rockford, IL | 7,088 |
| 32 | Portland-Vancouver, OR-WA | 51,388 | 96 | Springfield, MO | 15,113 | 160 | Flint, MI | 7,059 |
| 33 | Charlotte-Mecklenburg, NC-SC | 49,867 | 97 | El Paso, TX | 15,006 | 161 | Rockingham County, NH M.D. | 6,967 |
| 34 | Cincinnati, OH-KY-IN | 48,133 | 98 | North Port-Sarasota-Bradenton, FL | 14,885 | 162 | Spartanburg, SC | 6,898 |
| 35 | San Francisco-Redwood, CA M.D. | 47,520 | 99 | Chattanooga, TN-GA | 14,833 | 163 | Port St. Lucie, FL | 6,740 |
| 36 | Philadelphia, PA M.D. | 47,212 | 100 | Winston-Salem, NC | 14,769 | 164 | Medford, OR | 6,739 |
| 37 | Austin-Round Rock, TX | 46,713 | 101 | Gary, IN M.D. | 14,663 | 165 | Florence, SC | 6,729 |
| 38 | San Diego, CA | 45,034 | 102 | Grand Rapids-Wyoming, MI | 14,563 | 166 | South Bend-Mishawaka, IN-MI | 6,707 |
| 39 | Kansas City, MO-KS | 44,456 | 103 | Akron, OH | 14,520 | 167 | Vallejo-Fairfield, CA | 6,473 |
| 40 | Anaheim-Santa Ana-Irvine, CA M.D. | 44,001 | 104 | Corpus Christi, TX | 14,382 | 168 | Santa Maria-Santa Barbara, CA | 6,429 |
| 41 | Fort Lauderdale, FL M.D. | 43,855 | 105 | Augusta, GA-SC | 14,369 | 169 | Kingsport, TN-VA | 6,385 |
| 42 | Indianapolis, IN | 43,790 | 106 | Allentown, PA-NJ | 13,655 | 169 | Wilmington, NC | 6,385 |
| 43 | Virginia Beach-Norfolk, VA-NC | 39,937 | 107 | Lexington-Fayette, KY | 13,384 | 171 | Peoria, IL | 6,377 |
| 44 | Sacramento, CA | 38,144 | 108 | Deltona-Daytona Beach, FL | 13,372 | 172 | York-Hanover, PA | 6,334 |
| 45 | Tucson, AZ | 37,897 | 109 | Mobile, AL | 12,504 | 173 | Atlantic City, NJ | 6,226 |
| 46 | Memphis, TN-MS-AR | 36,837 | 110 | Syracuse, NY | 12,385 | 174 | Roanoke, VA | 6,180 |
| 47 | Salt Lake City, UT | 36,244 | 111 | Lakeland, FL | 12,280 | 175 | Amarillo, TX | 6,178 |
| 48 | Detroit-Dearborn-Livonia, MI M.D. | 35,484 | 112 | Fayetteville, NC | 12,166 | 176 | Waco, TX | 6,168 |
| 49 | Nashville-Davidson, TN | 34,923 | 113 | Springfield, MA | 12,130 | 177 | Fort Smith, AR-OK | 6,162 |
| 50 | Las Vegas-Henderson, NV | 34,302 | 114 | Myrtle Beach, SC-NC | 12,124 | 178 | Pueblo, CO | 6,112 |
| 51 | Milwaukee, WI | 33,908 | 115 | Lafayette, LA | 12,074 | 179 | Gainesville, FL | 6,095 |
| 52 | Oklahoma City, OK | 33,747 | 116 | Modesto, CA | 11,936 | 180 | Salinas, CA | 6,036 |
| 53 | Jacksonville, FL | 33,478 | 117 | Des Moines-West Des Moines, IA | 11,762 | 181 | Topeka, KS | 5,932 |
| 54 | Pittsburgh, PA | 33,343 | 118 | Worcester, MA-CT | 11,758 | 182 | Monroe, LA | 5,846 |
| 55 | Nassau-Suffolk, NY M.D. | 32,803 | 119 | Oxnard-Thousand Oaks, CA | 11,690 | 183 | Springfield, IL | 5,703 |
| 56 | Louisville, KY-IN | 30,252 | 120 | Ogden-Clearfield, UT | 11,614 | 184 | Santa Rosa, CA | 5,693 |
| 57 | West Palm Beach, FL M.D. | 30,030 | 121 | Brownsville-Harlingen, TX | 11,587 | 185 | Joplin, MO | 5,639 |
| 58 | Warren-Troy, MI M.D. | 29,938 | 122 | Shreveport-Bossier City, LA | 11,562 | 186 | Fort Collins, CO | 5,631 |
| 59 | Boston, MA M.D. | 29,920 | 123 | Lake Co.-Kenosha Co., IL-WI M.D. | 11,553 | 187 | Lake Charles, LA | 5,620 |
| 60 | Cambridge-Newton, MA M.D. | 29,160 | 124 | Madison, WI | 11,386 | 188 | Panama City, FL | 5,551 |
| 61 | Birmingham-Hoover, AL | 27,971 | 125 | Pensacola, FL | 11,099 | 189 | Ann Arbor, MI | 5,525 |
| 62 | New Orleans, LA | 27,676 | 126 | Palm Bay-Melbourne, FL | 10,952 | 190 | Boulder, CO | 5,514 |
| 63 | Montgomery County, PA M.D. | 26,866 | 127 | Anchorage, AK | 10,722 | 191 | Santa Cruz-Watsonville, CA | 5,477 |
| 64 | Newark, NJ-PA M.D. | 26,580 | 128 | Bridgeport-Stamford, CT | 10,644 | 192 | Tuscaloosa, AL | 5,422 |

Note: All listings are for Metropolitan Statistical Areas (M.S.A.s) except for those ending with "M.D." Listings with "M.D." are Metropolitan Divisions which are smaller parts of eleven large M.S.A.s. See explanatory note at beginning of metropolitan area section.

| RANK | METROPOLITAN AREA | THEFTS | RANK | METROPOLITAN AREA | THEFTS | RANK | METROPOLITAN AREA | THEFTS |
|---|---|---|---|---|---|---|---|---|
| 193 | Reading, PA | 5,421 | 254 | Charlottesville, VA | 3,439 | 317 | Sebastian-Vero Beach, FL | 2,215 |
| 194 | Warner Robins, GA | 5,376 | 256 | Burlington, NC | 3,433 | 318 | Eau Claire, WI | 2,212 |
| 195 | Binghamton, NY | 5,313 | 257 | Redding, CA | 3,396 | 319 | Sherman-Denison, TX | 2,189 |
| 196 | Bremerton-Silverdale, WA | 5,126 | 258 | Hot Springs, AR | 3,370 | 320 | Sebring, FL | 2,186 |
| 197 | Utica-Rome, NY | 5,101 | 259 | Rocky Mount, NC | 3,361 | 321 | Kankakee, IL | 2,160 |
| 198 | Houma, LA | 5,087 | 260 | Lawrence, KS | 3,334 | 322 | Columbus, IN | 2,142 |
| 199 | Longview, TX | 5,080 | 261 | Jackson, TN | 3,276 | 323 | Cape Girardeau, MO-IL | 2,136 |
| 200 | Yakima, WA | 4,958 | 262 | Bloomington, IN | 3,239 | 324 | Lewiston-Auburn, ME | 2,122 |
| 201 | Vineland-Bridgeton, NJ | 4,939 | 263 | Barnstable Town, MA | 3,219 | 325 | Pittsfield, MA | 2,095 |
| 202 | Alexandria, LA | 4,922 | 264 | Racine, WI | 3,180 | 326 | Grand Island, NE | 2,092 |
| 203 | Clarksville, TN-KY | 4,912 | 265 | Lynchburg, VA | 3,174 | 327 | Bismarck, ND | 2,081 |
| 204 | Trenton, NJ | 4,867 | 266 | Prescott, AZ | 3,158 | 328 | Winchester, VA-WV | 2,072 |
| 205 | Albany, GA | 4,813 | 267 | Florence-Muscle Shoals, AL | 3,103 | 329 | St. George, UT | 2,070 |
| 206 | Erie, PA | 4,804 | 268 | Grand Junction, CO | 3,101 | 330 | Cheyenne, WY | 2,069 |
| 207 | Billings, MT | 4,733 | 269 | Midland, TX | 3,056 | 331 | Carbondale-Marion, IL | 2,065 |
| 208 | Merced, CA | 4,657 | 270 | Brunswick, GA | 3,045 | 332 | Lebanon, PA | 2,049 |
| 209 | Las Cruces, NM | 4,637 | 271 | Ocean City, NJ | 3,044 | 333 | Pocatello, ID | 2,044 |
| 210 | Lake Havasu City-Kingman, AZ | 4,616 | 272 | San Rafael, CA M.D. | 3,009 | 334 | Cumberland, MD-WV | 2,031 |
| 211 | Muskegon, MI | 4,553 | 273 | Gainesville, GA | 3,005 | 335 | Mankato-North Mankato, MN | 1,995 |
| 212 | Olympia, WA | 4,548 | 274 | Bloomington, IL | 2,995 | 336 | La Crosse, WI-MN | 1,994 |
| 213 | Tyler, TX | 4,539 | 275 | San Angelo, TX | 2,994 | 337 | Homosassa Springs, FL | 1,989 |
| 214 | Kennewick-Richland, WA | 4,533 | 276 | Niles-Benton Harbor, MI | 2,983 | 338 | Farmington, NM | 1,969 |
| 215 | Odessa, TX | 4,498 | 277 | Albany, OR | 2,976 | 339 | Williamsport, PA | 1,949 |
| 216 | Columbia, MO | 4,497 | 278 | Janesville, WI | 2,969 | 340 | Owensboro, KY | 1,932 |
| 217 | Green Bay, WI | 4,474 | 279 | Rome, GA | 2,923 | 341 | Madera, CA | 1,930 |
| 218 | Crestview-Fort Walton Beach, FL | 4,469 | 280 | Jackson, MI | 2,910 | 342 | Watertown-Fort Drum, NY | 1,880 |
| 219 | Cedar Rapids, IA | 4,435 | 281 | Goldsboro, NC | 2,906 | 343 | Casper, WY | 1,879 |
| 220 | Athens-Clarke County, GA | 4,422 | 282 | Dothan, AL | 2,896 | 344 | Johnstown, PA | 1,853 |
| 221 | College Station-Bryan, TX | 4,383 | 283 | Jonesboro, AR | 2,892 | 345 | Corvallis, OR | 1,849 |
| 222 | Champaign-Urbana, IL | 4,326 | 284 | East Stroudsburg, PA | 2,886 | 346 | Decatur, IL | 1,832 |
| 223 | Kahului-Wailuku-Lahaina, HI | 4,314 | 285 | Dalton, GA | 2,879 | 347 | Idaho Falls, ID | 1,828 |
| 224 | Dutchess-Putnam, NY M.D. | 4,281 | 286 | Yuba City, CA | 2,866 | 348 | State College, PA | 1,824 |
| 225 | Sioux Falls, SD | 4,262 | 287 | Longview, WA | 2,859 | 349 | Kokomo, IN | 1,753 |
| 226 | Hammond, LA | 4,210 | 288 | Coeur d'Alene, ID | 2,845 | 350 | Sheboygan, WI | 1,740 |
| 227 | Lafayette, IN | 4,202 | 289 | Bowling Green, KY | 2,837 | 351 | Napa, CA | 1,732 |
| 228 | San Luis Obispo, CA | 4,167 | 290 | Muncie, IN | 2,821 | 352 | California-Lexington Park, MD | 1,730 |
| 229 | Texarkana, TX-AR | 4,132 | 291 | Anniston-Oxford, AL | 2,814 | 353 | Altoona, PA | 1,698 |
| 230 | Hagerstown-Martinsburg, MD-WV | 4,125 | 292 | Gadsden, AL | 2,805 | 354 | Grand Forks, ND-MN | 1,681 |
| 231 | Dover, DE | 4,104 | 293 | Blacksburg, VA | 2,795 | 354 | Morgantown, WV | 1,681 |
| 232 | Hilton Head Island, SC | 4,077 | 294 | Missoula, MT | 2,730 | 356 | Glens Falls, NY | 1,676 |
| 233 | Greeley, CO | 4,056 | 295 | Saginaw, MI | 2,708 | 357 | Elmira, NY | 1,670 |
| 234 | Springfield, OH | 4,010 | 296 | Decatur, AL | 2,698 | 358 | Elizabethtown-Fort Knox, KY | 1,640 |
| 235 | Mansfield, OH | 3,974 | 297 | Cleveland, TN | 2,669 | 359 | Bay City, MI | 1,636 |
| 236 | Greenville, NC | 3,958 | 298 | Morristown, TN | 2,652 | 360 | Staunton-Waynesboro, VA | 1,623 |
| 237 | Abilene, TX | 3,907 | 299 | Appleton, WI | 2,651 | 361 | Harrisonburg, VA | 1,603 |
| 238 | El Centro, CA | 3,886 | 300 | Norwich-New London, CT | 2,650 | 362 | Parkersburg-Vienna, WV | 1,586 |
| 239 | Naples-Marco Island, FL | 3,884 | 301 | Kingston, NY | 2,636 | 363 | Wausau, WI | 1,565 |
| 240 | Terre Haute, IN | 3,861 | 302 | Rochester, MN | 2,625 | 364 | Ames, IA | 1,561 |
| 241 | Wichita Falls, TX | 3,844 | 303 | Punta Gorda, FL | 2,511 | 365 | Lewiston, ID-WA | 1,531 |
| 242 | Johnson City, TN | 3,828 | 304 | Lima, OH | 2,499 | 366 | Hinesville, GA | 1,499 |
| 243 | St. Cloud, MN | 3,812 | 305 | Iowa City, IA | 2,466 | 367 | Fond du Lac, WI | 1,355 |
| 244 | Daphne-Fairhope-Foley, AL | 3,749 | 306 | Monroe, MI | 2,442 | 368 | Manhattan, KS | 1,336 |
| 245 | St. Joseph, MO-KS | 3,722 | 306 | Rapid City, SD | 2,442 | 369 | Dubuque, IA | 1,332 |
| 246 | Fargo, ND-MN | 3,694 | 308 | Jefferson City, MO | 2,418 | 370 | Logan, UT-ID | 1,227 |
| 247 | Mount Vernon-Anacortes, WA | 3,659 | 309 | Oshkosh-Neenah, WI | 2,416 | 371 | Fairbanks, AK | 1,190 |
| 248 | Chico, CA | 3,642 | 310 | Hanford-Corcoran, CA | 2,413 | 372 | Bloomsburg-Berwick, PA | 1,129 |
| 249 | Flagstaff, AZ | 3,594 | 311 | Great Falls, MT | 2,374 | 373 | Gettysburg, PA | 952 |
| 250 | Sioux City, IA-NE-SD | 3,549 | 312 | Chambersburg-Waynesboro, PA | 2,314 | 374 | The Villages, FL | 658 |
| 251 | Lawton, OK | 3,541 | 313 | Victoria, TX | 2,312 | 375 | Carson City, NV | 654 |
| 252 | Yuma, AZ | 3,449 | 314 | New Bern, NC | 2,298 | NA | Ocala, FL** | NA |
| 253 | Bend, OR | 3,443 | 315 | Sumter, SC | 2,277 | NA | Toledo, OH** | NA |
| 254 | Bangor, ME | 3,439 | 316 | Grants Pass, OR | 2,229 | | | |

Source: Reported data from the F.B.I. "Crime in the United States 2013"

*Larceny-theft is the unlawful taking of property. Attempts are included.

**Not available.

# 34. Larceny-Theft Rate in 2013
## National Rate = 1,899.4 Larceny-Thefts per 100,000 Population*

| RANK | METROPOLITAN AREA | RATE | RANK | METROPOLITAN AREA | RATE | RANK | METROPOLITAN AREA | RATE |
|---|---|---|---|---|---|---|---|---|
| 110 | Abilene, TX | 2,324.0 | 151 | Cheyenne, WY | 2,163.4 | 172 | Gary, IN M.D. | 2,070.7 |
| 174 | Akron, OH | 2,064.1 | 251 | Chicago (greater), IL-IN-WI | 1,716.4 | 374 | Gettysburg, PA | 938.5 |
| 228 | Albany-Schenectady-Troy, NY | 1,800.4 | 236 | Chicago-Naperville, IL M.D. | 1,769.2 | 348 | Glens Falls, NY | 1,304.7 |
| 27 | Albany, GA | 3,058.5 | 275 | Chico, CA | 1,637.8 | 111 | Goldsboro, NC | 2,323.3 |
| 78 | Albany, OR | 2,497.6 | 125 | Cincinnati, OH-KY-IN | 2,252.9 | 265 | Grand Forks, ND-MN | 1,672.6 |
| 38 | Albuquerque, NM | 2,910.6 | 241 | Clarksville, TN-KY | 1,761.0 | 79 | Grand Island, NE | 2,485.8 |
| 20 | Alexandria, LA | 3,182.1 | 126 | Cleveland, TN | 2,251.4 | 168 | Grand Junction, CO | 2,077.8 |
| 272 | Allentown, PA-NJ | 1,647.9 | 196 | Coeur d'Alene, ID | 1,972.6 | 318 | Grand Rapids-Wyoming, MI | 1,438.8 |
| 339 | Altoona, PA | 1,336.2 | 217 | College Station-Bryan, TX | 1,848.0 | 58 | Grants Pass, OR | 2,680.3 |
| 103 | Amarillo, TX | 2,373.4 | 129 | Colorado Springs, CO | 2,243.3 | 40 | Great Falls, MT | 2,888.2 |
| 257 | Ames, IA | 1,698.6 | 65 | Columbia, MO | 2,634.1 | 308 | Greeley, CO | 1,509.7 |
| 324 | Anaheim-Santa Ana-Irvine, CA M.D. | 1,410.9 | 73 | Columbia, SC | 2,552.2 | 319 | Green Bay, WI | 1,430.4 |
| 6 | Anchorage, AK | 3,408.6 | 23 | Columbus, GA-AL | 3,139.9 | 113 | Greensboro-High Point, NC | 2,313.2 |
| 290 | Ann Arbor, MI | 1,564.3 | 61 | Columbus, IN | 2,674.1 | 51 | Greenville-Anderson, SC | 2,708.7 |
| 91 | Anniston-Oxford, AL | 2,407.3 | 12 | Corpus Christi, TX | 3,254.0 | 121 | Greenville, NC | 2,270.1 |
| 366 | Appleton, WI | 1,155.3 | 159 | Corvallis, OR | 2,126.5 | 81 | Gulfport-Biloxi-Pascagoula, MS | 2,480.3 |
| 131 | Athens-Clarke County, GA | 2,239.7 | 237 | Crestview-Fort Walton Beach, FL | 1,768.9 | 284 | Hagerstown-Martinsburg, MD-WV | 1,600.4 |
| 146 | Atlanta, GA | 2,184.4 | 185 | Cumberland, MD-WV | 1,997.8 | 8 | Hammond, LA | 3,389.5 |
| 123 | Atlantic City, NJ | 2,255.0 | 171 | Dallas (greater), TX | 2,071.8 | 285 | Hanford-Corcoran, CA | 1,595.3 |
| 82 | Augusta, GA-SC | 2,477.7 | 206 | Dallas-Plano-Irving, TX M.D. | 1,916.5 | 358 | Harrisonburg, VA | 1,236.0 |
| 80 | Austin-Round Rock, TX | 2,485.7 | 183 | Dalton, GA | 2,014.7 | 273 | Hartford, CT | 1,646.1 |
| 202 | Bakersfield, CA | 1,954.4 | 204 | Daphne-Fairhope-Foley, AL | 1,939.3 | 170 | Hilton Head Island, SC | 2,071.9 |
| 155 | Baltimore, MD | 2,155.2 | 212 | Davenport, IA-IL | 1,886.4 | 227 | Hinesville, GA | 1,806.9 |
| 130 | Bangor, ME | 2,240.0 | 117 | Dayton, OH | 2,282.6 | 320 | Homosassa Springs, FL | 1,428.4 |
| 311 | Barnstable Town, MA | 1,491.3 | 244 | Decatur, AL | 1,748.4 | 4 | Hot Springs, AR | 3,468.4 |
| 52 | Baton Rouge, LA | 2,707.6 | 266 | Decatur, IL | 1,667.3 | 86 | Houma, LA | 2,430.2 |
| 299 | Bay City, MI | 1,532.1 | 134 | Deltona-Daytona Beach, FL | 2,231.9 | 108 | Houston, TX | 2,327.6 |
| 149 | Beaumont-Port Arthur, TX | 2,169.9 | 192 | Denver-Aurora, CO | 1,985.1 | 96 | Huntsville, AL | 2,391.9 |
| 164 | Bend, OR | 2,097.1 | 197 | Des Moines-West Des Moines, IA | 1,972.2 | 341 | Idaho Falls, ID | 1,328.9 |
| 42 | Billings, MT | 2,871.2 | 305 | Detroit (greater), MI | 1,522.6 | 128 | Indianapolis, IN | 2,249.6 |
| 157 | Binghamton, NY | 2,143.5 | 190 | Detroit-Dearborn-Livonia, MI M.D. | 1,986.2 | 298 | Iowa City, IA | 1,537.0 |
| 84 | Birmingham-Hoover, AL | 2,455.9 | 201 | Dothan, AL | 1,954.6 | 93 | Jacksonville, FL | 2,403.5 |
| 263 | Bismarck, ND | 1,675.0 | 88 | Dover, DE | 2,418.0 | 225 | Jackson, MI | 1,813.1 |
| 292 | Blacksburg, VA | 1,556.9 | 330 | Dubuque, IA | 1,391.1 | 221 | Jackson, MS | 1,830.6 |
| 286 | Bloomington, IL | 1,581.2 | 66 | Duluth, MN-WI | 2,628.8 | 77 | Jackson, TN | 2,506.5 |
| 194 | Bloomington, IN | 1,979.9 | 371 | Dutchess-Putnam, NY M.D. | 1,077.8 | 216 | Janesville, WI | 1,848.9 |
| 343 | Bloomsburg-Berwick, PA | 1,327.1 | 252 | East Stroudsburg, PA | 1,714.7 | 281 | Jefferson City, MO | 1,606.2 |
| 349 | Boise City, ID | 1,263.5 | 337 | Eau Claire, WI | 1,345.0 | 210 | Johnson City, TN | 1,900.3 |
| 323 | Boston (greater), MA-NH | 1,411.5 | 147 | El Centro, CA | 2,183.7 | 345 | Johnstown, PA | 1,315.3 |
| 297 | Boston, MA M.D. | 1,540.4 | 234 | El Paso, TX | 1,781.6 | 114 | Jonesboro, AR | 2,312.8 |
| 235 | Boulder, CO | 1,776.8 | 356 | Elgin, IL M.D. | 1,238.8 | 16 | Joplin, MO | 3,237.0 |
| 246 | Bowling Green, KY | 1,735.8 | 370 | Elizabethtown-Fort Knox, KY | 1,088.3 | 54 | Kahului-Wailuku-Lahaina, HI | 2,702.1 |
| 186 | Bremerton-Silverdale, WA | 1,995.4 | 213 | Elmira, NY | 1,875.6 | 207 | Kankakee, IL | 1,914.1 |
| 365 | Bridgeport-Stamford, CT | 1,155.6 | 253 | Erie, PA | 1,713.0 | 150 | Kansas City, MO-KS | 2,169.2 |
| 45 | Brownsville-Harlingen, TX | 2,759.2 | 53 | Eugene, OR | 2,706.3 | 271 | Kennewick-Richland, WA | 1,657.4 |
| 59 | Brunswick, GA | 2,677.1 | 5 | Fairbanks, AK | 3,425.3 | 173 | Kingsport, TN-VA | 2,064.7 |
| 180 | Buffalo-Niagara Falls, NY | 2,030.4 | 267 | Fargo, ND-MN | 1,662.7 | 316 | Kingston, NY | 1,449.9 |
| 142 | Burlington, NC | 2,211.8 | 294 | Farmington, NM | 1,543.7 | 140 | Knoxville, TN | 2,216.2 |
| 288 | California-Lexington Park, MD | 1,568.5 | 238 | Fayetteville-Springdale, AR-MO | 1,768.5 | 162 | Kokomo, IN | 2,109.3 |
| 351 | Cambridge-Newton, MA M.D. | 1,260.6 | 18 | Fayetteville, NC | 3,217.9 | 315 | La Crosse, WI-MN | 1,467.1 |
| 262 | Camden, NJ M.D. | 1,681.6 | 67 | Flagstaff, AZ | 2,623.4 | 182 | Lafayette, IN | 2,015.6 |
| 219 | Canton, OH | 1,839.9 | 258 | Flint, MI | 1,694.4 | 75 | Lafayette, LA | 2,530.4 |
| 310 | Cape Coral-Fort Myers, FL | 1,494.6 | 161 | Florence-Muscle Shoals, AL | 2,112.6 | 44 | Lake Charles, LA | 2,785.8 |
| 144 | Cape Girardeau, MO-IL | 2,190.5 | 13 | Florence, SC | 3,248.5 | 342 | Lake Co.-Kenosha Co., IL-WI M.D. | 1,328.5 |
| 277 | Carbondale-Marion, IL | 1,630.0 | 340 | Fond du Lac, WI | 1,329.0 | 127 | Lake Havasu City-Kingman, AZ | 2,250.6 |
| 361 | Carson City, NV | 1,190.5 | 233 | Fort Collins, CO | 1,782.5 | 198 | Lakeland, FL | 1,971.6 |
| 105 | Casper, WY | 2,349.0 | 100 | Fort Lauderdale, FL M.D. | 2,379.1 | 313 | Lancaster, PA | 1,478.0 |
| 261 | Cedar Rapids, IA | 1,682.6 | 143 | Fort Smith, AR-OK | 2,193.4 | 304 | Lansing-East Lansing, MI | 1,524.2 |
| 303 | Chambersburg-Waynesboro, PA | 1,525.9 | 160 | Fort Wayne, IN | 2,114.5 | 7 | Laredo, TX | 3,404.6 |
| 218 | Champaign-Urbana, IL | 1,847.0 | 101 | Fort Worth-Arlington, TX M.D. | 2,375.0 | 154 | Las Cruces, NM | 2,155.9 |
| 116 | Charleston-North Charleston, SC | 2,289.0 | 136 | Fresno, CA | 2,227.5 | 259 | Las Vegas-Henderson, NV | 1,693.2 |
| 158 | Charlotte-Mecklenburg, NC-SC | 2,141.0 | 55 | Gadsden, AL | 2,688.2 | 35 | Lawrence, KS | 2,940.8 |
| 301 | Charlottesville, VA | 1,530.7 | 124 | Gainesville, FL | 2,253.0 | 62 | Lawton, OK | 2,653.4 |
| 47 | Chattanooga, TN-GA | 2,740.8 | 282 | Gainesville, GA | 1,604.5 | 307 | Lebanon, PA | 1,510.1 |

Note: All listings are for Metropolitan Statistical Areas (M.S.A.s) except for those ending with "M.D." Listings with "M.D." are Metropolitan Divisions which are smaller parts of eleven large M.S.A.s. See explanatory note at beginning of metropolitan area section.

| RANK | METROPOLITAN AREA | RATE | RANK | METROPOLITAN AREA | RATE | RANK | METROPOLITAN AREA | RATE |
|---|---|---|---|---|---|---|---|---|
| 195 | Lewiston-Auburn, ME | 1,974.5 | 148 | Omaha-Council Bluffs, NE-IA | 2,173.4 | 306 | Sheboygan, WI | 1,513.7 |
| 83 | Lewiston, ID-WA | 2,476.5 | 106 | Orlando, FL | 2,335.4 | 231 | Sherman-Denison, TX | 1,783.6 |
| 48 | Lexington-Fayette, KY | 2,735.2 | 321 | Oshkosh-Neenah, WI | 1,425.5 | 71 | Shreveport-Bossier City, LA | 2,571.6 |
| 98 | Lima, OH | 2,380.0 | 270 | Owensboro, KY | 1,657.9 | 352 | Silver Spring-Frederick, MD M.D. | 1,260.5 |
| 69 | Lincoln, NE | 2,600.3 | 331 | Oxnard-Thousand Oaks, CA | 1,390.5 | 166 | Sioux City, IA-NE-SD | 2,094.5 |
| 10 | Little Rock, AR | 3,316.4 | 189 | Palm Bay-Melbourne, FL | 1,989.5 | 240 | Sioux Falls, SD | 1,763.8 |
| 373 | Logan, UT-ID | 944.9 | 36 | Panama City, FL | 2,934.3 | 163 | South Bend-Mishawaka, IN-MI | 2,101.2 |
| 109 | Longview, TX | 2,327.4 | 250 | Parkersburg-Vienna, WV | 1,716.5 | 152 | Spartanburg, SC | 2,158.6 |
| 43 | Longview, WA | 2,798.3 | 99 | Pensacola, FL | 2,379.6 | 1 | Spokane, WA | 3,923.8 |
| 326 | Los Angeles County, CA M.D. | 1,410.0 | 264 | Peoria, IL | 1,674.6 | 56 | Springfield, IL | 2,685.2 |
| 325 | Los Angeles (greater), CA | 1,410.2 | 220 | Philadelphia (greater) PA-NJ-MD-DE | 1,833.3 | 205 | Springfield, MA | 1,930.6 |
| 92 | Louisville, KY-IN | 2,405.9 | 133 | Philadelphia, PA M.D. | 2,232.8 | 9 | Springfield, MO | 3,373.4 |
| 34 | Lubbock, TX | 2,961.7 | 138 | Phoenix-Mesa-Scottsdale, AZ | 2,219.4 | 37 | Springfield, OH | 2,923.7 |
| 359 | Lynchburg, VA | 1,235.8 | 322 | Pittsburgh, PA | 1,412.4 | 362 | State College, PA | 1,173.7 |
| 19 | Macon, GA | 3,196.8 | 280 | Pittsfield, MA | 1,611.8 | 335 | Staunton-Waynesboro, VA | 1,363.1 |
| 350 | Madera, CA | 1,263.3 | 87 | Pocatello, ID | 2,419.5 | 90 | Stockton-Lodi, CA | 2,408.6 |
| 223 | Madison, WI | 1,818.7 | 295 | Port St. Lucie, FL | 1,542.9 | 188 | St. Cloud, MN | 1,990.3 |
| 222 | Manchester-Nashua, NH | 1,823.3 | 138 | Portland-Vancouver, OR-WA | 2,219.4 | 329 | St. George, UT | 1,399.4 |
| 338 | Manhattan, KS | 1,344.8 | 239 | Portland, ME | 1,767.5 | 39 | St. Joseph, MO-KS | 2,898.2 |
| 181 | Mankato-North Mankato, MN | 2,020.2 | 314 | Prescott, AZ | 1,474.0 | 208 | St. Louis, MO-IL | 1,912.9 |
| 14 | Mansfield, OH | 3,246.0 | 278 | Providence-Warwick, RI-MA | 1,621.0 | 165 | Sumter, SC | 2,094.7 |
| 50 | McAllen-Edinburg-Mission, TX | 2,720.3 | 289 | Provo-Orem, UT | 1,564.4 | 214 | Syracuse, NY | 1,873.5 |
| 15 | Medford, OR | 3,241.0 | 3 | Pueblo, CO | 3,765.9 | 68 | Tacoma, WA M.D. | 2,616.2 |
| 49 | Memphis, TN-MS-AR | 2,733.1 | 300 | Punta Gorda, FL | 1,531.7 | 102 | Tallahassee, FL | 2,374.2 |
| 242 | Merced, CA | 1,760.7 | 276 | Racine, WI | 1,633.2 | 200 | Tampa-St Petersburg, FL | 1,959.0 |
| 60 | Miami (greater), FL | 2,674.6 | 283 | Raleigh, NC | 1,600.9 | 135 | Terre Haute, IN | 2,231.8 |
| 24 | Miami-Dade County, FL M.D. | 3,135.8 | 247 | Rapid City, SD | 1,732.8 | 46 | Texarkana, TX-AR | 2,750.6 |
| 199 | Midland, TX | 1,961.8 | 347 | Reading, PA | 1,310.0 | 375 | The Villages, FL | 629.0 |
| 153 | Milwaukee, WI | 2,157.7 | 211 | Redding, CA | 1,894.6 | NA | Toledo, OH** | NA |
| 190 | Minneapolis-St. Paul, MN-WI | 1,986.2 | 243 | Reno, NV | 1,748.7 | 76 | Topeka, KS | 2,528.9 |
| 85 | Missoula, MT | 2,436.4 | 230 | Richmond, VA | 1,797.4 | 344 | Trenton, NJ | 1,317.9 |
| 30 | Mobile, AL | 3,019.8 | 296 | Riverside-San Bernardino, CA | 1,541.1 | 2 | Tucson, AZ | 3,791.0 |
| 119 | Modesto, CA | 2,275.3 | 192 | Roanoke, VA | 1,985.1 | 175 | Tulsa, OK | 2,058.3 |
| 11 | Monroe, LA | 3,278.9 | 354 | Rochester, MN | 1,243.2 | 112 | Tuscaloosa, AL | 2,313.6 |
| 279 | Monroe, MI | 1,618.3 | 229 | Rochester, NY | 1,799.9 | 167 | Tyler, TX | 2,089.8 |
| 332 | Montgomery County, PA M.D. | 1,380.4 | 176 | Rockford, IL | 2,055.6 | 254 | Utica-Rome, NY | 1,711.8 |
| 355 | Morgantown, WV | 1,241.9 | 274 | Rockingham County, NH M.D. | 1,645.0 | 302 | Vallejo-Fairfield, CA | 1,528.2 |
| 115 | Morristown, TN | 2,299.3 | 141 | Rocky Mount, NC | 2,213.3 | 104 | Victoria, TX | 2,361.6 |
| 26 | Mount Vernon-Anacortes, WA | 3,074.7 | 29 | Rome, GA | 3,040.9 | 25 | Vineland-Bridgeton, NJ | 3,120.4 |
| 94 | Muncie, IN | 2,399.2 | 249 | Sacramento, CA | 1,723.2 | 107 | Virginia Beach-Norfolk, VA-NC | 2,334.8 |
| 57 | Muskegon, MI | 2,682.0 | 334 | Saginaw, MI | 1,367.5 | 248 | Visalia-Porterville, CA | 1,727.6 |
| 31 | Myrtle Beach, SC-NC | 3,018.7 | 89 | Salem, OR | 2,416.5 | 97 | Waco, TX | 2,388.5 |
| 357 | Napa, CA | 1,237.3 | 328 | Salinas, CA | 1,400.8 | 41 | Warner Robins, GA | 2,871.3 |
| 367 | Naples-Marco Island, FL | 1,152.4 | 118 | Salisbury, MD-DE | 2,282.4 | 360 | Warren-Troy, MI M.D. | 1,192.7 |
| 184 | Nashville-Davidson, TN | 2,000.6 | 21 | Salt Lake City, UT | 3,174.4 | 260 | Washington (greater) DC-VA-MD-WV | 1,692.1 |
| 369 | Nassau-Suffolk, NY M.D. | 1,148.6 | 70 | San Angelo, TX | 2,576.3 | 226 | Washington, DC-VA-MD-WV M.D. | 1,808.1 |
| 232 | New Bern, NC | 1,783.4 | 17 | San Antonio, TX | 3,226.3 | 293 | Watertown-Fort Drum, NY | 1,545.3 |
| 169 | New Haven-Milford, CT | 2,075.0 | 327 | San Diego, CA | 1,404.6 | 364 | Wausau, WI | 1,158.9 |
| 132 | New Orleans, LA | 2,233.5 | 120 | San Francisco (greater), CA | 2,271.0 | 145 | West Palm Beach, FL M.D. | 2,187.6 |
| 353 | New York (greater), NY-NJ-PA | 1,254.4 | 32 | San Francisco-Redwood, CA M.D. | 3,006.2 | 74 | Wichita Falls, TX | 2,541.4 |
| 346 | New York-Jersey City, NY-NJ M.D. | 1,314.1 | 336 | San Jose, CA | 1,359.9 | 33 | Wichita, KS | 2,967.6 |
| 372 | Newark, NJ-PA M.D. | 1,064.2 | 309 | San Luis Obispo, CA | 1,505.3 | 269 | Williamsport, PA | 1,659.6 |
| 209 | Niles-Benton Harbor, MI | 1,912.4 | 363 | San Rafael, CA M.D. | 1,168.7 | 156 | Wilmington, DE-MD-NJ M.D. | 2,150.5 |
| 178 | North Port-Sarasota-Bradenton, FL | 2,043.5 | 179 | Santa Cruz-Watsonville, CA | 2,041.7 | 95 | Wilmington, NC | 2,392.5 |
| 224 | Norwich-New London, CT | 1,813.2 | 312 | Santa Maria-Santa Barbara, CA | 1,480.8 | 287 | Winchester, VA-WV | 1,571.1 |
| 203 | Oakland-Hayward, CA M.D. | 1,940.8 | 368 | Santa Rosa, CA | 1,150.4 | 122 | Winston-Salem, NC | 2,265.8 |
| NA | Ocala, FL** | NA | 177 | Savannah, GA | 2,049.7 | 333 | Worcester, MA-CT | 1,378.6 |
| 22 | Ocean City, NJ | 3,166.4 | 268 | Scranton--Wilkes-Barre, PA | 1,661.4 | 187 | Yakima, WA | 1,993.7 |
| 28 | Odessa, TX | 3,050.6 | 64 | Seattle (greater), WA | 2,639.6 | 317 | York-Hanover, PA | 1,445.0 |
| 215 | Ogden-Clearfield, UT | 1,871.3 | 63 | Seattle-Bellevue-Everett, WA M.D. | 2,646.5 | 256 | Yuba City, CA | 1,701.8 |
| 72 | Oklahoma City, OK | 2,565.3 | 291 | Sebastian-Vero Beach, FL | 1,561.1 | 255 | Yuma, AZ | 1,708.5 |
| 245 | Olympia, WA | 1,742.9 | 137 | Sebring, FL | 2,223.8 | | | |

Source: Reported data from the F.B.I. "Crime in the United States 2013"

*Larceny-theft is the unlawful taking of property. Attempts are included.

**Not available.

# 34. Larceny-Theft Rate in 2013 (continued)
## National Rate = 1,899.4 Larceny-Thefts per 100,000 Population*

| RANK | METROPOLITAN AREA | RATE | RANK | METROPOLITAN AREA | RATE | RANK | METROPOLITAN AREA | RATE |
|---|---|---|---|---|---|---|---|---|
| 1 | Spokane, WA | 3,923.8 | 65 | Columbia, MO | 2,634.1 | 129 | Colorado Springs, CO | 2,243.3 |
| 2 | Tucson, AZ | 3,791.0 | 66 | Duluth, MN-WI | 2,628.8 | 130 | Bangor, ME | 2,240.0 |
| 3 | Pueblo, CO | 3,765.9 | 67 | Flagstaff, AZ | 2,623.4 | 131 | Athens-Clarke County, GA | 2,239.7 |
| 4 | Hot Springs, AR | 3,468.4 | 68 | Tacoma, WA M.D. | 2,616.2 | 132 | New Orleans, LA | 2,233.5 |
| 5 | Fairbanks, AK | 3,425.3 | 69 | Lincoln, NE | 2,600.3 | 133 | Philadelphia, PA M.D. | 2,232.8 |
| 6 | Anchorage, AK | 3,408.6 | 70 | San Angelo, TX | 2,576.3 | 134 | Deltona-Daytona Beach, FL | 2,231.9 |
| 7 | Laredo, TX | 3,404.6 | 71 | Shreveport-Bossier City, LA | 2,571.6 | 135 | Terre Haute, IN | 2,231.8 |
| 8 | Hammond, LA | 3,389.5 | 72 | Oklahoma City, OK | 2,565.3 | 136 | Fresno, CA | 2,227.5 |
| 9 | Springfield, MO | 3,373.4 | 73 | Columbia, SC | 2,552.2 | 137 | Sebring, FL | 2,223.8 |
| 10 | Little Rock, AR | 3,316.4 | 74 | Wichita Falls, TX | 2,541.4 | 138 | Phoenix-Mesa-Scottsdale, AZ | 2,219.4 |
| 11 | Monroe, LA | 3,278.9 | 75 | Lafayette, LA | 2,530.4 | 138 | Portland-Vancouver, OR-WA | 2,219.4 |
| 12 | Corpus Christi, TX | 3,254.0 | 76 | Topeka, KS | 2,528.9 | 140 | Knoxville, TN | 2,216.2 |
| 13 | Florence, SC | 3,248.5 | 77 | Jackson, TN | 2,506.5 | 141 | Rocky Mount, NC | 2,213.3 |
| 14 | Mansfield, OH | 3,246.0 | 78 | Albany, OR | 2,497.6 | 142 | Burlington, NC | 2,211.8 |
| 15 | Medford, OR | 3,241.0 | 79 | Grand Island, NE | 2,485.8 | 143 | Fort Smith, AR-OK | 2,193.4 |
| 16 | Joplin, MO | 3,237.0 | 80 | Austin-Round Rock, TX | 2,485.7 | 144 | Cape Girardeau, MO-IL | 2,190.5 |
| 17 | San Antonio, TX | 3,226.3 | 81 | Gulfport-Biloxi-Pascagoula, MS | 2,480.3 | 145 | West Palm Beach, FL M.D. | 2,187.6 |
| 18 | Fayetteville, NC | 3,217.9 | 82 | Augusta, GA-SC | 2,477.7 | 146 | Atlanta, GA | 2,184.4 |
| 19 | Macon, GA | 3,196.8 | 83 | Lewiston, ID-WA | 2,476.5 | 147 | El Centro, CA | 2,183.7 |
| 20 | Alexandria, LA | 3,182.1 | 84 | Birmingham-Hoover, AL | 2,455.9 | 148 | Omaha-Council Bluffs, NE-IA | 2,173.4 |
| 21 | Salt Lake City, UT | 3,174.4 | 85 | Missoula, MT | 2,436.4 | 149 | Beaumont-Port Arthur, TX | 2,169.9 |
| 22 | Ocean City, NJ | 3,166.4 | 86 | Houma, LA | 2,430.2 | 150 | Kansas City, MO-KS | 2,169.2 |
| 23 | Columbus, GA-AL | 3,139.9 | 87 | Pocatello, ID | 2,419.5 | 151 | Cheyenne, WY | 2,163.4 |
| 24 | Miami-Dade County, FL M.D. | 3,135.8 | 88 | Dover, DE | 2,418.0 | 152 | Spartanburg, SC | 2,158.6 |
| 25 | Vineland-Bridgeton, NJ | 3,120.4 | 89 | Salem, OR | 2,416.5 | 153 | Milwaukee, WI | 2,157.7 |
| 26 | Mount Vernon-Anacortes, WA | 3,074.7 | 90 | Stockton-Lodi, CA | 2,408.6 | 154 | Las Cruces, NM | 2,155.9 |
| 27 | Albany, GA | 3,058.5 | 91 | Anniston-Oxford, AL | 2,407.3 | 155 | Baltimore, MD | 2,155.2 |
| 28 | Odessa, TX | 3,050.6 | 92 | Louisville, KY-IN | 2,405.9 | 156 | Wilmington, DE-MD-NJ M.D. | 2,150.5 |
| 29 | Rome, GA | 3,040.9 | 93 | Jacksonville, FL | 2,403.5 | 157 | Binghamton, NY | 2,143.5 |
| 30 | Mobile, AL | 3,019.8 | 94 | Muncie, IN | 2,399.2 | 158 | Charlotte-Mecklenburg, NC-SC | 2,141.0 |
| 31 | Myrtle Beach, SC-NC | 3,018.7 | 95 | Wilmington, NC | 2,392.5 | 159 | Corvallis, OR | 2,126.5 |
| 32 | San Francisco-Redwood, CA M.D. | 3,006.2 | 96 | Huntsville, AL | 2,391.9 | 160 | Fort Wayne, IN | 2,114.5 |
| 33 | Wichita, KS | 2,967.6 | 97 | Waco, TX | 2,388.5 | 161 | Florence-Muscle Shoals, AL | 2,112.6 |
| 34 | Lubbock, TX | 2,961.7 | 98 | Lima, OH | 2,380.0 | 162 | Kokomo, IN | 2,109.3 |
| 35 | Lawrence, KS | 2,940.8 | 99 | Pensacola, FL | 2,379.6 | 163 | South Bend-Mishawaka, IN-MI | 2,101.2 |
| 36 | Panama City, FL | 2,934.3 | 100 | Fort Lauderdale, FL M.D. | 2,379.1 | 164 | Bend, OR | 2,097.1 |
| 37 | Springfield, OH | 2,923.7 | 101 | Fort Worth-Arlington, TX M.D. | 2,375.0 | 165 | Sumter, SC | 2,094.7 |
| 38 | Albuquerque, NM | 2,910.6 | 102 | Tallahassee, FL | 2,374.2 | 166 | Sioux City, IA-NE-SD | 2,094.5 |
| 39 | St. Joseph, MO-KS | 2,898.2 | 103 | Amarillo, TX | 2,373.4 | 167 | Tyler, TX | 2,089.8 |
| 40 | Great Falls, MT | 2,888.2 | 104 | Victoria, TX | 2,361.6 | 168 | Grand Junction, CO | 2,077.8 |
| 41 | Warner Robins, GA | 2,871.3 | 105 | Casper, WY | 2,349.0 | 169 | New Haven-Milford, CT | 2,075.0 |
| 42 | Billings, MT | 2,871.2 | 106 | Orlando, FL | 2,335.4 | 170 | Hilton Head Island, SC | 2,071.9 |
| 43 | Longview, WA | 2,798.3 | 107 | Virginia Beach-Norfolk, VA-NC | 2,334.8 | 171 | Dallas (greater), TX | 2,071.8 |
| 44 | Lake Charles, LA | 2,785.8 | 108 | Houston, TX | 2,327.6 | 172 | Gary, IN M.D. | 2,070.7 |
| 45 | Brownsville-Harlingen, TX | 2,759.2 | 109 | Longview, TX | 2,327.4 | 173 | Kingsport, TN-VA | 2,064.7 |
| 46 | Texarkana, TX-AR | 2,750.6 | 110 | Abilene, TX | 2,324.0 | 174 | Akron, OH | 2,064.1 |
| 47 | Chattanooga, TN-GA | 2,740.8 | 111 | Goldsboro, NC | 2,323.3 | 175 | Tulsa, OK | 2,058.3 |
| 48 | Lexington-Fayette, KY | 2,735.2 | 112 | Tuscaloosa, AL | 2,313.6 | 176 | Rockford, IL | 2,055.6 |
| 49 | Memphis, TN-MS-AR | 2,733.1 | 113 | Greensboro-High Point, NC | 2,313.2 | 177 | Savannah, GA | 2,049.7 |
| 50 | McAllen-Edinburg-Mission, TX | 2,720.3 | 114 | Jonesboro, AR | 2,312.8 | 178 | North Port-Sarasota-Bradenton, FL | 2,043.5 |
| 51 | Greenville-Anderson, SC | 2,708.7 | 115 | Morristown, TN | 2,299.3 | 179 | Santa Cruz-Watsonville, CA | 2,041.7 |
| 52 | Baton Rouge, LA | 2,707.6 | 116 | Charleston-North Charleston, SC | 2,289.0 | 180 | Buffalo-Niagara Falls, NY | 2,030.4 |
| 53 | Eugene, OR | 2,706.3 | 117 | Dayton, OH | 2,282.6 | 181 | Mankato-North Mankato, MN | 2,020.2 |
| 54 | Kahului-Wailuku-Lahaina, HI | 2,702.1 | 118 | Salisbury, MD-DE | 2,282.4 | 182 | Lafayette, IN | 2,015.6 |
| 55 | Gadsden, AL | 2,688.2 | 119 | Modesto, CA | 2,275.3 | 183 | Dalton, GA | 2,014.7 |
| 56 | Springfield, IL | 2,685.2 | 120 | San Francisco (greater), CA | 2,271.0 | 184 | Nashville-Davidson, TN | 2,000.6 |
| 57 | Muskegon, MI | 2,682.0 | 121 | Greenville, NC | 2,270.1 | 185 | Cumberland, MD-WV | 1,997.8 |
| 58 | Grants Pass, OR | 2,680.3 | 122 | Winston-Salem, NC | 2,265.8 | 186 | Bremerton-Silverdale, WA | 1,995.4 |
| 59 | Brunswick, GA | 2,677.1 | 123 | Atlantic City, NJ | 2,255.0 | 187 | Yakima, WA | 1,993.7 |
| 60 | Miami (greater), FL | 2,674.6 | 124 | Gainesville, FL | 2,253.0 | 188 | St. Cloud, MN | 1,990.3 |
| 61 | Columbus, IN | 2,674.1 | 125 | Cincinnati, OH-KY-IN | 2,252.9 | 189 | Palm Bay-Melbourne, FL | 1,989.5 |
| 62 | Lawton, OK | 2,653.4 | 126 | Cleveland, TN | 2,251.4 | 190 | Detroit-Dearborn-Livonia, MI M.D. | 1,986.2 |
| 63 | Seattle-Bellevue-Everett, WA M.D. | 2,646.5 | 127 | Lake Havasu City-Kingman, AZ | 2,250.6 | 190 | Minneapolis-St. Paul, MN-WI | 1,986.2 |
| 64 | Seattle (greater), WA | 2,639.6 | 128 | Indianapolis, IN | 2,249.6 | 192 | Denver-Aurora, CO | 1,985.1 |

Note: All listings are for Metropolitan Statistical Areas (M.S.A.s) except for those ending with "M.D." Listings with "M.D." are Metropolitan Divisions which are smaller parts of eleven large M.S.A.s. See explanatory note at beginning of metropolitan area section.

| RANK | METROPOLITAN AREA | RATE | RANK | METROPOLITAN AREA | RATE | RANK | METROPOLITAN AREA | RATE |
|---|---|---|---|---|---|---|---|---|
| 192 | Roanoke, VA | 1,985.1 | 255 | Yuma, AZ | 1,708.5 | 317 | York-Hanover, PA | 1,445.0 |
| 194 | Bloomington, IN | 1,979.9 | 256 | Yuba City, CA | 1,701.8 | 318 | Grand Rapids-Wyoming, MI | 1,438.8 |
| 195 | Lewiston-Auburn, ME | 1,974.5 | 257 | Ames, IA | 1,698.6 | 319 | Green Bay, WI | 1,430.4 |
| 196 | Coeur d'Alene, ID | 1,972.6 | 258 | Flint, MI | 1,694.4 | 320 | Homosassa Springs, FL | 1,428.4 |
| 197 | Des Moines-West Des Moines, IA | 1,972.2 | 259 | Las Vegas-Henderson, NV | 1,693.2 | 321 | Oshkosh-Neenah, WI | 1,425.5 |
| 198 | Lakeland, FL | 1,971.6 | 260 | Washington (greater) DC-VA-MD-WV | 1,692.1 | 322 | Pittsburgh, PA | 1,412.4 |
| 199 | Midland, TX | 1,961.8 | 261 | Cedar Rapids, IA | 1,682.6 | 323 | Boston (greater), MA-NH | 1,411.5 |
| 200 | Tampa-St Petersburg, FL | 1,959.0 | 262 | Camden, NJ M.D. | 1,681.6 | 324 | Anaheim-Santa Ana-Irvine, CA M.D. | 1,410.9 |
| 201 | Dothan, AL | 1,954.6 | 263 | Bismarck, ND | 1,675.0 | 325 | Los Angeles (greater), CA | 1,410.2 |
| 202 | Bakersfield, CA | 1,954.4 | 264 | Peoria, IL | 1,674.6 | 326 | Los Angeles County, CA M.D. | 1,410.0 |
| 203 | Oakland-Hayward, CA M.D. | 1,940.8 | 265 | Grand Forks, ND-MN | 1,672.6 | 327 | San Diego, CA | 1,404.6 |
| 204 | Daphne-Fairhope-Foley, AL | 1,939.3 | 266 | Decatur, IL | 1,667.3 | 328 | Salinas, CA | 1,400.8 |
| 205 | Springfield, MA | 1,930.6 | 267 | Fargo, ND-MN | 1,662.7 | 329 | St. George, UT | 1,399.4 |
| 206 | Dallas-Plano-Irving, TX M.D. | 1,916.5 | 268 | Scranton--Wilkes-Barre, PA | 1,661.4 | 330 | Dubuque, IA | 1,391.1 |
| 207 | Kankakee, IL | 1,914.1 | 269 | Williamsport, PA | 1,659.6 | 331 | Oxnard-Thousand Oaks, CA | 1,390.5 |
| 208 | St. Louis, MO-IL | 1,912.9 | 270 | Owensboro, KY | 1,657.9 | 332 | Montgomery County, PA M.D. | 1,380.4 |
| 209 | Niles-Benton Harbor, MI | 1,912.4 | 271 | Kennewick-Richland, WA | 1,657.4 | 333 | Worcester, MA-CT | 1,378.6 |
| 210 | Johnson City, TN | 1,900.3 | 272 | Allentown, PA-NJ | 1,647.9 | 334 | Saginaw, MI | 1,367.5 |
| 211 | Redding, CA | 1,894.6 | 273 | Hartford, CT | 1,646.1 | 335 | Staunton-Waynesboro, VA | 1,363.1 |
| 212 | Davenport, IA-IL | 1,886.4 | 274 | Rockingham County, NH M.D. | 1,645.0 | 336 | San Jose, CA | 1,359.9 |
| 213 | Elmira, NY | 1,875.6 | 275 | Chico, CA | 1,637.8 | 337 | Eau Claire, WI | 1,345.0 |
| 214 | Syracuse, NY | 1,873.5 | 276 | Racine, WI | 1,633.2 | 338 | Manhattan, KS | 1,344.8 |
| 215 | Ogden-Clearfield, UT | 1,871.3 | 277 | Carbondale-Marion, IL | 1,630.0 | 339 | Altoona, PA | 1,336.2 |
| 216 | Janesville, WI | 1,848.9 | 278 | Providence-Warwick, RI-MA | 1,621.0 | 340 | Fond du Lac, WI | 1,329.0 |
| 217 | College Station-Bryan, TX | 1,848.0 | 279 | Monroe, MI | 1,618.3 | 341 | Idaho Falls, ID | 1,328.9 |
| 218 | Champaign-Urbana, IL | 1,847.0 | 280 | Pittsfield, MA | 1,611.8 | 342 | Lake Co.-Kenosha Co., IL-WI M.D. | 1,328.5 |
| 219 | Canton, OH | 1,839.9 | 281 | Jefferson City, MO | 1,606.2 | 343 | Bloomsburg-Berwick, PA | 1,327.1 |
| 220 | Philadelphia (greater) PA-NJ-MD-DE | 1,833.3 | 282 | Gainesville, GA | 1,604.5 | 344 | Trenton, NJ | 1,317.9 |
| 221 | Jackson, MS | 1,830.6 | 283 | Raleigh, NC | 1,600.9 | 345 | Johnstown, PA | 1,315.3 |
| 222 | Manchester-Nashua, NH | 1,823.3 | 284 | Hagerstown-Martinsburg, MD-WV | 1,600.4 | 346 | New York-Jersey City, NY-NJ M.D. | 1,314.1 |
| 223 | Madison, WI | 1,818.7 | 285 | Hanford-Corcoran, CA | 1,595.3 | 347 | Reading, PA | 1,310.0 |
| 224 | Norwich-New London, CT | 1,813.2 | 286 | Bloomington, IL | 1,581.2 | 348 | Glens Falls, NY | 1,304.7 |
| 225 | Jackson, MI | 1,813.1 | 287 | Winchester, VA-WV | 1,571.1 | 349 | Boise City, ID | 1,263.5 |
| 226 | Washington, DC-VA-MD-WV M.D. | 1,808.1 | 288 | California-Lexington Park, MD | 1,568.5 | 350 | Madera, CA | 1,263.3 |
| 227 | Hinesville, GA | 1,806.9 | 289 | Provo-Orem, UT | 1,564.4 | 351 | Cambridge-Newton, MA M.D. | 1,260.6 |
| 228 | Albany-Schenectady-Troy, NY | 1,800.4 | 290 | Ann Arbor, MI | 1,564.3 | 352 | Silver Spring-Frederick, MD M.D. | 1,260.5 |
| 229 | Rochester, NY | 1,799.9 | 291 | Sebastian-Vero Beach, FL | 1,561.1 | 353 | New York (greater), NY-NJ-PA | 1,254.4 |
| 230 | Richmond, VA | 1,797.4 | 292 | Blacksburg, VA | 1,556.9 | 354 | Rochester, MN | 1,243.2 |
| 231 | Sherman-Denison, TX | 1,783.6 | 293 | Watertown-Fort Drum, NY | 1,545.3 | 355 | Morgantown, WV | 1,241.9 |
| 232 | New Bern, NC | 1,783.4 | 294 | Farmington, NM | 1,543.7 | 356 | Elgin, IL M.D. | 1,238.8 |
| 233 | Fort Collins, CO | 1,782.5 | 295 | Port St. Lucie, FL | 1,542.9 | 357 | Napa, CA | 1,237.3 |
| 234 | El Paso, TX | 1,781.6 | 296 | Riverside-San Bernardino, CA | 1,541.1 | 358 | Harrisonburg, VA | 1,236.0 |
| 235 | Boulder, CO | 1,776.8 | 297 | Boston, MA M.D. | 1,540.4 | 359 | Lynchburg, VA | 1,235.8 |
| 236 | Chicago-Naperville, IL M.D. | 1,769.2 | 298 | Iowa City, IA | 1,537.0 | 360 | Warren-Troy, MI M.D. | 1,192.7 |
| 237 | Crestview-Fort Walton Beach, FL | 1,768.9 | 299 | Bay City, MI | 1,532.1 | 361 | Carson City, NV | 1,190.5 |
| 238 | Fayetteville-Springdale, AR-MO | 1,768.5 | 300 | Punta Gorda, FL | 1,531.7 | 362 | State College, PA | 1,173.7 |
| 239 | Portland, ME | 1,767.5 | 301 | Charlottesville, VA | 1,530.7 | 363 | San Rafael, CA M.D. | 1,168.7 |
| 240 | Sioux Falls, SD | 1,763.8 | 302 | Vallejo-Fairfield, CA | 1,528.2 | 364 | Wausau, WI | 1,158.9 |
| 241 | Clarksville, TN-KY | 1,761.0 | 303 | Chambersburg-Waynesboro, PA | 1,525.9 | 365 | Bridgeport-Stamford, CT | 1,155.6 |
| 242 | Merced, CA | 1,760.7 | 304 | Lansing-East Lansing, MI | 1,524.2 | 366 | Appleton, WI | 1,155.3 |
| 243 | Reno, NV | 1,748.7 | 305 | Detroit (greater), MI | 1,522.6 | 367 | Naples-Marco Island, FL | 1,152.4 |
| 244 | Decatur, AL | 1,748.4 | 306 | Sheboygan, WI | 1,513.7 | 368 | Santa Rosa, CA | 1,150.4 |
| 245 | Olympia, WA | 1,742.9 | 307 | Lebanon, PA | 1,510.1 | 369 | Nassau-Suffolk, NY M.D. | 1,148.6 |
| 246 | Bowling Green, KY | 1,735.8 | 308 | Greeley, CO | 1,509.7 | 370 | Elizabethtown-Fort Knox, KY | 1,088.3 |
| 247 | Rapid City, SD | 1,732.8 | 309 | San Luis Obispo, CA | 1,505.3 | 371 | Dutchess-Putnam, NY M.D. | 1,077.8 |
| 248 | Visalia-Porterville, CA | 1,727.6 | 310 | Cape Coral-Fort Myers, FL | 1,494.6 | 372 | Newark, NJ-PA M.D. | 1,064.2 |
| 249 | Sacramento, CA | 1,723.2 | 311 | Barnstable Town, MA | 1,491.3 | 373 | Logan, UT-ID | 944.9 |
| 250 | Parkersburg-Vienna, WV | 1,716.5 | 312 | Santa Maria-Santa Barbara, CA | 1,480.8 | 374 | Gettysburg, PA | 938.5 |
| 251 | Chicago (greater), IL-IN-WI | 1,716.4 | 313 | Lancaster, PA | 1,478.0 | 375 | The Villages, FL | 629.0 |
| 252 | East Stroudsburg, PA | 1,714.7 | 314 | Prescott, AZ | 1,474.0 | NA | Ocala, FL** | NA |
| 253 | Erie, PA | 1,713.0 | 315 | La Crosse, WI-MN | 1,467.1 | NA | Toledo, OH** | NA |
| 254 | Utica-Rome, NY | 1,711.8 | 316 | Kingston, NY | 1,449.9 | | | |

Source: Reported data from the F.B.I. "Crime in the United States 2013"

*Larceny-theft is the unlawful taking of property. Attempts are included.

**Not available.

# 35. Percent Change in Larceny-Theft Rate: 2012 to 2013
## National Percent Change = 3.4% Decrease*

| RANK | METROPOLITAN AREA | % CHANGE | RANK | METROPOLITAN AREA | % CHANGE | RANK | METROPOLITAN AREA | % CHANGE |
|---|---|---|---|---|---|---|---|---|
| 19 | Abilene, TX | 8.1 | 215 | Cheyenne, WY | (5.3) | 164 | Gary, IN M.D. | (3.4) |
| 103 | Akron, OH | (0.1) | 289 | Chicago (greater), IL-IN-WI | (9.1) | NA | Gettysburg, PA** | NA |
| 225 | Albany-Schenectady-Troy, NY | (5.7) | 296 | Chicago-Naperville, IL M.D. | (9.7) | 120 | Glens Falls, NY | (1.6) |
| 96 | Albany, GA | 0.5 | 6 | Chico, CA | 15.7 | 211 | Goldsboro, NC | (5.2) |
| 33 | Albany, OR | 5.3 | 228 | Cincinnati, OH-KY-IN | (5.8) | 142 | Grand Forks, ND-MN | (2.7) |
| NA | Albuquerque, NM** | NA | 127 | Clarksville, TN-KY | (2.1) | 284 | Grand Island, NE | (8.8) |
| 26 | Alexandria, LA | 6.7 | 57 | Cleveland, TN | 2.8 | 307 | Grand Junction, CO | (10.7) |
| 125 | Allentown, PA-NJ | (2.0) | 289 | Coeur d'Alene, ID | (9.1) | NA | Grand Rapids-Wyoming, MI** | NA |
| 51 | Altoona, PA | 3.3 | 243 | College Station-Bryan, TX | (6.4) | NA | Grants Pass, OR** | NA |
| 268 | Amarillo, TX | (7.8) | 96 | Colorado Springs, CO | 0.5 | 258 | Great Falls, MT | (7.3) |
| 106 | Ames, IA | (0.3) | 83 | Columbia, MO | 1.2 | 301 | Greeley, CO | (10.0) |
| 311 | Anaheim-Santa Ana-Irvine, CA M.D. | (11.0) | NA | Columbia, SC** | NA | 88 | Green Bay, WI | 1.0 |
| 6 | Anchorage, AK | 15.7 | 125 | Columbus, GA-AL | (2.0) | 146 | Greensboro-High Point, NC | (2.8) |
| 203 | Ann Arbor, MI | (4.7) | 146 | Columbus, IN | (2.8) | 68 | Greenville-Anderson, SC | 2.2 |
| 338 | Anniston-Oxford, AL | (18.2) | 65 | Corpus Christi, TX | 2.3 | 157 | Greenville, NC | (3.2) |
| 299 | Appleton, WI | (9.8) | 1 | Corvallis, OR | 26.0 | NA | Gulfport-Biloxi-Pascagoula, MS** | NA |
| 263 | Athens-Clarke County, GA | (7.6) | 315 | Crestview-Fort Walton Beach, FL | (11.9) | 89 | Hagerstown-Martinsburg, MD-WV | 0.9 |
| 68 | Atlanta, GA | 2.2 | 217 | Cumberland, MD-WV | (5.4) | 118 | Hammond, LA | (1.5) |
| 118 | Atlantic City, NJ | (1.5) | 142 | Dallas (greater), TX | (2.7) | 12 | Hanford-Corcoran, CA | 11.4 |
| 241 | Augusta, GA-SC | (6.3) | 225 | Dallas-Plano-Irving, TX M.D. | (5.7) | 6 | Harrisonburg, VA | 15.7 |
| 234 | Austin-Round Rock, TX | (6.1) | 65 | Dalton, GA | 2.3 | 257 | Hartford, CT | (7.2) |
| 198 | Bakersfield, CA | (4.5) | 210 | Daphne-Fairhope-Foley, AL | (5.1) | 122 | Hilton Head Island, SC | (1.9) |
| 53 | Baltimore, MD | 3.1 | 157 | Davenport, IA-IL | (3.2) | 270 | Hinesville, GA | (8.0) |
| 168 | Bangor, ME | (3.5) | 112 | Dayton, OH | (1.3) | 112 | Homosassa Springs, FL | (1.3) |
| 233 | Barnstable Town, MA | (6.0) | 289 | Decatur, AL | (9.1) | NA | Hot Springs, AR** | NA |
| 190 | Baton Rouge, LA | (4.1) | 44 | Decatur, IL | 4.0 | 93 | Houma, LA | 0.6 |
| 33 | Bay City, MI | 5.3 | 111 | Deltona-Daytona Beach, FL | (1.2) | 83 | Houston, TX | 1.2 |
| 38 | Beaumont-Port Arthur, TX | 4.7 | 75 | Denver-Aurora, CO | 1.8 | 33 | Huntsville, AL | 5.3 |
| NA | Bend, OR** | NA | 207 | Des Moines-West Des Moines, IA | (5.0) | 295 | Idaho Falls, ID | (9.6) |
| 17 | Billings, MT | 9.2 | 181 | Detroit (greater), MI | (3.8) | 217 | Indianapolis, IN | (5.4) |
| 79 | Binghamton, NY | 1.5 | 71 | Detroit-Dearborn-Livonia, MI M.D. | 2.1 | 55 | Iowa City, IA | 3.0 |
| 103 | Birmingham-Hoover, AL | (0.1) | 146 | Dothan, AL | (2.8) | 237 | Jacksonville, FL | (6.2) |
| 270 | Bismarck, ND | (8.0) | 331 | Dover, DE | (14.9) | NA | Jackson, MI** | NA |
| 277 | Blacksburg, VA | (8.3) | 102 | Dubuque, IA | 0.0 | 252 | Jackson, MS | (7.0) |
| 198 | Bloomington, IL | (4.5) | 18 | Duluth, MN-WI | 9.0 | 10 | Jackson, TN | 12.8 |
| 335 | Bloomington, IN | (16.8) | 309 | Dutchess-Putnam, NY M.D. | (10.8) | 340 | Janesville, WI | (20.6) |
| 337 | Bloomsburg-Berwick, PA | (18.1) | 278 | East Stroudsburg, PA | (8.4) | 287 | Jefferson City, MO | (9.0) |
| 332 | Boise City, ID | (15.1) | NA | Eau Claire, WI** | NA | 299 | Johnson City, TN | (9.8) |
| 151 | Boston (greater), MA-NH | (2.9) | 23 | El Centro, CA | 7.3 | 45 | Johnstown, PA | 3.9 |
| 127 | Boston, MA M.D. | (2.1) | 201 | El Paso, TX | (4.6) | 15 | Jonesboro, AR | 9.3 |
| 186 | Boulder, CO | (3.9) | 181 | Elgin, IL M.D. | (3.8) | 48 | Joplin, MO | 3.8 |
| 157 | Bowling Green, KY | (3.2) | 62 | Elizabethtown-Fort Knox, KY | 2.4 | 151 | Kahului-Wailuku-Lahaina, HI | (2.9) |
| 217 | Bremerton-Silverdale, WA | (5.4) | 211 | Elmira, NY | (5.2) | 258 | Kankakee, IL | (7.3) |
| 284 | Bridgeport-Stamford, CT | (8.8) | 294 | Erie, PA | (9.5) | 255 | Kansas City, MO-KS | (7.1) |
| 316 | Brownsville-Harlingen, TX | (12.0) | 192 | Eugene, OR | (4.2) | 168 | Kennewick-Richland, WA | (3.5) |
| 211 | Brunswick, GA | (5.2) | 263 | Fairbanks, AK | (7.6) | 241 | Kingsport, TN-VA | (6.3) |
| 196 | Buffalo-Niagara Falls, NY | (4.3) | 142 | Fargo, ND-MN | (2.7) | 255 | Kingston, NY | (7.1) |
| 153 | Burlington, NC | (3.0) | 328 | Farmington, NM | (14.4) | 225 | Knoxville, TN | (5.7) |
| 318 | California-Lexington Park, MD | (12.2) | 211 | Fayetteville-Springdale, AR-MO | (5.2) | 13 | Kokomo, IN | 11.3 |
| 139 | Cambridge-Newton, MA M.D. | (2.6) | 117 | Fayetteville, NC | (1.4) | NA | La Crosse, WI-MN** | NA |
| 243 | Camden, NJ M.D. | (6.4) | 109 | Flagstaff, AZ | (0.8) | 75 | Lafayette, IN | 1.8 |
| 109 | Canton, OH | (0.8) | 327 | Flint, MI | (14.0) | 40 | Lafayette, LA | 4.4 |
| 175 | Cape Coral-Fort Myers, FL | (3.6) | 36 | Florence-Muscle Shoals, AL | 5.0 | NA | Lake Charles, LA** | NA |
| 344 | Cape Girardeau, MO-IL | (23.7) | 79 | Florence, SC | 1.5 | 319 | Lake Co.-Kenosha Co., IL-WI M.D. | (12.3) |
| NA | Carbondale-Marion, IL** | NA | 270 | Fond du Lac, WI | (8.0) | 206 | Lake Havasu City-Kingman, AZ | (4.9) |
| 280 | Carson City, NV | (8.5) | 314 | Fort Collins, CO | (11.7) | 131 | Lakeland, FL | (2.3) |
| 38 | Casper, WY | 4.7 | 249 | Fort Lauderdale, FL M.D. | (6.8) | NA | Lancaster, PA** | NA |
| 136 | Cedar Rapids, IA | (2.5) | 30 | Fort Smith, AR-OK | 5.8 | 106 | Lansing-East Lansing, MI | (0.3) |
| NA | Chambersburg-Waynesboro, PA** | NA | 112 | Fort Wayne, IN | (1.3) | 101 | Laredo, TX | 0.2 |
| 93 | Champaign-Urbana, IL | 0.6 | 59 | Fort Worth-Arlington, TX M.D. | 2.7 | 40 | Las Cruces, NM | 4.4 |
| 157 | Charleston-North Charleston, SC | (3.2) | 326 | Fresno, CA | (13.8) | 86 | Las Vegas-Henderson, NV | 1.1 |
| NA | Charlotte-Mecklenburg, NC-SC** | NA | 134 | Gadsden, AL | (2.4) | 263 | Lawrence, KS | (7.6) |
| 71 | Charlottesville, VA | 2.1 | 231 | Gainesville, FL | (5.9) | 155 | Lawton, OK | (3.1) |
| NA | Chattanooga, TN-GA** | NA | 168 | Gainesville, GA | (3.5) | 164 | Lebanon, PA | (3.4) |

Note: All listings are for Metropolitan Statistical Areas (M.S.A.s) except for those ending with "M.D." Listings with "M.D." are Metropolitan Divisions which are smaller parts of eleven large M.S.A.s. See explanatory note at beginning of metropolitan area section.

| RANK | METROPOLITAN AREA | % CHANGE | RANK | METROPOLITAN AREA | % CHANGE | RANK | METROPOLITAN AREA | % CHANGE |
|---|---|---|---|---|---|---|---|---|
| 313 | Lewiston-Auburn, ME | (11.6) | 237 | Omaha-Council Bluffs, NE-IA | (6.2) | 311 | Sheboygan, WI | (11.0) |
| 217 | Lewiston, ID-WA | (5.4) | 60 | Orlando, FL | 2.5 | 320 | Sherman-Denison, TX | (12.4) |
| 263 | Lexington-Fayette, KY | (7.6) | 282 | Oshkosh-Neenah, WI | (8.6) | 50 | Shreveport-Bossier City, LA | 3.6 |
| 217 | Lima, OH | (5.4) | 339 | Owensboro, KY | (18.5) | 249 | Silver Spring-Frederick, MD M.D. | (6.8) |
| 289 | Lincoln, NE | (9.1) | 62 | Oxnard-Thousand Oaks, CA | 2.4 | 53 | Sioux City, IA-NE-SD | 3.1 |
| 168 | Little Rock, AR | (3.5) | 263 | Palm Bay-Melbourne, FL | (7.6) | 198 | Sioux Falls, SD | (4.5) |
| 341 | Logan, UT-ID | (22.2) | 139 | Panama City, FL | (2.6) | 57 | South Bend-Mishawaka, IN-MI | 2.8 |
| 262 | Longview, TX | (7.4) | 336 | Parkersburg-Vienna, WV | (17.2) | 207 | Spartanburg, SC | (5.0) |
| 24 | Longview, WA | 7.2 | 203 | Pensacola, FL | (4.7) | 36 | Spokane, WA | 5.0 |
| 112 | Los Angeles County, CA M.D. | (1.3) | 322 | Peoria, IL | (12.6) | 302 | Springfield, IL | (10.2) |
| 181 | Los Angeles (greater), CA | (3.8) | 179 | Philadelphia (greater) PA-NJ-MD-DE | (3.7) | 130 | Springfield, MA | (2.2) |
| 93 | Louisville, KY-IN | 0.6 | 168 | Philadelphia, PA M.D. | (3.5) | 134 | Springfield, MO | (2.4) |
| 196 | Lubbock, TX | (4.3) | 146 | Phoenix-Mesa-Scottsdale, AZ | (2.8) | 15 | Springfield, OH | 9.3 |
| 275 | Lynchburg, VA | (8.2) | NA | Pittsburgh, PA** | NA | 86 | State College, PA | 1.1 |
| 77 | Macon, GA | 1.6 | 28 | Pittsfield, MA | 6.0 | 246 | Staunton-Waynesboro, VA | (6.6) |
| 9 | Madera, CA | 13.7 | 5 | Pocatello, ID | 15.8 | 96 | Stockton-Lodi, CA | 0.5 |
| NA | Madison, WI** | NA | 207 | Port St. Lucie, FL | (5.0) | NA | St. Cloud, MN** | NA |
| 74 | Manchester-Nashua, NH | 2.0 | 168 | Portland-Vancouver, OR-WA | (3.5) | 237 | St. George, UT | (6.2) |
| 323 | Manhattan, KS | (12.7) | 258 | Portland, ME | (7.3) | 181 | St. Joseph, MO-KS | (3.8) |
| 275 | Mankato-North Mankato, MN | (8.2) | 164 | Prescott, AZ | (3.4) | 224 | St. Louis, MO-IL | (5.6) |
| 45 | Mansfield, OH | 3.9 | 179 | Providence-Warwick, RI-MA | (3.7) | 334 | Sumter, SC | (15.7) |
| 142 | McAllen-Edinburg-Mission, TX | (2.7) | 91 | Provo-Orem, UT | 0.8 | 45 | Syracuse, NY | 3.9 |
| 49 | Medford, OR | 3.7 | 11 | Pueblo, CO | 11.9 | 62 | Tacoma, WA M.D. | 2.4 |
| 121 | Memphis, TN-MS-AR | (1.8) | 92 | Punta Gorda, FL | 0.7 | 21 | Tallahassee, FL | 7.8 |
| 343 | Merced, CA | (23.6) | 324 | Racine, WI | (12.9) | 175 | Tampa-St Petersburg, FL | (3.6) |
| 192 | Miami (greater), FL | (4.2) | 252 | Raleigh, NC | (7.0) | 317 | Terre Haute, IN | (12.1) |
| 131 | Miami-Dade County, FL M.D. | (2.3) | 345 | Rapid City, SD | (28.4) | 157 | Texarkana, TX-AR | (3.2) |
| 42 | Midland, TX | 4.3 | 307 | Reading, PA | (10.7) | 252 | The Villages, FL | (7.0) |
| 280 | Milwaukee, WI | (8.5) | 237 | Redding, CA | (6.2) | NA | Toledo, OH** | NA |
| 223 | Minneapolis-St. Paul, MN-WI | (5.5) | 89 | Reno, NV | 0.9 | 258 | Topeka, KS | (7.3) |
| 302 | Missoula, MT | (10.2) | 203 | Richmond, VA | (4.7) | 168 | Trenton, NJ | (3.5) |
| 77 | Mobile, AL | 1.6 | 269 | Riverside-San Bernardino, CA | (7.9) | NA | Tucson, AZ** | NA |
| 192 | Modesto, CA | (4.2) | 71 | Roanoke, VA | 2.1 | 83 | Tulsa, OK | 1.2 |
| 43 | Monroe, LA | 4.2 | 231 | Rochester, MN | (5.9) | 55 | Tuscaloosa, AL | 3.0 |
| 306 | Monroe, MI | (10.6) | 278 | Rochester, NY | (8.4) | 163 | Tyler, TX | (3.3) |
| 112 | Montgomery County, PA M.D. | (1.3) | 325 | Rockford, IL | (13.4) | 157 | Utica-Rome, NY | (3.2) |
| 330 | Morgantown, WV | (14.7) | 247 | Rockingham County, NH M.D. | (6.7) | 108 | Vallejo-Fairfield, CA | (0.4) |
| 284 | Morristown, TN | (8.8) | 65 | Rocky Mount, NC | 2.3 | 103 | Victoria, TX | (0.1) |
| 32 | Mount Vernon-Anacortes, WA | 5.4 | 29 | Rome, GA | 5.9 | 19 | Vineland-Bridgeton, NJ | 8.1 |
| 22 | Muncie, IN | 7.7 | 175 | Sacramento, CA | (3.6) | 175 | Virginia Beach-Norfolk, VA-NC | (3.6) |
| NA | Muskegon, MI** | NA | 82 | Saginaw, MI | 1.3 | 333 | Visalia-Porterville, CA | (15.5) |
| NA | Myrtle Beach, SC-NC** | NA | 52 | Salem, OR | 3.2 | 201 | Waco, TX | (4.6) |
| 287 | Napa, CA | (9.0) | 27 | Salinas, CA | 6.3 | 68 | Warner Robins, GA | 2.2 |
| 136 | Naples-Marco Island, FL | (2.5) | 181 | Salisbury, MD-DE | (3.8) | 296 | Warren-Troy, MI M.D. | (9.7) |
| 234 | Nashville-Davidson, TN | (6.1) | 188 | Salt Lake City, UT | (4.0) | 164 | Washington (greater) DC-VA-MD-WV | (3.4) |
| 192 | Nassau-Suffolk, NY M.D. | (4.2) | NA | San Angelo, TX** | NA | 146 | Washington, DC-VA-MD-WV M.D. | (2.8) |
| 282 | New Bern, NC | (8.6) | 228 | San Antonio, TX | (5.8) | 329 | Watertown-Fort Drum, NY | (14.6) |
| 245 | New Haven-Milford, CT | (6.5) | 60 | San Diego, CA | 2.5 | 293 | Wausau, WI | (9.2) |
| 99 | New Orleans, LA | 0.3 | NA | San Francisco (greater), CA** | NA | 217 | West Palm Beach, FL M.D. | (5.4) |
| 139 | New York (greater), NY-NJ-PA | (2.6) | 4 | San Francisco-Redwood, CA M.D. | 20.3 | 190 | Wichita Falls, TX | (4.1) |
| 122 | New York-Jersey City, NY-NJ M.D. | (1.9) | 305 | San Jose, CA | (10.5) | 127 | Wichita, KS | (2.1) |
| 188 | Newark, NJ-PA M.D. | (4.0) | 155 | San Luis Obispo, CA | (3.1) | 99 | Williamsport, PA | 0.3 |
| NA | Niles-Benton Harbor, MI** | NA | NA | San Rafael, CA M.D.** | NA | 131 | Wilmington, DE-MD-NJ M.D. | (2.3) |
| 228 | North Port-Sarasota-Bradenton, FL | (5.8) | 309 | Santa Cruz-Watsonville, CA | (10.8) | 270 | Wilmington, NC | (8.0) |
| 81 | Norwich-New London, CT | 1.4 | 270 | Santa Maria-Santa Barbara, CA | (8.0) | 320 | Winchester, VA-WV | (12.4) |
| NA | Oakland-Hayward, CA M.D.** | NA | 215 | Santa Rosa, CA | (5.3) | 247 | Winston-Salem, NC | (6.7) |
| NA | Ocala, FL** | NA | 186 | Savannah, GA | (3.9) | 153 | Worcester, MA-CT | (3.0) |
| 234 | Ocean City, NJ | (6.1) | NA | Scranton--Wilkes-Barre, PA** | NA | 296 | Yakima, WA | (9.7) |
| 3 | Odessa, TX | 21.5 | 30 | Seattle (greater), WA | 5.8 | 304 | York-Hanover, PA | (10.4) |
| 136 | Ogden-Clearfield, UT | (2.5) | 25 | Seattle-Bellevue-Everett, WA M.D. | 6.8 | 122 | Yuba City, CA | (1.9) |
| 251 | Oklahoma City, OK | (6.9) | 342 | Sebastian-Vero Beach, FL | (22.3) | 14 | Yuma, AZ | 9.8 |
| NA | Olympia, WA** | NA | 2 | Sebring, FL | 25.8 | | | |

Source: CQ Press using reported data from the F.B.I. "Crime in the United States 2013"
*Larceny-theft is the unlawful taking of property. Attempts are included.
**Not available.

## 35. Percent Change in Larceny-Theft Rate: 2012 to 2013 (continued)
## National Percent Change = 3.4% Decrease*

| RANK | METROPOLITAN AREA | % CHANGE | RANK | METROPOLITAN AREA | % CHANGE | RANK | METROPOLITAN AREA | % CHANGE |
|---|---|---|---|---|---|---|---|---|
| 1 | Corvallis, OR | 26.0 | 65 | Corpus Christi, TX | 2.3 | 127 | Wichita, KS | (2.1) |
| 2 | Sebring, FL | 25.8 | 65 | Dalton, GA | 2.3 | 130 | Springfield, MA | (2.2) |
| 3 | Odessa, TX | 21.5 | 65 | Rocky Mount, NC | 2.3 | 131 | Lakeland, FL | (2.3) |
| 4 | San Francisco-Redwood, CA M.D. | 20.3 | 68 | Atlanta, GA | 2.2 | 131 | Miami-Dade County, FL M.D. | (2.3) |
| 5 | Pocatello, ID | 15.8 | 68 | Greenville-Anderson, SC | 2.2 | 131 | Wilmington, DE-MD-NJ M.D. | (2.3) |
| 6 | Anchorage, AK | 15.7 | 68 | Warner Robins, GA | 2.2 | 134 | Gadsden, AL | (2.4) |
| 6 | Chico, CA | 15.7 | 71 | Charlottesville, VA | 2.1 | 134 | Springfield, MO | (2.4) |
| 6 | Harrisonburg, VA | 15.7 | 71 | Detroit-Dearborn-Livonia, MI M.D. | 2.1 | 136 | Cedar Rapids, IA | (2.5) |
| 9 | Madera, CA | 13.7 | 71 | Roanoke, VA | 2.1 | 136 | Naples-Marco Island, FL | (2.5) |
| 10 | Jackson, TN | 12.8 | 74 | Manchester-Nashua, NH | 2.0 | 136 | Ogden-Clearfield, UT | (2.5) |
| 11 | Pueblo, CO | 11.9 | 75 | Denver-Aurora, CO | 1.8 | 139 | Cambridge-Newton, MA M.D. | (2.6) |
| 12 | Hanford-Corcoran, CA | 11.4 | 75 | Lafayette, IN | 1.8 | 139 | New York (greater), NY-NJ-PA | (2.6) |
| 13 | Kokomo, IN | 11.3 | 77 | Macon, GA | 1.6 | 139 | Panama City, FL | (2.6) |
| 14 | Yuma, AZ | 9.8 | 77 | Mobile, AL | 1.6 | 142 | Dallas (greater), TX | (2.7) |
| 15 | Jonesboro, AR | 9.3 | 79 | Binghamton, NY | 1.5 | 142 | Fargo, ND-MN | (2.7) |
| 15 | Springfield, OH | 9.3 | 79 | Florence, SC | 1.5 | 142 | Grand Forks, ND-MN | (2.7) |
| 17 | Billings, MT | 9.2 | 81 | Norwich-New London, CT | 1.4 | 142 | McAllen-Edinburg-Mission, TX | (2.7) |
| 18 | Duluth, MN-WI | 9.0 | 82 | Saginaw, MI | 1.3 | 146 | Columbus, IN | (2.8) |
| 19 | Abilene, TX | 8.1 | 83 | Columbia, MO | 1.2 | 146 | Dothan, AL | (2.8) |
| 19 | Vineland-Bridgeton, NJ | 8.1 | 83 | Houston, TX | 1.2 | 146 | Greensboro-High Point, NC | (2.8) |
| 21 | Tallahassee, FL | 7.8 | 83 | Tulsa, OK | 1.2 | 146 | Phoenix-Mesa-Scottsdale, AZ | (2.8) |
| 22 | Muncie, IN | 7.7 | 86 | Las Vegas-Henderson, NV | 1.1 | 146 | Washington, DC-VA-MD-WV M.D. | (2.8) |
| 23 | El Centro, CA | 7.3 | 86 | State College, PA | 1.1 | 151 | Boston (greater), MA-NH | (2.9) |
| 24 | Longview, WA | 7.2 | 88 | Green Bay, WI | 1.0 | 151 | Kahului-Wailuku-Lahaina, HI | (2.9) |
| 25 | Seattle-Bellevue-Everett, WA M.D. | 6.8 | 89 | Hagerstown-Martinsburg, MD-WV | 0.9 | 153 | Burlington, NC | (3.0) |
| 26 | Alexandria, LA | 6.7 | 89 | Reno, NV | 0.9 | 153 | Worcester, MA-CT | (3.0) |
| 27 | Salinas, CA | 6.3 | 91 | Provo-Orem, UT | 0.8 | 155 | Lawton, OK | (3.1) |
| 28 | Pittsfield, MA | 6.0 | 92 | Punta Gorda, FL | 0.7 | 155 | San Luis Obispo, CA | (3.1) |
| 29 | Rome, GA | 5.9 | 93 | Champaign-Urbana, IL | 0.6 | 157 | Bowling Green, KY | (3.2) |
| 30 | Fort Smith, AR-OK | 5.8 | 93 | Houma, LA | 0.6 | 157 | Charleston-North Charleston, SC | (3.2) |
| 30 | Seattle (greater), WA | 5.8 | 93 | Louisville, KY-IN | 0.6 | 157 | Davenport, IA-IL | (3.2) |
| 32 | Mount Vernon-Anacortes, WA | 5.4 | 96 | Albany, GA | 0.5 | 157 | Greenville, NC | (3.2) |
| 33 | Albany, OR | 5.3 | 96 | Colorado Springs, CO | 0.5 | 157 | Texarkana, TX-AR | (3.2) |
| 33 | Bay City, MI | 5.3 | 96 | Stockton-Lodi, CA | 0.5 | 157 | Utica-Rome, NY | (3.2) |
| 33 | Huntsville, AL | 5.3 | 99 | New Orleans, LA | 0.3 | 163 | Tyler, TX | (3.3) |
| 36 | Florence-Muscle Shoals, AL | 5.0 | 99 | Williamsport, PA | 0.3 | 164 | Gary, IN M.D. | (3.4) |
| 36 | Spokane, WA | 5.0 | 101 | Laredo, TX | 0.2 | 164 | Lebanon, PA | (3.4) |
| 38 | Beaumont-Port Arthur, TX | 4.7 | 102 | Dubuque, IA | 0.0 | 164 | Prescott, AZ | (3.4) |
| 38 | Casper, WY | 4.7 | 103 | Akron, OH | (0.1) | 164 | Washington (greater) DC-VA-MD-WV | (3.4) |
| 40 | Lafayette, LA | 4.4 | 103 | Birmingham-Hoover, AL | (0.1) | 168 | Bangor, ME | (3.5) |
| 40 | Las Cruces, NM | 4.4 | 103 | Victoria, TX | (0.1) | 168 | Gainesville, GA | (3.5) |
| 42 | Midland, TX | 4.3 | 106 | Ames, IA | (0.3) | 168 | Kennewick-Richland, WA | (3.5) |
| 43 | Monroe, LA | 4.2 | 106 | Lansing-East Lansing, MI | (0.3) | 168 | Little Rock, AR | (3.5) |
| 44 | Decatur, IL | 4.0 | 108 | Vallejo-Fairfield, CA | (0.4) | 168 | Philadelphia, PA M.D. | (3.5) |
| 45 | Johnstown, PA | 3.9 | 109 | Canton, OH | (0.8) | 168 | Portland-Vancouver, OR-WA | (3.5) |
| 45 | Mansfield, OH | 3.9 | 109 | Flagstaff, AZ | (0.8) | 168 | Trenton, NJ | (3.5) |
| 45 | Syracuse, NY | 3.9 | 111 | Deltona-Daytona Beach, FL | (1.2) | 175 | Cape Coral-Fort Myers, FL | (3.6) |
| 48 | Joplin, MO | 3.8 | 112 | Dayton, OH | (1.3) | 175 | Sacramento, CA | (3.6) |
| 49 | Medford, OR | 3.7 | 112 | Fort Wayne, IN | (1.3) | 175 | Tampa-St Petersburg, FL | (3.6) |
| 50 | Shreveport-Bossier City, LA | 3.6 | 112 | Homosassa Springs, FL | (1.3) | 175 | Virginia Beach-Norfolk, VA-NC | (3.6) |
| 51 | Altoona, PA | 3.3 | 112 | Los Angeles County, CA M.D. | (1.3) | 179 | Philadelphia (greater) PA-NJ-MD-DE | (3.7) |
| 52 | Salem, OR | 3.2 | 112 | Montgomery County, PA M.D. | (1.3) | 179 | Providence-Warwick, RI-MA | (3.7) |
| 53 | Baltimore, MD | 3.1 | 117 | Fayetteville, NC | (1.4) | 181 | Detroit (greater), MI | (3.8) |
| 53 | Sioux City, IA-NE-SD | 3.1 | 118 | Atlantic City, NJ | (1.5) | 181 | Elgin, IL M.D. | (3.8) |
| 55 | Iowa City, IA | 3.0 | 118 | Hammond, LA | (1.5) | 181 | Los Angeles (greater), CA | (3.8) |
| 55 | Tuscaloosa, AL | 3.0 | 120 | Glens Falls, NY | (1.6) | 181 | Salisbury, MD-DE | (3.8) |
| 57 | Cleveland, TN | 2.8 | 121 | Memphis, TN-MS-AR | (1.8) | 181 | St. Joseph, MO-KS | (3.8) |
| 57 | South Bend-Mishawaka, IN-MI | 2.8 | 122 | Hilton Head Island, SC | (1.9) | 186 | Boulder, CO | (3.9) |
| 59 | Fort Worth-Arlington, TX M.D. | 2.7 | 122 | New York-Jersey City, NY-NJ M.D. | (1.9) | 186 | Savannah, GA | (3.9) |
| 60 | Orlando, FL | 2.5 | 122 | Yuba City, CA | (1.9) | 188 | Newark, NJ-PA M.D. | (4.0) |
| 60 | San Diego, CA | 2.5 | 125 | Allentown, PA-NJ | (2.0) | 188 | Salt Lake City, UT | (4.0) |
| 62 | Elizabethtown-Fort Knox, KY | 2.4 | 125 | Columbus, GA-AL | (2.0) | 190 | Baton Rouge, LA | (4.1) |
| 62 | Oxnard-Thousand Oaks, CA | 2.4 | 127 | Boston, MA M.D. | (2.1) | 190 | Wichita Falls, TX | (4.1) |
| 62 | Tacoma, WA M.D. | 2.4 | 127 | Clarksville, TN-KY | (2.1) | 192 | Eugene, OR | (4.2) |

Note: All listings are for Metropolitan Statistical Areas (M.S.A.s) except for those ending with "M.D." Listings with "M.D." are Metropolitan Divisions which are smaller parts of eleven large M.S.A.s. See explanatory note at beginning of metropolitan area section.

| RANK | METROPOLITAN AREA | % CHANGE |
|---|---|---|
| 192 | Miami (greater), FL | (4.2) |
| 192 | Modesto, CA | (4.2) |
| 192 | Nassau-Suffolk, NY M.D. | (4.2) |
| 196 | Buffalo-Niagara Falls, NY | (4.3) |
| 196 | Lubbock, TX | (4.3) |
| 198 | Bakersfield, CA | (4.5) |
| 198 | Bloomington, IL | (4.5) |
| 198 | Sioux Falls, SD | (4.5) |
| 201 | El Paso, TX | (4.6) |
| 201 | Waco, TX | (4.6) |
| 203 | Ann Arbor, MI | (4.7) |
| 203 | Pensacola, FL | (4.7) |
| 203 | Richmond, VA | (4.7) |
| 206 | Lake Havasu City-Kingman, AZ | (4.9) |
| 207 | Des Moines-West Des Moines, IA | (5.0) |
| 207 | Port St. Lucie, FL | (5.0) |
| 207 | Spartanburg, SC | (5.0) |
| 210 | Daphne-Fairhope-Foley, AL | (5.1) |
| 211 | Brunswick, GA | (5.2) |
| 211 | Elmira, NY | (5.2) |
| 211 | Fayetteville-Springdale, AR-MO | (5.2) |
| 211 | Goldsboro, NC | (5.2) |
| 215 | Cheyenne, WY | (5.3) |
| 215 | Santa Rosa, CA | (5.3) |
| 217 | Bremerton-Silverdale, WA | (5.4) |
| 217 | Cumberland, MD-WV | (5.4) |
| 217 | Indianapolis, IN | (5.4) |
| 217 | Lewiston, ID-WA | (5.4) |
| 217 | Lima, OH | (5.4) |
| 217 | West Palm Beach, FL M.D. | (5.4) |
| 223 | Minneapolis-St. Paul, MN-WI | (5.5) |
| 224 | St. Louis, MO-IL | (5.6) |
| 225 | Albany-Schenectady-Troy, NY | (5.7) |
| 225 | Dallas-Plano-Irving, TX M.D. | (5.7) |
| 225 | Knoxville, TN | (5.7) |
| 228 | Cincinnati, OH-KY-IN | (5.8) |
| 228 | North Port-Sarasota-Bradenton, FL | (5.8) |
| 228 | San Antonio, TX | (5.8) |
| 231 | Gainesville, FL | (5.9) |
| 231 | Rochester, MN | (5.9) |
| 233 | Barnstable Town, MA | (6.0) |
| 234 | Austin-Round Rock, TX | (6.1) |
| 234 | Nashville-Davidson, TN | (6.1) |
| 234 | Ocean City, NJ | (6.1) |
| 237 | Jacksonville, FL | (6.2) |
| 237 | Omaha-Council Bluffs, NE-IA | (6.2) |
| 237 | Redding, CA | (6.2) |
| 237 | St. George, UT | (6.2) |
| 241 | Augusta, GA-SC | (6.3) |
| 241 | Kingsport, TN-VA | (6.3) |
| 243 | Camden, NJ M.D. | (6.4) |
| 243 | College Station-Bryan, TX | (6.4) |
| 245 | New Haven-Milford, CT | (6.5) |
| 246 | Staunton-Waynesboro, VA | (6.6) |
| 247 | Rockingham County, NH M.D. | (6.7) |
| 247 | Winston-Salem, NC | (6.7) |
| 249 | Fort Lauderdale, FL M.D. | (6.8) |
| 249 | Silver Spring-Frederick, MD M.D. | (6.8) |
| 251 | Oklahoma City, OK | (6.9) |
| 252 | Jackson, MS | (7.0) |
| 252 | Raleigh, NC | (7.0) |
| 252 | The Villages, FL | (7.0) |

| RANK | METROPOLITAN AREA | % CHANGE |
|---|---|---|
| 255 | Kansas City, MO-KS | (7.1) |
| 255 | Kingston, NY | (7.1) |
| 257 | Hartford, CT | (7.2) |
| 258 | Great Falls, MT | (7.3) |
| 258 | Kankakee, IL | (7.3) |
| 258 | Portland, ME | (7.3) |
| 258 | Topeka, KS | (7.3) |
| 262 | Longview, TX | (7.4) |
| 263 | Athens-Clarke County, GA | (7.6) |
| 263 | Fairbanks, AK | (7.6) |
| 263 | Lawrence, KS | (7.6) |
| 263 | Lexington-Fayette, KY | (7.6) |
| 263 | Palm Bay-Melbourne, FL | (7.6) |
| 268 | Amarillo, TX | (7.8) |
| 269 | Riverside-San Bernardino, CA | (7.9) |
| 270 | Bismarck, ND | (8.0) |
| 270 | Fond du Lac, WI | (8.0) |
| 270 | Hinesville, GA | (8.0) |
| 270 | Santa Maria-Santa Barbara, CA | (8.0) |
| 270 | Wilmington, NC | (8.0) |
| 275 | Lynchburg, VA | (8.2) |
| 275 | Mankato-North Mankato, MN | (8.2) |
| 277 | Blacksburg, VA | (8.3) |
| 278 | East Stroudsburg, PA | (8.4) |
| 278 | Rochester, NY | (8.4) |
| 280 | Carson City, NV | (8.5) |
| 280 | Milwaukee, WI | (8.5) |
| 282 | New Bern, NC | (8.6) |
| 282 | Oshkosh-Neenah, WI | (8.6) |
| 284 | Bridgeport-Stamford, CT | (8.8) |
| 284 | Grand Island, NE | (8.8) |
| 284 | Morristown, TN | (8.8) |
| 287 | Jefferson City, MO | (9.0) |
| 287 | Napa, CA | (9.0) |
| 289 | Chicago (greater), IL-IN-WI | (9.1) |
| 289 | Coeur d'Alene, ID | (9.1) |
| 289 | Decatur, AL | (9.1) |
| 289 | Lincoln, NE | (9.1) |
| 293 | Wausau, WI | (9.2) |
| 294 | Erie, PA | (9.5) |
| 295 | Idaho Falls, ID | (9.6) |
| 296 | Chicago-Naperville, IL M.D. | (9.7) |
| 296 | Warren-Troy, MI M.D. | (9.7) |
| 296 | Yakima, WA | (9.7) |
| 299 | Appleton, WI | (9.8) |
| 299 | Johnson City, TN | (9.8) |
| 301 | Greeley, CO | (10.0) |
| 302 | Missoula, MT | (10.2) |
| 302 | Springfield, IL | (10.2) |
| 304 | York-Hanover, PA | (10.4) |
| 305 | San Jose, CA | (10.5) |
| 306 | Monroe, MI | (10.6) |
| 307 | Grand Junction, CO | (10.7) |
| 307 | Reading, PA | (10.7) |
| 309 | Dutchess-Putnam, NY M.D. | (10.8) |
| 309 | Santa Cruz-Watsonville, CA | (10.8) |
| 311 | Anaheim-Santa Ana-Irvine, CA M.D. | (11.0) |
| 311 | Sheboygan, WI | (11.0) |
| 313 | Lewiston-Auburn, ME | (11.6) |
| 314 | Fort Collins, CO | (11.7) |
| 315 | Crestview-Fort Walton Beach, FL | (11.9) |
| 316 | Brownsville-Harlingen, TX | (12.0) |

| RANK | METROPOLITAN AREA | % CHANGE |
|---|---|---|
| 317 | Terre Haute, IN | (12.1) |
| 318 | California-Lexington Park, MD | (12.2) |
| 319 | Lake Co.-Kenosha Co., IL-WI M.D. | (12.3) |
| 320 | Sherman-Denison, TX | (12.4) |
| 320 | Winchester, VA-WV | (12.4) |
| 322 | Peoria, IL | (12.6) |
| 323 | Manhattan, KS | (12.7) |
| 324 | Racine, WI | (12.9) |
| 325 | Rockford, IL | (13.4) |
| 326 | Fresno, CA | (13.8) |
| 327 | Flint, MI | (14.0) |
| 328 | Farmington, NM | (14.4) |
| 329 | Watertown-Fort Drum, NY | (14.6) |
| 330 | Morgantown, WV | (14.7) |
| 331 | Dover, DE | (14.9) |
| 332 | Boise City, ID | (15.1) |
| 333 | Visalia-Porterville, CA | (15.5) |
| 334 | Sumter, SC | (15.7) |
| 335 | Bloomington, IN | (16.8) |
| 336 | Parkersburg-Vienna, WV | (17.2) |
| 337 | Bloomsburg-Berwick, PA | (18.1) |
| 338 | Anniston-Oxford, AL | (18.2) |
| 339 | Owensboro, KY | (18.5) |
| 340 | Janesville, WI | (20.6) |
| 341 | Logan, UT-ID | (22.2) |
| 342 | Sebastian-Vero Beach, FL | (22.3) |
| 343 | Merced, CA | (23.6) |
| 344 | Cape Girardeau, MO-IL | (23.7) |
| 345 | Rapid City, SD | (28.4) |
| NA | Albuquerque, NM** | NA |
| NA | Bend, OR** | NA |
| NA | Carbondale-Marion, IL** | NA |
| NA | Chambersburg-Waynesboro, PA** | NA |
| NA | Charlotte-Mecklenburg, NC-SC** | NA |
| NA | Chattanooga, TN-GA** | NA |
| NA | Columbia, SC** | NA |
| NA | Eau Claire, WI** | NA |
| NA | Gettysburg, PA** | NA |
| NA | Grand Rapids-Wyoming, MI** | NA |
| NA | Grants Pass, OR** | NA |
| NA | Gulfport-Biloxi-Pascagoula, MS** | NA |
| NA | Hot Springs, AR** | NA |
| NA | Jackson, MI** | NA |
| NA | La Crosse, WI-MN** | NA |
| NA | Lake Charles, LA** | NA |
| NA | Lancaster, PA** | NA |
| NA | Madison, WI** | NA |
| NA | Muskegon, MI** | NA |
| NA | Myrtle Beach, SC-NC** | NA |
| NA | Niles-Benton Harbor, MI** | NA |
| NA | Oakland-Hayward, CA M.D.** | NA |
| NA | Ocala, FL** | NA |
| NA | Olympia, WA** | NA |
| NA | Pittsburgh, PA** | NA |
| NA | San Angelo, TX** | NA |
| NA | San Francisco (greater), CA** | NA |
| NA | San Rafael, CA M.D.** | NA |
| NA | Scranton--Wilkes-Barre, PA** | NA |
| NA | St. Cloud, MN** | NA |
| NA | Toledo, OH** | NA |
| NA | Tucson, AZ** | NA |

Source: CQ Press using reported data from the F.B.I. "Crime in the United States 2013"
*Larceny-theft is the unlawful taking of property. Attempts are included.
**Not available.

## 36. Percent Change in Larceny-Theft Rate: 2009 to 2013
## National Percent Change = 8.0% Decrease*

| RANK | METROPOLITAN AREA | % CHANGE | RANK | METROPOLITAN AREA | % CHANGE | RANK | METROPOLITAN AREA | % CHANGE |
|---|---|---|---|---|---|---|---|---|
| 95 | Abilene, TX | (2.8) | 262 | Cheyenne, WY | (19.6) | NA | Gary, IN M.D.** | NA |
| 133 | Akron, OH | (6.1) | NA | Chicago (greater), IL-IN-WI** | NA | NA | Gettysburg, PA** | NA |
| 158 | Albany-Schenectady-Troy, NY | (8.8) | NA | Chicago-Naperville, IL M.D.** | NA | 77 | Glens Falls, NY | 0.2 |
| 24 | Albany, GA | 11.5 | 104 | Chico, CA | (3.7) | 188 | Goldsboro, NC | (12.3) |
| NA | Albany, OR** | NA | 112 | Cincinnati, OH-KY-IN | (4.3) | 136 | Grand Forks, ND-MN | (6.5) |
| 47 | Albuquerque, NM | 5.6 | 105 | Clarksville, TN-KY | (3.8) | NA | Grand Island, NE** | NA |
| 74 | Alexandria, LA | 0.6 | 32 | Cleveland, TN | 7.3 | 169 | Grand Junction, CO | (10.2) |
| 141 | Allentown, PA-NJ | (7.2) | 44 | Coeur d'Alene, ID | 5.9 | NA | Grand Rapids-Wyoming, MI** | NA |
| 148 | Altoona, PA | (7.8) | 308 | College Station-Bryan, TX | (40.2) | NA | Grants Pass, OR** | NA |
| 305 | Amarillo, TX | (29.7) | 18 | Colorado Springs, CO | 14.1 | 50 | Great Falls, MT | 4.6 |
| 243 | Ames, IA | (16.9) | 39 | Columbia, MO | 6.7 | 167 | Greeley, CO | (10.1) |
| 92 | Anaheim-Santa Ana-Irvine, CA M.D. | (2.1) | 119 | Columbia, SC | (4.9) | 86 | Green Bay, WI | (1.6) |
| 9 | Anchorage, AK | 21.4 | 259 | Columbus, GA-AL | (18.9) | 238 | Greensboro-High Point, NC | (16.6) |
| 217 | Ann Arbor, MI | (14.8) | 93 | Columbus, IN | (2.3) | NA | Greenville-Anderson, SC** | NA |
| 252 | Anniston-Oxford, AL | (18.3) | 204 | Corpus Christi, TX | (13.6) | NA | Greenville, NC** | NA |
| 306 | Appleton, WI | (30.4) | 111 | Corvallis, OR | (4.2) | NA | Gulfport-Biloxi-Pascagoula, MS** | NA |
| 197 | Athens-Clarke County, GA | (13.2) | NA | Crestview-Fort Walton Beach, FL** | NA | 79 | Hagerstown-Martinsburg, MD-WV | (0.2) |
| 66 | Atlanta, GA | 1.5 | 55 | Cumberland, MD-WV | 2.8 | NA | Hammond, LA** | NA |
| 209 | Atlantic City, NJ | (14.0) | 261 | Dallas (greater), TX | (19.1) | NA | Hanford-Corcoran, CA** | NA |
| 231 | Augusta, GA-SC | (16.2) | 276 | Dallas-Plano-Irving, TX M.D. | (21.3) | 52 | Harrisonburg, VA | 3.4 |
| 257 | Austin-Round Rock, TX | (18.8) | 138 | Dalton, GA | (6.6) | 250 | Hartford, CT | (18.2) |
| 136 | Bakersfield, CA | (6.5) | NA | Daphne-Fairhope-Foley, AL** | NA | NA | Hilton Head Island, SC** | NA |
| 128 | Baltimore, MD | (5.7) | NA | Davenport, IA-IL** | NA | 244 | Hinesville, GA | (17.4) |
| 228 | Bangor, ME | (15.7) | 81 | Dayton, OH | (0.5) | NA | Homosassa Springs, FL** | NA |
| 250 | Barnstable Town, MA | (18.2) | 289 | Decatur, AL | (24.1) | 142 | Hot Springs, AR | (7.3) |
| 134 | Baton Rouge, LA | (6.4) | 167 | Decatur, IL | (10.1) | 86 | Houma, LA | (1.6) |
| 199 | Bay City, MI | (13.3) | 144 | Deltona-Daytona Beach, FL | (7.6) | 190 | Houston, TX | (12.5) |
| 219 | Beaumont-Port Arthur, TX | (15.1) | 53 | Denver-Aurora, CO | 3.2 | 70 | Huntsville, AL | 1.2 |
| 30 | Bend, OR | 9.0 | 97 | Des Moines-West Des Moines, IA | (3.4) | 248 | Idaho Falls, ID | (18.1) |
| 76 | Billings, MT | 0.4 | 180 | Detroit (greater), MI | (11.6) | 157 | Indianapolis, IN | (8.7) |
| 56 | Binghamton, NY | 2.7 | 110 | Detroit-Dearborn-Livonia, MI M.D. | (4.1) | 42 | Iowa City, IA | 6.4 |
| 247 | Birmingham-Hoover, AL | (17.9) | 171 | Dothan, AL | (10.5) | 248 | Jacksonville, FL | (18.1) |
| 70 | Bismarck, ND | 1.2 | 121 | Dover, DE | (5.1) | 119 | Jackson, MI | (4.9) |
| 268 | Blacksburg, VA | (20.2) | 201 | Dubuque, IA | (13.4) | 252 | Jackson, MS | (18.3) |
| NA | Bloomington, IL** | NA | 82 | Duluth, MN-WI | (0.9) | 295 | Jackson, TN | (25.0) |
| 60 | Bloomington, IN | 2.4 | NA | Dutchess-Putnam, NY M.D.** | NA | 236 | Janesville, WI | (16.5) |
| NA | Bloomsburg-Berwick, PA** | NA | NA | East Stroudsburg, PA** | NA | 108 | Jefferson City, MO | (4.0) |
| 213 | Boise City, ID | (14.4) | 236 | Eau Claire, WI | (16.5) | 94 | Johnson City, TN | (2.4) |
| 165 | Boston (greater), MA-NH | (9.5) | NA | El Centro, CA** | NA | NA | Johnstown, PA** | NA |
| 186 | Boston, MA M.D. | (12.0) | 276 | El Paso, TX | (21.3) | 45 | Jonesboro, AR | 5.8 |
| 97 | Boulder, CO | (3.4) | NA | Elgin, IL M.D.** | NA | NA | Joplin, MO** | NA |
| NA | Bowling Green, KY** | NA | NA | Elizabethtown-Fort Knox, KY** | NA | NA | Kahului-Wailuku-Lahaina, HI** | NA |
| 23 | Bremerton-Silverdale, WA | 12.1 | 36 | Elmira, NY | 7.0 | NA | Kankakee, IL** | NA |
| 235 | Bridgeport-Stamford, CT | (16.4) | 64 | Erie, PA | 1.8 | 153 | Kansas City, MO-KS | (8.2) |
| 289 | Brownsville-Harlingen, TX | (24.1) | 85 | Eugene, OR | (1.5) | 162 | Kennewick-Richland, WA | (9.1) |
| 229 | Brunswick, GA | (15.8) | 66 | Fairbanks, AK | 1.5 | 199 | Kingsport, TN-VA | (13.3) |
| 128 | Buffalo-Niagara Falls, NY | (5.7) | 183 | Fargo, ND-MN | (11.9) | 73 | Kingston, NY | 0.8 |
| 218 | Burlington, NC | (14.9) | 148 | Farmington, NM | (7.8) | 134 | Knoxville, TN | (6.4) |
| NA | California-Lexington Park, MD** | NA | 89 | Fayetteville-Springdale, AR-MO | (1.9) | 219 | Kokomo, IN | (15.1) |
| NA | Cambridge-Newton, MA M.D.** | NA | 151 | Fayetteville, NC | (8.0) | NA | La Crosse, WI-MN** | NA |
| 122 | Camden, NJ M.D. | (5.3) | 147 | Flagstaff, AZ | (7.7) | 124 | Lafayette, IN | (5.5) |
| NA | Canton, OH** | NA | 281 | Flint, MI | (22.1) | NA | Lafayette, LA** | NA |
| 232 | Cape Coral-Fort Myers, FL | (16.3) | 90 | Florence-Muscle Shoals, AL | (2.0) | 12 | Lake Charles, LA | 19.2 |
| 193 | Cape Girardeau, MO-IL | (12.9) | 115 | Florence, SC | (4.5) | NA | Lake Co.-Kenosha Co., IL-WI M.D.** | NA |
| NA | Carbondale-Marion, IL** | NA | 175 | Fond du Lac, WI | (10.9) | 102 | Lake Havasu City-Kingman, AZ | (3.5) |
| 256 | Carson City, NV | (18.6) | 254 | Fort Collins, CO | (18.4) | 240 | Lakeland, FL | (16.8) |
| 274 | Casper, WY | (21.2) | 212 | Fort Lauderdale, FL M.D. | (14.2) | NA | Lancaster, PA** | NA |
| 240 | Cedar Rapids, IA | (16.8) | 75 | Fort Smith, AR-OK | 0.5 | 257 | Lansing-East Lansing, MI | (18.8) |
| NA | Chambersburg-Waynesboro, PA** | NA | 47 | Fort Wayne, IN | 5.6 | 266 | Laredo, TX | (19.9) |
| NA | Champaign-Urbana, IL** | NA | 226 | Fort Worth-Arlington, TX M.D. | (15.6) | 122 | Las Cruces, NM | (5.3) |
| 182 | Charleston-North Charleston, SC | (11.7) | 131 | Fresno, CA | (5.9) | 108 | Las Vegas-Henderson, NV | (4.0) |
| NA | Charlotte-Mecklenburg, NC-SC** | NA | 49 | Gadsden, AL | 4.9 | 226 | Lawrence, KS | (15.6) |
| 302 | Charlottesville, VA | (28.7) | 274 | Gainesville, FL | (21.2) | 202 | Lawton, OK | (13.5) |
| 152 | Chattanooga, TN-GA | (8.1) | 65 | Gainesville, GA | 1.7 | 15 | Lebanon, PA | 15.6 |

Note: All listings are for Metropolitan Statistical Areas (M.S.A.s) except for those ending with "M.D." Listings with "M.D." are Metropolitan Divisions which are smaller parts of eleven large M.S.A.s. See explanatory note at beginning of metropolitan area section.

| RANK | METROPOLITAN AREA | % CHANGE |
|---|---|---|
| 29 | Lewiston-Auburn, ME | 9.1 |
| 37 | Lewiston, ID-WA | 6.8 |
| 25 | Lexington-Fayette, KY | 11.2 |
| 194 | Lima, OH | (13.0) |
| 164 | Lincoln, NE | (9.4) |
| 96 | Little Rock, AR | (2.9) |
| 280 | Logan, UT-ID | (21.9) |
| 297 | Longview, TX | (26.0) |
| 34 | Longview, WA | 7.1 |
| 105 | Los Angeles County, CA M.D. | (3.8) |
| 97 | Los Angeles (greater), CA | (3.4) |
| 43 | Louisville, KY-IN | 6.2 |
| 224 | Lubbock, TX | (15.5) |
| 192 | Lynchburg, VA | (12.8) |
| 80 | Macon, GA | (0.4) |
| 7 | Madera, CA | 28.4 |
| NA | Madison, WI** | NA |
| 58 | Manchester-Nashua, NH | 2.6 |
| 283 | Manhattan, KS | (22.6) |
| 202 | Mankato-North Mankato, MN | (13.5) |
| 9 | Mansfield, OH | 21.4 |
| 289 | McAllen-Edinburg-Mission, TX | (24.1) |
| 2 | Medford, OR | 55.2 |
| 204 | Memphis, TN-MS-AR | (13.6) |
| 206 | Merced, CA | (13.7) |
| 194 | Miami (greater), FL | (13.0) |
| 158 | Miami-Dade County, FL M.D. | (8.8) |
| 268 | Midland, TX | (20.2) |
| 259 | Milwaukee, WI | (18.9) |
| 177 | Minneapolis-St. Paul, MN-WI | (11.2) |
| 13 | Missoula, MT | 18.4 |
| 90 | Mobile, AL | (2.0) |
| 124 | Modesto, CA | (5.5) |
| NA | Monroe, LA** | NA |
| 102 | Monroe, MI | (3.5) |
| NA | Montgomery County, PA M.D.** | NA |
| 299 | Morgantown, WV | (26.6) |
| 88 | Morristown, TN | (1.7) |
| 180 | Mount Vernon-Anacortes, WA | (11.6) |
| 17 | Muncie, IN | 14.7 |
| 210 | Muskegon, MI | (14.1) |
| NA | Myrtle Beach, SC-NC** | NA |
| 271 | Napa, CA | (20.7) |
| 219 | Naples-Marco Island, FL | (15.1) |
| 232 | Nashville-Davidson, TN | (16.3) |
| 215 | Nassau-Suffolk, NY M.D. | (14.7) |
| NA | New Bern, NC** | NA |
| 215 | New Haven-Milford, CT | (14.7) |
| 78 | New Orleans, LA | (0.1) |
| 126 | New York (greater), NY-NJ-PA | (5.6) |
| NA | New York-Jersey City, NY-NJ M.D.** | NA |
| 208 | Newark, NJ-PA M.D. | (13.9) |
| 232 | Niles-Benton Harbor, MI | (16.3) |
| 298 | North Port-Sarasota-Bradenton, FL | (26.2) |
| 171 | Norwich-New London, CT | (10.5) |
| 84 | Oakland-Hayward, CA M.D. | (1.3) |
| NA | Ocala, FL** | NA |
| 97 | Ocean City, NJ | (3.4) |
| 27 | Odessa, TX | 9.3 |
| 188 | Ogden-Clearfield, UT | (12.3) |
| 138 | Oklahoma City, OK | (6.6) |
| NA | Olympia, WA** | NA |

| RANK | METROPOLITAN AREA | % CHANGE |
|---|---|---|
| 162 | Omaha-Council Bluffs, NE-IA | (9.1) |
| 174 | Orlando, FL | (10.8) |
| 283 | Oshkosh-Neenah, WI | (22.6) |
| 281 | Owensboro, KY | (22.1) |
| 82 | Oxnard-Thousand Oaks, CA | (0.9) |
| 239 | Palm Bay-Melbourne, FL | (16.7) |
| 126 | Panama City, FL | (5.6) |
| NA | Parkersburg-Vienna, WV** | NA |
| 40 | Pensacola, FL | 6.6 |
| NA | Peoria, IL** | NA |
| 113 | Philadelphia (greater) PA-NJ-MD-DE | (4.4) |
| NA | Philadelphia, PA M.D.** | NA |
| 130 | Phoenix-Mesa-Scottsdale, AZ | (5.8) |
| NA | Pittsburgh, PA** | NA |
| 21 | Pittsfield, MA | 12.7 |
| 34 | Pocatello, ID | 7.1 |
| 254 | Port St. Lucie, FL | (18.4) |
| 66 | Portland-Vancouver, OR-WA | 1.5 |
| 117 | Portland, ME | (4.8) |
| 69 | Prescott, AZ | 1.3 |
| 144 | Providence-Warwick, RI-MA | (7.6) |
| 186 | Provo-Orem, UT | (12.0) |
| 1 | Pueblo, CO | 116.5 |
| 273 | Punta Gorda, FL | (21.1) |
| 240 | Racine, WI | (16.8) |
| 169 | Raleigh, NC | (10.2) |
| 283 | Rapid City, SD | (22.6) |
| 245 | Reading, PA | (17.6) |
| 11 | Redding, CA | 21.1 |
| 271 | Reno, NV | (20.7) |
| 154 | Richmond, VA | (8.5) |
| 113 | Riverside-San Bernardino, CA | (4.4) |
| 150 | Roanoke, VA | (7.9) |
| 296 | Rochester, MN | (25.6) |
| 197 | Rochester, NY | (13.2) |
| NA | Rockford, IL** | NA |
| 40 | Rockingham County, NH M.D. | 6.6 |
| 207 | Rocky Mount, NC | (13.8) |
| 3 | Rome, GA | 37.8 |
| 183 | Sacramento, CA | (11.9) |
| 265 | Saginaw, MI | (19.8) |
| 31 | Salem, OR | 8.5 |
| 155 | Salinas, CA | (8.6) |
| NA | Salisbury, MD-DE** | NA |
| 165 | Salt Lake City, UT | (9.5) |
| 222 | San Angelo, TX | (15.3) |
| 262 | San Antonio, TX | (19.6) |
| 59 | San Diego, CA | 2.5 |
| 27 | San Francisco (greater), CA | 9.3 |
| 5 | San Francisco-Redwood, CA M.D. | 34.6 |
| 210 | San Jose, CA | (14.1) |
| 105 | San Luis Obispo, CA | (3.8) |
| NA | San Rafael, CA M.D.** | NA |
| 270 | Santa Cruz-Watsonville, CA | (20.6) |
| 72 | Santa Maria-Santa Barbara, CA | 0.9 |
| 264 | Santa Rosa, CA | (19.7) |
| 293 | Savannah, GA | (24.9) |
| NA | Scranton--Wilkes-Barre, PA** | NA |
| 117 | Seattle (greater), WA | (4.8) |
| 97 | Seattle-Bellevue-Everett, WA M.D. | (3.4) |
| 300 | Sebastian-Vero Beach, FL | (26.9) |
| NA | Sebring, FL** | NA |

| RANK | METROPOLITAN AREA | % CHANGE |
|---|---|---|
| 301 | Sheboygan, WI | (27.5) |
| 286 | Sherman-Denison, TX | (22.7) |
| 140 | Shreveport-Bossier City, LA | (6.8) |
| 307 | Silver Spring-Frederick, MD M.D. | (32.2) |
| 14 | Sioux City, IA-NE-SD | 16.7 |
| 56 | Sioux Falls, SD | 2.7 |
| 292 | South Bend-Mishawaka, IN-MI | (24.4) |
| 230 | Spartanburg, SC | (16.1) |
| 6 | Spokane, WA | 34.4 |
| NA | Springfield, IL** | NA |
| 63 | Springfield, MA | 2.2 |
| 61 | Springfield, MO | 2.3 |
| 37 | Springfield, OH | 6.8 |
| 287 | State College, PA | (23.6) |
| NA | Staunton-Waynesboro, VA** | NA |
| 116 | Stockton-Lodi, CA | (4.7) |
| 53 | St. Cloud, MN | 3.2 |
| 26 | St. George, UT | 10.7 |
| 19 | St. Joseph, MO-KS | 14.0 |
| 213 | St. Louis, MO-IL | (14.4) |
| 20 | Sumter, SC | 12.8 |
| 45 | Syracuse, NY | 5.8 |
| 161 | Tacoma, WA M.D. | (9.0) |
| 22 | Tallahassee, FL | 12.6 |
| 288 | Tampa-St Petersburg, FL | (23.9) |
| NA | Terre Haute, IN** | NA |
| 51 | Texarkana, TX-AR | 4.1 |
| NA | The Villages, FL** | NA |
| NA | Toledo, OH** | NA |
| 143 | Topeka, KS | (7.5) |
| 173 | Trenton, NJ | (10.7) |
| NA | Tucson, AZ** | NA |
| 190 | Tulsa, OK | (12.5) |
| 276 | Tuscaloosa, AL | (21.3) |
| 303 | Tyler, TX | (29.3) |
| 183 | Utica-Rome, NY | (11.9) |
| 179 | Vallejo-Fairfield, CA | (11.3) |
| 303 | Victoria, TX | (29.3) |
| 4 | Vineland-Bridgeton, NJ | 36.8 |
| NA | Virginia Beach-Norfolk, VA-NC** | NA |
| 267 | Visalia-Porterville, CA | (20.0) |
| 293 | Waco, TX | (24.9) |
| NA | Warner Robins, GA** | NA |
| 246 | Warren-Troy, MI M.D. | (17.8) |
| 222 | Washington (greater) DC-VA-MD-WV | (15.3) |
| 177 | Washington, DC-VA-MD-WV M.D. | (11.2) |
| NA | Watertown-Fort Drum, NY** | NA |
| 158 | Wausau, WI | (8.8) |
| 279 | West Palm Beach, FL M.D. | (21.5) |
| 224 | Wichita Falls, TX | (15.5) |
| 61 | Wichita, KS | 2.3 |
| 16 | Williamsport, PA | 15.5 |
| 131 | Wilmington, DE-MD-NJ M.D. | (5.9) |
| 155 | Wilmington, NC | (8.6) |
| 196 | Winchester, VA-WV | (13.1) |
| NA | Winston-Salem, NC** | NA |
| 144 | Worcester, MA-CT | (7.6) |
| NA | Yakima, WA** | NA |
| 175 | York-Hanover, PA | (10.9) |
| 8 | Yuba City, CA | 23.7 |
| 33 | Yuma, AZ | 7.2 |

Source: CQ Press using reported data from the F.B.I. "Crime in the United States 2013"
*Larceny-theft is the unlawful taking of property. Attempts are included.
**Not available.

## 36. Percent Change in Larceny-Theft Rate: 2009 to 2013 (continued)
## National Percent Change = 8.0% Decrease*

| RANK | METROPOLITAN AREA | % CHANGE | RANK | METROPOLITAN AREA | % CHANGE | RANK | METROPOLITAN AREA | % CHANGE |
|---|---|---|---|---|---|---|---|---|
| 1 | Pueblo, CO | 116.5 | 65 | Gainesville, GA | 1.7 | 128 | Buffalo-Niagara Falls, NY | (5.7) |
| 2 | Medford, OR | 55.2 | 66 | Atlanta, GA | 1.5 | 130 | Phoenix-Mesa-Scottsdale, AZ | (5.8) |
| 3 | Rome, GA | 37.8 | 66 | Fairbanks, AK | 1.5 | 131 | Fresno, CA | (5.9) |
| 4 | Vineland-Bridgeton, NJ | 36.8 | 66 | Portland-Vancouver, OR-WA | 1.5 | 131 | Wilmington, DE-MD-NJ M.D. | (5.9) |
| 5 | San Francisco-Redwood, CA M.D. | 34.6 | 69 | Prescott, AZ | 1.3 | 133 | Akron, OH | (6.1) |
| 6 | Spokane, WA | 34.4 | 70 | Bismarck, ND | 1.2 | 134 | Baton Rouge, LA | (6.4) |
| 7 | Madera, CA | 28.4 | 70 | Huntsville, AL | 1.2 | 134 | Knoxville, TN | (6.4) |
| 8 | Yuba City, CA | 23.7 | 72 | Santa Maria-Santa Barbara, CA | 0.9 | 136 | Bakersfield, CA | (6.5) |
| 9 | Anchorage, AK | 21.4 | 73 | Kingston, NY | 0.8 | 136 | Grand Forks, ND-MN | (6.5) |
| 9 | Mansfield, OH | 21.4 | 74 | Alexandria, LA | 0.6 | 138 | Dalton, GA | (6.6) |
| 11 | Redding, CA | 21.1 | 75 | Fort Smith, AR-OK | 0.5 | 138 | Oklahoma City, OK | (6.6) |
| 12 | Lake Charles, LA | 19.2 | 76 | Billings, MT | 0.4 | 140 | Shreveport-Bossier City, LA | (6.8) |
| 13 | Missoula, MT | 18.4 | 77 | Glens Falls, NY | 0.2 | 141 | Allentown, PA-NJ | (7.2) |
| 14 | Sioux City, IA-NE-SD | 16.7 | 78 | New Orleans, LA | (0.1) | 142 | Hot Springs, AR | (7.3) |
| 15 | Lebanon, PA | 15.6 | 79 | Hagerstown-Martinsburg, MD-WV | (0.2) | 143 | Topeka, KS | (7.5) |
| 16 | Williamsport, PA | 15.5 | 80 | Macon, GA | (0.4) | 144 | Deltona-Daytona Beach, FL | (7.6) |
| 17 | Muncie, IN | 14.7 | 81 | Dayton, OH | (0.5) | 144 | Providence-Warwick, RI-MA | (7.6) |
| 18 | Colorado Springs, CO | 14.1 | 82 | Duluth, MN-WI | (0.9) | 144 | Worcester, MA-CT | (7.6) |
| 19 | St. Joseph, MO-KS | 14.0 | 82 | Oxnard-Thousand Oaks, CA | (0.9) | 147 | Flagstaff, AZ | (7.7) |
| 20 | Sumter, SC | 12.8 | 84 | Oakland-Hayward, CA M.D. | (1.3) | 148 | Altoona, PA | (7.8) |
| 21 | Pittsfield, MA | 12.7 | 85 | Eugene, OR | (1.5) | 148 | Farmington, NM | (7.8) |
| 22 | Tallahassee, FL | 12.6 | 86 | Green Bay, WI | (1.6) | 150 | Roanoke, VA | (7.9) |
| 23 | Bremerton-Silverdale, WA | 12.1 | 86 | Houma, LA | (1.6) | 151 | Fayetteville, NC | (8.0) |
| 24 | Albany, GA | 11.5 | 88 | Morristown, TN | (1.7) | 152 | Chattanooga, TN-GA | (8.1) |
| 25 | Lexington-Fayette, KY | 11.2 | 89 | Fayetteville-Springdale, AR-MO | (1.9) | 153 | Kansas City, MO-KS | (8.2) |
| 26 | St. George, UT | 10.7 | 90 | Florence-Muscle Shoals, AL | (2.0) | 154 | Richmond, VA | (8.5) |
| 27 | Odessa, TX | 9.3 | 90 | Mobile, AL | (2.0) | 155 | Salinas, CA | (8.6) |
| 27 | San Francisco (greater), CA | 9.3 | 92 | Anaheim-Santa Ana-Irvine, CA M.D. | (2.1) | 155 | Wilmington, NC | (8.6) |
| 29 | Lewiston-Auburn, ME | 9.1 | 93 | Columbus, IN | (2.3) | 157 | Indianapolis, IN | (8.7) |
| 30 | Bend, OR | 9.0 | 94 | Johnson City, TN | (2.4) | 158 | Albany-Schenectady-Troy, NY | (8.8) |
| 31 | Salem, OR | 8.5 | 95 | Abilene, TX | (2.8) | 158 | Miami-Dade County, FL M.D. | (8.8) |
| 32 | Cleveland, TN | 7.3 | 96 | Little Rock, AR | (2.9) | 158 | Wausau, WI | (8.8) |
| 33 | Yuma, AZ | 7.2 | 97 | Boulder, CO | (3.4) | 161 | Tacoma, WA M.D. | (9.0) |
| 34 | Longview, WA | 7.1 | 97 | Des Moines-West Des Moines, IA | (3.4) | 162 | Kennewick-Richland, WA | (9.1) |
| 34 | Pocatello, ID | 7.1 | 97 | Los Angeles (greater), CA | (3.4) | 162 | Omaha-Council Bluffs, NE-IA | (9.1) |
| 36 | Elmira, NY | 7.0 | 97 | Ocean City, NJ | (3.4) | 164 | Lincoln, NE | (9.4) |
| 37 | Lewiston, ID-WA | 6.8 | 97 | Seattle-Bellevue-Everett, WA M.D. | (3.4) | 165 | Boston (greater), MA-NH | (9.5) |
| 37 | Springfield, OH | 6.8 | 102 | Lake Havasu City-Kingman, AZ | (3.5) | 165 | Salt Lake City, UT | (9.5) |
| 39 | Columbia, MO | 6.7 | 102 | Monroe, MI | (3.5) | 167 | Decatur, IL | (10.1) |
| 40 | Pensacola, FL | 6.6 | 104 | Chico, CA | (3.7) | 167 | Greeley, CO | (10.1) |
| 40 | Rockingham County, NH M.D. | 6.6 | 105 | Clarksville, TN-KY | (3.8) | 169 | Grand Junction, CO | (10.2) |
| 42 | Iowa City, IA | 6.4 | 105 | Los Angeles County, CA M.D. | (3.8) | 169 | Raleigh, NC | (10.2) |
| 43 | Louisville, KY-IN | 6.2 | 105 | San Luis Obispo, CA | (3.8) | 171 | Dothan, AL | (10.5) |
| 44 | Coeur d'Alene, ID | 5.9 | 108 | Jefferson City, MO | (4.0) | 171 | Norwich-New London, CT | (10.5) |
| 45 | Jonesboro, AR | 5.8 | 108 | Las Vegas-Henderson, NV | (4.0) | 173 | Trenton, NJ | (10.7) |
| 45 | Syracuse, NY | 5.8 | 110 | Detroit-Dearborn-Livonia, MI M.D. | (4.1) | 174 | Orlando, FL | (10.8) |
| 47 | Albuquerque, NM | 5.6 | 111 | Corvallis, OR | (4.2) | 175 | Fond du Lac, WI | (10.9) |
| 47 | Fort Wayne, IN | 5.6 | 112 | Cincinnati, OH-KY-IN | (4.3) | 175 | York-Hanover, PA | (10.9) |
| 49 | Gadsden, AL | 4.9 | 113 | Philadelphia (greater) PA-NJ-MD-DE | (4.4) | 177 | Minneapolis-St. Paul, MN-WI | (11.2) |
| 50 | Great Falls, MT | 4.6 | 113 | Riverside-San Bernardino, CA | (4.4) | 177 | Washington, DC-VA-MD-WV M.D. | (11.2) |
| 51 | Texarkana, TX-AR | 4.1 | 115 | Florence, SC | (4.5) | 179 | Vallejo-Fairfield, CA | (11.3) |
| 52 | Harrisonburg, VA | 3.4 | 116 | Stockton-Lodi, CA | (4.7) | 180 | Detroit (greater), MI | (11.6) |
| 53 | Denver-Aurora, CO | 3.2 | 117 | Portland, ME | (4.8) | 180 | Mount Vernon-Anacortes, WA | (11.6) |
| 53 | St. Cloud, MN | 3.2 | 117 | Seattle (greater), WA | (4.8) | 182 | Charleston-North Charleston, SC | (11.7) |
| 55 | Cumberland, MD-WV | 2.8 | 119 | Columbia, SC | (4.9) | 183 | Fargo, ND-MN | (11.9) |
| 56 | Binghamton, NY | 2.7 | 119 | Jackson, MI | (4.9) | 183 | Sacramento, CA | (11.9) |
| 56 | Sioux Falls, SD | 2.7 | 121 | Dover, DE | (5.1) | 183 | Utica-Rome, NY | (11.9) |
| 58 | Manchester-Nashua, NH | 2.6 | 122 | Camden, NJ M.D. | (5.3) | 186 | Boston, MA M.D. | (12.0) |
| 59 | San Diego, CA | 2.5 | 122 | Las Cruces, NM | (5.3) | 186 | Provo-Orem, UT | (12.0) |
| 60 | Bloomington, IN | 2.4 | 124 | Lafayette, IN | (5.5) | 188 | Goldsboro, NC | (12.3) |
| 61 | Springfield, MO | 2.3 | 124 | Modesto, CA | (5.5) | 188 | Ogden-Clearfield, UT | (12.3) |
| 61 | Wichita, KS | 2.3 | 126 | New York (greater), NY-NJ-PA | (5.6) | 190 | Houston, TX | (12.5) |
| 63 | Springfield, MA | 2.2 | 126 | Panama City, FL | (5.6) | 190 | Tulsa, OK | (12.5) |
| 64 | Erie, PA | 1.8 | 128 | Baltimore, MD | (5.7) | 192 | Lynchburg, VA | (12.8) |

Note: All listings are for Metropolitan Statistical Areas (M.S.A.s) except for those ending with "M.D." Listings with "M.D." are Metropolitan Divisions which are smaller parts of eleven large M.S.A.s. See explanatory note at beginning of metropolitan area section.

| RANK | METROPOLITAN AREA | % CHANGE | RANK | METROPOLITAN AREA | % CHANGE | RANK | METROPOLITAN AREA | % CHANGE |
|---|---|---|---|---|---|---|---|---|
| 193 | Cape Girardeau, MO-IL | (12.9) | 254 | Port St. Lucie, FL | (18.4) | NA | Chambersburg-Waynesboro, PA** | NA |
| 194 | Lima, OH | (13.0) | 256 | Carson City, NV | (18.6) | NA | Champaign-Urbana, IL** | NA |
| 194 | Miami (greater), FL | (13.0) | 257 | Austin-Round Rock, TX | (18.8) | NA | Charlotte-Mecklenburg, NC-SC** | NA |
| 196 | Winchester, VA-WV | (13.1) | 257 | Lansing-East Lansing, MI | (18.8) | NA | Chicago (greater), IL-IN-WI** | NA |
| 197 | Athens-Clarke County, GA | (13.2) | 259 | Columbus, GA-AL | (18.9) | NA | Chicago-Naperville, IL M.D.** | NA |
| 197 | Rochester, NY | (13.2) | 259 | Milwaukee, WI | (18.9) | NA | Crestview-Fort Walton Beach, FL** | NA |
| 199 | Bay City, MI | (13.3) | 261 | Dallas (greater), TX | (19.1) | NA | Daphne-Fairhope-Foley, AL** | NA |
| 199 | Kingsport, TN-VA | (13.3) | 262 | Cheyenne, WY | (19.6) | NA | Davenport, IA-IL** | NA |
| 201 | Dubuque, IA | (13.4) | 262 | San Antonio, TX | (19.6) | NA | Dutchess-Putnam, NY M.D.** | NA |
| 202 | Lawton, OK | (13.5) | 264 | Santa Rosa, CA | (19.7) | NA | East Stroudsburg, PA** | NA |
| 202 | Mankato-North Mankato, MN | (13.5) | 265 | Saginaw, MI | (19.8) | NA | El Centro, CA** | NA |
| 204 | Corpus Christi, TX | (13.6) | 266 | Laredo, TX | (19.9) | NA | Elgin, IL M.D.** | NA |
| 204 | Memphis, TN-MS-AR | (13.6) | 267 | Visalia-Porterville, CA | (20.0) | NA | Elizabethtown-Fort Knox, KY** | NA |
| 206 | Merced, CA | (13.7) | 268 | Blacksburg, VA | (20.2) | NA | Gary, IN M.D.** | NA |
| 207 | Rocky Mount, NC | (13.8) | 268 | Midland, TX | (20.2) | NA | Gettysburg, PA** | NA |
| 208 | Newark, NJ-PA M.D. | (13.9) | 270 | Santa Cruz-Watsonville, CA | (20.6) | NA | Grand Island, NE** | NA |
| 209 | Atlantic City, NJ | (14.0) | 271 | Napa, CA | (20.7) | NA | Grand Rapids-Wyoming, MI** | NA |
| 210 | Muskegon, MI | (14.1) | 271 | Reno, NV | (20.7) | NA | Grants Pass, OR** | NA |
| 210 | San Jose, CA | (14.1) | 273 | Punta Gorda, FL | (21.1) | NA | Greenville-Anderson, SC** | NA |
| 212 | Fort Lauderdale, FL M.D. | (14.2) | 274 | Casper, WY | (21.2) | NA | Greenville, NC** | NA |
| 213 | Boise City, ID | (14.4) | 274 | Gainesville, FL | (21.2) | NA | Gulfport-Biloxi-Pascagoula, MS** | NA |
| 213 | St. Louis, MO-IL | (14.4) | 276 | Dallas-Plano-Irving, TX M.D. | (21.3) | NA | Hammond, LA** | NA |
| 215 | Nassau-Suffolk, NY M.D. | (14.7) | 276 | El Paso, TX | (21.3) | NA | Hanford-Corcoran, CA** | NA |
| 215 | New Haven-Milford, CT | (14.7) | 276 | Tuscaloosa, AL | (21.3) | NA | Hilton Head Island, SC** | NA |
| 217 | Ann Arbor, MI | (14.8) | 279 | West Palm Beach, FL M.D. | (21.5) | NA | Homosassa Springs, FL** | NA |
| 218 | Burlington, NC | (14.9) | 280 | Logan, UT-ID | (21.9) | NA | Johnstown, PA** | NA |
| 219 | Beaumont-Port Arthur, TX | (15.1) | 281 | Flint, MI | (22.1) | NA | Joplin, MO** | NA |
| 219 | Kokomo, IN | (15.1) | 281 | Owensboro, KY | (22.1) | NA | Kahului-Wailuku-Lahaina, HI** | NA |
| 219 | Naples-Marco Island, FL | (15.1) | 283 | Manhattan, KS | (22.6) | NA | Kankakee, IL** | NA |
| 222 | San Angelo, TX | (15.3) | 283 | Oshkosh-Neenah, WI | (22.6) | NA | La Crosse, WI-MN** | NA |
| 222 | Washington (greater) DC-VA-MD-WV | (15.3) | 283 | Rapid City, SD | (22.6) | NA | Lafayette, LA** | NA |
| 224 | Lubbock, TX | (15.5) | 286 | Sherman-Denison, TX | (22.7) | NA | Lake Co.-Kenosha Co., IL-WI M.D.** | NA |
| 224 | Wichita Falls, TX | (15.5) | 287 | State College, PA | (23.6) | NA | Lancaster, PA** | NA |
| 226 | Fort Worth-Arlington, TX M.D. | (15.6) | 288 | Tampa-St Petersburg, FL | (23.9) | NA | Madison, WI** | NA |
| 226 | Lawrence, KS | (15.6) | 289 | Brownsville-Harlingen, TX | (24.1) | NA | Monroe, LA** | NA |
| 228 | Bangor, ME | (15.7) | 289 | Decatur, AL | (24.1) | NA | Montgomery County, PA M.D.** | NA |
| 229 | Brunswick, GA | (15.8) | 289 | McAllen-Edinburg-Mission, TX | (24.1) | NA | Myrtle Beach, SC-NC** | NA |
| 230 | Spartanburg, SC | (16.1) | 292 | South Bend-Mishawaka, IN-MI | (24.4) | NA | New Bern, NC** | NA |
| 231 | Augusta, GA-SC | (16.2) | 293 | Savannah, GA | (24.9) | NA | New York-Jersey City, NY-NJ M.D.** | NA |
| 232 | Cape Coral-Fort Myers, FL | (16.3) | 293 | Waco, TX | (24.9) | NA | Ocala, FL** | NA |
| 232 | Nashville-Davidson, TN | (16.3) | 295 | Jackson, TN | (25.0) | NA | Olympia, WA** | NA |
| 232 | Niles-Benton Harbor, MI | (16.3) | 296 | Rochester, MN | (25.6) | NA | Parkersburg-Vienna, WV** | NA |
| 235 | Bridgeport-Stamford, CT | (16.4) | 297 | Longview, TX | (26.0) | NA | Peoria, IL** | NA |
| 236 | Eau Claire, WI | (16.5) | 298 | North Port-Sarasota-Bradenton, FL | (26.2) | NA | Philadelphia, PA M.D.** | NA |
| 236 | Janesville, WI | (16.5) | 299 | Morgantown, WV | (26.6) | NA | Pittsburgh, PA** | NA |
| 238 | Greensboro-High Point, NC | (16.6) | 300 | Sebastian-Vero Beach, FL | (26.9) | NA | Rockford, IL** | NA |
| 239 | Palm Bay-Melbourne, FL | (16.7) | 301 | Sheboygan, WI | (27.5) | NA | Salisbury, MD-DE** | NA |
| 240 | Cedar Rapids, IA | (16.8) | 302 | Charlottesville, VA | (28.7) | NA | San Rafael, CA M.D.** | NA |
| 240 | Lakeland, FL | (16.8) | 303 | Tyler, TX | (29.3) | NA | Scranton--Wilkes-Barre, PA** | NA |
| 240 | Racine, WI | (16.8) | 303 | Victoria, TX | (29.3) | NA | Sebring, FL** | NA |
| 243 | Ames, IA | (16.9) | 305 | Amarillo, TX | (29.7) | NA | Springfield, IL** | NA |
| 244 | Hinesville, GA | (17.4) | 306 | Appleton, WI | (30.4) | NA | Staunton-Waynesboro, VA** | NA |
| 245 | Reading, PA | (17.6) | 307 | Silver Spring-Frederick, MD M.D. | (32.2) | NA | Terre Haute, IN** | NA |
| 246 | Warren-Troy, MI M.D. | (17.8) | 308 | College Station-Bryan, TX | (40.2) | NA | The Villages, FL** | NA |
| 247 | Birmingham-Hoover, AL | (17.9) | NA | Albany, OR** | NA | NA | Toledo, OH** | NA |
| 248 | Idaho Falls, ID | (18.1) | NA | Bloomington, IL** | NA | NA | Tucson, AZ** | NA |
| 248 | Jacksonville, FL | (18.1) | NA | Bloomsburg-Berwick, PA** | NA | NA | Virginia Beach-Norfolk, VA-NC** | NA |
| 250 | Barnstable Town, MA | (18.2) | NA | Bowling Green, KY** | NA | NA | Warner Robins, GA** | NA |
| 250 | Hartford, CT | (18.2) | NA | California-Lexington Park, MD** | NA | NA | Watertown-Fort Drum, NY** | NA |
| 252 | Anniston-Oxford, AL | (18.3) | NA | Cambridge-Newton, MA M.D.** | NA | NA | Winston-Salem, NC** | NA |
| 252 | Jackson, MS | (18.3) | NA | Canton, OH** | NA | NA | Yakima, WA** | NA |
| 254 | Fort Collins, CO | (18.4) | NA | Carbondale-Marion, IL** | NA | | | |

Source: CQ Press using reported data from the F.B.I. "Crime in the United States 2013"
*Larceny-theft is the unlawful taking of property. Attempts are included.
**Not available.

# 37. Motor Vehicle Thefts in 2013
## National Total = 699,594 Motor Vehicle Thefts*

| RANK | METROPOLITAN AREA | THEFTS | RANK | METROPOLITAN AREA | THEFTS | RANK | METROPOLITAN AREA | THEFTS |
|---|---|---|---|---|---|---|---|---|
| 221 | Abilene, TX | 292 | 318 | Cheyenne, WY | 116 | 79 | Gary, IN M.D. | 2,092 |
| 126 | Akron, OH | 921 | 8 | Chicago (greater), IL-IN-WI | 19,191 | 371 | Gettysburg, PA | 40 |
| 154 | Albany-Schenectady-Troy, NY | 650 | 13 | Chicago-Naperville, IL M.D. | 16,452 | 373 | Glens Falls, NY | 31 |
| 221 | Albany, GA | 292 | 128 | Chico, CA | 896 | 263 | Goldsboro, NC | 226 |
| 221 | Albany, OR | 292 | 60 | Cincinnati, OH-KY-IN | 3,098 | 327 | Grand Forks, ND-MN | 108 |
| 52 | Albuquerque, NM | 3,849 | 231 | Clarksville, TN-KY | 278 | 308 | Grand Island, NE | 128 |
| 181 | Alexandria, LA | 432 | 253 | Cleveland, TN | 233 | 279 | Grand Junction, CO | 186 |
| 139 | Allentown, PA-NJ | 801 | 260 | Coeur d'Alene, ID | 228 | 145 | Grand Rapids-Wyoming, MI | 734 |
| 353 | Altoona, PA | 74 | 271 | College Station-Bryan, TX | 200 | 199 | Grants Pass, OR | 363 |
| 143 | Amarillo, TX | 743 | 77 | Colorado Springs, CO | 2,231 | 313 | Great Falls, MT | 122 |
| 364 | Ames, IA | 57 | 261 | Columbia, MO | 227 | 201 | Greeley, CO | 352 |
| 31 | Anaheim-Santa Ana-Irvine, CA M.D. | 7,233 | 69 | Columbia, SC | 2,678 | 290 | Green Bay, WI | 171 |
| 125 | Anchorage, AK | 927 | 97 | Columbus, GA-AL | 1,407 | 107 | Greensboro-High Point, NC | 1,173 |
| 196 | Ann Arbor, MI | 376 | 283 | Columbus, IN | 182 | 70 | Greenville-Anderson, SC | 2,599 |
| 277 | Anniston-Oxford, AL | 189 | 149 | Corpus Christi, TX | 700 | 269 | Greenville, NC | 204 |
| 358 | Appleton, WI | 68 | 349 | Corvallis, OR | 80 | 144 | Gulfport-Biloxi-Pascagoula, MS | 738 |
| 235 | Athens-Clarke County, GA | 274 | 240 | Crestview-Fort Walton Beach, FL | 263 | 237 | Hagerstown-Martinsburg, MD-WV | 270 |
| 10 | Atlanta, GA | 18,593 | 356 | Cumberland, MD-WV | 71 | 209 | Hammond, LA | 326 |
| 255 | Atlantic City, NJ | 232 | 12 | Dallas (greater), TX | 17,943 | 178 | Hanford-Corcoran, CA | 452 |
| 84 | Augusta, GA-SC | 1,707 | 17 | Dallas-Plano-Irving, TX M.D. | 12,998 | 363 | Harrisonburg, VA | 58 |
| 64 | Austin-Round Rock, TX | 2,983 | 255 | Dalton, GA | 232 | 86 | Hartford, CT | 1,679 |
| 41 | Bakersfield, CA | 5,802 | 269 | Daphne-Fairhope-Foley, AL | 204 | 232 | Hilton Head Island, SC | 277 |
| 32 | Baltimore, MD | 7,086 | 193 | Davenport, IA-IL | 383 | 326 | Hinesville, GA | 109 |
| 342 | Bangor, ME | 88 | 95 | Dayton, OH | 1,412 | 323 | Homosassa Springs, FL | 113 |
| 272 | Barnstable Town, MA | 199 | 247 | Decatur, AL | 242 | 242 | Hot Springs, AR | 261 |
| 116 | Baton Rouge, LA | 1,035 | 346 | Decatur, IL | 82 | 248 | Houma, LA | 239 |
| 320 | Bay City, MI | 114 | 111 | Deltona-Daytona Beach, FL | 1,109 | 4 | Houston, TX | 23,298 |
| 142 | Beaumont-Port Arthur, TX | 755 | 28 | Denver-Aurora, CO | 8,043 | 122 | Huntsville, AL | 998 |
| 285 | Bend, OR | 177 | 106 | Des Moines-West Des Moines, IA | 1,190 | 297 | Idaho Falls, ID | 164 |
| 153 | Billings, MT | 652 | 9 | Detroit (greater), MI | 19,168 | 35 | Indianapolis, IN | 6,496 |
| 300 | Binghamton, NY | 155 | 14 | Detroit-Dearborn-Livonia, MI M.D. | 15,514 | 307 | Iowa City, IA | 137 |
| 62 | Birmingham-Hoover, AL | 3,060 | 258 | Dothan, AL | 231 | 81 | Jacksonville, FL | 2,043 |
| 266 | Bismarck, ND | 221 | 281 | Dover, DE | 184 | 298 | Jackson, MI | 156 |
| 331 | Blacksburg, VA | 103 | 348 | Dubuque, IA | 81 | 94 | Jackson, MS | 1,439 |
| 337 | Bloomington, IL | 99 | 182 | Duluth, MN-WI | 430 | 250 | Jackson, TN | 236 |
| 255 | Bloomington, IN | 232 | 325 | Dutchess-Putnam, NY M.D. | 110 | 316 | Janesville, WI | 118 |
| 372 | Bloomsburg-Berwick, PA | 32 | 333 | East Stroudsburg, PA | 102 | 318 | Jefferson City, MO | 116 |
| 165 | Boise City, ID | 529 | 342 | Eau Claire, WI | 88 | 282 | Johnson City, TN | 183 |
| 39 | Boston (greater), MA-NH | 6,034 | 161 | El Centro, CA | 582 | 345 | Johnstown, PA | 87 |
| 67 | Boston, MA M.D. | 2,825 | 123 | El Paso, TX | 961 | 314 | Jonesboro, AR | 121 |
| 206 | Boulder, CO | 333 | 239 | Elgin, IL M.D. | 264 | 173 | Joplin, MO | 495 |
| 285 | Bowling Green, KY | 177 | 352 | Elizabethtown-Fort Knox, KY | 76 | 179 | Kahului-Wailuku-Lahaina, HI | 442 |
| 168 | Bremerton-Silverdale, WA | 512 | 374 | Elmira, NY | 27 | 349 | Kankakee, IL | 80 |
| 99 | Bridgeport-Stamford, CT | 1,319 | 287 | Erie, PA | 174 | 25 | Kansas City, MO-KS | 8,397 |
| 172 | Brownsville-Harlingen, TX | 496 | 121 | Eugene, OR | 1,006 | 185 | Kennewick-Richland, WA | 410 |
| 295 | Brunswick, GA | 167 | 320 | Fairbanks, AK | 114 | 197 | Kingsport, TN-VA | 371 |
| 93 | Buffalo-Niagara Falls, NY | 1,473 | 234 | Fargo, ND-MN | 276 | 367 | Kingston, NY | 55 |
| 264 | Burlington, NC | 225 | 294 | Farmington, NM | 168 | 89 | Knoxville, TN | 1,538 |
| 315 | California-Lexington Park, MD | 119 | 171 | Fayetteville-Springdale, AR-MO | 498 | 308 | Kokomo, IN | 128 |
| 65 | Cambridge-Newton, MA M.D. | 2,932 | 131 | Fayetteville, NC | 884 | 357 | La Crosse, WI-MN | 70 |
| 91 | Camden, NJ M.D. | 1,489 | 333 | Flagstaff, AZ | 102 | 215 | Lafayette, IN | 312 |
| 148 | Canton, OH | 703 | 141 | Flint, MI | 785 | 117 | Lafayette, LA | 1,027 |
| 136 | Cape Coral-Fort Myers, FL | 813 | 228 | Florence-Muscle Shoals, AL | 287 | 169 | Lake Charles, LA | 511 |
| 329 | Cape Girardeau, MO-IL | 107 | 164 | Florence, SC | 535 | 193 | Lake Co.-Kenosha Co., IL-WI M.D. | 383 |
| 306 | Carbondale-Marion, IL | 141 | 370 | Fond du Lac, WI | 46 | 186 | Lake Havasu City-Kingman, AZ | 405 |
| 358 | Carson City, NV | 68 | 246 | Fort Collins, CO | 247 | 127 | Lakeland, FL | 906 |
| 324 | Casper, WY | 111 | 51 | Fort Lauderdale, FL M.D. | 3,931 | 225 | Lancaster, PA | 290 |
| 195 | Cedar Rapids, IA | 380 | 184 | Fort Smith, AR-OK | 423 | 146 | Lansing-East Lansing, MI | 721 |
| 341 | Chambersburg-Waynesboro, PA | 89 | 167 | Fort Wayne, IN | 516 | 190 | Laredo, TX | 391 |
| 291 | Champaign-Urbana, IL | 170 | 45 | Fort Worth-Arlington, TX M.D. | 4,945 | 212 | Las Cruces, NM | 324 |
| 85 | Charleston-North Charleston, SC | 1,704 | 37 | Fresno, CA | 6,339 | 27 | Las Vegas-Henderson, NV | 8,246 |
| 54 | Charlotte-Mecklenburg, NC-SC | 3,600 | 217 | Gadsden, AL | 300 | 274 | Lawrence, KS | 196 |
| 288 | Charlottesville, VA | 173 | 198 | Gainesville, FL | 366 | 244 | Lawton, OK | 250 |
| 87 | Chattanooga, TN-GA | 1,644 | 221 | Gainesville, GA | 292 | 361 | Lebanon, PA | 66 |

Note: All listings are for Metropolitan Statistical Areas (M.S.A.s) except for those ending with "M.D." Listings with "M.D." are Metropolitan Divisions which are smaller parts of eleven large M.S.A.s. See explanatory note at beginning of metropolitan area section.

| RANK | METROPOLITAN AREA | THEFTS | RANK | METROPOLITAN AREA | THEFTS | RANK | METROPOLITAN AREA | THEFTS |
|---|---|---|---|---|---|---|---|---|
| 337 | Lewiston-Auburn, ME | 99 | 49 | Omaha-Council Bluffs, NE-IA | 4,086 | 362 | Sheboygan, WI | 61 |
| 340 | Lewiston, ID-WA | 93 | 46 | Orlando, FL | 4,575 | 289 | Sherman-Denison, TX | 172 |
| 119 | Lexington-Fayette, KY | 1,018 | 355 | Oshkosh-Neenah, WI | 72 | 134 | Shreveport-Bossier City, LA | 832 |
| 302 | Lima, OH | 147 | 310 | Owensboro, KY | 127 | 115 | Silver Spring-Frederick, MD M.D. | 1,063 |
| 209 | Lincoln, NE | 326 | 90 | Oxnard-Thousand Oaks, CA | 1,500 | 220 | Sioux City, IA-NE-SD | 295 |
| 74 | Little Rock, AR | 2,360 | 150 | Palm Bay-Melbourne, FL | 690 | 214 | Sioux Falls, SD | 317 |
| 369 | Logan, UT-ID | 48 | 213 | Panama City, FL | 322 | 162 | South Bend-Mishawaka, IN-MI | 559 |
| 191 | Longview, TX | 387 | 339 | Parkersburg-Vienna, WV | 96 | 160 | Spartanburg, SC | 598 |
| 227 | Longview, WA | 288 | 133 | Pensacola, FL | 855 | 58 | Spokane, WA | 3,330 |
| 2 | Los Angeles County, CA M.D. | 38,935 | 218 | Peoria, IL | 298 | 138 | Springfield, IL | 808 |
| 1 | Los Angeles (greater), CA | 46,168 | 21 | Philadelphia (greater) PA-NJ-MD-DE | 10,273 | 100 | Springfield, MA | 1,302 |
| 66 | Louisville, KY-IN | 2,848 | 36 | Philadelphia, PA M.D. | 6,461 | 92 | Springfield, MO | 1,483 |
| 124 | Lubbock, TX | 933 | NA | Phoenix-Mesa-Scottsdale, AZ** | NA | 230 | Springfield, OH | 283 |
| 268 | Lynchburg, VA | 206 | 83 | Pittsburgh, PA | 1,815 | 374 | State College, PA | 27 |
| 136 | Macon, GA | 813 | 335 | Pittsfield, MA | 101 | 351 | Staunton-Waynesboro, VA | 77 |
| 163 | Madera, CA | 550 | 336 | Pocatello, ID | 100 | 50 | Stockton-Lodi, CA | 3,996 |
| 180 | Madison, WI | 434 | 186 | Port St. Lucie, FL | 405 | 244 | St. Cloud, MN | 250 |
| 216 | Manchester-Nashua, NH | 310 | 33 | Portland-Vancouver, OR-WA | 6,871 | 316 | St. George, UT | 118 |
| 353 | Manhattan, KS | 74 | 204 | Portland, ME | 338 | 208 | St. Joseph, MO-KS | 330 |
| 331 | Mankato-North Mankato, MN | 103 | 252 | Prescott, AZ | 235 | 38 | St. Louis, MO-IL | 6,136 |
| 311 | Mansfield, OH | 125 | 61 | Providence-Warwick, RI-MA | 3,072 | 243 | Sumter, SC | 255 |
| 88 | McAllen-Edinburg-Mission, TX | 1,564 | 177 | Provo-Orem, UT | 455 | 156 | Syracuse, NY | 645 |
| 219 | Medford, OR | 296 | 159 | Pueblo, CO | 606 | 48 | Tacoma, WA M.D. | 4,267 |
| 56 | Memphis, TN-MS-AR | 3,517 | 320 | Punta Gorda, FL | 114 | 158 | Tallahassee, FL | 607 |
| 98 | Merced, CA | 1,342 | 303 | Racine, WI | 146 | 47 | Tampa-St Petersburg, FL | 4,411 |
| 15 | Miami (greater), FL | 14,980 | 102 | Raleigh, NC | 1,280 | 182 | Terre Haute, IN | 430 |
| 26 | Miami-Dade County, FL M.D. | 8,331 | 279 | Rapid City, SD | 186 | 225 | Texarkana, TX-AR | 290 |
| 238 | Midland, TX | 266 | 175 | Reading, PA | 478 | 364 | The Villages, FL | 57 |
| 44 | Milwaukee, WI | 4,986 | 112 | Redding, CA | 1,103 | 101 | Toledo, OH | 1,299 |
| 40 | Minneapolis-St. Paul, MN-WI | 5,989 | 105 | Reno, NV | 1,215 | 152 | Topeka, KS | 686 |
| 291 | Missoula, MT | 170 | 82 | Richmond, VA | 1,899 | 151 | Trenton, NJ | 688 |
| 104 | Mobile, AL | 1,228 | 6 | Riverside-San Bernardino, CA | 21,476 | 63 | Tucson, AZ | 3,030 |
| 57 | Modesto, CA | 3,469 | 211 | Roanoke, VA | 325 | 59 | Tulsa, OK | 3,264 |
| 250 | Monroe, LA | 236 | 304 | Rochester, MN | 144 | 200 | Tuscaloosa, AL | 361 |
| 253 | Monroe, MI | 233 | 120 | Rochester, NY | 1,015 | 202 | Tyler, TX | 346 |
| 103 | Montgomery County, PA M.D. | 1,229 | 170 | Rockford, IL | 500 | 278 | Utica-Rome, NY | 187 |
| 330 | Morgantown, WV | 106 | 232 | Rockingham County, NH M.D. | 277 | 73 | Vallejo-Fairfield, CA | 2,394 |
| 291 | Morristown, TN | 170 | 267 | Rocky Mount, NC | 212 | 327 | Victoria, TX | 108 |
| 204 | Mount Vernon-Anacortes, WA | 338 | 275 | Rome, GA | 190 | 275 | Vineland-Bridgeton, NJ | 190 |
| 284 | Muncie, IN | 179 | 24 | Sacramento, CA | 8,416 | 71 | Virginia Beach-Norfolk, VA-NC | 2,552 |
| 261 | Muskegon, MI | 227 | 264 | Saginaw, MI | 225 | NA | Visalia-Porterville, CA** | NA |
| 96 | Myrtle Beach, SC-NC | 1,409 | 109 | Salem, OR | 1,144 | 207 | Waco, TX | 331 |
| 249 | Napa, CA | 237 | 78 | Salinas, CA | 2,198 | 228 | Warner Robins, GA | 287 |
| 258 | Naples-Marco Island, FL | 231 | 189 | Salisbury, MD-DE | 395 | 53 | Warren-Troy, MI M.D. | 3,654 |
| 76 | Nashville-Davidson, TN | 2,255 | 42 | Salt Lake City, UT | 5,620 | 20 | Washington (greater) DC-VA-MD-WV | 11,008 |
| 80 | Nassau-Suffolk, NY M.D. | 2,065 | 273 | San Angelo, TX | 197 | 23 | Washington, DC-VA-MD-WV M.D. | 9,945 |
| 305 | New Bern, NC | 143 | 29 | San Antonio, TX | 7,705 | 346 | Watertown-Fort Drum, NY | 82 |
| 72 | New Haven-Milford, CT | 2,467 | 19 | San Diego, CA | 11,272 | 368 | Wausau, WI | 54 |
| 55 | New Orleans, LA | 3,530 | 3 | San Francisco (greater), CA | 28,500 | 68 | West Palm Beach, FL M.D. | 2,718 |
| 5 | New York (greater), NY-NJ-PA | 21,519 | 30 | San Francisco-Redwood, CA M.D. | 7,532 | 203 | Wichita Falls, TX | 339 |
| 18 | New York-Jersey City, NY-NJ M.D. | 12,671 | 22 | San Jose, CA | 10,269 | 75 | Wichita, KS | 2,281 |
| 34 | Newark, NJ-PA M.D. | 6,673 | 188 | San Luis Obispo, CA | 399 | 364 | Williamsport, PA | 57 |
| 296 | Niles-Benton Harbor, MI | 166 | 155 | San Rafael, CA M.D. | 649 | 113 | Wilmington, DE-MD-NJ M.D. | 1,094 |
| 140 | North Port-Sarasota-Bradenton, FL | 798 | 118 | Santa Cruz-Watsonville, CA | 1,023 | 174 | Wilmington, NC | 484 |
| 301 | Norwich-New London, CT | 153 | 108 | Santa Maria-Santa Barbara, CA | 1,146 | 311 | Winchester, VA-WV | 125 |
| 7 | Oakland-Hayward, CA M.D. | 20,319 | 146 | Santa Rosa, CA | 721 | 114 | Winston-Salem, NC | 1,070 |
| 236 | Ocala, FL | 273 | 132 | Savannah, GA | 870 | 129 | Worcester, MA-CT | 891 |
| 360 | Ocean City, NJ | 67 | 166 | Scranton--Wilkes-Barre, PA | 528 | 110 | Yakima, WA | 1,140 |
| 157 | Odessa, TX | 644 | 11 | Seattle (greater), WA | 18,291 | 241 | York-Hanover, PA | 262 |
| 130 | Ogden-Clearfield, UT | 886 | 16 | Seattle-Bellevue-Everett, WA M.D. | 14,024 | 135 | Yuba City, CA | 826 |
| 43 | Oklahoma City, OK | 5,434 | 342 | Sebastian-Vero Beach, FL | 88 | 191 | Yuma, AZ | 387 |
| 176 | Olympia, WA | 462 | 298 | Sebring, FL | 156 | | | |

Source: Reported data from the F.B.I. "Crime in the United States 2013"

*Motor vehicle theft includes the theft or attempted theft of a self-propelled vehicle.  Excludes motorboats, construction equipment, airplanes, and farming equipment.

**Not available.

# 37. Motor Vehicle Thefts in 2013 (continued)
## National Total = 699,594 Motor Vehicle Thefts*

| RANK | METROPOLITAN AREA | THEFTS | RANK | METROPOLITAN AREA | THEFTS | RANK | METROPOLITAN AREA | THEFTS |
|---|---|---|---|---|---|---|---|---|
| 1 | Los Angeles (greater), CA | 46,168 | 65 | Cambridge-Newton, MA M.D. | 2,932 | 129 | Worcester, MA-CT | 891 |
| 2 | Los Angeles County, CA M.D. | 38,935 | 66 | Louisville, KY-IN | 2,848 | 130 | Ogden-Clearfield, UT | 886 |
| 3 | San Francisco (greater), CA | 28,500 | 67 | Boston, MA M.D. | 2,825 | 131 | Fayetteville, NC | 884 |
| 4 | Houston, TX | 23,298 | 68 | West Palm Beach, FL M.D. | 2,718 | 132 | Savannah, GA | 870 |
| 5 | New York (greater), NY-NJ-PA | 21,519 | 69 | Columbia, SC | 2,678 | 133 | Pensacola, FL | 855 |
| 6 | Riverside-San Bernardino, CA | 21,476 | 70 | Greenville-Anderson, SC | 2,599 | 134 | Shreveport-Bossier City, LA | 832 |
| 7 | Oakland-Hayward, CA M.D. | 20,319 | 71 | Virginia Beach-Norfolk, VA-NC | 2,552 | 135 | Yuba City, CA | 826 |
| 8 | Chicago (greater), IL-IN-WI | 19,191 | 72 | New Haven-Milford, CT | 2,467 | 136 | Cape Coral-Fort Myers, FL | 813 |
| 9 | Detroit (greater), MI | 19,168 | 73 | Vallejo-Fairfield, CA | 2,394 | 136 | Macon, GA | 813 |
| 10 | Atlanta, GA | 18,593 | 74 | Little Rock, AR | 2,360 | 138 | Springfield, IL | 808 |
| 11 | Seattle (greater), WA | 18,291 | 75 | Wichita, KS | 2,281 | 139 | Allentown, PA-NJ | 801 |
| 12 | Dallas (greater), TX | 17,943 | 76 | Nashville-Davidson, TN | 2,255 | 140 | North Port-Sarasota-Bradenton, FL | 798 |
| 13 | Chicago-Naperville, IL M.D. | 16,452 | 77 | Colorado Springs, CO | 2,231 | 141 | Flint, MI | 785 |
| 14 | Detroit-Dearborn-Livonia, MI M.D. | 15,514 | 78 | Salinas, CA | 2,198 | 142 | Beaumont-Port Arthur, TX | 755 |
| 15 | Miami (greater), FL | 14,980 | 79 | Gary, IN M.D. | 2,092 | 143 | Amarillo, TX | 743 |
| 16 | Seattle-Bellevue-Everett, WA M.D. | 14,024 | 80 | Nassau-Suffolk, NY M.D. | 2,065 | 144 | Gulfport-Biloxi-Pascagoula, MS | 738 |
| 17 | Dallas-Plano-Irving, TX M.D. | 12,998 | 81 | Jacksonville, FL | 2,043 | 145 | Grand Rapids-Wyoming, MI | 734 |
| 18 | New York-Jersey City, NY-NJ M.D. | 12,671 | 82 | Richmond, VA | 1,899 | 146 | Lansing-East Lansing, MI | 721 |
| 19 | San Diego, CA | 11,272 | 83 | Pittsburgh, PA | 1,815 | 146 | Santa Rosa, CA | 721 |
| 20 | Washington (greater) DC-VA-MD-WV | 11,008 | 84 | Augusta, GA-SC | 1,707 | 148 | Canton, OH | 703 |
| 21 | Philadelphia (greater) PA-NJ-MD-DE | 10,273 | 85 | Charleston-North Charleston, SC | 1,704 | 149 | Corpus Christi, TX | 700 |
| 22 | San Jose, CA | 10,269 | 86 | Hartford, CT | 1,679 | 150 | Palm Bay-Melbourne, FL | 690 |
| 23 | Washington, DC-VA-MD-WV M.D. | 9,945 | 87 | Chattanooga, TN-GA | 1,644 | 151 | Trenton, NJ | 688 |
| 24 | Sacramento, CA | 8,416 | 88 | McAllen-Edinburg-Mission, TX | 1,564 | 152 | Topeka, KS | 686 |
| 25 | Kansas City, MO-KS | 8,397 | 89 | Knoxville, TN | 1,538 | 153 | Billings, MT | 652 |
| 26 | Miami-Dade County, FL M.D. | 8,331 | 90 | Oxnard-Thousand Oaks, CA | 1,500 | 154 | Albany-Schenectady-Troy, NY | 650 |
| 27 | Las Vegas-Henderson, NV | 8,246 | 91 | Camden, NJ M.D. | 1,489 | 155 | San Rafael, CA M.D. | 649 |
| 28 | Denver-Aurora, CO | 8,043 | 92 | Springfield, MO | 1,483 | 156 | Syracuse, NY | 645 |
| 29 | San Antonio, TX | 7,705 | 93 | Buffalo-Niagara Falls, NY | 1,473 | 157 | Odessa, TX | 644 |
| 30 | San Francisco-Redwood, CA M.D. | 7,532 | 94 | Jackson, MS | 1,439 | 158 | Tallahassee, FL | 607 |
| 31 | Anaheim-Santa Ana-Irvine, CA M.D. | 7,233 | 95 | Dayton, OH | 1,412 | 159 | Pueblo, CO | 606 |
| 32 | Baltimore, MD | 7,086 | 96 | Myrtle Beach, SC-NC | 1,409 | 160 | Spartanburg, SC | 598 |
| 33 | Portland-Vancouver, OR-WA | 6,871 | 97 | Columbus, GA-AL | 1,407 | 161 | El Centro, CA | 582 |
| 34 | Newark, NJ-PA M.D. | 6,673 | 98 | Merced, CA | 1,342 | 162 | South Bend-Mishawaka, IN-MI | 559 |
| 35 | Indianapolis, IN | 6,496 | 99 | Bridgeport-Stamford, CT | 1,319 | 163 | Madera, CA | 550 |
| 36 | Philadelphia, PA M.D. | 6,461 | 100 | Springfield, MA | 1,302 | 164 | Florence, SC | 535 |
| 37 | Fresno, CA | 6,339 | 101 | Toledo, OH | 1,299 | 165 | Boise City, ID | 529 |
| 38 | St. Louis, MO-IL | 6,136 | 102 | Raleigh, NC | 1,280 | 166 | Scranton--Wilkes-Barre, PA | 528 |
| 39 | Boston (greater), MA-NH | 6,034 | 103 | Montgomery County, PA M.D. | 1,229 | 167 | Fort Wayne, IN | 516 |
| 40 | Minneapolis-St. Paul, MN-WI | 5,989 | 104 | Mobile, AL | 1,228 | 168 | Bremerton-Silverdale, WA | 512 |
| 41 | Bakersfield, CA | 5,802 | 105 | Reno, NV | 1,215 | 169 | Lake Charles, LA | 511 |
| 42 | Salt Lake City, UT | 5,620 | 106 | Des Moines-West Des Moines, IA | 1,190 | 170 | Rockford, IL | 500 |
| 43 | Oklahoma City, OK | 5,434 | 107 | Greensboro-High Point, NC | 1,173 | 171 | Fayetteville-Springdale, AR-MO | 498 |
| 44 | Milwaukee, WI | 4,986 | 108 | Santa Maria-Santa Barbara, CA | 1,146 | 172 | Brownsville-Harlingen, TX | 496 |
| 45 | Fort Worth-Arlington, TX M.D. | 4,945 | 109 | Salem, OR | 1,144 | 173 | Joplin, MO | 495 |
| 46 | Orlando, FL | 4,575 | 110 | Yakima, WA | 1,140 | 174 | Wilmington, NC | 484 |
| 47 | Tampa-St Petersburg, FL | 4,411 | 111 | Deltona-Daytona Beach, FL | 1,109 | 175 | Reading, PA | 478 |
| 48 | Tacoma, WA M.D. | 4,267 | 112 | Redding, CA | 1,103 | 176 | Olympia, WA | 462 |
| 49 | Omaha-Council Bluffs, NE-IA | 4,086 | 113 | Wilmington, DE-MD-NJ M.D. | 1,094 | 177 | Provo-Orem, UT | 455 |
| 50 | Stockton-Lodi, CA | 3,996 | 114 | Winston-Salem, NC | 1,070 | 178 | Hanford-Corcoran, CA | 452 |
| 51 | Fort Lauderdale, FL M.D. | 3,931 | 115 | Silver Spring-Frederick, MD M.D. | 1,063 | 179 | Kahului-Wailuku-Lahaina, HI | 442 |
| 52 | Albuquerque, NM | 3,849 | 116 | Baton Rouge, LA | 1,035 | 180 | Madison, WI | 434 |
| 53 | Warren-Troy, MI M.D. | 3,654 | 117 | Lafayette, LA | 1,027 | 181 | Alexandria, LA | 432 |
| 54 | Charlotte-Mecklenburg, NC-SC | 3,600 | 118 | Santa Cruz-Watsonville, CA | 1,023 | 182 | Duluth, MN-WI | 430 |
| 55 | New Orleans, LA | 3,530 | 119 | Lexington-Fayette, KY | 1,018 | 182 | Terre Haute, IN | 430 |
| 56 | Memphis, TN-MS-AR | 3,517 | 120 | Rochester, NY | 1,015 | 184 | Fort Smith, AR-OK | 423 |
| 57 | Modesto, CA | 3,469 | 121 | Eugene, OR | 1,006 | 185 | Kennewick-Richland, WA | 410 |
| 58 | Spokane, WA | 3,330 | 122 | Huntsville, AL | 998 | 186 | Lake Havasu City-Kingman, AZ | 405 |
| 59 | Tulsa, OK | 3,264 | 123 | El Paso, TX | 961 | 186 | Port St. Lucie, FL | 405 |
| 60 | Cincinnati, OH-KY-IN | 3,098 | 124 | Lubbock, TX | 933 | 188 | San Luis Obispo, CA | 399 |
| 61 | Providence-Warwick, RI-MA | 3,072 | 125 | Anchorage, AK | 927 | 189 | Salisbury, MD-DE | 395 |
| 62 | Birmingham-Hoover, AL | 3,060 | 126 | Akron, OH | 921 | 190 | Laredo, TX | 391 |
| 63 | Tucson, AZ | 3,030 | 127 | Lakeland, FL | 906 | 191 | Longview, TX | 387 |
| 64 | Austin-Round Rock, TX | 2,983 | 128 | Chico, CA | 896 | 191 | Yuma, AZ | 387 |

Note: All listings are for Metropolitan Statistical Areas (M.S.A.s) except for those ending with "M.D." Listings with "M.D." are Metropolitan Divisions which are smaller parts of eleven large M.S.A.s. See explanatory note at beginning of metropolitan area section.

| RANK | METROPOLITAN AREA | THEFTS | RANK | METROPOLITAN AREA | THEFTS | RANK | METROPOLITAN AREA | THEFTS |
|---|---|---|---|---|---|---|---|---|
| 193 | Davenport, IA-IL | 383 | 255 | Atlantic City, NJ | 232 | 316 | St. George, UT | 118 |
| 193 | Lake Co.-Kenosha Co., IL-WI M.D. | 383 | 255 | Bloomington, IN | 232 | 318 | Cheyenne, WY | 116 |
| 195 | Cedar Rapids, IA | 380 | 255 | Dalton, GA | 232 | 318 | Jefferson City, MO | 116 |
| 196 | Ann Arbor, MI | 376 | 258 | Dothan, AL | 231 | 320 | Bay City, MI | 114 |
| 197 | Kingsport, TN-VA | 371 | 258 | Naples-Marco Island, FL | 231 | 320 | Fairbanks, AK | 114 |
| 198 | Gainesville, FL | 366 | 260 | Coeur d'Alene, ID | 228 | 320 | Punta Gorda, FL | 114 |
| 199 | Grants Pass, OR | 363 | 261 | Columbia, MO | 227 | 323 | Homosassa Springs, FL | 113 |
| 200 | Tuscaloosa, AL | 361 | 261 | Muskegon, MI | 227 | 324 | Casper, WY | 111 |
| 201 | Greeley, CO | 352 | 263 | Goldsboro, NC | 226 | 325 | Dutchess-Putnam, NY M.D. | 110 |
| 202 | Tyler, TX | 346 | 264 | Burlington, NC | 225 | 326 | Hinesville, GA | 109 |
| 203 | Wichita Falls, TX | 339 | 264 | Saginaw, MI | 225 | 327 | Grand Forks, ND-MN | 108 |
| 204 | Mount Vernon-Anacortes, WA | 338 | 266 | Bismarck, ND | 221 | 327 | Victoria, TX | 108 |
| 204 | Portland, ME | 338 | 267 | Rocky Mount, NC | 212 | 329 | Cape Girardeau, MO-IL | 107 |
| 206 | Boulder, CO | 333 | 268 | Lynchburg, VA | 206 | 330 | Morgantown, WV | 106 |
| 207 | Waco, TX | 331 | 269 | Daphne-Fairhope-Foley, AL | 204 | 331 | Blacksburg, VA | 103 |
| 208 | St. Joseph, MO-KS | 330 | 269 | Greenville, NC | 204 | 331 | Mankato-North Mankato, MN | 103 |
| 209 | Hammond, LA | 326 | 271 | College Station-Bryan, TX | 200 | 333 | East Stroudsburg, PA | 102 |
| 209 | Lincoln, NE | 326 | 272 | Barnstable Town, MA | 199 | 333 | Flagstaff, AZ | 102 |
| 211 | Roanoke, VA | 325 | 273 | San Angelo, TX | 197 | 335 | Pittsfield, MA | 101 |
| 212 | Las Cruces, NM | 324 | 274 | Lawrence, KS | 196 | 336 | Pocatello, ID | 100 |
| 213 | Panama City, FL | 322 | 275 | Rome, GA | 190 | 337 | Bloomington, IL | 99 |
| 214 | Sioux Falls, SD | 317 | 275 | Vineland-Bridgeton, NJ | 190 | 337 | Lewiston-Auburn, ME | 99 |
| 215 | Lafayette, IN | 312 | 277 | Anniston-Oxford, AL | 189 | 339 | Parkersburg-Vienna, WV | 96 |
| 216 | Manchester-Nashua, NH | 310 | 278 | Utica-Rome, NY | 187 | 340 | Lewiston, ID-WA | 93 |
| 217 | Gadsden, AL | 300 | 279 | Grand Junction, CO | 186 | 341 | Chambersburg-Waynesboro, PA | 89 |
| 218 | Peoria, IL | 298 | 279 | Rapid City, SD | 186 | 342 | Bangor, ME | 88 |
| 219 | Medford, OR | 296 | 281 | Dover, DE | 184 | 342 | Eau Claire, WI | 88 |
| 220 | Sioux City, IA-NE-SD | 295 | 282 | Johnson City, TN | 183 | 342 | Sebastian-Vero Beach, FL | 88 |
| 221 | Abilene, TX | 292 | 283 | Columbus, IN | 182 | 345 | Johnstown, PA | 87 |
| 221 | Albany, GA | 292 | 284 | Muncie, IN | 179 | 346 | Decatur, IL | 82 |
| 221 | Albany, OR | 292 | 285 | Bend, OR | 177 | 346 | Watertown-Fort Drum, NY | 82 |
| 221 | Gainesville, GA | 292 | 285 | Bowling Green, KY | 177 | 348 | Dubuque, IA | 81 |
| 225 | Lancaster, PA | 290 | 287 | Erie, PA | 174 | 349 | Corvallis, OR | 80 |
| 225 | Texarkana, TX-AR | 290 | 288 | Charlottesville, VA | 173 | 349 | Kankakee, IL | 80 |
| 227 | Longview, WA | 288 | 289 | Sherman-Denison, TX | 172 | 351 | Staunton-Waynesboro, VA | 77 |
| 228 | Florence-Muscle Shoals, AL | 287 | 290 | Green Bay, WI | 171 | 352 | Elizabethtown-Fort Knox, KY | 76 |
| 228 | Warner Robins, GA | 287 | 291 | Champaign-Urbana, IL | 170 | 353 | Altoona, PA | 74 |
| 230 | Springfield, OH | 283 | 291 | Missoula, MT | 170 | 353 | Manhattan, KS | 74 |
| 231 | Clarksville, TN-KY | 278 | 291 | Morristown, TN | 170 | 355 | Oshkosh-Neenah, WI | 72 |
| 232 | Hilton Head Island, SC | 277 | 294 | Farmington, NM | 168 | 356 | Cumberland, MD-WV | 71 |
| 232 | Rockingham County, NH M.D. | 277 | 295 | Brunswick, GA | 167 | 357 | La Crosse, WI-MN | 70 |
| 234 | Fargo, ND-MN | 276 | 296 | Niles-Benton Harbor, MI | 166 | 358 | Appleton, WI | 68 |
| 235 | Athens-Clarke County, GA | 274 | 297 | Idaho Falls, ID | 164 | 358 | Carson City, NV | 68 |
| 236 | Ocala, FL | 273 | 298 | Jackson, MI | 156 | 360 | Ocean City, NJ | 67 |
| 237 | Hagerstown-Martinsburg, MD-WV | 270 | 298 | Sebring, FL | 156 | 361 | Lebanon, PA | 66 |
| 238 | Midland, TX | 266 | 300 | Binghamton, NY | 155 | 362 | Sheboygan, WI | 61 |
| 239 | Elgin, IL M.D. | 264 | 301 | Norwich-New London, CT | 153 | 363 | Harrisonburg, VA | 58 |
| 240 | Crestview-Fort Walton Beach, FL | 263 | 302 | Lima, OH | 147 | 364 | Ames, IA | 57 |
| 241 | York-Hanover, PA | 262 | 303 | Racine, WI | 146 | 364 | The Villages, FL | 57 |
| 242 | Hot Springs, AR | 261 | 304 | Rochester, MN | 144 | 364 | Williamsport, PA | 57 |
| 243 | Sumter, SC | 255 | 305 | New Bern, NC | 143 | 367 | Kingston, NY | 55 |
| 244 | Lawton, OK | 250 | 306 | Carbondale-Marion, IL | 141 | 368 | Wausau, WI | 54 |
| 244 | St. Cloud, MN | 250 | 307 | Iowa City, IA | 137 | 369 | Logan, UT-ID | 48 |
| 246 | Fort Collins, CO | 247 | 308 | Grand Island, NE | 128 | 370 | Fond du Lac, WI | 46 |
| 247 | Decatur, AL | 242 | 308 | Kokomo, IN | 128 | 371 | Gettysburg, PA | 40 |
| 248 | Houma, LA | 239 | 310 | Owensboro, KY | 127 | 372 | Bloomsburg-Berwick, PA | 32 |
| 249 | Napa, CA | 237 | 311 | Mansfield, OH | 125 | 373 | Glens Falls, NY | 31 |
| 250 | Jackson, TN | 236 | 311 | Winchester, VA-WV | 125 | 374 | Elmira, NY | 27 |
| 250 | Monroe, LA | 236 | 313 | Great Falls, MT | 122 | 374 | State College, PA | 27 |
| 252 | Prescott, AZ | 235 | 314 | Jonesboro, AR | 121 | NA | Phoenix-Mesa-Scottsdale, AZ** | NA |
| 253 | Cleveland, TN | 233 | 315 | California-Lexington Park, MD | 119 | NA | Visalia-Porterville, CA** | NA |
| 253 | Monroe, MI | 233 | 316 | Janesville, WI | 118 | | | |

Source: Reported data from the F.B.I. "Crime in the United States 2013"

*Motor vehicle theft includes the theft or attempted theft of a self-propelled vehicle. Excludes motorboats, construction equipment, airplanes, and farming equipment.

**Not available.

# 38. Motor Vehicle Theft Rate in 2013
## National Rate = 221.3 Motor Vehicle Thefts per 100,000 Population*

| RANK | METROPOLITAN AREA | RATE | RANK | METROPOLITAN AREA | RATE | RANK | METROPOLITAN AREA | RATE |
|---|---|---|---|---|---|---|---|---|
| 154 | Abilene, TX | 173.7 | 242 | Cheyenne, WY | 121.3 | 67 | Gary, IN M.D. | 295.4 |
| 228 | Akron, OH | 130.9 | 119 | Chicago (greater), IL-IN-WI | 201.2 | 367 | Gettysburg, PA | 39.4 |
| 322 | Albany-Schenectady-Troy, NY | 74.1 | 107 | Chicago-Naperville, IL M.D. | 224.4 | 374 | Glens Falls, NY | 24.1 |
| 137 | Albany, GA | 185.6 | 31 | Chico, CA | 402.9 | 143 | Goldsboro, NC | 180.7 |
| 98 | Albany, OR | 245.1 | 204 | Cincinnati, OH-KY-IN | 145.0 | 266 | Grand Forks, ND-MN | 107.5 |
| 27 | Albuquerque, NM | 426.4 | 285 | Clarksville, TN-KY | 99.7 | 187 | Grand Island, NE | 152.1 |
| 80 | Alexandria, LA | 279.3 | 125 | Cleveland, TN | 196.5 | 237 | Grand Junction, CO | 124.6 |
| 289 | Allentown, PA-NJ | 96.7 | 171 | Coeur d'Alene, ID | 158.1 | 325 | Grand Rapids-Wyoming, MI | 72.5 |
| 348 | Altoona, PA | 58.2 | 302 | College Station-Bryan, TX | 84.3 | 26 | Grants Pass, OR | 436.5 |
| 74 | Amarillo, TX | 285.4 | 51 | Colorado Springs, CO | 328.7 | 196 | Great Falls, MT | 148.4 |
| 341 | Ames, IA | 62.0 | 221 | Columbia, MO | 133.0 | 227 | Greeley, CO | 131.0 |
| 103 | Anaheim-Santa Ana-Irvine, CA M.D. | 231.9 | 47 | Columbia, SC | 337.6 | 352 | Green Bay, WI | 54.7 |
| 68 | Anchorage, AK | 294.7 | 24 | Columbus, GA-AL | 445.6 | 171 | Greensboro-High Point, NC | 158.1 |
| 269 | Ann Arbor, MI | 106.5 | 105 | Columbus, IN | 227.2 | 60 | Greenville-Anderson, SC | 304.9 |
| 165 | Anniston-Oxford, AL | 161.7 | 170 | Corpus Christi, TX | 158.4 | 249 | Greenville, NC | 117.0 |
| 372 | Appleton, WI | 29.6 | 296 | Corvallis, OR | 92.0 | 127 | Gulfport-Biloxi-Pascagoula, MS | 193.0 |
| 217 | Athens-Clarke County, GA | 138.8 | 278 | Crestview-Fort Walton Beach, FL | 104.1 | 273 | Hagerstown-Martinsburg, MD-WV | 104.8 |
| 48 | Atlanta, GA | 337.4 | 328 | Cumberland, MD-WV | 69.8 | 88 | Hammond, LA | 262.5 |
| 303 | Atlantic City, NJ | 84.0 | 87 | Dallas (greater), TX | 263.3 | 63 | Hanford-Corcoran, CA | 298.8 |
| 69 | Augusta, GA-SC | 294.3 | 71 | Dallas-Plano-Irving, TX M.D. | 288.4 | 362 | Harrisonburg, VA | 44.7 |
| 168 | Austin-Round Rock, TX | 158.7 | 164 | Dalton, GA | 162.4 | 163 | Hartford, CT | 164.0 |
| 3 | Bakersfield, CA | 672.9 | 272 | Daphne-Fairhope-Foley, AL | 105.5 | 213 | Hilton Head Island, SC | 140.8 |
| 93 | Baltimore, MD | 255.7 | 284 | Davenport, IA-IL | 99.8 | 225 | Hinesville, GA | 131.4 |
| 350 | Bangor, ME | 57.3 | 150 | Dayton, OH | 175.8 | 305 | Homosassa Springs, FL | 81.2 |
| 294 | Barnstable Town, MA | 92.2 | 173 | Decatur, AL | 156.8 | 84 | Hot Springs, AR | 268.6 |
| 235 | Baton Rouge, LA | 126.3 | 319 | Decatur, IL | 74.6 | 251 | Houma, LA | 114.2 |
| 268 | Bay City, MI | 106.8 | 139 | Deltona-Daytona Beach, FL | 185.1 | 38 | Houston, TX | 370.9 |
| 136 | Beaumont-Port Arthur, TX | 185.9 | 64 | Denver-Aurora, CO | 298.6 | 104 | Huntsville, AL | 229.7 |
| 265 | Bend, OR | 107.8 | 120 | Des Moines-West Des Moines, IA | 199.5 | 245 | Idaho Falls, ID | 119.2 |
| 32 | Billings, MT | 395.5 | 23 | Detroit (greater), MI | 446.1 | 49 | Indianapolis, IN | 333.7 |
| 340 | Binghamton, NY | 62.5 | 1 | Detroit-Dearborn-Livonia, MI M.D. | 868.4 | 299 | Iowa City, IA | 85.4 |
| 83 | Birmingham-Hoover, AL | 268.7 | 174 | Dothan, AL | 155.9 | 199 | Jacksonville, FL | 146.7 |
| 147 | Bismarck, ND | 177.9 | 261 | Dover, DE | 108.4 | 287 | Jackson, MI | 97.2 |
| 349 | Blacksburg, VA | 57.4 | 300 | Dubuque, IA | 84.6 | 97 | Jackson, MS | 248.2 |
| 356 | Bloomington, IL | 52.3 | 182 | Duluth, MN-WI | 153.5 | 144 | Jackson, TN | 180.6 |
| 212 | Bloomington, IN | 141.8 | 373 | Dutchess-Putnam, NY M.D. | 27.7 | 323 | Janesville, WI | 73.5 |
| 368 | Bloomsburg-Berwick, PA | 37.6 | 345 | East Stroudsburg, PA | 60.6 | 314 | Jefferson City, MO | 77.1 |
| 304 | Boise City, ID | 81.7 | 354 | Eau Claire, WI | 53.5 | 297 | Johnson City, TN | 90.8 |
| 232 | Boston (greater), MA-NH | 129.0 | 53 | El Centro, CA | 327.0 | 344 | Johnstown, PA | 61.8 |
| 203 | Boston, MA M.D. | 145.4 | 252 | El Paso, TX | 114.1 | 288 | Jonesboro, AR | 96.8 |
| 267 | Boulder, CO | 107.3 | 365 | Elgin, IL M.D. | 42.0 | 76 | Joplin, MO | 284.1 |
| 262 | Bowling Green, KY | 108.3 | 358 | Elizabethtown-Fort Knox, KY | 50.4 | 82 | Kahului-Wailuku-Lahaina, HI | 276.9 |
| 121 | Bremerton-Silverdale, WA | 199.3 | 370 | Elmira, NY | 30.3 | 327 | Kankakee, IL | 70.9 |
| 209 | Bridgeport-Stamford, CT | 143.2 | 341 | Erie, PA | 62.0 | 29 | Kansas City, MO-KS | 409.7 |
| 248 | Brownsville-Harlingen, TX | 118.1 | 78 | Eugene, OR | 282.3 | 192 | Kennewick-Richland, WA | 149.9 |
| 198 | Brunswick, GA | 146.8 | 52 | Fairbanks, AK | 328.1 | 243 | Kingsport, TN-VA | 120.0 |
| 230 | Buffalo-Niagara Falls, NY | 129.8 | 238 | Fargo, ND-MN | 124.2 | 370 | Kingston, NY | 30.3 |
| 204 | Burlington, NC | 145.0 | 224 | Farmington, NM | 131.7 | 145 | Knoxville, TN | 180.4 |
| 263 | California-Lexington Park, MD | 107.9 | 283 | Fayetteville-Springdale, AR-MO | 102.0 | 179 | Kokomo, IN | 154.0 |
| 234 | Cambridge-Newton, MA M.D. | 126.8 | 102 | Fayetteville, NC | 233.8 | 357 | La Crosse, WI-MN | 51.5 |
| 246 | Camden, NJ M.D. | 118.4 | 320 | Flagstaff, AZ | 74.5 | 193 | Lafayette, IN | 149.7 |
| 153 | Canton, OH | 174.0 | 132 | Flint, MI | 188.4 | 110 | Lafayette, LA | 215.2 |
| 239 | Cape Coral-Fort Myers, FL | 123.9 | 126 | Florence-Muscle Shoals, AL | 195.4 | 94 | Lake Charles, LA | 253.3 |
| 257 | Cape Girardeau, MO-IL | 109.7 | 90 | Florence, SC | 258.3 | 363 | Lake Co.-Kenosha Co., IL-WI M.D. | 44.0 |
| 254 | Carbondale-Marion, IL | 111.3 | 361 | Fond du Lac, WI | 45.1 | 124 | Lake Havasu City-Kingman, AZ | 197.5 |
| 240 | Carson City, NV | 123.8 | 312 | Fort Collins, CO | 78.2 | 202 | Lakeland, FL | 145.5 |
| 217 | Casper, WY | 138.8 | 112 | Fort Lauderdale, FL M.D. | 213.3 | 351 | Lancaster, PA | 54.9 |
| 207 | Cedar Rapids, IA | 144.2 | 189 | Fort Smith, AR-OK | 150.6 | 177 | Lansing-East Lansing, MI | 154.5 |
| 347 | Chambersburg-Waynesboro, PA | 58.7 | 241 | Fort Wayne, IN | 121.7 | 195 | Laredo, TX | 148.7 |
| 324 | Champaign-Urbana, IL | 72.6 | 111 | Fort Worth-Arlington, TX M.D. | 214.3 | 189 | Las Cruces, NM | 150.6 |
| 99 | Charleston-North Charleston, SC | 239.7 | 4 | Fresno, CA | 664.3 | 30 | Las Vegas-Henderson, NV | 407.0 |
| 176 | Charlotte-Mecklenburg, NC-SC | 154.6 | 72 | Gadsden, AL | 287.5 | 156 | Lawrence, KS | 172.9 |
| 315 | Charlottesville, VA | 77.0 | 219 | Gainesville, FL | 135.3 | 133 | Lawton, OK | 187.3 |
| 61 | Chattanooga, TN-GA | 303.8 | 174 | Gainesville, GA | 155.9 | 359 | Lebanon, PA | 48.6 |

Note: All listings are for Metropolitan Statistical Areas (M.S.A.s) except for those ending with "M.D." Listings with "M.D." are Metropolitan Divisions which are smaller parts of eleven large M.S.A.s. See explanatory note at beginning of metropolitan area section.

| RANK | METROPOLITAN AREA | RATE | RANK | METROPOLITAN AREA | RATE | RANK | METROPOLITAN AREA | RATE |
|---|---|---|---|---|---|---|---|---|
| 295 | Lewiston-Auburn, ME | 92.1 | 22 | Omaha-Council Bluffs, NE-IA | 457.2 | 355 | Sheboygan, WI | 53.1 |
| 191 | Lewiston, ID-WA | 150.4 | 118 | Orlando, FL | 202.3 | 214 | Sherman-Denison, TX | 140.1 |
| 115 | Lexington-Fayette, KY | 208.0 | 364 | Oshkosh-Neenah, WI | 42.5 | 139 | Shreveport-Bossier City, LA | 185.1 |
| 215 | Lima, OH | 140.0 | 260 | Owensboro, KY | 109.0 | 301 | Silver Spring-Frederick, MD M.D. | 84.5 |
| 279 | Lincoln, NE | 104.0 | 146 | Oxnard-Thousand Oaks, CA | 178.4 | 152 | Sioux City, IA-NE-SD | 174.1 |
| 54 | Little Rock, AR | 326.4 | 236 | Palm Bay-Melbourne, FL | 125.3 | 226 | Sioux Falls, SD | 131.2 |
| 369 | Logan, UT-ID | 37.0 | 158 | Panama City, FL | 170.2 | 151 | South Bend-Mishawaka, IN-MI | 175.1 |
| 148 | Longview, TX | 177.3 | 280 | Parkersburg-Vienna, WV | 103.9 | 134 | Spartanburg, SC | 187.1 |
| 79 | Longview, WA | 281.9 | 141 | Pensacola, FL | 183.3 | 7 | Spokane, WA | 622.2 |
| 33 | Los Angeles County, CA M.D. | 388.5 | 310 | Peoria, IL | 78.3 | 35 | Springfield, IL | 380.4 |
| 42 | Los Angeles (greater), CA | 351.3 | 158 | Philadelphia (greater) PA-NJ-MD-DE | 170.2 | 116 | Springfield, MA | 207.2 |
| 106 | Louisville, KY-IN | 226.5 | 58 | Philadelphia, PA M.D. | 305.6 | 50 | Springfield, MO | 331.0 |
| 57 | Lubbock, TX | 310.2 | NA | Phoenix-Mesa-Scottsdale, AZ** | NA | 117 | Springfield, OH | 206.3 |
| 308 | Lynchburg, VA | 80.2 | 316 | Pittsburgh, PA | 76.9 | 375 | State College, PA | 17.4 |
| 44 | Macon, GA | 349.1 | 313 | Pittsfield, MA | 77.7 | 337 | Staunton-Waynesboro, VA | 64.7 |
| 39 | Madera, CA | 360.0 | 246 | Pocatello, ID | 118.4 | 10 | Stockton-Lodi, CA | 563.9 |
| 331 | Madison, WI | 69.3 | 293 | Port St. Lucie, FL | 92.7 | 229 | St. Cloud, MN | 130.5 |
| 317 | Manchester-Nashua, NH | 76.7 | 65 | Portland-Vancouver, OR-WA | 296.8 | 309 | St. George, UT | 79.8 |
| 320 | Manhattan, KS | 74.5 | 336 | Portland, ME | 65.1 | 91 | St. Joseph, MO-KS | 257.0 |
| 277 | Mankato-North Mankato, MN | 104.3 | 257 | Prescott, AZ | 109.7 | 109 | St. Louis, MO-IL | 218.9 |
| 282 | Mansfield, OH | 102.1 | 130 | Providence-Warwick, RI-MA | 191.4 | 101 | Sumter, SC | 234.6 |
| 131 | McAllen-Edinburg-Mission, TX | 190.9 | 306 | Provo-Orem, UT | 81.0 | 286 | Syracuse, NY | 97.6 |
| 211 | Medford, OR | 142.4 | 37 | Pueblo, CO | 373.4 | 12 | Tacoma, WA M.D. | 520.5 |
| 89 | Memphis, TN-MS-AR | 260.9 | 330 | Punta Gorda, FL | 69.5 | 166 | Tallahassee, FL | 160.2 |
| 15 | Merced, CA | 507.4 | 318 | Racine, WI | 75.0 | 181 | Tampa-St Petersburg, FL | 153.6 |
| 92 | Miami (greater), FL | 256.2 | 271 | Raleigh, NC | 105.8 | 96 | Terre Haute, IN | 248.6 |
| 56 | Miami-Dade County, FL M.D. | 316.7 | 223 | Rapid City, SD | 132.0 | 127 | Texarkana, TX-AR | 193.0 |
| 157 | Midland, TX | 170.8 | 250 | Reading, PA | 115.5 | 353 | The Villages, FL | 54.5 |
| 55 | Milwaukee, WI | 317.3 | 8 | Redding, CA | 615.3 | 113 | Toledo, OH | 213.1 |
| 155 | Minneapolis-St. Paul, MN-WI | 173.3 | 81 | Reno, NV | 277.2 | 70 | Topeka, KS | 292.5 |
| 188 | Missoula, MT | 151.7 | 184 | Richmond, VA | 152.9 | 135 | Trenton, NJ | 186.3 |
| 66 | Mobile, AL | 296.6 | 19 | Riverside-San Bernardino, CA | 489.0 | 62 | Tucson, AZ | 303.1 |
| 5 | Modesto, CA | 661.3 | 276 | Roanoke, VA | 104.4 | 45 | Tulsa, OK | 340.0 |
| 222 | Monroe, LA | 132.4 | 333 | Rochester, MN | 68.2 | 179 | Tuscaloosa, AL | 154.0 |
| 178 | Monroe, MI | 154.4 | 292 | Rochester, NY | 93.6 | 167 | Tyler, TX | 159.3 |
| 338 | Montgomery County, PA M.D. | 63.1 | 204 | Rockford, IL | 145.0 | 339 | Utica-Rome, NY | 62.8 |
| 310 | Morgantown, WV | 78.3 | 335 | Rockingham County, NH M.D. | 65.4 | 9 | Vallejo-Fairfield, CA | 565.2 |
| 197 | Morristown, TN | 147.4 | 216 | Rocky Mount, NC | 139.6 | 256 | Victoria, TX | 110.3 |
| 77 | Mount Vernon-Anacortes, WA | 284.0 | 123 | Rome, GA | 197.7 | 243 | Vineland-Bridgeton, NJ | 120.0 |
| 186 | Muncie, IN | 152.2 | 36 | Sacramento, CA | 380.2 | 194 | Virginia Beach-Norfolk, VA-NC | 149.2 |
| 220 | Muskegon, MI | 133.7 | 253 | Saginaw, MI | 113.6 | NA | Visalia-Porterville, CA** | NA |
| 43 | Myrtle Beach, SC-NC | 350.8 | 73 | Salem, OR | 286.8 | 233 | Waco, TX | 128.2 |
| 161 | Napa, CA | 169.3 | 13 | Salinas, CA | 510.1 | 183 | Warner Robins, GA | 153.3 |
| 332 | Naples-Marco Island, FL | 68.5 | 281 | Salisbury, MD-DE | 102.5 | 201 | Warren-Troy, MI M.D. | 145.6 |
| 231 | Nashville-Davidson, TN | 129.2 | 17 | Salt Lake City, UT | 492.2 | 138 | Washington (greater) DC-VA-MD-WV | 185.2 |
| 326 | Nassau-Suffolk, NY M.D. | 72.3 | 160 | San Angelo, TX | 169.5 | 114 | Washington, DC-VA-MD-WV M.D. | 212.3 |
| 255 | New Bern, NC | 111.0 | 46 | San Antonio, TX | 339.3 | 334 | Watertown-Fort Drum, NY | 67.4 |
| 59 | New Haven-Milford, CT | 305.0 | 41 | San Diego, CA | 351.6 | 366 | Wausau, WI | 40.0 |
| 75 | New Orleans, LA | 284.9 | 6 | San Francisco (greater), CA | 633.5 | 122 | West Palm Beach, FL M.D. | 198.0 |
| 263 | New York (greater), NY-NJ-PA | 107.9 | 20 | San Francisco-Redwood, CA M.D. | 476.5 | 108 | Wichita Falls, TX | 224.1 |
| 298 | New York-Jersey City, NY-NJ M.D. | 89.3 | 11 | San Jose, CA | 536.3 | 40 | Wichita, KS | 358.0 |
| 85 | Newark, NJ-PA M.D. | 267.2 | 208 | San Luis Obispo, CA | 144.1 | 360 | Williamsport, PA | 48.5 |
| 270 | Niles-Benton Harbor, MI | 106.4 | 95 | San Rafael, CA M.D. | 252.1 | 185 | Wilmington, DE-MD-NJ M.D. | 152.4 |
| 259 | North Port-Sarasota-Bradenton, FL | 109.6 | 34 | Santa Cruz-Watsonville, CA | 381.3 | 142 | Wilmington, NC | 181.4 |
| 274 | Norwich-New London, CT | 104.7 | 86 | Santa Maria-Santa Barbara, CA | 264.0 | 290 | Winchester, VA-WV | 94.8 |
| 2 | Oakland-Hayward, CA M.D. | 763.6 | 200 | Santa Rosa, CA | 145.7 | 162 | Winston-Salem, NC | 164.2 |
| 307 | Ocala, FL | 80.9 | 100 | Savannah, GA | 237.4 | 275 | Worcester, MA-CT | 104.5 |
| 329 | Ocean City, NJ | 69.7 | 291 | Scranton--Wilkes-Barre, PA | 93.7 | 21 | Yakima, WA | 458.4 |
| 25 | Odessa, TX | 436.8 | 14 | Seattle (greater), WA | 508.3 | 346 | York-Hanover, PA | 59.8 |
| 210 | Ogden-Clearfield, UT | 142.8 | 16 | Seattle-Bellevue-Everett, WA M.D. | 504.6 | 18 | Yuba City, CA | 490.5 |
| 28 | Oklahoma City, OK | 413.1 | 341 | Sebastian-Vero Beach, FL | 62.0 | 129 | Yuma, AZ | 191.7 |
| 149 | Olympia, WA | 177.0 | 168 | Sebring, FL | 158.7 | | | |

Source: Reported data from the F.B.I. "Crime in the United States 2013"

*Motor vehicle theft includes the theft or attempted theft of a self-propelled vehicle. Excludes motorboats, construction equipment, airplanes, and farming equipment.

**Not available.

# 38. Motor Vehicle Theft Rate in 2013 (continued)
## National Rate = 221.3 Motor Vehicle Thefts per 100,000 Population*

| RANK | METROPOLITAN AREA | RATE | RANK | METROPOLITAN AREA | RATE | RANK | METROPOLITAN AREA | RATE |
|---|---|---|---|---|---|---|---|---|
| 1 | Detroit-Dearborn-Livonia, MI M.D. | 868.4 | 65 | Portland-Vancouver, OR-WA | 296.8 | 129 | Yuma, AZ | 191.7 |
| 2 | Oakland-Hayward, CA M.D. | 763.6 | 66 | Mobile, AL | 296.6 | 130 | Providence-Warwick, RI-MA | 191.4 |
| 3 | Bakersfield, CA | 672.9 | 67 | Gary, IN M.D. | 295.4 | 131 | McAllen-Edinburg-Mission, TX | 190.9 |
| 4 | Fresno, CA | 664.3 | 68 | Anchorage, AK | 294.7 | 132 | Flint, MI | 188.4 |
| 5 | Modesto, CA | 661.3 | 69 | Augusta, GA-SC | 294.3 | 133 | Lawton, OK | 187.3 |
| 6 | San Francisco (greater), CA | 633.5 | 70 | Topeka, KS | 292.5 | 134 | Spartanburg, SC | 187.1 |
| 7 | Spokane, WA | 622.2 | 71 | Dallas-Plano-Irving, TX M.D. | 288.4 | 135 | Trenton, NJ | 186.3 |
| 8 | Redding, CA | 615.3 | 72 | Gadsden, AL | 287.5 | 136 | Beaumont-Port Arthur, TX | 185.9 |
| 9 | Vallejo-Fairfield, CA | 565.2 | 73 | Salem, OR | 286.8 | 137 | Albany, GA | 185.6 |
| 10 | Stockton-Lodi, CA | 563.9 | 74 | Amarillo, TX | 285.4 | 138 | Washington (greater) DC-VA-MD-WV | 185.2 |
| 11 | San Jose, CA | 536.3 | 75 | New Orleans, LA | 284.9 | 139 | Deltona-Daytona Beach, FL | 185.1 |
| 12 | Tacoma, WA M.D. | 520.5 | 76 | Joplin, MO | 284.1 | 139 | Shreveport-Bossier City, LA | 185.1 |
| 13 | Salinas, CA | 510.1 | 77 | Mount Vernon-Anacortes, WA | 284.0 | 141 | Pensacola, FL | 183.3 |
| 14 | Seattle (greater), WA | 508.3 | 78 | Eugene, OR | 282.3 | 142 | Wilmington, NC | 181.4 |
| 15 | Merced, CA | 507.4 | 79 | Longview, WA | 281.9 | 143 | Goldsboro, NC | 180.7 |
| 16 | Seattle-Bellevue-Everett, WA M.D. | 504.6 | 80 | Alexandria, LA | 279.3 | 144 | Jackson, TN | 180.6 |
| 17 | Salt Lake City, UT | 492.2 | 81 | Reno, NV | 277.2 | 145 | Knoxville, TN | 180.4 |
| 18 | Yuba City, CA | 490.5 | 82 | Kahului-Wailuku-Lahaina, HI | 276.9 | 146 | Oxnard-Thousand Oaks, CA | 178.4 |
| 19 | Riverside-San Bernardino, CA | 489.0 | 83 | Birmingham-Hoover, AL | 268.7 | 147 | Bismarck, ND | 177.9 |
| 20 | San Francisco-Redwood, CA M.D. | 476.5 | 84 | Hot Springs, AR | 268.6 | 148 | Longview, TX | 177.3 |
| 21 | Yakima, WA | 458.4 | 85 | Newark, NJ-PA M.D. | 267.2 | 149 | Olympia, WA | 177.0 |
| 22 | Omaha-Council Bluffs, NE-IA | 457.2 | 86 | Santa Maria-Santa Barbara, CA | 264.0 | 150 | Dayton, OH | 175.8 |
| 23 | Detroit (greater), MI | 446.1 | 87 | Dallas (greater), TX | 263.3 | 151 | South Bend-Mishawaka, IN-MI | 175.1 |
| 24 | Columbus, GA-AL | 445.6 | 88 | Hammond, LA | 262.5 | 152 | Sioux City, IA-NE-SD | 174.1 |
| 25 | Odessa, TX | 436.8 | 89 | Memphis, TN-MS-AR | 260.9 | 153 | Canton, OH | 174.0 |
| 26 | Grants Pass, OR | 436.5 | 90 | Florence, SC | 258.3 | 154 | Abilene, TX | 173.7 |
| 27 | Albuquerque, NM | 426.4 | 91 | St. Joseph, MO-KS | 257.0 | 155 | Minneapolis-St. Paul, MN-WI | 173.3 |
| 28 | Oklahoma City, OK | 413.1 | 92 | Miami (greater), FL | 256.2 | 156 | Lawrence, KS | 172.9 |
| 29 | Kansas City, MO-KS | 409.7 | 93 | Baltimore, MD | 255.7 | 157 | Midland, TX | 170.8 |
| 30 | Las Vegas-Henderson, NV | 407.0 | 94 | Lake Charles, LA | 253.3 | 158 | Panama City, FL | 170.2 |
| 31 | Chico, CA | 402.9 | 95 | San Rafael, CA M.D. | 252.1 | 158 | Philadelphia (greater) PA-NJ-MD-DE | 170.2 |
| 32 | Billings, MT | 395.5 | 96 | Terre Haute, IN | 248.6 | 160 | San Angelo, TX | 169.5 |
| 33 | Los Angeles County, CA M.D. | 388.5 | 97 | Jackson, MS | 248.2 | 161 | Napa, CA | 169.3 |
| 34 | Santa Cruz-Watsonville, CA | 381.3 | 98 | Albany, OR | 245.1 | 162 | Winston-Salem, NC | 164.2 |
| 35 | Springfield, IL | 380.4 | 99 | Charleston-North Charleston, SC | 239.7 | 163 | Hartford, CT | 164.0 |
| 36 | Sacramento, CA | 380.2 | 100 | Savannah, GA | 237.4 | 164 | Dalton, GA | 162.4 |
| 37 | Pueblo, CO | 373.4 | 101 | Sumter, SC | 234.6 | 165 | Anniston-Oxford, AL | 161.7 |
| 38 | Houston, TX | 370.9 | 102 | Fayetteville, NC | 233.8 | 166 | Tallahassee, FL | 160.2 |
| 39 | Madera, CA | 360.0 | 103 | Anaheim-Santa Ana-Irvine, CA M.D. | 231.9 | 167 | Tyler, TX | 159.3 |
| 40 | Wichita, KS | 358.0 | 104 | Huntsville, AL | 229.7 | 168 | Austin-Round Rock, TX | 158.7 |
| 41 | San Diego, CA | 351.6 | 105 | Columbus, IN | 227.2 | 168 | Sebring, FL | 158.7 |
| 42 | Los Angeles (greater), CA | 351.3 | 106 | Louisville, KY-IN | 226.5 | 170 | Corpus Christi, TX | 158.4 |
| 43 | Myrtle Beach, SC-NC | 350.8 | 107 | Chicago-Naperville, IL M.D. | 224.4 | 171 | Coeur d'Alene, ID | 158.1 |
| 44 | Macon, GA | 349.1 | 108 | Wichita Falls, TX | 224.1 | 171 | Greensboro-High Point, NC | 158.1 |
| 45 | Tulsa, OK | 340.0 | 109 | St. Louis, MO-IL | 218.9 | 173 | Decatur, AL | 156.8 |
| 46 | San Antonio, TX | 339.3 | 110 | Lafayette, LA | 215.2 | 174 | Dothan, AL | 155.9 |
| 47 | Columbia, SC | 337.6 | 111 | Fort Worth-Arlington, TX M.D. | 214.3 | 174 | Gainesville, GA | 155.9 |
| 48 | Atlanta, GA | 337.4 | 112 | Fort Lauderdale, FL M.D. | 213.3 | 176 | Charlotte-Mecklenburg, NC-SC | 154.6 |
| 49 | Indianapolis, IN | 333.7 | 113 | Toledo, OH | 213.1 | 177 | Lansing-East Lansing, MI | 154.5 |
| 50 | Springfield, MO | 331.0 | 114 | Washington, DC-VA-MD-WV M.D. | 212.3 | 178 | Monroe, MI | 154.4 |
| 51 | Colorado Springs, CO | 328.7 | 115 | Lexington-Fayette, KY | 208.0 | 179 | Kokomo, IN | 154.0 |
| 52 | Fairbanks, AK | 328.1 | 116 | Springfield, MA | 207.2 | 179 | Tuscaloosa, AL | 154.0 |
| 53 | El Centro, CA | 327.0 | 117 | Springfield, OH | 206.3 | 181 | Tampa-St Petersburg, FL | 153.6 |
| 54 | Little Rock, AR | 326.4 | 118 | Orlando, FL | 202.3 | 182 | Duluth, MN-WI | 153.5 |
| 55 | Milwaukee, WI | 317.3 | 119 | Chicago (greater), IL-IN-WI | 201.2 | 183 | Warner Robins, GA | 153.3 |
| 56 | Miami-Dade County, FL M.D. | 316.7 | 120 | Des Moines-West Des Moines, IA | 199.5 | 184 | Richmond, VA | 152.9 |
| 57 | Lubbock, TX | 310.2 | 121 | Bremerton-Silverdale, WA | 199.3 | 185 | Wilmington, DE-MD-NJ M.D. | 152.4 |
| 58 | Philadelphia, PA M.D. | 305.6 | 122 | West Palm Beach, FL M.D. | 198.0 | 186 | Muncie, IN | 152.2 |
| 59 | New Haven-Milford, CT | 305.0 | 123 | Rome, GA | 197.7 | 187 | Grand Island, NE | 152.1 |
| 60 | Greenville-Anderson, SC | 304.9 | 124 | Lake Havasu City-Kingman, AZ | 197.5 | 188 | Missoula, MT | 151.7 |
| 61 | Chattanooga, TN-GA | 303.8 | 125 | Cleveland, TN | 196.5 | 189 | Fort Smith, AR-OK | 150.6 |
| 62 | Tucson, AZ | 303.1 | 126 | Florence-Muscle Shoals, AL | 195.4 | 189 | Las Cruces, NM | 150.6 |
| 63 | Hanford-Corcoran, CA | 298.8 | 127 | Gulfport-Biloxi-Pascagoula, MS | 193.0 | 191 | Lewiston, ID-WA | 150.4 |
| 64 | Denver-Aurora, CO | 298.6 | 127 | Texarkana, TX-AR | 193.0 | 192 | Kennewick-Richland, WA | 149.9 |

Note: All listings are for Metropolitan Statistical Areas (M.S.A.s) except for those ending with "M.D." Listings with "M.D." are Metropolitan Divisions which are smaller parts of eleven large M.S.A.s. See explanatory note at beginning of metropolitan area section.

| RANK | METROPOLITAN AREA | RATE |
|---|---|---|
| 193 | Lafayette, IN | 149.7 |
| 194 | Virginia Beach-Norfolk, VA-NC | 149.2 |
| 195 | Laredo, TX | 148.7 |
| 196 | Great Falls, MT | 148.4 |
| 197 | Morristown, TN | 147.4 |
| 198 | Brunswick, GA | 146.8 |
| 199 | Jacksonville, FL | 146.7 |
| 200 | Santa Rosa, CA | 145.7 |
| 201 | Warren-Troy, MI M.D. | 145.6 |
| 202 | Lakeland, FL | 145.5 |
| 203 | Boston, MA M.D. | 145.4 |
| 204 | Burlington, NC | 145.0 |
| 204 | Cincinnati, OH-KY-IN | 145.0 |
| 204 | Rockford, IL | 145.0 |
| 207 | Cedar Rapids, IA | 144.2 |
| 208 | San Luis Obispo, CA | 144.1 |
| 209 | Bridgeport-Stamford, CT | 143.2 |
| 210 | Ogden-Clearfield, UT | 142.8 |
| 211 | Medford, OR | 142.4 |
| 212 | Bloomington, IN | 141.8 |
| 213 | Hilton Head Island, SC | 140.8 |
| 214 | Sherman-Denison, TX | 140.1 |
| 215 | Lima, OH | 140.0 |
| 216 | Rocky Mount, NC | 139.6 |
| 217 | Athens-Clarke County, GA | 138.8 |
| 217 | Casper, WY | 138.8 |
| 219 | Gainesville, FL | 135.3 |
| 220 | Muskegon, MI | 133.7 |
| 221 | Columbia, MO | 133.0 |
| 222 | Monroe, LA | 132.4 |
| 223 | Rapid City, SD | 132.0 |
| 224 | Farmington, NM | 131.7 |
| 225 | Hinesville, GA | 131.4 |
| 226 | Sioux Falls, SD | 131.2 |
| 227 | Greeley, CO | 131.0 |
| 228 | Akron, OH | 130.9 |
| 229 | St. Cloud, MN | 130.5 |
| 230 | Buffalo-Niagara Falls, NY | 129.8 |
| 231 | Nashville-Davidson, TN | 129.2 |
| 232 | Boston (greater), MA-NH | 129.0 |
| 233 | Waco, TX | 128.2 |
| 234 | Cambridge-Newton, MA M.D. | 126.8 |
| 235 | Baton Rouge, LA | 126.3 |
| 236 | Palm Bay-Melbourne, FL | 125.3 |
| 237 | Grand Junction, CO | 124.6 |
| 238 | Fargo, ND-MN | 124.2 |
| 239 | Cape Coral-Fort Myers, FL | 123.9 |
| 240 | Carson City, NV | 123.8 |
| 241 | Fort Wayne, IN | 121.7 |
| 242 | Cheyenne, WY | 121.3 |
| 243 | Kingsport, TN-VA | 120.0 |
| 243 | Vineland-Bridgeton, NJ | 120.0 |
| 245 | Idaho Falls, ID | 119.2 |
| 246 | Camden, NJ M.D. | 118.4 |
| 246 | Pocatello, ID | 118.4 |
| 248 | Brownsville-Harlingen, TX | 118.1 |
| 249 | Greenville, NC | 117.0 |
| 250 | Reading, PA | 115.5 |
| 251 | Houma, LA | 114.2 |
| 252 | El Paso, TX | 114.1 |
| 253 | Saginaw, MI | 113.6 |
| 254 | Carbondale-Marion, IL | 111.3 |

| RANK | METROPOLITAN AREA | RATE |
|---|---|---|
| 255 | New Bern, NC | 111.0 |
| 256 | Victoria, TX | 110.3 |
| 257 | Cape Girardeau, MO-IL | 109.7 |
| 257 | Prescott, AZ | 109.7 |
| 259 | North Port-Sarasota-Bradenton, FL | 109.6 |
| 260 | Owensboro, KY | 109.0 |
| 261 | Dover, DE | 108.4 |
| 262 | Bowling Green, KY | 108.3 |
| 263 | California-Lexington Park, MD | 107.9 |
| 263 | New York (greater), NY-NJ-PA | 107.9 |
| 265 | Bend, OR | 107.8 |
| 266 | Grand Forks, ND-MN | 107.5 |
| 267 | Boulder, CO | 107.3 |
| 268 | Bay City, MI | 106.8 |
| 269 | Ann Arbor, MI | 106.5 |
| 270 | Niles-Benton Harbor, MI | 106.4 |
| 271 | Raleigh, NC | 105.8 |
| 272 | Daphne-Fairhope-Foley, AL | 105.5 |
| 273 | Hagerstown-Martinsburg, MD-WV | 104.8 |
| 274 | Norwich-New London, CT | 104.7 |
| 275 | Worcester, MA-CT | 104.5 |
| 276 | Roanoke, VA | 104.4 |
| 277 | Mankato-North Mankato, MN | 104.3 |
| 278 | Crestview-Fort Walton Beach, FL | 104.1 |
| 279 | Lincoln, NE | 104.0 |
| 280 | Parkersburg-Vienna, WV | 103.9 |
| 281 | Salisbury, MD-DE | 102.5 |
| 282 | Mansfield, OH | 102.1 |
| 283 | Fayetteville-Springdale, AR-MO | 102.0 |
| 284 | Davenport, IA-IL | 99.8 |
| 285 | Clarksville, TN-KY | 99.7 |
| 286 | Syracuse, NY | 97.6 |
| 287 | Jackson, MI | 97.2 |
| 288 | Jonesboro, AR | 96.8 |
| 289 | Allentown, PA-NJ | 96.7 |
| 290 | Winchester, VA-WV | 94.8 |
| 291 | Scranton--Wilkes-Barre, PA | 93.7 |
| 292 | Rochester, NY | 93.6 |
| 293 | Port St. Lucie, FL | 92.7 |
| 294 | Barnstable Town, MA | 92.2 |
| 295 | Lewiston-Auburn, ME | 92.1 |
| 296 | Corvallis, OR | 92.0 |
| 297 | Johnson City, TN | 90.8 |
| 298 | New York-Jersey City, NY-NJ M.D. | 89.3 |
| 299 | Iowa City, IA | 85.4 |
| 300 | Dubuque, IA | 84.6 |
| 301 | Silver Spring-Frederick, MD M.D. | 84.5 |
| 302 | College Station-Bryan, TX | 84.3 |
| 303 | Atlantic City, NJ | 84.0 |
| 304 | Boise City, ID | 81.7 |
| 305 | Homosassa Springs, FL | 81.2 |
| 306 | Provo-Orem, UT | 81.0 |
| 307 | Ocala, FL | 80.9 |
| 308 | Lynchburg, VA | 80.2 |
| 309 | St. George, UT | 79.8 |
| 310 | Morgantown, WV | 78.3 |
| 310 | Peoria, IL | 78.3 |
| 312 | Fort Collins, CO | 78.2 |
| 313 | Pittsfield, MA | 77.7 |
| 314 | Jefferson City, MO | 77.1 |
| 315 | Charlottesville, VA | 77.0 |
| 316 | Pittsburgh, PA | 76.9 |

| RANK | METROPOLITAN AREA | RATE |
|---|---|---|
| 317 | Manchester-Nashua, NH | 76.7 |
| 318 | Racine, WI | 75.0 |
| 319 | Decatur, IL | 74.6 |
| 320 | Flagstaff, AZ | 74.5 |
| 320 | Manhattan, KS | 74.5 |
| 322 | Albany-Schenectady-Troy, NY | 74.1 |
| 323 | Janesville, WI | 73.5 |
| 324 | Champaign-Urbana, IL | 72.6 |
| 325 | Grand Rapids-Wyoming, MI | 72.5 |
| 326 | Nassau-Suffolk, NY M.D. | 72.3 |
| 327 | Kankakee, IL | 70.9 |
| 328 | Cumberland, MD-WV | 69.8 |
| 329 | Ocean City, NJ | 69.7 |
| 330 | Punta Gorda, FL | 69.5 |
| 331 | Madison, WI | 69.3 |
| 332 | Naples-Marco Island, FL | 68.5 |
| 333 | Rochester, MN | 68.2 |
| 334 | Watertown-Fort Drum, NY | 67.4 |
| 335 | Rockingham County, NH M.D. | 65.4 |
| 336 | Portland, ME | 65.1 |
| 337 | Staunton-Waynesboro, VA | 64.7 |
| 338 | Montgomery County, PA M.D. | 63.1 |
| 339 | Utica-Rome, NY | 62.8 |
| 340 | Binghamton, NY | 62.5 |
| 341 | Ames, IA | 62.0 |
| 341 | Erie, PA | 62.0 |
| 341 | Sebastian-Vero Beach, FL | 62.0 |
| 344 | Johnstown, PA | 61.8 |
| 345 | East Stroudsburg, PA | 60.6 |
| 346 | York-Hanover, PA | 59.8 |
| 347 | Chambersburg-Waynesboro, PA | 58.7 |
| 348 | Altoona, PA | 58.2 |
| 349 | Blacksburg, VA | 57.4 |
| 350 | Bangor, ME | 57.3 |
| 351 | Lancaster, PA | 54.9 |
| 352 | Green Bay, WI | 54.7 |
| 353 | The Villages, FL | 54.5 |
| 354 | Eau Claire, WI | 53.5 |
| 355 | Sheboygan, WI | 53.1 |
| 356 | Bloomington, IL | 52.3 |
| 357 | La Crosse, WI-MN | 51.5 |
| 358 | Elizabethtown-Fort Knox, KY | 50.4 |
| 359 | Lebanon, PA | 48.6 |
| 360 | Williamsport, PA | 48.5 |
| 361 | Fond du Lac, WI | 45.1 |
| 362 | Harrisonburg, VA | 44.7 |
| 363 | Lake Co.-Kenosha Co., IL-WI M.D. | 44.0 |
| 364 | Oshkosh-Neenah, WI | 42.5 |
| 365 | Elgin, IL M.D. | 42.0 |
| 366 | Wausau, WI | 40.0 |
| 367 | Gettysburg, PA | 39.4 |
| 368 | Bloomsburg-Berwick, PA | 37.6 |
| 369 | Logan, UT-ID | 37.0 |
| 370 | Elmira, NY | 30.3 |
| 370 | Kingston, NY | 30.3 |
| 372 | Appleton, WI | 29.6 |
| 373 | Dutchess-Putnam, NY M.D. | 27.7 |
| 374 | Glens Falls, NY | 24.1 |
| 375 | State College, PA | 17.4 |
| NA | Phoenix-Mesa-Scottsdale, AZ** | NA |
| NA | Visalia-Porterville, CA** | NA |

Source: Reported data from the F.B.I. "Crime in the United States 2013"

*Motor vehicle theft includes the theft or attempted theft of a self-propelled vehicle. Excludes motorboats, construction equipment, airplanes, and farming equipment.

**Not available.

## 39. Percent Change in Motor Vehicle Theft Rate: 2012 to 2013
## National Percent Change = 4.0% Decrease*

| RANK | METROPOLITAN AREA | % CHANGE | RANK | METROPOLITAN AREA | % CHANGE | RANK | METROPOLITAN AREA | % CHANGE |
|---|---|---|---|---|---|---|---|---|
| 7 | Abilene, TX | 43.8 | 300 | Cheyenne, WY | (20.8) | 143 | Gary, IN M.D. | (2.3) |
| 273 | Akron, OH | (15.5) | 302 | Chicago (greater), IL-IN-WI | (21.0) | NA | Gettysburg, PA** | NA |
| 136 | Albany-Schenectady-Troy, NY | (1.6) | 315 | Chicago-Naperville, IL M.D. | (23.2) | 345 | Glens Falls, NY | (44.2) |
| 238 | Albany, GA | (12.2) | 5 | Chico, CA | 51.1 | 271 | Goldsboro, NC | (15.4) |
| 9 | Albany, OR | 38.2 | 71 | Cincinnati, OH-KY-IN | 9.0 | 241 | Grand Forks, ND-MN | (12.8) |
| 64 | Albuquerque, NM | 11.4 | 296 | Clarksville, TN-KY | (19.8) | 36 | Grand Island, NE | 19.4 |
| NA | Alexandria, LA** | NA | 45 | Cleveland, TN | 16.3 | 333 | Grand Junction, CO | (29.4) |
| 200 | Allentown, PA-NJ | (8.4) | 284 | Coeur d'Alene, ID | (17.7) | NA | Grand Rapids-Wyoming, MI** | NA |
| 180 | Altoona, PA | (6.3) | 92 | College Station-Bryan, TX | 4.9 | NA | Grants Pass, OR** | NA |
| 76 | Amarillo, TX | 8.2 | 84 | Colorado Springs, CO | 5.9 | 307 | Great Falls, MT | (22.1) |
| 53 | Ames, IA | 14.0 | 69 | Columbia, MO | 10.4 | 63 | Greeley, CO | 11.5 |
| 114 | Anaheim-Santa Ana-Irvine, CA M.D. | 0.7 | NA | Columbia, SC** | NA | 266 | Green Bay, WI | (15.2) |
| 84 | Anchorage, AK | 5.9 | 28 | Columbus, GA-AL | 22.9 | 170 | Greensboro-High Point, NC | (4.9) |
| 274 | Ann Arbor, MI | (15.7) | 320 | Columbus, IN | (24.5) | 111 | Greenville-Anderson, SC | 1.3 |
| 18 | Anniston-Oxford, AL | 30.1 | 40 | Corpus Christi, TX | 17.9 | 84 | Greenville, NC | 5.9 |
| 289 | Appleton, WI | (18.7) | 11 | Corvallis, OR | 34.9 | NA | Gulfport-Biloxi-Pascagoula, MS** | NA |
| 307 | Athens-Clarke County, GA | (22.1) | 240 | Crestview-Fort Walton Beach, FL | (12.7) | 318 | Hagerstown-Martinsburg, MD-WV | (23.9) |
| 214 | Atlanta, GA | (10.1) | 285 | Cumberland, MD-WV | (17.8) | 6 | Hammond, LA | 48.5 |
| 314 | Atlantic City, NJ | (23.1) | 125 | Dallas (greater), TX | (0.3) | 51 | Hanford-Corcoran, CA | 14.5 |
| 257 | Augusta, GA-SC | (14.6) | 119 | Dallas-Plano-Irving, TX M.D. | 0.3 | 322 | Harrisonburg, VA | (24.7) |
| 168 | Austin-Round Rock, TX | (4.6) | 16 | Dalton, GA | 30.9 | 313 | Hartford, CT | (22.9) |
| 190 | Bakersfield, CA | (7.4) | 103 | Daphne-Fairhope-Foley, AL | 3.0 | 152 | Hilton Head Island, SC | (3.3) |
| 137 | Baltimore, MD | (1.7) | 281 | Davenport, IA-IL | (16.6) | 77 | Hinesville, GA | 8.1 |
| 340 | Bangor, ME | (36.1) | 153 | Dayton, OH | (3.4) | 266 | Homosassa Springs, FL | (15.2) |
| 21 | Barnstable Town, MA | 28.6 | 59 | Decatur, AL | 12.3 | NA | Hot Springs, AR** | NA |
| NA | Baton Rouge, LA** | NA | 259 | Decatur, IL | (14.8) | 324 | Houma, LA | (25.1) |
| 20 | Bay City, MI | 28.7 | 131 | Deltona-Daytona Beach, FL | (1.2) | 139 | Houston, TX | (2.0) |
| 163 | Beaumont-Port Arthur, TX | (4.4) | 117 | Denver-Aurora, CO | 0.6 | 114 | Huntsville, AL | 0.7 |
| NA | Bend, OR** | NA | 80 | Des Moines-West Des Moines, IA | 7.0 | 3 | Idaho Falls, ID | 52.6 |
| 19 | Billings, MT | 29.8 | 127 | Detroit (greater), MI | (1.0) | 70 | Indianapolis, IN | 9.6 |
| 64 | Binghamton, NY | 11.4 | 106 | Detroit-Dearborn-Livonia, MI M.D. | 2.5 | 17 | Iowa City, IA | 30.2 |
| 27 | Birmingham-Hoover, AL | 24.3 | 144 | Dothan, AL | (2.4) | 153 | Jacksonville, FL | (3.4) |
| 91 | Bismarck, ND | 5.4 | 254 | Dover, DE | (14.4) | NA | Jackson, MI** | NA |
| 293 | Blacksburg, VA | (19.4) | 87 | Dubuque, IA | 5.8 | 185 | Jackson, MS | (6.9) |
| 170 | Bloomington, IL | (4.9) | 90 | Duluth, MN-WI | 5.6 | 42 | Jackson, TN | 17.7 |
| 263 | Bloomington, IN | (15.0) | 342 | Dutchess-Putnam, NY M.D. | (39.1) | 300 | Janesville, WI | (20.8) |
| 142 | Bloomsburg-Berwick, PA | (2.1) | 99 | East Stroudsburg, PA | 4.1 | 290 | Jefferson City, MO | (18.8) |
| 31 | Boise City, ID | 20.9 | NA | Eau Claire, WI** | NA | 335 | Johnson City, TN | (29.9) |
| 147 | Boston (greater), MA-NH | (2.5) | 305 | El Centro, CA | (21.9) | 162 | Johnstown, PA | (4.3) |
| 166 | Boston, MA M.D. | (4.5) | 334 | El Paso, TX | (29.7) | 166 | Jonesboro, AR | (4.5) |
| 127 | Boulder, CO | (1.0) | 211 | Elgin, IL M.D. | (9.5) | 133 | Joplin, MO | (1.5) |
| 275 | Bowling Green, KY | (15.8) | 117 | Elizabethtown-Fort Knox, KY | 0.6 | 263 | Kahului-Wailuku-Lahaina, HI | (15.0) |
| 286 | Bremerton-Silverdale, WA | (18.2) | 344 | Elmira, NY | (41.2) | 309 | Kankakee, IL | (22.4) |
| 248 | Bridgeport-Stamford, CT | (13.9) | 282 | Erie, PA | (17.3) | 88 | Kansas City, MO-KS | 5.7 |
| 98 | Brownsville-Harlingen, TX | 4.3 | 44 | Eugene, OR | 16.6 | 203 | Kennewick-Richland, WA | (8.7) |
| 37 | Brunswick, GA | 18.9 | 159 | Fairbanks, AK | (3.8) | 323 | Kingsport, TN-VA | (24.8) |
| 245 | Buffalo-Niagara Falls, NY | (13.4) | 54 | Fargo, ND-MN | 13.7 | 331 | Kingston, NY | (27.9) |
| 215 | Burlington, NC | (10.2) | 194 | Farmington, NM | (7.6) | 316 | Knoxville, TN | (23.4) |
| 12 | California-Lexington Park, MD | 34.5 | 213 | Fayetteville-Springdale, AR-MO | (10.0) | 35 | Kokomo, IN | 19.6 |
| 122 | Cambridge-Newton, MA M.D. | 0.1 | 243 | Fayetteville, NC | (13.1) | NA | La Crosse, WI-MN** | NA |
| 329 | Camden, NJ M.D. | (27.1) | 245 | Flagstaff, AZ | (13.4) | 130 | Lafayette, IN | (1.1) |
| 163 | Canton, OH | (4.4) | 266 | Flint, MI | (15.2) | NA | Lafayette, LA** | NA |
| 249 | Cape Coral-Fort Myers, FL | (14.1) | 15 | Florence-Muscle Shoals, AL | 32.6 | NA | Lake Charles, LA** | NA |
| 219 | Cape Girardeau, MO-IL | (10.4) | 184 | Florence, SC | (6.5) | 278 | Lake Co.-Kenosha Co., IL-WI M.D. | (16.2) |
| NA | Carbondale-Marion, IL** | NA | 257 | Fond du Lac, WI | (14.6) | 207 | Lake Havasu City-Kingman, AZ | (9.0) |
| 227 | Carson City, NV | (10.9) | 156 | Fort Collins, CO | (3.5) | 71 | Lakeland, FL | 9.0 |
| 292 | Casper, WY | (19.2) | 238 | Fort Lauderdale, FL M.D. | (12.2) | NA | Lancaster, PA** | NA |
| 56 | Cedar Rapids, IA | 13.3 | 43 | Fort Smith, AR-OK | 17.6 | 24 | Lansing-East Lansing, MI | 26.6 |
| NA | Chambersburg-Waynesboro, PA** | NA | 206 | Fort Wayne, IN | (8.9) | 176 | Laredo, TX | (5.6) |
| 177 | Champaign-Urbana, IL | (5.7) | 138 | Fort Worth-Arlington, TX M.D. | (1.8) | 271 | Las Cruces, NM | (15.4) |
| 228 | Charleston-North Charleston, SC | (11.0) | 207 | Fresno, CA | (9.0) | 131 | Las Vegas-Henderson, NV | (1.2) |
| NA | Charlotte-Mecklenburg, NC-SC** | NA | 150 | Gadsden, AL | (2.9) | 224 | Lawrence, KS | (10.6) |
| 279 | Charlottesville, VA | (16.4) | 139 | Gainesville, FL | (2.0) | 321 | Lawton, OK | (24.6) |
| NA | Chattanooga, TN-GA** | NA | 228 | Gainesville, GA | (11.0) | 287 | Lebanon, PA | (18.3) |

Note: All listings are for Metropolitan Statistical Areas (M.S.A.s) except for those ending with "M.D." Listings with "M.D." are Metropolitan Divisions which are smaller parts of eleven large M.S.A.s. See explanatory note at beginning of metropolitan area section.

| RANK | METROPOLITAN AREA | % CHANGE | RANK | METROPOLITAN AREA | % CHANGE | RANK | METROPOLITAN AREA | % CHANGE |
|---|---|---|---|---|---|---|---|---|
| 161 | Lewiston-Auburn, ME | (3.9) | 81 | Omaha-Council Bluffs, NE-IA | 6.7 | 316 | Sheboygan, WI | (23.4) |
| 126 | Lewiston, ID-WA | (0.9) | 269 | Orlando, FL | (15.3) | 329 | Sherman-Denison, TX | (27.1) |
| 236 | Lexington-Fayette, KY | (12.1) | 299 | Oshkosh-Neenah, WI | (20.6) | NA | Shreveport-Bossier City, LA** | NA |
| 62 | Lima, OH | 11.6 | 251 | Owensboro, KY | (14.2) | 283 | Silver Spring-Frederick, MD M.D. | (17.6) |
| 157 | Lincoln, NE | (3.6) | 81 | Oxnard-Thousand Oaks, CA | 6.7 | 57 | Sioux City, IA-NE-SD | 12.8 |
| 144 | Little Rock, AR | (2.4) | 288 | Palm Bay-Melbourne, FL | (18.5) | 219 | Sioux Falls, SD | (10.4) |
| 336 | Logan, UT-ID | (30.7) | 88 | Panama City, FL | 5.7 | 153 | South Bend-Mishawaka, IN-MI | (3.4) |
| 326 | Longview, TX | (25.9) | 295 | Parkersburg-Vienna, WV | (19.6) | 207 | Spartanburg, SC | (9.0) |
| 25 | Longview, WA | 26.3 | 78 | Pensacola, FL | 8.0 | 67 | Spokane, WA | 10.7 |
| 163 | Los Angeles County, CA M.D. | (4.4) | 312 | Peoria, IL | (22.8) | 1 | Springfield, IL | 160.5 |
| 158 | Los Angeles (greater), CA | (3.7) | 251 | Philadelphia (greater) PA-NJ-MD-DE | (14.2) | 133 | Springfield, MA | (1.5) |
| 187 | Louisville, KY-IN | (7.1) | 186 | Philadelphia, PA M.D. | (7.0) | 100 | Springfield, MO | 4.0 |
| 61 | Lubbock, TX | 12.0 | NA | Phoenix-Mesa-Scottsdale, AZ** | NA | 10 | Springfield, OH | 35.3 |
| 49 | Lynchburg, VA | 15.1 | NA | Pittsburgh, PA** | NA | 341 | State College, PA | (38.7) |
| 93 | Macon, GA | 4.7 | 203 | Pittsfield, MA | (8.7) | 234 | Staunton-Waynesboro, VA | (11.9) |
| 251 | Madera, CA | (14.2) | 4 | Pocatello, ID | 51.2 | 212 | Stockton-Lodi, CA | (9.9) |
| NA | Madison, WI** | NA | 127 | Port St. Lucie, FL | (1.0) | NA | St. Cloud, MN** | NA |
| 228 | Manchester-Nashua, NH | (11.0) | 232 | Portland-Vancouver, OR-WA | (11.7) | 233 | St. George, UT | (11.8) |
| 95 | Manhattan, KS | 4.5 | 203 | Portland, ME | (8.7) | 306 | St. Joseph, MO-KS | (22.0) |
| 55 | Mankato-North Mankato, MN | 13.4 | 100 | Prescott, AZ | 4.0 | 236 | St. Louis, MO-IL | (12.1) |
| 280 | Mansfield, OH | (16.5) | 216 | Providence-Warwick, RI-MA | (10.3) | 327 | Sumter, SC | (26.2) |
| 73 | McAllen-Edinburg-Mission, TX | 8.8 | 32 | Provo-Orem, UT | 20.7 | 222 | Syracuse, NY | (10.5) |
| 179 | Medford, OR | (6.1) | 67 | Pueblo, CO | 10.7 | 95 | Tacoma, WA M.D. | 4.5 |
| 192 | Memphis, TN-MS-AR | (7.5) | 188 | Punta Gorda, FL | (7.3) | 276 | Tallahassee, FL | (16.0) |
| 139 | Merced, CA | (2.0) | 304 | Racine, WI | (21.5) | 120 | Tampa-St Petersburg, FL | 0.2 |
| 225 | Miami (greater), FL | (10.7) | 302 | Raleigh, NC | (21.0) | 103 | Terre Haute, IN | 3.0 |
| 244 | Miami-Dade County, FL M.D. | (13.3) | 338 | Rapid City, SD | (32.7) | 310 | Texarkana, TX-AR | (22.6) |
| 46 | Midland, TX | 15.5 | 343 | Reading, PA | (39.3) | 123 | The Villages, FL | 0.0 |
| 197 | Milwaukee, WI | (8.1) | 30 | Redding, CA | 22.3 | 297 | Toledo, OH | (20.0) |
| 222 | Minneapolis-St. Paul, MN-WI | (10.5) | 151 | Reno, NV | (3.0) | 190 | Topeka, KS | (7.4) |
| 48 | Missoula, MT | 15.3 | 197 | Richmond, VA | (8.1) | 159 | Trenton, NJ | (3.8) |
| 39 | Mobile, AL | 18.8 | 105 | Riverside-San Bernardino, CA | 2.6 | 277 | Tucson, AZ | (16.1) |
| 269 | Modesto, CA | (15.3) | 261 | Roanoke, VA | (14.9) | 102 | Tulsa, OK | 3.9 |
| 37 | Monroe, LA | 18.9 | 148 | Rochester, MN | (2.7) | 188 | Tuscaloosa, AL | (7.3) |
| 169 | Monroe, MI | (4.8) | 192 | Rochester, NY | (7.5) | 79 | Tyler, TX | 7.5 |
| 109 | Montgomery County, PA M.D. | 2.1 | 195 | Rockford, IL | (7.8) | 328 | Utica-Rome, NY | (27.0) |
| 172 | Morgantown, WV | (5.0) | 201 | Rockingham County, NH M.D. | (8.5) | 144 | Vallejo-Fairfield, CA | (2.4) |
| 180 | Morristown, TN | (6.3) | 256 | Rocky Mount, NC | (14.5) | 298 | Victoria, TX | (20.2) |
| 14 | Mount Vernon-Anacortes, WA | 32.8 | 23 | Rome, GA | 27.9 | 46 | Vineland-Bridgeton, NJ | 15.5 |
| 310 | Muncie, IN | (22.6) | 249 | Sacramento, CA | (14.1) | 108 | Virginia Beach-Norfolk, VA-NC | 2.2 |
| NA | Muskegon, MI** | NA | 120 | Saginaw, MI | 0.2 | NA | Visalia-Porterville, CA** | NA |
| NA | Myrtle Beach, SC-NC** | NA | 219 | Salem, OR | (10.4) | 52 | Waco, TX | 14.3 |
| 318 | Napa, CA | (23.9) | 29 | Salinas, CA | 22.4 | 107 | Warner Robins, GA | 2.3 |
| 180 | Naples-Marco Island, FL | (6.3) | 73 | Salisbury, MD-DE | 8.8 | 216 | Warren-Troy, MI M.D. | (10.3) |
| 259 | Nashville-Davidson, TN | (14.8) | 26 | Salt Lake City, UT | 25.0 | 265 | Washington (greater) DC-VA-MD-WV | (15.1) |
| 173 | Nassau-Suffolk, NY M.D. | (5.4) | NA | San Angelo, TX** | NA | 261 | Washington, DC-VA-MD-WV M.D. | (14.9) |
| 226 | New Bern, NC | (10.8) | 124 | San Antonio, TX | (0.1) | 346 | Watertown-Fort Drum, NY | (49.1) |
| 40 | New Haven-Milford, CT | 17.9 | 199 | San Diego, CA | (8.2) | 324 | Wausau, WI | (25.1) |
| 175 | New Orleans, LA | (5.5) | 113 | San Francisco (greater), CA | 0.9 | 112 | West Palm Beach, FL M.D. | 1.0 |
| 245 | New York (greater), NY-NJ-PA | (13.4) | 83 | San Francisco-Redwood, CA M.D. | 6.6 | 33 | Wichita Falls, TX | 20.4 |
| 228 | New York-Jersey City, NY-NJ M.D. | (11.0) | 207 | San Jose, CA | (9.0) | 75 | Wichita, KS | 8.7 |
| 291 | Newark, NJ-PA M.D. | (19.0) | 173 | San Luis Obispo, CA | (5.4) | 332 | Williamsport, PA | (29.1) |
| NA | Niles-Benton Harbor, MI** | NA | 66 | San Rafael, CA M.D. | 11.1 | 339 | Wilmington, DE-MD-NJ M.D. | (34.4) |
| 114 | North Port-Sarasota-Bradenton, FL | 0.7 | 94 | Santa Cruz-Watsonville, CA | 4.6 | 242 | Wilmington, NC | (12.9) |
| 234 | Norwich-New London, CT | (11.9) | 8 | Santa Maria-Santa Barbara, CA | 42.0 | 178 | Winchester, VA-WV | (5.8) |
| 133 | Oakland-Hayward, CA M.D. | (1.5) | 110 | Santa Rosa, CA | 1.7 | 180 | Winston-Salem, NC | (6.3) |
| 58 | Ocala, FL | 12.7 | 97 | Savannah, GA | 4.4 | 195 | Worcester, MA-CT | (7.8) |
| 293 | Ocean City, NJ | (19.4) | NA | Scranton--Wilkes-Barre, PA** | NA | 337 | Yakima, WA | (31.9) |
| 33 | Odessa, TX | 20.4 | 60 | Seattle (greater), WA | 12.1 | 216 | York-Hanover, PA | (10.3) |
| 13 | Ogden-Clearfield, UT | 33.3 | 50 | Seattle-Bellevue-Everett, WA M.D. | 14.7 | 2 | Yuba City, CA | 53.3 |
| 201 | Oklahoma City, OK | (8.5) | 254 | Sebastian-Vero Beach, FL | (14.4) | 148 | Yuma, AZ | (2.7) |
| NA | Olympia, WA** | NA | 22 | Sebring, FL | 28.0 | | | |

Source: CQ Press using reported data from the F.B.I. "Crime in the United States 2013"

*Motor vehicle theft includes the theft or attempted theft of a self-propelled vehicle. Excludes motorboats, construction equipment, airplanes, and farming equipment.

**Not available.

# 39. Percent Change in Motor Vehicle Theft Rate: 2012 to 2013 (continued)
## National Percent Change = 4.0% Decrease*

| RANK | METROPOLITAN AREA | % CHANGE | RANK | METROPOLITAN AREA | % CHANGE | RANK | METROPOLITAN AREA | % CHANGE |
|---|---|---|---|---|---|---|---|---|
| 1 | Springfield, IL | 160.5 | 64 | Binghamton, NY | 11.4 | 127 | Port St. Lucie, FL | (1.0) |
| 2 | Yuba City, CA | 53.3 | 66 | San Rafael, CA M.D. | 11.1 | 130 | Lafayette, IN | (1.1) |
| 3 | Idaho Falls, ID | 52.6 | 67 | Pueblo, CO | 10.7 | 131 | Deltona-Daytona Beach, FL | (1.2) |
| 4 | Pocatello, ID | 51.2 | 67 | Spokane, WA | 10.7 | 131 | Las Vegas-Henderson, NV | (1.2) |
| 5 | Chico, CA | 51.1 | 69 | Columbia, MO | 10.4 | 133 | Joplin, MO | (1.5) |
| 6 | Hammond, LA | 48.5 | 70 | Indianapolis, IN | 9.6 | 133 | Oakland-Hayward, CA M.D. | (1.5) |
| 7 | Abilene, TX | 43.8 | 71 | Cincinnati, OH-KY-IN | 9.0 | 133 | Springfield, MA | (1.5) |
| 8 | Santa Maria-Santa Barbara, CA | 42.0 | 71 | Lakeland, FL | 9.0 | 136 | Albany-Schenectady-Troy, NY | (1.6) |
| 9 | Albany, OR | 38.2 | 73 | McAllen-Edinburg-Mission, TX | 8.8 | 137 | Baltimore, MD | (1.7) |
| 10 | Springfield, OH | 35.3 | 73 | Salisbury, MD-DE | 8.8 | 138 | Fort Worth-Arlington, TX M.D. | (1.8) |
| 11 | Corvallis, OR | 34.9 | 75 | Wichita, KS | 8.7 | 139 | Gainesville, FL | (2.0) |
| 12 | California-Lexington Park, MD | 34.5 | 76 | Amarillo, TX | 8.2 | 139 | Houston, TX | (2.0) |
| 13 | Ogden-Clearfield, UT | 33.3 | 77 | Hinesville, GA | 8.1 | 139 | Merced, CA | (2.0) |
| 14 | Mount Vernon-Anacortes, WA | 32.8 | 78 | Pensacola, FL | 8.0 | 142 | Bloomsburg-Berwick, PA | (2.1) |
| 15 | Florence-Muscle Shoals, AL | 32.6 | 79 | Tyler, TX | 7.5 | 143 | Gary, IN M.D. | (2.3) |
| 16 | Dalton, GA | 30.9 | 80 | Des Moines-West Des Moines, IA | 7.0 | 144 | Dothan, AL | (2.4) |
| 17 | Iowa City, IA | 30.2 | 81 | Omaha-Council Bluffs, NE-IA | 6.7 | 144 | Little Rock, AR | (2.4) |
| 18 | Anniston-Oxford, AL | 30.1 | 81 | Oxnard-Thousand Oaks, CA | 6.7 | 144 | Vallejo-Fairfield, CA | (2.4) |
| 19 | Billings, MT | 29.8 | 83 | San Francisco-Redwood, CA M.D. | 6.6 | 147 | Boston (greater), MA-NH | (2.5) |
| 20 | Bay City, MI | 28.7 | 84 | Anchorage, AK | 5.9 | 148 | Rochester, MN | (2.7) |
| 21 | Barnstable Town, MA | 28.6 | 84 | Colorado Springs, CO | 5.9 | 148 | Yuma, AZ | (2.7) |
| 22 | Sebring, FL | 28.0 | 84 | Greenville, NC | 5.9 | 150 | Gadsden, AL | (2.9) |
| 23 | Rome, GA | 27.9 | 87 | Dubuque, IA | 5.8 | 151 | Reno, NV | (3.0) |
| 24 | Lansing-East Lansing, MI | 26.6 | 88 | Kansas City, MO-KS | 5.7 | 152 | Hilton Head Island, SC | (3.3) |
| 25 | Longview, WA | 26.3 | 88 | Panama City, FL | 5.7 | 153 | Dayton, OH | (3.4) |
| 26 | Salt Lake City, UT | 25.0 | 90 | Duluth, MN-WI | 5.6 | 153 | Jacksonville, FL | (3.4) |
| 27 | Birmingham-Hoover, AL | 24.3 | 91 | Bismarck, ND | 5.4 | 153 | South Bend-Mishawaka, IN-MI | (3.4) |
| 28 | Columbus, GA-AL | 22.9 | 92 | College Station-Bryan, TX | 4.9 | 156 | Fort Collins, CO | (3.5) |
| 29 | Salinas, CA | 22.4 | 93 | Macon, GA | 4.7 | 157 | Lincoln, NE | (3.6) |
| 30 | Redding, CA | 22.3 | 94 | Santa Cruz-Watsonville, CA | 4.6 | 158 | Los Angeles (greater), CA | (3.7) |
| 31 | Boise City, ID | 20.9 | 95 | Manhattan, KS | 4.5 | 159 | Fairbanks, AK | (3.8) |
| 32 | Provo-Orem, UT | 20.7 | 95 | Tacoma, WA M.D. | 4.5 | 159 | Trenton, NJ | (3.8) |
| 33 | Odessa, TX | 20.4 | 97 | Savannah, GA | 4.4 | 161 | Lewiston-Auburn, ME | (3.9) |
| 33 | Wichita Falls, TX | 20.4 | 98 | Brownsville-Harlingen, TX | 4.3 | 162 | Johnstown, PA | (4.3) |
| 35 | Kokomo, IN | 19.6 | 99 | East Stroudsburg, PA | 4.1 | 163 | Beaumont-Port Arthur, TX | (4.4) |
| 36 | Grand Island, NE | 19.4 | 100 | Prescott, AZ | 4.0 | 163 | Canton, OH | (4.4) |
| 37 | Brunswick, GA | 18.9 | 100 | Springfield, MO | 4.0 | 163 | Los Angeles County, CA M.D. | (4.4) |
| 37 | Monroe, LA | 18.9 | 102 | Tulsa, OK | 3.9 | 166 | Boston, MA M.D. | (4.5) |
| 39 | Mobile, AL | 18.8 | 103 | Daphne-Fairhope-Foley, AL | 3.0 | 166 | Jonesboro, AR | (4.5) |
| 40 | Corpus Christi, TX | 17.9 | 103 | Terre Haute, IN | 3.0 | 168 | Austin-Round Rock, TX | (4.6) |
| 40 | New Haven-Milford, CT | 17.9 | 105 | Riverside-San Bernardino, CA | 2.6 | 169 | Monroe, MI | (4.8) |
| 42 | Jackson, TN | 17.7 | 106 | Detroit-Dearborn-Livonia, MI M.D. | 2.5 | 170 | Bloomington, IL | (4.9) |
| 43 | Fort Smith, AR-OK | 17.6 | 107 | Warner Robins, GA | 2.3 | 170 | Greensboro-High Point, NC | (4.9) |
| 44 | Eugene, OR | 16.6 | 108 | Virginia Beach-Norfolk, VA-NC | 2.2 | 172 | Morgantown, WV | (5.0) |
| 45 | Cleveland, TN | 16.3 | 109 | Montgomery County, PA M.D. | 2.1 | 173 | Nassau-Suffolk, NY M.D. | (5.4) |
| 46 | Midland, TX | 15.5 | 110 | Santa Rosa, CA | 1.7 | 173 | San Luis Obispo, CA | (5.4) |
| 46 | Vineland-Bridgeton, NJ | 15.5 | 111 | Greenville-Anderson, SC | 1.3 | 175 | New Orleans, LA | (5.5) |
| 48 | Missoula, MT | 15.3 | 112 | West Palm Beach, FL M.D. | 1.0 | 176 | Laredo, TX | (5.6) |
| 49 | Lynchburg, VA | 15.1 | 113 | San Francisco (greater), CA | 0.9 | 177 | Champaign-Urbana, IL | (5.7) |
| 50 | Seattle-Bellevue-Everett, WA M.D. | 14.7 | 114 | Anaheim-Santa Ana-Irvine, CA M.D. | 0.7 | 178 | Winchester, VA-WV | (5.8) |
| 51 | Hanford-Corcoran, CA | 14.5 | 114 | Huntsville, AL | 0.7 | 179 | Medford, OR | (6.1) |
| 52 | Waco, TX | 14.3 | 114 | North Port-Sarasota-Bradenton, FL | 0.7 | 180 | Altoona, PA | (6.3) |
| 53 | Ames, IA | 14.0 | 117 | Denver-Aurora, CO | 0.6 | 180 | Morristown, TN | (6.3) |
| 54 | Fargo, ND-MN | 13.7 | 117 | Elizabethtown-Fort Knox, KY | 0.6 | 180 | Naples-Marco Island, FL | (6.3) |
| 55 | Mankato-North Mankato, MN | 13.4 | 119 | Dallas-Plano-Irving, TX M.D. | 0.3 | 180 | Winston-Salem, NC | (6.3) |
| 56 | Cedar Rapids, IA | 13.3 | 120 | Saginaw, MI | 0.2 | 184 | Florence, SC | (6.5) |
| 57 | Sioux City, IA-NE-SD | 12.8 | 120 | Tampa-St Petersburg, FL | 0.2 | 185 | Jackson, MS | (6.9) |
| 58 | Ocala, FL | 12.7 | 122 | Cambridge-Newton, MA M.D. | 0.1 | 186 | Philadelphia, PA M.D. | (7.0) |
| 59 | Decatur, AL | 12.3 | 123 | The Villages, FL | 0.0 | 187 | Louisville, KY-IN | (7.1) |
| 60 | Seattle (greater), WA | 12.1 | 124 | San Antonio, TX | (0.1) | 188 | Punta Gorda, FL | (7.3) |
| 61 | Lubbock, TX | 12.0 | 125 | Dallas (greater), TX | (0.3) | 188 | Tuscaloosa, AL | (7.3) |
| 62 | Lima, OH | 11.6 | 126 | Lewiston, ID-WA | (0.9) | 190 | Bakersfield, CA | (7.4) |
| 63 | Greeley, CO | 11.5 | 127 | Boulder, CO | (1.0) | 190 | Topeka, KS | (7.4) |
| 64 | Albuquerque, NM | 11.4 | 127 | Detroit (greater), MI | (1.0) | 192 | Memphis, TN-MS-AR | (7.5) |

Note: All listings are for Metropolitan Statistical Areas (M.S.A.s) except for those ending with "M.D." Listings with "M.D." are Metropolitan Divisions which are smaller parts of eleven large M.S.A.s. See explanatory note at beginning of metropolitan area section.

| RANK | METROPOLITAN AREA | % CHANGE | RANK | METROPOLITAN AREA | % CHANGE | RANK | METROPOLITAN AREA | % CHANGE |
|---|---|---|---|---|---|---|---|---|
| 192 | Rochester, NY | (7.5) | 254 | Sebastian-Vero Beach, FL | (14.4) | 316 | Sheboygan, WI | (23.4) |
| 194 | Farmington, NM | (7.6) | 256 | Rocky Mount, NC | (14.5) | 318 | Hagerstown-Martinsburg, MD-WV | (23.9) |
| 195 | Rockford, IL | (7.8) | 257 | Augusta, GA-SC | (14.6) | 318 | Napa, CA | (23.9) |
| 195 | Worcester, MA-CT | (7.8) | 257 | Fond du Lac, WI | (14.6) | 320 | Columbus, IN | (24.5) |
| 197 | Milwaukee, WI | (8.1) | 259 | Decatur, IL | (14.8) | 321 | Lawton, OK | (24.6) |
| 197 | Richmond, VA | (8.1) | 259 | Nashville-Davidson, TN | (14.8) | 322 | Harrisonburg, VA | (24.7) |
| 199 | San Diego, CA | (8.2) | 261 | Roanoke, VA | (14.9) | 323 | Kingsport, TN-VA | (24.8) |
| 200 | Allentown, PA-NJ | (8.4) | 261 | Washington, DC-VA-MD-WV M.D. | (14.9) | 324 | Houma, LA | (25.1) |
| 201 | Oklahoma City, OK | (8.5) | 263 | Bloomington, IN | (15.0) | 324 | Wausau, WI | (25.1) |
| 201 | Rockingham County, NH M.D. | (8.5) | 263 | Kahului-Wailuku-Lahaina, HI | (15.0) | 326 | Longview, TX | (25.9) |
| 203 | Kennewick-Richland, WA | (8.7) | 265 | Washington (greater) DC-VA-MD-WV | (15.1) | 327 | Sumter, SC | (26.2) |
| 203 | Pittsfield, MA | (8.7) | 266 | Flint, MI | (15.2) | 328 | Utica-Rome, NY | (27.0) |
| 203 | Portland, ME | (8.7) | 266 | Green Bay, WI | (15.2) | 329 | Camden, NJ M.D. | (27.1) |
| 206 | Fort Wayne, IN | (8.9) | 266 | Homosassa Springs, FL | (15.2) | 329 | Sherman-Denison, TX | (27.1) |
| 207 | Fresno, CA | (9.0) | 269 | Modesto, CA | (15.3) | 331 | Kingston, NY | (27.9) |
| 207 | Lake Havasu City-Kingman, AZ | (9.0) | 269 | Orlando, FL | (15.3) | 332 | Williamsport, PA | (29.1) |
| 207 | San Jose, CA | (9.0) | 271 | Goldsboro, NC | (15.4) | 333 | Grand Junction, CO | (29.4) |
| 207 | Spartanburg, SC | (9.0) | 271 | Las Cruces, NM | (15.4) | 334 | El Paso, TX | (29.7) |
| 211 | Elgin, IL M.D. | (9.5) | 273 | Akron, OH | (15.5) | 335 | Johnson City, TN | (29.9) |
| 212 | Stockton-Lodi, CA | (9.9) | 274 | Ann Arbor, MI | (15.7) | 336 | Logan, UT-ID | (30.7) |
| 213 | Fayetteville-Springdale, AR-MO | (10.0) | 275 | Bowling Green, KY | (15.8) | 337 | Yakima, WA | (31.9) |
| 214 | Atlanta, GA | (10.1) | 276 | Tallahassee, FL | (16.0) | 338 | Rapid City, SD | (32.7) |
| 215 | Burlington, NC | (10.2) | 277 | Tucson, AZ | (16.1) | 339 | Wilmington, DE-MD-NJ M.D. | (34.4) |
| 216 | Providence-Warwick, RI-MA | (10.3) | 278 | Lake Co.-Kenosha Co., IL-WI M.D. | (16.2) | 340 | Bangor, ME | (36.1) |
| 216 | Warren-Troy, MI M.D. | (10.3) | 279 | Charlottesville, VA | (16.4) | 341 | State College, PA | (38.7) |
| 216 | York-Hanover, PA | (10.3) | 280 | Mansfield, OH | (16.5) | 342 | Dutchess-Putnam, NY M.D. | (39.1) |
| 219 | Cape Girardeau, MO-IL | (10.4) | 281 | Davenport, IA-IL | (16.6) | 343 | Reading, PA | (39.3) |
| 219 | Salem, OR | (10.4) | 282 | Erie, PA | (17.3) | 344 | Elmira, NY | (41.2) |
| 219 | Sioux Falls, SD | (10.4) | 283 | Silver Spring-Frederick, MD M.D. | (17.6) | 345 | Glens Falls, NY | (44.2) |
| 222 | Minneapolis-St. Paul, MN-WI | (10.5) | 284 | Coeur d'Alene, ID | (17.7) | 346 | Watertown-Fort Drum, NY | (49.1) |
| 222 | Syracuse, NY | (10.5) | 285 | Cumberland, MD-WV | (17.8) | NA | Alexandria, LA** | NA |
| 224 | Lawrence, KS | (10.6) | 286 | Bremerton-Silverdale, WA | (18.2) | NA | Baton Rouge, LA** | NA |
| 225 | Miami (greater), FL | (10.7) | 287 | Lebanon, PA | (18.3) | NA | Bend, OR** | NA |
| 226 | New Bern, NC | (10.8) | 288 | Palm Bay-Melbourne, FL | (18.5) | NA | Carbondale-Marion, IL** | NA |
| 227 | Carson City, NV | (10.9) | 289 | Appleton, WI | (18.7) | NA | Chambersburg-Waynesboro, PA** | NA |
| 228 | Charleston-North Charleston, SC | (11.0) | 290 | Jefferson City, MO | (18.8) | NA | Charlotte-Mecklenburg, NC-SC** | NA |
| 228 | Gainesville, GA | (11.0) | 291 | Newark, NJ-PA M.D. | (19.0) | NA | Chattanooga, TN-GA** | NA |
| 228 | Manchester-Nashua, NH | (11.0) | 292 | Casper, WY | (19.2) | NA | Columbia, SC** | NA |
| 228 | New York-Jersey City, NY-NJ M.D. | (11.0) | 293 | Blacksburg, VA | (19.4) | NA | Eau Claire, WI** | NA |
| 232 | Portland-Vancouver, OR-WA | (11.7) | 293 | Ocean City, NJ | (19.4) | NA | Gettysburg, PA** | NA |
| 233 | St. George, UT | (11.8) | 295 | Parkersburg-Vienna, WV | (19.6) | NA | Grand Rapids-Wyoming, MI** | NA |
| 234 | Norwich-New London, CT | (11.9) | 296 | Clarksville, TN-KY | (19.8) | NA | Grants Pass, OR** | NA |
| 234 | Staunton-Waynesboro, VA | (11.9) | 297 | Toledo, OH | (20.0) | NA | Gulfport-Biloxi-Pascagoula, MS** | NA |
| 236 | Lexington-Fayette, KY | (12.1) | 298 | Victoria, TX | (20.2) | NA | Hot Springs, AR** | NA |
| 236 | St. Louis, MO-IL | (12.1) | 299 | Oshkosh-Neenah, WI | (20.6) | NA | Jackson, MI** | NA |
| 238 | Albany, GA | (12.2) | 300 | Cheyenne, WY | (20.8) | NA | La Crosse, WI-MN** | NA |
| 238 | Fort Lauderdale, FL M.D. | (12.2) | 300 | Janesville, WI | (20.8) | NA | Lafayette, LA** | NA |
| 240 | Crestview-Fort Walton Beach, FL | (12.7) | 302 | Chicago (greater), IL-IN-WI | (21.0) | NA | Lake Charles, LA** | NA |
| 241 | Grand Forks, ND-MN | (12.8) | 302 | Raleigh, NC | (21.0) | NA | Lancaster, PA** | NA |
| 242 | Wilmington, NC | (12.9) | 304 | Racine, WI | (21.5) | NA | Madison, WI** | NA |
| 243 | Fayetteville, NC | (13.1) | 305 | El Centro, CA | (21.9) | NA | Muskegon, MI** | NA |
| 244 | Miami-Dade County, FL M.D. | (13.3) | 306 | St. Joseph, MO-KS | (22.0) | NA | Myrtle Beach, SC-NC** | NA |
| 245 | Buffalo-Niagara Falls, NY | (13.4) | 307 | Athens-Clarke County, GA | (22.1) | NA | Niles-Benton Harbor, MI** | NA |
| 245 | Flagstaff, AZ | (13.4) | 307 | Great Falls, MT | (22.1) | NA | Olympia, WA** | NA |
| 245 | New York (greater), NY-NJ-PA | (13.4) | 309 | Kankakee, IL | (22.4) | NA | Phoenix-Mesa-Scottsdale, AZ** | NA |
| 248 | Bridgeport-Stamford, CT | (13.9) | 310 | Muncie, IN | (22.6) | NA | Pittsburgh, PA** | NA |
| 249 | Cape Coral-Fort Myers, FL | (14.1) | 310 | Texarkana, TX-AR | (22.6) | NA | San Angelo, TX** | NA |
| 249 | Sacramento, CA | (14.1) | 312 | Peoria, IL | (22.8) | NA | Scranton--Wilkes-Barre, PA** | NA |
| 251 | Madera, CA | (14.2) | 313 | Hartford, CT | (22.9) | NA | Shreveport-Bossier City, LA** | NA |
| 251 | Owensboro, KY | (14.2) | 314 | Atlantic City, NJ | (23.1) | NA | St. Cloud, MN** | NA |
| 251 | Philadelphia (greater) PA-NJ-MD-DE | (14.2) | 315 | Chicago-Naperville, IL M.D. | (23.2) | NA | Visalia-Porterville, CA** | NA |
| 254 | Dover, DE | (14.4) | 316 | Knoxville, TN | (23.4) | | | |

Source: CQ Press using reported data from the F.B.I. "Crime in the United States 2013"
*Motor vehicle theft includes the theft or attempted theft of a self-propelled vehicle. Excludes motorboats, construction equipment, airplanes, and farming equipment.
**Not available.

## 40. Percent Change in Motor Vehicle Theft Rate: 2009 to 2013
## National Percent Change = 14.6% Decrease*

| RANK | METROPOLITAN AREA | % CHANGE | RANK | METROPOLITAN AREA | % CHANGE | RANK | METROPOLITAN AREA | % CHANGE |
|---|---|---|---|---|---|---|---|---|
| 122 | Abilene, TX | (8.5) | 201 | Cheyenne, WY | (25.8) | NA | Gary, IN M.D.** | NA |
| 255 | Akron, OH | (34.7) | NA | Chicago (greater), IL-IN-WI** | NA | NA | Gettysburg, PA** | NA |
| 205 | Albany-Schenectady-Troy, NY | (26.3) | NA | Chicago-Naperville, IL M.D.** | NA | 288 | Glens Falls, NY | (43.4) |
| 221 | Albany, GA | (29.1) | 68 | Chico, CA | 6.2 | 227 | Goldsboro, NC | (30.2) |
| NA | Albany, OR** | NA | 140 | Cincinnati, OH-KY-IN | (12.4) | 111 | Grand Forks, ND-MN | (4.4) |
| 151 | Albuquerque, NM | (15.3) | 242 | Clarksville, TN-KY | (32.7) | NA | Grand Island, NE** | NA |
| 18 | Alexandria, LA | 39.6 | 37 | Cleveland, TN | 19.2 | 272 | Grand Junction, CO | (38.3) |
| 198 | Allentown, PA-NJ | (25.3) | 59 | Coeur d'Alene, ID | 10.4 | NA | Grand Rapids-Wyoming, MI** | NA |
| 257 | Altoona, PA | (35.0) | 298 | College Station-Bryan, TX | (49.8) | NA | Grants Pass, OR** | NA |
| 117 | Amarillo, TX | (7.1) | 10 | Colorado Springs, CO | 54.6 | 121 | Great Falls, MT | (8.3) |
| 151 | Ames, IA | (15.3) | 44 | Columbia, MO | 15.4 | 192 | Greeley, CO | (24.1) |
| 51 | Anaheim-Santa Ana-Irvine, CA M.D. | 12.1 | 103 | Columbia, SC | (3.5) | 252 | Green Bay, WI | (33.8) |
| 97 | Anchorage, AK | (1.8) | 209 | Columbus, GA-AL | (27.2) | 215 | Greensboro-High Point, NC | (28.1) |
| 238 | Ann Arbor, MI | (32.3) | 135 | Columbus, IN | (11.6) | NA | Greenville-Anderson, SC** | NA |
| 232 | Anniston-Oxford, AL | (31.4) | 142 | Corpus Christi, TX | (12.8) | NA | Greenville, NC** | NA |
| 303 | Appleton, WI | (52.8) | 144 | Corvallis, OR | (13.1) | NA | Gulfport-Biloxi-Pascagoula, MS** | NA |
| 220 | Athens-Clarke County, GA | (28.7) | NA | Crestview-Fort Walton Beach, FL** | NA | 201 | Hagerstown-Martinsburg, MD-WV | (25.8) |
| 157 | Atlanta, GA | (15.9) | 69 | Cumberland, MD-WV | 4.8 | NA | Hammond, LA** | NA |
| 273 | Atlantic City, NJ | (38.8) | 213 | Dallas (greater), TX | (27.9) | NA | Hanford-Corcoran, CA** | NA |
| 253 | Augusta, GA-SC | (34.2) | 230 | Dallas-Plano-Irving, TX M.D. | (31.0) | 277 | Harrisonburg, VA | (40.4) |
| 133 | Austin-Round Rock, TX | (11.0) | 37 | Dalton, GA | 19.2 | 237 | Hartford, CT | (32.2) |
| 60 | Bakersfield, CA | 9.7 | NA | Daphne-Fairhope-Foley, AL** | NA | NA | Hilton Head Island, SC** | NA |
| 186 | Baltimore, MD | (23.6) | NA | Davenport, IA-IL** | NA | 245 | Hinesville, GA | (32.9) |
| 245 | Bangor, ME | (32.9) | 138 | Dayton, OH | (12.0) | NA | Homosassa Springs, FL** | NA |
| 102 | Barnstable Town, MA | (3.4) | 9 | Decatur, AL | 54.9 | 230 | Hot Springs, AR | (31.0) |
| 299 | Baton Rouge, LA | (49.9) | 305 | Decatur, IL | (54.8) | 280 | Houma, LA | (40.6) |
| 67 | Bay City, MI | 6.6 | 259 | Deltona-Daytona Beach, FL | (35.1) | 141 | Houston, TX | (12.7) |
| 179 | Beaumont-Port Arthur, TX | (21.7) | 136 | Denver-Aurora, CO | (11.8) | 183 | Huntsville, AL | (22.3) |
| 77 | Bend, OR | 3.8 | 46 | Des Moines-West Des Moines, IA | 14.8 | 106 | Idaho Falls, ID | (3.8) |
| 4 | Billings, MT | 90.2 | 143 | Detroit (greater), MI | (12.9) | 66 | Indianapolis, IN | 6.9 |
| 31 | Binghamton, NY | 25.3 | 106 | Detroit-Dearborn-Livonia, MI M.D. | (3.8) | 87 | Iowa City, IA | 0.9 |
| 147 | Birmingham-Hoover, AL | (14.0) | 91 | Dothan, AL | (0.2) | 289 | Jacksonville, FL | (43.7) |
| 39 | Bismarck, ND | 18.9 | 229 | Dover, DE | (30.7) | 184 | Jackson, MI | (23.5) |
| 212 | Blacksburg, VA | (27.8) | 158 | Dubuque, IA | (16.3) | 263 | Jackson, MS | (36.2) |
| NA | Bloomington, IL** | NA | 101 | Duluth, MN-WI | (3.2) | 294 | Jackson, TN | (46.8) |
| 124 | Bloomington, IN | (9.5) | NA | Dutchess-Putnam, NY M.D.** | NA | 254 | Janesville, WI | (34.3) |
| NA | Bloomsburg-Berwick, PA** | NA | NA | East Stroudsburg, PA** | NA | 117 | Jefferson City, MO | (7.1) |
| 85 | Boise City, ID | 1.4 | 250 | Eau Claire, WI | (33.2) | 219 | Johnson City, TN | (28.6) |
| 195 | Boston (greater), MA-NH | (24.6) | 284 | El Centro, CA | (42.3) | NA | Johnstown, PA** | NA |
| 234 | Boston, MA M.D. | (31.9) | 307 | El Paso, TX | (60.0) | 170 | Jonesboro, AR | (20.1) |
| 96 | Boulder, CO | (0.7) | NA | Elgin, IL M.D.** | NA | NA | Joplin, MO** | NA |
| NA | Bowling Green, KY** | NA | NA | Elizabethtown-Fort Knox, KY** | NA | NA | Kahului-Wailuku-Lahaina, HI** | NA |
| 20 | Bremerton-Silverdale, WA | 38.6 | 281 | Elmira, NY | (41.2) | NA | Kankakee, IL** | NA |
| 248 | Bridgeport-Stamford, CT | (33.1) | 176 | Erie, PA | (21.2) | 50 | Kansas City, MO-KS | 12.2 |
| 279 | Brownsville-Harlingen, TX | (40.5) | 238 | Eugene, OR | (32.3) | 168 | Kennewick-Richland, WA | (18.9) |
| 214 | Brunswick, GA | (28.0) | 36 | Fairbanks, AK | 21.2 | 171 | Kingsport, TN-VA | (20.3) |
| 264 | Buffalo-Niagara Falls, NY | (36.3) | 206 | Fargo, ND-MN | (26.6) | 304 | Kingston, NY | (52.9) |
| 174 | Burlington, NC | (20.8) | 268 | Farmington, NM | (37.0) | 136 | Knoxville, TN | (11.8) |
| NA | California-Lexington Park, MD** | NA | 123 | Fayetteville-Springdale, AR-MO | (9.0) | 7 | Kokomo, IN | 60.9 |
| NA | Cambridge-Newton, MA M.D.** | NA | 217 | Fayetteville, NC | (28.5) | NA | La Crosse, WI-MN** | NA |
| 200 | Camden, NJ M.D. | (25.6) | 233 | Flagstaff, AZ | (31.7) | 99 | Lafayette, IN | (2.5) |
| NA | Canton, OH** | NA | 248 | Flint, MI | (33.1) | NA | Lafayette, LA** | NA |
| 274 | Cape Coral-Fort Myers, FL | (39.2) | 2 | Florence-Muscle Shoals, AL | 107.7 | 148 | Lake Charles, LA | (14.7) |
| 14 | Cape Girardeau, MO-IL | 49.0 | 182 | Florence, SC | (22.2) | NA | Lake Co.-Kenosha Co., IL-WI M.D.** | NA |
| NA | Carbondale-Marion, IL** | NA | 145 | Fond du Lac, WI | (13.6) | 129 | Lake Havasu City-Kingman, AZ | (10.5) |
| 178 | Carson City, NV | (21.6) | 282 | Fort Collins, CO | (41.3) | 192 | Lakeland, FL | (24.1) |
| 257 | Casper, WY | (35.0) | 210 | Fort Lauderdale, FL M.D. | (27.3) | NA | Lancaster, PA** | NA |
| 49 | Cedar Rapids, IA | 13.0 | 74 | Fort Smith, AR-OK | 4.1 | 13 | Lansing-East Lansing, MI | 49.9 |
| NA | Chambersburg-Waynesboro, PA** | NA | 120 | Fort Wayne, IN | (8.2) | 308 | Laredo, TX | (76.3) |
| NA | Champaign-Urbana, IL** | NA | 160 | Fort Worth-Arlington, TX M.D. | (16.7) | 187 | Las Cruces, NM | (23.8) |
| 184 | Charleston-North Charleston, SC | (23.5) | 55 | Fresno, CA | 11.1 | 216 | Las Vegas-Henderson, NV | (28.2) |
| NA | Charlotte-Mecklenburg, NC-SC** | NA | 15 | Gadsden, AL | 44.8 | 42 | Lawrence, KS | 17.2 |
| 296 | Charlottesville, VA | (48.5) | 301 | Gainesville, FL | (50.7) | 197 | Lawton, OK | (24.7) |
| 76 | Chattanooga, TN-GA | 3.9 | 125 | Gainesville, GA | (9.6) | 155 | Lebanon, PA | (15.6) |

Note: All listings are for Metropolitan Statistical Areas (M.S.A.s) except for those ending with "M.D." Listings with "M.D." are Metropolitan Divisions which are smaller parts of eleven large M.S.A.s. See explanatory note at beginning of metropolitan area section.

| RANK | METROPOLITAN AREA | % CHANGE | RANK | METROPOLITAN AREA | % CHANGE | RANK | METROPOLITAN AREA | % CHANGE |
|---|---|---|---|---|---|---|---|---|
| 21 | Lewiston-Auburn, ME | 35.0 | 28 | Omaha-Council Bluffs, NE-IA | 28.6 | 129 | Sheboygan, WI | (10.5) |
| 109 | Lewiston, ID-WA | (4.0) | 224 | Orlando, FL | (29.9) | 116 | Sherman-Denison, TX | (6.7) |
| 25 | Lexington-Fayette, KY | 31.3 | 286 | Oshkosh-Neenah, WI | (42.9) | 194 | Shreveport-Bossier City, LA | (24.4) |
| 276 | Lima, OH | (40.2) | 110 | Owensboro, KY | (4.3) | 297 | Silver Spring-Frederick, MD M.D. | (49.5) |
| 91 | Lincoln, NE | (0.2) | 33 | Oxnard-Thousand Oaks, CA | 23.6 | 35 | Sioux City, IA-NE-SD | 22.2 |
| 115 | Little Rock, AR | (6.4) | 226 | Palm Bay-Melbourne, FL | (30.0) | 113 | Sioux Falls, SD | (5.7) |
| 262 | Logan, UT-ID | (35.5) | 154 | Panama City, FL | (15.5) | 173 | South Bend-Mishawaka, IN-MI | (20.6) |
| 306 | Longview, TX | (56.4) | NA | Parkersburg-Vienna, WV** | NA | 240 | Spartanburg, SC | (32.5) |
| 199 | Longview, WA | (25.5) | 98 | Pensacola, FL | (2.1) | 27 | Spokane, WA | 29.5 |
| 166 | Los Angeles County, CA M.D. | (18.1) | NA | Peoria, IL** | NA | NA | Springfield, IL** | NA |
| 148 | Los Angeles (greater), CA | (14.7) | 181 | Philadelphia (greater) PA-NJ-MD-DE | (22.0) | 126 | Springfield, MA | (10.0) |
| 61 | Louisville, KY-IN | 9.2 | NA | Philadelphia, PA M.D.** | NA | 23 | Springfield, MO | 32.2 |
| 19 | Lubbock, TX | 39.0 | NA | Phoenix-Mesa-Scottsdale, AZ** | NA | 70 | Springfield, OH | 4.5 |
| 211 | Lynchburg, VA | (27.7) | NA | Pittsburgh, PA** | NA | 295 | State College, PA | (48.1) |
| 162 | Macon, GA | (17.1) | 73 | Pittsfield, MA | 4.2 | NA | Staunton-Waynesboro, VA** | NA |
| 71 | Madera, CA | 4.4 | 32 | Pocatello, ID | 25.0 | 103 | Stockton-Lodi, CA | (3.5) |
| NA | Madison, WI** | NA | 131 | Port St. Lucie, FL | (10.6) | 6 | St. Cloud, MN | 71.7 |
| 164 | Manchester-Nashua, NH | (17.7) | 105 | Portland-Vancouver, OR-WA | (3.6) | 131 | St. George, UT | (10.6) |
| 43 | Manhattan, KS | 16.6 | 175 | Portland, ME | (21.0) | 16 | St. Joseph, MO-KS | 40.9 |
| 112 | Mankato-North Mankato, MN | (5.4) | 75 | Prescott, AZ | 4.0 | 227 | St. Louis, MO-IL | (30.2) |
| 22 | Mansfield, OH | 32.9 | 127 | Providence-Warwick, RI-MA | (10.1) | 80 | Sumter, SC | 2.3 |
| 293 | McAllen-Edinburg-Mission, TX | (45.7) | 165 | Provo-Orem, UT | (18.0) | 87 | Syracuse, NY | 0.9 |
| 11 | Medford, OR | 53.8 | 12 | Pueblo, CO | 52.0 | 64 | Tacoma, WA M.D. | 8.0 |
| 268 | Memphis, TN-MS-AR | (37.0) | 282 | Punta Gorda, FL | (41.3) | 48 | Tallahassee, FL | 13.2 |
| 17 | Merced, CA | 40.2 | 267 | Racine, WI | (36.8) | 299 | Tampa-St Petersburg, FL | (49.9) |
| 234 | Miami (greater), FL | (31.9) | 245 | Raleigh, NC | (32.9) | NA | Terre Haute, IN** | NA |
| 260 | Miami-Dade County, FL M.D. | (35.3) | 79 | Rapid City, SD | 2.9 | 240 | Texarkana, TX-AR | (32.5) |
| 72 | Midland, TX | 4.3 | 302 | Reading, PA | (51.2) | NA | The Villages, FL** | NA |
| 139 | Milwaukee, WI | (12.3) | 1 | Redding, CA | 229.4 | 161 | Toledo, OH | (17.0) |
| 148 | Minneapolis-St. Paul, MN-WI | (14.7) | 80 | Reno, NV | 2.3 | 23 | Topeka, KS | 32.2 |
| 41 | Missoula, MT | 18.5 | 203 | Richmond, VA | (26.0) | 65 | Trenton, NJ | 7.6 |
| 189 | Mobile, AL | (24.0) | 56 | Riverside-San Bernardino, CA | 11.0 | 266 | Tucson, AZ | (36.5) |
| 89 | Modesto, CA | 0.4 | 223 | Roanoke, VA | (29.6) | 62 | Tulsa, OK | 8.8 |
| NA | Monroe, LA** | NA | 177 | Rochester, MN | (21.4) | 277 | Tuscaloosa, AL | (40.4) |
| 54 | Monroe, MI | 11.5 | 256 | Rochester, NY | (34.9) | 188 | Tyler, TX | (23.9) |
| NA | Montgomery County, PA M.D.** | NA | NA | Rockford, IL** | NA | 40 | Utica-Rome, NY | 18.7 |
| 221 | Morgantown, WV | (29.1) | 163 | Rockingham County, NH M.D. | (17.3) | 58 | Vallejo-Fairfield, CA | 10.5 |
| 93 | Morristown, TN | (0.4) | 242 | Rocky Mount, NC | (32.7) | 180 | Victoria, TX | (21.9) |
| 28 | Mount Vernon-Anacortes, WA | 28.6 | 78 | Rome, GA | 3.3 | 159 | Vineland-Bridgeton, NJ | (16.5) |
| 114 | Muncie, IN | (6.3) | 169 | Sacramento, CA | (19.2) | NA | Virginia Beach-Norfolk, VA-NC** | NA |
| 265 | Muskegon, MI | (36.4) | 217 | Saginaw, MI | (28.5) | NA | Visalia-Porterville, CA** | NA |
| NA | Myrtle Beach, SC-NC** | NA | 133 | Salem, OR | (11.0) | 270 | Waco, TX | (37.6) |
| 206 | Napa, CA | (26.6) | 45 | Salinas, CA | 14.9 | NA | Warner Robins, GA** | NA |
| 106 | Naples-Marco Island, FL | (3.8) | NA | Salisbury, MD-DE** | NA | 224 | Warren-Troy, MI M.D. | (29.9) |
| 234 | Nashville-Davidson, TN | (31.9) | 63 | Salt Lake City, UT | 8.4 | 291 | Washington (greater) DC-VA-MD-WV | (44.2) |
| 261 | Nassau-Suffolk, NY M.D. | (35.4) | 53 | San Angelo, TX | 11.7 | 290 | Washington, DC-VA-MD-WV M.D. | (43.8) |
| NA | New Bern, NC** | NA | 83 | San Antonio, TX | 2.1 | NA | Watertown-Fort Drum, NY** | NA |
| 90 | New Haven-Milford, CT | 0.0 | 189 | San Diego, CA | (24.0) | 151 | Wausau, WI | (15.3) |
| NA | New Orleans, LA** | NA | 86 | San Francisco (greater), CA | 1.1 | 204 | West Palm Beach, FL M.D. | (26.1) |
| 189 | New York (greater), NY-NJ-PA | (24.0) | 52 | San Francisco-Redwood, CA M.D. | 12.0 | 119 | Wichita Falls, TX | (7.4) |
| NA | New York-Jersey City, NY-NJ M.D.** | NA | 26 | San Jose, CA | 30.6 | 57 | Wichita, KS | 10.7 |
| 155 | Newark, NJ-PA M.D. | (15.6) | 80 | San Luis Obispo, CA | 2.3 | 251 | Williamsport, PA | (33.5) |
| 99 | Niles-Benton Harbor, MI | (2.5) | NA | San Rafael, CA M.D.** | NA | 271 | Wilmington, DE-MD-NJ M.D. | (38.1) |
| 275 | North Port-Sarasota-Bradenton, FL | (39.8) | 47 | Santa Cruz-Watsonville, CA | 13.4 | NA | Wilmington, NC** | NA |
| 128 | Norwich-New London, CT | (10.4) | 8 | Santa Maria-Santa Barbara, CA | 56.6 | 172 | Winchester, VA-WV | (20.4) |
| 95 | Oakland-Hayward, CA M.D. | (0.6) | 145 | Santa Rosa, CA | (13.6) | NA | Winston-Salem, NC** | NA |
| 208 | Ocala, FL | (27.1) | 285 | Savannah, GA | (42.6) | 244 | Worcester, MA-CT | (32.8) |
| 167 | Ocean City, NJ | (18.2) | NA | Scranton--Wilkes-Barre, PA** | NA | NA | Yakima, WA** | NA |
| 5 | Odessa, TX | 77.6 | 34 | Seattle (greater), WA | 22.4 | 287 | York-Hanover, PA | (43.0) |
| 84 | Ogden-Clearfield, UT | 1.9 | 30 | Seattle-Bellevue-Everett, WA M.D. | 27.8 | 3 | Yuba City, CA | 101.3 |
| 94 | Oklahoma City, OK | (0.5) | 292 | Sebastian-Vero Beach, FL | (45.2) | 195 | Yuma, AZ | (24.6) |
| NA | Olympia, WA** | NA | NA | Sebring, FL** | NA | | | |

Source: CQ Press using reported data from the F.B.I. "Crime in the United States 2013"

*Motor vehicle theft includes the theft or attempted theft of a self-propelled vehicle. Excludes motorboats, construction equipment, airplanes, and farming equipment.

**Not available.

## 40. Percent Change in Motor Vehicle Theft Rate: 2009 to 2013 (continued)
## National Percent Change = 14.6% Decrease*

| RANK | METROPOLITAN AREA | % CHANGE | RANK | METROPOLITAN AREA | % CHANGE | RANK | METROPOLITAN AREA | % CHANGE |
|---|---|---|---|---|---|---|---|---|
| 1 | Redding, CA | 229.4 | 65 | Trenton, NJ | 7.6 | 129 | Lake Havasu City-Kingman, AZ | (10.5) |
| 2 | Florence-Muscle Shoals, AL | 107.7 | 66 | Indianapolis, IN | 6.9 | 129 | Sheboygan, WI | (10.5) |
| 3 | Yuba City, CA | 101.3 | 67 | Bay City, MI | 6.6 | 131 | Port St. Lucie, FL | (10.6) |
| 4 | Billings, MT | 90.2 | 68 | Chico, CA | 6.2 | 131 | St. George, UT | (10.6) |
| 5 | Odessa, TX | 77.6 | 69 | Cumberland, MD-WV | 4.8 | 133 | Austin-Round Rock, TX | (11.0) |
| 6 | St. Cloud, MN | 71.7 | 70 | Springfield, OH | 4.5 | 133 | Salem, OR | (11.0) |
| 7 | Kokomo, IN | 60.9 | 71 | Madera, CA | 4.4 | 135 | Columbus, IN | (11.6) |
| 8 | Santa Maria-Santa Barbara, CA | 56.6 | 72 | Midland, TX | 4.3 | 136 | Denver-Aurora, CO | (11.8) |
| 9 | Decatur, AL | 54.9 | 73 | Pittsfield, MA | 4.2 | 136 | Knoxville, TN | (11.8) |
| 10 | Colorado Springs, CO | 54.6 | 74 | Fort Smith, AR-OK | 4.1 | 138 | Dayton, OH | (12.0) |
| 11 | Medford, OR | 53.8 | 75 | Prescott, AZ | 4.0 | 139 | Milwaukee, WI | (12.3) |
| 12 | Pueblo, CO | 52.0 | 76 | Chattanooga, TN-GA | 3.9 | 140 | Cincinnati, OH-KY-IN | (12.4) |
| 13 | Lansing-East Lansing, MI | 49.9 | 77 | Bend, OR | 3.8 | 141 | Houston, TX | (12.7) |
| 14 | Cape Girardeau, MO-IL | 49.0 | 78 | Rome, GA | 3.3 | 142 | Corpus Christi, TX | (12.8) |
| 15 | Gadsden, AL | 44.8 | 79 | Rapid City, SD | 2.9 | 143 | Detroit (greater), MI | (12.9) |
| 16 | St. Joseph, MO-KS | 40.9 | 80 | Reno, NV | 2.3 | 144 | Corvallis, OR | (13.1) |
| 17 | Merced, CA | 40.2 | 80 | San Luis Obispo, CA | 2.3 | 145 | Fond du Lac, WI | (13.6) |
| 18 | Alexandria, LA | 39.6 | 80 | Sumter, SC | 2.3 | 145 | Santa Rosa, CA | (13.6) |
| 19 | Lubbock, TX | 39.0 | 83 | San Antonio, TX | 2.1 | 147 | Birmingham-Hoover, AL | (14.0) |
| 20 | Bremerton-Silverdale, WA | 38.6 | 84 | Ogden-Clearfield, UT | 1.9 | 148 | Lake Charles, LA | (14.7) |
| 21 | Lewiston-Auburn, ME | 35.0 | 85 | Boise City, ID | 1.4 | 148 | Los Angeles (greater), CA | (14.7) |
| 22 | Mansfield, OH | 32.9 | 86 | San Francisco (greater), CA | 1.1 | 148 | Minneapolis-St. Paul, MN-WI | (14.7) |
| 23 | Springfield, MO | 32.2 | 87 | Iowa City, IA | 0.9 | 151 | Albuquerque, NM | (15.3) |
| 23 | Topeka, KS | 32.2 | 87 | Syracuse, NY | 0.9 | 151 | Ames, IA | (15.3) |
| 25 | Lexington-Fayette, KY | 31.3 | 89 | Modesto, CA | 0.4 | 151 | Wausau, WI | (15.3) |
| 26 | San Jose, CA | 30.6 | 90 | New Haven-Milford, CT | 0.0 | 154 | Panama City, FL | (15.5) |
| 27 | Spokane, WA | 29.5 | 91 | Dothan, AL | (0.2) | 155 | Lebanon, PA | (15.6) |
| 28 | Mount Vernon-Anacortes, WA | 28.6 | 91 | Lincoln, NE | (0.2) | 155 | Newark, NJ-PA M.D. | (15.6) |
| 28 | Omaha-Council Bluffs, NE-IA | 28.6 | 93 | Morristown, TN | (0.4) | 157 | Atlanta, GA | (15.9) |
| 30 | Seattle-Bellevue-Everett, WA M.D. | 27.8 | 94 | Oklahoma City, OK | (0.5) | 158 | Dubuque, IA | (16.3) |
| 31 | Binghamton, NY | 25.3 | 95 | Oakland-Hayward, CA M.D. | (0.6) | 159 | Vineland-Bridgeton, NJ | (16.5) |
| 32 | Pocatello, ID | 25.0 | 96 | Boulder, CO | (0.7) | 160 | Fort Worth-Arlington, TX M.D. | (16.7) |
| 33 | Oxnard-Thousand Oaks, CA | 23.6 | 97 | Anchorage, AK | (1.8) | 161 | Toledo, OH | (17.0) |
| 34 | Seattle (greater), WA | 22.4 | 98 | Pensacola, FL | (2.1) | 162 | Macon, GA | (17.1) |
| 35 | Sioux City, IA-NE-SD | 22.2 | 99 | Lafayette, IN | (2.5) | 163 | Rockingham County, NH M.D. | (17.3) |
| 36 | Fairbanks, AK | 21.2 | 99 | Niles-Benton Harbor, MI | (2.5) | 164 | Manchester-Nashua, NH | (17.7) |
| 37 | Cleveland, TN | 19.2 | 101 | Duluth, MN-WI | (3.2) | 165 | Provo-Orem, UT | (18.0) |
| 37 | Dalton, GA | 19.2 | 102 | Barnstable Town, MA | (3.4) | 166 | Los Angeles County, CA M.D. | (18.1) |
| 39 | Bismarck, ND | 18.9 | 103 | Columbia, SC | (3.5) | 167 | Ocean City, NJ | (18.2) |
| 40 | Utica-Rome, NY | 18.7 | 103 | Stockton-Lodi, CA | (3.5) | 168 | Kennewick-Richland, WA | (18.9) |
| 41 | Missoula, MT | 18.5 | 105 | Portland-Vancouver, OR-WA | (3.6) | 169 | Sacramento, CA | (19.2) |
| 42 | Lawrence, KS | 17.2 | 106 | Detroit-Dearborn-Livonia, MI M.D. | (3.8) | 170 | Jonesboro, AR | (20.1) |
| 43 | Manhattan, KS | 16.6 | 106 | Idaho Falls, ID | (3.8) | 171 | Kingsport, TN-VA | (20.3) |
| 44 | Columbia, MO | 15.4 | 106 | Naples-Marco Island, FL | (3.8) | 172 | Winchester, VA-WV | (20.4) |
| 45 | Salinas, CA | 14.9 | 109 | Lewiston, ID-WA | (4.0) | 173 | South Bend-Mishawaka, IN-MI | (20.6) |
| 46 | Des Moines-West Des Moines, IA | 14.8 | 110 | Owensboro, KY | (4.3) | 174 | Burlington, NC | (20.8) |
| 47 | Santa Cruz-Watsonville, CA | 13.4 | 111 | Grand Forks, ND-MN | (4.4) | 175 | Portland, ME | (21.0) |
| 48 | Tallahassee, FL | 13.2 | 112 | Mankato-North Mankato, MN | (5.4) | 176 | Erie, PA | (21.2) |
| 49 | Cedar Rapids, IA | 13.0 | 113 | Sioux Falls, SD | (5.7) | 177 | Rochester, MN | (21.4) |
| 50 | Kansas City, MO-KS | 12.2 | 114 | Muncie, IN | (6.3) | 178 | Carson City, NV | (21.6) |
| 51 | Anaheim-Santa Ana-Irvine, CA M.D. | 12.1 | 115 | Little Rock, AR | (6.4) | 179 | Beaumont-Port Arthur, TX | (21.7) |
| 52 | San Francisco-Redwood, CA M.D. | 12.0 | 116 | Sherman-Denison, TX | (6.7) | 180 | Victoria, TX | (21.9) |
| 53 | San Angelo, TX | 11.7 | 117 | Amarillo, TX | (7.1) | 181 | Philadelphia (greater) PA-NJ-MD-DE | (22.0) |
| 54 | Monroe, MI | 11.5 | 117 | Jefferson City, MO | (7.1) | 182 | Florence, SC | (22.2) |
| 55 | Fresno, CA | 11.1 | 119 | Wichita Falls, TX | (7.4) | 183 | Huntsville, AL | (22.3) |
| 56 | Riverside-San Bernardino, CA | 11.0 | 120 | Fort Wayne, IN | (8.2) | 184 | Charleston-North Charleston, SC | (23.5) |
| 57 | Wichita, KS | 10.7 | 121 | Great Falls, MT | (8.3) | 184 | Jackson, MI | (23.5) |
| 58 | Vallejo-Fairfield, CA | 10.5 | 122 | Abilene, TX | (8.5) | 186 | Baltimore, MD | (23.6) |
| 59 | Coeur d'Alene, ID | 10.4 | 123 | Fayetteville-Springdale, AR-MO | (9.0) | 187 | Las Cruces, NM | (23.8) |
| 60 | Bakersfield, CA | 9.7 | 124 | Bloomington, IN | (9.5) | 188 | Tyler, TX | (23.9) |
| 61 | Louisville, KY-IN | 9.2 | 125 | Gainesville, GA | (9.6) | 189 | Mobile, AL | (24.0) |
| 62 | Tulsa, OK | 8.8 | 126 | Springfield, MA | (10.0) | 189 | New York (greater), NY-NJ-PA | (24.0) |
| 63 | Salt Lake City, UT | 8.4 | 127 | Providence-Warwick, RI-MA | (10.1) | 189 | San Diego, CA | (24.0) |
| 64 | Tacoma, WA M.D. | 8.0 | 128 | Norwich-New London, CT | (10.4) | 192 | Greeley, CO | (24.1) |

Note: All listings are for Metropolitan Statistical Areas (M.S.A.s) except for those ending with "M.D." Listings with "M.D." are Metropolitan Divisions which are smaller parts of eleven large M.S.A.s. See explanatory note at beginning of metropolitan area section.

| RANK | METROPOLITAN AREA | % CHANGE | RANK | METROPOLITAN AREA | % CHANGE | RANK | METROPOLITAN AREA | % CHANGE |
|---|---|---|---|---|---|---|---|---|
| 192 | Lakeland, FL | (24.1) | 255 | Akron, OH | (34.7) | NA | Chambersburg-Waynesboro, PA** | NA |
| 194 | Shreveport-Bossier City, LA | (24.4) | 256 | Rochester, NY | (34.9) | NA | Champaign-Urbana, IL** | NA |
| 195 | Boston (greater), MA-NH | (24.6) | 257 | Altoona, PA | (35.0) | NA | Charlotte-Mecklenburg, NC-SC** | NA |
| 195 | Yuma, AZ | (24.6) | 257 | Casper, WY | (35.0) | NA | Chicago (greater), IL-IN-WI** | NA |
| 197 | Lawton, OK | (24.7) | 259 | Deltona-Daytona Beach, FL | (35.1) | NA | Chicago-Naperville, IL M.D.** | NA |
| 198 | Allentown, PA-NJ | (25.3) | 260 | Miami-Dade County, FL M.D. | (35.3) | NA | Crestview-Fort Walton Beach, FL** | NA |
| 199 | Longview, WA | (25.5) | 261 | Nassau-Suffolk, NY M.D. | (35.4) | NA | Daphne-Fairhope-Foley, AL** | NA |
| 200 | Camden, NJ M.D. | (25.6) | 262 | Logan, UT-ID | (35.5) | NA | Davenport, IA-IL** | NA |
| 201 | Cheyenne, WY | (25.8) | 263 | Jackson, MS | (36.2) | NA | Dutchess-Putnam, NY M.D.** | NA |
| 201 | Hagerstown-Martinsburg, MD-WV | (25.8) | 264 | Buffalo-Niagara Falls, NY | (36.3) | NA | East Stroudsburg, PA** | NA |
| 203 | Richmond, VA | (26.0) | 265 | Muskegon, MI | (36.4) | NA | Elgin, IL M.D.** | NA |
| 204 | West Palm Beach, FL M.D. | (26.1) | 266 | Tucson, AZ | (36.5) | NA | Elizabethtown-Fort Knox, KY** | NA |
| 205 | Albany-Schenectady-Troy, NY | (26.3) | 267 | Racine, WI | (36.8) | NA | Gary, IN M.D.** | NA |
| 206 | Fargo, ND-MN | (26.6) | 268 | Farmington, NM | (37.0) | NA | Gettysburg, PA** | NA |
| 206 | Napa, CA | (26.6) | 268 | Memphis, TN-MS-AR | (37.0) | NA | Grand Island, NE** | NA |
| 208 | Ocala, FL | (27.1) | 270 | Waco, TX | (37.6) | NA | Grand Rapids-Wyoming, MI** | NA |
| 209 | Columbus, GA-AL | (27.2) | 271 | Wilmington, DE-MD-NJ M.D. | (38.1) | NA | Grants Pass, OR** | NA |
| 210 | Fort Lauderdale, FL M.D. | (27.3) | 272 | Grand Junction, CO | (38.3) | NA | Greenville-Anderson, SC** | NA |
| 211 | Lynchburg, VA | (27.7) | 273 | Atlantic City, NJ | (38.8) | NA | Greenville, NC** | NA |
| 212 | Blacksburg, VA | (27.8) | 274 | Cape Coral-Fort Myers, FL | (39.2) | NA | Gulfport-Biloxi-Pascagoula, MS** | NA |
| 213 | Dallas (greater), TX | (27.9) | 275 | North Port-Sarasota-Bradenton, FL | (39.8) | NA | Hammond, LA** | NA |
| 214 | Brunswick, GA | (28.0) | 276 | Lima, OH | (40.2) | NA | Hanford-Corcoran, CA** | NA |
| 215 | Greensboro-High Point, NC | (28.1) | 277 | Harrisonburg, VA | (40.4) | NA | Hilton Head Island, SC** | NA |
| 216 | Las Vegas-Henderson, NV | (28.2) | 277 | Tuscaloosa, AL | (40.4) | NA | Homosassa Springs, FL** | NA |
| 217 | Fayetteville, NC | (28.5) | 279 | Brownsville-Harlingen, TX | (40.5) | NA | Johnstown, PA** | NA |
| 217 | Saginaw, MI | (28.5) | 280 | Houma, LA | (40.6) | NA | Joplin, MO** | NA |
| 219 | Johnson City, TN | (28.6) | 281 | Elmira, NY | (41.2) | NA | Kahului-Wailuku-Lahaina, HI** | NA |
| 220 | Athens-Clarke County, GA | (28.7) | 282 | Fort Collins, CO | (41.3) | NA | Kankakee, IL** | NA |
| 221 | Albany, GA | (29.1) | 282 | Punta Gorda, FL | (41.3) | NA | La Crosse, WI-MN** | NA |
| 221 | Morgantown, WV | (29.1) | 284 | El Centro, CA | (42.3) | NA | Lafayette, LA** | NA |
| 223 | Roanoke, VA | (29.6) | 285 | Savannah, GA | (42.6) | NA | Lake Co.-Kenosha Co., IL-WI M.D.** | NA |
| 224 | Orlando, FL | (29.9) | 286 | Oshkosh-Neenah, WI | (42.9) | NA | Lancaster, PA** | NA |
| 224 | Warren-Troy, MI M.D. | (29.9) | 287 | York-Hanover, PA | (43.0) | NA | Madison, WI** | NA |
| 226 | Palm Bay-Melbourne, FL | (30.0) | 288 | Glens Falls, NY | (43.4) | NA | Monroe, LA** | NA |
| 227 | Goldsboro, NC | (30.2) | 289 | Jacksonville, FL | (43.7) | NA | Montgomery County, PA M.D.** | NA |
| 227 | St. Louis, MO-IL | (30.2) | 290 | Washington, DC-VA-MD-WV M.D. | (43.8) | NA | Myrtle Beach, SC-NC** | NA |
| 229 | Dover, DE | (30.7) | 291 | Washington (greater) DC-VA-MD-WV | (44.2) | NA | New Bern, NC** | NA |
| 230 | Dallas-Plano-Irving, TX M.D. | (31.0) | 292 | Sebastian-Vero Beach, FL | (45.2) | NA | New Orleans, LA** | NA |
| 230 | Hot Springs, AR | (31.0) | 293 | McAllen-Edinburg-Mission, TX | (45.7) | NA | New York-Jersey City, NY-NJ M.D.** | NA |
| 232 | Anniston-Oxford, AL | (31.4) | 294 | Jackson, TN | (46.8) | NA | Olympia, WA** | NA |
| 233 | Flagstaff, AZ | (31.7) | 295 | State College, PA | (48.1) | NA | Parkersburg-Vienna, WV** | NA |
| 234 | Boston, MA M.D. | (31.9) | 296 | Charlottesville, VA | (48.5) | NA | Peoria, IL** | NA |
| 234 | Miami (greater), FL | (31.9) | 297 | Silver Spring-Frederick, MD M.D. | (49.5) | NA | Philadelphia, PA M.D.** | NA |
| 234 | Nashville-Davidson, TN | (31.9) | 298 | College Station-Bryan, TX | (49.8) | NA | Phoenix-Mesa-Scottsdale, AZ** | NA |
| 237 | Hartford, CT | (32.2) | 299 | Baton Rouge, LA | (49.9) | NA | Pittsburgh, PA** | NA |
| 238 | Ann Arbor, MI | (32.3) | 299 | Tampa-St Petersburg, FL | (49.9) | NA | Rockford, IL** | NA |
| 238 | Eugene, OR | (32.3) | 301 | Gainesville, FL | (50.7) | NA | Salisbury, MD-DE** | NA |
| 240 | Spartanburg, SC | (32.5) | 302 | Reading, PA | (51.2) | NA | San Rafael, CA M.D.** | NA |
| 240 | Texarkana, TX-AR | (32.5) | 303 | Appleton, WI | (52.8) | NA | Scranton--Wilkes-Barre, PA** | NA |
| 242 | Clarksville, TN-KY | (32.7) | 304 | Kingston, NY | (52.9) | NA | Sebring, FL** | NA |
| 242 | Rocky Mount, NC | (32.7) | 305 | Decatur, IL | (54.8) | NA | Springfield, IL** | NA |
| 244 | Worcester, MA-CT | (32.8) | 306 | Longview, TX | (56.4) | NA | Staunton-Waynesboro, VA** | NA |
| 245 | Bangor, ME | (32.9) | 307 | El Paso, TX | (60.0) | NA | Terre Haute, IN** | NA |
| 245 | Hinesville, GA | (32.9) | 308 | Laredo, TX | (76.3) | NA | The Villages, FL** | NA |
| 245 | Raleigh, NC | (32.9) | NA | Albany, OR** | NA | NA | Virginia Beach-Norfolk, VA-NC** | NA |
| 248 | Bridgeport-Stamford, CT | (33.1) | NA | Bloomington, IL** | NA | NA | Visalia-Porterville, CA** | NA |
| 248 | Flint, MI | (33.1) | NA | Bloomsburg-Berwick, PA** | NA | NA | Warner Robins, GA** | NA |
| 250 | Eau Claire, WI | (33.2) | NA | Bowling Green, KY** | NA | NA | Watertown-Fort Drum, NY** | NA |
| 251 | Williamsport, PA | (33.5) | NA | California-Lexington Park, MD** | NA | NA | Wilmington, NC** | NA |
| 252 | Green Bay, WI | (33.8) | NA | Cambridge-Newton, MA M.D.** | NA | NA | Winston-Salem, NC** | NA |
| 253 | Augusta, GA-SC | (34.2) | NA | Canton, OH** | NA | NA | Yakima, WA** | NA |
| 254 | Janesville, WI | (34.3) | NA | Carbondale-Marion, IL** | NA | | | |

Source: CQ Press using reported data from the F.B.I. "Crime in the United States 2013"

*Motor vehicle theft includes the theft or attempted theft of a self-propelled vehicle. Excludes motorboats, construction equipment, airplanes, and farming equipment.

**Not available.

# II. City Crime Statistics
## (for cities larger than 75,000 population)

**Please note the following for Tables 41 through 84 and 88 through 90:**

• All listings are for cities of 75,000 or more in population that reported data to the F.B.I. for 2012. The reported populations for crime reporting purposes may vary from Census populations.

# 41. Crimes in 2013
## National Total = 9,795,658 Crimes*

| RANK | CITY | CRIMES | RANK | CITY | CRIMES | RANK | CITY | CRIMES |
|---|---|---|---|---|---|---|---|---|
| 183 | Abilene, TX** | 5,246 | 366 | Chino, CA** | 2,302 | 230 | Fullerton, CA** | 4,231 |
| 87 | Akron, OH | 11,219 | 158 | Chula Vista, CA** | 5,879 | 161 | Gainesville, FL | 5,792 |
| 393 | Alameda, CA** | 2,060 | 382 | Cicero, IL** | 2,176 | 248 | Garden Grove, CA** | 3,852 |
| 177 | Albany, GA** | 5,410 | 45 | Cincinnati, OH | 20,057 | 104 | Garland, TX** | 8,885 |
| 204 | Albany, NY** | 4,881 | 308 | Citrus Heights, CA** | 2,973 | 166 | Gary, IN** | 5,602 |
| 24 | Albuquerque, NM** | 34,856 | 419 | Clarkstown, NY** | 1,580 | 256 | Gilbert, AZ | 3,665 |
| 289 | Alexandria, VA | 3,225 | 203 | Clarksville, TN | 4,889 | 64 | Glendale, AZ** | 14,531 |
| 402 | Alhambra, CA** | 1,937 | 200 | Clearwater, FL | 4,934 | 282 | Glendale, CA** | 3,379 |
| 197 | Allentown, PA | 4,952 | 31 | Cleveland, OH | 28,919 | 164 | Grand Prairie, TX** | 5,669 |
| 428 | Allen, TX | 1,267 | 412 | Clifton, NJ** | 1,696 | 122 | Grand Rapids, MI | 7,514 |
| 99 | Amarillo, TX | 9,440 | 358 | Clinton Twnshp, MI | 2,419 | 354 | Greece, NY** | 2,454 |
| 377 | Amherst, NY** | 2,225 | 265 | Clovis, CA** | 3,585 | 254 | Greeley, CO | 3,710 |
| 93 | Anaheim, CA** | 10,741 | 343 | College Station, TX** | 2,609 | 295 | Green Bay, WI | 3,174 |
| 65 | Anchorage, AK | 14,467 | 395 | Colonie, NY** | 2,053 | 74 | Greensboro, NC** | 12,986 |
| 326 | Ann Arbor, MI | 2,772 | 44 | Colorado Springs, CO | 20,068 | 221 | Greenville, NC** | 4,417 |
| 178 | Antioch, CA** | 5,386 | 207 | Columbia, MO | 4,775 | 188 | Gresham, OR** | 5,164 |
| 436 | Arlington Heights, IL** | 842 | 103 | Columbia, SC | 8,941 | 396 | Hamilton Twnshp, NJ** | 2,051 |
| 53 | Arlington, TX** | 16,837 | 68 | Columbus, GA** | 13,497 | 245 | Hammond, IN** | 3,889 |
| 321 | Arvada, CO | 2,829 | 252 | Compton, CA** | 3,780 | 208 | Hampton, VA | 4,765 |
| 218 | Athens-Clarke, GA** | 4,478 | 209 | Concord, CA** | 4,764 | 138 | Hartford, CT** | 6,509 |
| 26 | Atlanta, GA** | 33,045 | 338 | Concord, NC** | 2,671 | 322 | Hawthorne, CA** | 2,822 |
| 79 | Aurora, CO | 12,222 | 324 | Coral Springs, FL | 2,802 | 176 | Hayward, CA** | 5,433 |
| 266 | Aurora, IL** | 3,573 | 263 | Corona, CA** | 3,601 | 222 | Hemet, CA** | 4,410 |
| 13 | Austin, TX** | 44,790 | 55 | Corpus Christi, TX** | 16,540 | 162 | Henderson, NV** | 5,725 |
| 48 | Bakersfield, CA** | 18,671 | 251 | Costa Mesa, CA** | 3,808 | 336 | Hesperia, CA** | 2,701 |
| 418 | Baldwin Park, CA** | 1,590 | 403 | Cranston, RI | 1,906 | 125 | Hialeah, FL | 7,324 |
| 15 | Baltimore, MD** | 39,514 | 7 | Dallas, TX** | 60,604 | 194 | High Point, NC** | 5,045 |
| 67 | Baton Rouge, LA** | 13,545 | 394 | Daly City, CA** | 2,056 | 368 | Hillsboro, OR** | 2,301 |
| 123 | Beaumont, TX** | 7,417 | 423 | Danbury, CT** | 1,365 | 128 | Hollywood, FL | 7,270 |
| 417 | Beaverton, OR** | 1,595 | 201 | Davenport, IA | 4,902 | 339 | Hoover, AL | 2,670 |
| 237 | Bellevue, WA** | 4,074 | 255 | Davie, FL | 3,699 | 2 | Houston, TX** | 131,912 |
| 383 | Bellflower, CA** | 2,161 | 104 | Dayton, OH | 8,885 | 181 | Huntington Beach, CA** | 5,296 |
| 355 | Bend, OR | 2,449 | 273 | Dearborn, MI | 3,451 | 94 | Huntsville, AL | 10,723 |
| 154 | Berkeley, CA** | 5,939 | 333 | Decatur, IL** | 2,720 | 119 | Independence, MO | 7,651 |
| 378 | Bethlehem, PA | 2,193 | 337 | Deerfield Beach, FL | 2,691 | 11 | Indianapolis, IN | 55,085 |
| 150 | Billings, MT | 5,964 | 302 | Denton, TX | 3,115 | 296 | Indio, CA** | 3,167 |
| 52 | Birmingham, AL | 17,009 | 33 | Denver, CO | 27,798 | 272 | Inglewood, CA** | 3,457 |
| 369 | Bloomington, IL** | 2,300 | 89 | Des Moines, IA | 11,041 | 281 | Irvine, CA** | 3,398 |
| 317 | Bloomington, IN** | 2,881 | 10 | Detroit, MI | 55,339 | 135 | Irving, TX** | 6,705 |
| 279 | Bloomington, MN | 3,411 | 261 | Downey, CA** | 3,618 | 17 | Jacksonville, FL | 38,253 |
| 352 | Boca Raton, FL | 2,467 | 214 | Duluth, MN | 4,625 | 83 | Jackson, MS** | 11,915 |
| 180 | Boise, ID | 5,341 | 215 | Edinburg, TX** | 4,569 | 140 | Jersey City, NJ** | 6,491 |
| 40 | Boston, MA** | 22,890 | 422 | Edison Twnshp, NJ** | 1,368 | 439 | Johns Creek, GA** | 656 |
| 297 | Boulder, CO | 3,166 | 413 | Edmond, OK** | 1,682 | 253 | Joliet, IL** | 3,774 |
| 427 | Brick Twnshp, NJ** | 1,272 | 301 | El Cajon, CA** | 3,116 | 283 | Jurupa Valley, CA** | 3,332 |
| 160 | Bridgeport, CT** | 5,861 | 350 | El Monte, CA** | 2,522 | 115 | Kansas City, KS** | 7,959 |
| 226 | Brockton, MA | 4,351 | 50 | El Paso, TX** | 18,080 | 30 | Kansas City, MO | 30,512 |
| 379 | Broken Arrow, OK** | 2,181 | 384 | Elgin, IL** | 2,138 | 334 | Kennewick, WA | 2,718 |
| 335 | Brooklyn Park, MN | 2,704 | 213 | Elizabeth, NJ** | 4,654 | 331 | Kenosha, WI** | 2,736 |
| 113 | Brownsville, TX** | 8,311 | 275 | Elk Grove, CA** | 3,432 | 157 | Kent, WA | 5,919 |
| 340 | Bryan, TX** | 2,669 | 256 | Erie, PA | 3,665 | 172 | Killeen, TX** | 5,544 |
| 362 | Buena Park, CA** | 2,386 | 216 | Escondido, CA** | 4,561 | 75 | Knoxville, TN | 12,979 |
| 56 | Buffalo, NY** | 15,740 | 112 | Eugene, OR | 8,322 | 110 | Lafayette, LA** | 8,436 |
| 346 | Burbank, CA** | 2,601 | 389 | Evanston, IL** | 2,091 | 434 | Lake Forest, CA** | 918 |
| 287 | Cambridge, MA | 3,268 | 142 | Evansville, IN** | 6,423 | 159 | Lakeland, FL | 5,870 |
| 424 | Canton Twnshp, MI | 1,344 | 126 | Everett, WA** | 7,308 | 431 | Lakewood Twnshp, NJ** | 1,091 |
| 267 | Cape Coral, FL | 3,572 | 240 | Fairfield, CA** | 4,032 | 371 | Lakewood, CA** | 2,287 |
| 363 | Carlsbad, CA** | 2,306 | 284 | Fall River, MA | 3,308 | 121 | Lakewood, CO | 7,516 |
| 438 | Carmel, IN** | 764 | 258 | Fargo, ND | 3,655 | 227 | Lancaster, CA** | 4,327 |
| 299 | Carrollton, TX** | 3,145 | 429 | Farmington Hills, MI | 1,186 | 188 | Lansing, MI | 5,164 |
| 342 | Carson, CA** | 2,651 | 271 | Fayetteville, AR | 3,510 | 85 | Laredo, TX** | 11,509 |
| 380 | Cary, NC** | 2,177 | 69 | Fayetteville, NC** | 13,431 | 286 | Largo, FL | 3,276 |
| 192 | Cedar Rapids, IA | 5,099 | 174 | Federal Way, WA | 5,464 | 212 | Las Cruces, NM** | 4,681 |
| 425 | Centennial, CO | 1,335 | 436 | Fishers, IN** | 842 | 8 | Las Vegas, NV** | 59,342 |
| 313 | Champaign, IL** | 2,929 | 147 | Flint, MI | 6,168 | 243 | Lawrence, KS | 3,963 |
| 141 | Chandler, AZ** | 6,475 | 206 | Fontana, CA** | 4,813 | 304 | Lawrence, MA** | 3,049 |
| 278 | Charleston, SC | 3,423 | 233 | Fort Collins, CO | 4,165 | 152 | Lawton, OK** | 5,946 |
| 22 | Charlotte, NC** | 35,662 | 88 | Fort Lauderdale, FL | 11,106 | 398 | League City, TX** | 2,014 |
| 73 | Chattanooga, TN | 13,160 | 184 | Fort Smith, AR | 5,227 | 397 | Lee's Summit, MO | 2,049 |
| 320 | Cheektowaga, NY** | 2,847 | 92 | Fort Wayne, IN | 10,756 | 311 | Lewisville, TX | 2,964 |
| 132 | Chesapeake, VA | 6,925 | 16 | Fort Worth, TX | 38,692 | 70 | Lexington, KY | 13,393 |
| NA | Chicago, IL*** | NA | 223 | Fremont, CA** | 4,370 | 96 | Lincoln, NE** | 10,344 |
| 318 | Chico, CA** | 2,871 | 36 | Fresno, CA** | 25,136 | 49 | Little Rock, AR | 18,306 |
| 432 | Chino Hills, CA** | 1,080 | 344 | Frisco, TX | 2,607 | 388 | Livermore, CA** | 2,100 |

| RANK | CITY | CRIMES |
|---|---|---|
| 385 | Livonia, MI | 2,109 |
| 58 | Long Beach, CA** | 15,345 |
| 375 | Longmont, CO | 2,235 |
| 249 | Longview, TX | 3,823 |
| 3 | Los Angeles, CA** | 102,368 |
| 28 | Louisville, KY** | 32,424 |
| 241 | Lowell, MA | 4,004 |
| 71 | Lubbock, TX** | 13,386 |
| 364 | Lynchburg, VA | 2,304 |
| 290 | Lynn, MA | 3,212 |
| 124 | Macon, GA** | 7,383 |
| 108 | Madison, WI | 8,613 |
| 199 | Manchester, NH | 4,941 |
| 167 | McAllen, TX** | 5,595 |
| 288 | McKinney, TX | 3,262 |
| 181 | Medford, OR | 5,296 |
| 239 | Melbourne, FL | 4,034 |
| 12 | Memphis, TN | 50,698 |
| 407 | Menifee, CA** | 1,779 |
| 291 | Merced, CA** | 3,203 |
| 430 | Meridian, ID | 1,145 |
| 62 | Mesa, AZ** | 14,723 |
| 134 | Mesquite, TX** | 6,734 |
| 95 | Miami Beach, FL | 10,670 |
| 168 | Miami Gardens, FL | 5,581 |
| 35 | Miami, FL | 25,873 |
| 270 | Midland, TX** | 3,541 |
| 23 | Milwaukee, WI | 35,207 |
| 39 | Minneapolis, MN | 23,396 |
| 259 | Miramar, FL | 3,640 |
| 433 | Mission Viejo, CA** | 1,060 |
| 306 | Mission, TX** | 3,017 |
| 63 | Mobile, AL | 14,552 |
| 84 | Modesto, CA** | 11,693 |
| 137 | Moreno Valley, CA** | 6,510 |
| 404 | Mountain View, CA** | 1,863 |
| 210 | Murfreesboro, TN | 4,756 |
| 411 | Murrieta, CA** | 1,710 |
| 391 | Nampa, ID | 2,078 |
| 414 | Napa, CA** | 1,664 |
| 400 | Naperville, IL** | 1,974 |
| 357 | Nashua, NH | 2,430 |
| 29 | Nashville, TN | 31,072 |
| 219 | New Bedford, MA | 4,476 |
| 117 | New Haven, CT | 7,711 |
| 51 | New Orleans, LA** | 17,490 |
| 421 | New Rochelle, NY** | 1,566 |
| 1 | New York, NY** | 194,355 |
| 76 | Newark, NJ** | 12,481 |
| 376 | Newport Beach, CA** | 2,231 |
| 143 | Newport News, VA | 6,377 |
| 435 | Newton, MA | 881 |
| 78 | Norfolk, VA | 12,230 |
| 300 | Norman, OK** | 3,119 |
| 139 | North Charleston, SC | 6,497 |
| 116 | North Las Vegas, NV** | 7,775 |
| 341 | Norwalk, CA** | 2,653 |
| 401 | Norwalk, CT | 1,967 |
| 25 | Oakland, CA** | 33,160 |
| 191 | Oceanside, CA** | 5,128 |
| 175 | Odessa, TX** | 5,454 |
| 426 | O'Fallon, MO | 1,281 |
| 220 | Ogden, UT | 4,421 |
| 19 | Oklahoma City, OK** | 37,477 |
| 353 | Olathe, KS** | 2,458 |
| 41 | Omaha, NE** | 21,557 |
| 195 | Ontario, CA** | 4,960 |
| 349 | Orange, CA** | 2,565 |
| 385 | Orem, UT** | 2,112 |
| 46 | Orlando, FL | 18,805 |
| 250 | Overland Park, KS** | 3,814 |
| 162 | Oxnard, CA** | 5,725 |
| 359 | Palm Bay, FL | 2,409 |
| 235 | Palmdale, CA** | 4,103 |

| RANK | CITY | CRIMES |
|---|---|---|
| 231 | Pasadena, CA** | 4,213 |
| 149 | Pasadena, TX** | 6,093 |
| 165 | Paterson, NJ** | 5,656 |
| 390 | Pearland, TX | 2,080 |
| 228 | Pembroke Pines, FL | 4,298 |
| 236 | Peoria, AZ** | 4,084 |
| 186 | Peoria, IL** | 5,199 |
| 5 | Philadelphia, PA | 70,526 |
| 6 | Phoenix, AZ** | 69,577 |
| 77 | Pittsburgh, PA | 12,306 |
| 145 | Plano, TX | 6,319 |
| 276 | Plantation, FL | 3,427 |
| 185 | Pomona, CA** | 5,203 |
| 151 | Pompano Beach, FL | 5,948 |
| 328 | Port St. Lucie, FL | 2,764 |
| 27 | Portland, OR** | 32,574 |
| 153 | Portsmouth, VA | 5,945 |
| 102 | Providence, RI | 9,089 |
| 310 | Provo, UT | 2,970 |
| 109 | Pueblo, CO | 8,607 |
| 399 | Quincy, MA | 2,008 |
| 285 | Racine, WI** | 3,307 |
| 61 | Raleigh, NC** | 14,823 |
| 440 | Ramapo, NY** | 624 |
| 234 | Rancho Cucamon., CA** | 4,155 |
| 269 | Reading, PA | 3,542 |
| 224 | Redding, CA** | 4,359 |
| 392 | Redwood City, CA** | 2,061 |
| 111 | Reno, NV** | 8,334 |
| 187 | Renton, WA | 5,192 |
| 298 | Rialto, CA** | 3,151 |
| 316 | Richardson, TX** | 2,886 |
| 155 | Richmond, CA** | 5,938 |
| 97 | Richmond, VA | 10,031 |
| 82 | Riverside, CA** | 11,938 |
| 202 | Roanoke, VA | 4,901 |
| 326 | Rochester, MN | 2,772 |
| 80 | Rochester, NY** | 12,158 |
| 101 | Rockford, IL | 9,104 |
| 262 | Roseville, CA** | 3,604 |
| 374 | Roswell, GA** | 2,251 |
| 348 | Round Rock, TX** | 2,577 |
| 42 | Sacramento, CA** | 21,117 |
| 127 | Salem, OR | 7,302 |
| 144 | Salinas, CA** | 6,357 |
| 60 | Salt Lake City, UT | 14,936 |
| 247 | San Angelo, TX | 3,855 |
| 4 | San Antonio, TX** | 88,822 |
| 86 | San Bernardino, CA** | 11,338 |
| 21 | San Diego, CA** | 37,031 |
| 9 | San Francisco, CA** | 55,388 |
| 32 | San Jose, CA** | 28,725 |
| 225 | San Leandro, CA** | 4,354 |
| 415 | San Marcos, CA** | 1,614 |
| 364 | San Mateo, CA** | 2,304 |
| 314 | Sandy Springs, GA** | 2,925 |
| 303 | Sandy, UT | 3,076 |
| 120 | Santa Ana, CA** | 7,546 |
| 305 | Santa Barbara, CA** | 3,032 |
| 293 | Santa Clara, CA** | 3,195 |
| 307 | Santa Clarita, CA** | 2,989 |
| 277 | Santa Maria, CA** | 3,424 |
| 246 | Santa Monica, CA** | 3,868 |
| 238 | Santa Rosa, CA** | 4,047 |
| 100 | Savannah, GA** | 9,309 |
| 148 | Scottsdale, AZ** | 6,103 |
| 356 | Scranton, PA | 2,443 |
| 14 | Seattle, WA | 39,641 |
| 90 | Shreveport, LA** | 10,981 |
| 406 | Simi Valley, CA** | 1,841 |
| 242 | Sioux City, IA | 3,982 |
| 169 | Sioux Falls, SD | 5,566 |
| 410 | Somerville, MA | 1,716 |
| 171 | South Bend, IN | 5,554 |

| RANK | CITY | CRIMES |
|---|---|---|
| 294 | South Gate, CA** | 3,194 |
| 325 | Sparks, NV** | 2,793 |
| 172 | Spokane Valley, WA** | 5,544 |
| 43 | Spokane, WA** | 20,971 |
| 131 | Springfield, IL** | 7,096 |
| 106 | Springfield, MA | 8,786 |
| 54 | Springfield, MO | 16,585 |
| 372 | Stamford, CT | 2,272 |
| 332 | Sterling Heights, MI | 2,730 |
| 47 | Stockton, CA** | 18,702 |
| 405 | St. George, UT | 1,861 |
| 211 | St. Joseph, MO | 4,712 |
| 34 | St. Louis, MO | 26,164 |
| 72 | St. Paul, MN | 13,173 |
| 57 | St. Petersburg, FL | 15,560 |
| 319 | Suffolk, VA | 2,850 |
| 409 | Sugar Land, TX** | 1,721 |
| 347 | Sunnyvale, CA** | 2,578 |
| 268 | Sunrise, FL | 3,554 |
| 373 | Surprise, AZ** | 2,269 |
| 118 | Syracuse, NY** | 7,665 |
| 59 | Tacoma, WA | 15,076 |
| 98 | Tallahassee, FL | 9,514 |
| 91 | Tampa, FL | 10,920 |
| 312 | Temecula, CA** | 2,939 |
| 107 | Tempe, AZ** | 8,707 |
| 260 | Thornton, CO | 3,627 |
| 408 | Thousand Oaks, CA** | 1,743 |
| NA | Toledo, OH*** | NA |
| 323 | Toms River Twnshp, NJ** | 2,816 |
| 130 | Topeka, KS** | 7,098 |
| 308 | Torrance, CA** | 2,973 |
| 361 | Tracy, CA** | 2,388 |
| 274 | Trenton, NJ** | 3,443 |
| 416 | Troy, MI | 1,612 |
| 18 | Tucson, AZ** | 37,955 |
| 37 | Tulsa, OK** | 24,805 |
| 198 | Tuscaloosa, AL | 4,946 |
| 420 | Tustin, CA** | 1,573 |
| 217 | Tyler, TX | 4,492 |
| 360 | Upland, CA** | 2,397 |
| 366 | Upper Darby Twnshp, PA | 2,302 |
| 370 | Vacaville, CA** | 2,297 |
| 133 | Vallejo, CA** | 6,753 |
| 136 | Vancouver, WA | 6,526 |
| 229 | Ventura, CA** | 4,289 |
| 205 | Victorville, CA** | 4,816 |
| 81 | Virginia Beach, VA | 11,956 |
| 179 | Visalia, CA** | 5,353 |
| 351 | Vista, CA** | 2,490 |
| 156 | Waco, TX** | 5,937 |
| 232 | Warren, MI | 4,187 |
| 387 | Warwick, RI | 2,108 |
| 20 | Washington, DC | 37,449 |
| 193 | Waterbury, CT** | 5,046 |
| 315 | Waukegan, IL** | 2,914 |
| 263 | West Covina, CA** | 3,601 |
| 170 | West Palm Beach, FL | 5,564 |
| 129 | West Valley, UT | 7,263 |
| 329 | Westland, MI | 2,762 |
| 330 | Westminster, CA** | 2,759 |
| 292 | Westminster, CO | 3,201 |
| 345 | Whittier, CA** | 2,606 |
| 196 | Wichita Falls, TX** | 4,959 |
| 38 | Wichita, KS | 23,867 |
| 146 | Wilmington, NC** | 6,236 |
| 66 | Winston-Salem, NC** | 14,279 |
| 380 | Woodbridge Twnshp, NJ** | 2,177 |
| 114 | Worcester, MA | 7,989 |
| 190 | Yakima, WA | 5,155 |
| 280 | Yonkers, NY** | 3,404 |
| 244 | Yuma, AZ | 3,962 |

Source: CQ Press using reported data from the F.B.I. "Crime in the United States 2013"

*Includes murder, rape, robbery, aggravated assault, burglary, larceny-theft, and motor vehicle theft.

**Figures for these cities are based on the previous (legacy) definition of rape. See note on page vii.

***Not available.

# 41. Crimes in 2013 (continued)
## National Total = 9,795,658 Crimes*

| RANK | CITY | CRIMES | RANK | CITY | CRIMES | RANK | CITY | CRIMES |
|---|---|---|---|---|---|---|---|---|
| 1 | New York, NY** | 194,355 | 75 | Knoxville, TN | 12,979 | 149 | Pasadena, TX** | 6,093 |
| 2 | Houston, TX** | 131,912 | 76 | Newark, NJ** | 12,481 | 150 | Billings, MT | 5,964 |
| 3 | Los Angeles, CA** | 102,368 | 77 | Pittsburgh, PA | 12,306 | 151 | Pompano Beach, FL | 5,948 |
| 4 | San Antonio, TX** | 88,822 | 78 | Norfolk, VA | 12,230 | 152 | Lawton, OK** | 5,946 |
| 5 | Philadelphia, PA | 70,526 | 79 | Aurora, CO | 12,222 | 153 | Portsmouth, VA | 5,945 |
| 6 | Phoenix, AZ** | 69,577 | 80 | Rochester, NY** | 12,158 | 154 | Berkeley, CA** | 5,939 |
| 7 | Dallas, TX** | 60,604 | 81 | Virginia Beach, VA | 11,956 | 155 | Richmond, CA** | 5,938 |
| 8 | Las Vegas, NV** | 59,342 | 82 | Riverside, CA** | 11,938 | 156 | Waco, TX** | 5,937 |
| 9 | San Francisco, CA** | 55,388 | 83 | Jackson, MS** | 11,915 | 157 | Kent, WA | 5,919 |
| 10 | Detroit, MI | 55,339 | 84 | Modesto, CA** | 11,693 | 158 | Chula Vista, CA** | 5,879 |
| 11 | Indianapolis, IN | 55,085 | 85 | Laredo, TX** | 11,509 | 159 | Lakeland, FL | 5,870 |
| 12 | Memphis, TN | 50,698 | 86 | San Bernardino, CA** | 11,338 | 160 | Bridgeport, CT** | 5,861 |
| 13 | Austin, TX** | 44,790 | 87 | Akron, OH | 11,219 | 161 | Gainesville, FL | 5,792 |
| 14 | Seattle, WA | 39,641 | 88 | Fort Lauderdale, FL | 11,106 | 162 | Henderson, NV** | 5,725 |
| 15 | Baltimore, MD** | 39,514 | 89 | Des Moines, IA | 11,041 | 162 | Oxnard, CA** | 5,725 |
| 16 | Fort Worth, TX | 38,692 | 90 | Shreveport, LA** | 10,981 | 164 | Grand Prairie, TX** | 5,669 |
| 17 | Jacksonville, FL | 38,253 | 91 | Tampa, FL | 10,920 | 165 | Paterson, NJ** | 5,656 |
| 18 | Tucson, AZ** | 37,955 | 92 | Fort Wayne, IN | 10,756 | 166 | Gary, IN** | 5,602 |
| 19 | Oklahoma City, OK** | 37,477 | 93 | Anaheim, CA** | 10,741 | 167 | McAllen, TX** | 5,595 |
| 20 | Washington, DC | 37,449 | 94 | Huntsville, AL | 10,723 | 168 | Miami Gardens, FL | 5,581 |
| 21 | San Diego, CA** | 37,031 | 95 | Miami Beach, FL | 10,670 | 169 | Sioux Falls, SD | 5,566 |
| 22 | Charlotte, NC** | 35,662 | 96 | Lincoln, NE** | 10,344 | 170 | West Palm Beach, FL | 5,564 |
| 23 | Milwaukee, WI | 35,207 | 97 | Richmond, VA | 10,031 | 171 | South Bend, IN | 5,554 |
| 24 | Albuquerque, NM** | 34,856 | 98 | Tallahassee, FL | 9,514 | 172 | Killeen, TX** | 5,544 |
| 25 | Oakland, CA** | 33,160 | 99 | Amarillo, TX | 9,440 | 172 | Spokane Valley, WA** | 5,544 |
| 26 | Atlanta, GA** | 33,045 | 100 | Savannah, GA** | 9,309 | 174 | Federal Way, WA | 5,464 |
| 27 | Portland, OR** | 32,574 | 101 | Rockford, IL | 9,104 | 175 | Odessa, TX** | 5,454 |
| 28 | Louisville, KY** | 32,424 | 102 | Providence, RI | 9,089 | 176 | Hayward, CA** | 5,433 |
| 29 | Nashville, TN | 31,072 | 103 | Columbia, SC | 8,941 | 177 | Albany, GA** | 5,410 |
| 30 | Kansas City, MO | 30,512 | 104 | Dayton, OH | 8,885 | 178 | Antioch, CA** | 5,386 |
| 31 | Cleveland, OH | 28,919 | 104 | Garland, TX** | 8,885 | 179 | Visalia, CA** | 5,353 |
| 32 | San Jose, CA** | 28,725 | 106 | Springfield, MA | 8,786 | 180 | Boise, ID | 5,341 |
| 33 | Denver, CO | 27,798 | 107 | Tempe, AZ** | 8,707 | 181 | Huntington Beach, CA** | 5,296 |
| 34 | St. Louis, MO | 26,164 | 108 | Madison, WI | 8,613 | 181 | Medford, OR | 5,296 |
| 35 | Miami, FL | 25,873 | 109 | Pueblo, CO | 8,607 | 183 | Abilene, TX** | 5,246 |
| 36 | Fresno, CA** | 25,136 | 110 | Lafayette, LA** | 8,436 | 184 | Fort Smith, AR | 5,227 |
| 37 | Tulsa, OK** | 24,805 | 111 | Reno, NV** | 8,334 | 185 | Pomona, CA** | 5,203 |
| 38 | Wichita, KS | 23,867 | 112 | Eugene, OR | 8,322 | 186 | Peoria, IL** | 5,199 |
| 39 | Minneapolis, MN | 23,396 | 113 | Brownsville, TX** | 8,311 | 187 | Renton, WA | 5,192 |
| 40 | Boston, MA** | 22,890 | 114 | Worcester, MA | 7,989 | 188 | Gresham, OR** | 5,164 |
| 41 | Omaha, NE** | 21,557 | 115 | Kansas City, KS** | 7,959 | 188 | Lansing, MI | 5,164 |
| 42 | Sacramento, CA** | 21,117 | 116 | North Las Vegas, NV** | 7,775 | 190 | Yakima, WA | 5,155 |
| 43 | Spokane, WA** | 20,971 | 117 | New Haven, CT | 7,711 | 191 | Oceanside, CA** | 5,128 |
| 44 | Colorado Springs, CO | 20,068 | 118 | Syracuse, NY** | 7,665 | 192 | Cedar Rapids, IA | 5,099 |
| 45 | Cincinnati, OH | 20,057 | 119 | Independence, MO | 7,651 | 193 | Waterbury, CT** | 5,046 |
| 46 | Orlando, FL | 18,805 | 120 | Santa Ana, CA** | 7,546 | 194 | High Point, NC** | 5,045 |
| 47 | Stockton, CA** | 18,702 | 121 | Lakewood, CO | 7,516 | 195 | Ontario, CA** | 4,960 |
| 48 | Bakersfield, CA** | 18,671 | 122 | Grand Rapids, MI | 7,514 | 196 | Wichita Falls, TX** | 4,959 |
| 49 | Little Rock, AR | 18,306 | 123 | Beaumont, TX** | 7,417 | 197 | Allentown, PA | 4,952 |
| 50 | El Paso, TX** | 18,080 | 124 | Macon, GA** | 7,383 | 198 | Tuscaloosa, AL | 4,946 |
| 51 | New Orleans, LA** | 17,490 | 125 | Hialeah, FL | 7,324 | 199 | Manchester, NH | 4,941 |
| 52 | Birmingham, AL | 17,009 | 126 | Everett, WA** | 7,308 | 200 | Clearwater, FL | 4,934 |
| 53 | Arlington, TX** | 16,837 | 127 | Salem, OR | 7,302 | 201 | Davenport, IA | 4,902 |
| 54 | Springfield, MO | 16,585 | 128 | Hollywood, FL | 7,270 | 202 | Roanoke, VA | 4,901 |
| 55 | Corpus Christi, TX** | 16,540 | 129 | West Valley, UT | 7,263 | 203 | Clarksville, TN | 4,889 |
| 56 | Buffalo, NY** | 15,740 | 130 | Topeka, KS** | 7,098 | 204 | Albany, NY** | 4,881 |
| 57 | St. Petersburg, FL | 15,560 | 131 | Springfield, IL** | 7,096 | 205 | Victorville, CA** | 4,816 |
| 58 | Long Beach, CA** | 15,345 | 132 | Chesapeake, VA | 6,925 | 206 | Fontana, CA** | 4,813 |
| 59 | Tacoma, WA | 15,076 | 133 | Vallejo, CA** | 6,753 | 207 | Columbia, MO | 4,775 |
| 60 | Salt Lake City, UT | 14,936 | 134 | Mesquite, TX** | 6,734 | 208 | Hampton, VA | 4,765 |
| 61 | Raleigh, NC** | 14,823 | 135 | Irving, TX** | 6,705 | 209 | Concord, CA** | 4,764 |
| 62 | Mesa, AZ** | 14,723 | 136 | Vancouver, WA | 6,526 | 210 | Murfreesboro, TN | 4,756 |
| 63 | Mobile, AL | 14,552 | 137 | Moreno Valley, CA** | 6,510 | 211 | St. Joseph, MO | 4,712 |
| 64 | Glendale, AZ** | 14,531 | 138 | Hartford, CT** | 6,509 | 212 | Las Cruces, NM** | 4,681 |
| 65 | Anchorage, AK | 14,467 | 139 | North Charleston, SC | 6,497 | 213 | Elizabeth, NJ** | 4,654 |
| 66 | Winston-Salem, NC** | 14,279 | 140 | Jersey City, NJ** | 6,491 | 214 | Duluth, MN | 4,625 |
| 67 | Baton Rouge, LA** | 13,545 | 141 | Chandler, AZ** | 6,475 | 215 | Edinburg, TX** | 4,569 |
| 68 | Columbus, GA** | 13,497 | 142 | Evansville, IN** | 6,423 | 216 | Escondido, CA** | 4,561 |
| 69 | Fayetteville, NC** | 13,431 | 143 | Newport News, VA | 6,377 | 217 | Tyler, TX | 4,492 |
| 70 | Lexington, KY | 13,393 | 144 | Salinas, CA** | 6,357 | 218 | Athens-Clarke, GA** | 4,478 |
| 71 | Lubbock, TX** | 13,386 | 145 | Plano, TX | 6,319 | 219 | New Bedford, MA | 4,476 |
| 72 | St. Paul, MN | 13,173 | 146 | Wilmington, NC** | 6,236 | 220 | Ogden, UT | 4,421 |
| 73 | Chattanooga, TN | 13,160 | 147 | Flint, MI | 6,168 | 221 | Greenville, NC** | 4,417 |
| 74 | Greensboro, NC** | 12,986 | 148 | Scottsdale, AZ** | 6,103 | 222 | Hemet, CA** | 4,410 |

| RANK | CITY | CRIMES | RANK | CITY | CRIMES | RANK | CITY | CRIMES |
|---|---|---|---|---|---|---|---|---|
| 223 | Fremont, CA** | 4,370 | 297 | Boulder, CO | 3,166 | 371 | Lakewood, CA** | 2,287 |
| 224 | Redding, CA** | 4,359 | 298 | Rialto, CA** | 3,151 | 372 | Stamford, CT | 2,272 |
| 225 | San Leandro, CA** | 4,354 | 299 | Carrollton, TX** | 3,145 | 373 | Surprise, AZ** | 2,269 |
| 226 | Brockton, MA | 4,351 | 300 | Norman, OK** | 3,119 | 374 | Roswell, GA** | 2,251 |
| 227 | Lancaster, CA** | 4,327 | 301 | El Cajon, CA** | 3,116 | 375 | Longmont, CO | 2,235 |
| 228 | Pembroke Pines, FL | 4,298 | 302 | Denton, TX | 3,115 | 376 | Newport Beach, CA** | 2,231 |
| 229 | Ventura, CA** | 4,289 | 303 | Sandy, UT | 3,076 | 377 | Amherst, NY** | 2,225 |
| 230 | Fullerton, CA** | 4,231 | 304 | Lawrence, MA** | 3,049 | 378 | Bethlehem, PA | 2,193 |
| 231 | Pasadena, CA** | 4,213 | 305 | Santa Barbara, CA** | 3,032 | 379 | Broken Arrow, OK** | 2,181 |
| 232 | Warren, MI | 4,187 | 306 | Mission, TX** | 3,017 | 380 | Cary, NC** | 2,177 |
| 233 | Fort Collins, CO | 4,165 | 307 | Santa Clarita, CA** | 2,989 | 380 | Woodbridge Twnshp, NJ** | 2,177 |
| 234 | Rancho Cucamon., CA** | 4,155 | 308 | Citrus Heights, CA** | 2,973 | 382 | Cicero, IL** | 2,176 |
| 235 | Palmdale, CA** | 4,103 | 308 | Torrance, CA** | 2,973 | 383 | Bellflower, CA** | 2,161 |
| 236 | Peoria, AZ** | 4,084 | 310 | Provo, UT | 2,970 | 384 | Elgin, IL** | 2,138 |
| 237 | Bellevue, WA** | 4,074 | 311 | Lewisville, TX | 2,964 | 385 | Orem, UT** | 2,112 |
| 238 | Santa Rosa, CA** | 4,047 | 312 | Temecula, CA** | 2,939 | 385 | Livonia, MI | 2,109 |
| 239 | Melbourne, FL | 4,034 | 313 | Champaign, IL** | 2,929 | 387 | Warwick, RI | 2,108 |
| 240 | Fairfield, CA** | 4,032 | 314 | Sandy Springs, GA** | 2,925 | 388 | Livermore, CA** | 2,100 |
| 241 | Lowell, MA | 4,004 | 315 | Waukegan, IL** | 2,914 | 389 | Evanston, IL** | 2,091 |
| 242 | Sioux City, IA | 3,982 | 316 | Richardson, TX** | 2,886 | 390 | Pearland, TX | 2,080 |
| 243 | Lawrence, KS | 3,963 | 317 | Bloomington, IN** | 2,881 | 391 | Nampa, ID | 2,078 |
| 244 | Yuma, AZ | 3,962 | 318 | Chico, CA** | 2,871 | 392 | Redwood City, CA** | 2,061 |
| 245 | Hammond, IN** | 3,889 | 319 | Suffolk, VA | 2,850 | 393 | Alameda, CA** | 2,060 |
| 246 | Santa Monica, CA** | 3,868 | 320 | Cheektowaga, NY** | 2,847 | 394 | Daly City, CA** | 2,056 |
| 247 | San Angelo, TX | 3,855 | 321 | Arvada, CO | 2,829 | 395 | Colonie, NY** | 2,053 |
| 248 | Garden Grove, CA** | 3,852 | 322 | Hawthorne, CA** | 2,822 | 396 | Hamilton Twnshp, NJ** | 2,051 |
| 249 | Longview, TX | 3,823 | 323 | Toms River Twnshp, NJ** | 2,816 | 397 | Lee's Summit, MO | 2,049 |
| 250 | Overland Park, KS** | 3,814 | 324 | Coral Springs, FL | 2,802 | 398 | League City, TX** | 2,014 |
| 251 | Costa Mesa, CA** | 3,808 | 325 | Sparks, NV** | 2,793 | 399 | Quincy, MA | 2,008 |
| 252 | Compton, CA** | 3,780 | 326 | Ann Arbor, MI | 2,772 | 400 | Naperville, IL** | 1,974 |
| 253 | Joliet, IL** | 3,774 | 326 | Rochester, MN | 2,772 | 401 | Norwalk, CT | 1,967 |
| 254 | Greeley, CO | 3,710 | 328 | Port St. Lucie, FL | 2,764 | 402 | Alhambra, CA** | 1,937 |
| 255 | Davie, FL | 3,699 | 329 | Westland, MI | 2,762 | 403 | Cranston, RI | 1,906 |
| 256 | Erie, PA | 3,665 | 330 | Westminster, CA** | 2,759 | 404 | Mountain View, CA** | 1,863 |
| 256 | Gilbert, AZ | 3,665 | 331 | Kenosha, WI** | 2,736 | 405 | St. George, UT | 1,861 |
| 258 | Fargo, ND | 3,655 | 332 | Sterling Heights, MI | 2,730 | 406 | Simi Valley, CA** | 1,841 |
| 259 | Miramar, FL | 3,640 | 333 | Decatur, IL** | 2,720 | 407 | Menifee, CA** | 1,779 |
| 260 | Thornton, CO | 3,627 | 334 | Kennewick, WA | 2,718 | 408 | Thousand Oaks, CA** | 1,743 |
| 261 | Downey, CA** | 3,618 | 335 | Brooklyn Park, MN | 2,704 | 409 | Sugar Land, TX** | 1,721 |
| 262 | Roseville, CA** | 3,604 | 336 | Hesperia, CA** | 2,701 | 410 | Somerville, MA | 1,716 |
| 263 | Corona, CA** | 3,601 | 337 | Deerfield Beach, FL | 2,691 | 411 | Murrieta, CA** | 1,710 |
| 263 | West Covina, CA** | 3,601 | 338 | Concord, NC** | 2,671 | 412 | Clifton, NJ** | 1,696 |
| 265 | Clovis, CA** | 3,585 | 339 | Hoover, AL | 2,670 | 413 | Edmond, OK** | 1,682 |
| 266 | Aurora, IL** | 3,573 | 340 | Bryan, TX** | 2,669 | 414 | Napa, CA** | 1,664 |
| 267 | Cape Coral, FL | 3,572 | 341 | Norwalk, CA** | 2,653 | 415 | San Marcos, CA** | 1,614 |
| 268 | Sunrise, FL | 3,554 | 342 | Carson, CA** | 2,651 | 416 | Troy, MI | 1,612 |
| 269 | Reading, PA | 3,542 | 343 | College Station, TX** | 2,609 | 417 | Beaverton, OR** | 1,595 |
| 270 | Midland, TX** | 3,541 | 344 | Frisco, TX | 2,607 | 418 | Baldwin Park, CA** | 1,590 |
| 271 | Fayetteville, AR | 3,510 | 345 | Whittier, CA** | 2,606 | 419 | Clarkstown, NY** | 1,580 |
| 272 | Inglewood, CA** | 3,457 | 346 | Burbank, CA** | 2,601 | 420 | Tustin, CA** | 1,573 |
| 273 | Dearborn, MI | 3,451 | 347 | Sunnyvale, CA** | 2,578 | 421 | New Rochelle, NY** | 1,566 |
| 274 | Trenton, NJ** | 3,443 | 348 | Round Rock, TX** | 2,577 | 422 | Edison Twnshp, NJ** | 1,368 |
| 275 | Elk Grove, CA** | 3,432 | 349 | Orange, CA** | 2,565 | 423 | Danbury, CT** | 1,365 |
| 276 | Plantation, FL | 3,427 | 350 | El Monte, CA** | 2,522 | 424 | Canton Twnshp, MI | 1,344 |
| 277 | Santa Maria, CA** | 3,424 | 351 | Vista, CA** | 2,490 | 425 | Centennial, CO | 1,335 |
| 278 | Charleston, SC | 3,423 | 352 | Boca Raton, FL | 2,467 | 426 | O'Fallon, MO | 1,281 |
| 279 | Bloomington, MN | 3,411 | 353 | Olathe, KS** | 2,458 | 427 | Brick Twnshp, NJ** | 1,272 |
| 280 | Yonkers, NY** | 3,404 | 354 | Greece, NY** | 2,454 | 428 | Allen, TX | 1,267 |
| 281 | Irvine, CA** | 3,398 | 355 | Bend, OR | 2,449 | 429 | Farmington Hills, MI | 1,186 |
| 282 | Glendale, CA** | 3,379 | 356 | Scranton, PA | 2,443 | 430 | Meridian, ID | 1,145 |
| 283 | Jurupa Valley, CA** | 3,332 | 357 | Nashua, NH | 2,430 | 431 | Lakewood Twnshp, NJ** | 1,091 |
| 284 | Fall River, MA | 3,308 | 358 | Clinton Twnshp, MI | 2,419 | 432 | Chino Hills, CA** | 1,080 |
| 285 | Racine, WI** | 3,307 | 359 | Palm Bay, FL | 2,409 | 433 | Mission Viejo, CA** | 1,060 |
| 286 | Largo, FL | 3,276 | 360 | Upland, CA** | 2,397 | 434 | Lake Forest, CA** | 918 |
| 287 | Cambridge, MA | 3,268 | 361 | Tracy, CA** | 2,388 | 435 | Newton, MA | 881 |
| 288 | McKinney, TX | 3,262 | 362 | Buena Park, CA** | 2,386 | 436 | Arlington Heights, IL** | 842 |
| 289 | Alexandria, VA | 3,225 | 363 | Carlsbad, CA** | 2,306 | 436 | Fishers, IN** | 842 |
| 290 | Lynn, MA | 3,212 | 364 | Lynchburg, VA | 2,304 | 438 | Carmel, IN** | 764 |
| 291 | Merced, CA** | 3,203 | 364 | San Mateo, CA** | 2,304 | 439 | Johns Creek, GA** | 656 |
| 292 | Westminster, CO | 3,201 | 366 | Chino, CA** | 2,302 | 440 | Ramapo, NY** | 624 |
| 293 | Santa Clara, CA** | 3,195 | 366 | Upper Darby Twnshp, PA | 2,302 | NA | Chicago, IL*** | NA |
| 294 | South Gate, CA** | 3,194 | 368 | Hillsboro, OR** | 2,301 | NA | Toledo, OH*** | NA |
| 295 | Green Bay, WI | 3,174 | 369 | Bloomington, IL** | 2,300 | | | |
| 296 | Indio, CA** | 3,167 | 370 | Vacaville, CA** | 2,297 | | | |

Source: CQ Press using reported data from the F.B.I. "Crime in the United States 2013"

*Includes murder, rape, robbery, aggravated assault, burglary, larceny-theft, and motor vehicle theft.

**Figures for these cities are based on the previous (legacy) definition of rape. See note on page vii.

***Not available.

# 42. Crime Rate in 2013
## National Rate = 3,098.6 Crimes per 100,000 Population*

| RANK | CITY | RATE | RANK | CITY | RATE | RANK | CITY | RATE |
|---|---|---|---|---|---|---|---|---|
| 162 | Abilene, TX** | 4,393.6 | 294 | Chino, CA** | 2,852.4 | 273 | Fullerton, CA** | 3,029.2 |
| 74 | Akron, OH | 5,654.6 | 360 | Chula Vista, CA** | 2,304.8 | 148 | Gainesville, FL | 4,575.4 |
| 313 | Alameda, CA** | 2,703.2 | 326 | Cicero, IL** | 2,584.2 | 374 | Garden Grove, CA** | 2,195.3 |
| 21 | Albany, GA** | 6,992.8 | 26 | Cincinnati, OH | 6,764.8 | 205 | Garland, TX** | 3,769.9 |
| 114 | Albany, NY** | 4,982.8 | 227 | Citrus Heights, CA** | 3,483.8 | 19 | Gary, IN** | 7,107.4 |
| 42 | Albuquerque, NM** | 6,244.7 | 397 | Clarkstown, NY** | 1,957.7 | 415 | Gilbert, AZ | 1,627.2 |
| 377 | Alexandria, VA | 2,171.4 | 240 | Clarksville, TN | 3,357.9 | 44 | Glendale, AZ** | 6,209.7 |
| 364 | Alhambra, CA** | 2,286.6 | 151 | Clearwater, FL | 4,530.4 | 410 | Glendale, CA** | 1,729.6 |
| 173 | Allentown, PA | 4,151.7 | 14 | Cleveland, OH | 7,430.7 | 264 | Grand Prairie, TX** | 3,084.0 |
| 427 | Allen, TX | 1,387.9 | 393 | Clifton, NJ** | 1,994.8 | 193 | Grand Rapids, MI | 3,929.6 |
| 127 | Amarillo, TX | 4,802.2 | 344 | Clinton Twnshp, MI | 2,466.6 | 333 | Greece, NY** | 2,538.6 |
| 402 | Amherst, NY** | 1,880.9 | 215 | Clovis, CA** | 3,603.6 | 200 | Greeley, CO | 3,860.1 |
| 261 | Anaheim, CA** | 3,110.4 | 321 | College Station, TX** | 2,637.5 | 274 | Green Bay, WI | 3,019.8 |
| 123 | Anchorage, AK | 4,831.1 | 322 | Colonie, NY** | 2,624.8 | 139 | Greensboro, NC** | 4,648.8 |
| 352 | Ann Arbor, MI | 2,373.3 | 144 | Colorado Springs, CO | 4,601.6 | 111 | Greenville, NC** | 5,018.3 |
| 108 | Antioch, CA** | 5,059.8 | 172 | Columbia, MO | 4,167.1 | 135 | Gresham, OR** | 4,696.0 |
| 434 | Arlington Heights, IL** | 1,108.2 | 27 | Columbia, SC | 6,761.2 | 361 | Hamilton Twnshp, NJ** | 2,304.7 |
| 159 | Arlington, TX** | 4,445.2 | 28 | Columbus, GA** | 6,709.4 | 120 | Hammond, IN** | 4,902.4 |
| 329 | Arvada, CO | 2,553.4 | 199 | Compton, CA** | 3,860.8 | 228 | Hampton, VA | 3,479.4 |
| 206 | Athens-Clarke, GA** | 3,727.9 | 203 | Concord, CA** | 3,797.1 | 101 | Hartford, CT** | 5,210.2 |
| 17 | Atlanta, GA** | 7,326.7 | 254 | Concord, NC** | 3,222.0 | 248 | Hawthorne, CA** | 3,276.4 |
| 219 | Aurora, CO | 3,558.2 | 371 | Coral Springs, FL | 2,213.1 | 216 | Hayward, CA** | 3,599.1 |
| 408 | Aurora, IL** | 1,781.6 | 366 | Corona, CA** | 2,248.4 | 86 | Hemet, CA** | 5,397.9 |
| 100 | Austin, TX** | 5,213.1 | 96 | Corpus Christi, TX** | 5,258.8 | 381 | Henderson, NV** | 2,134.3 |
| 103 | Bakersfield, CA** | 5,159.7 | 238 | Costa Mesa, CA** | 3,383.7 | 286 | Hesperia, CA** | 2,916.2 |
| 389 | Baldwin Park, CA** | 2,071.8 | 354 | Cranston, RI | 2,361.3 | 259 | Hialeah, FL | 3,127.5 |
| 35 | Baltimore, MD** | 6,345.9 | 124 | Dallas, TX** | 4,828.9 | 134 | High Point, NC** | 4,703.5 |
| 62 | Baton Rouge, LA** | 5,883.7 | 396 | Daly City, CA** | 1,966.8 | 350 | Hillsboro, OR** | 2,389.1 |
| 41 | Beaumont, TX** | 6,276.2 | 414 | Danbury, CT** | 1,637.4 | 116 | Hollywood, FL | 4,957.6 |
| 412 | Beaverton, OR** | 1,705.0 | 126 | Davenport, IA | 4,813.7 | 257 | Hoover, AL | 3,173.3 |
| 256 | Bellevue, WA** | 3,190.8 | 202 | Davie, FL | 3,829.9 | 56 | Houston, TX** | 6,049.3 |
| 300 | Bellflower, CA** | 2,785.0 | 38 | Dayton, OH | 6,294.0 | 312 | Huntington Beach, CA** | 2,704.2 |
| 268 | Bend, OR | 3,064.1 | 217 | Dearborn, MI | 3,594.3 | 67 | Huntsville, AL | 5,804.4 |
| 105 | Berkeley, CA** | 5,110.3 | 214 | Decatur, IL** | 3,617.5 | 32 | Independence, MO | 6,518.1 |
| 285 | Bethlehem, PA | 2,918.7 | 232 | Deerfield Beach, FL | 3,441.0 | 33 | Indianapolis, IN | 6,478.9 |
| 79 | Billings, MT | 5,532.4 | 335 | Denton, TX | 2,527.2 | 190 | Indio, CA** | 3,946.8 |
| 8 | Birmingham, AL | 8,023.1 | 165 | Denver, CO | 4,283.3 | 263 | Inglewood, CA** | 3,095.7 |
| 282 | Bloomington, IL** | 2,946.5 | 93 | Des Moines, IA | 5,323.8 | 424 | Irvine, CA** | 1,440.9 |
| 226 | Bloomington, IN** | 3,495.7 | 10 | Detroit, MI | 7,906.8 | 284 | Irving, TX** | 2,936.1 |
| 196 | Bloomington, MN | 3,918.1 | 255 | Downey, CA** | 3,195.5 | 152 | Jacksonville, FL | 4,523.0 |
| 303 | Boca Raton, FL | 2,779.7 | 89 | Duluth, MN | 5,364.7 | 25 | Jackson, MS** | 6,768.4 |
| 339 | Boise, ID | 2,492.0 | 77 | Edinburg, TX** | 5,553.6 | 336 | Jersey City, NJ** | 2,526.8 |
| 220 | Boston, MA** | 3,555.5 | 430 | Edison Twnshp, NJ** | 1,350.2 | 439 | Johns Creek, GA** | 780.1 |
| 265 | Boulder, CO | 3,078.9 | 398 | Edmond, OK** | 1,956.4 | 331 | Joliet, IL** | 2,542.1 |
| 413 | Brick Twnshp, NJ** | 1,687.7 | 269 | El Cajon, CA** | 3,054.5 | 236 | Jurupa Valley, CA** | 3,396.9 |
| 183 | Bridgeport, CT** | 3,985.0 | 376 | El Monte, CA** | 2,181.8 | 87 | Kansas City, KS** | 5,391.6 |
| 143 | Brockton, MA | 4,606.8 | 316 | El Paso, TX** | 2,660.0 | 31 | Kansas City, MO | 6,554.5 |
| 384 | Broken Arrow, OK** | 2,118.4 | 401 | Elgin, IL** | 1,935.6 | 221 | Kennewick, WA | 3,552.6 |
| 230 | Brooklyn Park, MN | 3,451.0 | 210 | Elizabeth, NJ** | 3,662.6 | 309 | Kenosha, WI** | 2,724.6 |
| 147 | Brownsville, TX** | 4,576.8 | 382 | Elk Grove, CA** | 2,132.7 | 129 | Kent, WA | 4,759.6 |
| 237 | Bryan, TX** | 3,396.6 | 212 | Erie, PA | 3,635.4 | 179 | Killeen, TX** | 4,060.4 |
| 291 | Buena Park, CA** | 2,887.5 | 267 | Escondido, CA** | 3,068.3 | 20 | Knoxville, TN | 7,082.7 |
| 53 | Buffalo, NY** | 6,082.2 | 98 | Eugene, OR | 5,250.5 | 24 | Lafayette, LA** | 6,835.8 |
| 342 | Burbank, CA** | 2,483.6 | 305 | Evanston, IL** | 2,761.9 | 433 | Lake Forest, CA** | 1,157.1 |
| 271 | Cambridge, MA | 3,046.2 | 91 | Evansville, IN** | 5,339.9 | 65 | Lakeland, FL | 5,827.7 |
| 419 | Canton Twnshp, MI | 1,510.8 | 22 | Everett, WA** | 6,951.5 | 432 | Lakewood Twnshp, NJ** | 1,177.4 |
| 375 | Cape Coral, FL | 2,185.2 | 207 | Fairfield, CA** | 3,718.7 | 297 | Lakewood, CA** | 2,820.5 |
| 388 | Carlsbad, CA** | 2,086.8 | 209 | Fall River, MA | 3,707.7 | 104 | Lakewood, CO | 5,137.5 |
| 438 | Carmel, IN** | 900.1 | 246 | Fargo, ND | 3,289.8 | 310 | Lancaster, CA** | 2,707.9 |
| 343 | Carrollton, TX** | 2,467.5 | 420 | Farmington Hills, MI | 1,462.7 | 150 | Lansing, MI | 4,533.5 |
| 295 | Carson, CA** | 2,837.9 | 153 | Fayetteville, AR | 4,505.8 | 138 | Laredo, TX** | 4,652.9 |
| 421 | Cary, NC** | 1,462.0 | 30 | Fayetteville, NC** | 6,631.8 | 169 | Largo, FL | 4,204.7 |
| 186 | Cedar Rapids, IA | 3,963.7 | 61 | Federal Way, WA | 5,891.7 | 146 | Las Cruces, NM** | 4,588.9 |
| 431 | Centennial, CO | 1,274.2 | 437 | Fishers, IN** | 1,010.1 | 189 | Las Vegas, NV** | 3,954.9 |
| 223 | Champaign, IL** | 3,530.4 | 48 | Flint, MI | 6,171.6 | 161 | Lawrence, KS | 4,401.7 |
| 324 | Chandler, AZ** | 2,603.3 | 353 | Fontana, CA** | 2,366.0 | 195 | Lawrence, MA** | 3,918.4 |
| 314 | Charleston, SC | 2,690.9 | 304 | Fort Collins, CO | 2,775.4 | 58 | Lawton, OK** | 6,033.6 |
| 166 | Charlotte, NC** | 4,257.4 | 34 | Fort Lauderdale, FL | 6,442.1 | 367 | League City, TX** | 2,247.9 |
| 13 | Chattanooga, TN | 7,638.5 | 59 | Fort Smith, AR | 5,951.9 | 372 | Lee's Summit, MO | 2,208.8 |
| 213 | Cheektowaga, NY** | 3,633.2 | 168 | Fort Wayne, IN | 4,221.0 | 283 | Lewisville, TX | 2,943.1 |
| 277 | Chesapeake, VA | 3,003.3 | 119 | Fort Worth, TX | 4,903.7 | 164 | Lexington, KY | 4,338.3 |
| NA | Chicago, IL*** | NA | 400 | Fremont, CA** | 1,946.8 | 198 | Lincoln, NE** | 3,866.9 |
| 250 | Chico, CA** | 3,254.1 | 118 | Fresno, CA** | 4,939.5 | 4 | Little Rock, AR | 9,273.6 |
| 425 | Chino Hills, CA** | 1,403.6 | 395 | Frisco, TX | 1,978.5 | 341 | Livermore, CA** | 2,489.6 |

| RANK | CITY | RATE |
|---|---|---|
| 370 | Livonia, MI | 2,214.9 |
| 249 | Long Beach, CA** | 3,267.2 |
| 338 | Longmont, CO | 2,499.0 |
| 132 | Longview, TX | 4,703.9 |
| 320 | Los Angeles, CA** | 2,639.2 |
| 122 | Louisville, KY** | 4,831.3 |
| 211 | Lowell, MA | 3,658.3 |
| 75 | Lubbock, TX** | 5,627.3 |
| 280 | Lynchburg, VA | 2,963.1 |
| 225 | Lynn, MA | 3,500.1 |
| 7 | Macon, GA** | 8,097.4 |
| 222 | Madison, WI | 3,551.4 |
| 157 | Manchester, NH | 4,475.1 |
| 176 | McAllen, TX** | 4,108.9 |
| 369 | McKinney, TX | 2,221.0 |
| 23 | Medford, OR | 6,882.5 |
| 99 | Melbourne, FL | 5,220.2 |
| 12 | Memphis, TN | 7,708.5 |
| 379 | Menifee, CA** | 2,152.9 |
| 191 | Merced, CA** | 3,938.3 |
| 426 | Meridian, ID | 1,395.3 |
| 252 | Mesa, AZ** | 3,227.6 |
| 136 | Mesquite, TX** | 4,666.2 |
| 1 | Miami Beach, FL | 11,669.7 |
| 113 | Miami Gardens, FL | 4,988.8 |
| 46 | Miami, FL | 6,183.9 |
| 288 | Midland, TX** | 2,896.3 |
| 64 | Milwaukee, WI | 5,860.0 |
| 60 | Minneapolis, MN | 5,905.0 |
| 302 | Miramar, FL | 2,780.2 |
| 435 | Mission Viejo, CA** | 1,105.4 |
| 208 | Mission, TX** | 3,708.2 |
| 66 | Mobile, AL | 5,807.9 |
| 70 | Modesto, CA** | 5,724.8 |
| 251 | Moreno Valley, CA** | 3,234.2 |
| 349 | Mountain View, CA** | 2,407.0 |
| 175 | Murfreesboro, TN | 4,114.6 |
| 417 | Murrieta, CA** | 1,586.7 |
| 345 | Nampa, ID | 2,455.3 |
| 385 | Napa, CA** | 2,112.7 |
| 428 | Naperville, IL** | 1,368.7 |
| 299 | Nashua, NH | 2,791.4 |
| 121 | Nashville, TN | 4,888.0 |
| 132 | New Bedford, MA | 4,703.9 |
| 63 | New Haven, CT | 5,883.1 |
| 140 | New Orleans, LA** | 4,639.0 |
| 394 | New Rochelle, NY** | 1,987.3 |
| 357 | New York, NY** | 2,314.8 |
| 155 | Newark, NJ** | 4,485.6 |
| 330 | Newport Beach, CA** | 2,545.7 |
| 224 | Newport News, VA | 3,521.8 |
| 436 | Newton, MA | 1,014.2 |
| 117 | Norfolk, VA | 4,945.4 |
| 315 | Norman, OK** | 2,666.5 |
| 39 | North Charleston, SC | 6,288.0 |
| 231 | North Las Vegas, NV** | 3,445.9 |
| 340 | Norwalk, CA** | 2,490.7 |
| 368 | Norwalk, CT | 2,245.7 |
| 6 | Oakland, CA** | 8,210.2 |
| 279 | Oceanside, CA** | 2,972.3 |
| 110 | Odessa, TX** | 5,037.6 |
| 418 | O'Fallon, MO | 1,549.5 |
| 95 | Ogden, UT | 5,260.3 |
| 45 | Oklahoma City, OK** | 6,194.2 |
| 403 | Olathe, KS** | 1,871.5 |
| 107 | Omaha, NE** | 5,071.3 |
| 281 | Ontario, CA** | 2,949.9 |
| 406 | Orange, CA** | 1,828.2 |
| 358 | Orem, UT** | 2,309.8 |
| 15 | Orlando, FL | 7,425.8 |
| 386 | Overland Park, KS** | 2,112.4 |
| 296 | Oxnard, CA** | 2,825.8 |
| 359 | Palm Bay, FL | 2,307.7 |
| 323 | Palmdale, CA** | 2,621.4 |

| RANK | CITY | RATE |
|---|---|---|
| 272 | Pasadena, CA** | 3,030.9 |
| 184 | Pasadena, TX** | 3,977.3 |
| 197 | Paterson, NJ** | 3,898.5 |
| 383 | Pearland, TX | 2,118.5 |
| 319 | Pembroke Pines, FL | 2,652.0 |
| 337 | Peoria, AZ** | 2,526.6 |
| 156 | Peoria, IL** | 4,483.7 |
| 149 | Philadelphia, PA | 4,540.8 |
| 141 | Phoenix, AZ** | 4,631.9 |
| 181 | Pittsburgh, PA | 4,000.2 |
| 363 | Plano, TX | 2,291.2 |
| 201 | Plantation, FL | 3,853.6 |
| 234 | Pomona, CA** | 3,437.4 |
| 71 | Pompano Beach, FL | 5,720.8 |
| 416 | Port St. Lucie, FL | 1,627.1 |
| 90 | Portland, OR** | 5,347.6 |
| 50 | Portsmouth, VA | 6,127.7 |
| 106 | Providence, RI | 5,080.9 |
| 332 | Provo, UT | 2,539.8 |
| 9 | Pueblo, CO | 7,964.9 |
| 380 | Quincy, MA | 2,147.8 |
| 167 | Racine, WI** | 4,232.1 |
| 229 | Raleigh, NC** | 3,455.3 |
| 440 | Ramapo, NY** | 715.6 |
| 348 | Rancho Cucamon., CA** | 2,412.0 |
| 180 | Reading, PA | 4,020.1 |
| 128 | Redding, CA** | 4,788.3 |
| 325 | Redwood City, CA** | 2,585.7 |
| 218 | Reno, NV** | 3,583.6 |
| 88 | Renton, WA | 5,371.6 |
| 266 | Rialto, CA** | 3,073.5 |
| 306 | Richardson, TX** | 2,759.7 |
| 80 | Richmond, CA** | 5,531.9 |
| 131 | Richmond, VA | 4,713.2 |
| 204 | Riverside, CA** | 3,772.8 |
| 112 | Roanoke, VA | 5,004.7 |
| 334 | Rochester, MN | 2,527.5 |
| 69 | Rochester, NY** | 5,774.1 |
| 54 | Rockford, IL | 6,060.9 |
| 293 | Roseville, CA** | 2,855.0 |
| 355 | Roswell, GA** | 2,360.2 |
| 351 | Round Rock, TX** | 2,373.4 |
| 160 | Sacramento, CA** | 4,416.1 |
| 142 | Salem, OR | 4,614.7 |
| 177 | Salinas, CA** | 4,081.8 |
| 11 | Salt Lake City, UT | 7,850.9 |
| 182 | San Angelo, TX | 3,988.2 |
| 36 | San Antonio, TX** | 6,345.7 |
| 94 | San Bernardino, CA** | 5,290.2 |
| 308 | San Diego, CA** | 2,744.4 |
| 29 | San Francisco, CA** | 6,642.3 |
| 289 | San Jose, CA** | 2,895.2 |
| 115 | San Leandro, CA** | 4,976.6 |
| 405 | San Marcos, CA** | 1,840.1 |
| 362 | San Mateo, CA** | 2,293.9 |
| 290 | Sandy Springs, GA** | 2,890.9 |
| 235 | Sandy, UT | 3,419.9 |
| 365 | Santa Ana, CA** | 2,267.1 |
| 239 | Santa Barbara, CA** | 3,368.7 |
| 317 | Santa Clara, CA** | 2,659.2 |
| 423 | Santa Clarita, CA** | 1,458.4 |
| 241 | Santa Maria, CA** | 3,355.2 |
| 171 | Santa Monica, CA** | 4,182.2 |
| 356 | Santa Rosa, CA** | 2,358.9 |
| 187 | Savannah, GA** | 3,957.9 |
| 311 | Scottsdale, AZ** | 2,706.2 |
| 253 | Scranton, PA | 3,225.8 |
| 49 | Seattle, WA | 6,166.8 |
| 84 | Shreveport, LA** | 5,431.1 |
| 422 | Simi Valley, CA** | 1,458.6 |
| 125 | Sioux City, IA | 4,816.4 |
| 232 | Sioux Falls, SD | 3,441.0 |
| 373 | Somerville, MA | 2,206.6 |
| 81 | South Bend, IN | 5,514.8 |

| RANK | CITY | RATE |
|---|---|---|
| 243 | South Gate, CA** | 3,341.3 |
| 276 | Sparks, NV** | 3,010.7 |
| 51 | Spokane Valley, WA** | 6,103.4 |
| 3 | Spokane, WA** | 10,008.9 |
| 57 | Springfield, IL** | 6,046.8 |
| 72 | Springfield, MA | 5,720.6 |
| 2 | Springfield, MO | 10,171.0 |
| 407 | Stamford, CT | 1,805.0 |
| 387 | Sterling Heights, MI | 2,089.8 |
| 43 | Stockton, CA** | 6,238.2 |
| 346 | St. George, UT | 2,435.0 |
| 52 | St. Joseph, MO | 6,092.0 |
| 5 | St. Louis, MO | 8,213.1 |
| 158 | St. Paul, MN | 4,470.1 |
| 37 | St. Petersburg, FL | 6,297.5 |
| 245 | Suffolk, VA | 3,334.3 |
| 390 | Sugar Land, TX** | 2,062.1 |
| 409 | Sunnyvale, CA** | 1,740.0 |
| 192 | Sunrise, FL | 3,936.9 |
| 404 | Surprise, AZ** | 1,852.3 |
| 92 | Syracuse, NY** | 5,329.1 |
| 16 | Tacoma, WA | 7,418.3 |
| 109 | Tallahassee, FL | 5,041.5 |
| 262 | Tampa, FL | 3,108.3 |
| 307 | Temecula, CA** | 2,755.0 |
| 102 | Tempe, AZ** | 5,167.3 |
| 292 | Thornton, CO | 2,883.7 |
| 429 | Thousand Oaks, CA** | 1,352.4 |
| NA | Toledo, OH*** | NA |
| 270 | Toms River Twnshp, NJ** | 3,049.9 |
| 78 | Topeka, KS** | 5,544.9 |
| 391 | Torrance, CA** | 2,015.1 |
| 298 | Tracy, CA** | 2,803.7 |
| 178 | Trenton, NJ** | 4,077.5 |
| 399 | Troy, MI | 1,951.4 |
| 18 | Tucson, AZ** | 7,222.8 |
| 40 | Tulsa, OK** | 6,287.7 |
| 97 | Tuscaloosa, AL | 5,254.7 |
| 392 | Tustin, CA** | 1,995.3 |
| 154 | Tyler, TX | 4,490.5 |
| 258 | Upland, CA** | 3,169.0 |
| 301 | Upper Darby Twnshp, PA | 2,781.2 |
| 347 | Vacaville, CA** | 2,434.6 |
| 73 | Vallejo, CA** | 5,706.6 |
| 194 | Vancouver, WA | 3,918.7 |
| 185 | Ventura, CA** | 3,963.8 |
| 188 | Victorville, CA** | 3,957.3 |
| 318 | Virginia Beach, VA | 2,652.8 |
| 170 | Visalia, CA** | 4,187.8 |
| 328 | Vista, CA** | 2,574.7 |
| 137 | Waco, TX** | 4,653.9 |
| 260 | Warren, MI | 3,120.7 |
| 327 | Warwick, RI | 2,577.4 |
| 68 | Washington, DC | 5,793.0 |
| 145 | Waterbury, CT** | 4,597.2 |
| 247 | Waukegan, IL** | 3,282.9 |
| 244 | West Covina, CA** | 3,338.4 |
| 85 | West Palm Beach, FL | 5,427.8 |
| 83 | West Valley, UT | 5,445.6 |
| 242 | Westland, MI | 3,345.7 |
| 278 | Westminster, CA** | 3,002.7 |
| 287 | Westminster, CO | 2,907.5 |
| 275 | Whittier, CA** | 3,014.5 |
| 130 | Wichita Falls, TX** | 4,744.8 |
| 47 | Wichita, KS | 6,175.4 |
| 76 | Wilmington, NC** | 5,618.8 |
| 55 | Winston-Salem, NC** | 6,055.3 |
| 378 | Woodbridge Twnshp, NJ** | 2,164.7 |
| 163 | Worcester, MA | 4,354.8 |
| 82 | Yakima, WA | 5,508.1 |
| 411 | Yonkers, NY** | 1,709.4 |
| 174 | Yuma, AZ | 4,126.5 |

Source: CQ Press using reported data from the F.B.I. "Crime in the United States 2013"

*Includes murder, rape, robbery, aggravated assault, burglary, larceny-theft, and motor vehicle theft.

**Figures for these cities are based on the previous (legacy) definition of rape. See note on page vii.

***Not available.

# 42. Crime Rate in 2013 (continued)
## National Rate = 3,098.6 Crimes per 100,000 Population*

| RANK | CITY | RATE | RANK | CITY | RATE | RANK | CITY | RATE |
|---|---|---|---|---|---|---|---|---|
| 1 | Miami Beach, FL | 11,669.7 | 75 | Lubbock, TX** | 5,627.3 | 149 | Philadelphia, PA | 4,540.8 |
| 2 | Springfield, MO | 10,171.0 | 76 | Wilmington, NC** | 5,618.8 | 150 | Lansing, MI | 4,533.5 |
| 3 | Spokane, WA** | 10,008.9 | 77 | Edinburg, TX** | 5,553.6 | 151 | Clearwater, FL | 4,530.4 |
| 4 | Little Rock, AR | 9,273.6 | 78 | Topeka, KS** | 5,544.9 | 152 | Jacksonville, FL | 4,523.0 |
| 5 | St. Louis, MO | 8,213.1 | 79 | Billings, MT | 5,532.4 | 153 | Fayetteville, AR | 4,505.8 |
| 6 | Oakland, CA** | 8,210.2 | 80 | Richmond, CA** | 5,531.9 | 154 | Tyler, TX | 4,490.5 |
| 7 | Macon, GA** | 8,097.4 | 81 | South Bend, IN | 5,514.8 | 155 | Newark, NJ** | 4,485.6 |
| 8 | Birmingham, AL | 8,023.1 | 82 | Yakima, WA | 5,508.1 | 156 | Peoria, IL** | 4,483.7 |
| 9 | Pueblo, CO | 7,964.9 | 83 | West Valley, UT | 5,445.6 | 157 | Manchester, NH | 4,475.1 |
| 10 | Detroit, MI | 7,906.8 | 84 | Shreveport, LA** | 5,431.1 | 158 | St. Paul, MN | 4,470.1 |
| 11 | Salt Lake City, UT | 7,850.9 | 85 | West Palm Beach, FL | 5,427.8 | 159 | Arlington, TX** | 4,445.2 |
| 12 | Memphis, TN | 7,708.5 | 86 | Hemet, CA** | 5,397.9 | 160 | Sacramento, CA** | 4,416.1 |
| 13 | Chattanooga, TN | 7,638.5 | 87 | Kansas City, KS** | 5,391.6 | 161 | Lawrence, KS | 4,401.7 |
| 14 | Cleveland, OH | 7,430.7 | 88 | Renton, WA | 5,371.6 | 162 | Abilene, TX** | 4,393.6 |
| 15 | Orlando, FL | 7,425.8 | 89 | Duluth, MN | 5,364.7 | 163 | Worcester, MA | 4,354.8 |
| 16 | Tacoma, WA | 7,418.3 | 90 | Portland, OR** | 5,347.6 | 164 | Lexington, KY | 4,338.3 |
| 17 | Atlanta, GA** | 7,326.7 | 91 | Evansville, IN** | 5,339.9 | 165 | Denver, CO | 4,283.3 |
| 18 | Tucson, AZ** | 7,222.8 | 92 | Syracuse, NY** | 5,329.1 | 166 | Charlotte, NC** | 4,257.4 |
| 19 | Gary, IN** | 7,107.4 | 93 | Des Moines, IA | 5,323.8 | 167 | Racine, WI** | 4,232.1 |
| 20 | Knoxville, TN | 7,082.7 | 94 | San Bernardino, CA** | 5,290.2 | 168 | Fort Wayne, IN | 4,221.0 |
| 21 | Albany, GA** | 6,992.8 | 95 | Ogden, UT | 5,260.3 | 169 | Largo, FL | 4,204.7 |
| 22 | Everett, WA** | 6,951.5 | 96 | Corpus Christi, TX** | 5,258.8 | 170 | Visalia, CA** | 4,187.8 |
| 23 | Medford, OR | 6,882.5 | 97 | Tuscaloosa, AL | 5,254.7 | 171 | Santa Monica, CA** | 4,182.2 |
| 24 | Lafayette, LA** | 6,835.2 | 98 | Eugene, OR | 5,250.5 | 172 | Columbia, MO | 4,167.1 |
| 25 | Jackson, MS** | 6,768.4 | 99 | Melbourne, FL | 5,220.2 | 173 | Allentown, PA | 4,151.7 |
| 26 | Cincinnati, OH | 6,764.8 | 100 | Austin, TX** | 5,213.1 | 174 | Yuma, AZ | 4,126.5 |
| 27 | Columbia, SC | 6,761.2 | 101 | Hartford, CT** | 5,210.2 | 175 | Murfreesboro, TN | 4,114.6 |
| 28 | Columbus, GA** | 6,709.4 | 102 | Tempe, AZ** | 5,167.3 | 176 | McAllen, TX** | 4,108.9 |
| 29 | San Francisco, CA** | 6,642.3 | 103 | Bakersfield, CA** | 5,159.7 | 177 | Salinas, CA** | 4,081.8 |
| 30 | Fayetteville, NC** | 6,631.8 | 104 | Lakewood, CO | 5,137.5 | 178 | Trenton, NJ** | 4,077.5 |
| 31 | Kansas City, MO | 6,554.5 | 105 | Berkeley, CA** | 5,110.3 | 179 | Killeen, TX** | 4,060.4 |
| 32 | Independence, MO | 6,518.1 | 106 | Providence, RI | 5,080.9 | 180 | Reading, PA | 4,020.1 |
| 33 | Indianapolis, IN | 6,478.9 | 107 | Omaha, NE** | 5,071.3 | 181 | Pittsburgh, PA | 4,000.2 |
| 34 | Fort Lauderdale, FL | 6,442.1 | 108 | Antioch, CA** | 5,059.8 | 182 | San Angelo, TX | 3,988.2 |
| 35 | Baltimore, MD** | 6,345.9 | 109 | Tallahassee, FL | 5,041.5 | 183 | Bridgeport, CT** | 3,985.0 |
| 36 | San Antonio, TX** | 6,345.7 | 110 | Odessa, TX** | 5,037.6 | 184 | Pasadena, TX** | 3,977.3 |
| 37 | St. Petersburg, FL | 6,297.5 | 111 | Greenville, NC** | 5,018.3 | 185 | Ventura, CA** | 3,963.8 |
| 38 | Dayton, OH | 6,294.0 | 112 | Roanoke, VA | 5,004.7 | 186 | Cedar Rapids, IA | 3,963.7 |
| 39 | North Charleston, SC | 6,288.0 | 113 | Miami Gardens, FL | 4,988.8 | 187 | Savannah, GA** | 3,957.9 |
| 40 | Tulsa, OK** | 6,287.7 | 114 | Albany, NY** | 4,982.8 | 188 | Victorville, CA** | 3,957.3 |
| 41 | Beaumont, TX** | 6,276.2 | 115 | San Leandro, CA** | 4,976.6 | 189 | Las Vegas, NV** | 3,954.9 |
| 42 | Albuquerque, NM** | 6,244.7 | 116 | Hollywood, FL | 4,957.6 | 190 | Indio, CA** | 3,946.8 |
| 43 | Stockton, CA** | 6,238.2 | 117 | Norfolk, VA | 4,945.4 | 191 | Merced, CA** | 3,938.3 |
| 44 | Glendale, AZ** | 6,209.7 | 118 | Fresno, CA** | 4,939.5 | 192 | Sunrise, FL | 3,936.9 |
| 45 | Oklahoma City, OK** | 6,194.2 | 119 | Fort Worth, TX | 4,903.7 | 193 | Grand Rapids, MI | 3,929.6 |
| 46 | Miami, FL | 6,183.9 | 120 | Hammond, IN** | 4,902.4 | 194 | Vancouver, WA | 3,918.7 |
| 47 | Wichita, KS | 6,175.4 | 121 | Nashville, TN | 4,888.0 | 195 | Lawrence, MA** | 3,918.4 |
| 48 | Flint, MI | 6,171.6 | 122 | Louisville, KY** | 4,831.3 | 196 | Bloomington, MN | 3,918.1 |
| 49 | Seattle, WA | 6,166.8 | 123 | Anchorage, AK | 4,831.1 | 197 | Paterson, NJ** | 3,898.5 |
| 50 | Portsmouth, VA | 6,127.7 | 124 | Dallas, TX** | 4,828.9 | 198 | Lincoln, NE** | 3,866.0 |
| 51 | Spokane Valley, WA** | 6,103.4 | 125 | Sioux City, IA | 4,816.4 | 199 | Compton, CA** | 3,860.8 |
| 52 | St. Joseph, MO | 6,092.0 | 126 | Davenport, IA | 4,813.7 | 200 | Greeley, CO | 3,860.1 |
| 53 | Buffalo, NY** | 6,082.2 | 127 | Amarillo, TX | 4,802.2 | 201 | Plantation, FL | 3,853.6 |
| 54 | Rockford, IL | 6,060.9 | 128 | Redding, CA** | 4,788.3 | 202 | Davie, FL | 3,829.9 |
| 55 | Winston-Salem, NC** | 6,055.3 | 129 | Kent, WA | 4,759.6 | 203 | Concord, CA** | 3,797.1 |
| 56 | Houston, TX** | 6,049.3 | 130 | Wichita Falls, TX** | 4,744.8 | 204 | Riverside, CA** | 3,772.8 |
| 57 | Springfield, IL** | 6,046.8 | 131 | Richmond, VA | 4,713.2 | 205 | Garland, TX** | 3,769.9 |
| 58 | Lawton, OK** | 6,033.6 | 132 | Longview, TX | 4,703.9 | 206 | Athens-Clarke, GA** | 3,727.9 |
| 59 | Fort Smith, AR | 5,951.9 | 132 | New Bedford, MA | 4,703.9 | 207 | Fairfield, CA** | 3,718.7 |
| 60 | Minneapolis, MN | 5,905.0 | 134 | High Point, NC** | 4,703.5 | 208 | Mission, TX** | 3,708.2 |
| 61 | Federal Way, WA | 5,891.7 | 135 | Gresham, OR** | 4,696.0 | 209 | Fall River, MA | 3,707.7 |
| 62 | Baton Rouge, LA** | 5,883.7 | 136 | Mesquite, TX** | 4,666.2 | 210 | Elizabeth, NJ** | 3,662.6 |
| 63 | New Haven, CT | 5,883.1 | 137 | Waco, TX** | 4,653.9 | 211 | Lowell, MA | 3,658.3 |
| 64 | Milwaukee, WI | 5,860.0 | 138 | Laredo, TX** | 4,652.9 | 212 | Erie, PA | 3,635.4 |
| 65 | Lakeland, FL | 5,827.7 | 139 | Greensboro, NC** | 4,648.8 | 213 | Cheektowaga, NY** | 3,633.2 |
| 66 | Mobile, AL | 5,807.9 | 140 | New Orleans, LA** | 4,639.0 | 214 | Decatur, IL** | 3,617.5 |
| 67 | Huntsville, AL | 5,804.4 | 141 | Phoenix, AZ** | 4,631.9 | 215 | Clovis, CA** | 3,603.6 |
| 68 | Washington, DC | 5,793.0 | 142 | Salem, OR | 4,614.7 | 216 | Hayward, CA** | 3,599.1 |
| 69 | Rochester, NY** | 5,774.1 | 143 | Brockton, MA | 4,606.8 | 217 | Dearborn, MI | 3,594.3 |
| 70 | Modesto, CA** | 5,724.8 | 144 | Colorado Springs, CO | 4,601.6 | 218 | Reno, NV** | 3,583.6 |
| 71 | Pompano Beach, FL | 5,720.8 | 145 | Waterbury, CT** | 4,597.2 | 219 | Aurora, CO | 3,558.2 |
| 72 | Springfield, MA | 5,720.6 | 146 | Las Cruces, NM** | 4,588.9 | 220 | Boston, MA** | 3,555.5 |
| 73 | Vallejo, CA** | 5,706.6 | 147 | Brownsville, TX** | 4,576.8 | 221 | Kennewick, WA | 3,552.6 |
| 74 | Akron, OH | 5,654.6 | 148 | Gainesville, FL | 4,575.4 | 222 | Madison, WI | 3,551.4 |

| RANK | CITY | RATE |
|------|------|------|
| 223 | Champaign, IL** | 3,530.4 |
| 224 | Newport News, VA | 3,521.8 |
| 225 | Lynn, MA | 3,500.1 |
| 226 | Bloomington, IN** | 3,495.7 |
| 227 | Citrus Heights, CA** | 3,483.8 |
| 228 | Hampton, VA | 3,479.4 |
| 229 | Raleigh, NC** | 3,455.3 |
| 230 | Brooklyn Park, MN | 3,451.0 |
| 231 | North Las Vegas, NV** | 3,445.9 |
| 232 | Deerfield Beach, FL | 3,441.0 |
| 232 | Sioux Falls, SD | 3,441.0 |
| 234 | Pomona, CA** | 3,437.4 |
| 235 | Sandy, UT | 3,419.9 |
| 236 | Jurupa Valley, CA** | 3,396.9 |
| 237 | Bryan, TX** | 3,396.6 |
| 238 | Costa Mesa, CA** | 3,383.7 |
| 239 | Santa Barbara, CA** | 3,368.7 |
| 240 | Clarksville, TN | 3,357.9 |
| 241 | Santa Maria, CA** | 3,355.2 |
| 242 | Westland, MI | 3,345.7 |
| 243 | South Gate, CA** | 3,341.3 |
| 244 | West Covina, CA** | 3,338.4 |
| 245 | Suffolk, VA | 3,334.3 |
| 246 | Fargo, ND | 3,289.8 |
| 247 | Waukegan, IL** | 3,282.9 |
| 248 | Hawthorne, CA** | 3,276.4 |
| 249 | Long Beach, CA** | 3,267.2 |
| 250 | Chico, CA** | 3,254.1 |
| 251 | Moreno Valley, CA** | 3,234.2 |
| 252 | Mesa, AZ** | 3,227.6 |
| 253 | Scranton, PA | 3,225.8 |
| 254 | Concord, NC** | 3,222.0 |
| 255 | Downey, CA** | 3,195.5 |
| 256 | Bellevue, WA** | 3,190.8 |
| 257 | Hoover, AL | 3,173.3 |
| 258 | Upland, CA** | 3,169.0 |
| 259 | Hialeah, FL | 3,127.5 |
| 260 | Warren, MI | 3,120.7 |
| 261 | Anaheim, CA** | 3,110.4 |
| 262 | Tampa, FL | 3,108.3 |
| 263 | Inglewood, CA** | 3,095.7 |
| 264 | Grand Prairie, TX** | 3,084.0 |
| 265 | Boulder, CO | 3,078.9 |
| 266 | Rialto, CA** | 3,073.5 |
| 267 | Escondido, CA** | 3,068.3 |
| 268 | Bend, OR | 3,064.1 |
| 269 | El Cajon, CA** | 3,054.5 |
| 270 | Toms River Twnshp, NJ** | 3,049.9 |
| 271 | Cambridge, MA | 3,046.2 |
| 272 | Pasadena, CA** | 3,030.9 |
| 273 | Fullerton, CA** | 3,029.2 |
| 274 | Green Bay, WI | 3,019.8 |
| 275 | Whittier, CA** | 3,014.5 |
| 276 | Sparks, NV** | 3,010.7 |
| 277 | Chesapeake, VA | 3,003.3 |
| 278 | Westminster, CA** | 3,002.7 |
| 279 | Oceanside, CA** | 2,972.3 |
| 280 | Lynchburg, VA | 2,963.1 |
| 281 | Ontario, CA** | 2,949.9 |
| 282 | Bloomington, IL** | 2,946.5 |
| 283 | Lewisville, TX | 2,943.1 |
| 284 | Irving, TX** | 2,936.1 |
| 285 | Bethlehem, PA | 2,918.7 |
| 286 | Hesperia, CA** | 2,916.2 |
| 287 | Westminster, CO | 2,907.5 |
| 288 | Midland, TX** | 2,896.3 |
| 289 | San Jose, CA** | 2,895.2 |
| 290 | Sandy Springs, GA** | 2,890.9 |
| 291 | Buena Park, CA** | 2,887.5 |
| 292 | Thornton, CO | 2,883.7 |
| 293 | Roseville, CA** | 2,855.0 |
| 294 | Chino, CA** | 2,852.4 |
| 295 | Carson, CA** | 2,837.9 |
| 296 | Oxnard, CA** | 2,825.8 |

| RANK | CITY | RATE |
|------|------|------|
| 297 | Lakewood, CA** | 2,820.5 |
| 298 | Tracy, CA** | 2,803.7 |
| 299 | Nashua, NH | 2,791.4 |
| 300 | Bellflower, CA** | 2,785.0 |
| 301 | Upper Darby Twnshp, PA | 2,781.2 |
| 302 | Miramar, FL | 2,780.2 |
| 303 | Boca Raton, FL | 2,779.7 |
| 304 | Fort Collins, CO | 2,775.4 |
| 305 | Evanston, IL** | 2,761.9 |
| 306 | Richardson, TX** | 2,759.7 |
| 307 | Temecula, CA** | 2,755.0 |
| 308 | San Diego, CA** | 2,744.4 |
| 309 | Kenosha, WI** | 2,724.6 |
| 310 | Lancaster, CA** | 2,707.9 |
| 311 | Scottsdale, AZ** | 2,706.2 |
| 312 | Huntington Beach, CA** | 2,704.2 |
| 313 | Alameda, CA** | 2,703.2 |
| 314 | Charleston, SC | 2,690.9 |
| 315 | Norman, OK** | 2,666.5 |
| 316 | El Paso, TX** | 2,660.0 |
| 317 | Santa Clara, CA** | 2,659.2 |
| 318 | Virginia Beach, VA | 2,652.8 |
| 319 | Pembroke Pines, FL | 2,652.0 |
| 320 | Los Angeles, CA** | 2,639.2 |
| 321 | College Station, TX** | 2,637.5 |
| 322 | Colonie, NY** | 2,624.8 |
| 323 | Palmdale, CA** | 2,621.4 |
| 324 | Chandler, AZ** | 2,603.3 |
| 325 | Redwood City, CA** | 2,585.7 |
| 326 | Cicero, IL** | 2,584.2 |
| 327 | Warwick, RI | 2,577.4 |
| 328 | Vista, CA** | 2,574.7 |
| 329 | Arvada, CO | 2,553.4 |
| 330 | Newport Beach, CA** | 2,545.7 |
| 331 | Joliet, IL** | 2,542.1 |
| 332 | Provo, UT | 2,539.8 |
| 333 | Greece, NY** | 2,538.6 |
| 334 | Rochester, MN | 2,527.5 |
| 335 | Denton, TX | 2,527.2 |
| 336 | Jersey City, NJ** | 2,526.8 |
| 337 | Peoria, AZ** | 2,526.6 |
| 338 | Longmont, CO | 2,499.0 |
| 339 | Boise, ID | 2,492.0 |
| 340 | Norwalk, CA** | 2,490.7 |
| 341 | Livermore, CA** | 2,489.6 |
| 342 | Burbank, CA** | 2,483.6 |
| 343 | Carrollton, TX** | 2,467.5 |
| 344 | Clinton Twnshp, MI | 2,466.6 |
| 345 | Nampa, ID | 2,455.3 |
| 346 | St. George, UT | 2,435.0 |
| 347 | Vacaville, CA** | 2,434.6 |
| 348 | Rancho Cucamon., CA** | 2,412.0 |
| 349 | Mountain View, CA** | 2,407.0 |
| 350 | Hillsboro, OR** | 2,389.1 |
| 351 | Round Rock, TX** | 2,373.4 |
| 352 | Ann Arbor, MI | 2,373.3 |
| 353 | Fontana, CA** | 2,366.0 |
| 354 | Cranston, RI | 2,361.3 |
| 355 | Roswell, GA** | 2,360.2 |
| 356 | Santa Rosa, CA** | 2,358.9 |
| 357 | New York, NY** | 2,314.8 |
| 358 | Orem, UT** | 2,309.8 |
| 359 | Palm Bay, FL | 2,307.7 |
| 360 | Chula Vista, CA** | 2,304.8 |
| 361 | Hamilton Twnshp, NJ** | 2,304.7 |
| 362 | San Mateo, CA** | 2,293.9 |
| 363 | Plano, TX | 2,291.2 |
| 364 | Alhambra, CA** | 2,286.6 |
| 365 | Santa Ana, CA** | 2,267.1 |
| 366 | Corona, CA** | 2,248.4 |
| 367 | League City, TX** | 2,247.9 |
| 368 | Norwalk, CT | 2,245.7 |
| 369 | McKinney, TX | 2,221.0 |
| 370 | Livonia, MI | 2,214.9 |

| RANK | CITY | RATE |
|------|------|------|
| 371 | Coral Springs, FL | 2,213.1 |
| 372 | Lee's Summit, MO | 2,208.8 |
| 373 | Somerville, MA | 2,206.6 |
| 374 | Garden Grove, CA** | 2,195.3 |
| 375 | Cape Coral, FL | 2,185.2 |
| 376 | El Monte, CA** | 2,181.8 |
| 377 | Alexandria, VA | 2,171.4 |
| 378 | Woodbridge Twnshp, NJ** | 2,164.7 |
| 379 | Menifee, CA** | 2,152.9 |
| 380 | Quincy, MA | 2,147.8 |
| 381 | Henderson, NV** | 2,134.3 |
| 382 | Elk Grove, CA** | 2,132.7 |
| 383 | Pearland, TX | 2,118.5 |
| 384 | Broken Arrow, OK** | 2,118.4 |
| 385 | Napa, CA** | 2,112.7 |
| 386 | Overland Park, KS** | 2,112.4 |
| 387 | Sterling Heights, MI | 2,089.8 |
| 388 | Carlsbad, CA** | 2,086.8 |
| 389 | Baldwin Park, CA** | 2,071.8 |
| 390 | Sugar Land, TX** | 2,062.1 |
| 391 | Torrance, CA** | 2,015.1 |
| 392 | Tustin, CA** | 1,995.3 |
| 393 | Clifton, NJ** | 1,994.8 |
| 394 | New Rochelle, NY** | 1,987.3 |
| 395 | Frisco, TX | 1,978.5 |
| 396 | Daly City, CA** | 1,966.8 |
| 397 | Clarkstown, NY** | 1,957.7 |
| 398 | Edmond, OK** | 1,956.4 |
| 399 | Troy, MI | 1,951.4 |
| 400 | Fremont, CA** | 1,946.8 |
| 401 | Elgin, IL** | 1,935.6 |
| 402 | Amherst, NY** | 1,880.9 |
| 403 | Olathe, KS** | 1,871.5 |
| 404 | Surprise, AZ** | 1,852.3 |
| 405 | San Marcos, CA** | 1,840.1 |
| 406 | Orange, CA** | 1,828.2 |
| 407 | Stamford, CT | 1,805.0 |
| 408 | Aurora, IL** | 1,781.6 |
| 409 | Sunnyvale, CA** | 1,740.0 |
| 410 | Glendale, CA** | 1,729.6 |
| 411 | Yonkers, NY** | 1,709.4 |
| 412 | Beaverton, OR** | 1,705.0 |
| 413 | Brick Twnshp, NJ** | 1,687.7 |
| 414 | Danbury, CT** | 1,637.4 |
| 415 | Gilbert, AZ | 1,627.2 |
| 416 | Port St. Lucie, FL | 1,627.1 |
| 417 | Murrieta, CA** | 1,586.7 |
| 418 | O'Fallon, MO | 1,549.5 |
| 419 | Canton Twnshp, MI | 1,510.8 |
| 420 | Farmington Hills, MI | 1,462.7 |
| 421 | Cary, NC** | 1,462.0 |
| 422 | Simi Valley, CA** | 1,458.6 |
| 423 | Santa Clarita, CA** | 1,458.4 |
| 424 | Irvine, CA** | 1,440.9 |
| 425 | Chino Hills, CA** | 1,403.6 |
| 426 | Meridian, ID | 1,395.3 |
| 427 | Allen, TX | 1,387.9 |
| 428 | Naperville, IL** | 1,368.7 |
| 429 | Thousand Oaks, CA** | 1,352.4 |
| 430 | Edison Twnshp, NJ** | 1,350.2 |
| 431 | Centennial, CO | 1,274.2 |
| 432 | Lakewood Twnshp, NJ** | 1,177.4 |
| 433 | Lake Forest, CA** | 1,157.1 |
| 434 | Arlington Heights, IL** | 1,108.2 |
| 435 | Mission Viejo, CA** | 1,105.4 |
| 436 | Newton, MA | 1,014.2 |
| 437 | Fishers, IN** | 1,010.1 |
| 438 | Carmel, IN** | 900.1 |
| 439 | Johns Creek, GA** | 780.1 |
| 440 | Ramapo, NY** | 715.6 |
| NA | Chicago, IL*** | NA |
| NA | Toledo, OH*** | NA |

Source: CQ Press using reported data from the F.B.I. "Crime in the United States 2013"

*Includes murder, rape, robbery, aggravated assault, burglary, larceny-theft, and motor vehicle theft.

**Figures for these cities are based on the previous (legacy) definition of rape. See note on page vii.

***Not available.

# 43. Percent Change in Crime Rate: 2012 to 2013
## National Percent Change = 4.8% Decrease*

| RANK | CITY | % CHANGE | RANK | CITY | % CHANGE | RANK | CITY | % CHANGE |
|---|---|---|---|---|---|---|---|---|
| 30 | Abilene, TX** | 8.3 | 243 | Chino, CA** | (5.4) | 209 | Fullerton, CA** | (4.4) |
| 225 | Akron, OH | (4.9) | 89 | Chula Vista, CA** | 1.7 | 197 | Gainesville, FL | (4.0) |
| 127 | Alameda, CA** | (0.6) | 403 | Cicero, IL** | (16.2) | 385 | Garden Grove, CA** | (13.7) |
| 252 | Albany, GA** | (5.6) | 225 | Cincinnati, OH | (4.9) | 194 | Garland, TX** | (3.9) |
| 225 | Albany, NY** | (4.9) | 389 | Citrus Heights, CA** | (14.0) | 24 | Gary, IN** | 9.9 |
| 82 | Albuquerque, NM** | 2.1 | 135 | Clarkstown, NY** | (1.1) | 174 | Gilbert, AZ | (2.9) |
| 156 | Alexandria, VA | (2.0) | 116 | Clarksville, TN | (0.1) | 345 | Glendale, AZ** | (10.0) |
| 273 | Alhambra, CA** | (6.6) | 128 | Clearwater, FL | (0.8) | 74 | Glendale, CA** | 2.9 |
| 255 | Allentown, PA | (5.7) | 148 | Cleveland, OH | (1.7) | 165 | Grand Prairie, TX** | (2.4) |
| 410 | Allen, TX | (17.1) | 203 | Clifton, NJ** | (4.2) | 300 | Grand Rapids, MI | (7.7) |
| 288 | Amarillo, TX | (7.3) | 235 | Clinton Twnshp, MI | (5.1) | 314 | Greece, NY** | (8.5) |
| 261 | Amherst, NY** | (5.8) | 407 | Clovis, CA** | (16.9) | 95 | Greeley, CO | 1.3 |
| 252 | Anaheim, CA** | (5.6) | 363 | College Station, TX** | (11.8) | 307 | Green Bay, WI | (8.3) |
| 16 | Anchorage, AK | 11.0 | 246 | Colonie, NY** | (5.5) | 255 | Greensboro, NC** | (5.7) |
| 298 | Ann Arbor, MI | (7.6) | 112 | Colorado Springs, CO | 0.1 | 92 | Greenville, NC** | 1.4 |
| 319 | Antioch, CA** | (8.8) | 151 | Columbia, MO | (1.8) | 225 | Gresham, OR** | (4.9) |
| 412 | Arlington Heights, IL** | (17.9) | NA | Columbia, SC*** | NA | 237 | Hamilton Twnshp, NJ** | (5.2) |
| 132 | Arlington, TX** | (0.9) | 35 | Columbus, GA** | 7.4 | 184 | Hammond, IN** | (3.4) |
| 100 | Arvada, CO | 0.8 | 57 | Compton, CA** | 4.7 | 186 | Hampton, VA | (3.5) |
| 383 | Athens-Clarke, GA** | (13.4) | 65 | Concord, CA** | 3.7 | 271 | Hartford, CT** | (6.5) |
| 290 | Atlanta, GA** | (7.4) | NA | Concord, NC*** | NA | 121 | Hawthorne, CA** | (0.4) |
| 60 | Aurora, CO | 4.3 | 335 | Coral Springs, FL | (9.3) | 151 | Hayward, CA** | (1.8) |
| 387 | Aurora, IL** | (13.8) | 416 | Corona, CA** | (18.7) | 10 | Hemet, CA** | 12.6 |
| 290 | Austin, TX** | (7.4) | 84 | Corpus Christi, TX** | 2.0 | 156 | Henderson, NV** | (2.0) |
| 279 | Bakersfield, CA** | (6.8) | 364 | Costa Mesa, CA** | (12.0) | 287 | Hesperia, CA** | (7.2) |
| 389 | Baldwin Park, CA** | (14.0) | 281 | Cranston, RI | (6.9) | 322 | Hialeah, FL | (8.9) |
| 59 | Baltimore, MD** | 4.6 | 206 | Dallas, TX** | (4.3) | 98 | High Point, NC** | 1.0 |
| 271 | Baton Rouge, LA** | (6.5) | 104 | Daly City, CA** | 0.6 | 191 | Hillsboro, OR** | (3.7) |
| 40 | Beaumont, TX** | 6.9 | 419 | Danbury, CT** | (19.8) | 387 | Hollywood, FL | (13.8) |
| 165 | Beaverton, OR** | (2.4) | 63 | Davenport, IA | 3.8 | 7 | Hoover, AL | 15.3 |
| 25 | Bellevue, WA** | 9.7 | 241 | Davie, FL | (5.3) | 86 | Houston, TX** | 1.9 |
| 72 | Bellflower, CA** | 3.0 | 312 | Dayton, OH | (8.4) | 326 | Huntington Beach, CA** | (9.0) |
| NA | Bend, OR*** | NA | 176 | Dearborn, MI | (3.0) | 171 | Huntsville, AL | (2.7) |
| 231 | Berkeley, CA** | (5.0) | 146 | Decatur, IL** | (1.6) | 123 | Independence, MO | (0.5) |
| 103 | Bethlehem, PA | 0.7 | 246 | Deerfield Beach, FL | (5.5) | 209 | Indianapolis, IN | (4.4) |
| 8 | Billings, MT | 13.6 | 411 | Denton, TX | (17.2) | 209 | Indio, CA** | (4.4) |
| 235 | Birmingham, AL | (5.1) | 135 | Denver, CO | (1.1) | 115 | Inglewood, CA** | 0.0 |
| 57 | Bloomington, IL** | 4.7 | 163 | Des Moines, IA | (2.3) | 305 | Irvine, CA** | (8.2) |
| 414 | Bloomington, IN** | (18.2) | 116 | Detroit, MI | (0.1) | 186 | Irving, TX** | (3.5) |
| NA | Bloomington, MN*** | NA | 288 | Downey, CA** | (7.3) | 215 | Jacksonville, FL | (4.6) |
| 361 | Boca Raton, FL | (11.6) | NA | Duluth, MN*** | NA | 345 | Jackson, MS** | (10.0) |
| 356 | Boise, ID | (10.8) | 369 | Edinburg, TX** | (12.3) | 382 | Jersey City, NJ** | (13.2) |
| 231 | Boston, MA** | (5.0) | 398 | Edison Twnshp, NJ** | (14.9) | 25 | Johns Creek, GA** | 9.7 |
| 178 | Boulder, CO | (3.1) | 295 | Edmond, OK** | (7.5) | 381 | Joliet, IL** | (13.1) |
| 186 | Brick Twnshp, NJ** | (3.5) | 13 | El Cajon, CA** | 12.0 | 225 | Jurupa Valley, CA** | (4.9) |
| 402 | Bridgeport, CT** | (15.8) | 201 | El Monte, CA** | (4.1) | 255 | Kansas City, KS** | (5.7) |
| 53 | Brockton, MA | 5.4 | 278 | El Paso, TX** | (6.7) | 184 | Kansas City, MO | (3.4) |
| 322 | Broken Arrow, OK** | (8.9) | 252 | Elgin, IL** | (5.6) | 55 | Kennewick, WA | 5.1 |
| NA | Brooklyn Park, MN*** | NA | 385 | Elizabeth, NJ** | (13.7) | 405 | Kenosha, WI** | (16.8) |
| 262 | Brownsville, TX** | (5.9) | 369 | Elk Grove, CA** | (12.3) | 181 | Kent, WA | (3.3) |
| 206 | Bryan, TX** | (4.3) | 273 | Erie, PA | (6.6) | 305 | Killeen, TX** | (8.2) |
| 56 | Buena Park, CA** | 4.9 | 110 | Escondido, CA** | 0.2 | 290 | Knoxville, TN | (7.4) |
| 237 | Buffalo, NY** | (5.2) | 146 | Eugene, OR | (1.6) | 20 | Lafayette, LA** | 10.6 |
| 215 | Burbank, CA** | (4.6) | 339 | Evanston, IL** | (9.4) | 424 | Lake Forest, CA** | (23.3) |
| 295 | Cambridge, MA | (7.5) | 231 | Evansville, IN** | (5.0) | 78 | Lakeland, FL | 2.5 |
| NA | Canton Twnshp, MI*** | NA | 47 | Everett, WA** | 6.2 | 326 | Lakewood Twnshp, NJ** | (9.0) |
| 284 | Cape Coral, FL | (7.0) | 51 | Fairfield, CA** | 5.6 | 108 | Lakewood, CA** | 0.3 |
| 237 | Carlsbad, CA** | (5.2) | 330 | Fall River, MA | (9.1) | 86 | Lakewood, CO | 1.9 |
| 349 | Carmel, IN** | (10.1) | 14 | Fargo, ND | 11.9 | 135 | Lancaster, CA** | (1.1) |
| 396 | Carrollton, TX** | (14.5) | 366 | Farmington Hills, MI | (12.2) | 37 | Lansing, MI | 7.2 |
| 413 | Carson, CA** | (18.1) | 134 | Fayetteville, AR | (1.0) | 167 | Laredo, TX** | (2.5) |
| 86 | Cary, NC** | 1.9 | 220 | Fayetteville, NC** | (4.8) | 255 | Largo, FL | (5.7) |
| 110 | Cedar Rapids, IA | 0.2 | 108 | Federal Way, WA | 0.3 | 220 | Las Cruces, NM** | (4.8) |
| 409 | Centennial, CO | (17.0) | 197 | Fishers, IN** | (4.0) | 100 | Las Vegas, NV** | 0.8 |
| 404 | Champaign, IL** | (16.6) | 426 | Flint, MI | (25.5) | 349 | Lawrence, KS | (10.1) |
| 366 | Chandler, AZ** | (12.2) | 359 | Fontana, CA** | (11.1) | 19 | Lawrence, MA** | 10.7 |
| 331 | Charleston, SC | (9.2) | 312 | Fort Collins, CO | (8.4) | 171 | Lawton, OK** | (2.7) |
| 326 | Charlotte, NC** | (9.0) | 206 | Fort Lauderdale, FL | (4.3) | 42 | League City, TX** | 6.8 |
| NA | Chattanooga, TN*** | NA | 215 | Fort Smith, AR | (4.6) | 335 | Lee's Summit, MO | (9.3) |
| 197 | Cheektowaga, NY** | (4.0) | 65 | Fort Wayne, IN | 3.7 | NA | Lewisville, TX*** | NA |
| 203 | Chesapeake, VA | (4.2) | 84 | Fort Worth, TX | 2.0 | 335 | Lexington, KY | (9.3) |
| NA | Chicago, IL*** | NA | 273 | Fremont, CA** | (6.6) | 326 | Lincoln, NE** | (9.0) |
| 21 | Chico, CA** | 10.1 | 369 | Fresno, CA** | (12.3) | 135 | Little Rock, AR | (1.1) |
| 52 | Chino Hills, CA** | 5.5 | 285 | Frisco, TX | (7.1) | 161 | Livermore, CA** | (2.1) |

| RANK | CITY | % CHANGE | RANK | CITY | % CHANGE | RANK | CITY | % CHANGE |
|---|---|---|---|---|---|---|---|---|
| 268 | Livonia, MI | (6.3) | 18 | Pasadena, CA** | 10.8 | 68 | South Gate, CA** | 3.5 |
| 319 | Long Beach, CA** | (8.8) | 144 | Pasadena, TX** | (1.4) | 121 | Sparks, NV** | (0.4) |
| 255 | Longmont, CO | (5.7) | 290 | Paterson, NJ** | (7.4) | 15 | Spokane Valley, WA** | 11.3 |
| 407 | Longview, TX | (16.9) | 40 | Pearland, TX | 6.9 | 42 | Spokane, WA** | 6.8 |
| 197 | Los Angeles, CA** | (4.0) | 243 | Pembroke Pines, FL | (5.4) | 372 | Springfield, IL** | (12.4) |
| 141 | Louisville, KY** | (1.3) | 418 | Peoria, AZ** | (19.5) | 80 | Springfield, MA | 2.4 |
| 39 | Lowell, MA | 7.0 | 378 | Peoria, IL** | (13.0) | 89 | Springfield, MO | 1.7 |
| 265 | Lubbock, TX** | (6.2) | 273 | Philadelphia, PA | (6.6) | 151 | Stamford, CT | (1.8) |
| 174 | Lynchburg, VA | (2.9) | 156 | Phoenix, AZ** | (2.0) | 181 | Sterling Heights, MI | (3.3) |
| 192 | Lynn, MA | (3.8) | 203 | Pittsburgh, PA | (4.2) | 265 | Stockton, CA** | (6.2) |
| 71 | Macon, GA** | 3.2 | 303 | Plano, TX | (7.9) | 33 | St. George, UT | 7.5 |
| 167 | Madison, WI | (2.5) | 331 | Plantation, FL | (9.2) | 270 | St. Joseph, MO | (6.4) |
| 21 | Manchester, NH | 10.1 | 393 | Pomona, CA** | (14.3) | 243 | St. Louis, MO | (5.4) |
| 132 | McAllen, TX** | (0.9) | 358 | Pompano Beach, FL | (11.0) | 285 | St. Paul, MN | (7.1) |
| 89 | McKinney, TX | 1.7 | 422 | Port St. Lucie, FL | (20.0) | 46 | St. Petersburg, FL | 6.5 |
| 32 | Medford, OR | 8.1 | 218 | Portland, OR** | (4.7) | NA | Suffolk, VA*** | NA |
| 116 | Melbourne, FL | (0.1) | 12 | Portsmouth, VA | 12.2 | 67 | Sugar Land, TX** | 3.6 |
| 209 | Memphis, TN | (4.4) | 128 | Providence, RI | (0.8) | 307 | Sunnyvale, CA** | (8.3) |
| 399 | Menifee, CA** | (15.1) | 8 | Provo, UT | 13.6 | 128 | Sunrise, FL | (0.8) |
| 427 | Merced, CA** | (35.2) | 16 | Pueblo, CO | 11.0 | 401 | Surprise, AZ** | (15.6) |
| 415 | Meridian, ID | (18.4) | 72 | Quincy, MA | 3.0 | 49 | Syracuse, NY** | 5.8 |
| 315 | Mesa, AZ** | (8.6) | 262 | Racine, WI** | (5.9) | 63 | Tacoma, WA | 3.8 |
| 107 | Mesquite, TX** | 0.4 | 273 | Raleigh, NC** | (6.6) | 307 | Tallahassee, FL | (8.3) |
| 44 | Miami Beach, FL | 6.6 | 423 | Ramapo, NY** | (23.2) | 345 | Tampa, FL | (10.0) |
| 176 | Miami Gardens, FL | (3.0) | 377 | Rancho Cucamon., CA** | (12.8) | 11 | Temecula, CA** | 12.3 |
| 246 | Miami, FL | (5.5) | 419 | Reading, PA | (19.8) | 144 | Tempe, AZ** | (1.4) |
| 148 | Midland, TX** | (1.7) | 393 | Redding, CA** | (14.3) | 135 | Thornton, CO | (1.1) |
| 295 | Milwaukee, WI | (7.5) | 98 | Redwood City, CA** | 1.0 | 372 | Thousand Oaks, CA** | (12.4) |
| 128 | Minneapolis, MN | (0.8) | 201 | Reno, NV** | (4.1) | NA | Toledo, OH*** | NA |
| 123 | Miramar, FL | (0.5) | 62 | Renton, WA | 3.9 | 246 | Toms River Twnshp, NJ** | (5.5) |
| 405 | Mission Viejo, CA** | (16.8) | 425 | Rialto, CA** | (23.5) | 265 | Topeka, KS** | (6.2) |
| 3 | Mission, TX** | 20.7 | 351 | Richardson, TX** | (10.2) | 70 | Torrance, CA** | 3.4 |
| 27 | Mobile, AL | 8.9 | 220 | Richmond, CA** | (4.8) | 68 | Tracy, CA** | 3.5 |
| 322 | Modesto, CA** | (8.9) | 268 | Richmond, VA | (6.3) | 378 | Trenton, NJ** | (13.0) |
| 317 | Moreno Valley, CA** | (8.7) | 178 | Riverside, CA** | (3.1) | 300 | Troy, MI | (7.7) |
| 6 | Mountain View, CA** | 16.1 | 303 | Roanoke, VA | (7.9) | NA | Tucson, AZ*** | NA |
| 154 | Murfreesboro, TN | (1.9) | NA | Rochester, MN*** | NA | 95 | Tulsa, OK** | 1.3 |
| 231 | Murrieta, CA** | (5.0) | 307 | Rochester, NY** | (8.3) | 112 | Tuscaloosa, AL | 0.1 |
| 392 | Nampa, ID | (14.2) | 220 | Rockford, IL | (4.8) | 375 | Tustin, CA** | (12.6) |
| 354 | Napa, CA** | (10.7) | 156 | Roseville, CA** | (2.0) | 357 | Tyler, TX | (10.9) |
| 341 | Naperville, IL** | (9.6) | 5 | Roswell, GA** | 17.4 | 181 | Upland, CA** | (3.3) |
| 246 | Nashua, NH | (5.5) | 331 | Round Rock, TX** | (9.2) | 290 | Upper Darby Twnshp, PA | (7.4) |
| 342 | Nashville, TN | (9.7) | 353 | Sacramento, CA** | (10.4) | 106 | Vacaville, CA** | 0.5 |
| 36 | New Bedford, MA | 7.3 | 123 | Salem, OR | (0.5) | 112 | Vallejo, CA** | 0.1 |
| 319 | New Haven, CT | (8.8) | 47 | Salinas, CA** | 6.2 | 302 | Vancouver, WA | (7.8) |
| 97 | New Orleans, LA** | 1.1 | 186 | Salt Lake City, UT | (3.5) | 78 | Ventura, CA** | 2.5 |
| 148 | New Rochelle, NY** | (1.7) | NA | San Angelo, TX*** | NA | 315 | Victorville, CA** | (8.6) |
| 156 | New York, NY** | (2.0) | 163 | San Antonio, TX** | (2.3) | 220 | Virginia Beach, VA | (4.8) |
| 279 | Newark, NJ** | (6.8) | 331 | San Bernardino, CA** | (9.2) | 364 | Visalia, CA** | (12.0) |
| 141 | Newport Beach, CA** | (1.3) | 141 | San Diego, CA** | (1.3) | 54 | Vista, CA** | 5.3 |
| 140 | Newport News, VA | (1.2) | 1 | San Francisco, CA** | 22.0 | 298 | Waco, TX** | (7.6) |
| 335 | Newton, MA | (9.3) | 362 | San Jose, CA** | (11.7) | 281 | Warren, MI | (6.9) |
| 218 | Norfolk, VA | (4.7) | 33 | San Leandro, CA** | 7.5 | 209 | Warwick, RI | (4.4) |
| 255 | Norman, OK** | (5.7) | 317 | San Marcos, CA** | (8.7) | 119 | Washington, DC | (0.2) |
| 167 | North Charleston, SC | (2.5) | 44 | San Mateo, CA** | 6.6 | 100 | Waterbury, CT** | 0.8 |
| 49 | North Las Vegas, NV** | 5.8 | 190 | Sandy Springs, GA** | (3.6) | 246 | Waukegan, IL** | (5.5) |
| 366 | Norwalk, CA** | (12.2) | 23 | Sandy, UT | 10.0 | 76 | West Covina, CA** | 2.7 |
| 154 | Norwalk, CT | (1.9) | 384 | Santa Ana, CA** | (13.6) | 354 | West Palm Beach, FL | (10.7) |
| 209 | Oakland, CA** | (4.4) | 378 | Santa Barbara, CA** | (13.0) | 4 | West Valley, UT | 18.1 |
| 92 | Oceanside, CA** | 1.4 | 345 | Santa Clara, CA** | (10.0) | 92 | Westland, MI | 1.4 |
| 30 | Odessa, TX** | 8.3 | 400 | Santa Clarita, CA** | (15.2) | 375 | Westminster, CA** | (12.6) |
| 241 | O'Fallon, MO | (5.3) | 28 | Santa Maria, CA** | 8.8 | 81 | Westminster, CO | 2.2 |
| 75 | Ogden, UT | 2.8 | 104 | Santa Monica, CA** | 0.6 | 225 | Whittier, CA** | (4.9) |
| 342 | Oklahoma City, OK** | (9.7) | 340 | Santa Rosa, CA** | (9.5) | 322 | Wichita Falls, TX** | (8.9) |
| 344 | Olathe, KS** | (9.9) | 123 | Savannah, GA** | (0.5) | 120 | Wichita, KS | (0.3) |
| 162 | Omaha, NE** | (2.2) | 237 | Scottsdale, AZ** | (5.2) | 262 | Wilmington, NC** | (5.9) |
| 360 | Ontario, CA** | (11.4) | 374 | Scranton, PA | (12.5) | 281 | Winston-Salem, NC** | (6.9) |
| 389 | Orange, CA** | (14.0) | 29 | Seattle, WA | 8.4 | 60 | Woodbridge Twnshp, NJ** | 4.3 |
| 194 | Orem, UT** | (3.9) | 192 | Shreveport, LA** | (3.8) | 170 | Worcester, MA | (2.6) |
| 171 | Orlando, FL | (2.7) | 351 | Simi Valley, CA** | (10.2) | 417 | Yakima, WA | (18.8) |
| 393 | Overland Park, KS** | (14.3) | 38 | Sioux City, IA | 7.1 | 307 | Yonkers, NY** | (8.3) |
| 1 | Oxnard, CA** | 22.0 | 194 | Sioux Falls, SD | (3.9) | 82 | Yuma, AZ | 2.1 |
| 419 | Palm Bay, FL | (19.8) | 396 | Somerville, MA | (14.5) | | | |
| 180 | Palmdale, CA** | (3.2) | 77 | South Bend, IN | 2.6 | | | |

Source: CQ Press using reported data from the F.B.I. "Crime in the United States 2013"

*Includes murder, rape, robbery, aggravated assault, burglary, larceny-theft, and motor vehicle theft.

**Figures for these cities are based on the previous (legacy) definition of rape. See note on page vii.

***Not available.

# 43. Percent Change in Crime Rate: 2012 to 2013 (continued)
## National Percent Change = 4.8% Decrease*

| RANK | CITY | % CHANGE | RANK | CITY | % CHANGE | RANK | CITY | % CHANGE |
|---|---|---|---|---|---|---|---|---|
| 1 | Oxnard, CA** | 22.0 | 75 | Ogden, UT | 2.8 | 148 | Midland, TX** | (1.7) |
| 1 | San Francisco, CA** | 22.0 | 76 | West Covina, CA** | 2.7 | 148 | New Rochelle, NY** | (1.7) |
| 3 | Mission, TX** | 20.7 | 77 | South Bend, IN | 2.6 | 151 | Columbia, MO | (1.8) |
| 4 | West Valley, UT | 18.1 | 78 | Lakeland, FL | 2.5 | 151 | Hayward, CA** | (1.8) |
| 5 | Roswell, GA** | 17.4 | 78 | Ventura, CA** | 2.5 | 151 | Stamford, CT | (1.8) |
| 6 | Mountain View, CA** | 16.1 | 80 | Springfield, MA | 2.4 | 154 | Murfreesboro, TN | (1.9) |
| 7 | Hoover, AL | 15.3 | 81 | Westminster, CO | 2.2 | 154 | Norwalk, CT | (1.9) |
| 8 | Billings, MT | 13.6 | 82 | Albuquerque, NM** | 2.1 | 156 | Alexandria, VA | (2.0) |
| 8 | Provo, UT | 13.6 | 82 | Yuma, AZ | 2.1 | 156 | Henderson, NV** | (2.0) |
| 10 | Hemet, CA** | 12.6 | 84 | Corpus Christi, TX** | 2.0 | 156 | New York, NY** | (2.0) |
| 11 | Temecula, CA** | 12.3 | 84 | Fort Worth, TX | 2.0 | 156 | Phoenix, AZ** | (2.0) |
| 12 | Portsmouth, VA | 12.2 | 86 | Cary, NC** | 1.9 | 156 | Roseville, CA** | (2.0) |
| 13 | El Cajon, CA** | 12.0 | 86 | Houston, TX** | 1.9 | 161 | Livermore, CA** | (2.1) |
| 14 | Fargo, ND | 11.9 | 86 | Lakewood, CO | 1.9 | 162 | Omaha, NE** | (2.2) |
| 15 | Spokane Valley, WA** | 11.3 | 89 | Chula Vista, CA** | 1.7 | 163 | Des Moines, IA | (2.3) |
| 16 | Anchorage, AK | 11.0 | 89 | McKinney, TX | 1.7 | 163 | San Antonio, TX** | (2.3) |
| 16 | Pueblo, CO | 11.0 | 89 | Springfield, MO | 1.7 | 165 | Beaverton, OR** | (2.4) |
| 18 | Pasadena, CA** | 10.8 | 92 | Greenville, NC** | 1.4 | 165 | Grand Prairie, TX** | (2.4) |
| 19 | Lawrence, MA** | 10.7 | 92 | Oceanside, CA** | 1.4 | 167 | Laredo, TX** | (2.5) |
| 20 | Lafayette, LA** | 10.6 | 92 | Westland, MI | 1.4 | 167 | Madison, WI | (2.5) |
| 21 | Chico, CA** | 10.1 | 95 | Greeley, CO | 1.3 | 167 | North Charleston, SC | (2.5) |
| 21 | Manchester, NH | 10.1 | 95 | Tulsa, OK** | 1.3 | 170 | Worcester, MA | (2.6) |
| 23 | Sandy, UT | 10.0 | 97 | New Orleans, LA** | 1.1 | 171 | Huntsville, AL | (2.7) |
| 24 | Gary, IN** | 9.9 | 98 | High Point, NC** | 1.0 | 171 | Lawton, OK** | (2.7) |
| 25 | Bellevue, WA** | 9.7 | 98 | Redwood City, CA** | 1.0 | 171 | Orlando, FL | (2.7) |
| 25 | Johns Creek, GA** | 9.7 | 100 | Arvada, CO | 0.8 | 174 | Gilbert, AZ | (2.9) |
| 27 | Mobile, AL | 8.9 | 100 | Las Vegas, NV** | 0.8 | 174 | Lynchburg, VA | (2.9) |
| 28 | Santa Maria, CA** | 8.8 | 100 | Waterbury, CT** | 0.8 | 176 | Dearborn, MI | (3.0) |
| 29 | Seattle, WA | 8.4 | 103 | Bethlehem, PA | 0.7 | 176 | Miami Gardens, FL | (3.0) |
| 30 | Abilene, TX** | 8.3 | 104 | Daly City, CA** | 0.6 | 178 | Boulder, CO | (3.1) |
| 30 | Odessa, TX** | 8.3 | 104 | Santa Monica, CA** | 0.6 | 178 | Riverside, CA** | (3.1) |
| 32 | Medford, OR | 8.1 | 106 | Vacaville, CA** | 0.5 | 180 | Palmdale, CA** | (3.2) |
| 33 | San Leandro, CA** | 7.5 | 107 | Mesquite, TX** | 0.4 | 181 | Kent, WA | (3.3) |
| 33 | St. George, UT | 7.5 | 108 | Federal Way, WA | 0.3 | 181 | Sterling Heights, MI | (3.3) |
| 35 | Columbus, GA** | 7.4 | 108 | Lakewood, CA** | 0.3 | 181 | Upland, CA** | (3.3) |
| 36 | New Bedford, MA | 7.3 | 110 | Cedar Rapids, IA | 0.2 | 184 | Hammond, IN** | (3.4) |
| 37 | Lansing, MI | 7.2 | 110 | Escondido, CA** | 0.2 | 184 | Kansas City, MO | (3.4) |
| 38 | Sioux City, IA | 7.1 | 112 | Colorado Springs, CO | 0.1 | 186 | Brick Twnshp, NJ** | (3.5) |
| 39 | Lowell, MA | 7.0 | 112 | Tuscaloosa, AL | 0.1 | 186 | Hampton, VA | (3.5) |
| 40 | Beaumont, TX** | 6.9 | 112 | Vallejo, CA** | 0.1 | 186 | Irving, TX** | (3.5) |
| 40 | Pearland, TX | 6.9 | 115 | Inglewood, CA** | 0.0 | 186 | Salt Lake City, UT | (3.5) |
| 42 | League City, TX** | 6.8 | 116 | Clarksville, TN | (0.1) | 190 | Sandy Springs, GA** | (3.6) |
| 42 | Spokane, WA** | 6.8 | 116 | Detroit, MI | (0.1) | 191 | Hillsboro, OR** | (3.7) |
| 44 | Miami Beach, FL | 6.6 | 116 | Melbourne, FL | (0.1) | 192 | Lynn, MA | (3.8) |
| 44 | San Mateo, CA** | 6.6 | 119 | Washington, DC | (0.2) | 192 | Shreveport, LA** | (3.8) |
| 46 | St. Petersburg, FL | 6.5 | 120 | Wichita, KS | (0.3) | 194 | Garland, TX** | (3.9) |
| 47 | Everett, WA** | 6.2 | 121 | Hawthorne, CA** | (0.4) | 194 | Orem, UT** | (3.9) |
| 47 | Salinas, CA** | 6.2 | 121 | Sparks, NV** | (0.4) | 194 | Sioux Falls, SD | (3.9) |
| 49 | North Las Vegas, NV** | 5.8 | 123 | Independence, MO | (0.5) | 197 | Cheektowaga, NY** | (4.0) |
| 49 | Syracuse, NY** | 5.8 | 123 | Miramar, FL | (0.5) | 197 | Fishers, IN** | (4.0) |
| 51 | Fairfield, CA** | 5.6 | 123 | Salem, OR | (0.5) | 197 | Gainesville, FL | (4.0) |
| 52 | Chino Hills, CA** | 5.5 | 123 | Savannah, GA** | (0.5) | 197 | Los Angeles, CA** | (4.0) |
| 53 | Brockton, MA | 5.4 | 127 | Alameda, CA** | (0.6) | 201 | El Monte, CA** | (4.1) |
| 54 | Vista, CA** | 5.3 | 128 | Clearwater, FL | (0.8) | 201 | Reno, NV** | (4.1) |
| 55 | Kennewick, WA | 5.1 | 128 | Minneapolis, MN | (0.8) | 203 | Chesapeake, VA | (4.2) |
| 56 | Buena Park, CA** | 4.9 | 128 | Providence, RI | (0.8) | 203 | Clifton, NJ** | (4.2) |
| 57 | Bloomington, IL** | 4.7 | 128 | Sunrise, FL | (0.8) | 203 | Pittsburgh, PA | (4.2) |
| 57 | Compton, CA** | 4.7 | 132 | Arlington, TX** | (0.9) | 206 | Bryan, TX** | (4.3) |
| 59 | Baltimore, MD** | 4.6 | 132 | McAllen, TX** | (0.9) | 206 | Dallas, TX** | (4.3) |
| 60 | Aurora, CO | 4.3 | 134 | Fayetteville, AR | (1.0) | 206 | Fort Lauderdale, FL | (4.3) |
| 60 | Woodbridge Twnshp, NJ** | 4.3 | 135 | Clarkstown, NY** | (1.1) | 209 | Fullerton, CA** | (4.4) |
| 62 | Renton, WA | 3.9 | 135 | Denver, CO | (1.1) | 209 | Indianapolis, IN | (4.4) |
| 63 | Davenport, IA | 3.8 | 135 | Lancaster, CA** | (1.1) | 209 | Indio, CA** | (4.4) |
| 63 | Tacoma, WA | 3.8 | 135 | Little Rock, AR | (1.1) | 209 | Memphis, TN | (4.4) |
| 65 | Concord, CA** | 3.7 | 135 | Thornton, CO | (1.1) | 209 | Oakland, CA** | (4.4) |
| 65 | Fort Wayne, IN | 3.7 | 140 | Newport News, VA | (1.2) | 209 | Warwick, RI | (4.4) |
| 67 | Sugar Land, TX** | 3.6 | 141 | Louisville, KY** | (1.3) | 215 | Burbank, CA** | (4.6) |
| 68 | South Gate, CA** | 3.5 | 141 | Newport Beach, CA** | (1.3) | 215 | Fort Smith, AR | (4.6) |
| 68 | Tracy, CA** | 3.5 | 141 | San Diego, CA** | (1.3) | 215 | Jacksonville, FL | (4.6) |
| 70 | Torrance, CA** | 3.4 | 144 | Pasadena, CA** | (1.4) | 218 | Norfolk, VA | (4.7) |
| 71 | Macon, GA** | 3.2 | 144 | Tempe, AZ** | (1.4) | 218 | Portland, OR** | (4.7) |
| 72 | Bellflower, CA** | 3.0 | 146 | Decatur, IL** | (1.6) | 220 | Fayetteville, NC** | (4.8) |
| 72 | Quincy, MA | 3.0 | 146 | Eugene, OR | (1.6) | 220 | Las Cruces, NM** | (4.8) |
| 74 | Glendale, CA** | 2.9 | 148 | Cleveland, OH | (1.7) | 220 | Richmond, CA** | (4.8) |

| RANK | CITY | % CHANGE |
|---|---|---|
| 220 | Rockford, IL | (4.8) |
| 220 | Virginia Beach, VA | (4.8) |
| 225 | Akron, OH | (4.9) |
| 225 | Albany, NY** | (4.9) |
| 225 | Cincinnati, OH | (4.9) |
| 225 | Gresham, OR** | (4.9) |
| 225 | Jurupa Valley, CA** | (4.9) |
| 225 | Whittier, CA** | (4.9) |
| 231 | Berkeley, CA** | (5.0) |
| 231 | Boston, MA** | (5.0) |
| 231 | Evansville, IN** | (5.0) |
| 231 | Murrieta, CA** | (5.0) |
| 235 | Birmingham, AL | (5.1) |
| 235 | Clinton Twnshp, MI | (5.1) |
| 237 | Buffalo, NY** | (5.2) |
| 237 | Carlsbad, CA** | (5.2) |
| 237 | Hamilton Twnshp, NJ** | (5.2) |
| 237 | Scottsdale, AZ** | (5.2) |
| 241 | Davie, FL | (5.3) |
| 241 | O'Fallon, MO | (5.3) |
| 243 | Chino, CA** | (5.4) |
| 243 | Pembroke Pines, FL | (5.4) |
| 243 | St. Louis, MO | (5.4) |
| 246 | Colonie, NY** | (5.5) |
| 246 | Deerfield Beach, FL | (5.5) |
| 246 | Miami, FL | (5.5) |
| 246 | Nashua, NH | (5.5) |
| 246 | Toms River Twnshp, NJ** | (5.5) |
| 246 | Waukegan, IL** | (5.5) |
| 252 | Albany, GA** | (5.6) |
| 252 | Anaheim, CA** | (5.6) |
| 252 | Elgin, IL** | (5.6) |
| 255 | Allentown, PA | (5.7) |
| 255 | Greensboro, NC** | (5.7) |
| 255 | Kansas City, KS** | (5.7) |
| 255 | Largo, FL | (5.7) |
| 255 | Longmont, CO | (5.7) |
| 255 | Norman, OK** | (5.7) |
| 261 | Amherst, NY** | (5.8) |
| 262 | Brownsville, TX** | (5.9) |
| 262 | Racine, WI** | (5.9) |
| 262 | Wilmington, NC** | (5.9) |
| 265 | Lubbock, TX** | (6.2) |
| 265 | Stockton, CA** | (6.2) |
| 265 | Topeka, KS** | (6.2) |
| 268 | Livonia, MI | (6.3) |
| 268 | Richmond, VA | (6.3) |
| 270 | St. Joseph, MO | (6.4) |
| 271 | Baton Rouge, LA** | (6.5) |
| 271 | Hartford, CT** | (6.5) |
| 273 | Alhambra, CA** | (6.6) |
| 273 | Erie, PA | (6.6) |
| 273 | Fremont, CA** | (6.6) |
| 273 | Philadelphia, PA | (6.6) |
| 273 | Raleigh, NC** | (6.6) |
| 278 | El Paso, TX** | (6.7) |
| 279 | Bakersfield, CA** | (6.8) |
| 279 | Newark, NJ** | (6.8) |
| 281 | Cranston, RI | (6.9) |
| 281 | Warren, MI | (6.9) |
| 281 | Winston-Salem, NC** | (6.9) |
| 284 | Cape Coral, FL | (7.0) |
| 285 | Frisco, TX | (7.1) |
| 285 | St. Paul, MN | (7.1) |
| 287 | Hesperia, CA** | (7.2) |
| 288 | Amarillo, TX | (7.3) |
| 288 | Downey, CA** | (7.3) |
| 290 | Atlanta, GA** | (7.4) |
| 290 | Austin, TX** | (7.4) |
| 290 | Knoxville, TN | (7.4) |
| 290 | Paterson, NJ** | (7.4) |
| 290 | Upper Darby Twnshp, PA | (7.4) |
| 295 | Cambridge, MA | (7.5) |
| 295 | Edmond, OK** | (7.5) |
| 295 | Milwaukee, WI | (7.5) |
| 298 | Ann Arbor, MI | (7.6) |
| 298 | Waco, TX** | (7.6) |
| 300 | Grand Rapids, MI | (7.7) |
| 300 | Troy, MI | (7.7) |
| 302 | Vancouver, WA | (7.8) |
| 303 | Plano, TX | (7.9) |
| 303 | Roanoke, VA | (7.9) |
| 305 | Irvine, CA** | (8.2) |
| 305 | Killeen, TX** | (8.2) |
| 307 | Green Bay, WI | (8.3) |
| 307 | Rochester, NY** | (8.3) |
| 307 | Sunnyvale, CA** | (8.3) |
| 307 | Tallahassee, FL | (8.3) |
| 307 | Yonkers, NY** | (8.3) |
| 312 | Dayton, OH | (8.4) |
| 312 | Fort Collins, CO | (8.4) |
| 314 | Greece, NY** | (8.5) |
| 315 | Mesa, AZ** | (8.6) |
| 315 | Victorville, CA** | (8.6) |
| 317 | Moreno Valley, CA** | (8.7) |
| 317 | San Marcos, CA** | (8.7) |
| 319 | Antioch, CA** | (8.8) |
| 319 | Long Beach, CA** | (8.8) |
| 319 | New Haven, CT | (8.8) |
| 322 | Broken Arrow, OK** | (8.9) |
| 322 | Hialeah, FL | (8.9) |
| 322 | Modesto, CA** | (8.9) |
| 322 | Wichita Falls, TX** | (8.9) |
| 326 | Charlotte, NC** | (9.0) |
| 326 | Huntington Beach, CA** | (9.0) |
| 326 | Lakewood Twnshp, NJ** | (9.0) |
| 326 | Lincoln, NE** | (9.0) |
| 330 | Fall River, MA | (9.1) |
| 331 | Charleston, SC | (9.2) |
| 331 | Plantation, FL | (9.2) |
| 331 | Round Rock, TX** | (9.2) |
| 331 | San Bernardino, CA** | (9.2) |
| 335 | Coral Springs, FL | (9.3) |
| 335 | Lee's Summit, MO | (9.3) |
| 335 | Lexington, KY | (9.3) |
| 335 | Newton, MA | (9.3) |
| 339 | Evanston, IL** | (9.4) |
| 340 | Santa Rosa, CA** | (9.5) |
| 341 | Naperville, IL** | (9.6) |
| 342 | Nashville, TN | (9.7) |
| 342 | Oklahoma City, OK** | (9.7) |
| 344 | Olathe, KS** | (9.9) |
| 345 | Glendale, AZ** | (10.0) |
| 345 | Jackson, MS** | (10.0) |
| 345 | Santa Clara, CA** | (10.0) |
| 345 | Tampa, FL | (10.0) |
| 349 | Carmel, IN** | (10.1) |
| 349 | Lawrence, KS | (10.1) |
| 351 | Richardson, TX** | (10.2) |
| 351 | Simi Valley, CA** | (10.2) |
| 353 | Sacramento, CA** | (10.4) |
| 354 | Napa, CA** | (10.7) |
| 354 | West Palm Beach, FL | (10.7) |
| 356 | Boise, ID | (10.8) |
| 357 | Tyler, TX | (10.9) |
| 358 | Pompano Beach, FL | (11.0) |
| 359 | Fontana, CA** | (11.1) |
| 360 | Ontario, CA** | (11.4) |
| 361 | Boca Raton, FL | (11.6) |
| 362 | San Jose, CA** | (11.7) |
| 363 | College Station, TX** | (11.8) |
| 364 | Costa Mesa, CA** | (12.0) |
| 364 | Visalia, CA** | (12.0) |
| 366 | Chandler, AZ** | (12.2) |
| 366 | Farmington Hills, MI | (12.2) |
| 366 | Norwalk, CA** | (12.2) |
| 369 | Edinburg, TX** | (12.3) |
| 369 | Elk Grove, CA** | (12.3) |
| 369 | Fresno, CA** | (12.3) |
| 372 | Springfield, IL** | (12.4) |
| 372 | Thousand Oaks, CA** | (12.4) |
| 374 | Scranton, PA | (12.5) |
| 375 | Tustin, CA** | (12.6) |
| 375 | Westminster, CA** | (12.6) |
| 377 | Rancho Cucamon., CA** | (12.8) |
| 378 | Peoria, IL** | (13.0) |
| 378 | Santa Barbara, CA** | (13.0) |
| 378 | Trenton, NJ** | (13.0) |
| 381 | Joliet, IL** | (13.1) |
| 382 | Jersey City, NJ** | (13.2) |
| 383 | Athens-Clarke, GA** | (13.4) |
| 384 | Santa Ana, CA** | (13.6) |
| 385 | Elizabeth, NJ** | (13.7) |
| 385 | Garden Grove, CA** | (13.7) |
| 387 | Aurora, IL** | (13.8) |
| 387 | Hollywood, FL | (13.8) |
| 389 | Baldwin Park, CA** | (14.0) |
| 389 | Citrus Heights, CA** | (14.0) |
| 389 | Orange, CA** | (14.0) |
| 392 | Nampa, ID | (14.2) |
| 393 | Overland Park, KS** | (14.3) |
| 393 | Pomona, CA** | (14.3) |
| 393 | Redding, CA** | (14.3) |
| 396 | Carrollton, TX** | (14.5) |
| 396 | Somerville, MA | (14.5) |
| 398 | Edison Twnshp, NJ** | (14.9) |
| 399 | Menifee, CA** | (15.1) |
| 400 | Santa Clarita, CA** | (15.2) |
| 401 | Surprise, AZ** | (15.6) |
| 402 | Bridgeport, CT** | (15.8) |
| 403 | Cicero, IL** | (16.2) |
| 404 | Champaign, IL** | (16.6) |
| 405 | Kenosha, WI** | (16.8) |
| 405 | Mission Viejo, CA** | (16.8) |
| 407 | Clovis, CA** | (16.9) |
| 407 | Longview, TX | (16.9) |
| 409 | Centennial, CO | (17.0) |
| 410 | Allen, TX | (17.1) |
| 411 | Denton, TX | (17.2) |
| 412 | Arlington Heights, IL** | (17.9) |
| 413 | Carson, CA** | (18.1) |
| 414 | Bloomington, IN** | (18.2) |
| 415 | Meridian, ID | (18.4) |
| 416 | Corona, CA** | (18.7) |
| 417 | Yakima, WA | (18.8) |
| 418 | Peoria, AZ** | (19.5) |
| 419 | Danbury, CT** | (19.8) |
| 419 | Palm Bay, FL | (19.8) |
| 419 | Reading, PA | (19.8) |
| 422 | Port St. Lucie, FL | (20.0) |
| 423 | Ramapo, NY** | (23.2) |
| 424 | Lake Forest, CA** | (23.3) |
| 425 | Rialto, CA** | (23.5) |
| 426 | Flint, MI | (25.5) |
| 427 | Merced, CA** | (35.2) |
| NA | Bend, OR*** | NA |
| NA | Bloomington, MN*** | NA |
| NA | Brooklyn Park, MN*** | NA |
| NA | Canton Twnshp, MI*** | NA |
| NA | Chattanooga, TN*** | NA |
| NA | Chicago, IL*** | NA |
| NA | Columbia, SC*** | NA |
| NA | Concord, NC*** | NA |
| NA | Duluth, MN*** | NA |
| NA | Lewisville, TX*** | NA |
| NA | Rochester, MN*** | NA |
| NA | San Angelo, TX*** | NA |
| NA | Suffolk, VA*** | NA |
| NA | Toledo, OH*** | NA |
| NA | Tucson, AZ*** | NA |

Source: CQ Press using reported data from the F.B.I. "Crime in the United States 2013"

*Includes murder, rape, robbery, aggravated assault, burglary, larceny-theft, and motor vehicle theft.

**Figures for these cities are based on the previous (legacy) definition of rape. See note on page vii.

***Not available.

# 44. Percent Change in Crime Rate: 2009 to 2013
## National Percent Change = 10.8% Decrease*

| RANK | CITY | % CHANGE | RANK | CITY | % CHANGE | RANK | CITY | % CHANGE |
|---|---|---|---|---|---|---|---|---|
| 154 | Abilene, TX** | (6.7) | 47 | Chino, CA** | 5.4 | 165 | Fullerton, CA** | (7.7) |
| 146 | Akron, OH | (5.8) | 245 | Chula Vista, CA** | (13.8) | 397 | Gainesville, FL | (30.1) |
| 216 | Alameda, CA** | (11.7) | NA | Cicero, IL*** | NA | 140 | Garden Grove, CA** | (5.4) |
| 140 | Albany, GA** | (5.4) | 159 | Cincinnati, OH | (7.3) | 264 | Garland, TX** | (15.0) |
| 216 | Albany, NY** | (11.7) | 381 | Citrus Heights, CA** | (27.3) | 2 | Gary, IN** | 66.3 |
| 90 | Albuquerque, NM** | (0.3) | 345 | Clarkstown, NY** | (22.4) | 331 | Gilbert, AZ | (20.8) |
| 213 | Alexandria, VA | (11.4) | 353 | Clarksville, TN | (23.7) | 15 | Glendale, AZ** | 16.2 |
| 161 | Alhambra, CA** | (7.4) | 267 | Clearwater, FL | (15.4) | 274 | Glendale, CA** | (15.9) |
| 368 | Allentown, PA | (26.0) | 44 | Cleveland, OH | 5.9 | 410 | Grand Prairie, TX** | (40.0) |
| 366 | Allen, TX | (25.2) | 293 | Clifton, NJ** | (17.5) | 382 | Grand Rapids, MI | (27.4) |
| 386 | Amarillo, TX | (28.2) | 175 | Clinton Twnshp, MI | (8.3) | 229 | Greece, NY** | (12.6) |
| 173 | Amherst, NY** | (8.1) | 88 | Clovis, CA** | 0.0 | 81 | Greeley, CO | 0.6 |
| 19 | Anaheim, CA** | 13.9 | 406 | College Station, TX** | (34.0) | 137 | Green Bay, WI | (5.3) |
| 39 | Anchorage, AK | 6.9 | 231 | Colonie, NY** | (12.7) | 400 | Greensboro, NC** | (31.7) |
| 270 | Ann Arbor, MI | (15.7) | 25 | Colorado Springs, CO | 10.7 | NA | Greenville, NC*** | NA |
| 5 | Antioch, CA** | 44.3 | 117 | Columbia, MO | (3.0) | 26 | Gresham, OR** | 10.1 |
| NA | Arlington Heights, IL*** | NA | 128 | Columbia, SC | (4.2) | 28 | Hamilton Twnshp, NJ** | 9.9 |
| 371 | Arlington, TX** | (26.2) | 333 | Columbus, GA** | (21.1) | 282 | Hammond, IN** | (17.0) |
| 130 | Arvada, CO | (4.5) | 315 | Compton, CA** | (19.6) | 202 | Hampton, VA | (10.6) |
| 398 | Athens-Clarke, GA** | (30.2) | 37 | Concord, CA** | 7.7 | 287 | Hartford, CT** | (17.1) |
| 93 | Atlanta, GA** | (0.5) | 409 | Concord, NC** | (37.2) | 105 | Hawthorne, CA** | (1.5) |
| 90 | Aurora, CO | (0.3) | 258 | Coral Springs, FL | (14.6) | 93 | Hayward, CA** | (0.5) |
| NA | Aurora, IL*** | NA | 262 | Corona, CA** | (14.8) | 11 | Hemet, CA** | 21.6 |
| 349 | Austin, TX** | (23.0) | 303 | Corpus Christi, TX** | (18.2) | 121 | Henderson, NV** | (3.3) |
| 122 | Bakersfield, CA** | (3.6) | 66 | Costa Mesa, CA** | 2.8 | 8 | Hesperia, CA** | 32.1 |
| 298 | Baldwin Park, CA** | (17.9) | 245 | Cranston, RI | (13.8) | 388 | Hialeah, FL | (28.5) |
| 54 | Baltimore, MD** | 4.4 | 352 | Dallas, TX** | (23.6) | 308 | High Point, NC** | (18.8) |
| 325 | Baton Rouge, LA** | (20.3) | 88 | Daly City, CA** | 0.0 | 21 | Hillsboro, OR** | 13.5 |
| 144 | Beaumont, TX** | (5.6) | 338 | Danbury, CT** | (21.6) | 155 | Hollywood, FL | (6.9) |
| 203 | Beaverton, OR** | (10.8) | 290 | Davenport, IA | (17.4) | 124 | Hoover, AL | (3.9) |
| 117 | Bellevue, WA** | (3.0) | 321 | Davie, FL | (19.8) | 149 | Houston, TX** | (6.1) |
| 266 | Bellflower, CA** | (15.3) | 174 | Dayton, OH | (8.2) | 47 | Huntington Beach, CA** | 5.4 |
| 22 | Bend, OR | 12.9 | 404 | Dearborn, MI | (33.3) | 140 | Huntsville, AL | (5.4) |
| 377 | Berkeley, CA** | (27.0) | NA | Decatur, IL*** | NA | 81 | Independence, MO | 0.6 |
| 108 | Bethlehem, PA | (1.8) | NA | Deerfield Beach, FL*** | NA | 169 | Indianapolis, IN | (7.8) |
| 12 | Billings, MT | 20.1 | 224 | Denton, TX | (12.2) | 33 | Indio, CA** | 8.7 |
| 235 | Birmingham, AL | (13.0) | 43 | Denver, CO | 6.3 | 252 | Inglewood, CA** | (14.2) |
| NA | Bloomington, IL*** | NA | 38 | Des Moines, IA | 7.4 | 102 | Irvine, CA** | (1.3) |
| 395 | Bloomington, IN** | (29.9) | 51 | Detroit, MI | 4.9 | 407 | Irving, TX** | (34.2) |
| NA | Bloomington, MN*** | NA | 254 | Downey, CA** | (14.4) | 359 | Jacksonville, FL | (24.5) |
| 384 | Boca Raton, FL | (27.7) | NA | Duluth, MN*** | NA | 329 | Jackson, MS** | (20.4) |
| 305 | Boise, ID | (18.3) | 278 | Edinburg, TX** | (16.1) | 339 | Jersey City, NJ** | (21.7) |
| 295 | Boston, MA** | (17.6) | 413 | Edison Twnshp, NJ** | (45.4) | 412 | Johns Creek, GA** | (43.9) |
| 72 | Boulder, CO | 2.0 | 254 | Edmond, OK** | (14.4) | NA | Joliet, IL*** | NA |
| 218 | Brick Twnshp, NJ** | (11.8) | 172 | El Cajon, CA** | (8.0) | NA | Jurupa Valley, CA*** | NA |
| 356 | Bridgeport, CT** | (24.1) | 358 | El Monte, CA** | (24.2) | 218 | Kansas City, KS** | (11.8) |
| 79 | Brockton, MA | 1.0 | 347 | El Paso, TX** | (22.9) | 123 | Kansas City, MO | (3.7) |
| 182 | Broken Arrow, OK** | (9.0) | NA | Elgin, IL*** | NA | 205 | Kennewick, WA | (11.0) |
| NA | Brooklyn Park, MN*** | NA | 388 | Elizabeth, NJ** | (28.5) | 310 | Kenosha, WI** | (19.1) |
| 317 | Brownsville, TX** | (19.7) | 368 | Elk Grove, CA** | (26.0) | 158 | Kent, WA | (7.2) |
| 414 | Bryan, TX** | (47.2) | 34 | Erie, PA | 8.2 | 342 | Killeen, TX** | (21.8) |
| 63 | Buena Park, CA** | 3.0 | 152 | Escondido, CA** | (6.5) | 130 | Knoxville, TN | (4.5) |
| 209 | Buffalo, NY** | (11.2) | 229 | Eugene, OR | (12.6) | 183 | Lafayette, LA** | (9.1) |
| 222 | Burbank, CA** | (12.1) | NA | Evanston, IL*** | NA | 306 | Lake Forest, CA** | (18.6) |
| 250 | Cambridge, MA | (14.1) | 42 | Evansville, IN** | 6.4 | 92 | Lakeland, FL | (0.4) |
| 356 | Canton Twnshp, MI | (24.1) | 187 | Everett, WA** | (9.5) | NA | Lakewood Twnshp, NJ*** | NA |
| 335 | Cape Coral, FL | (21.3) | 46 | Fairfield, CA** | 5.5 | 205 | Lakewood, CA** | (11.0) |
| 150 | Carlsbad, CA** | (6.4) | 346 | Fall River, MA | (22.5) | 60 | Lakewood, CO | 3.2 |
| 403 | Carmel, IN** | (33.0) | 214 | Fargo, ND | (11.6) | 197 | Lancaster, CA** | (10.2) |
| 378 | Carrollton, TX** | (27.1) | 394 | Farmington Hills, MI | (29.8) | 77 | Lansing, MI | 1.2 |
| 157 | Carson, CA** | (7.1) | 53 | Fayetteville, AR | 4.7 | 393 | Laredo, TX** | (29.7) |
| 178 | Cary, NC** | (8.5) | 343 | Fayetteville, NC** | (21.9) | 290 | Largo, FL | (17.4) |
| 262 | Cedar Rapids, IA | (14.8) | 77 | Federal Way, WA | 1.2 | 258 | Las Cruces, NM** | (14.6) |
| 303 | Centennial, CO | (18.2) | 56 | Fishers, IN** | 3.9 | 199 | Las Vegas, NV** | (10.3) |
| NA | Champaign, IL*** | NA | 325 | Flint, MI | (20.3) | 279 | Lawrence, KS | (16.2) |
| 307 | Chandler, AZ** | (18.7) | 252 | Fontana, CA** | (14.2) | 55 | Lawrence, MA** | 4.1 |
| 404 | Charleston, SC | (33.3) | 362 | Fort Collins, CO | (24.9) | 191 | Lawton, OK** | (10.0) |
| 364 | Charlotte, NC** | (25.0) | 96 | Fort Lauderdale, FL | (0.6) | 354 | League City, TX** | (23.8) |
| 191 | Chattanooga, TN | (10.0) | 207 | Fort Smith, AR | (11.1) | 287 | Lee's Summit, MO | (17.1) |
| 74 | Cheektowaga, NY** | 1.6 | 58 | Fort Wayne, IN | 3.6 | 312 | Lewisville, TX | (19.3) |
| 339 | Chesapeake, VA | (21.7) | 214 | Fort Worth, TX | (11.6) | 34 | Lexington, KY | 8.2 |
| NA | Chicago, IL*** | NA | 385 | Fremont, CA** | (27.8) | 221 | Lincoln, NE** | (12.0) |
| 58 | Chico, CA** | 3.6 | 100 | Fresno, CA** | (0.8) | 137 | Little Rock, AR | (5.3) |
| 242 | Chino Hills, CA** | (13.6) | 101 | Frisco, TX | (1.1) | 41 | Livermore, CA** | 6.7 |

| RANK | CITY | % CHANGE | RANK | CITY | % CHANGE | RANK | CITY | % CHANGE |
|---|---|---|---|---|---|---|---|---|
| 282 | Livonia, MI | (17.0) | 147 | Pasadena, CA** | (5.9) | 65 | South Gate, CA** | 2.9 |
| 127 | Long Beach, CA** | (4.1) | 163 | Pasadena, TX** | (7.5) | 336 | Sparks, NV** | (21.4) |
| 314 | Longmont, CO | (19.4) | 30 | Paterson, NJ** | 9.6 | 4 | Spokane Valley, WA** | 50.1 |
| 411 | Longview, TX | (41.1) | 224 | Pearland, TX | (12.2) | 6 | Spokane, WA** | 40.7 |
| 250 | Los Angeles, CA** | (14.1) | 401 | Pembroke Pines, FL | (32.1) | NA | Springfield, IL*** | NA |
| 96 | Louisville, KY** | (0.6) | 322 | Peoria, AZ** | (20.0) | 156 | Springfield, MA | (7.0) |
| NA | Lowell, MA*** | NA | NA | Peoria, IL*** | NA | 52 | Springfield, MO | 4.8 |
| 281 | Lubbock, TX** | (16.9) | 150 | Philadelphia, PA | (6.4) | 242 | Stamford, CT | (13.6) |
| 258 | Lynchburg, VA | (14.6) | 93 | Phoenix, AZ** | (0.5) | 145 | Sterling Heights, MI | (5.7) |
| 245 | Lynn, MA | (13.8) | 277 | Pittsburgh, PA | (16.0) | 134 | Stockton, CA** | (4.7) |
| 130 | Macon, GA** | (4.5) | 370 | Plano, TX | (26.1) | 23 | St. George, UT | 12.5 |
| 134 | Madison, WI | (4.7) | 317 | Plantation, FL | (19.7) | 27 | St. Joseph, MO | 10.0 |
| 17 | Manchester, NH | 14.4 | 60 | Pomona, CA** | 3.2 | 332 | St. Louis, MO | (21.0) |
| 408 | McAllen, TX** | (34.9) | 129 | Pompano Beach, FL | (4.4) | 165 | St. Paul, MN | (7.7) |
| 300 | McKinney, TX | (18.1) | 402 | Port St. Lucie, FL | (32.8) | 362 | St. Petersburg, FL | (24.9) |
| 3 | Medford, OR | 59.8 | 75 | Portland, OR** | 1.3 | 20 | Suffolk, VA | 13.8 |
| 280 | Melbourne, FL | (16.8) | 116 | Portsmouth, VA | (2.6) | 239 | Sugar Land, TX** | (13.3) |
| 238 | Memphis, TN | (13.2) | 136 | Providence, RI | (4.9) | 339 | Sunnyvale, CA** | (21.7) |
| 119 | Menifee, CA** | (3.2) | 106 | Provo, UT | (1.7) | 297 | Sunrise, FL | (17.7) |
| 241 | Merced, CA** | (13.5) | 1 | Pueblo, CO | 95.5 | 347 | Surprise, AZ** | (22.9) |
| 210 | Meridian, ID | (11.3) | 119 | Quincy, MA | (3.2) | 67 | Syracuse, NY** | 2.7 |
| 274 | Mesa, AZ** | (15.9) | 226 | Racine, WI** | (12.3) | 171 | Tacoma, WA | (7.9) |
| 261 | Mesquite, TX** | (14.7) | 210 | Raleigh, NC** | (11.3) | 234 | Tallahassee, FL | (12.9) |
| 50 | Miami Beach, FL | 5.2 | 365 | Ramapo, NY** | (25.1) | 399 | Tampa, FL | (31.0) |
| 360 | Miami Gardens, FL | (24.6) | 57 | Rancho Cucamon., CA** | 3.8 | 24 | Temecula, CA** | 11.4 |
| 81 | Miami, FL | 0.6 | 392 | Reading, PA | (29.0) | 161 | Tempe, AZ** | (7.4) |
| 386 | Midland, TX** | (28.2) | 14 | Redding, CA** | 19.1 | 299 | Thornton, CO | (18.0) |
| 254 | Milwaukee, WI | (14.4) | 179 | Redwood City, CA** | (8.7) | 254 | Thousand Oaks, CA** | (14.4) |
| 71 | Minneapolis, MN | 2.2 | 349 | Reno, NV** | (23.0) | NA | Toledo, OH*** | NA |
| 373 | Miramar, FL | (26.8) | 372 | Renton, WA | (26.3) | 18 | Toms River Twnshp, NJ** | 14.3 |
| 282 | Mission Viejo, CA** | (17.0) | 199 | Rialto, CA** | (10.3) | 165 | Topeka, KS** | (7.7) |
| 374 | Mission, TX** | (26.9) | 367 | Richardson, TX** | (25.5) | 185 | Torrance, CA** | (9.2) |
| 210 | Mobile, AL | (11.3) | 70 | Richmond, CA** | 2.5 | 242 | Tracy, CA** | (13.6) |
| 87 | Modesto, CA** | 0.2 | 126 | Richmond, VA | (4.0) | 203 | Trenton, NJ** | (10.8) |
| 159 | Moreno Valley, CA** | (7.3) | 73 | Riverside, CA** | 1.7 | 323 | Troy, MI | (20.1) |
| 323 | Mountain View, CA** | (20.1) | 282 | Roanoke, VA | (17.0) | NA | Tucson, AZ*** | NA |
| 337 | Murfreesboro, TN | (21.5) | NA | Rochester, MN*** | NA | 222 | Tulsa, OK** | (12.1) |
| 69 | Murrieta, CA** | 2.6 | 181 | Rochester, NY** | (8.9) | 227 | Tuscaloosa, AL | (12.4) |
| 186 | Nampa, ID | (9.3) | 199 | Rockford, IL | (10.3) | 113 | Tustin, CA** | (2.0) |
| 383 | Napa, CA** | (27.6) | 329 | Roseville, CA** | (20.4) | 395 | Tyler, TX | (29.9) |
| NA | Naperville, IL*** | NA | 282 | Roswell, GA** | (17.0) | NA | Upland, CA*** | NA |
| 165 | Nashua, NH | (7.7) | 187 | Round Rock, TX** | (9.5) | 300 | Upper Darby Twnshp, PA | (18.1) |
| 290 | Nashville, TN | (17.4) | 293 | Sacramento, CA** | (17.5) | 148 | Vacaville, CA** | (6.0) |
| 103 | New Bedford, MA | (1.4) | 45 | Salem, OR | 5.6 | 80 | Vallejo, CA** | 0.8 |
| 333 | New Haven, CT | (21.1) | 124 | Salinas, CA** | (3.9) | 112 | Vancouver, WA | (1.9) |
| 85 | New Orleans, LA** | 0.3 | 195 | Salt Lake City, UT | (10.1) | 13 | Ventura, CA** | 20.0 |
| 115 | New Rochelle, NY** | (2.4) | 325 | San Angelo, TX | (20.3) | 108 | Victorville, CA** | (1.8) |
| 60 | New York, NY** | 3.2 | 227 | San Antonio, TX** | (12.4) | 309 | Virginia Beach, VA | (18.9) |
| 29 | Newark, NJ** | 9.7 | 137 | San Bernardino, CA** | (5.3) | 191 | Visalia, CA** | (10.0) |
| 248 | Newport Beach, CA** | (13.9) | 143 | San Diego, CA** | (5.5) | 248 | Vista, CA** | (13.9) |
| NA | Newport News, VA*** | NA | 7 | San Francisco, CA** | 32.9 | 380 | Waco, TX** | (27.2) |
| 315 | Newton, MA | (19.6) | 47 | San Jose, CA** | 5.4 | 179 | Warren, MI | (8.7) |
| 317 | Norfolk, VA | (19.7) | 85 | San Leandro, CA** | 0.3 | 351 | Warwick, RI | (23.5) |
| 374 | Norman, OK** | (26.9) | 169 | San Marcos, CA** | (7.8) | 84 | Washington, DC | 0.4 |
| 267 | North Charleston, SC | (15.4) | 270 | San Mateo, CA** | (15.7) | 300 | Waterbury, CT** | (18.1) |
| 113 | North Las Vegas, NV** | (2.0) | 361 | Sandy Springs, GA** | (24.7) | NA | Waukegan, IL*** | NA |
| 108 | Norwalk, CA** | (1.8) | 176 | Sandy, UT | (8.4) | 108 | West Covina, CA** | (1.8) |
| 269 | Norwalk, CT | (15.5) | 189 | Santa Ana, CA** | (9.8) | 232 | West Palm Beach, FL | (12.8) |
| 10 | Oakland, CA** | 23.2 | 232 | Santa Barbara, CA** | (12.8) | 99 | West Valley, UT | (0.7) |
| 39 | Oceanside, CA** | 6.9 | 164 | Santa Clara, CA** | (7.6) | 183 | Westland, MI | (9.1) |
| 67 | Odessa, TX** | 2.7 | 391 | Santa Clarita, CA** | (28.6) | 63 | Westminster, CA** | 3.0 |
| 195 | O'Fallon, MO | (10.1) | 16 | Santa Maria, CA** | 14.5 | 264 | Westminster, CO | (15.0) |
| 103 | Ogden, UT | (1.4) | 106 | Santa Monica, CA** | (1.7) | 75 | Whittier, CA** | 1.3 |
| 220 | Oklahoma City, OK** | (11.9) | 378 | Santa Rosa, CA** | (27.1) | 344 | Wichita Falls, TX** | (22.0) |
| 317 | Olathe, KS** | (19.7) | 388 | Savannah, GA** | (28.5) | 96 | Wichita, KS | (0.6) |
| 32 | Omaha, NE** | 8.8 | 197 | Scottsdale, AZ** | (10.2) | 311 | Wilmington, NC** | (19.2) |
| 236 | Ontario, CA** | (13.1) | 325 | Scranton, PA | (20.3) | 190 | Winston-Salem, NC** | (9.9) |
| 191 | Orange, CA** | (10.0) | 133 | Seattle, WA | (4.6) | 270 | Woodbridge Twnshp, NJ** | (15.7) |
| 270 | Orem, UT** | (15.7) | 207 | Shreveport, LA** | (11.1) | 176 | Worcester, MA | (8.4) |
| 240 | Orlando, FL | (13.4) | 295 | Simi Valley, CA** | (17.6) | NA | Yakima, WA*** | NA |
| 354 | Overland Park, KS** | (23.8) | 9 | Sioux City, IA | 25.3 | 274 | Yonkers, NY** | (15.9) |
| 31 | Oxnard, CA** | 9.0 | 36 | Sioux Falls, SD | 7.8 | 153 | Yuma, AZ | (6.6) |
| 312 | Palm Bay, FL | (19.3) | 374 | Somerville, MA | (26.9) | | | |
| 236 | Palmdale, CA** | (13.1) | 289 | South Bend, IN | (17.2) | | | |

Source: CQ Press using reported data from the F.B.I. "Crime in the United States 2013"

*Includes murder, rape, robbery, aggravated assault, burglary, larceny-theft, and motor vehicle theft.

**Figures for these cities are based on the previous (legacy) definition of rape. See note on page vii.

***Not available.

# 44. Percent Change in Crime Rate: 2009 to 2013 (continued)
## National Percent Change = 10.8% Decrease*

| RANK | CITY | % CHANGE | RANK | CITY | % CHANGE | RANK | CITY | % CHANGE |
|---|---|---|---|---|---|---|---|---|
| 1 | Pueblo, CO | 95.5 | 75 | Portland, OR** | 1.3 | 149 | Houston, TX** | (6.1) |
| 2 | Gary, IN** | 66.3 | 75 | Whittier, CA** | 1.3 | 150 | Carlsbad, CA** | (6.4) |
| 3 | Medford, OR | 59.8 | 77 | Federal Way, WA | 1.2 | 150 | Philadelphia, PA | (6.4) |
| 4 | Spokane Valley, WA** | 50.1 | 77 | Lansing, MI | 1.2 | 152 | Escondido, CA** | (6.5) |
| 5 | Antioch, CA** | 44.3 | 79 | Brockton, MA | 1.0 | 153 | Yuma, AZ | (6.6) |
| 6 | Spokane, WA** | 40.7 | 80 | Vallejo, CA** | 0.8 | 154 | Abilene, TX** | (6.7) |
| 7 | San Francisco, CA** | 32.9 | 81 | Greeley, CO | 0.6 | 155 | Hollywood, FL | (6.9) |
| 8 | Hesperia, CA** | 32.1 | 81 | Independence, MO | 0.6 | 156 | Springfield, MA | (7.0) |
| 9 | Sioux City, IA | 25.3 | 81 | Miami, FL | 0.6 | 157 | Carson, CA** | (7.1) |
| 10 | Oakland, CA** | 23.2 | 84 | Washington, DC | 0.4 | 158 | Kent, WA | (7.2) |
| 11 | Hemet, CA** | 21.6 | 85 | New Orleans, LA** | 0.3 | 159 | Cincinnati, OH | (7.3) |
| 12 | Billings, MT | 20.1 | 85 | San Leandro, CA** | 0.3 | 159 | Moreno Valley, CA** | (7.3) |
| 13 | Ventura, CA** | 20.0 | 87 | Modesto, CA** | 0.2 | 161 | Alhambra, CA** | (7.4) |
| 14 | Redding, CA** | 19.1 | 88 | Clovis, CA** | 0.0 | 161 | Tempe, AZ** | (7.4) |
| 15 | Glendale, AZ** | 16.2 | 88 | Daly City, CA** | 0.0 | 163 | Pasadena, TX** | (7.5) |
| 16 | Santa Maria, CA** | 14.5 | 90 | Albuquerque, NM** | (0.3) | 164 | Santa Clara, CA** | (7.6) |
| 17 | Manchester, NH | 14.4 | 90 | Aurora, CO | (0.3) | 165 | Fullerton, CA** | (7.7) |
| 18 | Toms River Twnshp, NJ** | 14.3 | 92 | Lakeland, FL | (0.4) | 165 | Nashua, NH | (7.7) |
| 19 | Anaheim, CA** | 13.9 | 93 | Atlanta, GA** | (0.5) | 165 | St. Paul, MN | (7.7) |
| 20 | Suffolk, VA | 13.8 | 93 | Hayward, CA** | (0.5) | 165 | Topeka, KS** | (7.7) |
| 21 | Hillsboro, OR** | 13.5 | 93 | Phoenix, AZ** | (0.5) | 169 | Indianapolis, IN | (7.8) |
| 22 | Bend, OR | 12.9 | 96 | Fort Lauderdale, FL | (0.6) | 169 | San Marcos, CA** | (7.8) |
| 23 | St. George, UT | 12.5 | 96 | Louisville, KY** | (0.6) | 171 | Tacoma, WA | (7.9) |
| 24 | Temecula, CA** | 11.4 | 96 | Wichita, KS | (0.6) | 172 | El Cajon, CA** | (8.0) |
| 25 | Colorado Springs, CO | 10.7 | 99 | West Valley, UT | (0.7) | 173 | Amherst, NY** | (8.1) |
| 26 | Gresham, OR** | 10.1 | 100 | Fresno, CA** | (0.8) | 174 | Dayton, OH | (8.2) |
| 27 | St. Joseph, MO | 10.0 | 101 | Frisco, TX | (1.1) | 175 | Clinton Twnshp, MI | (8.3) |
| 28 | Hamilton Twnshp, NJ** | 9.9 | 102 | Irvine, CA** | (1.3) | 176 | Sandy, UT | (8.4) |
| 29 | Newark, NJ** | 9.7 | 103 | New Bedford, MA | (1.4) | 176 | Worcester, MA | (8.4) |
| 30 | Paterson, NJ** | 9.6 | 103 | Ogden, UT | (1.4) | 178 | Cary, NC** | (8.5) |
| 31 | Oxnard, CA** | 9.0 | 105 | Hawthorne, CA** | (1.5) | 179 | Redwood City, CA** | (8.7) |
| 32 | Omaha, NE** | 8.8 | 106 | Provo, UT | (1.7) | 179 | Warren, MI | (8.7) |
| 33 | Indio, CA** | 8.7 | 106 | Santa Monica, CA** | (1.7) | 181 | Rochester, NY** | (8.9) |
| 34 | Erie, PA | 8.2 | 108 | Bethlehem, PA | (1.8) | 182 | Broken Arrow, OK** | (9.0) |
| 34 | Lexington, KY | 8.2 | 108 | Norwalk, CA** | (1.8) | 183 | Lafayette, LA** | (9.1) |
| 36 | Sioux Falls, SD | 7.8 | 108 | Victorville, CA** | (1.8) | 183 | Westland, MI | (9.1) |
| 37 | Concord, CA** | 7.7 | 108 | West Covina, CA** | (1.8) | 185 | Torrance, CA** | (9.2) |
| 38 | Des Moines, IA | 7.4 | 112 | Vancouver, WA | (1.9) | 186 | Nampa, ID | (9.3) |
| 39 | Anchorage, AK | 6.9 | 113 | North Las Vegas, NV** | (2.0) | 187 | Everett, WA** | (9.5) |
| 39 | Oceanside, CA** | 6.9 | 113 | Tustin, CA** | (2.0) | 187 | Round Rock, TX** | (9.5) |
| 41 | Livermore, CA** | 6.7 | 115 | New Rochelle, NY** | (2.4) | 189 | Santa Ana, CA** | (9.8) |
| 42 | Evansville, IN** | 6.4 | 116 | Portsmouth, VA | (2.6) | 190 | Winston-Salem, NC** | (9.9) |
| 43 | Denver, CO | 6.3 | 117 | Bellevue, WA** | (3.0) | 191 | Chattanooga, TN | (10.0) |
| 44 | Cleveland, OH | 5.9 | 117 | Columbia, MO | (3.0) | 191 | Lawton, OK** | (10.0) |
| 45 | Salem, OR | 5.6 | 119 | Menifee, CA** | (3.2) | 191 | Orange, CA** | (10.0) |
| 46 | Fairfield, CA** | 5.5 | 119 | Quincy, MA | (3.2) | 191 | Visalia, CA** | (10.0) |
| 47 | Chino, CA** | 5.4 | 121 | Henderson, NV** | (3.3) | 195 | O'Fallon, MO | (10.1) |
| 47 | Huntington Beach, CA** | 5.4 | 122 | Bakersfield, CA** | (3.6) | 195 | Salt Lake City, UT | (10.1) |
| 47 | San Jose, CA** | 5.4 | 123 | Kansas City, MO | (3.7) | 197 | Lancaster, CA** | (10.2) |
| 50 | Miami Beach, FL | 5.2 | 124 | Hoover, AL | (3.9) | 197 | Scottsdale, AZ** | (10.2) |
| 51 | Detroit, MI | 4.9 | 124 | Salinas, CA** | (3.9) | 199 | Las Vegas, NV** | (10.3) |
| 52 | Springfield, MO | 4.8 | 126 | Richmond, VA | (4.0) | 199 | Rialto, CA** | (10.3) |
| 53 | Fayetteville, AR | 4.7 | 127 | Long Beach, CA** | (4.1) | 199 | Rockford, IL | (10.3) |
| 54 | Baltimore, MD** | 4.4 | 128 | Columbia, SC | (4.2) | 202 | Hampton, VA | (10.6) |
| 55 | Lawrence, MA** | 4.1 | 129 | Pompano Beach, FL | (4.4) | 203 | Beaverton, OR** | (10.8) |
| 56 | Fishers, IN** | 3.9 | 130 | Arvada, CO | (4.5) | 203 | Trenton, NJ** | (10.8) |
| 57 | Rancho Cucamon., CA** | 3.8 | 130 | Knoxville, TN | (4.5) | 205 | Kennewick, WA | (11.0) |
| 58 | Chico, CA** | 3.6 | 130 | Macon, GA** | (4.5) | 205 | Lakewood, CA** | (11.0) |
| 58 | Fort Wayne, IN | 3.6 | 133 | Seattle, WA | (4.6) | 207 | Fort Smith, AR | (11.1) |
| 60 | Lakewood, CO | 3.2 | 134 | Madison, WI | (4.7) | 207 | Shreveport, LA** | (11.1) |
| 60 | New York, NY** | 3.2 | 134 | Stockton, CA** | (4.7) | 209 | Buffalo, NY** | (11.2) |
| 60 | Pomona, CA** | 3.2 | 136 | Providence, RI | (4.9) | 210 | Meridian, ID | (11.3) |
| 63 | Buena Park, CA** | 3.0 | 137 | Green Bay, WI | (5.3) | 210 | Mobile, AL | (11.3) |
| 63 | Westminster, CA** | 3.0 | 137 | Little Rock, AR | (5.3) | 210 | Raleigh, NC** | (11.3) |
| 65 | South Gate, CA** | 2.9 | 137 | San Bernardino, CA** | (5.3) | 213 | Alexandria, VA | (11.4) |
| 66 | Costa Mesa, CA** | 2.8 | 140 | Albany, GA** | (5.4) | 214 | Fargo, ND | (11.6) |
| 67 | Odessa, TX** | 2.7 | 140 | Garden Grove, CA** | (5.4) | 214 | Fort Worth, TX | (11.6) |
| 67 | Syracuse, NY** | 2.7 | 140 | Huntsville, AL | (5.4) | 216 | Alameda, CA** | (11.7) |
| 69 | Murrieta, CA** | 2.6 | 143 | San Diego, CA** | (5.5) | 216 | Albany, NY** | (11.7) |
| 70 | Richmond, CA** | 2.5 | 144 | Beaumont, TX** | (5.6) | 218 | Brick Twnshp, NJ** | (11.8) |
| 71 | Minneapolis, MN | 2.2 | 145 | Sterling Heights, MI | (5.7) | 218 | Kansas City, KS** | (11.8) |
| 72 | Boulder, CO | 2.0 | 146 | Akron, OH | (5.8) | 220 | Oklahoma City, OK** | (11.9) |
| 73 | Riverside, CA** | 1.7 | 147 | Pasadena, CA** | (5.9) | 221 | Lincoln, NE** | (12.0) |
| 74 | Cheektowaga, NY** | 1.6 | 148 | Vacaville, CA** | (6.0) | 222 | Burbank, CA** | (12.1) |

| RANK | CITY | % CHANGE | RANK | CITY | % CHANGE | RANK | CITY | % CHANGE |
|---|---|---|---|---|---|---|---|---|
| 222 | Tulsa, OK** | (12.1) | 297 | Sunrise, FL | (17.7) | 371 | Arlington, TX** | (26.2) |
| 224 | Denton, TX | (12.2) | 298 | Baldwin Park, CA** | (17.9) | 372 | Renton, WA | (26.3) |
| 224 | Pearland, TX | (12.2) | 299 | Thornton, CO | (18.0) | 373 | Miramar, FL | (26.8) |
| 226 | Racine, WI** | (12.3) | 300 | McKinney, TX | (18.1) | 374 | Mission, TX** | (26.9) |
| 227 | San Antonio, TX** | (12.4) | 300 | Upper Darby Twnshp, PA | (18.1) | 374 | Norman, OK** | (26.9) |
| 227 | Tuscaloosa, AL | (12.4) | 300 | Waterbury, CT** | (18.1) | 374 | Somerville, MA | (26.9) |
| 229 | Eugene, OR | (12.6) | 303 | Centennial, CO | (18.2) | 377 | Berkeley, CA** | (27.0) |
| 229 | Greece, NY** | (12.6) | 303 | Corpus Christi, TX** | (18.2) | 378 | Carrollton, TX** | (27.1) |
| 231 | Colonie, NY** | (12.7) | 305 | Boise, ID | (18.3) | 378 | Santa Rosa, CA** | (27.1) |
| 232 | Santa Barbara, CA** | (12.8) | 306 | Lake Forest, CA** | (18.6) | 380 | Waco, TX** | (27.2) |
| 232 | West Palm Beach, FL | (12.8) | 307 | Chandler, AZ** | (18.7) | 381 | Citrus Heights, CA** | (27.3) |
| 234 | Tallahassee, FL | (12.9) | 308 | High Point, NC** | (18.8) | 382 | Grand Rapids, MI | (27.4) |
| 235 | Birmingham, AL | (13.0) | 309 | Virginia Beach, VA | (18.9) | 383 | Napa, CA** | (27.6) |
| 236 | Ontario, CA** | (13.1) | 310 | Kenosha, WI** | (19.1) | 384 | Boca Raton, FL | (27.7) |
| 236 | Palmdale, CA** | (13.1) | 311 | Wilmington, NC** | (19.2) | 385 | Fremont, CA** | (27.8) |
| 238 | Memphis, TN | (13.2) | 312 | Lewisville, TX | (19.3) | 386 | Amarillo, TX | (28.2) |
| 239 | Sugar Land, TX** | (13.3) | 312 | Palm Bay, FL | (19.3) | 386 | Midland, TX** | (28.2) |
| 240 | Orlando, FL | (13.4) | 314 | Longmont, CO | (19.4) | 388 | Elizabeth, NJ** | (28.5) |
| 241 | Merced, CA** | (13.5) | 315 | Compton, CA** | (19.6) | 388 | Hialeah, FL | (28.5) |
| 242 | Chino Hills, CA** | (13.6) | 315 | Newton, MA | (19.6) | 388 | Savannah, GA** | (28.5) |
| 242 | Stamford, CT | (13.6) | 317 | Brownsville, TX** | (19.7) | 391 | Santa Clarita, CA** | (28.6) |
| 242 | Tracy, CA** | (13.6) | 317 | Norfolk, VA | (19.7) | 392 | Reading, PA | (29.0) |
| 245 | Chula Vista, CA** | (13.8) | 317 | Olathe, KS** | (19.7) | 393 | Laredo, TX** | (29.7) |
| 245 | Cranston, RI | (13.8) | 317 | Plantation, FL | (19.7) | 394 | Farmington Hills, MI | (29.8) |
| 245 | Lynn, MA | (13.8) | 321 | Davie, FL | (19.8) | 395 | Bloomington, IN** | (29.9) |
| 248 | Newport Beach, CA** | (13.9) | 322 | Peoria, AZ** | (20.0) | 395 | Tyler, TX | (29.9) |
| 248 | Vista, CA** | (13.9) | 323 | Mountain View, CA** | (20.1) | 397 | Gainesville, FL | (30.1) |
| 250 | Cambridge, MA | (14.1) | 323 | Troy, MI | (20.1) | 398 | Athens-Clarke, GA** | (30.2) |
| 250 | Los Angeles, CA** | (14.1) | 325 | Baton Rouge, LA** | (20.3) | 399 | Tampa, FL | (31.0) |
| 252 | Fontana, CA** | (14.2) | 325 | Flint, MI | (20.3) | 400 | Greensboro, NC** | (31.7) |
| 252 | Inglewood, CA** | (14.2) | 325 | San Angelo, TX | (20.3) | 401 | Pembroke Pines, FL | (32.1) |
| 254 | Downey, CA** | (14.4) | 325 | Scranton, PA | (20.3) | 402 | Port St. Lucie, FL | (32.8) |
| 254 | Edmond, OK** | (14.4) | 329 | Jackson, MS** | (20.4) | 403 | Carmel, IN** | (33.0) |
| 254 | Milwaukee, WI | (14.4) | 329 | Roseville, CA** | (20.4) | 404 | Charleston, SC | (33.3) |
| 254 | Thousand Oaks, CA** | (14.4) | 331 | Gilbert, AZ | (20.8) | 404 | Dearborn, MI | (33.3) |
| 258 | Coral Springs, FL | (14.6) | 332 | St. Louis, MO | (21.0) | 406 | College Station, TX** | (34.0) |
| 258 | Las Cruces, NM** | (14.6) | 333 | Columbus, GA** | (21.1) | 407 | Irving, TX** | (34.2) |
| 258 | Lynchburg, VA | (14.6) | 333 | New Haven, CT | (21.1) | 408 | McAllen, TX** | (34.9) |
| 261 | Mesquite, TX** | (14.7) | 335 | Cape Coral, FL | (21.3) | 409 | Concord, NC** | (37.2) |
| 262 | Cedar Rapids, IA | (14.8) | 336 | Sparks, NV** | (21.4) | 410 | Grand Prairie, TX** | (40.0) |
| 262 | Corona, CA** | (14.8) | 337 | Murfreesboro, TN | (21.5) | 411 | Longview, TX | (41.1) |
| 264 | Garland, TX** | (15.0) | 338 | Danbury, CT** | (21.6) | 412 | Johns Creek, GA** | (43.9) |
| 264 | Westminster, CO | (15.0) | 339 | Chesapeake, VA | (21.7) | 413 | Edison Twnshp, NJ** | (45.4) |
| 266 | Bellflower, CA** | (15.3) | 339 | Jersey City, NJ** | (21.7) | 414 | Bryan, TX** | (47.2) |
| 267 | Clearwater, FL | (15.4) | 339 | Sunnyvale, CA** | (21.7) | NA | Arlington Heights, IL*** | NA |
| 267 | North Charleston, SC | (15.4) | 342 | Killeen, TX** | (21.8) | NA | Aurora, IL*** | NA |
| 269 | Norwalk, CT | (15.5) | 343 | Fayetteville, NC** | (21.9) | NA | Bloomington, IL*** | NA |
| 270 | Ann Arbor, MI | (15.7) | 344 | Wichita Falls, TX** | (22.0) | NA | Bloomington, MN*** | NA |
| 270 | Orem, UT** | (15.7) | 345 | Clarkstown, NY** | (22.4) | NA | Brooklyn Park, MN*** | NA |
| 270 | San Mateo, CA** | (15.7) | 346 | Fall River, MA | (22.5) | NA | Champaign, IL*** | NA |
| 270 | Woodbridge Twnshp, NJ** | (15.7) | 347 | El Paso, TX** | (22.9) | NA | Chicago, IL*** | NA |
| 274 | Glendale, CA** | (15.9) | 347 | Surprise, AZ** | (22.9) | NA | Cicero, IL*** | NA |
| 274 | Mesa, AZ** | (15.9) | 349 | Austin, TX** | (23.0) | NA | Decatur, IL*** | NA |
| 274 | Yonkers, NY** | (15.9) | 349 | Reno, NV** | (23.0) | NA | Deerfield Beach, FL*** | NA |
| 277 | Pittsburgh, PA | (16.0) | 351 | Warwick, RI | (23.5) | NA | Duluth, MN*** | NA |
| 278 | Edinburg, TX** | (16.1) | 352 | Dallas, TX** | (23.6) | NA | Elgin, IL*** | NA |
| 279 | Lawrence, KS | (16.2) | 353 | Clarksville, TN | (23.7) | NA | Evanston, IL*** | NA |
| 280 | Melbourne, FL | (16.8) | 354 | League City, TX** | (23.8) | NA | Greenville, NC*** | NA |
| 281 | Lubbock, TX** | (16.9) | 354 | Overland Park, KS** | (23.8) | NA | Joliet, IL*** | NA |
| 282 | Hammond, IN** | (17.0) | 356 | Bridgeport, CT** | (24.1) | NA | Jurupa Valley, CA*** | NA |
| 282 | Livonia, MI | (17.0) | 356 | Canton Twnshp, MI | (24.1) | NA | Lakewood Twnshp, NJ*** | NA |
| 282 | Mission Viejo, CA** | (17.0) | 358 | El Monte, CA** | (24.2) | NA | Lowell, MA*** | NA |
| 282 | Roanoke, VA | (17.0) | 359 | Jacksonville, FL | (24.5) | NA | Naperville, IL*** | NA |
| 282 | Roswell, GA** | (17.0) | 360 | Miami Gardens, FL | (24.6) | NA | Newport News, VA*** | NA |
| 287 | Hartford, CT** | (17.1) | 361 | Sandy Springs, GA** | (24.7) | NA | Peoria, IL*** | NA |
| 287 | Lee's Summit, MO | (17.1) | 362 | Fort Collins, CO | (24.9) | NA | Rochester, MN*** | NA |
| 289 | South Bend, IN | (17.2) | 362 | St. Petersburg, FL | (24.9) | NA | Springfield, IL*** | NA |
| 290 | Davenport, IA | (17.4) | 364 | Charlotte, NC** | (25.0) | NA | Toledo, OH*** | NA |
| 290 | Largo, FL | (17.4) | 365 | Ramapo, NY** | (25.1) | NA | Tucson, AZ*** | NA |
| 290 | Nashville, TN | (17.4) | 366 | Allen, TX | (25.2) | NA | Upland, CA*** | NA |
| 293 | Clifton, NJ** | (17.5) | 367 | Richardson, TX** | (25.5) | NA | Waukegan, IL*** | NA |
| 293 | Sacramento, CA** | (17.5) | 368 | Allentown, PA | (26.0) | NA | Yakima, WA*** | NA |
| 295 | Boston, MA** | (17.6) | 368 | Elk Grove, CA** | (26.0) | | | |
| 295 | Simi Valley, CA** | (17.6) | 370 | Plano, TX | (26.1) | | | |

Source: CQ Press using reported data from the F.B.I. "Crime in the United States 2013"

*Includes murder, rape, robbery, aggravated assault, burglary, larceny-theft, and motor vehicle theft.

**Figures for these cities are based on the previous (legacy) definition of rape. See note on page vii.

***Not available.

# 45. Violent Crimes in 2013
## National Total = 1,163,146 Violent Crimes*

| RANK | CITY | CRIMES | RANK | CITY | CRIMES | RANK | CITY | CRIMES |
|---|---|---|---|---|---|---|---|---|
| 218 | Abilene, TX** | 477 | 316 | Chino, CA** | 258 | 258 | Fullerton, CA** | 372 |
| 81 | Akron, OH | 1,570 | 188 | Chula Vista, CA** | 595 | 144 | Gainesville, FL | 806 |
| 376 | Alameda, CA** | 158 | 273 | Cicero, IL** | 346 | 227 | Garden Grove, CA** | 455 |
| 152 | Albany, GA** | 749 | 47 | Cincinnati, OH | 2,826 | 209 | Garland, TX** | 514 |
| 146 | Albany, NY** | 791 | 288 | Citrus Heights, CA** | 320 | 136 | Gary, IN** | 883 |
| 29 | Albuquerque, NM** | 4,325 | 429 | Clarkstown, NY** | 65 | 349 | Gilbert, AZ | 193 |
| 316 | Alexandria, VA | 258 | 153 | Clarksville, TN | 748 | 134 | Glendale, AZ** | 905 |
| 371 | Alhambra, CA** | 163 | 181 | Clearwater, FL | 618 | 361 | Glendale, CA** | 181 |
| 178 | Allentown, PA | 628 | 19 | Cleveland, OH | 5,751 | 210 | Grand Prairie, TX** | 511 |
| 433 | Allen, TX | 62 | 364 | Clifton, NJ** | 175 | 99 | Grand Rapids, MI | 1,326 |
| 100 | Amarillo, TX | 1,286 | 298 | Clinton Twnshp, MI | 285 | 381 | Greece, NY** | 151 |
| 407 | Amherst, NY** | 107 | 361 | Clovis, CA** | 181 | 215 | Greeley, CO | 491 |
| 110 | Anaheim, CA** | 1,130 | 255 | College Station, TX** | 379 | 211 | Green Bay, WI | 500 |
| 52 | Anchorage, AK | 2,435 | 430 | Colonie, NY** | 63 | 89 | Greensboro, NC** | 1,449 |
| 323 | Ann Arbor, MI | 247 | 66 | Colorado Springs, CO | 1,893 | 203 | Greenville, NC** | 555 |
| 128 | Antioch, CA** | 946 | 239 | Columbia, MO | 416 | 183 | Gresham, OR** | 611 |
| 437 | Arlington Heights, IL** | 42 | 126 | Columbia, SC | 952 | 352 | Hamilton Twnshp, NJ** | 189 |
| 68 | Arlington, TX** | 1,837 | 120 | Columbus, GA** | 1,022 | 170 | Hammond, IN** | 654 |
| 371 | Arvada, CO | 163 | 101 | Compton, CA** | 1,242 | 296 | Hampton, VA | 292 |
| 245 | Athens-Clarke, GA** | 404 | 242 | Concord, CA** | 407 | 87 | Hartford, CT** | 1,473 |
| 20 | Atlanta, GA** | 5,517 | 402 | Concord, NC** | 122 | 196 | Hawthorne, CA** | 580 |
| 91 | Aurora, CO | 1,436 | 329 | Coral Springs, FL | 237 | 192 | Hayward, CA** | 589 |
| 185 | Aurora, IL** | 601 | 374 | Corona, CA** | 162 | 232 | Hemet, CA** | 447 |
| 41 | Austin, TX** | 3,123 | 63 | Corpus Christi, TX** | 1,939 | 260 | Henderson, NV** | 367 |
| 67 | Bakersfield, CA** | 1,857 | 321 | Costa Mesa, CA** | 252 | 259 | Hesperia, CA** | 371 |
| 340 | Baldwin Park, CA** | 220 | 381 | Cranston, RI | 151 | 149 | Hialeah, FL | 774 |
| 11 | Baltimore, MD** | 8,725 | 12 | Dallas, TX** | 8,330 | 201 | High Point, NC** | 556 |
| 58 | Baton Rouge, LA** | 2,127 | 336 | Daly City, CA** | 223 | 390 | Hillsboro, OR** | 141 |
| 103 | Beaumont, TX** | 1,225 | 405 | Danbury, CT** | 108 | 161 | Hollywood, FL | 720 |
| 400 | Beaverton, OR** | 124 | 170 | Davenport, IA | 654 | 422 | Hoover, AL | 74 |
| 399 | Bellevue, WA** | 125 | 291 | Davie, FL | 306 | 2 | Houston, TX** | 20,993 |
| 301 | Bellflower, CA** | 279 | 102 | Dayton, OH | 1,230 | 262 | Huntington Beach, CA** | 362 |
| 359 | Bend, OR | 182 | 272 | Dearborn, MI | 347 | 85 | Huntsville, AL | 1,507 |
| 199 | Berkeley, CA** | 562 | 270 | Decatur, IL** | 351 | 204 | Independence, MO | 543 |
| 358 | Bethlehem, PA | 183 | 292 | Deerfield Beach, FL | 305 | 8 | Indianapolis, IN | 10,479 |
| 266 | Billings, MT | 360 | 277 | Denton, TX | 338 | 223 | Indio, CA** | 468 |
| 46 | Birmingham, AL | 2,852 | 30 | Denver, CO | 4,087 | 156 | Inglewood, CA** | 739 |
| 250 | Bloomington, IL** | 399 | 119 | Des Moines, IA | 1,026 | 404 | Irvine, CA** | 113 |
| 304 | Bloomington, IN** | 275 | 5 | Detroit, MI | 14,504 | 206 | Irving, TX** | 530 |
| 397 | Bloomington, MN | 128 | 285 | Downey, CA** | 326 | 22 | Jacksonville, FL | 5,246 |
| 370 | Boca Raton, FL | 165 | 274 | Duluth, MN | 342 | 80 | Jackson, MS** | 1,631 |
| 186 | Boise, ID | 600 | 302 | Edinburg, TX** | 277 | 78 | Jersey City, NJ** | 1,655 |
| 25 | Boston, MA** | 5,037 | 401 | Edison Twnshp, NJ** | 123 | 438 | Johns Creek, GA** | 37 |
| 341 | Boulder, CO | 218 | 421 | Edmond, OK** | 87 | 200 | Joliet, IL** | 557 |
| 420 | Brick Twnshp, NJ** | 89 | 254 | El Cajon, CA** | 386 | 311 | Jurupa Valley, CA** | 267 |
| 95 | Bridgeport, CT** | 1,397 | 275 | El Monte, CA** | 340 | 158 | Kansas City, KS** | 731 |
| 108 | Brockton, MA | 1,162 | 50 | El Paso, TX** | 2,522 | 18 | Kansas City, MO | 5,864 |
| 386 | Broken Arrow, OK** | 147 | 330 | Elgin, IL** | 236 | 326 | Kennewick, WA | 240 |
| 322 | Brooklyn Park, MN | 248 | 124 | Elizabeth, NJ** | 999 | 306 | Kenosha, WI** | 274 |
| 220 | Brownsville, TX** | 473 | 222 | Elk Grove, CA** | 469 | 289 | Kent, WA | 319 |
| 267 | Bryan, TX** | 358 | 225 | Erie, PA | 457 | 151 | Killeen, TX** | 753 |
| 338 | Buena Park, CA** | 221 | 187 | Escondido, CA** | 596 | 83 | Knoxville, TN | 1,541 |
| 38 | Buffalo, NY** | 3,249 | 246 | Eugene, OR | 402 | 137 | Lafayette, LA** | 868 |
| 367 | Burbank, CA** | 171 | 352 | Evanston, IL** | 189 | 408 | Lake Forest, CA** | 105 |
| 264 | Cambridge, MA | 361 | 198 | Evansville, IN** | 564 | 224 | Lakeland, FL | 460 |
| 415 | Canton Twnshp, MI | 94 | 235 | Everett, WA** | 443 | 416 | Lakewood Twnshp, NJ** | 93 |
| 348 | Cape Coral, FL | 197 | 213 | Fairfield, CA** | 498 | 335 | Lakewood, CA** | 225 |
| 338 | Carlsbad, CA** | 221 | 130 | Fall River, MA | 944 | 180 | Lakewood, CO | 624 |
| 440 | Carmel, IN** | 20 | 233 | Fargo, ND | 446 | 139 | Lancaster, CA** | 832 |
| 356 | Carrollton, TX** | 185 | 426 | Farmington Hills, MI | 72 | 104 | Lansing, MI | 1,204 |
| 249 | Carson, CA** | 400 | 276 | Fayetteville, AR | 339 | 118 | Laredo, TX** | 1,027 |
| 410 | Cary, NC** | 102 | 107 | Fayetteville, NC** | 1,170 | 269 | Largo, FL | 352 |
| 252 | Cedar Rapids, IA | 392 | 297 | Federal Way, WA | 291 | 281 | Las Cruces, NM** | 332 |
| 390 | Centennial, CO | 141 | 441 | Fishers, IN** | 16 | 6 | Las Vegas, NV** | 11,374 |
| 170 | Champaign, IL** | 654 | 64 | Flint, MI | 1,907 | 277 | Lawrence, KS | 338 |
| 197 | Chandler, AZ** | 575 | 160 | Fontana, CA** | 725 | 148 | Lawrence, MA** | 776 |
| 331 | Charleston, SC | 231 | 268 | Fort Collins, CO | 357 | 132 | Lawton, OK** | 919 |
| 23 | Charlotte, NC** | 5,093 | 88 | Fort Lauderdale, FL | 1,456 | 414 | League City, TX** | 96 |
| 75 | Chattanooga, TN | 1,692 | 184 | Fort Smith, AR | 606 | 418 | Lee's Summit, MO | 91 |
| 376 | Cheektowaga, NY** | 158 | 127 | Fort Wayne, IN | 949 | 325 | Lewisville, TX | 243 |
| 157 | Chesapeake, VA | 737 | 28 | Fort Worth, TX | 4,420 | 128 | Lexington, KY | 946 |
| NA | Chicago, IL*** | NA | 307 | Fremont, CA** | 273 | 125 | Lincoln, NE** | 990 |
| 294 | Chico, CA** | 299 | 49 | Fresno, CA** | 2,552 | 48 | Little Rock, AR | 2,777 |
| 430 | Chino Hills, CA** | 63 | 411 | Frisco, TX | 100 | 309 | Livermore, CA** | 270 |

| RANK | CITY | CRIMES |
|---|---|---|
| 385 | Livonia, MI | 148 |
| 54 | Long Beach, CA** | 2,346 |
| 334 | Longmont, CO | 226 |
| 229 | Longview, TX | 451 |
| 4 | Los Angeles, CA** | 16,524 |
| 34 | Louisville, KY** | 3,644 |
| 179 | Lowell, MA | 625 |
| 69 | Lubbock, TX** | 1,829 |
| 284 | Lynchburg, VA | 330 |
| 142 | Lynn, MA | 814 |
| 195 | Macon, GA** | 583 |
| 135 | Madison, WI | 884 |
| 154 | Manchester, NH | 747 |
| 367 | McAllen, TX** | 171 |
| 345 | McKinney, TX | 207 |
| 217 | Medford, OR | 483 |
| 169 | Melbourne, FL | 657 |
| 7 | Memphis, TN | 10,894 |
| 413 | Menifee, CA** | 99 |
| 201 | Merced, CA** | 556 |
| 403 | Meridian, ID | 115 |
| 70 | Mesa, AZ** | 1,807 |
| 246 | Mesquite, TX** | 402 |
| 132 | Miami Beach, FL | 919 |
| 131 | Miami Gardens, FL | 921 |
| 27 | Miami, FL | 4,945 |
| 271 | Midland, TX** | 350 |
| 13 | Milwaukee, WI | 8,194 |
| 31 | Minneapolis, MN | 4,038 |
| 219 | Miramar, FL | 476 |
| 433 | Mission Viejo, CA** | 62 |
| 426 | Mission, TX** | 72 |
| 83 | Mobile, AL | 1,541 |
| 74 | Modesto, CA** | 1,704 |
| 175 | Moreno Valley, CA** | 638 |
| 378 | Mountain View, CA** | 157 |
| 162 | Murfreesboro, TN | 705 |
| 428 | Murrieta, CA** | 70 |
| 346 | Nampa, ID | 202 |
| 318 | Napa, CA** | 255 |
| 408 | Naperville, IL** | 105 |
| 359 | Nashua, NH | 182 |
| 17 | Nashville, TN | 6,612 |
| 116 | New Bedford, MA | 1,039 |
| 79 | New Haven, CT | 1,643 |
| 43 | New Orleans, LA** | 2,965 |
| 364 | New Rochelle, NY** | 175 |
| 1 | New York, NY** | 52,384 |
| 36 | Newark, NJ** | 3,516 |
| 425 | Newport Beach, CA** | 73 |
| 145 | Newport News, VA | 795 |
| 422 | Newton, MA | 74 |
| 93 | Norfolk, VA | 1,418 |
| 363 | Norman, OK** | 178 |
| 165 | North Charleston, SC | 693 |
| 71 | North Las Vegas, NV** | 1,806 |
| 242 | Norwalk, CA** | 407 |
| 327 | Norwalk, CT | 239 |
| 14 | Oakland, CA** | 7,984 |
| 177 | Oceanside, CA** | 634 |
| 115 | Odessa, TX** | 1,080 |
| 430 | O'Fallon, MO | 63 |
| 239 | Ogden, UT | 416 |
| 26 | Oklahoma City, OK** | 4,998 |
| 356 | Olathe, KS** | 185 |
| 51 | Omaha, NE** | 2,449 |
| 228 | Ontario, CA** | 453 |
| 386 | Orange, CA** | 147 |
| 439 | Orem, UT** | 33 |
| 55 | Orlando, FL | 2,316 |
| 299 | Overland Park, KS** | 284 |
| 173 | Oxnard, CA** | 651 |
| 229 | Palm Bay, FL | 451 |
| 150 | Palmdale, CA** | 759 |
| 236 | Pasadena, CA** | 434 |
| 190 | Pasadena, TX** | 592 |
| 82 | Paterson, NJ** | 1,555 |
| 379 | Pearland, TX | 152 |
| 304 | Pembroke Pines, FL | 275 |
| 319 | Peoria, AZ** | 254 |
| 147 | Peoria, IL** | 784 |
| 3 | Philadelphia, PA | 17,074 |
| 9 | Phoenix, AZ** | 9,492 |
| 56 | Pittsburgh, PA | 2,259 |
| 253 | Plano, TX | 389 |
| 290 | Plantation, FL | 311 |
| 143 | Pomona, CA** | 809 |
| 141 | Pompano Beach, FL | 819 |
| 293 | Port St. Lucie, FL | 303 |
| 44 | Portland, OR** | 2,941 |
| 191 | Portsmouth, VA | 590 |
| 113 | Providence, RI | 1,115 |
| 375 | Provo, UT | 160 |
| 122 | Pueblo, CO | 1,011 |
| 264 | Quincy, MA | 361 |
| 295 | Racine, WI** | 297 |
| 76 | Raleigh, NC** | 1,683 |
| 436 | Ramapo, NY** | 57 |
| 282 | Rancho Cucamon., CA** | 331 |
| 155 | Reading, PA | 743 |
| 194 | Redding, CA** | 585 |
| 351 | Redwood City, CA** | 190 |
| 109 | Reno, NV** | 1,154 |
| 319 | Renton, WA | 254 |
| 236 | Rialto, CA** | 434 |
| 397 | Richardson, TX** | 128 |
| 114 | Richmond, CA** | 1,112 |
| 98 | Richmond, VA | 1,327 |
| 97 | Riverside, CA** | 1,330 |
| 225 | Roanoke, VA | 457 |
| 342 | Rochester, MN | 214 |
| 59 | Rochester, NY** | 2,107 |
| 61 | Rockford, IL | 2,065 |
| 315 | Roseville, CA** | 261 |
| 388 | Roswell, GA** | 144 |
| 383 | Round Rock, TX** | 149 |
| 40 | Sacramento, CA** | 3,137 |
| 207 | Salem, OR | 520 |
| 123 | Salinas, CA** | 1,001 |
| 86 | Salt Lake City, UT | 1,475 |
| 313 | San Angelo, TX | 263 |
| 10 | San Antonio, TX** | 8,828 |
| 62 | San Bernardino, CA** | 1,949 |
| 21 | San Diego, CA** | 5,303 |
| 16 | San Francisco, CA** | 7,064 |
| 39 | San Jose, CA** | 3,215 |
| 251 | San Leandro, CA** | 394 |
| 342 | San Marcos, CA** | 214 |
| 327 | San Mateo, CA** | 239 |
| 355 | Sandy Springs, GA** | 186 |
| 394 | Sandy, UT | 134 |
| 112 | Santa Ana, CA** | 1,121 |
| 262 | Santa Barbara, CA** | 362 |
| 366 | Santa Clara, CA** | 172 |
| 303 | Santa Clarita, CA** | 276 |
| 216 | Santa Maria, CA** | 490 |
| 286 | Santa Monica, CA** | 324 |
| 205 | Santa Rosa, CA** | 541 |
| 138 | Savannah, GA** | 851 |
| 279 | Scottsdale, AZ** | 337 |
| 369 | Scranton, PA | 166 |
| 33 | Seattle, WA | 3,758 |
| 95 | Shreveport, LA** | 1,397 |
| 396 | Simi Valley, CA** | 132 |
| 286 | Sioux City, IA | 324 |
| 176 | Sioux Falls, SD | 636 |
| 350 | Somerville, MA | 191 |
| 168 | South Bend, IN | 664 |
| 214 | South Gate, CA** | 496 |
| 308 | Sparks, NV** | 271 |
| 331 | Spokane Valley, WA** | 231 |
| 90 | Spokane, WA** | 1,440 |
| 106 | Springfield, IL** | 1,191 |
| 77 | Springfield, MA | 1,673 |
| 65 | Springfield, MO | 1,894 |
| 280 | Stamford, CT | 334 |
| 324 | Sterling Heights, MI | 244 |
| 35 | Stockton, CA** | 3,622 |
| 395 | St. George, UT | 133 |
| 257 | St. Joseph, MO | 374 |
| 24 | St. Louis, MO | 5,077 |
| 57 | St. Paul, MN | 2,200 |
| 53 | St. Petersburg, FL | 2,379 |
| 310 | Suffolk, VA | 268 |
| 405 | Sugar Land, TX** | 108 |
| 388 | Sunnyvale, CA** | 144 |
| 312 | Sunrise, FL | 265 |
| 383 | Surprise, AZ** | 149 |
| 105 | Syracuse, NY** | 1,192 |
| 72 | Tacoma, WA | 1,766 |
| 94 | Tallahassee, FL | 1,398 |
| 60 | Tampa, FL | 2,097 |
| 418 | Temecula, CA** | 91 |
| 140 | Tempe, AZ** | 831 |
| 282 | Thornton, CO | 331 |
| 392 | Thousand Oaks, CA** | 139 |
| 45 | Toledo, OH | 2,902 |
| 422 | Toms River Twnshp, NJ** | 74 |
| 182 | Topeka, KS** | 612 |
| 354 | Torrance, CA** | 187 |
| 379 | Tracy, CA** | 152 |
| 111 | Trenton, NJ** | 1,122 |
| 433 | Troy, MI | 62 |
| 37 | Tucson, AZ** | 3,368 |
| 32 | Tulsa, OK** | 3,827 |
| 236 | Tuscaloosa, AL | 434 |
| 411 | Tustin, CA** | 100 |
| 256 | Tyler, TX | 376 |
| 371 | Upland, CA** | 163 |
| 231 | Upper Darby Twnshp, PA | 450 |
| 347 | Vacaville, CA** | 201 |
| 121 | Vallejo, CA** | 1,019 |
| 189 | Vancouver, WA | 593 |
| 314 | Ventura, CA** | 262 |
| 173 | Victorville, CA** | 651 |
| 159 | Virginia Beach, VA | 730 |
| 211 | Visalia, CA** | 500 |
| 234 | Vista, CA** | 445 |
| 208 | Waco, TX** | 515 |
| 167 | Warren, MI | 679 |
| 416 | Warwick, RI | 93 |
| 15 | Washington, DC | 7,880 |
| 241 | Waterbury, CT** | 410 |
| 244 | Waukegan, IL** | 405 |
| 331 | West Covina, CA** | 231 |
| 164 | West Palm Beach, FL | 701 |
| 163 | West Valley, UT | 703 |
| 261 | Westland, MI | 363 |
| 300 | Westminster, CA** | 283 |
| 342 | Westminster, CO | 214 |
| 336 | Whittier, CA** | 223 |
| 248 | Wichita Falls, TX** | 401 |
| 42 | Wichita, KS | 3,065 |
| 166 | Wilmington, NC** | 687 |
| 92 | Winston-Salem, NC** | 1,426 |
| 393 | Woodbridge Twnshp, NJ** | 135 |
| 73 | Worcester, MA | 1,750 |
| 221 | Yakima, WA | 471 |
| 117 | Yonkers, NY** | 1,036 |
| 193 | Yuma, AZ | 587 |

Source: Reported data from the F.B.I. "Crime in the United States 2013"

*Violent crimes are offenses of murder, rape, robbery, and aggravated assault.

**Figures for these cities are based on the previous (legacy) definition of rape. See note on page vii.

***Not available.

# 45. Violent Crimes in 2013 (continued)
## National Total = 1,163,146 Violent Crimes*

| RANK | CITY | CRIMES | RANK | CITY | CRIMES | RANK | CITY | CRIMES |
|---|---|---|---|---|---|---|---|---|
| 1 | New York, NY** | 52,384 | 75 | Chattanooga, TN | 1,692 | 149 | Hialeah, FL | 774 |
| 2 | Houston, TX** | 20,993 | 76 | Raleigh, NC** | 1,683 | 150 | Palmdale, CA** | 759 |
| 3 | Philadelphia, PA | 17,074 | 77 | Springfield, MA | 1,673 | 151 | Killeen, TX** | 753 |
| 4 | Los Angeles, CA** | 16,524 | 78 | Jersey City, NJ** | 1,655 | 152 | Albany, GA** | 749 |
| 5 | Detroit, MI | 14,504 | 79 | New Haven, CT | 1,643 | 153 | Clarksville, TN | 748 |
| 6 | Las Vegas, NV** | 11,374 | 80 | Jackson, MS** | 1,631 | 154 | Manchester, NH | 747 |
| 7 | Memphis, TN | 10,894 | 81 | Akron, OH | 1,570 | 155 | Reading, PA | 743 |
| 8 | Indianapolis, IN | 10,479 | 82 | Paterson, NJ** | 1,555 | 156 | Inglewood, CA** | 739 |
| 9 | Phoenix, AZ** | 9,492 | 83 | Knoxville, TN | 1,541 | 157 | Chesapeake, VA | 737 |
| 10 | San Antonio, TX** | 8,828 | 83 | Mobile, AL | 1,541 | 158 | Kansas City, KS** | 731 |
| 11 | Baltimore, MD** | 8,725 | 85 | Huntsville, AL | 1,507 | 159 | Virginia Beach, VA | 730 |
| 12 | Dallas, TX** | 8,330 | 86 | Salt Lake City, UT | 1,475 | 160 | Fontana, CA** | 725 |
| 13 | Milwaukee, WI | 8,194 | 87 | Hartford, CT** | 1,473 | 161 | Hollywood, FL | 720 |
| 14 | Oakland, CA** | 7,984 | 88 | Fort Lauderdale, FL | 1,456 | 162 | Murfreesboro, TN | 705 |
| 15 | Washington, DC | 7,880 | 89 | Greensboro, NC** | 1,449 | 163 | West Valley, UT | 703 |
| 16 | San Francisco, CA** | 7,064 | 90 | Spokane, WA** | 1,440 | 164 | West Palm Beach, FL | 701 |
| 17 | Nashville, TN | 6,612 | 91 | Aurora, CO | 1,436 | 165 | North Charleston, SC | 693 |
| 18 | Kansas City, MO | 5,864 | 92 | Winston-Salem, NC** | 1,426 | 166 | Wilmington, NC** | 687 |
| 19 | Cleveland, OH | 5,751 | 93 | Norfolk, VA | 1,418 | 167 | Warren, MI | 679 |
| 20 | Atlanta, GA** | 5,517 | 94 | Tallahassee, FL | 1,398 | 168 | South Bend, IN | 664 |
| 21 | San Diego, CA** | 5,303 | 95 | Bridgeport, CT** | 1,397 | 169 | Melbourne, FL | 657 |
| 22 | Jacksonville, FL | 5,246 | 95 | Shreveport, LA** | 1,397 | 170 | Champaign, IL** | 654 |
| 23 | Charlotte, NC** | 5,093 | 97 | Riverside, CA** | 1,330 | 170 | Davenport, IA | 654 |
| 24 | St. Louis, MO | 5,077 | 98 | Richmond, VA | 1,327 | 170 | Hammond, IN** | 654 |
| 25 | Boston, MA** | 5,037 | 99 | Grand Rapids, MI | 1,326 | 173 | Oxnard, CA** | 651 |
| 26 | Oklahoma City, OK** | 4,998 | 100 | Amarillo, TX | 1,286 | 173 | Victorville, CA** | 651 |
| 27 | Miami, FL | 4,945 | 101 | Compton, CA** | 1,242 | 175 | Moreno Valley, CA** | 638 |
| 28 | Fort Worth, TX | 4,420 | 102 | Dayton, OH | 1,230 | 176 | Sioux Falls, SD | 636 |
| 29 | Albuquerque, NM** | 4,325 | 103 | Beaumont, TX** | 1,225 | 177 | Oceanside, CA** | 634 |
| 30 | Denver, CO | 4,087 | 104 | Lansing, MI | 1,204 | 178 | Allentown, PA | 628 |
| 31 | Minneapolis, MN | 4,038 | 105 | Syracuse, NY** | 1,192 | 179 | Lowell, MA | 625 |
| 32 | Tulsa, OK** | 3,827 | 106 | Springfield, IL** | 1,191 | 180 | Lakewood, CO | 624 |
| 33 | Seattle, WA | 3,758 | 107 | Fayetteville, NC** | 1,170 | 181 | Clearwater, FL | 618 |
| 34 | Louisville, KY** | 3,644 | 108 | Brockton, MA | 1,162 | 182 | Topeka, KS** | 612 |
| 35 | Stockton, CA** | 3,622 | 109 | Reno, NV** | 1,154 | 183 | Gresham, OR** | 611 |
| 36 | Newark, NJ** | 3,516 | 110 | Anaheim, CA** | 1,130 | 184 | Fort Smith, AR | 606 |
| 37 | Tucson, AZ** | 3,368 | 111 | Trenton, NJ** | 1,122 | 185 | Aurora, IL** | 601 |
| 38 | Buffalo, NY** | 3,249 | 112 | Santa Ana, CA** | 1,121 | 186 | Boise, ID | 600 |
| 39 | San Jose, CA** | 3,215 | 113 | Providence, RI | 1,115 | 187 | Escondido, CA** | 596 |
| 40 | Sacramento, CA** | 3,137 | 114 | Richmond, CA** | 1,112 | 188 | Chula Vista, CA** | 595 |
| 41 | Austin, TX** | 3,123 | 115 | Odessa, TX** | 1,080 | 189 | Vancouver, WA | 593 |
| 42 | Wichita, KS | 3,065 | 116 | New Bedford, MA | 1,039 | 190 | Pasadena, TX** | 592 |
| 43 | New Orleans, LA** | 2,965 | 117 | Yonkers, NY** | 1,036 | 191 | Portsmouth, VA | 590 |
| 44 | Portland, OR** | 2,941 | 118 | Laredo, TX** | 1,027 | 192 | Hayward, CA** | 589 |
| 45 | Toledo, OH | 2,902 | 119 | Des Moines, IA | 1,026 | 193 | Yuma, AZ | 587 |
| 46 | Birmingham, AL | 2,852 | 120 | Columbus, GA** | 1,022 | 194 | Redding, CA** | 585 |
| 47 | Cincinnati, OH | 2,826 | 121 | Vallejo, CA** | 1,019 | 195 | Macon, GA** | 583 |
| 48 | Little Rock, AR | 2,777 | 122 | Pueblo, CO | 1,011 | 196 | Hawthorne, CA** | 580 |
| 49 | Fresno, CA** | 2,552 | 123 | Salinas, CA** | 1,001 | 197 | Chandler, AZ** | 575 |
| 50 | El Paso, TX** | 2,522 | 124 | Elizabeth, NJ** | 999 | 198 | Evansville, IN** | 564 |
| 51 | Omaha, NE** | 2,449 | 125 | Lincoln, NE** | 990 | 199 | Berkeley, CA** | 562 |
| 52 | Anchorage, AK | 2,435 | 126 | Columbia, SC | 952 | 200 | Joliet, IL** | 557 |
| 53 | St. Petersburg, FL | 2,379 | 127 | Fort Wayne, IN | 949 | 201 | High Point, NC** | 556 |
| 54 | Long Beach, CA** | 2,346 | 128 | Antioch, CA** | 946 | 201 | Merced, CA** | 556 |
| 55 | Orlando, FL | 2,316 | 128 | Lexington, KY | 946 | 203 | Greenville, NC** | 555 |
| 56 | Pittsburgh, PA | 2,259 | 130 | Fall River, MA | 944 | 204 | Independence, MO | 543 |
| 57 | St. Paul, MN | 2,200 | 131 | Miami Gardens, FL | 921 | 205 | Santa Rosa, CA** | 541 |
| 58 | Baton Rouge, LA** | 2,127 | 132 | Lawton, OK** | 919 | 206 | Irving, TX** | 530 |
| 59 | Rochester, NY** | 2,107 | 132 | Miami Beach, FL | 919 | 207 | Salem, OR | 520 |
| 60 | Tampa, FL | 2,097 | 134 | Glendale, AZ** | 905 | 208 | Waco, TX** | 515 |
| 61 | Rockford, IL | 2,065 | 135 | Madison, WI | 884 | 209 | Garland, TX** | 514 |
| 62 | San Bernardino, CA** | 1,949 | 136 | Gary, IN** | 883 | 210 | Grand Prairie, TX** | 511 |
| 63 | Corpus Christi, TX** | 1,939 | 137 | Lafayette, LA** | 868 | 211 | Green Bay, WI | 500 |
| 64 | Flint, MI | 1,907 | 138 | Savannah, GA** | 851 | 211 | Visalia, CA** | 500 |
| 65 | Springfield, MO | 1,894 | 139 | Lancaster, CA** | 832 | 213 | Fairfield, CA** | 498 |
| 66 | Colorado Springs, CO | 1,893 | 140 | Tempe, AZ** | 831 | 214 | South Gate, CA** | 496 |
| 67 | Bakersfield, CA** | 1,857 | 141 | Pompano Beach, FL | 819 | 215 | Greeley, CO | 491 |
| 68 | Arlington, TX** | 1,837 | 142 | Lynn, MA | 814 | 216 | Santa Maria, CA** | 490 |
| 69 | Lubbock, TX** | 1,829 | 143 | Pomona, CA** | 809 | 217 | Medford, OR | 483 |
| 70 | Mesa, AZ** | 1,807 | 144 | Gainesville, FL | 806 | 218 | Abilene, TX** | 477 |
| 71 | North Las Vegas, NV** | 1,806 | 145 | Newport News, VA | 795 | 219 | Miramar, FL | 476 |
| 72 | Tacoma, WA | 1,766 | 146 | Albany, NY** | 791 | 220 | Brownsville, TX** | 473 |
| 73 | Worcester, MA | 1,750 | 147 | Peoria, IL** | 784 | 221 | Yakima, WA | 471 |
| 74 | Modesto, CA** | 1,704 | 148 | Lawrence, MA** | 776 | 222 | Elk Grove, CA** | 469 |

| RANK | CITY | CRIMES | RANK | CITY | CRIMES | RANK | CITY | CRIMES |
|---|---|---|---|---|---|---|---|---|
| 223 | Indio, CA** | 468 | 297 | Federal Way, WA | 291 | 371 | Alhambra, CA** | 163 |
| 224 | Lakeland, FL | 460 | 298 | Clinton Twnshp, MI | 285 | 371 | Arvada, CO | 163 |
| 225 | Erie, PA | 457 | 299 | Overland Park, KS** | 284 | 371 | Upland, CA** | 163 |
| 225 | Roanoke, VA | 457 | 300 | Westminster, CA** | 283 | 374 | Corona, CA** | 162 |
| 227 | Garden Grove, CA** | 455 | 301 | Bellflower, CA** | 279 | 375 | Provo, UT | 160 |
| 228 | Ontario, CA** | 453 | 302 | Edinburg, TX** | 277 | 376 | Alameda, CA** | 158 |
| 229 | Longview, TX | 451 | 303 | Santa Clarita, CA** | 276 | 376 | Cheektowaga, NY** | 158 |
| 229 | Palm Bay, FL | 451 | 304 | Bloomington, IN** | 275 | 378 | Mountain View, CA** | 157 |
| 231 | Upper Darby Twnshp, PA | 450 | 304 | Pembroke Pines, FL | 275 | 379 | Pearland, TX | 152 |
| 232 | Hemet, CA** | 447 | 306 | Kenosha, WI** | 274 | 379 | Tracy, CA** | 152 |
| 233 | Fargo, ND | 446 | 307 | Fremont, CA** | 273 | 381 | Cranston, RI | 151 |
| 234 | Vista, CA** | 445 | 308 | Sparks, NV** | 271 | 381 | Greece, NY** | 151 |
| 235 | Everett, WA** | 443 | 309 | Livermore, CA** | 270 | 383 | Round Rock, TX** | 149 |
| 236 | Pasadena, CA** | 434 | 310 | Suffolk, VA | 268 | 383 | Surprise, AZ** | 149 |
| 236 | Rialto, CA** | 434 | 311 | Jurupa Valley, CA** | 267 | 385 | Livonia, MI | 148 |
| 236 | Tuscaloosa, AL | 434 | 312 | Sunrise, FL | 265 | 386 | Broken Arrow, OK** | 147 |
| 239 | Columbia, MO | 416 | 313 | San Angelo, TX | 263 | 386 | Orange, CA** | 147 |
| 239 | Ogden, UT | 416 | 314 | Ventura, CA** | 262 | 388 | Roswell, GA** | 144 |
| 241 | Waterbury, CT** | 410 | 315 | Roseville, CA** | 261 | 388 | Sunnyvale, CA** | 144 |
| 242 | Concord, CA** | 407 | 316 | Alexandria, VA | 258 | 390 | Centennial, CO | 141 |
| 242 | Norwalk, CA** | 407 | 316 | Chino, CA** | 258 | 390 | Hillsboro, OR** | 141 |
| 244 | Waukegan, IL** | 405 | 318 | Napa, CA** | 255 | 392 | Thousand Oaks, CA** | 139 |
| 245 | Athens-Clarke, GA** | 404 | 319 | Peoria, AZ** | 254 | 393 | Woodbridge Twnshp, NJ** | 135 |
| 246 | Eugene, OR | 402 | 319 | Renton, WA | 254 | 394 | Sandy, UT | 134 |
| 246 | Mesquite, TX** | 402 | 321 | Costa Mesa, CA** | 252 | 395 | St. George, UT | 133 |
| 248 | Wichita Falls, TX** | 401 | 322 | Brooklyn Park, MN | 248 | 396 | Simi Valley, CA** | 132 |
| 249 | Carson, CA** | 400 | 323 | Ann Arbor, MI | 247 | 397 | Bloomington, MN | 128 |
| 250 | Bloomington, IL** | 399 | 324 | Sterling Heights, MI | 244 | 397 | Richardson, TX** | 128 |
| 251 | San Leandro, CA** | 394 | 325 | Lewisville, TX | 243 | 399 | Bellevue, WA** | 125 |
| 252 | Cedar Rapids, IA | 392 | 326 | Kennewick, WA | 240 | 400 | Beaverton, OR** | 124 |
| 253 | Plano, TX | 389 | 327 | Norwalk, CT | 239 | 401 | Edison Twnshp, NJ** | 123 |
| 254 | El Cajon, CA** | 386 | 327 | San Mateo, CA** | 239 | 402 | Concord, NC** | 122 |
| 255 | College Station, TX** | 379 | 329 | Coral Springs, FL | 237 | 403 | Meridian, ID | 115 |
| 256 | Tyler, TX | 376 | 330 | Elgin, IL** | 236 | 404 | Irvine, CA** | 113 |
| 257 | St. Joseph, MO | 374 | 331 | Charleston, SC | 231 | 405 | Danbury, CT** | 108 |
| 258 | Fullerton, CA** | 372 | 331 | Spokane Valley, WA** | 231 | 405 | Sugar Land, TX** | 108 |
| 259 | Hesperia, CA** | 371 | 331 | West Covina, CA** | 231 | 407 | Amherst, NY** | 107 |
| 260 | Henderson, NV** | 367 | 334 | Longmont, CO | 226 | 408 | Lake Forest, CA** | 105 |
| 261 | Westland, MI | 363 | 335 | Lakewood, CA** | 225 | 408 | Naperville, IL** | 105 |
| 262 | Huntington Beach, CA** | 362 | 336 | Daly City, CA** | 223 | 410 | Cary, NC** | 102 |
| 262 | Santa Barbara, CA** | 362 | 336 | Whittier, CA** | 223 | 411 | Frisco, TX | 100 |
| 264 | Cambridge, MA | 361 | 338 | Buena Park, CA** | 221 | 411 | Tustin, CA** | 100 |
| 264 | Quincy, MA | 361 | 338 | Carlsbad, CA** | 221 | 413 | Menifee, CA** | 99 |
| 266 | Billings, MT | 360 | 340 | Baldwin Park, CA** | 220 | 414 | League City, TX** | 96 |
| 267 | Bryan, TX** | 358 | 341 | Boulder, CO | 218 | 415 | Canton Twnshp, MI | 94 |
| 268 | Fort Collins, CO | 357 | 342 | Rochester, MN | 214 | 416 | Lakewood Twnshp, NJ** | 93 |
| 269 | Largo, FL | 352 | 342 | San Marcos, CA** | 214 | 416 | Warwick, RI | 93 |
| 270 | Decatur, IL** | 351 | 342 | Westminster, CO | 214 | 418 | Lee's Summit, MO | 91 |
| 271 | Midland, TX** | 350 | 345 | McKinney, TX | 207 | 418 | Temecula, CA** | 91 |
| 272 | Dearborn, MI | 347 | 346 | Nampa, ID | 202 | 420 | Brick Twnshp, NJ** | 89 |
| 273 | Cicero, IL** | 346 | 347 | Vacaville, CA** | 201 | 421 | Edmond, OK** | 87 |
| 274 | Duluth, MN | 342 | 348 | Cape Coral, FL | 197 | 422 | Hoover, AL | 74 |
| 275 | El Monte, CA** | 340 | 349 | Gilbert, AZ | 193 | 422 | Newton, MA | 74 |
| 276 | Fayetteville, AR | 339 | 350 | Somerville, MA | 191 | 422 | Toms River Twnshp, NJ** | 74 |
| 277 | Denton, TX | 338 | 351 | Redwood City, CA** | 190 | 425 | Newport Beach, CA** | 73 |
| 277 | Lawrence, KS | 338 | 352 | Evanston, IL** | 189 | 426 | Farmington Hills, MI | 72 |
| 279 | Scottsdale, AZ** | 337 | 352 | Hamilton Twnshp, NJ** | 189 | 426 | Mission, TX** | 72 |
| 280 | Stamford, CT | 334 | 354 | Torrance, CA** | 187 | 428 | Murrieta, CA** | 70 |
| 281 | Las Cruces, NM** | 332 | 355 | Sandy Springs, GA** | 186 | 429 | Clarkstown, NY** | 65 |
| 282 | Rancho Cucamon., CA** | 331 | 356 | Carrollton, TX** | 185 | 430 | Chino Hills, CA** | 63 |
| 282 | Thornton, CO | 331 | 356 | Olathe, KS** | 185 | 430 | Colonie, NY** | 63 |
| 284 | Lynchburg, VA | 330 | 358 | Bethlehem, PA | 183 | 430 | O'Fallon, MO | 63 |
| 285 | Downey, CA** | 326 | 359 | Bend, OR | 182 | 433 | Allen, TX | 62 |
| 286 | Santa Monica, CA** | 324 | 359 | Nashua, NH | 182 | 433 | Mission Viejo, CA** | 62 |
| 286 | Sioux City, IA | 324 | 361 | Clovis, CA** | 181 | 433 | Troy, MI | 62 |
| 288 | Citrus Heights, CA** | 320 | 361 | Glendale, CA** | 181 | 436 | Ramapo, NY** | 57 |
| 289 | Kent, WA | 319 | 363 | Norman, OK** | 178 | 437 | Arlington Heights, IL** | 42 |
| 290 | Plantation, FL | 311 | 364 | Clifton, NJ** | 175 | 438 | Johns Creek, GA** | 37 |
| 291 | Davie, FL | 306 | 364 | New Rochelle, NY** | 175 | 439 | Orem, UT** | 33 |
| 292 | Deerfield Beach, FL | 305 | 366 | Santa Clara, CA** | 172 | 440 | Carmel, IN** | 20 |
| 293 | Port St. Lucie, FL | 303 | 367 | Burbank, CA** | 171 | 441 | Fishers, IN** | 16 |
| 294 | Chico, CA** | 299 | 367 | McAllen, TX** | 171 | NA | Chicago, IL*** | NA |
| 295 | Racine, WI** | 297 | 369 | Scranton, PA | 166 | | | |
| 296 | Hampton, VA | 292 | 370 | Boca Raton, FL | 165 | | | |

Source: Reported data from the F.B.I. "Crime in the United States 2013"

*Violent crimes are offenses of murder, rape, robbery, and aggravated assault.

**Figures for these cities are based on the previous (legacy) definition of rape. See note on page vii.

***Not available.

# 46. Violent Crime Rate in 2013
## National Rate = 367.9 Violent Crimes per 100,000 Population*

| RANK | CITY | RATE | RANK | CITY | RATE | RANK | CITY | RATE |
|---|---|---|---|---|---|---|---|---|
| 211 | Abilene, TX** | 399.5 | 265 | Chino, CA** | 319.7 | 298 | Fullerton, CA** | 266.3 |
| 77 | Akron, OH | 791.3 | 319 | Chula Vista, CA** | 233.3 | 113 | Gainesville, FL | 636.7 |
| 337 | Alameda, CA** | 207.3 | 205 | Cicero, IL** | 410.9 | 303 | Garden Grove, CA** | 259.3 |
| 45 | Albany, GA** | 968.1 | 49 | Cincinnati, OH | 953.1 | 326 | Garland, TX** | 218.1 |
| 74 | Albany, NY** | 807.5 | 232 | Citrus Heights, CA** | 375.0 | 26 | Gary, IN** | 1,120.3 |
| 84 | Albuquerque, NM** | 774.9 | 424 | Clarkstown, NY** | 80.5 | 419 | Gilbert, AZ | 85.7 |
| 358 | Alexandria, VA | 173.7 | 155 | Clarksville, TN | 513.7 | 221 | Glendale, AZ** | 386.7 |
| 345 | Alhambra, CA** | 192.4 | 138 | Clearwater, FL | 567.5 | 414 | Glendale, CA** | 92.6 |
| 149 | Allentown, PA | 526.5 | 6 | Cleveland, OH | 1,477.7 | 289 | Grand Prairie, TX** | 278.0 |
| 432 | Allen, TX | 67.9 | 339 | Clifton, NJ** | 205.8 | 92 | Grand Rapids, MI | 693.5 |
| 106 | Amarillo, TX | 654.2 | 283 | Clinton Twnshp, MI | 290.6 | 364 | Greece, NY** | 156.2 |
| 415 | Amherst, NY** | 90.5 | 353 | Clovis, CA** | 181.9 | 158 | Greeley, CO | 510.9 |
| 258 | Anaheim, CA** | 327.2 | 225 | College Station, TX** | 383.1 | 177 | Green Bay, WI | 475.7 |
| 73 | Anchorage, AK | 813.1 | 424 | Colonie, NY** | 80.5 | 153 | Greensboro, NC** | 518.7 |
| 335 | Ann Arbor, MI | 211.5 | 194 | Colorado Springs, CO | 434.1 | 116 | Greenville, NC** | 630.6 |
| 57 | Antioch, CA** | 888.7 | 241 | Columbia, MO | 363.0 | 140 | Gresham, OR** | 555.6 |
| 436 | Arlington Heights, IL** | 55.3 | 90 | Columbia, SC | 719.9 | 333 | Hamilton Twnshp, NJ** | 212.4 |
| 170 | Arlington, TX** | 485.0 | 159 | Columbus, GA** | 508.0 | 70 | Hammond, IN** | 824.4 |
| 372 | Arvada, CO | 147.1 | 13 | Compton, CA** | 1,268.6 | 331 | Hampton, VA | 213.2 |
| 253 | Athens-Clarke, GA** | 336.3 | 260 | Concord, CA** | 324.4 | 24 | Hartford, CT** | 1,179.1 |
| 20 | Atlanta, GA** | 1,223.2 | 371 | Concord, NC** | 147.2 | 100 | Hawthorne, CA** | 673.4 |
| 203 | Aurora, CO | 418.1 | 347 | Coral Springs, FL | 187.2 | 219 | Hayward, CA** | 390.2 |
| 278 | Aurora, IL** | 299.7 | 409 | Corona, CA** | 101.1 | 143 | Hemet, CA** | 547.1 |
| 240 | Austin, TX** | 363.5 | 124 | Corpus Christi, TX** | 616.5 | 383 | Henderson, NV** | 136.8 |
| 156 | Bakersfield, CA** | 513.2 | 323 | Costa Mesa, CA** | 223.9 | 210 | Hesperia, CA** | 400.6 |
| 285 | Baldwin Park, CA** | 286.7 | 348 | Cranston, RI | 187.1 | 256 | Hialeah, FL | 330.5 |
| 8 | Baltimore, MD** | 1,401.2 | 102 | Dallas, TX** | 663.7 | 154 | High Point, NC** | 518.4 |
| 54 | Baton Rouge, LA** | 923.9 | 330 | Daly City, CA** | 213.3 | 374 | Hillsboro, OR** | 146.4 |
| 34 | Beaumont, TX** | 1,036.6 | 390 | Danbury, CT** | 129.6 | 169 | Hollywood, FL | 491.0 |
| 388 | Beaverton, OR** | 132.5 | 110 | Davenport, IA | 642.2 | 418 | Hoover, AL | 87.9 |
| 412 | Bellevue, WA** | 97.9 | 268 | Davie, FL | 316.8 | 47 | Houston, TX** | 962.7 |
| 244 | Bellflower, CA** | 359.6 | 59 | Dayton, OH | 871.3 | 351 | Huntington Beach, CA** | 184.8 |
| 322 | Bend, OR | 227.7 | 243 | Dearborn, MI | 361.4 | 72 | Huntsville, AL | 815.7 |
| 172 | Berkeley, CA** | 483.6 | 179 | Decatur, IL** | 466.8 | 181 | Independence, MO | 462.6 |
| 312 | Bethlehem, PA | 243.6 | 220 | Deerfield Beach, FL | 390.0 | 18 | Indianapolis, IN | 1,232.5 |
| 254 | Billings, MT | 333.9 | 291 | Denton, TX | 274.2 | 133 | Indio, CA** | 583.2 |
| 11 | Birmingham, AL | 1,345.3 | 117 | Denver, CO | 629.8 | 103 | Inglewood, CA** | 661.8 |
| 157 | Bloomington, IL** | 511.1 | 167 | Des Moines, IA | 494.7 | 437 | Irvine, CA** | 47.9 |
| 255 | Bloomington, IN** | 333.7 | 1 | Detroit, MI | 2,072.3 | 320 | Irving, TX** | 232.1 |
| 373 | Bloomington, MN | 147.0 | 284 | Downey, CA** | 287.9 | 122 | Jacksonville, FL | 620.3 |
| 350 | Boca Raton, FL | 185.9 | 212 | Duluth, MN | 396.7 | 53 | Jackson, MS** | 926.5 |
| 287 | Boise, ID | 279.9 | 251 | Edinburg, TX** | 336.7 | 107 | Jersey City, NJ** | 644.3 |
| 82 | Boston, MA** | 782.4 | 398 | Edison Twnshp, NJ** | 121.4 | 438 | Johns Creek, GA** | 44.0 |
| 334 | Boulder, CO | 212.0 | 408 | Edmond, OK** | 101.2 | 231 | Joliet, IL** | 375.2 |
| 401 | Brick Twnshp, NJ** | 118.1 | 228 | El Cajon, CA** | 378.4 | 294 | Jurupa Valley, CA** | 272.2 |
| 50 | Bridgeport, CT** | 949.8 | 279 | El Monte, CA** | 294.1 | 165 | Kansas City, KS** | 495.2 |
| 19 | Brockton, MA | 1,230.3 | 235 | El Paso, TX** | 371.0 | 15 | Kansas City, MO | 1,259.7 |
| 377 | Broken Arrow, OK** | 142.8 | 329 | Elgin, IL** | 213.7 | 272 | Kennewick, WA | 313.7 |
| 269 | Brooklyn Park, MN | 316.5 | 81 | Elizabeth, NJ** | 786.2 | 292 | Kenosha, WI** | 272.9 |
| 302 | Brownsville, TX** | 260.5 | 282 | Elk Grove, CA** | 291.4 | 305 | Kent, WA | 256.5 |
| 187 | Bryan, TX** | 455.6 | 188 | Erie, PA | 453.3 | 142 | Killeen, TX** | 551.5 |
| 297 | Buena Park, CA** | 267.5 | 209 | Escondido, CA** | 400.9 | 66 | Knoxville, TN | 840.9 |
| 16 | Buffalo, NY** | 1,255.5 | 307 | Eugene, OR | 253.6 | 91 | Lafayette, LA** | 703.4 |
| 360 | Burbank, CA** | 163.3 | 309 | Evanston, IL** | 249.6 | 389 | Lake Forest, CA** | 132.3 |
| 252 | Cambridge, MA | 336.5 | 178 | Evansville, IN** | 468.9 | 185 | Lakeland, FL | 456.7 |
| 405 | Canton Twnshp, MI | 105.7 | 201 | Everett, WA** | 421.4 | 410 | Lakewood Twnshp, NJ** | 100.4 |
| 399 | Cape Coral, FL | 120.5 | 184 | Fairfield, CA** | 459.3 | 290 | Lakewood, CA** | 277.5 |
| 342 | Carlsbad, CA** | 200.0 | 31 | Fall River, MA | 1,058.1 | 197 | Lakewood, CO | 426.5 |
| 440 | Carmel, IN** | 23.6 | 208 | Fargo, ND | 401.4 | 150 | Lancaster, CA** | 520.7 |
| 375 | Carrollton, TX** | 145.1 | 416 | Farmington Hills, MI | 88.8 | 32 | Lansing, MI | 1,057.0 |
| 196 | Carson, CA** | 428.2 | 193 | Fayetteville, AR | 435.2 | 204 | Laredo, TX** | 415.2 |
| 431 | Cary, NC** | 68.5 | 134 | Fayetteville, NC** | 577.7 | 189 | Largo, FL | 451.8 |
| 277 | Cedar Rapids, IA | 304.7 | 271 | Federal Way, WA | 313.8 | 259 | Las Cruces, NM** | 325.5 |
| 386 | Centennial, CO | 134.6 | 441 | Fishers, IN** | 19.2 | 86 | Las Vegas, NV** | 758.0 |
| 78 | Champaign, IL** | 788.3 | 3 | Flint, MI | 1,908.1 | 230 | Lawrence, KS | 375.4 |
| 321 | Chandler, AZ** | 231.2 | 245 | Fontana, CA** | 356.4 | 42 | Lawrence, MA** | 997.3 |
| 354 | Charleston, SC | 181.6 | 318 | Fort Collins, CO | 237.9 | 52 | Lawton, OK** | 932.5 |
| 129 | Charlotte, NC** | 608.0 | 64 | Fort Lauderdale, FL | 844.6 | 404 | League City, TX** | 107.1 |
| 43 | Chattanooga, TN | 982.1 | 94 | Fort Smith, AR | 690.0 | 411 | Lee's Summit, MO | 98.1 |
| 341 | Cheektowaga, NY** | 201.6 | 234 | Fort Wayne, IN | 372.4 | 314 | Lewisville, TX | 241.3 |
| 266 | Chesapeake, VA | 319.6 | 139 | Fort Worth, TX | 560.2 | 276 | Lexington, KY | 306.4 |
| NA | Chicago, IL*** | NA | 396 | Fremont, CA** | 121.6 | 236 | Lincoln, NE** | 370.0 |
| 249 | Chico, CA** | 338.9 | 162 | Fresno, CA** | 501.5 | 7 | Little Rock, AR | 1,406.8 |
| 423 | Chino Hills, CA** | 81.9 | 428 | Frisco, TX | 75.9 | 264 | Livermore, CA** | 320.1 |

| RANK | CITY | RATE |
|---|---|---|
| 365 | Livonia, MI | 155.4 |
| 163 | Long Beach, CA** | 499.5 |
| 308 | Longmont, CO | 252.7 |
| 141 | Longview, TX | 554.9 |
| 198 | Los Angeles, CA** | 426.0 |
| 145 | Louisville, KY** | 543.0 |
| 137 | Lowell, MA | 571.0 |
| 85 | Lubbock, TX** | 768.9 |
| 199 | Lynchburg, VA | 424.4 |
| 58 | Lynn, MA | 887.0 |
| 112 | Macon, GA** | 639.4 |
| 238 | Madison, WI | 364.5 |
| 98 | Manchester, NH | 676.6 |
| 394 | McAllen, TX** | 125.6 |
| 379 | McKinney, TX | 140.9 |
| 118 | Medford, OR | 627.7 |
| 62 | Melbourne, FL | 850.2 |
| 4 | Memphis, TN | 1,656.4 |
| 400 | Menifee, CA** | 119.8 |
| 97 | Merced, CA** | 683.6 |
| 381 | Meridian, ID | 140.1 |
| 213 | Mesa, AZ** | 396.1 |
| 288 | Mesquite, TX** | 278.6 |
| 39 | Miami Beach, FL | 1,005.1 |
| 71 | Miami Gardens, FL | 823.3 |
| 23 | Miami, FL | 1,181.9 |
| 286 | Midland, TX** | 286.3 |
| 10 | Milwaukee, WI | 1,363.8 |
| 37 | Minneapolis, MN | 1,019.2 |
| 239 | Miramar, FL | 363.6 |
| 435 | Mission Viejo, CA** | 64.7 |
| 417 | Mission, TX** | 88.5 |
| 125 | Mobile, AL | 615.0 |
| 67 | Modesto, CA** | 834.3 |
| 267 | Moreno Valley, CA** | 317.0 |
| 340 | Mountain View, CA** | 202.8 |
| 127 | Murfreesboro, TN | 609.9 |
| 434 | Murrieta, CA** | 65.0 |
| 315 | Nampa, ID | 238.7 |
| 262 | Napa, CA** | 323.8 |
| 430 | Naperville, IL** | 72.8 |
| 336 | Nashua, NH | 209.1 |
| 33 | Nashville, TN | 1,040.2 |
| 28 | New Bedford, MA | 1,091.9 |
| 17 | New Haven, CT | 1,253.5 |
| 80 | New Orleans, LA** | 786.4 |
| 324 | New Rochelle, NY** | 222.1 |
| 119 | New York, NY** | 623.9 |
| 14 | Newark, NJ** | 1,263.6 |
| 422 | Newport Beach, CA** | 83.3 |
| 192 | Newport News, VA | 439.0 |
| 421 | Newton, MA | 85.2 |
| 136 | Norfolk, VA | 573.4 |
| 367 | Norman, OK** | 152.2 |
| 101 | North Charleston, SC | 670.7 |
| 75 | North Las Vegas, NV** | 800.4 |
| 226 | Norwalk, CA** | 382.1 |
| 292 | Norwalk, CT | 272.9 |
| 2 | Oakland, CA** | 1,976.8 |
| 237 | Oceanside, CA** | 367.5 |
| 41 | Odessa, TX** | 997.6 |
| 427 | O'Fallon, MO | 76.2 |
| 166 | Ogden, UT | 495.0 |
| 69 | Oklahoma City, OK** | 826.1 |
| 379 | Olathe, KS** | 140.9 |
| 135 | Omaha, NE** | 576.1 |
| 296 | Ontario, CA** | 269.4 |
| 406 | Orange, CA** | 104.8 |
| 439 | Orem, UT** | 36.1 |
| 55 | Orlando, FL | 914.6 |
| 362 | Overland Park, KS** | 157.3 |
| 263 | Oxnard, CA** | 321.3 |
| 195 | Palm Bay, FL | 432.0 |
| 171 | Palmdale, CA** | 484.9 |

| RANK | CITY | RATE |
|---|---|---|
| 274 | Pasadena, CA** | 312.2 |
| 222 | Pasadena, TX** | 386.4 |
| 30 | Paterson, NJ** | 1,071.8 |
| 366 | Pearland, TX | 154.8 |
| 359 | Pembroke Pines, FL | 169.7 |
| 363 | Peoria, AZ** | 157.1 |
| 99 | Peoria, IL** | 676.1 |
| 27 | Philadelphia, PA | 1,099.3 |
| 114 | Phoenix, AZ** | 631.9 |
| 89 | Pittsburgh, PA | 734.3 |
| 378 | Plano, TX | 141.0 |
| 248 | Plantation, FL | 349.7 |
| 147 | Pomona, CA** | 534.5 |
| 79 | Pompano Beach, FL | 787.7 |
| 356 | Port St. Lucie, FL | 178.4 |
| 174 | Portland, OR** | 482.8 |
| 128 | Portsmouth, VA | 608.1 |
| 121 | Providence, RI | 623.3 |
| 383 | Provo, UT | 136.8 |
| 51 | Pueblo, CO | 935.6 |
| 223 | Quincy, MA | 386.1 |
| 227 | Racine, WI** | 380.1 |
| 216 | Raleigh, NC** | 392.3 |
| 433 | Ramapo, NY** | 65.4 |
| 346 | Rancho Cucamon., CA** | 192.1 |
| 65 | Reading, PA | 843.3 |
| 109 | Redding, CA** | 642.6 |
| 316 | Redwood City, CA** | 238.4 |
| 164 | Reno, NV** | 496.2 |
| 301 | Renton, WA | 262.8 |
| 200 | Rialto, CA** | 423.3 |
| 395 | Richardson, TX** | 122.4 |
| 35 | Richmond, CA** | 1,036.0 |
| 120 | Richmond, VA | 623.5 |
| 202 | Riverside, CA** | 420.3 |
| 180 | Roanoke, VA | 466.7 |
| 343 | Rochester, MN | 195.1 |
| 40 | Rochester, NY** | 1,000.7 |
| 9 | Rockford, IL | 1,374.8 |
| 338 | Roseville, CA** | 206.8 |
| 368 | Roswell, GA** | 151.0 |
| 382 | Round Rock, TX** | 137.2 |
| 105 | Sacramento, CA** | 656.0 |
| 257 | Salem, OR | 328.6 |
| 108 | Salinas, CA** | 642.7 |
| 83 | Salt Lake City, UT | 775.3 |
| 295 | San Angelo, TX | 272.1 |
| 115 | San Antonio, TX** | 630.7 |
| 56 | San Bernardino, CA** | 909.4 |
| 215 | San Diego, CA** | 393.0 |
| 63 | San Francisco, CA** | 847.1 |
| 261 | San Jose, CA** | 324.0 |
| 190 | San Leandro, CA** | 450.3 |
| 311 | San Marcos, CA** | 244.0 |
| 317 | San Mateo, CA** | 238.0 |
| 352 | Sandy Springs, GA** | 183.8 |
| 370 | Sandy, UT | 149.0 |
| 250 | Santa Ana, CA** | 336.8 |
| 207 | Santa Barbara, CA** | 402.2 |
| 376 | Santa Clara, CA** | 143.2 |
| 385 | Santa Clarita, CA** | 134.7 |
| 175 | Santa Maria, CA** | 480.2 |
| 247 | Santa Monica, CA** | 350.3 |
| 270 | Santa Rosa, CA** | 315.3 |
| 242 | Savannah, GA** | 361.8 |
| 369 | Scottsdale, AZ** | 149.4 |
| 325 | Scranton, PA | 219.2 |
| 132 | Seattle, WA | 584.6 |
| 93 | Shreveport, LA** | 690.9 |
| 407 | Simi Valley, CA** | 104.6 |
| 217 | Sioux City, IA | 391.9 |
| 214 | Sioux Falls, SD | 393.2 |
| 310 | Somerville, MA | 245.6 |
| 104 | South Bend, IN | 659.3 |

| RANK | CITY | RATE |
|---|---|---|
| 152 | South Gate, CA** | 518.9 |
| 281 | Sparks, NV** | 292.1 |
| 306 | Spokane Valley, WA** | 254.3 |
| 95 | Spokane, WA** | 687.3 |
| 38 | Springfield, IL** | 1,014.9 |
| 29 | Springfield, MA | 1,089.3 |
| 25 | Springfield, MO | 1,161.5 |
| 299 | Stamford, CT | 265.3 |
| 349 | Sterling Heights, MI | 186.8 |
| 22 | Stockton, CA** | 1,208.2 |
| 357 | St. George, UT | 174.0 |
| 173 | St. Joseph, MO | 483.5 |
| 5 | St. Louis, MO | 1,593.7 |
| 87 | St. Paul, MN | 746.5 |
| 46 | St. Petersburg, FL | 962.8 |
| 273 | Suffolk, VA | 313.5 |
| 391 | Sugar Land, TX** | 129.4 |
| 413 | Sunnyvale, CA** | 97.2 |
| 280 | Sunrise, FL | 293.6 |
| 396 | Surprise, AZ** | 121.6 |
| 68 | Syracuse, NY** | 828.7 |
| 60 | Tacoma, WA | 869.0 |
| 88 | Tallahassee, FL | 740.8 |
| 131 | Tampa, FL | 596.9 |
| 420 | Temecula, CA** | 85.3 |
| 168 | Tempe, AZ** | 493.2 |
| 300 | Thornton, CO | 263.2 |
| 403 | Thousand Oaks, CA** | 107.8 |
| 36 | Toledo, OH | 1,025.3 |
| 426 | Toms River Twnshp, NJ** | 80.1 |
| 176 | Topeka, KS** | 478.1 |
| 392 | Torrance, CA** | 126.8 |
| 355 | Tracy, CA** | 178.5 |
| 12 | Trenton, NJ** | 1,328.8 |
| 429 | Troy, MI | 75.1 |
| 111 | Tucson, AZ** | 640.9 |
| 44 | Tulsa, OK** | 970.1 |
| 182 | Tuscaloosa, AL | 461.1 |
| 392 | Tustin, CA** | 126.8 |
| 229 | Tyler, TX | 375.9 |
| 327 | Upland, CA** | 215.5 |
| 144 | Upper Darby Twnshp, PA | 543.7 |
| 332 | Vacaville, CA** | 213.0 |
| 61 | Vallejo, CA** | 861.1 |
| 246 | Vancouver, WA | 356.1 |
| 313 | Ventura, CA** | 242.1 |
| 146 | Victorville, CA** | 534.9 |
| 361 | Virginia Beach, VA | 162.0 |
| 218 | Visalia, CA** | 391.2 |
| 183 | Vista, CA** | 460.1 |
| 206 | Waco, TX** | 403.7 |
| 160 | Warren, MI | 506.1 |
| 402 | Warwick, RI | 113.7 |
| 21 | Washington, DC | 1,219.0 |
| 233 | Waterbury, CT** | 373.5 |
| 186 | Waukegan, IL** | 456.3 |
| 328 | West Covina, CA** | 214.2 |
| 96 | West Palm Beach, FL | 683.8 |
| 148 | West Valley, UT | 527.1 |
| 191 | Westland, MI | 439.7 |
| 275 | Westminster, CA** | 308.0 |
| 344 | Westminster, CO | 194.4 |
| 304 | Whittier, CA** | 258.0 |
| 224 | Wichita Falls, TX** | 383.7 |
| 76 | Wichita, KS | 793.0 |
| 123 | Wilmington, NC** | 619.0 |
| 130 | Winston-Salem, NC** | 604.7 |
| 387 | Woodbridge Twnshp, NJ** | 134.2 |
| 48 | Worcester, MA | 953.9 |
| 161 | Yakima, WA | 503.3 |
| 151 | Yonkers, NY** | 520.3 |
| 126 | Yuma, AZ | 611.4 |

Source: Reported data from the F.B.I. "Crime in the United States 2013"

*Violent crimes are offenses of murder, rape, robbery, and aggravated assault.

**Figures for these cities are based on the previous (legacy) definition of rape. See note on page vii.

***Not available.

# 46. Violent Crime Rate in 2013 (continued)
## National Rate = 367.9 Violent Crimes per 100,000 Population*

| RANK | CITY | RATE | RANK | CITY | RATE | RANK | CITY | RATE |
|---|---|---|---|---|---|---|---|---|
| 1 | Detroit, MI | 2,072.3 | 75 | North Las Vegas, NV** | 800.4 | 149 | Allentown, PA | 526.5 |
| 2 | Oakland, CA** | 1,976.8 | 76 | Wichita, KS | 793.0 | 150 | Lancaster, CA** | 520.7 |
| 3 | Flint, MI | 1,908.1 | 77 | Akron, OH | 791.3 | 151 | Yonkers, NY** | 520.3 |
| 4 | Memphis, TN | 1,656.4 | 78 | Champaign, IL** | 788.3 | 152 | South Gate, CA** | 518.9 |
| 5 | St. Louis, MO | 1,593.7 | 79 | Pompano Beach, FL | 787.7 | 153 | Greensboro, NC** | 518.7 |
| 6 | Cleveland, OH | 1,477.7 | 80 | New Orleans, LA** | 786.4 | 154 | High Point, NC** | 518.4 |
| 7 | Little Rock, AR | 1,406.8 | 81 | Elizabeth, NJ** | 786.2 | 155 | Clarksville, TN | 513.7 |
| 8 | Baltimore, MD** | 1,401.2 | 82 | Boston, MA** | 782.4 | 156 | Bakersfield, CA** | 513.2 |
| 9 | Rockford, IL | 1,374.8 | 83 | Salt Lake City, UT | 775.3 | 157 | Bloomington, IL** | 511.1 |
| 10 | Milwaukee, WI | 1,363.8 | 84 | Albuquerque, NM** | 774.9 | 158 | Greeley, CO | 510.9 |
| 11 | Birmingham, AL | 1,345.3 | 85 | Lubbock, TX** | 768.9 | 159 | Columbus, GA** | 508.0 |
| 12 | Trenton, NJ** | 1,328.8 | 86 | Las Vegas, NV** | 758.0 | 160 | Warren, MI | 506.1 |
| 13 | Compton, CA** | 1,268.6 | 87 | St. Paul, MN | 746.5 | 161 | Yakima, WA | 503.3 |
| 14 | Newark, NJ** | 1,263.6 | 88 | Tallahassee, FL | 740.8 | 162 | Fresno, CA** | 501.5 |
| 15 | Kansas City, MO | 1,259.7 | 89 | Pittsburgh, PA | 734.3 | 163 | Long Beach, CA** | 499.5 |
| 16 | Buffalo, NY** | 1,255.5 | 90 | Columbia, SC | 719.9 | 164 | Reno, NV** | 496.2 |
| 17 | New Haven, CT | 1,253.5 | 91 | Lafayette, LA** | 703.4 | 165 | Kansas City, KS** | 495.2 |
| 18 | Indianapolis, IN | 1,232.5 | 92 | Grand Rapids, MI | 693.5 | 166 | Ogden, UT | 495.0 |
| 19 | Brockton, MA | 1,230.3 | 93 | Shreveport, LA** | 690.9 | 167 | Des Moines, IA | 494.7 |
| 20 | Atlanta, GA** | 1,223.2 | 94 | Fort Smith, AR | 690.0 | 168 | Tempe, AZ** | 493.2 |
| 21 | Washington, DC | 1,219.0 | 95 | Spokane, WA** | 687.3 | 169 | Hollywood, FL | 491.0 |
| 22 | Stockton, CA** | 1,208.2 | 96 | West Palm Beach, FL | 683.8 | 170 | Arlington, TX** | 485.0 |
| 23 | Miami, FL | 1,181.9 | 97 | Merced, CA** | 683.6 | 171 | Palmdale, CA** | 484.9 |
| 24 | Hartford, CT** | 1,179.1 | 98 | Manchester, NH | 676.6 | 172 | Berkeley, CA** | 483.6 |
| 25 | Springfield, MO | 1,161.5 | 99 | Peoria, IL** | 676.1 | 173 | St. Joseph, MO | 483.5 |
| 26 | Gary, IN** | 1,120.3 | 100 | Hawthorne, CA** | 673.4 | 174 | Portland, OR** | 482.8 |
| 27 | Philadelphia, PA | 1,099.3 | 101 | North Charleston, SC | 670.7 | 175 | Santa Maria, CA** | 480.2 |
| 28 | New Bedford, MA | 1,091.9 | 102 | Dallas, TX** | 663.7 | 176 | Topeka, KS** | 478.1 |
| 29 | Springfield, MA | 1,089.3 | 103 | Inglewood, CA** | 661.8 | 177 | Green Bay, WI | 475.7 |
| 30 | Paterson, NJ** | 1,071.8 | 104 | South Bend, IN | 659.3 | 178 | Evansville, IN** | 468.9 |
| 31 | Fall River, MA | 1,058.1 | 105 | Sacramento, CA** | 656.0 | 179 | Decatur, IL** | 466.8 |
| 32 | Lansing, MI | 1,057.0 | 106 | Amarillo, TX | 654.2 | 180 | Roanoke, VA | 466.7 |
| 33 | Nashville, TN | 1,040.2 | 107 | Jersey City, NJ** | 644.3 | 181 | Independence, MO | 462.6 |
| 34 | Beaumont, TX** | 1,036.6 | 108 | Salinas, CA** | 642.7 | 182 | Tuscaloosa, AL | 461.1 |
| 35 | Richmond, CA** | 1,036.0 | 109 | Redding, CA** | 642.6 | 183 | Vista, CA** | 460.1 |
| 36 | Toledo, OH | 1,025.3 | 110 | Davenport, IA | 642.2 | 184 | Fairfield, CA** | 459.3 |
| 37 | Minneapolis, MN | 1,019.2 | 111 | Tucson, AZ** | 640.9 | 185 | Lakeland, FL | 456.7 |
| 38 | Springfield, IL** | 1,014.9 | 112 | Macon, GA** | 639.4 | 186 | Waukegan, IL** | 456.3 |
| 39 | Miami Beach, FL | 1,005.1 | 113 | Gainesville, FL | 636.7 | 187 | Bryan, TX** | 455.6 |
| 40 | Rochester, NY** | 1,000.7 | 114 | Phoenix, AZ** | 631.9 | 188 | Erie, PA | 453.3 |
| 41 | Odessa, TX** | 997.6 | 115 | San Antonio, TX** | 630.7 | 189 | Largo, FL | 451.8 |
| 42 | Lawrence, MA** | 997.3 | 116 | Greenville, NC** | 630.6 | 190 | San Leandro, CA** | 450.3 |
| 43 | Chattanooga, TN | 982.1 | 117 | Denver, CO | 629.8 | 191 | Westland, MI | 439.7 |
| 44 | Tulsa, OK** | 970.1 | 118 | Medford, OR | 627.7 | 192 | Newport News, VA | 439.0 |
| 45 | Albany, GA** | 968.1 | 119 | New York, NY** | 623.9 | 193 | Fayetteville, AR | 435.2 |
| 46 | St. Petersburg, FL | 962.8 | 120 | Richmond, VA | 623.5 | 194 | Colorado Springs, CO | 434.1 |
| 47 | Houston, TX** | 962.7 | 121 | Providence, RI | 623.3 | 195 | Palm Bay, FL | 432.0 |
| 48 | Worcester, MA | 953.9 | 122 | Jacksonville, FL | 620.3 | 196 | Carson, CA** | 428.2 |
| 49 | Cincinnati, OH | 953.1 | 123 | Wilmington, NC** | 619.0 | 197 | Lakewood, CO | 426.5 |
| 50 | Bridgeport, CT** | 949.8 | 124 | Corpus Christi, TX** | 616.5 | 198 | Los Angeles, CA** | 426.0 |
| 51 | Pueblo, CO | 935.6 | 125 | Mobile, AL | 615.0 | 199 | Lynchburg, VA | 424.4 |
| 52 | Lawton, OK** | 932.5 | 126 | Yuma, AZ | 611.4 | 200 | Rialto, CA** | 423.3 |
| 53 | Jackson, MS** | 926.5 | 127 | Murfreesboro, TN | 609.9 | 201 | Everett, WA** | 421.4 |
| 54 | Baton Rouge, LA** | 923.9 | 128 | Portsmouth, VA | 608.1 | 202 | Riverside, CA** | 420.3 |
| 55 | Orlando, FL | 914.6 | 129 | Charlotte, NC** | 608.0 | 203 | Aurora, CO | 418.1 |
| 56 | San Bernardino, CA** | 909.4 | 130 | Winston-Salem, NC** | 604.7 | 204 | Laredo, TX** | 415.2 |
| 57 | Antioch, CA** | 888.7 | 131 | Tampa, FL | 596.9 | 205 | Cicero, IL** | 410.9 |
| 58 | Lynn, MA | 887.0 | 132 | Seattle, WA | 584.6 | 206 | Waco, TX** | 403.7 |
| 59 | Dayton, OH | 871.3 | 133 | Indio, CA** | 583.2 | 207 | Santa Barbara, CA** | 402.2 |
| 60 | Tacoma, WA | 869.0 | 134 | Fayetteville, NC** | 577.7 | 208 | Fargo, ND | 401.4 |
| 61 | Vallejo, CA** | 861.1 | 135 | Omaha, NE** | 576.1 | 209 | Escondido, CA** | 400.9 |
| 62 | Melbourne, FL | 850.2 | 136 | Norfolk, VA | 573.4 | 210 | Hesperia, CA** | 400.6 |
| 63 | San Francisco, CA** | 847.1 | 137 | Lowell, MA | 571.0 | 211 | Abilene, TX** | 399.5 |
| 64 | Fort Lauderdale, FL | 844.6 | 138 | Clearwater, FL | 567.5 | 212 | Duluth, MN | 396.7 |
| 65 | Reading, PA | 843.3 | 139 | Fort Worth, TX | 560.2 | 213 | Mesa, AZ** | 396.1 |
| 66 | Knoxville, TN | 840.9 | 140 | Gresham, OR** | 555.6 | 214 | Sioux Falls, SD | 393.2 |
| 67 | Modesto, CA** | 834.3 | 141 | Longview, TX | 554.9 | 215 | San Diego, CA** | 393.0 |
| 68 | Syracuse, NY** | 828.7 | 142 | Killeen, TX** | 551.5 | 216 | Raleigh, NC** | 392.3 |
| 69 | Oklahoma City, OK** | 826.1 | 143 | Hemet, CA** | 547.1 | 217 | Sioux City, IA | 391.9 |
| 70 | Hammond, IN** | 824.4 | 144 | Upper Darby Twnshp, PA | 543.7 | 218 | Visalia, CA** | 391.2 |
| 71 | Miami Gardens, FL | 823.3 | 145 | Louisville, KY** | 543.0 | 219 | Hayward, CA** | 390.2 |
| 72 | Huntsville, AL | 815.7 | 146 | Victorville, CA** | 534.9 | 220 | Deerfield Beach, FL | 390.0 |
| 73 | Anchorage, AK | 813.1 | 147 | Pomona, CA** | 534.5 | 221 | Glendale, AZ** | 386.7 |
| 74 | Albany, NY** | 807.5 | 148 | West Valley, UT | 527.1 | 222 | Pasadena, TX** | 386.4 |

| RANK | CITY | RATE |
|------|------|------|
| 223 | Quincy, MA | 386.1 |
| 224 | Wichita Falls, TX** | 383.7 |
| 225 | College Station, TX** | 383.1 |
| 226 | Norwalk, CA** | 382.1 |
| 227 | Racine, WI** | 380.1 |
| 228 | El Cajon, CA** | 378.4 |
| 229 | Tyler, TX | 375.9 |
| 230 | Lawrence, KS | 375.4 |
| 231 | Joliet, IL** | 375.2 |
| 232 | Citrus Heights, CA** | 375.0 |
| 233 | Waterbury, CT** | 373.5 |
| 234 | Fort Wayne, IN | 372.4 |
| 235 | El Paso, TX** | 371.0 |
| 236 | Lincoln, NE** | 370.0 |
| 237 | Oceanside, CA** | 367.5 |
| 238 | Madison, WI | 364.5 |
| 239 | Miramar, FL | 363.6 |
| 240 | Austin, TX** | 363.5 |
| 241 | Columbia, MO | 363.0 |
| 242 | Savannah, GA** | 361.8 |
| 243 | Dearborn, MI | 361.4 |
| 244 | Bellflower, CA** | 359.6 |
| 245 | Fontana, CA** | 356.4 |
| 246 | Vancouver, WA | 356.1 |
| 247 | Santa Monica, CA** | 350.3 |
| 248 | Plantation, FL | 349.7 |
| 249 | Chico, CA** | 338.9 |
| 250 | Santa Ana, CA** | 336.8 |
| 251 | Edinburg, TX** | 336.7 |
| 252 | Cambridge, MA | 336.5 |
| 253 | Athens-Clarke, GA** | 336.3 |
| 254 | Billings, MT | 333.9 |
| 255 | Bloomington, IN** | 333.7 |
| 256 | Hialeah, FL | 330.5 |
| 257 | Salem, OR | 328.6 |
| 258 | Anaheim, CA** | 327.2 |
| 259 | Las Cruces, NM** | 325.5 |
| 260 | Concord, CA** | 324.4 |
| 261 | San Jose, CA** | 324.0 |
| 262 | Napa, CA** | 323.8 |
| 263 | Oxnard, CA** | 321.3 |
| 264 | Livermore, CA** | 320.1 |
| 265 | Chino, CA** | 319.7 |
| 266 | Chesapeake, VA | 319.6 |
| 267 | Moreno Valley, CA** | 317.0 |
| 268 | Davie, FL | 316.8 |
| 269 | Brooklyn Park, MN | 316.5 |
| 270 | Santa Rosa, CA** | 315.3 |
| 271 | Federal Way, WA | 313.8 |
| 272 | Kennewick, WA | 313.7 |
| 273 | Suffolk, VA | 313.5 |
| 274 | Pasadena, CA** | 312.2 |
| 275 | Westminster, CA** | 308.0 |
| 276 | Lexington, KY | 306.4 |
| 277 | Cedar Rapids, IA | 304.7 |
| 278 | Aurora, IL** | 299.7 |
| 279 | El Monte, CA** | 294.1 |
| 280 | Sunrise, FL | 293.6 |
| 281 | Sparks, NV** | 292.1 |
| 282 | Elk Grove, CA** | 291.4 |
| 283 | Clinton Twnshp, MI | 290.6 |
| 284 | Downey, CA** | 287.9 |
| 285 | Baldwin Park, CA** | 286.7 |
| 286 | Midland, TX** | 286.3 |
| 287 | Boise, ID | 279.9 |
| 288 | Mesquite, TX** | 278.6 |
| 289 | Grand Prairie, TX** | 278.0 |
| 290 | Lakewood, CA** | 277.5 |
| 291 | Denton, TX | 274.2 |
| 292 | Kenosha, WI** | 272.9 |
| 292 | Norwalk, CT | 272.9 |
| 294 | Jurupa Valley, CA** | 272.2 |
| 295 | San Angelo, TX | 272.1 |
| 296 | Ontario, CA** | 269.4 |
| 297 | Buena Park, CA** | 267.5 |
| 298 | Fullerton, CA** | 266.3 |
| 299 | Stamford, CT | 265.3 |
| 300 | Thornton, CO | 263.2 |
| 301 | Renton, WA | 262.8 |
| 302 | Brownsville, TX** | 260.5 |
| 303 | Garden Grove, CA** | 259.3 |
| 304 | Whittier, CA** | 258.0 |
| 305 | Kent, WA | 256.5 |
| 306 | Spokane Valley, WA** | 254.3 |
| 307 | Eugene, OR | 253.6 |
| 308 | Longmont, CO | 252.7 |
| 309 | Evanston, IL** | 249.6 |
| 310 | Somerville, MA | 245.6 |
| 311 | San Marcos, CA** | 244.0 |
| 312 | Bethlehem, PA | 243.6 |
| 313 | Ventura, CA** | 242.1 |
| 314 | Lewisville, TX | 241.3 |
| 315 | Nampa, ID | 238.7 |
| 316 | Redwood City, CA** | 238.4 |
| 317 | San Mateo, CA** | 238.0 |
| 318 | Fort Collins, CO | 237.9 |
| 319 | Chula Vista, CA** | 233.3 |
| 320 | Irving, TX** | 232.1 |
| 321 | Chandler, AZ** | 231.2 |
| 322 | Bend, OR | 227.7 |
| 323 | Costa Mesa, CA** | 223.9 |
| 324 | New Rochelle, NY** | 222.1 |
| 325 | Scranton, PA | 219.2 |
| 326 | Garland, TX** | 218.1 |
| 327 | Upland, CA** | 215.5 |
| 328 | West Covina, CA** | 214.2 |
| 329 | Elgin, IL** | 213.7 |
| 330 | Daly City, CA** | 213.3 |
| 331 | Hampton, VA | 213.2 |
| 332 | Vacaville, CA** | 213.0 |
| 333 | Hamilton Twnshp, NJ** | 212.4 |
| 334 | Boulder, CO | 212.0 |
| 335 | Ann Arbor, MI | 211.5 |
| 336 | Nashua, NH | 209.1 |
| 337 | Alameda, CA** | 207.3 |
| 338 | Roseville, CA** | 206.8 |
| 339 | Clifton, NJ** | 205.8 |
| 340 | Mountain View, CA** | 202.8 |
| 341 | Cheektowaga, NY** | 201.6 |
| 342 | Carlsbad, CA** | 200.0 |
| 343 | Rochester, MN | 195.1 |
| 344 | Westminster, CO | 194.4 |
| 345 | Alhambra, CA** | 192.4 |
| 346 | Rancho Cucamon., CA** | 192.1 |
| 347 | Coral Springs, FL | 187.2 |
| 348 | Cranston, RI | 187.1 |
| 349 | Sterling Heights, MI | 186.8 |
| 350 | Boca Raton, FL | 185.9 |
| 351 | Huntington Beach, CA** | 184.8 |
| 352 | Sandy Springs, GA** | 183.8 |
| 353 | Clovis, CA** | 181.9 |
| 354 | Charleston, SC | 181.6 |
| 355 | Tracy, CA** | 178.5 |
| 356 | Port St. Lucie, FL | 178.4 |
| 357 | St. George, UT | 174.0 |
| 358 | Alexandria, VA | 173.7 |
| 359 | Pembroke Pines, FL | 169.7 |
| 360 | Burbank, CA** | 163.3 |
| 361 | Virginia Beach, VA | 162.0 |
| 362 | Overland Park, KS** | 157.3 |
| 363 | Peoria, AZ** | 157.1 |
| 364 | Greece, NY** | 156.2 |
| 365 | Livonia, MI | 155.4 |
| 366 | Pearland, TX | 154.8 |
| 367 | Norman, OK** | 152.2 |
| 368 | Roswell, GA** | 151.0 |
| 369 | Scottsdale, AZ** | 149.4 |
| 370 | Sandy, UT | 149.0 |
| 371 | Concord, NC** | 147.2 |
| 372 | Arvada, CO | 147.1 |
| 373 | Bloomington, MN | 147.0 |
| 374 | Hillsboro, OR** | 146.4 |
| 375 | Carrollton, TX** | 145.1 |
| 376 | Santa Clara, CA** | 143.2 |
| 377 | Broken Arrow, OK** | 142.8 |
| 378 | Plano, TX | 141.0 |
| 379 | McKinney, TX | 140.9 |
| 379 | Olathe, KS** | 140.9 |
| 381 | Meridian, ID | 140.1 |
| 382 | Round Rock, TX** | 137.2 |
| 383 | Henderson, NV** | 136.8 |
| 383 | Provo, UT | 136.8 |
| 385 | Santa Clarita, CA** | 134.7 |
| 386 | Centennial, CO | 134.6 |
| 387 | Woodbridge Twnshp, NJ** | 134.2 |
| 388 | Beaverton, OR** | 132.5 |
| 389 | Lake Forest, CA** | 132.3 |
| 390 | Danbury, CT** | 129.6 |
| 391 | Sugar Land, TX** | 129.4 |
| 392 | Torrance, CA** | 126.8 |
| 392 | Tustin, CA** | 126.8 |
| 394 | McAllen, TX** | 125.6 |
| 395 | Richardson, TX** | 122.4 |
| 396 | Fremont, CA** | 121.6 |
| 396 | Surprise, AZ** | 121.6 |
| 398 | Edison Twnshp, NJ** | 121.4 |
| 399 | Cape Coral, FL | 120.5 |
| 400 | Menifee, CA** | 119.8 |
| 401 | Brick Twnshp, NJ** | 118.1 |
| 402 | Warwick, RI | 113.7 |
| 403 | Thousand Oaks, CA** | 107.8 |
| 404 | League City, TX** | 107.1 |
| 405 | Canton Twnshp, MI | 105.7 |
| 406 | Orange, CA** | 104.8 |
| 407 | Simi Valley, CA** | 104.6 |
| 408 | Edmond, OK** | 101.2 |
| 409 | Corona, CA** | 101.1 |
| 410 | Lakewood Twnshp, NJ** | 100.4 |
| 411 | Lee's Summit, MO | 98.1 |
| 412 | Bellevue, WA** | 97.9 |
| 413 | Sunnyvale, CA** | 97.2 |
| 414 | Glendale, CA** | 92.6 |
| 415 | Amherst, NY** | 90.5 |
| 416 | Farmington Hills, MI | 88.8 |
| 417 | Mission, TX** | 88.5 |
| 418 | Hoover, AL | 87.9 |
| 419 | Gilbert, AZ | 85.7 |
| 420 | Temecula, CA** | 85.3 |
| 421 | Newton, MA | 85.2 |
| 422 | Newport Beach, CA** | 83.3 |
| 423 | Chino Hills, CA** | 81.9 |
| 424 | Clarkstown, NY** | 80.5 |
| 424 | Colonie, NY** | 80.5 |
| 426 | Toms River Twnshp, NJ** | 80.1 |
| 427 | O'Fallon, MO | 76.2 |
| 428 | Frisco, TX | 75.9 |
| 429 | Troy, MI | 75.1 |
| 430 | Naperville, IL** | 72.8 |
| 431 | Cary, NC** | 68.5 |
| 432 | Allen, TX | 67.9 |
| 433 | Ramapo, NY** | 65.4 |
| 434 | Murrieta, CA** | 65.0 |
| 435 | Mission Viejo, CA** | 64.7 |
| 436 | Arlington Heights, IL** | 55.3 |
| 437 | Irvine, CA** | 47.9 |
| 438 | Johns Creek, GA** | 44.0 |
| 439 | Orem, UT** | 36.1 |
| 440 | Carmel, IN** | 23.6 |
| 441 | Fishers, IN** | 19.2 |
| NA | Chicago, IL*** | NA |

Source: Reported data from the F.B.I. "Crime in the United States 2013"

*Violent crimes are offenses of murder, rape, robbery, and aggravated assault.

**Figures for these cities are based on the previous (legacy) definition of rape. See note on page vii.

***Not available.

# 47. Percent Change in Violent Crime Rate: 2012 to 2013
## National Percent Change = 5.1% Decrease*

| RANK | CITY | % CHANGE | RANK | CITY | % CHANGE | RANK | CITY | % CHANGE |
|---|---|---|---|---|---|---|---|---|
| 116 | Abilene, TX** | 1.5 | 322 | Chino, CA** | (12.3) | 389 | Fullerton, CA** | (18.4) |
| 301 | Akron, OH | (10.7) | 134 | Chula Vista, CA** | 0.3 | 225 | Gainesville, FL | (5.0) |
| 180 | Alameda, CA** | (2.2) | 270 | Cicero, IL** | (8.6) | 96 | Garden Grove, CA** | 3.4 |
| 248 | Albany, GA** | (6.5) | 180 | Cincinnati, OH | (2.2) | 226 | Garland, TX** | (5.1) |
| 160 | Albany, NY** | (1.1) | 196 | Citrus Heights, CA** | (3.0) | 7 | Gary, IN** | 23.8 |
| 96 | Albuquerque, NM** | 3.4 | 357 | Clarkstown, NY** | (15.1) | 296 | Gilbert, AZ | (10.4) |
| 93 | Alexandria, VA | 4.3 | 397 | Clarksville, TN | (19.4) | 402 | Glendale, AZ** | (21.3) |
| 55 | Alhambra, CA** | 9.1 | 348 | Clearwater, FL | (14.7) | 404 | Glendale, CA** | (22.5) |
| 209 | Allentown, PA | (3.8) | 73 | Cleveland, OH | 6.8 | 119 | Grand Prairie, TX** | 1.3 |
| 51 | Allen, TX | 9.7 | 231 | Clifton, NJ** | (5.3) | 291 | Grand Rapids, MI | (10.1) |
| 127 | Amarillo, TX | 0.6 | 198 | Clinton Twnshp, MI | (3.1) | 23 | Greece, NY** | 17.2 |
| 10 | Amherst, NY** | 21.0 | 393 | Clovis, CA** | (18.8) | 29 | Greeley, CO | 15.5 |
| 317 | Anaheim, CA** | (11.9) | 415 | College Station, TX** | (24.7) | 171 | Green Bay, WI | (1.8) |
| 173 | Anchorage, AK | (1.9) | 2 | Colonie, NY** | 36.2 | 262 | Greensboro, NC** | (7.9) |
| 70 | Ann Arbor, MI | 7.1 | 219 | Colorado Springs, CO | (4.7) | 11 | Greenville, NC** | 20.4 |
| 325 | Antioch, CA** | (12.6) | 365 | Columbia, MO | (15.6) | 8 | Gresham, OR** | 23.4 |
| 111 | Arlington Heights, IL** | 1.8 | NA | Columbia, SC*** | NA | 126 | Hamilton Twnshp, NJ** | 0.7 |
| 207 | Arlington, TX** | (3.6) | 134 | Columbus, GA** | 0.3 | 132 | Hammond, IN** | 0.4 |
| 116 | Arvada, CO | 1.5 | 108 | Compton, CA** | 2.1 | 247 | Hampton, VA | (6.4) |
| 333 | Athens-Clarke, GA** | (13.2) | 122 | Concord, CA** | 1.0 | 302 | Hartford, CT** | (10.8) |
| 309 | Atlanta, GA** | (11.3) | NA | Concord, NC*** | NA | 280 | Hawthorne, CA** | (9.4) |
| 168 | Aurora, CO | (1.7) | 106 | Coral Springs, FL | 2.2 | 241 | Hayward, CA** | (6.2) |
| 77 | Aurora, IL** | 6.4 | 414 | Corona, CA** | (24.3) | 53 | Hemet, CA** | 9.4 |
| 307 | Austin, TX** | (11.1) | 244 | Corpus Christi, TX** | (6.3) | 394 | Henderson, NV** | (19.0) |
| 234 | Bakersfield, CA** | (5.4) | 154 | Costa Mesa, CA** | (0.7) | 262 | Hesperia, CA** | (7.9) |
| 366 | Baldwin Park, CA** | (15.8) | 27 | Cranston, RI | 15.6 | 221 | Hialeah, FL | (4.9) |
| 141 | Baltimore, MD** | (0.3) | 168 | Dallas, TX** | (1.7) | 146 | High Point, NC** | (0.4) |
| 348 | Baton Rouge, LA** | (14.7) | 109 | Daly City, CA** | 2.0 | 408 | Hillsboro, OR** | (23.4) |
| 132 | Beaumont, TX** | 0.4 | 191 | Danbury, CT** | (2.6) | 42 | Hollywood, FL | 11.0 |
| 336 | Beaverton, OR** | (13.3) | 64 | Davenport, IA | 7.6 | 369 | Hoover, AL | (15.9) |
| 408 | Bellevue, WA** | (23.4) | 390 | Davie, FL | (18.5) | 196 | Houston, TX** | (3.0) |
| 262 | Bellflower, CA** | (7.9) | 298 | Dayton, OH | (10.5) | 32 | Huntington Beach, CA** | 14.9 |
| NA | Bend, OR*** | NA | 55 | Dearborn, MI | 9.1 | 316 | Huntsville, AL | (11.7) |
| 35 | Berkeley, CA** | 14.2 | 122 | Decatur, IL** | 1.0 | 121 | Independence, MO | 1.2 |
| 406 | Bethlehem, PA | (22.8) | 372 | Deerfield Beach, FL | (16.1) | 94 | Indianapolis, IN | 4.0 |
| 212 | Billings, MT | (4.0) | 315 | Denton, TX | (11.6) | 114 | Indio, CA** | 1.7 |
| 312 | Birmingham, AL | (11.4) | 105 | Denver, CO | 2.3 | 234 | Inglewood, CA** | (5.4) |
| 78 | Bloomington, IL** | 5.9 | 241 | Des Moines, IA | (6.2) | 231 | Irvine, CA** | (5.3) |
| 39 | Bloomington, IN** | 12.1 | 186 | Detroit, MI | (2.4) | 102 | Irving, TX** | 2.6 |
| NA | Bloomington, MN*** | NA | 343 | Downey, CA** | (14.1) | 128 | Jacksonville, FL | 0.5 |
| 175 | Boca Raton, FL | (2.0) | NA | Duluth, MN*** | NA | 184 | Jackson, MS** | (2.3) |
| 92 | Boise, ID | 4.4 | 413 | Edinburg, TX** | (24.2) | 321 | Jersey City, NJ** | (12.2) |
| 244 | Boston, MA** | (6.3) | 128 | Edison Twnshp, NJ** | 0.5 | 385 | Johns Creek, GA** | (18.1) |
| 348 | Boulder, CO | (14.7) | 151 | Edmond, OK** | (0.6) | 48 | Joliet, IL** | 10.1 |
| 44 | Brick Twnshp, NJ** | 10.6 | 81 | El Cajon, CA** | 5.6 | 354 | Jurupa Valley, CA** | (14.9) |
| 401 | Bridgeport, CT** | (21.2) | 343 | El Monte, CA** | (14.1) | 377 | Kansas City, KS** | (16.9) |
| 64 | Brockton, MA | 7.6 | 322 | El Paso, TX** | (12.3) | 141 | Kansas City, MO | (0.3) |
| 255 | Broken Arrow, OK** | (7.2) | 277 | Elgin, IL** | (9.2) | 83 | Kennewick, WA | 5.4 |
| NA | Brooklyn Park, MN*** | NA | 165 | Elizabeth, NJ** | (1.4) | 146 | Kenosha, WI** | (0.4) |
| 141 | Brownsville, TX** | (0.3) | 306 | Elk Grove, CA** | (11.0) | 429 | Kent, WA | (42.3) |
| 34 | Bryan, TX** | 14.6 | 124 | Erie, PA | 0.9 | 346 | Killeen, TX** | (14.5) |
| 70 | Buena Park, CA** | 7.1 | 237 | Escondido, CA** | (5.9) | 340 | Knoxville, TN | (13.6) |
| 191 | Buffalo, NY** | (2.6) | 252 | Eugene, OR | (6.8) | 43 | Lafayette, LA** | 10.9 |
| 419 | Burbank, CA** | (29.4) | 385 | Evanston, IL** | (18.1) | 177 | Lake Forest, CA** | (2.1) |
| 375 | Cambridge, MA | (16.5) | 159 | Evansville, IN** | (1.0) | 171 | Lakeland, FL | (1.8) |
| NA | Canton Twnshp, MI*** | NA | 259 | Everett, WA** | (7.7) | 345 | Lakewood Twnshp, NJ** | (14.4) |
| 371 | Cape Coral, FL | (16.0) | 60 | Fairfield, CA** | 8.4 | 149 | Lakewood, CA** | (0.5) |
| 391 | Carlsbad, CA** | (18.6) | 149 | Fall River, MA | (0.5) | 258 | Lakewood, CO | (7.6) |
| 1 | Carmel, IN** | 76.1 | 40 | Fargo, ND | 11.9 | 204 | Lancaster, CA** | (3.5) |
| 134 | Carrollton, TX** | 0.3 | 207 | Farmington Hills, MI | (3.6) | 37 | Lansing, MI | 12.5 |
| 407 | Carson, CA** | (23.2) | 363 | Fayetteville, AR | (15.4) | 167 | Laredo, TX** | (1.6) |
| 372 | Cary, NC** | (16.1) | 134 | Fayetteville, NC** | 0.3 | 286 | Largo, FL | (9.7) |
| 50 | Cedar Rapids, IA | 9.9 | 190 | Federal Way, WA | (2.5) | 382 | Las Cruces, NM** | (17.5) |
| 302 | Centennial, CO | (10.8) | 55 | Fishers, IN** | 9.1 | 201 | Las Vegas, NV** | (3.3) |
| 339 | Champaign, IL** | (13.5) | 424 | Flint, MI | (30.1) | 284 | Lawrence, KS | (9.5) |
| 300 | Chandler, AZ** | (10.6) | 366 | Fontana, CA** | (15.8) | 162 | Lawrence, MA** | (1.3) |
| 412 | Charleston, SC | (24.0) | 284 | Fort Collins, CO | (9.5) | 139 | Lawton, OK** | 0.1 |
| 241 | Charlotte, NC** | (6.2) | 248 | Fort Lauderdale, FL | (6.5) | 25 | League City, TX** | 16.8 |
| NA | Chattanooga, TN*** | NA | 320 | Fort Smith, AR | (12.1) | 381 | Lee's Summit, MO | (17.4) |
| 272 | Cheektowaga, NY** | (8.8) | 102 | Fort Wayne, IN | 2.6 | NA | Lewisville, TX*** | NA |
| 336 | Chesapeake, VA | (13.3) | 218 | Fort Worth, TX | (4.6) | 332 | Lexington, KY | (13.1) |
| NA | Chicago, IL*** | NA | 329 | Fremont, CA** | (13.0) | 253 | Lincoln, NE** | (6.9) |
| 88 | Chico, CA** | 4.7 | 259 | Fresno, CA** | (7.7) | 72 | Little Rock, AR | 6.9 |
| 173 | Chino Hills, CA** | (1.9) | 217 | Frisco, TX | (4.5) | 317 | Livermore, CA** | (11.9) |

| RANK | CITY | % CHANGE |
|---|---|---|
| 106 | Livonia, MI | 2.2 |
| 333 | Long Beach, CA** | (13.2) |
| 13 | Longmont, CO | 19.5 |
| 160 | Longview, TX | (1.1) |
| 313 | Los Angeles, CA** | (11.5) |
| 278 | Louisville, KY** | (9.3) |
| 78 | Lowell, MA | 5.9 |
| 254 | Lubbock, TX** | (7.0) |
| 9 | Lynchburg, VA | 22.9 |
| 62 | Lynn, MA | 8.1 |
| 111 | Macon, GA** | 1.8 |
| 204 | Madison, WI | (3.5) |
| 14 | Manchester, NH | 19.3 |
| 100 | McAllen, TX** | 2.7 |
| 356 | McKinney, TX | (15.0) |
| 38 | Medford, OR | 12.3 |
| 141 | Melbourne, FL | (0.3) |
| 234 | Memphis, TN | (5.4) |
| 47 | Menifee, CA** | 10.2 |
| 427 | Merced, CA** | (31.7) |
| 22 | Meridian, ID | 17.6 |
| 158 | Mesa, AZ** | (0.9) |
| 271 | Mesquite, TX** | (8.7) |
| 193 | Miami Beach, FL | (2.7) |
| 168 | Miami Gardens, FL | (1.7) |
| 125 | Miami, FL | 0.8 |
| 376 | Midland, TX** | (16.8) |
| 83 | Milwaukee, WI | 5.4 |
| 100 | Minneapolis, MN | 2.7 |
| 348 | Miramar, FL | (14.7) |
| 359 | Mission Viejo, CA** | (15.3) |
| 426 | Mission, TX** | (31.4) |
| 20 | Mobile, AL | 17.7 |
| 68 | Modesto, CA** | 7.4 |
| 296 | Moreno Valley, CA** | (10.4) |
| 151 | Mountain View, CA** | (0.6) |
| 184 | Murfreesboro, TN | (2.3) |
| 155 | Murrieta, CA** | (0.8) |
| 177 | Nampa, ID | (2.1) |
| 19 | Napa, CA** | 17.8 |
| 325 | Naperville, IL** | (12.6) |
| 305 | Nashua, NH | (10.9) |
| 346 | Nashville, TN | (14.5) |
| 111 | New Bedford, MA | 1.8 |
| 328 | New Haven, CT | (12.9) |
| 204 | New Orleans, LA** | (3.5) |
| 215 | New Rochelle, NY** | (4.3) |
| 186 | New York, NY** | (2.4) |
| 53 | Newark, NJ** | 9.4 |
| 418 | Newport Beach, CA** | (28.0) |
| 80 | Newport News, VA | 5.7 |
| 193 | Newton, MA | (2.7) |
| 81 | Norfolk, VA | 5.6 |
| 134 | Norman, OK** | 0.3 |
| 268 | North Charleston, SC | (8.4) |
| 86 | North Las Vegas, NV** | 4.8 |
| 231 | Norwalk, CA** | (5.3) |
| 329 | Norwalk, CT | (13.0) |
| 155 | Oakland, CA** | (0.8) |
| 340 | Oceanside, CA** | (13.6) |
| 244 | Odessa, TX** | (6.3) |
| 377 | O'Fallon, MO | (16.9) |
| 14 | Ogden, UT | 19.3 |
| 291 | Oklahoma City, OK** | (10.1) |
| 228 | Olathe, KS** | (5.2) |
| 198 | Omaha, NE** | (3.1) |
| 359 | Ontario, CA** | (15.3) |
| 59 | Orange, CA** | 8.5 |
| 395 | Orem, UT** | (19.1) |
| 291 | Orlando, FL | (10.1) |
| 180 | Overland Park, KS** | (2.2) |
| 66 | Oxnard, CA** | 7.5 |
| 388 | Palm Bay, FL | (18.3) |
| 256 | Palmdale, CA** | (7.3) |

| RANK | CITY | % CHANGE |
|---|---|---|
| 128 | Pasadena, CA** | 0.5 |
| 212 | Pasadena, TX** | (4.0) |
| 115 | Paterson, NJ** | 1.6 |
| 16 | Pearland, TX | 19.2 |
| 36 | Pembroke Pines, FL | 13.9 |
| 369 | Peoria, AZ** | (15.9) |
| 358 | Peoria, IL** | (15.2) |
| 228 | Philadelphia, PA | (5.2) |
| 155 | Phoenix, AZ** | (0.8) |
| 186 | Pittsburgh, PA | (2.4) |
| 63 | Plano, TX | 7.9 |
| 46 | Plantation, FL | 10.3 |
| 400 | Pomona, CA** | (20.7) |
| 410 | Pompano Beach, FL | (23.5) |
| 411 | Port St. Lucie, FL | (23.9) |
| 250 | Portland, OR** | (6.7) |
| 4 | Portsmouth, VA | 27.6 |
| 177 | Providence, RI | (2.1) |
| 69 | Provo, UT | 7.3 |
| 3 | Pueblo, CO | 28.0 |
| 286 | Quincy, MA | (9.7) |
| 398 | Racine, WI** | (19.7) |
| 256 | Raleigh, NC** | (7.3) |
| 424 | Ramapo, NY** | (30.1) |
| 119 | Rancho Cucamon., CA** | 1.3 |
| 288 | Reading, PA | (9.8) |
| 380 | Redding, CA** | (17.1) |
| 291 | Redwood City, CA** | (10.1) |
| 214 | Reno, NV** | (4.1) |
| 329 | Renton, WA | (13.0) |
| 364 | Rialto, CA** | (15.5) |
| 417 | Richardson, TX** | (26.1) |
| 228 | Richmond, CA** | (5.2) |
| 211 | Richmond, VA | (3.9) |
| 226 | Riverside, CA** | (5.1) |
| 366 | Roanoke, VA | (15.8) |
| NA | Rochester, MN*** | NA |
| 104 | Rochester, NY** | 2.5 |
| 128 | Rockford, IL | 0.5 |
| 336 | Roseville, CA** | (13.3) |
| 83 | Roswell, GA** | 5.4 |
| 96 | Round Rock, TX** | 3.4 |
| 308 | Sacramento, CA** | (11.2) |
| 266 | Salem, OR | (8.3) |
| 203 | Salinas, CA** | (3.4) |
| 33 | Salt Lake City, UT | 14.8 |
| NA | San Angelo, TX*** | NA |
| 6 | San Antonio, TX** | 25.4 |
| 201 | San Bernardino, CA** | (3.3) |
| 221 | San Diego, CA** | (4.9) |
| 12 | San Francisco, CA** | 20.3 |
| 302 | San Jose, CA** | (10.8) |
| 298 | San Leandro, CA** | (10.5) |
| 261 | San Marcos, CA** | (7.8) |
| 280 | San Mateo, CA** | (9.4) |
| 209 | Sandy Springs, GA** | (3.8) |
| 268 | Sandy, UT | (8.4) |
| 372 | Santa Ana, CA** | (16.1) |
| 146 | Santa Barbara, CA** | (0.4) |
| 405 | Santa Clara, CA** | (22.7) |
| 419 | Santa Clarita, CA** | (29.4) |
| 422 | Santa Maria, CA** | (29.6) |
| 395 | Santa Monica, CA** | (19.1) |
| 359 | Santa Rosa, CA** | (15.3) |
| 219 | Savannah, GA** | (4.7) |
| 116 | Scottsdale, AZ** | 1.5 |
| 428 | Scranton, PA | (33.8) |
| 180 | Seattle, WA | (2.2) |
| 289 | Shreveport, LA** | (9.9) |
| 238 | Simi Valley, CA** | (6.0) |
| 17 | Sioux City, IA | 19.1 |
| 162 | Sioux Falls, SD | (1.3) |
| 421 | Somerville, MA | (29.5) |
| 66 | South Bend, IN | 7.5 |

| RANK | CITY | % CHANGE |
|---|---|---|
| 289 | South Gate, CA** | (9.9) |
| 30 | Sparks, NV** | 15.3 |
| 18 | Spokane Valley, WA** | 18.3 |
| 76 | Spokane, WA** | 6.5 |
| 91 | Springfield, IL** | 4.5 |
| 86 | Springfield, MA | 4.8 |
| 24 | Springfield, MO | 17.1 |
| 239 | Stamford, CT | (6.1) |
| 90 | Sterling Heights, MI | 4.6 |
| 403 | Stockton, CA** | (22.0) |
| 354 | St. George, UT | (14.9) |
| 26 | St. Joseph, MO | 15.8 |
| 295 | St. Louis, MO | (10.3) |
| 99 | St. Paul, MN | 3.3 |
| 73 | St. Petersburg, FL | 6.8 |
| NA | Suffolk, VA*** | NA |
| 166 | Sugar Land, TX** | (1.5) |
| 384 | Sunnyvale, CA** | (17.9) |
| 41 | Sunrise, FL | 11.3 |
| 278 | Surprise, AZ** | (9.3) |
| 317 | Syracuse, NY** | (11.9) |
| 58 | Tacoma, WA | 9.0 |
| 333 | Tallahassee, FL | (13.2) |
| 200 | Tampa, FL | (3.2) |
| 276 | Temecula, CA** | (9.1) |
| 250 | Tempe, AZ** | (6.7) |
| 186 | Thornton, CO | (2.4) |
| 309 | Thousand Oaks, CA** | (11.3) |
| 324 | Toledo, OH | (12.5) |
| 274 | Toms River Twnshp, NJ** | (8.9) |
| 399 | Topeka, KS** | (20.2) |
| 162 | Torrance, CA** | (1.3) |
| 88 | Tracy, CA** | 4.7 |
| 280 | Trenton, NJ** | (9.4) |
| 109 | Troy, MI | 2.0 |
| 313 | Tucson, AZ** | (11.5) |
| 175 | Tulsa, OK** | (2.0) |
| 309 | Tuscaloosa, AL | (11.3) |
| 342 | Tustin, CA** | (13.9) |
| 423 | Tyler, TX | (29.8) |
| 49 | Upland, CA** | 10.0 |
| 327 | Upper Darby Twnshp, PA | (12.7) |
| 391 | Vacaville, CA** | (18.6) |
| 27 | Vallejo, CA** | 15.6 |
| 139 | Vancouver, WA | 0.1 |
| 359 | Ventura, CA** | (15.3) |
| 239 | Victorville, CA** | (6.1) |
| 216 | Virginia Beach, VA | (4.4) |
| 265 | Visalia, CA** | (8.2) |
| 221 | Vista, CA** | (4.9) |
| 387 | Waco, TX** | (18.2) |
| 221 | Warren, MI | (4.9) |
| 266 | Warwick, RI | (8.3) |
| 95 | Washington, DC | 3.5 |
| 5 | Waterbury, CT** | 25.8 |
| 195 | Waukegan, IL** | (2.8) |
| 383 | West Covina, CA** | (17.8) |
| 348 | West Palm Beach, FL | (14.7) |
| 20 | West Valley, UT | 17.7 |
| 60 | Westland, MI | 8.4 |
| 141 | Westminster, CA** | (0.3) |
| 416 | Westminster, CO | (25.1) |
| 280 | Whittier, CA** | (9.4) |
| 353 | Wichita Falls, TX** | (14.8) |
| 73 | Wichita, KS | 6.8 |
| 52 | Wilmington, NC** | 9.5 |
| 272 | Winston-Salem, NC** | (8.8) |
| 44 | Woodbridge Twnshp, NJ** | 10.6 |
| 151 | Worcester, MA | (0.6) |
| 377 | Yakima, WA | (16.9) |
| 274 | Yonkers, NY** | (8.9) |
| 31 | Yuma, AZ | 15.0 |

Source: CQ Press using reported data from the F.B.I. "Crime in the United States 2013"

*Violent crimes are offenses of murder, rape, robbery, and aggravated assault.

**Figures for these cities are based on the previous (legacy) definition of rape. See note on page vii.

***Not available.

## 47. Percent Change in Violent Crime Rate: 2012 to 2013 (continued)
## National Percent Change = 5.1% Decrease*

| RANK | CITY | % CHANGE | RANK | CITY | % CHANGE | RANK | CITY | % CHANGE |
|---|---|---|---|---|---|---|---|---|
| 1 | Carmel, IN** | 76.1 | 73 | Wichita, KS | 6.8 | 149 | Fall River, MA | (0.5) |
| 2 | Colonie, NY** | 36.2 | 76 | Spokane, WA** | 6.5 | 149 | Lakewood, CA** | (0.5) |
| 3 | Pueblo, CO | 28.0 | 77 | Aurora, IL** | 6.4 | 151 | Edmond, OK** | (0.6) |
| 4 | Portsmouth, VA | 27.6 | 78 | Bloomington, IL** | 5.9 | 151 | Mountain View, CA** | (0.6) |
| 5 | Waterbury, CT** | 25.8 | 78 | Lowell, MA | 5.9 | 151 | Worcester, MA | (0.6) |
| 6 | San Antonio, TX** | 25.4 | 80 | Newport News, VA | 5.7 | 154 | Costa Mesa, CA** | (0.7) |
| 7 | Gary, IN** | 23.8 | 81 | El Cajon, CA** | 5.6 | 155 | Murrieta, CA** | (0.8) |
| 8 | Gresham, OR** | 23.4 | 81 | Norfolk, VA | 5.6 | 155 | Oakland, CA** | (0.8) |
| 9 | Lynchburg, VA | 22.9 | 83 | Kennewick, WA | 5.4 | 155 | Phoenix, AZ** | (0.8) |
| 10 | Amherst, NY** | 21.0 | 83 | Milwaukee, WI | 5.4 | 158 | Mesa, AZ** | (0.9) |
| 11 | Greenville, NC** | 20.4 | 83 | Roswell, GA** | 5.4 | 159 | Evansville, IN** | (1.0) |
| 12 | San Francisco, CA** | 20.3 | 86 | North Las Vegas, NV** | 4.8 | 160 | Albany, NY** | (1.1) |
| 13 | Longmont, CO | 19.5 | 86 | Springfield, MA | 4.8 | 160 | Longview, TX | (1.1) |
| 14 | Manchester, NH | 19.3 | 88 | Chico, CA** | 4.7 | 162 | Lawrence, MA** | (1.3) |
| 14 | Ogden, UT | 19.3 | 88 | Tracy, CA** | 4.7 | 162 | Sioux Falls, SD | (1.3) |
| 16 | Pearland, TX | 19.2 | 90 | Sterling Heights, MI | 4.6 | 162 | Torrance, CA** | (1.3) |
| 17 | Sioux City, IA | 19.1 | 91 | Springfield, IL** | 4.5 | 165 | Elizabeth, NJ** | (1.4) |
| 18 | Spokane Valley, WA** | 18.3 | 92 | Boise, ID | 4.4 | 166 | Sugar Land, TX** | (1.5) |
| 19 | Napa, CA** | 17.8 | 93 | Alexandria, VA | 4.3 | 167 | Laredo, TX** | (1.6) |
| 20 | Mobile, AL | 17.7 | 94 | Indianapolis, IN | 4.0 | 168 | Aurora, CO | (1.7) |
| 20 | West Valley, UT | 17.7 | 95 | Washington, DC | 3.5 | 168 | Dallas, TX** | (1.7) |
| 22 | Meridian, ID | 17.6 | 96 | Albuquerque, NM** | 3.4 | 168 | Miami Gardens, FL | (1.7) |
| 23 | Greece, NY** | 17.2 | 96 | Garden Grove, CA** | 3.4 | 171 | Green Bay, WI | (1.8) |
| 24 | Springfield, MO | 17.1 | 96 | Round Rock, TX** | 3.4 | 171 | Lakeland, FL | (1.8) |
| 25 | League City, TX** | 16.8 | 99 | St. Paul, MN | 3.3 | 173 | Anchorage, AK | (1.9) |
| 26 | St. Joseph, MO | 15.8 | 100 | McAllen, TX** | 2.7 | 173 | Chino Hills, CA** | (1.9) |
| 27 | Cranston, RI | 15.6 | 100 | Minneapolis, MN | 2.7 | 175 | Boca Raton, FL | (2.0) |
| 27 | Vallejo, CA** | 15.6 | 102 | Fort Wayne, IN | 2.6 | 175 | Tulsa, OK** | (2.0) |
| 29 | Greeley, CO | 15.5 | 102 | Irving, TX** | 2.6 | 177 | Lake Forest, CA** | (2.1) |
| 30 | Sparks, NV** | 15.3 | 104 | Rochester, NY** | 2.5 | 177 | Nampa, ID | (2.1) |
| 31 | Yuma, AZ | 15.0 | 105 | Denver, CO | 2.3 | 177 | Providence, RI | (2.1) |
| 32 | Huntington Beach, CA** | 14.9 | 106 | Coral Springs, FL | 2.2 | 180 | Alameda, CA** | (2.2) |
| 33 | Salt Lake City, UT | 14.8 | 106 | Livonia, MI | 2.2 | 180 | Cincinnati, OH | (2.2) |
| 34 | Bryan, TX** | 14.6 | 108 | Compton, CA** | 2.1 | 180 | Overland Park, KS** | (2.2) |
| 35 | Berkeley, CA** | 14.2 | 109 | Daly City, CA** | 2.0 | 180 | Seattle, WA | (2.2) |
| 36 | Pembroke Pines, FL | 13.9 | 109 | Troy, MI | 2.0 | 184 | Jackson, MS** | (2.3) |
| 37 | Lansing, MI | 12.5 | 111 | Arlington Heights, IL** | 1.8 | 184 | Murfreesboro, TN | (2.3) |
| 38 | Medford, OR | 12.3 | 111 | Macon, GA** | 1.8 | 186 | Detroit, MI | (2.4) |
| 39 | Bloomington, IN** | 12.1 | 111 | New Bedford, MA | 1.8 | 186 | New York, NY** | (2.4) |
| 40 | Fargo, ND | 11.9 | 114 | Indio, CA** | 1.7 | 186 | Pittsburgh, PA | (2.4) |
| 41 | Sunrise, FL | 11.3 | 115 | Paterson, NJ** | 1.6 | 186 | Thornton, CO | (2.4) |
| 42 | Hollywood, FL | 11.0 | 116 | Abilene, TX** | 1.5 | 190 | Federal Way, WA | (2.5) |
| 43 | Lafayette, LA** | 10.9 | 116 | Arvada, CO | 1.5 | 191 | Buffalo, NY** | (2.6) |
| 44 | Brick Twnshp, NJ** | 10.6 | 116 | Scottsdale, AZ** | 1.5 | 191 | Danbury, CT** | (2.6) |
| 44 | Woodbridge Twnshp, NJ** | 10.6 | 119 | Grand Prairie, TX** | 1.3 | 193 | Miami Beach, FL | (2.7) |
| 46 | Plantation, FL | 10.3 | 119 | Rancho Cucamon., CA** | 1.3 | 193 | Newton, MA | (2.7) |
| 47 | Menifee, CA** | 10.2 | 121 | Independence, MO | 1.2 | 195 | Waukegan, IL** | (2.8) |
| 48 | Joliet, IL** | 10.1 | 122 | Concord, CA** | 1.0 | 196 | Citrus Heights, CA** | (3.0) |
| 49 | Upland, CA** | 10.0 | 122 | Decatur, IL** | 1.0 | 196 | Houston, TX** | (3.0) |
| 50 | Cedar Rapids, IA | 9.9 | 124 | Erie, PA | 0.9 | 198 | Clinton Twnshp, MI | (3.1) |
| 51 | Allen, TX | 9.7 | 125 | Miami, FL | 0.8 | 198 | Omaha, NE** | (3.1) |
| 52 | Wilmington, NC** | 9.5 | 126 | Hamilton Twnshp, NJ** | 0.7 | 200 | Tampa, FL | (3.2) |
| 53 | Hemet, CA** | 9.4 | 127 | Amarillo, TX | 0.6 | 201 | Las Vegas, NV** | (3.3) |
| 53 | Newark, NJ** | 9.4 | 128 | Edison Twnshp, NJ** | 0.5 | 201 | San Bernardino, CA** | (3.3) |
| 55 | Alhambra, CA** | 9.1 | 128 | Jacksonville, FL | 0.5 | 203 | Salinas, CA** | (3.4) |
| 55 | Dearborn, MI | 9.1 | 128 | Pasadena, CA** | 0.5 | 204 | Lancaster, CA** | (3.5) |
| 55 | Fishers, IN** | 9.1 | 128 | Rockford, IL | 0.5 | 204 | Madison, WI | (3.5) |
| 58 | Tacoma, WA | 9.0 | 132 | Beaumont, TX** | 0.4 | 204 | New Orleans, LA** | (3.5) |
| 59 | Orange, CA** | 8.5 | 132 | Hammond, IN** | 0.4 | 207 | Arlington, TX** | (3.6) |
| 60 | Fairfield, CA** | 8.4 | 134 | Carrollton, TX** | 0.3 | 207 | Farmington Hills, MI | (3.6) |
| 60 | Westland, MI | 8.4 | 134 | Chula Vista, CA** | 0.3 | 209 | Allentown, PA | (3.8) |
| 62 | Lynn, MA | 8.1 | 134 | Columbus, GA** | 0.3 | 209 | Sandy Springs, GA** | (3.8) |
| 63 | Plano, TX | 7.9 | 134 | Fayetteville, NC** | 0.3 | 211 | Richmond, VA | (3.9) |
| 64 | Brockton, MA | 7.6 | 134 | Norman, OK** | 0.3 | 212 | Billings, MT | (4.0) |
| 64 | Davenport, IA | 7.6 | 139 | Lawton, OK** | 0.1 | 212 | Pasadena, TX** | (4.0) |
| 66 | Oxnard, CA** | 7.5 | 139 | Vancouver, WA | 0.1 | 214 | Reno, NV** | (4.1) |
| 66 | South Bend, IN | 7.5 | 141 | Baltimore, MD** | (0.3) | 215 | New Rochelle, NY** | (4.3) |
| 68 | Modesto, CA** | 7.4 | 141 | Brownsville, TX** | (0.3) | 216 | Virginia Beach, VA | (4.4) |
| 69 | Provo, UT | 7.3 | 141 | Kansas City, MO | (0.3) | 217 | Frisco, TX | (4.5) |
| 70 | Ann Arbor, MI | 7.1 | 141 | Melbourne, FL | (0.3) | 218 | Fort Worth, TX | (4.6) |
| 70 | Buena Park, CA** | 7.1 | 141 | Westminster, CA** | (0.3) | 219 | Colorado Springs, CO | (4.7) |
| 72 | Little Rock, AR | 6.9 | 146 | High Point, NC** | (0.4) | 219 | Savannah, GA** | (4.7) |
| 73 | Cleveland, OH | 6.8 | 146 | Kenosha, WI** | (0.4) | 221 | Hialeah, FL | (4.9) |
| 73 | St. Petersburg, FL | 6.8 | 146 | Santa Barbara, CA** | (0.4) | 221 | San Diego, CA** | (4.9) |

| RANK | CITY | % CHANGE |
|------|------|----------|
| 221 | Vista, CA** | (4.9) |
| 221 | Warren, MI | (4.9) |
| 225 | Gainesville, FL | (5.0) |
| 226 | Garland, TX** | (5.1) |
| 226 | Riverside, CA** | (5.1) |
| 228 | Olathe, KS** | (5.2) |
| 228 | Philadelphia, PA | (5.2) |
| 228 | Richmond, CA** | (5.2) |
| 231 | Clifton, NJ** | (5.3) |
| 231 | Irvine, CA** | (5.3) |
| 231 | Norwalk, CA** | (5.3) |
| 234 | Bakersfield, CA** | (5.4) |
| 234 | Inglewood, CA** | (5.4) |
| 234 | Memphis, TN | (5.4) |
| 237 | Escondido, CA** | (5.9) |
| 238 | Simi Valley, CA** | (6.0) |
| 239 | Stamford, CT | (6.1) |
| 239 | Victorville, CA** | (6.1) |
| 241 | Charlotte, NC** | (6.2) |
| 241 | Des Moines, IA | (6.2) |
| 241 | Hayward, CA** | (6.2) |
| 244 | Boston, MA** | (6.3) |
| 244 | Corpus Christi, TX** | (6.3) |
| 244 | Odessa, TX** | (6.3) |
| 247 | Hampton, VA | (6.4) |
| 248 | Albany, GA** | (6.5) |
| 248 | Fort Lauderdale, FL | (6.5) |
| 250 | Portland, OR** | (6.7) |
| 250 | Tempe, AZ** | (6.7) |
| 252 | Eugene, OR | (6.8) |
| 253 | Lincoln, NE** | (6.9) |
| 254 | Lubbock, TX** | (7.0) |
| 255 | Broken Arrow, OK** | (7.2) |
| 256 | Palmdale, CA** | (7.3) |
| 256 | Raleigh, NC** | (7.3) |
| 258 | Lakewood, CO | (7.6) |
| 259 | Everett, WA** | (7.7) |
| 259 | Fresno, CA** | (7.7) |
| 261 | San Marcos, CA** | (7.8) |
| 262 | Bellflower, CA** | (7.9) |
| 262 | Greensboro, NC** | (7.9) |
| 262 | Hesperia, CA** | (7.9) |
| 265 | Visalia, CA** | (8.2) |
| 266 | Salem, OR | (8.3) |
| 266 | Warwick, RI | (8.3) |
| 268 | North Charleston, SC | (8.4) |
| 268 | Sandy, UT | (8.4) |
| 270 | Cicero, IL** | (8.6) |
| 271 | Mesquite, TX** | (8.7) |
| 272 | Cheektowaga, NY** | (8.8) |
| 272 | Winston-Salem, NC** | (8.8) |
| 274 | Toms River Twnshp, NJ** | (8.9) |
| 274 | Yonkers, NY** | (8.9) |
| 276 | Temecula, CA** | (9.1) |
| 277 | Elgin, IL** | (9.2) |
| 278 | Louisville, KY** | (9.3) |
| 278 | Surprise, AZ** | (9.3) |
| 280 | Hawthorne, CA** | (9.4) |
| 280 | San Mateo, CA** | (9.4) |
| 280 | Trenton, NJ** | (9.4) |
| 280 | Whittier, CA** | (9.4) |
| 284 | Fort Collins, CO | (9.5) |
| 284 | Lawrence, KS | (9.5) |
| 286 | Largo, FL | (9.7) |
| 286 | Quincy, MA | (9.7) |
| 288 | Reading, PA | (9.8) |
| 289 | Shreveport, LA** | (9.9) |
| 289 | South Gate, CA** | (9.9) |
| 291 | Grand Rapids, MI | (10.1) |
| 291 | Oklahoma City, OK** | (10.1) |
| 291 | Orlando, FL | (10.1) |
| 291 | Redwood City, CA** | (10.1) |
| 295 | St. Louis, MO | (10.3) |
| 296 | Gilbert, AZ | (10.4) |
| 296 | Moreno Valley, CA** | (10.4) |
| 298 | Dayton, OH | (10.5) |
| 298 | San Leandro, CA** | (10.5) |
| 300 | Chandler, AZ** | (10.6) |
| 301 | Akron, OH | (10.7) |
| 302 | Centennial, CO | (10.8) |
| 302 | Hartford, CT** | (10.8) |
| 302 | San Jose, CA** | (10.8) |
| 305 | Nashua, NH | (10.9) |
| 306 | Elk Grove, CA** | (11.0) |
| 307 | Austin, TX** | (11.1) |
| 308 | Sacramento, CA** | (11.2) |
| 309 | Atlanta, GA** | (11.3) |
| 309 | Thousand Oaks, CA** | (11.3) |
| 309 | Tuscaloosa, AL | (11.3) |
| 312 | Birmingham, AL | (11.4) |
| 313 | Los Angeles, CA** | (11.5) |
| 313 | Tucson, AZ** | (11.5) |
| 315 | Denton, TX | (11.6) |
| 316 | Huntsville, AL | (11.7) |
| 317 | Anaheim, CA** | (11.9) |
| 317 | Livermore, CA** | (11.9) |
| 317 | Syracuse, NY** | (11.9) |
| 320 | Fort Smith, AR | (12.1) |
| 321 | Jersey City, NJ** | (12.2) |
| 322 | Chino, CA** | (12.3) |
| 322 | El Paso, TX** | (12.3) |
| 324 | Toledo, OH | (12.5) |
| 325 | Antioch, CA** | (12.6) |
| 325 | Naperville, IL** | (12.6) |
| 327 | Upper Darby Twnshp, PA | (12.7) |
| 328 | New Haven, CT | (12.9) |
| 329 | Fremont, CA** | (13.0) |
| 329 | Norwalk, CT | (13.0) |
| 329 | Renton, WA | (13.0) |
| 332 | Lexington, KY | (13.1) |
| 333 | Athens-Clarke, GA** | (13.2) |
| 333 | Long Beach, CA** | (13.2) |
| 333 | Tallahassee, FL | (13.2) |
| 336 | Beaverton, OR** | (13.3) |
| 336 | Chesapeake, VA | (13.3) |
| 336 | Roseville, CA** | (13.3) |
| 339 | Champaign, IL** | (13.5) |
| 340 | Knoxville, TN | (13.6) |
| 340 | Oceanside, CA** | (13.6) |
| 342 | Tustin, CA** | (13.9) |
| 343 | Downey, CA** | (14.1) |
| 343 | El Monte, CA** | (14.1) |
| 345 | Lakewood Twnshp, NJ** | (14.4) |
| 346 | Killeen, TX** | (14.5) |
| 346 | Nashville, TN | (14.5) |
| 348 | Baton Rouge, LA** | (14.7) |
| 348 | Boulder, CO | (14.7) |
| 348 | Clearwater, FL | (14.7) |
| 348 | Miramar, FL | (14.7) |
| 348 | West Palm Beach, FL | (14.7) |
| 353 | Wichita Falls, TX** | (14.8) |
| 354 | Jurupa Valley, CA** | (14.9) |
| 354 | St. George, UT | (14.9) |
| 356 | McKinney, TX | (15.0) |
| 357 | Clarkstown, NY** | (15.1) |
| 358 | Peoria, IL** | (15.2) |
| 359 | Mission Viejo, CA** | (15.3) |
| 359 | Ontario, CA** | (15.3) |
| 359 | Santa Rosa, CA** | (15.3) |
| 359 | Ventura, CA** | (15.3) |
| 363 | Fayetteville, AR | (15.4) |
| 364 | Rialto, CA** | (15.5) |
| 365 | Columbia, MO | (15.6) |
| 366 | Baldwin Park, CA** | (15.8) |
| 366 | Fontana, CA** | (15.8) |
| 366 | Roanoke, VA | (15.8) |
| 369 | Hoover, AL | (15.9) |
| 369 | Peoria, AZ** | (15.9) |
| 371 | Cape Coral, FL | (16.0) |
| 372 | Cary, NC** | (16.1) |
| 372 | Deerfield Beach, FL | (16.1) |
| 372 | Santa Ana, CA** | (16.1) |
| 375 | Cambridge, MA | (16.5) |
| 376 | Midland, TX** | (16.8) |
| 377 | Kansas City, KS** | (16.9) |
| 377 | O'Fallon, MO | (16.9) |
| 377 | Yakima, WA | (16.9) |
| 380 | Redding, CA** | (17.1) |
| 381 | Lee's Summit, MO | (17.4) |
| 382 | Las Cruces, NM** | (17.5) |
| 383 | West Covina, CA** | (17.8) |
| 384 | Sunnyvale, CA** | (17.9) |
| 385 | Evanston, IL** | (18.1) |
| 385 | Johns Creek, GA** | (18.1) |
| 387 | Waco, TX** | (18.2) |
| 388 | Palm Bay, FL | (18.3) |
| 389 | Fullerton, CA** | (18.4) |
| 390 | Davie, FL | (18.5) |
| 391 | Carlsbad, CA** | (18.6) |
| 391 | Vacaville, CA** | (18.6) |
| 393 | Clovis, CA** | (18.8) |
| 394 | Henderson, NV** | (19.0) |
| 395 | Orem, UT** | (19.1) |
| 395 | Santa Monica, CA** | (19.1) |
| 397 | Clarksville, TN | (19.4) |
| 398 | Racine, WI** | (19.7) |
| 399 | Topeka, KS** | (20.2) |
| 400 | Pomona, CA** | (20.7) |
| 401 | Bridgeport, CT** | (21.2) |
| 402 | Glendale, AZ** | (21.3) |
| 403 | Stockton, CA** | (22.0) |
| 404 | Glendale, CA** | (22.5) |
| 405 | Santa Clara, CA** | (22.7) |
| 406 | Bethlehem, PA | (22.8) |
| 407 | Carson, CA** | (23.2) |
| 408 | Bellevue, WA** | (23.4) |
| 408 | Hillsboro, OR** | (23.4) |
| 410 | Pompano Beach, FL | (23.5) |
| 411 | Port St. Lucie, FL | (23.9) |
| 412 | Charleston, SC | (24.0) |
| 413 | Edinburg, TX** | (24.2) |
| 414 | Corona, CA** | (24.3) |
| 415 | College Station, TX** | (24.7) |
| 416 | Westminster, CO | (25.1) |
| 417 | Richardson, TX** | (26.1) |
| 418 | Newport Beach, CA** | (28.0) |
| 419 | Burbank, CA** | (29.4) |
| 419 | Santa Clarita, CA** | (29.4) |
| 421 | Somerville, MA | (29.5) |
| 422 | Santa Maria, CA** | (29.6) |
| 423 | Tyler, TX | (29.8) |
| 424 | Flint, MI | (30.1) |
| 424 | Ramapo, NY** | (30.1) |
| 426 | Mission, TX** | (31.4) |
| 427 | Merced, CA** | (31.7) |
| 428 | Scranton, PA | (33.8) |
| 429 | Kent, WA | (42.3) |
| NA | Bend, OR*** | NA |
| NA | Bloomington, MN*** | NA |
| NA | Brooklyn Park, MN*** | NA |
| NA | Canton Twnshp, MI*** | NA |
| NA | Chattanooga, TN*** | NA |
| NA | Chicago, IL*** | NA |
| NA | Columbia, SC*** | NA |
| NA | Concord, NC*** | NA |
| NA | Duluth, MN*** | NA |
| NA | Lewisville, TX*** | NA |
| NA | Rochester, MN*** | NA |
| NA | San Angelo, TX*** | NA |
| NA | Suffolk, VA*** | NA |

Source: CQ Press using reported data from the F.B.I. "Crime in the United States 2013"

*Violent crimes are offenses of murder, rape, robbery, and aggravated assault.

**Figures for these cities are based on the previous (legacy) definition of rape. See note on page vii.

***Not available.

# 48. Percent Change in Violent Crime Rate: 2009 to 2013
## National Percent Change = 14.8% Decrease*

| RANK | CITY | % CHANGE | RANK | CITY | % CHANGE | RANK | CITY | % CHANGE |
|---|---|---|---|---|---|---|---|---|
| 336 | Abilene, TX** | (29.2) | 5 | Chino, CA** | 60.1 | 365 | Fullerton, CA** | (32.9) |
| 196 | Akron, OH | (14.7) | 338 | Chula Vista, CA** | (29.8) | 383 | Gainesville, FL | (36.5) |
| 319 | Alameda, CA** | (26.7) | NA | Cicero, IL*** | NA | 252 | Garden Grove, CA** | (20.5) |
| 142 | Albany, GA** | (9.7) | 245 | Cincinnati, OH | (20.0) | 265 | Garland, TX** | (21.5) |
| 301 | Albany, NY** | (25.1) | 284 | Citrus Heights, CA** | (23.8) | 3 | Gary, IN** | 61.4 |
| 74 | Albuquerque, NM** | 0.7 | 349 | Clarkstown, NY** | (31.0) | 68 | Gilbert, AZ | 2.4 |
| 166 | Alexandria, VA | (11.6) | 276 | Clarksville, TN | (22.4) | 189 | Glendale, AZ** | (14.0) |
| 368 | Alhambra, CA** | (33.3) | 379 | Clearwater, FL | (35.3) | 390 | Glendale, CA** | (39.5) |
| 297 | Allentown, PA | (24.6) | 54 | Cleveland, OH | 5.9 | 170 | Grand Prairie, TX** | (12.6) |
| 294 | Allen, TX | (24.4) | 227 | Clifton, NJ** | (18.4) | 211 | Grand Rapids, MI | (16.6) |
| 269 | Amarillo, TX | (21.8) | 74 | Clinton Twnshp, MI | 0.7 | 8 | Greece, NY** | 48.6 |
| 278 | Amherst, NY** | (22.5) | 22 | Clovis, CA** | 22.8 | 49 | Greeley, CO | 7.8 |
| 123 | Anaheim, CA** | (7.2) | 2 | College Station, TX** | 94.0 | 70 | Green Bay, WI | 1.4 |
| 125 | Anchorage, AK | (7.4) | 65 | Colonie, NY** | 2.9 | 361 | Greensboro, NC** | (32.3) |
| 149 | Ann Arbor, MI | (10.4) | 160 | Colorado Springs, CO | (11.4) | NA | Greenville, NC*** | NA |
| 78 | Antioch, CA** | 0.3 | 312 | Columbia, MO | (25.7) | 7 | Gresham, OR** | 49.0 |
| NA | Arlington Heights, IL*** | NA | 350 | Columbia, SC | (31.2) | 119 | Hamilton Twnshp, NJ** | (6.2) |
| 263 | Arlington, TX** | (21.1) | 220 | Columbus, GA** | (17.9) | 201 | Hammond, IN** | (15.4) |
| 210 | Arvada, CO | (16.4) | 225 | Compton, CA** | (18.3) | 352 | Hampton, VA | (31.5) |
| 227 | Athens-Clarke, GA** | (18.4) | 87 | Concord, CA** | (1.1) | 134 | Hartford, CT** | (8.8) |
| 53 | Atlanta, GA** | 6.4 | 406 | Concord, NC** | (47.7) | 231 | Hawthorne, CA** | (18.9) |
| 153 | Aurora, CO | (11.1) | 342 | Coral Springs, FL | (30.4) | 301 | Hayward, CA** | (25.1) |
| NA | Aurora, IL*** | NA | 327 | Corona, CA** | (28.0) | 54 | Hemet, CA** | 5.9 |
| 344 | Austin, TX** | (30.5) | 301 | Corpus Christi, TX** | (25.1) | 396 | Henderson, NV** | (41.5) |
| 234 | Bakersfield, CA** | (19.1) | 231 | Costa Mesa, CA** | (18.9) | 22 | Hesperia, CA** | 22.8 |
| 298 | Baldwin Park, CA** | (24.7) | 20 | Cranston, RI | 25.1 | 309 | Hialeah, FL | (25.4) |
| 125 | Baltimore, MD** | (7.4) | 206 | Dallas, TX** | (16.2) | 259 | High Point, NC** | (20.7) |
| 324 | Baton Rouge, LA** | (27.0) | 143 | Daly City, CA** | (10.0) | 100 | Hillsboro, OR** | (3.8) |
| 35 | Beaumont, TX** | 14.0 | 252 | Danbury, CT** | (20.5) | 80 | Hollywood, FL | (0.1) |
| 375 | Beaverton, OR** | (34.6) | 168 | Davenport, IA | (12.1) | 330 | Hoover, AL | (28.2) |
| 294 | Bellevue, WA** | (24.4) | 376 | Davie, FL | (34.7) | 193 | Houston, TX** | (14.5) |
| 414 | Bellflower, CA** | (52.9) | 186 | Dayton, OH | (13.6) | 112 | Huntington Beach, CA** | (5.4) |
| 24 | Bend, OR | 22.3 | 138 | Dearborn, MI | (9.1) | 18 | Huntsville, AL | 25.2 |
| 249 | Berkeley, CA** | (20.4) | NA | Decatur, IL*** | NA | 296 | Independence, MO | (24.5) |
| 238 | Bethlehem, PA | (19.5) | NA | Deerfield Beach, FL*** | NA | 67 | Indianapolis, IN | 2.7 |
| 13 | Billings, MT | 35.9 | 38 | Denton, TX | 11.4 | 25 | Indio, CA** | 21.9 |
| 47 | Birmingham, AL | 8.8 | 45 | Denver, CO | 9.0 | 330 | Inglewood, CA** | (28.2) |
| NA | Bloomington, IL*** | NA | 134 | Des Moines, IA | (8.8) | 363 | Irvine, CA** | (32.4) |
| 374 | Bloomington, IN** | (34.5) | 57 | Detroit, MI | 5.4 | 272 | Irving, TX** | (22.2) |
| NA | Bloomington, MN*** | NA | 339 | Downey, CA** | (30.2) | 314 | Jacksonville, FL | (25.8) |
| 317 | Boca Raton, FL | (26.4) | NA | Duluth, MN*** | NA | 56 | Jackson, MS** | 5.7 |
| 50 | Boise, ID | 7.4 | 117 | Edinburg, TX** | (5.9) | 183 | Jersey City, NJ** | (13.4) |
| 263 | Boston, MA** | (21.1) | 415 | Edison Twnshp, NJ** | (54.3) | 411 | Johns Creek, GA** | (49.8) |
| 183 | Boulder, CO | (13.4) | 117 | Edmond, OK** | (5.9) | NA | Joliet, IL*** | NA |
| 301 | Brick Twnshp, NJ** | (25.1) | 291 | El Cajon, CA** | (24.1) | NA | Jurupa Valley, CA*** | NA |
| 201 | Bridgeport, CT** | (15.4) | 409 | El Monte, CA** | (49.7) | 301 | Kansas City, KS** | (25.1) |
| 84 | Brockton, MA | (0.6) | 231 | El Paso, TX** | (18.9) | 98 | Kansas City, MO | (3.1) |
| 301 | Broken Arrow, OK** | (25.1) | NA | Elgin, IL*** | NA | 217 | Kennewick, WA | (17.7) |
| NA | Brooklyn Park, MN*** | NA | 284 | Elizabeth, NJ** | (23.8) | 88 | Kenosha, WI** | (1.3) |
| 64 | Brownsville, TX** | 3.0 | 364 | Elk Grove, CA** | (32.6) | 416 | Kent, WA | (57.3) |
| 395 | Bryan, TX** | (41.3) | 82 | Erie, PA | (0.3) | 158 | Killeen, TX** | (11.3) |
| 188 | Buena Park, CA** | (13.9) | 169 | Escondido, CA** | (12.4) | 252 | Knoxville, TN | (20.5) |
| 189 | Buffalo, NY** | (14.0) | 225 | Eugene, OR | (18.3) | 330 | Lafayette, LA** | (28.2) |
| 368 | Burbank, CA** | (33.3) | NA | Evanston, IL*** | NA | 133 | Lake Forest, CA** | (8.4) |
| 342 | Cambridge, MA | (30.4) | 17 | Evansville, IN** | 25.6 | 164 | Lakeland, FL | (11.5) |
| 385 | Canton Twnshp, MI | (36.7) | 358 | Everett, WA** | (32.0) | 408 | Lakewood Twnshp, NJ** | (49.0) |
| 392 | Cape Coral, FL | (40.3) | 41 | Fairfield, CA** | 9.8 | 393 | Lakewood, CA** | (40.6) |
| 351 | Carlsbad, CA** | (31.4) | 150 | Fall River, MA | (10.5) | 177 | Lakewood, CO | (13.0) |
| 319 | Carmel, IN** | (26.7) | 21 | Fargo, ND | 24.3 | 255 | Lancaster, CA** | (20.6) |
| 316 | Carrollton, TX** | (26.0) | 381 | Farmington Hills, MI | (35.7) | 80 | Lansing, MI | (0.1) |
| 259 | Carson, CA** | (20.7) | 77 | Fayetteville, AR | 0.6 | 325 | Laredo, TX** | (27.2) |
| 346 | Cary, NC** | (30.6) | 259 | Fayetteville, NC** | (20.7) | 384 | Largo, FL | (36.6) |
| 95 | Cedar Rapids, IA | (2.6) | 333 | Federal Way, WA | (28.4) | 371 | Las Cruces, NM** | (34.0) |
| 141 | Centennial, CO | (9.6) | 72 | Fishers, IN** | 1.1 | 244 | Las Vegas, NV** | (19.9) |
| NA | Champaign, IL*** | NA | 108 | Flint, MI | (5.1) | 230 | Lawrence, KS | (18.8) |
| 245 | Chandler, AZ** | (20.0) | 262 | Fontana, CA** | (21.0) | 10 | Lawrence, MA** | 40.1 |
| 417 | Charleston, SC | (65.3) | 387 | Fort Collins, CO | (38.4) | 283 | Lawton, OK** | (23.7) |
| 204 | Charlotte, NC** | (15.9) | 62 | Fort Lauderdale, FL | 4.3 | 373 | League City, TX** | (34.3) |
| 112 | Chattanooga, TN | (5.4) | 214 | Fort Smith, AR | (17.5) | 255 | Lee's Summit, MO | (20.6) |
| 308 | Cheektowaga, NY** | (25.3) | 51 | Fort Wayne, IN | 7.0 | 15 | Lewisville, TX | 28.1 |
| 191 | Chesapeake, VA | (14.1) | 101 | Fort Worth, TX | (4.2) | 407 | Lexington, KY | (48.4) |
| NA | Chicago, IL*** | NA | 409 | Fremont, CA** | (49.7) | 236 | Lincoln, NE** | (19.2) |
| 125 | Chico, CA** | (7.4) | 217 | Fresno, CA** | (17.7) | 102 | Little Rock, AR | (4.3) |
| 390 | Chino Hills, CA** | (39.5) | 287 | Frisco, TX | (23.9) | 4 | Livermore, CA** | 60.9 |

| RANK | CITY | % CHANGE |
|---|---|---|
| 248 | Livonia, MI | (20.3) |
| 319 | Long Beach, CA** | (26.7) |
| 365 | Longmont, CO | (32.9) |
| 389 | Longview, TX | (39.1) |
| 357 | Los Angeles, CA** | (31.9) |
| 138 | Louisville, KY** | (9.1) |
| NA | Lowell, MA*** | NA |
| 216 | Lubbock, TX** | (17.6) |
| 128 | Lynchburg, VA | (7.7) |
| 88 | Lynn, MA | (1.3) |
| 206 | Macon, GA** | (16.2) |
| 79 | Madison, WI | 0.2 |
| 12 | Manchester, NH | 36.9 |
| 413 | McAllen, TX** | (52.1) |
| 289 | McKinney, TX | (24.0) |
| 1 | Medford, OR | 104.7 |
| 322 | Melbourne, FL | (26.9) |
| 132 | Memphis, TN | (8.3) |
| 30 | Menifee, CA** | 16.5 |
| 318 | Merced, CA** | (26.6) |
| 173 | Meridian, ID | (12.8) |
| 121 | Mesa, AZ** | (6.8) |
| 346 | Mesquite, TX** | (30.6) |
| 120 | Miami Beach, FL | (6.5) |
| 199 | Miami Gardens, FL | (15.0) |
| 84 | Miami, FL | (0.6) |
| 326 | Midland, TX** | (27.5) |
| 18 | Milwaukee, WI | 25.2 |
| 130 | Minneapolis, MN | (8.1) |
| 299 | Miramar, FL | (24.8) |
| 380 | Mission Viejo, CA** | (35.6) |
| 412 | Mission, TX** | (50.1) |
| 291 | Mobile, AL | (24.1) |
| 26 | Modesto, CA** | 20.2 |
| 360 | Moreno Valley, CA** | (32.1) |
| 238 | Mountain View, CA** | (19.5) |
| 124 | Murfreesboro, TN | (7.3) |
| 397 | Murrieta, CA** | (42.0) |
| 322 | Nampa, ID | (26.9) |
| 152 | Napa, CA** | (11.0) |
| NA | Naperville, IL*** | NA |
| 65 | Nashua, NH | 2.9 |
| 134 | Nashville, TN | (8.8) |
| 195 | New Bedford, MA | (14.6) |
| 335 | New Haven, CT | (29.0) |
| 71 | New Orleans, LA** | 1.2 |
| 234 | New Rochelle, NY** | (19.1) |
| 36 | New York, NY** | 13.1 |
| 13 | Newark, NJ** | 35.9 |
| 404 | Newport Beach, CA** | (46.7) |
| NA | Newport News, VA*** | NA |
| 281 | Newton, MA | (23.5) |
| 170 | Norfolk, VA | (12.6) |
| 69 | Norman, OK** | 1.6 |
| 378 | North Charleston, SC | (35.2) |
| 37 | North Las Vegas, NV** | 11.6 |
| 187 | Norwalk, CA** | (13.8) |
| 403 | Norwalk, CT | (46.6) |
| 29 | Oakland, CA** | 17.7 |
| 209 | Oceanside, CA** | (16.3) |
| 16 | Odessa, TX** | 26.5 |
| 116 | O'Fallon, MO | (5.6) |
| 60 | Ogden, UT | 5.1 |
| 154 | Oklahoma City, OK** | (11.2) |
| 372 | Olathe, KS** | (34.2) |
| 48 | Omaha, NE** | 8.0 |
| 382 | Ontario, CA** | (36.3) |
| 145 | Orange, CA** | (10.2) |
| 361 | Orem, UT** | (32.3) |
| 282 | Orlando, FL | (23.6) |
| 158 | Overland Park, KS** | (11.3) |
| 270 | Oxnard, CA** | (21.9) |
| 205 | Palm Bay, FL | (16.0) |
| 179 | Palmdale, CA** | (13.2) |

| RANK | CITY | % CHANGE |
|---|---|---|
| 122 | Pasadena, CA** | (6.9) |
| 240 | Pasadena, TX** | (19.6) |
| 28 | Paterson, NJ** | 17.9 |
| 57 | Pearland, TX | 5.4 |
| 217 | Pembroke Pines, FL | (17.7) |
| 240 | Peoria, AZ** | (19.6) |
| NA | Peoria, IL*** | NA |
| 154 | Philadelphia, PA | (11.2) |
| 32 | Phoenix, AZ** | 15.6 |
| 312 | Pittsburgh, PA | (25.7) |
| 213 | Plano, TX | (17.1) |
| 265 | Plantation, FL | (21.5) |
| 201 | Pomona, CA** | (15.4) |
| 271 | Pompano Beach, FL | (22.0) |
| 344 | Port St. Lucie, FL | (30.5) |
| 173 | Portland, OR** | (12.8) |
| 179 | Portsmouth, VA | (13.2) |
| 140 | Providence, RI | (9.5) |
| 93 | Provo, UT | (2.1) |
| 41 | Pueblo, CO | 9.8 |
| 96 | Quincy, MA | (2.9) |
| 339 | Racine, WI** | (30.2) |
| 249 | Raleigh, NC** | (20.4) |
| 249 | Ramapo, NY** | (20.4) |
| 86 | Rancho Cucamon., CA** | (0.8) |
| 164 | Reading, PA | (11.5) |
| 197 | Redding, CA** | (14.8) |
| 291 | Redwood City, CA** | (24.1) |
| 310 | Reno, NV** | (25.6) |
| 405 | Renton, WA | (46.8) |
| 276 | Rialto, CA** | (22.4) |
| 401 | Richardson, TX** | (45.4) |
| 97 | Richmond, CA** | (3.0) |
| 273 | Richmond, VA | (22.3) |
| 220 | Riverside, CA** | (17.9) |
| 358 | Roanoke, VA | (32.0) |
| NA | Rochester, MN*** | NA |
| 74 | Rochester, NY** | 0.7 |
| 57 | Rockford, IL | 5.4 |
| 307 | Roseville, CA** | (25.2) |
| 223 | Roswell, GA** | (18.1) |
| 27 | Round Rock, TX** | 18.5 |
| 315 | Sacramento, CA** | (25.9) |
| 160 | Salem, OR | (11.4) |
| 229 | Salinas, CA** | (18.5) |
| 41 | Salt Lake City, UT | 9.8 |
| 355 | San Angelo, TX | (31.8) |
| 40 | San Antonio, TX** | 10.5 |
| 105 | San Bernardino, CA** | (4.8) |
| 175 | San Diego, CA** | (12.9) |
| 33 | San Francisco, CA** | 15.1 |
| 144 | San Jose, CA** | (10.1) |
| 193 | San Leandro, CA** | (14.5) |
| 154 | San Marcos, CA** | (11.2) |
| 377 | San Mateo, CA** | (35.1) |
| 243 | Sandy Springs, GA** | (19.8) |
| 183 | Sandy, UT | (13.4) |
| 370 | Santa Ana, CA** | (33.8) |
| 237 | Santa Barbara, CA** | (19.4) |
| 110 | Santa Clara, CA** | (5.3) |
| 402 | Santa Clarita, CA** | (46.0) |
| 399 | Santa Maria, CA** | (42.9) |
| 265 | Santa Monica, CA** | (21.5) |
| 388 | Santa Rosa, CA** | (38.5) |
| 355 | Savannah, GA** | (31.8) |
| 175 | Scottsdale, AZ** | (12.9) |
| 400 | Scranton, PA | (44.5) |
| 134 | Seattle, WA | (8.8) |
| 273 | Shreveport, LA** | (22.3) |
| 222 | Simi Valley, CA** | (18.0) |
| 112 | Sioux City, IA | (5.4) |
| 11 | Sioux Falls, SD | 37.4 |
| 394 | Somerville, MA | (40.9) |
| 160 | South Bend, IN | (11.4) |

| RANK | CITY | % CHANGE |
|---|---|---|
| 160 | South Gate, CA** | (11.4) |
| 367 | Sparks, NV** | (33.1) |
| 212 | Spokane Valley, WA** | (16.8) |
| 41 | Spokane, WA** | 9.8 |
| NA | Springfield, IL*** | NA |
| 182 | Springfield, MA | (13.3) |
| 6 | Springfield, MO | 52.0 |
| 145 | Stamford, CT | (10.2) |
| 39 | Sterling Heights, MI | 11.3 |
| 104 | Stockton, CA** | (4.7) |
| 9 | St. George, UT | 42.6 |
| 206 | St. Joseph, MO | (16.2) |
| 280 | St. Louis, MO | (23.0) |
| 93 | St. Paul, MN | (2.1) |
| 337 | St. Petersburg, FL | (29.3) |
| 129 | Suffolk, VA | (7.9) |
| 110 | Sugar Land, TX** | (5.3) |
| 289 | Sunnyvale, CA** | (24.0) |
| 151 | Sunrise, FL | (10.6) |
| 34 | Surprise, AZ** | 14.7 |
| 200 | Syracuse, NY** | (15.3) |
| 167 | Tacoma, WA | (11.7) |
| 268 | Tallahassee, FL | (21.7) |
| 255 | Tampa, FL | (20.6) |
| 354 | Temecula, CA** | (31.7) |
| 108 | Tempe, AZ** | (5.1) |
| 61 | Thornton, CO | 4.4 |
| 223 | Thousand Oaks, CA** | (18.1) |
| 131 | Toledo, OH | (8.2) |
| 341 | Toms River Twnshp, NJ** | (30.3) |
| 214 | Topeka, KS** | (17.5) |
| 348 | Torrance, CA** | (30.9) |
| 102 | Tracy, CA** | (4.3) |
| 106 | Trenton, NJ** | (4.9) |
| 284 | Troy, MI | (23.8) |
| 91 | Tucson, AZ** | (1.4) |
| 178 | Tulsa, OK** | (13.1) |
| 72 | Tuscaloosa, AL | 1.1 |
| 83 | Tustin, CA** | (0.4) |
| 334 | Tyler, TX | (28.9) |
| NA | Upland, CA*** | NA |
| 198 | Upper Darby Twnshp, PA | (14.9) |
| 329 | Vacaville, CA** | (28.1) |
| 88 | Vallejo, CA** | (1.3) |
| 148 | Vancouver, WA | (10.3) |
| 353 | Ventura, CA** | (31.6) |
| 245 | Victorville, CA** | (20.0) |
| 273 | Virginia Beach, VA | (22.3) |
| 300 | Visalia, CA** | (25.0) |
| 192 | Vista, CA** | (14.3) |
| 398 | Waco, TX** | (42.8) |
| 179 | Warren, MI | (13.2) |
| 255 | Warwick, RI | (20.6) |
| 99 | Washington, DC | (3.6) |
| 52 | Waterbury, CT** | 6.6 |
| NA | Waukegan, IL*** | NA |
| 327 | West Covina, CA** | (28.0) |
| 287 | West Palm Beach, FL | (23.9) |
| 31 | West Valley, UT | 16.3 |
| 154 | Westland, MI | (11.2) |
| 63 | Westminster, CA** | 3.5 |
| 172 | Westminster, CO | (12.7) |
| 386 | Whittier, CA** | (37.1) |
| 310 | Wichita Falls, TX** | (25.6) |
| 145 | Wichita, KS | (10.2) |
| 279 | Wilmington, NC** | (22.9) |
| 242 | Winston-Salem, NC** | (19.7) |
| 112 | Woodbridge Twnshp, NJ** | (5.4) |
| 106 | Worcester, MA | (4.9) |
| NA | Yakima, WA*** | NA |
| 45 | Yonkers, NY** | 9.0 |
| 92 | Yuma, AZ | (1.9) |

Source: CQ Press using reported data from the F.B.I. "Crime in the United States 2013"

*Violent crimes are offenses of murder, rape, robbery, and aggravated assault.

**Figures for these cities are based on the previous (legacy) definition of rape. See note on page vii.

***Not available.

## 48. Percent Change in Violent Crime Rate: 2009 to 2013 (continued)
## National Percent Change = 14.8% Decrease*

| RANK | CITY | % CHANGE | RANK | CITY | % CHANGE | RANK | CITY | % CHANGE |
|---|---|---|---|---|---|---|---|---|
| 1 | Medford, OR | 104.7 | 74 | Clinton Twnshp, MI | 0.7 | 149 | Ann Arbor, MI | (10.4) |
| 2 | College Station, TX** | 94.0 | 74 | Rochester, NY** | 0.7 | 150 | Fall River, MA | (10.5) |
| 3 | Gary, IN** | 61.4 | 77 | Fayetteville, AR | 0.6 | 151 | Sunrise, FL | (10.6) |
| 4 | Livermore, CA** | 60.9 | 78 | Antioch, CA** | 0.3 | 152 | Napa, CA** | (11.0) |
| 5 | Chino, CA** | 60.1 | 79 | Madison, WI | 0.2 | 153 | Aurora, CO | (11.1) |
| 6 | Springfield, MO | 52.0 | 80 | Hollywood, FL | (0.1) | 154 | Oklahoma City, OK** | (11.2) |
| 7 | Gresham, OR** | 49.0 | 80 | Lansing, MI | (0.1) | 154 | Philadelphia, PA | (11.2) |
| 8 | Greece, NY** | 48.6 | 82 | Erie, PA | (0.3) | 154 | San Marcos, CA** | (11.2) |
| 9 | St. George, UT | 42.6 | 83 | Tustin, CA** | (0.4) | 154 | Westland, MI | (11.2) |
| 10 | Lawrence, MA** | 40.1 | 84 | Brockton, MA | (0.6) | 158 | Killeen, TX** | (11.3) |
| 11 | Sioux Falls, SD | 37.4 | 84 | Miami, FL | (0.6) | 158 | Overland Park, KS** | (11.3) |
| 12 | Manchester, NH | 36.9 | 86 | Rancho Cucamon., CA** | (0.8) | 160 | Colorado Springs, CO | (11.4) |
| 13 | Billings, MT | 35.9 | 87 | Concord, CA** | (1.1) | 160 | Salem, OR | (11.4) |
| 13 | Newark, NJ** | 35.9 | 88 | Kenosha, WI** | (1.3) | 160 | South Bend, IN | (11.4) |
| 15 | Lewisville, TX | 28.1 | 88 | Lynn, MA | (1.3) | 160 | South Gate, CA** | (11.4) |
| 16 | Odessa, TX** | 26.5 | 88 | Vallejo, CA** | (1.3) | 164 | Lakeland, FL | (11.5) |
| 17 | Evansville, IN** | 25.6 | 91 | Tucson, AZ** | (1.4) | 164 | Reading, PA | (11.5) |
| 18 | Huntsville, AL | 25.2 | 92 | Yuma, AZ | (1.9) | 166 | Alexandria, VA | (11.6) |
| 18 | Milwaukee, WI | 25.2 | 93 | Provo, UT | (2.1) | 167 | Tacoma, WA | (11.7) |
| 20 | Cranston, RI | 25.1 | 93 | St. Paul, MN | (2.1) | 168 | Davenport, IA | (12.1) |
| 21 | Fargo, ND | 24.3 | 95 | Cedar Rapids, IA | (2.6) | 169 | Escondido, CA** | (12.4) |
| 22 | Clovis, CA** | 22.8 | 96 | Quincy, MA | (2.9) | 170 | Grand Prairie, TX** | (12.6) |
| 22 | Hesperia, CA** | 22.8 | 97 | Richmond, CA** | (3.0) | 170 | Norfolk, VA | (12.6) |
| 24 | Bend, OR | 22.3 | 98 | Kansas City, MO | (3.1) | 172 | Westminster, CO | (12.7) |
| 25 | Indio, CA** | 21.9 | 99 | Washington, DC | (3.6) | 173 | Meridian, ID | (12.8) |
| 26 | Modesto, CA** | 20.2 | 100 | Hillsboro, OR** | (3.8) | 173 | Portland, OR** | (12.8) |
| 27 | Round Rock, TX** | 18.5 | 101 | Fort Worth, TX | (4.2) | 175 | San Diego, CA** | (12.9) |
| 28 | Paterson, NJ** | 17.9 | 102 | Little Rock, AR | (4.3) | 175 | Scottsdale, AZ** | (12.9) |
| 29 | Oakland, CA** | 17.7 | 102 | Tracy, CA** | (4.3) | 177 | Lakewood, CO | (13.0) |
| 30 | Menifee, CA** | 16.5 | 104 | Stockton, CA** | (4.7) | 178 | Tulsa, OK** | (13.1) |
| 31 | West Valley, UT | 16.3 | 105 | San Bernardino, CA** | (4.8) | 179 | Palmdale, CA** | (13.2) |
| 32 | Phoenix, AZ** | 15.6 | 106 | Trenton, NJ** | (4.9) | 179 | Portsmouth, VA | (13.2) |
| 33 | San Francisco, CA** | 15.1 | 106 | Worcester, MA | (4.9) | 179 | Warren, MI | (13.2) |
| 34 | Surprise, AZ** | 14.7 | 108 | Flint, MI | (5.1) | 182 | Springfield, MA | (13.3) |
| 35 | Beaumont, TX** | 14.0 | 108 | Tempe, AZ** | (5.1) | 183 | Boulder, CO | (13.4) |
| 36 | New York, NY** | 13.1 | 110 | Santa Clara, CA** | (5.3) | 183 | Jersey City, NJ** | (13.4) |
| 37 | North Las Vegas, NV** | 11.6 | 110 | Sugar Land, TX** | (5.3) | 183 | Sandy, UT | (13.4) |
| 38 | Denton, TX | 11.4 | 112 | Chattanooga, TN | (5.4) | 186 | Dayton, OH | (13.6) |
| 39 | Sterling Heights, MI | 11.3 | 112 | Huntington Beach, CA** | (5.4) | 187 | Norwalk, CA** | (13.8) |
| 40 | San Antonio, TX** | 10.5 | 112 | Sioux City, IA | (5.4) | 188 | Buena Park, CA** | (13.9) |
| 41 | Fairfield, CA** | 9.8 | 112 | Woodbridge Twnshp, NJ** | (5.4) | 189 | Buffalo, NY** | (14.0) |
| 41 | Pueblo, CO | 9.8 | 116 | O'Fallon, MO | (5.6) | 189 | Glendale, AZ** | (14.0) |
| 41 | Salt Lake City, UT | 9.8 | 117 | Edinburg, TX** | (5.9) | 191 | Chesapeake, VA | (14.1) |
| 41 | Spokane, WA** | 9.8 | 117 | Edmond, OK** | (5.9) | 192 | Vista, CA** | (14.3) |
| 45 | Denver, CO | 9.0 | 119 | Hamilton Twnshp, NJ** | (6.2) | 193 | Houston, TX** | (14.5) |
| 45 | Yonkers, NY** | 9.0 | 120 | Miami Beach, FL | (6.5) | 193 | San Leandro, CA** | (14.5) |
| 47 | Birmingham, AL | 8.8 | 121 | Mesa, AZ** | (6.8) | 195 | New Bedford, MA | (14.6) |
| 48 | Omaha, NE** | 8.0 | 122 | Pasadena, CA** | (6.9) | 196 | Akron, OH | (14.7) |
| 49 | Greeley, CO | 7.8 | 123 | Anaheim, CA** | (7.2) | 197 | Redding, CA** | (14.8) |
| 50 | Boise, ID | 7.4 | 124 | Murfreesboro, TN | (7.3) | 198 | Upper Darby Twnshp, PA | (14.9) |
| 51 | Fort Wayne, IN | 7.0 | 125 | Anchorage, AK | (7.4) | 199 | Miami Gardens, FL | (15.0) |
| 52 | Waterbury, CT** | 6.6 | 125 | Baltimore, MD** | (7.4) | 200 | Syracuse, NY** | (15.3) |
| 53 | Atlanta, GA** | 6.4 | 125 | Chico, CA** | (7.4) | 201 | Bridgeport, CT** | (15.4) |
| 54 | Cleveland, OH | 5.9 | 128 | Lynchburg, VA | (7.7) | 201 | Hammond, IN** | (15.4) |
| 54 | Hemet, CA** | 5.9 | 129 | Suffolk, VA | (7.9) | 201 | Pomona, CA** | (15.4) |
| 56 | Jackson, MS** | 5.7 | 130 | Minneapolis, MN | (8.1) | 204 | Charlotte, NC** | (15.9) |
| 57 | Detroit, MI | 5.4 | 131 | Toledo, OH | (8.2) | 205 | Palm Bay, FL | (16.0) |
| 57 | Pearland, TX | 5.4 | 132 | Memphis, TN | (8.3) | 206 | Dallas, TX** | (16.2) |
| 57 | Rockford, IL | 5.4 | 133 | Lake Forest, CA** | (8.4) | 206 | Macon, GA** | (16.2) |
| 60 | Ogden, UT | 5.1 | 134 | Des Moines, IA | (8.8) | 206 | St. Joseph, MO | (16.2) |
| 61 | Thornton, CO | 4.4 | 134 | Hartford, CT** | (8.8) | 209 | Oceanside, CA** | (16.3) |
| 62 | Fort Lauderdale, FL | 4.3 | 134 | Nashville, TN | (8.8) | 210 | Arvada, CO | (16.4) |
| 63 | Westminster, CA** | 3.5 | 134 | Seattle, WA | (8.8) | 211 | Grand Rapids, MI | (16.6) |
| 64 | Brownsville, TX** | 3.0 | 138 | Dearborn, MI | (9.1) | 212 | Spokane Valley, WA** | (16.8) |
| 65 | Colonie, NY** | 2.9 | 138 | Louisville, KY** | (9.1) | 213 | Plano, TX | (17.1) |
| 65 | Nashua, NH | 2.9 | 140 | Providence, RI | (9.5) | 214 | Fort Smith, AR | (17.5) |
| 67 | Indianapolis, IN | 2.7 | 141 | Centennial, CO | (9.6) | 214 | Topeka, KS** | (17.5) |
| 68 | Gilbert, AZ | 2.4 | 142 | Albany, GA** | (9.7) | 216 | Lubbock, TX** | (17.6) |
| 69 | Norman, OK** | 1.6 | 143 | Daly City, CA** | (10.0) | 217 | Fresno, CA** | (17.7) |
| 70 | Green Bay, WI | 1.4 | 144 | San Jose, CA** | (10.1) | 217 | Kennewick, WA | (17.7) |
| 71 | New Orleans, LA** | 1.2 | 145 | Orange, CA** | (10.2) | 217 | Pembroke Pines, FL | (17.7) |
| 72 | Fishers, IN** | 1.1 | 145 | Stamford, CT | (10.2) | 220 | Columbus, GA** | (17.9) |
| 72 | Tuscaloosa, AL | 1.1 | 145 | Wichita, KS | (10.2) | 220 | Riverside, CA** | (17.9) |
| 74 | Albuquerque, NM** | 0.7 | 148 | Vancouver, WA | (10.3) | 222 | Simi Valley, CA** | (18.0) |

| RANK | CITY | % CHANGE | RANK | CITY | % CHANGE | RANK | CITY | % CHANGE |
|---|---|---|---|---|---|---|---|---|
| 223 | Roswell, GA** | (18.1) | 297 | Allentown, PA | (24.6) | 371 | Las Cruces, NM** | (34.0) |
| 223 | Thousand Oaks, CA** | (18.1) | 298 | Baldwin Park, CA** | (24.7) | 372 | Olathe, KS** | (34.2) |
| 225 | Compton, CA** | (18.3) | 299 | Miramar, FL | (24.8) | 373 | League City, TX** | (34.3) |
| 225 | Eugene, OR | (18.3) | 300 | Visalia, CA** | (25.0) | 374 | Bloomington, IN** | (34.5) |
| 227 | Athens-Clarke, GA** | (18.4) | 301 | Albany, NY** | (25.1) | 375 | Beaverton, OR** | (34.6) |
| 227 | Clifton, NJ** | (18.4) | 301 | Brick Twnshp, NJ** | (25.1) | 376 | Davie, FL | (34.7) |
| 229 | Salinas, CA** | (18.5) | 301 | Broken Arrow, OK** | (25.1) | 377 | San Mateo, CA** | (35.1) |
| 230 | Lawrence, KS | (18.8) | 301 | Corpus Christi, TX** | (25.1) | 378 | North Charleston, SC | (35.2) |
| 231 | Costa Mesa, CA** | (18.9) | 301 | Hayward, CA** | (25.1) | 379 | Clearwater, FL | (35.3) |
| 231 | El Paso, TX** | (18.9) | 301 | Kansas City, KS** | (25.1) | 380 | Mission Viejo, CA** | (35.6) |
| 231 | Hawthorne, CA** | (18.9) | 307 | Roseville, CA** | (25.2) | 381 | Farmington Hills, MI | (35.7) |
| 234 | Bakersfield, CA** | (19.1) | 308 | Cheektowaga, NY** | (25.3) | 382 | Ontario, CA** | (36.3) |
| 234 | New Rochelle, NY** | (19.1) | 309 | Hialeah, FL | (25.4) | 383 | Gainesville, FL | (36.5) |
| 236 | Lincoln, NE** | (19.2) | 310 | Reno, NV** | (25.6) | 384 | Largo, FL | (36.6) |
| 237 | Santa Barbara, CA** | (19.4) | 310 | Wichita Falls, TX** | (25.6) | 385 | Canton Twnshp, MI | (36.7) |
| 238 | Bethlehem, PA | (19.5) | 312 | Columbia, MO | (25.7) | 386 | Whittier, CA** | (37.1) |
| 238 | Mountain View, CA** | (19.5) | 312 | Pittsburgh, PA | (25.7) | 387 | Fort Collins, CO | (38.4) |
| 240 | Pasadena, TX** | (19.6) | 314 | Jacksonville, FL | (25.8) | 388 | Santa Rosa, CA** | (38.5) |
| 240 | Peoria, AZ** | (19.6) | 315 | Sacramento, CA** | (25.9) | 389 | Longview, TX | (39.1) |
| 242 | Winston-Salem, NC** | (19.7) | 316 | Carrollton, TX** | (26.0) | 390 | Chino Hills, CA** | (39.5) |
| 243 | Sandy Springs, GA** | (19.8) | 317 | Boca Raton, FL | (26.4) | 390 | Glendale, CA** | (39.5) |
| 244 | Las Vegas, NV** | (19.9) | 318 | Merced, CA** | (26.6) | 392 | Cape Coral, FL | (40.3) |
| 245 | Chandler, AZ** | (20.0) | 319 | Alameda, CA** | (26.7) | 393 | Lakewood, CA** | (40.6) |
| 245 | Cincinnati, OH | (20.0) | 319 | Carmel, IN** | (26.7) | 394 | Somerville, MA | (40.9) |
| 245 | Victorville, CA** | (20.0) | 319 | Long Beach, CA** | (26.7) | 395 | Bryan, TX** | (41.3) |
| 248 | Livonia, MI | (20.3) | 322 | Melbourne, FL | (26.9) | 396 | Henderson, NV** | (41.5) |
| 249 | Berkeley, CA** | (20.4) | 322 | Nampa, ID | (26.9) | 397 | Murrieta, CA** | (42.0) |
| 249 | Raleigh, NC** | (20.4) | 324 | Baton Rouge, LA** | (27.0) | 398 | Waco, TX** | (42.8) |
| 249 | Ramapo, NY** | (20.4) | 325 | Laredo, TX** | (27.2) | 399 | Santa Maria, CA** | (42.9) |
| 252 | Danbury, CT** | (20.5) | 326 | Midland, TX** | (27.5) | 400 | Scranton, PA | (44.5) |
| 252 | Garden Grove, CA** | (20.5) | 327 | Corona, CA** | (28.0) | 401 | Richardson, TX** | (45.4) |
| 252 | Knoxville, TN | (20.5) | 327 | West Covina, CA** | (28.0) | 402 | Santa Clarita, CA** | (46.0) |
| 255 | Lancaster, CA** | (20.6) | 329 | Vacaville, CA** | (28.1) | 403 | Norwalk, CT | (46.6) |
| 255 | Lee's Summit, MO | (20.6) | 330 | Hoover, AL | (28.2) | 404 | Newport Beach, CA** | (46.7) |
| 255 | Tampa, FL | (20.6) | 330 | Inglewood, CA** | (28.2) | 405 | Renton, WA | (46.8) |
| 255 | Warwick, RI | (20.6) | 330 | Lafayette, LA** | (28.2) | 406 | Concord, NC** | (47.7) |
| 259 | Carson, CA** | (20.7) | 333 | Federal Way, WA | (28.4) | 407 | Lexington, KY | (48.4) |
| 259 | Fayetteville, NC** | (20.7) | 334 | Tyler, TX | (28.9) | 408 | Lakewood Twnshp, NJ** | (49.0) |
| 259 | High Point, NC** | (20.7) | 335 | New Haven, CT | (29.0) | 409 | El Monte, CA** | (49.7) |
| 262 | Fontana, CA** | (21.0) | 336 | Abilene, TX** | (29.2) | 409 | Fremont, CA** | (49.7) |
| 263 | Arlington, TX** | (21.1) | 337 | St. Petersburg, FL | (29.3) | 411 | Johns Creek, GA** | (49.8) |
| 263 | Boston, MA** | (21.1) | 338 | Chula Vista, CA** | (29.8) | 412 | Mission, TX** | (50.1) |
| 265 | Garland, TX** | (21.5) | 339 | Downey, CA** | (30.2) | 413 | McAllen, TX** | (52.1) |
| 265 | Plantation, FL | (21.5) | 339 | Racine, WI** | (30.2) | 414 | Bellflower, CA** | (52.9) |
| 265 | Santa Monica, CA** | (21.5) | 341 | Toms River Twnshp, NJ** | (30.3) | 415 | Edison Twnshp, NJ** | (54.3) |
| 268 | Tallahassee, FL | (21.7) | 342 | Cambridge, MA | (30.4) | 416 | Kent, WA | (57.3) |
| 269 | Amarillo, TX | (21.8) | 342 | Coral Springs, FL | (30.4) | 417 | Charleston, SC | (65.3) |
| 270 | Oxnard, CA** | (21.9) | 344 | Austin, TX** | (30.5) | NA | Arlington Heights, IL*** | NA |
| 271 | Pompano Beach, FL | (22.0) | 344 | Port St. Lucie, FL | (30.5) | NA | Aurora, IL*** | NA |
| 272 | Irving, TX** | (22.2) | 346 | Cary, NC** | (30.6) | NA | Bloomington, IL*** | NA |
| 273 | Richmond, VA | (22.3) | 346 | Mesquite, TX** | (30.6) | NA | Bloomington, MN*** | NA |
| 273 | Shreveport, LA** | (22.3) | 348 | Torrance, CA** | (30.9) | NA | Brooklyn Park, MN*** | NA |
| 273 | Virginia Beach, VA | (22.3) | 349 | Clarkstown, NY** | (31.0) | NA | Champaign, IL*** | NA |
| 276 | Clarksville, TN | (22.4) | 350 | Columbia, SC | (31.2) | NA | Chicago, IL*** | NA |
| 276 | Rialto, CA** | (22.4) | 351 | Carlsbad, CA** | (31.4) | NA | Cicero, IL*** | NA |
| 278 | Amherst, NY** | (22.5) | 352 | Hampton, VA | (31.5) | NA | Decatur, IL*** | NA |
| 279 | Wilmington, NC** | (22.9) | 353 | Ventura, CA** | (31.6) | NA | Deerfield Beach, FL*** | NA |
| 280 | St. Louis, MO | (23.0) | 354 | Temecula, CA** | (31.7) | NA | Duluth, MN*** | NA |
| 281 | Newton, MA | (23.5) | 355 | San Angelo, TX | (31.8) | NA | Elgin, IL*** | NA |
| 282 | Orlando, FL | (23.6) | 355 | Savannah, GA** | (31.8) | NA | Evanston, IL*** | NA |
| 283 | Lawton, OK** | (23.7) | 357 | Los Angeles, CA** | (31.9) | NA | Greenville, NC*** | NA |
| 284 | Citrus Heights, CA** | (23.8) | 358 | Everett, WA** | (32.0) | NA | Joliet, IL*** | NA |
| 284 | Elizabeth, NJ** | (23.8) | 358 | Roanoke, VA | (32.0) | NA | Jurupa Valley, CA*** | NA |
| 284 | Troy, MI | (23.8) | 360 | Moreno Valley, CA** | (32.1) | NA | Lowell, MA*** | NA |
| 287 | Frisco, TX | (23.9) | 361 | Greensboro, NC** | (32.3) | NA | Naperville, IL*** | NA |
| 287 | West Palm Beach, FL | (23.9) | 361 | Orem, UT** | (32.3) | NA | Newport News, VA*** | NA |
| 289 | McKinney, TX | (24.0) | 363 | Irvine, CA** | (32.4) | NA | Peoria, IL*** | NA |
| 289 | Sunnyvale, CA** | (24.0) | 364 | Elk Grove, CA** | (32.6) | NA | Rochester, MN*** | NA |
| 291 | El Cajon, CA** | (24.1) | 365 | Fullerton, CA** | (32.9) | NA | Springfield, IL*** | NA |
| 291 | Mobile, AL | (24.1) | 365 | Longmont, CO | (32.9) | NA | Upland, CA*** | NA |
| 291 | Redwood City, CA** | (24.1) | 367 | Sparks, NV** | (33.1) | NA | Waukegan, IL*** | NA |
| 294 | Allen, TX | (24.4) | 368 | Alhambra, CA** | (33.3) | NA | Yakima, WA*** | NA |
| 294 | Bellevue, WA** | (24.4) | 368 | Burbank, CA** | (33.3) | | | |
| 296 | Independence, MO | (24.5) | 370 | Santa Ana, CA** | (33.8) | | | |

Source: CQ Press using reported data from the F.B.I. "Crime in the United States 2013"

*Violent crimes are offenses of murder, rape, robbery, and aggravated assault.

**Figures for these cities are based on the previous (legacy) definition of rape. See note on page vii.

***Not available.

# 49. Murders in 2013
## National Total = 14,196 Murders*

| RANK | CITY | MURDERS | RANK | CITY | MURDERS | RANK | CITY | MURDERS |
|---|---|---|---|---|---|---|---|---|
| 330 | Abilene, TX | 1 | 217 | Chino, CA | 4 | 388 | Fullerton, CA | 0 |
| 76 | Akron, OH | 23 | 276 | Chula Vista, CA | 2 | 179 | Gainesville, FL | 6 |
| 388 | Alameda, CA | 0 | 244 | Cicero, IL | 3 | 197 | Garden Grove, CA | 5 |
| 155 | Albany, GA | 8 | 24 | Cincinnati, OH | 70 | 179 | Garland, TX | 6 |
| 155 | Albany, NY | 8 | 163 | Citrus Heights, CA | 7 | 30 | Gary, IN | 54 |
| 48 | Albuquerque, NM | 37 | 388 | Clarkstown, NY | 0 | 330 | Gilbert, AZ | 1 |
| 197 | Alexandria, VA | 5 | 179 | Clarksville, TN | 6 | 115 | Glendale, AZ | 13 |
| 330 | Alhambra, CA | 1 | 217 | Clearwater, FL | 4 | 330 | Glendale, CA | 1 |
| 121 | Allentown, PA | 12 | 29 | Cleveland, OH | 55 | 127 | Grand Prairie, TX | 11 |
| 388 | Allen, TX | 0 | 388 | Clifton, NJ | 0 | 96 | Grand Rapids, MI | 17 |
| 142 | Amarillo, TX | 9 | 197 | Clinton Twnshp, MI | 5 | 388 | Greece, NY | 0 |
| 330 | Amherst, NY | 1 | 388 | Clovis, CA | 0 | 276 | Greeley, CO | 2 |
| 127 | Anaheim, CA | 11 | 388 | College Station, TX | 0 | 276 | Green Bay, WI | 2 |
| 109 | Anchorage, AK | 14 | 388 | Colonie, NY | 0 | 67 | Greensboro, NC | 27 |
| 244 | Ann Arbor, MI | 3 | 68 | Colorado Springs, CO | 26 | 163 | Greenville, NC | 7 |
| 121 | Antioch, CA | 12 | 197 | Columbia, MO | 5 | 197 | Gresham, OR | 5 |
| 388 | Arlington Heights, IL | 0 | 155 | Columbia, SC | 8 | 330 | Hamilton Twnshp, NJ | 1 |
| 89 | Arlington, TX | 18 | 80 | Columbus, GA | 22 | 142 | Hammond, IN | 9 |
| 388 | Arvada, CO | 0 | 51 | Compton, CA | 36 | 80 | Hampton, VA | 22 |
| 276 | Athens-Clarke, GA | 2 | 330 | Concord, CA | 1 | 76 | Hartford, CT | 23 |
| 21 | Atlanta, GA | 84 | 163 | Concord, NC | 7 | 179 | Hawthorne, CA | 6 |
| 76 | Aurora, CO | 23 | 388 | Coral Springs, FL | 0 | 197 | Hayward, CA | 5 |
| 217 | Aurora, IL | 4 | 142 | Corona, CA | 9 | 217 | Hemet, CA | 4 |
| 68 | Austin, TX | 26 | 89 | Corpus Christi, TX | 18 | 155 | Henderson, NV | 8 |
| 73 | Bakersfield, CA | 24 | 330 | Costa Mesa, CA | 1 | 330 | Hesperia, CA | 1 |
| 197 | Baldwin Park, CA | 5 | 388 | Cranston, RI | 0 | 115 | Hialeah, FL | 13 |
| 6 | Baltimore, MD | 233 | 9 | Dallas, TX | 143 | 276 | High Point, NC | 2 |
| 32 | Baton Rouge, LA | 49 | 388 | Daly City, CA | 0 | 388 | Hillsboro, OR | 0 |
| 99 | Beaumont, TX | 16 | 276 | Danbury, CT | 2 | 99 | Hollywood, FL | 16 |
| 330 | Beaverton, OR | 1 | 276 | Davenport, IA | 2 | 276 | Hoover, AL | 2 |
| 330 | Bellevue, WA | 1 | 330 | Davie, FL | 1 | 7 | Houston, TX | 214 |
| 330 | Bellflower, CA | 1 | 62 | Dayton, OH | 28 | 276 | Huntington Beach, CA | 2 |
| 330 | Bend, OR | 1 | 276 | Dearborn, MI | 2 | 73 | Huntsville, AL | 24 |
| 217 | Berkeley, CA | 4 | 197 | Decatur, IL | 5 | 163 | Independence, MO | 7 |
| 217 | Bethlehem, PA | 4 | 276 | Deerfield Beach, FL | 2 | 10 | Indianapolis, IN | 129 |
| 217 | Billings, MT | 4 | 330 | Denton, TX | 1 | 330 | Indio, CA | 1 |
| 25 | Birmingham, AL | 63 | 43 | Denver, CO | 40 | 109 | Inglewood, CA | 14 |
| 276 | Bloomington, IL | 2 | 127 | Des Moines, IA | 11 | 276 | Irvine, CA | 2 |
| 276 | Bloomington, IN | 2 | 3 | Detroit, MI | 316 | 276 | Irving, TX | 2 |
| 330 | Bloomington, MN | 1 | 163 | Downey, CA | 7 | 19 | Jacksonville, FL | 93 |
| 217 | Boca Raton, FL | 4 | 276 | Duluth, MN | 2 | 31 | Jackson, MS | 50 |
| 244 | Boise, ID | 3 | 330 | Edinburg, TX | 1 | 85 | Jersey City, NJ | 20 |
| 45 | Boston, MA | 39 | 276 | Edison Twnshp, NJ | 2 | 217 | Johns Creek, GA | 4 |
| 388 | Boulder, CO | 0 | 388 | Edmond, OK | 0 | 135 | Joliet, IL | 10 |
| 330 | Brick Twnshp, NJ | 1 | 276 | El Cajon, CA | 2 | 244 | Jurupa Valley, CA | 3 |
| 127 | Bridgeport, CT | 11 | 244 | El Monte, CA | 3 | 62 | Kansas City, KS | 28 |
| 142 | Brockton, MA | 9 | 135 | El Paso, TX | 10 | 17 | Kansas City, MO | 99 |
| 388 | Broken Arrow, OK | 0 | 244 | Elgin, IL | 3 | 276 | Kennewick, WA | 2 |
| 244 | Brooklyn Park, MN | 3 | 163 | Elizabeth, NJ | 7 | 197 | Kenosha, WI | 5 |
| 330 | Brownsville, TX | 1 | 388 | Elk Grove, CA | 0 | 276 | Kent, WA | 2 |
| 276 | Bryan, TX | 2 | 244 | Erie, PA | 3 | 179 | Killeen, TX | 6 |
| 276 | Buena Park, CA | 2 | 179 | Escondido, CA | 6 | 89 | Knoxville, TN | 18 |
| 37 | Buffalo, NY | 47 | 388 | Eugene, OR | 0 | 155 | Lafayette, LA | 8 |
| 388 | Burbank, CA | 0 | 330 | Evanston, IL | 1 | 276 | Lake Forest, CA | 2 |
| 276 | Cambridge, MA | 2 | 197 | Evansville, IN | 5 | 163 | Lakeland, FL | 7 |
| 388 | Canton Twnshp, MI | 0 | 330 | Everett, WA | 1 | 276 | Lakewood Twnshp, NJ | 2 |
| 244 | Cape Coral, FL | 3 | 244 | Fairfield, CA | 3 | 276 | Lakewood, CA | 2 |
| 330 | Carlsbad, CA | 1 | 388 | Fall River, MA | 0 | 179 | Lakewood, CO | 6 |
| 388 | Carmel, IN | 0 | 244 | Fargo, ND | 3 | 142 | Lancaster, CA | 9 |
| 330 | Carrollton, TX | 1 | 330 | Farmington Hills, MI | 1 | 155 | Lansing, MI | 8 |
| 244 | Carson, CA | 3 | 244 | Fayetteville, AR | 3 | 244 | Laredo, TX | 3 |
| 330 | Cary, NC | 1 | 71 | Fayetteville, NC | 25 | 244 | Largo, FL | 3 |
| 217 | Cedar Rapids, IA | 4 | 179 | Federal Way, WA | 6 | 179 | Las Cruces, NM | 6 |
| 179 | Centennial, CO | 6 | 388 | Fishers, IN | 0 | 18 | Las Vegas, NV | 97 |
| 217 | Champaign, IL | 4 | 33 | Flint, MI | 48 | 330 | Lawrence, KS | 1 |
| 276 | Chandler, AZ | 2 | 135 | Fontana, CA | 10 | 330 | Lawrence, MA | 1 |
| 163 | Charleston, SC | 7 | 388 | Fort Collins, CO | 0 | 115 | Lawton, OK | 13 |
| 28 | Charlotte, NC | 59 | 115 | Fort Lauderdale, FL | 13 | 276 | League City, TX | 2 |
| 89 | Chattanooga, TN | 18 | 217 | Fort Smith, AR | 4 | 388 | Lee's Summit, MO | 0 |
| 388 | Cheektowaga, NY | 0 | 58 | Fort Wayne, IN | 31 | 330 | Lewisville, TX | 1 |
| 142 | Chesapeake, VA | 9 | 33 | Fort Worth, TX | 48 | 89 | Lexington, KY | 18 |
| 1 | Chicago, IL | 414 | 330 | Fremont, CA | 1 | 197 | Lincoln, NE | 5 |
| 276 | Chico, CA | 2 | 43 | Fresno, CA | 40 | 53 | Little Rock, AR | 35 |
| 388 | Chino Hills, CA | 0 | 388 | Frisco, TX | 0 | 388 | Livermore, CA | 0 |

| RANK | CITY | MURDERS |
|---|---|---|
| 388 | Livonia, MI | 0 |
| 55 | Long Beach, CA | 34 |
| 388 | Longmont, CO | 0 |
| 197 | Longview, TX | 5 |
| 4 | Los Angeles, CA | 251 |
| 33 | Louisville, KY | 48 |
| 217 | Lowell, MA | 4 |
| 197 | Lubbock, TX | 5 |
| 330 | Lynchburg, VA | 1 |
| 276 | Lynn, MA | 2 |
| 89 | Macon, GA | 18 |
| 197 | Madison, WI | 5 |
| 217 | Manchester, NH | 4 |
| 276 | McAllen, TX | 2 |
| 330 | McKinney, TX | 1 |
| 330 | Medford, OR | 1 |
| 179 | Melbourne, FL | 6 |
| 11 | Memphis, TN | 124 |
| 244 | Menifee, CA | 3 |
| 197 | Merced, CA | 5 |
| 388 | Meridian, ID | 0 |
| 80 | Mesa, AZ | 22 |
| 179 | Mesquite, TX | 6 |
| 217 | Miami Beach, FL | 4 |
| 76 | Miami Gardens, FL | 23 |
| 23 | Miami, FL | 71 |
| 197 | Midland, TX | 5 |
| 15 | Milwaukee, WI | 104 |
| 51 | Minneapolis, MN | 36 |
| 217 | Miramar, FL | 4 |
| 388 | Mission Viejo, CA | 0 |
| 388 | Mission, TX | 0 |
| 60 | Mobile, AL | 29 |
| 109 | Modesto, CA | 14 |
| 135 | Moreno Valley, CA | 10 |
| 388 | Mountain View, CA | 0 |
| 217 | Murfreesboro, TN | 4 |
| 330 | Murrieta, CA | 1 |
| 330 | Nampa, ID | 1 |
| 276 | Napa, CA | 2 |
| 388 | Naperville, IL | 0 |
| 179 | Nashua, NH | 6 |
| 53 | Nashville, TN | 35 |
| 179 | New Bedford, MA | 6 |
| 86 | New Haven, CT | 19 |
| 8 | New Orleans, LA | 156 |
| 388 | New Rochelle, NY | 0 |
| 2 | New York, NY | 335 |
| 14 | Newark, NJ | 112 |
| 276 | Newport Beach, CA | 2 |
| 103 | Newport News, VA | 15 |
| 388 | Newton, MA | 0 |
| 62 | Norfolk, VA | 28 |
| 217 | Norman, OK | 4 |
| 115 | North Charleston, SC | 13 |
| 163 | North Las Vegas, NV | 7 |
| 179 | Norwalk, CA | 6 |
| 388 | Norwalk, CT | 0 |
| 20 | Oakland, CA | 90 |
| 142 | Oceanside, CA | 9 |
| 276 | Odessa, TX | 2 |
| 330 | O'Fallon, MO | 1 |
| 276 | Ogden, UT | 2 |
| 26 | Oklahoma City, OK | 62 |
| 276 | Olathe, KS | 2 |
| 41 | Omaha, NE | 42 |
| 142 | Ontario, CA | 9 |
| 217 | Orange, CA | 4 |
| 276 | Orem, UT | 2 |
| 96 | Orlando, FL | 17 |
| 276 | Overland Park, KS | 2 |
| 103 | Oxnard, CA | 15 |
| 244 | Palm Bay, FL | 3 |
| 135 | Palmdale, CA | 10 |

| RANK | CITY | MURDERS |
|---|---|---|
| 244 | Pasadena, CA | 3 |
| 244 | Pasadena, TX | 3 |
| 89 | Paterson, NJ | 18 |
| 330 | Pearland, TX | 1 |
| 388 | Pembroke Pines, FL | 0 |
| 217 | Peoria, AZ | 4 |
| 99 | Peoria, IL | 16 |
| 5 | Philadelphia, PA | 247 |
| 13 | Phoenix, AZ | 118 |
| 39 | Pittsburgh, PA | 45 |
| 244 | Plano, TX | 3 |
| 276 | Plantation, FL | 2 |
| 60 | Pomona, CA | 29 |
| 163 | Pompano Beach, FL | 7 |
| 330 | Port St. Lucie, FL | 1 |
| 109 | Portland, OR | 14 |
| 121 | Portsmouth, VA | 12 |
| 121 | Providence, RI | 12 |
| 330 | Provo, UT | 1 |
| 276 | Pueblo, CO | 2 |
| 388 | Quincy, MA | 0 |
| 330 | Racine, WI | 1 |
| 121 | Raleigh, NC | 12 |
| 276 | Ramapo, NY | 2 |
| 330 | Rancho Cucamon., CA | 1 |
| 127 | Reading, PA | 11 |
| 276 | Redding, CA | 2 |
| 330 | Redwood City, CA | 1 |
| 109 | Reno, NV | 14 |
| 244 | Renton, WA | 3 |
| 217 | Rialto, CA | 4 |
| 276 | Richardson, TX | 2 |
| 99 | Richmond, CA | 16 |
| 48 | Richmond, VA | 37 |
| 135 | Riverside, CA | 10 |
| 142 | Roanoke, VA | 9 |
| 388 | Rochester, MN | 0 |
| 41 | Rochester, NY | 42 |
| 86 | Rockford, IL | 19 |
| 330 | Roseville, CA | 1 |
| 330 | Roswell, GA | 1 |
| 276 | Round Rock, TX | 2 |
| 55 | Sacramento, CA | 34 |
| 163 | Salem, OR | 7 |
| 73 | Salinas, CA | 24 |
| 163 | Salt Lake City, UT | 7 |
| 276 | San Angelo, TX | 2 |
| 22 | San Antonio, TX | 72 |
| 39 | San Bernardino, CA | 45 |
| 45 | San Diego, CA | 39 |
| 33 | San Francisco, CA | 48 |
| 47 | San Jose, CA | 38 |
| 244 | San Leandro, CA | 3 |
| 388 | San Marcos, CA | 0 |
| 388 | San Mateo, CA | 0 |
| 179 | Sandy Springs, GA | 6 |
| 330 | Sandy, UT | 1 |
| 115 | Santa Ana, CA | 13 |
| 276 | Santa Barbara, CA | 2 |
| 388 | Santa Clara, CA | 0 |
| 276 | Santa Clarita, CA | 2 |
| 244 | Santa Maria, CA | 3 |
| 163 | Santa Monica, CA | 7 |
| 244 | Santa Rosa, CA | 3 |
| 59 | Savannah, GA | 30 |
| 217 | Scottsdale, AZ | 4 |
| 276 | Scranton, PA | 2 |
| 86 | Seattle, WA | 19 |
| 68 | Shreveport, LA | 26 |
| 244 | Simi Valley, CA | 3 |
| 244 | Sioux City, IA | 3 |
| 244 | Sioux Falls, SD | 3 |
| 388 | Somerville, MA | 0 |
| 142 | South Bend, IN | 9 |

| RANK | CITY | MURDERS |
|---|---|---|
| 276 | South Gate, CA | 2 |
| 276 | Sparks, NV | 2 |
| 330 | Spokane Valley, WA | 1 |
| 127 | Spokane, WA | 11 |
| 217 | Springfield, IL | 4 |
| 80 | Springfield, MA | 22 |
| 121 | Springfield, MO | 12 |
| 330 | Stamford, CT | 1 |
| 388 | Sterling Heights, MI | 0 |
| 57 | Stockton, CA | 32 |
| 330 | St. George, UT | 1 |
| 330 | St. Joseph, MO | 1 |
| 12 | St. Louis, MO | 120 |
| 109 | St. Paul, MN | 14 |
| 103 | St. Petersburg, FL | 15 |
| 163 | Suffolk, VA | 7 |
| 330 | Sugar Land, TX | 1 |
| 217 | Sunnyvale, CA | 4 |
| 276 | Sunrise, FL | 2 |
| 388 | Surprise, AZ | 0 |
| 84 | Syracuse, NY | 21 |
| 135 | Tacoma, WA | 10 |
| 127 | Tallahassee, FL | 11 |
| 62 | Tampa, FL | 28 |
| 244 | Temecula, CA | 3 |
| 244 | Tempe, AZ | 3 |
| 197 | Thornton, CO | 5 |
| 388 | Thousand Oaks, CA | 0 |
| 62 | Toledo, OH | 28 |
| 330 | Toms River Twnshp, NJ | 1 |
| 127 | Topeka, KS | 11 |
| 330 | Torrance, CA | 1 |
| 388 | Tracy, CA | 0 |
| 48 | Trenton, NJ | 37 |
| 388 | Troy, MI | 0 |
| 37 | Tucson, AZ | 47 |
| 27 | Tulsa, OK | 60 |
| 155 | Tuscaloosa, AL | 8 |
| 330 | Tustin, CA | 1 |
| 197 | Tyler, TX | 5 |
| 388 | Upland, CA | 0 |
| 276 | Upper Darby Twnshp, PA | 2 |
| 330 | Vacaville, CA | 1 |
| 71 | Vallejo, CA | 25 |
| 276 | Vancouver, WA | 2 |
| 179 | Ventura, CA | 6 |
| 142 | Victorville, CA | 9 |
| 96 | Virginia Beach, VA | 17 |
| 155 | Visalia, CA | 8 |
| 330 | Vista, CA | 1 |
| 217 | Waco, TX | 4 |
| 244 | Warren, MI | 3 |
| 217 | Warwick, RI | 4 |
| 16 | Washington, DC | 103 |
| 197 | Waterbury, CT | 5 |
| 244 | Waukegan, IL | 3 |
| 330 | West Covina, CA | 1 |
| 103 | West Palm Beach, FL | 15 |
| 217 | West Valley, UT | 4 |
| 330 | Westland, MI | 1 |
| 388 | Westminster, CA | 0 |
| 276 | Westminster, CO | 2 |
| 244 | Whittier, CA | 3 |
| 163 | Wichita Falls, TX | 7 |
| 103 | Wichita, KS | 15 |
| 163 | Wilmington, NC | 7 |
| 103 | Winston-Salem, NC | 15 |
| 330 | Woodbridge Twnshp, NJ | 1 |
| 142 | Worcester, MA | 9 |
| 142 | Yakima, WA | 9 |
| 179 | Yonkers, NY | 6 |
| 197 | Yuma, AZ | 5 |

Source: Reported data from the F.B.I. "Crime in the United States 2013"

*Includes nonnegligent manslaughter.

# 49. Murders in 2013 (continued)
## National Total = 14,196 Murders*

| RANK | CITY | MURDERS | RANK | CITY | MURDERS | RANK | CITY | MURDERS |
|------|------|---------|------|------|---------|------|------|---------|
| 1 | Chicago, IL | 414 | 73 | Salinas, CA | 24 | 142 | Ontario, CA | 9 |
| 2 | New York, NY | 335 | 76 | Akron, OH | 23 | 142 | Roanoke, VA | 9 |
| 3 | Detroit, MI | 316 | 76 | Aurora, CO | 23 | 142 | South Bend, IN | 9 |
| 4 | Los Angeles, CA | 251 | 76 | Hartford, CT | 23 | 142 | Victorville, CA | 9 |
| 5 | Philadelphia, PA | 247 | 76 | Miami Gardens, FL | 23 | 142 | Worcester, MA | 9 |
| 6 | Baltimore, MD | 233 | 80 | Columbus, GA | 22 | 142 | Yakima, WA | 9 |
| 7 | Houston, TX | 214 | 80 | Hampton, VA | 22 | 155 | Albany, GA | 8 |
| 8 | New Orleans, LA | 156 | 80 | Mesa, AZ | 22 | 155 | Albany, NY | 8 |
| 9 | Dallas, TX | 143 | 80 | Springfield, MA | 22 | 155 | Columbia, SC | 8 |
| 10 | Indianapolis, IN | 129 | 84 | Syracuse, NY | 21 | 155 | Henderson, NV | 8 |
| 11 | Memphis, TN | 124 | 85 | Jersey City, NJ | 20 | 155 | Lafayette, LA | 8 |
| 12 | St. Louis, MO | 120 | 86 | New Haven, CT | 19 | 155 | Lansing, MI | 8 |
| 13 | Phoenix, AZ | 118 | 86 | Rockford, IL | 19 | 155 | Tuscaloosa, AL | 8 |
| 14 | Newark, NJ | 112 | 86 | Seattle, WA | 19 | 155 | Visalia, CA | 8 |
| 15 | Milwaukee, WI | 104 | 89 | Arlington, TX | 18 | 163 | Charleston, SC | 7 |
| 16 | Washington, DC | 103 | 89 | Chattanooga, TN | 18 | 163 | Citrus Heights, CA | 7 |
| 17 | Kansas City, MO | 99 | 89 | Corpus Christi, TX | 18 | 163 | Concord, NC | 7 |
| 18 | Las Vegas, NV | 97 | 89 | Knoxville, TN | 18 | 163 | Downey, CA | 7 |
| 19 | Jacksonville, FL | 93 | 89 | Lexington, KY | 18 | 163 | Elizabeth, NJ | 7 |
| 20 | Oakland, CA | 90 | 89 | Macon, GA | 18 | 163 | Greenville, NC | 7 |
| 21 | Atlanta, GA | 84 | 89 | Paterson, NJ | 18 | 163 | Independence, MO | 7 |
| 22 | San Antonio, TX | 72 | 96 | Grand Rapids, MI | 17 | 163 | Lakeland, FL | 7 |
| 23 | Miami, FL | 71 | 96 | Orlando, FL | 17 | 163 | North Las Vegas, NV | 7 |
| 24 | Cincinnati, OH | 70 | 96 | Virginia Beach, VA | 17 | 163 | Pompano Beach, FL | 7 |
| 25 | Birmingham, AL | 63 | 99 | Beaumont, TX | 16 | 163 | Salem, OR | 7 |
| 26 | Oklahoma City, OK | 62 | 99 | Hollywood, FL | 16 | 163 | Salt Lake City, UT | 7 |
| 27 | Tulsa, OK | 60 | 99 | Peoria, IL | 16 | 163 | Santa Monica, CA | 7 |
| 28 | Charlotte, NC | 59 | 99 | Richmond, CA | 16 | 163 | Suffolk, VA | 7 |
| 29 | Cleveland, OH | 55 | 103 | Newport News, VA | 15 | 163 | Wichita Falls, TX | 7 |
| 30 | Gary, IN | 54 | 103 | Oxnard, CA | 15 | 163 | Wilmington, NC | 7 |
| 31 | Jackson, MS | 50 | 103 | St. Petersburg, FL | 15 | 179 | Centennial, CO | 6 |
| 32 | Baton Rouge, LA | 49 | 103 | West Palm Beach, FL | 15 | 179 | Clarksville, TN | 6 |
| 33 | Flint, MI | 48 | 103 | Wichita, KS | 15 | 179 | Escondido, CA | 6 |
| 33 | Fort Worth, TX | 48 | 103 | Winston-Salem, NC | 15 | 179 | Federal Way, WA | 6 |
| 33 | Louisville, KY | 48 | 109 | Anchorage, AK | 14 | 179 | Gainesville, FL | 6 |
| 33 | San Francisco, CA | 48 | 109 | Inglewood, CA | 14 | 179 | Garland, TX | 6 |
| 37 | Buffalo, NY | 47 | 109 | Modesto, CA | 14 | 179 | Hawthorne, CA | 6 |
| 37 | Tucson, AZ | 47 | 109 | Portland, OR | 14 | 179 | Killeen, TX | 6 |
| 39 | Pittsburgh, PA | 45 | 109 | Reno, NV | 14 | 179 | Lakewood, CO | 6 |
| 39 | San Bernardino, CA | 45 | 109 | St. Paul, MN | 14 | 179 | Las Cruces, NM | 6 |
| 41 | Omaha, NE | 42 | 115 | Fort Lauderdale, FL | 13 | 179 | Melbourne, FL | 6 |
| 41 | Rochester, NY | 42 | 115 | Glendale, AZ | 13 | 179 | Mesquite, TX | 6 |
| 43 | Denver, CO | 40 | 115 | Hialeah, FL | 13 | 179 | Nashua, NH | 6 |
| 43 | Fresno, CA | 40 | 115 | Lawton, OK | 13 | 179 | New Bedford, MA | 6 |
| 45 | Boston, MA | 39 | 115 | North Charleston, SC | 13 | 179 | Norwalk, CA | 6 |
| 45 | San Diego, CA | 39 | 115 | Santa Ana, CA | 13 | 179 | Sandy Springs, GA | 6 |
| 47 | San Jose, CA | 38 | 121 | Allentown, PA | 12 | 179 | Ventura, CA | 6 |
| 48 | Albuquerque, NM | 37 | 121 | Antioch, CA | 12 | 179 | Yonkers, NY | 6 |
| 48 | Richmond, VA | 37 | 121 | Portsmouth, VA | 12 | 197 | Alexandria, VA | 5 |
| 48 | Trenton, NJ | 37 | 121 | Providence, RI | 12 | 197 | Baldwin Park, CA | 5 |
| 51 | Compton, CA | 36 | 121 | Raleigh, NC | 12 | 197 | Clinton Twnshp, MI | 5 |
| 51 | Minneapolis, MN | 36 | 121 | Springfield, MO | 12 | 197 | Columbia, MO | 5 |
| 53 | Little Rock, AR | 35 | 127 | Anaheim, CA | 11 | 197 | Decatur, IL | 5 |
| 53 | Nashville, TN | 35 | 127 | Bridgeport, CT | 11 | 197 | Evansville, IN | 5 |
| 55 | Long Beach, CA | 34 | 127 | Des Moines, IA | 11 | 197 | Garden Grove, CA | 5 |
| 55 | Sacramento, CA | 34 | 127 | Grand Prairie, TX | 11 | 197 | Gresham, OR | 5 |
| 57 | Stockton, CA | 32 | 127 | Reading, PA | 11 | 197 | Hayward, CA | 5 |
| 58 | Fort Wayne, IN | 31 | 127 | Spokane, WA | 11 | 197 | Kenosha, WI | 5 |
| 59 | Savannah, GA | 30 | 127 | Tallahassee, FL | 11 | 197 | Lincoln, NE | 5 |
| 60 | Mobile, AL | 29 | 127 | Topeka, KS | 11 | 197 | Longview, TX | 5 |
| 60 | Pomona, CA | 29 | 135 | El Paso, TX | 10 | 197 | Lubbock, TX | 5 |
| 62 | Dayton, OH | 28 | 135 | Fontana, CA | 10 | 197 | Madison, WI | 5 |
| 62 | Kansas City, KS | 28 | 135 | Joliet, IL | 10 | 197 | Merced, CA | 5 |
| 62 | Norfolk, VA | 28 | 135 | Moreno Valley, CA | 10 | 197 | Midland, TX | 5 |
| 62 | Tampa, FL | 28 | 135 | Palmdale, CA | 10 | 197 | Thornton, CO | 5 |
| 62 | Toledo, OH | 28 | 135 | Riverside, CA | 10 | 197 | Tyler, TX | 5 |
| 67 | Greensboro, NC | 27 | 135 | Tacoma, WA | 10 | 197 | Waterbury, CT | 5 |
| 68 | Austin, TX | 26 | 142 | Amarillo, TX | 9 | 197 | Yuma, AZ | 5 |
| 68 | Colorado Springs, CO | 26 | 142 | Brockton, MA | 9 | 217 | Aurora, IL | 4 |
| 68 | Shreveport, LA | 26 | 142 | Chesapeake, VA | 9 | 217 | Berkeley, CA | 4 |
| 71 | Fayetteville, NC | 25 | 142 | Corona, CA | 9 | 217 | Bethlehem, PA | 4 |
| 71 | Vallejo, CA | 25 | 142 | Hammond, IN | 9 | 217 | Billings, MT | 4 |
| 73 | Bakersfield, CA | 24 | 142 | Lancaster, CA | 9 | 217 | Boca Raton, FL | 4 |
| 73 | Huntsville, AL | 24 | 142 | Oceanside, CA | 9 | 217 | Cedar Rapids, IA | 4 |

| RANK | CITY | MURDERS | RANK | CITY | MURDERS | RANK | CITY | MURDERS |
|------|------|---------|------|------|---------|------|------|---------|
| 217 | Champaign, IL | 4 | 276 | Irvine, CA | 2 | 330 | Redwood City, CA | 1 |
| 217 | Chino, CA | 4 | 276 | Irving, TX | 2 | 330 | Roseville, CA | 1 |
| 217 | Clearwater, FL | 4 | 276 | Kennewick, WA | 2 | 330 | Roswell, GA | 1 |
| 217 | Fort Smith, AR | 4 | 276 | Kent, WA | 2 | 330 | Sandy, UT | 1 |
| 217 | Hemet, CA | 4 | 276 | Lake Forest, CA | 2 | 330 | Spokane Valley, WA | 1 |
| 217 | Johns Creek, GA | 4 | 276 | Lakewood Twnshp, NJ | 2 | 330 | Stamford, CT | 1 |
| 217 | Lowell, MA | 4 | 276 | Lakewood, CA | 2 | 330 | St. George, UT | 1 |
| 217 | Manchester, NH | 4 | 276 | League City, TX | 2 | 330 | St. Joseph, MO | 1 |
| 217 | Miami Beach, FL | 4 | 276 | Lynn, MA | 2 | 330 | Sugar Land, TX | 1 |
| 217 | Miramar, FL | 4 | 276 | McAllen, TX | 2 | 330 | Toms River Twnshp, NJ | 1 |
| 217 | Murfreesboro, TN | 4 | 276 | Napa, CA | 2 | 330 | Torrance, CA | 1 |
| 217 | Norman, OK | 4 | 276 | Newport Beach, CA | 2 | 330 | Tustin, CA | 1 |
| 217 | Orange, CA | 4 | 276 | Odessa, TX | 2 | 330 | Vacaville, CA | 1 |
| 217 | Peoria, AZ | 4 | 276 | Ogden, UT | 2 | 330 | Vista, CA | 1 |
| 217 | Rialto, CA | 4 | 276 | Olathe, KS | 2 | 330 | West Covina, CA | 1 |
| 217 | Scottsdale, AZ | 4 | 276 | Orem, UT | 2 | 330 | Westland, MI | 1 |
| 217 | Springfield, IL | 4 | 276 | Overland Park, KS | 2 | 330 | Woodbridge Twnshp, NJ | 1 |
| 217 | Sunnyvale, CA | 4 | 276 | Plantation, FL | 2 | 388 | Alameda, CA | 0 |
| 217 | Waco, TX | 4 | 276 | Pueblo, CO | 2 | 388 | Allen, TX | 0 |
| 217 | Warwick, RI | 4 | 276 | Ramapo, NY | 2 | 388 | Arlington Heights, IL | 0 |
| 217 | West Valley, UT | 4 | 276 | Redding, CA | 2 | 388 | Arvada, CO | 0 |
| 244 | Ann Arbor, MI | 3 | 276 | Richardson, TX | 2 | 388 | Boulder, CO | 0 |
| 244 | Boise, ID | 3 | 276 | Round Rock, TX | 2 | 388 | Broken Arrow, OK | 0 |
| 244 | Brooklyn Park, MN | 3 | 276 | San Angelo, TX | 2 | 388 | Burbank, CA | 0 |
| 244 | Cape Coral, FL | 3 | 276 | Santa Barbara, CA | 2 | 388 | Canton Twnshp, MI | 0 |
| 244 | Carson, CA | 3 | 276 | Santa Clarita, CA | 2 | 388 | Carmel, IN | 0 |
| 244 | Cicero, IL | 3 | 276 | Scranton, PA | 2 | 388 | Cheektowaga, NY | 0 |
| 244 | El Monte, CA | 3 | 276 | South Gate, CA | 2 | 388 | Chino Hills, CA | 0 |
| 244 | Elgin, IL | 3 | 276 | Sparks, NV | 2 | 388 | Clarkstown, NY | 0 |
| 244 | Erie, PA | 3 | 276 | Sunrise, FL | 2 | 388 | Clifton, NJ | 0 |
| 244 | Fairfield, CA | 3 | 276 | Upper Darby Twnshp, PA | 2 | 388 | Clovis, CA | 0 |
| 244 | Fargo, ND | 3 | 276 | Vancouver, WA | 2 | 388 | College Station, TX | 0 |
| 244 | Fayetteville, AR | 3 | 276 | Westminster, CO | 2 | 388 | Colonie, NY | 0 |
| 244 | Jurupa Valley, CA | 3 | 330 | Abilene, TX | 1 | 388 | Coral Springs, FL | 0 |
| 244 | Laredo, TX | 3 | 330 | Alhambra, CA | 1 | 388 | Cranston, RI | 0 |
| 244 | Largo, FL | 3 | 330 | Amherst, NY | 1 | 388 | Daly City, CA | 0 |
| 244 | Menifee, CA | 3 | 330 | Beaverton, OR | 1 | 388 | Edmond, OK | 0 |
| 244 | Palm Bay, FL | 3 | 330 | Bellevue, WA | 1 | 388 | Elk Grove, CA | 0 |
| 244 | Pasadena, CA | 3 | 330 | Bellflower, CA | 1 | 388 | Eugene, OR | 0 |
| 244 | Pasadena, TX | 3 | 330 | Bend, OR | 1 | 388 | Fall River, MA | 0 |
| 244 | Plano, TX | 3 | 330 | Bloomington, MN | 1 | 388 | Fishers, IN | 0 |
| 244 | Renton, WA | 3 | 330 | Brick Twnshp, NJ | 1 | 388 | Fort Collins, CO | 0 |
| 244 | San Leandro, CA | 3 | 330 | Brownsville, TX | 1 | 388 | Frisco, TX | 0 |
| 244 | Santa Maria, CA | 3 | 330 | Carlsbad, CA | 1 | 388 | Fullerton, CA | 0 |
| 244 | Santa Rosa, CA | 3 | 330 | Carrollton, TX | 1 | 388 | Greece, NY | 0 |
| 244 | Simi Valley, CA | 3 | 330 | Cary, NC | 1 | 388 | Hillsboro, OR | 0 |
| 244 | Sioux City, IA | 3 | 330 | Concord, CA | 1 | 388 | Lee's Summit, MO | 0 |
| 244 | Sioux Falls, SD | 3 | 330 | Costa Mesa, CA | 1 | 388 | Livermore, CA | 0 |
| 244 | Temecula, CA | 3 | 330 | Davie, FL | 1 | 388 | Livonia, MI | 0 |
| 244 | Tempe, AZ | 3 | 330 | Denton, TX | 1 | 388 | Longmont, CO | 0 |
| 244 | Warren, MI | 3 | 330 | Edinburg, TX | 1 | 388 | Meridian, ID | 0 |
| 244 | Waukegan, IL | 3 | 330 | Evanston, IL | 1 | 388 | Mission Viejo, CA | 0 |
| 244 | Whittier, CA | 3 | 330 | Everett, WA | 1 | 388 | Mission, TX | 0 |
| 276 | Athens-Clarke, GA | 2 | 330 | Farmington Hills, MI | 1 | 388 | Mountain View, CA | 0 |
| 276 | Bloomington, IL | 2 | 330 | Fremont, CA | 1 | 388 | Naperville, IL | 0 |
| 276 | Bloomington, IN | 2 | 330 | Gilbert, AZ | 1 | 388 | New Rochelle, NY | 0 |
| 276 | Bryan, TX | 2 | 330 | Glendale, CA | 1 | 388 | Newton, MA | 0 |
| 276 | Buena Park, CA | 2 | 330 | Hamilton Twnshp, NJ | 1 | 388 | Norwalk, CT | 0 |
| 276 | Cambridge, MA | 2 | 330 | Hesperia, CA | 1 | 388 | Pembroke Pines, FL | 0 |
| 276 | Chandler, AZ | 2 | 330 | Indio, CA | 1 | 388 | Quincy, MA | 0 |
| 276 | Chico, CA | 2 | 330 | Lawrence, KS | 1 | 388 | Rochester, MN | 0 |
| 276 | Chula Vista, CA | 2 | 330 | Lawrence, MA | 1 | 388 | San Marcos, CA | 0 |
| 276 | Danbury, CT | 2 | 330 | Lewisville, TX | 1 | 388 | San Mateo, CA | 0 |
| 276 | Davenport, IA | 2 | 330 | Lynchburg, VA | 1 | 388 | Santa Clara, CA | 0 |
| 276 | Dearborn, MI | 2 | 330 | McKinney, TX | 1 | 388 | Somerville, MA | 0 |
| 276 | Deerfield Beach, FL | 2 | 330 | Medford, OR | 1 | 388 | Sterling Heights, MI | 0 |
| 276 | Duluth, MN | 2 | 330 | Murrieta, CA | 1 | 388 | Surprise, AZ | 0 |
| 276 | Edison Twnshp, NJ | 2 | 330 | Nampa, ID | 1 | 388 | Thousand Oaks, CA | 0 |
| 276 | El Cajon, CA | 2 | 330 | O'Fallon, MO | 1 | 388 | Tracy, CA | 0 |
| 276 | Greeley, CO | 2 | 330 | Pearland, TX | 1 | 388 | Troy, MI | 0 |
| 276 | Green Bay, WI | 2 | 330 | Port St. Lucie, FL | 1 | 388 | Upland, CA | 0 |
| 276 | High Point, NC | 2 | 330 | Provo, UT | 1 | 388 | Westminster, CA | 0 |
| 276 | Hoover, AL | 2 | 330 | Racine, WI | 1 | | | |
| 276 | Huntington Beach, CA | 2 | 330 | Rancho Cucamon., CA | 1 | | | |

Source: Reported data from the F.B.I. "Crime in the United States 2013"
*Includes nonnegligent manslaughter.

# 50. Murder Rate in 2013
## National Rate = 4.5 Murders per 100,000 Population*

| RANK | CITY | RATE | RANK | CITY | RATE | RANK | CITY | RATE |
|---|---|---|---|---|---|---|---|---|
| 368 | Abilene, TX | 0.8 | 169 | Chino, CA | 5.0 | 388 | Fullerton, CA | 0.0 |
| 60 | Akron, OH | 11.6 | 368 | Chula Vista, CA | 0.8 | 183 | Gainesville, FL | 4.7 |
| 388 | Alameda, CA | 0.0 | 215 | Cicero, IL | 3.6 | 247 | Garden Grove, CA | 2.8 |
| 71 | Albany, GA | 10.3 | 12 | Cincinnati, OH | 23.6 | 260 | Garland, TX | 2.5 |
| 90 | Albany, NY | 8.2 | 90 | Citrus Heights, CA | 8.2 | 1 | Gary, IN | 68.5 |
| 120 | Albuquerque, NM | 6.6 | 388 | Clarkstown, NY | 0.0 | 386 | Gilbert, AZ | 0.4 |
| 221 | Alexandria, VA | 3.4 | 196 | Clarksville, TN | 4.1 | 152 | Glendale, AZ | 5.6 |
| 332 | Alhambra, CA | 1.2 | 211 | Clearwater, FL | 3.7 | 385 | Glendale, CA | 0.5 |
| 73 | Allentown, PA | 10.1 | 45 | Cleveland, OH | 14.1 | 140 | Grand Prairie, TX | 6.0 |
| 388 | Allen, TX | 0.0 | 388 | Clifton, NJ | 0.0 | 83 | Grand Rapids, MI | 8.9 |
| 185 | Amarillo, TX | 4.6 | 167 | Clinton Twnshp, MI | 5.1 | 388 | Greece, NY | 0.0 |
| 368 | Amherst, NY | 0.8 | 388 | Clovis, CA | 0.0 | 289 | Greeley, CO | 2.1 |
| 228 | Anaheim, CA | 3.2 | 388 | College Station, TX | 0.0 | 300 | Green Bay, WI | 1.9 |
| 183 | Anchorage, AK | 4.7 | 388 | Colonie, NY | 0.0 | 78 | Greensboro, NC | 9.7 |
| 254 | Ann Arbor, MI | 2.6 | 140 | Colorado Springs, CO | 6.0 | 93 | Greenville, NC | 8.0 |
| 63 | Antioch, CA | 11.3 | 190 | Columbia, MO | 4.4 | 188 | Gresham, OR | 4.5 |
| 388 | Arlington Heights, IL | 0.0 | 140 | Columbia, SC | 6.0 | 342 | Hamilton Twnshp, NJ | 1.1 |
| 178 | Arlington, TX | 4.8 | 67 | Columbus, GA | 10.9 | 63 | Hammond, IN | 11.3 |
| 388 | Arvada, CO | 0.0 | 9 | Compton, CA | 36.8 | 32 | Hampton, VA | 16.1 |
| 313 | Athens-Clarke, GA | 1.7 | 368 | Concord, CA | 0.8 | 26 | Hartford, CT | 18.4 |
| 25 | Atlanta, GA | 18.6 | 88 | Concord, NC | 8.4 | 108 | Hawthorne, CA | 7.0 |
| 114 | Aurora, CO | 6.7 | 388 | Coral Springs, FL | 0.0 | 227 | Hayward, CA | 3.3 |
| 295 | Aurora, IL | 2.0 | 152 | Corona, CA | 5.6 | 173 | Hemet, CA | 4.9 |
| 237 | Austin, TX | 3.0 | 150 | Corpus Christi, TX | 5.7 | 237 | Henderson, NV | 3.0 |
| 120 | Bakersfield, CA | 6.6 | 362 | Costa Mesa, CA | 0.9 | 342 | Hesperia, CA | 1.1 |
| 123 | Baldwin Park, CA | 6.5 | 388 | Cranston, RI | 0.0 | 152 | Hialeah, FL | 5.6 |
| 8 | Baltimore, MD | 37.4 | 62 | Dallas, TX | 11.4 | 300 | High Point, NC | 1.9 |
| 14 | Baton Rouge, LA | 21.3 | 388 | Daly City, CA | 0.0 | 388 | Hillsboro, OR | 0.0 |
| 47 | Beaumont, TX | 13.5 | 266 | Danbury, CT | 2.4 | 67 | Hollywood, FL | 10.9 |
| 342 | Beaverton, OR | 1.1 | 295 | Davenport, IA | 2.0 | 266 | Hoover, AL | 2.4 |
| 368 | Bellevue, WA | 0.8 | 353 | Davie, FL | 1.0 | 76 | Houston, TX | 9.8 |
| 320 | Bellflower, CA | 1.3 | 20 | Dayton, OH | 19.8 | 353 | Huntington Beach, CA | 1.0 |
| 320 | Bend, OR | 1.3 | 289 | Dearborn, MI | 2.1 | 49 | Huntsville, AL | 13.0 |
| 221 | Berkeley, CA | 3.4 | 120 | Decatur, IL | 6.6 | 140 | Independence, MO | 6.0 |
| 162 | Bethlehem, PA | 5.3 | 254 | Deerfield Beach, FL | 2.6 | 36 | Indianapolis, IN | 15.2 |
| 211 | Billings, MT | 3.7 | 368 | Denton, TX | 0.8 | 332 | Indio, CA | 1.2 |
| 10 | Birmingham, AL | 29.7 | 133 | Denver, CO | 6.2 | 54 | Inglewood, CA | 12.5 |
| 254 | Bloomington, IL | 2.6 | 162 | Des Moines, IA | 5.3 | 368 | Irvine, CA | 0.8 |
| 266 | Bloomington, IN | 2.4 | 3 | Detroit, MI | 45.2 | 362 | Irving, TX | 0.9 |
| 342 | Bloomington, MN | 1.1 | 133 | Downey, CA | 6.2 | 66 | Jacksonville, FL | 11.0 |
| 188 | Boca Raton, FL | 4.5 | 273 | Duluth, MN | 2.3 | 11 | Jackson, MS | 28.4 |
| 319 | Boise, ID | 1.4 | 332 | Edinburg, TX | 1.2 | 97 | Jersey City, NJ | 7.8 |
| 136 | Boston, MA | 6.1 | 295 | Edison Twnshp, NJ | 2.0 | 178 | Johns Creek, GA | 4.8 |
| 388 | Boulder, CO | 0.0 | 388 | Edmond, OK | 0.0 | 114 | Joliet, IL | 6.7 |
| 320 | Brick Twnshp, NJ | 1.3 | 295 | El Cajon, CA | 2.0 | 231 | Jurupa Valley, CA | 3.1 |
| 100 | Bridgeport, CT | 7.5 | 254 | El Monte, CA | 2.6 | 23 | Kansas City, KS | 19.0 |
| 80 | Brockton, MA | 9.5 | 316 | El Paso, TX | 1.5 | 14 | Kansas City, MO | 21.3 |
| 388 | Broken Arrow, OK | 0.0 | 251 | Elgin, IL | 2.7 | 254 | Kennewick, WA | 2.6 |
| 208 | Brooklyn Park, MN | 3.8 | 157 | Elizabeth, NJ | 5.5 | 169 | Kenosha, WI | 5.0 |
| 382 | Brownsville, TX | 0.6 | 388 | Elk Grove, CA | 0.0 | 315 | Kent, WA | 1.6 |
| 260 | Bryan, TX | 2.5 | 237 | Erie, PA | 3.0 | 190 | Killeen, TX | 4.4 |
| 266 | Buena Park, CA | 2.4 | 199 | Escondido, CA | 4.0 | 76 | Knoxville, TN | 9.8 |
| 27 | Buffalo, NY | 18.2 | 388 | Eugene, OR | 0.0 | 123 | Lafayette, LA | 6.5 |
| 388 | Burbank, CA | 0.0 | 320 | Evanston, IL | 1.3 | 260 | Lake Forest, CA | 2.5 |
| 300 | Cambridge, MA | 1.9 | 194 | Evansville, IN | 4.2 | 111 | Lakeland, FL | 6.9 |
| 388 | Canton Twnshp, MI | 0.0 | 353 | Everett, WA | 1.0 | 278 | Lakewood Twnshp, NJ | 2.2 |
| 307 | Cape Coral, FL | 1.8 | 247 | Fairfield, CA | 2.8 | 260 | Lakewood, CA | 2.5 |
| 362 | Carlsbad, CA | 0.9 | 388 | Fall River, MA | 0.0 | 196 | Lakewood, CO | 4.1 |
| 388 | Carmel, IN | 0.0 | 251 | Fargo, ND | 2.7 | 152 | Lancaster, CA | 5.6 |
| 368 | Carrollton, TX | 0.8 | 332 | Farmington Hills, MI | 1.2 | 108 | Lansing, MI | 7.0 |
| 228 | Carson, CA | 3.2 | 202 | Fayetteville, AR | 3.9 | 332 | Laredo, TX | 1.2 |
| 379 | Cary, NC | 0.7 | 58 | Fayetteville, NC | 12.3 | 202 | Largo, FL | 3.9 |
| 231 | Cedar Rapids, IA | 3.1 | 123 | Federal Way, WA | 6.5 | 145 | Las Cruces, NM | 5.9 |
| 150 | Centennial, CO | 5.7 | 388 | Fishers, IN | 0.0 | 123 | Las Vegas, NV | 6.5 |
| 178 | Champaign, IL | 4.8 | 2 | Flint, MI | 48.0 | 342 | Lawrence, KS | 1.1 |
| 368 | Chandler, AZ | 0.8 | 173 | Fontana, CA | 4.9 | 320 | Lawrence, MA | 1.3 |
| 157 | Charleston, SC | 5.5 | 388 | Fort Collins, CO | 0.0 | 48 | Lawton, OK | 13.2 |
| 108 | Charlotte, NC | 7.0 | 100 | Fort Lauderdale, FL | 7.5 | 278 | League City, TX | 2.2 |
| 70 | Chattanooga, TN | 10.4 | 185 | Fort Smith, AR | 4.6 | 388 | Lee's Summit, MO | 0.0 |
| 388 | Cheektowaga, NY | 0.0 | 59 | Fort Wayne, IN | 12.2 | 353 | Lewisville, TX | 1.0 |
| 202 | Chesapeake, VA | 3.9 | 136 | Fort Worth, TX | 6.1 | 147 | Lexington, KY | 5.8 |
| 36 | Chicago, IL | 15.2 | 386 | Fremont, CA | 0.4 | 300 | Lincoln, NE | 1.9 |
| 273 | Chico, CA | 2.3 | 95 | Fresno, CA | 7.9 | 28 | Little Rock, AR | 17.7 |
| 388 | Chino Hills, CA | 0.0 | 388 | Frisco, TX | 0.0 | 388 | Livermore, CA | 0.0 |

| RANK | CITY | RATE |
|------|------|------|
| 388 | Livonia, MI | 0.0 |
| 105 | Long Beach, CA | 7.2 |
| 388 | Longmont, CO | 0.0 |
| 133 | Longview, TX | 6.2 |
| 123 | Los Angeles, CA | 6.5 |
| 105 | Louisville, KY | 7.2 |
| 211 | Lowell, MA | 3.7 |
| 289 | Lubbock, TX | 2.1 |
| 320 | Lynchburg, VA | 1.3 |
| 278 | Lynn, MA | 2.2 |
| 21 | Macon, GA | 19.7 |
| 289 | Madison, WI | 2.1 |
| 215 | Manchester, NH | 3.6 |
| 316 | McAllen, TX | 1.5 |
| 379 | McKinney, TX | 0.7 |
| 320 | Medford, OR | 1.3 |
| 97 | Melbourne, FL | 7.8 |
| 24 | Memphis, TN | 18.9 |
| 215 | Menifee, CA | 3.6 |
| 136 | Merced, CA | 6.1 |
| 388 | Meridian, ID | 0.0 |
| 178 | Mesa, AZ | 4.8 |
| 194 | Mesquite, TX | 4.2 |
| 190 | Miami Beach, FL | 4.4 |
| 18 | Miami Gardens, FL | 20.6 |
| 31 | Miami, FL | 17.0 |
| 196 | Midland, TX | 4.1 |
| 30 | Milwaukee, WI | 17.3 |
| 82 | Minneapolis, MN | 9.1 |
| 231 | Miramar, FL | 3.1 |
| 388 | Mission Viejo, CA | 0.0 |
| 388 | Mission, TX | 0.0 |
| 60 | Mobile, AL | 11.6 |
| 111 | Modesto, CA | 6.9 |
| 169 | Moreno Valley, CA | 5.0 |
| 388 | Mountain View, CA | 0.0 |
| 219 | Murfreesboro, TN | 3.5 |
| 362 | Murrieta, CA | 0.9 |
| 332 | Nampa, ID | 1.2 |
| 260 | Napa, CA | 2.5 |
| 388 | Naperville, IL | 0.0 |
| 111 | Nashua, NH | 6.9 |
| 157 | Nashville, TN | 5.5 |
| 130 | New Bedford, MA | 6.3 |
| 43 | New Haven, CT | 14.5 |
| 5 | New Orleans, LA | 41.4 |
| 388 | New Rochelle, NY | 0.0 |
| 199 | New York, NY | 4.0 |
| 6 | Newark, NJ | 40.3 |
| 273 | Newport Beach, CA | 2.3 |
| 89 | Newport News, VA | 8.3 |
| 388 | Newton, MA | 0.0 |
| 63 | Norfolk, VA | 11.3 |
| 221 | Norman, OK | 3.4 |
| 52 | North Charleston, SC | 12.6 |
| 231 | North Las Vegas, NV | 3.1 |
| 152 | Norwalk, CA | 5.6 |
| 388 | Norwalk, CT | 0.0 |
| 13 | Oakland, CA | 22.3 |
| 164 | Oceanside, CA | 5.2 |
| 307 | Odessa, TX | 1.8 |
| 332 | O'Fallon, MO | 1.2 |
| 266 | Ogden, UT | 2.4 |
| 72 | Oklahoma City, OK | 10.2 |
| 316 | Olathe, KS | 1.5 |
| 74 | Omaha, NE | 9.9 |
| 161 | Ontario, CA | 5.4 |
| 243 | Orange, CA | 2.9 |
| 278 | Orem, UT | 2.2 |
| 114 | Orlando, FL | 6.7 |
| 342 | Overland Park, KS | 1.1 |
| 102 | Oxnard, CA | 7.4 |
| 243 | Palm Bay, FL | 2.9 |
| 128 | Palmdale, CA | 6.4 |
| 278 | Pasadena, CA | 2.2 |
| 295 | Pasadena, TX | 2.0 |
| 56 | Paterson, NJ | 12.4 |
| 353 | Pearland, TX | 1.0 |
| 388 | Pembroke Pines, FL | 0.0 |
| 260 | Peoria, AZ | 2.5 |
| 46 | Peoria, IL | 13.8 |
| 33 | Philadelphia, PA | 15.9 |
| 95 | Phoenix, AZ | 7.9 |
| 40 | Pittsburgh, PA | 14.6 |
| 342 | Plano, TX | 1.1 |
| 278 | Plantation, FL | 2.2 |
| 22 | Pomona, CA | 19.2 |
| 114 | Pompano Beach, FL | 6.7 |
| 382 | Port St. Lucie, FL | 0.6 |
| 273 | Portland, OR | 2.3 |
| 56 | Portsmouth, VA | 12.4 |
| 114 | Providence, RI | 6.7 |
| 362 | Provo, UT | 0.9 |
| 300 | Pueblo, CO | 1.9 |
| 388 | Quincy, MA | 0.0 |
| 320 | Racine, WI | 1.3 |
| 247 | Raleigh, NC | 2.8 |
| 273 | Ramapo, NY | 2.3 |
| 382 | Rancho Cucamon., CA | 0.6 |
| 54 | Reading, PA | 12.5 |
| 278 | Redding, CA | 2.2 |
| 320 | Redwood City, CA | 1.3 |
| 140 | Reno, NV | 6.0 |
| 231 | Renton, WA | 3.1 |
| 202 | Rialto, CA | 3.9 |
| 300 | Richardson, TX | 1.9 |
| 39 | Richmond, CA | 14.9 |
| 29 | Richmond, VA | 17.4 |
| 228 | Riverside, CA | 3.2 |
| 81 | Roanoke, VA | 9.2 |
| 388 | Rochester, MN | 0.0 |
| 19 | Rochester, NY | 19.9 |
| 52 | Rockford, IL | 12.6 |
| 368 | Roseville, CA | 0.8 |
| 353 | Roswell, GA | 1.0 |
| 307 | Round Rock, TX | 1.8 |
| 107 | Sacramento, CA | 7.1 |
| 190 | Salem, OR | 4.4 |
| 35 | Salinas, CA | 15.4 |
| 211 | Salt Lake City, UT | 3.7 |
| 289 | San Angelo, TX | 2.1 |
| 167 | San Antonio, TX | 5.1 |
| 17 | San Bernardino, CA | 21.0 |
| 243 | San Diego, CA | 2.9 |
| 147 | San Francisco, CA | 5.8 |
| 208 | San Jose, CA | 3.8 |
| 221 | San Leandro, CA | 3.4 |
| 388 | San Marcos, CA | 0.0 |
| 388 | San Mateo, CA | 0.0 |
| 145 | Sandy Springs, GA | 5.9 |
| 342 | Sandy, UT | 1.1 |
| 202 | Santa Ana, CA | 3.9 |
| 278 | Santa Barbara, CA | 2.2 |
| 388 | Santa Clara, CA | 0.0 |
| 353 | Santa Clarita, CA | 1.0 |
| 243 | Santa Maria, CA | 2.9 |
| 99 | Santa Monica, CA | 7.6 |
| 313 | Santa Rosa, CA | 1.7 |
| 51 | Savannah, GA | 12.8 |
| 307 | Scottsdale, AZ | 1.8 |
| 254 | Scranton, PA | 2.6 |
| 237 | Seattle, WA | 3.0 |
| 50 | Shreveport, LA | 12.9 |
| 266 | Simi Valley, CA | 2.4 |
| 215 | Sioux City, IA | 3.6 |
| 300 | Sioux Falls, SD | 1.9 |
| 388 | Somerville, MA | 0.0 |
| 83 | South Bend, IN | 8.9 |
| 289 | South Gate, CA | 2.1 |
| 278 | Sparks, NV | 2.2 |
| 342 | Spokane Valley, WA | 1.1 |
| 164 | Spokane, WA | 5.2 |
| 221 | Springfield, IL | 3.4 |
| 44 | Springfield, MA | 14.3 |
| 102 | Springfield, MO | 7.4 |
| 368 | Stamford, CT | 0.8 |
| 388 | Sterling Heights, MI | 0.0 |
| 69 | Stockton, CA | 10.7 |
| 320 | St. George, UT | 1.3 |
| 320 | St. Joseph, MO | 1.3 |
| 7 | St. Louis, MO | 37.7 |
| 178 | St. Paul, MN | 4.8 |
| 136 | St. Petersburg, FL | 6.1 |
| 90 | Suffolk, VA | 8.2 |
| 332 | Sugar Land, TX | 1.2 |
| 251 | Sunnyvale, CA | 2.7 |
| 278 | Sunrise, FL | 2.2 |
| 388 | Surprise, AZ | 0.0 |
| 40 | Syracuse, NY | 14.6 |
| 173 | Tacoma, WA | 4.9 |
| 147 | Tallahassee, FL | 5.8 |
| 93 | Tampa, FL | 8.0 |
| 247 | Temecula, CA | 2.8 |
| 307 | Tempe, AZ | 1.8 |
| 199 | Thornton, CO | 4.0 |
| 388 | Thousand Oaks, CA | 0.0 |
| 74 | Toledo, OH | 9.9 |
| 342 | Toms River Twnshp, NJ | 1.1 |
| 86 | Topeka, KS | 8.6 |
| 379 | Torrance, CA | 0.7 |
| 388 | Tracy, CA | 0.0 |
| 4 | Trenton, NJ | 43.8 |
| 388 | Troy, MI | 0.0 |
| 83 | Tucson, AZ | 8.9 |
| 36 | Tulsa, OK | 15.2 |
| 87 | Tuscaloosa, AL | 8.5 |
| 320 | Tustin, CA | 1.3 |
| 169 | Tyler, TX | 5.0 |
| 388 | Upland, CA | 0.0 |
| 266 | Upper Darby Twnshp, PA | 2.4 |
| 342 | Vacaville, CA | 1.1 |
| 16 | Vallejo, CA | 21.1 |
| 332 | Vancouver, WA | 1.2 |
| 157 | Ventura, CA | 5.5 |
| 102 | Victorville, CA | 7.4 |
| 208 | Virginia Beach, VA | 3.8 |
| 130 | Visalia, CA | 6.3 |
| 353 | Vista, CA | 1.0 |
| 231 | Waco, TX | 3.1 |
| 278 | Warren, MI | 2.2 |
| 173 | Warwick, RI | 4.9 |
| 33 | Washington, DC | 15.9 |
| 185 | Waterbury, CT | 4.6 |
| 221 | Waukegan, IL | 3.4 |
| 362 | West Covina, CA | 0.9 |
| 40 | West Palm Beach, FL | 14.6 |
| 237 | West Valley, UT | 3.0 |
| 332 | Westland, MI | 1.2 |
| 388 | Westminster, CA | 0.0 |
| 307 | Westminster, CO | 1.8 |
| 219 | Whittier, CA | 3.5 |
| 114 | Wichita Falls, TX | 6.7 |
| 202 | Wichita, KS | 3.9 |
| 130 | Wilmington, NC | 6.3 |
| 128 | Winston-Salem, NC | 6.4 |
| 353 | Woodbridge Twnshp, NJ | 1.0 |
| 173 | Worcester, MA | 4.9 |
| 79 | Yakima, WA | 9.6 |
| 237 | Yonkers, NY | 3.0 |
| 164 | Yuma, AZ | 5.2 |

Source: CQ Press using reported data from the F.B.I. "Crime in the United States 2013"

*Includes nonnegligent manslaughter.

# 50. Murder Rate in 2013 (continued)
## National Rate = 4.5 Murders per 100,000 Population*

| RANK | CITY | RATE | RANK | CITY | RATE | RANK | CITY | RATE |
|---|---|---|---|---|---|---|---|---|
| 1 | Gary, IN | 68.5 | 74 | Toledo, OH | 9.9 | 147 | Tallahassee, FL | 5.8 |
| 2 | Flint, MI | 48.0 | 76 | Houston, TX | 9.8 | 150 | Centennial, CO | 5.7 |
| 3 | Detroit, MI | 45.2 | 76 | Knoxville, TN | 9.8 | 150 | Corpus Christi, TX | 5.7 |
| 4 | Trenton, NJ | 43.8 | 78 | Greensboro, NC | 9.7 | 152 | Corona, CA | 5.6 |
| 5 | New Orleans, LA | 41.4 | 79 | Yakima, WA | 9.6 | 152 | Glendale, AZ | 5.6 |
| 6 | Newark, NJ | 40.3 | 80 | Brockton, MA | 9.5 | 152 | Hialeah, FL | 5.6 |
| 7 | St. Louis, MO | 37.7 | 81 | Roanoke, VA | 9.2 | 152 | Lancaster, CA | 5.6 |
| 8 | Baltimore, MD | 37.4 | 82 | Minneapolis, MN | 9.1 | 152 | Norwalk, CA | 5.6 |
| 9 | Compton, CA | 36.8 | 83 | Grand Rapids, MI | 8.9 | 157 | Charleston, SC | 5.5 |
| 10 | Birmingham, AL | 29.7 | 83 | South Bend, IN | 8.9 | 157 | Elizabeth, NJ | 5.5 |
| 11 | Jackson, MS | 28.4 | 83 | Tucson, AZ | 8.9 | 157 | Nashville, TN | 5.5 |
| 12 | Cincinnati, OH | 23.6 | 86 | Topeka, KS | 8.6 | 157 | Ventura, CA | 5.5 |
| 13 | Oakland, CA | 22.3 | 87 | Tuscaloosa, AL | 8.5 | 161 | Ontario, CA | 5.4 |
| 14 | Baton Rouge, LA | 21.3 | 88 | Concord, NC | 8.4 | 162 | Bethlehem, PA | 5.3 |
| 14 | Kansas City, MO | 21.3 | 89 | Newport News, VA | 8.3 | 162 | Des Moines, IA | 5.3 |
| 16 | Vallejo, CA | 21.1 | 90 | Albany, NY | 8.2 | 164 | Oceanside, CA | 5.2 |
| 17 | San Bernardino, CA | 21.0 | 90 | Citrus Heights, CA | 8.2 | 164 | Spokane, WA | 5.2 |
| 18 | Miami Gardens, FL | 20.6 | 90 | Suffolk, VA | 8.2 | 164 | Yuma, AZ | 5.2 |
| 19 | Rochester, NY | 19.9 | 93 | Greenville, NC | 8.0 | 167 | Clinton Twnshp, MI | 5.1 |
| 20 | Dayton, OH | 19.8 | 93 | Tampa, FL | 8.0 | 167 | San Antonio, TX | 5.1 |
| 21 | Macon, GA | 19.7 | 95 | Fresno, CA | 7.9 | 169 | Chino, CA | 5.0 |
| 22 | Pomona, CA | 19.2 | 95 | Phoenix, AZ | 7.9 | 169 | Kenosha, WI | 5.0 |
| 23 | Kansas City, KS | 19.0 | 97 | Jersey City, NJ | 7.8 | 169 | Moreno Valley, CA | 5.0 |
| 24 | Memphis, TN | 18.9 | 97 | Melbourne, FL | 7.8 | 169 | Tyler, TX | 5.0 |
| 25 | Atlanta, GA | 18.6 | 99 | Santa Monica, CA | 7.6 | 173 | Fontana, CA | 4.9 |
| 26 | Hartford, CT | 18.4 | 100 | Bridgeport, CT | 7.5 | 173 | Hemet, CA | 4.9 |
| 27 | Buffalo, NY | 18.2 | 100 | Fort Lauderdale, FL | 7.5 | 173 | Tacoma, WA | 4.9 |
| 28 | Little Rock, AR | 17.7 | 102 | Oxnard, CA | 7.4 | 173 | Warwick, RI | 4.9 |
| 29 | Richmond, VA | 17.4 | 102 | Springfield, MO | 7.4 | 173 | Worcester, MA | 4.9 |
| 30 | Milwaukee, WI | 17.3 | 102 | Victorville, CA | 7.4 | 178 | Arlington, TX | 4.8 |
| 31 | Miami, FL | 17.0 | 105 | Long Beach, CA | 7.2 | 178 | Champaign, IL | 4.8 |
| 32 | Hampton, VA | 16.1 | 105 | Louisville, KY | 7.2 | 178 | Johns Creek, GA | 4.8 |
| 33 | Philadelphia, PA | 15.9 | 107 | Sacramento, CA | 7.1 | 178 | Mesa, AZ | 4.8 |
| 33 | Washington, DC | 15.9 | 108 | Charlotte, NC | 7.0 | 178 | St. Paul, MN | 4.8 |
| 35 | Salinas, CA | 15.4 | 108 | Hawthorne, CA | 7.0 | 183 | Anchorage, AK | 4.7 |
| 36 | Chicago, IL | 15.2 | 108 | Lansing, MI | 7.0 | 183 | Gainesville, FL | 4.7 |
| 36 | Indianapolis, IN | 15.2 | 111 | Lakeland, FL | 6.9 | 185 | Amarillo, TX | 4.6 |
| 36 | Tulsa, OK | 15.2 | 111 | Modesto, CA | 6.9 | 185 | Fort Smith, AR | 4.6 |
| 39 | Richmond, CA | 14.9 | 111 | Nashua, NH | 6.9 | 185 | Waterbury, CT | 4.6 |
| 40 | Pittsburgh, PA | 14.6 | 114 | Aurora, CO | 6.7 | 188 | Boca Raton, FL | 4.5 |
| 40 | Syracuse, NY | 14.6 | 114 | Joliet, IL | 6.7 | 188 | Gresham, OR | 4.5 |
| 40 | West Palm Beach, FL | 14.6 | 114 | Orlando, FL | 6.7 | 190 | Columbia, MO | 4.4 |
| 43 | New Haven, CT | 14.5 | 114 | Pompano Beach, FL | 6.7 | 190 | Killeen, TX | 4.4 |
| 44 | Springfield, MA | 14.3 | 114 | Providence, RI | 6.7 | 190 | Miami Beach, FL | 4.4 |
| 45 | Cleveland, OH | 14.1 | 114 | Wichita Falls, TX | 6.7 | 190 | Salem, OR | 4.4 |
| 46 | Peoria, IL | 13.8 | 120 | Albuquerque, NM | 6.6 | 194 | Evansville, IN | 4.2 |
| 47 | Beaumont, TX | 13.5 | 120 | Bakersfield, CA | 6.6 | 194 | Mesquite, TX | 4.2 |
| 48 | Lawton, OK | 13.2 | 120 | Decatur, IL | 6.6 | 196 | Clarksville, TN | 4.1 |
| 49 | Huntsville, AL | 13.0 | 123 | Baldwin Park, CA | 6.5 | 196 | Lakewood, CO | 4.1 |
| 50 | Shreveport, LA | 12.9 | 123 | Federal Way, WA | 6.5 | 196 | Midland, TX | 4.1 |
| 51 | Savannah, GA | 12.8 | 123 | Lafayette, LA | 6.5 | 199 | Escondido, CA | 4.0 |
| 52 | North Charleston, SC | 12.6 | 123 | Las Vegas, NV | 6.5 | 199 | New York, NY | 4.0 |
| 52 | Rockford, IL | 12.6 | 123 | Los Angeles, CA | 6.5 | 199 | Thornton, CO | 4.0 |
| 54 | Inglewood, CA | 12.5 | 128 | Palmdale, CA | 6.4 | 202 | Chesapeake, VA | 3.9 |
| 54 | Reading, PA | 12.5 | 128 | Winston-Salem, NC | 6.4 | 202 | Fayetteville, AR | 3.9 |
| 56 | Paterson, NJ | 12.4 | 130 | New Bedford, MA | 6.3 | 202 | Largo, FL | 3.9 |
| 56 | Portsmouth, VA | 12.4 | 130 | Visalia, CA | 6.3 | 202 | Rialto, CA | 3.9 |
| 58 | Fayetteville, NC | 12.3 | 130 | Wilmington, NC | 6.3 | 202 | Santa Ana, CA | 3.9 |
| 59 | Fort Wayne, IN | 12.2 | 133 | Denver, CO | 6.2 | 202 | Wichita, KS | 3.9 |
| 60 | Akron, OH | 11.6 | 133 | Downey, CA | 6.2 | 208 | Brooklyn Park, MN | 3.8 |
| 60 | Mobile, AL | 11.6 | 133 | Longview, TX | 6.2 | 208 | San Jose, CA | 3.8 |
| 62 | Dallas, TX | 11.4 | 136 | Boston, MA | 6.1 | 208 | Virginia Beach, VA | 3.8 |
| 63 | Antioch, CA | 11.3 | 136 | Fort Worth, TX | 6.1 | 211 | Billings, MT | 3.7 |
| 63 | Hammond, IN | 11.3 | 136 | Merced, CA | 6.1 | 211 | Clearwater, FL | 3.7 |
| 63 | Norfolk, VA | 11.3 | 136 | St. Petersburg, FL | 6.1 | 211 | Lowell, MA | 3.7 |
| 66 | Jacksonville, FL | 11.0 | 140 | Colorado Springs, CO | 6.0 | 211 | Salt Lake City, UT | 3.7 |
| 67 | Columbus, GA | 10.9 | 140 | Columbia, SC | 6.0 | 215 | Cicero, IL | 3.6 |
| 67 | Hollywood, FL | 10.9 | 140 | Grand Prairie, TX | 6.0 | 215 | Manchester, NH | 3.6 |
| 69 | Stockton, CA | 10.7 | 140 | Independence, MO | 6.0 | 215 | Menifee, CA | 3.6 |
| 70 | Chattanooga, TN | 10.4 | 140 | Reno, NV | 6.0 | 215 | Sioux City, IA | 3.6 |
| 71 | Albany, GA | 10.3 | 145 | Las Cruces, NM | 5.9 | 219 | Murfreesboro, TN | 3.5 |
| 72 | Oklahoma City, OK | 10.2 | 145 | Sandy Springs, GA | 5.9 | 219 | Whittier, CA | 3.5 |
| 73 | Allentown, PA | 10.1 | 147 | Lexington, KY | 5.8 | 221 | Alexandria, VA | 3.4 |
| 74 | Omaha, NE | 9.9 | 147 | San Francisco, CA | 5.8 | 221 | Berkeley, CA | 3.4 |

| RANK | CITY | RATE | RANK | CITY | RATE | RANK | CITY | RATE |
|---|---|---|---|---|---|---|---|---|
| 221 | Norman, OK | 3.4 | 295 | Edison Twnshp, NJ | 2.0 | 368 | Carrollton, TX | 0.8 |
| 221 | San Leandro, CA | 3.4 | 295 | El Cajon, CA | 2.0 | 368 | Chandler, AZ | 0.8 |
| 221 | Springfield, IL | 3.4 | 295 | Pasadena, TX | 2.0 | 368 | Chula Vista, CA | 0.8 |
| 221 | Waukegan, IL | 3.4 | 300 | Cambridge, MA | 1.9 | 368 | Concord, CA | 0.8 |
| 227 | Hayward, CA | 3.3 | 300 | Green Bay, WI | 1.9 | 368 | Denton, TX | 0.8 |
| 228 | Anaheim, CA | 3.2 | 300 | High Point, NC | 1.9 | 368 | Irvine, CA | 0.8 |
| 228 | Carson, CA | 3.2 | 300 | Lincoln, NE | 1.9 | 368 | Roseville, CA | 0.8 |
| 228 | Riverside, CA | 3.2 | 300 | Pueblo, CO | 1.9 | 368 | Stamford, CT | 0.8 |
| 231 | Cedar Rapids, IA | 3.1 | 300 | Richardson, TX | 1.9 | 379 | Cary, NC | 0.7 |
| 231 | Jurupa Valley, CA | 3.1 | 300 | Sioux Falls, SD | 1.9 | 379 | McKinney, TX | 0.7 |
| 231 | Miramar, FL | 3.1 | 307 | Cape Coral, FL | 1.8 | 379 | Torrance, CA | 0.7 |
| 231 | North Las Vegas, NV | 3.1 | 307 | Odessa, TX | 1.8 | 382 | Brownsville, TX | 0.6 |
| 231 | Renton, WA | 3.1 | 307 | Round Rock, TX | 1.8 | 382 | Port St. Lucie, FL | 0.6 |
| 231 | Waco, TX | 3.1 | 307 | Scottsdale, AZ | 1.8 | 382 | Rancho Cucamon., CA | 0.6 |
| 237 | Austin, TX | 3.0 | 307 | Tempe, AZ | 1.8 | 385 | Glendale, CA | 0.5 |
| 237 | Erie, PA | 3.0 | 307 | Westminster, CO | 1.8 | 386 | Fremont, CA | 0.4 |
| 237 | Henderson, NV | 3.0 | 313 | Athens-Clarke, GA | 1.7 | 386 | Gilbert, AZ | 0.4 |
| 237 | Seattle, WA | 3.0 | 313 | Santa Rosa, CA | 1.7 | 388 | Alameda, CA | 0.0 |
| 237 | West Valley, UT | 3.0 | 315 | Kent, WA | 1.6 | 388 | Allen, TX | 0.0 |
| 237 | Yonkers, NY | 3.0 | 316 | El Paso, TX | 1.5 | 388 | Arlington Heights, IL | 0.0 |
| 243 | Orange, CA | 2.9 | 316 | McAllen, TX | 1.5 | 388 | Arvada, CO | 0.0 |
| 243 | Palm Bay, FL | 2.9 | 316 | Olathe, KS | 1.5 | 388 | Boulder, CO | 0.0 |
| 243 | San Diego, CA | 2.9 | 319 | Boise, ID | 1.4 | 388 | Broken Arrow, OK | 0.0 |
| 243 | Santa Maria, CA | 2.9 | 320 | Bellflower, CA | 1.3 | 388 | Burbank, CA | 0.0 |
| 247 | Fairfield, CA | 2.8 | 320 | Bend, OR | 1.3 | 388 | Canton Twnshp, MI | 0.0 |
| 247 | Garden Grove, CA | 2.8 | 320 | Brick Twnshp, NJ | 1.3 | 388 | Carmel, IN | 0.0 |
| 247 | Raleigh, NC | 2.8 | 320 | Evanston, IL | 1.3 | 388 | Cheektowaga, NY | 0.0 |
| 247 | Temecula, CA | 2.8 | 320 | Lawrence, MA | 1.3 | 388 | Chino Hills, CA | 0.0 |
| 251 | Elgin, IL | 2.7 | 320 | Lynchburg, VA | 1.3 | 388 | Clarkstown, NY | 0.0 |
| 251 | Fargo, ND | 2.7 | 320 | Medford, OR | 1.3 | 388 | Clifton, NJ | 0.0 |
| 251 | Sunnyvale, CA | 2.7 | 320 | Racine, WI | 1.3 | 388 | Clovis, CA | 0.0 |
| 254 | Ann Arbor, MI | 2.6 | 320 | Redwood City, CA | 1.3 | 388 | College Station, TX | 0.0 |
| 254 | Bloomington, IL | 2.6 | 320 | St. George, UT | 1.3 | 388 | Colonie, NY | 0.0 |
| 254 | Deerfield Beach, FL | 2.6 | 320 | St. Joseph, MO | 1.3 | 388 | Coral Springs, FL | 0.0 |
| 254 | El Monte, CA | 2.6 | 320 | Tustin, CA | 1.3 | 388 | Cranston, RI | 0.0 |
| 254 | Kennewick, WA | 2.6 | 332 | Alhambra, CA | 1.2 | 388 | Daly City, CA | 0.0 |
| 254 | Scranton, PA | 2.6 | 332 | Edinburg, TX | 1.2 | 388 | Edmond, OK | 0.0 |
| 260 | Bryan, TX | 2.5 | 332 | Farmington Hills, MI | 1.2 | 388 | Elk Grove, CA | 0.0 |
| 260 | Garland, TX | 2.5 | 332 | Indio, CA | 1.2 | 388 | Eugene, OR | 0.0 |
| 260 | Lake Forest, CA | 2.5 | 332 | Laredo, TX | 1.2 | 388 | Fall River, MA | 0.0 |
| 260 | Lakewood, CA | 2.5 | 332 | Nampa, ID | 1.2 | 388 | Fishers, IN | 0.0 |
| 260 | Napa, CA | 2.5 | 332 | O'Fallon, MO | 1.2 | 388 | Fort Collins, CO | 0.0 |
| 260 | Peoria, AZ | 2.5 | 332 | Sugar Land, TX | 1.2 | 388 | Frisco, TX | 0.0 |
| 266 | Bloomington, IN | 2.4 | 332 | Vancouver, WA | 1.2 | 388 | Fullerton, CA | 0.0 |
| 266 | Buena Park, CA | 2.4 | 332 | Westland, MI | 1.2 | 388 | Greece, NY | 0.0 |
| 266 | Danbury, CT | 2.4 | 342 | Beaverton, OR | 1.1 | 388 | Hillsboro, OR | 0.0 |
| 266 | Hoover, AL | 2.4 | 342 | Bloomington, MN | 1.1 | 388 | Lee's Summit, MO | 0.0 |
| 266 | Ogden, UT | 2.4 | 342 | Hamilton Twnshp, NJ | 1.1 | 388 | Livermore, CA | 0.0 |
| 266 | Simi Valley, CA | 2.4 | 342 | Hesperia, CA | 1.1 | 388 | Livonia, MI | 0.0 |
| 266 | Upper Darby Twnshp, PA | 2.4 | 342 | Lawrence, KS | 1.1 | 388 | Longmont, CO | 0.0 |
| 273 | Chico, CA | 2.3 | 342 | Overland Park, KS | 1.1 | 388 | Meridian, ID | 0.0 |
| 273 | Duluth, MN | 2.3 | 342 | Plano, TX | 1.1 | 388 | Mission Viejo, CA | 0.0 |
| 273 | Newport Beach, CA | 2.3 | 342 | Sandy, UT | 1.1 | 388 | Mission, TX | 0.0 |
| 273 | Portland, OR | 2.3 | 342 | Spokane Valley, WA | 1.1 | 388 | Mountain View, CA | 0.0 |
| 273 | Ramapo, NY | 2.3 | 342 | Toms River Twnshp, NJ | 1.1 | 388 | Naperville, IL | 0.0 |
| 278 | Lakewood Twnshp, NJ | 2.2 | 342 | Vacaville, CA | 1.1 | 388 | New Rochelle, NY | 0.0 |
| 278 | League City, TX | 2.2 | 353 | Davie, FL | 1.0 | 388 | Newton, MA | 0.0 |
| 278 | Lynn, MA | 2.2 | 353 | Everett, WA | 1.0 | 388 | Norwalk, CT | 0.0 |
| 278 | Orem, UT | 2.2 | 353 | Huntington Beach, CA | 1.0 | 388 | Pembroke Pines, FL | 0.0 |
| 278 | Pasadena, CA | 2.2 | 353 | Lewisville, TX | 1.0 | 388 | Quincy, MA | 0.0 |
| 278 | Plantation, FL | 2.2 | 353 | Pearland, TX | 1.0 | 388 | Rochester, MN | 0.0 |
| 278 | Redding, CA | 2.2 | 353 | Roswell, GA | 1.0 | 388 | San Marcos, CA | 0.0 |
| 278 | Santa Barbara, CA | 2.2 | 353 | Santa Clarita, CA | 1.0 | 388 | San Mateo, CA | 0.0 |
| 278 | Sparks, NV | 2.2 | 353 | Vista, CA | 1.0 | 388 | Santa Clara, CA | 0.0 |
| 278 | Sunrise, FL | 2.2 | 353 | Woodbridge Twnshp, NJ | 1.0 | 388 | Somerville, MA | 0.0 |
| 278 | Warren, MI | 2.2 | 362 | Carlsbad, CA | 0.9 | 388 | Sterling Heights, MI | 0.0 |
| 289 | Dearborn, MI | 2.1 | 362 | Costa Mesa, CA | 0.9 | 388 | Surprise, AZ | 0.0 |
| 289 | Greeley, CO | 2.1 | 362 | Irving, TX | 0.9 | 388 | Thousand Oaks, CA | 0.0 |
| 289 | Lubbock, TX | 2.1 | 362 | Murrieta, CA | 0.9 | 388 | Tracy, CA | 0.0 |
| 289 | Madison, WI | 2.1 | 362 | Provo, UT | 0.9 | 388 | Troy, MI | 0.0 |
| 289 | San Angelo, TX | 2.1 | 362 | West Covina, CA | 0.9 | 388 | Upland, CA | 0.0 |
| 289 | South Gate, CA | 2.1 | 368 | Abilene, TX | 0.8 | 388 | Westminster, CA | 0.0 |
| 295 | Aurora, IL | 2.0 | 368 | Amherst, NY | 0.8 | | | |
| 295 | Davenport, IA | 2.0 | 368 | Bellevue, WA | 0.8 | | | |

Source: CQ Press using reported data from the F.B.I. "Crime in the United States 2013"

*Includes nonnegligent manslaughter.

# 51. Percent Change in Murder Rate: 2012 to 2013
## National Percent Change = 5.1% Decrease*

| RANK | CITY | % CHANGE | RANK | CITY | % CHANGE | RANK | CITY | % CHANGE |
|---|---|---|---|---|---|---|---|---|
| 359 | Abilene, TX | (68.0) | 12 | Chino, CA | 284.6 | 152 | Fullerton, CA | 0.0 |
| 222 | Akron, OH | (4.1) | 364 | Chula Vista, CA | (75.0) | 152 | Gainesville, FL | 0.0 |
| 374 | Alameda, CA | (100.0) | 314 | Cicero, IL | (39.0) | 7 | Garden Grove, CA | 366.7 |
| 41 | Albany, GA | 102.0 | 81 | Cincinnati, OH | 52.3 | 250 | Garland, TX | (16.7) |
| 43 | Albany, NY | 100.0 | 14 | Citrus Heights, CA | 256.5 | 88 | Gary, IN | 48.9 |
| 237 | Albuquerque, NM | (10.8) | 152 | Clarkstown, NY | 0.0 | 371 | Gilbert, AZ | (82.6) |
| NA | Alexandria, VA*** | NA | 316 | Clarksville, TN | (43.8) | 139 | Glendale, AZ | 7.7 |
| NA | Alhambra, CA*** | NA | 101 | Clearwater, FL | 37.0 | NA | Glendale, CA*** | NA |
| 264 | Allentown, PA | (19.8) | 306 | Cleveland, OH | (33.8) | 1 | Grand Prairie, TX | 900.0 |
| 152 | Allen, TX | 0.0 | 152 | Clifton, NJ | 0.0 | 145 | Grand Rapids, MI | 6.0 |
| 236 | Amarillo, TX | (9.8) | NA | Clinton Twnshp, MI*** | NA | 152 | Greece, NY | 0.0 |
| NA | Amherst, NY*** | NA | 374 | Clovis, CA | (100.0) | 36 | Greeley, CO | 110.0 |
| 288 | Anaheim, CA | (27.3) | 374 | College Station, TX | (100.0) | 34 | Green Bay, WI | 111.1 |
| 227 | Anchorage, AK | (6.0) | 152 | Colonie, NY | 0.0 | 110 | Greensboro, NC | 27.6 |
| 26 | Ann Arbor, MI | 188.9 | 95 | Colorado Springs, CO | 42.9 | 218 | Greenville, NC | (1.2) |
| 116 | Antioch, CA | 18.9 | 71 | Columbia, MO | 63.0 | 114 | Gresham, OR | 21.6 |
| 374 | Arlington Heights, IL | (100.0) | NA | Columbia, SC** | NA | NA | Hamilton Twnshp, NJ*** | NA |
| 142 | Arlington, TX | 6.7 | 112 | Columbus, GA | 25.3 | 80 | Hammond, IN | 52.7 |
| 152 | Arvada, CO | 0.0 | 64 | Compton, CA | 72.0 | 30 | Hampton, VA | 147.7 |
| 349 | Athens-Clarke, GA | (60.5) | NA | Concord, CA*** | NA | 152 | Hartford, CT | 0.0 |
| 220 | Atlanta, GA | (2.1) | NA | Concord, NC** | NA | 247 | Hawthorne, CA | (14.6) |
| 272 | Aurora, CO | (22.1) | 374 | Coral Springs, FL | (100.0) | 263 | Hayward, CA | (19.5) |
| NA | Aurora, IL*** | NA | 2 | Corona, CA | 833.3 | 9 | Hemet, CA | 308.3 |
| 259 | Austin, TX | (18.9) | 130 | Corpus Christi, TX | 11.8 | 43 | Henderson, NV | 100.0 |
| 301 | Bakersfield, CA | (31.3) | 364 | Costa Mesa, CA | (75.0) | 372 | Hesperia, CA | (83.1) |
| 29 | Baldwin Park, CA | 150.0 | 374 | Cranston, RI | (100.0) | 16 | Hialeah, FL | 229.4 |
| 140 | Baltimore, MD | 7.2 | 229 | Dallas, TX | (8.1) | 346 | High Point, NC | (59.6) |
| 278 | Baton Rouge, LA | (25.3) | 152 | Daly City, CA | 0.0 | 374 | Hillsboro, OR | (100.0) |
| 113 | Beaumont, TX | 25.0 | 43 | Danbury, CT | 100.0 | 17 | Hollywood, FL | 220.6 |
| NA | Beaverton, OR*** | NA | 320 | Davenport, IA | (50.0) | 152 | Hoover, AL | 0.0 |
| 320 | Bellevue, WA | (50.0) | 370 | Davie, FL | (81.1) | 219 | Houston, TX | (2.0) |
| 372 | Bellflower, CA | (83.1) | 120 | Dayton, OH | 17.2 | 303 | Huntington Beach, CA | (33.3) |
| NA | Bend, OR** | NA | 36 | Dearborn, MI | 110.0 | 66 | Huntsville, AL | 71.1 |
| 269 | Berkeley, CA | (20.9) | 249 | Decatur, IL | (16.5) | 99 | Independence, MO | 39.5 |
| 55 | Bethlehem, PA | 96.3 | 320 | Deerfield Beach, FL | (50.0) | 105 | Indianapolis, IN | 31.0 |
| 104 | Billings, MT | 32.1 | 152 | Denton, TX | 0.0 | 335 | Indio, CA | (52.0) |
| 225 | Birmingham, AL | (5.4) | 152 | Denver, CO | 0.0 | 215 | Inglewood, CA | (0.8) |
| 43 | Bloomington, IL | 100.0 | 75 | Des Moines, IA | 55.9 | 239 | Irvine, CA | (11.1) |
| 309 | Bloomington, IN | (35.1) | 254 | Detroit, MI | (17.2) | 297 | Irving, TX | (30.8) |
| NA | Bloomington, MN*** | NA | 124 | Downey, CA | 17.0 | 216 | Jacksonville, FL | (0.9) |
| NA | Boca Raton, FL*** | NA | 152 | Duluth, MN | 0.0 | 268 | Jackson, MS | (20.7) |
| 27 | Boise, ID | 180.0 | 152 | Edinburg, TX | 0.0 | 61 | Jersey City, NJ | 77.3 |
| 302 | Boston, MA | (32.2) | NA | Edison Twnshp, NJ*** | NA | NA | Johns Creek, GA*** | NA |
| 152 | Boulder, CO | 0.0 | 374 | Edmond, OK | (100.0) | 235 | Joliet, IL | (9.5) |
| NA | Brick Twnshp, NJ*** | NA | 152 | El Cajon, CA | 0.0 | 18 | Jurupa Valley, CA | 210.0 |
| 331 | Bridgeport, CT | (50.3) | 280 | El Monte, CA | (25.7) | 60 | Kansas City, KS | 86.3 |
| 83 | Brockton, MA | 50.8 | 343 | El Paso, TX | (55.9) | 226 | Kansas City, MO | (5.8) |
| 374 | Broken Arrow, OK | (100.0) | 84 | Elgin, IL | 50.0 | 43 | Kennewick, WA | 100.0 |
| 285 | Brooklyn Park, MN | (26.9) | 332 | Elizabeth, NJ | (50.5) | 5 | Kenosha, WI | 400.0 |
| 355 | Brownsville, TX | (64.7) | 374 | Elk Grove, CA | (100.0) | 152 | Kent, WA | 0.0 |
| 58 | Bryan, TX | 92.3 | 350 | Erie, PA | (61.5) | 334 | Killeen, TX | (51.6) |
| 43 | Buena Park, CA | 100.0 | 119 | Escondido, CA | 17.6 | 217 | Knoxville, TN | (1.0) |
| 214 | Buffalo, NY | (0.5) | 152 | Eugene, OR | 0.0 | 289 | Lafayette, LA | (27.8) |
| 374 | Burbank, CA | (100.0) | 358 | Evanston, IL | (67.5) | NA | Lake Forest, CA*** | NA |
| 34 | Cambridge, MA | 111.1 | 312 | Evansville, IN | (38.2) | 299 | Lakeland, FL | (31.0) |
| NA | Canton Twnshp, MI** | NA | 133 | Everett, WA | 11.1 | 147 | Lakewood Twnshp, NJ | 4.8 |
| 290 | Cape Coral, FL | (28.0) | 353 | Fairfield, CA | (62.7) | 40 | Lakewood, CA | 108.3 |
| 338 | Carlsbad, CA | (52.6) | 374 | Fall River, MA | (100.0) | 25 | Lakewood, CO | 192.9 |
| 152 | Carmel, IN | 0.0 | 84 | Fargo, ND | 50.0 | 129 | Lancaster, CA | 12.0 |
| 320 | Carrollton, TX | (50.0) | 152 | Farmington Hills, MI | 0.0 | 311 | Lansing, MI | (38.1) |
| 345 | Carson, CA | (57.3) | 19 | Fayetteville, AR | 200.0 | 354 | Laredo, TX | (63.6) |
| NA | Cary, NC*** | NA | 125 | Fayetteville, NC | 15.0 | 19 | Largo, FL | 200.0 |
| 103 | Cedar Rapids, IA | 34.8 | 54 | Federal Way, WA | 97.0 | 118 | Las Cruces, NM | 18.0 |
| 4 | Centennial, CO | 470.0 | 152 | Fishers, IN | 0.0 | 111 | Las Vegas, NV | 27.5 |
| 106 | Champaign, IL | 29.7 | 274 | Flint, MI | (22.6) | NA | Lawrence, KS*** | NA |
| 320 | Chandler, AZ | (50.0) | 56 | Fontana, CA | 96.0 | 320 | Lawrence, MA | (50.0) |
| 315 | Charleston, SC | (43.3) | 374 | Fort Collins, CO | (100.0) | 152 | Lawton, OK | 0.0 |
| 137 | Charlotte, NC | 9.4 | 266 | Fort Lauderdale, FL | (20.2) | NA | League City, TX*** | NA |
| NA | Chattanooga, TN** | NA | 262 | Fort Smith, AR | (19.3) | 152 | Lee's Summit, MO | 0.0 |
| 152 | Cheektowaga, NY | 0.0 | 97 | Fort Wayne, IN | 41.9 | NA | Lewisville, TX** | NA |
| 284 | Chesapeake, VA | (26.4) | 141 | Fort Worth, TX | 7.0 | 93 | Lexington, KY | 45.0 |
| 256 | Chicago, IL | (17.8) | 342 | Fremont, CA | (55.6) | 63 | Lincoln, NE | 72.7 |
| 38 | Chico, CA | 109.1 | 271 | Fresno, CA | (21.8) | 276 | Little Rock, AR | (23.0) |
| 152 | Chino Hills, CA | 0.0 | 152 | Frisco, TX | 0.0 | 152 | Livermore, CA | 0.0 |

| RANK | CITY | % CHANGE | RANK | CITY | % CHANGE | RANK | CITY | % CHANGE |
|---|---|---|---|---|---|---|---|---|
| 374 | Livonia, MI | (100.0) | 313 | Pasadena, CA | (38.9) | 368 | South Gate, CA | (77.7) |
| 146 | Long Beach, CA | 5.9 | 350 | Pasadena, TX | (61.5) | 43 | Sparks, NV | 100.0 |
| 152 | Longmont, CO | 0.0 | 244 | Paterson, NJ | (13.3) | 152 | Spokane Valley, WA | 0.0 |
| 286 | Longview, TX | (27.1) | 233 | Pearland, TX | (9.1) | 248 | Spokane, WA | (14.8) |
| 250 | Los Angeles, CA | (16.7) | 374 | Pembroke Pines, FL | (100.0) | 347 | Springfield, IL | (60.0) |
| 274 | Louisville, KY | (22.6) | 344 | Peoria, AZ | (56.1) | 42 | Springfield, MA | 101.4 |
| NA | Lowell, MA*** | NA | 74 | Peoria, IL | 58.6 | 278 | Springfield, MO | (25.3) |
| 340 | Lubbock, TX | (54.3) | 282 | Philadelphia, PA | (26.0) | 369 | Stamford, CT | (80.0) |
| 357 | Lynchburg, VA | (66.7) | 224 | Phoenix, AZ | (4.8) | 374 | Sterling Heights, MI | (100.0) |
| 152 | Lynn, MA | 0.0 | 131 | Pittsburgh, PA | 11.5 | 341 | Stockton, CA | (54.9) |
| 243 | Macon, GA | (12.8) | 28 | Plano, TX | 175.0 | NA | St. George, UT*** | NA |
| 72 | Madison, WI | 61.5 | 337 | Plantation, FL | (52.2) | 152 | St. Joseph, MO | 0.0 |
| 11 | Manchester, NH | 300.0 | 65 | Pomona, CA | 71.4 | 144 | St. Louis, MO | 6.2 |
| 32 | McAllen, TX | 114.3 | 102 | Pompano Beach, FL | 36.7 | 142 | St. Paul, MN | 6.7 |
| NA | McKinney, TX*** | NA | 364 | Port St. Lucie, FL | (75.0) | 150 | St. Petersburg, FL | 1.7 |
| 320 | Medford, OR | (50.0) | 296 | Portland, OR | (30.3) | NA | Suffolk, VA** | NA |
| 152 | Melbourne, FL | 0.0 | 138 | Portsmouth, VA | 8.8 | NA | Sugar Land, TX*** | NA |
| 228 | Memphis, TN | (6.4) | 295 | Providence, RI | (30.2) | 109 | Sunnyvale, CA | 28.6 |
| 19 | Menifee, CA | 200.0 | NA | Provo, UT*** | NA | 43 | Sunrise, FL | 100.0 |
| 317 | Merced, CA | (45.0) | 361 | Pueblo, CO | (74.0) | 374 | Surprise, AZ | (100.0) |
| 152 | Meridian, ID | 0.0 | 152 | Quincy, MA | 0.0 | 82 | Syracuse, NY | 52.1 |
| 77 | Mesa, AZ | 54.8 | 363 | Racine, WI | (74.5) | 252 | Tacoma, WA | (16.9) |
| 19 | Mesquite, TX | 200.0 | 294 | Raleigh, NC | (30.0) | 237 | Tallahassee, FL | (10.8) |
| 265 | Miami Beach, FL | (20.0) | NA | Ramapo, NY*** | NA | 115 | Tampa, FL | 21.2 |
| 230 | Miami Gardens, FL | (8.4) | 364 | Rancho Cucamon., CA | (75.0) | NA | Temecula, CA*** | NA |
| 149 | Miami, FL | 1.8 | 282 | Reading, PA | (26.0) | 360 | Tempe, AZ | (72.7) |
| 122 | Midland, TX | 17.1 | 303 | Redding, CA | (33.3) | 5 | Thornton, CO | 400.0 |
| 127 | Milwaukee, WI | 13.8 | NA | Redwood City, CA*** | NA | 152 | Thousand Oaks, CA | 0.0 |
| 232 | Minneapolis, MN | (9.0) | 43 | Reno, NV | 100.0 | 287 | Toledo, OH | (27.2) |
| 57 | Miramar, FL | 93.8 | 90 | Renton, WA | 47.6 | 152 | Toms River Twnshp, NJ | 0.0 |
| 152 | Mission Viejo, CA | 0.0 | 152 | Rialto, CA | 0.0 | 281 | Topeka, KS | (25.9) |
| 374 | Mission, TX | (100.0) | 152 | Richardson, TX | 0.0 | 362 | Torrance, CA | (74.1) |
| 231 | Mobile, AL | (8.7) | 240 | Richmond, CA | (11.8) | 374 | Tracy, CA | (100.0) |
| 292 | Modesto, CA | (29.6) | 246 | Richmond, VA | (13.9) | 75 | Trenton, NJ | 55.9 |
| 43 | Moreno Valley, CA | 100.0 | 310 | Riverside, CA | (37.3) | 374 | Troy, MI | (100.0) |
| 152 | Mountain View, CA | 0.0 | 152 | Roanoke, VA | 0.0 | 136 | Tucson, AZ | 9.9 |
| 107 | Murfreesboro, TN | 29.6 | 374 | Rochester, MN | (100.0) | 94 | Tulsa, OK | 44.8 |
| 152 | Murrieta, CA | 0.0 | 122 | Rochester, NY | 17.1 | 53 | Tuscaloosa, AL | 97.7 |
| 320 | Nampa, ID | (50.0) | 33 | Rockford, IL | 113.6 | NA | Tustin, CA*** | NA |
| 152 | Napa, CA | 0.0 | 320 | Roseville, CA | (50.0) | 67 | Tyler, TX | 66.7 |
| 374 | Naperville, IL | (100.0) | 233 | Roswell, GA | (9.1) | 152 | Upland, CA | 0.0 |
| NA | Nashua, NH*** | NA | NA | Round Rock, TX*** | NA | 303 | Upper Darby Twnshp, PA | (33.3) |
| 317 | Nashville, TN | (45.0) | 152 | Sacramento, CA | 0.0 | 356 | Vacaville, CA | (65.6) |
| 19 | New Bedford, MA | 200.0 | 152 | Salem, OR | 0.0 | 61 | Vallejo, CA | 77.3 |
| 134 | New Haven, CT | 10.7 | 128 | Salinas, CA | 13.2 | 347 | Vancouver, WA | (60.0) |
| 273 | New Orleans, LA | (22.2) | 241 | Salt Lake City, UT | (11.9) | 3 | Ventura, CA | 511.1 |
| 152 | New Rochelle, NY | 0.0 | NA | San Angelo, TX** | NA | 92 | Victorville, CA | 45.1 |
| 270 | New York, NY | (21.6) | 267 | San Antonio, TX | (20.3) | 261 | Virginia Beach, VA | (19.1) |
| 120 | Newark, NJ | 17.2 | 222 | San Bernardino, CA | (4.1) | 72 | Visalia, CA | 61.5 |
| 38 | Newport Beach, CA | 109.1 | 253 | San Diego, CA | (17.1) | 152 | Vista, CA | 0.0 |
| 277 | Newport News, VA | (24.5) | 299 | San Francisco, CA | (31.0) | 307 | Waco, TX | (34.0) |
| 152 | Newton, MA | 0.0 | 255 | San Jose, CA | (17.4) | NA | Warren, MI*** | NA |
| 258 | Norfolk, VA | (18.7) | 89 | San Leandro, CA | 47.8 | 9 | Warwick, RI | 308.3 |
| 13 | Norman, OK | 277.8 | 374 | San Marcos, CA | (100.0) | 126 | Washington, DC | 14.4 |
| 221 | North Charleston, SC | (2.3) | 152 | San Mateo, CA | 0.0 | 148 | Waterbury, CT | 2.2 |
| 333 | North Las Vegas, NV | (50.8) | 59 | Sandy Springs, GA | 90.3 | 78 | Waukegan, IL | 54.5 |
| 319 | Norwalk, CA | (45.6) | 320 | Sandy, UT | (50.0) | 338 | West Covina, CA | (52.6) |
| 374 | Norwalk, CT | (100.0) | 117 | Santa Ana, CA | 18.2 | 242 | West Palm Beach, FL | (12.0) |
| 293 | Oakland, CA | (29.9) | NA | Santa Barbara, CA*** | NA | 8 | West Valley, UT | 328.6 |
| 135 | Oceanside, CA | 10.6 | 152 | Santa Clara, CA | 0.0 | 152 | Westland, MI | 0.0 |
| 352 | Odessa, TX | (62.5) | 67 | Santa Clarita, CA | 66.7 | 374 | Westminster, CA | (100.0) |
| 335 | O'Fallon, MO | (52.0) | NA | Santa Maria, CA*** | NA | 152 | Westminster, CO | 0.0 |
| 152 | Ogden, UT | 0.0 | 15 | Santa Monica, CA | 245.5 | NA | Whittier, CA*** | NA |
| 291 | Oklahoma City, OK | (28.7) | 98 | Santa Rosa, CA | 41.7 | 96 | Wichita Falls, TX | 42.6 |
| NA | Olathe, KS*** | NA | 108 | Savannah, GA | 29.3 | 308 | Wichita, KS | (35.0) |
| 151 | Omaha, NE | 1.0 | 100 | Scottsdale, AZ | 38.5 | 245 | Wilmington, NC | (13.7) |
| 19 | Ontario, CA | 200.0 | NA | Scranton, PA*** | NA | 31 | Winston-Salem, NC | 146.2 |
| 152 | Orange, CA | 0.0 | 259 | Seattle, WA | (18.9) | NA | Woodbridge Twnshp, NJ*** | NA |
| 152 | Orem, UT | 0.0 | 79 | Shreveport, LA | 53.6 | 132 | Worcester, MA | 11.4 |
| 298 | Orlando, FL | (30.9) | 152 | Simi Valley, CA | 0.0 | 257 | Yakima, WA | (18.6) |
| 152 | Overland Park, KS | 0.0 | 84 | Sioux City, IA | 50.0 | 84 | Yonkers, NY | 50.0 |
| 69 | Oxnard, CA | 64.4 | 91 | Sioux Falls, SD | 46.2 | 152 | Yuma, AZ | 0.0 |
| 152 | Palm Bay, FL | 0.0 | 152 | Somerville, MA | 0.0 | | | |
| 70 | Palmdale, CA | 64.1 | 320 | South Bend, IN | (50.0) | | | |

Source: CQ Press using reported data from the F.B.I. "Crime in the United States 2013"

*Includes nonnegligent manslaughter.  **Not available.  ***These cities had murder rates of 0 in 2012 but had at least one murder in 2013.  Calculating percent increase from zero results in an infinite number.  These are shown as "NA."

# 51. Percent Change in Murder Rate: 2012 to 2013 (continued)
## National Percent Change = 5.1% Decrease*

| RANK | CITY | % CHANGE | RANK | CITY | % CHANGE | RANK | CITY | % CHANGE |
|---|---|---|---|---|---|---|---|---|
| 1 | Grand Prairie, TX | 900.0 | 75 | Des Moines, IA | 55.9 | 149 | Miami, FL | 1.8 |
| 2 | Corona, CA | 833.3 | 75 | Trenton, NJ | 55.9 | 150 | St. Petersburg, FL | 1.7 |
| 3 | Ventura, CA | 511.1 | 77 | Mesa, AZ | 54.8 | 151 | Omaha, NE | 1.0 |
| 4 | Centennial, CO | 470.0 | 78 | Waukegan, IL | 54.5 | 152 | Allen, TX | 0.0 |
| 5 | Kenosha, WI | 400.0 | 79 | Shreveport, LA | 53.6 | 152 | Arvada, CO | 0.0 |
| 5 | Thornton, CO | 400.0 | 80 | Hammond, IN | 52.7 | 152 | Boulder, CO | 0.0 |
| 7 | Garden Grove, CA | 366.7 | 81 | Cincinnati, OH | 52.3 | 152 | Carmel, IN | 0.0 |
| 8 | West Valley, UT | 328.6 | 82 | Syracuse, NY | 52.1 | 152 | Cheektowaga, NY | 0.0 |
| 9 | Hemet, CA | 308.3 | 83 | Brockton, MA | 50.8 | 152 | Chino Hills, CA | 0.0 |
| 9 | Warwick, RI | 308.3 | 84 | Elgin, IL | 50.0 | 152 | Clarkstown, NY | 0.0 |
| 11 | Manchester, NH | 300.0 | 84 | Fargo, ND | 50.0 | 152 | Clifton, NJ | 0.0 |
| 12 | Chino, CA | 284.6 | 84 | Sioux City, IA | 50.0 | 152 | Colonie, NY | 0.0 |
| 13 | Norman, OK | 277.8 | 84 | Yonkers, NY | 50.0 | 152 | Daly City, CA | 0.0 |
| 14 | Citrus Heights, CA | 256.5 | 88 | Gary, IN | 48.9 | 152 | Denton, TX | 0.0 |
| 15 | Santa Monica, CA | 245.5 | 89 | San Leandro, CA | 47.8 | 152 | Denver, CO | 0.0 |
| 16 | Hialeah, FL | 229.4 | 90 | Renton, WA | 47.6 | 152 | Duluth, MN | 0.0 |
| 17 | Hollywood, FL | 220.6 | 91 | Sioux Falls, SD | 46.2 | 152 | Edinburg, TX | 0.0 |
| 18 | Jurupa Valley, CA | 210.0 | 92 | Victorville, CA | 45.1 | 152 | El Cajon, CA | 0.0 |
| 19 | Fayetteville, AR | 200.0 | 93 | Lexington, KY | 45.0 | 152 | Eugene, OR | 0.0 |
| 19 | Largo, FL | 200.0 | 94 | Tulsa, OK | 44.8 | 152 | Farmington Hills, MI | 0.0 |
| 19 | Menifee, CA | 200.0 | 95 | Colorado Springs, CO | 42.9 | 152 | Fishers, IN | 0.0 |
| 19 | Mesquite, TX | 200.0 | 96 | Wichita Falls, TX | 42.6 | 152 | Frisco, TX | 0.0 |
| 19 | New Bedford, MA | 200.0 | 97 | Fort Wayne, IN | 41.9 | 152 | Fullerton, CA | 0.0 |
| 19 | Ontario, CA | 200.0 | 98 | Santa Rosa, CA | 41.7 | 152 | Gainesville, FL | 0.0 |
| 25 | Lakewood, CO | 192.9 | 99 | Independence, MO | 39.5 | 152 | Greece, NY | 0.0 |
| 26 | Ann Arbor, MI | 188.9 | 100 | Scottsdale, AZ | 38.5 | 152 | Hartford, CT | 0.0 |
| 27 | Boise, ID | 180.0 | 101 | Clearwater, FL | 37.0 | 152 | Hoover, AL | 0.0 |
| 28 | Plano, TX | 175.0 | 102 | Pompano Beach, FL | 36.7 | 152 | Kent, WA | 0.0 |
| 29 | Baldwin Park, CA | 150.0 | 103 | Cedar Rapids, IA | 34.8 | 152 | Lawton, OK | 0.0 |
| 30 | Hampton, VA | 147.7 | 104 | Billings, MT | 32.1 | 152 | Lee's Summit, MO | 0.0 |
| 31 | Winston-Salem, NC | 146.2 | 105 | Indianapolis, IN | 31.0 | 152 | Livermore, CA | 0.0 |
| 32 | McAllen, TX | 114.3 | 106 | Champaign, IL | 29.7 | 152 | Longmont, CO | 0.0 |
| 33 | Rockford, IL | 113.6 | 107 | Murfreesboro, TN | 29.6 | 152 | Lynn, MA | 0.0 |
| 34 | Cambridge, MA | 111.1 | 108 | Savannah, GA | 29.3 | 152 | Melbourne, FL | 0.0 |
| 34 | Green Bay, WI | 111.1 | 109 | Sunnyvale, CA | 28.6 | 152 | Meridian, ID | 0.0 |
| 36 | Dearborn, MI | 110.0 | 110 | Greensboro, NC | 27.6 | 152 | Mission Viejo, CA | 0.0 |
| 36 | Greeley, CO | 110.0 | 111 | Las Vegas, NV | 27.5 | 152 | Mountain View, CA | 0.0 |
| 38 | Chico, CA | 109.1 | 112 | Columbus, GA | 25.3 | 152 | Murrieta, CA | 0.0 |
| 38 | Newport Beach, CA | 109.1 | 113 | Beaumont, TX | 25.0 | 152 | Napa, CA | 0.0 |
| 40 | Lakewood, CA | 108.3 | 114 | Gresham, OR | 21.6 | 152 | New Rochelle, NY | 0.0 |
| 41 | Albany, GA | 102.0 | 115 | Tampa, FL | 21.2 | 152 | Newton, MA | 0.0 |
| 42 | Springfield, MA | 101.4 | 116 | Antioch, CA | 18.9 | 152 | Ogden, UT | 0.0 |
| 43 | Albany, NY | 100.0 | 117 | Santa Ana, CA | 18.2 | 152 | Orange, CA | 0.0 |
| 43 | Bloomington, IL | 100.0 | 118 | Las Cruces, NM | 18.0 | 152 | Orem, UT | 0.0 |
| 43 | Buena Park, CA | 100.0 | 119 | Escondido, CA | 17.6 | 152 | Overland Park, KS | 0.0 |
| 43 | Danbury, CT | 100.0 | 120 | Dayton, OH | 17.2 | 152 | Palm Bay, FL | 0.0 |
| 43 | Henderson, NV | 100.0 | 120 | Newark, NJ | 17.2 | 152 | Quincy, MA | 0.0 |
| 43 | Kennewick, WA | 100.0 | 122 | Midland, TX | 17.1 | 152 | Rialto, CA | 0.0 |
| 43 | Moreno Valley, CA | 100.0 | 122 | Rochester, NY | 17.1 | 152 | Richardson, TX | 0.0 |
| 43 | Reno, NV | 100.0 | 124 | Downey, CA | 17.0 | 152 | Roanoke, VA | 0.0 |
| 43 | Sparks, NV | 100.0 | 125 | Fayetteville, NC | 15.0 | 152 | Sacramento, CA | 0.0 |
| 43 | Sunrise, FL | 100.0 | 126 | Washington, DC | 14.4 | 152 | Salem, OR | 0.0 |
| 53 | Tuscaloosa, AL | 97.7 | 127 | Milwaukee, WI | 13.8 | 152 | San Mateo, CA | 0.0 |
| 54 | Federal Way, WA | 97.0 | 128 | Salinas, CA | 13.2 | 152 | Santa Clara, CA | 0.0 |
| 55 | Bethlehem, PA | 96.3 | 129 | Lancaster, CA | 12.0 | 152 | Simi Valley, CA | 0.0 |
| 56 | Fontana, CA | 96.0 | 130 | Corpus Christi, TX | 11.8 | 152 | Somerville, MA | 0.0 |
| 57 | Miramar, FL | 93.8 | 131 | Pittsburgh, PA | 11.5 | 152 | Spokane Valley, WA | 0.0 |
| 58 | Bryan, TX | 92.3 | 132 | Worcester, MA | 11.4 | 152 | St. Joseph, MO | 0.0 |
| 59 | Sandy Springs, GA | 90.3 | 133 | Everett, WA | 11.1 | 152 | Thousand Oaks, CA | 0.0 |
| 60 | Kansas City, KS | 86.3 | 134 | New Haven, CT | 10.7 | 152 | Toms River Twnshp, NJ | 0.0 |
| 61 | Jersey City, NJ | 77.3 | 135 | Oceanside, CA | 10.6 | 152 | Upland, CA | 0.0 |
| 61 | Vallejo, CA | 77.3 | 136 | Tucson, AZ | 9.9 | 152 | Vista, CA | 0.0 |
| 63 | Lincoln, NE | 72.7 | 137 | Charlotte, NC | 9.4 | 152 | Westland, MI | 0.0 |
| 64 | Compton, CA | 72.0 | 138 | Portsmouth, VA | 8.8 | 152 | Westminster, CO | 0.0 |
| 65 | Pomona, CA | 71.4 | 139 | Glendale, AZ | 7.7 | 152 | Yuma, AZ | 0.0 |
| 66 | Huntsville, AL | 71.1 | 140 | Baltimore, MD | 7.2 | 214 | Buffalo, NY | (0.5) |
| 67 | Santa Clarita, CA | 66.7 | 141 | Fort Worth, TX | 7.0 | 215 | Inglewood, CA | (0.8) |
| 67 | Tyler, TX | 66.7 | 142 | Arlington, TX | 6.7 | 216 | Jacksonville, FL | (0.9) |
| 69 | Oxnard, CA | 64.4 | 142 | St. Paul, MN | 6.7 | 217 | Knoxville, TN | (1.0) |
| 70 | Palmdale, CA | 64.1 | 144 | St. Louis, MO | 6.2 | 218 | Greenville, NC | (1.2) |
| 71 | Columbia, MO | 63.0 | 145 | Grand Rapids, MI | 6.0 | 219 | Houston, TX | (2.0) |
| 72 | Madison, WI | 61.5 | 146 | Long Beach, CA | 5.9 | 220 | Atlanta, GA | (2.1) |
| 72 | Visalia, CA | 61.5 | 147 | Lakewood Twnshp, NJ | 4.8 | 221 | North Charleston, SC | (2.3) |
| 74 | Peoria, IL | 58.6 | 148 | Waterbury, CT | 2.2 | 222 | Akron, OH | (4.1) |

| RANK | CITY | % CHANGE | RANK | CITY | % CHANGE | RANK | CITY | % CHANGE |
|---|---|---|---|---|---|---|---|---|
| 222 | San Bernardino, CA | (4.1) | 297 | Irving, TX | (30.8) | 371 | Gilbert, AZ | (82.6) |
| 224 | Phoenix, AZ | (4.8) | 298 | Orlando, FL | (30.9) | 372 | Bellflower, CA | (83.1) |
| 225 | Birmingham, AL | (5.4) | 299 | Lakeland, FL | (31.0) | 372 | Hesperia, CA | (83.1) |
| 226 | Kansas City, MO | (5.8) | 299 | San Francisco, CA | (31.0) | 374 | Alameda, CA | (100.0) |
| 227 | Anchorage, AK | (6.0) | 301 | Bakersfield, CA | (31.3) | 374 | Arlington Heights, IL | (100.0) |
| 228 | Memphis, TN | (6.4) | 302 | Boston, MA | (32.2) | 374 | Broken Arrow, OK | (100.0) |
| 229 | Dallas, TX | (8.1) | 303 | Huntington Beach, CA | (33.3) | 374 | Burbank, CA | (100.0) |
| 230 | Miami Gardens, FL | (8.4) | 303 | Redding, CA | (33.3) | 374 | Clovis, CA | (100.0) |
| 231 | Mobile, AL | (8.7) | 303 | Upper Darby Twnshp, PA | (33.3) | 374 | College Station, TX | (100.0) |
| 232 | Minneapolis, MN | (9.0) | 306 | Cleveland, OH | (33.8) | 374 | Coral Springs, FL | (100.0) |
| 233 | Pearland, TX | (9.1) | 307 | Waco, TX | (34.0) | 374 | Cranston, RI | (100.0) |
| 233 | Roswell, GA | (9.1) | 308 | Wichita, KS | (35.0) | 374 | Edmond, OK | (100.0) |
| 235 | Joliet, IL | (9.5) | 309 | Bloomington, IN | (35.1) | 374 | Elk Grove, CA | (100.0) |
| 236 | Amarillo, TX | (9.8) | 310 | Riverside, CA | (37.3) | 374 | Fall River, MA | (100.0) |
| 237 | Albuquerque, NM | (10.8) | 311 | Lansing, MI | (38.1) | 374 | Fort Collins, CO | (100.0) |
| 237 | Tallahassee, FL | (10.8) | 312 | Evansville, IN | (38.2) | 374 | Hillsboro, OR | (100.0) |
| 239 | Irvine, CA | (11.1) | 313 | Pasadena, CA | (38.9) | 374 | Livonia, MI | (100.0) |
| 240 | Richmond, CA | (11.8) | 314 | Cicero, IL | (39.0) | 374 | Mission, TX | (100.0) |
| 241 | Salt Lake City, UT | (11.9) | 315 | Charleston, SC | (43.3) | 374 | Naperville, IL | (100.0) |
| 242 | West Palm Beach, FL | (12.0) | 316 | Clarksville, TN | (43.8) | 374 | Norwalk, CT | (100.0) |
| 243 | Macon, GA | (12.8) | 317 | Merced, CA | (45.0) | 374 | Pembroke Pines, FL | (100.0) |
| 244 | Paterson, NJ | (13.3) | 317 | Nashville, TN | (45.0) | 374 | Rochester, MN | (100.0) |
| 245 | Wilmington, NC | (13.7) | 319 | Norwalk, CA | (45.6) | 374 | San Marcos, CA | (100.0) |
| 246 | Richmond, VA | (13.9) | 320 | Bellevue, WA | (50.0) | 374 | Sterling Heights, MI | (100.0) |
| 247 | Hawthorne, CA | (14.6) | 320 | Carrollton, TX | (50.0) | 374 | Surprise, AZ | (100.0) |
| 248 | Spokane, WA | (14.8) | 320 | Chandler, AZ | (50.0) | 374 | Tracy, CA | (100.0) |
| 249 | Decatur, IL | (16.5) | 320 | Davenport, IA | (50.0) | 374 | Troy, MI | (100.0) |
| 250 | Garland, TX | (16.7) | 320 | Deerfield Beach, FL | (50.0) | 374 | Westminster, CA | (100.0) |
| 250 | Los Angeles, CA | (16.7) | 320 | Lawrence, MA | (50.0) | NA | Alexandria, VA*** | NA |
| 252 | Tacoma, WA | (16.9) | 320 | Medford, OR | (50.0) | NA | Alhambra, CA*** | NA |
| 253 | San Diego, CA | (17.1) | 320 | Nampa, ID | (50.0) | NA | Amherst, NY*** | NA |
| 254 | Detroit, MI | (17.2) | 320 | Roseville, CA | (50.0) | NA | Aurora, IL*** | NA |
| 255 | San Jose, CA | (17.4) | 320 | Sandy, UT | (50.0) | NA | Beaverton, OR** | NA |
| 256 | Chicago, IL | (17.8) | 320 | South Bend, IN | (50.0) | NA | Bend, OR** | NA |
| 257 | Yakima, WA | (18.6) | 331 | Bridgeport, CT | (50.3) | NA | Bloomington, MN*** | NA |
| 258 | Norfolk, VA | (18.7) | 332 | Elizabeth, NJ | (50.5) | NA | Boca Raton, FL*** | NA |
| 259 | Austin, TX | (18.9) | 333 | North Las Vegas, NV | (50.8) | NA | Brick Twnshp, NJ*** | NA |
| 259 | Seattle, WA | (18.9) | 334 | Killeen, TX | (51.6) | NA | Canton Twnshp, MI** | NA |
| 261 | Virginia Beach, VA | (19.1) | 335 | Indio, CA | (52.0) | NA | Cary, NC*** | NA |
| 262 | Fort Smith, AR | (19.3) | 335 | O'Fallon, MO | (52.0) | NA | Chattanooga, TN** | NA |
| 263 | Hayward, CA | (19.5) | 337 | Plantation, FL | (52.2) | NA | Clinton Twnshp, MI*** | NA |
| 264 | Allentown, PA | (19.8) | 338 | Carlsbad, CA | (52.6) | NA | Columbia, SC** | NA |
| 265 | Miami Beach, FL | (20.0) | 338 | West Covina, CA | (52.6) | NA | Concord, CA*** | NA |
| 266 | Fort Lauderdale, FL | (20.2) | 340 | Lubbock, TX | (54.3) | NA | Concord, NC** | NA |
| 267 | San Antonio, TX | (20.3) | 341 | Stockton, CA | (54.9) | NA | Edison Twnshp, NJ*** | NA |
| 268 | Jackson, MS | (20.7) | 342 | Fremont, CA | (55.6) | NA | Glendale, CA*** | NA |
| 269 | Berkeley, CA | (20.9) | 343 | El Paso, TX | (55.9) | NA | Hamilton Twnshp, NJ*** | NA |
| 270 | New York, NY | (21.6) | 344 | Peoria, AZ | (56.1) | NA | Johns Creek, GA*** | NA |
| 271 | Fresno, CA | (21.8) | 345 | Carson, CA | (57.3) | NA | Lake Forest, CA*** | NA |
| 272 | Aurora, CO | (22.1) | 346 | High Point, NC | (59.6) | NA | Lawrence, KS*** | NA |
| 273 | New Orleans, LA | (22.2) | 347 | Springfield, IL | (60.0) | NA | League City, TX*** | NA |
| 274 | Flint, MI | (22.6) | 347 | Vancouver, WA | (60.0) | NA | Lewisville, TX** | NA |
| 274 | Louisville, KY | (22.6) | 349 | Athens-Clarke, GA | (60.5) | NA | Lowell, MA*** | NA |
| 276 | Little Rock, AR | (23.0) | 350 | Erie, PA | (61.5) | NA | McKinney, TX*** | NA |
| 277 | Newport News, VA | (24.5) | 350 | Pasadena, TX | (61.5) | NA | Nashua, NH*** | NA |
| 278 | Baton Rouge, LA | (25.3) | 352 | Odessa, TX | (62.5) | NA | Olathe, KS*** | NA |
| 278 | Springfield, MO | (25.3) | 353 | Fairfield, CA | (62.7) | NA | Provo, UT*** | NA |
| 280 | El Monte, CA | (25.7) | 354 | Laredo, TX | (63.6) | NA | Ramapo, NY*** | NA |
| 281 | Topeka, KS | (25.9) | 355 | Brownsville, TX | (64.7) | NA | Redwood City, CA*** | NA |
| 282 | Philadelphia, PA | (26.0) | 356 | Vacaville, CA | (65.6) | NA | Round Rock, TX*** | NA |
| 282 | Reading, PA | (26.0) | 357 | Lynchburg, VA | (66.7) | NA | San Angelo, TX** | NA |
| 284 | Chesapeake, VA | (26.4) | 358 | Evanston, IL | (67.5) | NA | Santa Barbara, CA*** | NA |
| 285 | Brooklyn Park, MN | (26.9) | 359 | Abilene, TX | (68.0) | NA | Santa Maria, CA*** | NA |
| 286 | Longview, TX | (27.1) | 360 | Tempe, AZ | (72.7) | NA | Scranton, PA*** | NA |
| 287 | Toledo, OH | (27.2) | 361 | Pueblo, CO | (74.0) | NA | St. George, UT*** | NA |
| 288 | Anaheim, CA | (27.3) | 362 | Torrance, CA | (74.1) | NA | Suffolk, VA** | NA |
| 289 | Lafayette, LA | (27.8) | 363 | Racine, WI | (74.5) | NA | Sugar Land, TX*** | NA |
| 290 | Cape Coral, FL | (28.0) | 364 | Chula Vista, CA | (75.0) | NA | Temecula, CA*** | NA |
| 291 | Oklahoma City, OK | (28.7) | 364 | Costa Mesa, CA | (75.0) | NA | Tustin, CA*** | NA |
| 292 | Modesto, CA | (29.6) | 364 | Port St. Lucie, FL | (75.0) | NA | Warren, MI*** | NA |
| 293 | Oakland, CA | (29.9) | 364 | Rancho Cucamon., CA | (75.0) | NA | Whittier, CA*** | NA |
| 294 | Raleigh, NC | (30.0) | 368 | South Gate, CA | (77.7) | NA | Woodbridge Twnshp, NJ*** | NA |
| 295 | Providence, RI | (30.2) | 369 | Stamford, CT | (80.0) | | | |
| 296 | Portland, OR | (30.3) | 370 | Davie, FL | (81.1) | | | |

Source: CQ Press using reported data from the F.B.I. "Crime in the United States 2013"

*Includes nonnegligent manslaughter.  **Not available.  ***These cities had murder rates of 0 in 2012 but had at least one murder in 2013.  Calculating percent increase from zero results in an infinite number.  These are shown as "NA."

# 52. Percent Change in Murder Rate: 2009 to 2013
## National Percent Change = 10.5% Decrease*

| RANK | CITY | % CHANGE | RANK | CITY | % CHANGE | RANK | CITY | % CHANGE |
|---|---|---|---|---|---|---|---|---|
| 360 | Abilene, TX | (86.7) | 5 | Chino, CA | 316.7 | 363 | Fullerton, CA | (100.0) |
| 112 | Akron, OH | 19.6 | 321 | Chula Vista, CA | (55.6) | 41 | Gainesville, FL | 80.8 |
| 363 | Alameda, CA | (100.0) | NA | Cicero, IL** | NA | 243 | Garden Grove, CA | (22.2) |
| 177 | Albany, GA | (2.8) | 76 | Cincinnati, OH | 43.0 | 240 | Garland, TX | (21.9) |
| 218 | Albany, NY | (14.6) | NA | Citrus Heights, CA*** | NA | 89 | Gary, IN | 33.0 |
| 284 | Albuquerque, NM | (37.7) | 363 | Clarkstown, NY | (100.0) | 351 | Gilbert, AZ | (76.5) |
| 148 | Alexandria, VA | 0.0 | 346 | Clarksville, TN | (68.9) | 339 | Glendale, AZ | (66.7) |
| NA | Alhambra, CA*** | NA | 91 | Clearwater, FL | 32.1 | 339 | Glendale, CA | (66.7) |
| 225 | Allentown, PA | (16.5) | 261 | Cleveland, OH | (29.5) | 77 | Grand Prairie, TX | 42.9 |
| 363 | Allen, TX | (100.0) | 148 | Clifton, NJ | 0.0 | 37 | Grand Rapids, MI | 89.4 |
| 214 | Amarillo, TX | (13.2) | 3 | Clinton Twnshp, MI | 410.0 | 363 | Greece, NY | (100.0) |
| 208 | Amherst, NY | (11.1) | 363 | Clovis, CA | (100.0) | 274 | Greeley, CO | (34.4) |
| 115 | Anaheim, CA | 18.5 | 363 | College Station, TX | (100.0) | 36 | Green Bay, WI | 90.0 |
| 183 | Anchorage, AK | (4.1) | 148 | Colonie, NY | 0.0 | 143 | Greensboro, NC | 2.1 |
| 11 | Ann Arbor, MI | 188.9 | 54 | Colorado Springs, CO | 62.2 | NA | Greenville, NC** | NA |
| 17 | Antioch, CA | 130.6 | 63 | Columbia, MO | 51.7 | NA | Gresham, OR*** | NA |
| 363 | Arlington Heights, IL | (100.0) | 290 | Columbia, SC | (41.2) | NA | Hamilton Twnshp, NJ*** | NA |
| 64 | Arlington, TX | 50.0 | 59 | Columbus, GA | 55.7 | 241 | Hammond, IN | (22.1) |
| 363 | Arvada, CO | (100.0) | 184 | Compton, CA | (4.2) | 22 | Hampton, VA | 114.7 |
| 355 | Athens-Clarke, GA | (80.5) | 316 | Concord, CA | (52.9) | 263 | Hartford, CT | (30.8) |
| 101 | Atlanta, GA | 28.3 | 194 | Concord, NC | (5.6) | 68 | Hawthorne, CA | 48.9 |
| 175 | Aurora, CO | (1.5) | 363 | Coral Springs, FL | (100.0) | 267 | Hayward, CA | (32.7) |
| 264 | Aurora, IL | (31.0) | 127 | Corona, CA | 7.7 | 304 | Hemet, CA | (49.5) |
| 140 | Austin, TX | 3.4 | 86 | Corpus Christi, TX | 35.7 | 24 | Henderson, NV | 100.0 |
| 234 | Bakersfield, CA | (19.5) | 148 | Costa Mesa, CA | 0.0 | 344 | Hesperia, CA | (67.6) |
| 103 | Baldwin Park, CA | 25.0 | 363 | Cranston, RI | (100.0) | 69 | Hialeah, FL | 47.4 |
| 147 | Baltimore, MD | 0.3 | 209 | Dallas, TX | (11.6) | 275 | High Point, NC | (34.5) |
| 281 | Baton Rouge, LA | (36.6) | 363 | Daly City, CA | (100.0) | 363 | Hillsboro, OR | (100.0) |
| 10 | Beaumont, TX | 200.0 | 181 | Danbury, CT | (4.0) | 20 | Hollywood, FL | 122.4 |
| 298 | Beaverton, OR | (47.6) | 271 | Davenport, IA | (33.3) | 217 | Hoover, AL | (14.3) |
| 305 | Bellevue, WA | (50.0) | 352 | Davie, FL | (77.3) | 243 | Houston, TX | (22.2) |
| 345 | Bellflower, CA | (68.3) | 245 | Dayton, OH | (22.4) | 24 | Huntington Beach, CA | 100.0 |
| NA | Bend, OR*** | NA | 288 | Dearborn, MI | (40.0) | 43 | Huntsville, AL | 78.1 |
| 291 | Berkeley, CA | (42.4) | 52 | Decatur, IL | 65.0 | 15 | Independence, MO | 140.0 |
| 7 | Bethlehem, PA | 278.6 | NA | Deerfield Beach, FL** | NA | 104 | Indianapolis, IN | 23.6 |
| 31 | Billings, MT | 94.7 | 305 | Denton, TX | (50.0) | 353 | Indio, CA | (78.6) |
| 138 | Birmingham, AL | 3.8 | 178 | Denver, CO | (3.1) | 301 | Inglewood, CA | (47.9) |
| 180 | Bloomington, IL | (3.7) | 45 | Des Moines, IA | 76.7 | 293 | Irvine, CA | (42.9) |
| 293 | Bloomington, IN | (42.9) | 122 | Detroit, MI | 12.4 | 320 | Irving, TX | (55.0) |
| 323 | Bloomington, MN | (56.0) | 49 | Downey, CA | 67.6 | 207 | Jacksonville, FL | (9.8) |
| 30 | Boca Raton, FL | 95.7 | 280 | Duluth, MN | (36.1) | 90 | Jackson, MS | 32.7 |
| 329 | Boise, ID | (58.8) | 347 | Edinburg, TX | (70.0) | 268 | Jersey City, NJ | (32.8) |
| 249 | Boston, MA | (23.8) | 24 | Edison Twnshp, NJ | 100.0 | NA | Johns Creek, GA*** | NA |
| 363 | Boulder, CO | (100.0) | 363 | Edmond, OK | (100.0) | 220 | Joliet, IL | (15.2) |
| 148 | Brick Twnshp, NJ | 0.0 | 203 | El Cajon, CA | (9.1) | NA | Jurupa Valley, CA** | NA |
| 219 | Bridgeport, CT | (14.8) | 136 | El Monte, CA | 4.0 | 247 | Kansas City, KS | (22.8) |
| 142 | Brockton, MA | 2.2 | 238 | El Paso, TX | (21.1) | 141 | Kansas City, MO | 3.4 |
| 363 | Broken Arrow, OK | (100.0) | 179 | Elgin, IL | (3.6) | NA | Kennewick, WA*** | NA |
| NA | Brooklyn Park, MN*** | NA | 82 | Elizabeth, NJ | 37.5 | 107 | Kenosha, WI | 22.0 |
| 348 | Brownsville, TX | (72.7) | 363 | Elk Grove, CA | (100.0) | 88 | Kent, WA | 33.3 |
| 42 | Bryan, TX | 78.6 | 248 | Erie, PA | (23.1) | 128 | Killeen, TX | 7.3 |
| 181 | Buena Park, CA | (4.0) | 80 | Escondido, CA | 37.9 | 227 | Knoxville, TN | (16.9) |
| 230 | Buffalo, NY | (18.4) | 363 | Eugene, OR | (100.0) | 130 | Lafayette, LA | 6.6 |
| 363 | Burbank, CA | (100.0) | NA | Evanston, IL** | NA | NA | Lake Forest, CA*** | NA |
| 148 | Cambridge, MA | 0.0 | 55 | Evansville, IN | 61.5 | 99 | Lakeland, FL | 30.2 |
| 363 | Canton Twnshp, MI | (100.0) | 305 | Everett, WA | (50.0) | 58 | Lakewood Twnshp, NJ | 57.1 |
| 148 | Cape Coral, FL | 0.0 | 312 | Fairfield, CA | (50.9) | 35 | Lakewood, CA | 92.3 |
| 356 | Carlsbad, CA | (82.4) | 363 | Fall River, MA | (100.0) | 120 | Lakewood, CO | 13.9 |
| 148 | Carmel, IN | 0.0 | 100 | Fargo, ND | 28.6 | 224 | Lancaster, CA | (16.4) |
| 349 | Carrollton, TX | (74.2) | 201 | Farmington Hills, MI | (7.7) | 258 | Lansing, MI | (27.8) |
| 289 | Carson, CA | (40.7) | 75 | Fayetteville, AR | 44.4 | 358 | Laredo, TX | (84.0) |
| NA | Cary, NC*** | NA | 144 | Fayetteville, NC | 1.7 | 13 | Largo, FL | 178.6 |
| 6 | Cedar Rapids, IA | 287.5 | 126 | Federal Way, WA | 10.2 | 85 | Las Cruces, NM | 37.2 |
| 2 | Centennial, CO | 470.0 | 148 | Fishers, IN | 0.0 | 235 | Las Vegas, NV | (19.8) |
| NA | Champaign, IL** | NA | 67 | Flint, MI | 49.1 | NA | Lawrence, KS*** | NA |
| 330 | Chandler, AZ | (60.0) | 61 | Fontana, CA | 53.1 | 362 | Lawrence, MA | (89.8) |
| 262 | Charleston, SC | (30.4) | 363 | Fort Collins, CO | (100.0) | 92 | Lawton, OK | 32.0 |
| 198 | Charlotte, NC | (6.7) | 132 | Fort Lauderdale, FL | 5.6 | 232 | League City, TX | (18.5) |
| 134 | Chattanooga, TN | 5.1 | 94 | Fort Smith, AR | 31.4 | 363 | Lee's Summit, MO | (100.0) |
| 148 | Cheektowaga, NY | 0.0 | 48 | Fort Wayne, IN | 69.4 | 337 | Lewisville, TX | (65.5) |
| 257 | Chesapeake, VA | (27.8) | 148 | Fort Worth, TX | 0.0 | 93 | Lexington, KY | 31.8 |
| 193 | Chicago, IL | (5.6) | 330 | Fremont, CA | (60.0) | 114 | Lincoln, NE | 18.8 |
| 273 | Chico, CA | (34.3) | 205 | Fresno, CA | (9.2) | 133 | Little Rock, AR | 5.4 |
| 363 | Chino Hills, CA | (100.0) | 363 | Frisco, TX | (100.0) | 363 | Livermore, CA | (100.0) |

| RANK | CITY | % CHANGE | RANK | CITY | % CHANGE | RANK | CITY | % CHANGE |
|---|---|---|---|---|---|---|---|---|
| 363 | Livonia, MI | (100.0) | 282 | Pasadena, CA | (37.1) | 354 | South Gate, CA | (79.6) |
| 223 | Long Beach, CA | (16.3) | 333 | Pasadena, TX | (63.0) | 330 | Sparks, NV | (60.0) |
| 363 | Longmont, CO | (100.0) | 111 | Paterson, NJ | 20.4 | 202 | Spokane Valley, WA | (8.3) |
| 324 | Longview, TX | (56.3) | 203 | Pearland, TX | (9.1) | 62 | Spokane, WA | 52.9 |
| 235 | Los Angeles, CA | (19.8) | 363 | Pembroke Pines, FL | (100.0) | 339 | Springfield, IL | (66.7) |
| 254 | Louisville, KY | (26.5) | 302 | Peoria, AZ | (49.0) | 82 | Springfield, MA | 37.5 |
| NA | Lowell, MA** | NA | 174 | Peoria, IL | (1.4) | 31 | Springfield, MO | 94.7 |
| 334 | Lubbock, TX | (63.8) | 231 | Philadelphia, PA | (18.5) | 316 | Stamford, CT | (52.9) |
| NA | Lynchburg, VA*** | NA | 137 | Phoenix, AZ | 3.9 | 363 | Sterling Heights, MI | (100.0) |
| 305 | Lynn, MA | (50.0) | 116 | Pittsburgh, PA | 16.8 | 191 | Stockton, CA | (5.3) |
| 146 | Macon, GA | 1.0 | 255 | Plano, TX | (26.7) | NA | St. George, UT*** | NA |
| 105 | Madison, WI | 23.5 | 286 | Plantation, FL | (38.9) | 339 | St. Joseph, MO | (66.7) |
| 24 | Manchester, NH | 100.0 | 46 | Pomona, CA | 73.0 | 196 | St. Louis, MO | (6.5) |
| 305 | McAllen, TX | (50.0) | 220 | Pompano Beach, FL | (15.2) | 135 | St. Paul, MN | 4.3 |
| NA | McKinney, TX*** | NA | 148 | Port St. Lucie, FL | 0.0 | 87 | St. Petersburg, FL | 35.6 |
| 314 | Medford, OR | (51.9) | 266 | Portland, OR | (32.4) | 118 | Suffolk, VA | 15.5 |
| 145 | Melbourne, FL | 1.3 | 253 | Portsmouth, VA | (26.2) | NA | Sugar Land, TX*** | NA |
| 186 | Memphis, TN | (4.5) | 305 | Providence, RI | (50.0) | 8 | Sunnyvale, CA | 237.5 |
| NA | Menifee, CA*** | NA | 121 | Provo, UT | 12.5 | 313 | Sunrise, FL | (51.1) |
| 265 | Merced, CA | (31.5) | 359 | Pueblo, CO | (84.6) | 363 | Surprise, AZ | (100.0) |
| 148 | Meridian, ID | 0.0 | 363 | Quincy, MA | (100.0) | 123 | Syracuse, NY | 11.5 |
| 57 | Mesa, AZ | 60.0 | 335 | Racine, WI | (63.9) | 106 | Tacoma, WA | 22.5 |
| 125 | Mesquite, TX | 10.5 | 228 | Raleigh, NC | (17.6) | 47 | Tallahassee, FL | 70.6 |
| 296 | Miami Beach, FL | (47.0) | 44 | Ramapo, NY | 76.9 | 80 | Tampa, FL | 37.9 |
| 187 | Miami Gardens, FL | (5.1) | 148 | Rancho Cucamon., CA | 0.0 | 12 | Temecula, CA | 180.0 |
| 109 | Miami, FL | 20.6 | 222 | Reading, PA | (16.1) | 53 | Tempe, AZ | 63.6 |
| 70 | Midland, TX | 46.4 | 148 | Redding, CA | 0.0 | 4 | Thornton, CO | 344.4 |
| 74 | Milwaukee, WI | 45.4 | 199 | Redwood City, CA | (7.1) | 363 | Thousand Oaks, CA | (100.0) |
| 33 | Minneapolis, MN | 93.6 | 71 | Reno, NV | 46.3 | 210 | Toledo, OH | (12.4) |
| 315 | Miramar, FL | (52.3) | 148 | Renton, WA | 0.0 | 298 | Toms River Twnshp, NJ | (47.6) |
| 148 | Mission Viejo, CA | 0.0 | 276 | Rialto, CA | (35.0) | 131 | Topeka, KS | 6.2 |
| 363 | Mission, TX | (100.0) | NA | Richardson, TX*** | NA | 148 | Torrance, CA | 0.0 |
| 112 | Mobile, AL | 19.6 | 343 | Richmond, CA | (67.5) | 363 | Tracy, CA | (100.0) |
| 269 | Modesto, CA | (33.0) | 185 | Richmond, VA | (4.4) | 23 | Trenton, NJ | 112.6 |
| 50 | Moreno Valley, CA | 66.7 | 279 | Riverside, CA | (36.0) | 148 | Troy, MI | 0.0 |
| 148 | Mountain View, CA | 0.0 | 188 | Roanoke, VA | (5.2) | 79 | Tucson, AZ | 39.1 |
| 252 | Murfreesboro, TN | (25.5) | 363 | Rochester, MN | (100.0) | 216 | Tulsa, OK | (14.1) |
| NA | Murrieta, CA*** | NA | 72 | Rochester, NY | 46.3 | 60 | Tuscaloosa, AL | 54.5 |
| NA | Nampa, ID*** | NA | 189 | Rockford, IL | (5.3) | NA | Tustin, CA*** | NA |
| NA | Napa, CA*** | NA | 316 | Roseville, CA | (52.9) | 50 | Tyler, TX | 66.7 |
| 148 | Naperville, IL | 0.0 | 357 | Roswell, GA | (82.5) | NA | Upland, CA** | NA |
| 1 | Nashua, NH | 475.0 | 24 | Round Rock, TX | 100.0 | 40 | Upper Darby Twnshp, PA | 84.6 |
| 325 | Nashville, TN | (56.3) | 124 | Sacramento, CA | 10.9 | 148 | Vacaville, CA | 0.0 |
| 277 | New Bedford, MA | (35.1) | 82 | Salem, OR | 37.5 | 14 | Vallejo, CA | 142.5 |
| 66 | New Haven, CT | 49.5 | 250 | Salinas, CA | (23.8) | 339 | Vancouver, WA | (66.7) |
| 237 | New Orleans, LA | (19.9) | 21 | Salt Lake City, UT | 117.6 | 119 | Ventura, CA | 14.6 |
| 363 | New Rochelle, NY | (100.0) | 350 | San Angelo, TX | (75.9) | 213 | Victorville, CA | (12.9) |
| 259 | New York, NY | (28.6) | 260 | San Antonio, TX | (29.2) | 200 | Virginia Beach, VA | (7.3) |
| 78 | Newark, NJ | 40.4 | 95 | San Bernardino, CA | 31.3 | 211 | Visalia, CA | (12.5) |
| NA | Newport Beach, CA*** | NA | 196 | San Diego, CA | (6.5) | NA | Vista, CA*** | NA |
| NA | Newport News, VA** | NA | 139 | San Francisco, CA | 3.6 | 326 | Waco, TX | (56.9) |
| 363 | Newton, MA | (100.0) | 96 | San Jose, CA | 31.0 | 255 | Warren, MI | (26.7) |
| 241 | Norfolk, VA | (22.1) | 97 | San Leandro, CA | 30.8 | NA | Warwick, RI*** | NA |
| NA | Norman, OK*** | NA | 363 | San Marcos, CA | (100.0) | 270 | Washington, DC | (33.2) |
| 108 | North Charleston, SC | 21.2 | 363 | San Mateo, CA | (100.0) | 229 | Waterbury, CT | (17.9) |
| 328 | North Las Vegas, NV | (57.5) | 110 | Sandy Springs, GA | 20.4 | NA | Waukegan, IL** | NA |
| 321 | Norwalk, CA | (55.6) | 298 | Sandy, UT | (47.6) | 361 | West Covina, CA | (88.2) |
| 363 | Norwalk, CT | (100.0) | 297 | Santa Ana, CA | (47.3) | 246 | West Palm Beach, FL | (22.8) |
| 215 | Oakland, CA | (13.2) | 282 | Santa Barbara, CA | (37.1) | 195 | West Valley, UT | (6.3) |
| 18 | Oceanside, CA | 126.1 | 363 | Santa Clara, CA | (100.0) | 319 | Westland, MI | (53.8) |
| 336 | Odessa, TX | (64.0) | 337 | Santa Clarita, CA | (65.5) | 148 | Westminster, CA | 0.0 |
| 148 | O'Fallon, MO | 0.0 | 303 | Santa Maria, CA | (49.1) | 189 | Westminster, CO | (5.3) |
| 305 | Ogden, UT | (50.0) | 19 | Santa Monica, CA | 123.5 | 192 | Whittier, CA | (5.4) |
| 212 | Oklahoma City, OK | (12.8) | 97 | Santa Rosa, CA | 30.8 | 285 | Wichita Falls, TX | (38.5) |
| NA | Olathe, KS*** | NA | 206 | Savannah, GA | (9.2) | 292 | Wichita, KS | (42.6) |
| 73 | Omaha, NE | 45.6 | 327 | Scottsdale, AZ | (57.1) | 55 | Wilmington, NC | 61.5 |
| 38 | Ontario, CA | 86.2 | 39 | Scranton, PA | 85.7 | 176 | Winston-Salem, NC | (1.5) |
| 34 | Orange, CA | 93.3 | 233 | Seattle, WA | (18.9) | 148 | Woodbridge Twnshp, NJ | 0.0 |
| 24 | Orem, UT | 100.0 | 226 | Shreveport, LA | (16.8) | 102 | Worcester, MA | 25.6 |
| 295 | Orlando, FL | (43.7) | 64 | Simi Valley, CA | 50.0 | NA | Yakima, WA** | NA |
| 278 | Overland Park, KS | (35.3) | 148 | Sioux City, IA | 0.0 | 251 | Yonkers, NY | (25.0) |
| 129 | Oxnard, CA | 7.2 | 9 | Sioux Falls, SD | 216.7 | 16 | Yuma, AZ | 136.4 |
| 287 | Palm Bay, FL | (39.6) | 363 | Somerville, MA | (100.0) | | | |
| 117 | Palmdale, CA | 16.4 | 272 | South Bend, IN | (34.1) | | | |

Source: CQ Press using reported data from the F.B.I. "Crime in the United States 2013"

*Includes nonnegligent manslaughter.  **Not available.  ***These cities had murder rates of 0 in 2009 but had at least one murder in 2013.  Calculating percent increase from zero results in an infinite number.  These are shown as "NA."

# 52. Percent Change in Murder Rate: 2009 to 2013 (continued)
## National Percent Change = 10.5% Decrease*

| RANK | CITY | % CHANGE | RANK | CITY | % CHANGE | RANK | CITY | % CHANGE |
|---|---|---|---|---|---|---|---|---|
| 1 | Nashua, NH | 475.0 | 75 | Fayetteville, AR | 44.4 | 148 | Brick Twnshp, NJ | 0.0 |
| 2 | Centennial, CO | 470.0 | 76 | Cincinnati, OH | 43.0 | 148 | Cambridge, MA | 0.0 |
| 3 | Clinton Twnshp, MI | 410.0 | 77 | Grand Prairie, TX | 42.9 | 148 | Cape Coral, FL | 0.0 |
| 4 | Thornton, CO | 344.4 | 78 | Newark, NJ | 40.4 | 148 | Carmel, IN | 0.0 |
| 5 | Chino, CA | 316.7 | 79 | Tucson, AZ | 39.1 | 148 | Cheektowaga, NY | 0.0 |
| 6 | Cedar Rapids, IA | 287.5 | 80 | Escondido, CA | 37.9 | 148 | Clifton, NJ | 0.0 |
| 7 | Bethlehem, PA | 278.6 | 80 | Tampa, FL | 37.9 | 148 | Colonie, NY | 0.0 |
| 8 | Sunnyvale, CA | 237.5 | 82 | Elizabeth, NJ | 37.5 | 148 | Costa Mesa, CA | 0.0 |
| 9 | Sioux Falls, SD | 216.7 | 82 | Salem, OR | 37.5 | 148 | Fishers, IN | 0.0 |
| 10 | Beaumont, TX | 200.0 | 82 | Springfield, MA | 37.5 | 148 | Fort Worth, TX | 0.0 |
| 11 | Ann Arbor, MI | 188.9 | 85 | Las Cruces, NM | 37.2 | 148 | Meridian, ID | 0.0 |
| 12 | Temecula, CA | 180.0 | 86 | Corpus Christi, TX | 35.7 | 148 | Mission Viejo, CA | 0.0 |
| 13 | Largo, FL | 178.6 | 87 | St. Petersburg, FL | 35.6 | 148 | Mountain View, CA | 0.0 |
| 14 | Vallejo, CA | 142.5 | 88 | Kent, WA | 33.3 | 148 | Naperville, IL | 0.0 |
| 15 | Independence, MO | 140.0 | 89 | Gary, IN | 33.0 | 148 | O'Fallon, MO | 0.0 |
| 16 | Yuma, AZ | 136.4 | 90 | Jackson, MS | 32.7 | 148 | Port St. Lucie, FL | 0.0 |
| 17 | Antioch, CA | 130.6 | 91 | Clearwater, FL | 32.1 | 148 | Rancho Cucamon., CA | 0.0 |
| 18 | Oceanside, CA | 126.1 | 92 | Lawton, OK | 32.0 | 148 | Redding, CA | 0.0 |
| 19 | Santa Monica, CA | 123.5 | 93 | Lexington, KY | 31.8 | 148 | Renton, WA | 0.0 |
| 20 | Hollywood, FL | 122.4 | 94 | Fort Smith, AR | 31.4 | 148 | Sioux City, IA | 0.0 |
| 21 | Salt Lake City, UT | 117.6 | 95 | San Bernardino, CA | 31.3 | 148 | Torrance, CA | 0.0 |
| 22 | Hampton, VA | 114.7 | 96 | San Jose, CA | 31.0 | 148 | Troy, MI | 0.0 |
| 23 | Trenton, NJ | 112.6 | 97 | San Leandro, CA | 30.8 | 148 | Vacaville, CA | 0.0 |
| 24 | Edison Twnshp, NJ | 100.0 | 97 | Santa Rosa, CA | 30.8 | 148 | Westminster, CA | 0.0 |
| 24 | Henderson, NV | 100.0 | 99 | Lakeland, FL | 30.2 | 148 | Woodbridge Twnshp, NJ | 0.0 |
| 24 | Huntington Beach, CA | 100.0 | 100 | Fargo, ND | 28.6 | 174 | Peoria, IL | (1.4) |
| 24 | Manchester, NH | 100.0 | 101 | Atlanta, GA | 28.3 | 175 | Aurora, CO | (1.5) |
| 24 | Orem, UT | 100.0 | 102 | Worcester, MA | 25.6 | 176 | Winston-Salem, NC | (1.5) |
| 24 | Round Rock, TX | 100.0 | 103 | Baldwin Park, CA | 25.0 | 177 | Albany, GA | (2.8) |
| 30 | Boca Raton, FL | 95.7 | 104 | Indianapolis, IN | 23.6 | 178 | Denver, CO | (3.1) |
| 31 | Billings, MT | 94.7 | 105 | Madison, WI | 23.5 | 179 | Elgin, IL | (3.6) |
| 31 | Springfield, MO | 94.7 | 106 | Tacoma, WA | 22.5 | 180 | Bloomington, IL | (3.7) |
| 33 | Minneapolis, MN | 93.6 | 107 | Kenosha, WI | 22.0 | 181 | Buena Park, CA | (4.0) |
| 34 | Orange, CA | 93.3 | 108 | North Charleston, SC | 21.2 | 181 | Danbury, CT | (4.0) |
| 35 | Lakewood, CA | 92.3 | 109 | Miami, FL | 20.6 | 183 | Anchorage, AK | (4.1) |
| 36 | Green Bay, WI | 90.0 | 110 | Sandy Springs, GA | 20.4 | 184 | Compton, CA | (4.2) |
| 37 | Grand Rapids, MI | 89.4 | 111 | Paterson, NJ | 20.4 | 185 | Richmond, VA | (4.4) |
| 38 | Ontario, CA | 86.2 | 112 | Akron, OH | 19.6 | 186 | Memphis, TN | (4.5) |
| 39 | Scranton, PA | 85.7 | 112 | Mobile, AL | 19.6 | 187 | Miami Gardens, FL | (5.1) |
| 40 | Upper Darby Twnshp, PA | 84.6 | 114 | Lincoln, NE | 18.8 | 188 | Roanoke, VA | (5.2) |
| 41 | Gainesville, FL | 80.8 | 115 | Anaheim, CA | 18.5 | 189 | Rockford, IL | (5.3) |
| 42 | Bryan, TX | 78.6 | 116 | Pittsburgh, PA | 16.8 | 189 | Westminster, CO | (5.3) |
| 43 | Huntsville, AL | 78.1 | 117 | Palmdale, CA | 16.4 | 191 | Stockton, CA | (5.3) |
| 44 | Ramapo, NY | 76.9 | 118 | Suffolk, VA | 15.5 | 192 | Whittier, CA | (5.4) |
| 45 | Des Moines, IA | 76.7 | 119 | Ventura, CA | 14.6 | 193 | Chicago, IL | (5.6) |
| 46 | Pomona, CA | 73.0 | 120 | Lakewood, CO | 13.9 | 194 | Concord, NC | (5.6) |
| 47 | Tallahassee, FL | 70.6 | 121 | Provo, UT | 12.5 | 195 | West Valley, UT | (6.3) |
| 48 | Fort Wayne, IN | 69.4 | 122 | Detroit, MI | 12.4 | 196 | San Diego, CA | (6.5) |
| 49 | Downey, CA | 67.6 | 123 | Syracuse, NY | 11.5 | 196 | St. Louis, MO | (6.5) |
| 50 | Moreno Valley, CA | 66.7 | 124 | Sacramento, CA | 10.9 | 198 | Charlotte, NC | (6.7) |
| 50 | Tyler, TX | 66.7 | 125 | Mesquite, TX | 10.5 | 199 | Redwood City, CA | (7.1) |
| 52 | Decatur, IL | 65.0 | 126 | Federal Way, WA | 10.2 | 200 | Virginia Beach, VA | (7.3) |
| 53 | Tempe, AZ | 63.6 | 127 | Corona, CA | 7.7 | 201 | Farmington Hills, MI | (7.7) |
| 54 | Colorado Springs, CO | 62.2 | 128 | Killeen, TX | 7.3 | 202 | Spokane Valley, WA | (8.3) |
| 55 | Evansville, IN | 61.5 | 129 | Oxnard, CA | 7.2 | 203 | El Cajon, CA | (9.1) |
| 55 | Wilmington, NC | 61.5 | 130 | Lafayette, LA | 6.6 | 203 | Pearland, TX | (9.1) |
| 57 | Mesa, AZ | 60.0 | 131 | Topeka, KS | 6.2 | 205 | Fresno, CA | (9.2) |
| 58 | Lakewood Twnshp, NJ | 57.1 | 132 | Fort Lauderdale, FL | 5.6 | 206 | Savannah, GA | (9.2) |
| 59 | Columbus, GA | 55.7 | 133 | Little Rock, AR | 5.4 | 207 | Jacksonville, FL | (9.8) |
| 60 | Tuscaloosa, AL | 54.5 | 134 | Chattanooga, TN | 5.1 | 208 | Amherst, NY | (11.1) |
| 61 | Fontana, CA | 53.1 | 135 | St. Paul, MN | 4.3 | 209 | Dallas, TX | (11.6) |
| 62 | Spokane, WA | 52.9 | 136 | El Monte, CA | 4.0 | 210 | Toledo, OH | (12.4) |
| 63 | Columbia, MO | 51.7 | 137 | Phoenix, AZ | 3.9 | 211 | Visalia, CA | (12.5) |
| 64 | Arlington, TX | 50.0 | 138 | Birmingham, AL | 3.8 | 212 | Oklahoma City, OK | (12.8) |
| 64 | Simi Valley, CA | 50.0 | 139 | San Francisco, CA | 3.6 | 213 | Victorville, CA | (12.9) |
| 66 | New Haven, CT | 49.5 | 140 | Austin, TX | 3.4 | 214 | Amarillo, TX | (13.2) |
| 67 | Flint, MI | 49.1 | 141 | Kansas City, MO | 3.4 | 215 | Oakland, CA | (13.2) |
| 68 | Hawthorne, CA | 48.9 | 142 | Brockton, MA | 2.2 | 216 | Tulsa, OK | (14.1) |
| 69 | Hialeah, FL | 47.4 | 143 | Greensboro, NC | 2.1 | 217 | Hoover, AL | (14.3) |
| 70 | Midland, TX | 46.4 | 144 | Fayetteville, NC | 1.7 | 218 | Albany, NY | (14.6) |
| 71 | Reno, NV | 46.3 | 145 | Melbourne, FL | 1.3 | 219 | Bridgeport, CT | (14.8) |
| 72 | Rochester, NY | 46.3 | 146 | Macon, GA | 1.0 | 220 | Joliet, IL | (15.2) |
| 73 | Omaha, NE | 45.6 | 147 | Baltimore, MD | 0.3 | 220 | Pompano Beach, FL | (15.2) |
| 74 | Milwaukee, WI | 45.4 | 148 | Alexandria, VA | 0.0 | 222 | Reading, PA | (16.1) |

| RANK | CITY | % CHANGE | RANK | CITY | % CHANGE | RANK | CITY | % CHANGE |
|---|---|---|---|---|---|---|---|---|
| 223 | Long Beach, CA | (16.3) | 297 | Santa Ana, CA | (47.3) | 363 | Chino Hills, CA | (100.0) |
| 224 | Lancaster, CA | (16.4) | 298 | Beaverton, OR | (47.6) | 363 | Clarkstown, NY | (100.0) |
| 225 | Allentown, PA | (16.5) | 298 | Sandy, UT | (47.6) | 363 | Clovis, CA | (100.0) |
| 226 | Shreveport, LA | (16.8) | 298 | Toms River Twnshp, NJ | (47.6) | 363 | College Station, TX | (100.0) |
| 227 | Knoxville, TN | (16.9) | 301 | Inglewood, CA | (47.9) | 363 | Coral Springs, FL | (100.0) |
| 228 | Raleigh, NC | (17.6) | 302 | Peoria, AZ | (49.0) | 363 | Cranston, RI | (100.0) |
| 229 | Waterbury, CT | (17.9) | 303 | Santa Maria, CA | (49.1) | 363 | Daly City, CA | (100.0) |
| 230 | Buffalo, NY | (18.4) | 304 | Hemet, CA | (49.5) | 363 | Edmond, OK | (100.0) |
| 231 | Philadelphia, PA | (18.5) | 305 | Bellevue, WA | (50.0) | 363 | Elk Grove, CA | (100.0) |
| 232 | League City, TX | (18.5) | 305 | Denton, TX | (50.0) | 363 | Eugene, OR | (100.0) |
| 233 | Seattle, WA | (18.9) | 305 | Everett, WA | (50.0) | 363 | Fall River, MA | (100.0) |
| 234 | Bakersfield, CA | (19.5) | 305 | Lynn, MA | (50.0) | 363 | Fort Collins, CO | (100.0) |
| 235 | Las Vegas, NV | (19.8) | 305 | McAllen, TX | (50.0) | 363 | Frisco, TX | (100.0) |
| 235 | Los Angeles, CA | (19.8) | 305 | Ogden, UT | (50.0) | 363 | Fullerton, CA | (100.0) |
| 237 | New Orleans, LA | (19.9) | 305 | Providence, RI | (50.0) | 363 | Greece, NY | (100.0) |
| 238 | El Paso, TX | (21.1) | 312 | Fairfield, CA | (50.9) | 363 | Hillsboro, OR | (100.0) |
| 239 | Glendale, AZ | (21.1) | 313 | Sunrise, FL | (51.1) | 363 | Lee's Summit, MO | (100.0) |
| 240 | Garland, TX | (21.9) | 314 | Medford, OR | (51.9) | 363 | Livermore, CA | (100.0) |
| 241 | Hammond, IN | (22.1) | 315 | Miramar, FL | (52.3) | 363 | Livonia, MI | (100.0) |
| 241 | Norfolk, VA | (22.1) | 316 | Concord, CA | (52.9) | 363 | Longmont, CO | (100.0) |
| 243 | Garden Grove, CA | (22.2) | 316 | Roseville, CA | (52.9) | 363 | Mission, TX | (100.0) |
| 243 | Houston, TX | (22.2) | 316 | Stamford, CT | (52.9) | 363 | New Rochelle, NY | (100.0) |
| 245 | Dayton, OH | (22.4) | 319 | Westland, MI | (53.8) | 363 | Newton, MA | (100.0) |
| 246 | West Palm Beach, FL | (22.8) | 320 | Irving, TX | (55.0) | 363 | Norwalk, CT | (100.0) |
| 247 | Kansas City, KS | (22.8) | 321 | Chula Vista, CA | (55.6) | 363 | Pembroke Pines, FL | (100.0) |
| 248 | Erie, PA | (23.1) | 321 | Norwalk, CA | (55.6) | 363 | Quincy, MA | (100.0) |
| 249 | Boston, MA | (23.8) | 323 | Bloomington, MN | (56.0) | 363 | Rochester, MN | (100.0) |
| 250 | Salinas, CA | (23.8) | 324 | Longview, TX | (56.3) | 363 | San Marcos, CA | (100.0) |
| 251 | Yonkers, NY | (25.0) | 325 | Nashville, TN | (56.3) | 363 | San Mateo, CA | (100.0) |
| 252 | Murfreesboro, TN | (25.5) | 326 | Waco, TX | (56.9) | 363 | Santa Clara, CA | (100.0) |
| 253 | Portsmouth, VA | (26.2) | 327 | Scottsdale, AZ | (57.1) | 363 | Somerville, MA | (100.0) |
| 254 | Louisville, KY | (26.5) | 328 | North Las Vegas, NV | (57.5) | 363 | Sterling Heights, MI | (100.0) |
| 255 | Plano, TX | (26.7) | 329 | Boise, ID | (58.8) | 363 | Surprise, AZ | (100.0) |
| 255 | Warren, MI | (26.7) | 330 | Chandler, AZ | (60.0) | 363 | Thousand Oaks, CA | (100.0) |
| 257 | Chesapeake, VA | (27.8) | 330 | Fremont, CA | (60.0) | 363 | Tracy, CA | (100.0) |
| 258 | Lansing, MI | (27.8) | 330 | Sparks, NV | (60.0) | NA | Alhambra, CA*** | NA |
| 259 | New York, NY | (28.6) | 333 | Pasadena, TX | (63.0) | NA | Bend, OR*** | NA |
| 260 | San Antonio, TX | (29.2) | 334 | Lubbock, TX | (63.8) | NA | Brooklyn Park, MN*** | NA |
| 261 | Cleveland, OH | (29.5) | 335 | Racine, WI | (63.9) | NA | Cary, NC*** | NA |
| 262 | Charleston, SC | (30.4) | 336 | Odessa, TX | (64.0) | NA | Champaign, IL** | NA |
| 263 | Hartford, CT | (30.8) | 337 | Lewisville, TX | (65.5) | NA | Cicero, IL** | NA |
| 264 | Aurora, IL | (31.0) | 337 | Santa Clarita, CA | (65.5) | NA | Citrus Heights, CA*** | NA |
| 265 | Merced, CA | (31.5) | 339 | Glendale, CA | (66.7) | NA | Deerfield Beach, FL** | NA |
| 266 | Portland, OR | (32.4) | 339 | Springfield, IL | (66.7) | NA | Evanston, IL** | NA |
| 267 | Hayward, CA | (32.7) | 339 | St. Joseph, MO | (66.7) | NA | Greenville, NC** | NA |
| 268 | Jersey City, NJ | (32.8) | 339 | Vancouver, WA | (66.7) | NA | Gresham, OR*** | NA |
| 269 | Modesto, CA | (33.0) | 343 | Richmond, CA | (67.5) | NA | Hamilton Twnshp, NJ*** | NA |
| 270 | Washington, DC | (33.2) | 344 | Hesperia, CA | (67.6) | NA | Johns Creek, GA*** | NA |
| 271 | Davenport, IA | (33.3) | 345 | Bellflower, CA | (68.3) | NA | Jurupa Valley, CA** | NA |
| 272 | South Bend, IN | (34.1) | 346 | Clarksville, TN | (68.9) | NA | Kennewick, WA*** | NA |
| 273 | Chico, CA | (34.3) | 347 | Edinburg, TX | (70.0) | NA | Lake Forest, CA*** | NA |
| 274 | Greeley, CO | (34.4) | 348 | Brownsville, TX | (72.7) | NA | Lawrence, KS*** | NA |
| 275 | High Point, NC | (34.5) | 349 | Carrollton, TX | (74.2) | NA | Lowell, MA** | NA |
| 276 | Rialto, CA | (35.0) | 350 | San Angelo, TX | (75.9) | NA | Lynchburg, VA*** | NA |
| 277 | New Bedford, MA | (35.1) | 351 | Gilbert, AZ | (76.5) | NA | McKinney, TX*** | NA |
| 278 | Overland Park, KS | (35.3) | 352 | Davie, FL | (77.3) | NA | Menifee, CA*** | NA |
| 279 | Riverside, CA | (36.0) | 353 | Indio, CA | (78.6) | NA | Murrieta, CA*** | NA |
| 280 | Duluth, MN | (36.1) | 354 | South Gate, CA | (79.6) | NA | Nampa, ID*** | NA |
| 281 | Baton Rouge, LA | (36.6) | 355 | Athens-Clarke, GA | (80.5) | NA | Napa, CA*** | NA |
| 282 | Pasadena, CA | (37.1) | 356 | Carlsbad, CA | (82.4) | NA | Newport Beach, CA*** | NA |
| 282 | Santa Barbara, CA | (37.1) | 357 | Roswell, GA | (82.5) | NA | Newport News, VA** | NA |
| 284 | Albuquerque, NM | (37.7) | 358 | Laredo, TX | (84.0) | NA | Norman, OK*** | NA |
| 285 | Wichita Falls, TX | (38.5) | 359 | Pueblo, CO | (84.6) | NA | Olathe, KS*** | NA |
| 286 | Plantation, FL | (38.9) | 360 | Abilene, TX | (86.7) | NA | Richardson, TX*** | NA |
| 287 | Palm Bay, FL | (39.6) | 361 | West Covina, CA | (88.2) | NA | St. George, UT*** | NA |
| 288 | Dearborn, MI | (40.0) | 362 | Lawrence, MA | (89.8) | NA | Sugar Land, TX*** | NA |
| 289 | Carson, CA | (40.7) | 363 | Alameda, CA | (100.0) | NA | Tustin, CA*** | NA |
| 290 | Columbia, SC | (41.2) | 363 | Allen, TX | (100.0) | NA | Upland, CA** | NA |
| 291 | Berkeley, CA | (42.4) | 363 | Arlington Heights, IL | (100.0) | NA | Vista, CA*** | NA |
| 292 | Wichita, KS | (42.6) | 363 | Arvada, CO | (100.0) | NA | Warwick, RI*** | NA |
| 293 | Bloomington, IN | (42.9) | 363 | Boulder, CO | (100.0) | NA | Waukegan, IL** | NA |
| 293 | Irvine, CA | (42.9) | 363 | Broken Arrow, OK | (100.0) | NA | Yakima, WA** | NA |
| 295 | Orlando, FL | (43.7) | 363 | Burbank, CA | (100.0) | | | |
| 296 | Miami Beach, FL | (47.0) | 363 | Canton Twnshp, MI | (100.0) | | | |

Source: CQ Press using reported data from the F.B.I. "Crime in the United States 2013"

*Includes nonnegligent manslaughter. **Not available. ***These cities had murder rates of 0 in 2009 but had at least one murder in 2013. Calculating percent increase from zero results in an infinite number. These are shown as "NA."

## 53. Rapes in 2013
## National Total = 79,770 Rapes*

| RANK | CITY | RAPES | RANK | CITY | RAPES | RANK | CITY | RAPES |
|---|---|---|---|---|---|---|---|---|
| 222 | Abilene, TX** | 37 | 411 | Chino, CA** | 7 | 271 | Fullerton, CA** | 29 |
| 51 | Akron, OH | 160 | 271 | Chula Vista, CA** | 29 | 140 | Gainesville, FL | 62 |
| 393 | Alameda, CA** | 10 | 358 | Cicero, IL** | 14 | 347 | Garden Grove, CA** | 16 |
| 316 | Albany, GA** | 21 | 42 | Cincinnati, OH | 199 | 162 | Garland, TX** | 53 |
| 266 | Albany, NY** | 30 | 329 | Citrus Heights, CA** | 19 | 187 | Gary, IN** | 47 |
| 15 | Albuquerque, NM** | 439 | 405 | Clarkstown, NY** | 8 | 358 | Gilbert, AZ | 14 |
| 316 | Alexandria, VA | 21 | 98 | Clarksville, TN | 84 | 180 | Glendale, AZ** | 49 |
| 397 | Alhambra, CA** | 9 | 176 | Clearwater, FL | 50 | 405 | Glendale, CA** | 8 |
| 136 | Allentown, PA | 64 | 18 | Cleveland, OH | 417 | 158 | Grand Prairie, TX** | 54 |
| 370 | Allen, TX | 13 | 380 | Clifton, NJ** | 12 | 102 | Grand Rapids, MI | 82 |
| 39 | Amarillo, TX | 214 | 152 | Clinton Twnshp, MI | 56 | 397 | Greece, NY** | 9 |
| 411 | Amherst, NY** | 7 | 311 | Clovis, CA** | 23 | 120 | Greeley, CO | 74 |
| 102 | Anaheim, CA** | 82 | 241 | College Station, TX** | 34 | 167 | Green Bay, WI | 52 |
| 19 | Anchorage, AK | 408 | 441 | Colonie, NY** | 0 | 129 | Greensboro, NC** | 70 |
| 184 | Ann Arbor, MI | 48 | 25 | Colorado Springs, CO | 370 | 325 | Greenville, NC** | 20 |
| 299 | Antioch, CA** | 25 | 132 | Columbia, MO | 67 | 167 | Gresham, OR** | 52 |
| 411 | Arlington Heights, IL** | 7 | 147 | Columbia, SC | 58 | 405 | Hamilton Twnshp, NJ** | 8 |
| 76 | Arlington, TX** | 105 | 232 | Columbus, GA** | 36 | 222 | Hammond, IN** | 37 |
| 247 | Arvada, CO | 33 | 290 | Compton, CA** | 26 | 316 | Hampton, VA | 21 |
| 222 | Athens-Clarke, GA** | 37 | 380 | Concord, CA** | 12 | 162 | Hartford, CT** | 53 |
| 76 | Atlanta, GA** | 105 | 397 | Concord, NC** | 9 | 256 | Hawthorne, CA** | 32 |
| 35 | Aurora, CO | 224 | 305 | Coral Springs, FL | 24 | 247 | Hayward, CA** | 33 |
| 162 | Aurora, IL** | 53 | 358 | Corona, CA** | 14 | 305 | Hemet, CA** | 24 |
| 37 | Austin, TX** | 217 | 56 | Corpus Christi, TX** | 147 | 196 | Henderson, NV** | 45 |
| 200 | Bakersfield, CA** | 43 | 191 | Costa Mesa, CA** | 46 | 340 | Hesperia, CA** | 17 |
| 420 | Baldwin Park, CA** | 6 | 271 | Cranston, RI | 29 | 208 | Hialeah, FL | 41 |
| 28 | Baltimore, MD** | 298 | 10 | Dallas, TX** | 543 | 266 | High Point, NC** | 30 |
| 120 | Baton Rouge, LA** | 74 | 352 | Daly City, CA** | 15 | 271 | Hillsboro, OR** | 29 |
| 146 | Beaumont, TX** | 59 | 299 | Danbury, CT** | 25 | 139 | Hollywood, FL | 63 |
| 325 | Beaverton, OR** | 20 | 92 | Davenport, IA | 88 | 397 | Hoover, AL | 9 |
| 325 | Bellevue, WA** | 20 | 290 | Davie, FL | 26 | 8 | Houston, TX** | 618 |
| 397 | Bellflower, CA** | 9 | 74 | Dayton, OH | 107 | 259 | Huntington Beach, CA** | 31 |
| 316 | Bend, OR | 21 | 247 | Dearborn, MI | 33 | 95 | Huntsville, AL | 87 |
| 290 | Berkeley, CA** | 26 | 397 | Decatur, IL** | 9 | 174 | Independence, MO | 51 |
| 284 | Bethlehem, PA | 27 | 281 | Deerfield Beach, FL | 28 | 6 | Indianapolis, IN | 656 |
| 214 | Billings, MT | 39 | 85 | Denton, TX | 93 | 241 | Indio, CA** | 34 |
| 45 | Birmingham, AL | 178 | 12 | Denver, CO | 514 | 271 | Inglewood, CA** | 29 |
| 150 | Bloomington, IL** | 57 | 90 | Des Moines, IA | 90 | 380 | Irvine, CA** | 12 |
| 241 | Bloomington, IN** | 34 | 8 | Detroit, MI | 618 | 305 | Irving, TX** | 24 |
| 340 | Bloomington, MN | 17 | 380 | Downey, CA** | 12 | 13 | Jacksonville, FL | 452 |
| 405 | Boca Raton, FL | 8 | 167 | Duluth, MN | 52 | 73 | Jackson, MS** | 110 |
| 71 | Boise, ID | 123 | 266 | Edinburg, TX** | 30 | 236 | Jersey City, NJ** | 35 |
| 30 | Boston, MA** | 279 | 405 | Edison Twnshp, NJ** | 8 | 432 | Johns Creek, GA** | 4 |
| 221 | Boulder, CO | 38 | 352 | Edmond, OK** | 15 | 180 | Joliet, IL** | 49 |
| 432 | Brick Twnshp, NJ** | 4 | 271 | El Cajon, CA** | 29 | 380 | Jurupa Valley, CA** | 12 |
| 102 | Bridgeport, CT** | 82 | 358 | El Monte, CA** | 14 | 101 | Kansas City, KS** | 83 |
| 95 | Brockton, MA | 87 | 46 | El Paso, TX** | 176 | 23 | Kansas City, MO | 377 |
| 211 | Broken Arrow, OK** | 40 | 152 | Elgin, IL** | 56 | 241 | Kennewick, WA | 34 |
| 247 | Brooklyn Park, MN | 33 | 222 | Elizabeth, NJ** | 37 | 290 | Kenosha, WI** | 26 |
| 142 | Brownsville, TX** | 61 | 420 | Elk Grove, CA** | 6 | 147 | Kent, WA | 58 |
| 259 | Bryan, TX** | 31 | 145 | Erie, PA | 60 | 110 | Killeen, TX** | 78 |
| 370 | Buena Park, CA** | 13 | 214 | Escondido, CA** | 39 | 63 | Knoxville, TN | 139 |
| 57 | Buffalo, NY** | 145 | 130 | Eugene, OR | 68 | 340 | Lafayette, LA** | 17 |
| 370 | Burbank, CA** | 13 | 393 | Evanston, IL** | 10 | 380 | Lake Forest, CA** | 12 |
| 305 | Cambridge, MA | 24 | 158 | Evansville, IN** | 54 | 167 | Lakeland, FL | 52 |
| 335 | Canton Twnshp, MI | 18 | 205 | Everett, WA** | 42 | 427 | Lakewood Twnshp, NJ** | 5 |
| 411 | Cape Coral, FL | 7 | 370 | Fairfield, CA** | 13 | 387 | Lakewood, CA** | 11 |
| 311 | Carlsbad, CA** | 23 | 124 | Fall River, MA | 73 | 74 | Lakewood, CO | 107 |
| 432 | Carmel, IN** | 4 | 127 | Fargo, ND | 71 | 211 | Lancaster, CA** | 40 |
| 420 | Carrollton, TX** | 6 | 358 | Farmington Hills, MI | 14 | 68 | Lansing, MI | 127 |
| 352 | Carson, CA** | 15 | 247 | Fayetteville, AR | 33 | 118 | Laredo, TX** | 75 |
| 387 | Cary, NC** | 11 | 135 | Fayetteville, NC** | 65 | 187 | Largo, FL | 47 |
| 191 | Cedar Rapids, IA | 46 | 200 | Federal Way, WA | 43 | 284 | Las Cruces, NM** | 27 |
| 299 | Centennial, CO | 25 | 438 | Fishers, IN** | 2 | 4 | Las Vegas, NV** | 705 |
| 214 | Champaign, IL** | 39 | 57 | Flint, MI | 145 | 176 | Lawrence, KS | 50 |
| 167 | Chandler, AZ** | 52 | 247 | Fontana, CA** | 33 | 329 | Lawrence, MA** | 19 |
| 271 | Charleston, SC | 29 | 150 | Fort Collins, CO | 57 | 106 | Lawton, OK** | 80 |
| 34 | Charlotte, NC** | 230 | 124 | Fort Lauderdale, FL | 73 | 358 | League City, TX** | 14 |
| 136 | Chattanooga, TN | 64 | 108 | Fort Smith, AR | 79 | 335 | Lee's Summit, MO | 18 |
| 387 | Cheektowaga, NY** | 11 | 83 | Fort Wayne, IN | 95 | 184 | Lewisville, TX | 48 |
| 184 | Chesapeake, VA | 48 | 11 | Fort Worth, TX | 523 | 65 | Lexington, KY | 134 |
| NA | Chicago, IL*** | NA | 299 | Fremont, CA** | 25 | 61 | Lincoln, NE** | 142 |
| 208 | Chico, CA** | 41 | 162 | Fresno, CA** | 53 | 72 | Little Rock, AR | 119 |
| 427 | Chino Hills, CA** | 5 | 316 | Frisco, TX | 21 | 380 | Livermore, CA** | 12 |

| RANK | CITY | RAPES |
|---:|---|---:|
| 335 | Livonia, MI | 18 |
| 78 | Long Beach, CA** | 103 |
| 115 | Longmont, CO | 76 |
| 214 | Longview, TX | 39 |
| 3 | Los Angeles, CA** | 764 |
| 51 | Louisville, KY** | 160 |
| 211 | Lowell, MA | 40 |
| 92 | Lubbock, TX** | 88 |
| 232 | Lynchburg, VA | 36 |
| 214 | Lynn, MA | 39 |
| 191 | Macon, GA** | 46 |
| 115 | Madison, WI | 76 |
| 88 | Manchester, NH | 91 |
| 420 | McAllen, TX** | 6 |
| 167 | McKinney, TX | 52 |
| 222 | Medford, OR | 37 |
| 142 | Melbourne, FL | 61 |
| 16 | Memphis, TN | 437 |
| 420 | Menifee, CA** | 6 |
| 329 | Merced, CA** | 19 |
| 247 | Meridian, ID | 33 |
| 41 | Mesa, AZ** | 203 |
| 358 | Mesquite, TX** | 14 |
| 162 | Miami Beach, FL | 53 |
| 352 | Miami Gardens, FL | 15 |
| 82 | Miami, FL | 96 |
| 313 | Midland, TX** | 22 |
| 20 | Milwaukee, WI | 401 |
| 22 | Minneapolis, MN | 385 |
| 222 | Miramar, FL | 37 |
| 432 | Mission Viejo, CA** | 4 |
| 432 | Mission, TX** | 4 |
| 92 | Mobile, AL | 88 |
| 126 | Modesto, CA** | 72 |
| 259 | Moreno Valley, CA** | 31 |
| 370 | Mountain View, CA** | 13 |
| 158 | Murfreesboro, TN | 54 |
| 393 | Murrieta, CA** | 10 |
| 205 | Nampa, ID | 42 |
| 290 | Napa, CA** | 26 |
| 411 | Naperville, IL** | 7 |
| 256 | Nashua, NH | 32 |
| 16 | Nashville, TN | 437 |
| 80 | New Bedford, MA | 100 |
| 115 | New Haven, CT | 76 |
| 46 | New Orleans, LA** | 176 |
| 427 | New Rochelle, NY** | 5 |
| 2 | New York, NY** | 1,112 |
| 196 | Newark, NJ** | 45 |
| 411 | Newport Beach, CA** | 7 |
| 152 | Newport News, VA | 56 |
| 387 | Newton, MA | 11 |
| 65 | Norfolk, VA | 134 |
| 152 | Norman, OK** | 56 |
| 152 | North Charleston, SC | 56 |
| 97 | North Las Vegas, NV** | 85 |
| 347 | Norwalk, CA** | 16 |
| 358 | Norwalk, CT | 14 |
| 44 | Oakland, CA** | 180 |
| 208 | Oceanside, CA** | 41 |
| 152 | Odessa, TX** | 56 |
| 411 | O'Fallon, MO | 7 |
| 110 | Ogden, UT | 78 |
| 14 | Oklahoma City, OK** | 450 |
| 222 | Olathe, KS** | 37 |
| 43 | Omaha, NE** | 184 |
| 259 | Ontario, CA** | 31 |
| 405 | Orange, CA** | 8 |
| 370 | Orem, UT** | 13 |
| 70 | Orlando, FL | 126 |
| 247 | Overland Park, KS** | 33 |
| 393 | Oxnard, CA** | 10 |
| 316 | Palm Bay, FL | 21 |
| 284 | Palmdale, CA** | 27 |

| RANK | CITY | RAPES |
|---:|---|---:|
| 299 | Pasadena, CA** | 25 |
| 167 | Pasadena, TX** | 52 |
| 290 | Paterson, NJ** | 26 |
| 241 | Pearland, TX | 34 |
| 387 | Pembroke Pines, FL | 11 |
| 347 | Peoria, AZ** | 16 |
| 305 | Peoria, IL** | 24 |
| 1 | Philadelphia, PA | 1,279 |
| 7 | Phoenix, AZ** | 635 |
| 110 | Pittsburgh, PA | 78 |
| 98 | Plano, TX | 84 |
| 340 | Plantation, FL | 17 |
| 259 | Pomona, CA** | 31 |
| 136 | Pompano Beach, FL | 64 |
| 316 | Port St. Lucie, FL | 21 |
| 33 | Portland, OR** | 234 |
| 187 | Portsmouth, VA | 47 |
| 81 | Providence, RI | 97 |
| 102 | Provo, UT | 82 |
| 49 | Pueblo, CO | 165 |
| 236 | Quincy, MA | 35 |
| 316 | Racine, WI** | 21 |
| 108 | Raleigh, NC** | 79 |
| 427 | Ramapo, NY** | 5 |
| 358 | Rancho Cucamon., CA** | 14 |
| 176 | Reading, PA | 50 |
| 180 | Redding, CA** | 49 |
| 290 | Redwood City, CA** | 26 |
| 130 | Reno, NV** | 68 |
| 284 | Renton, WA | 27 |
| 329 | Rialto, CA** | 19 |
| 352 | Richardson, TX** | 15 |
| 236 | Richmond, CA** | 35 |
| 200 | Richmond, VA | 43 |
| 110 | Riverside, CA** | 78 |
| 198 | Roanoke, VA | 44 |
| 176 | Rochester, MN | 50 |
| 87 | Rochester, NY** | 92 |
| 57 | Rockford, IL | 145 |
| 370 | Roseville, CA** | 13 |
| 340 | Roswell, GA** | 17 |
| 305 | Round Rock, TX** | 24 |
| 83 | Sacramento, CA** | 95 |
| 187 | Salem, OR | 47 |
| 232 | Salinas, CA** | 36 |
| 40 | Salt Lake City, UT | 204 |
| 158 | San Angelo, TX | 54 |
| 5 | San Antonio, TX** | 663 |
| 120 | San Bernardino, CA** | 74 |
| 27 | San Diego, CA** | 316 |
| 50 | San Francisco, CA** | 161 |
| 31 | San Jose, CA** | 270 |
| 290 | San Leandro, CA** | 26 |
| 329 | San Marcos, CA** | 19 |
| 271 | San Mateo, CA** | 29 |
| 358 | Sandy Springs, GA** | 14 |
| 284 | Sandy, UT | 27 |
| 174 | Santa Ana, CA** | 51 |
| 256 | Santa Barbara, CA** | 32 |
| 370 | Santa Clara, CA** | 13 |
| 329 | Santa Clarita, CA** | 19 |
| 241 | Santa Maria, CA** | 34 |
| 284 | Santa Monica, CA** | 27 |
| 205 | Santa Rosa, CA** | 42 |
| 180 | Savannah, GA** | 49 |
| 222 | Scottsdale, AZ** | 37 |
| 335 | Scranton, PA | 18 |
| 55 | Seattle, WA | 153 |
| 98 | Shreveport, LA** | 84 |
| 397 | Simi Valley, CA** | 9 |
| 191 | Sioux City, IA | 46 |
| 64 | Sioux Falls, SD | 138 |
| 335 | Somerville, MA | 18 |
| 85 | South Bend, IN | 93 |

| RANK | CITY | RAPES |
|---:|---|---:|
| 352 | South Gate, CA** | 15 |
| 200 | Sparks, NV** | 43 |
| 236 | Spokane Valley, WA** | 35 |
| 48 | Spokane, WA** | 166 |
| 127 | Springfield, IL** | 71 |
| 91 | Springfield, MA | 89 |
| 29 | Springfield, MO | 281 |
| 281 | Stamford, CT | 28 |
| 266 | Sterling Heights, MI | 30 |
| 88 | Stockton, CA** | 91 |
| 214 | St. George, UT | 39 |
| 142 | St. Joseph, MO | 61 |
| 26 | St. Louis, MO | 333 |
| 36 | St. Paul, MN | 218 |
| 54 | St. Petersburg, FL | 155 |
| 222 | Suffolk, VA | 37 |
| 420 | Sugar Land, TX** | 6 |
| 347 | Sunnyvale, CA** | 16 |
| 313 | Sunrise, FL | 22 |
| 358 | Surprise, AZ** | 14 |
| 118 | Syracuse, NY** | 75 |
| 60 | Tacoma, WA | 144 |
| 51 | Tallahassee, FL | 160 |
| 110 | Tampa, FL | 78 |
| 387 | Temecula, CA** | 11 |
| 140 | Tempe, AZ** | 62 |
| 132 | Thornton, CO | 67 |
| 411 | Thousand Oaks, CA** | 7 |
| 67 | Toledo, OH | 129 |
| 427 | Toms River Twnshp, NJ** | 5 |
| 247 | Topeka, KS** | 33 |
| 347 | Torrance, CA** | 16 |
| 411 | Tracy, CA** | 7 |
| 370 | Trenton, NJ** | 13 |
| 340 | Troy, MI | 17 |
| 38 | Tucson, AZ** | 216 |
| 24 | Tulsa, OK** | 373 |
| 198 | Tuscaloosa, AL | 44 |
| 420 | Tustin, CA** | 6 |
| 200 | Tyler, TX | 43 |
| 397 | Upland, CA** | 9 |
| 325 | Upper Darby Twnshp, PA | 20 |
| 358 | Vacaville, CA** | 14 |
| 266 | Vallejo, CA** | 30 |
| 120 | Vancouver, WA | 74 |
| 316 | Ventura, CA** | 21 |
| 232 | Victorville, CA** | 36 |
| 62 | Virginia Beach, VA | 140 |
| 259 | Visalia, CA** | 31 |
| 281 | Vista, CA** | 28 |
| 147 | Waco, TX** | 58 |
| 68 | Warren, MI | 127 |
| 236 | Warwick, RI | 35 |
| 21 | Washington, DC | 393 |
| 438 | Waterbury, CT** | 2 |
| 259 | Waukegan, IL** | 31 |
| 438 | West Covina, CA** | 2 |
| 271 | West Palm Beach, FL | 29 |
| 79 | West Valley, UT | 102 |
| 134 | Westland, MI | 66 |
| 370 | Westminster, CA** | 13 |
| 290 | Westminster, CO | 26 |
| 340 | Whittier, CA** | 17 |
| 271 | Wichita Falls, TX** | 29 |
| 32 | Wichita, KS | 244 |
| 214 | Wilmington, NC** | 39 |
| 106 | Winston-Salem, NC** | 80 |
| 437 | Woodbridge Twnshp, NJ** | 3 |
| 313 | Worcester, MA | 22 |
| 222 | Yakima, WA | 37 |
| 299 | Yonkers, NY** | 25 |
| 191 | Yuma, AZ | 46 |

Source: Reported data from the F.B.I. "Crime in the United States 2013" *Revised definition: Rape is penetration, no matter how slight, of the vagina or anus with any body part or object, or oral penetration by a sex organ of another person, without the consent of the victim. Attempts or assaults to commit rape are also included; however, statutory rape and incest are excluded. **Figures for these cities are based on the previous (legacy) definition of rape. See note on page vii. ***Not available.

# 53. Rapes in 2013 (continued)
## National Total = 79,770 Rapes*

| RANK | CITY | RAPES | RANK | CITY | RAPES | RANK | CITY | RAPES |
|---|---|---|---|---|---|---|---|---|
| 1 | Philadelphia, PA | 1,279 | 74 | Lakewood, CO | 107 | 147 | Waco, TX** | 58 |
| 2 | New York, NY** | 1,112 | 76 | Arlington, TX** | 105 | 150 | Bloomington, IL** | 57 |
| 3 | Los Angeles, CA** | 764 | 76 | Atlanta, GA** | 105 | 150 | Fort Collins, CO | 57 |
| 4 | Las Vegas, NV** | 705 | 78 | Long Beach, CA** | 103 | 152 | Clinton Twnshp, MI | 56 |
| 5 | San Antonio, TX** | 663 | 79 | West Valley, UT | 102 | 152 | Elgin, IL** | 56 |
| 6 | Indianapolis, IN | 656 | 80 | New Bedford, MA | 100 | 152 | Newport News, VA | 56 |
| 7 | Phoenix, AZ** | 635 | 81 | Providence, RI | 97 | 152 | Norman, OK** | 56 |
| 8 | Detroit, MI | 618 | 82 | Miami, FL | 96 | 152 | North Charleston, SC | 56 |
| 8 | Houston, TX** | 618 | 83 | Fort Wayne, IN | 95 | 152 | Odessa, TX** | 56 |
| 10 | Dallas, TX** | 543 | 83 | Sacramento, CA** | 95 | 158 | Evansville, IN** | 54 |
| 11 | Fort Worth, TX | 523 | 85 | Denton, TX | 93 | 158 | Grand Prairie, TX** | 54 |
| 12 | Denver, CO | 514 | 85 | South Bend, IN | 93 | 158 | Murfreesboro, TN | 54 |
| 13 | Jacksonville, FL | 452 | 87 | Rochester, NY** | 92 | 158 | San Angelo, TX | 54 |
| 14 | Oklahoma City, OK** | 450 | 88 | Manchester, NH | 91 | 162 | Aurora, IL** | 53 |
| 15 | Albuquerque, NM** | 439 | 88 | Stockton, CA** | 91 | 162 | Fresno, CA** | 53 |
| 16 | Memphis, TN | 437 | 90 | Des Moines, IA | 90 | 162 | Garland, TX** | 53 |
| 16 | Nashville, TN | 437 | 91 | Springfield, MA | 89 | 162 | Hartford, CT** | 53 |
| 18 | Cleveland, OH | 417 | 92 | Davenport, IA | 88 | 162 | Miami Beach, FL | 53 |
| 19 | Anchorage, AK | 408 | 92 | Lubbock, TX** | 88 | 167 | Chandler, AZ** | 52 |
| 20 | Milwaukee, WI | 401 | 92 | Mobile, AL | 88 | 167 | Duluth, MN | 52 |
| 21 | Washington, DC | 393 | 95 | Brockton, MA | 87 | 167 | Green Bay, WI | 52 |
| 22 | Minneapolis, MN | 385 | 95 | Huntsville, AL | 87 | 167 | Gresham, OR** | 52 |
| 23 | Kansas City, MO | 377 | 97 | North Las Vegas, NV** | 85 | 167 | Lakeland, FL | 52 |
| 24 | Tulsa, OK** | 373 | 98 | Clarksville, TN | 84 | 167 | McKinney, TX | 52 |
| 25 | Colorado Springs, CO | 370 | 98 | Plano, TX | 84 | 167 | Pasadena, TX** | 52 |
| 26 | St. Louis, MO | 333 | 98 | Shreveport, LA** | 84 | 174 | Independence, MO | 51 |
| 27 | San Diego, CA** | 316 | 101 | Kansas City, KS** | 83 | 174 | Santa Ana, CA** | 51 |
| 28 | Baltimore, MD** | 298 | 102 | Anaheim, CA** | 82 | 176 | Clearwater, FL | 50 |
| 29 | Springfield, MO | 281 | 102 | Bridgeport, CT** | 82 | 176 | Lawrence, KS | 50 |
| 30 | Boston, MA** | 279 | 102 | Grand Rapids, MI | 82 | 176 | Reading, PA | 50 |
| 31 | San Jose, CA** | 270 | 102 | Provo, UT | 82 | 176 | Rochester, MN | 50 |
| 32 | Wichita, KS | 244 | 106 | Lawton, OK** | 80 | 180 | Glendale, AZ** | 49 |
| 33 | Portland, OR** | 234 | 106 | Winston-Salem, NC** | 80 | 180 | Joliet, IL** | 49 |
| 34 | Charlotte, NC** | 230 | 108 | Fort Smith, AR | 79 | 180 | Redding, CA** | 49 |
| 35 | Aurora, CO | 224 | 108 | Raleigh, NC** | 79 | 180 | Savannah, GA** | 49 |
| 36 | St. Paul, MN | 218 | 110 | Killeen, TX** | 78 | 184 | Ann Arbor, MI | 48 |
| 37 | Austin, TX** | 217 | 110 | Ogden, UT | 78 | 184 | Chesapeake, VA | 48 |
| 38 | Tucson, AZ** | 216 | 110 | Pittsburgh, PA | 78 | 184 | Lewisville, TX | 48 |
| 39 | Amarillo, TX | 214 | 110 | Riverside, CA** | 78 | 187 | Gary, IN** | 47 |
| 40 | Salt Lake City, UT | 204 | 110 | Tampa, FL | 78 | 187 | Largo, FL | 47 |
| 41 | Mesa, AZ** | 203 | 115 | Longmont, CO | 76 | 187 | Portsmouth, VA | 47 |
| 42 | Cincinnati, OH | 199 | 115 | Madison, WI | 76 | 187 | Salem, OR | 47 |
| 43 | Omaha, NE** | 184 | 115 | New Haven, CT | 76 | 191 | Cedar Rapids, IA | 46 |
| 44 | Oakland, CA** | 180 | 118 | Laredo, TX** | 75 | 191 | Costa Mesa, CA** | 46 |
| 45 | Birmingham, AL | 178 | 118 | Syracuse, NY** | 75 | 191 | Macon, GA** | 46 |
| 46 | El Paso, TX** | 176 | 120 | Baton Rouge, LA** | 74 | 191 | Sioux City, IA | 46 |
| 46 | New Orleans, LA** | 176 | 120 | Greeley, CO | 74 | 191 | Yuma, AZ | 46 |
| 48 | Spokane, WA** | 166 | 120 | San Bernardino, CA** | 74 | 196 | Henderson, NV** | 45 |
| 49 | Pueblo, CO | 165 | 120 | Vancouver, WA | 74 | 196 | Newark, NJ** | 45 |
| 50 | San Francisco, CA** | 161 | 124 | Fall River, MA | 73 | 198 | Roanoke, VA | 44 |
| 51 | Akron, OH | 160 | 124 | Fort Lauderdale, FL | 73 | 198 | Tuscaloosa, AL | 44 |
| 51 | Louisville, KY** | 160 | 126 | Modesto, CA** | 72 | 200 | Bakersfield, CA** | 43 |
| 51 | Tallahassee, FL | 160 | 127 | Fargo, ND | 71 | 200 | Federal Way, WA | 43 |
| 54 | St. Petersburg, FL | 155 | 127 | Springfield, IL** | 71 | 200 | Richmond, VA | 43 |
| 55 | Seattle, WA | 153 | 129 | Greensboro, NC** | 70 | 200 | Sparks, NV** | 43 |
| 56 | Corpus Christi, TX** | 147 | 130 | Eugene, OR | 68 | 200 | Tyler, TX | 43 |
| 57 | Buffalo, NY** | 145 | 130 | Reno, NV** | 68 | 205 | Everett, WA** | 42 |
| 57 | Flint, MI | 145 | 132 | Columbia, MO | 67 | 205 | Nampa, ID | 42 |
| 57 | Rockford, IL | 145 | 132 | Thornton, CO | 67 | 205 | Santa Rosa, CA** | 42 |
| 60 | Tacoma, WA | 144 | 134 | Westland, MI | 66 | 208 | Chico, CA** | 41 |
| 61 | Lincoln, NE** | 142 | 135 | Fayetteville, NC** | 65 | 208 | Hialeah, FL | 41 |
| 62 | Virginia Beach, VA | 140 | 136 | Allentown, PA | 64 | 208 | Oceanside, CA** | 41 |
| 63 | Knoxville, TN | 139 | 136 | Chattanooga, TN | 64 | 211 | Broken Arrow, OK** | 40 |
| 64 | Sioux Falls, SD | 138 | 136 | Pompano Beach, FL | 64 | 211 | Lancaster, CA** | 40 |
| 65 | Lexington, KY | 134 | 139 | Hollywood, FL | 63 | 211 | Lowell, MA | 40 |
| 65 | Norfolk, VA | 134 | 140 | Gainesville, FL | 62 | 214 | Billings, MT | 39 |
| 67 | Toledo, OH | 129 | 140 | Tempe, AZ** | 62 | 214 | Champaign, IL** | 39 |
| 68 | Lansing, MI | 127 | 142 | Brownsville, TX** | 61 | 214 | Escondido, CA** | 39 |
| 68 | Warren, MI | 127 | 142 | Melbourne, FL | 61 | 214 | Longview, TX | 39 |
| 70 | Orlando, FL | 126 | 142 | St. Joseph, MO | 61 | 214 | Lynn, MA | 39 |
| 71 | Boise, ID | 123 | 145 | Erie, PA | 60 | 214 | St. George, UT | 39 |
| 72 | Little Rock, AR | 119 | 146 | Beaumont, TX** | 59 | 214 | Wilmington, NC** | 39 |
| 73 | Jackson, MS** | 110 | 147 | Columbia, SC | 58 | 221 | Boulder, CO | 38 |
| 74 | Dayton, OH | 107 | 147 | Kent, WA | 58 | 222 | Abilene, TX** | 37 |

| RANK | CITY | RAPES | RANK | CITY | RAPES | RANK | CITY | RAPES |
|---|---|---|---|---|---|---|---|---|
| 222 | Athens-Clarke, GA** | 37 | 290 | San Leandro, CA** | 26 | 370 | Buena Park, CA** | 13 |
| 222 | Elizabeth, NJ** | 37 | 290 | Westminster, CO | 26 | 370 | Burbank, CA** | 13 |
| 222 | Hammond, IN** | 37 | 299 | Antioch, CA** | 25 | 370 | Fairfield, CA** | 13 |
| 222 | Medford, OR | 37 | 299 | Centennial, CO | 25 | 370 | Mountain View, CA** | 13 |
| 222 | Miramar, FL | 37 | 299 | Danbury, CT** | 25 | 370 | Orem, UT** | 13 |
| 222 | Olathe, KS** | 37 | 299 | Fremont, CA** | 25 | 370 | Roseville, CA** | 13 |
| 222 | Scottsdale, AZ** | 37 | 299 | Pasadena, CA** | 25 | 370 | Santa Clara, CA** | 13 |
| 222 | Suffolk, VA | 37 | 299 | Yonkers, NY** | 25 | 370 | Trenton, NJ** | 13 |
| 222 | Yakima, WA | 37 | 305 | Cambridge, MA | 24 | 370 | Westminster, CA** | 13 |
| 232 | Columbus, GA** | 36 | 305 | Coral Springs, FL | 24 | 380 | Clifton, NJ** | 12 |
| 232 | Lynchburg, VA | 36 | 305 | Hemet, CA** | 24 | 380 | Concord, CA** | 12 |
| 232 | Salinas, CA** | 36 | 305 | Irving, TX** | 24 | 380 | Downey, CA** | 12 |
| 232 | Victorville, CA** | 36 | 305 | Peoria, IL** | 24 | 380 | Irvine, CA** | 12 |
| 236 | Jersey City, NJ** | 35 | 305 | Round Rock, TX** | 24 | 380 | Jurupa Valley, CA** | 12 |
| 236 | Quincy, MA | 35 | 311 | Carlsbad, CA** | 23 | 380 | Lake Forest, CA** | 12 |
| 236 | Richmond, CA** | 35 | 311 | Clovis, CA** | 23 | 380 | Livermore, CA** | 12 |
| 236 | Spokane Valley, WA** | 35 | 313 | Midland, TX** | 22 | 387 | Cary, NC** | 11 |
| 236 | Warwick, RI | 35 | 313 | Sunrise, FL | 22 | 387 | Cheektowaga, NY** | 11 |
| 241 | Bloomington, IN** | 34 | 313 | Worcester, MA | 22 | 387 | Lakewood, CA** | 11 |
| 241 | College Station, TX** | 34 | 316 | Albany, GA** | 21 | 387 | Newton, MA | 11 |
| 241 | Indio, CA** | 34 | 316 | Alexandria, VA | 21 | 387 | Pembroke Pines, FL | 11 |
| 241 | Kennewick, WA | 34 | 316 | Bend, OR | 21 | 387 | Temecula, CA** | 11 |
| 241 | Pearland, TX | 34 | 316 | Frisco, TX | 21 | 393 | Alameda, CA** | 10 |
| 241 | Santa Maria, CA** | 34 | 316 | Hampton, VA | 21 | 393 | Evanston, IL** | 10 |
| 247 | Arvada, CO | 33 | 316 | Palm Bay, FL | 21 | 393 | Murrieta, CA** | 10 |
| 247 | Brooklyn Park, MN | 33 | 316 | Port St. Lucie, FL | 21 | 393 | Oxnard, CA** | 10 |
| 247 | Dearborn, MI | 33 | 316 | Racine, WI** | 21 | 397 | Alhambra, CA** | 9 |
| 247 | Fayetteville, AR | 33 | 316 | Ventura, CA** | 21 | 397 | Bellflower, CA** | 9 |
| 247 | Fontana, CA** | 33 | 325 | Beaverton, OR** | 20 | 397 | Concord, NC** | 9 |
| 247 | Hayward, CA** | 33 | 325 | Bellevue, WA** | 20 | 397 | Decatur, IL** | 9 |
| 247 | Meridian, ID | 33 | 325 | Greenville, NC** | 20 | 397 | Greece, NY** | 9 |
| 247 | Overland Park, KS** | 33 | 325 | Upper Darby Twnshp, PA | 20 | 397 | Hoover, AL | 9 |
| 247 | Topeka, KS** | 33 | 329 | Citrus Heights, CA** | 19 | 397 | Simi Valley, CA** | 9 |
| 256 | Hawthorne, CA** | 32 | 329 | Lawrence, MA** | 19 | 397 | Upland, CA** | 9 |
| 256 | Nashua, NH | 32 | 329 | Merced, CA** | 19 | 405 | Boca Raton, FL | 8 |
| 256 | Santa Barbara, CA** | 32 | 329 | Rialto, CA** | 19 | 405 | Clarkstown, NY** | 8 |
| 259 | Bryan, TX** | 31 | 329 | San Marcos, CA** | 19 | 405 | Edison Twnshp, NJ** | 8 |
| 259 | Huntington Beach, CA** | 31 | 329 | Santa Clarita, CA** | 19 | 405 | Glendale, CA** | 8 |
| 259 | Moreno Valley, CA** | 31 | 335 | Canton Twnshp, MI | 18 | 405 | Hamilton Twnshp, NJ** | 8 |
| 259 | Ontario, CA** | 31 | 335 | Lee's Summit, MO | 18 | 405 | Orange, CA** | 8 |
| 259 | Pomona, CA** | 31 | 335 | Livonia, MI | 18 | 411 | Amherst, NY** | 7 |
| 259 | Visalia, CA** | 31 | 335 | Scranton, PA | 18 | 411 | Arlington Heights, IL** | 7 |
| 259 | Waukegan, IL** | 31 | 335 | Somerville, MA | 18 | 411 | Cape Coral, FL | 7 |
| 266 | Albany, NY** | 30 | 340 | Bloomington, MN | 17 | 411 | Chino, CA** | 7 |
| 266 | Edinburg, TX** | 30 | 340 | Hesperia, CA** | 17 | 411 | Naperville, IL** | 7 |
| 266 | High Point, NC** | 30 | 340 | Lafayette, LA** | 17 | 411 | Newport Beach, CA** | 7 |
| 266 | Sterling Heights, MI | 30 | 340 | Plantation, FL | 17 | 411 | O'Fallon, MO | 7 |
| 266 | Vallejo, CA** | 30 | 340 | Roswell, GA** | 17 | 411 | Thousand Oaks, CA** | 7 |
| 271 | Charleston, SC | 29 | 340 | Troy, MI | 17 | 411 | Tracy, CA** | 7 |
| 271 | Chula Vista, CA** | 29 | 340 | Whittier, CA** | 17 | 420 | Baldwin Park, CA** | 6 |
| 271 | Cranston, RI | 29 | 347 | Garden Grove, CA** | 16 | 420 | Carrollton, TX** | 6 |
| 271 | El Cajon, CA** | 29 | 347 | Norwalk, CA** | 16 | 420 | Elk Grove, CA** | 6 |
| 271 | Fullerton, CA** | 29 | 347 | Peoria, AZ** | 16 | 420 | McAllen, TX** | 6 |
| 271 | Hillsboro, OR** | 29 | 347 | Sunnyvale, CA** | 16 | 420 | Menifee, CA** | 6 |
| 271 | Inglewood, CA** | 29 | 347 | Torrance, CA** | 16 | 420 | Sugar Land, TX** | 6 |
| 271 | San Mateo, CA** | 29 | 352 | Carson, CA** | 15 | 420 | Tustin, CA** | 6 |
| 271 | West Palm Beach, FL | 29 | 352 | Daly City, CA** | 15 | 427 | Chino Hills, CA** | 5 |
| 271 | Wichita Falls, TX** | 29 | 352 | Edmond, OK** | 15 | 427 | Lakewood Twnshp, NJ** | 5 |
| 281 | Deerfield Beach, FL | 28 | 352 | Miami Gardens, FL | 15 | 427 | New Rochelle, NY** | 5 |
| 281 | Stamford, CT | 28 | 352 | Richardson, TX** | 15 | 427 | Ramapo, NY** | 5 |
| 281 | Vista, CA** | 28 | 352 | South Gate, CA** | 15 | 427 | Toms River Twnshp, NJ** | 5 |
| 284 | Bethlehem, PA | 27 | 358 | Cicero, IL** | 14 | 432 | Brick Twnshp, NJ** | 4 |
| 284 | Las Cruces, NM** | 27 | 358 | Corona, CA** | 14 | 432 | Carmel, IN** | 4 |
| 284 | Palmdale, CA** | 27 | 358 | El Monte, CA** | 14 | 432 | Johns Creek, GA** | 4 |
| 284 | Renton, WA | 27 | 358 | Farmington Hills, MI | 14 | 432 | Mission Viejo, CA** | 4 |
| 284 | Sandy, UT | 27 | 358 | Gilbert, AZ | 14 | 432 | Mission, TX** | 4 |
| 284 | Santa Monica, CA** | 27 | 358 | League City, TX** | 14 | 437 | Woodbridge Twnshp, NJ** | 3 |
| 290 | Berkeley, CA** | 26 | 358 | Mesquite, TX** | 14 | 438 | Fishers, IN** | 2 |
| 290 | Compton, CA** | 26 | 358 | Norwalk, CT | 14 | 438 | Waterbury, CT** | 2 |
| 290 | Davie, FL | 26 | 358 | Rancho Cucamon., CA** | 14 | 438 | West Covina, CA** | 2 |
| 290 | Kenosha, WI** | 26 | 358 | Sandy Springs, GA** | 14 | 441 | Colonie, NY** | 0 |
| 290 | Napa, CA** | 26 | 358 | Surprise, AZ** | 14 | NA | Chicago, IL*** | NA |
| 290 | Paterson, NJ** | 26 | 358 | Vacaville, CA** | 14 | | | |
| 290 | Redwood City, CA** | 26 | 370 | Allen, TX | 13 | | | |

Source: Reported data from the F.B.I. "Crime in the United States 2013" *Revised definition: Rape is penetration, no matter how slight, of the vagina or anus with any body part or object, or oral penetration by a sex organ of another person, without the consent of the victim. Attempts or assaults to commit rape are also included; however, statutory rape and incest are excluded. **Figures for these cities are based on the previous (legacy) definition of rape. See note on page vii. ***Not available.

# 54. Rape Rate in 2013
## National Rate = 25.2 Rapes per 100,000 Population*

| RANK | CITY | RATE | RANK | CITY | RATE | RANK | CITY | RATE |
|---|---|---|---|---|---|---|---|---|
| 206 | Abilene, TX** | 31.0 | 401 | Chino, CA** | 8.7 | 292 | Fullerton, CA** | 20.8 |
| 31 | Akron, OH | 80.6 | 376 | Chula Vista, CA** | 11.4 | 101 | Gainesville, FL | 49.0 |
| 363 | Alameda, CA** | 13.1 | 328 | Cicero, IL** | 16.6 | 398 | Garden Grove, CA** | 9.1 |
| 238 | Albany, GA** | 27.1 | 51 | Cincinnati, OH | 67.1 | 279 | Garland, TX** | 22.5 |
| 209 | Albany, NY** | 30.6 | 282 | Citrus Heights, CA** | 22.3 | 66 | Gary, IN** | 59.6 |
| 37 | Albuquerque, NM** | 78.7 | 390 | Clarkstown, NY** | 9.9 | 417 | Gilbert, AZ | 6.2 |
| 352 | Alexandria, VA | 14.1 | 72 | Clarksville, TN | 57.7 | 290 | Glendale, AZ** | 20.9 |
| 384 | Alhambra, CA** | 10.6 | 124 | Clearwater, FL | 45.9 | 435 | Glendale, CA** | 4.1 |
| 87 | Allentown, PA | 53.7 | 8 | Cleveland, OH | 107.1 | 220 | Grand Prairie, TX** | 29.4 |
| 349 | Allen, TX | 14.2 | 352 | Clifton, NJ** | 14.1 | 145 | Grand Rapids, MI | 42.9 |
| 6 | Amarillo, TX | 108.9 | 74 | Clinton Twnshp, MI | 57.1 | 394 | Greece, NY** | 9.3 |
| 418 | Amherst, NY** | 5.9 | 272 | Clovis, CA** | 23.1 | 39 | Greeley, CO | 77.0 |
| 266 | Anaheim, CA** | 23.7 | 192 | College Station, TX** | 34.4 | 100 | Green Bay, WI | 49.5 |
| 4 | Anchorage, AK | 136.2 | 441 | Colonie, NY** | 0.0 | 253 | Greensboro, NC** | 25.1 |
| 157 | Ann Arbor, MI | 41.1 | 23 | Colorado Springs, CO | 84.8 | 278 | Greenville, NC** | 22.7 |
| 268 | Antioch, CA** | 23.5 | 68 | Columbia, MO | 58.5 | 110 | Gresham, OR** | 47.3 |
| 397 | Arlington Heights, IL** | 9.2 | 134 | Columbia, SC | 43.9 | 399 | Hamilton Twnshp, NJ** | 9.0 |
| 234 | Arlington, TX** | 27.7 | 319 | Columbus, GA** | 17.9 | 118 | Hammond, IN** | 46.6 |
| 216 | Arvada, CO | 29.8 | 241 | Compton, CA** | 26.6 | 342 | Hampton, VA | 15.3 |
| 208 | Athens-Clarke, GA** | 30.8 | 393 | Concord, CA** | 9.6 | 149 | Hartford, CT** | 42.4 |
| 271 | Atlanta, GA** | 23.3 | 379 | Concord, NC** | 10.9 | 171 | Hawthorne, CA** | 37.2 |
| 55 | Aurora, CO | 65.2 | 310 | Coral Springs, FL | 19.0 | 286 | Hayward, CA** | 21.9 |
| 243 | Aurora, IL** | 26.4 | 401 | Corona, CA** | 8.7 | 220 | Hemet, CA** | 29.4 |
| 252 | Austin, TX** | 25.3 | 114 | Corpus Christi, TX** | 46.7 | 326 | Henderson, NV** | 16.8 |
| 373 | Bakersfield, CA** | 11.9 | 159 | Costa Mesa, CA** | 40.9 | 313 | Hesperia, CA** | 18.4 |
| 408 | Baldwin Park, CA** | 7.8 | 180 | Cranston, RI | 35.9 | 322 | Hialeah, FL | 17.5 |
| 105 | Baltimore, MD** | 47.9 | 139 | Dallas, TX** | 43.3 | 232 | High Point, NC** | 28.0 |
| 202 | Baton Rouge, LA** | 32.1 | 347 | Daly City, CA** | 14.3 | 213 | Hillsboro, OR** | 30.1 |
| 97 | Beaumont, TX** | 49.9 | 214 | Danbury, CT** | 30.0 | 143 | Hollywood, FL | 43.0 |
| 289 | Beaverton, OR** | 21.4 | 20 | Davenport, IA | 86.4 | 383 | Hoover, AL | 10.7 |
| 336 | Bellevue, WA** | 15.7 | 239 | Davie, FL | 26.9 | 228 | Houston, TX** | 28.3 |
| 375 | Bellflower, CA** | 11.6 | 42 | Dayton, OH | 75.8 | 335 | Huntington Beach, CA** | 15.8 |
| 244 | Bend, OR | 26.3 | 192 | Dearborn, MI | 34.4 | 111 | Huntsville, AL | 47.1 |
| 280 | Berkeley, CA** | 22.4 | 370 | Decatur, IL** | 12.0 | 136 | Independence, MO | 43.4 |
| 180 | Bethlehem, PA | 35.9 | 182 | Deerfield Beach, FL | 35.8 | 38 | Indianapolis, IN | 77.2 |
| 179 | Billings, MT | 36.2 | 43 | Denton, TX | 75.5 | 149 | Indio, CA** | 42.4 |
| 25 | Birmingham, AL | 84.0 | 33 | Denver, CO | 79.2 | 246 | Inglewood, CA** | 26.0 |
| 47 | Bloomington, IL** | 73.0 | 136 | Des Moines, IA | 43.4 | 425 | Irvine, CA** | 5.1 |
| 156 | Bloomington, IN** | 41.3 | 19 | Detroit, MI | 88.3 | 386 | Irving, TX** | 10.5 |
| 305 | Bloomington, MN | 19.5 | 384 | Downey, CA** | 10.6 | 88 | Jacksonville, FL | 53.4 |
| 399 | Boca Raton, FL | 9.0 | 63 | Duluth, MN | 60.3 | 59 | Jackson, MS** | 62.5 |
| 73 | Boise, ID | 57.4 | 177 | Edinburg, TX** | 36.5 | 358 | Jersey City, NJ** | 13.6 |
| 139 | Boston, MA** | 43.3 | 407 | Edison Twnshp, NJ** | 7.9 | 429 | Johns Creek, GA** | 4.8 |
| 173 | Boulder, CO | 37.0 | 323 | Edmond, OK** | 17.4 | 198 | Joliet, IL** | 33.0 |
| 424 | Brick Twnshp, NJ** | 5.3 | 227 | El Cajon, CA** | 28.4 | 368 | Jurupa Valley, CA** | 12.2 |
| 80 | Bridgeport, CT** | 55.8 | 369 | El Monte, CA** | 12.1 | 77 | Kansas City, KS** | 56.2 |
| 17 | Brockton, MA | 92.1 | 247 | El Paso, TX** | 25.9 | 30 | Kansas City, MO | 81.0 |
| 164 | Broken Arrow, OK** | 38.9 | 95 | Elgin, IL** | 50.7 | 132 | Kennewick, WA | 44.4 |
| 154 | Brooklyn Park, MN | 42.1 | 224 | Elizabeth, NJ** | 29.1 | 247 | Kenosha, WI** | 25.9 |
| 196 | Brownsville, TX** | 33.6 | 436 | Elk Grove, CA** | 3.7 | 118 | Kent, WA | 46.6 |
| 162 | Bryan, TX** | 39.5 | 67 | Erie, PA | 59.5 | 74 | Killeen, TX** | 57.1 |
| 336 | Buena Park, CA** | 15.7 | 245 | Escondido, CA** | 26.2 | 41 | Knoxville, TN | 75.9 |
| 78 | Buffalo, NY** | 56.0 | 145 | Eugene, OR | 42.9 | 356 | Lafayette, LA** | 13.8 |
| 366 | Burbank, CA** | 12.4 | 361 | Evanston, IL** | 13.2 | 344 | Lake Forest, CA** | 15.1 |
| 280 | Cambridge, MA | 22.4 | 128 | Evansville, IN** | 44.9 | 93 | Lakeland, FL | 51.6 |
| 299 | Canton Twnshp, MI | 20.2 | 161 | Everett, WA** | 40.0 | 421 | Lakewood Twnshp, NJ** | 5.4 |
| 433 | Cape Coral, FL | 4.3 | 370 | Fairfield, CA** | 12.0 | 358 | Lakewood, CA** | 13.6 |
| 292 | Carlsbad, CA** | 20.8 | 28 | Fall River, MA | 81.8 | 46 | Lakewood, CO | 73.1 |
| 430 | Carmel, IN** | 4.7 | 56 | Fargo, ND | 63.9 | 254 | Lancaster, CA** | 25.0 |
| 430 | Carrollton, TX** | 4.7 | 324 | Farmington Hills, MI | 17.3 | 5 | Lansing, MI | 111.5 |
| 332 | Carson, CA** | 16.1 | 149 | Fayetteville, AR | 42.4 | 212 | Laredo, TX** | 30.3 |
| 410 | Cary, NC** | 7.4 | 202 | Fayetteville, NC** | 32.1 | 63 | Largo, FL | 60.3 |
| 182 | Cedar Rapids, IA | 35.8 | 121 | Federal Way, WA | 46.4 | 242 | Las Cruces, NM** | 26.5 |
| 261 | Centennial, CO | 23.9 | 438 | Fishers, IN** | 2.4 | 112 | Las Vegas, NV** | 47.0 |
| 112 | Champaign, IL** | 47.0 | 3 | Flint, MI | 145.1 | 82 | Lawrence, KS | 55.5 |
| 290 | Chandler, AZ** | 20.9 | 330 | Fontana, CA** | 16.2 | 257 | Lawrence, MA** | 24.4 |
| 277 | Charleston, SC | 22.8 | 167 | Fort Collins, CO | 38.0 | 29 | Lawton, OK** | 81.2 |
| 236 | Charlotte, NC** | 27.5 | 152 | Fort Lauderdale, FL | 42.3 | 339 | League City, TX** | 15.6 |
| 172 | Chattanooga, TN | 37.1 | 18 | Fort Smith, AR | 90.0 | 306 | Lee's Summit, MO | 19.4 |
| 355 | Cheektowaga, NY** | 14.0 | 170 | Fort Wayne, IN | 37.3 | 108 | Lewisville, TX | 47.7 |
| 292 | Chesapeake, VA | 20.8 | 54 | Fort Worth, TX | 66.3 | 136 | Lexington, KY | 43.4 |
| NA | Chicago, IL*** | NA | 378 | Fremont, CA** | 11.1 | 90 | Lincoln, NE** | 53.1 |
| 120 | Chico, CA** | 46.5 | 387 | Fresno, CA** | 10.4 | 63 | Little Rock, AR | 60.3 |
| 415 | Chino Hills, CA** | 6.5 | 334 | Frisco, TX | 15.9 | 349 | Livermore, CA** | 14.2 |

| RANK | CITY | RATE | RANK | CITY | RATE | RANK | CITY | RATE |
|---|---|---|---|---|---|---|---|---|
| 311 | Livonia, MI | 18.9 | 317 | Pasadena, CA** | 18.0 | 336 | South Gate, CA** | 15.7 |
| 286 | Long Beach, CA** | 21.9 | 194 | Pasadena, TX** | 33.9 | 121 | Sparks, NV** | 46.4 |
| 22 | Longmont, CO | 85.0 | 319 | Paterson, NJ** | 17.9 | 165 | Spokane Valley, WA** | 38.5 |
| 104 | Longview, TX | 48.0 | 190 | Pearland, TX | 34.6 | 33 | Spokane, WA** | 79.2 |
| 303 | Los Angeles, CA** | 19.7 | 414 | Pembroke Pines, FL | 6.8 | 62 | Springfield, IL** | 60.5 |
| 262 | Louisville, KY** | 23.8 | 390 | Peoria, AZ** | 9.9 | 71 | Springfield, MA | 57.9 |
| 177 | Lowell, MA | 36.5 | 296 | Peoria, IL** | 20.7 | 1 | Springfield, MO | 172.3 |
| 173 | Lubbock, TX** | 37.0 | 27 | Philadelphia, PA | 82.3 | 283 | Stamford, CT | 22.2 |
| 123 | Lynchburg, VA | 46.3 | 152 | Phoenix, AZ** | 42.3 | 275 | Sterling Heights, MI | 23.0 |
| 148 | Lynn, MA | 42.5 | 250 | Pittsburgh, PA | 25.4 | 211 | Stockton, CA** | 30.4 |
| 96 | Macon, GA** | 50.5 | 210 | Plano, TX | 30.5 | 94 | St. George, UT | 51.0 |
| 204 | Madison, WI | 31.3 | 309 | Plantation, FL | 19.1 | 35 | St. Joseph, MO | 78.9 |
| 26 | Manchester, NH | 82.4 | 298 | Pomona, CA** | 20.5 | 10 | St. Louis, MO | 104.5 |
| 432 | McAllen, TX** | 4.4 | 60 | Pompano Beach, FL | 61.6 | 45 | St. Paul, MN | 74.0 |
| 185 | McKinney, TX | 35.4 | 366 | Port St. Lucie, FL | 12.4 | 58 | St. Petersburg, FL | 62.7 |
| 103 | Medford, OR | 48.1 | 166 | Portland, OR** | 38.4 | 139 | Suffolk, VA | 43.3 |
| 35 | Melbourne, FL | 78.9 | 102 | Portsmouth, VA | 48.4 | 412 | Sugar Land, TX** | 7.2 |
| 53 | Memphis, TN | 66.4 | 83 | Providence, RI | 54.2 | 380 | Sunnyvale, CA** | 10.8 |
| 411 | Menifee, CA** | 7.3 | 49 | Provo, UT | 70.1 | 257 | Sunrise, FL | 24.4 |
| 269 | Merced, CA** | 23.4 | 2 | Pueblo, CO | 152.7 | 376 | Surprise, AZ** | 11.4 |
| 160 | Meridian, ID | 40.2 | 169 | Quincy, MA | 37.4 | 91 | Syracuse, NY** | 52.1 |
| 131 | Mesa, AZ** | 44.5 | 239 | Racine, WI** | 26.9 | 48 | Tacoma, WA | 70.9 |
| 392 | Mesquite, TX** | 9.7 | 313 | Raleigh, NC** | 18.4 | 23 | Tallahassee, FL | 84.8 |
| 69 | Miami Beach, FL | 58.0 | 419 | Ramapo, NY** | 5.7 | 283 | Tampa, FL | 22.2 |
| 360 | Miami Gardens, FL | 13.4 | 405 | Rancho Cucamon., CA** | 8.1 | 388 | Temecula, CA** | 10.3 |
| 276 | Miami, FL | 22.9 | 76 | Reading, PA | 56.7 | 175 | Tempe, AZ** | 36.8 |
| 317 | Midland, TX** | 18.0 | 86 | Redding, CA** | 53.8 | 89 | Thornton, CO | 53.3 |
| 52 | Milwaukee, WI | 66.7 | 200 | Redwood City, CA** | 32.6 | 421 | Thousand Oaks, CA** | 5.4 |
| 11 | Minneapolis, MN | 97.2 | 222 | Reno, NV** | 29.2 | 125 | Toledo, OH | 45.6 |
| 228 | Miramar, FL | 28.3 | 233 | Renton, WA | 27.9 | 421 | Toms River Twnshp, NJ** | 5.4 |
| 434 | Mission Viejo, CA** | 4.2 | 312 | Rialto, CA** | 18.5 | 249 | Topeka, KS** | 25.8 |
| 426 | Mission, TX** | 4.9 | 347 | Richardson, TX** | 14.3 | 380 | Torrance, CA** | 10.8 |
| 187 | Mobile, AL | 35.1 | 200 | Richmond, CA** | 32.6 | 404 | Tracy, CA** | 8.2 |
| 186 | Modesto, CA** | 35.3 | 299 | Richmond, VA | 20.2 | 340 | Trenton, NJ** | 15.4 |
| 340 | Moreno Valley, CA** | 15.4 | 255 | Riverside, CA** | 24.7 | 297 | Troy, MI | 20.6 |
| 326 | Mountain View, CA** | 16.8 | 128 | Roanoke, VA | 44.9 | 157 | Tucson, AZ** | 41.1 |
| 114 | Murfreesboro, TN | 46.7 | 125 | Rochester, MN | 45.6 | 14 | Tulsa, OK** | 94.6 |
| 394 | Murrieta, CA** | 9.3 | 135 | Rochester, NY** | 43.7 | 114 | Tuscaloosa, AL | 46.7 |
| 99 | Nampa, ID | 49.6 | 12 | Rockford, IL | 96.5 | 409 | Tustin, CA** | 7.6 |
| 198 | Napa, CA** | 33.0 | 388 | Roseville, CA** | 10.3 | 143 | Tyler, TX | 43.0 |
| 426 | Naperville, IL** | 4.9 | 321 | Roswell, GA** | 17.8 | 373 | Upland, CA** | 11.9 |
| 175 | Nashua, NH | 36.8 | 285 | Round Rock, TX** | 22.1 | 260 | Upper Darby Twnshp, PA | 24.2 |
| 50 | Nashville, TN | 68.7 | 302 | Sacramento, CA** | 19.9 | 346 | Vacaville, CA** | 14.8 |
| 9 | New Bedford, MA | 105.1 | 217 | Salem, OR | 29.7 | 250 | Vallejo, CA** | 25.4 |
| 69 | New Haven, CT | 58.0 | 272 | Salinas, CA** | 23.1 | 132 | Vancouver, WA | 44.4 |
| 114 | New Orleans, LA** | 46.7 | 7 | Salt Lake City, UT | 107.2 | 306 | Ventura, CA** | 19.4 |
| 416 | New Rochelle, NY** | 6.3 | 79 | San Angelo, TX | 55.9 | 219 | Victorville, CA** | 29.6 |
| 361 | New York, NY** | 13.2 | 109 | San Antonio, TX** | 47.4 | 205 | Virginia Beach, VA | 31.1 |
| 330 | Newark, NJ** | 16.2 | 191 | San Bernardino, CA** | 34.5 | 259 | Visalia, CA** | 24.3 |
| 406 | Newport Beach, CA** | 8.0 | 269 | San Diego, CA** | 23.4 | 225 | Vista, CA** | 29.0 |
| 207 | Newport News, VA | 30.9 | 308 | San Francisco, CA** | 19.3 | 127 | Waco, TX** | 45.5 |
| 364 | Newton, MA** | 12.7 | 237 | San Jose, CA** | 27.2 | 13 | Warren, MI | 94.7 |
| 83 | Norfolk, VA | 54.2 | 217 | San Leandro, CA** | 29.7 | 147 | Warwick, RI | 42.8 |
| 105 | Norman, OK** | 47.9 | 288 | San Marcos, CA** | 21.7 | 61 | Washington, DC | 60.8 |
| 83 | North Charleston, SC | 54.2 | 226 | San Mateo, CA** | 28.9 | 440 | Waterbury, CT** | 1.8 |
| 168 | North Las Vegas, NV** | 37.7 | 356 | Sandy Springs, GA** | 13.8 | 189 | Waukegan, IL** | 34.9 |
| 345 | Norwalk, CA** | 15.0 | 214 | Sandy, UT | 30.0 | 439 | West Covina, CA** | 1.9 |
| 333 | Norwalk, CT | 16.0 | 342 | Santa Ana, CA** | 15.3 | 228 | West Palm Beach, FL | 28.3 |
| 130 | Oakland, CA** | 44.6 | 184 | Santa Barbara, CA** | 35.6 | 40 | West Valley, UT | 76.5 |
| 262 | Oceanside, CA** | 23.8 | 380 | Santa Clara, CA** | 10.8 | 32 | Westland, MI | 79.9 |
| 92 | Odessa, TX** | 51.7 | 394 | Santa Clarita, CA** | 9.3 | 352 | Westminster, CA** | 14.1 |
| 403 | O'Fallon, MO | 8.5 | 197 | Santa Maria, CA** | 33.3 | 267 | Westminster, CO | 23.6 |
| 15 | Ogden, UT | 92.8 | 222 | Santa Monica, CA** | 29.2 | 303 | Whittier, CA** | 19.7 |
| 44 | Oklahoma City, OK** | 74.4 | 256 | Santa Rosa, CA** | 24.5 | 234 | Wichita Falls, TX** | 27.7 |
| 231 | Olathe, KS** | 28.2 | 292 | Savannah, GA** | 20.8 | 57 | Wichita, KS | 63.1 |
| 139 | Omaha, NE** | 43.3 | 329 | Scottsdale, AZ** | 16.4 | 187 | Wilmington, NC** | 35.1 |
| 313 | Ontario, CA** | 18.4 | 262 | Scranton, PA | 23.8 | 194 | Winston-Salem, NC** | 33.9 |
| 419 | Orange, CA** | 5.7 | 262 | Seattle, WA | 23.8 | 437 | Woodbridge Twnshp, NJ** | 3.0 |
| 349 | Orem, UT** | 14.2 | 155 | Shreveport, LA** | 41.5 | 370 | Worcester, MA | 12.0 |
| 98 | Orlando, FL | 49.8 | 413 | Simi Valley, CA** | 7.1 | 162 | Yakima, WA | 39.5 |
| 316 | Overland Park, KS** | 18.3 | 81 | Sioux City, IA | 55.6 | 365 | Yonkers, NY** | 12.6 |
| 426 | Oxnard, CA** | 4.9 | 21 | Sioux Falls, SD | 85.3 | 105 | Yuma, AZ | 47.9 |
| 301 | Palm Bay, FL | 20.1 | 272 | Somerville, MA | 23.1 | | | |
| 325 | Palmdale, CA** | 17.2 | 16 | South Bend, IN | 92.3 | | | |

Source: CQ Press using reported data from the F.B.I. "Crime in the United States 2013"  *Revised definition: Rape is penetration, no matter how slight, of the vagina or anus with any body part or object, or oral penetration by a sex organ of another person, without the consent of the victim. Attempts or assaults to commit rape are also included; however, statutory rape and incest are excluded. **Figures for these cities are based on the previous (legacy) definition of rape. See note on page vii. ***Not available.

# 54. Rape Rate in 2013 (continued)
## National Rate = 25.2 Rapes per 100,000 Population*

| RANK | CITY | RATE | RANK | CITY | RATE | RANK | CITY | RATE |
|------|------|------|------|------|------|------|------|------|
| 1 | Springfield, MO | 172.3 | 74 | Killeen, TX** | 57.1 | 149 | Fayetteville, AR | 42.4 |
| 2 | Pueblo, CO | 152.7 | 76 | Reading, PA | 56.7 | 149 | Hartford, CT** | 42.4 |
| 3 | Flint, MI | 145.1 | 77 | Kansas City, KS** | 56.2 | 149 | Indio, CA** | 42.4 |
| 4 | Anchorage, AK | 136.2 | 78 | Buffalo, NY** | 56.0 | 152 | Fort Lauderdale, FL | 42.3 |
| 5 | Lansing, MI | 111.5 | 79 | San Angelo, TX | 55.9 | 152 | Phoenix, AZ** | 42.3 |
| 6 | Amarillo, TX | 108.9 | 80 | Bridgeport, CT** | 55.8 | 154 | Brooklyn Park, MN | 42.1 |
| 7 | Salt Lake City, UT | 107.2 | 81 | Sioux City, IA | 55.6 | 155 | Shreveport, LA** | 41.5 |
| 8 | Cleveland, OH | 107.1 | 82 | Lawrence, KS | 55.5 | 156 | Bloomington, IN** | 41.3 |
| 9 | New Bedford, MA | 105.1 | 83 | Norfolk, VA | 54.2 | 157 | Ann Arbor, MI | 41.1 |
| 10 | St. Louis, MO | 104.5 | 83 | North Charleston, SC | 54.2 | 157 | Tucson, AZ** | 41.1 |
| 11 | Minneapolis, MN | 97.2 | 83 | Providence, RI | 54.2 | 159 | Costa Mesa, CA** | 40.9 |
| 12 | Rockford, IL | 96.5 | 86 | Redding, CA** | 53.8 | 160 | Meridian, ID | 40.2 |
| 13 | Warren, MI | 94.7 | 87 | Allentown, PA | 53.7 | 161 | Everett, WA** | 40.0 |
| 14 | Tulsa, OK** | 94.6 | 88 | Jacksonville, FL | 53.4 | 162 | Bryan, TX** | 39.5 |
| 15 | Ogden, UT | 92.8 | 89 | Thornton, CO | 53.3 | 162 | Yakima, WA | 39.5 |
| 16 | South Bend, IN | 92.3 | 90 | Lincoln, NE** | 53.1 | 164 | Broken Arrow, OK** | 38.9 |
| 17 | Brockton, MA | 92.1 | 91 | Syracuse, NY** | 52.1 | 165 | Spokane Valley, WA** | 38.5 |
| 18 | Fort Smith, AR | 90.0 | 92 | Odessa, TX** | 51.7 | 166 | Portland, OR** | 38.4 |
| 19 | Detroit, MI | 88.3 | 93 | Lakeland, FL | 51.6 | 167 | Fort Collins, CO | 38.0 |
| 20 | Davenport, IA | 86.4 | 94 | St. George, UT | 51.0 | 168 | North Las Vegas, NV** | 37.7 |
| 21 | Sioux Falls, SD | 85.3 | 95 | Elgin, IL** | 50.7 | 169 | Quincy, MA | 37.4 |
| 22 | Longmont, CO | 85.0 | 96 | Macon, GA** | 50.5 | 170 | Fort Wayne, IN | 37.3 |
| 23 | Colorado Springs, CO | 84.8 | 97 | Beaumont, TX** | 49.9 | 171 | Hawthorne, CA** | 37.2 |
| 23 | Tallahassee, FL | 84.8 | 98 | Orlando, FL | 49.8 | 172 | Chattanooga, TN | 37.1 |
| 25 | Birmingham, AL | 84.0 | 99 | Nampa, ID | 49.6 | 173 | Boulder, CO | 37.0 |
| 26 | Manchester, NH | 82.4 | 100 | Green Bay, WI | 49.5 | 173 | Lubbock, TX** | 37.0 |
| 27 | Philadelphia, PA | 82.3 | 101 | Gainesville, FL | 49.0 | 175 | Nashua, NH | 36.8 |
| 28 | Fall River, MA | 81.8 | 102 | Portsmouth, VA | 48.4 | 175 | Tempe, AZ** | 36.8 |
| 29 | Lawton, OK** | 81.2 | 103 | Medford, OR | 48.1 | 177 | Edinburg, TX** | 36.5 |
| 30 | Kansas City, MO | 81.0 | 104 | Longview, TX | 48.0 | 177 | Lowell, MA | 36.5 |
| 31 | Akron, OH | 80.6 | 105 | Baltimore, MD** | 47.9 | 179 | Billings, MT | 36.2 |
| 32 | Westland, MI | 79.9 | 105 | Norman, OK** | 47.9 | 180 | Bethlehem, PA | 35.9 |
| 33 | Denver, CO | 79.2 | 105 | Yuma, AZ | 47.9 | 180 | Cranston, RI | 35.9 |
| 33 | Spokane, WA** | 79.2 | 108 | Lewisville, TX | 47.7 | 182 | Cedar Rapids, IA | 35.8 |
| 35 | Melbourne, FL | 78.9 | 109 | San Antonio, TX** | 47.4 | 182 | Deerfield Beach, FL | 35.8 |
| 35 | St. Joseph, MO | 78.9 | 110 | Gresham, OR** | 47.3 | 184 | Santa Barbara, CA** | 35.6 |
| 37 | Albuquerque, NM** | 78.7 | 111 | Huntsville, AL | 47.1 | 185 | McKinney, TX | 35.4 |
| 38 | Indianapolis, IN | 77.2 | 112 | Champaign, IL** | 47.0 | 186 | Modesto, CA** | 35.3 |
| 39 | Greeley, CO | 77.0 | 112 | Las Vegas, NV** | 47.0 | 187 | Mobile, AL | 35.1 |
| 40 | West Valley, UT | 76.5 | 114 | Corpus Christi, TX** | 46.7 | 187 | Wilmington, NC** | 35.1 |
| 41 | Knoxville, TN | 75.9 | 114 | Murfreesboro, TN | 46.7 | 189 | Waukegan, IL** | 34.9 |
| 42 | Dayton, OH | 75.8 | 114 | New Orleans, LA** | 46.7 | 190 | Pearland, TX | 34.6 |
| 43 | Denton, TX | 75.5 | 114 | Tuscaloosa, AL | 46.7 | 191 | San Bernardino, CA** | 34.5 |
| 44 | Oklahoma City, OK** | 74.4 | 118 | Hammond, IN** | 46.6 | 192 | College Station, TX** | 34.4 |
| 45 | St. Paul, MN | 74.0 | 118 | Kent, WA | 46.6 | 192 | Dearborn, MI | 34.4 |
| 46 | Lakewood, CO | 73.1 | 120 | Chico, CA** | 46.5 | 194 | Pasadena, TX** | 33.9 |
| 47 | Bloomington, IL** | 73.0 | 121 | Federal Way, WA | 46.4 | 194 | Winston-Salem, NC** | 33.9 |
| 48 | Tacoma, WA | 70.9 | 121 | Sparks, NV** | 46.4 | 196 | Brownsville, TX** | 33.6 |
| 49 | Provo, UT | 70.1 | 123 | Lynchburg, VA | 46.3 | 197 | Santa Maria, CA** | 33.3 |
| 50 | Nashville, TN | 68.7 | 124 | Clearwater, FL | 45.9 | 198 | Joliet, IL** | 33.0 |
| 51 | Cincinnati, OH | 67.1 | 125 | Rochester, MN | 45.6 | 198 | Napa, CA** | 33.0 |
| 52 | Milwaukee, WI | 66.7 | 125 | Toledo, OH | 45.6 | 200 | Redwood City, CA** | 32.6 |
| 53 | Memphis, TN | 66.4 | 127 | Waco, TX** | 45.5 | 200 | Richmond, CA** | 32.6 |
| 54 | Fort Worth, TX | 66.3 | 128 | Evansville, IN** | 44.9 | 202 | Baton Rouge, LA** | 32.1 |
| 55 | Aurora, CO | 65.2 | 128 | Roanoke, VA | 44.9 | 202 | Fayetteville, NC** | 32.1 |
| 56 | Fargo, ND | 63.9 | 130 | Oakland, CA** | 44.6 | 204 | Madison, WI | 31.3 |
| 57 | Wichita, KS | 63.1 | 131 | Mesa, AZ** | 44.5 | 205 | Virginia Beach, VA | 31.1 |
| 58 | St. Petersburg, FL | 62.7 | 132 | Kennewick, WA | 44.4 | 206 | Abilene, TX** | 31.0 |
| 59 | Jackson, MS** | 62.5 | 132 | Vancouver, WA | 44.4 | 207 | Newport News, VA | 30.9 |
| 60 | Pompano Beach, FL | 61.6 | 134 | Columbia, SC | 43.9 | 208 | Athens-Clarke, GA** | 30.8 |
| 61 | Washington, DC | 60.8 | 135 | Rochester, NY** | 43.7 | 209 | Albany, NY** | 30.6 |
| 62 | Springfield, IL** | 60.5 | 136 | Des Moines, IA | 43.4 | 210 | Plano, TX | 30.5 |
| 63 | Duluth, MN | 60.3 | 136 | Independence, MO | 43.4 | 211 | Stockton, CA** | 30.4 |
| 63 | Largo, FL | 60.3 | 136 | Lexington, KY | 43.4 | 212 | Laredo, TX** | 30.3 |
| 63 | Little Rock, AR | 60.3 | 139 | Boston, MA** | 43.3 | 213 | Hillsboro, OR** | 30.1 |
| 66 | Gary, IN** | 59.6 | 139 | Dallas, TX** | 43.3 | 214 | Danbury, CT** | 30.0 |
| 67 | Erie, PA | 59.5 | 139 | Omaha, NE** | 43.3 | 214 | Sandy, UT | 30.0 |
| 68 | Columbia, MO | 58.5 | 139 | Suffolk, VA | 43.3 | 216 | Arvada, CO | 29.8 |
| 69 | Miami Beach, FL | 58.0 | 143 | Hollywood, FL | 43.0 | 217 | Salem, OR | 29.7 |
| 69 | New Haven, CT | 58.0 | 143 | Tyler, TX | 43.0 | 217 | San Leandro, CA** | 29.7 |
| 71 | Springfield, MA | 57.9 | 145 | Eugene, OR | 42.9 | 219 | Victorville, CA** | 29.6 |
| 72 | Clarksville, TN | 57.7 | 145 | Grand Rapids, MI | 42.9 | 220 | Grand Prairie, TX** | 29.4 |
| 73 | Boise, ID | 57.4 | 147 | Warwick, RI | 42.8 | 220 | Hemet, CA** | 29.4 |
| 74 | Clinton Twnshp, MI | 57.1 | 148 | Lynn, MA | 42.5 | 222 | Reno, NV** | 29.2 |

| RANK | CITY | RATE |
|---|---|---|
| 222 | Santa Monica, CA** | 29.2 |
| 224 | Elizabeth, NJ** | 29.1 |
| 225 | Vista, CA** | 29.0 |
| 226 | San Mateo, CA** | 28.9 |
| 227 | El Cajon, CA** | 28.4 |
| 228 | Houston, TX** | 28.3 |
| 228 | Miramar, FL | 28.3 |
| 228 | West Palm Beach, FL | 28.3 |
| 231 | Olathe, KS** | 28.2 |
| 232 | High Point, NC** | 28.0 |
| 233 | Renton, WA | 27.9 |
| 234 | Arlington, TX** | 27.7 |
| 234 | Wichita Falls, TX** | 27.7 |
| 236 | Charlotte, NC** | 27.5 |
| 237 | San Jose, CA** | 27.2 |
| 238 | Albany, GA** | 27.1 |
| 239 | Davie, FL | 26.9 |
| 239 | Racine, WI** | 26.9 |
| 241 | Compton, CA** | 26.6 |
| 242 | Las Cruces, NM** | 26.5 |
| 243 | Aurora, IL** | 26.4 |
| 244 | Bend, OR | 26.3 |
| 245 | Escondido, CA** | 26.2 |
| 246 | Inglewood, CA** | 26.0 |
| 247 | El Paso, TX** | 25.9 |
| 247 | Kenosha, WI** | 25.9 |
| 249 | Topeka, KS** | 25.8 |
| 250 | Pittsburgh, PA | 25.4 |
| 250 | Vallejo, CA** | 25.4 |
| 252 | Austin, TX** | 25.3 |
| 253 | Greensboro, NC** | 25.1 |
| 254 | Lancaster, CA** | 25.0 |
| 255 | Riverside, CA** | 24.7 |
| 256 | Santa Rosa, CA** | 24.5 |
| 257 | Lawrence, MA** | 24.4 |
| 257 | Sunrise, FL | 24.4 |
| 259 | Visalia, CA** | 24.3 |
| 260 | Upper Darby Twnshp, PA | 24.2 |
| 261 | Centennial, CO | 23.9 |
| 262 | Louisville, KY** | 23.8 |
| 262 | Oceanside, CA** | 23.8 |
| 262 | Scranton, PA | 23.8 |
| 262 | Seattle, WA | 23.8 |
| 266 | Anaheim, CA** | 23.7 |
| 267 | Westminster, CO | 23.6 |
| 268 | Antioch, CA** | 23.5 |
| 269 | Merced, CA** | 23.4 |
| 269 | San Diego, CA** | 23.4 |
| 271 | Atlanta, GA** | 23.3 |
| 272 | Clovis, CA** | 23.1 |
| 272 | Salinas, CA** | 23.1 |
| 272 | Somerville, MA | 23.1 |
| 275 | Sterling Heights, MI | 23.0 |
| 276 | Miami, FL | 22.9 |
| 277 | Charleston, SC | 22.8 |
| 278 | Greenville, NC** | 22.7 |
| 279 | Garland, TX** | 22.5 |
| 280 | Berkeley, CA** | 22.4 |
| 280 | Cambridge, MA | 22.4 |
| 282 | Citrus Heights, CA** | 22.3 |
| 283 | Stamford, CT | 22.2 |
| 283 | Tampa, FL | 22.2 |
| 285 | Round Rock, TX** | 22.1 |
| 286 | Hayward, CA** | 21.9 |
| 286 | Long Beach, CA** | 21.9 |
| 288 | San Marcos, CA** | 21.7 |
| 289 | Beaverton, OR** | 21.4 |
| 290 | Chandler, AZ** | 20.9 |
| 290 | Glendale, AZ** | 20.9 |
| 292 | Carlsbad, CA** | 20.8 |
| 292 | Chesapeake, VA | 20.8 |
| 292 | Fullerton, CA** | 20.8 |
| 292 | Savannah, GA** | 20.8 |
| 296 | Peoria, IL** | 20.7 |
| 297 | Troy, MI | 20.6 |
| 298 | Pomona, CA** | 20.5 |
| 299 | Canton Twnshp, MI | 20.2 |
| 299 | Richmond, VA | 20.2 |
| 301 | Palm Bay, FL | 20.1 |
| 302 | Sacramento, CA** | 19.9 |
| 303 | Los Angeles, CA** | 19.7 |
| 303 | Whittier, CA** | 19.7 |
| 305 | Bloomington, MN | 19.5 |
| 306 | Lee's Summit, MO | 19.4 |
| 306 | Ventura, CA** | 19.4 |
| 308 | San Francisco, CA** | 19.3 |
| 309 | Plantation, FL | 19.1 |
| 310 | Coral Springs, FL | 19.0 |
| 311 | Livonia, MI | 18.9 |
| 312 | Rialto, CA** | 18.5 |
| 313 | Hesperia, CA** | 18.4 |
| 313 | Ontario, CA** | 18.4 |
| 313 | Raleigh, NC** | 18.4 |
| 316 | Overland Park, KS** | 18.3 |
| 317 | Midland, TX** | 18.0 |
| 317 | Pasadena, CA** | 18.0 |
| 319 | Columbus, GA** | 17.9 |
| 319 | Paterson, NJ** | 17.9 |
| 321 | Roswell, GA** | 17.8 |
| 322 | Hialeah, FL | 17.5 |
| 323 | Edmond, OK** | 17.4 |
| 324 | Farmington Hills, MI | 17.3 |
| 325 | Palmdale, CA** | 17.2 |
| 326 | Henderson, NV** | 16.8 |
| 326 | Mountain View, CA** | 16.8 |
| 328 | Cicero, IL** | 16.6 |
| 329 | Scottsdale, AZ** | 16.4 |
| 330 | Fontana, CA** | 16.2 |
| 330 | Newark, NJ** | 16.2 |
| 332 | Carson, CA** | 16.1 |
| 333 | Norwalk, CT | 16.0 |
| 334 | Frisco, TX | 15.9 |
| 335 | Huntington Beach, CA** | 15.8 |
| 336 | Bellevue, WA** | 15.7 |
| 336 | Buena Park, CA** | 15.7 |
| 336 | South Gate, CA** | 15.7 |
| 339 | League City, TX** | 15.6 |
| 340 | Moreno Valley, CA** | 15.4 |
| 340 | Trenton, NJ** | 15.4 |
| 342 | Hampton, VA | 15.3 |
| 342 | Santa Ana, CA** | 15.3 |
| 344 | Lake Forest, CA** | 15.1 |
| 345 | Norwalk, CA** | 15.0 |
| 346 | Vacaville, CA** | 14.8 |
| 347 | Daly City, CA** | 14.3 |
| 347 | Richardson, TX** | 14.3 |
| 349 | Allen, TX | 14.2 |
| 349 | Livermore, CA** | 14.2 |
| 349 | Orem, UT** | 14.2 |
| 352 | Alexandria, VA | 14.1 |
| 352 | Clifton, NJ** | 14.1 |
| 352 | Westminster, CA** | 14.1 |
| 355 | Cheektowaga, NY** | 14.0 |
| 356 | Lafayette, LA** | 13.8 |
| 356 | Sandy Springs, GA** | 13.8 |
| 358 | Jersey City, NJ** | 13.6 |
| 358 | Lakewood, CA** | 13.6 |
| 360 | Miami Gardens, FL | 13.4 |
| 361 | Evanston, IL** | 13.2 |
| 361 | New York, NY** | 13.2 |
| 363 | Alameda, CA** | 13.1 |
| 364 | Newton, MA | 12.7 |
| 365 | Yonkers, NY** | 12.6 |
| 366 | Burbank, CA** | 12.4 |
| 366 | Port St. Lucie, FL | 12.4 |
| 368 | Jurupa Valley, CA** | 12.2 |
| 369 | El Monte, CA** | 12.1 |
| 370 | Decatur, IL** | 12.0 |
| 370 | Fairfield, CA** | 12.0 |
| 370 | Worcester, MA | 12.0 |
| 373 | Bakersfield, CA** | 11.9 |
| 373 | Upland, CA** | 11.9 |
| 375 | Bellflower, CA** | 11.6 |
| 376 | Chula Vista, CA** | 11.4 |
| 376 | Surprise, AZ** | 11.4 |
| 378 | Fremont, CA** | 11.1 |
| 379 | Concord, NC** | 10.9 |
| 380 | Santa Clara, CA** | 10.8 |
| 380 | Sunnyvale, CA** | 10.8 |
| 380 | Torrance, CA** | 10.8 |
| 383 | Hoover, AL | 10.7 |
| 384 | Alhambra, CA** | 10.6 |
| 384 | Downey, CA** | 10.6 |
| 386 | Irving, TX** | 10.5 |
| 387 | Fresno, CA** | 10.4 |
| 388 | Roseville, CA** | 10.3 |
| 388 | Temecula, CA** | 10.3 |
| 390 | Clarkstown, NY** | 9.9 |
| 390 | Peoria, AZ** | 9.9 |
| 392 | Mesquite, TX** | 9.7 |
| 393 | Concord, CA** | 9.6 |
| 394 | Greece, NY** | 9.3 |
| 394 | Murrieta, CA** | 9.3 |
| 394 | Santa Clarita, CA** | 9.3 |
| 397 | Arlington Heights, IL** | 9.2 |
| 398 | Garden Grove, CA** | 9.1 |
| 399 | Boca Raton, FL | 9.0 |
| 399 | Hamilton Twnshp, NJ** | 9.0 |
| 401 | Chino, CA** | 8.7 |
| 401 | Corona, CA** | 8.7 |
| 403 | O'Fallon, MO | 8.5 |
| 404 | Tracy, CA** | 8.2 |
| 405 | Rancho Cucamon., CA** | 8.1 |
| 406 | Newport Beach, CA** | 8.0 |
| 407 | Edison Twnshp, NJ** | 7.9 |
| 408 | Baldwin Park, CA** | 7.8 |
| 409 | Tustin, CA** | 7.6 |
| 410 | Cary, NC** | 7.4 |
| 411 | Menifee, CA** | 7.3 |
| 412 | Sugar Land, TX** | 7.2 |
| 413 | Simi Valley, CA** | 7.1 |
| 414 | Pembroke Pines, FL | 6.8 |
| 415 | Chino Hills, CA** | 6.5 |
| 416 | New Rochelle, NY** | 6.3 |
| 417 | Gilbert, AZ | 6.2 |
| 418 | Amherst, NY** | 5.9 |
| 419 | Orange, CA** | 5.7 |
| 419 | Ramapo, NY** | 5.7 |
| 421 | Lakewood Twnshp, NJ** | 5.4 |
| 421 | Thousand Oaks, CA** | 5.4 |
| 421 | Toms River Twnshp, NJ** | 5.4 |
| 424 | Brick Twnshp, NJ** | 5.3 |
| 425 | Irvine, CA** | 5.1 |
| 426 | Mission, TX** | 4.9 |
| 426 | Naperville, IL** | 4.9 |
| 426 | Oxnard, CA** | 4.9 |
| 429 | Johns Creek, GA** | 4.8 |
| 430 | Carmel, IN** | 4.7 |
| 430 | Carrollton, TX** | 4.7 |
| 432 | McAllen, TX** | 4.4 |
| 433 | Cape Coral, FL | 4.3 |
| 434 | Mission Viejo, CA** | 4.2 |
| 435 | Glendale, CA** | 4.1 |
| 436 | Elk Grove, CA** | 3.7 |
| 437 | Woodbridge Twnshp, NJ** | 3.0 |
| 438 | Fishers, IN** | 2.4 |
| 439 | West Covina, CA** | 1.9 |
| 440 | Waterbury, CT** | 1.8 |
| 441 | Colonie, NY** | 0.0 |
| NA | Chicago, IL*** | NA |

Source: CQ Press using reported data from the F.B.I. "Crime in the United States 2013" *Revised definition: Rape is penetration, no matter how slight, of the vagina or anus with any body part or object, or oral penetration by a sex organ of another person, without the consent of the victim. Attempts or assaults to commit rape are also included; however, statutory rape and incest are excluded. **Figures for these cities are based on the previous (legacy) definition of rape. See note on page vii. ***Not available.

# 55. Percent Change in Rape Rate: 2012 to 2013
## National Percent Change = 7.0% Decrease*

| RANK | CITY | % CHANGE | RANK | CITY | % CHANGE | RANK | CITY | % CHANGE |
|---|---|---|---|---|---|---|---|---|
| 263 | Abilene, TX** | (2.2) | 369 | Chino, CA** | (23.0) | 298 | Fullerton, CA** | (7.1) |
| 273 | Akron, OH | (4.3) | 325 | Chula Vista, CA** | (13.6) | 340 | Gainesville, FL | (16.0) |
| 206 | Alameda, CA** | 10.1 | 365 | Cicero, IL** | (22.4) | 242 | Garden Grove, CA** | 0.0 |
| 361 | Albany, GA** | (21.2) | 220 | Cincinnati, OH | 5.7 | 193 | Garland, TX** | 12.5 |
| 388 | Albany, NY** | (30.1) | 96 | Citrus Heights, CA** | 45.8 | 331 | Gary, IN** | (14.4) |
| 75 | Albuquerque, NM** | 56.8 | 28 | Clarkstown, NY** | 98.0 | 389 | Gilbert, AZ | (30.3) |
| 19 | Alexandria, VA | 127.4 | 51 | Clarksville, TN | 72.2 | 309 | Glendale, AZ** | (9.9) |
| 4 | Alhambra, CA** | 341.7 | 335 | Clearwater, FL | (15.0) | 124 | Glendale, CA** | 32.3 |
| 163 | Allentown, PA | 18.5 | 170 | Cleveland, OH | 16.2 | 214 | Grand Prairie, TX** | 6.9 |
| 178 | Allen, TX | 14.5 | 305 | Clifton, NJ** | (8.4) | 46 | Grand Rapids, MI | 77.3 |
| 34 | Amarillo, TX | 94.5 | 97 | Clinton Twnshp, MI | 45.7 | 418 | Greece, NY** | (50.0) |
| 262 | Amherst, NY** | (1.7) | 397 | Clovis, CA** | (33.6) | 40 | Greeley, CO | 85.5 |
| 251 | Anaheim, CA** | (0.4) | 264 | College Station, TX** | (2.3) | 155 | Green Bay, WI | 19.3 |
| 119 | Anchorage, AK | 34.5 | 242 | Colonie, NY** | 0.0 | 261 | Greensboro, NC** | (1.2) |
| 118 | Ann Arbor, MI | 35.2 | 230 | Colorado Springs, CO | 2.4 | 330 | Greenville, NC** | (14.3) |
| 333 | Antioch, CA** | (14.9) | 73 | Columbia, MO | 57.7 | 77 | Gresham, OR** | 55.1 |
| 259 | Arlington Heights, IL** | (1.1) | NA | Columbia, SC*** | NA | 356 | Hamilton Twnshp, NJ** | (19.6) |
| 364 | Arlington, TX** | (22.2) | 187 | Columbus, GA** | 13.3 | 24 | Hammond, IN** | 109.9 |
| 92 | Arvada, CO | 47.5 | 360 | Compton, CA** | (21.1) | 125 | Hampton, VA | 31.9 |
| 376 | Athens-Clarke, GA** | (24.7) | 405 | Concord, CA** | (36.8) | 31 | Hartford, CT** | 96.3 |
| 310 | Atlanta, GA** | (10.0) | NA | Concord, NC*** | NA | 145 | Hawthorne, CA** | 22.8 |
| 145 | Aurora, CO | 22.8 | 14 | Coral Springs, FL | 137.5 | 387 | Hayward, CA** | (29.8) |
| 351 | Aurora, IL** | (18.8) | 355 | Corona, CA** | (19.4) | 186 | Hemet, CA** | 13.5 |
| 240 | Austin, TX** | 0.8 | 357 | Corpus Christi, TX** | (20.7) | 382 | Henderson, NV** | (27.6) |
| 378 | Bakersfield, CA** | (25.6) | 98 | Costa Mesa, CA** | 44.0 | 242 | Hesperia, CA** | 0.0 |
| 152 | Baldwin Park, CA** | 20.0 | 45 | Cranston, RI | 80.4 | 233 | Hialeah, FL | 1.7 |
| 281 | Baltimore, MD** | (5.0) | 201 | Dallas, TX** | 10.7 | 74 | High Point, NC** | 57.3 |
| 169 | Baton Rouge, LA** | 16.3 | 64 | Daly City, CA** | 64.4 | 344 | Hillsboro, OR** | (16.6) |
| 359 | Beaumont, TX** | (21.0) | 217 | Danbury, CT** | 6.8 | 65 | Hollywood, FL | 64.1 |
| 290 | Beaverton, OR** | (6.1) | 22 | Davenport, IA | 118.7 | 393 | Hoover, AL | (32.3) |
| 370 | Bellevue, WA** | (23.8) | 199 | Davie, FL | 11.2 | 300 | Houston, TX** | (7.2) |
| 347 | Bellflower, CA** | (17.7) | 272 | Dayton, OH | (3.8) | 254 | Huntington Beach, CA** | (0.6) |
| NA | Bend, OR*** | NA | 107 | Dearborn, MI | 39.3 | 151 | Huntsville, AL | 20.2 |
| 399 | Berkeley, CA** | (33.9) | 424 | Decatur, IL** | (64.9) | 160 | Independence, MO | 18.6 |
| 102 | Bethlehem, PA | 42.5 | 69 | Deerfield Beach, FL | 62.7 | 91 | Indianapolis, IN | 48.5 |
| 235 | Billings, MT | 1.4 | 224 | Denton, TX | 4.4 | 86 | Indio, CA** | 51.4 |
| 165 | Birmingham, AL | 17.8 | 123 | Denver, CO | 32.4 | 211 | Inglewood, CA** | 7.4 |
| 121 | Bloomington, IL** | 33.9 | 310 | Des Moines, IA | (10.0) | 110 | Irvine, CA** | 37.8 |
| 36 | Bloomington, IN** | 87.7 | 104 | Detroit, MI | 41.5 | 322 | Irving, TX** | (13.2) |
| NA | Bloomington, MN*** | NA | 409 | Downey, CA** | (39.8) | 127 | Jacksonville, FL | 31.5 |
| 403 | Boca Raton, FL | (35.3) | NA | Duluth, MN*** | NA | 349 | Jackson, MS** | (18.5) |
| 70 | Boise, ID | 62.1 | 237 | Edinburg, TX** | 1.1 | 371 | Jersey City, NJ** | (24.0) |
| 208 | Boston, MA** | 9.6 | 316 | Edison Twnshp, NJ** | (11.2) | 129 | Johns Creek, GA** | 29.7 |
| 173 | Boulder, CO | 16.0 | 149 | Edmond, OK** | 20.8 | 67 | Joliet, IL** | 63.4 |
| 394 | Brick Twnshp, NJ** | (32.9) | 150 | El Cajon, CA** | 20.3 | 257 | Jurupa Valley, CA** | (0.8) |
| 428 | Bridgeport, CT** | (79.0) | 242 | El Monte, CA** | 0.0 | 265 | Kansas City, KS** | (2.6) |
| 42 | Brockton, MA | 82.7 | 279 | El Paso, TX** | (4.8) | 82 | Kansas City, MO | 52.8 |
| 160 | Broken Arrow, OK** | 18.6 | 346 | Elgin, IL** | (17.4) | 226 | Kennewick, WA | 3.5 |
| NA | Brooklyn Park, MN*** | NA | 256 | Elizabeth, NJ** | (0.7) | 384 | Kenosha, WI** | (28.1) |
| 72 | Brownsville, TX** | 60.0 | 426 | Elk Grove, CA** | (71.1) | 343 | Kent, WA | (16.3) |
| 242 | Bryan, TX** | 0.0 | 284 | Erie, PA | (5.3) | 303 | Killeen, TX** | (8.1) |
| 254 | Buena Park, CA** | (0.6) | 234 | Escondido, CA** | 1.6 | 170 | Knoxville, TN | 16.2 |
| 218 | Buffalo, NY** | 6.5 | 288 | Eugene, OR | (5.9) | 81 | Lafayette, LA** | 53.3 |
| 416 | Burbank, CA** | (45.6) | 10 | Evanston, IL** | 149.1 | 89 | Lake Forest, CA** | 49.5 |
| 153 | Cambridge, MA | 19.8 | 284 | Evansville, IN** | (5.3) | 76 | Lakeland, FL | 56.4 |
| NA | Canton Twnshp, MI*** | NA | 306 | Everett, WA** | (8.5) | 3 | Lakewood Twnshp, NJ** | 390.9 |
| 422 | Cape Coral, FL | (57.0) | 423 | Fairfield, CA** | (57.1) | 335 | Lakewood, CA** | (15.0) |
| 327 | Carlsbad, CA** | (13.7) | 105 | Fall River, MA | 41.3 | 183 | Lakewood, CO | 13.9 |
| 33 | Carmel, IN** | 95.8 | 232 | Fargo, ND | 1.8 | 380 | Lancaster, CA** | (26.3) |
| 341 | Carrollton, TX** | (16.1) | 302 | Farmington Hills, MI | (7.5) | 108 | Lansing, MI | 39.0 |
| 212 | Carson, CA** | 7.3 | 414 | Fayetteville, AR | (44.9) | 304 | Laredo, TX** | (8.2) |
| 282 | Cary, NC** | (5.1) | 286 | Fayetteville, NC** | (5.6) | 202 | Largo, FL | 10.4 |
| 214 | Cedar Rapids, IA | 6.9 | 258 | Federal Way, WA | (0.9) | 420 | Las Cruces, NM** | (52.8) |
| 407 | Centennial, CO | (37.9) | 41 | Fishers, IN** | 84.6 | 168 | Las Vegas, NV** | 16.6 |
| 377 | Champaign, IL** | (25.0) | 116 | Flint, MI | 36.5 | 279 | Lawrence, KS | (4.8) |
| 358 | Chandler, AZ** | (20.8) | 221 | Fontana, CA** | 5.2 | 374 | Lawrence, MA** | (24.2) |
| 90 | Charleston, SC | 49.0 | 133 | Fort Collins, CO | 28.4 | 23 | Lawton, OK** | 110.9 |
| 251 | Charlotte, NC** | (0.4) | 87 | Fort Lauderdale, FL | 50.5 | 341 | League City, TX** | (16.1) |
| NA | Chattanooga, TN*** | NA | 181 | Fort Smith, AR | 14.1 | 115 | Lee's Summit, MO | 36.6 |
| 410 | Cheektowaga, NY** | (41.7) | 228 | Fort Wayne, IN | 3.0 | NA | Lewisville, TX*** | NA |
| 126 | Chesapeake, VA | 31.6 | 128 | Fort Worth, TX | 30.5 | 131 | Lexington, KY | 28.8 |
| NA | Chicago, IL*** | NA | 49 | Fremont, CA** | 73.4 | 368 | Lincoln, NE** | (22.9) |
| 317 | Chico, CA** | (11.9) | 266 | Fresno, CA** | (2.8) | 327 | Little Rock, AR | (13.7) |
| 9 | Chino Hills, CA** | 150.0 | 11 | Frisco, TX | 144.6 | 363 | Livermore, CA** | (21.5) |

| RANK | CITY | % CHANGE |
|---|---|---|
| 275 | Livonia, MI | (4.5) |
| 312 | Long Beach, CA** | (10.6) |
| 2 | Longmont, CO | 585.5 |
| 103 | Longview, TX | 41.6 |
| 353 | Los Angeles, CA** | (18.9) |
| 324 | Louisville, KY** | (13.5) |
| 213 | Lowell, MA | 7.0 |
| 338 | Lubbock, TX** | (15.5) |
| 221 | Lynchburg, VA | 5.2 |
| 350 | Lynn, MA | (18.7) |
| 179 | Macon, GA** | 14.3 |
| 401 | Madison, WI | (34.8) |
| 136 | Manchester, NH | 26.0 |
| 27 | McAllen, TX** | 100.0 |
| 308 | McKinney, TX | (9.5) |
| 293 | Medford, OR | (6.2) |
| 135 | Melbourne, FL | 26.8 |
| 225 | Memphis, TN | 3.9 |
| 94 | Menifee, CA** | 46.0 |
| 375 | Merced, CA** | (24.3) |
| 12 | Meridian, ID | 139.3 |
| 167 | Mesa, AZ** | 16.8 |
| 242 | Mesquite, TX** | 0.0 |
| 137 | Miami Beach, FL | 25.8 |
| 297 | Miami Gardens, FL | (6.9) |
| 95 | Miami, FL | 45.9 |
| 259 | Midland, TX** | (1.1) |
| 48 | Milwaukee, WI | 73.7 |
| 288 | Minneapolis, MN | (5.9) |
| 175 | Miramar, FL | 15.0 |
| 117 | Mission Viejo, CA** | 35.5 |
| 398 | Mission, TX** | (33.8) |
| 32 | Mobile, AL | 96.1 |
| 147 | Modesto, CA** | 22.6 |
| 144 | Moreno Valley, CA** | 23.2 |
| 8 | Mountain View, CA** | 154.5 |
| 277 | Murfreesboro, TN | (4.7) |
| 142 | Murrieta, CA** | 24.0 |
| 290 | Nampa, ID | (6.1) |
| 82 | Napa, CA** | 52.8 |
| 242 | Naperville, IL** | 0.0 |
| 325 | Nashua, NH | (13.6) |
| 111 | Nashville, TN | 37.1 |
| 38 | New Bedford, MA | 87.0 |
| 111 | New Haven, CT | 37.1 |
| 141 | New Orleans, LA** | 24.5 |
| 62 | New Rochelle, NY** | 65.8 |
| 287 | New York, NY** | (5.7) |
| 348 | Newark, NJ** | (17.8) |
| 404 | Newport Beach, CA** | (36.5) |
| 194 | Newport News, VA | 12.4 |
| 21 | Newton, MA | 119.0 |
| 47 | Norfolk, VA | 77.1 |
| 223 | Norman, OK** | 5.0 |
| 312 | North Charleston, SC | (10.6) |
| 177 | North Las Vegas, NV** | 14.6 |
| 142 | Norwalk, CA** | 24.0 |
| 80 | Norwalk, CT | 53.8 |
| 400 | Oakland, CA** | (34.2) |
| 335 | Oceanside, CA** | (15.0) |
| 140 | Odessa, TX** | 24.6 |
| 111 | O'Fallon, MO | 37.1 |
| 5 | Ogden, UT | 215.6 |
| 183 | Oklahoma City, OK** | 13.9 |
| 277 | Olathe, KS** | (4.7) |
| 268 | Omaha, NE** | (3.1) |
| 329 | Ontario, CA** | (14.0) |
| 242 | Orange, CA** | 0.0 |
| 164 | Orem, UT** | 18.3 |
| 158 | Orlando, FL | 19.1 |
| 354 | Overland Park, KS** | (19.0) |
| 148 | Oxnard, CA** | 22.5 |
| 202 | Palm Bay, FL | 10.4 |
| 383 | Palmdale, CA** | (27.7) |

| RANK | CITY | % CHANGE |
|---|---|---|
| 157 | Pasadena, CA** | 19.2 |
| 239 | Pasadena, TX** | 0.9 |
| 155 | Paterson, NJ** | 19.3 |
| 43 | Pearland, TX | 82.1 |
| 367 | Pembroke Pines, FL | (22.7) |
| 402 | Peoria, AZ** | (34.9) |
| 276 | Peoria, IL** | (4.6) |
| 99 | Philadelphia, PA | 43.9 |
| 191 | Phoenix, AZ** | 13.1 |
| 59 | Pittsburgh, PA | 68.2 |
| 85 | Plano, TX | 51.7 |
| 82 | Plantation, FL | 52.8 |
| 419 | Pomona, CA** | (50.7) |
| 53 | Pompano Beach, FL | 71.6 |
| 421 | Port St. Lucie, FL | (55.6) |
| 253 | Portland, OR** | (0.5) |
| 180 | Portsmouth, VA | 14.2 |
| 176 | Providence, RI | 14.8 |
| 18 | Provo, UT | 127.6 |
| 1 | Pueblo, CO | 691.2 |
| 192 | Quincy, MA | 13.0 |
| 390 | Racine, WI** | (31.4) |
| 391 | Raleigh, NC** | (31.6) |
| 270 | Ramapo, NY** | (3.4) |
| 332 | Rancho Cucamon., CA** | (14.7) |
| 181 | Reading, PA | 14.1 |
| 379 | Redding, CA** | (25.8) |
| 30 | Redwood City, CA** | 96.4 |
| 26 | Reno, NV** | 104.2 |
| 268 | Renton, WA | (3.1) |
| 200 | Rialto, CA** | 10.8 |
| 415 | Richardson, TX** | (45.2) |
| 271 | Richmond, CA** | (3.6) |
| 202 | Richmond, VA | 10.4 |
| 231 | Riverside, CA** | 2.1 |
| 207 | Roanoke, VA | 9.8 |
| NA | Rochester, MN*** | NA |
| 345 | Rochester, NY** | (17.2) |
| 160 | Rockford, IL | 18.6 |
| 339 | Roseville, CA** | (15.6) |
| 16 | Roswell, GA** | 134.2 |
| 381 | Round Rock, TX** | (26.6) |
| 371 | Sacramento, CA** | (24.0) |
| 166 | Salem, OR | 16.9 |
| 322 | Salinas, CA** | (13.2) |
| 58 | Salt Lake City, UT | 69.1 |
| NA | San Angelo, TX*** | NA |
| 158 | San Antonio, TX** | 19.1 |
| 122 | San Bernardino, CA** | 32.7 |
| 227 | San Diego, CA** | 3.1 |
| 93 | San Francisco, CA** | 46.2 |
| 283 | San Jose, CA** | (5.2) |
| 52 | San Leandro, CA** | 71.7 |
| 56 | San Marcos, CA** | 69.5 |
| 20 | San Mateo, CA** | 120.6 |
| 7 | Sandy Springs, GA** | 170.6 |
| 188 | Sandy, UT | 13.2 |
| 301 | Santa Ana, CA** | (7.3) |
| 408 | Santa Barbara, CA** | (39.7) |
| 132 | Santa Clara, CA** | 28.6 |
| 413 | Santa Clarita, CA** | (44.3) |
| 71 | Santa Maria, CA** | 60.9 |
| 174 | Santa Monica, CA** | 15.9 |
| 406 | Santa Rosa, CA** | (37.5) |
| 35 | Savannah, GA | 92.6 |
| 320 | Scottsdale, AZ** | (12.8) |
| 361 | Scranton, PA | (21.2) |
| 139 | Seattle, WA | 25.3 |
| 307 | Shreveport, LA** | (8.8) |
| 130 | Simi Valley, CA** | 29.1 |
| 79 | Sioux City, IA | 54.4 |
| 266 | Sioux Falls, SD | (2.8) |
| 366 | Somerville, MA | (22.5) |
| 55 | South Bend, IN | 70.3 |

| RANK | CITY | % CHANGE |
|---|---|---|
| 241 | South Gate, CA** | 0.6 |
| 120 | Sparks, NV** | 34.1 |
| 188 | Spokane Valley, WA** | 13.2 |
| 25 | Spokane, WA** | 107.3 |
| 296 | Springfield, IL** | (6.8) |
| 17 | Springfield, MA | 129.8 |
| 29 | Springfield, MO | 96.7 |
| 202 | Stamford, CT | 10.4 |
| 38 | Sterling Heights, MI | 87.0 |
| 238 | Stockton, CA** | 1.0 |
| 101 | St. George, UT | 43.3 |
| 6 | St. Joseph, MO | 177.8 |
| 60 | St. Louis, MO | 67.5 |
| 134 | St. Paul, MN | 28.0 |
| 63 | St. Petersburg, FL | 65.4 |
| NA | Suffolk, VA*** | NA |
| 88 | Sugar Land, TX** | 50.0 |
| 198 | Sunnyvale, CA** | 11.3 |
| 196 | Sunrise, FL | 11.9 |
| 50 | Surprise, AZ** | 72.7 |
| 235 | Syracuse, NY** | 1.4 |
| 78 | Tacoma, WA | 54.5 |
| 114 | Tallahassee, FL | 36.8 |
| 44 | Tampa, FL | 80.5 |
| 219 | Temecula, CA** | 6.2 |
| 109 | Tempe, AZ** | 38.9 |
| 188 | Thornton, CO | 13.2 |
| 425 | Thousand Oaks, CA** | (69.7) |
| 373 | Toledo, OH | (24.1) |
| 66 | Toms River Twnshp, NJ** | 63.6 |
| 333 | Topeka, KS** | (14.9) |
| 290 | Torrance, CA** | (6.1) |
| 320 | Tracy, CA** | (12.8) |
| 412 | Trenton, NJ** | (43.0) |
| 37 | Troy, MI | 87.3 |
| 294 | Tucson, AZ** | (6.6) |
| 154 | Tulsa, OK** | 19.4 |
| 170 | Tuscaloosa, AL | 16.2 |
| 417 | Tustin, CA** | (46.5) |
| 274 | Tyler, TX | (4.4) |
| 195 | Upland, CA** | 12.3 |
| 138 | Upper Darby Twnshp, PA | 25.4 |
| 411 | Vacaville, CA** | (42.0) |
| 392 | Vallejo, CA** | (31.9) |
| 229 | Vancouver, WA | 2.5 |
| 318 | Ventura, CA** | (12.2) |
| 318 | Victorville, CA** | (12.2) |
| 13 | Virginia Beach, VA | 139.2 |
| 386 | Visalia, CA** | (29.6) |
| 197 | Vista, CA** | 11.5 |
| 298 | Waco, TX** | (7.1) |
| 106 | Warren, MI | 39.9 |
| 15 | Warwick, RI | 135.2 |
| 68 | Washington, DC | 63.0 |
| 427 | Waterbury, CT** | (71.4) |
| 396 | Waukegan, IL** | (33.5) |
| 429 | West Covina, CA** | (81.4) |
| 294 | West Palm Beach, FL | (6.6) |
| 185 | West Valley, UT | 13.7 |
| 209 | Westland, MI | 9.2 |
| 99 | Westminster, CA** | 43.9 |
| 315 | Westminster, CO | (10.9) |
| 54 | Whittier, CA** | 71.3 |
| 351 | Wichita Falls, TX** | (18.8) |
| 214 | Wichita, KS | 6.9 |
| 61 | Wilmington, NC** | 67.1 |
| 210 | Winston-Salem, NC** | 7.6 |
| 242 | Woodbridge Twnshp, NJ** | 0.0 |
| 395 | Worcester, MA | (33.3) |
| 385 | Yakima, WA | (29.1) |
| 312 | Yonkers, NY** | (10.6) |
| 57 | Yuma, AZ | 69.3 |

Source: CQ Press using reported data from the F.B.I. "Crime in the United States 2013"  *Revised definition: Rape is penetration, no matter how slight, of the vagina or anus with any body part or object, or oral penetration by a sex organ of another person, without the consent of the victim. Attempts or assaults to commit rape are also included; however, statutory rape and incest are excluded. **Figures for these cities are based on the previous (legacy) definition of rape. See note on page vii. ***Not available.

# 55. Percent Change in Rape Rate: 2012 to 2013 (continued)
## National Percent Change = 7.0% Decrease*

| RANK | CITY | % CHANGE | RANK | CITY | % CHANGE | RANK | CITY | % CHANGE |
|------|------|----------|------|------|----------|------|------|----------|
| 1 | Pueblo, CO | 691.2 | 75 | Albuquerque, NM** | 56.8 | 149 | Edmond, OK** | 20.8 |
| 2 | Longmont, CO | 585.5 | 76 | Lakeland, FL | 56.4 | 150 | El Cajon, CA** | 20.3 |
| 3 | Lakewood Twnshp, NJ** | 390.9 | 77 | Gresham, OR** | 55.1 | 151 | Huntsville, AL | 20.2 |
| 4 | Alhambra, CA** | 341.7 | 78 | Tacoma, WA | 54.5 | 152 | Baldwin Park, CA** | 20.0 |
| 5 | Ogden, UT | 215.6 | 79 | Sioux City, IA | 54.4 | 153 | Cambridge, MA | 19.8 |
| 6 | St. Joseph, MO | 177.8 | 80 | Norwalk, CT | 53.8 | 154 | Tulsa, OK** | 19.4 |
| 7 | Sandy Springs, GA** | 170.6 | 81 | Lafayette, LA** | 53.3 | 155 | Green Bay, WI | 19.3 |
| 8 | Mountain View, CA** | 154.5 | 82 | Kansas City, MO | 52.8 | 155 | Paterson, NJ** | 19.3 |
| 9 | Chino Hills, CA** | 150.0 | 82 | Napa, CA** | 52.8 | 157 | Pasadena, CA** | 19.2 |
| 10 | Evanston, IL** | 149.1 | 82 | Plantation, FL | 52.8 | 158 | Orlando, FL | 19.1 |
| 11 | Frisco, TX | 144.6 | 85 | Plano, TX | 51.7 | 158 | San Antonio, TX** | 19.1 |
| 12 | Meridian, ID | 139.3 | 86 | Indio, CA** | 51.4 | 160 | Broken Arrow, OK** | 18.6 |
| 13 | Virginia Beach, VA | 139.2 | 87 | Fort Lauderdale, FL | 50.5 | 160 | Independence, MO | 18.6 |
| 14 | Coral Springs, FL | 137.5 | 88 | Sugar Land, TX** | 50.0 | 160 | Rockford, IL | 18.6 |
| 15 | Warwick, RI | 135.2 | 89 | Lake Forest, CA** | 49.5 | 163 | Allentown, PA | 18.5 |
| 16 | Roswell, GA** | 134.2 | 90 | Charleston, SC | 49.0 | 164 | Orem, UT** | 18.3 |
| 17 | Springfield, MA | 129.8 | 91 | Indianapolis, IN | 48.5 | 165 | Birmingham, AL | 17.8 |
| 18 | Provo, UT | 127.6 | 92 | Arvada, CO | 47.5 | 166 | Salem, OR | 16.9 |
| 19 | Alexandria, VA | 127.4 | 93 | San Francisco, CA** | 46.2 | 167 | Mesa, AZ** | 16.8 |
| 20 | San Mateo, CA** | 120.6 | 94 | Menifee, CA** | 46.0 | 168 | Las Vegas, NV** | 16.6 |
| 21 | Newton, MA | 119.0 | 95 | Miami, FL | 45.9 | 169 | Baton Rouge, LA** | 16.3 |
| 22 | Davenport, IA | 118.7 | 96 | Citrus Heights, CA** | 45.8 | 170 | Cleveland, OH | 16.2 |
| 23 | Lawton, OK** | 110.9 | 97 | Clinton Twnshp, MI | 45.7 | 170 | Knoxville, TN | 16.2 |
| 24 | Hammond, IN** | 109.9 | 98 | Costa Mesa, CA** | 44.0 | 170 | Tuscaloosa, AL | 16.2 |
| 25 | Spokane, WA** | 107.3 | 99 | Philadelphia, PA | 43.9 | 173 | Boulder, CO | 16.0 |
| 26 | Reno, NV** | 104.2 | 99 | Westminster, CA** | 43.9 | 174 | Santa Monica, CA** | 15.9 |
| 27 | McAllen, TX** | 100.0 | 101 | St. George, UT | 43.3 | 175 | Miramar, FL | 15.0 |
| 28 | Clarkstown, NY** | 98.0 | 102 | Bethlehem, PA | 42.5 | 176 | Providence, RI | 14.8 |
| 29 | Springfield, MO | 96.7 | 103 | Longview, TX | 41.6 | 177 | North Las Vegas, NV** | 14.6 |
| 30 | Redwood City, CA** | 96.4 | 104 | Detroit, MI | 41.5 | 178 | Allen, TX | 14.5 |
| 31 | Hartford, CT** | 96.3 | 105 | Fall River, MA | 41.3 | 179 | Macon, GA** | 14.3 |
| 32 | Mobile, AL | 96.1 | 106 | Warren, MI | 39.9 | 180 | Portsmouth, VA | 14.2 |
| 33 | Carmel, IN** | 95.8 | 107 | Dearborn, MI | 39.3 | 181 | Fort Smith, AR | 14.1 |
| 34 | Amarillo, TX | 94.5 | 108 | Lansing, MI | 39.0 | 181 | Reading, PA | 14.1 |
| 35 | Savannah, GA** | 92.6 | 109 | Tempe, AZ** | 38.9 | 183 | Lakewood, CO | 13.9 |
| 36 | Bloomington, IN** | 87.7 | 110 | Irvine, CA** | 37.8 | 183 | Oklahoma City, OK** | 13.9 |
| 37 | Troy, MI | 87.3 | 111 | Nashville, TN | 37.1 | 185 | West Valley, UT | 13.7 |
| 38 | New Bedford, MA | 87.0 | 111 | New Haven, CT | 37.1 | 186 | Hemet, CA** | 13.5 |
| 38 | Sterling Heights, MI | 87.0 | 111 | O'Fallon, MO | 37.1 | 187 | Columbus, GA** | 13.3 |
| 40 | Greeley, CO | 85.5 | 114 | Tallahassee, FL | 36.8 | 188 | Sandy, UT | 13.2 |
| 41 | Fishers, IN** | 84.6 | 115 | Lee's Summit, MO | 36.6 | 188 | Spokane Valley, WA** | 13.2 |
| 42 | Brockton, MA | 82.7 | 116 | Flint, MI | 36.5 | 188 | Thornton, CO | 13.2 |
| 43 | Pearland, TX | 82.1 | 117 | Mission Viejo, CA** | 35.5 | 191 | Phoenix, AZ** | 13.1 |
| 44 | Tampa, FL | 80.5 | 118 | Ann Arbor, MI | 35.2 | 192 | Quincy, MA | 13.0 |
| 45 | Cranston, RI | 80.4 | 119 | Anchorage, AK | 34.5 | 193 | Garland, TX** | 12.5 |
| 46 | Grand Rapids, MI | 77.3 | 120 | Sparks, NV** | 34.1 | 194 | Newport News, VA | 12.4 |
| 47 | Norfolk, VA | 77.1 | 121 | Bloomington, IL** | 33.9 | 195 | Upland, CA** | 12.3 |
| 48 | Milwaukee, WI | 73.7 | 122 | San Bernardino, CA** | 32.7 | 196 | Sunrise, FL | 11.9 |
| 49 | Fremont, CA** | 73.4 | 123 | Denver, CO | 32.4 | 197 | Vista, CA** | 11.5 |
| 50 | Surprise, AZ** | 72.7 | 124 | Glendale, CA** | 32.3 | 198 | Sunnyvale, CA** | 11.3 |
| 51 | Clarksville, TN | 72.2 | 125 | Hampton, VA | 31.9 | 199 | Davie, FL | 11.2 |
| 52 | San Leandro, CA** | 71.7 | 126 | Chesapeake, VA | 31.6 | 200 | Rialto, CA** | 10.8 |
| 53 | Pompano Beach, FL | 71.6 | 127 | Jacksonville, FL | 31.5 | 201 | Dallas, TX** | 10.7 |
| 54 | Whittier, CA** | 71.3 | 128 | Fort Worth, TX | 30.5 | 202 | Largo, FL | 10.4 |
| 55 | South Bend, IN | 70.3 | 129 | Johns Creek, GA** | 29.7 | 202 | Palm Bay, FL | 10.4 |
| 56 | San Marcos, CA** | 69.5 | 130 | Simi Valley, CA** | 29.1 | 202 | Richmond, VA | 10.4 |
| 57 | Yuma, AZ | 69.3 | 131 | Lexington, KY | 28.8 | 202 | Stamford, CT | 10.4 |
| 58 | Salt Lake City, UT | 69.1 | 132 | Santa Clara, CA** | 28.6 | 206 | Alameda, CA** | 10.1 |
| 59 | Pittsburgh, PA | 68.2 | 133 | Fort Collins, CO | 28.4 | 207 | Roanoke, VA | 9.8 |
| 60 | St. Louis, MO | 67.5 | 134 | St. Paul, MN | 28.0 | 208 | Boston, MA** | 9.6 |
| 61 | Wilmington, NC** | 67.1 | 135 | Melbourne, FL | 26.8 | 209 | Westland, MI | 9.2 |
| 62 | New Rochelle, NY** | 65.8 | 136 | Manchester, NH | 26.0 | 210 | Winston-Salem, NC** | 7.6 |
| 63 | St. Petersburg, FL | 65.4 | 137 | Miami Beach, FL | 25.8 | 211 | Inglewood, CA** | 7.4 |
| 64 | Daly City, CA** | 64.4 | 138 | Upper Darby Twnshp, PA | 25.4 | 212 | Carson, CA** | 7.3 |
| 65 | Hollywood, FL | 64.1 | 139 | Seattle, WA | 25.3 | 213 | Lowell, MA | 7.0 |
| 66 | Toms River Twnshp, NJ** | 63.6 | 140 | Odessa, TX** | 24.6 | 214 | Cedar Rapids, IA | 6.9 |
| 67 | Joliet, IL** | 63.4 | 141 | New Orleans, LA** | 24.5 | 214 | Grand Prairie, TX** | 6.9 |
| 68 | Washington, DC | 63.0 | 142 | Murrieta, CA** | 24.0 | 214 | Wichita, KS | 6.9 |
| 69 | Deerfield Beach, FL | 62.7 | 142 | Norwalk, CA** | 24.0 | 217 | Danbury, CT** | 6.8 |
| 70 | Boise, ID | 62.1 | 144 | Moreno Valley, CA** | 23.2 | 218 | Buffalo, NY** | 6.5 |
| 71 | Santa Maria, CA** | 60.9 | 145 | Aurora, CO | 22.8 | 219 | Temecula, CA** | 6.2 |
| 72 | Brownsville, TX** | 60.0 | 145 | Hawthorne, CA** | 22.8 | 220 | Cincinnati, OH | 5.7 |
| 73 | Columbia, MO | 57.7 | 147 | Modesto, CA** | 22.6 | 221 | Fontana, CA** | 5.2 |
| 74 | High Point, NC** | 57.3 | 148 | Oxnard, CA** | 22.5 | 221 | Lynchburg, VA | 5.2 |

| RANK | CITY | % CHANGE | RANK | CITY | % CHANGE | RANK | CITY | % CHANGE |
|---|---|---|---|---|---|---|---|---|
| 223 | Norman, OK** | 5.0 | 297 | Miami Gardens, FL | (6.9) | 371 | Jersey City, NJ** | (24.0) |
| 224 | Denton, TX | 4.4 | 298 | Fullerton, CA** | (7.1) | 371 | Sacramento, CA** | (24.0) |
| 225 | Memphis, TN | 3.9 | 298 | Waco, TX** | (7.1) | 373 | Toledo, OH | (24.1) |
| 226 | Kennewick, WA | 3.5 | 300 | Houston, TX** | (7.2) | 374 | Lawrence, MA** | (24.2) |
| 227 | San Diego, CA** | 3.1 | 301 | Santa Ana, CA** | (7.3) | 375 | Merced, CA** | (24.3) |
| 228 | Fort Wayne, IN | 3.0 | 302 | Farmington Hills, MI | (7.5) | 376 | Athens-Clarke, GA** | (24.7) |
| 229 | Vancouver, WA | 2.5 | 303 | Killeen, TX** | (8.1) | 377 | Champaign, IL** | (25.0) |
| 230 | Colorado Springs, CO | 2.4 | 304 | Laredo, TX** | (8.2) | 378 | Bakersfield, CA** | (25.6) |
| 231 | Riverside, CA** | 2.1 | 305 | Clifton, NJ** | (8.4) | 379 | Redding, CA** | (25.8) |
| 232 | Fargo, ND | 1.8 | 306 | Everett, WA** | (8.5) | 380 | Lancaster, CA** | (26.3) |
| 233 | Hialeah, FL | 1.7 | 307 | Shreveport, LA** | (8.8) | 381 | Round Rock, TX** | (26.6) |
| 234 | Escondido, CA** | 1.6 | 308 | McKinney, TX | (9.5) | 382 | Henderson, NV** | (27.6) |
| 235 | Billings, MT | 1.4 | 309 | Glendale, AZ** | (9.9) | 383 | Palmdale, CA** | (27.7) |
| 235 | Syracuse, NY** | 1.4 | 310 | Atlanta, GA** | (10.0) | 384 | Kenosha, WI** | (28.1) |
| 237 | Edinburg, TX** | 1.1 | 310 | Des Moines, IA | (10.0) | 385 | Yakima, WA | (29.1) |
| 238 | Stockton, CA** | 1.0 | 312 | Long Beach, CA** | (10.6) | 386 | Visalia, CA** | (29.6) |
| 239 | Pasadena, TX** | 0.9 | 312 | North Charleston, SC | (10.6) | 387 | Hayward, CA** | (29.8) |
| 240 | Austin, TX** | 0.8 | 312 | Yonkers, NY** | (10.6) | 388 | Albany, NY** | (30.1) |
| 241 | South Gate, CA** | 0.6 | 315 | Westminster, CO | (10.9) | 389 | Gilbert, AZ | (30.3) |
| 242 | Bryan, TX** | 0.0 | 316 | Edison Twnshp, NJ** | (11.2) | 390 | Racine, WI** | (31.4) |
| 242 | Colonie, NY** | 0.0 | 317 | Chico, CA** | (11.9) | 391 | Raleigh, NC** | (31.6) |
| 242 | El Monte, CA** | 0.0 | 318 | Ventura, CA** | (12.2) | 392 | Vallejo, CA** | (31.9) |
| 242 | Garden Grove, CA** | 0.0 | 318 | Victorville, CA** | (12.2) | 393 | Hoover, AL | (32.3) |
| 242 | Hesperia, CA** | 0.0 | 320 | Scottsdale, AZ** | (12.8) | 394 | Brick Twnshp, NJ** | (32.9) |
| 242 | Mesquite, TX** | 0.0 | 320 | Tracy, CA** | (12.8) | 395 | Worcester, MA | (33.3) |
| 242 | Naperville, IL** | 0.0 | 322 | Irving, TX** | (13.2) | 396 | Waukegan, IL** | (33.5) |
| 242 | Orange, CA** | 0.0 | 322 | Salinas, CA** | (13.2) | 397 | Clovis, CA** | (33.6) |
| 242 | Woodbridge Twnshp, NJ** | 0.0 | 324 | Louisville, KY** | (13.5) | 398 | Mission, TX** | (33.8) |
| 251 | Anaheim, CA** | (0.4) | 325 | Chula Vista, CA** | (13.6) | 399 | Berkeley, CA** | (33.9) |
| 251 | Charlotte, NC** | (0.4) | 325 | Nashua, NH | (13.6) | 400 | Oakland, CA** | (34.2) |
| 253 | Portland, OR** | (0.5) | 327 | Carlsbad, CA** | (13.7) | 401 | Madison, WI | (34.8) |
| 254 | Buena Park, CA** | (0.6) | 327 | Little Rock, AR | (13.7) | 402 | Peoria, AZ** | (34.9) |
| 254 | Huntington Beach, CA** | (0.6) | 329 | Ontario, CA** | (14.0) | 403 | Boca Raton, FL | (35.3) |
| 256 | Elizabeth, NJ** | (0.7) | 330 | Greenville, NC** | (14.3) | 404 | Newport Beach, CA** | (36.5) |
| 257 | Jurupa Valley, CA** | (0.8) | 331 | Gary, IN** | (14.4) | 405 | Concord, CA** | (36.8) |
| 258 | Federal Way, WA | (0.9) | 332 | Rancho Cucamon., CA** | (14.7) | 406 | Santa Rosa, CA** | (37.5) |
| 259 | Arlington Heights, IL** | (1.1) | 333 | Antioch, CA** | (14.9) | 407 | Centennial, CO | (37.9) |
| 259 | Midland, TX** | (1.1) | 333 | Topeka, KS** | (14.9) | 408 | Santa Barbara, CA** | (39.7) |
| 261 | Greensboro, NC** | (1.2) | 335 | Clearwater, FL | (15.0) | 409 | Downey, CA** | (39.8) |
| 262 | Amherst, NY** | (1.7) | 335 | Lakewood, CA** | (15.0) | 410 | Cheektowaga, NY** | (41.7) |
| 263 | Abilene, TX** | (2.2) | 335 | Oceanside, CA** | (15.0) | 411 | Vacaville, CA** | (42.0) |
| 264 | College Station, TX** | (2.3) | 338 | Lubbock, TX** | (15.5) | 412 | Trenton, NJ** | (43.0) |
| 265 | Kansas City, KS** | (2.6) | 339 | Roseville, CA** | (15.6) | 413 | Santa Clarita, CA** | (44.3) |
| 266 | Fresno, CA** | (2.8) | 340 | Gainesville, FL | (16.0) | 414 | Fayetteville, AR | (44.9) |
| 266 | Sioux Falls, SD | (2.8) | 341 | Carrollton, TX** | (16.1) | 415 | Richardson, TX** | (45.2) |
| 268 | Omaha, NE** | (3.1) | 341 | League City, TX** | (16.1) | 416 | Burbank, CA** | (45.6) |
| 268 | Renton, WA | (3.1) | 343 | Kent, WA | (16.3) | 417 | Tustin, CA** | (46.5) |
| 270 | Ramapo, NY** | (3.4) | 344 | Hillsboro, OR** | (16.6) | 418 | Greece, NY** | (50.0) |
| 271 | Richmond, CA** | (3.6) | 345 | Rochester, NY** | (17.2) | 419 | Pomona, CA** | (50.7) |
| 272 | Dayton, OH | (3.8) | 346 | Elgin, IL** | (17.4) | 420 | Las Cruces, NM** | (52.8) |
| 273 | Akron, OH | (4.3) | 347 | Bellflower, CA** | (17.7) | 421 | Port St. Lucie, FL | (55.6) |
| 274 | Tyler, TX | (4.4) | 348 | Newark, NJ** | (17.8) | 422 | Cape Coral, FL | (57.0) |
| 275 | Livonia, MI | (4.5) | 349 | Jackson, MS** | (18.5) | 423 | Fairfield, CA** | (57.1) |
| 276 | Peoria, IL** | (4.6) | 350 | Lynn, MA | (18.7) | 424 | Decatur, IL** | (64.9) |
| 277 | Murfreesboro, TN | (4.7) | 351 | Aurora, IL** | (18.8) | 425 | Thousand Oaks, CA** | (69.7) |
| 277 | Olathe, KS** | (4.7) | 351 | Wichita Falls, TX** | (18.8) | 426 | Elk Grove, CA** | (71.1) |
| 279 | El Paso, TX** | (4.8) | 353 | Los Angeles, CA** | (18.9) | 427 | Waterbury, CT** | (71.4) |
| 279 | Lawrence, KS | (4.8) | 354 | Overland Park, KS** | (19.0) | 428 | Bridgeport, CT** | (79.0) |
| 281 | Baltimore, MD** | (5.0) | 355 | Corona, CA** | (19.4) | 429 | West Covina, CA** | (81.4) |
| 282 | Cary, NC** | (5.1) | 356 | Hamilton Twnshp, NJ** | (19.6) | NA | Bend, OR*** | NA |
| 283 | San Jose, CA** | (5.2) | 357 | Corpus Christi, TX** | (20.7) | NA | Bloomington, MN*** | NA |
| 284 | Erie, PA | (5.3) | 358 | Chandler, AZ** | (20.8) | NA | Brooklyn Park, MN*** | NA |
| 284 | Evansville, IN** | (5.3) | 359 | Beaumont, TX** | (21.0) | NA | Canton Twnshp, MI*** | NA |
| 286 | Fayetteville, NC** | (5.6) | 360 | Compton, CA** | (21.1) | NA | Chattanooga, TN*** | NA |
| 287 | New York, NY** | (5.7) | 361 | Albany, GA** | (21.2) | NA | Chicago, IL*** | NA |
| 288 | Eugene, OR | (5.9) | 361 | Scranton, PA | (21.2) | NA | Columbia, SC*** | NA |
| 288 | Minneapolis, MN | (5.9) | 363 | Livermore, CA** | (21.5) | NA | Concord, NC*** | NA |
| 290 | Beaverton, OR** | (6.1) | 364 | Arlington, TX** | (22.2) | NA | Duluth, MN*** | NA |
| 290 | Nampa, ID | (6.1) | 365 | Cicero, IL** | (22.4) | NA | Lewisville, TX*** | NA |
| 290 | Torrance, CA** | (6.1) | 366 | Somerville, MA | (22.5) | NA | Rochester, MN*** | NA |
| 293 | Medford, OR | (6.2) | 367 | Pembroke Pines, FL | (22.7) | NA | San Angelo, TX*** | NA |
| 294 | Tucson, AZ** | (6.6) | 368 | Lincoln, NE** | (22.9) | NA | Suffolk, VA*** | NA |
| 294 | West Palm Beach, FL | (6.6) | 369 | Chino, CA** | (23.0) | | | |
| 296 | Springfield, IL** | (6.8) | 370 | Bellevue, WA** | (23.8) | | | |

Source: CQ Press using reported data from the F.B.I. "Crime in the United States 2013" *Revised definition: Rape is penetration, no matter how slight, of the vagina or anus with any body part or object, or oral penetration by a sex organ of another person, without the consent of the victim. Attempts or assaults to commit rape are also included; however, statutory rape and incest are excluded. **Figures for these cities are based on the previous (legacy) definition of rape. See note on page vii. ***Not available.

# 56. Percent Change in Rape Rate: 2009 to 2013
## National Percent Change = 13.2% Decrease*

| RANK | CITY | % CHANGE | RANK | CITY | % CHANGE | RANK | CITY | % CHANGE |
|---|---|---|---|---|---|---|---|---|
| 411 | Abilene, TX** | (68.3) | 391 | Chino, CA** | (50.8) | 357 | Fullerton, CA** | (37.3) |
| 251 | Akron, OH | (11.9) | 387 | Chula Vista, CA** | (47.7) | 369 | Gainesville, FL | (40.5) |
| 323 | Alameda, CA** | (29.2) | NA | Cicero, IL*** | NA | 397 | Garden Grove, CA** | (55.6) |
| 400 | Albany, GA** | (56.4) | 222 | Cincinnati, OH | (4.8) | 241 | Garland, TX** | (8.9) |
| 372 | Albany, NY** | (41.6) | 314 | Citrus Heights, CA** | (27.6) | 131 | Gary, IN** | 20.6 |
| 112 | Albuquerque, NM** | 28.2 | 8 | Clarkstown, NY** | 160.5 | 351 | Gilbert, AZ | (34.7) |
| 47 | Alexandria, VA | 72.0 | 113 | Clarksville, TN | 27.7 | 206 | Glendale, AZ** | (1.4) |
| 365 | Alhambra, CA** | (39.4) | 153 | Clearwater, FL | 12.5 | 383 | Glendale, CA** | (46.1) |
| 284 | Allentown, PA | (20.0) | 124 | Cleveland, OH | 23.2 | 232 | Grand Prairie, TX** | (7.0) |
| 250 | Allen, TX | (11.8) | 161 | Clifton, NJ** | 10.2 | 181 | Grand Rapids, MI | 6.2 |
| 24 | Amarillo, TX | 107.8 | 22 | Clinton Twnshp, MI | 128.4 | 342 | Greece, NY** | (33.1) |
| 230 | Amherst, NY** | (6.3) | 218 | Clovis, CA** | (4.5) | 43 | Greeley, CO | 79.1 |
| 158 | Anaheim, CA** | 10.7 | 332 | College Station, TX** | (31.2) | 304 | Green Bay, WI | (24.4) |
| 91 | Anchorage, AK | 36.9 | 416 | Colonie, NY** | (100.0) | 272 | Greensboro, NC** | (16.3) |
| 60 | Ann Arbor, MI | 61.8 | 204 | Colorado Springs, CO | (1.1) | NA | Greenville, NC*** | NA |
| 369 | Antioch, CA** | (40.5) | 34 | Columbia, MO | 87.5 | 106 | Gresham, OR** | 31.0 |
| NA | Arlington Heights, IL*** | NA | 277 | Columbia, SC | (17.5) | 279 | Hamilton Twnshp, NJ** | (18.9) |
| 331 | Arlington, TX** | (30.9) | 321 | Columbus, GA** | (29.0) | 137 | Hammond, IN** | 18.3 |
| 174 | Arvada, CO | 7.2 | 328 | Compton, CA** | (30.7) | 275 | Hampton, VA | (17.3) |
| 269 | Athens-Clarke, GA** | (16.1) | 362 | Concord, CA** | (38.9) | 172 | Hartford, CT** | 7.3 |
| 218 | Atlanta, GA** | (4.5) | 396 | Concord, NC** | (54.0) | 236 | Hawthorne, CA** | (7.7) |
| 210 | Aurora, CO | (2.2) | 1 | Coral Springs, FL | 493.8 | 171 | Hayward, CA** | 7.4 |
| NA | Aurora, IL*** | NA | 162 | Corona, CA** | 10.1 | 120 | Hemet, CA** | 25.1 |
| 310 | Austin, TX** | (26.7) | 355 | Corpus Christi, TX** | (36.6) | 291 | Henderson, NV** | (21.5) |
| 280 | Bakersfield, CA** | (19.6) | 53 | Costa Mesa, CA** | 66.9 | 321 | Hesperia, CA** | (29.0) |
| 339 | Baldwin Park, CA** | (32.8) | 76 | Cranston, RI | 44.2 | 148 | Hialeah, FL | 14.4 |
| 31 | Baltimore, MD** | 93.9 | 146 | Dallas, TX** | 15.2 | 251 | High Point, NC** | (11.9) |
| 108 | Baton Rouge, LA** | 30.5 | 282 | Daly City, CA** | (19.7) | 229 | Hillsboro, OR** | (6.2) |
| 306 | Beaumont, TX** | (24.6) | 218 | Danbury, CT** | (4.5) | 70 | Hollywood, FL | 52.5 |
| 260 | Beaverton, OR** | (13.4) | 36 | Davenport, IA | 85.8 | 266 | Hoover, AL | (14.4) |
| 291 | Bellevue, WA** | (21.5) | 145 | Davie, FL | 15.5 | 293 | Houston, TX** | (21.8) |
| 385 | Bellflower, CA** | (47.0) | 114 | Dayton, OH | 27.4 | 194 | Huntington Beach, CA** | 1.3 |
| 71 | Bend, OR | 51.1 | 40 | Dearborn, MI | 83.0 | 225 | Huntsville, AL | (5.4) |
| 269 | Berkeley, CA** | (16.1) | NA | Decatur, IL*** | NA | 188 | Independence, MO | 4.1 |
| 58 | Bethlehem, PA | 62.4 | NA | Deerfield Beach, FL*** | NA | 92 | Indianapolis, IN | 36.6 |
| 94 | Billings, MT | 36.1 | 102 | Denton, TX | 32.2 | 96 | Indio, CA** | 35.5 |
| 213 | Birmingham, AL | (3.6) | 85 | Denver, CO | 39.7 | 237 | Inglewood, CA** | (8.5) |
| NA | Bloomington, IL*** | NA | 378 | Des Moines, IA | (44.1) | 403 | Irvine, CA** | (60.8) |
| 337 | Bloomington, IN** | (32.5) | 16 | Detroit, MI | 139.3 | 359 | Irving, TX** | (37.5) |
| NA | Bloomington, MN*** | NA | 354 | Downey, CA** | (36.5) | 27 | Jacksonville, FL | 98.5 |
| 410 | Boca Raton, FL | (67.7) | NA | Duluth, MN*** | NA | 258 | Jackson, MS** | (13.0) |
| 50 | Boise, ID | 69.3 | 93 | Edinburg, TX** | 36.2 | 341 | Jersey City, NJ** | (33.0) |
| 198 | Boston, MA** | 0.5 | 29 | Edison Twnshp, NJ** | 97.5 | 317 | Johns Creek, GA** | (28.4) |
| 144 | Boulder, CO | 15.6 | 254 | Edmond, OK** | (12.1) | NA | Joliet, IL*** | NA |
| 389 | Brick Twnshp, NJ** | (48.0) | 242 | El Cajon, CA** | (9.6) | NA | Jurupa Valley, CA*** | NA |
| 106 | Bridgeport, CT** | 31.0 | 182 | El Monte, CA** | 6.1 | 201 | Kansas City, KS** | (0.2) |
| 51 | Brockton, MA | 67.8 | 251 | El Paso, TX** | (11.9) | 80 | Kansas City, MO | 42.4 |
| 116 | Broken Arrow, OK** | 26.7 | NA | Elgin, IL*** | NA | 297 | Kennewick, WA | (23.2) |
| NA | Brooklyn Park, MN*** | NA | 275 | Elizabeth, NJ** | (17.3) | 327 | Kenosha, WI** | (29.8) |
| 20 | Brownsville, TX** | 131.7 | 408 | Elk Grove, CA** | (65.4) | 395 | Kent, WA | 52.1 |
| 255 | Bryan, TX** | (12.4) | 308 | Erie, PA | (25.5) | 201 | Killeen, TX** | (0.2) |
| 189 | Buena Park, CA** | 4.0 | 266 | Escondido, CA** | (14.4) | 216 | Knoxville, TN | (4.0) |
| 177 | Buffalo, NY** | 6.7 | 247 | Eugene, OR | (11.0) | 409 | Lafayette, LA** | (65.8) |
| 374 | Burbank, CA** | (41.8) | NA | Evanston, IL*** | NA | 5 | Lake Forest, CA** | 277.5 |
| 164 | Cambridge, MA | 9.8 | 259 | Evansville, IN** | (13.3) | 74 | Lakeland, FL | 47.4 |
| 286 | Canton Twnshp, MI | (20.5) | 296 | Everett, WA** | (22.8) | 379 | Lakewood Twnshp, NJ** | (44.3) |
| 398 | Cape Coral, FL | (55.7) | 382 | Fairfield, CA** | (45.5) | 384 | Lakewood, CA** | (46.7) |
| 290 | Carlsbad, CA** | (21.2) | 56 | Fall River, MA | 63.3 | 126 | Lakewood, CO | 22.4 |
| 59 | Carmel, IN** | 62.1 | 157 | Fargo, ND | 10.9 | 360 | Lancaster, CA** | (38.0) |
| 406 | Carrollton, TX** | (62.7) | 97 | Farmington Hills, MI | 35.2 | 82 | Lansing, MI | 42.0 |
| 179 | Carson, CA** | 6.6 | 345 | Fayetteville, AR | (33.6) | 227 | Laredo, TX** | (5.9) |
| 278 | Cary, NC** | (17.8) | 371 | Fayetteville, NC** | (40.6) | 223 | Largo, FL | (4.9) |
| 174 | Cedar Rapids, IA | 7.2 | 300 | Federal Way, WA | (23.4) | 168 | Las Cruces, NM** | 8.2 |
| 151 | Centennial, CO | 13.3 | NA | Fishers, IN*** | NA | 233 | Las Vegas, NV** | (7.3) |
| NA | Champaign, IL*** | NA | 44 | Flint, MI | 78.0 | 246 | Lawrence, KS | (10.8) |
| 141 | Chandler, AZ** | 16.1 | 342 | Fontana, CA** | (33.1) | 147 | Lawrence, MA** | 15.1 |
| 273 | Charleston, SC | (16.5) | 366 | Fort Collins, CO | (39.5) | 244 | Lawton, OK** | (10.0) |
| 326 | Charlotte, NC** | (29.5) | 87 | Fort Lauderdale, FL | 38.2 | 372 | League City, TX** | (41.6) |
| 130 | Chattanooga, TN | 20.8 | 123 | Fort Smith, AR | 23.6 | 187 | Lee's Summit, MO | 4.3 |
| 311 | Cheektowaga, NY** | (27.5) | 119 | Fort Wayne, IN | 25.2 | 18 | Lewisville, TX | 137.3 |
| 159 | Chesapeake, VA | 10.6 | 110 | Fort Worth, TX | 29.7 | 133 | Lexington, KY | 20.2 |
| NA | Chicago, IL*** | NA | 347 | Fremont, CA** | (33.9) | 172 | Lincoln, NE** | 7.3 |
| 230 | Chico, CA** | (6.3) | 375 | Fresno, CA** | (41.9) | 340 | Little Rock, AR | (32.9) |
| 15 | Chino Hills, CA** | 140.7 | 148 | Frisco, TX | 14.4 | 399 | Livermore, CA** | (55.8) |

| RANK | CITY | % CHANGE |
|------|------|----------|
| 176 | Livonia, MI | 6.8 |
| 294 | Long Beach, CA** | (22.3) |
| 4 | Longmont, CO | 364.5 |
| 100 | Longview, TX | 33.0 |
| 271 | Los Angeles, CA** | (16.2) |
| 350 | Louisville, KY** | (34.6) |
| NA | Lowell, MA*** | NA |
| 249 | Lubbock, TX** | (11.3) |
| 57 | Lynchburg, VA | 62.5 |
| 121 | Lynn, MA | 25.0 |
| 54 | Macon, GA** | 66.7 |
| 7 | Madison, WI | 163.0 |
| 117 | Manchester, NH | 26.2 |
| 413 | McAllen, TX** | (70.9) |
| 203 | McKinney, TX | (0.6) |
| 135 | Medford, OR | 18.8 |
| 9 | Melbourne, FL | 156.2 |
| 141 | Memphis, TN | 16.1 |
| 274 | Menifee, CA** | (17.0) |
| 335 | Merced, CA** | (31.8) |
| 89 | Meridian, ID | 37.2 |
| 48 | Mesa, AZ** | 70.5 |
| 303 | Mesquite, TX** | (24.2) |
| 134 | Miami Beach, FL | 19.1 |
| 386 | Miami Gardens, FL | (47.2) |
| 73 | Miami, FL | 47.7 |
| 405 | Midland, TX** | (61.9) |
| 28 | Milwaukee, WI | 97.9 |
| 243 | Minneapolis, MN | (9.9) |
| 255 | Miramar, FL | (12.4) |
| 289 | Mission Viejo, CA** | (20.8) |
| 392 | Mission, TX** | (51.0) |
| 19 | Mobile, AL | 134.0 |
| 105 | Modesto, CA** | 31.2 |
| 194 | Moreno Valley, CA** | 1.3 |
| 263 | Mountain View, CA** | (14.3) |
| 170 | Murfreesboro, TN | 7.6 |
| 376 | Murrieta, CA** | (42.6) |
| 177 | Nampa, ID | 6.7 |
| 139 | Napa, CA** | 17.4 |
| NA | Naperville, IL*** | NA |
| 115 | Nashua, NH | 27.3 |
| 63 | Nashville, TN | 60.1 |
| 74 | New Bedford, MA | 47.4 |
| 129 | New Haven, CT | 21.6 |
| 62 | New Orleans, LA** | 60.5 |
| 66 | New Rochelle, NY** | 57.5 |
| 98 | New York, NY** | 33.3 |
| 345 | Newark, NJ** | (33.6) |
| 65 | Newport Beach, CA** | 60.0 |
| NA | Newport News, VA*** | NA |
| 136 | Newton, MA | 18.7 |
| 122 | Norfolk, VA | 24.9 |
| 138 | Norman, OK** | 17.7 |
| 225 | North Charleston, SC | (5.4) |
| 46 | North Las Vegas, NV** | 72.1 |
| 215 | Norwalk, CA** | (3.8) |
| 98 | Norwalk, CT | 33.3 |
| 381 | Oakland, CA** | (44.7) |
| 348 | Oceanside, CA** | (34.4) |
| 79 | Odessa, TX** | 43.2 |
| 21 | O'Fallon, MO | 129.7 |
| 10 | Ogden, UT | 148.8 |
| 83 | Oklahoma City, OK** | 40.9 |
| 311 | Olathe, KS** | (27.5) |
| 199 | Omaha, NE** | 0.0 |
| 352 | Ontario, CA** | (35.0) |
| 318 | Orange, CA** | (28.8) |
| 221 | Orem, UT** | (4.7) |
| 199 | Orlando, FL | 0.0 |
| 150 | Overland Park, KS** | 13.7 |
| 404 | Oxnard, CA** | (61.7) |
| 283 | Palm Bay, FL | (19.9) |
| 361 | Palmdale, CA** | (38.6) |

| RANK | CITY | % CHANGE |
|------|------|----------|
| 191 | Pasadena, CA** | 3.4 |
| 247 | Pasadena, TX** | (11.0) |
| 233 | Paterson, NJ** | (7.3) |
| 68 | Pearland, TX | 53.1 |
| 206 | Pembroke Pines, FL | (1.4) |
| 412 | Peoria, AZ** | (69.3) |
| NA | Peoria, IL*** | NA |
| 81 | Philadelphia, PA | 42.1 |
| 111 | Phoenix, AZ** | 29.4 |
| 333 | Pittsburgh, PA | (31.7) |
| 37 | Plano, TX | 84.8 |
| 126 | Plantation, FL | 22.4 |
| 333 | Pomona, CA** | (31.7) |
| 163 | Pompano Beach, FL | 10.0 |
| 402 | Port St. Lucie, FL | (60.1) |
| 268 | Portland, OR** | (14.5) |
| 12 | Portsmouth, VA | 144.4 |
| 17 | Provo, UT | 139.2 |
| 35 | Providence, RI | 86.3 |
| 2 | Pueblo, CO | 419.4 |
| 42 | Quincy, MA | 80.7 |
| 356 | Racine, WI** | (36.9) |
| 306 | Raleigh, NC** | (24.6) |
| 165 | Ramapo, NY** | 9.6 |
| 316 | Rancho Cucamon., CA** | (28.3) |
| 26 | Reading, PA | 106.9 |
| 299 | Redding, CA** | (23.3) |
| 132 | Redwood City, CA** | 20.3 |
| 297 | Reno, NV** | (23.2) |
| 380 | Renton, WA | (44.5) |
| 348 | Rialto, CA** | (34.4) |
| 128 | Richardson, TX** | 22.2 |
| 302 | Richmond, CA** | (24.0) |
| 139 | Richmond, VA | 17.4 |
| 305 | Riverside, CA** | (24.5) |
| 61 | Roanoke, VA | 60.9 |
| NA | Rochester, MN*** | NA |
| 235 | Rochester, NY** | (7.4) |
| 94 | Rockford, IL | 36.1 |
| 262 | Roseville, CA** | (14.2) |
| 77 | Roswell, GA** | 43.5 |
| 180 | Round Rock, TX** | 6.3 |
| 388 | Sacramento, CA** | (47.8) |
| 352 | Salem, OR | (35.0) |
| 325 | Salinas, CA** | (29.4) |
| 31 | Salt Lake City, UT | 93.9 |
| 288 | San Angelo, TX | (20.6) |
| 190 | San Antonio, TX** | 3.7 |
| 152 | San Bernardino, CA** | 13.1 |
| 212 | San Diego, CA** | (3.3) |
| 257 | San Francisco, CA** | (12.7) |
| 197 | San Jose, CA** | 0.7 |
| 185 | San Leandro, CA** | 4.9 |
| 155 | San Marcos, CA** | 11.3 |
| 55 | San Mateo, CA** | 66.1 |
| 367 | Sandy Springs, GA** | (40.0) |
| 102 | Sandy, UT | 32.2 |
| 338 | Santa Ana, CA** | (32.6) |
| 184 | Santa Barbara, CA** | 5.3 |
| 367 | Santa Clara, CA** | (40.0) |
| 286 | Santa Clarita, CA** | (20.5) |
| 329 | Santa Maria, CA** | (30.8) |
| 38 | Santa Monica, CA** | 83.6 |
| 390 | Santa Rosa, CA** | (48.9) |
| 214 | Savannah, GA** | (3.7) |
| 25 | Scottsdale, AZ** | 107.6 |
| 393 | Scranton, PA | (51.1) |
| 84 | Seattle, WA | 40.8 |
| 344 | Shreveport, LA** | (33.2) |
| 260 | Simi Valley, CA** | (13.4) |
| 39 | Sioux City, IA | 83.5 |
| 193 | Sioux Falls, SD | 1.8 |
| 11 | Somerville, MA | 148.4 |
| 49 | South Bend, IN | 70.3 |

| RANK | CITY | % CHANGE |
|------|------|----------|
| 285 | South Gate, CA** | (20.3) |
| 183 | Sparks, NV** | 5.9 |
| 45 | Spokane Valley, WA** | 75.8 |
| 23 | Spokane, WA** | 114.1 |
| NA | Springfield, IL*** | NA |
| 300 | Springfield, MA | (23.4) |
| 14 | Springfield, MO | 141.0 |
| 263 | Stamford, CT | (14.3) |
| 167 | Sterling Heights, MI | 8.5 |
| 168 | Stockton, CA** | 8.2 |
| 6 | St. George, UT | 196.5 |
| 3 | St. Joseph, MO | 402.5 |
| 72 | St. Louis, MO | 48.4 |
| 118 | St. Paul, MN | 25.6 |
| 89 | St. Petersburg, FL | 37.2 |
| 155 | Suffolk, VA | 11.3 |
| 206 | Sugar Land, TX** | (1.4) |
| 109 | Sunnyvale, CA** | 30.1 |
| 67 | Sunrise, FL | 55.4 |
| 101 | Surprise, AZ** | 32.6 |
| 192 | Syracuse, NY** | 2.2 |
| 209 | Tacoma, WA | (2.1) |
| 125 | Tallahassee, FL | 23.1 |
| 217 | Tampa, FL | (4.3) |
| 309 | Temecula, CA** | (25.9) |
| 204 | Tempe, AZ** | (1.1) |
| 224 | Thornton, CO | (5.2) |
| 407 | Thousand Oaks, CA** | (64.9) |
| 280 | Toledo, OH | (19.6) |
| 104 | Toms River Twnshp, NJ** | 31.7 |
| 311 | Topeka, KS** | (27.5) |
| 363 | Torrance, CA** | (39.0) |
| 52 | Tracy, CA** | 67.3 |
| 393 | Trenton, NJ** | (51.1) |
| 211 | Troy, MI | (2.8) |
| 160 | Tucson, AZ** | 10.5 |
| 78 | Tulsa, OK** | 43.3 |
| 68 | Tuscaloosa, AL | 53.1 |
| 87 | Tustin, CA** | 38.2 |
| 295 | Tyler, TX | (22.4) |
| NA | Upland, CA*** | NA |
| 186 | Upper Darby Twnshp, PA | 4.8 |
| 238 | Vacaville, CA** | (8.6) |
| 329 | Vallejo, CA** | (30.8) |
| 357 | Vancouver, WA | (37.3) |
| 154 | Ventura, CA** | 12.1 |
| 315 | Victorville, CA** | (27.8) |
| 30 | Virginia Beach, VA | 94.4 |
| 377 | Visalia, CA** | (43.1) |
| 240 | Vista, CA** | (8.8) |
| 141 | Waco, TX** | 16.1 |
| 33 | Warren, MI | 88.6 |
| 86 | Warwick, RI | 39.0 |
| 13 | Washington, DC | 143.2 |
| 415 | Waterbury, CT** | (87.1) |
| NA | Waukegan, IL*** | NA |
| 414 | West Covina, CA** | (85.6) |
| 336 | West Palm Beach, FL | (32.1) |
| 166 | West Valley, UT | 9.4 |
| 63 | Westland, MI | 60.1 |
| 245 | Westminster, CA** | (10.2) |
| 228 | Westminster, CO | (6.0) |
| 196 | Whittier, CA** | 1.0 |
| 364 | Wichita Falls, TX** | (39.3) |
| 239 | Wichita, KS | (8.7) |
| 318 | Wilmington, NC** | (28.8) |
| 318 | Winston-Salem, NC** | (28.8) |
| 401 | Woodbridge Twnshp, NJ** | (57.7) |
| 263 | Worcester, MA | (14.3) |
| NA | Yakima, WA*** | NA |
| 323 | Yonkers, NY** | (29.2) |
| 41 | Yuma, AZ | 82.8 |

Source: CQ Press using reported data from the F.B.I. "Crime in the United States 2013" *Revised definition: Rape is penetration, no matter how slight, of the vagina or anus with any body part or object, or oral penetration by a sex organ of another person, without the consent of the victim. Attempts or assaults to commit rape are also included; however, statutory rape and incest are excluded. **Figures for these cities are based on the previous (legacy) definition of rape. See note on page vii. ***Not available.

# 56. Percent Change in Rape Rate: 2009 to 2013 (continued)
## National Percent Change = 13.2% Decrease*

| RANK | CITY | % CHANGE | RANK | CITY | % CHANGE | RANK | CITY | % CHANGE |
|---|---|---|---|---|---|---|---|---|
| 1 | Coral Springs, FL | 493.8 | 74 | New Bedford, MA | 47.4 | 148 | Hialeah, FL | 14.4 |
| 2 | Pueblo, CO | 419.4 | 76 | Cranston, RI | 44.2 | 150 | Overland Park, KS** | 13.7 |
| 3 | St. Joseph, MO | 402.5 | 77 | Roswell, GA** | 43.5 | 151 | Centennial, CO | 13.3 |
| 4 | Longmont, CO | 364.5 | 78 | Tulsa, OK** | 43.3 | 152 | San Bernardino, CA** | 13.1 |
| 5 | Lake Forest, CA** | 277.5 | 79 | Odessa, TX** | 43.2 | 153 | Clearwater, FL | 12.5 |
| 6 | St. George, UT | 196.5 | 80 | Kansas City, MO | 42.4 | 154 | Ventura, CA** | 12.1 |
| 7 | Madison, WI | 163.0 | 81 | Philadelphia, PA | 42.1 | 155 | San Marcos, CA** | 11.3 |
| 8 | Clarkstown, NY** | 160.5 | 82 | Lansing, MI | 42.0 | 155 | Suffolk, VA | 11.3 |
| 9 | Melbourne, FL | 156.2 | 83 | Oklahoma City, OK** | 40.9 | 157 | Fargo, ND | 10.9 |
| 10 | Ogden, UT | 148.8 | 84 | Seattle, WA | 40.8 | 158 | Anaheim, CA** | 10.7 |
| 11 | Somerville, MA | 148.4 | 85 | Denver, CO | 39.7 | 159 | Chesapeake, VA | 10.6 |
| 12 | Portsmouth, VA | 144.4 | 86 | Warwick, RI | 39.0 | 160 | Tucson, AZ** | 10.5 |
| 13 | Washington, DC | 143.2 | 87 | Fort Lauderdale, FL | 38.2 | 161 | Clifton, NJ** | 10.2 |
| 14 | Springfield, MO | 141.0 | 87 | Tustin, CA** | 38.2 | 162 | Corona, CA** | 10.1 |
| 15 | Chino Hills, CA** | 140.7 | 89 | Meridian, ID | 37.2 | 163 | Pompano Beach, FL | 10.0 |
| 16 | Detroit, MI | 139.3 | 89 | St. Petersburg, FL | 37.2 | 164 | Cambridge, MA | 9.8 |
| 17 | Provo, UT | 139.2 | 91 | Anchorage, AK | 36.9 | 165 | Ramapo, NY** | 9.6 |
| 18 | Lewisville, TX | 137.3 | 92 | Indianapolis, IN | 36.6 | 166 | West Valley, UT | 9.4 |
| 19 | Mobile, AL | 134.0 | 93 | Edinburg, TX** | 36.2 | 167 | Sterling Heights, MI | 8.5 |
| 20 | Brownsville, TX** | 131.7 | 94 | Billings, MT | 36.1 | 168 | Las Cruces, NM** | 8.2 |
| 21 | O'Fallon, MO | 129.7 | 94 | Rockford, IL | 36.1 | 168 | Stockton, CA** | 8.2 |
| 22 | Clinton Twnshp, MI | 128.4 | 96 | Indio, CA** | 35.5 | 170 | Murfreesboro, TN | 7.6 |
| 23 | Spokane, WA** | 114.1 | 97 | Farmington Hills, MI | 35.2 | 171 | Hayward, CA** | 7.4 |
| 24 | Amarillo, TX | 107.8 | 98 | New York, NY** | 33.3 | 172 | Hartford, CT** | 7.3 |
| 25 | Scottsdale, AZ** | 107.6 | 98 | Norwalk, CT | 33.3 | 172 | Lincoln, NE** | 7.3 |
| 26 | Reading, PA | 106.9 | 100 | Longview, TX | 33.0 | 174 | Arvada, CO | 7.2 |
| 27 | Jacksonville, FL | 98.5 | 101 | Surprise, AZ** | 32.6 | 174 | Cedar Rapids, IA | 7.2 |
| 28 | Milwaukee, WI | 97.9 | 102 | Denton, TX | 32.2 | 176 | Livonia, MI | 6.8 |
| 29 | Edison Twnshp, NJ** | 97.5 | 102 | Sandy, UT | 32.2 | 177 | Buffalo, NY** | 6.7 |
| 30 | Virginia Beach, VA | 94.4 | 104 | Toms River Twnshp, NJ** | 31.7 | 177 | Nampa, ID | 6.7 |
| 31 | Baltimore, MD** | 93.9 | 105 | Modesto, CA** | 31.2 | 179 | Carson, CA** | 6.6 |
| 31 | Salt Lake City, UT | 93.9 | 106 | Bridgeport, CT** | 31.0 | 180 | Round Rock, TX** | 6.3 |
| 33 | Warren, MI | 88.6 | 106 | Gresham, OR** | 31.0 | 181 | Grand Rapids, MI | 6.2 |
| 34 | Columbia, MO | 87.5 | 108 | Baton Rouge, LA** | 30.5 | 182 | El Monte, CA** | 6.1 |
| 35 | Providence, RI | 86.3 | 109 | Sunnyvale, CA** | 30.1 | 183 | Sparks, NV** | 5.9 |
| 36 | Davenport, IA | 85.8 | 110 | Fort Worth, TX | 29.7 | 184 | Santa Barbara, CA** | 5.3 |
| 37 | Plano, TX | 84.8 | 111 | Phoenix, AZ** | 29.4 | 185 | San Leandro, CA** | 4.9 |
| 38 | Santa Monica, CA** | 83.6 | 112 | Albuquerque, NM** | 28.2 | 186 | Upper Darby Twnshp, PA | 4.8 |
| 39 | Sioux City, IA | 83.5 | 113 | Clarksville, TN | 27.7 | 187 | Lee's Summit, MO | 4.3 |
| 40 | Dearborn, MI | 83.0 | 114 | Dayton, OH | 27.4 | 188 | Independence, MO | 4.1 |
| 41 | Yuma, AZ | 82.8 | 115 | Nashua, NH | 27.3 | 189 | Buena Park, CA** | 4.0 |
| 42 | Quincy, MA | 80.7 | 116 | Broken Arrow, OK** | 26.7 | 190 | San Antonio, TX** | 3.7 |
| 43 | Greeley, CO | 79.1 | 117 | Manchester, NH | 26.2 | 191 | Pasadena, CA** | 3.4 |
| 44 | Flint, MI | 78.0 | 118 | St. Paul, MN | 25.6 | 192 | Syracuse, NY** | 2.2 |
| 45 | Spokane Valley, WA** | 75.8 | 119 | Fort Wayne, IN | 25.2 | 193 | Sioux Falls, SD | 1.8 |
| 46 | North Las Vegas, NV** | 72.1 | 120 | Hemet, CA** | 25.1 | 194 | Huntington Beach, CA** | 1.3 |
| 47 | Alexandria, VA | 72.0 | 121 | Lynn, MA | 25.0 | 194 | Moreno Valley, CA** | 1.3 |
| 48 | Mesa, AZ** | 70.5 | 122 | Norfolk, VA | 24.9 | 196 | Whittier, CA** | 1.0 |
| 49 | South Bend, IN | 70.3 | 123 | Fort Smith, AR | 23.6 | 197 | San Jose, CA** | 0.7 |
| 50 | Boise, ID | 69.3 | 124 | Cleveland, OH | 23.2 | 198 | Boston, MA** | 0.5 |
| 51 | Brockton, MA | 67.8 | 125 | Tallahassee, FL | 23.1 | 199 | Omaha, NE** | 0.0 |
| 52 | Tracy, CA** | 67.3 | 126 | Lakewood, CO | 22.4 | 199 | Orlando, FL | 0.0 |
| 53 | Costa Mesa, CA** | 66.9 | 126 | Plantation, FL | 22.4 | 201 | Kansas City, KS** | (0.2) |
| 54 | Macon, GA** | 66.7 | 128 | Richardson, TX** | 22.2 | 201 | Killeen, TX** | (0.2) |
| 55 | San Mateo, CA** | 66.1 | 129 | New Haven, CT | 21.6 | 203 | McKinney, TX | (0.6) |
| 56 | Fall River, MA | 63.3 | 130 | Chattanooga, TN | 20.8 | 204 | Colorado Springs, CO | (1.1) |
| 57 | Lynchburg, VA | 62.5 | 131 | Gary, IN** | 20.6 | 204 | Tempe, AZ** | (1.1) |
| 58 | Bethlehem, PA | 62.4 | 132 | Redwood City, CA** | 20.3 | 206 | Glendale, AZ** | (1.4) |
| 59 | Carmel, IN** | 62.1 | 133 | Lexington, KY | 20.2 | 206 | Pembroke Pines, FL | (1.4) |
| 60 | Ann Arbor, MI | 61.8 | 134 | Miami Beach, FL | 19.1 | 206 | Sugar Land, TX** | (1.4) |
| 61 | Roanoke, VA | 60.9 | 135 | Medford, OR | 18.8 | 209 | Tacoma, WA | (2.1) |
| 62 | New Orleans, LA** | 60.5 | 136 | Newton, MA | 18.7 | 210 | Aurora, CO | (2.2) |
| 63 | Nashville, TN | 60.1 | 137 | Hammond, IN** | 18.3 | 211 | Troy, MI | (2.8) |
| 63 | Westland, MI | 60.1 | 138 | Norman, OK** | 17.7 | 212 | San Diego, CA** | (3.3) |
| 65 | Newport Beach, CA** | 60.0 | 139 | Napa, CA** | 17.4 | 213 | Birmingham, AL | (3.6) |
| 66 | New Rochelle, NY** | 57.5 | 139 | Richmond, VA | 17.4 | 214 | Savannah, GA** | (3.7) |
| 67 | Sunrise, FL | 55.4 | 141 | Chandler, AZ** | 16.1 | 215 | Norwalk, CA** | (3.8) |
| 68 | Pearland, TX | 53.1 | 141 | Memphis, TN | 16.1 | 216 | Knoxville, TN | (4.0) |
| 68 | Tuscaloosa, AL | 53.1 | 141 | Waco, TX** | 16.1 | 217 | Tampa, FL | (4.3) |
| 70 | Hollywood, FL | 52.5 | 144 | Boulder, CO | 15.6 | 218 | Atlanta, GA** | (4.5) |
| 71 | Bend, OR | 51.1 | 145 | Davie, FL | 15.5 | 218 | Clovis, CA** | (4.5) |
| 72 | St. Louis, MO | 48.4 | 146 | Dallas, TX** | 15.2 | 218 | Danbury, CT** | (4.5) |
| 73 | Miami, FL | 47.7 | 147 | Lawrence, MA** | 15.1 | 221 | Orem, UT** | (4.7) |
| 74 | Lakeland, FL | 47.4 | 148 | Frisco, TX | 14.4 | 222 | Cincinnati, OH | (4.8) |

| RANK | CITY | % CHANGE | RANK | CITY | % CHANGE | RANK | CITY | % CHANGE |
|---|---|---|---|---|---|---|---|---|
| 223 | Largo, FL | (4.9) | 297 | Kennewick, WA | (23.2) | 371 | Fayetteville, NC** | (40.6) |
| 224 | Thornton, CO | (5.2) | 297 | Reno, NV** | (23.2) | 372 | Albany, NY** | (41.6) |
| 225 | Huntsville, AL | (5.4) | 299 | Redding, CA** | (23.3) | 372 | League City, TX** | (41.6) |
| 225 | North Charleston, SC | (5.4) | 300 | Federal Way, WA | (23.4) | 374 | Burbank, CA** | (41.8) |
| 227 | Laredo, TX** | (5.9) | 300 | Springfield, MA | (23.4) | 375 | Fresno, CA** | (41.9) |
| 228 | Westminster, CO | (6.0) | 302 | Richmond, CA** | (24.0) | 376 | Murrieta, CA** | (42.6) |
| 229 | Hillsboro, OR** | (6.2) | 303 | Mesquite, TX** | (24.2) | 377 | Visalia, CA** | (43.1) |
| 230 | Amherst, NY** | (6.3) | 304 | Green Bay, WI | (24.4) | 378 | Des Moines, IA | (44.1) |
| 230 | Chico, CA** | (6.3) | 305 | Riverside, CA** | (24.5) | 379 | Lakewood Twnshp, NJ** | (44.3) |
| 232 | Grand Prairie, TX** | (7.0) | 306 | Beaumont, TX** | (24.6) | 380 | Renton, WA | (44.5) |
| 233 | Las Vegas, NV** | (7.3) | 306 | Raleigh, NC** | (24.6) | 381 | Oakland, CA** | (44.7) |
| 233 | Paterson, NJ** | (7.3) | 308 | Erie, PA | (25.5) | 382 | Fairfield, CA** | (45.5) |
| 235 | Rochester, NY** | (7.4) | 309 | Temecula, CA** | (25.9) | 383 | Glendale, CA** | (46.1) |
| 236 | Hawthorne, CA** | (7.7) | 310 | Austin, TX** | (26.7) | 384 | Lakewood, CA** | (46.7) |
| 237 | Inglewood, CA** | (8.5) | 311 | Cheektowaga, NY** | (27.5) | 385 | Bellflower, CA** | (47.0) |
| 238 | Vacaville, CA** | (8.6) | 311 | Olathe, KS** | (27.5) | 386 | Miami Gardens, FL | (47.2) |
| 239 | Wichita, KS | (8.7) | 311 | Topeka, KS** | (27.5) | 387 | Chula Vista, CA** | (47.7) |
| 240 | Vista, CA** | (8.8) | 314 | Citrus Heights, CA** | (27.6) | 388 | Sacramento, CA** | (47.8) |
| 241 | Garland, TX** | (8.9) | 315 | Victorville, CA** | (27.8) | 389 | Brick Twnshp, NJ** | (48.0) |
| 242 | El Cajon, CA** | (9.6) | 316 | Rancho Cucamon., CA** | (28.3) | 390 | Santa Rosa, CA** | (48.9) |
| 243 | Minneapolis, MN | (9.9) | 317 | Johns Creek, GA** | (28.4) | 391 | Chino, CA** | (50.8) |
| 244 | Lawton, OK** | (10.0) | 318 | Orange, CA** | (28.8) | 392 | Mission, TX** | (51.0) |
| 245 | Westminster, CA** | (10.2) | 318 | Wilmington, NC** | (28.8) | 393 | Scranton, PA | (51.1) |
| 246 | Lawrence, KS | (10.8) | 318 | Winston-Salem, NC** | (28.8) | 393 | Trenton, NJ** | (51.1) |
| 247 | Eugene, OR | (11.0) | 321 | Columbus, GA** | (29.0) | 395 | Kent, WA | (52.1) |
| 247 | Pasadena, TX** | (11.0) | 321 | Hesperia, CA** | (29.0) | 396 | Concord, NC** | (54.0) |
| 249 | Lubbock, TX** | (11.3) | 323 | Alameda, CA** | (29.2) | 397 | Garden Grove, CA** | (55.6) |
| 250 | Allen, TX | (11.8) | 323 | Yonkers, NY** | (29.2) | 398 | Cape Coral, FL | (55.7) |
| 251 | Akron, OH | (11.9) | 325 | Salinas, CA** | (29.4) | 399 | Livermore, CA** | (55.8) |
| 251 | El Paso, TX** | (11.9) | 326 | Charlotte, NC** | (29.5) | 400 | Albany, GA** | (56.4) |
| 251 | High Point, NC** | (11.9) | 327 | Kenosha, WI** | (29.8) | 401 | Woodbridge Twnshp, NJ** | (57.7) |
| 254 | Edmond, OK** | (12.1) | 328 | Compton, CA** | (30.7) | 402 | Port St. Lucie, FL | (60.1) |
| 255 | Bryan, TX** | (12.4) | 329 | Santa Maria, CA** | (30.8) | 403 | Irvine, CA** | (60.8) |
| 255 | Miramar, FL | (12.4) | 329 | Vallejo, CA** | (30.8) | 404 | Oxnard, CA** | (61.7) |
| 257 | San Francisco, CA** | (12.7) | 331 | Arlington, TX** | (30.9) | 405 | Midland, TX** | (61.9) |
| 258 | Jackson, MS** | (13.0) | 332 | College Station, TX** | (31.2) | 406 | Carrollton, TX** | (62.7) |
| 259 | Evansville, IN** | (13.3) | 333 | Pittsburgh, PA | (31.7) | 407 | Thousand Oaks, CA** | (64.9) |
| 260 | Beaverton, OR** | (13.4) | 333 | Pomona, CA** | (31.7) | 408 | Elk Grove, CA** | (65.4) |
| 260 | Simi Valley, CA** | (13.4) | 335 | Merced, CA** | (31.8) | 409 | Lafayette, LA** | (65.8) |
| 262 | Roseville, CA** | (14.2) | 336 | West Palm Beach, FL | (32.1) | 410 | Boca Raton, FL | (67.7) |
| 263 | Mountain View, CA** | (14.3) | 337 | Bloomington, IN** | (32.5) | 411 | Abilene, TX** | (68.3) |
| 263 | Stamford, CT | (14.3) | 338 | Santa Ana, CA** | (32.6) | 412 | Peoria, AZ** | (69.3) |
| 263 | Worcester, MA | (14.3) | 339 | Baldwin Park, CA** | (32.8) | 413 | McAllen, TX** | (70.9) |
| 266 | Escondido, CA** | (14.4) | 340 | Little Rock, AR | (32.9) | 414 | West Covina, CA** | (85.6) |
| 266 | Hoover, AL | (14.4) | 341 | Jersey City, NJ** | (33.0) | 415 | Waterbury, CT** | (87.1) |
| 268 | Portland, OR** | (14.5) | 342 | Fontana, CA** | (33.1) | 416 | Colonie, NY** | (100.0) |
| 269 | Athens-Clarke, GA** | (16.1) | 342 | Greece, NY** | (33.1) | NA | Arlington Heights, IL*** | NA |
| 269 | Berkeley, CA** | (16.1) | 344 | Shreveport, LA** | (33.2) | NA | Aurora, IL*** | NA |
| 271 | Los Angeles, CA** | (16.2) | 345 | Fayetteville, AR | (33.6) | NA | Bloomington, IL*** | NA |
| 272 | Greensboro, NC** | (16.3) | 345 | Newark, NJ** | (33.6) | NA | Bloomington, MN*** | NA |
| 273 | Charleston, SC | (16.5) | 347 | Fremont, CA** | (33.9) | NA | Brooklyn Park, MN*** | NA |
| 274 | Menifee, CA** | (17.0) | 348 | Oceanside, CA** | (34.4) | NA | Champaign, IL*** | NA |
| 275 | Elizabeth, NJ** | (17.3) | 348 | Rialto, CA** | (34.4) | NA | Chicago, IL*** | NA |
| 275 | Hampton, VA | (17.3) | 350 | Louisville, KY** | (34.6) | NA | Cicero, IL*** | NA |
| 277 | Columbia, SC | (17.5) | 351 | Gilbert, AZ | (34.7) | NA | Decatur, IL*** | NA |
| 278 | Cary, NC** | (17.8) | 352 | Ontario, CA** | (35.0) | NA | Deerfield Beach, FL*** | NA |
| 279 | Hamilton Twnshp, NJ** | (18.9) | 352 | Salem, OR | (35.0) | NA | Duluth, MN*** | NA |
| 280 | Bakersfield, CA** | (19.6) | 354 | Downey, CA** | (36.5) | NA | Elgin, IL*** | NA |
| 280 | Toledo, OH | (19.6) | 355 | Corpus Christi, TX** | (36.6) | NA | Evanston, IL*** | NA |
| 282 | Daly City, CA** | (19.7) | 356 | Racine, WI** | (36.9) | NA | Fishers, IN*** | NA |
| 283 | Palm Bay, FL | (19.9) | 357 | Fullerton, CA** | (37.3) | NA | Greenville, NC*** | NA |
| 284 | Allentown, PA | (20.0) | 357 | Vancouver, WA | (37.3) | NA | Joliet, IL*** | NA |
| 285 | South Gate, CA** | (20.3) | 359 | Irving, TX** | (37.5) | NA | Jurupa Valley, CA*** | NA |
| 286 | Canton Twnshp, MI | (20.5) | 360 | Lancaster, CA** | (38.0) | NA | Lowell, MA*** | NA |
| 286 | Santa Clarita, CA** | (20.5) | 361 | Palmdale, CA** | (38.6) | NA | Naperville, IL*** | NA |
| 288 | San Angelo, TX | (20.6) | 362 | Concord, CA** | (38.9) | NA | Newport News, VA*** | NA |
| 289 | Mission Viejo, CA** | (20.8) | 363 | Torrance, CA** | (39.0) | NA | Peoria, IL*** | NA |
| 290 | Carlsbad, CA** | (21.2) | 364 | Wichita Falls, TX** | (39.3) | NA | Rochester, MN*** | NA |
| 291 | Bellevue, WA** | (21.5) | 365 | Alhambra, CA** | (39.4) | NA | Springfield, IL*** | NA |
| 291 | Henderson, NV** | (21.5) | 366 | Fort Collins, CO | (39.5) | NA | Upland, CA*** | NA |
| 293 | Houston, TX** | (21.8) | 367 | Sandy Springs, GA** | (40.0) | NA | Waukegan, IL*** | NA |
| 294 | Long Beach, CA** | (22.3) | 367 | Santa Clara, CA** | (40.0) | NA | Yakima, WA*** | NA |
| 295 | Tyler, TX | (22.4) | 369 | Antioch, CA** | (40.5) | | | |
| 296 | Everett, WA** | (22.8) | 369 | Gainesville, FL | (40.5) | | | |

Source: CQ Press using reported data from the F.B.I. "Crime in the United States 2013"  *Revised definition: Rape is penetration, no matter how slight, of the vagina or anus with any body part or object, or oral penetration by a sex organ of another person, without the consent of the victim. Attempts or assaults to commit rape are also included; however, statutory rape and incest are excluded. **Figures for these cities are based on the previous (legacy) definition of rape. See note on page vii. ***Not available.

# 57. Robberies in 2013
## National Total = 345,031 Robberies*

| RANK | CITY | ROBBERY | RANK | CITY | ROBBERY | RANK | CITY | ROBBERY |
|---|---|---|---|---|---|---|---|---|
| 240 | Abilene, TX | 125 | 367 | Chino, CA | 47 | 260 | Fullerton, CA | 107 |
| 74 | Akron, OH | 528 | 153 | Chula Vista, CA | 248 | 215 | Gainesville, FL | 155 |
| 287 | Alameda, CA | 85 | 203 | Cicero, IL | 162 | 232 | Garden Grove, CA | 137 |
| 185 | Albany, GA | 183 | 27 | Cincinnati, OH | 1,610 | 158 | Garland, TX | 237 |
| 163 | Albany, NY | 227 | 303 | Citrus Heights, CA | 76 | 129 | Gary, IN | 327 |
| 42 | Albuquerque, NM | 1,046 | 424 | Clarkstown, NY | 17 | 367 | Gilbert, AZ | 47 |
| 251 | Alexandria, VA | 118 | 252 | Clarksville, TN | 115 | 123 | Glendale, AZ | 335 |
| 295 | Alhambra, CA | 81 | 189 | Clearwater, FL | 177 | 305 | Glendale, CA | 75 |
| 126 | Allentown, PA | 329 | 14 | Cleveland, OH | 3,490 | 215 | Grand Prairie, TX | 155 |
| 430 | Allen, TX | 13 | 344 | Clifton, NJ | 57 | 85 | Grand Rapids, MI | 471 |
| 155 | Amarillo, TX | 242 | 338 | Clinton Twnshp, MI | 60 | 338 | Greece, NY | 60 |
| 401 | Amherst, NY | 31 | 367 | Clovis, CA | 47 | 321 | Greeley, CO | 68 |
| 98 | Anaheim, CA | 437 | 387 | College Station, TX | 37 | 300 | Green Bay, WI | 79 |
| 77 | Anchorage, AK | 522 | 401 | Colonie, NY | 31 | 80 | Greensboro, NC | 496 |
| 361 | Ann Arbor, MI | 49 | 102 | Colorado Springs, CO | 418 | 191 | Greenville, NC | 175 |
| 122 | Antioch, CA | 352 | 255 | Columbia, MO | 112 | 142 | Gresham, OR | 275 |
| 437 | Arlington Heights, IL | 7 | 125 | Columbia, SC | 331 | 301 | Hamilton Twnshp, NJ | 78 |
| 71 | Arlington, TX | 562 | 83 | Columbus, GA | 481 | 161 | Hammond, IN | 228 |
| 393 | Arvada, CO | 34 | 121 | Compton, CA | 360 | 246 | Hampton, VA | 120 |
| 240 | Athens-Clarke, GA | 125 | 211 | Concord, CA | 159 | 72 | Hartford, CT | 557 |
| 19 | Atlanta, GA | 2,363 | 359 | Concord, NC | 50 | 135 | Hawthorne, CA | 299 |
| 86 | Aurora, CO | 468 | 271 | Coral Springs, FL | 99 | 124 | Hayward, CA | 333 |
| 249 | Aurora, IL | 119 | 327 | Corona, CA | 65 | 193 | Hemet, CA | 173 |
| 57 | Austin, TX | 763 | 112 | Corpus Christi, TX | 390 | 208 | Henderson, NV | 160 |
| 61 | Bakersfield, CA | 708 | 277 | Costa Mesa, CA | 94 | 292 | Hesperia, CA | 83 |
| 308 | Baldwin Park, CA | 74 | 379 | Cranston, RI | 42 | 159 | Hialeah, FL | 231 |
| 12 | Baltimore, MD | 3,734 | 8 | Dallas, TX | 4,202 | 188 | High Point, NC | 178 |
| 45 | Baton Rouge, LA | 974 | 282 | Daly City, CA | 90 | 347 | Hillsboro, OR | 55 |
| 101 | Beaumont, TX | 419 | 351 | Danbury, CT | 53 | 150 | Hollywood, FL | 253 |
| 410 | Beaverton, OR | 22 | 199 | Davenport, IA | 167 | 393 | Hoover, AL | 34 |
| 364 | Bellevue, WA | 48 | 280 | Davie, FL | 93 | 3 | Houston, TX | 9,891 |
| 263 | Bellflower, CA | 105 | 78 | Dayton, OH | 518 | 270 | Huntington Beach, CA | 100 |
| 410 | Bend, OR | 22 | 239 | Dearborn, MI | 126 | 111 | Huntsville, AL | 391 |
| 106 | Berkeley, CA | 410 | 290 | Decatur, IL | 84 | 244 | Independence, MO | 122 |
| 308 | Bethlehem, PA | 74 | 263 | Deerfield Beach, FL | 105 | 11 | Indianapolis, IN | 3,800 |
| 295 | Billings, MT | 81 | 354 | Denton, TX | 52 | 246 | Indio, CA | 120 |
| 46 | Birmingham, AL | 969 | 38 | Denver, CO | 1,132 | 130 | Inglewood, CA | 326 |
| 341 | Bloomington, IL | 59 | 169 | Des Moines, IA | 211 | 386 | Irvine, CA | 38 |
| 301 | Bloomington, IN | 78 | 7 | Detroit, MI | 4,774 | 184 | Irving, TX | 186 |
| 361 | Bloomington, MN | 49 | 196 | Downey, CA | 171 | 32 | Jacksonville, FL | 1,424 |
| 349 | Boca Raton, FL | 54 | 316 | Duluth, MN | 72 | 54 | Jackson, MS | 845 |
| 372 | Boise, ID | 45 | 359 | Edinburg, TX | 50 | 59 | Jersey City, NJ | 717 |
| 22 | Boston, MA | 1,868 | 346 | Edison Twnshp, NJ | 56 | 432 | Johns Creek, GA | 11 |
| 381 | Boulder, CO | 40 | 427 | Edmond, OK | 15 | 212 | Joliet, IL | 158 |
| 407 | Brick Twnshp, NJ | 24 | 225 | El Cajon, CA | 143 | 305 | Jurupa Valley, CA | 75 |
| 68 | Bridgeport, CT | 584 | 215 | El Monte, CA | 155 | 157 | Kansas City, KS | 238 |
| 161 | Brockton, MA | 228 | 92 | El Paso, TX | 457 | 25 | Kansas City, MO | 1,662 |
| 398 | Broken Arrow, OK | 32 | 332 | Elgin, IL | 63 | 377 | Kennewick, WA | 43 |
| 286 | Brooklyn Park, MN | 86 | 73 | Elizabeth, NJ | 554 | 267 | Kenosha, WI | 102 |
| 233 | Brownsville, TX | 136 | 271 | Elk Grove, CA | 99 | 208 | Kent, WA | 160 |
| 305 | Bryan, TX | 75 | 191 | Erie, PA | 175 | 197 | Killeen, TX | 170 |
| 299 | Buena Park, CA | 80 | 176 | Escondido, CA | 201 | 103 | Knoxville, TN | 415 |
| 33 | Buffalo, NY | 1,322 | 178 | Eugene, OR | 195 | 145 | Lafayette, LA | 272 |
| 356 | Burbank, CA | 51 | 332 | Evanston, IL | 63 | 408 | Lake Forest, CA | 23 |
| 253 | Cambridge, MA | 114 | 169 | Evansville, IN | 211 | 225 | Lakeland, FL | 143 |
| 425 | Canton Twnshp, MI | 16 | 179 | Everett, WA | 192 | 393 | Lakewood Twnshp, NJ | 34 |
| 381 | Cape Coral, FL | 40 | 202 | Fairfield, CA | 165 | 258 | Lakewood, CA | 110 |
| 374 | Carlsbad, CA | 44 | 165 | Fall River, MA | 225 | 254 | Lakewood, CO | 113 |
| 432 | Carmel, IN | 11 | 343 | Fargo, ND | 58 | 146 | Lancaster, CA | 261 |
| 313 | Carrollton, TX | 73 | 416 | Farmington Hills, MI | 21 | 148 | Lansing, MI | 256 |
| 221 | Carson, CA | 148 | 397 | Fayetteville, AR | 33 | 172 | Laredo, TX | 207 |
| 391 | Cary, NC | 35 | 67 | Fayetteville, NC | 586 | 277 | Largo, FL | 94 |
| 282 | Cedar Rapids, IA | 90 | 259 | Federal Way, WA | 108 | 308 | Las Cruces, NM | 74 |
| 421 | Centennial, CO | 20 | 437 | Fishers, IN | 7 | 10 | Las Vegas, NV | 4,072 |
| 249 | Champaign, IL | 119 | 95 | Flint, MI | 447 | 308 | Lawrence, KS | 74 |
| 203 | Chandler, AZ | 162 | 174 | Fontana, CA | 202 | 140 | Lawrence, MA | 283 |
| 316 | Charleston, SC | 72 | 387 | Fort Collins, CO | 37 | 198 | Lawton, OK | 168 |
| 24 | Charlotte, NC | 1,805 | 62 | Fort Lauderdale, FL | 701 | 410 | League City, TX | 22 |
| 116 | Chattanooga, TN | 385 | 277 | Fort Smith, AR | 94 | 427 | Lee's Summit, MO | 15 |
| 364 | Cheektowaga, NY | 48 | 95 | Fort Wayne, IN | 447 | 308 | Lewisville, TX | 74 |
| 215 | Chesapeake, VA | 155 | 34 | Fort Worth, TX | 1,256 | 88 | Lexington, KY | 467 |
| 2 | Chicago, IL | 11,815 | 233 | Fremont, CA | 136 | 168 | Lincoln, NE | 212 |
| 276 | Chico, CA | 95 | 52 | Fresno, CA | 903 | 49 | Little Rock, AR | 944 |
| 432 | Chino Hills, CA | 11 | 410 | Frisco, TX | 22 | 374 | Livermore, CA | 44 |

| RANK | CITY | ROBBERY |
|---|---|---|
| 393 | Livonia, MI | 34 |
| 39 | Long Beach, CA | 1,118 |
| 422 | Longmont, CO | 19 |
| 219 | Longview, TX | 152 |
| 4 | Los Angeles, CA | 7,885 |
| 31 | Louisville, KY | 1,427 |
| 179 | Lowell, MA | 192 |
| 114 | Lubbock, TX | 388 |
| 313 | Lynchburg, VA | 73 |
| 183 | Lynn, MA | 189 |
| 159 | Macon, GA | 231 |
| 136 | Madison, WI | 296 |
| 137 | Manchester, NH | 295 |
| 292 | McAllen, TX | 83 |
| 374 | McKinney, TX | 44 |
| 271 | Medford, OR | 99 |
| 233 | Melbourne, FL | 136 |
| 17 | Memphis, TN | 3,133 |
| 416 | Menifee, CA | 21 |
| 236 | Merced, CA | 133 |
| 442 | Meridian, ID | 5 |
| 84 | Mesa, AZ | 478 |
| 173 | Mesquite, TX | 204 |
| 117 | Miami Beach, FL | 377 |
| 131 | Miami Gardens, FL | 322 |
| 20 | Miami, FL | 2,216 |
| 332 | Midland, TX | 63 |
| 15 | Milwaukee, WI | 3,284 |
| 23 | Minneapolis, MN | 1,856 |
| 203 | Miramar, FL | 162 |
| 410 | Mission Viejo, CA | 22 |
| 398 | Mission, TX | 32 |
| 91 | Mobile, AL | 459 |
| 94 | Modesto, CA | 450 |
| 132 | Moreno Valley, CA | 312 |
| 398 | Mountain View, CA | 32 |
| 237 | Murfreesboro, TN | 130 |
| 416 | Murrieta, CA | 21 |
| 425 | Nampa, ID | 16 |
| 367 | Napa, CA | 47 |
| 416 | Naperville, IL | 21 |
| 336 | Nashua, NH | 61 |
| 26 | Nashville, TN | 1,611 |
| 148 | New Bedford, MA | 256 |
| 56 | New Haven, CT | 770 |
| 37 | New Orleans, LA | 1,138 |
| 295 | New Rochelle, NY | 81 |
| 1 | New York, NY | 19,170 |
| 18 | Newark, NJ | 2,433 |
| 430 | Newport Beach, CA | 13 |
| 154 | Newport News, VA | 246 |
| 423 | Newton, MA | 18 |
| 104 | Norfolk, VA | 414 |
| 371 | Norman, OK | 46 |
| 177 | North Charleston, SC | 196 |
| 89 | North Las Vegas, NV | 463 |
| 220 | Norwalk, CA | 150 |
| 336 | Norwalk, CT | 61 |
| 6 | Oakland, CA | 4,922 |
| 186 | Oceanside, CA | 182 |
| 225 | Odessa, TX | 143 |
| 441 | O'Fallon, MO | 6 |
| 257 | Ogden, UT | 111 |
| 35 | Oklahoma City, OK | 1,191 |
| 408 | Olathe, KS | 23 |
| 58 | Omaha, NE | 718 |
| 199 | Ontario, CA | 167 |
| 328 | Orange, CA | 64 |
| 437 | Orem, UT | 7 |
| 70 | Orlando, FL | 573 |
| 372 | Overland Park, KS | 45 |
| 127 | Oxnard, CA | 328 |
| 377 | Palm Bay, FL | 43 |
| 147 | Palmdale, CA | 257 |

| RANK | CITY | ROBBERY |
|---|---|---|
| 203 | Pasadena, CA | 162 |
| 179 | Pasadena, TX | 192 |
| 53 | Paterson, NJ | 848 |
| 405 | Pearland, TX | 29 |
| 284 | Pembroke Pines, FL | 87 |
| 341 | Peoria, AZ | 59 |
| 142 | Peoria, IL | 275 |
| 5 | Philadelphia, PA | 7,562 |
| 16 | Phoenix, AZ | 3,233 |
| 48 | Pittsburgh, PA | 956 |
| 261 | Plano, TX | 106 |
| 242 | Plantation, FL | 124 |
| 137 | Pomona, CA | 295 |
| 144 | Pompano Beach, FL | 273 |
| 381 | Port St. Lucie, FL | 40 |
| 51 | Portland, OR | 917 |
| 189 | Portsmouth, VA | 177 |
| 119 | Providence, RI | 365 |
| 416 | Provo, UT | 21 |
| 169 | Pueblo, CO | 211 |
| 284 | Quincy, MA | 87 |
| 187 | Racine, WI | 179 |
| 65 | Raleigh, NC | 605 |
| 436 | Ramapo, NY | 9 |
| 238 | Rancho Cucamon., CA | 128 |
| 127 | Reading, PA | 328 |
| 222 | Redding, CA | 146 |
| 324 | Redwood City, CA | 66 |
| 133 | Reno, NV | 305 |
| 268 | Renton, WA | 101 |
| 179 | Rialto, CA | 192 |
| 338 | Richardson, TX | 60 |
| 107 | Richmond, CA | 407 |
| 64 | Richmond, VA | 624 |
| 81 | Riverside, CA | 495 |
| 228 | Roanoke, VA | 142 |
| 349 | Rochester, MN | 54 |
| 50 | Rochester, NY | 918 |
| 110 | Rockford, IL | 394 |
| 328 | Roseville, CA | 64 |
| 316 | Roswell, GA | 72 |
| 387 | Round Rock, TX | 37 |
| 36 | Sacramento, CA | 1,158 |
| 231 | Salem, OR | 138 |
| 93 | Salinas, CA | 451 |
| 100 | Salt Lake City, UT | 422 |
| 410 | San Angelo, TX | 22 |
| 21 | San Antonio, TX | 2,192 |
| 55 | San Bernardino, CA | 794 |
| 30 | San Diego, CA | 1,456 |
| 8 | San Francisco, CA | 4,202 |
| 40 | San Jose, CA | 1,095 |
| 152 | San Leandro, CA | 251 |
| 335 | San Marcos, CA | 62 |
| 287 | San Mateo, CA | 85 |
| 263 | Sandy Springs, GA | 105 |
| 404 | Sandy, UT | 30 |
| 89 | Santa Ana, CA | 463 |
| 294 | Santa Barbara, CA | 82 |
| 347 | Santa Clara, CA | 55 |
| 275 | Santa Clarita, CA | 97 |
| 244 | Santa Maria, CA | 122 |
| 246 | Santa Monica, CA | 120 |
| 263 | Santa Rosa, CA | 105 |
| 104 | Savannah, GA | 414 |
| 268 | Scottsdale, AZ | 101 |
| 319 | Scranton, PA | 71 |
| 28 | Seattle, WA | 1,601 |
| 118 | Shreveport, LA | 376 |
| 401 | Simi Valley, CA | 31 |
| 381 | Sioux City, IA | 40 |
| 322 | Sioux Falls, SD | 67 |
| 356 | Somerville, MA | 51 |
| 120 | South Bend, IN | 363 |

| RANK | CITY | ROBBERY |
|---|---|---|
| 167 | South Gate, CA | 223 |
| 320 | Sparks, NV | 70 |
| 295 | Spokane Valley, WA | 81 |
| 78 | Spokane, WA | 518 |
| 139 | Springfield, IL | 287 |
| 66 | Springfield, MA | 598 |
| 109 | Springfield, MO | 395 |
| 208 | Stamford, CT | 160 |
| 406 | Sterling Heights, MI | 25 |
| 41 | Stockton, CA | 1,088 |
| 432 | St. George, UT | 11 |
| 287 | St. Joseph, MO | 85 |
| 29 | St. Louis, MO | 1,457 |
| 60 | St. Paul, MN | 716 |
| 63 | St. Petersburg, FL | 634 |
| 328 | Suffolk, VA | 64 |
| 391 | Sugar Land, TX | 35 |
| 356 | Sunnyvale, CA | 51 |
| 255 | Sunrise, FL | 112 |
| 361 | Surprise, AZ | 49 |
| 108 | Syracuse, NY | 400 |
| 76 | Tacoma, WA | 524 |
| 115 | Tallahassee, FL | 387 |
| 69 | Tampa, FL | 580 |
| 385 | Temecula, CA | 39 |
| 166 | Tempe, AZ | 224 |
| 351 | Thornton, CO | 53 |
| 379 | Thousand Oaks, CA | 42 |
| 47 | Toledo, OH | 962 |
| 364 | Toms River Twnshp, NJ | 48 |
| 194 | Topeka, KS | 172 |
| 303 | Torrance, CA | 76 |
| 344 | Tracy, CA | 57 |
| 75 | Trenton, NJ | 525 |
| 437 | Troy, MI | 7 |
| 43 | Tucson, AZ | 1,002 |
| 44 | Tulsa, OK | 994 |
| 207 | Tuscaloosa, AL | 161 |
| 390 | Tustin, CA | 36 |
| 351 | Tyler, TX | 53 |
| 322 | Upland, CA | 67 |
| 163 | Upper Darby Twnshp, PA | 227 |
| 324 | Vacaville, CA | 66 |
| 99 | Vallejo, CA | 424 |
| 222 | Vancouver, WA | 146 |
| 271 | Ventura, CA | 99 |
| 174 | Victorville, CA | 202 |
| 134 | Virginia Beach, VA | 304 |
| 213 | Visalia, CA | 156 |
| 230 | Vista, CA | 140 |
| 228 | Waco, TX | 142 |
| 201 | Warren, MI | 166 |
| 427 | Warwick, RI | 15 |
| 13 | Washington, DC | 3,660 |
| 155 | Waterbury, CT | 242 |
| 194 | Waukegan, IL | 172 |
| 261 | West Covina, CA | 106 |
| 141 | West Palm Beach, FL | 281 |
| 213 | West Valley, UT | 156 |
| 280 | Westland, MI | 93 |
| 290 | Westminster, CA | 84 |
| 354 | Westminster, CO | 52 |
| 313 | Whittier, CA | 73 |
| 242 | Wichita Falls, TX | 124 |
| 86 | Wichita, KS | 468 |
| 150 | Wilmington, NC | 253 |
| 97 | Winston-Salem, NC | 439 |
| 324 | Woodbridge Twnshp, NJ | 66 |
| 82 | Worcester, MA | 483 |
| 224 | Yakima, WA | 144 |
| 112 | Yonkers, NY | 390 |
| 328 | Yuma, AZ | 64 |

Source: Reported data from the F.B.I. "Crime in the United States 2013"

*Robbery is the taking of anything of value by force or threat of force. Attempts are included.

# 57. Robberies in 2013 (continued)
## National Total = 345,031 Robberies*

| RANK | CITY | ROBBERY | RANK | CITY | ROBBERY | RANK | CITY | ROBBERY |
|---|---|---|---|---|---|---|---|---|
| 1 | New York, NY | 19,170 | 75 | Trenton, NJ | 525 | 148 | New Bedford, MA | 256 |
| 2 | Chicago, IL | 11,815 | 76 | Tacoma, WA | 524 | 150 | Hollywood, FL | 253 |
| 3 | Houston, TX | 9,891 | 77 | Anchorage, AK | 522 | 150 | Wilmington, NC | 253 |
| 4 | Los Angeles, CA | 7,885 | 78 | Dayton, OH | 518 | 152 | San Leandro, CA | 251 |
| 5 | Philadelphia, PA | 7,562 | 78 | Spokane, WA | 518 | 153 | Chula Vista, CA | 248 |
| 6 | Oakland, CA | 4,922 | 80 | Greensboro, NC | 496 | 154 | Newport News, VA | 246 |
| 7 | Detroit, MI | 4,774 | 81 | Riverside, CA | 495 | 155 | Amarillo, TX | 242 |
| 8 | Dallas, TX | 4,202 | 82 | Worcester, MA | 483 | 155 | Waterbury, CT | 242 |
| 8 | San Francisco, CA | 4,202 | 83 | Columbus, GA | 481 | 157 | Kansas City, KS | 238 |
| 10 | Las Vegas, NV | 4,072 | 84 | Mesa, AZ | 478 | 158 | Garland, TX | 237 |
| 11 | Indianapolis, IN | 3,800 | 85 | Grand Rapids, MI | 471 | 159 | Hialeah, FL | 231 |
| 12 | Baltimore, MD | 3,734 | 86 | Aurora, CO | 468 | 159 | Macon, GA | 231 |
| 13 | Washington, DC | 3,660 | 86 | Wichita, KS | 468 | 161 | Brockton, MA | 228 |
| 14 | Cleveland, OH | 3,490 | 88 | Lexington, KY | 467 | 161 | Hammond, IN | 228 |
| 15 | Milwaukee, WI | 3,284 | 89 | North Las Vegas, NV | 463 | 163 | Albany, NY | 227 |
| 16 | Phoenix, AZ | 3,233 | 89 | Santa Ana, CA | 463 | 163 | Upper Darby Twnshp, PA | 227 |
| 17 | Memphis, TN | 3,133 | 91 | Mobile, AL | 459 | 165 | Fall River, MA | 225 |
| 18 | Newark, NJ | 2,433 | 92 | El Paso, TX | 457 | 166 | Tempe, AZ | 224 |
| 19 | Atlanta, GA | 2,363 | 93 | Salinas, CA | 451 | 167 | South Gate, CA | 223 |
| 20 | Miami, FL | 2,216 | 94 | Modesto, CA | 450 | 168 | Lincoln, NE | 212 |
| 21 | San Antonio, TX | 2,192 | 95 | Flint, MI | 447 | 169 | Des Moines, IA | 211 |
| 22 | Boston, MA | 1,868 | 95 | Fort Wayne, IN | 447 | 169 | Evansville, IN | 211 |
| 23 | Minneapolis, MN | 1,856 | 97 | Winston-Salem, NC | 439 | 169 | Pueblo, CO | 211 |
| 24 | Charlotte, NC | 1,805 | 98 | Anaheim, CA | 437 | 172 | Laredo, TX | 207 |
| 25 | Kansas City, MO | 1,662 | 99 | Vallejo, CA | 424 | 173 | Mesquite, TX | 204 |
| 26 | Nashville, TN | 1,611 | 100 | Salt Lake City, UT | 422 | 174 | Fontana, CA | 202 |
| 27 | Cincinnati, OH | 1,610 | 101 | Beaumont, TX | 419 | 174 | Victorville, CA | 202 |
| 28 | Seattle, WA | 1,601 | 102 | Colorado Springs, CO | 418 | 176 | Escondido, CA | 201 |
| 29 | St. Louis, MO | 1,457 | 103 | Knoxville, TN | 415 | 177 | North Charleston, SC | 196 |
| 30 | San Diego, CA | 1,456 | 104 | Norfolk, VA | 414 | 178 | Eugene, OR | 195 |
| 31 | Louisville, KY | 1,427 | 104 | Savannah, GA | 414 | 179 | Everett, WA | 192 |
| 32 | Jacksonville, FL | 1,424 | 106 | Berkeley, CA | 410 | 179 | Lowell, MA | 192 |
| 33 | Buffalo, NY | 1,322 | 107 | Richmond, CA | 407 | 179 | Pasadena, TX | 192 |
| 34 | Fort Worth, TX | 1,256 | 108 | Syracuse, NY | 400 | 179 | Rialto, CA | 192 |
| 35 | Oklahoma City, OK | 1,191 | 109 | Springfield, MO | 395 | 183 | Lynn, MA | 189 |
| 36 | Sacramento, CA | 1,158 | 110 | Rockford, IL | 394 | 184 | Irving, TX | 186 |
| 37 | New Orleans, LA | 1,138 | 111 | Huntsville, AL | 391 | 185 | Albany, GA | 183 |
| 38 | Denver, CO | 1,132 | 112 | Corpus Christi, TX | 390 | 186 | Oceanside, CA | 182 |
| 39 | Long Beach, CA | 1,118 | 112 | Yonkers, NY | 390 | 187 | Racine, WI | 179 |
| 40 | San Jose, CA | 1,095 | 114 | Lubbock, TX | 388 | 188 | High Point, NC | 178 |
| 41 | Stockton, CA | 1,088 | 115 | Tallahassee, FL | 387 | 189 | Clearwater, FL | 177 |
| 42 | Albuquerque, NM | 1,046 | 116 | Chattanooga, TN | 385 | 189 | Portsmouth, VA | 177 |
| 43 | Tucson, AZ | 1,002 | 117 | Miami Beach, FL | 377 | 191 | Erie, PA | 175 |
| 44 | Tulsa, OK | 994 | 118 | Shreveport, LA | 376 | 191 | Greenville, NC | 175 |
| 45 | Baton Rouge, LA | 974 | 119 | Providence, RI | 365 | 193 | Hemet, CA | 173 |
| 46 | Birmingham, AL | 969 | 120 | South Bend, IN | 363 | 194 | Topeka, KS | 172 |
| 47 | Toledo, OH | 962 | 121 | Compton, CA | 360 | 194 | Waukegan, IL | 172 |
| 48 | Pittsburgh, PA | 956 | 122 | Antioch, CA | 352 | 196 | Downey, CA | 171 |
| 49 | Little Rock, AR | 944 | 123 | Glendale, AZ | 335 | 197 | Killeen, TX | 170 |
| 50 | Rochester, NY | 918 | 124 | Hayward, CA | 333 | 198 | Lawton, OK | 168 |
| 51 | Portland, OR | 917 | 125 | Columbia, SC | 331 | 199 | Davenport, IA | 167 |
| 52 | Fresno, CA | 903 | 126 | Allentown, PA | 329 | 199 | Ontario, CA | 167 |
| 53 | Paterson, NJ | 848 | 127 | Oxnard, CA | 328 | 201 | Warren, MI | 166 |
| 54 | Jackson, MS | 845 | 127 | Reading, PA | 328 | 202 | Fairfield, CA | 165 |
| 55 | San Bernardino, CA | 794 | 129 | Gary, IN | 327 | 203 | Chandler, AZ | 162 |
| 56 | New Haven, CT | 770 | 130 | Inglewood, CA | 326 | 203 | Cicero, IL | 162 |
| 57 | Austin, TX | 763 | 131 | Miami Gardens, FL | 322 | 203 | Miramar, FL | 162 |
| 58 | Omaha, NE | 718 | 132 | Moreno Valley, CA | 312 | 203 | Pasadena, CA | 162 |
| 59 | Jersey City, NJ | 717 | 133 | Reno, NV | 305 | 207 | Tuscaloosa, AL | 161 |
| 60 | St. Paul, MN | 716 | 134 | Virginia Beach, VA | 304 | 208 | Henderson, NV | 160 |
| 61 | Bakersfield, CA | 708 | 135 | Hawthorne, CA | 299 | 208 | Kent, WA | 160 |
| 62 | Fort Lauderdale, FL | 701 | 136 | Madison, WI | 296 | 208 | Stamford, CT | 160 |
| 63 | St. Petersburg, FL | 634 | 137 | Manchester, NH | 295 | 211 | Concord, CA | 159 |
| 64 | Richmond, VA | 624 | 137 | Pomona, CA | 295 | 212 | Joliet, IL | 158 |
| 65 | Raleigh, NC | 605 | 139 | Springfield, IL | 287 | 213 | Visalia, CA | 156 |
| 66 | Springfield, MA | 598 | 140 | Lawrence, MA | 283 | 213 | West Valley, UT | 156 |
| 67 | Fayetteville, NC | 586 | 141 | West Palm Beach, FL | 281 | 215 | Chesapeake, VA | 155 |
| 68 | Bridgeport, CT | 584 | 142 | Gresham, OR | 275 | 215 | El Monte, CA | 155 |
| 69 | Tampa, FL | 580 | 142 | Peoria, IL | 275 | 215 | Gainesville, FL | 155 |
| 70 | Orlando, FL | 573 | 144 | Pompano Beach, FL | 273 | 215 | Grand Prairie, TX | 155 |
| 71 | Arlington, TX | 562 | 145 | Lafayette, LA | 272 | 219 | Longview, TX | 152 |
| 72 | Hartford, CT | 557 | 146 | Lancaster, CA | 261 | 220 | Norwalk, CA | 150 |
| 73 | Elizabeth, NJ | 554 | 147 | Palmdale, CA | 257 | 221 | Carson, CA | 148 |
| 74 | Akron, OH | 528 | 148 | Lansing, MI | 256 | 222 | Redding, CA | 146 |

| RANK | CITY | ROBBERY | RANK | CITY | ROBBERY | RANK | CITY | ROBBERY |
|---|---|---|---|---|---|---|---|---|
| 222 | Vancouver, WA | 146 | 295 | New Rochelle, NY | 81 | 371 | Norman, OK | 46 |
| 224 | Yakima, WA | 144 | 295 | Spokane Valley, WA | 81 | 372 | Boise, ID | 45 |
| 225 | El Cajon, CA | 143 | 299 | Buena Park, CA | 80 | 372 | Overland Park, KS | 45 |
| 225 | Lakeland, FL | 143 | 300 | Green Bay, WI | 79 | 374 | Carlsbad, CA | 44 |
| 225 | Odessa, TX | 143 | 301 | Bloomington, IN | 78 | 374 | Livermore, CA | 44 |
| 228 | Roanoke, VA | 142 | 301 | Hamilton Twnshp, NJ | 78 | 374 | McKinney, TX | 44 |
| 228 | Waco, TX | 142 | 303 | Citrus Heights, CA | 76 | 377 | Kennewick, WA | 43 |
| 230 | Vista, CA | 140 | 303 | Torrance, CA | 76 | 377 | Palm Bay, FL | 43 |
| 231 | Salem, OR | 138 | 305 | Bryan, TX | 75 | 379 | Cranston, RI | 42 |
| 232 | Garden Grove, CA | 137 | 305 | Glendale, CA | 75 | 379 | Thousand Oaks, CA | 42 |
| 233 | Brownsville, TX | 136 | 305 | Jurupa Valley, CA | 75 | 381 | Boulder, CO | 40 |
| 233 | Fremont, CA | 136 | 308 | Baldwin Park, CA | 74 | 381 | Cape Coral, FL | 40 |
| 233 | Melbourne, FL | 136 | 308 | Bethlehem, PA | 74 | 381 | Port St. Lucie, FL | 40 |
| 236 | Merced, CA | 133 | 308 | Las Cruces, NM | 74 | 381 | Sioux City, IA | 40 |
| 237 | Murfreesboro, TN | 130 | 308 | Lawrence, KS | 74 | 385 | Temecula, CA | 39 |
| 238 | Rancho Cucamon., CA | 128 | 308 | Lewisville, TX | 74 | 386 | Irvine, CA | 38 |
| 239 | Dearborn, MI | 126 | 313 | Carrollton, TX | 73 | 387 | College Station, TX | 37 |
| 240 | Abilene, TX | 125 | 313 | Lynchburg, VA | 73 | 387 | Fort Collins, CO | 37 |
| 240 | Athens-Clarke, GA | 125 | 313 | Whittier, CA | 73 | 387 | Round Rock, TX | 37 |
| 242 | Plantation, FL | 124 | 316 | Charleston, SC | 72 | 390 | Tustin, CA | 36 |
| 242 | Wichita Falls, TX | 124 | 316 | Duluth, MN | 72 | 391 | Cary, NC | 35 |
| 244 | Independence, MO | 122 | 316 | Roswell, GA | 72 | 391 | Sugar Land, TX | 35 |
| 244 | Santa Maria, CA | 122 | 319 | Scranton, PA | 71 | 393 | Arvada, CO | 34 |
| 246 | Hampton, VA | 120 | 320 | Sparks, NV | 70 | 393 | Hoover, AL | 34 |
| 246 | Indio, CA | 120 | 321 | Greeley, CO | 68 | 393 | Lakewood Twnshp, NJ | 34 |
| 246 | Santa Monica, CA | 120 | 322 | Sioux Falls, SD | 67 | 393 | Livonia, MI | 34 |
| 249 | Aurora, IL | 119 | 322 | Upland, CA | 67 | 397 | Fayetteville, AR | 33 |
| 249 | Champaign, IL | 119 | 324 | Redwood City, CA | 66 | 398 | Broken Arrow, OK | 32 |
| 251 | Alexandria, VA | 118 | 324 | Vacaville, CA | 66 | 398 | Mission, TX | 32 |
| 252 | Clarksville, TN | 115 | 324 | Woodbridge Twnshp, NJ | 66 | 398 | Mountain View, CA | 32 |
| 253 | Cambridge, MA | 114 | 327 | Corona, CA | 65 | 401 | Amherst, NY | 31 |
| 254 | Lakewood, CO | 113 | 328 | Orange, CA | 64 | 401 | Colonie, NY | 31 |
| 255 | Columbia, MO | 112 | 328 | Roseville, CA | 64 | 401 | Simi Valley, CA | 31 |
| 255 | Sunrise, FL | 112 | 328 | Suffolk, VA | 64 | 404 | Sandy, UT | 30 |
| 257 | Ogden, UT | 111 | 328 | Yuma, AZ | 64 | 405 | Pearland, TX | 29 |
| 258 | Lakewood, CA | 110 | 332 | Elgin, IL | 63 | 406 | Sterling Heights, MI | 25 |
| 259 | Federal Way, WA | 108 | 332 | Evanston, IL | 63 | 407 | Brick Twnshp, NJ | 24 |
| 260 | Fullerton, CA | 107 | 332 | Midland, TX | 63 | 408 | Lake Forest, CA | 23 |
| 261 | Plano, TX | 106 | 335 | San Marcos, CA | 62 | 408 | Olathe, KS | 23 |
| 261 | West Covina, CA | 106 | 336 | Nashua, NH | 61 | 410 | Beaverton, OR | 22 |
| 263 | Bellflower, CA | 105 | 336 | Norwalk, CT | 61 | 410 | Bend, OR | 22 |
| 263 | Deerfield Beach, FL | 105 | 338 | Clinton Twnshp, MI | 60 | 410 | Frisco, TX | 22 |
| 263 | Sandy Springs, GA | 105 | 338 | Greece, NY | 60 | 410 | League City, TX | 22 |
| 263 | Santa Rosa, CA | 105 | 338 | Richardson, TX | 60 | 410 | Mission Viejo, CA | 22 |
| 267 | Kenosha, WI | 102 | 341 | Bloomington, IL | 59 | 410 | San Angelo, TX | 22 |
| 268 | Renton, WA | 101 | 341 | Peoria, AZ | 59 | 416 | Farmington Hills, MI | 21 |
| 268 | Scottsdale, AZ | 101 | 343 | Fargo, ND | 58 | 416 | Menifee, CA | 21 |
| 270 | Huntington Beach, CA | 100 | 344 | Clifton, NJ | 57 | 416 | Murrieta, CA | 21 |
| 271 | Coral Springs, FL | 99 | 344 | Tracy, CA | 57 | 416 | Naperville, IL | 21 |
| 271 | Elk Grove, CA | 99 | 346 | Edison Twnshp, NJ | 56 | 416 | Provo, UT | 21 |
| 271 | Medford, OR | 99 | 347 | Hillsboro, OR | 55 | 421 | Centennial, CO | 20 |
| 271 | Ventura, CA | 99 | 347 | Santa Clara, CA | 55 | 422 | Longmont, CO | 19 |
| 275 | Santa Clarita, CA | 97 | 349 | Boca Raton, FL | 54 | 423 | Newton, MA | 18 |
| 276 | Chico, CA | 95 | 349 | Rochester, MN | 54 | 424 | Clarkstown, NY | 17 |
| 277 | Costa Mesa, CA | 94 | 351 | Danbury, CT | 53 | 425 | Canton Twnshp, MI | 16 |
| 277 | Fort Smith, AR | 94 | 351 | Thornton, CO | 53 | 425 | Nampa, ID | 16 |
| 277 | Largo, FL | 94 | 351 | Tyler, TX | 53 | 427 | Edmond, OK | 15 |
| 280 | Davie, FL | 93 | 354 | Denton, TX | 52 | 427 | Lee's Summit, MO | 15 |
| 280 | Westland, MI | 93 | 354 | Westminster, CO | 52 | 427 | Warwick, RI | 15 |
| 282 | Cedar Rapids, IA | 90 | 356 | Burbank, CA | 51 | 430 | Allen, TX | 13 |
| 282 | Daly City, CA | 90 | 356 | Somerville, MA | 51 | 430 | Newport Beach, CA | 13 |
| 284 | Pembroke Pines, FL | 87 | 356 | Sunnyvale, CA | 51 | 432 | Carmel, IN | 11 |
| 284 | Quincy, MA | 87 | 359 | Concord, NC | 50 | 432 | Chino Hills, CA | 11 |
| 286 | Brooklyn Park, MN | 86 | 359 | Edinburg, TX | 50 | 432 | Johns Creek, GA | 11 |
| 287 | Alameda, CA | 85 | 361 | Ann Arbor, MI | 49 | 432 | St. George, UT | 11 |
| 287 | San Mateo, CA | 85 | 361 | Bloomington, MN | 49 | 436 | Ramapo, NY | 9 |
| 287 | St. Joseph, MO | 85 | 361 | Surprise, AZ | 49 | 437 | Arlington Heights, IL | 7 |
| 290 | Decatur, IL | 84 | 364 | Bellevue, WA | 48 | 437 | Fishers, IN | 7 |
| 290 | Westminster, CA | 84 | 364 | Cheektowaga, NY | 48 | 437 | Orem, UT | 7 |
| 292 | Hesperia, CA | 83 | 364 | Toms River Twnshp, NJ | 48 | 437 | Troy, MI | 7 |
| 292 | McAllen, TX | 83 | 367 | Chino, CA | 47 | 441 | O'Fallon, MO | 6 |
| 294 | Santa Barbara, CA | 82 | 367 | Clovis, CA | 47 | 442 | Meridian, ID | 5 |
| 295 | Alhambra, CA | 81 | 367 | Gilbert, AZ | 47 | | | |
| 295 | Billings, MT | 81 | 367 | Napa, CA | 47 | | | |

Source: Reported data from the F.B.I. "Crime in the United States 2013"

*Robbery is the taking of anything of value by force or threat of force. Attempts are included.

# 58. Robbery Rate in 2013
## National Rate = 109.1 Robberies per 100,000 Population*

| RANK | CITY | RATE | RANK | CITY | RATE | RANK | CITY | RATE |
|---|---|---|---|---|---|---|---|---|
| 239 | Abilene, TX | 104.7 | 335 | Chino, CA | 58.2 | 294 | Fullerton, CA | 76.6 |
| 70 | Akron, OH | 266.1 | 254 | Chula Vista, CA | 97.2 | 214 | Gainesville, FL | 122.4 |
| 227 | Alameda, CA | 111.5 | 125 | Cicero, IL | 192.4 | 292 | Garden Grove, CA | 78.1 |
| 93 | Albany, GA | 236.5 | 11 | Cincinnati, OH | 543.0 | 247 | Garland, TX | 100.6 |
| 95 | Albany, NY | 231.7 | 270 | Citrus Heights, CA | 89.1 | 31 | Gary, IN | 414.9 |
| 128 | Albuquerque, NM | 187.4 | 413 | Clarkstown, NY | 21.1 | 415 | Gilbert, AZ | 20.9 |
| 288 | Alexandria, VA | 79.5 | 290 | Clarksville, TN | 79.0 | 179 | Glendale, AZ | 143.2 |
| 259 | Alhambra, CA | 95.6 | 160 | Clearwater, FL | 162.5 | 380 | Glendale, CA | 38.4 |
| 64 | Allentown, PA | 275.8 | 2 | Cleveland, OH | 896.8 | 280 | Grand Prairie, TX | 84.3 |
| 433 | Allen, TX | 14.2 | 315 | Clifton, NJ | 67.0 | 84 | Grand Rapids, MI | 246.3 |
| 212 | Amarillo, TX | 123.1 | 325 | Clinton Twnshp, MI | 61.2 | 322 | Greece, NY | 62.1 |
| 399 | Amherst, NY | 26.2 | 358 | Clovis, CA | 47.2 | 306 | Greeley, CO | 70.8 |
| 205 | Anaheim, CA | 126.5 | 383 | College Station, TX | 37.4 | 299 | Green Bay, WI | 75.2 |
| 144 | Anchorage, AK | 174.3 | 376 | Colonie, NY | 39.6 | 136 | Greensboro, NC | 177.6 |
| 367 | Ann Arbor, MI | 42.0 | 258 | Colorado Springs, CO | 95.8 | 118 | Greenville, NC | 198.8 |
| 51 | Antioch, CA | 330.7 | 253 | Columbia, MO | 97.7 | 81 | Gresham, OR | 250.1 |
| 437 | Arlington Heights, IL | 9.2 | 80 | Columbia, SC | 250.3 | 274 | Hamilton Twnshp, NJ | 87.6 |
| 175 | Arlington, TX | 148.4 | 90 | Columbus, GA | 239.1 | 60 | Hammond, IN | 287.4 |
| 394 | Arvada, CO | 30.7 | 39 | Compton, CA | 367.7 | 274 | Hampton, VA | 87.6 |
| 241 | Athens-Clarke, GA | 104.1 | 204 | Concord, CA | 126.7 | 26 | Hartford, CT | 445.9 |
| 13 | Atlanta, GA | 523.9 | 331 | Concord, NC | 60.3 | 48 | Hawthorne, CA | 347.1 |
| 187 | Aurora, CO | 136.3 | 291 | Coral Springs, FL | 78.2 | 104 | Hayward, CA | 220.6 |
| 334 | Aurora, IL | 59.3 | 372 | Corona, CA | 40.6 | 111 | Hemet, CA | 211.8 |
| 271 | Austin, TX | 88.8 | 209 | Corpus Christi, TX | 124.0 | 333 | Henderson, NV | 59.6 |
| 121 | Bakersfield, CA | 195.7 | 282 | Costa Mesa, CA | 83.5 | 268 | Hesperia, CA | 89.6 |
| 256 | Baldwin Park, CA | 96.4 | 348 | Cranston, RI | 52.0 | 250 | Hialeah, FL | 98.6 |
| 6 | Baltimore, MD | 599.7 | 50 | Dallas, TX | 334.8 | 152 | High Point, NC | 166.0 |
| 30 | Baton Rouge, LA | 423.1 | 277 | Daly City, CA | 86.1 | 338 | Hillsboro, OR | 57.1 |
| 46 | Beaumont, TX | 354.6 | 321 | Danbury, CT | 63.6 | 146 | Hollywood, FL | 172.5 |
| 407 | Beaverton, OR | 23.5 | 156 | Davenport, IA | 164.0 | 373 | Hoover, AL | 40.4 |
| 382 | Bellevue, WA | 37.6 | 257 | Davie, FL | 96.3 | 23 | Houston, TX | 453.6 |
| 190 | Bellflower, CA | 135.3 | 40 | Dayton, OH | 366.9 | 352 | Huntington Beach, CA | 51.1 |
| 398 | Bend, OR | 27.5 | 198 | Dearborn, MI | 131.2 | 112 | Huntsville, AL | 211.7 |
| 47 | Berkeley, CA | 352.8 | 226 | Decatur, IL | 111.7 | 242 | Independence, MO | 103.9 |
| 251 | Bethlehem, PA | 98.5 | 193 | Deerfield Beach, FL | 134.3 | 25 | Indianapolis, IN | 446.9 |
| 300 | Billings, MT | 75.1 | 365 | Denton, TX | 42.2 | 174 | Indio, CA | 149.5 |
| 22 | Birmingham, AL | 457.1 | 143 | Denver, CO | 174.4 | 55 | Inglewood, CA | 291.9 |
| 296 | Bloomington, IL | 75.6 | 245 | Des Moines, IA | 101.7 | 428 | Irvine, CA | 16.1 |
| 261 | Bloomington, IN | 94.6 | 4 | Detroit, MI | 682.1 | 287 | Irving, TX | 81.4 |
| 341 | Bloomington, MN | 56.3 | 172 | Downey, CA | 151.0 | 150 | Jacksonville, FL | 168.4 |
| 328 | Boca Raton, FL | 60.8 | 282 | Duluth, MN | 83.5 | 17 | Jackson, MS | 480.0 |
| 414 | Boise, ID | 21.0 | 328 | Edinburg, TX | 60.8 | 62 | Jersey City, NJ | 279.1 |
| 56 | Boston, MA | 290.2 | 343 | Edison Twnshp, NJ | 55.3 | 434 | Johns Creek, GA | 13.1 |
| 379 | Boulder, CO | 38.9 | 425 | Edmond, OK | 17.4 | 235 | Joliet, IL | 106.4 |
| 392 | Brick Twnshp, NJ | 31.8 | 184 | El Cajon, CA | 140.2 | 295 | Jurupa Valley, CA | 76.5 |
| 34 | Bridgeport, CT | 397.1 | 194 | El Monte, CA | 134.1 | 162 | Kansas City, KS | 161.2 |
| 89 | Brockton, MA | 241.4 | 313 | El Paso, TX | 67.2 | 45 | Kansas City, MO | 357.0 |
| 393 | Broken Arrow, OK | 31.1 | 339 | Elgin, IL | 57.0 | 342 | Kennewick, WA | 56.2 |
| 231 | Brooklyn Park, MN | 109.8 | 27 | Elizabeth, NJ | 436.0 | 246 | Kenosha, WI | 101.6 |
| 301 | Brownsville, TX | 74.9 | 323 | Elk Grove, CA | 61.5 | 201 | Kent, WA | 128.7 |
| 260 | Bryan, TX | 95.4 | 145 | Erie, PA | 173.6 | 207 | Killeen, TX | 124.5 |
| 255 | Buena Park, CA | 96.8 | 191 | Escondido, CA | 135.2 | 99 | Knoxville, TN | 226.5 |
| 14 | Buffalo, NY | 510.8 | 213 | Eugene, OR | 123.0 | 106 | Lafayette, LA | 220.4 |
| 355 | Burbank, CA | 48.7 | 284 | Evanston, IL | 83.2 | 397 | Lake Forest, CA | 29.0 |
| 236 | Cambridge, MA | 106.3 | 140 | Evansville, IN | 175.4 | 180 | Lakeland, FL | 142.0 |
| 422 | Canton Twnshp, MI | 18.0 | 134 | Everett, WA | 182.6 | 384 | Lakewood Twnshp, NJ | 36.7 |
| 406 | Cape Coral, FL | 24.5 | 170 | Fairfield, CA | 152.2 | 189 | Lakewood, CA | 135.7 |
| 375 | Carlsbad, CA | 39.8 | 78 | Fall River, MA | 252.2 | 293 | Lakewood, CO | 77.2 |
| 435 | Carmel, IN | 13.0 | 346 | Fargo, ND | 52.2 | 158 | Lancaster, CA | 163.3 |
| 337 | Carrollton, TX | 57.3 | 400 | Farmington Hills, MI | 25.9 | 101 | Lansing, MI | 224.7 |
| 165 | Carson, CA | 158.4 | 364 | Fayetteville, AR | 42.4 | 281 | Laredo, TX | 83.7 |
| 407 | Cary, NC | 23.5 | 58 | Fayetteville, NC | 289.3 | 218 | Largo, FL | 120.6 |
| 309 | Cedar Rapids, IA | 70.0 | 222 | Federal Way, WA | 116.5 | 305 | Las Cruces, NM | 72.5 |
| 418 | Centennial, CO | 19.1 | 439 | Fishers, IN | 8.4 | 67 | Las Vegas, NV | 271.4 |
| 178 | Champaign, IL | 143.4 | 24 | Flint, MI | 447.3 | 286 | Lawrence, KS | 82.2 |
| 320 | Chandler, AZ | 65.1 | 248 | Fontana, CA | 99.3 | 41 | Lawrence, MA | 363.7 |
| 340 | Charleston, SC | 56.6 | 403 | Fort Collins, CO | 24.7 | 148 | Lawton, OK | 170.5 |
| 108 | Charlotte, NC | 215.5 | 33 | Fort Lauderdale, FL | 406.6 | 404 | League City, TX | 24.6 |
| 102 | Chattanooga, TN | 223.5 | 234 | Fort Smith, AR | 107.0 | 427 | Lee's Summit, MO | 16.2 |
| 324 | Cheektowaga, NY | 61.3 | 140 | Fort Wayne, IN | 175.4 | 304 | Lewisville, TX | 73.5 |
| 313 | Chesapeake, VA | 67.2 | 164 | Fort Worth, TX | 159.2 | 171 | Lexington, KY | 151.3 |
| 29 | Chicago, IL | 434.3 | 330 | Fremont, CA | 60.6 | 289 | Lincoln, NE | 79.2 |
| 233 | Chico, CA | 107.7 | 137 | Fresno, CA | 177.4 | 18 | Little Rock, AR | 478.2 |
| 432 | Chino Hills, CA | 14.3 | 426 | Frisco, TX | 16.7 | 346 | Livermore, CA | 52.2 |

| RANK | CITY | RATE |
|---|---|---|
| 387 | Livonia, MI | 35.7 |
| 91 | Long Beach, CA | 238.0 |
| 412 | Longmont, CO | 21.2 |
| 130 | Longview, TX | 187.0 |
| 117 | Los Angeles, CA | 203.3 |
| 110 | Louisville, KY | 212.6 |
| 140 | Lowell, MA | 175.4 |
| 159 | Lubbock, TX | 163.1 |
| 262 | Lynchburg, VA | 93.9 |
| 113 | Lynn, MA | 206.0 |
| 76 | Macon, GA | 253.4 |
| 215 | Madison, WI | 122.1 |
| 69 | Manchester, NH | 267.2 |
| 327 | McAllen, TX | 61.0 |
| 395 | McKinney, TX | 30.0 |
| 201 | Medford, OR | 128.7 |
| 138 | Melbourne, FL | 176.0 |
| 19 | Memphis, TN | 476.4 |
| 401 | Menifee, CA | 25.4 |
| 157 | Merced, CA | 163.5 |
| 442 | Meridian, ID | 6.1 |
| 238 | Mesa, AZ | 104.8 |
| 181 | Mesquite, TX | 141.4 |
| 32 | Miami Beach, FL | 412.3 |
| 59 | Miami Gardens, FL | 287.8 |
| 12 | Miami, FL | 529.6 |
| 350 | Midland, TX | 51.5 |
| 10 | Milwaukee, WI | 546.6 |
| 20 | Minneapolis, MN | 468.4 |
| 210 | Miramar, FL | 123.7 |
| 410 | Mission Viejo, CA | 22.9 |
| 377 | Mission, TX | 39.3 |
| 133 | Mobile, AL | 183.2 |
| 107 | Modesto, CA | 220.3 |
| 168 | Moreno Valley, CA | 155.0 |
| 370 | Mountain View, CA | 41.3 |
| 225 | Murfreesboro, TN | 112.5 |
| 417 | Murrieta, CA | 19.5 |
| 420 | Nampa, ID | 18.9 |
| 332 | Napa, CA | 59.7 |
| 430 | Naperville, IL | 14.6 |
| 308 | Nashua, NH | 70.1 |
| 76 | Nashville, TN | 253.4 |
| 68 | New Bedford, MA | 269.0 |
| 7 | New Haven, CT | 587.5 |
| 53 | New Orleans, LA | 301.8 |
| 244 | New Rochelle, NY | 102.8 |
| 97 | New York, NY | 228.3 |
| 3 | Newark, NJ | 874.4 |
| 429 | Newport Beach, CA | 14.8 |
| 188 | Newport News, VA | 135.9 |
| 416 | Newton, MA | 20.7 |
| 151 | Norfolk, VA | 167.4 |
| 377 | Norman, OK | 39.3 |
| 127 | North Charleston, SC | 189.7 |
| 114 | North Las Vegas, NV | 205.2 |
| 183 | Norwalk, CA | 140.8 |
| 311 | Norwalk, CT | 69.6 |
| 1 | Oakland, CA | 1,218.7 |
| 237 | Oceanside, CA | 105.5 |
| 196 | Odessa, TX | 132.1 |
| 441 | O'Fallon, MO | 7.3 |
| 196 | Ogden, UT | 132.1 |
| 119 | Oklahoma City, OK | 196.8 |
| 424 | Olathe, KS | 17.5 |
| 149 | Omaha, NE | 168.9 |
| 248 | Ontario, CA | 99.3 |
| 362 | Orange, CA | 45.6 |
| 440 | Orem, UT | 7.7 |
| 100 | Orlando, FL | 226.3 |
| 402 | Overland Park, KS | 24.9 |
| 161 | Oxnard, CA | 161.9 |
| 371 | Palm Bay, FL | 41.2 |
| 155 | Palmdale, CA | 164.2 |

| RANK | CITY | RATE |
|---|---|---|
| 222 | Pasadena, CA | 116.5 |
| 206 | Pasadena, TX | 125.3 |
| 8 | Paterson, NJ | 584.5 |
| 396 | Pearland, TX | 29.5 |
| 344 | Pembroke Pines, FL | 53.7 |
| 386 | Peoria, AZ | 36.5 |
| 92 | Peoria, IL | 237.2 |
| 16 | Philadelphia, PA | 486.9 |
| 109 | Phoenix, AZ | 215.2 |
| 52 | Pittsburgh, PA | 310.8 |
| 380 | Plano, TX | 38.4 |
| 185 | Plantation, FL | 139.4 |
| 123 | Pomona, CA | 194.9 |
| 72 | Pompano Beach, FL | 262.6 |
| 407 | Port St. Lucie, FL | 23.5 |
| 173 | Portland, OR | 150.5 |
| 135 | Portsmouth, VA | 182.4 |
| 116 | Providence, RI | 204.0 |
| 422 | Provo, UT | 18.0 |
| 122 | Pueblo, CO | 195.3 |
| 264 | Quincy, MA | 93.1 |
| 96 | Racine, WI | 229.1 |
| 182 | Raleigh, NC | 141.0 |
| 436 | Ramapo, NY | 10.3 |
| 303 | Rancho Cucamon., CA | 74.3 |
| 37 | Reading, PA | 372.3 |
| 163 | Redding, CA | 160.4 |
| 285 | Redwood City, CA | 82.8 |
| 199 | Reno, NV | 131.1 |
| 240 | Renton, WA | 104.5 |
| 129 | Rialto, CA | 187.3 |
| 336 | Richardson, TX | 57.4 |
| 36 | Richmond, CA | 379.2 |
| 54 | Richmond, VA | 293.2 |
| 167 | Riverside, CA | 156.4 |
| 176 | Roanoke, VA | 145.0 |
| 354 | Rochester, MN | 49.2 |
| 27 | Rochester, NY | 436.0 |
| 73 | Rockford, IL | 262.3 |
| 353 | Roseville, CA | 50.7 |
| 297 | Roswell, GA | 75.5 |
| 389 | Round Rock, TX | 34.1 |
| 87 | Sacramento, CA | 242.2 |
| 276 | Salem, OR | 87.2 |
| 57 | Salinas, CA | 289.6 |
| 103 | Salt Lake City, UT | 221.8 |
| 411 | San Angelo, TX | 22.8 |
| 166 | San Antonio, TX | 156.6 |
| 38 | San Bernardino, CA | 370.5 |
| 232 | San Diego, CA | 107.9 |
| 15 | San Francisco, CA | 503.9 |
| 229 | San Jose, CA | 110.4 |
| 61 | San Leandro, CA | 286.9 |
| 307 | San Marcos, CA | 70.7 |
| 278 | San Mateo, CA | 84.6 |
| 243 | Sandy Springs, GA | 103.8 |
| 390 | Sandy, UT | 33.4 |
| 186 | Santa Ana, CA | 139.1 |
| 267 | Santa Barbara, CA | 91.1 |
| 360 | Santa Clara, CA | 45.8 |
| 357 | Santa Clarita, CA | 47.3 |
| 219 | Santa Maria, CA | 119.5 |
| 200 | Santa Monica, CA | 129.7 |
| 325 | Santa Rosa, CA | 61.2 |
| 138 | Savannah, GA | 176.0 |
| 363 | Scottsdale, AZ | 44.8 |
| 263 | Scranton, PA | 93.8 |
| 82 | Seattle, WA | 249.1 |
| 132 | Shreveport, LA | 186.0 |
| 404 | Simi Valley, CA | 24.6 |
| 356 | Sioux City, IA | 48.4 |
| 369 | Sioux Falls, SD | 41.4 |
| 318 | Somerville, MA | 65.6 |
| 43 | South Bend, IN | 360.4 |

| RANK | CITY | RATE |
|---|---|---|
| 94 | South Gate, CA | 233.3 |
| 297 | Sparks, NV | 75.5 |
| 269 | Spokane Valley, WA | 89.2 |
| 83 | Spokane, WA | 247.2 |
| 85 | Springfield, IL | 244.6 |
| 35 | Springfield, MA | 389.4 |
| 87 | Springfield, MO | 242.2 |
| 203 | Stamford, CT | 127.1 |
| 418 | Sterling Heights, MI | 19.1 |
| 42 | Stockton, CA | 362.9 |
| 431 | St. George, UT | 14.4 |
| 230 | St. Joseph, MO | 109.9 |
| 21 | St. Louis, MO | 457.4 |
| 86 | St. Paul, MN | 243.0 |
| 75 | St. Petersburg, FL | 256.6 |
| 301 | Suffolk, VA | 74.9 |
| 368 | Sugar Land, TX | 41.9 |
| 388 | Sunnyvale, CA | 34.4 |
| 208 | Sunrise, FL | 124.1 |
| 374 | Surprise, AZ | 40.0 |
| 63 | Syracuse, NY | 278.1 |
| 74 | Tacoma, WA | 257.8 |
| 115 | Tallahassee, FL | 205.1 |
| 154 | Tampa, FL | 165.1 |
| 385 | Temecula, CA | 36.6 |
| 195 | Tempe, AZ | 132.9 |
| 366 | Thornton, CO | 42.1 |
| 391 | Thousand Oaks, CA | 32.6 |
| 49 | Toledo, OH | 339.9 |
| 348 | Toms River Twnshp, NJ | 52.0 |
| 192 | Topeka, KS | 134.4 |
| 350 | Torrance, CA | 51.5 |
| 316 | Tracy, CA | 66.9 |
| 5 | Trenton, NJ | 621.8 |
| 438 | Troy, MI | 8.5 |
| 126 | Tucson, AZ | 190.7 |
| 79 | Tulsa, OK | 252.0 |
| 147 | Tuscaloosa, AL | 171.0 |
| 361 | Tustin, CA | 45.7 |
| 345 | Tyler, TX | 53.0 |
| 272 | Upland, CA | 88.6 |
| 65 | Upper Darby Twnshp, PA | 274.3 |
| 309 | Vacaville, CA | 70.0 |
| 44 | Vallejo, CA | 358.3 |
| 273 | Vancouver, WA | 87.7 |
| 265 | Ventura, CA | 91.5 |
| 152 | Victorville, CA | 166.0 |
| 312 | Virginia Beach, VA | 67.5 |
| 216 | Visalia, CA | 122.0 |
| 177 | Vista, CA | 144.8 |
| 228 | Waco, TX | 111.3 |
| 210 | Warren, MI | 123.7 |
| 421 | Warwick, RI | 18.3 |
| 9 | Washington, DC | 566.2 |
| 105 | Waterbury, CT | 220.5 |
| 124 | Waukegan, IL | 193.8 |
| 252 | West Covina, CA | 98.3 |
| 66 | West Palm Beach, FL | 274.1 |
| 221 | West Valley, UT | 117.0 |
| 224 | Westland, MI | 112.7 |
| 266 | Westminster, CA | 91.4 |
| 358 | Westminster, CO | 47.2 |
| 279 | Whittier, CA | 84.4 |
| 220 | Wichita Falls, TX | 118.6 |
| 217 | Wichita, KS | 121.1 |
| 98 | Wilmington, NC | 228.0 |
| 131 | Winston-Salem, NC | 186.2 |
| 318 | Woodbridge Twnshp, NJ | 65.6 |
| 71 | Worcester, MA | 263.3 |
| 169 | Yakima, WA | 153.9 |
| 120 | Yonkers, NY | 195.8 |
| 317 | Yuma, AZ | 66.7 |

Source: CQ Press using reported data from the F.B.I. "Crime in the United States 2013"
*Robbery is the taking of anything of value by force or threat of force. Attempts are included.

# 58. Robbery Rate in 2013 (continued)
## National Rate = 109.1 Robberies per 100,000 Population*

| RANK | CITY | RATE | RANK | CITY | RATE | RANK | CITY | RATE |
|---|---|---|---|---|---|---|---|---|
| 1 | Oakland, CA | 1,218.7 | 75 | St. Petersburg, FL | 256.6 | 149 | Omaha, NE | 168.9 |
| 2 | Cleveland, OH | 896.8 | 76 | Macon, GA | 253.4 | 150 | Jacksonville, FL | 168.4 |
| 3 | Newark, NJ | 874.4 | 76 | Nashville, TN | 253.4 | 151 | Norfolk, VA | 167.4 |
| 4 | Detroit, MI | 682.1 | 78 | Fall River, MA | 252.2 | 152 | High Point, NC | 166.0 |
| 5 | Trenton, NJ | 621.8 | 79 | Tulsa, OK | 252.0 | 152 | Victorville, CA | 166.0 |
| 6 | Baltimore, MD | 599.7 | 80 | Columbia, SC | 250.3 | 154 | Tampa, FL | 165.1 |
| 7 | New Haven, CT | 587.5 | 81 | Gresham, OR | 250.1 | 155 | Palmdale, CA | 164.2 |
| 8 | Paterson, NJ | 584.5 | 82 | Seattle, WA | 249.1 | 156 | Davenport, IA | 164.0 |
| 9 | Washington, DC | 566.2 | 83 | Spokane, WA | 247.2 | 157 | Merced, CA | 163.5 |
| 10 | Milwaukee, WI | 546.6 | 84 | Grand Rapids, MI | 246.3 | 158 | Lancaster, CA | 163.3 |
| 11 | Cincinnati, OH | 543.0 | 85 | Springfield, IL | 244.6 | 159 | Lubbock, TX | 163.1 |
| 12 | Miami, FL | 529.6 | 86 | St. Paul, MN | 243.0 | 160 | Clearwater, FL | 162.5 |
| 13 | Atlanta, GA | 523.9 | 87 | Sacramento, CA | 242.2 | 161 | Oxnard, CA | 161.9 |
| 14 | Buffalo, NY | 510.8 | 87 | Springfield, MO | 242.2 | 162 | Kansas City, KS | 161.2 |
| 15 | San Francisco, CA | 503.9 | 89 | Brockton, MA | 241.4 | 163 | Redding, CA | 160.4 |
| 16 | Philadelphia, PA | 486.9 | 90 | Columbus, GA | 239.1 | 164 | Fort Worth, TX | 159.2 |
| 17 | Jackson, MS | 480.0 | 91 | Long Beach, CA | 238.0 | 165 | Carson, CA | 158.4 |
| 18 | Little Rock, AR | 478.2 | 92 | Peoria, IL | 237.2 | 166 | San Antonio, TX | 156.6 |
| 19 | Memphis, TN | 476.4 | 93 | Albany, GA | 236.5 | 167 | Riverside, CA | 156.4 |
| 20 | Minneapolis, MN | 468.4 | 94 | South Gate, CA | 233.3 | 168 | Moreno Valley, CA | 155.0 |
| 21 | St. Louis, MO | 457.4 | 95 | Albany, NY | 231.7 | 169 | Yakima, WA | 153.9 |
| 22 | Birmingham, AL | 457.1 | 96 | Racine, WI | 229.1 | 170 | Fairfield, CA | 152.2 |
| 23 | Houston, TX | 453.6 | 97 | New York, NY | 228.3 | 171 | Lexington, KY | 151.3 |
| 24 | Flint, MI | 447.3 | 98 | Wilmington, NC | 228.0 | 172 | Downey, CA | 151.0 |
| 25 | Indianapolis, IN | 446.9 | 99 | Knoxville, TN | 226.5 | 173 | Portland, OR | 150.5 |
| 26 | Hartford, CT | 445.9 | 100 | Orlando, FL | 226.3 | 174 | Indio, CA | 149.5 |
| 27 | Elizabeth, NJ | 436.0 | 101 | Lansing, MI | 224.7 | 175 | Arlington, TX | 148.4 |
| 27 | Rochester, NY | 436.0 | 102 | Chattanooga, TN | 223.5 | 176 | Roanoke, VA | 145.0 |
| 29 | Chicago, IL | 434.3 | 103 | Salt Lake City, UT | 221.8 | 177 | Vista, CA | 144.8 |
| 30 | Baton Rouge, LA | 423.1 | 104 | Hayward, CA | 220.6 | 178 | Champaign, IL | 143.4 |
| 31 | Gary, IN | 414.9 | 105 | Waterbury, CT | 220.5 | 179 | Glendale, AZ | 143.2 |
| 32 | Miami Beach, FL | 412.3 | 106 | Lafayette, LA | 220.4 | 180 | Lakeland, FL | 142.0 |
| 33 | Fort Lauderdale, FL | 406.6 | 107 | Modesto, CA | 220.3 | 181 | Mesquite, TX | 141.4 |
| 34 | Bridgeport, CT | 397.1 | 108 | Charlotte, NC | 215.5 | 182 | Raleigh, NC | 141.0 |
| 35 | Springfield, MA | 389.4 | 109 | Phoenix, AZ | 215.2 | 183 | Norwalk, CA | 140.8 |
| 36 | Richmond, CA | 379.2 | 110 | Louisville, KY | 212.6 | 184 | El Cajon, CA | 140.2 |
| 37 | Reading, PA | 372.3 | 111 | Hemet, CA | 211.8 | 185 | Plantation, FL | 139.4 |
| 38 | San Bernardino, CA | 370.5 | 112 | Huntsville, AL | 211.7 | 186 | Santa Ana, CA | 139.1 |
| 39 | Compton, CA | 367.7 | 113 | Lynn, MA | 206.0 | 187 | Aurora, CO | 136.3 |
| 40 | Dayton, OH | 366.9 | 114 | North Las Vegas, NV | 205.2 | 188 | Newport News, VA | 135.9 |
| 41 | Lawrence, MA | 363.7 | 115 | Tallahassee, FL | 205.1 | 189 | Lakewood, CA | 135.7 |
| 42 | Stockton, CA | 362.9 | 116 | Providence, RI | 204.0 | 190 | Bellflower, CA | 135.3 |
| 43 | South Bend, IN | 360.4 | 117 | Los Angeles, CA | 203.3 | 191 | Escondido, CA | 135.2 |
| 44 | Vallejo, CA | 358.3 | 118 | Greenville, NC | 198.8 | 192 | Topeka, KS | 134.4 |
| 45 | Kansas City, MO | 357.0 | 119 | Oklahoma City, OK | 196.8 | 193 | Deerfield Beach, FL | 134.3 |
| 46 | Beaumont, TX | 354.6 | 120 | Yonkers, NY | 195.8 | 194 | El Monte, CA | 134.1 |
| 47 | Berkeley, CA | 352.8 | 121 | Bakersfield, CA | 195.7 | 195 | Tempe, AZ | 132.9 |
| 48 | Hawthorne, CA | 347.1 | 122 | Pueblo, CO | 195.3 | 196 | Odessa, TX | 132.1 |
| 49 | Toledo, OH | 339.9 | 123 | Pomona, CA | 194.9 | 196 | Ogden, UT | 132.1 |
| 50 | Dallas, TX | 334.8 | 124 | Waukegan, IL | 193.8 | 198 | Dearborn, MI | 131.2 |
| 51 | Antioch, CA | 330.7 | 125 | Cicero, IL | 192.4 | 199 | Reno, NV | 131.1 |
| 52 | Pittsburgh, PA | 310.8 | 126 | Tucson, AZ | 190.7 | 200 | Santa Monica, CA | 129.7 |
| 53 | New Orleans, LA | 301.8 | 127 | North Charleston, SC | 189.7 | 201 | Kent, WA | 128.7 |
| 54 | Richmond, VA | 293.2 | 128 | Albuquerque, NM | 187.4 | 201 | Medford, OR | 128.7 |
| 55 | Inglewood, CA | 291.9 | 129 | Rialto, CA | 187.3 | 203 | Stamford, CT | 127.1 |
| 56 | Boston, MA | 290.2 | 130 | Longview, TX | 187.0 | 204 | Concord, CA | 126.7 |
| 57 | Salinas, CA | 289.6 | 131 | Winston-Salem, NC | 186.2 | 205 | Anaheim, CA | 126.5 |
| 58 | Fayetteville, NC | 289.3 | 132 | Shreveport, LA | 186.0 | 206 | Pasadena, TX | 125.3 |
| 59 | Miami Gardens, FL | 287.8 | 133 | Mobile, AL | 183.2 | 207 | Killeen, TX | 124.5 |
| 60 | Hammond, IN | 287.4 | 134 | Everett, WA | 182.6 | 208 | Sunrise, FL | 124.1 |
| 61 | San Leandro, CA | 286.9 | 135 | Portsmouth, VA | 182.4 | 209 | Corpus Christi, TX | 124.0 |
| 62 | Jersey City, NJ | 279.1 | 136 | Greensboro, NC | 177.6 | 210 | Miramar, FL | 123.7 |
| 63 | Syracuse, NY | 278.1 | 137 | Fresno, CA | 177.4 | 210 | Warren, MI | 123.7 |
| 64 | Allentown, PA | 275.8 | 138 | Melbourne, FL | 176.0 | 212 | Amarillo, TX | 123.1 |
| 65 | Upper Darby Twnshp, PA | 274.3 | 138 | Savannah, GA | 176.0 | 213 | Eugene, OR | 123.0 |
| 66 | West Palm Beach, FL | 274.1 | 140 | Evansville, IN | 175.4 | 214 | Gainesville, FL | 122.4 |
| 67 | Las Vegas, NV | 271.4 | 140 | Fort Wayne, IN | 175.4 | 215 | Madison, WI | 122.1 |
| 68 | New Bedford, MA | 269.0 | 140 | Lowell, MA | 175.4 | 216 | Visalia, CA | 122.0 |
| 69 | Manchester, NH | 267.2 | 143 | Denver, CO | 174.4 | 217 | Wichita, KS | 121.1 |
| 70 | Akron, OH | 266.1 | 144 | Anchorage, AK | 174.3 | 218 | Largo, FL | 120.6 |
| 71 | Worcester, MA | 263.3 | 145 | Erie, PA | 173.6 | 219 | Santa Maria, CA | 119.5 |
| 72 | Pompano Beach, FL | 262.6 | 146 | Hollywood, FL | 172.5 | 220 | Wichita Falls, TX | 118.6 |
| 73 | Rockford, IL | 262.3 | 147 | Tuscaloosa, AL | 171.0 | 221 | West Valley, UT | 117.0 |
| 74 | Tacoma, WA | 257.8 | 148 | Lawton, OK | 170.5 | 222 | Federal Way, WA | 116.5 |

| RANK | CITY | RATE | RANK | CITY | RATE | RANK | CITY | RATE |
|------|------|------|------|------|------|------|------|------|
| 222 | Pasadena, CA | 116.5 | 297 | Roswell, GA | 75.5 | 371 | Palm Bay, FL | 41.2 |
| 224 | Westland, MI | 112.7 | 297 | Sparks, NV | 75.5 | 372 | Corona, CA | 40.6 |
| 225 | Murfreesboro, TN | 112.5 | 299 | Green Bay, WI | 75.2 | 373 | Hoover, AL | 40.4 |
| 226 | Decatur, IL | 111.7 | 300 | Billings, MT | 75.1 | 374 | Surprise, AZ | 40.0 |
| 227 | Alameda, CA | 111.5 | 301 | Brownsville, TX | 74.9 | 375 | Carlsbad, CA | 39.8 |
| 228 | Waco, TX | 111.3 | 301 | Suffolk, VA | 74.9 | 376 | Colonie, NY | 39.6 |
| 229 | San Jose, CA | 110.4 | 303 | Rancho Cucamon., CA | 74.3 | 377 | Mission, TX | 39.3 |
| 230 | St. Joseph, MO | 109.9 | 304 | Lewisville, TX | 73.5 | 377 | Norman, OK | 39.3 |
| 231 | Brooklyn Park, MN | 109.8 | 305 | Las Cruces, NM | 72.5 | 379 | Boulder, CO | 38.9 |
| 232 | San Diego, CA | 107.9 | 306 | Greeley, CO | 70.8 | 380 | Glendale, CA | 38.4 |
| 233 | Chico, CA | 107.7 | 307 | San Marcos, CA | 70.7 | 380 | Plano, TX | 38.4 |
| 234 | Fort Smith, AR | 107.0 | 308 | Nashua, NH | 70.1 | 382 | Bellevue, WA | 37.6 |
| 235 | Joliet, IL | 106.4 | 309 | Cedar Rapids, IA | 70.0 | 383 | College Station, TX | 37.4 |
| 236 | Cambridge, MA | 106.3 | 309 | Vacaville, CA | 70.0 | 384 | Lakewood Twnshp, NJ | 36.7 |
| 237 | Oceanside, CA | 105.5 | 311 | Norwalk, CT | 69.6 | 385 | Temecula, CA | 36.6 |
| 238 | Mesa, AZ | 104.8 | 312 | Virginia Beach, VA | 67.5 | 386 | Peoria, AZ | 36.5 |
| 239 | Abilene, TX | 104.7 | 313 | Chesapeake, VA | 67.2 | 387 | Livonia, MI | 35.7 |
| 240 | Renton, WA | 104.5 | 313 | El Paso, TX | 67.2 | 388 | Sunnyvale, CA | 34.4 |
| 241 | Athens-Clarke, GA | 104.1 | 315 | Clifton, NJ | 67.0 | 389 | Round Rock, TX | 34.1 |
| 242 | Independence, MO | 103.9 | 316 | Tracy, CA | 66.9 | 390 | Sandy, UT | 33.4 |
| 243 | Sandy Springs, GA | 103.8 | 317 | Yuma, AZ | 66.7 | 391 | Thousand Oaks, CA | 32.6 |
| 244 | New Rochelle, NY | 102.8 | 318 | Somerville, MA | 65.6 | 392 | Brick Twnshp, NJ | 31.8 |
| 245 | Des Moines, IA | 101.7 | 318 | Woodbridge Twnshp, NJ | 65.6 | 393 | Broken Arrow, OK | 31.1 |
| 246 | Kenosha, WI | 101.6 | 320 | Chandler, AZ | 65.1 | 394 | Arvada, CO | 30.7 |
| 247 | Garland, TX | 100.6 | 321 | Danbury, CT | 63.6 | 395 | McKinney, TX | 30.0 |
| 248 | Fontana, CA | 99.3 | 322 | Greece, NY | 62.1 | 396 | Pearland, TX | 29.5 |
| 248 | Ontario, CA | 99.3 | 323 | Elk Grove, CA | 61.5 | 397 | Lake Forest, CA | 29.0 |
| 250 | Hialeah, FL | 98.6 | 324 | Cheektowaga, NY | 61.3 | 398 | Bend, OR | 27.5 |
| 251 | Bethlehem, PA | 98.5 | 325 | Clinton Twnshp, MI | 61.2 | 399 | Amherst, NY | 26.2 |
| 252 | West Covina, CA | 98.3 | 325 | Santa Rosa, CA | 61.2 | 400 | Farmington Hills, MI | 25.9 |
| 253 | Columbia, MO | 97.7 | 327 | McAllen, TX | 61.0 | 401 | Menifee, CA | 25.4 |
| 254 | Chula Vista, CA | 97.2 | 328 | Boca Raton, FL | 60.8 | 402 | Overland Park, KS | 24.9 |
| 255 | Buena Park, CA | 96.8 | 328 | Edinburg, TX | 60.8 | 403 | Fort Collins, CO | 24.7 |
| 256 | Baldwin Park, CA | 96.4 | 330 | Fremont, CA | 60.6 | 404 | League City, TX | 24.6 |
| 257 | Davie, FL | 96.3 | 331 | Concord, NC | 60.3 | 404 | Simi Valley, CA | 24.6 |
| 258 | Colorado Springs, CO | 95.8 | 332 | Napa, CA | 59.7 | 406 | Cape Coral, FL | 24.5 |
| 259 | Alhambra, CA | 95.6 | 333 | Henderson, NV | 59.6 | 407 | Beaverton, OR | 23.5 |
| 260 | Bryan, TX | 95.4 | 334 | Aurora, IL | 59.3 | 407 | Cary, NC | 23.5 |
| 261 | Bloomington, IN | 94.6 | 335 | Chino, CA | 58.2 | 407 | Port St. Lucie, FL | 23.5 |
| 262 | Lynchburg, VA | 93.9 | 336 | Richardson, TX | 57.4 | 410 | Mission Viejo, CA | 22.9 |
| 263 | Scranton, PA | 93.8 | 337 | Carrollton, TX | 57.3 | 411 | San Angelo, TX | 22.8 |
| 264 | Quincy, MA | 93.1 | 338 | Hillsboro, OR | 57.1 | 412 | Longmont, CO | 21.2 |
| 265 | Ventura, CA | 91.5 | 339 | Elgin, IL | 57.0 | 413 | Clarkstown, NY | 21.1 |
| 266 | Westminster, CA | 91.4 | 340 | Charleston, SC | 56.6 | 414 | Boise, ID | 21.0 |
| 267 | Santa Barbara, CA | 91.1 | 341 | Bloomington, MN | 56.3 | 415 | Gilbert, AZ | 20.9 |
| 268 | Hesperia, CA | 89.6 | 342 | Kennewick, WA | 56.2 | 416 | Newton, MA | 20.7 |
| 269 | Spokane Valley, WA | 89.2 | 343 | Edison Twnshp, NJ | 55.3 | 417 | Murrieta, CA | 19.5 |
| 270 | Citrus Heights, CA | 89.1 | 344 | Pembroke Pines, FL | 53.7 | 418 | Centennial, CO | 19.1 |
| 271 | Austin, TX | 88.8 | 345 | Tyler, TX | 53.0 | 418 | Sterling Heights, MI | 19.1 |
| 272 | Upland, CA | 88.6 | 346 | Fargo, ND | 52.2 | 420 | Nampa, ID | 18.9 |
| 273 | Vancouver, WA | 87.7 | 346 | Livermore, CA | 52.2 | 421 | Warwick, RI | 18.3 |
| 274 | Hamilton Twnshp, NJ | 87.6 | 348 | Cranston, RI | 52.0 | 422 | Canton Twnshp, MI | 18.0 |
| 274 | Hampton, VA | 87.6 | 348 | Toms River Twnshp, NJ | 52.0 | 422 | Provo, UT | 18.0 |
| 276 | Salem, OR | 87.2 | 350 | Midland, TX | 51.5 | 424 | Olathe, KS | 17.5 |
| 277 | Daly City, CA | 86.1 | 350 | Torrance, CA | 51.5 | 425 | Edmond, OK | 17.4 |
| 278 | San Mateo, CA | 84.6 | 352 | Huntington Beach, CA | 51.1 | 426 | Frisco, TX | 16.7 |
| 279 | Whittier, CA | 84.4 | 353 | Roseville, CA | 50.7 | 427 | Lee's Summit, MO | 16.2 |
| 280 | Grand Prairie, TX | 84.3 | 354 | Rochester, MN | 49.2 | 428 | Irvine, CA | 16.1 |
| 281 | Laredo, TX | 83.7 | 355 | Burbank, CA | 48.7 | 429 | Newport Beach, CA | 14.8 |
| 282 | Costa Mesa, CA | 83.5 | 356 | Sioux City, IA | 48.4 | 430 | Naperville, IL | 14.6 |
| 282 | Duluth, MN | 83.5 | 357 | Santa Clarita, CA | 47.3 | 431 | St. George, UT | 14.4 |
| 284 | Evanston, IL | 83.2 | 358 | Clovis, CA | 47.2 | 432 | Chino Hills, CA | 14.3 |
| 285 | Redwood City, CA | 82.8 | 358 | Westminster, CO | 47.2 | 433 | Allen, TX | 14.2 |
| 286 | Lawrence, KS | 82.2 | 360 | Santa Clara, CA | 45.8 | 434 | Johns Creek, GA | 13.1 |
| 287 | Irving, TX | 81.4 | 361 | Tustin, CA | 45.7 | 435 | Carmel, IN | 13.0 |
| 288 | Alexandria, VA | 79.5 | 362 | Orange, CA | 45.6 | 436 | Ramapo, NY | 10.3 |
| 289 | Lincoln, NE | 79.2 | 363 | Scottsdale, AZ | 44.8 | 437 | Arlington Heights, IL | 9.2 |
| 290 | Clarksville, TN | 79.0 | 364 | Fayetteville, AR | 42.4 | 438 | Troy, MI | 8.5 |
| 291 | Coral Springs, FL | 78.2 | 365 | Denton, TX | 42.2 | 439 | Fishers, IN | 8.4 |
| 292 | Garden Grove, CA | 78.1 | 366 | Thornton, CO | 42.1 | 440 | Orem, UT | 7.7 |
| 293 | Lakewood, CO | 77.2 | 367 | Ann Arbor, MI | 42.0 | 441 | O'Fallon, MO | 7.3 |
| 294 | Fullerton, CA | 76.6 | 368 | Sugar Land, TX | 41.9 | 442 | Meridian, ID | 6.1 |
| 295 | Jurupa Valley, CA | 76.5 | 369 | Sioux Falls, SD | 41.4 | | | |
| 296 | Bloomington, IL | 75.6 | 370 | Mountain View, CA | 41.3 | | | |

Source: CQ Press using reported data from the F.B.I. "Crime in the United States 2013"

*Robbery is the taking of anything of value by force or threat of force. Attempts are included.

# 59. Percent Change in Robbery Rate: 2012 to 2013
## National Percent Change = 3.5% Decrease*

| RANK | CITY | % CHANGE | RANK | CITY | % CHANGE | RANK | CITY | % CHANGE |
|---|---|---|---|---|---|---|---|---|
| 177 | Abilene, TX | (1.1) | 276 | Chino, CA | (10.7) | 371 | Fullerton, CA | (22.5) |
| 260 | Akron, OH | (8.5) | 103 | Chula Vista, CA | 6.9 | 265 | Gainesville, FL | (9.1) |
| 116 | Alameda, CA | 5.2 | 281 | Cicero, IL | (11.4) | 149 | Garden Grove, CA | 1.3 |
| 336 | Albany, GA | (17.1) | 244 | Cincinnati, OH | (6.8) | 163 | Garland, TX | 0.2 |
| 261 | Albany, NY | (8.6) | 377 | Citrus Heights, CA | (24.2) | 33 | Gary, IN | 21.4 |
| 219 | Albuquerque, NM | (5.0) | 416 | Clarkstown, NY | (37.4) | 376 | Gilbert, AZ | (24.0) |
| 328 | Alexandria, VA | (16.0) | 87 | Clarksville, TN | 9.6 | 348 | Glendale, AZ | (19.2) |
| 32 | Alhambra, CA | 22.4 | 308 | Clearwater, FL | (13.8) | 403 | Glendale, CA | (30.7) |
| 288 | Allentown, PA | (12.0) | 92 | Cleveland, OH | 8.6 | 205 | Grand Prairie, TX | (4.2) |
| 186 | Allen, TX | (2.7) | 396 | Clifton, NJ | (29.1) | 149 | Grand Rapids, MI | 1.3 |
| 295 | Amarillo, TX | (12.9) | 142 | Clinton Twnshp, MI | 2.3 | 18 | Greece, NY | 30.7 |
| 84 | Amherst, NY | 10.1 | 346 | Clovis, CA | (19.0) | 105 | Greeley, CO | 6.5 |
| 175 | Anaheim, CA | (0.9) | 222 | College Station, TX | (5.1) | 257 | Green Bay, WI | (8.3) |
| 103 | Anchorage, AK | 6.9 | 105 | Colonie, NY | 6.5 | 285 | Greensboro, NC | (11.8) |
| 197 | Ann Arbor, MI | (3.4) | 360 | Colorado Springs, CO | (20.8) | 143 | Greenville, NC | 2.2 |
| 242 | Antioch, CA | (6.7) | 410 | Columbia, MO | (33.3) | 18 | Gresham, OR | 30.7 |
| 298 | Arlington Heights, IL | (13.2) | NA | Columbia, SC** | NA | 359 | Hamilton Twnshp, NJ | (20.4) |
| 112 | Arlington, TX | 5.8 | 79 | Columbus, GA | 10.9 | 35 | Hammond, IN | 21.3 |
| 61 | Arvada, CO | 15.4 | 325 | Compton, CA | (15.8) | 340 | Hampton, VA | (17.3) |
| 372 | Athens-Clarke, GA | (22.6) | 128 | Concord, CA | 3.7 | 292 | Hartford, CT | (12.8) |
| 159 | Atlanta, GA | 0.6 | NA | Concord, NC** | NA | 192 | Hawthorne, CA | (3.1) |
| 217 | Aurora, CO | (4.9) | 26 | Coral Springs, FL | 25.3 | 217 | Hayward, CA | (4.9) |
| 225 | Aurora, IL | (5.3) | 414 | Corona, CA | (37.3) | 47 | Hemet, CA | 17.8 |
| 380 | Austin, TX | (24.4) | 133 | Corpus Christi, TX | 3.3 | 262 | Henderson, NV | (8.7) |
| 168 | Bakersfield, CA | (0.2) | 68 | Costa Mesa, CA | 13.3 | 41 | Hesperia, CA | 19.9 |
| 149 | Baldwin Park, CA | 1.3 | 31 | Cranston, RI | 22.9 | 282 | Hialeah, FL | (11.6) |
| 124 | Baltimore, MD | 4.0 | 148 | Dallas, TX | 1.5 | 205 | High Point, NC | (4.2) |
| 223 | Baton Rouge, LA | (5.2) | 55 | Daly City, CA | 17.0 | 131 | Hillsboro, OR | 3.4 |
| 121 | Beaumont, TX | 4.6 | 60 | Danbury, CT | 15.6 | 271 | Hollywood, FL | (9.8) |
| 422 | Beaverton, OR | (39.7) | 85 | Davenport, IA | 9.9 | 392 | Hoover, AL | (27.7) |
| 398 | Bellevue, WA | (29.3) | 28 | Davie, FL | 23.6 | 116 | Houston, TX | 5.2 |
| 368 | Bellflower, CA | (21.9) | 342 | Dayton, OH | (17.6) | 40 | Huntington Beach, CA | 20.0 |
| NA | Bend, OR** | NA | 44 | Dearborn, MI | 19.2 | 316 | Huntsville, AL | (14.7) |
| 36 | Berkeley, CA | 21.1 | 355 | Decatur, IL | (19.8) | 203 | Independence, MO | (3.9) |
| 420 | Bethlehem, PA | (38.6) | 399 | Deerfield Beach, FL | (30.2) | 89 | Indianapolis, IN | 8.9 |
| 50 | Billings, MT | 17.5 | 421 | Denton, TX | (38.8) | 373 | Indio, CA | (23.3) |
| 172 | Birmingham, AL | (0.8) | 234 | Denver, CO | (5.9) | 292 | Inglewood, CA | (12.8) |
| 21 | Bloomington, IL | 29.5 | 322 | Des Moines, IA | (15.6) | 36 | Irvine, CA | 21.1 |
| 1 | Bloomington, IN | 84.0 | 170 | Detroit, MI | (0.4) | 14 | Irving, TX | 35.0 |
| 348 | Bloomington, MN | (19.2) | 269 | Downey, CA | (9.7) | 135 | Jacksonville, FL | 3.2 |
| 318 | Boca Raton, FL | (15.2) | 350 | Duluth, MN | (19.5) | 113 | Jackson, MS | 5.7 |
| 403 | Boise, ID | (30.7) | 183 | Edinburg, TX | (2.3) | 357 | Jersey City, NJ | (20.2) |
| 205 | Boston, MA | (4.2) | 225 | Edison Twnshp, NJ | (5.3) | 411 | Johns Creek, GA | (34.5) |
| 345 | Boulder, CO | (18.8) | 390 | Edmond, OK | (27.5) | 6 | Joliet, IL | 52.0 |
| 7 | Brick Twnshp, NJ | 50.7 | 187 | El Cajon, CA | (2.8) | 354 | Jurupa Valley, CA | (19.7) |
| 209 | Bridgeport, CT | (4.3) | 375 | El Monte, CA | (23.8) | 312 | Kansas City, KS | (14.3) |
| 144 | Brockton, MA | 2.1 | 200 | El Paso, TX | (3.6) | 159 | Kansas City, MO | 0.6 |
| 352 | Broken Arrow, OK | (19.6) | 344 | Elgin, IL | (18.1) | 29 | Kennewick, WA | 23.5 |
| 242 | Brooklyn Park, MN | (6.7) | 138 | Elizabeth, NJ | 2.9 | 195 | Kenosha, WI | (3.2) |
| 92 | Brownsville, TX | 8.6 | 153 | Elk Grove, CA | 1.2 | 346 | Kent, WA | (19.0) |
| 94 | Bryan, TX | 8.5 | 138 | Erie, PA | 2.9 | 401 | Killeen, TX | (30.4) |
| 127 | Buena Park, CA | 3.8 | 196 | Escondido, CA | (3.3) | 366 | Knoxville, TN | (21.8) |
| 197 | Buffalo, NY | (3.4) | 172 | Eugene, OR | (0.8) | 15 | Lafayette, LA | 34.1 |
| 433 | Burbank, CA | (53.9) | 361 | Evanston, IL | (21.2) | 64 | Lake Forest, CA | 14.6 |
| 325 | Cambridge, MA | (15.8) | 123 | Evansville, IN | 4.2 | 179 | Lakeland, FL | (1.5) |
| NA | Canton Twnshp, MI** | NA | 113 | Everett, WA | 5.7 | 383 | Lakewood Twnshp, NJ | (25.3) |
| 214 | Cape Coral, FL | (4.7) | 52 | Fairfield, CA | 17.3 | 96 | Lakewood, CA | 8.3 |
| 369 | Carlsbad, CA | (22.0) | 303 | Fall River, MA | (13.6) | 374 | Lakewood, CO | (23.6) |
| 2 | Carmel, IN | 78.1 | 27 | Fargo, ND | 24.6 | 334 | Lancaster, CA | (17.0) |
| 219 | Carrollton, TX | (5.0) | 3 | Farmington Hills, MI | 73.8 | 22 | Lansing, MI | 26.9 |
| 124 | Carson, CA | 4.0 | 357 | Fayetteville, AR | (20.2) | 70 | Laredo, TX | 12.3 |
| 66 | Cary, NC | 14.1 | 108 | Fayetteville, NC | 6.4 | 332 | Largo, FL | (16.7) |
| 245 | Cedar Rapids, IA | (7.3) | 154 | Federal Way, WA | 1.1 | 131 | Las Cruces, NM | 3.4 |
| 422 | Centennial, CO | (39.7) | 384 | Fishers, IN | (25.7) | 119 | Las Vegas, NV | 5.0 |
| 303 | Champaign, IL | (13.6) | 408 | Flint, MI | (32.5) | 11 | Lawrence, KS | 38.4 |
| 111 | Chandler, AZ | 6.0 | 406 | Fontana, CA | (31.5) | 24 | Lawrence, MA | 26.7 |
| 409 | Charleston, SC | (32.6) | 256 | Fort Collins, CO | (8.2) | 185 | Lawton, OK | (2.6) |
| 192 | Charlotte, NC | (3.1) | 333 | Fort Lauderdale, FL | (16.8) | 378 | League City, TX | (24.3) |
| NA | Chattanooga, TN** | NA | 179 | Fort Smith, AR | (1.5) | 417 | Lee's Summit, MO | (37.9) |
| 388 | Cheektowaga, NY | (26.5) | 157 | Fort Wayne, IN | 0.7 | NA | Lewisville, TX** | NA |
| 378 | Chesapeake, VA | (24.3) | 205 | Fort Worth, TX | (4.2) | 381 | Lexington, KY | (24.5) |
| 290 | Chicago, IL | (12.7) | 162 | Fremont, CA | 0.5 | 110 | Lincoln, NE | 6.2 |
| 178 | Chico, CA | (1.3) | 282 | Fresno, CA | (11.6) | 56 | Little Rock, AR | 16.2 |
| 430 | Chino Hills, CA | (50.2) | 313 | Frisco, TX | (14.4) | 12 | Livermore, CA | 35.2 |

| RANK | CITY | % CHANGE | RANK | CITY | % CHANGE | RANK | CITY | % CHANGE |
|---|---|---|---|---|---|---|---|---|
| 101 | Livonia, MI | 7.2 | 232 | Pasadena, CA | (5.6) | 321 | South Gate, CA | (15.5) |
| 269 | Long Beach, CA | (9.7) | 16 | Pasadena, TX | 31.8 | 141 | Sparks, NV | 2.6 |
| 413 | Longmont, CO | (37.1) | 157 | Paterson, NJ | 0.7 | 33 | Spokane Valley, WA | 21.4 |
| 47 | Longview, TX | 17.8 | 169 | Pearland, TX | (0.3) | 183 | Spokane, WA | (2.3) |
| 290 | Los Angeles, CA | (12.7) | 133 | Pembroke Pines, FL | 3.3 | 83 | Springfield, IL | 10.2 |
| 147 | Louisville, KY | 1.6 | 382 | Peoria, AZ | (24.9) | 78 | Springfield, MA | 11.0 |
| 88 | Lowell, MA | 9.4 | 322 | Peoria, IL | (15.6) | 80 | Springfield, MO | 10.4 |
| 45 | Lubbock, TX | 19.1 | 235 | Philadelphia, PA | (6.1) | 89 | Stamford, CT | 8.9 |
| 4 | Lynchburg, VA | 57.8 | 265 | Phoenix, AZ | (9.1) | 340 | Sterling Heights, MI | (17.3) |
| 76 | Lynn, MA | 11.3 | 314 | Pittsburgh, PA | (14.5) | 399 | Stockton, CA | (30.2) |
| 187 | Macon, GA | (2.8) | 212 | Plano, TX | (4.5) | 432 | St. George, UT | (52.6) |
| 39 | Madison, WI | 20.3 | 201 | Plantation, FL | (3.7) | 241 | St. Joseph, MO | (6.6) |
| 10 | Manchester, NH | 43.4 | 365 | Pomona, CA | (21.7) | 343 | St. Louis, MO | (18.0) |
| 8 | McAllen, TX | 47.7 | 412 | Pompano Beach, FL | (35.4) | 100 | St. Paul, MN | 7.3 |
| 394 | McKinney, TX | (28.6) | 393 | Port St. Lucie, FL | (28.1) | 89 | St. Petersburg, FL | 8.9 |
| 5 | Medford, OR | 52.9 | 225 | Portland, OR | (5.3) | NA | Suffolk, VA** | NA |
| 144 | Melbourne, FL | 2.1 | 190 | Portsmouth, VA | (3.0) | 235 | Sugar Land, TX | (6.1) |
| 247 | Memphis, TN | (7.4) | 163 | Providence, RI | 0.2 | 401 | Sunnyvale, CA | (30.4) |
| 320 | Menifee, CA | (15.3) | 80 | Provo, UT | 10.4 | 62 | Sunrise, FL | 15.1 |
| 419 | Merced, CA | (38.4) | 102 | Pueblo, CO | 7.0 | 369 | Surprise, AZ | (22.0) |
| 428 | Meridian, ID | (47.4) | 126 | Quincy, MA | 3.9 | 275 | Syracuse, NY | (10.6) |
| 156 | Mesa, AZ | 0.9 | 311 | Racine, WI | (14.2) | 98 | Tacoma, WA | 7.5 |
| 74 | Mesquite, TX | 11.9 | 277 | Raleigh, NC | (10.8) | 391 | Tallahassee, FL | (27.6) |
| 251 | Miami Beach, FL | (7.7) | 407 | Ramapo, NY | (32.2) | 155 | Tampa, FL | 1.0 |
| 300 | Miami Gardens, FL | (13.3) | 72 | Rancho Cucamon., CA | 12.2 | 395 | Temecula, CA | (28.7) |
| 120 | Miami, FL | 4.7 | 305 | Reading, PA | (13.7) | 292 | Tempe, AZ | (12.8) |
| 65 | Midland, TX | 14.4 | 75 | Redding, CA | 11.4 | 25 | Thornton, CO | 26.4 |
| 97 | Milwaukee, WI | 8.2 | 387 | Redwood City, CA | (26.2) | 258 | Thousand Oaks, CA | (8.4) |
| 109 | Minneapolis, MN | 6.3 | 250 | Reno, NV | (7.6) | 305 | Toledo, OH | (13.7) |
| 210 | Miramar, FL | (4.4) | 317 | Renton, WA | (14.8) | 43 | Toms River Twnshp, NJ | 19.8 |
| 366 | Mission Viejo, CA | (21.8) | 225 | Rialto, CA | (5.3) | 389 | Topeka, KS | (26.9) |
| 405 | Mission, TX | (31.2) | 385 | Richardson, TX | (25.9) | 339 | Torrance, CA | (17.2) |
| 163 | Mobile, AL | 0.2 | 135 | Richmond, CA | 3.2 | 308 | Tracy, CA | (13.8) |
| 163 | Modesto, CA | 0.2 | 201 | Richmond, VA | (3.7) | 255 | Trenton, NJ | (8.1) |
| 240 | Moreno Valley, CA | (6.5) | 223 | Riverside, CA | (5.2) | 427 | Troy, MI | (46.5) |
| 252 | Mountain View, CA | (7.8) | 159 | Roanoke, VA | 0.6 | 350 | Tucson, AZ | (19.5) |
| 233 | Murfreesboro, TN | (5.8) | 190 | Rochester, MN | (3.0) | 225 | Tulsa, OK | (5.3) |
| 176 | Murrieta, CA | (1.0) | 69 | Rochester, NY | 13.1 | 248 | Tuscaloosa, AL | (7.5) |
| 362 | Nampa, ID | (21.3) | 356 | Rockford, IL | (20.0) | 181 | Tustin, CA | (1.7) |
| 38 | Napa, CA | 20.4 | 385 | Roseville, CA | (25.9) | 424 | Tyler, TX | (42.4) |
| 297 | Naperville, IL | (13.1) | 80 | Roswell, GA | 10.4 | 167 | Upland, CA | (0.1) |
| 23 | Nashua, NH | 26.8 | 352 | Round Rock, TX | (19.6) | 324 | Upper Darby Twnshp, PA | (15.7) |
| 263 | Nashville, TN | (8.8) | 214 | Sacramento, CA | (4.7) | 272 | Vacaville, CA | (9.9) |
| 219 | New Bedford, MA | (5.0) | 171 | Salem, OR | (0.6) | 77 | Vallejo, CA | 11.2 |
| 267 | New Haven, CT | (9.6) | 258 | Salinas, CA | (8.4) | 318 | Vancouver, WA | (15.2) |
| 140 | New Orleans, LA | 2.8 | 13 | Salt Lake City, UT | 35.1 | 396 | Ventura, CA | (29.1) |
| 285 | New Rochelle, NY | (11.8) | NA | San Angelo, TX** | NA | 279 | Victorville, CA | (11.2) |
| 237 | New York, NY | (6.3) | 58 | San Antonio, TX | 15.9 | 245 | Virginia Beach, VA | (7.3) |
| 30 | Newark, NJ | 23.4 | 172 | San Bernardino, CA | (0.8) | 56 | Visalia, CA | 16.2 |
| 431 | Newport Beach, CA | (52.1) | 216 | San Diego, CA | (4.8) | 197 | Vista, CA | (3.4) |
| 264 | Newport News, VA | (8.9) | 46 | San Francisco, CA | 18.6 | 362 | Waco, TX | (21.3) |
| 115 | Newton, MA | 5.6 | 277 | San Jose, CA | (10.8) | 70 | Warren, MI | 12.3 |
| 329 | Norfolk, VA | (16.4) | 254 | San Leandro, CA | (8.0) | 429 | Warwick, RI | (48.0) |
| 336 | Norman, OK | (17.1) | 105 | San Marcos, CA | 6.5 | 203 | Washington, DC | (3.9) |
| 272 | North Charleston, SC | (9.9) | 128 | San Mateo, CA | 3.7 | 17 | Waterbury, CT | 31.7 |
| 53 | North Las Vegas, NV | 17.1 | 128 | Sandy Springs, GA | 3.7 | 95 | Waukegan, IL | 8.4 |
| 284 | Norwalk, CA | (11.7) | 305 | Sandy, UT | (13.7) | 182 | West Covina, CA | (1.8) |
| 279 | Norwalk, CT | (11.2) | 314 | Santa Ana, CA | (14.5) | 327 | West Palm Beach, FL | (15.9) |
| 72 | Oakland, CA | 12.2 | 308 | Santa Barbara, CA | (13.8) | 20 | West Valley, UT | 30.4 |
| 137 | Oceanside, CA | 3.1 | 274 | Santa Clara, CA | (10.4) | 51 | Westland, MI | 17.4 |
| 189 | Odessa, TX | (2.9) | 285 | Santa Clarita, CA | (11.8) | 212 | Westminster, CA | (4.5) |
| 9 | O'Fallon, MO | 46.0 | 330 | Santa Maria, CA | (16.6) | 149 | Westminster, CO | 1.3 |
| 53 | Ogden, UT | 17.1 | 364 | Santa Monica, CA | (21.6) | 267 | Whittier, CA | (9.6) |
| 192 | Oklahoma City, OK | (3.1) | 334 | Santa Rosa, CA | (17.0) | 330 | Wichita Falls, TX | (16.6) |
| 239 | Olathe, KS | (6.4) | 336 | Savannah, GA | (17.1) | 231 | Wichita, KS | (5.5) |
| 301 | Omaha, NE | (13.4) | 296 | Scottsdale, AZ | (13.0) | 210 | Wilmington, NC | (4.4) |
| 414 | Ontario, CA | (37.3) | 425 | Scranton, PA | (44.7) | 144 | Winston-Salem, NC | 2.1 |
| 47 | Orange, CA | 17.8 | 85 | Seattle, WA | 9.9 | 41 | Woodbridge Twnshp, NJ | 19.9 |
| 434 | Orem, UT | (66.2) | 298 | Shreveport, LA | (13.2) | 62 | Worcester, MA | 15.1 |
| 248 | Orlando, FL | (7.5) | 301 | Simi Valley, CA | (13.4) | 230 | Yakima, WA | (5.4) |
| 118 | Overland Park, KS | 5.1 | 289 | Sioux City, IA | (12.3) | 253 | Yonkers, NY | (7.9) |
| 98 | Oxnard, CA | 7.5 | 237 | Sioux Falls, SD | (6.3) | 122 | Yuma, AZ | 4.5 |
| 425 | Palm Bay, FL | (44.7) | 418 | Somerville, MA | (38.2) | | | |
| 67 | Palmdale, CA | 13.9 | 59 | South Bend, IN | 15.7 | | | |

Source: CQ Press using reported data from the F.B.I. "Crime in the United States 2013"

*Robbery is the taking of anything of value by force or threat of force. Attempts are included.

**Not available.

# 59. Percent Change in Robbery Rate: 2012 to 2013 (continued)
## National Percent Change = 3.5% Decrease*

| RANK | CITY | % CHANGE | RANK | CITY | % CHANGE | RANK | CITY | % CHANGE |
|---|---|---|---|---|---|---|---|---|
| 1 | Bloomington, IN | 84.0 | 75 | Redding, CA | 11.4 | 149 | Baldwin Park, CA | 1.3 |
| 2 | Carmel, IN | 78.1 | 76 | Lynn, MA | 11.3 | 149 | Garden Grove, CA | 1.3 |
| 3 | Farmington Hills, MI | 73.8 | 77 | Vallejo, CA | 11.2 | 149 | Grand Rapids, MI | 1.3 |
| 4 | Lynchburg, VA | 57.8 | 78 | Springfield, MA | 11.0 | 149 | Westminster, CO | 1.3 |
| 5 | Medford, OR | 52.9 | 79 | Columbus, GA | 10.9 | 153 | Elk Grove, CA | 1.2 |
| 6 | Joliet, IL | 52.0 | 80 | Provo, UT | 10.4 | 154 | Federal Way, WA | 1.1 |
| 7 | Brick Twnshp, NJ | 50.7 | 80 | Roswell, GA | 10.4 | 155 | Tampa, FL | 1.0 |
| 8 | McAllen, TX | 47.7 | 80 | Springfield, MO | 10.4 | 156 | Mesa, AZ | 0.9 |
| 9 | O'Fallon, MO | 46.0 | 83 | Springfield, IL | 10.2 | 157 | Fort Wayne, IN | 0.7 |
| 10 | Manchester, NH | 43.4 | 84 | Amherst, NY | 10.1 | 157 | Paterson, NJ | 0.7 |
| 11 | Lawrence, KS | 38.4 | 85 | Davenport, IA | 9.9 | 159 | Atlanta, GA | 0.6 |
| 12 | Livermore, CA | 35.2 | 85 | Seattle, WA | 9.9 | 159 | Kansas City, MO | 0.6 |
| 13 | Salt Lake City, UT | 35.1 | 87 | Clarksville, TN | 9.6 | 159 | Roanoke, VA | 0.6 |
| 14 | Irving, TX | 35.0 | 88 | Lowell, MA | 9.4 | 162 | Fremont, CA | 0.5 |
| 15 | Lafayette, LA | 34.1 | 89 | Indianapolis, IN | 8.9 | 163 | Garland, TX | 0.2 |
| 16 | Pasadena, TX | 31.8 | 89 | Stamford, CT | 8.9 | 163 | Mobile, AL | 0.2 |
| 17 | Waterbury, CT | 31.7 | 89 | St. Petersburg, FL | 8.9 | 163 | Modesto, CA | 0.2 |
| 18 | Greece, NY | 30.7 | 92 | Brownsville, TX | 8.6 | 163 | Providence, RI | 0.2 |
| 18 | Gresham, OR | 30.7 | 92 | Cleveland, OH | 8.6 | 167 | Upland, CA | (0.1) |
| 20 | West Valley, UT | 30.4 | 94 | Bryan, TX | 8.5 | 168 | Bakersfield, CA | (0.2) |
| 21 | Bloomington, IL | 29.5 | 95 | Waukegan, IL | 8.4 | 169 | Pearland, TX | (0.3) |
| 22 | Lansing, MI | 26.9 | 96 | Lakewood, CA | 8.3 | 170 | Detroit, MI | (0.4) |
| 23 | Nashua, NH | 26.8 | 97 | Milwaukee, WI | 8.2 | 171 | Salem, OR | (0.6) |
| 24 | Lawrence, MA | 26.7 | 98 | Oxnard, CA | 7.5 | 172 | Birmingham, AL | (0.8) |
| 25 | Thornton, CO | 26.4 | 98 | Tacoma, WA | 7.5 | 172 | Eugene, OR | (0.8) |
| 26 | Coral Springs, FL | 25.3 | 100 | St. Paul, MN | 7.3 | 172 | San Bernardino, CA | (0.8) |
| 27 | Fargo, ND | 24.6 | 101 | Livonia, MI | 7.2 | 175 | Anaheim, CA | (0.9) |
| 28 | Davie, FL | 23.6 | 102 | Pueblo, CO | 7.0 | 176 | Murrieta, CA | (1.0) |
| 29 | Kennewick, WA | 23.5 | 103 | Anchorage, AK | 6.9 | 177 | Abilene, TX | (1.1) |
| 30 | Newark, NJ | 23.4 | 103 | Chula Vista, CA | 6.9 | 178 | Chico, CA | (1.3) |
| 31 | Cranston, RI | 22.9 | 105 | Colonie, NY | 6.5 | 179 | Fort Smith, AR | (1.5) |
| 32 | Alhambra, CA | 22.4 | 105 | Greeley, CO | 6.5 | 179 | Lakeland, FL | (1.5) |
| 33 | Gary, IN | 21.4 | 105 | San Marcos, CA | 6.5 | 181 | Tustin, CA | (1.7) |
| 33 | Spokane Valley, WA | 21.4 | 108 | Fayetteville, NC | 6.4 | 182 | West Covina, CA | (1.8) |
| 35 | Hammond, IN | 21.3 | 109 | Minneapolis, MN | 6.3 | 183 | Edinburg, TX | (2.3) |
| 36 | Berkeley, CA | 21.1 | 110 | Lincoln, NE | 6.2 | 183 | Spokane, WA | (2.3) |
| 36 | Irvine, CA | 21.1 | 111 | Chandler, AZ | 6.0 | 185 | Lawton, OK | (2.6) |
| 38 | Napa, CA | 20.4 | 112 | Arlington, TX | 5.8 | 186 | Allen, TX | (2.7) |
| 39 | Madison, WI | 20.3 | 113 | Everett, WA | 5.7 | 187 | El Cajon, CA | (2.8) |
| 40 | Huntington Beach, CA | 20.0 | 113 | Jackson, MS | 5.7 | 187 | Macon, GA | (2.8) |
| 41 | Hesperia, CA | 19.9 | 115 | Newton, MA | 5.6 | 189 | Odessa, TX | (2.9) |
| 41 | Woodbridge Twnshp, NJ | 19.9 | 116 | Alameda, CA | 5.2 | 190 | Portsmouth, VA | (3.0) |
| 43 | Toms River Twnshp, NJ | 19.8 | 116 | Houston, TX | 5.2 | 190 | Rochester, MN | (3.0) |
| 44 | Dearborn, MI | 19.2 | 118 | Overland Park, KS | 5.1 | 192 | Charlotte, NC | (3.1) |
| 45 | Lubbock, TX | 19.1 | 119 | Las Vegas, NV | 5.0 | 192 | Hawthorne, CA | (3.1) |
| 46 | San Francisco, CA | 18.6 | 120 | Miami, FL | 4.7 | 192 | Oklahoma City, OK | (3.1) |
| 47 | Hemet, CA | 17.8 | 121 | Beaumont, TX | 4.6 | 195 | Kenosha, WI | (3.2) |
| 47 | Longview, TX | 17.8 | 122 | Yuma, AZ | 4.5 | 196 | Escondido, CA | (3.3) |
| 47 | Orange, CA | 17.8 | 123 | Evansville, IN | 4.2 | 197 | Ann Arbor, MI | (3.4) |
| 50 | Billings, MT | 17.5 | 124 | Baltimore, MD | 4.0 | 197 | Buffalo, NY | (3.4) |
| 51 | Westland, MI | 17.4 | 124 | Carson, CA | 4.0 | 197 | Vista, CA | (3.4) |
| 52 | Fairfield, CA | 17.3 | 126 | Quincy, MA | 3.9 | 200 | El Paso, TX | (3.6) |
| 53 | North Las Vegas, NV | 17.1 | 127 | Buena Park, CA | 3.8 | 201 | Plantation, FL | (3.7) |
| 53 | Ogden, UT | 17.1 | 128 | Concord, CA | 3.7 | 201 | Richmond, VA | (3.7) |
| 55 | Daly City, CA | 17.0 | 128 | San Mateo, CA | 3.7 | 203 | Independence, MO | (3.9) |
| 56 | Little Rock, AR | 16.2 | 128 | Sandy Springs, GA | 3.7 | 203 | Washington, DC | (3.9) |
| 56 | Visalia, CA | 16.2 | 131 | Hillsboro, OR | 3.4 | 205 | Boston, MA | (4.2) |
| 58 | San Antonio, TX | 15.9 | 131 | Las Cruces, NM | 3.4 | 205 | Fort Worth, TX | (4.2) |
| 59 | South Bend, IN | 15.7 | 133 | Corpus Christi, TX | 3.3 | 205 | Grand Prairie, TX | (4.2) |
| 60 | Danbury, CT | 15.6 | 133 | Pembroke Pines, FL | 3.3 | 205 | High Point, NC | (4.2) |
| 61 | Arvada, CO | 15.4 | 135 | Jacksonville, FL | 3.2 | 209 | Bridgeport, CT | (4.3) |
| 62 | Sunrise, FL | 15.1 | 135 | Richmond, CA | 3.2 | 210 | Miramar, FL | (4.4) |
| 62 | Worcester, MA | 15.1 | 137 | Oceanside, CA | 3.1 | 210 | Wilmington, NC | (4.4) |
| 64 | Lake Forest, CA | 14.6 | 138 | Elizabeth, NJ | 2.9 | 212 | Plano, TX | (4.5) |
| 65 | Midland, TX | 14.4 | 138 | Erie, PA | 2.9 | 212 | Westminster, CA | (4.5) |
| 66 | Cary, NC | 14.1 | 140 | New Orleans, LA | 2.8 | 214 | Cape Coral, FL | (4.7) |
| 67 | Palmdale, CA | 13.9 | 141 | Sparks, NV | 2.6 | 214 | Sacramento, CA | (4.7) |
| 68 | Costa Mesa, CA | 13.3 | 142 | Clinton Twnshp, MI | 2.3 | 216 | San Diego, CA | (4.8) |
| 69 | Rochester, NY | 13.1 | 143 | Greenville, NC | 2.2 | 217 | Aurora, CO | (4.9) |
| 70 | Laredo, TX | 12.3 | 144 | Brockton, MA | 2.1 | 217 | Hayward, CA | (4.9) |
| 70 | Warren, MI | 12.3 | 144 | Melbourne, FL | 2.1 | 219 | Albuquerque, NM | (5.0) |
| 72 | Oakland, CA | 12.2 | 144 | Winston-Salem, NC | 2.1 | 219 | Carrollton, TX | (5.0) |
| 72 | Rancho Cucamon., CA | 12.2 | 147 | Louisville, KY | 1.6 | 219 | New Bedford, MA | (5.0) |
| 74 | Mesquite, TX | 11.9 | 148 | Dallas, TX | 1.5 | 222 | College Station, TX | (5.1) |

| RANK | CITY | % CHANGE | RANK | CITY | % CHANGE | RANK | CITY | % CHANGE |
|------|------|----------|------|------|----------|------|------|----------|
| 223 | Baton Rouge, LA | (5.2) | 297 | Naperville, IL | (13.1) | 371 | Fullerton, CA | (22.5) |
| 223 | Riverside, CA | (5.2) | 298 | Arlington Heights, IL | (13.2) | 372 | Athens-Clarke, GA | (22.6) |
| 225 | Aurora, IL | (5.3) | 298 | Shreveport, LA | (13.2) | 373 | Indio, CA | (23.3) |
| 225 | Edison Twnshp, NJ | (5.3) | 300 | Miami Gardens, FL | (13.3) | 374 | Lakewood, CO | (23.6) |
| 225 | Portland, OR | (5.3) | 301 | Omaha, NE | (13.4) | 375 | El Monte, CA | (23.8) |
| 225 | Rialto, CA | (5.3) | 301 | Simi Valley, CA | (13.4) | 376 | Gilbert, AZ | (24.0) |
| 225 | Tulsa, OK | (5.3) | 303 | Champaign, IL | (13.6) | 377 | Citrus Heights, CA | (24.2) |
| 230 | Yakima, WA | (5.4) | 303 | Fall River, MA | (13.6) | 378 | Chesapeake, VA | (24.3) |
| 231 | Wichita, KS | (5.5) | 305 | Reading, PA | (13.7) | 378 | League City, TX | (24.3) |
| 232 | Pasadena, CA | (5.6) | 305 | Sandy, UT | (13.7) | 380 | Austin, TX | (24.4) |
| 233 | Murfreesboro, TN | (5.8) | 305 | Toledo, OH | (13.7) | 381 | Lexington, KY | (24.5) |
| 234 | Denver, CO | (5.9) | 308 | Clearwater, FL | (13.8) | 382 | Peoria, AZ | (24.9) |
| 235 | Philadelphia, PA | (6.1) | 308 | Santa Barbara, CA | (13.8) | 383 | Lakewood Twnshp, NJ | (25.3) |
| 235 | Sugar Land, TX | (6.1) | 308 | Tracy, CA | (13.8) | 384 | Fishers, IN | (25.7) |
| 237 | New York, NY | (6.3) | 311 | Racine, WI | (14.2) | 385 | Richardson, TX | (25.9) |
| 237 | Sioux Falls, SD | (6.3) | 312 | Kansas City, KS | (14.3) | 385 | Roseville, CA | (25.9) |
| 239 | Olathe, KS | (6.4) | 313 | Frisco, TX | (14.4) | 387 | Redwood City, CA | (26.2) |
| 240 | Moreno Valley, CA | (6.5) | 314 | Pittsburgh, PA | (14.5) | 388 | Cheektowaga, NY | (26.5) |
| 241 | St. Joseph, MO | (6.6) | 314 | Santa Ana, CA | (14.5) | 389 | Topeka, KS | (26.9) |
| 242 | Antioch, CA | (6.7) | 316 | Huntsville, AL | (14.7) | 390 | Edmond, OK | (27.5) |
| 242 | Brooklyn Park, MN | (6.7) | 317 | Renton, WA | (14.8) | 391 | Tallahassee, FL | (27.6) |
| 244 | Cincinnati, OH | (6.8) | 318 | Boca Raton, FL | (15.2) | 392 | Hoover, AL | (27.7) |
| 245 | Cedar Rapids, IA | (7.3) | 318 | Vancouver, WA | (15.2) | 393 | Port St. Lucie, FL | (28.1) |
| 245 | Virginia Beach, VA | (7.3) | 320 | Menifee, CA | (15.3) | 394 | McKinney, TX | (28.6) |
| 247 | Memphis, TN | (7.4) | 321 | South Gate, CA | (15.5) | 395 | Temecula, CA | (28.7) |
| 248 | Orlando, FL | (7.5) | 322 | Des Moines, IA | (15.6) | 396 | Clifton, NJ | (29.1) |
| 248 | Tuscaloosa, AL | (7.5) | 322 | Peoria, IL | (15.6) | 396 | Ventura, CA | (29.1) |
| 250 | Reno, NV | (7.6) | 324 | Upper Darby Twnshp, PA | (15.7) | 398 | Bellevue, WA | (29.3) |
| 251 | Miami Beach, FL | (7.7) | 325 | Cambridge, MA | (15.8) | 399 | Deerfield Beach, FL | (30.2) |
| 252 | Mountain View, CA | (7.8) | 325 | Compton, CA | (15.8) | 399 | Stockton, CA | (30.2) |
| 253 | Yonkers, NY | (7.9) | 327 | West Palm Beach, FL | (15.9) | 401 | Killeen, TX | (30.4) |
| 254 | San Leandro, CA | (8.0) | 328 | Alexandria, VA | (16.0) | 401 | Sunnyvale, CA | (30.4) |
| 255 | Trenton, NJ | (8.1) | 329 | Norfolk, VA | (16.4) | 403 | Boise, ID | (30.7) |
| 256 | Fort Collins, CO | (8.2) | 330 | Santa Maria, CA | (16.6) | 403 | Glendale, CA | (30.7) |
| 257 | Green Bay, WI | (8.3) | 330 | Wichita Falls, TX | (16.6) | 405 | Mission, TX | (31.2) |
| 258 | Salinas, CA | (8.4) | 332 | Largo, FL | (16.7) | 406 | Fontana, CA | (31.5) |
| 258 | Thousand Oaks, CA | (8.4) | 333 | Fort Lauderdale, FL | (16.8) | 407 | Ramapo, NY | (32.2) |
| 260 | Akron, OH | (8.5) | 334 | Lancaster, CA | (17.0) | 408 | Flint, MI | (32.5) |
| 261 | Albany, NY | (8.6) | 334 | Santa Rosa, CA | (17.0) | 409 | Charleston, SC | (32.6) |
| 262 | Henderson, NV | (8.7) | 336 | Albany, GA | (17.1) | 410 | Columbia, MO | (33.3) |
| 263 | Nashville, TN | (8.8) | 336 | Norman, OK | (17.1) | 411 | Johns Creek, GA | (34.5) |
| 264 | Newport News, VA | (8.9) | 336 | Savannah, GA | (17.1) | 412 | Pompano Beach, FL | (35.4) |
| 265 | Gainesville, FL | (9.1) | 339 | Torrance, CA | (17.2) | 413 | Longmont, CO | (37.1) |
| 265 | Phoenix, AZ | (9.1) | 340 | Hampton, VA | (17.3) | 414 | Corona, CA | (37.3) |
| 267 | New Haven, CT | (9.6) | 340 | Sterling Heights, MI | (17.3) | 414 | Ontario, CA | (37.3) |
| 267 | Whittier, CA | (9.6) | 342 | Dayton, OH | (17.6) | 416 | Clarkstown, NY | (37.4) |
| 269 | Downey, CA | (9.7) | 343 | St. Louis, MO | (18.0) | 417 | Lee's Summit, MO | (37.9) |
| 269 | Long Beach, CA | (9.7) | 344 | Elgin, IL | (18.1) | 418 | Somerville, MA | (38.2) |
| 271 | Hollywood, FL | (9.8) | 345 | Boulder, CO | (18.8) | 419 | Merced, CA | (38.4) |
| 272 | North Charleston, SC | (9.9) | 346 | Clovis, CA | (19.0) | 420 | Bethlehem, PA | (38.6) |
| 272 | Vacaville, CA | (9.9) | 346 | Kent, WA | (19.0) | 421 | Denton, TX | (38.8) |
| 274 | Santa Clara, CA | (10.4) | 348 | Bloomington, MN | (19.2) | 422 | Beaverton, OR | (39.7) |
| 275 | Syracuse, NY | (10.6) | 348 | Glendale, AZ | (19.2) | 422 | Centennial, CO | (39.7) |
| 276 | Chino, CA | (10.7) | 350 | Duluth, MN | (19.5) | 424 | Tyler, TX | (42.4) |
| 277 | Raleigh, NC | (10.8) | 350 | Tucson, AZ | (19.5) | 425 | Palm Bay, FL | (44.7) |
| 277 | San Jose, CA | (10.8) | 352 | Broken Arrow, OK | (19.6) | 425 | Scranton, PA | (44.7) |
| 279 | Norwalk, CT | (11.2) | 352 | Round Rock, TX | (19.6) | 427 | Troy, MI | (46.5) |
| 279 | Victorville, CA | (11.2) | 354 | Jurupa Valley, CA | (19.7) | 428 | Meridian, ID | (47.4) |
| 281 | Cicero, IL | (11.4) | 355 | Decatur, IL | (19.8) | 429 | Warwick, RI | (48.0) |
| 282 | Fresno, CA | (11.6) | 356 | Rockford, IL | (20.0) | 430 | Chino Hills, CA | (50.2) |
| 282 | Hialeah, FL | (11.6) | 357 | Fayetteville, AR | (20.2) | 431 | Newport Beach, CA | (52.1) |
| 284 | Norwalk, CA | (11.7) | 357 | Jersey City, NJ | (20.2) | 432 | St. George, UT | (52.6) |
| 285 | Greensboro, NC | (11.8) | 359 | Hamilton Twnshp, NJ | (20.4) | 433 | Burbank, CA | (53.9) |
| 285 | New Rochelle, NY | (11.8) | 360 | Colorado Springs, CO | (20.8) | 434 | Orem, UT | (66.2) |
| 285 | Santa Clarita, CA | (11.8) | 361 | Evanston, IL | (21.2) | NA | Bend, OR** | NA |
| 288 | Allentown, PA | (12.0) | 362 | Nampa, ID | (21.3) | NA | Canton Twnshp, MI** | NA |
| 289 | Sioux City, IA | (12.3) | 362 | Waco, TX | (21.3) | NA | Chattanooga, TN** | NA |
| 290 | Chicago, IL | (12.7) | 364 | Santa Monica, CA | (21.6) | NA | Columbia, SC** | NA |
| 290 | Los Angeles, CA | (12.7) | 365 | Pomona, CA | (21.7) | NA | Concord, NC** | NA |
| 292 | Hartford, CT | (12.8) | 366 | Knoxville, TN | (21.8) | NA | Lewisville, TX** | NA |
| 292 | Inglewood, CA | (12.8) | 366 | Mission Viejo, CA | (21.8) | NA | San Angelo, TX** | NA |
| 292 | Tempe, AZ | (12.8) | 368 | Bellflower, CA | (21.9) | NA | Suffolk, VA** | NA |
| 295 | Amarillo, TX | (12.9) | 369 | Carlsbad, CA | (22.0) | | | |
| 296 | Scottsdale, AZ | (13.0) | 369 | Surprise, AZ | (22.0) | | | |

Source: CQ Press using reported data from the F.B.I. "Crime in the United States 2013"

*Robbery is the taking of anything of value by force or threat of force. Attempts are included.

**Not available.

# 60. Percent Change in Robbery Rate: 2009 to 2013
## National Percent Change = 18.0% Decrease*

| RANK | CITY | % CHANGE | RANK | CITY | % CHANGE | RANK | CITY | % CHANGE |
|---|---|---|---|---|---|---|---|---|
| 127 | Abilene, TX | (10.9) | 277 | Chino, CA | (28.6) | 398 | Fullerton, CA | (46.3) |
| 246 | Akron, OH | (24.4) | 331 | Chula Vista, CA | (34.8) | 372 | Gainesville, FL | (41.0) |
| 123 | Alameda, CA | (9.8) | NA | Cicero, IL** | NA | 224 | Garden Grove, CA | (22.4) |
| 191 | Albany, GA | (19.0) | 204 | Cincinnati, OH | (20.3) | 269 | Garland, TX | (27.6) |
| 320 | Albany, NY | (33.8) | 376 | Citrus Heights, CA | (41.3) | 18 | Gary, IN | 36.7 |
| 124 | Albuquerque, NM | (9.9) | 317 | Clarkstown, NY | (33.4) | 180 | Gilbert, AZ | (18.0) |
| 177 | Alexandria, VA | (17.6) | 113 | Clarksville, TN | (8.5) | 137 | Glendale, AZ | (13.1) |
| 355 | Alhambra, CA | (38.2) | 354 | Clearwater, FL | (37.7) | 367 | Glendale, CA | (39.8) |
| 351 | Allentown, PA | (37.5) | 51 | Cleveland, OH | 8.3 | 274 | Grand Prairie, TX | (28.4) |
| 179 | Allen, TX | (17.9) | 406 | Clifton, NJ | (48.2) | 183 | Grand Rapids, MI | (18.2) |
| 321 | Amarillo, TX | (34.0) | 32 | Clinton Twnshp, MI | 17.5 | 14 | Greece, NY | 41.1 |
| 345 | Amherst, NY | (37.2) | 168 | Clovis, CA | (16.8) | 90 | Greeley, CO | (4.5) |
| 155 | Anaheim, CA | (15.7) | 21 | College Station, TX | 34.1 | 136 | Green Bay, WI | (12.9) |
| 102 | Anchorage, AK | (7.5) | 56 | Colonie, NY | 6.5 | 409 | Greensboro, NC | (50.5) |
| 242 | Ann Arbor, MI | (23.8) | 264 | Colorado Springs, CO | (26.7) | NA | Greenville, NC** | NA |
| 57 | Antioch, CA | 6.3 | 337 | Columbia, MO | (36.1) | 7 | Gresham, OR | 67.5 |
| 414 | Arlington Heights, IL | (52.1) | 154 | Columbia, SC | (15.6) | 258 | Hamilton Twnshp, NJ | (25.9) |
| 164 | Arlington, TX | (16.3) | 224 | Columbus, GA | (22.4) | 96 | Hammond, IN | (6.1) |
| 108 | Arvada, CO | (8.1) | 305 | Compton, CA | (32.2) | 325 | Hampton, VA | (34.4) |
| 236 | Athens-Clarke, GA | (23.1) | 269 | Concord, CA | (27.6) | 104 | Hartford, CT | (7.8) |
| 57 | Atlanta, GA | 6.3 | 373 | Concord, NC | (41.1) | 172 | Hawthorne, CA | (17.3) |
| 203 | Aurora, CO | (20.2) | 47 | Coral Springs, FL | 9.2 | 288 | Hayward, CA | (29.7) |
| 251 | Aurora, IL | (24.7) | 401 | Corona, CA | (47.1) | 23 | Hemet, CA | 25.7 |
| 413 | Austin, TX | (51.7) | 222 | Corpus Christi, TX | (22.3) | 362 | Henderson, NV | (39.2) |
| 107 | Bakersfield, CA | (8.0) | 195 | Costa Mesa, CA | (19.3) | 93 | Hesperia, CA | (5.2) |
| 315 | Baldwin Park, CA | (33.2) | 41 | Cranston, RI | 12.8 | 316 | Hialeah, FL | (33.3) |
| 66 | Baltimore, MD | 3.3 | 216 | Dallas, TX | (21.5) | 344 | High Point, NC | (37.0) |
| 168 | Baton Rouge, LA | (16.8) | 143 | Daly City, CA | (14.5) | 108 | Hillsboro, OR | (8.1) |
| 30 | Beaumont, TX | 17.7 | 74 | Danbury, CT | 1.4 | 231 | Hollywood, FL | (23.0) |
| 418 | Beaverton, OR | (53.4) | 252 | Davenport, IA | (25.0) | 321 | Hoover, AL | (34.0) |
| 231 | Bellevue, WA | (23.0) | 92 | Davie, FL | (4.6) | 119 | Houston, TX | (9.3) |
| 424 | Bellflower, CA | (59.3) | 268 | Dayton, OH | (27.1) | 231 | Huntington Beach, CA | (23.0) |
| 35 | Bend, OR | 16.5 | 80 | Dearborn, MI | (0.1) | 135 | Huntsville, AL | (12.7) |
| 198 | Berkeley, CA | (19.6) | 389 | Decatur, IL | (43.3) | 245 | Independence, MO | (24.0) |
| 257 | Bethlehem, PA | (25.8) | NA | Deerfield Beach, FL** | NA | 102 | Indianapolis, IN | (7.5) |
| 43 | Billings, MT | 11.6 | 318 | Denton, TX | (33.6) | 28 | Indio, CA | 19.4 |
| 121 | Birmingham, AL | (9.6) | 44 | Denver, CO | 11.5 | 305 | Inglewood, CA | (32.2) |
| 65 | Bloomington, IL | 3.4 | 180 | Des Moines, IA | (18.0) | 343 | Irvine, CA | (36.9) |
| 111 | Bloomington, IN | (8.2) | 64 | Detroit, MI | 4.8 | 231 | Irving, TX | (23.0) |
| 99 | Bloomington, MN | (7.1) | 295 | Downey, CA | (30.6) | 380 | Jacksonville, FL | (42.2) |
| 314 | Boca Raton, FL | (33.0) | 382 | Duluth, MN | (42.5) | 140 | Jackson, MS | (13.4) |
| 291 | Boise, ID | (30.0) | 324 | Edinburg, TX | (34.3) | 228 | Jersey City, NJ | (22.8) |
| 205 | Boston, MA | (20.4) | 389 | Edison Twnshp, NJ | (43.3) | 431 | Johns Creek, GA | (71.2) |
| 241 | Boulder, CO | (23.7) | 220 | Edmond, OK | (22.0) | 39 | Joliet, IL | 13.2 |
| 307 | Brick Twnshp, NJ | (32.3) | 384 | El Cajon, CA | (42.6) | NA | Jurupa Valley, CA** | NA |
| 206 | Bridgeport, CT | (20.5) | 396 | El Monte, CA | (46.0) | 273 | Kansas City, KS | (28.0) |
| 128 | Brockton, MA | (11.1) | 106 | El Paso, TX | (7.9) | 131 | Kansas City, MO | (12.2) |
| 208 | Broken Arrow, OK | (20.7) | 222 | Elgin, IL | (22.3) | 49 | Kennewick, WA | 8.9 |
| 271 | Brooklyn Park, MN | (27.7) | 274 | Elizabeth, NJ | (28.4) | 86 | Kenosha, WI | (2.7) |
| 130 | Brownsville, TX | (11.6) | 387 | Elk Grove, CA | (43.1) | 366 | Kent, WA | (39.7) |
| 393 | Bryan, TX | (45.5) | 10 | Erie, PA | 49.0 | 158 | Killeen, TX | (16.0) |
| 363 | Buena Park, CA | (39.4) | 254 | Escondido, CA | (25.4) | 338 | Knoxville, TN | (36.2) |
| 159 | Buffalo, NY | (16.1) | 101 | Eugene, OR | (7.4) | 132 | Lafayette, LA | (12.3) |
| 395 | Burbank, CA | (45.9) | NA | Evanston, IL** | NA | 267 | Lake Forest, CA | (27.0) |
| 360 | Cambridge, MA | (38.9) | 9 | Evansville, IN | 49.3 | 210 | Lakeland, FL | (20.8) |
| 385 | Canton Twnshp, MI | (42.9) | 304 | Everett, WA | (31.7) | 419 | Lakewood Twnshp, NJ | (54.3) |
| 420 | Cape Coral, FL | (56.3) | 177 | Fairfield, CA | (17.6) | 357 | Lakewood, CA | (38.5) |
| 259 | Carlsbad, CA | (26.0) | 148 | Fall River, MA | (15.1) | 340 | Lakewood, CO | (36.5) |
| 3 | Carmel, IN | 78.1 | 12 | Fargo, ND | 44.2 | 249 | Lancaster, CA | (24.6) |
| 373 | Carrollton, TX | (41.1) | 75 | Farmington Hills, MI | 1.2 | 80 | Lansing, MI | (0.1) |
| 126 | Carson, CA | (10.5) | 162 | Fayetteville, AR | (16.2) | 357 | Laredo, TX | (38.5) |
| 326 | Cary, NC | (34.5) | 70 | Fayetteville, NC | 2.5 | 323 | Largo, FL | (34.2) |
| 156 | Cedar Rapids, IA | (15.8) | 408 | Federal Way, WA | (50.4) | 280 | Las Cruces, NM | (29.0) |
| 172 | Centennial, CO | (17.3) | 415 | Fishers, IN | (52.5) | 170 | Las Vegas, NV | (16.9) |
| NA | Champaign, IL** | NA | 150 | Flint, MI | (15.3) | 82 | Lawrence, KS | (0.8) |
| 184 | Chandler, AZ | (18.6) | 342 | Fontana, CA | (36.8) | 11 | Lawrence, MA | 46.9 |
| 430 | Charleston, SC | (70.5) | 407 | Fort Collins, CO | (49.7) | 152 | Lawton, OK | (15.4) |
| 277 | Charlotte, NC | (28.6) | 50 | Fort Lauderdale, FL | 8.6 | 382 | League City, TX | (42.5) |
| 272 | Chattanooga, TN | (27.9) | 341 | Fort Smith, AR | (36.7) | 423 | Lee's Summit, MO | (59.1) |
| 375 | Cheektowaga, NY | (41.2) | 117 | Fort Wayne, IN | (9.0) | 70 | Lewisville, TX | 2.5 |
| 326 | Chesapeake, VA | (34.5) | 206 | Fort Worth, TX | (20.5) | 224 | Lexington, KY | (22.4) |
| 221 | Chicago, IL | (22.1) | 391 | Fremont, CA | (43.4) | 73 | Lincoln, NE | 2.3 |
| 261 | Chico, CA | (26.4) | 213 | Fresno, CA | (21.3) | 36 | Little Rock, AR | 13.8 |
| 411 | Chino Hills, CA | (51.5) | 17 | Frisco, TX | 39.2 | 238 | Livermore, CA | (23.2) |

| RANK | CITY | % CHANGE |
|---|---|---|
| 197 | Livonia, MI | (19.4) |
| 202 | Long Beach, CA | (20.0) |
| 422 | Longmont, CO | (57.8) |
| 216 | Longview, TX | (21.5) |
| 335 | Los Angeles, CA | (35.9) |
| 143 | Louisville, KY | (14.5) |
| NA | Lowell, MA** | NA |
| 33 | Lubbock, TX | 16.9 |
| 141 | Lynchburg, VA | (13.5) |
| 62 | Lynn, MA | 5.5 |
| 303 | Macon, GA | (31.6) |
| 213 | Madison, WI | (21.3) |
| 6 | Manchester, NH | 69.8 |
| 359 | McAllen, TX | (38.7) |
| 285 | McKinney, TX | (29.2) |
| 1 | Medford, OR | 297.2 |
| 277 | Melbourne, FL | (28.6) |
| 238 | Memphis, TN | (23.2) |
| 381 | Menifee, CA | (42.4) |
| 184 | Merced, CA | (18.6) |
| 429 | Meridian, ID | (68.9) |
| 195 | Mesa, AZ | (19.3) |
| 146 | Mesquite, TX | (14.6) |
| 176 | Miami Beach, FL | (17.5) |
| 120 | Miami Gardens, FL | (9.5) |
| 59 | Miami, FL | 6.0 |
| 328 | Midland, TX | (34.6) |
| 60 | Milwaukee, WI | 5.9 |
| 52 | Minneapolis, MN | 7.8 |
| 231 | Miramar, FL | (23.0) |
| 386 | Mission Viejo, CA | (43.0) |
| 313 | Mission, TX | (32.9) |
| 402 | Mobile, AL | (47.4) |
| 26 | Modesto, CA | 22.0 |
| 328 | Moreno Valley, CA | (34.6) |
| 345 | Mountain View, CA | (37.2) |
| 339 | Murfreesboro, TN | (36.3) |
| 365 | Murrieta, CA | (39.6) |
| 246 | Nampa, ID | (24.4) |
| 256 | Napa, CA | (25.7) |
| 88 | Naperville, IL | (3.9) |
| 8 | Nashua, NH | 59.7 |
| 216 | Nashville, TN | (21.5) |
| 264 | New Bedford, MA | (26.7) |
| 200 | New Haven, CT | (19.8) |
| 48 | New Orleans, LA | 9.0 |
| 90 | New Rochelle, NY | (4.5) |
| 67 | New York, NY | 3.1 |
| 2 | Newark, NJ | 85.1 |
| 426 | Newport Beach, CA | (63.0) |
| NA | Newport News, VA** | NA |
| 87 | Newton, MA | (2.8) |
| 351 | Norfolk, VA | (37.5) |
| 122 | Norman, OK | (9.7) |
| 412 | North Charleston, SC | (51.6) |
| 188 | North Las Vegas, NV | (18.7) |
| 188 | Norwalk, CA | (18.7) |
| 427 | Norwalk, CT | (63.1) |
| 5 | Oakland, CA | 70.1 |
| 184 | Oceanside, CA | (18.6) |
| 292 | Odessa, TX | (30.3) |
| 399 | O'Fallon, MO | (46.7) |
| 70 | Ogden, UT | 2.5 |
| 132 | Oklahoma City, OK | (12.3) |
| 410 | Olathe, KS | (51.0) |
| 159 | Omaha, NE | (16.1) |
| 368 | Ontario, CA | (39.9) |
| 108 | Orange, CA | (8.1) |
| 428 | Orem, UT | (67.2) |
| 295 | Orlando, FL | (30.6) |
| 150 | Overland Park, KS | (15.3) |
| 211 | Oxnard, CA | (21.0) |
| 371 | Palm Bay, FL | (40.8) |
| 117 | Palmdale, CA | (9.0) |

| RANK | CITY | % CHANGE |
|---|---|---|
| 104 | Pasadena, CA | (7.8) |
| 79 | Pasadena, TX | 0.1 |
| 20 | Paterson, NJ | 34.3 |
| 330 | Pearland, TX | (34.7) |
| 227 | Pembroke Pines, FL | (22.6) |
| 309 | Peoria, AZ | (32.5) |
| 319 | Peoria, IL | (33.7) |
| 166 | Philadelphia, PA | (16.6) |
| 113 | Phoenix, AZ | (8.5) |
| 280 | Pittsburgh, PA | (29.0) |
| 264 | Plano, TX | (26.7) |
| 307 | Plantation, FL | (32.3) |
| 138 | Pomona, CA | (13.2) |
| 236 | Pompano Beach, FL | (23.1) |
| 334 | Port St. Lucie, FL | (35.8) |
| 184 | Portland, OR | (18.6) |
| 403 | Portsmouth, VA | (47.5) |
| 129 | Providence, RI | (11.3) |
| 312 | Provo, UT | (32.8) |
| 24 | Pueblo, CO | 24.6 |
| 97 | Quincy, MA | (6.3) |
| 175 | Racine, WI | (17.4) |
| 299 | Raleigh, NC | (31.2) |
| 363 | Ramapo, NY | (39.4) |
| 55 | Rancho Cucamon., CA | 6.8 |
| 190 | Reading, PA | (18.9) |
| 4 | Redding, CA | 76.3 |
| 299 | Redwood City, CA | (31.2) |
| 285 | Reno, NV | (29.2) |
| 420 | Renton, WA | (56.3) |
| 172 | Rialto, CA | (17.3) |
| 396 | Richardson, TX | (46.0) |
| 89 | Richmond, CA | (4.4) |
| 290 | Richmond, VA | (29.9) |
| 288 | Riverside, CA | (29.7) |
| 262 | Roanoke, VA | (26.6) |
| 141 | Rochester, MN | (13.5) |
| 60 | Rochester, NY | 5.9 |
| 293 | Rockford, IL | (30.5) |
| 333 | Roseville, CA | (35.6) |
| 115 | Roswell, GA | (8.6) |
| 31 | Round Rock, TX | 17.6 |
| 282 | Sacramento, CA | (29.1) |
| 42 | Salem, OR | 11.9 |
| 45 | Salinas, CA | 9.8 |
| 85 | Salt Lake City, UT | (2.5) |
| 417 | San Angelo, TX | (53.3) |
| 200 | San Antonio, TX | (19.8) |
| 46 | San Bernardino, CA | 9.3 |
| 255 | San Diego, CA | (25.5) |
| 29 | San Francisco, CA | 19.2 |
| 69 | San Jose, CA | 2.8 |
| 146 | San Leandro, CA | (14.6) |
| 143 | San Marcos, CA | (14.5) |
| 282 | San Mateo, CA | (29.1) |
| 298 | Sandy Springs, GA | (31.0) |
| 15 | Sandy, UT | 40.9 |
| 394 | Santa Ana, CA | (45.7) |
| 274 | Santa Barbara, CA | (28.4) |
| 194 | Santa Clara, CA | (19.2) |
| 347 | Santa Clarita, CA | (37.3) |
| 13 | Santa Maria, CA | 43.1 |
| 287 | Santa Monica, CA | (29.5) |
| 400 | Santa Rosa, CA | (46.8) |
| 378 | Savannah, GA | (41.7) |
| 170 | Scottsdale, AZ | (16.9) |
| 353 | Scranton, PA | (37.6) |
| 162 | Seattle, WA | (16.2) |
| 240 | Shreveport, LA | (23.5) |
| 377 | Simi Valley, CA | (41.4) |
| 99 | Sioux City, IA | (7.1) |
| 16 | Sioux Falls, SD | 39.9 |
| 416 | Somerville, MA | (52.6) |
| 54 | South Bend, IN | 7.6 |

| RANK | CITY | % CHANGE |
|---|---|---|
| 349 | South Gate, CA | (37.4) |
| 356 | Sparks, NV | (38.4) |
| 25 | Spokane Valley, WA | 22.9 |
| 39 | Spokane, WA | 13.2 |
| 53 | Springfield, IL | 7.7 |
| 68 | Springfield, MA | 2.9 |
| 22 | Springfield, MO | 26.9 |
| 77 | Stamford, CT | 0.6 |
| 293 | Sterling Heights, MI | (30.5) |
| 156 | Stockton, CA | (15.8) |
| 164 | St. George, UT | (16.3) |
| 229 | St. Joseph, MO | (22.9) |
| 370 | St. Louis, MO | (40.3) |
| 83 | St. Paul, MN | (1.9) |
| 297 | St. Petersburg, FL | (30.7) |
| 216 | Suffolk, VA | (21.5) |
| 388 | Sugar Land, TX | (43.2) |
| 335 | Sunnyvale, CA | (35.9) |
| 84 | Sunrise, FL | (2.4) |
| 38 | Surprise, AZ | 13.3 |
| 94 | Syracuse, NY | (5.3) |
| 215 | Tacoma, WA | (21.4) |
| 249 | Tallahassee, FL | (24.6) |
| 347 | Tampa, FL | (37.3) |
| 349 | Temecula, CA | (37.4) |
| 229 | Tempe, AZ | (22.9) |
| 191 | Thornton, CO | (19.0) |
| 76 | Thousand Oaks, CA | 0.9 |
| 191 | Toledo, OH | (19.0) |
| 33 | Toms River Twnshp, NJ | 16.9 |
| 392 | Topeka, KS | (44.9) |
| 405 | Torrance, CA | (47.7) |
| 301 | Tracy, CA | (31.4) |
| 78 | Trenton, NJ | 0.3 |
| 403 | Troy, MI | (47.5) |
| 159 | Tucson, AZ | (16.1) |
| 138 | Tulsa, OK | (13.2) |
| 198 | Tuscaloosa, AL | (19.6) |
| 379 | Tustin, CA | (42.1) |
| 369 | Tyler, TX | (40.2) |
| NA | Upland, CA** | NA |
| 208 | Upper Darby Twnshp, PA | (20.7) |
| 309 | Vacaville, CA | (32.5) |
| 98 | Vallejo, CA | (6.6) |
| 112 | Vancouver, WA | (8.4) |
| 244 | Ventura, CA | (23.9) |
| 311 | Victorville, CA | (32.7) |
| 331 | Virginia Beach, VA | (34.8) |
| 182 | Visalia, CA | (18.1) |
| 116 | Vista, CA | (8.9) |
| 360 | Waco, TX | (38.9) |
| 211 | Warren, MI | (21.0) |
| 424 | Warwick, RI | (59.3) |
| 148 | Washington, DC | (15.1) |
| 19 | Waterbury, CT | 35.6 |
| NA | Waukegan, IL** | NA |
| 302 | West Covina, CA | (31.5) |
| 262 | West Palm Beach, FL | (26.6) |
| 95 | West Valley, UT | (6.0) |
| 125 | Westland, MI | (10.1) |
| 134 | Westminster, CA | (12.5) |
| 27 | Westminster, CO | 21.0 |
| 260 | Whittier, CA | (26.3) |
| 242 | Wichita Falls, TX | (23.8) |
| 153 | Wichita, KS | (15.5) |
| 246 | Wilmington, NC | (24.4) |
| 253 | Winston-Salem, NC | (25.2) |
| 62 | Woodbridge Twnshp, NJ | 5.5 |
| 37 | Worcester, MA | 13.5 |
| NA | Yakima, WA** | NA |
| 166 | Yonkers, NY | (16.6) |
| 282 | Yuma, AZ | (29.1) |

Source: CQ Press using reported data from the F.B.I. "Crime in the United States 2013"

*Robbery is the taking of anything of value by force or threat of force. Attempts are included.

**Not available.

# 60. Percent Change in Robbery Rate: 2009 to 2013 (continued)
## National Percent Change = 18.0% Decrease*

| RANK | CITY | % CHANGE | RANK | CITY | % CHANGE | RANK | CITY | % CHANGE |
|---|---|---|---|---|---|---|---|---|
| 1 | Medford, OR | 297.2 | 75 | Farmington Hills, MI | 1.2 | 148 | Washington, DC | (15.1) |
| 2 | Newark, NJ | 85.1 | 76 | Thousand Oaks, CA | 0.9 | 150 | Flint, MI | (15.3) |
| 3 | Carmel, IN | 78.1 | 77 | Stamford, CT | 0.6 | 150 | Overland Park, KS | (15.3) |
| 4 | Redding, CA | 76.3 | 78 | Trenton, NJ | 0.3 | 152 | Lawton, OK | (15.4) |
| 5 | Oakland, CA | 70.1 | 79 | Pasadena, TX | 0.1 | 153 | Wichita, KS | (15.5) |
| 6 | Manchester, NH | 69.8 | 80 | Dearborn, MI | (0.1) | 154 | Columbia, SC | (15.6) |
| 7 | Gresham, OR | 67.5 | 80 | Lansing, MI | (0.1) | 155 | Anaheim, CA | (15.7) |
| 8 | Nashua, NH | 59.7 | 82 | Lawrence, KS | (0.8) | 156 | Cedar Rapids, IA | (15.8) |
| 9 | Evansville, IN | 49.3 | 83 | St. Paul, MN | (1.9) | 156 | Stockton, CA | (15.8) |
| 10 | Erie, PA | 49.0 | 84 | Sunrise, FL | (2.4) | 158 | Killeen, TX | (16.0) |
| 11 | Lawrence, MA | 46.9 | 85 | Salt Lake City, UT | (2.5) | 159 | Buffalo, NY | (16.1) |
| 12 | Fargo, ND | 44.2 | 86 | Kenosha, WI | (2.7) | 159 | Omaha, NE | (16.1) |
| 13 | Santa Maria, CA | 43.1 | 87 | Newton, MA | (2.8) | 159 | Tucson, AZ | (16.1) |
| 14 | Greece, NY | 41.1 | 88 | Naperville, IL | (3.9) | 162 | Fayetteville, AR | (16.2) |
| 15 | Sandy, UT | 40.9 | 89 | Richmond, CA | (4.4) | 162 | Seattle, WA | (16.2) |
| 16 | Sioux Falls, SD | 39.9 | 90 | Greeley, CO | (4.5) | 164 | Arlington, TX | (16.3) |
| 17 | Frisco, TX | 39.2 | 90 | New Rochelle, NY | (4.5) | 164 | St. George, UT | (16.3) |
| 18 | Gary, IN | 36.7 | 92 | Davie, FL | (4.6) | 166 | Philadelphia, PA | (16.6) |
| 19 | Waterbury, CT | 35.6 | 93 | Hesperia, CA | (5.2) | 166 | Yonkers, NY | (16.6) |
| 20 | Paterson, NJ | 34.3 | 94 | Syracuse, NY | (5.3) | 168 | Baton Rouge, LA | (16.8) |
| 21 | College Station, TX | 34.1 | 95 | West Valley, UT | (6.0) | 168 | Clovis, CA | (16.8) |
| 22 | Springfield, MO | 26.9 | 96 | Hammond, IN | (6.1) | 170 | Las Vegas, NV | (16.9) |
| 23 | Hemet, CA | 25.7 | 97 | Quincy, MA | (6.3) | 170 | Scottsdale, AZ | (16.9) |
| 24 | Pueblo, CO | 24.6 | 98 | Vallejo, CA | (6.6) | 172 | Centennial, CO | (17.3) |
| 25 | Spokane Valley, WA | 22.9 | 99 | Bloomington, MN | (7.1) | 172 | Hawthorne, CA | (17.3) |
| 26 | Modesto, CA | 22.0 | 99 | Sioux City, IA | (7.1) | 172 | Rialto, CA | (17.3) |
| 27 | Westminster, CO | 21.0 | 101 | Eugene, OR | (7.4) | 175 | Racine, WI | (17.4) |
| 28 | Indio, CA | 19.4 | 102 | Anchorage, AK | (7.5) | 176 | Miami Beach, FL | (17.5) |
| 29 | San Francisco, CA | 19.2 | 102 | Indianapolis, IN | (7.5) | 177 | Alexandria, VA | (17.6) |
| 30 | Beaumont, TX | 17.7 | 104 | Hartford, CT | (7.8) | 177 | Fairfield, CA | (17.6) |
| 31 | Round Rock, TX | 17.6 | 104 | Pasadena, CA | (7.8) | 179 | Allen, TX | (17.9) |
| 32 | Clinton Twnshp, MI | 17.5 | 106 | El Paso, TX | (7.9) | 180 | Des Moines, IA | (18.0) |
| 33 | Lubbock, TX | 16.9 | 107 | Bakersfield, CA | (8.0) | 180 | Gilbert, AZ | (18.0) |
| 33 | Toms River Twnshp, NJ | 16.9 | 108 | Arvada, CO | (8.1) | 182 | Visalia, CA | (18.1) |
| 35 | Bend, OR | 16.5 | 108 | Hillsboro, OR | (8.1) | 183 | Grand Rapids, MI | (18.2) |
| 36 | Little Rock, AR | 13.8 | 108 | Orange, CA | (8.1) | 184 | Chandler, AZ | (18.6) |
| 37 | Worcester, MA | 13.5 | 111 | Bloomington, IN | (8.2) | 184 | Merced, CA | (18.6) |
| 38 | Surprise, AZ | 13.3 | 112 | Vancouver, WA | (8.4) | 184 | Oceanside, CA | (18.6) |
| 39 | Joliet, IL | 13.2 | 113 | Clarksville, TN | (8.5) | 184 | Portland, OR | (18.6) |
| 39 | Spokane, WA | 13.2 | 113 | Phoenix, AZ | (8.5) | 188 | North Las Vegas, NV | (18.7) |
| 41 | Cranston, RI | 12.8 | 115 | Roswell, GA | (8.6) | 188 | Norwalk, CA | (18.7) |
| 42 | Salem, OR | 11.9 | 116 | Vista, CA | (8.9) | 190 | Reading, PA | (18.9) |
| 43 | Billings, MT | 11.6 | 117 | Fort Wayne, IN | (9.0) | 191 | Albany, GA | (19.0) |
| 44 | Denver, CO | 11.5 | 117 | Palmdale, CA | (9.0) | 191 | Thornton, CO | (19.0) |
| 45 | Salinas, CA | 9.8 | 119 | Houston, TX | (9.3) | 191 | Toledo, OH | (19.0) |
| 46 | San Bernardino, CA | 9.3 | 120 | Miami Gardens, FL | (9.5) | 194 | Santa Clara, CA | (19.2) |
| 47 | Coral Springs, FL | 9.2 | 121 | Birmingham, AL | (9.6) | 195 | Costa Mesa, CA | (19.3) |
| 48 | New Orleans, LA | 9.0 | 122 | Norman, OK | (9.7) | 195 | Mesa, AZ | (19.3) |
| 49 | Kennewick, WA | 8.9 | 123 | Alameda, CA | (9.8) | 197 | Livonia, MI | (19.4) |
| 50 | Fort Lauderdale, FL | 8.6 | 124 | Albuquerque, NM | (9.9) | 198 | Berkeley, CA | (19.6) |
| 51 | Cleveland, OH | 8.3 | 125 | Westland, MI | (10.1) | 198 | Tuscaloosa, AL | (19.6) |
| 52 | Minneapolis, MN | 7.8 | 126 | Carson, CA | (10.5) | 200 | New Haven, CT | (19.8) |
| 53 | Springfield, IL | 7.7 | 127 | Abilene, TX | (10.9) | 200 | San Antonio, TX | (19.8) |
| 54 | South Bend, IN | 7.6 | 128 | Brockton, MA | (11.1) | 202 | Long Beach, CA | (20.0) |
| 55 | Rancho Cucamon., CA | 6.8 | 129 | Providence, RI | (11.3) | 203 | Aurora, CO | (20.2) |
| 56 | Colonie, NY | 6.5 | 130 | Brownsville, TX | (11.6) | 204 | Cincinnati, OH | (20.3) |
| 57 | Antioch, CA | 6.3 | 131 | Kansas City, MO | (12.2) | 205 | Boston, MA | (20.4) |
| 57 | Atlanta, GA | 6.3 | 132 | Lafayette, LA | (12.3) | 206 | Bridgeport, CT | (20.5) |
| 59 | Miami, FL | 6.0 | 132 | Oklahoma City, OK | (12.3) | 206 | Fort Worth, TX | (20.5) |
| 60 | Milwaukee, WI | 5.9 | 134 | Westminster, CA | (12.5) | 208 | Broken Arrow, OK | (20.7) |
| 60 | Rochester, NY | 5.9 | 135 | Huntsville, AL | (12.7) | 208 | Upper Darby Twnshp, PA | (20.7) |
| 62 | Lynn, MA | 5.5 | 136 | Green Bay, WI | (12.9) | 210 | Lakeland, FL | (20.8) |
| 62 | Woodbridge Twnshp, NJ | 5.5 | 137 | Glendale, AZ | (13.1) | 211 | Oxnard, CA | (21.0) |
| 64 | Detroit, MI | 4.8 | 138 | Pomona, CA | (13.2) | 211 | Warren, MI | (21.0) |
| 65 | Bloomington, IL | 3.4 | 138 | Tulsa, OK | (13.2) | 213 | Fresno, CA | (21.3) |
| 66 | Baltimore, MD | 3.3 | 140 | Jackson, MS | (13.4) | 213 | Madison, WI | (21.3) |
| 67 | New York, NY | 3.1 | 141 | Lynchburg, VA | (13.5) | 215 | Tacoma, WA | (21.4) |
| 68 | Springfield, MA | 2.9 | 141 | Rochester, MN | (13.5) | 216 | Dallas, TX | (21.5) |
| 69 | San Jose, CA | 2.8 | 143 | Daly City, CA | (14.5) | 216 | Longview, TX | (21.5) |
| 70 | Fayetteville, NC | 2.5 | 143 | Louisville, KY | (14.5) | 216 | Nashville, TN | (21.5) |
| 70 | Lewisville, TX | 2.5 | 143 | San Marcos, CA | (14.5) | 216 | Suffolk, VA | (21.5) |
| 70 | Ogden, UT | 2.5 | 146 | Mesquite, TX | (14.6) | 220 | Edmond, OK | (22.0) |
| 73 | Lincoln, NE | 2.3 | 146 | San Leandro, CA | (14.6) | 221 | Chicago, IL | (22.1) |
| 74 | Danbury, CT | 1.4 | 148 | Fall River, MA | (15.1) | 222 | Corpus Christi, TX | (22.3) |

| RANK | CITY | % CHANGE | RANK | CITY | % CHANGE | RANK | CITY | % CHANGE |
|---|---|---|---|---|---|---|---|---|
| 222 | Elgin, IL | (22.3) | 297 | St. Petersburg, FL | (30.7) | 371 | Palm Bay, FL | (40.8) |
| 224 | Columbus, GA | (22.4) | 298 | Sandy Springs, GA | (31.0) | 372 | Gainesville, FL | (41.0) |
| 224 | Garden Grove, CA | (22.4) | 299 | Raleigh, NC | (31.2) | 373 | Carrollton, TX | (41.1) |
| 224 | Lexington, KY | (22.4) | 299 | Redwood City, CA | (31.2) | 373 | Concord, NC | (41.1) |
| 227 | Pembroke Pines, FL | (22.6) | 301 | Tracy, CA | (31.4) | 375 | Cheektowaga, NY | (41.2) |
| 228 | Jersey City, NJ | (22.8) | 302 | West Covina, CA | (31.5) | 376 | Citrus Heights, CA | (41.3) |
| 229 | St. Joseph, MO | (22.9) | 303 | Macon, GA | (31.6) | 377 | Simi Valley, CA | (41.4) |
| 229 | Tempe, AZ | (22.9) | 304 | Everett, WA | (31.7) | 378 | Savannah, GA | (41.7) |
| 231 | Bellevue, WA | (23.0) | 305 | Compton, CA | (32.2) | 379 | Tustin, CA | (42.1) |
| 231 | Hollywood, FL | (23.0) | 305 | Inglewood, CA | (32.2) | 380 | Jacksonville, FL | (42.2) |
| 231 | Huntington Beach, CA | (23.0) | 307 | Brick Twnshp, NJ | (32.3) | 381 | Menifee, CA | (42.4) |
| 231 | Irving, TX | (23.0) | 307 | Plantation, FL | (32.3) | 382 | Duluth, MN | (42.5) |
| 231 | Miramar, FL | (23.0) | 309 | Peoria, AZ | (32.5) | 382 | League City, TX | (42.5) |
| 236 | Athens-Clarke, GA | (23.1) | 309 | Vacaville, CA | (32.5) | 384 | El Cajon, CA | (42.6) |
| 236 | Pompano Beach, FL | (23.1) | 311 | Victorville, CA | (32.7) | 385 | Canton Twnshp, MI | (42.9) |
| 238 | Livermore, CA | (23.2) | 312 | Provo, UT | (32.8) | 386 | Mission Viejo, CA | (43.0) |
| 238 | Memphis, TN | (23.2) | 313 | Mission, TX | (32.9) | 387 | Elk Grove, CA | (43.1) |
| 240 | Shreveport, LA | (23.5) | 314 | Boca Raton, FL | (33.0) | 388 | Sugar Land, TX | (43.2) |
| 241 | Boulder, CO | (23.7) | 315 | Baldwin Park, CA | (33.2) | 389 | Decatur, IL | (43.3) |
| 242 | Ann Arbor, MI | (23.8) | 316 | Hialeah, FL | (33.3) | 389 | Edison Twnshp, NJ | (43.3) |
| 242 | Wichita Falls, TX | (23.8) | 317 | Clarkstown, NY | (33.4) | 391 | Fremont, CA | (43.4) |
| 244 | Ventura, CA | (23.9) | 318 | Denton, TX | (33.6) | 392 | Topeka, KS | (44.9) |
| 245 | Independence, MO | (24.0) | 319 | Peoria, IL | (33.7) | 393 | Bryan, TX | (45.5) |
| 246 | Akron, OH | (24.4) | 320 | Albany, NY | (33.8) | 394 | Santa Ana, CA | (45.7) |
| 246 | Nampa, ID | (24.4) | 321 | Amarillo, TX | (34.0) | 395 | Burbank, CA | (45.9) |
| 246 | Wilmington, NC | (24.4) | 321 | Hoover, AL | (34.0) | 396 | El Monte, CA | (46.0) |
| 249 | Lancaster, CA | (24.6) | 323 | Largo, FL | (34.2) | 396 | Richardson, TX | (46.0) |
| 249 | Tallahassee, FL | (24.6) | 324 | Edinburg, TX | (34.3) | 398 | Fullerton, CA | (46.3) |
| 251 | Aurora, IL | (24.7) | 325 | Hampton, VA | (34.4) | 399 | O'Fallon, MO | (46.7) |
| 252 | Davenport, IA | (25.0) | 326 | Cary, NC | (34.5) | 400 | Santa Rosa, CA | (46.8) |
| 253 | Winston-Salem, NC | (25.2) | 326 | Chesapeake, VA | (34.5) | 401 | Corona, CA | (47.1) |
| 254 | Escondido, CA | (25.4) | 328 | Midland, TX | (34.6) | 402 | Mobile, AL | (47.4) |
| 255 | San Diego, CA | (25.5) | 328 | Moreno Valley, CA | (34.6) | 403 | Portsmouth, VA | (47.5) |
| 256 | Napa, CA | (25.7) | 330 | Pearland, TX | (34.7) | 403 | Troy, MI | (47.5) |
| 257 | Bethlehem, PA | (25.8) | 331 | Chula Vista, CA | (34.8) | 405 | Torrance, CA | (47.7) |
| 258 | Hamilton Twnshp, NJ | (25.9) | 331 | Virginia Beach, VA | (34.8) | 406 | Clifton, NJ | (48.2) |
| 259 | Carlsbad, CA | (26.0) | 333 | Roseville, CA | (35.6) | 407 | Fort Collins, CO | (49.7) |
| 260 | Whittier, CA | (26.3) | 334 | Port St. Lucie, FL | (35.8) | 408 | Federal Way, WA | (50.4) |
| 261 | Chico, CA | (26.4) | 335 | Los Angeles, CA | (35.9) | 409 | Greensboro, NC | (50.5) |
| 262 | Roanoke, VA | (26.6) | 335 | Sunnyvale, CA | (35.9) | 410 | Olathe, KS | (51.0) |
| 262 | West Palm Beach, FL | (26.6) | 337 | Columbia, MO | (36.1) | 411 | Chino Hills, CA | (51.5) |
| 264 | Colorado Springs, CO | (26.7) | 338 | Knoxville, TN | (36.2) | 412 | North Charleston, SC | (51.6) |
| 264 | New Bedford, MA | (26.7) | 339 | Murfreesboro, TN | (36.3) | 413 | Austin, TX | (51.7) |
| 264 | Plano, TX | (26.7) | 340 | Lakewood, CO | (36.5) | 414 | Arlington Heights, IL | (52.1) |
| 267 | Lake Forest, CA | (27.0) | 341 | Fort Smith, AR | (36.7) | 415 | Fishers, IN | (52.5) |
| 268 | Dayton, OH | (27.1) | 342 | Fontana, CA | (36.8) | 416 | Somerville, MA | (52.6) |
| 269 | Concord, CA | (27.6) | 343 | Irvine, CA | (36.9) | 417 | San Angelo, TX | (53.3) |
| 269 | Garland, TX | (27.6) | 344 | High Point, NC | (37.0) | 418 | Beaverton, OR | (53.4) |
| 271 | Brooklyn Park, MN | (27.7) | 345 | Amherst, NY | (37.2) | 419 | Lakewood Twnshp, NJ | (54.3) |
| 272 | Chattanooga, TN | (27.9) | 345 | Mountain View, CA | (37.2) | 420 | Cape Coral, FL | (56.3) |
| 273 | Kansas City, KS | (28.0) | 347 | Santa Clarita, CA | (37.3) | 420 | Renton, WA | (56.3) |
| 274 | Elizabeth, NJ | (28.4) | 347 | Tampa, FL | (37.3) | 422 | Longmont, CO | (57.8) |
| 274 | Grand Prairie, TX | (28.4) | 349 | South Gate, CA | (37.4) | 423 | Lee's Summit, MO | (59.1) |
| 274 | Santa Barbara, CA | (28.4) | 349 | Temecula, CA | (37.4) | 424 | Bellflower, CA | (59.3) |
| 277 | Charlotte, NC | (28.6) | 351 | Allentown, PA | (37.5) | 424 | Warwick, RI | (59.3) |
| 277 | Chino, CA | (28.6) | 351 | Norfolk, VA | (37.5) | 426 | Newport Beach, CA | (63.0) |
| 277 | Melbourne, FL | (28.6) | 353 | Scranton, PA | (37.6) | 427 | Norwalk, CT | (63.1) |
| 280 | Las Cruces, NM | (29.0) | 354 | Clearwater, FL | (37.7) | 428 | Orem, UT | (67.2) |
| 280 | Pittsburgh, PA | (29.0) | 355 | Alhambra, CA | (38.2) | 429 | Meridian, ID | (68.9) |
| 282 | Sacramento, CA | (29.1) | 356 | Sparks, NV | (38.4) | 430 | Charleston, SC | (70.5) |
| 282 | San Mateo, CA | (29.1) | 357 | Lakewood, CA | (38.5) | 431 | Johns Creek, GA | (71.2) |
| 282 | Yuma, AZ | (29.1) | 357 | Laredo, TX | (38.5) | NA | Champaign, IL** | NA |
| 285 | McKinney, TX | (29.2) | 359 | McAllen, TX | (38.7) | NA | Cicero, IL** | NA |
| 285 | Reno, NV | (29.2) | 360 | Cambridge, MA | (38.9) | NA | Deerfield Beach, FL** | NA |
| 287 | Santa Monica, CA | (29.5) | 360 | Waco, TX | (38.9) | NA | Evanston, IL** | NA |
| 288 | Hayward, CA | (29.7) | 362 | Henderson, NV | (39.2) | NA | Greenville, NC** | NA |
| 288 | Riverside, CA | (29.7) | 363 | Buena Park, CA | (39.4) | NA | Jurupa Valley, CA** | NA |
| 290 | Richmond, VA | (29.9) | 363 | Ramapo, NY | (39.4) | NA | Lowell, MA** | NA |
| 291 | Boise, ID | (30.0) | 365 | Murrieta, CA | (39.6) | NA | Newport News, VA** | NA |
| 292 | Odessa, TX | (30.3) | 366 | Kent, WA | (39.7) | NA | Upland, CA** | NA |
| 293 | Rockford, IL | (30.5) | 367 | Glendale, CA | (39.8) | NA | Waukegan, IL** | NA |
| 293 | Sterling Heights, MI | (30.5) | 368 | Ontario, CA | (39.9) | NA | Yakima, WA** | NA |
| 295 | Downey, CA | (30.6) | 369 | Tyler, TX | (40.2) | | | |
| 295 | Orlando, FL | (30.6) | 370 | St. Louis, MO | (40.3) | | | |

Source: CQ Press using reported data from the F.B.I. "Crime in the United States 2013"

*Robbery is the taking of anything of value by force or threat of force. Attempts are included.

**Not available.

# 61. Aggravated Assaults in 2013
## National Total = 724,149 Aggravated Assaults*

| RANK | CITY | ASSAULTS | RANK | CITY | ASSAULTS | RANK | CITY | ASSAULTS |
|---|---|---|---|---|---|---|---|---|
| 204 | Abilene, TX | 314 | 274 | Chino, CA | 200 | 244 | Fullerton, CA | 236 |
| 85 | Akron, OH | 859 | 203 | Chula Vista, CA | 316 | 122 | Gainesville, FL | 583 |
| 399 | Alameda, CA | 63 | 297 | Cicero, IL | 167 | 211 | Garden Grove, CA | 297 |
| 132 | Albany, GA | 537 | 79 | Cincinnati, OH | 947 | 261 | Garland, TX | 218 |
| 133 | Albany, NY | 526 | 261 | Citrus Heights, CA | 218 | 153 | Gary, IN | 455 |
| 24 | Albuquerque, NM | 2,803 | 424 | Clarkstown, NY | 40 | 324 | Gilbert, AZ | 131 |
| 342 | Alexandria, VA | 114 | 129 | Clarksville, TN | 543 | 137 | Glendale, AZ | 508 |
| 391 | Alhambra, CA | 72 | 174 | Clearwater, FL | 387 | 362 | Glendale, CA | 97 |
| 255 | Allentown, PA | 223 | 40 | Cleveland, OH | 1,789 | 213 | Grand Prairie, TX | 291 |
| 429 | Allen, TX | 36 | 354 | Clifton, NJ | 106 | 98 | Grand Rapids, MI | 756 |
| 93 | Amarillo, TX | 821 | 298 | Clinton Twnshp, MI | 164 | 378 | Greece, NY | 82 |
| 395 | Amherst, NY | 68 | 348 | Clovis, CA | 111 | 193 | Greeley, CO | 347 |
| 119 | Anaheim, CA | 600 | 208 | College Station, TX | 308 | 183 | Green Bay, WI | 367 |
| 53 | Anchorage, AK | 1,491 | 433 | Colonie, NY | 32 | 86 | Greensboro, NC | 856 |
| 310 | Ann Arbor, MI | 147 | 70 | Colorado Springs, CO | 1,079 | 191 | Greenville, NC | 353 |
| 126 | Antioch, CA | 557 | 250 | Columbia, MO | 232 | 218 | Gresham, OR | 279 |
| 435 | Arlington Heights, IL | 28 | 127 | Columbia, SC | 555 | 357 | Hamilton Twnshp, NJ | 102 |
| 65 | Arlington, TX | 1,152 | 145 | Columbus, GA | 483 | 178 | Hammond, IN | 380 |
| 364 | Arvada, CO | 96 | 94 | Compton, CA | 820 | 327 | Hampton, VA | 129 |
| 242 | Athens-Clarke, GA | 240 | 246 | Concord, CA | 235 | 89 | Hartford, CT | 840 |
| 22 | Atlanta, GA | 2,965 | 412 | Concord, NC | 56 | 239 | Hawthorne, CA | 243 |
| 103 | Aurora, CO | 721 | 342 | Coral Springs, FL | 114 | 261 | Hayward, CA | 218 |
| 161 | Aurora, IL | 425 | 389 | Corona, CA | 74 | 235 | Hemet, CA | 246 |
| 33 | Austin, TX | 2,117 | 55 | Corpus Christi, TX | 1,384 | 308 | Henderson, NV | 154 |
| 69 | Bakersfield, CA | 1,082 | 348 | Costa Mesa, CA | 111 | 223 | Hesperia, CA | 270 |
| 320 | Baldwin Park, CA | 135 | 381 | Cranston, RI | 80 | 143 | Hialeah, FL | 489 |
| 12 | Baltimore, MD | 4,460 | 17 | Dallas, TX | 3,442 | 194 | High Point, NC | 346 |
| 73 | Baton Rouge, LA | 1,030 | 340 | Daly City, CA | 118 | 407 | Hillsboro, OR | 57 |
| 102 | Beaumont, TX | 731 | 435 | Danbury, CT | 28 | 171 | Hollywood, FL | 388 |
| 380 | Beaverton, OR | 81 | 167 | Davenport, IA | 397 | 434 | Hoover, AL | 29 |
| 412 | Bellevue, WA | 56 | 283 | Davie, FL | 186 | 2 | Houston, TX | 10,270 |
| 298 | Bellflower, CA | 164 | 123 | Dayton, OH | 577 | 251 | Huntington Beach, CA | 229 |
| 317 | Bend, OR | 138 | 283 | Dearborn, MI | 186 | 74 | Huntsville, AL | 1,005 |
| 335 | Berkeley, CA | 122 | 232 | Decatur, IL | 253 | 185 | Independence, MO | 363 |
| 383 | Bethlehem, PA | 78 | 293 | Deerfield Beach, FL | 170 | 9 | Indianapolis, IN | 5,894 |
| 244 | Billings, MT | 236 | 280 | Denton, TX | 192 | 206 | Indio, CA | 313 |
| 46 | Birmingham, AL | 1,642 | 30 | Denver, CO | 2,401 | 182 | Inglewood, CA | 370 |
| 216 | Bloomington, IL | 281 | 105 | Des Moines, IA | 714 | 400 | Irvine, CA | 61 |
| 301 | Bloomington, IN | 161 | 3 | Detroit, MI | 8,796 | 201 | Irving, TX | 318 |
| 400 | Bloomington, MN | 61 | 318 | Downey, CA | 136 | 19 | Jacksonville, FL | 3,277 |
| 359 | Boca Raton, FL | 99 | 264 | Duluth, MN | 216 | 116 | Jackson, MS | 626 |
| 157 | Boise, ID | 429 | 277 | Edinburg, TX | 196 | 83 | Jersey City, NJ | 883 |
| 23 | Boston, MA | 2,851 | 407 | Edison Twnshp, NJ | 57 | 438 | Johns Creek, GA | 18 |
| 315 | Boulder, CO | 140 | 407 | Edmond, OK | 57 | 197 | Joliet, IL | 340 |
| 403 | Brick Twnshp, NJ | 60 | 267 | El Cajon, CA | 212 | 290 | Jurupa Valley, CA | 177 |
| 104 | Bridgeport, CT | 720 | 295 | El Monte, CA | 168 | 177 | Kansas City, KS | 382 |
| 91 | Brockton, MA | 838 | 37 | El Paso, TX | 1,879 | 14 | Kansas City, MO | 3,726 |
| 387 | Broken Arrow, OK | 75 | 342 | Elgin, IL | 114 | 301 | Kennewick, WA | 161 |
| 329 | Brooklyn Park, MN | 126 | 164 | Elizabeth, NJ | 401 | 314 | Kenosha, WI | 141 |
| 220 | Brownsville, TX | 275 | 184 | Elk Grove, CA | 364 | 359 | Kent, WA | 99 |
| 234 | Bryan, TX | 250 | 259 | Erie, PA | 219 | 139 | Killeen, TX | 499 |
| 329 | Buena Park, CA | 126 | 192 | Escondido, CA | 350 | 76 | Knoxville, TN | 969 |
| 44 | Buffalo, NY | 1,735 | 316 | Eugene, OR | 139 | 124 | Lafayette, LA | 571 |
| 353 | Burbank, CA | 107 | 341 | Evanston, IL | 115 | 395 | Lake Forest, CA | 68 |
| 256 | Cambridge, MA | 221 | 212 | Evansville, IN | 294 | 229 | Lakeland, FL | 258 |
| 403 | Canton Twnshp, MI | 60 | 268 | Everett, WA | 208 | 417 | Lakewood Twnshp, NJ | 52 |
| 310 | Cape Coral, FL | 147 | 202 | Fairfield, CA | 317 | 357 | Lakewood, CA | 102 |
| 309 | Carlsbad, CA | 153 | 112 | Fall River, MA | 646 | 166 | Lakewood, CO | 398 |
| 441 | Carmel, IN | 5 | 204 | Fargo, ND | 314 | 135 | Lancaster, CA | 522 |
| 355 | Carrollton, TX | 105 | 429 | Farmington Hills, MI | 36 | 95 | Lansing, MI | 813 |
| 249 | Carson, CA | 234 | 223 | Fayetteville, AR | 270 | 101 | Laredo, TX | 742 |
| 415 | Cary, NC | 55 | 140 | Fayetteville, NC | 494 | 268 | Largo, FL | 208 |
| 233 | Cedar Rapids, IA | 252 | 321 | Federal Way, WA | 134 | 253 | Las Cruces, NM | 225 |
| 368 | Centennial, CO | 90 | 440 | Fishers, IN | 7 | 7 | Las Vegas, NV | 6,500 |
| 141 | Champaign, IL | 492 | 57 | Flint, MI | 1,267 | 266 | Lawrence, KS | 213 |
| 186 | Chandler, AZ | 359 | 146 | Fontana, CA | 480 | 149 | Lawrence, MA | 473 |
| 332 | Charleston, SC | 123 | 226 | Fort Collins, CO | 263 | 110 | Lawton, OK | 658 |
| 21 | Charlotte, NC | 2,999 | 108 | Fort Lauderdale, FL | 669 | 405 | League City, TX | 58 |
| 61 | Chattanooga, TN | 1,225 | 157 | Fort Smith, AR | 429 | 405 | Lee's Summit, MO | 58 |
| 359 | Cheektowaga, NY | 99 | 179 | Fort Wayne, IN | 376 | 338 | Lewisville, TX | 120 |
| 134 | Chesapeake, VA | 525 | 27 | Fort Worth, TX | 2,593 | 200 | Lexington, KY | 327 |
| NA | Chicago, IL** | NA | 348 | Fremont, CA | 111 | 115 | Lincoln, NE | 631 |
| 301 | Chico, CA | 161 | 49 | Fresno, CA | 1,556 | 45 | Little Rock, AR | 1,679 |
| 421 | Chino Hills, CA | 47 | 407 | Frisco, TX | 57 | 265 | Livermore, CA | 214 |

| RANK | CITY | ASSAULTS | RANK | CITY | ASSAULTS | RANK | CITY | ASSAULTS |
|---|---|---|---|---|---|---|---|---|
| 364 | Livonia, MI | 96 | 238 | Pasadena, CA | 244 | 230 | South Gate, CA | 256 |
| 67 | Long Beach, CA | 1,091 | 196 | Pasadena, TX | 345 | 307 | Sparks, NV | 156 |
| 324 | Longmont, CO | 131 | 109 | Paterson, NJ | 663 | 342 | Spokane Valley, WA | 114 |
| 231 | Longview, TX | 255 | 372 | Pearland, TX | 88 | 100 | Spokane, WA | 745 |
| 5 | Los Angeles, CA | 7,624 | 290 | Pembroke Pines, FL | 177 | 92 | Springfield, IL | 829 |
| 35 | Louisville, KY | 2,009 | 292 | Peoria, AZ | 175 | 78 | Springfield, MA | 964 |
| 170 | Lowell, MA | 389 | 151 | Peoria, IL | 469 | 62 | Springfield, MO | 1,206 |
| 56 | Lubbock, TX | 1,348 | 4 | Philadelphia, PA | 7,986 | 312 | Stamford, CT | 145 |
| 258 | Lynchburg, VA | 220 | 10 | Phoenix, AZ | 5,506 | 281 | Sterling Heights, MI | 189 |
| 121 | Lynn, MA | 584 | 63 | Pittsburgh, PA | 1,180 | 29 | Stockton, CA | 2,411 |
| 214 | Macon, GA | 288 | 277 | Plano, TX | 196 | 378 | St. George, UT | 82 |
| 138 | Madison, WI | 507 | 295 | Plantation, FL | 168 | 252 | St. Joseph, MO | 227 |
| 188 | Manchester, NH | 357 | 154 | Pomona, CA | 454 | 20 | St. Louis, MO | 3,167 |
| 381 | McAllen, TX | 80 | 148 | Pompano Beach, FL | 475 | 58 | St. Paul, MN | 1,252 |
| 351 | McKinney, TX | 110 | 240 | Port St. Lucie, FL | 241 | 48 | St. Petersburg, FL | 1,575 |
| 194 | Medford, OR | 346 | 42 | Portland, OR | 1,776 | 305 | Suffolk, VA | 160 |
| 154 | Melbourne, FL | 454 | 189 | Portsmouth, VA | 354 | 397 | Sugar Land, TX | 66 |
| 6 | Memphis, TN | 7,200 | 113 | Providence, RI | 641 | 390 | Sunnyvale, CA | 73 |
| 394 | Menifee, CA | 69 | 412 | Provo, UT | 56 | 327 | Sunrise, FL | 129 |
| 165 | Merced, CA | 399 | 114 | Pueblo, CO | 633 | 375 | Surprise, AZ | 86 |
| 384 | Meridian, ID | 77 | 243 | Quincy, MA | 239 | 106 | Syracuse, NY | 696 |
| 66 | Mesa, AZ | 1,104 | 364 | Racine, WI | 96 | 68 | Tacoma, WA | 1,088 |
| 289 | Mesquite, TX | 178 | 75 | Raleigh, NC | 987 | 89 | Tallahassee, FL | 840 |
| 144 | Miami Beach, FL | 485 | 423 | Ramapo, NY | 41 | 54 | Tampa, FL | 1,411 |
| 125 | Miami Gardens, FL | 561 | 282 | Rancho Cucamon., CA | 188 | 426 | Temecula, CA | 38 |
| 28 | Miami, FL | 2,562 | 189 | Reading, PA | 354 | 130 | Tempe, AZ | 542 |
| 228 | Midland, TX | 260 | 171 | Redding, CA | 388 | 270 | Thornton, CO | 206 |
| 13 | Milwaukee, WI | 4,405 | 362 | Redwood City, CA | 97 | 368 | Thousand Oaks, CA | 90 |
| 43 | Minneapolis, MN | 1,761 | 97 | Reno, NV | 767 | 41 | Toledo, OH | 1,783 |
| 222 | Miramar, FL | 273 | 332 | Renton, WA | 123 | 437 | Toms River Twnshp, NJ | 20 |
| 429 | Mission Viejo, CA | 36 | 259 | Rialto, CA | 219 | 168 | Topeka, KS | 396 |
| 429 | Mission, TX | 36 | 418 | Richardson, TX | 51 | 367 | Torrance, CA | 94 |
| 77 | Mobile, AL | 965 | 111 | Richmond, CA | 654 | 372 | Tracy, CA | 88 |
| 64 | Modesto, CA | 1,168 | 117 | Richmond, VA | 623 | 128 | Trenton, NJ | 547 |
| 215 | Moreno Valley, CA | 285 | 99 | Riverside, CA | 747 | 426 | Troy, MI | 38 |
| 347 | Mountain View, CA | 112 | 227 | Roanoke, VA | 262 | 34 | Tucson, AZ | 2,103 |
| 136 | Murfreesboro, TN | 517 | 351 | Rochester, MN | 110 | 31 | Tulsa, OK | 2,400 |
| 426 | Murrieta, CA | 38 | 71 | Rochester, NY | 1,055 | 256 | Tuscaloosa, AL | 221 |
| 313 | Nampa, ID | 143 | 50 | Rockford, IL | 1,507 | 407 | Tustin, CA | 57 |
| 288 | Napa, CA | 180 | 287 | Roseville, CA | 183 | 220 | Tyler, TX | 275 |
| 384 | Naperville, IL | 77 | 416 | Roswell, GA | 54 | 374 | Upland, CA | 87 |
| 377 | Nashua, NH | 83 | 375 | Round Rock, TX | 86 | 273 | Upper Darby Twnshp, PA | 201 |
| 11 | Nashville, TN | 4,529 | 38 | Sacramento, CA | 1,850 | 338 | Vacaville, CA | 120 |
| 107 | New Bedford, MA | 677 | 199 | Salem, OR | 328 | 131 | Vallejo, CA | 540 |
| 96 | New Haven, CT | 778 | 142 | Salinas, CA | 490 | 181 | Vancouver, WA | 371 |
| 52 | New Orleans, LA | 1,495 | 87 | Salt Lake City, UT | 842 | 318 | Ventura, CA | 136 |
| 370 | New Rochelle, NY | 89 | 286 | San Angelo, TX | 185 | 162 | Victorville, CA | 404 |
| 1 | New York, NY | 31,767 | 8 | San Antonio, TX | 5,901 | 225 | Virginia Beach, VA | 269 |
| 80 | Newark, NJ | 926 | 72 | San Bernardino, CA | 1,036 | 209 | Visalia, CA | 305 |
| 418 | Newport Beach, CA | 51 | 16 | San Diego, CA | 3,492 | 219 | Vista, CA | 276 |
| 147 | Newport News, VA | 478 | 26 | San Francisco, CA | 2,653 | 207 | Waco, TX | 311 |
| 422 | Newton, MA | 45 | 39 | San Jose, CA | 1,812 | 176 | Warren, MI | 383 |
| 87 | Norfolk, VA | 842 | 342 | San Leandro, CA | 114 | 425 | Warwick, RI | 39 |
| 391 | Norman, OK | 72 | 323 | San Marcos, CA | 133 | 15 | Washington, DC | 3,724 |
| 159 | North Charleston, SC | 428 | 331 | San Mateo, CA | 125 | 301 | Waterbury, CT | 161 |
| 59 | North Las Vegas, NV | 1,251 | 400 | Sandy Springs, GA | 61 | 275 | Waukegan, IL | 199 |
| 246 | Norwalk, CA | 235 | 386 | Sandy, UT | 76 | 335 | West Covina, CA | 122 |
| 298 | Norwalk, CT | 164 | 120 | Santa Ana, CA | 594 | 179 | West Palm Beach, FL | 376 |
| 25 | Oakland, CA | 2,792 | 235 | Santa Barbara, CA | 246 | 156 | West Valley, UT | 441 |
| 163 | Oceanside, CA | 402 | 356 | Santa Clara, CA | 104 | 272 | Westland, MI | 203 |
| 84 | Odessa, TX | 879 | 306 | Santa Clarita, CA | 158 | 283 | Westminster, CA | 186 |
| 420 | O'Fallon, MO | 49 | 198 | Santa Maria, CA | 331 | 321 | Westminster, CO | 134 |
| 253 | Ogden, UT | 225 | 293 | Santa Monica, CA | 170 | 326 | Whittier, CA | 130 |
| 18 | Oklahoma City, OK | 3,295 | 169 | Santa Rosa, CA | 391 | 240 | Wichita Falls, TX | 241 |
| 332 | Olathe, KS | 123 | 187 | Savannah, GA | 358 | 32 | Wichita, KS | 2,338 |
| 51 | Omaha, NE | 1,505 | 279 | Scottsdale, AZ | 195 | 171 | Wilmington, NC | 388 |
| 235 | Ontario, CA | 246 | 387 | Scranton, PA | 75 | 82 | Winston-Salem, NC | 892 |
| 393 | Orange, CA | 71 | 36 | Seattle, WA | 1,985 | 398 | Woodbridge Twnshp, NJ | 65 |
| 439 | Orem, UT | 11 | 81 | Shreveport, LA | 911 | 60 | Worcester, MA | 1,236 |
| 47 | Orlando, FL | 1,600 | 370 | Simi Valley, CA | 89 | 216 | Yakima, WA | 281 |
| 271 | Overland Park, KS | 204 | 246 | Sioux City, IA | 235 | 118 | Yonkers, NY | 615 |
| 210 | Oxnard, CA | 298 | 159 | Sioux Falls, SD | 428 | 150 | Yuma, AZ | 472 |
| 175 | Palm Bay, FL | 384 | 335 | Somerville, MA | 122 | | | |
| 152 | Palmdale, CA | 465 | 275 | South Bend, IN | 199 | | | |

Source: Reported data from the F.B.I. "Crime in the United States 2013"

*Aggravated assault is an attack for the purpose of inflicting severe bodily injury.

**Not available.

# 61. Aggravated Assaults in 2013 (continued)
## National Total = 724,149 Aggravated Assaults*

| RANK | CITY | ASSAULTS | RANK | CITY | ASSAULTS | RANK | CITY | ASSAULTS |
|---|---|---|---|---|---|---|---|---|
| 1 | New York, NY | 31,767 | 75 | Raleigh, NC | 987 | 149 | Lawrence, MA | 473 |
| 2 | Houston, TX | 10,270 | 76 | Knoxville, TN | 969 | 150 | Yuma, AZ | 472 |
| 3 | Detroit, MI | 8,796 | 77 | Mobile, AL | 965 | 151 | Peoria, IL | 469 |
| 4 | Philadelphia, PA | 7,986 | 78 | Springfield, MA | 964 | 152 | Palmdale, CA | 465 |
| 5 | Los Angeles, CA | 7,624 | 79 | Cincinnati, OH | 947 | 153 | Gary, IN | 455 |
| 6 | Memphis, TN | 7,200 | 80 | Newark, NJ | 926 | 154 | Melbourne, FL | 454 |
| 7 | Las Vegas, NV | 6,500 | 81 | Shreveport, LA | 911 | 154 | Pomona, CA | 454 |
| 8 | San Antonio, TX | 5,901 | 82 | Winston-Salem, NC | 892 | 156 | West Valley, UT | 441 |
| 9 | Indianapolis, IN | 5,894 | 83 | Jersey City, NJ | 883 | 157 | Boise, ID | 429 |
| 10 | Phoenix, AZ | 5,506 | 84 | Odessa, TX | 879 | 157 | Fort Smith, AR | 429 |
| 11 | Nashville, TN | 4,529 | 85 | Akron, OH | 859 | 159 | North Charleston, SC | 428 |
| 12 | Baltimore, MD | 4,460 | 86 | Greensboro, NC | 856 | 159 | Sioux Falls, SD | 428 |
| 13 | Milwaukee, WI | 4,405 | 87 | Norfolk, VA | 842 | 161 | Aurora, IL | 425 |
| 14 | Kansas City, MO | 3,726 | 87 | Salt Lake City, UT | 842 | 162 | Victorville, CA | 404 |
| 15 | Washington, DC | 3,724 | 89 | Hartford, CT | 840 | 163 | Oceanside, CA | 402 |
| 16 | San Diego, CA | 3,492 | 89 | Tallahassee, FL | 840 | 164 | Elizabeth, NJ | 401 |
| 17 | Dallas, TX | 3,442 | 91 | Brockton, MA | 838 | 165 | Merced, CA | 399 |
| 18 | Oklahoma City, OK | 3,295 | 92 | Springfield, IL | 829 | 166 | Lakewood, CO | 398 |
| 19 | Jacksonville, FL | 3,277 | 93 | Amarillo, TX | 821 | 167 | Davenport, IA | 397 |
| 20 | St. Louis, MO | 3,167 | 94 | Compton, CA | 820 | 168 | Topeka, KS | 396 |
| 21 | Charlotte, NC | 2,999 | 95 | Lansing, MI | 813 | 169 | Santa Rosa, CA | 391 |
| 22 | Atlanta, GA | 2,965 | 96 | New Haven, CT | 778 | 170 | Lowell, MA | 389 |
| 23 | Boston, MA | 2,851 | 97 | Reno, NV | 767 | 171 | Hollywood, FL | 388 |
| 24 | Albuquerque, NM | 2,803 | 98 | Grand Rapids, MI | 756 | 171 | Redding, CA | 388 |
| 25 | Oakland, CA | 2,792 | 99 | Riverside, CA | 747 | 171 | Wilmington, NC | 388 |
| 26 | San Francisco, CA | 2,653 | 100 | Spokane, WA | 745 | 174 | Clearwater, FL | 387 |
| 27 | Fort Worth, TX | 2,593 | 101 | Laredo, TX | 742 | 175 | Palm Bay, FL | 384 |
| 28 | Miami, FL | 2,562 | 102 | Beaumont, TX | 731 | 176 | Warren, MI | 383 |
| 29 | Stockton, CA | 2,411 | 103 | Aurora, CO | 721 | 177 | Kansas City, KS | 382 |
| 30 | Denver, CO | 2,401 | 104 | Bridgeport, CT | 720 | 178 | Hammond, IN | 380 |
| 31 | Tulsa, OK | 2,400 | 105 | Des Moines, IA | 714 | 179 | Fort Wayne, IN | 376 |
| 32 | Wichita, KS | 2,338 | 106 | Syracuse, NY | 696 | 179 | West Palm Beach, FL | 376 |
| 33 | Austin, TX | 2,117 | 107 | New Bedford, MA | 677 | 181 | Vancouver, WA | 371 |
| 34 | Tucson, AZ | 2,103 | 108 | Fort Lauderdale, FL | 669 | 182 | Inglewood, CA | 370 |
| 35 | Louisville, KY | 2,009 | 109 | Paterson, NJ | 663 | 183 | Green Bay, WI | 367 |
| 36 | Seattle, WA | 1,985 | 110 | Lawton, OK | 658 | 184 | Elk Grove, CA | 364 |
| 37 | El Paso, TX | 1,879 | 111 | Richmond, CA | 654 | 185 | Independence, MO | 363 |
| 38 | Sacramento, CA | 1,850 | 112 | Fall River, MA | 646 | 186 | Chandler, AZ | 359 |
| 39 | San Jose, CA | 1,812 | 113 | Providence, RI | 641 | 187 | Savannah, GA | 358 |
| 40 | Cleveland, OH | 1,789 | 114 | Pueblo, CO | 633 | 188 | Manchester, NH | 357 |
| 41 | Toledo, OH | 1,783 | 115 | Lincoln, NE | 631 | 189 | Portsmouth, VA | 354 |
| 42 | Portland, OR | 1,776 | 116 | Jackson, MS | 626 | 189 | Reading, PA | 354 |
| 43 | Minneapolis, MN | 1,761 | 117 | Richmond, VA | 623 | 191 | Greenville, NC | 353 |
| 44 | Buffalo, NY | 1,735 | 118 | Yonkers, NY | 615 | 192 | Escondido, CA | 350 |
| 45 | Little Rock, AR | 1,679 | 119 | Anaheim, CA | 600 | 193 | Greeley, CO | 347 |
| 46 | Birmingham, AL | 1,642 | 120 | Santa Ana, CA | 594 | 194 | High Point, NC | 346 |
| 47 | Orlando, FL | 1,600 | 121 | Lynn, MA | 584 | 194 | Medford, OR | 346 |
| 48 | St. Petersburg, FL | 1,575 | 122 | Gainesville, FL | 583 | 196 | Pasadena, TX | 345 |
| 49 | Fresno, CA | 1,556 | 123 | Dayton, OH | 577 | 197 | Joliet, IL | 340 |
| 50 | Rockford, IL | 1,507 | 124 | Lafayette, LA | 571 | 198 | Santa Maria, CA | 331 |
| 51 | Omaha, NE | 1,505 | 125 | Miami Gardens, FL | 561 | 199 | Salem, OR | 328 |
| 52 | New Orleans, LA | 1,495 | 126 | Antioch, CA | 557 | 200 | Lexington, KY | 327 |
| 53 | Anchorage, AK | 1,491 | 127 | Columbia, SC | 555 | 201 | Irving, TX | 318 |
| 54 | Tampa, FL | 1,411 | 128 | Trenton, NJ | 547 | 202 | Fairfield, CA | 317 |
| 55 | Corpus Christi, TX | 1,384 | 129 | Clarksville, TN | 543 | 203 | Chula Vista, CA | 316 |
| 56 | Lubbock, TX | 1,348 | 130 | Tempe, AZ | 542 | 204 | Abilene, TX | 314 |
| 57 | Flint, MI | 1,267 | 131 | Vallejo, CA | 540 | 204 | Fargo, ND | 314 |
| 58 | St. Paul, MN | 1,252 | 132 | Albany, GA | 537 | 206 | Indio, CA | 313 |
| 59 | North Las Vegas, NV | 1,251 | 133 | Albany, NY | 526 | 207 | Waco, TX | 311 |
| 60 | Worcester, MA | 1,236 | 134 | Chesapeake, VA | 525 | 208 | College Station, TX | 308 |
| 61 | Chattanooga, TN | 1,225 | 135 | Lancaster, CA | 522 | 209 | Visalia, CA | 305 |
| 62 | Springfield, MO | 1,206 | 136 | Murfreesboro, TN | 517 | 210 | Oxnard, CA | 298 |
| 63 | Pittsburgh, PA | 1,180 | 137 | Glendale, AZ | 508 | 211 | Garden Grove, CA | 297 |
| 64 | Modesto, CA | 1,168 | 138 | Madison, WI | 507 | 212 | Evansville, IN | 294 |
| 65 | Arlington, TX | 1,152 | 139 | Killeen, TX | 499 | 213 | Grand Prairie, TX | 291 |
| 66 | Mesa, AZ | 1,104 | 140 | Fayetteville, NC | 494 | 214 | Macon, GA | 288 |
| 67 | Long Beach, CA | 1,091 | 141 | Champaign, IL | 492 | 215 | Moreno Valley, CA | 285 |
| 68 | Tacoma, WA | 1,088 | 142 | Salinas, CA | 490 | 216 | Bloomington, IL | 281 |
| 69 | Bakersfield, CA | 1,082 | 143 | Hialeah, FL | 489 | 216 | Yakima, WA | 281 |
| 70 | Colorado Springs, CO | 1,079 | 144 | Miami Beach, FL | 485 | 218 | Gresham, OR | 279 |
| 71 | Rochester, NY | 1,055 | 145 | Columbus, GA | 483 | 219 | Vista, CA | 276 |
| 72 | San Bernardino, CA | 1,036 | 146 | Fontana, CA | 480 | 220 | Brownsville, TX | 275 |
| 73 | Baton Rouge, LA | 1,030 | 147 | Newport News, VA | 478 | 220 | Tyler, TX | 275 |
| 74 | Huntsville, AL | 1,005 | 148 | Pompano Beach, FL | 475 | 222 | Miramar, FL | 273 |

| RANK | CITY | ASSAULTS |
|---|---|---|
| 223 | Fayetteville, AR | 270 |
| 223 | Hesperia, CA | 270 |
| 225 | Virginia Beach, VA | 269 |
| 226 | Fort Collins, CO | 263 |
| 227 | Roanoke, VA | 262 |
| 228 | Midland, TX | 260 |
| 229 | Lakeland, FL | 258 |
| 230 | South Gate, CA | 256 |
| 231 | Longview, TX | 255 |
| 232 | Decatur, IL | 253 |
| 233 | Cedar Rapids, IA | 252 |
| 234 | Bryan, TX | 250 |
| 235 | Hemet, CA | 246 |
| 235 | Ontario, CA | 246 |
| 235 | Santa Barbara, CA | 246 |
| 238 | Pasadena, CA | 244 |
| 239 | Hawthorne, CA | 243 |
| 240 | Port St. Lucie, FL | 241 |
| 240 | Wichita Falls, TX | 241 |
| 242 | Athens-Clarke, GA | 240 |
| 243 | Quincy, MA | 239 |
| 244 | Billings, MT | 236 |
| 244 | Fullerton, CA | 236 |
| 246 | Concord, CA | 235 |
| 246 | Norwalk, CA | 235 |
| 246 | Sioux City, IA | 235 |
| 249 | Carson, CA | 234 |
| 250 | Columbia, MO | 232 |
| 251 | Huntington Beach, CA | 229 |
| 252 | St. Joseph, MO | 227 |
| 253 | Las Cruces, NM | 225 |
| 253 | Ogden, UT | 225 |
| 255 | Allentown, PA | 223 |
| 256 | Cambridge, MA | 221 |
| 256 | Tuscaloosa, AL | 221 |
| 258 | Lynchburg, VA | 220 |
| 259 | Erie, PA | 219 |
| 259 | Rialto, CA | 219 |
| 261 | Citrus Heights, CA | 218 |
| 261 | Garland, TX | 218 |
| 261 | Hayward, CA | 218 |
| 264 | Duluth, MN | 216 |
| 265 | Livermore, CA | 214 |
| 266 | Lawrence, KS | 213 |
| 267 | El Cajon, CA | 212 |
| 268 | Everett, WA | 208 |
| 268 | Largo, FL | 208 |
| 270 | Thornton, CO | 206 |
| 271 | Overland Park, KS | 204 |
| 272 | Westland, MI | 203 |
| 273 | Upper Darby Twnshp, PA | 201 |
| 274 | Chino, CA | 200 |
| 275 | South Bend, IN | 199 |
| 275 | Waukegan, IL | 199 |
| 277 | Edinburg, TX | 196 |
| 277 | Plano, TX | 196 |
| 279 | Scottsdale, AZ | 195 |
| 280 | Denton, TX | 192 |
| 281 | Sterling Heights, MI | 189 |
| 282 | Rancho Cucamon., CA | 188 |
| 283 | Davie, FL | 186 |
| 283 | Dearborn, MI | 186 |
| 283 | Westminster, CA | 186 |
| 286 | San Angelo, TX | 185 |
| 287 | Roseville, CA | 183 |
| 288 | Napa, CA | 180 |
| 289 | Mesquite, TX | 178 |
| 290 | Jurupa Valley, CA | 177 |
| 290 | Pembroke Pines, FL | 177 |
| 292 | Peoria, AZ | 175 |
| 293 | Deerfield Beach, FL | 170 |
| 293 | Santa Monica, CA | 170 |
| 295 | El Monte, CA | 168 |
| 295 | Plantation, FL | 168 |
| 297 | Cicero, IL | 167 |
| 298 | Bellflower, CA | 164 |
| 298 | Clinton Twnshp, MI | 164 |
| 298 | Norwalk, CT | 164 |
| 301 | Bloomington, IN | 161 |
| 301 | Chico, CA | 161 |
| 301 | Kennewick, WA | 161 |
| 301 | Waterbury, CT | 161 |
| 305 | Suffolk, VA | 160 |
| 306 | Santa Clarita, CA | 158 |
| 307 | Sparks, NV | 156 |
| 308 | Henderson, NV | 154 |
| 309 | Carlsbad, CA | 153 |
| 310 | Ann Arbor, MI | 147 |
| 310 | Cape Coral, FL | 147 |
| 312 | Stamford, CT | 145 |
| 313 | Nampa, ID | 143 |
| 314 | Kenosha, WI | 141 |
| 315 | Boulder, CO | 140 |
| 316 | Eugene, OR | 139 |
| 317 | Bend, OR | 138 |
| 318 | Downey, CA | 136 |
| 318 | Ventura, CA | 136 |
| 320 | Baldwin Park, CA | 135 |
| 321 | Federal Way, WA | 134 |
| 321 | Westminster, CO | 134 |
| 323 | San Marcos, CA | 133 |
| 324 | Gilbert, AZ | 131 |
| 324 | Longmont, CO | 131 |
| 326 | Whittier, CA | 130 |
| 327 | Hampton, VA | 129 |
| 327 | Sunrise, FL | 129 |
| 329 | Brooklyn Park, MN | 126 |
| 329 | Buena Park, CA | 126 |
| 331 | San Mateo, CA | 125 |
| 332 | Charleston, SC | 123 |
| 332 | Olathe, KS | 123 |
| 332 | Renton, WA | 123 |
| 335 | Berkeley, CA | 122 |
| 335 | Somerville, MA | 122 |
| 335 | West Covina, CA | 122 |
| 338 | Lewisville, TX | 120 |
| 338 | Vacaville, CA | 120 |
| 340 | Daly City, CA | 118 |
| 341 | Evanston, IL | 115 |
| 342 | Alexandria, VA | 114 |
| 342 | Coral Springs, FL | 114 |
| 342 | Elgin, IL | 114 |
| 342 | San Leandro, CA | 114 |
| 342 | Spokane Valley, WA | 114 |
| 347 | Mountain View, CA | 112 |
| 348 | Clovis, CA | 111 |
| 348 | Costa Mesa, CA | 111 |
| 348 | Fremont, CA | 111 |
| 351 | McKinney, TX | 110 |
| 351 | Rochester, MN | 110 |
| 353 | Burbank, CA | 107 |
| 354 | Clifton, NJ | 106 |
| 355 | Carrollton, TX | 105 |
| 356 | Santa Clara, CA | 104 |
| 357 | Hamilton Twnshp, NJ | 102 |
| 357 | Lakewood, CA | 102 |
| 359 | Boca Raton, FL | 99 |
| 359 | Cheektowaga, NY | 99 |
| 359 | Kent, WA | 99 |
| 362 | Glendale, CA | 97 |
| 362 | Redwood City, CA | 97 |
| 364 | Arvada, CO | 96 |
| 364 | Livonia, MI | 96 |
| 364 | Racine, WI | 96 |
| 367 | Torrance, CA | 94 |
| 368 | Centennial, CO | 90 |
| 368 | Thousand Oaks, CA | 90 |
| 370 | New Rochelle, NY | 89 |
| 370 | Simi Valley, CA | 89 |
| 372 | Pearland, TX | 88 |
| 372 | Tracy, CA | 88 |
| 374 | Upland, CA | 87 |
| 375 | Round Rock, TX | 86 |
| 375 | Surprise, AZ | 86 |
| 377 | Nashua, NH | 83 |
| 378 | Greece, NY | 82 |
| 378 | St. George, UT | 82 |
| 380 | Beaverton, OR | 81 |
| 381 | Cranston, RI | 80 |
| 381 | McAllen, TX | 80 |
| 383 | Bethlehem, PA | 78 |
| 384 | Meridian, ID | 77 |
| 384 | Naperville, IL | 77 |
| 386 | Sandy, UT | 76 |
| 387 | Broken Arrow, OK | 75 |
| 387 | Scranton, PA | 75 |
| 389 | Corona, CA | 74 |
| 390 | Sunnyvale, CA | 73 |
| 391 | Alhambra, CA | 72 |
| 391 | Norman, OK | 72 |
| 393 | Orange, CA | 71 |
| 394 | Menifee, CA | 69 |
| 395 | Amherst, NY | 68 |
| 395 | Lake Forest, CA | 68 |
| 397 | Sugar Land, TX | 66 |
| 398 | Woodbridge Twnshp, NJ | 65 |
| 399 | Alameda, CA | 63 |
| 400 | Bloomington, MN | 61 |
| 400 | Irvine, CA | 61 |
| 400 | Sandy Springs, GA | 61 |
| 403 | Brick Twnshp, NJ | 60 |
| 403 | Canton Twnshp, MI | 60 |
| 405 | League City, TX | 58 |
| 405 | Lee's Summit, MO | 58 |
| 407 | Edison Twnshp, NJ | 57 |
| 407 | Edmond, OK | 57 |
| 407 | Frisco, TX | 57 |
| 407 | Hillsboro, OR | 57 |
| 407 | Tustin, CA | 57 |
| 412 | Bellevue, WA | 56 |
| 412 | Concord, NC | 56 |
| 412 | Provo, UT | 56 |
| 415 | Cary, NC | 55 |
| 416 | Roswell, GA | 54 |
| 417 | Lakewood Twnshp, NJ | 52 |
| 418 | Newport Beach, CA | 51 |
| 418 | Richardson, TX | 51 |
| 420 | O'Fallon, MO | 49 |
| 421 | Chino Hills, CA | 47 |
| 422 | Newton, MA | 45 |
| 423 | Ramapo, NY | 41 |
| 424 | Clarkstown, NY | 40 |
| 425 | Warwick, RI | 39 |
| 426 | Murrieta, CA | 38 |
| 426 | Temecula, CA | 38 |
| 426 | Troy, MI | 38 |
| 429 | Allen, TX | 36 |
| 429 | Farmington Hills, MI | 36 |
| 429 | Mission Viejo, CA | 36 |
| 429 | Mission, TX | 36 |
| 433 | Colonie, NY | 32 |
| 434 | Hoover, AL | 29 |
| 435 | Arlington Heights, IL | 28 |
| 435 | Danbury, CT | 28 |
| 437 | Toms River Twnshp, NJ | 20 |
| 438 | Johns Creek, GA | 18 |
| 439 | Orem, UT | 11 |
| 440 | Fishers, IN | 7 |
| 441 | Carmel, IN | 5 |
| NA | Chicago, IL** | NA |

Source: Reported data from the F.B.I. "Crime in the United States 2013"

*Aggravated assault is an attack for the purpose of inflicting severe bodily injury.

**Not available.

# 62. Aggravated Assault Rate in 2013
## National Rate = 229.1 Aggravated Assaults per 100,000 Population*

| RANK | CITY | RATE | RANK | CITY | RATE | RANK | CITY | RATE |
|---|---|---|---|---|---|---|---|---|
| 190 | Abilene, TX | 263.0 | 200 | Chino, CA | 247.8 | 277 | Fullerton, CA | 169.0 |
| 87 | Akron, OH | 433.0 | 321 | Chula Vista, CA | 123.9 | 72 | Gainesville, FL | 460.5 |
| 373 | Alameda, CA | 82.7 | 252 | Cicero, IL | 198.3 | 276 | Garden Grove, CA | 169.3 |
| 22 | Albany, GA | 694.1 | 145 | Cincinnati, OH | 319.4 | 358 | Garland, TX | 92.5 |
| 53 | Albany, NY | 537.0 | 195 | Citrus Heights, CA | 255.5 | 46 | Gary, IN | 577.3 |
| 59 | Albuquerque, NM | 502.2 | 414 | Clarkstown, NY | 49.6 | 403 | Gilbert, AZ | 58.2 |
| 380 | Alexandria, VA | 76.8 | 111 | Clarksville, TN | 372.9 | 235 | Glendale, AZ | 217.1 |
| 369 | Alhambra, CA | 85.0 | 125 | Clearwater, FL | 355.3 | 413 | Glendale, CA | 49.7 |
| 265 | Allentown, PA | 187.0 | 73 | Cleveland, OH | 459.7 | 283 | Grand Prairie, TX | 158.3 |
| 428 | Allen, TX | 39.4 | 319 | Clifton, NJ | 124.7 | 101 | Grand Rapids, MI | 395.4 |
| 92 | Amarillo, TX | 417.6 | 280 | Clinton Twnshp, MI | 167.2 | 370 | Greece, NY | 84.8 |
| 405 | Amherst, NY | 57.5 | 336 | Clovis, CA | 111.6 | 118 | Greeley, CO | 361.0 |
| 274 | Anaheim, CA | 173.8 | 152 | College Station, TX | 311.4 | 128 | Green Bay, WI | 349.2 |
| 62 | Anchorage, AK | 497.9 | 427 | Colonie, NY | 40.9 | 157 | Greensboro, NC | 306.4 |
| 315 | Ann Arbor, MI | 125.9 | 201 | Colorado Springs, CO | 247.4 | 98 | Greenville, NC | 401.1 |
| 57 | Antioch, CA | 523.3 | 248 | Columbia, MO | 202.5 | 196 | Gresham, OR | 253.7 |
| 430 | Arlington Heights, IL | 36.9 | 91 | Columbia, SC | 419.7 | 331 | Hamilton Twnshp, NJ | 114.6 |
| 159 | Arlington, TX | 304.1 | 209 | Columbus, GA | 240.1 | 69 | Hammond, IN | 479.0 |
| 363 | Arvada, CO | 86.6 | 8 | Compton, CA | 837.5 | 355 | Hampton, VA | 94.2 |
| 251 | Athens-Clarke, GA | 199.8 | 262 | Concord, CA | 187.3 | 26 | Hartford, CT | 672.4 |
| 29 | Atlanta, GA | 657.4 | 389 | Concord, NC | 67.6 | 177 | Hawthorne, CA | 282.1 |
| 241 | Aurora, CO | 209.9 | 359 | Coral Springs, FL | 90.0 | 302 | Hayward, CA | 144.4 |
| 238 | Aurora, IL | 211.9 | 421 | Corona, CA | 46.2 | 160 | Hemet, CA | 301.1 |
| 202 | Austin, TX | 246.4 | 85 | Corpus Christi, TX | 440.0 | 406 | Henderson, NV | 57.4 |
| 165 | Bakersfield, CA | 299.0 | 352 | Costa Mesa, CA | 98.6 | 171 | Hesperia, CA | 291.5 |
| 271 | Baldwin Park, CA | 175.9 | 350 | Cranston, RI | 99.1 | 243 | Hialeah, FL | 208.8 |
| 16 | Baltimore, MD | 716.3 | 180 | Dallas, TX | 274.3 | 143 | High Point, NC | 322.6 |
| 79 | Baton Rouge, LA | 447.4 | 334 | Daly City, CA | 112.9 | 401 | Hillsboro, OR | 59.2 |
| 36 | Beaumont, TX | 618.6 | 435 | Danbury, CT | 33.6 | 187 | Hollywood, FL | 264.6 |
| 363 | Beaverton, OR | 86.6 | 103 | Davenport, IA | 389.9 | 434 | Hoover, AL | 34.5 |
| 425 | Bellevue, WA | 43.9 | 259 | Davie, FL | 192.6 | 70 | Houston, TX | 471.0 |
| 239 | Bellflower, CA | 211.4 | 94 | Dayton, OH | 408.7 | 328 | Huntington Beach, CA | 116.9 |
| 275 | Bend, OR | 172.7 | 258 | Dearborn, MI | 193.7 | 52 | Huntsville, AL | 544.0 |
| 343 | Berkeley, CA | 105.0 | 133 | Decatur, IL | 336.5 | 154 | Independence, MO | 309.2 |
| 344 | Bethlehem, PA | 103.8 | 233 | Deerfield Beach, FL | 217.4 | 23 | Indianapolis, IN | 693.2 |
| 232 | Billings, MT | 218.9 | 285 | Denton, TX | 155.8 | 102 | Indio, CA | 390.1 |
| 12 | Birmingham, AL | 774.5 | 112 | Denver, CO | 370.0 | 136 | Inglewood, CA | 331.3 |
| 119 | Bloomington, IL | 360.0 | 130 | Des Moines, IA | 344.3 | 436 | Irvine, CA | 25.9 |
| 257 | Bloomington, IN | 195.4 | 2 | Detroit, MI | 1,256.8 | 308 | Irving, TX | 139.2 |
| 387 | Bloomington, MN | 70.1 | 326 | Downey, CA | 120.1 | 105 | Jacksonville, FL | 387.5 |
| 336 | Boca Raton, FL | 111.6 | 198 | Duluth, MN | 250.5 | 122 | Jackson, MS | 355.6 |
| 250 | Boise, ID | 200.2 | 211 | Edinburg, TX | 238.2 | 131 | Jersey City, NJ | 343.7 |
| 83 | Boston, MA | 442.8 | 408 | Edison Twnshp, NJ | 56.3 | 438 | Johns Creek, GA | 21.4 |
| 310 | Boulder, CO | 136.1 | 391 | Edmond, OK | 66.3 | 222 | Joliet, IL | 229.0 |
| 375 | Brick Twnshp, NJ | 79.6 | 245 | El Cajon, CA | 207.8 | 269 | Jurupa Valley, CA | 180.4 |
| 65 | Bridgeport, CT | 489.5 | 297 | El Monte, CA | 145.3 | 191 | Kansas City, KS | 258.8 |
| 6 | Brockton, MA | 887.3 | 178 | El Paso, TX | 276.4 | 11 | Kansas City, MO | 800.4 |
| 382 | Broken Arrow, OK | 72.8 | 346 | Elgin, IL | 103.2 | 240 | Kennewick, WA | 210.4 |
| 282 | Brooklyn Park, MN | 160.8 | 149 | Elizabeth, NJ | 315.6 | 307 | Kenosha, WI | 140.4 |
| 290 | Brownsville, TX | 151.4 | 226 | Elk Grove, CA | 226.2 | 375 | Kent, WA | 79.6 |
| 146 | Bryan, TX | 318.2 | 234 | Erie, PA | 217.2 | 116 | Killeen, TX | 365.5 |
| 286 | Buena Park, CA | 152.5 | 216 | Escondido, CA | 235.5 | 56 | Knoxville, TN | 528.8 |
| 27 | Buffalo, NY | 670.4 | 362 | Eugene, OR | 87.7 | 71 | Lafayette, LA | 462.7 |
| 347 | Burbank, CA | 102.2 | 288 | Evanston, IL | 151.9 | 368 | Lake Forest, CA | 85.7 |
| 247 | Cambridge, MA | 206.0 | 204 | Evansville, IN | 244.4 | 193 | Lakeland, FL | 256.1 |
| 390 | Canton Twnshp, MI | 67.4 | 253 | Everett, WA | 197.9 | 409 | Lakewood Twnshp, NJ | 56.1 |
| 360 | Cape Coral, FL | 89.9 | 169 | Fairfield, CA | 292.4 | 316 | Lakewood, CA | 125.8 |
| 309 | Carlsbad, CA | 138.5 | 15 | Fall River, MA | 724.1 | 182 | Lakewood, CO | 272.0 |
| 441 | Carmel, IN | 5.9 | 176 | Fargo, ND | 282.6 | 140 | Lancaster, CA | 326.7 |
| 374 | Carrollton, TX | 82.4 | 423 | Farmington Hills, MI | 44.4 | 17 | Lansing, MI | 713.7 |
| 198 | Carson, CA | 250.5 | 129 | Fayetteville, AR | 346.6 | 162 | Laredo, TX | 300.0 |
| 430 | Cary, NC | 36.9 | 205 | Fayetteville, NC | 243.9 | 186 | Largo, FL | 267.0 |
| 256 | Cedar Rapids, IA | 195.9 | 301 | Federal Way, WA | 144.5 | 230 | Las Cruces, NM | 220.6 |
| 367 | Centennial, CO | 85.9 | 440 | Fishers, IN | 8.4 | 86 | Las Vegas, NV | 433.2 |
| 43 | Champaign, IL | 593.0 | 1 | Flint, MI | 1,267.7 | 212 | Lawrence, KS | 236.6 |
| 303 | Chandler, AZ | 144.3 | 214 | Fontana, CA | 236.0 | 40 | Lawrence, MA | 607.9 |
| 353 | Charleston, SC | 96.7 | 273 | Fort Collins, CO | 175.3 | 28 | Lawton, OK | 667.7 |
| 121 | Charlotte, NC | 358.0 | 104 | Fort Lauderdale, FL | 388.1 | 392 | League City, TX | 64.7 |
| 20 | Chattanooga, TN | 711.0 | 66 | Fort Smith, AR | 488.5 | 395 | Lee's Summit, MO | 62.5 |
| 314 | Cheektowaga, NY | 126.3 | 292 | Fort Wayne, IN | 147.6 | 327 | Lewisville, TX | 119.2 |
| 225 | Chesapeake, VA | 227.7 | 139 | Fort Worth, TX | 328.6 | 342 | Lexington, KY | 105.9 |
| NA | Chicago, IL** | NA | 415 | Fremont, CA | 49.4 | 215 | Lincoln, NE | 235.9 |
| 268 | Chico, CA | 182.5 | 158 | Fresno, CA | 305.8 | 7 | Little Rock, AR | 850.6 |
| 397 | Chino Hills, CA | 61.1 | 426 | Frisco, TX | 43.3 | 196 | Livermore, CA | 253.7 |

| RANK | CITY | RATE |
|---|---|---|
| 348 | Livonia, MI | 100.8 |
| 219 | Long Beach, CA | 232.3 |
| 295 | Longmont, CO | 146.5 |
| 151 | Longview, TX | 313.8 |
| 255 | Los Angeles, CA | 196.6 |
| 164 | Louisville, KY | 299.4 |
| 124 | Lowell, MA | 355.4 |
| 49 | Lubbock, TX | 566.7 |
| 175 | Lynchburg, VA | 282.9 |
| 32 | Lynn, MA | 636.4 |
| 148 | Macon, GA | 315.9 |
| 242 | Madison, WI | 209.1 |
| 142 | Manchester, NH | 323.3 |
| 402 | McAllen, TX | 58.8 |
| 381 | McKinney, TX | 74.9 |
| 78 | Medford, OR | 449.6 |
| 44 | Melbourne, FL | 587.5 |
| 3 | Memphis, TN | 1,094.1 |
| 372 | Menifee, CA | 83.5 |
| 64 | Merced, CA | 490.6 |
| 356 | Meridian, ID | 93.8 |
| 208 | Mesa, AZ | 242.0 |
| 322 | Mesquite, TX | 123.3 |
| 55 | Miami Beach, FL | 530.4 |
| 60 | Miami Gardens, FL | 501.5 |
| 37 | Miami, FL | 612.3 |
| 237 | Midland, TX | 212.7 |
| 14 | Milwaukee, WI | 733.2 |
| 82 | Minneapolis, MN | 444.5 |
| 244 | Miramar, FL | 208.5 |
| 429 | Mission Viejo, CA | 37.5 |
| 424 | Mission, TX | 44.2 |
| 107 | Mobile, AL | 385.1 |
| 48 | Modesto, CA | 571.8 |
| 306 | Moreno Valley, CA | 141.6 |
| 299 | Mountain View, CA | 144.7 |
| 80 | Murfreesboro, TN | 447.3 |
| 433 | Murrieta, CA | 35.3 |
| 277 | Nampa, ID | 169.0 |
| 223 | Napa, CA | 228.5 |
| 410 | Naperville, IL | 53.4 |
| 354 | Nashua, NH | 95.3 |
| 18 | Nashville, TN | 712.5 |
| 19 | New Bedford, MA | 711.5 |
| 42 | New Haven, CT | 593.6 |
| 100 | New Orleans, LA | 396.5 |
| 334 | New Rochelle, NY | 112.9 |
| 109 | New York, NY | 378.4 |
| 134 | Newark, NJ | 332.8 |
| 403 | Newport Beach, CA | 58.2 |
| 189 | Newport News, VA | 264.0 |
| 411 | Newton, MA | 51.8 |
| 132 | Norfolk, VA | 340.5 |
| 396 | Norman, OK | 61.6 |
| 93 | North Charleston, SC | 414.2 |
| 50 | North Las Vegas, NV | 554.4 |
| 230 | Norwalk, CA | 220.6 |
| 263 | Norwalk, CT | 187.2 |
| 24 | Oakland, CA | 691.3 |
| 218 | Oceanside, CA | 233.0 |
| 9 | Odessa, TX | 811.9 |
| 400 | O'Fallon, MO | 59.3 |
| 184 | Ogden, UT | 267.7 |
| 51 | Oklahoma City, OK | 544.6 |
| 357 | Olathe, KS | 93.6 |
| 126 | Omaha, NE | 354.1 |
| 296 | Ontario, CA | 146.3 |
| 412 | Orange, CA | 50.6 |
| 439 | Orem, UT | 12.0 |
| 33 | Orlando, FL | 631.8 |
| 333 | Overland Park, KS | 113.0 |
| 293 | Oxnard, CA | 147.1 |
| 113 | Palm Bay, FL | 367.8 |
| 166 | Palmdale, CA | 297.1 |

| RANK | CITY | RATE |
|---|---|---|
| 272 | Pasadena, CA | 175.5 |
| 227 | Pasadena, TX | 225.2 |
| 74 | Paterson, NJ | 457.0 |
| 361 | Pearland, TX | 89.6 |
| 338 | Pembroke Pines, FL | 109.2 |
| 340 | Peoria, AZ | 108.3 |
| 95 | Peoria, IL | 404.5 |
| 58 | Philadelphia, PA | 514.2 |
| 115 | Phoenix, AZ | 366.5 |
| 108 | Pittsburgh, PA | 383.6 |
| 384 | Plano, TX | 71.1 |
| 261 | Plantation, FL | 188.9 |
| 163 | Pomona, CA | 299.9 |
| 75 | Pompano Beach, FL | 456.9 |
| 305 | Port St. Lucie, FL | 141.9 |
| 170 | Portland, OR | 291.6 |
| 117 | Portsmouth, VA | 364.9 |
| 120 | Providence, RI | 358.3 |
| 418 | Provo, UT | 47.9 |
| 45 | Pueblo, CO | 585.8 |
| 194 | Quincy, MA | 255.6 |
| 323 | Racine, WI | 122.9 |
| 221 | Raleigh, NC | 230.1 |
| 420 | Ramapo, NY | 47.0 |
| 339 | Rancho Cucamon., CA | 109.1 |
| 96 | Reading, PA | 401.8 |
| 88 | Redding, CA | 426.2 |
| 324 | Redwood City, CA | 121.7 |
| 138 | Reno, NV | 329.8 |
| 312 | Renton, WA | 127.3 |
| 236 | Rialto, CA | 213.6 |
| 417 | Richardson, TX | 48.8 |
| 38 | Richmond, CA | 609.3 |
| 168 | Richmond, VA | 292.7 |
| 213 | Riverside, CA | 236.1 |
| 185 | Roanoke, VA | 267.5 |
| 349 | Rochester, MN | 100.3 |
| 61 | Rochester, NY | 501.0 |
| 4 | Rockford, IL | 1,003.3 |
| 298 | Roseville, CA | 145.0 |
| 407 | Roswell, GA | 56.6 |
| 377 | Round Rock, TX | 79.2 |
| 106 | Sacramento, CA | 386.9 |
| 246 | Salem, OR | 207.3 |
| 150 | Salinas, CA | 314.6 |
| 84 | Salt Lake City, UT | 442.6 |
| 260 | San Angelo, TX | 191.4 |
| 90 | San Antonio, TX | 421.6 |
| 68 | San Bernardino, CA | 483.4 |
| 191 | San Diego, CA | 258.8 |
| 146 | San Francisco, CA | 318.2 |
| 267 | San Jose, CA | 182.6 |
| 311 | San Leandro, CA | 130.3 |
| 289 | San Marcos, CA | 151.6 |
| 320 | San Mateo, CA | 124.5 |
| 398 | Sandy Springs, GA | 60.3 |
| 371 | Sandy, UT | 84.5 |
| 270 | Santa Ana, CA | 178.5 |
| 181 | Santa Barbara, CA | 273.3 |
| 363 | Santa Clara, CA | 86.6 |
| 379 | Santa Clarita, CA | 77.1 |
| 141 | Santa Maria, CA | 324.3 |
| 266 | Santa Monica, CA | 183.8 |
| 224 | Santa Rosa, CA | 227.9 |
| 287 | Savannah, GA | 152.2 |
| 366 | Scottsdale, AZ | 86.5 |
| 351 | Scranton, PA | 99.0 |
| 155 | Seattle, WA | 308.8 |
| 77 | Shreveport, LA | 450.6 |
| 385 | Simi Valley, CA | 70.5 |
| 174 | Sioux City, IA | 284.2 |
| 187 | Sioux Falls, SD | 264.6 |
| 284 | Somerville, MA | 156.9 |
| 254 | South Bend, IN | 197.6 |

| RANK | CITY | RATE |
|---|---|---|
| 183 | South Gate, CA | 267.8 |
| 279 | Sparks, NV | 168.2 |
| 318 | Spokane Valley, WA | 125.5 |
| 122 | Spokane, WA | 355.6 |
| 21 | Springfield, IL | 706.4 |
| 35 | Springfield, MA | 627.7 |
| 13 | Springfield, MO | 739.6 |
| 329 | Stamford, CT | 115.2 |
| 299 | Sterling Heights, MI | 144.7 |
| 10 | Stockton, CA | 804.2 |
| 341 | St. George, UT | 107.3 |
| 167 | St. Joseph, MO | 293.5 |
| 5 | St. Louis, MO | 994.2 |
| 89 | St. Paul, MN | 424.9 |
| 31 | St. Petersburg, FL | 637.4 |
| 263 | Suffolk, VA | 187.2 |
| 378 | Sugar Land, TX | 79.1 |
| 416 | Sunnyvale, CA | 49.3 |
| 304 | Sunrise, FL | 142.9 |
| 386 | Surprise, AZ | 70.2 |
| 67 | Syracuse, NY | 483.9 |
| 54 | Tacoma, WA | 535.4 |
| 81 | Tallahassee, FL | 445.1 |
| 97 | Tampa, FL | 401.6 |
| 432 | Temecula, CA | 35.6 |
| 144 | Tempe, AZ | 321.7 |
| 281 | Thornton, CO | 163.8 |
| 388 | Thousand Oaks, CA | 69.8 |
| 34 | Toledo, OH | 630.0 |
| 437 | Toms River Twnshp, NJ | 21.7 |
| 153 | Topeka, KS | 309.4 |
| 394 | Torrance, CA | 63.7 |
| 345 | Tracy, CA | 103.3 |
| 30 | Trenton, NJ | 647.8 |
| 422 | Troy, MI | 46.0 |
| 99 | Tucson, AZ | 400.2 |
| 39 | Tulsa, OK | 608.4 |
| 217 | Tuscaloosa, AL | 234.8 |
| 383 | Tustin, CA | 72.3 |
| 179 | Tyler, TX | 274.9 |
| 330 | Upland, CA | 115.0 |
| 207 | Upper Darby Twnshp, PA | 242.8 |
| 313 | Vacaville, CA | 127.2 |
| 76 | Vallejo, CA | 456.3 |
| 229 | Vancouver, WA | 222.8 |
| 317 | Ventura, CA | 125.7 |
| 135 | Victorville, CA | 332.0 |
| 399 | Virginia Beach, VA | 59.7 |
| 210 | Visalia, CA | 238.6 |
| 173 | Vista, CA | 285.4 |
| 206 | Waco, TX | 243.8 |
| 172 | Warren, MI | 285.5 |
| 419 | Warwick, RI | 47.7 |
| 47 | Washington, DC | 576.1 |
| 294 | Waterbury, CT | 146.7 |
| 228 | Waukegan, IL | 224.2 |
| 332 | West Covina, CA | 113.1 |
| 114 | West Palm Beach, FL | 366.8 |
| 137 | West Valley, UT | 330.7 |
| 203 | Westland, MI | 245.9 |
| 249 | Westminster, CA | 202.4 |
| 324 | Westminster, CO | 121.7 |
| 291 | Whittier, CA | 150.4 |
| 220 | Wichita Falls, TX | 230.6 |
| 41 | Wichita, KS | 604.9 |
| 127 | Wilmington, NC | 349.6 |
| 110 | Winston-Salem, NC | 378.3 |
| 393 | Woodbridge Twnshp, NJ | 64.6 |
| 25 | Worcester, MA | 673.7 |
| 161 | Yakima, WA | 300.2 |
| 155 | Yonkers, NY | 308.8 |
| 63 | Yuma, AZ | 491.6 |

Source: CQ Press using reported data from the F.B.I. "Crime in the United States 2013"

*Aggravated assault is an attack for the purpose of inflicting severe bodily injury.

**Not available.

# 62. Aggravated Assault Rate in 2013 (continued)
## National Rate = 229.1 Aggravated Assaults per 100,000 Population*

| RANK CITY | RATE | RANK CITY | RATE | RANK CITY | RATE |
|---|---|---|---|---|---|
| 1 Flint, MI | 1,267.7 | 75 Pompano Beach, FL | 456.9 | 149 Elizabeth, NJ | 315.6 |
| 2 Detroit, MI | 1,256.8 | 76 Vallejo, CA | 456.3 | 150 Salinas, CA | 314.6 |
| 3 Memphis, TN | 1,094.7 | 77 Shreveport, LA | 450.6 | 151 Longview, TX | 313.8 |
| 4 Rockford, IL | 1,003.3 | 78 Medford, OR | 449.6 | 152 College Station, TX | 311.4 |
| 5 St. Louis, MO | 994.2 | 79 Baton Rouge, LA | 447.4 | 153 Topeka, KS | 309.4 |
| 6 Brockton, MA | 887.3 | 80 Murfreesboro, TN | 447.3 | 154 Independence, MO | 309.2 |
| 7 Little Rock, AR | 850.6 | 81 Tallahassee, FL | 445.1 | 155 Seattle, WA | 308.8 |
| 8 Compton, CA | 837.5 | 82 Minneapolis, MN | 444.5 | 155 Yonkers, NY | 308.8 |
| 9 Odessa, TX | 811.9 | 83 Boston, MA | 442.8 | 157 Greensboro, NC | 306.4 |
| 10 Stockton, CA | 804.2 | 84 Salt Lake City, UT | 442.6 | 158 Fresno, CA | 305.8 |
| 11 Kansas City, MO | 800.4 | 85 Corpus Christi, TX | 440.0 | 159 Arlington, TX | 304.1 |
| 12 Birmingham, AL | 774.5 | 86 Las Vegas, NV | 433.2 | 160 Hemet, CA | 301.1 |
| 13 Springfield, MO | 739.6 | 87 Akron, OH | 433.0 | 161 Yakima, WA | 300.2 |
| 14 Milwaukee, WI | 733.2 | 88 Redding, CA | 426.2 | 162 Laredo, TX | 300.0 |
| 15 Fall River, MA | 724.1 | 89 St. Paul, MN | 424.9 | 163 Pomona, CA | 299.9 |
| 16 Baltimore, MD | 716.3 | 90 San Antonio, TX | 421.6 | 164 Louisville, KY | 299.4 |
| 17 Lansing, MI | 713.7 | 91 Columbia, SC | 419.7 | 165 Bakersfield, CA | 299.0 |
| 18 Nashville, TN | 712.5 | 92 Amarillo, TX | 417.6 | 166 Palmdale, CA | 297.1 |
| 19 New Bedford, MA | 711.5 | 93 North Charleston, SC | 414.2 | 167 St. Joseph, MO | 293.5 |
| 20 Chattanooga, TN | 711.0 | 94 Dayton, OH | 408.7 | 168 Richmond, VA | 292.7 |
| 21 Springfield, IL | 706.4 | 95 Peoria, IL | 404.5 | 169 Fairfield, CA | 292.4 |
| 22 Albany, GA | 694.1 | 96 Reading, PA | 401.8 | 170 Portland, OR | 291.6 |
| 23 Indianapolis, IN | 693.2 | 97 Tampa, FL | 401.6 | 171 Hesperia, CA | 291.5 |
| 24 Oakland, CA | 691.3 | 98 Greenville, NC | 401.1 | 172 Warren, MI | 285.5 |
| 25 Worcester, MA | 673.7 | 99 Tucson, AZ | 400.2 | 173 Vista, CA | 285.4 |
| 26 Hartford, CT | 672.4 | 100 New Orleans, LA | 396.5 | 174 Sioux City, IA | 284.2 |
| 27 Buffalo, NY | 670.4 | 101 Grand Rapids, MI | 395.4 | 175 Lynchburg, VA | 282.9 |
| 28 Lawton, OK | 667.7 | 102 Indio, CA | 390.1 | 176 Fargo, ND | 282.6 |
| 29 Atlanta, GA | 657.4 | 103 Davenport, IA | 389.9 | 177 Hawthorne, CA | 282.1 |
| 30 Trenton, NJ | 647.8 | 104 Fort Lauderdale, FL | 388.1 | 178 El Paso, TX | 276.4 |
| 31 St. Petersburg, FL | 637.4 | 105 Jacksonville, FL | 387.5 | 179 Tyler, TX | 274.9 |
| 32 Lynn, MA | 636.4 | 106 Sacramento, CA | 386.9 | 180 Dallas, TX | 274.3 |
| 33 Orlando, FL | 631.8 | 107 Mobile, AL | 385.1 | 181 Santa Barbara, CA | 273.3 |
| 34 Toledo, OH | 630.0 | 108 Pittsburgh, PA | 383.6 | 182 Lakewood, CO | 272.0 |
| 35 Springfield, MA | 627.7 | 109 New York, NY | 378.4 | 183 South Gate, CA | 267.8 |
| 36 Beaumont, TX | 618.6 | 110 Winston-Salem, NC | 378.3 | 184 Ogden, UT | 267.7 |
| 37 Miami, FL | 612.3 | 111 Clarksville, TN | 372.9 | 185 Roanoke, VA | 267.5 |
| 38 Richmond, CA | 609.3 | 112 Denver, CO | 370.0 | 186 Largo, FL | 267.0 |
| 39 Tulsa, OK | 608.4 | 113 Palm Bay, FL | 367.8 | 187 Hollywood, FL | 264.6 |
| 40 Lawrence, MA | 607.9 | 114 West Palm Beach, FL | 366.8 | 187 Sioux Falls, SD | 264.6 |
| 41 Wichita, KS | 604.9 | 115 Phoenix, AZ | 366.5 | 189 Newport News, VA | 264.0 |
| 42 New Haven, CT | 593.6 | 116 Killeen, TX | 365.5 | 190 Abilene, TX | 263.0 |
| 43 Champaign, IL | 593.0 | 117 Portsmouth, VA | 364.9 | 191 Kansas City, KS | 258.8 |
| 44 Melbourne, FL | 587.5 | 118 Greeley, CO | 361.0 | 191 San Diego, CA | 258.8 |
| 45 Pueblo, CO | 585.8 | 119 Bloomington, IL | 360.0 | 193 Lakeland, FL | 256.1 |
| 46 Gary, IN | 577.3 | 120 Providence, RI | 358.3 | 194 Quincy, MA | 255.6 |
| 47 Washington, DC | 576.1 | 121 Charlotte, NC | 358.0 | 195 Citrus Heights, CA | 255.5 |
| 48 Modesto, CA | 571.8 | 122 Jackson, MS | 355.6 | 196 Gresham, OR | 253.7 |
| 49 Lubbock, TX | 566.7 | 122 Spokane, WA | 355.6 | 196 Livermore, CA | 253.7 |
| 50 North Las Vegas, NV | 554.4 | 124 Lowell, MA | 355.4 | 198 Carson, CA | 250.5 |
| 51 Oklahoma City, OK | 544.6 | 125 Clearwater, FL | 355.3 | 198 Duluth, MN | 250.5 |
| 52 Huntsville, AL | 544.0 | 126 Omaha, NE | 354.1 | 200 Chino, CA | 247.8 |
| 53 Albany, NY | 537.0 | 127 Wilmington, NC | 349.6 | 201 Colorado Springs, CO | 247.4 |
| 54 Tacoma, WA | 535.4 | 128 Green Bay, WI | 349.2 | 202 Austin, TX | 246.4 |
| 55 Miami Beach, FL | 530.4 | 129 Fayetteville, AR | 346.6 | 203 Westland, MI | 245.9 |
| 56 Knoxville, TN | 528.8 | 130 Des Moines, IA | 344.3 | 204 Evansville, IN | 244.4 |
| 57 Antioch, CA | 523.3 | 131 Jersey City, NJ | 343.7 | 205 Fayetteville, NC | 243.9 |
| 58 Philadelphia, PA | 514.2 | 132 Norfolk, VA | 340.5 | 206 Waco, TX | 243.8 |
| 59 Albuquerque, NM | 502.2 | 133 Decatur, IL | 336.5 | 207 Upper Darby Twnshp, PA | 242.8 |
| 60 Miami Gardens, FL | 501.5 | 134 Newark, NJ | 332.8 | 208 Mesa, AZ | 242.0 |
| 61 Rochester, NY | 501.0 | 135 Victorville, CA | 332.0 | 209 Columbus, GA | 240.1 |
| 62 Anchorage, AK | 497.9 | 136 Inglewood, CA | 331.3 | 210 Visalia, CA | 238.6 |
| 63 Yuma, AZ | 491.6 | 137 West Valley, UT | 330.7 | 211 Edinburg, TX | 238.2 |
| 64 Merced, CA | 490.6 | 138 Reno, NV | 329.8 | 212 Lawrence, KS | 236.6 |
| 65 Bridgeport, CT | 489.5 | 139 Fort Worth, TX | 328.6 | 213 Riverside, CA | 236.1 |
| 66 Fort Smith, AR | 488.5 | 140 Lancaster, CA | 326.7 | 214 Fontana, CA | 236.0 |
| 67 Syracuse, NY | 483.9 | 141 Santa Maria, CA | 324.3 | 215 Lincoln, NE | 235.8 |
| 68 San Bernardino, CA | 483.4 | 142 Manchester, NH | 323.3 | 216 Escondido, CA | 235.5 |
| 69 Hammond, IN | 479.0 | 143 High Point, NC | 322.6 | 217 Tuscaloosa, AL | 234.8 |
| 70 Houston, TX | 471.0 | 144 Tempe, AZ | 321.7 | 218 Oceanside, CA | 233.0 |
| 71 Lafayette, LA | 462.7 | 145 Cincinnati, OH | 319.4 | 219 Long Beach, CA | 232.3 |
| 72 Gainesville, FL | 460.5 | 146 Bryan, TX | 318.2 | 220 Wichita Falls, TX | 230.6 |
| 73 Cleveland, OH | 459.7 | 146 San Francisco, CA | 318.2 | 221 Raleigh, NC | 230.1 |
| 74 Paterson, NJ | 457.0 | 148 Macon, GA | 315.9 | 222 Joliet, IL | 229.0 |

| RANK CITY | RATE | RANK CITY | RATE | RANK CITY | RATE |
|---|---|---|---|---|---|
| 223 Napa, CA | 228.5 | 297 El Monte, CA | 145.3 | 371 Sandy, UT | 84.5 |
| 224 Santa Rosa, CA | 227.9 | 298 Roseville, CA | 145.0 | 372 Menifee, CA | 83.5 |
| 225 Chesapeake, VA | 227.7 | 299 Mountain View, CA | 144.7 | 373 Alameda, CA | 82.7 |
| 226 Elk Grove, CA | 226.2 | 299 Sterling Heights, MI | 144.7 | 374 Carrollton, TX | 82.4 |
| 227 Pasadena, TX | 225.2 | 301 Federal Way, WA | 144.5 | 375 Brick Twnshp, NJ | 79.6 |
| 228 Waukegan, IL | 224.2 | 302 Hayward, CA | 144.4 | 375 Kent, WA | 79.6 |
| 229 Vancouver, WA | 222.8 | 303 Chandler, AZ | 144.3 | 377 Round Rock, TX | 79.2 |
| 230 Las Cruces, NM | 220.6 | 304 Sunrise, FL | 142.9 | 378 Sugar Land, TX | 79.1 |
| 230 Norwalk, CA | 220.6 | 305 Port St. Lucie, FL | 141.9 | 379 Santa Clarita, CA | 77.1 |
| 232 Billings, MT | 218.9 | 306 Moreno Valley, CA | 141.6 | 380 Alexandria, VA | 76.8 |
| 233 Deerfield Beach, FL | 217.4 | 307 Kenosha, WI | 140.4 | 381 McKinney, TX | 74.9 |
| 234 Erie, PA | 217.2 | 308 Irving, TX | 139.2 | 382 Broken Arrow, OK | 72.8 |
| 235 Glendale, AZ | 217.1 | 309 Carlsbad, CA | 138.5 | 383 Tustin, CA | 72.3 |
| 236 Rialto, CA | 213.6 | 310 Boulder, CO | 136.1 | 384 Plano, TX | 71.1 |
| 237 Midland, TX | 212.7 | 311 San Leandro, CA | 130.3 | 385 Simi Valley, CA | 70.5 |
| 238 Aurora, IL | 211.9 | 312 Renton, WA | 127.3 | 386 Surprise, AZ | 70.2 |
| 239 Bellflower, CA | 211.4 | 313 Vacaville, CA | 127.2 | 387 Bloomington, MN | 70.1 |
| 240 Kennewick, WA | 210.4 | 314 Cheektowaga, NY | 126.3 | 388 Thousand Oaks, CA | 69.8 |
| 241 Aurora, CO | 209.9 | 315 Ann Arbor, MI | 125.9 | 389 Concord, NC | 67.6 |
| 242 Madison, WI | 209.1 | 316 Lakewood, CA | 125.8 | 390 Canton Twnshp, MI | 67.4 |
| 243 Hialeah, FL | 208.8 | 317 Ventura, CA | 125.7 | 391 Edmond, OK | 66.3 |
| 244 Miramar, FL | 208.5 | 318 Spokane Valley, WA | 125.5 | 392 League City, TX | 64.7 |
| 245 El Cajon, CA | 207.8 | 319 Clifton, NJ | 124.7 | 393 Woodbridge Twnshp, NJ | 64.6 |
| 246 Salem, OR | 207.3 | 320 San Mateo, CA | 124.5 | 394 Torrance, CA | 63.7 |
| 247 Cambridge, MA | 206.0 | 321 Chula Vista, CA | 123.9 | 395 Lee's Summit, MO | 62.5 |
| 248 Columbia, MO | 202.5 | 322 Mesquite, TX | 123.3 | 396 Norman, OK | 61.6 |
| 249 Westminster, CA | 202.4 | 323 Racine, WI | 122.9 | 397 Chino Hills, CA | 61.1 |
| 250 Boise, ID | 200.2 | 324 Redwood City, CA | 121.7 | 398 Sandy Springs, GA | 60.3 |
| 251 Athens-Clarke, GA | 199.8 | 324 Westminster, CO | 121.7 | 399 Virginia Beach, VA | 59.7 |
| 252 Cicero, IL | 198.3 | 326 Downey, CA | 120.1 | 400 O'Fallon, MO | 59.3 |
| 253 Everett, WA | 197.9 | 327 Lewisville, TX | 119.2 | 401 Hillsboro, OR | 59.2 |
| 254 South Bend, IN | 197.6 | 328 Huntington Beach, CA | 116.9 | 402 McAllen, TX | 58.8 |
| 255 Los Angeles, CA | 196.6 | 329 Stamford, CT | 115.2 | 403 Gilbert, AZ | 58.2 |
| 256 Cedar Rapids, IA | 195.9 | 330 Upland, CA | 115.0 | 403 Newport Beach, CA | 58.2 |
| 257 Bloomington, IN | 195.4 | 331 Hamilton Twnshp, NJ | 114.6 | 405 Amherst, NY | 57.5 |
| 258 Dearborn, MI | 193.7 | 332 West Covina, CA | 113.1 | 406 Henderson, NV | 57.4 |
| 259 Davie, FL | 192.6 | 333 Overland Park, KS | 113.0 | 407 Roswell, GA | 56.6 |
| 260 San Angelo, TX | 191.4 | 334 Daly City, CA | 112.9 | 408 Edison Twnshp, NJ | 56.3 |
| 261 Plantation, FL | 188.9 | 334 New Rochelle, NY | 112.9 | 409 Lakewood Twnshp, NJ | 56.1 |
| 262 Concord, CA | 187.3 | 336 Boca Raton, FL | 111.6 | 410 Naperville, IL | 53.4 |
| 263 Norwalk, CT | 187.2 | 336 Clovis, CA | 111.6 | 411 Newton, MA | 51.8 |
| 263 Suffolk, VA | 187.2 | 338 Pembroke Pines, FL | 109.2 | 412 Orange, CA | 50.6 |
| 265 Allentown, PA | 187.0 | 339 Rancho Cucamon., CA | 109.1 | 413 Glendale, CA | 49.7 |
| 266 Santa Monica, CA | 183.8 | 340 Peoria, AZ | 108.3 | 414 Clarkstown, NY | 49.6 |
| 267 San Jose, CA | 182.6 | 341 St. George, UT | 107.3 | 415 Fremont, CA | 49.4 |
| 268 Chico, CA | 182.5 | 342 Lexington, KY | 105.9 | 416 Sunnyvale, CA | 49.3 |
| 269 Jurupa Valley, CA | 180.4 | 343 Berkeley, CA | 105.0 | 417 Richardson, TX | 48.8 |
| 270 Santa Ana, CA | 178.5 | 344 Bethlehem, PA | 103.8 | 418 Provo, UT | 47.9 |
| 271 Baldwin Park, CA | 175.9 | 345 Tracy, CA | 103.3 | 419 Warwick, RI | 47.7 |
| 272 Pasadena, CA | 175.5 | 346 Elgin, IL | 103.2 | 420 Ramapo, NY | 47.0 |
| 273 Fort Collins, CO | 175.3 | 347 Burbank, CA | 102.2 | 421 Corona, CA | 46.2 |
| 274 Anaheim, CA | 173.8 | 348 Livonia, MI | 100.8 | 422 Troy, MI | 46.0 |
| 275 Bend, OR | 172.7 | 349 Rochester, MN | 100.3 | 423 Farmington Hills, MI | 44.4 |
| 276 Garden Grove, CA | 169.3 | 350 Cranston, RI | 99.1 | 424 Mission, TX | 44.2 |
| 277 Fullerton, CA | 169.0 | 351 Scranton, PA | 99.0 | 425 Bellevue, WA | 43.9 |
| 277 Nampa, ID | 169.0 | 352 Costa Mesa, CA | 98.6 | 426 Frisco, TX | 43.3 |
| 279 Sparks, NV | 168.2 | 353 Charleston, SC | 96.7 | 427 Colonie, NY | 40.9 |
| 280 Clinton Twnshp, MI | 167.2 | 354 Nashua, NH | 95.3 | 428 Allen, TX | 39.4 |
| 281 Thornton, CO | 163.8 | 355 Hampton, VA | 94.2 | 429 Mission Viejo, CA | 37.5 |
| 282 Brooklyn Park, MN | 160.8 | 356 Meridian, ID | 93.8 | 430 Arlington Heights, IL | 36.9 |
| 283 Grand Prairie, TX | 158.3 | 357 Olathe, KS | 93.6 | 430 Cary, NC | 36.9 |
| 284 Somerville, MA | 156.9 | 358 Garland, TX | 92.5 | 432 Temecula, CA | 35.6 |
| 285 Denton, TX | 155.8 | 359 Coral Springs, FL | 90.0 | 433 Murrieta, CA | 35.3 |
| 286 Buena Park, CA | 152.5 | 360 Cape Coral, FL | 89.9 | 434 Hoover, AL | 34.5 |
| 287 Savannah, GA | 152.2 | 361 Pearland, TX | 89.6 | 435 Danbury, CT | 33.6 |
| 288 Evanston, IL | 151.9 | 362 Eugene, OR | 87.7 | 436 Irvine, CA | 25.9 |
| 289 San Marcos, CA | 151.6 | 363 Arvada, CO | 86.6 | 437 Toms River Twnshp, NJ | 21.7 |
| 290 Brownsville, TX | 151.4 | 363 Beaverton, OR | 86.6 | 438 Johns Creek, GA | 21.4 |
| 291 Whittier, CA | 150.4 | 363 Santa Clara, CA | 86.6 | 439 Orem, UT | 12.0 |
| 292 Fort Wayne, IN | 147.6 | 366 Scottsdale, AZ | 86.5 | 440 Fishers, IN | 8.4 |
| 293 Oxnard, CA | 147.1 | 367 Centennial, CO | 85.9 | 441 Carmel, IN | 5.9 |
| 294 Waterbury, CT | 146.7 | 368 Lake Forest, CA | 85.7 | NA Chicago, IL** | NA |
| 295 Longmont, CO | 146.5 | 369 Alhambra, CA | 85.0 | | |
| 296 Ontario, CA | 146.3 | 370 Greece, NY | 84.8 | | |

Source: CQ Press using reported data from the F.B.I. "Crime in the United States 2013"

*Aggravated assault is an attack for the purpose of inflicting severe bodily injury.

**Not available.

## 63. Percent Change in Aggravated Assault Rate: 2012 to 2013
## National Percent Change = 5.6% Decrease*

| RANK | CITY | % CHANGE | RANK | CITY | % CHANGE | RANK | CITY | % CHANGE |
|---|---|---|---|---|---|---|---|---|
| 99 | Abilene, TX | 3.7 | 302 | Chino, CA | (13.7) | 351 | Fullerton, CA | (17.6) |
| 299 | Akron, OH | (13.3) | 157 | Chula Vista, CA | (1.1) | 164 | Gainesville, FL | (2.5) |
| 268 | Alameda, CA | (10.9) | 173 | Cicero, IL | (3.4) | 105 | Garden Grove, CA | 3.3 |
| 161 | Albany, GA | (2.3) | 126 | Cincinnati, OH | 1.9 | 295 | Garland, TX | (13.1) |
| 96 | Albany, NY | 4.2 | 129 | Citrus Heights, CA | 1.6 | 11 | Gary, IN | 29.0 |
| 131 | Albuquerque, NM | 1.5 | 281 | Clarkstown, NY | (11.6) | 119 | Gilbert, AZ | 2.3 |
| 33 | Alexandria, VA | 16.7 | 413 | Clarksville, TN | (28.9) | 394 | Glendale, AZ | (24.0) |
| 276 | Alhambra, CA | (11.4) | 328 | Clearwater, FL | (15.4) | 361 | Glendale, CA | (18.7) |
| 82 | Allentown, PA | 6.3 | 102 | Cleveland, OH | 3.4 | 145 | Grand Prairie, TX | (0.1) |
| 49 | Allen, TX | 12.9 | 36 | Clifton, NJ | 16.0 | 380 | Grand Rapids, MI | (20.2) |
| 218 | Amarillo, TX | (6.7) | 339 | Clinton Twnshp, MI | (16.8) | 14 | Greece, NY | 26.2 |
| 13 | Amherst, NY | 27.5 | 292 | Clovis, CA | (12.7) | 66 | Greeley, CO | 8.3 |
| 371 | Anaheim, CA | (19.3) | 411 | College Station, TX | (27.7) | 171 | Green Bay, WI | (3.0) |
| 270 | Anchorage, AK | (11.0) | 1 | Colonie, NY | 87.6 | 220 | Greensboro, NC | (6.8) |
| 110 | Ann Arbor, MI | 2.7 | 144 | Colorado Springs, CO | 0.0 | 7 | Greenville, NC | 36.1 |
| 335 | Antioch, CA | (16.4) | 341 | Columbia, MO | (17.0) | 48 | Gresham, OR | 13.0 |
| 56 | Arlington Heights, IL | 11.5 | NA | Columbia, SC** | NA | 12 | Hamilton Twnshp, NJ | 27.6 |
| 210 | Arlington, TX | (5.9) | 259 | Columbus, GA | (9.9) | 301 | Hammond, IN | (13.6) |
| 284 | Arvada, CO | (11.7) | 54 | Compton, CA | 11.6 | 251 | Hampton, VA | (9.2) |
| 182 | Athens-Clarke, GA | (3.8) | 124 | Concord, CA | 2.0 | 293 | Hartford, CT | (12.8) |
| 367 | Atlanta, GA | (19.2) | NA | Concord, NC** | NA | 360 | Hawthorne, CA | (18.6) |
| 191 | Aurora, CO | (4.7) | 375 | Coral Springs, FL | (19.6) | 170 | Hayward, CA | (2.8) |
| 43 | Aurora, IL | 13.5 | 367 | Corona, CA | (19.2) | 110 | Hemet, CA | 2.7 |
| 215 | Austin, TX | (6.2) | 226 | Corpus Christi, TX | (7.2) | 409 | Henderson, NV | (27.2) |
| 220 | Bakersfield, CA | (6.8) | 352 | Costa Mesa, CA | (17.8) | 295 | Hesperia, CA | (13.1) |
| 402 | Baldwin Park, CA | (25.5) | 122 | Cranston, RI | 2.1 | 182 | Hialeah, FL | (3.8) |
| 180 | Baltimore, MD | (3.7) | 217 | Dallas, TX | (6.6) | 152 | High Point, NC | (0.7) |
| 387 | Baton Rouge, LA | (22.9) | 270 | Daly City, CA | (11.0) | 430 | Hillsboro, OR | (39.4) |
| 145 | Beaumont, TX | (0.1) | 419 | Danbury, CT | (31.1) | 24 | Hollywood, FL | 19.4 |
| 193 | Beaverton, OR | (4.8) | 176 | Davenport, IA | (3.5) | 43 | Hoover, AL | 13.5 |
| 332 | Bellevue, WA | (16.2) | 422 | Davie, FL | (31.5) | 253 | Houston, TX | (9.6) |
| 66 | Bellflower, CA | 8.3 | 207 | Dayton, OH | (5.5) | 34 | Huntington Beach, CA | 16.1 |
| NA | Bend, OR** | NA | 155 | Dearborn, MI | (0.9) | 300 | Huntsville, AL | (13.4) |
| 53 | Berkeley, CA | 11.8 | 23 | Decatur, IL | 19.7 | 143 | Independence, MO | 0.3 |
| 359 | Bethlehem, PA | (18.5) | 276 | Deerfield Beach, FL | (11.4) | 165 | Indianapolis, IN | (2.6) |
| 266 | Billings, MT | (10.8) | 228 | Denton, TX | (7.3) | 51 | Indio, CA | 12.2 |
| 364 | Birmingham, AL | (18.8) | 131 | Denver, CO | 1.5 | 138 | Inglewood, CA | 0.9 |
| 161 | Bloomington, IL | (2.3) | 172 | Des Moines, IA | (3.1) | 383 | Irvine, CA | (20.6) |
| 276 | Bloomington, IN | (11.4) | 194 | Detroit, MI | (4.9) | 249 | Irving, TX | (8.8) |
| 210 | Bloomington, MN | (5.9) | 345 | Downey, CA | (17.3) | 180 | Jacksonville, FL | (3.7) |
| 74 | Boca Raton, FL | 7.2 | 122 | Duluth, MN | 2.1 | 220 | Jackson, MS | (6.8) |
| 153 | Boise, ID | (0.8) | 418 | Edinburg, TX | (30.9) | 201 | Jersey City, NJ | (5.1) |
| 245 | Boston, MA | (8.4) | 87 | Edison Twnshp, NJ | 5.2 | 412 | Johns Creek, GA | (28.7) |
| 371 | Boulder, CO | (19.3) | 65 | Edmond, OK | 8.5 | 209 | Joliet, IL | (5.8) |
| 119 | Brick Twnshp, NJ | 2.3 | 59 | El Cajon, CA | 10.2 | 316 | Jurupa Valley, CA | (14.5) |
| 186 | Bridgeport, CT | (3.9) | 178 | El Monte, CA | (3.6) | 393 | Kansas City, KS | (23.8) |
| 94 | Brockton, MA | 4.4 | 311 | El Paso, TX | (14.4) | 186 | Kansas City, MO | (3.9) |
| 262 | Broken Arrow, OK | (10.6) | 140 | Elgin, IL | 0.6 | 137 | Kennewick, WA | 1.2 |
| 124 | Brooklyn Park, MN | 2.0 | 204 | Elizabeth, NJ | (5.3) | 79 | Kenosha, WI | 6.4 |
| 264 | Brownsville, TX | (10.7) | 264 | Elk Grove, CA | (10.7) | 433 | Kent, WA | (65.2) |
| 27 | Bryan, TX | 18.3 | 100 | Erie, PA | 3.5 | 229 | Killeen, TX | (7.4) |
| 63 | Buena Park, CA | 9.4 | 245 | Escondido, CA | (8.4) | 295 | Knoxville, TN | (13.1) |
| 166 | Buffalo, NY | (2.7) | 311 | Eugene, OR | (14.4) | 117 | Lafayette, LA | 2.4 |
| 135 | Burbank, CA | 1.3 | 378 | Evanston, IL | (20.0) | 307 | Lake Forest, CA | (14.1) |
| 377 | Cambridge, MA | (19.9) | 166 | Evansville, IN | (2.7) | 239 | Lakeland, FL | (7.9) |
| NA | Canton Twnshp, MI** | NA | 345 | Everett, WA | (17.3) | 304 | Lakewood Twnshp, NJ | (13.8) |
| 316 | Cape Coral, FL | (14.5) | 47 | Fairfield, CA | 13.1 | 234 | Lakewood, CA | (7.8) |
| 353 | Carlsbad, CA | (17.9) | 126 | Fall River, MA | 1.9 | 234 | Lakewood, CO | (7.8) |
| 3 | Carmel, IN | 59.5 | 52 | Fargo, ND | 12.1 | 71 | Lancaster, CA | 7.4 |
| 77 | Carrollton, TX | 6.9 | 385 | Farmington Hills, MI | (22.5) | 82 | Lansing, MI | 6.3 |
| 426 | Carson, CA | (34.6) | 253 | Fayetteville, AR | (9.6) | 178 | Laredo, TX | (3.6) |
| 417 | Cary, NC | (30.6) | 210 | Fayetteville, NC | (5.9) | 268 | Largo, FL | (10.9) |
| 28 | Cedar Rapids, IA | 18.1 | 233 | Federal Way, WA | (7.7) | 334 | Las Cruces, NM | (16.3) |
| 70 | Centennial, CO | 7.6 | 2 | Fishers, IN | 68.0 | 258 | Las Vegas, NV | (9.8) |
| 291 | Champaign, IL | (12.6) | 424 | Flint, MI | (33.2) | 382 | Lawrence, KS | (20.4) |
| 321 | Chandler, AZ | (14.8) | 252 | Fontana, CA | (9.4) | 287 | Lawrence, MA | (11.8) |
| 403 | Charleston, SC | (25.6) | 316 | Fort Collins, CO | (14.5) | 203 | Lawton, OK | (5.2) |
| 247 | Charlotte, NC | (8.6) | 107 | Fort Lauderdale, FL | 2.9 | 4 | League City, TX | 59.4 |
| NA | Chattanooga, TN** | NA | 350 | Fort Smith, AR | (17.5) | 381 | Lee's Summit, MO | (20.3) |
| 57 | Cheektowaga, NY | 11.1 | 113 | Fort Wayne, IN | 2.6 | NA | Lewisville, TX** | NA |
| 289 | Chesapeake, VA | (12.1) | 259 | Fort Worth, TX | (9.9) | 229 | Lexington, KY | (7.4) |
| NA | Chicago, IL** | NA | 423 | Fremont, CA | (31.6) | 220 | Lincoln, NE | (6.8) |
| 43 | Chico, CA | 13.5 | 194 | Fresno, CA | (4.9) | 90 | Little Rock, AR | 4.9 |
| 31 | Chino Hills, CA | 17.0 | 367 | Frisco, TX | (19.2) | 345 | Livermore, CA | (17.3) |

| RANK | CITY | % CHANGE | RANK | CITY | % CHANGE | RANK | CITY | % CHANGE |
|---|---|---|---|---|---|---|---|---|
| 87 | Livonia, MI | 5.2 | 97 | Pasadena, CA | 4.1 | 166 | South Gate, CA | (2.7) |
| 343 | Long Beach, CA | (17.2) | 331 | Pasadena, TX | (16.1) | 32 | Sparks, NV | 16.8 |
| 276 | Longmont, CO | (11.4) | 110 | Paterson, NJ | 2.7 | 29 | Spokane Valley, WA | 18.0 |
| 293 | Longview, TX | (12.8) | 54 | Pearland, TX | 11.6 | 121 | Spokane, WA | 2.2 |
| 250 | Los Angeles, CA | (9.0) | 15 | Pembroke Pines, FL | 25.5 | 92 | Springfield, IL | 4.5 |
| 324 | Louisville, KY | (15.1) | 234 | Peoria, AZ | (7.8) | 190 | Springfield, MA | (4.3) |
| 106 | Lowell, MA | 3.1 | 338 | Peoria, IL | (16.7) | 61 | Springfield, MO | 9.6 |
| 284 | Lubbock, TX | (11.7) | 247 | Philadelphia, PA | (8.6) | 361 | Stamford, CT | (18.7) |
| 26 | Lynchburg, VA | 18.9 | 102 | Phoenix, AZ | 3.4 | 102 | Sterling Heights, MI | 3.4 |
| 62 | Lynn, MA | 9.5 | 79 | Pittsburgh, PA | 6.4 | 349 | Stockton, CA | (17.4) |
| 89 | Macon, GA | 5.1 | 133 | Plano, TX | 1.4 | 386 | St. George, UT | (22.6) |
| 234 | Madison, WI | (7.8) | 21 | Plantation, FL | 21.8 | 64 | St. Joseph, MO | 8.6 |
| 108 | Manchester, NH | 2.8 | 373 | Pomona, CA | (19.4) | 274 | St. Louis, MO | (11.3) |
| 400 | McAllen, TX | (24.7) | 384 | Pompano Beach, FL | (21.4) | 160 | St. Paul, MN | (2.1) |
| 281 | McKinney, TX | (11.6) | 345 | Port St. Lucie, FL | (17.3) | 115 | St. Petersburg, FL | 2.5 |
| 78 | Medford, OR | 6.8 | 234 | Portland, OR | (7.8) | NA | Suffolk, VA** | NA |
| 182 | Melbourne, FL | (3.8) | 6 | Portsmouth, VA | 55.5 | 176 | Sugar Land, TX | (3.5) |
| 194 | Memphis, TN | (4.9) | 194 | Providence, RI | (4.9) | 302 | Sunnyvale, CA | (13.7) |
| 37 | Menifee, CA | 15.2 | 431 | Provo, UT | (40.4) | 71 | Sunrise, FL | 7.4 |
| 414 | Merced, CA | (29.2) | 50 | Pueblo, CO | 12.3 | 191 | Surprise, AZ | (4.7) |
| 100 | Meridian, ID | 3.5 | 332 | Quincy, MA | (16.2) | 321 | Syracuse, NY | (14.8) |
| 194 | Mesa, AZ | (4.9) | 396 | Racine, WI | (24.1) | 84 | Tacoma, WA | 6.0 |
| 407 | Mesquite, TX | (26.5) | 159 | Raleigh, NC | (1.8) | 273 | Tallahassee, FL | (11.2) |
| 153 | Miami Beach, FL | (0.8) | 427 | Ramapo, NY | (35.3) | 231 | Tampa, FL | (7.5) |
| 76 | Miami Gardens, FL | 7.0 | 161 | Rancho Cucamon., CA | (2.3) | 68 | Temecula, CA | 8.2 |
| 173 | Miami, FL | (3.4) | 243 | Reading, PA | (8.1) | 216 | Tempe, AZ | (6.3) |
| 390 | Midland, TX | (23.4) | 389 | Redding, CA | (23.2) | 295 | Thornton, CO | (13.1) |
| 149 | Milwaukee, WI | (0.4) | 266 | Redwood City, CA | (10.8) | 115 | Thousand Oaks, CA | 2.5 |
| 133 | Minneapolis, MN | 1.4 | 239 | Reno, NV | (7.9) | 262 | Toledo, OH | (10.6) |
| 387 | Miramar, FL | (22.9) | 308 | Renton, WA | (14.2) | 432 | Toms River Twnshp, NJ | (46.0) |
| 320 | Mission Viejo, CA | (14.6) | 399 | Rialto, CA | (24.4) | 342 | Topeka, KS | (17.1) |
| 410 | Mission, TX | (27.3) | 361 | Richardson, TX | (18.7) | 19 | Torrance, CA | 22.3 |
| 16 | Mobile, AL | 24.7 | 253 | Richmond, CA | (9.6) | 9 | Tracy, CA | 31.1 |
| 58 | Modesto, CA | 10.3 | 189 | Richmond, VA | (4.2) | 288 | Trenton, NJ | (11.9) |
| 355 | Moreno Valley, CA | (18.1) | 201 | Riverside, CA | (5.1) | 95 | Troy, MI | 4.3 |
| 204 | Mountain View, CA | (5.3) | 404 | Roanoke, VA | (25.7) | 243 | Tucson, AZ | (8.1) |
| 158 | Murfreesboro, TN | (1.4) | 91 | Rochester, MN | 4.7 | 188 | Tulsa, OK | (4.0) |
| 208 | Murrieta, CA | (5.6) | 182 | Rochester, NY | (3.8) | 366 | Tuscaloosa, AL | (19.1) |
| 108 | Nampa, ID | 2.8 | 85 | Rockford, IL | 5.3 | 337 | Tustin, CA | (16.5) |
| 42 | Napa, CA | 13.7 | 226 | Roseville, CA | (7.2) | 416 | Tyler, TX | (30.5) |
| 261 | Naperville, IL | (10.3) | 316 | Roswell, GA | (14.5) | 25 | Upland, CA | 19.0 |
| 415 | Nashua, NH | (30.4) | 8 | Round Rock, TX | 31.6 | 281 | Upper Darby Twnshp, PA | (11.6) |
| 365 | Nashville, TN | (18.9) | 309 | Sacramento, CA | (14.3) | 355 | Vacaville, CA | (18.1) |
| 166 | New Bedford, MA | (2.7) | 305 | Salem, OR | (13.9) | 19 | Vallejo, CA | 22.3 |
| 367 | New Haven, CT | (19.2) | 128 | Salinas, CA | 1.8 | 69 | Vancouver, WA | 8.1 |
| 242 | New Orleans, LA | (8.0) | 147 | Salt Lake City, UT | (0.2) | 210 | Ventura, CA | (5.9) |
| 135 | New Rochelle, NY | 1.3 | NA | San Angelo, TX** | NA | 173 | Victorville, CA | (3.4) |
| 141 | New York, NY | 0.5 | 10 | San Antonio, TX | 31.0 | 398 | Virginia Beach, VA | (24.3) |
| 324 | Newark, NJ | (15.1) | 224 | San Bernardino, CA | (6.9) | 330 | Visalia, CA | (15.7) |
| 354 | Newport Beach, CA | (18.0) | 206 | San Diego, CA | (5.4) | 225 | Vista, CA | (7.0) |
| 34 | Newport News, VA | 16.1 | 18 | San Francisco, CA | 23.4 | 357 | Waco, TX | (18.4) |
| 340 | Newton, MA | (16.9) | 280 | San Jose, CA | (11.5) | 373 | Warren, MI | (19.4) |
| 40 | Norfolk, VA | 14.1 | 394 | San Leandro, CA | (24.0) | 421 | Warwick, RI | (31.2) |
| 79 | Norman, OK | 6.4 | 343 | San Marcos, CA | (17.2) | 74 | Washington, DC | 7.2 |
| 231 | North Charleston, SC | (7.5) | 405 | San Mateo, CA | (26.0) | 17 | Waterbury, CT | 23.7 |
| 138 | North Las Vegas, NV | 0.9 | 408 | Sandy Springs, GA | (27.1) | 194 | Waukegan, IL | (4.9) |
| 151 | Norwalk, CA | (0.5) | 272 | Sandy, UT | (11.1) | 392 | West Covina, CA | (23.7) |
| 329 | Norwalk, CT | (15.5) | 357 | Santa Ana, CA | (18.4) | 311 | West Palm Beach, FL | (14.4) |
| 311 | Oakland, CA | (14.4) | 39 | Santa Barbara, CA | 14.3 | 41 | West Valley, UT | 14.0 |
| 376 | Oceanside, CA | (19.8) | 419 | Santa Clara, CA | (31.1) | 92 | Westland, MI | 4.5 |
| 239 | Odessa, TX | (7.9) | 428 | Santa Clarita, CA | (35.7) | 141 | Westminster, CA | 0.5 |
| 396 | O'Fallon, MO | (24.1) | 429 | Santa Maria, CA | (37.4) | 425 | Westminster, CO | (34.0) |
| 156 | Ogden, UT | (1.0) | 390 | Santa Monica, CA | (23.4) | 335 | Whittier, CA | (16.4) |
| 311 | Oklahoma City, OK | (14.4) | 284 | Santa Rosa, CA | (11.7) | 309 | Wichita Falls, TX | (14.3) |
| 218 | Olathe, KS | (6.7) | 98 | Savannah, GA | 3.8 | 60 | Wichita, KS | 10.1 |
| 113 | Omaha, NE | 2.6 | 38 | Scottsdale, AZ | 14.4 | 30 | Wilmington, NC | 17.3 |
| 73 | Ontario, CA | 7.3 | 400 | Scranton, PA | (24.7) | 326 | Winston-Salem, NC | (15.3) |
| 117 | Orange, CA | 2.4 | 274 | Seattle, WA | (11.3) | 129 | Woodbridge Twnshp, NJ | 1.6 |
| 5 | Orem, UT | 57.9 | 253 | Shreveport, LA | (9.6) | 194 | Worcester, MA | (4.9) |
| 290 | Orlando, FL | (12.4) | 214 | Simi Valley, CA | (6.0) | 379 | Yakima, WA | (20.1) |
| 149 | Overland Park, KS | (0.4) | 22 | Sioux City, IA | 20.8 | 257 | Yonkers, NY | (9.7) |
| 85 | Oxnard, CA | 5.3 | 147 | Sioux Falls, SD | (0.2) | 46 | Yuma, AZ | 13.2 |
| 323 | Palm Bay, FL | (15.0) | 406 | Somerville, MA | (26.1) | | | |
| 326 | Palmdale, CA | (15.3) | 306 | South Bend, IN | (14.0) | | | |

Source: CQ Press using reported data from the F.B.I. "Crime in the United States 2013"

*Aggravated assault is an attack for the purpose of inflicting severe bodily injury.

**Not available.

## 63. Percent Change in Aggravated Assault Rate: 2012 to 2013 (continued)
## National Percent Change = 5.6% Decrease*

| RANK | CITY | % CHANGE | RANK | CITY | % CHANGE | RANK | CITY | % CHANGE |
|---|---|---|---|---|---|---|---|---|
| 1 | Colonie, NY | 87.6 | 74 | Washington, DC | 7.2 | 149 | Milwaukee, WI | (0.4) |
| 2 | Fishers, IN | 68.0 | 76 | Miami Gardens, FL | 7.0 | 149 | Overland Park, KS | (0.4) |
| 3 | Carmel, IN | 59.5 | 77 | Carrollton, TX | 6.9 | 151 | Norwalk, CA | (0.5) |
| 4 | League City, TX | 59.4 | 78 | Medford, OR | 6.8 | 152 | High Point, NC | (0.7) |
| 5 | Orem, UT | 57.9 | 79 | Kenosha, WI | 6.4 | 153 | Boise, ID | (0.8) |
| 6 | Portsmouth, VA | 55.5 | 79 | Norman, OK | 6.4 | 153 | Miami Beach, FL | (0.8) |
| 7 | Greenville, NC | 36.1 | 79 | Pittsburgh, PA | 6.4 | 155 | Dearborn, MI | (0.9) |
| 8 | Round Rock, TX | 31.6 | 82 | Allentown, PA | 6.3 | 156 | Ogden, UT | (1.0) |
| 9 | Tracy, CA | 31.1 | 82 | Lansing, MI | 6.3 | 157 | Chula Vista, CA | (1.1) |
| 10 | San Antonio, TX | 31.0 | 84 | Tacoma, WA | 6.0 | 158 | Murfreesboro, TN | (1.4) |
| 11 | Gary, IN | 29.0 | 85 | Oxnard, CA | 5.3 | 159 | Raleigh, NC | (1.8) |
| 12 | Hamilton Twnshp, NJ | 27.6 | 85 | Rockford, IL | 5.3 | 160 | St. Paul, MN | (2.1) |
| 13 | Amherst, NY | 27.5 | 87 | Edison Twnshp, NJ | 5.2 | 161 | Albany, GA | (2.3) |
| 14 | Greece, NY | 26.2 | 87 | Livonia, MI | 5.2 | 161 | Bloomington, IL | (2.3) |
| 15 | Pembroke Pines, FL | 25.5 | 89 | Macon, GA | 5.1 | 161 | Rancho Cucamon., CA | (2.3) |
| 16 | Mobile, AL | 24.7 | 90 | Little Rock, AR | 4.9 | 164 | Gainesville, FL | (2.5) |
| 17 | Waterbury, CT | 23.7 | 91 | Rochester, MN | 4.7 | 165 | Indianapolis, IN | (2.6) |
| 18 | San Francisco, CA | 23.4 | 92 | Springfield, IL | 4.5 | 166 | Buffalo, NY | (2.7) |
| 19 | Torrance, CA | 22.3 | 92 | Westland, MI | 4.5 | 166 | Evansville, IN | (2.7) |
| 19 | Vallejo, CA | 22.3 | 94 | Brockton, MA | 4.4 | 166 | New Bedford, MA | (2.7) |
| 21 | Plantation, FL | 21.8 | 95 | Troy, MI | 4.3 | 166 | South Gate, CA | (2.7) |
| 22 | Sioux City, IA | 20.8 | 96 | Albany, NY | 4.2 | 170 | Hayward, CA | (2.8) |
| 23 | Decatur, IL | 19.7 | 97 | Pasadena, CA | 4.1 | 171 | Green Bay, WI | (3.0) |
| 24 | Hollywood, FL | 19.4 | 98 | Savannah, GA | 3.8 | 172 | Des Moines, IA | (3.1) |
| 25 | Upland, CA | 19.0 | 99 | Abilene, TX | 3.7 | 173 | Cicero, IL | (3.4) |
| 26 | Lynchburg, VA | 18.9 | 100 | Erie, PA | 3.5 | 173 | Miami, FL | (3.4) |
| 27 | Bryan, TX | 18.3 | 100 | Meridian, ID | 3.5 | 173 | Victorville, CA | (3.4) |
| 28 | Cedar Rapids, IA | 18.1 | 102 | Cleveland, OH | 3.4 | 176 | Davenport, IA | (3.5) |
| 29 | Spokane Valley, WA | 18.0 | 102 | Phoenix, AZ | 3.4 | 176 | Sugar Land, TX | (3.5) |
| 30 | Wilmington, NC | 17.3 | 102 | Sterling Heights, MI | 3.4 | 178 | El Monte, CA | (3.6) |
| 31 | Chino Hills, CA | 17.0 | 105 | Garden Grove, CA | 3.3 | 178 | Laredo, TX | (3.6) |
| 32 | Sparks, NV | 16.8 | 106 | Lowell, MA | 3.1 | 180 | Baltimore, MD | (3.7) |
| 33 | Alexandria, VA | 16.7 | 107 | Fort Lauderdale, FL | 2.9 | 180 | Jacksonville, FL | (3.7) |
| 34 | Huntington Beach, CA | 16.1 | 108 | Manchester, NH | 2.8 | 182 | Athens-Clarke, GA | (3.8) |
| 34 | Newport News, VA | 16.1 | 108 | Nampa, ID | 2.8 | 182 | Hialeah, FL | (3.8) |
| 36 | Clifton, NJ | 16.0 | 110 | Ann Arbor, MI | 2.7 | 182 | Melbourne, FL | (3.8) |
| 37 | Menifee, CA | 15.2 | 110 | Hemet, CA | 2.7 | 182 | Rochester, NY | (3.8) |
| 38 | Scottsdale, AZ | 14.4 | 110 | Paterson, NJ | 2.7 | 186 | Bridgeport, CT | (3.9) |
| 39 | Santa Barbara, CA | 14.3 | 113 | Fort Wayne, IN | 2.6 | 186 | Kansas City, MO | (3.9) |
| 40 | Norfolk, VA | 14.1 | 113 | Omaha, NE | 2.6 | 188 | Tulsa, OK | (4.0) |
| 41 | West Valley, UT | 14.0 | 115 | St. Petersburg, FL | 2.5 | 189 | Richmond, VA | (4.2) |
| 42 | Napa, CA | 13.7 | 115 | Thousand Oaks, CA | 2.5 | 190 | Springfield, MA | (4.3) |
| 43 | Aurora, IL | 13.5 | 117 | Lafayette, LA | 2.4 | 191 | Aurora, CO | (4.7) |
| 43 | Chico, CA | 13.5 | 117 | Orange, CA | 2.4 | 191 | Surprise, AZ | (4.7) |
| 43 | Hoover, AL | 13.5 | 119 | Brick Twnshp, NJ | 2.3 | 193 | Beaverton, OR | (4.8) |
| 46 | Yuma, AZ | 13.2 | 119 | Gilbert, AZ | 2.3 | 194 | Detroit, MI | (4.9) |
| 47 | Fairfield, CA | 13.1 | 121 | Spokane, WA | 2.2 | 194 | Fresno, CA | (4.9) |
| 48 | Gresham, OR | 13.0 | 122 | Cranston, RI | 2.1 | 194 | Memphis, TN | (4.9) |
| 49 | Allen, TX | 12.9 | 122 | Duluth, MN | 2.1 | 194 | Mesa, AZ | (4.9) |
| 50 | Pueblo, CO | 12.3 | 124 | Brooklyn Park, MN | 2.0 | 194 | Providence, RI | (4.9) |
| 51 | Indio, CA | 12.2 | 124 | Concord, CA | 2.0 | 194 | Waukegan, IL | (4.9) |
| 52 | Fargo, ND | 12.1 | 126 | Cincinnati, OH | 1.9 | 194 | Worcester, MA | (4.9) |
| 53 | Berkeley, CA | 11.8 | 126 | Fall River, MA | 1.9 | 201 | Jersey City, NJ | (5.1) |
| 54 | Compton, CA | 11.6 | 128 | Salinas, CA | 1.8 | 201 | Riverside, CA | (5.1) |
| 54 | Pearland, TX | 11.6 | 129 | Citrus Heights, CA | 1.6 | 203 | Lawton, OK | (5.2) |
| 56 | Arlington Heights, IL | 11.5 | 129 | Woodbridge Twnshp, NJ | 1.6 | 204 | Elizabeth, NJ | (5.3) |
| 57 | Cheektowaga, NY | 11.1 | 131 | Albuquerque, NM | 1.5 | 204 | Mountain View, CA | (5.3) |
| 58 | Modesto, CA | 10.3 | 131 | Denver, CO | 1.5 | 206 | San Diego, CA | (5.4) |
| 59 | El Cajon, CA | 10.2 | 133 | Minneapolis, MN | 1.4 | 207 | Dayton, OH | (5.5) |
| 60 | Wichita, KS | 10.1 | 133 | Plano, TX | 1.4 | 208 | Murrieta, CA | (5.6) |
| 61 | Springfield, MO | 9.6 | 135 | Burbank, CA | 1.3 | 209 | Joliet, IL | (5.8) |
| 62 | Lynn, MA | 9.5 | 135 | New Rochelle, NY | 1.3 | 210 | Arlington, TX | (5.9) |
| 63 | Buena Park, CA | 9.4 | 137 | Kennewick, WA | 1.2 | 210 | Bloomington, MN | (5.9) |
| 64 | St. Joseph, MO | 8.6 | 138 | Inglewood, CA | 0.9 | 210 | Fayetteville, NC | (5.9) |
| 65 | Edmond, OK | 8.5 | 138 | North Las Vegas, NV | 0.9 | 210 | Ventura, CA | (5.9) |
| 66 | Bellflower, CA | 8.3 | 140 | Elgin, IL | 0.6 | 214 | Simi Valley, CA | (6.0) |
| 66 | Greeley, CO | 8.3 | 141 | New York, NY | 0.5 | 215 | Austin, TX | (6.2) |
| 68 | Temecula, CA | 8.2 | 141 | Westminster, CA | 0.5 | 216 | Tempe, AZ | (6.3) |
| 69 | Vancouver, WA | 8.1 | 143 | Independence, MO | 0.3 | 217 | Dallas, TX | (6.6) |
| 70 | Centennial, CO | 7.6 | 144 | Colorado Springs, CO | 0.0 | 218 | Amarillo, TX | (6.7) |
| 71 | Lancaster, CA | 7.4 | 145 | Beaumont, TX | (0.1) | 218 | Olathe, KS | (6.7) |
| 71 | Sunrise, FL | 7.4 | 145 | Grand Prairie, TX | (0.1) | 220 | Bakersfield, CA | (6.8) |
| 73 | Ontario, CA | 7.3 | 147 | Salt Lake City, UT | (0.2) | 220 | Greensboro, NC | (6.8) |
| 74 | Boca Raton, FL | 7.2 | 147 | Sioux Falls, SD | (0.2) | 220 | Jackson, MS | (6.8) |

| RANK | CITY | % CHANGE | RANK | CITY | % CHANGE | RANK | CITY | % CHANGE |
|---|---|---|---|---|---|---|---|---|
| 220 | Lincoln, NE | (6.8) | 295 | Knoxville, TN | (13.1) | 371 | Anaheim, CA | (19.3) |
| 224 | San Bernardino, CA | (6.9) | 295 | Thornton, CO | (13.1) | 371 | Boulder, CO | (19.3) |
| 225 | Vista, CA | (7.0) | 299 | Akron, OH | (13.3) | 373 | Pomona, CA | (19.4) |
| 226 | Corpus Christi, TX | (7.2) | 300 | Huntsville, AL | (13.4) | 373 | Warren, MI | (19.4) |
| 226 | Roseville, CA | (7.2) | 301 | Hammond, IN | (13.6) | 375 | Coral Springs, FL | (19.6) |
| 228 | Denton, TX | (7.3) | 302 | Chino, CA | (13.7) | 376 | Oceanside, CA | (19.8) |
| 229 | Killeen, TX | (7.4) | 302 | Sunnyvale, CA | (13.7) | 377 | Cambridge, MA | (19.9) |
| 229 | Lexington, KY | (7.4) | 304 | Lakewood Twnshp, NJ | (13.8) | 378 | Evanston, IL | (20.0) |
| 231 | North Charleston, SC | (7.5) | 305 | Salem, OR | (13.9) | 379 | Yakima, WA | (20.1) |
| 231 | Tampa, FL | (7.5) | 306 | South Bend, IN | (14.0) | 380 | Grand Rapids, MI | (20.2) |
| 233 | Federal Way, WA | (7.7) | 307 | Lake Forest, CA | (14.1) | 381 | Lee's Summit, MO | (20.3) |
| 234 | Lakewood, CA | (7.8) | 308 | Renton, WA | (14.2) | 382 | Lawrence, KS | (20.4) |
| 234 | Lakewood, CO | (7.8) | 309 | Sacramento, CA | (14.3) | 383 | Irvine, CA | (20.6) |
| 234 | Madison, WI | (7.8) | 309 | Wichita Falls, TX | (14.3) | 384 | Pompano Beach, FL | (21.4) |
| 234 | Peoria, AZ | (7.8) | 311 | El Paso, TX | (14.4) | 385 | Farmington Hills, MI | (22.5) |
| 234 | Portland, OR | (7.8) | 311 | Eugene, OR | (14.4) | 386 | St. George, UT | (22.6) |
| 239 | Lakeland, FL | (7.9) | 311 | Oakland, CA | (14.4) | 387 | Baton Rouge, LA | (22.9) |
| 239 | Odessa, TX | (7.9) | 311 | Oklahoma City, OK | (14.4) | 387 | Miramar, FL | (22.9) |
| 239 | Reno, NV | (7.9) | 311 | West Palm Beach, FL | (14.4) | 389 | Redding, CA | (23.2) |
| 242 | New Orleans, LA | (8.0) | 316 | Cape Coral, FL | (14.5) | 390 | Midland, TX | (23.4) |
| 243 | Reading, PA | (8.1) | 316 | Fort Collins, CO | (14.5) | 390 | Santa Monica, CA | (23.4) |
| 243 | Tucson, AZ | (8.1) | 316 | Jurupa Valley, CA | (14.5) | 392 | West Covina, CA | (23.7) |
| 245 | Boston, MA | (8.4) | 316 | Roswell, GA | (14.5) | 393 | Kansas City, KS | (23.8) |
| 245 | Escondido, CA | (8.4) | 320 | Mission Viejo, CA | (14.6) | 394 | Glendale, AZ | (24.0) |
| 247 | Charlotte, NC | (8.6) | 321 | Chandler, AZ | (14.8) | 394 | San Leandro, CA | (24.0) |
| 247 | Philadelphia, PA | (8.6) | 321 | Syracuse, NY | (14.8) | 396 | O'Fallon, MO | (24.1) |
| 249 | Irving, TX | (8.8) | 323 | Palm Bay, FL | (15.0) | 396 | Racine, WI | (24.1) |
| 250 | Los Angeles, CA | (9.0) | 324 | Louisville, KY | (15.1) | 398 | Virginia Beach, VA | (24.3) |
| 251 | Hampton, VA | (9.2) | 324 | Newark, NJ | (15.1) | 399 | Rialto, CA | (24.4) |
| 252 | Fontana, CA | (9.4) | 326 | Palmdale, CA | (15.3) | 400 | McAllen, TX | (24.7) |
| 253 | Fayetteville, AR | (9.6) | 326 | Winston-Salem, NC | (15.3) | 400 | Scranton, PA | (24.7) |
| 253 | Houston, TX | (9.6) | 328 | Clearwater, FL | (15.4) | 402 | Baldwin Park, CA | (25.5) |
| 253 | Richmond, CA | (9.6) | 329 | Norwalk, CT | (15.5) | 403 | Charleston, SC | (25.6) |
| 253 | Shreveport, LA | (9.6) | 330 | Visalia, CA | (15.7) | 404 | Roanoke, VA | (25.7) |
| 257 | Yonkers, NY | (9.7) | 331 | Pasadena, TX | (16.1) | 405 | San Mateo, CA | (26.0) |
| 258 | Las Vegas, NV | (9.8) | 332 | Bellevue, WA | (16.2) | 406 | Somerville, MA | (26.1) |
| 259 | Columbus, GA | (9.9) | 332 | Quincy, MA | (16.2) | 407 | Mesquite, TX | (26.5) |
| 259 | Fort Worth, TX | (9.9) | 334 | Las Cruces, NM | (16.3) | 408 | Sandy Springs, GA | (27.1) |
| 261 | Naperville, IL | (10.3) | 335 | Antioch, CA | (16.4) | 409 | Henderson, NV | (27.2) |
| 262 | Broken Arrow, OK | (10.6) | 335 | Whittier, CA | (16.4) | 410 | Mission, TX | (27.3) |
| 262 | Toledo, OH | (10.6) | 337 | Tustin, CA | (16.5) | 411 | College Station, TX | (27.7) |
| 264 | Brownsville, TX | (10.7) | 338 | Peoria, IL | (16.7) | 412 | Johns Creek, GA | (28.7) |
| 264 | Elk Grove, CA | (10.7) | 339 | Clinton Twnshp, MI | (16.8) | 413 | Clarksville, TN | (28.9) |
| 266 | Billings, MT | (10.8) | 340 | Newton, MA | (16.9) | 414 | Merced, CA | (29.2) |
| 266 | Redwood City, CA | (10.8) | 341 | Columbia, MO | (17.0) | 415 | Nashua, NH | (30.4) |
| 268 | Alameda, CA | (10.9) | 342 | Topeka, KS | (17.1) | 416 | Tyler, TX | (30.5) |
| 268 | Largo, FL | (10.9) | 343 | Long Beach, CA | (17.2) | 417 | Cary, NC | (30.6) |
| 270 | Anchorage, AK | (11.0) | 343 | San Marcos, CA | (17.2) | 418 | Edinburg, TX | (30.9) |
| 270 | Daly City, CA | (11.0) | 345 | Downey, CA | (17.3) | 419 | Danbury, CT | (31.1) |
| 272 | Sandy, UT | (11.1) | 345 | Everett, WA | (17.3) | 419 | Santa Clara, CA | (31.1) |
| 273 | Tallahassee, FL | (11.2) | 345 | Livermore, CA | (17.3) | 421 | Warwick, RI | (31.2) |
| 274 | Seattle, WA | (11.3) | 345 | Port St. Lucie, FL | (17.3) | 422 | Davie, FL | (31.5) |
| 274 | St. Louis, MO | (11.3) | 349 | Stockton, CA | (17.4) | 423 | Fremont, CA | (31.6) |
| 276 | Alhambra, CA | (11.4) | 350 | Fort Smith, AR | (17.5) | 424 | Flint, MI | (33.2) |
| 276 | Bloomington, IN | (11.4) | 351 | Fullerton, CA | (17.6) | 425 | Westminster, CO | (34.0) |
| 276 | Deerfield Beach, FL | (11.4) | 352 | Costa Mesa, CA | (17.8) | 426 | Carson, CA | (34.6) |
| 276 | Longmont, CO | (11.4) | 353 | Carlsbad, CA | (17.9) | 427 | Ramapo, NY | (35.3) |
| 280 | San Jose, CA | (11.5) | 354 | Newport Beach, CA | (18.0) | 428 | Santa Clarita, CA | (35.7) |
| 281 | Clarkstown, NY | (11.6) | 355 | Moreno Valley, CA | (18.1) | 429 | Santa Maria, CA | (37.4) |
| 281 | McKinney, TX | (11.6) | 355 | Vacaville, CA | (18.1) | 430 | Hillsboro, OR | (39.4) |
| 281 | Upper Darby Twnshp, PA | (11.6) | 357 | Santa Ana, CA | (18.4) | 431 | Provo, UT | (40.4) |
| 284 | Arvada, CO | (11.7) | 357 | Waco, TX | (18.4) | 432 | Toms River Twnshp, NJ | (46.0) |
| 284 | Lubbock, TX | (11.7) | 359 | Bethlehem, PA | (18.5) | 433 | Kent, WA | (65.2) |
| 284 | Santa Rosa, CA | (11.7) | 360 | Hawthorne, CA | (18.6) | NA | Bend, OR** | NA |
| 287 | Lawrence, MA | (11.8) | 361 | Glendale, CA | (18.7) | NA | Canton Twnshp, MI** | NA |
| 288 | Trenton, NJ | (11.9) | 361 | Richardson, TX | (18.7) | NA | Chattanooga, TN** | NA |
| 289 | Chesapeake, VA | (12.1) | 361 | Stamford, CT | (18.7) | NA | Chicago, IL** | NA |
| 290 | Orlando, FL | (12.4) | 364 | Birmingham, AL | (18.8) | NA | Columbia, SC** | NA |
| 291 | Champaign, IL | (12.6) | 365 | Nashville, TN | (18.9) | NA | Concord, NC** | NA |
| 292 | Clovis, CA | (12.7) | 366 | Tuscaloosa, AL | (19.1) | NA | Lewisville, TX** | NA |
| 293 | Hartford, CT | (12.8) | 367 | Atlanta, GA | (19.2) | NA | San Angelo, TX** | NA |
| 293 | Longview, TX | (12.8) | 367 | Corona, CA | (19.2) | NA | Suffolk, VA** | NA |
| 295 | Garland, TX | (13.1) | 367 | Frisco, TX | (19.2) | | | |
| 295 | Hesperia, CA | (13.1) | 367 | New Haven, CT | (19.2) | | | |

Source: CQ Press using reported data from the F.B.I. "Crime in the United States 2013"

*Aggravated assault is an attack for the purpose of inflicting severe bodily injury.

**Not available.

# 64. Percent Change in Aggravated Assault Rate: 2009 to 2013
## National Percent Change = 13.4% Decrease*

| RANK | CITY | % CHANGE | RANK | CITY | % CHANGE | RANK | CITY | % CHANGE |
|---|---|---|---|---|---|---|---|---|
| 285 | Abilene, TX | (23.4) | 4 | Chino, CA | 149.5 | 283 | Fullerton, CA | (23.1) |
| 152 | Akron, OH | (8.8) | 272 | Chula Vista, CA | (22.4) | 368 | Gainesville, FL | (35.2) |
| 382 | Alameda, CA | (38.7) | NA | Cicero, IL** | NA | 217 | Garden Grove, CA | (15.9) |
| 111 | Albany, GA | (1.9) | 300 | Cincinnati, OH | (24.7) | 222 | Garland, TX | (16.7) |
| 246 | Albany, NY | (19.3) | 230 | Citrus Heights, CA | (17.4) | 5 | Gary, IN | 99.1 |
| 92 | Albuquerque, NM | 2.6 | 375 | Clarkstown, NY | (37.8) | 38 | Gilbert, AZ | 23.8 |
| 183 | Alexandria, VA | (13.0) | 323 | Clarksville, TN | (27.9) | 215 | Glendale, AZ | (15.5) |
| 315 | Alhambra, CA | (26.9) | 377 | Clearwater, FL | (37.9) | 377 | Glendale, CA | (37.9) |
| 75 | Allentown, PA | 5.6 | 103 | Cleveland, OH | (0.2) | 122 | Grand Prairie, TX | (3.8) |
| 316 | Allen, TX | (27.2) | 59 | Clifton, NJ | 13.3 | 243 | Grand Rapids, MI | (18.5) |
| 340 | Amarillo, TX | (29.6) | 255 | Clinton Twnshp, MI | (20.6) | 7 | Greece, NY | 83.9 |
| 213 | Amherst, NY | (15.3) | 8 | Clovis, CA | 68.6 | 94 | Greeley, CO | 2.1 |
| 116 | Anaheim, CA | (2.5) | 2 | College Station, TX | 168.0 | 63 | Green Bay, WI | 10.4 |
| 206 | Anchorage, AK | (14.9) | 89 | Colonie, NY | 3.0 | 225 | Greensboro, NC | (16.8) |
| 245 | Ann Arbor, MI | (18.7) | 149 | Colorado Springs, CO | (8.3) | NA | Greenville, NC** | NA |
| 107 | Antioch, CA | (1.3) | 354 | Columbia, MO | (32.8) | 25 | Gresham, OR | 35.4 |
| 334 | Arlington Heights, IL | (29.0) | 384 | Columbia, SC | (38.9) | 51 | Hamilton Twnshp, NJ | 17.9 |
| 278 | Arlington, TX | (22.8) | 196 | Columbus, GA | (13.9) | 269 | Hammond, IN | (22.0) |
| 285 | Arvada, CO | (23.4) | 162 | Compton, CA | (10.3) | 375 | Hampton, VA | (37.8) |
| 191 | Athens-Clarke, GA | (13.7) | 24 | Concord, CA | 38.2 | 157 | Hartford, CT | (9.4) |
| 71 | Atlanta, GA | 6.3 | 417 | Concord, NC | (53.9) | 278 | Hawthorne, CA | (22.8) |
| 142 | Aurora, CO | (7.2) | 416 | Coral Springs, FL | (53.3) | 256 | Hayward, CA | (20.7) |
| 342 | Aurora, IL | (30.1) | 150 | Corona, CA | (8.5) | 128 | Hemet, CA | (4.4) |
| 240 | Austin, TX | (18.4) | 302 | Corpus Christi, TX | (24.8) | 410 | Henderson, NV | (49.0) |
| 305 | Bakersfield, CA | (25.0) | 357 | Costa Mesa, CA | (33.0) | 18 | Hesperia, CA | 44.0 |
| 248 | Baldwin Park, CA | (19.8) | 29 | Cranston, RI | 30.4 | 294 | Hialeah, FL | (24.3) |
| 233 | Baltimore, MD | (17.7) | 183 | Dallas, TX | (13.0) | 157 | High Point, NC | (9.4) |
| 371 | Baton Rouge, LA | (35.9) | 123 | Daly City, CA | (3.9) | 65 | Hillsboro, OR | 9.8 |
| 53 | Beaumont, TX | 15.2 | 412 | Danbury, CT | (49.5) | 61 | Hollywood, FL | 12.8 |
| 345 | Beaverton, OR | (31.0) | 216 | Davenport, IA | (15.8) | 302 | Hoover, AL | (24.8) |
| 308 | Bellevue, WA | (25.8) | 405 | Davie, FL | (45.9) | 239 | Houston, TX | (18.3) |
| 407 | Bellflower, CA | (47.8) | 118 | Dayton, OH | (2.6) | 84 | Huntington Beach, CA | 3.5 |
| 49 | Bend, OR | 18.9 | 254 | Dearborn, MI | (20.5) | 12 | Huntsville, AL | 54.5 |
| 281 | Berkeley, CA | (23.0) | 382 | Decatur, IL | (38.7) | 329 | Independence, MO | (28.5) |
| 335 | Bethlehem, PA | (29.1) | NA | Deerfield Beach, FL** | NA | 70 | Indianapolis, IN | 7.0 |
| 16 | Billings, MT | 46.0 | 34 | Denton, TX | 25.7 | 39 | Indio, CA | 23.3 |
| 33 | Birmingham, AL | 25.9 | 85 | Denver, CO | 3.4 | 298 | Inglewood, CA | (24.6) |
| 151 | Bloomington, IL | (8.6) | 95 | Des Moines, IA | 2.0 | 222 | Irvine, CA | (16.7) |
| 398 | Bloomington, IN | (42.7) | 97 | Detroit, MI | 1.4 | 252 | Irving, TX | (20.0) |
| 199 | Bloomington, MN | (14.1) | 346 | Downey, CA | (31.3) | 285 | Jacksonville, FL | (23.4) |
| 209 | Boca Raton, FL | (15.1) | 78 | Duluth, MN | 4.8 | 11 | Jackson, MS | 55.1 |
| 83 | Boise, ID | 3.6 | 96 | Edinburg, TX | 1.6 | 110 | Jersey City, NJ | (1.8) |
| 283 | Boston, MA | (23.1) | 425 | Edison Twnshp, NJ | (65.5) | 388 | Johns Creek, GA | (39.5) |
| 187 | Boulder, CO | (13.3) | 76 | Edmond, OK | 5.2 | 67 | Joliet, IL | 9.5 |
| 248 | Brick Twnshp, NJ | (19.8) | 133 | El Cajon, CA | (5.8) | NA | Jurupa Valley, CA** | NA |
| 202 | Bridgeport, CT | (14.3) | 421 | El Monte, CA | (55.0) | 319 | Kansas City, KS | (27.5) |
| 109 | Brockton, MA | (1.6) | 266 | El Paso, TX | (21.7) | 114 | Kansas City, MO | (2.0) |
| 381 | Broken Arrow, OK | (38.6) | 363 | Elgin, IL | (33.5) | 275 | Kennewick, WA | (22.6) |
| 265 | Brooklyn Park, MN | (21.5) | 231 | Elizabeth, NJ | (17.5) | 69 | Kenosha, WI | 7.1 |
| 102 | Brownsville, TX | (0.1) | 316 | Elk Grove, CA | (27.2) | 429 | Kent, WA | (72.5) |
| 397 | Bryan, TX | (42.6) | 205 | Erie, PA | (14.6) | 173 | Killeen, TX | (11.3) |
| 57 | Buena Park, CA | 14.4 | 120 | Escondido, CA | (3.1) | 190 | Knoxville, TN | (13.6) |
| 189 | Buffalo, NY | (13.5) | 350 | Eugene, OR | (31.9) | 351 | Lafayette, LA | (32.1) |
| 281 | Burbank, CA | (23.0) | NA | Evanston, IL** | NA | 206 | Lake Forest, CA | (14.9) |
| 327 | Cambridge, MA | (28.2) | 44 | Evansville, IN | 21.4 | 191 | Lakeland, FL | (13.7) |
| 379 | Canton Twnshp, MI | (38.1) | 364 | Everett, WA | (33.7) | 406 | Lakewood Twnshp, NJ | (46.7) |
| 360 | Cape Coral, FL | (33.2) | 20 | Fairfield, CA | 42.1 | 398 | Lakewood, CA | (42.7) |
| 354 | Carlsbad, CA | (32.8) | 181 | Fall River, MA | (12.8) | 168 | Lakewood, CO | (10.8) |
| 430 | Carmel, IN | (73.1) | 37 | Fargo, ND | 24.5 | 225 | Lancaster, CA | (16.8) |
| 106 | Carrollton, TX | (1.0) | 420 | Farmington Hills, MI | (54.9) | 125 | Lansing, MI | (4.2) |
| 314 | Carson, CA | (26.8) | 64 | Fayetteville, AR | 9.9 | 291 | Laredo, TX | (23.9) |
| 347 | Cary, NC | (31.4) | 371 | Fayetteville, NC | (35.9) | 396 | Largo, FL | (42.5) |
| 100 | Cedar Rapids, IA | 0.1 | 73 | Federal Way, WA | 5.9 | 386 | Las Cruces, NM | (39.2) |
| 228 | Centennial, CO | (17.1) | 1 | Fishers, IN | 500.0 | 280 | Las Vegas, NV | (22.9) |
| NA | Champaign, IL** | NA | 145 | Flint, MI | (7.3) | 307 | Lawrence, KS | (25.4) |
| 290 | Chandler, AZ | (23.7) | 176 | Fontana, CA | (11.6) | 21 | Lawrence, MA | 41.3 |
| 427 | Charleston, SC | (67.4) | 370 | Fort Collins, CO | (35.8) | 319 | Lawton, OK | (27.5) |
| 131 | Charlotte, NC | (4.6) | 115 | Fort Lauderdale, FL | (2.3) | 332 | League City, TX | (28.8) |
| 86 | Chattanooga, TN | 3.3 | 229 | Fort Smith, AR | (17.3) | 116 | Lee's Summit, MO | (2.5) |
| 194 | Cheektowaga, NY | (13.8) | 36 | Fort Wayne, IN | 24.7 | 32 | Lewisville, TX | 27.2 |
| 145 | Chesapeake, VA | (7.3) | 99 | Fort Worth, TX | 0.3 | 428 | Lexington, KY | (70.4) |
| NA | Chicago, IL** | NA | 422 | Fremont, CA | (57.7) | 328 | Lincoln, NE | (28.4) |
| 66 | Chico, CA | 9.7 | 204 | Fresno, CA | (14.4) | 161 | Little Rock, AR | (9.8) |
| 380 | Chino Hills, CA | (38.3) | 389 | Frisco, TX | (39.9) | 3 | Livermore, CA | 166.5 |

| RANK | CITY | % CHANGE |
|---|---|---|
| 271 | Livonia, MI | (22.3) |
| 357 | Long Beach, CA | (33.0) |
| 415 | Longmont, CO | (52.3) |
| 413 | Longview, TX | (49.6) |
| 333 | Los Angeles, CA | (28.9) |
| 104 | Louisville, KY | (0.9) |
| NA | Lowell, MA** | NA |
| 292 | Lubbock, TX | (24.0) |
| 179 | Lynchburg, VA | (12.4) |
| 126 | Lynn, MA | (4.3) |
| 148 | Macon, GA | (7.7) |
| 68 | Madison, WI | 7.3 |
| 47 | Manchester, NH | 19.9 |
| 424 | McAllen, TX | (59.4) |
| 343 | McKinney, TX | (30.3) |
| 6 | Medford, OR | 94.6 |
| 359 | Melbourne, FL | (33.1) |
| 107 | Memphis, TN | (1.3) |
| 10 | Menifee, CA | 67.3 |
| 330 | Merced, CA | (28.6) |
| 219 | Meridian, ID | (16.1) |
| 155 | Mesa, AZ | (9.0) |
| 400 | Mesquite, TX | (43.9) |
| 93 | Miami Beach, FL | 2.3 |
| 227 | Miami Gardens, FL | (16.9) |
| 142 | Miami, FL | (7.2) |
| 252 | Midland, TX | (20.0) |
| 23 | Milwaukee, WI | 39.2 |
| 258 | Minneapolis, MN | (20.8) |
| 313 | Miramar, FL | (26.6) |
| 349 | Mission Viejo, CA | (31.8) |
| 423 | Mission, TX | (58.7) |
| 177 | Mobile, AL | (11.9) |
| 46 | Modesto, CA | 20.1 |
| 360 | Moreno Valley, CA | (33.2) |
| 185 | Mountain View, CA | (13.1) |
| 87 | Murfreesboro, TN | 3.2 |
| 402 | Murrieta, CA | (44.6) |
| 365 | Nampa, ID | (33.8) |
| 165 | Napa, CA | (10.6) |
| 104 | Naperville, IL | (0.9) |
| 312 | Nashua, NH | (26.4) |
| 139 | Nashville, TN | (6.5) |
| 202 | New Bedford, MA | (14.3) |
| 385 | New Haven, CT | (39.1) |
| 132 | New Orleans, LA | (5.4) |
| 339 | New Rochelle, NY | (29.5) |
| 45 | New York, NY | 20.2 |
| 234 | Newark, NJ | (17.8) |
| 407 | Newport Beach, CA | (47.8) |
| NA | Newport News, VA** | NA |
| 365 | Newton, MA | (33.8) |
| 87 | Norfolk, VA | 3.2 |
| 136 | Norman, OK | (6.1) |
| 324 | North Charleston, SC | (28.0) |
| 31 | North Las Vegas, NV | 27.3 |
| 154 | Norwalk, CA | (8.9) |
| 387 | Norwalk, CT | (39.4) |
| 246 | Oakland, CA | (19.3) |
| 198 | Oceanside, CA | (14.0) |
| 17 | Odessa, TX | 45.4 |
| 130 | O'Fallon, MO | (4.5) |
| 166 | Ogden, UT | (10.7) |
| 209 | Oklahoma City, OK | (15.1) |
| 356 | Olathe, KS | (32.9) |
| 35 | Omaha, NE | 25.6 |
| 369 | Ontario, CA | (35.4) |
| 178 | Orange, CA | (12.2) |
| 191 | Orem, UT | (13.7) |
| 267 | Orlando, FL | (21.9) |
| 185 | Overland Park, KS | (13.1) |
| 264 | Oxnard, CA | (21.3) |
| 173 | Palm Bay, FL | (11.3) |
| 196 | Palmdale, CA | (13.9) |

| RANK | CITY | % CHANGE |
|---|---|---|
| 140 | Pasadena, CA | (6.7) |
| 321 | Pasadena, TX | (27.7) |
| 91 | Paterson, NJ | 2.9 |
| 54 | Pearland, TX | 15.0 |
| 199 | Pembroke Pines, FL | (14.1) |
| 82 | Peoria, AZ | 4.1 |
| 221 | Peoria, IL | (16.6) |
| 170 | Philadelphia, PA | (10.9) |
| 26 | Phoenix, AZ | 35.2 |
| 288 | Pittsburgh, PA | (23.5) |
| 331 | Plano, TX | (28.7) |
| 201 | Plantation, FL | (14.2) |
| 237 | Pomona, CA | (18.1) |
| 297 | Pompano Beach, FL | (24.5) |
| 298 | Port St. Lucie, FL | (24.6) |
| 155 | Portland, OR | (9.0) |
| 52 | Portsmouth, VA | 15.5 |
| 194 | Providence, RI | (13.8) |
| 394 | Provo, UT | (42.2) |
| 163 | Pueblo, CO | (10.4) |
| 136 | Quincy, MA | (6.1) |
| 401 | Racine, WI | (44.5) |
| 175 | Raleigh, NC | (11.5) |
| 251 | Ramapo, NY | (19.9) |
| 119 | Rancho Cucamon., CA | (2.7) |
| 172 | Reading, PA | (11.0) |
| 322 | Redding, CA | (27.8) |
| 311 | Redwood City, CA | (26.3) |
| 304 | Reno, NV | (24.9) |
| 374 | Renton, WA | (36.8) |
| 305 | Rialto, CA | (25.0) |
| 419 | Richardson, TX | (54.0) |
| 80 | Richmond, CA | 4.7 |
| 219 | Richmond, VA | (16.1) |
| 138 | Riverside, CA | (6.2) |
| 393 | Roanoke, VA | (40.7) |
| 324 | Rochester, MN | (28.0) |
| 123 | Rochester, NY | (3.9) |
| 48 | Rockford, IL | 19.0 |
| 263 | Roseville, CA | (21.2) |
| 353 | Roswell, GA | (32.4) |
| 43 | Round Rock, TX | 21.7 |
| 275 | Sacramento, CA | (22.6) |
| 208 | Salem, OR | (15.0) |
| 362 | Salinas, CA | (33.3) |
| 77 | Salt Lake City, UT | 5.0 |
| 337 | San Angelo, TX | (29.3) |
| 28 | San Antonio, TX | 30.6 |
| 212 | San Bernardino, CA | (15.2) |
| 142 | San Diego, CA | (7.2) |
| 62 | San Francisco, CA | 11.5 |
| 238 | San Jose, CA | (18.2) |
| 240 | San Leandro, CA | (18.4) |
| 170 | San Marcos, CA | (10.9) |
| 404 | San Mateo, CA | (45.3) |
| 50 | Sandy Springs, GA | 18.5 |
| 348 | Sandy, UT | (31.7) |
| 248 | Santa Ana, CA | (19.8) |
| 240 | Santa Barbara, CA | (18.4) |
| 42 | Santa Clara, CA | 21.8 |
| 414 | Santa Clarita, CA | (51.7) |
| 417 | Santa Maria, CA | (53.9) |
| 296 | Santa Monica, CA | (24.4) |
| 367 | Santa Rosa, CA | (34.7) |
| 260 | Savannah, GA | (21.0) |
| 235 | Scottsdale, AZ | (17.9) |
| 411 | Scranton, PA | (49.2) |
| 126 | Seattle, WA | (4.3) |
| 258 | Shreveport, LA | (20.8) |
| 141 | Simi Valley, CA | (6.9) |
| 188 | Sioux City, IA | (13.4) |
| 13 | Sioux Falls, SD | 53.7 |
| 391 | Somerville, MA | (40.5) |
| 394 | South Bend, IN | (42.2) |

| RANK | CITY | % CHANGE |
|---|---|---|
| 15 | South Gate, CA | 46.3 |
| 373 | Sparks, NV | (36.5) |
| 390 | Spokane Valley, WA | (40.2) |
| 120 | Spokane, WA | (3.1) |
| 275 | Springfield, IL | (22.6) |
| 256 | Springfield, MA | (20.7) |
| 14 | Springfield, MO | 48.5 |
| 243 | Stamford, CT | (18.5) |
| 40 | Sterling Heights, MI | 22.9 |
| 98 | Stockton, CA | 0.9 |
| 41 | St. George, UT | 22.6 |
| 336 | St. Joseph, MO | (29.2) |
| 222 | St. Louis, MO | (16.7) |
| 134 | St. Paul, MN | (5.9) |
| 352 | St. Petersburg, FL | (32.2) |
| 134 | Suffolk, VA | (5.9) |
| 19 | Sugar Land, TX | 42.3 |
| 294 | Sunnyvale, CA | (24.3) |
| 260 | Sunrise, FL | (21.0) |
| 55 | Surprise, AZ | 14.9 |
| 270 | Syracuse, NY | (22.1) |
| 147 | Tacoma, WA | (7.6) |
| 309 | Tallahassee, FL | (26.0) |
| 180 | Tampa, FL | (12.7) |
| 344 | Temecula, CA | (30.9) |
| 81 | Tempe, AZ | 4.2 |
| 56 | Thornton, CO | 14.5 |
| 213 | Thousand Oaks, CA | (15.3) |
| 100 | Toledo, OH | 0.1 |
| 426 | Toms River Twnshp, NJ | (66.2) |
| 72 | Topeka, KS | 6.1 |
| 128 | Torrance, CA | (4.4) |
| 27 | Tracy, CA | 32.4 |
| 166 | Trenton, NJ | (10.7) |
| 300 | Troy, MI | (24.7) |
| 74 | Tucson, AZ | 5.7 |
| 236 | Tulsa, OK | (18.0) |
| 59 | Tuscaloosa, AL | 13.3 |
| 9 | Tustin, CA | 68.5 |
| 324 | Tyler, TX | (28.0) |
| NA | Upland, CA** | NA |
| 160 | Upper Darby Twnshp, PA | (9.7) |
| 318 | Vacaville, CA | (27.4) |
| 89 | Vallejo, CA | 3.0 |
| 111 | Vancouver, WA | (1.9) |
| 392 | Ventura, CA | (40.6) |
| 168 | Victorville, CA | (10.8) |
| 340 | Virginia Beach, VA | (29.6) |
| 310 | Visalia, CA | (26.1) |
| 232 | Vista, CA | (17.6) |
| 409 | Waco, TX | (48.9) |
| 288 | Warren, MI | (23.5) |
| 337 | Warwick, RI | (29.3) |
| 78 | Washington, DC | 4.8 |
| 181 | Waterbury, CT | (12.8) |
| NA | Waukegan, IL** | NA |
| 209 | West Covina, CA | (15.1) |
| 260 | West Palm Beach, FL | (21.0) |
| 30 | West Valley, UT | 29.4 |
| 274 | Westland, MI | (22.5) |
| 58 | Westminster, CA | 14.1 |
| 272 | Westminster, CO | (22.4) |
| 403 | Whittier, CA | (44.9) |
| 292 | Wichita Falls, TX | (24.0) |
| 152 | Wichita, KS | (8.8) |
| 267 | Wilmington, NC | (21.9) |
| 217 | Winston-Salem, NC | (15.9) |
| 159 | Woodbridge Twnshp, NJ | (9.5) |
| 164 | Worcester, MA | (10.5) |
| NA | Yakima, WA** | NA |
| 22 | Yonkers, NY | 40.0 |
| 111 | Yuma, AZ | (1.9) |

Source: CQ Press using reported data from the F.B.I. "Crime in the United States 2013"
*Aggravated assault is an attack for the purpose of inflicting severe bodily injury.
**Not available.

# 64. Percent Change in Aggravated Assault Rate: 2009 to 2013 (continued)
## National Percent Change = 13.4% Decrease*

| RANK | CITY | % CHANGE | RANK | CITY | % CHANGE | RANK | CITY | % CHANGE |
|---|---|---|---|---|---|---|---|---|
| 1 | Fishers, IN | 500.0 | 75 | Allentown, PA | 5.6 | 149 | Colorado Springs, CO | (8.3) |
| 2 | College Station, TX | 168.0 | 76 | Edmond, OK | 5.2 | 150 | Corona, CA | (8.5) |
| 3 | Livermore, CA | 166.5 | 77 | Salt Lake City, UT | 5.0 | 151 | Bloomington, IL | (8.6) |
| 4 | Chino, CA | 149.5 | 78 | Duluth, MN | 4.8 | 152 | Akron, OH | (8.8) |
| 5 | Gary, IN | 99.1 | 78 | Washington, DC | 4.8 | 152 | Wichita, KS | (8.8) |
| 6 | Medford, OR | 94.6 | 80 | Richmond, CA | 4.7 | 154 | Norwalk, CA | (8.9) |
| 7 | Greece, NY | 83.9 | 81 | Tempe, AZ | 4.2 | 155 | Mesa, AZ | (9.0) |
| 8 | Clovis, CA | 68.6 | 82 | Peoria, AZ | 4.1 | 155 | Portland, OR | (9.0) |
| 9 | Tustin, CA | 68.5 | 83 | Boise, ID | 3.6 | 157 | Hartford, CT | (9.4) |
| 10 | Menifee, CA | 67.3 | 84 | Huntington Beach, CA | 3.5 | 157 | High Point, NC | (9.4) |
| 11 | Jackson, MS | 55.1 | 85 | Denver, CO | 3.4 | 159 | Woodbridge Twnshp, NJ | (9.5) |
| 12 | Huntsville, AL | 54.5 | 86 | Chattanooga, TN | 3.3 | 160 | Upper Darby Twnshp, PA | (9.7) |
| 13 | Sioux Falls, SD | 53.7 | 87 | Murfreesboro, TN | 3.2 | 161 | Little Rock, AR | (9.8) |
| 14 | Springfield, MO | 48.5 | 87 | Norfolk, VA | 3.2 | 162 | Compton, CA | (10.3) |
| 15 | South Gate, CA | 46.3 | 89 | Colonie, NY | 3.0 | 163 | Pueblo, CO | (10.4) |
| 16 | Billings, MT | 46.0 | 89 | Vallejo, CA | 3.0 | 164 | Worcester, MA | (10.5) |
| 17 | Odessa, TX | 45.4 | 91 | Paterson, NJ | 2.9 | 165 | Napa, CA | (10.6) |
| 18 | Hesperia, CA | 44.0 | 92 | Albuquerque, NM | 2.6 | 166 | Ogden, UT | (10.7) |
| 19 | Sugar Land, TX | 42.3 | 93 | Miami Beach, FL | 2.3 | 166 | Trenton, NJ | (10.7) |
| 20 | Fairfield, CA | 42.1 | 94 | Greeley, CO | 2.1 | 168 | Lakewood, CO | (10.8) |
| 21 | Lawrence, MA | 41.3 | 95 | Des Moines, IA | 2.0 | 168 | Victorville, CA | (10.8) |
| 22 | Yonkers, NY | 40.0 | 96 | Edinburg, TX | 1.6 | 170 | Philadelphia, PA | (10.9) |
| 23 | Milwaukee, WI | 39.2 | 97 | Detroit, MI | 1.4 | 170 | San Marcos, CA | (10.9) |
| 24 | Concord, CA | 38.2 | 98 | Stockton, CA | 0.9 | 172 | Reading, PA | (11.0) |
| 25 | Gresham, OR | 35.4 | 99 | Fort Worth, TX | 0.3 | 173 | Killeen, TX | (11.3) |
| 26 | Phoenix, AZ | 35.2 | 100 | Cedar Rapids, IA | 0.1 | 173 | Palm Bay, FL | (11.3) |
| 27 | Tracy, CA | 32.4 | 100 | Toledo, OH | 0.1 | 175 | Raleigh, NC | (11.5) |
| 28 | San Antonio, TX | 30.6 | 102 | Brownsville, TX | (0.1) | 176 | Fontana, CA | (11.6) |
| 29 | Cranston, RI | 30.4 | 103 | Cleveland, OH | (0.2) | 177 | Mobile, AL | (11.9) |
| 30 | West Valley, UT | 29.4 | 104 | Louisville, KY | (0.9) | 178 | Orange, CA | (12.2) |
| 31 | North Las Vegas, NV | 27.3 | 104 | Naperville, IL | (0.9) | 179 | Lynchburg, VA | (12.4) |
| 32 | Lewisville, TX | 27.2 | 106 | Carrollton, TX | (1.0) | 180 | Tampa, FL | (12.7) |
| 33 | Birmingham, AL | 25.9 | 107 | Antioch, CA | (1.3) | 181 | Fall River, MA | (12.8) |
| 34 | Denton, TX | 25.7 | 107 | Memphis, TN | (1.3) | 181 | Waterbury, CT | (12.8) |
| 35 | Omaha, NE | 25.6 | 109 | Brockton, MA | (1.6) | 183 | Alexandria, VA | (13.0) |
| 36 | Fort Wayne, IN | 24.7 | 110 | Jersey City, NJ | (1.8) | 183 | Dallas, TX | (13.0) |
| 37 | Fargo, ND | 24.5 | 111 | Albany, GA | (1.9) | 185 | Mountain View, CA | (13.1) |
| 38 | Gilbert, AZ | 23.8 | 111 | Vancouver, WA | (1.9) | 185 | Overland Park, KS | (13.1) |
| 39 | Indio, CA | 23.3 | 111 | Yuma, AZ | (1.9) | 187 | Boulder, CO | (13.3) |
| 40 | Sterling Heights, MI | 22.9 | 114 | Kansas City, MO | (2.0) | 188 | Sioux City, IA | (13.4) |
| 41 | St. George, UT | 22.6 | 115 | Fort Lauderdale, FL | (2.3) | 189 | Buffalo, NY | (13.5) |
| 42 | Santa Clara, CA | 21.8 | 116 | Anaheim, CA | (2.5) | 190 | Knoxville, TN | (13.6) |
| 43 | Round Rock, TX | 21.7 | 116 | Lee's Summit, MO | (2.5) | 191 | Athens-Clarke, GA | (13.7) |
| 44 | Evansville, IN | 21.4 | 118 | Dayton, OH | (2.6) | 191 | Lakeland, FL | (13.7) |
| 45 | New York, NY | 20.2 | 119 | Rancho Cucamon., CA | (2.7) | 191 | Orem, UT | (13.7) |
| 46 | Modesto, CA | 20.1 | 120 | Escondido, CA | (3.1) | 194 | Cheektowaga, NY | (13.8) |
| 47 | Manchester, NH | 19.9 | 120 | Spokane, WA | (3.1) | 194 | Providence, RI | (13.8) |
| 48 | Rockford, IL | 19.0 | 122 | Grand Prairie, TX | (3.8) | 196 | Columbus, GA | (13.9) |
| 49 | Bend, OR | 18.9 | 123 | Daly City, CA | (3.9) | 196 | Palmdale, CA | (13.9) |
| 50 | Sandy Springs, GA | 18.5 | 123 | Rochester, NY | (3.9) | 198 | Oceanside, CA | (14.0) |
| 51 | Hamilton Twnshp, NJ | 17.9 | 125 | Lansing, MI | (4.2) | 199 | Bloomington, MN | (14.1) |
| 52 | Portsmouth, VA | 15.5 | 126 | Lynn, MA | (4.3) | 199 | Pembroke Pines, FL | (14.1) |
| 53 | Beaumont, TX | 15.2 | 126 | Seattle, WA | (4.3) | 201 | Plantation, FL | (14.2) |
| 54 | Pearland, TX | 15.0 | 128 | Hemet, CA | (4.4) | 202 | Bridgeport, CT | (14.3) |
| 55 | Surprise, AZ | 14.9 | 128 | Torrance, CA | (4.4) | 202 | New Bedford, MA | (14.3) |
| 56 | Thornton, CO | 14.5 | 130 | O'Fallon, MO | (4.5) | 204 | Fresno, CA | (14.4) |
| 57 | Buena Park, CA | 14.4 | 131 | Charlotte, NC | (4.6) | 205 | Erie, PA | (14.6) |
| 58 | Westminster, CA | 14.1 | 132 | New Orleans, LA | (5.4) | 206 | Anchorage, AK | (14.9) |
| 59 | Clifton, NJ | 13.3 | 133 | El Cajon, CA | (5.8) | 206 | Lake Forest, CA | (14.9) |
| 59 | Tuscaloosa, AL | 13.3 | 134 | St. Paul, MN | (5.9) | 208 | Salem, OR | (15.0) |
| 61 | Hollywood, FL | 12.8 | 134 | Suffolk, VA | (5.9) | 209 | Boca Raton, FL | (15.1) |
| 62 | San Francisco, CA | 11.5 | 136 | Norman, OK | (6.1) | 209 | Oklahoma City, OK | (15.1) |
| 63 | Green Bay, WI | 10.4 | 136 | Quincy, MA | (6.1) | 209 | West Covina, CA | (15.1) |
| 64 | Fayetteville, AR | 9.9 | 138 | Riverside, CA | (6.2) | 212 | San Bernardino, CA | (15.2) |
| 65 | Hillsboro, OR | 9.8 | 139 | Nashville, TN | (6.5) | 213 | Amherst, NY | (15.3) |
| 66 | Chico, CA | 9.7 | 140 | Pasadena, CA | (6.7) | 213 | Thousand Oaks, CA | (15.3) |
| 67 | Joliet, IL | 9.5 | 141 | Simi Valley, CA | (6.9) | 215 | Glendale, AZ | (15.5) |
| 68 | Madison, WI | 7.3 | 142 | Aurora, CO | (7.2) | 216 | Davenport, IA | (15.8) |
| 69 | Kenosha, WI | 7.1 | 142 | Miami, FL | (7.2) | 217 | Garden Grove, CA | (15.9) |
| 70 | Indianapolis, IN | 7.0 | 142 | San Diego, CA | (7.2) | 217 | Winston-Salem, NC | (15.9) |
| 71 | Atlanta, GA | 6.3 | 145 | Chesapeake, VA | (7.3) | 219 | Meridian, ID | (16.1) |
| 72 | Topeka, KS | 6.1 | 145 | Flint, MI | (7.3) | 219 | Richmond, VA | (16.1) |
| 73 | Federal Way, WA | 5.9 | 147 | Tacoma, WA | (7.6) | 221 | Peoria, IL | (16.6) |
| 74 | Tucson, AZ | 5.7 | 148 | Macon, GA | (7.7) | 222 | Garland, TX | (16.7) |

| RANK | CITY | % CHANGE | RANK | CITY | % CHANGE | RANK | CITY | % CHANGE |
|---|---|---|---|---|---|---|---|---|
| 222 | Irvine, CA | (16.7) | 297 | Pompano Beach, FL | (24.5) | 371 | Baton Rouge, LA | (35.9) |
| 222 | St. Louis, MO | (16.7) | 298 | Inglewood, CA | (24.6) | 371 | Fayetteville, NC | (35.9) |
| 225 | Greensboro, NC | (16.8) | 298 | Port St. Lucie, FL | (24.6) | 373 | Sparks, NV | (36.5) |
| 225 | Lancaster, CA | (16.8) | 300 | Cincinnati, OH | (24.7) | 374 | Renton, WA | (36.8) |
| 227 | Miami Gardens, FL | (16.9) | 300 | Troy, MI | (24.7) | 375 | Clarkstown, NY | (37.8) |
| 228 | Centennial, CO | (17.1) | 302 | Corpus Christi, TX | (24.8) | 375 | Hampton, VA | (37.8) |
| 229 | Fort Smith, AR | (17.3) | 302 | Hoover, AL | (24.8) | 377 | Clearwater, FL | (37.9) |
| 230 | Citrus Heights, CA | (17.4) | 304 | Reno, NV | (24.9) | 377 | Glendale, CA | (37.9) |
| 231 | Elizabeth, NJ | (17.5) | 305 | Bakersfield, CA | (25.0) | 379 | Canton Twnshp, MI | (38.1) |
| 232 | Vista, CA | (17.6) | 305 | Rialto, CA | (25.0) | 380 | Chino Hills, CA | (38.3) |
| 233 | Baltimore, MD | (17.7) | 307 | Lawrence, KS | (25.4) | 381 | Broken Arrow, OK | (38.6) |
| 234 | Newark, NJ | (17.8) | 308 | Bellevue, WA | (25.8) | 382 | Alameda, CA | (38.7) |
| 235 | Scottsdale, AZ | (17.9) | 309 | Tallahassee, FL | (26.0) | 382 | Decatur, IL | (38.7) |
| 236 | Tulsa, OK | (18.0) | 310 | Visalia, CA | (26.1) | 384 | Columbia, SC | (38.9) |
| 237 | Pomona, CA | (18.1) | 311 | Redwood City, CA | (26.3) | 385 | New Haven, CT | (39.1) |
| 238 | San Jose, CA | (18.2) | 312 | Nashua, NH | (26.4) | 386 | Las Cruces, NM | (39.2) |
| 239 | Houston, TX | (18.3) | 313 | Miramar, FL | (26.6) | 387 | Norwalk, CT | (39.4) |
| 240 | Austin, TX | (18.4) | 314 | Carson, CA | (26.8) | 388 | Johns Creek, GA | (39.5) |
| 240 | San Leandro, CA | (18.4) | 315 | Alhambra, CA | (26.9) | 389 | Frisco, TX | (39.9) |
| 240 | Santa Barbara, CA | (18.4) | 316 | Allen, TX | (27.2) | 390 | Spokane Valley, WA | (40.2) |
| 243 | Grand Rapids, MI | (18.5) | 316 | Elk Grove, CA | (27.2) | 391 | Somerville, MA | (40.5) |
| 243 | Stamford, CT | (18.5) | 318 | Vacaville, CA | (27.4) | 392 | Ventura, CA | (40.6) |
| 245 | Ann Arbor, MI | (18.7) | 319 | Kansas City, KS | (27.5) | 393 | Roanoke, VA | (40.7) |
| 246 | Albany, NY | (19.3) | 319 | Lawton, OK | (27.5) | 394 | Provo, UT | (42.2) |
| 246 | Oakland, CA | (19.3) | 321 | Pasadena, TX | (27.7) | 394 | South Bend, IN | (42.2) |
| 248 | Baldwin Park, CA | (19.8) | 322 | Redding, CA | (27.8) | 396 | Largo, FL | (42.5) |
| 248 | Brick Twnshp, NJ | (19.8) | 323 | Clarksville, TN | (27.9) | 397 | Bryan, TX | (42.6) |
| 248 | Santa Ana, CA | (19.8) | 324 | North Charleston, SC | (28.0) | 398 | Bloomington, IN | (42.7) |
| 251 | Ramapo, NY | (19.9) | 324 | Rochester, MN | (28.0) | 398 | Lakewood, CA | (42.7) |
| 252 | Irving, TX | (20.0) | 324 | Tyler, TX | (28.0) | 400 | Mesquite, TX | (43.9) |
| 252 | Midland, TX | (20.0) | 327 | Cambridge, MA | (28.2) | 401 | Racine, WI | (44.5) |
| 254 | Dearborn, MI | (20.5) | 328 | Lincoln, NE | (28.4) | 402 | Murrieta, CA | (44.6) |
| 255 | Clinton Twnshp, MI | (20.6) | 329 | Independence, MO | (28.5) | 403 | Whittier, CA | (44.9) |
| 256 | Hayward, CA | (20.7) | 330 | Merced, CA | (28.6) | 404 | San Mateo, CA | (45.3) |
| 256 | Springfield, MA | (20.7) | 331 | Plano, TX | (28.7) | 405 | Davie, FL | (45.9) |
| 258 | Minneapolis, MN | (20.8) | 332 | League City, TX | (28.8) | 406 | Lakewood Twnshp, NJ | (46.7) |
| 258 | Shreveport, LA | (20.8) | 333 | Los Angeles, CA | (28.9) | 407 | Bellflower, CA | (47.8) |
| 260 | Savannah, GA | (21.0) | 334 | Arlington Heights, IL | (29.0) | 407 | Newport Beach, CA | (47.8) |
| 260 | Sunrise, FL | (21.0) | 335 | Bethlehem, PA | (29.1) | 409 | Waco, TX | (48.9) |
| 260 | West Palm Beach, FL | (21.0) | 336 | St. Joseph, MO | (29.2) | 410 | Henderson, NV | (49.0) |
| 263 | Roseville, CA | (21.2) | 337 | San Angelo, TX | (29.3) | 411 | Scranton, PA | (49.2) |
| 264 | Oxnard, CA | (21.3) | 337 | Warwick, RI | (29.3) | 412 | Danbury, CT | (49.5) |
| 265 | Brooklyn Park, MN | (21.5) | 339 | New Rochelle, NY | (29.5) | 413 | Longview, TX | (49.6) |
| 266 | El Paso, TX | (21.7) | 340 | Amarillo, TX | (29.6) | 414 | Santa Clarita, CA | (51.7) |
| 267 | Orlando, FL | (21.9) | 340 | Virginia Beach, VA | (29.6) | 415 | Longmont, CO | (52.3) |
| 267 | Wilmington, NC | (21.9) | 342 | Aurora, IL | (30.1) | 416 | Coral Springs, FL | (53.3) |
| 269 | Hammond, IN | (22.0) | 343 | McKinney, TX | (30.3) | 417 | Concord, NC | (53.9) |
| 270 | Syracuse, NY | (22.1) | 344 | Temecula, CA | (30.9) | 417 | Santa Maria, CA | (53.9) |
| 271 | Livonia, MI | (22.3) | 345 | Beaverton, OR | (31.0) | 419 | Richardson, TX | (54.0) |
| 272 | Chula Vista, CA | (22.4) | 346 | Downey, CA | (31.3) | 420 | Farmington Hills, MI | (54.9) |
| 272 | Westminster, CO | (22.4) | 347 | Cary, NC | (31.4) | 421 | El Monte, CA | (55.0) |
| 274 | Westland, MI | (22.5) | 348 | Sandy, UT | (31.7) | 422 | Fremont, CA | (57.7) |
| 275 | Kennewick, WA | (22.6) | 349 | Mission Viejo, CA | (31.8) | 423 | Mission, TX | (58.7) |
| 275 | Sacramento, CA | (22.6) | 350 | Eugene, OR | (31.9) | 424 | McAllen, TX | (59.4) |
| 275 | Springfield, IL | (22.6) | 351 | Lafayette, LA | (32.1) | 425 | Edison Twnshp, NJ | (65.5) |
| 278 | Arlington, TX | (22.8) | 352 | St. Petersburg, FL | (32.2) | 426 | Toms River Twnshp, NJ | (66.2) |
| 278 | Hawthorne, CA | (22.8) | 353 | Roswell, GA | (32.4) | 427 | Charleston, SC | (67.4) |
| 280 | Las Vegas, NV | (22.9) | 354 | Carlsbad, CA | (32.8) | 428 | Lexington, KY | (70.4) |
| 281 | Berkeley, CA | (23.0) | 354 | Columbia, MO | (32.8) | 429 | Kent, WA | (72.5) |
| 281 | Burbank, CA | (23.0) | 356 | Olathe, KS | (32.9) | 430 | Carmel, IN | (73.1) |
| 283 | Boston, MA | (23.1) | 357 | Costa Mesa, CA | (33.0) | NA | Champaign, IL** | NA |
| 283 | Fullerton, CA | (23.1) | 357 | Long Beach, CA | (33.0) | NA | Chicago, IL** | NA |
| 285 | Abilene, TX | (23.4) | 359 | Melbourne, FL | (33.1) | NA | Cicero, IL** | NA |
| 285 | Arvada, CO | (23.4) | 360 | Cape Coral, FL | (33.2) | NA | Deerfield Beach, FL** | NA |
| 285 | Jacksonville, FL | (23.4) | 360 | Moreno Valley, CA | (33.2) | NA | Evanston, IL** | NA |
| 288 | Pittsburgh, PA | (23.5) | 362 | Salinas, CA | (33.3) | NA | Greenville, NC** | NA |
| 288 | Warren, MI | (23.5) | 363 | Elgin, IL | (33.5) | NA | Jurupa Valley, CA** | NA |
| 290 | Chandler, AZ | (23.7) | 364 | Everett, WA | (33.7) | NA | Lowell, MA** | NA |
| 291 | Laredo, TX | (23.9) | 365 | Nampa, ID | (33.8) | NA | Newport News, VA** | NA |
| 292 | Lubbock, TX | (24.0) | 365 | Newton, MA | (33.8) | NA | Upland, CA** | NA |
| 292 | Wichita Falls, TX | (24.0) | 367 | Santa Rosa, CA | (34.7) | NA | Waukegan, IL** | NA |
| 294 | Hialeah, FL | (24.3) | 368 | Gainesville, FL | (35.2) | NA | Yakima, WA** | NA |
| 294 | Sunnyvale, CA | (24.3) | 369 | Ontario, CA | (35.4) | | | |
| 296 | Santa Monica, CA | (24.4) | 370 | Fort Collins, CO | (35.8) | | | |

Source: CQ Press using reported data from the F.B.I. "Crime in the United States 2013"

*Aggravated assault is an attack for the purpose of inflicting severe bodily injury.

**Not available.

# 65. Property Crimes in 2013
## National Total = 8,632,512 Property Crimes*

| RANK | CITY | CRIMES | RANK | CITY | CRIMES | RANK | CITY | CRIMES |
|---|---|---|---|---|---|---|---|---|
| 176 | Abilene, TX | 4,769 | 374 | Chino, CA | 2,044 | 227 | Fullerton, CA | 3,859 |
| 90 | Akron, OH | 9,649 | 157 | Chula Vista, CA | 5,284 | 164 | Gainesville, FL | 4,986 |
| 388 | Alameda, CA | 1,902 | 399 | Cicero, IL | 1,830 | 248 | Garden Grove, CA | 3,397 |
| 181 | Albany, GA | 4,661 | 46 | Cincinnati, OH | 17,231 | 100 | Garland, TX | 8,371 |
| 214 | Albany, NY | 4,090 | 311 | Citrus Heights, CA | 2,653 | 178 | Gary, IN | 4,719 |
| 23 | Albuquerque, NM | 30,531 | 416 | Clarkstown, NY | 1,515 | 244 | Gilbert, AZ | 3,472 |
| 282 | Alexandria, VA | 2,967 | 210 | Clarksville, TN | 4,141 | 57 | Glendale, AZ | 13,626 |
| 401 | Alhambra, CA | 1,774 | 203 | Clearwater, FL | 4,316 | 268 | Glendale, CA | 3,198 |
| 202 | Allentown, PA | 4,324 | 34 | Cleveland, OH | 23,168 | 159 | Grand Prairie, TX | 5,158 |
| 427 | Allen, TX | 1,205 | 415 | Clifton, NJ | 1,521 | 130 | Grand Rapids, MI | 6,188 |
| 101 | Amarillo, TX | 8,154 | 363 | Clinton Twnshp, MI | 2,134 | 345 | Greece, NY | 2,303 |
| 365 | Amherst, NY | 2,118 | 247 | Clovis, CA | 3,404 | 264 | Greeley, CO | 3,219 |
| 91 | Anaheim, CA | 9,611 | 358 | College Station, TX | 2,230 | 308 | Green Bay, WI | 2,674 |
| 70 | Anchorage, AK | 12,032 | 380 | Colonie, NY | 1,990 | 72 | Greensboro, NC | 11,537 |
| 321 | Ann Arbor, MI | 2,525 | 43 | Colorado Springs, CO | 18,175 | 226 | Greenville, NC | 3,862 |
| 194 | Antioch, CA | 4,440 | 198 | Columbia, MO | 4,359 | 186 | Gresham, OR | 4,553 |
| 438 | Arlington Heights, IL | 800 | 103 | Columbia, SC | 7,989 | 396 | Hamilton Twnshp, NJ | 1,862 |
| 52 | Arlington, TX | 15,000 | 67 | Columbus, GA | 12,475 | 263 | Hammond, IN | 3,235 |
| 310 | Arvada, CO | 2,666 | 320 | Compton, CA | 2,538 | 191 | Hampton, VA | 4,473 |
| 216 | Athens-Clarke, GA | 4,074 | 199 | Concord, CA | 4,357 | 162 | Hartford, CT | 5,036 |
| 27 | Atlanta, GA | 27,528 | 319 | Concord, NC | 2,549 | 355 | Hawthorne, CA | 2,242 |
| 79 | Aurora, CO | 10,786 | 317 | Coral Springs, FL | 2,565 | 171 | Hayward, CA | 4,844 |
| 281 | Aurora, IL | 2,972 | 245 | Corona, CA | 3,439 | 222 | Hemet, CA | 3,963 |
| 12 | Austin, TX | 41,667 | 54 | Corpus Christi, TX | 14,601 | 153 | Henderson, NV | 5,358 |
| 47 | Bakersfield, CA | 16,814 | 237 | Costa Mesa, CA | 3,556 | 342 | Hesperia, CA | 2,330 |
| 422 | Baldwin Park, CA | 1,370 | 402 | Cranston, RI | 1,755 | 122 | Hialeah, FL | 6,550 |
| 21 | Baltimore, MD | 30,789 | 8 | Dallas, TX | 52,274 | 190 | High Point, NC | 4,489 |
| 75 | Baton Rouge, LA | 11,418 | 398 | Daly City, CA | 1,833 | 361 | Hillsboro, OR | 2,160 |
| 129 | Beaumont, TX | 6,192 | 423 | Danbury, CT | 1,257 | 122 | Hollywood, FL | 6,550 |
| 418 | Beaverton, OR | 1,471 | 207 | Davenport, IA | 4,248 | 314 | Hoover, AL | 2,596 |
| 225 | Bellevue, WA | 3,949 | 249 | Davie, FL | 3,393 | 2 | Houston, TX | 110,919 |
| 392 | Bellflower, CA | 1,882 | 109 | Dayton, OH | 7,655 | 166 | Huntington Beach, CA | 4,934 |
| 351 | Bend, OR | 2,267 | 275 | Dearborn, MI | 3,104 | 95 | Huntsville, AL | 9,216 |
| 152 | Berkeley, CA | 5,377 | 339 | Decatur, IL | 2,369 | 115 | Independence, MO | 7,108 |
| 378 | Bethlehem, PA | 2,010 | 337 | Deerfield Beach, FL | 2,386 | 11 | Indianapolis, IN | 44,606 |
| 144 | Billings, MT | 5,604 | 296 | Denton, TX | 2,777 | 305 | Indio, CA | 2,699 |
| 56 | Birmingham, AL | 14,157 | 33 | Denver, CO | 23,711 | 302 | Inglewood, CA | 2,718 |
| 391 | Bloomington, IL | 1,901 | 85 | Des Moines, IA | 10,015 | 261 | Irvine, CA | 3,285 |
| 313 | Bloomington, IN | 2,606 | 13 | Detroit, MI | 40,835 | 132 | Irving, TX | 6,175 |
| 262 | Bloomington, MN | 3,283 | 259 | Downey, CA | 3,292 | 18 | Jacksonville, FL | 33,007 |
| 346 | Boca Raton, FL | 2,302 | 205 | Duluth, MN | 4,283 | 82 | Jackson, MS | 10,284 |
| 177 | Boise, ID | 4,741 | 204 | Edinburg, TX | 4,292 | 172 | Jersey City, NJ | 4,836 |
| 45 | Boston, MA | 17,853 | 425 | Edison Twnshp, NJ | 1,245 | 440 | Johns Creek, GA | 619 |
| 285 | Boulder, CO | 2,948 | 412 | Edmond, OK | 1,595 | 265 | Joliet, IL | 3,217 |
| 429 | Brick Twnshp, NJ | 1,183 | 300 | El Cajon, CA | 2,730 | 276 | Jurupa Valley, CA | 3,065 |
| 192 | Bridgeport, CT | 4,464 | 359 | El Monte, CA | 2,182 | 112 | Kansas City, KS | 7,228 |
| 271 | Brockton, MA | 3,189 | 49 | El Paso, TX | 15,558 | 31 | Kansas City, MO | 24,648 |
| 376 | Broken Arrow, OK | 2,034 | 388 | Elgin, IL | 1,902 | 326 | Kennewick, WA | 2,478 |
| 330 | Brooklyn Park, MN | 2,456 | 234 | Elizabeth, NJ | 3,655 | 328 | Kenosha, WI | 2,462 |
| 107 | Brownsville, TX | 7,838 | 283 | Elk Grove, CA | 2,963 | 145 | Kent, WA | 5,600 |
| 344 | Bryan, TX | 2,311 | 267 | Erie, PA | 3,208 | 175 | Killeen, TX | 4,791 |
| 360 | Buena Park, CA | 2,165 | 221 | Escondido, CA | 3,965 | 74 | Knoxville, TN | 11,438 |
| 66 | Buffalo, NY | 12,491 | 105 | Eugene, OR | 7,920 | 111 | Lafayette, LA | 7,568 |
| 332 | Burbank, CA | 2,430 | 388 | Evanston, IL | 1,902 | 436 | Lake Forest, CA | 813 |
| 291 | Cambridge, MA | 2,907 | 140 | Evansville, IN | 5,859 | 151 | Lakeland, FL | 5,410 |
| 424 | Canton Twnshp, MI | 1,250 | 118 | Everett, WA | 6,865 | 433 | Lakewood Twnshp, NJ | 998 |
| 252 | Cape Coral, FL | 3,375 | 239 | Fairfield, CA | 3,534 | 372 | Lakewood, CA | 2,062 |
| 368 | Carlsbad, CA | 2,085 | 341 | Fall River, MA | 2,364 | 117 | Lakewood, CO | 6,892 |
| 439 | Carmel, IN | 744 | 266 | Fargo, ND | 3,209 | 243 | Lancaster, CA | 3,495 |
| 284 | Carrollton, TX | 2,960 | 430 | Farmington Hills, MI | 1,114 | 223 | Lansing, MI | 3,960 |
| 352 | Carson, CA | 2,251 | 272 | Fayetteville, AR | 3,171 | 81 | Laredo, TX | 10,482 |
| 370 | Cary, NC | 2,075 | 69 | Fayetteville, NC | 12,261 | 290 | Largo, FL | 2,924 |
| 179 | Cedar Rapids, IA | 4,707 | 158 | Federal Way, WA | 5,173 | 200 | Las Cruces, NM | 4,349 |
| 428 | Centennial, CO | 1,194 | 435 | Fishers, IN | 826 | 10 | Las Vegas, NV | 47,968 |
| 348 | Champaign, IL | 2,275 | 206 | Flint, MI | 4,261 | 235 | Lawrence, KS | 3,625 |
| 138 | Chandler, AZ | 5,900 | 215 | Fontana, CA | 4,088 | 349 | Lawrence, MA | 2,273 |
| 269 | Charleston, SC | 3,192 | 230 | Fort Collins, CO | 3,808 | 163 | Lawton, OK | 5,027 |
| 22 | Charlotte, NC | 30,569 | 89 | Fort Lauderdale, FL | 9,650 | 387 | League City, TX | 1,918 |
| 73 | Chattanooga, TN | 11,468 | 184 | Fort Smith, AR | 4,621 | 383 | Lee's Summit, MO | 1,958 |
| 307 | Cheektowaga, NY | 2,689 | 87 | Fort Wayne, IN | 9,807 | 301 | Lewisville, TX | 2,721 |
| 130 | Chesapeake, VA | 6,188 | 17 | Fort Worth, TX | 34,272 | 68 | Lexington, KY | 12,447 |
| 3 | Chicago, IL | 95,908 | 213 | Fremont, CA | 4,097 | 94 | Lincoln, NE | 9,354 |
| 316 | Chico, CA | 2,572 | 35 | Fresno, CA | 22,584 | 50 | Little Rock, AR | 15,529 |
| 432 | Chino Hills, CA | 1,017 | 324 | Frisco, TX | 2,507 | 399 | Livermore, CA | 1,830 |

| RANK | CITY | CRIMES | RANK | CITY | CRIMES | RANK | CITY | CRIMES |
|---|---|---|---|---|---|---|---|---|
| 382 | Livonia, MI | 1,961 | 231 | Pasadena, CA | 3,779 | 306 | South Gate, CA | 2,698 |
| 63 | Long Beach, CA | 12,999 | 148 | Pasadena, TX | 5,501 | 322 | Sparks, NV | 2,522 |
| 379 | Longmont, CO | 2,009 | 212 | Paterson, NJ | 4,101 | 156 | Spokane Valley, WA | 5,313 |
| 254 | Longview, TX | 3,372 | 386 | Pearland, TX | 1,928 | 40 | Spokane, WA | 19,531 |
| 4 | Los Angeles, CA | 85,844 | 219 | Pembroke Pines, FL | 4,023 | 137 | Springfield, IL | 5,905 |
| 26 | Louisville, KY | 28,780 | 228 | Peoria, AZ | 3,830 | 114 | Springfield, MA | 7,113 |
| 250 | Lowell, MA | 3,379 | 195 | Peoria, IL | 4,415 | 53 | Springfield, MO | 14,691 |
| 71 | Lubbock, TX | 11,557 | 7 | Philadelphia, PA | 53,452 | 385 | Stamford, CT | 1,938 |
| 381 | Lynchburg, VA | 1,974 | 6 | Phoenix, AZ | 60,085 | 325 | Sterling Heights, MI | 2,486 |
| 336 | Lynn, MA | 2,398 | 84 | Pittsburgh, PA | 10,047 | 51 | Stockton, CA | 15,080 |
| 119 | Macon, GA | 6,800 | 136 | Plano, TX | 5,930 | 403 | St. George, UT | 1,728 |
| 108 | Madison, WI | 7,729 | 274 | Plantation, FL | 3,116 | 201 | St. Joseph, MO | 4,338 |
| 208 | Manchester, NH | 4,194 | 196 | Pomona, CA | 4,394 | 36 | St. Louis, MO | 21,087 |
| 149 | McAllen, TX | 5,424 | 160 | Pompano Beach, FL | 5,129 | 77 | St. Paul, MN | 10,973 |
| 277 | McKinney, TX | 3,055 | 329 | Port St. Lucie, FL | 2,461 | 60 | St. Petersburg, FL | 13,181 |
| 174 | Medford, OR | 4,813 | 24 | Portland, OR | 29,633 | 315 | Suffolk, VA | 2,582 |
| 251 | Melbourne, FL | 3,377 | 155 | Portsmouth, VA | 5,355 | 410 | Sugar Land, TX | 1,613 |
| 14 | Memphis, TN | 39,804 | 104 | Providence, RI | 7,974 | 331 | Sunnyvale, CA | 2,434 |
| 407 | Menifee, CA | 1,680 | 293 | Provo, UT | 2,810 | 260 | Sunrise, FL | 3,289 |
| 312 | Merced, CA | 2,647 | 110 | Pueblo, CO | 7,596 | 364 | Surprise, AZ | 2,120 |
| 431 | Meridian, ID | 1,030 | 408 | Quincy, MA | 1,647 | 125 | Syracuse, NY | 6,473 |
| 64 | Mesa, AZ | 12,916 | 279 | Racine, WI | 3,010 | 59 | Tacoma, WA | 13,310 |
| 127 | Mesquite, TX | 6,332 | 61 | Raleigh, NC | 13,140 | 102 | Tallahassee, FL | 8,116 |
| 88 | Miami Beach, FL | 9,751 | 441 | Ramapo, NY | 567 | 97 | Tampa, FL | 8,823 |
| 182 | Miami Gardens, FL | 4,660 | 229 | Rancho Cucamon., CA | 3,824 | 292 | Temecula, CA | 2,848 |
| 38 | Miami, FL | 20,928 | 294 | Reading, PA | 2,799 | 106 | Tempe, AZ | 7,876 |
| 270 | Midland, TX | 3,191 | 232 | Redding, CA | 3,774 | 258 | Thornton, CO | 3,296 |
| 28 | Milwaukee, WI | 27,013 | 394 | Redwood City, CA | 1,871 | 411 | Thousand Oaks, CA | 1,604 |
| 41 | Minneapolis, MN | 19,358 | 113 | Reno, NV | 7,180 | NA | Toledo, OH** | NA |
| 273 | Miramar, FL | 3,164 | 165 | Renton, WA | 4,938 | 298 | Toms River Twnshp, NJ | 2,742 |
| 433 | Mission Viejo, CA | 998 | 303 | Rialto, CA | 2,717 | 124 | Topeka, KS | 6,486 |
| 286 | Mission, TX | 2,945 | 297 | Richardson, TX | 2,758 | 295 | Torrance, CA | 2,786 |
| 62 | Mobile, AL | 13,011 | 173 | Richmond, CA | 4,826 | 356 | Tracy, CA | 2,236 |
| 86 | Modesto, CA | 9,989 | 98 | Richmond, VA | 8,704 | 343 | Trenton, NJ | 2,321 |
| 139 | Moreno Valley, CA | 5,872 | 80 | Riverside, CA | 10,608 | 413 | Troy, MI | 1,550 |
| 406 | Mountain View, CA | 1,706 | 193 | Roanoke, VA | 4,444 | 16 | Tucson, AZ | 34,587 |
| 217 | Murfreesboro, TN | 4,051 | 318 | Rochester, MN | 2,558 | 37 | Tulsa, OK | 20,978 |
| 409 | Murrieta, CA | 1,640 | 83 | Rochester, NY | 10,051 | 187 | Tuscaloosa, AL | 4,512 |
| 393 | Nampa, ID | 1,876 | 116 | Rockford, IL | 7,039 | 417 | Tustin, CA | 1,473 |
| 419 | Napa, CA | 1,409 | 257 | Roseville, CA | 3,343 | 211 | Tyler, TX | 4,116 |
| 395 | Naperville, IL | 1,869 | 366 | Roswell, GA | 2,107 | 357 | Upland, CA | 2,234 |
| 353 | Nashua, NH | 2,248 | 333 | Round Rock, TX | 2,428 | 397 | Upper Darby Twnshp, PA | 1,852 |
| 32 | Nashville, TN | 24,460 | 44 | Sacramento, CA | 17,980 | 367 | Vacaville, CA | 2,096 |
| 246 | New Bedford, MA | 3,437 | 120 | Salem, OR | 6,782 | 143 | Vallejo, CA | 5,734 |
| 133 | New Haven, CT | 6,068 | 154 | Salinas, CA | 5,356 | 135 | Vancouver, WA | 5,933 |
| 55 | New Orleans, LA | 14,525 | 58 | Salt Lake City, UT | 13,461 | 218 | Ventura, CA | 4,027 |
| 421 | New Rochelle, NY | 1,391 | 236 | San Angelo, TX | 3,592 | 209 | Victorville, CA | 4,165 |
| 1 | New York, NY | 141,971 | 5 | San Antonio, TX | 79,994 | 76 | Virginia Beach, VA | 11,226 |
| 96 | Newark, NJ | 8,965 | 93 | San Bernardino, CA | 9,389 | 170 | Visalia, CA | 4,853 |
| 362 | Newport Beach, CA | 2,158 | 20 | San Diego, CA | 31,728 | 373 | Vista, CA | 2,045 |
| 146 | Newport News, VA | 5,582 | 9 | San Francisco, CA | 48,324 | 150 | Waco, TX | 5,422 |
| 437 | Newton, MA | 807 | 29 | San Jose, CA | 25,510 | 241 | Warren, MI | 3,508 |
| 78 | Norfolk, VA | 10,812 | 223 | San Leandro, CA | 3,960 | 377 | Warwick, RI | 2,015 |
| 288 | Norman, OK | 2,941 | 420 | San Marcos, CA | 1,400 | 25 | Washington, DC | 29,569 |
| 141 | North Charleston, SC | 5,804 | 371 | San Mateo, CA | 2,065 | 183 | Waterbury, CT | 4,636 |
| 134 | North Las Vegas, NV | 5,969 | 299 | Sandy Springs, GA | 2,739 | 323 | Waukegan, IL | 2,509 |
| 354 | Norwalk, CA | 2,246 | 287 | Sandy, UT | 2,942 | 255 | West Covina, CA | 3,370 |
| 403 | Norwalk, CT | 1,728 | 126 | Santa Ana, CA | 6,425 | 169 | West Palm Beach, FL | 4,863 |
| 30 | Oakland, CA | 25,176 | 309 | Santa Barbara, CA | 2,670 | 121 | West Valley, UT | 6,560 |
| 189 | Oceanside, CA | 4,494 | 278 | Santa Clara, CA | 3,023 | 335 | Westland, MI | 2,399 |
| 197 | Odessa, TX | 4,374 | 304 | Santa Clarita, CA | 2,713 | 327 | Westminster, CA | 2,476 |
| 426 | O'Fallon, MO | 1,218 | 289 | Santa Maria, CA | 2,934 | 280 | Westminster, CO | 2,987 |
| 220 | Ogden, UT | 4,005 | 238 | Santa Monica, CA | 3,544 | 338 | Whittier, CA | 2,383 |
| 19 | Oklahoma City, OK | 32,479 | 242 | Santa Rosa, CA | 3,506 | 185 | Wichita Falls, TX | 4,558 |
| 349 | Olathe, KS | 2,273 | 99 | Savannah, GA | 8,458 | 39 | Wichita, KS | 20,802 |
| 42 | Omaha, NE | 19,108 | 142 | Scottsdale, AZ | 5,766 | 147 | Wilmington, NC | 5,549 |
| 188 | Ontario, CA | 4,507 | 347 | Scranton, PA | 2,277 | 65 | Winston-Salem, NC | 12,853 |
| 334 | Orange, CA | 2,418 | 15 | Seattle, WA | 35,883 | 375 | Woodbridge Twnshp, NJ | 2,042 |
| 369 | Orem, UT | 2,079 | 92 | Shreveport, LA | 9,584 | 128 | Worcester, MA | 6,239 |
| 48 | Orlando, FL | 16,489 | 405 | Simi Valley, CA | 1,709 | 180 | Yakima, WA | 4,684 |
| 240 | Overland Park, KS | 3,530 | 233 | Sioux City, IA | 3,658 | 340 | Yonkers, NY | 2,368 |
| 161 | Oxnard, CA | 5,074 | 167 | Sioux Falls, SD | 4,930 | 252 | Yuma, AZ | 3,375 |
| 383 | Palm Bay, FL | 1,958 | 414 | Somerville, MA | 1,525 | | | |
| 256 | Palmdale, CA | 3,344 | 168 | South Bend, IN | 4,890 | | | |

Source: Reported data from the F.B.I. "Crime in the United States 2013"

*Property crimes are offenses of burglary, larceny-theft, and motor vehicle theft. Attempts are included.

**Not available.

# 65. Property Crimes in 2013 (continued)
## National Total = 8,632,512 Property Crimes*

| RANK | CITY | CRIMES | RANK | CITY | CRIMES | RANK | CITY | CRIMES |
|---|---|---|---|---|---|---|---|---|
| 1 | New York, NY | 141,971 | 75 | Baton Rouge, LA | 11,418 | 149 | McAllen, TX | 5,424 |
| 2 | Houston, TX | 110,919 | 76 | Virginia Beach, VA | 11,226 | 150 | Waco, TX | 5,422 |
| 3 | Chicago, IL | 95,908 | 77 | St. Paul, MN | 10,973 | 151 | Lakeland, FL | 5,410 |
| 4 | Los Angeles, CA | 85,844 | 78 | Norfolk, VA | 10,812 | 152 | Berkeley, CA | 5,377 |
| 5 | San Antonio, TX | 79,994 | 79 | Aurora, CO | 10,786 | 153 | Henderson, NV | 5,358 |
| 6 | Phoenix, AZ | 60,085 | 80 | Riverside, CA | 10,608 | 154 | Salinas, CA | 5,356 |
| 7 | Philadelphia, PA | 53,452 | 81 | Laredo, TX | 10,482 | 155 | Portsmouth, VA | 5,355 |
| 8 | Dallas, TX | 52,274 | 82 | Jackson, MS | 10,284 | 156 | Spokane Valley, WA | 5,313 |
| 9 | San Francisco, CA | 48,324 | 83 | Rochester, NY | 10,051 | 157 | Chula Vista, CA | 5,284 |
| 10 | Las Vegas, NV | 47,968 | 84 | Pittsburgh, PA | 10,047 | 158 | Federal Way, WA | 5,173 |
| 11 | Indianapolis, IN | 44,606 | 85 | Des Moines, IA | 10,015 | 159 | Grand Prairie, TX | 5,158 |
| 12 | Austin, TX | 41,667 | 86 | Modesto, CA | 9,989 | 160 | Pompano Beach, FL | 5,129 |
| 13 | Detroit, MI | 40,835 | 87 | Fort Wayne, IN | 9,807 | 161 | Oxnard, CA | 5,074 |
| 14 | Memphis, TN | 39,804 | 88 | Miami Beach, FL | 9,751 | 162 | Hartford, CT | 5,036 |
| 15 | Seattle, WA | 35,883 | 89 | Fort Lauderdale, FL | 9,650 | 163 | Lawton, OK | 5,027 |
| 16 | Tucson, AZ | 34,587 | 90 | Akron, OH | 9,649 | 164 | Gainesville, FL | 4,986 |
| 17 | Fort Worth, TX | 34,272 | 91 | Anaheim, CA | 9,611 | 165 | Renton, WA | 4,938 |
| 18 | Jacksonville, FL | 33,007 | 92 | Shreveport, LA | 9,584 | 166 | Huntington Beach, CA | 4,934 |
| 19 | Oklahoma City, OK | 32,479 | 93 | San Bernardino, CA | 9,389 | 167 | Sioux Falls, SD | 4,930 |
| 20 | San Diego, CA | 31,728 | 94 | Lincoln, NE | 9,354 | 168 | South Bend, IN | 4,890 |
| 21 | Baltimore, MD | 30,789 | 95 | Huntsville, AL | 9,216 | 169 | West Palm Beach, FL | 4,863 |
| 22 | Charlotte, NC | 30,569 | 96 | Newark, NJ | 8,965 | 170 | Visalia, CA | 4,853 |
| 23 | Albuquerque, NM | 30,531 | 97 | Tampa, FL | 8,823 | 171 | Hayward, CA | 4,844 |
| 24 | Portland, OR | 29,633 | 98 | Richmond, VA | 8,704 | 172 | Jersey City, NJ | 4,836 |
| 25 | Washington, DC | 29,569 | 99 | Savannah, GA | 8,458 | 173 | Richmond, CA | 4,826 |
| 26 | Louisville, KY | 28,780 | 100 | Garland, TX | 8,371 | 174 | Medford, OR | 4,813 |
| 27 | Atlanta, GA | 27,528 | 101 | Amarillo, TX | 8,154 | 175 | Killeen, TX | 4,791 |
| 28 | Milwaukee, WI | 27,013 | 102 | Tallahassee, FL | 8,116 | 176 | Abilene, TX | 4,769 |
| 29 | San Jose, CA | 25,510 | 103 | Columbia, SC | 7,989 | 177 | Boise, ID | 4,741 |
| 30 | Oakland, CA | 25,176 | 104 | Providence, RI | 7,974 | 178 | Gary, IN | 4,719 |
| 31 | Kansas City, MO | 24,648 | 105 | Eugene, OR | 7,920 | 179 | Cedar Rapids, IA | 4,707 |
| 32 | Nashville, TN | 24,460 | 106 | Tempe, AZ | 7,876 | 180 | Yakima, WA | 4,684 |
| 33 | Denver, CO | 23,711 | 107 | Brownsville, TX | 7,838 | 181 | Albany, GA | 4,661 |
| 34 | Cleveland, OH | 23,168 | 108 | Madison, WI | 7,729 | 182 | Miami Gardens, FL | 4,660 |
| 35 | Fresno, CA | 22,584 | 109 | Dayton, OH | 7,655 | 183 | Waterbury, CT | 4,636 |
| 36 | St. Louis, MO | 21,087 | 110 | Pueblo, CO | 7,596 | 184 | Fort Smith, AR | 4,621 |
| 37 | Tulsa, OK | 20,978 | 111 | Lafayette, LA | 7,568 | 185 | Wichita Falls, TX | 4,558 |
| 38 | Miami, FL | 20,928 | 112 | Kansas City, KS | 7,228 | 186 | Gresham, OR | 4,553 |
| 39 | Wichita, KS | 20,802 | 113 | Reno, NV | 7,180 | 187 | Tuscaloosa, AL | 4,512 |
| 40 | Spokane, WA | 19,531 | 114 | Springfield, MA | 7,113 | 188 | Ontario, CA | 4,507 |
| 41 | Minneapolis, MN | 19,358 | 115 | Independence, MO | 7,108 | 189 | Oceanside, CA | 4,494 |
| 42 | Omaha, NE | 19,108 | 116 | Rockford, IL | 7,039 | 190 | High Point, NC | 4,489 |
| 43 | Colorado Springs, CO | 18,175 | 117 | Lakewood, CO | 6,892 | 191 | Hampton, VA | 4,473 |
| 44 | Sacramento, CA | 17,980 | 118 | Everett, WA | 6,865 | 192 | Bridgeport, CT | 4,464 |
| 45 | Boston, MA | 17,853 | 119 | Macon, GA | 6,800 | 193 | Roanoke, VA | 4,444 |
| 46 | Cincinnati, OH | 17,231 | 120 | Salem, OR | 6,782 | 194 | Antioch, CA | 4,440 |
| 47 | Bakersfield, CA | 16,814 | 121 | West Valley, UT | 6,560 | 195 | Peoria, IL | 4,415 |
| 48 | Orlando, FL | 16,489 | 122 | Hialeah, FL | 6,550 | 196 | Pomona, CA | 4,394 |
| 49 | El Paso, TX | 15,558 | 122 | Hollywood, FL | 6,550 | 197 | Odessa, TX | 4,374 |
| 50 | Little Rock, AR | 15,529 | 124 | Topeka, KS | 6,486 | 198 | Columbia, MO | 4,359 |
| 51 | Stockton, CA | 15,080 | 125 | Syracuse, NY | 6,473 | 199 | Concord, CA | 4,357 |
| 52 | Arlington, TX | 15,000 | 126 | Santa Ana, CA | 6,425 | 200 | Las Cruces, NM | 4,349 |
| 53 | Springfield, MO | 14,691 | 127 | Mesquite, TX | 6,332 | 201 | St. Joseph, MO | 4,338 |
| 54 | Corpus Christi, TX | 14,601 | 128 | Worcester, MA | 6,239 | 202 | Allentown, PA | 4,324 |
| 55 | New Orleans, LA | 14,525 | 129 | Beaumont, TX | 6,192 | 203 | Clearwater, FL | 4,316 |
| 56 | Birmingham, AL | 14,157 | 130 | Chesapeake, VA | 6,188 | 204 | Edinburg, TX | 4,292 |
| 57 | Glendale, AZ | 13,626 | 130 | Grand Rapids, MI | 6,188 | 205 | Duluth, MN | 4,283 |
| 58 | Salt Lake City, UT | 13,461 | 132 | Irving, TX | 6,175 | 206 | Flint, MI | 4,261 |
| 59 | Tacoma, WA | 13,310 | 133 | New Haven, CT | 6,068 | 207 | Davenport, IA | 4,248 |
| 60 | St. Petersburg, FL | 13,181 | 134 | North Las Vegas, NV | 5,969 | 208 | Manchester, NH | 4,194 |
| 61 | Raleigh, NC | 13,140 | 135 | Vancouver, WA | 5,933 | 209 | Victorville, CA | 4,165 |
| 62 | Mobile, AL | 13,011 | 136 | Plano, TX | 5,930 | 210 | Clarksville, TN | 4,141 |
| 63 | Long Beach, CA | 12,999 | 137 | Springfield, IL | 5,905 | 211 | Tyler, TX | 4,116 |
| 64 | Mesa, AZ | 12,916 | 138 | Chandler, AZ | 5,900 | 212 | Paterson, NJ | 4,101 |
| 65 | Winston-Salem, NC | 12,853 | 139 | Moreno Valley, CA | 5,872 | 213 | Fremont, CA | 4,097 |
| 66 | Buffalo, NY | 12,491 | 140 | Evansville, IN | 5,859 | 214 | Albany, NY | 4,090 |
| 67 | Columbus, GA | 12,475 | 141 | North Charleston, SC | 5,804 | 215 | Fontana, CA | 4,088 |
| 68 | Lexington, KY | 12,447 | 142 | Scottsdale, AZ | 5,766 | 216 | Athens-Clarke, GA | 4,074 |
| 69 | Fayetteville, NC | 12,261 | 143 | Vallejo, CA | 5,734 | 217 | Murfreesboro, TN | 4,051 |
| 70 | Anchorage, AK | 12,032 | 144 | Billings, MT | 5,604 | 218 | Ventura, CA | 4,027 |
| 71 | Lubbock, TX | 11,557 | 145 | Kent, WA | 5,600 | 219 | Pembroke Pines, FL | 4,023 |
| 72 | Greensboro, NC | 11,537 | 146 | Newport News, VA | 5,582 | 220 | Ogden, UT | 4,005 |
| 73 | Chattanooga, TN | 11,468 | 147 | Wilmington, NC | 5,549 | 221 | Escondido, CA | 3,965 |
| 74 | Knoxville, TN | 11,438 | 148 | Pasadena, TX | 5,501 | 222 | Hemet, CA | 3,963 |

| RANK | CITY | CRIMES | RANK | CITY | CRIMES | RANK | CITY | CRIMES |
|---|---|---|---|---|---|---|---|---|
| 223 | Lansing, MI | 3,960 | 297 | Richardson, TX | 2,758 | 371 | San Mateo, CA | 2,065 |
| 223 | San Leandro, CA | 3,960 | 298 | Toms River Twnshp, NJ | 2,742 | 372 | Lakewood, CA | 2,062 |
| 225 | Bellevue, WA | 3,949 | 299 | Sandy Springs, GA | 2,739 | 373 | Vista, CA | 2,045 |
| 226 | Greenville, NC | 3,862 | 300 | El Cajon, CA | 2,730 | 374 | Chino, CA | 2,044 |
| 227 | Fullerton, CA | 3,859 | 301 | Lewisville, TX | 2,721 | 375 | Woodbridge Twnshp, NJ | 2,042 |
| 228 | Peoria, AZ | 3,830 | 302 | Inglewood, CA | 2,718 | 376 | Broken Arrow, OK | 2,034 |
| 229 | Rancho Cucamon., CA | 3,824 | 303 | Rialto, CA | 2,717 | 377 | Warwick, RI | 2,015 |
| 230 | Fort Collins, CO | 3,808 | 304 | Santa Clarita, CA | 2,713 | 378 | Bethlehem, PA | 2,010 |
| 231 | Pasadena, CA | 3,779 | 305 | Indio, CA | 2,699 | 379 | Longmont, CO | 2,009 |
| 232 | Redding, CA | 3,774 | 306 | South Gate, CA | 2,698 | 380 | Colonie, NY | 1,990 |
| 233 | Sioux City, IA | 3,658 | 307 | Cheektowaga, NY | 2,689 | 381 | Lynchburg, VA | 1,974 |
| 234 | Elizabeth, NJ | 3,655 | 308 | Green Bay, WI | 2,674 | 382 | Livonia, MI | 1,961 |
| 235 | Lawrence, KS | 3,625 | 309 | Santa Barbara, CA | 2,670 | 383 | Lee's Summit, MO | 1,958 |
| 236 | San Angelo, TX | 3,592 | 310 | Arvada, CO | 2,666 | 383 | Palm Bay, FL | 1,958 |
| 237 | Costa Mesa, CA | 3,556 | 311 | Citrus Heights, CA | 2,653 | 385 | Stamford, CT | 1,938 |
| 238 | Santa Monica, CA | 3,544 | 312 | Merced, CA | 2,647 | 386 | Pearland, TX | 1,928 |
| 239 | Fairfield, CA | 3,534 | 313 | Bloomington, IN | 2,606 | 387 | League City, TX | 1,918 |
| 240 | Overland Park, KS | 3,530 | 314 | Hoover, AL | 2,596 | 388 | Alameda, CA | 1,902 |
| 241 | Warren, MI | 3,508 | 315 | Suffolk, VA | 2,582 | 388 | Elgin, IL | 1,902 |
| 242 | Santa Rosa, CA | 3,506 | 316 | Chico, CA | 2,572 | 388 | Evanston, IL | 1,902 |
| 243 | Lancaster, CA | 3,495 | 317 | Coral Springs, FL | 2,565 | 391 | Bloomington, IL | 1,901 |
| 244 | Gilbert, AZ | 3,472 | 318 | Rochester, MN | 2,558 | 392 | Bellflower, CA | 1,882 |
| 245 | Corona, CA | 3,439 | 319 | Concord, NC | 2,549 | 393 | Nampa, ID | 1,876 |
| 246 | New Bedford, MA | 3,437 | 320 | Compton, CA | 2,538 | 394 | Redwood City, CA | 1,871 |
| 247 | Clovis, CA | 3,404 | 321 | Ann Arbor, MI | 2,525 | 395 | Naperville, IL | 1,869 |
| 248 | Garden Grove, CA | 3,397 | 322 | Sparks, NV | 2,522 | 396 | Hamilton Twnshp, NJ | 1,862 |
| 249 | Davie, FL | 3,393 | 323 | Waukegan, IL | 2,509 | 397 | Upper Darby Twnshp, PA | 1,852 |
| 250 | Lowell, MA | 3,379 | 324 | Frisco, TX | 2,507 | 398 | Daly City, CA | 1,833 |
| 251 | Melbourne, FL | 3,377 | 325 | Sterling Heights, MI | 2,486 | 399 | Cicero, IL | 1,830 |
| 252 | Cape Coral, FL | 3,375 | 326 | Kennewick, WA | 2,478 | 399 | Livermore, CA | 1,830 |
| 252 | Yuma, AZ | 3,375 | 327 | Westminster, CA | 2,476 | 401 | Alhambra, CA | 1,774 |
| 254 | Longview, TX | 3,372 | 328 | Kenosha, WI | 2,462 | 402 | Cranston, RI | 1,755 |
| 255 | West Covina, CA | 3,370 | 329 | Port St. Lucie, FL | 2,461 | 403 | Norwalk, CT | 1,728 |
| 256 | Palmdale, CA | 3,344 | 330 | Brooklyn Park, MN | 2,456 | 403 | St. George, UT | 1,728 |
| 257 | Roseville, CA | 3,343 | 331 | Sunnyvale, CA | 2,434 | 405 | Simi Valley, CA | 1,709 |
| 258 | Thornton, CO | 3,296 | 332 | Burbank, CA | 2,430 | 406 | Mountain View, CA | 1,706 |
| 259 | Downey, CA | 3,292 | 333 | Round Rock, TX | 2,428 | 407 | Menifee, CA | 1,680 |
| 260 | Sunrise, FL | 3,289 | 334 | Orange, CA | 2,418 | 408 | Quincy, MA | 1,647 |
| 261 | Irvine, CA | 3,285 | 335 | Westland, MI | 2,399 | 409 | Murrieta, CA | 1,640 |
| 262 | Bloomington, MN | 3,283 | 336 | Lynn, MA | 2,398 | 410 | Sugar Land, TX | 1,613 |
| 263 | Hammond, IN | 3,235 | 337 | Deerfield Beach, FL | 2,386 | 411 | Thousand Oaks, CA | 1,604 |
| 264 | Greeley, CO | 3,219 | 338 | Whittier, CA | 2,383 | 412 | Edmond, OK | 1,595 |
| 265 | Joliet, IL | 3,217 | 339 | Decatur, IL | 2,369 | 413 | Troy, MI | 1,550 |
| 266 | Fargo, ND | 3,209 | 340 | Yonkers, NY | 2,368 | 414 | Somerville, MA | 1,525 |
| 267 | Erie, PA | 3,208 | 341 | Fall River, MA | 2,364 | 415 | Clifton, NJ | 1,521 |
| 268 | Glendale, CA | 3,198 | 342 | Hesperia, CA | 2,330 | 416 | Clarkstown, NY | 1,515 |
| 269 | Charleston, SC | 3,192 | 343 | Trenton, NJ | 2,321 | 417 | Tustin, CA | 1,473 |
| 270 | Midland, TX | 3,191 | 344 | Bryan, TX | 2,311 | 418 | Beaverton, OR | 1,471 |
| 271 | Brockton, MA | 3,189 | 345 | Greece, NY | 2,303 | 419 | Napa, CA | 1,409 |
| 272 | Fayetteville, AR | 3,171 | 346 | Boca Raton, FL | 2,302 | 420 | San Marcos, CA | 1,400 |
| 273 | Miramar, FL | 3,164 | 347 | Scranton, PA | 2,277 | 421 | New Rochelle, NY | 1,391 |
| 274 | Plantation, FL | 3,116 | 348 | Champaign, IL | 2,275 | 422 | Baldwin Park, CA | 1,370 |
| 275 | Dearborn, MI | 3,104 | 349 | Lawrence, MA | 2,273 | 423 | Danbury, CT | 1,257 |
| 276 | Jurupa Valley, CA | 3,065 | 349 | Olathe, KS | 2,273 | 424 | Canton Twnshp, MI | 1,250 |
| 277 | McKinney, TX | 3,055 | 351 | Bend, OR | 2,267 | 425 | Edison Twnshp, NJ | 1,245 |
| 278 | Santa Clara, CA | 3,023 | 352 | Carson, CA | 2,251 | 426 | O'Fallon, MO | 1,218 |
| 279 | Racine, WI | 3,010 | 353 | Nashua, NH | 2,248 | 427 | Allen, TX | 1,205 |
| 280 | Westminster, CO | 2,987 | 354 | Norwalk, CA | 2,246 | 428 | Centennial, CO | 1,194 |
| 281 | Aurora, IL | 2,972 | 355 | Hawthorne, CA | 2,242 | 429 | Brick Twnshp, NJ | 1,183 |
| 282 | Alexandria, VA | 2,967 | 356 | Tracy, CA | 2,236 | 430 | Farmington Hills, MI | 1,114 |
| 283 | Elk Grove, CA | 2,963 | 357 | Upland, CA | 2,234 | 431 | Meridian, ID | 1,030 |
| 284 | Carrollton, TX | 2,960 | 358 | College Station, TX | 2,230 | 432 | Chino Hills, CA | 1,017 |
| 285 | Boulder, CO | 2,948 | 359 | El Monte, CA | 2,182 | 433 | Lakewood Twnshp, NJ | 998 |
| 286 | Mission, TX | 2,945 | 360 | Buena Park, CA | 2,165 | 433 | Mission Viejo, CA | 998 |
| 287 | Sandy, UT | 2,942 | 361 | Hillsboro, OR | 2,160 | 435 | Fishers, IN | 826 |
| 288 | Norman, OK | 2,941 | 362 | Newport Beach, CA | 2,158 | 436 | Lake Forest, CA | 813 |
| 289 | Santa Maria, CA | 2,934 | 363 | Clinton Twnshp, MI | 2,134 | 437 | Newton, MA | 807 |
| 290 | Largo, FL | 2,924 | 364 | Surprise, AZ | 2,120 | 438 | Arlington Heights, IL | 800 |
| 291 | Cambridge, MA | 2,907 | 365 | Amherst, NY | 2,118 | 439 | Carmel, IN | 744 |
| 292 | Temecula, CA | 2,848 | 366 | Roswell, GA | 2,107 | 440 | Johns Creek, GA | 619 |
| 293 | Provo, UT | 2,810 | 367 | Vacaville, CA | 2,096 | 441 | Ramapo, NY | 567 |
| 294 | Reading, PA | 2,799 | 368 | Carlsbad, CA | 2,085 | NA | Toledo, OH** | NA |
| 295 | Torrance, CA | 2,786 | 369 | Orem, UT | 2,079 | | | |
| 296 | Denton, TX | 2,777 | 370 | Cary, NC | 2,075 | | | |

Source: Reported data from the F.B.I. "Crime in the United States 2013"

*Property crimes are offenses of burglary, larceny-theft, and motor vehicle theft. Attempts are included.

**Not available.

# 66. Property Crime Rate in 2013
## National Rate = 2,730.7 Property Crimes per 100,000 Population*

| RANK | CITY | RATE | RANK | CITY | RATE | RANK | CITY | RATE |
|---|---|---|---|---|---|---|---|---|
| 148 | Abilene, TX | 3,994.1 | 300 | Chino, CA | 2,532.7 | 259 | Fullerton, CA | 2,762.8 |
| 77 | Akron, OH | 4,863.3 | 363 | Chula Vista, CA | 2,071.6 | 152 | Gainesville, FL | 3,938.7 |
| 309 | Alameda, CA | 2,495.9 | 349 | Cicero, IL | 2,173.3 | 379 | Garden Grove, CA | 1,936.0 |
| 25 | Albany, GA | 6,024.7 | 32 | Cincinnati, OH | 5,811.6 | 179 | Garland, TX | 3,551.8 |
| 127 | Albany, NY | 4,175.3 | 221 | Citrus Heights, CA | 3,108.9 | 26 | Gary, IN | 5,987.1 |
| 41 | Albuquerque, NM | 5,469.9 | 388 | Clarkstown, NY | 1,877.2 | 412 | Gilbert, AZ | 1,541.5 |
| 372 | Alexandria, VA | 1,997.7 | 248 | Clarksville, TN | 2,844.1 | 31 | Glendale, AZ | 5,822.9 |
| 360 | Alhambra, CA | 2,094.2 | 150 | Clearwater, FL | 3,963.0 | 408 | Glendale, CA | 1,636.9 |
| 173 | Allentown, PA | 3,625.2 | 27 | Cleveland, OH | 5,953.0 | 254 | Grand Prairie, TX | 2,806.0 |
| 426 | Allen, TX | 1,320.0 | 397 | Clifton, NJ | 1,788.9 | 206 | Grand Rapids, MI | 3,236.2 |
| 134 | Amarillo, TX | 4,148.0 | 347 | Clinton Twnshp, MI | 2,176.0 | 322 | Greece, NY | 2,382.4 |
| 395 | Amherst, NY | 1,790.4 | 193 | Clovis, CA | 3,421.7 | 199 | Greeley, CO | 3,349.3 |
| 256 | Anaheim, CA | 2,783.2 | 333 | College Station, TX | 2,254.4 | 296 | Green Bay, WI | 2,544.1 |
| 146 | Anchorage, AK | 4,018.0 | 295 | Colonie, NY | 2,544.3 | 137 | Greensboro, NC | 4,130.0 |
| 352 | Ann Arbor, MI | 2,161.8 | 130 | Colorado Springs, CO | 4,167.5 | 110 | Greenville, NC | 4,387.7 |
| 129 | Antioch, CA | 4,171.1 | 160 | Columbia, MO | 3,804.1 | 136 | Gresham, OR | 4,140.4 |
| 434 | Arlington Heights, IL | 1,052.9 | 24 | Columbia, SC | 6,041.3 | 361 | Hamilton Twnshp, NJ | 2,092.3 |
| 151 | Arlington, TX | 3,960.2 | 18 | Columbus, GA | 6,201.4 | 140 | Hammond, IN | 4,078.0 |
| 320 | Arvada, CO | 2,406.3 | 291 | Compton, CA | 2,592.3 | 201 | Hampton, VA | 3,266.2 |
| 195 | Athens-Clarke, GA | 3,391.6 | 188 | Concord, CA | 3,472.7 | 144 | Hartford, CT | 4,031.2 |
| 20 | Atlanta, GA | 6,103.5 | 227 | Concord, NC | 3,074.8 | 289 | Hawthorne, CA | 2,603.0 |
| 217 | Aurora, CO | 3,140.2 | 370 | Coral Springs, FL | 2,025.9 | 209 | Hayward, CA | 3,208.9 |
| 416 | Aurora, IL | 1,481.9 | 354 | Corona, CA | 2,147.2 | 80 | Hemet, CA | 4,850.8 |
| 81 | Austin, TX | 4,849.6 | 94 | Corpus Christi, TX | 4,642.3 | 373 | Henderson, NV | 1,997.5 |
| 93 | Bakersfield, CA | 4,646.6 | 215 | Costa Mesa, CA | 3,159.8 | 303 | Hesperia, CA | 2,515.6 |
| 398 | Baldwin Park, CA | 1,785.1 | 348 | Cranston, RI | 2,174.2 | 255 | Hialeah, FL | 2,797.0 |
| 69 | Baltimore, MD | 4,944.7 | 132 | Dallas, TX | 4,165.2 | 126 | High Point, NC | 4,185.1 |
| 68 | Baton Rouge, LA | 4,959.8 | 401 | Daly City, CA | 1,753.5 | 336 | Hillsboro, OR | 2,242.7 |
| 52 | Beaumont, TX | 5,239.6 | 415 | Danbury, CT | 1,507.9 | 106 | Hollywood, FL | 4,466.6 |
| 410 | Beaverton, OR | 1,572.4 | 128 | Davenport, IA | 4,171.5 | 225 | Hoover, AL | 3,085.4 |
| 222 | Bellevue, WA | 3,092.9 | 182 | Davie, FL | 3,513.1 | 58 | Houston, TX | 5,086.6 |
| 317 | Bellflower, CA | 2,425.4 | 43 | Dayton, OH | 5,422.7 | 301 | Huntington Beach, CA | 2,519.4 |
| 249 | Bend, OR | 2,836.4 | 207 | Dearborn, MI | 3,232.9 | 66 | Huntsville, AL | 4,988.7 |
| 97 | Berkeley, CA | 4,626.7 | 216 | Decatur, IL | 3,150.7 | 21 | Independence, MO | 6,055.5 |
| 274 | Bethlehem, PA | 2,675.2 | 229 | Deerfield Beach, FL | 3,051.0 | 51 | Indianapolis, IN | 5,246.4 |
| 54 | Billings, MT | 5,198.4 | 334 | Denton, TX | 2,253.0 | 197 | Indio, CA | 3,363.5 |
| 8 | Birmingham, AL | 6,677.8 | 170 | Denver, CO | 3,653.6 | 316 | Inglewood, CA | 2,433.9 |
| 315 | Bloomington, IL | 2,435.3 | 83 | Des Moines, IA | 4,829.0 | 421 | Irvine, CA | 1,393.0 |
| 214 | Bloomington, IN | 3,162.0 | 30 | Detroit, MI | 5,834.5 | 268 | Irving, TX | 2,704.0 |
| 163 | Bloomington, MN | 3,771.1 | 241 | Downey, CA | 2,907.6 | 153 | Jacksonville, FL | 3,902.7 |
| 290 | Boca Raton, FL | 2,593.8 | 67 | Duluth, MN | 4,968.0 | 29 | Jackson, MS | 5,841.9 |
| 343 | Boise, ID | 2,212.0 | 53 | Edinburg, TX | 5,216.9 | 387 | Jersey City, NJ | 1,882.5 |
| 257 | Boston, MA | 2,773.1 | 430 | Edison Twnshp, NJ | 1,228.8 | 440 | Johns Creek, GA | 736.1 |
| 247 | Boulder, CO | 2,866.9 | 392 | Edmond, OK | 1,855.2 | 351 | Joliet, IL | 2,166.9 |
| 411 | Brick Twnshp, NJ | 1,569.6 | 273 | El Cajon, CA | 2,676.2 | 219 | Jurupa Valley, CA | 3,124.7 |
| 231 | Bridgeport, CT | 3,035.2 | 385 | El Monte, CA | 1,887.7 | 72 | Kansas City, KS | 4,896.4 |
| 196 | Brockton, MA | 3,376.5 | 330 | El Paso, TX | 2,289.0 | 49 | Kansas City, MO | 5,294.8 |
| 374 | Broken Arrow, OK | 1,975.6 | 405 | Elgin, IL | 1,722.0 | 205 | Kennewick, WA | 3,238.9 |
| 218 | Brooklyn Park, MN | 3,134.5 | 245 | Elizabeth, NJ | 2,876.4 | 314 | Kenosha, WI | 2,451.8 |
| 117 | Brownsville, TX | 4,316.3 | 393 | Elk Grove, CA | 1,841.2 | 101 | Kent, WA | 4,503.1 |
| 237 | Bryan, TX | 2,941.0 | 212 | Erie, PA | 3,182.1 | 183 | Killeen, TX | 3,508.9 |
| 284 | Buena Park, CA | 2,620.1 | 276 | Escondido, CA | 2,667.3 | 16 | Knoxville, TN | 6,241.8 |
| 84 | Buffalo, NY | 4,826.7 | 65 | Eugene, OR | 4,996.9 | 19 | Lafayette, LA | 6,132.5 |
| 329 | Burbank, CA | 2,320.3 | 305 | Evanston, IL | 2,512.3 | 436 | Lake Forest, CA | 1,024.8 |
| 266 | Cambridge, MA | 2,709.7 | 75 | Evansville, IN | 4,871.0 | 45 | Lakeland, FL | 5,371.1 |
| 419 | Canton Twnshp, MI | 1,405.2 | 13 | Everett, WA | 6,530.1 | 433 | Lakewood Twnshp, NJ | 1,077.0 |
| 364 | Cape Coral, FL | 2,064.7 | 203 | Fairfield, CA | 3,259.4 | 297 | Lakewood, CA | 2,543.0 |
| 386 | Carlsbad, CA | 1,886.8 | 278 | Fall River, MA | 2,649.6 | 90 | Lakewood, CO | 4,710.9 |
| 439 | Carmel, IN | 876.5 | 244 | Fargo, ND | 2,888.4 | 346 | Lancaster, CA | 2,187.2 |
| 328 | Carrollton, TX | 2,322.3 | 422 | Farmington Hills, MI | 1,373.9 | 187 | Lansing, MI | 3,476.5 |
| 319 | Carson, CA | 2,409.7 | 141 | Fayetteville, AR | 4,070.6 | 124 | Laredo, TX | 4,237.7 |
| 420 | Cary, NC | 1,393.5 | 22 | Fayetteville, NC | 6,054.1 | 165 | Largo, FL | 3,752.9 |
| 169 | Cedar Rapids, IA | 3,659.0 | 39 | Federal Way, WA | 5,577.9 | 122 | Las Cruces, NM | 4,263.4 |
| 432 | Centennial, CO | 1,139.6 | 437 | Fishers, IN | 990.9 | 210 | Las Vegas, NV | 3,196.9 |
| 262 | Champaign, IL | 2,742.1 | 121 | Flint, MI | 4,263.5 | 145 | Lawrence, KS | 4,026.3 |
| 323 | Chandler, AZ | 2,372.2 | 371 | Fontana, CA | 2,009.6 | 238 | Lawrence, MA | 2,921.1 |
| 307 | Charleston, SC | 2,509.3 | 299 | Fort Collins, CO | 2,537.6 | 57 | Lawton, OK | 5,101.1 |
| 171 | Charlotte, NC | 3,649.4 | 37 | Fort Lauderdale, FL | 5,597.5 | 355 | League City, TX | 2,140.7 |
| 9 | Chattanooga, TN | 6,656.4 | 50 | Fort Smith, AR | 5,261.8 | 358 | Lee's Summit, MO | 2,110.7 |
| 191 | Cheektowaga, NY | 3,431.6 | 156 | Fort Wayne, IN | 3,848.6 | 269 | Lewisville, TX | 2,701.8 |
| 271 | Chesapeake, VA | 2,683.7 | 116 | Fort Worth, TX | 4,343.5 | 143 | Lexington, KY | 4,031.9 |
| 180 | Chicago, IL | 3,525.3 | 394 | Fremont, CA | 1,825.1 | 186 | Lincoln, NE | 3,496.0 |
| 240 | Chico, CA | 2,915.2 | 108 | Fresno, CA | 4,438.0 | 4 | Little Rock, AR | 7,866.8 |
| 425 | Chino Hills, CA | 1,321.8 | 383 | Frisco, TX | 1,902.6 | 350 | Livermore, CA | 2,169.5 |

| RANK | CITY | RATE | RANK | CITY | RATE | RANK | CITY | RATE |
|---|---|---|---|---|---|---|---|---|
| 365 | Livonia, MI | 2,059.4 | 263 | Pasadena, CA | 2,718.6 | 253 | South Gate, CA | 2,822.4 |
| 258 | Long Beach, CA | 2,767.7 | 177 | Pasadena, TX | 3,590.8 | 263 | Sparks, NV | 2,718.6 |
| 335 | Longmont, CO | 2,246.3 | 251 | Paterson, NJ | 2,826.7 | 28 | Spokane Valley, WA | 5,849.1 |
| 133 | Longview, TX | 4,149.0 | 376 | Pearland, TX | 1,963.7 | 2 | Spokane, WA | 9,321.6 |
| 342 | Los Angeles, CA | 2,213.2 | 311 | Pembroke Pines, FL | 2,482.4 | 60 | Springfield, IL | 5,031.9 |
| 119 | Louisville, KY | 4,288.4 | 324 | Peoria, AZ | 2,369.4 | 95 | Springfield, MA | 4,631.3 |
| 224 | Lowell, MA | 3,087.3 | 159 | Peoria, IL | 3,807.6 | 3 | Springfield, MO | 9,009.5 |
| 78 | Lubbock, TX | 4,858.4 | 189 | Philadelphia, PA | 3,441.5 | 413 | Stamford, CT | 1,539.6 |
| 298 | Lynchburg, VA | 2,538.7 | 147 | Phoenix, AZ | 4,000.0 | 382 | Sterling Heights, MI | 1,903.0 |
| 286 | Lynn, MA | 2,613.1 | 202 | Pittsburgh, PA | 3,265.9 | 61 | Stockton, CA | 5,030.1 |
| 5 | Macon, GA | 7,458.0 | 353 | Plano, TX | 2,150.1 | 332 | St. George, UT | 2,261.0 |
| 211 | Madison, WI | 3,186.9 | 185 | Plantation, FL | 3,503.9 | 36 | St. Joseph, MO | 5,608.5 |
| 161 | Manchester, NH | 3,798.5 | 243 | Pomona, CA | 2,902.6 | 10 | St. Louis, MO | 6,619.4 |
| 149 | McAllen, TX | 3,983.3 | 70 | Pompano Beach, FL | 4,933.1 | 166 | St. Paul, MN | 3,723.6 |
| 362 | McKinney, TX | 2,080.1 | 418 | Port St. Lucie, FL | 1,448.7 | 47 | St. Petersburg, FL | 5,334.6 |
| 15 | Medford, OR | 6,254.8 | 76 | Portland, OR | 4,864.8 | 232 | Suffolk, VA | 3,020.8 |
| 114 | Melbourne, FL | 4,370.0 | 40 | Portsmouth, VA | 5,519.6 | 380 | Sugar Land, TX | 1,932.7 |
| 23 | Memphis, TN | 6,052.1 | 107 | Providence, RI | 4,457.6 | 407 | Sunnyvale, CA | 1,642.8 |
| 368 | Menifee, CA | 2,033.1 | 321 | Provo, UT | 2,403.0 | 172 | Sunrise, FL | 3,643.4 |
| 204 | Merced, CA | 3,254.7 | 7 | Pueblo, CO | 7,029.3 | 402 | Surprise, AZ | 1,730.7 |
| 428 | Meridian, ID | 1,255.1 | 400 | Quincy, MA | 1,761.7 | 102 | Syracuse, NY | 4,500.3 |
| 250 | Mesa, AZ | 2,831.5 | 155 | Racine, WI | 3,852.0 | 12 | Tacoma, WA | 6,549.4 |
| 110 | Mesquite, TX | 4,387.7 | 228 | Raleigh, NC | 3,063.0 | 118 | Tallahassee, FL | 4,300.7 |
| 1 | Miami Beach, FL | 10,664.6 | 441 | Ramapo, NY | 650.2 | 306 | Tampa, FL | 2,511.4 |
| 131 | Miami Gardens, FL | 4,165.5 | 340 | Rancho Cucamon., CA | 2,219.9 | 275 | Temecula, CA | 2,669.7 |
| 63 | Miami, FL | 5,002.0 | 213 | Reading, PA | 3,176.8 | 92 | Tempe, AZ | 4,674.2 |
| 287 | Midland, TX | 2,610.0 | 135 | Redding, CA | 4,145.7 | 283 | Thornton, CO | 2,620.6 |
| 103 | Milwaukee, WI | 4,496.1 | 326 | Redwood City, CA | 2,347.3 | 429 | Thousand Oaks, CA | 1,244.5 |
| 74 | Minneapolis, MN | 4,885.8 | 223 | Reno, NV | 3,087.4 | NA | Toledo, OH** | NA |
| 318 | Miramar, FL | 2,416.6 | 56 | Renton, WA | 5,108.8 | 234 | Toms River Twnshp, NJ | 2,969.7 |
| 435 | Mission Viejo, CA | 1,040.7 | 277 | Rialto, CA | 2,650.2 | 59 | Topeka, KS | 5,066.8 |
| 174 | Mission, TX | 3,619.7 | 281 | Richardson, TX | 2,637.3 | 384 | Torrance, CA | 1,888.4 |
| 55 | Mobile, AL | 5,192.8 | 104 | Richmond, CA | 4,496.0 | 282 | Tracy, CA | 2,625.2 |
| 73 | Modesto, CA | 4,890.5 | 139 | Richmond, VA | 4,089.6 | 261 | Trenton, NJ | 2,748.7 |
| 239 | Moreno Valley, CA | 2,917.3 | 198 | Riverside, CA | 3,352.5 | 389 | Troy, MI | 1,876.3 |
| 345 | Mountain View, CA | 2,204.2 | 99 | Roanoke, VA | 4,538.1 | 11 | Tucson, AZ | 6,581.9 |
| 184 | Murfreesboro, TN | 3,504.7 | 327 | Rochester, MN | 2,332.3 | 48 | Tulsa, OK | 5,317.6 |
| 414 | Murrieta, CA | 1,521.8 | 86 | Rochester, NY | 4,773.4 | 85 | Tuscaloosa, AL | 4,793.6 |
| 341 | Nampa, ID | 2,216.6 | 91 | Rockford, IL | 4,686.1 | 391 | Tustin, CA | 1,868.4 |
| 396 | Napa, CA | 1,789.0 | 279 | Roseville, CA | 2,648.2 | 138 | Tyler, TX | 4,114.6 |
| 427 | Naperville, IL | 1,295.9 | 344 | Roswell, GA | 2,209.2 | 236 | Upland, CA | 2,953.5 |
| 292 | Nashua, NH | 2,582.4 | 338 | Round Rock, TX | 2,236.2 | 337 | Upper Darby Twnshp, PA | 2,237.5 |
| 157 | Nashville, TN | 3,847.9 | 164 | Sacramento, CA | 3,760.1 | 339 | Vacaville, CA | 2,221.6 |
| 175 | New Bedford, MA | 3,612.0 | 120 | Salem, OR | 4,286.1 | 82 | Vallejo, CA | 4,845.5 |
| 96 | New Haven, CT | 4,629.6 | 190 | Salinas, CA | 3,439.0 | 178 | Vancouver, WA | 3,562.6 |
| 154 | New Orleans, LA | 3,852.6 | 6 | Salt Lake City, UT | 7,075.6 | 167 | Ventura, CA | 3,721.7 |
| 399 | New Rochelle, NY | 1,765.2 | 168 | San Angelo, TX | 3,716.1 | 192 | Victorville, CA | 3,422.4 |
| 406 | New York, NY | 1,690.9 | 34 | San Antonio, TX | 5,715.0 | 310 | Virginia Beach, VA | 2,490.9 |
| 208 | Newark, NJ | 3,222.0 | 112 | San Bernardino, CA | 4,380.8 | 162 | Visalia, CA | 3,796.6 |
| 313 | Newport Beach, CA | 2,462.4 | 325 | San Diego, CA | 2,351.4 | 357 | Vista, CA | 2,114.5 |
| 226 | Newport News, VA | 3,082.7 | 33 | San Francisco, CA | 5,795.2 | 123 | Waco, TX | 4,250.2 |
| 438 | Newton, MA | 929.0 | 293 | San Jose, CA | 2,571.2 | 285 | Warren, MI | 2,614.7 |
| 113 | Norfolk, VA | 4,372.0 | 100 | San Leandro, CA | 4,526.2 | 312 | Warwick, RI | 2,463.7 |
| 304 | Norman, OK | 2,514.3 | 409 | San Marcos, CA | 1,596.1 | 98 | Washington, DC | 4,574.1 |
| 35 | North Charleston, SC | 5,617.3 | 366 | San Mateo, CA | 2,056.0 | 125 | Waterbury, CT | 4,223.6 |
| 280 | North Las Vegas, NV | 2,645.5 | 267 | Sandy Springs, GA | 2,707.1 | 252 | Waukegan, IL | 2,826.6 |
| 359 | Norwalk, CA | 2,108.6 | 200 | Sandy, UT | 3,271.0 | 220 | West Covina, CA | 3,124.2 |
| 375 | Norwalk, CT | 1,972.8 | 381 | Santa Ana, CA | 1,930.3 | 88 | West Palm Beach, FL | 4,743.9 |
| 17 | Oakland, CA | 6,233.4 | 235 | Santa Barbara, CA | 2,966.5 | 71 | West Valley, UT | 4,918.5 |
| 288 | Oceanside, CA | 2,604.8 | 302 | Santa Clara, CA | 2,516.0 | 242 | Westland, MI | 2,906.0 |
| 142 | Odessa, TX | 4,040.1 | 424 | Santa Clarita, CA | 1,323.7 | 270 | Westminster, CA | 2,694.7 |
| 417 | O'Fallon, MO | 1,473.3 | 246 | Santa Maria, CA | 2,875.0 | 265 | Westminster, CO | 2,713.2 |
| 87 | Ogden, UT | 4,765.3 | 158 | Santa Monica, CA | 3,831.8 | 260 | Whittier, CA | 2,756.5 |
| 46 | Oklahoma City, OK | 5,368.1 | 367 | Santa Rosa, CA | 2,043.6 | 115 | Wichita Falls, TX | 4,361.1 |
| 403 | Olathe, KS | 1,730.6 | 176 | Savannah, GA | 3,596.1 | 44 | Wichita, KS | 5,382.3 |
| 105 | Omaha, NE | 4,495.2 | 294 | Scottsdale, AZ | 2,556.7 | 64 | Wilmington, NC | 4,999.8 |
| 272 | Ontario, CA | 2,680.4 | 233 | Scranton, PA | 3,006.7 | 42 | Winston-Salem, NC | 5,450.6 |
| 404 | Orange, CA | 1,723.4 | 38 | Seattle, WA | 5,582.2 | 369 | Woodbridge Twnshp, NJ | 2,030.5 |
| 331 | Orem, UT | 2,273.7 | 89 | Shreveport, LA | 4,740.1 | 194 | Worcester, MA | 3,400.9 |
| 14 | Orlando, FL | 6,511.3 | 423 | Simi Valley, CA | 1,354.0 | 62 | Yakima, WA | 5,004.9 |
| 378 | Overland Park, KS | 1,955.1 | 109 | Sioux City, IA | 4,424.5 | 431 | Yonkers, NY | 1,189.1 |
| 308 | Oxnard, CA | 2,504.5 | 230 | Sioux Falls, SD | 3,047.8 | 181 | Yuma, AZ | 3,515.1 |
| 390 | Palm Bay, FL | 1,875.6 | 377 | Somerville, MA | 1,961.0 | | | |
| 356 | Palmdale, CA | 2,136.4 | 79 | South Bend, IN | 4,855.5 | | | |

Source: CQ Press using reported data from the F.B.I. "Crime in the United States 2013"

*Property crimes are offenses of burglary, larceny-theft, and motor vehicle theft. Attempts are included.

**Not available.

# 66. Property Crime Rate in 2013 (continued)
## National Rate = 2,730.7 Property Crimes per 100,000 Population*

| RANK | CITY | RATE | RANK | CITY | RATE | RANK | CITY | RATE |
|---|---|---|---|---|---|---|---|---|
| 1 | Miami Beach, FL | 10,664.6 | 75 | Evansville, IN | 4,871.0 | 149 | McAllen, TX | 3,983.3 |
| 2 | Spokane, WA | 9,321.6 | 76 | Portland, OR | 4,864.8 | 150 | Clearwater, FL | 3,963.0 |
| 3 | Springfield, MO | 9,009.5 | 77 | Akron, OH | 4,863.3 | 151 | Arlington, TX | 3,960.2 |
| 4 | Little Rock, AR | 7,866.8 | 78 | Lubbock, TX | 4,858.4 | 152 | Gainesville, FL | 3,938.7 |
| 5 | Macon, GA | 7,458.0 | 79 | South Bend, IN | 4,855.5 | 153 | Jacksonville, FL | 3,902.7 |
| 6 | Salt Lake City, UT | 7,075.6 | 80 | Hemet, CA | 4,850.8 | 154 | New Orleans, LA | 3,852.6 |
| 7 | Pueblo, CO | 7,029.3 | 81 | Austin, TX | 4,849.6 | 155 | Racine, WI | 3,852.0 |
| 8 | Birmingham, AL | 6,677.8 | 82 | Vallejo, CA | 4,845.5 | 156 | Fort Wayne, IN | 3,848.6 |
| 9 | Chattanooga, TN | 6,656.4 | 83 | Des Moines, IA | 4,829.0 | 157 | Nashville, TN | 3,847.9 |
| 10 | St. Louis, MO | 6,619.4 | 84 | Buffalo, NY | 4,826.7 | 158 | Santa Monica, CA | 3,831.8 |
| 11 | Tucson, AZ | 6,581.9 | 85 | Tuscaloosa, AL | 4,793.6 | 159 | Peoria, IL | 3,807.6 |
| 12 | Tacoma, WA | 6,549.4 | 86 | Rochester, NY | 4,773.4 | 160 | Columbia, MO | 3,804.1 |
| 13 | Everett, WA | 6,530.1 | 87 | Ogden, UT | 4,765.3 | 161 | Manchester, NH | 3,798.5 |
| 14 | Orlando, FL | 6,511.3 | 88 | West Palm Beach, FL | 4,743.9 | 162 | Visalia, CA | 3,796.6 |
| 15 | Medford, OR | 6,254.8 | 89 | Shreveport, LA | 4,740.1 | 163 | Bloomington, MN | 3,771.1 |
| 16 | Knoxville, TN | 6,241.8 | 90 | Lakewood, CO | 4,710.9 | 164 | Sacramento, CA | 3,760.1 |
| 17 | Oakland, CA | 6,233.4 | 91 | Rockford, IL | 4,686.1 | 165 | Largo, FL | 3,752.9 |
| 18 | Columbus, GA | 6,201.4 | 92 | Tempe, AZ | 4,674.2 | 166 | St. Paul, MN | 3,723.6 |
| 19 | Lafayette, LA | 6,132.5 | 93 | Bakersfield, CA | 4,646.6 | 167 | Ventura, CA | 3,721.7 |
| 20 | Atlanta, GA | 6,103.5 | 94 | Corpus Christi, TX | 4,642.3 | 168 | San Angelo, TX | 3,716.1 |
| 21 | Independence, MO | 6,055.5 | 95 | Springfield, MA | 4,631.3 | 169 | Cedar Rapids, IA | 3,659.0 |
| 22 | Fayetteville, NC | 6,054.1 | 96 | New Haven, CT | 4,629.6 | 170 | Denver, CO | 3,653.6 |
| 23 | Memphis, TN | 6,052.1 | 97 | Berkeley, CA | 4,626.7 | 171 | Charlotte, NC | 3,649.4 |
| 24 | Columbia, SC | 6,041.3 | 98 | Washington, DC | 4,574.1 | 172 | Sunrise, FL | 3,643.4 |
| 25 | Albany, GA | 6,024.7 | 99 | Roanoke, VA | 4,538.1 | 173 | Allentown, PA | 3,625.2 |
| 26 | Gary, IN | 5,987.1 | 100 | San Leandro, CA | 4,526.2 | 174 | Mission, TX | 3,619.7 |
| 27 | Cleveland, OH | 5,953.0 | 101 | Kent, WA | 4,503.1 | 175 | New Bedford, MA | 3,612.0 |
| 28 | Spokane Valley, WA | 5,849.1 | 102 | Syracuse, NY | 4,500.3 | 176 | Savannah, GA | 3,596.1 |
| 29 | Jackson, MS | 5,841.9 | 103 | Milwaukee, WI | 4,496.1 | 177 | Pasadena, TX | 3,590.8 |
| 30 | Detroit, MI | 5,834.5 | 104 | Richmond, CA | 4,496.0 | 178 | Vancouver, WA | 3,562.6 |
| 31 | Glendale, AZ | 5,822.9 | 105 | Omaha, NE | 4,495.2 | 179 | Garland, TX | 3,551.8 |
| 32 | Cincinnati, OH | 5,811.6 | 106 | Hollywood, FL | 4,466.6 | 180 | Chicago, IL | 3,525.3 |
| 33 | San Francisco, CA | 5,795.2 | 107 | Providence, RI | 4,457.6 | 181 | Yuma, AZ | 3,515.1 |
| 34 | San Antonio, TX | 5,715.0 | 108 | Fresno, CA | 4,438.0 | 182 | Davie, FL | 3,513.1 |
| 35 | North Charleston, SC | 5,617.3 | 109 | Sioux City, IA | 4,424.5 | 183 | Killeen, TX | 3,508.9 |
| 36 | St. Joseph, MO | 5,608.5 | 110 | Greenville, NC | 4,387.7 | 184 | Murfreesboro, TN | 3,504.7 |
| 37 | Fort Lauderdale, FL | 5,597.5 | 110 | Mesquite, TX | 4,387.7 | 185 | Plantation, FL | 3,503.9 |
| 38 | Seattle, WA | 5,582.2 | 112 | San Bernardino, CA | 4,380.8 | 186 | Lincoln, NE | 3,496.0 |
| 39 | Federal Way, WA | 5,577.9 | 113 | Norfolk, VA | 4,372.0 | 187 | Lansing, MI | 3,476.5 |
| 40 | Portsmouth, VA | 5,519.6 | 114 | Melbourne, FL | 4,370.0 | 188 | Concord, CA | 3,472.7 |
| 41 | Albuquerque, NM | 5,469.9 | 115 | Wichita Falls, TX | 4,361.1 | 189 | Philadelphia, PA | 3,441.5 |
| 42 | Winston-Salem, NC | 5,450.6 | 116 | Fort Worth, TX | 4,343.5 | 190 | Salinas, CA | 3,439.0 |
| 43 | Dayton, OH | 5,422.7 | 117 | Brownsville, TX | 4,316.3 | 191 | Cheektowaga, NY | 3,431.6 |
| 44 | Wichita, KS | 5,382.3 | 118 | Tallahassee, FL | 4,300.7 | 192 | Victorville, CA | 3,422.4 |
| 45 | Lakeland, FL | 5,371.1 | 119 | Louisville, KY | 4,288.4 | 193 | Clovis, CA | 3,421.7 |
| 46 | Oklahoma City, OK | 5,368.1 | 120 | Salem, OR | 4,286.1 | 194 | Worcester, MA | 3,400.9 |
| 47 | St. Petersburg, FL | 5,334.6 | 121 | Flint, MI | 4,263.5 | 195 | Athens-Clarke, GA | 3,391.6 |
| 48 | Tulsa, OK | 5,317.6 | 122 | Las Cruces, NM | 4,263.4 | 196 | Brockton, MA | 3,376.5 |
| 49 | Kansas City, MO | 5,294.8 | 123 | Waco, TX | 4,250.2 | 197 | Indio, CA | 3,363.5 |
| 50 | Fort Smith, AR | 5,261.8 | 124 | Laredo, TX | 4,237.7 | 198 | Riverside, CA | 3,352.5 |
| 51 | Indianapolis, IN | 5,246.4 | 125 | Waterbury, CT | 4,223.6 | 199 | Greeley, CO | 3,349.3 |
| 52 | Beaumont, TX | 5,239.6 | 126 | High Point, NC | 4,185.1 | 200 | Sandy, UT | 3,271.0 |
| 53 | Edinburg, TX | 5,216.9 | 127 | Albany, NY | 4,175.3 | 201 | Hampton, VA | 3,266.2 |
| 54 | Billings, MT | 5,198.4 | 128 | Davenport, IA | 4,171.5 | 202 | Pittsburgh, PA | 3,265.9 |
| 55 | Mobile, AL | 5,192.8 | 129 | Antioch, CA | 4,171.1 | 203 | Fairfield, CA | 3,259.4 |
| 56 | Renton, WA | 5,108.8 | 130 | Colorado Springs, CO | 4,167.5 | 204 | Merced, CA | 3,254.7 |
| 57 | Lawton, OK | 5,101.1 | 131 | Miami Gardens, FL | 4,165.5 | 205 | Kennewick, WA | 3,238.9 |
| 58 | Houston, TX | 5,086.6 | 132 | Dallas, TX | 4,165.2 | 206 | Grand Rapids, MI | 3,236.2 |
| 59 | Topeka, KS | 5,066.8 | 133 | Longview, TX | 4,149.0 | 207 | Dearborn, MI | 3,232.9 |
| 60 | Springfield, IL | 5,031.9 | 134 | Amarillo, TX | 4,148.0 | 208 | Newark, NJ | 3,222.0 |
| 61 | Stockton, CA | 5,030.1 | 135 | Redding, CA | 4,145.7 | 209 | Hayward, CA | 3,208.9 |
| 62 | Yakima, WA | 5,004.9 | 136 | Gresham, OR | 4,140.4 | 210 | Las Vegas, NV | 3,196.9 |
| 63 | Miami, FL | 5,002.0 | 137 | Greensboro, NC | 4,130.0 | 211 | Madison, WI | 3,186.9 |
| 64 | Wilmington, NC | 4,999.8 | 138 | Tyler, TX | 4,114.6 | 212 | Erie, PA | 3,182.1 |
| 65 | Eugene, OR | 4,996.9 | 139 | Richmond, VA | 4,089.6 | 213 | Reading, PA | 3,176.8 |
| 66 | Huntsville, AL | 4,988.7 | 140 | Hammond, IN | 4,078.0 | 214 | Bloomington, IN | 3,162.0 |
| 67 | Duluth, MN | 4,968.0 | 141 | Fayetteville, AR | 4,070.6 | 215 | Costa Mesa, CA | 3,159.8 |
| 68 | Baton Rouge, LA | 4,959.8 | 142 | Odessa, TX | 4,040.1 | 216 | Decatur, IL | 3,150.7 |
| 69 | Baltimore, MD | 4,944.7 | 143 | Lexington, KY | 4,031.9 | 217 | Aurora, CO | 3,140.2 |
| 70 | Pompano Beach, FL | 4,933.1 | 144 | Hartford, CT | 4,031.2 | 218 | Brooklyn Park, MN | 3,134.5 |
| 71 | West Valley, UT | 4,918.5 | 145 | Lawrence, KS | 4,026.3 | 219 | Jurupa Valley, CA | 3,124.7 |
| 72 | Kansas City, KS | 4,896.4 | 146 | Anchorage, AK | 4,018.0 | 220 | West Covina, CA | 3,124.2 |
| 73 | Modesto, CA | 4,890.5 | 147 | Phoenix, AZ | 4,000.0 | 221 | Citrus Heights, CA | 3,108.9 |
| 74 | Minneapolis, MN | 4,885.8 | 148 | Abilene, TX | 3,994.1 | 222 | Bellevue, WA | 3,092.9 |

| RANK | CITY | RATE | RANK | CITY | RATE | RANK | CITY | RATE |
|---|---|---|---|---|---|---|---|---|
| 223 | Reno, NV | 3,087.4 | 297 | Lakewood, CA | 2,543.0 | 371 | Fontana, CA | 2,009.6 |
| 224 | Lowell, MA | 3,087.3 | 298 | Lynchburg, VA | 2,538.7 | 372 | Alexandria, VA | 1,997.7 |
| 225 | Hoover, AL | 3,085.4 | 299 | Fort Collins, CO | 2,537.6 | 373 | Henderson, NV | 1,997.5 |
| 226 | Newport News, VA | 3,082.7 | 300 | Chino, CA | 2,532.7 | 374 | Broken Arrow, OK | 1,975.6 |
| 227 | Concord, NC | 3,074.8 | 301 | Huntington Beach, CA | 2,519.4 | 375 | Norwalk, CT | 1,972.8 |
| 228 | Raleigh, NC | 3,063.0 | 302 | Santa Clara, CA | 2,516.0 | 376 | Pearland, TX | 1,963.7 |
| 229 | Deerfield Beach, FL | 3,051.0 | 303 | Hesperia, CA | 2,515.6 | 377 | Somerville, MA | 1,961.0 |
| 230 | Sioux Falls, SD | 3,047.8 | 304 | Norman, OK | 2,514.3 | 378 | Overland Park, KS | 1,955.1 |
| 231 | Bridgeport, CT | 3,035.2 | 305 | Evanston, IL | 2,512.3 | 379 | Garden Grove, CA | 1,936.0 |
| 232 | Suffolk, VA | 3,020.8 | 306 | Tampa, FL | 2,511.4 | 380 | Sugar Land, TX | 1,932.7 |
| 233 | Scranton, PA | 3,006.7 | 307 | Charleston, SC | 2,509.3 | 381 | Santa Ana, CA | 1,930.3 |
| 234 | Toms River Twnshp, NJ | 2,969.7 | 308 | Oxnard, CA | 2,504.5 | 382 | Sterling Heights, MI | 1,903.0 |
| 235 | Santa Barbara, CA | 2,966.5 | 309 | Alameda, CA | 2,495.9 | 383 | Frisco, TX | 1,902.6 |
| 236 | Upland, CA | 2,953.5 | 310 | Virginia Beach, VA | 2,490.9 | 384 | Torrance, CA | 1,888.4 |
| 237 | Bryan, TX | 2,941.0 | 311 | Pembroke Pines, FL | 2,482.4 | 385 | El Monte, CA | 1,887.7 |
| 238 | Lawrence, MA | 2,921.1 | 312 | Warwick, RI | 2,463.7 | 386 | Carlsbad, CA | 1,886.8 |
| 239 | Moreno Valley, CA | 2,917.3 | 313 | Newport Beach, CA | 2,462.4 | 387 | Jersey City, NJ | 1,882.5 |
| 240 | Chico, CA | 2,915.2 | 314 | Kenosha, WI | 2,451.8 | 388 | Clarkstown, NY | 1,877.2 |
| 241 | Downey, CA | 2,907.6 | 315 | Bloomington, IL | 2,435.3 | 389 | Troy, MI | 1,876.3 |
| 242 | Westland, MI | 2,906.0 | 316 | Inglewood, CA | 2,433.9 | 390 | Palm Bay, FL | 1,875.6 |
| 243 | Pomona, CA | 2,902.9 | 317 | Bellflower, CA | 2,425.4 | 391 | Tustin, CA | 1,868.4 |
| 244 | Fargo, ND | 2,888.4 | 318 | Miramar, FL | 2,416.6 | 392 | Edmond, OK | 1,855.2 |
| 245 | Elizabeth, NJ | 2,876.4 | 319 | Carson, CA | 2,409.7 | 393 | Elk Grove, CA | 1,841.2 |
| 246 | Santa Maria, CA | 2,875.0 | 320 | Arvada, CO | 2,406.3 | 394 | Fremont, CA | 1,825.1 |
| 247 | Boulder, CO | 2,866.9 | 321 | Provo, UT | 2,403.0 | 395 | Amherst, NY | 1,790.4 |
| 248 | Clarksville, TN | 2,844.1 | 322 | Greece, NY | 2,382.4 | 396 | Napa, CA | 1,789.0 |
| 249 | Bend, OR | 2,836.4 | 323 | Chandler, AZ | 2,372.2 | 397 | Clifton, NJ | 1,788.9 |
| 250 | Mesa, AZ | 2,831.5 | 324 | Peoria, AZ | 2,369.4 | 398 | Baldwin Park, CA | 1,785.1 |
| 251 | Paterson, NJ | 2,826.7 | 325 | San Diego, CA | 2,351.4 | 399 | New Rochelle, NY | 1,765.2 |
| 252 | Waukegan, IL | 2,826.6 | 326 | Redwood City, CA | 2,347.3 | 400 | Quincy, MA | 1,761.7 |
| 253 | South Gate, CA | 2,822.4 | 327 | Rochester, MN | 2,332.3 | 401 | Daly City, CA | 1,753.5 |
| 254 | Grand Prairie, TX | 2,806.0 | 328 | Carrollton, TX | 2,322.3 | 402 | Surprise, AZ | 1,730.7 |
| 255 | Hialeah, FL | 2,797.0 | 329 | Burbank, CA | 2,320.3 | 403 | Olathe, KS | 1,730.6 |
| 256 | Anaheim, CA | 2,783.2 | 330 | El Paso, TX | 2,289.0 | 404 | Orange, CA | 1,723.4 |
| 257 | Boston, MA | 2,773.1 | 331 | Orem, UT | 2,273.7 | 405 | Elgin, IL | 1,722.0 |
| 258 | Long Beach, CA | 2,767.7 | 332 | St. George, UT | 2,261.0 | 406 | New York, NY | 1,690.9 |
| 259 | Fullerton, CA | 2,762.8 | 333 | College Station, TX | 2,254.4 | 407 | Sunnyvale, CA | 1,642.8 |
| 260 | Whittier, CA | 2,756.5 | 334 | Denton, TX | 2,253.0 | 408 | Glendale, CA | 1,636.9 |
| 261 | Trenton, NJ | 2,748.7 | 335 | Longmont, CO | 2,246.3 | 409 | San Marcos, CA | 1,596.1 |
| 262 | Champaign, IL | 2,742.1 | 336 | Hillsboro, OR | 2,242.7 | 410 | Beaverton, OR | 1,572.4 |
| 263 | Pasadena, CA | 2,718.6 | 337 | Upper Darby Twnshp, PA | 2,237.5 | 411 | Brick Twnshp, NJ | 1,569.6 |
| 263 | Sparks, NV | 2,718.6 | 338 | Round Rock, TX | 2,236.2 | 412 | Gilbert, AZ | 1,541.5 |
| 265 | Westminster, CO | 2,713.2 | 339 | Vacaville, CA | 2,221.6 | 413 | Stamford, CT | 1,539.6 |
| 266 | Cambridge, MA | 2,709.7 | 340 | Rancho Cucamon., CA | 2,219.9 | 414 | Murrieta, CA | 1,521.8 |
| 267 | Sandy Springs, GA | 2,707.1 | 341 | Nampa, ID | 2,216.6 | 415 | Danbury, CT | 1,507.9 |
| 268 | Irving, TX | 2,704.0 | 342 | Los Angeles, CA | 2,213.2 | 416 | Aurora, IL | 1,481.9 |
| 269 | Lewisville, TX | 2,701.8 | 343 | Boise, ID | 2,212.0 | 417 | O'Fallon, MO | 1,473.3 |
| 270 | Westminster, CA | 2,694.7 | 344 | Roswell, GA | 2,209.2 | 418 | Port St. Lucie, FL | 1,448.7 |
| 271 | Chesapeake, VA | 2,683.7 | 345 | Mountain View, CA | 2,204.2 | 419 | Canton Twnshp, MI | 1,405.2 |
| 272 | Ontario, CA | 2,680.4 | 346 | Lancaster, CA | 2,187.2 | 420 | Cary, NC | 1,393.5 |
| 273 | El Cajon, CA | 2,676.2 | 347 | Clinton Twnshp, MI | 2,176.0 | 421 | Irvine, CA | 1,393.0 |
| 274 | Bethlehem, PA | 2,675.2 | 348 | Cranston, RI | 2,174.2 | 422 | Farmington Hills, MI | 1,373.9 |
| 275 | Temecula, CA | 2,669.7 | 349 | Cicero, IL | 2,173.3 | 423 | Simi Valley, CA | 1,354.0 |
| 276 | Escondido, CA | 2,667.3 | 350 | Livermore, CA | 2,169.5 | 424 | Santa Clarita, CA | 1,323.7 |
| 277 | Rialto, CA | 2,650.2 | 351 | Joliet, IL | 2,166.9 | 425 | Chino Hills, CA | 1,321.8 |
| 278 | Fall River, MA | 2,649.6 | 352 | Ann Arbor, MI | 2,161.8 | 426 | Allen, TX | 1,320.0 |
| 279 | Roseville, CA | 2,648.2 | 353 | Plano, TX | 2,150.1 | 427 | Naperville, IL | 1,295.9 |
| 280 | North Las Vegas, NV | 2,645.5 | 354 | Corona, CA | 2,147.2 | 428 | Meridian, ID | 1,255.1 |
| 281 | Richardson, TX | 2,637.3 | 355 | League City, TX | 2,140.7 | 429 | Thousand Oaks, CA | 1,244.5 |
| 282 | Tracy, CA | 2,625.2 | 356 | Palmdale, CA | 2,136.4 | 430 | Edison Twnshp, NJ | 1,228.8 |
| 283 | Thornton, CO | 2,620.6 | 357 | Vista, CA | 2,114.5 | 431 | Yonkers, NY | 1,189.1 |
| 284 | Buena Park, CA | 2,620.1 | 358 | Lee's Summit, MO | 2,110.7 | 432 | Centennial, CO | 1,139.6 |
| 285 | Warren, MI | 2,614.7 | 359 | Norwalk, CA | 2,108.6 | 433 | Lakewood Twnshp, NJ | 1,077.0 |
| 286 | Lynn, MA | 2,613.1 | 360 | Alhambra, CA | 2,094.2 | 434 | Arlington Heights, IL | 1,052.9 |
| 287 | Midland, TX | 2,610.0 | 361 | Hamilton Twnshp, NJ | 2,092.3 | 435 | Mission Viejo, CA | 1,040.7 |
| 288 | Oceanside, CA | 2,604.8 | 362 | McKinney, TX | 2,080.1 | 436 | Lake Forest, CA | 1,024.8 |
| 289 | Hawthorne, CA | 2,603.0 | 363 | Chula Vista, CA | 2,071.6 | 437 | Fishers, IN | 990.9 |
| 290 | Boca Raton, FL | 2,593.8 | 364 | Cape Coral, FL | 2,064.7 | 438 | Newton, MA | 929.0 |
| 291 | Compton, CA | 2,592.3 | 365 | Livonia, MI | 2,059.4 | 439 | Carmel, IN | 876.5 |
| 292 | Nashua, NH | 2,582.4 | 366 | San Mateo, CA | 2,056.0 | 440 | Johns Creek, GA | 736.1 |
| 293 | San Jose, CA | 2,571.2 | 367 | Santa Rosa, CA | 2,043.6 | 441 | Ramapo, NY | 650.2 |
| 294 | Scottsdale, AZ | 2,556.7 | 368 | Menifee, CA | 2,033.1 | NA | Toledo, OH** | NA |
| 295 | Colonie, NY | 2,544.3 | 369 | Woodbridge Twnshp, NJ | 2,030.5 | | | |
| 296 | Green Bay, WI | 2,544.1 | 370 | Coral Springs, FL | 2,025.9 | | | |

Source: CQ Press using reported data from the F.B.I. "Crime in the United States 2013"

*Property crimes are offenses of burglary, larceny-theft, and motor vehicle theft. Attempts are included.

**Not available.

# 67. Percent Change in Property Crime Rate: 2012 to 2013
## National Percent Change = 4.8% Decrease*

| RANK | CITY | % CHANGE | RANK | CITY | % CHANGE | RANK | CITY | % CHANGE |
|---|---|---|---|---|---|---|---|---|
| 33 | Abilene, TX | 9.0 | 221 | Chino, CA | (4.5) | 180 | Fullerton, CA | (2.8) |
| 197 | Akron, OH | (3.8) | 96 | Chula Vista, CA | 1.9 | 197 | Gainesville, FL | (3.8) |
| 127 | Alameda, CA | (0.4) | 412 | Cicero, IL | (17.5) | 400 | Garden Grove, CA | (15.6) |
| 242 | Albany, GA | (5.4) | 239 | Cincinnati, OH | (5.3) | 197 | Garland, TX | (3.8) |
| 247 | Albany, NY | (5.5) | 394 | Citrus Heights, CA | (15.1) | 41 | Gary, IN | 7.7 |
| 96 | Albuquerque, NM | 1.9 | 127 | Clarkstown, NY | (0.4) | 176 | Gilbert, AZ | (2.5) |
| 176 | Alexandria, VA | (2.5) | 69 | Clarksville, TN | 4.4 | 330 | Glendale, AZ | (9.2) |
| 297 | Alhambra, CA | (7.8) | 101 | Clearwater, FL | 1.5 | 63 | Glendale, CA | 4.8 |
| 256 | Allentown, PA | (6.0) | 191 | Cleveland, OH | (3.6) | 180 | Grand Prairie, TX | (2.8) |
| 415 | Allen, TX | (18.2) | 205 | Clifton, NJ | (4.1) | 284 | Grand Rapids, MI | (7.1) |
| 312 | Amarillo, TX | (8.4) | 239 | Clinton Twnshp, MI | (5.3) | 341 | Greece, NY | (9.8) |
| 278 | Amherst, NY | (6.9) | 407 | Clovis, CA | (16.8) | 132 | Greeley, CO | (0.6) |
| 229 | Anaheim, CA | (4.8) | 330 | College Station, TX | (9.2) | 335 | Green Bay, WI | (9.4) |
| 11 | Anchorage, AK | 14.0 | 266 | Colonie, NY | (6.4) | 247 | Greensboro, NC | (5.5) |
| 322 | Ann Arbor, MI | (8.8) | 109 | Colorado Springs, CO | 0.7 | 140 | Greenville, NC | (0.9) |
| 301 | Antioch, CA | (7.9) | 126 | Columbia, MO | (0.3) | 297 | Gresham, OR | (7.8) |
| 419 | Arlington Heights, IL | (18.8) | NA | Columbia, SC** | NA | 251 | Hamilton Twnshp, NJ | (5.7) |
| 132 | Arlington, TX | (0.6) | 38 | Columbus, GA | 8.0 | 210 | Hammond, IN | (4.2) |
| 109 | Arvada, CO | 0.7 | 55 | Compton, CA | 6.0 | 188 | Hampton, VA | (3.3) |
| 382 | Athens-Clarke, GA | (13.4) | 70 | Concord, CA | 4.0 | 234 | Hartford, CT | (5.1) |
| 272 | Atlanta, GA | (6.6) | NA | Concord, NC** | NA | 91 | Hawthorne, CA | 2.3 |
| 59 | Aurora, CO | 5.2 | 345 | Coral Springs, FL | (10.2) | 149 | Hayward, CA | (1.3) |
| 409 | Aurora, IL | (17.0) | 417 | Corona, CA | (18.5) | 14 | Hemet, CA | 13.0 |
| 284 | Austin, TX | (7.1) | 81 | Corpus Christi, TX | 3.2 | 132 | Henderson, NV | (0.6) |
| 278 | Bakersfield, CA | (6.9) | 376 | Costa Mesa, CA | (12.7) | 284 | Hesperia, CA | (7.1) |
| 385 | Baldwin Park, CA | (13.7) | 314 | Cranston, RI | (8.5) | 335 | Hialeah, FL | (9.4) |
| 52 | Baltimore, MD | 6.1 | 229 | Dallas, TX | (4.8) | 105 | High Point, NC | 1.2 |
| 229 | Baton Rouge, LA | (4.8) | 113 | Daly City, CA | 0.5 | 164 | Hillsboro, OR | (2.0) |
| 36 | Beaumont, TX | 8.2 | 425 | Danbury, CT | (20.9) | 401 | Hollywood, FL | (15.8) |
| 153 | Beaverton, OR | (1.4) | 80 | Davenport, IA | 3.3 | 8 | Hoover, AL | 16.5 |
| 21 | Bellevue, WA | 11.3 | 202 | Davie, FL | (4.0) | 84 | Houston, TX | 2.9 |
| 63 | Bellflower, CA | 4.8 | 308 | Dayton, OH | (8.1) | 348 | Huntington Beach, CA | (10.3) |
| NA | Bend, OR** | NA | 210 | Dearborn, MI | (4.2) | 142 | Huntsville, AL | (1.0) |
| 272 | Berkeley, CA | (6.6) | 164 | Decatur, IL | (2.0) | 132 | Independence, MO | (0.6) |
| 77 | Bethlehem, PA | 3.5 | 200 | Deerfield Beach, FL | (3.9) | 260 | Indianapolis, IN | (6.2) |
| 10 | Billings, MT | 14.9 | 414 | Denton, TX | (17.8) | 242 | Indio, CA | (5.4) |
| 194 | Birmingham, AL | (3.7) | 157 | Denver, CO | (1.6) | 101 | Inglewood, CA | 1.5 |
| 67 | Bloomington, IL | 4.5 | 162 | Des Moines, IA | (1.9) | 309 | Irvine, CA | (8.3) |
| 424 | Bloomington, IN | (20.4) | 109 | Detroit, MI | 0.7 | 202 | Irving, TX | (4.0) |
| 137 | Bloomington, MN | (0.7) | 272 | Downey, CA | (6.6) | 242 | Jacksonville, FL | (5.4) |
| 368 | Boca Raton, FL | (12.3) | 20 | Duluth, MN | 11.7 | 359 | Jackson, MS | (11.1) |
| 369 | Boise, ID | (12.4) | 362 | Edinburg, TX | (11.4) | 384 | Jersey City, NJ | (13.6) |
| 226 | Boston, MA | (4.7) | 404 | Edison Twnshp, NJ | (16.2) | 18 | Johns Creek, GA | 12.0 |
| 167 | Boulder, CO | (2.1) | 297 | Edmond, OK | (7.8) | 403 | Joliet, IL | (16.1) |
| 218 | Brick Twnshp, NJ | (4.4) | 15 | El Cajon, CA | 12.9 | 200 | Jurupa Valley, CA | (3.9) |
| 389 | Bridgeport, CT | (14.0) | 173 | El Monte, CA | (2.3) | 218 | Kansas City, KS | (4.4) |
| 65 | Brockton, MA | 4.6 | 252 | El Paso, TX | (5.8) | 210 | Kansas City, MO | (4.2) |
| 326 | Broken Arrow, OK | (9.0) | 237 | Elgin, IL | (5.2) | 60 | Kennewick, WA | 5.1 |
| 297 | Brooklyn Park, MN | (7.8) | 406 | Elizabeth, NJ | (16.5) | 416 | Kenosha, WI | (18.3) |
| 260 | Brownsville, TX | (6.2) | 374 | Elk Grove, CA | (12.6) | 112 | Kent, WA | 0.6 |
| 277 | Bryan, TX | (6.7) | 294 | Erie, PA | (7.6) | 284 | Killeen, TX | (7.1) |
| 65 | Buena Park, CA | 4.6 | 106 | Escondido, CA | 1.1 | 269 | Knoxville, TN | (6.5) |
| 252 | Buffalo, NY | (5.8) | 149 | Eugene, OR | (1.3) | 26 | Lafayette, LA | 10.5 |
| 168 | Burbank, CA | (2.2) | 314 | Evanston, IL | (8.5) | 431 | Lake Forest, CA | (25.4) |
| 260 | Cambridge, MA | (6.2) | 242 | Evansville, IN | (5.4) | 84 | Lakeland, FL | 2.9 |
| NA | Canton Twnshp, MI** | NA | 44 | Everett, WA | 7.2 | 314 | Lakewood Twnshp, NJ | (8.5) |
| 266 | Cape Coral, FL | (6.4) | 58 | Fairfield, CA | 5.3 | 115 | Lakewood, CA | 0.4 |
| 189 | Carlsbad, CA | (3.5) | 366 | Fall River, MA | (12.1) | 84 | Lakewood, CO | 2.9 |
| 360 | Carmel, IN | (11.2) | 19 | Fargo, ND | 11.9 | 129 | Lancaster, CA | (0.5) |
| 398 | Carrollton, TX | (15.3) | 376 | Farmington Hills, MI | (12.7) | 57 | Lansing, MI | 5.6 |
| 410 | Carson, CA | (17.1) | 108 | Fayetteville, AR | 0.8 | 179 | Laredo, TX | (2.6) |
| 84 | Cary, NC | 2.9 | 239 | Fayetteville, NC | (5.3) | 234 | Largo, FL | (5.1) |
| 129 | Cedar Rapids, IA | (0.5) | 113 | Federal Way, WA | 0.5 | 194 | Las Cruces, NM | (3.7) |
| 413 | Centennial, CO | (17.6) | 210 | Fishers, IN | (4.2) | 96 | Las Vegas, NV | 1.9 |
| 411 | Champaign, IL | (17.4) | 429 | Flint, MI | (23.2) | 345 | Lawrence, KS | (10.2) |
| 369 | Chandler, AZ | (12.4) | 345 | Fontana, CA | (10.2) | 9 | Lawrence, MA | 15.4 |
| 301 | Charleston, SC | (7.9) | 309 | Fort Collins, CO | (8.3) | 186 | Lawton, OK | (3.2) |
| 338 | Charlotte, NC | (9.5) | 202 | Fort Lauderdale, FL | (4.0) | 49 | League City, TX | 6.3 |
| NA | Chattanooga, TN** | NA | 189 | Fort Smith, AR | (3.5) | 325 | Lee's Summit, MO | (8.9) |
| 194 | Cheektowaga, NY | (3.7) | 75 | Fort Wayne, IN | 3.8 | NA | Lewisville, TX** | NA |
| 184 | Chesapeake, VA | (3.0) | 84 | Fort Worth, TX | 2.9 | 326 | Lexington, KY | (9.0) |
| 394 | Chicago, IL | (15.1) | 260 | Fremont, CA | (6.2) | 330 | Lincoln, NE | (9.2) |
| 24 | Chico, CA | 10.8 | 376 | Fresno, CA | (12.7) | 174 | Little Rock, AR | (2.4) |
| 55 | Chino Hills, CA | 6.0 | 289 | Frisco, TX | (7.2) | 129 | Livermore, CA | (0.5) |

| RANK | CITY | % CHANGE | RANK | CITY | % CHANGE | RANK | CITY | % CHANGE |
|---|---|---|---|---|---|---|---|---|
| 278 | Livonia, MI | (6.9) | 17 | Pasadena, CA | 12.1 | 47 | South Gate, CA | 6.4 |
| 305 | Long Beach, CA | (8.0) | 146 | Pasadena, TX | (1.1) | 162 | Sparks, NV | (1.9) |
| 301 | Longmont, CO | (7.9) | 352 | Paterson, NJ | (10.4) | 22 | Spokane Valley, WA | 11.0 |
| 418 | Longview, TX | (18.7) | 52 | Pearland, TX | 6.1 | 46 | Spokane, WA | 6.8 |
| 176 | Los Angeles, CA | (2.5) | 266 | Pembroke Pines, FL | (6.4) | 394 | Springfield, IL | (15.1) |
| 121 | Louisville, KY | (0.1) | 422 | Peoria, AZ | (19.7) | 96 | Springfield, MA | 1.9 |
| 44 | Lowell, MA | 7.2 | 374 | Peoria, IL | (12.6) | 120 | Springfield, MO | 0.0 |
| 259 | Lubbock, TX | (6.1) | 284 | Philadelphia, PA | (7.1) | 142 | Stamford, CT | (1.0) |
| 260 | Lynchburg, VA | (6.2) | 168 | Phoenix, AZ | (2.2) | 205 | Sterling Heights, MI | (4.1) |
| 291 | Lynn, MA | (7.3) | 226 | Pittsburgh, PA | (4.7) | 153 | Stockton, CA | (1.4) |
| 79 | Macon, GA | 3.4 | 322 | Plano, TX | (8.8) | 28 | St. George, UT | 9.8 |
| 174 | Madison, WI | (2.4) | 356 | Plantation, FL | (10.7) | 301 | St. Joseph, MO | (7.9) |
| 35 | Manchester, NH | 8.6 | 379 | Pomona, CA | (13.0) | 205 | St. Louis, MO | (4.1) |
| 146 | McAllen, TX | (1.1) | 319 | Pompano Beach, FL | (8.6) | 326 | St. Paul, MN | (9.0) |
| 83 | McKinney, TX | 3.1 | 421 | Port St. Lucie, FL | (19.5) | 47 | St. Petersburg, FL | 6.4 |
| 41 | Medford, OR | 7.7 | 221 | Portland, OR | (4.5) | NA | Suffolk, VA** | NA |
| 121 | Melbourne, FL | (0.1) | 24 | Portsmouth, VA | 10.8 | 70 | Sugar Land, TX | 4.0 |
| 205 | Memphis, TN | (4.1) | 132 | Providence, RI | (0.6) | 295 | Sunnyvale, CA | (7.7) |
| 404 | Menifee, CA | (16.2) | 12 | Provo, UT | 13.9 | 157 | Sunrise, FL | (1.6) |
| 432 | Merced, CA | (35.9) | 31 | Pueblo, CO | 9.1 | 402 | Surprise, AZ | (16.0) |
| 426 | Meridian, ID | (21.2) | 49 | Quincy, MA | 6.3 | 27 | Syracuse, NY | 9.9 |
| 339 | Mesa, AZ | (9.6) | 216 | Racine, WI | (4.3) | 81 | Tacoma, WA | 3.2 |
| 106 | Mesquite, TX | 1.1 | 269 | Raleigh, NC | (6.5) | 292 | Tallahassee, FL | (7.4) |
| 43 | Miami Beach, FL | 7.6 | 428 | Ramapo, NY | (22.4) | 362 | Tampa, FL | (11.4) |
| 186 | Miami Gardens, FL | (3.2) | 386 | Rancho Cucamon., CA | (13.9) | 13 | Temecula, CA | 13.2 |
| 278 | Miami, FL | (6.9) | 427 | Reading, PA | (22.1) | 139 | Tempe, AZ | (0.8) |
| 117 | Midland, TX | 0.3 | 386 | Redding, CA | (13.9) | 140 | Thornton, CO | (0.9) |
| 357 | Milwaukee, WI | (10.8) | 91 | Redwood City, CA | 2.3 | 372 | Thousand Oaks, CA | (12.5) |
| 155 | Minneapolis, MN | (1.5) | 205 | Reno, NV | (4.1) | NA | Toledo, OH** | NA |
| 94 | Miramar, FL | 2.0 | 61 | Renton, WA | 5.0 | 242 | Toms River Twnshp, NJ | (5.4) |
| 408 | Mission Viejo, CA | (16.9) | 430 | Rialto, CA | (24.6) | 223 | Topeka, KS | (4.6) |
| 2 | Mission, TX | 23.0 | 334 | Richardson, TX | (9.3) | 75 | Torrance, CA | 3.8 |
| 39 | Mobile, AL | 7.9 | 226 | Richmond, CA | (4.7) | 77 | Tracy, CA | 3.5 |
| 360 | Modesto, CA | (11.2) | 272 | Richmond, VA | (6.6) | 392 | Trenton, NJ | (14.6) |
| 319 | Moreno Valley, CA | (8.6) | 180 | Riverside, CA | (2.8) | 305 | Troy, MI | (8.0) |
| 7 | Mountain View, CA | 17.9 | 283 | Roanoke, VA | (7.0) | NA | Tucson, AZ** | NA |
| 159 | Murfreesboro, TN | (1.8) | 278 | Rochester, MN | (6.9) | 96 | Tulsa, OK | 1.9 |
| 237 | Murrieta, CA | (5.2) | 348 | Rochester, NY | (10.3) | 103 | Tuscaloosa, AL | 1.4 |
| 398 | Nampa, ID | (15.3) | 260 | Rockford, IL | (6.2) | 372 | Tustin, CA | (12.5) |
| 390 | Napa, CA | (14.4) | 142 | Roseville, CA | (1.0) | 319 | Tyler, TX | (8.6) |
| 335 | Naperville, IL | (9.4) | 5 | Roswell, GA | 18.3 | 210 | Upland, CA | (4.2) |
| 233 | Nashua, NH | (5.0) | 342 | Round Rock, TX | (9.9) | 256 | Upper Darby Twnshp, PA | (6.0) |
| 309 | Nashville, TN | (8.3) | 348 | Sacramento, CA | (10.3) | 90 | Vacaville, CA | 2.8 |
| 31 | New Bedford, MA | 9.1 | 118 | Salem, OR | 0.2 | 168 | Vallejo, CA | (2.2) |
| 295 | New Haven, CT | (7.7) | 36 | Salinas, CA | 8.2 | 314 | Vancouver, WA | (8.5) |
| 93 | New Orleans, LA | 2.1 | 234 | Salt Lake City, UT | (5.1) | 72 | Ventura, CA | 3.9 |
| 149 | New Rochelle, NY | (1.3) | NA | San Angelo, TX** | NA | 326 | Victorville, CA | (9.0) |
| 159 | New York, NY | (1.8) | 223 | San Antonio, TX | (4.6) | 229 | Virginia Beach, VA | (4.8) |
| 365 | Newark, NJ | (11.9) | 352 | San Bernardino, CA | (10.4) | 369 | Visalia, CA | (12.4) |
| 121 | Newport Beach, CA | (0.1) | 137 | San Diego, CA | (0.7) | 40 | Vista, CA | 7.8 |
| 168 | Newport News, VA | (2.2) | 3 | San Francisco, CA | 22.2 | 269 | Waco, TX | (6.5) |
| 342 | Newton, MA | (9.9) | 364 | San Jose, CA | (11.8) | 289 | Warren, MI | (7.2) |
| 252 | Norfolk, VA | (5.8) | 29 | San Leandro, CA | 9.7 | 210 | Warwick, RI | (4.2) |
| 256 | Norman, OK | (6.0) | 322 | San Marcos, CA | (8.8) | 148 | Washington, DC | (1.2) |
| 159 | North Charleston, SC | (1.8) | 34 | San Mateo, CA | 8.8 | 142 | Waterbury, CT | (1.0) |
| 52 | North Las Vegas, NV | 6.1 | 191 | Sandy Springs, GA | (3.6) | 255 | Waukegan, IL | (5.9) |
| 381 | Norwalk, CA | (13.3) | 22 | Sandy, UT | 11.0 | 67 | West Covina, CA | 4.5 |
| 125 | Norwalk, CT | (0.2) | 380 | Santa Ana, CA | (13.1) | 344 | West Palm Beach, FL | (10.1) |
| 247 | Oakland, CA | (5.5) | 390 | Santa Barbara, CA | (14.4) | 6 | West Valley, UT | 18.1 |
| 72 | Oceanside, CA | 3.9 | 330 | Santa Clara, CA | (9.2) | 115 | Westland, MI | 0.4 |
| 16 | Odessa, TX | 12.6 | 383 | Santa Clarita, CA | (13.5) | 386 | Westminster, CA | (13.9) |
| 223 | O'Fallon, MO | (4.6) | 4 | Santa Maria, CA | 19.7 | 62 | Westminster, CO | 4.9 |
| 104 | Ogden, UT | 1.3 | 84 | Santa Monica, CA | 2.9 | 218 | Whittier, CA | (4.4) |
| 340 | Oklahoma City, OK | (9.7) | 314 | Santa Rosa, CA | (8.5) | 312 | Wichita Falls, TX | (8.4) |
| 348 | Olathe, KS | (10.3) | 121 | Savannah, GA | (0.1) | 149 | Wichita, KS | (1.3) |
| 164 | Omaha, NE | (2.0) | 247 | Scottsdale, AZ | (5.5) | 293 | Wilmington, NC | (7.5) |
| 358 | Ontario, CA | (11.0) | 352 | Scranton, PA | (10.4) | 272 | Winston-Salem, NC | (6.6) |
| 393 | Orange, CA | (15.0) | 30 | Seattle, WA | 9.6 | 72 | Woodbridge Twnshp, NJ | 3.9 |
| 191 | Orem, UT | (3.6) | 180 | Shreveport, LA | (2.8) | 185 | Worcester, MA | (3.1) |
| 155 | Orlando, FL | (1.5) | 355 | Simi Valley, CA | (10.5) | 420 | Yakima, WA | (19.0) |
| 394 | Overland Park, KS | (15.1) | 51 | Sioux City, IA | 6.2 | 305 | Yonkers, NY | (8.0) |
| 1 | Oxnard, CA | 24.1 | 216 | Sioux Falls, SD | (4.3) | 118 | Yuma, AZ | 0.2 |
| 423 | Palm Bay, FL | (20.1) | 367 | Somerville, MA | (12.2) | | | |
| 168 | Palmdale, CA | (2.2) | 94 | South Bend, IN | 2.0 | | | |

Source: CQ Press using reported data from the F.B.I. "Crime in the United States 2013"

*Property crimes are offenses of burglary, larceny-theft, and motor vehicle theft. Attempts are included.

**Not available.

# 67. Percent Change in Property Crime Rate: 2012 to 2013 (continued)
## National Percent Change = 4.8% Decrease*

| RANK | CITY | % CHANGE | RANK | CITY | % CHANGE | RANK | CITY | % CHANGE |
|---|---|---|---|---|---|---|---|---|
| 1 | Oxnard, CA | 24.1 | 75 | Fort Wayne, IN | 3.8 | 149 | Eugene, OR | (1.3) |
| 2 | Mission, TX | 23.0 | 75 | Torrance, CA | 3.8 | 149 | Hayward, CA | (1.3) |
| 3 | San Francisco, CA | 22.2 | 77 | Bethlehem, PA | 3.5 | 149 | New Rochelle, NY | (1.3) |
| 4 | Santa Maria, CA | 19.7 | 77 | Tracy, CA | 3.5 | 149 | Wichita, KS | (1.3) |
| 5 | Roswell, GA | 18.3 | 79 | Macon, GA | 3.4 | 153 | Beaverton, OR | (1.4) |
| 6 | West Valley, UT | 18.1 | 80 | Davenport, IA | 3.3 | 153 | Stockton, CA | (1.4) |
| 7 | Mountain View, CA | 17.9 | 81 | Corpus Christi, TX | 3.2 | 155 | Minneapolis, MN | (1.5) |
| 8 | Hoover, AL | 16.5 | 81 | Tacoma, WA | 3.2 | 155 | Orlando, FL | (1.5) |
| 9 | Lawrence, MA | 15.4 | 83 | McKinney, TX | 3.1 | 157 | Denver, CO | (1.6) |
| 10 | Billings, MT | 14.9 | 84 | Cary, NC | 2.9 | 157 | Sunrise, FL | (1.6) |
| 11 | Anchorage, AK | 14.0 | 84 | Fort Worth, TX | 2.9 | 159 | Murfreesboro, TN | (1.8) |
| 12 | Provo, UT | 13.9 | 84 | Houston, TX | 2.9 | 159 | New York, NY | (1.8) |
| 13 | Temecula, CA | 13.2 | 84 | Lakeland, FL | 2.9 | 159 | North Charleston, SC | (1.8) |
| 14 | Hemet, CA | 13.0 | 84 | Lakewood, CO | 2.9 | 162 | Des Moines, IA | (1.9) |
| 15 | El Cajon, CA | 12.9 | 84 | Santa Monica, CA | 2.9 | 162 | Sparks, NV | (1.9) |
| 16 | Odessa, TX | 12.6 | 90 | Vacaville, CA | 2.8 | 164 | Decatur, IL | (2.0) |
| 17 | Pasadena, CA | 12.1 | 91 | Hawthorne, CA | 2.3 | 164 | Hillsboro, OR | (2.0) |
| 18 | Johns Creek, GA | 12.0 | 91 | Redwood City, CA | 2.3 | 164 | Omaha, NE | (2.0) |
| 19 | Fargo, ND | 11.9 | 93 | New Orleans, LA | 2.1 | 167 | Boulder, CO | (2.1) |
| 20 | Duluth, MN | 11.7 | 94 | Miramar, FL | 2.0 | 168 | Burbank, CA | (2.2) |
| 21 | Bellevue, WA | 11.3 | 94 | South Bend, IN | 2.0 | 168 | Newport News, VA | (2.2) |
| 22 | Sandy, UT | 11.0 | 96 | Albuquerque, NM | 1.9 | 168 | Palmdale, CA | (2.2) |
| 22 | Spokane Valley, WA | 11.0 | 96 | Chula Vista, CA | 1.9 | 168 | Phoenix, AZ | (2.2) |
| 24 | Chico, CA | 10.8 | 96 | Las Vegas, NV | 1.9 | 168 | Vallejo, CA | (2.2) |
| 24 | Portsmouth, VA | 10.8 | 96 | Springfield, MA | 1.9 | 173 | El Monte, CA | (2.3) |
| 26 | Lafayette, LA | 10.5 | 96 | Tulsa, OK | 1.9 | 174 | Little Rock, AR | (2.4) |
| 27 | Syracuse, NY | 9.9 | 101 | Clearwater, FL | 1.5 | 174 | Madison, WI | (2.4) |
| 28 | St. George, UT | 9.8 | 101 | Inglewood, CA | 1.5 | 176 | Alexandria, VA | (2.5) |
| 29 | San Leandro, CA | 9.7 | 103 | Tuscaloosa, AL | 1.4 | 176 | Gilbert, AZ | (2.5) |
| 30 | Seattle, WA | 9.6 | 104 | Ogden, UT | 1.3 | 176 | Los Angeles, CA | (2.5) |
| 31 | New Bedford, MA | 9.1 | 105 | High Point, NC | 1.2 | 179 | Laredo, TX | (2.6) |
| 31 | Pueblo, CO | 9.1 | 106 | Escondido, CA | 1.1 | 180 | Fullerton, CA | (2.8) |
| 33 | Abilene, TX | 9.0 | 106 | Mesquite, TX | 1.1 | 180 | Grand Prairie, TX | (2.8) |
| 34 | San Mateo, CA | 8.8 | 108 | Fayetteville, AR | 0.8 | 180 | Riverside, CA | (2.8) |
| 35 | Manchester, NH | 8.6 | 109 | Arvada, CO | 0.7 | 180 | Shreveport, LA | (2.8) |
| 36 | Beaumont, TX | 8.2 | 109 | Colorado Springs, CO | 0.7 | 184 | Chesapeake, VA | (3.0) |
| 36 | Salinas, CA | 8.2 | 109 | Detroit, MI | 0.7 | 185 | Worcester, MA | (3.1) |
| 38 | Columbus, GA | 8.0 | 112 | Kent, WA | 0.6 | 186 | Lawton, OK | (3.2) |
| 39 | Mobile, AL | 7.9 | 113 | Daly City, CA | 0.5 | 186 | Miami Gardens, FL | (3.2) |
| 40 | Vista, CA | 7.8 | 113 | Federal Way, WA | 0.5 | 188 | Hampton, VA | (3.3) |
| 41 | Gary, IN | 7.7 | 115 | Lakewood, CA | 0.4 | 189 | Carlsbad, CA | (3.5) |
| 41 | Medford, OR | 7.7 | 115 | Westland, MI | 0.4 | 189 | Fort Smith, AR | (3.5) |
| 43 | Miami Beach, FL | 7.6 | 117 | Midland, TX | 0.3 | 191 | Cleveland, OH | (3.6) |
| 44 | Everett, WA | 7.2 | 118 | Salem, OR | 0.2 | 191 | Orem, UT | (3.6) |
| 44 | Lowell, MA | 7.2 | 118 | Yuma, AZ | 0.2 | 191 | Sandy Springs, GA | (3.6) |
| 46 | Spokane, WA | 6.8 | 120 | Springfield, MO | 0.0 | 194 | Birmingham, AL | (3.7) |
| 47 | South Gate, CA | 6.4 | 121 | Louisville, KY | (0.1) | 194 | Cheektowaga, NY | (3.7) |
| 47 | St. Petersburg, FL | 6.4 | 121 | Melbourne, FL | (0.1) | 194 | Las Cruces, NM | (3.7) |
| 49 | League City, TX | 6.3 | 121 | Newport Beach, CA | (0.1) | 197 | Akron, OH | (3.8) |
| 49 | Quincy, MA | 6.3 | 121 | Savannah, GA | (0.1) | 197 | Gainesville, FL | (3.8) |
| 51 | Sioux City, IA | 6.2 | 125 | Norwalk, CT | (0.2) | 197 | Garland, TX | (3.8) |
| 52 | Baltimore, MD | 6.1 | 126 | Columbia, MO | (0.3) | 200 | Deerfield Beach, FL | (3.9) |
| 52 | North Las Vegas, NV | 6.1 | 127 | Alameda, CA | (0.4) | 200 | Jurupa Valley, CA | (3.9) |
| 52 | Pearland, TX | 6.1 | 127 | Clarkstown, NY | (0.4) | 202 | Davie, FL | (4.0) |
| 55 | Chino Hills, CA | 6.0 | 129 | Cedar Rapids, IA | (0.5) | 202 | Fort Lauderdale, FL | (4.0) |
| 55 | Compton, CA | 6.0 | 129 | Lancaster, CA | (0.5) | 202 | Irving, TX | (4.0) |
| 57 | Lansing, MI | 5.6 | 129 | Livermore, CA | (0.5) | 205 | Clifton, NJ | (4.1) |
| 58 | Fairfield, CA | 5.3 | 132 | Arlington, TX | (0.6) | 205 | Memphis, TN | (4.1) |
| 59 | Aurora, CO | 5.2 | 132 | Greeley, CO | (0.6) | 205 | Reno, NV | (4.1) |
| 60 | Kennewick, WA | 5.1 | 132 | Henderson, NV | (0.6) | 205 | Sterling Heights, MI | (4.1) |
| 61 | Renton, WA | 5.0 | 132 | Independence, MO | (0.6) | 205 | St. Louis, MO | (4.1) |
| 62 | Westminster, CO | 4.9 | 132 | Providence, RI | (0.6) | 210 | Dearborn, MI | (4.2) |
| 63 | Bellflower, CA | 4.8 | 137 | Bloomington, MN | (0.7) | 210 | Fishers, IN | (4.2) |
| 63 | Glendale, CA | 4.8 | 137 | San Diego, CA | (0.7) | 210 | Hammond, IN | (4.2) |
| 65 | Brockton, MA | 4.6 | 139 | Tempe, AZ | (0.8) | 210 | Kansas City, MO | (4.2) |
| 65 | Buena Park, CA | 4.6 | 140 | Greenville, NC | (0.9) | 210 | Upland, CA | (4.2) |
| 67 | Bloomington, IL | 4.5 | 140 | Thornton, CO | (0.9) | 210 | Warwick, RI | (4.2) |
| 67 | West Covina, CA | 4.5 | 142 | Huntsville, AL | (1.0) | 216 | Racine, WI | (4.3) |
| 69 | Clarksville, TN | 4.4 | 142 | Roseville, CA | (1.0) | 216 | Sioux Falls, SD | (4.3) |
| 70 | Concord, CA | 4.0 | 142 | Stamford, CT | (1.0) | 218 | Brick Twnshp, NJ | (4.4) |
| 70 | Sugar Land, TX | 4.0 | 142 | Waterbury, CT | (1.0) | 218 | Kansas City, KS | (4.4) |
| 72 | Oceanside, CA | 3.9 | 146 | McAllen, TX | (1.1) | 218 | Whittier, CA | (4.4) |
| 72 | Ventura, CA | 3.9 | 146 | Pasadena, TX | (1.1) | 221 | Chino, CA | (4.5) |
| 72 | Woodbridge Twnshp, NJ | 3.9 | 148 | Washington, DC | (1.2) | 221 | Portland, OR | (4.5) |

| RANK | CITY | % CHANGE | RANK | CITY | % CHANGE | RANK | CITY | % CHANGE |
|---|---|---|---|---|---|---|---|---|
| 223 | O'Fallon, MO | (4.6) | 297 | Alhambra, CA | (7.8) | 369 | Visalia, CA | (12.4) |
| 223 | San Antonio, TX | (4.6) | 297 | Brooklyn Park, MN | (7.8) | 372 | Thousand Oaks, CA | (12.5) |
| 223 | Topeka, KS | (4.6) | 297 | Edmond, OK | (7.8) | 372 | Tustin, CA | (12.5) |
| 226 | Boston, MA | (4.7) | 297 | Gresham, OR | (7.8) | 374 | Elk Grove, CA | (12.6) |
| 226 | Pittsburgh, PA | (4.7) | 301 | Antioch, CA | (7.9) | 374 | Peoria, IL | (12.6) |
| 226 | Richmond, CA | (4.7) | 301 | Charleston, SC | (7.9) | 376 | Costa Mesa, CA | (12.7) |
| 229 | Anaheim, CA | (4.8) | 301 | Longmont, CO | (7.9) | 376 | Farmington Hills, MI | (12.7) |
| 229 | Baton Rouge, LA | (4.8) | 301 | St. Joseph, MO | (7.9) | 376 | Fresno, CA | (12.7) |
| 229 | Dallas, TX | (4.8) | 305 | Long Beach, CA | (8.0) | 379 | Pomona, CA | (13.0) |
| 229 | Virginia Beach, VA | (4.8) | 305 | Troy, MI | (8.0) | 380 | Santa Ana, CA | (13.1) |
| 233 | Nashua, NH | (5.0) | 305 | Yonkers, NY | (8.0) | 381 | Norwalk, CA | (13.3) |
| 234 | Hartford, CT | (5.1) | 308 | Dayton, OH | (8.1) | 382 | Athens-Clarke, GA | (13.4) |
| 234 | Largo, FL | (5.1) | 309 | Fort Collins, CO | (8.3) | 383 | Santa Clarita, CA | (13.5) |
| 234 | Salt Lake City, UT | (5.1) | 309 | Irvine, CA | (8.3) | 384 | Jersey City, NJ | (13.6) |
| 237 | Elgin, IL | (5.2) | 309 | Nashville, TN | (8.3) | 385 | Baldwin Park, CA | (13.7) |
| 237 | Murrieta, CA | (5.2) | 312 | Amarillo, TX | (8.4) | 386 | Rancho Cucamon., CA | (13.9) |
| 239 | Cincinnati, OH | (5.3) | 312 | Wichita Falls, TX | (8.4) | 386 | Redding, CA | (13.9) |
| 239 | Clinton Twnshp, MI | (5.3) | 314 | Cranston, RI | (8.5) | 386 | Westminster, CA | (13.9) |
| 239 | Fayetteville, NC | (5.3) | 314 | Evanston, IL | (8.5) | 389 | Bridgeport, CT | (14.0) |
| 242 | Albany, GA | (5.4) | 314 | Lakewood Twnshp, NJ | (8.5) | 390 | Napa, CA | (14.4) |
| 242 | Evansville, IN | (5.4) | 314 | Santa Rosa, CA | (8.5) | 390 | Santa Barbara, CA | (14.4) |
| 242 | Indio, CA | (5.4) | 314 | Vancouver, WA | (8.5) | 392 | Trenton, NJ | (14.6) |
| 242 | Jacksonville, FL | (5.4) | 319 | Moreno Valley, CA | (8.6) | 393 | Orange, CA | (15.0) |
| 242 | Toms River Twnshp, NJ | (5.4) | 319 | Pompano Beach, FL | (8.6) | 394 | Chicago, IL | (15.1) |
| 247 | Albany, NY | (5.5) | 319 | Tyler, TX | (8.6) | 394 | Citrus Heights, CA | (15.1) |
| 247 | Greensboro, NC | (5.5) | 322 | Ann Arbor, MI | (8.8) | 394 | Overland Park, KS | (15.1) |
| 247 | Oakland, CA | (5.5) | 322 | Plano, TX | (8.8) | 394 | Springfield, IL | (15.1) |
| 247 | Scottsdale, AZ | (5.5) | 322 | San Marcos, CA | (8.8) | 398 | Carrollton, TX | (15.3) |
| 251 | Hamilton Twnshp, NJ | (5.7) | 325 | Lee's Summit, MO | (8.9) | 398 | Nampa, ID | (15.3) |
| 252 | Buffalo, NY | (5.8) | 326 | Broken Arrow, OK | (9.0) | 400 | Garden Grove, CA | (15.6) |
| 252 | El Paso, TX | (5.8) | 326 | Lexington, KY | (9.0) | 401 | Hollywood, FL | (15.8) |
| 252 | Norfolk, VA | (5.8) | 326 | St. Paul, MN | (9.0) | 402 | Surprise, AZ | (16.0) |
| 255 | Waukegan, IL | (5.9) | 326 | Victorville, CA | (9.0) | 403 | Joliet, IL | (16.1) |
| 256 | Allentown, PA | (6.0) | 330 | College Station, TX | (9.2) | 404 | Edison Twnshp, NJ | (16.2) |
| 256 | Norman, OK | (6.0) | 330 | Glendale, AZ | (9.2) | 404 | Menifee, CA | (16.2) |
| 256 | Upper Darby Twnshp, PA | (6.0) | 330 | Lincoln, NE | (9.2) | 406 | Elizabeth, NJ | (16.5) |
| 259 | Lubbock, TX | (6.1) | 330 | Santa Clara, CA | (9.2) | 407 | Clovis, CA | (16.8) |
| 260 | Brownsville, TX | (6.2) | 334 | Richardson, TX | (9.3) | 408 | Mission Viejo, CA | (16.9) |
| 260 | Cambridge, MA | (6.2) | 335 | Green Bay, WI | (9.4) | 409 | Aurora, IL | (17.0) |
| 260 | Fremont, CA | (6.2) | 335 | Hialeah, FL | (9.4) | 410 | Carson, CA | (17.1) |
| 260 | Indianapolis, IN | (6.2) | 335 | Naperville, IL | (9.4) | 411 | Champaign, IL | (17.4) |
| 260 | Lynchburg, VA | (6.2) | 338 | Charlotte, NC | (9.5) | 412 | Cicero, IL | (17.5) |
| 260 | Rockford, IL | (6.2) | 339 | Mesa, AZ | (9.6) | 413 | Centennial, CO | (17.6) |
| 266 | Cape Coral, FL | (6.4) | 340 | Oklahoma City, OK | (9.7) | 414 | Denton, TX | (17.8) |
| 266 | Colonie, NY | (6.4) | 341 | Greece, NY | (9.8) | 415 | Allen, TX | (18.2) |
| 266 | Pembroke Pines, FL | (6.4) | 342 | Newton, MA | (9.9) | 416 | Kenosha, WI | (18.3) |
| 269 | Knoxville, TN | (6.5) | 342 | Round Rock, TX | (9.9) | 417 | Corona, CA | (18.5) |
| 269 | Raleigh, NC | (6.5) | 344 | West Palm Beach, FL | (10.1) | 418 | Longview, TX | (18.7) |
| 269 | Waco, TX | (6.5) | 345 | Coral Springs, FL | (10.2) | 419 | Arlington Heights, IL | (18.8) |
| 272 | Atlanta, GA | (6.6) | 345 | Fontana, CA | (10.2) | 420 | Yakima, WA | (19.0) |
| 272 | Berkeley, CA | (6.6) | 345 | Lawrence, KS | (10.2) | 421 | Port St. Lucie, FL | (19.5) |
| 272 | Downey, CA | (6.6) | 348 | Huntington Beach, CA | (10.3) | 422 | Peoria, AZ | (19.7) |
| 272 | Richmond, VA | (6.6) | 348 | Olathe, KS | (10.3) | 423 | Palm Bay, FL | (20.1) |
| 272 | Winston-Salem, NC | (6.6) | 348 | Rochester, NY | (10.3) | 424 | Bloomington, IN | (20.4) |
| 277 | Bryan, TX | (6.7) | 348 | Sacramento, CA | (10.3) | 425 | Danbury, CT | (20.9) |
| 278 | Amherst, NY | (6.9) | 352 | Paterson, NJ | (10.4) | 426 | Meridian, ID | (21.2) |
| 278 | Bakersfield, CA | (6.9) | 352 | San Bernardino, CA | (10.4) | 427 | Reading, PA | (22.1) |
| 278 | Livonia, MI | (6.9) | 352 | Scranton, PA | (10.4) | 428 | Ramapo, NY | (22.4) |
| 278 | Miami, FL | (6.9) | 355 | Simi Valley, CA | (10.5) | 429 | Flint, MI | (23.2) |
| 278 | Rochester, MN | (6.9) | 356 | Plantation, FL | (10.7) | 430 | Rialto, CA | (24.6) |
| 283 | Roanoke, VA | (7.0) | 357 | Milwaukee, WI | (10.8) | 431 | Lake Forest, CA | (25.4) |
| 284 | Austin, TX | (7.1) | 358 | Ontario, CA | (11.0) | 432 | Merced, CA | (35.9) |
| 284 | Grand Rapids, MI | (7.1) | 359 | Jackson, MS | (11.1) | NA | Bend, OR** | NA |
| 284 | Hesperia, CA | (7.1) | 360 | Carmel, IN | (11.2) | NA | Canton Twnshp, MI** | NA |
| 284 | Killeen, TX | (7.1) | 360 | Modesto, CA | (11.2) | NA | Chattanooga, TN** | NA |
| 284 | Philadelphia, PA | (7.1) | 362 | Edinburg, TX | (11.4) | NA | Columbia, SC** | NA |
| 289 | Frisco, TX | (7.2) | 362 | Tampa, FL | (11.4) | NA | Concord, NC** | NA |
| 289 | Warren, MI | (7.2) | 364 | San Jose, CA | (11.8) | NA | Lewisville, TX** | NA |
| 291 | Lynn, MA | (7.3) | 365 | Newark, NJ | (11.9) | NA | San Angelo, TX** | NA |
| 292 | Tallahassee, FL | (7.4) | 366 | Fall River, MA | (12.1) | NA | Suffolk, VA** | NA |
| 293 | Wilmington, NC | (7.5) | 367 | Somerville, MA | (12.2) | NA | Toledo, OH** | NA |
| 294 | Erie, PA | (7.6) | 368 | Boca Raton, FL | (12.3) | NA | Tucson, AZ** | NA |
| 295 | New Haven, CT | (7.7) | 369 | Boise, ID | (12.4) | | | |
| 295 | Sunnyvale, CA | (7.7) | 369 | Chandler, AZ | (12.4) | | | |

Source: CQ Press using reported data from the F.B.I. "Crime in the United States 2013"

*Property crimes are offenses of burglary, larceny-theft, and motor vehicle theft. Attempts are included.

**Not available.

# 68. Percent Change in Property Crime Rate: 2009 to 2013
## National Percent Change = 10.2% Decrease*

| RANK | CITY | % CHANGE | RANK | CITY | % CHANGE | RANK | CITY | % CHANGE |
|---|---|---|---|---|---|---|---|---|
| 134 | Abilene, TX | (3.6) | 88 | Chino, CA | 1.0 | 146 | Fullerton, CA | (4.3) |
| 143 | Akron, OH | (4.2) | 230 | Chula Vista, CA | (11.5) | 400 | Gainesville, FL | (28.9) |
| 215 | Alameda, CA | (10.2) | NA | Cicero, IL** | NA | 128 | Garden Grove, CA | (2.9) |
| 149 | Albany, GA | (4.7) | 152 | Cincinnati, OH | (4.8) | 267 | Garland, TX | (14.6) |
| 192 | Albany, NY | (8.5) | 394 | Citrus Heights, CA | (27.7) | 2 | Gary, IN | 67.3 |
| 105 | Albuquerque, NM | (0.4) | 347 | Clarkstown, NY | (22.0) | 344 | Gilbert, AZ | (21.8) |
| 229 | Alexandria, VA | (11.4) | 364 | Clarksville, TN | (24.0) | 16 | Glendale, AZ | 18.9 |
| 137 | Alhambra, CA | (3.9) | 230 | Clearwater, FL | (11.5) | 256 | Glendale, CA | (14.0) |
| 384 | Allentown, PA | (26.2) | 49 | Cleveland, OH | 5.9 | 425 | Grand Prairie, TX | (41.8) |
| 378 | Allen, TX | (25.3) | 299 | Clifton, NJ | (17.5) | 403 | Grand Rapids, MI | (29.3) |
| 402 | Amarillo, TX | (29.1) | 201 | Clinton Twnshp, MI | (9.3) | 269 | Greece, NY | (14.9) |
| 173 | Amherst, NY | (7.2) | 111 | Clovis, CA | (0.9) | 105 | Greeley, CO | (0.4) |
| 18 | Anaheim, CA | 17.0 | 423 | College Station, TX | (40.6) | 166 | Green Bay, WI | (6.4) |
| 31 | Anchorage, AK | 10.3 | 247 | Colonie, NY | (13.1) | 411 | Greensboro, NC | (31.7) |
| 281 | Ann Arbor, MI | (16.2) | 23 | Colorado Springs, CO | 13.7 | NA | Greenville, NC** | NA |
| 3 | Antioch, CA | 59.2 | 104 | Columbia, MO | (0.1) | 45 | Gresham, OR | 6.4 |
| 422 | Arlington Heights, IL | (39.2) | 97 | Columbia, SC | 0.5 | 27 | Hamilton Twnshp, NJ | 11.8 |
| 390 | Arlington, TX | (26.8) | 340 | Columbus, GA | (21.4) | 295 | Hammond, IN | (17.3) |
| 135 | Arvada, CO | (3.7) | 333 | Compton, CA | (20.2) | 196 | Hampton, VA | (8.8) |
| 410 | Athens-Clarke, GA | (31.2) | 35 | Concord, CA | 8.6 | 318 | Hartford, CT | (19.2) |
| 117 | Atlanta, GA | (1.8) | 420 | Concord, NC | (36.5) | 62 | Hawthorne, CA | 4.3 |
| 84 | Aurora, CO | 1.4 | 245 | Coral Springs, FL | (12.8) | 67 | Hayward, CA | 3.6 |
| 421 | Aurora, IL | (38.5) | 258 | Corona, CA | (14.1) | 14 | Hemet, CA | 23.6 |
| 351 | Austin, TX | (22.4) | 294 | Corpus Christi, TX | (17.2) | 86 | Henderson, NV | 1.2 |
| 115 | Bakersfield, CA | (1.5) | 58 | Costa Mesa, CA | 4.8 | 9 | Hesperia, CA | 33.7 |
| 288 | Baldwin Park, CA | (16.7) | 280 | Cranston, RI | (16.0) | 400 | Hialeah, FL | (28.9) |
| 36 | Baltimore, MD | 8.3 | 369 | Dallas, TX | (24.7) | 311 | High Point, NC | (18.5) |
| 316 | Baton Rouge, LA | (18.9) | 85 | Daly City, CA | 1.3 | 21 | Hillsboro, OR | 14.8 |
| 196 | Beaumont, TX | (8.8) | 342 | Danbury, CT | (21.7) | 180 | Hollywood, FL | (7.5) |
| 187 | Beaverton, OR | (7.9) | 307 | Davenport, IA | (18.2) | 129 | Hoover, AL | (3.0) |
| 121 | Bellevue, WA | (2.1) | 306 | Davie, FL | (18.1) | 148 | Houston, TX | (4.4) |
| 137 | Bellflower, CA | (3.9) | 175 | Dayton, OH | (7.3) | 46 | Huntington Beach, CA | 6.3 |
| 26 | Bend, OR | 12.2 | 419 | Dearborn, MI | (35.2) | 199 | Huntsville, AL | (9.0) |
| 393 | Berkeley, CA | (27.6) | 354 | Decatur, IL | (22.6) | 70 | Independence, MO | 3.3 |
| 99 | Bethlehem, PA | 0.2 | NA | Deerfield Beach, FL** | NA | 207 | Indianapolis, IN | (10.0) |
| 15 | Billings, MT | 19.2 | 264 | Denton, TX | (14.4) | 43 | Indio, CA | 6.7 |
| 283 | Birmingham, AL | (16.4) | 50 | Denver, CO | 5.8 | 203 | Inglewood, CA | (9.5) |
| 152 | Bloomington, IL | (4.8) | 33 | Des Moines, IA | 9.4 | 98 | Irvine, CA | 0.3 |
| 403 | Bloomington, IN | (29.3) | 58 | Detroit, MI | 4.8 | 418 | Irving, TX | (35.0) |
| 161 | Bloomington, MN | (5.7) | 242 | Downey, CA | (12.5) | 367 | Jacksonville, FL | (24.3) |
| 395 | Boca Raton, FL | (27.8) | 117 | Duluth, MN | (1.8) | 358 | Jackson, MS | (23.4) |
| 338 | Boise, ID | (20.7) | 285 | Edinburg, TX | (16.6) | 366 | Jersey City, NJ | (24.2) |
| 285 | Boston, MA | (16.6) | 427 | Edison Twnshp, NJ | (44.3) | 426 | Johns Creek, GA | (43.5) |
| 70 | Boulder, CO | 3.3 | 268 | Edmond, OK | (14.8) | 275 | Joliet, IL | (15.6) |
| 221 | Brick Twnshp, NJ | (10.7) | 154 | El Cajon, CA | (5.2) | NA | Jurupa Valley, CA** | NA |
| 387 | Bridgeport, CT | (26.5) | 304 | El Monte, CA | (17.8) | 212 | Kansas City, KS | (10.1) |
| 78 | Brockton, MA | 1.6 | 360 | El Paso, TX | (23.5) | 137 | Kansas City, MO | (3.9) |
| 180 | Broken Arrow, OK | (7.5) | 297 | Elgin, IL | (17.4) | 217 | Kennewick, WA | (10.3) |
| 350 | Brooklyn Park, MN | (22.1) | 406 | Elizabeth, NJ | (29.7) | 335 | Kenosha, WI | (20.6) |
| 339 | Brownsville, TX | (20.8) | 373 | Elk Grove, CA | (24.8) | 109 | Kent, WA | (0.6) |
| 428 | Bryan, TX | (48.0) | 32 | Erie, PA | 9.5 | 356 | Killeen, TX | (23.2) |
| 52 | Buena Park, CA | 5.1 | 158 | Escondido, CA | (5.5) | 119 | Knoxville, TN | (1.9) |
| 219 | Buffalo, NY | (10.5) | 240 | Eugene, OR | (12.3) | 165 | Lafayette, LA | (6.3) |
| 207 | Burbank, CA | (10.0) | NA | Evanston, IL** | NA | 324 | Lake Forest, CA | (19.7) |
| 230 | Cambridge, MA | (11.5) | 54 | Evansville, IN | 4.9 | 93 | Lakeland, FL | 0.7 |
| 355 | Canton Twnshp, MI | (22.9) | 180 | Everett, WA | (7.5) | NA | Lakewood Twnshp, NJ** | NA |
| 326 | Cape Coral, FL | (19.8) | 54 | Fairfield, CA | 4.9 | 163 | Lakewood, CA | (5.9) |
| 125 | Carlsbad, CA | (2.6) | 387 | Fall River, MA | (26.5) | 54 | Lakewood, CO | 4.9 |
| 414 | Carmel, IN | (33.1) | 270 | Fargo, ND | (15.0) | 173 | Lancaster, CA | (7.2) |
| 391 | Carrollton, TX | (27.1) | 405 | Farmington Hills, MI | (29.4) | 83 | Lansing, MI | 1.5 |
| 143 | Carson, CA | (4.2) | 51 | Fayetteville, AR | 5.2 | 407 | Laredo, TX | (29.9) |
| 171 | Cary, NC | (7.0) | 347 | Fayetteville, NC | (22.0) | 262 | Largo, FL | (14.2) |
| 277 | Cedar Rapids, IA | (15.7) | 67 | Federal Way, WA | 3.6 | 243 | Las Cruces, NM | (12.7) |
| 318 | Centennial, CO | (19.2) | 64 | Fishers, IN | 4.0 | 183 | Las Vegas, NV | (7.6) |
| NA | Champaign, IL** | NA | 380 | Flint, MI | (25.6) | 279 | Lawrence, KS | (15.9) |
| 311 | Chandler, AZ | (18.5) | 246 | Fontana, CA | (12.9) | 146 | Lawrence, MA | (4.3) |
| 399 | Charleston, SC | (28.5) | 358 | Fort Collins, CO | (23.4) | 169 | Lawton, OK | (6.9) |
| 386 | Charlotte, NC | (26.3) | 114 | Fort Lauderdale, FL | (1.3) | 356 | League City, TX | (23.2) |
| 220 | Chattanooga, TN | (10.6) | 215 | Fort Smith, AR | (10.2) | 291 | Lee's Summit, MO | (16.9) |
| 66 | Cheektowaga, NY | 3.8 | 72 | Fort Wayne, IN | 3.2 | 345 | Lewisville, TX | (21.9) |
| 352 | Chesapeake, VA | (22.5) | 241 | Fort Worth, TX | (12.4) | 17 | Lexington, KY | 18.0 |
| 285 | Chicago, IL | (16.6) | 381 | Fremont, CA | (25.7) | 225 | Lincoln, NE | (11.1) |
| 53 | Chico, CA | 5.0 | 78 | Fresno, CA | 1.6 | 158 | Little Rock, AR | (5.5) |
| 227 | Chino Hills, CA | (11.2) | 102 | Frisco, TX | 0.1 | 78 | Livermore, CA | 1.6 |

| RANK | CITY | % CHANGE | RANK | CITY | % CHANGE | RANK | CITY | % CHANGE |
|---|---|---|---|---|---|---|---|---|
| 288 | Livonia, MI | (16.7) | 162 | Pasadena, CA | (5.8) | 47 | South Gate, CA | 6.1 |
| 78 | Long Beach, CA | 1.6 | 163 | Pasadena, TX | (5.9) | 328 | Sparks, NV | (20.0) |
| 300 | Longmont, CO | (17.6) | 41 | Paterson, NJ | 6.8 | 5 | Spokane Valley, WA | 55.6 |
| 424 | Longview, TX | (41.4) | 249 | Pearland, TX | (13.3) | 6 | Spokane, WA | 43.7 |
| 205 | Los Angeles, CA | (9.6) | 413 | Pembroke Pines, FL | (32.9) | 295 | Springfield, IL | (17.3) |
| 95 | Louisville, KY | 0.6 | 332 | Peoria, AZ | (20.1) | 156 | Springfield, MA | (5.4) |
| NA | Lowell, MA** | NA | 310 | Peoria, IL | (18.4) | 93 | Springfield, MO | 0.7 |
| 290 | Lubbock, TX | (16.8) | 149 | Philadelphia, PA | (4.7) | 258 | Stamford, CT | (14.1) |
| 275 | Lynchburg, VA | (15.6) | 125 | Phoenix, AZ | (2.6) | 172 | Sterling Heights, MI | (7.1) |
| 297 | Lynn, MA | (17.4) | 250 | Pittsburgh, PA | (13.4) | 149 | Stockton, CA | (4.7) |
| 131 | Macon, GA | (3.3) | 389 | Plano, TX | (26.6) | 30 | St. George, UT | 10.7 |
| 154 | Madison, WI | (5.2) | 322 | Plantation, FL | (19.5) | 25 | St. Joseph, MO | 13.0 |
| 29 | Manchester, NH | 11.1 | 38 | Pomona, CA | 7.6 | 335 | St. Louis, MO | (20.6) |
| 417 | McAllen, TX | (34.1) | 110 | Pompano Beach, FL | (0.8) | 194 | St. Paul, MN | (8.7) |
| 303 | McKinney, TX | (17.7) | 414 | Port St. Lucie, FL | (33.1) | 364 | St. Petersburg, FL | (24.0) |
| 4 | Medford, OR | 56.4 | 73 | Portland, OR | 3.0 | 19 | Suffolk, VA | 16.6 |
| 266 | Melbourne, FL | (14.5) | 113 | Portsmouth, VA | (1.2) | 254 | Sugar Land, TX | (13.8) |
| 264 | Memphis, TN | (14.4) | 143 | Providence, RI | (4.2) | 341 | Sunnyvale, CA | (21.6) |
| 140 | Menifee, CA | (4.1) | 116 | Provo, UT | (1.6) | 307 | Sunrise, FL | (18.2) |
| 212 | Merced, CA | (10.1) | 1 | Pueblo, CO | 118.2 | 369 | Surprise, AZ | (24.7) |
| 225 | Meridian, ID | (11.1) | 131 | Quincy, MA | (3.3) | 41 | Syracuse, NY | 6.8 |
| 293 | Mesa, AZ | (17.1) | 207 | Racine, WI | (10.0) | 178 | Tacoma, WA | (7.4) |
| 250 | Mesquite, TX | (13.4) | 207 | Raleigh, NC | (10.0) | 227 | Tallahassee, FL | (11.2) |
| 44 | Miami Beach, FL | 6.5 | 379 | Ramapo, NY | (25.5) | 414 | Tampa, FL | (33.1) |
| 384 | Miami Gardens, FL | (26.2) | 63 | Rancho Cucamon., CA | 4.2 | 23 | Temecula, CA | 13.7 |
| 90 | Miami, FL | 0.9 | 412 | Reading, PA | (32.6) | 184 | Tempe, AZ | (7.7) |
| 397 | Midland, TX | (28.2) | 11 | Redding, CA | 27.0 | 324 | Thornton, CO | (19.7) |
| 345 | Milwaukee, WI | (21.9) | 167 | Redwood City, CA | (6.7) | 258 | Thousand Oaks, CA | (14.1) |
| 61 | Minneapolis, MN | 4.7 | 352 | Reno, NV | (22.5) | NA | Toledo, OH** | NA |
| 391 | Miramar, FL | (27.1) | 373 | Renton, WA | (24.8) | 20 | Toms River Twnshp, NJ | 16.3 |
| 274 | Mission Viejo, CA | (15.5) | 188 | Rialto, CA | (8.0) | 167 | Topeka, KS | (6.7) |
| 382 | Mission, TX | (26.0) | 367 | Richardson, TX | (24.3) | 175 | Torrance, CA | (7.3) |
| 203 | Mobile, AL | (9.5) | 65 | Richmond, CA | 3.9 | 258 | Tracy, CA | (14.1) |
| 125 | Modesto, CA | (2.6) | 107 | Richmond, VA | (0.5) | 252 | Trenton, NJ | (13.5) |
| 133 | Moreno Valley, CA | (3.5) | 58 | Riverside, CA | 4.8 | NA | Tucson, AZ** | NA |
| 333 | Mountain View, CA | (20.2) | 271 | Roanoke, VA | (15.1) | 235 | Tulsa, OK | (11.9) |
| 360 | Murfreesboro, TN | (23.5) | 284 | Rochester, MN | (16.5) | 252 | Tuscaloosa, AL | (13.5) |
| 47 | Murrieta, CA | 6.1 | 221 | Rochester, NY | (10.7) | 121 | Tustin, CA | (2.1) |
| 169 | Nampa, ID | (6.9) | 256 | Rockford, IL | (14.0) | 408 | Tyler, TX | (30.0) |
| 408 | Napa, CA | (30.0) | 328 | Roseville, CA | (20.0) | NA | Upland, CA** | NA |
| 347 | Naperville, IL | (22.0) | 291 | Roswell, GA | (16.9) | 316 | Upper Darby Twnshp, PA | (18.9) |
| 192 | Nashua, NH | (8.5) | 223 | Round Rock, TX | (10.8) | 130 | Vacaville, CA | (3.1) |
| 322 | Nashville, TN | (19.5) | 278 | Sacramento, CA | (15.8) | 86 | Vallejo, CA | 1.2 |
| 69 | New Bedford, MA | 3.4 | 40 | Salem, OR | 7.2 | 112 | Vancouver, WA | (1.0) |
| 313 | New Haven, CT | (18.7) | 107 | Salinas, CA | (0.5) | 12 | Ventura, CA | 26.2 |
| 99 | New Orleans, LA | 0.2 | 233 | Salt Lake City, UT | (11.8) | 77 | Victorville, CA | 1.8 |
| 99 | New Rochelle, NY | 0.2 | 321 | San Angelo, TX | (19.3) | 313 | Virginia Beach, VA | (18.7) |
| 103 | New York, NY | 0.0 | 263 | San Antonio, TX | (14.3) | 189 | Visalia, CA | (8.1) |
| 76 | Newark, NJ | 2.0 | 156 | San Bernardino, CA | (5.4) | 254 | Vista, CA | (13.8) |
| 238 | Newport Beach, CA | (12.1) | 140 | San Diego, CA | (4.1) | 377 | Waco, TX | (25.2) |
| NA | Newport News, VA** | NA | 8 | San Francisco, CA | 36.0 | 186 | Warren, MI | (7.8) |
| 318 | Newton, MA | (19.2) | 37 | San Jose, CA | 7.8 | 362 | Warwick, RI | (23.6) |
| 335 | Norfolk, VA | (20.6) | 75 | San Leandro, CA | 2.1 | 78 | Washington, DC | 1.6 |
| 396 | Norman, OK | (28.1) | 175 | San Marcos, CA | (7.3) | 326 | Waterbury, CT | (19.8) |
| 239 | North Charleston, SC | (12.2) | 243 | San Mateo, CA | (12.7) | NA | Waukegan, IL** | NA |
| 158 | North Las Vegas, NV | (5.5) | 375 | Sandy Springs, GA | (25.0) | 91 | West Covina, CA | 0.8 |
| 91 | Norwalk, CA | 0.8 | 191 | Sandy, UT | (8.2) | 224 | West Palm Beach, FL | (10.9) |
| 189 | Norwalk, CT | (8.1) | 135 | Santa Ana, CA | (3.7) | 124 | West Valley, UT | (2.2) |
| 13 | Oakland, CA | 25.0 | 235 | Santa Barbara, CA | (11.9) | 196 | Westland, MI | (8.8) |
| 28 | Oceanside, CA | 11.2 | 184 | Santa Clara, CA | (7.7) | 73 | Westminster, CA | 3.0 |
| 119 | Odessa, TX | (1.9) | 383 | Santa Clarita, CA | (26.1) | 272 | Westminster, CO | (15.2) |
| 217 | O'Fallon, MO | (10.3) | 7 | Santa Maria, CA | 37.6 | 39 | Whittier, CA | 7.5 |
| 121 | Ogden, UT | (2.1) | 95 | Santa Monica, CA | 0.6 | 342 | Wichita Falls, TX | (21.7) |
| 237 | Oklahoma City, OK | (12.0) | 375 | Santa Rosa, CA | (25.0) | 88 | Wichita, KS | 1.0 |
| 307 | Olathe, KS | (18.2) | 397 | Savannah, GA | (28.2) | 313 | Wilmington, NC | (18.7) |
| 34 | Omaha, NE | 8.9 | 212 | Scottsdale, AZ | (10.1) | 194 | Winston-Salem, NC | (8.7) |
| 206 | Ontario, CA | (9.8) | 300 | Scranton, PA | (17.6) | 282 | Woodbridge Twnshp, NJ | (16.3) |
| 207 | Orange, CA | (10.0) | 140 | Seattle, WA | (4.1) | 201 | Worcester, MA | (9.3) |
| 273 | Orem, UT | (15.4) | 200 | Shreveport, LA | (9.2) | NA | Yakima, WA** | NA |
| 233 | Orlando, FL | (11.8) | 300 | Simi Valley, CA | (17.6) | 362 | Yonkers, NY | (23.6) |
| 369 | Overland Park, KS | (24.7) | 10 | Sioux City, IA | 29.0 | 178 | Yuma, AZ | (7.4) |
| 21 | Oxnard, CA | 14.8 | 54 | Sioux Falls, SD | 4.9 | | | |
| 328 | Palm Bay, FL | (20.0) | 369 | Somerville, MA | (24.7) | | | |
| 247 | Palmdale, CA | (13.1) | 305 | South Bend, IN | (17.9) | | | |

Source: CQ Press using reported data from the F.B.I. "Crime in the United States 2013"

*Property crimes are offenses of burglary, larceny-theft, and motor vehicle theft. Attempts are included.

**Not available.

# 68. Percent Change in Property Crime Rate: 2009 to 2013 (continued)
## National Percent Change = 10.2% Decrease*

| RANK | CITY | % CHANGE | RANK | CITY | % CHANGE | RANK | CITY | % CHANGE |
|---|---|---|---|---|---|---|---|---|
| 1 | Pueblo, CO | 118.2 | 75 | San Leandro, CA | 2.1 | 149 | Albany, GA | (4.7) |
| 2 | Gary, IN | 67.3 | 76 | Newark, NJ | 2.0 | 149 | Philadelphia, PA | (4.7) |
| 3 | Antioch, CA | 59.2 | 77 | Victorville, CA | 1.8 | 149 | Stockton, CA | (4.7) |
| 4 | Medford, OR | 56.4 | 78 | Brockton, MA | 1.6 | 152 | Bloomington, IL | (4.8) |
| 5 | Spokane Valley, WA | 55.6 | 78 | Fresno, CA | 1.6 | 152 | Cincinnati, OH | (4.8) |
| 6 | Spokane, WA | 43.7 | 78 | Livermore, CA | 1.6 | 154 | El Cajon, CA | (5.2) |
| 7 | Santa Maria, CA | 37.6 | 78 | Long Beach, CA | 1.6 | 154 | Madison, WI | (5.2) |
| 8 | San Francisco, CA | 36.0 | 78 | Washington, DC | 1.6 | 156 | San Bernardino, CA | (5.4) |
| 9 | Hesperia, CA | 33.7 | 83 | Lansing, MI | 1.5 | 156 | Springfield, MA | (5.4) |
| 10 | Sioux City, IA | 29.0 | 84 | Aurora, CO | 1.4 | 158 | Escondido, CA | (5.5) |
| 11 | Redding, CA | 27.0 | 85 | Daly City, CA | 1.3 | 158 | Little Rock, AR | (5.5) |
| 12 | Ventura, CA | 26.2 | 86 | Henderson, NV | 1.2 | 158 | North Las Vegas, NV | (5.5) |
| 13 | Oakland, CA | 25.0 | 86 | Vallejo, CA | 1.2 | 161 | Bloomington, MN | (5.7) |
| 14 | Hemet, CA | 23.6 | 88 | Chino, CA | 1.0 | 162 | Pasadena, CA | (5.8) |
| 15 | Billings, MT | 19.2 | 88 | Wichita, KS | 1.0 | 163 | Lakewood, CA | (5.9) |
| 16 | Glendale, AZ | 18.9 | 90 | Miami, FL | 0.9 | 163 | Pasadena, TX | (5.9) |
| 17 | Lexington, KY | 18.0 | 91 | Norwalk, CA | 0.8 | 165 | Lafayette, LA | (6.3) |
| 18 | Anaheim, CA | 17.0 | 91 | West Covina, CA | 0.8 | 166 | Green Bay, WI | (6.4) |
| 19 | Suffolk, VA | 16.6 | 93 | Lakeland, FL | 0.7 | 167 | Redwood City, CA | (6.7) |
| 20 | Toms River Twnshp, NJ | 16.3 | 93 | Springfield, MO | 0.7 | 167 | Topeka, KS | (6.7) |
| 21 | Hillsboro, OR | 14.8 | 95 | Louisville, KY | 0.6 | 169 | Lawton, OK | (6.9) |
| 21 | Oxnard, CA | 14.8 | 95 | Santa Monica, CA | 0.6 | 169 | Nampa, ID | (6.9) |
| 23 | Colorado Springs, CO | 13.7 | 97 | Columbia, SC | 0.5 | 171 | Cary, NC | (7.0) |
| 23 | Temecula, CA | 13.7 | 98 | Irvine, CA | 0.3 | 172 | Sterling Heights, MI | (7.1) |
| 25 | St. Joseph, MO | 13.0 | 99 | Bethlehem, PA | 0.2 | 173 | Amherst, NY | (7.2) |
| 26 | Bend, OR | 12.2 | 99 | New Orleans, LA | 0.2 | 173 | Lancaster, CA | (7.2) |
| 27 | Hamilton Twnshp, NJ | 11.8 | 99 | New Rochelle, NY | 0.2 | 175 | Dayton, OH | (7.3) |
| 28 | Oceanside, CA | 11.2 | 102 | Frisco, TX | 0.1 | 175 | San Marcos, CA | (7.3) |
| 29 | Manchester, NH | 11.1 | 103 | New York, NY | 0.0 | 175 | Torrance, CA | (7.3) |
| 30 | St. George, UT | 10.7 | 104 | Columbia, MO | (0.1) | 178 | Tacoma, WA | (7.4) |
| 31 | Anchorage, AK | 10.3 | 105 | Albuquerque, NM | (0.4) | 178 | Yuma, AZ | (7.4) |
| 32 | Erie, PA | 9.5 | 105 | Greeley, CO | (0.4) | 180 | Broken Arrow, OK | (7.5) |
| 33 | Des Moines, IA | 9.4 | 107 | Richmond, VA | (0.5) | 180 | Everett, WA | (7.5) |
| 34 | Omaha, NE | 8.9 | 107 | Salinas, CA | (0.5) | 180 | Hollywood, FL | (7.5) |
| 35 | Concord, CA | 8.6 | 109 | Kent, WA | (0.6) | 183 | Las Vegas, NV | (7.6) |
| 36 | Baltimore, MD | 8.3 | 110 | Pompano Beach, FL | (0.8) | 184 | Santa Clara, CA | (7.7) |
| 37 | San Jose, CA | 7.8 | 111 | Clovis, CA | (0.9) | 184 | Tempe, AZ | (7.7) |
| 38 | Pomona, CA | 7.6 | 112 | Vancouver, WA | (1.0) | 186 | Warren, MI | (7.8) |
| 39 | Whittier, CA | 7.5 | 113 | Portsmouth, VA | (1.2) | 187 | Beaverton, OR | (7.9) |
| 40 | Salem, OR | 7.2 | 114 | Fort Lauderdale, FL | (1.3) | 188 | Rialto, CA | (8.0) |
| 41 | Paterson, NJ | 6.8 | 115 | Bakersfield, CA | (1.5) | 189 | Norwalk, CT | (8.1) |
| 41 | Syracuse, NY | 6.8 | 116 | Provo, UT | (1.6) | 189 | Visalia, CA | (8.1) |
| 43 | Indio, CA | 6.7 | 117 | Atlanta, GA | (1.8) | 191 | Sandy, UT | (8.2) |
| 44 | Miami Beach, FL | 6.5 | 117 | Duluth, MN | (1.8) | 192 | Albany, NY | (8.5) |
| 45 | Gresham, OR | 6.4 | 119 | Knoxville, TN | (1.9) | 192 | Nashua, NH | (8.5) |
| 46 | Huntington Beach, CA | 6.3 | 119 | Odessa, TX | (1.9) | 194 | St. Paul, MN | (8.7) |
| 47 | Murrieta, CA | 6.1 | 121 | Bellevue, WA | (2.1) | 194 | Winston-Salem, NC | (8.7) |
| 47 | South Gate, CA | 6.1 | 121 | Ogden, UT | (2.1) | 196 | Beaumont, TX | (8.8) |
| 49 | Cleveland, OH | 5.9 | 121 | Tustin, CA | (2.1) | 196 | Hampton, VA | (8.8) |
| 50 | Denver, CO | 5.8 | 124 | West Valley, UT | (2.2) | 196 | Westland, MI | (8.8) |
| 51 | Fayetteville, AR | 5.2 | 125 | Carlsbad, CA | (2.6) | 199 | Huntsville, AL | (9.0) |
| 52 | Buena Park, CA | 5.1 | 125 | Modesto, CA | (2.6) | 200 | Shreveport, LA | (9.2) |
| 53 | Chico, CA | 5.0 | 125 | Phoenix, AZ | (2.6) | 201 | Clinton Twnshp, MI | (9.3) |
| 54 | Evansville, IN | 4.9 | 128 | Garden Grove, CA | (2.9) | 201 | Worcester, MA | (9.3) |
| 54 | Fairfield, CA | 4.9 | 129 | Hoover, AL | (3.0) | 203 | Inglewood, CA | (9.5) |
| 54 | Lakewood, CO | 4.9 | 130 | Vacaville, CA | (3.1) | 203 | Mobile, AL | (9.5) |
| 54 | Sioux Falls, SD | 4.9 | 131 | Macon, GA | (3.3) | 205 | Los Angeles, CA | (9.6) |
| 58 | Costa Mesa, CA | 4.8 | 131 | Quincy, MA | (3.3) | 206 | Ontario, CA | (9.8) |
| 58 | Detroit, MI | 4.8 | 133 | Moreno Valley, CA | (3.5) | 207 | Burbank, CA | (10.0) |
| 58 | Riverside, CA | 4.8 | 134 | Abilene, TX | (3.6) | 207 | Indianapolis, IN | (10.0) |
| 61 | Minneapolis, MN | 4.7 | 135 | Arvada, CO | (3.7) | 207 | Orange, CA | (10.0) |
| 62 | Hawthorne, CA | 4.3 | 135 | Santa Ana, CA | (3.7) | 207 | Racine, WI | (10.0) |
| 63 | Rancho Cucamon., CA | 4.2 | 137 | Alhambra, CA | (3.9) | 207 | Raleigh, NC | (10.0) |
| 64 | Fishers, IN | 4.0 | 137 | Bellflower, CA | (3.9) | 212 | Kansas City, KS | (10.1) |
| 65 | Richmond, CA | 3.9 | 137 | Kansas City, MO | (3.9) | 212 | Merced, CA | (10.1) |
| 66 | Cheektowaga, NY | 3.8 | 140 | Menifee, CA | (4.1) | 212 | Scottsdale, AZ | (10.1) |
| 67 | Federal Way, WA | 3.6 | 140 | San Diego, CA | (4.1) | 215 | Alameda, CA | (10.2) |
| 67 | Hayward, CA | 3.6 | 140 | Seattle, WA | (4.1) | 215 | Fort Smith, AR | (10.2) |
| 69 | New Bedford, MA | 3.4 | 143 | Akron, OH | (4.2) | 217 | Kennewick, WA | (10.3) |
| 70 | Boulder, CO | 3.3 | 143 | Carson, CA | (4.2) | 217 | O'Fallon, MO | (10.3) |
| 70 | Independence, MO | 3.3 | 143 | Providence, RI | (4.2) | 219 | Buffalo, NY | (10.5) |
| 72 | Fort Wayne, IN | 3.2 | 146 | Fullerton, CA | (4.3) | 220 | Chattanooga, TN | (10.6) |
| 73 | Portland, OR | 3.0 | 146 | Lawrence, MA | (4.3) | 221 | Brick Twnshp, NJ | (10.7) |
| 73 | Westminster, CA | 3.0 | 148 | Houston, TX | (4.4) | 221 | Rochester, NY | (10.7) |

| RANK | CITY | % CHANGE | RANK | CITY | % CHANGE | RANK | CITY | % CHANGE |
|---|---|---|---|---|---|---|---|---|
| 223 | Round Rock, TX | (10.8) | 297 | Elgin, IL | (17.4) | 369 | Somerville, MA | (24.7) |
| 224 | West Palm Beach, FL | (10.9) | 297 | Lynn, MA | (17.4) | 369 | Surprise, AZ | (24.7) |
| 225 | Lincoln, NE | (11.1) | 299 | Clifton, NJ | (17.5) | 373 | Elk Grove, CA | (24.8) |
| 225 | Meridian, ID | (11.1) | 300 | Longmont, CO | (17.6) | 373 | Renton, WA | (24.8) |
| 227 | Chino Hills, CA | (11.2) | 300 | Scranton, PA | (17.6) | 375 | Sandy Springs, GA | (25.0) |
| 227 | Tallahassee, FL | (11.2) | 300 | Simi Valley, CA | (17.6) | 375 | Santa Rosa, CA | (25.0) |
| 229 | Alexandria, VA | (11.4) | 303 | McKinney, TX | (17.7) | 377 | Waco, TX | (25.2) |
| 230 | Cambridge, MA | (11.5) | 304 | El Monte, CA | (17.8) | 378 | Allen, TX | (25.3) |
| 230 | Chula Vista, CA | (11.5) | 305 | South Bend, IN | (17.9) | 379 | Ramapo, NY | (25.5) |
| 230 | Clearwater, FL | (11.5) | 306 | Davie, FL | (18.1) | 380 | Flint, MI | (25.6) |
| 233 | Orlando, FL | (11.8) | 307 | Davenport, IA | (18.2) | 381 | Fremont, CA | (25.7) |
| 233 | Salt Lake City, UT | (11.8) | 307 | Olathe, KS | (18.2) | 382 | Mission, TX | (26.0) |
| 235 | Santa Barbara, CA | (11.9) | 307 | Sunrise, FL | (18.2) | 383 | Santa Clarita, CA | (26.1) |
| 235 | Tulsa, OK | (11.9) | 310 | Peoria, IL | (18.4) | 384 | Allentown, PA | (26.2) |
| 237 | Oklahoma City, OK | (12.0) | 311 | Chandler, AZ | (18.5) | 384 | Miami Gardens, FL | (26.2) |
| 238 | Newport Beach, CA | (12.1) | 311 | High Point, NC | (18.5) | 386 | Charlotte, NC | (26.3) |
| 239 | North Charleston, SC | (12.2) | 313 | New Haven, CT | (18.7) | 387 | Bridgeport, CT | (26.5) |
| 240 | Eugene, OR | (12.3) | 313 | Virginia Beach, VA | (18.7) | 387 | Fall River, MA | (26.5) |
| 241 | Fort Worth, TX | (12.4) | 313 | Wilmington, NC | (18.7) | 389 | Plano, TX | (26.6) |
| 242 | Downey, CA | (12.5) | 316 | Baton Rouge, LA | (18.9) | 390 | Arlington, TX | (26.8) |
| 243 | Las Cruces, NM | (12.7) | 316 | Upper Darby Twnshp, PA | (18.9) | 391 | Carrollton, TX | (27.1) |
| 243 | San Mateo, CA | (12.7) | 318 | Centennial, CO | (19.2) | 391 | Miramar, FL | (27.1) |
| 245 | Coral Springs, FL | (12.8) | 318 | Hartford, CT | (19.2) | 393 | Berkeley, CA | (27.6) |
| 246 | Fontana, CA | (12.9) | 318 | Newton, MA | (19.2) | 394 | Citrus Heights, CA | (27.7) |
| 247 | Colonie, NY | (13.1) | 321 | San Angelo, TX | (19.3) | 395 | Boca Raton, FL | (27.8) |
| 247 | Palmdale, CA | (13.1) | 322 | Nashville, TN | (19.5) | 396 | Norman, OK | (28.1) |
| 249 | Pearland, TX | (13.3) | 322 | Plantation, FL | (19.5) | 397 | Midland, TX | (28.2) |
| 250 | Mesquite, TX | (13.4) | 324 | Lake Forest, CA | (19.7) | 397 | Savannah, GA | (28.2) |
| 250 | Pittsburgh, PA | (13.4) | 324 | Thornton, CO | (19.7) | 399 | Charleston, SC | (28.5) |
| 252 | Trenton, NJ | (13.5) | 326 | Cape Coral, FL | (19.8) | 400 | Gainesville, FL | (28.9) |
| 252 | Tuscaloosa, AL | (13.5) | 326 | Waterbury, CT | (19.8) | 400 | Hialeah, FL | (28.9) |
| 254 | Sugar Land, TX | (13.8) | 328 | Palm Bay, FL | (20.0) | 402 | Amarillo, TX | (29.1) |
| 254 | Vista, CA | (13.8) | 328 | Roseville, CA | (20.0) | 403 | Bloomington, IN | (29.3) |
| 256 | Glendale, CA | (14.0) | 328 | Sparks, NV | (20.0) | 403 | Grand Rapids, MI | (29.3) |
| 256 | Rockford, IL | (14.0) | 328 | Troy, MI | (20.0) | 405 | Farmington Hills, MI | (29.4) |
| 258 | Corona, CA | (14.1) | 332 | Peoria, AZ | (20.1) | 406 | Elizabeth, NJ | (29.7) |
| 258 | Stamford, CT | (14.1) | 333 | Compton, CA | (20.2) | 407 | Laredo, TX | (29.9) |
| 258 | Thousand Oaks, CA | (14.1) | 333 | Mountain View, CA | (20.2) | 408 | Napa, CA | (30.0) |
| 258 | Tracy, CA | (14.1) | 335 | Kenosha, WI | (20.6) | 408 | Tyler, TX | (30.0) |
| 262 | Largo, FL | (14.2) | 335 | Norfolk, VA | (20.6) | 410 | Athens-Clarke, GA | (31.2) |
| 263 | San Antonio, TX | (14.3) | 335 | St. Louis, MO | (20.6) | 411 | Greensboro, NC | (31.7) |
| 264 | Denton, TX | (14.4) | 338 | Boise, ID | (20.7) | 412 | Reading, PA | (32.6) |
| 264 | Memphis, TN | (14.4) | 339 | Brownsville, TX | (20.8) | 413 | Pembroke Pines, FL | (32.9) |
| 266 | Melbourne, FL | (14.5) | 340 | Columbus, GA | (21.4) | 414 | Carmel, IN | (33.1) |
| 267 | Garland, TX | (14.6) | 341 | Sunnyvale, CA | (21.6) | 414 | Port St. Lucie, FL | (33.1) |
| 268 | Edmond, OK | (14.8) | 342 | Danbury, CT | (21.7) | 414 | Tampa, FL | (33.1) |
| 269 | Greece, NY | (14.9) | 342 | Wichita Falls, TX | (21.7) | 417 | McAllen, TX | (34.1) |
| 270 | Fargo, ND | (15.0) | 344 | Gilbert, AZ | (21.8) | 418 | Irving, TX | (35.0) |
| 271 | Roanoke, VA | (15.1) | 345 | Lewisville, TX | (21.9) | 419 | Dearborn, MI | (35.2) |
| 272 | Westminster, CO | (15.2) | 345 | Milwaukee, WI | (21.9) | 420 | Concord, NC | (36.5) |
| 273 | Orem, UT | (15.4) | 347 | Clarkstown, NY | (22.0) | 421 | Aurora, IL | (38.5) |
| 274 | Mission Viejo, CA | (15.5) | 347 | Fayetteville, NC | (22.0) | 422 | Arlington Heights, IL | (39.2) |
| 275 | Joliet, IL | (15.6) | 347 | Naperville, IL | (22.0) | 423 | College Station, TX | (40.6) |
| 275 | Lynchburg, VA | (15.6) | 350 | Brooklyn Park, MN | (22.1) | 424 | Longview, TX | (41.4) |
| 277 | Cedar Rapids, IA | (15.7) | 351 | Austin, TX | (22.4) | 425 | Grand Prairie, TX | (41.8) |
| 278 | Sacramento, CA | (15.8) | 352 | Chesapeake, VA | (22.5) | 426 | Johns Creek, GA | (43.5) |
| 279 | Lawrence, KS | (15.9) | 352 | Reno, NV | (22.5) | 427 | Edison Twnshp, NJ | (44.3) |
| 280 | Cranston, RI | (16.0) | 354 | Decatur, IL | (22.6) | 428 | Bryan, TX | (48.0) |
| 281 | Ann Arbor, MI | (16.2) | 355 | Canton Twnshp, MI | (22.9) | NA | Champaign, IL** | NA |
| 282 | Woodbridge Twnshp, NJ | (16.3) | 356 | Killeen, TX | (23.2) | NA | Cicero, IL** | NA |
| 283 | Birmingham, AL | (16.4) | 356 | League City, TX | (23.2) | NA | Deerfield Beach, FL** | NA |
| 284 | Rochester, MN | (16.5) | 358 | Fort Collins, CO | (23.4) | NA | Evanston, IL** | NA |
| 285 | Boston, MA | (16.6) | 358 | Jackson, MS | (23.4) | NA | Greenville, NC** | NA |
| 285 | Chicago, IL | (16.6) | 360 | El Paso, TX | (23.5) | NA | Jurupa Valley, CA** | NA |
| 285 | Edinburg, TX | (16.6) | 360 | Murfreesboro, TN | (23.5) | NA | Lakewood Twnshp, NJ** | NA |
| 288 | Baldwin Park, CA | (16.7) | 362 | Warwick, RI | (23.6) | NA | Lowell, MA** | NA |
| 288 | Livonia, MI | (16.7) | 362 | Yonkers, NY | (23.6) | NA | Newport News, VA** | NA |
| 290 | Lubbock, TX | (16.8) | 364 | Clarksville, TN | (24.0) | NA | Toledo, OH** | NA |
| 291 | Lee's Summit, MO | (16.9) | 364 | St. Petersburg, FL | (24.0) | NA | Tucson, AZ** | NA |
| 291 | Roswell, GA | (16.9) | 366 | Jersey City, NJ | (24.2) | NA | Upland, CA** | NA |
| 293 | Mesa, AZ | (17.1) | 367 | Jacksonville, FL | (24.3) | NA | Waukegan, IL** | NA |
| 294 | Corpus Christi, TX | (17.2) | 367 | Richardson, TX | (24.3) | NA | Yakima, WA** | NA |
| 295 | Hammond, IN | (17.3) | 369 | Dallas, TX | (24.7) | | | |
| 295 | Springfield, IL | (17.3) | 369 | Overland Park, KS | (24.7) | | | |

Source: CQ Press using reported data from the F.B.I. "Crime in the United States 2013"

*Property crimes are offenses of burglary, larceny-theft, and motor vehicle theft. Attempts are included.

**Not available.

# 69. Burglaries in 2013
## National Total = 1,928,465 Burglaries*

| RANK | CITY | BURGLARY | RANK | CITY | BURGLARY | RANK | CITY | BURGLARY |
|---|---|---|---|---|---|---|---|---|
| 169 | Abilene, TX | 1,055 | 309 | Chino, CA | 518 | 270 | Fullerton, CA | 627 |
| 63 | Akron, OH | 3,096 | 191 | Chula Vista, CA | 971 | 234 | Gainesville, FL | 742 |
| 399 | Alameda, CA | 287 | 317 | Cicero, IL | 503 | 266 | Garden Grove, CA | 637 |
| 136 | Albany, GA | 1,319 | 30 | Cincinnati, OH | 5,467 | 92 | Garland, TX | 2,053 |
| 249 | Albany, NY | 705 | 322 | Citrus Heights, CA | 483 | 122 | Gary, IN | 1,454 |
| 18 | Albuquerque, NM | 7,297 | 440 | Clarkstown, NY | 99 | 260 | Gilbert, AZ | 647 |
| 413 | Alexandria, VA | 249 | 176 | Clarksville, TN | 1,020 | 77 | Glendale, AZ | 2,410 |
| 379 | Alhambra, CA | 344 | 212 | Clearwater, FL | 851 | 295 | Glendale, CA | 563 |
| 142 | Allentown, PA | 1,263 | 14 | Cleveland, OH | 8,259 | 161 | Grand Prairie, TX | 1,120 |
| 432 | Allen, TX | 170 | 372 | Clifton, NJ | 358 | 113 | Grand Rapids, MI | 1,621 |
| 108 | Amarillo, TX | 1,816 | 348 | Clinton Twnshp, MI | 420 | 382 | Greece, NY | 332 |
| 423 | Amherst, NY | 204 | 204 | Clovis, CA | 879 | 326 | Greeley, CO | 475 |
| 125 | Anaheim, CA | 1,412 | 342 | College Station, TX | 432 | 285 | Green Bay, WI | 575 |
| 137 | Anchorage, AK | 1,318 | 427 | Colonie, NY | 186 | 66 | Greensboro, NC | 2,972 |
| 353 | Ann Arbor, MI | 410 | 50 | Colorado Springs, CO | 3,726 | 152 | Greenville, NC | 1,157 |
| 135 | Antioch, CA | 1,351 | 251 | Columbia, MO | 703 | 199 | Gresham, OR | 920 |
| 439 | Arlington Heights, IL | 125 | 129 | Columbia, SC | 1,398 | 337 | Hamilton Twnshp, NJ | 448 |
| 61 | Arlington, TX | 3,181 | 55 | Columbus, GA | 3,355 | 276 | Hammond, IN | 608 |
| 383 | Arvada, CO | 331 | 281 | Compton, CA | 579 | 242 | Hampton, VA | 722 |
| 192 | Athens-Clarke, GA | 967 | 215 | Concord, CA | 825 | 187 | Hartford, CT | 981 |
| 26 | Atlanta, GA | 5,938 | 352 | Concord, NC | 414 | 308 | Hawthorne, CA | 523 |
| 97 | Aurora, CO | 1,981 | 364 | Coral Springs, FL | 389 | 172 | Hayward, CA | 1,051 |
| 283 | Aurora, IL | 576 | 262 | Corona, CA | 644 | 162 | Hemet, CA | 1,110 |
| 21 | Austin, TX | 6,550 | 74 | Corpus Christi, TX | 2,595 | 128 | Henderson, NV | 1,405 |
| 37 | Bakersfield, CA | 4,605 | 313 | Costa Mesa, CA | 512 | 209 | Hesperia, CA | 869 |
| 406 | Baldwin Park, CA | 280 | 389 | Cranston, RI | 309 | 230 | Hialeah, FL | 763 |
| 16 | Baltimore, MD | 7,391 | 8 | Dallas, TX | 14,516 | 147 | High Point, NC | 1,206 |
| 58 | Baton Rouge, LA | 3,264 | 375 | Daly City, CA | 352 | 388 | Hillsboro, OR | 311 |
| 101 | Beaumont, TX | 1,922 | 419 | Danbury, CT | 221 | 118 | Hollywood, FL | 1,500 |
| 430 | Beaverton, OR | 175 | 193 | Davenport, IA | 961 | 379 | Hoover, AL | 344 |
| 254 | Bellevue, WA | 688 | 258 | Davie, FL | 651 | 1 | Houston, TX | 23,733 |
| 345 | Bellflower, CA | 427 | 72 | Dayton, OH | 2,613 | 223 | Huntington Beach, CA | 793 |
| 407 | Bend, OR | 267 | 360 | Dearborn, MI | 399 | 104 | Huntsville, AL | 1,884 |
| 169 | Berkeley, CA | 1,055 | 223 | Decatur, IL | 793 | 150 | Independence, MO | 1,167 |
| 369 | Bethlehem, PA | 365 | 271 | Deerfield Beach, FL | 624 | 9 | Indianapolis, IN | 13,445 |
| 185 | Billings, MT | 989 | 329 | Denton, TX | 472 | 226 | Indio, CA | 792 |
| 42 | Birmingham, AL | 4,018 | 36 | Denver, CO | 4,918 | 266 | Inglewood, CA | 637 |
| 357 | Bloomington, IL | 402 | 84 | Des Moines, IA | 2,311 | 280 | Irvine, CA | 583 |
| 311 | Bloomington, IN | 516 | 11 | Detroit, MI | 11,754 | 155 | Irving, TX | 1,137 |
| 424 | Bloomington, MN | 193 | 288 | Downey, CA | 573 | 19 | Jacksonville, FL | 7,069 |
| 331 | Boca Raton, FL | 464 | 264 | Duluth, MN | 643 | 54 | Jackson, MS | 3,366 |
| 215 | Boise, ID | 825 | 238 | Edinburg, TX | 738 | 171 | Jersey City, NJ | 1,052 |
| 63 | Boston, MA | 3,096 | 401 | Edison Twnshp, NJ | 285 | 437 | Johns Creek, GA | 136 |
| 274 | Boulder, CO | 612 | 389 | Edmond, OK | 309 | 240 | Joliet, IL | 724 |
| 412 | Brick Twnshp, NJ | 252 | 320 | El Cajon, CA | 493 | 290 | Jurupa Valley, CA | 570 |
| 149 | Bridgeport, CT | 1,191 | 291 | El Monte, CA | 568 | 114 | Kansas City, KS | 1,617 |
| 210 | Brockton, MA | 865 | 110 | El Paso, TX | 1,771 | 24 | Kansas City, MO | 6,412 |
| 354 | Broken Arrow, OK | 409 | 376 | Elgin, IL | 351 | 339 | Kennewick, WA | 444 |
| 347 | Brooklyn Park, MN | 421 | 223 | Elizabeth, NJ | 793 | 295 | Kenosha, WI | 563 |
| 154 | Brownsville, TX | 1,140 | 299 | Elk Grove, CA | 544 | 168 | Kent, WA | 1,061 |
| 300 | Bryan, TX | 539 | 177 | Erie, PA | 1,017 | 130 | Killeen, TX | 1,396 |
| 370 | Buena Park, CA | 361 | 244 | Escondido, CA | 717 | 85 | Knoxville, TN | 2,275 |
| 53 | Buffalo, NY | 3,458 | 115 | Eugene, OR | 1,539 | 139 | Lafayette, LA | 1,276 |
| 401 | Burbank, CA | 285 | 370 | Evanston, IL | 361 | 434 | Lake Forest, CA | 150 |
| 359 | Cambridge, MA | 401 | 180 | Evansville, IN | 996 | 157 | Lakeland, FL | 1,130 |
| 431 | Canton Twnshp, MI | 173 | 158 | Everett, WA | 1,129 | 427 | Lakewood Twnshp, NJ | 186 |
| 220 | Cape Coral, FL | 803 | 239 | Fairfield, CA | 735 | 351 | Lakewood, CA | 419 |
| 307 | Carlsbad, CA | 525 | 253 | Fall River, MA | 698 | 206 | Lakewood, CO | 872 |
| 438 | Carmel, IN | 128 | 252 | Fargo, ND | 701 | 167 | Lancaster, CA | 1,062 |
| 248 | Carrollton, TX | 706 | 414 | Farmington Hills, MI | 245 | 141 | Lansing, MI | 1,268 |
| 312 | Carson, CA | 514 | 302 | Fayetteville, AR | 538 | 123 | Laredo, TX | 1,425 |
| 361 | Cary, NC | 392 | 57 | Fayetteville, NC | 3,279 | 259 | Largo, FL | 650 |
| 188 | Cedar Rapids, IA | 977 | 205 | Federal Way, WA | 874 | 240 | Las Cruces, NM | 724 |
| 427 | Centennial, CO | 186 | 442 | Fishers, IN | 78 | 7 | Las Vegas, NV | 14,785 |
| 316 | Champaign, IL | 506 | 100 | Flint, MI | 1,941 | 320 | Lawrence, KS | 493 |
| 183 | Chandler, AZ | 993 | 206 | Fontana, CA | 872 | 341 | Lawrence, MA | 433 |
| 392 | Charleston, SC | 305 | 304 | Fort Collins, CO | 531 | 119 | Lawton, OK | 1,485 |
| 23 | Charlotte, NC | 6,439 | 71 | Fort Lauderdale, FL | 2,654 | 366 | League City, TX | 386 |
| 82 | Chattanooga, TN | 2,317 | 189 | Fort Smith, AR | 975 | 407 | Lee's Summit, MO | 267 |
| 378 | Cheektowaga, NY | 345 | 78 | Fort Wayne, IN | 2,396 | 318 | Lewisville, TX | 501 |
| 165 | Chesapeake, VA | 1,076 | 13 | Fort Worth, TX | 8,316 | 76 | Lexington, KY | 2,574 |
| 2 | Chicago, IL | 17,775 | 196 | Fremont, CA | 944 | 124 | Lincoln, NE | 1,423 |
| 272 | Chico, CA | 622 | 32 | Fresno, CA | 5,223 | 48 | Little Rock, AR | 3,794 |
| 387 | Chino Hills, CA | 315 | 368 | Frisco, TX | 374 | 365 | Livermore, CA | 387 |

| RANK | CITY | BURGLARY | RANK | CITY | BURGLARY | RANK | CITY | BURGLARY |
|---|---|---|---|---|---|---|---|---|
| 401 | Livonia, MI | 285 | 198 | Pasadena, CA | 939 | 355 | South Gate, CA | 406 |
| 49 | Long Beach, CA | 3,776 | 178 | Pasadena, TX | 1,011 | 297 | Sparks, NV | 559 |
| 410 | Longmont, CO | 266 | 134 | Paterson, NJ | 1,368 | 193 | Spokane Valley, WA | 961 |
| 268 | Longview, TX | 630 | 399 | Pearland, TX | 287 | 45 | Spokane, WA | 3,889 |
| 5 | Los Angeles, CA | 15,728 | 227 | Pembroke Pines, FL | 775 | 138 | Springfield, IL | 1,300 |
| 20 | Louisville, KY | 6,920 | 244 | Peoria, AZ | 717 | 79 | Springfield, MA | 2,360 |
| 232 | Lowell, MA | 759 | 160 | Peoria, IL | 1,123 | 83 | Springfield, MO | 2,313 |
| 73 | Lubbock, TX | 2,608 | 12 | Philadelphia, PA | 10,408 | 373 | Stamford, CT | 354 |
| 377 | Lynchburg, VA | 349 | 3 | Phoenix, AZ | 16,747 | 384 | Sterling Heights, MI | 330 |
| 314 | Lynn, MA | 510 | 87 | Pittsburgh, PA | 2,173 | 40 | Stockton, CA | 4,189 |
| 96 | Macon, GA | 1,993 | 196 | Plano, TX | 944 | 326 | St. George, UT | 475 |
| 131 | Madison, WI | 1,382 | 246 | Plantation, FL | 711 | 218 | St. Joseph, MO | 805 |
| 201 | Manchester, NH | 894 | 213 | Pomona, CA | 847 | 39 | St. Louis, MO | 4,305 |
| 303 | McAllen, TX | 536 | 144 | Pompano Beach, FL | 1,220 | 68 | St. Paul, MN | 2,769 |
| 324 | McKinney, TX | 476 | 242 | Port St. Lucie, FL | 722 | 69 | St. Petersburg, FL | 2,742 |
| 285 | Medford, OR | 575 | 41 | Portland, OR | 4,128 | 319 | Suffolk, VA | 500 |
| 237 | Melbourne, FL | 741 | 116 | Portsmouth, VA | 1,535 | 411 | Sugar Land, TX | 256 |
| 10 | Memphis, TN | 11,825 | 105 | Providence, RI | 1,828 | 287 | Sunnyvale, CA | 574 |
| 362 | Menifee, CA | 391 | 385 | Provo, UT | 329 | 228 | Sunrise, FL | 773 |
| 262 | Merced, CA | 644 | 103 | Pueblo, CO | 1,900 | 357 | Surprise, AZ | 402 |
| 424 | Meridian, ID | 193 | 332 | Quincy, MA | 461 | 109 | Syracuse, NY | 1,781 |
| 81 | Mesa, AZ | 2,357 | 146 | Racine, WI | 1,211 | 65 | Tacoma, WA | 3,086 |
| 131 | Mesquite, TX | 1,382 | 62 | Raleigh, NC | 3,157 | 89 | Tallahassee, FL | 2,082 |
| 195 | Miami Beach, FL | 950 | 441 | Ramapo, NY | 88 | 99 | Tampa, FL | 1,950 |
| 159 | Miami Gardens, FL | 1,128 | 133 | Rancho Cucamon., CA | 1,374 | 246 | Temecula, CA | 711 |
| 43 | Miami, FL | 3,993 | 174 | Reading, PA | 1,040 | 139 | Tempe, AZ | 1,276 |
| 291 | Midland, TX | 568 | 234 | Redding, CA | 742 | 343 | Thornton, CO | 431 |
| 22 | Milwaukee, WI | 6,491 | 315 | Redwood City, CA | 507 | 398 | Thousand Oaks, CA | 291 |
| 38 | Minneapolis, MN | 4,601 | 126 | Reno, NV | 1,411 | 31 | Toledo, OH | 5,357 |
| 166 | Miramar, FL | 1,070 | 211 | Renton, WA | 859 | 305 | Toms River Twnshp, NJ | 527 |
| 433 | Mission Viejo, CA | 156 | 222 | Rialto, CA | 798 | 143 | Topeka, KS | 1,238 |
| 338 | Mission, TX | 447 | 300 | Richardson, TX | 539 | 278 | Torrance, CA | 591 |
| 59 | Mobile, AL | 3,207 | 112 | Richmond, CA | 1,631 | 374 | Tracy, CA | 353 |
| 86 | Modesto, CA | 2,251 | 107 | Richmond, VA | 1,817 | 180 | Trenton, NJ | 996 |
| 106 | Moreno Valley, CA | 1,822 | 98 | Riverside, CA | 1,978 | 418 | Troy, MI | 222 |
| 397 | Mountain View, CA | 294 | 269 | Roanoke, VA | 628 | 35 | Tucson, AZ | 4,957 |
| 234 | Murfreesboro, TN | 742 | 344 | Rochester, MN | 429 | 27 | Tulsa, OK | 5,935 |
| 401 | Murrieta, CA | 285 | 75 | Rochester, NY | 2,587 | 151 | Tuscaloosa, AL | 1,165 |
| 340 | Nampa, ID | 434 | 95 | Rockford, IL | 2,001 | 421 | Tustin, CA | 213 |
| 393 | Napa, CA | 304 | 323 | Roseville, CA | 482 | 215 | Tyler, TX | 825 |
| 416 | Naperville, IL | 225 | 324 | Roswell, GA | 476 | 279 | Upland, CA | 589 |
| 386 | Nashua, NH | 323 | 395 | Round Rock, TX | 297 | 416 | Upper Darby Twnshp, PA | 225 |
| 29 | Nashville, TN | 5,613 | 46 | Sacramento, CA | 3,886 | 407 | Vacaville, CA | 267 |
| 200 | New Bedford, MA | 916 | 186 | Salem, OR | 983 | 66 | Vallejo, CA | 2,972 |
| 164 | New Haven, CT | 1,082 | 153 | Salinas, CA | 1,148 | 179 | Vancouver, WA | 1,007 |
| 60 | New Orleans, LA | 3,203 | 91 | Salt Lake City, UT | 2,068 | 233 | Ventura, CA | 745 |
| 434 | New Rochelle, NY | 150 | 255 | San Angelo, TX | 682 | 121 | Victorville, CA | 1,461 |
| 4 | New York, NY | 16,606 | 6 | San Antonio, TX | 14,850 | 127 | Virginia Beach, VA | 1,407 |
| 90 | Newark, NJ | 2,074 | 70 | San Bernardino, CA | 2,673 | 145 | Visalia, CA | 1,218 |
| 336 | Newport Beach, CA | 454 | 25 | San Diego, CA | 6,355 | 363 | Vista, CA | 390 |
| 184 | Newport News, VA | 991 | 28 | San Francisco, CA | 5,931 | 117 | Waco, TX | 1,508 |
| 422 | Newton, MA | 205 | 33 | San Jose, CA | 5,173 | 203 | Warren, MI | 887 |
| 94 | Norfolk, VA | 2,039 | 231 | San Leandro, CA | 761 | 405 | Warwick, RI | 282 |
| 274 | Norman, OK | 612 | 394 | San Marcos, CA | 299 | 56 | Washington, DC | 3,314 |
| 202 | North Charleston, SC | 892 | 389 | San Mateo, CA | 309 | 293 | Waterbury, CT | 566 |
| 93 | North Las Vegas, NV | 2,050 | 306 | Sandy Springs, GA | 526 | 256 | Waukegan, IL | 681 |
| 348 | Norwalk, CA | 420 | 283 | Sandy, UT | 576 | 273 | West Covina, CA | 615 |
| 414 | Norwalk, CT | 245 | 220 | Santa Ana, CA | 803 | 175 | West Palm Beach, FL | 1,024 |
| 34 | Oakland, CA | 5,058 | 334 | Santa Barbara, CA | 459 | 156 | West Valley, UT | 1,132 |
| 257 | Oceanside, CA | 677 | 332 | Santa Clara, CA | 461 | 294 | Westland, MI | 564 |
| 229 | Odessa, TX | 764 | 250 | Santa Clarita, CA | 704 | 348 | Westminster, CA | 420 |
| 436 | O'Fallon, MO | 139 | 260 | Santa Maria, CA | 647 | 367 | Westminster, CO | 382 |
| 282 | Ogden, UT | 578 | 288 | Santa Monica, CA | 573 | 335 | Whittier, CA | 455 |
| 15 | Oklahoma City, OK | 8,016 | 265 | Santa Rosa, CA | 638 | 182 | Wichita Falls, TX | 995 |
| 420 | Olathe, KS | 217 | 88 | Savannah, GA | 2,125 | 44 | Wichita, KS | 3,933 |
| 51 | Omaha, NE | 3,509 | 163 | Scottsdale, AZ | 1,093 | 111 | Wilmington, NC | 1,645 |
| 214 | Ontario, CA | 830 | 298 | Scranton, PA | 549 | 47 | Winston-Salem, NC | 3,883 |
| 328 | Orange, CA | 473 | 17 | Seattle, WA | 7,384 | 396 | Woodbridge Twnshp, NJ | 296 |
| 426 | Orem, UT | 192 | 79 | Shreveport, LA | 2,360 | 102 | Worcester, MA | 1,916 |
| 52 | Orlando, FL | 3,485 | 379 | Simi Valley, CA | 344 | 148 | Yakima, WA | 1,194 |
| 356 | Overland Park, KS | 404 | 277 | Sioux City, IA | 604 | 330 | Yonkers, NY | 470 |
| 190 | Oxnard, CA | 974 | 208 | Sioux Falls, SD | 870 | 218 | Yuma, AZ | 805 |
| 310 | Palm Bay, FL | 517 | 346 | Somerville, MA | 426 | | | |
| 173 | Palmdale, CA | 1,049 | 120 | South Bend, IN | 1,468 | | | |

Source: Reported data from the F.B.I. "Crime in the United States 2013"

*Burglary is the unlawful entry of a structure to commit a felony or theft. Attempts are included.

# 69. Burglaries in 2013 (continued)
## National Total = 1,928,465 Burglaries*

| RANK | CITY | BURGLARY | RANK | CITY | BURGLARY | RANK | CITY | BURGLARY |
|---|---|---|---|---|---|---|---|---|
| 1 | Houston, TX | 23,733 | 75 | Rochester, NY | 2,587 | 149 | Bridgeport, CT | 1,191 |
| 2 | Chicago, IL | 17,775 | 76 | Lexington, KY | 2,574 | 150 | Independence, MO | 1,167 |
| 3 | Phoenix, AZ | 16,747 | 77 | Glendale, AZ | 2,410 | 151 | Tuscaloosa, AL | 1,165 |
| 4 | New York, NY | 16,606 | 78 | Fort Wayne, IN | 2,396 | 152 | Greenville, NC | 1,157 |
| 5 | Los Angeles, CA | 15,728 | 79 | Shreveport, LA | 2,360 | 153 | Salinas, CA | 1,148 |
| 6 | San Antonio, TX | 14,850 | 79 | Springfield, MA | 2,360 | 154 | Brownsville, TX | 1,140 |
| 7 | Las Vegas, NV | 14,785 | 81 | Mesa, AZ | 2,357 | 155 | Irving, TX | 1,137 |
| 8 | Dallas, TX | 14,516 | 82 | Chattanooga, TN | 2,317 | 156 | West Valley, UT | 1,132 |
| 9 | Indianapolis, IN | 13,445 | 83 | Springfield, MO | 2,313 | 157 | Lakeland, FL | 1,130 |
| 10 | Memphis, TN | 11,825 | 84 | Des Moines, IA | 2,311 | 158 | Everett, WA | 1,129 |
| 11 | Detroit, MI | 11,754 | 85 | Knoxville, TN | 2,275 | 159 | Miami Gardens, FL | 1,128 |
| 12 | Philadelphia, PA | 10,408 | 86 | Modesto, CA | 2,251 | 160 | Peoria, IL | 1,123 |
| 13 | Fort Worth, TX | 8,316 | 87 | Pittsburgh, PA | 2,173 | 161 | Grand Prairie, TX | 1,120 |
| 14 | Cleveland, OH | 8,259 | 88 | Savannah, GA | 2,125 | 162 | Hemet, CA | 1,110 |
| 15 | Oklahoma City, OK | 8,016 | 89 | Tallahassee, FL | 2,082 | 163 | Scottsdale, AZ | 1,093 |
| 16 | Baltimore, MD | 7,391 | 90 | Newark, NJ | 2,074 | 164 | New Haven, CT | 1,082 |
| 17 | Seattle, WA | 7,384 | 91 | Salt Lake City, UT | 2,068 | 165 | Chesapeake, VA | 1,076 |
| 18 | Albuquerque, NM | 7,297 | 92 | Garland, TX | 2,053 | 166 | Miramar, FL | 1,070 |
| 19 | Jacksonville, FL | 7,069 | 93 | North Las Vegas, NV | 2,050 | 167 | Lancaster, CA | 1,062 |
| 20 | Louisville, KY | 6,920 | 94 | Norfolk, VA | 2,039 | 168 | Kent, WA | 1,061 |
| 21 | Austin, TX | 6,550 | 95 | Rockford, IL | 2,001 | 169 | Abilene, TX | 1,055 |
| 22 | Milwaukee, WI | 6,491 | 96 | Macon, GA | 1,993 | 169 | Berkeley, CA | 1,055 |
| 23 | Charlotte, NC | 6,439 | 97 | Aurora, CO | 1,981 | 171 | Jersey City, NJ | 1,052 |
| 24 | Kansas City, MO | 6,412 | 98 | Riverside, CA | 1,978 | 172 | Hayward, CA | 1,051 |
| 25 | San Diego, CA | 6,355 | 99 | Tampa, FL | 1,950 | 173 | Palmdale, CA | 1,049 |
| 26 | Atlanta, GA | 5,938 | 100 | Flint, MI | 1,941 | 174 | Reading, PA | 1,040 |
| 27 | Tulsa, OK | 5,935 | 101 | Beaumont, TX | 1,922 | 175 | West Palm Beach, FL | 1,024 |
| 28 | San Francisco, CA | 5,931 | 102 | Worcester, MA | 1,916 | 176 | Clarksville, TN | 1,020 |
| 29 | Nashville, TN | 5,613 | 103 | Pueblo, CO | 1,900 | 177 | Erie, PA | 1,017 |
| 30 | Cincinnati, OH | 5,467 | 104 | Huntsville, AL | 1,884 | 178 | Pasadena, TX | 1,011 |
| 31 | Toledo, OH | 5,357 | 105 | Providence, RI | 1,828 | 179 | Vancouver, WA | 1,007 |
| 32 | Fresno, CA | 5,223 | 106 | Moreno Valley, CA | 1,822 | 180 | Evansville, IN | 996 |
| 33 | San Jose, CA | 5,173 | 107 | Richmond, VA | 1,817 | 180 | Trenton, NJ | 996 |
| 34 | Oakland, CA | 5,058 | 108 | Amarillo, TX | 1,816 | 182 | Wichita Falls, TX | 995 |
| 35 | Tucson, AZ | 4,957 | 109 | Syracuse, NY | 1,781 | 183 | Chandler, AZ | 993 |
| 36 | Denver, CO | 4,918 | 110 | El Paso, TX | 1,771 | 184 | Newport News, VA | 991 |
| 37 | Bakersfield, CA | 4,605 | 111 | Wilmington, NC | 1,645 | 185 | Billings, MT | 989 |
| 38 | Minneapolis, MN | 4,601 | 112 | Richmond, CA | 1,631 | 186 | Salem, OR | 983 |
| 39 | St. Louis, MO | 4,305 | 113 | Grand Rapids, MI | 1,621 | 187 | Hartford, CT | 981 |
| 40 | Stockton, CA | 4,189 | 114 | Kansas City, KS | 1,617 | 188 | Cedar Rapids, IA | 977 |
| 41 | Portland, OR | 4,128 | 115 | Eugene, OR | 1,539 | 189 | Fort Smith, AR | 975 |
| 42 | Birmingham, AL | 4,018 | 116 | Portsmouth, VA | 1,535 | 190 | Oxnard, CA | 974 |
| 43 | Miami, FL | 3,993 | 117 | Waco, TX | 1,508 | 191 | Chula Vista, CA | 971 |
| 44 | Wichita, KS | 3,933 | 118 | Hollywood, FL | 1,500 | 192 | Athens-Clarke, GA | 967 |
| 45 | Spokane, WA | 3,889 | 119 | Lawton, OK | 1,485 | 193 | Davenport, IA | 961 |
| 46 | Sacramento, CA | 3,886 | 120 | South Bend, IN | 1,468 | 193 | Spokane Valley, WA | 961 |
| 47 | Winston-Salem, NC | 3,883 | 121 | Victorville, CA | 1,461 | 195 | Miami Beach, FL | 950 |
| 48 | Little Rock, AR | 3,794 | 122 | Gary, IN | 1,454 | 196 | Fremont, CA | 944 |
| 49 | Long Beach, CA | 3,776 | 123 | Laredo, TX | 1,425 | 196 | Plano, TX | 944 |
| 50 | Colorado Springs, CO | 3,726 | 124 | Lincoln, NE | 1,423 | 198 | Pasadena, CA | 939 |
| 51 | Omaha, NE | 3,509 | 125 | Anaheim, CA | 1,412 | 199 | Gresham, OR | 920 |
| 52 | Orlando, FL | 3,485 | 126 | Reno, NV | 1,411 | 200 | New Bedford, MA | 916 |
| 53 | Buffalo, NY | 3,458 | 127 | Virginia Beach, VA | 1,407 | 201 | Manchester, NH | 894 |
| 54 | Jackson, MS | 3,366 | 128 | Henderson, NV | 1,405 | 202 | North Charleston, SC | 892 |
| 55 | Columbus, GA | 3,355 | 129 | Columbia, SC | 1,398 | 203 | Warren, MI | 887 |
| 56 | Washington, DC | 3,314 | 130 | Killeen, TX | 1,396 | 204 | Clovis, CA | 879 |
| 57 | Fayetteville, NC | 3,279 | 131 | Madison, WI | 1,382 | 205 | Federal Way, WA | 874 |
| 58 | Baton Rouge, LA | 3,264 | 131 | Mesquite, TX | 1,382 | 206 | Fontana, CA | 872 |
| 59 | Mobile, AL | 3,207 | 133 | Rancho Cucamon., CA | 1,374 | 206 | Lakewood, CO | 872 |
| 60 | New Orleans, LA | 3,203 | 134 | Paterson, NJ | 1,368 | 208 | Sioux Falls, SD | 870 |
| 61 | Arlington, TX | 3,181 | 135 | Antioch, CA | 1,351 | 209 | Hesperia, CA | 869 |
| 62 | Raleigh, NC | 3,157 | 136 | Albany, GA | 1,319 | 210 | Brockton, MA | 865 |
| 63 | Akron, OH | 3,096 | 137 | Anchorage, AK | 1,318 | 211 | Renton, WA | 859 |
| 63 | Boston, MA | 3,096 | 138 | Springfield, IL | 1,300 | 212 | Clearwater, FL | 851 |
| 65 | Tacoma, WA | 3,086 | 139 | Lafayette, LA | 1,276 | 213 | Pomona, CA | 847 |
| 66 | Greensboro, NC | 2,972 | 139 | Tempe, AZ | 1,276 | 214 | Ontario, CA | 830 |
| 66 | Vallejo, CA | 2,972 | 141 | Lansing, MI | 1,268 | 215 | Boise, ID | 825 |
| 68 | St. Paul, MN | 2,769 | 142 | Allentown, PA | 1,263 | 215 | Concord, CA | 825 |
| 69 | St. Petersburg, FL | 2,742 | 143 | Topeka, KS | 1,238 | 215 | Tyler, TX | 825 |
| 70 | San Bernardino, CA | 2,673 | 144 | Pompano Beach, FL | 1,220 | 218 | St. Joseph, MO | 805 |
| 71 | Fort Lauderdale, FL | 2,654 | 145 | Visalia, CA | 1,218 | 218 | Yuma, AZ | 805 |
| 72 | Dayton, OH | 2,613 | 146 | Racine, WI | 1,211 | 220 | Cape Coral, FL | 803 |
| 73 | Lubbock, TX | 2,608 | 147 | High Point, NC | 1,206 | 220 | Santa Ana, CA | 803 |
| 74 | Corpus Christi, TX | 2,595 | 148 | Yakima, WA | 1,194 | 222 | Rialto, CA | 798 |

| RANK | CITY | BURGLARY | RANK | CITY | BURGLARY | RANK | CITY | BURGLARY |
|---|---|---|---|---|---|---|---|---|
| 223 | Decatur, IL | 793 | 297 | Sparks, NV | 559 | 370 | Evanston, IL | 361 |
| 223 | Elizabeth, NJ | 793 | 298 | Scranton, PA | 549 | 372 | Clifton, NJ | 358 |
| 223 | Huntington Beach, CA | 793 | 299 | Elk Grove, CA | 544 | 373 | Stamford, CT | 354 |
| 226 | Indio, CA | 792 | 300 | Bryan, TX | 539 | 374 | Tracy, CA | 353 |
| 227 | Pembroke Pines, FL | 775 | 300 | Richardson, TX | 539 | 375 | Daly City, CA | 352 |
| 228 | Sunrise, FL | 773 | 302 | Fayetteville, AR | 538 | 376 | Elgin, IL | 351 |
| 229 | Odessa, TX | 764 | 303 | McAllen, TX | 536 | 377 | Lynchburg, VA | 349 |
| 230 | Hialeah, FL | 763 | 304 | Fort Collins, CO | 531 | 378 | Cheektowaga, NY | 345 |
| 231 | San Leandro, CA | 761 | 305 | Toms River Twnshp, NJ | 527 | 379 | Alhambra, CA | 344 |
| 232 | Lowell, MA | 759 | 306 | Sandy Springs, GA | 526 | 379 | Hoover, AL | 344 |
| 233 | Ventura, CA | 745 | 307 | Carlsbad, CA | 525 | 379 | Simi Valley, CA | 344 |
| 234 | Gainesville, FL | 742 | 308 | Hawthorne, CA | 523 | 382 | Greece, NY | 332 |
| 234 | Murfreesboro, TN | 742 | 309 | Chino, CA | 518 | 383 | Arvada, CO | 331 |
| 234 | Redding, CA | 742 | 310 | Palm Bay, FL | 517 | 384 | Sterling Heights, MI | 330 |
| 237 | Melbourne, FL | 741 | 311 | Bloomington, IN | 516 | 385 | Provo, UT | 329 |
| 238 | Edinburg, TX | 738 | 312 | Carson, CA | 514 | 386 | Nashua, NH | 323 |
| 239 | Fairfield, CA | 735 | 313 | Costa Mesa, CA | 512 | 387 | Chino Hills, CA | 315 |
| 240 | Joliet, IL | 724 | 314 | Lynn, MA | 510 | 388 | Hillsboro, OR | 311 |
| 240 | Las Cruces, NM | 724 | 315 | Redwood City, CA | 507 | 389 | Cranston, RI | 309 |
| 242 | Hampton, VA | 722 | 316 | Champaign, IL | 506 | 389 | Edmond, OK | 309 |
| 242 | Port St. Lucie, FL | 722 | 317 | Cicero, IL | 503 | 389 | San Mateo, CA | 309 |
| 244 | Escondido, CA | 717 | 318 | Lewisville, TX | 501 | 392 | Charleston, SC | 305 |
| 244 | Peoria, AZ | 717 | 319 | Suffolk, VA | 500 | 393 | Napa, CA | 304 |
| 246 | Plantation, FL | 711 | 320 | El Cajon, CA | 493 | 394 | San Marcos, CA | 299 |
| 246 | Temecula, CA | 711 | 320 | Lawrence, KS | 493 | 395 | Round Rock, TX | 297 |
| 248 | Carrollton, TX | 706 | 322 | Citrus Heights, CA | 483 | 396 | Woodbridge Twnshp, NJ | 296 |
| 249 | Albany, NY | 705 | 323 | Roseville, CA | 482 | 397 | Mountain View, CA | 294 |
| 250 | Santa Clarita, CA | 704 | 324 | McKinney, TX | 476 | 398 | Thousand Oaks, CA | 291 |
| 251 | Columbia, MO | 703 | 324 | Roswell, GA | 476 | 399 | Alameda, CA | 287 |
| 252 | Fargo, ND | 701 | 326 | Greeley, CO | 475 | 399 | Pearland, TX | 287 |
| 253 | Fall River, MA | 698 | 326 | St. George, UT | 475 | 401 | Burbank, CA | 285 |
| 254 | Bellevue, WA | 688 | 328 | Orange, CA | 473 | 401 | Edison Twnshp, NJ | 285 |
| 255 | San Angelo, TX | 682 | 329 | Denton, TX | 472 | 401 | Livonia, MI | 285 |
| 256 | Waukegan, IL | 681 | 330 | Yonkers, NY | 470 | 401 | Murrieta, CA | 285 |
| 257 | Oceanside, CA | 677 | 331 | Boca Raton, FL | 464 | 405 | Warwick, RI | 282 |
| 258 | Davie, FL | 651 | 332 | Quincy, MA | 461 | 406 | Baldwin Park, CA | 280 |
| 259 | Largo, FL | 650 | 332 | Santa Clara, CA | 461 | 407 | Bend, OR | 267 |
| 260 | Gilbert, AZ | 647 | 334 | Santa Barbara, CA | 459 | 407 | Lee's Summit, MO | 267 |
| 260 | Santa Maria, CA | 647 | 335 | Whittier, CA | 455 | 407 | Vacaville, CA | 267 |
| 262 | Corona, CA | 644 | 336 | Newport Beach, CA | 454 | 410 | Longmont, CO | 266 |
| 262 | Merced, CA | 644 | 337 | Hamilton Twnshp, NJ | 448 | 411 | Sugar Land, TX | 256 |
| 264 | Duluth, MN | 643 | 338 | Mission, TX | 447 | 412 | Brick Twnshp, NJ | 252 |
| 265 | Santa Rosa, CA | 638 | 339 | Kennewick, WA | 444 | 413 | Alexandria, VA | 249 |
| 266 | Garden Grove, CA | 637 | 340 | Nampa, ID | 434 | 414 | Farmington Hills, MI | 245 |
| 266 | Inglewood, CA | 637 | 341 | Lawrence, MA | 433 | 414 | Norwalk, CT | 245 |
| 268 | Longview, TX | 630 | 342 | College Station, TX | 432 | 416 | Naperville, IL | 225 |
| 269 | Roanoke, VA | 628 | 343 | Thornton, CO | 431 | 416 | Upper Darby Twnshp, PA | 225 |
| 270 | Fullerton, CA | 627 | 344 | Rochester, MN | 429 | 418 | Troy, MI | 222 |
| 271 | Deerfield Beach, FL | 624 | 345 | Bellflower, CA | 427 | 419 | Danbury, CT | 221 |
| 272 | Chico, CA | 622 | 346 | Somerville, MA | 426 | 420 | Olathe, KS | 217 |
| 273 | West Covina, CA | 615 | 347 | Brooklyn Park, MN | 421 | 421 | Tustin, CA | 213 |
| 274 | Boulder, CO | 612 | 348 | Clinton Twnshp, MI | 420 | 422 | Newton, MA | 205 |
| 274 | Norman, OK | 612 | 348 | Norwalk, CA | 420 | 423 | Amherst, NY | 204 |
| 276 | Hammond, IN | 608 | 348 | Westminster, CA | 420 | 424 | Bloomington, MN | 193 |
| 277 | Sioux City, IA | 604 | 351 | Lakewood, CA | 419 | 424 | Meridian, ID | 193 |
| 278 | Torrance, CA | 591 | 352 | Concord, NC | 414 | 426 | Orem, UT | 192 |
| 279 | Upland, CA | 589 | 353 | Ann Arbor, MI | 410 | 427 | Centennial, CO | 186 |
| 280 | Irvine, CA | 583 | 354 | Broken Arrow, OK | 409 | 427 | Colonie, NY | 186 |
| 281 | Compton, CA | 579 | 355 | South Gate, CA | 406 | 427 | Lakewood Twnshp, NJ | 186 |
| 282 | Ogden, UT | 578 | 356 | Overland Park, KS | 404 | 430 | Beaverton, OR | 175 |
| 283 | Aurora, IL | 576 | 357 | Bloomington, IL | 402 | 431 | Canton Twnshp, MI | 173 |
| 283 | Sandy, UT | 576 | 357 | Surprise, AZ | 402 | 432 | Allen, TX | 170 |
| 285 | Green Bay, WI | 575 | 359 | Cambridge, MA | 401 | 433 | Mission Viejo, CA | 156 |
| 285 | Medford, OR | 575 | 360 | Dearborn, MI | 399 | 434 | Lake Forest, CA | 150 |
| 287 | Sunnyvale, CA | 574 | 361 | Cary, NC | 392 | 434 | New Rochelle, NY | 150 |
| 288 | Downey, CA | 573 | 362 | Menifee, CA | 391 | 436 | O'Fallon, MO | 139 |
| 288 | Santa Monica, CA | 573 | 363 | Vista, CA | 390 | 437 | Johns Creek, GA | 136 |
| 290 | Jurupa Valley, CA | 570 | 364 | Coral Springs, FL | 389 | 438 | Carmel, IN | 128 |
| 291 | El Monte, CA | 568 | 365 | Livermore, CA | 387 | 439 | Arlington Heights, IL | 125 |
| 291 | Midland, TX | 568 | 366 | League City, TX | 386 | 440 | Clarkstown, NY | 99 |
| 293 | Waterbury, CT | 566 | 367 | Westminster, CO | 382 | 441 | Ramapo, NY | 88 |
| 294 | Westland, MI | 564 | 368 | Frisco, TX | 374 | 442 | Fishers, IN | 78 |
| 295 | Glendale, CA | 563 | 369 | Bethlehem, PA | 365 | | | |
| 295 | Kenosha, WI | 563 | 370 | Buena Park, CA | 361 | | | |

Source: Reported data from the F.B.I. "Crime in the United States 2013"

*Burglary is the unlawful entry of a structure to commit a felony or theft. Attempts are included.

# 70. Burglary Rate in 2013
## National Rate = 610.0 Burglaries per 100,000 Population*

| RANK | CITY | RATE | RANK | CITY | RATE | RANK | CITY | RATE |
|---|---|---|---|---|---|---|---|---|
| 133 | Abilene, TX | 883.6 | 216 | Chino, CA | 641.9 | 314 | Fullerton, CA | 448.9 |
| 23 | Akron, OH | 1,560.4 | 353 | Chula Vista, CA | 380.7 | 241 | Gainesville, FL | 586.1 |
| 355 | Alameda, CA | 376.6 | 237 | Cicero, IL | 597.4 | 360 | Garden Grove, CA | 363.0 |
| 15 | Albany, GA | 1,704.9 | 12 | Cincinnati, OH | 1,843.9 | 136 | Garland, TX | 871.1 |
| 189 | Albany, NY | 719.7 | 251 | Citrus Heights, CA | 566.0 | 11 | Gary, IN | 1,844.7 |
| 46 | Albuquerque, NM | 1,307.3 | 440 | Clarkstown, NY | 122.7 | 393 | Gilbert, AZ | 287.3 |
| 433 | Alexandria, VA | 167.7 | 196 | Clarksville, TN | 700.6 | 95 | Glendale, AZ | 1,029.9 |
| 334 | Alhambra, CA | 406.1 | 171 | Clearwater, FL | 781.4 | 391 | Glendale, CA | 288.2 |
| 85 | Allentown, PA | 1,058.9 | 3 | Cleveland, OH | 2,122.1 | 232 | Grand Prairie, TX | 609.3 |
| 429 | Allen, TX | 186.2 | 326 | Clifton, NJ | 421.1 | 145 | Grand Rapids, MI | 847.3 |
| 124 | Amarillo, TX | 923.8 | 323 | Clinton Twnshp, MI | 428.3 | 367 | Greece, NY | 343.4 |
| 431 | Amherst, NY | 172.4 | 133 | Clovis, CA | 883.6 | 292 | Greeley, CO | 494.2 |
| 332 | Anaheim, CA | 408.9 | 320 | College Station, TX | 436.7 | 264 | Green Bay, WI | 547.1 |
| 318 | Anchorage, AK | 440.1 | 415 | Colonie, NY | 237.8 | 83 | Greensboro, NC | 1,063.9 |
| 363 | Ann Arbor, MI | 351.0 | 140 | Colorado Springs, CO | 854.4 | 45 | Greenville, NC | 1,314.5 |
| 50 | Antioch, CA | 1,269.2 | 230 | Columbia, MO | 613.5 | 148 | Gresham, OR | 836.6 |
| 435 | Arlington Heights, IL | 164.5 | 87 | Columbia, SC | 1,057.2 | 286 | Hamilton Twnshp, NJ | 503.4 |
| 146 | Arlington, TX | 839.8 | 17 | Columbus, GA | 1,667.8 | 177 | Hammond, IN | 766.4 |
| 387 | Arvada, CO | 298.8 | 240 | Compton, CA | 591.4 | 269 | Hampton, VA | 527.2 |
| 163 | Athens-Clarke, GA | 805.0 | 214 | Concord, CA | 657.6 | 169 | Hartford, CT | 785.3 |
| 44 | Atlanta, GA | 1,316.6 | 287 | Concord, NC | 499.4 | 233 | Hawthorne, CA | 607.2 |
| 245 | Aurora, CO | 576.7 | 383 | Coral Springs, FL | 307.2 | 197 | Hayward, CA | 696.2 |
| 394 | Aurora, IL | 287.2 | 338 | Corona, CA | 402.1 | 38 | Hemet, CA | 1,358.7 |
| 178 | Austin, TX | 762.4 | 155 | Corpus Christi, TX | 825.1 | 271 | Henderson, NV | 523.8 |
| 49 | Bakersfield, CA | 1,272.6 | 313 | Costa Mesa, CA | 455.0 | 123 | Hesperia, CA | 938.2 |
| 359 | Baldwin Park, CA | 364.8 | 351 | Cranston, RI | 382.8 | 377 | Hialeah, FL | 325.8 |
| 58 | Baltimore, MD | 1,187.0 | 65 | Dallas, TX | 1,156.6 | 67 | High Point, NC | 1,124.4 |
| 34 | Baton Rouge, LA | 1,417.8 | 373 | Daly City, CA | 336.7 | 379 | Hillsboro, OR | 322.9 |
| 19 | Beaumont, TX | 1,626.4 | 407 | Danbury, CT | 265.1 | 97 | Hollywood, FL | 1,022.9 |
| 428 | Beaverton, OR | 187.1 | 117 | Davenport, IA | 943.7 | 333 | Hoover, AL | 408.8 |
| 265 | Bellevue, WA | 538.9 | 207 | Davie, FL | 674.0 | 79 | Houston, TX | 1,088.4 |
| 258 | Bellflower, CA | 550.3 | 10 | Dayton, OH | 1,851.0 | 336 | Huntington Beach, CA | 404.9 |
| 375 | Bend, OR | 334.1 | 328 | Dearborn, MI | 415.6 | 100 | Huntsville, AL | 1,019.8 |
| 128 | Berkeley, CA | 907.8 | 88 | Decatur, IL | 1,054.7 | 105 | Independence, MO | 994.2 |
| 298 | Bethlehem, PA | 485.8 | 166 | Deerfield Beach, FL | 797.9 | 22 | Indianapolis, IN | 1,581.4 |
| 125 | Billings, MT | 917.4 | 350 | Denton, TX | 382.9 | 106 | Indio, CA | 987.0 |
| 7 | Birmingham, AL | 1,895.3 | 180 | Denver, CO | 757.8 | 248 | Inglewood, CA | 570.4 |
| 281 | Bloomington, IL | 515.0 | 70 | Des Moines, IA | 1,114.3 | 412 | Irvine, CA | 247.2 |
| 224 | Bloomington, IN | 626.1 | 16 | Detroit, MI | 1,679.4 | 289 | Irving, TX | 497.9 |
| 421 | Bloomington, MN | 221.7 | 285 | Downey, CA | 506.1 | 149 | Jacksonville, FL | 835.8 |
| 273 | Boca Raton, FL | 522.8 | 183 | Duluth, MN | 745.8 | 6 | Jackson, MS | 1,912.1 |
| 348 | Boise, ID | 384.9 | 131 | Edinburg, TX | 897.0 | 330 | Jersey City, NJ | 409.5 |
| 302 | Boston, MA | 480.9 | 397 | Edison Twnshp, NJ | 281.3 | 437 | Johns Creek, GA | 161.7 |
| 239 | Boulder, CO | 595.2 | 361 | Edmond, OK | 359.4 | 297 | Joliet, IL | 487.7 |
| 374 | Brick Twnshp, NJ | 334.3 | 300 | El Cajon, CA | 483.3 | 243 | Jurupa Valley, CA | 581.1 |
| 161 | Bridgeport, CT | 809.8 | 295 | El Monte, CA | 491.4 | 78 | Kansas City, KS | 1,095.4 |
| 126 | Brockton, MA | 915.8 | 410 | El Paso, TX | 260.6 | 36 | Kansas City, MO | 1,377.4 |
| 341 | Broken Arrow, OK | 397.3 | 380 | Elgin, IL | 317.8 | 244 | Kennewick, WA | 580.3 |
| 267 | Brooklyn Park, MN | 537.3 | 226 | Elizabeth, NJ | 624.1 | 252 | Kenosha, WI | 560.7 |
| 223 | Brownsville, TX | 627.8 | 371 | Elk Grove, CA | 338.0 | 142 | Kent, WA | 853.2 |
| 202 | Bryan, TX | 685.9 | 102 | Erie, PA | 1,008.8 | 98 | Killeen, TX | 1,022.4 |
| 319 | Buena Park, CA | 436.9 | 301 | Escondido, CA | 482.3 | 53 | Knoxville, TN | 1,241.5 |
| 41 | Buffalo, NY | 1,336.2 | 108 | Eugene, OR | 971.0 | 93 | Lafayette, LA | 1,034.0 |
| 403 | Burbank, CA | 272.1 | 305 | Evanston, IL | 476.8 | 427 | Lake Forest, CA | 189.1 |
| 356 | Cambridge, MA | 373.8 | 152 | Evansville, IN | 828.0 | 68 | Lakeland, FL | 1,121.9 |
| 425 | Canton Twnshp, MI | 194.5 | 82 | Everett, WA | 1,073.9 | 423 | Lakewood Twnshp, NJ | 200.7 |
| 296 | Cape Coral, FL | 491.2 | 204 | Fairfield, CA | 677.9 | 277 | Lakewood, CA | 516.7 |
| 306 | Carlsbad, CA | 475.1 | 170 | Fall River, MA | 782.3 | 238 | Lakewood, CO | 596.0 |
| 439 | Carmel, IN | 150.8 | 222 | Fargo, ND | 631.0 | 211 | Lancaster, CA | 664.6 |
| 257 | Carrollton, TX | 553.9 | 385 | Farmington Hills, MI | 302.2 | 71 | Lansing, MI | 1,113.2 |
| 259 | Carson, CA | 550.2 | 199 | Fayetteville, AR | 690.6 | 246 | Laredo, TX | 576.1 |
| 409 | Cary, NC | 263.3 | 20 | Fayetteville, NC | 1,619.1 | 150 | Largo, FL | 834.3 |
| 179 | Cedar Rapids, IA | 759.5 | 120 | Federal Way, WA | 942.4 | 191 | Las Cruces, NM | 709.8 |
| 430 | Centennial, CO | 177.5 | 442 | Fishers, IN | 93.6 | 107 | Las Vegas, NV | 985.4 |
| 231 | Champaign, IL | 609.9 | 4 | Flint, MI | 1,942.1 | 262 | Lawrence, KS | 547.6 |
| 340 | Chandler, AZ | 399.2 | 322 | Fontana, CA | 428.7 | 254 | Lawrence, MA | 556.5 |
| 414 | Charleston, SC | 239.8 | 362 | Fort Collins, CO | 353.8 | 29 | Lawton, OK | 1,506.9 |
| 175 | Charlotte, NC | 768.7 | 25 | Fort Lauderdale, FL | 1,539.5 | 321 | League City, TX | 430.8 |
| 40 | Chattanooga, TN | 1,344.9 | 72 | Fort Smith, AR | 1,110.2 | 392 | Lee's Summit, MO | 287.8 |
| 317 | Cheektowaga, NY | 440.3 | 121 | Fort Wayne, IN | 940.3 | 290 | Lewisville, TX | 497.5 |
| 309 | Chesapeake, VA | 466.7 | 89 | Fort Worth, TX | 1,053.9 | 151 | Lexington, KY | 833.8 |
| 215 | Chicago, IL | 653.4 | 327 | Fremont, CA | 420.5 | 268 | Lincoln, NE | 531.8 |
| 195 | Chico, CA | 705.0 | 96 | Fresno, CA | 1,026.4 | 5 | Little Rock, AR | 1,922.0 |
| 331 | Chino Hills, CA | 409.4 | 395 | Frisco, TX | 283.8 | 311 | Livermore, CA | 458.8 |

| RANK | CITY | RATE |
|---|---|---|
| 386 | Livonia, MI | 299.3 |
| 164 | Long Beach, CA | 804.0 |
| 388 | Longmont, CO | 297.4 |
| 174 | Longview, TX | 775.2 |
| 335 | Los Angeles, CA | 405.5 |
| 94 | Louisville, KY | 1,031.1 |
| 198 | Lowell, MA | 693.5 |
| 77 | Lubbock, TX | 1,096.4 |
| 315 | Lynchburg, VA | 448.8 |
| 255 | Lynn, MA | 555.7 |
| 2 | Macon, GA | 2,185.9 |
| 250 | Madison, WI | 569.8 |
| 162 | Manchester, NH | 809.7 |
| 343 | McAllen, TX | 393.6 |
| 378 | McKinney, TX | 324.1 |
| 182 | Medford, OR | 747.2 |
| 112 | Melbourne, FL | 958.9 |
| 13 | Memphis, TN | 1,798.0 |
| 307 | Menifee, CA | 473.2 |
| 168 | Merced, CA | 791.8 |
| 418 | Meridian, ID | 235.2 |
| 277 | Mesa, AZ | 516.7 |
| 113 | Mesquite, TX | 957.6 |
| 92 | Miami Beach, FL | 1,039.0 |
| 103 | Miami Gardens, FL | 1,008.3 |
| 114 | Miami, FL | 954.4 |
| 310 | Midland, TX | 464.6 |
| 81 | Milwaukee, WI | 1,080.4 |
| 64 | Minneapolis, MN | 1,161.3 |
| 158 | Miramar, FL | 817.3 |
| 436 | Mission Viejo, CA | 162.7 |
| 260 | Mission, TX | 549.4 |
| 47 | Mobile, AL | 1,279.9 |
| 76 | Modesto, CA | 1,102.1 |
| 129 | Moreno Valley, CA | 905.2 |
| 354 | Mountain View, CA | 379.8 |
| 216 | Murfreesboro, TN | 641.9 |
| 408 | Murrieta, CA | 264.5 |
| 282 | Nampa, ID | 512.8 |
| 347 | Napa, CA | 386.0 |
| 438 | Naperville, IL | 156.0 |
| 358 | Nashua, NH | 371.0 |
| 135 | Nashville, TN | 883.0 |
| 111 | New Bedford, MA | 962.6 |
| 153 | New Haven, CT | 825.5 |
| 143 | New Orleans, LA | 849.6 |
| 426 | New Rochelle, NY | 190.4 |
| 424 | New York, NY | 197.8 |
| 184 | Newark, NJ | 745.4 |
| 276 | Newport Beach, CA | 518.0 |
| 263 | Newport News, VA | 547.3 |
| 416 | Newton, MA | 236.0 |
| 157 | Norfolk, VA | 824.5 |
| 272 | Norman, OK | 523.2 |
| 138 | North Charleston, SC | 863.3 |
| 127 | North Las Vegas, NV | 908.6 |
| 342 | Norwalk, CA | 394.3 |
| 400 | Norwalk, CT | 279.7 |
| 51 | Oakland, CA | 1,252.3 |
| 344 | Oceanside, CA | 392.4 |
| 193 | Odessa, TX | 705.7 |
| 432 | O'Fallon, MO | 168.1 |
| 201 | Ogden, UT | 687.7 |
| 43 | Oklahoma City, OK | 1,324.9 |
| 434 | Olathe, KS | 165.2 |
| 153 | Omaha, NE | 825.5 |
| 293 | Ontario, CA | 493.6 |
| 372 | Orange, CA | 337.1 |
| 422 | Orem, UT | 210.0 |
| 37 | Orlando, FL | 1,376.2 |
| 420 | Overland Park, KS | 223.8 |
| 303 | Oxnard, CA | 480.8 |
| 291 | Palm Bay, FL | 495.3 |
| 208 | Palmdale, CA | 670.2 |

| RANK | CITY | RATE |
|---|---|---|
| 206 | Pasadena, CA | 675.5 |
| 213 | Pasadena, TX | 659.9 |
| 119 | Paterson, NJ | 942.9 |
| 390 | Pearland, TX | 292.3 |
| 304 | Pembroke Pines, FL | 478.2 |
| 316 | Peoria, AZ | 443.6 |
| 109 | Peoria, IL | 968.5 |
| 209 | Philadelphia, PA | 670.1 |
| 69 | Phoenix, AZ | 1,114.9 |
| 192 | Pittsburgh, PA | 706.4 |
| 369 | Plano, TX | 342.3 |
| 165 | Plantation, FL | 799.5 |
| 253 | Pomona, CA | 559.6 |
| 62 | Pompano Beach, FL | 1,173.4 |
| 324 | Port St. Lucie, FL | 425.0 |
| 205 | Portland, OR | 677.7 |
| 21 | Portsmouth, VA | 1,582.2 |
| 99 | Providence, RI | 1,021.9 |
| 397 | Provo, UT | 281.3 |
| 14 | Pueblo, CO | 1,758.2 |
| 294 | Quincy, MA | 493.1 |
| 24 | Racine, WI | 1,549.8 |
| 186 | Raleigh, NC | 735.9 |
| 441 | Ramapo, NY | 100.9 |
| 167 | Rancho Cucamon., CA | 797.6 |
| 60 | Reading, PA | 1,180.4 |
| 159 | Redding, CA | 815.1 |
| 220 | Redwood City, CA | 636.1 |
| 234 | Reno, NV | 606.7 |
| 132 | Renton, WA | 888.7 |
| 173 | Rialto, CA | 778.4 |
| 280 | Richardson, TX | 515.4 |
| 27 | Richmond, CA | 1,519.5 |
| 141 | Richmond, VA | 853.7 |
| 225 | Riverside, CA | 625.1 |
| 218 | Roanoke, VA | 641.3 |
| 345 | Rochester, MN | 391.2 |
| 56 | Rochester, NY | 1,228.6 |
| 42 | Rockford, IL | 1,332.1 |
| 352 | Roseville, CA | 381.8 |
| 288 | Roswell, GA | 499.1 |
| 401 | Round Rock, TX | 273.5 |
| 160 | Sacramento, CA | 812.7 |
| 228 | Salem, OR | 621.2 |
| 185 | Salinas, CA | 737.1 |
| 80 | Salt Lake City, UT | 1,087.0 |
| 194 | San Angelo, TX | 705.6 |
| 84 | San Antonio, TX | 1,060.9 |
| 52 | San Bernardino, CA | 1,247.2 |
| 308 | San Diego, CA | 471.0 |
| 190 | San Francisco, CA | 711.3 |
| 274 | San Jose, CA | 521.4 |
| 137 | San Leandro, CA | 869.8 |
| 370 | San Marcos, CA | 340.9 |
| 382 | San Mateo, CA | 307.6 |
| 275 | Sandy Springs, GA | 519.9 |
| 219 | Sandy, UT | 640.4 |
| 413 | Santa Ana, CA | 241.3 |
| 284 | Santa Barbara, CA | 510.0 |
| 349 | Santa Clara, CA | 383.7 |
| 366 | Santa Clarita, CA | 343.5 |
| 221 | Santa Maria, CA | 634.0 |
| 229 | Santa Monica, CA | 619.5 |
| 357 | Santa Rosa, CA | 371.9 |
| 130 | Savannah, GA | 903.5 |
| 299 | Scottsdale, AZ | 484.7 |
| 188 | Scranton, PA | 724.9 |
| 66 | Seattle, WA | 1,148.7 |
| 63 | Shreveport, LA | 1,167.2 |
| 402 | Simi Valley, CA | 272.6 |
| 187 | Sioux City, IA | 730.6 |
| 266 | Sioux Falls, SD | 537.9 |
| 261 | Somerville, MA | 547.8 |
| 32 | South Bend, IN | 1,457.6 |

| RANK | CITY | RATE |
|---|---|---|
| 325 | South Gate, CA | 424.7 |
| 236 | Sparks, NV | 602.6 |
| 86 | Spokane Valley, WA | 1,058.0 |
| 9 | Spokane, WA | 1,856.1 |
| 74 | Springfield, IL | 1,107.8 |
| 26 | Springfield, MA | 1,536.6 |
| 33 | Springfield, MO | 1,418.5 |
| 399 | Stamford, CT | 281.2 |
| 411 | Sterling Heights, MI | 252.6 |
| 35 | Stockton, CA | 1,397.3 |
| 227 | St. George, UT | 621.5 |
| 91 | St. Joseph, MO | 1,040.8 |
| 39 | St. Louis, MO | 1,351.4 |
| 122 | St. Paul, MN | 939.6 |
| 73 | St. Petersburg, FL | 1,109.7 |
| 242 | Suffolk, VA | 585.0 |
| 384 | Sugar Land, TX | 306.7 |
| 346 | Sunnyvale, CA | 387.4 |
| 139 | Sunrise, FL | 856.3 |
| 376 | Surprise, AZ | 328.2 |
| 54 | Syracuse, NY | 1,238.2 |
| 28 | Tacoma, WA | 1,518.5 |
| 75 | Tallahassee, FL | 1,103.3 |
| 256 | Tampa, FL | 555.1 |
| 210 | Temecula, CA | 666.5 |
| 181 | Tempe, AZ | 757.3 |
| 368 | Thornton, CO | 342.7 |
| 419 | Thousand Oaks, CA | 225.8 |
| 8 | Toledo, OH | 1,892.7 |
| 247 | Toms River Twnshp, NJ | 570.8 |
| 110 | Topeka, KS | 967.1 |
| 339 | Torrance, CA | 400.6 |
| 329 | Tracy, CA | 414.4 |
| 61 | Trenton, NJ | 1,179.5 |
| 406 | Troy, MI | 268.7 |
| 118 | Tucson, AZ | 943.3 |
| 30 | Tulsa, OK | 1,504.4 |
| 55 | Tuscaloosa, AL | 1,237.7 |
| 405 | Tustin, CA | 270.2 |
| 156 | Tyler, TX | 824.7 |
| 172 | Upland, CA | 778.7 |
| 404 | Upper Darby Twnshp, PA | 271.8 |
| 396 | Vacaville, CA | 283.0 |
| 1 | Vallejo, CA | 2,511.5 |
| 235 | Vancouver, WA | 604.7 |
| 200 | Ventura, CA | 688.5 |
| 57 | Victorville, CA | 1,200.5 |
| 381 | Virginia Beach, VA | 312.2 |
| 115 | Visalia, CA | 952.9 |
| 337 | Vista, CA | 403.3 |
| 59 | Waco, TX | 1,182.1 |
| 212 | Warren, MI | 661.1 |
| 365 | Warwick, RI | 344.8 |
| 283 | Washington, DC | 512.6 |
| 279 | Waterbury, CT | 515.7 |
| 176 | Waukegan, IL | 767.2 |
| 249 | West Covina, CA | 570.1 |
| 104 | West Palm Beach, FL | 998.9 |
| 144 | West Valley, UT | 848.7 |
| 203 | Westland, MI | 683.2 |
| 312 | Westminster, CA | 457.1 |
| 364 | Westminster, CO | 347.0 |
| 270 | Whittier, CA | 526.3 |
| 116 | Wichita Falls, TX | 952.0 |
| 101 | Wichita, KS | 1,017.6 |
| 31 | Wilmington, NC | 1,482.2 |
| 18 | Winston-Salem, NC | 1,646.7 |
| 389 | Woodbridge Twnshp, NJ | 294.3 |
| 90 | Worcester, MA | 1,044.4 |
| 48 | Yakima, WA | 1,275.8 |
| 416 | Yonkers, NY | 236.0 |
| 147 | Yuma, AZ | 838.4 |

Source: CQ Press using reported data from the F.B.I. "Crime in the United States 2013"

*Burglary is the unlawful entry of a structure to commit a felony or theft. Attempts are included.

# 70. Burglary Rate in 2013 (continued)
## National Rate = 610.0 Burglaries per 100,000 Population*

| RANK | CITY | RATE | RANK | CITY | RATE | RANK | CITY | RATE |
|---|---|---|---|---|---|---|---|---|
| 1 | Vallejo, CA | 2,511.5 | 75 | Tallahassee, FL | 1,103.3 | 149 | Jacksonville, FL | 835.8 |
| 2 | Macon, GA | 2,185.9 | 76 | Modesto, CA | 1,102.1 | 150 | Largo, FL | 834.3 |
| 3 | Cleveland, OH | 2,122.1 | 77 | Lubbock, TX | 1,096.4 | 151 | Lexington, KY | 833.8 |
| 4 | Flint, MI | 1,942.1 | 78 | Kansas City, KS | 1,095.4 | 152 | Evansville, IN | 828.0 |
| 5 | Little Rock, AR | 1,922.0 | 79 | Houston, TX | 1,088.4 | 153 | New Haven, CT | 825.5 |
| 6 | Jackson, MS | 1,912.1 | 80 | Salt Lake City, UT | 1,087.0 | 153 | Omaha, NE | 825.5 |
| 7 | Birmingham, AL | 1,895.3 | 81 | Milwaukee, WI | 1,080.4 | 155 | Corpus Christi, TX | 825.1 |
| 8 | Toledo, OH | 1,892.7 | 82 | Everett, WA | 1,073.9 | 156 | Tyler, TX | 824.7 |
| 9 | Spokane, WA | 1,856.1 | 83 | Greensboro, NC | 1,063.9 | 157 | Norfolk, VA | 824.5 |
| 10 | Dayton, OH | 1,851.0 | 84 | San Antonio, TX | 1,060.9 | 158 | Miramar, FL | 817.3 |
| 11 | Gary, IN | 1,844.7 | 85 | Allentown, PA | 1,058.9 | 159 | Redding, CA | 815.1 |
| 12 | Cincinnati, OH | 1,843.9 | 86 | Spokane Valley, WA | 1,058.0 | 160 | Sacramento, CA | 812.7 |
| 13 | Memphis, TN | 1,798.0 | 87 | Columbia, SC | 1,057.2 | 161 | Bridgeport, CT | 809.8 |
| 14 | Pueblo, CO | 1,758.2 | 88 | Decatur, IL | 1,054.7 | 162 | Manchester, NH | 809.7 |
| 15 | Albany, GA | 1,704.9 | 89 | Fort Worth, TX | 1,053.9 | 163 | Athens-Clarke, GA | 805.0 |
| 16 | Detroit, MI | 1,679.4 | 90 | Worcester, MA | 1,044.4 | 164 | Long Beach, CA | 804.0 |
| 17 | Columbus, GA | 1,667.8 | 91 | St. Joseph, MO | 1,040.8 | 165 | Plantation, FL | 799.5 |
| 18 | Winston-Salem, NC | 1,646.7 | 92 | Miami Beach, FL | 1,039.0 | 166 | Deerfield Beach, FL | 797.9 |
| 19 | Beaumont, TX | 1,626.4 | 93 | Lafayette, LA | 1,034.0 | 167 | Rancho Cucamon., CA | 797.6 |
| 20 | Fayetteville, NC | 1,619.1 | 94 | Louisville, KY | 1,031.1 | 168 | Merced, CA | 791.8 |
| 21 | Portsmouth, VA | 1,582.2 | 95 | Glendale, AZ | 1,029.9 | 169 | Hartford, CT | 785.3 |
| 22 | Indianapolis, IN | 1,581.4 | 96 | Fresno, CA | 1,026.4 | 170 | Fall River, MA | 782.3 |
| 23 | Akron, OH | 1,560.4 | 97 | Hollywood, FL | 1,022.9 | 171 | Clearwater, FL | 781.4 |
| 24 | Racine, WI | 1,549.8 | 98 | Killeen, TX | 1,022.4 | 172 | Upland, CA | 778.7 |
| 25 | Fort Lauderdale, FL | 1,539.5 | 99 | Providence, RI | 1,021.9 | 173 | Rialto, CA | 778.4 |
| 26 | Springfield, MA | 1,536.6 | 100 | Huntsville, AL | 1,019.8 | 174 | Longview, TX | 775.2 |
| 27 | Richmond, CA | 1,519.5 | 101 | Wichita, KS | 1,017.6 | 175 | Charlotte, NC | 768.7 |
| 28 | Tacoma, WA | 1,518.5 | 102 | Erie, PA | 1,008.8 | 176 | Waukegan, IL | 767.2 |
| 29 | Lawton, OK | 1,506.9 | 103 | Miami Gardens, FL | 1,008.3 | 177 | Hammond, IN | 766.4 |
| 30 | Tulsa, OK | 1,504.4 | 104 | West Palm Beach, FL | 998.9 | 178 | Austin, TX | 762.4 |
| 31 | Wilmington, NC | 1,482.2 | 105 | Independence, MO | 994.2 | 179 | Cedar Rapids, IA | 759.5 |
| 32 | South Bend, IN | 1,457.6 | 106 | Indio, CA | 987.0 | 180 | Denver, CO | 757.8 |
| 33 | Springfield, MO | 1,418.5 | 107 | Las Vegas, NV | 985.4 | 181 | Tempe, AZ | 757.3 |
| 34 | Baton Rouge, LA | 1,417.8 | 108 | Eugene, OR | 971.0 | 182 | Medford, OR | 747.2 |
| 35 | Stockton, CA | 1,397.3 | 109 | Peoria, IL | 968.5 | 183 | Duluth, MN | 745.8 |
| 36 | Kansas City, MO | 1,377.4 | 110 | Topeka, KS | 967.1 | 184 | Newark, NJ | 745.4 |
| 37 | Orlando, FL | 1,376.2 | 111 | New Bedford, MA | 962.6 | 185 | Salinas, CA | 737.1 |
| 38 | Hemet, CA | 1,358.7 | 112 | Melbourne, FL | 958.9 | 186 | Raleigh, NC | 735.9 |
| 39 | St. Louis, MO | 1,351.4 | 113 | Mesquite, TX | 957.6 | 187 | Sioux City, IA | 730.6 |
| 40 | Chattanooga, TN | 1,344.9 | 114 | Miami, FL | 954.4 | 188 | Scranton, PA | 724.9 |
| 41 | Buffalo, NY | 1,336.2 | 115 | Visalia, CA | 952.9 | 189 | Albany, NY | 719.7 |
| 42 | Rockford, IL | 1,332.1 | 116 | Wichita Falls, TX | 952.0 | 190 | San Francisco, CA | 711.3 |
| 43 | Oklahoma City, OK | 1,324.9 | 117 | Davenport, IA | 943.7 | 191 | Las Cruces, NM | 709.8 |
| 44 | Atlanta, GA | 1,316.6 | 118 | Tucson, AZ | 943.3 | 192 | Pittsburgh, PA | 706.4 |
| 45 | Greenville, NC | 1,314.5 | 119 | Paterson, NJ | 942.9 | 193 | Odessa, TX | 705.7 |
| 46 | Albuquerque, NM | 1,307.3 | 120 | Federal Way, WA | 942.4 | 194 | San Angelo, TX | 705.6 |
| 47 | Mobile, AL | 1,279.9 | 121 | Fort Wayne, IN | 940.3 | 195 | Chico, CA | 705.0 |
| 48 | Yakima, WA | 1,275.8 | 122 | St. Paul, MN | 939.6 | 196 | Clarksville, TN | 700.6 |
| 49 | Bakersfield, CA | 1,272.6 | 123 | Hesperia, CA | 938.2 | 197 | Hayward, CA | 696.2 |
| 50 | Antioch, CA | 1,269.2 | 124 | Amarillo, TX | 923.8 | 198 | Lowell, MA | 693.5 |
| 51 | Oakland, CA | 1,252.3 | 125 | Billings, MT | 917.4 | 199 | Fayetteville, AR | 690.6 |
| 52 | San Bernardino, CA | 1,247.2 | 126 | Brockton, MA | 915.8 | 200 | Ventura, CA | 688.5 |
| 53 | Knoxville, TN | 1,241.5 | 127 | North Las Vegas, NV | 908.6 | 201 | Ogden, UT | 687.7 |
| 54 | Syracuse, NY | 1,238.2 | 128 | Berkeley, CA | 907.8 | 202 | Bryan, TX | 685.9 |
| 55 | Tuscaloosa, AL | 1,237.7 | 129 | Moreno Valley, CA | 905.2 | 203 | Westland, MI | 683.2 |
| 56 | Rochester, NY | 1,228.6 | 130 | Savannah, GA | 903.5 | 204 | Fairfield, CA | 677.9 |
| 57 | Victorville, CA | 1,200.5 | 131 | Edinburg, TX | 897.0 | 205 | Portland, OR | 677.7 |
| 58 | Baltimore, MD | 1,187.0 | 132 | Renton, WA | 888.7 | 206 | Pasadena, CA | 675.5 |
| 59 | Waco, TX | 1,182.1 | 133 | Abilene, TX | 883.6 | 207 | Davie, FL | 674.0 |
| 60 | Reading, PA | 1,180.4 | 133 | Clovis, CA | 883.6 | 208 | Palmdale, CA | 670.2 |
| 61 | Trenton, NJ | 1,179.5 | 135 | Nashville, TN | 883.0 | 209 | Philadelphia, PA | 670.1 |
| 62 | Pompano Beach, FL | 1,173.4 | 136 | Garland, TX | 871.1 | 210 | Temecula, CA | 666.5 |
| 63 | Shreveport, LA | 1,167.2 | 137 | San Leandro, CA | 869.8 | 211 | Lancaster, CA | 664.6 |
| 64 | Minneapolis, MN | 1,161.3 | 138 | North Charleston, SC | 863.3 | 212 | Warren, MI | 661.1 |
| 65 | Dallas, TX | 1,156.6 | 139 | Sunrise, FL | 856.3 | 213 | Pasadena, TX | 659.9 |
| 66 | Seattle, WA | 1,148.7 | 140 | Colorado Springs, CO | 854.4 | 214 | Concord, CA | 657.6 |
| 67 | High Point, NC | 1,124.4 | 141 | Richmond, VA | 853.7 | 215 | Chicago, IL | 653.4 |
| 68 | Lakeland, FL | 1,121.9 | 142 | Kent, WA | 853.2 | 216 | Chino, CA | 641.9 |
| 69 | Phoenix, AZ | 1,114.9 | 143 | New Orleans, LA | 849.6 | 216 | Murfreesboro, TN | 641.9 |
| 70 | Des Moines, IA | 1,114.3 | 144 | West Valley, UT | 848.7 | 218 | Roanoke, VA | 641.3 |
| 71 | Lansing, MI | 1,113.2 | 145 | Grand Rapids, MI | 847.7 | 219 | Sandy, UT | 640.4 |
| 72 | Fort Smith, AR | 1,110.2 | 146 | Arlington, TX | 839.8 | 220 | Redwood City, CA | 636.1 |
| 73 | St. Petersburg, FL | 1,109.7 | 147 | Yuma, AZ | 838.4 | 221 | Santa Maria, CA | 634.0 |
| 74 | Springfield, IL | 1,107.8 | 148 | Gresham, OR | 836.6 | 222 | Fargo, ND | 631.0 |

| RANK | CITY | RATE | RANK | CITY | RATE | RANK | CITY | RATE |
|------|------|------|------|------|------|------|------|------|
| 223 | Brownsville, TX | 627.8 | 297 | Joliet, IL | 487.7 | 371 | Elk Grove, CA | 338.0 |
| 224 | Bloomington, IN | 626.1 | 298 | Bethlehem, PA | 485.8 | 372 | Orange, CA | 337.1 |
| 225 | Riverside, CA | 625.1 | 299 | Scottsdale, AZ | 484.7 | 373 | Daly City, CA | 336.7 |
| 226 | Elizabeth, NJ | 624.1 | 300 | El Cajon, CA | 483.3 | 374 | Brick Twnshp, NJ | 334.3 |
| 227 | St. George, UT | 621.5 | 301 | Escondido, CA | 482.3 | 375 | Bend, OR | 334.1 |
| 228 | Salem, OR | 621.2 | 302 | Boston, MA | 480.9 | 376 | Surprise, AZ | 328.2 |
| 229 | Santa Monica, CA | 619.5 | 303 | Oxnard, CA | 480.8 | 377 | Hialeah, FL | 325.8 |
| 230 | Columbia, MO | 613.5 | 304 | Pembroke Pines, FL | 478.2 | 378 | McKinney, TX | 324.1 |
| 231 | Champaign, IL | 609.9 | 305 | Evanston, IL | 476.8 | 379 | Hillsboro, OR | 322.9 |
| 232 | Grand Prairie, TX | 609.3 | 306 | Carlsbad, CA | 475.1 | 380 | Elgin, IL | 317.8 |
| 233 | Hawthorne, CA | 607.2 | 307 | Menifee, CA | 473.2 | 381 | Virginia Beach, VA | 312.2 |
| 234 | Reno, NV | 606.7 | 308 | San Diego, CA | 471.0 | 382 | San Mateo, CA | 307.6 |
| 235 | Vancouver, WA | 604.7 | 309 | Chesapeake, VA | 466.7 | 383 | Coral Springs, FL | 307.2 |
| 236 | Sparks, NV | 602.6 | 310 | Midland, TX | 464.6 | 384 | Sugar Land, TX | 306.7 |
| 237 | Cicero, IL | 597.4 | 311 | Livermore, CA | 458.8 | 385 | Farmington Hills, MI | 302.2 |
| 238 | Lakewood, CO | 596.0 | 312 | Westminster, CA | 457.1 | 386 | Livonia, MI | 299.3 |
| 239 | Boulder, CO | 595.2 | 313 | Costa Mesa, CA | 455.0 | 387 | Arvada, CO | 298.8 |
| 240 | Compton, CA | 591.4 | 314 | Fullerton, CA | 448.9 | 388 | Longmont, CO | 297.4 |
| 241 | Gainesville, FL | 586.1 | 315 | Lynchburg, VA | 448.8 | 389 | Woodbridge Twnshp, NJ | 294.3 |
| 242 | Suffolk, VA | 585.0 | 316 | Peoria, AZ | 443.6 | 390 | Pearland, TX | 292.3 |
| 243 | Jurupa Valley, CA | 581.1 | 317 | Cheektowaga, NY | 440.3 | 391 | Glendale, CA | 288.2 |
| 244 | Kennewick, WA | 580.3 | 318 | Anchorage, AK | 440.1 | 392 | Lee's Summit, MO | 287.8 |
| 245 | Aurora, CO | 576.7 | 319 | Buena Park, CA | 436.9 | 393 | Gilbert, AZ | 287.3 |
| 246 | Laredo, TX | 576.1 | 320 | College Station, TX | 436.7 | 394 | Aurora, IL | 287.2 |
| 247 | Toms River Twnshp, NJ | 570.8 | 321 | League City, TX | 430.8 | 395 | Frisco, TX | 283.8 |
| 248 | Inglewood, CA | 570.4 | 322 | Fontana, CA | 428.7 | 396 | Vacaville, CA | 283.0 |
| 249 | West Covina, CA | 570.1 | 323 | Clinton Twnshp, MI | 428.3 | 397 | Edison Twnshp, NJ | 281.3 |
| 250 | Madison, WI | 569.8 | 324 | Port St. Lucie, FL | 425.0 | 397 | Provo, UT | 281.3 |
| 251 | Citrus Heights, CA | 566.0 | 325 | South Gate, CA | 424.7 | 399 | Stamford, CT | 281.2 |
| 252 | Kenosha, WI | 560.7 | 326 | Clifton, NJ | 421.1 | 400 | Norwalk, CT | 279.7 |
| 253 | Pomona, CA | 559.6 | 327 | Fremont, CA | 420.5 | 401 | Round Rock, TX | 273.5 |
| 254 | Lawrence, MA | 556.5 | 328 | Dearborn, MI | 415.6 | 402 | Simi Valley, CA | 272.6 |
| 255 | Lynn, MA | 555.7 | 329 | Tracy, CA | 414.4 | 403 | Burbank, CA | 272.1 |
| 256 | Tampa, FL | 555.1 | 330 | Jersey City, NJ | 409.5 | 404 | Upper Darby Twnshp, PA | 271.8 |
| 257 | Carrollton, TX | 553.9 | 331 | Chino Hills, CA | 409.4 | 405 | Tustin, CA | 270.2 |
| 258 | Bellflower, CA | 550.3 | 332 | Anaheim, CA | 408.9 | 406 | Troy, MI | 268.7 |
| 259 | Carson, CA | 550.2 | 333 | Hoover, AL | 408.8 | 407 | Danbury, CT | 265.1 |
| 260 | Mission, TX | 549.4 | 334 | Alhambra, CA | 406.1 | 408 | Murrieta, CA | 264.5 |
| 261 | Somerville, MA | 547.8 | 335 | Los Angeles, CA | 405.5 | 409 | Cary, NC | 263.3 |
| 262 | Lawrence, KS | 547.6 | 336 | Huntington Beach, CA | 404.9 | 410 | El Paso, TX | 260.6 |
| 263 | Newport News, VA | 547.3 | 337 | Vista, CA | 403.3 | 411 | Sterling Heights, MI | 252.6 |
| 264 | Green Bay, WI | 547.1 | 338 | Corona, CA | 402.1 | 412 | Irvine, CA | 247.2 |
| 265 | Bellevue, WA | 538.9 | 339 | Torrance, CA | 400.6 | 413 | Santa Ana, CA | 241.3 |
| 266 | Sioux Falls, SD | 537.9 | 340 | Chandler, AZ | 399.2 | 414 | Charleston, SC | 239.8 |
| 267 | Brooklyn Park, MN | 537.3 | 341 | Broken Arrow, OK | 397.3 | 415 | Colonie, NY | 237.8 |
| 268 | Lincoln, NE | 531.8 | 342 | Norwalk, CA | 394.3 | 416 | Newton, MA | 236.0 |
| 269 | Hampton, VA | 527.2 | 343 | McAllen, TX | 393.6 | 416 | Yonkers, NY | 236.0 |
| 270 | Whittier, CA | 526.3 | 344 | Oceanside, CA | 392.4 | 418 | Meridian, ID | 235.2 |
| 271 | Henderson, NV | 523.8 | 345 | Rochester, MN | 391.2 | 419 | Thousand Oaks, CA | 225.8 |
| 272 | Norman, OK | 523.2 | 346 | Sunnyvale, CA | 387.4 | 420 | Overland Park, KS | 223.8 |
| 273 | Boca Raton, FL | 522.8 | 347 | Napa, CA | 386.0 | 421 | Bloomington, MN | 221.7 |
| 274 | San Jose, CA | 521.4 | 348 | Boise, ID | 384.9 | 422 | Orem, UT | 210.0 |
| 275 | Sandy Springs, GA | 519.9 | 349 | Santa Clara, CA | 383.7 | 423 | Lakewood Twnshp, NJ | 200.7 |
| 276 | Newport Beach, CA | 518.0 | 350 | Denton, TX | 382.9 | 424 | New York, NY | 197.8 |
| 277 | Lakewood, CA | 516.7 | 351 | Cranston, RI | 382.8 | 425 | Canton Twnshp, MI | 194.5 |
| 277 | Mesa, AZ | 516.7 | 352 | Roseville, CA | 381.8 | 426 | New Rochelle, NY | 190.4 |
| 279 | Waterbury, CT | 515.7 | 353 | Chula Vista, CA | 380.7 | 427 | Lake Forest, CA | 189.1 |
| 280 | Richardson, TX | 515.4 | 354 | Mountain View, CA | 379.8 | 428 | Beaverton, OR | 187.1 |
| 281 | Bloomington, IL | 515.0 | 355 | Alameda, CA | 376.6 | 429 | Allen, TX | 186.2 |
| 282 | Nampa, ID | 512.8 | 356 | Cambridge, MA | 373.8 | 430 | Centennial, CO | 177.5 |
| 283 | Washington, DC | 512.6 | 357 | Santa Rosa, CA | 371.9 | 431 | Amherst, NY | 172.4 |
| 284 | Santa Barbara, CA | 510.0 | 358 | Nashua, NH | 371.0 | 432 | O'Fallon, MO | 168.1 |
| 285 | Downey, CA | 506.1 | 359 | Baldwin Park, CA | 364.8 | 433 | Alexandria, VA | 167.7 |
| 286 | Hamilton Twnshp, NJ | 503.4 | 360 | Garden Grove, CA | 363.0 | 434 | Olathe, KS | 165.2 |
| 287 | Concord, NC | 499.4 | 361 | Edmond, OK | 359.4 | 435 | Arlington Heights, IL | 164.5 |
| 288 | Roswell, GA | 499.1 | 362 | Fort Collins, CO | 353.8 | 436 | Mission Viejo, CA | 162.7 |
| 289 | Irving, TX | 497.9 | 363 | Ann Arbor, MI | 351.0 | 437 | Johns Creek, GA | 161.7 |
| 290 | Lewisville, TX | 497.5 | 364 | Westminster, CO | 347.0 | 438 | Naperville, IL | 156.0 |
| 291 | Palm Bay, FL | 495.3 | 365 | Warwick, RI | 344.8 | 439 | Carmel, IN | 150.8 |
| 292 | Greeley, CO | 494.2 | 366 | Santa Clarita, CA | 343.5 | 440 | Clarkstown, NY | 122.7 |
| 293 | Ontario, CA | 493.6 | 367 | Greece, NY | 343.4 | 441 | Ramapo, NY | 100.9 |
| 294 | Quincy, MA | 493.1 | 368 | Thornton, CO | 342.7 | 442 | Fishers, IN | 93.6 |
| 295 | El Monte, CA | 491.4 | 369 | Plano, TX | 342.3 | | | |
| 296 | Cape Coral, FL | 491.2 | 370 | San Marcos, CA | 340.9 | | | |

Source: CQ Press using reported data from the F.B.I. "Crime in the United States 2013"

*Burglary is the unlawful entry of a structure to commit a felony or theft. Attempts are included.

# 71. Percent Change in Burglary Rate: 2012 to 2013
## National Percent Change = 9.3% Decrease*

| RANK | CITY | % CHANGE | RANK | CITY | % CHANGE | RANK | CITY | % CHANGE |
|---|---|---|---|---|---|---|---|---|
| 82 | Abilene, TX | 2.2 | 218 | Chino, CA | (8.9) | 333 | Fullerton, CA | (16.2) |
| 228 | Akron, OH | (9.7) | 78 | Chula Vista, CA | 2.7 | 404 | Gainesville, FL | (26.2) |
| 149 | Alameda, CA | (4.0) | 418 | Cicero, IL | (29.2) | 335 | Garden Grove, CA | (16.5) |
| 163 | Albany, GA | (4.9) | 111 | Cincinnati, OH | (0.4) | 203 | Garland, TX | (7.7) |
| 363 | Albany, NY | (20.3) | 389 | Citrus Heights, CA | (22.9) | 221 | Gary, IN | (9.2) |
| 47 | Albuquerque, NM | 8.4 | 207 | Clarkstown, NY | (8.0) | 321 | Gilbert, AZ | (15.2) |
| 282 | Alexandria, VA | (12.9) | 125 | Clarksville, TN | (1.4) | 326 | Glendale, AZ | (15.7) |
| 60 | Alhambra, CA | 5.5 | 192 | Clearwater, FL | (7.1) | 42 | Glendale, CA | 8.9 |
| 91 | Allentown, PA | 1.3 | 309 | Cleveland, OH | (14.2) | 318 | Grand Prairie, TX | (14.7) |
| 390 | Allen, TX | (23.1) | 111 | Clifton, NJ | (0.4) | 330 | Grand Rapids, MI | (16.0) |
| 285 | Amarillo, TX | (13.0) | 282 | Clinton Twnshp, MI | (12.9) | 352 | Greece, NY | (19.0) |
| 171 | Amherst, NY | (5.3) | 225 | Clovis, CA | (9.5) | 266 | Greeley, CO | (12.2) |
| 266 | Anaheim, CA | (12.2) | 408 | College Station, TX | (26.8) | 257 | Green Bay, WI | (11.9) |
| 28 | Anchorage, AK | 13.7 | 295 | Colonie, NY | (13.5) | 266 | Greensboro, NC | (12.2) |
| 434 | Ann Arbor, MI | (43.5) | 89 | Colorado Springs, CO | 1.4 | 95 | Greenville, NC | 1.1 |
| 392 | Antioch, CA | (23.4) | 293 | Columbia, MO | (13.4) | 82 | Gresham, OR | 2.2 |
| 250 | Arlington Heights, IL | (11.3) | NA | Columbia, SC** | NA | 212 | Hamilton Twnshp, NJ | (8.3) |
| 235 | Arlington, TX | (10.1) | 15 | Columbus, GA | 20.8 | 429 | Hammond, IN | (33.7) |
| 335 | Arvada, CO | (16.5) | 97 | Compton, CA | 1.0 | 151 | Hampton, VA | (4.1) |
| 343 | Athens-Clarke, GA | (17.7) | 116 | Concord, CA | (0.7) | 185 | Hartford, CT | (6.4) |
| 192 | Atlanta, GA | (7.1) | NA | Concord, NC** | NA | 225 | Hawthorne, CA | (9.5) |
| 43 | Aurora, CO | 8.5 | 425 | Coral Springs, FL | (32.9) | 200 | Hayward, CA | (7.5) |
| 433 | Aurora, IL | (39.2) | 407 | Corona, CA | (26.5) | 66 | Hemet, CA | 4.9 |
| 269 | Austin, TX | (12.3) | 62 | Corpus Christi, TX | 5.2 | 128 | Henderson, NV | (2.0) |
| 224 | Bakersfield, CA | (9.4) | 391 | Costa Mesa, CA | (23.3) | 173 | Hesperia, CA | (5.5) |
| 335 | Baldwin Park, CA | (16.5) | 375 | Cranston, RI | (21.6) | 410 | Hialeah, FL | (27.5) |
| 156 | Baltimore, MD | (4.5) | 242 | Dallas, TX | (10.8) | 95 | High Point, NC | 1.1 |
| 309 | Baton Rouge, LA | (14.2) | 257 | Daly City, CA | (11.9) | 178 | Hillsboro, OR | (5.9) |
| 53 | Beaumont, TX | 7.1 | 399 | Danbury, CT | (24.4) | 396 | Hollywood, FL | (24.1) |
| 257 | Beaverton, OR | (11.9) | 51 | Davenport, IA | 7.3 | 314 | Hoover, AL | (14.4) |
| 120 | Bellevue, WA | (0.9) | 151 | Davie, FL | (4.1) | 245 | Houston, TX | (11.0) |
| 77 | Bellflower, CA | 2.8 | 295 | Dayton, OH | (13.5) | 124 | Huntington Beach, CA | (1.1) |
| NA | Bend, OR** | NA | 274 | Dearborn, MI | (12.5) | 295 | Huntsville, AL | (13.5) |
| 49 | Berkeley, CA | 7.5 | 280 | Decatur, IL | (12.8) | 190 | Independence, MO | (6.8) |
| 136 | Bethlehem, PA | (2.9) | 70 | Deerfield Beach, FL | 4.0 | 236 | Indianapolis, IN | (10.2) |
| 11 | Billings, MT | 23.1 | 413 | Denton, TX | (27.9) | 199 | Indio, CA | (7.3) |
| 305 | Birmingham, AL | (14.1) | 192 | Denver, CO | (7.1) | 126 | Inglewood, CA | (1.6) |
| 33 | Bloomington, IL | 11.2 | 209 | Des Moines, IA | (8.1) | 174 | Irvine, CA | (5.6) |
| 345 | Bloomington, IN | (17.8) | 261 | Detroit, MI | (12.0) | 279 | Irving, TX | (12.7) |
| 340 | Bloomington, MN | (17.4) | 309 | Downey, CA | (14.2) | 204 | Jacksonville, FL | (7.9) |
| 204 | Boca Raton, FL | (7.9) | 99 | Duluth, MN | 0.9 | 348 | Jackson, MS | (18.4) |
| 242 | Boise, ID | (10.8) | 328 | Edinburg, TX | (15.9) | 411 | Jersey City, NJ | (27.8) |
| 215 | Boston, MA | (8.8) | 339 | Edison Twnshp, NJ | (16.7) | 8 | Johns Creek, GA | 24.5 |
| 6 | Boulder, CO | 26.4 | 122 | Edmond, OK | (1.0) | 396 | Joliet, IL | (24.1) |
| 154 | Brick Twnshp, NJ | (4.4) | 106 | El Cajon, CA | (0.1) | 387 | Jurupa Valley, CA | (22.4) |
| 305 | Bridgeport, CT | (14.1) | 116 | El Monte, CA | (0.7) | 219 | Kansas City, KS | (9.0) |
| 55 | Brockton, MA | 6.9 | 141 | El Paso, TX | (3.6) | 210 | Kansas City, MO | (8.2) |
| 54 | Broken Arrow, OK | 7.0 | 135 | Elgin, IL | (2.8) | 116 | Kennewick, WA | (0.7) |
| 326 | Brooklyn Park, MN | (15.7) | 361 | Elizabeth, NJ | (20.2) | 369 | Kenosha, WI | (20.7) |
| 116 | Brownsville, TX | (0.7) | 375 | Elk Grove, CA | (21.6) | 328 | Kent, WA | (15.9) |
| 43 | Bryan, TX | 8.5 | 182 | Erie, PA | (6.1) | 232 | Killeen, TX | (9.9) |
| 61 | Buena Park, CA | 5.4 | 191 | Escondido, CA | (7.0) | 373 | Knoxville, TN | (21.5) |
| 256 | Buffalo, NY | (11.8) | 91 | Eugene, OR | 1.3 | 156 | Lafayette, LA | (4.5) |
| 402 | Burbank, CA | (25.4) | 322 | Evanston, IL | (15.3) | 431 | Lake Forest, CA | (34.0) |
| 363 | Cambridge, MA | (20.3) | 295 | Evansville, IN | (13.5) | 295 | Lakeland, FL | (13.5) |
| NA | Canton Twnshp, MI** | NA | 136 | Everett, WA | (2.9) | 420 | Lakewood Twnshp, NJ | (31.3) |
| 215 | Cape Coral, FL | (8.8) | 50 | Fairfield, CA | 7.4 | 29 | Lakewood, CA | 13.3 |
| 73 | Carlsbad, CA | 3.1 | 222 | Fall River, MA | (9.3) | 162 | Lakewood, CO | (4.8) |
| 40 | Carmel, IN | 9.2 | 2 | Fargo, ND | 53.6 | 89 | Lancaster, CA | 1.4 |
| 241 | Carrollton, TX | (10.6) | 63 | Farmington Hills, MI | 5.1 | 132 | Lansing, MI | (2.3) |
| 317 | Carson, CA | (14.6) | 72 | Fayetteville, AR | 3.3 | 343 | Laredo, TX | (17.7) |
| 103 | Cary, NC | 0.3 | 349 | Fayetteville, NC | (18.8) | 25 | Largo, FL | 14.5 |
| 97 | Cedar Rapids, IA | 1.0 | 210 | Federal Way, WA | (8.2) | 417 | Las Cruces, NM | (28.5) |
| 427 | Centennial, CO | (33.3) | 406 | Fishers, IN | (26.4) | 80 | Las Vegas, NV | 2.5 |
| 420 | Champaign, IL | (31.3) | 429 | Flint, MI | (33.7) | 353 | Lawrence, KS | (19.1) |
| 324 | Chandler, AZ | (15.5) | 375 | Fontana, CA | (21.6) | 354 | Lawrence, MA | (19.4) |
| 367 | Charleston, SC | (20.6) | 261 | Fort Collins, CO | (12.0) | 159 | Lawton, OK | (4.6) |
| 357 | Charlotte, NC | (19.9) | 244 | Fort Lauderdale, FL | (10.9) | 9 | League City, TX | 24.1 |
| NA | Chattanooga, TN** | NA | 214 | Fort Smith, AR | (8.7) | 102 | Lee's Summit, MO | 0.5 |
| 73 | Cheektowaga, NY | 3.1 | 19 | Fort Wayne, IN | 19.2 | NA | Lewisville, TX** | NA |
| 78 | Chesapeake, VA | 2.7 | 146 | Fort Worth, TX | (3.9) | 255 | Lexington, KY | (11.7) |
| 383 | Chicago, IL | (22.2) | 379 | Fremont, CA | (21.7) | 287 | Lincoln, NE | (13.1) |
| 370 | Chico, CA | (21.1) | 261 | Fresno, CA | (12.0) | 248 | Little Rock, AR | (11.2) |
| 238 | Chino Hills, CA | (10.4) | 366 | Frisco, TX | (20.5) | 12 | Livermore, CA | 22.5 |

| RANK | CITY | % CHANGE | RANK | CITY | % CHANGE | RANK | CITY | % CHANGE |
|---|---|---|---|---|---|---|---|---|
| 245 | Livonia, MI | (11.0) | 59 | Pasadena, CA | 5.7 | 114 | South Gate, CA | (0.6) |
| 114 | Long Beach, CA | (0.6) | 84 | Pasadena, TX | 2.1 | 213 | Sparks, NV | (8.6) |
| 405 | Longmont, CO | (26.3) | 313 | Paterson, NJ | (14.3) | 43 | Spokane Valley, WA | 8.5 |
| 423 | Longview, TX | (32.6) | 106 | Pearland, TX | (0.1) | 76 | Spokane, WA | 2.9 |
| 159 | Los Angeles, CA | (4.6) | 228 | Pembroke Pines, FL | (9.7) | 385 | Springfield, IL | (22.3) |
| 128 | Louisville, KY | (2.0) | 399 | Peoria, AZ | (24.4) | 80 | Springfield, MA | 2.5 |
| 250 | Lowell, MA | (11.3) | 371 | Peoria, IL | (21.4) | 73 | Springfield, MO | 3.1 |
| 331 | Lubbock, TX | (16.1) | 305 | Philadelphia, PA | (14.1) | 17 | Stamford, CT | 20.4 |
| 163 | Lynchburg, VA | (4.9) | 200 | Phoenix, AZ | (7.5) | 207 | Sterling Heights, MI | (8.0) |
| 409 | Lynn, MA | (26.9) | 287 | Pittsburgh, PA | (13.1) | 172 | Stockton, CA | (5.4) |
| 34 | Macon, GA | 11.0 | 314 | Plano, TX | (14.4) | 3 | St. George, UT | 53.4 |
| 324 | Madison, WI | (15.5) | 106 | Plantation, FL | (0.1) | 350 | St. Joseph, MO | (18.9) |
| 65 | Manchester, NH | 5.0 | 178 | Pomona, CA | (5.9) | 301 | St. Louis, MO | (13.6) |
| 57 | McAllen, TX | 6.2 | 175 | Pompano Beach, FL | (5.8) | 292 | St. Paul, MN | (13.3) |
| 219 | McKinney, TX | (9.0) | 269 | Port St. Lucie, FL | (12.3) | 180 | St. Petersburg, FL | (6.0) |
| 20 | Medford, OR | 19.1 | 222 | Portland, OR | (9.3) | NA | Suffolk, VA** | NA |
| 27 | Melbourne, FL | 14.1 | 7 | Portsmouth, VA | 25.7 | 261 | Sugar Land, TX | (12.0) |
| 180 | Memphis, TN | (6.0) | 175 | Providence, RI | (5.8) | 57 | Sunnyvale, CA | 6.2 |
| 401 | Menifee, CA | (25.3) | 40 | Provo, UT | 9.2 | 186 | Sunrise, FL | (6.6) |
| 425 | Merced, CA | (32.9) | 93 | Pueblo, CO | 1.2 | 394 | Surprise, AZ | (23.6) |
| 340 | Meridian, ID | (17.4) | 186 | Quincy, MA | (6.6) | 161 | Syracuse, NY | (4.7) |
| 285 | Mesa, AZ | (13.0) | 32 | Racine, WI | 11.3 | 71 | Tacoma, WA | 3.8 |
| 254 | Mesquite, TX | (11.6) | 85 | Raleigh, NC | 2.0 | 383 | Tallahassee, FL | (22.2) |
| 228 | Miami Beach, FL | (9.7) | 432 | Ramapo, NY | (37.1) | 371 | Tampa, FL | (21.4) |
| 287 | Miami Gardens, FL | (13.1) | 200 | Rancho Cucamon., CA | (7.5) | 21 | Temecula, CA | 17.2 |
| 192 | Miami, FL | (7.1) | 411 | Reading, PA | (27.8) | 100 | Tempe, AZ | 0.6 |
| 146 | Midland, TX | (3.9) | 422 | Redding, CA | (31.8) | 252 | Thornton, CO | (11.4) |
| 198 | Milwaukee, WI | (7.2) | 167 | Redwood City, CA | (5.1) | 66 | Thousand Oaks, CA | 4.9 |
| 168 | Minneapolis, MN | (5.2) | 314 | Reno, NV | (14.4) | 355 | Toledo, OH | (19.5) |
| 18 | Miramar, FL | 19.5 | 192 | Renton, WA | (7.1) | 345 | Toms River Twnshp, NJ | (17.8) |
| 415 | Mission Viejo, CA | (28.0) | 257 | Rialto, CA | (11.9) | 133 | Topeka, KS | (2.4) |
| 68 | Mission, TX | 4.6 | 395 | Richardson, TX | (23.7) | 31 | Torrance, CA | 12.0 |
| 23 | Mobile, AL | 15.1 | 63 | Richmond, CA | 5.1 | 9 | Tracy, CA | 24.1 |
| 269 | Modesto, CA | (12.3) | 277 | Richmond, VA | (12.6) | 382 | Trenton, NJ | (22.1) |
| 238 | Moreno Valley, CA | (10.4) | 280 | Riverside, CA | (12.8) | 14 | Troy, MI | 21.1 |
| 1 | Mountain View, CA | 62.0 | 427 | Roanoke, VA | (33.3) | 106 | Tucson, AZ | (0.1) |
| 381 | Murfreesboro, TN | (21.9) | 309 | Rochester, MN | (14.2) | 144 | Tulsa, OK | (3.7) |
| 419 | Murrieta, CA | (30.7) | 274 | Rochester, NY | (12.5) | 144 | Tuscaloosa, AL | (3.7) |
| 333 | Nampa, ID | (16.2) | 215 | Rockford, IL | (8.8) | 282 | Tustin, CA | (12.9) |
| 287 | Napa, CA | (13.1) | 227 | Roseville, CA | (9.6) | 355 | Tyler, TX | (19.5) |
| 277 | Naperville, IL | (12.6) | 22 | Roswell, GA | 15.3 | 192 | Upland, CA | (7.1) |
| 305 | Nashua, NH | (14.1) | 295 | Round Rock, TX | (13.5) | 93 | Upper Darby Twnshp, PA | 1.2 |
| 154 | Nashville, TN | (4.4) | 293 | Sacramento, CA | (13.4) | 338 | Vacaville, CA | (16.6) |
| 113 | New Bedford, MA | (0.5) | 184 | Salem, OR | (6.3) | 37 | Vallejo, CA | 10.2 |
| 403 | New Haven, CT | (26.1) | 186 | Salinas, CA | (6.6) | 141 | Vancouver, WA | (3.6) |
| 232 | New Orleans, LA | (9.9) | 24 | Salt Lake City, UT | 14.7 | 149 | Ventura, CA | (4.0) |
| 342 | New Rochelle, NY | (17.5) | NA | San Angelo, TX** | NA | 387 | Victorville, CA | (22.4) |
| 261 | New York, NY | (12.0) | 186 | San Antonio, TX | (6.6) | 248 | Virginia Beach, VA | (11.2) |
| 138 | Newark, NJ | (3.0) | 156 | San Bernardino, CA | (4.5) | 120 | Visalia, CA | (0.9) |
| 88 | Newport Beach, CA | 1.6 | 56 | San Diego, CA | 6.8 | 253 | Vista, CA | (11.5) |
| 140 | Newport News, VA | (3.4) | 38 | San Francisco, CA | 9.8 | 127 | Waco, TX | (1.9) |
| 35 | Newton, MA | 10.6 | 131 | San Jose, CA | (2.2) | 247 | Warren, MI | (11.1) |
| 240 | Norfolk, VA | (10.5) | 48 | San Leandro, CA | 8.1 | 320 | Warwick, RI | (15.1) |
| 168 | Norman, OK | (5.2) | 359 | San Marcos, CA | (20.1) | 204 | Washington, DC | (7.9) |
| 86 | North Charleston, SC | 1.8 | 52 | San Mateo, CA | 7.2 | 303 | Waterbury, CT | (13.9) |
| 4 | North Las Vegas, NV | 29.5 | 416 | Sandy Springs, GA | (28.2) | 38 | Waukegan, IL | 9.8 |
| 373 | Norwalk, CA | (21.5) | 5 | Sandy, UT | 27.8 | 30 | West Covina, CA | 12.6 |
| 138 | Norwalk, CT | (3.0) | 385 | Santa Ana, CA | (22.3) | 367 | West Palm Beach, FL | (20.6) |
| 350 | Oakland, CA | (18.9) | 347 | Santa Barbara, CA | (17.9) | 16 | West Valley, UT | 20.7 |
| 359 | Oceanside, CA | (20.1) | 375 | Santa Clara, CA | (21.6) | 122 | Westland, MI | (1.0) |
| 166 | Odessa, TX | (5.0) | 106 | Santa Clarita, CA | (0.1) | 231 | Westminster, CA | (9.8) |
| 43 | O'Fallon, MO | 8.5 | 232 | Santa Maria, CA | (9.9) | 146 | Westminster, CO | (3.9) |
| 363 | Ogden, UT | (20.3) | 141 | Santa Monica, CA | (3.6) | 87 | Whittier, CA | 1.7 |
| 357 | Oklahoma City, OK | (19.9) | 269 | Santa Rosa, CA | (12.3) | 361 | Wichita Falls, TX | (20.2) |
| 423 | Olathe, KS | (32.6) | 103 | Savannah, GA | 0.3 | 103 | Wichita, KS | 0.3 |
| 69 | Omaha, NE | 4.2 | 302 | Scottsdale, AZ | (13.7) | 153 | Wilmington, NC | (4.3) |
| 379 | Ontario, CA | (21.7) | 303 | Scranton, PA | (13.9) | 318 | Winston-Salem, NC | (14.7) |
| 175 | Orange, CA | (5.8) | 36 | Seattle, WA | 10.4 | 273 | Woodbridge Twnshp, NJ | (12.4) |
| 163 | Orem, UT | (4.9) | 134 | Shreveport, LA | (2.7) | 183 | Worcester, MA | (6.2) |
| 236 | Orlando, FL | (10.2) | 291 | Simi Valley, CA | (13.2) | 398 | Yakima, WA | (24.2) |
| 392 | Overland Park, KS | (23.4) | 128 | Sioux City, IA | (2.0) | 274 | Yonkers, NY | (12.5) |
| 26 | Oxnard, CA | 14.4 | 168 | Sioux Falls, SD | (5.2) | 331 | Yuma, AZ | (16.1) |
| 413 | Palm Bay, FL | (27.9) | 13 | Somerville, MA | 21.5 | | | |
| 100 | Palmdale, CA | 0.6 | 322 | South Bend, IN | (15.3) | | | |

Source: CQ Press using reported data from the F.B.I. "Crime in the United States 2013"

*Burglary is the unlawful entry of a structure to commit a felony or theft. Attempts are included.

**Not available.

## 71. Percent Change in Burglary Rate: 2012 to 2013 (continued)
## National Percent Change = 9.3% Decrease*

| RANK | CITY | % CHANGE | RANK | CITY | % CHANGE | RANK | CITY | % CHANGE |
|---|---|---|---|---|---|---|---|---|
| 1 | Mountain View, CA | 62.0 | 73 | Springfield, MO | 3.1 | 149 | Alameda, CA | (4.0) |
| 2 | Fargo, ND | 53.6 | 76 | Spokane, WA | 2.9 | 149 | Ventura, CA | (4.0) |
| 3 | St. George, UT | 53.4 | 77 | Bellflower, CA | 2.8 | 151 | Davie, FL | (4.1) |
| 4 | North Las Vegas, NV | 29.5 | 78 | Chesapeake, VA | 2.7 | 151 | Hampton, VA | (4.1) |
| 5 | Sandy, UT | 27.8 | 78 | Chula Vista, CA | 2.7 | 153 | Wilmington, NC | (4.3) |
| 6 | Boulder, CO | 26.4 | 80 | Las Vegas, NV | 2.5 | 154 | Brick Twnshp, NJ | (4.4) |
| 7 | Portsmouth, VA | 25.7 | 80 | Springfield, MA | 2.5 | 154 | Nashville, TN | (4.4) |
| 8 | Johns Creek, GA | 24.5 | 82 | Abilene, TX | 2.2 | 156 | Baltimore, MD | (4.5) |
| 9 | League City, TX | 24.1 | 82 | Gresham, OR | 2.2 | 156 | Lafayette, LA | (4.5) |
| 9 | Tracy, CA | 24.1 | 84 | Pasadena, TX | 2.1 | 156 | San Bernardino, CA | (4.5) |
| 11 | Billings, MT | 23.1 | 85 | Raleigh, NC | 2.0 | 159 | Lawton, OK | (4.6) |
| 12 | Livermore, CA | 22.5 | 86 | North Charleston, SC | 1.8 | 159 | Los Angeles, CA | (4.6) |
| 13 | Somerville, MA | 21.5 | 87 | Whittier, CA | 1.7 | 161 | Syracuse, NY | (4.7) |
| 14 | Troy, MI | 21.1 | 88 | Newport Beach, CA | 1.6 | 162 | Lakewood, CO | (4.8) |
| 15 | Columbus, GA | 20.8 | 89 | Colorado Springs, CO | 1.4 | 163 | Albany, GA | (4.9) |
| 16 | West Valley, UT | 20.7 | 89 | Lancaster, CA | 1.4 | 163 | Lynchburg, VA | (4.9) |
| 17 | Stamford, CT | 20.4 | 91 | Allentown, PA | 1.3 | 163 | Orem, UT | (4.9) |
| 18 | Miramar, FL | 19.5 | 91 | Eugene, OR | 1.3 | 166 | Odessa, TX | (5.0) |
| 19 | Fort Wayne, IN | 19.2 | 93 | Pueblo, CO | 1.2 | 167 | Redwood City, CA | (5.1) |
| 20 | Medford, OR | 19.1 | 93 | Upper Darby Twnshp, PA | 1.2 | 168 | Minneapolis, MN | (5.2) |
| 21 | Temecula, CA | 17.2 | 95 | Greenville, NC | 1.1 | 168 | Norman, OK | (5.2) |
| 22 | Roswell, GA | 15.3 | 95 | High Point, NC | 1.1 | 168 | Sioux Falls, SD | (5.2) |
| 23 | Mobile, AL | 15.1 | 97 | Cedar Rapids, IA | 1.0 | 171 | Amherst, NY | (5.3) |
| 24 | Salt Lake City, UT | 14.7 | 97 | Compton, CA | 1.0 | 172 | Stockton, CA | (5.4) |
| 25 | Largo, FL | 14.5 | 99 | Duluth, MN | 0.9 | 173 | Hesperia, CA | (5.5) |
| 26 | Oxnard, CA | 14.4 | 100 | Palmdale, CA | 0.6 | 174 | Irvine, CA | (5.6) |
| 27 | Melbourne, FL | 14.1 | 100 | Tempe, AZ | 0.6 | 175 | Orange, CA | (5.8) |
| 28 | Anchorage, AK | 13.7 | 102 | Lee's Summit, MO | 0.5 | 175 | Pompano Beach, FL | (5.8) |
| 29 | Lakewood, CA | 13.3 | 103 | Cary, NC | 0.3 | 175 | Providence, RI | (5.8) |
| 30 | West Covina, CA | 12.6 | 103 | Savannah, GA | 0.3 | 178 | Hillsboro, OR | (5.9) |
| 31 | Torrance, CA | 12.0 | 103 | Wichita, KS | 0.3 | 178 | Pomona, CA | (5.9) |
| 32 | Racine, WI | 11.3 | 106 | El Cajon, CA | (0.1) | 180 | Memphis, TN | (6.0) |
| 33 | Bloomington, IL | 11.2 | 106 | Pearland, TX | (0.1) | 180 | St. Petersburg, FL | (6.0) |
| 34 | Macon, GA | 11.0 | 106 | Plantation, FL | (0.1) | 182 | Erie, PA | (6.1) |
| 35 | Newton, MA | 10.6 | 106 | Santa Clarita, CA | (0.1) | 183 | Worcester, MA | (6.2) |
| 36 | Seattle, WA | 10.4 | 106 | Tucson, AZ | (0.1) | 184 | Salem, OR | (6.3) |
| 37 | Vallejo, CA | 10.2 | 111 | Cincinnati, OH | (0.4) | 185 | Hartford, CT | (6.4) |
| 38 | San Francisco, CA | 9.8 | 111 | Clifton, NJ | (0.4) | 186 | Quincy, MA | (6.6) |
| 38 | Waukegan, IL | 9.8 | 113 | New Bedford, MA | (0.5) | 186 | Salinas, CA | (6.6) |
| 40 | Carmel, IN | 9.2 | 114 | Long Beach, CA | (0.6) | 186 | San Antonio, TX | (6.6) |
| 40 | Provo, UT | 9.2 | 114 | South Gate, CA | (0.6) | 186 | Sunrise, FL | (6.6) |
| 42 | Glendale, CA | 8.9 | 116 | Brownsville, TX | (0.7) | 190 | Independence, MO | (6.8) |
| 43 | Aurora, CO | 8.5 | 116 | Concord, CA | (0.7) | 191 | Escondido, CA | (7.0) |
| 43 | Bryan, TX | 8.5 | 116 | El Monte, CA | (0.7) | 192 | Atlanta, GA | (7.1) |
| 43 | O'Fallon, MO | 8.5 | 116 | Kennewick, WA | (0.7) | 192 | Clearwater, FL | (7.1) |
| 43 | Spokane Valley, WA | 8.5 | 120 | Bellevue, WA | (0.9) | 192 | Denver, CO | (7.1) |
| 47 | Albuquerque, NM | 8.4 | 120 | Visalia, CA | (0.9) | 192 | Miami, FL | (7.1) |
| 48 | San Leandro, CA | 8.1 | 122 | Edmond, OK | (1.0) | 192 | Renton, WA | (7.1) |
| 49 | Berkeley, CA | 7.5 | 122 | Westland, MI | (1.0) | 192 | Upland, CA | (7.1) |
| 50 | Fairfield, CA | 7.4 | 124 | Huntington Beach, CA | (1.1) | 198 | Milwaukee, WI | (7.2) |
| 51 | Davenport, IA | 7.3 | 125 | Clarksville, TN | (1.4) | 199 | Indio, CA | (7.3) |
| 52 | San Mateo, CA | 7.2 | 126 | Inglewood, CA | (1.6) | 200 | Hayward, CA | (7.5) |
| 53 | Beaumont, TX | 7.1 | 127 | Waco, TX | (1.9) | 200 | Phoenix, AZ | (7.5) |
| 54 | Broken Arrow, OK | 7.0 | 128 | Henderson, NV | (2.0) | 200 | Rancho Cucamon., CA | (7.5) |
| 55 | Brockton, MA | 6.9 | 128 | Louisville, KY | (2.0) | 203 | Garland, TX | (7.7) |
| 56 | San Diego, CA | 6.8 | 128 | Sioux City, IA | (2.0) | 204 | Boca Raton, FL | (7.9) |
| 57 | McAllen, TX | 6.2 | 131 | San Jose, CA | (2.2) | 204 | Jacksonville, FL | (7.9) |
| 57 | Sunnyvale, CA | 6.2 | 132 | Lansing, MI | (2.3) | 204 | Washington, DC | (7.9) |
| 59 | Pasadena, CA | 5.7 | 133 | Topeka, KS | (2.4) | 207 | Clarkstown, NY | (8.0) |
| 60 | Alhambra, CA | 5.5 | 134 | Shreveport, LA | (2.7) | 207 | Sterling Heights, MI | (8.0) |
| 61 | Buena Park, CA | 5.4 | 135 | Elgin, IL | (2.8) | 209 | Des Moines, IA | (8.1) |
| 62 | Corpus Christi, TX | 5.2 | 136 | Bethlehem, PA | (2.9) | 210 | Federal Way, WA | (8.2) |
| 63 | Farmington Hills, MI | 5.1 | 136 | Everett, WA | (2.9) | 210 | Kansas City, MO | (8.2) |
| 63 | Richmond, CA | 5.1 | 138 | Newark, NJ | (3.0) | 212 | Hamilton Twnshp, NJ | (8.3) |
| 65 | Manchester, NH | 5.0 | 138 | Norwalk, CT | (3.0) | 213 | Sparks, NV | (8.6) |
| 66 | Hemet, CA | 4.9 | 140 | Newport News, VA | (3.4) | 214 | Fort Smith, AR | (8.7) |
| 66 | Thousand Oaks, CA | 4.9 | 141 | El Paso, TX | (3.6) | 215 | Boston, MA | (8.8) |
| 68 | Mission, TX | 4.6 | 141 | Santa Monica, CA | (3.6) | 215 | Cape Coral, FL | (8.8) |
| 69 | Omaha, NE | 4.2 | 141 | Vancouver, WA | (3.6) | 215 | Rockford, IL | (8.8) |
| 70 | Deerfield Beach, FL | 4.0 | 144 | Tulsa, OK | (3.7) | 218 | Chino, CA | (8.9) |
| 71 | Tacoma, WA | 3.8 | 144 | Tuscaloosa, AL | (3.7) | 219 | Kansas City, KS | (9.0) |
| 72 | Fayetteville, AR | 3.3 | 146 | Fort Worth, TX | (3.9) | 219 | McKinney, TX | (9.0) |
| 73 | Carlsbad, CA | 3.1 | 146 | Midland, TX | (3.9) | 221 | Gary, IN | (9.2) |
| 73 | Cheektowaga, NY | 3.1 | 146 | Westminster, CO | (3.9) | 222 | Fall River, MA | (9.3) |

| RANK | CITY | % CHANGE | RANK | CITY | % CHANGE | RANK | CITY | % CHANGE |
|---|---|---|---|---|---|---|---|---|
| 222 | Portland, OR | (9.3) | 295 | Evansville, IN | (13.5) | 371 | Peoria, IL | (21.4) |
| 224 | Bakersfield, CA | (9.4) | 295 | Huntsville, AL | (13.5) | 371 | Tampa, FL | (21.4) |
| 225 | Clovis, CA | (9.5) | 295 | Lakeland, FL | (13.5) | 373 | Knoxville, TN | (21.5) |
| 225 | Hawthorne, CA | (9.5) | 295 | Round Rock, TX | (13.5) | 373 | Norwalk, CA | (21.5) |
| 227 | Roseville, CA | (9.6) | 301 | St. Louis, MO | (13.6) | 375 | Cranston, RI | (21.6) |
| 228 | Akron, OH | (9.7) | 302 | Scottsdale, AZ | (13.7) | 375 | Elk Grove, CA | (21.6) |
| 228 | Miami Beach, FL | (9.7) | 303 | Scranton, PA | (13.9) | 375 | Fontana, CA | (21.6) |
| 228 | Pembroke Pines, FL | (9.7) | 303 | Waterbury, CT | (13.9) | 375 | Santa Clara, CA | (21.6) |
| 231 | Westminster, CA | (9.8) | 305 | Birmingham, AL | (14.1) | 379 | Fremont, CA | (21.7) |
| 232 | Killeen, TX | (9.9) | 305 | Bridgeport, CT | (14.1) | 379 | Ontario, CA | (21.7) |
| 232 | New Orleans, LA | (9.9) | 305 | Nashua, NH | (14.1) | 381 | Murfreesboro, TN | (21.9) |
| 232 | Santa Maria, CA | (9.9) | 305 | Philadelphia, PA | (14.1) | 382 | Trenton, NJ | (22.1) |
| 235 | Arlington, TX | (10.1) | 309 | Baton Rouge, LA | (14.2) | 383 | Chicago, IL | (22.2) |
| 236 | Indianapolis, IN | (10.2) | 309 | Cleveland, OH | (14.2) | 383 | Tallahassee, FL | (22.2) |
| 236 | Orlando, FL | (10.2) | 309 | Downey, CA | (14.2) | 385 | Santa Ana, CA | (22.3) |
| 238 | Chino Hills, CA | (10.4) | 309 | Rochester, MN | (14.2) | 385 | Springfield, IL | (22.3) |
| 238 | Moreno Valley, CA | (10.4) | 313 | Paterson, NJ | (14.3) | 387 | Jurupa Valley, CA | (22.4) |
| 240 | Norfolk, VA | (10.5) | 314 | Hoover, AL | (14.4) | 387 | Victorville, CA | (22.4) |
| 241 | Carrollton, TX | (10.6) | 314 | Plano, TX | (14.4) | 389 | Citrus Heights, CA | (22.9) |
| 242 | Boise, ID | (10.8) | 314 | Reno, NV | (14.4) | 390 | Allen, TX | (23.1) |
| 242 | Dallas, TX | (10.8) | 317 | Carson, CA | (14.6) | 391 | Costa Mesa, CA | (23.3) |
| 244 | Fort Lauderdale, FL | (10.9) | 318 | Grand Prairie, TX | (14.7) | 392 | Antioch, CA | (23.4) |
| 245 | Houston, TX | (11.0) | 318 | Winston-Salem, NC | (14.7) | 392 | Overland Park, KS | (23.4) |
| 245 | Livonia, MI | (11.0) | 320 | Warwick, RI | (15.1) | 394 | Surprise, AZ | (23.6) |
| 247 | Warren, MI | (11.1) | 321 | Gilbert, AZ | (15.2) | 395 | Richardson, TX | (23.7) |
| 248 | Little Rock, AR | (11.2) | 322 | Evanston, IL | (15.3) | 396 | Hollywood, FL | (24.1) |
| 248 | Virginia Beach, VA | (11.2) | 322 | South Bend, IN | (15.3) | 396 | Joliet, IL | (24.1) |
| 250 | Arlington Heights, IL | (11.3) | 324 | Chandler, AZ | (15.5) | 398 | Yakima, WA | (24.2) |
| 250 | Lowell, MA | (11.3) | 324 | Madison, WI | (15.5) | 399 | Danbury, CT | (24.4) |
| 252 | Thornton, CO | (11.4) | 326 | Brooklyn Park, MN | (15.7) | 399 | Peoria, AZ | (24.4) |
| 253 | Vista, CA | (11.5) | 326 | Glendale, AZ | (15.7) | 401 | Menifee, CA | (25.3) |
| 254 | Mesquite, TX | (11.6) | 328 | Edinburg, TX | (15.9) | 402 | Burbank, CA | (25.4) |
| 255 | Lexington, KY | (11.7) | 328 | Kent, WA | (15.9) | 403 | New Haven, CT | (26.1) |
| 256 | Buffalo, NY | (11.8) | 330 | Grand Rapids, MI | (16.0) | 404 | Gainesville, FL | (26.2) |
| 257 | Beaverton, OR | (11.9) | 331 | Lubbock, TX | (16.1) | 405 | Longmont, CO | (26.3) |
| 257 | Daly City, CA | (11.9) | 331 | Yuma, AZ | (16.1) | 406 | Fishers, IN | (26.4) |
| 257 | Green Bay, WI | (11.9) | 333 | Fullerton, CA | (16.2) | 407 | Corona, CA | (26.5) |
| 257 | Rialto, CA | (11.9) | 333 | Nampa, ID | (16.2) | 408 | College Station, TX | (26.8) |
| 261 | Detroit, MI | (12.0) | 335 | Arvada, CO | (16.5) | 409 | Lynn, MA | (26.9) |
| 261 | Fort Collins, CO | (12.0) | 335 | Baldwin Park, CA | (16.5) | 410 | Hialeah, FL | (27.5) |
| 261 | Fresno, CA | (12.0) | 335 | Garden Grove, CA | (16.5) | 411 | Jersey City, NJ | (27.8) |
| 261 | New York, NY | (12.0) | 338 | Vacaville, CA | (16.6) | 411 | Reading, PA | (27.8) |
| 261 | Sugar Land, TX | (12.0) | 339 | Edison Twnshp, NJ | (16.7) | 413 | Denton, TX | (27.9) |
| 266 | Anaheim, CA | (12.2) | 340 | Bloomington, MN | (17.4) | 413 | Palm Bay, FL | (27.9) |
| 266 | Greeley, CO | (12.2) | 340 | Meridian, ID | (17.4) | 415 | Mission Viejo, CA | (28.0) |
| 266 | Greensboro, NC | (12.2) | 342 | New Rochelle, NY | (17.5) | 416 | Sandy Springs, GA | (28.2) |
| 269 | Austin, TX | (12.3) | 343 | Athens-Clarke, GA | (17.7) | 417 | Las Cruces, NM | (28.5) |
| 269 | Modesto, CA | (12.3) | 343 | Laredo, TX | (17.7) | 418 | Cicero, IL | (29.2) |
| 269 | Port St. Lucie, FL | (12.3) | 345 | Bloomington, IN | (17.8) | 419 | Murrieta, CA | (30.7) |
| 269 | Santa Rosa, CA | (12.3) | 345 | Toms River Twnshp, NJ | (17.8) | 420 | Champaign, IL | (31.3) |
| 273 | Woodbridge Twnshp, NJ | (12.4) | 347 | Santa Barbara, CA | (17.9) | 420 | Lakewood Twnshp, NJ | (31.3) |
| 274 | Dearborn, MI | (12.5) | 348 | Jackson, MS | (18.4) | 422 | Redding, CA | (31.8) |
| 274 | Rochester, NY | (12.5) | 349 | Fayetteville, NC | (18.8) | 423 | Longview, TX | (32.6) |
| 274 | Yonkers, NY | (12.5) | 350 | Oakland, CA | (18.9) | 423 | Olathe, KS | (32.6) |
| 277 | Naperville, IL | (12.6) | 350 | St. Joseph, MO | (18.9) | 425 | Coral Springs, FL | (32.9) |
| 277 | Richmond, VA | (12.6) | 352 | Greece, NY | (19.0) | 425 | Merced, CA | (32.9) |
| 279 | Irving, TX | (12.7) | 353 | Lawrence, KS | (19.1) | 427 | Centennial, CO | (33.3) |
| 280 | Decatur, IL | (12.8) | 354 | Lawrence, MA | (19.4) | 427 | Roanoke, VA | (33.3) |
| 280 | Riverside, CA | (12.8) | 355 | Toledo, OH | (19.5) | 429 | Flint, MI | (33.7) |
| 282 | Alexandria, VA | (12.9) | 355 | Tyler, TX | (19.5) | 429 | Hammond, IN | (33.7) |
| 282 | Clinton Twnshp, MI | (12.9) | 357 | Charlotte, NC | (19.9) | 431 | Lake Forest, CA | (34.0) |
| 282 | Tustin, CA | (12.9) | 357 | Oklahoma City, OK | (19.9) | 432 | Ramapo, NY | (37.1) |
| 285 | Amarillo, TX | (13.0) | 359 | Oceanside, CA | (20.1) | 433 | Aurora, IL | (39.2) |
| 285 | Mesa, AZ | (13.0) | 359 | San Marcos, CA | (20.1) | 434 | Ann Arbor, MI | (43.5) |
| 287 | Lincoln, NE | (13.1) | 361 | Elizabeth, NJ | (20.2) | NA | Bend, OR** | NA |
| 287 | Miami Gardens, FL | (13.1) | 361 | Wichita Falls, TX | (20.2) | NA | Canton Twnshp, MI** | NA |
| 287 | Napa, CA | (13.1) | 363 | Albany, NY | (20.3) | NA | Chattanooga, TN** | NA |
| 287 | Pittsburgh, PA | (13.1) | 363 | Cambridge, MA | (20.3) | NA | Columbia, SC** | NA |
| 291 | Simi Valley, CA | (13.2) | 363 | Ogden, UT | (20.3) | NA | Concord, NC** | NA |
| 292 | St. Paul, MN | (13.3) | 366 | Frisco, TX | (20.5) | NA | Lewisville, TX** | NA |
| 293 | Columbia, MO | (13.4) | 367 | Charleston, SC | (20.6) | NA | San Angelo, TX** | NA |
| 293 | Sacramento, CA | (13.4) | 367 | West Palm Beach, FL | (20.6) | NA | Suffolk, VA** | NA |
| 295 | Colonie, NY | (13.5) | 369 | Kenosha, WI | (20.7) | | | |
| 295 | Dayton, OH | (13.5) | 370 | Chico, CA | (21.1) | | | |

Source: CQ Press using reported data from the F.B.I. "Crime in the United States 2013"

*Burglary is the unlawful entry of a structure to commit a felony or theft. Attempts are included.

**Not available.

# 72. Percent Change in Burglary Rate: 2009 to 2013
## National Percent Change = 15.0% Decrease*

| RANK | CITY | % CHANGE | RANK | CITY | % CHANGE | RANK | CITY | % CHANGE |
|---|---|---|---|---|---|---|---|---|
| 270 | Abilene, TX | (20.8) | 103 | Chino, CA | 0.0 | 300 | Fullerton, CA | (23.7) |
| 216 | Akron, OH | (14.3) | 138 | Chula Vista, CA | (6.1) | 429 | Gainesville, FL | (54.6) |
| 248 | Alameda, CA | (18.4) | NA | Cicero, IL** | NA | 192 | Garden Grove, CA | (12.4) |
| 181 | Albany, GA | (11.0) | 117 | Cincinnati, OH | (2.2) | 207 | Garland, TX | (13.6) |
| 295 | Albany, NY | (23.2) | 360 | Citrus Heights, CA | (32.0) | 30 | Gary, IN | 17.6 |
| 56 | Albuquerque, NM | 8.8 | 338 | Clarkstown, NY | (28.8) | 371 | Gilbert, AZ | (34.1) |
| 344 | Alexandria, VA | (29.4) | 418 | Clarksville, TN | (45.7) | 86 | Glendale, AZ | 3.0 |
| 121 | Alhambra, CA | (3.0) | 88 | Clearwater, FL | 2.7 | 178 | Glendale, CA | (10.4) |
| 259 | Allentown, PA | (19.6) | 114 | Cleveland, OH | (1.3) | 426 | Grand Prairie, TX | (51.8) |
| 408 | Allen, TX | (40.7) | 44 | Clifton, NJ | 11.9 | 368 | Grand Rapids, MI | (33.4) |
| 359 | Amarillo, TX | (31.9) | 269 | Clinton Twnshp, MI | (20.7) | 150 | Greece, NY | (7.2) |
| 263 | Amherst, NY | (20.0) | 26 | Clovis, CA | 19.4 | 277 | Greeley, CO | (21.4) |
| 135 | Anaheim, CA | (5.7) | 402 | College Station, TX | (38.7) | 205 | Green Bay, WI | (13.4) |
| 289 | Anchorage, AK | (22.7) | 175 | Colonie, NY | (9.5) | 413 | Greensboro, NC | (43.8) |
| 371 | Ann Arbor, MI | (34.1) | 80 | Colorado Springs, CO | 3.8 | NA | Greenville, NC** | NA |
| 4 | Antioch, CA | 55.9 | 169 | Columbia, MO | (9.0) | 5 | Gresham, OR | 49.8 |
| 348 | Arlington Heights, IL | (29.7) | 258 | Columbia, SC | (19.4) | 9 | Hamilton Twnshp, NJ | 42.4 |
| 383 | Arlington, TX | (34.9) | 247 | Columbus, GA | (18.1) | 400 | Hammond, IN | (37.8) |
| 261 | Arvada, CO | (19.8) | 325 | Compton, CA | (27.7) | 160 | Hampton, VA | (7.9) |
| 428 | Athens-Clarke, GA | (51.9) | 115 | Concord, CA | (1.5) | 214 | Hartford, CT | (14.2) |
| 264 | Atlanta, GA | (20.1) | 390 | Concord, NC | (36.1) | 280 | Hawthorne, CA | (21.7) |
| 168 | Aurora, CO | (8.9) | 335 | Coral Springs, FL | (28.6) | 97 | Hayward, CA | 1.1 |
| 368 | Aurora, IL | (33.4) | 102 | Corona, CA | 0.1 | 39 | Hemet, CA | 13.7 |
| 363 | Austin, TX | (33.0) | 267 | Corpus Christi, TX | (20.3) | 118 | Henderson, NV | (2.8) |
| 58 | Bakersfield, CA | 8.3 | 120 | Costa Mesa, CA | (2.9) | 1 | Hesperia, CA | 75.2 |
| 288 | Baldwin Park, CA | (22.5) | 315 | Cranston, RI | (26.0) | 398 | Hialeah, FL | (37.7) |
| 118 | Baltimore, MD | (2.8) | 295 | Dallas, TX | (23.2) | 267 | High Point, NC | (20.3) |
| 313 | Baton Rouge, LA | (25.9) | 61 | Daly City, CA | 7.6 | 13 | Hillsboro, OR | 32.7 |
| 60 | Beaumont, TX | 7.7 | 124 | Danbury, CT | (3.5) | 212 | Hollywood, FL | (14.1) |
| 290 | Beaverton, OR | (22.8) | 200 | Davenport, IA | (13.0) | 363 | Hoover, AL | (33.0) |
| 57 | Bellevue, WA | 8.5 | 184 | Davie, FL | (11.4) | 228 | Houston, TX | (15.5) |
| 112 | Bellflower, CA | (1.0) | 195 | Dayton, OH | (12.7) | 48 | Huntington Beach, CA | 11.0 |
| 220 | Bend, OR | (14.8) | 423 | Dearborn, MI | (50.2) | 325 | Huntsville, AL | (27.7) |
| 221 | Berkeley, CA | (14.9) | 407 | Decatur, IL | (40.6) | 165 | Independence, MO | (8.5) |
| 126 | Bethlehem, PA | (3.7) | NA | Deerfield Beach, FL** | NA | 228 | Indianapolis, IN | (15.5) |
| 14 | Billings, MT | 28.6 | 351 | Denton, TX | (30.1) | 131 | Indio, CA | (4.7) |
| 212 | Birmingham, AL | (14.1) | 127 | Denver, CO | (3.8) | 138 | Inglewood, CA | (6.1) |
| 188 | Bloomington, IL | (11.7) | 24 | Des Moines, IA | 19.8 | 49 | Irvine, CA | 10.9 |
| 420 | Bloomington, IN | (49.1) | 260 | Detroit, MI | (19.7) | 419 | Irving, TX | (47.3) |
| 388 | Bloomington, MN | (35.3) | 79 | Downey, CA | 3.9 | 406 | Jacksonville, FL | (40.1) |
| 252 | Boca Raton, FL | (18.9) | 110 | Duluth, MN | (0.8) | 325 | Jackson, MS | (27.7) |
| 303 | Boise, ID | (24.0) | 248 | Edinburg, TX | (18.4) | 347 | Jersey City, NJ | (29.6) |
| 95 | Boston, MA | 1.6 | 370 | Edison Twnshp, NJ | (33.9) | 425 | Johns Creek, GA | (51.3) |
| 73 | Boulder, CO | 5.6 | 283 | Edmond, OK | (22.1) | 242 | Joliet, IL | (18.0) |
| 234 | Brick Twnshp, NJ | (16.5) | 162 | El Cajon, CA | (8.2) | NA | Jurupa Valley, CA** | NA |
| 209 | Bridgeport, CT | (13.7) | 146 | El Monte, CA | (6.6) | 251 | Kansas City, KS | (18.8) |
| 36 | Brockton, MA | 14.4 | 253 | El Paso, TX | (19.0) | 157 | Kansas City, MO | (7.7) |
| 183 | Broken Arrow, OK | (11.3) | 294 | Elgin, IL | (23.1) | 75 | Kennewick, WA | 5.5 |
| 361 | Brooklyn Park, MN | (32.5) | 285 | Elizabeth, NJ | (22.2) | 157 | Kenosha, WI | (7.7) |
| 333 | Brownsville, TX | (28.5) | 414 | Elk Grove, CA | (44.7) | 201 | Kent, WA | (13.1) |
| 430 | Bryan, TX | (56.0) | 83 | Erie, PA | 3.4 | 339 | Killeen, TX | (28.9) |
| 275 | Buena Park, CA | (21.2) | 221 | Escondido, CA | (14.9) | 180 | Knoxville, TN | (10.9) |
| 172 | Buffalo, NY | (9.2) | 276 | Eugene, OR | (21.3) | 232 | Lafayette, LA | (16.3) |
| 412 | Burbank, CA | (43.7) | NA | Evanston, IL** | NA | 266 | Lake Forest, CA | (20.2) |
| 184 | Cambridge, MA | (11.4) | 207 | Evansville, IN | (13.6) | 224 | Lakeland, FL | (15.1) |
| 416 | Canton Twnshp, MI | (45.3) | 127 | Everett, WA | (3.8) | NA | Lakewood Twnshp, NJ** | NA |
| 392 | Cape Coral, FL | (36.3) | 170 | Fairfield, CA | (9.1) | 16 | Lakewood, CA | 28.1 |
| 76 | Carlsbad, CA | 4.9 | 150 | Fall River, MA | (7.2) | 149 | Lakewood, CO | (7.0) |
| 397 | Carmel, IN | (37.5) | 153 | Fargo, ND | (7.3) | 242 | Lancaster, CA | (18.0) |
| 383 | Carrollton, TX | (34.9) | 159 | Farmington Hills, MI | (7.8) | 136 | Lansing, MI | (5.8) |
| 64 | Carson, CA | 7.3 | 63 | Fayetteville, AR | 7.4 | 404 | Laredo, TX | (39.6) |
| 307 | Cary, NC | (24.9) | 374 | Fayetteville, NC | (34.3) | 32 | Largo, FL | 16.7 |
| 298 | Cedar Rapids, IA | (23.5) | 67 | Federal Way, WA | 7.1 | 356 | Las Cruces, NM | (30.8) |
| 376 | Centennial, CO | (34.4) | 253 | Fishers, IN | (19.0) | 98 | Las Vegas, NV | 0.4 |
| NA | Champaign, IL** | NA | 340 | Flint, MI | (29.1) | 319 | Lawrence, KS | (26.5) |
| 311 | Chandler, AZ | (25.7) | 292 | Fontana, CA | (23.0) | 355 | Lawrence, MA | (30.5) |
| 426 | Charleston, SC | (51.8) | 382 | Fort Collins, CO | (34.8) | 144 | Lawton, OK | (6.5) |
| 403 | Charlotte, NC | (39.1) | 122 | Fort Lauderdale, FL | (3.1) | 343 | League City, TX | (29.3) |
| 286 | Chattanooga, TN | (22.3) | 228 | Fort Smith, AR | (15.5) | 381 | Lee's Summit, MO | (34.7) |
| 91 | Cheektowaga, NY | 2.5 | 78 | Fort Wayne, IN | 4.3 | 270 | Lewisville, TX | (20.8) |
| 273 | Chesapeake, VA | (20.9) | 308 | Fort Worth, TX | (25.2) | 94 | Lexington, KY | 1.8 |
| 348 | Chicago, IL | (29.7) | 332 | Fremont, CA | (28.4) | 233 | Lincoln, NE | (16.4) |
| 197 | Chico, CA | (12.8) | 45 | Fresno, CA | 11.7 | 238 | Little Rock, AR | (17.1) |
| 23 | Chino Hills, CA | 21.8 | 210 | Frisco, TX | (13.9) | 133 | Livermore, CA | (5.5) |

| RANK | CITY | % CHANGE |
|---|---|---|
| 270 | Livonia, MI | (20.8) |
| 25 | Long Beach, CA | 19.7 |
| 396 | Longmont, CO | (37.2) |
| 424 | Longview, TX | (50.5) |
| 226 | Los Angeles, CA | (15.3) |
| 161 | Louisville, KY | (8.1) |
| NA | Lowell, MA** | NA |
| 378 | Lubbock, TX | (34.5) |
| 181 | Lynchburg, VA | (11.0) |
| 374 | Lynn, MA | (34.3) |
| 47 | Macon, GA | 11.2 |
| 191 | Madison, WI | (12.3) |
| 34 | Manchester, NH | 15.8 |
| 376 | McAllen, TX | (34.4) |
| 405 | McKinney, TX | (39.8) |
| 2 | Medford, OR | 70.7 |
| 96 | Melbourne, FL | 1.3 |
| 210 | Memphis, TN | (13.9) |
| 242 | Menifee, CA | (18.0) |
| 162 | Merced, CA | (8.2) |
| 312 | Meridian, ID | (25.8) |
| 273 | Mesa, AZ | (20.9) |
| 164 | Mesquite, TX | (8.4) |
| 323 | Miami Beach, FL | (27.5) |
| 365 | Miami Gardens, FL | (33.1) |
| 240 | Miami, FL | (17.6) |
| 415 | Midland, TX | (44.8) |
| 103 | Milwaukee, WI | 0.0 |
| 142 | Minneapolis, MN | (6.3) |
| 202 | Miramar, FL | (13.2) |
| 354 | Mission Viejo, CA | (30.4) |
| 361 | Mission, TX | (32.5) |
| 225 | Mobile, AL | (15.2) |
| 116 | Modesto, CA | (1.6) |
| 188 | Moreno Valley, CA | (11.7) |
| 66 | Mountain View, CA | 7.2 |
| 421 | Murfreesboro, TN | (49.5) |
| 409 | Murrieta, CA | (40.9) |
| 165 | Nampa, ID | (8.5) |
| 351 | Napa, CA | (30.1) |
| 300 | Naperville, IL | (23.7) |
| 226 | Nashua, NH | (15.3) |
| 219 | Nashville, TN | (14.7) |
| 283 | New Bedford, MA | (22.1) |
| 335 | New Haven, CT | (28.6) |
| 308 | New Orleans, LA | (25.2) |
| 333 | New Rochelle, NY | (28.5) |
| 186 | New York, NY | (11.5) |
| 68 | Newark, NJ | 6.9 |
| 256 | Newport Beach, CA | (19.2) |
| NA | Newport News, VA** | NA |
| 70 | Newton, MA | 6.5 |
| 147 | Norfolk, VA | (6.7) |
| 315 | Norman, OK | (26.0) |
| 255 | North Charleston, SC | (19.1) |
| 51 | North Las Vegas, NV | 10.5 |
| 92 | Norwalk, CA | 2.4 |
| 313 | Norwalk, CT | (25.9) |
| 73 | Oakland, CA | 5.6 |
| 197 | Oceanside, CA | (12.8) |
| 386 | Odessa, TX | (35.0) |
| 137 | O'Fallon, MO | (6.0) |
| 315 | Ogden, UT | (26.0) |
| 353 | Oklahoma City, OK | (30.3) |
| 393 | Olathe, KS | (36.5) |
| 41 | Omaha, NE | 13.3 |
| 203 | Ontario, CA | (13.3) |
| 64 | Orange, CA | 7.3 |
| 179 | Orem, UT | (10.5) |
| 214 | Orlando, FL | (14.2) |
| 321 | Overland Park, KS | (27.2) |
| 17 | Oxnard, CA | 27.9 |
| 290 | Palm Bay, FL | (22.8) |
| 172 | Palmdale, CA | (9.2) |

| RANK | CITY | % CHANGE |
|---|---|---|
| 29 | Pasadena, CA | 18.1 |
| 264 | Pasadena, TX | (20.1) |
| 52 | Paterson, NJ | 10.1 |
| 365 | Pearland, TX | (33.1) |
| 391 | Pembroke Pines, FL | (36.2) |
| 383 | Peoria, AZ | (34.9) |
| 357 | Peoria, IL | (31.1) |
| 133 | Philadelphia, PA | (5.5) |
| 54 | Phoenix, AZ | 9.4 |
| 278 | Pittsburgh, PA | (21.5) |
| 395 | Plano, TX | (36.8) |
| 111 | Plantation, FL | (0.9) |
| 98 | Pomona, CA | 0.4 |
| 21 | Pompano Beach, FL | 23.1 |
| 394 | Port St. Lucie, FL | (36.7) |
| 87 | Portland, OR | 2.9 |
| 11 | Portsmouth, VA | 34.9 |
| 129 | Providence, RI | (3.9) |
| 239 | Provo, UT | (17.4) |
| 10 | Pueblo, CO | 41.2 |
| 107 | Quincy, MA | (0.4) |
| 35 | Racine, WI | 15.0 |
| 142 | Raleigh, NC | (6.3) |
| 241 | Ramapo, NY | (17.8) |
| 3 | Rancho Cucamon., CA | 63.8 |
| 329 | Reading, PA | (28.1) |
| 132 | Redding, CA | (5.0) |
| 61 | Redwood City, CA | 7.6 |
| 322 | Reno, NV | (27.4) |
| 344 | Renton, WA | (29.4) |
| 123 | Rialto, CA | (3.4) |
| 411 | Richardson, TX | (42.4) |
| 76 | Richmond, CA | 4.9 |
| 46 | Richmond, VA | 11.6 |
| 150 | Riverside, CA | (7.2) |
| 379 | Roanoke, VA | (34.6) |
| 101 | Rochester, MN | 0.2 |
| 199 | Rochester, NY | (12.9) |
| 217 | Rockford, IL | (14.4) |
| 223 | Roseville, CA | (15.0) |
| 304 | Roswell, GA | (24.5) |
| 320 | Round Rock, TX | (26.6) |
| 310 | Sacramento, CA | (25.6) |
| 106 | Salem, OR | (0.2) |
| 297 | Salinas, CA | (23.4) |
| 176 | Salt Lake City, UT | (9.6) |
| 379 | San Angelo, TX | (34.6) |
| 261 | San Antonio, TX | (19.8) |
| 72 | San Bernardino, CA | 6.0 |
| 154 | San Diego, CA | (7.5) |
| 50 | San Francisco, CA | 10.8 |
| 12 | San Jose, CA | 33.0 |
| 20 | San Leandro, CA | 23.5 |
| 167 | San Marcos, CA | (8.7) |
| 82 | San Mateo, CA | 3.5 |
| 421 | Sandy Springs, GA | (49.5) |
| 53 | Sandy, UT | 10.0 |
| 344 | Santa Ana, CA | (29.4) |
| 331 | Santa Barbara, CA | (28.3) |
| 107 | Santa Clara, CA | (0.4) |
| 235 | Santa Clarita, CA | (16.6) |
| 103 | Santa Maria, CA | 0.0 |
| 70 | Santa Monica, CA | 6.5 |
| 242 | Santa Rosa, CA | (18.0) |
| 323 | Savannah, GA | (27.5) |
| 203 | Scottsdale, AZ | (13.3) |
| 250 | Scranton, PA | (18.6) |
| 85 | Seattle, WA | 3.2 |
| 218 | Shreveport, LA | (14.6) |
| 187 | Simi Valley, CA | (11.6) |
| 124 | Sioux City, IA | (3.5) |
| 37 | Sioux Falls, SD | 14.1 |
| 236 | Somerville, MA | (16.7) |
| 328 | South Bend, IN | (27.8) |

| RANK | CITY | % CHANGE |
|---|---|---|
| 55 | South Gate, CA | 8.9 |
| 387 | Sparks, NV | (35.2) |
| 6 | Spokane Valley, WA | 49.0 |
| 7 | Spokane, WA | 46.8 |
| 299 | Springfield, IL | (23.6) |
| 37 | Springfield, MA | 14.1 |
| 130 | Springfield, MO | (4.0) |
| 172 | Stamford, CT | (9.2) |
| 190 | Sterling Heights, MI | (11.8) |
| 89 | Stockton, CA | 2.6 |
| 8 | St. George, UT | 45.5 |
| 242 | St. Joseph, MO | (18.0) |
| 350 | St. Louis, MO | (29.8) |
| 177 | St. Paul, MN | (10.1) |
| 398 | St. Petersburg, FL | (37.7) |
| 69 | Suffolk, VA | 6.8 |
| 138 | Sugar Land, TX | (6.1) |
| 27 | Sunnyvale, CA | 18.8 |
| 89 | Sunrise, FL | 2.6 |
| 389 | Surprise, AZ | (35.4) |
| 195 | Syracuse, NY | (12.7) |
| 84 | Tacoma, WA | 3.3 |
| 401 | Tallahassee, FL | (38.5) |
| 416 | Tampa, FL | (45.3) |
| 31 | Temecula, CA | 16.8 |
| 170 | Tempe, AZ | (9.1) |
| 410 | Thornton, CO | (41.1) |
| 206 | Thousand Oaks, CA | (13.5) |
| 358 | Toledo, OH | (31.7) |
| 39 | Toms River Twnshp, NJ | 13.7 |
| 330 | Topeka, KS | (28.2) |
| 17 | Torrance, CA | 27.9 |
| 335 | Tracy, CA | (28.6) |
| 28 | Trenton, NJ | 18.2 |
| 147 | Troy, MI | (6.7) |
| 93 | Tucson, AZ | 2.1 |
| 193 | Tulsa, OK | (12.6) |
| 305 | Tuscaloosa, AL | (24.7) |
| 144 | Tustin, CA | (6.5) |
| 279 | Tyler, TX | (21.6) |
| NA | Upland, CA** | NA |
| 300 | Upper Darby Twnshp, PA | (23.7) |
| 373 | Vacaville, CA | (34.2) |
| 22 | Vallejo, CA | 21.9 |
| 42 | Vancouver, WA | 12.7 |
| 33 | Ventura, CA | 16.4 |
| 43 | Victorville, CA | 12.2 |
| 367 | Virginia Beach, VA | (33.3) |
| 138 | Visalia, CA | (6.1) |
| 340 | Vista, CA | (29.1) |
| 281 | Waco, TX | (22.0) |
| 109 | Warren, MI | (0.5) |
| 257 | Warwick, RI | (19.3) |
| 237 | Washington, DC | (16.8) |
| 318 | Waterbury, CT | (26.3) |
| NA | Waukegan, IL** | NA |
| 15 | West Covina, CA | 28.4 |
| 281 | West Palm Beach, FL | (22.0) |
| 113 | West Valley, UT | (1.1) |
| 193 | Westland, MI | (12.6) |
| 100 | Westminster, CA | 0.3 |
| 286 | Westminster, CO | (22.3) |
| 59 | Whittier, CA | 8.0 |
| 306 | Wichita Falls, TX | (24.8) |
| 154 | Wichita, KS | (7.5) |
| 154 | Wilmington, NC | (7.5) |
| 231 | Winston-Salem, NC | (16.1) |
| 80 | Woodbridge Twnshp, NJ | 3.8 |
| 19 | Worcester, MA | 25.5 |
| NA | Yakima, WA** | NA |
| 292 | Yonkers, NY | (23.0) |
| 342 | Yuma, AZ | (29.2) |

Source: CQ Press using reported data from the F.B.I. "Crime in the United States 2013"

*Burglary is the unlawful entry of a structure to commit a felony or theft. Attempts are included.

**Not available.

## 72. Percent Change in Burglary Rate: 2009 to 2013 (continued)
## National Percent Change = 15.0% Decrease*

| RANK | CITY | % CHANGE | RANK | CITY | % CHANGE | RANK | CITY | % CHANGE |
|---|---|---|---|---|---|---|---|---|
| 1 | Hesperia, CA | 75.2 | 75 | Kennewick, WA | 5.5 | 149 | Lakewood, CO | (7.0) |
| 2 | Medford, OR | 70.7 | 76 | Carlsbad, CA | 4.9 | 150 | Fall River, MA | (7.2) |
| 3 | Rancho Cucamon., CA | 63.8 | 76 | Richmond, CA | 4.9 | 150 | Greece, NY | (7.2) |
| 4 | Antioch, CA | 55.9 | 78 | Fort Wayne, IN | 4.3 | 150 | Riverside, CA | (7.2) |
| 5 | Gresham, OR | 49.8 | 79 | Downey, CA | 3.9 | 153 | Fargo, ND | (7.3) |
| 6 | Spokane Valley, WA | 49.0 | 80 | Colorado Springs, CO | 3.8 | 154 | San Diego, CA | (7.5) |
| 7 | Spokane, WA | 46.8 | 80 | Woodbridge Twnshp, NJ | 3.8 | 154 | Wichita, KS | (7.5) |
| 8 | St. George, UT | 45.5 | 82 | San Mateo, CA | 3.5 | 154 | Wilmington, NC | (7.5) |
| 9 | Hamilton Twnshp, NJ | 42.4 | 83 | Erie, PA | 3.4 | 157 | Kansas City, MO | (7.7) |
| 10 | Pueblo, CO | 41.2 | 84 | Tacoma, WA | 3.3 | 157 | Kenosha, WI | (7.7) |
| 11 | Portsmouth, VA | 34.9 | 85 | Seattle, WA | 3.2 | 159 | Farmington Hills, MI | (7.8) |
| 12 | San Jose, CA | 33.0 | 86 | Glendale, AZ | 3.0 | 160 | Hampton, VA | (7.9) |
| 13 | Hillsboro, OR | 32.7 | 87 | Portland, OR | 2.9 | 161 | Louisville, KY | (8.1) |
| 14 | Billings, MT | 28.6 | 88 | Clearwater, FL | 2.7 | 162 | El Cajon, CA | (8.2) |
| 15 | West Covina, CA | 28.4 | 89 | Stockton, CA | 2.6 | 162 | Merced, CA | (8.2) |
| 16 | Lakewood, CA | 28.1 | 89 | Sunrise, FL | 2.6 | 164 | Mesquite, TX | (8.4) |
| 17 | Oxnard, CA | 27.9 | 91 | Cheektowaga, NY | 2.5 | 165 | Independence, MO | (8.5) |
| 17 | Torrance, CA | 27.9 | 92 | Norwalk, CA | 2.4 | 165 | Nampa, ID | (8.5) |
| 19 | Worcester, MA | 25.5 | 93 | Tucson, AZ | 2.1 | 167 | San Marcos, CA | (8.7) |
| 20 | San Leandro, CA | 23.5 | 94 | Lexington, KY | 1.8 | 168 | Aurora, CO | (8.9) |
| 21 | Pompano Beach, FL | 23.1 | 95 | Boston, MA | 1.6 | 169 | Columbia, MO | (9.0) |
| 22 | Vallejo, CA | 21.9 | 96 | Melbourne, FL | 1.3 | 170 | Fairfield, CA | (9.1) |
| 23 | Chino Hills, CA | 21.8 | 97 | Hayward, CA | 1.1 | 170 | Tempe, AZ | (9.1) |
| 24 | Des Moines, IA | 19.8 | 98 | Las Vegas, NV | 0.4 | 172 | Buffalo, NY | (9.2) |
| 25 | Long Beach, CA | 19.7 | 98 | Pomona, CA | 0.4 | 172 | Palmdale, CA | (9.2) |
| 26 | Clovis, CA | 19.4 | 100 | Westminster, CA | 0.3 | 172 | Stamford, CT | (9.2) |
| 27 | Sunnyvale, CA | 18.8 | 101 | Rochester, MN | 0.2 | 175 | Colonie, NY | (9.5) |
| 28 | Trenton, NJ | 18.2 | 102 | Corona, CA | 0.1 | 176 | Salt Lake City, UT | (9.6) |
| 29 | Pasadena, CA | 18.1 | 103 | Chino, CA | 0.0 | 177 | St. Paul, MN | (10.1) |
| 30 | Gary, IN | 17.6 | 103 | Milwaukee, WI | 0.0 | 178 | Glendale, CA | (10.4) |
| 31 | Temecula, CA | 16.8 | 103 | Santa Maria, CA | 0.0 | 179 | Orem, UT | (10.5) |
| 32 | Largo, FL | 16.7 | 106 | Salem, OR | (0.2) | 180 | Knoxville, TN | (10.9) |
| 33 | Ventura, CA | 16.4 | 107 | Quincy, MA | (0.4) | 181 | Albany, GA | (11.0) |
| 34 | Manchester, NH | 15.8 | 107 | Santa Clara, CA | (0.4) | 181 | Lynchburg, VA | (11.0) |
| 35 | Racine, WI | 15.0 | 109 | Warren, MI | (0.5) | 183 | Broken Arrow, OK | (11.3) |
| 36 | Brockton, MA | 14.4 | 110 | Duluth, MN | (0.8) | 184 | Cambridge, MA | (11.4) |
| 37 | Sioux Falls, SD | 14.1 | 111 | Plantation, FL | (0.9) | 184 | Davie, FL | (11.4) |
| 37 | Springfield, MA | 14.1 | 112 | Bellflower, CA | (1.0) | 186 | New York, NY | (11.5) |
| 39 | Hemet, CA | 13.7 | 113 | West Valley, UT | (1.1) | 187 | Simi Valley, CA | (11.6) |
| 39 | Toms River Twnshp, NJ | 13.7 | 114 | Cleveland, OH | (1.3) | 188 | Bloomington, IL | (11.7) |
| 41 | Omaha, NE | 13.3 | 115 | Concord, CA | (1.5) | 188 | Moreno Valley, CA | (11.7) |
| 42 | Vancouver, WA | 12.7 | 116 | Modesto, CA | (1.6) | 190 | Sterling Heights, MI | (11.8) |
| 43 | Victorville, CA | 12.2 | 117 | Cincinnati, OH | (2.2) | 191 | Madison, WI | (12.3) |
| 44 | Clifton, NJ | 11.9 | 118 | Baltimore, MD | (2.8) | 192 | Garden Grove, CA | (12.4) |
| 45 | Fresno, CA | 11.7 | 118 | Henderson, NV | (2.8) | 193 | Tulsa, OK | (12.6) |
| 46 | Richmond, VA | 11.6 | 120 | Costa Mesa, CA | (2.9) | 193 | Westland, MI | (12.6) |
| 47 | Macon, GA | 11.2 | 121 | Alhambra, CA | (3.0) | 195 | Dayton, OH | (12.7) |
| 48 | Huntington Beach, CA | 11.0 | 122 | Fort Lauderdale, FL | (3.1) | 195 | Syracuse, NY | (12.7) |
| 49 | Irvine, CA | 10.9 | 123 | Rialto, CA | (3.4) | 197 | Chico, CA | (12.8) |
| 50 | San Francisco, CA | 10.8 | 124 | Danbury, CT | (3.5) | 197 | Oceanside, CA | (12.8) |
| 51 | North Las Vegas, NV | 10.5 | 124 | Sioux City, IA | (3.5) | 199 | Rochester, NY | (12.9) |
| 52 | Paterson, NJ | 10.1 | 126 | Bethlehem, PA | (3.7) | 200 | Davenport, IA | (13.0) |
| 53 | Sandy, UT | 10.0 | 127 | Denver, CO | (3.8) | 201 | Kent, WA | (13.1) |
| 54 | Phoenix, AZ | 9.4 | 127 | Everett, WA | (3.8) | 202 | Miramar, FL | (13.2) |
| 55 | South Gate, CA | 8.9 | 129 | Providence, RI | (3.9) | 203 | Ontario, CA | (13.3) |
| 56 | Albuquerque, NM | 8.8 | 130 | Springfield, MO | (4.0) | 203 | Scottsdale, AZ | (13.3) |
| 57 | Bellevue, WA | 8.5 | 131 | Indio, CA | (4.7) | 205 | Green Bay, WI | (13.4) |
| 58 | Bakersfield, CA | 8.3 | 132 | Redding, CA | (5.0) | 206 | Thousand Oaks, CA | (13.5) |
| 59 | Whittier, CA | 8.0 | 133 | Livermore, CA | (5.5) | 207 | Evansville, IN | (13.6) |
| 60 | Beaumont, TX | 7.7 | 133 | Philadelphia, PA | (5.5) | 207 | Garland, TX | (13.6) |
| 61 | Daly City, CA | 7.6 | 135 | Anaheim, CA | (5.7) | 209 | Bridgeport, CT | (13.7) |
| 61 | Redwood City, CA | 7.6 | 136 | Lansing, MI | (5.8) | 210 | Frisco, TX | (13.9) |
| 63 | Fayetteville, AR | 7.4 | 137 | O'Fallon, MO | (6.0) | 210 | Memphis, TN | (13.9) |
| 64 | Carson, CA | 7.3 | 138 | Chula Vista, CA | (6.1) | 212 | Birmingham, AL | (14.1) |
| 64 | Orange, CA | 7.3 | 138 | Inglewood, CA | (6.1) | 212 | Hollywood, FL | (14.1) |
| 66 | Mountain View, CA | 7.2 | 138 | Sugar Land, TX | (6.1) | 214 | Hartford, CT | (14.2) |
| 67 | Federal Way, WA | 7.1 | 138 | Visalia, CA | (6.1) | 214 | Orlando, FL | (14.2) |
| 68 | Newark, NJ | 6.9 | 142 | Minneapolis, MN | (6.3) | 216 | Akron, OH | (14.3) |
| 69 | Suffolk, VA | 6.8 | 142 | Raleigh, NC | (6.3) | 217 | Rockford, IL | (14.4) |
| 70 | Newton, MA | 6.5 | 144 | Lawton, OK | (6.5) | 218 | Shreveport, LA | (14.6) |
| 70 | Santa Monica, CA | 6.5 | 144 | Tustin, CA | (6.5) | 219 | Nashville, TN | (14.7) |
| 72 | San Bernardino, CA | 6.0 | 146 | El Monte, CA | (6.6) | 220 | Bend, OR | (14.8) |
| 73 | Boulder, CO | 5.6 | 147 | Norfolk, VA | (6.7) | 221 | Berkeley, CA | (14.9) |
| 73 | Oakland, CA | 5.6 | 147 | Troy, MI | (6.7) | 221 | Escondido, CA | (14.9) |

| RANK | CITY | % CHANGE | RANK | CITY | % CHANGE | RANK | CITY | % CHANGE |
|---|---|---|---|---|---|---|---|---|
| 223 | Roseville, CA | (15.0) | 297 | Salinas, CA | (23.4) | 371 | Ann Arbor, MI | (34.1) |
| 224 | Lakeland, FL | (15.1) | 298 | Cedar Rapids, IA | (23.5) | 371 | Gilbert, AZ | (34.1) |
| 225 | Mobile, AL | (15.2) | 299 | Springfield, IL | (23.6) | 373 | Vacaville, CA | (34.2) |
| 226 | Los Angeles, CA | (15.3) | 300 | Fullerton, CA | (23.7) | 374 | Fayetteville, NC | (34.3) |
| 226 | Nashua, NH | (15.3) | 300 | Naperville, IL | (23.7) | 374 | Lynn, MA | (34.3) |
| 228 | Fort Smith, AR | (15.5) | 300 | Upper Darby Twnshp, PA | (23.7) | 376 | Centennial, CO | (34.4) |
| 228 | Houston, TX | (15.5) | 303 | Boise, ID | (24.0) | 376 | McAllen, TX | (34.4) |
| 228 | Indianapolis, IN | (15.5) | 304 | Roswell, GA | (24.5) | 378 | Lubbock, TX | (34.5) |
| 231 | Winston-Salem, NC | (16.1) | 305 | Tuscaloosa, AL | (24.7) | 379 | Roanoke, VA | (34.6) |
| 232 | Lafayette, LA | (16.3) | 306 | Wichita Falls, TX | (24.8) | 379 | San Angelo, TX | (34.6) |
| 233 | Lincoln, NE | (16.4) | 307 | Cary, NC | (24.9) | 381 | Lee's Summit, MO | (34.7) |
| 234 | Brick Twnshp, NJ | (16.5) | 308 | Fort Worth, TX | (25.2) | 382 | Fort Collins, CO | (34.8) |
| 235 | Santa Clarita, CA | (16.6) | 308 | New Orleans, LA | (25.2) | 383 | Arlington, TX | (34.9) |
| 236 | Somerville, MA | (16.7) | 310 | Sacramento, CA | (25.6) | 383 | Carrollton, TX | (34.9) |
| 237 | Washington, DC | (16.8) | 311 | Chandler, AZ | (25.7) | 383 | Peoria, AZ | (34.9) |
| 238 | Little Rock, AR | (17.1) | 312 | Meridian, ID | (25.8) | 386 | Odessa, TX | (35.0) |
| 239 | Provo, UT | (17.4) | 313 | Baton Rouge, LA | (25.9) | 387 | Sparks, NV | (35.2) |
| 240 | Miami, FL | (17.6) | 313 | Norwalk, CT | (25.9) | 388 | Bloomington, MN | (35.3) |
| 241 | Ramapo, NY | (17.8) | 315 | Cranston, RI | (26.0) | 389 | Surprise, AZ | (35.4) |
| 242 | Joliet, IL | (18.0) | 315 | Norman, OK | (26.0) | 390 | Concord, NC | (36.1) |
| 242 | Lancaster, CA | (18.0) | 315 | Ogden, UT | (26.0) | 391 | Pembroke Pines, FL | (36.2) |
| 242 | Menifee, CA | (18.0) | 318 | Waterbury, CT | (26.3) | 392 | Cape Coral, FL | (36.3) |
| 242 | Santa Rosa, CA | (18.0) | 319 | Lawrence, KS | (26.5) | 393 | Olathe, KS | (36.5) |
| 242 | St. Joseph, MO | (18.0) | 320 | Round Rock, TX | (26.6) | 394 | Port St. Lucie, FL | (36.7) |
| 247 | Columbus, GA | (18.1) | 321 | Overland Park, KS | (27.2) | 395 | Plano, TX | (36.8) |
| 248 | Alameda, CA | (18.4) | 322 | Reno, NV | (27.4) | 396 | Longmont, CO | (37.2) |
| 248 | Edinburg, TX | (18.4) | 323 | Miami Beach, FL | (27.5) | 397 | Carmel, IN | (37.5) |
| 250 | Scranton, PA | (18.6) | 323 | Savannah, GA | (27.5) | 398 | Hialeah, FL | (37.7) |
| 251 | Kansas City, KS | (18.8) | 325 | Compton, CA | (27.7) | 398 | St. Petersburg, FL | (37.7) |
| 252 | Boca Raton, FL | (18.9) | 325 | Huntsville, AL | (27.7) | 400 | Hammond, IN | (37.8) |
| 253 | El Paso, TX | (19.0) | 325 | Jackson, MS | (27.7) | 401 | Tallahassee, FL | (38.5) |
| 253 | Fishers, IN | (19.0) | 328 | South Bend, IN | (27.8) | 402 | College Station, TX | (38.7) |
| 255 | North Charleston, SC | (19.1) | 329 | Reading, PA | (28.1) | 403 | Charlotte, NC | (39.1) |
| 256 | Newport Beach, CA | (19.2) | 330 | Topeka, KS | (28.2) | 404 | Laredo, TX | (39.6) |
| 257 | Warwick, RI | (19.3) | 331 | Santa Barbara, CA | (28.3) | 405 | McKinney, TX | (39.8) |
| 258 | Columbia, SC | (19.4) | 332 | Fremont, CA | (28.4) | 406 | Jacksonville, FL | (40.1) |
| 259 | Allentown, PA | (19.6) | 333 | Brownsville, TX | (28.5) | 407 | Decatur, IL | (40.6) |
| 260 | Detroit, MI | (19.7) | 333 | New Rochelle, NY | (28.5) | 408 | Allen, TX | (40.7) |
| 261 | Arvada, CO | (19.8) | 335 | Coral Springs, FL | (28.6) | 409 | Murrieta, CA | (40.9) |
| 261 | San Antonio, TX | (19.8) | 335 | New Haven, CT | (28.6) | 410 | Thornton, CO | (41.1) |
| 263 | Amherst, NY | (20.0) | 335 | Tracy, CA | (28.6) | 411 | Richardson, TX | (42.4) |
| 264 | Atlanta, GA | (20.1) | 338 | Clarkstown, NY | (28.8) | 412 | Burbank, CA | (43.7) |
| 264 | Pasadena, TX | (20.1) | 339 | Killeen, TX | (28.9) | 413 | Greensboro, NC | (43.8) |
| 266 | Lake Forest, CA | (20.2) | 340 | Flint, MI | (29.1) | 414 | Elk Grove, CA | (44.7) |
| 267 | Corpus Christi, TX | (20.3) | 340 | Vista, CA | (29.1) | 415 | Midland, TX | (44.8) |
| 267 | High Point, NC | (20.3) | 342 | Yuma, AZ | (29.2) | 416 | Canton Twnshp, MI | (45.3) |
| 269 | Clinton Twnshp, MI | (20.7) | 343 | League City, TX | (29.3) | 416 | Tampa, FL | (45.3) |
| 270 | Abilene, TX | (20.8) | 344 | Alexandria, VA | (29.4) | 418 | Clarksville, TN | (45.7) |
| 270 | Lewisville, TX | (20.8) | 344 | Renton, WA | (29.4) | 419 | Irving, TX | (47.3) |
| 270 | Livonia, MI | (20.8) | 344 | Santa Ana, CA | (29.4) | 420 | Bloomington, IN | (49.1) |
| 273 | Chesapeake, VA | (20.9) | 347 | Jersey City, NJ | (29.6) | 421 | Murfreesboro, TN | (49.5) |
| 273 | Mesa, AZ | (20.9) | 348 | Arlington Heights, IL | (29.7) | 421 | Sandy Springs, GA | (49.5) |
| 275 | Buena Park, CA | (21.2) | 348 | Chicago, IL | (29.7) | 423 | Dearborn, MI | (50.2) |
| 276 | Eugene, OR | (21.3) | 350 | St. Louis, MO | (29.8) | 424 | Longview, TX | (50.5) |
| 277 | Greeley, CO | (21.4) | 351 | Denton, TX | (30.1) | 425 | Johns Creek, GA | (51.3) |
| 278 | Pittsburgh, PA | (21.5) | 351 | Napa, CA | (30.1) | 426 | Charleston, SC | (51.8) |
| 279 | Tyler, TX | (21.6) | 353 | Oklahoma City, OK | (30.3) | 426 | Grand Prairie, TX | (51.8) |
| 280 | Hawthorne, CA | (21.7) | 354 | Mission Viejo, CA | (30.4) | 428 | Athens-Clarke, GA | (51.9) |
| 281 | Waco, TX | (22.0) | 355 | Lawrence, MA | (30.5) | 429 | Gainesville, FL | (54.6) |
| 281 | West Palm Beach, FL | (22.0) | 356 | Las Cruces, NM | (30.8) | 430 | Bryan, TX | (56.0) |
| 283 | Edmond, OK | (22.1) | 357 | Peoria, IL | (31.1) | NA | Champaign, IL** | NA |
| 283 | New Bedford, MA | (22.1) | 358 | Toledo, OH | (31.7) | NA | Cicero, IL** | NA |
| 285 | Elizabeth, NJ | (22.2) | 359 | Amarillo, TX | (31.9) | NA | Deerfield Beach, FL** | NA |
| 286 | Chattanooga, TN | (22.3) | 360 | Citrus Heights, CA | (32.0) | NA | Evanston, IL** | NA |
| 286 | Westminster, CO | (22.3) | 361 | Brooklyn Park, MN | (32.5) | NA | Greenville, NC** | NA |
| 288 | Baldwin Park, CA | (22.5) | 361 | Mission, TX | (32.5) | NA | Jurupa Valley, CA** | NA |
| 289 | Anchorage, AK | (22.7) | 363 | Austin, TX | (33.0) | NA | Lakewood Twnshp, NJ** | NA |
| 290 | Beaverton, OR | (22.8) | 363 | Hoover, AL | (33.0) | NA | Lowell, MA** | NA |
| 290 | Palm Bay, FL | (22.8) | 365 | Miami Gardens, FL | (33.1) | NA | Newport News, VA** | NA |
| 292 | Fontana, CA | (23.0) | 365 | Pearland, TX | (33.1) | NA | Upland, CA** | NA |
| 292 | Yonkers, NY | (23.0) | 367 | Virginia Beach, VA | (33.3) | NA | Waukegan, IL** | NA |
| 294 | Elgin, IL | (23.1) | 368 | Aurora, IL | (33.4) | NA | Yakima, WA** | NA |
| 295 | Albany, NY | (23.2) | 368 | Grand Rapids, MI | (33.4) | | | |
| 295 | Dallas, TX | (23.2) | 370 | Edison Twnshp, NJ | (33.9) | | | |

Source: CQ Press using reported data from the F.B.I. "Crime in the United States 2013"

*Burglary is the unlawful entry of a structure to commit a felony or theft. Attempts are included.

**Not available.

# 73. Larceny-Thefts in 2013
## National Total = 6,004,453 Larceny-Thefts*

| RANK | CITY | THEFTS | RANK | CITY | THEFTS | RANK | CITY | THEFTS |
|---|---|---|---|---|---|---|---|---|
| 164 | Abilene, TX | 3,460 | 394 | Chino, CA | 1,249 | 210 | Fullerton, CA | 2,873 |
| 99 | Akron, OH | 5,922 | 160 | Chula Vista, CA | 3,532 | 142 | Gainesville, FL | 4,000 |
| 388 | Alameda, CA | 1,285 | 414 | Cicero, IL | 1,044 | 264 | Garden Grove, CA | 2,221 |
| 185 | Albany, GA | 3,169 | 52 | Cincinnati, OH | 10,488 | 103 | Garland, TX | 5,671 |
| 180 | Albany, NY | 3,243 | 318 | Citrus Heights, CA | 1,825 | 231 | Gary, IN | 2,533 |
| 22 | Albuquerque, NM | 20,229 | 377 | Clarkstown, NY | 1,388 | 220 | Gilbert, AZ | 2,672 |
| 241 | Alexandria, VA | 2,427 | 204 | Clarksville, TN | 2,965 | 53 | Glendale, AZ | 10,166 |
| 401 | Alhambra, CA | 1,196 | 178 | Clearwater, FL | 3,284 | 245 | Glendale, CA | 2,384 |
| 218 | Allentown, PA | 2,724 | 50 | Cleveland, OH | 10,784 | 167 | Grand Prairie, TX | 3,448 |
| 418 | Allen, TX | 985 | 411 | Clifton, NJ | 1,060 | 131 | Grand Rapids, MI | 4,315 |
| 104 | Amarillo, TX | 5,643 | 365 | Clinton Twnshp, MI | 1,480 | 303 | Greece, NY | 1,925 |
| 307 | Amherst, NY | 1,882 | 266 | Clovis, CA | 2,220 | 227 | Greeley, CO | 2,558 |
| 89 | Anaheim, CA | 6,518 | 324 | College Station, TX | 1,750 | 294 | Green Bay, WI | 2,001 |
| 54 | Anchorage, AK | 9,845 | 323 | Colonie, NY | 1,753 | 75 | Greensboro, NC | 8,063 |
| 293 | Ann Arbor, MI | 2,021 | 42 | Colorado Springs, CO | 12,521 | 225 | Greenville, NC | 2,573 |
| 312 | Antioch, CA | 1,872 | 162 | Columbia, MO | 3,490 | 191 | Gresham, OR | 3,123 |
| 435 | Arlington Heights, IL | 659 | 101 | Columbia, SC | 5,800 | 389 | Hamilton Twnshp, NJ | 1,283 |
| 49 | Arlington, TX | 10,879 | 76 | Columbus, GA | 8,012 | 264 | Hammond, IN | 2,221 |
| 276 | Arvada, CO | 2,138 | 405 | Compton, CA | 1,160 | 161 | Hampton, VA | 3,525 |
| 207 | Athens-Clarke, GA | 2,912 | 214 | Concord, CA | 2,764 | 172 | Hartford, CT | 3,416 |
| 28 | Atlanta, GA | 17,158 | 290 | Concord, NC | 2,033 | 382 | Hawthorne, CA | 1,333 |
| 78 | Aurora, CO | 7,805 | 285 | Coral Springs, FL | 2,067 | 278 | Hayward, CA | 2,122 |
| 257 | Aurora, IL | 2,285 | 253 | Corona, CA | 2,305 | 255 | Hemet, CA | 2,294 |
| 9 | Austin, TX | 32,948 | 46 | Corpus Christi, TX | 11,519 | 172 | Henderson, NV | 3,416 |
| 60 | Bakersfield, CA | 9,272 | 215 | Costa Mesa, CA | 2,748 | 413 | Hesperia, CA | 1,052 |
| 433 | Baldwin Park, CA | 727 | 387 | Cranston, RI | 1,306 | 112 | Hialeah, FL | 5,079 |
| 25 | Baltimore, MD | 18,946 | 10 | Dallas, TX | 30,374 | 203 | High Point, NC | 2,970 |
| 79 | Baton Rouge, LA | 7,648 | 402 | Daly City, CA | 1,190 | 327 | Hillsboro, OR | 1,723 |
| 144 | Beaumont, TX | 3,987 | 421 | Danbury, CT | 972 | 122 | Hollywood, FL | 4,478 |
| 400 | Beaverton, OR | 1,213 | 196 | Davenport, IA | 3,048 | 275 | Hoover, AL | 2,144 |
| 201 | Bellevue, WA | 3,013 | 236 | Davie, FL | 2,480 | 2 | Houston, TX | 73,591 |
| 422 | Bellflower, CA | 968 | 127 | Dayton, OH | 4,427 | 149 | Huntington Beach, CA | 3,796 |
| 305 | Bend, OR | 1,913 | 251 | Dearborn, MI | 2,328 | 88 | Huntsville, AL | 6,629 |
| 154 | Berkeley, CA | 3,658 | 361 | Decatur, IL | 1,512 | 110 | Independence, MO | 5,149 |
| 348 | Bethlehem, PA | 1,601 | 347 | Deerfield Beach, FL | 1,606 | 13 | Indianapolis, IN | 26,156 |
| 139 | Billings, MT | 4,074 | 268 | Denton, TX | 2,203 | 381 | Indio, CA | 1,335 |
| 66 | Birmingham, AL | 8,661 | 30 | Denver, CO | 15,306 | 373 | Inglewood, CA | 1,441 |
| 371 | Bloomington, IL | 1,446 | 86 | Des Moines, IA | 6,854 | 228 | Irvine, CA | 2,553 |
| 300 | Bloomington, IN | 1,942 | 27 | Detroit, MI | 17,188 | 125 | Irving, TX | 4,444 |
| 202 | Bloomington, MN | 2,990 | 311 | Downey, CA | 1,873 | 15 | Jacksonville, FL | 24,361 |
| 325 | Boca Raton, FL | 1,744 | 163 | Duluth, MN | 3,484 | 100 | Jackson, MS | 5,864 |
| 152 | Boise, ID | 3,703 | 177 | Edinburg, TX | 3,299 | 197 | Jersey City, NJ | 3,046 |
| 39 | Boston, MA | 13,147 | 428 | Edison Twnshp, NJ | 854 | 440 | Johns Creek, GA | 468 |
| 262 | Boulder, CO | 2,236 | 398 | Edmond, OK | 1,230 | 249 | Joliet, IL | 2,337 |
| 426 | Brick Twnshp, NJ | 911 | 320 | El Cajon, CA | 1,775 | 326 | Jurupa Valley, CA | 1,732 |
| 222 | Bridgeport, CT | 2,610 | 415 | El Monte, CA | 1,038 | 121 | Kansas City, KS | 4,566 |
| 279 | Brockton, MA | 2,100 | 40 | El Paso, TX | 12,993 | 33 | Kansas City, MO | 13,949 |
| 363 | Broken Arrow, OK | 1,490 | 369 | Elgin, IL | 1,462 | 309 | Kennewick, WA | 1,876 |
| 310 | Brooklyn Park, MN | 1,875 | 314 | Elizabeth, NJ | 1,861 | 317 | Kenosha, WI | 1,826 |
| 91 | Brownsville, TX | 6,441 | 263 | Elk Grove, CA | 2,229 | 153 | Kent, WA | 3,669 |
| 333 | Bryan, TX | 1,683 | 280 | Erie, PA | 2,093 | 184 | Killeen, TX | 3,189 |
| 375 | Buena Park, CA | 1,435 | 237 | Escondido, CA | 2,476 | 68 | Knoxville, TN | 8,424 |
| 74 | Buffalo, NY | 8,076 | 102 | Eugene, OR | 5,773 | 97 | Lafayette, LA | 5,995 |
| 302 | Burbank, CA | 1,926 | 367 | Evanston, IL | 1,474 | 436 | Lake Forest, CA | 620 |
| 243 | Cambridge, MA | 2,402 | 129 | Evansville, IN | 4,371 | 137 | Lakeland, FL | 4,082 |
| 422 | Canton Twnshp, MI | 968 | 116 | Everett, WA | 4,702 | 432 | Lakewood Twnshp, NJ | 768 |
| 241 | Cape Coral, FL | 2,427 | 272 | Fairfield, CA | 2,170 | 380 | Lakewood, CA | 1,356 |
| 374 | Carlsbad, CA | 1,436 | 372 | Fall River, MA | 1,443 | 107 | Lakewood, CO | 5,397 |
| 439 | Carmel, IN | 573 | 248 | Fargo, ND | 2,342 | 291 | Lancaster, CA | 2,030 |
| 288 | Carrollton, TX | 2,048 | 431 | Farmington Hills, MI | 773 | 250 | Lansing, MI | 2,329 |
| 395 | Carson, CA | 1,248 | 238 | Fayetteville, AR | 2,473 | 65 | Laredo, TX | 8,685 |
| 342 | Cary, NC | 1,623 | 70 | Fayetteville, NC | 8,351 | 277 | Largo, FL | 2,134 |
| 170 | Cedar Rapids, IA | 3,433 | 159 | Federal Way, WA | 3,535 | 165 | Las Cruces, NM | 3,454 |
| 424 | Centennial, CO | 936 | 434 | Fishers, IN | 719 | 12 | Las Vegas, NV | 26,548 |
| 331 | Champaign, IL | 1,698 | 295 | Flint, MI | 2,000 | 205 | Lawrence, KS | 2,959 |
| 120 | Chandler, AZ | 4,628 | 267 | Fontana, CA | 2,217 | 416 | Lawrence, MA | 1,012 |
| 216 | Charleston, SC | 2,725 | 189 | Fort Collins, CO | 3,137 | 176 | Lawton, OK | 3,313 |
| 19 | Charlotte, NC | 22,274 | 92 | Fort Lauderdale, FL | 6,429 | 366 | League City, TX | 1,476 |
| 72 | Chattanooga, TN | 8,165 | 168 | Fort Smith, AR | 3,447 | 352 | Lee's Summit, MO | 1,582 |
| 259 | Cheektowaga, NY | 2,271 | 82 | Fort Wayne, IN | 7,025 | 304 | Lewisville, TX | 1,921 |
| 114 | Chesapeake, VA | 4,832 | 17 | Fort Worth, TX | 23,557 | 63 | Lexington, KY | 9,042 |
| 3 | Chicago, IL | 65,497 | 234 | Fremont, CA | 2,484 | 80 | Lincoln, NE | 7,625 |
| 354 | Chico, CA | 1,568 | 36 | Fresno, CA | 13,304 | 51 | Little Rock, AR | 10,655 |
| 437 | Chino Hills, CA | 615 | 283 | Frisco, TX | 2,075 | 391 | Livermore, CA | 1,275 |

| RANK | CITY | THEFTS | RANK | CITY | THEFTS | RANK | CITY | THEFTS |
|---|---|---|---|---|---|---|---|---|
| 362 | Livonia, MI | 1,498 | 228 | Pasadena, CA | 2,553 | 378 | South Gate, CA | 1,379 |
| 84 | Long Beach, CA | 6,868 | 145 | Pasadena, TX | 3,980 | 329 | Sparks, NV | 1,710 |
| 341 | Longmont, CO | 1,634 | 296 | Paterson, NJ | 1,984 | 148 | Spokane Valley, WA | 3,862 |
| 230 | Longview, TX | 2,542 | 359 | Pearland, TX | 1,541 | 35 | Spokane, WA | 13,352 |
| 5 | Los Angeles, CA | 55,734 | 198 | Pembroke Pines, FL | 3,042 | 126 | Springfield, IL | 4,439 |
| 23 | Louisville, KY | 19,835 | 208 | Peoria, AZ | 2,906 | 141 | Springfield, MA | 4,018 |
| 254 | Lowell, MA | 2,300 | 193 | Peoria, IL | 3,098 | 48 | Springfield, MO | 11,232 |
| 73 | Lubbock, TX | 8,103 | 6 | Philadelphia, PA | 37,253 | 375 | Stamford, CT | 1,435 |
| 360 | Lynchburg, VA | 1,538 | 7 | Phoenix, AZ | 36,983 | 299 | Sterling Heights, MI | 1,957 |
| 340 | Lynn, MA | 1,635 | 81 | Pittsburgh, PA | 7,258 | 64 | Stockton, CA | 8,748 |
| 130 | Macon, GA | 4,318 | 115 | Plano, TX | 4,730 | 403 | St. George, UT | 1,184 |
| 96 | Madison, WI | 6,094 | 260 | Plantation, FL | 2,256 | 181 | St. Joseph, MO | 3,237 |
| 188 | Manchester, NH | 3,141 | 223 | Pomona, CA | 2,591 | 34 | St. Louis, MO | 13,452 |
| 119 | McAllen, TX | 4,652 | 157 | Pompano Beach, FL | 3,580 | 90 | St. Paul, MN | 6,443 |
| 240 | McKinney, TX | 2,450 | 336 | Port St. Lucie, FL | 1,666 | 58 | St. Petersburg, FL | 9,315 |
| 138 | Medford, OR | 4,075 | 20 | Portland, OR | 22,216 | 297 | Suffolk, VA | 1,980 |
| 232 | Melbourne, FL | 2,526 | 156 | Portsmouth, VA | 3,615 | 386 | Sugar Land, TX | 1,311 |
| 14 | Memphis, TN | 25,295 | 108 | Providence, RI | 5,184 | 370 | Sunnyvale, CA | 1,456 |
| 419 | Menifee, CA | 979 | 246 | Provo, UT | 2,373 | 244 | Sunrise, FL | 2,392 |
| 346 | Merced, CA | 1,608 | 109 | Pueblo, CO | 5,168 | 353 | Surprise, AZ | 1,572 |
| 429 | Meridian, ID | 812 | 410 | Quincy, MA | 1,113 | 132 | Syracuse, NY | 4,298 |
| 55 | Mesa, AZ | 9,607 | 330 | Racine, WI | 1,704 | 71 | Tacoma, WA | 8,200 |
| 135 | Mesquite, TX | 4,184 | 59 | Raleigh, NC | 9,278 | 106 | Tallahassee, FL | 5,594 |
| 67 | Miami Beach, FL | 8,425 | 441 | Ramapo, NY | 466 | 94 | Tampa, FL | 6,320 |
| 195 | Miami Gardens, FL | 3,054 | 298 | Rancho Cucamon., CA | 1,972 | 306 | Temecula, CA | 1,897 |
| 31 | Miami, FL | 15,021 | 368 | Reading, PA | 1,465 | 95 | Tempe, AZ | 6,113 |
| 239 | Midland, TX | 2,459 | 235 | Redding, CA | 2,483 | 233 | Thornton, CO | 2,513 |
| 29 | Milwaukee, WI | 16,138 | 409 | Redwood City, CA | 1,138 | 399 | Thousand Oaks, CA | 1,222 |
| 38 | Minneapolis, MN | 13,182 | 113 | Reno, NV | 4,901 | NA | Toledo, OH** | NA |
| 313 | Miramar, FL | 1,862 | 174 | Renton, WA | 3,396 | 269 | Toms River Twnshp, NJ | 2,192 |
| 430 | Mission Viejo, CA | 802 | 407 | Rialto, CA | 1,148 | 117 | Topeka, KS | 4,679 |
| 252 | Mission, TX | 2,321 | 284 | Richardson, TX | 2,068 | 316 | Torrance, CA | 1,833 |
| 62 | Mobile, AL | 9,123 | 332 | Richmond, CA | 1,685 | 338 | Tracy, CA | 1,648 |
| 93 | Modesto, CA | 6,349 | 98 | Richmond, VA | 5,949 | 427 | Trenton, NJ | 909 |
| 182 | Moreno Valley, CA | 3,224 | 83 | Riverside, CA | 6,912 | 393 | Troy, MI | 1,250 |
| 390 | Mountain View, CA | 1,277 | 155 | Roanoke, VA | 3,636 | 11 | Tucson, AZ | 27,440 |
| 190 | Murfreesboro, TN | 3,131 | 292 | Rochester, MN | 2,026 | 41 | Tulsa, OK | 12,654 |
| 406 | Murrieta, CA | 1,149 | 85 | Rochester, NY | 6,855 | 183 | Tuscaloosa, AL | 3,196 |
| 385 | Nampa, ID | 1,319 | 118 | Rockford, IL | 4,666 | 408 | Tustin, CA | 1,147 |
| 420 | Napa, CA | 975 | 221 | Roseville, CA | 2,623 | 192 | Tyler, TX | 3,111 |
| 345 | Naperville, IL | 1,610 | 356 | Roswell, GA | 1,556 | 396 | Upland, CA | 1,246 |
| 315 | Nashua, NH | 1,857 | 282 | Round Rock, TX | 2,086 | 364 | Upper Darby Twnshp, PA | 1,487 |
| 26 | Nashville, TN | 17,650 | 47 | Sacramento, CA | 11,233 | 351 | Vacaville, CA | 1,598 |
| 270 | New Bedford, MA | 2,186 | 111 | Salem, OR | 5,143 | 357 | Vallejo, CA | 1,553 |
| 134 | New Haven, CT | 4,233 | 219 | Salinas, CA | 2,720 | 146 | Vancouver, WA | 3,950 |
| 61 | New Orleans, LA | 9,179 | 56 | Salt Lake City, UT | 9,517 | 199 | Ventura, CA | 3,025 |
| 404 | New Rochelle, NY | 1,172 | 216 | San Angelo, TX | 2,725 | 285 | Victorville, CA | 2,067 |
| 1 | New York, NY | 117,931 | 4 | San Antonio, TX | 58,567 | 57 | Virginia Beach, VA | 9,374 |
| 143 | Newark, NJ | 3,997 | 140 | San Bernardino, CA | 4,025 | 200 | Visalia, CA | 3,016 |
| 350 | Newport Beach, CA | 1,600 | 24 | San Diego, CA | 19,230 | 383 | Vista, CA | 1,326 |
| 133 | Newport News, VA | 4,247 | 8 | San Francisco, CA | 36,527 | 151 | Waco, TX | 3,751 |
| 438 | Newton, MA | 584 | 44 | San Jose, CA | 12,411 | 289 | Warren, MI | 2,037 |
| 77 | Norfolk, VA | 8,006 | 256 | San Leandro, CA | 2,287 | 338 | Warwick, RI | 1,648 |
| 274 | Norman, OK | 2,161 | 425 | San Marcos, CA | 931 | 18 | Washington, DC | 23,108 |
| 128 | North Charleston, SC | 4,409 | 348 | San Mateo, CA | 1,601 | 175 | Waterbury, CT | 3,381 |
| 206 | North Las Vegas, NV | 2,936 | 287 | Sandy Springs, GA | 2,063 | 321 | Waukegan, IL | 1,766 |
| 392 | Norwalk, CA | 1,262 | 271 | Sandy, UT | 2,173 | 261 | West Covina, CA | 2,254 |
| 379 | Norwalk, CT | 1,377 | 136 | Santa Ana, CA | 4,163 | 166 | West Palm Beach, FL | 3,453 |
| 37 | Oakland, CA | 13,285 | 281 | Santa Barbara, CA | 2,091 | 124 | West Valley, UT | 4,447 |
| 171 | Oceanside, CA | 3,417 | 273 | Santa Clara, CA | 2,169 | 357 | Westland, MI | 1,553 |
| 187 | Odessa, TX | 3,147 | 322 | Santa Clarita, CA | 1,760 | 328 | Westminster, CA | 1,720 |
| 412 | O'Fallon, MO | 1,059 | 355 | Santa Maria, CA | 1,557 | 258 | Westminster, CO | 2,283 |
| 186 | Ogden, UT | 3,153 | 213 | Santa Monica, CA | 2,806 | 334 | Whittier, CA | 1,675 |
| 21 | Oklahoma City, OK | 20,387 | 226 | Santa Rosa, CA | 2,559 | 179 | Wichita Falls, TX | 3,277 |
| 308 | Olathe, KS | 1,877 | 105 | Savannah, GA | 5,608 | 32 | Wichita, KS | 14,885 |
| 43 | Omaha, NE | 12,519 | 123 | Scottsdale, AZ | 4,465 | 158 | Wilmington, NC | 3,569 |
| 224 | Ontario, CA | 2,586 | 344 | Scranton, PA | 1,614 | 69 | Winston-Salem, NC | 8,359 |
| 335 | Orange, CA | 1,673 | 16 | Seattle, WA | 24,189 | 343 | Woodbridge Twnshp, NJ | 1,622 |
| 319 | Orem, UT | 1,789 | 87 | Shreveport, LA | 6,720 | 147 | Worcester, MA | 3,924 |
| 45 | Orlando, FL | 11,984 | 397 | Simi Valley, CA | 1,233 | 209 | Yakima, WA | 2,896 |
| 211 | Overland Park, KS | 2,846 | 212 | Sioux City, IA | 2,814 | 337 | Yonkers, NY | 1,662 |
| 169 | Oxnard, CA | 3,436 | 149 | Sioux Falls, SD | 3,796 | 247 | Yuma, AZ | 2,348 |
| 383 | Palm Bay, FL | 1,326 | 417 | Somerville, MA | 998 | | | |
| 301 | Palmdale, CA | 1,928 | 194 | South Bend, IN | 3,096 | | | |

Source: Reported data from the F.B.I. "Crime in the United States 2013"

*Larceny-theft is the unlawful taking of property. Attempts are included.

**Not available.

# 73. Larceny-Thefts in 2013 (continued)
## National Total = 6,004,453 Larceny-Thefts*

| RANK | CITY | THEFTS | RANK | CITY | THEFTS | RANK | CITY | THEFTS |
|---|---|---|---|---|---|---|---|---|
| 1 | New York, NY | 117,931 | 75 | Greensboro, NC | 8,063 | 149 | Huntington Beach, CA | 3,796 |
| 2 | Houston, TX | 73,591 | 76 | Columbus, GA | 8,012 | 149 | Sioux Falls, SD | 3,796 |
| 3 | Chicago, IL | 65,497 | 77 | Norfolk, VA | 8,006 | 151 | Waco, TX | 3,751 |
| 4 | San Antonio, TX | 58,567 | 78 | Aurora, CO | 7,805 | 152 | Boise, ID | 3,703 |
| 5 | Los Angeles, CA | 55,734 | 79 | Baton Rouge, LA | 7,648 | 153 | Kent, WA | 3,669 |
| 6 | Philadelphia, PA | 37,253 | 80 | Lincoln, NE | 7,625 | 154 | Berkeley, CA | 3,658 |
| 7 | Phoenix, AZ | 36,983 | 81 | Pittsburgh, PA | 7,258 | 155 | Roanoke, VA | 3,636 |
| 8 | San Francisco, CA | 36,527 | 82 | Fort Wayne, IN | 7,025 | 156 | Portsmouth, VA | 3,615 |
| 9 | Austin, TX | 32,948 | 83 | Riverside, CA | 6,912 | 157 | Pompano Beach, FL | 3,580 |
| 10 | Dallas, TX | 30,374 | 84 | Long Beach, CA | 6,868 | 158 | Wilmington, NC | 3,569 |
| 11 | Tucson, AZ | 27,440 | 85 | Rochester, NY | 6,855 | 159 | Federal Way, WA | 3,535 |
| 12 | Las Vegas, NV | 26,548 | 86 | Des Moines, IA | 6,854 | 160 | Chula Vista, CA | 3,532 |
| 13 | Indianapolis, IN | 26,156 | 87 | Shreveport, LA | 6,720 | 161 | Hampton, VA | 3,525 |
| 14 | Memphis, TN | 25,295 | 88 | Huntsville, AL | 6,629 | 162 | Columbia, MO | 3,490 |
| 15 | Jacksonville, FL | 24,361 | 89 | Anaheim, CA | 6,518 | 163 | Duluth, MN | 3,484 |
| 16 | Seattle, WA | 24,189 | 90 | St. Paul, MN | 6,443 | 164 | Abilene, TX | 3,460 |
| 17 | Fort Worth, TX | 23,557 | 91 | Brownsville, TX | 6,441 | 165 | Las Cruces, NM | 3,454 |
| 18 | Washington, DC | 23,108 | 92 | Fort Lauderdale, FL | 6,429 | 166 | West Palm Beach, FL | 3,453 |
| 19 | Charlotte, NC | 22,274 | 93 | Modesto, CA | 6,349 | 167 | Grand Prairie, TX | 3,448 |
| 20 | Portland, OR | 22,216 | 94 | Tampa, FL | 6,320 | 168 | Fort Smith, AR | 3,447 |
| 21 | Oklahoma City, OK | 20,387 | 95 | Tempe, AZ | 6,113 | 169 | Oxnard, CA | 3,436 |
| 22 | Albuquerque, NM | 20,229 | 96 | Madison, WI | 6,094 | 170 | Cedar Rapids, IA | 3,433 |
| 23 | Louisville, KY | 19,835 | 97 | Lafayette, LA | 5,995 | 171 | Oceanside, CA | 3,417 |
| 24 | San Diego, CA | 19,230 | 98 | Richmond, VA | 5,949 | 172 | Hartford, CT | 3,416 |
| 25 | Baltimore, MD | 18,946 | 99 | Akron, OH | 5,922 | 172 | Henderson, NV | 3,416 |
| 26 | Nashville, TN | 17,650 | 100 | Jackson, MS | 5,864 | 174 | Renton, WA | 3,396 |
| 27 | Detroit, MI | 17,188 | 101 | Columbia, SC | 5,800 | 175 | Waterbury, CT | 3,381 |
| 28 | Atlanta, GA | 17,158 | 102 | Eugene, OR | 5,773 | 176 | Lawton, OK | 3,313 |
| 29 | Milwaukee, WI | 16,138 | 103 | Garland, TX | 5,671 | 177 | Edinburg, TX | 3,299 |
| 30 | Denver, CO | 15,306 | 104 | Amarillo, TX | 5,643 | 178 | Clearwater, FL | 3,284 |
| 31 | Miami, FL | 15,021 | 105 | Savannah, GA | 5,608 | 179 | Wichita Falls, TX | 3,277 |
| 32 | Wichita, KS | 14,885 | 106 | Tallahassee, FL | 5,594 | 180 | Albany, NY | 3,243 |
| 33 | Kansas City, MO | 13,949 | 107 | Lakewood, CO | 5,397 | 181 | St. Joseph, MO | 3,237 |
| 34 | St. Louis, MO | 13,452 | 108 | Providence, RI | 5,184 | 182 | Moreno Valley, CA | 3,224 |
| 35 | Spokane, WA | 13,352 | 109 | Pueblo, CO | 5,168 | 183 | Tuscaloosa, AL | 3,196 |
| 36 | Fresno, CA | 13,304 | 110 | Independence, MO | 5,149 | 184 | Killeen, TX | 3,189 |
| 37 | Oakland, CA | 13,285 | 111 | Salem, OR | 5,143 | 185 | Albany, GA | 3,169 |
| 38 | Minneapolis, MN | 13,182 | 112 | Hialeah, FL | 5,079 | 186 | Ogden, UT | 3,153 |
| 39 | Boston, MA | 13,147 | 113 | Reno, NV | 4,901 | 187 | Odessa, TX | 3,147 |
| 40 | El Paso, TX | 12,993 | 114 | Chesapeake, VA | 4,832 | 188 | Manchester, NH | 3,141 |
| 41 | Tulsa, OK | 12,654 | 115 | Plano, TX | 4,730 | 189 | Fort Collins, CO | 3,137 |
| 42 | Colorado Springs, CO | 12,521 | 116 | Everett, WA | 4,702 | 190 | Murfreesboro, TN | 3,131 |
| 43 | Omaha, NE | 12,519 | 117 | Topeka, KS | 4,679 | 191 | Gresham, OR | 3,123 |
| 44 | San Jose, CA | 12,411 | 118 | Rockford, IL | 4,666 | 192 | Tyler, TX | 3,111 |
| 45 | Orlando, FL | 11,984 | 119 | McAllen, TX | 4,652 | 193 | Peoria, IL | 3,098 |
| 46 | Corpus Christi, TX | 11,519 | 120 | Chandler, AZ | 4,628 | 194 | South Bend, IN | 3,096 |
| 47 | Sacramento, CA | 11,233 | 121 | Kansas City, KS | 4,566 | 195 | Miami Gardens, FL | 3,054 |
| 48 | Springfield, MO | 11,232 | 122 | Hollywood, FL | 4,478 | 196 | Davenport, IA | 3,048 |
| 49 | Arlington, TX | 10,879 | 123 | Scottsdale, AZ | 4,465 | 197 | Jersey City, NJ | 3,046 |
| 50 | Cleveland, OH | 10,784 | 124 | West Valley, UT | 4,447 | 198 | Pembroke Pines, FL | 3,042 |
| 51 | Little Rock, AR | 10,655 | 125 | Irving, TX | 4,444 | 199 | Ventura, CA | 3,025 |
| 52 | Cincinnati, OH | 10,488 | 126 | Springfield, IL | 4,439 | 200 | Visalia, CA | 3,016 |
| 53 | Glendale, AZ | 10,166 | 127 | Dayton, OH | 4,427 | 201 | Bellevue, WA | 3,013 |
| 54 | Anchorage, AK | 9,845 | 128 | North Charleston, SC | 4,409 | 202 | Bloomington, MN | 2,990 |
| 55 | Mesa, AZ | 9,607 | 129 | Evansville, IN | 4,371 | 203 | High Point, NC | 2,970 |
| 56 | Salt Lake City, UT | 9,517 | 130 | Macon, GA | 4,318 | 204 | Clarksville, TN | 2,965 |
| 57 | Virginia Beach, VA | 9,374 | 131 | Grand Rapids, MI | 4,315 | 205 | Lawrence, KS | 2,959 |
| 58 | St. Petersburg, FL | 9,315 | 132 | Syracuse, NY | 4,298 | 206 | North Las Vegas, NV | 2,936 |
| 59 | Raleigh, NC | 9,278 | 133 | Newport News, VA | 4,247 | 207 | Athens-Clarke, GA | 2,912 |
| 60 | Bakersfield, CA | 9,272 | 134 | New Haven, CT | 4,233 | 208 | Peoria, AZ | 2,906 |
| 61 | New Orleans, LA | 9,179 | 135 | Mesquite, TX | 4,184 | 209 | Yakima, WA | 2,896 |
| 62 | Mobile, AL | 9,123 | 136 | Santa Ana, CA | 4,163 | 210 | Fullerton, CA | 2,873 |
| 63 | Lexington, KY | 9,042 | 137 | Lakeland, FL | 4,082 | 211 | Overland Park, KS | 2,846 |
| 64 | Stockton, CA | 8,748 | 138 | Medford, OR | 4,075 | 212 | Sioux City, IA | 2,814 |
| 65 | Laredo, TX | 8,685 | 139 | Billings, MT | 4,074 | 213 | Santa Monica, CA | 2,806 |
| 66 | Birmingham, AL | 8,661 | 140 | San Bernardino, CA | 4,025 | 214 | Concord, CA | 2,764 |
| 67 | Miami Beach, FL | 8,425 | 141 | Springfield, MA | 4,018 | 215 | Costa Mesa, CA | 2,748 |
| 68 | Knoxville, TN | 8,424 | 142 | Gainesville, FL | 4,000 | 216 | Charleston, SC | 2,725 |
| 69 | Winston-Salem, NC | 8,359 | 143 | Newark, NJ | 3,997 | 216 | San Angelo, TX | 2,725 |
| 70 | Fayetteville, NC | 8,351 | 144 | Beaumont, TX | 3,987 | 218 | Allentown, PA | 2,724 |
| 71 | Tacoma, WA | 8,200 | 145 | Pasadena, TX | 3,980 | 219 | Salinas, CA | 2,720 |
| 72 | Chattanooga, TN | 8,165 | 146 | Vancouver, WA | 3,950 | 220 | Gilbert, AZ | 2,672 |
| 73 | Lubbock, TX | 8,103 | 147 | Worcester, MA | 3,924 | 221 | Roseville, CA | 2,623 |
| 74 | Buffalo, NY | 8,076 | 148 | Spokane Valley, WA | 3,862 | 222 | Bridgeport, CT | 2,610 |

| RANK | CITY | THEFTS | RANK | CITY | THEFTS | RANK | CITY | THEFTS |
|---|---|---|---|---|---|---|---|---|
| 223 | Pomona, CA | 2,591 | 297 | Suffolk, VA | 1,980 | 371 | Bloomington, IL | 1,446 |
| 224 | Ontario, CA | 2,586 | 298 | Rancho Cucamon., CA | 1,972 | 372 | Fall River, MA | 1,443 |
| 225 | Greenville, NC | 2,573 | 299 | Sterling Heights, MI | 1,957 | 373 | Inglewood, CA | 1,441 |
| 226 | Santa Rosa, CA | 2,559 | 300 | Bloomington, IN | 1,942 | 374 | Carlsbad, CA | 1,436 |
| 227 | Greeley, CO | 2,558 | 301 | Palmdale, CA | 1,928 | 375 | Buena Park, CA | 1,435 |
| 228 | Irvine, CA | 2,553 | 302 | Burbank, CA | 1,926 | 375 | Stamford, CT | 1,435 |
| 228 | Pasadena, CA | 2,553 | 303 | Greece, NY | 1,925 | 377 | Clarkstown, NY | 1,388 |
| 230 | Longview, TX | 2,542 | 304 | Lewisville, TX | 1,921 | 378 | South Gate, CA | 1,379 |
| 231 | Gary, IN | 2,533 | 305 | Bend, OR | 1,913 | 379 | Norwalk, CT | 1,377 |
| 232 | Melbourne, FL | 2,526 | 306 | Temecula, CA | 1,897 | 380 | Lakewood, CA | 1,356 |
| 233 | Thornton, CO | 2,513 | 307 | Amherst, NY | 1,882 | 381 | Indio, CA | 1,335 |
| 234 | Fremont, CA | 2,484 | 308 | Olathe, KS | 1,877 | 382 | Hawthorne, CA | 1,333 |
| 235 | Redding, CA | 2,483 | 309 | Kennewick, WA | 1,876 | 383 | Palm Bay, FL | 1,326 |
| 236 | Davie, FL | 2,480 | 310 | Brooklyn Park, MN | 1,875 | 383 | Vista, CA | 1,326 |
| 237 | Escondido, CA | 2,476 | 311 | Downey, CA | 1,873 | 385 | Nampa, ID | 1,319 |
| 238 | Fayetteville, AR | 2,473 | 312 | Antioch, CA | 1,872 | 386 | Sugar Land, TX | 1,311 |
| 239 | Midland, TX | 2,459 | 313 | Miramar, FL | 1,862 | 387 | Cranston, RI | 1,306 |
| 240 | McKinney, TX | 2,450 | 314 | Elizabeth, NJ | 1,861 | 388 | Alameda, CA | 1,285 |
| 241 | Alexandria, VA | 2,427 | 315 | Nashua, NH | 1,857 | 389 | Hamilton Twnshp, NJ | 1,283 |
| 241 | Cape Coral, FL | 2,427 | 316 | Torrance, CA | 1,833 | 390 | Mountain View, CA | 1,277 |
| 243 | Cambridge, MA | 2,402 | 317 | Kenosha, WI | 1,826 | 391 | Livermore, CA | 1,275 |
| 244 | Sunrise, FL | 2,392 | 318 | Citrus Heights, CA | 1,825 | 392 | Norwalk, CA | 1,262 |
| 245 | Glendale, CA | 2,384 | 319 | Orem, UT | 1,789 | 393 | Troy, MI | 1,250 |
| 246 | Provo, UT | 2,373 | 320 | El Cajon, CA | 1,775 | 394 | Chino, CA | 1,249 |
| 247 | Yuma, AZ | 2,348 | 321 | Waukegan, IL | 1,766 | 395 | Carson, CA | 1,248 |
| 248 | Fargo, ND | 2,342 | 322 | Santa Clarita, CA | 1,760 | 396 | Upland, CA | 1,246 |
| 249 | Joliet, IL | 2,337 | 323 | Colonie, NY | 1,753 | 397 | Simi Valley, CA | 1,233 |
| 250 | Lansing, MI | 2,329 | 324 | College Station, TX | 1,750 | 398 | Edmond, OK | 1,230 |
| 251 | Dearborn, MI | 2,328 | 325 | Boca Raton, FL | 1,744 | 399 | Thousand Oaks, CA | 1,222 |
| 252 | Mission, TX | 2,321 | 326 | Jurupa Valley, CA | 1,732 | 400 | Beaverton, OR | 1,213 |
| 253 | Corona, CA | 2,305 | 327 | Hillsboro, OR | 1,723 | 401 | Alhambra, CA | 1,196 |
| 254 | Lowell, MA | 2,300 | 328 | Westminster, CA | 1,720 | 402 | Daly City, CA | 1,190 |
| 255 | Hemet, CA | 2,294 | 329 | Sparks, NV | 1,710 | 403 | St. George, UT | 1,184 |
| 256 | San Leandro, CA | 2,287 | 330 | Racine, WI | 1,704 | 404 | New Rochelle, NY | 1,172 |
| 257 | Aurora, IL | 2,285 | 331 | Champaign, IL | 1,698 | 405 | Compton, CA | 1,160 |
| 258 | Westminster, CO | 2,283 | 332 | Richmond, CA | 1,685 | 406 | Murrieta, CA | 1,149 |
| 259 | Cheektowaga, NY | 2,271 | 333 | Bryan, TX | 1,683 | 407 | Rialto, CA | 1,148 |
| 260 | Plantation, FL | 2,256 | 334 | Whittier, CA | 1,675 | 408 | Tustin, CA | 1,147 |
| 261 | West Covina, CA | 2,254 | 335 | Orange, CA | 1,673 | 409 | Redwood City, CA | 1,138 |
| 262 | Boulder, CO | 2,236 | 336 | Port St. Lucie, FL | 1,666 | 410 | Quincy, MA | 1,113 |
| 263 | Elk Grove, CA | 2,229 | 337 | Yonkers, NY | 1,662 | 411 | Clifton, NJ | 1,060 |
| 264 | Garden Grove, CA | 2,221 | 338 | Tracy, CA | 1,648 | 412 | O'Fallon, MO | 1,059 |
| 264 | Hammond, IN | 2,221 | 338 | Warwick, RI | 1,648 | 413 | Hesperia, CA | 1,052 |
| 266 | Clovis, CA | 2,220 | 340 | Lynn, MA | 1,635 | 414 | Cicero, IL | 1,044 |
| 267 | Fontana, CA | 2,217 | 341 | Longmont, CO | 1,634 | 415 | El Monte, CA | 1,038 |
| 268 | Denton, TX | 2,203 | 342 | Cary, NC | 1,623 | 416 | Lawrence, MA | 1,012 |
| 269 | Toms River Twnshp, NJ | 2,192 | 343 | Woodbridge Twnshp, NJ | 1,622 | 417 | Somerville, MA | 998 |
| 270 | New Bedford, MA | 2,186 | 344 | Scranton, PA | 1,614 | 418 | Allen, TX | 985 |
| 271 | Sandy, UT | 2,173 | 345 | Naperville, IL | 1,610 | 419 | Menifee, CA | 979 |
| 272 | Fairfield, CA | 2,170 | 346 | Merced, CA | 1,608 | 420 | Napa, CA | 975 |
| 273 | Santa Clara, CA | 2,169 | 347 | Deerfield Beach, FL | 1,606 | 421 | Danbury, CT | 972 |
| 274 | Norman, OK | 2,161 | 348 | Bethlehem, PA | 1,601 | 422 | Bellflower, CA | 968 |
| 275 | Hoover, AL | 2,144 | 348 | San Mateo, CA | 1,601 | 422 | Canton Twnshp, MI | 968 |
| 276 | Arvada, CO | 2,138 | 350 | Newport Beach, CA | 1,600 | 424 | Centennial, CO | 936 |
| 277 | Largo, FL | 2,134 | 351 | Vacaville, CA | 1,598 | 425 | San Marcos, CA | 931 |
| 278 | Hayward, CA | 2,122 | 352 | Lee's Summit, MO | 1,582 | 426 | Brick Twnshp, NJ | 911 |
| 279 | Brockton, MA | 2,100 | 353 | Surprise, AZ | 1,572 | 427 | Trenton, NJ | 909 |
| 280 | Erie, PA | 2,093 | 354 | Chico, CA | 1,568 | 428 | Edison Twnshp, NJ | 854 |
| 281 | Santa Barbara, CA | 2,091 | 355 | Santa Maria, CA | 1,557 | 429 | Meridian, ID | 812 |
| 282 | Round Rock, TX | 2,086 | 356 | Roswell, GA | 1,556 | 430 | Mission Viejo, CA | 802 |
| 283 | Frisco, TX | 2,075 | 357 | Vallejo, CA | 1,553 | 431 | Farmington Hills, MI | 773 |
| 284 | Richardson, TX | 2,068 | 357 | Westland, MI | 1,553 | 432 | Lakewood Twnshp, NJ | 768 |
| 285 | Coral Springs, FL | 2,067 | 359 | Pearland, TX | 1,541 | 433 | Baldwin Park, CA | 727 |
| 285 | Victorville, CA | 2,067 | 360 | Lynchburg, VA | 1,538 | 434 | Fishers, IN | 719 |
| 287 | Sandy Springs, GA | 2,063 | 361 | Decatur, IL | 1,512 | 435 | Arlington Heights, IL | 659 |
| 288 | Carrollton, TX | 2,048 | 362 | Livonia, MI | 1,498 | 436 | Lake Forest, CA | 620 |
| 289 | Warren, MI | 2,037 | 363 | Broken Arrow, OK | 1,490 | 437 | Chino Hills, CA | 615 |
| 290 | Concord, NC | 2,033 | 364 | Upper Darby Twnshp, PA | 1,487 | 438 | Newton, MA | 584 |
| 291 | Lancaster, CA | 2,030 | 365 | Clinton Twnshp, MI | 1,480 | 439 | Carmel, IN | 573 |
| 292 | Rochester, MN | 2,026 | 366 | League City, TX | 1,476 | 440 | Johns Creek, GA | 468 |
| 293 | Ann Arbor, MI | 2,021 | 367 | Evanston, IL | 1,474 | 441 | Ramapo, NY | 466 |
| 294 | Green Bay, WI | 2,001 | 368 | Reading, PA | 1,465 | NA | Toledo, OH** | NA |
| 295 | Flint, MI | 2,000 | 369 | Elgin, IL | 1,462 | | | |
| 296 | Paterson, NJ | 1,984 | 370 | Sunnyvale, CA | 1,456 | | | |

Source: Reported data from the F.B.I. "Crime in the United States 2013"

*Larceny-theft is the unlawful taking of property. Attempts are included.

**Not available.

# 74. Larceny-Theft Rate in 2013
## National Rate = 1,899.4 Larceny-Thefts per 100,000 Population*

| RANK | CITY | RATE | RANK | CITY | RATE | RANK | CITY | RATE |
|---|---|---|---|---|---|---|---|---|
| 130 | Abilene, TX | 2,897.8 | 338 | Chino, CA | 1,547.6 | 233 | Fullerton, CA | 2,056.9 |
| 117 | Akron, OH | 2,984.8 | 368 | Chula Vista, CA | 1,384.7 | 94 | Gainesville, FL | 3,159.8 |
| 308 | Alameda, CA | 1,686.2 | 391 | Cicero, IL | 1,239.8 | 385 | Garden Grove, CA | 1,265.8 |
| 25 | Albany, GA | 4,096.2 | 60 | Cincinnati, OH | 3,537.4 | 182 | Garland, TX | 2,406.2 |
| 80 | Albany, NY | 3,310.7 | 218 | Citrus Heights, CA | 2,138.6 | 91 | Gary, IN | 3,213.7 |
| 54 | Albuquerque, NM | 3,624.2 | 301 | Clarkstown, NY | 1,719.8 | 398 | Gilbert, AZ | 1,186.3 |
| 318 | Alexandria, VA | 1,634.1 | 239 | Clarksville, TN | 2,036.4 | 18 | Glendale, AZ | 4,344.3 |
| 364 | Alhambra, CA | 1,411.9 | 112 | Clearwater, FL | 3,015.4 | 394 | Glendale, CA | 1,220.3 |
| 201 | Allentown, PA | 2,283.8 | 146 | Cleveland, OH | 2,770.9 | 270 | Grand Prairie, TX | 1,875.7 |
| 416 | Allen, TX | 1,079.0 | 389 | Clifton, NJ | 1,246.7 | 203 | Grand Rapids, MI | 2,256.6 |
| 135 | Amarillo, TX | 2,870.6 | 345 | Clinton Twnshp, MI | 1,509.1 | 247 | Greece, NY | 1,991.4 |
| 327 | Amherst, NY | 1,590.9 | 206 | Clovis, CA | 2,231.5 | 157 | Greeley, CO | 2,661.5 |
| 266 | Anaheim, CA | 1,887.5 | 293 | College Station, TX | 1,769.1 | 265 | Green Bay, WI | 1,903.8 |
| 83 | Anchorage, AK | 3,287.6 | 204 | Colonie, NY | 2,241.3 | 131 | Greensboro, NC | 2,886.4 |
| 299 | Ann Arbor, MI | 1,730.3 | 134 | Colorado Springs, CO | 2,871.1 | 124 | Greenville, NC | 2,923.3 |
| 295 | Antioch, CA | 1,758.6 | 109 | Columbia, MO | 3,045.7 | 139 | Gresham, OR | 2,840.0 |
| 429 | Arlington Heights, IL | 867.4 | 16 | Columbia, SC | 4,386.0 | 355 | Hamilton Twnshp, NJ | 1,441.7 |
| 133 | Arlington, TX | 2,872.2 | 31 | Columbus, GA | 3,982.8 | 142 | Hammond, IN | 2,799.7 |
| 261 | Arvada, CO | 1,929.7 | 400 | Compton, CA | 1,184.8 | 164 | Hampton, VA | 2,574.0 |
| 178 | Athens-Clarke, GA | 2,424.2 | 208 | Concord, CA | 2,203.0 | 150 | Hartford, CT | 2,734.4 |
| 37 | Atlanta, GA | 3,804.3 | 172 | Concord, NC | 2,452.4 | 338 | Hawthorne, CA | 1,547.6 |
| 202 | Aurora, CO | 2,272.3 | 319 | Coral Springs, FL | 1,632.6 | 365 | Hayward, CA | 1,405.7 |
| 406 | Aurora, IL | 1,139.4 | 356 | Corona, CA | 1,439.2 | 141 | Hemet, CA | 2,807.9 |
| 35 | Austin, TX | 3,834.8 | 47 | Corpus Christi, TX | 3,662.4 | 382 | Henderson, NV | 1,273.5 |
| 166 | Bakersfield, CA | 2,562.3 | 175 | Costa Mesa, CA | 2,441.8 | 408 | Hesperia, CA | 1,135.8 |
| 426 | Baldwin Park, CA | 947.3 | 321 | Cranston, RI | 1,618.0 | 213 | Hialeah, FL | 2,168.8 |
| 110 | Baltimore, MD | 3,042.7 | 179 | Dallas, TX | 2,420.2 | 147 | High Point, NC | 2,768.9 |
| 79 | Baton Rouge, LA | 3,322.2 | 407 | Daly City, CA | 1,138.4 | 286 | Hillsboro, OR | 1,789.0 |
| 71 | Beaumont, TX | 3,373.8 | 403 | Danbury, CT | 1,166.0 | 108 | Hollywood, FL | 3,053.7 |
| 377 | Beaverton, OR | 1,296.6 | 114 | Davenport, IA | 2,993.1 | 167 | Hoover, AL | 2,548.2 |
| 189 | Bellevue, WA | 2,359.8 | 165 | Davie, FL | 2,567.8 | 70 | Houston, TX | 3,374.8 |
| 388 | Bellflower, CA | 1,247.5 | 96 | Dayton, OH | 3,136.0 | 258 | Huntington Beach, CA | 1,938.3 |
| 184 | Bend, OR | 2,393.5 | 177 | Dearborn, MI | 2,424.7 | 56 | Huntsville, AL | 3,588.3 |
| 95 | Berkeley, CA | 3,147.6 | 243 | Decatur, IL | 2,010.9 | 15 | Independence, MO | 4,386.6 |
| 221 | Bethlehem, PA | 2,130.8 | 234 | Deerfield Beach, FL | 2,053.6 | 106 | Indianapolis, IN | 3,076.4 |
| 39 | Billings, MT | 3,779.2 | 287 | Denton, TX | 1,787.3 | 312 | Indio, CA | 1,663.7 |
| 26 | Birmingham, AL | 4,085.4 | 192 | Denver, CO | 2,358.5 | 378 | Inglewood, CA | 1,290.4 |
| 273 | Bloomington, IL | 1,852.4 | 81 | Des Moines, IA | 3,304.9 | 415 | Irvine, CA | 1,082.6 |
| 193 | Bloomington, IN | 2,356.4 | 171 | Detroit, MI | 2,455.8 | 257 | Irving, TX | 1,946.0 |
| 64 | Bloomington, MN | 3,434.5 | 314 | Downey, CA | 1,654.3 | 132 | Jacksonville, FL | 2,880.4 |
| 254 | Boca Raton, FL | 1,965.1 | 28 | Duluth, MN | 4,041.2 | 76 | Jackson, MS | 3,331.1 |
| 300 | Boise, ID | 1,727.7 | 30 | Edinburg, TX | 4,009.9 | 399 | Jersey City, NJ | 1,185.7 |
| 237 | Boston, MA | 2,042.1 | 432 | Edison Twnshp, NJ | 842.9 | 440 | Johns Creek, GA | 556.5 |
| 212 | Boulder, CO | 2,174.5 | 359 | Edmond, OK | 1,430.7 | 330 | Joliet, IL | 1,574.1 |
| 395 | Brick Twnshp, NJ | 1,208.7 | 297 | El Cajon, CA | 1,740.0 | 294 | Jurupa Valley, CA | 1,765.7 |
| 291 | Bridgeport, CT | 1,774.6 | 427 | El Monte, CA | 898.0 | 104 | Kansas City, KS | 3,093.1 |
| 207 | Brockton, MA | 2,223.4 | 263 | El Paso, TX | 1,911.6 | 113 | Kansas City, MO | 2,996.5 |
| 353 | Broken Arrow, OK | 1,447.2 | 372 | Elgin, IL | 1,323.6 | 173 | Kennewick, WA | 2,452.0 |
| 185 | Brooklyn Park, MN | 2,393.0 | 350 | Elizabeth, NJ | 1,464.6 | 281 | Kenosha, WI | 1,818.4 |
| 58 | Brownsville, TX | 3,547.0 | 367 | Elk Grove, CA | 1,385.1 | 120 | Kent, WA | 2,950.3 |
| 216 | Bryan, TX | 2,141.8 | 231 | Erie, PA | 2,076.1 | 197 | Killeen, TX | 2,335.6 |
| 298 | Buena Park, CA | 1,736.6 | 311 | Escondido, CA | 1,665.7 | 13 | Knoxville, TN | 4,597.0 |
| 99 | Buffalo, NY | 3,120.7 | 50 | Eugene, OR | 3,642.3 | 8 | Lafayette, LA | 4,857.8 |
| 277 | Burbank, CA | 1,839.1 | 256 | Evanston, IL | 1,946.9 | 437 | Lake Forest, CA | 781.5 |
| 205 | Cambridge, MA | 2,239.0 | 52 | Evansville, IN | 3,633.9 | 27 | Lakeland, FL | 4,052.6 |
| 414 | Canton Twnshp, MI | 1,088.2 | 14 | Everett, WA | 4,472.6 | 435 | Lakewood Twnshp, NJ | 828.8 |
| 349 | Cape Coral, FL | 1,484.8 | 244 | Fairfield, CA | 2,001.4 | 309 | Lakewood, CA | 1,672.3 |
| 376 | Carlsbad, CA | 1,299.5 | 322 | Fall River, MA | 1,617.4 | 46 | Lakewood, CO | 3,689.0 |
| 438 | Carmel, IN | 675.1 | 222 | Fargo, ND | 2,108.0 | 383 | Lancaster, CA | 1,270.4 |
| 324 | Carrollton, TX | 1,606.8 | 424 | Farmington Hills, MI | 953.3 | 236 | Lansing, MI | 2,044.7 |
| 371 | Carson, CA | 1,336.0 | 93 | Fayetteville, AR | 3,174.6 | 62 | Laredo, TX | 3,511.2 |
| 412 | Cary, NC | 1,090.0 | 24 | Fayetteville, NC | 4,123.5 | 149 | Largo, FL | 2,739.0 |
| 156 | Cedar Rapids, IA | 2,668.6 | 36 | Federal Way, WA | 3,811.7 | 69 | Las Cruces, NM | 3,386.0 |
| 428 | Centennial, CO | 893.4 | 430 | Fishers, IN | 862.5 | 292 | Las Vegas, NV | 1,769.3 |
| 235 | Champaign, IL | 2,046.6 | 245 | Flint, MI | 2,001.2 | 84 | Lawrence, KS | 3,286.5 |
| 272 | Chandler, AZ | 1,860.7 | 413 | Fontana, CA | 1,089.8 | 375 | Lawrence, MA | 1,300.6 |
| 215 | Charleston, SC | 2,142.2 | 227 | Fort Collins, CO | 2,090.4 | 74 | Lawton, OK | 3,361.8 |
| 158 | Charlotte, NC | 2,659.1 | 43 | Fort Lauderdale, FL | 3,729.2 | 316 | League City, TX | 1,647.4 |
| 10 | Chattanooga, TN | 4,739.2 | 32 | Fort Smith, AR | 3,925.0 | 304 | Lee's Summit, MO | 1,705.4 |
| 128 | Cheektowaga, NY | 2,898.1 | 148 | Fort Wayne, IN | 2,756.8 | 264 | Lewisville, TX | 1,907.5 |
| 226 | Chesapeake, VA | 2,095.6 | 116 | Fort Worth, TX | 2,985.5 | 123 | Lexington, KY | 2,928.9 |
| 181 | Chicago, IL | 2,407.5 | 411 | Fremont, CA | 1,106.6 | 137 | Lincoln, NE | 2,849.8 |
| 290 | Chico, CA | 1,777.3 | 161 | Fresno, CA | 2,614.4 | 4 | Little Rock, AR | 5,397.7 |
| 436 | Chino Hills, CA | 799.3 | 329 | Frisco, TX | 1,574.7 | 344 | Livermore, CA | 1,511.6 |

| RANK | CITY | RATE |
|---|---|---|
| 331 | Livonia, MI | 1,573.2 |
| 351 | Long Beach, CA | 1,462.3 |
| 279 | Longmont, CO | 1,827.0 |
| 98 | Longview, TX | 3,127.7 |
| 357 | Los Angeles, CA | 1,436.9 |
| 119 | Louisville, KY | 2,955.5 |
| 225 | Lowell, MA | 2,101.4 |
| 66 | Lubbock, TX | 3,406.4 |
| 251 | Lynchburg, VA | 1,978.0 |
| 288 | Lynn, MA | 1,781.6 |
| 11 | Macon, GA | 4,735.8 |
| 169 | Madison, WI | 2,512.8 |
| 138 | Manchester, NH | 2,844.8 |
| 65 | McAllen, TX | 3,416.3 |
| 310 | McKinney, TX | 1,668.2 |
| 5 | Medford, OR | 5,295.7 |
| 85 | Melbourne, FL | 3,268.8 |
| 34 | Memphis, TN | 3,846.0 |
| 402 | Menifee, CA | 1,184.7 |
| 253 | Merced, CA | 1,977.2 |
| 420 | Meridian, ID | 989.5 |
| 224 | Mesa, AZ | 2,106.1 |
| 127 | Mesquite, TX | 2,899.3 |
| 1 | Miami Beach, FL | 9,214.4 |
| 151 | Miami Gardens, FL | 2,730.0 |
| 55 | Miami, FL | 3,590.2 |
| 242 | Midland, TX | 2,011.3 |
| 154 | Milwaukee, WI | 2,686.1 |
| 77 | Minneapolis, MN | 3,327.1 |
| 363 | Miramar, FL | 1,422.2 |
| 433 | Mission Viejo, CA | 836.3 |
| 136 | Mission, TX | 2,852.8 |
| 51 | Mobile, AL | 3,641.1 |
| 101 | Modesto, CA | 3,108.4 |
| 325 | Moreno Valley, CA | 1,601.7 |
| 315 | Mountain View, CA | 1,649.9 |
| 153 | Murfreesboro, TN | 2,708.8 |
| 418 | Murrieta, CA | 1,066.2 |
| 336 | Nampa, ID | 1,558.5 |
| 392 | Napa, CA | 1,237.9 |
| 410 | Naperville, IL | 1,116.3 |
| 219 | Nashua, NH | 2,133.2 |
| 145 | Nashville, TN | 2,776.6 |
| 200 | New Bedford, MA | 2,297.3 |
| 89 | New Haven, CT | 3,229.5 |
| 176 | New Orleans, LA | 2,434.6 |
| 348 | New Rochelle, NY | 1,487.3 |
| 366 | New York, NY | 1,404.6 |
| 358 | Newark, NJ | 1,436.5 |
| 280 | Newport Beach, CA | 1,825.7 |
| 196 | Newport News, VA | 2,345.4 |
| 439 | Newton, MA | 672.3 |
| 88 | Norfolk, VA | 3,237.3 |
| 274 | Norman, OK | 1,847.5 |
| 19 | North Charleston, SC | 4,267.2 |
| 374 | North Las Vegas, NV | 1,301.2 |
| 400 | Norwalk, CA | 1,184.8 |
| 332 | Norwalk, CT | 1,572.1 |
| 82 | Oakland, CA | 3,289.3 |
| 249 | Oceanside, CA | 1,980.6 |
| 126 | Odessa, TX | 2,906.8 |
| 381 | O'Fallon, MO | 1,281.0 |
| 42 | Ogden, UT | 3,751.6 |
| 72 | Oklahoma City, OK | 3,369.6 |
| 360 | Olathe, KS | 1,429.1 |
| 121 | Omaha, NE | 2,945.1 |
| 340 | Ontario, CA | 1,538.0 |
| 396 | Orange, CA | 1,192.4 |
| 255 | Orem, UT | 1,956.5 |
| 12 | Orlando, FL | 4,732.3 |
| 328 | Overland Park, KS | 1,576.3 |
| 306 | Oxnard, CA | 1,696.0 |
| 384 | Palm Bay, FL | 1,270.2 |
| 393 | Palmdale, CA | 1,231.8 |

| RANK | CITY | RATE |
|---|---|---|
| 278 | Pasadena, CA | 1,836.7 |
| 163 | Pasadena, TX | 2,598.0 |
| 370 | Paterson, NJ | 1,367.5 |
| 335 | Pearland, TX | 1,569.5 |
| 269 | Pembroke Pines, FL | 1,877.0 |
| 284 | Peoria, AZ | 1,797.8 |
| 155 | Peoria, IL | 2,671.8 |
| 183 | Philadelphia, PA | 2,398.5 |
| 170 | Phoenix, AZ | 2,462.0 |
| 191 | Pittsburgh, PA | 2,359.3 |
| 302 | Plano, TX | 1,715.0 |
| 168 | Plantation, FL | 2,536.9 |
| 303 | Pomona, CA | 1,711.7 |
| 63 | Pompano Beach, FL | 3,443.3 |
| 422 | Port St. Lucie, FL | 980.7 |
| 49 | Portland, OR | 3,647.1 |
| 44 | Portsmouth, VA | 3,726.1 |
| 129 | Providence, RI | 2,897.9 |
| 240 | Provo, UT | 2,029.3 |
| 9 | Pueblo, CO | 4,782.4 |
| 397 | Quincy, MA | 1,190.5 |
| 211 | Racine, WI | 2,180.7 |
| 214 | Raleigh, NC | 2,162.7 |
| 441 | Ramapo, NY | 534.4 |
| 404 | Rancho Cucamon., CA | 1,144.8 |
| 313 | Reading, PA | 1,662.8 |
| 152 | Redding, CA | 2,727.5 |
| 361 | Redwood City, CA | 1,427.7 |
| 223 | Reno, NV | 2,107.4 |
| 61 | Renton, WA | 3,513.5 |
| 409 | Rialto, CA | 1,119.8 |
| 252 | Richardson, TX | 1,977.5 |
| 334 | Richmond, CA | 1,569.8 |
| 144 | Richmond, VA | 2,795.2 |
| 210 | Riverside, CA | 2,184.4 |
| 45 | Roanoke, VA | 3,713.0 |
| 275 | Rochester, MN | 1,847.3 |
| 86 | Rochester, NY | 3,255.6 |
| 102 | Rockford, IL | 3,106.3 |
| 230 | Roseville, CA | 2,077.8 |
| 320 | Roswell, GA | 1,631.5 |
| 262 | Round Rock, TX | 1,921.2 |
| 194 | Sacramento, CA | 2,349.1 |
| 87 | Salem, OR | 3,250.2 |
| 296 | Salinas, CA | 1,746.5 |
| 7 | Salt Lake City, UT | 5,002.5 |
| 140 | San Angelo, TX | 2,819.1 |
| 23 | San Antonio, TX | 4,184.2 |
| 268 | San Bernardino, CA | 1,878.0 |
| 362 | San Diego, CA | 1,425.2 |
| 17 | San Francisco, CA | 4,380.5 |
| 386 | San Jose, CA | 1,250.9 |
| 162 | San Leandro, CA | 2,614.0 |
| 419 | San Marcos, CA | 1,061.4 |
| 326 | San Mateo, CA | 1,594.0 |
| 238 | Sandy Springs, GA | 2,038.9 |
| 180 | Sandy, UT | 2,416.0 |
| 387 | Santa Ana, CA | 1,250.7 |
| 198 | Santa Barbara, CA | 2,323.2 |
| 282 | Santa Clara, CA | 1,805.2 |
| 431 | Santa Clarita, CA | 858.7 |
| 341 | Santa Maria, CA | 1,525.7 |
| 111 | Santa Monica, CA | 3,033.9 |
| 347 | Santa Rosa, CA | 1,491.6 |
| 186 | Savannah, GA | 2,384.4 |
| 250 | Scottsdale, AZ | 1,979.8 |
| 220 | Scranton, PA | 2,131.2 |
| 41 | Seattle, WA | 3,763.0 |
| 78 | Shreveport, LA | 3,323.6 |
| 423 | Simi Valley, CA | 976.9 |
| 67 | Sioux City, IA | 3,403.6 |
| 195 | Sioux Falls, SD | 2,346.8 |
| 379 | Somerville, MA | 1,283.3 |
| 107 | South Bend, IN | 3,074.1 |

| RANK | CITY | RATE |
|---|---|---|
| 354 | South Gate, CA | 1,442.6 |
| 276 | Sparks, NV | 1,843.3 |
| 20 | Spokane Valley, WA | 4,251.7 |
| 3 | Spokane, WA | 6,372.5 |
| 38 | Springfield, IL | 3,782.7 |
| 160 | Springfield, MA | 2,616.1 |
| 2 | Springfield, MO | 6,888.2 |
| 405 | Stamford, CT | 1,140.0 |
| 346 | Sterling Heights, MI | 1,498.1 |
| 125 | Stockton, CA | 2,918.0 |
| 337 | St. George, UT | 1,549.2 |
| 22 | St. Joseph, MO | 4,185.0 |
| 21 | St. Louis, MO | 4,222.7 |
| 209 | St. Paul, MN | 2,186.4 |
| 40 | St. Petersburg, FL | 3,770.0 |
| 199 | Suffolk, VA | 2,316.5 |
| 333 | Sugar Land, TX | 1,570.8 |
| 421 | Sunnyvale, CA | 982.7 |
| 159 | Sunrise, FL | 2,649.7 |
| 379 | Surprise, AZ | 1,283.3 |
| 115 | Syracuse, NY | 2,988.2 |
| 29 | Tacoma, WA | 4,034.9 |
| 118 | Tallahassee, FL | 2,964.3 |
| 283 | Tampa, FL | 1,799.0 |
| 289 | Temecula, CA | 1,778.2 |
| 53 | Tempe, AZ | 3,627.9 |
| 246 | Thornton, CO | 1,998.0 |
| 425 | Thousand Oaks, CA | 948.1 |
| NA | Toledo, OH** | NA |
| 187 | Toms River Twnshp, NJ | 2,374.0 |
| 48 | Topeka, KS | 3,655.2 |
| 390 | Torrance, CA | 1,242.4 |
| 260 | Tracy, CA | 1,934.9 |
| 417 | Trenton, NJ | 1,076.5 |
| 343 | Troy, MI | 1,513.2 |
| 6 | Tucson, AZ | 5,221.8 |
| 92 | Tulsa, OK | 3,207.6 |
| 68 | Tuscaloosa, AL | 3,395.4 |
| 352 | Tustin, CA | 1,454.9 |
| 100 | Tyler, TX | 3,110.0 |
| 317 | Upland, CA | 1,647.3 |
| 285 | Upper Darby Twnshp, PA | 1,796.5 |
| 307 | Vacaville, CA | 1,693.7 |
| 373 | Vallejo, CA | 1,312.4 |
| 188 | Vancouver, WA | 2,371.9 |
| 143 | Ventura, CA | 2,795.6 |
| 305 | Victorville, CA | 1,698.5 |
| 229 | Virginia Beach, VA | 2,079.9 |
| 190 | Visalia, CA | 2,359.5 |
| 369 | Vista, CA | 1,371.1 |
| 122 | Waco, TX | 2,940.3 |
| 342 | Warren, MI | 1,518.3 |
| 241 | Warwick, RI | 2,014.9 |
| 57 | Washington, DC | 3,574.6 |
| 105 | Waterbury, CT | 3,080.3 |
| 248 | Waukegan, IL | 1,989.6 |
| 228 | West Covina, CA | 2,089.6 |
| 73 | West Palm Beach, FL | 3,368.5 |
| 75 | West Valley, UT | 3,334.3 |
| 267 | Westland, MI | 1,881.2 |
| 271 | Westminster, CA | 1,871.9 |
| 232 | Westminster, CO | 2,073.7 |
| 259 | Whittier, CA | 1,937.5 |
| 97 | Wichita Falls, TX | 3,135.5 |
| 33 | Wichita, KS | 3,851.4 |
| 90 | Wilmington, NC | 3,215.7 |
| 59 | Winston-Salem, NC | 3,544.8 |
| 323 | Woodbridge Twnshp, NJ | 1,612.8 |
| 217 | Worcester, MA | 2,139.0 |
| 103 | Yakima, WA | 3,094.4 |
| 434 | Yonkers, NY | 834.6 |
| 174 | Yuma, AZ | 2,445.5 |

Source: CQ Press using reported data from the F.B.I. "Crime in the United States 2013"
*Larceny-theft is the unlawful taking of property. Attempts are included.
**Not available.

# 74. Larceny-Theft Rate in 2013 (continued)
## National Rate = 1,899.4 Larceny-Thefts per 100,000 Population*

| RANK | CITY | RATE | RANK | CITY | RATE | RANK | CITY | RATE |
|---|---|---|---|---|---|---|---|---|
| 1 | Miami Beach, FL | 9,214.4 | 75 | West Valley, UT | 3,334.3 | 149 | Largo, FL | 2,739.0 |
| 2 | Springfield, MO | 6,888.2 | 76 | Jackson, MS | 3,331.1 | 150 | Hartford, CT | 2,734.4 |
| 3 | Spokane, WA | 6,372.5 | 77 | Minneapolis, MN | 3,327.1 | 151 | Miami Gardens, FL | 2,730.0 |
| 4 | Little Rock, AR | 5,397.7 | 78 | Shreveport, LA | 3,323.6 | 152 | Redding, CA | 2,727.5 |
| 5 | Medford, OR | 5,295.7 | 79 | Baton Rouge, LA | 3,322.2 | 153 | Murfreesboro, TN | 2,708.8 |
| 6 | Tucson, AZ | 5,221.8 | 80 | Albany, NY | 3,310.7 | 154 | Milwaukee, WI | 2,686.1 |
| 7 | Salt Lake City, UT | 5,002.5 | 81 | Des Moines, IA | 3,304.9 | 155 | Peoria, IL | 2,671.8 |
| 8 | Lafayette, LA | 4,857.8 | 82 | Oakland, CA | 3,289.3 | 156 | Cedar Rapids, IA | 2,668.6 |
| 9 | Pueblo, CO | 4,782.4 | 83 | Anchorage, AK | 3,287.6 | 157 | Greeley, CO | 2,661.5 |
| 10 | Chattanooga, TN | 4,739.2 | 84 | Lawrence, KS | 3,286.5 | 158 | Charlotte, NC | 2,659.1 |
| 11 | Macon, GA | 4,735.8 | 85 | Melbourne, FL | 3,268.8 | 159 | Sunrise, FL | 2,649.7 |
| 12 | Orlando, FL | 4,732.3 | 86 | Rochester, NY | 3,255.6 | 160 | Springfield, MA | 2,616.1 |
| 13 | Knoxville, TN | 4,597.0 | 87 | Salem, OR | 3,250.2 | 161 | Fresno, CA | 2,614.4 |
| 14 | Everett, WA | 4,472.6 | 88 | Norfolk, VA | 3,237.3 | 162 | San Leandro, CA | 2,614.0 |
| 15 | Independence, MO | 4,386.6 | 89 | New Haven, CT | 3,229.5 | 163 | Pasadena, TX | 2,598.0 |
| 16 | Columbia, SC | 4,386.0 | 90 | Wilmington, NC | 3,215.7 | 164 | Hampton, VA | 2,574.0 |
| 17 | San Francisco, CA | 4,380.5 | 91 | Gary, IN | 3,213.7 | 165 | Davie, FL | 2,567.8 |
| 18 | Glendale, AZ | 4,344.3 | 92 | Tulsa, OK | 3,207.6 | 166 | Bakersfield, CA | 2,562.3 |
| 19 | North Charleston, SC | 4,267.2 | 93 | Fayetteville, AR | 3,174.6 | 167 | Hoover, AL | 2,548.2 |
| 20 | Spokane Valley, WA | 4,251.7 | 94 | Gainesville, FL | 3,159.8 | 168 | Plantation, FL | 2,536.9 |
| 21 | St. Louis, MO | 4,222.7 | 95 | Berkeley, CA | 3,147.6 | 169 | Madison, WI | 2,512.8 |
| 22 | St. Joseph, MO | 4,185.0 | 96 | Dayton, OH | 3,136.0 | 170 | Phoenix, AZ | 2,462.0 |
| 23 | San Antonio, TX | 4,184.2 | 97 | Wichita Falls, TX | 3,135.5 | 171 | Detroit, MI | 2,455.8 |
| 24 | Fayetteville, NC | 4,123.5 | 98 | Longview, TX | 3,127.7 | 172 | Concord, NC | 2,452.4 |
| 25 | Albany, GA | 4,096.2 | 99 | Buffalo, NY | 3,120.7 | 173 | Kennewick, WA | 2,452.0 |
| 26 | Birmingham, AL | 4,085.4 | 100 | Tyler, TX | 3,110.0 | 174 | Yuma, AZ | 2,445.5 |
| 27 | Lakeland, FL | 4,052.6 | 101 | Modesto, CA | 3,108.4 | 175 | Costa Mesa, CA | 2,441.8 |
| 28 | Duluth, MN | 4,041.2 | 102 | Rockford, IL | 3,106.3 | 176 | New Orleans, LA | 2,434.6 |
| 29 | Tacoma, WA | 4,034.9 | 103 | Yakima, WA | 3,094.4 | 177 | Dearborn, MI | 2,424.7 |
| 30 | Edinburg, TX | 4,009.9 | 104 | Kansas City, KS | 3,093.1 | 178 | Athens-Clarke, GA | 2,424.2 |
| 31 | Columbus, GA | 3,982.8 | 105 | Waterbury, CT | 3,080.3 | 179 | Dallas, TX | 2,420.2 |
| 32 | Fort Smith, AR | 3,925.0 | 106 | Indianapolis, IN | 3,076.4 | 180 | Sandy, UT | 2,416.0 |
| 33 | Wichita, KS | 3,851.4 | 107 | South Bend, IN | 3,074.1 | 181 | Chicago, IL | 2,407.5 |
| 34 | Memphis, TN | 3,846.0 | 108 | Hollywood, FL | 3,053.7 | 182 | Garland, TX | 2,406.2 |
| 35 | Austin, TX | 3,834.8 | 109 | Columbia, MO | 3,045.7 | 183 | Philadelphia, PA | 2,398.5 |
| 36 | Federal Way, WA | 3,811.7 | 110 | Baltimore, MD | 3,042.7 | 184 | Bend, OR | 2,393.5 |
| 37 | Atlanta, GA | 3,804.3 | 111 | Santa Monica, CA | 3,033.9 | 185 | Brooklyn Park, MN | 2,393.0 |
| 38 | Springfield, IL | 3,782.7 | 112 | Clearwater, FL | 3,015.4 | 186 | Savannah, GA | 2,384.4 |
| 39 | Billings, MT | 3,779.2 | 113 | Kansas City, MO | 2,996.5 | 187 | Toms River Twnshp, NJ | 2,374.0 |
| 40 | St. Petersburg, FL | 3,770.0 | 114 | Davenport, IA | 2,993.1 | 188 | Vancouver, WA | 2,371.9 |
| 41 | Seattle, WA | 3,763.0 | 115 | Syracuse, NY | 2,988.2 | 189 | Bellevue, WA | 2,359.8 |
| 42 | Ogden, UT | 3,751.6 | 116 | Fort Worth, TX | 2,985.5 | 190 | Visalia, CA | 2,359.5 |
| 43 | Fort Lauderdale, FL | 3,729.2 | 117 | Akron, OH | 2,984.8 | 191 | Pittsburgh, PA | 2,359.3 |
| 44 | Portsmouth, VA | 3,726.1 | 118 | Tallahassee, FL | 2,964.3 | 192 | Denver, CO | 2,358.5 |
| 45 | Roanoke, VA | 3,713.0 | 119 | Louisville, KY | 2,955.5 | 193 | Bloomington, IN | 2,356.4 |
| 46 | Lakewood, CO | 3,689.0 | 120 | Kent, WA | 2,950.3 | 194 | Sacramento, CA | 2,349.1 |
| 47 | Corpus Christi, TX | 3,662.4 | 121 | Omaha, NE | 2,945.1 | 195 | Sioux Falls, SD | 2,346.8 |
| 48 | Topeka, KS | 3,655.2 | 122 | Waco, TX | 2,940.3 | 196 | Newport News, VA | 2,345.4 |
| 49 | Portland, OR | 3,647.1 | 123 | Lexington, KY | 2,928.9 | 197 | Killeen, TX | 2,335.6 |
| 50 | Eugene, OR | 3,642.3 | 124 | Greenville, NC | 2,923.3 | 198 | Santa Barbara, CA | 2,323.2 |
| 51 | Mobile, AL | 3,641.1 | 125 | Stockton, CA | 2,918.0 | 199 | Suffolk, VA | 2,316.5 |
| 52 | Evansville, IN | 3,633.9 | 126 | Odessa, TX | 2,906.8 | 200 | New Bedford, MA | 2,297.3 |
| 53 | Tempe, AZ | 3,627.9 | 127 | Mesquite, TX | 2,899.3 | 201 | Allentown, PA | 2,283.8 |
| 54 | Albuquerque, NM | 3,624.2 | 128 | Cheektowaga, NY | 2,898.1 | 202 | Aurora, CO | 2,272.3 |
| 55 | Miami, FL | 3,590.2 | 129 | Providence, RI | 2,897.9 | 203 | Grand Rapids, MI | 2,256.6 |
| 56 | Huntsville, AL | 3,588.3 | 130 | Abilene, TX | 2,897.8 | 204 | Colonie, NY | 2,241.3 |
| 57 | Washington, DC | 3,574.6 | 131 | Greensboro, NC | 2,886.4 | 205 | Cambridge, MA | 2,239.0 |
| 58 | Brownsville, TX | 3,547.0 | 132 | Jacksonville, FL | 2,880.4 | 206 | Clovis, CA | 2,231.5 |
| 59 | Winston-Salem, NC | 3,544.8 | 133 | Arlington, TX | 2,872.2 | 207 | Brockton, MA | 2,223.4 |
| 60 | Cincinnati, OH | 3,537.4 | 134 | Colorado Springs, CO | 2,871.1 | 208 | Concord, CA | 2,203.0 |
| 61 | Renton, WA | 3,513.5 | 135 | Amarillo, TX | 2,870.6 | 209 | St. Paul, MN | 2,186.4 |
| 62 | Laredo, TX | 3,511.2 | 136 | Mission, TX | 2,852.8 | 210 | Riverside, CA | 2,184.4 |
| 63 | Pompano Beach, FL | 3,443.3 | 137 | Lincoln, NE | 2,849.8 | 211 | Racine, WI | 2,180.7 |
| 64 | Bloomington, MN | 3,434.5 | 138 | Manchester, NH | 2,844.8 | 212 | Boulder, CO | 2,174.5 |
| 65 | McAllen, TX | 3,416.3 | 139 | Gresham, OR | 2,840.0 | 213 | Hialeah, FL | 2,168.8 |
| 66 | Lubbock, TX | 3,406.4 | 140 | San Angelo, TX | 2,819.1 | 214 | Raleigh, NC | 2,162.7 |
| 67 | Sioux City, IA | 3,403.6 | 141 | Hemet, CA | 2,807.9 | 215 | Charleston, SC | 2,142.2 |
| 68 | Tuscaloosa, AL | 3,395.4 | 142 | Hammond, IN | 2,799.7 | 216 | Bryan, TX | 2,141.8 |
| 69 | Las Cruces, NM | 3,386.0 | 143 | Ventura, CA | 2,795.6 | 217 | Worcester, MA | 2,139.0 |
| 70 | Houston, TX | 3,374.8 | 144 | Richmond, VA | 2,795.2 | 218 | Citrus Heights, CA | 2,138.6 |
| 71 | Beaumont, TX | 3,373.8 | 145 | Nashville, TN | 2,776.6 | 219 | Nashua, NH | 2,133.2 |
| 72 | Oklahoma City, OK | 3,369.6 | 146 | Cleveland, OH | 2,770.9 | 220 | Scranton, PA | 2,131.2 |
| 73 | West Palm Beach, FL | 3,368.5 | 147 | High Point, NC | 2,768.9 | 221 | Bethlehem, PA | 2,130.8 |
| 74 | Lawton, OK | 3,361.8 | 148 | Fort Wayne, IN | 2,756.8 | 222 | Fargo, ND | 2,108.0 |

| RANK | CITY | RATE | RANK | CITY | RATE | RANK | CITY | RATE |
|---|---|---|---|---|---|---|---|---|
| 223 | Reno, NV | 2,107.4 | 297 | El Cajon, CA | 1,740.0 | 371 | Carson, CA | 1,336.0 |
| 224 | Mesa, AZ | 2,106.1 | 298 | Buena Park, CA | 1,736.6 | 372 | Elgin, IL | 1,323.6 |
| 225 | Lowell, MA | 2,101.4 | 299 | Ann Arbor, MI | 1,730.3 | 373 | Vallejo, CA | 1,312.4 |
| 226 | Chesapeake, VA | 2,095.6 | 300 | Boise, ID | 1,727.7 | 374 | North Las Vegas, NV | 1,301.2 |
| 227 | Fort Collins, CO | 2,090.4 | 301 | Clarkstown, NY | 1,719.8 | 375 | Lawrence, MA | 1,300.6 |
| 228 | West Covina, CA | 2,089.6 | 302 | Plano, TX | 1,715.0 | 376 | Carlsbad, CA | 1,299.5 |
| 229 | Virginia Beach, VA | 2,079.9 | 303 | Pomona, CA | 1,711.7 | 377 | Beaverton, OR | 1,296.6 |
| 230 | Roseville, CA | 2,077.9 | 304 | Lee's Summit, MO | 1,705.4 | 378 | Inglewood, CA | 1,290.4 |
| 231 | Erie, PA | 2,076.1 | 305 | Victorville, CA | 1,698.5 | 379 | Somerville, MA | 1,283.3 |
| 232 | Westminster, CO | 2,073.7 | 306 | Oxnard, CA | 1,696.0 | 379 | Surprise, AZ | 1,283.3 |
| 233 | Fullerton, CA | 2,056.9 | 307 | Vacaville, CA | 1,693.7 | 381 | O'Fallon, MO | 1,281.0 |
| 234 | Deerfield Beach, FL | 2,053.6 | 308 | Alameda, CA | 1,686.2 | 382 | Henderson, NV | 1,273.5 |
| 235 | Champaign, IL | 2,046.6 | 309 | Lakewood, CA | 1,672.3 | 383 | Lancaster, CA | 1,270.4 |
| 236 | Lansing, MI | 2,044.7 | 310 | McKinney, TX | 1,668.2 | 384 | Palm Bay, FL | 1,270.2 |
| 237 | Boston, MA | 2,042.1 | 311 | Escondido, CA | 1,665.7 | 385 | Garden Grove, CA | 1,265.8 |
| 238 | Sandy Springs, GA | 2,038.9 | 312 | Indio, CA | 1,663.7 | 386 | San Jose, CA | 1,250.9 |
| 239 | Clarksville, TN | 2,036.4 | 313 | Reading, PA | 1,662.8 | 387 | Santa Ana, CA | 1,250.7 |
| 240 | Provo, UT | 2,029.3 | 314 | Downey, CA | 1,654.3 | 388 | Bellflower, CA | 1,247.5 |
| 241 | Warwick, RI | 2,014.9 | 315 | Mountain View, CA | 1,649.9 | 389 | Clifton, NJ | 1,246.7 |
| 242 | Midland, TX | 2,011.3 | 316 | League City, TX | 1,647.4 | 390 | Torrance, CA | 1,242.4 |
| 243 | Decatur, IL | 2,010.9 | 317 | Upland, CA | 1,647.3 | 391 | Cicero, IL | 1,239.8 |
| 244 | Fairfield, CA | 2,001.4 | 318 | Alexandria, VA | 1,634.1 | 392 | Napa, CA | 1,237.9 |
| 245 | Flint, MI | 2,001.2 | 319 | Coral Springs, FL | 1,632.6 | 393 | Palmdale, CA | 1,231.8 |
| 246 | Thornton, CO | 1,998.0 | 320 | Roswell, GA | 1,631.5 | 394 | Glendale, CA | 1,220.3 |
| 247 | Greece, NY | 1,991.4 | 321 | Cranston, RI | 1,618.0 | 395 | Brick Twnshp, NJ | 1,208.7 |
| 248 | Waukegan, IL | 1,989.6 | 322 | Fall River, MA | 1,617.4 | 396 | Orange, CA | 1,192.4 |
| 249 | Oceanside, CA | 1,980.6 | 323 | Woodbridge Twnshp, NJ | 1,612.8 | 397 | Quincy, MA | 1,190.5 |
| 250 | Scottsdale, AZ | 1,979.8 | 324 | Carrollton, TX | 1,606.8 | 398 | Gilbert, AZ | 1,186.3 |
| 251 | Lynchburg, VA | 1,978.0 | 325 | Moreno Valley, CA | 1,601.7 | 399 | Jersey City, NJ | 1,185.7 |
| 252 | Richardson, TX | 1,977.5 | 326 | San Mateo, CA | 1,594.0 | 400 | Compton, CA | 1,184.8 |
| 253 | Merced, CA | 1,977.2 | 327 | Amherst, NY | 1,590.9 | 400 | Norwalk, CA | 1,184.8 |
| 254 | Boca Raton, FL | 1,965.1 | 328 | Overland Park, KS | 1,576.3 | 402 | Menifee, CA | 1,184.7 |
| 255 | Orem, UT | 1,956.5 | 329 | Frisco, TX | 1,574.7 | 403 | Danbury, CT | 1,166.0 |
| 256 | Evanston, IL | 1,946.9 | 330 | Joliet, IL | 1,574.1 | 404 | Rancho Cucamon., CA | 1,144.8 |
| 257 | Irving, TX | 1,946.0 | 331 | Livonia, MI | 1,573.2 | 405 | Stamford, CT | 1,140.0 |
| 258 | Huntington Beach, CA | 1,938.3 | 332 | Norwalk, CT | 1,572.1 | 406 | Aurora, IL | 1,139.4 |
| 259 | Whittier, CA | 1,937.5 | 333 | Sugar Land, TX | 1,570.8 | 407 | Daly City, CA | 1,138.4 |
| 260 | Tracy, CA | 1,934.9 | 334 | Richmond, CA | 1,569.8 | 408 | Hesperia, CA | 1,135.8 |
| 261 | Arvada, CO | 1,929.7 | 335 | Pearland, TX | 1,569.5 | 409 | Rialto, CA | 1,119.8 |
| 262 | Round Rock, TX | 1,921.2 | 336 | Nampa, ID | 1,558.5 | 410 | Naperville, IL | 1,116.3 |
| 263 | El Paso, TX | 1,911.6 | 337 | St. George, UT | 1,549.2 | 411 | Fremont, CA | 1,106.6 |
| 264 | Lewisville, TX | 1,907.5 | 338 | Chino, CA | 1,547.6 | 412 | Cary, NC | 1,090.0 |
| 265 | Green Bay, WI | 1,903.8 | 338 | Hawthorne, CA | 1,547.6 | 413 | Fontana, CA | 1,089.8 |
| 266 | Anaheim, CA | 1,887.5 | 340 | Ontario, CA | 1,538.0 | 414 | Canton Twnshp, MI | 1,088.2 |
| 267 | Westland, MI | 1,881.2 | 341 | Santa Maria, CA | 1,525.7 | 415 | Irvine, CA | 1,082.6 |
| 268 | San Bernardino, CA | 1,878.0 | 342 | Warren, MI | 1,518.3 | 416 | Allen, TX | 1,079.0 |
| 269 | Pembroke Pines, FL | 1,877.0 | 343 | Troy, MI | 1,513.2 | 417 | Trenton, NJ | 1,076.5 |
| 270 | Grand Prairie, TX | 1,875.7 | 344 | Livermore, CA | 1,511.6 | 418 | Murrieta, CA | 1,066.2 |
| 271 | Westminster, CA | 1,871.9 | 345 | Clinton Twnshp, MI | 1,509.1 | 419 | San Marcos, CA | 1,061.4 |
| 272 | Chandler, AZ | 1,860.7 | 346 | Sterling Heights, MI | 1,498.1 | 420 | Meridian, ID | 989.5 |
| 273 | Bloomington, IL | 1,852.4 | 347 | Santa Rosa, CA | 1,491.6 | 421 | Sunnyvale, CA | 982.7 |
| 274 | Norman, OK | 1,847.5 | 348 | New Rochelle, NY | 1,487.3 | 422 | Port St. Lucie, FL | 980.7 |
| 275 | Rochester, MN | 1,847.3 | 349 | Cape Coral, FL | 1,484.8 | 423 | Simi Valley, CA | 976.9 |
| 276 | Sparks, NV | 1,843.3 | 350 | Elizabeth, NJ | 1,464.6 | 424 | Farmington Hills, MI | 953.3 |
| 277 | Burbank, CA | 1,839.1 | 351 | Long Beach, CA | 1,462.3 | 425 | Thousand Oaks, CA | 948.1 |
| 278 | Pasadena, CA | 1,836.7 | 352 | Tustin, CA | 1,454.9 | 426 | Baldwin Park, CA | 947.3 |
| 279 | Longmont, CO | 1,827.0 | 353 | Broken Arrow, OK | 1,447.2 | 427 | El Monte, CA | 898.0 |
| 280 | Newport Beach, CA | 1,825.7 | 354 | South Gate, CA | 1,442.6 | 428 | Centennial, CO | 893.4 |
| 281 | Kenosha, WI | 1,818.4 | 355 | Hamilton Twnshp, NJ | 1,441.7 | 429 | Arlington Heights, IL | 867.4 |
| 282 | Santa Clara, CA | 1,805.2 | 356 | Corona, CA | 1,439.2 | 430 | Fishers, IN | 862.5 |
| 283 | Tampa, FL | 1,799.0 | 357 | Los Angeles, CA | 1,436.9 | 431 | Santa Clarita, CA | 858.7 |
| 284 | Peoria, AZ | 1,797.8 | 358 | Newark, NJ | 1,436.5 | 432 | Edison Twnshp, NJ | 842.9 |
| 285 | Upper Darby Twnshp, PA | 1,796.5 | 359 | Edmond, OK | 1,430.7 | 433 | Mission Viejo, CA | 836.3 |
| 286 | Hillsboro, OR | 1,789.0 | 360 | Olathe, KS | 1,429.1 | 434 | Yonkers, NY | 834.6 |
| 287 | Denton, TX | 1,787.3 | 361 | Redwood City, CA | 1,427.7 | 435 | Lakewood Twnshp, NJ | 828.8 |
| 288 | Lynn, MA | 1,781.6 | 362 | San Diego, CA | 1,425.2 | 436 | Chino Hills, CA | 799.3 |
| 289 | Temecula, CA | 1,778.2 | 363 | Miramar, FL | 1,422.2 | 437 | Lake Forest, CA | 781.5 |
| 290 | Chico, CA | 1,777.3 | 364 | Alhambra, CA | 1,411.9 | 438 | Carmel, IN | 675.1 |
| 291 | Bridgeport, CT | 1,774.6 | 365 | Hayward, CA | 1,405.7 | 439 | Newton, MA | 672.3 |
| 292 | Las Vegas, NV | 1,769.3 | 366 | New York, NY | 1,404.6 | 440 | Johns Creek, GA | 556.5 |
| 293 | College Station, TX | 1,769.1 | 367 | Elk Grove, CA | 1,385.1 | 441 | Ramapo, NY | 534.4 |
| 294 | Jurupa Valley, CA | 1,765.7 | 368 | Chula Vista, CA | 1,384.7 | NA | Toledo, OH** | NA |
| 295 | Antioch, CA | 1,758.6 | 369 | Vista, CA | 1,371.1 | | | |
| 296 | Salinas, CA | 1,746.5 | 370 | Paterson, NJ | 1,367.5 | | | |

Source: CQ Press using reported data from the F.B.I. "Crime in the United States 2013"

*Larceny-theft is the unlawful taking of property. Attempts are included.

**Not available.

## 75. Percent Change in Larceny-Theft Rate: 2012 to 2013
## National Percent Change = 3.4% Decrease*

| RANK | CITY | % CHANGE | RANK | CITY | % CHANGE | RANK | CITY | % CHANGE |
|---|---|---|---|---|---|---|---|---|
| 46 | Abilene, TX | 9.1 | 284 | Chino, CA | (6.4) | 169 | Fullerton, CA | (0.8) |
| 143 | Akron, OH | 0.6 | 39 | Chula Vista, CA | 9.7 | 126 | Gainesville, FL | 1.5 |
| 197 | Alameda, CA | (2.2) | 393 | Cicero, IL | (14.7) | 405 | Garden Grove, CA | (16.5) |
| 248 | Albany, GA | (4.5) | 344 | Cincinnati, OH | (9.6) | 227 | Garland, TX | (3.6) |
| 188 | Albany, NY | (1.5) | 347 | Citrus Heights, CA | (9.8) | 5 | Gary, IN | 25.2 |
| 177 | Albuquerque, NM | (1.1) | 154 | Clarkstown, NY | 0.0 | 122 | Gilbert, AZ | 1.8 |
| 154 | Alexandria, VA | 0.0 | 56 | Clarksville, TN | 7.7 | 292 | Glendale, AZ | (6.8) |
| 358 | Alhambra, CA | (10.9) | 93 | Clearwater, FL | 4.0 | 59 | Glendale, CA | 7.2 |
| 334 | Allentown, PA | (8.8) | 136 | Cleveland, OH | 1.0 | 108 | Grand Prairie, TX | 2.8 |
| 415 | Allen, TX | (18.3) | 197 | Clifton, NJ | (2.2) | 220 | Grand Rapids, MI | (3.3) |
| 334 | Amarillo, TX | (8.8) | 293 | Clinton Twnshp, MI | (6.9) | 293 | Greece, NY | (6.9) |
| 293 | Amherst, NY | (6.9) | 418 | Clovis, CA | (18.7) | 152 | Greeley, CO | 0.1 |
| 305 | Anaheim, CA | (7.4) | 214 | College Station, TX | (3.0) | 329 | Green Bay, WI | (8.6) |
| 21 | Anchorage, AK | 15.0 | 273 | Colonie, NY | (5.5) | 197 | Greensboro, NC | (2.2) |
| 83 | Ann Arbor, MI | 4.8 | 162 | Colorado Springs, CO | (0.4) | 197 | Greenville, NC | (2.2) |
| 232 | Antioch, CA | (3.8) | 117 | Columbia, MO | 2.3 | 258 | Gresham, OR | (4.9) |
| 423 | Arlington Heights, IL | (20.3) | NA | Columbia, SC** | NA | 268 | Hamilton Twnshp, NJ | (5.3) |
| 110 | Arlington, TX | 2.6 | 129 | Columbus, GA | 1.3 | 71 | Hammond, IN | 5.8 |
| 87 | Arvada, CO | 4.5 | 18 | Compton, CA | 15.5 | 203 | Hampton, VA | (2.4) |
| 366 | Athens-Clarke, GA | (11.3) | 114 | Concord, CA | 2.4 | 183 | Hartford, CT | (1.3) |
| 223 | Atlanta, GA | (3.4) | NA | Concord, NC** | NA | 15 | Hawthorne, CA | 16.5 |
| 96 | Aurora, CO | 3.9 | 210 | Coral Springs, FL | (2.7) | 293 | Hayward, CA | (6.9) |
| 334 | Aurora, IL | (8.8) | 413 | Corona, CA | (18.1) | 14 | Hemet, CA | 16.6 |
| 278 | Austin, TX | (5.8) | 112 | Corpus Christi, TX | 2.5 | 173 | Henderson, NV | (0.9) |
| 248 | Bakersfield, CA | (4.5) | 347 | Costa Mesa, CA | (9.8) | 368 | Hesperia, CA | (11.5) |
| 400 | Baldwin Park, CA | (15.7) | 251 | Cranston, RI | (4.6) | 287 | Hialeah, FL | (6.5) |
| 43 | Baltimore, MD | 9.4 | 224 | Dallas, TX | (3.5) | 148 | High Point, NC | 0.5 |
| 169 | Baton Rouge, LA | (0.8) | 120 | Daly City, CA | 2.2 | 194 | Hillsboro, OR | (1.9) |
| 45 | Beaumont, TX | 9.2 | 425 | Danbury, CT | (20.5) | 379 | Hollywood, FL | (12.9) |
| 109 | Beaverton, OR | 2.7 | 93 | Davenport, IA | 4.0 | 6 | Hoover, AL | 23.3 |
| 29 | Bellevue, WA | 12.3 | 258 | Davie, FL | (4.9) | 51 | Houston, TX | 8.1 |
| 39 | Bellflower, CA | 9.7 | 239 | Dayton, OH | (4.1) | 381 | Huntington Beach, CA | (13.3) |
| NA | Bend, OR** | NA | 245 | Dearborn, MI | (4.3) | 106 | Huntsville, AL | 3.2 |
| 367 | Berkeley, CA | (11.4) | 70 | Decatur, IL | 5.9 | 141 | Independence, MO | 0.7 |
| 53 | Bethlehem, PA | 8.0 | 269 | Deerfield Beach, FL | (5.4) | 283 | Indianapolis, IN | (6.3) |
| 32 | Billings, MT | 11.4 | 385 | Denton, TX | (14.0) | 358 | Indio, CA | (10.9) |
| 227 | Birmingham, AL | (3.6) | 121 | Denver, CO | 1.9 | 101 | Inglewood, CA | 3.6 |
| 117 | Bloomington, IL | 2.3 | 173 | Des Moines, IA | (0.9) | 342 | Irvine, CA | (9.4) |
| 427 | Bloomington, IN | (22.2) | 47 | Detroit, MI | 8.7 | 203 | Irving, TX | (2.4) |
| 158 | Bloomington, MN | (0.1) | 188 | Downey, CA | (1.5) | 253 | Jacksonville, FL | (4.7) |
| 382 | Boca Raton, FL | (13.5) | 19 | Duluth, MN | 15.2 | 301 | Jackson, MS | (7.1) |
| 389 | Boise, ID | (14.4) | 371 | Edinburg, TX | (12.1) | 342 | Jersey City, NJ | (9.4) |
| 236 | Boston, MA | (3.9) | 410 | Edison Twnshp, NJ | (17.3) | 39 | Johns Creek, GA | 9.7 |
| 291 | Boulder, CO | (6.7) | 351 | Edmond, OK | (10.2) | 386 | Joliet, IL | (14.2) |
| 258 | Brick Twnshp, NJ | (4.9) | 16 | El Cajon, CA | 16.1 | 215 | Jurupa Valley, CA | (3.2) |
| 358 | Bridgeport, CT | (10.9) | 241 | El Monte, CA | (4.2) | 158 | Kansas City, KS | (0.1) |
| 103 | Brockton, MA | 3.4 | 232 | El Paso, TX | (3.8) | 310 | Kansas City, MO | (7.8) |
| 386 | Broken Arrow, OK | (14.2) | 287 | Elgin, IL | (6.5) | 80 | Kennewick, WA | 5.1 |
| 306 | Brooklyn Park, MN | (7.5) | 401 | Elizabeth, NJ | (15.8) | 409 | Kenosha, WI | (17.1) |
| 317 | Brownsville, TX | (8.0) | 349 | Elk Grove, CA | (10.0) | 62 | Kent, WA | 7.1 |
| 361 | Bryan, TX | (11.0) | 324 | Erie, PA | (8.4) | 287 | Killeen, TX | (6.5) |
| 129 | Buena Park, CA | 1.3 | 99 | Escondido, CA | 3.8 | 152 | Knoxville, TN | 0.1 |
| 197 | Buffalo, NY | (2.2) | 258 | Eugene, OR | (4.9) | 23 | Lafayette, LA | 13.8 |
| 134 | Burbank, CA | 1.1 | 303 | Evanston, IL | (7.2) | 429 | Lake Forest, CA | (22.5) |
| 224 | Cambridge, MA | (3.5) | 263 | Evansville, IN | (5.2) | 48 | Lakeland, FL | 8.4 |
| NA | Canton Twnshp, MI** | NA | 37 | Everett, WA | 10.0 | 175 | Lakewood Twnshp, NJ | (1.0) |
| 293 | Cape Coral, FL | (6.9) | 154 | Fairfield, CA | 0.0 | 186 | Lakewood, CA | (1.4) |
| 241 | Carlsbad, CA | (4.2) | 375 | Fall River, MA | (12.5) | 88 | Lakewood, CO | 4.3 |
| 396 | Carmel, IN | (14.9) | 96 | Fargo, ND | 3.9 | 186 | Lancaster, CA | (1.4) |
| 397 | Carrollton, TX | (15.2) | 399 | Farmington Hills, MI | (15.6) | 67 | Lansing, MI | 6.4 |
| 421 | Carson, CA | (20.1) | 165 | Fayetteville, AR | (0.5) | 149 | Laredo, TX | 0.4 |
| 91 | Cary, NC | 4.1 | 114 | Fayetteville, NC | 2.4 | 355 | Largo, FL | (10.6) |
| 197 | Cedar Rapids, IA | (2.2) | 89 | Federal Way, WA | 4.2 | 77 | Las Cruces, NM | 5.2 |
| 388 | Centennial, CO | (14.3) | 181 | Fishers, IN | (1.2) | 110 | Las Vegas, NV | 2.6 |
| 373 | Champaign, IL | (12.3) | 310 | Flint, MI | (7.8) | 319 | Lawrence, KS | (8.1) |
| 376 | Chandler, AZ | (12.6) | 324 | Fontana, CA | (8.4) | 1 | Lawrence, MA | 35.9 |
| 238 | Charleston, SC | (4.0) | 317 | Fort Collins, CO | (8.0) | 169 | Lawton, OK | (0.8) |
| 263 | Charlotte, NC | (5.2) | 169 | Fort Lauderdale, FL | (0.8) | 96 | League City, TX | 3.9 |
| NA | Chattanooga, TN** | NA | 206 | Fort Smith, AR | (2.6) | 356 | Lee's Summit, MO | (10.8) |
| 241 | Cheektowaga, NY | (4.2) | 154 | Fort Wayne, IN | 0.0 | NA | Lewisville, TX** | NA |
| 241 | Chesapeake, VA | (4.2) | 69 | Fort Worth, TX | 6.2 | 322 | Lexington, KY | (8.2) |
| 353 | Chicago, IL | (10.3) | 215 | Fremont, CA | (3.2) | 332 | Lincoln, NE | (8.7) |
| 7 | Chico, CA | 22.9 | 394 | Fresno, CA | (14.8) | 134 | Little Rock, AR | 1.1 |
| 25 | Chino Hills, CA | 13.2 | 251 | Frisco, TX | (4.6) | 262 | Livermore, CA | (5.1) |

| RANK | CITY | % CHANGE | RANK | CITY | % CHANGE | RANK | CITY | % CHANGE |
|---|---|---|---|---|---|---|---|---|
| 275 | Livonia, MI | (5.6) | 22 | Pasadena, CA | 14.4 | 23 | South Gate, CA | 13.8 |
| 356 | Long Beach, CA | (10.8) | 192 | Pasadena, TX | (1.7) | 162 | Sparks, NV | (0.4) |
| 253 | Longmont, CO | (4.7) | 256 | Paterson, NJ | (4.8) | 34 | Spokane Valley, WA | 11.3 |
| 374 | Longview, TX | (12.4) | 65 | Pearland, TX | 6.7 | 58 | Spokane, WA | 7.3 |
| 177 | Los Angeles, CA | (1.1) | 275 | Pembroke Pines, FL | (5.6) | 370 | Springfield, IL | (12.0) |
| 127 | Louisville, KY | 1.4 | 413 | Peoria, AZ | (18.1) | 114 | Springfield, MA | 2.4 |
| 20 | Lowell, MA | 15.1 | 329 | Peoria, IL | (8.6) | 183 | Springfield, MO | (1.3) |
| 239 | Lubbock, TX | (4.1) | 246 | Philadelphia, PA | (4.4) | 232 | Stamford, CT | (3.8) |
| 310 | Lynchburg, VA | (7.8) | 112 | Phoenix, AZ | 2.5 | 269 | Sterling Heights, MI | (5.4) |
| 127 | Lynn, MA | 1.4 | 215 | Pittsburgh, PA | (3.2) | 84 | Stockton, CA | 4.7 |
| 143 | Macon, GA | 0.6 | 293 | Plano, TX | (6.9) | 143 | St. George, UT | 0.6 |
| 132 | Madison, WI | 1.2 | 378 | Plantation, FL | (12.8) | 215 | St. Joseph, MO | (3.2) |
| 38 | Manchester, NH | 9.9 | 394 | Pomona, CA | (14.8) | 165 | St. Louis, MO | (0.5) |
| 203 | McAllen, TX | (2.4) | 327 | Pompano Beach, FL | (8.5) | 324 | St. Paul, MN | (8.4) |
| 77 | McKinney, TX | 5.2 | 427 | Port St. Lucie, FL | (22.2) | 50 | St. Petersburg, FL | 8.3 |
| 63 | Medford, OR | 7.0 | 206 | Portland, OR | (2.6) | NA | Suffolk, VA** | NA |
| 220 | Melbourne, FL | (3.3) | 68 | Portsmouth, VA | 6.3 | 63 | Sugar Land, TX | 7.0 |
| 206 | Memphis, TN | (2.6) | 75 | Providence, RI | 5.5 | 407 | Sunnyvale, CA | (16.8) |
| 391 | Menifee, CA | (14.5) | 17 | Provo, UT | 15.6 | 136 | Sunrise, FL | 1.0 |
| 432 | Merced, CA | (41.2) | 28 | Pueblo, CO | 12.4 | 404 | Surprise, AZ | (16.3) |
| 430 | Meridian, ID | (22.8) | 9 | Quincy, MA | 18.3 | 10 | Syracuse, NY | 17.9 |
| 350 | Mesa, AZ | (10.1) | 369 | Racine, WI | (11.6) | 117 | Tacoma, WA | 2.3 |
| 89 | Mesquite, TX | 4.2 | 304 | Raleigh, NC | (7.3) | 143 | Tallahassee, FL | 0.6 |
| 34 | Miami Beach, FL | 11.3 | 419 | Ramapo, NY | (18.9) | 319 | Tampa, FL | (8.1) |
| 188 | Miami Gardens, FL | (1.5) | 422 | Rancho Cucamon., CA | (20.2) | 31 | Temecula, CA | 12.1 |
| 211 | Miami, FL | (2.8) | 344 | Reading, PA | (9.6) | 175 | Tempe, AZ | (1.0) |
| 143 | Midland, TX | 0.6 | 363 | Redding, CA | (11.1) | 132 | Thornton, CO | 1.2 |
| 377 | Milwaukee, WI | (12.7) | 158 | Redwood City, CA | (0.1) | 406 | Thousand Oaks, CA | (16.7) |
| 122 | Minneapolis, MN | 1.8 | 177 | Reno, NV | (1.1) | NA | Toledo, OH** | NA |
| 277 | Miramar, FL | (5.7) | 53 | Renton, WA | 8.0 | 183 | Toms River Twnshp, NJ | (1.3) |
| 392 | Mission Viejo, CA | (14.6) | 431 | Rialto, CA | (36.7) | 263 | Topeka, KS | (5.2) |
| 2 | Mission, TX | 28.5 | 279 | Richardson, TX | (6.1) | 138 | Torrance, CA | 0.8 |
| 85 | Mobile, AL | 4.6 | 103 | Richmond, CA | 3.4 | 100 | Tracy, CA | 3.7 |
| 314 | Modesto, CA | (7.9) | 269 | Richmond, VA | (5.4) | 293 | Trenton, NJ | (6.9) |
| 306 | Moreno Valley, CA | (7.5) | 224 | Riverside, CA | (3.5) | 353 | Troy, MI | (10.3) |
| 36 | Mountain View, CA | 11.2 | 129 | Roanoke, VA | 1.3 | NA | Tucson, AZ** | NA |
| 82 | Murfreesboro, TN | 4.9 | 279 | Rochester, MN | (6.1) | 77 | Tulsa, OK | 5.2 |
| 215 | Murrieta, CA | (3.2) | 351 | Rochester, NY | (10.2) | 76 | Tuscaloosa, AL | 5.3 |
| 415 | Nampa, ID | (18.3) | 269 | Rockford, IL | (5.4) | 372 | Tustin, CA | (12.2) |
| 341 | Napa, CA | (9.3) | 141 | Roseville, CA | 0.7 | 301 | Tyler, TX | (7.1) |
| 334 | Naperville, IL | (8.8) | 8 | Roswell, GA | 22.4 | 284 | Upland, CA | (6.4) |
| 206 | Nashua, NH | (2.6) | 319 | Round Rock, TX | (8.1) | 338 | Upper Darby Twnshp, PA | (9.0) |
| 332 | Nashville, TN | (8.7) | 310 | Sacramento, CA | (7.8) | 105 | Vacaville, CA | 3.3 |
| 26 | New Bedford, MA | 13.1 | 106 | Salem, OR | 3.2 | 314 | Vallejo, CA | (7.9) |
| 227 | New Haven, CT | (3.6) | 102 | Salinas, CA | 3.5 | 339 | Vancouver, WA | (9.1) |
| 39 | New Orleans, LA | 9.7 | 363 | Salt Lake City, UT | (11.1) | 57 | Ventura, CA | 7.4 |
| 138 | New Rochelle, NY | 0.8 | NA | San Angelo, TX** | NA | 122 | Victorville, CA | 1.8 |
| 149 | New York, NY | 0.4 | 256 | San Antonio, TX | (4.8) | 231 | Virginia Beach, VA | (3.7) |
| 196 | Newark, NJ | (2.1) | 420 | San Bernardino, CA | (19.1) | 423 | Visalia, CA | (20.3) |
| 177 | Newport Beach, CA | (1.1) | 168 | San Diego, CA | (0.6) | 11 | Vista, CA | 17.8 |
| 236 | Newport News, VA | (3.9) | 4 | San Francisco, CA | 27.2 | 329 | Waco, TX | (8.6) |
| 403 | Newton, MA | (15.9) | 401 | San Jose, CA | (15.8) | 165 | Warren, MI | (0.5) |
| 273 | Norfolk, VA | (5.5) | 48 | San Leandro, CA | 8.4 | 193 | Warwick, RI | (1.8) |
| 287 | Norman, OK | (6.5) | 149 | San Marcos, CA | 0.4 | 122 | Washington, DC | 1.8 |
| 188 | North Charleston, SC | (1.5) | 44 | San Mateo, CA | 9.3 | 232 | Waterbury, CT | (3.8) |
| 248 | North Las Vegas, NV | (4.5) | 65 | Sandy Springs, GA | 6.7 | 361 | Waukegan, IL | (11.0) |
| 410 | Norwalk, CA | (17.3) | 73 | Sandy, UT | 5.6 | 73 | West Covina, CA | 5.6 |
| 138 | Norwalk, CT | 0.8 | 380 | Santa Ana, CA | (13.0) | 340 | West Palm Beach, FL | (9.2) |
| 162 | Oakland, CA | (0.4) | 384 | Santa Barbara, CA | (13.9) | 29 | West Valley, UT | 12.3 |
| 27 | Oceanside, CA | 12.9 | 263 | Santa Clara, CA | (5.2) | 91 | Westland, MI | 4.1 |
| 12 | Odessa, TX | 17.4 | 398 | Santa Clarita, CA | (15.5) | 412 | Westminster, CA | (17.5) |
| 279 | O'Fallon, MO | (6.1) | 13 | Santa Maria, CA | 17.2 | 71 | Westminster, CO | 5.8 |
| 85 | Ogden, UT | 4.6 | 80 | Santa Monica, CA | 5.1 | 246 | Whittier, CA | (4.4) |
| 263 | Oklahoma City, OK | (5.2) | 322 | Santa Rosa, CA | (8.2) | 284 | Wichita Falls, TX | (6.4) |
| 309 | Olathe, KS | (7.6) | 181 | Savannah, GA | (1.2) | 213 | Wichita, KS | (2.9) |
| 282 | Omaha, NE | (6.2) | 211 | Scottsdale, AZ | (2.8) | 327 | Wilmington, NC | (8.5) |
| 389 | Ontario, CA | (14.4) | 346 | Scranton, PA | (9.7) | 195 | Winston-Salem, NC | (2.0) |
| 417 | Orange, CA | (18.5) | 55 | Seattle, WA | 7.9 | 59 | Woodbridge Twnshp, NJ | 7.2 |
| 253 | Orem, UT | (4.7) | 227 | Shreveport, LA | (3.6) | 161 | Worcester, MA | (0.2) |
| 93 | Orlando, FL | 4.0 | 365 | Simi Valley, CA | (11.2) | 293 | Yakima, WA | (6.9) |
| 383 | Overland Park, KS | (13.8) | 59 | Sioux City, IA | 7.2 | 314 | Yonkers, NY | (7.9) |
| 3 | Oxnard, CA | 27.8 | 220 | Sioux Falls, SD | (3.3) | 51 | Yuma, AZ | 8.1 |
| 408 | Palm Bay, FL | (17.0) | 426 | Somerville, MA | (20.6) | | | |
| 306 | Palmdale, CA | (7.5) | 32 | South Bend, IN | 11.4 | | | |

Source: CQ Press using reported data from the F.B.I. "Crime in the United States 2013"

*Larceny-theft is the unlawful taking of property. Attempts are included.

**Not available.

## 75. Percent Change in Larceny-Theft Rate: 2012 to 2013 (continued)
## National Percent Change = 3.4% Decrease*

| RANK | CITY | % CHANGE | RANK | CITY | % CHANGE | RANK | CITY | % CHANGE |
|---|---|---|---|---|---|---|---|---|
| 1 | Lawrence, MA | 35.9 | 75 | Providence, RI | 5.5 | 149 | Laredo, TX | 0.4 |
| 2 | Mission, TX | 28.5 | 76 | Tuscaloosa, AL | 5.3 | 149 | New York, NY | 0.4 |
| 3 | Oxnard, CA | 27.8 | 77 | Las Cruces, NM | 5.2 | 149 | San Marcos, CA | 0.4 |
| 4 | San Francisco, CA | 27.2 | 77 | McKinney, TX | 5.2 | 152 | Greeley, CO | 0.1 |
| 5 | Gary, IN | 25.2 | 77 | Tulsa, OK | 5.2 | 152 | Knoxville, TN | 0.1 |
| 6 | Hoover, AL | 23.3 | 80 | Kennewick, WA | 5.1 | 154 | Alexandria, VA | 0.0 |
| 7 | Chico, CA | 22.9 | 80 | Santa Monica, CA | 5.1 | 154 | Clarkstown, NY | 0.0 |
| 8 | Roswell, GA | 22.4 | 82 | Murfreesboro, TN | 4.9 | 154 | Fairfield, CA | 0.0 |
| 9 | Quincy, MA | 18.3 | 83 | Ann Arbor, MI | 4.8 | 154 | Fort Wayne, IN | 0.0 |
| 10 | Syracuse, NY | 17.9 | 84 | Stockton, CA | 4.7 | 158 | Bloomington, MN | (0.1) |
| 11 | Vista, CA | 17.8 | 85 | Mobile, AL | 4.6 | 158 | Kansas City, KS | (0.1) |
| 12 | Odessa, TX | 17.4 | 85 | Ogden, UT | 4.6 | 158 | Redwood City, CA | (0.1) |
| 13 | Santa Maria, CA | 17.2 | 87 | Arvada, CO | 4.5 | 161 | Worcester, MA | (0.2) |
| 14 | Hemet, CA | 16.6 | 88 | Lakewood, CO | 4.3 | 162 | Colorado Springs, CO | (0.4) |
| 15 | Hawthorne, CA | 16.5 | 89 | Federal Way, WA | 4.2 | 162 | Oakland, CA | (0.4) |
| 16 | El Cajon, CA | 16.1 | 89 | Mesquite, TX | 4.2 | 162 | Sparks, NV | (0.4) |
| 17 | Provo, UT | 15.6 | 91 | Cary, NC | 4.1 | 165 | Fayetteville, AR | (0.5) |
| 18 | Compton, CA | 15.5 | 91 | Westland, MI | 4.1 | 165 | St. Louis, MO | (0.5) |
| 19 | Duluth, MN | 15.2 | 93 | Clearwater, FL | 4.0 | 165 | Warren, MI | (0.5) |
| 20 | Lowell, MA | 15.1 | 93 | Davenport, IA | 4.0 | 168 | San Diego, CA | (0.6) |
| 21 | Anchorage, AK | 15.0 | 93 | Orlando, FL | 4.0 | 169 | Baton Rouge, LA | (0.8) |
| 22 | Pasadena, CA | 14.4 | 96 | Aurora, CO | 3.9 | 169 | Fort Lauderdale, FL | (0.8) |
| 23 | Lafayette, LA | 13.8 | 96 | Fargo, ND | 3.9 | 169 | Fullerton, CA | (0.8) |
| 23 | South Gate, CA | 13.8 | 96 | League City, TX | 3.9 | 169 | Lawton, OK | (0.8) |
| 25 | Chino Hills, CA | 13.2 | 99 | Escondido, CA | 3.8 | 173 | Des Moines, IA | (0.9) |
| 26 | New Bedford, MA | 13.1 | 100 | Tracy, CA | 3.7 | 173 | Henderson, NV | (0.9) |
| 27 | Oceanside, CA | 12.9 | 101 | Inglewood, CA | 3.6 | 175 | Lakewood Twnshp, NJ | (1.0) |
| 28 | Pueblo, CO | 12.4 | 102 | Salinas, CA | 3.5 | 175 | Tempe, AZ | (1.0) |
| 29 | Bellevue, WA | 12.3 | 103 | Brockton, MA | 3.4 | 177 | Albuquerque, NM | (1.1) |
| 29 | West Valley, UT | 12.3 | 103 | Richmond, CA | 3.4 | 177 | Los Angeles, CA | (1.1) |
| 31 | Temecula, CA | 12.1 | 105 | Vacaville, CA | 3.3 | 177 | Newport Beach, CA | (1.1) |
| 32 | Billings, MT | 11.4 | 106 | Huntsville, AL | 3.2 | 177 | Reno, NV | (1.1) |
| 32 | South Bend, IN | 11.4 | 106 | Salem, OR | 3.2 | 181 | Fishers, IN | (1.2) |
| 34 | Miami Beach, FL | 11.3 | 108 | Grand Prairie, TX | 2.8 | 181 | Savannah, GA | (1.2) |
| 34 | Spokane Valley, WA | 11.3 | 109 | Beaverton, OR | 2.7 | 183 | Hartford, CT | (1.3) |
| 36 | Mountain View, CA | 11.2 | 110 | Arlington, TX | 2.6 | 183 | Springfield, MO | (1.3) |
| 37 | Everett, WA | 10.0 | 110 | Las Vegas, NV | 2.6 | 183 | Toms River Twnshp, NJ | (1.3) |
| 38 | Manchester, NH | 9.9 | 112 | Corpus Christi, TX | 2.5 | 186 | Lakewood, CA | (1.4) |
| 39 | Bellflower, CA | 9.7 | 112 | Phoenix, AZ | 2.5 | 186 | Lancaster, CA | (1.4) |
| 39 | Chula Vista, CA | 9.7 | 114 | Concord, CA | 2.4 | 188 | Albany, NY | (1.5) |
| 39 | Johns Creek, GA | 9.7 | 114 | Fayetteville, NC | 2.4 | 188 | Downey, CA | (1.5) |
| 39 | New Orleans, LA | 9.7 | 114 | Springfield, MA | 2.4 | 188 | Miami Gardens, FL | (1.5) |
| 43 | Baltimore, MD | 9.4 | 117 | Bloomington, IL | 2.3 | 188 | North Charleston, SC | (1.5) |
| 44 | San Mateo, CA | 9.3 | 117 | Columbia, MO | 2.3 | 192 | Pasadena, TX | (1.7) |
| 45 | Beaumont, TX | 9.2 | 117 | Tacoma, WA | 2.3 | 193 | Warwick, RI | (1.8) |
| 46 | Abilene, TX | 9.1 | 120 | Daly City, CA | 2.2 | 194 | Hillsboro, OR | (1.9) |
| 47 | Detroit, MI | 8.7 | 121 | Denver, CO | 1.9 | 195 | Winston-Salem, NC | (2.0) |
| 48 | Lakeland, FL | 8.4 | 122 | Gilbert, AZ | 1.8 | 196 | Newark, NJ | (2.1) |
| 48 | San Leandro, CA | 8.4 | 122 | Minneapolis, MN | 1.8 | 197 | Alameda, CA | (2.2) |
| 50 | St. Petersburg, FL | 8.3 | 122 | Victorville, CA | 1.8 | 197 | Buffalo, NY | (2.2) |
| 51 | Houston, TX | 8.1 | 122 | Washington, DC | 1.8 | 197 | Cedar Rapids, IA | (2.2) |
| 51 | Yuma, AZ | 8.1 | 126 | Gainesville, FL | 1.5 | 197 | Clifton, NJ | (2.2) |
| 53 | Bethlehem, PA | 8.0 | 127 | Louisville, KY | 1.4 | 197 | Greensboro, NC | (2.2) |
| 53 | Renton, WA | 8.0 | 127 | Lynn, MA | 1.4 | 197 | Greenville, NC | (2.2) |
| 55 | Seattle, WA | 7.9 | 129 | Buena Park, CA | 1.3 | 203 | Hampton, VA | (2.4) |
| 56 | Clarksville, TN | 7.7 | 129 | Columbus, GA | 1.3 | 203 | Irving, TX | (2.4) |
| 57 | Ventura, CA | 7.4 | 129 | Roanoke, VA | 1.3 | 203 | McAllen, TX | (2.4) |
| 58 | Spokane, WA | 7.3 | 132 | Madison, WI | 1.2 | 206 | Fort Smith, AR | (2.6) |
| 59 | Glendale, CA | 7.2 | 132 | Thornton, CO | 1.2 | 206 | Memphis, TN | (2.6) |
| 59 | Sioux City, IA | 7.2 | 134 | Burbank, CA | 1.1 | 206 | Nashua, NH | (2.6) |
| 59 | Woodbridge Twnshp, NJ | 7.2 | 134 | Little Rock, AR | 1.1 | 206 | Portland, OR | (2.6) |
| 62 | Kent, WA | 7.1 | 136 | Cleveland, OH | 1.0 | 210 | Coral Springs, FL | (2.7) |
| 63 | Medford, OR | 7.0 | 136 | Sunrise, FL | 1.0 | 211 | Miami, FL | (2.8) |
| 63 | Sugar Land, TX | 7.0 | 138 | New Rochelle, NY | 0.8 | 211 | Scottsdale, AZ | (2.8) |
| 65 | Pearland, TX | 6.7 | 138 | Norwalk, CT | 0.8 | 213 | Wichita, KS | (2.9) |
| 65 | Sandy Springs, GA | 6.7 | 138 | Torrance, CA | 0.8 | 214 | College Station, TX | (3.0) |
| 67 | Lansing, MI | 6.4 | 141 | Independence, MO | 0.7 | 215 | Fremont, CA | (3.2) |
| 68 | Portsmouth, VA | 6.3 | 141 | Roseville, CA | 0.7 | 215 | Jurupa Valley, CA | (3.2) |
| 69 | Fort Worth, TX | 6.2 | 143 | Akron, OH | 0.6 | 215 | Murrieta, CA | (3.2) |
| 70 | Decatur, IL | 5.9 | 143 | Macon, GA | 0.6 | 215 | Pittsburgh, PA | (3.2) |
| 71 | Hammond, IN | 5.8 | 143 | Midland, TX | 0.6 | 215 | St. Joseph, MO | (3.2) |
| 71 | Westminster, CO | 5.8 | 143 | St. George, UT | 0.6 | 220 | Grand Rapids, MI | (3.3) |
| 73 | Sandy, UT | 5.6 | 143 | Tallahassee, FL | 0.6 | 220 | Melbourne, FL | (3.3) |
| 73 | West Covina, CA | 5.6 | 148 | High Point, NC | 0.5 | 220 | Sioux Falls, SD | (3.3) |

| RANK | CITY | % CHANGE |
|---|---|---|
| 223 | Atlanta, GA | (3.4) |
| 224 | Cambridge, MA | (3.5) |
| 224 | Dallas, TX | (3.5) |
| 224 | Riverside, CA | (3.5) |
| 227 | Birmingham, AL | (3.6) |
| 227 | Garland, TX | (3.6) |
| 227 | New Haven, CT | (3.6) |
| 227 | Shreveport, LA | (3.6) |
| 231 | Virginia Beach, VA | (3.7) |
| 232 | Antioch, CA | (3.8) |
| 232 | El Paso, TX | (3.8) |
| 232 | Stamford, CT | (3.8) |
| 232 | Waterbury, CT | (3.8) |
| 236 | Boston, MA | (3.9) |
| 236 | Newport News, VA | (3.9) |
| 238 | Charleston, SC | (4.0) |
| 239 | Dayton, OH | (4.1) |
| 239 | Lubbock, TX | (4.1) |
| 241 | Carlsbad, CA | (4.2) |
| 241 | Cheektowaga, NY | (4.2) |
| 241 | Chesapeake, VA | (4.2) |
| 241 | El Monte, CA | (4.2) |
| 245 | Dearborn, MI | (4.3) |
| 246 | Philadelphia, PA | (4.4) |
| 246 | Whittier, CA | (4.4) |
| 248 | Albany, GA | (4.5) |
| 248 | Bakersfield, CA | (4.5) |
| 248 | North Las Vegas, NV | (4.5) |
| 251 | Cranston, RI | (4.6) |
| 251 | Frisco, TX | (4.6) |
| 253 | Jacksonville, FL | (4.7) |
| 253 | Longmont, CO | (4.7) |
| 253 | Orem, UT | (4.7) |
| 256 | Paterson, NJ | (4.8) |
| 256 | San Antonio, TX | (4.8) |
| 258 | Brick Twnshp, NJ | (4.9) |
| 258 | Davie, FL | (4.9) |
| 258 | Eugene, OR | (4.9) |
| 258 | Gresham, OR | (4.9) |
| 262 | Livermore, CA | (5.1) |
| 263 | Charlotte, NC | (5.2) |
| 263 | Evansville, IN | (5.2) |
| 263 | Oklahoma City, OK | (5.2) |
| 263 | Santa Clara, CA | (5.2) |
| 263 | Topeka, KS | (5.2) |
| 268 | Hamilton Twnshp, NJ | (5.3) |
| 269 | Deerfield Beach, FL | (5.4) |
| 269 | Richmond, VA | (5.4) |
| 269 | Rockford, IL | (5.4) |
| 269 | Sterling Heights, MI | (5.4) |
| 273 | Colonie, NY | (5.5) |
| 273 | Norfolk, VA | (5.5) |
| 275 | Livonia, MI | (5.6) |
| 275 | Pembroke Pines, FL | (5.6) |
| 277 | Miramar, FL | (5.7) |
| 278 | Austin, TX | (5.8) |
| 279 | O'Fallon, MO | (6.1) |
| 279 | Richardson, TX | (6.1) |
| 279 | Rochester, MN | (6.1) |
| 282 | Omaha, NE | (6.2) |
| 283 | Indianapolis, IN | (6.3) |
| 284 | Chino, CA | (6.4) |
| 284 | Upland, CA | (6.4) |
| 284 | Wichita Falls, TX | (6.4) |
| 287 | Elgin, IL | (6.5) |
| 287 | Hialeah, FL | (6.5) |
| 287 | Killeen, TX | (6.5) |
| 287 | Norman, OK | (6.5) |
| 291 | Boulder, CO | (6.7) |
| 292 | Glendale, AZ | (6.8) |
| 293 | Amherst, NY | (6.9) |
| 293 | Cape Coral, FL | (6.9) |
| 293 | Clinton Twnshp, MI | (6.9) |
| 293 | Greece, NY | (6.9) |

| RANK | CITY | % CHANGE |
|---|---|---|
| 293 | Hayward, CA | (6.9) |
| 293 | Plano, TX | (6.9) |
| 293 | Trenton, NJ | (6.9) |
| 293 | Yakima, WA | (6.9) |
| 301 | Jackson, MS | (7.1) |
| 301 | Tyler, TX | (7.1) |
| 303 | Evanston, IL | (7.2) |
| 304 | Raleigh, NC | (7.3) |
| 305 | Anaheim, CA | (7.4) |
| 306 | Brooklyn Park, MN | (7.5) |
| 306 | Moreno Valley, CA | (7.5) |
| 306 | Palmdale, CA | (7.5) |
| 309 | Olathe, KS | (7.6) |
| 310 | Flint, MI | (7.8) |
| 310 | Kansas City, MO | (7.8) |
| 310 | Lynchburg, VA | (7.8) |
| 310 | Sacramento, CA | (7.8) |
| 314 | Modesto, CA | (7.9) |
| 314 | Vallejo, CA | (7.9) |
| 314 | Yonkers, NY | (7.9) |
| 317 | Brownsville, TX | (8.0) |
| 317 | Fort Collins, CO | (8.0) |
| 319 | Lawrence, KS | (8.1) |
| 319 | Round Rock, TX | (8.1) |
| 319 | Tampa, FL | (8.1) |
| 322 | Lexington, KY | (8.2) |
| 322 | Santa Rosa, CA | (8.2) |
| 324 | Erie, PA | (8.4) |
| 324 | Fontana, CA | (8.4) |
| 324 | St. Paul, MN | (8.4) |
| 327 | Pompano Beach, FL | (8.5) |
| 327 | Wilmington, NC | (8.5) |
| 329 | Green Bay, WI | (8.6) |
| 329 | Peoria, IL | (8.6) |
| 329 | Waco, TX | (8.6) |
| 332 | Lincoln, NE | (8.7) |
| 332 | Nashville, TN | (8.7) |
| 334 | Allentown, PA | (8.8) |
| 334 | Amarillo, TX | (8.8) |
| 334 | Aurora, IL | (8.8) |
| 334 | Naperville, IL | (8.8) |
| 338 | Upper Darby Twnshp, PA | (9.0) |
| 339 | Vancouver, WA | (9.1) |
| 340 | West Palm Beach, FL | (9.2) |
| 341 | Napa, CA | (9.3) |
| 342 | Irvine, CA | (9.4) |
| 342 | Jersey City, NJ | (9.4) |
| 344 | Cincinnati, OH | (9.6) |
| 344 | Reading, PA | (9.6) |
| 346 | Scranton, PA | (9.7) |
| 347 | Citrus Heights, CA | (9.8) |
| 347 | Costa Mesa, CA | (9.8) |
| 349 | Elk Grove, CA | (10.0) |
| 350 | Mesa, AZ | (10.1) |
| 351 | Edmond, OK | (10.2) |
| 351 | Rochester, NY | (10.2) |
| 353 | Chicago, IL | (10.3) |
| 353 | Troy, MI | (10.3) |
| 355 | Largo, FL | (10.6) |
| 356 | Lee's Summit, MO | (10.8) |
| 356 | Long Beach, CA | (10.8) |
| 358 | Alhambra, CA | (10.9) |
| 358 | Bridgeport, CT | (10.9) |
| 358 | Indio, CA | (10.9) |
| 361 | Bryan, TX | (11.0) |
| 361 | Waukegan, IL | (11.0) |
| 363 | Redding, CA | (11.1) |
| 363 | Salt Lake City, UT | (11.1) |
| 365 | Simi Valley, CA | (11.2) |
| 366 | Athens-Clarke, GA | (11.3) |
| 367 | Berkeley, CA | (11.4) |
| 368 | Hesperia, CA | (11.5) |
| 369 | Racine, WI | (11.6) |
| 370 | Springfield, IL | (12.0) |

| RANK | CITY | % CHANGE |
|---|---|---|
| 371 | Edinburg, TX | (12.1) |
| 372 | Tustin, CA | (12.2) |
| 373 | Champaign, IL | (12.3) |
| 374 | Longview, TX | (12.4) |
| 375 | Fall River, MA | (12.5) |
| 376 | Chandler, AZ | (12.6) |
| 377 | Milwaukee, WI | (12.7) |
| 378 | Plantation, FL | (12.8) |
| 379 | Hollywood, FL | (12.9) |
| 380 | Santa Ana, CA | (13.0) |
| 381 | Huntington Beach, CA | (13.3) |
| 382 | Boca Raton, FL | (13.5) |
| 383 | Overland Park, KS | (13.8) |
| 384 | Santa Barbara, CA | (13.9) |
| 385 | Denton, TX | (14.0) |
| 386 | Broken Arrow, OK | (14.2) |
| 386 | Joliet, IL | (14.2) |
| 388 | Centennial, CO | (14.3) |
| 389 | Boise, ID | (14.4) |
| 389 | Ontario, CA | (14.4) |
| 391 | Menifee, CA | (14.5) |
| 392 | Mission Viejo, CA | (14.6) |
| 393 | Cicero, IL | (14.7) |
| 394 | Fresno, CA | (14.8) |
| 394 | Pomona, CA | (14.8) |
| 396 | Carmel, IN | (14.9) |
| 397 | Carrollton, TX | (15.2) |
| 398 | Santa Clarita, CA | (15.5) |
| 399 | Farmington Hills, MI | (15.6) |
| 400 | Baldwin Park, CA | (15.7) |
| 401 | Elizabeth, NJ | (15.8) |
| 401 | San Jose, CA | (15.8) |
| 403 | Newton, MA | (15.9) |
| 404 | Surprise, AZ | (16.3) |
| 405 | Garden Grove, CA | (16.5) |
| 406 | Thousand Oaks, CA | (16.7) |
| 407 | Sunnyvale, CA | (16.8) |
| 408 | Palm Bay, FL | (17.0) |
| 409 | Kenosha, WI | (17.1) |
| 410 | Edison Twnshp, NJ | (17.3) |
| 410 | Norwalk, CA | (17.3) |
| 412 | Westminster, CA | (17.5) |
| 413 | Corona, CA | (18.1) |
| 413 | Peoria, AZ | (18.1) |
| 415 | Allen, TX | (18.3) |
| 415 | Nampa, ID | (18.3) |
| 417 | Orange, CA | (18.5) |
| 418 | Clovis, CA | (18.7) |
| 419 | Ramapo, NY | (18.9) |
| 420 | San Bernardino, CA | (19.1) |
| 421 | Carson, CA | (20.1) |
| 422 | Rancho Cucamon., CA | (20.2) |
| 423 | Arlington Heights, IL | (20.3) |
| 423 | Visalia, CA | (20.3) |
| 425 | Danbury, CT | (20.5) |
| 426 | Somerville, MA | (20.6) |
| 427 | Bloomington, IN | (22.2) |
| 427 | Port St. Lucie, FL | (22.2) |
| 429 | Lake Forest, CA | (22.5) |
| 430 | Meridian, ID | (22.8) |
| 431 | Rialto, CA | (36.7) |
| 432 | Merced, CA | (41.2) |
| NA | Bend, OR** | NA |
| NA | Canton Twnshp, MI** | NA |
| NA | Chattanooga, TN** | NA |
| NA | Columbia, SC** | NA |
| NA | Concord, NC** | NA |
| NA | Lewisville, TX** | NA |
| NA | San Angelo, TX** | NA |
| NA | Suffolk, VA** | NA |
| NA | Toledo, OH** | NA |
| NA | Tucson, AZ** | NA |

Source: CQ Press using reported data from the F.B.I. "Crime in the United States 2013"

*Larceny-theft is the unlawful taking of property. Attempts are included.

**Not available.

# 76. Percent Change in Larceny-Theft Rate: 2009 to 2013
## National Percent Change = 8.0% Decrease*

| RANK | CITY | % CHANGE | RANK | CITY | % CHANGE | RANK | CITY | % CHANGE |
|---|---|---|---|---|---|---|---|---|
| 91 | Abilene, TX | 3.4 | 148 | Chino, CA | (2.7) | 110 | Fullerton, CA | 1.5 |
| 59 | Akron, OH | 7.0 | 105 | Chula Vista, CA | 2.1 | 323 | Gainesville, FL | (18.3) |
| 276 | Alameda, CA | (14.6) | NA | Cicero, IL** | NA | 141 | Garden Grove, CA | (2.1) |
| 109 | Albany, GA | 1.8 | 170 | Cincinnati, OH | (5.7) | 270 | Garland, TX | (14.2) |
| 139 | Albany, NY | (1.8) | 394 | Citrus Heights, CA | (26.3) | 2 | Gary, IN | 186.2 |
| 131 | Albuquerque, NM | (0.7) | 342 | Clarkstown, NY | (20.6) | 315 | Gilbert, AZ | (17.6) |
| 209 | Alexandria, VA | (8.6) | 230 | Clarksville, TN | (10.5) | 11 | Glendale, AZ | 34.9 |
| 121 | Alhambra, CA | 0.4 | 245 | Clearwater, FL | (12.1) | 238 | Glendale, CA | (11.5) |
| 396 | Allentown, PA | (27.6) | 49 | Cleveland, OH | 9.4 | 419 | Grand Prairie, TX | (34.8) |
| 361 | Allen, TX | (21.7) | 340 | Clifton, NJ | (20.1) | 396 | Grand Rapids, MI | (27.6) |
| 403 | Amarillo, TX | (30.2) | 188 | Clinton Twnshp, MI | (6.8) | 284 | Greece, NY | (15.2) |
| 165 | Amherst, NY | (4.8) | 170 | Clovis, CA | (5.7) | 79 | Greeley, CO | 4.4 |
| 37 | Anaheim, CA | 13.4 | 426 | College Station, TX | (41.0) | 151 | Green Bay, WI | (3.0) |
| 27 | Anchorage, AK | 18.9 | 270 | Colonie, NY | (14.2) | 383 | Greensboro, NC | (24.4) |
| 233 | Ann Arbor, MI | (10.7) | 42 | Colorado Springs, CO | 11.3 | NA | Greenville, NC** | NA |
| 3 | Antioch, CA | 64.6 | 111 | Columbia, MO | 1.4 | 65 | Gresham, OR | 5.9 |
| 425 | Arlington Heights, IL | (40.8) | 69 | Columbia, SC | 5.4 | 101 | Hamilton Twnshp, NJ | 2.3 |
| 373 | Arlington, TX | (23.2) | 346 | Columbus, GA | (20.9) | 199 | Hammond, IN | (7.9) |
| 112 | Arvada, CO | 1.3 | 319 | Compton, CA | (17.9) | 179 | Hampton, VA | (6.1) |
| 330 | Athens-Clarke, GA | (19.6) | 22 | Concord, CA | 21.1 | 303 | Hartford, CT | (16.5) |
| 56 | Atlanta, GA | 7.8 | 417 | Concord, NC | (34.3) | 17 | Hawthorne, CA | 22.9 |
| 55 | Aurora, CO | 8.0 | 197 | Coral Springs, FL | (7.7) | 112 | Hayward, CA | 1.3 |
| 423 | Aurora, IL | (39.0) | 305 | Corona, CA | (16.6) | 17 | Hemet, CA | 22.9 |
| 341 | Austin, TX | (20.4) | 299 | Corpus Christi, TX | (16.0) | 63 | Henderson, NV | 6.2 |
| 216 | Bakersfield, CA | (9.2) | 71 | Costa Mesa, CA | 5.2 | 42 | Hesperia, CA | 11.3 |
| 153 | Baldwin Park, CA | (3.4) | 238 | Cranston, RI | (11.5) | 380 | Hialeah, FL | (24.0) |
| 34 | Baltimore, MD | 16.1 | 388 | Dallas, TX | (24.7) | 343 | High Point, NC | (20.7) |
| 248 | Baton Rouge, LA | (12.3) | 99 | Daly City, CA | 2.4 | 38 | Hillsboro, OR | 13.1 |
| 284 | Beaumont, TX | (15.2) | 377 | Danbury, CT | (23.7) | 155 | Hollywood, FL | (3.5) |
| 138 | Beaverton, OR | (1.7) | 361 | Davenport, IA | (21.7) | 83 | Hoover, AL | 4.0 |
| 183 | Bellevue, WA | (6.3) | 321 | Davie, FL | (18.1) | 128 | Houston, TX | (0.4) |
| 48 | Bellflower, CA | 10.4 | 148 | Dayton, OH | (2.7) | 77 | Huntington Beach, CA | 4.7 |
| 31 | Bend, OR | 17.4 | 402 | Dearborn, MI | (30.1) | 120 | Huntsville, AL | 0.5 |
| 412 | Berkeley, CA | (31.7) | 158 | Decatur, IL | (3.7) | 79 | Independence, MO | 4.4 |
| 60 | Bethlehem, PA | 6.8 | NA | Deerfield Beach, FL** | NA | 223 | Indianapolis, IN | (9.7) |
| 44 | Billings, MT | 10.9 | 196 | Denton, TX | (7.5) | 67 | Indio, CA | 5.7 |
| 329 | Birmingham, AL | (19.5) | 39 | Denver, CO | 12.9 | 225 | Inglewood, CA | (9.9) |
| 133 | Bloomington, IL | (1.0) | 66 | Des Moines, IA | 5.8 | 136 | Irvine, CA | (1.3) |
| 368 | Bloomington, IN | (22.5) | 24 | Detroit, MI | 20.1 | 411 | Irving, TX | (31.2) |
| 145 | Bloomington, MN | (2.4) | 289 | Downey, CA | (15.4) | 296 | Jacksonville, FL | (15.9) |
| 401 | Boca Raton, FL | (28.9) | 133 | Duluth, MN | (1.0) | 317 | Jackson, MS | (17.7) |
| 356 | Boise, ID | (21.4) | 308 | Edinburg, TX | (16.8) | 377 | Jersey City, NJ | (23.7) |
| 318 | Boston, MA | (17.8) | 429 | Edison Twnshp, NJ | (47.2) | 424 | Johns Creek, GA | (40.1) |
| 84 | Boulder, CO | 3.9 | 248 | Edmond, OK | (12.3) | 305 | Joliet, IL | (16.6) |
| 191 | Brick Twnshp, NJ | (7.2) | 97 | El Cajon, CA | 3.0 | NA | Jurupa Valley, CA** | NA |
| 399 | Bridgeport, CT | (28.5) | 364 | El Monte, CA | (21.9) | 193 | Kansas City, KS | (7.3) |
| 72 | Brockton, MA | 5.0 | 328 | El Paso, TX | (19.2) | 214 | Kansas City, MO | (8.9) |
| 200 | Broken Arrow, OK | (8.1) | 288 | Elgin, IL | (15.3) | 262 | Kennewick, WA | (13.4) |
| 330 | Brooklyn Park, MN | (19.6) | 427 | Elizabeth, NJ | (42.2) | 370 | Kenosha, WI | (22.7) |
| 327 | Brownsville, TX | (19.1) | 219 | Elk Grove, CA | (9.5) | 78 | Kent, WA | 4.5 |
| 428 | Bryan, TX | (44.3) | 33 | Erie, PA | 16.3 | 349 | Killeen, TX | (21.0) |
| 23 | Buena Park, CA | 20.6 | 164 | Escondido, CA | (4.7) | 127 | Knoxville, TN | (0.1) |
| 183 | Buffalo, NY | (6.3) | 179 | Eugene, OR | (6.1) | 137 | Lafayette, LA | (1.4) |
| 86 | Burbank, CA | 3.8 | NA | Evanston, IL** | NA | 322 | Lake Forest, CA | (18.2) |
| 212 | Cambridge, MA | (8.8) | 81 | Evansville, IN | 4.2 | 51 | Lakeland, FL | 8.7 |
| 333 | Canton Twnshp, MI | (19.7) | 259 | Everett, WA | (13.2) | 263 | Lakewood Twnshp, NJ | (13.6) |
| 254 | Cape Coral, FL | (12.6) | 117 | Fairfield, CA | 0.7 | 185 | Lakewood, CA | (6.5) |
| 157 | Carlsbad, CA | (3.6) | 407 | Fall River, MA | (30.7) | 54 | Lakewood, CO | 8.3 |
| 416 | Carmel, IN | (34.1) | 269 | Fargo, ND | (14.1) | 93 | Lancaster, CA | 3.3 |
| 365 | Carrollton, TX | (22.2) | 417 | Farmington Hills, MI | (34.3) | 133 | Lansing, MI | (1.0) |
| 235 | Carson, CA | (10.9) | 91 | Fayetteville, AR | 3.4 | 346 | Laredo, TX | (20.9) |
| 123 | Cary, NC | 0.3 | 281 | Fayetteville, NC | (15.1) | 337 | Largo, FL | (19.8) |
| 291 | Cedar Rapids, IA | (15.5) | 129 | Federal Way, WA | (0.6) | 178 | Las Cruces, NM | (6.0) |
| 294 | Centennial, CO | (15.7) | 58 | Fishers, IN | 7.1 | 153 | Las Vegas, NV | (3.4) |
| NA | Champaign, IL** | NA | 302 | Flint, MI | (16.1) | 281 | Lawrence, KS | (15.1) |
| 279 | Chandler, AZ | (14.9) | 277 | Fontana, CA | (14.7) | 359 | Lawrence, MA | (21.6) |
| 370 | Charleston, SC | (22.7) | 333 | Fort Collins, CO | (19.7) | 188 | Lawton, OK | (6.8) |
| 325 | Charlotte, NC | (18.5) | 118 | Fort Lauderdale, FL | 0.6 | 356 | League City, TX | (21.4) |
| 209 | Chattanooga, TN | (8.6) | 214 | Fort Smith, AR | (8.9) | 245 | Lee's Summit, MO | (12.1) |
| 68 | Cheektowaga, NY | 5.6 | 86 | Fort Wayne, IN | 3.8 | 349 | Lewisville, TX | (21.0) |
| 363 | Chesapeake, VA | (21.8) | 206 | Fort Worth, TX | (8.3) | 19 | Lexington, KY | 21.3 |
| 254 | Chicago, IL | (12.6) | 407 | Fremont, CA | (30.7) | 229 | Lincoln, NE | (10.4) |
| 45 | Chico, CA | 10.8 | 173 | Fresno, CA | (5.8) | 125 | Little Rock, AR | 0.1 |
| 344 | Chino Hills, CA | (20.8) | 76 | Frisco, TX | 4.8 | 98 | Livermore, CA | 2.7 |

| RANK | CITY | % CHANGE |
|---|---|---|
| 227 | Livonia, MI | (10.2) |
| 169 | Long Beach, CA | (5.3) |
| 259 | Longmont, CO | (13.2) |
| 422 | Longview, TX | (36.8) |
| 158 | Los Angeles, CA | (3.7) |
| 95 | Louisville, KY | 3.1 |
| NA | Lowell, MA** | NA |
| 261 | Lubbock, TX | (13.3) |
| 296 | Lynchburg, VA | (15.9) |
| 158 | Lynn, MA | (3.7) |
| 186 | Macon, GA | (6.6) |
| 141 | Madison, WI | (2.1) |
| 45 | Manchester, NH | 10.8 |
| 415 | McAllen, TX | (33.2) |
| 251 | McKinney, TX | (12.5) |
| 4 | Medford, OR | 54.4 |
| 308 | Melbourne, FL | (16.8) |
| 240 | Memphis, TN | (11.7) |
| 124 | Menifee, CA | 0.2 |
| 324 | Merced, CA | (18.4) |
| 193 | Meridian, ID | (7.3) |
| 284 | Mesa, AZ | (15.2) |
| 313 | Mesquite, TX | (17.3) |
| 28 | Miami Beach, FL | 18.2 |
| 373 | Miami Gardens, FL | (23.2) |
| 41 | Miami, FL | 12.4 |
| 377 | Midland, TX | (23.7) |
| 406 | Milwaukee, WI | (30.6) |
| 40 | Minneapolis, MN | 12.5 |
| 409 | Miramar, FL | (30.8) |
| 243 | Mission Viejo, CA | (12.0) |
| 354 | Mission, TX | (21.3) |
| 166 | Mobile, AL | (5.2) |
| 163 | Modesto, CA | (4.2) |
| 101 | Moreno Valley, CA | 2.3 |
| 382 | Mountain View, CA | (24.2) |
| 263 | Murfreesboro, TN | (13.6) |
| 14 | Murrieta, CA | 26.9 |
| 200 | Nampa, ID | (8.1) |
| 404 | Napa, CA | (30.4) |
| 351 | Naperville, IL | (21.1) |
| 176 | Nashua, NH | (5.9) |
| 337 | Nashville, TN | (19.8) |
| 30 | New Bedford, MA | 17.8 |
| 241 | New Haven, CT | (11.9) |
| 15 | New Orleans, LA | 25.9 |
| 52 | New Rochelle, NY | 8.6 |
| 75 | New York, NY | 4.9 |
| 64 | Newark, NJ | 6.1 |
| 212 | Newport Beach, CA | (8.8) |
| NA | Newport News, VA** | NA |
| 386 | Newton, MA | (24.6) |
| 373 | Norfolk, VA | (23.2) |
| 405 | Norman, OK | (30.5) |
| 216 | North Charleston, SC | (9.2) |
| 241 | North Las Vegas, NV | (11.9) |
| 62 | Norwalk, CA | 6.3 |
| 95 | Norwalk, CT | 3.1 |
| 7 | Oakland, CA | 50.7 |
| 19 | Oceanside, CA | 21.3 |
| 101 | Odessa, TX | 2.3 |
| 232 | O'Fallon, MO | (10.6) |
| 69 | Ogden, UT | 5.4 |
| 162 | Oklahoma City, OK | (4.0) |
| 312 | Olathe, KS | (17.1) |
| 115 | Omaha, NE | 0.8 |
| 310 | Ontario, CA | (16.9) |
| 303 | Orange, CA | (16.5) |
| 299 | Orem, UT | (16.0) |
| 224 | Orlando, FL | (9.8) |
| 384 | Overland Park, KS | (24.5) |
| 53 | Oxnard, CA | 8.5 |
| 320 | Palm Bay, FL | (18.0) |
| 237 | Palmdale, CA | (11.2) |

| RANK | CITY | % CHANGE |
|---|---|---|
| 251 | Pasadena, CA | (12.5) |
| 155 | Pasadena, TX | (3.5) |
| 115 | Paterson, NJ | 0.8 |
| 204 | Pearland, TX | (8.2) |
| 410 | Pembroke Pines, FL | (30.9) |
| 230 | Peoria, AZ | (10.5) |
| 220 | Peoria, IL | (9.6) |
| 143 | Philadelphia, PA | (2.2) |
| 132 | Phoenix, AZ | (0.8) |
| 218 | Pittsburgh, PA | (9.4) |
| 369 | Plano, TX | (22.6) |
| 366 | Plantation, FL | (22.3) |
| 35 | Pomona, CA | 15.4 |
| 166 | Pompano Beach, FL | (5.2) |
| 414 | Port St. Lucie, FL | (32.6) |
| 81 | Portland, OR | 4.2 |
| 220 | Portsmouth, VA | (9.6) |
| 143 | Providence, RI | (2.2) |
| 99 | Provo, UT | 2.4 |
| 1 | Pueblo, CO | 190.0 |
| 121 | Quincy, MA | 0.4 |
| 346 | Racine, WI | (20.9) |
| 233 | Raleigh, NC | (10.7) |
| 384 | Ramapo, NY | (24.5) |
| 313 | Rancho Cucamon., CA | (17.3) |
| 400 | Reading, PA | (28.6) |
| 16 | Redding, CA | 24.9 |
| 243 | Redwood City, CA | (12.0) |
| 389 | Reno, NV | (25.0) |
| 395 | Renton, WA | (26.5) |
| 339 | Rialto, CA | (20.0) |
| 274 | Richardson, TX | (14.4) |
| 72 | Richmond, CA | 5.0 |
| 145 | Richmond, VA | (2.4) |
| 72 | Riverside, CA | 5.0 |
| 207 | Roanoke, VA | (8.4) |
| 333 | Rochester, MN | (19.7) |
| 182 | Rochester, NY | (6.2) |
| 267 | Rockford, IL | (13.9) |
| 330 | Roseville, CA | (19.6) |
| 247 | Roswell, GA | (12.2) |
| 173 | Round Rock, TX | (5.8) |
| 170 | Sacramento, CA | (5.7) |
| 50 | Salem, OR | 9.3 |
| 107 | Salinas, CA | 1.9 |
| 311 | Salt Lake City, UT | (17.0) |
| 296 | San Angelo, TX | (15.9) |
| 281 | San Antonio, TX | (15.1) |
| 358 | San Bernardino, CA | (21.5) |
| 86 | San Diego, CA | 3.8 |
| 9 | San Francisco, CA | 45.4 |
| 251 | San Jose, CA | (12.5) |
| 93 | San Leandro, CA | 3.3 |
| 152 | San Marcos, CA | (3.1) |
| 275 | San Mateo, CA | (14.5) |
| 225 | Sandy Springs, GA | (9.9) |
| 256 | Sandy, UT | (12.7) |
| 107 | Santa Ana, CA | 1.9 |
| 208 | Santa Barbara, CA | (8.5) |
| 200 | Santa Clara, CA | (8.1) |
| 398 | Santa Clarita, CA | (27.8) |
| 5 | Santa Maria, CA | 54.3 |
| 90 | Santa Monica, CA | 3.6 |
| 393 | Santa Rosa, CA | (26.2) |
| 392 | Savannah, GA | (26.1) |
| 204 | Scottsdale, AZ | (8.2) |
| 305 | Scranton, PA | (16.6) |
| 220 | Seattle, WA | (9.6) |
| 176 | Shreveport, LA | (5.9) |
| 354 | Simi Valley, CA | (21.3) |
| 10 | Sioux City, IA | 38.0 |
| 84 | Sioux Falls, SD | 3.9 |
| 391 | Somerville, MA | (25.9) |
| 270 | South Bend, IN | (14.2) |

| RANK | CITY | % CHANGE |
|---|---|---|
| 12 | South Gate, CA | 30.3 |
| 299 | Sparks, NV | (16.0) |
| 6 | Spokane Valley, WA | 54.1 |
| 8 | Spokane, WA | 45.9 |
| 273 | Springfield, IL | (14.3) |
| 258 | Springfield, MA | (13.0) |
| 129 | Springfield, MO | (0.6) |
| 278 | Stamford, CT | (14.8) |
| 195 | Sterling Heights, MI | (7.4) |
| 200 | Stockton, CA | (8.1) |
| 104 | St. George, UT | 2.2 |
| 21 | St. Joseph, MO | 21.2 |
| 294 | St. Louis, MO | (15.7) |
| 211 | St. Paul, MN | (8.7) |
| 256 | St. Petersburg, FL | (12.7) |
| 25 | Suffolk, VA | 19.9 |
| 265 | Sugar Land, TX | (13.7) |
| 420 | Sunnyvale, CA | (35.9) |
| 359 | Sunrise, FL | (21.6) |
| 353 | Surprise, AZ | (21.2) |
| 32 | Syracuse, NY | 17.3 |
| 284 | Tacoma, WA | (15.2) |
| 86 | Tallahassee, FL | 3.8 |
| 376 | Tampa, FL | (23.3) |
| 36 | Temecula, CA | 14.0 |
| 161 | Tempe, AZ | (3.8) |
| 268 | Thornton, CO | (14.0) |
| 289 | Thousand Oaks, CA | (15.4) |
| NA | Toledo, OH** | NA |
| 29 | Toms River Twnshp, NJ | 18.0 |
| 147 | Topeka, KS | (2.6) |
| 266 | Torrance, CA | (13.8) |
| 197 | Tracy, CA | (7.7) |
| 421 | Trenton, NJ | (36.4) |
| 367 | Troy, MI | (22.4) |
| NA | Tucson, AZ** | NA |
| 280 | Tulsa, OK | (15.0) |
| 191 | Tuscaloosa, AL | (7.2) |
| 114 | Tustin, CA | 1.2 |
| 413 | Tyler, TX | (32.1) |
| NA | Upland, CA** | NA |
| 333 | Upper Darby Twnshp, PA | (19.7) |
| 126 | Vacaville, CA | 0.0 |
| 326 | Vallejo, CA | (19.0) |
| 173 | Vancouver, WA | (5.8) |
| 13 | Ventura, CA | 27.7 |
| 228 | Victorville, CA | (10.3) |
| 292 | Virginia Beach, VA | (15.6) |
| 250 | Visalia, CA | (12.4) |
| 187 | Vista, CA | (6.7) |
| 386 | Waco, TX | (24.6) |
| 60 | Warren, MI | 6.8 |
| 381 | Warwick, RI | (24.1) |
| 26 | Washington, DC | 19.0 |
| 390 | Waterbury, CT | (25.5) |
| NA | Waukegan, IL** | NA |
| 118 | West Covina, CA | 0.6 |
| 190 | West Palm Beach, FL | (6.9) |
| 166 | West Valley, UT | (5.2) |
| 179 | Westland, MI | (6.1) |
| 140 | Westminster, CA | (2.0) |
| 236 | Westminster, CO | (11.1) |
| 45 | Whittier, CA | 10.8 |
| 351 | Wichita Falls, TX | (21.1) |
| 106 | Wichita, KS | 2.0 |
| 344 | Wilmington, NC | (20.8) |
| 150 | Winston-Salem, NC | (2.9) |
| 315 | Woodbridge Twnshp, NJ | (17.6) |
| 292 | Worcester, MA | (15.6) |
| NA | Yakima, WA** | NA |
| 370 | Yonkers, NY | (22.7) |
| 56 | Yuma, AZ | 7.8 |

Source: CQ Press using reported data from the F.B.I. "Crime in the United States 2013"

*Larceny-theft is the unlawful taking of property. Attempts are included.

**Not available.

## 76. Percent Change in Larceny-Theft Rate: 2009 to 2013 (continued)
## National Percent Change = 8.0% Decrease*

| RANK | CITY | % CHANGE | RANK | CITY | % CHANGE | RANK | CITY | % CHANGE |
|---|---|---|---|---|---|---|---|---|
| 1 | Pueblo, CO | 190.0 | 75 | New York, NY | 4.9 | 148 | Dayton, OH | (2.7) |
| 2 | Gary, IN | 186.2 | 76 | Frisco, TX | 4.8 | 150 | Winston-Salem, NC | (2.9) |
| 3 | Antioch, CA | 64.6 | 77 | Huntington Beach, CA | 4.7 | 151 | Green Bay, WI | (3.0) |
| 4 | Medford, OR | 54.4 | 78 | Kent, WA | 4.5 | 152 | San Marcos, CA | (3.1) |
| 5 | Santa Maria, CA | 54.3 | 79 | Greeley, CO | 4.4 | 153 | Baldwin Park, CA | (3.4) |
| 6 | Spokane Valley, WA | 54.1 | 79 | Independence, MO | 4.4 | 153 | Las Vegas, NV | (3.4) |
| 7 | Oakland, CA | 50.7 | 81 | Evansville, IN | 4.2 | 155 | Hollywood, FL | (3.5) |
| 8 | Spokane, WA | 45.9 | 81 | Portland, OR | 4.2 | 155 | Pasadena, TX | (3.5) |
| 9 | San Francisco, CA | 45.4 | 83 | Hoover, AL | 4.0 | 157 | Carlsbad, CA | (3.6) |
| 10 | Sioux City, IA | 38.0 | 84 | Boulder, CO | 3.9 | 158 | Decatur, IL | (3.7) |
| 11 | Glendale, AZ | 34.9 | 84 | Sioux Falls, SD | 3.9 | 158 | Los Angeles, CA | (3.7) |
| 12 | South Gate, CA | 30.3 | 86 | Burbank, CA | 3.8 | 158 | Lynn, MA | (3.7) |
| 13 | Ventura, CA | 27.7 | 86 | Fort Wayne, IN | 3.8 | 161 | Tempe, AZ | (3.8) |
| 14 | Murrieta, CA | 26.9 | 86 | San Diego, CA | 3.8 | 162 | Oklahoma City, OK | (4.0) |
| 15 | New Orleans, LA | 25.9 | 86 | Tallahassee, FL | 3.8 | 163 | Modesto, CA | (4.2) |
| 16 | Redding, CA | 24.9 | 90 | Santa Monica, CA | 3.6 | 164 | Escondido, CA | (4.7) |
| 17 | Hawthorne, CA | 22.9 | 91 | Abilene, TX | 3.4 | 165 | Amherst, NY | (4.8) |
| 17 | Hemet, CA | 22.9 | 91 | Fayetteville, AR | 3.4 | 166 | Mobile, AL | (5.2) |
| 19 | Lexington, KY | 21.3 | 93 | Lancaster, CA | 3.3 | 166 | Pompano Beach, FL | (5.2) |
| 19 | Oceanside, CA | 21.3 | 93 | San Leandro, CA | 3.3 | 166 | West Valley, UT | (5.2) |
| 21 | St. Joseph, MO | 21.2 | 95 | Louisville, KY | 3.1 | 169 | Long Beach, CA | (5.3) |
| 22 | Concord, CA | 21.1 | 95 | Norwalk, CT | 3.1 | 170 | Cincinnati, OH | (5.7) |
| 23 | Buena Park, CA | 20.6 | 97 | El Cajon, CA | 3.0 | 170 | Clovis, CA | (5.7) |
| 24 | Detroit, MI | 20.1 | 98 | Livermore, CA | 2.7 | 170 | Sacramento, CA | (5.7) |
| 25 | Suffolk, VA | 19.9 | 99 | Daly City, CA | 2.4 | 173 | Fresno, CA | (5.8) |
| 26 | Washington, DC | 19.0 | 99 | Provo, UT | 2.4 | 173 | Round Rock, TX | (5.8) |
| 27 | Anchorage, AK | 18.9 | 101 | Hamilton Twnshp, NJ | 2.3 | 173 | Vancouver, WA | (5.8) |
| 28 | Miami Beach, FL | 18.2 | 101 | Moreno Valley, CA | 2.3 | 176 | Nashua, NH | (5.9) |
| 29 | Toms River Twnshp, NJ | 18.0 | 101 | Odessa, TX | 2.3 | 176 | Shreveport, LA | (5.9) |
| 30 | New Bedford, MA | 17.8 | 104 | St. George, UT | 2.2 | 178 | Las Cruces, NM | (6.0) |
| 31 | Bend, OR | 17.4 | 105 | Chula Vista, CA | 2.1 | 179 | Eugene, OR | (6.1) |
| 32 | Syracuse, NY | 17.3 | 106 | Wichita, KS | 2.0 | 179 | Hampton, VA | (6.1) |
| 33 | Erie, PA | 16.3 | 107 | Salinas, CA | 1.9 | 179 | Westland, MI | (6.1) |
| 34 | Baltimore, MD | 16.1 | 107 | Santa Ana, CA | 1.9 | 182 | Rochester, NY | (6.2) |
| 35 | Pomona, CA | 15.4 | 109 | Albany, GA | 1.8 | 183 | Bellevue, WA | (6.3) |
| 36 | Temecula, CA | 14.0 | 110 | Fullerton, CA | 1.5 | 183 | Buffalo, NY | (6.3) |
| 37 | Anaheim, CA | 13.4 | 111 | Columbia, MO | 1.4 | 185 | Lakewood, CA | (6.5) |
| 38 | Hillsboro, OR | 13.1 | 112 | Arvada, CO | 1.3 | 186 | Macon, GA | (6.6) |
| 39 | Denver, CO | 12.9 | 112 | Hayward, CA | 1.3 | 187 | Vista, CA | (6.7) |
| 40 | Minneapolis, MN | 12.5 | 114 | Tustin, CA | 1.2 | 188 | Clinton Twnshp, MI | (6.8) |
| 41 | Miami, FL | 12.4 | 115 | Omaha, NE | 0.8 | 188 | Lawton, OK | (6.8) |
| 42 | Colorado Springs, CO | 11.3 | 115 | Paterson, NJ | 0.8 | 190 | West Palm Beach, FL | (6.9) |
| 42 | Hesperia, CA | 11.3 | 117 | Fairfield, CA | 0.7 | 191 | Brick Twnshp, NJ | (7.2) |
| 44 | Billings, MT | 10.9 | 118 | Fort Lauderdale, FL | 0.6 | 191 | Tuscaloosa, AL | (7.2) |
| 45 | Chico, CA | 10.8 | 118 | West Covina, CA | 0.6 | 193 | Kansas City, KS | (7.3) |
| 45 | Manchester, NH | 10.8 | 120 | Huntsville, AL | 0.5 | 193 | Meridian, ID | (7.3) |
| 45 | Whittier, CA | 10.8 | 121 | Alhambra, CA | 0.4 | 195 | Sterling Heights, MI | (7.4) |
| 48 | Bellflower, CA | 10.4 | 121 | Quincy, MA | 0.4 | 196 | Denton, TX | (7.5) |
| 49 | Cleveland, OH | 9.4 | 123 | Cary, NC | 0.3 | 197 | Coral Springs, FL | (7.7) |
| 50 | Salem, OR | 9.3 | 124 | Menifee, CA | 0.2 | 197 | Tracy, CA | (7.7) |
| 51 | Lakeland, FL | 8.7 | 125 | Little Rock, AR | 0.1 | 199 | Hammond, IN | (7.9) |
| 52 | New Rochelle, NY | 8.6 | 126 | Vacaville, CA | 0.0 | 200 | Broken Arrow, OK | (8.1) |
| 53 | Oxnard, CA | 8.5 | 127 | Knoxville, TN | (0.1) | 200 | Nampa, ID | (8.1) |
| 54 | Lakewood, CO | 8.3 | 128 | Houston, TX | (0.4) | 200 | Santa Clara, CA | (8.1) |
| 55 | Aurora, CO | 8.0 | 129 | Federal Way, WA | (0.6) | 200 | Stockton, CA | (8.1) |
| 56 | Atlanta, GA | 7.8 | 129 | Springfield, MO | (0.6) | 204 | Pearland, TX | (8.2) |
| 56 | Yuma, AZ | 7.8 | 131 | Albuquerque, NM | (0.7) | 204 | Scottsdale, AZ | (8.2) |
| 58 | Fishers, IN | 7.1 | 132 | Phoenix, AZ | (0.8) | 206 | Fort Worth, TX | (8.3) |
| 59 | Akron, OH | 7.0 | 133 | Bloomington, IL | (1.0) | 207 | Roanoke, VA | (8.4) |
| 60 | Bethlehem, PA | 6.8 | 133 | Duluth, MN | (1.0) | 208 | Santa Barbara, CA | (8.5) |
| 60 | Warren, MI | 6.8 | 133 | Lansing, MI | (1.0) | 209 | Alexandria, VA | (8.6) |
| 62 | Norwalk, CA | 6.3 | 136 | Irvine, CA | (1.3) | 209 | Chattanooga, TN | (8.6) |
| 63 | Henderson, NV | 6.2 | 137 | Lafayette, LA | (1.4) | 211 | St. Paul, MN | (8.7) |
| 64 | Newark, NJ | 6.1 | 138 | Beaverton, OR | (1.7) | 212 | Cambridge, MA | (8.8) |
| 65 | Gresham, OR | 5.9 | 139 | Albany, NY | (1.8) | 212 | Newport Beach, CA | (8.8) |
| 66 | Des Moines, IA | 5.8 | 140 | Westminster, CA | (2.0) | 214 | Fort Smith, AR | (8.9) |
| 67 | Indio, CA | 5.7 | 141 | Garden Grove, CA | (2.1) | 214 | Kansas City, MO | (8.9) |
| 68 | Cheektowaga, NY | 5.6 | 141 | Madison, WI | (2.1) | 216 | Bakersfield, CA | (9.2) |
| 69 | Columbia, SC | 5.4 | 143 | Philadelphia, PA | (2.2) | 216 | North Charleston, SC | (9.2) |
| 69 | Ogden, UT | 5.4 | 143 | Providence, RI | (2.2) | 218 | Pittsburgh, PA | (9.4) |
| 71 | Costa Mesa, CA | 5.2 | 145 | Bloomington, MN | (2.4) | 219 | Elk Grove, CA | (9.5) |
| 72 | Brockton, MA | 5.0 | 145 | Richmond, VA | (2.4) | 220 | Peoria, IL | (9.6) |
| 72 | Richmond, CA | 5.0 | 147 | Topeka, KS | (2.6) | 220 | Portsmouth, VA | (9.6) |
| 72 | Riverside, CA | 5.0 | 148 | Chino, CA | (2.7) | 220 | Seattle, WA | (9.6) |

| RANK | CITY | % CHANGE | RANK | CITY | % CHANGE | RANK | CITY | % CHANGE |
|---|---|---|---|---|---|---|---|---|
| 223 | Indianapolis, IN | (9.7) | 296 | Lynchburg, VA | (15.9) | 370 | Kenosha, WI | (22.7) |
| 224 | Orlando, FL | (9.8) | 296 | San Angelo, TX | (15.9) | 370 | Yonkers, NY | (22.7) |
| 225 | Inglewood, CA | (9.9) | 299 | Corpus Christi, TX | (16.0) | 373 | Arlington, TX | (23.2) |
| 225 | Sandy Springs, GA | (9.9) | 299 | Orem, UT | (16.0) | 373 | Miami Gardens, FL | (23.2) |
| 227 | Livonia, MI | (10.2) | 299 | Sparks, NV | (16.0) | 373 | Norfolk, VA | (23.2) |
| 228 | Victorville, CA | (10.3) | 302 | Flint, MI | (16.1) | 376 | Tampa, FL | (23.3) |
| 229 | Lincoln, NE | (10.4) | 303 | Hartford, CT | (16.5) | 377 | Danbury, CT | (23.7) |
| 230 | Clarksville, TN | (10.5) | 303 | Orange, CA | (16.5) | 377 | Jersey City, NJ | (23.7) |
| 230 | Peoria, AZ | (10.5) | 305 | Corona, CA | (16.6) | 377 | Midland, TX | (23.7) |
| 232 | O'Fallon, MO | (10.6) | 305 | Joliet, IL | (16.6) | 380 | Hialeah, FL | (24.0) |
| 233 | Ann Arbor, MI | (10.7) | 305 | Scranton, PA | (16.6) | 381 | Warwick, RI | (24.1) |
| 233 | Raleigh, NC | (10.7) | 308 | Edinburg, TX | (16.8) | 382 | Mountain View, CA | (24.2) |
| 235 | Carson, CA | (10.9) | 308 | Melbourne, FL | (16.8) | 383 | Greensboro, NC | (24.4) |
| 236 | Westminster, CO | (11.1) | 310 | Ontario, CA | (16.9) | 384 | Overland Park, KS | (24.5) |
| 237 | Palmdale, CA | (11.2) | 311 | Salt Lake City, UT | (17.0) | 384 | Ramapo, NY | (24.5) |
| 238 | Cranston, RI | (11.5) | 312 | Olathe, KS | (17.1) | 386 | Newton, MA | (24.6) |
| 238 | Glendale, CA | (11.5) | 313 | Mesquite, TX | (17.3) | 386 | Waco, TX | (24.6) |
| 240 | Memphis, TN | (11.7) | 313 | Rancho Cucamon., CA | (17.3) | 388 | Dallas, TX | (24.7) |
| 241 | New Haven, CT | (11.9) | 315 | Gilbert, AZ | (17.6) | 389 | Reno, NV | (25.0) |
| 241 | North Las Vegas, NV | (11.9) | 315 | Woodbridge Twnshp, NJ | (17.6) | 390 | Waterbury, CT | (25.5) |
| 243 | Mission Viejo, CA | (12.0) | 317 | Jackson, MS | (17.7) | 391 | Somerville, MA | (25.9) |
| 243 | Redwood City, CA | (12.0) | 318 | Boston, MA | (17.8) | 392 | Savannah, GA | (26.1) |
| 245 | Clearwater, FL | (12.1) | 319 | Compton, CA | (17.9) | 393 | Santa Rosa, CA | (26.2) |
| 245 | Lee's Summit, MO | (12.1) | 320 | Palm Bay, FL | (18.0) | 394 | Citrus Heights, CA | (26.3) |
| 247 | Roswell, GA | (12.2) | 321 | Davie, FL | (18.1) | 395 | Renton, WA | (26.5) |
| 248 | Baton Rouge, LA | (12.3) | 322 | Lake Forest, CA | (18.2) | 396 | Allentown, PA | (27.6) |
| 248 | Edmond, OK | (12.3) | 323 | Gainesville, FL | (18.3) | 396 | Grand Rapids, MI | (27.6) |
| 250 | Visalia, CA | (12.4) | 324 | Merced, CA | (18.4) | 398 | Santa Clarita, CA | (27.8) |
| 251 | McKinney, TX | (12.5) | 325 | Charlotte, NC | (18.5) | 399 | Bridgeport, CT | (28.5) |
| 251 | Pasadena, CA | (12.5) | 326 | Vallejo, CA | (19.0) | 400 | Reading, PA | (28.6) |
| 251 | San Jose, CA | (12.5) | 327 | Brownsville, TX | (19.1) | 401 | Boca Raton, FL | (28.9) |
| 254 | Cape Coral, FL | (12.6) | 328 | El Paso, TX | (19.2) | 402 | Dearborn, MI | (30.1) |
| 254 | Chicago, IL | (12.6) | 329 | Birmingham, AL | (19.5) | 403 | Amarillo, TX | (30.2) |
| 256 | Sandy, UT | (12.7) | 330 | Athens-Clarke, GA | (19.6) | 404 | Napa, CA | (30.4) |
| 256 | St. Petersburg, FL | (12.7) | 330 | Brooklyn Park, MN | (19.6) | 405 | Norman, OK | (30.5) |
| 258 | Springfield, MA | (13.0) | 330 | Roseville, CA | (19.6) | 406 | Milwaukee, WI | (30.6) |
| 259 | Everett, WA | (13.2) | 333 | Canton Twnshp, MI | (19.7) | 407 | Fall River, MA | (30.7) |
| 259 | Longmont, CO | (13.2) | 333 | Fort Collins, CO | (19.7) | 407 | Fremont, CA | (30.7) |
| 261 | Lubbock, TX | (13.3) | 333 | Rochester, MN | (19.7) | 409 | Miramar, FL | (30.8) |
| 262 | Kennewick, WA | (13.4) | 333 | Upper Darby Twnshp, PA | (19.7) | 410 | Pembroke Pines, FL | (30.9) |
| 263 | Lakewood Twnshp, NJ | (13.6) | 337 | Largo, FL | (19.8) | 411 | Irving, TX | (31.2) |
| 263 | Murfreesboro, TN | (13.6) | 337 | Nashville, TN | (19.8) | 412 | Berkeley, CA | (31.7) |
| 265 | Sugar Land, TX | (13.7) | 339 | Rialto, CA | (20.0) | 413 | Tyler, TX | (32.1) |
| 266 | Torrance, CA | (13.8) | 340 | Clifton, NJ | (20.1) | 414 | Port St. Lucie, FL | (32.6) |
| 267 | Rockford, IL | (13.9) | 341 | Austin, TX | (20.4) | 415 | McAllen, TX | (33.2) |
| 268 | Thornton, CO | (14.0) | 342 | Clarkstown, NY | (20.6) | 416 | Carmel, IN | (34.1) |
| 269 | Fargo, ND | (14.1) | 343 | High Point, NC | (20.7) | 417 | Concord, NC | (34.3) |
| 270 | Colonie, NY | (14.2) | 344 | Chino Hills, CA | (20.8) | 417 | Farmington Hills, MI | (34.3) |
| 270 | Garland, TX | (14.2) | 344 | Wilmington, NC | (20.8) | 419 | Grand Prairie, TX | (34.8) |
| 270 | South Bend, IN | (14.2) | 346 | Columbus, GA | (20.9) | 420 | Sunnyvale, CA | (35.9) |
| 273 | Springfield, IL | (14.3) | 346 | Laredo, TX | (20.9) | 421 | Trenton, NJ | (36.4) |
| 274 | Richardson, TX | (14.4) | 346 | Racine, WI | (20.9) | 422 | Longview, TX | (36.8) |
| 275 | San Mateo, CA | (14.5) | 349 | Killeen, TX | (21.0) | 423 | Aurora, IL | (39.0) |
| 276 | Alameda, CA | (14.6) | 349 | Lewisville, TX | (21.0) | 424 | Johns Creek, GA | (40.1) |
| 277 | Fontana, CA | (14.7) | 351 | Naperville, IL | (21.1) | 425 | Arlington Heights, IL | (40.8) |
| 278 | Stamford, CT | (14.8) | 351 | Wichita Falls, TX | (21.1) | 426 | College Station, TX | (41.0) |
| 279 | Chandler, AZ | (14.9) | 353 | Surprise, AZ | (21.2) | 427 | Elizabeth, NJ | (42.2) |
| 280 | Tulsa, OK | (15.0) | 354 | Mission, TX | (21.3) | 428 | Bryan, TX | (44.3) |
| 281 | Fayetteville, NC | (15.1) | 354 | Simi Valley, CA | (21.3) | 429 | Edison Twnshp, NJ | (47.2) |
| 281 | Lawrence, KS | (15.1) | 356 | Boise, ID | (21.4) | NA | Champaign, IL** | NA |
| 281 | San Antonio, TX | (15.1) | 356 | League City, TX | (21.4) | NA | Cicero, IL** | NA |
| 284 | Beaumont, TX | (15.2) | 358 | San Bernardino, CA | (21.5) | NA | Deerfield Beach, FL** | NA |
| 284 | Greece, NY | (15.2) | 359 | Lawrence, MA | (21.6) | NA | Evanston, IL** | NA |
| 284 | Mesa, AZ | (15.2) | 359 | Sunrise, FL | (21.6) | NA | Greenville, NC** | NA |
| 284 | Tacoma, WA | (15.2) | 361 | Allen, TX | (21.7) | NA | Jurupa Valley, CA** | NA |
| 288 | Elgin, IL | (15.3) | 361 | Davenport, IA | (21.7) | NA | Lowell, MA** | NA |
| 289 | Downey, CA | (15.4) | 363 | Chesapeake, VA | (21.8) | NA | Newport News, VA** | NA |
| 289 | Thousand Oaks, CA | (15.4) | 364 | El Monte, CA | (21.9) | NA | Toledo, OH** | NA |
| 291 | Cedar Rapids, IA | (15.5) | 365 | Carrollton, TX | (22.2) | NA | Tucson, AZ** | NA |
| 292 | Virginia Beach, VA | (15.6) | 366 | Plantation, FL | (22.3) | NA | Upland, CA** | NA |
| 292 | Worcester, MA | (15.6) | 367 | Troy, MI | (22.4) | NA | Waukegan, IL** | NA |
| 294 | Centennial, CO | (15.7) | 368 | Bloomington, IN | (22.5) | NA | Yakima, WA** | NA |
| 294 | St. Louis, MO | (15.7) | 369 | Plano, TX | (22.6) | | | |
| 296 | Jacksonville, FL | (15.9) | 370 | Charleston, SC | (22.7) | | | |

Source: CQ Press using reported data from the F.B.I. "Crime in the United States 2013"

*Larceny-theft is the unlawful taking of property. Attempts are included.

**Not available.

# 77. Motor Vehicle Thefts in 2013
## National Total = 699,594 Motor Vehicle Thefts*

| RANK | CITY | THEFTS | RANK | CITY | THEFTS | RANK | CITY | THEFTS |
|---|---|---|---|---|---|---|---|---|
| 256 | Abilene, TX | 254 | 247 | Chino, CA | 277 | 209 | Fullerton, CA | 359 |
| 137 | Akron, OH | 631 | 105 | Chula Vista, CA | 781 | 265 | Gainesville, FL | 244 |
| 218 | Alameda, CA | 330 | 241 | Cicero, IL | 283 | 161 | Garden Grove, CA | 539 |
| 310 | Albany, GA | 173 | 62 | Cincinnati, OH | 1,276 | 133 | Garland, TX | 647 |
| 343 | Albany, NY | 142 | 211 | Citrus Heights, CA | 345 | 118 | Gary, IN | 732 |
| 29 | Albuquerque, NM | 3,005 | 434 | Clarkstown, NY | 28 | 333 | Gilbert, AZ | 153 |
| 236 | Alexandria, VA | 291 | 328 | Clarksville, TN | 156 | 73 | Glendale, AZ | 1,050 |
| 273 | Alhambra, CA | 234 | 303 | Clearwater, FL | 181 | 262 | Glendale, CA | 251 |
| 214 | Allentown, PA | 337 | 21 | Cleveland, OH | 4,125 | 149 | Grand Prairie, TX | 590 |
| 421 | Allen, TX | 50 | 376 | Clifton, NJ | 103 | 261 | Grand Rapids, MI | 252 |
| 124 | Amarillo, TX | 695 | 273 | Clinton Twnshp, MI | 234 | 423 | Greece, NY | 46 |
| 432 | Amherst, NY | 32 | 229 | Clovis, CA | 305 | 301 | Greeley, CO | 186 |
| 52 | Anaheim, CA | 1,681 | 422 | College Station, TX | 48 | 385 | Green Bay, WI | 98 |
| 93 | Anchorage, AK | 869 | 420 | Colonie, NY | 51 | 169 | Greensboro, NC | 502 |
| 390 | Ann Arbor, MI | 94 | 46 | Colorado Springs, CO | 1,928 | 350 | Greenville, NC | 132 |
| 63 | Antioch, CA | 1,217 | 316 | Columbia, MO | 166 | 164 | Gresham, OR | 510 |
| 440 | Arlington Heights, IL | 16 | 104 | Columbia, SC | 791 | 352 | Hamilton Twnshp, NJ | 131 |
| 88 | Arlington, TX | 940 | 68 | Columbus, GA | 1,108 | 187 | Hammond, IN | 406 |
| 296 | Arvada, CO | 197 | 101 | Compton, CA | 799 | 278 | Hampton, VA | 226 |
| 297 | Athens-Clarke, GA | 195 | 108 | Concord, CA | 768 | 135 | Hartford, CT | 639 |
| 17 | Atlanta, GA | 4,432 | 378 | Concord, NC | 102 | 196 | Hawthorne, CA | 386 |
| 78 | Aurora, CO | 1,000 | 366 | Coral Springs, FL | 109 | 53 | Hayward, CA | 1,671 |
| 364 | Aurora, IL | 111 | 172 | Corona, CA | 490 | 157 | Hemet, CA | 559 |
| 40 | Austin, TX | 2,169 | 176 | Corpus Christi, TX | 487 | 162 | Henderson, NV | 537 |
| 30 | Bakersfield, CA | 2,937 | 233 | Costa Mesa, CA | 296 | 186 | Hesperia, CA | 409 |
| 206 | Baldwin Park, CA | 363 | 344 | Cranston, RI | 140 | 121 | Hialeah, FL | 708 |
| 16 | Baltimore, MD | 4,452 | 7 | Dallas, TX | 7,384 | 225 | High Point, NC | 313 |
| 166 | Baton Rouge, LA | 506 | 236 | Daly City, CA | 291 | 355 | Hillsboro, OR | 126 |
| 241 | Beaumont, TX | 283 | 412 | Danbury, CT | 64 | 152 | Hollywood, FL | 572 |
| 399 | Beaverton, OR | 83 | 268 | Davenport, IA | 239 | 370 | Hoover, AL | 108 |
| 264 | Bellevue, WA | 248 | 251 | Davie, FL | 262 | 2 | Houston, TX | 13,595 |
| 176 | Bellflower, CA | 487 | 143 | Dayton, OH | 615 | 211 | Huntington Beach, CA | 345 |
| 395 | Bend, OR | 87 | 200 | Dearborn, MI | 377 | 123 | Huntsville, AL | 703 |
| 129 | Berkeley, CA | 664 | 412 | Decatur, IL | 64 | 103 | Independence, MO | 792 |
| 426 | Bethlehem, PA | 44 | 328 | Deerfield Beach, FL | 156 | 15 | Indianapolis, IN | 5,005 |
| 160 | Billings, MT | 541 | 378 | Denton, TX | 102 | 152 | Indio, CA | 572 |
| 59 | Birmingham, AL | 1,478 | 24 | Denver, CO | 3,487 | 134 | Inglewood, CA | 640 |
| 419 | Bloomington, IL | 53 | 95 | Des Moines, IA | 850 | 337 | Irvine, CA | 149 |
| 340 | Bloomington, IN | 148 | 4 | Detroit, MI | 11,893 | 147 | Irving, TX | 594 |
| 382 | Bloomington, MN | 100 | 96 | Downey, CA | 846 | 55 | Jacksonville, FL | 1,577 |
| 390 | Boca Raton, FL | 94 | 328 | Duluth, MN | 156 | 72 | Jackson, MS | 1,054 |
| 284 | Boise, ID | 213 | 255 | Edinburg, TX | 255 | 116 | Jersey City, NJ | 738 |
| 54 | Boston, MA | 1,610 | 372 | Edison Twnshp, NJ | 106 | 441 | Johns Creek, GA | 15 |
| 382 | Boulder, CO | 100 | 417 | Edmond, OK | 56 | 328 | Joliet, IL | 156 |
| 437 | Brick Twnshp, NJ | 20 | 182 | El Cajon, CA | 462 | 112 | Jurupa Valley, CA | 763 |
| 131 | Bridgeport, CT | 663 | 151 | El Monte, CA | 576 | 74 | Kansas City, KS | 1,045 |
| 280 | Brockton, MA | 224 | 102 | El Paso, TX | 794 | 20 | Kansas City, MO | 4,287 |
| 348 | Broken Arrow, OK | 135 | 393 | Elgin, IL | 89 | 327 | Kennewick, WA | 158 |
| 324 | Brooklyn Park, MN | 160 | 77 | Elizabeth, NJ | 1,001 | 402 | Kenosha, WI | 73 |
| 252 | Brownsville, TX | 257 | 300 | Elk Grove, CA | 190 | 92 | Kent, WA | 870 |
| 393 | Bryan, TX | 89 | 385 | Erie, PA | 98 | 287 | Killeen, TX | 206 |
| 204 | Buena Park, CA | 369 | 106 | Escondido, CA | 772 | 115 | Knoxville, TN | 739 |
| 85 | Buffalo, NY | 957 | 146 | Eugene, OR | 608 | 231 | Lafayette, LA | 297 |
| 283 | Burbank, CA | 219 | 411 | Evanston, IL | 67 | 428 | Lake Forest, CA | 43 |
| 374 | Cambridge, MA | 104 | 171 | Evansville, IN | 492 | 295 | Lakeland, FL | 198 |
| 366 | Canton Twnshp, MI | 109 | 75 | Everett, WA | 1,034 | 426 | Lakewood Twnshp, NJ | 44 |
| 342 | Cape Coral, FL | 145 | 139 | Fairfield, CA | 629 | 238 | Lakewood, CA | 287 |
| 356 | Carlsbad, CA | 124 | 281 | Fall River, MA | 223 | 140 | Lakewood, CO | 623 |
| 428 | Carmel, IN | 43 | 316 | Fargo, ND | 166 | 189 | Lancaster, CA | 403 |
| 287 | Carrollton, TX | 206 | 388 | Farmington Hills, MI | 96 | 206 | Lansing, MI | 363 |
| 174 | Carson, CA | 489 | 324 | Fayetteville, AR | 160 | 202 | Laredo, TX | 372 |
| 415 | Cary, NC | 60 | 137 | Fayetteville, NC | 631 | 344 | Largo, FL | 140 |
| 231 | Cedar Rapids, IA | 297 | 111 | Federal Way, WA | 764 | 312 | Las Cruces, NM | 171 |
| 406 | Centennial, CO | 72 | 433 | Fishers, IN | 29 | 9 | Las Vegas, NV | 6,635 |
| 407 | Champaign, IL | 71 | 223 | Flint, MI | 320 | 310 | Lawrence, KS | 173 |
| 246 | Chandler, AZ | 279 | 79 | Fontana, CA | 999 | 99 | Lawrence, MA | 828 |
| 323 | Charleston, SC | 162 | 344 | Fort Collins, CO | 140 | 277 | Lawton, OK | 229 |
| 49 | Charlotte, NC | 1,856 | 155 | Fort Lauderdale, FL | 567 | 417 | League City, TX | 56 |
| 80 | Chattanooga, TN | 986 | 293 | Fort Smith, AR | 199 | 366 | Lee's Summit, MO | 109 |
| 402 | Cheektowaga, NY | 73 | 196 | Fort Wayne, IN | 386 | 230 | Lewisville, TX | 299 |
| 244 | Chesapeake, VA | 280 | 35 | Fort Worth, TX | 2,399 | 98 | Lexington, KY | 831 |
| 3 | Chicago, IL | 12,636 | 128 | Fremont, CA | 669 | 228 | Lincoln, NE | 306 |
| 199 | Chico, CA | 382 | 23 | Fresno, CA | 4,057 | 70 | Little Rock, AR | 1,080 |
| 395 | Chino Hills, CA | 87 | 416 | Frisco, TX | 58 | 314 | Livermore, CA | 168 |

| RANK | CITY | THEFTS | RANK | CITY | THEFTS | RANK | CITY | THEFTS |
|---|---|---|---|---|---|---|---|---|
| 307 | Livonia, MI | 178 | 238 | Pasadena, CA | 287 | 90 | South Gate, CA | 913 |
| 37 | Long Beach, CA | 2,355 | 164 | Pasadena, TX | 510 | 257 | Sparks, NV | 253 |
| 366 | Longmont, CO | 109 | 114 | Paterson, NJ | 749 | 172 | Spokane Valley, WA | 490 |
| 292 | Longview, TX | 200 | 382 | Pearland, TX | 100 | 38 | Spokane, WA | 2,290 |
| 1 | Los Angeles, CA | 14,382 | 287 | Pembroke Pines, FL | 206 | 316 | Springfield, IL | 166 |
| 43 | Louisville, KY | 2,025 | 286 | Peoria, AZ | 207 | 117 | Springfield, MA | 735 |
| 223 | Lowell, MA | 320 | 298 | Peoria, IL | 194 | 66 | Springfield, MO | 1,146 |
| 96 | Lubbock, TX | 846 | 14 | Philadelphia, PA | 5,791 | 337 | Stamford, CT | 149 |
| 395 | Lynchburg, VA | 87 | 11 | Phoenix, AZ | 6,355 | 293 | Sterling Heights, MI | 199 |
| 257 | Lynn, MA | 253 | 142 | Pittsburgh, PA | 616 | 41 | Stockton, CA | 2,143 |
| 174 | Macon, GA | 489 | 254 | Plano, TX | 256 | 408 | St. George, UT | 69 |
| 257 | Madison, WI | 253 | 337 | Plantation, FL | 149 | 233 | St. Joseph, MO | 296 |
| 326 | Manchester, NH | 159 | 86 | Pomona, CA | 956 | 25 | St. Louis, MO | 3,330 |
| 270 | McAllen, TX | 236 | 219 | Pompano Beach, FL | 329 | 50 | St. Paul, MN | 1,761 |
| 354 | McKinney, TX | 129 | 402 | Port St. Lucie, FL | 73 | 67 | St. Petersburg, FL | 1,124 |
| 321 | Medford, OR | 163 | 26 | Portland, OR | 3,289 | 378 | Suffolk, VA | 102 |
| 365 | Melbourne, FL | 110 | 291 | Portsmouth, VA | 205 | 423 | Sugar Land, TX | 46 |
| 34 | Memphis, TN | 2,684 | 84 | Providence, RI | 962 | 188 | Sunnyvale, CA | 404 |
| 226 | Menifee, CA | 310 | 370 | Provo, UT | 108 | 356 | Sunrise, FL | 124 |
| 193 | Merced, CA | 395 | 163 | Pueblo, CO | 528 | 341 | Surprise, AZ | 146 |
| 435 | Meridian, ID | 25 | 402 | Quincy, MA | 73 | 194 | Syracuse, NY | 394 |
| 87 | Mesa, AZ | 952 | 389 | Racine, WI | 95 | 44 | Tacoma, WA | 2,024 |
| 110 | Mesquite, TX | 766 | 122 | Raleigh, NC | 705 | 184 | Tallahassee, FL | 440 |
| 201 | Miami Beach, FL | 376 | 442 | Ramapo, NY | 13 | 158 | Tampa, FL | 553 |
| 179 | Miami Gardens, FL | 478 | 179 | Rancho Cucamon., CA | 478 | 266 | Temecula, CA | 240 |
| 47 | Miami, FL | 1,914 | 235 | Reading, PA | 294 | 176 | Tempe, AZ | 487 |
| 320 | Midland, TX | 164 | 159 | Redding, CA | 549 | 210 | Thornton, CO | 352 |
| 18 | Milwaukee, WI | 4,384 | 278 | Redwood City, CA | 226 | 392 | Thousand Oaks, CA | 91 |
| 56 | Minneapolis, MN | 1,575 | 94 | Reno, NV | 868 | 71 | Toledo, OH | 1,064 |
| 275 | Miramar, FL | 232 | 126 | Renton, WA | 683 | 436 | Toms River Twnshp, NJ | 23 |
| 430 | Mission Viejo, CA | 40 | 107 | Rialto, CA | 771 | 154 | Topeka, KS | 569 |
| 309 | Mission, TX | 177 | 334 | Richardson, TX | 151 | 208 | Torrance, CA | 362 |
| 127 | Mobile, AL | 681 | 57 | Richmond, CA | 1,510 | 272 | Tracy, CA | 235 |
| 61 | Modesto, CA | 1,389 | 89 | Richmond, VA | 938 | 185 | Trenton, NJ | 416 |
| 100 | Moreno Valley, CA | 826 | 51 | Riverside, CA | 1,718 | 400 | Troy, MI | 78 |
| 348 | Mountain View, CA | 135 | 304 | Roanoke, VA | 180 | 39 | Tucson, AZ | 2,190 |
| 307 | Murfreesboro, TN | 178 | 376 | Rochester, MN | 103 | 36 | Tulsa, OK | 2,389 |
| 287 | Murrieta, CA | 206 | 145 | Rochester, NY | 609 | 334 | Tuscaloosa, AL | 151 |
| 359 | Nampa, ID | 123 | 202 | Rockford, IL | 372 | 363 | Tustin, CA | 113 |
| 353 | Napa, CA | 130 | 269 | Roseville, CA | 238 | 304 | Tyler, TX | 180 |
| 431 | Naperville, IL | 34 | 401 | Roswell, GA | 75 | 191 | Upland, CA | 399 |
| 410 | Nashua, NH | 68 | 425 | Round Rock, TX | 45 | 344 | Upper Darby Twnshp, PA | 140 |
| 65 | Nashville, TN | 1,197 | 32 | Sacramento, CA | 2,861 | 276 | Vacaville, CA | 231 |
| 216 | New Bedford, MA | 335 | 132 | Salem, OR | 656 | 64 | Vallejo, CA | 1,209 |
| 113 | New Haven, CT | 753 | 58 | Salinas, CA | 1,488 | 83 | Vancouver, WA | 976 |
| 41 | New Orleans, LA | 2,143 | 48 | Salt Lake City, UT | 1,876 | 252 | Ventura, CA | 257 |
| 408 | New Rochelle, NY | 69 | 302 | San Angelo, TX | 185 | 136 | Victorville, CA | 637 |
| 6 | New York, NY | 7,434 | 10 | San Antonio, TX | 6,577 | 183 | Virginia Beach, VA | 445 |
| 31 | Newark, NJ | 2,894 | 33 | San Bernardino, CA | 2,691 | 141 | Visalia, CA | 619 |
| 374 | Newport Beach, CA | 104 | 12 | San Diego, CA | 6,143 | 219 | Vista, CA | 329 |
| 213 | Newport News, VA | 344 | 13 | San Francisco, CA | 5,866 | 321 | Waco, TX | 163 |
| 439 | Newton, MA | 18 | 5 | San Jose, CA | 7,926 | 150 | Warren, MI | 584 |
| 109 | Norfolk, VA | 767 | 91 | San Leandro, CA | 912 | 398 | Warwick, RI | 85 |
| 314 | Norman, OK | 168 | 313 | San Marcos, CA | 170 | 27 | Washington, DC | 3,147 |
| 168 | North Charleston, SC | 503 | 332 | San Mateo, CA | 155 | 125 | Waterbury, CT | 689 |
| 81 | North Las Vegas, NV | 983 | 336 | Sandy Springs, GA | 150 | 414 | Waukegan, IL | 62 |
| 156 | Norwalk, CA | 564 | 299 | Sandy, UT | 193 | 170 | West Covina, CA | 501 |
| 372 | Norwalk, CT | 106 | 60 | Santa Ana, CA | 1,459 | 196 | West Palm Beach, FL | 386 |
| 8 | Oakland, CA | 6,833 | 360 | Santa Barbara, CA | 120 | 82 | West Valley, UT | 981 |
| 190 | Oceanside, CA | 400 | 195 | Santa Clara, CA | 393 | 243 | Westland, MI | 282 |
| 181 | Odessa, TX | 463 | 263 | Santa Clarita, CA | 249 | 215 | Westminster, CA | 336 |
| 437 | O'Fallon, MO | 20 | 119 | Santa Maria, CA | 730 | 222 | Westminster, CO | 322 |
| 248 | Ogden, UT | 274 | 319 | Santa Monica, CA | 165 | 257 | Whittier, CA | 253 |
| 22 | Oklahoma City, OK | 4,076 | 227 | Santa Rosa, CA | 309 | 240 | Wichita Falls, TX | 286 |
| 306 | Olathe, KS | 179 | 120 | Savannah, GA | 725 | 45 | Wichita, KS | 1,984 |
| 28 | Omaha, NE | 3,080 | 285 | Scottsdale, AZ | 208 | 216 | Wilmington, NC | 335 |
| 69 | Ontario, CA | 1,091 | 362 | Scranton, PA | 114 | 144 | Winston-Salem, NC | 611 |
| 249 | Orange, CA | 272 | 19 | Seattle, WA | 4,310 | 356 | Woodbridge Twnshp, NJ | 124 |
| 385 | Orem, UT | 98 | 167 | Shreveport, LA | 504 | 191 | Worcester, MA | 399 |
| 76 | Orlando, FL | 1,020 | 350 | Simi Valley, CA | 132 | 147 | Yakima, WA | 594 |
| 244 | Overland Park, KS | 280 | 266 | Sioux City, IA | 240 | 270 | Yonkers, NY | 236 |
| 129 | Oxnard, CA | 664 | 250 | Sioux Falls, SD | 264 | 282 | Yuma, AZ | 222 |
| 361 | Palm Bay, FL | 115 | 381 | Somerville, MA | 101 | | | |
| 205 | Palmdale, CA | 367 | 221 | South Bend, IN | 326 | | | |

Source: Reported data from the F.B.I. "Crime in the United States 2013"

*Motor vehicle theft includes the theft or attempted theft of a self-propelled vehicle. Excludes motorboats, construction equipment, airplanes, and farming equipment.

# 77. Motor Vehicle Thefts in 2013 (continued)
## National Total = 699,594 Motor Vehicle Thefts*

| RANK | CITY | THEFTS | RANK | CITY | THEFTS | RANK | CITY | THEFTS |
|---|---|---|---|---|---|---|---|---|
| 1 | Los Angeles, CA | 14,382 | 75 | Everett, WA | 1,034 | 149 | Grand Prairie, TX | 590 |
| 2 | Houston, TX | 13,595 | 76 | Orlando, FL | 1,020 | 150 | Warren, MI | 584 |
| 3 | Chicago, IL | 12,636 | 77 | Elizabeth, NJ | 1,001 | 151 | El Monte, CA | 576 |
| 4 | Detroit, MI | 11,893 | 78 | Aurora, CO | 1,000 | 152 | Hollywood, FL | 572 |
| 5 | San Jose, CA | 7,926 | 79 | Fontana, CA | 999 | 152 | Indio, CA | 572 |
| 6 | New York, NY | 7,434 | 80 | Chattanooga, TN | 986 | 154 | Topeka, KS | 569 |
| 7 | Dallas, TX | 7,384 | 81 | North Las Vegas, NV | 983 | 155 | Fort Lauderdale, FL | 567 |
| 8 | Oakland, CA | 6,833 | 82 | West Valley, UT | 981 | 156 | Norwalk, CA | 564 |
| 9 | Las Vegas, NV | 6,635 | 83 | Vancouver, WA | 976 | 157 | Hemet, CA | 559 |
| 10 | San Antonio, TX | 6,577 | 84 | Providence, RI | 962 | 158 | Tampa, FL | 553 |
| 11 | Phoenix, AZ | 6,355 | 85 | Buffalo, NY | 957 | 159 | Redding, CA | 549 |
| 12 | San Diego, CA | 6,143 | 86 | Pomona, CA | 956 | 160 | Billings, MT | 541 |
| 13 | San Francisco, CA | 5,866 | 87 | Mesa, AZ | 952 | 161 | Garden Grove, CA | 539 |
| 14 | Philadelphia, PA | 5,791 | 88 | Arlington, TX | 940 | 162 | Henderson, NV | 537 |
| 15 | Indianapolis, IN | 5,005 | 89 | Richmond, VA | 938 | 163 | Pueblo, CO | 528 |
| 16 | Baltimore, MD | 4,452 | 90 | South Gate, CA | 913 | 164 | Gresham, OR | 510 |
| 17 | Atlanta, GA | 4,432 | 91 | San Leandro, CA | 912 | 164 | Pasadena, TX | 510 |
| 18 | Milwaukee, WI | 4,384 | 92 | Kent, WA | 870 | 166 | Baton Rouge, LA | 506 |
| 19 | Seattle, WA | 4,310 | 93 | Anchorage, AK | 869 | 167 | Shreveport, LA | 504 |
| 20 | Kansas City, MO | 4,287 | 94 | Reno, NV | 868 | 168 | North Charleston, SC | 503 |
| 21 | Cleveland, OH | 4,125 | 95 | Des Moines, IA | 850 | 169 | Greensboro, NC | 502 |
| 22 | Oklahoma City, OK | 4,076 | 96 | Downey, CA | 846 | 170 | West Covina, CA | 501 |
| 23 | Fresno, CA | 4,057 | 96 | Lubbock, TX | 846 | 171 | Evansville, IN | 492 |
| 24 | Denver, CO | 3,487 | 98 | Lexington, KY | 831 | 172 | Corona, CA | 490 |
| 25 | St. Louis, MO | 3,330 | 99 | Lawrence, MA | 828 | 172 | Spokane Valley, WA | 490 |
| 26 | Portland, OR | 3,289 | 100 | Moreno Valley, CA | 826 | 174 | Carson, CA | 489 |
| 27 | Washington, DC | 3,147 | 101 | Compton, CA | 799 | 174 | Macon, GA | 489 |
| 28 | Omaha, NE | 3,080 | 102 | El Paso, TX | 794 | 176 | Bellflower, CA | 487 |
| 29 | Albuquerque, NM | 3,005 | 103 | Independence, MO | 792 | 176 | Corpus Christi, TX | 487 |
| 30 | Bakersfield, CA | 2,937 | 104 | Columbia, SC | 791 | 176 | Tempe, AZ | 487 |
| 31 | Newark, NJ | 2,894 | 105 | Chula Vista, CA | 781 | 179 | Miami Gardens, FL | 478 |
| 32 | Sacramento, CA | 2,861 | 106 | Escondido, CA | 772 | 179 | Rancho Cucamon., CA | 478 |
| 33 | San Bernardino, CA | 2,691 | 107 | Rialto, CA | 771 | 181 | Odessa, TX | 463 |
| 34 | Memphis, TN | 2,684 | 108 | Concord, CA | 768 | 182 | El Cajon, CA | 462 |
| 35 | Fort Worth, TX | 2,399 | 109 | Norfolk, VA | 767 | 183 | Virginia Beach, VA | 445 |
| 36 | Tulsa, OK | 2,389 | 110 | Mesquite, TX | 766 | 184 | Tallahassee, FL | 440 |
| 37 | Long Beach, CA | 2,355 | 111 | Federal Way, WA | 764 | 185 | Trenton, NJ | 416 |
| 38 | Spokane, WA | 2,290 | 112 | Jurupa Valley, CA | 763 | 186 | Hesperia, CA | 409 |
| 39 | Tucson, AZ | 2,190 | 113 | New Haven, CT | 753 | 187 | Hammond, IN | 406 |
| 40 | Austin, TX | 2,169 | 114 | Paterson, NJ | 749 | 188 | Sunnyvale, CA | 404 |
| 41 | New Orleans, LA | 2,143 | 115 | Knoxville, TN | 739 | 189 | Lancaster, CA | 403 |
| 41 | Stockton, CA | 2,143 | 116 | Jersey City, NJ | 738 | 190 | Oceanside, CA | 400 |
| 43 | Louisville, KY | 2,025 | 117 | Springfield, MA | 735 | 191 | Upland, CA | 399 |
| 44 | Tacoma, WA | 2,024 | 118 | Gary, IN | 732 | 191 | Worcester, MA | 399 |
| 45 | Wichita, KS | 1,984 | 119 | Santa Maria, CA | 730 | 193 | Merced, CA | 395 |
| 46 | Colorado Springs, CO | 1,928 | 120 | Savannah, GA | 725 | 194 | Syracuse, NY | 394 |
| 47 | Miami, FL | 1,914 | 121 | Hialeah, FL | 708 | 195 | Santa Clara, CA | 393 |
| 48 | Salt Lake City, UT | 1,876 | 122 | Raleigh, NC | 705 | 196 | Fort Wayne, IN | 386 |
| 49 | Charlotte, NC | 1,856 | 123 | Huntsville, AL | 703 | 196 | Hawthorne, CA | 386 |
| 50 | St. Paul, MN | 1,761 | 124 | Amarillo, TX | 695 | 196 | West Palm Beach, FL | 386 |
| 51 | Riverside, CA | 1,718 | 125 | Waterbury, CT | 689 | 199 | Chico, CA | 382 |
| 52 | Anaheim, CA | 1,681 | 126 | Renton, WA | 683 | 200 | Dearborn, MI | 377 |
| 53 | Hayward, CA | 1,671 | 127 | Mobile, AL | 681 | 201 | Miami Beach, FL | 376 |
| 54 | Boston, MA | 1,610 | 128 | Fremont, CA | 669 | 202 | Laredo, TX | 372 |
| 55 | Jacksonville, FL | 1,577 | 129 | Berkeley, CA | 664 | 202 | Rockford, IL | 372 |
| 56 | Minneapolis, MN | 1,575 | 129 | Oxnard, CA | 664 | 204 | Buena Park, CA | 369 |
| 57 | Richmond, CA | 1,510 | 131 | Bridgeport, CT | 663 | 205 | Palmdale, CA | 367 |
| 58 | Salinas, CA | 1,488 | 132 | Salem, OR | 656 | 206 | Baldwin Park, CA | 363 |
| 59 | Birmingham, AL | 1,478 | 133 | Garland, TX | 647 | 206 | Lansing, MI | 363 |
| 60 | Santa Ana, CA | 1,459 | 134 | Inglewood, CA | 640 | 208 | Torrance, CA | 362 |
| 61 | Modesto, CA | 1,389 | 135 | Hartford, CT | 639 | 209 | Fullerton, CA | 359 |
| 62 | Cincinnati, OH | 1,276 | 136 | Victorville, CA | 637 | 210 | Thornton, CO | 352 |
| 63 | Antioch, CA | 1,217 | 137 | Akron, OH | 631 | 211 | Citrus Heights, CA | 345 |
| 64 | Vallejo, CA | 1,209 | 137 | Fayetteville, NC | 631 | 211 | Huntington Beach, CA | 345 |
| 65 | Nashville, TN | 1,197 | 139 | Fairfield, CA | 629 | 213 | Newport News, VA | 344 |
| 66 | Springfield, MO | 1,146 | 140 | Lakewood, CO | 623 | 214 | Allentown, PA | 337 |
| 67 | St. Petersburg, FL | 1,124 | 141 | Visalia, CA | 619 | 215 | Westminster, CA | 336 |
| 68 | Columbus, GA | 1,108 | 142 | Pittsburgh, PA | 616 | 216 | New Bedford, MA | 335 |
| 69 | Ontario, CA | 1,091 | 143 | Dayton, OH | 615 | 216 | Wilmington, NC | 335 |
| 70 | Little Rock, AR | 1,080 | 144 | Winston-Salem, NC | 611 | 218 | Alameda, CA | 330 |
| 71 | Toledo, OH | 1,064 | 145 | Rochester, NY | 609 | 219 | Pompano Beach, FL | 329 |
| 72 | Jackson, MS | 1,054 | 146 | Eugene, OR | 608 | 219 | Vista, CA | 329 |
| 73 | Glendale, AZ | 1,050 | 147 | Irving, TX | 594 | 221 | South Bend, IN | 326 |
| 74 | Kansas City, KS | 1,045 | 147 | Yakima, WA | 594 | 222 | Westminster, CO | 322 |

| RANK | CITY | THEFTS | RANK | CITY | THEFTS | RANK | CITY | THEFTS |
|---|---|---|---|---|---|---|---|---|
| 223 | Flint, MI | 320 | 297 | Athens-Clarke, GA | 195 | 370 | Provo, UT | 108 |
| 223 | Lowell, MA | 320 | 298 | Peoria, IL | 194 | 372 | Edison Twnshp, NJ | 106 |
| 225 | High Point, NC | 313 | 299 | Sandy, UT | 193 | 372 | Norwalk, CT | 106 |
| 226 | Menifee, CA | 310 | 300 | Elk Grove, CA | 190 | 374 | Cambridge, MA | 104 |
| 227 | Santa Rosa, CA | 309 | 301 | Greeley, CO | 186 | 374 | Newport Beach, CA | 104 |
| 228 | Lincoln, NE | 306 | 302 | San Angelo, TX | 185 | 376 | Clifton, NJ | 103 |
| 229 | Clovis, CA | 305 | 303 | Clearwater, FL | 181 | 376 | Rochester, MN | 103 |
| 230 | Lewisville, TX | 299 | 304 | Roanoke, VA | 180 | 378 | Concord, NC | 102 |
| 231 | Cedar Rapids, IA | 297 | 304 | Tyler, TX | 180 | 378 | Denton, TX | 102 |
| 231 | Lafayette, LA | 297 | 306 | Olathe, KS | 179 | 378 | Suffolk, VA | 102 |
| 233 | Costa Mesa, CA | 296 | 307 | Livonia, MI | 178 | 381 | Somerville, MA | 101 |
| 233 | St. Joseph, MO | 296 | 307 | Murfreesboro, TN | 178 | 382 | Bloomington, MN | 100 |
| 235 | Reading, PA | 294 | 309 | Mission, TX | 177 | 382 | Boulder, CO | 100 |
| 236 | Alexandria, VA | 291 | 310 | Albany, GA | 173 | 382 | Pearland, TX | 100 |
| 236 | Daly City, CA | 291 | 310 | Lawrence, KS | 173 | 385 | Erie, PA | 98 |
| 238 | Lakewood, CA | 287 | 312 | Las Cruces, NM | 171 | 385 | Green Bay, WI | 98 |
| 238 | Pasadena, CA | 287 | 313 | San Marcos, CA | 170 | 385 | Orem, UT | 98 |
| 240 | Wichita Falls, TX | 286 | 314 | Livermore, CA | 168 | 388 | Farmington Hills, MI | 96 |
| 241 | Beaumont, TX | 283 | 314 | Norman, OK | 168 | 389 | Racine, WI | 95 |
| 241 | Cicero, IL | 283 | 316 | Columbia, MO | 166 | 390 | Ann Arbor, MI | 94 |
| 243 | Westland, MI | 282 | 316 | Fargo, ND | 166 | 390 | Boca Raton, FL | 94 |
| 244 | Chesapeake, VA | 280 | 316 | Springfield, IL | 166 | 392 | Thousand Oaks, CA | 91 |
| 244 | Overland Park, KS | 280 | 319 | Santa Monica, CA | 165 | 393 | Bryan, TX | 89 |
| 246 | Chandler, AZ | 279 | 320 | Midland, TX | 164 | 393 | Elgin, IL | 89 |
| 247 | Chino, CA | 277 | 321 | Medford, OR | 163 | 395 | Bend, OR | 87 |
| 248 | Ogden, UT | 274 | 321 | Waco, TX | 163 | 395 | Chino Hills, CA | 87 |
| 249 | Orange, CA | 272 | 323 | Charleston, SC | 162 | 395 | Lynchburg, VA | 87 |
| 250 | Sioux Falls, SD | 264 | 324 | Brooklyn Park, MN | 160 | 398 | Warwick, RI | 85 |
| 251 | Davie, FL | 262 | 324 | Fayetteville, AR | 160 | 399 | Beaverton, OR | 83 |
| 252 | Brownsville, TX | 257 | 326 | Manchester, NH | 159 | 400 | Troy, MI | 78 |
| 252 | Ventura, CA | 257 | 327 | Kennewick, WA | 158 | 401 | Roswell, GA | 75 |
| 254 | Plano, TX | 256 | 328 | Clarksville, TN | 156 | 402 | Cheektowaga, NY | 73 |
| 255 | Edinburg, TX | 255 | 328 | Deerfield Beach, FL | 156 | 402 | Kenosha, WI | 73 |
| 256 | Abilene, TX | 254 | 328 | Duluth, MN | 156 | 402 | Port St. Lucie, FL | 73 |
| 257 | Lynn, MA | 253 | 328 | Joliet, IL | 156 | 402 | Quincy, MA | 73 |
| 257 | Madison, WI | 253 | 332 | San Mateo, CA | 155 | 406 | Centennial, CO | 72 |
| 257 | Sparks, NV | 253 | 333 | Gilbert, AZ | 153 | 407 | Champaign, IL | 71 |
| 257 | Whittier, CA | 253 | 334 | Richardson, TX | 151 | 408 | New Rochelle, NY | 69 |
| 261 | Grand Rapids, MI | 252 | 334 | Tuscaloosa, AL | 151 | 408 | St. George, UT | 69 |
| 262 | Glendale, CA | 251 | 336 | Sandy Springs, GA | 150 | 410 | Nashua, NH | 68 |
| 263 | Santa Clarita, CA | 249 | 337 | Irvine, CA | 149 | 411 | Evanston, IL | 67 |
| 264 | Bellevue, WA | 248 | 337 | Plantation, FL | 149 | 412 | Danbury, CT | 64 |
| 265 | Gainesville, FL | 244 | 337 | Stamford, CT | 149 | 412 | Decatur, IL | 64 |
| 266 | Sioux City, IA | 240 | 340 | Bloomington, IN | 148 | 414 | Waukegan, IL | 62 |
| 266 | Temecula, CA | 240 | 341 | Surprise, AZ | 146 | 415 | Cary, NC | 60 |
| 268 | Davenport, IA | 239 | 342 | Cape Coral, FL | 145 | 416 | Frisco, TX | 58 |
| 269 | Roseville, CA | 238 | 343 | Albany, NY | 142 | 417 | Edmond, OK | 56 |
| 270 | McAllen, TX | 236 | 344 | Cranston, RI | 140 | 417 | League City, TX | 56 |
| 270 | Yonkers, NY | 236 | 344 | Fort Collins, CO | 140 | 419 | Bloomington, IL | 53 |
| 272 | Tracy, CA | 235 | 344 | Largo, FL | 140 | 420 | Colonie, NY | 51 |
| 273 | Alhambra, CA | 234 | 344 | Upper Darby Twnshp, PA | 140 | 421 | Allen, TX | 50 |
| 273 | Clinton Twnshp, MI | 234 | 348 | Broken Arrow, OK | 135 | 422 | College Station, TX | 48 |
| 275 | Miramar, FL | 232 | 348 | Mountain View, CA | 135 | 423 | Greece, NY | 46 |
| 276 | Vacaville, CA | 231 | 350 | Greenville, NC | 132 | 423 | Sugar Land, TX | 46 |
| 277 | Lawton, OK | 229 | 350 | Simi Valley, CA | 132 | 425 | Round Rock, TX | 45 |
| 278 | Hampton, VA | 226 | 352 | Hamilton Twnshp, NJ | 131 | 426 | Bethlehem, PA | 44 |
| 278 | Redwood City, CA | 226 | 353 | Napa, CA | 130 | 426 | Lakewood Twnshp, NJ | 44 |
| 280 | Brockton, MA | 224 | 354 | McKinney, TX | 129 | 428 | Carmel, IN | 43 |
| 281 | Fall River, MA | 223 | 355 | Hillsboro, OR | 126 | 428 | Lake Forest, CA | 43 |
| 282 | Yuma, AZ | 222 | 356 | Carlsbad, CA | 124 | 430 | Mission Viejo, CA | 40 |
| 283 | Burbank, CA | 219 | 356 | Sunrise, FL | 124 | 431 | Naperville, IL | 34 |
| 284 | Boise, ID | 213 | 356 | Woodbridge Twnshp, NJ | 124 | 432 | Amherst, NY | 32 |
| 285 | Scottsdale, AZ | 208 | 359 | Nampa, ID | 123 | 433 | Fishers, IN | 29 |
| 286 | Peoria, AZ | 207 | 360 | Santa Barbara, CA | 120 | 434 | Clarkstown, NY | 28 |
| 287 | Carrollton, TX | 206 | 361 | Palm Bay, FL | 115 | 435 | Meridian, ID | 25 |
| 287 | Killeen, TX | 206 | 362 | Scranton, PA | 114 | 436 | Toms River Twnshp, NJ | 23 |
| 287 | Murrieta, CA | 206 | 363 | Tustin, CA | 113 | 437 | Brick Twnshp, NJ | 20 |
| 287 | Pembroke Pines, FL | 206 | 364 | Aurora, IL | 111 | 437 | O'Fallon, MO | 20 |
| 291 | Portsmouth, VA | 205 | 365 | Melbourne, FL | 110 | 439 | Newton, MA | 18 |
| 292 | Longview, TX | 200 | 366 | Canton Twnshp, MI | 109 | 440 | Arlington Heights, IL | 16 |
| 293 | Fort Smith, AR | 199 | 366 | Coral Springs, FL | 109 | 441 | Johns Creek, GA | 15 |
| 293 | Sterling Heights, MI | 199 | 366 | Lee's Summit, MO | 109 | 442 | Ramapo, NY | 13 |
| 295 | Lakeland, FL | 198 | 366 | Longmont, CO | 109 | | | |
| 296 | Arvada, CO | 197 | 370 | Hoover, AL | 108 | | | |

Source: Reported data from the F.B.I. "Crime in the United States 2013"

*Motor vehicle theft includes the theft or attempted theft of a self-propelled vehicle. Excludes motorboats, construction equipment, airplanes, and farming equipment.

# 78. Motor Vehicle Theft Rate in 2013
## National Rate = 221.3 Motor Vehicle Thefts per 100,000 Population*

| RANK | CITY | RATE | RANK | CITY | RATE | RANK | CITY | RATE |
|---|---|---|---|---|---|---|---|---|
| 249 | Abilene, TX | 212.7 | 159 | Chino, CA | 343.2 | 218 | Fullerton, CA | 257.0 |
| 173 | Akron, OH | 318.0 | 181 | Chula Vista, CA | 306.2 | 268 | Gainesville, FL | 192.7 |
| 124 | Alameda, CA | 433.0 | 162 | Cicero, IL | 336.1 | 179 | Garden Grove, CA | 307.2 |
| 243 | Albany, GA | 223.6 | 126 | Cincinnati, OH | 430.4 | 207 | Garland, TX | 274.5 |
| 318 | Albany, NY | 145.0 | 138 | Citrus Heights, CA | 404.3 | 20 | Gary, IN | 928.7 |
| 76 | Albuquerque, NM | 538.4 | 432 | Clarkstown, NY | 34.7 | 411 | Gilbert, AZ | 67.9 |
| 263 | Alexandria, VA | 195.9 | 369 | Clarksville, TN | 107.1 | 112 | Glendale, AZ | 448.7 |
| 204 | Alhambra, CA | 276.2 | 295 | Clearwater, FL | 166.2 | 335 | Glendale, CA | 128.5 |
| 200 | Allentown, PA | 282.5 | 9 | Cleveland, OH | 1,059.9 | 170 | Grand Prairie, TX | 321.0 |
| 420 | Allen, TX | 54.8 | 348 | Clifton, NJ | 121.1 | 331 | Grand Rapids, MI | 131.8 |
| 157 | Amarillo, TX | 353.6 | 231 | Clinton Twnshp, MI | 238.6 | 424 | Greece, NY | 47.6 |
| 434 | Amherst, NY | 27.1 | 180 | Clovis, CA | 306.6 | 267 | Greeley, CO | 193.5 |
| 96 | Anaheim, CA | 486.8 | 423 | College Station, TX | 48.5 | 385 | Green Bay, WI | 93.2 |
| 195 | Anchorage, AK | 290.2 | 413 | Colonie, NY | 65.2 | 281 | Greensboro, NC | 179.7 |
| 402 | Ann Arbor, MI | 80.5 | 117 | Colorado Springs, CO | 442.1 | 313 | Greenville, NC | 150.0 |
| 5 | Antioch, CA | 1,143.3 | 319 | Columbia, MO | 144.9 | 106 | Gresham, OR | 463.8 |
| 439 | Arlington Heights, IL | 21.1 | 60 | Columbia, SC | 598.2 | 316 | Hamilton Twnshp, NJ | 147.2 |
| 224 | Arlington, TX | 248.2 | 71 | Columbus, GA | 550.8 | 88 | Hammond, IN | 511.8 |
| 285 | Arvada, CO | 177.8 | 23 | Compton, CA | 816.1 | 297 | Hampton, VA | 165.0 |
| 300 | Athens-Clarke, GA | 162.3 | 55 | Concord, CA | 612.1 | 89 | Hartford, CT | 511.5 |
| 17 | Atlanta, GA | 982.7 | 342 | Concord, NC | 123.0 | 113 | Hawthorne, CA | 448.1 |
| 193 | Aurora, CO | 291.1 | 397 | Coral Springs, FL | 86.1 | 6 | Hayward, CA | 1,107.0 |
| 418 | Aurora, IL | 55.3 | 182 | Corona, CA | 305.9 | 44 | Hemet, CA | 684.2 |
| 219 | Austin, TX | 252.5 | 305 | Corpus Christi, TX | 154.8 | 258 | Henderson, NV | 200.2 |
| 24 | Bakersfield, CA | 811.6 | 215 | Costa Mesa, CA | 263.0 | 118 | Hesperia, CA | 441.6 |
| 102 | Baldwin Park, CA | 473.0 | 289 | Cranston, RI | 173.4 | 184 | Hialeah, FL | 302.3 |
| 35 | Baltimore, MD | 715.0 | 63 | Dallas, TX | 588.4 | 192 | High Point, NC | 291.8 |
| 245 | Baton Rouge, LA | 219.8 | 202 | Daly City, CA | 278.4 | 333 | Hillsboro, OR | 130.8 |
| 230 | Beaumont, TX | 239.5 | 406 | Danbury, CT | 76.8 | 143 | Hollywood, FL | 390.1 |
| 391 | Beaverton, OR | 88.7 | 234 | Davenport, IA | 234.7 | 336 | Hoover, AL | 128.4 |
| 264 | Bellevue, WA | 194.2 | 213 | Davie, FL | 271.3 | 54 | Houston, TX | 623.5 |
| 53 | Bellflower, CA | 627.6 | 121 | Dayton, OH | 435.7 | 287 | Huntington Beach, CA | 176.2 |
| 367 | Bend, OR | 108.9 | 142 | Dearborn, MI | 392.7 | 146 | Huntsville, AL | 380.5 |
| 69 | Berkeley, CA | 571.3 | 399 | Decatur, IL | 85.1 | 46 | Independence, MO | 674.7 |
| 417 | Bethlehem, PA | 58.6 | 260 | Deerfield Beach, FL | 199.5 | 62 | Indianapolis, IN | 588.7 |
| 90 | Billings, MT | 501.8 | 400 | Denton, TX | 82.8 | 37 | Indio, CA | 712.8 |
| 43 | Birmingham, AL | 697.2 | 78 | Denver, CO | 537.3 | 67 | Inglewood, CA | 573.1 |
| 411 | Bloomington, IL | 67.9 | 135 | Des Moines, IA | 409.9 | 415 | Irvine, CA | 63.2 |
| 283 | Bloomington, IN | 179.6 | 1 | Detroit, MI | 1,699.3 | 216 | Irving, TX | 260.1 |
| 359 | Bloomington, MN | 114.9 | 30 | Downey, CA | 747.2 | 276 | Jacksonville, FL | 186.5 |
| 370 | Boca Raton, FL | 105.9 | 278 | Duluth, MN | 181.0 | 58 | Jackson, MS | 598.7 |
| 377 | Boise, ID | 99.4 | 177 | Edinburg, TX | 310.0 | 198 | Jersey City, NJ | 287.3 |
| 221 | Boston, MA | 250.1 | 372 | Edison Twnshp, NJ | 104.6 | 441 | Johns Creek, GA | 17.8 |
| 379 | Boulder, CO | 97.2 | 414 | Edmond, OK | 65.1 | 371 | Joliet, IL | 105.1 |
| 435 | Brick Twnshp, NJ | 26.5 | 110 | El Cajon, CA | 452.9 | 28 | Jurupa Valley, CA | 777.9 |
| 111 | Bridgeport, CT | 450.8 | 92 | El Monte, CA | 498.3 | 38 | Kansas City, KS | 707.9 |
| 233 | Brockton, MA | 237.2 | 358 | El Paso, TX | 116.8 | 21 | Kansas City, MO | 920.9 |
| 332 | Broken Arrow, OK | 131.1 | 401 | Elgin, IL | 80.6 | 254 | Kennewick, WA | 206.5 |
| 257 | Brooklyn Park, MN | 204.2 | 27 | Elizabeth, NJ | 787.8 | 407 | Kenosha, WI | 72.7 |
| 325 | Brownsville, TX | 141.5 | 356 | Elk Grove, CA | 118.1 | 42 | Kent, WA | 699.6 |
| 361 | Bryan, TX | 113.3 | 379 | Erie, PA | 97.2 | 310 | Killeen, TX | 150.9 |
| 114 | Buena Park, CA | 446.6 | 85 | Escondido, CA | 519.3 | 139 | Knoxville, TN | 403.3 |
| 153 | Buffalo, NY | 369.8 | 144 | Eugene, OR | 383.6 | 229 | Lafayette, LA | 240.7 |
| 252 | Burbank, CA | 209.1 | 393 | Evanston, IL | 88.5 | 421 | Lake Forest, CA | 54.2 |
| 381 | Cambridge, MA | 96.9 | 136 | Evansville, IN | 409.0 | 262 | Lakeland, FL | 196.6 |
| 343 | Canton Twnshp, MI | 122.5 | 16 | Everett, WA | 983.6 | 425 | Lakewood Twnshp, NJ | 47.5 |
| 391 | Cape Coral, FL | 88.7 | 65 | Fairfield, CA | 580.1 | 156 | Lakewood, CA | 353.9 |
| 363 | Carlsbad, CA | 112.2 | 222 | Fall River, MA | 249.9 | 129 | Lakewood, CO | 425.8 |
| 422 | Carmel, IN | 50.7 | 314 | Fargo, ND | 149.4 | 220 | Lancaster, CA | 252.2 |
| 301 | Carrollton, TX | 161.6 | 354 | Farmington Hills, MI | 118.4 | 172 | Lansing, MI | 318.7 |
| 83 | Carson, CA | 523.5 | 256 | Fayetteville, AR | 205.4 | 312 | Laredo, TX | 150.4 |
| 430 | Cary, NC | 40.3 | 175 | Fayetteville, NC | 311.6 | 281 | Largo, FL | 179.7 |
| 240 | Cedar Rapids, IA | 230.9 | 22 | Federal Way, WA | 823.8 | 292 | Las Cruces, NM | 167.6 |
| 410 | Centennial, CO | 68.7 | 431 | Fishers, IN | 34.8 | 116 | Las Vegas, NV | 442.2 |
| 398 | Champaign, IL | 85.6 | 171 | Flint, MI | 320.2 | 269 | Lawrence, KS | 192.1 |
| 363 | Chandler, AZ | 112.2 | 94 | Fontana, CA | 491.1 | 8 | Lawrence, MA | 1,064.1 |
| 339 | Charleston, SC | 127.4 | 384 | Fort Collins, CO | 93.3 | 237 | Lawton, OK | 232.4 |
| 244 | Charlotte, NC | 221.6 | 165 | Fort Lauderdale, FL | 328.9 | 416 | League City, TX | 62.5 |
| 68 | Chattanooga, TN | 572.3 | 241 | Fort Smith, AR | 226.6 | 357 | Lee's Summit, MO | 117.5 |
| 385 | Cheektowaga, NY | 93.2 | 309 | Fort Wayne, IN | 151.5 | 188 | Lewisville, TX | 296.9 |
| 347 | Chesapeake, VA | 121.4 | 183 | Fort Worth, TX | 304.0 | 214 | Lexington, KY | 269.2 |
| 104 | Chicago, IL | 464.5 | 187 | Fremont, CA | 298.0 | 360 | Lincoln, NE | 114.4 |
| 124 | Chico, CA | 433.0 | 26 | Fresno, CA | 797.2 | 72 | Little Rock, AR | 547.1 |
| 362 | Chino Hills, CA | 113.1 | 426 | Frisco, TX | 44.0 | 261 | Livermore, CA | 199.2 |

| RANK | CITY | RATE | RANK | CITY | RATE | RANK | CITY | RATE |
|------|------|------|------|------|------|------|------|------|
| 275 | Livonia, MI | 186.9 | 254 | Pasadena, CA | 206.5 | 19 | South Gate, CA | 955.1 |
| 91 | Long Beach, CA | 501.4 | 164 | Pasadena, TX | 332.9 | 210 | Sparks, NV | 272.7 |
| 344 | Longmont, CO | 121.9 | 86 | Paterson, NJ | 516.3 | 75 | Spokane Valley, WA | 539.4 |
| 226 | Longview, TX | 246.1 | 376 | Pearland, TX | 101.9 | 7 | Spokane, WA | 1,093.0 |
| 152 | Los Angeles, CA | 370.8 | 340 | Pembroke Pines, FL | 127.1 | 325 | Springfield, IL | 141.5 |
| 186 | Louisville, KY | 301.7 | 337 | Peoria, AZ | 128.1 | 101 | Springfield, MA | 478.6 |
| 191 | Lowell, MA | 292.4 | 294 | Peoria, IL | 167.3 | 41 | Springfield, MO | 702.8 |
| 155 | Lubbock, TX | 355.6 | 151 | Philadelphia, PA | 372.9 | 354 | Stamford, CT | 118.4 |
| 365 | Lynchburg, VA | 111.9 | 130 | Phoenix, AZ | 423.1 | 308 | Sterling Heights, MI | 152.3 |
| 206 | Lynn, MA | 275.7 | 258 | Pittsburgh, PA | 200.2 | 36 | Stockton, CA | 714.8 |
| 79 | Macon, GA | 536.3 | 387 | Plano, TX | 92.8 | 390 | St. George, UT | 90.3 |
| 374 | Madison, WI | 104.3 | 293 | Plantation, FL | 167.5 | 145 | St. Joseph, MO | 382.7 |
| 321 | Manchester, NH | 144.0 | 51 | Pomona, CA | 631.6 | 10 | St. Louis, MO | 1,045.3 |
| 290 | McAllen, TX | 173.3 | 174 | Pompano Beach, FL | 316.4 | 61 | St. Paul, MN | 597.6 |
| 395 | McKinney, TX | 87.8 | 427 | Port St. Lucie, FL | 43.0 | 109 | St. Petersburg, FL | 454.9 |
| 250 | Medford, OR | 211.8 | 74 | Portland, OR | 539.9 | 350 | Suffolk, VA | 119.3 |
| 324 | Melbourne, FL | 142.3 | 251 | Portsmouth, VA | 211.3 | 419 | Sugar Land, TX | 55.1 |
| 137 | Memphis, TN | 408.1 | 77 | Providence, RI | 537.8 | 210 | Sunnyvale, CA | 272.7 |
| 149 | Menifee, CA | 375.1 | 388 | Provo, UT | 92.4 | 327 | Sunrise, FL | 137.4 |
| 99 | Merced, CA | 485.7 | 95 | Pueblo, CO | 488.6 | 351 | Surprise, AZ | 119.2 |
| 433 | Meridian, ID | 30.5 | 404 | Quincy, MA | 78.1 | 208 | Syracuse, NY | 273.9 |
| 253 | Mesa, AZ | 208.7 | 345 | Racine, WI | 121.6 | 14 | Tacoma, WA | 995.9 |
| 80 | Mesquite, TX | 530.8 | 298 | Raleigh, NC | 164.3 | 236 | Tallahassee, FL | 233.2 |
| 133 | Miami Beach, FL | 411.2 | 442 | Ramapo, NY | 14.9 | 303 | Tampa, FL | 157.4 |
| 128 | Miami Gardens, FL | 427.3 | 203 | Rancho Cucamon., CA | 277.5 | 242 | Temecula, CA | 225.0 |
| 107 | Miami, FL | 457.5 | 163 | Reading, PA | 333.7 | 197 | Tempe, AZ | 289.0 |
| 329 | Midland, TX | 134.1 | 57 | Redding, CA | 603.1 | 201 | Thornton, CO | 279.9 |
| 32 | Milwaukee, WI | 729.7 | 199 | Redwood City, CA | 283.5 | 408 | Thousand Oaks, CA | 70.6 |
| 141 | Minneapolis, MN | 397.5 | 150 | Reno, NV | 373.2 | 148 | Toledo, OH | 375.9 |
| 286 | Miramar, FL | 177.2 | 39 | Renton, WA | 706.6 | 436 | Toms River Twnshp, NJ | 24.9 |
| 428 | Mission Viejo, CA | 41.7 | 29 | Rialto, CA | 752.0 | 115 | Topeka, KS | 444.5 |
| 246 | Mission, TX | 217.6 | 320 | Richardson, TX | 144.4 | 227 | Torrance, CA | 245.4 |
| 212 | Mobile, AL | 271.8 | 3 | Richmond, CA | 1,406.7 | 205 | Tracy, CA | 275.9 |
| 45 | Modesto, CA | 680.0 | 119 | Richmond, VA | 440.7 | 93 | Trenton, NJ | 492.7 |
| 134 | Moreno Valley, CA | 410.4 | 73 | Riverside, CA | 542.9 | 382 | Troy, MI | 94.4 |
| 288 | Mountain View, CA | 174.4 | 277 | Roanoke, VA | 183.8 | 131 | Tucson, AZ | 416.8 |
| 307 | Murfreesboro, TN | 154.0 | 383 | Rochester, MN | 93.9 | 56 | Tulsa, OK | 605.6 |
| 271 | Murrieta, CA | 191.2 | 196 | Rochester, NY | 289.2 | 302 | Tuscaloosa, AL | 160.4 |
| 317 | Nampa, ID | 145.3 | 225 | Rockford, IL | 247.7 | 323 | Tustin, CA | 143.3 |
| 296 | Napa, CA | 165.1 | 273 | Roseville, CA | 188.5 | 280 | Tyler, TX | 179.9 |
| 438 | Naperville, IL | 23.6 | 403 | Roswell, GA | 78.6 | 82 | Upland, CA | 527.5 |
| 404 | Nashua, NH | 78.1 | 429 | Round Rock, TX | 41.4 | 291 | Upper Darby Twnshp, PA | 169.1 |
| 274 | Nashville, TN | 188.3 | 59 | Sacramento, CA | 598.3 | 228 | Vacaville, CA | 244.8 |
| 158 | New Bedford, MA | 352.1 | 132 | Salem, OR | 414.6 | 13 | Vallejo, CA | 1,021.7 |
| 66 | New Haven, CT | 574.5 | 18 | Salinas, CA | 955.4 | 64 | Vancouver, WA | 586.1 |
| 70 | New Orleans, LA | 568.4 | 15 | Salt Lake City, UT | 986.1 | 232 | Ventura, CA | 237.5 |
| 396 | New Rochelle, NY | 87.6 | 270 | San Angelo, TX | 191.4 | 84 | Victorville, CA | 523.4 |
| 393 | New York, NY | 88.5 | 103 | San Antonio, TX | 469.9 | 378 | Virginia Beach, VA | 98.7 |
| 12 | Newark, NJ | 1,040.1 | 4 | San Bernardino, CA | 1,255.6 | 100 | Visalia, CA | 484.3 |
| 352 | Newport Beach, CA | 118.7 | 108 | San Diego, CA | 455.3 | 161 | Vista, CA | 340.2 |
| 272 | Newport News, VA | 190.0 | 40 | San Francisco, CA | 703.5 | 338 | Waco, TX | 127.8 |
| 440 | Newton, MA | 20.7 | 25 | San Jose, CA | 798.9 | 123 | Warren, MI | 435.3 |
| 176 | Norfolk, VA | 310.1 | 11 | San Leandro, CA | 1,042.4 | 375 | Warwick, RI | 103.9 |
| 322 | Norman, OK | 143.6 | 266 | San Marcos, CA | 193.8 | 96 | Washington, DC | 486.8 |
| 96 | North Charleston, SC | 486.8 | 306 | San Mateo, CA | 154.3 | 52 | Waterbury, CT | 627.7 |
| 121 | North Las Vegas, NV | 435.7 | 315 | Sandy Springs, GA | 148.3 | 409 | Waukegan, IL | 69.8 |
| 81 | Norwalk, CA | 529.5 | 248 | Sandy, UT | 214.6 | 104 | West Covina, CA | 464.5 |
| 349 | Norwalk, CT | 121.0 | 120 | Santa Ana, CA | 438.3 | 147 | West Palm Beach, FL | 376.5 |
| 2 | Oakland, CA | 1,691.8 | 330 | Santa Barbara, CA | 133.3 | 31 | West Valley, UT | 735.5 |
| 238 | Oceanside, CA | 231.9 | 167 | Santa Clara, CA | 327.1 | 160 | Westland, MI | 341.6 |
| 127 | Odessa, TX | 427.7 | 346 | Santa Clarita, CA | 121.5 | 154 | Westminster, CA | 365.7 |
| 437 | O'Fallon, MO | 24.2 | 34 | Santa Maria, CA | 715.3 | 190 | Westminster, CO | 292.5 |
| 168 | Ogden, UT | 326.0 | 284 | Santa Monica, CA | 178.4 | 189 | Whittier, CA | 292.7 |
| 47 | Oklahoma City, OK | 673.7 | 279 | Santa Rosa, CA | 180.1 | 209 | Wichita Falls, TX | 273.6 |
| 328 | Olathe, KS | 136.3 | 178 | Savannah, GA | 308.2 | 87 | Wichita, KS | 513.3 |
| 33 | Omaha, NE | 724.6 | 389 | Scottsdale, AZ | 92.2 | 185 | Wilmington, NC | 301.8 |
| 49 | Ontario, CA | 648.8 | 311 | Scranton, PA | 150.5 | 217 | Winston-Salem, NC | 259.1 |
| 265 | Orange, CA | 193.9 | 48 | Seattle, WA | 670.5 | 341 | Woodbridge Twnshp, NJ | 123.3 |
| 368 | Orem, UT | 107.2 | 223 | Shreveport, LA | 249.3 | 247 | Worcester, MA | 217.5 |
| 140 | Orlando, FL | 402.8 | 372 | Simi Valley, CA | 104.6 | 50 | Yakima, WA | 634.7 |
| 304 | Overland Park, KS | 155.1 | 194 | Sioux City, IA | 290.3 | 353 | Yonkers, NY | 118.5 |
| 166 | Oxnard, CA | 327.7 | 299 | Sioux Falls, SD | 163.2 | 239 | Yuma, AZ | 231.2 |
| 366 | Palm Bay, FL | 110.2 | 334 | Somerville, MA | 129.9 | | | |
| 235 | Palmdale, CA | 234.5 | 169 | South Bend, IN | 323.7 | | | |

Source: CQ Press using reported data from the F.B.I. "Crime in the United States 2013"

*Motor vehicle theft includes the theft or attempted theft of a self-propelled vehicle. Excludes motorboats, construction equipment, airplanes, and farming equipment.

# 78. Motor Vehicle Theft Rate in 2013 (continued)
## National Rate = 221.3 Motor Vehicle Thefts per 100,000 Population*

| RANK | CITY | RATE | RANK | CITY | RATE | RANK | CITY | RATE |
|---|---|---|---|---|---|---|---|---|
| 1 | Detroit, MI | 1,699.3 | 75 | Spokane Valley, WA | 539.4 | 149 | Menifee, CA | 375.1 |
| 2 | Oakland, CA | 1,691.8 | 76 | Albuquerque, NM | 538.4 | 150 | Reno, NV | 373.2 |
| 3 | Richmond, CA | 1,406.7 | 77 | Providence, RI | 537.8 | 151 | Philadelphia, PA | 372.9 |
| 4 | San Bernardino, CA | 1,255.6 | 78 | Denver, CO | 537.3 | 152 | Los Angeles, CA | 370.8 |
| 5 | Antioch, CA | 1,143.3 | 79 | Macon, GA | 536.3 | 153 | Buffalo, NY | 369.8 |
| 6 | Hayward, CA | 1,107.0 | 80 | Mesquite, TX | 530.8 | 154 | Westminster, CA | 365.7 |
| 7 | Spokane, WA | 1,093.0 | 81 | Norwalk, CA | 529.5 | 155 | Lubbock, TX | 355.6 |
| 8 | Lawrence, MA | 1,064.1 | 82 | Upland, CA | 527.5 | 156 | Lakewood, CA | 353.9 |
| 9 | Cleveland, OH | 1,059.9 | 83 | Carson, CA | 523.5 | 157 | Amarillo, TX | 353.6 |
| 10 | St. Louis, MO | 1,045.3 | 84 | Victorville, CA | 523.4 | 158 | New Bedford, MA | 352.1 |
| 11 | San Leandro, CA | 1,042.4 | 85 | Escondido, CA | 519.3 | 159 | Chino, CA | 343.2 |
| 12 | Newark, NJ | 1,040.1 | 86 | Paterson, NJ | 516.3 | 160 | Westland, MI | 341.6 |
| 13 | Vallejo, CA | 1,021.7 | 87 | Wichita, KS | 513.3 | 161 | Vista, CA | 340.2 |
| 14 | Tacoma, WA | 995.9 | 88 | Hammond, IN | 511.8 | 162 | Cicero, IL | 336.1 |
| 15 | Salt Lake City, UT | 986.1 | 89 | Hartford, CT | 511.5 | 163 | Reading, PA | 333.7 |
| 16 | Everett, WA | 983.6 | 90 | Billings, MT | 501.8 | 164 | Pasadena, TX | 332.9 |
| 17 | Atlanta, GA | 982.7 | 91 | Long Beach, CA | 501.4 | 165 | Fort Lauderdale, FL | 328.9 |
| 18 | Salinas, CA | 955.4 | 92 | El Monte, CA | 498.3 | 166 | Oxnard, CA | 327.7 |
| 19 | South Gate, CA | 955.1 | 93 | Trenton, NJ | 492.7 | 167 | Santa Clara, CA | 327.1 |
| 20 | Gary, IN | 928.7 | 94 | Fontana, CA | 491.1 | 168 | Ogden, UT | 326.0 |
| 21 | Kansas City, MO | 920.9 | 95 | Pueblo, CO | 488.6 | 169 | South Bend, IN | 323.7 |
| 22 | Federal Way, WA | 823.8 | 96 | Anaheim, CA | 486.8 | 170 | Grand Prairie, TX | 321.0 |
| 23 | Compton, CA | 816.1 | 96 | North Charleston, SC | 486.8 | 171 | Flint, MI | 320.2 |
| 24 | Bakersfield, CA | 811.6 | 96 | Washington, DC | 486.8 | 172 | Lansing, MI | 318.7 |
| 25 | San Jose, CA | 798.9 | 99 | Merced, CA | 485.7 | 173 | Akron, OH | 318.0 |
| 26 | Fresno, CA | 797.2 | 100 | Visalia, CA | 484.3 | 174 | Pompano Beach, FL | 316.4 |
| 27 | Elizabeth, NJ | 787.8 | 101 | Springfield, MA | 478.6 | 175 | Fayetteville, NC | 311.6 |
| 28 | Jurupa Valley, CA | 777.9 | 102 | Baldwin Park, CA | 473.0 | 176 | Norfolk, VA | 310.1 |
| 29 | Rialto, CA | 752.0 | 103 | San Antonio, TX | 469.9 | 177 | Edinburg, TX | 310.0 |
| 30 | Downey, CA | 747.2 | 104 | Chicago, IL | 464.5 | 178 | Savannah, GA | 308.2 |
| 31 | West Valley, UT | 735.5 | 104 | West Covina, CA | 464.5 | 179 | Garden Grove, CA | 307.2 |
| 32 | Milwaukee, WI | 729.7 | 106 | Gresham, OR | 463.8 | 180 | Clovis, CA | 306.6 |
| 33 | Omaha, NE | 724.6 | 107 | Miami, FL | 457.5 | 181 | Chula Vista, CA | 306.2 |
| 34 | Santa Maria, CA | 715.3 | 108 | San Diego, CA | 455.3 | 182 | Corona, CA | 305.9 |
| 35 | Baltimore, MD | 715.0 | 109 | St. Petersburg, FL | 454.9 | 183 | Fort Worth, TX | 304.0 |
| 36 | Stockton, CA | 714.8 | 110 | El Cajon, CA | 452.9 | 184 | Hialeah, FL | 302.3 |
| 37 | Indio, CA | 712.8 | 111 | Bridgeport, CT | 450.8 | 185 | Wilmington, NC | 301.8 |
| 38 | Kansas City, KS | 707.9 | 112 | Glendale, AZ | 448.7 | 186 | Louisville, KY | 301.7 |
| 39 | Renton, WA | 706.6 | 113 | Hawthorne, CA | 448.1 | 187 | Fremont, CA | 298.0 |
| 40 | San Francisco, CA | 703.5 | 114 | Buena Park, CA | 446.6 | 188 | Lewisville, TX | 296.9 |
| 41 | Springfield, MO | 702.8 | 115 | Topeka, KS | 444.5 | 189 | Whittier, CA | 292.7 |
| 42 | Kent, WA | 699.6 | 116 | Las Vegas, NV | 442.2 | 190 | Westminster, CO | 292.5 |
| 43 | Birmingham, AL | 697.2 | 117 | Colorado Springs, CO | 442.1 | 191 | Lowell, MA | 292.4 |
| 44 | Hemet, CA | 684.2 | 118 | Hesperia, CA | 441.6 | 192 | High Point, NC | 291.8 |
| 45 | Modesto, CA | 680.0 | 119 | Richmond, VA | 440.7 | 193 | Aurora, CO | 291.1 |
| 46 | Independence, MO | 674.7 | 120 | Santa Ana, CA | 438.3 | 194 | Sioux City, IA | 290.3 |
| 47 | Oklahoma City, OK | 673.7 | 121 | Dayton, OH | 435.7 | 195 | Anchorage, AK | 290.2 |
| 48 | Seattle, WA | 670.5 | 121 | North Las Vegas, NV | 435.7 | 196 | Rochester, NY | 289.2 |
| 49 | Ontario, CA | 648.8 | 123 | Warren, MI | 435.3 | 197 | Tempe, AZ | 289.0 |
| 50 | Yakima, WA | 634.7 | 124 | Alameda, CA | 433.0 | 198 | Jersey City, NJ | 287.3 |
| 51 | Pomona, CA | 631.6 | 124 | Chico, CA | 433.0 | 199 | Redwood City, CA | 283.5 |
| 52 | Waterbury, CT | 627.7 | 126 | Cincinnati, OH | 430.4 | 200 | Allentown, PA | 282.5 |
| 53 | Bellflower, CA | 627.6 | 127 | Odessa, TX | 427.7 | 201 | Thornton, CO | 279.9 |
| 54 | Houston, TX | 623.5 | 128 | Miami Gardens, FL | 427.3 | 202 | Daly City, CA | 278.4 |
| 55 | Concord, CA | 612.1 | 129 | Lakewood, CO | 425.8 | 203 | Rancho Cucamon., CA | 277.5 |
| 56 | Tulsa, OK | 605.6 | 130 | Phoenix, AZ | 423.1 | 204 | Alhambra, CA | 276.2 |
| 57 | Redding, CA | 603.1 | 131 | Tucson, AZ | 416.8 | 205 | Tracy, CA | 275.9 |
| 58 | Jackson, MS | 598.7 | 132 | Salem, OR | 414.6 | 206 | Lynn, MA | 275.7 |
| 59 | Sacramento, CA | 598.3 | 133 | Miami Beach, FL | 411.2 | 207 | Garland, TX | 274.5 |
| 60 | Columbia, SC | 598.2 | 134 | Moreno Valley, CA | 410.4 | 208 | Syracuse, NY | 273.9 |
| 61 | St. Paul, MN | 597.6 | 135 | Des Moines, IA | 409.9 | 209 | Wichita Falls, TX | 273.6 |
| 62 | Indianapolis, IN | 588.7 | 136 | Evansville, IN | 409.0 | 210 | Sparks, NV | 272.7 |
| 63 | Dallas, TX | 588.4 | 137 | Memphis, TN | 408.1 | 210 | Sunnyvale, CA | 272.7 |
| 64 | Vancouver, WA | 586.1 | 138 | Citrus Heights, CA | 404.3 | 212 | Mobile, AL | 271.8 |
| 65 | Fairfield, CA | 580.1 | 139 | Knoxville, TN | 403.3 | 213 | Davie, FL | 271.3 |
| 66 | New Haven, CT | 574.5 | 140 | Orlando, FL | 402.8 | 214 | Lexington, KY | 269.2 |
| 67 | Inglewood, CA | 573.1 | 141 | Minneapolis, MN | 397.5 | 215 | Costa Mesa, CA | 263.0 |
| 68 | Chattanooga, TN | 572.3 | 142 | Dearborn, MI | 392.7 | 216 | Irving, TX | 260.1 |
| 69 | Berkeley, CA | 571.3 | 143 | Hollywood, FL | 390.1 | 217 | Winston-Salem, NC | 259.1 |
| 70 | New Orleans, LA | 568.4 | 144 | Eugene, OR | 383.6 | 218 | Fullerton, CA | 257.0 |
| 71 | Columbus, GA | 550.8 | 145 | St. Joseph, MO | 382.7 | 219 | Austin, TX | 252.5 |
| 72 | Little Rock, AR | 547.1 | 146 | Huntsville, AL | 380.5 | 220 | Lancaster, CA | 252.2 |
| 73 | Riverside, CA | 542.9 | 147 | West Palm Beach, FL | 376.5 | 221 | Boston, MA | 250.1 |
| 74 | Portland, OR | 539.9 | 148 | Toledo, OH | 375.9 | 222 | Fall River, MA | 249.9 |

| RANK | CITY | RATE | RANK | CITY | RATE | RANK | CITY | RATE |
|---|---|---|---|---|---|---|---|---|
| 223 | Shreveport, LA | 249.3 | 297 | Hampton, VA | 165.0 | 371 | Joliet, IL | 105.1 |
| 224 | Arlington, TX | 248.2 | 298 | Raleigh, NC | 164.3 | 372 | Edison Twnshp, NJ | 104.6 |
| 225 | Rockford, IL | 247.7 | 299 | Sioux Falls, SD | 163.2 | 372 | Simi Valley, CA | 104.6 |
| 226 | Longview, TX | 246.1 | 300 | Athens-Clarke, GA | 162.3 | 374 | Madison, WI | 104.3 |
| 227 | Torrance, CA | 245.4 | 301 | Carrollton, TX | 161.6 | 375 | Warwick, RI | 103.9 |
| 228 | Vacaville, CA | 244.8 | 302 | Tuscaloosa, AL | 160.4 | 376 | Pearland, TX | 101.9 |
| 229 | Lafayette, LA | 240.7 | 303 | Tampa, FL | 157.4 | 377 | Boise, ID | 99.4 |
| 230 | Beaumont, TX | 239.5 | 304 | Overland Park, KS | 155.1 | 378 | Virginia Beach, VA | 98.7 |
| 231 | Clinton Twnshp, MI | 238.6 | 305 | Corpus Christi, TX | 154.8 | 379 | Boulder, CO | 97.2 |
| 232 | Ventura, CA | 237.5 | 306 | San Mateo, CA | 154.3 | 379 | Erie, PA | 97.2 |
| 233 | Brockton, MA | 237.2 | 307 | Murfreesboro, TN | 154.0 | 381 | Cambridge, MA | 96.9 |
| 234 | Davenport, IA | 234.7 | 308 | Sterling Heights, MI | 152.3 | 382 | Troy, MI | 94.4 |
| 235 | Palmdale, CA | 234.5 | 309 | Fort Wayne, IN | 151.5 | 383 | Rochester, MN | 93.9 |
| 236 | Tallahassee, FL | 233.2 | 310 | Killeen, TX | 150.9 | 384 | Fort Collins, CO | 93.3 |
| 237 | Lawton, OK | 232.4 | 311 | Scranton, PA | 150.5 | 385 | Cheektowaga, NY | 93.2 |
| 238 | Oceanside, CA | 231.9 | 312 | Laredo, TX | 150.4 | 385 | Green Bay, WI | 93.2 |
| 239 | Yuma, AZ | 231.2 | 313 | Greenville, NC | 150.0 | 387 | Plano, TX | 92.8 |
| 240 | Cedar Rapids, IA | 230.9 | 314 | Fargo, ND | 149.4 | 388 | Provo, UT | 92.4 |
| 241 | Fort Smith, AR | 226.6 | 315 | Sandy Springs, GA | 148.3 | 389 | Scottsdale, AZ | 92.2 |
| 242 | Temecula, CA | 225.0 | 316 | Hamilton Twnshp, NJ | 147.2 | 390 | St. George, UT | 90.3 |
| 243 | Albany, GA | 223.6 | 317 | Nampa, ID | 145.3 | 391 | Beaverton, OR | 88.7 |
| 244 | Charlotte, NC | 221.6 | 318 | Albany, NY | 145.0 | 391 | Cape Coral, FL | 88.7 |
| 245 | Baton Rouge, LA | 219.8 | 319 | Columbia, MO | 144.9 | 393 | Evanston, IL | 88.5 |
| 246 | Mission, TX | 217.6 | 320 | Richardson, TX | 144.4 | 393 | New York, NY | 88.5 |
| 247 | Worcester, MA | 217.5 | 321 | Manchester, NH | 144.0 | 395 | McKinney, TX | 87.8 |
| 248 | Sandy, UT | 214.6 | 322 | Norman, OK | 143.6 | 396 | New Rochelle, NY | 87.6 |
| 249 | Abilene, TX | 212.7 | 323 | Tustin, CA | 143.3 | 397 | Coral Springs, FL | 86.1 |
| 250 | Medford, OR | 211.8 | 324 | Melbourne, FL | 142.3 | 398 | Champaign, IL | 85.6 |
| 251 | Portsmouth, VA | 211.3 | 325 | Brownsville, TX | 141.5 | 399 | Decatur, IL | 85.1 |
| 252 | Burbank, CA | 209.1 | 325 | Springfield, IL | 141.5 | 400 | Denton, TX | 82.8 |
| 253 | Mesa, AZ | 208.7 | 327 | Sunrise, FL | 137.4 | 401 | Elgin, IL | 80.6 |
| 254 | Kennewick, WA | 206.5 | 328 | Olathe, KS | 136.3 | 402 | Ann Arbor, MI | 80.5 |
| 254 | Pasadena, CA | 206.5 | 329 | Midland, TX | 134.1 | 403 | Roswell, GA | 78.6 |
| 256 | Fayetteville, AR | 205.4 | 330 | Santa Barbara, CA | 133.3 | 404 | Nashua, NH | 78.1 |
| 257 | Brooklyn Park, MN | 204.2 | 331 | Grand Rapids, MI | 131.8 | 404 | Quincy, MA | 78.1 |
| 258 | Henderson, NV | 200.2 | 332 | Broken Arrow, OK | 131.1 | 406 | Danbury, CT | 76.8 |
| 258 | Pittsburgh, PA | 200.2 | 333 | Hillsboro, OR | 130.8 | 407 | Kenosha, WI | 72.7 |
| 260 | Deerfield Beach, FL | 199.5 | 334 | Somerville, MA | 129.9 | 408 | Thousand Oaks, CA | 70.6 |
| 261 | Livermore, CA | 199.2 | 335 | Glendale, CA | 128.5 | 409 | Waukegan, IL | 69.8 |
| 262 | Lakeland, FL | 196.6 | 336 | Hoover, AL | 128.4 | 410 | Centennial, CO | 68.7 |
| 263 | Alexandria, VA | 195.9 | 337 | Peoria, AZ | 128.1 | 411 | Bloomington, IL | 67.9 |
| 264 | Bellevue, WA | 194.2 | 338 | Waco, TX | 127.8 | 411 | Gilbert, AZ | 67.9 |
| 265 | Orange, CA | 193.9 | 339 | Charleston, SC | 127.4 | 413 | Colonie, NY | 65.2 |
| 266 | San Marcos, CA | 193.8 | 340 | Pembroke Pines, FL | 127.1 | 414 | Edmond, OK | 65.1 |
| 267 | Greeley, CO | 193.5 | 341 | Woodbridge Twnshp, NJ | 123.3 | 415 | Irvine, CA | 63.2 |
| 268 | Gainesville, FL | 192.7 | 342 | Concord, NC | 123.0 | 416 | League City, TX | 62.5 |
| 269 | Lawrence, KS | 192.1 | 343 | Canton Twnshp, MI | 122.5 | 417 | Bethlehem, PA | 58.6 |
| 270 | San Angelo, TX | 191.4 | 344 | Longmont, CO | 121.9 | 418 | Aurora, IL | 55.3 |
| 271 | Murrieta, CA | 191.2 | 345 | Racine, WI | 121.6 | 419 | Sugar Land, TX | 55.1 |
| 272 | Newport News, VA | 190.0 | 346 | Santa Clarita, CA | 121.5 | 420 | Allen, TX | 54.8 |
| 273 | Roseville, CA | 188.5 | 347 | Chesapeake, VA | 121.4 | 421 | Lake Forest, CA | 54.2 |
| 274 | Nashville, TN | 188.3 | 348 | Clifton, NJ | 121.1 | 422 | Carmel, IN | 50.7 |
| 275 | Livonia, MI | 186.9 | 349 | Norwalk, CT | 121.0 | 423 | College Station, TX | 48.5 |
| 276 | Jacksonville, FL | 186.5 | 350 | Suffolk, VA | 119.3 | 424 | Greece, NY | 47.6 |
| 277 | Roanoke, VA | 183.8 | 351 | Surprise, AZ | 119.2 | 425 | Lakewood Twnshp, NJ | 47.5 |
| 278 | Duluth, MN | 181.0 | 352 | Newport Beach, CA | 118.7 | 426 | Frisco, TX | 44.0 |
| 279 | Santa Rosa, CA | 180.1 | 353 | Yonkers, NY | 118.5 | 427 | Port St. Lucie, FL | 43.0 |
| 280 | Tyler, TX | 179.9 | 354 | Farmington Hills, MI | 118.4 | 428 | Mission Viejo, CA | 41.7 |
| 281 | Greensboro, NC | 179.7 | 354 | Stamford, CT | 118.4 | 429 | Round Rock, TX | 41.4 |
| 281 | Largo, FL | 179.7 | 356 | Elk Grove, CA | 118.1 | 430 | Cary, NC | 40.3 |
| 283 | Bloomington, IN | 179.6 | 357 | Lee's Summit, MO | 117.5 | 431 | Fishers, IN | 34.8 |
| 284 | Santa Monica, CA | 178.4 | 358 | El Paso, TX | 116.8 | 432 | Clarkstown, NY | 34.7 |
| 285 | Arvada, CO | 177.8 | 359 | Bloomington, MN | 114.9 | 433 | Meridian, ID | 30.5 |
| 286 | Miramar, FL | 177.2 | 360 | Lincoln, NE | 114.4 | 434 | Amherst, NY | 27.1 |
| 287 | Huntington Beach, CA | 176.2 | 361 | Bryan, TX | 113.3 | 435 | Brick Twnshp, NJ | 26.5 |
| 288 | Mountain View, CA | 174.4 | 362 | Chino Hills, CA | 113.1 | 436 | Toms River Twnshp, NJ | 24.9 |
| 289 | Cranston, RI | 173.4 | 363 | Carlsbad, CA | 112.2 | 437 | O'Fallon, MO | 24.2 |
| 290 | McAllen, TX | 173.3 | 363 | Chandler, AZ | 112.2 | 438 | Naperville, IL | 23.6 |
| 291 | Upper Darby Twnshp, PA | 169.1 | 365 | Lynchburg, VA | 111.9 | 439 | Arlington Heights, IL | 21.1 |
| 292 | Las Cruces, NM | 167.6 | 366 | Palm Bay, FL | 110.2 | 440 | Newton, MA | 20.7 |
| 293 | Plantation, FL | 167.5 | 367 | Bend, OR | 108.9 | 441 | Johns Creek, GA | 17.8 |
| 294 | Peoria, IL | 167.3 | 368 | Orem, UT | 107.2 | 442 | Ramapo, NY | 14.9 |
| 295 | Clearwater, FL | 166.2 | 369 | Clarksville, TN | 107.1 | | | |
| 296 | Napa, CA | 165.1 | 370 | Boca Raton, FL | 105.9 | | | |

Source: CQ Press using reported data from the F.B.I. "Crime in the United States 2013"

*Motor vehicle theft includes the theft or attempted theft of a self-propelled vehicle. Excludes motorboats, construction equipment, airplanes, and farming equipment.

# 79. Percent Change in Motor Vehicle Theft Rate: 2012 to 2013
## National Percent Change = 4.0% Decrease*

| RANK | CITY | % CHANGE | RANK | CITY | % CHANGE | RANK | CITY | % CHANGE |
|---|---|---|---|---|---|---|---|---|
| 5 | Abilene, TX | 49.2 | 59 | Chino, CA | 16.5 | 106 | Fullerton, CA | 10.2 |
| 322 | Akron, OH | (12.5) | 397 | Chula Vista, CA | (23.7) | 170 | Gainesville, FL | 2.4 |
| 99 | Alameda, CA | 10.8 | 190 | Cicero, IL | (0.6) | 303 | Garden Grove, CA | (10.5) |
| 387 | Albany, GA | (21.6) | 67 | Cincinnati, OH | 15.9 | 114 | Garland, TX | 9.1 |
| 262 | Albany, NY | (7.5) | 413 | Citrus Heights, CA | (27.6) | 230 | Gary, IN | (3.6) |
| 120 | Albuquerque, NM | 8.7 | 96 | Clarkstown, NY | 11.2 | 311 | Gilbert, AZ | (11.2) |
| 318 | Alexandria, VA | (12.3) | 317 | Clarksville, TN | (11.9) | 339 | Glendale, AZ | (14.6) |
| 274 | Alhambra, CA | (8.5) | 166 | Clearwater, FL | 3.2 | 372 | Glendale, CA | (18.9) |
| 272 | Allentown, PA | (8.4) | 98 | Cleveland, OH | 11.0 | 264 | Grand Prairie, TX | (7.7) |
| 102 | Allen, TX | 10.5 | 410 | Clifton, NJ | (27.3) | 253 | Grand Rapids, MI | (6.6) |
| 102 | Amarillo, TX | 10.5 | 25 | Clinton Twnshp, MI | 27.9 | 429 | Greece, NY | (40.2) |
| 335 | Amherst, NY | (14.0) | 392 | Clovis, CA | (22.1) | 19 | Greeley, CO | 32.1 |
| 59 | Anaheim, CA | 16.5 | 390 | College Station, TX | (21.9) | 285 | Green Bay, WI | (9.3) |
| 157 | Anchorage, AK | 4.5 | 285 | Colonie, NY | (9.3) | 318 | Greensboro, NC | (12.3) |
| 370 | Ann Arbor, MI | (18.8) | 146 | Colorado Springs, CO | 6.0 | 109 | Greenville, NC | 9.5 |
| 109 | Antioch, CA | 9.5 | 88 | Columbia, MO | 12.2 | 423 | Gresham, OR | (32.4) |
| 247 | Arlington Heights, IL | (6.2) | NA | Columbia, SC** | NA | 190 | Hamilton Twnshp, NJ | (0.6) |
| 196 | Arlington, TX | (0.9) | 26 | Columbus, GA | 27.7 | 84 | Hammond, IN | 12.4 |
| 230 | Arvada, CO | (3.6) | 215 | Compton, CA | (2.3) | 327 | Hampton, VA | (13.2) |
| 385 | Athens-Clarke, GA | (21.2) | 62 | Concord, CA | 16.3 | 379 | Hartford, CT | (20.2) |
| 358 | Atlanta, GA | (16.6) | NA | Concord, NC** | NA | 364 | Hawthorne, CA | (17.9) |
| 112 | Aurora, CO | 9.2 | 415 | Coral Springs, FL | (28.3) | 89 | Hayward, CA | 12.1 |
| 321 | Aurora, IL | (12.4) | 254 | Corona, CA | (6.7) | 65 | Hemet, CA | 16.0 |
| 282 | Austin, TX | (9.1) | 112 | Corpus Christi, TX | 9.2 | 150 | Henderson, NV | 5.3 |
| 299 | Bakersfield, CA | (10.4) | 364 | Costa Mesa, CA | (17.9) | 172 | Hesperia, CA | 2.0 |
| 255 | Baldwin Park, CA | (6.8) | 288 | Cranston, RI | (9.5) | 235 | Hialeah, FL | (4.4) |
| 85 | Baltimore, MD | 12.3 | 163 | Dallas, TX | 3.4 | 116 | High Point, NC | 9.0 |
| 149 | Baton Rouge, LA | 5.6 | 90 | Daly City, CA | 11.9 | 135 | Hillsboro, OR | 7.0 |
| 164 | Beaumont, TX | 3.3 | 346 | Danbury, CT | (15.0) | 336 | Hollywood, FL | (14.1) |
| 403 | Beaverton, OR | (25.6) | 360 | Davenport, IA | (16.9) | 36 | Hoover, AL | 24.4 |
| 8 | Bellevue, WA | 44.8 | 136 | Davie, FL | 6.9 | 161 | Houston, TX | 3.9 |
| 210 | Bellflower, CA | (2.0) | 304 | Dayton, OH | (10.6) | 136 | Huntington Beach, CA | 6.9 |
| NA | Bend, OR** | NA | 136 | Dearborn, MI | 6.9 | 206 | Huntsville, AL | (1.6) |
| 168 | Berkeley, CA | 2.5 | 384 | Decatur, IL | (21.0) | 178 | Independence, MO | 1.2 |
| 434 | Bethlehem, PA | (46.8) | 354 | Deerfield Beach, FL | (16.0) | 131 | Indianapolis, IN | 7.3 |
| 22 | Billings, MT | 29.9 | 427 | Denton, TX | (37.3) | 77 | Indio, CA | 14.4 |
| 9 | Birmingham, AL | 42.7 | 269 | Denver, CO | (8.0) | 185 | Inglewood, CA | 0.1 |
| 49 | Bloomington, IL | 18.9 | 120 | Des Moines, IA | 8.7 | 174 | Irvine, CA | 1.8 |
| 222 | Bloomington, IN | (2.9) | 157 | Detroit, MI | 4.5 | 164 | Irving, TX | 3.3 |
| 28 | Bloomington, MN | 26.3 | 314 | Downey, CA | (11.5) | 235 | Jacksonville, FL | (4.4) |
| 285 | Boca Raton, FL | (9.3) | 275 | Duluth, MN | (8.6) | 261 | Jackson, MS | (7.3) |
| 16 | Boise, ID | 34.0 | 47 | Edinburg, TX | 19.1 | 243 | Jersey City, NJ | (5.2) |
| 222 | Boston, MA | (2.9) | 240 | Edison Twnshp, NJ | (4.8) | 310 | Johns Creek, GA | (11.0) |
| 399 | Boulder, CO | (23.9) | 68 | Edmond, OK | 15.6 | 202 | Joliet, IL | (1.2) |
| 29 | Brick Twnshp, NJ | 25.6 | 54 | El Cajon, CA | 17.1 | 78 | Jurupa Valley, CA | 14.3 |
| 401 | Bridgeport, CT | (24.2) | 190 | El Monte, CA | (0.6) | 331 | Kansas City, KS | (13.7) |
| 130 | Brockton, MA | 7.5 | 422 | El Paso, TX | (32.0) | 48 | Kansas City, MO | 19.0 |
| 75 | Broken Arrow, OK | 14.8 | 94 | Elgin, IL | 11.3 | 33 | Kennewick, WA | 25.2 |
| 55 | Brooklyn Park, MN | 17.0 | 344 | Elizabeth, NJ | (14.7) | 404 | Kenosha, WI | (25.8) |
| 35 | Brownsville, TX | 24.5 | 325 | Elk Grove, CA | (12.9) | 200 | Kent, WA | (1.1) |
| 180 | Bryan, TX | 1.1 | 239 | Erie, PA | (4.7) | 162 | Killeen, TX | 3.7 |
| 46 | Buena Park, CA | 19.3 | 181 | Escondido, CA | 1.0 | 377 | Knoxville, TN | (19.6) |
| 318 | Buffalo, NY | (12.3) | 10 | Eugene, OR | 39.4 | 41 | Lafayette, LA | 22.7 |
| 104 | Burbank, CA | 10.4 | 152 | Evanston, IL | 5.1 | 421 | Lake Forest, CA | (31.9) |
| 224 | Cambridge, MA | (3.1) | 71 | Evansville, IN | 15.1 | 143 | Lakeland, FL | 6.2 |
| NA | Canton Twnshp, MI** | NA | 139 | Everett, WA | 6.8 | 176 | Lakewood Twnshp, NJ | 1.3 |
| 37 | Cape Coral, FL | 24.2 | 34 | Fairfield, CA | 25.0 | 259 | Lakewood, CA | (7.1) |
| 370 | Carlsbad, CA | (18.8) | 364 | Fall River, MA | (17.9) | 168 | Lakewood, CO | 2.5 |
| 291 | Carmel, IN | (9.8) | 147 | Fargo, ND | 5.9 | 190 | Lancaster, CA | (0.6) |
| 418 | Carrollton, TX | (29.4) | 402 | Farmington Hills, MI | (24.5) | 11 | Lansing, MI | 38.4 |
| 312 | Carson, CA | (11.3) | 61 | Fayetteville, AR | 16.4 | 224 | Laredo, TX | (3.1) |
| 291 | Cary, NC | (9.8) | 347 | Fayetteville, NC | (15.1) | 118 | Largo, FL | 8.9 |
| 57 | Cedar Rapids, IA | 16.7 | 242 | Federal Way, WA | (5.0) | 389 | Las Cruces, NM | (21.8) |
| 260 | Centennial, CO | (7.2) | 170 | Fishers, IN | 2.4 | 212 | Las Vegas, NV | (2.1) |
| 336 | Champaign, IL | (14.1) | 417 | Flint, MI | (29.1) | 351 | Lawrence, KS | (15.6) |
| 142 | Chandler, AZ | 6.4 | 208 | Fontana, CA | (1.9) | 45 | Lawrence, MA | 20.5 |
| 424 | Charleston, SC | (32.8) | 214 | Fort Collins, CO | (2.2) | 396 | Lawton, OK | (23.2) |
| 355 | Charlotte, NC | (16.2) | 240 | Fort Lauderdale, FL | (4.8) | 391 | League City, TX | (22.0) |
| NA | Chattanooga, TN** | NA | 123 | Fort Smith, AR | 8.3 | 186 | Lee's Summit, MO | (0.1) |
| 348 | Cheektowaga, NY | (15.2) | 255 | Fort Wayne, IN | (6.8) | NA | Lewisville, TX** | NA |
| 197 | Chesapeake, VA | (1.0) | 229 | Fort Worth, TX | (3.4) | 295 | Lexington, KY | (10.0) |
| 406 | Chicago, IL | (26.0) | 85 | Fremont, CA | 12.3 | 221 | Lincoln, NE | (2.8) |
| 6 | Chico, CA | 48.4 | 247 | Fresno, CA | (6.2) | 210 | Little Rock, AR | (2.0) |
| 18 | Chino Hills, CA | 33.4 | 183 | Frisco, TX | 0.5 | 249 | Livermore, CA | (6.3) |

| RANK | CITY | % CHANGE |
|---|---|---|
| 297 | Livonia, MI | (10.3) |
| 299 | Long Beach, CA | (10.4) |
| 166 | Longmont, CO | 3.2 |
| 425 | Longview, TX | (35.7) |
| 243 | Los Angeles, CA | (5.2) |
| 270 | Louisville, KY | (8.1) |
| 128 | Lowell, MA | 7.6 |
| 83 | Lubbock, TX | 13.2 |
| 32 | Lynchburg, VA | 25.4 |
| 275 | Lynn, MA | (8.6) |
| 188 | Macon, GA | (0.4) |
| 216 | Madison, WI | (2.4) |
| 153 | Manchester, NH | 5.0 |
| 93 | McAllen, TX | 11.5 |
| 58 | McKinney, TX | 16.6 |
| 281 | Medford, OR | (9.0) |
| 266 | Melbourne, FL | (7.8) |
| 289 | Memphis, TN | (9.6) |
| 268 | Menifee, CA | (7.9) |
| 289 | Merced, CA | (9.6) |
| 52 | Meridian, ID | 17.8 |
| 143 | Mesa, AZ | 6.2 |
| 90 | Mesquite, TX | 11.9 |
| 352 | Miami Beach, FL | (15.7) |
| 73 | Miami Gardens, FL | 15.0 |
| 419 | Miami, FL | (30.1) |
| 80 | Midland, TX | 14.0 |
| 280 | Milwaukee, WI | (8.9) |
| 339 | Minneapolis, MN | (14.6) |
| 181 | Miramar, FL | 1.0 |
| 314 | Mission Viejo, CA | (11.5) |
| 106 | Mission, TX | 10.2 |
| 39 | Mobile, AL | 23.8 |
| 394 | Modesto, CA | (22.6) |
| 275 | Moreno Valley, CA | (8.6) |
| 64 | Mountain View, CA | 16.2 |
| 246 | Murfreesboro, TN | (6.0) |
| 2 | Murrieta, CA | 57.1 |
| 3 | Nampa, ID | 51.4 |
| 430 | Napa, CA | (41.3) |
| 362 | Naperville, IL | (17.8) |
| 374 | Nashua, NH | (19.2) |
| 367 | Nashville, TN | (18.3) |
| 85 | New Bedford, MA | 12.3 |
| 157 | New Haven, CT | 4.5 |
| 257 | New Orleans, LA | (6.9) |
| 151 | New Rochelle, NY | 5.2 |
| 299 | New York, NY | (10.4) |
| 408 | Newark, NJ | (26.8) |
| 114 | Newport Beach, CA | 9.1 |
| 20 | Newport News, VA | 31.7 |
| 90 | Newton, MA | 11.9 |
| 155 | Norfolk, VA | 4.6 |
| 228 | Norman, OK | (3.2) |
| 284 | North Charleston, SC | (9.2) |
| 178 | North Las Vegas, NV | 1.2 |
| 141 | Norwalk, CA | 6.6 |
| 245 | Norwalk, CT | (5.5) |
| 224 | Oakland, CA | (3.1) |
| 307 | Oceanside, CA | (10.8) |
| 65 | Odessa, TX | 16.0 |
| 257 | O'Fallon, MO | (6.9) |
| 24 | Ogden, UT | 28.4 |
| 271 | Oklahoma City, OK | (8.3) |
| 197 | Olathe, KS | (1.0) |
| 105 | Omaha, NE | 10.3 |
| 94 | Ontario, CA | 11.3 |
| 249 | Orange, CA | (6.3) |
| 27 | Orem, UT | 26.4 |
| 399 | Orlando, FL | (23.9) |
| 348 | Overland Park, KS | (15.2) |
| 44 | Oxnard, CA | 21.1 |
| 353 | Palm Bay, FL | (15.8) |
| 29 | Palmdale, CA | 25.6 |

| RANK | CITY | % CHANGE |
|---|---|---|
| 71 | Pasadena, CA | 15.1 |
| 207 | Pasadena, TX | (1.8) |
| 355 | Paterson, NJ | (16.2) |
| 62 | Pearland, TX | 16.3 |
| 251 | Pembroke Pines, FL | (6.4) |
| 398 | Peoria, AZ | (23.8) |
| 359 | Peoria, IL | (16.8) |
| 297 | Philadelphia, PA | (10.3) |
| 322 | Phoenix, AZ | (12.5) |
| 74 | Pittsburgh, PA | 14.9 |
| 375 | Plano, TX | (19.3) |
| 393 | Plantation, FL | (22.3) |
| 332 | Pomona, CA | (13.8) |
| 373 | Pompano Beach, FL | (19.1) |
| 382 | Port St. Lucie, FL | (20.4) |
| 293 | Portland, OR | (9.9) |
| 224 | Portsmouth, VA | (3.1) |
| 362 | Providence, RI | (17.8) |
| 235 | Provo, UT | (4.4) |
| 125 | Pueblo, CO | 8.1 |
| 426 | Quincy, MA | (36.9) |
| 406 | Racine, WI | (26.0) |
| 404 | Raleigh, NC | (25.8) |
| 381 | Ramapo, NY | (20.3) |
| 200 | Rancho Cucamon., CA | (1.1) |
| 432 | Reading, PA | (44.9) |
| 111 | Redding, CA | 9.3 |
| 7 | Redwood City, CA | 45.4 |
| 216 | Reno, NV | (2.4) |
| 131 | Renton, WA | 7.3 |
| 324 | Rialto, CA | (12.7) |
| 81 | Richardson, TX | 13.8 |
| 131 | Torrance, CA | 7.3 |
| 378 | Richmond, CA | (19.8) |
| 212 | Richmond, VA | (2.1) |
| 69 | Riverside, CA | 15.3 |
| 412 | Roanoke, VA | (27.5) |
| 76 | Rochester, MN | 14.5 |
| 204 | Rochester, NY | (1.4) |
| 197 | Rockford, IL | (1.0) |
| 190 | Roseville, CA | (0.6) |
| 395 | Roswell, GA | (22.9) |
| 431 | Round Rock, TX | (43.6) |
| 345 | Sacramento, CA | (14.8) |
| 304 | Salem, OR | (10.6) |
| 14 | Salinas, CA | 36.3 |
| 96 | Salt Lake City, UT | 11.2 |
| NA | San Angelo, TX** | NA |
| 173 | San Antonio, TX | 1.9 |
| 188 | San Bernardino, CA | (0.4) |
| 266 | San Diego, CA | (7.8) |
| 125 | San Francisco, CA | 8.1 |
| 309 | San Jose, CA | (10.9) |
| 78 | San Leandro, CA | 14.3 |
| 411 | San Marcos, CA | (27.4) |
| 134 | San Mateo, CA | 7.2 |
| 339 | Sandy Springs, GA | (14.6) |
| 13 | Sandy, UT | 36.6 |
| 263 | Santa Ana, CA | (7.6) |
| 293 | Santa Barbara, CA | (9.9) |
| 326 | Santa Clara, CA | (13.1) |
| 416 | Santa Clarita, CA | (28.4) |
| 1 | Santa Maria, CA | 81.0 |
| 275 | Santa Monica, CA | (8.6) |
| 219 | Santa Rosa, CA | (2.6) |
| 124 | Savannah, GA | 8.2 |
| 339 | Scottsdale, AZ | (14.6) |
| 202 | Scranton, PA | (1.2) |
| 51 | Seattle, WA | 18.2 |
| 122 | Shreveport, LA | 8.6 |
| 139 | Simi Valley, CA | 6.8 |
| 50 | Sioux City, IA | 18.5 |
| 330 | Sioux Falls, SD | (13.6) |
| 388 | Somerville, MA | (21.7) |
| 70 | South Bend, IN | 15.2 |

| RANK | CITY | % CHANGE |
|---|---|---|
| 187 | South Gate, CA | (0.2) |
| 153 | Sparks, NV | 5.0 |
| 81 | Spokane Valley, WA | 13.8 |
| 101 | Spokane, WA | 10.7 |
| 420 | Springfield, IL | (31.5) |
| 220 | Springfield, MA | (2.7) |
| 128 | Springfield, MO | 7.6 |
| 329 | Stamford, CT | (13.5) |
| 42 | Sterling Heights, MI | 22.2 |
| 339 | Stockton, CA | (14.6) |
| 386 | St. George, UT | (21.3) |
| 379 | St. Joseph, MO | (20.2) |
| 238 | St. Louis, MO | (4.5) |
| 232 | St. Paul, MN | (3.8) |
| 23 | St. Petersburg, FL | 29.0 |
| NA | Suffolk, VA** | NA |
| 21 | Sugar Land, TX | 30.6 |
| 56 | Sunnyvale, CA | 16.9 |
| 357 | Sunrise, FL | (16.3) |
| 43 | Surprise, AZ | 22.0 |
| 155 | Syracuse, NY | 4.6 |
| 147 | Tacoma, WA | 5.9 |
| 361 | Tallahassee, FL | (17.5) |
| 282 | Tampa, FL | (9.1) |
| 108 | Temecula, CA | 9.8 |
| 208 | Tempe, AZ | (1.9) |
| 205 | Thornton, CO | (1.5) |
| 176 | Thousand Oaks, CA | 1.3 |
| 376 | Toledo, OH | (19.4) |
| 428 | Toms River Twnshp, NJ | (39.6) |
| 234 | Topeka, KS | (4.1) |
| 131 | Torrance, CA | 7.3 |
| 367 | Tracy, CA | (18.3) |
| 299 | Trenton, NJ | (10.4) |
| 414 | Troy, MI | (28.0) |
| 312 | Tucson, AZ | (11.3) |
| 184 | Tulsa, OK | 0.2 |
| 409 | Tuscaloosa, AL | (27.0) |
| 350 | Tustin, CA | (15.4) |
| 12 | Tyler, TX | 37.4 |
| 118 | Upland, CA | 8.9 |
| 37 | Upper Darby Twnshp, PA | 24.2 |
| 17 | Vacaville, CA | 33.7 |
| 367 | Vallejo, CA | (18.3) |
| 304 | Vancouver, WA | (10.6) |
| 275 | Ventura, CA | (8.6) |
| 233 | Victorville, CA | (4.0) |
| 272 | Virginia Beach, VA | (8.4) |
| 53 | Visalia, CA | 17.5 |
| 190 | Vista, CA | (0.6) |
| 145 | Waco, TX | 6.1 |
| 383 | Warren, MI | (20.9) |
| 295 | Warwick, RI | (10.0) |
| 328 | Washington, DC | (13.3) |
| 15 | Waterbury, CT | 35.2 |
| 216 | Waukegan, IL | (2.4) |
| 264 | West Covina, CA | (7.7) |
| 40 | West Palm Beach, FL | 22.8 |
| 4 | West Valley, UT | 49.7 |
| 332 | Westland, MI | (13.8) |
| 160 | Westminster, CA | 4.1 |
| 99 | Westminster, CO | 10.8 |
| 334 | Whittier, CA | (13.9) |
| 31 | Wichita Falls, TX | 25.5 |
| 116 | Wichita, KS | 9.0 |
| 314 | Wilmington, NC | (11.5) |
| 307 | Winston-Salem, NC | (10.8) |
| 127 | Woodbridge Twnshp, NJ | 7.9 |
| 338 | Worcester, MA | (14.3) |
| 433 | Yakima, WA | (45.8) |
| 174 | Yonkers, NY | 1.8 |
| 251 | Yuma, AZ | (6.4) |

Source: CQ Press using reported data from the F.B.I. "Crime in the United States 2013"

*Motor vehicle theft includes the theft or attempted theft of a self-propelled vehicle. Excludes motorboats, construction equipment, airplanes, and farming equipment.

**Not available.

# 79. Percent Change in Motor Vehicle Theft Rate: 2012 to 2013 (continued)
## National Percent Change = 4.0% Decrease*

| RANK | CITY | % CHANGE | RANK | CITY | % CHANGE | RANK | CITY | % CHANGE |
|---|---|---|---|---|---|---|---|---|
| 1 | Santa Maria, CA | 81.0 | 75 | Broken Arrow, OK | 14.8 | 149 | Baton Rouge, LA | 5.6 |
| 2 | Murrieta, CA | 57.1 | 76 | Rochester, MN | 14.5 | 150 | Henderson, NV | 5.3 |
| 3 | Nampa, ID | 51.4 | 77 | Indio, CA | 14.4 | 151 | New Rochelle, NY | 5.2 |
| 4 | West Valley, UT | 49.7 | 78 | Jurupa Valley, CA | 14.3 | 152 | Evanston, IL | 5.1 |
| 5 | Abilene, TX | 49.2 | 78 | San Leandro, CA | 14.3 | 153 | Manchester, NH | 5.0 |
| 6 | Chico, CA | 48.4 | 80 | Midland, TX | 14.0 | 153 | Sparks, NV | 5.0 |
| 7 | Redwood City, CA | 45.4 | 81 | Richardson, TX | 13.8 | 155 | Norfolk, VA | 4.6 |
| 8 | Bellevue, WA | 44.8 | 81 | Spokane Valley, WA | 13.8 | 155 | Syracuse, NY | 4.6 |
| 9 | Birmingham, AL | 42.7 | 83 | Lubbock, TX | 13.2 | 157 | Anchorage, AK | 4.5 |
| 10 | Eugene, OR | 39.4 | 84 | Hammond, IN | 12.4 | 157 | Detroit, MI | 4.5 |
| 11 | Lansing, MI | 38.4 | 85 | Baltimore, MD | 12.3 | 157 | New Haven, CT | 4.5 |
| 12 | Tyler, TX | 37.4 | 85 | Fremont, CA | 12.3 | 160 | Westminster, CA | 4.1 |
| 13 | Sandy, UT | 36.6 | 85 | New Bedford, MA | 12.3 | 161 | Houston, TX | 3.9 |
| 14 | Salinas, CA | 36.3 | 88 | Columbia, MO | 12.2 | 162 | Killeen, TX | 3.7 |
| 15 | Waterbury, CT | 35.2 | 89 | Hayward, CA | 12.1 | 163 | Dallas, TX | 3.4 |
| 16 | Boise, ID | 34.0 | 90 | Daly City, CA | 11.9 | 164 | Beaumont, TX | 3.3 |
| 17 | Vacaville, CA | 33.7 | 90 | Mesquite, TX | 11.9 | 164 | Irving, TX | 3.3 |
| 18 | Chino Hills, CA | 33.4 | 90 | Newton, MA | 11.9 | 166 | Clearwater, FL | 3.2 |
| 19 | Greeley, CO | 32.1 | 93 | McAllen, TX | 11.5 | 166 | Longmont, CO | 3.2 |
| 20 | Newport News, VA | 31.7 | 94 | Elgin, IL | 11.3 | 168 | Berkeley, CA | 2.5 |
| 21 | Sugar Land, TX | 30.6 | 94 | Ontario, CA | 11.3 | 168 | Lakewood, CO | 2.5 |
| 22 | Billings, MT | 29.9 | 96 | Clarkstown, NY | 11.2 | 170 | Fishers, IN | 2.4 |
| 23 | St. Petersburg, FL | 29.0 | 96 | Salt Lake City, UT | 11.2 | 170 | Gainesville, FL | 2.4 |
| 24 | Ogden, UT | 28.4 | 98 | Cleveland, OH | 11.0 | 172 | Hesperia, CA | 2.0 |
| 25 | Clinton Twnshp, MI | 27.9 | 99 | Alameda, CA | 10.8 | 173 | San Antonio, TX | 1.9 |
| 26 | Columbus, GA | 27.7 | 99 | Westminster, CO | 10.8 | 174 | Irvine, CA | 1.8 |
| 27 | Orem, UT | 26.4 | 101 | Spokane, WA | 10.7 | 174 | Yonkers, NY | 1.8 |
| 28 | Bloomington, MN | 26.3 | 102 | Allen, TX | 10.5 | 176 | Lakewood Twnshp, NJ | 1.3 |
| 29 | Brick Twnshp, NJ | 25.6 | 102 | Amarillo, TX | 10.5 | 176 | Thousand Oaks, CA | 1.3 |
| 29 | Palmdale, CA | 25.6 | 104 | Burbank, CA | 10.4 | 178 | Independence, MO | 1.2 |
| 31 | Wichita Falls, TX | 25.5 | 105 | Omaha, NE | 10.3 | 178 | North Las Vegas, NV | 1.2 |
| 32 | Lynchburg, VA | 25.4 | 106 | Fullerton, CA | 10.2 | 180 | Bryan, TX | 1.1 |
| 33 | Kennewick, WA | 25.2 | 106 | Mission, TX | 10.2 | 181 | Escondido, CA | 1.0 |
| 34 | Fairfield, CA | 25.0 | 108 | Temecula, CA | 9.8 | 181 | Miramar, FL | 1.0 |
| 35 | Brownsville, TX | 24.5 | 109 | Antioch, CA | 9.5 | 183 | Frisco, TX | 0.5 |
| 36 | Hoover, AL | 24.4 | 109 | Greenville, NC | 9.5 | 184 | Tulsa, OK | 0.2 |
| 37 | Cape Coral, FL | 24.2 | 111 | Redding, CA | 9.3 | 185 | Inglewood, CA | 0.1 |
| 37 | Upper Darby Twnshp, PA | 24.2 | 112 | Aurora, CO | 9.2 | 186 | Lee's Summit, MO | (0.1) |
| 39 | Mobile, AL | 23.8 | 112 | Corpus Christi, TX | 9.2 | 187 | South Gate, CA | (0.2) |
| 40 | West Palm Beach, FL | 22.8 | 114 | Garland, TX | 9.1 | 188 | Macon, GA | (0.4) |
| 41 | Lafayette, LA | 22.7 | 114 | Newport Beach, CA | 9.1 | 188 | San Bernardino, CA | (0.4) |
| 42 | Sterling Heights, MI | 22.2 | 116 | High Point, NC | 9.0 | 190 | Cicero, IL | (0.6) |
| 43 | Surprise, AZ | 22.0 | 116 | Wichita, KS | 9.0 | 190 | El Monte, CA | (0.6) |
| 44 | Oxnard, CA | 21.1 | 118 | Largo, FL | 8.9 | 190 | Hamilton Twnshp, NJ | (0.6) |
| 45 | Lawrence, MA | 20.5 | 118 | Upland, CA | 8.9 | 190 | Lancaster, CA | (0.6) |
| 46 | Buena Park, CA | 19.3 | 120 | Albuquerque, NM | 8.7 | 190 | Roseville, CA | (0.6) |
| 47 | Edinburg, TX | 19.1 | 120 | Des Moines, IA | 8.7 | 190 | Vista, CA | (0.6) |
| 48 | Kansas City, MO | 19.0 | 122 | Shreveport, LA | 8.6 | 196 | Arlington, TX | (0.9) |
| 49 | Bloomington, IL | 18.9 | 123 | Fort Smith, AR | 8.3 | 197 | Chesapeake, VA | (1.0) |
| 50 | Sioux City, IA | 18.5 | 124 | Savannah, GA | 8.2 | 197 | Olathe, KS | (1.0) |
| 51 | Seattle, WA | 18.2 | 125 | Pueblo, CO | 8.1 | 197 | Rockford, IL | (1.0) |
| 52 | Meridian, ID | 17.8 | 125 | San Francisco, CA | 8.1 | 200 | Kent, WA | (1.1) |
| 53 | Visalia, CA | 17.5 | 127 | Woodbridge Twnshp, NJ | 7.9 | 200 | Rancho Cucamon., CA | (1.1) |
| 54 | El Cajon, CA | 17.1 | 128 | Lowell, MA | 7.6 | 202 | Joliet, IL | (1.2) |
| 55 | Brooklyn Park, MN | 17.0 | 128 | Springfield, MO | 7.6 | 202 | Scranton, PA | (1.2) |
| 56 | Sunnyvale, CA | 16.9 | 130 | Brockton, MA | 7.5 | 204 | Rochester, NY | (1.4) |
| 57 | Cedar Rapids, IA | 16.7 | 131 | Indianapolis, IN | 7.3 | 205 | Thornton, CO | (1.5) |
| 58 | McKinney, TX | 16.6 | 131 | Renton, WA | 7.3 | 206 | Huntsville, AL | (1.6) |
| 59 | Anaheim, CA | 16.5 | 131 | Torrance, CA | 7.3 | 207 | Pasadena, TX | (1.8) |
| 59 | Chino, CA | 16.5 | 134 | San Mateo, CA | 7.2 | 208 | Fontana, CA | (1.9) |
| 61 | Fayetteville, AR | 16.4 | 135 | Hillsboro, OR | 7.0 | 208 | Tempe, AZ | (1.9) |
| 62 | Concord, CA | 16.3 | 136 | Davie, FL | 6.9 | 210 | Bellflower, CA | (2.0) |
| 62 | Pearland, TX | 16.3 | 136 | Dearborn, MI | 6.9 | 210 | Little Rock, AR | (2.0) |
| 64 | Mountain View, CA | 16.2 | 136 | Huntington Beach, CA | 6.9 | 212 | Las Vegas, NV | (2.1) |
| 65 | Hemet, CA | 16.0 | 139 | Everett, WA | 6.8 | 212 | Richmond, VA | (2.1) |
| 65 | Odessa, TX | 16.0 | 139 | Simi Valley, CA | 6.8 | 214 | Fort Collins, CO | (2.2) |
| 67 | Cincinnati, OH | 15.9 | 141 | Norwalk, CA | 6.6 | 215 | Compton, CA | (2.3) |
| 68 | Edmond, OK | 15.6 | 142 | Chandler, AZ | 6.4 | 216 | Madison, WI | (2.4) |
| 69 | Riverside, CA | 15.3 | 143 | Lakeland, FL | 6.2 | 216 | Reno, NV | (2.4) |
| 70 | South Bend, IN | 15.2 | 143 | Mesa, AZ | 6.2 | 216 | Waukegan, IL | (2.4) |
| 71 | Evansville, IN | 15.1 | 145 | Waco, TX | 6.1 | 219 | Santa Rosa, CA | (2.6) |
| 71 | Pasadena, CA | 15.1 | 146 | Colorado Springs, CO | 6.0 | 220 | Springfield, MA | (2.7) |
| 73 | Miami Gardens, FL | 15.0 | 147 | Fargo, ND | 5.9 | 221 | Lincoln, NE | (2.8) |
| 74 | Pittsburgh, PA | 14.9 | 147 | Tacoma, WA | 5.9 | 222 | Bloomington, IN | (2.9) |

| RANK | CITY | % CHANGE | RANK | CITY | % CHANGE | RANK | CITY | % CHANGE |
|---|---|---|---|---|---|---|---|---|
| 222 | Boston, MA | (2.9) | 297 | Livonia, MI | (10.3) | 370 | Carlsbad, CA | (18.8) |
| 224 | Cambridge, MA | (3.1) | 297 | Philadelphia, PA | (10.3) | 372 | Glendale, CA | (18.9) |
| 224 | Laredo, TX | (3.1) | 299 | Bakersfield, CA | (10.4) | 373 | Pompano Beach, FL | (19.1) |
| 224 | Oakland, CA | (3.1) | 299 | Long Beach, CA | (10.4) | 374 | Nashua, NH | (19.2) |
| 224 | Portsmouth, VA | (3.1) | 299 | New York, NY | (10.4) | 375 | Plano, TX | (19.3) |
| 228 | Norman, OK | (3.2) | 299 | Trenton, NJ | (10.4) | 376 | Toledo, OH | (19.4) |
| 229 | Fort Worth, TX | (3.4) | 303 | Garden Grove, CA | (10.5) | 377 | Knoxville, TN | (19.6) |
| 230 | Arvada, CO | (3.6) | 304 | Dayton, OH | (10.6) | 378 | Richmond, CA | (19.8) |
| 230 | Gary, IN | (3.6) | 304 | Salem, OR | (10.6) | 379 | Hartford, CT | (20.2) |
| 232 | St. Paul, MN | (3.8) | 304 | Vancouver, WA | (10.6) | 379 | St. Joseph, MO | (20.2) |
| 233 | Victorville, CA | (4.0) | 307 | Oceanside, CA | (10.8) | 381 | Ramapo, NY | (20.3) |
| 234 | Topeka, KS | (4.1) | 307 | Winston-Salem, NC | (10.8) | 382 | Port St. Lucie, FL | (20.4) |
| 235 | Hialeah, FL | (4.4) | 309 | San Jose, CA | (10.9) | 383 | Warren, MI | (20.9) |
| 235 | Jacksonville, FL | (4.4) | 310 | Johns Creek, GA | (11.0) | 384 | Decatur, IL | (21.0) |
| 235 | Provo, UT | (4.4) | 311 | Gilbert, AZ | (11.2) | 385 | Athens-Clarke, GA | (21.2) |
| 238 | St. Louis, MO | (4.5) | 312 | Carson, CA | (11.3) | 386 | St. George, UT | (21.3) |
| 239 | Erie, PA | (4.7) | 312 | Tucson, AZ | (11.3) | 387 | Albany, GA | (21.6) |
| 240 | Edison Twnshp, NJ | (4.8) | 314 | Downey, CA | (11.5) | 388 | Somerville, MA | (21.7) |
| 240 | Fort Lauderdale, FL | (4.8) | 314 | Mission Viejo, CA | (11.5) | 389 | Las Cruces, NM | (21.8) |
| 242 | Federal Way, WA | (5.0) | 314 | Wilmington, NC | (11.5) | 390 | College Station, TX | (21.9) |
| 243 | Jersey City, NJ | (5.2) | 317 | Clarksville, TN | (11.9) | 391 | League City, TX | (22.0) |
| 243 | Los Angeles, CA | (5.2) | 318 | Alexandria, VA | (12.3) | 392 | Clovis, CA | (22.1) |
| 245 | Norwalk, CT | (5.5) | 318 | Buffalo, NY | (12.3) | 393 | Plantation, FL | (22.3) |
| 246 | Murfreesboro, TN | (6.0) | 318 | Greensboro, NC | (12.3) | 394 | Modesto, CA | (22.6) |
| 247 | Arlington Heights, IL | (6.2) | 321 | Aurora, IL | (12.4) | 395 | Roswell, GA | (22.9) |
| 247 | Fresno, CA | (6.2) | 322 | Akron, OH | (12.5) | 396 | Lawton, OK | (23.2) |
| 249 | Livermore, CA | (6.3) | 322 | Phoenix, AZ | (12.5) | 397 | Chula Vista, CA | (23.7) |
| 249 | Orange, CA | (6.3) | 324 | Rialto, CA | (12.7) | 398 | Peoria, AZ | (23.8) |
| 251 | Pembroke Pines, FL | (6.4) | 325 | Elk Grove, CA | (12.9) | 399 | Boulder, CO | (23.9) |
| 251 | Yuma, AZ | (6.4) | 326 | Santa Clara, CA | (13.1) | 399 | Orlando, FL | (23.9) |
| 253 | Grand Rapids, MI | (6.6) | 327 | Hampton, VA | (13.2) | 401 | Bridgeport, CT | (24.2) |
| 254 | Corona, CA | (6.7) | 328 | Washington, DC | (13.3) | 402 | Farmington Hills, MI | (24.5) |
| 255 | Baldwin Park, CA | (6.8) | 329 | Stamford, CT | (13.5) | 403 | Beaverton, OR | (25.6) |
| 255 | Fort Wayne, IN | (6.8) | 330 | Sioux Falls, SD | (13.6) | 404 | Kenosha, WI | (25.8) |
| 257 | New Orleans, LA | (6.9) | 331 | Kansas City, KS | (13.7) | 404 | Raleigh, NC | (25.8) |
| 257 | O'Fallon, MO | (6.9) | 332 | Pomona, CA | (13.8) | 406 | Chicago, IL | (26.0) |
| 259 | Lakewood, CA | (7.1) | 332 | Westland, MI | (13.8) | 406 | Racine, WI | (26.0) |
| 260 | Centennial, CO | (7.2) | 334 | Whittier, CA | (13.9) | 408 | Newark, NJ | (26.8) |
| 261 | Jackson, MS | (7.3) | 335 | Amherst, NY | (14.0) | 409 | Tuscaloosa, AL | (27.0) |
| 262 | Albany, NY | (7.5) | 336 | Champaign, IL | (14.1) | 410 | Clifton, NJ | (27.3) |
| 263 | Santa Ana, CA | (7.6) | 336 | Hollywood, FL | (14.1) | 411 | San Marcos, CA | (27.4) |
| 264 | Grand Prairie, TX | (7.7) | 338 | Worcester, MA | (14.3) | 412 | Roanoke, VA | (27.5) |
| 264 | West Covina, CA | (7.7) | 339 | Glendale, AZ | (14.6) | 413 | Citrus Heights, CA | (27.6) |
| 266 | Melbourne, FL | (7.8) | 339 | Minneapolis, MN | (14.6) | 414 | Troy, MI | (28.0) |
| 266 | San Diego, CA | (7.8) | 339 | Sandy Springs, GA | (14.6) | 415 | Coral Springs, FL | (28.3) |
| 268 | Menifee, CA | (7.9) | 339 | Scottsdale, AZ | (14.6) | 416 | Santa Clarita, CA | (28.4) |
| 269 | Denver, CO | (8.0) | 339 | Stockton, CA | (14.6) | 417 | Flint, MI | (29.1) |
| 270 | Louisville, KY | (8.1) | 344 | Elizabeth, NJ | (14.7) | 418 | Carrollton, TX | (29.4) |
| 271 | Oklahoma City, OK | (8.3) | 345 | Sacramento, CA | (14.8) | 419 | Miami, FL | (30.1) |
| 272 | Allentown, PA | (8.4) | 346 | Danbury, CT | (15.0) | 420 | Springfield, IL | (31.5) |
| 272 | Virginia Beach, VA | (8.4) | 347 | Fayetteville, NC | (15.1) | 421 | Lake Forest, CA | (31.9) |
| 274 | Alhambra, CA | (8.5) | 348 | Cheektowaga, NY | (15.2) | 422 | El Paso, TX | (32.0) |
| 275 | Duluth, MN | (8.6) | 348 | Overland Park, KS | (15.2) | 423 | Gresham, OR | (32.4) |
| 275 | Lynn, MA | (8.6) | 350 | Tustin, CA | (15.4) | 424 | Charleston, SC | (32.8) |
| 275 | Moreno Valley, CA | (8.6) | 351 | Lawrence, KS | (15.6) | 425 | Longview, TX | (35.7) |
| 275 | Santa Monica, CA | (8.6) | 352 | Miami Beach, FL | (15.7) | 426 | Quincy, MA | (36.9) |
| 275 | Ventura, CA | (8.6) | 353 | Palm Bay, FL | (15.8) | 427 | Denton, TX | (37.3) |
| 280 | Milwaukee, WI | (8.9) | 354 | Deerfield Beach, FL | (16.0) | 428 | Toms River Twnshp, NJ | (39.6) |
| 281 | Medford, OR | (9.0) | 355 | Charlotte, NC | (16.2) | 429 | Greece, NY | (40.2) |
| 282 | Austin, TX | (9.1) | 355 | Paterson, NJ | (16.2) | 430 | Napa, CA | (41.3) |
| 282 | Tampa, FL | (9.1) | 357 | Sunrise, FL | (16.3) | 431 | Round Rock, TX | (43.6) |
| 284 | North Charleston, SC | (9.2) | 358 | Atlanta, GA | (16.6) | 432 | Reading, PA | (44.9) |
| 285 | Boca Raton, FL | (9.3) | 359 | Peoria, IL | (16.8) | 433 | Yakima, WA | (45.8) |
| 285 | Colonie, NY | (9.3) | 360 | Davenport, IA | (16.9) | 434 | Bethlehem, PA | (46.8) |
| 285 | Green Bay, WI | (9.3) | 361 | Tallahassee, FL | (17.5) | NA | Bend, OR** | NA |
| 288 | Cranston, RI | (9.5) | 362 | Naperville, IL | (17.8) | NA | Canton Twnshp, MI** | NA |
| 289 | Memphis, TN | (9.6) | 362 | Providence, RI | (17.8) | NA | Chattanooga, TN** | NA |
| 289 | Merced, CA | (9.6) | 364 | Costa Mesa, CA | (17.9) | NA | Columbia, SC** | NA |
| 291 | Carmel, IN | (9.8) | 364 | Fall River, MA | (17.9) | NA | Concord, NC** | NA |
| 291 | Cary, NC | (9.8) | 364 | Hawthorne, CA | (17.9) | NA | Lewisville, TX** | NA |
| 293 | Portland, OR | (9.9) | 367 | Nashville, TN | (18.3) | NA | San Angelo, TX** | NA |
| 293 | Santa Barbara, CA | (9.9) | 367 | Tracy, CA | (18.3) | NA | Suffolk, VA** | NA |
| 295 | Lexington, KY | (10.0) | 367 | Vallejo, CA | (18.3) | | | |
| 295 | Warwick, RI | (10.0) | 370 | Ann Arbor, MI | (18.8) | | | |

Source: CQ Press using reported data from the F.B.I. "Crime in the United States 2013"

*Motor vehicle theft includes the theft or attempted theft of a self-propelled vehicle. Excludes motorboats, construction equipment, airplanes, and farming equipment.

**Not available.

# 80. Percent Change in Motor Vehicle Theft Rate: 2009 to 2013
## National Percent Change = 14.6% Decrease*

| RANK | CITY | % CHANGE | RANK | CITY | % CHANGE | RANK | CITY | % CHANGE |
|---|---|---|---|---|---|---|---|---|
| 151 | Abilene, TX | (5.4) | 41 | Chino, CA | 24.7 | 152 | Fullerton, CA | (5.7) |
| 312 | Akron, OH | (31.8) | 400 | Chula Vista, CA | (47.2) | 409 | Gainesville, FL | (49.5) |
| 38 | Alameda, CA | 27.0 | NA | Cicero, IL** | NA | 102 | Garden Grove, CA | 7.5 |
| 366 | Albany, GA | (41.4) | 163 | Cincinnati, OH | (7.8) | 236 | Garland, TX | (20.2) |
| 378 | Albany, NY | (43.3) | 288 | Citrus Heights, CA | (28.7) | 111 | Gary, IN | 4.5 |
| 210 | Albuquerque, NM | (16.0) | 402 | Clarkstown, NY | (47.3) | 299 | Gilbert, AZ | (29.7) |
| 205 | Alexandria, VA | (14.8) | 358 | Clarksville, TN | (39.4) | 324 | Glendale, AZ | (33.6) |
| 245 | Alhambra, CA | (22.2) | 369 | Clearwater, FL | (41.8) | 339 | Glendale, CA | (36.1) |
| 333 | Allentown, PA | (35.6) | 76 | Cleveland, OH | 12.9 | 416 | Grand Prairie, TX | (52.9) |
| 270 | Allen, TX | (25.5) | 403 | Clifton, NJ | (47.4) | 309 | Grand Rapids, MI | (31.5) |
| 153 | Amarillo, TX | (6.0) | 135 | Clinton Twnshp, MI | (1.3) | 373 | Greece, NY | (42.4) |
| 353 | Amherst, NY | (37.7) | 183 | Clovis, CA | (11.5) | 109 | Greeley, CO | 4.7 |
| 8 | Anaheim, CA | 73.1 | 381 | College Station, TX | (43.6) | 263 | Green Bay, WI | (24.8) |
| 150 | Anchorage, AK | (5.3) | 51 | Colonie, NY | 21.2 | 397 | Greensboro, NC | (46.2) |
| 277 | Ann Arbor, MI | (26.3) | 9 | Colorado Springs, CO | 67.3 | NA | Greenville, NC** | NA |
| 13 | Antioch, CA | 55.0 | 79 | Columbia, MO | 12.6 | 293 | Gresham, OR | (29.0) |
| 335 | Arlington Heights, IL | (35.7) | 89 | Columbia, SC | 10.9 | 27 | Hamilton Twnshp, NJ | 35.9 |
| 330 | Arlington, TX | (34.6) | 318 | Columbus, GA | (32.4) | 246 | Hammond, IN | (22.4) |
| 229 | Arvada, CO | (19.0) | 217 | Compton, CA | (17.4) | 354 | Hampton, VA | (38.2) |
| 316 | Athens-Clarke, GA | (32.1) | 197 | Concord, CA | (13.8) | 339 | Hartford, CT | (36.1) |
| 149 | Atlanta, GA | (5.1) | 428 | Concord, NC | (63.3) | 138 | Hawthorne, CA | (2.6) |
| 230 | Aurora, CO | (19.1) | 302 | Coral Springs, FL | (30.2) | 97 | Hayward, CA | 8.4 |
| 410 | Aurora, IL | (50.3) | 218 | Corona, CA | (17.6) | 14 | Hemet, CA | 54.3 |
| 189 | Austin, TX | (12.5) | 271 | Corpus Christi, TX | (25.6) | 207 | Henderson, NV | (15.3) |
| 75 | Bakersfield, CA | 13.0 | 63 | Costa Mesa, CA | 16.8 | 29 | Hesperia, CA | 35.4 |
| 310 | Baldwin Park, CA | (31.6) | 293 | Cranston, RI | (29.0) | 393 | Hialeah, FL | (45.7) |
| 134 | Baltimore, MD | (1.2) | 281 | Dallas, TX | (27.4) | 43 | High Point, NC | 24.0 |
| 400 | Baton Rouge, LA | (47.2) | 167 | Daly City, CA | (9.0) | 126 | Hillsboro, OR | 1.9 |
| 153 | Beaumont, TX | (6.0) | 351 | Danbury, CT | (37.5) | 220 | Hollywood, FL | (17.9) |
| 357 | Beaverton, OR | (39.2) | 45 | Davenport, IA | 23.6 | 106 | Hoover, AL | 6.1 |
| 28 | Bellevue, WA | 35.7 | 308 | Davie, FL | (31.1) | 139 | Houston, TX | (2.9) |
| 264 | Bellflower, CA | (25.1) | 197 | Dayton, OH | (13.8) | 68 | Huntington Beach, CA | 14.9 |
| 80 | Bend, OR | 12.5 | 373 | Dearborn, MI | (42.4) | 254 | Huntsville, AL | (24.1) |
| 237 | Berkeley, CA | (20.5) | 424 | Decatur, IL | (58.5) | 61 | Independence, MO | 17.3 |
| 430 | Bethlehem, PA | (65.8) | NA | Deerfield Beach, FL** | NA | 103 | Indianapolis, IN | 6.8 |
| 3 | Billings, MT | 109.1 | 390 | Denton, TX | (44.9) | 33 | Indio, CA | 31.2 |
| 132 | Birmingham, AL | (0.6) | 160 | Denver, CO | (6.8) | 183 | Inglewood, CA | (11.5) |
| 335 | Bloomington, IL | (35.7) | 72 | Des Moines, IA | 13.3 | 168 | Irvine, CA | (9.1) |
| 187 | Bloomington, IN | (12.2) | 55 | Detroit, MI | 18.6 | 320 | Irving, TX | (32.8) |
| 214 | Bloomington, MN | (17.0) | 206 | Downey, CA | (15.0) | 387 | Jacksonville, FL | (44.5) |
| 373 | Boca Raton, FL | (42.4) | 233 | Duluth, MN | (19.9) | 339 | Jackson, MS | (36.1) |
| 59 | Boise, ID | 17.9 | 166 | Edinburg, TX | (8.6) | 218 | Jersey City, NJ | (17.6) |
| 311 | Boston, MA | (31.7) | 379 | Edison Twnshp, NJ | (43.5) | 423 | Johns Creek, GA | (57.8) |
| 226 | Boulder, CO | (18.3) | 260 | Edmond, OK | (24.7) | 40 | Joliet, IL | 26.0 |
| 411 | Brick Twnshp, NJ | (50.4) | 265 | El Cajon, CA | (25.2) | NA | Jurupa Valley, CA** | NA |
| 343 | Bridgeport, CT | (36.4) | 231 | El Monte, CA | (19.6) | 161 | Kansas City, KS | (6.9) |
| 369 | Brockton, MA | (41.8) | 427 | El Paso, TX | (61.8) | 39 | Kansas City, MO | 26.5 |
| 69 | Broken Arrow, OK | 14.6 | 265 | Elgin, IL | (25.2) | 177 | Kennewick, WA | (10.7) |
| 227 | Brooklyn Park, MN | (18.6) | 113 | Elizabeth, NJ | 3.9 | 387 | Kenosha, WI | (44.5) |
| 260 | Brownsville, TX | (24.7) | 426 | Elk Grove, CA | (61.6) | 140 | Kent, WA | (3.4) |
| 420 | Bryan, TX | (55.2) | 324 | Erie, PA | (33.6) | 200 | Killeen, TX | (14.1) |
| 172 | Buena Park, CA | (10.3) | 125 | Escondido, CA | 2.1 | 91 | Knoxville, TN | 10.4 |
| 349 | Buffalo, NY | (37.1) | 330 | Eugene, OR | (34.6) | 345 | Lafayette, LA | (36.6) |
| 333 | Burbank, CA | (35.6) | NA | Evanston, IL** | NA | 339 | Lake Forest, CA | (36.1) |
| 404 | Cambridge, MA | (47.8) | 4 | Evansville, IN | 107.7 | 307 | Lakeland, FL | (30.8) |
| 93 | Canton Twnshp, MI | 10.1 | 42 | Everett, WA | 24.3 | 171 | Lakewood Twnshp, NJ | (9.7) |
| 211 | Cape Coral, FL | (16.2) | 12 | Fairfield, CA | 55.4 | 306 | Lakewood, CA | (30.7) |
| 223 | Carlsbad, CA | (18.2) | 367 | Fall River, MA | (41.6) | 144 | Lakewood, CO | (4.2) |
| 82 | Carmel, IN | 11.9 | 376 | Fargo, ND | (43.0) | 237 | Lancaster, CA | (20.5) |
| 359 | Carrollton, TX | (40.0) | 290 | Farmington Hills, MI | (28.8) | 7 | Lansing, MI | 79.8 |
| 114 | Carson, CA | 3.8 | 36 | Fayetteville, AR | 29.7 | 431 | Laredo, TX | (77.0) |
| 328 | Cary, NC | (34.3) | 290 | Fayetteville, NC | (28.8) | 280 | Largo, FL | (27.2) |
| 47 | Cedar Rapids, IA | 23.4 | 44 | Federal Way, WA | 23.7 | 329 | Las Cruces, NM | (34.4) |
| 196 | Centennial, CO | (13.6) | 104 | Fishers, IN | 6.7 | 312 | Las Vegas, NV | (31.8) |
| NA | Champaign, IL** | NA | 399 | Flint, MI | (47.1) | 76 | Lawrence, KS | 12.9 |
| 361 | Chandler, AZ | (40.5) | 116 | Fontana, CA | 3.7 | 6 | Lawrence, MA | 79.9 |
| 398 | Charleston, SC | (46.9) | 384 | Fort Collins, CO | (43.8) | 179 | Lawton, OK | (10.8) |
| 408 | Charlotte, NC | (48.4) | 188 | Fort Lauderdale, FL | (12.4) | 258 | League City, TX | (24.6) |
| 98 | Chattanooga, TN | 8.1 | 147 | Fort Smith, AR | (4.9) | 274 | Lee's Summit, MO | (25.9) |
| 293 | Cheektowaga, NY | (29.0) | 177 | Fort Wayne, IN | (10.7) | 290 | Lewisville, TX | (28.8) |
| 347 | Chesapeake, VA | (36.8) | 119 | Fort Worth, TX | 3.2 | 19 | Lexington, KY | 46.9 |
| 204 | Chicago, IL | (14.5) | 94 | Fremont, CA | 9.6 | 133 | Lincoln, NE | (1.0) |
| 53 | Chico, CA | 19.1 | 57 | Fresno, CA | 18.2 | 175 | Little Rock, AR | (10.5) |
| 241 | Chino Hills, CA | (21.1) | 335 | Frisco, TX | (35.7) | 78 | Livermore, CA | 12.7 |

| RANK | CITY | % CHANGE | RANK | CITY | % CHANGE | RANK | CITY | % CHANGE |
|---|---|---|---|---|---|---|---|---|
| 394 | Livonia, MI | (45.8) | 145 | Pasadena, CA | (4.4) | 220 | South Gate, CA | (17.9) |
| 136 | Long Beach, CA | (1.5) | 90 | Pasadena, TX | 10.7 | 131 | Sparks, NV | 0.5 |
| 215 | Longmont, CO | (17.2) | 54 | Paterson, NJ | 19.0 | 5 | Spokane Valley, WA | 85.0 |
| 422 | Longview, TX | (56.5) | 200 | Pearland, TX | (14.1) | 37 | Spokane, WA | 27.7 |
| 246 | Los Angeles, CA | (22.4) | 394 | Pembroke Pines, FL | (45.8) | 347 | Springfield, IL | (36.8) |
| 92 | Louisville, KY | 10.2 | 417 | Peoria, AZ | (53.1) | 186 | Springfield, MA | (12.0) |
| NA | Lowell, MA** | NA | 392 | Peoria, IL | (45.2) | 33 | Springfield, MO | 31.2 |
| 17 | Lubbock, TX | 50.7 | 216 | Philadelphia, PA | (17.3) | 223 | Stamford, CT | (18.2) |
| 271 | Lynchburg, VA | (25.6) | 303 | Phoenix, AZ | (30.3) | 108 | Sterling Heights, MI | 4.9 |
| 365 | Lynn, MA | (41.0) | 260 | Pittsburgh, PA | (24.7) | 141 | Stockton, CA | (3.9) |
| 239 | Macon, GA | (20.8) | 396 | Plano, TX | (46.0) | 169 | St. George, UT | (9.2) |
| 296 | Madison, WI | (29.3) | 361 | Plantation, FL | (40.5) | 11 | St. Joseph, MO | 58.1 |
| 143 | Manchester, NH | (4.0) | 141 | Pomona, CA | (3.9) | 265 | St. Louis, MO | (25.2) |
| 406 | McAllen, TX | (47.9) | 228 | Pompano Beach, FL | (18.8) | 156 | St. Paul, MN | (6.4) |
| 107 | McKinney, TX | 5.5 | 65 | Port St. Lucie, FL | 15.6 | 413 | St. Petersburg, FL | (50.6) |
| 10 | Medford, OR | 60.0 | 146 | Portland, OR | (4.6) | 100 | Suffolk, VA | 7.8 |
| 360 | Melbourne, FL | (40.1) | 285 | Portsmouth, VA | (27.9) | 367 | Sugar Land, TX | (41.6) |
| 332 | Memphis, TN | (35.0) | 202 | Providence, RI | (14.3) | 66 | Sunnyvale, CA | 15.5 |
| 114 | Menifee, CA | 3.8 | 253 | Provo, UT | (23.9) | 383 | Sunrise, FL | (43.7) |
| 23 | Merced, CA | 44.2 | 18 | Pueblo, CO | 49.1 | 268 | Surprise, AZ | (25.3) |
| 96 | Meridian, ID | 9.3 | 387 | Quincy, MA | (44.5) | 86 | Syracuse, NY | 11.2 |
| 258 | Mesa, AZ | (24.6) | 314 | Racine, WI | (32.0) | 61 | Tacoma, WA | 17.3 |
| 123 | Mesquite, TX | 2.6 | 211 | Raleigh, NC | (16.2) | 52 | Tallahassee, FL | 20.2 |
| 406 | Miami Beach, FL | (47.9) | 429 | Ramapo, NY | (65.4) | 425 | Tampa, FL | (60.1) |
| 279 | Miami Gardens, FL | (27.1) | 105 | Rancho Cucamon., CA | 6.6 | 119 | Temecula, CA | 3.2 |
| 255 | Miami, FL | (24.4) | 419 | Reading, PA | (54.9) | 349 | Tempe, AZ | (37.1) |
| 207 | Midland, TX | (15.3) | 1 | Redding, CA | 169.7 | 242 | Thornton, CO | (21.8) |
| 169 | Milwaukee, WI | (9.2) | 157 | Redwood City, CA | (6.5) | 112 | Thousand Oaks, CA | 4.0 |
| 209 | Minneapolis, MN | (15.4) | 95 | Reno, NV | 9.5 | 223 | Toledo, OH | (18.2) |
| 386 | Miramar, FL | (44.2) | 159 | Renton, WA | (6.6) | 345 | Toms River Twnshp, NJ | (36.6) |
| 172 | Mission Viejo, CA | (10.3) | 84 | Rialto, CA | 11.6 | 31 | Topeka, KS | 34.8 |
| 414 | Mission, TX | (52.0) | 404 | Richardson, TX | (47.8) | 190 | Torrance, CA | (13.0) |
| 298 | Mobile, AL | (29.6) | 127 | Richmond, CA | 1.5 | 282 | Tracy, CA | (27.5) |
| 116 | Modesto, CA | 3.7 | 164 | Richmond, VA | (7.9) | 127 | Trenton, NJ | 1.5 |
| 148 | Moreno Valley, CA | (5.0) | 50 | Riverside, CA | 22.3 | 180 | Troy, MI | (10.9) |
| 256 | Mountain View, CA | (24.5) | 364 | Roanoke, VA | (40.6) | 338 | Tucson, AZ | (35.9) |
| 182 | Murfreesboro, TN | (11.3) | 165 | Rochester, MN | (8.0) | 81 | Tulsa, OK | 12.4 |
| 35 | Murrieta, CA | 30.7 | 354 | Rochester, NY | (38.2) | 322 | Tuscaloosa, AL | (33.1) |
| 56 | Nampa, ID | 18.3 | 191 | Rockford, IL | (13.1) | 240 | Tustin, CA | (20.9) |
| 273 | Napa, CA | (25.7) | 314 | Roseville, CA | (32.0) | 276 | Tyler, TX | (26.2) |
| 385 | Naperville, IL | (43.9) | 379 | Roswell, GA | (43.5) | NA | Upland, CA** | NA |
| 326 | Nashua, NH | (33.7) | 421 | Round Rock, TX | (56.4) | 119 | Upper Darby Twnshp, PA | 3.2 |
| 323 | Nashville, TN | (33.4) | 316 | Sacramento, CA | (32.1) | 22 | Vacaville, CA | 44.3 |
| 70 | New Bedford, MA | 14.4 | 124 | Salem, OR | 2.4 | 162 | Vallejo, CA | (7.6) |
| 327 | New Haven, CT | (34.2) | 49 | Salinas, CA | 22.4 | 101 | Vancouver, WA | 7.7 |
| 278 | New Orleans, LA | (26.8) | 45 | Salt Lake City, UT | 23.6 | 26 | Ventura, CA | 39.5 |
| 300 | New Rochelle, NY | (30.0) | 88 | San Angelo, TX | 11.1 | 32 | Victorville, CA | 31.3 |
| 304 | New York, NY | (30.5) | 86 | San Antonio, TX | 11.2 | 252 | Virginia Beach, VA | (23.8) |
| 155 | Newark, NJ | (6.1) | 57 | San Bernardino, CA | 18.2 | 71 | Visalia, CA | 14.0 |
| 268 | Newport Beach, CA | (25.3) | 234 | San Diego, CA | (20.1) | 220 | Vista, CA | (17.9) |
| NA | Newport News, VA** | NA | 64 | San Francisco, CA | 16.0 | 415 | Waco, TX | (52.1) |
| 381 | Newton, MA | (43.6) | 24 | San Jose, CA | 41.7 | 371 | Warren, MI | (42.0) |
| 250 | Norfolk, VA | (23.3) | 191 | San Leandro, CA | (13.1) | 286 | Warwick, RI | (28.0) |
| 99 | Norman, OK | 7.9 | 251 | San Marcos, CA | (23.4) | 390 | Washington, DC | (44.9) |
| 249 | North Charleston, SC | (22.9) | 234 | San Mateo, CA | (20.1) | 21 | Waterbury, CT | 44.8 |
| 191 | North Las Vegas, NV | (13.1) | 418 | Sandy Springs, GA | (53.3) | NA | Waukegan, IL** | NA |
| 176 | Norwalk, CA | (10.6) | 129 | Sandy, UT | 1.1 | 232 | West Covina, CA | (19.8) |
| 411 | Norwalk, CT | (50.4) | 130 | Santa Ana, CA | 0.9 | 185 | West Palm Beach, FL | (11.6) |
| 110 | Oakland, CA | 4.6 | 67 | Santa Barbara, CA | 15.4 | 82 | West Valley, UT | 11.9 |
| 172 | Oceanside, CA | (10.3) | 191 | Santa Clara, CA | (13.1) | 203 | Westland, MI | (14.4) |
| 2 | Odessa, TX | 123.5 | 343 | Santa Clarita, CA | (36.4) | 20 | Westminster, CA | 45.4 |
| 243 | O'Fallon, MO | (21.9) | 15 | Santa Maria, CA | 53.2 | 305 | Westminster, CO | (30.6) |
| 197 | Ogden, UT | (13.8) | 361 | Santa Monica, CA | (40.5) | 181 | Whittier, CA | (11.0) |
| 137 | Oklahoma City, OK | (1.9) | 284 | Santa Rosa, CA | (27.7) | 213 | Wichita Falls, TX | (16.4) |
| 116 | Olathe, KS | 3.7 | 372 | Savannah, GA | (42.2) | 72 | Wichita, KS | 13.3 |
| 16 | Omaha, NE | 51.1 | 286 | Scottsdale, AZ | (28.0) | 352 | Wilmington, NC | (37.6) |
| 59 | Ontario, CA | 17.9 | 274 | Scranton, PA | (25.9) | 283 | Winston-Salem, NC | (27.6) |
| 74 | Orange, CA | 13.1 | 48 | Seattle, WA | 22.9 | 320 | Woodbridge Twnshp, NJ | (32.8) |
| 195 | Orem, UT | (13.3) | 246 | Shreveport, LA | (22.4) | 377 | Worcester, MA | (43.2) |
| 256 | Orlando, FL | (24.5) | 85 | Simi Valley, CA | 11.5 | NA | Yakima, WA** | NA |
| 243 | Overland Park, KS | (21.9) | 25 | Sioux City, IA | 40.2 | 301 | Yonkers, NY | (30.1) |
| 30 | Oxnard, CA | 35.2 | 157 | Sioux Falls, SD | (6.5) | 319 | Yuma, AZ | (32.7) |
| 288 | Palm Bay, FL | (28.7) | 356 | Somerville, MA | (39.0) | | | |
| 297 | Palmdale, CA | (29.5) | 122 | South Bend, IN | 2.9 | | | |

Source: CQ Press using reported data from the F.B.I. "Crime in the United States 2013"

*Motor vehicle theft includes the theft or attempted theft of a self-propelled vehicle. Excludes motorboats, construction equipment, airplanes, and farming equipment.

**Not available.

# 80. Percent Change in Motor Vehicle Theft Rate: 2009 to 2013 (continued)
## National Percent Change = 14.6% Decrease*

| RANK | CITY | % CHANGE | RANK | CITY | % CHANGE | RANK | CITY | % CHANGE |
|---|---|---|---|---|---|---|---|---|
| 1 | Redding, CA | 169.7 | 75 | Bakersfield, CA | 13.0 | 149 | Atlanta, GA | (5.1) |
| 2 | Odessa, TX | 123.5 | 76 | Cleveland, OH | 12.9 | 150 | Anchorage, AK | (5.3) |
| 3 | Billings, MT | 109.1 | 76 | Lawrence, KS | 12.9 | 151 | Abilene, TX | (5.4) |
| 4 | Evansville, IN | 107.7 | 78 | Livermore, CA | 12.7 | 152 | Fullerton, CA | (5.7) |
| 5 | Spokane Valley, WA | 85.0 | 79 | Columbia, MO | 12.6 | 153 | Amarillo, TX | (6.0) |
| 6 | Lawrence, MA | 79.9 | 80 | Bend, OR | 12.5 | 153 | Beaumont, TX | (6.0) |
| 7 | Lansing, MI | 79.8 | 81 | Tulsa, OK | 12.4 | 155 | Newark, NJ | (6.1) |
| 8 | Anaheim, CA | 73.1 | 82 | Carmel, IN | 11.9 | 156 | St. Paul, MN | (6.4) |
| 9 | Colorado Springs, CO | 67.3 | 82 | West Valley, UT | 11.9 | 157 | Redwood City, CA | (6.5) |
| 10 | Medford, OR | 60.0 | 84 | Rialto, CA | 11.6 | 157 | Sioux Falls, SD | (6.5) |
| 11 | St. Joseph, MO | 58.1 | 85 | Simi Valley, CA | 11.5 | 159 | Renton, WA | (6.6) |
| 12 | Fairfield, CA | 55.4 | 86 | San Antonio, TX | 11.2 | 160 | Denver, CO | (6.8) |
| 13 | Antioch, CA | 55.0 | 86 | Syracuse, NY | 11.2 | 161 | Kansas City, KS | (6.9) |
| 14 | Hemet, CA | 54.3 | 88 | San Angelo, TX | 11.1 | 162 | Vallejo, CA | (7.6) |
| 15 | Santa Maria, CA | 53.2 | 89 | Columbia, SC | 10.9 | 163 | Cincinnati, OH | (7.8) |
| 16 | Omaha, NE | 51.1 | 90 | Pasadena, TX | 10.7 | 164 | Richmond, VA | (7.9) |
| 17 | Lubbock, TX | 50.7 | 91 | Knoxville, TN | 10.4 | 165 | Rochester, MN | (8.0) |
| 18 | Pueblo, CO | 49.1 | 92 | Louisville, KY | 10.2 | 166 | Edinburg, TX | (8.6) |
| 19 | Lexington, KY | 46.9 | 93 | Canton Twnshp, MI | 10.1 | 167 | Daly City, CA | (9.0) |
| 20 | Westminster, CA | 45.4 | 94 | Fremont, CA | 9.6 | 168 | Irvine, CA | (9.1) |
| 21 | Waterbury, CT | 44.8 | 95 | Reno, NV | 9.5 | 169 | Milwaukee, WI | (9.2) |
| 22 | Vacaville, CA | 44.3 | 96 | Meridian, ID | 9.3 | 169 | St. George, UT | (9.2) |
| 23 | Merced, CA | 44.2 | 97 | Hayward, CA | 8.4 | 171 | Lakewood Twnshp, NJ | (9.7) |
| 24 | San Jose, CA | 41.7 | 98 | Chattanooga, TN | 8.1 | 172 | Buena Park, CA | (10.3) |
| 25 | Sioux City, IA | 40.2 | 99 | Norman, OK | 7.9 | 172 | Mission Viejo, CA | (10.3) |
| 26 | Ventura, CA | 39.5 | 100 | Suffolk, VA | 7.8 | 172 | Oceanside, CA | (10.3) |
| 27 | Hamilton Twnshp, NJ | 35.9 | 101 | Vancouver, WA | 7.7 | 175 | Little Rock, AR | (10.5) |
| 28 | Bellevue, WA | 35.7 | 102 | Garden Grove, CA | 7.5 | 176 | Norwalk, CA | (10.6) |
| 29 | Hesperia, CA | 35.4 | 103 | Indianapolis, IN | 6.8 | 177 | Fort Wayne, IN | (10.7) |
| 30 | Oxnard, CA | 35.2 | 104 | Fishers, IN | 6.7 | 177 | Kennewick, WA | (10.7) |
| 31 | Topeka, KS | 34.8 | 105 | Rancho Cucamon., CA | 6.6 | 179 | Lawton, OK | (10.8) |
| 32 | Victorville, CA | 31.3 | 106 | Hoover, AL | 6.1 | 180 | Troy, MI | (10.9) |
| 33 | Indio, CA | 31.2 | 107 | McKinney, TX | 5.5 | 181 | Whittier, CA | (11.0) |
| 33 | Springfield, MO | 31.2 | 108 | Sterling Heights, MI | 4.9 | 182 | Murfreesboro, TN | (11.3) |
| 35 | Murrieta, CA | 30.7 | 109 | Greeley, CO | 4.7 | 183 | Clovis, CA | (11.5) |
| 36 | Fayetteville, AR | 29.7 | 110 | Oakland, CA | 4.6 | 183 | Inglewood, CA | (11.5) |
| 37 | Spokane, WA | 27.7 | 111 | Gary, IN | 4.5 | 185 | West Palm Beach, FL | (11.6) |
| 38 | Alameda, CA | 27.0 | 112 | Thousand Oaks, CA | 4.0 | 186 | Springfield, MA | (12.0) |
| 39 | Kansas City, MO | 26.5 | 113 | Elizabeth, NJ | 3.9 | 187 | Bloomington, IN | (12.2) |
| 40 | Joliet, IL | 26.0 | 114 | Carson, CA | 3.8 | 188 | Fort Lauderdale, FL | (12.4) |
| 41 | Chino, CA | 24.7 | 114 | Menifee, CA | 3.8 | 189 | Austin, TX | (12.5) |
| 42 | Everett, WA | 24.3 | 116 | Fontana, CA | 3.7 | 190 | Torrance, CA | (13.0) |
| 43 | High Point, NC | 24.0 | 116 | Modesto, CA | 3.7 | 191 | North Las Vegas, NV | (13.1) |
| 44 | Federal Way, WA | 23.7 | 116 | Olathe, KS | 3.7 | 191 | Rockford, IL | (13.1) |
| 45 | Davenport, IA | 23.6 | 119 | Fort Worth, TX | 3.2 | 191 | San Leandro, CA | (13.1) |
| 45 | Salt Lake City, UT | 23.6 | 119 | Temecula, CA | 3.2 | 191 | Santa Clara, CA | (13.1) |
| 47 | Cedar Rapids, IA | 23.4 | 119 | Upper Darby Twnshp, PA | 3.2 | 195 | Orem, UT | (13.3) |
| 48 | Seattle, WA | 22.9 | 122 | South Bend, IN | 2.9 | 196 | Centennial, CO | (13.6) |
| 49 | Salinas, CA | 22.4 | 123 | Mesquite, TX | 2.6 | 197 | Concord, CA | (13.8) |
| 50 | Riverside, CA | 22.3 | 124 | Salem, OR | 2.4 | 197 | Dayton, OH | (13.8) |
| 51 | Colonie, NY | 21.2 | 125 | Escondido, CA | 2.1 | 197 | Ogden, UT | (13.8) |
| 52 | Tallahassee, FL | 20.2 | 126 | Hillsboro, OR | 1.9 | 200 | Killeen, TX | (14.1) |
| 53 | Chico, CA | 19.1 | 127 | Richmond, CA | 1.5 | 200 | Pearland, TX | (14.1) |
| 54 | Paterson, NJ | 19.0 | 127 | Trenton, NJ | 1.5 | 202 | Providence, RI | (14.3) |
| 55 | Detroit, MI | 18.6 | 129 | Sandy, UT | 1.1 | 203 | Westland, MI | (14.4) |
| 56 | Nampa, ID | 18.3 | 130 | Santa Ana, CA | 0.9 | 204 | Chicago, IL | (14.5) |
| 57 | Fresno, CA | 18.2 | 131 | Sparks, NV | 0.5 | 205 | Alexandria, VA | (14.8) |
| 57 | San Bernardino, CA | 18.2 | 132 | Birmingham, AL | (0.6) | 206 | Downey, CA | (15.0) |
| 59 | Boise, ID | 17.9 | 133 | Lincoln, NE | (1.0) | 207 | Henderson, NV | (15.3) |
| 59 | Ontario, CA | 17.9 | 134 | Baltimore, MD | (1.2) | 207 | Midland, TX | (15.3) |
| 61 | Independence, MO | 17.3 | 135 | Clinton Twnshp, MI | (1.3) | 209 | Minneapolis, MN | (15.4) |
| 61 | Tacoma, WA | 17.3 | 136 | Long Beach, CA | (1.5) | 210 | Albuquerque, NM | (16.0) |
| 63 | Costa Mesa, CA | 16.8 | 137 | Oklahoma City, OK | (1.9) | 211 | Cape Coral, FL | (16.2) |
| 64 | San Francisco, CA | 16.0 | 138 | Hawthorne, CA | (2.6) | 211 | Raleigh, NC | (16.2) |
| 65 | Port St. Lucie, FL | 15.6 | 139 | Houston, TX | (2.9) | 213 | Wichita Falls, TX | (16.4) |
| 66 | Sunnyvale, CA | 15.5 | 140 | Kent, WA | (3.4) | 214 | Bloomington, MN | (17.0) |
| 67 | Santa Barbara, CA | 15.4 | 141 | Pomona, CA | (3.9) | 215 | Longmont, CO | (17.2) |
| 68 | Huntington Beach, CA | 14.9 | 141 | Stockton, CA | (3.9) | 216 | Philadelphia, PA | (17.3) |
| 69 | Broken Arrow, OK | 14.6 | 143 | Manchester, NH | (4.0) | 217 | Compton, CA | (17.4) |
| 70 | New Bedford, MA | 14.4 | 144 | Lakewood, CO | (4.2) | 218 | Corona, CA | (17.6) |
| 71 | Visalia, CA | 14.0 | 145 | Pasadena, CA | (4.4) | 218 | Jersey City, NJ | (17.6) |
| 72 | Des Moines, IA | 13.3 | 146 | Portland, OR | (4.6) | 220 | Hollywood, FL | (17.9) |
| 72 | Wichita, KS | 13.3 | 147 | Fort Smith, AR | (4.9) | 220 | South Gate, CA | (17.9) |
| 74 | Orange, CA | 13.1 | 148 | Moreno Valley, CA | (5.0) | 220 | Vista, CA | (17.9) |

| RANK | CITY | % CHANGE | RANK | CITY | % CHANGE | RANK | CITY | % CHANGE |
|---|---|---|---|---|---|---|---|---|
| 223 | Carlsbad, CA | (18.2) | 297 | Palmdale, CA | (29.5) | 371 | Warren, MI | (42.0) |
| 223 | Stamford, CT | (18.2) | 298 | Mobile, AL | (29.6) | 372 | Savannah, GA | (42.2) |
| 223 | Toledo, OH | (18.2) | 299 | Gilbert, AZ | (29.7) | 373 | Boca Raton, FL | (42.4) |
| 226 | Boulder, CO | (18.3) | 300 | New Rochelle, NY | (30.0) | 373 | Dearborn, MI | (42.4) |
| 227 | Brooklyn Park, MN | (18.6) | 301 | Yonkers, NY | (30.1) | 373 | Greece, NY | (42.4) |
| 228 | Pompano Beach, FL | (18.8) | 302 | Coral Springs, FL | (30.2) | 376 | Fargo, ND | (43.0) |
| 229 | Arvada, CO | (19.0) | 303 | Phoenix, AZ | (30.3) | 377 | Worcester, MA | (43.2) |
| 230 | Aurora, CO | (19.1) | 304 | New York, NY | (30.5) | 378 | Albany, NY | (43.3) |
| 231 | El Monte, CA | (19.6) | 305 | Westminster, CO | (30.6) | 379 | Edison Twnshp, NJ | (43.5) |
| 232 | West Covina, CA | (19.8) | 306 | Lakewood, CA | (30.7) | 379 | Roswell, GA | (43.5) |
| 233 | Duluth, MN | (19.9) | 307 | Lakeland, FL | (30.8) | 381 | College Station, TX | (43.6) |
| 234 | San Diego, CA | (20.1) | 308 | Davie, FL | (31.1) | 381 | Newton, MA | (43.6) |
| 234 | San Mateo, CA | (20.1) | 309 | Grand Rapids, MI | (31.5) | 383 | Sunrise, FL | (43.7) |
| 236 | Garland, TX | (20.2) | 310 | Baldwin Park, CA | (31.6) | 384 | Fort Collins, CO | (43.8) |
| 237 | Berkeley, CA | (20.5) | 311 | Boston, MA | (31.7) | 385 | Naperville, IL | (43.9) |
| 237 | Lancaster, CA | (20.5) | 312 | Akron, OH | (31.8) | 386 | Miramar, FL | (44.2) |
| 239 | Macon, GA | (20.8) | 312 | Las Vegas, NV | (31.8) | 387 | Jacksonville, FL | (44.5) |
| 240 | Tustin, CA | (20.9) | 314 | Racine, WI | (32.0) | 387 | Kenosha, WI | (44.5) |
| 241 | Chino Hills, CA | (21.1) | 314 | Roseville, CA | (32.0) | 387 | Quincy, MA | (44.5) |
| 242 | Thornton, CO | (21.8) | 316 | Athens-Clarke, GA | (32.1) | 390 | Denton, TX | (44.9) |
| 243 | O'Fallon, MO | (21.9) | 316 | Sacramento, CA | (32.1) | 390 | Washington, DC | (44.9) |
| 243 | Overland Park, KS | (21.9) | 318 | Columbus, GA | (32.4) | 392 | Peoria, IL | (45.2) |
| 245 | Alhambra, CA | (22.2) | 319 | Yuma, AZ | (32.7) | 393 | Hialeah, FL | (45.7) |
| 246 | Hammond, IN | (22.4) | 320 | Irving, TX | (32.8) | 394 | Livonia, MI | (45.8) |
| 246 | Los Angeles, CA | (22.4) | 320 | Woodbridge Twnshp, NJ | (32.8) | 394 | Pembroke Pines, FL | (45.8) |
| 246 | Shreveport, LA | (22.4) | 322 | Tuscaloosa, AL | (33.1) | 396 | Plano, TX | (46.0) |
| 249 | North Charleston, SC | (22.9) | 323 | Nashville, TN | (33.4) | 397 | Greensboro, NC | (46.2) |
| 250 | Norfolk, VA | (23.3) | 324 | Erie, PA | (33.6) | 398 | Charleston, SC | (46.9) |
| 251 | San Marcos, CA | (23.4) | 324 | Glendale, AZ | (33.6) | 399 | Flint, MI | (47.1) |
| 252 | Virginia Beach, VA | (23.8) | 326 | Nashua, NH | (33.7) | 400 | Baton Rouge, LA | (47.2) |
| 253 | Provo, UT | (23.9) | 327 | New Haven, CT | (34.2) | 400 | Chula Vista, CA | (47.2) |
| 254 | Huntsville, AL | (24.1) | 328 | Cary, NC | (34.3) | 402 | Clarkstown, NY | (47.3) |
| 255 | Miami, FL | (24.4) | 329 | Las Cruces, NM | (34.4) | 403 | Clifton, NJ | (47.4) |
| 256 | Mountain View, CA | (24.5) | 330 | Arlington, TX | (34.6) | 404 | Cambridge, MA | (47.8) |
| 256 | Orlando, FL | (24.5) | 330 | Eugene, OR | (34.6) | 404 | Richardson, TX | (47.8) |
| 258 | League City, TX | (24.6) | 332 | Memphis, TN | (35.0) | 406 | McAllen, TX | (47.9) |
| 258 | Mesa, AZ | (24.6) | 333 | Allentown, PA | (35.6) | 406 | Miami Beach, FL | (47.9) |
| 260 | Brownsville, TX | (24.7) | 333 | Burbank, CA | (35.6) | 408 | Charlotte, NC | (48.4) |
| 260 | Edmond, OK | (24.7) | 335 | Arlington Heights, IL | (35.7) | 409 | Gainesville, FL | (49.5) |
| 260 | Pittsburgh, PA | (24.7) | 335 | Bloomington, IL | (35.7) | 410 | Aurora, IL | (50.3) |
| 263 | Green Bay, WI | (24.8) | 335 | Frisco, TX | (35.7) | 411 | Brick Twnshp, NJ | (50.4) |
| 264 | Bellflower, CA | (25.1) | 338 | Tucson, AZ | (35.9) | 411 | Norwalk, CT | (50.4) |
| 265 | El Cajon, CA | (25.2) | 339 | Glendale, CA | (36.1) | 413 | St. Petersburg, FL | (50.6) |
| 265 | Elgin, IL | (25.2) | 339 | Hartford, CT | (36.1) | 414 | Mission, TX | (52.0) |
| 265 | St. Louis, MO | (25.2) | 339 | Jackson, MS | (36.1) | 415 | Waco, TX | (52.1) |
| 268 | Newport Beach, CA | (25.3) | 339 | Lake Forest, CA | (36.1) | 416 | Grand Prairie, TX | (52.9) |
| 268 | Surprise, AZ | (25.3) | 343 | Bridgeport, CT | (36.4) | 417 | Peoria, AZ | (53.1) |
| 270 | Allen, TX | (25.5) | 343 | Santa Clarita, CA | (36.4) | 418 | Sandy Springs, GA | (53.3) |
| 271 | Corpus Christi, TX | (25.6) | 345 | Lafayette, LA | (36.6) | 419 | Reading, PA | (54.9) |
| 271 | Lynchburg, VA | (25.6) | 345 | Toms River Twnshp, NJ | (36.6) | 420 | Bryan, TX | (55.2) |
| 273 | Napa, CA | (25.7) | 347 | Chesapeake, VA | (36.8) | 421 | Round Rock, TX | (56.4) |
| 274 | Lee's Summit, MO | (25.9) | 347 | Springfield, IL | (36.8) | 422 | Longview, TX | (56.5) |
| 274 | Scranton, PA | (25.9) | 349 | Buffalo, NY | (37.1) | 423 | Johns Creek, GA | (57.8) |
| 276 | Tyler, TX | (26.2) | 349 | Tempe, AZ | (37.1) | 424 | Decatur, IL | (58.5) |
| 277 | Ann Arbor, MI | (26.3) | 351 | Danbury, CT | (37.5) | 425 | Tampa, FL | (60.1) |
| 278 | New Orleans, LA | (26.8) | 352 | Wilmington, NC | (37.6) | 426 | Elk Grove, CA | (61.6) |
| 279 | Miami Gardens, FL | (27.1) | 353 | Amherst, NY | (37.7) | 427 | El Paso, TX | (61.8) |
| 280 | Largo, FL | (27.2) | 354 | Hampton, VA | (38.2) | 428 | Concord, NC | (63.3) |
| 281 | Dallas, TX | (27.4) | 354 | Rochester, NY | (38.2) | 429 | Ramapo, NY | (65.4) |
| 282 | Tracy, CA | (27.5) | 356 | Somerville, MA | (39.0) | 430 | Bethlehem, PA | (65.8) |
| 283 | Winston-Salem, NC | (27.6) | 357 | Beaverton, OR | (39.2) | 431 | Laredo, TX | (77.0) |
| 284 | Santa Rosa, CA | (27.7) | 358 | Clarksville, TN | (39.4) | NA | Champaign, IL** | NA |
| 285 | Portsmouth, VA | (27.9) | 359 | Carrollton, TX | (40.0) | NA | Cicero, IL** | NA |
| 286 | Scottsdale, AZ | (28.0) | 360 | Melbourne, FL | (40.1) | NA | Deerfield Beach, FL** | NA |
| 286 | Warwick, RI | (28.0) | 361 | Chandler, AZ | (40.5) | NA | Evanston, IL** | NA |
| 288 | Citrus Heights, CA | (28.7) | 361 | Plantation, FL | (40.5) | NA | Greenville, NC** | NA |
| 288 | Palm Bay, FL | (28.7) | 361 | Santa Monica, CA | (40.5) | NA | Jurupa Valley, CA** | NA |
| 290 | Farmington Hills, MI | (28.8) | 364 | Roanoke, VA | (40.6) | NA | Lowell, MA** | NA |
| 290 | Fayetteville, NC | (28.8) | 365 | Lynn, MA | (41.0) | NA | Newport News, VA** | NA |
| 290 | Lewisville, TX | (28.8) | 366 | Albany, GA | (41.4) | NA | Upland, CA** | NA |
| 293 | Cheektowaga, NY | (29.0) | 367 | Fall River, MA | (41.6) | NA | Waukegan, IL** | NA |
| 293 | Cranston, RI | (29.0) | 367 | Sugar Land, TX | (41.6) | NA | Yakima, WA** | NA |
| 293 | Gresham, OR | (29.0) | 369 | Brockton, MA | (41.8) | | | |
| 296 | Madison, WI | (29.3) | 369 | Clearwater, FL | (41.8) | | | |

Source: CQ Press using reported data from the F.B.I. "Crime in the United States 2013"

*Motor vehicle theft includes the theft or attempted theft of a self-propelled vehicle. Excludes motorboats, construction equipment, airplanes, and farming equipment.

**Not available.

# 81. Police Officers in 2013
## National Total = 626,942 Officers*

| RANK | CITY | OFFICERS | RANK | CITY | OFFICERS | RANK | CITY | OFFICERS |
|---|---|---|---|---|---|---|---|---|
| 221 | Abilene, TX | 170 | 360 | Chino, CA | 92 | 289 | Fullerton, CA | 135 |
| 82 | Akron, OH | 412 | 179 | Chula Vista, CA | 202 | 122 | Gainesville, FL | 294 |
| 377 | Alameda, CA | 81 | 252 | Cicero, IL | 154 | 252 | Garden Grove, CA | 154 |
| NA | Albany, GA** | NA | 35 | Cincinnati, OH | 961 | 115 | Garland, TX | 317 |
| 110 | Albany, NY | 332 | 364 | Citrus Heights, CA | 89 | 168 | Gary, IN | 220 |
| NA | Albuquerque, NM** | NA | 237 | Clarkstown, NY | 163 | 161 | Gilbert, AZ | 226 |
| 119 | Alexandria, VA | 307 | 132 | Clarksville, TN | 268 | 90 | Glendale, AZ | 383 |
| 372 | Alhambra, CA | 83 | 157 | Clearwater, FL | 230 | 151 | Glendale, CA | 241 |
| 174 | Allentown, PA | 211 | 21 | Cleveland, OH | 1,476 | 166 | Grand Prairie, TX | 221 |
| 323 | Allen, TX | 117 | 273 | Clifton, NJ | 145 | 127 | Grand Rapids, MI | 282 |
| 106 | Amarillo, TX | 339 | 378 | Clinton Twnshp, MI | 80 | 349 | Greece, NY | 98 |
| 258 | Amherst, NY | 152 | 357 | Clovis, CA | 93 | 273 | Greeley, CO | 145 |
| 99 | Anaheim, CA | 361 | 305 | College Station, TX | 127 | 199 | Green Bay, WI | 186 |
| 105 | Anchorage, AK | 344 | 338 | Colonie, NY | 107 | 55 | Greensboro, NC | 666 |
| 322 | Ann Arbor, MI | 118 | 56 | Colorado Springs, CO | 649 | 212 | Greenville, NC | 177 |
| 372 | Antioch, CA | 83 | 258 | Columbia, MO | 152 | 315 | Gresham, OR | 121 |
| NA | Arlington Heights, IL** | NA | 93 | Columbia, SC | 374 | 228 | Hamilton Twnshp, NJ | 168 |
| 58 | Arlington, TX | 624 | 72 | Columbus, GA | 454 | 175 | Hammond, IN | 207 |
| 241 | Arvada, CO | 161 | NA | Compton, CA** | NA | 131 | Hampton, VA | 277 |
| 154 | Athens-Clarke, GA | 235 | 267 | Concord, CA | 148 | 71 | Hartford, CT | 455 |
| 16 | Atlanta, GA | 1,855 | 250 | Concord, NC | 156 | 352 | Hawthorne, CA | 96 |
| 54 | Aurora, CO | 675 | 178 | Coral Springs, FL | 203 | 210 | Hayward, CA | 179 |
| NA | Aurora, IL** | NA | 263 | Corona, CA | 150 | 389 | Hemet, CA | 58 |
| 17 | Austin, TX | 1,675 | 73 | Corpus Christi, TX | 449 | 112 | Henderson, NV | 327 |
| 106 | Bakersfield, CA | 339 | 323 | Costa Mesa, CA | 117 | NA | Hesperia, CA** | NA |
| 386 | Baldwin Park, CA | 64 | 279 | Cranston, RI | 141 | NA | Hialeah, FL** | NA |
| 7 | Baltimore, MD | 2,829 | 5 | Dallas, TX | 3,474 | 172 | High Point, NC | 216 |
| NA | Baton Rouge, LA** | NA | 343 | Daly City, CA | 104 | 297 | Hillsboro, OR | 131 |
| 142 | Beaumont, TX | 253 | 277 | Danbury, CT | 144 | 122 | Hollywood, FL | 294 |
| 288 | Beaverton, OR | 137 | 234 | Davenport, IA | 164 | 246 | Hoover, AL | 158 |
| 221 | Bellevue, WA | 170 | 219 | Davie, FL | 171 | NA | Houston, TX** | NA |
| NA | Bellflower, CA** | NA | 102 | Dayton, OH | 347 | 191 | Huntington Beach, CA | 193 |
| 367 | Bend, OR | 85 | 206 | Dearborn, MI | 182 | 91 | Huntsville, AL | 377 |
| 229 | Berkeley, CA | 167 | NA | Decatur, IL** | NA | 181 | Independence, MO | 201 |
| 266 | Bethlehem, PA | 149 | NA | Deerfield Beach, FL** | NA | 20 | Indianapolis, IN | 1,539 |
| 285 | Billings, MT | 139 | 255 | Denton, TX | 153 | 388 | Indio, CA | 59 |
| 40 | Birmingham, AL | 836 | 22 | Denver, CO | 1,395 | 240 | Inglewood, CA | 162 |
| NA | Bloomington, IL** | NA | 96 | Des Moines, IA | 366 | 189 | Irvine, CA | 194 |
| 353 | Bloomington, IN | 95 | 9 | Detroit, MI | 2,356 | 111 | Irving, TX | 329 |
| 333 | Bloomington, MN | 111 | 337 | Downey, CA | 109 | 19 | Jacksonville, FL | 1,581 |
| 194 | Boca Raton, FL | 191 | 255 | Duluth, MN | 153 | 74 | Jackson, MS | 442 |
| 128 | Boise, ID | 280 | 307 | Edinburg, TX | 125 | 45 | Jersey City, NJ | 770 |
| 13 | Boston, MA | 2,131 | 243 | Edison Twnshp, NJ | 160 | 387 | Johns Creek, GA | 62 |
| 218 | Boulder, CO | 172 | 329 | Edmond, OK | 113 | 139 | Joliet, IL | 256 |
| 300 | Brick Twnshp, NJ | 130 | 319 | El Cajon, CA | 119 | NA | Jurupa Valley, CA** | NA |
| 83 | Bridgeport, CT | 411 | 326 | El Monte, CA | 115 | 91 | Kansas City, KS | 377 |
| 207 | Brockton, MA | 180 | 30 | El Paso, TX | 1,069 | 24 | Kansas City, MO | 1,367 |
| 300 | Broken Arrow, OK | 130 | 207 | Elgin, IL | 180 | 357 | Kennewick, WA | 93 |
| 343 | Brooklyn Park, MN | 104 | 115 | Elizabeth, NJ | 317 | 184 | Kenosha, WI | 199 |
| 150 | Brownsville, TX | 244 | 309 | Elk Grove, CA | 123 | 286 | Kent, WA | 138 |
| 286 | Bryan, TX | 138 | 221 | Erie, PA | 170 | 154 | Killeen, TX | 235 |
| 371 | Buena Park, CA | 84 | 263 | Escondido, CA | 150 | 87 | Knoxville, TN | 393 |
| 49 | Buffalo, NY | 741 | 187 | Eugene, OR | 196 | NA | Lafayette, LA** | NA |
| 267 | Burbank, CA | 148 | 231 | Evanston, IL | 165 | NA | Lake Forest, CA** | NA |
| 134 | Cambridge, MA | 267 | 124 | Evansville, IN | 286 | 175 | Lakeland, FL | 207 |
| 382 | Canton Twnshp, MI | 76 | 204 | Everett, WA | 183 | 316 | Lakewood Twnshp, NJ | 120 |
| 166 | Cape Coral, FL | 221 | 333 | Fairfield, CA | 111 | NA | Lakewood, CA** | NA |
| 332 | Carlsbad, CA | 112 | 163 | Fall River, MA | 224 | 136 | Lakewood, CO | 264 |
| 333 | Carmel, IN | 111 | 278 | Fargo, ND | 143 | NA | Lancaster, CA** | NA |
| 251 | Carrollton, TX | 155 | 343 | Farmington Hills, MI | 104 | 201 | Lansing, MI | 185 |
| NA | Carson, CA** | NA | 326 | Fayetteville, AR | 115 | NA | Laredo, TX** | NA |
| 202 | Cary, NC | 184 | 98 | Fayetteville, NC | 362 | 292 | Largo, FL | 134 |
| 177 | Cedar Rapids, IA | 204 | 319 | Federal Way, WA | 119 | NA | Las Cruces, NM** | NA |
| 319 | Centennial, CO | 119 | NA | Fishers, IN** | NA | 8 | Las Vegas, NV | 2,444 |
| 310 | Champaign, IL | 122 | 310 | Flint, MI | 122 | 273 | Lawrence, KS | 145 |
| 113 | Chandler, AZ | 322 | 224 | Fontana, CA | 169 | 325 | Lawrence, MA | 116 |
| 77 | Charleston, SC | 433 | 189 | Fort Collins, CO | 194 | 245 | Lawton, OK | 159 |
| 18 | Charlotte, NC | 1,587 | 69 | Fort Lauderdale, FL | 491 | 338 | League City, TX | 107 |
| 78 | Chattanooga, TN | 432 | 237 | Fort Smith, AR | 163 | 292 | Lee's Summit, MO | 134 |
| 303 | Cheektowaga, NY | 129 | 79 | Fort Wayne, IN | 429 | 267 | Lewisville, TX | 148 |
| 89 | Chesapeake, VA | 384 | NA | Fort Worth, TX** | NA | 63 | Lexington, KY | 557 |
| NA | Chicago, IL** | NA | 224 | Fremont, CA | 169 | 114 | Lincoln, NE | 321 |
| 372 | Chico, CA | 83 | 53 | Fresno, CA | 701 | 63 | Little Rock, AR | 557 |
| NA | Chino Hills, CA** | NA | 267 | Frisco, TX | 148 | 367 | Livermore, CA | 85 |

| RANK | CITY | OFFICERS |
|------|------|----------|
| 310 | Livonia, MI | 122 |
| 43 | Long Beach, CA | 775 |
| 294 | Longmont, CO | 133 |
| 243 | Longview, TX | 160 |
| 2 | Los Angeles, CA | 9,843 |
| 28 | Louisville, KY | 1,200 |
| 157 | Lowell, MA | 230 |
| 86 | Lubbock, TX | 399 |
| 224 | Lynchburg, VA | 169 |
| 204 | Lynn, MA | 183 |
| NA | Macon, GA** | NA |
| 70 | Madison, WI | 462 |
| 170 | Manchester, NH | 217 |
| 135 | McAllen, TX | 266 |
| 231 | McKinney, TX | 165 |
| 348 | Medford, OR | 101 |
| 246 | Melbourne, FL | 158 |
| 10 | Memphis, TN | 2,319 |
| NA | Menifee, CA** | NA |
| 378 | Merced, CA | 80 |
| 372 | Meridian, ID | 83 |
| 47 | Mesa, AZ | 765 |
| NA | Mesquite, TX** | NA |
| 94 | Miami Beach, FL | 373 |
| 173 | Miami Gardens, FL | 212 |
| 31 | Miami, FL | 1,066 |
| 215 | Midland, TX | 176 |
| 15 | Milwaukee, WI | 1,862 |
| 39 | Minneapolis, MN | 844 |
| 186 | Miramar, FL | 197 |
| NA | Mission Viejo, CA** | NA |
| 279 | Mission, TX | 141 |
| 68 | Mobile, AL | 521 |
| 170 | Modesto, CA | 217 |
| NA | Moreno Valley, CA** | NA |
| 357 | Mountain View, CA | 93 |
| 164 | Murfreesboro, TN | 223 |
| 367 | Murrieta, CA | 85 |
| 342 | Nampa, ID | 105 |
| 384 | Napa, CA | 68 |
| NA | Naperville, IL** | NA |
| 212 | Nashua, NH | 177 |
| 23 | Nashville, TN | 1,368 |
| 137 | New Bedford, MA | 261 |
| 88 | New Haven, CT | 385 |
| 27 | New Orleans, LA | 1,210 |
| 252 | New Rochelle, NY | 154 |
| 1 | New York, NY | 34,822 |
| 32 | Newark, NJ | 1,007 |
| 289 | Newport Beach, CA | 135 |
| 81 | Newport News, VA | 426 |
| 297 | Newton, MA | 131 |
| 48 | Norfolk, VA | 763 |
| 237 | Norman, OK | 163 |
| 108 | North Charleston, SC | 338 |
| 132 | North Las Vegas, NV | 268 |
| NA | Norwalk, CA** | NA |
| 212 | Norwalk, CT | 177 |
| 57 | Oakland, CA | 639 |
| 182 | Oceanside, CA | 200 |
| 283 | Odessa, TX | 140 |
| 329 | O'Fallon, MO | 113 |
| 297 | Ogden, UT | 131 |
| 32 | Oklahoma City, OK | 1,007 |
| 234 | Olathe, KS | 164 |
| 46 | Omaha, NE | 767 |
| 157 | Ontario, CA | 230 |
| 258 | Orange, CA | 152 |
| NA | Orem, UT** | NA |
| 51 | Orlando, FL | 718 |
| 146 | Overland Park, KS | 247 |
| 160 | Oxnard, CA | 227 |
| 255 | Palm Bay, FL | 153 |
| NA | Palmdale, CA** | NA |
| 161 | Pasadena, CA | 226 |
| 139 | Pasadena, TX | 256 |
| 97 | Paterson, NJ | 365 |
| 273 | Pearland, TX | 145 |
| 156 | Pembroke Pines, FL | 234 |
| 210 | Peoria, AZ | 179 |
| NA | Peoria, IL** | NA |
| 3 | Philadelphia, PA | 6,508 |
| 6 | Phoenix, AZ | 2,890 |
| 38 | Pittsburgh, PA | 861 |
| 102 | Plano, TX | 347 |
| 262 | Plantation, FL | 151 |
| 249 | Pomona, CA | 157 |
| NA | Pompano Beach, FL** | NA |
| 169 | Port St. Lucie, FL | 219 |
| 37 | Portland, OR | 938 |
| 146 | Portsmouth, VA | 247 |
| 84 | Providence, RI | 410 |
| 347 | Provo, UT | 102 |
| 202 | Pueblo, CO | 184 |
| 192 | Quincy, MA | 192 |
| 182 | Racine, WI | 200 |
| 44 | Raleigh, NC | 773 |
| 338 | Ramapo, NY | 107 |
| NA | Rancho Cucamon., CA** | NA |
| 234 | Reading, PA | 164 |
| 349 | Redding, CA | 98 |
| 354 | Redwood City, CA | 94 |
| 120 | Reno, NV | 297 |
| 326 | Renton, WA | 115 |
| 354 | Rialto, CA | 94 |
| 272 | Richardson, TX | 146 |
| 199 | Richmond, CA | 186 |
| 52 | Richmond, VA | 703 |
| 95 | Riverside, CA | 367 |
| 143 | Roanoke, VA | 252 |
| 294 | Rochester, MN | 133 |
| 50 | Rochester, NY | 735 |
| NA | Rockford, IL** | NA |
| 310 | Roseville, CA | 122 |
| NA | Roswell, GA** | NA |
| NA | Round Rock, TX** | NA |
| 60 | Sacramento, CA | 612 |
| 197 | Salem, OR | 187 |
| 279 | Salinas, CA | 141 |
| NA | Salt Lake City, UT** | NA |
| 229 | San Angelo, TX | 167 |
| 11 | San Antonio, TX | 2,312 |
| 148 | San Bernardino, CA | 246 |
| 14 | San Diego, CA | 1,875 |
| 12 | San Francisco, CA | 2,150 |
| 29 | San Jose, CA | 1,077 |
| 364 | San Leandro, CA | 89 |
| NA | San Marcos, CA** | NA |
| 338 | San Mateo, CA | 107 |
| NA | Sandy Springs, GA** | NA |
| 333 | Sandy, UT | 111 |
| 115 | Santa Ana, CA | 317 |
| 283 | Santa Barbara, CA | 140 |
| 294 | Santa Clara, CA | 133 |
| NA | Santa Clarita, CA** | NA |
| 354 | Santa Maria, CA | 94 |
| 179 | Santa Monica, CA | 202 |
| 241 | Santa Rosa, CA | 161 |
| 62 | Savannah, GA | 563 |
| 84 | Scottsdale, AZ | 410 |
| 263 | Scranton, PA | 150 |
| 25 | Seattle, WA | 1,294 |
| NA | Shreveport, LA** | NA |
| 310 | Simi Valley, CA | 122 |
| 316 | Sioux City, IA | 120 |
| 149 | Sioux Falls, SD | 245 |
| 307 | Somerville, MA | 125 |
| 143 | South Bend, IN | 252 |
| 383 | South Gate, CA | 69 |
| 343 | Sparks, NV | 104 |
| 349 | Spokane Valley, WA | 98 |
| 128 | Spokane, WA | 280 |
| 152 | Springfield, IL | 239 |
| 74 | Springfield, MA | 442 |
| 118 | Springfield, MO | 316 |
| 126 | Stamford, CT | 283 |
| 271 | Sterling Heights, MI | 147 |
| 101 | Stockton, CA | 351 |
| NA | St. George, UT** | NA |
| 329 | St. Joseph, MO | 113 |
| 26 | St. Louis, MO | 1,287 |
| 61 | St. Paul, MN | 587 |
| 66 | St. Petersburg, FL | 533 |
| 217 | Suffolk, VA | 175 |
| NA | Sugar Land, TX** | NA |
| 187 | Sunnyvale, CA | 196 |
| 224 | Sunrise, FL | 169 |
| 303 | Surprise, AZ | 129 |
| 76 | Syracuse, NY | 440 |
| 109 | Tacoma, WA | 334 |
| 100 | Tallahassee, FL | 355 |
| 36 | Tampa, FL | 952 |
| NA | Temecula, CA** | NA |
| 104 | Tempe, AZ | 345 |
| 246 | Thornton, CO | 158 |
| NA | Thousand Oaks, CA** | NA |
| 67 | Toledo, OH | 532 |
| 258 | Toms River Twnshp, NJ | 152 |
| 121 | Topeka, KS | 295 |
| 165 | Torrance, CA | 222 |
| 378 | Tracy, CA | 80 |
| 153 | Trenton, NJ | 237 |
| 362 | Troy, MI | 91 |
| 34 | Tucson, AZ | 983 |
| 42 | Tulsa, OK | 780 |
| 125 | Tuscaloosa, AL | 285 |
| 366 | Tustin, CA | 87 |
| 194 | Tyler, TX | 191 |
| 384 | Upland, CA | 68 |
| 306 | Upper Darby Twnshp, PA | 126 |
| 360 | Vacaville, CA | 92 |
| 376 | Vallejo, CA | 82 |
| 197 | Vancouver, WA | 187 |
| 300 | Ventura, CA | 130 |
| NA | Victorville, CA** | NA |
| 41 | Virginia Beach, VA | 782 |
| 289 | Visalia, CA | 135 |
| NA | Vista, CA** | NA |
| 145 | Waco, TX | 248 |
| 185 | Warren, MI | 198 |
| 231 | Warwick, RI | 165 |
| 4 | Washington, DC | 3,976 |
| 130 | Waterbury, CT | 279 |
| NA | Waukegan, IL** | NA |
| 363 | West Covina, CA | 90 |
| 137 | West Palm Beach, FL | 261 |
| 207 | West Valley, UT | 180 |
| 381 | Westland, MI | 77 |
| 367 | Westminster, CA | 85 |
| 215 | Westminster, CO | 176 |
| 316 | Whittier, CA | 120 |
| 192 | Wichita Falls, TX | 192 |
| NA | Wichita, KS** | NA |
| 141 | Wilmington, NC | 255 |
| 65 | Winston-Salem, NC | 544 |
| 194 | Woodbridge Twnshp, NJ | 191 |
| 79 | Worcester, MA | 429 |
| 279 | Yakima, WA | 141 |
| 59 | Yonkers, NY | 616 |
| 219 | Yuma, AZ | 171 |

Source: Reported data from the F.B.I. "Crime in the United States 2013"

*Sworn officers only, does not include civilian employees.

**Not available

# 81. Police Officers in 2013 (continued)
## National Total = 626,942 Officers*

| RANK | CITY | OFFICERS | RANK | CITY | OFFICERS | RANK | CITY | OFFICERS |
|------|------|----------|------|------|----------|------|------|----------|
| 1 | New York, NY | 34,822 | 74 | Springfield, MA | 442 | 149 | Sioux Falls, SD | 245 |
| 2 | Los Angeles, CA | 9,843 | 76 | Syracuse, NY | 440 | 150 | Brownsville, TX | 244 |
| 3 | Philadelphia, PA | 6,508 | 77 | Charleston, SC | 433 | 151 | Glendale, CA | 241 |
| 4 | Washington, DC | 3,976 | 78 | Chattanooga, TN | 432 | 152 | Springfield, IL | 239 |
| 5 | Dallas, TX | 3,474 | 79 | Fort Wayne, IN | 429 | 153 | Trenton, NJ | 237 |
| 6 | Phoenix, AZ | 2,890 | 79 | Worcester, MA | 429 | 154 | Athens-Clarke, GA | 235 |
| 7 | Baltimore, MD | 2,829 | 81 | Newport News, VA | 426 | 154 | Killeen, TX | 235 |
| 8 | Las Vegas, NV | 2,444 | 82 | Akron, OH | 412 | 156 | Pembroke Pines, FL | 234 |
| 9 | Detroit, MI | 2,356 | 83 | Bridgeport, CT | 411 | 157 | Clearwater, FL | 230 |
| 10 | Memphis, TN | 2,319 | 84 | Providence, RI | 410 | 157 | Lowell, MA | 230 |
| 11 | San Antonio, TX | 2,312 | 84 | Scottsdale, AZ | 410 | 157 | Ontario, CA | 230 |
| 12 | San Francisco, CA | 2,150 | 86 | Lubbock, TX | 399 | 160 | Oxnard, CA | 227 |
| 13 | Boston, MA | 2,131 | 87 | Knoxville, TN | 393 | 161 | Gilbert, AZ | 226 |
| 14 | San Diego, CA | 1,875 | 88 | New Haven, CT | 385 | 161 | Pasadena, CA | 226 |
| 15 | Milwaukee, WI | 1,862 | 89 | Chesapeake, VA | 384 | 163 | Fall River, MA | 224 |
| 16 | Atlanta, GA | 1,855 | 90 | Glendale, AZ | 383 | 164 | Murfreesboro, TN | 223 |
| 17 | Austin, TX | 1,675 | 91 | Huntsville, AL | 377 | 165 | Torrance, CA | 222 |
| 18 | Charlotte, NC | 1,587 | 91 | Kansas City, KS | 377 | 166 | Cape Coral, FL | 221 |
| 19 | Jacksonville, FL | 1,581 | 93 | Columbia, SC | 374 | 166 | Grand Prairie, TX | 221 |
| 20 | Indianapolis, IN | 1,539 | 94 | Miami Beach, FL | 373 | 168 | Gary, IN | 220 |
| 21 | Cleveland, OH | 1,476 | 95 | Riverside, CA | 367 | 169 | Port St. Lucie, FL | 219 |
| 22 | Denver, CO | 1,395 | 96 | Des Moines, IA | 366 | 170 | Manchester, NH | 217 |
| 23 | Nashville, TN | 1,368 | 97 | Paterson, NJ | 365 | 170 | Modesto, CA | 217 |
| 24 | Kansas City, MO | 1,367 | 98 | Fayetteville, NC | 362 | 172 | High Point, NC | 216 |
| 25 | Seattle, WA | 1,294 | 99 | Anaheim, CA | 361 | 173 | Miami Gardens, FL | 212 |
| 26 | St. Louis, MO | 1,287 | 100 | Tallahassee, FL | 355 | 174 | Allentown, PA | 211 |
| 27 | New Orleans, LA | 1,210 | 101 | Stockton, CA | 351 | 175 | Hammond, IN | 207 |
| 28 | Louisville, KY | 1,200 | 102 | Dayton, OH | 347 | 175 | Lakeland, FL | 207 |
| 29 | San Jose, CA | 1,077 | 102 | Plano, TX | 347 | 177 | Cedar Rapids, IA | 204 |
| 30 | El Paso, TX | 1,069 | 104 | Tempe, AZ | 345 | 178 | Coral Springs, FL | 203 |
| 31 | Miami, FL | 1,066 | 105 | Anchorage, AK | 344 | 179 | Chula Vista, CA | 202 |
| 32 | Newark, NJ | 1,007 | 106 | Amarillo, TX | 339 | 179 | Santa Monica, CA | 202 |
| 32 | Oklahoma City, OK | 1,007 | 106 | Bakersfield, CA | 339 | 181 | Independence, MO | 201 |
| 34 | Tucson, AZ | 983 | 108 | North Charleston, SC | 338 | 182 | Oceanside, CA | 200 |
| 35 | Cincinnati, OH | 961 | 109 | Tacoma, WA | 334 | 182 | Racine, WI | 200 |
| 36 | Tampa, FL | 952 | 110 | Albany, NY | 332 | 184 | Kenosha, WI | 199 |
| 37 | Portland, OR | 938 | 111 | Irving, TX | 329 | 185 | Warren, MI | 198 |
| 38 | Pittsburgh, PA | 861 | 112 | Henderson, NV | 327 | 186 | Miramar, FL | 197 |
| 39 | Minneapolis, MN | 844 | 113 | Chandler, AZ | 322 | 187 | Eugene, OR | 196 |
| 40 | Birmingham, AL | 836 | 114 | Lincoln, NE | 321 | 187 | Sunnyvale, CA | 196 |
| 41 | Virginia Beach, VA | 782 | 115 | Elizabeth, NJ | 317 | 189 | Fort Collins, CO | 194 |
| 42 | Tulsa, OK | 780 | 115 | Garland, TX | 317 | 189 | Irvine, CA | 194 |
| 43 | Long Beach, CA | 775 | 115 | Santa Ana, CA | 317 | 191 | Huntington Beach, CA | 193 |
| 44 | Raleigh, NC | 773 | 118 | Springfield, MO | 316 | 192 | Quincy, MA | 192 |
| 45 | Jersey City, NJ | 770 | 119 | Alexandria, VA | 307 | 192 | Wichita Falls, TX | 192 |
| 46 | Omaha, NE | 767 | 120 | Reno, NV | 297 | 194 | Boca Raton, FL | 191 |
| 47 | Mesa, AZ | 765 | 121 | Topeka, KS | 295 | 194 | Tyler, TX | 191 |
| 48 | Norfolk, VA | 763 | 122 | Gainesville, FL | 294 | 194 | Woodbridge Twnshp, NJ | 191 |
| 49 | Buffalo, NY | 741 | 122 | Hollywood, FL | 294 | 197 | Salem, OR | 187 |
| 50 | Rochester, NY | 735 | 124 | Evansville, IN | 286 | 197 | Vancouver, WA | 187 |
| 51 | Orlando, FL | 718 | 125 | Tuscaloosa, AL | 285 | 199 | Green Bay, WI | 186 |
| 52 | Richmond, VA | 703 | 126 | Stamford, CT | 283 | 199 | Richmond, CA | 186 |
| 53 | Fresno, CA | 701 | 127 | Grand Rapids, MI | 282 | 201 | Lansing, MI | 185 |
| 54 | Aurora, CO | 675 | 128 | Boise, ID | 280 | 202 | Cary, NC | 184 |
| 55 | Greensboro, NC | 666 | 128 | Spokane, WA | 280 | 202 | Pueblo, CO | 184 |
| 56 | Colorado Springs, CO | 649 | 130 | Waterbury, CT | 279 | 204 | Everett, WA | 183 |
| 57 | Oakland, CA | 639 | 131 | Hampton, VA | 277 | 204 | Lynn, MA | 183 |
| 58 | Arlington, TX | 624 | 132 | Clarksville, TN | 268 | 206 | Dearborn, MI | 182 |
| 59 | Yonkers, NY | 616 | 132 | North Las Vegas, NV | 268 | 207 | Brockton, MA | 180 |
| 60 | Sacramento, CA | 612 | 134 | Cambridge, MA | 267 | 207 | Elgin, IL | 180 |
| 61 | St. Paul, MN | 587 | 135 | McAllen, TX | 266 | 207 | West Valley, UT | 180 |
| 62 | Savannah, GA | 563 | 136 | Lakewood, CO | 264 | 210 | Hayward, CA | 179 |
| 63 | Lexington, KY | 557 | 137 | New Bedford, MA | 261 | 210 | Peoria, AZ | 179 |
| 63 | Little Rock, AR | 557 | 137 | West Palm Beach, FL | 261 | 212 | Greenville, NC | 177 |
| 65 | Winston-Salem, NC | 544 | 139 | Joliet, IL | 256 | 212 | Nashua, NH | 177 |
| 66 | St. Petersburg, FL | 533 | 139 | Pasadena, TX | 256 | 212 | Norwalk, CT | 177 |
| 67 | Toledo, OH | 532 | 141 | Wilmington, NC | 255 | 215 | Midland, TX | 176 |
| 68 | Mobile, AL | 521 | 142 | Beaumont, TX | 253 | 215 | Westminster, CO | 176 |
| 69 | Fort Lauderdale, FL | 491 | 143 | Roanoke, VA | 252 | 217 | Suffolk, VA | 175 |
| 70 | Madison, WI | 462 | 143 | South Bend, IN | 252 | 218 | Boulder, CO | 172 |
| 71 | Hartford, CT | 455 | 145 | Waco, TX | 248 | 219 | Davie, FL | 171 |
| 72 | Columbus, GA | 454 | 146 | Overland Park, KS | 247 | 219 | Yuma, AZ | 171 |
| 73 | Corpus Christi, TX | 449 | 146 | Portsmouth, VA | 247 | 221 | Abilene, TX | 170 |
| 74 | Jackson, MS | 442 | 148 | San Bernardino, CA | 246 | 221 | Bellevue, WA | 170 |

| RANK | CITY | OFFICERS | RANK | CITY | OFFICERS | RANK | CITY | OFFICERS |
|---|---|---|---|---|---|---|---|---|
| 221 | Erie, PA | 170 | 297 | Hillsboro, OR | 131 | 371 | Buena Park, CA | 84 |
| 224 | Fontana, CA | 169 | 297 | Newton, MA | 131 | 372 | Alhambra, CA | 83 |
| 224 | Fremont, CA | 169 | 297 | Ogden, UT | 131 | 372 | Antioch, CA | 83 |
| 224 | Lynchburg, VA | 169 | 300 | Brick Twnshp, NJ | 130 | 372 | Chico, CA | 83 |
| 224 | Sunrise, FL | 169 | 300 | Broken Arrow, OK | 130 | 372 | Meridian, ID | 83 |
| 228 | Hamilton Twnshp, NJ | 168 | 300 | Ventura, CA | 130 | 376 | Vallejo, CA | 82 |
| 229 | Berkeley, CA | 167 | 303 | Cheektowaga, NY | 129 | 377 | Alameda, CA | 81 |
| 229 | San Angelo, TX | 167 | 303 | Surprise, AZ | 129 | 378 | Clinton Twnshp, MI | 80 |
| 231 | Evanston, IL | 165 | 305 | College Station, TX | 127 | 378 | Merced, CA | 80 |
| 231 | McKinney, TX | 165 | 306 | Upper Darby Twnshp, PA | 126 | 378 | Tracy, CA | 80 |
| 231 | Warwick, RI | 165 | 307 | Edinburg, TX | 125 | 381 | Westland, MI | 77 |
| 234 | Davenport, IA | 164 | 307 | Somerville, MA | 125 | 382 | Canton Twnshp, MI | 76 |
| 234 | Olathe, KS | 164 | 309 | Elk Grove, CA | 123 | 383 | South Gate, CA | 69 |
| 234 | Reading, PA | 164 | 310 | Champaign, IL | 122 | 384 | Napa, CA | 68 |
| 237 | Clarkstown, NY | 163 | 310 | Flint, MI | 122 | 384 | Upland, CA | 68 |
| 237 | Fort Smith, AR | 163 | 310 | Livonia, MI | 122 | 386 | Baldwin Park, CA | 64 |
| 237 | Norman, OK | 163 | 310 | Roseville, CA | 122 | 387 | Johns Creek, GA | 62 |
| 240 | Inglewood, CA | 162 | 310 | Simi Valley, CA | 122 | 388 | Indio, CA | 59 |
| 241 | Arvada, CO | 161 | 315 | Gresham, OR | 121 | 389 | Hemet, CA | 58 |
| 241 | Santa Rosa, CA | 161 | 316 | Lakewood Twnshp, NJ | 120 | NA | Albany, GA** | NA |
| 243 | Edison Twnshp, NJ | 160 | 316 | Sioux City, IA | 120 | NA | Albuquerque, NM** | NA |
| 243 | Longview, TX | 160 | 316 | Whittier, CA | 120 | NA | Arlington Heights, IL** | NA |
| 245 | Lawton, OK | 159 | 319 | Centennial, CO | 119 | NA | Aurora, IL** | NA |
| 246 | Hoover, AL | 158 | 319 | El Cajon, CA | 119 | NA | Baton Rouge, LA** | NA |
| 246 | Melbourne, FL | 158 | 319 | Federal Way, WA | 119 | NA | Bellflower, CA** | NA |
| 246 | Thornton, CO | 158 | 322 | Ann Arbor, MI | 118 | NA | Bloomington, IL** | NA |
| 249 | Pomona, CA | 157 | 323 | Allen, TX | 117 | NA | Carson, CA** | NA |
| 250 | Concord, NC | 156 | 323 | Costa Mesa, CA | 117 | NA | Chicago, IL** | NA |
| 251 | Carrollton, TX | 155 | 325 | Lawrence, MA | 116 | NA | Chino Hills, CA** | NA |
| 252 | Cicero, IL | 154 | 326 | El Monte, CA | 115 | NA | Compton, CA** | NA |
| 252 | Garden Grove, CA | 154 | 326 | Fayetteville, AR | 115 | NA | Decatur, IL** | NA |
| 252 | New Rochelle, NY | 154 | 326 | Renton, WA | 115 | NA | Deerfield Beach, FL** | NA |
| 255 | Denton, TX | 153 | 329 | Edmond, OK | 113 | NA | Fishers, IN** | NA |
| 255 | Duluth, MN | 153 | 329 | O'Fallon, MO | 113 | NA | Fort Worth, TX** | NA |
| 255 | Palm Bay, FL | 153 | 329 | St. Joseph, MO | 113 | NA | Hesperia, CA** | NA |
| 258 | Amherst, NY | 152 | 332 | Carlsbad, CA | 112 | NA | Hialeah, FL** | NA |
| 258 | Columbia, MO | 152 | 333 | Bloomington, MN | 111 | NA | Houston, TX** | NA |
| 258 | Orange, CA | 152 | 333 | Carmel, IN | 111 | NA | Jurupa Valley, CA** | NA |
| 258 | Toms River Twnshp, NJ | 152 | 333 | Fairfield, CA | 111 | NA | Lafayette, LA** | NA |
| 262 | Plantation, FL | 151 | 333 | Sandy, UT | 111 | NA | Lake Forest, CA** | NA |
| 263 | Corona, CA | 150 | 337 | Downey, CA | 109 | NA | Lakewood, CA** | NA |
| 263 | Escondido, CA | 150 | 338 | Colonie, NY | 107 | NA | Lancaster, CA** | NA |
| 263 | Scranton, PA | 150 | 338 | League City, TX | 107 | NA | Laredo, TX** | NA |
| 266 | Bethlehem, PA | 149 | 338 | Ramapo, NY | 107 | NA | Las Cruces, NM** | NA |
| 267 | Burbank, CA | 148 | 338 | San Mateo, CA | 107 | NA | Macon, GA** | NA |
| 267 | Concord, CA | 148 | 342 | Nampa, ID | 105 | NA | Menifee, CA** | NA |
| 267 | Frisco, TX | 148 | 343 | Brooklyn Park, MN | 104 | NA | Mesquite, TX** | NA |
| 267 | Lewisville, TX | 148 | 343 | Daly City, CA | 104 | NA | Mission Viejo, CA** | NA |
| 271 | Sterling Heights, MI | 147 | 343 | Farmington Hills, MI | 104 | NA | Moreno Valley, CA** | NA |
| 272 | Richardson, TX | 146 | 343 | Sparks, NV | 104 | NA | Naperville, IL** | NA |
| 273 | Clifton, NJ | 145 | 347 | Provo, UT | 102 | NA | Norwalk, CA** | NA |
| 273 | Greeley, CO | 145 | 348 | Medford, OR | 101 | NA | Orem, UT** | NA |
| 273 | Lawrence, KS | 145 | 349 | Greece, NY | 98 | NA | Palmdale, CA** | NA |
| 273 | Pearland, TX | 145 | 349 | Redding, CA | 98 | NA | Peoria, IL** | NA |
| 277 | Danbury, CT | 144 | 349 | Spokane Valley, WA | 98 | NA | Pompano Beach, FL** | NA |
| 278 | Fargo, ND | 143 | 352 | Hawthorne, CA | 96 | NA | Rancho Cucamon., CA** | NA |
| 279 | Cranston, RI | 141 | 353 | Bloomington, IN | 95 | NA | Rockford, IL** | NA |
| 279 | Mission, TX | 141 | 354 | Redwood City, CA | 94 | NA | Roswell, GA** | NA |
| 279 | Salinas, CA | 141 | 354 | Rialto, CA | 94 | NA | Round Rock, TX** | NA |
| 279 | Yakima, WA | 141 | 354 | Santa Maria, CA | 94 | NA | Salt Lake City, UT** | NA |
| 283 | Odessa, TX | 140 | 357 | Clovis, CA | 93 | NA | San Marcos, CA** | NA |
| 283 | Santa Barbara, CA | 140 | 357 | Kennewick, WA | 93 | NA | Sandy Springs, GA** | NA |
| 285 | Billings, MT | 139 | 357 | Mountain View, CA | 93 | NA | Santa Clarita, CA** | NA |
| 286 | Bryan, TX | 138 | 360 | Chino, CA | 92 | NA | Shreveport, LA** | NA |
| 286 | Kent, WA | 138 | 360 | Vacaville, CA | 92 | NA | St. George, UT** | NA |
| 288 | Beaverton, OR | 137 | 362 | Troy, MI | 91 | NA | Sugar Land, TX** | NA |
| 289 | Fullerton, CA | 135 | 363 | West Covina, CA | 90 | NA | Temecula, CA** | NA |
| 289 | Newport Beach, CA | 135 | 364 | Citrus Heights, CA | 89 | NA | Thousand Oaks, CA** | NA |
| 289 | Visalia, CA | 135 | 364 | San Leandro, CA | 89 | NA | Victorville, CA** | NA |
| 292 | Largo, FL | 134 | 366 | Tustin, CA | 87 | NA | Vista, CA** | NA |
| 292 | Lee's Summit, MO | 134 | 367 | Bend, OR | 85 | NA | Waukegan, IL** | NA |
| 294 | Longmont, CO | 133 | 367 | Livermore, CA | 85 | NA | Wichita, KS** | NA |
| 294 | Rochester, MN | 133 | 367 | Murrieta, CA | 85 | | | |
| 294 | Santa Clara, CA | 133 | 367 | Westminster, CA | 85 | | | |

Source: Reported data from the F.B.I. "Crime in the United States 2013"

*Sworn officers only, does not include civilian employees.

**Not available

# 82. Rate of Police Officers in 2013
## National Rate = 233 Officers per 100,000 Population*

| RANK | CITY | RATE | RANK | CITY | RATE | RANK | CITY | RATE |
|---|---|---|---|---|---|---|---|---|
| 234 | Abilene, TX | 142 | 309 | Chino, CA | 114 | 354 | Fullerton, CA | 97 |
| 85 | Akron, OH | 208 | 380 | Chula Vista, CA | 79 | 66 | Gainesville, FL | 232 |
| 329 | Alameda, CA | 106 | 140 | Cicero, IL | 183 | 371 | Garden Grove, CA | 88 |
| NA | Albany, GA** | NA | 20 | Cincinnati, OH | 324 | 246 | Garland, TX | 135 |
| 15 | Albany, NY | 339 | 335 | Citrus Heights, CA | 104 | 38 | Gary, IN | 279 |
| NA | Albuquerque, NM** | NA | 96 | Clarkstown, NY | 202 | 347 | Gilbert, AZ | 100 |
| 87 | Alexandria, VA | 207 | 138 | Clarksville, TN | 184 | 185 | Glendale, AZ | 164 |
| 351 | Alhambra, CA | 98 | 83 | Clearwater, FL | 211 | 283 | Glendale, CA | 123 |
| 150 | Allentown, PA | 177 | 9 | Cleveland, OH | 379 | 291 | Grand Prairie, TX | 120 |
| 266 | Allen, TX | 128 | 168 | Clifton, NJ | 171 | 219 | Grand Rapids, MI | 147 |
| 163 | Amarillo, TX | 172 | 378 | Clinton Twnshp, MI | 82 | 341 | Greece, NY | 101 |
| 266 | Amherst, NY | 128 | 364 | Clovis, CA | 93 | 207 | Greeley, CO | 151 |
| 333 | Anaheim, CA | 105 | 266 | College Station, TX | 128 | 150 | Green Bay, WI | 177 |
| 306 | Anchorage, AK | 115 | 241 | Colonie, NY | 137 | 62 | Greensboro, NC | 238 |
| 341 | Ann Arbor, MI | 101 | 213 | Colorado Springs, CO | 149 | 100 | Greenville, NC | 201 |
| 382 | Antioch, CA | 78 | 251 | Columbia, MO | 133 | 321 | Gresham, OR | 110 |
| NA | Arlington Heights, IL** | NA | 34 | Columbia, SC | 283 | 127 | Hamilton Twnshp, NJ | 189 |
| 180 | Arlington, TX | 165 | 71 | Columbus, GA | 226 | 43 | Hammond, IN | 261 |
| 225 | Arvada, CO | 145 | NA | Compton, CA** | NA | 96 | Hampton, VA | 202 |
| 113 | Athens-Clarke, GA | 196 | 299 | Concord, CA | 118 | 10 | Hartford, CT | 364 |
| 5 | Atlanta, GA | 411 | 129 | Concord, NC | 188 | 317 | Hawthorne, CA | 111 |
| 110 | Aurora, CO | 197 | 195 | Coral Springs, FL | 160 | 295 | Hayward, CA | 119 |
| NA | Aurora, IL** | NA | 359 | Corona, CA | 94 | 388 | Hemet, CA | 71 |
| 114 | Austin, TX | 195 | 233 | Corpus Christi, TX | 143 | 286 | Henderson, NV | 122 |
| 359 | Bakersfield, CA | 94 | 335 | Costa Mesa, CA | 104 | NA | Hesperia, CA** | NA |
| 375 | Baldwin Park, CA | 83 | 156 | Cranston, RI | 175 | NA | Hialeah, FL** | NA |
| 2 | Baltimore, MD | 454 | 40 | Dallas, TX | 277 | 100 | High Point, NC | 201 |
| NA | Baton Rouge, LA** | NA | 348 | Daly City, CA | 99 | 245 | Hillsboro, OR | 136 |
| 80 | Beaumont, TX | 214 | 159 | Danbury, CT | 173 | 103 | Hollywood, FL | 200 |
| 223 | Beaverton, OR | 146 | 191 | Davenport, IA | 161 | 129 | Hoover, AL | 188 |
| 251 | Bellevue, WA | 133 | 150 | Davie, FL | 177 | NA | Houston, TX** | NA |
| NA | Bellflower, CA** | NA | 60 | Dayton, OH | 246 | 348 | Huntington Beach, CA | 99 |
| 329 | Bend, OR | 106 | 123 | Dearborn, MI | 190 | 92 | Huntsville, AL | 204 |
| 228 | Berkeley, CA | 144 | NA | Decatur, IL** | NA | 168 | Independence, MO | 171 |
| 106 | Bethlehem, PA | 198 | NA | Deerfield Beach, FL** | NA | 142 | Indianapolis, IN | 181 |
| 260 | Billings, MT | 129 | 279 | Denton, TX | 124 | 385 | Indio, CA | 74 |
| 8 | Birmingham, AL | 394 | 77 | Denver, CO | 215 | 225 | Inglewood, CA | 145 |
| NA | Bloomington, IL** | NA | 154 | Des Moines, IA | 176 | 378 | Irvine, CA | 82 |
| 306 | Bloomington, IN | 115 | 16 | Detroit, MI | 337 | 228 | Irving, TX | 144 |
| 266 | Bloomington, MN | 128 | 357 | Downey, CA | 96 | 133 | Jacksonville, FL | 187 |
| 77 | Boca Raton, FL | 215 | 150 | Duluth, MN | 177 | 54 | Jackson, MS | 251 |
| 255 | Boise, ID | 131 | 205 | Edinburg, TX | 152 | 27 | Jersey City, NJ | 300 |
| 17 | Boston, MA | 331 | 198 | Edison Twnshp, NJ | 158 | 385 | Johns Creek, GA | 74 |
| 176 | Boulder, CO | 167 | 255 | Edmond, OK | 131 | 163 | Joliet, IL | 172 |
| 163 | Brick Twnshp, NJ | 172 | 302 | El Cajon, CA | 117 | NA | Jurupa Valley, CA** | NA |
| 38 | Bridgeport, CT | 279 | 348 | El Monte, CA | 99 | 47 | Kansas City, KS | 255 |
| 121 | Brockton, MA | 191 | 200 | El Paso, TX | 157 | 28 | Kansas City, MO | 294 |
| 275 | Broken Arrow, OK | 126 | 187 | Elgin, IL | 163 | 286 | Kennewick, WA | 122 |
| 251 | Brooklyn Park, MN | 133 | 58 | Elizabeth, NJ | 249 | 106 | Kenosha, WI | 198 |
| 249 | Brownsville, TX | 134 | 383 | Elk Grove, CA | 76 | 317 | Kent, WA | 111 |
| 154 | Bryan, TX | 176 | 172 | Erie, PA | 169 | 163 | Killeen, TX | 172 |
| 338 | Buena Park, CA | 102 | 341 | Escondido, CA | 101 | 80 | Knoxville, TN | 214 |
| 31 | Buffalo, NY | 286 | 279 | Eugene, OR | 124 | NA | Lafayette, LA** | NA |
| 235 | Burbank, CA | 141 | 73 | Evanston, IL | 218 | NA | Lake Forest, CA** | NA |
| 58 | Cambridge, MA | 249 | 62 | Evansville, IN | 238 | 88 | Lakeland, FL | 206 |
| 374 | Canton Twnshp, MI | 85 | 157 | Everett, WA | 174 | 259 | Lakewood Twnshp, NJ | 130 |
| 246 | Cape Coral, FL | 135 | 338 | Fairfield, CA | 102 | NA | Lakewood, CA** | NA |
| 341 | Carlsbad, CA | 101 | 54 | Fall River, MA | 251 | 143 | Lakewood, CO | 180 |
| 255 | Carmel, IN | 131 | 260 | Fargo, ND | 129 | NA | Lancaster, CA** | NA |
| 286 | Carrollton, TX | 122 | 266 | Farmington Hills, MI | 128 | 190 | Lansing, MI | 162 |
| NA | Carson, CA** | NA | 216 | Fayetteville, AR | 148 | NA | Laredo, TX** | NA |
| 279 | Cary, NC | 124 | 147 | Fayetteville, NC | 179 | 163 | Largo, FL | 172 |
| 197 | Cedar Rapids, IA | 159 | 266 | Federal Way, WA | 128 | NA | Las Cruces, NM** | NA |
| 309 | Centennial, CO | 114 | NA | Fishers, IN** | NA | 187 | Las Vegas, NV | 163 |
| 219 | Champaign, IL | 147 | 286 | Flint, MI | 122 | 191 | Lawrence, KS | 161 |
| 260 | Chandler, AZ | 129 | 375 | Fontana, CA | 83 | 213 | Lawrence, MA | 149 |
| 14 | Charleston, SC | 340 | 260 | Fort Collins, CO | 129 | 191 | Lawton, OK | 161 |
| 127 | Charlotte, NC | 189 | 32 | Fort Lauderdale, FL | 285 | 295 | League City, TX | 119 |
| 54 | Chattanooga, TN | 251 | 136 | Fort Smith, AR | 186 | 228 | Lee's Summit, MO | 144 |
| 180 | Cheektowaga, NY | 165 | 173 | Fort Wayne, IN | 168 | 219 | Lewisville, TX | 147 |
| 176 | Chesapeake, VA | 167 | NA | Fort Worth, TX** | NA | 143 | Lexington, KY | 180 |
| NA | Chicago, IL** | NA | 384 | Fremont, CA | 75 | 291 | Lincoln, NE | 120 |
| 359 | Chico, CA | 94 | 240 | Fresno, CA | 138 | 35 | Little Rock, AR | 282 |
| NA | Chino Hills, CA** | NA | 312 | Frisco, TX | 112 | 341 | Livermore, CA | 101 |

| RANK | CITY | RATE | RANK | CITY | RATE | RANK | CITY | RATE |
|---|---|---|---|---|---|---|---|---|
| 266 | Livonia, MI | 128 | 187 | Pasadena, CA | 163 | 387 | South Gate, CA | 72 |
| 180 | Long Beach, CA | 165 | 176 | Pasadena, TX | 167 | 312 | Sparks, NV | 112 |
| 213 | Longmont, CO | 149 | 53 | Paterson, NJ | 252 | 325 | Spokane Valley, WA | 108 |
| 110 | Longview, TX | 197 | 216 | Pearland, TX | 148 | 249 | Spokane, WA | 134 |
| 51 | Los Angeles, CA | 254 | 228 | Pembroke Pines, FL | 144 | 92 | Springfield, IL | 204 |
| 147 | Louisville, KY | 179 | 317 | Peoria, AZ | 111 | 30 | Springfield, MA | 288 |
| 84 | Lowell, MA | 210 | NA | Peoria, IL** | NA | 117 | Springfield, MO | 194 |
| 173 | Lubbock, TX | 168 | 3 | Philadelphia, PA | 419 | 72 | Stamford, CT | 225 |
| 75 | Lynchburg, VA | 217 | 120 | Phoenix, AZ | 192 | 311 | Sterling Heights, MI | 113 |
| 104 | Lynn, MA | 199 | 37 | Pittsburgh, PA | 280 | 302 | Stockton, CA | 117 |
| NA | Macon, GA** | NA | 275 | Plano, TX | 126 | NA | St. George, UT** | NA |
| 123 | Madison, WI | 190 | 170 | Plantation, FL | 170 | 223 | St. Joseph, MO | 146 |
| 110 | Manchester, NH | 197 | 335 | Pomona, CA | 104 | 7 | St. Louis, MO | 404 |
| 114 | McAllen, TX | 195 | NA | Pompano Beach, FL** | NA | 104 | St. Paul, MN | 199 |
| 312 | McKinney, TX | 112 | 260 | Port St. Lucie, FL | 129 | 76 | St. Petersburg, FL | 216 |
| 255 | Medford, OR | 131 | 203 | Portland, OR | 154 | 89 | Suffolk, VA | 205 |
| 92 | Melbourne, FL | 204 | 47 | Portsmouth, VA | 255 | NA | Sugar Land, TX** | NA |
| 12 | Memphis, TN | 353 | 70 | Providence, RI | 229 | 254 | Sunnyvale, CA | 132 |
| NA | Menifee, CA** | NA | 372 | Provo, UT | 87 | 133 | Sunrise, FL | 187 |
| 351 | Merced, CA | 98 | 170 | Pueblo, CO | 170 | 333 | Surprise, AZ | 105 |
| 341 | Meridian, ID | 101 | 89 | Quincy, MA | 205 | 25 | Syracuse, NY | 306 |
| 173 | Mesa, AZ | 168 | 46 | Racine, WI | 256 | 185 | Tacoma, WA | 164 |
| NA | Mesquite, TX** | NA | 143 | Raleigh, NC | 180 | 129 | Tallahassee, FL | 188 |
| 6 | Miami Beach, FL | 408 | 283 | Ramapo, NY | 123 | 42 | Tampa, FL | 271 |
| 123 | Miami Gardens, FL | 190 | NA | Rancho Cucamon., CA** | NA | NA | Temecula, CA** | NA |
| 47 | Miami, FL | 255 | 136 | Reading, PA | 186 | 89 | Tempe, AZ | 205 |
| 228 | Midland, TX | 144 | 325 | Redding, CA | 108 | 275 | Thornton, CO | 126 |
| 22 | Milwaukee, WI | 310 | 299 | Redwood City, CA | 118 | NA | Thousand Oaks, CA** | NA |
| 82 | Minneapolis, MN | 213 | 266 | Reno, NV | 128 | 129 | Toledo, OH | 188 |
| 211 | Miramar, FL | 150 | 295 | Renton, WA | 119 | 180 | Toms River Twnshp, NJ | 165 |
| NA | Mission Viejo, CA** | NA | 367 | Rialto, CA | 92 | 211 | Torrance, CA | 150 |
| 159 | Mission, TX | 173 | 236 | Richardson, TX | 140 | 359 | Tracy, CA | 94 |
| 85 | Mobile, AL | 208 | 159 | Richmond, CA | 173 | 36 | Trenton, NJ | 281 |
| 329 | Modesto, CA | 106 | 18 | Richmond, VA | 330 | 321 | Troy, MI | 110 |
| NA | Moreno Valley, CA** | NA | 304 | Riverside, CA | 116 | 133 | Tucson, AZ | 187 |
| 291 | Mountain View, CA | 120 | 45 | Roanoke, VA | 257 | 106 | Tulsa, OK | 198 |
| 119 | Murfreesboro, TN | 193 | 290 | Rochester, MN | 121 | 26 | Tuscaloosa, AL | 303 |
| 380 | Murrieta, CA | 79 | 13 | Rochester, NY | 349 | 321 | Tustin, CA | 110 |
| 279 | Nampa, ID | 124 | NA | Rockford, IL** | NA | 121 | Tyler, TX | 191 |
| 373 | Napa, CA | 86 | 354 | Roseville, CA | 97 | 370 | Upland, CA | 90 |
| NA | Naperville, IL** | NA | NA | Roswell, GA** | NA | 205 | Upper Darby Twnshp, PA | 152 |
| 95 | Nashua, NH | 203 | NA | Round Rock, TX** | NA | 351 | Vacaville, CA | 98 |
| 77 | Nashville, TN | 215 | 266 | Sacramento, CA | 128 | 389 | Vallejo, CA | 69 |
| 41 | New Bedford, MA | 274 | 299 | Salem, OR | 118 | 312 | Vancouver, WA | 112 |
| 28 | New Haven, CT | 294 | 369 | Salinas, CA | 91 | 291 | Ventura, CA | 120 |
| 21 | New Orleans, LA | 321 | NA | Salt Lake City, UT** | NA | NA | Victorville, CA** | NA |
| 114 | New Rochelle, NY | 195 | 159 | San Angelo, TX | 173 | 157 | Virginia Beach, VA | 174 |
| 4 | New York, NY | 415 | 180 | San Antonio, TX | 165 | 329 | Visalia, CA | 106 |
| 11 | Newark, NJ | 362 | 306 | San Bernardino, CA | 115 | NA | Vista, CA** | NA |
| 203 | Newport Beach, CA | 154 | 237 | San Diego, CA | 139 | 117 | Waco, TX | 194 |
| 64 | Newport News, VA | 235 | 44 | San Francisco, CA | 258 | 216 | Warren, MI | 148 |
| 207 | Newton, MA | 151 | 324 | San Jose, CA | 109 | 96 | Warwick, RI | 202 |
| 23 | Norfolk, VA | 309 | 338 | San Leandro, CA | 102 | 1 | Washington, DC | 615 |
| 237 | Norman, OK | 139 | NA | San Marcos, CA** | NA | 51 | Waterbury, CT | 254 |
| 19 | North Charleston, SC | 327 | 328 | San Mateo, CA | 107 | NA | Waukegan, IL** | NA |
| 295 | North Las Vegas, NV | 119 | NA | Sandy Springs, GA** | NA | 375 | West Covina, CA | 83 |
| NA | Norwalk, CA** | NA | 283 | Sandy, UT | 123 | 47 | West Palm Beach, FL | 255 |
| 96 | Norwalk, CT | 202 | 358 | Santa Ana, CA | 95 | 246 | West Valley, UT | 135 |
| 198 | Oakland, CA | 158 | 201 | Santa Barbara, CA | 156 | 364 | Westland, MI | 93 |
| 304 | Oceanside, CA | 116 | 317 | Santa Clara, CA | 111 | 364 | Westminster, CA | 93 |
| 260 | Odessa, TX | 129 | NA | Santa Clarita, CA** | NA | 195 | Westminster, CO | 160 |
| 241 | O'Fallon, MO | 137 | 367 | Santa Maria, CA | 92 | 237 | Whittier, CA | 139 |
| 201 | Ogden, UT | 156 | 73 | Santa Monica, CA | 218 | 138 | Wichita Falls, TX | 184 |
| 179 | Oklahoma City, OK | 166 | 359 | Santa Rosa, CA | 94 | NA | Wichita, KS** | NA |
| 278 | Olathe, KS | 125 | 61 | Savannah, GA | 239 | 68 | Wilmington, NC | 230 |
| 143 | Omaha, NE | 180 | 141 | Scottsdale, AZ | 182 | 67 | Winston-Salem, NC | 231 |
| 241 | Ontario, CA | 137 | 106 | Scranton, PA | 198 | 123 | Woodbridge Twnshp, NJ | 190 |
| 325 | Orange, CA | 108 | 100 | Seattle, WA | 201 | 65 | Worcester, MA | 234 |
| NA | Orem, UT** | NA | NA | Shreveport, LA** | NA | 207 | Yakima, WA | 151 |
| 33 | Orlando, FL | 284 | 354 | Simi Valley, CA | 97 | 23 | Yonkers, NY | 309 |
| 241 | Overland Park, KS | 137 | 225 | Sioux City, IA | 145 | 149 | Yuma, AZ | 178 |
| 312 | Oxnard, CA | 112 | 207 | Sioux Falls, SD | 151 | | | |
| 219 | Palm Bay, FL | 147 | 191 | Somerville, MA | 161 | | | |
| NA | Palmdale, CA** | NA | 57 | South Bend, IN | 250 | | | |

Source: CQ Press using reported data from the F.B.I. "Crime in the United States 2013"

*Sworn officers only, does not include civilian employees.

**Not available

# 82. Rate of Police Officers in 2013 (continued)
## National Rate = 233 Officers per 100,000 Population*

| RANK CITY | RATE | RANK CITY | RATE | RANK CITY | RATE |
|---|---|---|---|---|---|
| 1 Washington, DC | 615 | 75 Lynchburg, VA | 217 | 149 Yuma, AZ | 178 |
| 2 Baltimore, MD | 454 | 76 St. Petersburg, FL | 216 | 150 Allentown, PA | 177 |
| 3 Philadelphia, PA | 419 | 77 Boca Raton, FL | 215 | 150 Davie, FL | 177 |
| 4 New York, NY | 415 | 77 Denver, CO | 215 | 150 Duluth, MN | 177 |
| 5 Atlanta, GA | 411 | 77 Nashville, TN | 215 | 150 Green Bay, WI | 177 |
| 6 Miami Beach, FL | 408 | 80 Beaumont, TX | 214 | 154 Bryan, TX | 176 |
| 7 St. Louis, MO | 404 | 80 Knoxville, TN | 214 | 154 Des Moines, IA | 176 |
| 8 Birmingham, AL | 394 | 82 Minneapolis, MN | 213 | 156 Cranston, RI | 175 |
| 9 Cleveland, OH | 379 | 83 Clearwater, FL | 211 | 157 Everett, WA | 174 |
| 10 Hartford, CT | 364 | 84 Lowell, MA | 210 | 157 Virginia Beach, VA | 174 |
| 11 Newark, NJ | 362 | 85 Akron, OH | 208 | 159 Danbury, CT | 173 |
| 12 Memphis, TN | 353 | 85 Mobile, AL | 208 | 159 Mission, TX | 173 |
| 13 Rochester, NY | 349 | 87 Alexandria, VA | 207 | 159 Richmond, CA | 173 |
| 14 Charleston, SC | 340 | 88 Lakeland, FL | 206 | 159 San Angelo, TX | 173 |
| 15 Albany, NY | 339 | 89 Quincy, MA | 205 | 163 Amarillo, TX | 172 |
| 16 Detroit, MI | 337 | 89 Suffolk, VA | 205 | 163 Brick Twnshp, NJ | 172 |
| 17 Boston, MA | 331 | 89 Tempe, AZ | 205 | 163 Joliet, IL | 172 |
| 18 Richmond, VA | 330 | 92 Huntsville, AL | 204 | 163 Killeen, TX | 172 |
| 19 North Charleston, SC | 327 | 92 Melbourne, FL | 204 | 163 Largo, FL | 172 |
| 20 Cincinnati, OH | 324 | 92 Springfield, IL | 204 | 168 Clifton, NJ | 171 |
| 21 New Orleans, LA | 321 | 95 Nashua, NH | 203 | 168 Independence, MO | 171 |
| 22 Milwaukee, WI | 310 | 96 Clarkstown, NY | 202 | 170 Plantation, FL | 170 |
| 23 Norfolk, VA | 309 | 96 Hampton, VA | 202 | 170 Pueblo, CO | 170 |
| 23 Yonkers, NY | 309 | 96 Norwalk, CT | 202 | 172 Erie, PA | 169 |
| 25 Syracuse, NY | 306 | 96 Warwick, RI | 202 | 173 Fort Wayne, IN | 168 |
| 26 Tuscaloosa, AL | 303 | 100 Greenville, NC | 201 | 173 Lubbock, TX | 168 |
| 27 Jersey City, NJ | 300 | 100 High Point, NC | 201 | 173 Mesa, AZ | 168 |
| 28 Kansas City, MO | 294 | 100 Seattle, WA | 201 | 176 Boulder, CO | 167 |
| 28 New Haven, CT | 294 | 103 Hollywood, FL | 200 | 176 Chesapeake, VA | 167 |
| 30 Springfield, MA | 288 | 104 Lynn, MA | 199 | 176 Pasadena, TX | 167 |
| 31 Buffalo, NY | 286 | 104 St. Paul, MN | 199 | 179 Oklahoma City, OK | 166 |
| 32 Fort Lauderdale, FL | 285 | 106 Bethlehem, PA | 198 | 180 Arlington, TX | 165 |
| 33 Orlando, FL | 284 | 106 Kenosha, WI | 198 | 180 Cheektowaga, NY | 165 |
| 34 Columbia, SC | 283 | 106 Scranton, PA | 198 | 180 Long Beach, CA | 165 |
| 35 Little Rock, AR | 282 | 106 Tulsa, OK | 198 | 180 San Antonio, TX | 165 |
| 36 Trenton, NJ | 281 | 110 Aurora, CO | 197 | 180 Toms River Twnshp, NJ | 165 |
| 37 Pittsburgh, PA | 280 | 110 Longview, TX | 197 | 185 Glendale, AZ | 164 |
| 38 Bridgeport, CT | 279 | 110 Manchester, NH | 197 | 185 Tacoma, WA | 164 |
| 38 Gary, IN | 279 | 113 Athens-Clarke, GA | 196 | 187 Elgin, IL | 163 |
| 40 Dallas, TX | 277 | 114 Austin, TX | 195 | 187 Las Vegas, NV | 163 |
| 41 New Bedford, MA | 274 | 114 McAllen, TX | 195 | 187 Pasadena, CA | 163 |
| 42 Tampa, FL | 271 | 114 New Rochelle, NY | 195 | 190 Lansing, MI | 162 |
| 43 Hammond, IN | 261 | 117 Springfield, MO | 194 | 191 Davenport, IA | 161 |
| 44 San Francisco, CA | 258 | 117 Waco, TX | 194 | 191 Lawrence, KS | 161 |
| 45 Roanoke, VA | 257 | 119 Murfreesboro, TN | 193 | 191 Lawton, OK | 161 |
| 46 Racine, WI | 256 | 120 Phoenix, AZ | 192 | 191 Somerville, MA | 161 |
| 47 Kansas City, KS | 255 | 121 Brockton, MA | 191 | 195 Coral Springs, FL | 160 |
| 47 Miami, FL | 255 | 121 Tyler, TX | 191 | 195 Westminster, CO | 160 |
| 47 Portsmouth, VA | 255 | 123 Dearborn, MI | 190 | 197 Cedar Rapids, IA | 159 |
| 47 West Palm Beach, FL | 255 | 123 Madison, WI | 190 | 198 Edison Twnshp, NJ | 158 |
| 51 Los Angeles, CA | 254 | 123 Miami Gardens, FL | 190 | 198 Oakland, CA | 158 |
| 51 Waterbury, CT | 254 | 123 Woodbridge Twnshp, NJ | 190 | 200 El Paso, TX | 157 |
| 53 Paterson, NJ | 252 | 127 Charlotte, NC | 189 | 201 Ogden, UT | 156 |
| 54 Chattanooga, TN | 251 | 127 Hamilton Twnshp, NJ | 189 | 201 Santa Barbara, CA | 156 |
| 54 Fall River, MA | 251 | 129 Concord, NC | 188 | 203 Newport Beach, CA | 154 |
| 54 Jackson, MS | 251 | 129 Hoover, AL | 188 | 203 Portland, OR | 154 |
| 57 South Bend, IN | 250 | 129 Tallahassee, FL | 188 | 205 Edinburg, TX | 152 |
| 58 Cambridge, MA | 249 | 129 Toledo, OH | 188 | 205 Upper Darby Twnshp, PA | 152 |
| 58 Elizabeth, NJ | 249 | 133 Jacksonville, FL | 187 | 207 Greeley, CO | 151 |
| 60 Dayton, OH | 246 | 133 Sunrise, FL | 187 | 207 Newton, MA | 151 |
| 61 Savannah, GA | 239 | 133 Tucson, AZ | 187 | 207 Sioux Falls, SD | 151 |
| 62 Evansville, IN | 238 | 136 Fort Smith, AR | 186 | 207 Yakima, WA | 151 |
| 62 Greensboro, NC | 238 | 136 Reading, PA | 186 | 211 Miramar, FL | 150 |
| 64 Newport News, VA | 235 | 138 Clarksville, TN | 184 | 211 Torrance, CA | 150 |
| 65 Worcester, MA | 234 | 138 Wichita Falls, TX | 184 | 213 Colorado Springs, CO | 149 |
| 66 Gainesville, FL | 232 | 140 Cicero, IL | 183 | 213 Lawrence, MA | 149 |
| 67 Winston-Salem, NC | 231 | 141 Scottsdale, AZ | 182 | 213 Longmont, CO | 149 |
| 68 Topeka, KS | 230 | 142 Indianapolis, IN | 181 | 216 Fayetteville, AR | 148 |
| 68 Wilmington, NC | 230 | 143 Lakewood, CO | 180 | 216 Pearland, TX | 148 |
| 70 Providence, RI | 229 | 143 Lexington, KY | 180 | 216 Warren, MI | 148 |
| 71 Columbus, GA | 226 | 143 Omaha, NE | 180 | 219 Champaign, IL | 147 |
| 72 Stamford, CT | 225 | 143 Raleigh, NC | 180 | 219 Grand Rapids, MI | 147 |
| 73 Evanston, IL | 218 | 147 Fayetteville, NC | 179 | 219 Lewisville, TX | 147 |
| 73 Santa Monica, CA | 218 | 147 Louisville, KY | 179 | 219 Palm Bay, FL | 147 |

| RANK | CITY | RATE | RANK | CITY | RATE | RANK | CITY | RATE |
|---|---|---|---|---|---|---|---|---|
| 223 | Beaverton, OR | 146 | 295 | North Las Vegas, NV | 119 | 371 | Garden Grove, CA | 88 |
| 223 | St. Joseph, MO | 146 | 295 | Renton, WA | 119 | 372 | Provo, UT | 87 |
| 225 | Arvada, CO | 145 | 299 | Concord, CA | 118 | 373 | Napa, CA | 86 |
| 225 | Inglewood, CA | 145 | 299 | Redwood City, CA | 118 | 374 | Canton Twnshp, MI | 85 |
| 225 | Sioux City, IA | 145 | 299 | Salem, OR | 118 | 375 | Baldwin Park, CA | 83 |
| 228 | Berkeley, CA | 144 | 302 | El Cajon, CA | 117 | 375 | Fontana, CA | 83 |
| 228 | Irving, TX | 144 | 302 | Stockton, CA | 117 | 375 | West Covina, CA | 83 |
| 228 | Lee's Summit, MO | 144 | 304 | Oceanside, CA | 116 | 378 | Clinton Twnshp, MI | 82 |
| 228 | Midland, TX | 144 | 304 | Riverside, CA | 116 | 378 | Irvine, CA | 82 |
| 228 | Pembroke Pines, FL | 144 | 306 | Anchorage, AK | 115 | 380 | Chula Vista, CA | 79 |
| 233 | Corpus Christi, TX | 143 | 306 | Bloomington, IN | 115 | 380 | Murrieta, CA | 79 |
| 234 | Abilene, TX | 142 | 306 | San Bernardino, CA | 115 | 382 | Antioch, CA | 78 |
| 235 | Burbank, CA | 141 | 309 | Centennial, CO | 114 | 383 | Elk Grove, CA | 76 |
| 236 | Richardson, TX | 140 | 309 | Chino, CA | 114 | 384 | Fremont, CA | 75 |
| 237 | Norman, OK | 139 | 311 | Sterling Heights, MI | 113 | 385 | Indio, CA | 74 |
| 237 | San Diego, CA | 139 | 312 | Frisco, TX | 112 | 385 | Johns Creek, GA | 74 |
| 237 | Whittier, CA | 139 | 312 | McKinney, TX | 112 | 387 | South Gate, CA | 72 |
| 240 | Fresno, CA | 138 | 312 | Oxnard, CA | 112 | 388 | Hemet, CA | 71 |
| 241 | Colonie, NY | 137 | 312 | Sparks, NV | 112 | 389 | Vallejo, CA | 69 |
| 241 | O'Fallon, MO | 137 | 312 | Vancouver, WA | 112 | NA | Albany, GA** | NA |
| 241 | Ontario, CA | 137 | 317 | Hawthorne, CA | 111 | NA | Albuquerque, NM** | NA |
| 241 | Overland Park, KS | 137 | 317 | Kent, WA | 111 | NA | Arlington Heights, IL** | NA |
| 245 | Hillsboro, OR | 136 | 317 | Peoria, AZ | 111 | NA | Aurora, IL** | NA |
| 246 | Cape Coral, FL | 135 | 317 | Santa Clara, CA | 111 | NA | Baton Rouge, LA** | NA |
| 246 | Garland, TX | 135 | 321 | Gresham, OR | 110 | NA | Bellflower, CA** | NA |
| 246 | West Valley, UT | 135 | 321 | Troy, MI | 110 | NA | Bloomington, IL** | NA |
| 249 | Brownsville, TX | 134 | 321 | Tustin, CA | 110 | NA | Carson, CA** | NA |
| 249 | Spokane, WA | 134 | 324 | San Jose, CA | 109 | NA | Chicago, IL** | NA |
| 251 | Bellevue, WA | 133 | 325 | Orange, CA | 108 | NA | Chino Hills, CA** | NA |
| 251 | Brooklyn Park, MN | 133 | 325 | Redding, CA | 108 | NA | Compton, CA** | NA |
| 251 | Columbia, MO | 133 | 325 | Spokane Valley, WA | 108 | NA | Decatur, IL** | NA |
| 254 | Sunnyvale, CA | 132 | 328 | San Mateo, CA | 107 | NA | Deerfield Beach, FL** | NA |
| 255 | Boise, ID | 131 | 329 | Alameda, CA | 106 | NA | Fishers, IN** | NA |
| 255 | Carmel, IN | 131 | 329 | Bend, OR | 106 | NA | Fort Worth, TX** | NA |
| 255 | Edmond, OK | 131 | 329 | Modesto, CA | 106 | NA | Hesperia, CA** | NA |
| 255 | Medford, OR | 131 | 329 | Visalia, CA | 106 | NA | Hialeah, FL** | NA |
| 259 | Lakewood Twnshp, NJ | 130 | 333 | Anaheim, CA | 105 | NA | Houston, TX** | NA |
| 260 | Billings, MT | 129 | 333 | Surprise, AZ | 105 | NA | Jurupa Valley, CA** | NA |
| 260 | Chandler, AZ | 129 | 335 | Citrus Heights, CA | 104 | NA | Lafayette, LA** | NA |
| 260 | Fargo, ND | 129 | 335 | Costa Mesa, CA | 104 | NA | Lake Forest, CA** | NA |
| 260 | Fort Collins, CO | 129 | 335 | Pomona, CA | 104 | NA | Lakewood, CA** | NA |
| 260 | Odessa, TX | 129 | 338 | Buena Park, CA | 102 | NA | Lancaster, CA** | NA |
| 260 | Port St. Lucie, FL | 129 | 338 | Fairfield, CA | 102 | NA | Laredo, TX** | NA |
| 266 | Allen, TX | 128 | 338 | San Leandro, CA | 102 | NA | Las Cruces, NM** | NA |
| 266 | Amherst, NY | 128 | 341 | Ann Arbor, MI | 101 | NA | Macon, GA** | NA |
| 266 | Bloomington, MN | 128 | 341 | Carlsbad, CA | 101 | NA | Menifee, CA** | NA |
| 266 | College Station, TX | 128 | 341 | Escondido, CA | 101 | NA | Mesquite, TX** | NA |
| 266 | Farmington Hills, MI | 128 | 341 | Greece, NY | 101 | NA | Mission Viejo, CA** | NA |
| 266 | Federal Way, WA | 128 | 341 | Livermore, CA | 101 | NA | Moreno Valley, CA** | NA |
| 266 | Livonia, MI | 128 | 341 | Meridian, ID | 101 | NA | Naperville, IL** | NA |
| 266 | Reno, NV | 128 | 347 | Gilbert, AZ | 100 | NA | Norwalk, CA** | NA |
| 266 | Sacramento, CA | 128 | 348 | Daly City, CA | 99 | NA | Orem, UT** | NA |
| 275 | Broken Arrow, OK | 126 | 348 | El Monte, CA | 99 | NA | Palmdale, CA** | NA |
| 275 | Plano, TX | 126 | 348 | Huntington Beach, CA | 99 | NA | Peoria, IL** | NA |
| 275 | Thornton, CO | 126 | 351 | Alhambra, CA | 98 | NA | Pompano Beach, FL** | NA |
| 278 | Olathe, KS | 125 | 351 | Merced, CA | 98 | NA | Rancho Cucamon., CA** | NA |
| 279 | Cary, NC | 124 | 351 | Vacaville, CA | 98 | NA | Rockford, IL** | NA |
| 279 | Denton, TX | 124 | 354 | Fullerton, CA | 97 | NA | Roswell, GA** | NA |
| 279 | Eugene, OR | 124 | 354 | Roseville, CA | 97 | NA | Round Rock, TX** | NA |
| 279 | Nampa, ID | 124 | 354 | Simi Valley, CA | 97 | NA | Salt Lake City, UT** | NA |
| 283 | Glendale, CA | 123 | 357 | Downey, CA | 96 | NA | San Marcos, CA** | NA |
| 283 | Ramapo, NY | 123 | 358 | Santa Ana, CA | 95 | NA | Sandy Springs, GA** | NA |
| 283 | Sandy, UT | 123 | 359 | Bakersfield, CA | 94 | NA | Santa Clarita, CA** | NA |
| 286 | Carrollton, TX | 122 | 359 | Chico, CA | 94 | NA | Shreveport, LA** | NA |
| 286 | Flint, MI | 122 | 359 | Corona, CA | 94 | NA | St. George, UT** | NA |
| 286 | Henderson, NV | 122 | 359 | Santa Rosa, CA | 94 | NA | Sugar Land, TX** | NA |
| 286 | Kennewick, WA | 122 | 359 | Tracy, CA | 94 | NA | Temecula, CA** | NA |
| 290 | Rochester, MN | 121 | 364 | Clovis, CA | 93 | NA | Thousand Oaks, CA** | NA |
| 291 | Grand Prairie, TX | 120 | 364 | Westland, MI | 93 | NA | Victorville, CA** | NA |
| 291 | Lincoln, NE | 120 | 364 | Westminster, CA | 93 | NA | Vista, CA** | NA |
| 291 | Mountain View, CA | 120 | 367 | Rialto, CA | 92 | NA | Waukegan, IL** | NA |
| 291 | Ventura, CA | 120 | 367 | Santa Maria, CA | 92 | NA | Wichita, KS** | NA |
| 295 | Hayward, CA | 119 | 369 | Salinas, CA | 91 | | | |
| 295 | League City, TX | 119 | 370 | Upland, CA | 90 | | | |

Source: CQ Press using reported data from the F.B.I. "Crime in the United States 2013"

*Sworn officers only, does not include civilian employees.

**Not available

# 83. Percent Change in Rate of Police Officers: 2012 to 2013
## National Percent Change = 0.9% Decrease*

| RANK | CITY | % CHANGE | RANK | CITY | % CHANGE | RANK | CITY | % CHANGE |
|---|---|---|---|---|---|---|---|---|
| NA | Abilene, TX** | NA | 366 | Chino, CA | (10.9) | 269 | Fullerton, CA | (3.0) |
| 210 | Akron, OH | (1.4) | 340 | Chula Vista, CA | (6.0) | 134 | Gainesville, FL | 0.4 |
| 187 | Alameda, CA | (0.9) | 76 | Cicero, IL | 1.7 | 102 | Garden Grove, CA | 1.1 |
| NA | Albany, GA** | NA | 277 | Cincinnati, OH | (3.3) | 57 | Garland, TX | 2.3 |
| NA | Albany, NY** | NA | 30 | Citrus Heights, CA | 4.0 | 311 | Gary, IN | (4.5) |
| NA | Albuquerque, NM** | NA | 70 | Clarkstown, NY | 2.0 | 293 | Gilbert, AZ | (3.8) |
| 314 | Alexandria, VA | (4.6) | 341 | Clarksville, TN | (6.1) | 285 | Glendale, AZ | (3.5) |
| 105 | Alhambra, CA | 1.0 | 105 | Clearwater, FL | 1.0 | 137 | Glendale, CA | 0.0 |
| 125 | Allentown, PA | 0.6 | 115 | Cleveland, OH | 0.8 | 115 | Grand Prairie, TX | 0.8 |
| 214 | Allen, TX | (1.5) | 125 | Clifton, NJ | 0.6 | 311 | Grand Rapids, MI | (4.5) |
| 20 | Amarillo, TX | 4.9 | 360 | Clinton Twnshp, MI | (8.9) | 137 | Greece, NY | 0.0 |
| 214 | Amherst, NY | (1.5) | 102 | Clovis, CA | 1.1 | 137 | Greeley, CO | 0.0 |
| 105 | Anaheim, CA | 1.0 | 46 | College Station, TX | 3.2 | 57 | Green Bay, WI | 2.3 |
| 353 | Anchorage, AK | (7.3) | 120 | Colonie, NY | 0.7 | 16 | Greensboro, NC | 5.8 |
| 197 | Ann Arbor, MI | (1.0) | 120 | Colorado Springs, CO | 0.7 | 281 | Greenville, NC | (3.4) |
| 323 | Antioch, CA | (4.9) | 335 | Columbia, MO | (5.7) | 187 | Gresham, OR | (0.9) |
| NA | Arlington Heights, IL** | NA | NA | Columbia, SC** | NA | 82 | Hamilton Twnshp, NJ | 1.6 |
| 125 | Arlington, TX | 0.6 | 327 | Columbus, GA | (5.0) | 70 | Hammond, IN | 2.0 |
| 277 | Arvada, CO | (3.3) | NA | Compton, CA** | NA | 130 | Hampton, VA | 0.5 |
| 281 | Athens-Clarke, GA | (3.4) | 53 | Concord, CA | 2.6 | 317 | Hartford, CT | (4.7) |
| 96 | Atlanta, GA | 1.2 | NA | Concord, NC** | NA | 187 | Hawthorne, CA | (0.9) |
| 66 | Aurora, CO | 2.1 | 93 | Coral Springs, FL | 1.3 | 219 | Hayward, CA | (1.7) |
| NA | Aurora, IL** | NA | 137 | Corona, CA | 0.0 | 90 | Hemet, CA | 1.4 |
| 137 | Austin, TX | 0.0 | 37 | Corpus Christi, TX | 3.6 | 218 | Henderson, NV | (1.6) |
| 302 | Bakersfield, CA | (4.1) | 359 | Costa Mesa, CA | (8.8) | NA | Hesperia, CA** | NA |
| 349 | Baldwin Park, CA | (6.7) | 76 | Cranston, RI | 1.7 | NA | Hialeah, FL** | NA |
| 304 | Baltimore, MD | (4.2) | NA | Dallas, TX** | NA | 137 | High Point, NC | 0.0 |
| NA | Baton Rouge, LA** | NA | 297 | Daly City, CA | (3.9) | 240 | Hillsboro, OR | (2.2) |
| NA | Beaumont, TX** | NA | 245 | Danbury, CT | (2.3) | 168 | Hollywood, FL | (0.5) |
| 210 | Beaverton, OR | (1.4) | 137 | Davenport, IA | 0.0 | NA | Hoover, AL** | NA |
| 214 | Bellevue, WA | (1.5) | 57 | Davie, FL | 2.3 | NA | Houston, TX** | NA |
| NA | Bellflower, CA** | NA | 66 | Dayton, OH | 2.1 | 197 | Huntington Beach, CA | (1.0) |
| NA | Bend, OR** | NA | 137 | Dearborn, MI | 0.0 | 346 | Huntsville, AL | (6.4) |
| 281 | Berkeley, CA | (3.4) | NA | Decatur, IL** | NA | 14 | Independence, MO | 6.2 |
| 168 | Bethlehem, PA | (0.5) | NA | Deerfield Beach, FL** | NA | 317 | Indianapolis, IN | (4.7) |
| 269 | Billings, MT | (3.0) | 248 | Denton, TX | (2.4) | 354 | Indio, CA | (7.5) |
| 269 | Birmingham, AL | (3.0) | 256 | Denver, CO | (2.7) | 362 | Inglewood, CA | (9.4) |
| NA | Bloomington, IL** | NA | NA | Des Moines, IA** | NA | 366 | Irvine, CA | (10.9) |
| NA | Bloomington, IN** | NA | 352 | Detroit, MI | (7.2) | 231 | Irving, TX | (2.0) |
| 179 | Bloomington, MN | (0.8) | 66 | Downey, CA | 2.1 | 61 | Jacksonville, FL | 2.2 |
| 187 | Boca Raton, FL | (0.9) | 4 | Duluth, MN | 7.3 | 334 | Jackson, MS | (5.6) |
| 240 | Boise, ID | (2.2) | NA | Edinburg, TX** | NA | 332 | Jersey City, NJ | (5.4) |
| 237 | Boston, MA | (2.1) | 321 | Edison Twnshp, NJ | (4.8) | 253 | Johns Creek, GA | (2.6) |
| 285 | Boulder, CO | (3.5) | 214 | Edmond, OK | (1.5) | 37 | Joliet, IL | 3.6 |
| 125 | Brick Twnshp, NJ | 0.6 | 9 | El Cajon, CA | 6.4 | NA | Jurupa Valley, CA** | NA |
| 223 | Bridgeport, CT | (1.8) | 231 | El Monte, CA | (2.0) | 12 | Kansas City, KS | 6.3 |
| 7 | Brockton, MA | 6.7 | 53 | El Paso, TX | 2.6 | 4 | Kansas City, MO | 7.3 |
| 19 | Broken Arrow, OK | 5.0 | 203 | Elgin, IL | (1.2) | 25 | Kennewick, WA | 4.3 |
| 240 | Brooklyn Park, MN | (2.2) | 285 | Elizabeth, NJ | (3.5) | 168 | Kenosha, WI | (0.5) |
| 137 | Brownsville, TX | 0.0 | 344 | Elk Grove, CA | (6.2) | 21 | Kent, WA | 4.7 |
| 137 | Bryan, TX | 0.0 | 173 | Erie, PA | (0.6) | 201 | Killeen, TX | (1.1) |
| 105 | Buena Park, CA | 1.0 | 137 | Escondido, CA | 0.0 | 323 | Knoxville, TN | (4.9) |
| 197 | Buffalo, NY | (1.0) | 42 | Eugene, OR | 3.3 | NA | Lafayette, LA** | NA |
| 281 | Burbank, CA | (3.4) | 137 | Evanston, IL | 0.0 | NA | Lake Forest, CA** | NA |
| 285 | Cambridge, MA | (3.5) | 219 | Evansville, IN | (1.7) | 329 | Lakeland, FL | (5.1) |
| NA | Canton Twnshp, MI** | NA | 323 | Everett, WA | (4.9) | 30 | Lakewood Twnshp, NJ | 4.0 |
| 137 | Cape Coral, FL | 0.0 | 346 | Fairfield, CA | (6.4) | NA | Lakewood, CA** | NA |
| 264 | Carlsbad, CA | (2.9) | 42 | Fall River, MA | 3.3 | 201 | Lakewood, CO | (1.1) |
| 179 | Carmel, IN | (0.8) | 115 | Fargo, ND | 0.8 | NA | Lancaster, CA** | NA |
| 297 | Carrollton, TX | (3.9) | 137 | Farmington Hills, MI | 0.0 | 248 | Lansing, MI | (2.4) |
| NA | Carson, CA** | NA | 297 | Fayetteville, AR | (3.9) | NA | Laredo, TX** | NA |
| 274 | Cary, NC | (3.1) | 57 | Fayetteville, NC | 2.3 | 96 | Largo, FL | 1.2 |
| 93 | Cedar Rapids, IA | 1.3 | 293 | Federal Way, WA | (3.8) | NA | Las Cruces, NM** | NA |
| 114 | Centennial, CO | 0.9 | NA | Fishers, IN** | NA | 338 | Las Vegas, NV | (5.8) |
| 8 | Champaign, IL | 6.5 | 25 | Flint, MI | 4.3 | 317 | Lawrence, KS | (4.7) |
| 179 | Chandler, AZ | (0.8) | 349 | Fontana, CA | (6.7) | 208 | Lawrence, MA | (1.3) |
| 23 | Charleston, SC | 4.6 | 55 | Fort Collins, CO | 2.4 | 351 | Lawton, OK | (6.9) |
| 365 | Charlotte, NC | (10.8) | 256 | Fort Lauderdale, FL | (2.7) | 277 | League City, TX | (3.3) |
| NA | Chattanooga, TN** | NA | 237 | Fort Smith, AR | (2.1) | 90 | Lee's Summit, MO | 1.4 |
| 74 | Cheektowaga, NY | 1.9 | 223 | Fort Wayne, IN | (1.8) | NA | Lewisville, TX** | NA |
| 24 | Chesapeake, VA | 4.4 | NA | Fort Worth, TX** | NA | 2 | Lexington, KY | 8.4 |
| NA | Chicago, IL** | NA | 345 | Fremont, CA | (6.3) | 179 | Lincoln, NE | (0.8) |
| 358 | Chico, CA | (8.7) | 321 | Fresno, CA | (4.8) | 9 | Little Rock, AR | 6.4 |
| NA | Chino Hills, CA** | NA | 253 | Frisco, TX | (2.6) | 70 | Livermore, CA | 2.0 |

| RANK | CITY | % CHANGE | RANK | CITY | % CHANGE | RANK | CITY | % CHANGE |
|---|---|---|---|---|---|---|---|---|
| 82 | Livonia, MI | 1.6 | 203 | Pasadena, CA | (1.2) | 256 | South Gate, CA | (2.7) |
| 264 | Long Beach, CA | (2.9) | 285 | Pasadena, TX | (3.5) | 308 | Sparks, NV | (4.3) |
| 208 | Longmont, CO | (1.3) | 137 | Paterson, NJ | 0.0 | 187 | Spokane Valley, WA | (0.9) |
| 34 | Longview, TX | 3.7 | 40 | Pearland, TX | 3.5 | 49 | Spokane, WA | 3.1 |
| 226 | Los Angeles, CA | (1.9) | NA | Pembroke Pines, FL** | NA | 304 | Springfield, IL | (4.2) |
| 293 | Louisville, KY | (3.8) | 329 | Peoria, AZ | (5.1) | 1 | Springfield, MA | 21.0 |
| 90 | Lowell, MA | 1.4 | NA | Peoria, IL** | NA | 231 | Springfield, MO | (2.0) |
| 173 | Lubbock, TX | (0.6) | 203 | Philadelphia, PA | (1.2) | 34 | Stamford, CT | 3.7 |
| 341 | Lynchburg, VA | (6.1) | 311 | Phoenix, AZ | (4.5) | 219 | Sterling Heights, MI | (1.7) |
| 66 | Lynn, MA | 2.1 | 210 | Pittsburgh, PA | (1.4) | 17 | Stockton, CA | 5.4 |
| NA | Macon, GA** | NA | 82 | Plano, TX | 1.6 | NA | St. George, UT** | NA |
| 82 | Madison, WI | 1.6 | 364 | Plantation, FL | (10.5) | 231 | St. Joseph, MO | (2.0) |
| 87 | Manchester, NH | 1.5 | 30 | Pomona, CA | 4.0 | 256 | St. Louis, MO | (2.7) |
| 137 | McAllen, TX | 0.0 | NA | Pompano Beach, FL** | NA | 264 | St. Paul, MN | (2.9) |
| 223 | McKinney, TX | (1.8) | NA | Port St. Lucie, FL** | NA | 187 | St. Petersburg, FL | (0.9) |
| 240 | Medford, OR | (2.2) | 323 | Portland, OR | (4.9) | NA | Suffolk, VA** | NA |
| NA | Melbourne, FL** | NA | 226 | Portsmouth, VA | (1.9) | NA | Sugar Land, TX** | NA |
| 293 | Memphis, TN | (3.8) | 314 | Providence, RI | (4.6) | 335 | Sunnyvale, CA | (5.7) |
| NA | Menifee, CA** | NA | 96 | Provo, UT | 1.2 | 348 | Sunrise, FL | (6.5) |
| 297 | Merced, CA | (3.9) | 173 | Pueblo, CO | (0.6) | 226 | Surprise, AZ | (1.9) |
| 361 | Meridian, ID | (9.0) | 105 | Quincy, MA | 1.0 | 317 | Syracuse, NY | (4.7) |
| 264 | Mesa, AZ | (2.9) | 55 | Racine, WI | 2.4 | 335 | Tacoma, WA | (5.7) |
| NA | Mesquite, TX** | NA | 76 | Raleigh, NC | 1.7 | 130 | Tallahassee, FL | 0.5 |
| 137 | Miami Beach, FL | 0.0 | 179 | Ramapo, NY | (0.8) | 178 | Tampa, FL | (0.7) |
| 3 | Miami Gardens, FL | 8.0 | NA | Rancho Cucamon., CA** | NA | NA | Temecula, CA** | NA |
| 134 | Miami, FL | 0.4 | 168 | Reading, PA | (0.5) | 87 | Tempe, AZ | 1.5 |
| 231 | Midland, TX | (2.0) | 137 | Redding, CA | 0.0 | 115 | Thornton, CO | 0.8 |
| 251 | Milwaukee, WI | (2.5) | 12 | Redwood City, CA | 6.3 | NA | Thousand Oaks, CA** | NA |
| 245 | Minneapolis, MN | (2.3) | 179 | Reno, NV | (0.8) | 333 | Toledo, OH | (5.5) |
| 231 | Miramar, FL | (2.0) | 301 | Renton, WA | (4.0) | 96 | Toms River Twnshp, NJ | 1.2 |
| NA | Mission Viejo, CA** | NA | 61 | Rialto, CA | 2.2 | 61 | Topeka, KS | 2.2 |
| 263 | Mission, TX | (2.8) | 302 | Richardson, TX | (4.1) | 9 | Torrance, CA | 6.4 |
| 292 | Mobile, AL | (3.7) | 96 | Richmond, CA | 1.2 | 61 | Tracy, CA | 2.2 |
| 137 | Modesto, CA | 0.0 | 314 | Richmond, VA | (4.6) | 120 | Trenton, NJ | 0.7 |
| NA | Moreno Valley, CA** | NA | 187 | Riverside, CA | (0.9) | 137 | Troy, MI | 0.0 |
| 275 | Mountain View, CA | (3.2) | 226 | Roanoke, VA | (1.9) | 33 | Tucson, AZ | 3.9 |
| 269 | Murfreesboro, TN | (3.0) | 179 | Rochester, MN | (0.8) | 105 | Tulsa, OK | 1.0 |
| 137 | Murrieta, CA | 0.0 | 166 | Rochester, NY | (0.3) | 245 | Tuscaloosa, AL | (2.3) |
| 354 | Nampa, ID | (7.5) | NA | Rockford, IL** | NA | 187 | Tustin, CA | (0.9) |
| 96 | Napa, CA | 1.2 | 46 | Roseville, CA | 3.2 | 82 | Tyler, TX | 1.6 |
| NA | Naperville, IL** | NA | NA | Roswell, GA** | NA | 275 | Upland, CA | (3.2) |
| 87 | Nashua, NH | 1.5 | NA | Round Rock, TX** | NA | 137 | Upper Darby Twnshp, PA | 0.0 |
| 74 | Nashville, TN | 1.9 | 269 | Sacramento, CA | (3.0) | 46 | Vacaville, CA | 3.2 |
| 27 | New Bedford, MA | 4.2 | 179 | Salem, OR | (0.8) | 368 | Vallejo, CA | (11.5) |
| 341 | New Haven, CT | (6.1) | 304 | Salinas, CA | (4.2) | 21 | Vancouver, WA | 4.7 |
| 356 | New Orleans, LA | (8.3) | NA | Salt Lake City, UT** | NA | 14 | Ventura, CA | 6.2 |
| 285 | New Rochelle, NY | (3.5) | NA | San Angelo, TX** | NA | NA | Victorville, CA** | NA |
| 168 | New York, NY | (0.5) | 137 | San Antonio, TX | 0.0 | 173 | Virginia Beach, VA | (0.6) |
| 327 | Newark, NJ | (5.0) | 362 | San Bernardino, CA | (9.4) | 105 | Visalia, CA | 1.0 |
| 70 | Newport Beach, CA | 2.0 | 137 | San Diego, CA | 0.0 | NA | Vista, CA** | NA |
| 61 | Newport News, VA | 2.2 | 253 | San Francisco, CA | (2.6) | 34 | Waco, TX | 3.7 |
| 310 | Newton, MA | (4.4) | 256 | San Jose, CA | (2.7) | 120 | Warren, MI | 0.7 |
| 42 | Norfolk, VA | 3.3 | 226 | San Leandro, CA | (1.9) | 264 | Warwick, RI | (2.9) |
| 137 | Norman, OK | 0.0 | NA | San Marcos, CA** | NA | 130 | Washington, DC | 0.5 |
| 28 | North Charleston, SC | 4.1 | 52 | San Mateo, CA | 2.9 | 134 | Waterbury, CT | 0.4 |
| 219 | North Las Vegas, NV | (1.7) | NA | Sandy Springs, GA** | NA | NA | Waukegan, IL** | NA |
| NA | Norwalk, CA** | NA | 76 | Sandy, UT | 1.7 | 137 | West Covina, CA | 0.0 |
| 37 | Norwalk, CT | 3.6 | 197 | Santa Ana, CA | (1.0) | 203 | West Palm Beach, FL | (1.2) |
| 125 | Oakland, CA | 0.6 | 17 | Santa Barbara, CA | 5.4 | 308 | West Valley, UT | (4.3) |
| 251 | Oceanside, CA | (2.5) | 285 | Santa Clara, CA | (3.5) | 102 | Westland, MI | 1.1 |
| 357 | Odessa, TX | (8.5) | NA | Santa Clarita, CA** | NA | 237 | Westminster, CA | (2.1) |
| 50 | O'Fallon, MO | 3.0 | 137 | Santa Maria, CA | 0.0 | 304 | Westminster, CO | (4.2) |
| 137 | Ogden, UT | 0.0 | 240 | Santa Monica, CA | (2.2) | 210 | Whittier, CA | (1.4) |
| 203 | Oklahoma City, OK | (1.2) | 137 | Santa Rosa, CA | 0.0 | 76 | Wichita Falls, TX | 1.7 |
| NA | Olathe, KS** | NA | 339 | Savannah, GA | (5.9) | NA | Wichita, KS** | NA |
| 331 | Omaha, NE | (5.3) | 76 | Scottsdale, AZ | 1.7 | 167 | Wilmington, NC | (0.4) |
| 50 | Ontario, CA | 3.0 | 130 | Scranton, PA | 0.5 | 187 | Winston-Salem, NC | (0.9) |
| 256 | Orange, CA | (2.7) | 248 | Seattle, WA | (2.4) | 42 | Woodbridge Twnshp, NJ | 3.3 |
| NA | Orem, UT** | NA | NA | Shreveport, LA** | NA | 40 | Worcester, MA | 3.5 |
| 256 | Orlando, FL | (2.7) | 105 | Simi Valley, CA | 1.0 | 93 | Yakima, WA | 1.3 |
| NA | Overland Park, KS** | NA | 277 | Sioux City, IA | (3.3) | 105 | Yonkers, NY | 1.0 |
| 187 | Oxnard, CA | (0.9) | 28 | Sioux Falls, SD | 4.1 | 6 | Yuma, AZ | 7.2 |
| 120 | Palm Bay, FL | 0.7 | 173 | Somerville, MA | (0.6) | | | |
| NA | Palmdale, CA** | NA | 115 | South Bend, IN | 0.8 | | | |

Source: CQ Press using reported data from the F.B.I. "Crime in the United States 2013"

*Sworn officers only, does not include civilian employees.

**Not available

## 83. Percent Change in Rate of Police Officers: 2012 to 2013 (continued)
### National Percent Change = 0.9% Decrease*

| RANK | CITY | % CHANGE | RANK | CITY | % CHANGE | RANK | CITY | % CHANGE |
|---|---|---|---|---|---|---|---|---|
| 1 | Springfield, MA | 21.0 | 74 | Nashville, TN | 1.9 | 137 | Greeley, CO | 0.0 |
| 2 | Lexington, KY | 8.4 | 76 | Cicero, IL | 1.7 | 137 | High Point, NC | 0.0 |
| 3 | Miami Gardens, FL | 8.0 | 76 | Cranston, RI | 1.7 | 137 | McAllen, TX | 0.0 |
| 4 | Duluth, MN | 7.3 | 76 | Raleigh, NC | 1.7 | 137 | Miami Beach, FL | 0.0 |
| 4 | Kansas City, MO | 7.3 | 76 | Sandy, UT | 1.7 | 137 | Modesto, CA | 0.0 |
| 6 | Yuma, AZ | 7.2 | 76 | Scottsdale, AZ | 1.7 | 137 | Murrieta, CA | 0.0 |
| 7 | Brockton, MA | 6.7 | 76 | Wichita Falls, TX | 1.7 | 137 | Norman, OK | 0.0 |
| 8 | Champaign, IL | 6.5 | 82 | Hamilton Twnshp, NJ | 1.6 | 137 | Ogden, UT | 0.0 |
| 9 | El Cajon, CA | 6.4 | 82 | Livonia, MI | 1.6 | 137 | Paterson, NJ | 0.0 |
| 9 | Little Rock, AR | 6.4 | 82 | Madison, WI | 1.6 | 137 | Redding, CA | 0.0 |
| 9 | Torrance, CA | 6.4 | 82 | Plano, TX | 1.6 | 137 | San Antonio, TX | 0.0 |
| 12 | Kansas City, KS | 6.3 | 82 | Tyler, TX | 1.6 | 137 | San Diego, CA | 0.0 |
| 12 | Redwood City, CA | 6.3 | 87 | Manchester, NH | 1.5 | 137 | Santa Maria, CA | 0.0 |
| 14 | Independence, MO | 6.2 | 87 | Nashua, NH | 1.5 | 137 | Santa Rosa, CA | 0.0 |
| 14 | Ventura, CA | 6.2 | 87 | Tempe, AZ | 1.5 | 137 | Troy, MI | 0.0 |
| 16 | Greensboro, NC | 5.8 | 90 | Hemet, CA | 1.4 | 137 | Upper Darby Twnshp, PA | 0.0 |
| 17 | Santa Barbara, CA | 5.4 | 90 | Lee's Summit, MO | 1.4 | 137 | West Covina, CA | 0.0 |
| 17 | Stockton, CA | 5.4 | 90 | Lowell, MA | 1.4 | 166 | Rochester, NY | (0.3) |
| 19 | Broken Arrow, OK | 5.0 | 93 | Cedar Rapids, IA | 1.3 | 167 | Wilmington, NC | (0.4) |
| 20 | Amarillo, TX | 4.9 | 93 | Coral Springs, FL | 1.3 | 168 | Bethlehem, PA | (0.5) |
| 21 | Kent, WA | 4.7 | 93 | Yakima, WA | 1.3 | 168 | Hollywood, FL | (0.5) |
| 21 | Vancouver, WA | 4.7 | 96 | Atlanta, GA | 1.2 | 168 | Kenosha, WI | (0.5) |
| 23 | Charleston, SC | 4.6 | 96 | Largo, FL | 1.2 | 168 | New York, NY | (0.5) |
| 24 | Chesapeake, VA | 4.4 | 96 | Napa, CA | 1.2 | 168 | Reading, PA | (0.5) |
| 25 | Flint, MI | 4.3 | 96 | Provo, UT | 1.2 | 173 | Erie, PA | (0.6) |
| 25 | Kennewick, WA | 4.3 | 96 | Richmond, CA | 1.2 | 173 | Lubbock, TX | (0.6) |
| 27 | New Bedford, MA | 4.2 | 96 | Toms River Twnshp, NJ | 1.2 | 173 | Pueblo, CO | (0.6) |
| 28 | North Charleston, SC | 4.1 | 102 | Clovis, CA | 1.1 | 173 | Somerville, MA | (0.6) |
| 28 | Sioux Falls, SD | 4.1 | 102 | Garden Grove, CA | 1.1 | 173 | Virginia Beach, VA | (0.6) |
| 30 | Citrus Heights, CA | 4.0 | 102 | Westland, MI | 1.1 | 178 | Tampa, FL | (0.7) |
| 30 | Lakewood Twnshp, NJ | 4.0 | 105 | Alhambra, CA | 1.0 | 179 | Bloomington, MN | (0.8) |
| 30 | Pomona, CA | 4.0 | 105 | Anaheim, CA | 1.0 | 179 | Carmel, IN | (0.8) |
| 33 | Tucson, AZ | 3.9 | 105 | Buena Park, CA | 1.0 | 179 | Chandler, AZ | (0.8) |
| 34 | Longview, TX | 3.7 | 105 | Clearwater, FL | 1.0 | 179 | Lincoln, NE | (0.8) |
| 34 | Stamford, CT | 3.7 | 105 | Quincy, MA | 1.0 | 179 | Ramapo, NY | (0.8) |
| 34 | Waco, TX | 3.7 | 105 | Simi Valley, CA | 1.0 | 179 | Reno, NV | (0.8) |
| 37 | Corpus Christi, TX | 3.6 | 105 | Tulsa, OK | 1.0 | 179 | Rochester, MN | (0.8) |
| 37 | Joliet, IL | 3.6 | 105 | Visalia, CA | 1.0 | 179 | Salem, OR | (0.8) |
| 37 | Norwalk, CT | 3.6 | 105 | Yonkers, NY | 1.0 | 187 | Alameda, CA | (0.9) |
| 40 | Pearland, TX | 3.5 | 114 | Centennial, CO | 0.9 | 187 | Boca Raton, FL | (0.9) |
| 40 | Worcester, MA | 3.5 | 115 | Cleveland, OH | 0.8 | 187 | Gresham, OR | (0.9) |
| 42 | Eugene, OR | 3.3 | 115 | Fargo, ND | 0.8 | 187 | Hawthorne, CA | (0.9) |
| 42 | Fall River, MA | 3.3 | 115 | Grand Prairie, TX | 0.8 | 187 | Oxnard, CA | (0.9) |
| 42 | Norfolk, VA | 3.3 | 115 | South Bend, IN | 0.8 | 187 | Riverside, CA | (0.9) |
| 42 | Woodbridge Twnshp, NJ | 3.3 | 115 | Thornton, CO | 0.8 | 187 | Spokane Valley, WA | (0.9) |
| 46 | College Station, TX | 3.2 | 120 | Colonie, NY | 0.7 | 187 | St. Petersburg, FL | (0.9) |
| 46 | Roseville, CA | 3.2 | 120 | Colorado Springs, CO | 0.7 | 187 | Tustin, CA | (0.9) |
| 46 | Vacaville, CA | 3.2 | 120 | Palm Bay, FL | 0.7 | 187 | Winston-Salem, NC | (0.9) |
| 49 | Spokane, WA | 3.1 | 120 | Trenton, NJ | 0.7 | 197 | Ann Arbor, MI | (1.0) |
| 50 | O'Fallon, MO | 3.0 | 120 | Warren, MI | 0.7 | 197 | Buffalo, NY | (1.0) |
| 50 | Ontario, CA | 3.0 | 125 | Allentown, PA | 0.6 | 197 | Huntington Beach, CA | (1.0) |
| 52 | San Mateo, CA | 2.9 | 125 | Arlington, TX | 0.6 | 197 | Santa Ana, CA | (1.0) |
| 53 | Concord, CA | 2.6 | 125 | Brick Twnshp, NJ | 0.6 | 201 | Killeen, TX | (1.1) |
| 53 | El Paso, TX | 2.6 | 125 | Clifton, NJ | 0.6 | 201 | Lakewood, CO | (1.1) |
| 55 | Fort Collins, CO | 2.4 | 125 | Oakland, CA | 0.6 | 203 | Elgin, IL | (1.2) |
| 55 | Racine, WI | 2.4 | 130 | Hampton, VA | 0.5 | 203 | Oklahoma City, OK | (1.2) |
| 57 | Davie, FL | 2.3 | 130 | Scranton, PA | 0.5 | 203 | Pasadena, CA | (1.2) |
| 57 | Fayetteville, NC | 2.3 | 130 | Tallahassee, FL | 0.5 | 203 | Philadelphia, PA | (1.2) |
| 57 | Garland, TX | 2.3 | 130 | Washington, DC | 0.5 | 203 | West Palm Beach, FL | (1.2) |
| 57 | Green Bay, WI | 2.3 | 134 | Gainesville, FL | 0.4 | 208 | Lawrence, MA | (1.3) |
| 61 | Jacksonville, FL | 2.2 | 134 | Miami, FL | 0.4 | 208 | Longmont, CO | (1.3) |
| 61 | Newport News, VA | 2.2 | 134 | Waterbury, CT | 0.4 | 210 | Akron, OH | (1.4) |
| 61 | Rialto, CA | 2.2 | 137 | Austin, TX | 0.0 | 210 | Beaverton, OR | (1.4) |
| 61 | Topeka, KS | 2.2 | 137 | Brownsville, TX | 0.0 | 210 | Pittsburgh, PA | (1.4) |
| 61 | Tracy, CA | 2.2 | 137 | Bryan, TX | 0.0 | 210 | Whittier, CA | (1.4) |
| 66 | Aurora, CO | 2.1 | 137 | Cape Coral, FL | 0.0 | 214 | Allen, TX | (1.5) |
| 66 | Dayton, OH | 2.1 | 137 | Corona, CA | 0.0 | 214 | Amherst, NY | (1.5) |
| 66 | Downey, CA | 2.1 | 137 | Davenport, IA | 0.0 | 214 | Bellevue, WA | (1.5) |
| 66 | Lynn, MA | 2.1 | 137 | Dearborn, MI | 0.0 | 214 | Edmond, OK | (1.5) |
| 70 | Clarkstown, NY | 2.0 | 137 | Escondido, CA | 0.0 | 218 | Henderson, NV | (1.6) |
| 70 | Hammond, IN | 2.0 | 137 | Evanston, IL | 0.0 | 219 | Evansville, IN | (1.7) |
| 70 | Livermore, CA | 2.0 | 137 | Farmington Hills, MI | 0.0 | 219 | Hayward, CA | (1.7) |
| 70 | Newport Beach, CA | 2.0 | 137 | Glendale, CA | 0.0 | 219 | North Las Vegas, NV | (1.7) |
| 74 | Cheektowaga, NY | 1.9 | 137 | Greece, NY | 0.0 | 219 | Sterling Heights, MI | (1.7) |

| RANK | CITY | % CHANGE | RANK | CITY | % CHANGE | RANK | CITY | % CHANGE |
|---|---|---|---|---|---|---|---|---|
| 223 | Bridgeport, CT | (1.8) | 297 | Carrollton, TX | (3.9) | NA | Albany, NY** | NA |
| 223 | Fort Wayne, IN | (1.8) | 297 | Daly City, CA | (3.9) | NA | Albuquerque, NM** | NA |
| 223 | McKinney, TX | (1.8) | 297 | Fayetteville, AR | (3.9) | NA | Arlington Heights, IL** | NA |
| 226 | Los Angeles, CA | (1.9) | 297 | Merced, CA | (3.9) | NA | Aurora, IL** | NA |
| 226 | Portsmouth, VA | (1.9) | 301 | Renton, WA | (4.0) | NA | Baton Rouge, LA** | NA |
| 226 | Roanoke, VA | (1.9) | 302 | Bakersfield, CA | (4.1) | NA | Beaumont, TX** | NA |
| 226 | San Leandro, CA | (1.9) | 302 | Richardson, TX | (4.1) | NA | Bellflower, CA** | NA |
| 226 | Surprise, AZ | (1.9) | 304 | Baltimore, MD | (4.2) | NA | Bend, OR** | NA |
| 231 | El Monte, CA | (2.0) | 304 | Salinas, CA | (4.2) | NA | Bloomington, IL** | NA |
| 231 | Irving, TX | (2.0) | 304 | Springfield, IL | (4.2) | NA | Bloomington, IN** | NA |
| 231 | Midland, TX | (2.0) | 304 | Westminster, CO | (4.2) | NA | Canton Twnshp, MI** | NA |
| 231 | Miramar, FL | (2.0) | 308 | Sparks, NV | (4.3) | NA | Carson, CA** | NA |
| 231 | Springfield, MO | (2.0) | 308 | West Valley, UT | (4.3) | NA | Chattanooga, TN** | NA |
| 231 | St. Joseph, MO | (2.0) | 310 | Newton, MA | (4.4) | NA | Chicago, IL** | NA |
| 237 | Boston, MA | (2.1) | 311 | Gary, IN | (4.5) | NA | Chino Hills, CA** | NA |
| 237 | Fort Smith, AR | (2.1) | 311 | Grand Rapids, MI | (4.5) | NA | Columbia, SC** | NA |
| 237 | Westminster, CA | (2.1) | 311 | Phoenix, AZ | (4.5) | NA | Compton, CA** | NA |
| 240 | Boise, ID | (2.2) | 314 | Alexandria, VA | (4.6) | NA | Concord, NC** | NA |
| 240 | Brooklyn Park, MN | (2.2) | 314 | Providence, RI | (4.6) | NA | Dallas, TX** | NA |
| 240 | Hillsboro, OR | (2.2) | 314 | Richmond, VA | (4.6) | NA | Decatur, IL** | NA |
| 240 | Medford, OR | (2.2) | 317 | Hartford, CT | (4.7) | NA | Deerfield Beach, FL** | NA |
| 240 | Santa Monica, CA | (2.2) | 317 | Indianapolis, IN | (4.7) | NA | Des Moines, IA** | NA |
| 245 | Danbury, CT | (2.3) | 317 | Lawrence, KS | (4.7) | NA | Edinburg, TX** | NA |
| 245 | Minneapolis, MN | (2.3) | 317 | Syracuse, NY | (4.7) | NA | Fishers, IN** | NA |
| 245 | Tuscaloosa, AL | (2.3) | 321 | Edison Twnshp, NJ | (4.8) | NA | Fort Worth, TX** | NA |
| 248 | Denton, TX | (2.4) | 321 | Fresno, CA | (4.8) | NA | Hesperia, CA** | NA |
| 248 | Lansing, MI | (2.4) | 323 | Antioch, CA | (4.9) | NA | Hialeah, FL** | NA |
| 248 | Seattle, WA | (2.4) | 323 | Everett, WA | (4.9) | NA | Hoover, AL** | NA |
| 251 | Milwaukee, WI | (2.5) | 323 | Knoxville, TN | (4.9) | NA | Houston, TX** | NA |
| 251 | Oceanside, CA | (2.5) | 323 | Portland, OR | (4.9) | NA | Jurupa Valley, CA** | NA |
| 253 | Frisco, TX | (2.6) | 327 | Columbus, GA | (5.0) | NA | Lafayette, LA** | NA |
| 253 | Johns Creek, GA | (2.6) | 327 | Newark, NJ | (5.0) | NA | Lake Forest, CA** | NA |
| 253 | San Francisco, CA | (2.6) | 329 | Lakeland, FL | (5.1) | NA | Lakewood, CA** | NA |
| 256 | Denver, CO | (2.7) | 329 | Peoria, AZ | (5.1) | NA | Lancaster, CA** | NA |
| 256 | Fort Lauderdale, FL | (2.7) | 331 | Omaha, NE | (5.3) | NA | Laredo, TX** | NA |
| 256 | Orange, CA | (2.7) | 332 | Jersey City, NJ | (5.4) | NA | Las Cruces, NM** | NA |
| 256 | Orlando, FL | (2.7) | 333 | Toledo, OH | (5.5) | NA | Lewisville, TX** | NA |
| 256 | San Jose, CA | (2.7) | 334 | Jackson, MS | (5.6) | NA | Macon, GA** | NA |
| 256 | South Gate, CA | (2.7) | 335 | Columbia, MO | (5.7) | NA | Melbourne, FL** | NA |
| 256 | St. Louis, MO | (2.7) | 335 | Sunnyvale, CA | (5.7) | NA | Menifee, CA** | NA |
| 263 | Mission, TX | (2.8) | 335 | Tacoma, WA | (5.7) | NA | Mesquite, TX** | NA |
| 264 | Carlsbad, CA | (2.9) | 338 | Las Vegas, NV | (5.8) | NA | Mission Viejo, CA** | NA |
| 264 | Long Beach, CA | (2.9) | 339 | Savannah, GA | (5.9) | NA | Moreno Valley, CA** | NA |
| 264 | Mesa, AZ | (2.9) | 340 | Chula Vista, CA | (6.0) | NA | Naperville, IL** | NA |
| 264 | St. Paul, MN | (2.9) | 341 | Clarksville, TN | (6.1) | NA | Norwalk, CA** | NA |
| 264 | Warwick, RI | (2.9) | 341 | Lynchburg, VA | (6.1) | NA | Olathe, KS** | NA |
| 269 | Billings, MT | (3.0) | 341 | New Haven, CT | (6.1) | NA | Orem, UT** | NA |
| 269 | Birmingham, AL | (3.0) | 344 | Elk Grove, CA | (6.2) | NA | Overland Park, KS** | NA |
| 269 | Fullerton, CA | (3.0) | 345 | Fremont, CA | (6.3) | NA | Palmdale, CA** | NA |
| 269 | Murfreesboro, TN | (3.0) | 346 | Fairfield, CA | (6.4) | NA | Pembroke Pines, FL** | NA |
| 269 | Sacramento, CA | (3.0) | 346 | Huntsville, AL | (6.4) | NA | Peoria, IL** | NA |
| 274 | Cary, NC | (3.1) | 348 | Sunrise, FL | (6.5) | NA | Pompano Beach, FL** | NA |
| 275 | Mountain View, CA | (3.2) | 349 | Baldwin Park, CA | (6.7) | NA | Port St. Lucie, FL** | NA |
| 275 | Upland, CA | (3.2) | 349 | Fontana, CA | (6.7) | NA | Rancho Cucamon., CA** | NA |
| 277 | Arvada, CO | (3.3) | 351 | Lawton, OK | (6.9) | NA | Rockford, IL** | NA |
| 277 | Cincinnati, OH | (3.3) | 352 | Detroit, MI | (7.2) | NA | Roswell, GA** | NA |
| 277 | League City, TX | (3.3) | 353 | Anchorage, AK | (7.3) | NA | Round Rock, TX** | NA |
| 277 | Sioux City, IA | (3.3) | 354 | Indio, CA | (7.5) | NA | Salt Lake City, UT** | NA |
| 281 | Athens-Clarke, GA | (3.4) | 354 | Nampa, ID | (7.5) | NA | San Angelo, TX** | NA |
| 281 | Berkeley, CA | (3.4) | 356 | New Orleans, LA | (8.3) | NA | San Marcos, CA** | NA |
| 281 | Burbank, CA | (3.4) | 357 | Odessa, TX | (8.5) | NA | Sandy Springs, GA** | NA |
| 281 | Greenville, NC | (3.4) | 358 | Chico, CA | (8.7) | NA | Santa Clarita, CA** | NA |
| 285 | Boulder, CO | (3.5) | 359 | Costa Mesa, CA | (8.8) | NA | Shreveport, LA** | NA |
| 285 | Cambridge, MA | (3.5) | 360 | Clinton Twnshp, MI | (8.9) | NA | St. George, UT** | NA |
| 285 | Elizabeth, NJ | (3.5) | 361 | Meridian, ID | (9.0) | NA | Suffolk, VA** | NA |
| 285 | Glendale, AZ | (3.5) | 362 | Inglewood, CA | (9.4) | NA | Sugar Land, TX** | NA |
| 285 | New Rochelle, NY | (3.5) | 362 | San Bernardino, CA | (9.4) | NA | Temecula, CA** | NA |
| 285 | Pasadena, TX | (3.5) | 364 | Plantation, FL | (10.5) | NA | Thousand Oaks, CA** | NA |
| 285 | Santa Clara, CA | (3.5) | 365 | Charlotte, NC | (10.8) | NA | Victorville, CA** | NA |
| 292 | Mobile, AL | (3.7) | 366 | Chino, CA | (10.9) | NA | Vista, CA** | NA |
| 293 | Federal Way, WA | (3.8) | 366 | Irvine, CA | (10.9) | NA | Waukegan, IL** | NA |
| 293 | Gilbert, AZ | (3.8) | 368 | Vallejo, CA | (11.5) | NA | Wichita, KS** | NA |
| 293 | Louisville, KY | (3.8) | NA | Abilene, TX** | NA | | | |
| 293 | Memphis, TN | (3.8) | NA | Albany, GA** | NA | | | |

Source: CQ Press using reported data from the F.B.I. "Crime in the United States 2013"

*Sworn officers only, does not include civilian employees.

**Not available

# 84. Percent Change in Rate of Police Officers: 2009 to 2013
## National Percent Change = 4.5% Decrease*

| RANK | CITY | % CHANGE | RANK | CITY | % CHANGE | RANK | CITY | % CHANGE |
|---|---|---|---|---|---|---|---|---|
| 234 | Abilene, TX | (8.4) | 94 | Chino, CA | (0.9) | 343 | Fullerton, CA | (17.8) |
| 202 | Akron, OH | (6.7) | 364 | Chula Vista, CA | (23.3) | 231 | Gainesville, FL | (8.3) |
| 343 | Alameda, CA | (17.8) | 88 | Cicero, IL | (0.5) | 292 | Garden Grove, CA | (12.0) |
| NA | Albany, GA** | NA | 128 | Cincinnati, OH | (3.0) | 221 | Garland, TX | (7.5) |
| 129 | Albany, NY | (3.1) | 65 | Citrus Heights, CA | 1.0 | 2 | Gary, IN | 14.8 |
| NA | Albuquerque, NM** | NA | 174 | Clarkstown, NY | (5.6) | 42 | Gilbert, AZ | 3.1 |
| 150 | Alexandria, VA | (4.2) | 187 | Clarksville, TN | (6.1) | 78 | Glendale, AZ | 0.0 |
| 65 | Alhambra, CA | 1.0 | 273 | Clearwater, FL | (10.2) | 187 | Glendale, CA | (6.1) |
| 190 | Allentown, PA | (6.3) | 98 | Cleveland, OH | (1.0) | 252 | Grand Prairie, TX | (9.1) |
| 23 | Allen, TX | 4.9 | 209 | Clifton, NJ | (7.1) | 296 | Grand Rapids, MI | (12.5) |
| 22 | Amarillo, TX | 5.5 | 374 | Clinton Twnshp, MI | (26.8) | 2 | Greece, NY | 14.8 |
| 213 | Amherst, NY | (7.2) | 159 | Clovis, CA | (5.1) | 130 | Greeley, CO | (3.2) |
| 302 | Anaheim, CA | (13.2) | 78 | College Station, TX | 0.0 | 101 | Green Bay, WI | (1.1) |
| 323 | Anchorage, AK | (14.8) | 93 | Colonie, NY | (0.7) | 78 | Greensboro, NC | 0.0 |
| 200 | Ann Arbor, MI | (6.5) | 252 | Colorado Springs, CO | (9.1) | 259 | Greenville, NC | (9.5) |
| 382 | Antioch, CA | (31.0) | 270 | Columbia, MO | (10.1) | 252 | Gresham, OR | (9.1) |
| NA | Arlington Heights, IL** | NA | 24 | Columbia, SC | 4.8 | 120 | Hamilton Twnshp, NJ | (2.6) |
| 69 | Arlington, TX | 0.6 | 242 | Columbus, GA | (8.9) | 140 | Hammond, IN | (3.7) |
| 106 | Arvada, CO | (1.4) | NA | Compton, CA** | NA | 14 | Hampton, VA | 6.3 |
| 118 | Athens-Clarke, GA | (2.5) | 190 | Concord, CA | (6.3) | 67 | Hartford, CT | 0.8 |
| 1 | Atlanta, GA | 51.1 | 340 | Concord, NC | (17.5) | 159 | Hawthorne, CA | (5.1) |
| 57 | Aurora, CO | 1.5 | 16 | Coral Springs, FL | 6.0 | 236 | Hayward, CA | (8.5) |
| NA | Aurora, IL** | NA | 340 | Corona, CA | (17.5) | 369 | Hemet, CA | (24.5) |
| 145 | Austin, TX | (3.9) | 224 | Corpus Christi, TX | (7.7) | 284 | Henderson, NV | (10.9) |
| 225 | Bakersfield, CA | (7.8) | 378 | Costa Mesa, CA | (28.3) | NA | Hesperia, CA** | NA |
| 319 | Baldwin Park, CA | (14.4) | 90 | Cranston, RI | (0.6) | NA | Hialeah, FL** | NA |
| 142 | Baltimore, MD | (3.8) | 78 | Dallas, TX | 0.0 | 154 | High Point, NC | (4.7) |
| NA | Baton Rouge, LA** | NA | 231 | Daly City, CA | (8.3) | 28 | Hillsboro, OR | 4.6 |
| 262 | Beaumont, TX | (9.7) | 185 | Danbury, CT | (6.0) | 275 | Hollywood, FL | (10.3) |
| 58 | Beaverton, OR | 1.4 | 59 | Davenport, IA | 1.3 | 321 | Hoover, AL | (14.5) |
| 158 | Bellevue, WA | (5.0) | 121 | Davie, FL | (2.7) | NA | Houston, TX** | NA |
| NA | Bellflower, CA** | NA | 169 | Dayton, OH | (5.4) | 329 | Huntington Beach, CA | (15.4) |
| 122 | Bend, OR | (2.8) | 332 | Dearborn, MI | (15.9) | 302 | Huntsville, AL | (13.2) |
| 352 | Berkeley, CA | (19.1) | NA | Decatur, IL** | NA | 45 | Independence, MO | 2.4 |
| 267 | Bethlehem, PA | (10.0) | NA | Deerfield Beach, FL** | NA | 246 | Indianapolis, IN | (9.0) |
| 159 | Billings, MT | (5.1) | 78 | Denton, TX | 0.0 | 221 | Indio, CA | (7.5) |
| 24 | Birmingham, AL | 4.8 | 315 | Denver, CO | (14.0) | 309 | Inglewood, CA | (13.7) |
| NA | Bloomington, IL** | NA | 218 | Des Moines, IA | (7.4) | 242 | Irvine, CA | (8.9) |
| 273 | Bloomington, IN | (10.2) | 29 | Detroit, MI | 4.3 | 326 | Irving, TX | (15.3) |
| 238 | Bloomington, MN | (8.6) | 306 | Downey, CA | (13.5) | 305 | Jacksonville, FL | (13.4) |
| 138 | Boca Raton, FL | (3.6) | 43 | Duluth, MN | 2.9 | 282 | Jackson, MS | (10.7) |
| 199 | Boise, ID | (6.4) | 130 | Edinburg, TX | (3.2) | 347 | Jersey City, NJ | (18.3) |
| 163 | Boston, MA | (5.2) | 342 | Edison Twnshp, NJ | (17.7) | 371 | Johns Creek, GA | (25.3) |
| 69 | Boulder, CO | 0.6 | 209 | Edmond, OK | (7.1) | 134 | Joliet, IL | (3.4) |
| 10 | Brick Twnshp, NJ | 6.8 | 227 | El Cajon, CA | (7.9) | NA | Jurupa Valley, CA** | NA |
| 215 | Bridgeport, CT | (7.3) | 155 | El Monte, CA | (4.8) | NA | Kansas City, KS** | NA |
| 50 | Brockton, MA | 2.1 | 304 | El Paso, TX | (13.3) | 45 | Kansas City, MO | 2.4 |
| 116 | Broken Arrow, OK | (2.3) | 117 | Elgin, IL | (2.4) | 275 | Kennewick, WA | (10.3) |
| 223 | Brooklyn Park, MN | (7.6) | 209 | Elizabeth, NJ | (7.1) | 126 | Kenosha, WI | (2.9) |
| 107 | Brownsville, TX | (1.5) | 330 | Elk Grove, CA | (15.6) | 373 | Kent, WA | (26.5) |
| 24 | Bryan, TX | 4.8 | 29 | Erie, PA | 4.3 | 122 | Killeen, TX | (2.8) |
| 262 | Buena Park, CA | (9.7) | 294 | Escondido, CA | (12.2) | 45 | Knoxville, TN | 2.4 |
| 134 | Buffalo, NY | (3.4) | 109 | Eugene, OR | (1.6) | NA | Lafayette, LA** | NA |
| 246 | Burbank, CA | (9.0) | 40 | Evanston, IL | 3.3 | NA | Lake Forest, CA** | NA |
| 177 | Cambridge, MA | (5.7) | 78 | Evansville, IN | 0.0 | 292 | Lakeland, FL | (12.0) |
| 347 | Canton Twnshp, MI | (18.3) | 313 | Everett, WA | (13.9) | 381 | Lakewood Twnshp, NJ | (30.1) |
| 190 | Cape Coral, FL | (6.3) | 300 | Fairfield, CA | (12.8) | NA | Lakewood, CA** | NA |
| 246 | Carlsbad, CA | (9.0) | 5 | Fall River, MA | 13.1 | 229 | Lakewood, CO | (8.2) |
| 333 | Carmel, IN | (16.0) | 257 | Fargo, ND | (9.2) | NA | Lancaster, CA** | NA |
| 130 | Carrollton, TX | (3.2) | 306 | Farmington Hills, MI | (13.5) | 371 | Lansing, MI | (25.3) |
| NA | Carson, CA** | NA | 190 | Fayetteville, AR | (6.3) | NA | Laredo, TX** | NA |
| 54 | Cary, NC | 1.6 | 270 | Fayetteville, NC | (10.1) | 246 | Largo, FL | (9.0) |
| 59 | Cedar Rapids, IA | 1.3 | 349 | Federal Way, WA | (18.5) | NA | Las Cruces, NM** | NA |
| 94 | Centennial, CO | (0.9) | NA | Fishers, IN** | NA | 346 | Las Vegas, NV | (18.1) |
| 104 | Champaign, IL | (1.3) | 375 | Flint, MI | (26.9) | 7 | Lawrence, KS | 8.1 |
| 67 | Chandler, AZ | 0.8 | 356 | Fontana, CA | (20.2) | 377 | Lawrence, MA | (28.0) |
| 94 | Charleston, SC | (0.9) | 19 | Fort Collins, CO | 5.7 | 280 | Lawton, OK | (10.6) |
| 267 | Charlotte, NC | (10.0) | 11 | Fort Lauderdale, FL | 6.7 | 319 | League City, TX | (14.4) |
| 75 | Chattanooga, TN | 0.4 | 114 | Fort Smith, AR | (2.1) | 183 | Lee's Summit, MO | (5.9) |
| 61 | Cheektowaga, NY | 1.2 | 202 | Fort Wayne, IN | (6.7) | 2 | Lewisville, TX | 14.8 |
| 69 | Chesapeake, VA | 0.6 | NA | Fort Worth, TX** | NA | 130 | Lexington, KY | (3.2) |
| NA | Chicago, IL** | NA | 311 | Fremont, CA | (13.8) | 147 | Lincoln, NE | (4.0) |
| 334 | Chico, CA | (16.1) | 354 | Fresno, CA | (19.8) | 63 | Little Rock, AR | 1.1 |
| NA | Chino Hills, CA** | NA | 242 | Frisco, TX | (8.9) | 246 | Livermore, CA | (9.0) |

| RANK | CITY | % CHANGE |
|------|------|----------|
| 359 | Livonia, MI | (22.0) |
| 355 | Long Beach, CA | (19.9) |
| 177 | Longmont, CO | (5.7) |
| 267 | Longview, TX | (10.0) |
| 113 | Los Angeles, CA | (1.9) |
| 190 | Louisville, KY | (6.3) |
| 45 | Lowell, MA | 2.4 |
| 19 | Lubbock, TX | 5.7 |
| 163 | Lynchburg, VA | (5.2) |
| 27 | Lynn, MA | 4.7 |
| NA | Macon, GA** | NA |
| 73 | Madison, WI | 0.5 |
| 73 | Manchester, NH | 0.5 |
| 98 | McAllen, TX | (1.0) |
| 202 | McKinney, TX | (6.7) |
| 180 | Medford, OR | (5.8) |
| 150 | Melbourne, FL | (4.2) |
| 9 | Memphis, TN | 7.0 |
| NA | Menifee, CA** | NA |
| 360 | Merced, CA | (22.2) |
| 215 | Meridian, ID | (7.3) |
| 103 | Mesa, AZ | (1.2) |
| NA | Mesquite, TX** | NA |
| 180 | Miami Beach, FL | (5.8) |
| 15 | Miami Gardens, FL | 6.1 |
| 157 | Miami, FL | (4.9) |
| 242 | Midland, TX | (8.9) |
| 118 | Milwaukee, WI | (2.5) |
| 229 | Minneapolis, MN | (8.2) |
| 311 | Miramar, FL | (13.8) |
| NA | Mission Viejo, CA** | NA |
| NA | Mission, TX** | NA |
| 183 | Mobile, AL | (5.9) |
| 289 | Modesto, CA | (11.7) |
| NA | Moreno Valley, CA** | NA |
| 252 | Mountain View, CA | (9.1) |
| 190 | Murfreesboro, TN | (6.3) |
| 228 | Murrieta, CA | (8.1) |
| 321 | Nampa, ID | (14.5) |
| 259 | Napa, CA | (9.5) |
| NA | Naperville, IL** | NA |
| 36 | Nashua, NH | 3.6 |
| 236 | Nashville, TN | (8.5) |
| 122 | New Bedford, MA | (2.8) |
| 315 | New Haven, CT | (14.0) |
| NA | New Orleans, LA** | NA |
| 363 | New Rochelle, NY | (22.9) |
| 88 | New York, NY | (0.5) |
| 360 | Newark, NJ | (22.2) |
| 286 | Newport Beach, CA | (11.5) |
| 32 | Newport News, VA | 4.0 |
| 218 | Newton, MA | (7.4) |
| 140 | Norfolk, VA | (3.7) |
| 169 | Norman, OK | (5.4) |
| 77 | North Charleston, SC | 0.3 |
| 265 | North Las Vegas, NV | (9.8) |
| NA | Norwalk, CA** | NA |
| 142 | Norwalk, CT | (3.8) |
| 353 | Oakland, CA | (19.4) |
| 148 | Oceanside, CA | (4.1) |
| 335 | Odessa, TX | (16.2) |
| 78 | O'Fallon, MO | 0.0 |
| 90 | Ogden, UT | (0.6) |
| 289 | Oklahoma City, OK | (11.7) |
| NA | Olathe, KS** | NA |
| 38 | Omaha, NE | 3.4 |
| 8 | Ontario, CA | 7.9 |
| 207 | Orange, CA | (6.9) |
| NA | Orem, UT** | NA |
| 225 | Orlando, FL | (7.8) |
| 171 | Overland Park, KS | (5.5) |
| 262 | Oxnard, CA | (9.7) |
| 163 | Palm Bay, FL | (5.2) |
| NA | Palmdale, CA** | NA |

| RANK | CITY | % CHANGE |
|------|------|----------|
| 138 | Pasadena, CA | (3.6) |
| 257 | Pasadena, TX | (9.2) |
| 370 | Paterson, NJ | (25.2) |
| 31 | Pearland, TX | 4.2 |
| 231 | Pembroke Pines, FL | (8.3) |
| 94 | Peoria, AZ | (0.9) |
| NA | Peoria, IL** | NA |
| 136 | Philadelphia, PA | (3.5) |
| 190 | Phoenix, AZ | (6.3) |
| 153 | Pittsburgh, PA | (4.4) |
| 54 | Plano, TX | 1.6 |
| 350 | Plantation, FL | (18.7) |
| 275 | Pomona, CA | (10.3) |
| NA | Pompano Beach, FL** | NA |
| 287 | Port St. Lucie, FL | (11.6) |
| 266 | Portland, OR | (9.9) |
| 11 | Portsmouth, VA | 6.7 |
| 336 | Providence, RI | (16.4) |
| 36 | Provo, UT | 3.6 |
| 279 | Pueblo, CO | (10.5) |
| 19 | Quincy, MA | 5.7 |
| 17 | Racine, WI | 5.8 |
| 32 | Raleigh, NC | 4.0 |
| 358 | Ramapo, NY | (20.6) |
| NA | Rancho Cucamon., CA** | NA |
| 366 | Reading, PA | (23.8) |
| 294 | Redding, CA | (12.2) |
| 209 | Redwood City, CA | (7.1) |
| 365 | Reno, NV | (23.4) |
| 385 | Renton, WA | (38.3) |
| 345 | Rialto, CA | (17.9) |
| 114 | Richardson, TX | (2.1) |
| 101 | Richmond, CA | (1.1) |
| 215 | Richmond, VA | (7.3) |
| 177 | Riverside, CA | (5.7) |
| 163 | Roanoke, VA | (5.2) |
| 109 | Rochester, MN | (1.6) |
| 213 | Rochester, NY | (7.2) |
| NA | Rockford, IL** | NA |
| 202 | Roseville, CA | (6.7) |
| NA | Roswell, GA** | NA |
| NA | Round Rock, TX** | NA |
| 317 | Sacramento, CA | (14.1) |
| 285 | Salem, OR | (11.3) |
| 356 | Salinas, CA | (20.2) |
| NA | Salt Lake City, UT** | NA |
| 61 | San Angelo, TX | 1.2 |
| 69 | San Antonio, TX | 0.6 |
| 380 | San Bernardino, CA | (29.0) |
| 136 | San Diego, CA | (3.5) |
| 287 | San Francisco, CA | (11.6) |
| 367 | San Jose, CA | (24.3) |
| 308 | San Leandro, CA | (13.6) |
| NA | San Marcos, CA** | NA |
| 309 | San Mateo, CA | (13.7) |
| NA | Sandy Springs, GA** | NA |
| 38 | Sandy, UT | 3.4 |
| 240 | Santa Ana, CA | (8.7) |
| 51 | Santa Barbara, CA | 2.0 |
| 326 | Santa Clara, CA | (15.3) |
| NA | Santa Clarita, CA** | NA |
| 376 | Santa Maria, CA | (27.6) |
| 174 | Santa Monica, CA | (5.6) |
| 301 | Santa Rosa, CA | (13.0) |
| 325 | Savannah, GA | (15.2) |
| 49 | Scottsdale, AZ | 2.2 |
| 167 | Scranton, PA | (5.3) |
| 275 | Seattle, WA | (10.3) |
| NA | Shreveport, LA** | NA |
| 98 | Simi Valley, CA | (1.0) |
| 180 | Sioux City, IA | (5.8) |
| 6 | Sioux Falls, SD | 9.4 |
| 167 | Somerville, MA | (5.3) |
| 35 | South Bend, IN | 3.7 |

| RANK | CITY | % CHANGE |
|------|------|----------|
| 339 | South Gate, CA | (17.2) |
| 159 | Sparks, NV | (5.1) |
| 207 | Spokane Valley, WA | (6.9) |
| 190 | Spokane, WA | (6.3) |
| 270 | Springfield, IL | (10.1) |
| 111 | Springfield, MA | (1.7) |
| 41 | Springfield, MO | 3.2 |
| 171 | Stamford, CT | (5.5) |
| 331 | Sterling Heights, MI | (15.7) |
| 282 | Stockton, CA | (10.7) |
| NA | St. George, UT** | NA |
| 145 | St. Joseph, MO | (3.9) |
| 51 | St. Louis, MO | 2.0 |
| 252 | St. Paul, MN | (9.1) |
| 112 | St. Petersburg, FL | (1.8) |
| 142 | Suffolk, VA | (3.8) |
| NA | Sugar Land, TX** | NA |
| 351 | Sunnyvale, CA | (19.0) |
| 148 | Sunrise, FL | (4.1) |
| 296 | Surprise, AZ | (12.5) |
| 337 | Syracuse, NY | (16.8) |
| 337 | Tacoma, WA | (16.8) |
| 171 | Tallahassee, FL | (5.5) |
| 126 | Tampa, FL | (2.9) |
| NA | Temecula, CA** | NA |
| 51 | Tempe, AZ | 2.0 |
| 185 | Thornton, CO | (6.0) |
| NA | Thousand Oaks, CA** | NA |
| 261 | Toledo, OH | (9.6) |
| 78 | Toms River Twnshp, NJ | 0.0 |
| 75 | Topeka, KS | 0.4 |
| 190 | Torrance, CA | (6.3) |
| 326 | Tracy, CA | (15.3) |
| 384 | Trenton, NJ | (37.6) |
| 383 | Troy, MI | (31.3) |
| 63 | Tucson, AZ | 1.1 |
| 189 | Tulsa, OK | (6.2) |
| 87 | Tuscaloosa, AL | (0.3) |
| 298 | Tustin, CA | (12.7) |
| 34 | Tyler, TX | 3.8 |
| 318 | Upland, CA | (14.3) |
| 174 | Upper Darby Twnshp, PA | (5.6) |
| 323 | Vacaville, CA | (14.8) |
| 379 | Vallejo, CA | (28.9) |
| 202 | Vancouver, WA | (6.7) |
| 155 | Ventura, CA | (4.8) |
| NA | Victorville, CA** | NA |
| 122 | Virginia Beach, VA | (2.8) |
| 78 | Visalia, CA | 0.0 |
| NA | Vista, CA** | NA |
| 107 | Waco, TX | (1.5) |
| 291 | Warren, MI | (11.9) |
| 17 | Warwick, RI | 5.8 |
| 246 | Washington, DC | (9.0) |
| 201 | Waterbury, CT | (6.6) |
| NA | Waukegan, IL** | NA |
| 362 | West Covina, CA | (22.4) |
| 298 | West Palm Beach, FL | (12.7) |
| 280 | West Valley, UT | (10.6) |
| 368 | Westland, MI | (24.4) |
| 313 | Westminster, CA | (13.9) |
| 90 | Westminster, CO | (0.6) |
| 238 | Whittier, CA | (8.6) |
| 150 | Wichita Falls, TX | (4.2) |
| NA | Wichita, KS** | NA |
| 234 | Wilmington, NC | (8.4) |
| 44 | Winston-Salem, NC | 2.7 |
| 240 | Woodbridge Twnshp, NJ | (8.7) |
| 104 | Worcester, MA | (1.3) |
| 218 | Yakima, WA | (7.4) |
| 54 | Yonkers, NY | 1.6 |
| 13 | Yuma, AZ | 6.6 |

Source: CQ Press using reported data from the F.B.I. "Crime in the United States 2013"

*Sworn officers only, does not include civilian employees.

**Not available

## 84. Percent Change in Rate of Police Officers: 2009 to 2013 (continued)
## National Percent Change = 4.5% Decrease*

| RANK | CITY | % CHANGE | RANK | CITY | % CHANGE | RANK | CITY | % CHANGE |
|---|---|---|---|---|---|---|---|---|
| 1 | Atlanta, GA | 51.1 | 75 | Chattanooga, TN | 0.4 | 148 | Sunrise, FL | (4.1) |
| 2 | Gary, IN | 14.8 | 75 | Topeka, KS | 0.4 | 150 | Alexandria, VA | (4.2) |
| 2 | Greece, NY | 14.8 | 77 | North Charleston, SC | 0.3 | 150 | Melbourne, FL | (4.2) |
| 2 | Lewisville, TX | 14.8 | 78 | College Station, TX | 0.0 | 150 | Wichita Falls, TX | (4.2) |
| 5 | Fall River, MA | 13.1 | 78 | Dallas, TX | 0.0 | 153 | Pittsburgh, PA | (4.4) |
| 6 | Sioux Falls, SD | 9.4 | 78 | Denton, TX | 0.0 | 154 | High Point, NC | (4.7) |
| 7 | Lawrence, KS | 8.1 | 78 | Evansville, IN | 0.0 | 155 | El Monte, CA | (4.8) |
| 8 | Ontario, CA | 7.9 | 78 | Glendale, AZ | 0.0 | 155 | Ventura, CA | (4.8) |
| 9 | Memphis, TN | 7.0 | 78 | Greensboro, NC | 0.0 | 157 | Miami, FL | (4.9) |
| 10 | Brick Twnshp, NJ | 6.8 | 78 | O'Fallon, MO | 0.0 | 158 | Bellevue, WA | (5.0) |
| 11 | Fort Lauderdale, FL | 6.7 | 78 | Toms River Twnshp, NJ | 0.0 | 159 | Billings, MT | (5.1) |
| 11 | Portsmouth, VA | 6.7 | 78 | Visalia, CA | 0.0 | 159 | Clovis, CA | (5.1) |
| 13 | Yuma, AZ | 6.6 | 87 | Tuscaloosa, AL | (0.3) | 159 | Hawthorne, CA | (5.1) |
| 14 | Hampton, VA | 6.3 | 88 | Cicero, IL | (0.5) | 159 | Sparks, NV | (5.1) |
| 15 | Miami Gardens, FL | 6.1 | 88 | New York, NY | (0.5) | 163 | Boston, MA | (5.2) |
| 16 | Coral Springs, FL | 6.0 | 90 | Cranston, RI | (0.6) | 163 | Lynchburg, VA | (5.2) |
| 17 | Racine, WI | 5.8 | 90 | Ogden, UT | (0.6) | 163 | Palm Bay, FL | (5.2) |
| 17 | Warwick, RI | 5.8 | 90 | Westminster, CO | (0.6) | 163 | Roanoke, VA | (5.2) |
| 19 | Fort Collins, CO | 5.7 | 93 | Colonie, NY | (0.7) | 167 | Scranton, PA | (5.3) |
| 19 | Lubbock, TX | 5.7 | 94 | Centennial, CO | (0.9) | 167 | Somerville, MA | (5.3) |
| 19 | Quincy, MA | 5.7 | 94 | Charleston, SC | (0.9) | 169 | Dayton, OH | (5.4) |
| 22 | Amarillo, TX | 5.5 | 94 | Chino, CA | (0.9) | 169 | Norman, OK | (5.4) |
| 23 | Allen, TX | 4.9 | 94 | Peoria, AZ | (0.9) | 171 | Overland Park, KS | (5.5) |
| 24 | Birmingham, AL | 4.8 | 98 | Cleveland, OH | (1.0) | 171 | Stamford, CT | (5.5) |
| 24 | Bryan, TX | 4.8 | 98 | McAllen, TX | (1.0) | 171 | Tallahassee, FL | (5.5) |
| 24 | Columbia, SC | 4.8 | 98 | Simi Valley, CA | (1.0) | 174 | Clarkstown, NY | (5.6) |
| 27 | Lynn, MA | 4.7 | 101 | Green Bay, WI | (1.1) | 174 | Santa Monica, CA | (5.6) |
| 28 | Hillsboro, OR | 4.6 | 101 | Richmond, CA | (1.1) | 174 | Upper Darby Twnshp, PA | (5.6) |
| 29 | Detroit, MI | 4.3 | 103 | Mesa, AZ | (1.2) | 177 | Cambridge, MA | (5.7) |
| 29 | Erie, PA | 4.3 | 104 | Champaign, IL | (1.3) | 177 | Longmont, CO | (5.7) |
| 31 | Pearland, TX | 4.2 | 104 | Worcester, MA | (1.3) | 177 | Riverside, CA | (5.7) |
| 32 | Newport News, VA | 4.0 | 106 | Arvada, CO | (1.4) | 180 | Medford, OR | (5.8) |
| 32 | Raleigh, NC | 4.0 | 107 | Brownsville, TX | (1.5) | 180 | Miami Beach, FL | (5.8) |
| 34 | Tyler, TX | 3.8 | 107 | Waco, TX | (1.5) | 180 | Sioux City, IA | (5.8) |
| 35 | South Bend, IN | 3.7 | 109 | Eugene, OR | (1.6) | 183 | Lee's Summit, MO | (5.9) |
| 36 | Nashua, NH | 3.6 | 109 | Rochester, MN | (1.6) | 183 | Mobile, AL | (5.9) |
| 36 | Provo, UT | 3.6 | 111 | Springfield, MA | (1.7) | 185 | Danbury, CT | (6.0) |
| 38 | Omaha, NE | 3.4 | 112 | St. Petersburg, FL | (1.8) | 185 | Thornton, CO | (6.0) |
| 38 | Sandy, UT | 3.4 | 113 | Los Angeles, CA | (1.9) | 187 | Clarksville, TN | (6.1) |
| 40 | Evanston, IL | 3.3 | 114 | Fort Smith, AR | (2.1) | 187 | Glendale, CA | (6.1) |
| 41 | Springfield, MO | 3.2 | 114 | Richardson, TX | (2.1) | 189 | Tulsa, OK | (6.2) |
| 42 | Gilbert, AZ | 3.1 | 116 | Broken Arrow, OK | (2.3) | 190 | Allentown, PA | (6.3) |
| 43 | Duluth, MN | 2.9 | 117 | Elgin, IL | (2.4) | 190 | Cape Coral, FL | (6.3) |
| 44 | Winston-Salem, NC | 2.7 | 118 | Athens-Clarke, GA | (2.5) | 190 | Concord, CA | (6.3) |
| 45 | Independence, MO | 2.4 | 118 | Milwaukee, WI | (2.5) | 190 | Fayetteville, AR | (6.3) |
| 45 | Kansas City, MO | 2.4 | 120 | Hamilton Twnshp, NJ | (2.6) | 190 | Louisville, KY | (6.3) |
| 45 | Knoxville, TN | 2.4 | 121 | Davie, FL | (2.7) | 190 | Murfreesboro, TN | (6.3) |
| 45 | Lowell, MA | 2.4 | 122 | Bend, OR | (2.8) | 190 | Phoenix, AZ | (6.3) |
| 49 | Scottsdale, AZ | 2.2 | 122 | Killeen, TX | (2.8) | 190 | Spokane, WA | (6.3) |
| 50 | Brockton, MA | 2.1 | 122 | New Bedford, MA | (2.8) | 190 | Torrance, CA | (6.3) |
| 51 | Santa Barbara, CA | 2.0 | 122 | Virginia Beach, VA | (2.8) | 199 | Boise, ID | (6.4) |
| 51 | St. Louis, MO | 2.0 | 126 | Kenosha, WI | (2.9) | 200 | Ann Arbor, MI | (6.5) |
| 51 | Tempe, AZ | 2.0 | 126 | Tampa, FL | (2.9) | 201 | Waterbury, CT | (6.6) |
| 54 | Cary, NC | 1.6 | 128 | Cincinnati, OH | (3.0) | 202 | Akron, OH | (6.7) |
| 54 | Plano, TX | 1.6 | 129 | Albany, NY | (3.1) | 202 | Fort Wayne, IN | (6.7) |
| 54 | Yonkers, NY | 1.6 | 130 | Carrollton, TX | (3.2) | 202 | McKinney, TX | (6.7) |
| 57 | Aurora, CO | 1.5 | 130 | Edinburg, TX | (3.2) | 202 | Roseville, CA | (6.7) |
| 58 | Beaverton, OR | 1.4 | 130 | Greeley, CO | (3.2) | 202 | Vancouver, WA | (6.7) |
| 59 | Cedar Rapids, IA | 1.3 | 130 | Lexington, KY | (3.2) | 207 | Orange, CA | (6.9) |
| 59 | Davenport, IA | 1.3 | 134 | Buffalo, NY | (3.4) | 207 | Spokane Valley, WA | (6.9) |
| 61 | Cheektowaga, NY | 1.2 | 134 | Joliet, IL | (3.4) | 209 | Clifton, NJ | (7.1) |
| 61 | San Angelo, TX | 1.2 | 136 | Philadelphia, PA | (3.5) | 209 | Edmond, OK | (7.1) |
| 63 | Little Rock, AR | 1.1 | 136 | San Diego, CA | (3.5) | 209 | Elizabeth, NJ | (7.1) |
| 63 | Tucson, AZ | 1.1 | 138 | Boca Raton, FL | (3.6) | 209 | Redwood City, CA | (7.1) |
| 65 | Alhambra, CA | 1.0 | 138 | Pasadena, CA | (3.6) | 213 | Amherst, NY | (7.2) |
| 65 | Citrus Heights, CA | 1.0 | 140 | Hammond, IN | (3.7) | 213 | Rochester, NY | (7.2) |
| 67 | Chandler, AZ | 0.8 | 140 | Norfolk, VA | (3.7) | 215 | Bridgeport, CT | (7.3) |
| 67 | Hartford, CT | 0.8 | 142 | Baltimore, MD | (3.8) | 215 | Meridian, ID | (7.3) |
| 69 | Arlington, TX | 0.6 | 142 | Norwalk, CT | (3.8) | 215 | Richmond, VA | (7.3) |
| 69 | Boulder, CO | 0.6 | 142 | Suffolk, VA | (3.8) | 218 | Des Moines, IA | (7.4) |
| 69 | Chesapeake, VA | 0.6 | 145 | Austin, TX | (3.9) | 218 | Newton, MA | (7.4) |
| 69 | San Antonio, TX | 0.6 | 145 | St. Joseph, MO | (3.9) | 218 | Yakima, WA | (7.4) |
| 73 | Madison, WI | 0.5 | 147 | Lincoln, NE | (4.0) | 221 | Garland, TX | (7.5) |
| 73 | Manchester, NH | 0.5 | 148 | Oceanside, CA | (4.1) | 221 | Indio, CA | (7.5) |

| RANK | CITY | % CHANGE | RANK | CITY | % CHANGE | RANK | CITY | % CHANGE |
|---|---|---|---|---|---|---|---|---|
| 223 | Brooklyn Park, MN | (7.6) | 296 | Surprise, AZ | (12.5) | 371 | Johns Creek, GA | (25.3) |
| 224 | Corpus Christi, TX | (7.7) | 298 | Tustin, CA | (12.7) | 371 | Lansing, MI | (25.3) |
| 225 | Bakersfield, CA | (7.8) | 298 | West Palm Beach, FL | (12.7) | 373 | Kent, WA | (26.5) |
| 225 | Orlando, FL | (7.8) | 300 | Fairfield, CA | (12.8) | 374 | Clinton Twnshp, MI | (26.8) |
| 227 | El Cajon, CA | (7.9) | 301 | Santa Rosa, CA | (13.0) | 375 | Flint, MI | (26.9) |
| 228 | Murrieta, CA | (8.1) | 302 | Anaheim, CA | (13.2) | 376 | Santa Maria, CA | (27.6) |
| 229 | Lakewood, CO | (8.2) | 302 | Huntsville, AL | (13.2) | 377 | Lawrence, MA | (28.0) |
| 229 | Minneapolis, MN | (8.2) | 304 | El Paso, TX | (13.3) | 378 | Costa Mesa, CA | (28.3) |
| 231 | Daly City, CA | (8.3) | 305 | Jacksonville, FL | (13.4) | 379 | Vallejo, CA | (28.9) |
| 231 | Gainesville, FL | (8.3) | 306 | Downey, CA | (13.5) | 380 | San Bernardino, CA | (29.0) |
| 231 | Pembroke Pines, FL | (8.3) | 306 | Farmington Hills, MI | (13.5) | 381 | Lakewood Twnshp, NJ | (30.1) |
| 234 | Abilene, TX | (8.4) | 308 | San Leandro, CA | (13.6) | 382 | Antioch, CA | (31.0) |
| 234 | Wilmington, NC | (8.4) | 309 | Inglewood, CA | (13.7) | 383 | Troy, MI | (31.3) |
| 236 | Hayward, CA | (8.5) | 309 | San Mateo, CA | (13.7) | 384 | Trenton, NJ | (37.6) |
| 236 | Nashville, TN | (8.5) | 311 | Fremont, CA | (13.8) | 385 | Renton, WA | (38.3) |
| 238 | Bloomington, MN | (8.6) | 311 | Miramar, FL | (13.8) | NA | Albany, GA** | NA |
| 238 | Whittier, CA | (8.6) | 313 | Everett, WA | (13.9) | NA | Albuquerque, NM** | NA |
| 240 | Santa Ana, CA | (8.7) | 313 | Westminster, CA | (13.9) | NA | Arlington Heights, IL** | NA |
| 240 | Woodbridge Twnshp, NJ | (8.7) | 315 | Denver, CO | (14.0) | NA | Aurora, IL** | NA |
| 242 | Columbus, GA | (8.9) | 315 | New Haven, CT | (14.0) | NA | Baton Rouge, LA** | NA |
| 242 | Frisco, TX | (8.9) | 317 | Sacramento, CA | (14.1) | NA | Bellflower, CA** | NA |
| 242 | Irvine, CA | (8.9) | 318 | Upland, CA | (14.3) | NA | Bloomington, IL** | NA |
| 242 | Midland, TX | (8.9) | 319 | Baldwin Park, CA | (14.4) | NA | Carson, CA** | NA |
| 246 | Burbank, CA | (9.0) | 319 | League City, TX | (14.4) | NA | Chicago, IL** | NA |
| 246 | Carlsbad, CA | (9.0) | 321 | Hoover, AL | (14.5) | NA | Chino Hills, CA** | NA |
| 246 | Indianapolis, IN | (9.0) | 321 | Nampa, ID | (14.5) | NA | Compton, CA** | NA |
| 246 | Largo, FL | (9.0) | 323 | Anchorage, AK | (14.8) | NA | Decatur, IL** | NA |
| 246 | Livermore, CA | (9.0) | 323 | Vacaville, CA | (14.8) | NA | Deerfield Beach, FL** | NA |
| 246 | Washington, DC | (9.0) | 325 | Savannah, GA | (15.2) | NA | Fishers, IN** | NA |
| 252 | Colorado Springs, CO | (9.1) | 326 | Irving, TX | (15.3) | NA | Fort Worth, TX** | NA |
| 252 | Grand Prairie, TX | (9.1) | 326 | Santa Clara, CA | (15.3) | NA | Hesperia, CA** | NA |
| 252 | Gresham, OR | (9.1) | 326 | Tracy, CA | (15.3) | NA | Hialeah, FL** | NA |
| 252 | Mountain View, CA | (9.1) | 329 | Huntington Beach, CA | (15.4) | NA | Houston, TX** | NA |
| 252 | St. Paul, MN | (9.1) | 330 | Elk Grove, CA | (15.6) | NA | Jurupa Valley, CA** | NA |
| 257 | Fargo, ND | (9.2) | 331 | Sterling Heights, MI | (15.7) | NA | Kansas City, KS** | NA |
| 257 | Pasadena, TX | (9.2) | 332 | Dearborn, MI | (15.9) | NA | Lafayette, LA** | NA |
| 259 | Greenville, NC | (9.5) | 333 | Carmel, IN | (16.0) | NA | Lake Forest, CA** | NA |
| 259 | Napa, CA | (9.5) | 334 | Chico, CA | (16.1) | NA | Lakewood, CA** | NA |
| 261 | Toledo, OH | (9.6) | 335 | Odessa, TX | (16.2) | NA | Lancaster, CA** | NA |
| 262 | Beaumont, TX | (9.7) | 336 | Providence, RI | (16.4) | NA | Laredo, TX** | NA |
| 262 | Buena Park, CA | (9.7) | 337 | Syracuse, NY | (16.8) | NA | Las Cruces, NM** | NA |
| 262 | Oxnard, CA | (9.7) | 337 | Tacoma, WA | (16.8) | NA | Macon, GA** | NA |
| 265 | North Las Vegas, NV | (9.8) | 339 | South Gate, CA | (17.2) | NA | Menifee, CA** | NA |
| 266 | Portland, OR | (9.9) | 340 | Concord, NC | (17.5) | NA | Mesquite, TX** | NA |
| 267 | Bethlehem, PA | (10.0) | 340 | Corona, CA | (17.5) | NA | Mission Viejo, CA** | NA |
| 267 | Charlotte, NC | (10.0) | 342 | Edison Twnshp, NJ | (17.7) | NA | Mission, TX** | NA |
| 267 | Longview, TX | (10.0) | 343 | Alameda, CA | (17.8) | NA | Moreno Valley, CA** | NA |
| 270 | Columbia, MO | (10.1) | 343 | Fullerton, CA | (17.8) | NA | Naperville, IL** | NA |
| 270 | Fayetteville, NC | (10.1) | 345 | Rialto, CA | (17.9) | NA | New Orleans, LA** | NA |
| 270 | Springfield, IL | (10.1) | 346 | Las Vegas, NV | (18.1) | NA | Norwalk, CA** | NA |
| 273 | Bloomington, IN | (10.2) | 347 | Canton Twnshp, MI | (18.3) | NA | Olathe, KS** | NA |
| 273 | Clearwater, FL | (10.2) | 347 | Jersey City, NJ | (18.3) | NA | Orem, UT** | NA |
| 275 | Hollywood, FL | (10.3) | 349 | Federal Way, WA | (18.5) | NA | Palmdale, CA** | NA |
| 275 | Kennewick, WA | (10.3) | 350 | Plantation, FL | (18.7) | NA | Peoria, IL** | NA |
| 275 | Pomona, CA | (10.3) | 351 | Sunnyvale, CA | (19.0) | NA | Pompano Beach, FL** | NA |
| 275 | Seattle, WA | (10.3) | 352 | Berkeley, CA | (19.1) | NA | Rancho Cucamon., CA** | NA |
| 279 | Pueblo, CO | (10.5) | 353 | Oakland, CA | (19.4) | NA | Rockford, IL** | NA |
| 280 | Lawton, OK | (10.6) | 354 | Fresno, CA | (19.8) | NA | Roswell, GA** | NA |
| 280 | West Valley, UT | (10.6) | 355 | Long Beach, CA | (19.9) | NA | Round Rock, TX** | NA |
| 282 | Jackson, MS | (10.7) | 356 | Fontana, CA | (20.2) | NA | Salt Lake City, UT** | NA |
| 282 | Stockton, CA | (10.7) | 356 | Salinas, CA | (20.2) | NA | San Marcos, CA** | NA |
| 284 | Henderson, NV | (10.9) | 358 | Ramapo, NY | (20.6) | NA | Sandy Springs, GA** | NA |
| 285 | Salem, OR | (11.3) | 359 | Livonia, MI | (22.0) | NA | Santa Clarita, CA** | NA |
| 286 | Newport Beach, CA | (11.5) | 360 | Merced, CA | (22.2) | NA | Shreveport, LA** | NA |
| 287 | Port St. Lucie, FL | (11.6) | 360 | Newark, NJ | (22.2) | NA | St. George, UT** | NA |
| 287 | San Francisco, CA | (11.6) | 362 | West Covina, CA | (22.4) | NA | Sugar Land, TX** | NA |
| 289 | Modesto, CA | (11.7) | 363 | New Rochelle, NY | (22.9) | NA | Temecula, CA** | NA |
| 289 | Oklahoma City, OK | (11.7) | 364 | Chula Vista, CA | (23.3) | NA | Thousand Oaks, CA** | NA |
| 291 | Warren, MI | (11.9) | 365 | Reno, NV | (23.4) | NA | Victorville, CA** | NA |
| 292 | Garden Grove, CA | (12.0) | 366 | Reading, PA | (23.8) | NA | Vista, CA** | NA |
| 292 | Lakeland, FL | (12.0) | 367 | San Jose, CA | (24.3) | NA | Waukegan, IL** | NA |
| 294 | Escondido, CA | (12.2) | 368 | Westland, MI | (24.4) | NA | Wichita, KS** | NA |
| 294 | Redding, CA | (12.2) | 369 | Hemet, CA | (24.5) | | | |
| 296 | Grand Rapids, MI | (12.5) | 370 | Paterson, NJ | (25.2) | | | |

Source: CQ Press using reported data from the F.B.I. "Crime in the United States 2013"

*Sworn officers only, does not include civilian employees.

**Not available

# III. Metropolitan and City Populations

---

**Please note the following for Tables 1 through 40 and 85 through 87:**

- All listings are for Metropolitan Statistical Areas (M.S.A.s) except for those ending with "M.D."
- Listings with "M.D." are Metropolitan Divisions, which are smaller parts of eleven large M.S.A.s. These eleven M.S.A.s divided into M.D.s are identified using "(greater)" following the metropolitan area name.
- For example, the "Dallas (greater)" M.S.A. includes the two M.D.s of Dallas-Plano-Irving and Fort Worth-Arlington. The data for the M.D.s are included in the data for the overall M.S.A. as well.
- The name of a M.S.A. or M.D. is subject to change based on the changing proportional size of the large cities included within it. Percent changes are calculated in this book if the M.S.A. or M.D. has not substantially changed, despite the changes in name. Furthermore, the Office of Management and Budget (OMB) redefined a number of M.S.A.s in 2013; if the redefined M.S.A. had a population change of 5% or greater from the previous definition, its data are treated as not comparable and are not included in the tables showing change over time.
- Some M.S.A. and M.D. names are abbreviated to preserve space within the tables.

**Please note the following for Tables 41 through 84 and 88 through 90:**
- All listings are for cities of 75,000 or more in population that reported data to the F.B.I. for 2013. The reported populations for crime reporting purposes may vary from Census populations.

# 85. Metropolitan Population in 2013
## National Total = 316,128,839*

| RANK | METROPOLITAN AREA | POP | RANK | METROPOLITAN AREA | POP | RANK | METROPOLITAN AREA | POP |
|---|---|---|---|---|---|---|---|---|
| 255 | Abilene, TX | 168,117 | 361 | Cheyenne, WY | 95,635 | 101 | Gary, IN M.D. | 708,116 |
| 102 | Akron, OH | 703,468 | 5 | Chicago (greater), IL-IN-WI | 9,538,161 | 350 | Gettysburg, PA | 101,443 |
| 80 | Albany-Schenectady-Troy, NY | 876,869 | 6 | Chicago-Naperville, IL M.D. | 7,331,456 | 312 | Glens Falls, NY | 128,459 |
| 268 | Albany, GA | 157,365 | 213 | Chico, CA | 222,365 | 317 | Goldsboro, NC | 125,081 |
| 324 | Albany, OR | 119,155 | 42 | Cincinnati, OH-KY-IN | 2,136,525 | 351 | Grand Forks, ND-MN | 100,500 |
| 78 | Albuquerque, NM | 902,627 | 184 | Clarksville, TN-KY | 278,930 | 368 | Grand Island, NE | 84,159 |
| 273 | Alexandria, LA | 154,678 | 327 | Cleveland, TN | 118,551 | 285 | Grand Junction, CO | 149,245 |
| 88 | Allentown, PA-NJ | 828,654 | 291 | Coeur d'Alene, ID | 144,225 | 73 | Grand Rapids-Wyoming, MI | 1,012,133 |
| 315 | Altoona, PA | 127,076 | 206 | College Station-Bryan, TX | 237,174 | 369 | Grants Pass, OR | 83,162 |
| 196 | Amarillo, TX | 260,305 | 103 | Colorado Springs, CO | 678,821 | 372 | Great Falls, MT | 82,197 |
| 363 | Ames, IA | 91,897 | 248 | Columbia, MO | 170,724 | 189 | Greeley, CO | 268,670 |
| 23 | Anaheim-Santa Ana-Irvine, CA M.D. | 3,118,731 | 94 | Columbia, SC | 793,289 | 175 | Green Bay, WI | 312,769 |
| 173 | Anchorage, AK | 314,553 | 172 | Columbus, GA-AL | 315,743 | 95 | Greensboro-High Point, NC | 742,007 |
| 165 | Ann Arbor, MI | 353,189 | 373 | Columbus, IN | 80,102 | 84 | Greenville-Anderson, SC | 852,405 |
| 330 | Anniston-Oxford, AL | 116,893 | 136 | Corpus Christi, TX | 441,984 | 245 | Greenville, NC | 174,355 |
| 211 | Appleton, WI | 229,465 | 365 | Corvallis, OR | 86,952 | 158 | Gulfport-Biloxi-Pascagoula, MS | 382,406 |
| 231 | Athens-Clarke County, GA | 197,437 | 202 | Crestview-Fort Walton Beach, FL | 252,641 | 198 | Hagerstown-Martinsburg, MD-WV | 257,750 |
| 12 | Atlanta, GA | 5,511,212 | 349 | Cumberland, MD-WV | 101,663 | 320 | Hammond, LA | 124,208 |
| 186 | Atlantic City, NJ | 276,095 | 7 | Dallas (greater), TX | 6,814,175 | 279 | Hanford-Corcoran, CA | 151,256 |
| 117 | Augusta, GA-SC | 579,933 | 15 | Dallas-Plano-Irving, TX M.D. | 4,506,295 | 310 | Harrisonburg, VA | 129,689 |
| 50 | Austin-Round Rock, TX | 1,879,235 | 292 | Dalton, GA | 142,901 | 72 | Hartford, CT | 1,023,807 |
| 82 | Bakersfield, CA | 862,202 | 234 | Daphne-Fairhope-Foley, AL | 193,322 | 232 | Hilton Head Island, SC | 196,780 |
| 28 | Baltimore, MD | 2,771,247 | 157 | Davenport, IA-IL | 383,796 | 371 | Hinesville, GA | 82,962 |
| 275 | Bangor, ME | 153,530 | 93 | Dayton, OH | 802,990 | 297 | Homosassa Springs, FL | 139,242 |
| 217 | Barnstable Town, MA | 215,847 | 274 | Decatur, AL | 154,311 | 357 | Hot Springs, AR | 97,163 |
| 90 | Baton Rouge, LA | 819,681 | 340 | Decatur, IL | 109,877 | 222 | Houma, LA | 209,328 |
| 343 | Bay City, MI | 106,781 | 115 | Deltona-Daytona Beach, FL | 599,128 | 8 | Houston, TX | 6,281,279 |
| 150 | Beaumont-Port Arthur, TX | 406,050 | 29 | Denver-Aurora, CO | 2,693,369 | 140 | Huntsville, AL | 434,500 |
| 258 | Bend, OR | 164,183 | 116 | Des Moines-West Des Moines, IA | 596,382 | 298 | Idaho Falls, ID | 137,561 |
| 256 | Billings, MT | 164,846 | 19 | Detroit (greater), MI | 4,296,628 | 46 | Indianapolis, IN | 1,946,607 |
| 204 | Binghamton, NY | 247,869 | 52 | Detroit-Dearborn-Livonia, MI M.D. | 1,786,498 | 265 | Iowa City, IA | 160,439 |
| 69 | Birmingham-Hoover, AL | 1,138,940 | 286 | Dothan, AL | 148,166 | 58 | Jacksonville, FL | 1,392,914 |
| 319 | Bismarck, ND | 124,238 | 250 | Dover, DE | 169,725 | 264 | Jackson, MI | 160,498 |
| 241 | Blacksburg, VA | 179,521 | 360 | Dubuque, IA | 95,753 | 118 | Jackson, MS | 579,868 |
| 236 | Bloomington, IL | 189,408 | 183 | Duluth, MN-WI | 280,163 | 307 | Jackson, TN | 130,702 |
| 260 | Bloomington, IN | 163,596 | 155 | Dutchess-Putnam, NY M.D. | 397,186 | 263 | Janesville, WI | 160,586 |
| 366 | Bloomsburg-Berwick, PA | 85,071 | 254 | East Stroudsburg, PA | 168,309 | 283 | Jefferson City, MO | 150,542 |
| 107 | Boise City, ID | 647,858 | 257 | Eau Claire, WI | 164,463 | 229 | Johnson City, TN | 201,439 |
| 14 | Boston (greater), MA-NH | 4,679,143 | 244 | El Centro, CA | 177,955 | 295 | Johnstown, PA | 140,876 |
| 48 | Boston, MA M.D. | 1,942,405 | 86 | El Paso, TX | 842,271 | 318 | Jonesboro, AR | 125,041 |
| 177 | Boulder, CO | 310,333 | 109 | Elgin, IL M.D. | 628,978 | 246 | Joplin, MO | 174,207 |
| 261 | Bowling Green, KY | 163,437 | 282 | Elizabethtown-Fort Knox, KY | 150,699 | 266 | Kahului-Wailuku-Lahaina, HI | 159,652 |
| 200 | Bremerton-Silverdale, WA | 256,890 | 364 | Elmira, NY | 89,040 | 337 | Kankakee, IL | 112,844 |
| 77 | Bridgeport-Stamford, CT | 921,059 | 182 | Erie, PA | 280,450 | 44 | Kansas City, MO-KS | 2,049,436 |
| 146 | Brownsville-Harlingen, TX | 419,944 | 164 | Eugene, OR | 356,321 | 187 | Kennewick-Richland, WA | 273,507 |
| 335 | Brunswick, GA | 113,744 | 377 | Fairbanks, AK | 34,741 | 178 | Kingsport, TN-VA | 309,240 |
| 70 | Buffalo-Niagara Falls, NY | 1,135,074 | 214 | Fargo, ND-MN | 222,166 | 240 | Kingston, NY | 181,804 |
| 272 | Burlington, NC | 155,214 | 314 | Farmington, NM | 127,552 | 85 | Knoxville, TN | 852,347 |
| 339 | California-Lexington Park, MD | 110,294 | 129 | Fayetteville-Springdale, AR-MO | 488,051 | 370 | Kokomo, IN | 83,108 |
| 37 | Cambridge-Newton, MA M.D. | 2,313,211 | 161 | Fayetteville, NC | 378,067 | 301 | La Crosse, WI-MN | 135,914 |
| 64 | Camden, NJ M.D. | 1,257,382 | 300 | Flagstaff, AZ | 136,999 | 223 | Lafayette, IN | 208,478 |
| 151 | Canton, OH | 404,048 | 147 | Flint, MI | 416,606 | 130 | Lafayette, LA | 477,151 |
| 105 | Cape Coral-Fort Myers, FL | 656,243 | 289 | Florence-Muscle Shoals, AL | 146,880 | 228 | Lake Charles, LA | 201,735 |
| 356 | Cape Girardeau, MO-IL | 97,510 | 225 | Florence, SC | 207,144 | 81 | Lake Co.-Kenosha Co., IL-WI M.D. | 869,611 |
| 316 | Carbondale-Marion, IL | 126,687 | 348 | Fond du Lac, WI | 101,960 | 226 | Lake Havasu City-Kingman, AZ | 205,099 |
| 376 | Carson City, NV | 54,937 | 171 | Fort Collins, CO | 315,907 | 112 | Lakeland, FL | 622,846 |
| 374 | Casper, WY | 79,993 | 51 | Fort Lauderdale, FL M.D. | 1,843,375 | 124 | Lancaster, PA | 528,698 |
| 193 | Cedar Rapids, IA | 263,588 | 181 | Fort Smith, AR-OK | 280,934 | 131 | Lansing-East Lansing, MI | 466,728 |
| 278 | Chambersburg-Waynesboro, PA | 151,646 | 143 | Fort Wayne, IN | 424,081 | 194 | Laredo, TX | 262,936 |
| 209 | Champaign-Urbana, IL | 234,223 | 38 | Fort Worth-Arlington, TX M.D. | 2,307,880 | 218 | Las Cruces, NM | 215,083 |
| 99 | Charleston-North Charleston, SC | 710,846 | 76 | Fresno, CA | 954,305 | 45 | Las Vegas-Henderson, NV | 2,025,864 |
| 35 | Charlotte-Mecklenburg, NC-SC | 2,329,109 | 346 | Gadsden, AL | 104,345 | 336 | Lawrence, KS | 113,372 |
| 212 | Charlottesville, VA | 224,663 | 188 | Gainesville, FL | 270,523 | 305 | Lawton, OK | 133,449 |
| 122 | Chattanooga, TN-GA | 541,195 | 238 | Gainesville, GA | 187,290 | 302 | Lebanon, PA | 135,689 |

Note: All listings are for Metropolitan Statistical Areas (M.S.A.s) except for those ending with "M.D." Listings with "M.D." are Metropolitan Divisions which are smaller parts of eleven large M.S.A.s. See explanatory note at beginning of metropolitan area section.

| RANK | METROPOLITAN AREA | POP | RANK | METROPOLITAN AREA | POP | RANK | METROPOLITAN AREA | POP |
|---|---|---|---|---|---|---|---|---|
| 342 | Lewiston-Auburn, ME | 107,469 | 79 | Omaha-Council Bluffs, NE-IA | 893,630 | 334 | Sheboygan, WI | 114,951 |
| 375 | Lewiston, ID-WA | 61,820 | 40 | Orlando, FL | 2,261,201 | 321 | Sherman-Denison, TX | 122,729 |
| 128 | Lexington-Fayette, KY | 489,329 | 251 | Oshkosh-Neenah, WI | 169,484 | 134 | Shreveport-Bossier City, LA | 449,602 |
| 344 | Lima, OH | 105,002 | 331 | Owensboro, KY | 116,530 | 62 | Silver Spring-Frederick, MD M.D. | 1,258,323 |
| 174 | Lincoln, NE | 313,545 | 87 | Oxnard-Thousand Oaks, CA | 840,678 | 252 | Sioux City, IA-NE-SD | 169,444 |
| 97 | Little Rock, AR | 723,132 | 121 | Palm Bay-Melbourne, FL | 550,499 | 205 | Sioux Falls, SD | 241,643 |
| 309 | Logan, UT-ID | 129,858 | 237 | Panama City, FL | 189,176 | 170 | South Bend-Mishawaka, IN-MI | 319,204 |
| 215 | Longview, TX | 218,274 | 362 | Parkersburg-Vienna, WV | 92,396 | 169 | Spartanburg, SC | 319,563 |
| 347 | Longview, WA | 102,169 | 132 | Pensacola, FL | 466,427 | 123 | Spokane, WA | 535,166 |
| 4 | Los Angeles County, CA M.D. | 10,022,399 | 159 | Peoria, IL | 380,809 | 220 | Springfield, IL | 212,387 |
| 3 | Los Angeles (greater), CA | 13,141,130 | 9 | Philadelphia (greater) PA-NJ-MD-DE | 6,036,138 | 110 | Springfield, MA | 628,316 |
| 63 | Louisville, KY-IN | 1,257,388 | 43 | Philadelphia, PA M.D. | 2,114,504 | 135 | Springfield, MO | 448,011 |
| 179 | Lubbock, TX | 300,769 | 18 | Phoenix-Mesa-Scottsdale, AZ | 4,386,981 | 299 | Springfield, OH | 137,153 |
| 201 | Lynchburg, VA | 256,835 | 34 | Pittsburgh, PA | 2,360,685 | 271 | State College, PA | 155,409 |
| 210 | Macon, GA | 232,892 | 308 | Pittsfield, MA | 129,977 | 325 | Staunton-Waynesboro, VA | 119,067 |
| 276 | Madera, CA | 152,772 | 367 | Pocatello, ID | 84,482 | 100 | Stockton-Lodi, CA | 708,679 |
| 111 | Madison, WI | 626,047 | 139 | Port St. Lucie, FL | 436,841 | 235 | St. Cloud, MN | 191,531 |
| 152 | Manchester-Nashua, NH | 403,992 | 36 | Portland-Vancouver, OR-WA | 2,315,358 | 287 | St. George, UT | 147,923 |
| 352 | Manhattan, KS | 99,347 | 126 | Portland, ME | 518,977 | 313 | St. Joseph, MO-KS | 128,425 |
| 353 | Mankato-North Mankato, MN | 98,755 | 219 | Prescott, AZ | 214,243 | 26 | St. Louis, MO-IL | 2,803,655 |
| 322 | Mansfield, OH | 122,427 | 55 | Providence-Warwick, RI-MA | 1,604,757 | 341 | Sumter, SC | 108,703 |
| 91 | McAllen-Edinburg-Mission, TX | 819,252 | 120 | Provo-Orem, UT | 561,483 | 104 | Syracuse, NY | 661,048 |
| 224 | Medford, OR | 207,927 | 262 | Pueblo, CO | 162,300 | 89 | Tacoma, WA M.D. | 819,740 |
| 60 | Memphis, TN-MS-AR | 1,347,803 | 259 | Punta Gorda, FL | 163,934 | 160 | Tallahassee, FL | 378,864 |
| 192 | Merced, CA | 264,498 | 233 | Racine, WI | 194,711 | 24 | Tampa-St Petersburg, FL | 2,872,186 |
| 11 | Miami (greater), FL | 5,846,679 | 67 | Raleigh, NC | 1,209,877 | 247 | Terre Haute, IN | 172,996 |
| 31 | Miami-Dade County, FL M.D. | 2,630,552 | 294 | Rapid City, SD | 140,926 | 284 | Texarkana, TX-AR | 150,224 |
| 270 | Midland, TX | 155,778 | 149 | Reading, PA | 413,820 | 345 | The Villages, FL | 104,608 |
| 57 | Milwaukee, WI | 1,571,468 | 242 | Redding, CA | 179,250 | 114 | Toledo, OH | 609,674 |
| 21 | Minneapolis-St. Paul, MN-WI | 3,455,982 | 137 | Reno, NV | 438,372 | 207 | Topeka, KS | 234,566 |
| 338 | Missoula, MT | 112,051 | 65 | Richmond, VA | 1,242,277 | 162 | Trenton, NJ | 369,292 |
| 148 | Mobile, AL | 414,070 | 17 | Riverside-San Bernardino, CA | 4,392,057 | 74 | Tucson, AZ | 999,664 |
| 125 | Modesto, CA | 524,583 | 176 | Roanoke, VA | 311,327 | 75 | Tulsa, OK | 960,098 |
| 243 | Monroe, LA | 178,294 | 221 | Rochester, MN | 211,141 | 208 | Tuscaloosa, AL | 234,358 |
| 281 | Monroe, MI | 150,897 | 71 | Rochester, NY | 1,084,351 | 216 | Tyler, TX | 217,202 |
| 47 | Montgomery County, PA M.D. | 1,946,242 | 166 | Rockford, IL | 344,806 | 180 | Utica-Rome, NY | 297,990 |
| 303 | Morgantown, WV | 135,362 | 145 | Rockingham County, NH M.D. | 423,527 | 144 | Vallejo-Fairfield, CA | 423,574 |
| 333 | Morristown, TN | 115,337 | 277 | Rocky Mount, NC | 151,852 | 355 | Victoria, TX | 97,898 |
| 326 | Mount Vernon-Anacortes, WA | 119,004 | 359 | Rome, GA | 96,122 | 267 | Vineland-Bridgeton, NJ | 158,281 |
| 328 | Muncie, IN | 117,579 | 41 | Sacramento, CA | 2,213,600 | 54 | Virginia Beach-Norfolk, VA-NC | 1,710,528 |
| 249 | Muskegon, MI | 169,764 | 230 | Saginaw, MI | 198,026 | 133 | Visalia-Porterville, CA | 455,552 |
| 153 | Myrtle Beach, SC-NC | 401,625 | 154 | Salem, OR | 398,927 | 197 | Waco, TX | 258,233 |
| 296 | Napa, CA | 139,982 | 142 | Salinas, CA | 430,882 | 239 | Warner Robins, GA | 187,233 |
| 168 | Naples-Marco Island, FL | 337,025 | 156 | Salisbury, MD-DE | 385,257 | 32 | Warren-Troy, MI M.D. | 2,510,130 |
| 53 | Nashville-Davidson, TN | 1,745,622 | 68 | Salt Lake City, UT | 1,141,757 | 10 | Washington (greater) DC-VA-MD-WV | 5,943,171 |
| 25 | Nassau-Suffolk, NY M.D. | 2,856,018 | 332 | San Angelo, TX | 116,215 | 13 | Washington, DC-VA-MD-WV M.D. | 4,684,848 |
| 311 | New Bern, NC | 128,857 | 39 | San Antonio, TX | 2,271,017 | 323 | Watertown-Fort Drum, NY | 121,663 |
| 92 | New Haven-Milford, CT | 808,809 | 22 | San Diego, CA | 3,206,175 | 304 | Wausau, WI | 135,041 |
| 66 | New Orleans, LA | 1,239,126 | 16 | San Francisco (greater), CA | 4,499,119 | 59 | West Palm Beach, FL M.D. | 1,372,752 |
| 1 | New York (greater), NY-NJ-PA | 19,936,617 | 56 | San Francisco-Redwood, CA M.D. | 1,580,707 | 280 | Wichita Falls, TX | 151,253 |
| 2 | New York-Jersey City, NY-NJ M.D. | 14,185,877 | 49 | San Jose, CA | 1,914,750 | 108 | Wichita, KS | 637,215 |
| 33 | Newark, NJ-PA M.D. | 2,497,536 | 185 | San Luis Obispo, CA | 276,816 | 329 | Williamsport, PA | 117,439 |
| 269 | Niles-Benton Harbor, MI | 155,981 | 199 | San Rafael, CA M.D. | 257,458 | 98 | Wilmington, DE-MD-NJ M.D. | 718,010 |
| 96 | North Port-Sarasota-Bradenton, FL | 728,392 | 190 | Santa Cruz-Watsonville, CA | 268,260 | 191 | Wilmington, NC | 266,872 |
| 290 | Norwich-New London, CT | 146,149 | 141 | Santa Maria-Santa Barbara, CA | 434,144 | 306 | Winchester, VA-WV | 131,881 |
| 30 | Oakland-Hayward, CA M.D. | 2,660,954 | 127 | Santa Rosa, CA | 494,862 | 106 | Winston-Salem, NC | 651,819 |
| 167 | Ocala, FL | 337,649 | 163 | Savannah, GA | 366,493 | 83 | Worcester, MA-CT | 852,899 |
| 358 | Ocean City, NJ | 96,133 | 119 | Scranton--Wilkes-Barre, PA | 563,315 | 203 | Yakima, WA | 248,678 |
| 288 | Odessa, TX | 147,448 | 20 | Seattle (greater), WA | 3,598,765 | 138 | York-Hanover, PA | 438,349 |
| 113 | Ogden-Clearfield, UT | 620,648 | 27 | Seattle-Bellevue-Everett, WA M.D. | 2,779,025 | 253 | Yuba City, CA | 168,410 |
| 61 | Oklahoma City, OK | 1,315,519 | 293 | Sebastian-Vero Beach, FL | 141,889 | 227 | Yuma, AZ | 201,878 |
| 195 | Olympia, WA | 260,949 | 354 | Sebring, FL | 98,300 | | | |

Source: Reported data from the F.B.I. "Crime in the United States 2013"
*Estimates as of July 2013 based on U.S. Bureau of the Census figures.

# 85. Metropolitan Population in 2013 (continued)
## National Total = 316,128,839*

| RANK | METROPOLITAN AREA | POP | RANK | METROPOLITAN AREA | POP | RANK | METROPOLITAN AREA | POP |
|---|---|---|---|---|---|---|---|---|
| 1 | New York (greater), NY-NJ-PA | 19,936,617 | 65 | Richmond, VA | 1,242,277 | 129 | Fayetteville-Springdale, AR-MO | 488,051 |
| 2 | New York-Jersey City, NY-NJ M.D. | 14,185,877 | 66 | New Orleans, LA | 1,239,126 | 130 | Lafayette, LA | 477,151 |
| 3 | Los Angeles (greater), CA | 13,141,130 | 67 | Raleigh, NC | 1,209,877 | 131 | Lansing-East Lansing, MI | 466,728 |
| 4 | Los Angeles County, CA M.D. | 10,022,399 | 68 | Salt Lake City, UT | 1,141,757 | 132 | Pensacola, FL | 466,427 |
| 5 | Chicago (greater), IL-IN-WI | 9,538,161 | 69 | Birmingham-Hoover, AL | 1,138,940 | 133 | Visalia-Porterville, CA | 455,552 |
| 6 | Chicago-Naperville, IL M.D. | 7,331,456 | 70 | Buffalo-Niagara Falls, NY | 1,135,074 | 134 | Shreveport-Bossier City, LA | 449,602 |
| 7 | Dallas (greater), TX | 6,814,175 | 71 | Rochester, NY | 1,084,351 | 135 | Springfield, MO | 448,011 |
| 8 | Houston, TX | 6,281,279 | 72 | Hartford, CT | 1,023,807 | 136 | Corpus Christi, TX | 441,984 |
| 9 | Philadelphia (greater) PA-NJ-MD-DE | 6,036,138 | 73 | Grand Rapids-Wyoming, MI | 1,012,133 | 137 | Reno, NV | 438,372 |
| 10 | Washington (greater) DC-VA-MD-WV | 5,943,171 | 74 | Tucson, AZ | 999,664 | 138 | York-Hanover, PA | 438,349 |
| 11 | Miami (greater), FL | 5,846,679 | 75 | Tulsa, OK | 960,098 | 139 | Port St. Lucie, FL | 436,841 |
| 12 | Atlanta, GA | 5,511,212 | 76 | Fresno, CA | 954,305 | 140 | Huntsville, AL | 434,500 |
| 13 | Washington, DC-VA-MD-WV M.D. | 4,684,848 | 77 | Bridgeport-Stamford, CT | 921,059 | 141 | Santa Maria-Santa Barbara, CA | 434,144 |
| 14 | Boston (greater), MA-NH | 4,679,143 | 78 | Albuquerque, NM | 902,627 | 142 | Salinas, CA | 430,882 |
| 15 | Dallas-Plano-Irving, TX M.D. | 4,506,295 | 79 | Omaha-Council Bluffs, NE-IA | 893,630 | 143 | Fort Wayne, IN | 424,081 |
| 16 | San Francisco (greater), CA | 4,499,119 | 80 | Albany-Schenectady-Troy, NY | 876,869 | 144 | Vallejo-Fairfield, CA | 423,574 |
| 17 | Riverside-San Bernardino, CA | 4,392,057 | 81 | Lake Co.-Kenosha Co., IL-WI M.D. | 869,611 | 145 | Rockingham County, NH M.D. | 423,527 |
| 18 | Phoenix-Mesa-Scottsdale, AZ | 4,386,981 | 82 | Bakersfield, CA | 862,202 | 146 | Brownsville-Harlingen, TX | 419,944 |
| 19 | Detroit (greater), MI | 4,296,628 | 83 | Worcester, MA-CT | 852,899 | 147 | Flint, MI | 416,606 |
| 20 | Seattle (greater), WA | 3,598,765 | 84 | Greenville-Anderson, SC | 852,405 | 148 | Mobile, AL | 414,070 |
| 21 | Minneapolis-St. Paul, MN-WI | 3,455,982 | 85 | Knoxville, TN | 852,347 | 149 | Reading, PA | 413,820 |
| 22 | San Diego, CA | 3,206,175 | 86 | El Paso, TX | 842,271 | 150 | Beaumont-Port Arthur, TX | 406,050 |
| 23 | Anaheim-Santa Ana-Irvine, CA M.D. | 3,118,731 | 87 | Oxnard-Thousand Oaks, CA | 840,678 | 151 | Canton, OH | 404,048 |
| 24 | Tampa-St Petersburg, FL | 2,872,186 | 88 | Allentown, PA-NJ | 828,654 | 152 | Manchester-Nashua, NH | 403,992 |
| 25 | Nassau-Suffolk, NY M.D. | 2,856,018 | 89 | Tacoma, WA M.D. | 819,740 | 153 | Myrtle Beach, SC-NC | 401,625 |
| 26 | St. Louis, MO-IL | 2,803,655 | 90 | Baton Rouge, LA | 819,681 | 154 | Salem, OR | 398,927 |
| 27 | Seattle-Bellevue-Everett, WA M.D. | 2,779,025 | 91 | McAllen-Edinburg-Mission, TX | 819,252 | 155 | Dutchess-Putnam, NY M.D. | 397,186 |
| 28 | Baltimore, MD | 2,771,247 | 92 | New Haven-Milford, CT | 808,809 | 156 | Salisbury, MD-DE | 385,257 |
| 29 | Denver-Aurora, CO | 2,693,369 | 93 | Dayton, OH | 802,990 | 157 | Davenport, IA-IL | 383,796 |
| 30 | Oakland-Hayward, CA M.D. | 2,660,954 | 94 | Columbia, SC | 793,289 | 158 | Gulfport-Biloxi-Pascagoula, MS | 382,406 |
| 31 | Miami-Dade County, FL M.D. | 2,630,552 | 95 | Greensboro-High Point, NC | 742,007 | 159 | Peoria, IL | 380,809 |
| 32 | Warren-Troy, MI M.D. | 2,510,130 | 96 | North Port-Sarasota-Bradenton, FL | 728,392 | 160 | Tallahassee, FL | 378,864 |
| 33 | Newark, NJ-PA M.D. | 2,497,536 | 97 | Little Rock, AR | 723,132 | 161 | Fayetteville, NC | 378,067 |
| 34 | Pittsburgh, PA | 2,360,685 | 98 | Wilmington, DE-MD-NJ M.D. | 718,010 | 162 | Trenton, NJ | 369,292 |
| 35 | Charlotte-Mecklenburg, NC-SC | 2,329,109 | 99 | Charleston-North Charleston, SC | 710,846 | 163 | Savannah, GA | 366,493 |
| 36 | Portland-Vancouver, OR-WA | 2,315,358 | 100 | Stockton-Lodi, CA | 708,679 | 164 | Eugene, OR | 356,321 |
| 37 | Cambridge-Newton, MA M.D. | 2,313,211 | 101 | Gary, IN M.D. | 708,116 | 165 | Ann Arbor, MI | 353,189 |
| 38 | Fort Worth-Arlington, TX M.D. | 2,307,880 | 102 | Akron, OH | 703,468 | 166 | Rockford, IL | 344,806 |
| 39 | San Antonio, TX | 2,271,017 | 103 | Colorado Springs, CO | 678,821 | 167 | Ocala, FL | 337,649 |
| 40 | Orlando, FL | 2,261,201 | 104 | Syracuse, NY | 661,048 | 168 | Naples-Marco Island, FL | 337,025 |
| 41 | Sacramento, CA | 2,213,600 | 105 | Cape Coral-Fort Myers, FL | 656,243 | 169 | Spartanburg, SC | 319,563 |
| 42 | Cincinnati, OH-KY-IN | 2,136,525 | 106 | Winston-Salem, NC | 651,819 | 170 | South Bend-Mishawaka, IN-MI | 319,204 |
| 43 | Philadelphia, PA M.D. | 2,114,504 | 107 | Boise City, ID | 647,858 | 171 | Fort Collins, CO | 315,907 |
| 44 | Kansas City, MO-KS | 2,049,436 | 108 | Wichita, KS | 637,215 | 172 | Columbus, GA-AL | 315,743 |
| 45 | Las Vegas-Henderson, NV | 2,025,864 | 109 | Elgin, IL M.D. | 628,978 | 173 | Anchorage, AK | 314,553 |
| 46 | Indianapolis, IN | 1,946,607 | 110 | Springfield, MA | 628,316 | 174 | Lincoln, NE | 313,545 |
| 47 | Montgomery County, PA M.D. | 1,946,242 | 111 | Madison, WI | 626,047 | 175 | Green Bay, WI | 312,769 |
| 48 | Boston, MA M.D. | 1,942,405 | 112 | Lakeland, FL | 622,846 | 176 | Roanoke, VA | 311,327 |
| 49 | San Jose, CA | 1,914,750 | 113 | Ogden-Clearfield, UT | 620,648 | 177 | Boulder, CO | 310,533 |
| 50 | Austin-Round Rock, TX | 1,879,235 | 114 | Toledo, OH | 609,674 | 178 | Kingsport, TN-VA | 309,240 |
| 51 | Fort Lauderdale, FL M.D. | 1,843,375 | 115 | Deltona-Daytona Beach, FL | 599,128 | 179 | Lubbock, TX | 300,769 |
| 52 | Detroit-Dearborn-Livonia, MI M.D. | 1,786,498 | 116 | Des Moines-West Des Moines, IA | 596,382 | 180 | Utica-Rome, NY | 297,990 |
| 53 | Nashville-Davidson, TN | 1,745,622 | 117 | Augusta, GA-SC | 579,933 | 181 | Fort Smith, AR-OK | 280,934 |
| 54 | Virginia Beach-Norfolk, VA-NC | 1,710,528 | 118 | Jackson, MS | 579,868 | 182 | Erie, PA | 280,450 |
| 55 | Providence-Warwick, RI-MA | 1,604,757 | 119 | Scranton--Wilkes-Barre, PA | 563,315 | 183 | Duluth, MN-WI | 280,163 |
| 56 | San Francisco-Redwood, CA M.D. | 1,580,707 | 120 | Provo-Orem, UT | 561,483 | 184 | Clarksville, TN-KY | 278,930 |
| 57 | Milwaukee, WI | 1,571,468 | 121 | Palm Bay-Melbourne, FL | 550,499 | 185 | San Luis Obispo, CA | 276,816 |
| 58 | Jacksonville, FL | 1,392,914 | 122 | Chattanooga, TN-GA | 541,195 | 186 | Atlantic City, NJ | 276,095 |
| 59 | West Palm Beach, FL M.D. | 1,372,752 | 123 | Spokane, WA | 535,166 | 187 | Kennewick-Richland, WA | 273,507 |
| 60 | Memphis, TN-MS-AR | 1,347,803 | 124 | Lancaster, PA | 528,698 | 188 | Gainesville, FL | 270,523 |
| 61 | Oklahoma City, OK | 1,315,519 | 125 | Modesto, CA | 524,583 | 189 | Greeley, CO | 268,670 |
| 62 | Silver Spring-Frederick, MD M.D. | 1,258,323 | 126 | Portland, ME | 518,977 | 190 | Santa Cruz-Watsonville, CA | 268,260 |
| 63 | Louisville, KY-IN | 1,257,388 | 127 | Santa Rosa, CA | 494,862 | 191 | Wilmington, NC | 266,872 |
| 64 | Camden, NJ M.D. | 1,257,382 | 128 | Lexington-Fayette, KY | 489,329 | 192 | Merced, CA | 264,498 |

Note: All listings are for Metropolitan Statistical Areas (M.S.A.s) except for those ending with "M.D." Listings with "M.D." are Metropolitan Divisions which are smaller parts of eleven large M.S.A.s. See explanatory note at beginning of metropolitan area section.

| RANK | METROPOLITAN AREA | POP | RANK | METROPOLITAN AREA | POP | RANK | METROPOLITAN AREA | POP |
|---|---|---|---|---|---|---|---|---|
| 193 | Cedar Rapids, IA | 263,588 | 255 | Abilene, TX | 168,117 | 317 | Goldsboro, NC | 125,081 |
| 194 | Laredo, TX | 262,936 | 256 | Billings, MT | 164,846 | 318 | Jonesboro, AR | 125,041 |
| 195 | Olympia, WA | 260,949 | 257 | Eau Claire, WI | 164,463 | 319 | Bismarck, ND | 124,238 |
| 196 | Amarillo, TX | 260,305 | 258 | Bend, OR | 164,183 | 320 | Hammond, LA | 124,208 |
| 197 | Waco, TX | 258,233 | 259 | Punta Gorda, FL | 163,934 | 321 | Sherman-Denison, TX | 122,729 |
| 198 | Hagerstown-Martinsburg, MD-WV | 257,750 | 260 | Bloomington, IN | 163,596 | 322 | Mansfield, OH | 122,427 |
| 199 | San Rafael, CA M.D. | 257,458 | 261 | Bowling Green, KY | 163,437 | 323 | Watertown-Fort Drum, NY | 121,663 |
| 200 | Bremerton-Silverdale, WA | 256,890 | 262 | Pueblo, CO | 162,300 | 324 | Albany, OR | 119,155 |
| 201 | Lynchburg, VA | 256,835 | 263 | Janesville, WI | 160,586 | 325 | Staunton-Waynesboro, VA | 119,067 |
| 202 | Crestview-Fort Walton Beach, FL | 252,641 | 264 | Jackson, MI | 160,498 | 326 | Mount Vernon-Anacortes, WA | 119,004 |
| 203 | Yakima, WA | 248,678 | 265 | Iowa City, IA | 160,439 | 327 | Cleveland, TN | 118,551 |
| 204 | Binghamton, NY | 247,869 | 266 | Kahului-Wailuku-Lahaina, HI | 159,652 | 328 | Muncie, IN | 117,579 |
| 205 | Sioux Falls, SD | 241,643 | 267 | Vineland-Bridgeton, NJ | 158,281 | 329 | Williamsport, PA | 117,439 |
| 206 | College Station-Bryan, TX | 237,174 | 268 | Albany, GA | 157,365 | 330 | Anniston-Oxford, AL | 116,893 |
| 207 | Topeka, KS | 234,566 | 269 | Niles-Benton Harbor, MI | 155,981 | 331 | Owensboro, KY | 116,530 |
| 208 | Tuscaloosa, AL | 234,358 | 270 | Midland, TX | 155,778 | 332 | San Angelo, TX | 116,215 |
| 209 | Champaign-Urbana, IL | 234,223 | 271 | State College, PA | 155,409 | 333 | Morristown, TN | 115,337 |
| 210 | Macon, GA | 232,892 | 272 | Burlington, NC | 155,214 | 334 | Sheboygan, WI | 114,951 |
| 211 | Appleton, WI | 229,465 | 273 | Alexandria, LA | 154,678 | 335 | Brunswick, GA | 113,744 |
| 212 | Charlottesville, VA | 224,663 | 274 | Decatur, AL | 154,311 | 336 | Lawrence, KS | 113,372 |
| 213 | Chico, CA | 222,365 | 275 | Bangor, ME | 153,530 | 337 | Kankakee, IL | 112,844 |
| 214 | Fargo, ND-MN | 222,166 | 276 | Madera, CA | 152,772 | 338 | Missoula, MT | 112,051 |
| 215 | Longview, TX | 218,274 | 277 | Rocky Mount, NC | 151,852 | 339 | California-Lexington Park, MD | 110,294 |
| 216 | Tyler, TX | 217,202 | 278 | Chambersburg-Waynesboro, PA | 151,646 | 340 | Decatur, IL | 109,877 |
| 217 | Barnstable Town, MA | 215,847 | 279 | Hanford-Corcoran, CA | 151,256 | 341 | Sumter, SC | 108,703 |
| 218 | Las Cruces, NM | 215,083 | 280 | Wichita Falls, TX | 151,253 | 342 | Lewiston-Auburn, ME | 107,469 |
| 219 | Prescott, AZ | 214,243 | 281 | Monroe, MI | 150,897 | 343 | Bay City, MI | 106,781 |
| 220 | Springfield, IL | 212,387 | 282 | Elizabethtown-Fort Knox, KY | 150,699 | 344 | Lima, OH | 105,002 |
| 221 | Rochester, MN | 211,141 | 283 | Jefferson City, MO | 150,542 | 345 | The Villages, FL | 104,608 |
| 222 | Houma, LA | 209,328 | 284 | Texarkana, TX-AR | 150,224 | 346 | Gadsden, AL | 104,345 |
| 223 | Lafayette, IN | 208,478 | 285 | Grand Junction, CO | 149,245 | 347 | Longview, WA | 102,169 |
| 224 | Medford, OR | 207,927 | 286 | Dothan, AL | 148,166 | 348 | Fond du Lac, WI | 101,960 |
| 225 | Florence, SC | 207,144 | 287 | St. George, UT | 147,923 | 349 | Cumberland, MD-WV | 101,663 |
| 226 | Lake Havasu City-Kingman, AZ | 205,099 | 288 | Odessa, TX | 147,448 | 350 | Gettysburg, PA | 101,443 |
| 227 | Yuma, AZ | 201,878 | 289 | Florence-Muscle Shoals, AL | 146,880 | 351 | Grand Forks, ND-MN | 100,500 |
| 228 | Lake Charles, LA | 201,735 | 290 | Norwich-New London, CT | 146,149 | 352 | Manhattan, KS | 99,347 |
| 229 | Johnson City, TN | 201,439 | 291 | Coeur d'Alene, ID | 144,225 | 353 | Mankato-North Mankato, MN | 98,755 |
| 230 | Saginaw, MI | 198,026 | 292 | Dalton, GA | 142,901 | 354 | Sebring, FL | 98,300 |
| 231 | Athens-Clarke County, GA | 197,437 | 293 | Sebastian-Vero Beach, FL | 141,889 | 355 | Victoria, TX | 97,898 |
| 232 | Hilton Head Island, SC | 196,780 | 294 | Rapid City, SD | 140,926 | 356 | Cape Girardeau, MO-IL | 97,510 |
| 233 | Racine, WI | 194,711 | 295 | Johnstown, PA | 140,876 | 357 | Hot Springs, AR | 97,163 |
| 234 | Daphne-Fairhope-Foley, AL | 193,322 | 296 | Napa, CA | 139,982 | 358 | Ocean City, NJ | 96,133 |
| 235 | St. Cloud, MN | 191,531 | 297 | Homosassa Springs, FL | 139,242 | 359 | Rome, GA | 96,122 |
| 236 | Bloomington, IL | 189,408 | 298 | Idaho Falls, ID | 137,561 | 360 | Dubuque, IA | 95,753 |
| 237 | Panama City, FL | 189,176 | 299 | Springfield, OH | 137,153 | 361 | Cheyenne, WY | 95,635 |
| 238 | Gainesville, GA | 187,290 | 300 | Flagstaff, AZ | 136,999 | 362 | Parkersburg-Vienna, WV | 92,396 |
| 239 | Warner Robins, GA | 187,233 | 301 | La Crosse, WI-MN | 135,914 | 363 | Ames, IA | 91,897 |
| 240 | Kingston, NY | 181,804 | 302 | Lebanon, PA | 135,689 | 364 | Elmira, NY | 89,040 |
| 241 | Blacksburg, VA | 179,521 | 303 | Morgantown, WV | 135,362 | 365 | Corvallis, OR | 86,952 |
| 242 | Redding, CA | 179,250 | 304 | Wausau, WI | 135,041 | 366 | Bloomsburg-Berwick, PA | 85,071 |
| 243 | Monroe, LA | 178,294 | 305 | Lawton, OK | 133,449 | 367 | Pocatello, ID | 84,482 |
| 244 | El Centro, CA | 177,955 | 306 | Winchester, VA-WV | 131,881 | 368 | Grand Island, NE | 84,159 |
| 245 | Greenville, NC | 174,355 | 307 | Jackson, TN | 130,702 | 369 | Grants Pass, OR | 83,162 |
| 246 | Joplin, MO | 174,207 | 308 | Pittsfield, MA | 129,977 | 370 | Kokomo, IN | 83,108 |
| 247 | Terre Haute, IN | 172,996 | 309 | Logan, UT-ID | 129,858 | 371 | Hinesville, GA | 82,962 |
| 248 | Columbia, MO | 170,724 | 310 | Harrisonburg, VA | 129,689 | 372 | Great Falls, MT | 82,197 |
| 249 | Muskegon, MI | 169,764 | 311 | New Bern, NC | 128,857 | 373 | Columbus, IN | 80,102 |
| 250 | Dover, DE | 169,725 | 312 | Glens Falls, NY | 128,459 | 374 | Casper, WY | 79,993 |
| 251 | Oshkosh-Neenah, WI | 169,484 | 313 | St. Joseph, MO-KS | 128,425 | 375 | Lewiston, ID-WA | 61,820 |
| 252 | Sioux City, IA-NE-SD | 169,444 | 314 | Farmington, NM | 127,552 | 376 | Carson City, NV | 54,937 |
| 253 | Yuba City, CA | 168,410 | 315 | Altoona, PA | 127,076 | 377 | Fairbanks, AK | 34,741 |
| 254 | East Stroudsburg, PA | 168,309 | 316 | Carbondale-Marion, IL | 126,687 | | | |

Source: Reported data from the F.B.I. "Crime in the United States 2013"
*Estimates as of July 2013 based on U.S. Bureau of the Census figures.

# 86. Metropolitan Population in 2012
## National Total = 313,873,685*

| RANK | METROPOLITAN AREA | POP | RANK | METROPOLITAN AREA | POP | RANK | METROPOLITAN AREA | POP |
|---|---|---|---|---|---|---|---|---|
| 243 | Abilene, TX | 168,908 | 345 | Cheyenne, WY | 94,026 | 96 | Gary, IN M.D. | 710,891 |
| 98 | Akron, OH | 701,412 | 5 | Chicago (greater), IL-IN-WI | 9,511,421 | 334 | Gettysburg, PA | 101,598 |
| 78 | Albany-Schenectady-Troy, NY | 876,182 | 6 | Chicago-Naperville, IL M.D. | 7,300,952 | 296 | Glens Falls, NY | 129,692 |
| 253 | Albany, GA | 159,370 | 207 | Chico, CA | 222,309 | 303 | Goldsboro, NC | 124,923 |
| 311 | Albany, OR | 118,961 | 42 | Cincinnati, OH-KY-IN | 2,123,695 | 336 | Grand Forks, ND-MN | 99,784 |
| 76 | Albuquerque, NM | 900,072 | 183 | Clarksville, TN-KY | 266,196 | 352 | Grand Island, NE | 83,197 |
| 257 | Alexandria, LA | 155,419 | 315 | Cleveland, TN | 117,799 | 271 | Grand Junction, CO | 149,118 |
| 86 | Allentown, PA-NJ | 826,611 | 280 | Coeur d'Alene, ID | 142,089 | NA | Grand Rapids-Wyoming, MI** | NA |
| 302 | Altoona, PA | 127,305 | 201 | College Station-Bryan, TX | 235,092 | NA | Grants Pass, OR** | NA |
| 190 | Amarillo, TX | 259,729 | 100 | Colorado Springs, CO | 669,453 | 354 | Great Falls, MT | 82,406 |
| 347 | Ames, IA | 90,011 | 246 | Columbia, MO | 165,938 | 185 | Greeley, CO | 262,216 |
| 23 | Anaheim-Santa Ana-Irvine, CA M.D. | 3,084,081 | NA | Columbia, SC** | NA | 168 | Green Bay, WI | 310,262 |
| 165 | Anchorage, AK | 313,529 | 171 | Columbus, GA-AL | 304,291 | 92 | Greensboro-High Point, NC | 738,208 |
| 160 | Ann Arbor, MI | 348,215 | 356 | Columbus, IN | 78,114 | 83 | Greenville-Anderson, SC | 843,836 |
| 313 | Anniston-Oxford, AL | 118,270 | 132 | Corpus Christi, TX | 437,841 | 239 | Greenville, NC | 172,830 |
| 205 | Appleton, WI | 227,986 | 349 | Corvallis, OR | 86,538 | NA | Gulfport-Biloxi-Pascagoula, MS** | NA |
| 225 | Athens-Clarke County, GA | 195,380 | 198 | Crestview-Fort Walton Beach, FL | 242,539 | 195 | Hagerstown-Martinsburg, MD-WV | 255,387 |
| 12 | Atlanta, GA | 5,434,540 | 331 | Cumberland, MD-WV | 103,606 | 305 | Hammond, LA | 123,296 |
| 178 | Atlantic City, NJ | 275,689 | 7 | Dallas (greater), TX | 6,680,025 | 258 | Hanford-Corcoran, CA | 155,191 |
| 114 | Augusta, GA-SC | 575,582 | 16 | Dallas-Plano-Irving, TX M.D. | 4,405,585 | 300 | Harrisonburg, VA | 127,957 |
| 49 | Austin-Round Rock, TX | 1,810,230 | 276 | Dalton, GA | 144,264 | 71 | Hartford, CT | 1,023,883 |
| 80 | Bakersfield, CA | 859,608 | 228 | Daphne-Fairhope-Foley, AL | 187,467 | 226 | Hilton Head Island, SC | 191,685 |
| 27 | Baltimore, MD | 2,755,459 | 151 | Davenport, IA-IL | 382,090 | 355 | Hinesville, GA | 81,447 |
| 263 | Bangor, ME | 153,902 | 91 | Dayton, OH | 803,255 | 281 | Homosassa Springs, FL | 141,942 |
| 209 | Barnstable Town, MA | 217,689 | 261 | Decatur, AL | 154,689 | NA | Hot Springs, AR** | NA |
| 88 | Baton Rouge, LA | 813,022 | 324 | Decatur, IL | 110,782 | 216 | Houma, LA | 209,817 |
| 328 | Bay City, MI | 107,188 | 112 | Deltona-Daytona Beach, FL | 600,260 | 8 | Houston, TX | 6,150,496 |
| 146 | Beaumont-Port Arthur, TX | 411,053 | 29 | Denver-Aurora, CO | 2,635,467 | 137 | Huntsville, AL | 427,189 |
| NA | Bend, OR** | NA | 113 | Des Moines-West Des Moines, IA | 582,506 | 287 | Idaho Falls, ID | 135,809 |
| 249 | Billings, MT | 162,082 | 19 | Detroit (greater), MI | 4,288,943 | 46 | Indianapolis, IN | 1,915,784 |
| 196 | Binghamton, NY | 251,424 | 51 | Detroit-Dearborn-Livonia, MI M.D. | 1,803,403 | 256 | Iowa City, IA | 155,494 |
| 68 | Birmingham-Hoover, AL | 1,136,805 | 274 | Dothan, AL | 147,151 | 57 | Jacksonville, FL | 1,378,810 |
| 309 | Bismarck, ND | 119,673 | 245 | Dover, DE | 166,643 | NA | Jackson, MI** | NA |
| 233 | Blacksburg, VA | 179,827 | 344 | Dubuque, IA | 95,015 | 115 | Jackson, MS | 574,517 |
| 229 | Bloomington, IL | 187,221 | 177 | Duluth, MN-WI | 281,439 | 295 | Jackson, TN | 131,023 |
| 250 | Bloomington, IN | 161,803 | 149 | Dutchess-Putnam, NY M.D. | 400,079 | 252 | Janesville, WI | 160,502 |
| 350 | Bloomsburg-Berwick, PA | 85,911 | 240 | East Stroudsburg, PA | 170,157 | 270 | Jefferson City, MO | 150,764 |
| 105 | Boise City, ID | 631,917 | NA | Eau Claire, WI** | NA | 222 | Johnson City, TN | 201,468 |
| 13 | Boston (greater), MA-NH | 4,629,025 | 236 | El Centro, CA | 178,699 | 277 | Johnstown, PA | 143,961 |
| 45 | Boston, MA M.D. | 1,920,886 | 85 | El Paso, TX | 836,557 | 306 | Jonesboro, AR | 123,295 |
| 172 | Boulder, CO | 303,520 | 107 | Elgin, IL M.D. | 625,305 | 237 | Joplin, MO | 177,182 |
| 251 | Bowling Green, KY | 160,980 | 266 | Elizabethtown-Fort Knox, KY | 151,716 | 254 | Kahului-Wailuku-Lahaina, HI | 158,760 |
| 193 | Bremerton-Silverdale, WA | 257,130 | 348 | Elmira, NY | 89,320 | 321 | Kankakee, IL | 113,751 |
| 75 | Bridgeport-Stamford, CT | 910,707 | 176 | Erie, PA | 281,440 | 43 | Kansas City, MO-KS | 2,033,239 |
| 143 | Brownsville-Harlingen, TX | 420,325 | 158 | Eugene, OR | 355,926 | 182 | Kennewick-Richland, WA | 266,723 |
| 320 | Brunswick, GA | 114,128 | 360 | Fairbanks, AK | 34,603 | 166 | Kingsport, TN-VA | 312,616 |
| 67 | Buffalo-Niagara Falls, NY | 1,140,160 | 211 | Fargo, ND-MN | 216,055 | 232 | Kingston, NY | 183,433 |
| 260 | Burlington, NC | 154,810 | 299 | Farmington, NM | 128,404 | 82 | Knoxville, TN | 850,421 |
| 325 | California-Lexington Park, MD | 108,522 | 125 | Fayetteville-Springdale, AR-MO | 475,585 | 353 | Kokomo, IN | 83,059 |
| 35 | Cambridge-Newton, MA M.D. | 2,287,271 | 154 | Fayetteville, NC | 377,864 | 288 | La Crosse, WI-MN | 134,905 |
| 61 | Camden, NJ M.D. | 1,258,086 | 286 | Flagstaff, AZ | 135,979 | 220 | Lafayette, IN | 204,246 |
| 147 | Canton, OH | 403,843 | 139 | Flint, MI | 422,387 | 126 | Lafayette, LA | 473,751 |
| 103 | Cape Coral-Fort Myers, FL | 639,944 | 272 | Florence-Muscle Shoals, AL | 147,885 | NA | Lake Charles, LA** | NA |
| 339 | Cape Girardeau, MO-IL | 97,195 | 217 | Florence, SC | 208,121 | 79 | Lake Co.-Kenosha Co., IL-WI M.D. | 874,273 |
| NA | Carbondale-Marion, IL** | NA | 333 | Fond du Lac, WI | 102,340 | 219 | Lake Havasu City-Kingman, AZ | 204,559 |
| 359 | Carson City, NV | 56,164 | 169 | Fort Collins, CO | 309,752 | 108 | Lakeland, FL | 617,808 |
| 357 | Casper, WY | 77,475 | 50 | Fort Lauderdale, FL M.D. | 1,804,461 | 120 | Lancaster, PA | 524,442 |
| 187 | Cedar Rapids, IA | 261,586 | 175 | Fort Smith, AR-OK | 283,329 | 127 | Lansing-East Lansing, MI | 465,476 |
| 269 | Chambersburg-Waynesboro, PA | 151,055 | 141 | Fort Wayne, IN | 420,767 | 189 | Laredo, TX | 260,337 |
| 204 | Champaign-Urbana, IL | 232,445 | 37 | Fort Worth-Arlington, TX M.D. | 2,274,440 | 213 | Las Cruces, NM | 213,938 |
| 99 | Charleston-North Charleston, SC | 688,607 | 74 | Fresno, CA | 951,648 | 44 | Las Vegas-Henderson, NV | 1,995,735 |
| NA | Charlotte-Mecklenburg, NC-SC** | NA | 330 | Gadsden, AL | 104,722 | 322 | Lawrence, KS | 112,784 |
| 206 | Charlottesville, VA | 223,598 | 180 | Gainesville, FL | 270,003 | 291 | Lawton, OK | 132,806 |
| NA | Chattanooga, TN-GA** | NA | 231 | Gainesville, GA | 185,005 | 290 | Lebanon, PA | 134,529 |

Note: All listings are for Metropolitan Statistical Areas (M.S.A.s) except for those ending with "M.D."  Listings with "M.D." are Metropolitan Divisions which are smaller parts of eleven large M.S.A.s.  See explanatory note at beginning of metropolitan area section.

| RANK | METROPOLITAN AREA | POP |
|---|---|---|
| 327 | Lewiston-Auburn, ME | 107,479 |
| 358 | Lewiston, ID-WA | 61,959 |
| 124 | Lexington-Fayette, KY | 480,457 |
| 329 | Lima, OH | 106,087 |
| 170 | Lincoln, NE | 308,646 |
| 95 | Little Rock, AR | 712,592 |
| 298 | Logan, UT-ID | 129,186 |
| 208 | Longview, TX | 219,910 |
| 332 | Longview, WA | 103,483 |
| 4 | Los Angeles County, CA M.D. | 9,980,757 |
| 3 | Los Angeles (greater), CA | 13,064,838 |
| 62 | Louisville, KY-IN | 1,248,616 |
| 173 | Lubbock, TX | 300,321 |
| 194 | Lynchburg, VA | 256,973 |
| 200 | Macon, GA | 235,405 |
| 262 | Madera, CA | 154,343 |
| 109 | Madison, WI | 614,928 |
| 148 | Manchester-Nashua, NH | 402,466 |
| 343 | Manhattan, KS | 95,402 |
| 338 | Mankato-North Mankato, MN | 97,827 |
| 304 | Mansfield, OH | 123,502 |
| 90 | McAllen-Edinburg-Mission, TX | 809,759 |
| 218 | Medford, OR | 206,276 |
| 59 | Memphis, TN-MS-AR | 1,343,608 |
| 184 | Merced, CA | 262,308 |
| 11 | Miami (greater), FL | 5,747,489 |
| 31 | Miami-Dade County, FL M.D. | 2,589,623 |
| 273 | Midland, TX | 147,417 |
| 55 | Milwaukee, WI | 1,566,214 |
| 21 | Minneapolis-St. Paul, MN-WI | 3,408,532 |
| 323 | Missoula, MT | 110,904 |
| 144 | Mobile, AL | 414,233 |
| 121 | Modesto, CA | 523,330 |
| 235 | Monroe, LA | 178,701 |
| 267 | Monroe, MI | 151,670 |
| 47 | Montgomery County, PA M.D. | 1,892,483 |
| 292 | Morgantown, WV | 132,255 |
| 317 | Morristown, TN | 115,676 |
| 310 | Mount Vernon-Anacortes, WA | 119,267 |
| 314 | Muncie, IN | 118,029 |
| NA | Muskegon, MI** | NA |
| NA | Myrtle Beach, SC-NC** | NA |
| 283 | Napa, CA | 139,368 |
| 162 | Naples-Marco Island, FL | 332,611 |
| 52 | Nashville-Davidson, TN | 1,712,682 |
| 25 | Nassau-Suffolk, NY M.D. | 2,858,599 |
| 297 | New Bern, NC | 129,271 |
| 89 | New Haven-Milford, CT | 809,772 |
| 65 | New Orleans, LA | 1,220,047 |
| 1 | New York (greater), NY-NJ-PA | 19,791,750 |
| 2 | New York-Jersey City, NY-NJ M.D. | 14,043,153 |
| 32 | Newark, NJ-PA M.D. | 2,489,919 |
| NA | Niles-Benton Harbor, MI** | NA |
| 93 | North Port-Sarasota-Bradenton, FL | 719,034 |
| 275 | Norwich-New London, CT | 146,391 |
| 30 | Oakland-Hayward, CA M.D. | 2,620,044 |
| 161 | Ocala, FL | 337,066 |
| 340 | Ocean City, NJ | 97,077 |
| 279 | Odessa, TX | 142,209 |
| 110 | Ogden-Clearfield, UT | 614,396 |
| 60 | Oklahoma City, OK | 1,285,907 |
| 191 | Olympia, WA | 259,107 |

| RANK | METROPOLITAN AREA | POP |
|---|---|---|
| 77 | Omaha-Council Bluffs, NE-IA | 882,865 |
| 39 | Orlando, FL | 2,200,987 |
| 244 | Oshkosh-Neenah, WI | 168,129 |
| 318 | Owensboro, KY | 115,625 |
| 84 | Oxnard-Thousand Oaks, CA | 839,484 |
| 117 | Palm Bay-Melbourne, FL | 550,983 |
| 227 | Panama City, FL | 188,234 |
| 346 | Parkersburg-Vienna, WV | 92,884 |
| 128 | Pensacola, FL | 459,402 |
| 153 | Peoria, IL | 379,733 |
| 9 | Philadelphia (greater) PA-NJ-MD-DE | 6,012,363 |
| 41 | Philadelphia, PA M.D. | 2,144,972 |
| 18 | Phoenix-Mesa-Scottsdale, AZ | 4,309,766 |
| 34 | Pittsburgh, PA | 2,363,571 |
| 293 | Pittsfield, MA | 131,619 |
| 351 | Pocatello, ID | 84,258 |
| 135 | Port St. Lucie, FL | 433,712 |
| 36 | Portland-Vancouver, OR-WA | 2,279,873 |
| 122 | Portland, ME | 516,198 |
| 212 | Prescott, AZ | 214,201 |
| 54 | Providence-Warwick, RI-MA | 1,604,098 |
| 118 | Provo-Orem, UT | 548,142 |
| 247 | Pueblo, CO | 162,766 |
| 248 | Punta Gorda, FL | 162,701 |
| 224 | Racine, WI | 195,888 |
| 66 | Raleigh, NC | 1,175,043 |
| 284 | Rapid City, SD | 138,237 |
| 145 | Reading, PA | 413,447 |
| 234 | Redding, CA | 179,423 |
| 134 | Reno, NV | 435,223 |
| 64 | Richmond, VA | 1,232,458 |
| 17 | Riverside-San Bernardino, CA | 4,344,917 |
| 167 | Roanoke, VA | 312,265 |
| 215 | Rochester, MN | 209,826 |
| 70 | Rochester, NY | 1,086,565 |
| 159 | Rockford, IL | 348,522 |
| 140 | Rockingham County, NH M.D. | 420,868 |
| 264 | Rocky Mount, NC | 153,664 |
| 341 | Rome, GA | 97,013 |
| 40 | Sacramento, CA | 2,196,416 |
| 223 | Saginaw, MI | 199,233 |
| 150 | Salem, OR | 397,669 |
| 138 | Salinas, CA | 425,810 |
| 152 | Salisbury, MD-DE | 381,281 |
| 69 | Salt Lake City, UT | 1,123,286 |
| NA | San Angelo, TX** | NA |
| 38 | San Antonio, TX | 2,227,800 |
| 22 | San Diego, CA | 3,169,187 |
| 15 | San Francisco (greater), CA | 4,431,755 |
| 56 | San Francisco-Redwood, CA M.D. | 1,554,315 |
| 48 | San Jose, CA | 1,882,748 |
| 179 | San Luis Obispo, CA | 274,491 |
| 192 | San Rafael, CA M.D. | 257,396 |
| 181 | Santa Cruz-Watsonville, CA | 266,749 |
| 136 | Santa Maria-Santa Barbara, CA | 430,836 |
| 123 | Santa Rosa, CA | 492,642 |
| 157 | Savannah, GA | 359,371 |
| 116 | Scranton--Wilkes-Barre, PA | 564,136 |
| 20 | Seattle (greater), WA | 3,534,349 |
| 28 | Seattle-Bellevue-Everett, WA M.D. | 2,718,523 |
| 282 | Sebastian-Vero Beach, FL | 140,789 |
| 335 | Sebring, FL | 99,976 |

| RANK | METROPOLITAN AREA | POP |
|---|---|---|
| 319 | Sheboygan, WI | 115,444 |
| 307 | Sherman-Denison, TX | 123,237 |
| 130 | Shreveport-Bossier City, LA | 447,514 |
| 63 | Silver Spring-Frederick, MD M.D. | 1,238,384 |
| 241 | Sioux City, IA-NE-SD | 169,806 |
| 202 | Sioux Falls, SD | 235,045 |
| 163 | South Bend-Mishawaka, IN-MI | 319,561 |
| 164 | Spartanburg, SC | 318,548 |
| 119 | Spokane, WA | 535,393 |
| 214 | Springfield, IL | 211,646 |
| 106 | Springfield, MA | 627,135 |
| 131 | Springfield, MO | 440,970 |
| 285 | Springfield, OH | 137,682 |
| 259 | State College, PA | 154,973 |
| 308 | Staunton-Waynesboro, VA | 119,937 |
| 97 | Stockton-Lodi, CA | 702,670 |
| NA | St. Cloud, MN** | NA |
| 278 | St. George, UT | 143,580 |
| 301 | St. Joseph, MO-KS | 127,840 |
| 26 | St. Louis, MO-IL | 2,798,017 |
| 326 | Sumter, SC | 108,482 |
| 101 | Syracuse, NY | 666,129 |
| 87 | Tacoma, WA M.D. | 815,826 |
| 155 | Tallahassee, FL | 374,804 |
| 24 | Tampa-St Petersburg, FL | 2,863,265 |
| 238 | Terre Haute, IN | 173,204 |
| 268 | Texarkana, TX-AR | 151,153 |
| 337 | The Villages, FL | 99,090 |
| 111 | Toledo, OH | 608,831 |
| 199 | Topeka, KS | 235,846 |
| 156 | Trenton, NJ | 368,870 |
| 72 | Tucson, AZ | 1,000,369 |
| 73 | Tulsa, OK | 952,785 |
| 203 | Tuscaloosa, AL | 232,913 |
| 210 | Tyler, TX | 216,577 |
| 174 | Utica-Rome, NY | 300,058 |
| 142 | Vallejo-Fairfield, CA | 420,333 |
| 342 | Victoria, TX | 96,207 |
| 255 | Vineland-Bridgeton, NJ | 157,869 |
| 53 | Virginia Beach-Norfolk, VA-NC | 1,703,542 |
| 129 | Visalia-Porterville, CA | 453,419 |
| 188 | Waco, TX | 260,350 |
| 230 | Warner Robins, GA | 185,441 |
| 33 | Warren-Troy, MI M.D. | 2,485,540 |
| 10 | Washington (greater) DC-VA-MD-WV | 5,826,080 |
| 14 | Washington, DC-VA-MD-WV M.D. | 4,587,696 |
| 312 | Watertown-Fort Drum, NY | 118,546 |
| 289 | Wausau, WI | 134,744 |
| 58 | West Palm Beach, FL M.D. | 1,353,405 |
| 265 | Wichita Falls, TX | 152,511 |
| 104 | Wichita, KS | 636,615 |
| 316 | Williamsport, PA | 116,936 |
| 94 | Wilmington, DE-MD-NJ M.D. | 716,822 |
| 186 | Wilmington, NC | 262,160 |
| 294 | Winchester, VA-WV | 131,237 |
| 102 | Winston-Salem, NC | 651,110 |
| 81 | Worcester, MA-CT | 851,171 |
| 197 | Yakima, WA | 249,564 |
| 133 | York-Hanover, PA | 437,478 |
| 242 | Yuba City, CA | 169,050 |
| 221 | Yuma, AZ | 203,062 |

Source: Reported data from the F.B.I. "Crime in the United States 2012"
*Estimates as of July 2012 based on U.S. Bureau of the Census figures.
**Not available (comparable metro area not included in 2012 crime statistics).

# 86. Metropolitan Population in 2012 (continued)
## National Total = 313,873,685*

| RANK | METROPOLITAN AREA | POP | RANK | METROPOLITAN AREA | POP | RANK | METROPOLITAN AREA | POP |
|---|---|---|---|---|---|---|---|---|
| 1 | New York (greater), NY-NJ-PA | 19,791,750 | 65 | New Orleans, LA | 1,220,047 | 129 | Visalia-Porterville, CA | 453,419 |
| 2 | New York-Jersey City, NY-NJ M.D. | 14,043,153 | 66 | Raleigh, NC | 1,175,043 | 130 | Shreveport-Bossier City, LA | 447,514 |
| 3 | Los Angeles (greater), CA | 13,064,838 | 67 | Buffalo-Niagara Falls, NY | 1,140,160 | 131 | Springfield, MO | 440,970 |
| 4 | Los Angeles County, CA M.D. | 9,980,757 | 68 | Birmingham-Hoover, AL | 1,136,805 | 132 | Corpus Christi, TX | 437,841 |
| 5 | Chicago (greater), IL-IN-WI | 9,511,421 | 69 | Salt Lake City, UT | 1,123,286 | 133 | York-Hanover, PA | 437,478 |
| 6 | Chicago-Naperville, IL M.D. | 7,300,952 | 70 | Rochester, NY | 1,086,565 | 134 | Reno, NV | 435,223 |
| 7 | Dallas (greater), TX | 6,680,025 | 71 | Hartford, CT | 1,023,883 | 135 | Port St. Lucie, FL | 433,712 |
| 8 | Houston, TX | 6,150,496 | 72 | Tucson, AZ | 1,000,369 | 136 | Santa Maria-Santa Barbara, CA | 430,836 |
| 9 | Philadelphia (greater) PA-NJ-MD-DE | 6,012,363 | 73 | Tulsa, OK | 952,785 | 137 | Huntsville, AL | 427,189 |
| 10 | Washington (greater) DC-VA-MD-WV | 5,826,080 | 74 | Fresno, CA | 951,648 | 138 | Salinas, CA | 425,810 |
| 11 | Miami (greater), FL | 5,747,489 | 75 | Bridgeport-Stamford, CT | 910,707 | 139 | Flint, MI | 422,387 |
| 12 | Atlanta, GA | 5,434,540 | 76 | Albuquerque, NM | 900,072 | 140 | Rockingham County, NH M.D. | 420,868 |
| 13 | Boston (greater), MA-NH | 4,629,025 | 77 | Omaha-Council Bluffs, NE-IA | 882,865 | 141 | Fort Wayne, IN | 420,767 |
| 14 | Washington, DC-VA-MD-WV M.D. | 4,587,696 | 78 | Albany-Schenectady-Troy, NY | 876,182 | 142 | Vallejo-Fairfield, CA | 420,333 |
| 15 | San Francisco (greater), CA | 4,431,755 | 79 | Lake Co.-Kenosha Co., IL-WI M.D. | 874,273 | 143 | Brownsville-Harlingen, TX | 420,325 |
| 16 | Dallas-Plano-Irving, TX M.D. | 4,405,585 | 80 | Bakersfield, CA | 859,608 | 144 | Mobile, AL | 414,233 |
| 17 | Riverside-San Bernardino, CA | 4,344,917 | 81 | Worcester, MA-CT | 851,171 | 145 | Reading, PA | 413,447 |
| 18 | Phoenix-Mesa-Scottsdale, AZ | 4,309,766 | 82 | Knoxville, TN | 850,421 | 146 | Beaumont-Port Arthur, TX | 411,053 |
| 19 | Detroit (greater), MI | 4,288,943 | 83 | Greenville-Anderson, SC | 843,836 | 147 | Canton, OH | 403,843 |
| 20 | Seattle (greater), WA | 3,534,349 | 84 | Oxnard-Thousand Oaks, CA | 839,484 | 148 | Manchester-Nashua, NH | 402,466 |
| 21 | Minneapolis-St. Paul, MN-WI | 3,408,532 | 85 | El Paso, TX | 836,557 | 149 | Dutchess-Putnam, NY M.D. | 400,079 |
| 22 | San Diego, CA | 3,169,187 | 86 | Allentown, PA-NJ | 826,611 | 150 | Salem, OR | 397,669 |
| 23 | Anaheim-Santa Ana-Irvine, CA M.D. | 3,084,081 | 87 | Tacoma, WA M.D. | 815,826 | 151 | Davenport, IA-IL | 382,090 |
| 24 | Tampa-St Petersburg, FL | 2,863,265 | 88 | Baton Rouge, LA | 813,022 | 152 | Salisbury, MD-DE | 381,281 |
| 25 | Nassau-Suffolk, NY M.D. | 2,858,599 | 89 | New Haven-Milford, CT | 809,772 | 153 | Peoria, IL | 379,733 |
| 26 | St. Louis, MO-IL | 2,798,017 | 90 | McAllen-Edinburg-Mission, TX | 809,759 | 154 | Fayetteville, NC | 377,864 |
| 27 | Baltimore, MD | 2,755,459 | 91 | Dayton, OH | 803,255 | 155 | Tallahassee, FL | 374,804 |
| 28 | Seattle-Bellevue-Everett, WA M.D. | 2,718,523 | 92 | Greensboro-High Point, NC | 738,208 | 156 | Trenton, NJ | 368,870 |
| 29 | Denver-Aurora, CO | 2,635,467 | 93 | North Port-Sarasota-Bradenton, FL | 719,034 | 157 | Savannah, GA | 359,371 |
| 30 | Oakland-Hayward, CA M.D. | 2,620,044 | 94 | Wilmington, DE-MD-NJ M.D. | 716,822 | 158 | Eugene, OR | 355,926 |
| 31 | Miami-Dade County, FL M.D. | 2,589,623 | 95 | Little Rock, AR | 712,592 | 159 | Rockford, IL | 348,522 |
| 32 | Newark, NJ-PA M.D. | 2,489,919 | 96 | Gary, IN M.D. | 710,891 | 160 | Ann Arbor, MI | 348,215 |
| 33 | Warren-Troy, MI M.D. | 2,485,540 | 97 | Stockton-Lodi, CA | 702,670 | 161 | Ocala, FL | 337,066 |
| 34 | Pittsburgh, PA | 2,363,571 | 98 | Akron, OH | 701,412 | 162 | Naples-Marco Island, FL | 332,611 |
| 35 | Cambridge-Newton, MA M.D. | 2,287,271 | 99 | Charleston-North Charleston, SC | 688,607 | 163 | South Bend-Mishawaka, IN-MI | 319,561 |
| 36 | Portland-Vancouver, OR-WA | 2,279,873 | 100 | Colorado Springs, CO | 669,453 | 164 | Spartanburg, SC | 318,548 |
| 37 | Fort Worth-Arlington, TX M.D. | 2,274,440 | 101 | Syracuse, NY | 666,129 | 165 | Anchorage, AK | 313,529 |
| 38 | San Antonio, TX | 2,227,800 | 102 | Winston-Salem, NC | 651,110 | 166 | Kingsport, TN-VA | 312,616 |
| 39 | Orlando, FL | 2,200,987 | 103 | Cape Coral-Fort Myers, FL | 639,944 | 167 | Roanoke, VA | 312,265 |
| 40 | Sacramento, CA | 2,196,416 | 104 | Wichita, KS | 636,615 | 168 | Green Bay, WI | 310,262 |
| 41 | Philadelphia, PA M.D. | 2,144,972 | 105 | Boise City, ID | 631,917 | 169 | Fort Collins, CO | 309,752 |
| 42 | Cincinnati, OH-KY-IN | 2,123,695 | 106 | Springfield, MA | 627,135 | 170 | Lincoln, NE | 308,646 |
| 43 | Kansas City, MO-KS | 2,033,239 | 107 | Elgin, IL M.D. | 625,305 | 171 | Columbus, GA-AL | 304,291 |
| 44 | Las Vegas-Henderson, NV | 1,995,735 | 108 | Lakeland, FL | 617,808 | 172 | Boulder, CO | 303,520 |
| 45 | Boston, MA M.D. | 1,920,886 | 109 | Madison, WI | 614,928 | 173 | Lubbock, TX | 300,321 |
| 46 | Indianapolis, IN | 1,915,784 | 110 | Ogden-Clearfield, UT | 614,396 | 174 | Utica-Rome, NY | 300,058 |
| 47 | Montgomery County, PA M.D. | 1,892,483 | 111 | Toledo, OH | 608,831 | 175 | Fort Smith, AR-OK | 283,329 |
| 48 | San Jose, CA | 1,882,748 | 112 | Deltona-Daytona Beach, FL | 600,260 | 176 | Erie, PA | 281,440 |
| 49 | Austin-Round Rock, TX | 1,810,230 | 113 | Des Moines-West Des Moines, IA | 582,506 | 177 | Duluth, MN-WI | 281,439 |
| 50 | Fort Lauderdale, FL M.D. | 1,804,461 | 114 | Augusta, GA-SC | 575,582 | 178 | Atlantic City, NJ | 275,689 |
| 51 | Detroit-Dearborn-Livonia, MI M.D. | 1,803,403 | 115 | Jackson, MS | 574,517 | 179 | San Luis Obispo, CA | 274,491 |
| 52 | Nashville-Davidson, TN | 1,712,682 | 116 | Scranton--Wilkes-Barre, PA | 564,136 | 180 | Gainesville, FL | 270,003 |
| 53 | Virginia Beach-Norfolk, VA-NC | 1,703,542 | 117 | Palm Bay-Melbourne, FL | 550,983 | 181 | Santa Cruz-Watsonville, CA | 266,749 |
| 54 | Providence-Warwick, RI-MA | 1,604,098 | 118 | Provo-Orem, UT | 548,142 | 182 | Kennewick-Richland, WA | 266,723 |
| 55 | Milwaukee, WI | 1,566,214 | 119 | Spokane, WA | 535,393 | 183 | Clarksville, TN-KY | 266,196 |
| 56 | San Francisco-Redwood, CA M.D. | 1,554,315 | 120 | Lancaster, PA | 524,442 | 184 | Merced, CA | 262,308 |
| 57 | Jacksonville, FL | 1,378,810 | 121 | Modesto, CA | 523,330 | 185 | Greeley, CO | 262,216 |
| 58 | West Palm Beach, FL M.D. | 1,353,405 | 122 | Portland, ME | 516,198 | 186 | Wilmington, NC | 262,160 |
| 59 | Memphis, TN-MS-AR | 1,343,608 | 123 | Santa Rosa, CA | 492,642 | 187 | Cedar Rapids, IA | 261,586 |
| 60 | Oklahoma City, OK | 1,285,907 | 124 | Lexington-Fayette, KY | 480,457 | 188 | Waco, TX | 260,350 |
| 61 | Camden, NJ M.D. | 1,258,086 | 125 | Fayetteville-Springdale, AR-MO | 475,585 | 189 | Laredo, TX | 260,337 |
| 62 | Louisville, KY-IN | 1,248,616 | 126 | Lafayette, LA | 473,751 | 190 | Amarillo, TX | 259,729 |
| 63 | Silver Spring-Frederick, MD M.D. | 1,238,384 | 127 | Lansing-East Lansing, MI | 465,476 | 191 | Olympia, WA | 259,107 |
| 64 | Richmond, VA | 1,232,458 | 128 | Pensacola, FL | 459,402 | 192 | San Rafael, CA M.D. | 257,396 |

Note: All listings are for Metropolitan Statistical Areas (M.S.A.s) except for those ending with "M.D." Listings with "M.D." are Metropolitan Divisions which are smaller parts of eleven large M.S.A.s. See explanatory note at beginning of metropolitan area section.

| RANK | METROPOLITAN AREA | POP | RANK | METROPOLITAN AREA | POP | RANK | METROPOLITAN AREA | POP |
|---|---|---|---|---|---|---|---|---|
| 193 | Bremerton-Silverdale, WA | 257,130 | 255 | Vineland-Bridgeton, NJ | 157,869 | 317 | Morristown, TN | 115,676 |
| 194 | Lynchburg, VA | 256,973 | 256 | Iowa City, IA | 155,494 | 318 | Owensboro, KY | 115,625 |
| 195 | Hagerstown-Martinsburg, MD-WV | 255,387 | 257 | Alexandria, LA | 155,419 | 319 | Sheboygan, WI | 115,444 |
| 196 | Binghamton, NY | 251,424 | 258 | Hanford-Corcoran, CA | 155,191 | 320 | Brunswick, GA | 114,128 |
| 197 | Yakima, WA | 249,564 | 259 | State College, PA | 154,973 | 321 | Kankakee, IL | 113,751 |
| 198 | Crestview-Fort Walton Beach, FL | 242,539 | 260 | Burlington, NC | 154,810 | 322 | Lawrence, KS | 112,784 |
| 199 | Topeka, KS | 235,846 | 261 | Decatur, AL | 154,689 | 323 | Missoula, MT | 110,904 |
| 200 | Macon, GA | 235,405 | 262 | Madera, CA | 154,343 | 324 | Decatur, IL | 110,782 |
| 201 | College Station-Bryan, TX | 235,092 | 263 | Bangor, ME | 153,902 | 325 | California-Lexington Park, MD | 108,522 |
| 202 | Sioux Falls, SD | 235,045 | 264 | Rocky Mount, NC | 153,664 | 326 | Sumter, SC | 108,482 |
| 203 | Tuscaloosa, AL | 232,913 | 265 | Wichita Falls, TX | 152,511 | 327 | Lewiston-Auburn, ME | 107,479 |
| 204 | Champaign-Urbana, IL | 232,445 | 266 | Elizabethtown-Fort Knox, KY | 151,716 | 328 | Bay City, MI | 107,188 |
| 205 | Appleton, WI | 227,986 | 267 | Monroe, MI | 151,670 | 329 | Lima, OH | 106,087 |
| 206 | Charlottesville, VA | 223,598 | 268 | Texarkana, TX-AR | 151,153 | 330 | Gadsden, AL | 104,722 |
| 207 | Chico, CA | 222,309 | 269 | Chambersburg-Waynesboro, PA | 151,055 | 331 | Cumberland, MD-WV | 103,606 |
| 208 | Longview, TX | 219,910 | 270 | Jefferson City, MO | 150,764 | 332 | Longview, WA | 103,483 |
| 209 | Barnstable Town, MA | 217,689 | 271 | Grand Junction, CO | 149,118 | 333 | Fond du Lac, WI | 102,340 |
| 210 | Tyler, TX | 216,577 | 272 | Florence-Muscle Shoals, AL | 147,885 | 334 | Gettysburg, PA | 101,598 |
| 211 | Fargo, ND-MN | 216,055 | 273 | Midland, TX | 147,417 | 335 | Sebring, FL | 99,976 |
| 212 | Prescott, AZ | 214,201 | 274 | Dothan, AL | 147,151 | 336 | Grand Forks, ND-MN | 99,784 |
| 213 | Las Cruces, NM | 213,938 | 275 | Norwich-New London, CT | 146,391 | 337 | The Villages, FL | 99,090 |
| 214 | Springfield, IL | 211,646 | 276 | Dalton, GA | 144,264 | 338 | Mankato-North Mankato, MN | 97,827 |
| 215 | Rochester, MN | 209,826 | 277 | Johnstown, PA | 143,961 | 339 | Cape Girardeau, MO-IL | 97,195 |
| 216 | Houma, LA | 209,817 | 278 | St. George, UT | 143,580 | 340 | Ocean City, NJ | 97,077 |
| 217 | Florence, SC | 208,121 | 279 | Odessa, TX | 142,209 | 341 | Rome, GA | 97,013 |
| 218 | Medford, OR | 206,276 | 280 | Coeur d'Alene, ID | 142,089 | 342 | Victoria, TX | 96,207 |
| 219 | Lake Havasu City-Kingman, AZ | 204,559 | 281 | Homosassa Springs, FL | 141,942 | 343 | Manhattan, KS | 95,402 |
| 220 | Lafayette, IN | 204,246 | 282 | Sebastian-Vero Beach, FL | 140,789 | 344 | Dubuque, IA | 95,015 |
| 221 | Yuma, AZ | 203,062 | 283 | Napa, CA | 139,368 | 345 | Cheyenne, WY | 94,026 |
| 222 | Johnson City, TN | 201,468 | 284 | Rapid City, SD | 138,237 | 346 | Parkersburg-Vienna, WV | 92,884 |
| 223 | Saginaw, MI | 199,233 | 285 | Springfield, OH | 137,682 | 347 | Ames, IA | 90,011 |
| 224 | Racine, WI | 195,888 | 286 | Flagstaff, AZ | 135,979 | 348 | Elmira, NY | 89,320 |
| 225 | Athens-Clarke County, GA | 195,380 | 287 | Idaho Falls, ID | 135,809 | 349 | Corvallis, OR | 86,538 |
| 226 | Hilton Head Island, SC | 191,685 | 288 | La Crosse, WI-MN | 134,905 | 350 | Bloomsburg-Berwick, PA | 85,911 |
| 227 | Panama City, FL | 188,234 | 289 | Wausau, WI | 134,744 | 351 | Pocatello, ID | 84,258 |
| 228 | Daphne-Fairhope-Foley, AL | 187,467 | 290 | Lebanon, PA | 134,529 | 352 | Grand Island, NE | 83,197 |
| 229 | Bloomington, IL | 187,221 | 291 | Lawton, OK | 132,806 | 353 | Kokomo, IN | 83,059 |
| 230 | Warner Robins, GA | 185,441 | 292 | Morgantown, WV | 132,255 | 354 | Great Falls, MT | 82,406 |
| 231 | Gainesville, GA | 185,005 | 293 | Pittsfield, MA | 131,619 | 355 | Hinesville, GA | 81,447 |
| 232 | Kingston, NY | 183,433 | 294 | Winchester, VA-WV | 131,237 | 356 | Columbus, IN | 78,114 |
| 233 | Blacksburg, VA | 179,827 | 295 | Jackson, TN | 131,023 | 357 | Casper, WY | 77,475 |
| 234 | Redding, CA | 179,423 | 296 | Glens Falls, NY | 129,692 | 358 | Lewiston, ID-WA | 61,959 |
| 235 | Monroe, LA | 178,701 | 297 | New Bern, NC | 129,271 | 359 | Carson City, NV | 56,164 |
| 236 | El Centro, CA | 178,699 | 298 | Logan, UT-ID | 129,186 | 360 | Fairbanks, AK | 34,603 |
| 237 | Joplin, MO | 177,182 | 299 | Farmington, NM | 128,404 | NA | Bend, OR** | NA |
| 238 | Terre Haute, IN | 173,204 | 300 | Harrisonburg, VA | 127,957 | NA | Carbondale-Marion, IL** | NA |
| 239 | Greenville, NC | 172,830 | 301 | St. Joseph, MO-KS | 127,840 | NA | Charlotte-Mecklenburg, NC-SC** | NA |
| 240 | East Stroudsburg, PA | 170,157 | 302 | Altoona, PA | 127,305 | NA | Chattanooga, TN-GA** | NA |
| 241 | Sioux City, IA-NE-SD | 169,806 | 303 | Goldsboro, NC | 124,923 | NA | Columbia, SC** | NA |
| 242 | Yuba City, CA | 169,050 | 304 | Mansfield, OH | 123,502 | NA | Eau Claire, WI** | NA |
| 243 | Abilene, TX | 168,908 | 305 | Hammond, LA | 123,296 | NA | Grand Rapids-Wyoming, MI** | NA |
| 244 | Oshkosh-Neenah, WI | 168,129 | 306 | Jonesboro, AR | 123,295 | NA | Grants Pass, OR** | NA |
| 245 | Dover, DE | 166,643 | 307 | Sherman-Denison, TX | 123,237 | NA | Gulfport-Biloxi-Pascagoula, MS** | NA |
| 246 | Columbia, MO | 165,938 | 308 | Staunton-Waynesboro, VA | 119,937 | NA | Hot Springs, AR** | NA |
| 247 | Pueblo, CO | 162,766 | 309 | Bismarck, ND | 119,673 | NA | Jackson, MI** | NA |
| 248 | Punta Gorda, FL | 162,701 | 310 | Mount Vernon-Anacortes, WA | 119,267 | NA | Lake Charles, LA** | NA |
| 249 | Billings, MT | 162,082 | 311 | Albany, OR | 118,961 | NA | Muskegon, MI** | NA |
| 250 | Bloomington, IN | 161,803 | 312 | Watertown-Fort Drum, NY | 118,546 | NA | Myrtle Beach, SC-NC** | NA |
| 251 | Bowling Green, KY | 160,980 | 313 | Anniston-Oxford, AL | 118,270 | NA | Niles-Benton Harbor, MI** | NA |
| 252 | Janesville, WI | 160,502 | 314 | Muncie, IN | 118,029 | NA | San Angelo, TX** | NA |
| 253 | Albany, GA | 159,370 | 315 | Cleveland, TN | 117,799 | NA | St. Cloud, MN** | NA |
| 254 | Kahului-Wailuku-Lahaina, HI | 158,760 | 316 | Williamsport, PA | 116,936 | | | |

Source: Reported data from the F.B.I. "Crime in the United States 2013"
*Estimates as of July 2012 based on U.S. Bureau of the Census figures.
**Not available (comparable metro area not included in 2012 crime statistics).

# 87. Metropolitan Population in 2009
## National Total = 307,006,550*

| RANK | METROPOLITAN AREA | POP | RANK | METROPOLITAN AREA | POP | RANK | METROPOLITAN AREA | POP |
|---|---|---|---|---|---|---|---|---|
| 226 | Abilene, TX | 159,632 | 314 | Cheyenne, WY | 89,355 | NA | Gary, IN M.D.** | NA |
| 88 | Akron, OH | 700,932 | NA | Chicago (greater), IL-IN-WI** | NA | NA | Gettysburg, PA** | NA |
| 71 | Albany-Schenectady-Troy, NY | 856,725 | NA | Chicago-Naperville, IL M.D.** | NA | 264 | Glens Falls, NY | 129,238 |
| 218 | Albany, GA | 165,165 | 187 | Chico, CA | 221,473 | 287 | Goldsboro, NC | 113,890 |
| NA | Albany, OR** | NA | 32 | Cincinnati, OH-KY-IN | 2,178,158 | 308 | Grand Forks, ND-MN | 97,848 |
| 70 | Albuquerque, NM | 862,190 | 168 | Clarksville, TN-KY | 265,303 | NA | Grand Island, NE** | NA |
| 231 | Alexandria, LA | 154,999 | 289 | Cleveland, TN | 113,409 | 243 | Grand Junction, CO | 146,602 |
| 74 | Allentown, PA-NJ | 817,689 | 249 | Coeur d'Alene, ID | 140,410 | 81 | Grand Rapids-Wyoming, MI | 777,531 |
| 269 | Altoona, PA | 125,069 | 189 | College Station-Bryan, TX | 210,281 | NA | Grants Pass, OR** | NA |
| 176 | Amarillo, TX | 246,040 | 96 | Colorado Springs, CO | 628,075 | 318 | Great Falls, MT | 82,193 |
| 317 | Ames, IA | 87,399 | 216 | Columbia, MO | 166,465 | 170 | Greeley, CO | 259,011 |
| 19 | Anaheim-Santa Ana-Irvine, CA M.D. | 3,017,883 | 84 | Columbia, SC | 741,623 | 153 | Green Bay, WI | 305,045 |
| 152 | Anchorage, AK | 305,284 | 160 | Columbus, GA-AL | 287,607 | 85 | Greensboro-High Point, NC | 713,890 |
| 145 | Ann Arbor, MI | 348,606 | 320 | Columbus, IN | 75,902 | NA | Greenville-Anderson, SC** | NA |
| 286 | Anniston-Oxford, AL | 114,155 | 127 | Corpus Christi, TX | 417,198 | NA | Greenville, NC** | NA |
| 186 | Appleton, WI | 221,608 | 319 | Corvallis, OR | 82,116 | NA | Gulfport-Biloxi-Pascagoula, MS** | NA |
| 206 | Athens-Clarke County, GA | 191,096 | 213 | Crestview-Fort Walton Beach, FL | 179,103 | 166 | Hagerstown-Martinsburg, MD-WV | 269,769 |
| 8 | Atlanta, GA | 5,494,398 | 306 | Cumberland, MD-WV | 99,133 | NA | Hammond, LA** | NA |
| 165 | Atlantic City, NJ | 272,593 | 4 | Dallas (greater), TX | 6,449,790 | NA | Hanford-Corcoran, CA** | NA |
| 108 | Augusta, GA-SC | 537,765 | 13 | Dallas-Plano-Irving, TX M.D. | 4,330,070 | 276 | Harrisonburg, VA | 120,036 |
| 47 | Austin-Round Rock, TX | 1,705,541 | 255 | Dalton, GA | 135,102 | 66 | Hartford, CT | 1,007,503 |
| 75 | Bakersfield, CA | 814,516 | NA | Daphne-Fairhope-Foley, AL** | NA | NA | Hilton Head Island, SC** | NA |
| 24 | Baltimore, MD | 2,693,099 | NA | Davenport, IA-IL** | NA | 322 | Hinesville, GA | 69,456 |
| 239 | Bangor, ME | 148,774 | 73 | Dayton, OH | 837,876 | NA | Homosassa Springs, FL** | NA |
| 185 | Barnstable Town, MA | 224,302 | 235 | Decatur, AL | 151,260 | 307 | Hot Springs, AR | 98,925 |
| 80 | Baton Rouge, LA | 787,715 | 295 | Decatur, IL | 107,232 | 194 | Houma, LA | 203,180 |
| 298 | Bay City, MI | 106,777 | 113 | Deltona-Daytona Beach, FL | 499,859 | 6 | Houston, TX | 5,858,967 |
| 140 | Beaumont-Port Arthur, TX | 377,984 | 26 | Denver-Aurora, CO | 2,550,871 | 136 | Huntsville, AL | 403,661 |
| 220 | Bend, OR | 163,637 | 102 | Des Moines-West Des Moines, IA | 564,422 | 270 | Idaho Falls, ID | 125,056 |
| 232 | Billings, MT | 153,443 | 11 | Detroit (greater), MI | 4,404,383 | 46 | Indianapolis, IN | 1,742,101 |
| 177 | Binghamton, NY | 244,367 | 39 | Detroit-Dearborn-Livonia, MI M.D. | 1,930,388 | 234 | Iowa City, IA | 151,283 |
| 60 | Birmingham-Hoover, AL | 1,130,745 | 248 | Dothan, AL | 142,752 | 51 | Jacksonville, FL | 1,324,985 |
| 297 | Bismarck, ND | 106,952 | 227 | Dover, DE | 159,218 | 225 | Jackson, MI | 159,695 |
| 224 | Blacksburg, VA | 159,705 | 313 | Dubuque, IA | 92,984 | 105 | Jackson, MS | 542,259 |
| NA | Bloomington, IL** | NA | 163 | Duluth, MN-WI | 274,899 | 288 | Jackson, TN | 113,615 |
| 210 | Bloomington, IN | 185,191 | NA | Dutchess-Putnam, NY M.D.** | NA | 222 | Janesville, WI | 161,011 |
| NA | Bloomsburg-Berwick, PA** | NA | NA | East Stroudsburg, PA** | NA | 240 | Jefferson City, MO | 147,055 |
| 97 | Boise City, ID | 614,020 | 223 | Eau Claire, WI | 159,822 | 201 | Johnson City, TN | 198,071 |
| 10 | Boston (greater), MA-NH | 4,586,485 | 217 | El Centro, CA | 165,988 | NA | Johnstown, PA** | NA |
| 40 | Boston, MA M.D. | 1,912,393 | 82 | El Paso, TX | 749,958 | 280 | Jonesboro, AR | 118,932 |
| 157 | Boulder, CO | 296,153 | NA | Elgin, IL M.D.** | NA | NA | Joplin, MO** | NA |
| 278 | Bowling Green, KY | 119,746 | 291 | Elizabethtown-Fort Knox, KY | 112,967 | NA | Kahului-Wailuku-Lahaina, HI** | NA |
| 180 | Bremerton-Silverdale, WA | 242,027 | 316 | Elmira, NY | 87,431 | NA | Kankakee, IL** | NA |
| 69 | Bridgeport-Stamford, CT | 878,051 | 162 | Erie, PA | 279,714 | 38 | Kansas City, MO-KS | 2,060,705 |
| 137 | Brownsville-Harlingen, TX | 399,958 | 146 | Eugene, OR | 348,528 | 178 | Kennewick-Richland, WA | 242,824 |
| 302 | Brunswick, GA | 103,525 | 325 | Fairbanks, AK | 38,034 | 151 | Kingsport, TN-VA | 306,401 |
| 63 | Buffalo-Niagara Falls, NY | 1,119,104 | 198 | Fargo, ND-MN | 199,348 | 211 | Kingston, NY | 182,041 |
| 237 | Burlington, NC | 150,252 | 273 | Farmington, NM | 123,809 | 87 | Knoxville, TN | 702,038 |
| NA | California-Lexington Park, MD** | NA | 118 | Fayetteville-Springdale, AR-MO | 457,820 | 305 | Kokomo, IN | 99,224 |
| NA | Cambridge-Newton, MA M.D.** | NA | 142 | Fayetteville, NC | 358,986 | 259 | La Crosse, WI-MN | 132,407 |
| 54 | Camden, NJ M.D. | 1,257,180 | 265 | Flagstaff, AZ | 128,458 | 204 | Lafayette, IN | 194,848 |
| NA | Canton, OH** | NA | 124 | Flint, MI | 426,176 | NA | Lafayette, LA** | NA |
| 99 | Cape Coral-Fort Myers, FL | 607,216 | 245 | Florence-Muscle Shoals, AL | 144,517 | 205 | Lake Charles, LA | 194,066 |
| 311 | Cape Girardeau, MO-IL | 93,713 | 196 | Florence, SC | 201,707 | NA | Lake Co.-Kenosha Co., IL-WI M.D.** | NA |
| NA | Carbondale-Marion, IL** | NA | 304 | Fond du Lac, WI | 99,634 | 199 | Lake Havasu City-Kingman, AZ | 199,041 |
| 324 | Carson City, NV | 54,462 | 156 | Fort Collins, CO | 298,107 | 100 | Lakeland, FL | 587,062 |
| 321 | Casper, WY | 74,856 | 45 | Fort Lauderdale, FL M.D. | 1,749,470 | 112 | Lancaster, PA | 507,174 |
| 171 | Cedar Rapids, IA | 257,120 | 158 | Fort Smith, AR-OK | 294,314 | 120 | Lansing-East Lansing, MI | 452,842 |
| NA | Chambersburg-Waynesboro, PA** | NA | 128 | Fort Wayne, IN | 414,144 | 179 | Laredo, TX | 242,446 |
| NA | Champaign-Urbana, IL** | NA | 35 | Fort Worth-Arlington, TX M.D. | 2,119,720 | 192 | Las Cruces, NM | 205,347 |
| 93 | Charleston-North Charleston, SC | 659,704 | 68 | Fresno, CA | 918,710 | 41 | Las Vegas-Henderson, NV | 1,903,935 |
| 44 | Charlotte-Mecklenburg, NC-SC | 1,752,202 | 301 | Gadsden, AL | 103,760 | 282 | Lawrence, KS | 116,602 |
| 202 | Charlottesville, VA | 197,483 | 169 | Gainesville, FL | 259,242 | 292 | Lawton, OK | 112,142 |
| 109 | Chattanooga, TN-GA | 523,787 | 207 | Gainesville, GA | 189,639 | 263 | Lebanon, PA | 130,248 |

Note: All listings are for Metropolitan Statistical Areas (M.S.A.s) except for those ending with "M.D." Listings with "M.D." are Metropolitan Divisions which are smaller parts of eleven large M.S.A.s. See explanatory note at beginning of metropolitan area section.

| RANK | METROPOLITAN AREA | POP | RANK | METROPOLITAN AREA | POP | RANK | METROPOLITAN AREA | POP |
|---|---|---|---|---|---|---|---|---|
| 296 | Lewiston-Auburn, ME | 107,004 | 72 | Omaha-Council Bluffs, NE-IA | 847,725 | 284 | Sheboygan, WI | 114,705 |
| 323 | Lewiston, ID-WA | 60,637 | 36 | Orlando, FL | 2,087,292 | 277 | Sherman-Denison, TX | 119,831 |
| 115 | Lexington-Fayette, KY | 470,843 | 221 | Oshkosh-Neenah, WI | 162,596 | 139 | Shreveport-Bossier City, LA | 393,564 |
| 299 | Lima, OH | 105,110 | 290 | Owensboro, KY | 113,253 | 58 | Silver Spring-Frederick, MD M.D. | 1,194,257 |
| 155 | Lincoln, NE | 299,461 | 77 | Oxnard-Thousand Oaks, CA | 799,696 | 247 | Sioux City, IA-NE-SD | 143,132 |
| 91 | Little Rock, AR | 685,389 | 107 | Palm Bay-Melbourne, FL | 538,696 | 181 | Sioux Falls, SD | 239,252 |
| 266 | Logan, UT-ID | 127,116 | 219 | Panama City, FL | 164,328 | 150 | South Bend-Mishawaka, IN-MI | 317,097 |
| 191 | Longview, TX | 206,197 | NA | Parkersburg-Vienna, WV** | NA | 161 | Spartanburg, SC | 285,421 |
| 303 | Longview, WA | 102,816 | 119 | Pensacola, FL | 453,889 | 116 | Spokane, WA | 470,570 |
| 3 | Los Angeles County, CA M.D. | 9,863,786 | NA | Peoria, IL** | NA | NA | Springfield, IL** | NA |
| 2 | Los Angeles (greater), CA | 12,881,669 | 5 | Philadelphia (greater) PA-NJ-MD-DE | 5,970,355 | 89 | Springfield, MA | 697,676 |
| 55 | Louisville, KY-IN | 1,256,252 | NA | Philadelphia, PA M.D.** | NA | 121 | Springfield, MO | 433,099 |
| 164 | Lubbock, TX | 273,291 | 12 | Phoenix-Mesa-Scottsdale, AZ | 4,362,725 | 250 | Springfield, OH | 139,752 |
| 175 | Lynchburg, VA | 248,706 | 30 | Pittsburgh, PA | 2,348,787 | 244 | State College, PA | 146,172 |
| 183 | Macon, GA | 230,750 | 261 | Pittsfield, MA | 131,299 | NA | Staunton-Waynesboro, VA** | NA |
| 236 | Madera, CA | 150,856 | 315 | Pocatello, ID | 88,737 | 92 | Stockton-Lodi, CA | 682,784 |
| 101 | Madison, WI | 568,019 | 129 | Port St. Lucie, FL | 410,941 | 208 | St. Cloud, MN | 189,562 |
| 135 | Manchester-Nashua, NH | 404,309 | 31 | Portland-Vancouver, OR-WA | 2,239,268 | 246 | St. George, UT | 143,274 |
| 274 | Manhattan, KS | 123,597 | 111 | Portland, ME | 515,866 | 267 | St. Joseph, MO-KS | 126,650 |
| 312 | Mankato-North Mankato, MN | 93,372 | 188 | Prescott, AZ | 218,897 | 22 | St. Louis, MO-IL | 2,829,698 |
| 271 | Mansfield, OH | 124,956 | 48 | Providence-Warwick, RI-MA | 1,607,064 | 300 | Sumter, SC | 104,675 |
| 83 | McAllen-Edinburg-Mission, TX | 746,767 | 103 | Provo-Orem, UT | 559,579 | 95 | Syracuse, NY | 642,939 |
| 195 | Medford, OR | 203,007 | 228 | Pueblo, CO | 158,754 | 76 | Tacoma, WA M.D. | 799,945 |
| 52 | Memphis, TN-MS-AR | 1,299,027 | 238 | Punta Gorda, FL | 149,640 | 143 | Tallahassee, FL | 358,382 |
| 174 | Merced, CA | 249,432 | 197 | Racine, WI | 200,613 | 23 | Tampa-St Petersburg, FL | 2,750,962 |
| 7 | Miami (greater), FL | 5,501,220 | 61 | Raleigh, NC | 1,127,897 | NA | Terre Haute, IN** | NA |
| 28 | Miami-Dade County, FL M.D. | 2,482,417 | 272 | Rapid City, SD | 123,903 | 253 | Texarkana, TX-AR | 136,443 |
| 262 | Midland, TX | 131,294 | 131 | Reading, PA | 407,999 | NA | The Villages, FL** | NA |
| 50 | Milwaukee, WI | 1,553,875 | 212 | Redding, CA | 181,512 | 94 | Toledo, OH | 649,954 |
| 18 | Minneapolis-St. Paul, MN-WI | 3,266,869 | 126 | Reno, NV | 418,246 | 184 | Topeka, KS | 230,405 |
| 294 | Missoula, MT | 108,586 | 56 | Richmond, VA | 1,245,391 | 141 | Trenton, NJ | 366,219 |
| 130 | Mobile, AL | 408,816 | 16 | Riverside-San Bernardino, CA | 4,208,217 | 65 | Tucson, AZ | 1,020,210 |
| 110 | Modesto, CA | 516,191 | 154 | Roanoke, VA | 300,340 | 67 | Tulsa, OK | 928,117 |
| NA | Monroe, LA** | NA | 209 | Rochester, MN | 185,487 | 190 | Tuscaloosa, AL | 209,255 |
| 233 | Monroe, MI | 153,073 | 64 | Rochester, NY | 1,032,945 | 193 | Tyler, TX | 204,582 |
| NA | Montgomery County, PA M.D.** | NA | NA | Rockford, IL** | NA | 159 | Utica-Rome, NY | 293,084 |
| 279 | Morgantown, WV | 119,585 | 125 | Rockingham County, NH M.D. | 422,505 | 133 | Vallejo-Fairfield, CA | 407,294 |
| 252 | Morristown, TN | 137,792 | 242 | Rocky Mount, NC | 146,985 | 283 | Victoria, TX | 114,735 |
| 275 | Mount Vernon-Anacortes, WA | 120,438 | 309 | Rome, GA | 96,145 | 230 | Vineland-Bridgeton, NJ | 157,963 |
| 285 | Muncie, IN | 114,435 | 33 | Sacramento, CA | 2,139,517 | NA | Virginia Beach-Norfolk, VA-NC** | NA |
| 214 | Muskegon, MI | 174,071 | 200 | Saginaw, MI | 198,943 | 122 | Visalia-Porterville, CA | 431,712 |
| NA | Myrtle Beach, SC-NC** | NA | 138 | Salem, OR | 396,094 | 182 | Waco, TX | 232,320 |
| 256 | Napa, CA | 133,996 | 132 | Salinas, CA | 407,403 | 254 | Warner Robins, GA | 135,248 |
| 149 | Naples-Marco Island, FL | 320,093 | NA | Salisbury, MD-DE** | NA | 29 | Warren-Troy, MI M.D. | 2,473,995 |
| 49 | Nashville-Davidson, TN | 1,584,715 | 62 | Salt Lake City, UT | 1,126,937 | 9 | Washington (greater) DC-VA-MD-WV | 5,452,184 |
| 21 | Nassau-Suffolk, NY M.D. | 2,874,918 | 293 | San Angelo, TX | 110,104 | 15 | Washington, DC-VA-MD-WV M.D. | 4,257,927 |
| NA | New Bern, NC** | NA | 37 | San Antonio, TX | 2,072,016 | NA | Watertown-Fort Drum, NY** | NA |
| 79 | New Haven-Milford, CT | 794,705 | 20 | San Diego, CA | 3,010,824 | 260 | Wausau, WI | 131,469 |
| 59 | New Orleans, LA | 1,179,206 | 14 | San Francisco (greater), CA | 4,275,475 | 53 | West Palm Beach, FL M.D. | 1,269,333 |
| 1 | New York (greater), NY-NJ-PA | 19,075,412 | 43 | San Francisco-Redwood, CA M.D. | 1,768,528 | 241 | Wichita Falls, TX | 147,018 |
| NA | New York-Jersey City, NY-NJ M.D.** | NA | 42 | San Jose, CA | 1,821,945 | 98 | Wichita, KS | 608,013 |
| 34 | Newark, NJ-PA M.D. | 2,122,829 | 167 | San Luis Obispo, CA | 266,382 | 281 | Williamsport, PA | 116,606 |
| 229 | Niles-Benton Harbor, MI | 158,501 | NA | San Rafael, CA M.D.** | NA | 86 | Wilmington, DE-MD-NJ M.D. | 702,146 |
| 90 | North Port-Sarasota-Bradenton, FL | 693,167 | 172 | Santa Cruz-Watsonville, CA | 251,964 | 144 | Wilmington, NC | 356,659 |
| 251 | Norwich-New London, CT | 138,611 | 134 | Santa Maria-Santa Barbara, CA | 404,613 | 268 | Winchester, VA-WV | 125,112 |
| 27 | Oakland-Hayward, CA M.D. | 2,506,947 | 117 | Santa Rosa, CA | 465,831 | 114 | Winston-Salem, NC | 474,159 |
| 148 | Ocala, FL | 335,426 | 147 | Savannah, GA | 337,908 | 78 | Worcester, MA-CT | 795,340 |
| 310 | Ocean City, NJ | 95,099 | 104 | Scranton--Wilkes-Barre, PA | 549,402 | NA | Yakima, WA** | NA |
| 258 | Odessa, TX | 133,400 | 17 | Seattle (greater), WA | 3,398,863 | 123 | York-Hanover, PA | 430,605 |
| 106 | Ogden-Clearfield, UT | 539,260 | 25 | Seattle-Bellevue-Everett, WA M.D. | 2,598,918 | 215 | Yuba City, CA | 167,852 |
| 57 | Oklahoma City, OK | 1,226,361 | 257 | Sebastian-Vero Beach, FL | 133,420 | 203 | Yuma, AZ | 196,196 |
| 173 | Olympia, WA | 251,133 | NA | Sebring, FL** | NA | | | |

Source: Reported data from the F.B.I. "Crime in the United States 2009"

*Estimates as of July 2009 based on U.S. Bureau of the Census figures.

**Not available (comparable metro area not included in 2009 crime statistics).

# 87. Metropolitan Population in 2009 (continued)
## National Total = 307,006,550*

| RANK | METROPOLITAN AREA | POP | RANK | METROPOLITAN AREA | POP | RANK | METROPOLITAN AREA | POP |
|---|---|---|---|---|---|---|---|---|
| 1 | New York (greater), NY-NJ-PA | 19,075,412 | 65 | Tucson, AZ | 1,020,210 | 129 | Port St. Lucie, FL | 410,941 |
| 2 | Los Angeles (greater), CA | 12,881,669 | 66 | Hartford, CT | 1,007,503 | 130 | Mobile, AL | 408,816 |
| 3 | Los Angeles County, CA M.D. | 9,863,786 | 67 | Tulsa, OK | 928,117 | 131 | Reading, PA | 407,999 |
| 4 | Dallas (greater), TX | 6,449,790 | 68 | Fresno, CA | 918,710 | 132 | Salinas, CA | 407,403 |
| 5 | Philadelphia (greater) PA-NJ-MD-DE | 5,970,355 | 69 | Bridgeport-Stamford, CT | 878,051 | 133 | Vallejo-Fairfield, CA | 407,294 |
| 6 | Houston, TX | 5,858,967 | 70 | Albuquerque, NM | 862,190 | 134 | Santa Maria-Santa Barbara, CA | 404,613 |
| 7 | Miami (greater), FL | 5,501,220 | 71 | Albany-Schenectady-Troy, NY | 856,725 | 135 | Manchester-Nashua, NH | 404,309 |
| 8 | Atlanta, GA | 5,494,398 | 72 | Omaha-Council Bluffs, NE-IA | 847,725 | 136 | Huntsville, AL | 403,661 |
| 9 | Washington (greater) DC-VA-MD-WV | 5,452,184 | 73 | Dayton, OH | 837,876 | 137 | Brownsville-Harlingen, TX | 399,958 |
| 10 | Boston (greater), MA-NH | 4,586,485 | 74 | Allentown, PA-NJ | 817,689 | 138 | Salem, OR | 396,094 |
| 11 | Detroit (greater), MI | 4,404,383 | 75 | Bakersfield, CA | 814,516 | 139 | Shreveport-Bossier City, LA | 393,564 |
| 12 | Phoenix-Mesa-Scottsdale, AZ | 4,362,725 | 76 | Tacoma, WA M.D. | 799,945 | 140 | Beaumont-Port Arthur, TX | 377,984 |
| 13 | Dallas-Plano-Irving, TX M.D. | 4,330,070 | 77 | Oxnard-Thousand Oaks, CA | 799,696 | 141 | Trenton, NJ | 366,219 |
| 14 | San Francisco (greater), CA | 4,275,475 | 78 | Worcester, MA-CT | 795,340 | 142 | Fayetteville, NC | 358,986 |
| 15 | Washington, DC-VA-MD-WV M.D. | 4,257,927 | 79 | New Haven-Milford, CT | 794,705 | 143 | Tallahassee, FL | 358,382 |
| 16 | Riverside-San Bernardino, CA | 4,208,217 | 80 | Baton Rouge, LA | 787,715 | 144 | Wilmington, NC | 356,659 |
| 17 | Seattle (greater), WA | 3,398,863 | 81 | Grand Rapids-Wyoming, MI | 777,531 | 145 | Ann Arbor, MI | 348,606 |
| 18 | Minneapolis-St. Paul, MN-WI | 3,266,869 | 82 | El Paso, TX | 749,958 | 146 | Eugene, OR | 348,528 |
| 19 | Anaheim-Santa Ana-Irvine, CA M.D. | 3,017,883 | 83 | McAllen-Edinburg-Mission, TX | 746,767 | 147 | Savannah, GA | 337,908 |
| 20 | San Diego, CA | 3,010,824 | 84 | Columbia, SC | 741,623 | 148 | Ocala, FL | 335,426 |
| 21 | Nassau-Suffolk, NY M.D. | 2,874,918 | 85 | Greensboro-High Point, NC | 713,890 | 149 | Naples-Marco Island, FL | 320,093 |
| 22 | St. Louis, MO-IL | 2,829,698 | 86 | Wilmington, DE-MD-NJ M.D. | 702,146 | 150 | South Bend-Mishawaka, IN-MI | 317,097 |
| 23 | Tampa-St Petersburg, FL | 2,750,962 | 87 | Knoxville, TN | 702,038 | 151 | Kingsport, TN-VA | 306,401 |
| 24 | Baltimore, MD | 2,693,099 | 88 | Akron, OH | 700,932 | 152 | Anchorage, AK | 305,284 |
| 25 | Seattle-Bellevue-Everett, WA M.D. | 2,598,918 | 89 | Springfield, MA | 697,676 | 153 | Green Bay, WI | 305,045 |
| 26 | Denver-Aurora, CO | 2,550,871 | 90 | North Port-Sarasota-Bradenton, FL | 693,167 | 154 | Roanoke, VA | 300,340 |
| 27 | Oakland-Hayward, CA M.D. | 2,506,947 | 91 | Little Rock, AR | 685,389 | 155 | Lincoln, NE | 299,461 |
| 28 | Miami-Dade County, FL M.D. | 2,482,417 | 92 | Stockton-Lodi, CA | 682,784 | 156 | Fort Collins, CO | 298,101 |
| 29 | Warren-Troy, MI M.D. | 2,473,995 | 93 | Charleston-North Charleston, SC | 659,704 | 157 | Boulder, CO | 296,153 |
| 30 | Pittsburgh, PA | 2,348,787 | 94 | Toledo, OH | 649,954 | 158 | Fort Smith, AR-OK | 294,314 |
| 31 | Portland-Vancouver, OR-WA | 2,239,268 | 95 | Syracuse, NY | 642,939 | 159 | Utica-Rome, NY | 293,084 |
| 32 | Cincinnati, OH-KY-IN | 2,178,158 | 96 | Colorado Springs, CO | 628,075 | 160 | Columbus, GA-AL | 287,607 |
| 33 | Sacramento, CA | 2,139,517 | 97 | Boise City, ID | 614,020 | 161 | Spartanburg, SC | 285,421 |
| 34 | Newark, NJ-PA M.D. | 2,122,829 | 98 | Wichita, KS | 608,013 | 162 | Erie, PA | 279,714 |
| 35 | Fort Worth-Arlington, TX M.D. | 2,119,720 | 99 | Cape Coral-Fort Myers, FL | 607,216 | 163 | Duluth, MN-WI | 274,899 |
| 36 | Orlando, FL | 2,087,292 | 100 | Lakeland, FL | 587,062 | 164 | Lubbock, TX | 273,291 |
| 37 | San Antonio, TX | 2,072,016 | 101 | Madison, WI | 568,019 | 165 | Atlantic City, NJ | 272,593 |
| 38 | Kansas City, MO-KS | 2,060,705 | 102 | Des Moines-West Des Moines, IA | 564,422 | 166 | Hagerstown-Martinsburg, MD-WV | 269,769 |
| 39 | Detroit-Dearborn-Livonia, MI M.D. | 1,930,388 | 103 | Provo-Orem, UT | 559,579 | 167 | San Luis Obispo, CA | 266,382 |
| 40 | Boston, MA M.D. | 1,912,393 | 104 | Scranton--Wilkes-Barre, PA | 549,402 | 168 | Clarksville, TN-KY | 265,303 |
| 41 | Las Vegas-Henderson, NV | 1,903,935 | 105 | Jackson, MS | 542,259 | 169 | Gainesville, FL | 259,242 |
| 42 | San Jose, CA | 1,821,945 | 106 | Ogden-Clearfield, UT | 539,260 | 170 | Greeley, CO | 259,011 |
| 43 | San Francisco-Redwood, CA M.D. | 1,768,528 | 107 | Palm Bay-Melbourne, FL | 538,696 | 171 | Cedar Rapids, IA | 257,120 |
| 44 | Charlotte-Mecklenburg, NC-SC | 1,752,202 | 108 | Augusta, GA-SC | 537,765 | 172 | Santa Cruz-Watsonville, CA | 251,964 |
| 45 | Fort Lauderdale, FL M.D. | 1,749,470 | 109 | Chattanooga, TN-GA | 523,787 | 173 | Olympia, WA | 251,133 |
| 46 | Indianapolis, IN | 1,742,101 | 110 | Modesto, CA | 516,191 | 174 | Merced, CA | 249,432 |
| 47 | Austin-Round Rock, TX | 1,705,541 | 111 | Portland, ME | 515,866 | 175 | Lynchburg, VA | 248,706 |
| 48 | Providence-Warwick, RI-MA | 1,607,064 | 112 | Lancaster, PA | 507,174 | 176 | Amarillo, TX | 246,040 |
| 49 | Nashville-Davidson, TN | 1,584,715 | 113 | Deltona-Daytona Beach, FL | 499,859 | 177 | Binghamton, NY | 244,367 |
| 50 | Milwaukee, WI | 1,553,875 | 114 | Winston-Salem, NC | 474,159 | 178 | Kennewick-Richland, WA | 242,824 |
| 51 | Jacksonville, FL | 1,324,985 | 115 | Lexington-Fayette, KY | 470,843 | 179 | Laredo, TX | 242,446 |
| 52 | Memphis, TN-MS-AR | 1,299,027 | 116 | Spokane, WA | 470,570 | 180 | Bremerton-Silverdale, WA | 242,027 |
| 53 | West Palm Beach, FL M.D. | 1,269,333 | 117 | Santa Rosa, CA | 465,831 | 181 | Sioux Falls, SD | 239,252 |
| 54 | Camden, NJ M.D. | 1,257,180 | 118 | Fayetteville-Springdale, AR-MO | 457,820 | 182 | Waco, TX | 232,320 |
| 55 | Louisville, KY-IN | 1,256,252 | 119 | Pensacola, FL | 453,889 | 183 | Macon, GA | 230,750 |
| 56 | Richmond, VA | 1,245,391 | 120 | Lansing-East Lansing, MI | 452,842 | 184 | Topeka, KS | 230,405 |
| 57 | Oklahoma City, OK | 1,226,361 | 121 | Springfield, MO | 433,099 | 185 | Barnstable Town, MA | 224,302 |
| 58 | Silver Spring-Frederick, MD M.D. | 1,194,257 | 122 | Visalia-Porterville, CA | 431,712 | 186 | Appleton, WI | 221,608 |
| 59 | New Orleans, LA | 1,179,206 | 123 | York-Hanover, PA | 430,605 | 187 | Chico, CA | 221,473 |
| 60 | Birmingham-Hoover, AL | 1,130,745 | 124 | Flint, MI | 426,176 | 188 | Prescott, AZ | 218,897 |
| 61 | Raleigh, NC | 1,127,897 | 125 | Rockingham County, NH M.D. | 422,505 | 189 | College Station-Bryan, TX | 210,281 |
| 62 | Salt Lake City, UT | 1,126,937 | 126 | Reno, NV | 418,246 | 190 | Tuscaloosa, AL | 209,255 |
| 63 | Buffalo-Niagara Falls, NY | 1,119,104 | 127 | Corpus Christi, TX | 417,198 | 191 | Longview, TX | 206,197 |
| 64 | Rochester, NY | 1,032,945 | 128 | Fort Wayne, IN | 414,144 | 192 | Las Cruces, NM | 205,347 |

Note: All listings are for Metropolitan Statistical Areas (M.S.A.s) except for those ending with "M.D." Listings with "M.D." are Metropolitan Divisions which are smaller parts of eleven large M.S.A.s. See explanatory note at beginning of metropolitan area section.

| RANK | METROPOLITAN AREA | POP | RANK | METROPOLITAN AREA | POP | RANK | METROPOLITAN AREA | POP |
|---|---|---|---|---|---|---|---|---|
| 193 | Tyler, TX | 204,582 | 255 | Dalton, GA | 135,102 | 317 | Ames, IA | 87,399 |
| 194 | Houma, LA | 203,180 | 256 | Napa, CA | 133,996 | 318 | Great Falls, MT | 82,193 |
| 195 | Medford, OR | 203,007 | 257 | Sebastian-Vero Beach, FL | 133,420 | 319 | Corvallis, OR | 82,116 |
| 196 | Florence, SC | 201,707 | 258 | Odessa, TX | 133,400 | 320 | Columbus, IN | 75,902 |
| 197 | Racine, WI | 200,613 | 259 | La Crosse, WI-MN | 132,407 | 321 | Casper, WY | 74,856 |
| 198 | Fargo, ND-MN | 199,348 | 260 | Wausau, WI | 131,469 | 322 | Hinesville, GA | 69,456 |
| 199 | Lake Havasu City-Kingman, AZ | 199,041 | 261 | Pittsfield, MA | 131,299 | 323 | Lewiston, ID-WA | 60,637 |
| 200 | Saginaw, MI | 198,943 | 262 | Midland, TX | 131,294 | 324 | Carson City, NV | 54,462 |
| 201 | Johnson City, TN | 198,071 | 263 | Lebanon, PA | 130,248 | 325 | Fairbanks, AK | 38,034 |
| 202 | Charlottesville, VA | 197,483 | 264 | Glens Falls, NY | 129,238 | NA | Albany, OR** | NA |
| 203 | Yuma, AZ | 196,196 | 265 | Flagstaff, AZ | 128,458 | NA | Bloomington, IL** | NA |
| 204 | Lafayette, IN | 194,848 | 266 | Logan, UT-ID | 127,116 | NA | Bloomsburg-Berwick, PA** | NA |
| 205 | Lake Charles, LA | 194,066 | 267 | St. Joseph, MO-KS | 126,650 | NA | California-Lexington Park, MD** | NA |
| 206 | Athens-Clarke County, GA | 191,096 | 268 | Winchester, VA-WV | 125,112 | NA | Cambridge-Newton, MA M.D.** | NA |
| 207 | Gainesville, GA | 189,639 | 269 | Altoona, PA | 125,069 | NA | Canton, OH** | NA |
| 208 | St. Cloud, MN | 189,562 | 270 | Idaho Falls, ID | 125,056 | NA | Carbondale-Marion, IL** | NA |
| 209 | Rochester, MN | 185,487 | 271 | Mansfield, OH | 124,956 | NA | Chambersburg-Waynesboro, PA** | NA |
| 210 | Bloomington, IN | 185,191 | 272 | Rapid City, SD | 123,903 | NA | Champaign-Urbana, IL** | NA |
| 211 | Kingston, NY | 182,041 | 273 | Farmington, NM | 123,809 | NA | Chicago (greater), IL-IN-WI** | NA |
| 212 | Redding, CA | 181,512 | 274 | Manhattan, KS | 123,597 | NA | Chicago-Naperville, IL M.D.** | NA |
| 213 | Crestview-Fort Walton Beach, FL | 179,103 | 275 | Mount Vernon-Anacortes, WA | 120,438 | NA | Daphne-Fairhope-Foley, AL** | NA |
| 214 | Muskegon, MI | 174,071 | 276 | Harrisonburg, VA | 120,036 | NA | Davenport, IA-IL** | NA |
| 215 | Yuba City, CA | 167,852 | 277 | Sherman-Denison, TX | 119,831 | NA | Dutchess-Putnam, NY M.D.** | NA |
| 216 | Columbia, MO | 166,465 | 278 | Bowling Green, KY | 119,746 | NA | East Stroudsburg, PA** | NA |
| 217 | El Centro, CA | 165,988 | 279 | Morgantown, WV | 119,585 | NA | Elgin, IL M.D.** | NA |
| 218 | Albany, GA | 165,165 | 280 | Jonesboro, AR | 118,932 | NA | Gary, IN M.D.** | NA |
| 219 | Panama City, FL | 164,328 | 281 | Williamsport, PA | 116,606 | NA | Gettysburg, PA** | NA |
| 220 | Bend, OR | 163,637 | 282 | Lawrence, KS | 116,602 | NA | Grand Island, NE** | NA |
| 221 | Oshkosh-Neenah, WI | 162,596 | 283 | Victoria, TX | 114,735 | NA | Grants Pass, OR** | NA |
| 222 | Janesville, WI | 161,011 | 284 | Sheboygan, WI | 114,705 | NA | Greenville-Anderson, SC** | NA |
| 223 | Eau Claire, WI | 159,822 | 285 | Muncie, IN | 114,435 | NA | Greenville, NC** | NA |
| 224 | Blacksburg, VA | 159,705 | 286 | Anniston-Oxford, AL | 114,155 | NA | Gulfport-Biloxi-Pascagoula, MS** | NA |
| 225 | Jackson, MI | 159,695 | 287 | Goldsboro, NC | 113,890 | NA | Hammond, LA** | NA |
| 226 | Abilene, TX | 159,632 | 288 | Jackson, TN | 113,615 | NA | Hanford-Corcoran, CA** | NA |
| 227 | Dover, DE | 159,218 | 289 | Cleveland, TN | 113,409 | NA | Hilton Head Island, SC** | NA |
| 228 | Pueblo, CO | 158,754 | 290 | Owensboro, KY | 113,253 | NA | Homosassa Springs, FL** | NA |
| 229 | Niles-Benton Harbor, MI | 158,501 | 291 | Elizabethtown-Fort Knox, KY | 112,967 | NA | Johnstown, PA** | NA |
| 230 | Vineland-Bridgeton, NJ | 157,963 | 292 | Lawton, OK | 112,142 | NA | Joplin, MO** | NA |
| 231 | Alexandria, LA | 154,999 | 293 | San Angelo, TX | 110,104 | NA | Kahului-Wailuku-Lahaina, HI** | NA |
| 232 | Billings, MT | 153,443 | 294 | Missoula, MT | 108,586 | NA | Kankakee, IL** | NA |
| 233 | Monroe, MI | 153,073 | 295 | Decatur, IL | 107,232 | NA | Lafayette, LA** | NA |
| 234 | Iowa City, IA | 151,283 | 296 | Lewiston-Auburn, ME | 107,004 | NA | Lake Co.-Kenosha Co., IL-WI M.D.** | NA |
| 235 | Decatur, AL | 151,260 | 297 | Bismarck, ND | 106,952 | NA | Monroe, LA** | NA |
| 236 | Madera, CA | 150,856 | 298 | Bay City, MI | 106,777 | NA | Montgomery County, PA M.D.** | NA |
| 237 | Burlington, NC | 150,252 | 299 | Lima, OH | 105,110 | NA | Myrtle Beach, SC-NC** | NA |
| 238 | Punta Gorda, FL | 149,640 | 300 | Sumter, SC | 104,675 | NA | New Bern, NC** | NA |
| 239 | Bangor, ME | 148,774 | 301 | Gadsden, AL | 103,760 | NA | New York-Jersey City, NY-NJ M.D.** | NA |
| 240 | Jefferson City, MO | 147,055 | 302 | Brunswick, GA | 103,525 | NA | Parkersburg-Vienna, WV** | NA |
| 241 | Wichita Falls, TX | 147,018 | 303 | Longview, WA | 102,816 | NA | Peoria, IL** | NA |
| 242 | Rocky Mount, NC | 146,985 | 304 | Fond du Lac, WI | 99,634 | NA | Philadelphia, PA M.D.** | NA |
| 243 | Grand Junction, CO | 146,602 | 305 | Kokomo, IN | 99,224 | NA | Rockford, IL** | NA |
| 244 | State College, PA | 146,172 | 306 | Cumberland, MD-WV | 99,133 | NA | Salisbury, MD-DE** | NA |
| 245 | Florence-Muscle Shoals, AL | 144,517 | 307 | Hot Springs, AR | 98,925 | NA | San Rafael, CA M.D.** | NA |
| 246 | St. George, UT | 143,274 | 308 | Grand Forks, ND-MN | 97,848 | NA | Sebring, FL** | NA |
| 247 | Sioux City, IA-NE-SD | 143,132 | 309 | Rome, GA | 96,145 | NA | Springfield, IL** | NA |
| 248 | Dothan, AL | 142,752 | 310 | Ocean City, NJ | 95,099 | NA | Staunton-Waynesboro, VA** | NA |
| 249 | Coeur d'Alene, ID | 140,410 | 311 | Cape Girardeau, MO-IL | 93,713 | NA | Terre Haute, IN** | NA |
| 250 | Springfield, OH | 139,752 | 312 | Mankato-North Mankato, MN | 93,372 | NA | The Villages, FL** | NA |
| 251 | Norwich-New London, CT | 138,611 | 313 | Dubuque, IA | 92,984 | NA | Virginia Beach-Norfolk, VA-NC** | NA |
| 252 | Morristown, TN | 137,792 | 314 | Cheyenne, WY | 89,355 | NA | Watertown-Fort Drum, NY** | NA |
| 253 | Texarkana, TX-AR | 136,443 | 315 | Pocatello, ID | 88,737 | NA | Yakima, WA** | NA |
| 254 | Warner Robins, GA | 135,248 | 316 | Elmira, NY | 87,431 | | | |

Source: Reported data from the F.B.I. "Crime in the United States 2009"

*Estimates as of July 2009 based on U.S. Bureau of the Census figures.

**Not available (comparable metro area not included in 2009 crime statistics).

## 88. City Population in 2013
## National Total = 316,128,839*

| RANK | CITY | POP | RANK | CITY | POP | RANK | CITY | POP |
|---|---|---|---|---|---|---|---|---|
| 217 | Abilene, TX | 119,401 | 403 | Chino, CA | 80,704 | 178 | Fullerton, CA | 139,676 |
| 115 | Akron, OH | 198,405 | 73 | Chula Vista, CA | 255,073 | 201 | Gainesville, FL | 126,589 |
| 435 | Alameda, CA | 76,206 | 375 | Cicero, IL | 84,204 | 132 | Garden Grove, CA | 175,469 |
| 427 | Albany, GA | 77,365 | 63 | Cincinnati, OH | 296,491 | 85 | Garland, TX | 235,683 |
| 298 | Albany, NY | 97,956 | 367 | Citrus Heights, CA | 85,337 | 410 | Gary, IN | 78,819 |
| 31 | Albuquerque, NM | 558,165 | 402 | Clarkstown, NY | 80,705 | 95 | Gilbert, AZ | 225,232 |
| 162 | Alexandria, VA | 148,519 | 171 | Clarksville, TN | 145,599 | 88 | Glendale, AZ | 234,006 |
| 371 | Alhambra, CA | 84,710 | 248 | Clearwater, FL | 108,908 | 119 | Glendale, CA | 195,366 |
| 218 | Allentown, PA | 119,277 | 47 | Cleveland, OH | 389,181 | 124 | Grand Prairie, TX | 183,822 |
| 334 | Allen, TX | 91,289 | 369 | Clifton, NJ | 85,022 | 120 | Grand Rapids, MI | 191,213 |
| 117 | Amarillo, TX | 196,577 | 297 | Clinton Twnshp, MI | 98,071 | 303 | Greece, NY | 96,667 |
| 220 | Amherst, NY | 118,296 | 292 | Clovis, CA | 99,483 | 308 | Greeley, CO | 96,111 |
| 53 | Anaheim, CA | 345,320 | 293 | College Station, TX | 98,919 | 264 | Green Bay, WI | 105,107 |
| 62 | Anchorage, AK | 299,455 | 416 | Colonie, NY | 78,215 | 66 | Greensboro, NC | 279,343 |
| 226 | Ann Arbor, MI | 116,799 | 40 | Colorado Springs, CO | 436,108 | 352 | Greenville, NC | 88,018 |
| 262 | Antioch, CA | 106,447 | 231 | Columbia, MO | 114,587 | 244 | Gresham, OR | 109,965 |
| 436 | Arlington Heights, IL | 75,978 | 185 | Columbia, SC | 132,240 | 345 | Hamilton Twnshp, NJ | 88,993 |
| 49 | Arlington, TX | 378,765 | 112 | Columbus, GA | 201,165 | 408 | Hammond, IN | 79,329 |
| 239 | Arvada, CO | 110,792 | 300 | Compton, CA | 97,907 | 180 | Hampton, VA | 136,949 |
| 216 | Athens-Clarke, GA | 120,122 | 206 | Concord, CA | 125,464 | 207 | Hartford, CT | 124,927 |
| 38 | Atlanta, GA | 451,020 | 383 | Concord, NC | 82,899 | 364 | Hawthorne, CA | 86,132 |
| 54 | Aurora, CO | 343,484 | 200 | Coral Springs, FL | 126,608 | 157 | Hayward, CA | 150,955 |
| 113 | Aurora, IL | 200,551 | 148 | Corona, CA | 160,159 | 395 | Hemet, CA | 81,698 |
| 12 | Austin, TX | 859,180 | 58 | Corpus Christi, TX | 314,523 | 69 | Henderson, NV | 268,237 |
| 51 | Bakersfield, CA | 361,859 | 234 | Costa Mesa, CA | 112,538 | 327 | Hesperia, CA | 92,621 |
| 432 | Baldwin Park, CA | 76,745 | 401 | Cranston, RI | 80,718 | 87 | Hialeah, FL | 234,182 |
| 27 | Baltimore, MD | 622,671 | 10 | Dallas, TX | 1,255,015 | 259 | High Point, NC | 107,261 |
| 91 | Baton Rouge, LA | 230,212 | 268 | Daly City, CA | 104,536 | 307 | Hillsboro, OR | 96,313 |
| 221 | Beaumont, TX | 118,177 | 380 | Danbury, CT | 83,363 | 169 | Hollywood, FL | 146,643 |
| 320 | Beaverton, OR | 93,551 | 280 | Davenport, IA | 101,834 | 376 | Hoover, AL | 84,139 |
| 195 | Bellevue, WA | 127,678 | 306 | Davie, FL | 96,581 | 4 | Houston, TX | 2,180,606 |
| 425 | Bellflower, CA | 77,594 | 176 | Dayton, OH | 141,167 | 118 | Huntington Beach, CA | 195,842 |
| 405 | Bend, OR | 79,926 | 310 | Dearborn, MI | 96,012 | 123 | Huntsville, AL | 184,738 |
| 227 | Berkeley, CA | 116,217 | 441 | Decatur, IL | 75,190 | 222 | Independence, MO | 117,381 |
| 442 | Bethlehem, PA | 75,135 | 417 | Deerfield Beach, FL | 78,203 | 13 | Indianapolis, IN | 850,220 |
| 255 | Billings, MT | 107,802 | 210 | Denton, TX | 123,260 | 404 | Indio, CA | 80,243 |
| 100 | Birmingham, AL | 212,001 | 22 | Denver, CO | 648,981 | 236 | Inglewood, CA | 111,672 |
| 419 | Bloomington, IL | 78,060 | 103 | Des Moines, IA | 207,391 | 83 | Irvine, CA | 235,830 |
| 391 | Bloomington, IN | 82,415 | 18 | Detroit, MI | 699,889 | 92 | Irving, TX | 228,367 |
| 359 | Bloomington, MN | 87,057 | 233 | Downey, CA | 113,222 | 14 | Jacksonville, FL | 845,745 |
| 349 | Boca Raton, FL | 88,749 | 363 | Duluth, MN | 86,211 | 131 | Jackson, MS | 176,039 |
| 97 | Boise, ID | 214,330 | 392 | Edinburg, TX | 82,271 | 72 | Jersey City, NJ | 256,886 |
| 24 | Boston, MA | 643,799 | 281 | Edison Twnshp, NJ | 101,316 | 377 | Johns Creek, GA | 84,093 |
| 274 | Boulder, CO | 102,828 | 365 | Edmond, OK | 85,974 | 163 | Joliet, IL | 148,462 |
| 440 | Brick Twnshp, NJ | 75,371 | 278 | El Cajon, CA | 102,012 | 296 | Jurupa Valley, CA | 98,090 |
| 167 | Bridgeport, CT | 147,076 | 229 | El Monte, CA | 115,591 | 165 | Kansas City, KS | 147,618 |
| 316 | Brockton, MA | 94,448 | 19 | El Paso, TX | 679,700 | 36 | Kansas City, MO | 465,514 |
| 273 | Broken Arrow, OK | 102,956 | 241 | Elgin, IL | 110,454 | 433 | Kennewick, WA | 76,508 |
| 415 | Brooklyn Park, MN | 78,353 | 199 | Elizabeth, NJ | 127,067 | 289 | Kenosha, WI | 100,418 |
| 127 | Brownsville, TX | 181,590 | 147 | Elk Grove, CA | 160,925 | 208 | Kent, WA | 124,359 |
| 413 | Bryan, TX | 78,578 | 283 | Erie, PA | 100,814 | 181 | Killeen, TX | 136,539 |
| 388 | Buena Park, CA | 82,632 | 161 | Escondido, CA | 148,650 | 126 | Knoxville, TN | 183,249 |
| 71 | Buffalo, NY | 258,789 | 150 | Eugene, OR | 158,499 | 209 | Lafayette, LA | 123,409 |
| 266 | Burbank, CA | 104,727 | 438 | Evanston, IL | 75,709 | 407 | Lake Forest, CA | 79,336 |
| 258 | Cambridge, MA | 107,282 | 214 | Evansville, IN | 120,284 | 284 | Lakeland, FL | 100,725 |
| 346 | Canton Twnshp, MI | 88,958 | 263 | Everett, WA | 105,129 | 326 | Lakewood Twnshp, NJ | 92,664 |
| 142 | Cape Coral, FL | 163,461 | 250 | Fairfield, CA | 108,425 | 399 | Lakewood, CA | 81,086 |
| 240 | Carlsbad, CA | 110,505 | 344 | Fall River, MA | 89,220 | 170 | Lakewood, CO | 146,298 |
| 370 | Carmel, IN | 84,880 | 237 | Fargo, ND | 111,101 | 149 | Lancaster, CA | 159,792 |
| 197 | Carrollton, TX | 127,459 | 400 | Farmington Hills, MI | 81,084 | 232 | Lansing, MI | 113,907 |
| 322 | Carson, CA | 93,415 | 421 | Fayetteville, AR | 77,900 | 78 | Laredo, TX | 247,353 |
| 160 | Cary, NC | 148,905 | 109 | Fayetteville, NC | 202,524 | 420 | Largo, FL | 77,913 |
| 192 | Cedar Rapids, IA | 128,642 | 325 | Federal Way, WA | 92,741 | 279 | Las Cruces, NM | 102,007 |
| 265 | Centennial, CO | 104,771 | 381 | Fishers, IN | 83,358 | 7 | Las Vegas, NV | 1,500,455 |
| 382 | Champaign, IL | 82,966 | 291 | Flint, MI | 99,941 | 339 | Lawrence, KS | 90,034 |
| 77 | Chandler, AZ | 248,718 | 106 | Fontana, CA | 203,427 | 422 | Lawrence, MA | 77,812 |
| 198 | Charleston, SC | 127,206 | 159 | Fort Collins, CO | 150,066 | 294 | Lawton, OK | 98,548 |
| 15 | Charlotte, NC | 837,638 | 134 | Fort Lauderdale, FL | 172,398 | 342 | League City, TX | 89,596 |
| 135 | Chattanooga, TN | 172,286 | 353 | Fort Smith, AR | 87,821 | 324 | Lee's Summit, MO | 92,765 |
| 414 | Cheektowaga, NY | 78,361 | 74 | Fort Wayne, IN | 254,820 | 286 | Lewisville, TX | 100,710 |
| 90 | Chesapeake, VA | 230,577 | 17 | Fort Worth, TX | 789,035 | 59 | Lexington, KY | 308,712 |
| 3 | Chicago, IL | 2,720,554 | 96 | Fremont, CA | 224,475 | 70 | Lincoln, NE | 267,565 |
| 350 | Chico, CA | 88,226 | 33 | Fresno, CA | 508,876 | 116 | Little Rock, AR | 197,399 |
| 431 | Chino Hills, CA | 76,943 | 186 | Frisco, TX | 131,769 | 374 | Livermore, CA | 84,350 |

| RANK | CITY | POP | RANK | CITY | POP | RANK | CITY | POP |
|---|---|---|---|---|---|---|---|---|
| 314 | Livonia, MI | 95,220 | 179 | Pasadena, CA | 139,003 | 312 | South Gate, CA | 95,591 |
| 35 | Long Beach, CA | 469,665 | 155 | Pasadena, TX | 153,195 | 323 | Sparks, NV | 92,768 |
| 343 | Longmont, CO | 89,434 | 172 | Paterson, NJ | 145,082 | 337 | Spokane Valley, WA | 90,835 |
| 398 | Longview, TX | 81,273 | 295 | Pearland, TX | 98,183 | 102 | Spokane, WA | 209,524 |
| 2 | Los Angeles, CA | 3,878,725 | 144 | Pembroke Pines, FL | 162,064 | 223 | Springfield, IL | 117,351 |
| 20 | Louisville, KY | 671,120 | 146 | Peoria, AZ | 161,641 | 154 | Springfield, MA | 153,586 |
| 247 | Lowell, MA | 109,449 | 228 | Peoria, IL | 115,953 | 143 | Springfield, MO | 163,062 |
| 82 | Lubbock, TX | 237,875 | 5 | Philadelphia, PA | 1,553,153 | 204 | Stamford, CT | 125,876 |
| 424 | Lynchburg, VA | 77,757 | 6 | Phoenix, AZ | 1,502,139 | 190 | Sterling Heights, MI | 130,634 |
| 331 | Lynn, MA | 91,769 | 60 | Pittsburgh, PA | 307,632 | 61 | Stockton, CA | 299,796 |
| 335 | Macon, GA | 91,177 | 68 | Plano, TX | 275,795 | 434 | St. George, UT | 76,427 |
| 81 | Madison, WI | 242,523 | 347 | Plantation, FL | 88,929 | 428 | St. Joseph, MO | 77,347 |
| 242 | Manchester, NH | 110,411 | 156 | Pomona, CA | 151,366 | 56 | St. Louis, MO | 318,563 |
| 182 | McAllen, TX | 136,169 | 271 | Pompano Beach, FL | 103,971 | 64 | St. Paul, MN | 294,690 |
| 168 | McKinney, TX | 146,869 | 138 | Port St. Lucie, FL | 169,877 | 80 | St. Petersburg, FL | 247,084 |
| 430 | Medford, OR | 76,949 | 28 | Portland, OR | 609,136 | 366 | Suffolk, VA | 85,475 |
| 429 | Melbourne, FL | 77,277 | 301 | Portsmouth, VA | 97,018 | 379 | Sugar Land, TX | 83,460 |
| 21 | Memphis, TN | 657,691 | 130 | Providence, RI | 178,887 | 164 | Sunnyvale, CA | 148,160 |
| 387 | Menifee, CA | 82,634 | 225 | Provo, UT | 116,937 | 338 | Sunrise, FL | 90,274 |
| 397 | Merced, CA | 81,329 | 253 | Pueblo, CO | 108,062 | 211 | Surprise, AZ | 122,497 |
| 393 | Meridian, ID | 82,064 | 321 | Quincy, MA | 93,490 | 175 | Syracuse, NY | 143,834 |
| 37 | Mesa, AZ | 456,155 | 418 | Racine, WI | 78,141 | 107 | Tacoma, WA | 203,226 |
| 173 | Mesquite, TX | 144,313 | 41 | Raleigh, NC | 428,993 | 122 | Tallahassee, FL | 188,714 |
| 333 | Miami Beach, FL | 91,433 | 358 | Ramapo, NY | 87,204 | 52 | Tampa, FL | 351,314 |
| 235 | Miami Gardens, FL | 111,870 | 136 | Rancho Cucamon., CA | 172,262 | 260 | Temecula, CA | 106,680 |
| 43 | Miami, FL | 418,394 | 351 | Reading, PA | 88,107 | 139 | Tempe, AZ | 168,501 |
| 212 | Midland, TX | 122,259 | 336 | Redding, CA | 91,035 | 205 | Thornton, CO | 125,775 |
| 30 | Milwaukee, WI | 600,805 | 406 | Redwood City, CA | 79,707 | 191 | Thousand Oaks, CA | 128,884 |
| 45 | Minneapolis, MN | 396,206 | 89 | Reno, NV | 232,561 | 65 | Toledo, OH | 283,035 |
| 189 | Miramar, FL | 130,926 | 305 | Renton, WA | 96,657 | 329 | Toms River Twnshp, NJ | 92,332 |
| 311 | Mission Viejo, CA | 95,895 | 275 | Rialto, CA | 102,520 | 193 | Topeka, KS | 128,009 |
| 396 | Mission, TX | 81,360 | 267 | Richardson, TX | 104,577 | 166 | Torrance, CA | 147,534 |
| 76 | Mobile, AL | 250,557 | 257 | Richmond, CA | 107,341 | 368 | Tracy, CA | 85,174 |
| 105 | Modesto, CA | 204,252 | 99 | Richmond, VA | 212,830 | 373 | Trenton, NJ | 84,439 |
| 111 | Moreno Valley, CA | 201,284 | 57 | Riverside, CA | 316,423 | 389 | Troy, MI | 82,608 |
| 426 | Mountain View, CA | 77,399 | 299 | Roanoke, VA | 97,927 | 32 | Tucson, AZ | 525,486 |
| 230 | Murfreesboro, TN | 115,587 | 246 | Rochester, MN | 109,675 | 46 | Tulsa, OK | 394,498 |
| 256 | Murrieta, CA | 107,768 | 101 | Rochester, NY | 210,562 | 318 | Tuscaloosa, AL | 94,126 |
| 372 | Nampa, ID | 84,634 | 158 | Rockford, IL | 150,209 | 409 | Tustin, CA | 78,836 |
| 412 | Napa, CA | 78,761 | 202 | Roseville, CA | 126,236 | 290 | Tyler, TX | 100,033 |
| 174 | Naperville, IL | 144,221 | 313 | Roswell, GA | 95,373 | 439 | Upland, CA | 75,640 |
| 360 | Nashua, NH | 87,052 | 249 | Round Rock, TX | 108,577 | 384 | Upper Darby Twnshp, PA | 82,771 |
| 26 | Nashville, TN | 635,673 | 34 | Sacramento, CA | 478,182 | 317 | Vacaville, CA | 94,347 |
| 315 | New Bedford, MA | 95,156 | 151 | Salem, OR | 158,234 | 219 | Vallejo, CA | 118,336 |
| 188 | New Haven, CT | 131,071 | 153 | Salinas, CA | 155,742 | 141 | Vancouver, WA | 166,535 |
| 50 | New Orleans, LA | 377,022 | 121 | Salt Lake City, UT | 190,246 | 252 | Ventura, CA | 108,204 |
| 411 | New Rochelle, NY | 78,800 | 304 | San Angelo, TX | 96,661 | 213 | Victorville, CA | 121,699 |
| 1 | New York, NY | 8,396,126 | 8 | San Antonio, TX | 1,399,725 | 39 | Virginia Beach, VA | 450,687 |
| 67 | Newark, NJ | 278,246 | 98 | San Bernardino, CA | 214,322 | 194 | Visalia, CA | 127,824 |
| 355 | Newport Beach, CA | 87,639 | 9 | San Diego, CA | 1,349,306 | 302 | Vista, CA | 96,712 |
| 128 | Newport News, VA | 181,074 | 16 | San Francisco, CA | 833,863 | 196 | Waco, TX | 127,570 |
| 361 | Newton, MA | 86,867 | 11 | San Jose, CA | 992,143 | 183 | Warren, MI | 134,167 |
| 79 | Norfolk, VA | 247,303 | 357 | San Leandro, CA | 87,490 | 394 | Warwick, RI | 81,789 |
| 224 | Norman, OK | 116,970 | 354 | San Marcos, CA | 87,712 | 23 | Washington, DC | 646,449 |
| 272 | North Charleston, SC | 103,324 | 288 | San Mateo, CA | 100,440 | 245 | Waterbury, CT | 109,763 |
| 93 | North Las Vegas, NV | 225,632 | 282 | Sandy Springs, GA | 101,180 | 348 | Waukegan, IL | 88,763 |
| 261 | Norwalk, CA | 106,518 | 341 | Sandy, UT | 89,943 | 254 | West Covina, CA | 107,867 |
| 356 | Norwalk, CT | 87,590 | 55 | Santa Ana, CA | 332,848 | 276 | West Palm Beach, FL | 102,510 |
| 44 | Oakland, CA | 403,887 | 340 | Santa Barbara, CA | 90,006 | 184 | West Valley, UT | 133,373 |
| 133 | Oceanside, CA | 172,525 | 215 | Santa Clara, CA | 120,150 | 390 | Westland, MI | 82,554 |
| 251 | Odessa, TX | 108,265 | 104 | Santa Clarita, CA | 204,951 | 330 | Westminster, CA | 91,885 |
| 386 | O'Fallon, MO | 82,672 | 277 | Santa Maria, CA | 102,051 | 243 | Westminster, CO | 110,093 |
| 378 | Ogden, UT | 84,045 | 328 | Santa Monica, CA | 92,488 | 362 | Whittier, CA | 86,450 |
| 29 | Oklahoma City, OK | 605,034 | 137 | Santa Rosa, CA | 171,564 | 269 | Wichita Falls, TX | 104,514 |
| 187 | Olathe, KS | 131,342 | 86 | Savannah, GA | 235,200 | 48 | Wichita, KS | 386,486 |
| 42 | Omaha, NE | 425,076 | 94 | Scottsdale, AZ | 225,523 | 238 | Wilmington, NC | 110,985 |
| 140 | Ontario, CA | 168,144 | 437 | Scranton, PA | 75,732 | 84 | Winston-Salem, NC | 235,811 |
| 177 | Orange, CA | 140,304 | 25 | Seattle, WA | 642,814 | 287 | Woodbridge Twnshp, NJ | 100,568 |
| 332 | Orem, UT | 91,438 | 110 | Shreveport, LA | 202,189 | 125 | Worcester, MA | 183,454 |
| 75 | Orlando, FL | 253,238 | 203 | Simi Valley, CA | 126,215 | 319 | Yakima, WA | 93,589 |
| 129 | Overland Park, KS | 180,555 | 385 | Sioux City, IA | 82,676 | 114 | Yonkers, NY | 199,134 |
| 108 | Oxnard, CA | 202,594 | 145 | Sioux Falls, SD | 161,754 | 309 | Yuma, AZ | 96,014 |
| 270 | Palm Bay, FL | 104,391 | 423 | Somerville, MA | 77,768 | | | |
| 152 | Palmdale, CA | 156,522 | 285 | South Bend, IN | 100,711 | | | |

Source: Reported data from the F.B.I. "Crime in the United States 2013"

*Estimates as of July 2013 based on U.S. Bureau of the Census figures. Charlotte, Indianapolis, Las Vegas, Louisville, Mobile, and Savannah include areas under their police department but outside the city limits. All populations are for area covered by police department.

# 88. City Population in 2013 (continued)
## National Total = 316,128,839*

| RANK | CITY | POP | RANK | CITY | POP | RANK | CITY | POP |
|---|---|---|---|---|---|---|---|---|
| 1 | New York, NY | 8,396,126 | 75 | Orlando, FL | 253,238 | 149 | Lancaster, CA | 159,792 |
| 2 | Los Angeles, CA | 3,878,725 | 76 | Mobile, AL | 250,557 | 150 | Eugene, OR | 158,499 |
| 3 | Chicago, IL | 2,720,554 | 77 | Chandler, AZ | 248,718 | 151 | Salem, OR | 158,234 |
| 4 | Houston, TX | 2,180,606 | 78 | Laredo, TX | 247,353 | 152 | Palmdale, CA | 156,522 |
| 5 | Philadelphia, PA | 1,553,153 | 79 | Norfolk, VA | 247,303 | 153 | Salinas, CA | 155,742 |
| 6 | Phoenix, AZ | 1,502,139 | 80 | St. Petersburg, FL | 247,084 | 154 | Springfield, MA | 153,586 |
| 7 | Las Vegas, NV | 1,500,455 | 81 | Madison, WI | 242,523 | 155 | Pasadena, TX | 153,195 |
| 8 | San Antonio, TX | 1,399,725 | 82 | Lubbock, TX | 237,875 | 156 | Pomona, CA | 151,366 |
| 9 | San Diego, CA | 1,349,306 | 83 | Irvine, CA | 235,830 | 157 | Hayward, CA | 150,955 |
| 10 | Dallas, TX | 1,255,015 | 84 | Winston-Salem, NC | 235,811 | 158 | Rockford, IL | 150,209 |
| 11 | San Jose, CA | 992,143 | 85 | Garland, TX | 235,683 | 159 | Fort Collins, CO | 150,066 |
| 12 | Austin, TX | 859,180 | 86 | Savannah, GA | 235,200 | 160 | Cary, NC | 148,905 |
| 13 | Indianapolis, IN | 850,220 | 87 | Hialeah, FL | 234,182 | 161 | Escondido, CA | 148,650 |
| 14 | Jacksonville, FL | 845,745 | 88 | Glendale, AZ | 234,006 | 162 | Alexandria, VA | 148,519 |
| 15 | Charlotte, NC | 837,638 | 89 | Reno, NV | 232,561 | 163 | Joliet, IL | 148,462 |
| 16 | San Francisco, CA | 833,863 | 90 | Chesapeake, VA | 230,577 | 164 | Sunnyvale, CA | 148,160 |
| 17 | Fort Worth, TX | 789,035 | 91 | Baton Rouge, LA | 230,212 | 165 | Kansas City, KS | 147,618 |
| 18 | Detroit, MI | 699,889 | 92 | Irving, TX | 228,367 | 166 | Torrance, CA | 147,534 |
| 19 | El Paso, TX | 679,700 | 93 | North Las Vegas, NV | 225,632 | 167 | Bridgeport, CT | 147,076 |
| 20 | Louisville, KY | 671,120 | 94 | Scottsdale, AZ | 225,523 | 168 | McKinney, TX | 146,869 |
| 21 | Memphis, TN | 657,691 | 95 | Gilbert, AZ | 225,232 | 169 | Hollywood, FL | 146,643 |
| 22 | Denver, CO | 648,981 | 96 | Fremont, CA | 224,475 | 170 | Lakewood, CO | 146,298 |
| 23 | Washington, DC | 646,449 | 97 | Boise, ID | 214,330 | 171 | Clarksville, TN | 145,599 |
| 24 | Boston, MA | 643,799 | 98 | San Bernardino, CA | 214,322 | 172 | Paterson, NJ | 145,082 |
| 25 | Seattle, WA | 642,814 | 99 | Richmond, VA | 212,830 | 173 | Mesquite, TX | 144,313 |
| 26 | Nashville, TN | 635,673 | 100 | Birmingham, AL | 212,001 | 174 | Naperville, IL | 144,221 |
| 27 | Baltimore, MD | 622,671 | 101 | Rochester, NY | 210,562 | 175 | Syracuse, NY | 143,834 |
| 28 | Portland, OR | 609,136 | 102 | Spokane, WA | 209,524 | 176 | Dayton, OH | 141,167 |
| 29 | Oklahoma City, OK | 605,034 | 103 | Des Moines, IA | 207,391 | 177 | Orange, CA | 140,304 |
| 30 | Milwaukee, WI | 600,805 | 104 | Santa Clarita, CA | 204,951 | 178 | Fullerton, CA | 139,676 |
| 31 | Albuquerque, NM | 558,165 | 105 | Modesto, CA | 204,252 | 179 | Pasadena, CA | 139,003 |
| 32 | Tucson, AZ | 525,486 | 106 | Fontana, CA | 203,427 | 180 | Hampton, VA | 136,949 |
| 33 | Fresno, CA | 508,876 | 107 | Tacoma, WA | 203,226 | 181 | Killeen, TX | 136,539 |
| 34 | Sacramento, CA | 478,182 | 108 | Oxnard, CA | 202,594 | 182 | McAllen, TX | 136,169 |
| 35 | Long Beach, CA | 469,665 | 109 | Fayetteville, NC | 202,524 | 183 | Warren, MI | 134,167 |
| 36 | Kansas City, MO | 465,514 | 110 | Shreveport, LA | 202,189 | 184 | West Valley, UT | 133,373 |
| 37 | Mesa, AZ | 456,155 | 111 | Moreno Valley, CA | 201,284 | 185 | Columbia, SC | 132,240 |
| 38 | Atlanta, GA | 451,020 | 112 | Columbus, GA | 201,165 | 186 | Frisco, TX | 131,769 |
| 39 | Virginia Beach, VA | 450,687 | 113 | Aurora, IL | 200,551 | 187 | Olathe, KS | 131,342 |
| 40 | Colorado Springs, CO | 436,108 | 114 | Yonkers, NY | 199,134 | 188 | New Haven, CT | 131,071 |
| 41 | Raleigh, NC | 428,993 | 115 | Akron, OH | 198,405 | 189 | Miramar, FL | 130,926 |
| 42 | Omaha, NE | 425,076 | 116 | Little Rock, AR | 197,399 | 190 | Sterling Heights, MI | 130,634 |
| 43 | Miami, FL | 418,394 | 117 | Amarillo, TX | 196,577 | 191 | Thousand Oaks, CA | 128,884 |
| 44 | Oakland, CA | 403,887 | 118 | Huntington Beach, CA | 195,842 | 192 | Cedar Rapids, IA | 128,642 |
| 45 | Minneapolis, MN | 396,206 | 119 | Glendale, CA | 195,366 | 193 | Topeka, KS | 128,009 |
| 46 | Tulsa, OK | 394,498 | 120 | Grand Rapids, MI | 191,213 | 194 | Visalia, CA | 127,824 |
| 47 | Cleveland, OH | 389,181 | 121 | Salt Lake City, UT | 190,246 | 195 | Bellevue, WA | 127,678 |
| 48 | Wichita, KS | 386,486 | 122 | Tallahassee, FL | 188,714 | 196 | Waco, TX | 127,570 |
| 49 | Arlington, TX | 378,765 | 123 | Huntsville, AL | 184,738 | 197 | Carrollton, TX | 127,459 |
| 50 | New Orleans, LA | 377,022 | 124 | Grand Prairie, TX | 183,822 | 198 | Charleston, SC | 127,206 |
| 51 | Bakersfield, CA | 361,859 | 125 | Worcester, MA | 183,454 | 199 | Elizabeth, NJ | 127,067 |
| 52 | Tampa, FL | 351,314 | 126 | Knoxville, TN | 183,249 | 200 | Coral Springs, FL | 126,608 |
| 53 | Anaheim, CA | 345,320 | 127 | Brownsville, TX | 181,590 | 201 | Gainesville, FL | 126,589 |
| 54 | Aurora, CO | 343,484 | 128 | Newport News, VA | 181,074 | 202 | Roseville, CA | 126,236 |
| 55 | Santa Ana, CA | 332,848 | 129 | Overland Park, KS | 180,555 | 203 | Simi Valley, CA | 126,215 |
| 56 | St. Louis, MO | 318,563 | 130 | Providence, RI | 178,887 | 204 | Stamford, CT | 125,876 |
| 57 | Riverside, CA | 316,423 | 131 | Jackson, MS | 176,039 | 205 | Thornton, CO | 125,775 |
| 58 | Corpus Christi, TX | 314,523 | 132 | Garden Grove, CA | 175,469 | 206 | Concord, CA | 125,464 |
| 59 | Lexington, KY | 308,712 | 133 | Oceanside, CA | 172,525 | 207 | Hartford, CT | 124,927 |
| 60 | Pittsburgh, PA | 307,632 | 134 | Fort Lauderdale, FL | 172,398 | 208 | Kent, WA | 124,359 |
| 61 | Stockton, CA | 299,796 | 135 | Chattanooga, TN | 172,286 | 209 | Lafayette, LA | 123,409 |
| 62 | Anchorage, AK | 299,455 | 136 | Rancho Cucamon., CA | 172,262 | 210 | Denton, TX | 123,260 |
| 63 | Cincinnati, OH | 296,491 | 137 | Santa Rosa, CA | 171,564 | 211 | Surprise, AZ | 122,497 |
| 64 | St. Paul, MN | 294,690 | 138 | Port St. Lucie, FL | 169,877 | 212 | Midland, TX | 122,259 |
| 65 | Toledo, OH | 283,035 | 139 | Tempe, AZ | 168,501 | 213 | Victorville, CA | 121,699 |
| 66 | Greensboro, NC | 279,343 | 140 | Ontario, CA | 168,144 | 214 | Evansville, IN | 120,284 |
| 67 | Newark, NJ | 278,246 | 141 | Vancouver, WA | 166,535 | 215 | Santa Clara, CA | 120,150 |
| 68 | Plano, TX | 275,795 | 142 | Cape Coral, FL | 163,461 | 216 | Athens-Clarke, GA | 120,122 |
| 69 | Henderson, NV | 268,237 | 143 | Springfield, MO | 163,062 | 217 | Abilene, TX | 119,401 |
| 70 | Lincoln, NE | 267,565 | 144 | Pembroke Pines, FL | 162,064 | 218 | Allentown, PA | 119,277 |
| 71 | Buffalo, NY | 258,789 | 145 | Sioux Falls, SD | 161,754 | 219 | Vallejo, CA | 118,336 |
| 72 | Jersey City, NJ | 256,886 | 146 | Peoria, AZ | 161,641 | 220 | Amherst, NY | 118,296 |
| 73 | Chula Vista, CA | 255,073 | 147 | Elk Grove, CA | 160,925 | 221 | Beaumont, TX | 118,177 |
| 74 | Fort Wayne, IN | 254,820 | 148 | Corona, CA | 160,159 | 222 | Independence, MO | 117,381 |

| RANK | CITY | POP | RANK | CITY | POP | RANK | CITY | POP |
|---|---|---|---|---|---|---|---|---|
| 223 | Springfield, IL | 117,351 | 297 | Clinton Twnshp, MI | 98,071 | 371 | Alhambra, CA | 84,710 |
| 224 | Norman, OK | 116,970 | 298 | Albany, NY | 97,956 | 372 | Nampa, ID | 84,634 |
| 225 | Provo, UT | 116,937 | 299 | Roanoke, VA | 97,927 | 373 | Trenton, NJ | 84,439 |
| 226 | Ann Arbor, MI | 116,799 | 300 | Compton, CA | 97,907 | 374 | Livermore, CA | 84,350 |
| 227 | Berkeley, CA | 116,217 | 301 | Portsmouth, VA | 97,018 | 375 | Cicero, IL | 84,204 |
| 228 | Peoria, IL | 115,953 | 302 | Vista, CA | 96,712 | 376 | Hoover, AL | 84,139 |
| 229 | El Monte, CA | 115,591 | 303 | Greece, NY | 96,667 | 377 | Johns Creek, GA | 84,093 |
| 230 | Murfreesboro, TN | 115,587 | 304 | San Angelo, TX | 96,661 | 378 | Ogden, UT | 84,045 |
| 231 | Columbia, MO | 114,587 | 305 | Renton, WA | 96,657 | 379 | Sugar Land, TX | 83,460 |
| 232 | Lansing, MI | 113,907 | 306 | Davie, FL | 96,581 | 380 | Danbury, CT | 83,363 |
| 233 | Downey, CA | 113,222 | 307 | Hillsboro, OR | 96,313 | 381 | Fishers, IN | 83,358 |
| 234 | Costa Mesa, CA | 112,538 | 308 | Greeley, CO | 96,111 | 382 | Champaign, IL | 82,966 |
| 235 | Miami Gardens, FL | 111,870 | 309 | Yuma, AZ | 96,014 | 383 | Concord, NC | 82,899 |
| 236 | Inglewood, CA | 111,672 | 310 | Dearborn, MI | 96,012 | 384 | Upper Darby Twnshp, PA | 82,771 |
| 237 | Fargo, ND | 111,101 | 311 | Mission Viejo, CA | 95,895 | 385 | Sioux City, IA | 82,676 |
| 238 | Wilmington, NC | 110,985 | 312 | South Gate, CA | 95,591 | 386 | O'Fallon, MO | 82,672 |
| 239 | Arvada, CO | 110,792 | 313 | Roswell, GA | 95,373 | 387 | Menifee, CA | 82,634 |
| 240 | Carlsbad, CA | 110,505 | 314 | Livonia, MI | 95,220 | 388 | Buena Park, CA | 82,632 |
| 241 | Elgin, IL | 110,454 | 315 | New Bedford, MA | 95,156 | 389 | Troy, MI | 82,608 |
| 242 | Manchester, NH | 110,411 | 316 | Brockton, MA | 94,448 | 390 | Westland, MI | 82,554 |
| 243 | Westminster, CO | 110,093 | 317 | Vacaville, CA | 94,347 | 391 | Bloomington, IN | 82,415 |
| 244 | Gresham, OR | 109,965 | 318 | Tuscaloosa, AL | 94,126 | 392 | Edinburg, TX | 82,271 |
| 245 | Waterbury, CT | 109,763 | 319 | Yakima, WA | 93,589 | 393 | Meridian, ID | 82,064 |
| 246 | Rochester, MN | 109,675 | 320 | Beaverton, OR | 93,551 | 394 | Warwick, RI | 81,789 |
| 247 | Lowell, MA | 109,449 | 321 | Quincy, MA | 93,490 | 395 | Hemet, CA | 81,698 |
| 248 | Clearwater, FL | 108,908 | 322 | Carson, CA | 93,415 | 396 | Mission, TX | 81,360 |
| 249 | Round Rock, TX | 108,577 | 323 | Sparks, NV | 92,768 | 397 | Merced, CA | 81,329 |
| 250 | Fairfield, CA | 108,425 | 324 | Lee's Summit, MO | 92,765 | 398 | Longview, TX | 81,273 |
| 251 | Odessa, TX | 108,265 | 325 | Federal Way, WA | 92,741 | 399 | Lakewood, CA | 81,086 |
| 252 | Ventura, CA | 108,204 | 326 | Lakewood Twnshp, NJ | 92,664 | 400 | Farmington Hills, MI | 81,084 |
| 253 | Pueblo, CO | 108,062 | 327 | Hesperia, CA | 92,621 | 401 | Cranston, RI | 80,718 |
| 254 | West Covina, CA | 107,867 | 328 | Santa Monica, CA | 92,488 | 402 | Clarkstown, NY | 80,705 |
| 255 | Billings, MT | 107,802 | 329 | Toms River Twnshp, NJ | 92,332 | 403 | Chino, CA | 80,704 |
| 256 | Murrieta, CA | 107,768 | 330 | Westminster, CA | 91,885 | 404 | Indio, CA | 80,243 |
| 257 | Richmond, CA | 107,341 | 331 | Lynn, MA | 91,769 | 405 | Bend, OR | 79,926 |
| 258 | Cambridge, MA | 107,282 | 332 | Orem, UT | 91,438 | 406 | Redwood City, CA | 79,707 |
| 259 | High Point, NC | 107,261 | 333 | Miami Beach, FL | 91,433 | 407 | Lake Forest, CA | 79,336 |
| 260 | Temecula, CA | 106,680 | 334 | Allen, TX | 91,289 | 408 | Hammond, IN | 79,329 |
| 261 | Norwalk, CA | 106,518 | 335 | Macon, GA | 91,177 | 409 | Tustin, CA | 78,836 |
| 262 | Antioch, CA | 106,447 | 336 | Redding, CA | 91,035 | 410 | Gary, IN | 78,819 |
| 263 | Everett, WA | 105,129 | 337 | Spokane Valley, WA | 90,835 | 411 | New Rochelle, NY | 78,800 |
| 264 | Green Bay, WI | 105,107 | 338 | Sunrise, FL | 90,274 | 412 | Napa, CA | 78,761 |
| 265 | Centennial, CO | 104,771 | 339 | Lawrence, KS | 90,034 | 413 | Bryan, TX | 78,578 |
| 266 | Burbank, CA | 104,727 | 340 | Santa Barbara, CA | 90,006 | 414 | Cheektowaga, NY | 78,361 |
| 267 | Richardson, TX | 104,577 | 341 | Sandy, UT | 89,943 | 415 | Brooklyn Park, MN | 78,353 |
| 268 | Daly City, CA | 104,536 | 342 | League City, TX | 89,596 | 416 | Colonie, NY | 78,215 |
| 269 | Wichita Falls, TX | 104,514 | 343 | Longmont, CO | 89,434 | 417 | Deerfield Beach, FL | 78,203 |
| 270 | Palm Bay, FL | 104,391 | 344 | Fall River, MA | 89,220 | 418 | Racine, WI | 78,141 |
| 271 | Pompano Beach, FL | 103,971 | 345 | Hamilton Twnshp, NJ | 88,993 | 419 | Bloomington, IL | 78,060 |
| 272 | North Charleston, SC | 103,324 | 346 | Canton Twnshp, MI | 88,958 | 420 | Largo, FL | 77,913 |
| 273 | Broken Arrow, OK | 102,956 | 347 | Plantation, FL | 88,929 | 421 | Fayetteville, AR | 77,900 |
| 274 | Boulder, CO | 102,828 | 348 | Waukegan, IL | 88,763 | 422 | Lawrence, MA | 77,812 |
| 275 | Rialto, CA | 102,520 | 349 | Boca Raton, FL | 88,749 | 423 | Somerville, MA | 77,768 |
| 276 | West Palm Beach, FL | 102,510 | 350 | Chico, CA | 88,226 | 424 | Lynchburg, VA | 77,757 |
| 277 | Santa Maria, CA | 102,051 | 351 | Reading, PA | 88,107 | 425 | Bellflower, CA | 77,594 |
| 278 | El Cajon, CA | 102,012 | 352 | Greenville, NC | 88,018 | 426 | Mountain View, CA | 77,399 |
| 279 | Las Cruces, NM | 102,007 | 353 | Fort Smith, AR | 87,821 | 427 | Albany, GA | 77,365 |
| 280 | Davenport, IA | 101,834 | 354 | San Marcos, CA | 87,712 | 428 | St. Joseph, MO | 77,347 |
| 281 | Edison Twnshp, NJ | 101,316 | 355 | Newport Beach, CA | 87,639 | 429 | Melbourne, FL | 77,277 |
| 282 | Sandy Springs, GA | 101,180 | 356 | Norwalk, CT | 87,590 | 430 | Medford, OR | 76,949 |
| 283 | Erie, PA | 100,814 | 357 | San Leandro, CA | 87,490 | 431 | Chino Hills, CA | 76,943 |
| 284 | Lakeland, FL | 100,725 | 358 | Ramapo, NY | 87,204 | 432 | Baldwin Park, CA | 76,745 |
| 285 | South Bend, IN | 100,711 | 359 | Bloomington, MN | 87,057 | 433 | Kennewick, WA | 76,508 |
| 286 | Lewisville, TX | 100,710 | 360 | Nashua, NH | 87,052 | 434 | St. George, UT | 76,427 |
| 287 | Woodbridge Twnshp, NJ | 100,568 | 361 | Newton, MA | 86,867 | 435 | Alameda, CA | 76,206 |
| 288 | San Mateo, CA | 100,440 | 362 | Whittier, CA | 86,450 | 436 | Arlington Heights, IL | 75,978 |
| 289 | Kenosha, WI | 100,418 | 363 | Duluth, MN | 86,211 | 437 | Scranton, PA | 75,732 |
| 290 | Tyler, TX | 100,033 | 364 | Hawthorne, CA | 86,132 | 438 | Evanston, IL | 75,709 |
| 291 | Flint, MI | 99,941 | 365 | Edmond, OK | 85,974 | 439 | Upland, CA | 75,640 |
| 292 | Clovis, CA | 99,483 | 366 | Suffolk, VA | 85,475 | 440 | Brick Twnshp, NJ | 75,371 |
| 293 | College Station, TX | 98,919 | 367 | Citrus Heights, CA | 85,337 | 441 | Decatur, IL | 75,190 |
| 294 | Lawton, OK | 98,548 | 368 | Tracy, CA | 85,174 | 442 | Bethlehem, PA | 75,135 |
| 295 | Pearland, TX | 98,183 | 369 | Clifton, NJ | 85,022 | | | |
| 296 | Jurupa Valley, CA | 98,090 | 370 | Carmel, IN | 84,880 | | | |

Source: Reported data from the F.B.I. "Crime in the United States 2013"

*Estimates as of July 2013 based on U.S. Bureau of the Census figures. Charlotte, Indianapolis, Las Vegas, Louisville, Mobile, and Savannah include areas under their police department but outside the city limits. All populations are for area covered by police department.

# 89. City Population in 2012
## National Total = 313,873,685*

| RANK | CITY | POP | RANK | CITY | POP | RANK | CITY | POP |
|---|---|---|---|---|---|---|---|---|
| 210 | Abilene, TX | 119,886 | 396 | Chino, CA | 79,792 | 176 | Fullerton, CA | 138,455 |
| 113 | Akron, OH | 198,390 | 75 | Chula Vista, CA | 249,830 | 192 | Gainesville, FL | 127,036 |
| 430 | Alameda, CA | 75,467 | 366 | Cicero, IL | 84,300 | 132 | Garden Grove, CA | 175,079 |
| 403 | Albany, GA | 78,512 | 63 | Cincinnati, OH | 296,204 | 83 | Garland, TX | 234,984 |
| 289 | Albany, NY | 98,187 | 360 | Citrus Heights, CA | 85,112 | 389 | Gary, IN | 80,472 |
| 31 | Albuquerque, NM | 553,684 | 393 | Clarkstown, NY | 80,186 | 97 | Gilbert, AZ | 214,264 |
| 167 | Alexandria, VA | 145,892 | 179 | Clarksville, TN | 137,356 | 86 | Glendale, AZ | 232,997 |
| 365 | Alhambra, CA | 84,469 | 240 | Clearwater, FL | 109,255 | 117 | Glendale, CA | 194,902 |
| 212 | Allentown, PA | 119,334 | 46 | Cleveland, OH | 393,781 | 125 | Grand Prairie, TX | 181,782 |
| 340 | Allen, TX | 88,783 | 363 | Clifton, NJ | 84,684 | 120 | Grand Rapids, MI | 189,953 |
| 114 | Amarillo, TX | 196,576 | 296 | Clinton Twnshp, MI | 97,001 | 297 | Greece, NY | 96,752 |
| 217 | Amherst, NY | 117,591 | 292 | Clovis, CA | 97,828 | 300 | Greeley, CO | 96,276 |
| 53 | Anaheim, CA | 344,526 | 299 | College Station, TX | 96,567 | 258 | Green Bay, WI | 106,080 |
| 61 | Anchorage, AK | 299,143 | 409 | Colonie, NY | 77,853 | 67 | Greensboro, NC | 276,134 |
| 225 | Ann Arbor, MI | 115,008 | 40 | Colorado Springs, CO | 432,287 | 348 | Greenville, NC | 86,869 |
| 262 | Antioch, CA | 105,009 | 234 | Columbia, MO | 110,646 | 247 | Gresham, OR | 108,202 |
| 431 | Arlington Heights, IL | 75,463 | NA | Columbia, SC** | NA | 338 | Hamilton Twnshp, NJ | 89,111 |
| 49 | Arlington, TX | 379,295 | 115 | Columbus, GA | 196,178 | 385 | Hammond, IN | 81,010 |
| 243 | Arvada, CO | 109,029 | 290 | Compton, CA | 98,057 | 178 | Hampton, VA | 137,905 |
| 218 | Athens-Clarke, GA | 117,457 | 197 | Concord, CA | 125,205 | 198 | Hartford, CT | 125,203 |
| 39 | Atlanta, GA | 437,041 | NA | Concord, NC** | NA | 357 | Hawthorne, CA | 85,692 |
| 54 | Aurora, CO | 336,952 | 199 | Coral Springs, FL | 125,021 | 160 | Hayward, CA | 147,424 |
| 110 | Aurora, IL | 199,765 | 149 | Corona, CA | 157,342 | 384 | Hemet, CA | 81,213 |
| 14 | Austin, TX | 832,901 | 58 | Corpus Christi, TX | 312,565 | 70 | Henderson, NV | 263,469 |
| 51 | Bakersfield, CA | 355,696 | 230 | Costa Mesa, CA | 112,635 | 319 | Hesperia, CA | 92,383 |
| 421 | Baldwin Park, CA | 76,644 | 392 | Cranston, RI | 80,315 | 85 | Hialeah, FL | 233,107 |
| 26 | Baltimore, MD | 625,474 | 10 | Dallas, TX | 1,241,549 | 254 | High Point, NC | 106,801 |
| 87 | Baton Rouge, LA | 231,500 | 267 | Daly City, CA | 103,311 | 310 | Hillsboro, OR | 94,119 |
| 209 | Beaumont, TX | 120,323 | 378 | Danbury, CT | 81,891 | 168 | Hollywood, FL | 145,313 |
| 320 | Beaverton, OR | 92,276 | 277 | Davenport, IA | 101,193 | 376 | Hoover, AL | 82,332 |
| 195 | Bellevue, WA | 126,022 | 308 | Davie, FL | 94,952 | 4 | Houston, TX | 2,177,273 |
| 408 | Bellflower, CA | 77,886 | 172 | Dayton, OH | 142,139 | 118 | Huntington Beach, CA | 194,677 |
| NA | Bend, OR** | NA | 295 | Dearborn, MI | 97,215 | 122 | Huntsville, AL | 183,691 |
| 226 | Berkeley, CA | 114,961 | 423 | Decatur, IL | 76,131 | 219 | Independence, MO | 117,433 |
| 432 | Bethlehem, PA | 75,388 | 411 | Deerfield Beach, FL | 77,431 | 13 | Indianapolis, IN | 838,650 |
| 255 | Billings, MT | 106,371 | 213 | Denton, TX | 118,942 | 404 | Indio, CA | 78,501 |
| 98 | Birmingham, AL | 213,266 | 24 | Denver, CO | 628,545 | 232 | Inglewood, CA | 111,488 |
| 419 | Bloomington, IL | 77,107 | 103 | Des Moines, IA | 207,400 | 95 | Irvine, CA | 217,528 |
| 380 | Bloomington, IN | 81,636 | 18 | Detroit, MI | 707,096 | 91 | Irving, TX | 224,007 |
| 364 | Bloomington, MN | 84,596 | 229 | Downey, CA | 113,628 | 12 | Jacksonville, FL | 840,660 |
| 354 | Boca Raton, FL | 86,493 | 350 | Duluth, MN | 86,830 | 131 | Jackson, MS | 175,939 |
| 101 | Boise, ID | 211,569 | 390 | Edinburg, TX | 80,332 | 73 | Jersey City, NJ | 251,554 |
| 23 | Boston, MA | 630,648 | 278 | Edison Twnshp, NJ | 101,007 | 395 | Johns Creek, GA | 80,037 |
| 282 | Boulder, CO | 100,257 | 367 | Edmond, OK | 83,473 | 158 | Joliet, IL | 148,471 |
| 427 | Brick Twnshp, NJ | 75,809 | 272 | El Cajon, CA | 101,864 | 294 | Jurupa Valley, CA | 97,577 |
| 165 | Bridgeport, CT | 146,030 | 223 | El Monte, CA | 115,356 | 162 | Kansas City, KS | 147,201 |
| 307 | Brockton, MA | 95,156 | 19 | El Paso, TX | 675,536 | 36 | Kansas City, MO | 464,073 |
| 279 | Broken Arrow, OK | 100,688 | 241 | Elgin, IL | 109,155 | 420 | Kennewick, WA | 76,971 |
| 414 | Brooklyn Park, MN | 77,346 | 194 | Elizabeth, NJ | 126,281 | 284 | Kenosha, WI | 99,993 |
| 127 | Brownsville, TX | 181,102 | 150 | Elk Grove, CA | 156,344 | 207 | Kent, WA | 122,102 |
| 405 | Bryan, TX | 78,479 | 271 | Erie, PA | 101,972 | 183 | Killeen, TX | 131,965 |
| 375 | Buena Park, CA | 82,505 | 161 | Escondido, CA | 147,386 | 124 | Knoxville, TN | 182,254 |
| 71 | Buffalo, NY | 262,434 | 147 | Eugene, OR | 158,043 | 206 | Lafayette, LA | 122,852 |
| 261 | Burbank, CA | 105,057 | 434 | Evanston, IL | 74,820 | 399 | Lake Forest, CA | 79,166 |
| 252 | Cambridge, MA | 106,981 | 215 | Evansville, IN | 118,194 | 285 | Lakeland, FL | 99,934 |
| NA | Canton Twnshp, MI** | NA | 260 | Everett, WA | 105,318 | 312 | Lakewood Twnshp, NJ | 93,742 |
| 143 | Cape Coral, FL | 159,625 | 251 | Fairfield, CA | 107,110 | 382 | Lakewood, CA | 81,382 |
| 248 | Carlsbad, CA | 107,879 | 335 | Fall River, MA | 89,753 | 164 | Lakewood, CO | 146,404 |
| 379 | Carmel, IN | 81,819 | 237 | Fargo, ND | 109,813 | 144 | Lancaster, CA | 159,155 |
| 200 | Carrollton, TX | 124,477 | 391 | Farmington Hills, MI | 80,316 | 227 | Lansing, MI | 114,688 |
| 316 | Carson, CA | 93,233 | 433 | Fayetteville, AR | 75,387 | 78 | Laredo, TX | 245,558 |
| 173 | Cary, NC | 141,016 | 104 | Fayetteville, NC | 205,966 | 401 | Largo, FL | 78,783 |
| 190 | Cedar Rapids, IA | 128,401 | 323 | Federal Way, WA | 91,978 | 286 | Las Cruces, NM | 99,824 |
| 264 | Centennial, CO | 104,022 | 397 | Fishers, IN | 79,375 | 7 | Las Vegas, NV | 1,479,393 |
| 383 | Champaign, IL | 81,329 | 273 | Flint, MI | 101,632 | 337 | Lawrence, KS | 89,180 |
| 80 | Chandler, AZ | 242,721 | 109 | Fontana, CA | 200,874 | 410 | Lawrence, MA | 77,661 |
| 202 | Charleston, SC | 123,856 | 157 | Fort Collins, CO | 148,792 | 288 | Lawton, OK | 98,781 |
| 16 | Charlotte, NC | 808,504 | 135 | Fort Lauderdale, FL | 170,827 | 355 | League City, TX | 86,127 |
| NA | Chattanooga, TN** | NA | 343 | Fort Smith, AR | 87,483 | 328 | Lee's Summit, MO | 91,840 |
| 398 | Cheektowaga, NY | 79,178 | 72 | Fort Wayne, IN | 256,625 | NA | Lewisville, TX** | NA |
| 90 | Chesapeake, VA | 227,531 | 17 | Fort Worth, TX | 770,101 | 60 | Lexington, KY | 302,332 |
| 3 | Chicago, IL | 2,708,382 | 94 | Fremont, CA | 218,927 | 69 | Lincoln, NE | 264,175 |
| 346 | Chico, CA | 87,090 | 33 | Fresno, CA | 506,011 | 116 | Little Rock, AR | 196,055 |
| 422 | Chino Hills, CA | 76,632 | 203 | Frisco, TX | 123,205 | 373 | Livermore, CA | 82,800 |

| RANK | CITY | POP | RANK | CITY | POP | RANK | CITY | POP |
|---|---|---|---|---|---|---|---|---|
| 303 | Livonia, MI | 96,028 | 175 | Pasadena, CA | 139,382 | 304 | South Gate, CA | 95,966 |
| 35 | Long Beach, CA | 469,893 | 152 | Pasadena, TX | 154,562 | 318 | Sparks, NV | 92,387 |
| 339 | Longmont, CO | 88,925 | 163 | Paterson, NJ | 147,148 | 330 | Spokane Valley, WA | 91,164 |
| 374 | Longview, TX | 82,554 | 309 | Pearland, TX | 94,702 | 99 | Spokane, WA | 212,163 |
| 2 | Los Angeles, CA | 3,855,122 | 142 | Pembroke Pines, FL | 159,744 | 220 | Springfield, IL | 117,131 |
| 20 | Louisville, KY | 666,200 | 146 | Peoria, AZ | 158,347 | 153 | Springfield, MA | 154,518 |
| 245 | Lowell, MA | 108,539 | 224 | Peoria, IL | 115,288 | 141 | Springfield, MO | 160,962 |
| 82 | Lubbock, TX | 237,241 | 5 | Philadelphia, PA | 1,538,957 | 201 | Stamford, CT | 124,201 |
| 413 | Lynchburg, VA | 77,347 | 6 | Phoenix, AZ | 1,485,509 | 184 | Sterling Heights, MI | 129,974 |
| 327 | Lynn, MA | 91,846 | 59 | Pittsburgh, PA | 312,112 | 62 | Stockton, CA | 299,105 |
| 317 | Macon, GA | 92,836 | 68 | Plano, TX | 273,816 | 428 | St. George, UT | 75,780 |
| 81 | Madison, WI | 237,508 | 342 | Plantation, FL | 87,705 | 415 | St. Joseph, MO | 77,330 |
| 236 | Manchester, NH | 110,040 | 156 | Pomona, CA | 151,511 | 56 | St. Louis, MO | 318,667 |
| 180 | McAllen, TX | 135,745 | 269 | Pompano Beach, FL | 103,003 | 64 | St. Paul, MN | 290,700 |
| 177 | McKinney, TX | 138,105 | 137 | Port St. Lucie, FL | 168,416 | 76 | St. Petersburg, FL | 248,340 |
| 425 | Medford, OR | 76,037 | 29 | Portland, OR | 598,037 | NA | Suffolk, VA** | NA |
| 418 | Melbourne, FL | 77,133 | 298 | Portsmouth, VA | 96,739 | 372 | Sugar Land, TX | 82,924 |
| 21 | Memphis, TN | 657,436 | 129 | Providence, RI | 177,882 | 170 | Sunnyvale, CA | 143,606 |
| 394 | Menifee, CA | 80,047 | 221 | Provo, UT | 116,879 | 345 | Sunrise, FL | 87,168 |
| 386 | Merced, CA | 80,976 | 242 | Pueblo, CO | 109,065 | 208 | Surprise, AZ | 120,793 |
| 416 | Meridian, ID | 77,270 | 313 | Quincy, MA | 93,736 | 166 | Syracuse, NY | 145,934 |
| 37 | Mesa, AZ | 451,391 | 400 | Racine, WI | 79,055 | 106 | Tacoma, WA | 202,646 |
| 169 | Mesquite, TX | 144,811 | 41 | Raleigh, NC | 420,594 | 121 | Tallahassee, FL | 185,461 |
| 331 | Miami Beach, FL | 91,066 | 358 | Ramapo, NY | 85,448 | 52 | Tampa, FL | 350,758 |
| 233 | Miami Gardens, FL | 111,177 | 136 | Rancho Cucamon., CA | 169,276 | 266 | Temecula, CA | 103,414 |
| 43 | Miami, FL | 414,327 | 341 | Reading, PA | 88,557 | 140 | Tempe, AZ | 166,061 |
| 222 | Midland, TX | 115,637 | 332 | Redding, CA | 90,974 | 204 | Thornton, CO | 123,115 |
| 28 | Milwaukee, WI | 599,395 | 406 | Redwood City, CA | 78,466 | 186 | Thousand Oaks, CA | 129,171 |
| 47 | Minneapolis, MN | 390,240 | 89 | Reno, NV | 230,486 | 65 | Toledo, OH | 286,020 |
| 196 | Miramar, FL | 125,998 | 314 | Renton, WA | 93,722 | 322 | Toms River Twnshp, NJ | 92,131 |
| 305 | Mission Viejo, CA | 95,599 | 274 | Rialto, CA | 101,595 | 187 | Topeka, KS | 128,843 |
| 388 | Mission, TX | 80,557 | 268 | Richardson, TX | 103,266 | 159 | Torrance, CA | 147,851 |
| 74 | Mobile, AL | 251,516 | 256 | Richmond, CA | 106,357 | 362 | Tracy, CA | 85,047 |
| 105 | Modesto, CA | 204,631 | 102 | Richmond, VA | 207,799 | 359 | Trenton, NJ | 85,317 |
| 111 | Moreno Valley, CA | 199,673 | 57 | Riverside, CA | 313,532 | 381 | Troy, MI | 81,567 |
| 426 | Mountain View, CA | 75,933 | 293 | Roanoke, VA | 97,780 | 32 | Tucson, AZ | 531,535 |
| 231 | Murfreesboro, TN | 112,247 | 244 | Rochester, MN | 108,582 | 45 | Tulsa, OK | 398,904 |
| 253 | Murrieta, CA | 106,839 | 100 | Rochester, NY | 211,993 | 324 | Tuscaloosa, AL | 91,973 |
| 368 | Nampa, ID | 83,316 | 155 | Rockford, IL | 152,293 | 412 | Tustin, CA | 77,400 |
| 402 | Napa, CA | 78,589 | 205 | Roseville, CA | 122,896 | 283 | Tyler, TX | 100,040 |
| 171 | Naperville, IL | 142,840 | 321 | Roswell, GA | 92,141 | 429 | Upland, CA | 75,531 |
| 347 | Nashua, NH | 86,870 | 257 | Round Rock, TX | 106,232 | 371 | Upper Darby Twnshp, PA | 82,978 |
| 27 | Nashville, TN | 620,886 | 34 | Sacramento, CA | 476,557 | 311 | Vacaville, CA | 93,951 |
| 302 | New Bedford, MA | 96,031 | 148 | Salem, OR | 157,353 | 216 | Vallejo, CA | 117,912 |
| 185 | New Haven, CT | 129,934 | 154 | Salinas, CA | 154,413 | 139 | Vancouver, WA | 166,375 |
| 50 | New Orleans, LA | 362,874 | 119 | Salt Lake City, UT | 192,465 | 246 | Ventura, CA | 108,511 |
| 407 | New Rochelle, NY | 78,025 | NA | San Angelo, TX** | NA | 214 | Victorville, CA | 118,687 |
| 1 | New York, NY | 8,289,415 | 8 | San Antonio, TX | 1,380,123 | 38 | Virginia Beach, VA | 447,588 |
| 66 | Newark, NJ | 278,906 | 96 | San Bernardino, CA | 214,987 | 191 | Visalia, CA | 127,604 |
| 344 | Newport Beach, CA | 87,286 | 9 | San Diego, CA | 1,338,477 | 301 | Vista, CA | 96,087 |
| 126 | Newport News, VA | 181,591 | 15 | San Francisco, CA | 820,363 | 188 | Waco, TX | 128,595 |
| 352 | Newton, MA | 86,710 | 11 | San Jose, CA | 976,459 | 181 | Warren, MI | 134,340 |
| 79 | Norfolk, VA | 245,303 | 348 | San Leandro, CA | 86,869 | 377 | Warwick, RI | 82,282 |
| 228 | Norman, OK | 113,969 | 356 | San Marcos, CA | 85,810 | 22 | Washington, DC | 632,323 |
| 280 | North Charleston, SC | 100,675 | 287 | San Mateo, CA | 99,303 | 235 | Waterbury, CT | 110,486 |
| 93 | North Las Vegas, NV | 221,884 | 291 | Sandy Springs, GA | 97,890 | 336 | Waukegan, IL | 89,468 |
| 250 | Norwalk, CA | 107,295 | 333 | Sandy, UT | 90,405 | 249 | West Covina, CA | 107,861 |
| 353 | Norwalk, CT | 86,693 | 55 | Santa Ana, CA | 332,482 | 270 | West Palm Beach, FL | 102,422 |
| 44 | Oakland, CA | 399,487 | 334 | Santa Barbara, CA | 89,871 | 182 | West Valley, UT | 133,725 |
| 133 | Oceanside, CA | 171,141 | 211 | Santa Clara, CA | 119,360 | 369 | Westland, MI | 83,299 |
| 265 | Odessa, TX | 103,635 | 128 | Santa Clarita, CA | 179,248 | 326 | Westminster, CA | 91,908 |
| 387 | O'Fallon, MO | 80,670 | 276 | Santa Maria, CA | 101,207 | 238 | Westminster, CO | 109,461 |
| 361 | Ogden, UT | 85,083 | 329 | Santa Monica, CA | 91,215 | 351 | Whittier, CA | 86,740 |
| 30 | Oklahoma City, OK | 595,607 | 134 | Santa Rosa, CA | 170,862 | 259 | Wichita Falls, TX | 105,488 |
| 189 | Olathe, KS | 128,560 | 88 | Savannah, GA | 231,285 | 48 | Wichita, KS | 386,409 |
| 42 | Omaha, NE | 417,970 | 92 | Scottsdale, AZ | 223,432 | 239 | Wilmington, NC | 109,370 |
| 138 | Ontario, CA | 167,933 | 424 | Scranton, PA | 76,118 | 84 | Winston-Salem, NC | 234,687 |
| 174 | Orange, CA | 139,692 | 25 | Seattle, WA | 626,865 | 281 | Woodbridge Twnshp, NJ | 100,612 |
| 325 | Orem, UT | 91,953 | 107 | Shreveport, LA | 202,164 | 123 | Worcester, MA | 183,247 |
| 77 | Orlando, FL | 246,513 | 193 | Simi Valley, CA | 126,686 | 315 | Yakima, WA | 93,419 |
| 130 | Overland Park, KS | 177,085 | 370 | Sioux City, IA | 83,289 | 112 | Yonkers, NY | 198,464 |
| 108 | Oxnard, CA | 201,797 | 145 | Sioux Falls, SD | 158,354 | 306 | Yuma, AZ | 95,568 |
| 263 | Palm Bay, FL | 104,635 | 417 | Somerville, MA | 77,200 | | | |
| 151 | Palmdale, CA | 155,294 | 275 | South Bend, IN | 101,398 | | | |

Source: Reported data from the F.B.I. "Crime in the United States 2012"

*Estimates as of July 2012 based on U.S. Bureau of the Census figures. Charlotte, Indianapolis, Las Vegas, Louisville, Mobile, and Savannah include areas under their police department but outside the city limits. All populations are for area covered by police department.

**Not available.

# 89. City Population in 2012 (continued)
## National Total = 313,873,685*

| RANK | CITY | POP | RANK | CITY | POP | RANK | CITY | POP |
|---|---|---|---|---|---|---|---|---|
| 1 | New York, NY | 8,289,415 | 75 | Chula Vista, CA | 249,830 | 149 | Corona, CA | 157,342 |
| 2 | Los Angeles, CA | 3,855,122 | 76 | St. Petersburg, FL | 248,340 | 150 | Elk Grove, CA | 156,344 |
| 3 | Chicago, IL | 2,708,382 | 77 | Orlando, FL | 246,513 | 151 | Palmdale, CA | 155,294 |
| 4 | Houston, TX | 2,177,273 | 78 | Laredo, TX | 245,558 | 152 | Pasadena, TX | 154,562 |
| 5 | Philadelphia, PA | 1,538,957 | 79 | Norfolk, VA | 245,303 | 153 | Springfield, MA | 154,518 |
| 6 | Phoenix, AZ | 1,485,509 | 80 | Chandler, AZ | 242,721 | 154 | Salinas, CA | 154,413 |
| 7 | Las Vegas, NV | 1,479,393 | 81 | Madison, WI | 237,508 | 155 | Rockford, IL | 152,293 |
| 8 | San Antonio, TX | 1,380,123 | 82 | Lubbock, TX | 237,241 | 156 | Pomona, CA | 151,511 |
| 9 | San Diego, CA | 1,338,477 | 83 | Garland, TX | 234,984 | 157 | Fort Collins, CO | 148,792 |
| 10 | Dallas, TX | 1,241,549 | 84 | Winston-Salem, NC | 234,687 | 158 | Joliet, IL | 148,471 |
| 11 | San Jose, CA | 976,459 | 85 | Hialeah, FL | 233,107 | 159 | Torrance, CA | 147,851 |
| 12 | Jacksonville, FL | 840,660 | 86 | Glendale, AZ | 232,997 | 160 | Hayward, CA | 147,424 |
| 13 | Indianapolis, IN | 838,650 | 87 | Baton Rouge, LA | 231,500 | 161 | Escondido, CA | 147,386 |
| 14 | Austin, TX | 832,901 | 88 | Savannah, GA | 231,285 | 162 | Kansas City, KS | 147,201 |
| 15 | San Francisco, CA | 820,363 | 89 | Reno, NV | 230,486 | 163 | Paterson, NJ | 147,148 |
| 16 | Charlotte, NC | 808,504 | 90 | Chesapeake, VA | 227,531 | 164 | Lakewood, CO | 146,404 |
| 17 | Fort Worth, TX | 770,101 | 91 | Irving, TX | 224,007 | 165 | Bridgeport, CT | 146,030 |
| 18 | Detroit, MI | 707,096 | 92 | Scottsdale, AZ | 223,432 | 166 | Syracuse, NY | 145,934 |
| 19 | El Paso, TX | 675,536 | 93 | North Las Vegas, NV | 221,884 | 167 | Alexandria, VA | 145,892 |
| 20 | Louisville, KY | 666,200 | 94 | Fremont, CA | 218,927 | 168 | Hollywood, FL | 145,313 |
| 21 | Memphis, TN | 657,436 | 95 | Irvine, CA | 217,528 | 169 | Mesquite, TX | 144,811 |
| 22 | Washington, DC | 632,323 | 96 | San Bernardino, CA | 214,987 | 170 | Sunnyvale, CA | 143,606 |
| 23 | Boston, MA | 630,648 | 97 | Gilbert, AZ | 214,264 | 171 | Naperville, IL | 142,840 |
| 24 | Denver, CO | 628,545 | 98 | Birmingham, AL | 213,266 | 172 | Dayton, OH | 142,139 |
| 25 | Seattle, WA | 626,865 | 99 | Spokane, WA | 212,163 | 173 | Cary, NC | 141,016 |
| 26 | Baltimore, MD | 625,474 | 100 | Rochester, NY | 211,993 | 174 | Orange, CA | 139,692 |
| 27 | Nashville, TN | 620,886 | 101 | Boise, ID | 211,569 | 175 | Pasadena, CA | 139,382 |
| 28 | Milwaukee, WI | 599,395 | 102 | Richmond, VA | 207,799 | 176 | Fullerton, CA | 138,455 |
| 29 | Portland, OR | 598,037 | 103 | Des Moines, IA | 207,400 | 177 | McKinney, TX | 138,105 |
| 30 | Oklahoma City, OK | 595,607 | 104 | Fayetteville, NC | 205,966 | 178 | Hampton, VA | 137,905 |
| 31 | Albuquerque, NM | 553,684 | 105 | Modesto, CA | 204,631 | 179 | Clarksville, TN | 137,356 |
| 32 | Tucson, AZ | 531,535 | 106 | Tacoma, WA | 202,646 | 180 | McAllen, TX | 135,745 |
| 33 | Fresno, CA | 506,011 | 107 | Shreveport, LA | 202,164 | 181 | Warren, MI | 134,340 |
| 34 | Sacramento, CA | 476,557 | 108 | Oxnard, CA | 201,797 | 182 | West Valley, UT | 133,725 |
| 35 | Long Beach, CA | 469,893 | 109 | Fontana, CA | 200,874 | 183 | Killeen, TX | 131,965 |
| 36 | Kansas City, MO | 464,073 | 110 | Aurora, IL | 199,765 | 184 | Sterling Heights, MI | 129,974 |
| 37 | Mesa, AZ | 451,391 | 111 | Moreno Valley, CA | 199,673 | 185 | New Haven, CT | 129,934 |
| 38 | Virginia Beach, VA | 447,588 | 112 | Yonkers, NY | 198,464 | 186 | Thousand Oaks, CA | 129,171 |
| 39 | Atlanta, GA | 437,041 | 113 | Akron, OH | 198,390 | 187 | Topeka, KS | 128,843 |
| 40 | Colorado Springs, CO | 432,287 | 114 | Amarillo, TX | 196,576 | 188 | Waco, TX | 128,595 |
| 41 | Raleigh, NC | 420,594 | 115 | Columbus, GA | 196,178 | 189 | Olathe, KS | 128,560 |
| 42 | Omaha, NE | 417,970 | 116 | Little Rock, AR | 196,055 | 190 | Cedar Rapids, IA | 128,401 |
| 43 | Miami, FL | 414,327 | 117 | Glendale, CA | 194,902 | 191 | Visalia, CA | 127,604 |
| 44 | Oakland, CA | 399,487 | 118 | Huntington Beach, CA | 194,677 | 192 | Gainesville, FL | 127,036 |
| 45 | Tulsa, OK | 398,904 | 119 | Salt Lake City, UT | 192,465 | 193 | Simi Valley, CA | 126,686 |
| 46 | Cleveland, OH | 393,781 | 120 | Grand Rapids, MI | 189,953 | 194 | Elizabeth, NJ | 126,281 |
| 47 | Minneapolis, MN | 390,240 | 121 | Tallahassee, FL | 185,461 | 195 | Bellevue, WA | 126,022 |
| 48 | Wichita, KS | 386,409 | 122 | Huntsville, AL | 183,691 | 196 | Miramar, FL | 125,998 |
| 49 | Arlington, TX | 379,295 | 123 | Worcester, MA | 183,247 | 197 | Concord, CA | 125,205 |
| 50 | New Orleans, LA | 362,874 | 124 | Knoxville, TN | 182,254 | 198 | Hartford, CT | 125,203 |
| 51 | Bakersfield, CA | 355,696 | 125 | Grand Prairie, TX | 181,782 | 199 | Coral Springs, FL | 125,021 |
| 52 | Tampa, FL | 350,758 | 126 | Newport News, VA | 181,591 | 200 | Carrollton, TX | 124,477 |
| 53 | Anaheim, CA | 344,526 | 127 | Brownsville, TX | 181,102 | 201 | Stamford, CT | 124,201 |
| 54 | Aurora, CO | 336,952 | 128 | Santa Clarita, CA | 179,248 | 202 | Charleston, SC | 123,856 |
| 55 | Santa Ana, CA | 332,482 | 129 | Providence, RI | 177,882 | 203 | Frisco, TX | 123,205 |
| 56 | St. Louis, MO | 318,667 | 130 | Overland Park, KS | 177,085 | 204 | Thornton, CO | 123,115 |
| 57 | Riverside, CA | 313,532 | 131 | Jackson, MS | 175,939 | 205 | Roseville, CA | 122,896 |
| 58 | Corpus Christi, TX | 312,565 | 132 | Garden Grove, CA | 175,079 | 206 | Lafayette, LA | 122,852 |
| 59 | Pittsburgh, PA | 312,112 | 133 | Oceanside, CA | 171,141 | 207 | Kent, WA | 122,102 |
| 60 | Lexington, KY | 302,332 | 134 | Santa Rosa, CA | 170,862 | 208 | Surprise, AZ | 120,793 |
| 61 | Anchorage, AK | 299,143 | 135 | Fort Lauderdale, FL | 170,827 | 209 | Beaumont, TX | 120,323 |
| 62 | Stockton, CA | 299,105 | 136 | Rancho Cucamon., CA | 169,276 | 210 | Abilene, TX | 119,886 |
| 63 | Cincinnati, OH | 296,204 | 137 | Port St. Lucie, FL | 168,416 | 211 | Santa Clara, CA | 119,360 |
| 64 | St. Paul, MN | 290,700 | 138 | Ontario, CA | 167,933 | 212 | Allentown, PA | 119,334 |
| 65 | Toledo, OH | 286,020 | 139 | Vancouver, WA | 166,375 | 213 | Denton, TX | 118,942 |
| 66 | Newark, NJ | 278,906 | 140 | Tempe, AZ | 166,061 | 214 | Victorville, CA | 118,687 |
| 67 | Greensboro, NC | 276,134 | 141 | Springfield, MO | 160,962 | 215 | Evansville, IN | 118,194 |
| 68 | Plano, TX | 273,816 | 142 | Pembroke Pines, FL | 159,744 | 216 | Vallejo, CA | 117,912 |
| 69 | Lincoln, NE | 264,175 | 143 | Cape Coral, FL | 159,625 | 217 | Amherst, NY | 117,591 |
| 70 | Henderson, NV | 263,469 | 144 | Lancaster, CA | 159,155 | 218 | Athens-Clarke, GA | 117,457 |
| 71 | Buffalo, NY | 262,434 | 145 | Sioux Falls, SD | 158,354 | 219 | Independence, MO | 117,433 |
| 72 | Fort Wayne, IN | 256,625 | 146 | Peoria, AZ | 158,347 | 220 | Springfield, IL | 117,131 |
| 73 | Jersey City, NJ | 251,554 | 147 | Eugene, OR | 158,043 | 221 | Provo, UT | 116,879 |
| 74 | Mobile, AL | 251,516 | 148 | Salem, OR | 157,353 | 222 | Midland, TX | 115,637 |

| RANK | CITY | POP |
|---|---|---|
| 223 | El Monte, CA | 115,356 |
| 224 | Peoria, IL | 115,288 |
| 225 | Ann Arbor, MI | 115,008 |
| 226 | Berkeley, CA | 114,961 |
| 227 | Lansing, MI | 114,688 |
| 228 | Norman, OK | 113,969 |
| 229 | Downey, CA | 113,628 |
| 230 | Costa Mesa, CA | 112,635 |
| 231 | Murfreesboro, TN | 112,247 |
| 232 | Inglewood, CA | 111,488 |
| 233 | Miami Gardens, FL | 111,177 |
| 234 | Columbia, MO | 110,646 |
| 235 | Waterbury, CT | 110,486 |
| 236 | Manchester, NH | 110,040 |
| 237 | Fargo, ND | 109,813 |
| 238 | Westminster, CO | 109,461 |
| 239 | Wilmington, NC | 109,370 |
| 240 | Clearwater, FL | 109,255 |
| 241 | Elgin, IL | 109,155 |
| 242 | Pueblo, CO | 109,065 |
| 243 | Arvada, CO | 109,029 |
| 244 | Rochester, MN | 108,582 |
| 245 | Lowell, MA | 108,539 |
| 246 | Ventura, CA | 108,511 |
| 247 | Gresham, OR | 108,202 |
| 248 | Carlsbad, CA | 107,879 |
| 249 | West Covina, CA | 107,861 |
| 250 | Norwalk, CA | 107,295 |
| 251 | Fairfield, CA | 107,110 |
| 252 | Cambridge, MA | 106,981 |
| 253 | Murrieta, CA | 106,839 |
| 254 | High Point, NC | 106,801 |
| 255 | Billings, MT | 106,371 |
| 256 | Richmond, CA | 106,357 |
| 257 | Round Rock, TX | 106,232 |
| 258 | Green Bay, WI | 106,080 |
| 259 | Wichita Falls, TX | 105,488 |
| 260 | Everett, WA | 105,318 |
| 261 | Burbank, CA | 105,057 |
| 262 | Antioch, CA | 105,009 |
| 263 | Palm Bay, FL | 104,635 |
| 264 | Centennial, CO | 104,022 |
| 265 | Odessa, TX | 103,635 |
| 266 | Temecula, CA | 103,414 |
| 267 | Daly City, CA | 103,311 |
| 268 | Richardson, TX | 103,266 |
| 269 | Pompano Beach, FL | 103,003 |
| 270 | West Palm Beach, FL | 102,422 |
| 271 | Erie, PA | 101,972 |
| 272 | El Cajon, CA | 101,864 |
| 273 | Flint, MI | 101,632 |
| 274 | Rialto, CA | 101,595 |
| 275 | South Bend, IN | 101,398 |
| 276 | Santa Maria, CA | 101,207 |
| 277 | Davenport, IA | 101,193 |
| 278 | Edison Twnshp, NJ | 101,007 |
| 279 | Broken Arrow, OK | 100,688 |
| 280 | North Charleston, SC | 100,675 |
| 281 | Woodbridge Twnshp, NJ | 100,612 |
| 282 | Boulder, CO | 100,257 |
| 283 | Tyler, TX | 100,040 |
| 284 | Kenosha, WI | 99,993 |
| 285 | Lakeland, FL | 99,934 |
| 286 | Las Cruces, NM | 99,824 |
| 287 | San Mateo, CA | 99,303 |
| 288 | Lawton, OK | 98,781 |
| 289 | Albany, NY | 98,187 |
| 290 | Compton, CA | 98,057 |
| 291 | Sandy Springs, GA | 97,890 |
| 292 | Clovis, CA | 97,828 |
| 293 | Roanoke, VA | 97,780 |
| 294 | Jurupa Valley, CA | 97,577 |
| 295 | Dearborn, MI | 97,215 |
| 296 | Clinton Twnshp, MI | 97,001 |
| 297 | Greece, NY | 96,752 |
| 298 | Portsmouth, VA | 96,739 |
| 299 | College Station, TX | 96,567 |
| 300 | Greeley, CO | 96,276 |
| 301 | Vista, CA | 96,087 |
| 302 | New Bedford, MA | 96,031 |
| 303 | Livonia, MI | 96,028 |
| 304 | South Gate, CA | 95,966 |
| 305 | Mission Viejo, CA | 95,599 |
| 306 | Yuma, AZ | 95,568 |
| 307 | Brockton, MA | 95,156 |
| 308 | Davie, FL | 94,952 |
| 309 | Pearland, TX | 94,702 |
| 310 | Hillsboro, OR | 94,119 |
| 311 | Vacaville, CA | 93,951 |
| 312 | Lakewood Twnshp, NJ | 93,742 |
| 313 | Quincy, MA | 93,736 |
| 314 | Renton, WA | 93,722 |
| 315 | Yakima, WA | 93,419 |
| 316 | Carson, CA | 93,233 |
| 317 | Macon, GA | 92,836 |
| 318 | Sparks, NV | 92,387 |
| 319 | Hesperia, CA | 92,383 |
| 320 | Beaverton, OR | 92,276 |
| 321 | Roswell, GA | 92,141 |
| 322 | Toms River Twnshp, NJ | 92,131 |
| 323 | Federal Way, WA | 91,978 |
| 324 | Tuscaloosa, AL | 91,973 |
| 325 | Orem, UT | 91,953 |
| 326 | Westminster, CA | 91,908 |
| 327 | Lynn, MA | 91,846 |
| 328 | Lee's Summit, MO | 91,840 |
| 329 | Santa Monica, CA | 91,215 |
| 330 | Spokane Valley, WA | 91,164 |
| 331 | Miami Beach, FL | 91,066 |
| 332 | Redding, CA | 90,974 |
| 333 | Sandy, UT | 90,405 |
| 334 | Santa Barbara, CA | 89,871 |
| 335 | Fall River, MA | 89,753 |
| 336 | Waukegan, IL | 89,468 |
| 337 | Lawrence, KS | 89,180 |
| 338 | Hamilton Twnshp, NJ | 89,111 |
| 339 | Longmont, CO | 88,925 |
| 340 | Allen, TX | 88,783 |
| 341 | Reading, PA | 88,557 |
| 342 | Plantation, FL | 87,705 |
| 343 | Fort Smith, AR | 87,483 |
| 344 | Newport Beach, CA | 87,286 |
| 345 | Sunrise, FL | 87,168 |
| 346 | Chico, CA | 87,090 |
| 347 | Nashua, NH | 86,870 |
| 348 | Greenville, NC | 86,869 |
| 348 | San Leandro, CA | 86,869 |
| 350 | Duluth, MN | 86,830 |
| 351 | Whittier, CA | 86,740 |
| 352 | Newton, MA | 86,710 |
| 353 | Norwalk, CT | 86,693 |
| 354 | Boca Raton, FL | 86,493 |
| 355 | League City, TX | 86,127 |
| 356 | San Marcos, CA | 85,810 |
| 357 | Hawthorne, CA | 85,692 |
| 358 | Ramapo, NY | 85,448 |
| 359 | Trenton, NJ | 85,317 |
| 360 | Citrus Heights, CA | 85,112 |
| 361 | Ogden, UT | 85,083 |
| 362 | Tracy, CA | 85,047 |
| 363 | Clifton, NJ | 84,684 |
| 364 | Bloomington, MN | 84,596 |
| 365 | Alhambra, CA | 84,469 |
| 366 | Cicero, IL | 84,300 |
| 367 | Edmond, OK | 83,473 |
| 368 | Nampa, ID | 83,316 |
| 369 | Westland, MI | 83,299 |
| 370 | Sioux City, IA | 83,289 |
| 371 | Upper Darby Twnshp, PA | 82,978 |
| 372 | Sugar Land, TX | 82,924 |
| 373 | Livermore, CA | 82,800 |
| 374 | Longview, TX | 82,554 |
| 375 | Buena Park, CA | 82,505 |
| 376 | Hoover, AL | 82,332 |
| 377 | Warwick, RI | 82,282 |
| 378 | Danbury, CT | 81,891 |
| 379 | Carmel, IN | 81,819 |
| 380 | Bloomington, IN | 81,636 |
| 381 | Troy, MI | 81,567 |
| 382 | Lakewood, CA | 81,382 |
| 383 | Champaign, IL | 81,329 |
| 384 | Hemet, CA | 81,213 |
| 385 | Hammond, IN | 81,010 |
| 386 | Merced, CA | 80,976 |
| 387 | O'Fallon, MO | 80,670 |
| 388 | Mission, TX | 80,557 |
| 389 | Gary, IN | 80,472 |
| 390 | Edinburg, TX | 80,332 |
| 391 | Farmington Hills, MI | 80,316 |
| 392 | Cranston, RI | 80,315 |
| 393 | Clarkstown, NY | 80,186 |
| 394 | Menifee, CA | 80,047 |
| 395 | Johns Creek, GA | 80,037 |
| 396 | Chino, CA | 79,792 |
| 397 | Fishers, IN | 79,375 |
| 398 | Cheektowaga, NY | 79,178 |
| 399 | Lake Forest, CA | 79,166 |
| 400 | Racine, WI | 79,055 |
| 401 | Largo, FL | 78,783 |
| 402 | Napa, CA | 78,589 |
| 403 | Albany, GA | 78,512 |
| 404 | Indio, CA | 78,501 |
| 405 | Bryan, TX | 78,479 |
| 406 | Redwood City, CA | 78,466 |
| 407 | New Rochelle, NY | 78,025 |
| 408 | Bellflower, CA | 77,886 |
| 409 | Colonie, NY | 77,853 |
| 410 | Lawrence, MA | 77,661 |
| 411 | Deerfield Beach, FL | 77,431 |
| 412 | Tustin, CA | 77,400 |
| 413 | Lynchburg, VA | 77,347 |
| 414 | Brooklyn Park, MN | 77,346 |
| 415 | St. Joseph, MO | 77,330 |
| 416 | Meridian, ID | 77,270 |
| 417 | Somerville, MA | 77,200 |
| 418 | Melbourne, FL | 77,133 |
| 419 | Bloomington, IL | 77,107 |
| 420 | Kennewick, WA | 76,971 |
| 421 | Baldwin Park, CA | 76,644 |
| 422 | Chino Hills, CA | 76,632 |
| 423 | Decatur, IL | 76,131 |
| 424 | Scranton, PA | 76,118 |
| 425 | Medford, OR | 76,037 |
| 426 | Mountain View, CA | 75,933 |
| 427 | Brick Twnshp, NJ | 75,809 |
| 428 | St. George, UT | 75,780 |
| 429 | Upland, CA | 75,531 |
| 430 | Alameda, CA | 75,467 |
| 431 | Arlington Heights, IL | 75,463 |
| 432 | Bethlehem, PA | 75,388 |
| 433 | Fayetteville, AR | 75,387 |
| 434 | Evanston, IL | 74,820 |
| NA | Bend, OR** | NA |
| NA | Canton Twnshp, MI** | NA |
| NA | Chattanooga, TN** | NA |
| NA | Columbia, SC** | NA |
| NA | Concord, NC** | NA |
| NA | Lewisville, TX** | NA |
| NA | San Angelo, TX** | NA |
| NA | Suffolk, VA** | NA |

Source: Reported data from the F.B.I. "Crime in the United States 2012"

*Estimates as of July 2012 based on U.S. Bureau of the Census figures. Charlotte, Indianapolis, Las Vegas, Louisville, Mobile, and Savannah include areas under their police department but outside the city limits. All populations are for area covered by police department.

**Not available.

# 90. City Population in 2009
## National Total = 307,006,550*

| RANK | CITY | POP | RANK | CITY | POP | RANK | CITY | POP |
|---|---|---|---|---|---|---|---|---|
| 210 | Abilene, TX | 116,557 | 346 | Chino, CA | 84,626 | 179 | Fullerton, CA | 132,478 |
| 96 | Akron, OH | 206,497 | 87 | Chula Vista, CA | 224,841 | 212 | Gainesville, FL | 115,265 |
| 433 | Alameda, CA | 70,372 | 380 | Cicero, IL | 79,870 | 137 | Garden Grove, CA | 165,837 |
| 401 | Albany, GA | 75,734 | 55 | Cincinnati, OH | 333,568 | 92 | Garland, TX | 218,872 |
| 300 | Albany, NY | 93,445 | 350 | Citrus Heights, CA | 84,333 | 292 | Gary, IN | 95,219 |
| 33 | Albuquerque, NM | 530,636 | 383 | Clarkstown, NY | 78,899 | 83 | Gilbert, AZ | 231,799 |
| 157 | Alexandria, VA | 146,145 | 200 | Clarksville, TN | 121,661 | 71 | Glendale, AZ | 255,080 |
| 338 | Alhambra, CA | 85,956 | 243 | Clearwater, FL | 105,383 | 108 | Glendale, CA | 197,384 |
| 238 | Allentown, PA | 107,326 | 41 | Cleveland, OH | 429,238 | 139 | Grand Prairie, TX | 164,766 |
| 334 | Allen, TX | 86,901 | 389 | Clifton, NJ | 78,124 | 112 | Grand Rapids, MI | 192,901 |
| 115 | Amarillo, TX | 188,767 | 290 | Clinton Twnshp, MI | 95,956 | 301 | Greece, NY | 93,274 |
| 225 | Amherst, NY | 110,399 | 291 | Clovis, CA | 95,229 | 304 | Greeley, CO | 93,070 |
| 54 | Anaheim, CA | 335,970 | 337 | College Station, TX | 86,072 | 271 | Green Bay, WI | 100,836 |
| 64 | Anchorage, AK | 283,300 | 392 | Colonie, NY | 78,003 | 73 | Greensboro, NC | 253,191 |
| 215 | Ann Arbor, MI | 114,367 | 45 | Colorado Springs, CO | 401,626 | 369 | Greenville, NC | 81,814 |
| 265 | Antioch, CA | 101,243 | 258 | Columbia, MO | 102,588 | 260 | Gresham, OR | 102,463 |
| 418 | Arlington Heights, IL | 73,061 | 183 | Columbia, SC | 127,884 | 321 | Hamilton Twnshp, NJ | 90,491 |
| 48 | Arlington, TX | 379,104 | 117 | Columbus, GA | 186,224 | 400 | Hammond, IN | 76,085 |
| 233 | Arvada, CO | 107,943 | 297 | Compton, CA | 93,872 | 158 | Hampton, VA | 145,932 |
| 213 | Athens-Clarke, GA | 114,540 | 202 | Concord, CA | 121,042 | 193 | Hartford, CT | 124,049 |
| 31 | Atlanta, GA | 552,901 | 437 | Concord, NC | 67,478 | 351 | Hawthorne, CA | 84,314 |
| 57 | Aurora, CO | 324,014 | 186 | Coral Springs, FL | 125,656 | 164 | Hayward, CA | 142,227 |
| 127 | Aurora, IL | 175,135 | 151 | Corona, CA | 152,438 | 422 | Hemet, CA | 72,417 |
| 17 | Austin, TX | 768,970 | 63 | Corpus Christi, TX | 287,507 | 69 | Henderson, NV | 261,883 |
| 56 | Bakersfield, CA | 330,897 | 228 | Costa Mesa, CA | 110,150 | 328 | Hesperia, CA | 88,904 |
| 397 | Baldwin Park, CA | 77,539 | 377 | Cranston, RI | 80,223 | 95 | Hialeah, FL | 208,874 |
| 20 | Baltimore, MD | 638,755 | 10 | Dallas, TX | 1,290,266 | 251 | High Point, NC | 103,675 |
| 89 | Baton Rouge, LA | 223,187 | 264 | Daly City, CA | 101,284 | 287 | Hillsboro, OR | 96,563 |
| 227 | Beaumont, TX | 110,237 | 381 | Danbury, CT | 79,729 | 166 | Hollywood, FL | 141,597 |
| 302 | Beaverton, OR | 93,221 | 267 | Davenport, IA | 101,116 | 426 | Hoover, AL | 71,919 |
| 188 | Bellevue, WA | 125,054 | 323 | Davie, FL | 90,147 | 4 | Houston, TX | 2,273,771 |
| 419 | Bellflower, CA | 73,038 | 150 | Dayton, OH | 152,965 | 111 | Huntington Beach, CA | 192,911 |
| 373 | Bend, OR | 80,550 | 342 | Dearborn, MI | 85,305 | 123 | Huntsville, AL | 178,601 |
| 266 | Berkeley, CA | 101,190 | 402 | Decatur, IL | 75,651 | 199 | Independence, MO | 122,174 |
| 423 | Bethlehem, PA | 72,349 | NA | Deerfield Beach, FL** | NA | 13 | Indianapolis, IN | 813,471 |
| 242 | Billings, MT | 105,427 | 191 | Denton, TX | 124,308 | 325 | Indio, CA | 89,459 |
| 85 | Birmingham, AL | 227,373 | 25 | Denver, CO | 604,680 | 220 | Inglewood, CA | 112,712 |
| 414 | Bloomington, IL | 73,897 | 110 | Des Moines, IA | 196,794 | 93 | Irvine, CA | 215,673 |
| 427 | Bloomington, IN | 71,845 | 12 | Detroit, MI | 908,441 | 103 | Irving, TX | 202,447 |
| 372 | Bloomington, MN | 80,864 | 237 | Downey, CA | 107,598 | 14 | Jacksonville, FL | 810,064 |
| 338 | Boca Raton, FL | 85,956 | 355 | Duluth, MN | 84,071 | 132 | Jackson, MS | 172,799 |
| 97 | Boise, ID | 206,437 | 410 | Edinburg, TX | 74,611 | 77 | Jersey City, NJ | 240,858 |
| 22 | Boston, MA | 624,222 | 277 | Edison Twnshp, NJ | 99,356 | 440 | Johns Creek, GA | 59,305 |
| 273 | Boulder, CO | 100,035 | 371 | Edmond, OK | 80,889 | 153 | Joliet, IL | 151,103 |
| 385 | Brick Twnshp, NJ | 78,666 | 308 | El Cajon, CA | 92,466 | NA | Jurupa Valley, CA** | NA |
| 174 | Bridgeport, CT | 136,049 | 198 | El Monte, CA | 122,428 | 165 | Kansas City, KS | 142,102 |
| 288 | Brockton, MA | 96,471 | 23 | El Paso, TX | 618,812 | 34 | Kansas City, MO | 484,684 |
| 294 | Broken Arrow, OK | 94,415 | 236 | Elgin, IL | 107,686 | 438 | Kennewick, WA | 64,009 |
| 429 | Brooklyn Park, MN | 71,740 | 189 | Elizabeth, NJ | 124,910 | 282 | Kenosha, WI | 97,657 |
| 122 | Brownsville, TX | 179,491 | 169 | Elk Grove, CA | 140,576 | 349 | Kent, WA | 84,363 |
| 417 | Bryan, TX | 73,111 | 250 | Erie, PA | 103,837 | 203 | Killeen, TX | 120,670 |
| 382 | Buena Park, CA | 79,525 | 171 | Escondido, CA | 137,432 | 118 | Knoxville, TN | 185,850 |
| 68 | Buffalo, NY | 268,655 | 152 | Eugene, OR | 151,383 | 217 | Lafayette, LA | 113,868 |
| 254 | Burbank, CA | 103,248 | 390 | Evanston, IL | 78,101 | 403 | Lake Forest, CA | 75,509 |
| 255 | Cambridge, MA | 102,866 | 211 | Evansville, IN | 115,770 | 295 | Lakeland, FL | 94,322 |
| 361 | Canton Twnshp, MI | 82,634 | 280 | Everett, WA | 98,431 | 425 | Lakewood Twnshp, NJ | 72,206 |
| 141 | Cape Coral, FL | 164,344 | 248 | Fairfield, CA | 104,478 | 386 | Lakewood, CA | 78,334 |
| 279 | Carlsbad, CA | 98,482 | 312 | Fall River, MA | 91,901 | 168 | Lakewood, CO | 140,618 |
| 435 | Carmel, IN | 68,424 | 298 | Fargo, ND | 93,830 | 154 | Lancaster, CA | 148,742 |
| 185 | Carrollton, TX | 127,432 | 388 | Farmington Hills, MI | 78,140 | 219 | Lansing, MI | 113,392 |
| 305 | Carson, CA | 92,635 | 405 | Fayetteville, AR | 75,120 | 86 | Laredo, TX | 226,944 |
| 175 | Cary, NC | 133,757 | 129 | Fayetteville, NC | 173,995 | 420 | Largo, FL | 72,567 |
| 182 | Cedar Rapids, IA | 128,779 | 353 | Federal Way, WA | 84,219 | 296 | Las Cruces, NM | 94,024 |
| 276 | Centennial, CO | 99,385 | 416 | Fishers, IN | 73,538 | 7 | Las Vegas, NV | 1,377,282 |
| 375 | Champaign, IL | 80,467 | 222 | Flint, MI | 111,657 | 313 | Lawrence, KS | 91,703 |
| 70 | Chandler, AZ | 256,091 | 113 | Fontana, CA | 190,303 | 432 | Lawrence, MA | 70,670 |
| 218 | Charleston, SC | 113,681 | 170 | Fort Collins, CO | 138,487 | 324 | Lawton, OK | 89,835 |
| 16 | Charlotte, NC | 777,708 | 119 | Fort Lauderdale, FL | 182,942 | 407 | League City, TX | 74,801 |
| 133 | Chattanooga, TN | 172,536 | 343 | Fort Smith, AR | 85,175 | 340 | Lee's Summit, MO | 85,792 |
| 394 | Cheektowaga, NY | 77,772 | 74 | Fort Wayne, IN | 251,584 | 247 | Lewisville, TX | 104,601 |
| 88 | Chesapeake, VA | 223,261 | 18 | Fort Worth, TX | 723,456 | 60 | Lexington, KY | 296,406 |
| 3 | Chicago, IL | 2,848,431 | 102 | Fremont, CA | 202,714 | 72 | Lincoln, NE | 254,438 |
| 345 | Chico, CA | 84,724 | 35 | Fresno, CA | 481,370 | 114 | Little Rock, AR | 190,205 |
| 409 | Chino Hills, CA | 74,650 | 231 | Frisco, TX | 108,244 | 370 | Livermore, CA | 80,915 |

| RANK | CITY | POP | RANK | CITY | POP | RANK | CITY | POP |
|---|---|---|---|---|---|---|---|---|
| 322 | Livonia, MI | 90,232 | 162 | Pasadena, CA | 144,063 | 284 | South Gate, CA | 96,651 |
| 38 | Long Beach, CA | 463,969 | 155 | Pasadena, TX | 146,963 | 316 | Sparks, NV | 91,421 |
| 332 | Longmont, CO | 87,611 | 160 | Paterson, NJ | 144,943 | 335 | Spokane Valley, WA | 86,756 |
| 396 | Longview, TX | 77,663 | 329 | Pearland, TX | 88,528 | 101 | Spokane, WA | 202,932 |
| 2 | Los Angeles, CA | 3,848,776 | 159 | Pembroke Pines, FL | 145,514 | 206 | Springfield, IL | 117,973 |
| 21 | Louisville, KY | 631,260 | 140 | Peoria, AZ | 164,366 | 148 | Springfield, MA | 153,533 |
| 221 | Lowell, MA | 111,772 | 216 | Peoria, IL | 114,241 | 145 | Springfield, MO | 156,659 |
| 90 | Lubbock, TX | 222,884 | 6 | Philadelphia, PA | 1,547,605 | 204 | Stamford, CT | 119,507 |
| 415 | Lynchburg, VA | 73,735 | 5 | Phoenix, AZ | 1,597,397 | 184 | Sterling Heights, MI | 127,440 |
| 319 | Lynn, MA | 91,149 | 58 | Pittsburgh, PA | 312,232 | 61 | Stockton, CA | 292,212 |
| 309 | Macon, GA | 92,299 | 67 | Plano, TX | 272,747 | 404 | St. George, UT | 75,391 |
| 81 | Madison, WI | 234,461 | 357 | Plantation, FL | 83,544 | 399 | St. Joseph, MO | 76,436 |
| 229 | Manchester, NH | 108,671 | 149 | Pomona, CA | 153,217 | 50 | St. Louis, MO | 355,208 |
| 178 | McAllen, TX | 132,598 | 262 | Pompano Beach, FL | 101,840 | 65 | St. Paul, MN | 280,194 |
| 180 | McKinney, TX | 132,146 | 142 | Port St. Lucie, FL | 164,069 | 76 | St. Petersburg, FL | 244,933 |
| 412 | Medford, OR | 74,042 | 29 | Portland, OR | 560,908 | 344 | Suffolk, VA | 84,929 |
| 393 | Melbourne, FL | 77,854 | 268 | Portsmouth, VA | 100,970 | 360 | Sugar Land, TX | 82,696 |
| 19 | Memphis, TN | 667,421 | 134 | Providence, RI | 171,664 | 181 | Sunnyvale, CA | 132,144 |
| 436 | Menifee, CA | 68,083 | 205 | Provo, UT | 119,472 | 327 | Sunrise, FL | 88,936 |
| 384 | Merced, CA | 78,693 | 244 | Pueblo, CO | 105,271 | 246 | Surprise, AZ | 104,692 |
| 430 | Meridian, ID | 71,581 | 286 | Quincy, MA | 96,580 | 172 | Syracuse, NY | 137,208 |
| 36 | Mesa, AZ | 470,833 | 366 | Racine, WI | 82,232 | 107 | Tacoma, WA | 197,557 |
| 177 | Mesquite, TX | 132,941 | 43 | Raleigh, NC | 406,005 | 128 | Tallahassee, FL | 174,183 |
| 352 | Miami Beach, FL | 84,260 | 398 | Ramapo, NY | 76,611 | 51 | Tampa, FL | 345,233 |
| 226 | Miami Gardens, FL | 110,346 | 126 | Rancho Cucamon., CA | 176,676 | 269 | Temecula, CA | 100,922 |
| 42 | Miami, FL | 419,205 | 376 | Reading, PA | 80,418 | 125 | Tempe, AZ | 177,486 |
| 234 | Midland, TX | 107,933 | 318 | Redding, CA | 91,242 | 207 | Thornton, CO | 117,415 |
| 26 | Milwaukee, WI | 604,673 | 413 | Redwood City, CA | 73,905 | 194 | Thousand Oaks, CA | 123,735 |
| 47 | Minneapolis, MN | 382,618 | 91 | Reno, NV | 221,010 | 62 | Toledo, OH | 291,066 |
| 230 | Miramar, FL | 108,375 | 439 | Renton, WA | 63,599 | 285 | Toms River Twnshp, NJ | 96,614 |
| 293 | Mission Viejo, CA | 94,552 | 275 | Rialto, CA | 99,386 | 196 | Topeka, KS | 123,449 |
| 434 | Mission, TX | 69,997 | 257 | Richardson, TX | 102,675 | 167 | Torrance, CA | 141,109 |
| 75 | Mobile, AL | 246,171 | 259 | Richmond, CA | 102,566 | 368 | Tracy, CA | 82,019 |
| 99 | Modesto, CA | 204,474 | 100 | Richmond, VA | 203,233 | 362 | Trenton, NJ | 82,609 |
| 109 | Moreno Valley, CA | 197,114 | 59 | Riverside, CA | 299,871 | 378 | Troy, MI | 80,182 |
| 431 | Mountain View, CA | 71,423 | 303 | Roanoke, VA | 93,110 | 32 | Tucson, AZ | 547,981 |
| 240 | Murfreesboro, TN | 105,910 | 261 | Rochester, MN | 101,884 | 46 | Tulsa, OK | 384,851 |
| 245 | Murrieta, CA | 105,238 | 98 | Rochester, NY | 205,537 | 314 | Tuscaloosa, AL | 91,688 |
| 356 | Nampa, ID | 83,875 | 144 | Rockford, IL | 157,943 | 424 | Tustin, CA | 72,286 |
| 408 | Napa, CA | 74,736 | 209 | Roseville, CA | 116,846 | 278 | Tyler, TX | 99,279 |
| 161 | Naperville, IL | 144,731 | 330 | Roswell, GA | 88,371 | 421 | Upland, CA | 72,461 |
| 336 | Nashua, NH | 86,554 | 224 | Round Rock, TX | 110,531 | 391 | Upper Darby Twnshp, PA | 78,088 |
| 24 | Nashville, TN | 610,176 | 37 | Sacramento, CA | 470,308 | 307 | Vacaville, CA | 92,538 |
| 306 | New Bedford, MA | 92,621 | 147 | Salem, OR | 155,329 | 214 | Vallejo, CA | 114,443 |
| 195 | New Haven, CT | 123,659 | 163 | Salinas, CA | 143,660 | 138 | Vancouver, WA | 165,147 |
| 53 | New Orleans, LA | 336,425 | 120 | Salt Lake City, UT | 180,724 | 249 | Ventura, CA | 103,997 |
| 411 | New Rochelle, NY | 74,320 | 310 | San Angelo, TX | 92,269 | 208 | Victorville, CA | 117,150 |
| 1 | New York, NY | 8,400,907 | 8 | San Antonio, TX | 1,373,936 | 40 | Virginia Beach, VA | 436,175 |
| 66 | Newark, NJ | 279,203 | 105 | San Bernardino, CA | 199,683 | 192 | Visalia, CA | 124,263 |
| 379 | Newport Beach, CA | 79,912 | 9 | San Diego, CA | 1,314,773 | 317 | Vista, CA | 91,252 |
| 121 | Newport News, VA | 180,174 | 15 | San Francisco, CA | 809,755 | 187 | Waco, TX | 125,098 |
| 348 | Newton, MA | 84,427 | 11 | San Jose, CA | 954,009 | 176 | Warren, MI | 133,485 |
| 80 | Norfolk, VA | 235,097 | 395 | San Leandro, CA | 77,676 | 347 | Warwick, RI | 84,488 |
| 232 | Norman, OK | 108,152 | 365 | San Marcos, CA | 82,258 | 28 | Washington, DC | 599,657 |
| 289 | North Charleston, SC | 95,982 | 311 | San Mateo, CA | 92,208 | 239 | Waterbury, CT | 107,007 |
| 82 | North Las Vegas, NV | 232,631 | 364 | Sandy Springs, GA | 82,435 | 320 | Waukegan, IL | 91,059 |
| 256 | Norwalk, CA | 102,807 | 283 | Sandy, UT | 97,031 | 241 | West Covina, CA | 105,846 |
| 358 | Norwalk, CT | 83,198 | 52 | Santa Ana, CA | 339,196 | 272 | West Palm Beach, FL | 100,763 |
| 44 | Oakland, CA | 404,553 | 341 | Santa Barbara, CA | 85,715 | 190 | West Valley, UT | 124,472 |
| 136 | Oceanside, CA | 170,579 | 223 | Santa Clara, CA | 111,106 | 387 | Westland, MI | 78,149 |
| 274 | Odessa, TX | 99,770 | 135 | Santa Clarita, CA | 171,112 | 326 | Westminster, CA | 89,057 |
| 374 | O'Fallon, MO | 80,528 | 333 | Santa Maria, CA | 87,381 | 235 | Westminster, CO | 107,705 |
| 359 | Ogden, UT | 83,016 | 331 | Santa Monica, CA | 88,038 | 367 | Whittier, CA | 82,096 |
| 30 | Oklahoma City, OK | 556,939 | 146 | Santa Rosa, CA | 156,541 | 270 | Wichita Falls, TX | 100,884 |
| 197 | Olathe, KS | 123,321 | 94 | Savannah, GA | 212,711 | 49 | Wichita, KS | 367,635 |
| 39 | Omaha, NE | 443,037 | 78 | Scottsdale, AZ | 239,115 | 263 | Wilmington, NC | 101,438 |
| 131 | Ontario, CA | 173,212 | 428 | Scranton, PA | 71,843 | 84 | Winston-Salem, NC | 230,978 |
| 173 | Orange, CA | 137,132 | 27 | Seattle, WA | 602,531 | 281 | Woodbridge Twnshp, NJ | 98,013 |
| 299 | Orem, UT | 93,785 | 106 | Shreveport, LA | 199,629 | 124 | Worcester, MA | 178,474 |
| 79 | Orlando, FL | 235,109 | 201 | Simi Valley, CA | 121,538 | 354 | Yakima, WA | 84,167 |
| 130 | Overland Park, KS | 173,688 | 363 | Sioux City, IA | 82,573 | 104 | Yonkers, NY | 202,192 |
| 116 | Oxnard, CA | 187,357 | 143 | Sioux Falls, SD | 158,672 | 315 | Yuma, AZ | 91,433 |
| 252 | Palm Bay, FL | 103,475 | 406 | Somerville, MA | 75,112 | | | |
| 156 | Palmdale, CA | 146,377 | 253 | South Bend, IN | 103,326 | | | |

Source: Reported data from the F.B.I. "Crime in the United States 2009"

*Estimates as of July 2009 based on U.S. Bureau of the Census figures. Charlotte, Indianapolis, Las Vegas, Louisville, Mobile, and Savannah include areas under their police department but outside the city limits. All populations are for area covered by police department.

**Not available.

# 90. City Population in 2009 (continued)
## National Total = 307,006,550*

| RANK | CITY | POP | RANK | CITY | POP | RANK | CITY | POP |
|---|---|---|---|---|---|---|---|---|
| 1 | New York, NY | 8,400,907 | 75 | Mobile, AL | 246,171 | 149 | Pomona, CA | 153,217 |
| 2 | Los Angeles, CA | 3,848,776 | 76 | St. Petersburg, FL | 244,933 | 150 | Dayton, OH | 152,965 |
| 3 | Chicago, IL | 2,848,431 | 77 | Jersey City, NJ | 240,858 | 151 | Corona, CA | 152,438 |
| 4 | Houston, TX | 2,273,771 | 78 | Scottsdale, AZ | 239,115 | 152 | Eugene, OR | 151,383 |
| 5 | Phoenix, AZ | 1,597,397 | 79 | Orlando, FL | 235,109 | 153 | Joliet, IL | 151,103 |
| 6 | Philadelphia, PA | 1,547,605 | 80 | Norfolk, VA | 235,097 | 154 | Lancaster, CA | 148,742 |
| 7 | Las Vegas, NV | 1,377,282 | 81 | Madison, WI | 234,461 | 155 | Pasadena, TX | 146,963 |
| 8 | San Antonio, TX | 1,373,936 | 82 | North Las Vegas, NV | 232,631 | 156 | Palmdale, CA | 146,377 |
| 9 | San Diego, CA | 1,314,773 | 83 | Gilbert, AZ | 231,799 | 157 | Alexandria, VA | 146,145 |
| 10 | Dallas, TX | 1,290,266 | 84 | Winston-Salem, NC | 230,978 | 158 | Hampton, VA | 145,932 |
| 11 | San Jose, CA | 954,009 | 85 | Birmingham, AL | 227,373 | 159 | Pembroke Pines, FL | 145,514 |
| 12 | Detroit, MI | 908,441 | 86 | Laredo, TX | 226,944 | 160 | Paterson, NJ | 144,943 |
| 13 | Indianapolis, IN | 813,471 | 87 | Chula Vista, CA | 224,841 | 161 | Naperville, IL | 144,731 |
| 14 | Jacksonville, FL | 810,064 | 88 | Chesapeake, VA | 223,261 | 162 | Pasadena, CA | 144,063 |
| 15 | San Francisco, CA | 809,755 | 89 | Baton Rouge, LA | 223,187 | 163 | Salinas, CA | 143,660 |
| 16 | Charlotte, NC | 777,708 | 90 | Lubbock, TX | 222,884 | 164 | Hayward, CA | 142,227 |
| 17 | Austin, TX | 768,970 | 91 | Reno, NV | 221,010 | 165 | Kansas City, KS | 142,102 |
| 18 | Fort Worth, TX | 723,456 | 92 | Garland, TX | 218,872 | 166 | Hollywood, FL | 141,597 |
| 19 | Memphis, TN | 667,421 | 93 | Irvine, CA | 215,673 | 167 | Torrance, CA | 141,109 |
| 20 | Baltimore, MD | 638,755 | 94 | Savannah, GA | 212,711 | 168 | Lakewood, CO | 140,618 |
| 21 | Louisville, KY | 631,260 | 95 | Hialeah, FL | 208,874 | 169 | Elk Grove, CA | 140,576 |
| 22 | Boston, MA | 624,222 | 96 | Akron, OH | 206,497 | 170 | Fort Collins, CO | 138,487 |
| 23 | El Paso, TX | 618,812 | 97 | Boise, ID | 206,437 | 171 | Escondido, CA | 137,432 |
| 24 | Nashville, TN | 610,176 | 98 | Rochester, NY | 205,537 | 172 | Syracuse, NY | 137,208 |
| 25 | Denver, CO | 604,680 | 99 | Modesto, CA | 204,474 | 173 | Orange, CA | 137,132 |
| 26 | Milwaukee, WI | 604,673 | 100 | Richmond, VA | 203,233 | 174 | Bridgeport, CT | 136,049 |
| 27 | Seattle, WA | 602,531 | 101 | Spokane, WA | 202,932 | 175 | Cary, NC | 133,757 |
| 28 | Washington, DC | 599,657 | 102 | Fremont, CA | 202,714 | 176 | Warren, MI | 133,485 |
| 29 | Portland, OR | 560,908 | 103 | Irving, TX | 202,447 | 177 | Mesquite, TX | 132,941 |
| 30 | Oklahoma City, OK | 556,939 | 104 | Yonkers, NY | 202,192 | 178 | McAllen, TX | 132,598 |
| 31 | Atlanta, GA | 552,901 | 105 | San Bernardino, CA | 199,683 | 179 | Fullerton, CA | 132,478 |
| 32 | Tucson, AZ | 547,981 | 106 | Shreveport, LA | 199,629 | 180 | McKinney, TX | 132,146 |
| 33 | Albuquerque, NM | 530,636 | 107 | Tacoma, WA | 197,557 | 181 | Sunnyvale, CA | 132,144 |
| 34 | Kansas City, MO | 484,684 | 108 | Glendale, CA | 197,384 | 182 | Cedar Rapids, IA | 128,779 |
| 35 | Fresno, CA | 481,370 | 109 | Moreno Valley, CA | 197,114 | 183 | Columbia, SC | 127,884 |
| 36 | Mesa, AZ | 470,833 | 110 | Des Moines, IA | 196,794 | 184 | Sterling Heights, MI | 127,440 |
| 37 | Sacramento, CA | 470,308 | 111 | Huntington Beach, CA | 192,911 | 185 | Carrollton, TX | 127,432 |
| 38 | Long Beach, CA | 463,969 | 112 | Grand Rapids, MI | 192,901 | 186 | Coral Springs, FL | 125,656 |
| 39 | Omaha, NE | 443,037 | 113 | Fontana, CA | 190,303 | 187 | Waco, TX | 125,098 |
| 40 | Virginia Beach, VA | 436,175 | 114 | Little Rock, AR | 190,205 | 188 | Bellevue, WA | 125,054 |
| 41 | Cleveland, OH | 429,238 | 115 | Amarillo, TX | 188,767 | 189 | Elizabeth, NJ | 124,910 |
| 42 | Miami, FL | 419,205 | 116 | Oxnard, CA | 187,357 | 190 | West Valley, UT | 124,472 |
| 43 | Raleigh, NC | 406,005 | 117 | Columbus, GA | 186,224 | 191 | Denton, TX | 124,308 |
| 44 | Oakland, CA | 404,553 | 118 | Knoxville, TN | 185,850 | 192 | Visalia, CA | 124,263 |
| 45 | Colorado Springs, CO | 401,626 | 119 | Fort Lauderdale, FL | 182,942 | 193 | Hartford, CT | 124,049 |
| 46 | Tulsa, OK | 384,851 | 120 | Salt Lake City, UT | 180,724 | 194 | Thousand Oaks, CA | 123,735 |
| 47 | Minneapolis, MN | 382,618 | 121 | Newport News, VA | 180,174 | 195 | New Haven, CT | 123,659 |
| 48 | Arlington, TX | 379,104 | 122 | Brownsville, TX | 179,491 | 196 | Topeka, KS | 123,449 |
| 49 | Wichita, KS | 367,635 | 123 | Huntsville, AL | 178,601 | 197 | Olathe, KS | 123,321 |
| 50 | St. Louis, MO | 355,208 | 124 | Worcester, MA | 178,474 | 198 | El Monte, CA | 122,428 |
| 51 | Tampa, FL | 345,233 | 125 | Tempe, AZ | 177,486 | 199 | Independence, MO | 122,174 |
| 52 | Santa Ana, CA | 339,196 | 126 | Rancho Cucamon., CA | 176,676 | 200 | Clarksville, TN | 121,661 |
| 53 | New Orleans, LA | 336,425 | 127 | Aurora, IL | 175,135 | 201 | Simi Valley, CA | 121,538 |
| 54 | Anaheim, CA | 335,970 | 128 | Tallahassee, FL | 174,183 | 202 | Concord, CA | 121,042 |
| 55 | Cincinnati, OH | 333,568 | 129 | Fayetteville, NC | 173,995 | 203 | Killeen, TX | 120,670 |
| 56 | Bakersfield, CA | 330,897 | 130 | Overland Park, KS | 173,688 | 204 | Stamford, CT | 119,507 |
| 57 | Aurora, CO | 324,014 | 131 | Ontario, CA | 173,212 | 205 | Provo, UT | 119,472 |
| 58 | Pittsburgh, PA | 312,232 | 132 | Jackson, MS | 172,799 | 206 | Springfield, IL | 117,973 |
| 59 | Riverside, CA | 299,871 | 133 | Chattanooga, TN | 172,536 | 207 | Thornton, CO | 117,415 |
| 60 | Lexington, KY | 296,406 | 134 | Providence, RI | 171,664 | 208 | Victorville, CA | 117,150 |
| 61 | Stockton, CA | 292,212 | 135 | Santa Clarita, CA | 171,112 | 209 | Roseville, CA | 116,846 |
| 62 | Toledo, OH | 291,066 | 136 | Oceanside, CA | 170,579 | 210 | Abilene, TX | 116,557 |
| 63 | Corpus Christi, TX | 287,507 | 137 | Garden Grove, CA | 165,837 | 211 | Evansville, IN | 115,770 |
| 64 | Anchorage, AK | 283,300 | 138 | Vancouver, WA | 165,147 | 212 | Gainesville, FL | 115,265 |
| 65 | St. Paul, MN | 280,194 | 139 | Grand Prairie, TX | 164,766 | 213 | Athens-Clarke, GA | 114,540 |
| 66 | Newark, NJ | 279,203 | 140 | Peoria, AZ | 164,366 | 214 | Vallejo, CA | 114,443 |
| 67 | Plano, TX | 272,747 | 141 | Cape Coral, FL | 164,344 | 215 | Ann Arbor, MI | 114,367 |
| 68 | Buffalo, NY | 268,655 | 142 | Port St. Lucie, FL | 164,069 | 216 | Peoria, IL | 114,241 |
| 69 | Henderson, NV | 261,883 | 143 | Sioux Falls, SD | 158,672 | 217 | Lafayette, LA | 113,868 |
| 70 | Chandler, AZ | 256,091 | 144 | Rockford, IL | 157,943 | 218 | Charleston, SC | 113,681 |
| 71 | Glendale, AZ | 255,080 | 145 | Springfield, MO | 156,659 | 219 | Lansing, MI | 113,392 |
| 72 | Lincoln, NE | 254,438 | 146 | Santa Rosa, CA | 156,541 | 220 | Inglewood, CA | 112,712 |
| 73 | Greensboro, NC | 253,191 | 147 | Salem, OR | 155,329 | 221 | Lowell, MA | 111,772 |
| 74 | Fort Wayne, IN | 251,584 | 148 | Springfield, MA | 153,533 | 222 | Flint, MI | 111,657 |

| RANK | CITY | POP |
|---|---|---|
| 223 | Santa Clara, CA | 111,106 |
| 224 | Round Rock, TX | 110,531 |
| 225 | Amherst, NY | 110,399 |
| 226 | Miami Gardens, FL | 110,346 |
| 227 | Beaumont, TX | 110,237 |
| 228 | Costa Mesa, CA | 110,150 |
| 229 | Manchester, NH | 108,671 |
| 230 | Miramar, FL | 108,375 |
| 231 | Frisco, TX | 108,244 |
| 232 | Norman, OK | 108,152 |
| 233 | Arvada, CO | 107,943 |
| 234 | Midland, TX | 107,933 |
| 235 | Westminster, CO | 107,705 |
| 236 | Elgin, IL | 107,686 |
| 237 | Downey, CA | 107,598 |
| 238 | Allentown, PA | 107,326 |
| 239 | Waterbury, CT | 107,007 |
| 240 | Murfreesboro, TN | 105,910 |
| 241 | West Covina, CA | 105,846 |
| 242 | Billings, MT | 105,427 |
| 243 | Clearwater, FL | 105,383 |
| 244 | Pueblo, CO | 105,271 |
| 245 | Murrieta, CA | 105,238 |
| 246 | Surprise, AZ | 104,692 |
| 247 | Lewisville, TX | 104,601 |
| 248 | Fairfield, CA | 104,478 |
| 249 | Ventura, CA | 103,997 |
| 250 | Erie, PA | 103,837 |
| 251 | High Point, NC | 103,675 |
| 252 | Palm Bay, FL | 103,475 |
| 253 | South Bend, IN | 103,326 |
| 254 | Burbank, CA | 103,248 |
| 255 | Cambridge, MA | 102,866 |
| 256 | Norwalk, CA | 102,807 |
| 257 | Richardson, TX | 102,675 |
| 258 | Columbia, MO | 102,588 |
| 259 | Richmond, CA | 102,566 |
| 260 | Gresham, OR | 102,463 |
| 261 | Rochester, MN | 101,884 |
| 262 | Pompano Beach, FL | 101,840 |
| 263 | Wilmington, NC | 101,438 |
| 264 | Daly City, CA | 101,284 |
| 265 | Antioch, CA | 101,243 |
| 266 | Berkeley, CA | 101,190 |
| 267 | Davenport, IA | 101,116 |
| 268 | Portsmouth, VA | 100,970 |
| 269 | Temecula, CA | 100,922 |
| 270 | Wichita Falls, TX | 100,884 |
| 271 | Green Bay, WI | 100,836 |
| 272 | West Palm Beach, FL | 100,763 |
| 273 | Boulder, CO | 100,035 |
| 274 | Odessa, TX | 99,770 |
| 275 | Rialto, CA | 99,386 |
| 276 | Centennial, CO | 99,385 |
| 277 | Edison Twnshp, NJ | 99,356 |
| 278 | Tyler, TX | 99,279 |
| 279 | Carlsbad, CA | 98,482 |
| 280 | Everett, WA | 98,431 |
| 281 | Woodbridge Twnshp, NJ | 98,013 |
| 282 | Kenosha, WI | 97,657 |
| 283 | Sandy, UT | 97,031 |
| 284 | South Gate, CA | 96,651 |
| 285 | Toms River Twnshp, NJ | 96,614 |
| 286 | Quincy, MA | 96,580 |
| 287 | Hillsboro, OR | 96,563 |
| 288 | Brockton, MA | 96,471 |
| 289 | North Charleston, SC | 95,982 |
| 290 | Clinton Twnshp, MI | 95,956 |
| 291 | Clovis, CA | 95,229 |
| 292 | Gary, IN | 95,219 |
| 293 | Mission Viejo, CA | 94,552 |
| 294 | Broken Arrow, OK | 94,415 |
| 295 | Lakeland, FL | 94,322 |
| 296 | Las Cruces, NM | 94,024 |

| RANK | CITY | POP |
|---|---|---|
| 297 | Compton, CA | 93,872 |
| 298 | Fargo, ND | 93,830 |
| 299 | Orem, UT | 93,785 |
| 300 | Albany, NY | 93,445 |
| 301 | Greece, NY | 93,274 |
| 302 | Beaverton, OR | 93,221 |
| 303 | Roanoke, VA | 93,110 |
| 304 | Greeley, CO | 93,070 |
| 305 | Carson, CA | 92,635 |
| 306 | New Bedford, MA | 92,621 |
| 307 | Vacaville, CA | 92,538 |
| 308 | El Cajon, CA | 92,466 |
| 309 | Macon, GA | 92,299 |
| 310 | San Angelo, TX | 92,269 |
| 311 | San Mateo, CA | 92,208 |
| 312 | Fall River, MA | 91,901 |
| 313 | Lawrence, KS | 91,703 |
| 314 | Tuscaloosa, AL | 91,688 |
| 315 | Yuma, AZ | 91,433 |
| 316 | Sparks, NV | 91,421 |
| 317 | Vista, CA | 91,252 |
| 318 | Redding, CA | 91,242 |
| 319 | Lynn, MA | 91,149 |
| 320 | Waukegan, IL | 91,059 |
| 321 | Hamilton Twnshp, NJ | 90,491 |
| 322 | Livonia, MI | 90,232 |
| 323 | Davie, FL | 90,147 |
| 324 | Lawton, OK | 89,835 |
| 325 | Indio, CA | 89,459 |
| 326 | Westminster, CA | 89,057 |
| 327 | Sunrise, FL | 88,936 |
| 328 | Hesperia, CA | 88,904 |
| 329 | Pearland, TX | 88,528 |
| 330 | Roswell, GA | 88,371 |
| 331 | Santa Monica, CA | 88,038 |
| 332 | Longmont, CO | 87,611 |
| 333 | Santa Maria, CA | 87,381 |
| 334 | Allen, TX | 86,901 |
| 335 | Spokane Valley, WA | 86,756 |
| 336 | Nashua, NH | 86,554 |
| 337 | College Station, TX | 86,072 |
| 338 | Alhambra, CA | 85,956 |
| 338 | Boca Raton, FL | 85,956 |
| 340 | Lee's Summit, MO | 85,792 |
| 341 | Santa Barbara, CA | 85,715 |
| 342 | Dearborn, MI | 85,305 |
| 343 | Fort Smith, AR | 85,175 |
| 344 | Suffolk, VA | 84,929 |
| 345 | Chico, CA | 84,724 |
| 346 | Chino, CA | 84,626 |
| 347 | Warwick, RI | 84,488 |
| 348 | Newton, MA | 84,427 |
| 349 | Kent, WA | 84,363 |
| 350 | Citrus Heights, CA | 84,333 |
| 351 | Hawthorne, CA | 84,314 |
| 352 | Miami Beach, FL | 84,260 |
| 353 | Federal Way, WA | 84,219 |
| 354 | Yakima, WA | 84,167 |
| 355 | Duluth, MN | 84,071 |
| 356 | Nampa, ID | 83,875 |
| 357 | Plantation, FL | 83,544 |
| 358 | Norwalk, CT | 83,198 |
| 359 | Ogden, UT | 83,016 |
| 360 | Sugar Land, TX | 82,696 |
| 361 | Canton Twnshp, MI | 82,634 |
| 362 | Trenton, NJ | 82,609 |
| 363 | Sioux City, IA | 82,573 |
| 364 | Sandy Springs, GA | 82,435 |
| 365 | San Marcos, CA | 82,258 |
| 366 | Racine, WI | 82,232 |
| 367 | Whittier, CA | 82,096 |
| 368 | Tracy, CA | 82,019 |
| 369 | Greenville, NC | 81,814 |
| 370 | Livermore, CA | 80,915 |

| RANK | CITY | POP |
|---|---|---|
| 371 | Edmond, OK | 80,889 |
| 372 | Bloomington, MN | 80,864 |
| 373 | Bend, OR | 80,550 |
| 374 | O'Fallon, MO | 80,528 |
| 375 | Champaign, IL | 80,467 |
| 376 | Reading, PA | 80,418 |
| 377 | Cranston, RI | 80,223 |
| 378 | Troy, MI | 80,182 |
| 379 | Newport Beach, CA | 79,912 |
| 380 | Cicero, IL | 79,870 |
| 381 | Danbury, CT | 79,729 |
| 382 | Buena Park, CA | 79,525 |
| 383 | Clarkstown, NY | 78,899 |
| 384 | Merced, CA | 78,693 |
| 385 | Brick Twnshp, NJ | 78,666 |
| 386 | Lakewood, CA | 78,334 |
| 387 | Westland, MI | 78,149 |
| 388 | Farmington Hills, MI | 78,140 |
| 389 | Clifton, NJ | 78,124 |
| 390 | Evanston, IL | 78,101 |
| 391 | Upper Darby Twnshp, PA | 78,088 |
| 392 | Colonie, NY | 78,003 |
| 393 | Melbourne, FL | 77,854 |
| 394 | Cheektowaga, NY | 77,772 |
| 395 | San Leandro, CA | 77,676 |
| 396 | Longview, TX | 77,663 |
| 397 | Baldwin Park, CA | 77,539 |
| 398 | Ramapo, NY | 76,611 |
| 399 | St. Joseph, MO | 76,436 |
| 400 | Hammond, IN | 76,085 |
| 401 | Albany, GA | 75,734 |
| 402 | Decatur, IL | 75,651 |
| 403 | Lake Forest, CA | 75,509 |
| 404 | St. George, UT | 75,391 |
| 405 | Fayetteville, AR | 75,120 |
| 406 | Somerville, MA | 75,112 |
| 407 | League City, TX | 74,801 |
| 408 | Napa, CA | 74,736 |
| 409 | Chino Hills, CA | 74,650 |
| 410 | Edinburg, TX | 74,611 |
| 411 | New Rochelle, NY | 74,320 |
| 412 | Medford, OR | 74,042 |
| 413 | Redwood City, CA | 73,905 |
| 414 | Bloomington, IL | 73,897 |
| 415 | Lynchburg, VA | 73,735 |
| 416 | Fishers, IN | 73,538 |
| 417 | Bryan, TX | 73,111 |
| 418 | Arlington Heights, IL | 73,061 |
| 419 | Bellflower, CA | 73,038 |
| 420 | Largo, FL | 72,567 |
| 421 | Upland, CA | 72,461 |
| 422 | Hemet, CA | 72,417 |
| 423 | Bethlehem, PA | 72,349 |
| 424 | Tustin, CA | 72,286 |
| 425 | Lakewood Twnshp, NJ | 72,206 |
| 426 | Hoover, AL | 71,919 |
| 427 | Bloomington, IN | 71,845 |
| 428 | Scranton, PA | 71,843 |
| 429 | Brooklyn Park, MN | 71,740 |
| 430 | Meridian, ID | 71,581 |
| 431 | Mountain View, CA | 71,423 |
| 432 | Lawrence, MA | 70,670 |
| 433 | Alameda, CA | 70,372 |
| 434 | Mission, TX | 69,997 |
| 435 | Carmel, IN | 68,424 |
| 436 | Menifee, CA | 68,083 |
| 437 | Concord, NC | 67,478 |
| 438 | Kennewick, WA | 64,009 |
| 439 | Renton, WA | 63,599 |
| 440 | Johns Creek, GA | 59,305 |
| NA | Deerfield Beach, FL** | NA |
| NA | Jurupa Valley, CA** | NA |

Source: Reported data from the F.B.I. "Crime in the United States 2009"

*Estimates as of July 2009 based on U.S. Bureau of the Census figures. Charlotte, Indianapolis, Las Vegas, Louisville, Mobile, and Savannah include areas under their police department but outside the city limits. All populations are for area covered by police department.

**Not available.

# Appendix

# Descriptions of Metropolitan Areas in 2013

**Note: The name of a Metropolitan Statistical Area (MSA) and Metropolitan Division (M.D.) is subject to change based on the changing proportional size of the largest cities included within them. Percent changes are calculated in this book if the MSA or M.D. has not substantially changed, despite the changes in name. In the tables in this book, some MSA and M.D. names are abbreviated to preserve space.**

Abilene, TX includes Callahan, Jones, and Taylor Counties

Akron, OH includes Portage and Summit Counties

Albany, GA includes Baker, Dougherty, Lee, Terrell, and Worth Counties

Albany, OR includes Linn County

Albany-Schenectady-Troy, NY includes Albany, Rensselaer, Saratoga, Schenectady, and Schoharie Counties

Albuquerque, NM includes Bernalillo, Sandoval, Torrance, and Valencia Counties

Alexandria, LA includes Grant and Rapides Parishes

Allentown-Bethlehem-Easton, PA-NJ includes Warren County, NJ and Carbon, Lehigh, and Northampton Counties, PA

Altoona, PA includes Blair County

Amarillo, TX includes Armstrong, Carson, Oldham, Potter, and Randall Counties

Ames, IA includes Story County

Anchorage, AK includes Anchorage Municipality and Matanuska-Susitna Borough

Ann Arbor, MI includes Washtenaw County

Anniston-Oxford-Jacksonville, AL includes Calhoun County

Appleton, WI includes Calumet and Outagamie Counties

Asheville, NC includes Buncombe, Haywood, Henderson, and Madison Counties

Athens-Clarke County, GA includes Clarke, Madison, Oconee, and Oglethorpe Counties

Atlanta-Sandy Springs-Roswell, GA includes Barrow, Bartow, Butts, Carroll, Cherokee, Clayton, Cobb, Coweta, Dawson, DeKalb, Douglas, Fayette, Forsyth, Fulton, Gwinnett, Haralson, Heard, Henry, Jasper, Lamar, Meriwether, Morgan, Newton, Paulding, Pickens, Pike, Rockdale, Spalding, and Walton Counties

Atlantic City-Hammonton, NJ includes Atlantic County

Auburn-Opelika, AL includes Lee County

Augusta-Richmond County, GA-SC includes Burke, Columbia, Lincoln, McDuffie, and Richmond Counties, GA and Aiken and Edgefield Counties, SC

Austin-Round Rock, TX includes Bastrop, Caldwell, Hays, Travis, and Williamson Counties

Bakersfield, CA includes Kern County

Baltimore-Columbia-Towson, MD includes Anne Arundel, Baltimore, Carroll, Harford, Howard, and Queen Anne's Counties and Baltimore City

Bangor, ME includes Penobscot County

Barnstable Town, MA includes Barnstable County

Baton Rouge, LA includes Ascension, East Baton Rouge, East Feliciana, Iberville, Livingston, Pointe Coupee, St. Helena, West Baton Rouge, and West Feliciana Parishes

Bay City, MI includes Bay County

Beaumont-Port Arthur, TX includes Hardin, Jefferson, Newton, and Orange Counties

Beckley, WV includes Fayette and Raleigh Counties

Bellingham, WA includes Whatcom County

Billings, MT includes Carbon, Golden Valley, and Yellowstone Counties

Binghamton, NY includes Broome and Tioga Counties

Birmingham-Hoover, AL includes Bibb, Blount, Chilton, Jefferson, St. Clair, Shelby, and Walker Counties

Bismarck, ND includes Burleigh, Morton, Oliver, and Sioux Counties

Blacksburg-Christiansburg-Radford, VA includes Floyd, Giles, Montgomery, and Pulaski Counties and Radford City

Bloomington, IL includes DeWitt and McLean Counties

Bloomington, IN includes Monroe and Owen Counties

Bloomsburg-Berwick, PA includes Columbia and Montour Counties

Boise City, ID includes Ada, Boise, Canyon, Gem, and Owyhee Counties

Boston-Cambridge-Newton, MA-NH includes the Metropolitan Divisions of Boston, MA; Cambridge-Newton-Framingham, MA; and Rockingham County-Strafford County, NH
- Boston, MA Metropolitan Division includes Norfolk, Plymouth, and Suffolk Counties
- Cambridge-Newton-Framingham, MA Metropolitan Division includes Essex and Middlesex Counties
- Rockingham County-Strafford County, NH Metropolitan Division includes Rockingham and Strafford Counties

Boulder, CO includes Boulder County

Bowling Green, KY includes Allen, Butler, Edmonson, and Warren Counties

Bremerton-Silverdale, WA includes Kitsap County

Bridgeport-Stamford-Norwalk, CT includes Fairfield County

Brownsville-Harlingen, TX includes Cameron County

Brunswick, GA includes Brantley, Glynn,

and McIntosh Counties

Buffalo-Cheektowaga-Niagara Falls, NY includes Erie and Niagara Counties

Burlington, NC includes Alamance County

California-Lexington Park, MD includes St. Mary's County

Canton-Massillon, OH includes Carroll and Stark Counties

Cape Coral-Fort Myers, FL includes Lee County

Cape Girardeau, MO-IL includes Alexander County, IL and Bollinger and Cape Girardeau Counties, MO

Carson City, NV includes Carson City

Casper, WY includes Natrona County

Cedar Rapids, IA includes Benton, Jones, and Linn Counties

Chambersburg-Waynesboro, PA includes Franklin County

Champaign-Urbana, IL includes Champaign, Ford, and Piatt Counties

Charleston-North Charleston, SC includes Berkeley, Charleston, and Dorchester Counties

Charlottesville, VA includes Albemarle, Buckingham, Fluvanna, Greene, and Nelson Counties and Charlottesville City

Cheyenne, WY includes Laramie County

Chicago-Naperville-Elgin, IL-IN-WI includes the Metropolitan Divisions of Chicago-Naperville-Arlington Heights, IL; Elgin, IL; Gary, IN; and Lake County-Kenosha County, IL-WI
- Chicago-Naperville-Arlington Heights, IL Metropolitan Division includes Cook, DuPage, Grundy, Kendall, McHenry, and Will Counties
- Elgin, IL Metropolitan Division includes DeKalb and Kane Counties
- Gary, IN Metropolitan Division includes Jasper, Lake, Newton, and Porter Counties
- Lake County-Kenosha County, IL-WI Metropolitan Division includes Lake

County, IL and Kenosha County, WI

Chico, CA includes Butte County

Cincinnati, OH-KY-IN includes Dearborn, Ohio, and Union Counties, IN; Boone, Bracken, Campbell, Gallatin, Grant, Kenton, and Pendleton Counties, KY; and Brown, Butler, Clermont, Hamilton, and Warren Counties, OH

Clarksville, TN-KY includes Christian and Trigg Counties, KY and Montgomery County, TN

Cleveland, TN includes Bradley and Polk Counties

Coeur d'Alene, ID includes Kootenai County

College Station-Bryan, TX includes Brazos, Burleson, and Robertson Counties

Colorado Springs, CO includes El Paso and Teller Counties

Columbia, MO includes Boone County

Columbus, GA-AL includes Russell County, AL and Chattahoochee, Harris, Marion, and Muscogee Counties, GA

Columbus, IN includes Bartholomew County

Corpus Christi, TX includes Aransas, Nueces, and San Patricio Counties

Corvallis, OR includes Benton County

Crestview-Fort Walton Beach-Destin, FL includes Okaloosa and Walton Counties

Cumberland, MD-WV includes Allegany County, MD and Mineral County, WV

Dallas-Fort Worth-Arlington, TX includes the Metropolitan Divisions of Dallas-Plano-Irving and Fort Worth-Arlington
- Dallas-Plano-Irving, TX Metropolitan Division includes Collin, Dallas, Denton, Ellis, Hunt, Kaufman, and Rockwall Counties
- Fort Worth-Arlington, TX Metropolitan Division includes Hood, Johnson, Parker, Somervell, Tarrant, and Wise Counties

Dalton, GA includes Murray and Whitfield Counties

Danville, IL includes Vermilion County

Daphne-Fairhope-Foley, AL includes Baldwin County

Davenport-Moline-Rock Island, IA-IL includes Henry, Mercer, and Rock Island Counties, IL and Scott County, IA

Dayton, OH includes Greene, Miami, and Montgomery Counties

Decatur, AL includes Lawrence and Morgan Counties

Decatur, IL includes Macon County

Deltona-Daytona Beach-Ormond Beach, FL includes Flagler and Volusia Counties

Denver-Aurora-Lakewood, CO includes Adams, Arapahoe, Broomfield, Clear Creek, Denver, Douglas, Elbert, Gilpin, Jefferson, and Park Counties

Des Moines-West Des Moines, IA includes Dallas, Guthrie, Madison, Polk, and Warren Counties

Detroit-Warren-Dearborn, MI includes the Metropolitan Divisions of Detroit-Dearborn-Livonia and Warren-Troy-Farmington Hills
- Detroit-Dearborn-Livonia, MI Metropolitan Division includes Wayne County
- Warren-Troy-Farmington Hills, MI Metropolitan Division includes Lapeer, Livingston, Macomb, Oakland, and St. Clair Counties

Dothan, AL includes Geneva, Henry, and Houston Counties

Dover, DE includes Kent County

Dubuque, IA includes Dubuque County

Duluth, MN-WI includes Carlton and St. Louis Counties, MN and Douglas County, WI

Durham-Chapel Hill, NC includes Chatham, Durham, Orange, and Person Counties

# Descriptions of Metropolitan Areas in 2013 (continued)

East Stroudsburg, PA includes Monroe County

El Centro, CA includes Imperial County

Elizabethtown-Fort Knox, KY includes Hardin, Larue, and Meade Counties

Elmira, NY includes Chemung County

El Paso, TX includes El Paso and Hudspeth Counties

Erie, PA includes Erie County

Eugene, OR includes Lane County

Fairbanks, AK includes Fairbanks North Star Borough

Fargo, ND-MN includes Clay County, MN and Cass County, ND

Farmington, NM includes San Juan County

Fayetteville, NC includes Cumberland and Hoke Counties

Fayetteville-Springdale-Rogers, AR-MO includes Benton, Madison, and Washington Counties, AR and McDonald County, MO

Flagstaff, AZ includes Coconino County

Flint, MI includes Genesee County

Florence, SC includes Darlington and Florence Counties

Florence-Muscle Shoals, AL includes Colbert and Lauderdale Counties

Fond du Lac, WI includes Fond du Lac County

Fort Collins, CO includes Larimer County

Fort Smith, AR-OK includes Crawford and Sebastian Counties, AR and Le Flore and Sequoyah Counties, OK

Fort Wayne, IN includes Allen, Wells, and Whitley Counties

Fresno, CA includes Fresno County

Gadsden, AL includes Etowah County

Gainesville, FL includes Alachua and Gilchrist Counties

Gainesville, GA includes Hall County

Gettysburg, PA includes Adams County

Glens Falls, NY includes Warren and Washington Counties

Goldsboro, NC includes Wayne County

Grand Forks, ND-MN includes Polk County, MN and Grand Forks County, ND

Grand Island, NE includes Hall, Hamilton, Howard, and Merrick Counties

Grand Junction, CO includes Mesa County

Great Falls, MT includes Cascade County

Greeley, CO includes Weld County

Green Bay, WI includes Brown, Kewaunee, and Oconto Counties

Greensboro-High Point, NC includes Guilford, Randolph, and Rockingham Counties

Greenville, NC includes Pitt County

Greenville-Anderson-Mauldin, SC includes Anderson, Greenville, Laurens, and Pickens Counties

Hagerstown-Martinsburg, MD-WV includes Washington County, MD and Berkeley County, WV

Hammond, LA includes Tangipahoa Parish

Hanford-Corcoran, CA includes Kings County

Harrisburg-Carlisle, PA includes Cumberland, Dauphin, and Perry Counties

Harrisonburg, VA includes Rockingham County and Harrisonburg City

Hartford-West Hartford-East Hartford, CT includes Hartford, Middlesex, and Tolland Counties

Hattiesburg, MS includes Forrest, Lamar, and Perry Counties

Hickory-Lenoir-Morganton, NC includes Alexander, Burke, Caldwell, and Catawba Counties

Hilton Head Island-Bluffton-Beaufort, SC includes Beaufort and Jasper Counties

Hinesville, GA includes Liberty and Long Counties

Homosassa Spring, FL includes Citrus County

Houma-Thibodaux, LA includes Lafourche and Terrebonne Parishes

Houston-The Woodlands-Sugar Land, TX includes Austin, Brazoria, Chambers, Fort Bend, Galveston, Harris, Liberty, Montgomery, and Waller Counties

Huntsville, AL includes Limestone and Madison Counties

Idaho Falls, ID includes Bonneville, Butte, and Jefferson Counties

Indianapolis-Carmel-Anderson, IN includes Boone, Brown, Hamilton, Hancock, Hendricks, Johnson, Madison, Marion, Morgan, Putnam, and Shelby Counties

Iowa City, IA includes Johnson and Washington Counties

Jackson, MS includes Copiah, Hinds, Madison, Rankin, Simpson, and Yazoo Counties

Jackson, TN includes Chester, Crockett, and Madison Counties

Jacksonville, FL includes Baker, Clay, Duval, Nassau, and St. Johns Counties

Janesville-Beloit, WI includes Rock County

Jefferson City, MO includes Callaway, Cole, Moniteau, and Osage Counties

Johnson City, TN includes Carter, Unicoi, and Washington Counties

Johnstown, PA includes Cambria County

Jonesboro, AR includes Craighead and Poinsett Counties

# Descriptions of Metropolitan Areas in 2013 (continued)

Joplin, MO includes Jasper and Newton Counties

Kahului-Wailuku-Lahaina, HI includes Kalawao and Maui Counties

Kalamazoo-Portage, MI includes Kalamazoo and Van Buren Counties

Kankakee, IL includes Kankakee County

Kansas City, MO-KS includes Johnson, Leavenworth, Linn, Miami, and Wyandotte Counties, KS and Bates, Caldwell, Cass, Clay, Clinton, Jackson, Lafayette, Platte, and Ray Counties, MO

Kennewick-Richland, WA includes Benton and Franklin Counties

Killeen-Temple, TX includes Bell, Coryell, and Lampasas Counties

Kingsport-Bristol-Bristol, TN-VA includes Hawkins and Sullivan Counties, TN and Scott and Washington Counties and Bristol City, VA

Kingston, NY includes Ulster County

Knoxville, TN includes Anderson, Blount, Campbell, Grainger, Knox, Loudon, Morgan, Roane, and Union Counties

Kokomo, IN includes Howard County

La Crosse-Onalaska, WI-MN includes Houston County, MN and La Crosse County, WI

Lafayette, LA includes Acadia, Iberia, Lafayette, St. Martin, and Vermilion Parishes

Lafayette-West Lafayette, IN includes Benton, Carroll, and Tippecanoe Counties

Lake Havasu City-Kingman, AZ includes Mohave County

Lakeland-Winter Haven, FL includes Polk County

Lancaster, PA includes Lancaster County

Lansing-East Lansing, MI includes Clinton, Eaton, and Ingham Counties

Laredo, TX includes Webb County

Las Cruces, NM includes Dona Ana County

Las Vegas-Henderson-Paradise, NV includes Clark County

Lawrence, KS includes Douglas County

Lawton, OK includes Comanche and Cotton Counties

Lebanon, PA includes Lebanon County

Lewiston, ID-WA includes Nez Perce County, ID and Asotin County, WA

Lewiston-Auburn, ME includes Androscoggin County

Lexington-Fayette, KY includes Bourbon, Clark, Fayette, Jessamine, Scott, and Woodford Counties

Lima, OH includes Allen County

Lincoln, NE includes Lancaster and Seward Counties

Little Rock-North Little Rock-Conway, AR includes Faulkner, Grant, Lonoke, Perry, Pulaski, and Saline Counties

Logan, UT-ID includes Franklin County, ID and Cache County, UT

Longview, TX includes Gregg, Rusk, and Upshur Counties

Longview, WA includes Cowlitz County

Los Angeles-Long Beach-Anaheim, CA includes the Metropolitan Divisions of Anaheim-Santa Ana-Irvine and Los Angeles-Long Beach-Glendale
- Anaheim-Santa Ana-Irvine, CA Metropolitan Division includes Orange County
- Los Angeles-Long Beach-Glendale, CA Metropolitan Division includes Los Angeles County

Louisville/Jefferson County, KY-IN includes Clark, Floyd, Harrison, Scott, and Washington Counties, IN and Bullitt, Henry, Jefferson, Oldham, Shelby, Spencer, and Trimble Counties, KY

Lubbock, TX includes Crosby, Lubbock, and Lynn Counties

Lynchburg, VA includes Amherst, Appomattox, Bedford, and Campbell Counties and Bedford and Lynchburg Cities

Macon, GA includes Bibb, Crawford, Jones, Monroe, and Twiggs Counties

Madera, CA includes Madera County

Madison, WI includes Columbia, Dane, Green, and Iowa Counties

Manchester-Nashua, NH includes Hillsborough County

Manhattan, KS includes Pottawatomie and Riley Counties

Mankato-North Mankato, MN includes Blue Earth and Nicollet Counties

Mansfield, OH includes Richland County

McAllen-Edinburg-Mission, TX includes Hidalgo County

Medford, OR includes Jackson County

Memphis, TN-MS-AR includes Crittenden County, AR; Benton, DeSoto, Marshall, Tate, and Tunica Counties, MS; and Fayette, Shelby, and Tipton Counties, TN

Merced, CA includes Merced County

Miami-Fort Lauderdale-West Palm Beach, FL includes the Metropolitan Divisions of Fort Lauderdale-Pompano Beach-Deerfield Beach, Miami-Miami Beach-Kendall, and West Palm Beach-Boca Raton-Delray Beach
- Fort Lauderdale-Pompano Beach-Deerfield Beach, FL Metropolitan Division includes Broward County
- Miami-Miami Beach-Kendall, FL Metropolitan Division includes Miami-Dade County
- West Palm Beach-Boca Raton-Delray Beach, FL Metropolitan Division includes Palm Beach County

Michigan City-La Porte, IN includes La Porte County

Midland, MI includes Midland County

Midland, TX includes Martin and Midland Counties

# Descriptions of Metropolitan Areas in 2013 (continued)

Milwaukee-Waukesha-West Allis, WI includes Milwaukee, Ozaukee, Washington, and Waukesha Counties

Minneapolis-St. Paul-Bloomington, MN-WI includes Anoka, Carver, Chisago, Dakota, Hennepin, Isanti, Le Sueur, Mille Lacs, Ramsey, Scott, Sherburne, Sibley, Washington, and Wright Counties, MN and Pierce and St. Croix Counties, WI

Missoula, MT includes Missoula County

Mobile, AL includes Mobile County

Modesto, CA includes Stanislaus County

Monroe, LA includes Ouachita and Union Parishes

Monroe, MI includes Monroe County

Montgomery, AL includes Autauga, Elmore, Lowndes, and Montgomery Counties

Morgantown, WV includes Monongalia and Preston Counties

Morristown, TN includes Hamblen and Jefferson Counties

Mount Vernon-Anacortes, WA includes Skagit County

Muncie, IN includes Delaware County

Napa, CA includes Napa County

Naples-Immokalee-Marco Island, FL includes Collier County

Nashville-Davidson--Murfreesboro--Franklin, TN includes Cannon, Cheatham, Davidson, Dickson, Hickman, Macon, Maury, Robertson, Rutherford, Smith, Sumner, Trousdale, Williamson, and Wilson Counties

New Bern, NC includes Craven, Jones, and Pamlico Counties

New Haven-Milford, CT includes New Haven County

New Orleans-Metairie, LA includes Jefferson, Orleans, Plaquemines, St. Bernard, St. Charles, St. James, St. John the Baptist, and St. Tammany Parishes

New York-Newark-Jersey City, NY-NJ-PA includes the Metropolitan Divisions of Dutchess County-Putnam County, NY; Nassau County-Suffolk County, NY; Newark, NJ-PA; and New York-Jersey City-White Plains, NY-NJ

- Dutchess County-Putnam County, NY Metropolitan Division includes Dutchess and Putnam Counties1
- Nassau County-Suffolk County, NY Metropolitan Division includes Nassau and Suffolk Counties1
- Newark, NJ-PA Metropolitan Division includes Essex, Hunterdon, Morris, Somerset, Sussex, and Union Counties, NJ and Pike County, PA
- New York-Jersey City-White Plains, NY-NJ Metropolitan Division includes Bergen, Hudson, Middlesex, Monmouth, Ocean, and Passaic Counties, NJ and Bronx, Kings, New York, Orange, Queens, Richmond, Rockland, and Westchester Counties, NY1

North Port-Sarasota-Bradenton, FL includes Manatee and Sarasota Counties

Norwich-New London, CT includes New London County

Ocala, FL includes Marion County

Ocean City, NJ includes Cape May County

Odessa, TX includes Ector County

Ogden-Clearfield, UT includes Box Elder, Davis, Morgan, and Weber Counties

Oklahoma City, OK includes Canadian, Cleveland, Grady, Lincoln, Logan, McClain, and Oklahoma Counties

Olympia-Tumwater, WA includes Thurston County

Omaha-Council Bluffs, NE-IA includes Harrison, Mills, and Pottawattamie Counties, IA and Cass, Douglas, Sarpy, Saunders, and Washington Counties, NE

Orlando-Kissimmee-Sanford, FL includes Lake, Orange, Osceola, and Seminole Counties

Oshkosh-Neenah, WI includes Winnebago County

Owensboro, KY includes Daviess,

Hancock, and McLean Counties

Oxnard-Thousand Oaks-Ventura, CA includes Ventura County

Palm Bay-Melbourne-Titusville, FL includes Brevard County

Panama City, FL includes Bay and Gulf Counties

Parkersburg-Vienna, WV includes Wirt and Wood Counties

Pensacola-Ferry Pass-Brent, FL includes Escambia and Santa Rosa Counties

Peoria, IL includes Marshall, Peoria, Stark, Tazewell, and Woodford Counties

Philadelphia-Camden-Wilmington, PA-NJ-DE-MD includes the Metropolitan Divisions of Camden, NJ; Montgomery County-Bucks County-Chester County, PA; Philadelphia, PA; and Wilmington, DE-MD-NJ

- Camden, NJ Metropolitan Division includes Burlington, Camden, and Gloucester Counties
- Montgomery County-Bucks County-Chester County, PA Metropolitan Division includes Bucks, Chester, and Montgomery Counties
- Philadelphia, PA Metropolitan Division includes Delaware and Philadelphia Counties
- Wilmington, DE-MD-NJ Metropolitan Division includes New Castle County, DE; Cecil County, MD; and Salem County, NJ
- Phoenix-Mesa-Scottsdale, AZ includes Maricopa and Pinal Counties

Pine Bluff, AR includes Cleveland, Jefferson, and Lincoln Counties

Pittsburgh, PA includes Allegheny, Armstrong, Beaver, Butler, Fayette, Washington, and Westmoreland Counties

Pittsfield, MA includes Berkshire County

Pocatello, ID includes Bannock County

Portland-South Portland, ME includes Cumberland, Sagadahoc, and York Counties

Portland-Vancouver-Hillsboro, OR-WA includes Clackamas, Columbia,

# Descriptions of Metropolitan Areas in 2013 (continued)

Multnomah, Washington, and Yamhill Counties, OR and Clark and Skamania Counties, WA

Port St. Lucie, FL includes Martin and St. Lucie Counties

Prescott, AZ includes Yavapai County

Providence-Warwick, RI-MA includes Bristol County, MA and Bristol, Kent, Newport, Providence, and Washington Counties RI

Provo-Orem, UT includes Juab and Utah Counties

Pueblo, CO includes Pueblo County

Punta Gorda, FL includes Charlotte County

Racine, WI includes Racine County

Raleigh, NC includes Franklin, Johnston, and Wake Counties

Rapid City, SD includes Custer, Meade, and Pennington Counties

Reading, PA includes Berks County

Redding, CA includes Shasta County

Reno, NV includes Storey and Washoe Counties

Richmond, VA includes Amelia, Caroline, Charles City, Chesterfield, Dinwiddie, Goochland, Hanover, Henrico, King William, New Kent, Powhatan, Prince George, and Sussex Counties and Colonial Heights, Hopewell, Petersburg, and Richmond Cities

Riverside-San Bernardino-Ontario, CA includes Riverside and San Bernardino Counties

Roanoke, VA includes Botetourt, Craig, Franklin, and Roanoke Counties and Roanoke and Salem Cities

Rochester, MN includes Dodge, Fillmore, Olmsted, and Wabasha Counties

Rochester, NY includes Livingston, Monroe, Ontario, Orleans, Wayne, and Yates Counties

Rockford, IL includes Boone and Winnebago Counties

Rocky Mount, NC includes Edgecombe and Nash Counties

Rome, GA includes Floyd County

Sacramento--Roseville--Arden-Arcade, CA includes El Dorado, Placer, Sacramento, and Yolo Counties

Saginaw, MI includes Saginaw County

Salem, OR includes Marion and Polk Counties

Salinas, CA includes Monterey County

Salisbury, MD-DE includes Sussex County, DE and Somerset, Wicomico, and Worcester Counties, MD

Salt Lake City, UT includes Salt Lake and Tooele Counties

San Antonio-New Braunfels, TX includes Atascosa, Bandera, Bexar, Comal, Guadalupe, Kendall, Medina, and Wilson Counties

San Diego-Carlsbad, CA includes San Diego County

San Francisco-Oakland-Hayward, CA includes the Metropolitan Divisions of Oakland-Hayward-Berkeley, San Francisco-Redwood City-South San Francisco, and San Rafael
- Oakland-Hayward-Berkeley, CA Metropolitan Division includes Alameda and Contra Costa Counties
- San Francisco-Redwood City-South San Francisco, CA Metropolitan Division includes San Francisco and San Mateo Counties
- San Rafael, CA Metropolitan Division includes Marin County

San Jose-Sunnyvale-Santa Clara, CA includes San Benito and Santa Clara Counties

San Luis Obispo-Paso Robles-Arroyo Grande, CA includes San Luis Obispo County

Santa Cruz-Watsonville, CA includes Santa Cruz County

Santa Fe, NM includes Santa Fe County

Santa Maria-Santa Barbara, CA includes Santa Barbara County

Santa Rosa, CA includes Sonoma County

Savannah, GA includes Bryan, Chatham, and Effingham Counties

Scranton--Wilkes-Barre--Hazleton, PA includes Lackawanna, Luzerne, and Wyoming Counties

Seattle-Tacoma-Bellevue, WA includes the Metropolitan Divisions of Seattle-Bellevue-Everett and Tacoma-Lakewood
- Seattle-Bellevue-Everett, WA Metropolitan Division includes King and Snohomish Counties
- Tacoma-Lakewood, WA Metropolitan Division includes Pierce County

Sebastian-Vero Beach, FL includes Indian River County

Sebring, FL includes Highlands County

Sheboygan, WI includes Sheboygan County

Sherman-Denison, TX includes Grayson County

Shreveport-Bossier City, LA includes Bossier, Caddo, De Soto, and Webster Parishes

Sierra Vista-Douglas, AZ includes Cochise County

Sioux City, IA-NE-SD includes Plymouth and Woodbury Counties, IA; Dakota and Dixon Counties, NE; and Union County, SD

Sioux Falls, SD includes Lincoln, McCook, Minnehaha, and Turner Counties

South Bend-Mishawaka, IN-MI includes St. Joseph County, IN and Cass County, MI

Spartanburg, SC includes Spartanburg and Union Counties

Spokane-Spokane Valley, WA includes Pend Oreille, Spokane, and Stevens Counties

# Descriptions of Metropolitan Areas in 2013 (continued)

Springfield, IL includes Menard and Sangamon Counties

Springfield, MA includes Hampden and Hampshire Counties

Springfield, MO includes Christian, Dallas, Greene, Polk, and Webster Counties

Springfield, OH includes Clark County

State College, PA includes Centre County

Staunton-Waynesboro, VA includes Augusta County and Staunton and Waynesboro Cities

St. George, UT includes Washington County

St. Joseph, MO-KS includes Doniphan County, KS and Andrew, Buchanan, and De Kalb Counties, MO

St. Louis, MO-IL includes Bond, Calhoun, Clinton, Jersey, Macoupin, Madison, Monroe, and St. Clair Counties, IL and Franklin, Jefferson, Lincoln, St. Charles, St. Louis, and Warren Counties and St. Louis City, MO

Stockton-Lodi, CA includes San Joaquin County

Sumter, SC includes Sumter County

Syracuse, NY includes Madison, Onondaga, and Oswego Counties

Tallahassee, FL includes Gadsden, Jefferson, Leon, and Wakulla Counties

Tampa-St. Petersburg-Clearwater, FL includes Hernando, Hillsborough, Pasco, and Pinellas Counties

Terre Haute, IN includes Clay, Sullivan, Vermillion, and Vigo Counties

Texarkana, TX-AR includes Little River and Miller Counties, AR and Bowie County, TX

The Villages, FL includes Sumter County

Toledo, OH includes Fulton, Lucas, and Wood Counties

Topeka, KS includes Jackson, Jefferson, Osage, Shawnee, and Wabaunsee Counties

Trenton, NJ includes Mercer County

Tucson, AZ includes Pima County

Tulsa, OK includes Creek, Okmulgee, Osage, Pawnee, Rogers, Tulsa, and Wagoner Counties

Tuscaloosa, AL includes Hale, Pickens, and Tuscaloosa Counties

Tyler, TX includes Smith County

Utica-Rome, NY includes Herkimer and Oneida Counties

Valdosta, GA includes Brooks, Echols, Lanier, and Lowndes Counties

Vallejo-Fairfield, CA includes Solano County

Victoria, TX includes Goliad and Victoria Counties

Vineland-Bridgeton, NJ includes Cumberland County

Virginia Beach-Norfolk-Newport News, VA-NC includes Currituck and Gates Counties, NC and Gloucester, Isle of Wight, James City, Mathews, and York Counties and Chesapeake, Hampton, Newport News, Norfolk, Poquoson, Portsmouth, Suffolk, Virginia Beach, and Williamsburg Cities, VA

Visalia-Porterville, CA includes Tulare County

Waco, TX includes Falls and McLennan Counties

Walla Walla, WA includes Columbia and Walla Walla Counties

Warner Robins, GA includes Houston, Peach, and Pulaski Counties

Washington-Arlington-Alexandria, DC-VA-MD-WV includes the Metropolitan Divisions of Silver Spring-Frederick-Rockville, MD and Washington-Arlington-Alexandria, DC-VA-MD-WV
- Silver Spring-Frederick-Rockville, MD Metropolitan Division includes Frederick and Montgomery Counties
- Washington-Arlington-Alexandria, DC-VA-MD-WV Metropolitan Division includes District of Columbia; Calvert,

Charles, and Prince George's Counties, MD; Arlington, Clarke, Culpeper, Fairfax, Fauquier, Loudoun, Prince William, Rapppahannock, Spotsylvania, Stafford, and Warren Counties and Alexandria, Fairfax, Falls Church, Fredericksburg, Manassas, and Manassas Park Cities, VA; and Jefferson County, WV

Waterloo-Cedar Falls, IA includes Black Hawk, Bremer, and Grundy Counties

Watertown-Fort Drum, NY includes Jefferson County

Wausau, WI includes Marathon County

Wheeling, WV-OH includes Belmont County, OH and Marshall and Ohio Counties, WV

Wichita, KS includes Butler, Harvey, Kingman, Sedgewick, and Sumner Counties

Wichita Falls, TX includes Archer, Clay, and Wichita Counties

Williamsport, PA includes Lycoming County

Wilmington, NC includes New Hanover and Pender Counties

Winchester, VA-WV includes Frederick County and Winchester City, VA and Hampshire County, WV

Winston-Salem, NC includes Davidson, Davie, Forsyth, Stokes, and Yadkin Counties

Worcester, MA-CT includes Windham County, CT and Worcester County, MA

Yakima, WA includes Yakima County

York-Hanover, PA includes York County

Youngstown-Warren-Boardman, OH-PA includes Mahoning and Trumbull Counties, OH and Mercer County, PA

Yuba City, CA includes Sutter and Yuba Counties

Yuma, AZ includes Yuma County

# County Index: 2013

| COUNTY: | IS IN METROPOLITAN: | COUNTY: | IS IN METROPOLITAN: |
|---|---|---|---|
| Acadia, LA | Lafayette, LA | Blue Earth, MN | Mankato-North Mankato, MN |
| Adams, CO | Denver-Aurora-Lakewood, CO | Boise, ID | Boise City, ID |
| Adams, PA | Gettysburg, PA | Bollinger, MO | Cape Girardeau, MO-IL |
| Ada, ID | Boise City, ID | Bond, IL | St. Louis, MO-IL |
| Aiken, SC | Augusta-Richmond County, GA-SC | Bonneville, ID | Idaho Falls, ID |
| Alachua, FL | Gainesville, FL | Boone, IL | Rockford, IL |
| Alamance, NC | Burlington, NC | Boone, IN | Indianapolis-Carmel-Anderson, IN |
| Alameda, CA | San Francisco-Oakland-Hayward, CA | Boone, KY | Cincinnati, OH-KY-IN |
| Albany, NY | Albany-Schenectady-Troy, NY | Boone, MO | Columbia, MO |
| Albemarle, VA | Charlottesville, VA | Boone, WV | Charleston, WV |
| Alexander, IL | Cape Girardeau, MO-IL | Bossier, LA | Shreveport-Bossier City, LA |
| Alexander, NC | Hickory-Lenoir-Morganton, NC | Botetourt, VA | Roanoke, VA |
| Alexandria city, VA | Washington-Arlington-Alexandria, DC-VA-MD-WV | Boulder, CO | Boulder, CO |
| Allegany, MD | Cumberland, MD-WV | Bourbon, KY | Lexington-Fayette, KY |
| Allegheny, PA | Pittsburgh, PA | Bowie, TX | Texarkana, TX-AR |
| Allen, IN | Fort Wayne, IN | Box Elder, UT | Ogden-Clearfield, UT |
| Allen, KY | Bowling Green, KY | Boyd, KY | Huntington-Ashland, WV-KY-OH |
| Allen, OH | Lima, OH | Bracken, KY | Cincinnati, OH-KY-IN |
| Amelia, VA | Richmond, VA | Bradley, TN | Cleveland, TN |
| Amherst, VA | Lynchburg, VA | Brantley, GA | Brunswick, GA |
| Anchorage city, AK | Anchorage, AK | Brazoria, TX | Houston-The Woodlands-Sugar Land, TX |
| Anderson, SC | Greenville-Anderson-Mauldin, SC | Brazos, TX | College Station-Bryan, TX |
| Anderson, TN | Knoxville, TN | Bremer, IA | Waterloo-Cedar Falls, IA |
| Andrew, MO | St. Joseph, MO-KS | Brevard, FL | Palm Bay-Melbourne-Titusville, FL |
| Androscoggin, ME | Lewiston-Auburn, ME | Bristol city, VA | Kingsport-Bristol-Bristol, TN-VA |
| Anne Arundel, MD | Baltimore-Columbia-Towson, MD | Bristol, MA | Providence-Warwick, RI-MA |
| Anoka, MN | Minneapolis-St. Paul-Bloomington, MN-WI | Bristol, RI | Providence-Warwick, RI-MA |
| Appomattox, VA | Lynchburg, VA | Bronx, NY | New York-Newark-Jersey City, NY-NJ-PA |
| Aransas, TX | Corpus Christi, TX | Brooke, WV | Weirton-Steubenville, WV-OH |
| Arapahoe, CO | Denver-Aurora-Lakewood, CO | Brooks, GA | Valdosta, GA |
| Archer, TX | Wichita Falls, TX | Broome, NY | Binghamton, NY |
| Arlington, VA | Washington-Arlington-Alexandria, DC-VA-MD-WV | Broomfield, CO | Denver-Aurora-Lakewood, CO |
| Armstrong, PA | Pittsburgh, PA | Broward, FL | Miami-Fort Lauderdale-West Palm Beach, FL |
| Armstrong, TX | Amarillo, TX | Brown, IN | Indianapolis-Carmel-Anderson, IN |
| Ascension, LA | Baton Rouge, LA | Brown, OH | Cincinnati, OH-KY-IN |
| Asotin, WA | Lewiston, ID-WA | Brown, WI | Green Bay, WI |
| Atascosa, TX | San Antonio-New Braunfels, TX | Brunswick, NC | Myrtle Beach-Conway-North Myrtle Beach, SC-NC |
| Atlantic, NJ | Atlantic City-Hammonton, NJ | Bryan, GA | Savannah, GA |
| Augusta, VA | Staunton-Waynesboro, VA | Buchanan, MO | St. Joseph, MO-KS |
| Austin, TX | Houston-The Woodlands-Sugar Land, TX | Buckingham, VA | Charlottesville, VA |
| Autauga, AL | Montgomery, AL | Bucks, PA | Philadelphia-Camden-Wilmington, PA-NJ-DE-MD |
| Baker, FL | Jacksonville, FL | Bullitt, KY | Louisville/Jefferson County, KY-IN |
| Baker, GA | Albany, GA | Buncombe, NC | Asheville, NC |
| Baldwin, AL | Daphne-Fairhope-Foley, AL | Burke, GA | Augusta-Richmond County, GA-SC |
| Baltimore city, MD | Baltimore-Columbia-Towson, MD | Burke, NC | Hickory-Lenoir-Morganton, NC |
| Baltimore, MD | Baltimore-Columbia-Towson, MD | Burleigh, ND | Bismarck, ND |
| Bandera, TX | San Antonio-New Braunfels, TX | Burleson, TX | College Station-Bryan, TX |
| Bannock, ID | Pocatello, ID | Burlington, NJ | Philadelphia-Camden-Wilmington, PA-NJ-DE-MD |
| Barnstable, MA | Barnstable Town, MA | Butler, KS | Wichita, KS |
| Barrow, GA | Atlanta-Sandy Springs-Roswell, GA | Butler, KY | Bowling Green, KY |
| Barry, MI | Grand Rapids-Wyoming, MI | Butler, OH | Cincinnati, OH-KY-IN |
| Bartholomew, IN | Columbus, IN | Butler, PA | Pittsburgh, PA |
| Bartow, GA | Atlanta-Sandy Springs-Roswell, GA | Butte, CA | Chico, CA |
| Bastrop, TX | Austin-Round Rock, TX | Butte, ID | Idaho Falls, ID |
| Bates, MO | Kansas City, MO-KS | Butts, GA | Atlanta-Sandy Springs-Roswell, GA |
| Bay, FL | Panama City, FL | Cabarrus, NC | Charlotte-Concord-Gastonia, NC-SC |
| Bay, MI | Bay City, MI | Cabell, WV | Huntington-Ashland, WV-KY-OH |
| Beaufort, SC | Hilton Head Island-Bluffton-Beaufort, SC | Cache, UT | Logan, UT-ID |
| Beaver, PA | Pittsburgh, PA | Caddo, LA | Shreveport-Bossier City, LA |
| Bedford city, VA | Lynchburg, VA | Calcasieu, LA | Lake Charles, LA |
| Bedford, VA | Lynchburg, VA | Caldwell, MO | Kansas City, MO-KS |
| Bell, TX | Killeen-Temple, TX | Caldwell, NC | Hickory-Lenoir-Morganton, NC |
| Belmont, OH | Wheeling, WV-OH | Caldwell, TX | Austin-Round Rock, TX |
| Benton, AR | Fayetteville-Springdale-Rogers, AR-MO | Calhoun, AL | Anniston-Oxford-Jacksonville, AL |
| Benton, IA | Cedar Rapids, IA | Calhoun, IL | St. Louis, MO-IL |
| Benton, IN | Lafayette-West Lafayette, IN | Calhoun, MI | Battle Creek, MI |
| Benton, MN | St. Cloud, MN | Calhoun, SC | Columbia, SC |
| Benton, MS | Memphis, TN-MS-AR | Callahan, TX | Abilene, TX |
| Benton, OR | Corvallis, OR | Callaway, MO | Jefferson City, MO |
| Benton, WA | Kennewick-Richland, WA | Calumet, WI | Appleton, WI |
| Bergen, NJ | New York-Newark-Jersey City, NY-NJ-PA | Calvert, MD | Washington-Arlington-Alexandria DC-VA-MD-WV |
| Berkeley, SC | Charleston-North Charleston, SC | Cambria, PA | Johnstown, PA |
| Berkeley, WV | Hagerstown-Martinsburg, MD-WV | Camden, NJ | Philadelphia-Camden-Wilmington, PA-NJ-DE-MD |
| Berkshire, MA | Pittsfield, MA | Cameron, LA | Lake Charles, LA |
| Berks, PA | Reading, PA | Cameron, TX | Brownsville-Harlingen, TX |
| Bernalillo, NM | Albuquerque, NM | Campbell, KY | Cincinnati, OH-KY-IN |
| Berrien, MI | Niles-Benton Harbor, MI | Campbell, TN | Knoxville, TN |
| Bexar, TX | San Antonio-New Braunfels, TX | Campbell, VA | Lynchburg, VA |
| Bibb, AL | Birmingham-Hoover, AL | Canadian, OK | Oklahoma City, OK |
| Bibb, GA | Macon, GA | Cannon, TN | Nashville-Davidson--Murfreesboro--Franklin, TN |
| Black Hawk, IA | Waterloo-Cedar Falls, IA | Canyon, ID | Boise City, ID |
| Blair, PA | Altoona, PA | Cape Girardeau, MO | Cape Girardeau, MO-IL |
| Blount, AL | Birmingham-Hoover, AL | Cape May, NJ | Ocean City, NJ |
| Blount, TN | Knoxville, TN | Carbon, MT | Billings, MT |

# County Index: 2013 (continued)

| COUNTY: | IS IN METROPOLITAN: | COUNTY: | IS IN METROPOLITAN: |
|---|---|---|---|
| Carbon, PA | Allentown-Bethlehem-Easton, PA-NJ | Cook, IL | Chicago-Naperville-Elgin, IL-IN-WI |
| Carlton, MN | Duluth, MN-WI | Copiah, MS | Jackson, MS |
| Caroline, VA | Richmond, VA | Coryell, TX | Killeen-Temple, TX |
| Carroll, GA | Atlanta-Sandy Springs-Roswell, GA | Cotton, OK | Lawton, OK |
| Carroll, IN | Lafayette-West Lafayette, IN | Coweta, GA | Atlanta-Sandy Springs-Roswell, GA |
| Carroll, MD | Baltimore-Columbia-Towson, MD | Cowlitz, WA | Longview, WA |
| Carroll, OH | Canton-Massillon, OH | Craighead, AR | Jonesboro, AR |
| Carson City, NV | Carson City, NV | Craig, VA | Roanoke, VA |
| Carson, TX | Amarillo, TX | Craven, NC | New Bern, NC |
| Carter, TN | Johnson City, TN | Crawford, AR | Fort Smith, AR-OK |
| Carver, MN | Minneapolis-St. Paul-Bloomington, MN-WI | Crawford, GA | Macon, GA |
| Cascade, MT | Great Falls, MT | Creek, OK | Tulsa, OK |
| Cass, MI | South Bend-Mishawaka, IN-MI | Crittenden, AR | Memphis, TN-MS-AR |
| Cass, MO | Kansas City, MO-KS | Crockett, TN | Jackson, TN |
| Cass, ND | Fargo, ND-MN | Crosby, TX | Lubbock, TX |
| Cass, NE | Omaha-Council Bluffs, NE-IA | Culpeper, VA | Washington-Arlington-Alexandria, DC-VA-MD-WV |
| Catawba, NC | Hickory-Lenoir-Morganton, NC | Cumberland, ME | Portland-South Portland, ME |
| Catoosa, GA | Chattanooga, TN-GA | Cumberland, NC | Fayetteville, NC |
| Cecil, MD | Philadelphia-Camden-Wilmington, PA-NJ-DE-MD | Cumberland, NJ | Vineland-Bridgeton, NJ |
| Centre, PA | State College, PA | Cumberland, PA | Harrisburg-Carlisle, PA |
| Chambers, TX | Houston-The Woodlands-Sugar Land, TX | Currituck, NC | Virginia Beach-Norfolk-Newport News, VA-NC |
| Champaign, IL | Champaign-Urbana, IL | Custer, SD | Rapid City, SD |
| Charles City, VA | Richmond, VA | Cuyahoga, OH | Cleveland-Elyria, OH |
| Charleston, SC | Charleston-North Charleston, SC | Dade, GA | Chattanooga, TN-GA |
| Charles, MD | Washington-Arlington-Alexandria, DC-VA-MD-WV | Dakota, MN | Minneapolis-St. Paul-Bloomington, MN-WI |
| Charlottesville city, VA | Charlottesville, VA | Dakota, NE | Sioux City, IA-NE-SD |
| Charlotte, FL | Punta Gorda, FL | Dallas, IA | Des Moines-West Des Moines, IA |
| Chatham, GA | Savannah, GA | Dallas, MO | Springfield, MO |
| Chatham, NC | Durham-Chapel Hill, NC | Dallas, TX | Dallas-Fort Worth-Arlington, TX |
| Chattahoochee, GA | Columbus, GA-AL | Dane, WI | Madison, WI |
| Cheatham, TN | Nashville-Davidson--Murfreesboro--Franklin, TN | Darlington, SC | Florence, SC |
| Chelan, WA | Wenatchee, WA | Dauphin, PA | Harrisburg-Carlisle, PA |
| Chemung, NY | Elmira, NY | Davidson, NC | Winston-Salem, NC |
| Cherokee, GA | Atlanta-Sandy Springs-Roswell, GA | Davidson, TN | Nashville-Davidson--Murfreesboro--Franklin, TN |
| Chesapeake city, VA | Virginia Beach-Norfolk-Newport News, VA-NC | Daviess, KY | Owensboro, KY |
| Chesterfield, VA | Richmond, VA | Davie, NC | Winston-Salem, NC |
| Chester, PA | Philadelphia-Camden-Wilmington, PA-NJ-DE-MD | Davis, UT | Ogden-Clearfield, UT |
| Chester, SC | Charlotte-Concord-Gastonia, NC-SC | Dawson, GA | Atlanta-Sandy Springs-Roswell, GA |
| Chester, TN | Jackson, TN | De Soto, LA | Shreveport-Bossier City, LA |
| Chilton, AL | Birmingham-Hoover, AL | De Witt, IL | Bloomington, IL |
| Chippewa, WI | Eau Claire, WI | Dearborn, IN | Cincinnati, OH-KY-IN |
| Chisago, MN | Minneapolis-St. Paul-Bloomington, MN-WI | DeKalb, GA | Atlanta-Sandy Springs-Roswell, GA |
| Chittenden, VT | Burlington-South Burlington, VT | DeKalb, IL | Chicago-Naperville-Elgin, IL-IN-WI |
| Christian, KY | Clarksville, TN-KY | DeKalb, MO | St. Joseph, MO-KS |
| Christian, MO | Springfield, MO | Delaware, IN | Muncie, IN |
| Citrus, FL | Homosassa Springs, FL | Delaware, OH | Columbus, OH |
| Clackamas, OR | Portland-Vancouver-Hillsboro, OR-WA | Delaware, PA | Philadelphia-Camden-Wilmington, PA-NJ-DE-MD |
| Clarke, GA | Athens-Clarke County, GA | Denton, TX | Dallas-Fort Worth-Arlington, TX |
| Clarke, VA | Washington-Arlington-Alexandria, DC-VA-MD-WV | Denver, CO | Denver-Aurora-Lakewood, CO |
| Clark, IN | Louisville/Jefferson County, KY-IN | Deschutes, OR | Bend-Redmond, OR |
| Clark, KY | Lexington-Fayette, KY | DeSoto, MS | Memphis, TN-MS-AR |
| Clark, NV | Las Vegas-Henderson-Paradise, NV | Dickson, TN | Nashville-Davidson--Murfreesboro--Franklin, TN |
| Clark, OH | Springfield, OH | Dinwiddie, VA | Richmond, VA |
| Clark, WA | Portland-Vancouver-Hillsboro, OR-WA | District of Columbia, DC | Washington-Arlington-Alexandria, DC-VA-MD-WV |
| Clayton, GA | Atlanta-Sandy Springs-Roswell, GA | Dixon, NE | Sioux City, IA-NE-SD |
| Clay, FL | Jacksonville, FL | Dodge, MN | Rochester, MN |
| Clay, IN | Terre Haute, IN | Doniphan, KS | St. Joseph, MO-KS |
| Clay, MN | Fargo, ND-MN | Doña Ana, NM | Las Cruces, NM |
| Clay, MO | Kansas City, MO-KS | Dorchester, SC | Charleston-North Charleston, SC |
| Clay, TX | Wichita Falls, TX | Dougherty, GA | Albany, GA |
| Clay, WV | Charleston, WV | Douglas, CO | Denver-Aurora-Lakewood, CO |
| Clear Creek, CO | Denver-Aurora-Lakewood, CO | Douglas, GA | Atlanta-Sandy Springs-Roswell, GA |
| Clermont, OH | Cincinnati, OH-KY-IN | Douglas, KS | Lawrence, KS |
| Cleveland, AR | Pine Bluff, AR | Douglas, NE | Omaha-Council Bluffs, NE-IA |
| Cleveland, OK | Oklahoma City, OK | Douglas, WA | Wenatchee, WA |
| Clinton, IL | St. Louis, MO-IL | Douglas, WI | Duluth, MN-WI |
| Clinton, MI | Lansing-East Lansing, MI | Dubuque, IA | Dubuque, IA |
| Clinton, MO | Kansas City, MO-KS | DuPage, IL | Chicago-Naperville-Elgin, IL-IN-WI |
| Cobb, GA | Atlanta-Sandy Springs-Roswell, GA | Durham, NC | Durham-Chapel Hill, NC |
| Cochise, AZ | Sierra Vista-Douglas, AZ | Dutchess, NY | New York-Newark-Jersey City, NY-NJ-PA |
| Coconino, AZ | Flagstaff, AZ | Duval, FL | Jacksonville, FL |
| Colbert, AL | Florence-Muscle Shoals, AL | East Baton Rouge, LA | Baton Rouge, LA |
| Cole, MO | Jefferson City, MO | East Feliciana, LA | Baton Rouge, LA |
| Collier, FL | Naples-Immokalee-Marco Island, FL | Eaton, MI | Lansing-East Lansing, MI |
| Collin, TX | Dallas-Fort Worth-Arlington, TX | Eau Claire, WI | Eau Claire, WI |
| Colonial Heights city, VA | Richmond, VA | Echols, GA | Valdosta, GA |
| Columbia, GA | Augusta-Richmond County, GA-SC | Ector, TX | Odessa, TX |
| Columbia, OR | Portland-Vancouver-Hillsboro, OR-WA | Edgecombe, NC | Rocky Mount, NC |
| Columbia, PA | Bloomsburg-Berwick, PA | Edgefield, SC | Augusta-Richmond County, GA-SC |
| Columbia, WA | Walla Walla, WA | Edmonson, KY | Bowling Green, KY |
| Columbia, WI | Madison, WI | Effingham, GA | Savannah, GA |
| Comal, TX | San Antonio-New Braunfels, TX | El Dorado, CA | Sacramento--Roseville--Arden-Arcade, CA |
| Comanche, OK | Lawton, OK | El Paso, CO | Colorado Springs, CO |
| Contra Costa, CA | San Francisco-Oakland-Hayward, CA | El Paso, TX | El Paso, TX |

# County Index: 2013 (continued)

| COUNTY: | IS IN METROPOLITAN: |
|---|---|
| Elbert, CO | Denver-Aurora-Lakewood, CO |
| Elkhart, IN | Elkhart-Goshen, IN |
| Ellis, TX | Dallas-Fort Worth-Arlington, TX |
| Elmore, AL | Montgomery, AL |
| Erie, NY | Buffalo-Cheektowaga-Niagara Falls, NY |
| Erie, PA | Erie, PA |
| Escambia, FL | Pensacola-Ferry Pass-Brent, FL |
| Essex, MA | Boston-Cambridge-Newton, MA-NH |
| Essex, NJ | New York-Newark-Jersey City, NY-NJ-PA |
| Etowah, AL | Gadsden, AL |
| Fairbanks North Star, AK | Fairbanks, AK |
| Fairfax city, VA | Washington-Arlington-Alexandria, DC-VA-MD-WV |
| Fairfax, VA | Washington-Arlington-Alexandria, DC-VA-MD-WV |
| Fairfield, CT | Bridgeport-Stamford-Norwalk, CT |
| Fairfield, OH | Columbus, OH |
| Fairfield, SC | Columbia, SC |
| Falls Church city, VA | Washington-Arlington-Alexandria, DC-VA-MD-WV |
| Falls, TX | Waco, TX |
| Faulkner, AR | Little Rock-North Little Rock-Conway, AR |
| Fauquier, VA | Washington-Arlington-Alexandria, DC-VA-MD-WV |
| Fayette, GA | Atlanta-Sandy Springs-Roswell, GA |
| Fayette, KY | Lexington-Fayette, KY |
| Fayette, PA | Pittsburgh, PA |
| Fayette, TN | Memphis, TN-MS-AR |
| Fayette, WV | Beckley, WV |
| Fillmore, MN | Rochester, MN |
| Flagler, FL | Deltona-Daytona Beach-Ormond Beach, FL |
| Florence, SC | Florence, SC |
| Floyd, GA | Rome, GA |
| Floyd, IN | Louisville/Jefferson County, KY-IN |
| Floyd, VA | Blacksburg-Christiansburg-Radford, VA |
| Fluvanna, VA | Charlottesville, VA |
| Fond du Lac, WI | Fond du Lac, WI |
| Ford, IL | Champaign-Urbana, IL |
| Forrest, MS | Hattiesburg, MS |
| Forsyth, GA | Atlanta-Sandy Springs-Roswell, GA |
| Forsyth, NC | Winston-Salem, NC |
| Fort Bend, TX | Houston-The Woodlands-Sugar Land, TX |
| Franklin, ID | Logan, UT-ID |
| Franklin, MO | St. Louis, MO-IL |
| Franklin, NC | Raleigh, NC |
| Franklin, OH | Columbus, OH |
| Franklin, PA | Chambersburg-Waynesboro, PA |
| Franklin, VA | Roanoke, VA |
| Franklin, VT | Burlington-South Burlington, VT |
| Franklin, WA | Kennewick-Richland, WA |
| Fredericksburg city, VA | Washington-Arlington-Alexandria, DC-VA-MD-WV |
| Frederick, MD | Washington-Arlington-Alexandria, DC-VA-MD-WV |
| Frederick, VA | Winchester, VA-WV |
| Fresno, CA | Fresno, CA |
| Fulton, GA | Atlanta-Sandy Springs-Roswell, GA |
| Fulton, OH | Toledo, OH |
| Gadsden, FL | Tallahassee, FL |
| Gallatin, KY | Cincinnati, OH-KY-IN |
| Galveston, TX | Houston-The Woodlands-Sugar Land, TX |
| Garland, AR | Hot Springs, AR |
| Gaston, NC | Charlotte-Concord-Gastonia, NC-SC |
| Gates, NC | Virginia Beach-Norfolk-Newport News, VA-NC |
| Geauga, OH | Cleveland-Elyria, OH |
| Gem, ID | Boise City, ID |
| Genesee, MI | Flint, MI |
| Geneva, AL | Dothan, AL |
| Gilchrist, FL | Gainesville, FL |
| Giles, VA | Blacksburg-Christiansburg-Radford, VA |
| Gilpin, CO | Denver-Aurora-Lakewood, CO |
| Gloucester, NJ | Philadelphia-Camden-Wilmington, PA-NJ-DE-MD |
| Gloucester, VA | Virginia Beach-Norfolk-Newport News, VA-NC |
| Glynn, GA | Brunswick, GA |
| Golden Valley, MT | Billings, MT |
| Goliad, TX | Victoria, TX |
| Goochland, VA | Richmond, VA |
| Grady, OK | Oklahoma City, OK |
| Grainger, TN | Knoxville, TN |
| Grand Forks, ND | Grand Forks, ND-MN |
| Grand Isle, VT | Burlington-South Burlington, VT |
| Grant, AR | Little Rock-North Little Rock-Conway, AR |
| Grant, KY | Cincinnati, OH-KY-IN |
| Grant, LA | Alexandria, LA |
| Grayson, TX | Sherman-Denison, TX |
| Greene, MO | Springfield, MO |
| Greene, OH | Dayton, OH |
| Greene, VA | Charlottesville, VA |
| Greenup, KY | Huntington-Ashland, WV-KY-OH |
| Greenville, SC | Greenville-Anderson-Mauldin, SC |

| COUNTY: | IS IN METROPOLITAN: |
|---|---|
| Green, WI | Madison, WI |
| Gregg, TX | Longview, TX |
| Grundy, IA | Waterloo-Cedar Falls, IA |
| Grundy, IL | Chicago-Naperville-Elgin, IL-IN-WI |
| Guadalupe, TX | San Antonio-New Braunfels, TX |
| Guilford, NC | Greensboro-High Point, NC |
| Gulf, FL | Panama City, FL |
| Guthrie, IA | Des Moines-West Des Moines, IA |
| Gwinnett, GA | Atlanta-Sandy Springs-Roswell, GA |
| Hale, AL | Tuscaloosa, AL |
| Hall, GA | Gainesville, GA |
| Hall, NE | Grand Island, NE |
| Hamblen, TN | Morristown, TN |
| Hamilton, IN | Indianapolis-Carmel-Anderson, IN |
| Hamilton, NE | Grand Island, NE |
| Hamilton, OH | Cincinnati, OH-KY-IN |
| Hamilton, TN | Chattanooga, TN-GA |
| Hampden, MA | Springfield, MA |
| Hampshire, MA | Springfield, MA |
| Hampshire, WV | Winchester, VA-WV |
| Hampton city, VA | Virginia Beach-Norfolk-Newport News, VA-NC |
| Hancock, IN | Indianapolis-Carmel-Anderson, IN |
| Hancock, KY | Owensboro, KY |
| Hancock, MS | Gulfport-Biloxi-Pascagoula, MS |
| Hancock, WV | Weirton-Steubenville, WV-OH |
| Hanover, VA | Richmond, VA |
| Haralson, GA | Atlanta-Sandy Springs-Roswell, GA |
| Hardin, KY | Elizabethtown-Fort Knox, KY |
| Hardin, TX | Beaumont-Port Arthur, TX |
| Harford, MD | Baltimore-Columbia-Towson, MD |
| Harrisonburg city, VA | Harrisonburg, VA |
| Harrison, IA | Omaha-Council Bluffs, NE-IA |
| Harrison, IN | Louisville/Jefferson County, KY-IN |
| Harrison, MS | Gulfport-Biloxi-Pascagoula, MS |
| Harris, GA | Columbus, GA-AL |
| Harris, TX | Houston-The Woodlands-Sugar Land, TX |
| Hartford, CT | Hartford-West Hartford-East Hartford, CT |
| Harvey, KS | Wichita, KS |
| Hawkins, TN | Kingsport-Bristol-Bristol, TN-VA |
| Hays, TX | Austin-Round Rock, TX |
| Haywood, NC | Asheville, NC |
| Heard, GA | Atlanta-Sandy Springs-Roswell, GA |
| Henderson, KY | Evansville, IN-KY |
| Henderson, NC | Asheville, NC |
| Hendricks, IN | Indianapolis-Carmel-Anderson, IN |
| Hennepin, MN | Minneapolis-St. Paul-Bloomington, MN-WI |
| Henrico, VA | Richmond, VA |
| Henry, AL | Dothan, AL |
| Henry, GA | Atlanta-Sandy Springs-Roswell, GA |
| Henry, IL | Davenport-Moline-Rock Island, IA-IL |
| Henry, KY | Louisville/Jefferson County, KY-IN |
| Herkimer, NY | Utica-Rome, NY |
| Hernando, FL | Tampa-St. Petersburg-Clearwater, FL |
| Hickman, TN | Nashville-Davidson--Murfreesboro--Franklin, TN |
| Hidalgo, TX | McAllen-Edinburg-Mission, TX |
| Highlands, FL | Sebring, FL |
| Hillsborough, FL | Tampa-St. Petersburg-Clearwater, FL |
| Hillsborough, NH | Manchester-Nashua, NH |
| Hinds, MS | Jackson, MS |
| Hocking, OH | Columbus, OH |
| Hoke, NC | Fayetteville, NC |
| Honolulu, HI | Urban Honolulu, HI |
| Hood, TX | Dallas-Fort Worth-Arlington, TX |
| Hopewell city, VA | Richmond, VA |
| Horry, SC | Myrtle Beach-Conway-North Myrtle Beach, SC-NC |
| Houston, AL | Dothan, AL |
| Houston, GA | Warner Robins, GA |
| Houston, MN | La Crosse-Onalaska, WI-MN |
| Howard, IN | Kokomo, IN |
| Howard, MD | Baltimore-Columbia-Towson, MD |
| Howard, NE | Grand Island, NE |
| Hudson, NJ | New York-Newark-Jersey City, NY-NJ-PA |
| Hudspeth, TX | El Paso, TX |
| Hunterdon, NJ | New York-Newark-Jersey City, NY-NJ-PA |
| Hunt, TX | Dallas-Fort Worth-Arlington, TX |
| Iberia, LA | Lafayette, LA |
| Iberville, LA | Baton Rouge, LA |
| Imperial, CA | El Centro, CA |
| Indian River, FL | Sebastian-Vero Beach, FL |
| Ingham, MI | Lansing-East Lansing, MI |
| Iowa, WI | Madison, WI |
| Iredell, NC | Charlotte-Concord-Gastonia, NC-SC |
| Irion, TX | San Angelo, TX |
| Isanti, MN | Minneapolis-St. Paul-Bloomington, MN-WI |

# County Index: 2013 (continued)

| COUNTY: | IS IN METROPOLITAN: |
|---|---|
| Isle of Wight, VA | Virginia Beach-Norfolk-Newport News, VA-NC |
| Jackson, IL | Carbondale-Marion, IL |
| Jackson, KS | Topeka, KS |
| Jackson, MI | Jackson, MI |
| Jackson, MO | Kansas City, MO-KS |
| Jackson, MS | Gulfport-Biloxi-Pascagoula, MS |
| Jackson, OR | Medford, OR |
| James City, VA | Virginia Beach-Norfolk-Newport News, VA-NC |
| Jasper, GA | Atlanta-Sandy Springs-Roswell, GA |
| Jasper, IN | Chicago-Naperville-Elgin, IL-IN-WI |
| Jasper, MO | Joplin, MO |
| Jasper, SC | Hilton Head Island-Bluffton-Beaufort, SC |
| Jefferson, AL | Birmingham-Hoover, AL |
| Jefferson, AR | Pine Bluff, AR |
| Jefferson, CO | Denver-Aurora-Lakewood, CO |
| Jefferson, FL | Tallahassee, FL |
| Jefferson, ID | Idaho Falls, ID |
| Jefferson, KS | Topeka, KS |
| Jefferson, KY | Louisville/Jefferson County, KY-IN |
| Jefferson, LA | New Orleans-Metairie, LA |
| Jefferson, MO | St. Louis, MO-IL |
| Jefferson, NY | Watertown-Fort Drum, NY |
| Jefferson, OH | Weirton-Steubenville, WV-OH |
| Jefferson, TN | Morristown, TN |
| Jefferson, TX | Beaumont-Port Arthur, TX |
| Jefferson, WV | Washington-Arlington-Alexandria, DC-VA-MD-WV |
| Jersey, IL | St. Louis, MO-IL |
| Jessamine, KY | Lexington-Fayette, KY |
| Johnson, IA | Iowa City, IA |
| Johnson, IN | Indianapolis-Carmel-Anderson, IN |
| Johnson, KS | Kansas City, MO-KS |
| Johnson, TX | Dallas-Fort Worth-Arlington, TX |
| Johnston, NC | Raleigh, NC |
| Jones, GA | Macon, GA |
| Jones, IA | Cedar Rapids, IA |
| Jones, NC | New Bern, NC |
| Jones, TX | Abilene, TX |
| Josephine, OR | Grants Pass, OR |
| Juab, UT | Provo-Orem, UT |
| Kalamazoo, MI | Kalamazoo-Portage, MI |
| Kalawao, HI | Kahului-Wailuku-Lahaina, HI |
| Kanawha, WV | Charleston, WV |
| Kane, IL | Chicago-Naperville-Elgin, IL-IN-WI |
| Kankakee, IL | Kankakee, IL |
| Kaufman, TX | Dallas-Fort Worth-Arlington, TX |
| Kendall, IL | Chicago-Naperville-Elgin, IL-IN-WI |
| Kendall, TX | San Antonio-New Braunfels, TX |
| Kenosha, WI | Chicago-Naperville-Elgin, IL-IN-WI |
| Kenton, KY | Cincinnati, OH-KY-IN |
| Kent, DE | Dover, DE |
| Kent, MI | Grand Rapids-Wyoming, MI |
| Kent, RI | Providence-Warwick, RI-MA |
| Kern, CA | Bakersfield, CA |
| Kershaw, SC | Columbia, SC |
| Kewaunee, WI | Green Bay, WI |
| King William, VA | Richmond, VA |
| Kingman, KS | Wichita, KS |
| Kings, CA | Hanford-Corcoran, CA |
| Kings, NY | New York-Newark-Jersey City, NY-NJ-PA |
| King, WA | Seattle-Tacoma-Bellevue, WA |
| Kitsap, WA | Bremerton-Silverdale, WA |
| Knox, TN | Knoxville, TN |
| Kootenai, ID | Coeur d'Alene, ID |
| La Crosse, WI | La Crosse-Onalaska, WI-MN |
| Lackawanna, PA | Scranton--Wilkes-Barre--Hazleton, PA |
| Lafayette, LA | Lafayette, LA |
| Lafayette, MO | Kansas City, MO-KS |
| Lafourche, LA | Houma-Thibodaux, LA |
| Lake, FL | Orlando-Kissimmee-Sanford, FL |
| Lake, IL | Chicago-Naperville-Elgin, IL-IN-WI |
| Lake, IN | Chicago-Naperville-Elgin, IL-IN-WI |
| Lake, OH | Cleveland-Elyria, OH |
| Lamar, GA | Atlanta-Sandy Springs-Roswell, GA |
| Lamar, MS | Hattiesburg, MS |
| Lampasas, TX | Killeen-Temple, TX |
| Lancaster, NE | Lincoln, NE |
| Lancaster, PA | Lancaster, PA |
| Lancaster, SC | Charlotte-Concord-Gastonia, NC-SC |
| Lane, OR | Eugene, OR |
| Lanier, GA | Valdosta, GA |
| Lapeer, MI | Detroit-Warren-Dearborn, MI |
| LaPorte, IN | Michigan City-La Porte, IN |
| Laramie, WY | Cheyenne, WY |
| Larimer, CO | Fort Collins, CO |

| COUNTY: | IS IN METROPOLITAN: |
|---|---|
| Larue, KY | Elizabethtown-Fort Knox, KY |
| Lauderdale, AL | Florence-Muscle Shoals, AL |
| Laurens, SC | Greenville-Anderson-Mauldin, SC |
| Lawrence, AL | Decatur, AL |
| Lawrence, OH | Huntington-Ashland, WV-KY-OH |
| Le Flore, OK | Fort Smith, AR-OK |
| Le Sueur, MN | Minneapolis-St. Paul-Bloomington, MN-WI |
| Leavenworth, KS | Kansas City, MO-KS |
| Lebanon, PA | Lebanon, PA |
| Lee, AL | Auburn-Opelika, AL |
| Lee, FL | Cape Coral-Fort Myers, FL |
| Lee, GA | Albany, GA |
| Lehigh, PA | Allentown-Bethlehem-Easton, PA-NJ |
| Leon, FL | Tallahassee, FL |
| Lexington, SC | Columbia, SC |
| Liberty, GA | Hinesville, GA |
| Liberty, TX | Houston-The Woodlands-Sugar Land, TX |
| Licking, OH | Columbus, OH |
| Limestone, AL | Huntsville, AL |
| Lincoln, AR | Pine Bluff, AR |
| Lincoln, GA | Augusta-Richmond County, GA-SC |
| Lincoln, MO | St. Louis, MO-IL |
| Lincoln, NC | Charlotte-Concord-Gastonia, NC-SC |
| Lincoln, OK | Oklahoma City, OK |
| Lincoln, SD | Sioux Falls, SD |
| Lincoln, WV | Huntington-Ashland, WV-KY-OH |
| Linn, IA | Cedar Rapids, IA |
| Linn, KS | Kansas City, MO-KS |
| Linn, OR | Albany, OR |
| Little River, AR | Texarkana, TX-AR |
| Livingston, LA | Baton Rouge, LA |
| Livingston, MI | Detroit-Warren-Dearborn, MI |
| Livingston, NY | Rochester, NY |
| Logan, OK | Oklahoma City, OK |
| Long, GA | Hinesville, GA |
| Lonoke, AR | Little Rock-North Little Rock-Conway, AR |
| Lorain, OH | Cleveland-Elyria, OH |
| Los Angeles, CA | Los Angeles-Long Beach-Anaheim, CA |
| Loudon, TN | Knoxville, TN |
| Loudoun, VA | Washington-Arlington-Alexandria, DC-VA-MD-WV |
| Lowndes, AL | Montgomery, AL |
| Lowndes, GA | Valdosta, GA |
| Lubbock, TX | Lubbock, TX |
| Lucas, OH | Toledo, OH |
| Luzerne, PA | Scranton--Wilkes-Barre--Hazleton, PA |
| Lycoming, PA | Williamsport, PA |
| Lynchburg city, VA | Lynchburg, VA |
| Lynn, TX | Lubbock, TX |
| Macomb, MI | Detroit-Warren-Dearborn, MI |
| Macon, IL | Decatur, IL |
| Macon, TN | Nashville-Davidson--Murfreesboro--Franklin, TN |
| Macoupin, IL | St. Louis, MO-IL |
| Madera, CA | Madera, CA |
| Madison, AL | Huntsville, AL |
| Madison, AR | Fayetteville-Springdale-Rogers, AR-MO |
| Madison, GA | Athens-Clarke County, GA |
| Madison, IA | Des Moines-West Des Moines, IA |
| Madison, IL | St. Louis, MO-IL |
| Madison, IN | Indianapolis-Carmel-Anderson, IN |
| Madison, MS | Jackson, MS |
| Madison, NC | Asheville, NC |
| Madison, NY | Syracuse, NY |
| Madison, OH | Columbus, OH |
| Madison, TN | Jackson, TN |
| Mahoning, OH | Youngstown-Warren-Boardman, OH-PA |
| Manassas city, VA | Washington-Arlington-Alexandria, DC-VA-MD-WV |
| Manassas Park city, VA | Washington-Arlington-Alexandria, DC-VA-MD-WV |
| Manatee, FL | North Port-Sarasota-Bradenton, FL |
| Marathon, WI | Wausau, WI |
| Maricopa, AZ | Phoenix-Mesa-Scottsdale, AZ |
| Marin, CA | San Francisco-Oakland-Hayward, CA |
| Marion, FL | Ocala, FL |
| Marion, GA | Columbus, GA-AL |
| Marion, IN | Indianapolis-Carmel-Anderson, IN |
| Marion, OR | Salem, OR |
| Marion, TN | Chattanooga, TN-GA |
| Marshall, IL | Peoria, IL |
| Marshall, MS | Memphis, TN-MS-AR |
| Marshall, WV | Wheeling, WV-OH |
| Martin, FL | Port St. Lucie, FL |
| Martin, TX | Midland, TX |
| Matanuska-Susitna, AK | Anchorage, AK |
| Mathews, VA | Virginia Beach-Norfolk-Newport News, VA-NC |
| Maui, HI | Kahului-Wailuku-Lahaina, HI |

# County Index: 2013 (continued)

| COUNTY: | IS IN METROPOLITAN: | COUNTY: | IS IN METROPOLITAN: |
|---------|---------------------|---------|---------------------|
| Maury, TN | Nashville-Davidson--Murfreesboro--Franklin, TN | Newport, RI | Providence-Warwick, RI-MA |
| McClain, OK | Oklahoma City, OK | Newton, GA | Atlanta-Sandy Springs-Roswell, GA |
| McCook, SD | Sioux Falls, SD | Newton, IN | Chicago-Naperville-Elgin, IL-IN-WI |
| McDonald, MO | Fayetteville-Springdale-Rogers, AR-MO | Newton, MO | Joplin, MO |
| McDuffie, GA | Augusta-Richmond County, GA-SC | Newton, TX | Beaumont-Port Arthur, TX |
| McHenry, IL | Chicago-Naperville-Elgin, IL-IN-WI | Nez Perce, ID | Lewiston, ID-WA |
| McIntosh, GA | Brunswick, GA | Niagara, NY | Buffalo-Cheektowaga-Niagara Falls, NY |
| McLean, IL | Bloomington, IL | Nicollet, MN | Mankato-North Mankato, MN |
| McLean, KY | Owensboro, KY | Norfolk city, VA | Virginia Beach-Norfolk-Newport News, VA-NC |
| McLennan, TX | Waco, TX | Norfolk, MA | Boston-Cambridge-Newton, MA-NH |
| Meade, KY | Elizabethtown-Fort Knox, KY | Northampton, PA | Allentown-Bethlehem-Easton, PA-NJ |
| Meade, SD | Rapid City, SD | Nueces, TX | Corpus Christi, TX |
| Mecklenburg, NC | Charlotte-Concord-Gastonia, NC-SC | Oakland, MI | Detroit-Warren-Dearborn, MI |
| Medina, OH | Cleveland-Elyria, OH | Ocean, NJ | New York-Newark-Jersey City, NY-NJ-PA |
| Medina, TX | San Antonio-New Braunfels, TX | Oconee, GA | Athens-Clarke County, GA |
| Menard, IL | Springfield, IL | Oconto, WI | Green Bay, WI |
| Merced, CA | Merced, CA | Oglethorpe, GA | Athens-Clarke County, GA |
| Mercer, IL | Davenport-Moline-Rock Island, IA-IL | Ohio, IN | Cincinnati, OH-KY-IN |
| Mercer, NJ | Trenton, NJ | Ohio, WV | Wheeling, WV-OH |
| Mercer, PA | Youngstown-Warren-Boardman, OH-PA | Okaloosa, FL | Crestview-Fort Walton Beach-Destin, FL |
| Meriwether, GA | Atlanta-Sandy Springs-Roswell, GA | Oklahoma, OK | Oklahoma City, OK |
| Merrick, NE | Grand Island, NE | Okmulgee, OK | Tulsa, OK |
| Mesa, CO | Grand Junction, CO | Oldham, KY | Louisville/Jefferson County, KY-IN |
| Miami-Dade, FL | Miami-Fort Lauderdale-West Palm Beach, FL | Oldham, TX | Amarillo, TX |
| Miami, KS | Kansas City, MO-KS | Oliver, ND | Bismarck, ND |
| Miami, OH | Dayton, OH | Olmsted, MN | Rochester, MN |
| Middlesex, CT | Hartford-West Hartford-East Hartford, CT | Oneida, NY | Utica-Rome, NY |
| Middlesex, MA | Boston-Cambridge-Newton, MA-NH | Onondaga, NY | Syracuse, NY |
| Middlesex, NJ | New York-Newark-Jersey City, NY-NJ-PA | Onslow, NC | Jacksonville, NC |
| Midland, MI | Midland, MI | Ontario, NY | Rochester, NY |
| Midland, TX | Midland, TX | Orange, CA | Los Angeles-Long Beach-Anaheim, CA |
| Mille Lacs, MN | Minneapolis-St. Paul-Bloomington, MN-WI | Orange, FL | Orlando-Kissimmee-Sanford, FL |
| Miller, AR | Texarkana, TX-AR | Orange, NC | Durham-Chapel Hill, NC |
| Mills, IA | Omaha-Council Bluffs, NE-IA | Orange, NY | New York-Newark-Jersey City, NY-NJ-PA |
| Milwaukee, WI | Milwaukee-Waukesha-West Allis, WI | Orange, TX | Beaumont-Port Arthur, TX |
| Mineral, WV | Cumberland, MD-WV | Orleans, LA | New Orleans-Metairie, LA |
| Minnehaha, SD | Sioux Falls, SD | Orleans, NY | Rochester, NY |
| Missoula, MT | Missoula, MT | Osage, KS | Topeka, KS |
| Mobile, AL | Mobile, AL | Osage, MO | Jefferson City, MO |
| Mohave, AZ | Lake Havasu City-Kingman, AZ | Osage, OK | Tulsa, OK |
| Moniteau, MO | Jefferson City, MO | Osceola, FL | Orlando-Kissimmee-Sanford, FL |
| Monmouth, NJ | New York-Newark-Jersey City, NY-NJ-PA | Oswego, NY | Syracuse, NY |
| Monongalia, WV | Morgantown, WV | Ottawa, MI | Grand Rapids-Wyoming, MI |
| Monroe, GA | Macon, GA | Ouachita, LA | Monroe, LA |
| Monroe, IL | St. Louis, MO-IL | Outagamie, WI | Appleton, WI |
| Monroe, IN | Bloomington, IN | Owen, IN | Bloomington, IN |
| Monroe, MI | Monroe, MI | Owyhee, ID | Boise City, ID |
| Monroe, NY | Rochester, NY | Ozaukee, WI | Milwaukee-Waukesha-West Allis, WI |
| Monroe, PA | East Stroudsburg, PA | Palm Beach, FL | Miami-Fort Lauderdale-West Palm Beach, FL |
| Montcalm, MI | Grand Rapids-Wyoming, MI | Pamlico, NC | New Bern, NC |
| Monterey, CA | Salinas, CA | Parker, TX | Dallas-Fort Worth-Arlington, TX |
| Montgomery, AL | Montgomery, AL | Park, CO | Denver-Aurora-Lakewood, CO |
| Montgomery, MD | Washington-Arlington-Alexandria, DC-VA-MD-WV | Pasco, FL | Tampa-St. Petersburg-Clearwater, FL |
| Montgomery, OH | Dayton, OH | Passaic, NJ | New York-Newark-Jersey City, NY-NJ-PA |
| Montgomery, PA | Philadelphia-Camden-Wilmington, PA-NJ-DE-MD | Paulding, GA | Atlanta-Sandy Springs-Roswell, GA |
| Montgomery, TN | Clarksville, TN-KY | Pawnee, OK | Tulsa, OK |
| Montgomery, TX | Houston-The Woodlands-Sugar Land, TX | Peach, GA | Warner Robins, GA |
| Montgomery, VA | Blacksburg-Christiansburg-Radford, VA | Pend Oreille, WA | Spokane-Spokane Valley, WA |
| Montour, PA | Bloomsburg-Berwick, PA | Pender, NC | Wilmington, NC |
| Morgan, AL | Decatur, AL | Pendleton, KY | Cincinnati, OH-KY-IN |
| Morgan, GA | Atlanta-Sandy Springs-Roswell, GA | Pennington, SD | Rapid City, SD |
| Morgan, IN | Indianapolis-Carmel-Anderson, IN | Penobscot, ME | Bangor, ME |
| Morgan, TN | Knoxville, TN | Peoria, IL | Peoria, IL |
| Morgan, UT | Ogden-Clearfield, UT | Perry, AR | Little Rock-North Little Rock-Conway, AR |
| Morris, NJ | New York-Newark-Jersey City, NY-NJ-PA | Perry, MS | Hattiesburg, MS |
| Morrow, OH | Columbus, OH | Perry, OH | Columbus, OH |
| Morton, ND | Bismarck, ND | Perry, PA | Harrisburg-Carlisle, PA |
| Multnomah, OR | Portland-Vancouver-Hillsboro, OR-WA | Person, NC | Durham-Chapel Hill, NC |
| Murray, GA | Dalton, GA | Petersburg city, VA | Richmond, VA |
| Muscogee, GA | Columbus, GA-AL | Philadelphia, PA | Philadelphia-Camden-Wilmington, PA-NJ-DE-MD |
| Muskegon, MI | Muskegon, MI | Piatt, IL | Champaign-Urbana, IL |
| Napa, CA | Napa, CA | Pickaway, OH | Columbus, OH |
| Nash, NC | Rocky Mount, NC | Pickens, AL | Tuscaloosa, AL |
| Nassau, FL | Jacksonville, FL | Pickens, GA | Atlanta-Sandy Springs-Roswell, GA |
| Nassau, NY | New York-Newark-Jersey City, NY-NJ-PA | Pickens, SC | Greenville-Anderson-Mauldin, SC |
| Natrona, WY | Casper, WY | Pierce, WA | Seattle-Tacoma-Bellevue, WA |
| Nelson, VA | Charlottesville, VA | Pierce, WI | Minneapolis-St. Paul-Bloomington, MN-WI |
| New Castle, DE | Philadelphia-Camden-Wilmington, PA-NJ-DE-MD | Pike, GA | Atlanta-Sandy Springs-Roswell, GA |
| New Hanover, NC | Wilmington, NC | Pike, PA | New York-Newark-Jersey City, NY-NJ-PA |
| New Haven, CT | New Haven-Milford, CT | Pima, AZ | Tucson, AZ |
| New Kent, VA | Richmond, VA | Pinal, AZ | Phoenix-Mesa-Scottsdale, AZ |
| New London, CT | Norwich-New London, CT | Pinellas, FL | Tampa-St. Petersburg-Clearwater, FL |
| New York, NY | New York-Newark-Jersey City, NY-NJ-PA | Pitt, NC | Greenville, NC |
| Newport News city, VA | Virginia Beach-Norfolk-Newport News, VA-NC | Placer, CA | Sacramento--Roseville--Arden-Arcade, CA |

# County Index: 2013 (continued)

| COUNTY: | IS IN METROPOLITAN: | COUNTY: | IS IN METROPOLITAN: |
|---|---|---|---|
| Plaquemines, LA | New Orleans-Metairie, LA | San Juan, NM | Farmington, NM |
| Platte, MO | Kansas City, MO-KS | San Luis Obispo, CA | San Luis Obispo-Paso Robles-Arroyo Grande, CA |
| Plymouth, IA | Sioux City, IA-NE-SD | San Mateo, CA | San Francisco-Oakland-Hayward, CA |
| Plymouth, MA | Boston-Cambridge-Newton, MA-NH | San Patricio, TX | Corpus Christi, TX |
| Poinsett, AR | Jonesboro, AR | Sandoval, NM | Albuquerque, NM |
| Pointe Coupee, LA | Baton Rouge, LA | Sangamon, IL | Springfield, IL |
| Polk, FL | Lakeland-Winter Haven, FL | Santa Barbara, CA | Santa Maria-Santa Barbara, CA |
| Polk, IA | Des Moines-West Des Moines, IA | Santa Clara, CA | San Jose-Sunnyvale-Santa Clara, CA |
| Polk, MN | Grand Forks, ND-MN | Santa Cruz, CA | Santa Cruz-Watsonville, CA |
| Polk, MO | Springfield, MO | Santa Fe, NM | Santa Fe, NM |
| Polk, OR | Salem, OR | Santa Rosa, FL | Pensacola-Ferry Pass-Brent, FL |
| Polk, TN | Cleveland, TN | Sarasota, FL | North Port-Sarasota-Bradenton, FL |
| Poquoson city, VA | Virginia Beach-Norfolk-Newport News, VA-NC | Saratoga, NY | Albany-Schenectady-Troy, NY |
| Portage, OH | Akron, OH | Sarpy, NE | Omaha-Council Bluffs, NE-IA |
| Porter, IN | Chicago-Naperville-Elgin, IL-IN-WI | Saunders, NE | Omaha-Council Bluffs, NE-IA |
| Portsmouth city, VA | Virginia Beach-Norfolk-Newport News, VA-NC | Schenectady, NY | Albany-Schenectady-Troy, NY |
| Posey, IN | Evansville, IN-KY | Schoharie, NY | Albany-Schenectady-Troy, NY |
| Pottawatomie, KS | Manhattan, KS | Scott, IA | Davenport-Moline-Rock Island, IA-IL |
| Pottawattamie, IA | Omaha-Council Bluffs, NE-IA | Scott, IN | Louisville/Jefferson County, KY-IN |
| Potter, TX | Amarillo, TX | Scott, KY | Lexington-Fayette, KY |
| Powhatan, VA | Richmond, VA | Scott, MN | Minneapolis-St. Paul-Bloomington, MN-WI |
| Preston, WV | Morgantown, WV | Scott, VA | Kingsport-Bristol-Bristol, TN-VA |
| Prince George's, MD | Washington-Arlington-Alexandria, DC-VA-MD-WV | Sebastian, AR | Fort Smith, AR-OK |
| Prince George, VA | Richmond, VA | Sedgwick, KS | Wichita, KS |
| Prince William, VA | Washington-Arlington-Alexandria, DC-VA-MD-WV | Seminole, FL | Orlando-Kissimmee-Sanford, FL |
| Providence, RI | Providence-Warwick, RI-MA | Sequatchie, TN | Chattanooga, TN-GA |
| Pueblo, CO | Pueblo, CO | Sequoyah, OK | Fort Smith, AR-OK |
| Pulaski, AR | Little Rock-North Little Rock-Conway, AR | Seward, NE | Lincoln, NE |
| Pulaski, GA | Warner Robins, GA | Shasta, CA | Redding, CA |
| Pulaski, VA | Blacksburg-Christiansburg-Radford, VA | Shawnee, KS | Topeka, KS |
| Putnam, IN | Indianapolis-Carmel-Anderson, IN | Sheboygan, WI | Sheboygan, WI |
| Putnam, NY | New York-Newark-Jersey City, NY-NJ-PA | Shelby, AL | Birmingham-Hoover, AL |
| Putnam, WV | Huntington-Ashland, WV-KY-OH | Shelby, IN | Indianapolis-Carmel-Anderson, IN |
| Queen Anne's, MD | Baltimore-Columbia-Towson, MD | Shelby, KY | Louisville/Jefferson County, KY-IN |
| Queens, NY | New York-Newark-Jersey City, NY-NJ-PA | Shelby, TN | Memphis, TN-MS-AR |
| Racine, WI | Racine, WI | Sherburne, MN | Minneapolis-St. Paul-Bloomington, MN-WI |
| Radford city, VA | Blacksburg-Christiansburg-Radford, VA | Sibley, MN | Minneapolis-St. Paul-Bloomington, MN-WI |
| Raleigh, WV | Beckley, WV | Simpson, MS | Jackson, MS |
| Ramsey, MN | Minneapolis-St. Paul-Bloomington, MN-WI | Sioux, ND | Bismarck, ND |
| Randall, TX | Amarillo, TX | Skagit, WA | Mount Vernon-Anacortes, WA |
| Randolph, NC | Greensboro-High Point, NC | Skamania, WA | Portland-Vancouver-Hillsboro, OR-WA |
| Rankin, MS | Jackson, MS | Smith, TN | Nashville-Davidson--Murfreesboro--Franklin, TN |
| Rapides, LA | Alexandria, LA | Smith, TX | Tyler, TX |
| Rappahannock, VA | Washington-Arlington-Alexandria, DC-VA-MD-WV | Snohomish, WA | Seattle-Tacoma-Bellevue, WA |
| Ray, MO | Kansas City, MO-KS | Solano, CA | Vallejo-Fairfield, CA |
| Rensselaer, NY | Albany-Schenectady-Troy, NY | Somerset, MD | Salisbury, MD-DE |
| Richland, OH | Mansfield, OH | Somerset, NJ | New York-Newark-Jersey City, NY-NJ-PA |
| Richland, SC | Columbia, SC | Somervell, TX | Dallas-Fort Worth-Arlington, TX |
| Richmond city, VA | Richmond, VA | Sonoma, CA | Santa Rosa, CA |
| Richmond, GA | Augusta-Richmond County, GA-SC | Spalding, GA | Atlanta-Sandy Springs-Roswell, GA |
| Richmond, NY | New York-Newark-Jersey City, NY-NJ-PA | Spartanburg, SC | Spartanburg, SC |
| Riley, KS | Manhattan, KS | Spencer, KY | Louisville/Jefferson County, KY-IN |
| Riverside, CA | Riverside-San Bernardino-Ontario, CA | Spokane, WA | Spokane-Spokane Valley, WA |
| Roane, TN | Knoxville, TN | Spotsylvania, VA | Washington-Arlington-Alexandria, DC-VA-MD-WV |
| Roanoke city, VA | Roanoke, VA | Stafford, VA | Washington-Arlington-Alexandria, DC-VA-MD-WV |
| Roanoke, VA | Roanoke, VA | Stanislaus, CA | Modesto, CA |
| Robertson, TN | Nashville-Davidson--Murfreesboro--Franklin, TN | Stark, IL | Peoria, IL |
| Robertson, TX | College Station-Bryan, TX | Stark, OH | Canton-Massillon, OH |
| Rock Island, IL | Davenport-Moline-Rock Island, IA-IL | Staunton city, VA | Staunton-Waynesboro, VA |
| Rockdale, GA | Atlanta-Sandy Springs-Roswell, GA | Stearns, MN | St. Cloud, MN |
| Rockingham, NC | Greensboro-High Point, NC | Stevens, WA | Spokane-Spokane Valley, WA |
| Rockingham, NH | Boston-Cambridge-Newton, MA-NH | Stokes, NC | Winston-Salem, NC |
| Rockingham, VA | Harrisonburg, VA | Storey, NV | Reno, NV |
| Rockland, NY | New York-Newark-Jersey City, NY-NJ-PA | Story, IA | Ames, IA |
| Rockwall, TX | Dallas-Fort Worth-Arlington, TX | Strafford, NH | Boston-Cambridge-Newton, MA-NH |
| Rock, WI | Janesville-Beloit, WI | St. Bernard, LA | New Orleans-Metairie, LA |
| Rogers, OK | Tulsa, OK | St. Charles, LA | New Orleans-Metairie, LA |
| Rowan, NC | Charlotte-Concord-Gastonia, NC-SC | St. Charles, MO | St. Louis, MO-IL |
| Rusk, TX | Longview, TX | St. Clair, AL | Birmingham-Hoover, AL |
| Russell, AL | Columbus, GA-AL | St. Clair, IL | St. Louis, MO-IL |
| Rutherford, TN | Nashville-Davidson--Murfreesboro--Franklin, TN | St. Clair, MI | Detroit-Warren-Dearborn, MI |
| Sacramento, CA | Sacramento--Roseville--Arden-Arcade, CA | St. Croix, WI | Minneapolis-St. Paul-Bloomington, MN-WI |
| Sagadahoc, ME | Portland-South Portland, ME | St. Helena, LA | Baton Rouge, LA |
| Saginaw, MI | Saginaw, MI | St. James, LA | New Orleans-Metairie, LA |
| Salem city, VA | Roanoke, VA | St. John the Baptist, LA | New Orleans-Metairie, LA |
| Salem, NJ | Philadelphia-Camden-Wilmington, PA-NJ-DE-MD | St. Johns, FL | Jacksonville, FL |
| Saline, AR | Little Rock-North Little Rock-Conway, AR | St. Joseph, IN | South Bend-Mishawaka, IN-MI |
| Salt Lake, UT | Salt Lake City, UT | St. Louis city, MO | St. Louis, MO-IL |
| Saluda, SC | Columbia, SC | St. Louis, MN | Duluth, MN-WI |
| San Benito, CA | San Jose-Sunnyvale-Santa Clara, CA | St. Louis, MO | St. Louis, MO-IL |
| San Bernardino, CA | Riverside-San Bernardino-Ontario, CA | St. Lucie, FL | Port St. Lucie, FL |
| San Diego, CA | San Diego-Carlsbad, CA | St. Martin, LA | Lafayette, LA |
| San Francisco, CA | San Francisco-Oakland-Hayward, CA | St. Mary's, MD | California-Lexington Park, MD |
| San Joaquin, CA | Stockton-Lodi, CA | St. Tammany, LA | New Orleans-Metairie, LA |

# County Index: 2013 (continued)

| COUNTY: | IS IN METROPOLITAN: |
|---------|---------------------|
| Suffolk city, VA | Virginia Beach-Norfolk-Newport News, VA-NC |
| Suffolk, MA | Boston-Cambridge-Newton, MA-NH |
| Suffolk, NY | New York-Newark-Jersey City, NY-NJ-PA |
| Sullivan, IN | Terre Haute, IN |
| Sullivan, TN | Kingsport-Bristol-Bristol, TN-VA |
| Summit, OH | Akron, OH |
| Sumner, KS | Wichita, KS |
| Sumner, TN | Nashville-Davidson--Murfreesboro--Franklin, TN |
| Sumter, FL | The Villages, FL |
| Sumter, SC | Sumter, SC |
| Sussex, DE | Salisbury, MD-DE |
| Sussex, NJ | New York-Newark-Jersey City, NY-NJ-PA |
| Sussex, VA | Richmond, VA |
| Sutter, CA | Yuba City, CA |
| Tangipahoa, LA | Hammond, LA |
| Tarrant, TX | Dallas-Fort Worth-Arlington, TX |
| Tate, MS | Memphis, TN-MS-AR |
| Taylor, TX | Abilene, TX |
| Tazewell, IL | Peoria, IL |
| Teller, CO | Colorado Springs, CO |
| Terrebonne, LA | Houma-Thibodaux, LA |
| Terrell, GA | Albany, GA |
| Thurston, WA | Olympia-Tumwater, WA |
| Tioga, NY | Binghamton, NY |
| Tippecanoe, IN | Lafayette-West Lafayette, IN |
| Tipton, TN | Memphis, TN-MS-AR |
| Tolland, CT | Hartford-West Hartford-East Hartford, CT |
| Tom Green, TX | San Angelo, TX |
| Tompkins, NY | Ithaca, NY |
| Tooele, UT | Salt Lake City, UT |
| Torrance, NM | Albuquerque, NM |
| Travis, TX | Austin-Round Rock, TX |
| Trigg, KY | Clarksville, TN-KY |
| Trimble, KY | Louisville/Jefferson County, KY-IN |
| Trousdale, TN | Nashville-Davidson--Murfreesboro--Franklin, TN |
| Trumbull, OH | Youngstown-Warren-Boardman, OH-PA |
| Tulare, CA | Visalia-Porterville, CA |
| Tulsa, OK | Tulsa, OK |
| Tunica, MS | Memphis, TN-MS-AR |
| Turner, SD | Sioux Falls, SD |
| Tuscaloosa, AL | Tuscaloosa, AL |
| Twiggs, GA | Macon, GA |
| Ulster, NY | Kingston, NY |
| Unicoi, TN | Johnson City, TN |
| Union, IN | Cincinnati, OH-KY-IN |
| Union, LA | Monroe, LA |
| Union, NC | Charlotte-Concord-Gastonia, NC-SC |
| Union, NJ | New York-Newark-Jersey City, NY-NJ-PA |
| Union, OH | Columbus, OH |
| Union, SC | Spartanburg, SC |
| Union, SD | Sioux City, IA-NE-SD |
| Union, TN | Knoxville, TN |
| Upshur, TX | Longview, TX |
| Utah, UT | Provo-Orem, UT |
| Valencia, NM | Albuquerque, NM |
| Van Buren, MI | Kalamazoo-Portage, MI |
| Vanderburgh, IN | Evansville, IN-KY |
| Ventura, CA | Oxnard-Thousand Oaks-Ventura, CA |
| Vermilion, IL | Danville, IL |
| Vermilion, LA | Lafayette, LA |
| Vermillion, IN | Terre Haute, IN |
| Victoria, TX | Victoria, TX |
| Vigo, IN | Terre Haute, IN |
| Virginia Beach city, VA | Virginia Beach-Norfolk-Newport News, VA-NC |
| Volusia, FL | Deltona-Daytona Beach-Ormond Beach, FL |
| Wabasha, MN | Rochester, MN |
| Wabaunsee, KS | Topeka, KS |
| Wagoner, OK | Tulsa, OK |
| Wake, NC | Raleigh, NC |
| Wakulla, FL | Tallahassee, FL |
| Walker, AL | Birmingham-Hoover, AL |
| Walker, GA | Chattanooga, TN-GA |
| Walla Walla, WA | Walla Walla, WA |
| Waller, TX | Houston-The Woodlands-Sugar Land, TX |
| Walton, FL | Crestview-Fort Walton Beach-Destin, FL |
| Walton, GA | Atlanta-Sandy Springs-Roswell, GA |
| Warren, IA | Des Moines-West Des Moines, IA |
| Warren, KY | Bowling Green, KY |
| Warren, MO | St. Louis, MO-IL |
| Warren, NJ | Allentown-Bethlehem-Easton, PA-NJ |
| Warren, NY | Glens Falls, NY |
| Warren, OH | Cincinnati, OH-KY-IN |
| Warren, VA | Washington-Arlington-Alexandria, DC-VA-MD-WV |
| Warrick, IN | Evansville, IN-KY |

| COUNTY: | IS IN METROPOLITAN: |
|---------|---------------------|
| Washington, AR | Fayetteville-Springdale-Rogers, AR-MO |
| Washington, IA | Iowa City, IA |
| Washington, IN | Louisville/Jefferson County, KY-IN |
| Washington, MD | Hagerstown-Martinsburg, MD-WV |
| Washington, MN | Minneapolis-St. Paul-Bloomington, MN-WI |
| Washington, NE | Omaha-Council Bluffs, NE-IA |
| Washington, NY | Glens Falls, NY |
| Washington, OR | Portland-Vancouver-Hillsboro, OR-WA |
| Washington, PA | Pittsburgh, PA |
| Washington, RI | Providence-Warwick, RI-MA |
| Washington, TN | Johnson City, TN |
| Washington, UT | St. George, UT |
| Washington, VA | Kingsport-Bristol-Bristol, TN-VA |
| Washington, WI | Milwaukee-Waukesha-West Allis, WI |
| Washoe, NV | Reno, NV |
| Washtenaw, MI | Ann Arbor, MI |
| Waukesha, WI | Milwaukee-Waukesha-West Allis, WI |
| Waynesboro city, VA | Staunton-Waynesboro, VA |
| Wayne, MI | Detroit-Warren-Dearborn, MI |
| Wayne, NC | Goldsboro, NC |
| Wayne, NY | Rochester, NY |
| Wayne, WV | Huntington-Ashland, WV-KY-OH |
| Webb, TX | Laredo, TX |
| Weber, UT | Ogden-Clearfield, UT |
| Webster, LA | Shreveport-Bossier City, LA |
| Webster, MO | Springfield, MO |
| Weld, CO | Greeley, CO |
| Wells, IN | Fort Wayne, IN |
| West Baton Rouge, LA | Baton Rouge, LA |
| West Feliciana, LA | Baton Rouge, LA |
| Westchester, NY | New York-Newark-Jersey City, NY-NJ-PA |
| Westmoreland, PA | Pittsburgh, PA |
| Whatcom, WA | Bellingham, WA |
| Whitfield, GA | Dalton, GA |
| Whitley, IN | Fort Wayne, IN |
| Wichita, TX | Wichita Falls, TX |
| Wicomico, MD | Salisbury, MD-DE |
| Williamsburg city, VA | Virginia Beach-Norfolk-Newport News, VA-NC |
| Williamson, IL | Carbondale-Marion, IL |
| Williamson, TN | Nashville-Davidson--Murfreesboro--Franklin, TN |
| Williamson, TX | Austin-Round Rock, TX |
| Will, IL | Chicago-Naperville-Elgin, IL-IN-WI |
| Wilson, TN | Nashville-Davidson--Murfreesboro--Franklin, TN |
| Wilson, TX | San Antonio-New Braunfels, TX |
| Winchester city, VA | Winchester, VA-WV |
| Windham, CT | Worcester, MA-CT |
| Winnebago, IL | Rockford, IL |
| Winnebago, WI | Oshkosh-Neenah, WI |
| Wirt, WV | Parkersburg-Vienna, WV |
| Wise, TX | Dallas-Fort Worth-Arlington, TX |
| Woodbury, IA | Sioux City, IA-NE-SD |
| Woodford, IL | Peoria, IL |
| Woodford, KY | Lexington-Fayette, KY |
| Wood, OH | Toledo, OH |
| Wood, WV | Parkersburg-Vienna, WV |
| Worcester, MA | Worcester, MA-CT |
| Worcester, MD | Salisbury, MD-DE |
| Worth, GA | Albany, GA |
| Wright, MN | Minneapolis-St. Paul-Bloomington, MN-WI |
| Wyandotte, KS | Kansas City, MO-KS |
| Wyoming, PA | Scranton--Wilkes-Barre--Hazleton, PA |
| Yadkin, NC | Winston-Salem, NC |
| Yakima, WA | Yakima, WA |
| Yamhill, OR | Portland-Vancouver-Hillsboro, OR-WA |
| Yates, NY | Rochester, NY |
| Yavapai, AZ | Prescott, AZ |
| Yazoo, MS | Jackson, MS |
| Yellowstone, MT | Billings, MT |
| Yolo, CA | Sacramento--Roseville--Arden-Arcade, CA |
| York, ME | Portland-South Portland, ME |
| York, PA | York-Hanover, PA |
| York, SC | Charlotte-Concord-Gastonia, NC-SC |
| York, VA | Virginia Beach-Norfolk-Newport News, VA-NC |
| Yuba, CA | Yuba City, CA |
| Yuma, AZ | Yuma, AZ |

# National Crime Trends: 1994 to 2013

In the 20 years from 1994 to 2013, crime rates in the United States fell significantly. The total crime rate dropped 42.3 percent: from 5,373.8 crimes per 100,000 population in 1994 to a rate of 3,098.6 in 2013. Violent crime rates also decreased, falling 48.4 percent from 1994 to 2013. In addition, property crime rates dropped 41.4 percent.

Among individual crime categories, each recorded declines from 1994 to 2013. The nation's motor vehicle theft rate posted the largest decrease, falling 62.6 percent from 1994 to 2013. The smallest decline was in the rape rate, which dropped 35.9 percent during that same 20-year time frame.

The table below shows rates for each category of crime for every year since 1994. Trends for each individual crime are shown in graphs on the following pages. Violent crimes are murder, rape, robbery, and aggravated assault. Property crimes consist of burglary, larceny-theft, and motor vehicle theft. The total crime rate is simply the sum of the seven specific crimes and was calculated by the editors. All rates are crimes per 100,000 population for the year shown.

| Year | Crime | Violent Crime | Property Crime | Murder | Rape* | Robbery | Assault | Burglary | Larceny-Theft | Motor Vehicle Theft |
|------|-------|---------------|----------------|--------|-------|---------|---------|----------|---------------|---------------------|
| 1994 | 5,373.8 | 713.6 | 4,660.2 | 9.0 | 39.3 | 237.8 | 427.6 | 1,042.1 | 3,026.9 | 591.3 |
| 1995 | 5,275.0 | 684.5 | 4,590.5 | 8.2 | 37.1 | 220.9 | 418.3 | 987.0 | 3,043.2 | 560.3 |
| 1996 | 5,087.6 | 636.6 | 4,451.0 | 7.4 | 36.3 | 201.9 | 391.0 | 945.0 | 2,980.3 | 525.7 |
| 1997 | 4,927.3 | 611.0 | 4,316.3 | 6.8 | 35.9 | 186.2 | 382.1 | 918.8 | 2,891.8 | 505.7 |
| 1998 | 4,620.1 | 567.6 | 4,052.5 | 6.3 | 34.5 | 165.5 | 361.4 | 863.2 | 2,729.5 | 459.9 |
| 1999 | 4,266.6 | 523.0 | 3,743.6 | 5.7 | 32.8 | 150.1 | 334.3 | 770.4 | 2,550.7 | 422.5 |
| 2000 | 4,124.8 | 506.5 | 3,618.3 | 5.5 | 32.0 | 145.0 | 324.0 | 728.8 | 2,477.3 | 412.2 |
| 2001 | 4,162.6 | 504.5 | 3,658.1 | 5.6 | 31.8 | 148.5 | 318.6 | 741.8 | 2,485.7 | 430.5 |
| 2002 | 4,125.0 | 494.4 | 3,630.6 | 5.6 | 33.1 | 146.1 | 309.5 | 747.0 | 2,450.7 | 432.9 |
| 2003 | 4,067.0 | 475.8 | 3,591.2 | 5.7 | 32.3 | 142.5 | 295.4 | 741.0 | 2,416.5 | 433.7 |
| 2004 | 3,977.3 | 463.2 | 3,514.1 | 5.5 | 32.4 | 136.7 | 288.6 | 730.3 | 2,362.3 | 421.5 |
| 2005 | 3,900.5 | 469.0 | 3,431.5 | 5.6 | 31.8 | 140.8 | 290.8 | 726.9 | 2,287.8 | 416.8 |
| 2006 | 3,825.9 | 479.3 | 3,346.6 | 5.8 | 31.6 | 150.0 | 292.0 | 733.1 | 2,213.2 | 400.2 |
| 2007 | 3,748.2 | 471.8 | 3,276.4 | 5.7 | 30.6 | 148.3 | 287.2 | 726.1 | 2,185.4 | 364.9 |
| 2008 | 3,673.2 | 458.6 | 3,214.6 | 5.4 | 29.8 | 145.9 | 277.5 | 733.0 | 2,166.1 | 315.4 |
| 2009 | 3,473.2 | 431.9 | 3,041.3 | 5.0 | 29.1 | 133.1 | 264.7 | 717.7 | 2,064.5 | 259.2 |
| 2010 | 3,350.4 | 404.5 | 2,945.9 | 4.8 | 27.7 | 119.3 | 252.8 | 701.0 | 2,005.8 | 239.1 |
| 2011 | 3,292.5 | 387.1 | 2,905.4 | 4.7 | 27.0 | 113.9 | 241.5 | 701.3 | 1,974.1 | 230.0 |
| 2012 | 3,255.8 | 387.8 | 2,868.0 | 4.7 | 27.1 | 113.1 | 242.8 | 672.2 | 1,965.4 | 230.4 |
| 2013 | 3,098.6 | 367.9 | 2,730.7 | 4.5 | 25.2 | 109.1 | 229.1 | 610.0 | 610.0 | 221.3 |

*The figures shown in this column for the offense of rape were estimated using the legacy Uniform Crime Reporting definition of rape. The definition was changed for offenses reported beginning in 2013. See note on page vii for further explanation.

Source: Reported data from the F.B.I. Data for 2012 are revised from that which appeared in the previous edition of *City Crime Rankings*. "Crime in the United States 2013" (Uniform Crime Reports, November 10, 2014)

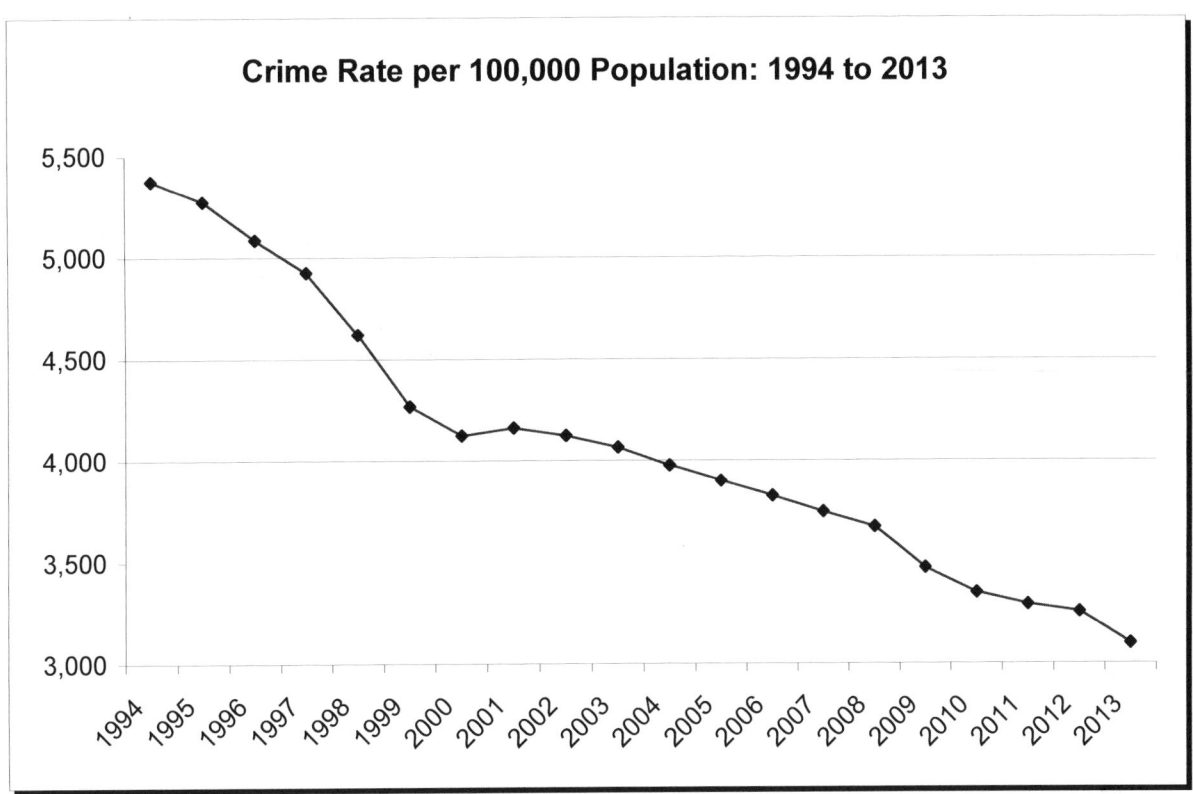

Crime Rate per 100,000 Population: 1994 to 2013

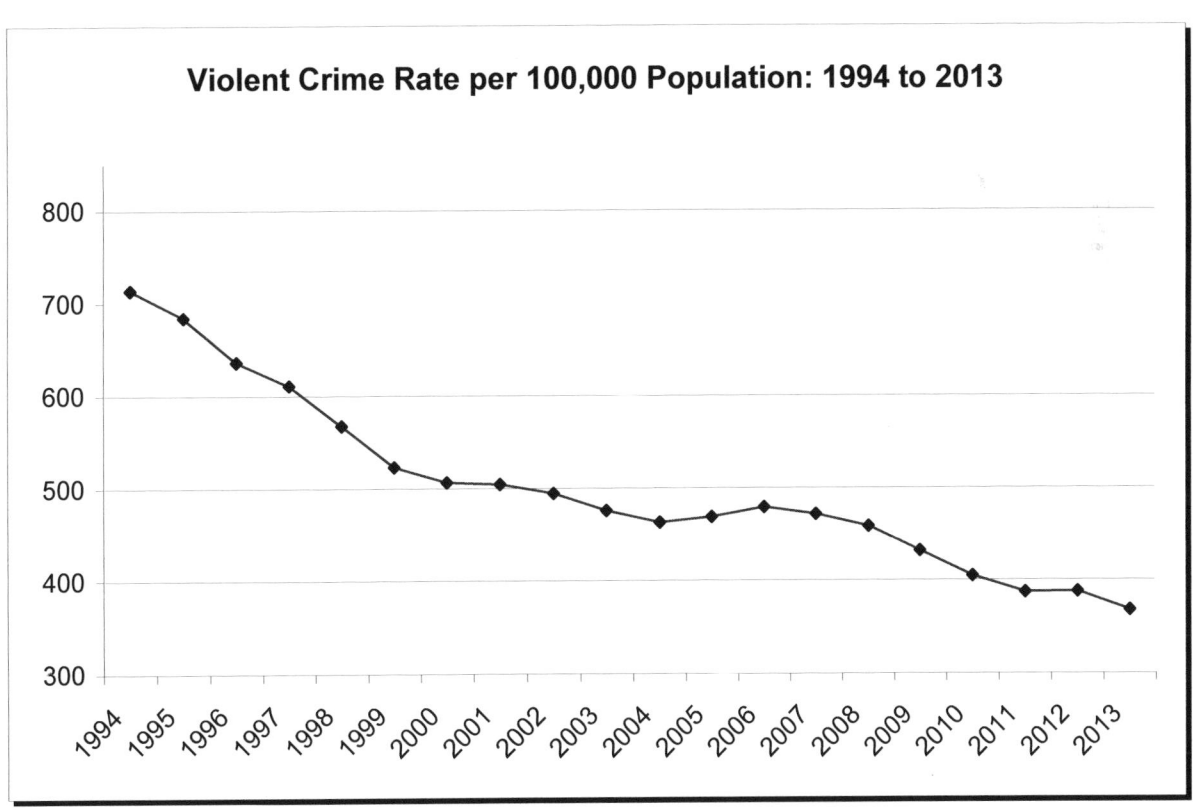

Violent Crime Rate per 100,000 Population: 1994 to 2013

Source: Reported data from the F.B.I.

"Crime in the United States 2013" (Uniform Crime Reports, November 10, 2014)

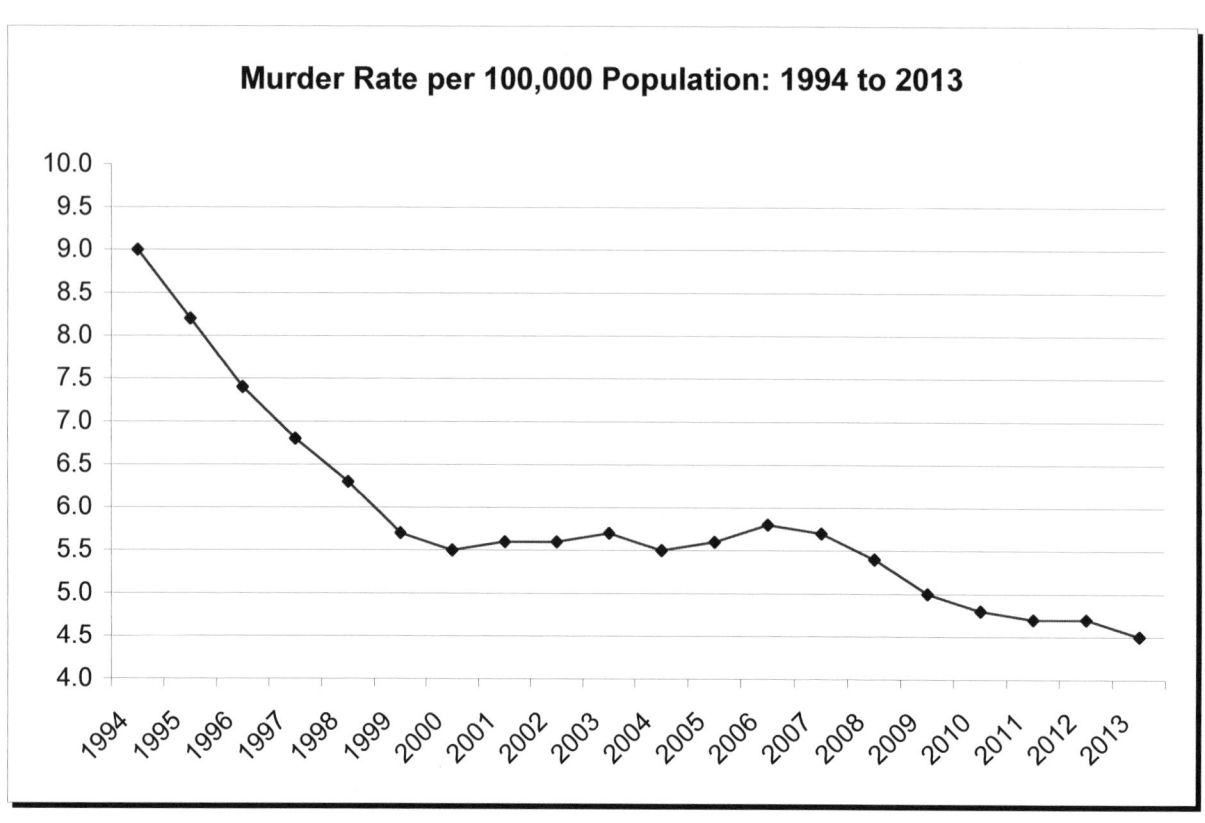

**Murder Rate per 100,000 Population: 1994 to 2013**

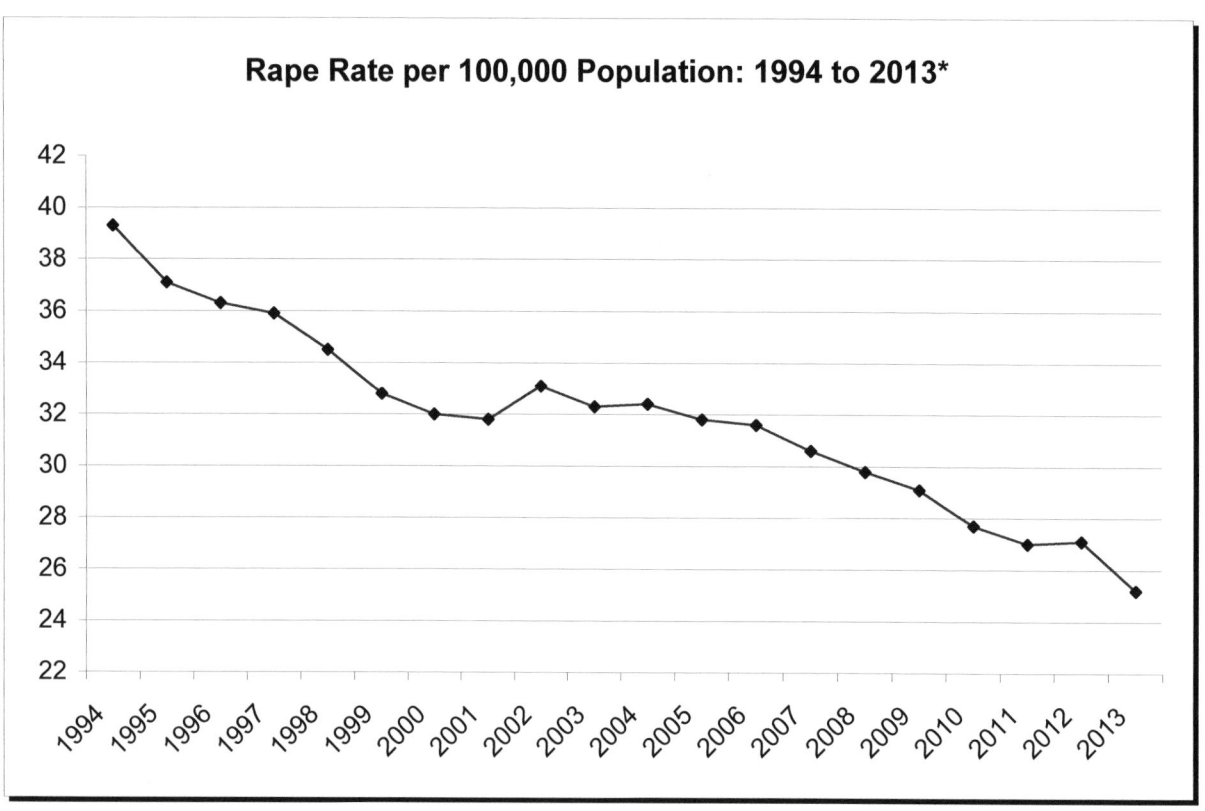

**Rape Rate per 100,000 Population: 1994 to 2013\***

Source: Reported data from the F.B.I.

"Crime in the United States 2013" (Uniform Crime Reports, November 10, 2014)

\*The figures shown in this chart for the offense of rape were estimated using the legacy Uniform Crime Reporting definition of rape. The definition was changed for offenses reported beginning in 2013. See note on page vii for further explanation.

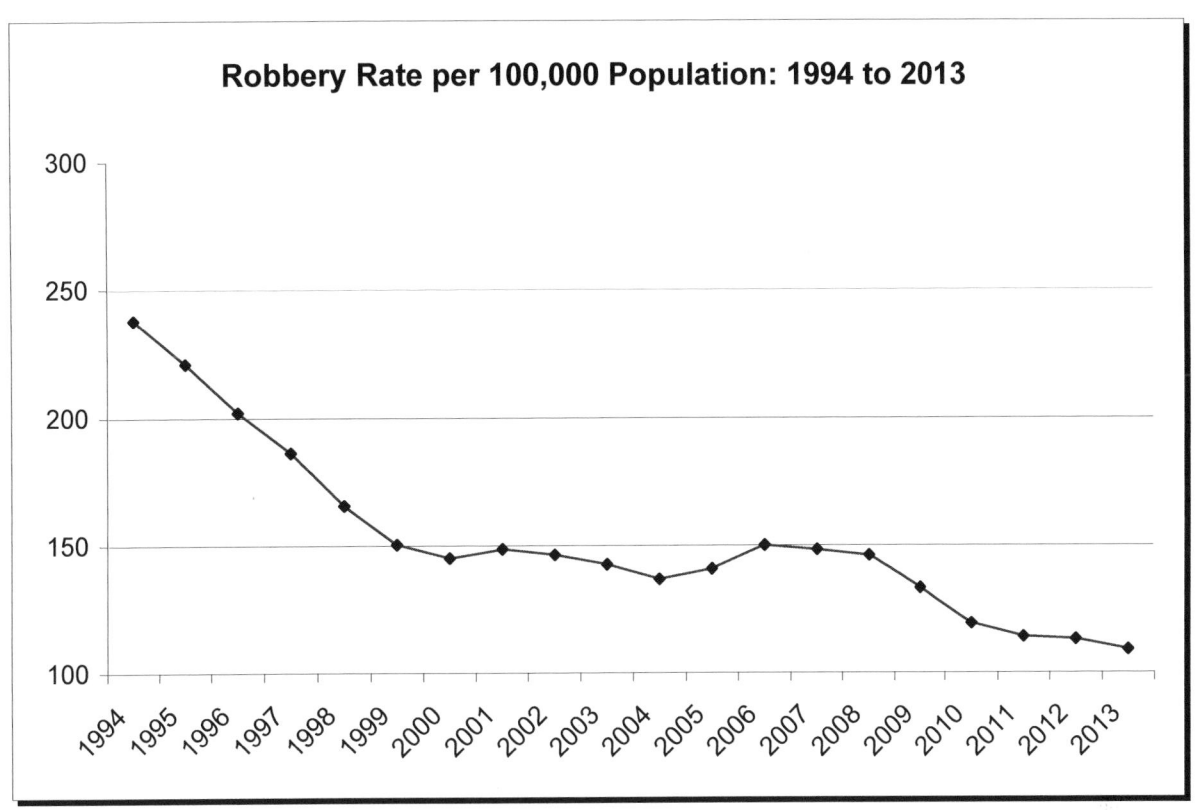

**Robbery Rate per 100,000 Population: 1994 to 2013**

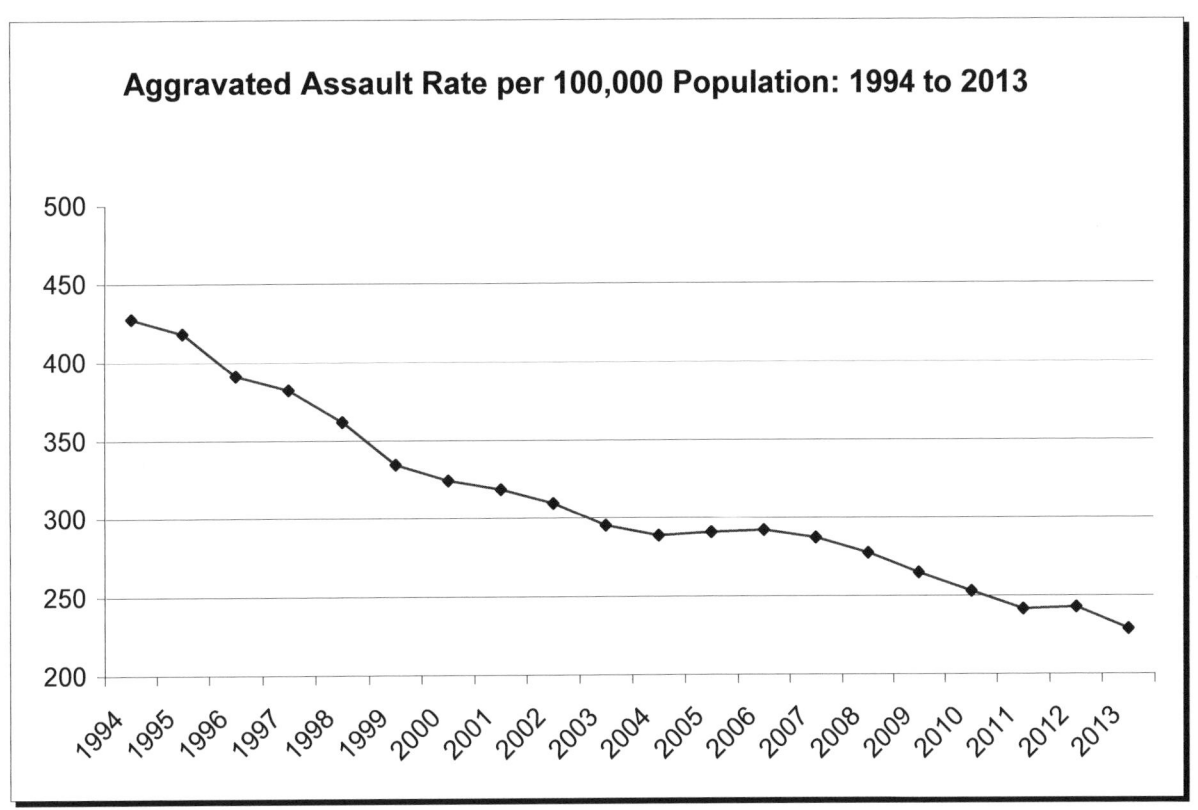

**Aggravated Assault Rate per 100,000 Population: 1994 to 2013**

Source: Reported data from the F.B.I.

"Crime in the United States 2013" (Uniform Crime Reports, November 10, 2014)

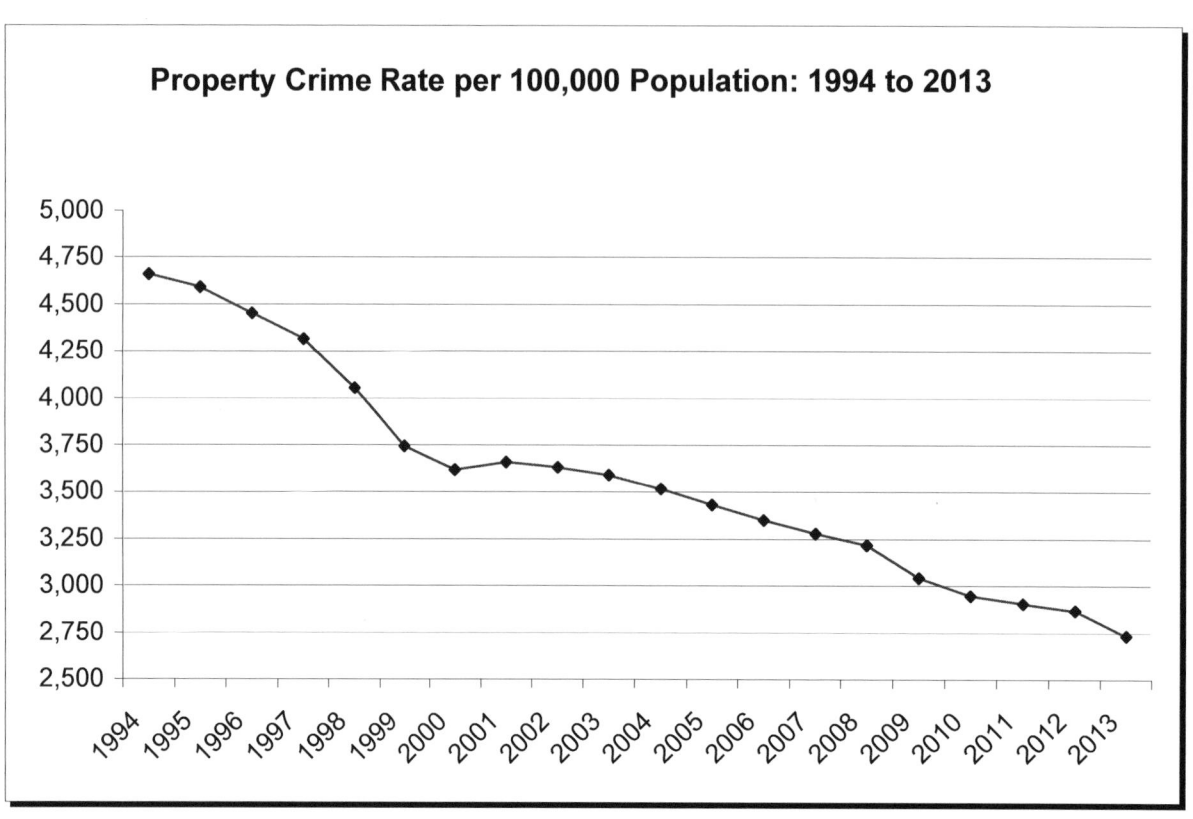

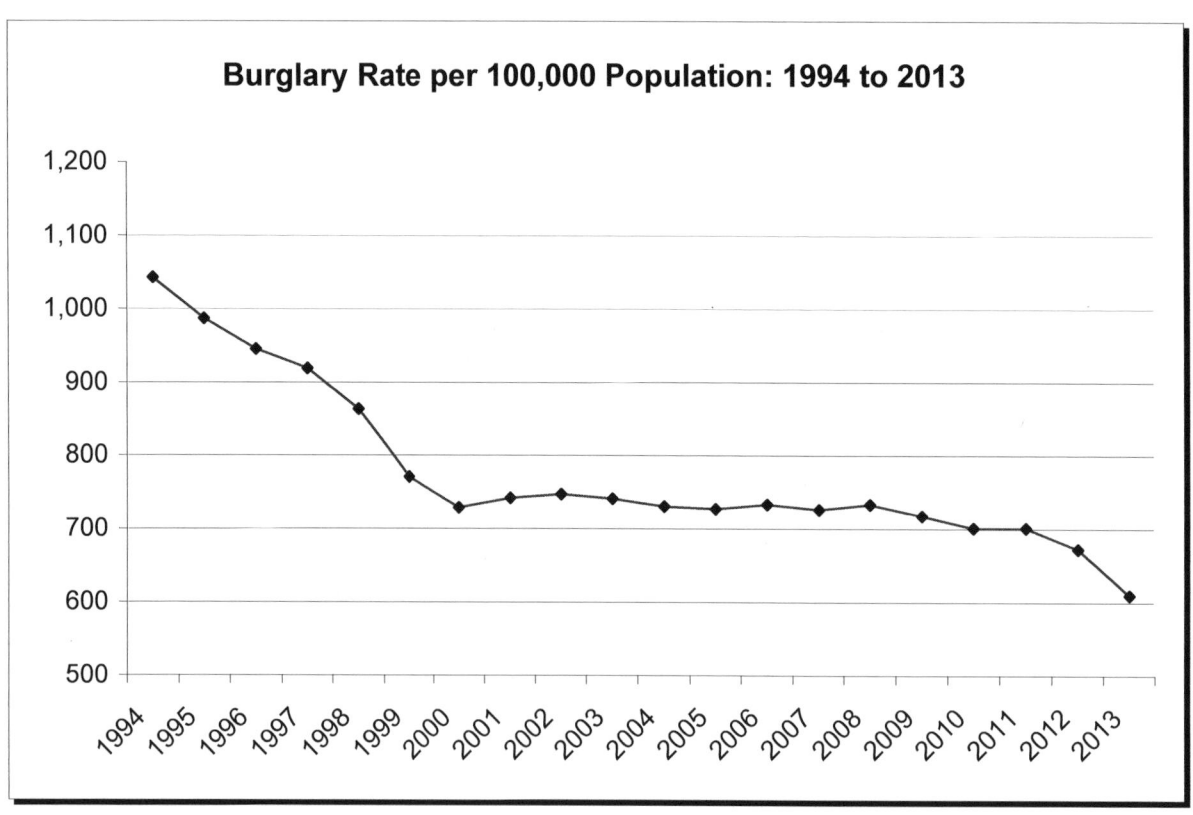

Source: Reported data from the F.B.I.

"Crime in the United States 2013" (Uniform Crime Reports, November 10, 2014)

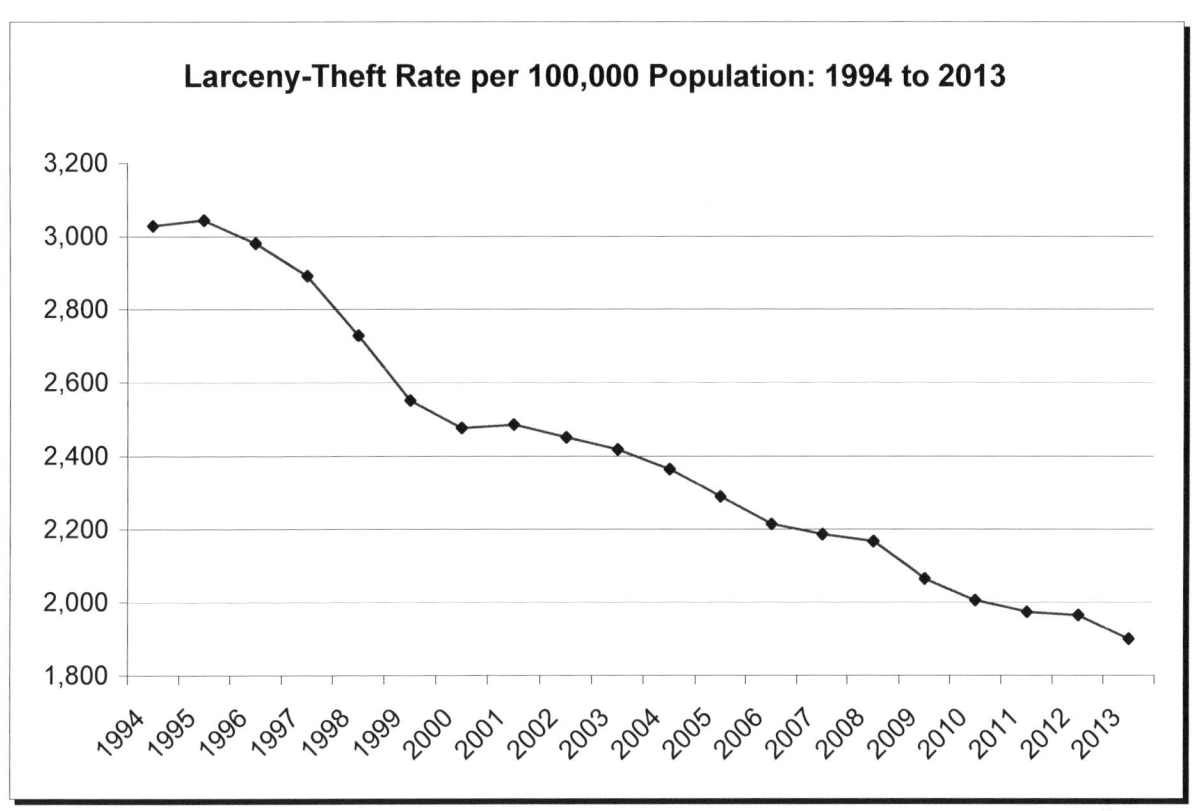

Larceny-Theft Rate per 100,000 Population: 1994 to 2013

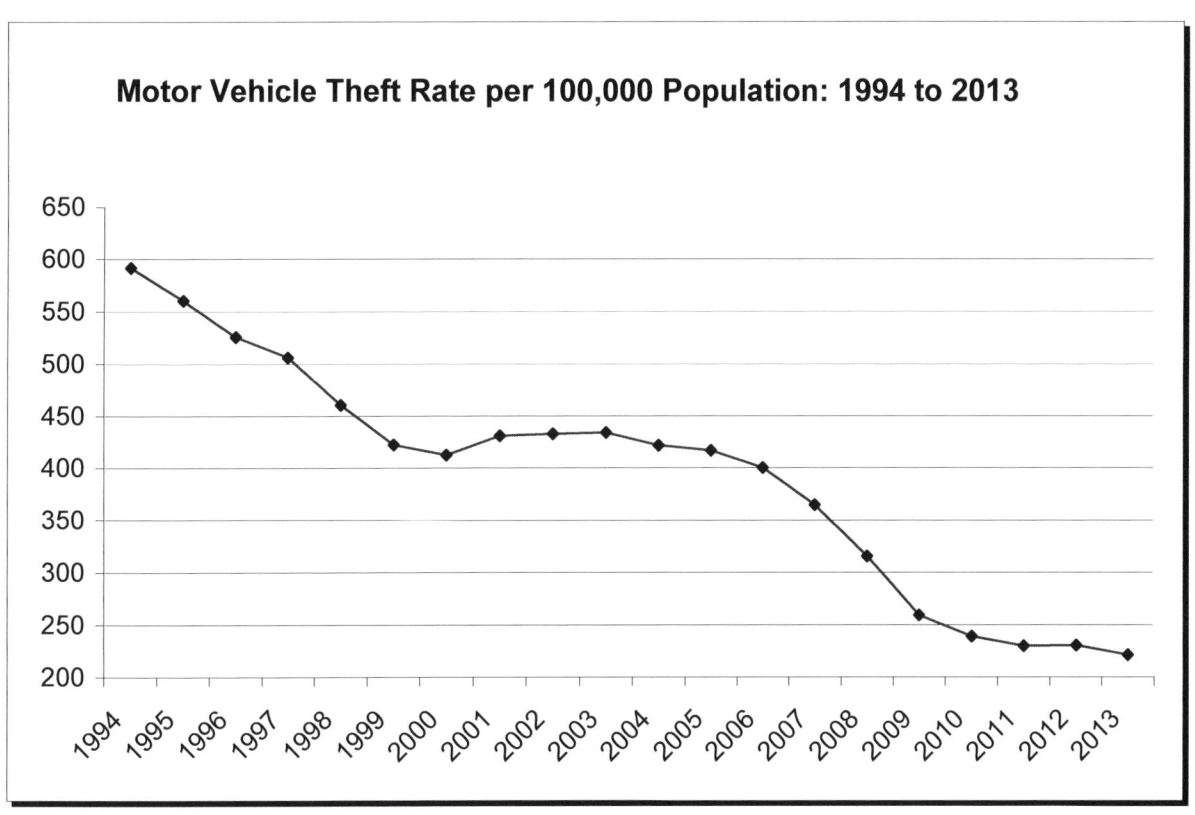

Motor Vehicle Theft Rate per 100,000 Population: 1994 to 2013

Source: Reported data from the F.B.I.

"Crime in the United States 2013" (Uniform Crime Reports, November 10, 2014)

# National, Metropolitan, and City Crime Statistics Summary: 2013

|  | NATIONAL | METRO* | CITY* |
|---|---|---|---|
| Population 2013 | 316,128,839 | 269,190,260 | 89,424,575 |
| Police (Sworn Officers) | 626,942 |  |  |
| Rate of Police Officers (per 100,000 Population) | 233 |  |  |
|  |  |  |  |
| Crimes in 2013 | 9,795,658 | 8,649,357 | 3,777,213 |
| Crime Rate in 2013 (per 100,000 Population) | 3,098.6 | 3,213.1 | 4,223.9 |
| Percent Change in Crime Rate: 2012 to 2013 | (4.8) | (4.3) | (2.5) |
| Percent Change in Crime Rate: 2009 to 2013 | (10.8) | (16.3) | (10.4) |
|  |  |  |  |
| Violent Crimes in 2013 | 1,163,146 | 1,069,788 | 548,396 |
| Violent Crime Rate in 2013 (per 100,000 Population) | 367.9 | 397.4 | 613.2 |
| Percent Change in Violent Crime Rate: 2012 to 2013 | (5.1) | (2.9) | (6.3) |
| Percent Change in Violent Crime Rate: 2009 to 2013 | (14.8) | (13.4) | (14.7) |
|  |  |  |  |
| Murders in 2013 | 14,196 | 12,548 | 7,162 |
| Murder Rate in 2013 (per 100,000 Population) | 4.5 | 4.7 | 8.0 |
| Percent Change in Murder Rate: 2012 to 2013 | (5.1) | (4.1) | (7.0) |
| Percent Change in Murder Rate: 2009 to 2013 | (10.5) | (9.6) | (11.1) |
|  |  |  |  |
| Rapes in 2013** | 79,770 | 66,640 | 23,473 |
| Rape Rate in 2013 (per 100,000 Population) | 25.2 | 24.8 | 26.2 |
| Percent Change in Rape Rate: 2012 to 2013 | (7.0) | (6.1) | (17.6) |
| Percent Change in Rape Rate: 2009 to 2013 | (13.2) | (12.1) | (21.8) |
|  |  |  |  |
| Robberies in 2013 | 345,031 | 332,161 | 211,405 |
| Robbery Rate in 2013 (per 100,000 Population) | 109.1 | 123.4 | 236.4 |
| Percent Change in Robbery Rate: 2012 to 2013 | (3.5) | (3.5) | (2.2) |
| Percent Change in Robbery Rate: 2009 to 2013 | (18.0) | (18.9) | (15.9) |
|  |  |  |  |
| Aggravated Assaults in 2013 | 724,149 | 634,340 | 306,356 |
| Aggravated Assault Rate in 2013 (per 100,000 Population) | 229.1 | 235.6 | 342.6 |
| Percent Change in Aggravated Assault Rate: 2012 to 2013 | (5.6) | (5.8) | (8.0) |
| Percent Change in Aggravated Assault Rate: 2009 to 2013 | (13.4) | (13.8) | (13.3) |
|  |  |  |  |
| Property Crimes in 2013 | 8,632,512 | 7,579,569 | 3,228,817 |
| Property Crime Rate in 2013 (per 100,000 Population) | 2,730.7 | 2,815.7 | 3,610.7 |
| Percent Change in Property Crime Rate: 2012 to 2013 | (4.8) | (4.5) | (1.8) |
| Percent Change in Property Crime Rate: 2009 to 2013 | (10.2) | (10.9) | (9.6) |
|  |  |  |  |
| Burglaries in 2013 | 1,928,465 | 1,650,943 | 701,340 |
| Burglary Rate in 2013 (per 100,000 Population) | 610.0 | 613.3 | 784.3 |
| Percent Change in Burglary Rate: 2012 to 2013 | (9.3) | (9.3) | (7.1) |
| Percent Change in Burglary Rate: 2009 to 2013 | (15.0) | (15.7) | (15.6) |
|  |  |  |  |
| Larceny-Thefts in 2013 | 6,004,453 | 5,280,799 | 2,174,160 |
| Larceny-Theft Rate in 2013 (per 100,000 Population) | 1,899.4 | 1,961.7 | 2,431.3 |
| Percent Change in Larceny-Theft Rate: 2012 to 2013 | (3.4) | (3.0) | 0.2 |
| Percent Change in Larceny-Theft Rate: 2009 to 2013 | (8.0) | (8.6) | (6.9) |
|  |  |  |  |
| Motor Vehicle Thefts in 2013 | 699,594 | 647,827 | 353,317 |
| Motor Vehicle Theft Rate in 2013 (per 100,000 Population) | 221.3 | 240.7 | 395.1 |
| Percent Change in Motor Vehicle Theft Rate: 2012 to 2013 | (4.0) | (4.0) | (2.6) |
| Percent Change in Motor Vehicle Theft Rate: 2009 to 2013 | (14.6) | (15.8) | (12.9) |

Source: CQ Press using reported data from the F.B.I.
    "Crime in the United States 2013" (Uniform Crime Reports, November 10, 2014)
*Metro includes population and crime for all metropolitan statistical areas. City statistics are for cities of 100,000 or more in population.
**The figures shown in this table for the offense of rape were estimated using the legacy Uniform Crime Reporting definition of rape. The definition was changed for offenses reported beginning in 2013. See note on page vii for further explanation.